TABLE OF CONTENTS

TABLE OF CONTENTS (Continued)

SECTION 4 — EXECUTIVE

TABLE OF CONTENTS (Continued)

SECTION 5 — JUDICIARY

SECTION 6 — LOCAL GOVERNMENT

TABLE OF CONTENTS (Continued)

TABLE OF CONTENTS (Continued)

SECTION 9 — APPENDIX

Commonwealth of Pennsylvania
GOVERNOR'S OFFICE
Harrisburg

THE GOVERNOR

To My Fellow Pennsylvanians:

Two hundred years ago, our state played host to the framers of the United States Constitution. Our delegates played a leading role in the crafting of a document which has endured for two centuries as a model for democratic governments throughout the world.

This year, as we celebrate the constitutional bicentennial, we remember that Pennsylvania was the birthplace not only of representative government, but also of social diversity and religious tolerance. Indeed, a hundred years before the constitutional convention, William Penn established our commonwealth as a haven of freedom and opportunity for all people.

In our own time, we have rededicated ourselves to the goal of providing genuine opportunity for all our citizens; jobs for our workers, a world-class education for our children, and a cleaner environment for both this generation and those to follow. These are the goals my administration brings to our leadership of state government. But the key to our success — like that of the U.S. Constitution — is a concerned and well-informed citizenry.

This 108th edition of *The Pennsylvania Manual* provides the most complete citizen's guide to the history, structure, people and responsibilities of our state government. It describes an enterprise reinvigorated by new energy, new ideas and new leaders, working to fulfill the agenda of a new Pennsylvania Partnership.

I hope this new edition of the *Manual* encourages all Pennsylvanians to join in the great partnership, to participate in the democratic process, and to share their ideas with their elected and appointed officials. Together, we will make Pennsylvania a commonwealth that works.

Yours truly,

Robert P. Casey
Governor

GOVERNOR ROBERT P. CASEY

LIEUTENANT GOVERNOR MARK S. SINGEL

PENNSYLVANIA PARTNERSHIP

"Two centuries ago, in 1787, a troubled people who were the children of destiny gathered in Pennsylvania. In the turbulent wake of a revolution only just ended, their infant nation would surely perish unless they could form a new political and social partnership unlike anything the world had ever seen.

Torn by faction, paralyzed by petty partisanship, unsure of their course, and uncertain of their possibilities, they convened in Pennsylvania to invent the future.

During a long summer of sometimes bitter debates, a former Governor of Pennsylvania, Dr. Benjamin Franklin, took to musing about a wooden carving on the back of the chair of the convention's presiding officer, George Washington.

The carving was a representation of the sun, and in it Franklin saw a metaphor for the infant nation; but, he wondered, had the artist meant to carve it as a sun that was rising or setting?

Finally, on September 17, 1787, the Constitution was born, and Dr. Franklin told his fellow delegates: 'Now at length I have the happiness to know that it is a rising and not a setting sun.'

What that sun was rising on, of course, was a future made possible by a great constitutional partnership. The genius of that partnership is that it has proved to have room for all of us, and a place for each of us.

I believe that once again, it is within our power to determine whether Pennsylvania's sun is to set or to rise. I believe that the choice is ours, if we will but make it. I believe the future is ours, if we will but reach for it.

That is why I call for a new Pennsylvania Partnership:

— A Pennsylvania Partnership which must be as bold and stunning as that which two centuries ago fashioned in Philadelphia the Constitution which I have just sworn to uphold.

— A Pennsylvania Partnership which brings into the same house the men and women of labor and business, of politics and education, of cities and suburbs, of factories and farms.

— A Pennsylvania Partnership which knows that if the sun does not rise for all of us, it will surely set on most of us."

From the Inaugural Address of
Governor Robert P. Casey
January 20, 1987

For over a century, Pennsylvania has been America's workhorse. But during the last decade, changes in the world marketplace damaged Pennsylvania's ability to compete in many traditional industries. While some parts of the state have begun to regain their economic vitality with a dynamic mix of high technology and service industries, many regions have not been given the support necessary to reclaim the jobs lost to other countries and other states.

Farm, Lancaster County

Pennsylvania retains extraordinary strengths: a rich inventory of major universities and private colleges; renowned teaching hospitals and scientific research centers; world-class skills in computer software, robotics, biotechnology, plant automation, diamond coating and other new technologies. Governor Casey's new Pennsylvania Economic Development Partnership builds on these strengths to create a fertile environment for business growth and job creation throughout the entire state.

The Economic Development Partnership recognizes that when it comes to growth and opportunity, better schools and a cleaner environment, private sector needs and public goals are in harmony. The partnership brings together presidents of Pennsylvania's leading universities,

Pittsburgh Point

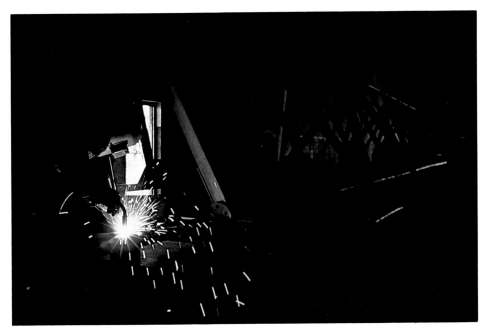

Steel fabrication

the chief executives of our major corporations, the entrepreneurs of our most innovative growth companies, and leaders from labor, small business, high technology and agribusiness to help state government target its energies and its resources on creating jobs, improving education, and cleaning up the environment. It is a partnership which brings a concern for people to the task of rebuilding Pennsylvania's economy, and a business-like efficiency to helping our citizens to help themselves.

Ohiopyle Falls, Fayette County

The most logical place to start any unified program for stimulating economic growth and opportunity is with young people. "The good education of youth," wrote Benjamin Franklin, "has been esteemed by wise men in all ages as the surest foundation of the happiness both of private families and of Commonwealths." Today education remains foremost on the agenda of Pennsylvania and its families. The focus on public education must be intensified so that our children are prepared to meet and beat competition from around the nation, and around the world. We challenge teachers and students alike not to be average, but to be great. The minds of our children are Pennsylvania's most vital raw material, and Governor Casey is committed to investing unprecedented resources in their development.

Computer training - Harrisburg Elementary School

Philadelphia Art Museum

Middle Creek Waterfowl Area

As William Penn himself realized over three hundred years ago, a clean environment is itself an irreplaceable asset in promoting the growth of the Commonwealth. He wrote of Pennsylvania: "The air is sweet and clear, the heavens serene, like the south parts of France . . . The waters are generally good . . . The woods are adorned with lovely flowers. I have seen the gardens of London best stored with that sort of beauty, but I think they may be improved by our woods."

Over three centuries later, we have again come to realize the natural beauty and environmental quality are a fundamental part of Pennsylvania's heritage. They are at the center of our new efforts to attract people and business to our Commonwealth. Good environmental policy is still good economic policy. We cannot tolerate pollution as the price of prosperity. In the end, our standard of living depends on our quality of life. So we are moving forward to clean up, to conserve, to maintain the land and water and air, and to regain the natural glory that is Pennsylvania.

Like a good family, Pennsylvania is both strong and compassionate. Good families stay together, grow together, work together, and move into the future together. And like any good family, the family of Pennsylvania must leave no one out and no one behind.

We are a frugal people, but we are a caring people, too. And we want Pennsylvania to be judged as much by our concern for our neighbors as by our dedication to wise management of the public purse. We insist that government be sensible without being insensitive.

These are the challenges of the new Pennsylvania Partnership.

As Governor Casey said at his inaugural in January 1987:

"Our cause is nothing less than to redeem the promise of Pennsylvania for ourselves and our children — and their children yet to be born. Our cause is nothing less than the creation of a new Pennsylvania, rooted in our long and rich heritage, striving for a future of greater prosperity and justice for all.

"Along the way, in countless decisions and debates, let this be our guiding star: to build a Pennsylvania future worthy of our people and our past. What I pledge to you — what I ask of all of us — is a constant commitment to initiative and innovation, and to the enduring values of family, community, and concern for one another."

Warrendale Electronics School

Penn State "Old Main"

PENNSYLVANIA: PAST AND PRESENT

BY
SYLVESTER K. STEVENS
AND
DONALD H. KENT

REVISED BY
LOUIS M. WADDELL

SECTION 1 - PENNSYLVANIA: PAST AND PRESENT

PHYSICAL AND NATURAL PROPERTIES

William Penn, as proprietor of Penn's Woods, was an aggressive and active promoter of his new land. "The country itself," he wrote, "its soil, air, water, seasons and produce, both natural and artificial, is not to be despised." Pennsylvania still contains a rich diversity of natural and geological features.

One of the original thirteen colonies, Pennsylvania is today surrounded by the states of New York, New Jersey, Delaware, Maryland, West Virginia and Ohio. It has a land area of 45,333 square miles and 891 square miles of the area of Lake Erie. It ranks thirty-second in area among the 50 states. Pennsylvania has an average width of 285 miles, east to west, and an average north-to-south distance of 156 miles.

Only the Delaware River on the east and about 40 miles of Lake Erie in the northwest corner form natural boundaries. Elsewhere borders are based on those established in the charter granted to William Penn by King Charles II of England, although it was 1787 before land and border disputes were settled and Pennsylvania held clear title to its land. The most famous border dispute was with Maryland and was ultimately settled when the English Crown accepted the Mason-Dixon line in 1769, a border which, in subsequent years, became the symbolic demarcation in the United States between the North and the South.

A dissected plateau covers Pennsylvania's northern and western sections, ranging from about 2,000 feet above sea level in the northern tier of counties to about 1,200 feet south of Pittsburgh. A broad belt of wide valleys, alternating with narrow mountains, stretches across the state from the south-central boundary to the northeast corner. To the east of this section is the Great Valley, which is divided into southern, central and eastern sections — the Cumberland, Lebanon and Lehigh valleys, respectively. Further to the east is a line of discontinuous mountains, as well as lowlands of irregular form and a deeply dissected plateau of moderate height which gradually slopes to the Delaware River. There is also another lowland along the shores of Lake Erie. Pennsylvania's highest peak is Mt. Davis on Negro Mountain in Somerset County, with an elevation of 3,213 feet above sea level.

Pennsylvania has three major river systems — the Delaware, the Susquehanna and the Ohio. The Delaware's important tributaries are the Schuylkill and Lehigh rivers. The Susquehanna has North and West branches as does the Juniata River. In the west, the Ohio River begins at the confluence of the Allegheny and the Monongahela, and its tributaries include the Youghiogheny, Beaver and Clarion rivers. The Ohio system provides 35 percent of all the water emptying into the Gulf of Mexico.

The state has a great variety of soils, ranging from extremely rich in Lancaster County to very poor in the mountain regions. Through advanced agricultural methods, a large part of Pennsylvania soil which was only marginally fertile has been made very productive. Originally almost all of Pennsylvania, which was a transition zone between northern and southern primeval forests, was covered by dense growth of hickory, locust, black walnut, maple, beech, birch, cherry, and conifers. Because much land was cleared by settlement and by lumber operations, very little virgin timber remains, but even today half the state is wooded.

Animal and bird life, including the wild pigeon, panther, black bear and Canada lynx, was abundant in the primeval forest. The first of these is now extinct, the second has been exterminated, and the last two are no longer abundant. Raccoons, squirrels, rabbits, skunks and woodchucks are still common, as are most of the smaller birds. Today, deer, pheasants, rabbits, ducks and turkeys are popular with hunters. Pennsylvania's rivers were originally filled with sturgeon, shad, salmon, trout, perch and, surprisingly, mussels. State and federal agencies keep streams and ponds well-stocked, and trout, salmon and walleyed pike are caught in enormous numbers.

Pennsylvania ranks second in value of mineral production among all the states. Coal, petroleum, natural gas and cement are the principal products. Others are fire clay, iron ore, lime, slate and stone.

In spite of its proximity to the ocean, Pennsylvania has a continental climate because the prevailing winds are from the west. This makes for extremes of heat and cold, but not with so marked a variation as in the central states. There are minor climatic differences within the state because of altitude and geological features. The frost-free period, for example, is longest in southeastern Pennsylvania, in the Ohio and Monongahela valleys in southwestern Pennsylvania, and in the region bordering Lake Erie. The higher lands have only three to five months free from frost. Rainfall throughout the state is usually adequate for temperate zone crops.

Pennsylvania's location and its characteristics of climate, waters, minerals, flora and fauna helped shape the growth not only of the state, but of the entire nation. Midway between the North and the South, the fledgling colony prospered and became the keystone of the young nation.

SYMBOLS

"Commonwealth"

Pennsylvania shares with Virginia, Kentucky, and Massachusetts the designation "Commonwealth." The word is of English derivation and refers to the common "weal" or well-being of the public. The State Seal of Pennsylvania does not use the term, but it is a traditional, official designation used in referring to the state, and legal processes are in the name of the Commonwealth. In 1776, our first state constitution referred to Pennsylvania as both "Commonwealth" and "State," a pattern of usage that was perpetuated in the constitutions of 1790, 1838, and 1874, and in the revisions of 1968. Today, "State" and "Commonwealth" are correctly used interchangeably. The distinction between them has been held to have no legal significance.

"Keystone State"

The word "keystone" comes from architecture and refers to the central, wedge-shaped stone in an arch which holds all the other stones in place. The use of the term "Keystone State" as applied to Pennsylvania cannot be traced to any single source. Apparently, it came into use shortly after the Revolution and was commonly accepted soon after 1800. The early common use of the term may be attributed to the strategic geographical location of Pennsylvania in the original union dominated by the states of the Atlantic seaboard. The modern persistence of this designation for Pennsylvania is justified in view of the key position of Pennsylvania in the economic, social and political development of the United States.

State Seal

The State Seal is the symbol used by the Commonwealth to authenticate certain documents. It is impressed upon the document by an instrument known as a seal-press, or stamp. The State Seal has two faces: the obverse, which is the more familiar face and the one most often referred to as the "State Seal," and the reverse, or counter-seal, which is used less frequently. The State Seal is in the custody of the Secretary of the Commonwealth. When Pennsylvania was still a province of England, its seals were those of William Penn and his descendants. The transition from this provincial seal to a state seal began when the State Constitutional Convention of 1776 directed that "all commissions shall be . . . sealed with the State Seal," and appointed a committee to prepare such a seal for future use. By 1778 there was in use a seal similar to the present one. The seal received legal recognition from the General Assembly in 1791, when it was designated the official State Seal.

The obverse of the seal contains a shield, upon which are emblazoned a sailing ship, a plough, and three sheaves of wheat. To the left of the shield is a stalk of Indian corn; to the right, an olive branch. The shield's crest is an eagle, and the entire design is encircled by the inscription "Seal of the State of Pennsylvania." These three symbols — the plough, the ship, and the sheaves of wheat — have, despite minor changes through the years, remained the traditional emblems of Pennsylvania's State Seal. They were first found in the individual seals of several colonial Pennsylvania counties, which mounted their own identifying crests above the

OBVERSE   REVERSE

existing Penn Coat of Arms. Chester County's crest was a plough; Philadelphia County's crest was a ship under full sail; Sussex County, Delaware (then a part of provincial Pennsylvania) used a sheaf of wheat as its crest. The shield of the City of Philadelphia contained both a sheaf of wheat and a ship under sail. It was a combination of these sources that provided the three emblems now forming the obverse of the State Seal. The reverse of this first seal shows a woman, who represents liberty. Her left hand holds a wand topped by a liberty cap, a French symbol of liberty. In her right hand is a drawn sword. She is trampling upon Tyranny, represented by a lion. The entire design is encircled by the legend "Both Can't Survive."

Coat of Arms

Pennsylvania's Coat of Arms, while not used in the same official capacity as the State Seal (although it contains the emblems of the seal), is perhaps a more familiar symbol of the Commonwealth of Pennsylvania. It appears on countless documents, letterheads, and publications, and forms the design on Pennsylvania's State Flag. Provincial Pennsylvania's coat of arms was that of the Penn family. A state coat of arms first appeared on state paper money issued in 1777. This first coat of arms was nearly identical to the State Seal, without the inscription. In 1778, Caleb Lownes of Philadelphia prepared a coat of arms. Heraldic in design, it consisted of: a shield, which displayed the emblems of the State Seal — the ship, plough, and sheaves of wheat; an eagle for the crest; two black horses as supporters; and the motto "Virtue, Liberty and Independence." An olive branch and cornstalk were crossed below the shield. Behind each horse was a stalk of corn but these were omitted after 1805.

Numerous modifications were made to this coat of arms between 1778 and 1873, chiefly in the position and color of the supporting horses. In 1874, the legislature noted these variations and lack of uniformity, and appointed a commission to establish an official coat of arms for the Commonwealth. In 1875, the commission reported that it had adopted, almost unchanged, the coat of arms originally designed by Caleb Lownes 96 years earlier. This is the coat of arms in use today.

State Flag

Pennsylvania's State Flag is composed of a blue field, on which is embroidered the State Coat of Arms. The flag is flown from all state buildings, and further display on any public

The **Brook Trout** is the state fish as adopted by the General Assembly on March 9, 1970.

building within the Commonwealth is provided for by law. The first State Flag bearing the State Coat of Arms was authorized by the General Assembly in 1799. During the Civil War, many Pennsylvania regiments carried flags modeled after the U.S. Flag, but substituted Pennsylvania's Coat of Arms for the field of stars. An act of the General Assembly of June 13, 1907, standardized the flag and required that the blue field match the blue of Old Glory.

The **Whitetail Deer** is the official state animal by an act of the General Assembly of October 2, 1959.

The **Ruffed Grouse** is the state game bird by an act of the General Assembly of June 22, 1931. The Pennsylvania ruffed grouse, sometimes called the partridge, is distinguished by its plump body, feathered legs, and mottled reddish-brown color. This protective coloring makes it possible for the ruffed grouse to conceal itself in the wilds.

The **Great Dane** is the state dog as approved by the General Assembly on August 15, 1965.

The **Mountain Laurel** is the state flower as approved by the General Assembly on May 5, 1933. The mountain laurel is in full bloom in mid-June, when Pennsylvania's woodlands are filled with its distinctive pink flower.

The **Firefly** is the state insect as enacted by the General Assembly on April 10, 1974.

Milk is the official state beverage by an act of the General Assembly of April 29, 1982.

The **Hemlock** is the state tree by an act of the General Assembly of June 23, 1931.

The **Penngift Crownvetch** is the official beautification and conservation plant by an act of the General Assembly of June 17, 1982.

CAPITOL

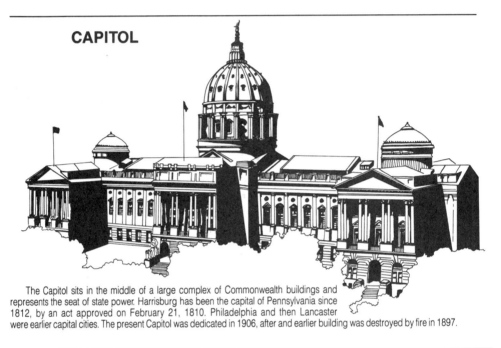

The Capitol sits in the middle of a large complex of Commonwealth buildings and represents the seat of state power. Harrisburg has been the capital of Pennsylvania since 1812, by an act approved on February 21, 1810. Philadelphia and then Lancaster were earlier capital cities. The present Capitol was dedicated in 1906, after and earlier building was destroyed by fire in 1897.

GOVERNOR'S RESIDENCE

Built in 1968, the Governor's Residence is the home of Pennsylvania's first family. Extensively damaged during a flood in 1972, the building and grounds have been restored and refurbished.

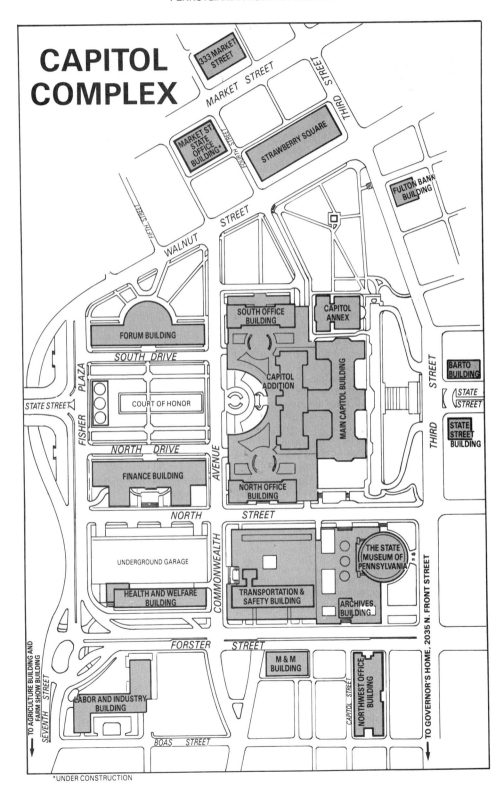

CAPITOL COMPLEX

333 MARKET STREET

MARKET STREET

MARKET ST STATE OFFICE BUILDING*

STRAWBERRY SQUARE

THIRD STREET

FOURTH STREET

FULTON BANK BUILDING

FIFTH STREET

WALNUT STREET

FORUM BUILDING

SOUTH OFFICE BUILDING

CAPITOL ANNEX

PLAZA

SOUTH DRIVE

FISHER

COURT OF HONOR

CAPITOL ADDITION

MAIN CAPITOL BUILDING

THIRD STREET

BARTO BUILDING

STATE STREET

STATE STREET BUILDING

STATE STREET

NORTH DRIVE

FINANCE BUILDING

AVENUE

NORTH OFFICE BUILDING

NORTH STREET

UNDERGROUND GARAGE

COMMONWEALTH

THE STATE MUSEUM OF PENNSYLVANIA

HEALTH AND WELFARE BUILDING

TRANSPORTATION & SAFETY BUILDING

ARCHIVES BUILDING

FORSTER STREET

M & M BUILDING

CAPITOL STREET

NORTHWEST OFFICE BUILDING

TO AGRICULTURE BUILDING AND FARM SHOW BUILDING

SEVENTH STREET

LABOR AND INDUSTRY BUILDING

TO GOVERNOR'S HOME, 2035 N. FRONT STREET

BOAS STREET

*UNDER CONSTRUCTION

PENNSYLVANIA HISTORY

PENNSYLVANIA ON THE EVE OF COLONIZATION

Indians: The First Inhabitants.

When first discovered by Europeans, Pennsylvania, like the rest of the continent, was inhabited by groups of American Indians, people of Mongoloid ancestry unaware of European culture. The life of the Indians reflected Stone Age backgrounds, especially in material arts and crafts. Tools, weapons, and household equipment were made from stone, wood, and bark. Transportation was on foot or by canoe. Houses were made of bark, clothing from the skins of animals. The rudiments of a more complex civilization were at hand in the arts of weaving, pottery, and agriculture, although hunting and food gathering prevailed. Some Indians formed confederacies such as the league of the Five Nations, which was made up of certain New York-Pennsylvania groups of Iroquoian speech. The other large linguistic group in Pennsylvania was the Algonkian, represented by the Delawares, Shawnees, and other tribes.

The Delawares, calling themselves Leni-Lenape or "real men," originally occupied the basin of the Delaware River and were the most important of several tribes that spoke an Algonkian language. Under the pressure of white settlement, they began to drift westward to the Wyoming Valley, to the Allegheny and, finally, to eastern Ohio. Many of them took the French side in the French and Indian War, joined in Pontiac's War, and fought on the British side in the Revolutionary War. Afterwards, some fled to Ontario and the rest wandered west. Their descendants now live on reservations in Oklahoma and Ontario. The Munsees were a division of the Delawares who lived on the upper Delaware River, above the Lehigh River.

The Susquehannocks were a powerful Iroquoian-speaking tribe who lived along the Susquehanna in Pennsylvania and Maryland. An energetic people living in Algonkian-speaking tribes' territory, they engaged in many wars. In the end they fell victim to new diseases brought by European settlers, and to attacks by Marylanders and by the Iroquois which destroyed them as a nation by 1675. A few descendants were among the Conestoga Indians who were massacred in 1763 in Lancaster County.

The Shawnees were an important Algonkian-speaking tribe who came to Pennsylvania from the west in the 1690s, some groups settling on the lower Susquehanna and others with the Munsees near Easton. In the course of time they moved to the Wyoming Valley and the Ohio Valley, where they joined other Shawnees who had gone there directly. They were allies of the French in the French and Indian War and of the British in the Revolution, being almost constantly at war with settlers for forty years preceding the Treaty of Greenville in 1795. After Wayne's victory at Fallen Timbers (1794), they settled near the Delawares in Indiana, and their descendants now live in Oklahoma.

The Iroquois Confederacy of Iroquoian-speaking tribes, at first known as the Five Nations, included the Mohawks, Oneidas, Onondagas, Cayugas and Senecas. After about 1723 when the Tuscaroras from the South were admitted to the confederacy, it was called the Six Nations. The five original tribes, when first known to Europeans, held much of New York State from Lake Champlain to the Genesee River. From this central position they gradually extended their power. As middlemen in the fur trade with the western Indians, as intermediaries skilled in dealing with the whites, and as the largest single group of Indians in northeastern America, they gained influence over Indian tribes from Illinois and Lake Michigan to the eastern seaboard. During the colonial wars their alliance or their neutrality was eagerly sought by both the French and the British. The Senecas, the westernmost tribe, established villages on the upper Allegheny in the 1730s. Small groups of Iroquois also scattered westward into Ohio, and became known as Mingoes. During the Revolution most of the Six Nations took the British side, but the Oneidas and many Tuscaroras were pro-American. Gen. John Sullivan's expedition up the Susquehanna River and Gen. Daniel Brodhead's expedition up the Allegheny River laid waste their villages and cornfields in 1779 and disrupted their society. Those who were most pro-British moved to Canada after the Revolution, but the rest worked out peaceful relations with the United States under the leadership of such chiefs as Cornplanter. The General Assembly recognized this noted chief by granting him a tract of land on the upper Allegheny in 1791.

Other Tribes which cannot be identified with certainty occupied western Pennsylvania before the Europeans arrived, but were eliminated by wars and diseases in the seventeenth century, long before the Delawares, Shawnees, and Senecas began to move there. The Eries, a great Iroquoian-speaking tribe, lived along the south shore of Lake Erie, but were wiped out by the Iroquois about 1654. The Mahicans, an Algonkian-speaking tribe related to the Mohegans of Connecticut, lived in the upper Hudson Valley of New York, but were driven out by pressure from the Iroquois and from the white settlers, some joining the Delawares in the Wyoming Valley about 1730 and some settling at Stockbridge, Massachusetts. Two Algonkian-speaking tribes, the Conoys and the Nanticokes, moved northward from Maryland early in the eighteenth century, settling in southern New York, and eventually moved west with the Delawares with whom they merged. The Saponis, Siouan-speaking tribes from Virginia and North Carolina, moved northward to seek Iroquois protection and were eventually absorbed into the Cayugas. In the latter part of the eighteenth century there were temporary villages of Wyandots, Chippewas, Missisaugas, and Ottawas in western Pennsylvania.

European Background and Early Settlements

The rise of nation-states in Europe coincided with the age of discovery and brought a desire for territorial gains beyond the seas, first by Spain and Portugal, and later by England, France, the Netherlands, and Sweden. Wars in southern Germany caused many Germans to migrate, eventually to Pennsylvania. The struggle in England between the Crown and Parliament also had a pronounced effect on migration to America. The Reformation led to religious ferment and division, and minorities of various faiths sought refuge in America. Such an impulse brought Quakers, Puritans, and Catholics from England, German Pietists from the Rhineland, Scotch Calvinists via Ireland, and Huguenots from France. Also, great economic changes took place in Europe in the seventeenth century. The old manorial system was breaking down, creating a large class of landless men ready to seek new homes. An increase in commerce and trade led to an accumulation of capital available for colonial ventures. The Swedish and Dutch colonies were financed in this way, and William Penn's colony was also a business enterprise.

Exploration

The English based their claims in North America on the discoveries of the Cabots (1497), while the French pointed to the voyage of Verrazano in 1524. The Spanish claim was founded on Columbus' discovery of the West Indies, but there is evidence that Spanish ships sailed up the coast of North America as early as 1520. It is uncertain, however, that any of these explorers touched land that became Pennsylvania. Captain John Smith journeyed from Virginia up the Susquehanna River in 1608, visiting the Susquehannock Indians. In 1609 Henry Hudson, an Englishman in the Dutch service, sailed the *Half Moon* into Delaware Bay, thus giving the Dutch a claim to the area. In 1610 Captain Samuel Argall of Virginia visited the bay and named it for Lord de la Warr, governor of Virginia. After Hudson's time, the Dutch navigators Cornelis Hendricksen (1616) and Cornelis Jacobsen (1623) explored the Delaware region more thoroughly, and trading posts were established in 1623 and in later years, though not on Pennsylvania soil until 1647.

The Colony of New Sweden, 1638-1655

The Swedes were the first to make permanent settlement, beginning with the expedition of 1637-1638 which occupied the site of Wilmington, Delaware. In 1643 Governor Johan Printz of New Sweden established his capital at Tinicum Island within the present limits of Pennsylvania, where there is now a state park bearing his name.

Dutch Dominion on the Delaware, 1655-1664, and the Duke of York's Rule, 1664-1681

Trouble broke out between the Swedes and the Dutch, who had trading posts in the region. In 1655 Governor Peter Stuyvesant of New Netherlands seized New Sweden and made it part of the Dutch colony. In 1664 the English seized the Dutch possessions in the name of the Duke of York, the king's brother. Except when it was recaptured by the Dutch in 1673-1674, the Delaware region remained under his jurisdiction until 1681. English laws and civil government were introduced by *The Duke of Yorke's Laws* in 1676.

THE QUAKER PROVINCE: 1681-1776

The Founding of Pennsylvania

William Penn and the Quakers

Penn was born in London on October 24, 1644, the son of Admiral Sir William Penn. With high social position and an excellent education, he shocked his upper-class associates by his conversion to the beliefs of the Society of Friends, or Quakers, then a persecuted sect. He used his inherited wealth and rank to benefit and protect his fellow believers. Despite the unpopularity of his religion, he was socially acceptable in the king's court because he was trusted by the Duke of York, later King James II. The origins of the Society of Friends lie in the intense religious ferment of seventeenth-century England. George Fox, the son of a Leicestershire weaver, is credited with founding it in 1647, though there was no definite organization before 1668. The Society's rejections of rituals and oaths, its opposition to war, and its simplicity of speech and dress soon attracted attention, usually hostile.

The Charter

King Charles II owed William Penn 16,000 pounds, money which Admiral Penn had lent him. Seeking a haven in the New World for persecuted Friends, Penn asked the King to grant him land in the territory between Lord Baltimore's province of Maryland and the Duke of York's province of New York. With the Duke's support, Penn's petition was granted. The King signed the Charter of Pennsylvania on March 4, 1681, and it was officially proclaimed on April 2. The King named the new colony in honor of William Penn's father. It was to include the land between the 39th and 42nd degrees of north latitude and from the Delaware River westward for five degrees of longitude. Other provisions assured its people the protection of English laws, and kept it subject to the government in England to a certain degree. Provincial laws could be annulled by the King. In 1682 the Duke of York deeded to Penn his claim to the three lower counties on the Delaware, which are now the State of Delaware.

The New Colony

In April 1681, Penn made his cousin William Markham deputy governor of the province and sent him to take control. In England Penn drew up the *First Frame of Government,* his proposed constitution for Pennsylvania. Penn's preface to *First Frame of Government* has become famous as the summation of his governmental ideals. Later, in October 1682, the Proprietor arrived in Pennsylvania on the ship *Welcome*. He visited Philadelphia, just laid out as the capital city, created the three originial counties, and summoned a General Assembly to Chester on December 4. This first Assembly united the Delaware counties with Pennsylvania, adopted a naturalization act and, on December 7, adopted the *Great Law*, a humanitarian code which became the fundamental basis of Pennsylvania law, and which guaranteed liberty of conscience. The second Assembly in 1683 reviewed and amended Penn's *First Frame* with his cooperation and created the *Second Frame of Government*. By the time of Penn's return to England late in 1684, the foundations of the Quaker Province were well established.

In 1986 William Penn and his wife, Hannah Callowhill Penn, were made the third and fourth honorary citizens of the United States, by act of Congress.

Population and Immigration

Indians
Although William Penn was granted all the land in Pennsylvania by the King, he and his heirs chose not to grant or settle any part of it without first buying the claims of Indians who lived there. In this manner, all of Pennsylvania, except the northwestern third, was purchased by 1768. The Commonwealth bought the Six Nations' claims to the remainder of the land in 1784 and 1789, and the claims of the Delawares and Wyandots in 1785. The defeat of the French and Indian war alliance by 1760, the withdrawal of the French, the crushing of Chief Pontiac's Indian alliance in 1764, and the failure of all attempts by Indians and colonists to live side by side, led the Indians to migrate westward, gradually leaving Pennsylvania.

English
English Quakers were the dominant element, although many English settlers were Anglican. The English settled heavily in the southeastern counties, which soon lost frontier characteristics and became the center of a thriving agricultural and commercial society. Philadelphia became the metropolis of the British colonies and a center of intellectual and commercial life.

Germans
Thousands of Germans were also attracted to the colony and, by the time of the Revolution, comprised a third of the population. The volume of German immigration increased after 1727, coming largely from the Rhineland. The Pennsylvania Germans settled most heavily in the interior counties of Northampton, Berks, Lancaster, and Lehigh, and neighboring areas. Their skill and industry transformed this region into a rich farming country, contributing greatly to the expanding prosperity of the province.

Scotch-Irish
Another important immigrant group was the Scotch-Irish, who migrated from about 1717 until the Revolution in a series of waves caused by hardships in Ireland. They were primarily frontiersmen, pushing first into the Cumberland Valley region and then farther into central and western Pennsylvania. They, with immigrants from old Scotland, numbered about one-fourth of the population by 1776.

Blacks
Despite Quaker opposition to slavery, about 4,000 slaves were brought to Pennsylvania by 1730, most of them owned by English, Welsh, and Scotch-Irish colonists. The census of 1790 showed that the number of Blacks had increased to about 10,000, of whom about 6,300 had received their freedom.

Others
Many Quakers were Irish and Welsh, and they settled in the area immediately outside of Philadelphia. French Huguenot and Jewish settlers, together with Dutch, Swedes, and other groups, contributed in smaller numbers to the development of colonial Pennsylvania. The mixture of various national groups in the Quaker Province helped to create its broad-minded tolerance and cosmopolitan outlook.

Politics
Pennsylvania's political history ran a rocky course during the provincial era. There was a natural conflict between the proprietary and popular elements in the government which began under Penn and grew stronger under his successors. As a result of the English Revolution of 1688 which overthrew King James II, Penn was deprived of his province from 1692 until 1694. A popular party led by David Lloyd demanded greater powers for the Assembly, and in 1696 *Markham's Frame of Government* granted some of these. In December 1699, the Proprietor again visited Pennsylvania and, just before his return to England in 1701, agreed with the Assembly on a revised constitution, the *Charter of Privileges,* which remained in effect until 1776. This gave the Assembly full legislative powers and permitted the three Delaware counties to have a separate legislature.

Deputy or lieutenant governors (addressed as "governor") resided in Pennsylvania and represented the Penn family proprietors who remained themselves in England until 1773. After 1763 these governors were members of the Penn family. From 1773 until independence John Penn was both a proprietor and the governor.

William Penn's heirs, who eventually abandoned Quakerism, were often in conflict with the Assembly, which was usually dominated by the Quakers until 1756. One after another, governors defending the proprietors' prerogatives wore themselves out on the rock of an Assembly vigilant in the defense of its rights. The people of the frontier areas contended with the people of the older, southeastern region for more adequate representation in the Assembly and better protection in time of war. Such controversies were preparing the people for their part in the Revolution.

The Colonial Wars

As part of the British Empire, Pennsylvania was involved in the wars between Great Britain and France for dominance in North America. These wars ended the long period when Pennsylvania was virtually without defense. The government built forts and furnished men and supplies to help defend the empire of which it was part. The territory claimed for New France included western Pennsylvania. The Longueuil and Celoron expeditions of the French in 1739 and 1749 traversed this region, and French traders competed with Pennsylvanians for Indian trade. The French efforts in 1753 and 1754 to establish control over the upper Ohio Valley led to the last and conclusive colonial war, the French and Indian War (1754-1763). French forts at Erie (Fort Presque Isle), Waterford (Fort LeBoeuf), Pittsburgh (Fort Duquesne) and Franklin (Fort Machault) threatened all the middle colonies. In 1753 Washington failed to persuade the French to leave. In the ensuing war Gen. Braddock's British and colonial army was slaughtered on the Monongahela in 1755, but Gen. John Forbes recaptured the site of Pittsburgh in 1758. After the war, the Indians rose up against the British colonies in Pontiac's War, but in August 1763, Colonel Henry Bouquet defeated them at Bushy Run, ending a threat to the frontier in this region.

Economics

Agriculture

From its beginning Pennsylvania ranked as a leading agricultural area and produced surpluses for export, adding to its wealth. By the 1750s an exceptionally prosperous farming area had developed in southeastern Pennsylvania. Wheat and corn were the leading crops, though rye, hemp, and flax were also important.

Manufacturing

The abundant natural resources of the colony made for early development of industries. Arts and crafts, as well as home manufactures, grew rapidly. Sawmills and gristmills were usually the first to appear, using the power of the numerous streams. Textile products were spun and woven mainly in the homes, though factory production was not unknown. Shipbuilding became important on the Delaware. The province early gained importance in iron manufacture, producing pig iron as well as finished products. Printing, publishing and the related industry of papermaking, as well as tanning, were significant industries.

Commerce and Transportation

The rivers were important as early arteries of commerce, and were soon supplemented by roads in the southeastern area. The Conestoga wagon, developed in Pennsylvania for land travel, played an important part in expansion to the West. Stagecoach lines by 1776 reached from Philadelphia into the southcentral region. Trade with the Indians for furs was important in the early period. Later, the transport and sale of farm products to Philadelphia and Baltimore by water and road formed an important business. Philadelphia became one of the most important centers in the colonies for the conduct of foreign trade, and the commercial metropolis of an expanding hinterland. By 1776 the province's imports and exports were worth several million dollars.

Society and Culture

The Arts and Learning

Philadelphia was known in colonial times as the "Athens of America" because of its rich cultural and intellectual life. By 1750 it had become the intellectual capital of America. Because of the liberality of Penn's principles and the freedom of expression that prevailed, the province was noted for the variety and strength of its intellectual and educational institutions and interests. An academy which held its first classes in 1740 became the College of Philadelphia in 1755, and ultimately grew into the University of Pennsylvania. It was the only nondenominational college of the colonial period. The arts and sciences flourished, and the public buildings of Philadelphia were the marvel of the colonies. Many fine old buildings in the Philadelphia area still bear witness to the richness of Pennsylvania's civilization in the eighteenth century. Such men of intellect as Benjamin Franklin, David Rittenhouse, John Bartram and Benjamin West achieved international renown. Newspapers and magazines flourished, as did law and medicine. Pennsylvania can claim America's first hospital, first library, and first insurance company.

Religion

Quakers held their first meeting at Upland (now Chester) in 1675, and came to Pennsylvania in great numbers after William Penn received his Charter. Most numerous in the southeastern counties, the Quakers gradually declined in number but retained considerable influence. The Pennsylvania Germans belonged largely to the Lutheran and Reformed churches, but there were also several smaller sects: Mennonites, Amish, German Baptist Brethren or "Dunkers," Schwenkfelders, and Moravians. Although the Lutheran Church was established by the Swedes on Tinicum Island in 1643, it began its growth to become the largest of the Protestant denominations in

Pennsylvania upon the arrival of Henry Melchior Muhlenberg in 1742. The Reformed Church owed its expansion to Michael Schlatter, who arrived in 1746. The Moravians did notable missionary work among the Indians. The Church of England held services in Philadelphia as early as 1695. The first Catholic congregation was organized in Philadelphia in 1720 and the first chapel was erected in 1733; Pennsylvania had the second largest Catholic population among the colonies. The Scotch brought Presbyterianism; its first congregation was organized in Philadelphia in 1698. Scotch-Irish immigrants swelled its numbers. Methodism began late in the colonial period. St. George's Church built in Philadelphia in 1769, is the oldest Methodist building in America. There was a significant Jewish population in colonial Pennsylvania. Its Mikveh Israel congregation was established in Philadelphia in 1740.

Pennsylvania on the Eve of the Revolution

By 1776 the Province of Pennsylvania had become the third largest English colony in America, though next to the last to be founded. Philadelphia had become the largest English-speaking city in the world next to London. There were originally three counties: Philadelphia, Chester, and Bucks. By 1773 there were eleven, with the creation of Westmoreland west of the Alleghenies. Settlement had moved far to the west.

The American Revolution had urban origins, and Philadelphia was a center of ferment. Groups of artisans and mechanics, many loyal to Benjamin Franklin, formed grassroots leadership. Philadelphia was a center of resistance to the Stamp Act (1765) and moved quickly to support Boston against the impact of the Intolerable Acts, in 1774.

INDEPENDENCE TO THE CIVIL WAR: 1776-1861

Pennsylvania in the Revolution

Pennsylvanians may well take pride in the dominant role played by their state in the early development of the national government. At the same time that Pennsylvania was molding its own statehood, it was providing leadership and a meeting place for the men concerned with building a nation.

Philadelphia was the nation's capital during the Revolution, except when the British threat caused the capital to be moved to Baltimore, Lancaster, and York. While Congress was sitting in York (October 1777 - June 1778), it approved the Articles of Confederation, the first step toward a national government. After the war the capital was moved to New York, but from 1790 until the opening of the District of Columbia in 1800, Philadelphia was again the capital. In 1787 the U.S. Constitutional Convention met in Philadelphia.

The Declaration of Independence

The movement to defend American rights grew into the movement for independence in the meetings of the Continental Congress at Carpenters' Hall and the State House (Independence Hall) in Philadelphia. The spirit of independence ran high, as shown by spontaneous declarations of frontiersmen in the western areas, and by the political events which displaced the old provincial government.

The War for Independence

Pennsylvania troops took part in almost all the campaigns of the Revolution. A rifle battalion joined in the siege of Boston in August 1775. Others fought bravely in the ill-fated Canadian campaign of 1776 and in the New York and New Jersey campaigns. The British naturally considered Philadelphia of key importance and, in the summer of 1777, invaded the state and captured the capital. The battles of Brandywine, Germantown, and Whitemarsh were important engagements of this period. Following these battles, Washington went into winter quarters at Valley Forge from December 1777 to June 1778. News of the French alliance, which Benjamin Franklin had helped to negotiate, and the adoption of new strategy caused the British to leave Philadelphia in the spring of 1778. Frontier Pennsylvania suffered heavily from British and Indian raids, until they were answered in 1779 by John Sullivan's and David Brodhead's expeditions against the Six Nations Indians.

Pennsylvania soldiers formed a major portion of Washington's army, and such military leaders as Arthur St. Clair, Anthony Wayne, and Daniel Brodhead gave valuable service. Pennsylvania also aided in the creation of the Continental navy, many ships being built or purchased in Philadelphia and manned by Pennsylvania sailors. The Irish-born John Barry became first in a long list of Pennsylvania's naval heroes.

The Arsenal of Independence

The products of Pennsylvania farms, factories, and mines were essential to the success of the Revolutionary armies. At Carlisle a Continental ordnance arsenal turned out cannons, swords, pikes, and muskets. The state actively encouraged the manufacture of gunpowder. Pennsylvania's financial support, both from its government and from individuals, was of great importance. By 1780 the state had contributed more than $6 million to the Congress and, when the

American states had reached financial exhaustion, 90 Philadelphians subscribed a loan of 300,000 pounds to supply the army. Later, in 1782, the Bank of North America was chartered to support government fiscal needs. Robert Morris and Haym Salomon were important financial supporters of the Revolution.

Founding a Commonwealth

A Pennsylvania Revolution
Pennsylvania's part in the American Revolution was complicated by political changes within the state, constituting a Pennsylvania revolution of which not all patriots approved. The temper of the people outran the conservatism of the Provincial Assembly. Extralegal committees gradually took over the reins of government, and in June 1776 these committees called a state convention to meet on July 15, 1776.

The Constitution of 1776
The convention superseded the old government completely, established a Council of Safety to rule in the interim, and drew up the first state constitution, adopted on September 28, 1776. This provided an assembly of one house, and a supreme executive council instead of a governor. The Declaration of Rights section has been copied in subsequent constitutions without significant change.

Many patriot leaders were bitterly opposed to the new Pennsylvania constitution. Led by such men as John Dickinson, James Wilson, Robert Morris, and Frederick Muhlenberg, they carried on a long fight with the Constitutional party, a radical group. Joseph Reed, George Bryan, William Findley, and other radicals governed Pennsylvania until 1790. Its most noteworthy accomplishments were the act for the gradual abolition of slavery (1780) and an act of 1779 which took over the public lands owned by the Penn family (but allowed them some compensation in recognition of the services of the founder). The conservatives gradually gained more strength, helped by the Constitutionalists' poor financial administration.

The Constitution of 1790
By 1789 the conservatives felt strong enough to rewrite the state constitution, and the Assembly called a convention to meet in November. In the convention both the conservative majority and the radical minority showed a tendency to compromise and to settle their differences along moderate lines. As a result, the new constitution embodied the best ideas of both parties and was adopted with little objection. It provided for a second legislative house, the State Senate, and for a strong governor with extensive appointing powers.

Founding a Nation

Pennsylvania and the United States Constitution
Because of a lack of central power, as well as financial difficulties, the Articles of Confederation could no longer bind together the newly independent states. As a result, the Federal Constitutional Convention met in Philadelphia in 1787. The structure that evolved remains the basis of our government today.

The Pennsylvania Assembly sent eight delegates to the Federal Convention. Four of these had been signers of the Declaration of Independence. The delegation included the venerable Benjamin Franklin, whose counsels of moderation on several occasions kept the convention from dissolving; the brilliant Gouverneur Morris, who spoke more often than any other member; and the able lawyer James Wilson, who, next to Madison of Virginia, was the principal architect of the Constitution. Pennsylvania's delegation supported every move to strengthen the national government and signed the finished Constitution on September 17. The conservatives in the Pennsylvania Assembly took swift action to call a ratifying convention, which met in Philadelphia on November 21. The Federalists, favoring ratification, elected a majority of delegates and, led by Wilson, made Pennsylvania the second state to ratify, on December 12, 1787.

Population and Immigration

Large areas of the northern and western parts of the state were undistributed or undeveloped in 1790, and many other sections were thinly populated. The state adopted generous land policies, distributed free "Donation Lands" to Revolutionary veterans and offered other lands at reasonable prices to actual settlers. Conflicting methods of land distribution and the activities of land companies and of unduly optimistic speculators caused much legal confusion. By 1860, with the possible exception of the northern tier counties, population was scattered throughout the state. There was increased urbanization, although rural life remained strong and agriculture involved large numbers of people. The immigrant tide swelled because of large numbers of Irish fleeing the potato famine of the late 1840s, and Germans fleeing the political turbulence of their homeland about the same time. As a result of the Gradual Emancipation Act of 1780, the 3,737 Black slave population of 1790 dropped to 64 by 1840, and by 1850 all Pennsylvania blacks were free unless they were fugitives from the South. The Black community had 6,500 free people in 1790, rising to 57,000 in 1860. Philadelphia was their population and cultural center.

Political Developments

Reaction Against the Federalist Party

From 1790 to 1800 Philadelphia was the capital of the United States. While Washington was president, the state supported the Federalist Party, but grew gradually suspicious of its aristocratic goals. From the beginning, Senator William Maclay of Pennsylvania was an outspoken critic of the party. When Thomas Jefferson organized the Democrat-Republican Party, he had many supporters in Pennsylvania. Thomas Mifflin, Pennsylvania's first governor under the Constitution of 1790, was a moderate who avoided commitment to any party, but leaned toward the Jeffersonians. The so-called Whiskey Rebellion in Western Pennsylvania in 1794 hastened the reaction against the Federalists, as well as provided a test of national unity. The insurrection was suppressed by an army assembled at Carlisle and Fort Cumberland and headed by President Washington. Partly as a result, Jefferson drew more votes than Adams in Pennsylvania in the presidential election in 1796. It was a foreboding sign for the Federalists, who were defeated in the national election of 1800.

Democrat Dominance: The Keystone State Slogan

In 1799 Mifflin was succeeded by Thomas McKean, a conservative Democrat-Republican, who served until 1808. In 1803, boasting of their voting strength, the Jeffersonians—whose formal party name was "Republicans," but were popularly termed Democrats—published an essay in the *Aurora* of Philadelphia saying that Pennsylvania was the Keystone in the Democratic arch.

McKean's opposition to measures advocated by the liberal element in his party led to a split in its ranks and even an attempt to impeach him. His successor, Simon Snyder of Selinsgrove, represented the liberal wing. Snyder, who served three terms until 1817, was the first governor to come from common, nonaristocratic origins. In this period, the capital was transferred from Philadelphia to Lancaster in 1799 and finally to Harrisburg in 1812. During the War of 1812 Pennsylvanians General Jacob Brown and Commodore Stephen Decatur were major military leaders. Stephen Girard, Albert Gallatin, and Alexander James Dallas helped organize national war finances, and Gallatin served as peace commissioner at Ghent. Oliver Hazard Perry's fleet, which won the Battle of Lake Erie in 1813, was built at Erie by Daniel Dobbins, a native Pennsylvanian. The trend toward more popular government continued under Governor William Findlay from 1817 to 1820. In 1820 a coalition of Federalists and conservative Democrats elected Joseph Hiester. The conservatives lost strength and, in 1823, the regular Democrat candidate, J. Andrew Shulze, won overwhelmingly. His successor, George Wolf, also a Democrat, signed the Free School Act of 1834, which reflected the democratic trend. In 1835, a coalition of opposing factions elected Joseph Ritner, a member of the Antimasonic Party, because there had been another split in the majority party, the Democrats.

The Constitution of 1838

In 1837 a convention was called to revise the state's laws and draft a new constitution. The resulting constitution reduced the governor's appointive power, increased the number of elective offices and shortened terms of office. The voters were given a greater voice in government and were better protected from abuses of power. However, free blacks were disenfranchised. The burning of Pennsylvania Hall in Philadelphia, a center for many reform activities, in the same year, showed that the new constitution coincided with an awakened hostility toward abolition and racial equality.

The annexation of Texas and the war with Mexico which ensued in 1846 were generally supported in Pennsylvania. More men enlisted than could be accepted by the armed forces, but many Pennsylvanians were opposed to any expansion of slavery into the territory taken from Mexico. David Wilmot of Bradford County became a national figure in 1846 by his presentation in Congress of the Wilmot Proviso opposing slavery extension, and his action was supported almost unanimously by the Pennsylvania Assembly.

Shifting Tides

Following the adoption of the new constitution in 1838, six governors followed in succession, two of whom were Whigs. President Andrew Jackson's struggle with the Bank of the United States had a special impact on Pennsylvania, where the Bank was located. State debts which were incurred for internal improvements, such as the canal system, also caused much controversy.

Pennsylvania and the Antislavery Movement

The Quakers were the first group to express organized opposition to slavery. It slowly disappeared in Pennsylvania under the Gradual Emancipation Act of 1780, but nationally the issue of slavery became acute after 1820. Many Pennsylvanians were averse to the return of fugitive slaves to their masters. Under an act of 1826 which was passed to restrain this, a Maryland agent was convicted of kidnapping in 1837, but the United States Supreme Court declared the act unconstitutional in 1842. The state forbade the use of its jails to detain fugitive blacks in 1847. The expression "underground railroad" may have originated in Pennsylvania where numerous citizens aided the escape of slaves to freedom in Canada. Anna Dickinson, Lucretia Mott, Ann Preston, and Jane Swisshelm were among Pennsylvania women who led the antislavery cause. Thaddeus Stevens was an uncompromising foe of slavery in Congress.

Pennsylvania abolitionist leaders were both black and white. Black leaders included those who made political appeals, James Forten and Robert Purvis; underground railroad workers, Robert Porter and William Still; publication activists, John B. Vashon and his son George; and the organizer of the Christiana Riot of 1851 against fugitive slave hunters, William Parker.

Blacks made some cultural advances during this period. William Whipper organized reading rooms in Philadelphia. In 1794 Rev. Absolam Jones founded St. Thomas African Episcopal Church, and Rev. Richard Allen opened the Mother Bethel African Methodist Episcopal Church, both in Philadelphia. The first Black church in Pittsburgh (A.M.E.) was founded in 1822.

Women
Courageous individual women worked not only for their own cause, but also for other reforms. But the status of the whole female population changed little during this period. Catherine Smith, for example, manufactured musket barrels for the Revolutionary Army, and the mythical battle heroine Molly Pitcher was probably also a Pennsylvanian. Sara Franklin Bache and Ester De Berdt Reed organized a group of 2,200 Pennsylvania women to collect money, buy cloth, and sew clothing for Revolutionary soldiers. Lucretia Mott, a Quaker preacher and teacher, was one of four women to participate at the formation of the American Anti-Slavery Society in Philadelphia in 1833, and became president of the Female Anti-Slavery Society. With Elizabeth Cady Stanton she launched the campaign for women's rights at Seneca Falls, New York, in 1848. Jane Grey Swisshelm, abolitionist and advocate of women's rights, used newspapers and lectures. In 1848, she launched her abolitionist paper, *The Saturday Visiter,* which featured antislavery propaganda and women's rights. Her essays influenced the state legislature to grant married women the right to own property, in 1848.

Disruption of the Democracy
The political winds began to shift due to the Southern domination of the Democratic Party, rising abolition sentiment and a desire to promote Pennsylvania's growing industries by raising tariffs. In 1856 Pennsylvania took the lead in the organization of the new Republican Party, with former Democratic leader Simon Cameron throwing his support to the new party. Congressmen David Wilmot and Galusha Grow typified the national statesmanship of Pennsylvania in the period. Despite the new party's emergence in 1856, the Democratic candidate James Buchanan became the only native Pennsylvanian ever to be elected President. In 1860 the Republicans emerged as the dominant party in the state and nation with the election of Governor Andrew Gregg Curtin, and of President Abraham Lincoln.

Industry

By 1861 the factory system had largely replaced the domestic system of home manufacture, and the foundation of the state's industrial greatness was established. The change was most noticeable after 1840, because of a shift to machinery and factories in the textile industry. By 1860 there were more than 200 textile mills. Leathermaking, lumbering, shipbuilding, publishing, and tobacco and paper manufacture also prospered in the 1800s.

Pennsylvania's outstanding industrial achievements were in iron and steel. Its production of iron was notable even in colonial times, and the charcoal furnaces of the state spread into the Juniata and western regions during the mid-1800s. Foundries, rolling mills, and machine shops became numerous and, by the Civil War, the state rolled about half the nation's iron, aiding the development of the railroads. The Baldwin Works were established in Philadelphia in 1842 and the Bethlehem Company was organized in 1862. The Cambria Works at Johnstown were established in 1854 and, by the end of the Civil War, were the largest mills in the country. William Kelly, a native of Pittsburgh, is regarded as the inventor of the Bessemer process of making steel.

Although much importance is given to the discovery of gold in California, the discovery and development of Pennsylvania's mineral and energy resources far overshadowed that event. Cornwall, in Lebanon County, provided iron ore from colonial times, and ore was also found in many other sections of Pennsylvania in which the charcoal iron industry flourished. The use of anthracite coal began on a large scale after 1820 with the organization of important mining companies.

Labor
After the Revolution the use of indentured servants sharply declined. The growth of industrial factories up to 1860, however, enlarged the gulf between skilled and unskilled labor, and immigrants were as much subordinated by this as they had been under indenture. Local, specialized labor unions had brief successes, especially in Philadelphia where in 1845 a city ordinance placed a ten-hour limit on the laborer's day. The state's mechanics' lien law of 1854 was another victory for the rights of labor.

Transportation

Roads
The settlement of new regions of the state was accompanied by provisions for new roads. The original Lancaster Pike connecting Philadelphia with Lancaster was completed in 1794. U.S. Route 40, which passes through Somerset, Fayette, and Washington counties, was built between 1811 and 1818. In addition, between 1790 and 1840, private companies built many turnpikes for which they collected tolls. By 1832 the state led the nation in improved roads, having more than 3,000 miles. Pennsylvania's Conestoga wagon became the typical transport of westward moving pioneers, and U.S. Route 40 — the National or Cumberland Road — was a major route for western movement before 1850.

Waterways

Most of the state's major cities were built along important river routes. In the 1790s the state made extensive studies for improving the navigation of all major streams, and canals began to supplement natural waterways. Canals extending the use of the Delaware and the Schuylkill rivers were chartered before 1815, and the Lehigh canal was completed in 1838. The vast system named the State Works of Pennsylvania soon overshadowed privately constructed canals. The system linked the east and the west by 1834, but the expense nearly made the state financially insolvent. The benefits to the economic progress of distant regions, however, provided ample justification for the high cost.

Although canals declined rapidly with the advent of the railroad, Pennsylvania's ports and waterways remained active. The steamboat originated with experiments by John Fitch of Philadelphia from 1787 to 1790, and Lancaster County native Robert Fulton established it as a practical medium of transportation on the Ohio, Allegheny, and Monongahela rivers.

Railroads

Railroads, first built in 1827, operated at first by horsepower or cables and connected anthracite fields with canals or rivers. The Columbia and Philadelphia Railroad, completed in 1834 as part of the State Works, was the world's first to be built by a government. Pennsylvania's first railroad built as a common carrier was the Philadelphia, Germantown, and Norristown Railroad, completed in 1835.

Major railroads chartered in the state included the Philadelphia and Reading (1833) and the Lehigh Valley (1846, reincorporated 1853). However, the most important of all was the Pennsylvania Railroad, chartered April 13, 1846, and completed to Pittsburgh by 1852. It absorbed so many short railroad lines by 1860 that it had a near-monopoly of rail traffic through Pennsylvania from Chicago. And whereas Pennsylvania had reached its maximum of 954 canal miles by 1840, total railroad trackage had already grown by 1860 to 2,598 miles. In this, as in the capital invested in railroads, Pennsylvania led all other states on the eve of the Civil War.

Culture

Education

The Constitution of 1790 provided the basis for a public system of education, and several acts were passed in accordance with it. It was not until the Free School Act of 1834, however, that a genuinely democratic system of public schools was initiated. By 1865 the number of public schools had quadrupled. In 1852 a state association of teachers was organized. Five years later the Normal School Act was passed and a separate government department was created for the supervision of schools. These were significant advances in social progress. Numerous private schools supplemented the public system. There also was a rapid development of academies, corresponding to modern high schools. Many academies received public aid.

Science

The traditions of scientific inquiry established in Pennsylvania by Franklin, Rittenhouse, and Bartram continued. The American Philosophical Society was the first of many organizations founded in Philadelphia to encourage scientific work. The Academy of Natural Sciences was founded in 1812 and the Franklin Institute in 1824. The American Association of Geologists, formed in Philadelphia in 1840, later grew into the American Association for the Advancement of Science. The scientific leadership of Pennsylvania was represented by many individuals of whom only a few can be named. James Woodhouse (1770-1809) pioneered in chemical analysis, plant chemistry, and the scientific study of industrial processes. Isaac Hayes (1796-1879) of Philadelphia pioneered in the study of astigmatism and color blindness. The Moravian clergyman Lewis David von Schweinitz (1780-1834) made great contributions to botany, discovering more than 1,200 species of fungi.

Literature and the Arts

Charles Brockden Brown (1771-1810) was the first American novelist of distinction and the first to follow a purely literary career. Hugh Henry Brackenridge of Pittsburgh gave the West its first literary work in his satire *Modern Chivalry*. Philadelphia continued as an important center for printing with Lippincott and Curtis taking the lead and, for the magazine, with the publication of the *Saturday Evening Post*. Barnard Taylor, who began his literary career before the Civil War, published his most notable work in 1870-71 — the famous translation of Goethe's *Faust*.

In architecture, the historic red brick of southeastern Pennsylvania was supplemented by buildings in the Greek Revival style. The New England influence was strong in the domestic architecture of the northern tier counties. Thomas U. Walter and William Strickland gave Pennsylvania an important role in the architectural history of the early 1800s. Walter designed the Treasury Building and the Capitol Dome in Washington. The nation's first institution of art — the Pennsylvania Academy of the Fine Arts — was founded in Philadelphia in 1805, although by then such painters as Gilbert Stuart, Benjamin West, and the Peale family had already made Philadelphia famous.

Philadelphia was the theatrical center of America until 1830, a leader in music publishing and piano manufacture and the birthplace of American opera. William Henry Fry's *Lenora* (1845) was probably the first publicly performed opera by an American composer. Stephen Foster became the songwriter for the nation.

Religion

In the years between independence and the Civil War, religion flourished in the Commonwealth. In addition to the growth of worship, religion led the way to enlargement of the educational system. In this period churches threw off European ties and established governing bodies in the United States. In 1789 John Carroll of Maryland became the first Catholic bishop in America. In 1820 the establishment of a national Lutheran synod was the last of the breaks from Europe by a major Protestant denomination. Some new churches were formed: Jacob Albright formed the Evangelical Association, a Pennsylvania German parallel to Methodism; Richard Allen formed the African Methodist Episcopal Church in 1816; and John Winebrenner founded the Church of God in Harrisburg in 1830. Isaac Leeser, who founded Conservative Judaism in America, did most of his important writing in Philadelphia in this period. Presbyterianism, which was the largest Protestant denomination before 1860, drifted westward and had its stronghold in western Pennsylvania. Quakers, although decreasing in number, led many humanitarian and reform movements. Although anti-Catholic riots occurred at Kensington in 1844, German and Irish immigrants enlarged the number of Catholics in the state.

THE ERA OF INDUSTRIAL ASCENDANCY: 1861-1945

After 1861 Pennsylvania's influence on national politics diminished gradually, but its industrial complex grew at an amazing pace.

Civil War

During the Civil War, Pennsylvania played an important role in preserving the Union. Southern forces invaded Pennsylvania three times by way of the Cumberland Valley, a natural highway from Virginia to the North. This made Pennsylvania's defense efforts doubly important.

Pennsylvania's industrial enterprise and natural resources were essential factors in the economic strength of the northern cause. Its railroad system, iron and steel industry, and agricultural wealth were vital to the war effort. The shipbuilders of Pennsylvania, led by the famous Cramp yards, contributed to naval strength and the merchant marine. Thomas Scott as assistant secretary of war directed telegraph and railway services. Engineer Herman Haupt directed railroad movement of troops and was commended by President Lincoln. Jay Cooke helped in financing the Union effort, and Thaddeus Stevens was an important congressional leader. Simon Cameron was the Secretary of War until January 1862.

No man made a greater impression as a state governor during the Civil War than Pennsylvania's Andrew Curtin. In his first inaugural he denied the right of the South to secede, and throughout the war was active in support of the national draft. In September 1862 he was the host at Altoona to a conference of northern governors which pledged support to Lincoln's policies.

Nearly 350,000 Pennsylvanians served in the Union forces including 8,600 black volunteers. At the beginning, Lincoln's call for 14 regiments of volunteers was answered by 25. In May 1861 the Assembly, at Curtin's suggestion, created the Pennsylvania Reserve Corps of 15 regiments enlisted for three years' service. They were mustered into the Army of the Potomac after the first Battle of Bull Run, and thousands of other Pennsylvanians followed them. Camp Curtin at Harrisburg was one of the great troop concentration centers of the war. Admiral David D. Porter opened the Mississippi, and Rear Admiral John A. Dahlgren made innovations in ordnance which greatly improved naval armament. Army leaders from Pennsylvania were numerous and able, including such outstanding officers as George B. McClellan, George G. Meade, John F. Reynolds, Winfield S. Hancock, John W. Geary, and John F. Hartranft.

After the Battle of Antietam, General J.E.B. Stewart's cavalry rode around General George McClellan's army and reached Chambersburg on October 10, 1862. There they seized supplies and horses, and burned a large storehouse before retiring as rapidly as they had come.

In June 1863 General Robert E. Lee turned his 75,000 men northward on a major invasion of Pennsylvania. The state called up reserves and volunteers for emergency duty. At Pittsburgh the citizens fortified the surrounding hills, and at Harrisburg fortifications were thrown up on both sides of the Susquehanna. Confederate forces captured Carlisle and advanced to within three miles of Harrisburg; the bridge at Wrightsville had to be burned to prevent their crossing. These outlying forces were recalled when the Union army under General George G. Meade met Lee's army at Gettysburg. In a bitterly fought engagement on the first three days of July, the Union army threw back the Confederate forces, a major turning point of the struggle to save the Union. Not only was the battle fought on Pennsylvania soil, but nearly a third of General Meade's army were Pennsylvania troops. Governor Curtin led the movement to establish the battlefield as a memorial park.

In 1864, in retaliation for Union raids on Virginia, a Confederate force under General John McCausland advanced to Chambersburg and threatened to burn the town unless a large ransom was paid. The citizens refused, and Chambersburg was burned on July 20, leaving two-thirds of its people homeless and causing damage of almost two million dollars.

Republican Dominance

After the Civil War the Republican party was dominant. The war was viewed as a victory for its principles. Conflicts between conservatives and liberals took place within the party. A series of political managers or bosses—Simon and J. Donald Cameron, Matthew Quay, and Boies Penrose—assured Republican control of the state, although reformers were shocked by their methods. These bosses sat in Congress. Other Republican leaders prevailed in most cities. From 1861 to 1883 Republicans held the governorship. Then, a factional split within the Republicans led to the election of Democrat Robert E. Pattison, and his reelection in 1891. After that, Republicans held the governor's office until 1935. The death of Senator Penrose in 1921 ended the era of Republican state bosses in Congress. Joseph R. Grundy of the Pennsylvania Manufacturers Association, and Andrew W. Mellon, U.S. Secretary of the Treasury (1921-1932), were typical of Republican leadership after Penrose. While Pennsylvania's government was closely allied to industry and big business, it also spawned progressive programs. Governor Gifford Pinchot was a remarkable reformer. On balance, the Republican system's justification was that in assisting industry it fostered prosperity for all—"the full dinner pail." The enormous adjustments necessary for dealing with the unemployment and economic chaos of the 1930s led to the revival of the Democratic party. Democrats captured Pittsburgh in 1933, and the administration of Governor George H. Earle (1935-1939) was modeled on the New Deal of President Roosevelt. But the state returned to Republican administration in 1940 and remained so until 1954.

The Constitution of 1874

The fourth constitution of the Commonwealth was partly a result of a nationwide reform movement in the 1870s and partly a result of specific corrections to the previous constitution. It provided for the popular election of judges, the state treasurer and the auditor general. It created the office of lieutenant governor and a department of internal affairs which combined several offices under an elected secretary. The head of the public school system received the title of superintendent of public instruction. The General Assembly was required to provide efficient public education for no less than one million dollars per year. The governor's term was lengthened from three to four years, but he could no longer succeed himself. He was empowered to veto individual items within appropriations bills. The membership of the General Assembly was increased, but its powers were limited by a prohibition of special or local legislation about certain specified subjects, a constitutional debt limit, and other restrictions. Sessions of the General Assembly became biennial.

New State Agencies

Although the new constitution was detailed, it provided flexibility in the creation of new agencies. Thus in 1873, even while the new constitution was being discussed, the Insurance Department was created to supervise and regulate insurance companies. In the following years, many other agencies were created, sometimes as full fledged departments and sometimes as boards, bureaus, or commissions, while existing agencies were often changed or abolished. For example, the factory inspectorship of 1889 eventually became the Department of Labor and Industry in 1913. The Board of Public Charities (1869), the Committee on Lunacy (1883), the Mothers' Assistance Fund (1913), and the Prison Labor Commission (1915) were consolidated into the Department of Welfare in 1921. By 1922 there were 139 separate state agencies, demonstrating the need for simplification, consolidation, and reorganization. The administrative codes of 1923 and 1929 accomplished these goals. The judicial branch of government was also changed by the creation of the Superior Court in 1895 to relieve the mounting caseload of the Supreme Court.

The Spanish-American War

By 1895 the island of Cuba was in a state of revolution, its people desiring to break away from Spanish rule. News of harsh methods used to suppress Cuban outbreaks aroused anger in the United States. When the battleship *Maine* blew up in Havana harbor, war became inevitable in 1898. Congressman Robert Adams of Philadelphia wrote the resolutions declaring war on Spain and recognizing the independence of Cuba. President McKinley's call for volunteers was answered with enthusiasm throughout the Commonwealth. Pennsylvania military leaders included Brigadier General Abraham K. Arnold and Brigadier General James M. Bell. Major General John R. Brooks, a native of Pottsville, served as military governor in Cuba and Puerto Rico. Although no Pennsylvania troops fought in Cuba, units from the Commonwealth saw action in Puerto Rico. A Pennsylvania regiment was the first American organization to engage in land combat in the Philippine Islands. It remained there for the Filipino Insurrection.

The First World War

Pennsylvania's resources and manpower were of great value to the war effort of 1917-1918. The shipyards of Philadelphia and Chester were decisive in maintaining maritime transport. Pennsylvania's mills and factories provided a large part of the war materials for the nation. Nearly 3,000 separate firms held contracts for war supplies of various types. Pennsylvanians subscribed to nearly three billion dollars worth of Liberty and Victory Bonds, and paid well over a billion dollars in federal taxes during the war. Civilian resources were organized through a State Defense Council with local affiliates. Pennsylvania furnished more than 300,000 men for the armed forces, and the 28th Division won special distinction. The Saint Mihiel drive and the Argonne offensive were among the famous campaigns of the war in which Pennsylvania troops took part. General Tasker H. Bliss, a native of Lewisburg, was appointed chief of staff in 1917, and later was made a member of the Supreme War Council and the American Peace Commission. He was succeeded as chief of staff by another Pennsylvania West Point graduate, General Peyton C. March, originally from Easton. Admiral William S. Sims, a Pennsylvania graduate of the Naval Academy, was in charge of American naval operations.

Population

Large areas of the northern and western parts of the state were unsettled or thinly populated in 1800. By Civil War days, with the exception of the northern tier counties, population was scattered throughout the state. There was increased urbanization, although rural life remained strong and agriculture involved large numbers of people. The immigrant tide continued after the Civil War and brought about a remarkable change in the composition of the population. While most of the state's pre-1861 population was composed of ethnic groups from northern Europe such as the English, Irish, Scotch-Irish, and Germans, the later period brought increased numbers of Slavic, Italian, Finn, Scandinavian, and Jewish immigrants. At the height of this "new immigration" between 1900 and 1910, the Commonwealth witnessed the largest population increase of any decade in its history. Black migration from the South intensified after 1917, when World War I curtailed European immigration, and again during World War II. By World War II almost five percent of the state's population was Black. In 1940 the Commonwealth was the second largest state in the nation with a population two-thirds that of New York.

Women

The status of women began to improve by the 1860s. In 1861 the first school for nurses in America opened in Pennsylvania. Pennsylvania played a prominent part in the suffrage movement. Philadelphia was a hotbed of feminist agitation. In 1868 women in Philadelphia organized a Pennsylvania Women's Suffrage Association. On July 4, 1876, Susan B. Anthony read her famous "Declaration of Rights for Women" at the Washington statue in front of Independence Hall. Well-known Pennsylvania feminists such as Lucretia Mott, Ann Davies, Florence Kelley, Ann Preston, and Emma Guffey Miller were all active in the long battle which culminated in women receiving the vote.

The General Assembly approved a suffrage amendment to the state Constitution in 1913 and again in 1915, but Pennsylvania's male voters rejected the amendment by 55,000 votes. On June 4, 1919, the Nineteenth Amendment to the U.S. Constitution was approved by Congress. Just ten days later, Pennsylvania became the seventh state to ratify it. By August 1920, the amendment became law and women could vote.

Florence Kelley was a Philadelphia-born lawyer who championed the fight for better working conditions for women and children. For 32 years she was the leader of the National Consumer's League, which demanded consumer protection as well as improved working conditions. Isabel Darlington was the first female lawyer admitted to practice before the Pennsylvania Supreme and Superior Courts.

Sarah C. F. Hallowell was active in the work of the Philadelphia Centennial Exposition and in charge of a newspaper, the *New Century,* published by the Women's Executive Committee and staffed entirely by women who worked as editors, reporters, correspondents, and compositors.

When the ten greatest American painters of all time were exhibited in a special section of the Chicago Century of Progress Art Exhibition, Mary Stevenson Cassatt was the only woman represented. Born in Pittsburgh, she received her only formal training at the Pennsylvania Academy of the Fine Arts. This institution has always regarded her as one of its most important alumnae, granting her its gold medal of honor in 1914.

From the 1890s to 1906 Ida Tarbell from Erie worked for the publisher S.S. McClure, as a feature writer and editor of *McClure's Magazine.* It was during this time that she published her *History of the Standard Oil Company,* a muckraking account which brought her to the forefront of her profession.

Because of the Quakers' traditional high view of women's capacity, Philadelphia had long been a center for female education. The founding of Women's Medical College there in 1850 led to entrance of women into the medical profession. Hannah E. Myers Longshore was the first female M.D. to establish a successful private practice. Beaver College in Jenkintown was the first women's college of higher education in the state. Women were very successful in the teaching profession. Mollie Woods Hare pioneered in teaching the mentally retarded before World War I. In 1887 Ella M. Boyce was made school superintendent of Bradford, the first woman to hold such a position in the United States.

Labor

Pennsylvanians played an important role in the development of the labor movement, and the Commonwealth was the site of some of the largest strikes in the history of American labor. William H. Sylvis, from Indiana County, was a founder of the Iron-Molders' International Union and he later led the National Labor Union in 1868-69. Uriah Stephens of Philadelphia and Terence V. Powderly of Scranton were leaders of the Knights of Labor, the most important national union between 1871 and 1886. At their peak in the mid-1880s, the Knights had about 700,000 members. Pennsylvanians played an important role in the formation of the Amalgamated Association of Iron and Steel Workers in 1876. Pennsylvania's anthracite miners in Schuylkill, Carbon, and Northumberland counties organized the Workingmen's Benevolent Association in 1868.

From the Civil War until 1877 the secret group named the Molly Maguires was powerful in the anthracite region, working for miners of Irish descent and sympathetic to a miners' union. In 1877 private resources led by railroad executive Franklin B. Gowen smashed the Mollies, using a private force, the coal and iron police. But continued problems in the anthracite area gave rise to the United Mine Workers union. At first a union for skilled miners opposed to immigrant mine laborers, under the leadership of John Mitchell it grew to encompass all coal mine workers. The anthracite strike of 1902 in which President Theodore Roosevelt intervened set the pattern for non-violent arbitration in labor relations. After Mitchell, John L. Lewis led the union for many years and membership spread throughout the bituminous areas. Intervention in the anthracite strikes of the 1920s by Governor Gifford Pinchot brought the 8-hour day, but no permanent end to labor discontent; many customers began to shift to other heating sources at that time. In 1929 the coal and iron police were subjected to higher standards of conduct.

Pittsburgh was the scene of major violence and property destruction during the Great Railroad Strike of 1877. Historically significant and violent strikes in the steel industry occurred at Homestead, Pennsylvania, in 1892 and throughout the greater Pittsburgh district and Monongahela River Valley in 1919. During the later 1930s western Pennsylvania was a major center of strength in the formation of the Steel Workers Organization Committee (S.W.O.C.), which in 1942 became the United Steelworkers of America. Since the labor legislation of President Franklin D. Roosevelt's New Deal, unions have flourished and workers have received fairer treatment. It was a dispute over the right of S.W.O.C. to organize workers at the Aliquippa plant of Jones and Laughlin Steel Corporation that led, in 1936, to the U.S. Supreme Court's decision upholding the constitutionality of the Wagner Labor Relations Act and its agency, the National Labor Relations Board. This was a major advance for the cause of labor.

Industry

Manufacturing

The manufacture of steel and iron products was the largest single industry. The story of Andrew Carnegie, Henry C. Frick, Charles M. Schwab, Eugene Grace, and other "iron men" of Pennsylvania is in a large measure the story of modern American business. Concentrated for the most part in western Pennsylvania, but with important centers also at Bethlehem, Harrisburg, Lewistown, Carlisle, and Morrisville, Pennsylvania's steel industry furnished the rails for the nation's railway empire, the structural steel for its modern cities, and the armament for national defense.

The career of Andrew Carnegie, Scotch immigrant, coincided with the rise of Pennsylvania's steel industry. Starting as a telegrapher for the Pennsylvania Railroad, he handled messages for the Army during the Civil War and entered railroad management thereafter. In 1873 he began to build new steel mills. His success in steel went on and on. Carnegie balanced his own success and ability by pledging to pay the world back through benevolent distribution of his wealth. In 1901 he sold Carnegie Steel Corporation to J. P. Morgan's new giant corporation, U. S. Steel, and spent the rest of his life managing his enormous charitable foundation.

Charles M. Schwab was born in Williamsburg and attended St. Francis College. He taught himself metallurgy in a chemistry lab in his own basement and rose to be Carnegie's managing president. Schwab decided that he preferred to invest his own savings, so he bought Bethlehem Steel Company. He successfully advanced its interests until his death in 1939, making sure that the giant he had helped spawn, U.S. Steel, always had strong competition.

U.S. Steel Corporation was concentrated within a circle of 100-mile radius around Pittsburgh. By sheer size it set industry standards, its ownership spilling over into the coal, coke, limestone, and iron ore industries. By 1900 the steel industry had begun its inevitable migration west of Pennsylvania, but 60 percent of the nation's production still came from our state. It had slipped below 50 percent by 1916, but our steel industry received new life as a result of World War I. In the 1920s the growth of the auto industry gave steel renewed vigor, and World War II revived the industry once again. By this time the aluminum industry was also growing in western Pennsylvania, where Andrew W. Mellon was the main financier of the giant Alcoa Corporation.

In the nineteenth century, textiles and clothing, especially worsteds and silk, grew from a base in Philadelphia so that the state led the nation by 1900. Willingness to invest in new technology and new styles was largely responsible. By the 1920s, competition from the South and overseas made inroads into textile production. In 1900 the state also led the nation in tanning leather.

Food processing grew into a major industry. 1905 was the year of the Hershey Chocolate factory and the incorporation of H. J. Heinz Co. Henry J. Heinz was known as "The Good Provider." He led a movement for model factories based on the principle that workers deserve clean, pleasant work conditions with some chance for self-improvement. Also, he fought for federal legislation outlawing commercially processed foods that had false labels and harmful chemical adulterations. This culminated in the passage of federal legislation in 1906.

During this period Pennsylvania dominated the manufacture of railroad equipment. In the twentieth century electrical equipment manufacture became prominent. George Westinghouse was a leader in both these fields. His air brake, patented in 1869, revolutionized railroading and was followed by numerous Westinghouse inventions of signals, switches, and other safety features on trains. His Union Switch and Signal Company was formed in Pittsburgh in 1882, and about the time he turned to improving natural gas transmission and controls. Then he moved into improving the nation's use of electricity by perfecting a means for generating large amounts of power in the more practical form of alternating current. Eventually all his laboratory and manufacturing plants were moved out of Pittsburgh to nearby Turtle Creek Valley.

Representative of America's "Management Revolution" was the Philadelphia genius Frederick Winslow Taylor, who abandoned a law career because of poor eyesight and worked as a laboring mechanic. He excelled at organizing work shops. Then he advanced to making improvements in the organization of major corporations like Bethlehem Steel, for which he worked from 1898 to 1901. While there he developed a revolutionary method for producing fine tool steel. He set up his own management consulting company in Philadelphia, becoming America's first efficiency engineer. His crowning achievement was the publication, in 1911, of *Scientific Management.*

Lumber, Petroleum, Natural Gas and Coal

Pennsylvania has exercised leadership in the extractive industries of lumber, petroleum, natural gas, and coal. Large amounts of the natural stands of timber were exhausted before conservation concepts were recognized. In the 1860s the state led the nation in lumber production, but by 1900 it was in fourth place. Within that period Williamsport's log boom on the Susquehanna had been the world's largest lumber pile. Twentieth-century timber conservation planning owes much to Gifford Pinchot, the nation's first professional forester.

Following the discovery of oil near Titusville in 1859, production and marketing of oil grew. The oil producing counties extended from Tioga west to Crawford, and south to the West Virginia line. By 1891 Warren, Venango, and McKean were the leaders, as they still are today. Once practical methods of transmitting and burning natural gas were developed, Pennsylvania became a leading producer in that area, also. John D. Rockefeller's Standard Oil Company was always foremost in the refining and marketing of petroleum. The early lead Pennsylvania had achieved in drilling for oil made the Keystone state the natural battleground for competing investors. Rockefeller founded Standard Oil in 1868 and, as a result of a freight price rebate deal with the New York Central Railroad, it grew to be the world's largest refinery by 1870. To overcome Pennsylvania's small, independent refiners, he engaged in secret agreements with such powerful interests as the Pennsylvania Railroad. He allowed the independent refiners to survive—they finally merged into the Pure Oil Company, just before 1900—as long as they did not undersell Standard Oil. The organization of refiners in Pennsylvania before 1900 is one reason why the state has continued to be a leading refining area even though the raw petroleum is now almost entirely imported.

Anthracite coal was the main fuel used to smelt iron until the 1880s, when the manufacture of coke from bituminous was developed to a degree that it replaced anthracite. But production of anthracite continued to increase as it was used for heating and other purposes. The bituminous and coke industries were responsible for the late nineteenth-century industrial growth of westen Pennsylvania; the iron ore deposits there would not have merited such growth. World War I caused two years (1917-1918) of the largest production of both types of coal the state has ever seen. The market decline of the 1920s created business and labor problems. Mobilization for World War II revived the industry.

Agriculture

The prosperous farms of the Pennsylvania Germans have always been a bulwark of our agricultural economy. The settlement and development of western and northern Pennsylvania was initially based on agriculture. Cereals and livestock continued to be the mainstays of the farmer. The rise of agricultural societies, such as the Grange, and of county fairs led to improvements in farm methods and machinery. Pennsylvania turned toward a market-oriented approach in the mid-1800s. While the number of farms has declined since 1930, farm production has increased dramatically to meet consumer demands.

In 1880 the pattern of increasing total area farmed in Pennsylvania (which began in the colonial period) ended, and total farm acreage has declined ever since, but this trend has been outweighed by improved farming methods. In 1874 a dairymen's association was formed; in 1876 a State Board of Agriculture was created which was made a department in 1895. In 1887 the federal government established an agricultural experiment station at the Agricultural College of Pennsylvania, in Centre County (the predecessor of the Pennsylvania State University) and cooperation between the college's faculty and working farmers, so important for improving production, began. In 1895 a state veterinarian was appointed who eventually eliminated bouvine tuberculosis. The nature of farm products changed because of competition from expanding agriculture in the West, distances from markets, and changing consumption patterns of the American diet.

Transportation

Railways

Pennsylvania pioneered early rail development. By 1860 mileage had increased to 2,598, and the Reading, Lehigh, and Pennsylvania systems were developing. The Pennsylvania Railroad, chartered in 1846, reached Pittsburgh in 1852. Alexander Cassatt, Thomas Scott, and John A. Roebling who was the surveyor of the Pennsylvania's route, were leaders in development. After 1865 the Pennsylvania Railroad extended its lines to New York, Washington, Buffalo, Chicago, and St. Louis, becoming one of the great trunk-line railroads of the nation, and developed a network of subsidiary lines within the state. The Reading and Lehigh Valley systems also expanded to become great carriers of freight and important links in the industrial economy of the Middle Atlantic region. Numerous smaller lines grew, to serve districts or special purposes. For example, the

Bessemer and Lake Erie carried Lake Superior ore to the steel mills of Pittsburgh. All the important trunk lines of the eastern United States passed through Pennsylvania and had subsidiary feeders in the state. The Commonwealth had more than 10,000 miles of railroad. As early as 1915 the state's railroads had ceased to expand, and after World War I both passenger and freight service were reduced.

Urban Transit

Pennsylvania has a long tradition of urban public transport, beginning with horsecars in Pittsburgh and Philadelphia in the 1850s. The first of many Pittsburgh inclines — two of which operate today — opened in 1870. Philadelphia's first streetcar system began in 1892, and the Market Street Elevated train began operation in 1907. The Market Street subway was one of the first in the nation and remains in operation today. Transit use increased steadily in Pennsylvania until the end of World War II.

Roads

Although 1,700 state-owned bridges were built before 1900, attention to building roads had lapsed during the canal and railroad era. It sprang anew with the advent of the automobile. Charles and Frank Duryea experimented with automobiles in Reading, and Robert Allison of Port Carbon was supposedly the first purchaser of an automobile on March 24, 1898. Between 1903 and 1911 Pennsylvania took the lead in creating a modern road system, establishing a department of highways, licensing automobiles, and taking over more than 8,000 miles of highway for maintenance and improvement. Operators' license fees, fines for violation of driving regulations, and a gasoline tax swelled the Motor Fund, thus making the motoring public the chief supporters of the system. Most highway construction consisted of improvements to existing routes. This included widening, laying hard surfaces, and relocation to eliminate sharp curves or grades. Repair garages and filling stations became numerous. The world's first "drive-in gas station" opened in Pittsburgh in 1913. Outstanding was the Lincoln Highway which was designated in 1913. It connected the state's two largest cities and stretched from New York City to San Francisco. In 1916 the federal government instituted grants to states for highway construction, beginning a great primary highway construction effort which peaked in the 1930s. By 1928 the transcontinental system of U.S.-numbered, through highways was in use in Pennsylvania, and at about the same time an expanded state-numbered system came into being. Campaigning in 1930, Governor Gifford Pinchot promised to "get the farmers out of the mud." The following year, the state took over 20,156 miles of township roads and began paving them, using light construction costing less than $7,000 a mile. As the depression deepened, this road-building program became an important means of providing work relief. Special federal programs also benefited the state's highways during depression years. In 1940 Pennsylvania opened the first high-speed, multi-lane highway in the country, the Pennsylvania Turnpike, which set the pattern for modern super-highways throughout the nation. The Turnpike initially connected Pittsburgh and Harrisburg, and was later expanded from the western boundary to the Delaware River, as well as northward into the anthracite region.

Aviation

In 1925 Philadelphia Congressman Clyde Kelly introduced the Airmail Act which set the American aviation industry on the road to progress. In 1927 Governor Pinchot created a State Bureau of Aeronautics. When in 1939 All American Aviation, a Pennsylvania company, was licensed to carry mail to 54 communities in Pennsylvania, Ohio, Delaware and West Virginia, the organization that became Allegheny Airlines entered a period of rapid expansion. By the beginning of World War II passenger service was in its infancy, although the very reliable DC-3 plane had been developed. The Hog Island site of the present Philadelphia International Airport was developed in the late 1930s with city and federal WPA assistance.

Society and Culture

Pennsylvania made rapid progress in social and cultural fields through continually expanding educational and cultural opportunities. While Philadelphia lost the preeminent position which it had earlier enjoyed as the center of most new enterprises, the wealth and position of the state as a whole exerted a powerful influence in almost every phase of the nation's social and cultural development.

Communication, Performing Arts and the Media

Philadelphia was the birthplace of many publications and served as the center of publishing in the early national period. By 1840 Pennsylvania was the home of more newspapers than any other state. In the 1900s economic pressures forced many newspapers and magazines into bankruptcy, failure or consolidation. Today most cities have only one newspaper, although Philadelphia and Pittsburgh continue to support a number of major dailies.

The telegraph and the telephone became widespread after the Civil War. Following Samuel Morse's development of the telegraph in the 1840s, the state was interlaced by a network of telegraph lines. Alexander Graham Bell's telephone was first demonstrated publicly at the Philadelphia Centennial Exhibition in 1876. By the end of the century, the telephone had become universal. Pennsylvanian Daniel Drawbaugh claimed to have invented a working telephone 10 years before Bell, but his claim did not hold up in patent litigation. The Commonwealth now has thousands of miles of telegraph and telephone lines and almost 10 million telephones.

Pennsylvania played a key role in the development of a major twentieth-century contribution to the dissemination of ideas and information — the radio. The first commercial broadcast station in the world was KDKA in Pittsburgh, which started a daily schedule of broadcasting on November 2, 1920. The first church service broadcast by radio was from that station a year later and the first public address by radio was made by Herbert Hoover at the Duquesne Club in Pittsburgh in 1921. Radio quickly became a fixture in most homes, but lost its dominance in the broadcasting market with the advent of television in the 1950s.

Philadelphia was the theatrical capital of America before 1830, a leader in music publishing and piano manufacture and the birthplace of American opera. Edwin Forest, Joseph Jefferson, the Drews, and the Barrymores were important stage actors in the late 1800s and the early 1900s. The first all-motion-picture theater in the world was opened on Smithfield Street in Pittsburgh on June 19, 1905, by John P. Harris and Harry Davis. The name "nickelodeon" was coined there. The Warner brothers began their career in western Pennsylvania.

Education

In 1857 The Normal School Act was passed and a separate state department was created for the supervision of public schools. In 1860 there were only six public high schools in the state. Beginning in 1887 the Assembly passed general laws authorizing the establishment of high schools. They had enrolled only two percent of the public school population when the state began to appropriate money for high schools in 1895. Ten years later the system was firmly established. By 1895 every school district was authorized to establish a high school. Initially high schools offered only two-year courses. Between 1913 and 1920 the state assumed control over all the normal schools, which were given college status in 1927. Probably the most important school legislation since 1834 was the Edmonds Act in 1921, which established minimum salary standards and qualifications for teachers and county superintendents, centralized teacher certification, set up a state Council of Education, provided for consolidation of rural schools, increased state aid to education, and made other improvements.

In 1790 there were only three institutions of university or college rank. Today there are almost 200 institutions of higher education, a majority of which have been founded since 1865. Most higher education before 1900 was sponsored by churches. The development of higher education for women, the broadening of the curriculum, and the decline of purely denominational control were important trends of the twentieth century.

Science and Invention

The tradition of scientific inquiry established in Pennsylvania by Franklin, Rittenhouse, and Bartram continued. The scientific leadership of Pennsylvania was represented by many individuals. Isaac Hayes (1796-1879) of Philadelphia pioneered in the study of astigmatism and color blindness. The four Rogers brothers of Philadelphia were a remarkable scientific family. James (1802-1852) and Robert (1813-1884) were noted chemists; William (1804-1882) was the state geologist of Virginia and later president of the Massachusetts Institute of Technology; and Henry (1808-1866) directed the first geological survey of Pennsylvania (1836-1847). Spencer Baird (1823-1887) of Reading was a leader in the natural sciences and the secretary of the Smithsonian Institution. Joseph Saxton (1799-1873) of Huntingdon was the father of photography in America.

Pennsylvanians also led in invention and the application of science in industry and daily life. John A. Roebling, who came to America in 1839 and spent most of his active life in Pennsylvania, led in the development of steel wire rope and steel bridges, and his engineering work was carried forward by his son Washington. William Kelly (1811-1888) exhibited leadership in invention. Edward G. Acheson (1856-1931), chemist and inventor, contributed to the development of carborundum as an abrasive and a graphite as a lubricant. Henry P. Armsby (1853-1921), director of the Pennsylvania State University Agricultural Experiment Station, was internationally known for his contributions to nutritional science. Edgar Fahs Smith (1854-1928) of the University of Pennsylvania was a leading American chemist and helped to found the American Chemical Society. In the field of medicine, the Hahnemann Medical College, Jefferson Medical College, and the University of Pennsylvania Medical School made Philadelphia one of the outstanding medical centers of the nation. Medical colleges were established at the University of Pittsburgh in 1885 and at Temple University in 1901. These institutions made noteworthy contributions to medical science.

John A. Brashear (1840-1920) of Pittsburgh was important in the development of astronomical precision instruments which made great contributions to knowledge. The inventor George Westinghouse (1846-1914), while not a native of the state, spent the greater portion of his life here. The earliest successful experiment of Thomas A. Edison with electric lighting was made at Sunbury. John R. Carson (1887-1940) and Dr. Harry Davis (1868-1931) of Pittsburgh were notable for contributions to the development of radio. Elihu Thomson (1853-1937), one of the founders of General Electric, continued the Franklin tradition in electrical science. The world's first computer was developed at the University of Pennsylvania. In recent times, the engineering schools of the state's universities and such institutions as the Franklin Institute and the Mellon Institute have placed Pennsylvania in the forefront of modern industrial research and invention.

The Second World War

In World War II 1.25 million Pennsylvanians served in the armed forces, or about one-eighth of the population. Also, one out of every seven members of the armed forces in World War II was a Pennsylvanian. The chief of staff, General of the Army George C. Marshall, was a native of Uniontown, and the commander of the Army Air Forces was General of the Army Henry H. Arnold, born in Gladwyne. Pennsylvania also had three full generals: Jacob L. Devers, York, commander of the Sixth Army

Group; Joseph T. McNarney, Emporium, Deputy Allied Commander in the Mediterranean; and Carl Spaatz, Boyertown, commander of the American Strategic Air Forces in Europe. Lieutenant General Lewis H. Brereton, Pittsburgh, commanded the First Allied Airborne Army, and Lieutenant General Alexander M. Patch, Lebanon, commanded the Seventh Army. The Chief of Naval Operations at the outbreak of hostilities was Admiral Harold R. Stark, Wilkes-Barre, who later became commander of American naval forces in European waters. Admiral Richard S. Edwards, Philadelphia, was deputy chief of naval operations, and an adopted Philadelphian, Admiral Thomas C. Kinkaid, commanded the Seventh Fleet in the South Pacific.

Altogether, there were 130 generals and admirals from Pennsylvania. More Congressional Medals of Honor were awarded to Pennsylvanians than to citizens of any other state. There were 40 military and naval installations in Pennsylvania, including two large camps, Indiantown Gap and Camp Reynolds. All the Army's doctors received training at Carlisle Barracks, and the Navy's photographic reconnaissance pilots were instructed at the Harrisburg Airport. The Philadelphia Navy Yard built two of the world's largest battleships and many lesser vessels. Among a dozen military depots in the state were Mechanicsburg Naval Supply Depot, Middletown Air Depot, Letterkenny Ordnance Depot, Frankford Arsenal and Philadelphia Quartermaster Depot.

Pennsylvania's industrial resources made her the "Arsenal of America." Planes, tanks, armored cars, guns, and shells poured out of her factories. Ships were launched in the Delaware and Ohio rivers and on Lake Erie. Steady streams of war goods flowed over her railroads and highways. Pennsylvania oil lubricated the machines of war and her coal kept the steel mills going. Food from her fields fed war workers and soldiers. In total war production, Pennsylvania ranked sixth among the states, in shipbuilding fifth, and in ordnance fourth. It furnished almost one-third of the nation's steel. More money was spent to expand production capacity in Pennsylvania than in any other state. Three hundred Pennsylvania firms were honored with production awards.

Pennsylvanians paid over two billion dollars a year in taxes, and were second only to New Yorkers in the purchase of war bonds. Under the leadership of the State Council of Defense more than a million and a half people were organized to protect the state against enemy attack and to aid in the war effort.

MATURITY: 1945-1987

Population

The 1980 U.S. Census showed that Pennsylvania had a population of slightly less than 12 million people, in which women outnumbered men by about one-half million. Of the 48 states whose populations had grown since 1970, Pennsylvania had the lowest rate of growth, six-tenths of one percent. Of the 15 states that have lost population since 1970 due to migration, Pennsylvania is fifth, just behind Michigan. The census shows that the resident Black population is slightly less than nine percent of the total resident population. In terms of Census Bureau definitions of urban areas, Pennsylvania has the nineteenth most urban population of all the states; it is 69 percent urbanized. The degree of urbanization grew by five percent in the 1960s, but dropped by almost one percent from 1970 to 1980. Philadelphia is the fourth largest metropolitan area in the nation, and Pittsburgh is the thirteenth. Pennsylvania dropped from second to the third most populous state in 1950, falling then behind California in addition to N.Y., and in 1980 dropped to fourth place, behind Texas as well. The average age of Pennsylvanians is 32.1 years.

Labor

Except for the primary metals and apparel industries, unemployment is higher than the national average. The entire decade following World War II was a period of frequent labor disagreements and strikes. Fringe benefits for wage earners were points of heated dispute; they were scarcely dreamt of before 1941. The steel strikes of 1952 and 1959-1960 required the intervention of Presidents Truman and Eisenhower. The outcome in 1960 was a triumph for the Taft-Hartley Labor Relations Act which was less favorable to labor's power to bargain than the preceding Wagner Labor Act. Although the merger of the AFL and the CIO in 1955 gave organized labor more strength, the recessions of the 1970s prevented expansion of unionization into many manufacturing areas and may have diminished membership in traditional factory forces. Unionization of office workers, however, has gone on, in line with the increasing involvement of workers in the service sector of the economy. Pennsylvania is not considered to be among the right-to-work states. In 1970 the Public Employees Relations Act established collective bargaining for teachers and other public workers. Both state and federal involvement have assisted in retraining workers laid off due to industrial technological change. Today Pennsylvania has the fifth largest civilian work force in the nation.

Women

After World War II Pennsylvania women continued to add to their record of achievement. Rachel Carson whose *Silent Spring* (1962) did much to awaken the nation to environmental dangers was born in Springdale and educated at Chatham College. The theories of anthropologist Margaret Mead continue to provoke discussion and research in that field of science. Catherine Drinker Bowen's historical and biographical works have received general acclaim. Jean Collins Kerr, dramatist and drama critic, has influenced a generation of cinema and television audiences. Actresses Lizabeth Scott and Grace Kelly were national idols in the 1950s. Hulda Magalhaes of Bucknell University has had a remarkable career in biological research and teaching. Kathryn O'Hay Granahan was the first female member of Congress from Philadelphia and the Treasurer of the United States from 1962 to 1966. Elizabeth Nath Marshall, four times mayor of York, was largely responsible for urban renewal there. The remarkable career of Genevieve Blatt includes twelve years as Secretary of Internal Affairs, and judgeship on the Commonwealth Court since 1972. In June 1964 the state's Commission for Women was created.

Industry

Diversity came to Pennsylvania as the coal, steel and railroad industries declined. Ironically, Pennsylvania's early preeminence in industrial development poses a major liability in plants and equipment. Its enormous capital investment, past and present, is in plants and equipment now less efficient than that of newer industrial areas. In steel, Pennsylvania's integrated mills are less efficient than the South's minimills and the new steel complexes abroad, especially since nature has placed western Pennsylvania at a geographic disadvantage to the Great Lakes-Midwest steel area for many decades. The proximity of steel plants to sources of ore and coal is not, however, as important a cost factor in corporate competition as it was forty years ago. Our steel industry began to contract in 1963, although we still lead the nation in specialty steel production.

The production and distribution of chemicals, food, and electrical machinery and equipment are important elements of Pennsylvania's industrial life. The state is also a leader in the cement industry, providing more than 10 percent of the nation's supply. Pennsylvania also produces quantities of clay products—brick, tile, and fire clay—as well as glass, limestone, and slate. However, by 1980 the apparels industry showed marked decline. Electronic data processing has developed tremendously, especially in the Pittsburgh area.

Today Pennsylvania remains the sixth most productive state. A major area of growth is the service sector, including trade, medical and health services, education, food, entertainment, and financial institutions. Pennsylvania's labor pool has 5,490,500 people, ranking fourth in the nation.

Energy Resources

The coal industry has continued to decline since World War II. Improved technology has meant less jobs for workers, but more important is coal's displacement by other fuels that are apparently more attractive. The energy crisis of the late 1970s brought only a partial return of old customers. Although one of John D. Rockefeller's associates once joked that he could drink all the oil that was not produced in Pennsylvania, Pennsylvania now barely produces one-thousandth of the nation's crude oil. Natural gas, however, is still a major product. Large amounts of nuclear energy are still being produced although many object to it as a health hazard. They point to the nuclear plant accident on Three Mile Island in March 1979.

Agriculture

While the number of farms and the acreage farmed have generally declined over the past 50 years, farm production has increased dramatically due to technical improvements. The state government has fostered many agricultural developments. Pennsylvania's 55,535 farms are the backbone of the state's economy, and today the state boasts the largest rural population in the nation. By the mid-1980s the financial pressures on the family farms threaten their continued existence. Pennsylvania is an important food distribution center with farm and food products supplied for markets from New England to the Mississippi River. Pennsylvania agriculture continues to grow strong through the statewide efforts of farm and commodity organizations, agricultural extension services, strong vocational agricultural programs, and the Pennsylvania Department of Agriculture, all of which keep farmers informed of new developments and assist them in promoting and marketing farm products. Today Pennsylvania farmers sell more than $2.85 billion in crop and livestock products annually, and agribusiness and food-related industries account for an annual $25 billion in sales. Six million acres of land are used for crops and pasture, and another three million acres is in farm woodlands — one-third of the state's total land area. Agricultural diversity in the Commonwealth is demonstrated by the fact that Pennsylvania ranks among the top ten states in such varied products as milk, poultry and eggs, ice cream, peaches, apples, grapes, cherries, sweet corn, potatoes, mushrooms, hay, cheese, maple syrup, cabbage, snap beans, Christmas trees and floriculture crops, pretzels, potato chips, sausage, wheat flour, and bakery products. The state is nineteenth in the nation in total farm income, although in total farm acreage it is thirty-seventh in the nation. In livestock Pennsylvania is ranked fifth in milk cows, seventeenth in total cattle, fifteenth in hogs, and twenty-fourth in sheep. Before the avian flu epidemic of 1983 it was fifth in the nation in the number of chickens. It ranks seventh in non-citrus fruits.

Transportation

The Pennsylvania Turnpike, which set the pattern for modern super-highways throughout the nation, was expanded from the western boundary to the Delaware River, as well as northward into the anthracite region. A far-reaching federal highway act was passed in 1956 authorizing the federal government to pay 90 percent of the costs of new roads connecting the nation's principal urban centers. More turnpike miles would probably have been built, had it not been for the toll-free interstate highway system established by the Federal Highway Act of 1956; of the 1,567 miles of interstate road authorized for Pennsylvania, most are now completed and in use. Pennsylvania took advantage of these funds to build an interstate system that today totals more than 1,500 miles. The most outstanding example of the system is Interstate 80, known as the Keystone Shortway, which is 313 miles long and transverses fifteen northern Pennsylvania counties. The state now has more than 45,000 miles of improved roads. The state is seventh in the nation in number of registered vehicles.

Waterways
Waterways have always been of major importance to Pennsylvania, and the state's three ports — Philadelphia, Pittsburgh, and Erie — accommodated more than 144,000,000 tons of cargo in 1973. The nation's largest industrial port, Philadelphia, has listed more than 1,250 arrivals and departures of oceangoing vessels per year. At the confluence of the Monongahela, Allegheny, and Ohio rivers, the port of Pittsburgh has seen a growing interstate movement of goods between western Pennsylvania and ports on the Ohio and Mississippi rivers and the Gulf intracoastal canal. The port of Erie was formerly of limited importance, but the emergence of the St. Lawrence Seaway produced a trend toward growth and development.

Aviation
Constant expansion of passenger service has been the story of aviation in Pennsylvania since World War II. Today there are sixteen major airports, five of which have been granted international status. Pittsburgh, the second largest, was built in 1951. Instrument landing systems became standard at airports in all the smaller cities following the Bradford Regional Airport accidents of 1968-1969. In the 1970s automated radar terminal systems were installed at all the major airports, to handle the increased volume of traffic with safety.

The expansion of All American Aviation to Allegheny Airlines, and then to U.S. Air, is typical of progress in the industry. The energy crises beginning in the late 1970s caused reorganization involving commuter lines, using smaller craft, operating as feeders from smaller cities to the major airports. Deregulation and the trend toward corporate mergers in the 1980s have caused further reorganizaiton of the industry.

Two aircraft manufacturers reached their apex during this period. Piper Aircraft Corporation of Lock Haven outdistanced its competitors and produced America's most popular light airplane. Vertol Division of Boeing Corporation, successor to Piasecki Helicopter Corporation, located in Delaware County, was a major manufacturer of helicopters.

Railroads
After World War II both its passenger and freight service were gradually reduced. The railroads' steepening decline was climaxed by the 1968 merger of the once mighty Pennsylvania Railroad into the Penn Central, and the bankruptcy of this new line a little over two years later. Even in 1975, however, 85 percent of raw materials, 35 percent of farm commodities, and 46 percent of manufactured products were listed as being moved by rail. The recent creation of the Amtrak passenger rail system and the consolidation of various lines including the Penn Central into Conrail for freight service are important efforts toward revitalization. Meanwhile, in the area of mass transit, several intrastate corridors in Pennsylvania have been under study, and in time there may be high-speed rail transit service between several of the state's largest cities.

Culture

Literature
A major figure in the American literary scene, Pearl S. Buck (1872-1973) won both a Nobel Prize and a Pulitzer Prize. She made her home in Perkasie. Christopher Morely (1890-1957) and John O'Hara (1905-1970) were other famous twentieth-century novelists.

Among living writers associated with Pennsylvania are L. Sprague deCamp, author of science fiction, and John Updike, who won the Pulitzer Prize for fiction in 1982, for *Rabbit Is Rich,* and received the 1983 Governor's Distinguished Pennsylvania Artist Award. James A. Michener, recipient of the 1981 Governor's Distinguished Pennsylvania Artist Award, is the author of 27 novels including the Pulitzer Prize winner *Tales of the South Pacific.* Marianne Moore (1887-1972), who was educated at Bryn Mawr College and taught at the United States Indian School in Carlisle, was a famous poet and the winner of many international awards. Poet Gerald Stern, born in Pittsburgh and now living in Easton, received the prestigious Lamont Poetry Prize for *Lucky Leaf,* as well as a 1980 Hazlett Memorial Award for Excellence in the Arts.

Performing Arts and Media
Among the famous Pennsylvanians who have starred in the movies were W. C. Fields, Gene Kelly, Joe E. Brown, Richard Gere, Tom Mix, Jack Palance, and James Stewart, who received the first Governor's Distinguished Pennsylvania Artist Award in 1980. In 1984 Bill Cosby received this award.

In the field of dance the Pennsylvania Ballet, founded by Barbara Weisberger in 1964, has an international reputation, and the Pittsburgh Ballet is also widely known. Band leaders Fred Waring and Les Brown have distinguished themselves in the 1940s and 1950s.

The Curtis Institute in Philadelphia has a world reputation for the advanced study of music. Distinguished singers who are Pennsylvanians by birth or association include Louis Homer, Paul Athouse, Dusolina Giannini, Mario Lanza, Helen Jepson, Perry Como, Bobby Vinton, and Marian Anderson (who received the 1982 Governor's Distinguished Pennsylvania Artist Award). Leopold Stowkowski rose to fame as the conductor of the Philadelphia Orchestra. Victor Herbert was conductor of the Pittsburgh Symphony during part of his career. Eugene Ormandy, conductor of the world-renowned Philadelphia

Orchestra for 44 years, received the 1980 Hazlett Memorial Award for Excellence in the Arts in the field of music. The Pittsburgh Symphony is proud to have had Andre Previn (recipient of the 1983 Hazlett Memorial Award for Excellence in the Arts) as its conductor. Samuel Barber, Peter Mennin, and Charles Wakefield Cadman are among the better known Pennsylvania symphonic composers.

Television grew rapidly and today Philadelphia is the fourth largest television market in the country and Pittsburgh is the eleventh largest. Each city has three major network stations, a public broadcasting station and smaller independent stations. WQED in Pittsburgh pioneered community-sponsored education television when it began broadcasting in 1954.

Religion
Although current statistics for many religious bodies in the state are not available, the Roman Catholic Church, which by 1937 had forty percent of the state's entire religious membership, is the largest group. Philadelphia is the only Catholic archdiocese; there are dioceses in seven other Pennsylvania cities.

The Lutherans and Methodists are the largest Protestant denominations. Four other denominations have more than one hundred thousand adherents each: Presbyterians, United Church of Christ, Episcopalians and American Baptists. The Quakers, so important in colonial times, had only 13,174 adherents in 1980. Significant smaller Protestant denominations are: Christian Scientists, Mormons, Seventh-Day Adventists, Jehovah's Witnesses, Assembly of God, Disciples of Christ, Church of the Brethren, Nazarene Church, Evangelical Congregational, and Church of God.

Nearly half the Jewish population is in Philadelphia, but other strong Jewish communities are in Pittsburgh and Harrisburg.

Philadelphia was the home of Bishop Richard Allen, who founded the African Methodist Episcopal (A.M.E.) Church in 1816; today it is a leading Protestant denomination with churches around the world. Blacks in Pennsylvania have belonged to many of the same churches (both Protestant and Catholic) as whites. Nonetheless, predominantly Black denominations include the African Methodist Episcopal and A.M.E. Zion Churches and two National Baptist Conventions.

Many churches descended from the Greek Orthodox and Russian Orthodox traditions are represented in Pennsylvania. Many are distinguished by ties to the national and ethnic divisions of Eastern Europe.

The German sects — the Mennonites and the Amish, for example — brought distinction to the Commonwealth through the appellation "Pennsylvania Dutch," but there are today more Plain People in Ohio and Indiana than there are in Pennsylvania.

Education
Pennsylvania has persistently pursued excellence in education. The state is seventh in the nation in the number of public elementary schools, fourth in the number of public secondary schools, third in the number of private elementary and secondary schools, fifth in the number of public institutions of higher education, and second in the number of private institutions of higher education. We lead the nation in the number of postsecondary vocational/technical schools. In total enrollment for institutions of higher education the state is sixth. It is third in total enrollment in private institutions of higher education. In 1983-1984 Pennsylvania stood fourth in the nation in state general expenditures for elementary and secondary education, and twelfth for higher education.

School consolidation became a major goal after World War II. By 1968 the number of school districts had been compressed from over 2,000 to 742. Centralization and improved spending had the desired effects. In the 1970s programs for exceptional and for disadvantaged students were becoming available, and the vocational-technical secondary school option assisted many youths in finding career areas. In 1974 Pennsylvania's Human Relations Commission ordered that racial imbalance in public schools be eliminated by the end of the year.

Political Developments

Two-Party State
The New Deal, the rising influence of labor, and the growing urbanization of the state ended a long period of Republican dominance. In stride with the New Deal, the Democrats fielded a successful gubernatorial candidate in 1934, but the Republicans dominated the next four gubernatorial elections. The Democrats, however, took control of the two major cities, Pittsburgh in 1933 and Philadelphia in 1951, and achieved electoral majorities in seven of the eleven presidential elections from 1936 to 1976. In 1954 and 1958 the Democrats elected George M. Leader and David L. Lawrence successively as governors. They were followed in 1962 by Republican William W. Scranton, Jr., and in 1966 by Republican Raymond P. Shafer. In 1970 the Democrats elected Milton Shapp and regained firm control of the legislature for the first time since 1936. Shapp became the first governor eligible to succeed himself under the 1968 Constitution, and he was reelected in 1974. In 1978 Republican Dick Thornburgh was elected governor. Within two years, the Republicans became the majority party when, in addition to the governorship, they held both U.S. Senate seats, supported President Ronald Reagan's candidacy in 1980, and won majorities in both houses of the state legislature. In 1982 Thornburgh was reelected to a second term; President Ronald Reagan was reelected in 1984. In 1985 the Democrats became the majority party in the House of Representatives. In 1986 the Democrat Robert P. Casey of Scranton, a former State Auditor General, defeated Lieutenant Governor William W. Scranton III for the governorship, becoming the forty-second person to hold that office.

Government Modernization

After the Second World War, there was a renewed effort to reorganize state government. The Chesterman Committee in 1953 proposed the consolidation of various departments. The Leader Administration in 1955 set up an Office of Administration to provide a closer check on the operation of various agencies. A government reorganization act permitted the governor to transfer functions from one department to another, subject to approval of the General Assembly. New departments continued to be created, the most recent of which is the Department of Corrections (1984). Establishment of the departments of Environmental Resources in 1970 and Aging in 1979 were major steps forward. In 1978 a constitutional amendment made the Attorney General an elected official. As a result the new office of General Counsel was created to serve the executive branch.

A series of important constitutional amendments culminated in the calling of a Constitutional Convention in 1967-1968, which revised the 1874 constitution. A significant provision prohibits the denial to any person of his civil rights. The General Assembly now meets annually and is a continuing body. The governor and other elective state officers are eligible to succeed themselves for one additional term. A unified judicial system has been established under the Supreme Court, a Commonwealth Court was created, and the inferior courts were modernized. Broad extensions of county and local home rule are possible. (See Section 2) In 1971 the voters amended the state constitution to guarantee that equal rights could not be denied because of sex and in 1972 the Pennsylvania General Assembly ratified the equal rights amendment to the United States Constitution.

The Cold War, Korean Conflict and Vietnam Involvement

After the end of World War II, the United Nations was established as a parliament of governments in which disputes between nations could be settled peacefully. Nevertheless, the United States and Communist countries started an arms race that led to a "cold war," resulting in several undeclared limited wars. From 1950 to 1953, individual Pennsylvanians were among the many Americans who fought with the South Koreans against the North Koreans and their Red Chinese allies. Pennsylvania's 28th Infantry Division was one of four National Guard divisions called to active duty during the crisis, being deployed to Germany to help deflect any expansion of the conflict.

Pennsylvania served their country faithfully during the Korean and Vietnam conflicts. In Korea, Pfc. Melvin L. Brown of Mahaffey, Sfc. William S. Sitman of Bellwood, and Cpl. Clifton T. Speicher of Gray gave their lives in self-sacrificing combat deeds for which they were awarded the Congressional Medal of Honor. Major General John Huston Church (1892-1953) commanded the 24th Infantry Division in the first year of fighting. Lieutenant General Henry Aurand commanded the U.S. Army-Pacific (which included the Korean operation) from 1949 to 1952. General Lyman L. Lemnitzer, a native of Honesdale, was Chairman of the Joint Chiefs of Staff during the Cuban Missile Crisis of 1962 which brought the Cold War to an end. In 1964 a conflict against expanding communism developed in Vietnam. American troops fought beside the South Vietnamese against the North Vietnamese and their communist supporters until 1973, and many Pennsylvanians served and died there. Cpl. Michael J. Crescenz of Philadelphia and Sgt. Glenn H. English, Jr., a native of Altoona, were mortally wounded while performing courageous acts for which they were awarded the Congressional Medal of Honor. Major General Charles W. Eifler, a native of Altoona, directed the First Logistical command in south Vietnam until May 1967.

CONSTITUTION
OF
PENNSYLVANIA

SECTION 2 - CONSTITUTION

CONSTITUTION
of the
COMMONWEALTH OF PENNSYLVANIA

PREAMBLE

WE, the people of the Commonwealth of Pennsylvania, grateful to Almighty God for the blessings of civil and religious liberty, and humbly invoking His guidance, do ordain and establish this Constitution.

Article I
DECLARATION OF RIGHTS

That the general, great and essential principles of liberty and free government may be recognized and unalterably established, WE DECLARE THAT —

Inherent Rights of Mankind
Section 1. All men are born equally free and independent, and have certain inherent and indefeasible rights, among which are those of enjoying and defending life and liberty, of acquiring, possessing and protecting property and reputation, and of pursuing their own happiness.

Political Powers
Section 2. All power is inherent in the people, and all free governments are founded on their authority and instituted for their peace, safety and happiness. For the advancement of these ends they have at all times an inalienable and indefeasible right to alter, reform or abolish their government in such manner as they may think proper.

Religious Freedom
Section 3. All men have a natural and indefeasible right to worship Almighty God according to the dictates of their own consciences; no man can of right be compelled to attend, erect or support any place of worship or to maintain any ministry against his consent; no human authority can, in any case whatever, control or interfere with the rights of conscience, and no preference shall ever be given by law to any religious establishments or modes of worship.

Religion
Section 4. No person who acknowledges the being of a God and a future state of rewards and punishments shall, on account of his religious sentiments, be disqualified to hold any office or place of trust or profit under this Commonwealth.

Elections
Section 5. Elections shall be free and equal; and no power, civil or military, shall at any time interfere to prevent the free exercise of the right of suffrage.

Trial by Jury
Section 6.[1] Trial by jury shall be as heretofore, and the right thereof remain inviolate. The General Assembly may provide, however, by law, that a verdict may be rendered by not less than five-sixths of the jury in any civil case.

Freedom of Press and Speech; Libels
Section 7. The printing press shall be free to every person who may undertake to examine the proceedings of the Legislature or any branch of government, and no law shall ever be made to restrain the right thereof. The free communication of thoughts and opinions is one of the invaluable rights of man, and every citizen may freely speak, write and print on any subject, being responsible for the abuse of that liberty. No conviction shall be had in any prosecution for the publication of papers relating to the official conduct of officers or men in public capacity, or to any other matter proper for public investigation or information, where the fact that such publication was not maliciously or negligently made shall be established to the satisfaction of the jury; and in all indictments for libels the jury shall have the right to determine the law and the facts, under the direction of the court, as in other cases.

Security From Searches and Seizures
Section 8. The people shall be secure in their persons, houses, papers and possessions from unreasonable searches and seizures, and no warrant to search any place or to seize any person or things shall issue without describing them as nearly as may be, nor without probable cause, supported by oath or affirmation subscribed to by the affiant.

[1] *Amended May 18, 1971.*

Rights of Accused in Criminal Prosecutions

Section 9.[2] In all criminal prosecutions the accused hath a right to be heard by himself and his counsel, to demand the nature and cause of the accusation against him, to meet the witnesses face to face, to have compulsory process for obtaining witnesses in his favor, and, in prosecutions by indictment or information, a speedy public trial by an impartial jury of the vicinage; he cannot be compelled to give evidence against himself, nor can he be deprived of his life, liberty or property, unless by the judgment of his peers or the law of the land. The use of a suppressed voluntary admission or voluntary confession to impeach the credibility of a person may be permitted and shall not be construed as compelling a person to give evidence against himself.

Initiation of Criminal Proceedings; Twice in Jeopardy; Eminent Domain

Section 10.[3] Except as hereinafter provided no person shall, for any indictable offense, be proceeded against criminally by information, except in cases arising in the land or naval forces, or in the militia, when in actual service, in time of war or public danger, or by leave of the court for oppression or misdemeanor in office. Each of the several courts of common pleas may, with the approval of the Supreme Court, provide for the initiation of criminal proceedings therein by information filed in the manner provided by law. No person shall, for the same offense, be twice put in jeopardy of life or limb; nor shall private property be taken or applied to public use, without authority of law and without just compensation being first made or secured.

Courts to Be Open; Suits Against the Commonwealth

Section 11. All courts shall be open; and every man for an injury done him in his lands, goods, person or reputation shall have remedy by due course of law, and right and justice administered without sale, denial or delay. Suits may be brought against the Commonwealth in such manner, in such courts and in such cases as the Legislature may by law direct.

Power of Suspending Laws

Section 12. No power of suspending laws shall be exercised unless by the Legislature or by its authority.

Bail, Fines and Punishments

Section 13. Excessive bail shall not be required, nor excessive fines imposed, nor cruel punishments inflicted.

Prisoners to Be Bailable; Habeas Corpus

Section 14. All prisoners shall be bailable by sufficient sureties, unless for capital offenses when the proof is evident or presumption great; and the privilege of the writ of habeas corpus shall not be suspended, unless when in case of rebellion or invasion the public safety may require it.

Special Criminal Tribunals

Section 15. No commission shall issue creating special temporary criminal tribunals to try particular individuals or particular classes of cases.

Insolvent Debtors

Section 16. The person of a debtor, where there is not strong presumption of fraud, shall not be continued in prison after delivering up his estate for the benefit of his creditors in such manner as shall be prescribed by law.

Ex Post Facto Laws; Impairment of Contracts

Section 17. No ex post facto law, nor any law impairing the obligation of contracts, or making irrevocable any grant of special privileges or immunities, shall be passed.

Attainder

Section 18. No person shall be attainted of treason or felony by the Legislature.

Attainder Limited

Section 19. No attainder shall work corruption of blood, nor, except during the life of the offender, forefeiture of estate to the Commonwealth.

Right of Petition

Section 20. The citizens have a right in a peaceable manner to assemble together for their common good, and to apply to those invested with the powers of government for redress of grievances or other proper purposes by petition, address or remonstrance.

Right to Bear Arms

Section 21. The right of the citizens to bear arms in defense of themselves and the State shall not be questioned.

Standing Army; Military Subordinate to Civil Power

Section 22. No standing army shall, in time of peace, be kept up without the consent of the Legislature, and the military shall in all cases and at all times be in strict subordination to the civil power.

[2]Amended Nov. 6, 1984.   [3]Amended Nov. 6, 1973.

Quartering of Troops

Section 23. No soldier shall in time of peace be quartered in any house without the consent of the owner, nor in time of war but in a manner to be prescribed by law.

Titles and Offices

Section 24. The Legislature shall not grant any title of nobility or hereditary distinction, nor create any office the appointment to which shall be for a longer term than during good behavior.

Reservation of Powers in People

Section 25. To guard against transgressions of the high powers which we have delegated, we declare that everything in this article is excepted out of the general powers of government and shall forever remain inviolate.

No Discrimination by Commonwealth and Its Political Subdivisions

Section 26. Neither the Commonwealth nor any political subdivision thereof shall deny to any person the enjoyment of any civil right, nor discriminate against any person in the exercise of any civil right.

Natural Resources and the Public Estate

Section 27.[4] The people have a right to clean air, pure water, and to the preservation of the natural, scenic, historic and esthetic values of the environment. Pennsylvania's public natural resources are the common property of all the people, including generations yet to come. As trustee of these resources, the Commonwealth shall conserve and maintain them for the benefit of all the people.

Prohibition Against Denial or Abridgment of Equality of Rights Because of Sex

Section 28.[5] Equality of rights under the law shall not be denied or abridged in the Commonwealth of Pennsylvania because of the sex of the individual.

Article II

THE LEGISLATURE

Legislative Power

Section 1. The legislative power of this Commonwealth shall be vested in a General Assembly, which shall consist of a Senate and a House of Representatives.

Election of Members; Vacancies

Section 2. Members of the General Assembly shall be chosen at the general election every second year. Their term of service shall begin on the first day of December next after their election. Whenever a vacancy shall occur in either House, the presiding officer thereof shall issue a writ of election to fill such vacancy for the remainder of the term.

Terms of Members

Section 3. Senators shall be elected for the term of four years and Representatives for the term of two years.

Sessions

Section 4. The General Assembly shall be a continuing body during the term for which its Representatives are elected. It shall meet at twelve o'clock noon on the first Tuesday of January each year. Special sessions shall be called by the Governor on petition of a majority of the members elected to each House or may be called by the Governor whenever in his opinion the public interest requires.

Qualifications of Members

Section 5. Senators shall be at least twenty-five years of age and Representatives twenty-one years of age. They shall have been citizens and inhabitants of the State four years, and inhabitants of their respective districts one year next before their election (unless absent on the public business of the United States or of this State) and shall reside in their respective districts during their terms of service.

Disqualification to Hold Other Office

Section 6. No Senator or Representative shall, during the time for which he was elected, be appointed to any civil office under this Commonwealth to which a salary, fee or perquisite is attached. No member of Congress or other person holding any office (except of attorney-at-law or in the national guard or in a reserve component of the armed forces of the United States) under the United States or this Commonwealth to which a salary, fee or perquisite is attached shall be a member of either House during his continuance in office.

4,5Adopted May 18, 1971.

Ineligibility by Criminal Convictions

Section 7. No person hereafter convicted of embezzlement of public moneys, bribery, perjury or other infamous crime, shall be eligible to the General Assembly, or capable of holding any office of trust or profit in this Commonwealth.

Compensation

Section 8. The members of the General Assembly shall receive such salary and mileage for regular and special sessions as shall be fixed by law, and no other compensation whatever, whether for service upon committee or otherwise. No member of either House shall during the term for which he may have been elected, receive any increase of salary, or mileage, under any law passed during such term.

Election of Officers; Judge of Election and Qualifications of Members

Section 9. The Senate shall, at the beginning and close of each regular session and at such other times as may be necessary, elect one of its members President pro tempore, who shall perform the duties of the Lieutenant Governor, in any case of absence or disability of that officer, and whenever the said office of Lieutenant Governor shall be vacant. The House of Representatives shall elect one of its members as Speaker. Each House shall choose its other officers, and shall judge of the election and qualifications of its members.

Quorum

Section 10. A majority of each House shall constitute a quorum, but a smaller number may adjourn from day to day and compel the attendance of absent members.

Powers of Each House; Expulsion

Section 11. Each House shall have power to determine the rules of its proceedings and punish its members or other persons for contempt or disorderly behavior in its presence, to enforce obedience to its process, to protect its members against violence or offers of bribes or private solicitation, and, with the concurrence of two-thirds, to expel a member, but not a second time for the same cause, and shall have all other powers necessary for the Legislature of a free State. A member expelled for corruption shall not thereafter be eligible to either House, and punishment for contempt or disorderly behavior shall not bar an indictment for the same offense.

Journals; Yeas and Nays

Section 12. Each House shall keep a journal of its proceedings and from time to time publish the same, except such parts as require secrecy, and the yeas and nays of the members on any question shall, at the desire of any two of them, be entered on the journal.

Open Sessions

Section 13. The sessions of each House and of committees of the whole shall be open, unless when the business is such as ought to be kept secret.

Adjournments

Section 14. Neither House shall, without the consent of the other, adjourn for more than three days, nor to any other place than that in which the two Houses shall be sitting.

Privileges of Members

Section 15. The members of the General Assembly shall in all cases, except treason, felony, violation of their oath of office, and breach of surety of the peace, be privileged from arrest during their attendance at the sessions of their respective Houses and in going to and returning from the same; and for any speech or debate in either House they shall not be questioned in any other place.

Legislative Districts

Section 16. The Commonwealth shall be divided into fifty senatorial and two hundred three representative districts, which shall be composed of compact and contiguous territory as nearly equal in population as practicable. Each senatorial district shall elect one Senator, and each representative district one Representative. Unless absolutely necessary no county, city, incorporated town, borough, township or ward shall be divided in forming either a senatorial or representative district.

Legislative Reapportionment Commission

Section 17.[1] (a) In each year following the year of the Federal decennial census, a Legislative Reapportionment Commission shall be constituted for the purpose of reapportioning the Commonwealth. The commission shall act by a majority of its entire membership.

(b) The commission shall consist of five members: four of whom shall be the majority and minority leaders of both the Senate and the House of Representatives, or deputies appointed by each of them, and a chairman selected as hereinafter provided. No later than 60 days following the official reporting of the Federal decennial census as required by Federal law, the four members shall be certified by the President Pro Tempore of the Senate and the Speaker of the House of Representatives to the elections officer of the Commonwealth who under law shall have supervision over elections.

The four members within 45 days after their certification shall select the fifth member, who shall serve as chairman of the commission, and shall immediately certify his name to such elections officer. The chairman shall be a citizen of the Commonwealth other than a local, State or Federal official holding an office to which compensation is attached.

[1] Section 17 amended Nov. 3, 1981.

If the four members fail to select the fifth member within the time prescribed, a majority of the entire membership of the Supreme Court within thirty days thereafter shall appoint the chairman as aforesaid and certify his appointment to such elections officer.

Any vacancy in the commission shall be filled within fifteen days in the same manner in which such position was originally filled.

(c) No later than ninety days after either the commission has been duly certified or the population data for the Commonwealth as determined by the Federal decennial census are available, whichever is later in time, the commission shall file a preliminary reapportionment plan with such elections officer.

The commission shall have thirty days after filing the preliminary plan to make corrections in the plan.

Any person aggrieved by the preliminary plan shall have the same thirty-day period to file exceptions with the commission in which case the commission shall have thirty days after the date the exceptions were filed to prepare and file with such elections officer a revised reapportionment plan. If no exceptions are filed within thirty days, or if filed and acted upon, the commission's plan shall be final and have the force of law.

(d) Any aggrieved person may file an appeal from the final plan directly to the Supreme Court within thirty days after the filing thereof. If the appellant establishes that the final plan is contrary to law, the Supreme Court shall issue an order remanding the plan to the commission and directing the commission to reapportion the Commonwealth in a manner not inconsistent with such order.

(e) When the Supreme Court has finally decided an appeal or when the last day for filing an appeal has passed with no appeal taken, the reapportionment plan shall have the force of law and the districts therein provided shall be used thereafter in elections to the General Assembly until the next reapportionment as required under this section 17.

(f) The General Assembly shall appropriate sufficient funds for the compensation and expenses of members and staff appointed by the commission, and other necessary expenses. The members of the commission shall be entitled to such compensation for their services as the General Assembly from time to time shall determine, but no part thereof shall be paid until a preliminary plan is filed. If a preliminary plan is filed but the commission fails to file a revised or final plan within the time prescribed, the commission members shall forfeit all right to compensation not paid.

(g) If a preliminary, revised or final reapportionment plan is not filed by the commission within the time prescribed by this section, unless the time be extended by the Supreme Court for cause shown, the Supreme Court shall immediately proceed on its own motion to reapportion the Commonwealth.

(h) Any reapportionment plan filed by the commission, or ordered or prepared by the Supreme Court upon the failure of the commission to act, shall be published by the elections officer once in at least one newspaper of general circulation in each senatorial and representative district. The publication shall contain a map of the Commonwealth showing the complete reapportionment of the General Assembly by districts, and a map showing the reapportionment districts in the area normally served by the newspaper in which the publication is made. The publication shall also state the population of the senatorial and representative districts having the smallest and largest population and the percentage variation of such districts from the average population for senatorial and representative districts.

Article III
LEGISLATION

A. Procedure

Passage of Laws
   Section 1. No law shall be passed except by bill, and no bill shall be so altered or amended, on its passage through either House, as to change its original purpose.

Reference to Committee; Printing
   Section 2. No bill shall be considered unless referred to a committee, printed for the use of the members and returned therefrom.

Form of Bills
   Section 3. No bill shall be passed containing more than one subject, which shall be clearly expressed in its title, except a general appropriation bill or a bill codifying or compiling the law or a part thereof.

Consideration of Bills
   Section 4. Every bill shall be considered on three different days in each House. All amendments made thereto shall be printed for the use of the members before the final vote is taken on the bill and before the final vote is taken, upon written request addressed to the presiding officer of either House by at least twenty-five per cent of the members elected to that House, any bill shall be read at length in that House. No bill shall become a law, unless on its final passage the vote is taken by yeas and nays, the names of the persons voting for and against it are entered on the journal, and a majority of the members elected to each House is recorded thereon as voting in its favor.

Concurring in Amendments; Conference Committee Reports

Section 5. No amendment to bills by one House shall be concurred in by the other, except by the vote of a majority of the members elected thereto, taken by yeas and nays, and the names of those voting for and against recorded upon the journal thereof; and reports of committees of conference shall be adopted in either House only by the vote of a majority of the members elected thereto, taken by yeas and nays, and the names of those voting recorded upon the journals.

Revival and Amendment of Laws

Section 6. No law shall be revived, amended, or the provisions thereof extended or conferred, by reference to its title only, but so much thereof as is revived, amended, extended or conferred shall be re-enacted and published at length.

Notice of Local and Special Bills

Section 7. No local or special bill shall be passed unless notice of the intention to apply therefor shall have been published in the locality where the matter or the thing to be effected may be situated, which notice shall be at least thirty days prior to the introduction into the General Assembly of such bill and in the manner to be provided by law; the evidence of such notice having been published, shall be exhibited in the General Assembly, before such act shall be passed.

Signing of Bills

Section 8. The presiding officer of each House shall, in the presence of the House over which he presides, sign all bills and joint resolutions passed by the General Assembly, after their titles have been publicly read immediately before signing; and the fact of signing shall be entered on the journal.

Action on Concurrent Orders and Resolutions

Section 9. Every order, resolution or vote, to which the concurrence of both Houses may be necessary, except on the question of adjournment, shall be presented to the Governor and before it shall take effect be approved by him, or being disapproved, shall be repassed by two-thirds of both Houses according to the rules and limitations prescribed in case of a bill.

Revenue Bills

Section 10. All bills for raising revenue shall originate in the House of Representatives, but the Senate may propose amendments as in other bills.

Appropriation Bills

Section 11. The general appropriation bill shall embrace nothing but appropriations for the executive, legislative and judicial departments of the Commonwealth, for the public debt and for public schools. All other appropriations shall be made by separate bills, each embracing but one subject.

Legislation Designated by Governor at Special Sessions

Section 12. When the General Assembly shall be convened in special session, there shall be no legislation upon subjects other than those designated in the proclamation of the Governor calling such session.

Vote Denied Members with Personal Interest

Section 13. A member who has a personal or private interest in any measure or bill proposed or pending before the General Assembly shall disclose the fact to the House of which he is a member, and shall not vote thereon.

B. Education

Public School System

Section 14. The General Assembly shall provide for the maintenance and support of a thorough and efficient system of public education to serve the needs of the Commonwealth.

Public School Money Not Available to Sectarian Schools

Section 15. No money raised for the support of the public schools of the Commonwealth shall be appropriated to or used for the support of any sectarian school.

C. National Guard

National Guard to be Organized and Maintained

Section 16. The citizens of this Commonwealth shall be armed, organized and disciplined for its defense when and in such manner as may be directed by law. The General Assembly shall provide for maintaining the National Guard by appropriations from the Treasury of the Commonwealth, and may exempt from State military service persons having conscientious scruples against bearing arms.

D. Other Legislation Specifically Authorized

Appointment of Legislative Officers and Employees

Section 17. The General Assembly shall prescribe by law the number, duties and compensation of the officers and employees of each House, and no payment shall be made from the State Treasury, or be in any way authorized, to any person, except to an acting officer or employee elected or appointed in pursuance of law.

Compensation Laws Allowed to General Assembly

Section 18. The General Assembly may enact laws requiring the payment by employers, or employers and employees jointly, of reasonable compensation for injuries to employees arising in the course of their employment, and for occupational diseases of employees, whether or not such injuries or diseases result in death, and regardless of fault of employer or employee, and fixing the basis of ascertainment of such compensation and the maximum and minimum limits thereof, and providing special or general remedies for the collection thereof; but in no other cases shall the General Assembly limit the amount to be recovered for injuries resulting in death, or for injuries to persons or property, and in case of death from such injuries, the right of action shall survive, and the General Assembly shall prescribe for whose benefit such actions shall be prosecuted. No act shall prescribe any limitations of time within which suits may be brought against corporations for injuries to persons or property, or for other causes different from those fixed by general laws regulating actions against natural persons, and such acts now existing are avoided.

Appropriations for Support of Widows and Orphans of Persons Who Served in the Armed Forces

Section 19. The General Assembly may make appropriations of money to institutions wherein the widows of persons who served in the armed forces are supported or assisted, or the orphans of persons who served in the armed forces are maintained and educated; but such appropriations shall be applied exclusively to the support of such widows and orphans.

Classification of Municipalities

Section 20. The Legislature shall have power to classify counties, cities, boroughs, school districts, and townships according to population, and all laws passed relating to each class, and all laws passed relating to, and regulating procedure and proceedings in court with reference to, any class, shall be deemed general legislation within the meaning of this Constitution.

Land Title Registration

Section 21. Laws may be passed providing for a system of registering, transferring, insuring of and guaranteeing land titles by the State, or by the counties thereof, and for settling and determining adverse or other claims to and interest in lands the titles to which are so registered, transferred, insured, and guaranteed; and for the creation and collection of indemnity funds; and for carrying the system and powers hereby provided for into effect by such existing courts as may be designated by the Legislature. Such laws may provide for continuing the registering, transferring, insuring, and guaranteeing such titles after the first or original registration has been perfected by the court, and provision may be made for raising the necessary funds for expenses and salaries of officers, which shall be paid out of the treasury of the several counties.

State Purchases

Section 22. The General Assembly shall maintain by law a system of competitive bidding under which all purchases of materials, printing, supplies or other personal property used by the government of this Commonwealth shall so far as practicable be made. The law shall provide that no officer or employee of the Commonwealth shall be in any way interested in any purchase made by the Commonwealth under contract or otherwise.

Change of Venue

Section 23. The power to change the venue in civil and criminal cases shall be vested in the courts, to be exercised in such manner as shall be provided by law.

Paying Out Public Moneys

Section 24. No money shall be paid out of the treasury, except on appropriations made by law and on warrant issued by the proper officers; but cash refunds of taxes, licenses, fees and other charges paid or collected, but not legally due, may be paid, as provided by law, without appropriation from the fund into which they were paid on warrant of the proper officer.

Emergency Seats of Government

Section 25. The General Assembly may provide, by law, during any session, for the continuity of the executive, legislative, and judicial functions of the government of the Commonwealth, and its political subdivisions, and the establishment of emergency seats thereof and any such laws heretofore enacted are validated. Such legislation shall become effective in the event of an attack by an enemy of the United States.

Extra Compensation Prohibited; Claims Against the Commonwealth; Pensions

Section 26. No bill shall be passed giving any extra compensation to any public officer, servant, employee, agent or contractor, after services shall have been rendered or contract made, nor providing for the payment of any claim against the Commonwealth without previous authority of law: Provided, however, that nothing in this Constitution shall be construed to prohibit the General Assembly from authorizing the increase of retirement allowances or pensions of members of a retirement or pension system now in effect or hereafter legally constituted by the Commonwealth, its political subdivisions, agencies or instrumentalities, after the termination of the services of said member.

Changes in Term of Office or Salary Prohibited

Section 27. No law shall extend the term of any public officer, or increase or diminish his salary or emoluments, after his election or appointment.

E. Restrictions on Legislative Power

Change of Permanent Location of State Capital

Section 28. No law changing the permanent location of the Capital of the State shall be valid until the same shall have been submitted to the qualified electors of the Commonwealth at a general election and ratified and approved by them.

Appropriations for Public Assistance, Military Service, Scholarships

Section 29. No appropriation shall be made for charitable, educational or benevolent purposes to any person or community nor to any denomination and sectarian institution, corporation or association: Provided, that appropriations may be made for pensions or gratuities for military service and to blind persons twenty-one years of age and upwards and for assistance to mothers having dependent children and to aged persons without adequate means of support and in the form of scholarship grants or loans for higher educational purposes to residents of the Commonwealth enrolled in institutions of higher learning except that no scholarship, grants or loans for higher educational purposes shall be given to persons enrolled in a theological seminary or school of theology.

Charitable and Educational Appropriations

Section 30. No appropriation shall be made to any charitable or educational institution not under the absolute control of the Commonwealth, other than normal schools established by law for the professional training of teachers for the public schools of the State, except by a vote of two-thirds of all the members elected to each House.

Delegation of Certain Powers Prohibited

Section 31. The General Assembly shall not delegate to any special commission, private corporation or association, any power to make, supervise or interfere with any municipal improvement, money, property or effects, whether held in trust or otherwise, or to levy taxes or perform any municipal function whatever. Notwithstanding the foregoing limitation or any other provision of the Constitution, the General Assembly may enact laws which provide that the findings of panels or commissions, selected and acting in accordance with law for the adjustment or settlement of grievances or disputes or for collective bargaining between policemen and firemen and their public employers shall be binding upon all parties and shall constitute a mandate to the head of the political subdivision which is the employer, or to the appropriate officer of the Commonwealth if the Commonwealth is the employer, with respect to matters which can be remedied by administrative action, and to the lawmaking body of such political subdivision or of the Commonwealth, with respect to matters which require legislative action, to take the action necessary to carry out such findings.

Certain Local and Special Laws

Section 32. The General Assembly shall pass no local or special law in any case which has been or can be provided for by general law and specifically the General Assembly shall not pass any local or special law:
1. Regulating the affairs of counties, cities, townships, wards, boroughs or school districts:
2. Vacating roads, town plats, streets or alleys:
3. Locating or changing county seats, erecting new counties or changing county lines:
4. Erecting new townships or boroughs, changing township lines, borough limits or school districts:
5. Remitting fines, penalties and forfeitures, or refunding moneys legally paid into the treasury:
6. Exempting property from taxation:
7. Regulating labor, trade, mining or manufacturing:
8. Creating corporations, or amending, renewing or extending the charters thereof:
Nor shall the General Assembly indirectly enact any special or local law by the partial repeal of a general law; but laws repealing local or special acts may be passed.

Article IV
THE EXECUTIVE

Executive Department

Section 1. The Executive Department of this Commonwealth shall consist of a Governor, Lieutenant Governor, Attorney General, Auditor General, State Treasurer, and Superintendent of Public Instruction and such other officers as the General Assembly may from time to time prescribe.

Duties of Governor; Election Procedure; Tie or Contest

Section 2. The supreme executive power shall be vested in the Governor, who shall take care that the laws be faithfully executed; he shall be chosen on the day of the general election, by the qualified electors of the Commonwealth, at the places where they shall vote for Representatives. The returns of every election for Governor shall be sealed up and transmitted to the seat of government, directed to the President of the Senate, who shall open and publish them in the presence of the members of both Houses of the

General Assembly. The person having the highest number of votes shall be Governor, but if two or more be equal and highest in votes, one of them shall be chosen Governor by the joint vote of the members of both Houses. Contested elections shall be determined by a committee, to be selected from both Houses of the General Assembly, and formed and regulated in such manner as shall be directed by law.

Terms of Office of Governor; Number of Terms

Section 3. The Governor shall hold his office during four years from the third Tuesday of January next ensuing his election. Except for the Governor who may be in office when this amendment is adopted, he shall be eligible to succeed himself for one additional term.

Lieutenant Governor

Section 4. A Lieutenant Governor shall be chosen jointly with the Governor by the casting by each voter of a single vote applicable to both offices, for the same term, and subject to the same provisions as the Governor; he shall be President of the Senate. As such, he may vote in case of a tie on any question except the final passage of a bill or joint resolution, the adoption of a conference report or the concurrence in amendments made by the House of Representatives.

Attorney General

Section 4.1.[1] An Attorney General shall be chosen by the qualified electors of the Commonwealth on the day the general election is held for the Auditor General and State Treasurer; he shall hold his office during four years from the third Tuesday of January next ensuing his election and shall not be eligible to serve continuously for more than two successive terms; he shall be the chief law officer of the Commonwealth and shall exercise such powers and perform such duties as may be imposed by law.

Qualifications of Governor, Lieutenant Governor and Attorney General

Section 5.[2] No person shall be eligible to the office of Governor, Lieutenant Governor or Attorney General except a citizen of the United States, who shall have attained the age of thirty years, and have been seven years next preceding his election an inhabitant of this Commonwealth, unless he shall have been absent on the public business of the United States or of this Commonwealth. No person shall be eligible to the office of Attorney General except a member of the bar of the Supreme Court of Pennsylvania.

Disqualification for Offices of Governor, Lieutenant Governor and Attorney General

Section 6.[3] No member of Congress or person holding any office (except of attorney-at-law or in the National Guard or in a reserve component of the armed forces of the United States) under the United States or this Commonwealth shall exercise the office of Governor, Lieutenant Governor or Attorney General.

Military Power

Section 7. The Governor shall be commander-in-chief of the military forces of the Commonwealth, except when they shall be called into actual service of the United States.

Appointing Power

Section 8.[4] (a) The Governor shall appoint a Secretary of Education and such other officers as he shall be authorized by law to appoint. The appointment of the Secretary of Education and of such other officers as may be specified by law, shall be subject to the consent of two-thirds or a majority of the members elected to the Senate as is specified by law.

(b) The Governor shall fill vacancies in offices to which he appoints by nominating to the Senate a proper person to fill the vacancy within 90 days of the first day of the vacancy and not thereafter. The Senate shall act on each executive nomination within 25 legislative days of its submission. If the Senate has not voted upon a nomination within 15 legislative days following such submission, any five members of the Senate may, in writing, request the presiding officer of the Senate to place the nomination before the entire Senate body whereby the nomination must be voted upon prior to the expiration of five legislative days or 25 legislative days following submission by the Governor, whichever occurs first. If the nomination is made during a recess or after adjournment sine die, the Senate shall act upon it within 25 legislative days after its return or reconvening. If the Senate for any reason fails to act upon a nomination submitted to it within the required 25 legislative days, the nominee shall take office as if the appointment had been consented to by the Senate. The Governor shall in a similar manner fill vacancies in the offices of Auditor General, State Treasurer, justice, judge, justice of the peace and in any other elective office he is authorized to fill. In the case of a vacancy in an elective office, a person shall be elected to the office on the next election day appropriate to the office unless the first day of the vacancy is within two calendar months immediately preceding the election day in which case the election shall be held on the second succeeding election day appropriate to the office.

(c) In acting on executive nominations, the Senate shall sit with open doors. The votes shall be taken by yeas and nays and shall be entered on the journal.

Pardoning Power; Board of Pardons

Section 9.[5] (a) In all criminal cases except impeachment, the Governor shall have power to remit fines and forfeitures, to grant reprieves, commutation of sentences and pardons; but no pardon shall be granted, nor sentence commuted, except on the recommendation in writing of a majority of the Board of Pardons, after full hearing in open session, upon due public notice. The recommendation, with the reasons therefor at length, shall be delivered to the Governor and a copy thereof shall be kept on file in the office of the Lieutenant Governor in a docket kept for that purpose.

---

[1]Amended May 16, 1978   [2],[3]Amended May 16, 1978.   [4]Amended May 20, 1975, and May 16, 1978.   [5]Amended May 20, 1975.

(b) The Board of Pardons shall consist of the Lieutenant Governor who shall be chairman, the Attorney General and three members appointed by the Governor with the consent of two-thirds or a majority of the members elected to the Senate as is specified by law for terms of six years. The three members appointed by the Governor shall be residents of Pennsylvania and shall be recognized leaders in their fields; one shall be a member of the bar, one a penologist, and the third a doctor of medicine, psychiatrist or psychologist. The board shall keep records of its actions, which shall at all times be open for public inspection.

Information from Department Officials
Section 10. The Governor may require information in writing from the officers of the Executive Department, upon any subject relating to the duties of their respective offices.

Messages to the General Assembly
Section 11. He shall, from time to time, give to the General Assembly information of the state of the Commonwealth, and recommend to their consideration such measures as he may judge expedient.

Power to Convene and Adjourn the General Assembly
Section 12. He may, on extraordinary occasions, convene the General Assembly, and in case of disagreement between the two Houses, with respect to the time of adjournment, adjourn them to such time as he shall think proper, not exceeding four months. He shall have power to convene the Senate in extraordinary session by proclamation for the transaction of Executive business.

When Lieutenant Governor to Act as Governor
Section 13. In the case of the death, conviction on impeachment, failure to qualify or resignation of the Governor, the Lieutenant Governor shall become Governor for the remainder of the term and in the case of the disability of the Governor, the powers, duties and emoluments of the office shall devolve upon the Lieutenant Governor until the disability is removed.

Vacancy in Office of Lieutenant Governor
Section 14. In case of the death, conviction on impeachment, failure to qualify or resignation of the Lieutenant Governor, or in case he should become Governor under section 13 of this article, the President pro tempore of the Senate shall become Lieutenant Governor for the remainder of the term. In case of the disability of the Lieutenant Governor, the powers, duties and emoluments of the office shall devolve upon the President pro tempore of the Senate until the disability is removed. Should there be no Lieutenant Governor, the President pro tempore of the Senate shall become Governor if a vacancy shall occur in the office of Governor and in case of the disability of the Governor, the powers, duties and emoluments of the office shall devolve upon the President pro tempore of the Senate until the disability is removed. His seat as Senator shall become vacant whenever he shall become Governor and shall be filled by election as any other vacancy in the Senate.

Approval of Bills; Vetoes
Section 15. Every bill which shall have passed both Houses shall be presented to the Governor; if he approves he shall sign it, but if he shall not approve he shall return it with his objections to the House in which it shall have originated, which House shall enter the objections at large upon their journal, and proceed to re-consider it. If after such re-consideration, two-thirds of all the members elected to that House shall agree to pass the bill, it shall be sent with the objections to the other House by which likewise it shall be re-considered, and if approved by two-thirds of all the members elected to that House it shall be a law; but in such cases the votes of both Houses shall be determined by yeas and nays, and the names of the members voting for and against the bill shall be entered on the journals of each House, respectively. If any bill shall not be returned by the Governor within ten days after it shall have been presented to him, the same shall be a law in like manner as if he had signed it, unless the General Assembly, by their adjournment, prevent its return, in which case it shall be a law, unless he shall file the same, with his objections, in the office of the Secretary of the Commonwealth, and give notice thereof by public proclamation within thirty days after such adjournment.

Partial Disapproval of Appropriation Bills
Section 16. The Governor shall have power to disapprove of any item or items of any bill, making appropriations of money, embracing distinct items, and the part or parts of the bill approved shall be the law, and the item or items of appropriation disapproved shall be void, unless re-passed according to the rules and limitations prescribed for the passage of other bills over the Executive veto.

Contested Elections of Governor, Lieutenant Governor and Attorney General; When Succeeded
Section 17.[6] The Chief Justice of the Supreme Court shall preside upon the trial of any contested election of Governor, Lieutenant Governor or Attorney General and shall decide questions regarding the admissibility of evidence, and shall, upon request of the committee, pronounce his opinion upon other questions of law involved in the trial. The Governor, Lieutenant Governor and Attorney General shall exercise the duties of their respective offices until their successors shall be duly qualified.

Terms of Office of Auditor General and State Treasurer; Number of Terms; Eligibility of State Treasurer to become Auditor General
Section 18. The terms of the Auditor General and of the State Treasurer shall each be four years from the third Tuesday of January next ensuing his election. They shall be chosen by the qualified electors of the Commonwealth at general elections but shall not be eligible to serve continuously for more than two successive terms. The State Treasurer shall not be eligible to the office of Auditor General until four years after he has been State Treasurer.

[6]Amended May 16, 1978.

State Seal; Commissions

Section 19. The present Great Seal of Pennsylvania shall be the seal of the State. All commissions shall be in the name and by authority of the Commonwealth of Pennsylvania, and be sealed with the State seal and signed by the Governor.

Article V
THE JUDICIARY

Unified Judicial System

Section 1. The judicial power of the Commonwealth shall be vested in a unified judicial system consisting of the Supreme Court, the Superior Court, the Commonwealth Court, courts of common pleas, community courts, municipal and traffic courts in the City of Philadelphia, such other courts as may be provided by law and justices of the peace. All courts and justices of the peace and their jurisdiction shall be in this unified judicial system.

Supreme Court

Section 2. The Supreme Court (a) shall be the highest court of the Commonwealth and in this court shall be reposed the supreme judicial power of the Commonwealth;

(b) shall consist of seven justices, one of whom shall be the Chief Justice; and

(c) shall have such jurisdiction as shall be provided by law.

Superior Court

Section 3.[1] The Superior Court shall be a statewide court, and shall consist of the number of judges, which shall be not less than seven judges, and have such jurisdiction as shall be provided by this Constitution or by the General Assembly. One of its judges shall be the president judge.

Commonwealth Court

Section 4. The Commonwealth Court shall be a statewide court, and shall consist of the number of judges and have such jurisdiction as shall be provided by law. One of its judges shall be the president judge.

Courts of Common Pleas

Section 5. There shall be one court of common pleas for each judicial district (a) having such divisions and consisting of such number of judges as shall be provided by law, one of whom shall be the president judge; and

(b) having unlimited original jurisdiction in all cases except as may otherwise be provided by law.

Community Courts; Philadelphia Municipal Court and Traffic Court

Section 6. (a) In any judicial district a majority of the electors voting thereon may approve the establishment or discontinuance of a community court. Where a community court is approved, one community court shall be established; its divisions, number of judges and jurisdiction shall be as provided by law.

(b) The question whether a community court shall be established or discontinued in any judicial district shall be placed upon the ballot in a primary election by petition which shall be in the form prescribed by the officer of the Commonwealth who under law shall have supervision over elections. The petition shall be filed with that officer and shall be signed by a number of electors equal to five percent of the total votes cast for all candidates for the office occupied by a single official for which the highest number of votes was cast in that judicial district at the last preceding general or municipal election. The manner of signing such petitions, the time of circulating them, the affidavits of the persons circulating them and all other details not contained herein shall be governed by the general laws relating to elections. The question shall not be placed upon the ballot in a judicial district more than once in any five-year period.

(c) In the City of Philadelphia there shall be a municipal court and a traffic court. The number of judges and the jurisdiction of each shall be as provided by law. These courts shall exist so long as a community court has not been established or in the event one has been discontinued under this section.

Justices of the Peace; Magisterial Districts

Section 7. (a) In any judicial district, other than the City of Philadelphia, where a community court has not been established or where one has been discontinued there shall be one justice of the peace in each magisterial district. The jurisdiction of the justice of the peace shall be as provided by law.

(b) The General Assembly shall by law establish classes of magisterial districts solely on the basis of population and population density and shall fix the salaries to be paid justices of the peace in each class. The number and boundaries of magisterial districts of each class within each judicial district shall be established by the Supreme Court or by the courts of common pleas under the direction of the Supreme Court as required for the efficient administration of justice within each magisterial district.

[1]Amended Nov. 6, 1979.

Other Courts

Section 8. The General Assembly may establish additional courts or divisions of existing courts, as needed, or abolish any statutory court or division thereof.

Right of Appeal

Section 9. There shall be a right of appeal in all cases to a court of record from a court not of record; and there shall also be a right of appeal from a court of record or from an administrative agency to a court of record or to an appellate court, the selection of such court to be as provided by law; and there shall be such other rights of appeal as may be provided by law.

Judicial Administration

Section 10.(a) The Supreme Court shall exercise general supervisory and administrative authority over all the courts and justices of the peace, including authority to temporarily assign judges and justices of the peace from one court or district to another as it deems appropriate.

(b) The Supreme Court shall appoint a court administrator and may appoint such subordinate administrators and staff as may be necessary and proper for the prompt and proper disposition of the business of all courts and justices of the peace.

(c) The Supreme Court shall have the power to prescribe general rules governing practice, procedure and the conduct of all courts, justices of the peace and all officers serving process or enforcing orders, judgments or decrees of any court or justice of the peace, including the power to provide for assignment and reassignment of classes or classes of appeals among the several courts as the needs of justice shall require, and for admission to the bar and to practice law, and the administration of all courts and supervision of all officers of the Judicial Branch, if such rules are consistent with this Constitution and neither abridge, enlarge nor modify the substantive rights of any litigant, nor affect the right of the General Assembly to determine the jurisdiction of any court or justice of the peace, nor suspend nor alter any statute of limitation or repose. All laws shall be suspended to the extent that they are inconsistent with rules prescribed under these provisions.

(d) The Chief Justice and president judges of all courts with seven or less judges shall be the justice or judge longest in continuous service on their respective courts; and in the event of his resignation from this postion the justice or judge next longest in continuous service shall be the Chief Justice or president judge. The president judges of all other courts shall be selected for five-year terms by the members of their respective courts, except that the president judge of the traffic court in the City of Philadelphia shall be appointed by the Governor. A Chief Justice or president judge may resign such position and remain a member of the court. In the event of a tie vote for office of president judge in a court which elects its president judge, the Supreme Court shall appoint as president judge one of the judges receiving the highest number of votes.

(e) Should any two or more justices or judges of the same court assume office at the same time, they shall cast lots forthwith for priority of commission, and certify the results to the Governor who shall issue their commissions accordingly.

Judicial Districts; Boundaries

Section 11. The number and boundaries of judicial districts shall be changed by the General Assembly only with the advice and consent of the Supreme Court.

Qualifications of Justices, Judges and Justices of the Peace

Section 12. (a) Justices, judges and justices of the peace shall be citizens of the Commonwealth. Justices and judges, except the judges of the traffic court in the City of Philadelphia, shall be members of the bar of the Supreme Court. Justices and judges of statewide courts, for a period of one year preceding their election or appointment and during their continuance in office, shall reside within the Commonwealth. Other judges and justices of the peace, for a period of one year preceding their election or appointment and during their continuance in office, shall reside within their respective districts, except as provided in this article for temporary assignments.

(b) Judges of the traffic court in the City of Philadelphia and justices of the peace shall be members of the bar of the Supreme Court or shall complete a course of training and instruction in the duties of their respective offices and pass an examination prior to assuming office. Such courses and examinations shall be as provided by law.

Election of Justices, Judges and Justices of the Peace; Vacancies

Section 13.[2] (a) Justices, judges and justices of the peace shall be elected at the municipal election next preceding the commencement of their respective terms of office by the electors of the Commonwealth or the respective districts in which they are to serve.

(b) A vacancy in the office of justice, judge or justice of the peace shall be filled by appointment by the Governor. The appointment shall be with the advice and consent of two-thirds of the members elected to the Senate, except in the case of justices of the peace which shall be by a majority. The person so appointed shall serve for a term ending on the first Monday of January following the next municipal election more than ten months after the vacancy occurs or for the remainder of the unexpired term whichever is less, except in the case of persons selected as additional judges to the Superior Court, where the General Assembly may stagger and fix the length of the initial terms of such additional judges by reference to any of the first, second and third municipal elections more than ten months after the additional judges are selected. The manner by which any additional judges are selected shall be provided by this section for the filling of vacancies in judicial offices.

(c) The provisions of section thirteen (b) shall not apply either in the case of a vacancy to be filled by retention election as provided in section fifteen (b), or in the case of a vacancy created by failure of a justice or judge to file a declaration for retention election as provided in section fifteen (b). In the case of a vacancy occurring at the expiration of an appointive term under section thirteen (b), the vacancy shall be filled by election as provided in section thirteen (a).

[2]Section 13 amended May 20, 1975; May 16, 1978; and Nov. 6, 1979.

(d) At the primary election in 1969, the electors of the Commonwealth may elect to have the justices and judges of the Supreme, Superior, Commonwealth and all other statewide courts appointed by the Governor from a list of persons qualified for the offices submitted to him by the Judicial Qualifications Commission. If a majority vote of those voting on the question is in favor of this method of appointment, then whenever any vacancy occurs thereafter for any reason in such court, the Governor shall fill the vacancy by appointment in the manner prescribed in this subsection. Such appointment shall not require the consent of the Senate.

(e) Each justice or judge appointed by the Governor under section thirteen (d) shall hold office for an initial term ending the first Monday of January following the next municipal election more than twenty-four months following the appointment.

Judicial Qualifications Commission

Section 14. (a) Should the method of judicial selection be adopted as provided in section thirteen (d), there shall be a Judicial Qualifications Commission, composed of four non-lawyer electors appointed by the Governor and three non-judge members of the bar of the Supreme Court appointed by the Supreme Court. No more than four members shall be of the same political party. The members of the commission shall serve for terms of seven years, with one member being selected each year. The commission shall consider all names submitted to it and recommend to the Governor not fewer than ten nor more than twenty of those qualified for each vacancy to be filled.

(b) During his term, no member shall hold a public office or public appointment for which he receives compensation, nor shall he hold office in a political party or political organization.

(c) A vacancy on the commission shall be filled by the appointing authority for the balance of the term.

Tenure of Justices, Judges and Justices of the Peace

Section 15. (a) The regular term of office of justices and judges shall be ten years and the regular term of office for judges of the municipal court and traffic court in the City of Philadelphia and of justices of the peace shall be six years. The tenure of any justice or judge shall not be affected by changes in judicial districts or by reduction in the number of judges.

(b) A justice or judge elected under section thirteen (a), appointed under section thirteen (d) or retained under this section fifteen (b) may file a declaration of candidacy for retention election with the officer of the Commonwealth who under law shall have supervision over elections on or before the first Monday of January of the year preceding the year in which his term of office expires. If no declaration is filed, a vacancy shall exist upon the expiration of the term of office of such justice or judge, to be filled by election under section thirteen (a) or by appointment under section thirteen (d) if applicable. If a justice or judge files a declaration, his name shall be submitted to the electors without party designation, on a separate judicial ballot or in a separate column on voting machines, at the municipal election immediately preceding the expiration of the term of office of the justice or judge, to determine only the question whether he shall be retained in office. If a majority is against retention, a vacancy shall exist upon the expiration of his term of office, to be filled by appointment under section thirteen (b) or under section thirteen (d) if applicable. If a majority favors retention, the justice or judge shall serve for the regular term of office provided herein, unless sooner removed or retired. At the expiration of each term a justice or judge shall be eligible for retention as provided herein subject only to the retirement provisions of this article.

Compensation and Retirement of Justices, Judges and Justices of the Peace

Section 16. (a) Justices, judges and justices of the peace shall be compensated by the Commonwealth as provided by law. Their compensation shall not be diminished during their terms of office, unless by law applying generally to all salaried officers of the Commonwealth.

(b) Justices, judges and justices of the peace shall be retired upon attaining the age of seventy years. Former and retired justices, judges and justices of the peace shall receive such compensation as shall be provided by law. No compensation shall be paid to any justice, judge or justice of the peace who is suspended or removed from office under section eighteen of this article or under Article VI.

(c) A former or retired justice or judge may, with his consent, be assigned by the Supreme Court on temporary judicial service as may be prescribed by rule of the Supreme Court.

Prohibited Activities

Section 17. (a) Justices and judges shall devote full time to their judicial duties, and shall not engage in the practice of law, hold office in a political party or political organization, or hold an office or position of profit in the government of the United States, the Commonwealth or any municipal corporation or political subdivision thereof, except in the armed service of the United States or the Commonwealth.

(b) Justices and judges shall not engage in any activity prohibited by law and shall not violate any canon of legal or judicial ethics prescribed by the Supreme Court. Justices of the peace shall be governed by rules or canons which shall be prescribed by the Supreme Court.

(c) No justice, judge or justice of the peace shall be paid or accept for the performance of any judicial duty or for any service connected with his office, any fee, emolument of perquisite other than the salary and expenses provided by law.

(d) No duties shall be imposed by law upon the Supreme Court or any of the justices thereof or the Superior Court or any of the judges thereof, except such as are judicial, nor shall any of them exercise any power of appointment except as provided in this Constitution.

Suspension, Removal, Discipline and Compulsory Retirement

Section 18. (a) There shall be a Judicial Inquiry and Review Board having nine members as follows: three judges of the courts of common pleas from different judicial districts and two judges of the Superior Court, all of whom shall be selected by the Supreme Court; and two non-judge members of the bar of the Supreme Court and two non-lawyer electors, all of whom shall be selected by the Governor.

(b) The members shall serve for terms of four years, provided that a member, rather than his successor, shall continue to participate in any hearing in progress at the end of his term. A vacancy on the board shall be filled by the respective appointing authority for the balance of the term. The respective appointing authority may remove a member only for cause. No member shall serve more than four consecutive years; he may be reappointed after a lapse of one year. Annually the members of the board shall elect a chairman. The board shall act only with the concurrence of a majority of its members.

(c) A member shall not hold office in a political party or political organization. Members, other than judges, shall be compensated for their services as the Supreme Court shall prescribe. All members shall be reimbursed for expenses necessarily incurred in the discharge of their official duties.

(d) Under the procedure prescribed herein, any justice or judge may be suspended, removed from office or otherwise disciplined for violation of section seventeen of this article, misconduct in office, neglect of duty, failure to perform his duties, or conduct which prejudices the proper administration of justice or brings the judicial office into disrepute, and may be retired for disability seriously interfering with the performance of his duties.

(e) The board shall keep informed as to matters relating to grounds for suspension, removal, discipline, or compulsory retirement of justices or judges. It shall receive complaints or reports, formal or informal, from any source pertaining to such matters, and shall make such preliminary investigations as it deems necessary.

(f) The board, after such investigation, may order a hearing concerning the suspension, removal, discipline or compulsory retirement of a justice or judge. The board's orders for attendance of or testimony by witnesses or for the production of documents at any hearing or investigation shall be enforceable by contempt proceedings.

(g) If, after hearing, the board finds good cause therefor, it shall recommend to the Supreme Court the suspension, removal, discipline or compulsory retirement of the justice or judge.

(h) The Supreme Court shall review the record of the board's proceedings on the law and facts and may permit the introduction of additional evidence. It shall order suspension, removal, discipline or compulsory retirement, or wholly reject the recommendation, as it finds just and proper. Upon an order for compulsory retirement, the justice or judge shall be retired with the same rights and privileges were he retired under section sixteen of this article. Upon an order for suspension or removal, the justice or judge shall be suspended or removed from office, and his salary shall cease from the date of such order. All papers filed with and proceedings before the board shall be confidential but upon being filed by the board in the Supreme Court, the record shall lose its confidential character. The filing of papers with and the giving of testimony before the board shall be privileged.

(i) No justice or judge shall participate as a member of the board or of the Supreme Court in any proceeding involving his suspension, removal, discipline or compulsory retirement.

(j) The Supreme Court shall prescribe rules of procedure under this section.

(k) The Supreme Court shall prescribe rules of procedure for the suspension, removal, discipline and compulsory retirement of justices of the peace.

(l) A justice, judge or justice of the peace convicted of misbehavior in office by a court, disbarred as a member of the bar of the Supreme Court or removed under this section eighteen shall forfeit automatically his judicial office and thereafter be ineligible for judicial office.

(m) A justice or judge who shall file for nomination for or election to any public office other than a judicial office shall forfeit automatically his judicial office.

(n) This section is in addition to and not in substitution for the provisions for impeachment for misbehavior in office contained in Article VI. No justice, judge or justice of the peace against whom impeachment proceedings are pending in the Senate shall exercise any of the duties of his office until he has been acquitted.

COURTS OTHER THAN IN THE CITY OF PHILADELPHIA AND ALLEGHENY COUNTY

The Supreme Court

Section 1. The Supreme Court shall exercise all the powers and, until otherwise provided by law, jurisdiction now vested in the present Supreme Court and, until otherwise provided by law, the accused in all cases of felonious homicide shall have the right of appeal to the Supreme Court.

The Superior Court

Section 2. Until otherwise provided by law, the Superior Court shall exercise all the jurisdiction now vested in the present Superior Court. The present terms of all judges of the Superior Court which would otherwise expire on the first Monday of January in an odd-numbered year shall be extended to expire in the even-numbered year next following.

Commonwealth Court

Section 3. The Commonwealth Court shall come into existence on January 1, 1970. Notwithstanding anything to the contrary in this article, the General Assembly shall stagger the initial terms of judges of the Commonwealth Court.

The Courts of Common Pleas

Section 4. Until otherwise provided by law, the several courts of common pleas shall exercise the jurisdiction now vested in the present courts of common pleas. The courts of oyer and terminer and general jail delivery, quarter sessions of the peace, and orphans' courts are abolished and the several courts of common pleas shall also exercise the jurisdiction of these courts. Orphans' courts in judicial districts having separate orphans' courts shall become orphans' court divisions of the courts of common pleas and the court of common pleas in those judicial districts shall exercise the jurisdiction presently exercised by the separate orphans' courts through their respective orphans' court division.

Orphans' Court Judges

Section 5. In those judicial districts having separate orphans' courts, the present judges thereof shall become judges of the orphans' court division of the court of common pleas and the present president judge shall become the president judge of the orphans' court division of the court of common pleas for the remainder of his term without diminution in salary.

Courts of Common Pleas in Multi-County Judicial Districts

Section 6. Courts of common pleas in multi-county judicial districts are abolished as separate courts and are hereby constituted as branches of the single court of common pleas established under this article in each such judicial district.

Community Courts

Section 7. In a judicial district which establishes a community court, a person serving as a justice of the peace at such time:

(a) May complete his term exercising the jurisdiction provided by law and with the compensation provided by law, and

(b) Upon completion of his term, his office is abolished and no judicial function of the kind heretofore exercised by a justice of the peace shall thereafter be exercised other than by the community court.

JUSTICES, JUDGES AND JUSTICES OF THE PEACE

Justices, Judges and Justices of the Peace

Section 8. Notwithstanding any provision in the article, a present justice, judge or justice of the peace may complete his term of office.

Associate Judges

Section 9. The office of associate judge not learned in the law is abolished, but a present associate judge may complete his term.

Retention Election of Present Justices and Judges

Section 10. A present judge who was originally elected to office and seeks retention in the 1969 municipal election and is otherwise eligible may file his declaration of candidacy by February 1, 1969.

Selection of President Judges

Section 11.[3] (a) Except in the City of Philadelphia, section ten (d) of the article shall become effective upon the expiration of the term of the present president judge, or upon earlier vacancy.

(b) Notwithstanding section ten (d) of the article the president judge of the Superior Court shall be the judge longest in continuous service on such court if such judge was a member of such court on the first Monday of January 1977. If no such judge exists or is willing to serve as president judge the president judge shall be selected as provided by this article.

MAGISTRATES, ALDERMEN AND JUSTICES OF THE PEACE AND MAGISTERIAL DISTRICTS OTHER THAN IN THE CITY OF PHILADELPHIA

Magistrates, Aldermen and Justices of the Peace

Section 12. An alderman, justice of the peace or magistrate:

(a) May complete his term, exercising the jurisdiction provided by law and with the method of compensation provided by law prior to the adoption of this article;

(b) Shall be deemed to have taken and passed the examination required by this article for justices of the peace if he has completed one full term of office before creation of a magisterial district, and

(c) At the completion of his term, his office is abolished.

(d) Except for officers completing their terms, after the first Monday in January, 1970, no judicial function of the kind heretofore exercised by these officers, by mayors and like officers in municipalities shall be exercised by any officer other than the one justice of the peace elected or appointed to serve in that magisterial district.

Magisterial Districts

Section 13. So that the provisions of this article regarding the establishment of magisterial districts and the instruction and examination of justices of the peace may be self-executing, until otherwise provided by law in a manner agreeable to this article, the following provisions shall be in force:

(a) The Supreme Court or the courts of common pleas under the direction of the Supreme Court shall fix the number and boundaries of magisterial districts of each class within each judicial district by January 1, 1969, and these magisterial districts, except where a community court has been adopted, shall come into existence on January 1, 1970, the justices of the peace thereof to be elected at the municipal election in 1969. These justices of the peace shall retain no fine, costs or any other sum that shall be delivered into their hands for the performance of any judicial duty or for any service connected with their offices, but shall remit the same to the Commonwealth, county, municipal subdivision, school district or otherwise as may be provided by law.

(b) Classes of magisterial districts.

(i) Magisterial districts of the first class shall have a population density of more than five thousand persons per square mile and a population of not less than sixty-five thousand persons.

(ii) Magisterial districts of the second class shall have a population density of between one thousand and five thousand persons per square mile and a population of between twenty thousand persons and sixty-five thousand persons.

3Section 11 amended Nov. 6, 1979.

(iii) Magisterial districts of the third class shall have a population density of between two hundred and one thousand persons per square mile and a population of between twelve thousand persons and twenty thousand persons.

(iv) Magisterial districts of the fourth class shall have a population density of between seventy and two hundred persons per square mile and a population of between seven thousand five hundred persons and twelve thousand persons.

(v) Magisterial districts of the fifth class shall have a population density of under seventy persons per square mile and a population of between four thousand persons and seven thousand five hundred persons.

(c) Salaries of justices of the peace.

The salaries of the justices of the peace shall be as follows:

(i) In first class magisterial districts, twelve thousand dollars per year,

(ii) In second class magisterial districts, ten thousand dollars per year,

(iii) In third class magisterial districts, eight thousand dollars per year,

(iv) In fourth and fifth class magisterial districts, five thousand dollars per year.

(v) The salaries here fixed shall be paid by the State Treasurer and for such payment this article and schedule shall be sufficient warrant.

(d) Course of training, instruction and examination. The course of training and instruction and examination in civil and criminal law and procedure for a justice of the peace shall be devised by the Department of Public Instruction, and it shall administer this course and examination to insure that justices of the peace are competent to perform their duties.

Magisterial Districts

Section 14.   Effective immediately upon establishment of magisterial districts and until otherwise prescribed the civil and criminal procedural rules relating to venue shall apply to magisterial districts; all proceedings before aldermen, magistrates and justices of the peace shall be brought in and only in a magisterial district in which occurs an event which would give rise to venue in a court of record; the court of common pleas upon its own motion or on application at any stage of proceedings shall transfer any proceeding in any magisterial district to the justice of the peace for the magisterial district in which proper venue lies.

PROTHONOTARIES AND CLERKS OTHER THAN IN THE CITY OF PHILADELPHIA

Prothonotaries, Clerks of Courts, Clerks of Orphans' Courts

Section 15.   Until otherwise provided by law, the offices of prothonotary and clerk of courts shall become the offices of prothonotary and clerk of courts of the court of common pleas of the judicial district, and in multi-county judicial districts of their county's branch of the court of common pleas, and the clerk of the orphans' court in a judicial district now having a separate orphans' court shall become the clerk of the orphans' court division of the court of common pleas, and these officers shall continue to perform the duties of the office and to maintain and be responsible for the records, books and dockets as heretofore. In judicial districts where the clerk of the orphans' court is not the register of wills, he shall continue to perform the duties of the office and to maintain and be responsible for the records, books and dockets as heretofore until otherwise provided by law.

THE CITY OF PHILADELPHIA

Courts and Judges

Section 16.   Until otherwise provided by law:

(a) The court of common pleas shall consist of a trial division, orphans' court division and family court division.

(b) The judges of the court of common pleas shall become judges of the trial division of the court of common pleas provided for in this article and their tenure shall not otherwise be affected.

(c) The judges of the county court shall become judges of the family court division of the court of common pleas and their tenure shall not otherwise be affected.

(d) The judges of the orphans' court shall become judges of the orphans' court division of the court of common pleas and their tenure shall not otherwise be affected.

(e) As designated by the Governor, twenty-two of the present magistrates shall become judges of the municipal court and six shall become judges of the traffic court, and their tenure shall not otherwise be affected.

(f) One of the judges of the court of common pleas shall be president judge and he shall be selected in the manner provided in section ten (d) of this article. He shall be the administrative head of the court and shall supervise the court's judicial business.

(g) Each division of the court of common pleas shall be presided over by an administrative judge, who shall be one of its judges and shall be elected for a term of five years by a majority vote of the judges of that division. He shall assist the president judge in supervising the judicial business of the court and shall be responsible to him. Subject to the foregoing, the judges of the court of common pleas shall prescribe rules defining the duties of the administrative judges. The president judge shall have the power to assign judges from each division to each other division of the court when required to expedite the business of the court.

(h) Until all members of the municipal court are members of the bar of the Supreme Court, the president judge of the court of common pleas shall appoint one of the judges of the municipal court as president judge for a five-year term or at the pleasure of the president judge of the court of common pleas. The president judge of the municipal court shall be eligible to succeed himself as president judge for any number of terms and shall be the administrative head of that court and shall supervise the judicial business of the court. He shall promulgate all administrative rules and regulations and make all judicial assignments. The president judge of the court of common pleas may assign temporarily judges of the municipal court who are members of the bar of the Supreme Court to the court of common pleas when required to expedite the business of the court.

(i) The Governor shall appoint one of the judges of the traffic court as president judge for a term of five years or at the pleasure of the Governor. The president judge of the traffic court shall be eligible to succeed himself as president judge for any number of terms, shall be the executive and administrative head of the traffic court, and shall supervise the judicial business of the court, shall promulgate all administrative rules and regulations, and shall make all judicial assignments.

(j) The exercise of all supervisory and administrative powers detailed in this section sixteen shall be subject to the supervisory and administrative control of the Supreme Court.

(k) The prothonotary shall continue to exercise the duties of that office for the trial division of the court of common pleas and for the municipal court.

(l) The clerk of quarter sessions shall continue to exercise the duties of that office for the trial division of the court of common pleas and for the municipal court.

(m) That officer serving as clerk to the county court shall continue to exercise the duties of that office for the family division of the court of common pleas.

(n) The register of wills shall serve ex officio as clerk of the orphans' court division of the court of common pleas.

(o) The court of common pleas shall have unlimited original jurisdiction in all cases except those cases assigned by this schedule to the municipal court and to the traffic court. The court of common pleas shall have all the jurisdiction now vested in the court of common pleas, the court of oyer and terminer and general jail delivery, courts of quarter sessions of the peace, orphans' court, and county court. Jurisdiction in all of the foregoing cases shall be exercised through the trial division of the court of common pleas except in those cases which are assigned by this schedule to the orphans' court and family court divisions of the court of common pleas. The court of common pleas through the trial division shall also hear and determine appeals from the municipal court and traffic court.

(p) The court of common pleas through the orphans' court division shall exercise the jurisidiction heretofore exercised by the orphans' court.

(q) The court of common pleas through the family court division of the court of common pleas shall exercise jurisdiction in the following matters:

(i) Domestic Relations: desertion or nonsupport of wives, children and indigent parents, including children born out of wedlock; proceedings for custody of children; divorce and annulment and property matters relating thereto.

(ii) Juvenile Matters: dependent, delinquent and neglected children and children under eighteen years of age, suffering from epilepsy, nervous or mental defects, incorrigible, runaway and disorderly minors eighteen to twenty years of age and preliminary hearings in criminal cases where the victim is a juvenile.

(iii) Adoptions and Delayed Birth Certificates.

(r) The municipal court shall have jurisdiction in the following matters:

(i) Committing magistrates' jurisdiction in all criminal matters.

(ii) All summary offenses, except those under the motor vehicle laws.

(iii) All criminal offenses for which no prison term may be imposed or which are punishable by a term of imprisonment of not more than two years, and indictable offenses under the motor vehicle laws for which no prison term may be imposed or punishable by a term of imprisonment of not more than three years. In these cases, the defendant shall have no right of trial by jury in that court, but he shall have the right of appeal for trial de novo including the right to trial by jury to the trial division of the court of common pleas. Until there are a sufficient number of judges who are members of the bar of the Supreme Court serving in the municipal court to handle such matters, the trial division of the court of common pleas shall have concurrent jurisdiction over such matters, the assignment of cases to the respective courts to be determined by rule prescribed by the president judge of the court of common pleas.

(iv) Matters arising under The Landlord and Tenant Act of 1951.

(v) All civil claims involving less than five hundred dollars. In these cases, the parties shall have no right of trial by jury in that court but shall have the right of appeal for a trial de novo including the right to trial by jury to the trial division of the court of common pleas, it being the purpose of this subsection to establish an expeditious small claims procedure whereby it shall not be necessary for the litigants to obtain counsel. This limited grant of civil jurisdiction shall be co-extensive with the civil jurisdiction of the trial division of the court of common pleas.

(vi) As commissioners to preside at arraignments, fix and accept bail, issue warrants and perform duties of a similar nature.

The grant of jurisdiction under clauses (iii) and (v) of this subsection may be exercised only by those judges who are members of the bar of the Supreme Court.

(s) The traffic court shall have exclusive jurisdiction of all summary offenses under the motor vehicle laws.

(t) The courts of oyer and terminer and general jail delivery, quarter sessions of the peace, the county court, the orphans' court and the ten separate courts of common pleas are abolished and their jurisdiction and powers shall be exercised by the court of common pleas provided for in this article through the divisions established by this schedule.

(u) The office of magistrate, the board of magistrates and the present traffic court are abolished.

(v) Those judges appointed to the municipal court in accordance with subsection (e) of this section who are not members of the bar of the Supreme Court shall be eligible to complete their present terms and to be elected to and serve for one additional term, but not thereafter.

(w) The causes, proceedings, books, dockets and records of the abolished courts shall become those of the court or division thereof to which, under this schedule, jurisdiction of the proceedings or matters concerned has been transferred, and that court or division thereof shall determine and conclude such proceedings as if it had assumed jurisdiction in the first instance.

(x) The present president judges of the abolished courts and chief magistrate shall continue to receive the compensation to which they are now entitled as president judges and chief magistrate until the end of their present terms as president judges and chief magistrate respectively.

(y) The offices of prothonotary and register of wills in the City of Philadelphia shall no longer be considered constitutional offices under this article, but their powers and functions shall continue as at present until these offices are covered in the Home Rule Charter by a referendum in the manner provided by law.

(z) If a community court is established in the City of Philadelphia, a person serving as a judge of the municipal or traffic court at that time:

(i) Notwithstanding the provisions of subsection (v) of this section, may complete his term exercising the jurisdiction provided by law and with the compensation provided by law; and

(ii) At the completion of his term, his office is abolished and no jurisdiction of the kind exercised by those officers immediately after the effective date of this article and schedule shall thereafter be exercised other than by the community court.

ALLEGHENY COUNTY

Courts
Section 17. Until otherwise provided by law:

(a) The court of common pleas shall consist of a trial division, an orphans' court division and a family court division; the courts of oyer and terminer and general jail delivery and quarter sessions of the peace, the county court, the orphans' court, and the juvenile court are abolished and their present jurisdiction shall be exercised by the court of common pleas. Until otherwise provided by rule of the court of common pleas and, except as otherwise provided in this schedule, the court of common pleas shall exercise the jurisdiction of the present court of common pleas and the present county court through the trial division. Until otherwise provided by rule of the court of common pleas, the jurisdiction of the present orphans' court, except as otherwise provided in this schedule, shall be exercised by the court of common pleas through the orphans' court division.

(b) Until otherwise provided by rule of the court of common pleas, the court of common pleas shall exercise jurisdiction in the following matters through the family court division:

(i) Domestic Relations: Desertion or nonsupport of wives, children and indigent parents, including children born out of wedlock; proceedings, including habeas corpus, for custody of children; divorce and annulment and property matters relating thereto.

(ii) Juvenile Matters: All matters now within the jurisdiction of the juvenile court.

(iii) Adoptions and Delayed Birth Certificates.

Judges
Section 18. Until otherwise provided by law, the present judges of the court of common pleas shall continue to act as the judges of that court; the present judges of the county court shall become judges of the court of common pleas; the present judges of the orphans' court shall become judges of the orphans' court division of the court of common pleas; the present judges of the juvenile court shall become judges of the family court division of the court of common pleas.

President Judges
Section 19. The present president judge of the court of common pleas may complete his term as president judge; the present president judge of the orphans' court shall be the president judge of the orphans' court division of the court of common pleas for the remainder of his term as president judge, and the present president judge of the county court shall be the president judge of the family court division of the court of common pleas for the remainder of his term as president judge, all these without diminution of salary as president judge. The president judge of the trial division shall be selected pursuant to section twenty of this schedule.

President Judges; Court Division
Section 20. Until otherwise provided by law, the trial division, the orphans' court division and the family court division of the court of common pleas shall each be presided over by a president judge, who shall be one of the judges of such division and shall be elected for a term of five years by a majority vote of the judges of that division. He shall assist the president judge of the court of common pleas in supervising the judicial business of the court and shall be responsible to him. Subject to the foregoing, the judges of the court of common pleas shall prescribe rules defining the duties of the president judges. The president judge of the court of common pleas shall have the power to assign judges from one division to another division of the court when required to expedite the business of the court. The exercise of these supervisory and administrative powers, however, shall be subject to the supervisory and administrative powers of the Supreme Court.

THE CITY OF PITTSBURGH

Inferior Courts
Section 21. Upon the establishment of magisterial districts pursuant to this article and schedule, and unless otherwise provided by law, the police magistrates, including those serving in the traffic court, the housing court and the city court shall continue as at present. Such magistrates shall be part of the unified judicial system and shall be subject to the general supervisory and administrative authority of the Supreme Court. Such magistrates shall be subject to the provisions of this article and schedule regarding educational requirements and prohibited activities of justices of the peace.

CAUSES, PROCEEDINGS, BOOKS AND RECORDS

Causes, Proceedings, Books and Records

Section 22. All causes and proceedings pending in any abolished court or office of the justice of the peace shall be determined and concluded by the court to which jurisdiction of the proceedings has been transferred under this schedule and all books, dockets and records of any abolished court or office of the justice of the peace shall become those of the court to which, under this schedule, jurisdiction of the proceedings concerned has been transferred.

COMMISSION AND BOARD

Judicial Qualifications Commission

Section 23. The selection of the first members of the Judicial Qualifications Commission provided for in section fourteen (a) of this article shall be made as follows: The Governor shall appoint the four non-lawyer members for terms of, respectively, one year, three years, five years and seven years, no more than two of whom shall be members of the same political party. The Supreme Court shall appoint the three non-judge members of the bar of the Supreme Court of Pennsylvania for terms, respectively, of two years, four years and six years, no more than two of whom shall be members of the same political party.

Judicial Inquiry and Review Board

Section 24. The selection of the first members of the Judicial Inquiry and Review Board shall be made as follows: one judge of the Superior Court, one non-judge member of the bar of the Supreme Court, and one non-lawyer member shall be selected for two-year terms; one judge of the Superior Court, one non-judge member of the bar of the Supreme Court, and one non-lawyer member shall be selected for four-year terms; one judge of the court of common pleas shall be selected for a term of two years, one for a term of three years, and one for a term of four years.

GENERAL PROVISIONS

Dispensing with Trial by Jury

Section 25. Until otherwise provided by law, the parties, by agreement filed, may in any civil case dispense with trial by jury, and submit the decision of such case to the court having jurisdiction thereof, and such court shall hear and determine the same; and the judgment thereon shall be subject to writ of error as in other cases.

Writs of Certiorari

Section 26. Unless and until changed by rule of the Supreme Court, in addition to the right of appeal under section nine of this article, the judges of the courts of common pleas, within their respective judicial districts, shall have power to issue writs of certiorari to the municipal court in the City of Philadelphia, justices of the peace and inferior courts not of record and to cause their proceedings to be brought before them, and right and justice to be done.

Judicial Districts

Section 27. Until changed in accordance with section eleven of this article, the number and boundaries of judicial districts shall remain as at present.

Referendum

Section 28. The officer of the Commonwealth who under law shall have supervision over elections shall cause the question provided for in section thirteen (d) of this article to be placed on the ballot in the 1969 primary election throughout the Commonwealth.

Persons Specially Admitted by Local Rules

Section 29. Any person now specially admitted to practice may continue to practice in the court of common pleas or in that division of the court of common pleas and the municipal court in the City of Philadelphia which substantially includes the practice for which such person was previously specially admitted.

Article VI

PUBLIC OFFICERS

Selection of Officers Not Otherwise Provided for in Constitution

Section 1. All officers, whose selection is not provided for in this Constitution, shall be elected or appointed as may be directed by law.

Incompatible Offices

Section 2. No member of Congress from this State, nor any person holding or exercising any office or appointment of trust or profit under the United States, shall at the same time hold or exercise any office in this State to which a salary, fees or perquisites shall be attached. The General Assembly may by law declare what offices are incompatible.

Oath of Office

Section 3. Senators, Representatives and all judicial, State and county officers shall, before entering on the duties of their respective offices, take and subscribe the following oath or affirmation before a person authorized to administer oaths.

"I do solemnly swear (or affirm) that I will support, obey and defend the Constitution of the United States and the Constitution of this Commonwealth and that I will discharge the duties of my office with fidelity."

The oath or affirmation shall be administered to a member of the Senate or to a member of the House of Representatives in the hall of the House to which he shall have been elected.

Any person refusing to take the oath or affirmation shall forfeit his office.

Power of Impeachment
Section 4. The House of Representatives shall have the sole power of impeachment.

Trial of Impeachments
Section 5. All impeachments shall be tried by the Senate. When sitting for that purpose the Senators shall be upon oath or affirmation. No person shall be convicted without the concurrence of two-thirds of the members present.

Officers Liable to Impeachment
Section 6. The Governor and all other civil officers shall be liable to impeachment for any misbehavior in office, but judgment in such cases shall not extend further than to removal from office and disqualification to hold any office of trust or profit under this Commonwealth. The person accused, whether convicted or acquitted, shall nevertheless be liable to indictment, trial, judgment and punishment according to law.

Removal of Civil Officers
Section 7. All civil officers shall hold their offices on the condition that they behave themselves well while in office, and shall be removed on conviction of misbehavior in office or of any infamous crime. Appointed civil officers, other than judges of the courts of record, may be removed at the pleasure of the power by which they shall have been appointed. All civil officers elected by the people, except the Governor, the Lieutenant Governor, members of the General Assembly and judges of the courts of record, shall be removed by the Governor for reasonable cause, after due notice and full hearing, on the address of two-thirds of the Senate.

Article VII

ELECTIONS

Qualifications of Electors
Section 1. Every citizen 21 years of age, possessing the following qualifications, shall be entitled to vote at all elections subject, however, to such laws requiring and regulating the registration of electors as the General Assembly may enact.

1. He or she shall have been a citizen of the United States at least one month.

2. He or she shall have resided in the State ninety (90) days immediately preceding the election.

3. He or she shall have resided in the election district where he or she shall offer to vote at least sixty (60) days immediately preceding the election, except that if qualified to vote in an election district prior to removal of residence, he or she may, if a resident of Pennsylvania, vote in the election district from which he or she removed his or her residence within sixty (60) days preceding the election.

General Election Day
Section 2. The general election shall be held biennially on the Tuesday next following the first Monday of November in each even-numbered year, but the General Assembly may by law fix a different day, two-thirds of all the members of each House consenting thereto: Provided, that such election shall always be held in an even-numbered year.

Municipal Election Day; Offices to Be Filled on Election Days
Section 3. All judges elected by the electors of the State at large may be elected at either a general or municipal election, as circumstances may require. All elections for judges of the courts for the several judicial districts, and for county, city, ward, borough, and township officers, for regular terms of service, shall be held on the municipal election day; namely, the Tuesday next following the first Monday of November in each odd-numbered year, but the General Assembly may by law fix a different day, two-thirds of all the members of each House consenting thereto: Provided, That such elections shall be held in an odd-numbered year: Provided further, That all judges for the courts of the several judicial districts holding office at the present time, whose terms of office may end in an odd-numbered year, shall continue to hold their offices until the first Monday of January in the next succeeding even-numbered year.

Method of Elections; Secrecy in Voting
Section 4. All elections by the citizens shall be by ballot or by such other method as may be prescribed by law: Provided, That secrecy in voting be preserved.

Electors Privileged from Arrest
Section 5. Electors shall in all cases except treason, felony and breach or surety of the peace, be privileged from arrest during their attendance on elections and in going to and returning therefrom.

Election and Registration Laws
Section 6. All laws regulating the holding of elections by the citizens, or for the registration of electors, shall be uniform throughout the State, except that laws regulating and requiring the registration of electors may be enacted to apply to cities only, provided that such laws be uniform for cities of the same class, and except further, that the General Assembly shall by general law, permit the use of voting machines, or other mechanical devices for registering or recording and computing the vote, at all elections

Editor's Note: Under 1971 statutory amendment, the voting age in Pennsylvania is now 18 years of age.   25 P.S. §2811

or primaries, in any county, city, borough, incorporated town or township of the Commonwealth, at the option of the electors of such county, city, borough, incorporated town or township, without being obliged to require the use of such voting machines or mechanical devices in any other county, city, borough, incorporated town or township, under such regulations with reference thereto as the General Assembly may from time to time prescribe. The General Assembly may, from time to time, prescribe the number and duties of election officers in any political subdivison of the Commonwealth in which voting machines or other mechanical devices authorized by this section may be used.

Bribery of Electors

Section 7. Any person who shall give, or promise or offer to give, to an elector, any money, reward or other valuable consideration for his vote at an election, or for withholding the same, or who shall give or promise to give such consideration to any other person or party for such elector's vote or for the withholding thereof, and any elector who shall receive or agree to receive, for himself or for another, any money, reward or other valuable consideration for his vote at an election, or for withholding the same, shall thereby forfeit the right to vote at such election, and any elector whose right to vote shall be challenged for such cause before the election officers, shall be required to swear or affirm that the matter of the challenge is untrue before his vote shall be received.

Witnesses in Contested Elections

Section 8. In trials of contested elections and in proceedings for the investigation of elections, no person shall be permitted to withhold his testimony upon the ground that it may criminate himself or subject him to public infamy; but such testimony shall not afterwards be used against him in any judicial proceedings except for perjury in giving such testimony.

Fixing Election Districts

Section 9. Townships and wards of cities or boroughs shall form or be divided into election districts of compact and contiguous territory and their boundaries fixed and changed in such manner as may be provided by law.

Viva Voce Elections

Section 10. All elections by persons in a representative capacity shall be viva voce or by automatic recording device publicly indicating how each person voted.

Election Officers

Section 11. District election boards shall consist of a judge and two inspectors, who shall be chosen at municipal elections for such terms as may be provided by law. Each elector shall have the right to vote for the judge and one inspector, and each inspector shall appoint one clerk. The first election board for any new district shall be selected, and vacancies in election boards filled, as shall be provided by law. Election officers shall be privileged from arrest upon days of election, and while engaged in making up and transmitting returns, except upon warrant of a court of record or judge thereof, for an election fraud, for felony, or for wanton breach of the peace. In cities they may claim exemption from jury duty during their terms of service.

Disqualifications for Service as Election Officer

Section 12. No person shall be qualified to serve as an election officer who shall hold, or shall within two months have held any office, appointment or employment in or under the government of the United States, or of this State, or of any city, or county, or of any municipal board, commission or trust in any city, save only notaries public and persons in the National Guard or in a reserve component of the armed forces of the United States; nor shall any election officer be eligibile to any civil office to be filled at an election at which he shall serve, save only to such subordinate municipal or local offices, below the grade of city or county offices, as shall be designated by general law.

Contested Elections

Section 13. The trial and determination of contested elections of electors of President and Vice-President, members of the General Assembly, and of all public officers, whether State, judicial, municipal or local, and contests involving questions submitted to the electors at any election shall be by the courts of law, or by one or more of the law judges thereof. The General Assembly shall, by general law, designate the courts and judges by whom the several classes of election contests shall be tried, and regulate the manner of trial and all matters incident thereto; but no such law assigning jurisdiction, or regulating its exercise, shall apply to any contest arising out of an election held before its passage.

Absentee Voting

Section 14.[1] The Legislature shall, by general law, provide a manner in which, and the time and place at which, qualified electors who may, on the occurrence of any election, be absent from the State or county of their residence, because their duties, occupation or business require them to be elsewhere or who, on the occurrence of any election, are unable to attend at their proper polling places because of illness or physical disability or who will not attend a polling place because of the observance of a religious holiday or who cannot vote because of election day duties, in the case of a county employee, may vote, and for the return and canvass of their votes in the election district in which they respectively reside.

[1] Amended Nov. 5, 1985.

Article VIII

TAXATION AND FINANCE

Uniformity of Taxation

Section 1. All taxes shall be uniform, upon the same class of subjects, within the territorial limits of the authority levying the tax, and shall be levied and collected under general laws.

Exemptions and Special Provisions

Section 2.[1] (a) The General Assembly may by law exempt from taxation:

(i) Actual places of regularly stated religious worship:

(ii) Actual places of burial, when used or held by a person or organization deriving no private or corporate profit therefrom and no substantial part of whose activity consists of selling personal property in connection therewith;

(iii) That portion of public property which is actually and regularly used for public purposes;

(iv) That portion of the property owned and occupied by any branch, post or camp of honorably discharged servicemen or servicewomen which is actually and regularly used for benevolent, charitable or patriotic purposes; and

(v) Institutions of purely public charity, but in the case of any real property tax exemptions only that portion of real property of such institution which is actually and regularly used for the purposes of the institution.

(b) The General Assembly may, by law:

(i) Establish standards and qualifications for private forest reserves, agriculture reserves, and land actively devoted to agriculture use, and make special provision for the taxation thereof;

(ii) Establish as a class or classes of subjects of taxation the property or privileges of persons who, because of age, disability, infirmity or poverty are determined to be in need of tax exemption or of special tax provisions, and for any such class or classes, uniform standards and qualifications. The Commonwealth, or any other taxing authority, may adopt or employ such class or classes and standards and qualifications, and except as herein provided may impose taxes, grant exemptions, or make special tax provisions in accordance therewith. No exemption or special provision shall be made under this clause with respect to taxes upon the sale or use of personal property, and no exemption from any tax upon real property shall be granted by the General Assembly under this clause unless the General Assembly shall provide for the reimbursement of local taxing authorities by or through the Commonwealth for revenue losses occasioned by such exemption;

(iii) Establish standards and qualifications by which local taxing authorities may make uniform special tax provisions applicable to a taxpayer for a limited period of time to encourage improvement of deteriorating property or areas by an individual, association or corporation, or to encourage industrial development by a non-profit corporation; and

(iv) Make special tax provisions on any increase in value of real estate resulting from residential construction. Such special tax provisions shall be applicable for a period not to exceed two years.

(v) Establish standards and qualifications by which local taxing authorities in counties of the first and second class may make uniform special real property tax provisions applicable to taxpayers who are long-time owner-occupants as shall be defined by the General Assembly of residences in areas where real property values have risen markedly as a consequence of the refurbishing or renovating of other deteriorating residences or the construction of new residences.

(c) Citizens and residents of this Commonwealth, who served in any war or armed conflict in which the United States was engaged and were honorably discharged or released under honorable circumstances from active service, shall be exempt from the payment of all real property taxes upon the residence occupied by the said citizens and residents of this Commonwealth imposed by the Commonwealth of Pennsylvania or any of its political subdivisions if, as a result of military service, they are blind, paraplegic or double or quadruple amputees or have a service-connected disability declared by the United States Veterans' Administration or its successor to be a total or 100% permanent disability, and if the State Veterans' Commission determines that such persons are in need of the tax exemptions granted herein. This exemption shall be extended to the unmarried surviving spouse upon the death of an eligible veteran provided that the State Veterans' Commission determines that such person is in need of the exemption.

Reciprocal Exemptions

Section 3. Taxation laws may grant exemptions or rebates to residents, or estates of residents, of other States which grant similar exemptions or rebates to residents, or estates of residents, of Pennsylvania.

Public Utilities

Section 4. The real property of public utilities is subject to real estate taxes imposed by local taxing authorities. Payment to the Commonwealth of gross receipts taxes or other special taxes in replacement of gross receipts taxes by a public utility and the distribution by the Commonwealth to the local taxing authorities of the amount as herein provided shall, however, be in lieu of local taxes upon its real property which is used or useful in furnishing its public utility service. The amount raised annually by such gross receipts or other special taxes shall not be less than the gross amount of real estate taxes which the local taxing authorities could have imposed upon such real property but for the exemption herein provided. This gross amount shall be determined in the manner provided by law. An amount equivalent to such real estate taxes shall be distributed annually among all local taxing authorities in the proportion which the total tax receipts of each local taxing authority bear to the total tax receipts of all local taxing authorities, or in such other equitable proportions as may be provided by law.

Notwithstanding the provisions of this section, any law which presently subjects real property of public utilities to local real estate taxation by local taxing authorities shall remain in full force and effect.

[1] Section 2 amended May 15, 1973; Nov. 8, 1977; Nov. 6, 1984; Nov. 5, 1985.

Exemption from Taxation Restricted

Section 5. All laws exempting property from taxation, other than the property above enumerated, shall be void.

Taxation of Corporations

Section 6. The power to tax corporations and corporate property shall not be surrendered or suspended by any contract or grant to which the Commonwealth shall be a party.

Commonwealth Indebtedness

Section 7. (a) No debt shall be incurred by or on behalf of the Commonwealth except by law and in accordance with the provisions of this section.

(1) Debt may be incurred without limit to suppress insurrection, rehabilitate areas affected by man-made or natural disaster, or to implement unissued authority approved by the electors prior to the adoption of this article.

(2) The Governor, State Treasurer and Auditor General, acting jointly, may (i) issue tax anticipation notes having a maturity within the fiscal year of issue and payable exclusively from revenues received in the same fiscal year, and (ii) incur debt for the purpose of refunding other debt, if such refunding debt matures within the term of the original debt.

(3) Debt may be incurred without limit for purposes specifically itemized in the law authorizing such debt, if the question whether the debt shall be incurred has been submitted to the electors and approved by a majority of those voting on the question.

(4) Debt may be incurred without the approval of the electors for capital projects specifically itemized in a capital budget, if such debt will not cause the amount of all net debt outstanding to exceed one and three-quarters times the average of the annual tax revenues deposited in the previous five fiscal years as certified by the Auditor General. For the purposes of this subsection, debt outstanding shall not include debt incurred under clauses (1) and (2) (i), or debt incurred under clause (2) (ii) if the original debt would not be so considered, or debt incurred under subsection (3) unless the General Assembly shall so provide in the law authorizing such debt.

(b) All debt incurred for capital projects shall mature within a period not to exceed the estimated useful life of the projects as stated in the authorizing law, and when so stated shall be conclusive. All debt, except indebtedness permitted by clause (2) (i), shall be amortized in substantial and regular amounts, the first of which shall be due prior to the expiration of a period equal to one-tenth the term of the debt.

(c) As used in this section, debt shall mean the issued and outstanding obligations of the Commonwealth and shall include obligations of its agencies or authorities to the extent they are to be repaid from lease rentals or other charges payable directly or indirectly from revenues of the Commonwealth. Debts shall not include either (1) that portion of obligations to be repaid from charges made to the public for the use of the capital projects financed, as determined by the Auditor General, or (2) obligations to be repaid from lease rentals or other charges payable by a school district or other local taxing authority, or (3) obligations to be repaid by agencies or authorities created for the joint benefit of the Commonwealth and one or more other State governments.

(d) If sufficient funds are not appropriated for the timely payment of the interest upon and installments of principal of all debt, the State Treasurer shall set apart from the first revenues thereafter received applicable to the appropriate fund a sum sufficient to pay such interest and installments of principal, and shall so apply the money so set apart. The State Treasurer may be required to set aside and apply such revenues at the suit of any holder of Commonwealth obligations.

Commonwealth Credit Not to Be Pledged

Section 8. The credit of the Commonwealth shall not be pledged or loaned to any individual, company, corporation or association nor shall the Commonwealth become a joint owner or stockholder in any company, corporation or association.

Municipal Debt Not to be Assumed by Commonwealth

Section 9. The Commonwealth shall not assume the debt, or any part thereof, of any county, city, borough, incorporated town, township or any similar general purpose unit of government unless such debt shall have been incurred to enable the Commonwealth to suppress insurrection or to assist the Commonwealth in the discharge of any portion of its present indebtedness.

Audit

Section 10. The financial affairs of any entity funded or financially aided by the Commonwealth, and all departments, boards, commissions, agencies, instrumentalities, authorities and institutions of the Commonwealth, shall be subject to audits made in accordance with generally accepted auditing standards.

Any Commonwealth officer whose approval is necessary for any transaction relative to the financial affairs of the Commonwealth shall not be charged with the function of auditing that transaction after its occurrence.

Gasoline Taxes and Motor License Fees Restricted

Section 11.[2] (a) All proceeds from gasoline and other motor fuel excise taxes, motor vehicle registration fees and license taxes, operators' license fees and other excise taxes imposed on products used in motor transportation after providing therefrom for (a) cost of administration and collection, (b) payment of obligations incurred in the construction and reconstruction of public highways and bridges shall be appropriated by the General Assembly to agencies of the State or political subdivisions thereof; and used solely for construction, reconstruction, maintenance and repair of and safety on public highways and bridges and costs and expenses incident thereto, and for the payment of obligations incurred for such purposes, and shall not be diverted by transfer or otherwise

[2]*Section 11 amended Nov. 3, 1981.*

to any other purpose, except that loans may be made by the State from the proceeds of such taxes and fees for a single period not exceeding eight months, but no such loan shall be made within the period of one year from any preceding loan, and every loan made in any fiscal year shall be repayable within one month after the beginning of the next fiscal year.

(b) All proceeds from aviation fuel excise taxes, after providing therefrom for the cost of administration and collection, shall be appropriated by the General Assembly to agencies of the State or political subdivisions thereof and used solely for: the purchase, construction, reconstruction, operation and maintenance of airports and other air navigation facilities; aircraft accident investigation; the operation, maintenance and other costs of aircraft owned or leased by the Commonwealth; any other purpose reasonably related to air navigation including but not limited to the reimbursement of airport property owners for property tax expenditures; and costs and expenses incident thereto and for the payment of obligations incurred for such purposes, and shall not be diverted by transfer or otherwise to any other purpose.

Governor's Budgets and Financial Plan

Section 12. Annually, at the times set by law, the Governor shall submit to the General Assembly:

(a) A balanced operating budget for the ensuing fiscal year setting forth in detail (i) proposed expenditures classified by department or agency and by program and (ii) estimated revenues from all sources. If estimated revenues and available surplus are less than proposed expenditures, the Governor shall recommend specific additional sources of revenue sufficient to pay the deficiency and the estimated revenue to be derived from each source;

(b) A capital budget for the ensuing fiscal year setting forth in detail proposed expenditures to be financed from the proceeds of obligations of the Commonwealth or of its agencies or authorities or from operating funds; and

(c) A financial plan for not less than the next succeeding five fiscal years, which plan shall include for each such fiscal year:

(i) Projected operating expenditures classified by department or agency and by program, in reasonable detail, and estimated revenues, by major categories, from existing and additional sources, and

(ii) Projected expenditures for capital projects specifically itemized by purpose, and the proposed sources of financing each.

Appropriations

Section 13. (a) Operating budget appropriations made by the General Assembly shall not exceed the actual and estimated revenues and surplus available in the same fiscal year.

(b) The General Assembly shall adopt a capital budget for the ensuing fiscal year.

Surplus

Section 14. All surplus of operating funds at the end of the fiscal year shall be appropriated during the ensuing fiscal year by the General Assembly.

Project "70"

Section 15. In addition to the purposes stated in Article VIII, section seven of this Constitution, the Commonwealth may be authorized by law to create debt and to issue bonds to the amount of $70,000,000 for the acquisition of land for State parks, reservoirs and other conservation and recreation and historical preservation purposes, and for participation by the Commonwealth with political subdivisions in the acquisition of land for parks, reservoirs and other conservation and recreation and historical preservation purposes, subject to such conditions and limitations as the General Assembly may prescribe.

Land and Water Conservation and Reclamation Fund

Section 16. In addition to the purposes stated in Article VIII, section seven of this Constitution, the Commonwealth may be authorized by law to create a debt and issue bonds in the amount of $500,000,000 for a Land and Water Conservation and Reclamation Fund to be used for the conservation and reclamation of land and water resources of the Commonwealth, including the elimination of acid mine drainage, sewage, and other pollution from the streams of the Commonwealth, the provision of State financial assistance to political subdivisions and municipal authorities of the Commonwealth of Pennsylvania for the construction of sewage treatment plants, the restoration of abandoned strip-mined areas, the control and extinguishment of surface and underground mine fires, the alleviation and prevention of subsidence resulting from mining operations, and the acquisition of additional lands and the reclamation and development of park and recreational lands acquired pursuant to the authority of Article VIII, section 15 of this Constitution, subject to such conditions and liabilities as the General Assembly may prescribe.

Special Emergency Legislation.

Section 17. [3](a) Notwithstanding any provisions of this Constitution to the contrary, the General Assembly shall have the authority to enact laws providing for tax rebates, credits, exemptions, grants-in-aid, State supplementations, or otherwise provide special provisions for individuals, corporations, associations or nonprofit institutions, including nonpublic schools (whether sectarian or nonsectarian) in order to alleviate the danger, damage, suffering or hardship faced by such individuals, corporations, associations, institutions or nonpublic schools as a result of Great Storms or Floods of September 1971, of June 1972, or of 1974, or of 1975 or of 1976.

[4](b) Notwithstanding the provisions of Article III, section 29 subsequent to a Presidential declaration of an emergency or of a major disaster in any part of this Commonwealth, the General Assembly shall have the authority by a vote of two-thirds of all members elected to each House to make appropriations limited to moneys required for Federal emergency or major disaster relief. This subsection may apply retroactively to any Presidential declaration of an emergency or of a major disaster in 1976 or 1977.

[3]Adopted Nov. 7, 1972, amended Nov. 4, 1975, Nov. 8, 1977.   [4]Adopted Nov. 8, 1977.

Article IX

LOCAL GOVERNMENT

Local Government

Section 1. The General Assembly shall provide by general law for local government within the Commonwealth. Such general law shall be uniform as to all classes of local government regarding procedural matters.

Home Rule

Section 2. Municipalities shall have the right and power to frame and adopt home rule charters. Adoption, amendment or repeal of a home rule charter shall be by referendum. The General Assembly shall provide the procedure by which a home rule charter may be framed and its adoption, amendment or repeal presented to the electors. If the General Assembly does not so provide, a home rule charter or a procedure for framing and presenting a home rule charter may be presented to the electors by initiative or by the governing body of the municipality. A municipality which has a home rule charter may exercise any power or perform any function not denied by this Constitution, by its home rule charter or by the General Assembly at any time.

Optional Plans

Section 3. Municipalities shall have the right and power to adopt optional forms of government as provided by law. The General Assembly shall provide optional forms of government for all municipalities. An optional form of government shall be presented to the electors by initiative, by the governing body of the municipality, or by the General Assembly. Adoption or repeal of an optional form of government shall be by referendum.

County Government

Section 4. County officers shall consist of commissioners, controllers or auditors, district attorneys, public defenders, treasurers, sheriffs, registers of wills, recorders of deeds, prothonotaries, clerks of the courts, and such others as may from time to time be provided by law.

County officers, except for public defenders who shall be appointed as shall be provided by law, shall be elected at the municipal elections and shall hold their offices for the term of four years, beginning on the first Monday of January next after their election, and until their successors shall be duly qualified; all vacancies shall be filled in such a manner as may be provided by law.

County officers shall be paid only by salary as provided by law for services performed for the county or any other governmental unit. Fees incidental to the conduct of any county office shall be payable directly to the county or the Commonwealth, or as otherwise provided by law.

Three county commissioners shall be elected in each county. In the election of these officers each qualified elector shall vote for no more than two persons, and the three persons receiving the highest number of votes shall be elected.

Provisions for county government in this section shall apply to every county except a county which has adopted a home rule charter or an optional form of government. One of the optional forms of county government provided by law shall include the provisions of this section.

Intergovernmental Cooperation

Section 5. A municipality by act of its governing body may, or upon being required by initiative and referendum in the area affected shall, cooperate or agree in the exercise of any function, power or responsibility with, or delegate or transfer any function, power or responsibility to, one or more other governmental units including other municipalities or districts, the Federal government, any other state or its governmental units, or any newly created governmental unit.

Area Government

Section 6. The General Assembly shall provide for the establishment and dissolution of government of areas involving two or more municipalities or parts thereof.

Area-wide Powers

Section 7. The General Assembly may grant powers to area governments or to municipalities within a given geographical area in which there exists intergovernmental cooperation or area government and designate the classes of municipalities subject to such legislation.

Consolidation, Merger or Boundary Change

Section 8. Uniform Legislation. — — The General Assembly shall, within two years following the adoption of this article, enact uniform legislation establishing the procedure for consolidation, merger or change of the boundaries of municipalities.

Initiative. — — The electors of any municipality shall have the right, by initiative and referendum, to consolidate, merge and change boundaries by a majority vote of those voting thereon in each municipality, without the approval of any governing body.

Study. — — The General Assembly shall designate an agency of the Commonwealth to study consolidation, merger and boundary changes, advise municipalities on all problems which might be connected therewith, and initiate local referendum.

Legislative Power. — — Nothing herein shall prohibit or prevent the General Assembly from providing additional methods for consolidation, merger or change of boundaries.

Appropriation for Public Purposes

Section 9. The General Assembly shall not authorize any municipality or incorporated district to become a stockholder in any company, association or corporation, or to obtain or appropriate money for, or to loan its credit to, any corporation, association, institution or individual. The General Assembly may provide standards by which municipalities or school districts may give financial assistance or lease property to public service, industrial or commercial enterprises if it shall find that such assistance or leasing is necessary to the health, safety or welfare of the Commonwealth or any municipality or school district. Existing authority of any municipality or incorporated district to obtain or appropriate money for, or to loan its credit to, any corporation, association, institution or individual, is preserved.

Local Government Debt

Section 10. Subject only to the restrictions imposed by this section, the General Assembly shall prescribe the debt limits of all units of local government including municipalities and school districts. For such purposes, the debt limit base shall be a percentage of the total revenue, as defined by the General Assembly, of the unit of local government computed over a specific period immediately preceding the year of borrowing. The debt limit to be prescribed in every such case shall exclude all indebtedness (1) for any project to the extent that it is self-liquidating or self-supporting or which has heretofore been defined as self-liquidating or self-supporting, or (2) which has been approved by referendum held in such manner as shall be provided by law. The provisions of this paragraph shall not apply to the City or County of Philadelphia.

Any unit of local government, including municipalities and school districts, incurring any indebtedness, shall at or before the time of so doing adopt a covenant, which shall be binding upon it so long as any such indebtedness shall remain unpaid, to make payments out of its sinking fund or any other of its revenues or funds at such time and in such annual amounts specified in such covenant as shall be sufficient for the payment of the interest thereon and the principal thereof when due.

Local Reapportionment

Section 11. Within the year following that in which the Federal decennial census is officially reported as required by Federal law, and at such other times as the governing body of any municipality shall deem necessary, each municipality having a governing body not entirely elected at large shall be reapportioned, by its governing body or as shall otherwise be provided by uniform law, into districts which shall be composed of compact and contiguous territory as nearly equal in population as practicable, for the purpose of describing the districts for those not elected at large.

Philadelphia Debt

Section 12. The debt of the City of Philadelphia may be increased in such amount that the total debt of said city shall not exceed thirteen and one-half percent of the average of the annual assessed valuations of the taxable realty therein, during the ten years immediately preceding the year in which such increase is made, but said city shall not increase its indebtedness to an amount exceeding three percent upon such average assessed valuation of realty, without the consent of the electors thereof at a public election held in such manner as shall be provided by law.

In ascertaining the debt-incurring capacity of the City of Philadelphia at any time, there shall be deducted from the debt of said city so much of such debt as shall have been incurred, or is about to be incurred, and the proceeds thereof expended, or about to be expended, upon any public improvement, or in construction, purchase or condemnation of any public utility, or part thereof, or facility therefor, if such public improvement or public utility, or part thereof, or facility therefor, whether separately, or in connection with any other public improvement or public utility, or part thereof, or facility therefor, may reasonably be expected to yield revenue in excess of operating expenses sufficient to pay the interest and sinking fund charges thereon. The method of determining such amount, so to be deducted, shall be as now prescribed, or which may hereafter be prescribed by law.

In incurring indebtedness for any purpose the City of Philadelphia may issue its obligations maturing not later than fifty years from the date thereof, with provision for a sinking fund to be in equal or graded annual or other periodical installments. Where any indebtedness shall be or shall have been incurred by said City of Philadelphia for the purpose of the construction or improvement of public works or utilities of any character, from which income or revenue is to be derived by said city, or for the reclamation of land to be used in the construction of wharves or docks owned or to be owned by said city, such obligations may be in an amount sufficient to provide for, and may include the amount of the interest and sinking fund charges accruing and which may accrue thereon throughout the period of construction, and until the expiration of one year after the completion of the work for which said indebtedness shall have been incurred.

No debt shall be incurred by, or on behalf of, the County of Philadelphia.

Abolition of County Offices in Philadelphia

Section 13. (a) In Philadelphia all county offices are hereby abolished, and the city shall henceforth perform all functions of county government within its area through officers selected in such manner as may be provided by law.

(b) Local and special laws, regulating the affairs of the City of Philadelphia and creating offices or prescribing the powers and duties of officers of the City of Philadelphia, shall be valid notwithstanding the provisions of section thirty-two of Article III of this Constitution.

(c) All laws applicable to the County of Philadelphia shall apply to the City of Philadelphia.

(d) The City of Philadelphia shall have, assume and take over all powers, property, obligations and indebtedness of the County of Philadelphia.

(e) The provisions of section two of this article shall apply with full force and effect to the functions of the county government hereafter to be performed by the city government.

(f) Upon adoption of this amendment all county officers shall become officers of the City of Philadelphia, and until the General Assembly shall otherwise provide, shall continue to perform their duties and be elected, appointed, compensated and organized in such manner as may be provided by the provisions of this Constitution and the laws of the Commonwealth in effect at the time this amendment becomes effective, but such officers serving when this amendment becomes effective shall be permitted to complete their terms.

Definitions

Section 14. As used in this article, the following words shall have the following meanings:

"Municipality" means a county, city, borough, incorporated town, township or any similar general purpose unit of government which shall hereafter be created by the General Assembly.

"Initiative" means the filing with the applicable election officials at least ninety days prior to the next primary or general election of a petition containing a proposal for referendum signed by electors comprising five percent of the number of electors voting for the office of Governor in the last gubernatorial general election in each municipality or area affected. The applicable election official shall place the proposal on the ballot in a manner fairly representing the content of the petition for decision by referendum at said election. Initiative on a similar question shall not be submitted more often than once in five years. No enabling law shall be required for initiative.

"Referendum" means approval of a question placed on the ballot, by initiative or otherwise, by a majority vote of the electors voting thereon.

Article X

PRIVATE CORPORATIONS

Certain Unused Charters Void

Section 1. The charters and privileges granted prior to 1874 to private corporations which had not been organized in good faith and commenced business prior to 1874 shall be void.

Certain Charters to Be Subject to the Constitution

Section 2. Private corporations which have accepted or accept the Constitution of this Commonwealth or the benefits of any law passed by the General Assembly after 1873 governing the affairs of corporations shall hold their charters subject to the provisions of the Constitution of this Commonwealth.

Revocation, Amendment and Repeal of Charters and Corporation Laws

Section 3. All charters of private corporations and all present and future common or statutory law with respect to the formation or regulation of private corporations or prescribing powers, rights, duties or liabilities of private corporations or their officers, directors or shareholders may be revoked, amended or repealed.

Compensation for Property Taken by Corporations Under Right of Eminent Domain

Section 4. Municipal and other corporations invested with the privilege of taking private property for public use shall make just compensation for property taken, injured or destroyed by the construction or enlargement of their works, highways or improvements and compensation shall be paid or secured before the taking, injury or destruction.

Article XI

AMENDMENTS

Proposal of Amendments by the General Assembly and Their Adoption

Section 1. Amendments to this Constitution may be proposed in the Senate or House of Representatives; and if the same shall be agreed to by a majority of the members elected to each House, such proposed amendment or amendments shall be entered on their journals with the yeas and nays taken thereon, and the Secretary of the Commonwealth shall cause the same to be published three months before the next general election, in at least two newspapers in every county in which such newspapers shall be published; and if, in the General Assembly next afterwards chosen, such proposed amendment or amendments shall be agreed to by a majority of the members elected to each House, the Secretary of the Commonwealth shall cause the same again to be published in the manner aforesaid; and such proposed amendment or amendments shall be submitted to the qualified electors of the State in such manner, and at such time at least three months after being so agreed to by the two Houses, as the General Assembly shall prescribe; and, if such amendment or amendments shall be approved by a majority of those voting thereon, such amendment or amendments shall become a part of the Constitution; but no amendment or amendments shall be submitted oftener than once in five years. When two or more amendments shall be submitted they shall be voted upon separately.

(a) In the event a major emergency threatens or is about to threaten the Commonwealth and if the safety or welfare of the Commonwealth requires prompt amendment of this Constitution, such amendments to this Constitution may be proposed in the Senate or House of Representatives at any regular or special session of the General Assembly, and if agreed to by at least two-thirds of the members elected to each House, a proposed amendment shall be entered on the journal of each House with the yeas and nays taken thereon and the official in charge of statewide elections shall promptly publish such proposed amendment in at least two newspapers in every county in which such newspapers are published. Such amendment shall then be submitted to the qualified electors of the Commonwealth in such manner, and at such time, at least one month after being agreed to by both Houses as the General Assembly prescribes.

(b) If an emergency amendment is approved by a majority of the qualified electors voting thereon, it shall become part of this Constitution. When two or more emergency amendments are submitted they shall be voted on separately.

SCHEDULES TO
CONSTITUTION OF PENNSYLVANIA

Schedule
1. Adopted with the Constitution
2. Amendments of November 2, 1909

SCHEDULE NO. 1
(ADOPTED WITH THE CONSTITUTION)

That no inconvenience may arise from the changes in the Constitution of the Commonwealth, and in order to carry the same into complete operation, it is hereby declared, that:

When to Take Effect
Section 1. This Constitution shall take effect on the first day of January, in the year one thousand eight hundred and seventy-four, for all purposes not otherwise provided for therein.

Former Laws Remain in Force
Section 2. All laws in force in this Commonwealth at the time of the adoption of this Constitution not inconsistent therewith, and all rights, actions, prosecutions and contracts shall continue as if this Constitution had not been adopted.

Election of Senators
Section 3. At the general election in the years one thousand eight hundred and seventy-four and one thousand eight hundred and seventy-five, Senators shall be elected in all districts where there shall be vacancies. Those elected in the year one thousand eight hundred and seventy-four shall serve for two years, and those elected in the year one thousand eight hundred and seventy-five shall serve for one year. Senators now elected and those whose terms are unexpired shall represent the districts in which they reside until the end of the terms for which they were elected.

Election of Senators *(continued)*
Section 4. At the general election in the year one thousand eight hundred and seventy-six, Senators shall be elected from even-numbered districts to serve for two years, and from odd-numbered districts to serve for four years.

Election of Governor
Section 5. The first election of Governor under this Constitution shall be at the general election in the year one thousand eight hundred and seventy-five, when a Governor shall be elected for three years; and the term of the Governor elected in the year one thousand eight hundred and seventy-eight and of those thereafter elected shall be for four years, according to the provisions of this Constitution.

Election of Lieutenant Governor
Section 6. At the general election in the year one thousand eight hundred and seventy-four, a Lieutenant Governor shall be elected according to the provisions of this Constitution.

Secretary of Internal Affairs
Section 7. The Secretary of Internal Affairs shall be elected at the first general election after the adoption of this Constitution; and, when the said officer shall be duly elected and qualified, the office of Surveyor General shall be abolished. The Surveyor General in office at the time of the adoption of this Constitution shall continue in office until the expiration of the term for which he was elected.

Superintendent of Public Instruction
Section 8. When the Superintendent of Public Instruction shall be duly qualified the office of Superintendent of Common Schools shall cease.

Eligibility of Present Officers
Section 9. Nothing contained in this Constitution shall be construed to render any person now holding any State office for a first official term ineligible for re-election at the end of such term.

Judges of Supreme Court

Section 10. The judges of the Supreme Court in office when this Constitution shall take effect shall continue until their commissions severally expire. Two judges in addition to the number now composing the said court shall be elected at the first general election after the adoption of this Constitution.

Courts of Record

Section 11. All courts of record and all existing courts which are not specified in this Constitution shall continue in existence until the first day of December, in the year one thousand eight hundred and seventy-five, without abridgement of their present jurisdiction, but no longer. The court of first criminal jurisdiction for the counties of Schuylkill, Lebanon and Dauphin is hereby abolished, and all causes and proceedings pending therein in the county of Schuylkill shall be tried and disposed of in the courts of oyer and terminer and quarter sessions of the peace of said county.

Register's Courts Abolished

Section 12. The register's courts now in existence shall be abolished on the first day of January next succeeding the adoption of this Constitution.

Judicial Districts

Section 13. The General Assembly shall, at the next session after the adoption of this Constitution, designate the several judicial districts as required by this Constitution. The judges in commission when such designation shall be made shall continue during their unexpired terms judges of the new districts in which they reside; but, when there shall be two judges residing in the same district, the president judge shall elect to which district he shall be assigned, and the additional law judge shall be assigned to the other district.

Decennial Adjustment of Judicial Districts

Section 14. The General Assembly shall, at the next succeeding session after each decennial census and not oftener, designate the several judicial districts as required by this Constitution.

Judges in Commission

Section 15. Judges learned in the law of any court of record holding commissions in force at the adoption of this Constitution shall hold their respective offices until the expiration of the terms for which they were commissioned, and until their successors shall be duly qualified. The Governor shall commission the president judge of the court of first criminal jurisdiction for the counties of Schuylkill, Lebanon and Dauphin as a judge of the court of common pleas of Schuylkill county, for the unexpired term of his office.

President Judges; Casting Lots; Associate Judges

Section 16. After the expiration of the term of any president judge of any court of common pleas, in commission at the adoption of this Constitution, the judge of such court learned in the law and oldest in commission shall be the president judge thereof; and when two or more judges are elected at the same time in any judicial district they shall decide by lot which shall be president judge; but when the president judge of a court shall be re-elected he shall continue to be president judge of that court. Associate judges not learned in the law, elected after the adoption of this Constitution, shall be commissioned to hold their offices for the term of five years from the first day of January next after their election.

Compensation of Judges

Section 17. The General Assembly, at the first session after the adoption of this Constitution, shall fix and determine the compensation of the judges of the Supreme Court and of the judges of the several judicial districts of the Commonwealth; and the provisions of the fifteenth section of the article on Legislation shall not be deemed inconsistent herewith. Nothing contained in this Constitution shall be held to reduce the compensation now paid to any law judge of this Commonwealth now in commission.

Courts of Philadelphia and Allegheny Counties; Organization in Philadelphia

Section 18. The courts of common pleas in the counties of Philadelphia and Allegheny shall be composed of the present judges of the district court and court of common pleas of said counties until their offices shall severally end, and of such other judges as may from time to time be selected. For the purpose of first organization in Philadelphia the judges of the court number one shall be Judges Allison, Pierce and Paxson; of the court number two, Judges Hare, Mitchell and one other judge to be elected; of the court number three, Judges Ludlow, Finletter and Lynd; and of the court number four, Judges Thayer, Briggs and one other judge to be elected. The judge first named shall be the president judge of said courts respectively, and thereafter the president judge shall be the judge oldest in commission; but any president judge, re-elected in the same court or district, shall continue to be president judge thereof. The additional judges for courts numbers two and four shall be voted for and elected at the first general election after the adoption of this Constitution, in the same manner as the two additional judges of the Supreme Court, and they shall decide by lot to which court they shall belong. Their term of office shall commence on the first Monday of January, in the year one thousand eight hundred and seventy-five.

Organization of Courts in Allegheny County

Section 19. In the county of Allegheny, for the purpose of first organization under this Constitution, the judge of the court of common pleas, at the time of the adoption of this Constitution, shall be the judges of the court number one, and the judges of the district court, at the same date, shall be the judges of the common pleas number two. The president judges of the common pleas and district court shall be president judge of said courts number one and two, respectively, until their offices shall end; and thereafter the judge oldest in commission shall be president judge; but any president judge re-elected in the same court, or district, shall continue to be president judge thereof.

When Re-Organization of Courts to Take Effect

Section 20. The organization of the courts of common pleas under this Constitution for the counties of Philadelphia and Allegheny shall take effect on the first Monday of January, one thousand eight hundred and seventy-five, and existing courts in said counties shall continue with their present powers and jurisdiction until that date, but no new suits shall be instituted in the courts of nisi prius after the adoption of this Constitution.

Causes Pending in Philadelphia; Transfer of Records

Section 21. The causes and proceedings pending in the court of nisi prius, court of common pleas, and district court in Philadelphia shall be tried and disposed of in the court of common pleas. The records and dockets of said courts shall be transferred to the prothonotary's office of said county.

Causes Pending in Allegheny County

Section 22. The causes and proceedings pending in the court of common pleas in the county of Allegheny shall be tried and disposed of in the court number one; and the causes and proceedings pending in the district court shall be tried and disposed of in the court number two.

Prothonotary of Philadelphia County

Section 23. The prothonotary of the court of common pleas of Philadelphia shall be first appointed by the judges of said court on the first Monday of December, in the year one thousand eight hundred and seventy-five, and the present prothonotary of the district court in said county shall be the prothonotary of the said court of common pleas until said date when his commission shall expire, and the present clerk of the court of oyer and terminer and quarter sessions of the peace in Philadelphia shall be the clerk of such court until the expiration of his present commission on the first Monday of December, in the year one thousand eight hundred and seventy-five.

Aldermen

Section 24. In cities containing over fifty thousand inhabitants, except Philadelphia, all aldermen in office at the time of the adoption of this Constitution shall continue in office until the expiration of their commissions, and at the election for city and ward officers in the year one thousand eight hundred and seventy-five one alderman shall be elected in each ward as provided in this Constitution.

Magistrates in Philadelphia

Section 25. In Philadelphia magistrates in lieu of aldermen shall be chosen, as required in this Constitution, at the election in said city for city and ward officers in the year one thousand eight hundred and seventy-five; their term of office shall commence on the first Monday of April succeeding their election. The terms of office of aldermen in said city holding or entitled to commissions at the time of the adoption of this Constitution shall not be affected thereby.

Term of Present Officers

Section 26. All persons in office in this Commonwealth at the time of the adoption of this Constitution, and at the first election under it, shall hold their respective offices until the term for which they have been elected or appointed shall expire, and until their successors shall be duly qualified, unless otherwise provided in this Constitution.

Oath of Office

Section 27. The seventh article of this Constitution prescribing an oath of office shall take effect on and after the first day of January, one thousand eight hundred and seventy-five.

County Commissioners and Auditors

Section 28. The terms of office of county commissioners and county auditors, chosen prior to the year one thousand eight hundred and seventy-five, which shall not have expired before the first Monday of January in the year one thousand eight hundred and seventy-six, shall expire on that day.

Compensation of Present Officers

Section 29. All State, county, city, ward, borough and township officers in office at the time of the adoption of this Constitution, whose compensation is not provided for by salaries alone, shall continue to receive the compensation allowed them by law until the expiration of their respective terms of office.

Renewal of Oath of Office

Section 30. All State and judicial officers heretofore elected, sworn, affirmed, or in office when this Constitution shall take effect, shall severally, within one month after such adoption, take and subscribe an oath, or affirmation to support this Constitution.

Enforcing Legislation

Section 31. The General Assembly at its first session, or as soon as may be after the adoption of this Constitution, shall pass such laws as may be necessary to carry the same into full force and effect.

An Ordinance Declared Valid

Section 32. The ordinance passed by this Convention, entitled "An ordinance for submitting the amended Constitution of Pennsylvania to a vote of the electors thereof," shall be held to be valid for all the purposes thereof.

City Commissioners of Philadelphia

Section 33. The words "county commissioners," wherever used in this Constitution and in any ordinance accompanying the same, shall be held to include the commissioners for the city of Philadelphia.

SCHEDULE NO. 2
(AMENDMENTS OF NOVEMBER 2, 1909)

Adoption. The provisions of Schedule No. 2 were adopted November 2, 1909, P.L. 948, J.R.1.

Partial Repeal of Schedule. See section 2 of Proposal No. 7 of 1968 in the appendix to the Constitution for provisions relating to the partial repeal of Schedule No. 2.

Adjustments of Terms of Public Officers

Section 1. That no inconvenience may arise from the changes in the Constitution of the Commonwealth, and in order to carry the same into complete operation, it is hereby declared that —

In the case of officers elected by the people, all terms of office fixed by act of Assembly at an odd number of years shall each be lengthened one year, but the Legislature may change the length of the term, provided the terms for which such officers are elected shall always be for an even number of years.

The above extension of official terms shall not affect officers elected at the general election of one thousand nine hundred and eight; nor any city, ward, borough, township, or election division officers, whose terms of office, under existing law, end in the year one thousand nine hundred and ten.

In the year one thousand nine hundred and ten the municipal election shall be held on the third Tuesday of February as heretofore; but all officers chosen at that election to an office the regular term of which is two years, and also all election officers and assessors chosen at that election, shall serve until the first Monday of December in the year one thousand nine hundred and eleven. All officers chosen at that election to offices the term of which is now four years, or is made four years by the operation of these amendments or this schedule, shall serve until the first Monday of December in the year one thousand nine hundred and thirteen. All justices of the peace, magistrates, and aldermen, chosen at that election, shall serve until the first Monday of December in the year one thousand nine hundred and fifteen. After the year nineteen hundred and ten, and until the Legislature shall otherwise provide, all terms of city, ward, borough, township, and election division officers shall begin on the first Monday of December in an odd-numbered year.

All city, ward, borough, and township officers holding office at the date of the approval of these amendments, whose terms of office may end in the year one thousand nine hundred and eleven, shall continue to hold their offices until the first Monday of December of that year.

All judges of the courts for the several judicial districts, and also all county officers, holding office at the date of the approval of these amendments, whose terms of office may end in the year one thousand nine hundred and eleven, shall continue to hold their offices until the first Monday of January, one thousand nine hundred and twelve.

APPENDIX

Supplementary Provisions of Constitutional Amendments

1967, MAY 16, P.L. 1044, J.R.4

Schedule. Terms of State Treasurer and Auditor General

That no inconvenience may arise from changes in Article IV of the Constitution of this Commonwealth, it is hereby declared that the State Treasurer and Auditor General first elected after this amended article becomes effective shall serve terms beginning the first Tuesday in May next following their election and expiring four years from the third Tuesday in January next ensuing their election.

Explanatory Note. Joint Resolution No. 4 added section 18 and made other changes in Article IV.

1968, APRIL 23, P.L.APP.3, PROP. NO.1

Schedule. Effective Date of Amendment

The foregoing amendment to Article II of the Constitution of Pennsylvania if approved by the electorate voting on April 23, 1968, shall become effective the year following that in which the next Federal decennial census is officially reported as required by Federal Law.

Explanatory Note. Proposal No.1 amended and consolidated sections 16 and 17 into section 16 of Article II.

1968, APRIL 23, P.L.APP.3, PROP. NO.2

Schedule. Effective Date of Amendment

The foregoing amendment to Article II of the Constitution of Pennsylvania if approved by the electorate voting on April 23, 1968, shall become effective the year following that in which the next Federal decennial census is officially reported as required by Federal law.

Explanatory Note. Proposal No.2 amended and renumbered section 18 to section 17 of Article II.

1968, APRIL 23, P.L.APP.5, PROP. NO.3

Repeals

Section 4. Effective when the last bonds have been issued under their authority, sections 24 and 25 of Article VIII of the Constitution of Pennsylvania are hereby repealed.

References in Text. Sections 24 and 25 were renumbered sections 15 and 16, respectively, of Article VIII by Proposal No.5 of 1968.

1968, APRIL 23, P.L.APP.7, PROP. NO.4

Effective Date of Amendments

Section 3. The following schedule is adopted: Sections 10, 12, 13 and 14 of Article VIII shall take effect as soon as possible, but no later than July 1, 1970.

1968, APRIL 23, P.L.APP.9, PROP. NO.5

Effective Date of Amendments

Section 4. Sections 1 and 2 shall take effect as soon as possible, but no later than July 1, 1970. Section 4 shall take effect July 1, 1970, unless the General Assembly earlier provides enabling legislation in accordance therewith.

References in Text. Proposal No. 5 amended section 1, added sections 2 and 4 and renumbered or amended other sections of Article VIII.

1968, APRIL 23, P.L.APP.11, PROP. NO.6

Effective Date and Interpretation of Amendments

Section 3. This new article and the repeal of existing sections shall take effect on the date of approval by the electorate, except that the following sections shall take effect on the effective date of legislation adopted pursuant to the sections or the date indicated below, whichever shall first occur.

The first, third and fourth paragraphs of section 8 shall take effect two years after the effective date. The second sentence of section 1, the fourth sentence of section 2, all of section 3, the third paragraph of section 4, and the first paragraph of section 10 shall take effect four years after the effective date. The second sentence of section 1 and the first paragraph of section 8 on Uniform Legislation shall be construed so as to be consistent with the jurisdiction of this Convention.

Explanatory Note. Proposal No.6 added present Article IX and repealed sections in Articles VIII, XIII, XIV and XV.

1968, APRIL 23, P.L.APP.16, PROP. NO.7

Repeals

Section 2. Article V of the Constitution of Pennsylvania is repealed in its entirety, and those provisions of Schedules No.1 and No.2 are repealed to the extent they are inconsistent with this article and attached schedule.

Explanatory Note. Proposal No.7 added present Article V.

1972, NOVEMBER 7, 1ST SP.SESS., P.L.1970, J.R.1

Preamble

Section 1. Millions of Pennsylvanians have suffered greatly from the ravages of the most disastrous flood in the history of the Commonwealth. This flood has left devastation in its wake. Thousands of people have been left homeless and countless industrial and commercial establishments and public facilities have been damaged or destroyed.

It is imperative that the victims of this disaster immediately receive the fullest possible aid from both the public and private sectors in order to clean up and rebuild the affected areas of the Commonwealth.

In addition, many Pennsylvanians suffered greatly as a result of the Great Storm or Flood of September, 1971.

The General Assembly desires to alleviate such storm or economic deprivation caused by the flood, but is limited in its efforts by rigid restrictions in the Constitution of the Commonwealth of Pennsylvania. The safety and welfare of the Commonwealth requires prompt amendment to the Constitution of the Commonwealth of Pennsylvania.

The following amendment to the Constitution of the Commonwealth of Pennsylvania is proposed in accordance with the emergency provisions contained in subsections (a) and (b) of section 1 of the eleventh article thereof:

That Article VIII of the Constitution of the Commonwealth of Pennsylvania be amended by adding a new section to read:

Explanatory Note. Joint Resolution No.1 added section 17 of Article VIII.

1975, NOVEMBER 4, P.L. 622, J.R.2

Preamble

Section 1. Many Pennsylvanians have suffered greatly from the ravages of great storms or floods in the last few years. The great storms or floods of 1974 and 1975 are additional major disasters causing loss of life and great damage and destruction to property of individuals, industrial and commercial establishments and public facilities.

It is imperative that the victims of these disasters immediately receive the fullest possible aid from both the public and private sectors in order to clean up and rebuild the affected areas of the Commonwealth and that persons in the Commonwealth be eligible for the maximum available aid from the government of the United States.

The General Assembly desires to alleviate such storm or economic deprivation caused by the floods but is limited in its efforts by rigid restrictions in the Constitution of the Commonwealth of Pennsylvania. The safety and welfare of the Commonwealth requires prompt amendment to the Constitution of the Commonwealth of Pennsylvania.

The following amendment to the Constitution of the Commonwealth of Pennsylvania is proposed in accordance with the emergency provisions contained in subsections (a) and (b) of section 1 of the eleventh article thereof:

That section 17 of Article VIII of the Constitution of the Commonwealth of Pennsylvania be amended to read:
* * *

1977, NOVEMBER 8, P.L. 362, J.R. 2

Preamble

Many Pennsylvanians have suffered greatly from the ravages of Great Storms and Floods in recent years. The Great Storms or Floods of 1974, 1975, 1976 and 1977 were additional major disasters causing loss of life and great damage and destruction to property of individuals, industrial and commercial establishments and public facilities.

It is imperative that the victims of these disasters receive the fullest possible aid from both the Federal Government and the Commonwealth in order to accomplish a speedy recovery.

The Congress of the United States, through enactment of the Disaster Relief Act of 1974, Public Law 93-288, has authorized the making of certain disaster relief grants. The General Assembly wishes to make such Federal disaster relief grants, or other grants made available from Federal programs hereafter enacted, available to eligible individuals and families in order to alleviate the deprivation caused by storms or floods which have occurred in the past and seeks to address those emergencies of future years. However, the General Assembly is limited by rigid restrictions in the Constitution of the Commonwealth of Pennsylvania. The safety and welfare of the Commonwealth requries the prompt amendment to the Constitution to aid those already inflicted by the Great Storms of 1976 or 1977 and any future emergency that may strike Commonwealth citizens.

Therefore, the following amendment to the Constitution of the Commonwealth of Pennsylvania is proposed in accordance with the emergency provisions of Article XI thereof:

That section 17 of Article VIII be amended to read:
* * *

1978, MAY 16, 1977 P.L. 365, J.R.4

Vacancy in Existing Office of Attorney General.

Upon approval of this amendment by the electors, there shall be a vacancy in the office of Attorney General which shall be filled as provided herein.
* * *

Explanatory Note. Joint Resolution No.4 added section 4.1 and amended sections 5, 6, 8 and 17 of Article IV.

1987-88 GENERAL ASSEMBLY

SECTION 3 - GENERAL ASSEMBLY

LEGISLATIVE PRACTICE AND PROCEDURE

TIME OF MEETING

The General Assembly convenes annually on the first Tuesday of January at 12 o'clock Noon.*

OFFICERS OF THE PRECEDING SESSION WHO ARE AUTHORIZED TO BE PRESENT AT THE ORGANIZATION OF THE LEGISLATURE.

The Lieutenant Governor who by the Constitution is made President of the Senate, presides at the opening of the Senate.

ORGANIZATION OF THE SENATE

Convening in odd numbered years.

At twelve o'clock N., on the day fixed for the meeting of the General Assembly, the twenty-five Senators whose terms of office have not expired and the twenty-five Senators elect, together with the returning officers of the Senate, assemble in the Senate Chamber and are called to order by the President of the Senate (the Lieutenant Governor), in the following form: "This being the day fixed by the Constitution for the meeting of the General Assembly, the Senate will come to order."

The custom is to call upon the chaplain, any minister of the Gospel who may be present to open the proceedings with prayer, after which the Secretary of the Commonwealth, being introduced by the Sergeant-at-Arms, presents to the Senate the returns of the election for Senators held at the previous November election. The Clerk proceeds to open and read the returns as presented. After which the newly elected Senators present themselves in front of the Clerk's desk, where the requisite oath of office is administered to them by any person authorized to administer oaths and is signed by the Senators in a book prepared for the purpose.

The next proceeding is the election of the President pro tempore. Nominations are made from the floor by any Senator, the President announces the nominations for said office. After the nominations have been made the clerks proceed with the election by calling the roll of the Senate, the Senators voting for their choice by a viva voce vote. The President announces the result of the vote and declares who has been elected; he then appoints a committee of three Senators (usually the defeated candidate, and two of the Senators who nominated the successful candidate) to escort the President pro tempore to the chair at which time the oath of office is administered usually by the same judge who administered the oath to the Senators. The next order of business is the election of the Secretary and Chief Clerk after which the Senate is ready to proceed with any business that may be presented.

ORGANIZATION OF THE HOUSE

The members elected and returned together with the returning officers of the House of Representatives, meet in the Hall of the House of Representatives, on the day fixed for the meeting of the General Assembly, and at eleven-thirty A.M. of that day in odd numbered years one of the oldest members, that is, one who has been a member for previous years and

*See Article II, Section 4 of the Pennsylvania Constitution.

returned elected to the present session, announces from the Speaker's rostrum, "that the members of the House of Representatives will meet this day at twelve o'clock N., for the purpose of organization." When that time arrives the Clerk arises and says, "This being the day appointed by the Constitution for the meeting of the General Assembly, and there appearing to be present a sufficient number of ladies and gentlemen elected members to constitute a quorum they will come to order."

Following the Invocation, the Secretary of the Commonwealth presents himself at the bar of the House. The Sergeant-at-Arms immediately announces: "The Secretary of the Commonwealth." The clerk then announces to the House, "The Secretary of the Commonwealth." When this is done, the Secretary of the Commonwealth advances a few feet within the bar of the House, and says, "Mr. Chief Clerk, I have the honor to present the returns of the late election of members of the House of Representatives for the several cities and counties of this Commonwealth, agreeable to the provisions of the Constitution and laws relating to the elections of this Commonwealth."

As soon as the Secretary of the Commonwealth retires, a member rises in his place, and presents a resolution "that the returns of the elections be opened and read." This resolution being read by the Clerk, and agreed to by a majority of those present, the Clerk proceeds with reading the returns from the several counties in the Commonwealth in alphabetical order.

When the returns are all read, and the names of the members returned as such announced, the roll of the members is taken to establish the presence of a quorum. The oath of office is then administered by a Justice of the Supreme Court or a judge of another court learned in the law, and is signed by the members in a book prepared for the purpose.

A resolution is then presented by a member, "that the members present do now, in conformity with the ninth section of the second article of the Constitution, proceed to the election of a Speaker." If any one candidate receives a majority of all the votes cast, he is declared elected Speaker. The House is then ready to proceed with the business of the Session. Committees on the part of the House are then appointed to notify the Senate and the Governor that the House is organized and ready to proceed with the business of the session.

THE GENERAL POWERS AND DUTIES OF THE PRESIDENT OF THE SENATE AND THE SPEAKER OF THE HOUSE

There are certain duties pertaining to the offices of President and Speaker which are not necessary to be specified by rule, being so obviously proper and right as to be indisputable.

1. He calls the legislative body to order at the time fixed for the meeting, and ascertains the presence of a quorum.

2. He announces the business and lays it before the body, in the order in which it is to be acted upon.

3. He states and puts to a vote all questions which are regularly moved and announces the result.

4. He recognizes members entitled to the floor.

5. He receives any propositions made by members and puts them to the legislative body and declares the determination of the body.

6. He decides all questions of order, subject to an appeal to the legislative body.

7. He preserves order and decorum in debate and at all other times.

8. He restrains members when engaged in debate within the rules of order.

9. He is representative of the body itself, in its powers, its proceedings and its dignity.

10. Under the rules he has the general direction of the hall.

11. He receives and announces to the legislative body all messages from other branches of the Government, and also any other appropriate communications.

12. He gives notices and signs in the presence of the body all acts, orders, addresses and joint resolutions.

13. When a legislative body is engaged in its judicial function, it is the duty of the presiding officers to conduct the proceedings, to put questions to parties and witnesses, and to pronounce the sentence or judgment.

14. When the legislative body is engaged in any of its high administrative functions, or in matters of state or ceremony, as for example, when a member or other person is to be reprimanded or thanked, the presiding officer is the mouth piece and organ of the body.

15. He has general charge and supervision of the legislative chamber; galleries; committees, caucus and conference rooms assigned to the House.

16. The President pro tempore of the Senate and the Speaker of the House are always members, and may present petitions, memorials and remonstrances sent to them. They possess the right to vote as other members, on all questions before the body, and may leave the chair and address the body on any question. The president of the Senate is the Lieutenant Governor, and he votes only when there is a tie on any question except in those instances where the Constitution requires the vote of "a majority of the members elected" to decide a question.

BILL IN PLACE OR INTRODUCED

All bills read in place in the Senate and introduced in the House of Representatives must be presented in quintuplicate. Before presenting a bill, it is the duty of the member to sign his name to each copy and insert the date of introduction.

FORM OF INDORSEMENT ON BILL COVER:
(Senate or H.R. No.)
Title of the Bill.
Name of the member.
Date.

In the Senate when the order of business of reading bills in place is reached the Senator who desires to present a bill arises, and, addressing the Chair, says: "Mr. President, I read in place and present to the Chair, a bill." The President says: "The Senator from _____ County, Mr. _____ reads in place and presents to the Chair a bill." To expedite the business of the Senate, a Member may introduce a bill by first endorsing it as described above and then depositing the original copy together with the four copies properly endorsed, with the Secretary/Parliamentarian of the Senate. The

Secretary/Parliamentarian presents the bills that have been left in his custody to the Lieutenant Governor for reference by him to the appropriate committees. The next legislative day, the bills are announced to the Senate by the Lieutenant Governor, with the appropriate committee references thereon.

To expedite the business of the House of Representatives, a Member who desires to introduce a bill, first endorses the same as described above and then deposits the original copy together with the four copies properly endorsed, with the Chief Clerk. At the close of each day the Chief Clerk presents all the bills that have been left in his custody during the day to the Speaker for reference by him to appropriate committees. The next succeeding legislative day the bills are announced to the House by the Speaker, with the appropriate committee references thereon.

All bills and joint resolutions presented in either the Senate or House of Representatives must be presented in quintuplicate—one copy for the committee, one for the printer, one for the computer, one for the press and one for indexing.

RESOLUTIONS

In general, the parliamentary meaning of "resolution" is the written expression of the will of the Senate or House in regard to any subject before it, either public or private; as, for example, that the use of the hall be granted for a particular purpose; that the Senate or House will adjourn at a particular time; that certain departments of the government be required to furnish statements, et cetera. If information is desired from any of the departments, or from the Executive, the resolution assumes the form of a request, as for example: "Resolved, That the Auditor General be requested to furnish the Senate or House with a statement," et cetera.

This however, is but an expression of will; the Senate or House, by the resolution doing nothing more than declaring it to be its will that the Auditor General furnish the statement.

When a member is desirous of bringing before the Senate or House any proposition for its determination, he presents it in the form of a written resolution, and as soon as the President announces that "original resolutions are now in order in the Senate," he arises in place and says, "Mr. President, I offer the following resolution." The President then says, "The Senator from _____ County offers the following resolution. The resolution will be read by the Clerk."

As soon as it has been read by the Clerk, if it be a resolution that can be considered without reference to committee, it is voted on immediately.

In the Senate, resolutions on the following subjects, after being read, must be referred to an appropriate committee without debate (unless by unanimous consent the Senate shall otherwise direct), and, if favorably reported by the committee, shall lie over for one day for consideration, after which they may be called up under their appropriate order of business, viz: All Senate and House concurrent resolutions (excepting resolutions in reference to adjournments and those recalling bills from Governor, which are regarded as privileged); resolutions containing calls for information from the heads of departments, or to alter the rules; and resolutions giving rise to debate, (except such as relate to the disposition of matters immediately before the Senate, to the business of the day on which offered, and to adjournment or taking a recess).

In the House all resolutions (except those privileged under the Rules) are introduced by Members filing them with the Chief Clerk. They are then referred to appropriate committees by the

Speaker. When a resolution is reported from committee and placed on the Calendar, it may be called up for consideration under the regular order of business for resolutions. The only resolutions which are considered privileged and receive the immediate consideration of the House are those:

Recalling from or returning bills to the Governor.

Recalling from or returning bills to the Senate.

Originated by the Committee on Rules.

Providing for a joint Session of the Senate and House and its procedure.

Placing bills negatived by committees on the calendar.

Adjournment or recess.

Concurrent resolutions are those on which the consideration of both Senate and House is required.

Joint resolutions, being in the nature of bills, cannot be submitted to the House under the head of original resolutions. They are deposited with the Chief Clerk, who presents them to the Speaker for reference to committees, after which they follow the same procedure as bills under the Rules of the House.

ACTION ON BILLS BY STANDING COMMITTEES

When a bill has been referred to a standing committee, the committee as soon as it has completed its consideration, makes a report of the result of its deliberations to the House and this report varies according to the circumstances.

Suppose, for example, a bill has been, in the usual course of business, referred to the appropriate committee. Should the committee agree to report the bill affirmatively, it would assign it to the Chairman to be reported, endorsing thereon his name, the name of the committee and the words "as committed." In case the committee made amendments, he would then endorse on the bill the words "as amended."

AMENDING BILLS IN COMMITTEE

Whenever a committee to whom a bill has been referred for their consideration makes amendments to it, they should be typewritten and securely attached to the bill. Amendments are prepared by the Legislative Reference Bureau when requested by the committees.

No part of any bill should be mutilated by writing in or striking out amendments.

ACTION ON BILLS IN THE SENATE AND HOUSE

When a bill is reported from committee in the Senate or House it is reprinted if amended. Bills are usually read for the first time in the Senate and House on the day they are reported from committee.

When the order of business "Bills on Second Consideration" is reached in the Senate, bills are called up for consideration by the President, and are considered as a whole and subject to amendment and debate.

The next step is the transcribing of the bill, and the President says, "This bill has now been considered a second time, and agreed to." The bill being thus agreed to, lies over and comes up on the calendar of bills on third consideration.

Bills on second consideration in the House must be called up by a sponsor and are considered as a whole and are subject to amendment and debate.

When a bill is reached on third consideration, the President or Speaker says, "This bill has now been considered a third time; the question is on agreeing to the bill a third time." If agreed to, the next question is on its final passage, when the President or

Speaker says, "This bill has been considered three times on three different days, and agreed to, the question is now on its final passage. Agreeable to the provisions of the Constitution the yeas and nays will be taken on the final passage of the bill." If the bill passes, an order follows, of course, which should always be stated by the Speaker in the case of House bills, "The Clerk will present the same to the Senate for concurrence"; in the case of Senate bills without amendment, "The Clerk will return the same to the Senate with information that the House of Representatives has passed the same without amendment"; in case of Senate bills with amendments, "The Clerk will return the same to the Senate with information that the House of Representatives has passed the same with amendments, in which the concurrence of the Senate is requested."

When a bill in the House is on third consideration, it is subject to amendment in the same manner as on second consideration.

A bill on third consideration in the Senate may be amended by obtaining unanimous consent.

FORMS OF MESSAGES FROM ONE BODY TO THE OTHER

When the Clerk has but one bill to take from the House to the Senate for concurrence the form is:

"The Clerk of the House of Representatives (being introduced) presented for concurrence, Bill No. 1, entitled 'An act for the protection of laborers'."

If there be two or more bills, the form is:

"The Clerk of the House of Representatives (being introduced) presented for concurrence, bills numbered and entitled as follows:

"No. 1. 'An act for the protection of laborers.'

"No. 2. 'An act relative to insurance companies'."

If there be in connection with bills for concurrence, Senate bills, without amendment, the form is:

"The Clerk of the House of Representatives (being introduced) presented for concurrence bills numbered and entitled as follows:

"No. 1. 'An act for the protection of laborers.'

"No. 2. 'An act relative to insurance companies.'

"He also returned bills from the Senate, numbered and entitled as follows:

"No. 20. 'An act relative to brokers.'

"No. 21. 'An act relative to banks.'

"With information that the House of Representatives has passed the same without amendments."

If the Senate bills have amendments, the form is:

"The Clerk of the House of Representatives (being introduced) presented for concurrence, bills numbered and entitled as follows:

"No. 1. 'An act for the protection of laborers.'

"No. 2. 'An act relative to insurance companies.'

"He also returned bills from the Senate, numbered and entitled as follows:

"No. 20. 'An act relative to brokers.'

"No. 21. 'An act relative to banks.'

"With information that the House of Representatives has passed the same with an amendment (or amendments) in which the concurrence of the Senate is requested."

But suppose the Senate has passed a bill from the House, No. 1, for example, with amendments, and the House has concurred in them, the following would be added to the above message:

"He also informed the Senate that the House of Representatives has concurred in the amendments made by the Senate to the bill from the House of Representatives, entitled:

"No. 1. 'An act for the protection of laborers'."

Should the House non-concur in the amendments made by the Senate to the bill then the information is the same, except that the word non-concurred is used instead of concurred.

If the House, however, concurs in the Senate amendments with an amendment, the information in the message is:

"He also informed the Senate that the House of Representatives has concurred in the amendments made by the Senate to the bill from the House of Representatives, entitled:

"No. 1. 'An act for the protection of laborers.'

"With an amendment (or amendments) in which the concurrence of the Senate is requested."

But suppose the House should concur in one amendment made by the Senate to the bill and non-concur in the other, the information to be given would be:

"He also informed the Senate that the House of Representatives has non-concurred in the first amendment made by the Senate to the bill from the House of Representatives, entitled:

"No. 1. 'An act for the protection of laborers,' and has concurred in the second."

And if the House should concur with an amendment, then is added: "And has concurred in the second, with an amendment in which the concurrence of the Senate is requested."

Suppose again, that the House of Representatives concur in the amendments made by the Senate to amendments made by the House of Representatives to said bill, the information would be:

"He also informed the Senate that the House of Representatives has concurred in the amendment made by the Senate to the amendments made by the House of Representatives to bill from the House of Representatives, entitled:

"No. 1. 'An act for the protection of laborers.' "

And if the House should non-concur, then the message varies accordingly.

If, in these cases, the House or Senate should recede, insist or adhere to any amendments made by them, respectively, to a bill then the form used is precisely the same as those already given, except the words recede, insist or adhere, are used, as the case may be.

If the House insists, then follows the appointment of the committee of conference, and the information to be given is:

"He informed the Senate that the House of Representatives insists upon its amendments, non-concurred in by the Senate, to bill No. 1, entitled (here, state the title) and has appointed Messrs. A., B. and C. a committee of conference, to confer with a similar committee of the Senate; if the Senate should appoint such committee, on the subject of the difference existing between the two Houses on said bill."

If the Senate should have already appointed a committee then the words used, instead of "if the Senate should appoint a committee," change the form to suit the circumstances.

If the House should pass a resolution, which requires the concurrence of the Senate, the form of the message is:

"The Clerk of the House of Representatives (being introduced) presented the following extract from the Journal of the House of Representatives":

(Here follows the resolution, with the date of its passage.)

The same form is used by the Clerk of the Senate using the word "Senate," instead of "House of Representatives," et cetera.

CERTIFICATES ATTACHED TO BILLS PASSED OVER VETO, AND TO BILLS HELD TEN DAYS

The following forms are used when bills become laws, in any of the modes prescribed by the Constitution, other than by the approval of the Governor.

When a bill has not been returned by the Governor within ten days after it has been presented to him for his approval, the following certificate is attached, which the clerks of the Senate and House of Representatives both sign, the clerk of the body in which the bill originated signing first, and they send the bill to the office of the Secretary of the Commonwealth.

"We do certify that the bill (here insert title) was presented to the Governor on the _____ day of _____, one thousand nine hundred and _____, and was not returned within ten days after it has been presented to him; wherefore it has, agreeable to the Constitution of this Commonwealth, become a law in like manner as if he had signed it.

"We do certify that the bill, entitled (here insert title), which has been disapproved by the Governor, and returned with his objections to the House of Representatives (or Senate), in which it originated, was passed by two-thirds of all the members elected to the House of Representatives on the _____ day of _____, one thousand nine hundred and _____, and the foregoing is the act so passed by the House.

"Speaker of the House of Representatives.

"Clerk of the House.

"Harrisburg (date)."

"We do certify that the bill (here insert title), which has been disapproved by the Governor, and returned with his objections to the House of Representatives (or Senate), in which it originated, was passed by two-thirds of all the members elected to the Senate on the _____ day of _____, one thousand nine hundred and _____, and the foregoing is the act so passed by the Senate.

"President of the Senate.

"Secretary/Parliamentarian of the Senate.

"Harrisburg (date)."

The Speaker and Clerk of the body in which the bill originated sign the first certificate and then the President and the Clerk of the other body the second.

OATH OF PUBLIC OFFICERS

Senators, Representatives and all judicial, State and county officers shall, before entering on the duties of their respective offices, take and subscribe the following oath or affirmation before a person authorized to administer oaths.

"I do solemnly swear (or affirm) that I will support, obey and defend the Constitution of the United States and the Constitution of this Commonwealth and that I will discharge the duties of my office with fidelity."

The oath or affirmation shall be administered to a member of the Senate or to a member of the House of Representatives in the hall of the House to which he shall have been elected.

Any person refusing to take the oath or affirmation shall forfeit his office.

COUNTING THE VOTE FOR STATE ELECTIVE OFFICERS

When the General Assembly meets after an election for Governor and Lieutenant Governor or Auditor General, State Treasurer and Attorney General, the two bodies, by a resolution, fix the time and place for opening and publishing the returns of the election. The time is usually the day the General Assembly organizes, and the place — the House of Representatives, in the presence of the two bodies. Each body appoints a Teller and notifies the other in advance of the meeting.

A committee from the House of Representatives awaits on the Senate a few minutes before the meeting, and escorts the President and members of the Senate to the place of meeting, when the President of the Senate, or in his absence, the President pro tempore takes the chair of the Speaker of the House, and after order is restored, says, "This being the day and hour agreed upon for opening and publishing the returns of the election for Governor (held on Tuesday next following the first Monday in November last), the clerk of the Senate will read over the returns from the several counties and the tellers take down the number of votes given for each person voted for as Governor." The clerk then proceeds to read aloud the returns, and the tellers note down the number of votes, and so on until all the returns from the several counties are read over. A computation is then made. When this is done the result is announced by the President of the Senate, and the certificate of election signed by the President of the Senate and the Speaker of the House of Representatives and attested by the tellers, as follows:

FORM OF CERTIFICATE OF ELECTION OF STATE OFFICERS:

"We, the President of the Senate and Speaker of the House of Representatives of the Commonwealth of Pennsylvania, do certify that the President of the Senate, did on the _____ ____ day of _____, A.D., one thousand nine hundred and _____, in the Hall of the House of Representatives at the State Capitol, open the returns of the election for Governor of this Commonwealth, and publish the same in the presence of both Houses of the General Assembly, conformably to the provisions of the Constitution and law of said Commonwealth, and upon counting the votes by a teller appointed on the part of each House it appeared that _____ had the highest number of votes; whereupon the said _____ was declared to have been duly elected Governor of the Commonwealth.

"In testimony whereof, we have hereunto set our hands and affixed our seals the day and year above written.

"_____(Seal)

"_____(Seal)"

DISPOSITION OF CERTIFICATE

This certificate is to be deposited in the office of the Secretary of the Commonwealth and a duplicate, signed by the President of the Senate and Speaker of the House of Representatives, and attested by the tellers, transmitted to the Governor-elect.

ACTION AFTER RETURNS ARE ANNOUNCED AND CERTIFICATES SIGNED

The Committee of introduction then conducts the President and members of the Senate to their Chamber and retire. The tellers make out a report of the number of votes given for each person voted for, including a copy of the certificate, and this report is made to the Senate and House, respectively, and entered on the Journals. The same form of proceeding is followed in counting the vote for Lieutenant Governor, State Treasurer, Auditor General, and Attorney General.

INAUGURATION OF GOVERNOR AND LIEUTENANT GOVERNOR

The oath of office is administered to the Governor in the presence of the General Assembly and officers of the Commonwealth by some person authorized to administer oaths (usually the Chief Justice of the Supreme Court) on the third Tuesday of January following his election

The Lieutenant Governor takes the oath of office on the same day in the presence of the Senate in the Senate Chamber, but prior to the induction of the Governor.

SALARIES OF THE GENERAL ASSEMBLY

SENATE

Salaries

Members of the Senate elected at the General Election of 1984, and thereafter, will receive a salary in the amount of $35,000 per annum plus $27,500 per annum for legislative and district office operations.

In addition to the above, each Senator shall receive mileage at the rate of twenty cents ($.20) per mile circular between the Senator's home and the State Capitol for each week a Senator was in actual attendance at the Session.

No other compensation shall be allowed.

Officers

The Senate shall at the beginning and close of each regular session elect one of its members President Pro Tempore. The President Pro Tempore shall receive, in addition to his salary as a member of the Senate, the sum of $19,600.

The Senate shall at the beginning of each regular biennial session elect the following officers, who shall serve for two years or until their successors are elected and qualified unless sooner removed by a majority vote of all the members of the Senate: one Secretary and one Chief Clerk.

In addition, the President of the Senate (Lieutenant Governor), President Pro Tempore, Secretary, Chief Clerk, Majority Leader and Minority Leader each appoint their office personnel as provided by act of the General Assembly.

HOUSE OF REPRESENTATIVES

Salaries

Members of the House of Representatives elected at the General Election of 1986, and thereafter, will receive a salary of $35,000 per annum payable in equal monthly installments. They may also receive up to $21,000 annually in allowable reimbursement for legislative, district office and postage expenses.

In addition to the above, each Member receives constitutional mileage at the rate of twenty cents ($.20) per circular mile between the Member's home and the State Capitol for each week of actual attendance at Session.

Officers

At the beginning of each Regular Session in odd-numbered years, the House of Representatives elects a Speaker as provided by the Constitution. The Speaker appoints a Parliamentarian and determines the salary.

The Bipartisan Management Committee is responsible for the overall administration of the House. It consists of the Speaker as chairman, the Majority Leader, the Minority Leader, the Majority Whip and the Minority Whip. The Committee appoints an Executive Director and other necessary staff. A Chief Clerk and a Comptroller are selected by the Bipartisan Management Committee subject to confirmation and removal solely on the affirmative vote of two-thirds of the Members of the House of Representatives in office at the time of any such vote. All the foregoing officers are compensated in the amounts determined by the Committee.

Other employees necessary to perform the work of the House are selected by appropriate appointing authorities and compensated in amounts determined by such authorities.

SENATE OFFICERS AND EMPLOYES
1987 SESSION

	Main Capitol
LIEUTENANT GOVERNOR AND PRESIDENT OF THE SENATE Mark S. Singel, State House, Ft. Indiantown Gap, Annville 17003	Room 200
Executive Assistant Joseph R. Powers, 3503 North Third Street, Harrisburg 17110	Room 200
Press Secretary Veronica Varga, 86 Beacon Drive, Harrisburg 17112	Room 200
Administrative Assistant/Scheduling Lynn A. Corbett, 218 Pine Street, Harrisburg 17101	Room 200
Administrative Assistants Bonita F. Truax, 200 Shamokin Street, B-5, Harrisburg 17110 Myra A. Kline, 312 W. Orchard Drive, Palmyra 17078 John Lord, 916 Green Street, Harrisburg 17102	Room 38 CAx. Room 38 CAx. Room 38 CAx.
Personal Secretary Jean Brannon, R.D. #5, 116 Locust Lane, Dillsburg 17019	Room 200
Secretary Karen Stefanic, 3908 Greenbriar Terrace, Harrisburg 17109	Room 200
Receptionist Jennifer Glass, 44 Winter Lane, Enola 17025	Room 200
PRESIDENT PRO TEMPORE Robert C. Jubelirer, P.O. Box 2023, Altoona 16603	Room 292
Executive Secretary Anne M. Serano, 650 Santanna Drive, Harrisburg 17109	Room 292
Counsel to President Pro Tempore Frederick D. Giles, R. D. #2, Box 4600, Grantville 17028	Room 292
Staff Administrator Michael S. Long, 865 Lovers Lane, Lebanon 17042	Room 292
Communications Office - Director David A. Atkinson, 2638 Gateway Drive, Harrisburg 17110	Room 292
Policy Development & Research Office - Director Charles E. Greenawalt, II, Ph.D., 223 North Harrison Street, Palmyra 17078	611 North Office Building
SECRETARY Mark R. Corrigan, 209 Briarcliff Road, Harrisburg 17104	Room 462
Assistant Secretary Helen R. Huffman, 1422 North Second Street, Harrisburg 17102	Room 462
Administrative Officers	
Chief Official Reporter Albert S. Marshal, R. D. #5, Hummelstown 17036	Room 644
Chief of Senate Security & Chief Sergeant-at-Arms Charles D. Hippensteel, Jr., 1919 Manada Street, Harrisburg 17104	Room B34-A
Documents' Room Supervisor Donald Free, 660 Boas Street, Harrisburg 17102	Room B34-A

Legislative Printing Coordinator
Jack O. Sanders, 6215 Warren Avenue, Linglestown 17112 — Room B38

Librarian
Thomas J. Duszak, 1016 Green Street, Harrisburg 17102 — Room 157

Page Services Director
Suzanne Bell, 625 Bosler Avenue, Lemoyne 17043 — Room B55

Administrative Assistants
Edward E. Holtzman, 2143 Derry Street, Harrisburg 17104 — Room 462
Marian T. O'Neill, 2 Richland Lane, Camp Hill 17011 — Room 462
Jill Raudensky, 325 Blacksmith Road, Camp Hill 17011 — Room 462
Gail W. Weber, 900 Lancelot Avenue, Mechanicsburg 17055 — Room 462

CHIEF CLERK
Gary E. Crowell, 857 Hillside Drive, Camp Hill 17011 — Room 350

Executive Secretary
Cynthia S. Confer, 3517 Rutherford Street, Harrisburg 17111 — Room 350

Assistant Chief Clerk
Ralph J. Fulginiti, 710 South 25th Street, Harrisburg 17111 — Senate Chamber

Purchasing Agent
Sandra Magera, 221-Q Evans Avenue, Harrisburg 17109 — Room 350

Director, Mail Services
William J. Whalen, 1415 Caracas Avenue, Hershey 17033 — Room B54

Superintendent of the Senate Chamber
Ronald Smith, 812 Green Street, Harrisburg 17102 — Senate Chamber

MAJORITY LEADER
John Stauffer, 1215 Dorothy Avenue, Phoenixville 19460 — Room 362

General Counsel
Stephen C. MacNett, 208 Liberty Street, Harrisburg 17101 — Room 362

Legal Counsel
Gregg L. Warner, 2319 North Second Street, Harrisburg 17110 — Room 362

Administrative Assistant
Debra A. Drais, R. D. #28, C-3, York 17404 — Room 362

MAJORITY WHIP
F. Joseph Loeper, 403 Burmont Road, Drexel Hill 19026 — Room 178

Legislative Aide
David W. Woods, 232 Sedgewood Road, Springfield 19064 — Room 159

Secretary
Ellen M. Bevan, 215 Verbeke Street, Harrisburg 17102 — Room 178

MAJORITY CAUCUS CHAIRMAN
William J. Moore, Center Square, P.O. Box 308, New Bloomfield 17068 — Room 350

Administrative Officer
Anne Anstine, R.D. #1, 325 Locust Grove Road, Mifflintown 17059 — Room 350

MAJORITY CAUCUS SECRETARY
David J. Brightbill, Senate Post Office, Harrisburg 17120 — Room 281

Research Analyst
Peter Calcara, 1911 West Market Street, York 17404   Room 281

Legislative Assistant
Mark Snoberger, 133 Hillside Street, Lebanon 17042   Room 281

MAJORITY POLICY COMMITTEE CHAIRMAN
Roy W. Wilt, Senate Post Office, Harrisburg 17120   Room 281

Administrative Assistant
Susie H. Stoner, 1 Brentwood Road, Camp Hill 17011   Room 281

MAJORITY CAUCUS ADMINISTRATOR
Ralph W. Hess, Post Office Box 226, Spring Grove 17362   Room 351

Executive Secretary
Martha T. Myers, 500 DeWitt Avenue, Harrisburg 17109   Room 351

MINORITY LEADER
Edward P. Zemprelli, 528 St. Clair Avenue, Clairton 15025   Room 535

Chief Counsel
Michael T. McCarthy, 3813 Candlelight Drive, Camp Hill 17011   Room 535

Executive Assistant
Michael C. McLaughlin, 4841 Spring Top Drive, Harrisburg 17111   Room 535

Executive Secretary
Charlotte O'Neal, 2909 Heather Place, Harrisburg 17104   Room 535

MINORITY WHIP
J. William Lincoln, R. D. #1, Box 14, Dunbar 15431   Room 171

Executive Assistant
Catherine Hammond, R. D. #2, Box 880, Annville 17003   Room 171

Legislative Aide
Sharon C. McDermott, 521 Lamp Post Lane, Camp Hill 17011   Room 171

MINORITY CAUCUS CHAIRMAN
Robert J. Mellow, 300 Scranton Life Building, 538 Spruce Street, Scranton 18503   Room 169

Executive Assistant
Thomas A. Browning, 416 Academy Street, Peckville 18452   Room B-48

Executive Secretary
Gloria J. See, 980-C King Russ Road, Harrisburg 17109   Room B-48

MINORITY CAUCUS SECRETARY
James E. Ross, Fort McIntosh Office Building, First Floor, 855 Second Street, Beaver 15009   Room 535

Executive Assistant
Jeanette D'Eramo, 2311 North Front Street, Harrisburg 17110   Room 535

MINORITY POLICY COMMITTEE CHAIRMAN
Patrick J. Stapleton, 710 Croyland Avenue, Indiana 15701   Room 458

Executive Director
Robert E. Quigley, 301 South York Street, Mechanicsburg 17055   Room 463

Administrative Assistant
Casey Stine, 623 State Street, Lemoyne 17043   Room 463

MINORITY CAUCUS ADMINISTRATOR
Freeman Hankins, 4116 Haverford Avenue, Philadelphia 19104   Room 458

Counsel
Larry S. Diehl, P.O. Box 408, Harrisburg 17108   Room 458

Legislative Assistant
Gina H. McBean, 225 Verbeke Street, Harrisburg 17102   Room 458

MAJORITY APPROPRIATIONS COMMITTEE CHAIRMAN
Richard A. Tilghman, 406 Gatcombe Lane, Bryn Mawr 19010   Room 281

Executive Director
William H. Clouser, R. D. #3, P.O. Box 27, Newport 17074   Room 281

Executive Secretary
Helen S. Gleichman, 380 Regent Street, Camp Hill 17011   Room 281

MINORITY APPROPRIATIONS COMMITTEE CHAIRMAN
Vincent J. Fumo, 1208 Tasker Street, Philadelphia 19148   Room 545

Executive Director
Paul S. Dlugolecki, 303 Monroe Street, Mechanicsburg 17055   Room 545

SENATE OF PENNSYLVANIA
OFFICERS

ROBERT C. JUBELIRER

President Pro Tempore
30th District

Bedford, Blair, Fulton, and Huntingdon Counties

Robert C. Jubelirer (R) was born Feb. 9, 1937, in Altoona, the son of the late Judge Samuel H. and Dorothy Brett Jubelirer; grad., Pa. St. Univ.; Dickinson Law Schl.; attorney; adm. to practice, Blair Co., St., Federal Courts; Pa. and Blair Co. Bar Assns.; Altoona Council Navy League; past Hon. Chmn. of Tuckahoe District Penns Woods Council BSA; chmn., Blair Co. Multiple Sclerosis Society; bd. mem., Allegheny Chptr. Natl. Multiple Sclerosis Soc.; mem., adv. council, Hollidaysburg Veterans Home; mem., Pa. Council on the Arts; Pa. Chptr., Natl. Com. on Youth Suicide Prevention; Altoona Chamber of Commerce; Altoona Rotary Club; mem., all Masonic bodies; elected to the State Senate in 1974; reelected 1978, 1982, 1986; elected Majority Leader, 1981 and 1983; elected President Pro-Tempore, 1985, 1986 and 1987; wife, Mary-Jo; 4 children; home address: 222 Beaumont Dr., Altoona.

MARK R. CORRIGAN

Secretary of the Senate

Mark R. Corrigan was born Aug. 19, 1951, the son of Ronald and Carolyn McTish Corrigan; Univ. de Montpellier, France (Certificat Pratique de la Langue Francaise); Shippensburg Univ. (B.S.); Pa. St. Univ. Grad. Schl.; Dickinson Schl. of Law (J.D.) 1979; attorney; mem., Bar of the Supreme Court of Pa.; school teacher, Harrisburg City Schools, 1973-76; Law Clerk, Pa. Dept. of Education, 1976-79; Legal Counsel to Senator J. Doyle Corman, Senate of Pa., 1979-81; elected Secretary of the Senate, June 30, 1981; re-elected 1983, 1985, 1987.

GARY E. CROWELL

Chief Clerk of the Senate

Gary E. Crowell was born April 21, 1943, in DuBois, the son of Jules and Helen Hagerman Crowell; Pa. St. Univ. (B.S.) 1965; U.S. Marine Corps, 1965-69; St. Manpower Services Co.; Commonwealth Health and Welfare Fund; asst. personnel dir., Dept. of Forests and Waters, 1969-70; dir., Manpower Planning, Civil Service Comm., 1970-71; personnel dir., Justice Dept., 1971-74; dep. dir., Office of Drug Law Enforcement, 1974-75; dir., Office of Mgmt. Services, Justice Dept., 1975-76; dep. secretary, Dept. of General Services, 1976-83; bd. mem., Keystone Area Co., B.S.A.; pres., West Shore Vikings Football Assn.; exec. dir., Independent Regulatory Review Comm., 1983-86; elected Chief Clerk of the Senate, April 22, 1986; married Donna Sellers; 1 child, Errin; home address: 857 Hillside Dr., Camp Hill.

SENATE OF PENNSYLVANIA

MEMBERS

ROY C. AFFLERBACH, II   16th District

Lehigh (part) County

Roy C. Afflerbach, II (D) was born Feb. 6, 1945, in Allentown, the son of Roy, Sr. and Dorothy Zeigler Afflerbach; Kutztown Univ. (B.A.) 1973; grad. studies, Kutztown Univ., Muhlenberg Coll.; U.S. Air Force, 1963-67; pres., County Cabs, Inc., 1970-72; Senate staff, 1970-73; Admin. Asst. to Sen. Maj. Whip 1973-77; Exec. Asst. to Sen. Maj. Leader, 1977-78; exec. dir., Sen. Dem. Policy Comm., 1979-82; exec. dir., Sen. Business & Commerce Comm., 1979-80; exec. dir., Sen. Finance Comm., 1981-82; selected "One of Ten Outstanding Legislators in the United States" by Assn. of Governmental Employees; Outstanding Young Men of America; Community Leaders of America; first elected to the House of Representatives, Nov. 2, 1982; nominated for reelection by both Dem. and Rep. parties in 1984; reelected 1984; elected to the Senate, Nov. 4, 1986; married Barbara A. Kasper of Northampton; 1 child, Darci; home address: 1222 Lehigh St., Allentown.

ANTHONY BUZZ ANDREZESKI   49th District

Erie (part) County

Anthony Buzz Andrezeski (D) was born Nov. 8, 1947, in Erie, the son of Anthony F. and Esther Walczak Andrezeski; Gannon Univ. (B.A.) 1970, (Masters degree, Guidance & Counseling) 1974; chmn., Erie Co. Council, 1980; Co. councilman, 2nd Dist., 1978-80; chmn., Erie Co. Election Bd., 1979-80; Democratic committeeman; Erie Employment Task Force; ex-officio mem., Erie Conference on Community Development; founder, Sexual Harassment in the Workplace Task Force; mem., Right to Life, Inc.; ex. bd., Economic Futures, Inc.; mem., St. Peter's Cathedral Usher's Society; E. Side Federation of Polish Am. Societies; Huzar's Club; founder, Children's Lobby; elected to the State Senate in 1980; reelected 1984; married Kathleen Knecht; 3 children: Anthony Edward, Jonathan Gabriel, Rachel Marie; home address: 713 W. 10th St., Erie.

GIBSON E. ARMSTRONG   13th District

Lancaster (part) County

Gibson E. Armstrong (R) was born Aug. 28, 1943, in Butler, the son of S. Gibson and Helen Burns Armstrong; Westminster Coll. (BBA) 1965; Capt., Intelligence Officer, Naval Nuclear Weapons Courier, U.S. Marine Corps, 1966-69; rec., Vietnam commendation ribbons; voted Outstanding Young Men of America, 1979; Outstanding Service Award, Friendship Force Internatl., 1983; selected to *Who's Who in Politics*; served on Gov. Thornburgh's Blue Ribbon Panel on Worker's Compensation; voted "Legislator of the Year," 1986; bd. mem., Saint Joseph's Hosp.; bd. mem., Water Street Rescue Mission; mem., Willow Street Lions Club; Manheim VFW; member of the House of Representatives, 1976-84; elected to State Senate, Nov. 6, 1984; married Martha Wilson; 4 children: Gibson C., Erik, Kristian, Erin; home address: Seven Springs Farm, Refton.

CLARENCE D. BELL   9th District

Delaware (part) County

Clarence D. Bell (R) was born Feb. 4, 1914, in Upland, the son of Samuel R. and Belle Hanna Bell; grad., Swarthmore Coll.; Harvard Law Sch.; U.S. Army Command and General Staff Coll.; Maj. Gen., Pa. Natl. Guard (Ret.); served 38 yrs. active Army, Natl. Guard, Army Reserve; 62 mos. active duty, W.W. II; attorney; adm. to practice, Delaware Co., St., Fed. courts; past chmn., Natl. Army Affairs Comm., ROA; past st. pres., Reserve Officers' Assn.; past pres., Pa. Exchange Clubs; past v. pres., St. Highway and Bridge Auth.; mem., Pa. Historical & Museum Comm.; frmr. mem., Aeronautics Comm., Local Govt. Comm., Bicentennial Comm.; Pa. Interst. Coop. Comm.; chmn., Legis. Budget and Finance Comm.; Masonic bodies; rec., awards presented by DAV, Jewish War Veterans, Am. Legion, VFW, K. of C., B'nai B'rith; Legion of Merit, U.S. Army; Pa. Distinguished Service Medal (2 awards); served in House of Representatives, 1955-60; elected to State Senate 1960; reelected to 8 successive terms; married Mary Isabel James; 2 children; home address: 400 West 24th Street, Upland.

LEONARD J. BODACK   38th District

Allegheny (part) County

Leonard J. Bodack (D) was born Aug. 10, 1932, in Pgh., the son of Joseph J. (dec.) and Mary L. Spehar Bodack (dec.); att. Pittsburgh Acad., Point Park Coll.; U.S. Marine Corp., Sgt. (1950-54); A.F.U.; C.F.U.; K.S.K.J.; P.N.A.; Arsenal Board of Trade; Alleg. Co. Democratic Committee; past v. comdr., Slovenian Vets.; past v. Commandant, Marine Corps League, Alleg. Co. detachment; Am. Legion, Post 715, Legionnaire of the Yr. 1979-80; V.F.W. Post 278; Slovenian Home, Pgh.; L.O.O.M. Lodge 46; Moose; Lions Club; elected to the State Senate in 1978; reelected 1982, 1986; married Shirley M. Wagner; father of 6 children: Leonard, Cheryl, Mark, James, Carol, Patricia; home address: 4922 Hatfield Street, Pittsburgh.

DAVID J. BRIGHTBILL   Republican Caucus Secretary
                                                        48th District

Lebanon, Berks (part), and Lehigh (part) Counties

David J. Brightbill (R) was born in Lebanon, the son of Jonathan McMichael and Verda McGill Brightbill; Pa. St. Univ., 1964; Duquesne Univ. Schl. of Law (J.D. cum laude) 1970; attorney; Lebanon bd. of schl. dirs., 1966-67; Lebanon Co. dist. atty., 1977-81; author, "International Shoe and Long Arm Jurisdiction — How About Pennsylvania," *Duquesne Law Review*, 1970; elected to the State Senate, Nov. 2, 1982, 1986; 3 children: John David, Jonathan Daniel, Andrew James.

J. DOYLE CORMAN   34th District

Cameron, Centre, Clearfield (part),
Clinton, Juniata (part), and
Mifflin Counties

J. Doyle Corman (R) was born Sept. 17, 1932, the son of Jacob Doyle and Mary McClincy Corman; Indiana U. of Pa. (B.S. Ed.) 1957; U.S. Army, 1954-56, Spc. 3rd class, radio operator; insurance broker, realtor, pres., Corman Assocs.; Centre Co. Bd. of Realtors; Central Counties Independent Ins. Agents Assn.; Centre Co. Commissioner, 1968-77; Rep. St. Comm.; pres., SEDA (11-co./org.) 1973, 1974, 1976; Masonic bodies; BPOE 1094; Kiwanis; United Way; Cameron Co. Historical Society; Mt. Nittany Sportsman's Club; Pleasant Gap Fire Co. No. 1; American Legion Post –867; NCAA; PIAA; YMCA swimming official; Methodist Ch.; elected to the State Senate in special election May 17, 1977; reelected 1978, 1982, 1986; married Rebecca Kay Davis; 5 children: Katherine Elizabeth, Sharon Rebecca, Melissa Ann, Jacob Doyle III, Kevin Thomas; home address: 1230 Sylvan Circle, Bellefonte.

D. MICHAEL FISHER   37th District

Allegheny (part) and Washington (part) Counties

D. Michael Fisher (R) was born Nov. 7, 1944, in Pgh., the son of C. Francis and Dolores Darby Fisher; S. Hills Catholic H.S., 1962, outstand. grad. award, 1977; Georgetown Univ. (A.B.) 1966; Georgetown Law Center (J.D.) 1969; U.S. Army Reserves, 1969-75; atty.; Allegheny Co., Pa. Bar Assns.; Am. Arbitration Assn.; adm. to practice before all Pa. and Federal Cts.; Elks; Am. Legion; Bethel Park C. of C.; Rotary; asst. dist. atty., Alleg. Co., 1970-74; mem., Pa. House of Representatives, 1975-80; St. Louise de Marillac Ch., parish Council, 1975-78; alternate delegate, Republican Natl. Convention, 1972; Outstanding Young Man of Am., U.S. Jaycees, 1977-78-79; 1980 Man of the Year, Upper St. Clair Repub. Club; author, *Report on Medical and Mental Health,* Pa. Correctional System, 1980; author, 1985, PCCD Prison and Jail Overcrowding Task Force Report and Senate Act 195 Task Force Report; Environmental Quality Bd., 1981; Pa. Comm. on Crime and Delinquency, 1979-pres., Vice Chairman, 1982-pres.; Gov. Energy Council, 1981-1986; Pa. Energy Develop. Authority, 1984-pres.; elected to the State Senate in 1980; reelected 1984; married Carol Hudak; 2 children: Michelle Lynn and Brett Michael; home address: 339 Alamo Dr., Pittsburgh.

VINCENT J. FUMO   **Democratic Appropriations Committee Chairman**
1st District

Philadelphia (part) County

Vincent J. Fumo (D) was born May 8, 1943, in Phila., the son of Vincent E. and Helen Rodgers Fumo; Villanova Univ. (B.S.) 1964; Temple Univ. Schl. of Law (J.D.) 1972; Univ. of Pa., Wharton Schl. (M.B.A.) 1984; lawyer, businessman; mem., Am., Pa., and Phila. Bar Assns. (frmr. chmn., Private Practice Com. of Criminal Justice Section); Lawyers Club of Phila.; Phila. Justinian Society; A.C.L.U.; A.D.A.; U.S. Power Squadrons (advanced pilot); K. of C. (4th Degree); Natl. Sheriff's Assn.; F & AM (3rd Degree); Order of Sons of Italy; Natl. Rifle Assn. (life mem.); founder, past pres., Moore St. Civic Assn.; American Mensa Society; licensed motor boat operator, Charter Boat Capt., U.S.C.G.; pres., Pa. Savings Assn.; frmr. depty. comm. and comm., Bur. of Professional and Occupational Affairs, 1971-73; member of Senate, April 8, 1978, to date; Majority Caucus Sec., 1979-80; Dem. Chmn., Senate Appropriations Com., 1985-86, reelected 1987-88; 2 children: Vincent E., II, and Nichole S.; district office address: 1208 Tasker St., Philadelphia.

STEWART J. GREENLEAF   **12th District**

Montgomery (part) County

Stewart John Greenleaf (R) was born Oct. 4, 1939, in Phila., the son of Stewart William and Belford Denner Greenleaf; Univ. of Pa. (B.A.) 1961; Univ. of Toledo Law Schl. (J.D.) 1966; lawyer; bd. of dirs., Montgomery Co. Bar Assn.; mem., Montgomery Co., Pa. Bar Assns.; adm. to practice, U.S. Supreme Ct., Fed. Dist. Ct. of E. Pa., Pa. Supreme, Superior Cts.; trial asst., chief of appeals div., Montgomery Co. dist. atty's. office (7 yrs.); asst. dist. atty., Montgomery Co.; Judicial Law Clerk, Montgomery Co. Ct. of Common Pleas; Upper Moreland Twp. Commissioner, 1971-75 (bd. pres., 1973-75); Presbyterian; elected to the House of Representatives, 1976; elected to the State Senate, 1978; reelected 1982, 1986; married Cecilia Kelly Finley.

JAMES C. GREENWOOD   **10th District**

Bucks (part) County

James C. Greenwood (R) was born May 4, 1951; Council Rock H.S., 1969; Dickinson Coll. (B.A., honors) 1973; chmn., Pa. Legislative Children's Caucus; bd. dir., Pa. Trauma Systems Foundation; bd. dir., TODAY Inc., Drug and Alcohol Treatment Program; hon. bd. mem., Bucks Co. Assn. of Retarded Citizens; bd. dir., Parents Anonymous; mem., Central Bucks Chamber of Commerce; mem., Bucks Co. Conservation Alliance; mem., League of Women Voters; awards: Humane Society of United States; Natl. Head Injury Foundation; legis. asst., Pa. State Rep. John S. Renninger, 1972-76; campaign coordinator, Renninger for Congress, 1976; caseworker, Bucks Co. Children & Youth Social Service Agency, 1977-80; elected to the House of Representatives, Nov. 1980; reelected 1982, 1984; elected to the Senate, 1986; married Christina Paugh; 3 children: Robert, Andrew, Laura; home address: River Road, Erwinna.

FREEMAN HANKINS   **Democratic Caucus Administrator**
7th District

Philadelphia (part) County

Freeman Hankins (D) was born Sept. 30, 1917, in Brunswick, Ga., the son of Oliver and Anna (Pyles) Hankins; grad., Dolan's Coll. of Embalming, 1945; att., Selden Institute, Brunswick, Ga., and Temple U.; funeral dir.; former basketball player; ldr., Phila. Sixth Ward Dem. Comm.; 2nd v. chmn., Phila. Dem. Comm., 1971-76; treas., Metropolitan Baptist Ch.; mem., bds. of trustees, Lincoln U. and Stephen Smith Geriatric Cntr.; Am. Legion; NAACP; Natl. Funeral Assn.; Pa. Funeral Dirs. Assn.; Keystone Funeral Dirs. Assn.; Masonic bodies; Pa. Advsry. Comm. on Prison Education; pres., Rafters Charities; U.S. Army Medical Corps, 1944-47; mem., House of Representatives, 1961-67; chmn., Senate Prison Inquiry Comm., 1973-76; mem., PHEAA Bd., 1970-pres.; chmn., Ins. Com. 1972-80; min. chmn., Banking & Ins., 1980-86; min. chmn., Military & Veterans Affairs Com., 1987-pres.; Dem. Caucus Admn., 1987-pres.; elected to State Senate, Nov. 29, 1967; reelected 1968, 1972, 1976, 1980, 1984; married Dorothy Days, April 20, 1939; 1 daughter, Bernadette; home address: 4075 Haverford Ave., Philadelphia.

EDWARD W. HELFRICK   27th District

Columbia, Montour, Luzerne (part), Northumberland (part), Snyder, Union (part) Counties

Edward W. Helfrick (R) was born Mar. 11, 1928, in Pottsville, the son of Edward and Elizabeth Rosenberger Helfrick; Mt. Carmel H.S., 1945; U.S. Army, paratrooper, 11th Airborne Div., 1945-46; mining contractor; Am. Legion Post #804; V.F.W.; K. of C.; Elks; Eagles; Ralpho, Atlas, Kulpmont W. End Fire Cos.; mem., House of Representatives, 1977-80; Queen of Most Holy Rosary Ch.; trustee, Anthracite Health and Welfare Fund; dir., 1st Natl. Trust Bank; elected to the State Senate in 1980; reelected 1984; married Rosemarie Ciokajlo; 5 children: Mary Rose, Kathy, Diane, Edward Jr., Susan; home address: R.D. 1, Elysburg.

RALPH W. HESS   Republican Caucus Administrator
                                                     28th District

York (part) County

Ralph W. Hess (R) was born Dec. 25, 1939, in Fawn Grove, the son of Avon W. and Marian Jamison Hess; att., Western Maryland Coll., Pa. St. Univ.-York campus, Oklahoma St. Univ.; grad., Millersville Univ. (B.S.) 1962; San Diego St. Univ. (M.S.) 1969; active, reserve duty, U.S. Army; mem., bd. of dirs., York Co. Mental Health Center, York Co. Blind Center; Spring Grove Sportsmen's Club; Spring Grove Lions Club; York Co. Republican Men's Club; Young Republicans of York Co.; Mount Zion United Ch. of Christ; elected to the State Senate in 1970; reelected 1974, 1978, 1982, 1986; Minority Caucus Administrator, 1977-80; Majority Caucus Administrator, 1981-82; 1983-84; 1985-86; 1987-88; married Ruth Sprenkle on Dec. 25, 1963; 2 children; home address: P.O. Box 226, Spring Grove.

EDWIN G. HOLL   24th District

Bucks (part) and Montgomery (part) Counties

Edwin G. Holl (R) was born in Chester, the son of Paul T. and Margaret (Rupp) Holl; grad., Taylor School in Phila.; att. Temple Univ.; heads E.G. Holl Co., industrial equipment and supplies; mem. and past pres., Lansdale Lions Club, Dist. Gov. Cabinet; past pres., Lansdale Youth Council; founding pres., trustee, North Penn Y.M.C.A.; past chm., Lansdale Recreation Comm.; chm. of bd., Valley Forge Council, B.S.A.; founder, past pres., mem. U.S. Navy League; chm., past pres., North Penn United Way; Col. in Civil Air Patrol, PA Wing; mem., Montgomery Co. Rep. Exec. Com.; North Penn C. of C.; Montgomery Co. Health & Welfare Council; Moose; Elks; Lansdale Historical Society; Manufacturers Golf & Country Club of Oreland; Union League; Trinity Lutheran Church of Lansdale; Montgomery Co. Health and Mental Retardation Clinic; Arthur P. Noyes Foundation; 32nd Degree Mason; Natl. Council, B.S.A.; licensed FAA Commercial Pilot and Flight Instructor; rec., awards for Outstanding Community Service, Lansdale Lions Club, North Penn Junior C. of C.; Service to Youth from Y.M.C.A.; Silver Beaver Award, B.S.A.; 1968 Outstanding Citizen Award North Penn C. of C.; Natl. POW/MIA Award, 1973; Service Award, Tuberculosis and Respiratory Disease Assn., 1973; 1980 Pottstown Comm. Counseling Services Award; 1981 DAR Honor Medal; Life Membership FOP; North Penn C. of C. Humanitarian Award; Senior Member of the Year, Civil Air Patrol, 1984; Citation for "Outstanding Contribution" in passage of Child Car Restraint Safety Seat Bill, American Acad. of Pediatrics, PA Highway Users Conference, 1984; Award for Outstanding Support to Civil Air Patrol, 1984; Trail Award, Neskenno Dist., B.S.A., 1984; Natl. Distinguished Service Award Medal, Civil Air Patrol, 1984; Take Pride in Pa., 1986, for Historical and Environmental Protection; honored for 22 years of service to Montgomery Co. Comm. Coll.; Member of Legislature, 26 years; 2 children: Sandra K. and Paul E.; address: 210 S. Broad Street, Lansdale.

JOHN D. HOPPER   31st District

Cumberland (part) and York (part) Counties

John D. Hopper (R) was born on Jan. 9, 1923, in Charleston, W. Va., the son of Ellis S. and Adra Dunfee Hopper; Dickinson Coll. (A.B.) 1948; Dickinson Schl. of Law (LL.B.) 1951; Am. Coll. of Life Underwriters (CLU) 1959; U.S. Air Force, Sr. pilot, WW II; Maj., Air Force Reserves, inactive; bd. of trustees, Central Pa. Chapter, M.S.; bds. of dirs., PHEAA, Keystone State Games, West Shore Div., Dauphin Deposit Trust Co., Holy Spirit Hospital; bd. of trustees, Dickinson Coll.; mem., Pa. Bar Assn.; U.S. Air Force Assn.; campaign chmn. (1965), pres. (1969) Tri Co. United Way; past pres., Dickinson Coll. Natl. Alum. Assn.; 1975-76 chmn., M.S. "Dinner of Champions"; frmr. v. p., Camp Hill Schl. Bd.; pres. (1962-63) Hbg. Assn. Life Underwriters; (1971-72) Pa. Assn. Life Underwriters; past trustee, Natl. Assn. Life Underwriters, (1974-78) life mem., Pa. Leaders' Round Table, Million Dollar Round Table of NALU; named to Dickinson Coll. Sports Hall of Fame, 1973; one of 5 individuals in U.S. selected by NCAA for silver anniv. award, 1973; Elder, Camp Hill Presbyterian Ch.; elected to State Senate in 1976; reelected 1980, 1984; married Ann Bowman; 4 children; home address: 2304 Chestnut Street, Camp Hill.

ROXANNE H. JONES   3rd District

Philadelphia (part) County

Roxanne H. Jones (D) was born May 3, 1928, in South Carolina, the daughter of Gilford and Mary Beatrice Bruton Harper; Howard H.S., Wilm.; state senator; chair, Southwark Chapt., Phila. Welfare Rights Org., 1967; chair, Philadelphia Welfare Rights, 1968; founder, Philadelphia Citizens In Action (PCIA), 1967; bd. mem., Americans For Democratic Action; Lincoln Univ.; co-chair, Coalition of Concerned Citizens; mem., State Transp. Adv. Com.; Pa. Legislative Black Caucus; rec., OIC Top Fundraiser, 1966; Chapel of Four Chaplains Service Award, 1969; Community Legal Services Award, 1969; Phila. Comm. on Human Relations Award, 1970; Natl. Welfare Rights Org. Award, 1972; Bright Hope Baptist Ch. Outstanding Woman, 1981; Black Social Workers Community Service Award, 1983; Women United for Roxanne Jones Award, 1984; Certificate of Merit, Defense Logistics Agency, 1985; Women of the Year Award, Beta Delta Zeta Chapt., 1985; Women's Day Award, Metropolitan AME Ch., 1985; Mary Church Terrell Award, 1985; mem., United House of Prayer For All People; 1st black woman elected to the State Senate, Nov. 1984; minority chmn., Urban Affairs & Housing; mem., Dem. Policy Com.; married James H. Jones (dec.); 2 daughters: Patricia and Wanda; 4 grandchildren; home address: 3133 North Broad St., Philadelphia.

JAMES R. KELLEY   39th District

Westmoreland (part) and Indiana (part) Counties

James R. Kelley (D), B.A. and J.D. degrees; attorney-at-law; member of State Senate since June 1974; former Westmoreland County Commissioner; office address: 111 West Second St., Greensburg.

CHARLES D. LEMMOND, JR.   20th District

Luzerne (part), Monroe (part), Pike
Susquehanna, Wayne, and Wyoming Counties

Charles D. Lemmond, Jr. (R) was born Jan. 17, 1929, the son of Charles D. and Ruth Zierdt Lemmond; grad., Harvard Coll. (A.B.) 1952; Univ. of Pa. Law Schl. (LL.B.) 1955; U.S. Army, 1946-47; attorney/legislator; Pa. and Am. Bar Assns.; Wilkes-Barre Law Lib. Assn.; judge, Court of Common Pleas, Luzerne Co.; 1st asst. D.A. and asst. D.A. of Luzerne Co.; solicitor for various boroughs, twps. and school districts in N.E. Pa.; past Potentate, Irem Temple; mem., Kingston Lodge 395 F. & A.M., Caldwell Consistory; 33rd deg. Mason; trustee, Wyoming Conf. of United Methodist Churches; mem., First United Methodist Ch. of Wilkes-Barre; bd. mem., Nesbitt Memorial Hosp.; mem., adv. bd., Pa. State Univ., Wilkes-Barre Campus; mem., adv. bd., Northeast Tier of Ben Franklin Partnership Program; mem., Salvation Army Adv. Bd.; mem., bd. dirs., Wyoming Seminary; mem., bd. dirs., First Eastern Bank. N.A.; elected to the State Senate, November 1985; reelected 1986; married Barbara Northrup; 4 children: Charles N., Judy, John, David; home address: 58 Lehman Ave., Dallas.

H. CRAIG LEWIS   6th District

Bucks (part) County

H. Craig Lewis (D) was born July 22, 1944, in Hazleton, the son of Harold W. and Dorothy M. Lewis; grad., Millersville Univ.; att., Univ. of Nebraska Grad. Schl.; grad., Temple Univ. Schl. of Law (J.D.); attorney; Bar of the Supreme Court of Pa.; elected to the State Senate in 1974; reelected 1978, 1982, 1986; 2 children: Janet and Craig Robert.

J. WILLIAM LINCOLN

Democratic Whip
32nd District

Fayette and Somerset (part) Counties

J. William Lincoln (D) was born Oct. 27, 1940, in Lemont Furnace, the son of Philip and Catherine Goodwin Lincoln; att., Pa. St. Univ.; St. Aloysius Ch.; elected to the House of Representatives, 1972; reelected 1974, 1976; elected to the State Senate in 1978; reelected 1982, 1986; married Sandra Gambone; 4 sons; home address: 20 Front St.,Dunbar.

F. JOSEPH LOEPER

Republican Whip
26th District

Delaware (part) County

F. Joseph Loeper, Jr. (R) was born Dec. 23, 1944, in Upper Darby, the son of F. Joseph and J. Isabel Martin Loeper (both dec.); West Chester Univ. (B.S.) 1966; Temple Univ. (M.S.) 1970; chmn., Eastern Pa. Dist. and Leg. Com., Pa. Recreation and Park Society; frmr. chmn. bd., Am. Red Cross Eastern Del. Co. Branch; past pres., Garrettford-Drexel Hill Fire Co.; Upper Darby Twp. Firemen's Relief Assn.; Upper Darby Young Rep. Club; mem., Natl. Ed. Assn. (life mem.); Upper Darby Assn. of Supvrs. and Administrators; bd. of trustees, Schl. of the Holy Child, Drexel; Del. Co. Firemen's Assn.; Rotary Club of Upper Darby; bd. dir., Del. Co. Assn. for Retarded Citizens and S.E. Pa. Ch. Am. Red Cross; Rep. leader, Upper Darby Twp. 3rd Councilmanic Dist.; rec., St. Charles Catholic Youth Assn. Award, 1971; Outstanding Young Man of America, 1976, 1979; Who's Who in Government, 1977; Who's Who in the East, 1980; Pa. Recreation and Park Soc. Gov. Service Award, 1982, 1984; Chapel of Four Chaplains Legion of Honor Membership for Disting. Service, 1982; Del. Co. Savings & Loan League Gov. Award, 1984; rec., 1984 YMCA Youth and Gov. Award; elected to the State Senate in 1978; reelected 1982, 1986; elected Maj. Caucus Sec., 1981-1984; elected Majority Whip, 1985; reelected 1987; married Joann Eisenacher; 3 children: F. Joseph III, James H., and Joanne M.; address: 403 Burmont Road, Drexel Hill.

FRANCIS J. LYNCH

2nd District

Philadelphia (part) County

Francis J. Lynch (D) was born in Phila.; att., Roman Catholic high school; Banks Business Coll., St. John's Night Schl.; infantryman, Army, 1942-46, wounded in France; Am. Legion; VFW; ward leader (15th Ward Phila. Co.); Delegate, Natl. Dem. Conv. 1964; Dem. State Comm., 1971-1972; Pa. Trans. Comm.; Natl. Comm. on Uniform Traffic Laws and Ordinances; elected to Pa. House of Representatives, 1966; reelected 1968, 1970, 1972; elected State Senator, special election, March 26, 1973; reelected 1974, 1978, 1982, 1986; chmn., Sen. Transp. Com., 1976-80; Dem. Caucus Administrator; married Anne M. Neilon; 2 daughters: Margaret Mary Strykowski and Anne Marie Zimba; home address: 4207 Disston Street, Philadelphia.

ROGER A. MADIGAN

23rd District

Bradford, Lycoming, Sullivan, Tioga, and Union (part) Counties

Roger A. Madigan (R) was born Jan. 25, 1930, in Burlington Twp., Bradford Co., the son of State Senator Albert E. and Ada Allen Madigan; Pa. St. Univ. (B.S. Dairy Production) 1951; insurance consultant, farmer; treas., Bradford-Sullivan-Wyoming Co. Libraries, 1955-64; treas., Bradford Co. 4-H Development Fund, 1967-76; sec., Bradford Co. Vo-Tech Schl. Auth., 1967-present; past pres., Troy Rotary Club; trustee, Luthers Mills Un. Methodist Ch.; dir., First Bank of Troy, 1956-present; Williamsport Consistory, IREM Temple; Bradford Co. Shrine Club, Bradford Lodge 100F; Sparks Club; PAMIC; PFA; Grange; Pa. Holstein Assn.; Delta Theta Sigma; Union Lodge 102 F&AM; Union Chapter 168, PHP; elected to the House of Representatives, 1976; reelected 1978, 1980, 1982; elected to the Senate of Pennsylvania, 1984; married Peggy E. Goble; 4 children: Vicki Lynne, Annette Kay, Paul Jay, Steven Gary; home address: R.D. 3, Box 114, Towanda.

ROBERT J. MELLOW   **Democratic Caucus Chairman**
                                                            22nd District
Lackawanna and Monroe (part) Counties

Robert J. Mellow (D) was born Dec. 10, 1942, in Peckville, the son of James and Alice Generotti Mellow; att., Lackawanna Co. Jr. Coll., U. of Scranton; grad., Bethel Coll. (B.S.); Pa. Natl. Guard, 1962-68; att. grad. schl., Marywood Coll.; accounting; Natl., Pa. Society of Public Accountants; U. of Scranton Purple Club; Valley View Cougar Club; Young Democrats of Lackawanna Co.; PIAA; K of C., Italian-Am. Dem. Assn., Grtr. Scranton C of C; Blakely-Peckville Lions Club; Scranton Elks; pres., Chic Feldman Foundation; mem., bd. of dir., Economic Development Council of Northeastern Pa.; mem., adv. bd., Worthington-Scranton Campus, Pa. State Univ.; Distinguished Pennsylvanian Award, 1982; General State Authority, ex. bd.; Catholic; elected to the State Senate in 1970; reelected 1974, 1978, 1982, 1986; elected Democratic Caucus Chmn., 1985; reelected 1987; v. chmn., Ethics & Official Conduct, 1987-88; married Diane Pullman on August 27, 1966; 2 daughters: Melissa and Tressa; home address: 920 Main Street, Peckville.

WILLIAM J. MOORE   **Republican Caucus Chairman**
                                                            33rd District
Adams, Cumberland (part), Franklin, Juniata (part), and Perry Counties

William J. Moore (R), Univ. of Pa. (A.B.) Earth Sciences; att., Univ. of Md. (engineering); grad., U.S. Army Command and General Staff Coll.; frmr., instructor, YMCA boxing, wrestling, self-defense; war veteran; Lt. Colonel, U.S. Army Res.; member, Infantry Schl. Hall of Fame, Ft. Benning, Ga., 1981; Leg. Comm., Veterans of Foreign Wars, Dept. of Pa.; frmr. mem., Am. Assn. of Petroleum Geologists; frmr. Party Chief-Geophysical; frmr. schl. bd. pres.; chmn., W. J. Moore, Inc.; past pres., county Industrial Develop. Authority; past pres., Perry Co. Boy Scout Comm.; dir., CCNB Bank, N.A.; mem., Harrisburg Ex. Club; Co. chmn., Heart Fund, United Fund; Newport Lodge F&AM; Zembo Temple; past Lay Leader, Keboch United Methodist Ch., New Bloomfield; served in House of Representatives 1971-72; elected to State Senate in 1972; reelected 1976, 1980, 1984; elected Minority Caucus Secretary, 1976-78; elected Majority Caucus Chmn., 1980-pres.; married Sally Jane Keith; 2 children: Stephen and William, Jr.; resides in New Bloomfield, Perry County.

RAPHAEL J. MUSTO   **14th District**
Luzerne (part) County

Raphael J. Musto (D) was born Mar. 30, 1929, in Pittston, the son of Rose Frushon Musto and the late Representative James Musto; Kings Coll., (B.S.) 1971; U.S. Army, 1951-53; Knights of Columbus; dir., Pittston C of C; Lions; Pittston Twp. Vol. Fire Co.; bd. dir., Economic Develop. Council of NE Pa.; elected to the House of Representatives in a special election to fill his late father's unexpired term, 1971; elected to the U.S. Congress in a special election, 1980; elected to the State Senate, Nov. 2, 1982; reelected 1986; married Frances Panzetta; 4 children: James, Raphael Jr., Michael, Frances Anne; home address: 260 Market St., Pittston.

MICHAEL A. O'PAKE   **11th District**
Berks (part) and Montgomery (part) Counties

Michael A. O'Pake (D) was born Feb. 2, 1940, in Reading, the son of Michael E. and Anna Masler O'Pake; grad., Reading Central Catholic H.S., Valedictorian 1957; St. Joseph's Univ. (A.B., summa cum laude) 1961; Univ. of Pa. Law Schl. (J.D.) 1964; past chmn., Eastern Region, Council of State Govts.; chmn., Special Sen. Com. to Investigate Drug Law Enforcement, Task Force on an Elected Atty. Gen., Special Sen. Com. to Investigate State Procurement Practices, and Special Sen. Com. to Investigate Medicaid Fraud; mem., U.S. Supreme, Pa. Supreme, Superior and Berks Co. Cts.; Natl. Exec. Bd., Council of State Govts.; adv. bd., Ben Franklin Partnership Prog.; bd. dir., Parents Anonymous of Pa.; adv. bd., Pa. St. Univ. Berks Campus; St. Joseph's Univ. President's Adv. Council; bd. dir., Support Center for Child Advocates; Reading Optimist Club (pres., 1968); Pa. Com. for Effective Justice; Pa. Comm. on Crime and Delinquency; adv. com., Juvenile Justice and Delinquency Prevention; Governor's Task Force on Max. Security Psych. Care; Jt. St. Govt. Task Force to Study Children's Civil Rights and Duties; Transition Task Force to Establish Dept. of Aging; mem. task force: Update Master Plan for Higher Ed., Mental Health of Juvenile Offenders, Eminent Domain, Life Care Retirement Communities, Permanency Planning for Children in Placement, Third Party Real Estate Brokerage, Review Pa. Mental Health Commitment Procedures Law, Private Prisons; frmr. law clerk to Judge Robert Lee Jacobs, Pa. Superior Ct.; winner, Internatl. Oratorical Contest of Optimist Internatl. 1956, Keedy Cup (best appellate advocacy at Univ. of Pa. Law Schl.) 1964; nominated, Outstanding Young Men in America 1969, 1974, 1977; rec.; Dist. Service Award, Reading Jaycees 1969, Pa. Dist. Attys. Award 1978, Pa. Elem. Schl. Principals' Service to Children Award 1978, B'nai B'rith Humanitarian Award 1980, Natl. Org. for Victim Assistance Award 1984; Pa. Assn. of Home Economists' Friend of the Year Award 1984, Outstanding Pa. Award, Tenth Annual Pa. Child Abuse Conf. 1986; mem., House of Representatives, 1969-72; Senate 1973 to date.

FRANK A. PECORA
44th District

Allegheny (part) and Westmoreland (part) Counties

Frank A. Pecora (R) was born Aug. 8, 1930, in Pgh., the son of Frank L. and Elizabeth Cristillo Pecora; att., Westinghouse H.S.; Robert Morris Coll.; rep., Pgh. Burial Vault Inc.; Penn Hills Twp. Comm., 1971-75, elected councilman-at-large, 1975; reelected, 1977; past pres., Penn Hills Taxpayers League; co-founder, Concerned Taxpayers of Allegheny Co.; Penn Hills Chamber of Commerce; hon. mem., Kiwanis; Loyal Order of Moose, Perry Lodge #796, F. & A.M.; Shiloh Chapter #257 Royal Arch Masons; Penn Hills Caravan #20 of Syria Temple, A.A.O.N.M.S.; Syria Temple A.A.O.N.M.S. of Pittsburgh; Ancient Accepted Scottish Rite of Freemasonry, Northern Masonic; Jurisdiction, U.S.A., Valley of Pittsburgh, Dist. of Pa.; Gourgas Lodge of Perfection; Pittsburgh Chapter of Rose Croix; Pa. Council of Princes of Jerusalem; Pa. Consistory; first Penn Hills citizen to represent the 44th senatorial district; elected to the State Senate in 1978, reelected 1982, 1986; married Barbara Gigliotti; 2 children: Frank and Barbara; home address: 5970 Poketa Rd., Verona.

JOHN E. PETERSON
25th District

Clarion (part), Elk, Erie (part), Forest, McKean, Potter, Venango (part), and Warren Counties

John E. Peterson (R) was born Dec. 25, 1938, the son of Mary Elizabeth Baker Peterson and the late Axel Benjamin Peterson; grad., Titusville H.S.; Public Affairs Leadership Training, Pa. St. Univ.; frmr. U.S. Army Specialist; frmr. Food Merchant; frmr. bd. dir., Titusville Hosp.; District Rep. for 23rd U.S. Congressional Dist., 1975; pres., Pleasantville Borough Council, 1971-1977; past pres., Titusville Area Chamber of Commerce; past pres., Pleasantville Lions Club; chmn., Pastor Parish Com., Layleader, Sunday schl. teacher, Pleasantville United Methodist Ch.; past pres., Pleasantville P.T.A.; mem., Venango Co. Industrial Board; mem., adv. bd., Univ. of Pgh., Titusville Campus and Bradford Campus; mem., bd. advisors, Foxview Manor, Inc.; elected to the House of Rep., Nov. 28, 1977; reelected 1978, 1980, 1982; elected to Senate, Nov. 1984; married Saundra June Watson; 2 children: Richard and Florence Waychoff; home address: Box 289, 248 N. Main St., Pleasantville.

JOHN W. REGOLI
40th District

Allegheny (part), Armstrong (part), and Westmoreland (part) Counties

John W. Regoli (D) was born June 4, 1938; grad., Arizona State Univ. (B.A., education); U.S. Army, 1961-63; mem., Penn State Univ. Adv. Bd.; Municipal Sanitary Authority; Knights of Columbus; Loyal Order of Moose; American Legion; Sons of Italy and Italian Sons and Daughters of America; Westmoreland Co. Commissioner, 1975, 1979, 1983; Arnold Chamber of Commerce Community Service Award; Allekiski Community Development Corp. Public Service Award; Southwestern Bldg. Trades Council Govt. Service Award; elected to the State Senate in 1986; married Gloria "Dolly" Zampogna; 3 children: John, Jr., David, Sharon; home address: 293 Elmtree Road, New Kensington.

JEANETTE F. REIBMAN
18th District

Monroe (part) and Northampton Counties

Jeanette F. Reibman (D) was born in Fort Wayne, Ind., the daughter of Meir and Pearl Schwartz Fichman; Hunter Coll. (A.B.) 1937; Indiana Univ. Law Schl. (LL.B.) 1940; (Hon.) L.L.D., Lafayette Coll., 1969; Wilson Coll., 1974; Cedar Crest Coll, Lehigh Univ., 1977; attorney, U.S. War Dept., U.S. War Production Bd. during WW II; extensive service in ed., adv. groups; bd. of dirs., Forks of the Delaware United Fund, Mercersburg Acad.; Northampton Co. Family Counseling Service; Northampton Co. chmn., Cancer Crusade (1962); Easton City Chmn., Heart Drive (1969-72); cited for outstanding service, U.S. War Dept., Pa. Dept. of Public Instruction, Am. Legion, Jr. Historians of Pa., FFA, Natl. Honorary Ed. Frat.; Pa. Library Assn.; named Disting. Daughter of Pa. (1969); Alumni Hall of Fame, Hunter Coll. (1974); mem. of Bar, U.S. Supreme Court; Pa. Citizen's Comm. on Basic Ed.; bd. of trustees, Lafayette Coll.; St. Luke's Hospital, Bethlehem; Commonwealth Bd.; Camphill Special Schls., Inc.; Water Facilities Loan Board; Council on the Arts; PHEAA; Com. on Arts, Tourism & Cultural Resources, Natl. Conf. of State Legislators; mem., State Comm. on Child Support, 1985; social services; Gov't. Comm.; Ed. Comm. of the States; Pa. commissioner; Pa. Planning Comm., Internatl. Women's Year; delegate, Natl. Conference of I.W.Y. (1977); rec., St. of Israel City of Jerusalem Peace Award (1977); Myrtle Wreath Award, Hadassah, E. Region; rec., Pa. Assn. Univs. & Colls. Disting. Friend of Public Higher Educ. Award, 1982; Pa. Assn. for Gifted Educ. Award for outstanding services to the gifted child, 1984; Pa. Psychologists Assn. Award for outstanding service, 1984; Disting. Cit. Award, Minsi Trail Council, Boy Scouts of America, 1984; appt., Gov. Comm. on Financing of Higher Educ., 1983; Am. Schl. Counselor Assn. Legislator of the Year Award, 1986; Natl. Assn. of Social Workers, Pa. Chptr., 1986; served Pa. House of Representatives, 1955-56, 1959-66; elected to the State Senate, 1966; reelected 1970, 1974, 1978, 1982, 1986; married Nathan L. Reibman, Easton lawyer; 3 sons; home office address: 711 Lehigh St., Easton.

JAMES JOHN RHOADES
29th District

Schuylkill, Carbon, and Monroe (part) Counties

James John Rhoades (R) was born in Waterbury, CT., the son of Earl and Stella Krankowski Rhoades; Mahanoy City H.S., 1959; East Stroudsburg Univ. (B.S.) 1964; Lehigh Univ. (M.Ed.) 1976; grad. studies, Bloomsburg Univ., East Stroudsburg Univ.; frmr. schl. principal; PHEAA Board member; MILRITE Co.; Lions; B.P.O.E.; Travelers Protective Assn.; Humane Fire Co. #1; Schuyl. Co. Chptr., Natl. Football Found. and Hall of Fame; Jerry Wolman Chpt., Pa. Sports Hall of Fame; Natl. Rifle Assn.; St. Canicus Ch.; elected to the State Senate in 1980; reelected 1984; married Mary Edith Holland; 3 children: James Jr., Alisa Ann, Michael David; home address: 1000 E. Center St., Mahanoy City.

M. JOSEPH ROCKS
4th District

Philadelphia (part) County

M. Joseph Rocks (D) was born June 6, 1947, the son of Joseph F. and Catherine Gilchrist Rocks; West Catholic Boys H. S., 1961-65; Community Coll. of Phila. (A.S.) 1967; Defense Language Inst., Monterey, Ca., German Linguist; U. of Iowa (B.A.) 1972; att., Univ. of Md.; served with U.S. Army Security Agency; Trustee, Comm. Coll. of Phila.; mem., bd. dir., Rudolphy Residence for the Blind-Phila.; Center for Early Childhood Services, Inc.; bd. mem., PHEAA, PA School Employ. Ret. Bd.; Assn. for Retarded Citizens; Shalom and Friendly Sons of St. Patrick; mem., Therapeutic Center at Fox Chase (The Bridge); Knights of Columbus Cor MARIAE Council 4th Degree; 21st Ward Comm. Council; PA Jobs Coordinating Council; Pa. St. Unemploy. Comp. Adv. Council; St. Ed. Adv. Bd. on Block Grants; Am. Legion; frmr. v. pres., Samuel LePera Inc., General Contractors; special asst., Senate Education Comm., 1973; budget analyst, House of Rep., 1974-75; S.E. reg. dir., Leg. Service, House of Rep., 1976-78; elected to the House of Representatives in 1978; reelected 1980; elected to Senate in 1982, reelected 1986; married Nancy LePera; 3 children: Michael Joseph III, Patricia Ann, Andrew Patrick; home address: 940 Cathedral Rd. Philadelphia.

JAMES A. ROMANELLI
43rd District

Allegheny (part) County

James A. Romanelli (D) was born July 8, 1929, in Pgh., the son of Dominick T. and Sarah McWilliams Romanelli; att., Univ. of Pgh. Schl. of Local Govt.; grad. course Civil Law and Procedure; completed course of Grtr. Pgh. Bd. of Realtors, Duquesne Univ.; licensed real estate salesman; bd. dir.: South Side Hospital; South Side C. of C.; Squirrel Hill Urban Coalition; Urban League of Pgh.; Generations Together; American Wind Symphony; Kiwanis Club of Oakland; bd. trustees, Pgh. History and Landmarks Foundation; mem., Lions; South Side Community Council; BPOE; Moose; Variety Club Tent 1; Italian Sons and Daughters of Am.; Pgh. Press Club; Pgh. Athletic Assn.; Penn's SW Assn.; Air Force Assn. of Pa. Chpt. 225; Allegheny Club; Peoples Oakland Mental Health Steering Comm.; Duquesne Tamburitzans Adv. Comm.; Pa. Society; Carrick Businesssman's Assn.; Knights of Columbus, 4th Degree, Homestead Council #2201; South Hills Italian Club; Wilkins Twp. Italian Club; Sacred Heart Church; Subalpine Italian Club; St. Adalbert's Alumni Assn.; Zionists of Am.; elected to the House of Representatives in 1972; reelected 1974; elected to State Senate in special election, Nov. 1975; reelected 1976, 1980, 1984; married Alexandra M. Gorskey; home address: 5847 Aylesboro Ave., Pittsburgh.

JAMES E. ROSS
Democratic Caucus Secretary
47th District

Beaver (part) and Lawrence (part) Counties

James E. Ross (D) was born Jan. 23, 1921, in Beaver Falls and raised in Koppel; att., Beaver Co. schls.; grad., Ellwood City H.S.; extension courses, Pa. St. Univ. (labor management, community devel.); Coast Guard, Pacific Theater, W.W. II, 4 battle stars; frmr. millworker and construction foreman; workmen's compensation referee, Labor and Industry Dept., 3 1/2 yrs.; treas., Democratic Party of Beaver Co., 2 yrs.; Beaver Co., commissioner, 1960-72; chmn., Smoke Control Assn., W. Pa.; past exec. bd. mem. and pres., Construction Union Local 833; trustee, Pa. St. Univ. Branch Campus; bd. of dirs., Beaver Co. Retarded Children's Assn.; mem., Beaver Co. Conference on Community Devel.; Governor's Ed. Comm.; Pa. Emergency Management Council; High Speed Rail Compact; awards: Pa. Planning Assn. Award (1971), Pa. St. Univ. Bronze Medal; mem., Koppel Italian Club, Rochester; Rochester Elks, Center Twp. VFW, New Brighton Am. Legion, New Brighton SOI, Koppel Italian Wolves Club, Ambridge Eagles, Beaver Falls Moose; elected to State Senate, 1972; reelected 1976, 1980, 1984; Majority Caucus Secretary, 1977-78; Majority Caucus Chmn., 1979-80; Democratic Caucus Chmn., 1980-1984; Democratic Caucus Sec., 1985-present; married Dorothy Moravec; 8 daughters and 1 son; home address: 200 Fourth St., Beaver.

FRANK A. SALVATORE
5th District

Philadelphia (part) County

Frank A. (Hank) Salvatore (R) was born June 2, 1922, in Phila., the son of Peter and Dominica Salvatore; att. Northeast H.S., Phila.; St. Joseph's Coll. of Industrial Relations; Fells Inst. of the Univ. of Pa.; WW II vet.; extensive action in South Pacific, 1942-45; field auditor, Pa. Dept. of Revenue; Archbishop Ryan Men's Club; B'rith Sholom; Sons of Italy (Vince Lombardi Lodge); Phila. Assn. for Retarded Children, Inc.; Counselling or Referral Assistance Services (CORA); K of C; Bustleton Lions Club; Knights of Pythias; Frankford Hospital Adv. Bd.; The Benjamin Rush Center for Mental Health and Mental Retardation; Greater Northeast Lodge #71; Shaare Shamayin Men's Club; Bustleton/Somerton Synagogue Men's Club; Phila. Boosters Club; Sunshine Foundation; elected to the House of Representatives in 1972; reelected to 5 successive terms; Republican Administrator from 1979 to 1984; elected to the State Senate, 1984; married to Gloria Leggiere; 5 children; home address: 316 Buxmont St., Philadelphia.

EUGENE F. SCANLON
42nd District

Allegheny (part) County

Eugene F. Scanlon (D) was born Dec. 19, 1924, in Pgh., the son of William and Marie Garrity Scanlon; Univ. of Pgh. (B.A.) 1950; Univ. of Pgh. Law Schl. (J.D.) 1953; attorney; Army Capt., W.W. II, 1943-46, and Korean War, 1950-52; Allegheny Co., Pa., Am. Bar Assns.; K. of C., Knights of Equity, Elks; dpty. atty. gen., 1955-63; Case Editor, Univ. of Pgh. Law Review (author of several articles, Vol. 14); Trustee, Univ. of Pgh.; bd. mem., Stadium Auth. of City of Pgh.; mem., Natl. Honor Society; Roman Catholic; served in the Pa. House of Representatives, 1968-1974; elected to the State Senate, 1974, elected Majority Whip, 1977; reelected 1978; elected Minority Whip, 1980; reelected 1982, 1986; married Ann Boyle on Jan. 11, 1947; 2 children; home address: 1431 Termon Ave., Pgh.

TIM SHAFFER
21st District

Butler, Clarion (part), Lawrence (part), and Venango (part) Counties

Tim Shaffer (R) was born Oct. 2, 1945, in Butler, the son of John M. and Jean Kaufman Shaffer; Pa. St. Univ (B.A.) 1966; Duquesne Law Schl. (J.D.) 1974, Law Review; U.S. Army, 1st Lt., 1967-70, Vietnam Vet. (rec., Bronze Star); Butler Co. Bar Assn.; Butler Co. solicitor, 1976-78; Am. Legion; V.F.W.; Grange; League of Women Voters; Ducks Unlimited; Butler Area C. of C.; Butler City Hunting and Fishing Club; Polish Nat'l. Alliance; Loyal Order of Moose; Harmony Historical Society; W. Pa. Conservancy; Butler Co. Historical Society; N.F.I.B.; dir., Midwestern Pa. Heart Assn.; elected to the State Senate in 1980; reelected 1984; home address: Prospect.

JOHN J. SHUMAKER
15th District

Dauphin and Northumberland (part) Counties

John J. Shumaker (R) was born Mar. 13, 1929, in Harrisburg, the son of John and Esther Jeffries Shumaker; Dickinson Coll. (B.A.) 1951, and its law schl. (J.D.)1956; U.S. Navy, 1951-53; Retired Reserve (Cmdr. Naval Intelligence) frmr. Officer in Charge, Naval Reserve Intell. Unit, 1966-68, 1972-73; attorney; chmn., Dauphin Co. Young Republicans (3 years); chmn., Dauphin Co. Republican Adv. Comm.; frmr. chmn., Susquehanna Twp. Republican Comm.; co-founder, pres., Penn National Race Course since 1968; founded Shumaker Agency (gen. insurance) 1954; chmn., Susquehanna Twp. Auth., 1968-75; frmr. pres., Pa. Municipal Authorities Assn., 1975; Pa. Crime Comm., 1967-69; Regional III Planning Co. of Pa. Justice Comm., 1969-73; chmn., Pa. Council of Natl. Co. on Crime & Delinquency, 1966-1968; Natl. Trustee, Natl. Co. on Crime & Delinquency, 1962-75; Pa. Co. on Crime & Delinquency, 1964-72; pres., Grtr. Hbg. C of C, 1968-69; pres., Dauphin Co. Unit, Am. Cancer Society, 1965-67; Dist. Gov., Rotary Internatl. Dist. 739, 1970-71; trustee, Colonial Park United Methodist Ch.; bd. dirs., Hbg. Horse Show Assn, Inc.; Tri- Co. Easter Seal Society for the Handicapped, Inc.; dir. bd. of trustees, Community General Osteopathic Hospital; dir., Community General Osteopathic Hospital Foundation, Inc.; bd. dirs., Dauphin Co. Fire Training Center, Inc.; the Uptown Late Start Senior Citizens Center, Inc.; exec. bd., Keystone Area Co., BSA; ex. bd., Tri-County Opportunities Industrialization Center Inc. (OIC); prof. mem., Am. Correctional Assn.; Am. Legion; elected to the State Senate, Mar. 22, 1983; reelected 1984; married Judith Rine Strohecker; 3 children: Lori, Lisa, Lianne; home address: P.O. Box 68, Grantville.

PATRICK J. STAPLETON   Democratic Policy Committee Chairman
41st District

Armstrong (part), Clarion (part), Clearfield (part), Indiana (part), and Jefferson Counties

Patrick James Stapleton (D) was born in Indiana, Pa., the son of Patrick and Bertha Stadtmiller Stapleton; att., Penn St. Univ.; grad., Indiana Univ. of Pa. (B.S.) 1950; U.S. Navy, 4 1/2 yrs.; restaurant owner; chmn., council of trustees, Indiana Univ. of Pa.; Co. Commissioner, 1962-69; past pres., Pa. St. Assn. of Commissioners; dir., S.W. Pa. Economic Dev. Dist.; mem., adv. bd., LPN Assn. of Pa.; mem., Community Adv. Bd. of WPSX-TV; rec., Centennial Award of Merit, U. of Pa. Vet. Schl.; past pres., Am. Red Cross Bloodmobile; past pres., Comprehensive Health; K. of C.; VFW; Am. Legion; Council at Large, Boy Scouts of Am.; St. Bernard's Ch.; rec., YMCA Decade of Service Award; elected to the State Senate in special election, May 1970; reelected 1972, 1976, 1980, 1984; married Madeline Feidler on June 10, 1950; 1 son; home address: 710 Croyland Ave., Indiana.

JOHN STAUFFER   Republican Leader
19th District

Chester (part) and Montgomery (part) Counties

John Stauffer (R) was born May 28, 1925, in Phoenixville, son of the late John and Alice Funk Stauffer; grad., Phoenixville H.S.; Pa. St. Planning Bd., 1968-71, pres. (1962-64); borough council of Phoenixville, 1959-64; extensive service in transpo. advisory groups; area chmn., District 7, Chester Co. Republican Comm., 1966; past v. pres., Kiwanis Club of Phoenixville; charter mem., Phoenixville Junior C. of C.; chmn., Joint St. Gov. Comm. Task Force on Schl. Construction Costs and Intergov. Fiscal Affairs; Legislative Data Processing Comm., 1977-82; Washington Mem'l. Chapel (Episcopal) Valley Forge; special award, Schuylkill Valley Highway Assn., 1967; B'nai B'rith Citizenship Citation, 1971; Phoenixville Inter-Service Club Council Ambassadorship Award, 1972; Phoenixville C. of C. Outstanding Citizen Award, 1974; Disting. Service Award, United Vets' Council of Phila., 1976; Pomona Grange Award for Public Service, 1982; Centennial Award, Univ. of Pa. Veterinary Schl., 1984; Pa. Jewish Coalition's "Senator of the Year" Award-1985; Hon. Doctor of Laws, Pa. Coll. of Optometry; served in Pa. House of Representatives, 1964-70; elected to State Senate in 1970; reelected 1972, 1976, 1980, 1984; elected Senate Republican Whip, 1976, 1978, 1980, 1982; elected Senate Republican Leader, 1984, 1986; married Mary Elizabeth Bergantz on May 29, 1946; father of 3 children; home address: 1215 Dorothy Ave., Phoenixville.

WILLIAM J. STEWART   35th District

Cambria, Clearfield (part), and Somerset (part) Counties

William J. Stewart (D) was born July 12, 1950, in Johnstown, the son of Charles J. and Pauline Bowman Stewart; att. Grtr. Johnstown H.S.; U. of Pgh. at Johnstown; Pa. Natl. Guard, 1969-76; two Pa. Service Ribbons; retail businessman 10 yrs.; mem., Elks, Knights of Columbus; Adv. Bd., Univ. of Pgh. at Johnstown; bd. of dirs.: Cambria Residential Services, TOUCH, OWL, JARI; Cambria Co. Transit Auth.; St. Columba R.C. Ch.; elected to the House of Representatives, 1976; reelected 5 successive terms; elected to State Senate in special election, March 24, 1987; married Kathryn T. Greene; 2 children: Patrick and Christopher; home address: R.D. #5, Box 2, Johnstown.

J. BARRY STOUT   46th District

Beaver (part), Greene, and Washington (part) Counties

J. Barry Stout (D) was born Nov. 7, 1936, in Washington Co., the son of William B. and Mary Watkins Stout; Washington and Jefferson Coll. (B.A.) 1964; assoc., Thompson Funeral Home, Bentleyville; U.S. Army Corps of Engineers, 1959-62; Atlas Railroad Construction Co., Eighty Four; NFDA, PFDA, Southwestern Funeral Directors Assn., Bentleyville Boosters Club, F&AM Shrine, FOE, LOOM, St. Library Assn.; frmr. pres., Bentleyville Public Library; Bentleyville Planning Comm.; dpty coroner, Washington Co.; Young Democrats; financial chmn., exec. comm., Bentleyville Sesquicentennial, 1965-66; Booster Club that built "Caramel Park" for Boys Baseball, Bentleyville area; Bentleyville Vol. Fire Dept.; Washington Co. Library Award; Presbyterian Ch.; Electoral Coll. 1976, for the 22nd dist.; elected to the House of Representatives in 1970; reelected 1972, 1974; elected to State Senate in special election, May 17, 1977; reelected 1978, 1982, 1986; married Lenore Ann Thompson on July 18, 1959; 6 children; home address: 214 Piersol Avenue, Bentleyville.

RICHARD A. TILGHMAN

Republican Appropriations Committee Chairman
17th District

Delaware (part), Montgomery (part), and Philadelphia (part) Counties

Richard A. Tilghman (R) was born Mar. 8, 1920, in Manchester, England, the son of Benjamin Chew and Eliza Middleton Fox Tilghman; att. Fountain Valley Schl., Princeton Univ.; additional studies, Berlitz Schl. of Languages; U.S. Marine Corps, Maj., W.W. II; rec., Silver Star for action in Iwo Jima; legislator; Bryn Mawr Civic Assn.; VFW; Episcopal Ch.; served in Pa. House of Representatives, 1967-68; elected to the State Senate in 1968; reelected in 1972, 1976, 1980, 1984; married Diana Disston on Feb. 26, 1944; 3 children; home address: 406 Gatcombe Lane, Bryn Mawr.

NOAH W. WENGER

36th District

Chester (part) and Lancaster (part) Counties

Noah W. Wenger (R) was born Oct. 20, 1934, in New Holland, the son of Elam Z. and Hettie Weaver Wenger; grad. Lancaster Co. public schls.; farmer; Director, Ephrata Natl. Bank; Pa. Farmers' Assn.; Ephrata Young Farmers; Gov.'s Advsry. Comm. on Solid Waste Management; chmn., Pa. Agricultural and Stabilization Comm.; v. chmn., Cocalico Schl. Auth., 1971-84; chrt. mem., Pa. Agriculture Repub. Comm.; Reinholds Lions Club; Stevens Fire Co.; Shoeneck Fire Co.; Outstanding Community Service Award, Ephrata Area Young Farmers, 1976; Evangelical Assembly of God; elected to the House of Representatives, 1976; reelected 2 successive terms; elected to the State Senate, 1982; reelected 1986; married Barbara Ann Bundrick; 3 children, Nancy, Brenda, Pamela; home address: 1325 Wollups Hill Rd., Stevens.

HARDY WILLIAMS

8th District

Philadelphia (part) County

Hardy Williams (D) was born April 14, 1931, in Phila., the son of James (dec.d) and Frances Connix Williams; Pa. St. Univ., and the Univ. of Pa. Law Schl.; Lieut., U.S. Army, 1952-54; attorney; Phila. Bar Assn.; Barristers' Club of Phila.; Am. Arbitration Assn.; Omega Psi Phi; Task Force on Mental Health Laws; mem., bd. dirs., Pa. Trauma Systems Fd.; bd. mem., Community Legal Services of Phila.; bd. mem., Stephen Smith Home; White Rock Baptist Ch.; asst. city solicitor, 1962-68; rec.: Distinguished Son of West Phila. H.S.; Distinguished Citizen's Award, Club VIP; Distinguished Service Award; elected to the House of Representatives, 1970; reelected 1972, 1976, 1978, 1980; elected to State Senate, Nov. 2, 1982; reelected 1986; Pa. Commission on Sentencing; Pa. Historical and Museum Commission; chmn., Pa. Senate Phila. Delegation; 3 children: Lisa Dawn, Anthony Hardy, Clifford Kelley; home address: 5939 Cobbs Creek Pkwy., Philadelphia.

ROY W. WILT

Republican Policy Committee Chairman
50th District

Crawford, Mercer, and Venango (part) Counties

Roy W. Wilt (R) was born July 4, 1935, in Pgh., the son of Raymond E. and Marcella Newman Wilt; Thiel Coll. (B.A.) 1959, Michigan St. Univ. (M.A.) 1967; Doctor of Humanities, Thiel Coll., 1985; U.S. Army Reserves and Natl. Guard, 1960-66; former Dean of Men, Thiel Coll.; St. John's Lutheran Ch.; elected to House of Representatives in 1968, reelected to 6 successive terms; elected to the State Senate in special election, March 31, 1981; reelected 1982, 1986; appt., Majority Policy Committee Chmn.; ex. com. chmn., mem., bd. dirs., PHEAA; mem., Joint Water & Air Pollution Control & Conservation Com.; mem., Great Lakes Comm.; chmn., Natural Resources Com. of Great Lakes Commission; married Sonya Mugnani on Aug. 6, 1960; 2 sons: Roy Jr. and Rod; address: 262 Leech Rd., Greenville.

EDWARD P. ZEMPRELLI

Democratic Leader
45th District

Allegheny (part), Washington (part), and
Westmoreland (part) Counties

Edward P. Zemprelli (D) was born May 11, 1925, in Clairton, the son of John and Mary Mercurio Zemprelli; att. Clairton public schls.; Pa. St. Univ., (B.A.) 1945; Univ. of Pgh. Law Schl. (LL.B.) 1949; Allegheny Co., Am. Bar Assns.; bd. of trustees, Clairton Public Library, Univ. of Pgh., and Pa. St. Univ.; K. of C. 4th Degree; Sons of Columbus; Italian Sons and Daughters of Am.; Clairton Sportsmen's Club; solicitor, City of Clairton, 1952-60; served in Pa. House of Representatives, 1963-68; elected to the State Senate in 1968; reelected in 1972, 1976, 1980, 1984; Senate Majority Leader, 1979; Senate Democratic Floor Leader, 1981; married Margaret Antoinette on April 23, 1949; 1 daughter; home address: 1244 Bickerton Drive, Clairton.

ALPHABETICAL LIST OF SENATORS

Name		District	Expires Nov. 30	Home Office Address	Capitol Address: Harrisburg Zip Code 17120	Occupation
AFFLERBACH, ROY C.	(D)	16	1990	Office: Crown Tower, Suite 110, 33 South Seventh Street, Allentown 18101	Senate of Pa.	State Senator
ANDREZESKI, ANTHONY B.	(D)	49	1988	Office: 460 East 26th Street, Erie 16504	Senate of Pa.	State Senator
ARMSTRONG, GIBSON E.	(R)	13	1988	Office: Senate Post Office, Harrisburg 17120	Senate of Pa.	Stockbroker
BELL, CLARENCE D.	(R)	9	1988	Office: 344 West Front Street, Media 19063	Senate of Pa.	Attorney
BODACK, LEONARD J.	(D)	38	1990	Office: 4211 Butler Street, Pittsburgh 15201	Senate of Pa.	State Senator
BRIGHTBILL, DAVID J.	(R)	48	1990	Office: Senate Post Office, Harrisburg 17120	Senate of Pa.	Lawyer
CORMAN, J. DOYLE	(R)	34	1990	Office: 220 W. High Street, Bellefonte 16823	Senate of Pa.	State Senator
FISHER, D. MICHAEL	(R)	37	1988	Office: 71 McMurray Road, Suite 103, Pittsburgh 15241	Senate of Pa.	Attorney
FUMO, VINCENT J.	(D)	1	1988	1208 Tasker Street, Philadelphia 19148	Senate of Pa.	Lawyer
GREENLEAF, STEWART J.	(R)	12	1990	Office: 27 North York Road, Willow Grove 19090-3419	Senate of Pa.	Attorney
GREENWOOD, JAMES C.	(R)	10	1990	Office: 76 East State Street, Doylestown 18901	Senate of Pa.	State Senator
HANKINS, FREEMAN	(D)	7	1988	Office: 4116 Haverford Ave., Philadelphia 19104	Senate of Pa.	Funeral Director
HELFRICK, EDWARD W.	(R)	27	1988	Office: 23 East 2nd Street, Mt. Carmel 17851	Senate of Pa.	Mining Contractor
HESS, RALPH W.	(R)	28	1990	P.O. Box 226, Spring Grove 17362	Senate of Pa.	State Senator
HOLL, EDWIN G.	(R)	24	1990	Office: 210 S. Broad Street, Lansdale 19446	Senate of Pa.	Business Executive
HOPPER, JOHN D.	(R)	31	1988	Office: Senate Post Office, Harrisburg 17120	Senate of Pa.	Insurance Executive
JONES, ROXANNE H.	(D)	3	1988	Office: 3133 N. Broad Street, Philadelphia 19132	Senate of Pa.	State Senator
JUBELIRER, ROBERT C.	(R)	30	1990	Office: 309 E. Plank Rd., Rear, P.O. Box 2023, Altoona 16603	Senate of Pa.	Legislator-Attorney
KELLEY, JAMES R.	(D)	39	1988	Office: 111 W. 2nd Street, Greensburg 15601	Senate of Pa.	Attorney
LEMMOND, CHARLES D., JR.	(R)	20	1990	Office: 701 Market Street, Kingston 18704	Senate of Pa.	State Senator-Attorney
LEWIS, H. CRAIG	(D)	6	1990	Office: 50 Trenton Road, Fairless Hills 19030	Senate of Pa.	Attorney
LINCOLN, J. WILLIAM	(D)	32	1990	Office: R.D. #1, Box 14, Dunbar 15431	Senate of Pa.	State Senator
LOEPER, F. JOSEPH	(R)	26	1990	Office: 403 Burmont Rd., Drexel Hill 19026	Senate of Pa.	State Senator
LYNCH, FRANCIS J.	(R)	2	1990	Office: 1423 E. Luzerne Street, Philadelphia 19124	Senate of Pa.	State Senator
MADIGAN, ROGER A.	(R)	23	1988	R. D. #3, Box 114, Towanda 18848	Senate of Pa.	Insurance Consultant
MELLOW, ROBERT J.	(D)	22	1990	Office: Scranton Life Bldg., Suite 300, 538 Spruce Street, Scranton 18503	Senate of Pa.	State Senator
MOORE, WILLIAM J.	(R)	33	1988	Office: Center Square, P.O. Box 308, New Bloomfield 17068	Senate of Pa.	State Senator
MUSTO, RAPHAEL J.	(D)	14	1990	Office: P.O. Box 786, Pittston 18640	Senate of Pa.	State Senator
O'PAKE, MICHAEL A.	(D)	11	1988	Office: 645 Penn Street, Suite 100, Reading 19601	Senate of Pa.	State Senator-Lawyer
PECORA, FRANK A.	(R)	44	1990	Office: 15 Duff Road, Pittsburgh 15235	Senate of Pa.	State Senator
PETERSON, JOHN E.	(R)	25	1988	Office: P.O. Box 289, Pleasantville 16341	Senate of Pa.	State Senator
REGOLI, JOHN W.	(D)	40	1990	Office: Senate Post Office, Harrisburg 17120	Senate of Pa.	State Senator
REIBMAN, JEANETTE F.	(D)	18	1990	Office: 711 Lehigh Street, Easton 18042	Senate of Pa.	Housewife - Lawyer
RHOADES, JAMES J.	(R)	29	1988	Office: 32 East Centre Street, Mahanoy City 17948	Senate of Pa.	State Senator

ALPHABETICAL LIST OF SENATORS

Name	District	Expires Nov. 30	Home Office Address	Capitol Address: Harrisburg Zip Code 17120	Occupation
ROCKS, M. JOSEPH	(D) 4	1990	Office: 7623 Ridge Avenue, Philadelphia 19128	Senate of Pa.	State Senator
ROMANELLI, JAMES A.	(D) 43	1988	Office: 1901 East Carson Street, Pittsburgh 15203	Senate of Pa.	State Senator
ROSS, JAMES E.	(D) 47	1988	Office: Fort McIntosh Office Building, First Floor, 855 Second Street, Beaver 15009	Senate of Pa.	State Senator
SALVATORE, FRANK A.	(R) 5	1988	7711 Castor Avenue, Philadelphia 19152	Senate of Pa.	State Senator
SCANLON, EUGENE F.	(D) 42	1990	Office: 1212 Manor Building, Pittsburgh 15219	Senate of Pa.	Attorney
SHAFFER, TIM	(R) 21	1988	Office: 259 South Main Street, Butler 16001	Senate of Pa.	State Senator
					Attorney at Law
SHUMAKER, JOHN J.	(R) 15	1988	Office: Senate Post Office, Harrisburg 17120	Senate of Pa.	Attorney at Law
STAPLETON, PATRICK J.	(D) 41	1988	710 Croyland Ave., Indiana 15701	Senate of Pa.	State Senator
STAUFFER, JOHN	(R) 19	1988	Office: Senate Post Office, Harrisburg 17120	Senate of Pa.	State Senator
STEWART, WILLIAM J.	(D) 35	1988	Office: 915 Menoher Boulevard, Suite D., Easy Grade Highway, Johnstown 15905	Senate of Pa.	State Senator
STOUT, J. BARRY	(D) 46	1990	Route 136 & Mitchell Road, R. D. #4, Box 108, Eighty Four 15330	Senate of Pa.	State Senator
TILGHMAN, RICHARD A.	(R) 17	1988	406 Gatcombe Lane, Bryn Mawr 19010	Senate of Pa.	State Senator
WENGER, NOAH W.	(R) 36	1990	Office: 1248 West Main Street, Ephrata 17522	Senate of Pa.	Farmer
WILLIAMS, HARDY	(D) 8	1990	Office: 5630 Chestnut Street, Philadelphia 19139	Senate of Pa.	Attorney
WILT, ROY W.	(R) 50	1990	Office: Senate Post Office, Harrisburg 17120	Senate of Pa.	Farmer
ZEMPRELLI, EDWARD P.	(D) 45	1988	Office: 528 St. Clair Avenue, Clairton 15025	Senate of Pa.	Attorney

RECAPITULATION

Republicans 26
Democrats. 24

Total **50**

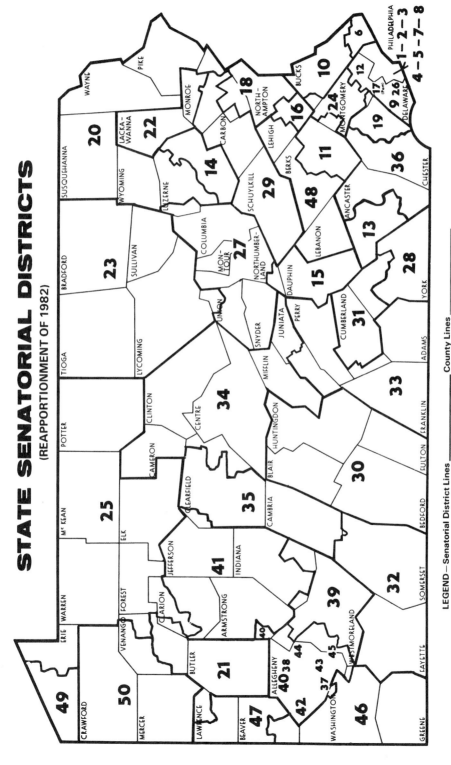

STATE SENATORIAL DISTRICTS
(REAPPORTIONMENT OF 1982)

LEGEND — Senatorial District Lines _____ County Lines _____

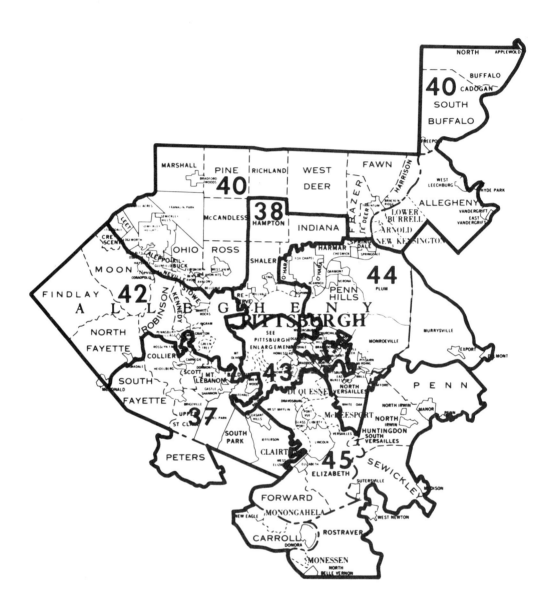

ALLEGHENY COUNTY
SENATE APPORTIONMENT

**PHILADELPHIA
SENATE APPORTIONMENT**

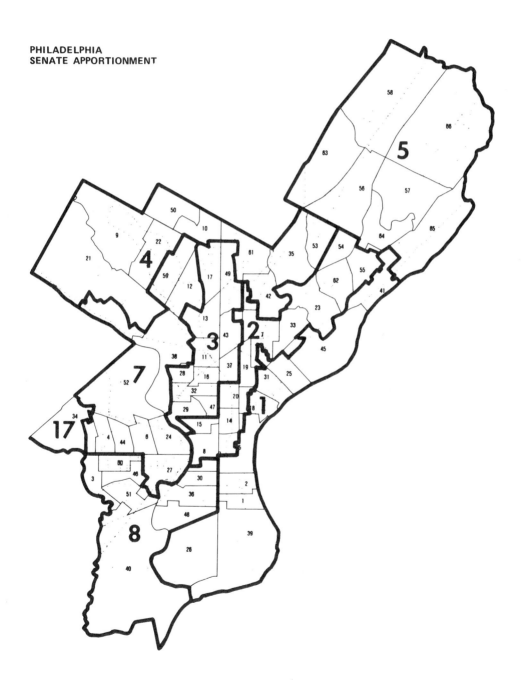

SENATE DISTRICTS

Terms in the even numbered districts expire
November 30, 1990 — Odd-numbered districts expire November 30, 1988

1st. **Philadelphia** County. Part of **Philadelphia** County consisting of the *City* of Philadelphia (part, wards 01, 02, 05 [part, divisions 01, 02, 03, 04, 05, 06, 07, 08, 09, 10, 11, 12, 14, 16, 17, 18, 21, 22, 24, 25 and 26], 07 [part, divisions 14, 15, 18, 19, 23 and 24], 18 [part, divisions 01, 02, 03, 04, 05, 06, 07, 08, 10, 11, 12, 13, 16, 17 and 21], 25, 26, 31, 35, 39, 41 and 45 [part, divisions 01, 02, 03, 04, 05, 06, 07, 08, 13, 14, 15, 18, 20, 21, 22, 23, 24, 25, 26, 27 and 28]). Total population: 236,657. **Vincent J. Fumo (D)**

2nd. **Philadelphia** County. Part of **Philadelphia** County consisting of the *City* of Philadelphia (part, wards 05 [part, divisions 13, 15, 19, 20 and 23], 07 [part, divisions 01, 02, 03, 04, 05, 06, 07, 08, 09, 10, 11, 12, 13, 16, 17, 20, 21 and 22], 08 [part, divisions 07, 09, 13, 15, 16, 17, 18, 19, 20, 21, 22, 23, 24, 25, 26, 27 and 29], 14, 15, 18 [part, divisions 09, 14, 15, 18, 19 and 20], 19, 20, 23, 33, 42 [part, divisions 03, 04, 07, 13, 17 and 21] 43 [part, divisions 02, 03, 04, 05 and 06] 45 [part, divisions 09, 10, 11, 12, 16, 17 and 19], 54, 55 [part, divisions 01, 02, 03, 04, 05, 06, 07, 08, 09, 10, 11, 12, 13, 14, 15, 16, 17, 18, 20, 21, 22, 25, 26, 27, 28 and 29] and 62). Total population: 236,856. **Francis J. Lynch (D)**

3rd. **Philadelphia** County. Part of **Philadelphia** County consisting of the *City* of Philadelphia (part, wards 11, 13, 16, 17, 28 [part, divisions 01, 02, 03, 04, 05, 06, 07, 08, 09, 10, 11, 12, 13, 14, 15, 18 and 19], 29, 32, 37, 43 [part, divisions 01, 07, 08, 09, 10, 11, 12, 13, 14, 15, 16, 17, 18, 19, 20, 21, 22, 23, 24, 25 and 26], 47 and 49). Total population: 238,378. **Roxanne H. Jones (D)**

4th. **Philadelphia** County. Part of **Philadelphia** County consisting of the *City* of Philadelphia (part, wards 09, 10, 21 [part, divisions 21, 22, 23, 24, 25, 26, 27, 28, 29, 30, 31, 32, 33, 34, 35, 37, 38, 39, 40, 41 and 42], 22, 35, 42 [part, divisions 01, 02, 05, 06, 08, 09, 10, 11, 12, 14, 15, 16, 18, 19, 20, 22, 23, 24 and 25], 50, 53 and 61). Total population: 238,053. **M. Joseph Rocks (D)**

5th. **Philadelphia** County. Part of **Philadelphia** County consisting of the *City* of Philadelphia (part, wards 55 [part, divisions 19, 23 and 24], 56, 57, 58, 63, 64, 65 and 66). Total population: 237,373. **Frank A. Salvatore (R)**

6th. **Bucks** County. Part of **Bucks** County consisting of the *Townships* of Bensalem, Bristol, Falls, Lower Southampton, Middletown and Upper Southampton and the *Boroughs* of Bristol, Hulmeville, Langhorne, Langhorne Manor, Penndel and Tullytown. Total population: 235,233. **H. Craig Lewis (D)**

7th. **Philadelphia** County. Part of **Philadelphia** County consisting of the *City* of Philadelphia (part, wards 04, 06, 12, 21 [part, divisions 01, 02, 03, 04, 05, 06, 07, 08, 09, 10, 11, 12, 13, 14, 15, 16, 17, 18, 19, 20 and 36], 24, 27 [part, divisions 01, 02, 03, 05, 06, 07, 08, 09, 10, 11, 13, 14, 15, 16, 18 and 19], 28 [part, divisions 16 and 17], 34 [part, divisions 01, 02, 03, 04, 05, 06, 07, 08, 09, 10, 11, 35, 36, 38 and 42], 38, 44, 52 and 59). Total population: 236,762. **Freeman Hankins (D)**

8th. **Philadelphia** County. Part of **Philadelphia** County consisting of the *City* of Philadelphia (part, wards 03, 08 [part, divisions 01, 02, 03, 04, 05, 06, 08, 10, 11, 12, 14 and 28], 27 [part, divisions 04, 12 and 17], 30, 36, 40, 46, 48, 51 and 60). Total population: 237,793. **Hardy Williams (D)**

9th. **Delaware** County. Part of **Delaware** County consisting of the *City* of Chester and the *Townships* of Aston, Bethel, Birmingham, Chester, Concord, Edgemont, Lower Chichester, Middletown, Nether Providence, Newtown, Ridley, Thornbury, Tinicum, Upper Chichester and Upper Providence and the *Boroughs* of Brookhaven, Chester Heights, Eddystone, Marcus Hook, Media, Morton, Norwood, Parkside, Prospect Park, Ridley Park, Rose Valley, Rutledge, Trainer and Upland. Total population: 238,691. **Clarence D. Bell (R)**

10th. **Bucks** County. Part of **Bucks** County consisting of the *Townships* of Bedminster, Bridgeton, Buckingham, Doylestown, Durham, East Rockhill, Haycock, Hilltown, Lower Makefield, New Britain, Newtown, Nockamixon, Northampton, Plumstead, Richland, Solebury, Springfield, Tinicum, Upper Makefield, Warminster, Warrington, Warwick, West Rockhill and Wrightstown and the *Boroughs* of Chalfont, Doylestown, Dublin, Ivyland, Morrisville, New Britain, New Hope, Newtown, Perkasie,

Quakertown, Richlandtown, Riegelsville, Sellersville, Silverdale, Telford (Bucks County Portion) and Yardley. Total population: 237,144. **James C. Greenwood (R)**

11th. **Berks** and **Montgomery** Counties. Part of **Berks** County consisting of the *City* of Reading and the *Townships* of Alsace, Amity, Brecknock, Caernarvon, Colebrookdale, Cumru, District, Douglass, Earl, Exeter, Hereford, Longswamp, Lower Alsace, Maidencreek, Muhlenberg, Oley, Ontelaunee, Pike, Richmond, Robeson, Rockland, Ruscombmanor, Union and Washington and the *Boroughs* of Adamstown (Berks County Portion), Bally, Bechtelsville, Birdsboro, Boyertown, Fleetwood, Kenhorst, Laureldale, Mohnton, Mt. Penn, Shillington, St. Lawrence, Temple, Topton and West Reading and part of **Montgomery** County consisting of the *Townships* of Douglass, New Hanover and West Pottsgrove. Total population: 235,529. **Michael A. O'Pake (D)**

12th. **Montgomery** County. Part of **Montgomery** County consisting of the *Townships* of Abington, Cheltenham, East Norriton, Horsham, Lower Gwynedd, Lower Moreland, Upper Dublin, Upper Gwynedd, Upper Moreland and Whitpain and the *Boroughs* of Ambler, Bryn Athyn, Hatboro, Jenkintown, North Wales and Rockledge. Total population: 238,143. **Stewart J. Greenleaf (R)**

13th. **Lancaster** County. Part of **Lancaster** County consisting of the *City* of Lancaster and the *Townships* of Conestoga, Conoy, East Donegal, East Hempfield, Lancaster, Manheim, Manor, Mt. Joy, Penn, Pequea, Rapho, Strasburg, Warwick, West Donegal, West Hempfield and West Lampeter and the *Boroughs* of Columbia, East Petersburg, Elizabethtown, Lititz, Manheim, Marietta, Millersville, Mountville, Mt. Joy and Strasburg. Total population: 235,171. **Gibson E. Armstrong (R)**

14th. **Luzerne** County. Part of **Luzerne** County consisting of the *Cities* of Hazleton, Nanticoke, Pittston and Wilkes-Barre and the *Townships* of Bear Creek, Black Creek, Buck, Butler, Conyngham, Dennison, Dorrance, Fairview, Foster, Hanover, Hazle, Hollenback, Jenkins, Nescopeck, Newport, Pittston, Plains, Rice, Slocum, Sugarloaf, Wilkes-Barre and Wright and the *Boroughs* of Ashley, Avoca, Conyngham, Dupont, Duryea, Freeland, Hughestown, Jeddo, Laflin, Laurel Run, Nescopeck, Nuangola, Penn Lake Park, Sugar Notch, Swoyersville, Warrior Run, West Hazleton,. West Wyoming, White Haven, Wyoming and Yatesville. Total population: 238,272. **Raphael J. Musto (D)**

15th. **Dauphin** and **Northumberland** Counties. All of **Dauphin** County and part of **Northumberland** County consisting of the *Townships* of Jackson, Jordan and Lower Mahanoy and the *Borough* of Herndon. Total population: 236,001. **John J. Shumaker (R)**

16th. **Lehigh** County: part of **Lehigh** County consisting of the *Cities* of Allentown and Bethlehem (Lehigh County Portion) and the *Townships* of Hanover, Lower Macungie, Lower Milford, Salisbury, South Whitehall, Upper Milford, Upper Saucon and Whitehall and the *Boroughs* of Alburtis, Catasauqua, Coopersburg, Coplay, Emmaus, Fountain Hill and Macungie. Total population: 238,835. **Roy C. Afflerbach (D)**

17th. **Delaware, Montgomery** and **Philadelphia** Counties. Part of **Delaware** County consisting of the *Townships* of Haverford and Radnor; part of **Montgomery** County consisting of the *Townships* of Lower Merion, Plymouth, Springfield and Whitemarsh and the *Boroughs* of Bridgeport, Conshohocken, Narberth and West Conshohocken and part of **Philadelphia** County consisting of the *City* of Philadelphia (part, ward 34 [part, divisions 12, 13, 14, 15, 16, 17, 18, 19, 20, 21, 22, 23, 24, 25, 26, 27, 28, 29, 30, 31, 32, 33, 34, 37, 39, 40, 41 and 43]). Total population: 237,957. **Richard A. Tilghman (R)**

18th. **Monroe** and **Northampton** Counties: part of **Monroe** County consisting of the *Townships* of Chestnuthill, Eldred, Hamilton and Ross and the *Borough* of Delaware Water Gap and All of **Northampton** County. Total population: 239,262. **Jeanette F. Reibman (D)**

19th. **Chester** and **Montgomery** Counties: part of **Chester** County consisting of the *Townships* of Birmingham, Caln, Charlestown, East Bradford, East Brandywine, East Caln, East Coventry, East Goshen,

East Pikeland, East Vincent, East Whiteland, Easttown, Pennsbury, Pocopson, Schuylkill, Thornbury, Tredyffrin, Upper Uwchlan, Uwchlan, West Bradford, West Goshen, West Pikeland, West Vincent, West Whiteland, Westtown and Willistown and the *Boroughs* of Downingtown, Malvern, Phoenixville, Spring City and West Chester and part of **Montgomery** County consisting of the *Township* of Upper Merion and the *Borough* of Royersford. Total population: 238,008. **John Stauffer (R)**

20th. **Luzerne, Monroe, Pike, Susquehanna, Wayne** and **Wyoming** Counties. Part of **Luzerne** County consisting of the *Townships* of Dallas, Exeter, Franklin, Hunlock, Jackson, Kingston, Lake, Lehman, Plymouth, Ross, Salem and Union and the *Boroughs* of Courtdale, Dallas, Edwardsville, Exeter, Forty Fort, Harveys Lake, Kingston, Larksville, Luzerne, Plymouth, Pringle, Shickshinny and West Pittston; part of **Monroe** County consisting of the *Townships* of Middle Smithfield and Smithfield and the *Boroughs* of East Stroudsburg and Stroudsburg; All of **Pike** County; All of **Susquehanna** County; All of **Wayne** County and All of **Wyoming** County. Total population: 239,450. **Charles D. Lemmond, Jr. (R)**

21st. **Butler, Clarion, Lawrence** and **Venango** Counties. All of **Butler** County; part of **Clarion** County consisting of the *Townships* of Ashland and Salem; part of **Lawrence** County consisting of the *City* of New Castle and the *Townships* of Hickory, Neshannock, Plain Grove, Scott, Union, Washington and Wilmington and the *Boroughs* of New Wilmington, South New Castle and Volant and part of **Venango** County consisting of the *City* of Franklin and the *Townships* of Clinton, Cranberry, Irwin, Pine Grove, Richland, Rockland, Sandycreek, Scrubgrass and Victory and the *Boroughs* of Barkeyville, Clintonville and Emlenton. Total population: 237,206. **Tim Shaffer (R)**

22nd. **Lackawanna** and **Monroe** Counties. All of **Lackawanna** County and part of **Monroe** County consisting of the *Townships* of Barrett, Coolbaugh, Paradise and Price. Total population: 237,841. **Robert J. Mellow (D)**

23rd. **Bradford, Lycoming, Sullivan, Tioga** and **Union** Counties. All of **Bradford** County; All of **Lycoming** County; All of **Sullivan** County; All of **Tioga** County and part of **Union** County consisting of the *Townships* of Gregg, Kelly and White Deer. Total population: 237,102. **Roger A. Madigan (R)**

24th. **Bucks** and **Montgomery** Counties. Part of **Bucks** County consisting of the *Township* of Milford and the *Borough* of Trumbauersville and part of **Montgomery** County consisting of the *Townships* of Franconia, Hatfield, Limerick, Lower Frederick, Lower Pottsgrove, Lower Providence, Lower Salford, Marlborough, Montgomery, Perkiomen, Salford, Skippack, Towamencin, Upper Frederick, Upper Hanover, Upper Pottsgrove, Upper Providence, Upper Salford, West Norriton and Worcester and the *Boroughs* of Collegeville, East Greenville, Green Lane, Hatfield, Lansdale, Norristown, Pennsburg, Pottstown, Red Hill, Schwenksville, Souderton, Telford (Montgomery County Portion) and Trappe. Total population: 235,673. **Edwin G. Holl (R)**

25th. **Clarion, Elk, Erie, Forest, McKean, Potter, Venango** and **Warren** Counties. Part of **Clarion** County consisting of the *Townships* of Beaver, Elk, Farmington, Highland, Knox, Licking, Paint, Perry, Piney, Richland and Washington and the *Boroughs* of Callensburg, Foxburg, Knox, Shippenville, Sligo and St. Petersburg; All of **Elk** County; part of **Erie** County consisting of the *City* of Corry and the *Townships* of Amity, Concord, Greene, Greenfield, Le Boeuf, North East, Union, Venango, Waterford and Wayne and the *Boroughs* of Elgin, Mill Village, North East, Union City, Waterford and Wattsburg; All of **Forest** County; All of **McKean** County; All of **Potter** County; part of **Venango** County consisting of the *City* of Oil City and the *Townships* of Allegheny, Cornplanter and President and the *Boroughs* of Pleasantville and Rouseville and All of **Warren** County. Total population: 239,661. **John E. Peterson (R)**

26th. **Delaware** County. Part of **Delaware** County consisting of the *Townships* of Darby, Marple, Springfield and Upper Darby and the *Boroughs* of Aldan, Clifton Heights, Collingdale, Colwyn, Darby, East Lansdowne, Folcroft, Glenolden, Lansdowne, Millbourne, Sharon Hill, Swarthmore and Yeadon. Total population: 236,291. **F. Joseph Loeper (R)**

27th. **Columbia, Luzerne, Montour, Northumberland, Snyder** and **Union** Counties. All of **Columbia** County; part of **Luzerne** County consisting of the *Townships* of Fairmount and Huntingdon and the *Borough* of New Columbus; All of **Montour** County; part of

Northumberland County consisting of the *Cities* of Shamokin and Sunbury and the *Townships* of Coal, Delaware, East Cameron, East Chillisquaque, Lewis, Little Mahanoy, Lower Augusta, Mt. Carmel, Point, Ralpho, Rockefeller, Rush, Shamokin, Turbot, Upper Augusta, Upper Mahanoy, Washington, West Cameron, West Chillisquaque and Zerbe and the *Boroughs* of Kulpmont, Marion Heights, Mc Ewensville, Milton, Mt. Carmel, Northumberland, Riverside, Snydertown, Turbotville and Watsontown; All of **Snyder** County and part of **Union** County consisting of the *Townships* of Buffalo, East Buffalo, Hartley, Lewis, Limestone, Union and West Buffalo and the *Boroughs* of Hartleton, Lewisburg, Mifflinburg and New Berlin. Total population: 236,672. **Edward W. Helfrick (R)**

28th. **York** County. Part of **York** County consisting of the *City* of York and the *Townships* of Chanceford, Codorus, Dover, East Hopewell, Fawn, Heidelberg, Hellam, Hopewell, Jackson, Lower Chanceford, Lower Windsor, Manheim, North Codorus, North Hopewell, Paradise, Peach Bottom, Penn, Shrewsbury, Spring Garden, Springfield, Warrington, Washington, West Manchester, West Manheim, Windsor and York and the *Boroughs* of Cross Roads, Dallastown, Delta, Dover, East Prospect, Fawn Grove, Felton, Glen Rock, Hallam, Hanover, Jacobus, Jefferson, Loganville, New Freedom, New Salem, Railroad, Red Lion, Seven Valleys, Shrewsbury, Spring Grove, Stewartstown, Wellsville, West York, Windsor, Winterstown, Wrightsville, Yoe and Yorkana. Total population: 238,692. **Ralph W. Hess (R)**

29th. **Carbon, Monroe** and **Schuylkill** Counties. All of **Carbon** County; Part of **Monroe** County consisting of the *Townships* of Jackson, Pocono, Polk, Stroud, Tobyhanna and Tunkhannock and the *Borough* of Mt. Pocono and All of **Schuylkill** County. Total population: 239,397. **James J. Rhoades (R)**

30th. **Bedford, Blair, Fulton** and **Huntingdon** Counties. All of **Bedford** County; All of **Blair** County; All of **Fulton** County and All of **Huntingdon** County. Total population: 238,500. **Robert C. Jubelirer (R)**

31st. **Cumberland** and **York** Counties. Part of **Cumberland** County consisting of the *Townships* of Cooke, Dickinson, East Pennsboro, Hampden, Lower Allen, Lower Frankford, Lower Mifflin, Middlesex, Monroe, North Middleton, North Newton, Penn, Silver Spring, South Middleton, South Newton, Upper Allen, Upper Frankford and West Pennsboro and the *Boroughs* of Camp Hill, Carlisle, Lemoyne, Mechanicsburg, Mt. Holly Springs, New Cumberland, Newville, Shiremanstown, West Fairview and Wormleysburg and Part of **York** County consisting of the *Townships* of Carroll, Conewago, East Manchester, Fairview, Franklin, Manchester, Monaghan, Newberry and Springettsbury and the *Boroughs* of Dillsburg, Franklintown, Goldsboro, Lewisberry, Manchester, Mt. Wolf, North York and York Haven. Total population: 238,114. **John D. Hopper (R)**

32nd. **Fayette** and **Somerset** Counties. All of **Fayette** County and part of **Somerset** County consisting of the *Townships* of Addison, Allegheny, Black, Brothers Valley, Conemaugh, Elk Lick, Fairhope, Greenville, Jefferson, Jenner, Larimer, Lincoln, Lower Turkeyfoot, Middlecreek, Milford, Northampton, Ogle, Paint, Quemahoning, Shade, Somerset, Southampton, Stonycreek, Summit and Upper Turkeyfoot and the *Boroughs* of Addison, Benson, Berlin, Boswell, Callimont, Casselman, Central City, Confluence, Garrett, Hooversville, Indian Lake, Jennerstown, Meyersdale, New Baltimore, New Centerville, Paint, Rockwood, Salisbury, Seven Springs, Shanksville, Somerset, Stoystown, Ursina and Wellersburg. Total population: 236,053. **J. William Lincoln (D)**

33rd. **Adams, Cumberland, Franklin, Juniata** and **Perry** Counties. All of **Adams** County; Part of **Cumberland** County consisting of the *Townships* of Hopewell, Shippensburg, Southampton and Upper Mifflin and the *Boroughs* of Newburg and Shippensburg (Cumberland County Portion); All of **Franklin** County; Part of **Juniata** County consisting of the *Townships* of Beale, Lack, Milford, Spruce Hill, Turbett and Tuscarora and the *Boroughs* of Mifflin, Mifflintown and Port Royal and All of **Perry** County. Total population: 239,160. **William J. Moore (R)**

34th. **Cameron, Centre, Clearfield, Clinton, Juniata,** and **Mifflin** Counties. All of **Cameron** County; All of **Centre** County; part of **Clearfield** County consisting of the *Townships* of Bradford, Cooper, Decatur, Graham, Karthaus, Morris and Woodward and the *Boroughs* of Brisbin, Chester Hill, Houtzdale and Osceola; all of **Clinton** County; part of **Juniata** County consisting of the *Townships* of Delaware, Fayette, Fermanagh, Greenwood, Monroe, Susquehanna and Walker and the *Borough* of

Thompsontown and All of **Mifflin** County. Total population: 237,591. **J. Doyle Corman (R)**

35th. **Cambria, Clearfield** and **Somerset** Counties. All of **Cambria** County; part of **Clearfield** County consisting of the *Townships* of Beccaria, Bell, Bigler, Bloom, Boggs, Brady, Burnside, Chest, Covington, Ferguson, Girard, Goshen, Greenwood, Gulich, Huston, Jordan, Knox, Lawrence, Penn, Pike, Pine and Union and the *Boroughs* of Burnside, Clearfield, Coalport, Curwensville, Glenhope, Grampian, Irvona, Lumber City, Mahaffey, New Washington, Newburg, Ramey, Troutville, Wallaceton and Westover and part of **Somerset** County consisting of the *Borough* of Windber. Total population: 235,069. **William J. Stewart (D)**

36th. **Chester** and **Lancaster** Counties. Part of **Chester** County consisting of the *City* of Coatesville and the *Townships* of East Fallowfield, East Marlborough, East Nantmeal, East Nottingham, Elk, Franklin, Highland, Honeybrook, Kennett, London Britain, London Grove, Londonderry, Lower Oxford, New Garden, New London, Newlin, North Coventry, Penn, Sadsbury, South Coventry, Upper Oxford, Valley, Wallace, Warwick, West Brandywine, West Caln, West Fallowfield, West Marlborough, West Nantmeal, West Nottingham and West Sadsbury and the *Boroughs* of Atglen, Avondale, Elverson, Honey Brook, Kennett Square, Modena, Oxford, Parkesburg, South Coatesville and West Grove; and part of **Lancaster** County consisting of the *Townships* of Bart, Brecknock, Caernarvon, Clay, Colerain, Drumore, Earl, East Cocalico, East Drumore, East Earl, East Lampeter, Eden, Elizabeth, Ephrata, Fulton, Leacock, Little Britain, Martic, Paradise, Providence, Sadsbury, Salisbury, Upper Leacock, West Cocalico and West Earl and the *Boroughs* of Adamstown (Lancaster County Portion), Akron, Christiana, Denver, Ephrata, New Holland, Quarryville, and Terre Hill. Total population: 236,208. **Noah W. Wenger (R)**

37th. **Allegheny** and **Washington** Counties. Part of **Allegheny** County consisting of the *Townships* of Baldwin, Collier, Mt. Lebanon, Scott, South Fayette, South Park and Upper St. Clair and the *Boroughs* of Bethel Park, Brentwood, Bridgeville, Carnegie, Castle Shannon, Dormont, Heidelberg, Jefferson, Pleasant Hills, Rosslyn Farms, Thornburg and Whitehall and part of **Washington** County consisting of the *Township* of Peters. Total population: 238,471. **D. Michael Fisher (R)**

38th. **Allegheny** County. Part of **Allegheny** County consisting of the *City* of Pittsburgh (part, Wards 02, 05, 06, 08, 09, 10, 11, 12, 13, 22, 23, 24 and 25) and the *Townships* of Hampton, Indiana, Reserve and Shaler and the *Boroughs* of Aspinwall, Etna, Millvale, Sharpsburg and Wilkinsburg. Total population: 238,826. **Leonard J. Bodack (D)**

39th. **Indiana** and **Westmoreland** Counties. Part of **Indiana** County consisting of the *Townships* of Brush Valley, Buffington, Conemaugh, East Wheatfield and West Wheatfield and the *Boroughs* of Armagh and Saltsburg and part of **Westmoreland** County consisting of the *Cities* of Greensburg and Jeannette and the *Townships* of Bell, Cook, Derry, Donegal, East Huntingdon, Fairfield, Hempfield, Ligonier, Loyalhanna, Mt. Pleasant, Salem, South Huntingdon, St. Clair, Unity, Upper Burrell and Washington and the *Boroughs* of Adamsburg, Arona, Avonmore, Bolivar, Derry, Donegal, Hunker, Latrobe, Ligonier, Mt. Pleasant, New Alexandria, New Florence, New Stanton, Oklahoma, Scottdale, Seward, Smithton, South Greensburg, Southwest Greensburg, West Newton, Youngstown and Youngwood. Total population: 235,791. **James R. Kelley (D)**

40th. **Allegheny, Armstrong** and **Westmoreland** Counties. Part of **Allegheny** County consisting of the *Townships* of Aleppo, East Deer, Fawn, Frazer, Harrison, Kilbuck, Leet, Marshall, McCandless, Neville, Ohio, Pine, Richland, Ross and West Deer and the *Boroughs* of Avalon, Bell Acres, Bellevue, Ben Avon, Ben Avon Heights, Brackenridge, Bradford Woods, Edgeworth, Emsworth, Franklin Park, Glenfield, Haysville, Leetsdale, Osborne, Sewickley, Sewickley Heights, Sewickley Hills, Tarentum and West View; part of **Armstrong** County consisting of the *Townships* of Cadogan, North Buffalo and South Buffalo and the *Boroughs* of Applewold and Freeport and part of **Westmoreland** County consisting of the *Cities* of Arnold, Lower Burrell and New Kensington and the *Township* of Allegheny and the *Boroughs* of East Vandergrift, Hyde Park, Vandergrift and West Leechburg. Total population: 236,736. **John W. Regoli (D)**

41st. **Armstrong, Clarion, Clearfield, Indiana** and **Jefferson** Counties. Part of **Armstrong** County consisting of the *Townships* of Bethel, Boggs, Bradys Bend, Burrell, Cowanshannock, East Franklin, Gilpin,

Hovey, Kiskiminetas, Kittanning, Madison, Mahoning, Manor, Parks, Perry, Pine, Plumcreek, Rayburn, Redbank, South Bend, Sugarcreek, Valley, Washington, Wayne and West Franklin and the *Boroughs* of Apollo, Atwood, Dayton, Elderton, Ford City, Ford Cliff, Kittanning, Leechburg, Manorville, North Apollo, Parker City, Rural Valley, South Bethlehem, West Kittanning and Worthington; part of **Clarion** County consisting of the *Townships* of Brady, Clarion, Limestone, Madison, Millcreek, Monroe, Porter, Red Bank and Toby and the *Boroughs* of Clarion, East Brady, Hawthorn, New Bethlehem, Rimersburg and Strattanville; part of **Clearfield** County consisting of the *City* of DuBois and the *Township* of Sandy and the *Borough* of Falls Creek (Clearfield County Portion); part of **Indiana** County consisting of the *Townships* of Armstrong, Banks, Blacklick, Burrell, Canoe, Center, Cherryhill, East Mahoning, Grant, Green, Montgomery, North Mahoning, Pine, Rayne, South Mahoning, Washington, West Mahoning, White and Young and the *Boroughs* of Blairsville, Cherry Tree, Clymer, Creekside, Ernest, Glen Campbell, Homer City, Indiana, Jacksonville, Marion Center, Plumville, Shelocta and Smicksburg and All of **Jefferson** County. Total population: 238,122. **Patrick J. Stapleton (D)**

42nd. **Allegheny** County. Part of **Allegheny** County consisting of the *City* of Pittsburgh (part, wards 18, 19, 20, 21, 26, 27, 28, 30 and 32) and the *Townships* of Crescent, Findlay, Kennedy, Moon, North Fayette, Robinson and Stowe and the *Boroughs* of Coraopolis, Crafton, Green Tree, Ingram, McDonald (Allegheny County Portion), McKees Rocks, Oakdale and Pennsbury Village. Total population: 236,113. **Eugene F. Scanlon (D)**

43rd. **Allegheny** County. Part of **Allegheny** County consisting of the *City* of Pittsburgh (part, Wards 01, 03, 04, 07, 14, 15, 16, 17, 29 and 31) and the *Township* of Wilkins and the *Boroughs* of Baldwin, Braddock, Chalfant, East Pittsburgh, Homestead, Mt. Oliver, Munhall, North Braddock, Rankin, Turtle Creek, West Homestead, Whitaker and Wilmerding. Total population: 238,722. **James A. Romanelli (D)**

44th. **Allegheny** and **Westmoreland** Counties. Part of **Allegheny** County consisting of the *Townships* of Harmar, North Versailles, O'Hara, Penn Hills and Springdale and the *Boroughs* of Blawnox, Braddock Hills, Cheswick, Churchill, East McKeesport, Edgewood, Forest Hills, Fox Chapel,˙ Monroeville, Oakmont, Pitcairn, Plum, Springdale, Swissvale, Trafford (Allegheny County Portion), Verona, Wall and White Oak and part of **Westmoreland** County consisting of the *Boroughs* of Delmont, Export, Murrysville and Trafford (Westmoreland County Portion). Total population: 236,929. **Frank A. Pecora (R)**

45th. **Allegheny, Washington** and **Westmoreland** Counties. Part of **Allegheny** County consisting of the *Cities* of Clairton, Duquesne and McKeesport and the *Townships* of Elizabeth, Forward and South Versailles and the *Boroughs* of Dravosburg, Elizabeth, Glassport, Liberty, Lincoln, Port Vue, Versailles, West Elizabeth and West Mifflin; part of **Washington** County consisting of the *City* of Monongahela and the *Township* of Carroll and the *Boroughs* of Donora and New Eagle and part of **Westmoreland** County consisting of the *City* of Monessen and the *Townships* of North Huntingdon, Penn, Rostraver and Sewickley and the *Boroughs* of Irwin, Madison, Manor, North Belle Vernon, North Irwin, Penn and Sutersville. Total population: 237,549. **Edward P. Zemprelli (D)**

46th. **Beaver, Greene** and **Washington** Counties. Part of **Beaver** County consisting of the *Townships* of Greene, Hanover, Independence, Potter and Raccoon and the *Boroughs* of Frankfort Springs, Georgetown, Hookstown, Industry and Shippingport; All of **Greene** County and part of **Washington** County consisting of the *City* of Washington and the *Townships* of Amwell, Blaine, Buffalo, Canton, Cecil, Chartiers, Cross Creek, Donegal, East Bethlehem, East Finley, Fallowfield, Hanover, Hopewell, Independence, Jefferson, Morris, Mt. Pleasant, North Bethlehem, North Franklin, North Strabane, Nottingham, Robinson, Smith, Somerset, South Franklin, South Strabane, Union, West Bethlehem, West Finley and West Pike Run and the *Boroughs* of Allenport, Beallsville, Bentleyville, Burgettstown, California, Canonsburg, Centerville, Charleroi, Claysville, Coal Center, Cokeburg, Deemston, Dunlevy, East Washington, Elco, Ellsworth, Finleyville, Green Hills, Houston, Long Branch, Marianna, McDonald (Washington County Portion), Midway, North Charleroi, Roscoe, Speers, Stockdale, Twilight, West Alexander, West Brownsville and West Middletown. Total population: 237,099. **J. Barry Stout (D)**

47th. **Beaver** and **Lawrence** Counties. Part of **Beaver** County consisting of the *City* of Beaver Falls and the *Townships* of Brighton,

Center, Chippewa, Darlington, Daugherty, Franklin, Harmony, Hopewell, Marion, New Sewickley, North Sewickley, Patterson, Pulaski, Rochester, South Beaver, Vanport and White and the *Boroughs* of Aliquippa, Ambridge, Baden, Beaver, Big Beaver, Bridgewater, Conway, Darlington, East Rochester, Eastvale, Economy, Ellwood City (Beaver County Portion), Fallston, Freedom, Glasgow, Homewood, Koppel, Midland, Monaca, New Brighton, New Galilee, Ohioville, Patterson Heights, Rochester, South Heights and West Mayfield and part of **Lawrence** County consisting of the *Townships* of Little Beaver, Mahoning, North Beaver, Perry, Pulaski, Shenango, Slippery Rock, Taylor and Wayne and the *Boroughs* of Bessemer, Ellport, Ellwood City (Lawrence County Portion), Enon Valley, New Beaver, Snpj and Wampum. Total population: 235,111. **James E. Ross (D)**

48th. **Berks, Lebanon** and **Lehigh** Counties. Part of **Berks** County consisting of the *Townships* of Albany, Bern, Bethel, Centre, Greenwich, Heidelberg, Jefferson, Lower Heidelberg, Marion, Maxatawny, North Heidelberg, Penn, Perry, South Heidelberg, Spring, Tilden, Tulpehocken, Upper Bern, Upper Tulpehocken and Windsor and the *Boroughs* of Bernville, Centerport, Hamburg, Kutztown, Leesport, Lenhartsville, Lyons, Robesonia, Shoemakersville, Sinking Spring, Strausstown, Wernersville, West Lawn, Womelsdorf, Wyomissing and Wyomissing Hills; All of **Lebanon** County and part of **Lehigh** County consisting of the *Townships* of Heidelberg, Lowhill, Lynn, North Whitehall, Upper Macungie, Washington and Weisenberg and the *Borough* of Slatington. Total population: 236,220. **David J. Brightbill (R)**

49th. **Erie** County. Part of **Erie** County consisting of the *City* of Erie and the *Townships* of Conneaut, Elk Creek, Fairview, Franklin, Girard, Harborcreek, Lawrence Park, McKean, Millcreek, Springfield, Summit and Washington and the *Boroughs* of Albion, Cranesville, Edinboro, Fairview, Girard, Lake City, McKean, Platea and Wesleyville. Total population: 236,491. **Anthony B. Andrezeski (D)**

50th. **Crawford, Mercer** and **Venango** Counties. All of **Crawford** County; All of **Mercer** County and part of **Venango** County consisting of the *Townships* of Canal, Cherrytree, Frenchcreek, Jackson, Mineral, Oakland, Oil Creek and Plum and the *Boroughs* of Cooperstown, Polk, Sugar Creek and Utica. Total population: 235,750. **Roy W. Wilt (R)**

Population of all districts: 11,866,728

STANDING COMMITTEES OF THE SENATE OF PENNSYLVANIA
SESSIONS OF 1987 and 1988

AGING AND YOUTH (10)
Hopper, *Chairman*
Greenwood, *Vice Chairman*

Loeper	Salvatore	O'Pake
Rhoades	Andrezeski,	Rocks
Shaffer	*Minority Chm.*	Jubelirer, ex-officio
	Reibman	

AGRICULTURE AND RURAL AFFAIRS (10)
Helfrick, *Chairman*
Wenger, *Vice Chairman*

Rhoades	Peterson	Kelley
Wilt	Stapleton,	Afflerbach
Madigan	*Minority Chm.*	Jubelirer, ex-officio
	O'Pake	

APPROPRIATIONS (20)
Tilghman, *Chairman*
Bell, *Vice Chairman*

Holl	Shaffer	Hankins
Stauffer	Rhoades	Stapleton
Hess	Wenger	Lewis
Moore	Brightbill	Romanelli
Corman	Armstrong	Stout
Loeper	Fumo,	Musto
	Minority Chm.	Jubelirer, ex-officio

BANKING AND INSURANCE (10)
Holl, *Chairman*
Helfrick, *Vice Chairman*

Hess	Salvatore	Lewis
Loeper	Lynch,	Scanlon
Pecora	*Minority Chm.*	Jubelirer, ex-officio
	O'Pake	

COMMUNITY AND ECONOMIC DEVELOPMENT (10)
Shaffer, *Chairman*
Salvatore, *Vice Chairman*

Pecora	Greenwood	Jones
Armstrong	Romanelli,	Stewart
Peterson	*Minority Chm.*	Jubelirer, ex-officio
	Ross	

CONSUMER PROTECTION AND PROFESSIONAL LICENSURE (10)
Bell, *Chairman*
Shumaker, *Vice Chairman*

Moore	Peterson	Hankins
Greenleaf	Bodack,	Andrezeski
Armstrong	*Minority Chm.*	Jubelirer, ex-officio
	Reibman	

EDUCATION (10)
Hess, *Chairman*
Rhoades, *Vice Chairman*

Greenleaf	Madigan	Rocks
Shumaker	Reibman,	Regoli
Armstrong	*Minority Chm.*	Jubelirer, ex-officio
	Lincoln	

ENVIRONMENTAL RESOURCES AND ENERGY (10)
Fisher, *Chairman*
Brightbill, *Vice Chairman*

Holl	Greenwood	Kelley
Greenleaf	Musto,	Lincoln
Rhoades	*Minority Chm.*	Jubelirer, ex-officio
	Stapleton	

FINANCE (10)
Armstrong, *Chairman*
Moore, *Vice Chairman*

Tilghman	Helfrick	Fumo
Stauffer	Kelley,	Andrezeski
Loeper	*Minority Chm.*	Jubelirer, ex-officio
	Lynch	

GAME AND FISHERIES (10)

Rhoades, *Chairman*
Madigan, *Vice Chairman*

Moore	Peterson	Andrezeski
Helfrick	Regoli,	Stewart
Wilt	*Minority Chm.*	Jubelirer, ex-officio
	Stout	

JUDICIARY (10)

Greenleaf, *Chairman*
Fisher, *Vice Chairman*

Hopper	Lemmond	Rocks
Brightbill	O'Pake	Williams
Shumaker	*Minority Chm.*	Jubelirer, ex-officio
	Lewis	

LABOR AND INDUSTRY (10)

Madigan, *Chairman*
Hopper, *Vice Chairman*

Moore	Brightbill	Bodack
Corman	Rocks,	Musto
Wenger	*Minority Chm.*	Jubelirer, ex-officio
	Lynch	

LAW AND JUSTICE (10)

Shumaker, *Chairman*
Greenleaf, *Vice Chairman*

Tilghman	Salvatore	Fumo
Shaffer	Scanlon,	Musto
Fisher	*Minority Chm.*	Jubelirer, ex-officio
	Mellow	

LOCAL GOVERNMENT (10)

Pecora, *Chairman*
Corman, *Vice Chairman*

Wenger	Greenwood	Stout
Madigan	Afflerbach,	Regoli
Lemmond	*Minority Chm.*	Jubelirer, ex-officio
	Reibman	

MILITARY AND VETERANS AFFAIRS (10)

Wilt, *Chairman*
Pecora, *Vice Chairman*

Bell	Lemmond	Ross
Hopper	Hankins,	Bodack
Helfrick	*Minority Chm.*	Jubelirer, ex-officio
	Stapleton	

PUBLIC HEALTH AND WELFARE (10)

Peterson, *Chairman*
Lemmond, *Vice Chairman*

Hopper	Greenwood	Afflerbach
Corman	Williams,	Stewart
Brightbill	*Minority Chm.*	Jubelirer, ex-officio
	Jones	

RULES AND EXECUTIVE NOMINATIONS (15)

Stauffer, *Chairman*
Loeper, *Vice Chairman*

Bell	Fisher	Mellow
Holl	Wilt	Ross
Tilghman	Brightbill	Bodack
Hess	Zemprelli,	Williams
Moore	*Minority Chm.*	Jubelirer, ex-officio

STATE GOVERNMENT (10)

Wenger, *Chairman*
Lemmond, *Vice Chairman*

Bell	Shaffer	Fumo
Hess	Lewis,	Stewart
Pecora	*Minority Chm.*	Jubelirer, ex-officio
	Mellow	

TRANSPORTATION (10)

Corman, *Chairman*
Holl, *Vice Chairman*

Bell	Wilt	Scanlon
Stauffer	Stout,	Romanelli
Fisher	*Minority Chm.*	Jubelirer, ex-officio
	Lynch	

URBAN AFFAIRS AND HOUSING (10)

Salvatore, *Chairman*
Shaffer, *Vice Chairman*

Tilghman	Lemmond	Romanelli
Pecora	Jones,	Williams
Shumaker	*Minority Chm.*	Jubelirer, ex-officio
	Zemprelli	

SENATE STANDING COMMITTEE ASSIGNMENTS

Afflerbach, Roy C.
Local Government,
  Minority Chairman
Agriculture & Rural Affairs
Public Health & Welfare

Andrezeski, Anthony B.
Aging & Youth,
  Minority Chairman
Consumer Protection &
  Professional Licensure
Finance
Game & Fisheries

Armstrong, Gibson E.
Finance, *Chairman*
Appropriations
Community & Economic Development
Consumer Protection &
  Professional Licensure
Education

Bell, Clarence D.
Consumer Protection &
  Professional Licensure, *Chairman*
Appropriations, *Vice Chairman*
Military & Veterans Affairs
Rules & Executive Nominations
State Government
Transportation

Bodack, Leonard J.
Consumer Protection & Professional
  Licensure, *Minority Chairman*
Labor & Industry
Military & Veterans Affairs
Rules & Executive Nominations

Brightbill, David J.
Environmental Resources & Energy,
  Vice Chairman
Appropriations
Judiciary
Labor & Industry
Public Health & Welfare
Rules & Executive Nominations

Corman, J. Doyle
Transportation, *Chairman*
Local Government, *Vice Chairman*
Appropriations
Labor & Industry
Public Health & Welfare

Fisher, D. Michael
Environmental Resources & Energy,
  Chairman
Judiciary, *Vice Chairman*
Law & Justice
Rules & Executive Nominations
Transportation

Fumo, Vincent J.
Appropriations, *Minority Chairman*
Finance
Law & Justice
State Government

Greenleaf, Stewart J.
Judiciary, *Chairman*
Law & Justice, *Vice Chairman*
Consumer Protection &
  Professional Licensure
Education
Environmental Resources & Energy

Greenwood, James C.
Aging & Youth, *Vice Chairman*
Community & Economic Development
Environmental Resources & Energy
Local Government
Public Health & Welfare

Hankins, Freeman
Military & Veterans Affairs,
  Minority Chairman
Appropriations
Consumer Protection &
  Professional Licensure

Helfrick, Edward W.
Agriculture & Rural Affairs, *Chairman*
Banking & Insurance, *Vice Chairman*
Finance
Game & Fisheries
Military & Veterans Affairs

Hess, Ralph W.
Education, *Chairman*
Appropriations
Banking & Insurance
Rules & Executive Nominations
State Government

Holl, Edwin G.
Banking & Insurance, *Chairman*
Transportation, *Vice Chairman*
Appropriations
Environmental Resources & Energy
Rules & Executive Nominations

Hopper, John D.
Aging & Youth, *Chairman*
Labor & Industry, *Vice Chairman*
Judiciary
Military & Veterans Affairs
Public Health & Welfare

Jones, Roxanne H.
Urban Affairs & Housing, *Minority Chairman*
Community & Economic Development
Public Health & Welfare

Jubelirer, Robert C.
President Pro Tempore and Member ex-
  officio of all Standing Committees

Kelley, James R.
Finance, *Minority Chairman*
Agriculture & Rural Affairs
Environmental Resources & Energy

Lemmond, Charles D., Jr.
Public Health & Welfare, *Vice Chairman*
State Government, *Vice Chairman*
Judiciary
Local Government
Military & Veterans Affairs
Urban Affairs & Housing

Lewis, H. Craig
State Government, *Minority Chairman*
Appropriations
Banking & Insurance
Judiciary

Lincoln, J. William
Education
Environmental Resources & Energy

Loeper, F. Joseph
Rules & Executive Nominations,
  Vice Chairman
Aging & Youth
Appropriations
Banking & Insurance
Finance

Lynch, Francis J.
Banking & Insurance, *Minority Chairman*
Finance
Labor & Industry
Transportation

Madigan, Roger A.
Labor & Industry, *Chairman*
Game & Fisheries, *Vice Chairman*
Agriculture & Rural Affairs
Education
Local Government

Mellow, Robert J.
Law & Justice
Rules & Executive Nominations
State Government

Moore, William J.
Finance, *Vice Chairman*
Appropriations
Consumer Protection &
  Professional Licensure
Game & Fisheries
Labor & Industry
Rules & Executive Nominations

Musto, Raphael J.
Environmental Resources & Energy,
  Minority Chairman
Appropriations
Labor & Industry
Law & Justice

O'Pake, Michael A.
Judiciary, *Minority Chairman*
Aging & Youth
Agriculture & Rural Affairs
Banking & Insurance

Pecora, Frank A.
Local Government, *Chairman*
Military & Veterans Affairs,
  Vice Chairman
Banking & Insurance
Community & Economic Development
State Government
Urban Affairs & Housing

Peterson, John E.
Public Health & Welfare, *Chairman*
Agriculture & Rural Affairs
Community & Economic Development
Consumer Protection &
   Professional Licensure
Game & Fisheries

Regoli, John W.
Game & Fisheries, *Minority Chairman*
Education
Local Government

Reibman, Jeanette F.
Education, *Minority Chairman*
Aging & Youth
Consumer Protection &
   Professional Licensure
Local Government

Rhoades, James J.
Game & Fisheries, *Chairman*
Education, *Vice Chairman*
Aging & Youth
Agriculture & Rural Affairs
Appropriations
Environmental Resources & Energy

Rocks, M. Joseph
Labor & Industry, *Minority Chairman*
Aging & Youth
Education
Judiciary

Romanelli, James A.
Community & Economic Development,
   Minority Chairman
Appropriations
Transportation
Urban Affairs & Housing

Ross, James E.
Community & Economic Development
Military & Veterans Affairs
Rules & Executive Nominations

Salvatore, Frank A.
Urban Affairs & Housing, *Chairman*
Community & Economic Development,
   Vice Chairman
Aging & Youth
Banking & Insurance
Law & Justice

Scanlon, Eugene F.
Law & Justice, *Minority Chairman*
Banking & Insurance
Transportation

Shaffer, Tim
Community & Economic Development,
   Chairman
Urban Affairs & Housing, *Vice Chairman*
Aging & Youth
Appropriations
Law & Justice
State Government

Shumaker, John J.
Law & Justice, *Chairman*
Consumer Protection & Professional
   Licensure, *Vice Chairman*
Education
Judiciary
Urban Affairs & Housing

Stapleton, Patrick J.
Agriculture & Rural Affairs,
   Minority Chairman
Appropriations
Environmental Resources & Energy
Military & Veterans Affairs

Stauffer, John
Rules & Executive Nominations,
   Chairman
Appropriations
Finance
Transportation

Stewart, William J.
Community & Economic Development
Game & Fisheries
Public Health & Welfare
State Government

Stout, J. Barry
Transportation, *Minority Chairman*
Appropriations
Game & Fisheries
Local Government

Tilghman, Richard A.
Appropriations, *Chairman*
Finance
Law & Justice
Rules & Executive Nominations
Urban Affairs & Housing

Wenger, Noah W.
State Government, *Chairman*
Agriculture & Rural Affairs,
   Vice Chairman
Appropriations
Labor & Industry
Local Government

Williams, Hardy
Public Health & Welfare, *Minority Chairman*
Judiciary
Rules & Executive Nominations
Urban Affairs & Housing

Wilt, Roy W.
Military & Veterans Affairs, *Chairman*
Agriculture & Rural Affairs
Game & Fisheries
Rules & Executive Nominations
Transportation

Zemprelli, Edward P.
Rules & Executive Nominations,
   Minority Chairman
Urban Affairs & Housing

RULES OF THE SENATE OF PENNSYLVANIA
(OPERATING RULES FOR 1987 SESSION)

I SESSIONS

Regular and Special
1. The General Assembly shall be a continuing body during the term for which its Representatives are elected. It shall meet at twelve o'clock noon on the first Tuesday of January each year. Special sessions shall be called by the Governor on petition of a majority of the members elected to each House or may be called by the Governor whenever in his opinion the public interest requires. (Const. of Pa., Art. 2, Sec. 4)

Weekly
2. The Senate shall convene its weekly sessions on Monday unless the Senate shall otherwise direct.

II PRESIDENT
The Lieutenant Governor shall be President of the Senate. (Const. of Pa., Art. 4, Sec. 4)

III DUTIES OF THE PRESIDENT
1. **The President shall —**

(a) take the chair on every legislative day precisely at the hour to which the Senate stands adjourned, immediately call the Senators to order, and on the appearance of a quorum proceed with the Order of Business of the Senate;

(b) while in session have general direction of the Senate Chamber. It shall be his duty to preserve order and decorum, and, in case of disturbance or disorderly conduct in the Chamber or galleries, may cause the same to be cleared. When in his opinion there arises a case of extreme disturbance or emergency he shall, with the concurrence of the President Pro Tempore, the Majority and Minority Leaders, adjourn the Senate. Such adjournment shall not extend beyond the limitation imposed by Article 2, Section 14 of the Constitution;

(c) during debate, prevent personal reflections and confine Senators, in debate, to the question;

(d) decide, when two or more Senators arise, who shall be first to speak;

(e) in the presence of the Senate, sign all bills and joint resolutions which have passed both Houses after their titles have been read;

(f) sign resolutions, orders, writs, warrants and subpoenas issued by order of the Senate and shall be attested by the Secretary of the Senate, or, in his absence, by the Chief Clerk the fact of signing shall be entered in the Journal;

(g) refer to the appropriate standing committee, every bill and joint resolution which may be introduced in the Senate or received from the House of Representatives. Such referral shall be at his convenience but not later than the succeeding legislative day;

(h) decide all points of order, subject to appeal, giving, however, any member called to order the right to extenuate or justify. Debate shall not be permitted unless there be an appeal from a decision of the President in which event he shall submit the question to the whole Senate for decision. He shall submit points of order involving the constitutionality of any matter to the Senate for decision. Questions of order submitted to the Senate may be debated;

(i) deliver to the House with appropriate message all Senate and House bills within twenty-four hours after final passage thereof in the Senate. All Senate Bills returned by the House after final passage therein without amendment, and all conference committee reports or Senate Bills received from the House and adopted by the Senate, shall be signed by the presiding officer within one legislative day after receipt or adoption. The same shall be delivered to the House within twenty-four hours thereafter.

IV PRESIDENT PRO TEMPORE
1. At the beginning and close of each regular session and at such other times as may be necessary, the Senate shall elect one of its members President Pro Tempore, who shall perform the duties of the Lieutenant Governor in any case of absence or disability of that officer, and whenever said office shall be vacant. (Const. of Pa., Art. 2, Sec. 9)

V DUTIES OF PRESIDENT PRO TEMPORE
1. **The President Pro Tempore shall —**

(a) appoint the Chairmen, Vice-Chairmen and members of the Standing Committees of the Senate as soon after his election as possible;

(b) appoint members to special committees whenever authorized;

(c) fill all vacancies occurring in standing and special committees;

(d) appoint and have under his direction such Senate employes as are authorized by law;

(e) vote last on all questions when occupying the Chair.

2. **He may —**

(a) name any Senator to preside in the absence of the President, or if both the President and President Pro Tempore are absent the Majority Leader, or his designee, shall preside. The Majority Leader, during such time, shall be vested with all powers of the President. This authority shall not extend beyond a day's adjournment.

VI OTHER OFFICERS
1. Each House shall choose its other officers. (Const. of Pa., Art. 2, Sec. 9)

VII DUTIES OF THE SECRETARY-PARLIAMENTARIAN
1. At the beginning of each regular session convening in an odd-numbered year and at other times as may be necessary, the Senate shall elect a Secretary-Parliamentarian of the Senate.

2. **The Secretary-Parliamentarian of the Senate shall —**

(a) assist the presiding officer in conducting the business of the session;

(b) act in the capacity of Parliamentarian;

(c) have under his direction the following functions: (1) Amending bills in the Senate; (2) preparing and publishing the Senate Calendar; (3) publication of the Senate History; (4) numbering Senate bills as they are introduced and causing them to be distributed to the chairman of the committee to which they are referred and receiving a receipt for same; (5) printing of bills;

(d) keep a record of the Senate action on a bill on a special record sheet attached to the bill after it has been reported from committee;

(e) transmit all bills, joint resolutions, concurrent resolutions and appropriate memorials to the House of Representatives within twenty-four hours of final passage, and each shall be accompanied by a message stating the title to the measure being transmitted and requesting concurrence of the House;

(f) attest all writs, warrants and subpoenas issued by order of the Senate; certify as to the passage of Senate Bills and the approval of executive nominations;

(g) be in charge of the Senate Library and assist Senators by making reference material available to them;

(h) perform any duties assigned to the Senate Librarian by any statute;

(i) supervise the Chief Sergeant-at-Arms and the Senate Bill Room, the Senate Print Shop, the Official Reporter's Office and the Senate Page Service.

VIII DUTIES OF THE CHIEF CLERK
1. At the beginning of each regular session convening in an odd-numbered year and whenever necessary, the Senate shall elect a Chief Clerk of the Senate.

2. The Chief Clerk shall be the chief fiscal officer of the Senate and shall perform those duties prescribed in section 2.4 of the act of January 10, 1968 (1967 P.L. 925, No. 417), referred to as the Legislative Officers and Employes Law. In addition he shall perform those powers and duties prescribed in the Financial Operating Rules of the Senate. In the absence

of the Secretary, the Chief Clerk shall attest all writs, warrants and subpoenas issued by order of the Senate and shall certify as to the passage of Senate Bills and the approval of executive nominations.

IX DUTIES OF THE LIBRARIAN

Rule IX deleted pursuant to Senate Resolution Number 54, Adopted July 1, 1981.

X DUTIES OF THE SERGEANT-AT-ARMS

1. The Chief Sergeant-at-Arms shall —

(a) be constantly in attendance during the sessions of the Senate except when absent in discharging his other duties;

(b) have charge of and direct the work of the Assistant Sergeant-at-Arms;

(c) serve all subpoenas and warrants issued by the Senate or any duly authorized officer or committee;

(d) be in charge of assembling and distributing bills, calendars, histories, and journals as they are printed;

(e) be empowered to reasonably limit the number of bills distributed to any one person at any one time;

(f) maintain order, at the direction of the presiding officer, in the Senate Chamber and adjoining rooms;

(g) see that no person, except those authorized to do so, disturbs or interferes with the desks of the Senators or officers, or with books, papers, etc., thereat;

(h) exclude from the floor all persons not entitled to the privilege of the same;

(i) have charge of all entrances to the Chamber during the sessions of the Senate and shall see that the doors are properly attended;

(j) announce, upon recognition by the presiding officer, all important messages and committees;

(k) escort the Senate to all Joint meetings with the mace;

(l) escort the Senate Committee appointed to attend funeral services of members or former members of the Senate with the mace.

XI ORDER OF BUSINESS

1. The Order of Business to be observed in taking up business shall be as follows:

First	— Call to Order.
Second	— Prayer by the Chaplain of the Senate.
Third	— Reading of the Journal of the preceding day.
Fourth	— Asking of leaves of absence. No Senator shall absent himself without leave of the Senate, first obtained, unless prevented from attendance by sickness, or other sufficient cause.
Fifth	— Reading of Communications.
Sixth	— Receiving reports of committees.
Seventh	— Reading of bills in place at which time they shall not be subject to debate or remarks. All bills in place shall be accompanied by three copies of the same. Bills not introduced at this time will be accepted and will be referred to committee and processed not later than the next succeeding legislative day.
Eighth	— Offering of original resolutions.
Ninth	— Consideration of Executive Nominations.
Tenth	— Consideration of the Calendar. Any bill or resolution on the calendar not finally acted upon within ten legislative days shall be recommitted to the committee which reported the same to the calendar; any bill or resolution on the calendar which cannot, by its status, be recommitted shall be removed from the calendar and laid on the table, unless the Senate shall otherwise direct.
Eleventh	— Unfinished Business. Reports of Committees. Congratulatory and condolence resolutions.
Twelfth	— First consideration of bills reported from committee and in this state shall not be subject to amendment or a vote thereon.
Thirteenth	— Introduction of Petitions and Remonstrances.
Fourteenth	— Announcements by the Secretary.
Fifteenth	— Adjournment.

Special Order of Business

2. Any subject may, by a vote of a majority of the members present, be made a special order; and when the time so fixed for its consideration arrives, the presiding officer shall lay it before the Senate.

XII ORDER AND DECORUM

Recognition

1. When any Senator desires to speak or deliver any matter to the Senate, he shall rise at his desk and respectfully address himself to "Mr. President," and on being recognized, may address the Senate preferably at a microphone conveniently located on the floor, and shall confine himself to the question under debate, avoiding personalities.

Speaking Out of Order

2. If any Senator, in speaking or otherwise shall transgress the rules of the Senate, the President shall, or any Senator may through the Chair, call him to order.

Time of Speaking

3. No Senator shall speak more than once on one question, to the prevention of any other who has not spoken and is desirous to speak; nor more than twice without leave of the Senate.

Decorum

4. While the President is putting a question no member shall walk out or across the hall nor when a Senator is speaking pass between him and the Chair, and during the session of the Senate no Senator shall remain at the clerk's desk during the calling of the roll or the tabulating thereof.

Order and Privilege

5. No Senator speaking shall be interrupted by another except by a call to order, or by a question of privilege, or by a call for the previous question, without the consent of the Senator speaking, and no Senator shall speak on a question after it is put to a vote.

Questions of Order

6. The presiding officer shall decide all questions of order, subject to appeal by any member. No debate shall be allowed on questions of order, unless there be an appeal. A second point of order on the same general subject, but not the same point, is not in order while an appeal is pending, but when the first appeal is decided, laid on the table or otherwise disposed of, the second point of order is in order and is subject to appeal. While an appeal is pending no other business is in order. It is within the discretion of the presiding officer as to whether he will vacate the Chair on an appeal from his decision.

Question When Interrupted

7. A question regularly before the Senate can be interrupted only by a call for the previous question, for amendment, postponement, to lay on the table, commitment, or adjournment.

XIII MOTIONS

Putting a Motion

1. When a motion is made, it shall, before debate, be stated by the President. Every motion made to the Senate and entertained by the President shall be reduced to writing on the demand of any member, and shall be entered on the Journal with the name of the Senator making it unless it is withdrawn the same day. A motion may be withdrawn by the member making it before amendment, postponement, an order to lie on the table, or decision.

Precedence of Motions

2. Motions shall take precedence in the following order:

1. Adjourn.
2. Previous question.
3. Recess.
4. Privilege.
5. Orders of the day.
6. Lay on the table.
7. Limit, close or extend limit on debate.

8. Postpone.
9. Commit or recommit.
10. Amend.
11. Main motion.

Non-Debatable Motions
3. Non-debatable motions are:
1. Adjourn or recess.
2. Previous question.
3. Lay on table.
4. Orders of the day.
5. Limit, close or extend limit on debate.

Motions Which Permit Limited Debate
4. On the motion to postpone, the question of postponement is open to debate, but the main question is not.

5. The motion to commit or recommit to committee is debatable as to the propriety of the reference, but the main question is not open to debate.

6. The motion to amend is debatable on the amendments only and does not open the main question to debate.

Seconding Motions
7. All motions except for the previous questions (which shall be moved by not less than four Senators) and reconsideration, may be made without a second.

Motion to Adjourn or Recess
8. A motion to adjourn shall always be in order, excepting when on the call for the previous question, the main question shall have been ordered to be now put, or when a Member has the floor and shall be decided without debate.

A motion to adjourn, adopted and not having a reconvening time, the Senate will meet the following day at 10:00 A.M.

Motion for Previous Question
9. Pending the consideration of any question before the Senate, a Senator may call for the previous question, and if seconded by four Senators, the President shall submit the question: "Shall the main question now be put?" If a majority vote is in favor of it, the main question shall be ordered, the effect of which shall cut off all further amendments and debate, and bring the Senate to a direct vote. First upon the pending amendments and motions, if there be any, then upon the main proposition. The previous question may be ordered on any pending amendment or motion before the Senate.

Motion to Lay on Table
10. The motion to lay on the table is not debatable and the effect of the adoption of this motion is to place on the table the pending question and everything adhering to it. Questions laid on the table remain there for the entire session unless taken up before the session closes.

Motion to Take from Table
11. A motion to take from the table, a bill or other subject, is in order under the same order of business in which the matter was tabled. It shall be decided without debate or amendment.

Reconsideration
12. When a question has once been made and carried in the affirmative or negative, it shall be in order for any two members to move the reconsideration thereof. When the Senate has been equally divided on a question, or a bill shall have failed to pass, by reason of not having a constitutional majority, it shall be in order for any two members to move the reconsideration thereof.

Provided, however, that no motion for the reconsideration of any vote shall be in order after a bill, resolution, report, amendment or motion upon which the vote was taken shall have gone out of the possession of the Senate.

Provided, further, that no motion for reconsideration shall be in order unless made on the same day on which the vote was taken, or within the next five days of actual session of the Senate thereafter.

A motion to reconsider the same question cannot be reconsidered a third time. Identical bills cannot be considered at the same session.

When a bill, resolution, report, amendment, order, or message, upon which a vote has been taken, shall have gone out of the possession of the Senate and been communicated to the House of Representatives, or to the Governor, the motion to reconsider shall not be in order until a resolution has been passed to request the House or Governor to return the same and the same shall have been returned to the possession of the Senate.

XIV BILLS
Passage of Bills
1. (a) No law shall be passed except by bill, and no bill shall be so altered or amended, on its passage through either House, as to change its original purpose. (Const. of Pa., Art. 3, Sec. 1)

(b) No alteration or amendment shall be considered which is not appropriate and closely allied to the original purpose of the bill.

Reference and Printing
2. No bill shall be considered unless referred to a committee, printed for the use of the members and returned therefrom. (Const. of Pa., Art. 3, Sec. 2)

Form of Bills
3. No bill shall be passed containing more than one subject, which shall be clearly expressed in its title, except a general appropriation bill or a bill codifying or compiling the law or a part thereof. (Const. of Pa., Art. 3, Sec. 3)

Consideration of Bills
4. Every bill shall be considered on three different days in each House. All amendments made thereto shall be printed for the use of the members before the final vote is taken on the bill and before the final vote is taken, upon written request addressed to the presiding officer of either House by at least twenty-five per cent of the members elected to that House, any bill shall be read at length in that House. No bill shall become a law, unless on its final passage the vote is taken by yeas and nays, the names of the persons voting for and against it are entered on the Journal, and a majority of the members elected to each House is recorded thereon as voting in its favor. (Const. of Pa., Art. 3, Sec. 4)

Local and Special Bills
5. No local or special bill shall be passed unless notice of the intention to apply therefor shall have been published in the locality where the matter or the thing to be effected may be situated, which notice shall be at least thirty days prior to the introduction into the General Assembly of such bill and in the manner to be provided by law; the evidence of such notice having been published, shall be exhibited in the General Assembly, before such act shall be passed. (Const. of Pa., Art. 3, Sec. 7)

Revenue Bills
6. All bills for raising revenue shall originate in the House of Representatives, but the Senate may propose amendments as in other bills. (Const. of Pa., Art. 3, Sec. 10)

Appropriation Bills
7. (a) The general appropriation bill shall embrace nothing but appropriations for the executive, legislative and judicial departments of the Commonwealth, for the public debt and for public schools. All other appropriations shall be made by separate bills, each embracing but one subject. (Const. of Pa., Art. 3, Sec. 11)

(b) No appropriation shall be made for charitable, educational or benevolent purposes to any person or community nor to any denomination and sectarian institution, corporation or association: Provided, That appropriations may be made for pensions or gratuities for military service and to blind persons twenty-one years of age and upwards and for assistance to mothers having dependent children and to aged persons without adequate means of support and in the form of scholarship grants or loans for higher educational purposes to residents of the Commonwealth enrolled in institutions of higher learning except that no scholarship, grants or loans for higher educational purposes shall be given to persons enrolled in a theological seminary or school of theology. (Const. of Pa., Art. 3, Sec. 29)

Charitable and Educational Appropriations

8. No appropriation shall be made to any charitable or educational institution not under the absolute control of the Commonwealth, other than normal schools established by law for the professional training of teachers for the public schools of the State, except by a vote of two-thirds of all the members elected to each House. (Const. of Pa., Art. 3, Sec. 30)

Land Transfer Legislation

8.1 No bills granting or conveying Commonwealth land or taking title thereto shall be reported by any Committee of the Senate unless there has been filed with the Secretary-Parliamentarian and the Chairman of the reporting Committee, a memorandum from the Department of General Services indicating the use to which the property is presently employed, the full consideration for the transfer, if any, a departmental appraisal of the property, including its valuation and a list of recorded liens and encumbrances, if any, the use to which the property will be employed upon its transfer, the date by which the land is needed for its new use, and the senatorial district or districts in which the land is located. The memorandum shall be filed within 60 days after a request is made for same and contain a statement by a responsible person in the Department of General Services indicating whether or not the departments involved favor the transfer which is the subject of the bill under consideration.

Consideration — Second Regular Session

9. All bills, joint resolutions, resolutions, concurrent resolutions, or other matters pending before the Senate upon the adjournment sine die of a first regular session convening in an odd-numbered year shall maintain their status and be pending before a second regular session convening in an even-numbered year but not beyond adjournment sine die or November 30th of such year whichever first occurs.

Introduction

10. All bills shall be introduced in quintuplicate. A sponsor may be added after a bill has been printed but the addition of sponsors shall not require that the bill be reprinted. All bills shall be examined by the Legislative Reference Bureau for correctness as to form and shall be imprinted with the stamp of the Bureau, before being accepted by the President for introduction.

Character of Bills in Place — Etcetera

11. No member shall read in place, nor shall any committee report any bill for the action of the Senate, proposing to legislate upon any of the subjects prohibited by the thirty-second section of the third article of the Constitution; nor shall any bill be read in place or reported from a committee, reviving, amending, or extending the provisions of any law, by reference to its title only, but the whole shall be reenacted in words by such bill.

Reference to Committee by President

12. Every bill and joint resolution which may be introduced by a Senator or which may be received from the House of Representatives, shall, after being presented to the Chair, be referred by the President to the appropriate committee, but not later than the succeeding legislative day.

Printing of Amended Bills

13. All bills reported or re-reported from committee, if amended by the committee, and all bills on the Calendar, if amended by the Senate, shall be reprinted and a new printer's number assigned thereto before any action is taken thereon.

Any bill or resolution re-reported from committee as amended shall not be finally considered until it has appeared on the Senate Calendar for two legislative days. Such bills shall appear under a separate heading on the Senate Calendar.

First Consideration

14. Bills on first consideration shall not be subject to amendment, debate or a vote thereon.

Second Consideration

15. Bills on second consideration shall be subject to amendment, debate and a vote thereon.

Third Consideration and Final Passage

16. (a) Bills on third consideration shall not be amended unless by unanimous consent and are subject to debate. Bills on final passage may not be amended but are open to debate. The vote on final passage shall be taken by a roll call and the names of the elected Senators voting for and against recorded and entered in the Journal. No bill shall be declared passed unless a majority of all Senators elected to the Senate shall be recorded as voting for the same.

(b) No bill which may require an expenditure of Commonwealth funds or funds of any political subdivision shall be given third consideration reading on the Calendar until it has been referred to the Appropriations Committee, and a fiscal note has been attached thereto.

(c) In obtaining the information required by these rules, the Appropriations Committee may utilize the services of the Budget Office and any other State agency as may be necessary.

17. It shall not be in order, by suspension of this rule or otherwise, to consider a bill on final passage unless it is printed, together with amendments, if any, and placed on the desks of the Senators.

Appropriation Bills for Charitable Purposes

18. No bills appropriating money for charitable or benevolent purposes shall be considered finally until after the general appropriation bill shall have been reported from committee.

Pre-Filing

19. Senators may, on days when the Senate is not in session or in the period between sine die adjournment of a First Regular Session and the convening of a Second Regular Session, introduce bills, joint resolutions and resolutions by filing the same with the Secretary-Parliamentarian of the Senate. The Secretary-Parliamentarian of the Senate shall notify the President of the fact of such filing. The President shall refer the bills, joint resolutions or resolutions to the appropriate committees as soon as possible but not later than two weeks from the time of notification of filing. Upon referral, the Parliamentarian of the Senate shall deliver said bills, joint resolutions or resolutions to the committees to which they have been referred. The Secretary-Parliamentarian of the Senate shall have the bills or joint resolutions printed for distribution and notification of such filing shall be given to the Members and news media in the usual manner.

20. Any Member of the Senate or Member-elect of the Senate may file bills with the Secretary-Parliamentarian of the Senate commencing on December 15 of each even numbered year. The Secretary-Parliamentarian of the Senate shall number the bills in the order received, print and distribute such measures in the usual custom and give notification of such filing to the Members and news media.

21. Upon the naming of the committees and subcommittees of the Senate at the convening of a First Regular Session the President shall refer all pre-filed measures to the proper committee, announcing the number, sponsors and committee referred to the Senate.

XV AMENDMENTS
When in Order

1. Amendments shall be in order when a bill is reported or re-reported from committee, on second consideration and by unanimous consent on third consideration. No amendments shall be received by the presiding officer or considered by the Senate which destroys the general sense of the original bill, or is not appropriate and closely allied to the original purpose of the bill. Any member upon request must be furnished a copy of a proposed amendment and be given a reasonable opportunity to consider same before being required to vote thereon.

2. Amendments offered on the floor shall be read by the clerk and stated by the presiding officer to the Senate before being acted upon. Amendments shall be presented in ten typewritten copies, the original of which shall be signed by the Sponsor.

Amendments Reconsidering-Revert to Prior Print

3. Amendments adopted or defeated may not be again considered without reconsidering the vote by which said amendments were adopted or defeated, unless a majority vote of the Senators present shall decide to revert to a prior printer's number. If such a motion is made to a bill on third consideration and carried it shall not be in order to vote on the final passage of said bill until a copy of the reverted printer's number is placed on the Senator's desk.

Concurrence in House Amendments

4. No amendments to bills by the House shall be concurred in by the Senate, except by the vote of a majority of the members elected to the Senate, taken by yeas and nays. (Const. of Pa., Art. 3, Sec. 5)

5. The vote on concurring in bills amended by the House shall not be taken until said bills have been placed on the files of Senators and particularly referred to on their calendars unless by unanimous consent the Senate shall decide otherwise.

XVI COMMITTEES

1. There shall be the following permanent Standing committees, the Chairmen, the Vice-Chairmen and members thereof to be appointed by the President Pro Tempore as soon as possible after his election in sessions convening in odd-numbered years. The composition of each Standing Committee shall reasonably reflect the party composition of the Senate membership.

Aging and Youth — 10 members
Agriculture and Rural Affairs — 10 members
Appropriations — 20 members
Banking and Insurance — 10 members
Community and Economic Development — 10 members
Consumer Protection and Professional Licensure —
   10 members
Education — 10 members
Environmental Resources and Energy — 10 members
Finance — 10 members
Game and Fisheries — 10 members
Judiciary — 10 members
Labor and Industry — 10 members
Law and Justice — 10 members
Local Government — 10 members
Military and Veterans Affairs — 10 members
Public Health and Welfare — 10 members
Rules and Executive Nominations — 15 members
State Government — 10 members
Transportation — 10 members
Urban Affairs and Housing — 10 members

President Pro Tempore-ex-officio

2. The President Pro Tempore shall be ex-officio and a voting member of all standing committees and subcommittees and not included in the number of committee members herein provided. Except that, the President Pro Tempore shall not be an ex-officio member of the Committee on Ethics and Official Conduct.

Committees' Function Between Sessions

3. Permanent standing committees shall exist and function both during and between sessions. Such power shall not extend beyond November 30th of any even-numbered year.

Subcommittees

4. Each standing committee or the chairman thereof may appoint, from time to time, a subcommittee to study or investigate a matter falling within the jurisdiction of the standing committee or to consider a bill or resolution referred to it. Subcommittees shall be regulated by the Senate Rules of Procedure and shall be in existence for only that time necessary to complete their assignments and report to their standing committees. Their reports, whether favorable or unfavorable, shall be considered by the standing committee.

Powers and Responsibilities

5. Permanent standing committees are authorized:

(a) to maintain a continuous review of the work of the Commonwealth agencies concerned with their subject areas and the performance of the functions of government within each such subject area, and for this purpose to request reports from time to time, in such form as the standing committee or select subcommittee shall designate, concerning the operation of any Commonwealth agency and presenting any proposal or recommendation such agency may have with regard to existing laws or proposed legislation in its subject area. The standing committee or subcommittee is authorized to require public officials and employes and private individuals to appear before the standing committee or subcommittee for the purpose of submitting information to it;

(b) in order to carry out its duties, each standing committee or sub-committee is empowered with the right and authority to inspect and investigate the books, records, papers, documents, data, operation, and physical plant of any public agency in this Commonwealth;

(c) in order to carry out its duties, each standing committee or subcommittee may issue subpoenas duces tecum and other necessary process to compel the attendance of witnesses and the production of any books, letters, or other documentary evidence desired by such committee. The Chairman may administer all oaths and affirmations in the manner prescribed by law to witnesses who shall appear before such committee for the purpose of testifying in any matter about which such committee may desire evidence. The Chairman shall administer an oath or affirmation in the manner prescribed by law to all witnesses who shall appear at a formal hearing of such committee to testify in any matter which such committee may desire evidence.

Notice of Meetings

6. (a) The chairman of a committee or subcommittee, or, in his absence, the vice-chairman with the approval of the chairman, shall provide each member of the committee with written notice of committee meetings, which shall include the date, time and place of the meeting and the number of each bill which may be considered. During session notice of meetings of standing committee may be published in the daily calendar. If notice of publication in the daily calendar of standing committee or subcommittee meetings has been ordered by a committee chairman such information shall be delivered to the Secretary's office in writing by the end of the session on the day preceding its intended publication.

(b) Whenever the Chairman of any Standing Committee shall refuse to call a regular meeting, then a majority plus one of its members of the Standing Committee may vote to call a meeting by giving two days written notice to the Secretary of the Senate, setting the time and place for such meeting. Such notice shall be read in the Senate and the same posted by the Secretary in the Senate. Thereafter, the meeting shall be held at the time and place specified in the notice. In addition, all provisions of the act of July 19, 1974 (P.L. 486, No. 175), referred to as the Sunshine Law, relative to notice of meetings shall be complied with.

(c) When the majority plus one of the members of a Standing Committee believe that a certain bill or resolution in the possession of the Standing Committee should be considered and acted upon by such Committee, they may request the Chairman to include the same as part of the business of a committee meeting. Upon failure of the Chairman to comply with such request, the membership may require that such bill be considered by written motion made and approved by a majority plus one vote of the entire membership to which such committee is entitled.

7. A committee meeting may be held during a session only if approval is granted by the Majority and Minority Leaders and if notice of the bills to be considered is given during session.

8. Before any standing committee or subcommittee of the Senate holds a meeting while the Legislature is in recess, a notice of said meeting, stating date, time and place, shall be filed with the Secretary of the Senate at least seven (7) days prior thereto.

Bills Recommitted

9. Any bill or resolution reported by any standing committee without prior notice having been given as required by these rules shall be recommitted to the committee reporting the same.

Public Meetings or Hearings

10. (a) The Chairman of a standing committee may hold hearings open to the public and in doing so shall make public announcement of the date, the place, and the subject matter of the hearing in ample time to permit participation by the public. All subcommittees may hold public hearings with the permission of the parent standing committee.

(b) The Chairman of a standing committee shall have the power to designate whether or not a meeting of the committee for the purpose of transacting committee business shall be open to the public or shall be held in executive session and therefore closed to the public.

11. All permanent standing committees, and with permission of the parent committee, subcommittees, may, have their hearings reported and transcribed if payment for such service is being made from committee funds. The Chairman shall contact the Secretary to make arrangements for such reporting and transcribing. However, if payment is expected to be made from a source other than committee funds, approval must be first obtained from the President Pro Tempore. The President Pro Tempore shall notify the Secretary of the Senate if permission is granted.

Subcommittee Reports

12. It shall be the duty of a subcommittee to report all measures referred to them directly to the parent standing committee. The subcommittee shall report all measures either (a) favorably, (b) favorably with amendments, or (c) unfavorably.

13. Such reports shall also reflect (a) the time and place of the meeting at which the action was taken, (b) the name and address of each person (if any) addressing the committee relative to each measure and the interest represented (proponent or opponent), and (c) the vote of each member of the subcommittee on the motion to report each measure.

14. Subcommittee may not report a bill directly to the Senate but must be reported back to the parent committee who in turn shall be authorized to report to the Senate if it is so ordered.

15. When a bill with a favorable report by a subcommittee is considered by the parent committee, no additional testimony of witnesses shall be permitted except upon vote of a majority of members of the parent committee as provided by these rules.

Quorum of Committee

16. A committee or subcommittee is actually assembled only when a quorum constituting a majority of the members of that committee is present in person. A majority of the quorum of the whole committee shall be required to report any measure to the floor for action by the whole Senate. Any measure reported in violation of this Rule shall be immediately recommitted by the President when it is called to his attention by a Senator.

Discharging Committees

17. (a) No committee shall be discharged from consideration of any measure within ten legislative days of its reference without unanimous consent of the Senate or after such ten-day period except by majority vote of all members elected to the Senate.

(b) Such discharge shall be by resolution which shall lie over one day for consideration upon introduction and which shall be considered under the Order of Business of Resolutions.

XVII   COMMITTEE OFFICERS
Chairman — Ex-officio

1. The Chairman of each standing committee shall be ex-officio a member of each subcommittee which is part of his standing committee with the right to attend meetings of such subcommittees and vote on any matter before such committees.

Calling Committee to Order

2. The Chairman, or, in his absence, the majority Vice-Chairman shall call the committee to order at the hour provided by these Rules. Upon the appearance of a quorum, the committee shall proceed with the order of business. Any member of the committee may question the existence of a quorum.

The Chairman Control of the Committee Room

3. The Chairman or Vice-Chairman shall preserve order and decorum and shall have general control of the committee room. In case of a disturbance or disorderly conduct in the committee room, he may cause the same to be cleared.

Chairman's Authority to Sign Notices, etc.
Decide Questions of Order

4. The Chairman shall sign all notices, vouchers, subpoenas or reports required or permitted by these Rules. He shall decide all questions of order relative to parliamentary procedure, subject to an appeal by any Senator to the committee.

Vote of Chairman, Vice-Chairman

5. The Chairman and Vice-Chairman shall vote on all matters before such committee provided that the name of the Chairman shall be called last.

Temporary Appointment of Alternate to Chairman

6. The Chairman may name any member of the committee to perform the duties of the Chair provided that such substitution shall not extend beyond such meeting. In his absence and omission to make such appointment, the Vice-Chairman shall act during his absence.

Performance of Duties by Vice-Chairman

7. Upon the death of the Chairman, the Vice-Chairman shall perform the duties of the office until and unless the President Pro Tempore shall appoint a successor. Upon and during disability, or incapacity of the Chairman, the Vice-Chairman shall perform his duties.

Chairman's Duty to Report

8. The Chairman shall report any bill to the floor of the Senate within four legislative days of the committee's vote to report it.

XVIII   COMMITTEE MEMBERS
Members, Attendance, Voting

1. Every member of a committee shall be in attendance during each of its meetings, unless excused or necessarily prevented and shall vote on each question, except that no member of a committee shall be required or permitted to vote on any questions immediately concerning his private rights as distinct from the public interest.

2. The Chairman may excuse any Senator for just cause from attendance on the meetings of his committee for any stated period, and such excused absence shall be noted on the records of such committee.

3. Any member of a committee who is otherwise engaged in legislative duties may have his vote recorded on measures pending before the committee by communicating in writing to the Chairman: (a) the nature of the legislative duties that prohibits his attendance and; (b) the manner in which he desires to be voted on such measures pending before the committee.

XIX   COMMITTEE VOTING
Taking the Vote

1. The Chairman shall declare all votes and the said votes and the results thereof shall be open to the public. In all cases where the committee shall be equally divided, the question shall be lost.

XX   MOTIONS IN COMMITTEES

1. All motions made in committee shall be governed and take the same precedence as those set forth in these Rules.

XXI   CONFERENCE COMMITTEES

1. The President Pro Tempore shall appoint three Senators to comprise a Committee of Conference. Two shall be from the majority party and one from the minority party.

2. The deliberations of the committee shall be confined to the subject of difference between the two houses, unless both Houses shall direct a free conference, and if their authority has been exceeded it shall be the duty of the presiding officer to call it to the attention of the Senate who shall then decide the question by a majority vote of those present.

Report of Conference Committee

3. Reports of Conference Committees shall be prepared in triplicate by the Legislative Reference Bureau and shall be signed by the members or a majority of the members of the committee. Every report of a Committee of Conference shall be printed together with the bill as amended by the committee, placed on the files of Senators and particularly referred to on their calendars before action shall be taken on such report.

Report of Conference Committee — Adoption

4. Reports of Committees of Conference shall be adopted only by the vote of a majority of the members elected to the Senate, taken by yeas and nays. (Const. of Pa., Art. 3, Sec. 5)

XXII VOTING

1. Must be Present and Vote

(a) Except as may be otherwise provided by this rule, no Senator shall be permitted to vote on any question unless he is present in the Senate Chamber at the time the roll is being called, or prior to the announcement of the vote: Provided, however, That if a Senator is performing a legislative duty to which he was duly appointed by the Senate or any officer thereof, he may be voted by his respective floor leader.

Harrisburg Assignment

(b) A Senator who is performing a legislative assignment in the Harrisburg area (as defined in the Financial Operating Rules of the Senate) on behalf of the body of the Senate and to which he or she was duly appointed by the Senate or the appropriate officer thereof, may be voted by his or her respective floor leader. A specific reason must be given by the Senator and it must be announced by the respective floor leader.

Legislative Leave

(c) A Senator who is performing a legislative assignment outside of the Harrisburg area on behalf of the body of the Senate and to which he or she was duly appointed by the Senate or the appropriate officer thereof, may be voted by his or her respective floor leader. A specific reason for the legislative leave must be given in writing by the Senator and it must be announced by the respective floor leader.

Personal or Private Interest

2. Senators who have a personal or private interest in any measure or bill proposed or pending before the Senate shall disclose the fact to the Senate, and shall not vote thereon.

Senators Must be Present

3. Every Senator shall be present within the Senate Chamber during the sessions of the Senate, unless duly excused or necessarily prevented, and shall be recorded as voting on each question stated from the Chair which requires a roll call vote unless excused by the Senate. The refusal of any Senator to vote shall be deemed a contempt unless he be excused by the Senate or unless he has a direct personal or pecuniary interest in connection with the pending question.

Excused from Voting

4. A Senator desiring to be excused from voting shall, when his name is called, make a brief statement of the reasons for making such request, and the question on excusing him shall then be decided by the Chair without debate.

Changing Vote

5. No Senator may vote or change his vote after the result is announced by the Chair. Before the announcement of the final result, however, a Senator may change his vote, or may vote, if previously absent from the Chamber. Should a Senator be erroneously recorded on any vote, he may at any time, with the permission of the Senate, make a statement to that effect which shall be entered in the Journal. Similarly, should the Senator be absent when a vote is taken on any question, he may later, with the permission of the Senate, make a statement for entry upon the Journal, indicating how he would have voted had he been present when the roll was taken and the reasons therefor shall be submitted in writing or delivered orally not to exceed five minutes.

Persons Allowed at Desk During Roll Call

6. No Senator or other person except the majority or minority leader or other persons designated by them, shall be permitted at the Reading Clerk's desk during the recording, counting or verification of a roll call vote.

Two-Thirds Vote

7. When bills or other matters, which require a two-thirds vote are under consideration the concurrence of two-thirds of all the Senators elected shall not be requisite to decide any question or amendment short of the final question and on any question short of the final one, a majority of Senators voting shall be sufficient to pass the same.

Majority Vote Defined

8. A majority of the Senators elected shall mean a majority of the Senators elected, living, sworn and seated.

Majority Vote

9. When bills or other matters, which require a vote of the majority of all Senators elected are under consideration, the concurrence of a majority of all the Senators elected shall not be requisite to decide any question or amendment short of the final question; and on any question short of a final one a majority of Senators voting shall be sufficient to pass the same.

Announcement of Vote

10. Upon completion of a roll call vote or a voice vote the result shall be announced immediately unless the majority or minority leader requests a delay.

Explanation of Vote

11. Any Senator may, with the consent of the Senate, make an explanation of his vote on any question and have the explanation printed in the Journal.

Tie Vote

12. In the case of a tie vote the President of the Senate may cast his vote to break such tie so long as by doing so it does not violate any provisions of the Constitution of Pennsylvania. In the event there is a tie vote on a question requiring a constitutional majority, the question falls.

Verifying Vote

13. Any Senator may demand a verification of a vote immediately upon the completion of a roll call or after the announcement of vote by the presiding officer. In verifying a vote the Clerk shall first read the affirmative roll at which time any additions or corrections shall be made. Upon the completion and verification of the affirmative roll call, the Clerk shall proceed with the reading of the negative roll at which time any additions or corrections shall be made. Upon the completion and verification of the negative roll call the roll call shall be declared verified. It shall not be in order for a Senator to change his vote after the verified roll call is announced. A demand for a verification shall not be in order when all Senators vote one way. The demand for a verification of a vote is not debatable.

Voice Vote

14. Unless otherwise ordered or demanded, a voice vote may be taken. Any Senator who doubts the accuracy of a voice vote may demand a roll call vote. Such request must be made immediately upon the announcement of the vote by the presiding officer and shall not be in order after other business has intervened. The demand for a verification of a voice vote shall not be in order.

XXIII CORRESPONDENTS

Admission to Press Gallery —
Committee on Correspondents

1. Admission to and administration of the Press Galleries of the Senate and House of Representatives shall be vested in a Committee on Correspondents consisting of the President Pro Tempore of the Senate, or his designee; the Speaker of the House of Representatives, or his designee; the Supervisor of the Capitol Newsroom; the President of the Pennsylvania Legislative Correspondents' Association, or his designee and the Executive Director of the Pennsylvania Association of Broadcasters, or his designee.

Application to Press Gallery

2. Persons desiring admission to the press sections of the Senate and House of Representatives shall make application to the Chairman of the Committee on Correspondents. Such applications shall state the newspaper, press association or licensed radio or television station, its location, times of publication or hours of broadcasting, and be signed by the applicant.

Committee to Verify Statement

3. The Committee on Correspondents shall verify the statements made in such application, and, if the application is approved by the Committee, shall issue a correspondent's card signed by the members of the Committee.

Exclusive Use of Gallery

4. The Gallery assigned to newspaper correspondents or recognized press association correspondents or representatives of licensed radio and television stations, systems or news-gathering agencies shall be for their exclusive use and persons not holding correspondents cards shall not be entitled to admission thereto. Employes of the General Assembly, representatives and employes of state departments, boards, commissions and agencies, visitors and members of the families of correspondents entitled to admission to the press gallery shall, at no time, be permitted to occupy seats or be entitled to the privilege of the press gallery.

Photographs in Senate Chamber — Hearings

5. Accredited photographers of newspapers, wire, newsreel services and licensed television stations, systems or news-gathering agencies, may be authorized by the President Pro Tempore to take photographs in the Senate, and by the Speaker of the House to take photographs in the House of Representatives. Applications to take photographs at public hearings of committees must be approved by the Committee Chairman or Co-Chairman conducting such hearing.

Photographs — Notice to be Given

6. No photographs shall be taken in the Senate or House of Representatives during sessions, being at ease or recessed, without prior notice to the Senators in the Senate or the Representatives in the House of Representatives. When possible, such notice shall be given at the beginning of the session, at ease or recess, during which the photographs are scheduled to be taken.

Correspondents — Number Limited

7. No more than one representative of each newspaper, press association or licensed radio or television station, system or news-gathering agency shall be admitted to the press gallery at one time. Members of the Pennsylvania Legislative Correspondents' Association and representatives of licensed radio and television stations, systems or news-gathering agencies, assigned to the Senate and/or House of Representatives on a daily basis shall have permanent assigned seating in the press gallery with identification plates. Visiting representatives of daily newspapers, press associations, Sunday newspapers as well as radio and television stations, systems or news-gathering agencies shall coordinate seating accommodations with the supervisor of the Capitol Newsroom.

Order and Decorum of Press

8. Persons assigned to the press gallery on a permanent or temporary basis, shall, at all times, refrain from loud talking or causing any disturbance which tends to interrupt the proceedings of the Senate or House of Representatives.

9. Persons assigned to the press gallery on a permanent or temporary basis shall not walk onto the floor of the Senate or House of Representatives nor approach the rostrum or the clerks desks during session or while being at ease.

10. Persons assigned to the press gallery on a permanent or temporary basis wishing to confer with a Senator or Representative shall disclose this fact by having a message delivered by a Page to the Senator or Representative. Such conversation shall be conducted off the floor of the Senate or House of Representatives.

XXIV RADIO AND TELEVISION

1. Filming, televising or broadcasting of any sessions of the Senate, within the Senate Chamber is prohibited except by resolution, which upon introduction shall be referred to the Committee on Rules. Violation of this rule shall be dealt with as the Committee on Rules shall direct.

XXV RECORDS OF THE SENATE

1. The records of the Senate may be inspected by the Members, but no paper shall be withdrawn therefrom without the consent of the Senate.

XXVI WHO PRIVILEGED TO THE FLOOR OF THE SENATE

1. No person shall be admitted within the Senate Chamber (galleries and press boxes excepted) during its sessions, unless invited by the President or a Member of the Senate, except the Members and staff authorized by the Majority and Minority Leader. Such authorized staff shall be restricted to the area immediate to the Majority and Minority Leaders' desks and shall be allowed to advise members being interrogated only when such Member is using the microphones at the Leaders' desks.

Rear Entrance Closed During Session

2. No person or persons shall, during a session, be permitted to enter through the rear door of the Senate Chamber nor be present in the rooms immediately to the rear of the Senate Chamber except Senators, officers and employes expressly authorized.

Telephone Facilities

3. No person or persons other than Senators or their staff shall, at any time, be permitted to use the telephone facilities in or adjacent to the Senate Chamber.

XXVII RULES

1. These rules shall be in full force and effect until altered, changed, amended or repealed as provided herein.

Dispensing with Rules

2. The consent of a majority of the Senators elected shall be necessary to suspend any Rule except that part of Rule which requires unanimous consent to be given to consider the confirmation of a nomination which has been reported from a committee on that day shall not be suspended.

Altering, Changing or Amending — Vote

3. The consent of a majority of the Senators elected shall be necessary to alter, change or amend these Rules.

Alterations, Changing or Amending — Resolution

4. All alterations, changes or amendments to Senate Rules shall be by resolution which shall not be considered unless first referred to and reported from the Rules Committee.

XXVIII MASON'S MANUAL OF LEGISLATIVE PROCEDURE TO GOVERN SENATE

1. The Rules of Parliamentary Practice comprised in Mason's Manual of Legislative Procedure shall govern the Senate in all cases to which they are applicable, and in which they are not inconsistent with the Standing Rules and Orders of the Senate.

XXIX QUORUM

Majority Constitutes a Quorum

1. A majority of Senators elected shall constitute a quorum, but a smaller number may adjourn from day to day, and compel the attendance of absent members. (Const. of Pa., Art. 2, Sec. 10)

When Less than a Quorum is Present

2. When, upon a call, which may be demanded by not less than four Senators, it is found that less than a quorum is present, it shall be the duty of the President to order the doors of the Senate to be closed, and to direct the clerk to call the roll of the Senate and note the absentees after which the names of the absentees shall be again called, and those for whose absence no excuse, or an insufficient excuse is made, may by order of a majority of the Senators present, be sent for and taken into custody by the Sergeant-at-Arms, or his assistants appointed for the purpose, and brought before the bar of the Senate, where, unless excused by a majority of the Senators present they shall be reproved by the President for neglect of duty.

When Less than a Quorum Vote But Present

3. When less than a quorum vote upon any subject under the consideration of the Senate not less than four Senators may demand a call of the Senate, when it shall be the duty of the President forthwith to order

the doors of the Senate to be closed, the roll of the Senators to be called, and if it is ascertained that a quorum is present, either by answering to their names, or by their presence in the Senate, the President shall again order the yeas and nays, and if any Senator or Senators present refuse to vote the name or names of such Senator or Senators shall be entered on the Journal as "Present but not voting," and such refusal to vote shall be deemed a contempt, and, unless purged, the President shall direct the Sergeant-at-Arms to bring such Senator or Senators before the bar of the Senate, where he or they shall be publicly reprimanded by the President.

XXX EXECUTIVE NOMINATIONS
Presentation and Reference
1. All nominations by the Governor or the Attorney General shall be submitted to the Secretary-Parliamentarian of the Senate. All nominees shall file the financial statements required pursuant to the act of October 4, 1978 (P.L. 883, No. 170), referred to as the Public Official and Employee Ethics Law, with the Secretary-Parliamentarian of the Senate. Copies of the nominations and financial statements shall be furnished by the Secretary-Parliamentarian of the Senate to the Majority and Minority Caucus Secretaries or their designees.

2. Nominations shall, after being read, without a motion, be referred by the presiding officer to the Committee on Rules and Executive Nominations. After having been reported by the committee, the final question on every nomination shall be: "Will the Senate advise and consent to this nomination?" Which question shall not be put on the day on which the nomination or nominations are reported from committee, unless by unanimous consent.

3. The Committee on Rules and Executive Nominations shall refer nominations to appropriate standing committees of the Senate, which shall hold public hearings for all nominees for offices which have Statewide jurisdiction and to which salaries are attached; scrutinize the qualifications of nominees and report back their recommendations. Public hearings may be held for nominees for any other office.

Information Concerning Nominations
4. All information, communication or remarks made by a Senator when acting upon nominations in committee, concerning the character or qualifications of the person nominated, shall be kept secret. If, however, charges shall be made against a person nominated, the committee may, in its discretion, notify such nominee thereof, but the name of the person making such charges shall not be disclosed.

Consideration
5. When the consideration of executive nominations is reached in the order of business, a Senator may make a motion to go into executive session for the purpose of confirming the nominations which have been reported from a committee at a previous session and, if unanimous consent be given, also those which may be reported on the day the motion is made; and on the motion being agreed to, such nomination or nominations shall be considered the first order of the day until finally disposed of, unless the same shall be postponed by a majority of the Senate; but such business when once commenced shall not be postponed for more than five days, except in case of an adjournment of the Senate for a longer period.

Executive Session
6. When in executive session, no message shall be received from the Governor, unless it be relative to the nomination under consideration, nor from the House of Representatives, nor shall any other business be considered, except executive business, and the executive session shall not adjourn pending the consideration of the nomination until a time fixed by a majority vote of those present for the next meeting of the executive session to resume the consideration thereof.

Reconsideration
7. When a nomination is confirmed or rejected by the Senate, any two Senators may move for a reconsideration on the same day on which the vote was taken, or on either of the next two days of actual session of the Senate; but if a notification of the confirmation or rejection of a nomination shall have been sent to the Governor before the expiration of the time within which a motion to reconsider may be made, the motion to reconsider shall be accompanied by a motion to request the Governor to return such notification to the Senate. A motion to reconsider the vote on a nomination may be laid on the table without prejudice to the nomination.

XXXI RESOLUTIONS
Introduction
1. All resolutions, Senate and concurrent, shall be introduced by presenting ten copies thereof to the President.

Consideration
2. The following resolutions after they have been read, shall be referred to an appropriate committee, without debate (unless by unanimous consent the Senate shall otherwise direct) and if favorably reported by the committee, shall lie over one day for consideration, after which they may be called up as, of course, under their appropriate order of business;

3. All Senate and House concurrent resolutions, excepting resolutions in reference to adjournments and those recalling bills from the Governor which shall be regarded as privileged;

4. Resolutions containing calls for information from the heads of departments, or to alter the rules;

5. Resolutions giving rise to debate, except such as relate to the disposition of matters immediately before the Senate, such as relate to the business of the day on which they were offered, and such as relate to adjournment or taking a recess.

Printing in Senate History
6. Congratulatory and condolence resolutions shall be given to the Secretary-Parliamentarian and shall be considered under the order of unfinished business in the daily order of business.

7. All resolutions shall be adopted by a majority vote of the Senators present.

Joint Resolutions
8. Joint Resolutions shall be limited to constitutional amendments and shall be adopted by a vote of a majority of the Senators elected to the Senate;

A joint resolution when passed by both Houses, shall not be transmitted to the Governor for his approval or disapproval but shall be filed in the Office of the Secretary-Parliamentarian of the Commonwealth in accordance with Article 9, Section 1 of the Constitution of Pennsylvania.

XXXII LOUNGING IN THE SENATE PROHIBITED
1. The Secretary-Parliamentarian of the Senate shall cause the doors of the Senate Chamber closed to all persons except persons who are entitled under the rule of the Senate; and he shall call on any officer of the Senate to aid him in enforcing this order; and on days when the Senate is not in session the officers are hereby required to strictly prohibit any lounging within the Senate Chamber by any person not connected with the Legislature, and that henceforth no officer, nor any other person, be permitted to occupy the seat of a Senator at any time; it shall be the duty of the President to see that this rule is enforced, and a persistent disregard of it by any officer shall be cause of dismissal by the President.

XXXIII VETO
Passing over Veto
1. When any bill is not approved by the Governor he shall return it with his objection to the House in which such bill originated. Thereupon such House shall enter the objections upon their Journal and proceed to reconsider it. If after such reconsideration, two-thirds of all the Members elected to that House shall agree to pass the bill, it shall be sent with the objections to the other House by which likewise it shall be reconsidered, and if approved by two-thirds of all the members elected to that House it shall become a law. (Const. of Pa., Art. 4, Sec. 15)

2. A bill vetoed in a first regular session and not finally acted upon may be brought up for consideration in a second regular session.

XXXIV DIVISION OF A QUESTION
1. Any Senator may call for a division of a question by the Senate if the question includes points so distinct and separate that, one of them being taken away, the other will stand as a complete proposition. The motion to strike out and insert is strictly one proposition, and, therefore indivisible.

XXXV ACCOUNTING FOR APPROPRIATIONS

Rule XXXV repealed in its entirety, pursuant to Senate Resolutions, Numbers 53 and 54, adopted July 1, 1981.

XXXVI SENATE EXPENDITURES

1. Repealed, pursuant to Senate Resolutions, Numbers 53 and 54, adopted July 1, 1981.

2. Repealed, pursuant to Senate Resolutions, Numbers 53 and 54, adopted July 1, 1981.

3. Repealed, pursuant to Senate Resolutions, Numbers 53 and 54, adopted July 1, 1981.

4. Counsel employed by a committee chairman or minority chairman for the committee may not represent the committee chairman or a member of the chairman's staff, or any member of the committee or of a committee member's staff, in any private legal proceeding while employed by the Senate. Nor may any Senate funds be used to pay private legal counsel for any Senator, officer or staff member.

5. Repealed, pursuant to Senate Resolutions, Numbers 53 and 54, adopted July 1, 1981.

6. Repealed, pursuant to Senate Resolutions, Number 53 and 54, adopted July 1, 1981.

XXXVII COMMITTEE ON ETHICS AND OFFICIAL CONDUCT

1. In addition to the committees created by Rule XVI, there shall be a Committee on Ethics and Official Conduct which shall be composed of six members appointed by the President Pro Tempore. Three members shall be of the Majority Party and three members shall be of the Minority Party. The Minority Party members will be appointed on the recommendation of the Minority Leader.

2. The President Pro Tempore shall appoint one of the Majority Party members as Chairman and, on the recommendation of the Minority Leader, one of the Minority Party members as Vice-Chairman. A quorum for this committee shall be four members and the committee shall have such duties, powers, procedure and jurisdiction as are prescribed and authorized in this Rule.

3. The committee shall receive complaints against members, officers and employees of the Senate alleging illegal or unethical conduct or violation of any statute, rule or regulation governing the use of moneys appropriated to the Senate. Any such complaint must be in writing, verified by the person filing the complaint and must set forth in detail the conduct in question and the section of the "Legislative Code of Ethics" or the statute, rule or regulation violated. The committee shall make a preliminary investigation of the complaint, and if it is determined by a majority of the committee that a violation may have occurred, the person against whom the complaint has been brought shall be notified in writing and given a copy of the complaint. Within ten days after receipt of the complaint, such person may file a written answer thereto with the committee. Upon receipt of the answer, by vote of a majority of the committee, the committee shall either dismiss the complaint within ten days or proceed with a formal investigation, which may include hearings, not more than twenty days after notice in writing to the persons so charged. Failure of the person charged to file an answer shall not be deemed to be an admission or create an inference or presumption that the complaint is true, and such failure to file an answer shall not prohibit a majority of the committee from either proceeding with a formal investigation or dismissing the complaint.

4. In addition to action on formal complaints as provided in section 3, a majority of the committee may initiate a preliminary investigation of a suspected violation of the "Legislative Code of Ethics" or a violation of any other statute, rule or regulation governing the use of moneys appropriated to the Senate by a member, officer or employee of the Senate. If it is determined by a majority of the committee that a violation may have occurred, the person in question shall be notified in writing of the conduct in question and the section of the "Legislative Code of Ethics" or other statute, rule or regulation violated. Within ten days, such person may file a written answer thereto. Upon receipt of the answer, by vote of a majority of the committee, the committee shall either dismiss the charges within ten days or proceed with a formal investigation which may include hearings, not more than twenty days after notice in writing to the person so charged. Failure of the person charged to file an answer shall not be deemed to be an admission or create an inference or presumption that the charge is true, and

such failure to file an answer shall not prohibit a majority of the committee from either proceeding with a formal investigation or dismissing the charge.

5. The chairman shall notify all members of the committee at least twenty-four hours in advance of the date, time and place of a regular meeting. Whenever the chairman shall refuse to call a regular meeting, a majority of the committee may call a meeting by giving two days' written notice to the Majority and Minority Leaders of the Senate setting forth the time and place for such meeting. Thereafter, the meeting shall be held at the time and place specified in such notice.

The committee shall conduct its investigations, hearings and meetings relating to a specific investigation or a specific member, officer or employee of the Senate in closed session and the fact that such investigation is being conducted or is to be conducted or that hearings or such meetings are being held or are to be held shall be confidential information unless the person subject to investigation advises the committee in writing that he elects that such meetings or hearings shall be held publicly: Provided, however, That whenever the committee is conducting an investigation of an employee of the Senate the committee shall inform the Senator or officer supervising such employee of the investigation. In the event of such an election, the committee shall furnish such person a public meeting or hearing. All other meetings of the committee shall be open to the public and notice of such meetings shall be given as generally provided in these rules for the convening of committees.

In the event that the committee shall elect to proceed with a formal investigation of the conduct of any member, officer or employee of the Senate, the committee may employ independent counsel.

All constitutional rights of any person under investigation shall be preserved, and such person shall be entitled to present evidence, cross-examine witnesses, face the accuser, and be represented by counsel.

The chairman may continue any hearing for reasonable cause, and upon the vote of a majority of the committee or upon the request of the person subject to investigation, the chairman shall issue subpoenas for the attendance and testimony of witnesses and the production of documentary evidence relating to any matter under formal investigation by the committee. The committee may administer oaths or affirmations and examine and receive evidence.

6. All testimony, documents, records, data, statements or information received by the committee in the course of any investigation shall be private and confidential except in the case of public meetings or hearings or in a report to the Senate. No report shall be made to the Senate unless a majority of the committee has made a finding of unethical or illegal conduct or violation of the statutes, rules and regulations relating to Senate funds on the part of the person under investigation. No finding of unethical or illegal conduct or violation of the statutes, rules and regulations relating to Senate funds shall be valid unless signed by at least a majority of the committee. Any such report may include a minority report. No action shall be taken on any finding of illegal or unethical conduct or violation of the statutes, rules or regulations relating to Senate funds nor shall such finding or report containing such finding be made public sooner than seven days after a copy of the finding is sent by certified mail to the member, officer or employee under investigation.

7. In the event, the committee finds that a member, officer, or employee of the Senate has violated a statute, rule or regulation relating to use of Senate funds, the committee may order such member, officer, or employee to reimburse the Senate for the funds wrongly expended and to take other remedial action. If the member, officer, or employee, does reimburse the Senate or take such other remedial action as may have been required, no formal report shall be made to the Senate unless the committee is requested in writing to file a formal report by the member, officer, or employee who is the subject of the order. If the member, officer, or employee fails to reimburse the Senate or take the required remedial action within seven days of receipt of the order, the committee, unless it shall, by majority vote thereof, extend such time for good cause, shall within seven days file its formal report with the Senate along with its recommendation of action by the Senate to secure reimbursement, effect the recommended remedial action, or initiate appropriate disciplinary action.

Any member, officer, or employee of the Senate who is the subject of an order of reimbursement or remedial action, may appeal the committee's order to the Senate within seven days of receipt of the order, by filing notice thereof with the Secretary-Parliamentarian of the Senate who shall cause such notice to be distributed to the members of the Senate along with a copy of the report of the committee involving such member, officer, or employee.

Notice of the appeal shall be placed on the Senate Calendar and shall be acted on by the Senate within ten legislative days. A vote by a majority of the members elected shall be necessary to sustain an appeal or modify the committee report or order; otherwise it shall become effective and the members, officers, and employees of the Senate shall take such action as is necessary to secure compliance.

8. The committee, whether or not at the request of a member, officer or employee concerned about an ethical problem or question concerning the use of Senate funds relating to himself alone or in conjunction with others, may render advisory opinions with regard to questions pertaining to legislative ethics, decorum, or use of Senate funds. Such advisory opinions, with such deletions and changes as shall be necessary to protect the identity of the persons involved or seeking them, may be published and shall be distributed to all members, officers and employees of the Senate. No order for reimbursement or remedial action may be made when the member, officer, or employee has relied on a written advisory opinion, whether addressed to him or not, which is reasonably construed as being applicable to the complained of conduct.

9. In the event that a member of the committee shall be under investigation, said member shall be temporarily replaced on the committee in a like manner as said member's original appointment.

Any member of the committee breaching the confidentiality of materials and events as set forth in this Rule shall be removed immediately from the committee and replaced by another member of the Senate appointed in a like manner as said member's original appointment.

10. The committee may adopt rules of procedure for the orderly conduct of its affairs, investigations, hearings and meetings, which rules are not inconsistent with this Rule.

11. The committee may meet with a committee of the House of Representatives to hold investigations or hearings involving employees of the two Houses jointly, or officers or employees of the Legislative Reference Bureau, the Joint State Government Commission, the Local Government Commission, the Joint Legislative Air, Soil and Water Conservation and Control Commission, the Legislative Budget and Finance Committee and the Legislative Data Processing Committee: Provided, however, That no action may be taken at a joint meeting unless it is approved by a majority of each committee.

12. The Legislative Audit Advisory Commission shall submit copies of its reports to the committee which shall review them and proceed, where appropriate, as provided in section 7.

13. Whenever the committee shall employ independent counsel or shall incur other expenses pursuant to its duties under this rule, payment of costs of such independent counsel or other expenses incurred by the committee pursuant to this rule, shall be paid by the Chief Clerk upon submission of vouchers and necessary documentation which vouchers shall be signed by both the chairman and vice chairman of the committee. Included in such allowable expense items shall be travel and per diem for the members of the committee. The Chief Clerk shall pay such expenses out of funds appropriated to the Chief Clerk for incidental expenses.

XXXVIII STATUS OF MEMBERS INDICTED OR CONVICTED OF A CRIME

1. When an indictment is returned against a member of the Senate, and the gravamen of the indictment is directly related to the member's conduct as a committee chairman, ranking minority committee member or in a position of leadership, the member shall be relieved of such committee chairmanship, ranking minority committee member status, or leadership position until the indictment is disposed of, but the member shall otherwise continue to function as a Senator, including voting, and shall continue to be paid.

2. If, during the same legislative session, the indictment is quashed, or the court finds that the member is not guilty of the offense alleged, the member shall immediately be restored to the committee chairmanship, ranking minority committee member status, or leadership position retroactively from which he was suspended.

3. Upon a finding or verdict of guilt by a judge or jury, plea or admission of guilt or plea of nolo contendere of a member of the Senate of a crime, the gravamen of which relates to the member's conduct as a Senator, and upon imposition of sentence, the Secretary-Parliamentarian of the Senate shall prepare a resolution of expulsion under the sponsorship of the Chairman and Vice-Chairman of the Senate Committee on Ethics and Official Conduct. The resolution shall be printed and placed on the calendar for the next day of Senate session.

XXXIX STATUS OF OFFICERS OR EMPLOYEES INDICTED OR CONVICTED OF A CRIME

1. Whenever any officer or employee of the Senate is indicted or otherwise charged before a court of record with the commission of a felony or misdemeanor the gravamen of which relates to the officer's or employee's conduct or status as an officer or employee of the Commonwealth or the disposition of public funds, such employee shall immediately be suspended without pay and benefits by the Chief Clerk. After a finding or a verdict of guilt by a judge or a jury, plea or admission of guilt, or plea of nolo contendere, and upon imposition of sentence, the employment shall be terminated.

2. If the indictment is quashed, or the court finds that the officer or employee is not guilty of the offense alleged, the suspension without pay shall be terminated, and the officer or employee shall receive compensation for the period of time during which the officer or employee was suspended which compenation shall be reduced by the amount of any compensation said officer or employee earned from other employment during the period of suspension.

3. If the officer or employee or the supervising Senator of such employee disagrees with the decision of the Chief Clerk as to whether an indictment for particular conduct shall be a crime requiring suspension or dismissal, the officer or employee in question or the supervising Senator, may appeal the suspension to the Committee on Ethics and Official Conduct which shall determine whether the conduct charged is an offense requiring suspension. Whenever an appeal of a suspension shall be taken to the committee, the suspension shall remain effective pending a decision by the committee.

INDEX TO RULES OF THE SENATE

DECISIONS OF THE SENATE ON POINTS OF ORDER

SECTION 1

ADJOURNMENT

"From Day to Day" by Less Than a Quorum Means from Day to Day as Fixed by the Orders

1 (a). The Senate having fixed an order for sessions, on Tuesdays and Fridays only, on a motion to adjourn, less than a quorum voting, Mr. Gordon submitted the point of order that under the Constitution it was only competent for less than quorum to adjourn from day to day. The President decided that the phrase "from day to day" signified from day to day as fixed in the regular order of the Senate. Whereupon, the President decided the resolution carried, and adjourned the Senate until Friday morning next at eleven o'clock. (Senate Journal, extra session, 1883, p. 157.)

Senate May Adjourn For Three Days, Exclusive of Sunday

1 (b). The question having been raised on the change of time of the convening of the Senate, the Chair (Lieutenant-Governor Daniel B. Strickler) ruled that the Senate may at its pleasure adjourn for any period within three days, Sunday not being regarded as a legislative day. (Legislative Journal, March 14, 1949, pp. 1199, 1200, 1201.)

Adjournment to a Definite Time is Debatable

1 (c). The point of order was raised that the motion to adjourn is not debatable. The President ruled that a motion to adjourn to a definite time is debatable. (Legislative Journal, 1937, pp. 5389-5390.)

Two Succeeding Motions Out of Order

1 (d). Mr. Rosenfeld made a motion to adjourn immediately after a previous motion to adjourn was defeated.

The Chair, Lieutenant-Governor Lloyd H. Wood, ruled the motion out of order because of a lack of intervening business between the two motions. (Legislative Journal, December 10, 1951, p. 5963.)

Motion to Adjourn Not Debatable

1 (e). A point of order being raised that a motion to adjourn was not debatable, the Chair (Lieutenant-Governor Daniel B. Strickler), upheld the motion and ruled that a motion to adjourn was not debatable. (Legislative Journal, March 10, 1949, p. 1188.) (Legislative Journal, March 14, 1949, pp. 1199, 1200, 1201.)

Adjournment, Sine Die, Needs House Concurrence

1 (g). On December 31, 1973 the Senate adopted a resolution (not concurrent) to adjourn sine die. The next Regular Session was to convene at 12:00 o'clock Noon the next day (January 1, 1974). The resolution was adopted and the Senate adjourned sine die.

After adjournment the Governor made approximately 680 appointments in accordance with Article 4, Section 8 (b) of the Constitution of Pennsylvania.

In January, Senators Frame, Tilghman and Wood instituted quo warranto action in the Commonwealth Court to test the rights of certain of these appointees to hold office since the House of Representatives did not concur in the adjournment sine die. The plaintiffs also petitioned the Supreme Court to assume plenary jurisdiction of the matter. Their petition was granted by the Supreme Court on February 22, 1974. The Majority Opinion was handed down on October 25, 1974 and is as follows: (Senate Journal, 1973, page 1292):

Opinion of the Court

Roberts, J.   Filed: October 25, 1974

We are presented with challenges to the validity of certain appointments made by the Governor without the consent of the Senate. We hold that, because the appointments were not made "during the recess of the Senate," they are invalid.

At 2:30 p.m. on December 31, 1973, the Pennsylvania Senate voted to adjourn its 1973 session. The adjournment resolution, adopted by a vote of 24-22, purported to adjourn the Senate sine die. The resolution did not contemplate, provide for, or receive the consent of the House of Representatives. In fact, the House met and conducted business on December 31 and the morning of January 1, 1974. At noon that day, the one hundred fifty-seventh General Assembly expired and the one hundred fifty-eighth was mandated to begin.

Several hours after the adjournment of the Senate, the Governor, pursuant to article IV, section 8 (b) of the Constitution, made approximately 680 appointments, including defendants Grace Hatch as a member of the Civil Service Commission, Robert E. Sutherland as a member of the Pennsylvania Game Commission, Peter Elish as a member of the Milk Marketing Board, and Egidio Cerilli as a member of the Pennsylvania Turnpike Commission.

In January, 1974, plaintiffs, three members of the Senate, instituted these actions in quo warranto in the Commonwealth Court to test the rights of the named defendants to hold the offices to which they had been appointed on December 31. Plaintiffs also petitioned this Court to assume plenary jurisdiction of the matter; we granted their petition on February 6, 1974, and heard argument on April 22, 1974.

This controversy depends for its resolution on the construction of article IV, section 8 of our Constitution, which in pertinent part provides:

"(a) The Governor shall appoint an Attorney General, a Superintendent of Public Instruction and such other officers as he shall be authorized by law to appoint. The appointment of the Attorney General, the Superintendent of Public Instruction and of such other officers as may be specified by law, shall be subject to the consent of two-thirds of the members elected to the Senate.

"(b) Except as may now or hereafter be otherwise provided in this Constitution as to appellate and other judges, he may, during the recess of the Senate, fill vacancies happening in offices to which he appoints by granting commissions expiring at the end of its session ... If the vacancy happens during the session of the Senate except as otherwise provided in this Constitution, he shall nominate to the Senate, before its final adjournment, a proper person to fill the vacancy."

The procedure established by section 8 (a) is the submission of appointments to the Senate for the consent of two-thirds of its members. Section 8 (b) creates an exception to that general rule, exempting certain appointments from the requirement of senatorial confirmation. The Governor, it is provided, may fill vacancies in offices to which he appoints without submitting the appointments to the Senate by granting temporary commissions "during the recess of the Senate." If the Senate is not in recess when the appointments are made, the general requirement of senatorial confirmation is applicable. That requirement is suspended only during "the recess of the Senate." Thus, the validity of an unconfirmed appointment depends on whether the Governor's power to issue temporary commissions was triggered by "the recess of the Senate."

The phrase "recess of the Senate" in this context does not include an interruption or break following a daily meeting. If it did, the Governor would have a choice in the appointment procedure he could utilize. Obviously, unless the Senate undertook 24-hour sittings, there would be a "recess of the Senate" for at least some period of time every day of the year when unconfirmed appointments could be made.

The relationship of the temporary appointment power and the permanent appointment power indicates, however, that the Governor is not to have that option. It is clear that the draftsmen preferred appointments be made by gubernatorial nomination-senatorial consent for traditional checks-and-balances purposes. However, public necessity might require a position be filled after the Senate had terminated its session, when the constitutionally preferred procedure could not be followed. To provide an appointment process for occasions when the preferred procedure is thus inadequate, the Constitution permits the Governor to issue temporary commissions "during the recess of the Senate." The exception was designed for use only when the preferred procedure could not be employed. It follows that "recess of the Senate" must be limited to those periods of time when the Senate is unable to consent to apppointments.

Inability to consent does not result from a break between one day's session and the next. Neither does it result from a Friday-to-Monday interruption. Indeed, we are unable to say that any interruption during a session of the Senate renders the Senate unable to consent to appointments. Therefore, we conclude that "recess of the Senate" refers only to the final sine die adjournment at the end of the session.

This conclusion is consistent with our cases dealing with recess appointments. In *Stroup v. Kapleau,* 455 Pa. 171, 313 A.2d 237 (1973), the majority referred to the "final adjournment of the Senate" as the trigger which activates the temporary appointment power. In *Creamer v. Twelve Common Pleas Judges,* 443 Pa. 484, 493, 281 A.2d 57, 61 (1971) (Opinion in Support of the Per Curiam Order), three Justices, in comparing article IV, section 8 and article V, section 13, concluded that "recess of the Senate" and "sine die adjournment of the Senate" differed editorially only and not in substance and interpreted both to mean final adjournment. *Ritenour v. Peirce,* 442 Pa. 1, 10, 272 A.2d 900, 905 (1971), also recognized final adjournment as the circumstance which suspended the senatorial-confirmation requirement.

Therefore, only if the Senate had finally adjourned on the afternoon of December 31, 1973, a "recess of the Senate" existed which activated the Governor's power to issue temporary commissions and the appointments of defendants are valid. If the Senate had not finally adjourned, the requirement of senatorial confirmation was not suspended by a "recess of the Senate" and the appointments are invalid. Thus, the narrow question for decision is whether the Senate's unilateral adjournment on December 31 was a final adjournment.

We hold that the Senate's attempt to adjourn sine die failed because of the absence of consent by the House of Representatives. Our holding rests on a conclusion that the Constitution prohibits either house from adjourning sine die without the consent of the other.

The entire constitutional scheme is clearly predicated on the assumption that adjournment may not be a unilateral act on the part of one of the houses of the General Assembly. Article III, section 9 provides:

"Every order, resolution or vote, to which the concurrence of both Houses may be necessary, except on the question of adjournment, shall be presented to the Governor ...."

Article IV, section 12 states:

"[The Governor] may, on extraordinary occasions, convene the General Assembly, and in case of disagreement between the two Houses, with respect to the time of adjournment, adjourn them to such time as he shall think proper ...."

The exclusion of adjournment resolutions from article III, section 9 and the provision for adjournment by the Governor in article IV, section 12 would be utterly superfluous if the Constitution did not contemplate that adjournment of a house of the General Assembly required the consent of the other house.

The reason of policy for this requirement is not difficult to discern. Because each house is powerless to enact legislation alone, each has a strong interest in insuring that bills passed by it are considered by the other house. The greatest threat to this interest is the possibility that the other house might adjourn, thus disabling itself from the consideration of bills. Protection against this possibility is provided each house by the Constitution in the form of a power to refuse to consent to the adjournment of the other house.

An exception to the consent requirement demonstrates that protection of each house's interest in the consideration of its bills by the other is its underlying policy. Article II, section 14 states:

"Neither House shall, without the consent of the other, adjourn for more than three days. .."

The draftsmen foresaw that protection of the interest of each house in having its bills considered by the other, if unqualified, would be gained at the expense of flexibility in the administration of the legislative calendar. Accordingly, the Constitution provides an exception to the consent requirement for adjournments of less than four days. This exception clearly reflects the perception that adjournments of less than four days present a minimal threat to each house's interest in the consideration by the other of its bills.

Defendants argue that the Senate's adjournment in this case was effective despite the absence of the consent of the House of Representatives under article II, section 14 because its duration was not more than three days. We disagree. Sine die adjournments are vastly different from the short recesses envisioned by article II, section 14 in two important respects. First, article II, section 14, as pointed out above, was designed to provide flexibility in the legislative calendar. However, sine die adjournments are unrelated to flexibility in the calendar, representing as they do the end of the legislative calendar for the session. Because the purpose of the exception to the consent requirement would not be served by its application to sine die adjournments, we conclude that the Constitution does not intend its application. Hence, section 14 does not expand the power of the Governor to make unconfirmed appointments.

Second, at the time the consent exception was inserted into the Constitution, a sine die adjournment by one house posed a far more drastic threat to the interests of the other than a short recess contemplated by Article II, section 14. Recesses of less than four days pose a minimal danger that one house will so absent itself as to disable it from consideration of legislation. However, at the time the consent requirement and the three-day exception were inserted in the Constitution, a sine die adjournment represented the greatest threat to the interests of the other house. This was so because unenacted bills pending at the end of a session expired, requiring reintroduction and repassage of the bill in the originating house in order to obtain consideration by the other house. The absence of one house prevented legislation initiated by the other from ever being enacted into law. Accordingly, in contrast to a three-day intra-session recess, a sine die adjournment by one house was the ultimate threat to the interest in having the bills of the other enacted.

It is true that, since the constitutional amendment of 1967, a sine die adjournment at the end of a session does not terminate all then-pending business. Article II, section 4 now provides that "The General Assembly shall be a continuing body during the term for which its Representatives are elected." But there is no evidence that suggests that the change in article II, section 4 was intended to affect the consent requirement or the inapplicability of the three-day exception.

Nothing in our prior cases dealing with the recess appointment power of the Governor suggests that that power is triggered by a unilateral adjournment of the Senate. In fact, a conclusion that a unilateral adjournment is sufficient would be an unwarranted and constitutionally impermissible extension of our decisions. In those cases, it is clear that the respective recesses of the Senate had been consented to by the House of Representatives; see *Stroup v. Kapleau,* 455 Pa. 171, 173, 313 A.2d 237, 238 (1973); *Creamer v. Twelve Common Pleas Judges,* 443 Pa. 484, 500-501 n. *, 281 A.2d 57, 65 n.4 (1971) (Opinion Supporting in Part and Opposing in Part the Per Curiam Order); *Ritenour v. Peirce,* 442 Pa. 1, 4 n.5, 272 A.2d 900, 902 n.5 (1971). Our discussion in *Stroup* at 183, 313 A.2d at 243, assumed that House consent was in fact necessary for final adjournment of the Senate.

In summary, we hold that the consent of the House of Representatives is a prerequisite for a valid final adjournment of the Senate. Since it was not obtained in this instance, there was no "recess of the Senate" within the meaning of article IV, section 8. Therefore, the recess appointment power under section 8 (b) was not operative. Because defendants' appointments were not submitted to the Senate for its consent as required by section 8 (a), their appointments are invalid.

Judgments of quo warranto are entered, declaring the defendants are unlawfully holding the offices which they occupy and they are accordingly ousted and excluded therefrom.

Delaying Adjournment Pending Signing of Bills In Order

1 (h). The Senate agreed to a motion providing for the Senate to adjourn upon the completion of signing bills by the presiding officer which have been transmitted from the House. The motion carried by a 28-19 vote.

Senator Bell raised a point of order that this motion was out of order in that the Chair could not sign bills after the Senate has adjourned.

The Chair, Lt. Gov. Ernest P. Kline, ruled the motion was in order as it was a decision of the whole Senate.

Senator Bell appealed the ruling of the Chair and the Senate sustained the decision of the Chair (Senate Journal, July 24, 1975, pages 727-729.) (See also: Senate Journal, Dec. 14, 1983, p. 1539.)

Motion to Adjourn Out of Order During Executive Session Without a Motion for Executive Session to Rise

1 (i). The President, ruled that a motion to adjourn was out of order without a prior motion that executive session do now rise. (Senate Journal, 1979, p. 436.)

Motion to Adjourn May Not Interrupt Speaker

1 (j). The President held that a motion to adjourn is out of order if it interrupts a speaker. A speaker may be interrupted only by a call of order, a question of privilege, or a call for the previous question. (Senate Journal, 1980, p. 1935.)

Revision or Amendment of Sine Die Adjournment Resolution Possible But Must Have Concurrence of the House

1 (k). On parliamentary inquiry from Senator Zemprelli, the President held that under the currently adopted adjournment sine die resolution, the session terminates at the exact time indicated. The President went on to decide that any revision or amendatory resolution would require the concurrence of the House of Representatives. (Senate Journal, 1980, pp. 2233-4.)

Motion to Adjourn Takes Precedence Over Motion For Previous Question

1 (l). A motion for the previous question was followed by a motion to adjourn. The President pro tempore, on point of order from Senator Mellow, decided that under Rule XIII, Section 8, a motion to adjourn is always in order except when the motion for the previous question had been voted on in the affirmative. There had been no vote on the motion for the previous question; so, the motion to adjourn was in order. (Senate Journal, 1984, p. 2243.)

SECTION 2

AMENDMENTS

Amendment on Third Reading by Unanimous Consent Only

2 (b). Senator Dent, having offered amendments to Senate Bill No. 23, which was on the third reading calendar, Senator Tallman objected.

The Chair, Lieutenant-Governor John C. Bell, sustained the objection and ruled that under Rule 17 of the Senate Rules, the amendments could not be considered on third reading in the face of the objection of a Senator. Rule 17 provides "No amendments shall be permitted to a bill on third reading except by unanimous consent." (Legislative Journal, February 9, 1943, pp. 273 and 274.)

To Title in Order, When Concurring in House Amendments

2 (c). The Speaker decided that, in concurring in amendments made by the House of Representatives, it was in order for the Senate to amend the title to correspond with the amendments made by the House of Representatives. (Senate Journal, 1861, p. 254.) (See also Senate Journals, 1874, p. 692, and 1889, p. 364.)

Cannot be Made to Bills That Will Change Original Purpose

2 (g). The President pro tempore decided that the bill was so amended as to repeal the whole act of 1868, and then to extend it to the whole State, and was so altered in its passage as to be changed from its original purpose, and therefore is unconstitutional. (Senate Journal, 1879, p. 389.) (See also Senate Journal, 1974, page 1310.) (See also Senate Journal, 1974, page 1465.)

Not Germane to Resolution, Out of Order

2 (h). The President decided it out of order to amend a resolution to print the report of the Pennsylvania State College, by adding a provision for the appointment of a committee to investigate its accounts. (Senate Journal, 1875, p. 202.)

The President pro tempore (Mr. Penrose in the Chair) was of the opinion that the original resolution of the Senator from Lebanon pertained to a question of law or jurisdiction, whilst the substitute or amendment of the Senator from Bucks raised a question of fact. He therefore decided the point of order raised by the Senator from Lebanon to be well taken and that the amendment of the Senator from Bucks was not germane and therefore not in order. (Senate Journal, Extra Session, 1891, p. 624.)

Can be Made to Resolution Regulating Senate Business

2 (i). A resolution fixing an afternoon session for certain business pending an amendment was offered fixing a session at a different time, on which the President ruled that the purpose of both the resolution and the proposed amendment being to regulate the business of the Senate, the amendment was germane, and therefore ruled the point of order to be not well taken. (Senate Journal, 1881, p. 1014.)

Senate Can Re-insert Matter Stricken Out in Committee of the Whole

2 (j). Mr. Gordon submitted the point of order "that the motion of the Senator from Delaware (Mr. Cooper) was not in order, as it proposed to insert in the bill a provision just stricken out in the Committee of the Whole." Decided not well taken. Decision sustained by the Senate. (Senate Journal, 1883, p. 625.)

Bills on Concurring in House Amendments to be Noted on Senate Calendar

2 (k). Mr. Buckman raised the point of order that the Senate Rules provide bills amended in the House shall not be considered until properly noted on the Senate Calendar. The President decided the point of order well taken and ordered the amended bills noted in the Calendar. (Legislative Journal, 1937, p. 1993.)

To Amend Senate Bill Returned from House with Amendments, When in Order

2 (l). Mr. Gordon submitted the point of order that, as the question before the Senate was on concurring in the amendments made by the House of Representatives to said bill, and the amendment proposed by Mr. Hughes, not being an amendment to the amendments made by the House, the motion was not in order. The President decided the point of order well taken, and ruled the motion out of order. (Senate Journal, 1883, p. 1241.)

House Amendments to Senate Bill

2 (n). Mr. Ealy raised the point of order that in considering amendments made by the House to a Senate bill, the Senate had to consider them as a whole and could not separate them and act upon them in this manner.

The Chair (Lieutenant-Governor Samuel S. Lewis) declared the point of order well taken and ruled that the Senate must either concur or nonconcur in the bill as amended by the House. (Legislative Journal, May 12, 1941, p. 2083.)

Germane to Original Purpose of Bill, Defined

2 (o). Senator Weiner questioned the germaneness of amendments offered by Senator Scott. The bill (House Bill 1082, Printer's No. 1199) being amended was an amendment of the Election Code providing for the opening and closing of polls. Senator Scott's amendments proposed to include in the bill provisions relating to the resident requirement of watchers. Senator Seyler asked for a ruling by the Chair. After a conference with the Presiding Officer and the leadership, Senator Seyler withdrew his request and Senator Weiner moved the amendments be laid on the table pending an opinion from the Attorney General.

OPINION

June 19, 1961

Constitutionality of proposed Amendment to House Bill No. 1082, Printer's No. 1199

Article III, Section 1 of the Constitution of the Commonwealth of Pennsylvania reads as follows:

"No law shall be passed except by bill, and no bill shall be so altered or amended on its passage through either House, as to change its original purpose."

In 82 C.J.S., Statutes, Section 30, it is said:

A Constitutional provision that a bill shall not be so altered or amended, in the course of its enactment, as to change its original purpose does not prevent the insertion of amendments germane to, and within the scope of, the original.

"A constitutional provision that a bill shall not be so altered or amended, in the course of its enactment, as to change its original purpose is not to be so construed as to prevent the introduction of matter merely extending the purpose or scope of operation of the bill, or limiting it, or the substitution of a measure or insertion of amendments having the same purpose as the original or germane to, and within the scope of, the original; and a bill thus limited and extended by the amendments of the two houses in its scope or purpose, or otherwise amended, but embracing no matter not germane to the original purpose or the subject of legislation as expressed in the title of the act which it purports to amend, may become a valid law. Also, such a restriction should not be so embraced as to prevent the substitution for a bill which is essentially amendatory in character in another related to the same subject and having the same general effect on existing laws, although some changes may be proposed by the substitute which would not have resulted from the passage of the original.

"The 'purpose' contemplated in such a constitutional provision is the general purpose of the bill, and not the mere details through which and by which that purpose is manifested and effectuated. Such a constitutional provision should be given a reasonable construction so as not unnecessarily to embarrass proper legislation. . ."

In 158 A.L.R., in the annotation appearing at page 421, in discussing constitutional provisions against changing the purpose of the bill during passage, it is said:

"III Types of alterations or amendments which do not change original purpose:

"a. Immaterial changes, 424.

"b. Extension of scope, 426.

"c. Limitation of scope, 428.

"d. Changes in time, 428.

"e. Substitution of other measures having the same purpose as original measures, 429.

"f. Additions of matters germane to original purpose, 429."

In the case of Black Hawk Consol. Mines Co. v. Gallegos, 191 P. 2d 996 (1948), the Court at page 1005 said:

"The purpose of Article 4, Section 15 of the New Mexico Constitution prohibiting the altering or amending a bill on its passage so as to change its purpose is, solely to prohibit amendments not germane to subject of legislation expressed in the title of act purported to be amended.

"See Stein v. Leeper, 78 Ala. 517; Hall v. Steel, 82 Ala. 562, 2 So. 650; Alabama State Bridge Corp. v. Smith, 217 Ala. 311, 116 So. 695." (Emphasis supplied.)

In Cone v. Garner, 3 S. W. 2d 1 (1927), the Constitution of the State of Arkansas reads:

"No law shall be passed except by bill, and no bill shall be so altered or amended on its passage through either house as to change its purpose."

At page 4 the Court said:

"It is said that the object of this section of the Constitution was that the Senate and House of Representatives of the state might not be hampered or embarrassed in amending and perfecting their bills and thus be driven to accomplish by a number of bills that which might well be accomplished by one bill, but the purpose of the section was to forbid amendments which should not be germane to the subject of legislation expressed in the title of the act which it purports to amend. Hickey v. State, 114 Ark. 526, 170 S.W. 562."

In a later case, the Supreme Court of Arkansas, in Pope v. Oliver, 117 S. W. 2d 1072 (1938), said, in speaking of an alleged violation of Section 21 of Article V of the State Constitution, that:

". . .The purpose of this provision in our Constitution is to prevent amendments to a bill which would not be germane to the subject of the legislation expressed in the title of the Act, which it purports to amend. Loftin v. Watson, 32 Ark. 414; Hickey v. State, 114 Ark. 526, 170 S. W. 562; Cone v. Garner, 175 Ark. 860, 3 S. W. 2d 1; Matthews v. Byrd, 187 Ark. 458, 60 S. W. 2d 909." (Emphasis supplied.)

It may well be argued that since the purpose of House Bill No. 1082 was to amend the Election Code that any other amendment included in the bill concerning elections was but an extension of the scope of the original amendment.

The initial amendment in the bill regulated the time for opening and closing polls. The Election Code provides for the appointment of watchers and also provides they may, with certain exceptions, be present during the time when the polls are open as well as closed. The second amendment was well within the subject of the original amendment and was certainly germane to the general subject of elections in the Commonwealth of Pennsylvania.

It is, therefore, the opinion of the writer that the proposed amendment to House Bill No. 1082, Printer's No. 1199, as proposed by Senator Scott is not in violation of Article III, Section 1 of the Constitution of the Commonwealth of Pennsylvania.

/s/Harrington Adams
Deputy Attorney General
/s/Anne X. Alpern
Attorney General

(Legislative Journal, June 13, 1961, p. 2250-52. Legislative Journal, June 20, 1961, p. 2399.)

House Amendments to Senate Bill — Procedure of House Not to be Questioned — Germaneness

2 (p). The Senate had under consideration the amendments placed in Senate Bill 1400 by the House. The Senate passed the bill which amended the Administrative Code by providing for the Commissioner of Corrections to deputize certain individuals. The House amended the bill by adding the provision which restricted powers of certain departments, boards and commissions.

Senator Coppersmith raised the point of order that the amendments were not germane to the original subject in that it had nothing to do with school children.

The President, Lieutenant Governor Ernest P. Kline, ruled the point of order not well taken and gave his reasons as follows:

"...the Chair would like to quote for the record the Rule, which is Rule XV, covering amendments, when in order.

" 'Amendments shall be in order when a bill is reported or re-reported from committee, on second consideration and by unanimous consent on third consideration. No amendment shall be received by the presiding officer or considered by the Senate which destroys the general sense of the original bill, or is not appropriate and closely allied to the original purpose of the bill. Any member upon request. ..' and so on.

"It would be the ruling of the Chair that the gentleman's point of order is not well taken and the bill is in order for two reasons:

"First, it is an amendment to the Administrative Code, and it has been the history of this Chair to broadly rule that so long as the amendments are in their proper context within the statutory structure of the Commonwealth, they will be accepted and considered; and secondly, the fact of the matter is that this Senate is not now considering an amendment, we are considering a bill on concurrence in House amendments, and it would be improper for me, as the presiding officer of this Chamber, to rule the amendment out of order.

"The gentleman's point is not well taken and it is the ruling of the Chair that from that point of order the bill is, indeed, in proper form."

Senator Coppersmith then raised a second point of order that the House Journal showed that the bill was passed by the House without, as the Constitution requires that, all amendments made to a bill must be printed for the use of the members before the final vote is taken on the bill. The bill was passed by the House without the amendments being printed in the bill but rather copies of the amendments were made available to the Members. He also referred to a letter from the Speaker regarding the Constitutional duties of the Senate regarding the passage of bills.

The President, Lieutenant Governor Ernest P. Kline, ruled the point of order not well taken and gave his reasons as follows:

"First, as it relates to his suggestion that I consider the letter sent to me earlier by the Speaker of the House, I can understand the position of the Speaker of the House and, frankly, although the issue has never been drawn in this House, I share his concern about the propriety of accepting a bill on final passage that may not have met what I would consider to be the constitutional requirements. However, when a piece of legislation reaches this Chamber in proper, final constitutional order from the House of

Representatives, it should be accepted and acted upon without regard to any action that may have taken place in the House prior to final passage. To have this Senate look behind the final action of the House of Representatives would set, I think, a dangerous precedent which could disrupt the long established and, I believe, desperately needed independence of each House of this Legislature.

"I would like to quote to you from Jefferson's Manual which warns in part: 'It is a breach of order in debate to notice what has been said on the same subject in the other House, or the particular votes or majorities on it there; because the opinion of each House should be left to its own independency, not to be influenced by the proceedings of the other; and the quoting them might beget reflections leading to a misunderstanding between the two Houses.'

"The United States Congress invokes that concept so vigorously that it prohibits the insertion of quotes from the record and specific votes from the other Chamber. We have not been that rigid in our interpretation of the debate that goes on on this floor, but I do believe that we should maintain the independence of each House. Our duty is to judge the merits of each issue, not the parliamentary conduct of the other House. For that reason it would be the ruling of this Chair that the bill is in order as it came from the House and, further, that the Senate cannot take exception nor stand in judgment of actions taken by the House prior to final passage of a bill."

The decision of the Chair was appealed during which the question arose as to what Constitutional responsibility the Senate had in regards to any House procedure.

The following occurred:

The PRESIDENT. The Chair would like to point out to the Members that the ruling was very carefully explained and did say that when a piece of legislation reaches this Chamber in final, proper constitutional order, which presumes a great deal of things, the ruling goes to the question of, essentially, whether or not this Chamber should go behind the final action of the House which, when we get it, we presume is constitutional and decide whether their actions were indeed proper.

Senator REIBMAN. Mr. President, you indicated that this Body would presume that the other Body passed the bill in constitutional form. Is not that a rebuttable presumption if the House Journal indicates that it was not in proper form? Would that not be proper evidence?

The PRESIDENT. My response to that, Senator, would be that, first of all, I do not think this Body should stand in judgment of the actions of the House in that regard. That is the thin line that I do not think this Senate should transgress, as to whether or not they should decide whether the actions of the House are constitutional or not on those kinds of issues as they relate particularly to the House Rules.

In my ruling I have tried to avoid discussing the actual question, satisfied that when the bill reached here, it reached here in proper constitutional form. I do not think this is the time nor the place in which to stand in judgment of the House action which got it here.

Senator REIBMAN. Mr. President, I am a little puzzled. You said that we would not stand in judgment of the House Rules, but this is not a question of the House Rules, this is a question of constitutionality. The Constitution very plainly says that the amendments must be in print. The House Journal, which is the best evidence, says that it is not. I think that we cannot be a party to an unconstitutional action. If the House does it, I do not think we have to concur in an unconstitutional action.

The PRESIDENT. Senator, in an effort to be responsive to what you are saying, I will get into some of the questions involved here.

The House Rules do require, as does the Constitution, that the ". . . amendments made thereto shall be printed for the use of the members ..."

It has been, as is my understanding, the ruling of the House that the printing of the amendments, in the same form that we take it from the Legislative Reference Bureau in the seven copies, meets that constitutional requirement. That has been the traditional decision of the House and, frankly, the decision of this Senate from time to time, and I do not think we should be deciding whether or not the House is correct in making that kind of interpretation of their own Rules.

The decision of the Chair was sustained by the Senate (43-5) (Senate Journal 1974, p. 2525.)

Appropriation to Harrisburg for Fire Protection of State Buildings — Amendments to Extend to Other Municipalities In Order

2 (q). The Senate had under consideration House Bill 191 which appropriated money to the City of Harrisburg for fire protection to the State buildings in Harrisburg. Senator Murphy offered an amendment to extend coverage to all communities requesting an appropriation for protection of State buildings in their areas.

A point of order was raised by Senator Bell that the amendments were not germane to the subject matter in the bill.

The President, Lieutenant Governor Ernest P. Kline, stated:

"The gentleman raises a point of order as to whether or not the amendments are germane, and it is the ruling of the Chair that the amendments are in order and are germane.

"Our Rules state that: 'No amendments shall be received by the presiding officer or considered by the Senate which destroys the general sense of the original bill, or is not appropriate and closely allied to the original purpose of the bill.'

"The original intent of the bill is to provide funds for the City of Harrisburg for the purpose of fire protection and, as the Chair interprets the amendments, the intent is closely allied to that because they extend that protection to all other cities, boroughs and townships, limiting it to fire protection, and thereby follows generally the intent of the original bill." (Senate Journal, 1974, p. 1838.)

To Amend House Amendments to Senate Bill Not in Order

2 (r). The Senate had under consideration the concurrence in House amendments to Senate Bill 737. Senator Coppersmith offered amendments to the House amendments. Senator Bell asked the Chair to rule whether or not the amendments were in order. The President, Lieutenant Governor Ernest P. Kline, stated:

"From the standpoint of presenting amendments on the question of their precedence over a motion to concur in the amendments, they are in order, Senator, and that is why Senator Coppersmith was proper in presenting the amendment at that time.

"The question you raise is one that, as long as I have been in the Senate and in all of my research, has never really been decided by this Body, and that is the question of whether or not this Body wants to begin now the practice of amending House amendments to a Senate bill, and I take it that is the point you raise. . . In line with a long-standing practice in legislative bodies and in line with a practice that has been used in this Senate before, it would be the position of the Chair that this matter should not be decided by the Chair, but, rather, submitted to the Body for its advice on this issue. I would like to take just a moment as the Presiding Officer to explain to you precisely what is at issue and what is involved:

"Senator Bell calls to the attention of the Members Senate Rule XV which covers amendments and reads:

'Amendments shall be in order when a bill is reported or re-reported from committee, on second consideration and by unanimous consent on third consideration.'

"The question which the Chair intends to submit, without ruling, to the Members is whether or not Senator Coppersmith's amendment to House amendments is in order at this time. This question is fully debatable."

After considerable debate Senator Stauffer raised a parliamentary inquiry asking if the Senate Rules were silent on this situation, would Mason's Manual prevail.

The president, Lieutenant Governor Ernest P. Kline, replied:

"It would be my position that where the Rules are totally silent Mason's and/or Jefferson's would prevail. The point which is at issue here, as I understand it, is that the Rules are not silent. The Rule clearly states when an amendment is in order, and the Body could determine that to be the exclusive time at which an amendment could be received. Technically, the Rules are not totally silent, but as a direct answer to your question, where the Rules are silent we refer to Mason's and/or Jefferson's.

"Senator, it is the Chair's position that our Rule is not specifically clear to cover you, and that is the reason for the Chair's action. Under a procedure in Mason's Legislative Manual which reads, 'A point of order is decided by the presiding officer without debate unless in doubtful cases he submits the question to the body for advice or decision.'

"It is my judgment that that Rule is not so clear as to permit the Chair to make a ruling that can be challenged, and for that reason I chose the course of submitting it to the full Body."

Senator Frame raised objection to have the Senate decide this question. He stated that he thought it was the Chair's responsibility to make a ruling.

In answer to Senator Frame the President, Lieutenant Governor Ernest P. Kline, replied:

"Senator Frame, the Chair would like to point out to you that I would much prefer to do things in a democratic manner, rather than in a dictatorial, heavyhanded manner. When these issues come up that are so closely divided, it is my preference to submit the matter to the full Body and let you Senators decide how you wish to rule your Chamber, rather than my trying to superimpose my own personal judgment on you.

"I am surprised that anyone would question that — my decision to ask the Senate for advice in this matter seems like a very orderly, sensible, democratic thing to do. It surprises me that anyone would be concerned about my choosing that course. The Rules are made by the Senators collectively. It is my job to interpret them and, when they are clear, I do my best to interpret them subject to appeal. In an issue such as this, which is of such profound importance to this Senate, I have chosen the course of submitting them to the Senate and asking for its advice on the matter."

The Senate decided the amendments were out of order (1-45) (Senate Journal, 1974, p. 1496.) (Senate Journal, July 18, 1977, p. 670.) The Senate reversed this decision on October 19, 1977 (Senate Journal, October 19, 1977, p. 981.)

Appropriation Bills, Additional Subject, Prohibited

2 (s). The Senate had under consideration Senate Bill 394 which appropriated moneys to the Land and Water Development Fund when Senator Ewing offered an amendment that provided that a finding by the Department of Community Affairs that exclusionary zoning or development policies exist in a political subdivision shall not serve as a basis for denial of requests for grants-in-aid made pursuant to this act.

Senator Lamb raised the point of order that the amendment was in violation of Senate Rule XV which provides that:

"No amendment shall be received by the presiding officer or considered by the Senate which destroys the general sense of the original bill, or is not appropriate and closely allied to the original purpose of the bill"

and the Constitution of Pennsylvania, Art. III, Sec. 11 which provides that:

"The general appropriation bill shall embrace nothing but appropriations for the executive, legislative and judicial departments of the Commonwealth, for the public debt and for public schools. All other appropriations shall be made by separate bills, each embracing but one subject."

The President, Lieutenant Governor Ernest P. Kline, ruled the amendments out of order.

Senator Ewing appealed the ruling of the Chair and the following debate took place on the appeal:

Senator STROUP. Mr. President and Members of the Senate, the interpretation being placed upon Rule XV.1 by the Chair is, in my considered opinion, extremely restrictive and certainly in derogation of the intent of the Rule as adopted by this Body. The major purpose of the Rule was to implement Article III, Section 1, of our Constitution, which reads as follows:

"No law shall be passed except by bill, and no bill shall be so altered or amended, on its passage through either House, as to change its original purpose."

That portion of the Rule itself, relative to that which we are now considering the interpretation, reads as follows:

"No amendments shall be received by the presiding officer or considered by the Senate which" — and notice the word — "destroys the general sense of the original bill, or is not appropriate and closely allied to the original purpose of the bill."

In considering the interpretation of the Rule in the light of the Constitution which was the guide in the adoption of the Rule by this Body, one must consider the language, and I quote, "which destroys the general sense of the original bill." So, one must ask one's self this question, and the query is: Does the amendment offered by Senator Ewing in any way destroy the original purpose of the bill? The answer to that query must in all logic be that the amendment offered in no way destroys the appropriation or the amount of the appropriation. That section of the bill remains untouched and the appropriation remains the same. It is not taken out, it is not destroyed.

Mr. President, the second portion of the Rule which one must consider is the language, and I am quoting, "or is not appropriate and closely allied to the original purpose of the bill." The query then is: Is it not appropriate to prescribe the procedure by which funds in appropriation bills shall be expended? To limit this Body in its effort to further direct expenditure of appropriation moneys is entirely contrary to the purpose of Article III, Section 1, and the intention of the Rule as it was adopted. The intention of the rule was to make it impossible to destroy a bill that came out on the floor, or was in committee, in which you took the whole portion of the bill out, gutted it and left only the frame of the original bill and portions of the title, perhaps. That was the intention of this Rule. That is what we are trying to do to follow the Constitution.

Now, Mr. President, a further query might be asked and I am quoting: "Is the method of expenditure of the funds closely allied to the original purpose of the bill?" Again, I submit to you in all logic, and I think in common sense, too, the method of procedure by which funds may be expended is not only appropriate and closely allied, but is entirely germane to the appropriation of funds.

The Chair has further called our attention to Article III, Section 11, and the forepart of the first sentence of that particular part of the Constitution deals with general appropriation bills. We do not have a general appropriation bill before us, but I read with pertinency the relevant portion which the Chair interprets as follows: "All other appropriations shall be made by separate bills, each embracing but one subject."

So we rest, I believe the Chair rests, the entire decision upon this particular item, one subject.

Here we get into a semantic situation of reference and modification and language, and I maintain that the words "one subject" refer to one subject of appropriations, and nothing more. Therefore, I maintain that the appeal from the Chair should be sustained by this Body and I further say to you that to continue this type of restrictive and very limited interpretation is placing a halter around the neck of the Members of this Body. Such was not the intent of the adoption of the Rule.

Senator LAMB. Mr. President, I believe and feel that the Chair has correctly interpreted Rule XV and the Constitution and I would ask the Members on this side to sustain the ruling of the Chair.

Senator BELL. Mr. President, it is a well-known interpretation of the constitutional law processes that we may interpret the Constitution as an entire piece of cloth, you do not piecemeal it; and to interpret the Constitution as an entire piece of cloth, let me refer to Article VIII, Section 16, which deals with the $500 million for a Land and Water Conservation and Reclamation Fund. I understand this pertains to this bill.

The Constitution reads that this money and I will now go into Section 16: "....The provision of State financial assistance to political subdivisions and municipal authorities of the Commonwealth of Pennsylvania for the construction" — and then it goes through a series of things and it ends, — "subject to such conditions and liabilities as the General Assembly may prescribe."

Mr. President, this clearly is a condition that is being sought to be inserted into this bill.

Senator ROVNER. Mr. President, I rise to agree with my colleagues, Senator Ewing, Senator Stroup and Senator Bell, and feel that what we are doing here today is going to frustrate the legislative processes of Pennsylvania, because it is certainly unfair that just because the majority disagrees with something it will not be considered.

I know last year, for instance, many people in this room wanted no-fault insurance. They knew they could not pass no-fault insurance through the committee system, but yet it was the proper thing to do because the people of Pennsylvania wanted to hear a debate on no-fault insurance at that time. Mr. President, even though you should not have the Rule, it is certainly germane for the Majority to begin consideration and have discussions and, whenever the Majority disagrees with something the Minority wants to do, not to accept that amendment, I say that is a sorry day for the people of Pennsylvania.

Therefore, Mr. President, I hope the Members today will appeal the ruling of the Chair so that we can at least consider Senator Ewing's amendment.

The Senate sustained the decision. (Senate Journal, 1973, p. 422.)

Appropriation Bill — Stop Gap to General Appropriation Bill — Constitutional

2 (t). The Senate had under consideration HB 1147 which the Senate had amended. The House of Representatives passed the bill providing for the paying of the general costs of government from June 30, 1973 to August 1, 1973. This was due to the failure of the General Assembly enacting a General Appropriation Bill for the 1973-74 fiscal period. The Senate Appropriations Committee amended the bill making it a General Appropriation Bill.

A point of order was raised by Senator Stroup that the amendments changed the original purpose of the bill and were unconstitutional and in violation of Senate Rules.

Senator STROUP. Mr. President, my point of order is, first, the question of the violation of the Rules of this Senate that is now before us in consideration of House Bill No. 1147, and, secondly, the question of the constitutionality of the consideration by this Senate of House Bill No. 1147 as it has been altered by the Appropriations Committee at Printer's No. 1488.

May I submit to you, first of all, Mr. President, and to you my colleagues, that the Rules of this Senate are very specifically set forth as we adopted them in this Body only several months ago. The Rules to which I refer are based on the Constitution of Pennsylvania and that is the reason they were inserted in our Rules in this Body.

The first Rule is Section 1, subsection (b) of Article XIV of the Rules of this Body, which reads specifically as follows:

"No alteration or amendment shall be considered which is not appropriate and closely allied to the original purpose of the bill."

Then if I may, I refer you to Rule No. XV, which reads as follows, and I quote the pertinent part of that Rule:

"No amendments shall be received by the presiding officer or considered by the Senate which destroys the general sense of the original bill, or is not appropriate and closely allied to the original purpose of the bill."

Now such, beyond any question of effective contravention, are the Rules of this Body...Article III, Section 1, of the Constitution of 1968 — and some of you in this Body were members of that Constitutional Convention — states as follows:

"No law shall be passed except by bill, and no bill shall be so altered or amended, on its passage through either House, as to change its original purpose."

It cannot be more clearly stated in the Constitution and the Rules that we adopted are based on the Constitution, that particular segment of the Constitution which we inserted in our Rules.

Mr. President, the subject and the purpose of House Bill No. 1147, Printer's No. 1391, which I now consider with you as it passed the House was clearly expressed in the title of the bill as follows — that title is now stricken from the bill which is before us right now read as follows:

"Making an appropriation to the State Treasurer for the purpose of paying salaries and wages of State officers and employees and other ordinary and general expenses in the interim between June 30, 1973 and August 1, 1973, and for the payment of bills incurred and remaining unpaid at the close of the fiscal year ending June 30, 1973."

That was for a period of one month. That is House Bill No. 1147 and its title as it came to us from the other Body.

However, mind you, the Senate Appropriations Committee has totally altered House Bill No. 1147 as it passed the other Body. It has entirely deleted the title of that bill and in its stead has rewritten the title of a new bill and you can see it in front of us as follows:

"To provide for the expenses of the Executive, Legislative and Judicial Departments of the Commonwealth, the public debt and for public schools for the fiscal year July 1, 1973 to June 30, 1974 ..."

This is a complete alteration and change. Making House Bill No. 1147 a General Appropriations bill is the effect of the complete change of the bill which came from the House, contrary to our Rules and contrary to our Constitution.

Now, very clearly, the purpose of House Bill No. 1147 as it was passed by the House was to appropriate — we all know this — $100 million to the State Treasurer for the purpose of salaries and wages of employees and other ordinary expenses just for a thirty-day period. Moreover, no legislative purpose is expressed by the original bill. House Bill No. 1147, to appropriate funds for either the public debt or for public schools, or for the expenses of the Executive, Legislative and Judicial Departments of the Commonwealth for the entire fiscal year.

I submit to you, Mr. President and my colleagues, the altered purpose expressed in its substituted title is to provide for the public debt, for the public schools and the expenses of the three branches of government for an entire year.

Further, the bill as it has been amended by the Appropriations Committee contains an appropriation in excess of $630 million for public assistance and medical assistance programs, a purpose which was expressly prohibited in House Bill No. 1147 as it came from the other Body. I ask you to look at the bill and you will see it there. It is impossible, I submit, in all considered opinion to conceive a more flagrant alteration of a bill in its passage through either House in the General Assembly or one that more obviously contravenes Article III, Section 1, of our Constitution, or of the Rules of this Body based on that Constitution. Now, any contention that this bill in its altered form does not change its original purpose is just beyond the bounds of common reason and utterly at variance with all the facts which are before us. Palpably, my colleagues, the Committee has altered this bill in violation of both the Constitution and the Rules of the Senate, there is no question about that that one can raise effectively whatsoever. It has increased the original appropriation of the bill from $100 million to more than $3.5 billion. It has appropriated money for other purposes. Patently, the bill now before us is not either appropriate to or closely allied to the original purpose of the bill as required by the Rules of the Senate and by our Constitution.

Now may I submit to you in case you are of the opinion, some of you, that we in this Body when we take our oath of office should not consider constitutionality. May I consider with you the Supreme Court decision in 85 Pa. 401 at page 412 in 1877, which upon being Shepherdized, has never been changed. This is the law of this Commonwealth, Mr. President. It is the law of the Commonwealth, my colleagues. This is what the Court said and it still stands unchanged:

"In regard to the passage of the law and the alleged disregard of the forms of legislation required by the constitution, we think the subject is not within the pale of judicial inquiry. So far as the duty and the conscience of the members of the legislature are involved the law is mandatory. They are bound by their oaths to obey the constitutional mode of proceedings, and any intentional disregard is a breach of duty and a violation of their oaths."

Mr. President, I feel very strongly about this situation here tonight, and I feel if we have rules and regulations and if we have a Constitution, it is our duty and our obligation to adhere to it. We must rise up and consider it, or else we are in utter disregard of the Rules we write and adopt based upon the Constitution of Pennsylvania.

There is no question that House Bill No. 1147 has been changed and completely altered and gutted, which is in violation of Article XIV, Section 1 (b), of the Rules of the Senate and Article XV.

Now, may I express the considered opinion, Mr. President, that the Chair might be consistent in its rulings with similar points of order on this identical question as submitted to the Chair previously in this Session.

The President, Lieutenant Governor Ernest P. Kline, ruled the amendments were in order and in doing so stated:

The PRESIDENT. The Chair understands Senator Stroup's presentation to be made in the form of asking for a ruling on the propriety of considering House Bill No. 1147 as it relates to the constitutional points raised by Senator Stroup and to the points connected with our Rules.

The constitutional points the Senator stated are clear and the Rules are clear. The Chair wishes to point out that in the opinion of this Presiding Officer the original purpose of House Bill No. 1147 was to fund on an interim basis the ordinary and general expenses of government for a thirty-one day period, and it is a reasonable exercise of legislative authority for the Senate to so amend this bill to include the funding of general government for the full year. It deals specifically with government expenses.

The gentleman referred to Senate Bill No. 765, which brings up an entirely different question where a Senate bill, which was intended to replace checks for the State Treasurer, was changed considerably to cover two subjects, which is specifically prohibited in any kind of bill except a General Appropriations bill, and transmitted to this Senate.

The question before us is the propriety of House Bill No. 1147, and it is the ruling of this Chair that the action taken by the Appropriations Committee was in order and the bill is properly before the Senate on constitutional grounds and is within the Rules of the Senate because it deals specifically with funding the general and ordinary expenses of the government.

Senator Ewing appealed the ruling of the Chair and the Senate sustained the decision. (Senate Journal, 1973, p. 753).

Not Germane — Changing Resolution of Censure to Expulsion

2 (u). The Senate was considering a resolution of censure when Senator Andrews presented amendments changing it to a resolution of expulsion.

The Chair, Lt. Gov. Ernest P. Kline, ruled the amendments out of order because they were not germane in that they changed the original purpose of the resolution.

Senator Andrews appealed the ruling of the Chair and the Senate sustained the decision of the Chair. (Senate Journal, April 22, 1975, pages 274-275.)

Germane — Changing Amendment to Constitution

2 (v). The Senate was considering Senate Bill 982 amending the Constitution relating to confirmation proceedings and the president judge of the Superior Court. Senator Nolan offered amendments striking out the title and text of said bill and inserting provisions to amend the Constitution to provide for the election of an Attorney General. The President, Lieutenant Governor Ernest P. Kline, ruled the amendments destroyed the original purpose of the bill and were, therefore, out of order, being in violation of the Constitution and Senate Rules. The decision was appealed and after much debate, the Senate reversed the decision. (Senate Journal, October 11, 1977, p. 905.)

Amendments to Amended Bill Not Yet Reprinted Which Gut Bill and Insert New Language Not in Order

2 (w). The President, in response to a parliamentary inquiry from Senator Gekas, held that after amendments have been adopted to any particular bill, another amendment which purports to gut the entire bill or insert totally new language is out of order until the bill is printed and the amendment could be drawn to that new printer's number. (Senate Journal, 1980, p. 1377.)

Secondary Amendments Not Germane To Main Amendment Are Out of Order

2 (x). On point of order, Senator Kelley objected to amendments made to an amendment. He stated that they were not germane to the main amendment and operated to change the main amendment. The President decided the amendments were germane and in order. On appeal, the Senate (22-28) did not sustain the decision of the Chair, and the amendments were found not germane and out of order. (Senate Journal, 1980, pp. 1397-9.)

Members Entitled to Copies of Amendments When Being Discussed

2 (y). The President, on a point of order raised by Senator Holl, decided that the members are entitled to copies of the amendments which are being discussed. (Senate Journal, 1980, p. 1635.)

Land Transfer Legislation Rules Not Applicable to Amendments on the Senate Floor

2 (z). Amendments were offered to a bill on the floor of the Senate. These amendments authorized the transfer of Commonwealth land. Senator Mellow raised a point of order that the amendments were out of order under Senate Rule XIV Section 8.1. The President held that the amendments were in order because the rule does not speak to amendments offered on the floor — it only applied to bills being reported from committee. On appeal, the Senate (26-24) upheld the decision of the Chair. (Senate Journal, 1982, pp. 1784-5.)

Amendments to House Amendments in Order if: Senate Rule XV is Suspended; They Amend the Amendments; and they are Germane to the Bill

2 (bb). There was a motion to suspend Senate Rule XV for the purpose of amending House amendments to a bill which was before the Senate on concurrence in those amendments. The President, responding to parliamentary inquiries, held: Any amendment subsequent to the suspension of Rule XV would be in order as long as it amends the amendments and not the original bill, and as long as the amendments are germane to the bill. (Senate Journal, 1983, pp. 280-1.)

Amendment of Senate Resolution Must Be Germane to the Resolution

2 (cc). A Member offered an amendment altering Senate Rule XXIV to a Senate Resolution providing for a special judicial study committee. Senator Jubelirer rose to a point of order to object to the amendment as not being germane. The President ruled the amendment was not in order because it was not germane to the resolution, and the rules require that any amendment to any proposition before the body be germane. (Senate Journal, 1983, p. 780.)

Amendment Can Be Withdrawn by Maker Before Action is Taken

2 (dd). An amendment to a bill was offered by Senator Street. During debate on the amendment, Senator Street withdrew his amendment. On point of order from Senator Williams, the Presiding Officer (Robert J. Kusse) decided that an amendment may be withdrawn at any time prior to action on the amendment; therefore, Senator Street's withdrawal was permitted. (Senate Journal, 1984, p. 2235.)

Amendment Which Adds a Bill Calling For a Non-Binding Referendum to a Joint Resolution Providing For a Constitutional Amendment Is Out of Order

2 (ee). The President pro tempore decided that an amendment which would add a bill calling for a non-binding referendum to a joint resolution providing for a constitutional amendment was incompatible, not germane, and out of order. On appeal, the Senate (26-22) upheld the decision of the Chair. (Senate Journal, 1984, pp. 2648-50.)

SECTION 3

APPEALS

Chairman May Vacate Chair on an Appeal From a Decision

3 (a). Mr. Walker raised the question that on an appeal from a decision of the Chair, the Presiding Officer must vacate the Chair and permit a Member of the Senate to preside.

The Presiding Officer ruled that he may vacate the Chair and that it is within the discretion of the Chair to decide whether he shall step down. (Legislative Journal, December 13, 1951, p. 6188.)

SECTION 4

BILLS

Consideration of, in Numerical Order

4 (a). The Senate decided that when bills on first reading are the pending order, it was not in order to proceed to the consideration of a bill not first in numerical order, without dispensing with the orders of the day. (Senate Journal, 1845, pp. 160-70.)

Negatived by the Senate, Not in Order to Introduce and Consider Similar Ones During the Same Session

4 (c). The President decided that it was not in order to consider a certain bill, as one containing similar provisions had been voted down at the present session of the Senate. (Senate Journal, 1878, p. 855.)

Negatived by the Senate, Not in Order to Consider Bill of Similar Character from the House During the Same Session

4 (d). The President decided that it is not in order to introduce into the Senate from the House of Representatives, or consider a bill which is in substance, in nature, or intent and purpose the same as a Senate Bill which has been defeated in the Senate during the present session. An appeal was taken. The Senate sustained the decision. (Senate Journal, 1878, p. 834.)

House Bill Negatived by Senate — Not in Order for Senate to Consider Bill of Similar Import from House at Same Session

4 (e). The Senate decided that it was not in order to consider a House bill similar in character to a House bill which has been negatived by the Senate at same session. (Senate Journal, 1907, pp. 2116, 2636.)

Unanimous Consent Required to Have Bill Go Over in Order

4 (g). Mr. Harris submitted the point of order that a request for a bill to go over in its order required unanimous consent. The President decided the point of order well taken. (Legislative Journal, 1933, p. 4695.)

Showing No Evidence of Consideration by Committee, Can be Considered by Senate If According to the Records Regularly Reported

4 (h). Mr. Govin submitted the point of order that there was no evidence of marks on the bill to indicate that it had been regularly considered and reported from committee, and therefore should not have been placed upon the calendar for consideration by the Senate. Whereupon, the President decided that as the absence of marks and date of reporting the bill on the back thereof did not vitiate the fact that, according to the record, the bill had been regularly reported, therefore, the point of order was not well taken. (Senate Journal, 1893, p. 1066.)

When Amendments Can Be Made to — What in Order on Final Passage of

4 (i). The Speaker decided that a bill having been reported, it can be amended only when upon its second or third reading, and that, upon the final passage of a bill, nothing is in order but discussion upon it, and the final vote upon it by yeas and nays, as required by the Constitution, except privileged questions, such as motion to reconsider. (Senate Journal, 1874, p. 192.)

Regularly Before the Senate, Can Be Disposed of by a Simple Majority

4 (j). The Speaker decided that when a bill was regularly before the Senate, a simple majority could make such a disposition of it as they saw proper. (Senate Journal, 1874, p. 722.)

Passed Both Houses, but Not Sent to the Governor Cannot Be Taken Up

4 (k). Mr. White submitted the point of order that a bill having passed the Senate, been sent to the House and returned from that body as having been therein passed without amendment, it is not in order for the Senate to take up the bill and amend it further. The Speaker decided the point of order well taken. Bills which have passed both Houses and have not been sent to the Governor cannot be taken up again and acted on. (Senate Journal, 1874, p. 908.)

Sent to Printer, Cannot Be Considered Until Returned to the Senate — Error by Printer in Not Properly Showing Amendments, Prevents Consideration of

4 (l). The President pro tempore decided that a bill having been sent to the printer to be printed, it was not in possession of the Senate, and therefore it was not in order to consider it under the rules. (Senate Journal, 1875, p. 477.)

In order to consider bill amended by the Senate which amendments were stricken out by the House and are not shown in bill when returned to Senate by error of printer in omitting brackets. Appeals from decisions of the Chair that the bill cannot be considered in a committee of conference because it was not the bill that was sent to the House, through error made by the printer. A vote on appeal was decision of Chair sustained that decision. (Legislative Journal, June 7, 1923, pp. 4294, 4295.)

Motion to Recommit, for Amending to Change Character of, Not in Order

4 (m). The President decided that a motion to recommit a bill to a committee, with instruction to the committee to amend the said bill so as to change its character was not in order. (Senate Journal, 1875, p. 357.)

Merits of, Not Debatable on Motion to Recommit, Postpone or Reconsider

4 (n). The President decided that the merits of a bill were not debatable on a motion to recommit (Legislative Journal, 1933, pp. 5644, 3036, 3572, 4123, 6275) nor on a motion to postpone (Legislative Journal, 1933, p. 2133) nor on a motion to reconsider the vote by which a bill passed second reading. (Legislative Journal, 1935, p. 4128.) (Legislative Journal, pp. 1843, 3190, 5714.) (Legislative Journal, February 28, 1949, pp. 756, 757, 758.) (Legislative Journal, April 13, 1949, p. 3123.)

Negatived by Committee Similar One Can Be Acted on by Senate

4 (o). The President decided that it was competent for the Senate to consider a bill similar to one which had previously been reported with a negative recommendation, if the said bill had not been acted upon by the Senate. (Senate Journal, 1876, p. 906.)

General, Local and Special — Class Legislation

4 (p). The Senate having under consideration "An act to secure the operatives and laborers engaged in and about coal mines and manufactories of iron and steel the payment of their wages at regular intervals and in lawful money of the United States," the President pro tempore decided that the Constitution prohibits legislation of a local or special character regulating labor, trade, mining or manufacturing. A general law is one that applies to all persons. A local law is one that operates within a limited territory. A special law is one that is not confined in its operation by territory, but is limited to a particular class, sect, trade or interest. Under the Constitution, the Legislature has not the power to make arbitrary distinctions in order to escape the prohibition of the fundamental law, but the subject must have some natural or necessary quality to constitute a class. This view is sustained by Sedgwick on statutes, and a decision by Judge Folgar, in 4 Heard, New York Report. The bill before us proposes to legislate for a particular and special body to operate in particular localities. Overruled by the Senate. (Senate Journal, 1879, pp. 667, 695.)

After Reconsideration of Vote on, Can Be Acted on Only When Reached in their Regular Order, Unless Regular Order is Dispensed With

4 (q). The vote negativing a bill on final passage having been reconsidered, the President pro tempore decided that the bill could not be considered until the order of "bills on final passage" was reached, except by two-thirds vote. (Senate Journal, 1879, p. 599.)

A bill being on third reading, and the vote by which it passed second reading having been reconsidered, the President pro tempore decided that the bill could not be considered on second reading until that was reached, except by suspending the orders. (Senate Journal, 1879, p. 613.)

Objection to Consideration of, Reconsidered Must Be Made at the Proper Time

4 (r). The order of business being bills on third reading, the President pro tempore (Mr. Reyburn in the chair), was of the opinion that the objection of the Senator from Elk (Mr. Hall) was raised too late, and the ruling of 1879, cited by him, did not apply, the Senate having already reconsidered the several votes by which the bill had passed second reading, and the bill being already under consideration, worked a suspension of the orders. He therefore decided the point of order to that effect submitted by the Senator from Venango (Mr. Lee) to be well taken. (Senate Journal 1883, p. 554.)

Amending Laws, Must Recite in Full the Part to Be Amended

4 (s). The Senate decided that a bill proposing to amend an act, failing to recite the section in full intended to be amended conflicted with Section 6, Article III of the Constitution, and was therefore, not in order. (Senate Journal, 1879, p. 620.)

Raising Revenue, Must Originate in the House

4 (t). A point of order was submitted by Mr. Lee that the amendment of the Senator from Delaware is not in order, because it adds a proviso to the bill which virtually makes it a bill for raising revenue, and all bills for raising revenue, by the Constitution, must originate in the House of Representatives, and the amendment is not germane and changes the purpose of the bill. Decided well taken by Senate. (Senate Journal, 1883, p. 711.)

Appropriating Money for the Erection of Monuments Does Not Require a Two-thirds Vote

4 (v).   Mr. Stober raised the point of order that the bill under consideration appropriated money for the erection of a monument and required a two-thirds vote. The President decided the point of order not well taken, as this was an appropriation for the erection of a monument and not to a charitable institution of the State. (Senate Journal, 1903, p. 825.)

Objections to Consideration of, Must Be Raised at the Proper Time

4 (w).   A bill being under consideration, Mr. Lee submitted the point of order that the bill, as amended, was not properly on the calendar, as contemplated by the rules, it having been imperfectly printed, and the bill could, therefore, not be considered at this time. Decided not well taken. (Senate Journal, 1883, p. 635.)

Merits of, Not Debatable on Motion to Suspend Rule for Purpose of Discharging Committee

4 (x).   A point of order was raised that a motion to suspend the rules for the purpose of discharging a committee from a particular bill, is not debatable, and if debatable the particular reason for the consideration of a particular bill is not debatable. The debate can be only upon the reason for the suspension of the rule and not upon the merits of a bill. The chair ruled that the question to suspend the rules is debatable, but that the question can be debated only insofar as the reason for the discharge of the committee may be essential. Therefore, the merits of the bill cannot be discussed on a motion to suspend the rules. (Senate Journal, 1919, pp. 2763-64.)

Merits of, Debatable on Motion to Postpone Consideration of, to a Fixed Time

4 (y).   Mr. McNeil submitted the point of order that it was not in order to discuss the merits of the main question on a motion to postpone the consideration of the same until a definite time. The President pro tempore decided that the merits of the main question could be incidentally discussed on a motion to postpone to a day fixed, and the point of order was, therefore, not well taken (Senate Journal, 1885, p. 664.)

Merits of Other Bill Not Debatable

4 (z).   The President decided that the merits of another bill not under consideration were not debatable, but that the remarks had to be limited to the bill under discussion and related subjects. (Legislative Journal, 1935, p. 5859.)

Constitutionality of, to Be Determined by the Senate.

4 (aa).   Mr. McDonald submitted the point of order "that the bill was not in order for the reason that it was contrary to Article III, section 6, of the Constitution." The President pro tempore decided that as the question of the constitutionality of the bill is a matter which will be decided by the Senate in the consideration and final disposition of the bill, it is not in the province of the Chair; by decision, as to the constitutionality of the bill, to assume the duty and power properly vested in the Senate. (Senate Journal, 1893, p. 209.)

Postponed Cannot Be Called Up the Same Day It Was Proposed

4 (bb).   Mr. Freed asked if he could call up a bill just placed on the Postponed Calendar.

The Chair, Lieutenant-Governor Lloyd H. Wood, ruled a bill placed on the Postponed Calendar could not be called up until it properly appeared on the Calendar. (Legislative Journal, June 26, 1951, p. 348.)

Carrying Appropriations Need Not Be Referred to Appropriations Committee

4 (cc).   Mr. Seyler raised the question of parliamentary inquiry as to whether it was customary that any bill which carried an appropriation is referred to the Appropriations Committee before final passage.

The Chair, Lieutenant-Governor John Morgan Davis, ruled that this was done in some instances but not in all. Therefore it might be termed customary rather than mandatory. (Legislative Journal, 1959, p. 451.)

Over in Order — Reason for Motion Debatable

4 (dd).   Mr. Seyler raised the point of information if it was in order to debate a motion to put a bill over in order.

The Presiding Officer ruled the reason for the motion is debatable. (Legislative Journal, 1959, p. 1251.) (See also Mason's Manual, sec. 494, p. 332.) (Senate Journal, 1971, p. 372.)

Re-reported From Committee As Amended — Must Appear on Calendar Two Days

4 (ee).   Senate Bill 851 was re-reported from committee as amended and was called up for consideration the next day.

Senator Coppersmith raised the point of order that since it had not appeared on the Calendar for two days it could not be considered.

The President, Lieutenant Governor Ernest P. Kline, ruled the point of order well taken and quoted Senate Rule 13, Section 13 as follows:

"Any bill or resolution re-reported from committee as amended shall not be finally considered until it has appeared on the Senate Calendar for two legislative days." (Senate Journal, 1973, p. 1128.)

Over in Order — Precedence over Reverting to Prior Printer's No.

4 (ff).   Senator Hager moved to have House Bill 406 reverted to a prior printer's no. Senator Smith, after some debate, moved that the bill go over in its order. The President, Lieutenant Governor Ernest P. Kline, ruled the motion to have the bill go over in its order took precedence over the motion to revert. (Senate Journal, November 14, 1978, p. 1097.)

Appropriation — Preferred and Nonpreferred — What Determines

4 (gg).   The Senate was considering several appropriation bills under the headings of "Preferred" and "Nonpreferred." Senator Kelley raised a point of parliamentary inquiry as to what or who determines whether a bill is preferred or nonpreferred. The Presiding Officer, Senator Scanlon, stated that the Constitution of Pennsylvania by providing any appropriation to any charitable or educational institution not under the absolute control of the Commonwealth would need a two-thirds vote of the Senate and as such would be under the category of nonpreferred appropriation. All others, such as State department, boards and commissions and the like would need only a majority vote of the elected Senators and would, therefore, be under the category of preferred. The Secretary of the Senate when preparing the calendar decides, under these provisions, which are preferred and nonpreferred. (Senate Journal, November 15, 1978, p. 1146.)

Bills Transferring Existing Appropriations Need Not Be Referred to Appropriations Committee Before Third Consideration

4 (hh).   Senator Stauffer inquired whether a bill needed to be referred to the Appropriations Committee for a fiscal note under Senate Rule XIV, Section 16(b). The President held that it did not require such a note because the funds were being transferred from an existing appropriation and the bill merely added the authority to act. (Senate Journal, 1979, p. 756.)

Bills Other Than General Appropriation Bill Shall Embrace But One Subject

4 (ii).   An amendment was offered adding appropriations for higher education assistance to a bill which called for appropriations for a special election. Senator Jubelirer raised a point of order that the amendment violated the Senate Rules. The President held that this bill was clearly not a general appropriations bill (which can contain more than one subject), and that under Rule XIV, Section 7(a), the bill could contain only one subject. Thus the amendment was out of order. The decision of the Chair was upheld on appeal (25-20). (Senate Journal, 1981, pp. 258-9.)

If Tabled, Bill Will Not Appear on Calendar

4 (jj).   On parliamentary inquiry from Senator Kelley, the President held that if a bill was tabled it would not appear on the calendar, but that a motion to bring it from the table can be entertained at any time. (Senate Journal, 1981, pp. 661-2.)

Land Transfer Legislation Rules Not Applicable to Bill Where Title to Lands Rested With Borough

4 (kk).   Senator Kelley, by point of order, objected to the consideration of a bill, stating that it violated the land transfer legislation provisions of the Senate Rules (Rule XIV, Section 8.1). The President held that the Senator's point was not well-taken because the title to the land in the bill was held by the Borough, not the Commonwealth, notwithstanding the fact that

Commonwealth bond money was used in the acquisition of the land. (Senate Journal, 1982, p. 2068.)

Appropriation Bill is Preferred if Made to State Owned Entity — Non-preferred if Made to Entity Not State Owned

4 (ll).   On parliamentary inquiry from Senator Lincoln regarding the status of a bill appropriating money for Cheyney State Hospital, the President held the bill became a "Preferred" appropriations bill rather than a "non-preferred" because the appropriation was to a state-owned entity. The President continued to state that if the appropriation is to some entity which is not owned by the state, then it must be non-preferred. (Senate Journal, 1982, p. 2748.)

Bills Requiring Expenditure of Funds May Not be Given Third Consideration Until Referred to Appropriations Committee

4 (mm).   In answering a series of parliamentary inquiries, the President held that no bill which may require an expenditure of Commonwealth funds or funds of any political subdivision shall be given Third Consideration reading on the calendar until it has been referred to the Appropriations Committee, and a fiscal note attached. The President noted that a motion to suspend this rule would be in order, however. (Senate Journal. 1983, pp. 42-5.)

Bills Requiring Expenditure of Commonwealth Funds Must Be Referred to Committee on Appropriations

4 (nn).   On point of order raised by Senator Lewis questioning whether a certain bill requiring an expense of state or municipal funds should be referred to the Appropriations Committee, the Presiding Officer (William J. Moore) decided that the Senate Rules provide that where an expenditure of Commonwealth funds is required, the bill must be rereferred to the Committee on Appropriations. (Senate Journal, 1983, p. 1429.)

SECTION 5

CALL OF THE HOUSE

Is the Order When a Motion to Adjourn Fails, and Less Than a Quorum Vote

5 (a).   Mr. Gordon submitted the following point of order, viz.: "I raised the point of order that upon the motion to adjourn, fourteen Senators having voted 'no' and eleven Senators having voted 'aye'; the motion to adjourn is therefore lost, and the question disposed of, and that, therefore, the Senate may proceed to consider other business, as under the ruling of the Chair, it is not necessary that quorum vote upon the motion to adjourn, and that a call of the Senate, as directed in the thirty-sixth rule, is not necessary, as that rule clearly only contemplates subjects before the Senate upon which it was necessary that a quorum vote, in order that the subject might be disposed of, as that rule directs that when a call of the Senate is made and a quorum disclosed to be present, the yeas and nays should be again taken upon the question on which the absence of a quorum was directed. In this case that rule would not apply as if the call showed a quorum present, the yeas and nays could not be again taken, for the original question — the motion to adjourn — is disposed of." The President decided that the motion to adjourn was lost, a majority having voted "no"; but less than a quorum having voted, nothing was in order but a call of the House. (Senate Journal, extra session, 1883, p. 162.)

Chair May Take Judicial Notice a Quorum Is Not Present

5 (b).   Mr. Law raised the point of order the Chair should not rule he took judicial notice a quorum was not present as no member from the floor had suggested the absence of a quorum. The President ruled he can take judicial notice to the fact a quorum was not present. (Legislative Journal, 1937, p. 5389.)

Senate Has No Power to Enforce Presence of Senators if There is a Quorum Present

5 (c).   Twenty Senators walked out of the chamber at the beginning of a roll call vote to protest the ruling of the President (upheld on appeal) that a constitutional majority consisted of Senators elected, living, sworn, and seated. On parliamentary inquiry from Senator Gekas, the President held

there were no provisions in the rules to enforce the presence of Senators if there is a quorum present. The President noted such powers did exist if a quorum would not be present. (Senate Journal, 1981, p. 113.)

SECTION 6

CHANGE OF TIME FOR CONVENING

Senate May Change by Majority Vote

6 (a).   The question having been raised, it was ruled by the presiding officer that the Senate may by a majority vote change the time for convening after the weekly adjournment from that set forth in concurrent adjournment resolution previously adopted by both Houses. (Legislative Journal, March 4, 1919, pp. 1199, 1200.)

SECTION 7

COMMITTEES

Powers of, Over Bills

7 (a).   The Speaker decided that the committee to whom a bill had been referred had full power over the same, except that it could not change the title or subject thereof. (Senate Journal, 1857, p. 842.).

Mr. Flinn submitted the point of order, that after a bill has been reported by a standing committee and passed any reading in the Senate and recommitted to a standing committee that such committee has not the power to report such bill with a negative recommendation, because the Senate as a body had acted favorably upon the bill by passing it on a reading, and a part of the Senate, as represented by a standing committee, cannot negative that which the whole Senate has approved by passing through a reading, and that any such bill so reported negatively by any standing committee should be placed upon the calendar for the consideration of the Senate in regular order. The President decided the point of order not well taken. (Senate Journal, 1899, p. 1933.)

Report of a Bill by a Minority of a Standing Committee in Order Only by Consent of Majority

7 (b).   Mr. Greer submitted the point of order that a minority of a standing committee cannot make a report from such committee (of a bill) without the consent of a majority thereof. The President decided that the point of order, as a general proposition was well taken; but the bill having been reported, and ordered to be printed and placed upon the calendar, the point of order is submitted too late. (Senate Journal, 1883, p. 1030.)

Motion to Recommit, Only, Debatable

7 (c).   Mr. Henry I. Wilson raised the point of order that the merits of a bill which a Senator had moved to recommit could not be discussed.

The Chair (Lieutenant-Governor Samuel S. Lewis) ruled that the point of order was well taken, and that, upon a motion to recommit, the subject matter of the bill may not be discussed. (Legislative Journal, April 8, 1941, p. 1223.)

Reference Cannot Bind Committee

7 (d).   Mr. Thomas B. Wilson raised the point of order that a motion referring a bill to a committee could not carry with it binding instructions to the committee to report the bill out. The Chair (Lieutenant-Governor Samuel S. Lewis) declared the point of order well taken. (Legislative Journal, February 24, 1941, p. 413.)

Report Objected to Not in Order

7 (e).   Mr. Holland objected to the reporting of a bill from Committee.

The Chair, Lieutenant-Governor Lloyd H.Wood, ruled the gentleman out of order. (Legislative Journal, December 5, 1951, p. 5872.)

Meeting During Session — Not Announced at Beginning — Suspension of Rule

7 (f).   Senator Lamb asked for a recess of the Senate to hold an immediate meeting of the Finance Committee.

Senator raised the point of order that since Senate Rule 16, Section 7, required that "A committee meeting may be held during a session only if approval is granted by the Majority and Minority Leaders and if notice of the bills to be considered is given at the beginning of session," and since no notice was given the meeting could not be held.

The President, Lieutenant Governor Ernest P. Kline, ruled the point of order well taken.

Senator Lamb then made a motion to suspend Rule 16, Section 7. The motion carried. (Senate Journal, 1973, p. 1158.)

Committee on Executive Nominations Not Subject to Senate Rule Regarding Notice of Meetings

7 (g).   Senator Ross reported several Executive Nominations from the Committee on Rules and Executive Nominations. Senator Romanelli rose to a point of order that since the meeting was not held in compliance with the Senate Rule regarding "Notice of Meetings," the report was, therefore, not in order.

The Presiding Officer, Senator Zemprelli, ruled the point of order not well taken in as much as the rule referred to by Senator Romanelli, dealt with the consideration of bills only. During debate mention was made that the report may also violate the Sunshine Law (1974, P.L. 486, No. 175). The Chair ruled that the Sunshine Law did not apply to the consideration of Executive Nominations.

Senator Romanelli appealed the decision of the Chair. The Senate sustained the decision (33.3). (Senate Journal, April 19, 1978, p. 455.) (Compilers note: The Pennsylvania Supreme Court and the Commonwealth Court handed down decisions stating that "Committee of State Senate which was meeting to consider executive nominations was not conducting a meeting 'where bills are considered' nor was it conducting a hearing 'where testimony was taken,' so that the meeting did not come within notice requirements of the Sunshine Law, even though the committee was an 'agency' and was, when it decided to refer the nomination to the Senate floor, taking 'formal action.' " Consumers Ed. and Protective Assn. Intern. Inc. v. Nolan, 346 A2d 871, 21 Pa. Cmwlth. 566, 1975, affirmed 368 A2d 675, 470 Pa. 372.)

After Committee Action, No Time Limit Compels Chairman to Report Bill to Floor

7 (h).   Senator Zemprelli inquired how long a committee chairman had to report a bill back to the floor of the Senate after the committee had authorized the report. The President pro tempore found that the Rules of the Senate are silent on the subject and that there is no secondary authority which states any such time limit; thus, the chair would not speculate on any time limit. (Senate Journal, 1984, p. 1663.)

SECTION 8

COMMITTEE OF THE WHOLE
(RESERVED)

SECTION 9

COMMITTEE OF
CONFERENCE — REPORTS

Conference Committee Reports to Be Noted on Calendar

9 (a).   Mr. Buckman raised the point of order that under Rule 21 of the Senate the Conference Committee report cannot be voted upon unless it is noted on the calendar. The President ruled Conference Committee reports would be noted on the calendar in the future. (Legislative Journal, 1937, p. 3435.)

Senate Can Instruct

9 (b).   The Speaker decided that it was not in order for the Senate to instruct a committee of conference. The Senate reversed the decision. (Senate Journal, 1868, pp. 430-431.)

Power of, Over Whole Bill

9 (d).   The Speaker decided that, in a committee of conference, on the appropriation bill, the difference between the two Houses on said bill extended to the whole bill, and not to any particular parts of it, although both may have separately voted for some parts of it. The Senate sustained the decision. (Senate Journal, 1873, p. 1056.)

Mr. McCracken submitted the point of order that the committee of conference in amending the bill in certain particulars concerning which no difference existed between the two Houses, exceeded the authority conferred upon it, in violation of joint rule three, which says that a committee of conference "shall not have power or control over any part of a bill, resolution or order, except such parts upon which a difference exists between the two Houses." The Senate decided the point of order not well taken. (Senate Journal, extra session, 1883, p. 75.)

Report of Disagreement of, Discharges

9 (e).   The question being propounded to the Chair, viz.: Does the report of a committee of conference on its final disagreement operate as a discharge of the committee without further action of the Senate? Decided in the affirmative by the Senate. (Senate Journal, extra session, 1883, p. 48.)

Being Dissolved, Not Subject to Instruction

9 (f).   Mr. Cooper submitted the point of order that as the committee of conference on the part of the Senate had been dissolved, the resolution was not in order. The President decided the point of order well taken, and ruled the resolution out of order. (Senate Journal, extra session, 1883, p. 55.)

Motion to Appoint, Once Negatived, Not Again in Order Without Reconsideration

9 (g).   And the question being, Will the Senate agree to the first division, viz.: "That a committee of conference on Congressional apportionment be appointed?" Mr. McCracken submitted the point of order that the Senate has refused to appoint a committee of conference; and that it is proposed by this resolution to do something that the Senate has already refused to do without reconsidering the previous action of the Senate, and is, therefore, not in order. The President decided the point of order well taken. (Senate Journal, extra session, 1883, p. 56.)

Power of Senate Over — Motion to Return Bill to House While Considering Conference Report, Out of Order, Reports of, Not Amendable

9 (h).   Mr. Hughes submitted the point of order that the resolution contains a proposition in violation of the established method of legislation, in that it authorizes a conference committee to consider a bill which has not been presented or considered at this session (extraordinary), in violation of the joint rule three, which expressly says that a committee of conference shall not have power or control over any part of a bill, except such parts upon which a difference exists between the two Houses, and therefore it is not in order. The President decided the point of order not well taken. (Senate Journal, extra session, 1883, p. 61.)

The conference committee having amended the bill in part, a motion was made to return the bill to the House of Representatives. The point of order was raised that the motion is out of order as there is nothing before the Senate but the adoption or rejection of conference report, and the Senate in consideration of such report cannot go beyond an inquiry into the regularity of the proceedings of either House during the passage of the bill, and that when a bill is in committee of conference, it is not in the custody of either House and neither House has the right or authority to transmit the bill back to the other House for any purpose. The President of the Senate ruled the point of order well taken. (Legislative Journal, June 12, 1923, p. 4678.)

Mr. Shapiro submitted the point of order that the report of a conference committee was not amendable. The President decided the point of order well taken. (Legislative Journal, extra session, 1933, p. 997.)

Discharge of Committee

9 (i).   Senate members of a conference committee of the House and Senate appointed to consider a Congressional Reapportionment Bill, having stated to the Senate, in reply to questions that the committee had not been able to agree, Senator Coleman raised the point of order that "the conferees appointed by the President pro tempore on the part of the Senate to consider Senate Bill No. 507, having made their report to the Senate Body that they are hopelessly dead-locked, that the committee is automatically discharged and that the bill is in the physical possession of the Senate and the question recurs on the adoption of the amendments inserted by the House." The Chair (Lieutenant-Governor Samuel S. Lewis) ruled that the point of order was not well taken. (Legislative Journal, July 12, 1941, p. 5500.)

Conference Report Rejected by Senate — Status

9 (j). A parliamentary inquiry was raised by Senator R. D. Fleming as to whether a rejection of the Conference Report on Senate Bill 30 by the Senate would constitute the killing of the bill. The Chair, Lt. Gov. Ernest P. Kline, stated that if the report was rejected, the question would immediately recur on the concurrence in the amendments placed in the bill by the House. (Senate Journal, June 20, 1971, p. 1501.) also (Senate Journal, 1973, p. 847.)

Committee of Conference Did Not Exceed Authority Under Senate Rule XXI

9 (k). On a point of order raised by Senator Bell, the President, being in doubt, put the question before the Senate as to whether a Report of the Committee of Conference violated Senate Rule XXI, Section 2 (Conference Committee exceeding its authority). The Senate (30-19) decided the report did not violate the Rule. (Senate Journal, 1980, pp. 2245-6.)

SECTION 10

CONSTITUTIONAL QUESTIONS

Constitutionality of Bills to be Determined by the Senate

10 (a). Mr. McDonald submitted the point of order "that the bill was not in order for the reason that it was contrary to Article III, section 6, of the Constitution." The President Pro Tempore decided that as the question of the constitutionality of the bill is a matter which will be decided by the Senate in the consideration and final disposition of the bill, it is not in the province of the Chair, by decision, as to the constitutionality of the bill, to assume the duty and power properly vested in the Senate. (Senate Journal, 1893, p. 209.)

10 (b). Mr. Weiner submitted the point of order that "the bill was not in order for the reason that it was in violation of Article III, Section 14 of the Constitution." The Chair, Lieutenant-Governor John Morgan Davis, decided the point of order not well taken and quoted from Mason's Manual, page 242:

"It is not the duty of the Presiding Officer to rule upon any question which is not presented in the course of proceedings. It is not his right to rule upon the constitutionality or legal effect or expediency of a proposed bill, as that authority belongs to the House."

Declaring a Seat Vacant on Constitutional Point of Order — Not in Order

10 (c). Upon the completion of a roll call, Senator Ewing raised a Constitutional Point of Order that Senator Frank Mazzei, having been convicted of an infamous crime, is no longer a Member of the Senate pursuant to Art. 2, Sec. 7 and Art. 6, Sec. 7 of the Constitution and should not be recorded as voting.

After much debate the Chair, Lt. Gov. Ernest P. Kline, ruled the point of order not well taken because it would in effect expel Senator Mazzei by a simple majority vote instead of the two-thirds required by the Constitution.

Senator appealed the decision of the Chair and after much debate the Senate sustained the decision of the Chair. (Senate Journal, April 21, 1975, pages 252-258.)

Points of Order to be Determined by Senate

10 (d). The President, Lieutenant Governor Ernest P. Kline, voted in the affirmative on motion for the previous question (see TIE VOTE, 36(e). Senator Nolan raised a Constitutional Point of Order that he, the President, could not vote, and asked for a ruling by the Chair. The President ruled that on a Constitutional Point of Order the Chair must submit the question to the Senate for decision. Senator Nolan, after much debate, withdrew his point of order. (Senate Journal, August 10, 1977, p. 822.) (Compilers note: See Senate Rule 3, Sec. 1h.)

Senate May Act on Nominations Submitted by Former Governor When Those Nominations Have Been Recalled by the Current Governor

10 (e). A constitutional point of order was raised by Senator Hager that consideration of nominations submitted by Governor Shapp before he left office, but recalled by Governor Thornburgh, violated Article IV, Section 8 of the Constitution of Pennsylvania. The Senate (23-26) held the point of order was not well-taken, and consideration of the nominees was thus constitutional. (Senate Journal, 1979, p. 153.)

Bill Dealing With Three Separate Areas of Appropriation Was Constitutional

10 (f). A constitutional point of order was raised by Senator Kelley, that a bill which dealt with: one, general appropriation; two, the Motor License Fund; and three, federal augumentation monies; violated Article III, Section 11 of the Constitution of Pennsylvania (providing what general appropriations bills shall embrace). The Senate (5-44) held the point of order not well-taken, and thus the bill was constitutional. (Senate Journal, 1979, pp. 195-6.)

Senate Amendment Which Would Raise Revenue Not Unconstitutional

10 (g). A constitutional point of order was raised by Senator Early that proposed amendments to a Senate bill to charge fees on the purchase and use of studded snow tires were unconstitutional under Article III, Section 10 of the Constitution of Pennsylvania which provides that all bills raising revenue shall originate in the House. The Senate (3-46) decided that the point of order was not well-taken, thereby declaring the amendments constitutional. (Senate Journal, 1979, pp. 200-1.)

Bill Not Violative of Impairment of Contracts Provision

10 (h). Senator Hager raised a constitutional point of order stating that the bill under consideration was unconstitutional because it violated Article I, Section 17 of the Constitution of Pennsylvania by impairing the obligations of contracts already existing. The Senate (23-25) decided the point was not well-taken and that the bill did not violate the Constitution. (Senate Journal, 1979, pp. 432-3.)

Partial Passage Meets Requirement That Proposed Constitutional Amendment Be Passed by Two Consecutive General Assemblies

10 (i). Senator Lewis inquired whether if the next session of the General Assembly were to pass only part of a proposed constitutional amendment, that part would then meet the "approval of two consecutive sessions" requirement. The President decided that passage of a portion the second time would meet this requirement of passage by two consecutive assemblies as to that portion. (Senate Journal, 1980, pp. 1911-2.)

Bills Shall Not Be so Altered or Amended as to Change Their Original Purpose

10 (j). Senator Hager raised a constitutional point of order stating that certain amendments, which reinstate the function that the bill's original purpose was to eliminate, alter the original intention of the bill thus violating Article III, Section 1 of the Constitution of Pennsylvania. The Senate (25-23) held that the amendment altered the original purpose and was thus unconstitutional. However, the vote on the constitutional point of order was later reconsidered (Senate Journal, 1981, p. 605) and the point was withdrawn. (Senate Journal, 1981, pp. 559-61.)

Constitutional Point of Order Shall Be Submitted to the Senate for Decision

10 (k). On a point of order, Senator Zemprelli asked whether the chair can rule on constitutionality. The President held that the Rules of the Senate state that the President shall submit points of order involving the constitutionality of any matter to the Senate for decision, thus the proper place for decision is with the members of the Senate. (Senate Journal, 1981, p. 1397.)

No Bill Shall be Altered so as to Change Its Original Purpose

10 (l). Senator Stauffer raised a constitutional point of order stating that amendments providing a salary increase for the District Attorney in Philadelphia, when made to a bill dealing with the depth of graves under the Vital Statistics Law, is violative of Article III, Section 1 of the Constitution of Pennsylvania which states no bill shall be altered to change its original purpose. The Senate (25-22) sustained the point of order and decided the amendments unconstitutional. (Senate Journal, 1981, pp. 1397-8.)

Not Unconstitutional for Senator to Vote on Executive Nomination When Corporation He Was Associated With is Undergoing Federal Investigation

10 (m). Senator Fumo raised a constitutional point of order stating that Article III, Section 13 of the Constitution of Pennsylvania, providing that members shall not vote on matters which a member has a personal or private interest in, makes it unconstitutional for a particular Senator to vote on the executive nomination of a Secretary of Labor and Industry. At the time, a corporation which a Senator had been associated with was undergoing federal investigation for misuse of federal grant funds. The Senate (21-27) did not sustain the point of order, so the member could vote on the matter. (Senate Journal, 1982, pp. 1648-55.)

Bill Not Unconstitutional Based on Equal Protection and Equal Application of Law

10 (n). Senator Williams raised a constitutional point of order that a bill (S.B. 661) was unconstitutional based on equal protection and unequal application of a law because of provisions requiring suspensions of Liquor Control Board agents who plead the Fifth Amendment after having been given immunity to testify. The Senate (23-26) decided that the Senator's point was not well-taken and that the bill was constitutional. (Senate Journal, 1983, pp. 799-801.)

Not In Order to Raise Possible Constitutional Violation of the House

10 (o). The President pro tempore, on parliamentary inquiry from Senator Kelley, decided that each house of the General Assembly determines constitutionality for itself, and the Senate must accept a bill as it comes from the House. Therefore, a constitutional point of order in the Senate would not be allowed if it raised a violation by the House of the constitutional prohibition that no bill be amended to change its original purpose. (Senate Journal, 1984, p. 2661.)

SECTION 11

DEBATE

Inflammatory and Derogatory Remarks May Be Expunged

11 (a). The point of order having been raised on a motion to expunge remarks from the record, the President ruled that the motion was in order, and that it was the prerogative of the Senate to expunge inflammatory and derogatory remarks from the record. (Legislative Journal, 1935, p. 1417.)

Speaking More Than Twice on a Bill

11 (b). The President decided that a point of order that a Senator might not speak more than twice on the same subject was well taken, but recognized the Senator to allow an interrogation. (Legislative Journal, 1935, p. 5639.)

Discussion on Motion Limited — Appeal from Ruling Can be Withdrawn

11 (c). Senator Watkins raised the point of order that Senator Holland could not, during consideration of a request that a bill go over in order, discuss other matters on a question of personal privilege.

The Chair, Lieutenant-Governor John C. Bell, sustained the point of order.

Senator Holland and three other Senators joined in an appeal from the decision of the Chair and then requested permission to withdraw the appeal.

The Chair, President pro tempore Ely, decided, when objection was raised to the withdrawal, that the appeal could be withdrawn. (Legislative Journal, April 13, 1943, pp. 1766 and 1767.)

Order of Debate on Bills

11 (d). On a question of order raised by Senator Watkins, the Chair, Lieutenant-Governor John C. Bell, ruled that a Senator could not under a question of personal privilege debate a bill that had already gone over in order, unless by consent of the Senate. (Legislative Journal, April 6, 1943, pp. 1940, 1941 and 1942.)

Bill on Second Reading

11 (e). On a question of order raised by Senator Seyler as to whether a bill was debatable on second reading, the Chair, Lieutenant-Governor Roy Furman, ruled, in effect, that on second reading the matter of consideration of amendments was the principal subject of discussion. However, in this discussion, it would be only natural and proper to digress at times, and discuss the entire section of the bill. This same procedure could continue until all sections of the bill were amended and approved.

Finally, when the question is put, "Will the Senate agree to and pass the bill on second reading" or "second reading as amended," it is proper then to discuss the entire bill. This can be done by any Senator or Senators who are given recognition by the Chair.

A roll call vote may also be demanded as to each section and/or the entire bill. (Legislative Journal, 1957, p. 321.) also (Senate Journal, 1973, p. 932.)

Not in Order After Bill Has Passed Second Reading

11 (f). Senate Bills 1, 2 and 3 had just passed second reading when Senators Weiner and Sesler rose to debate and interrogate certain Senators regarding the bills. Senator Berger raised the point of order that since the bills had passed second reading and were being prepared for third reading, that they were not properly before the Senate for debate. The Chair, Lieutenant-Governor Raymond P. Shafer, ruled the point of order well taken stating that the bills were not subject to debate, the bills having passed second reading. Senator Weiner then asked the Chair whether asking a Member of the Senate what a particular measure means to him as a sponsor is debating the bill. The Chair then quoted from Mason's Manual "Questions addressed to Members must relate only to a question before the body." As the gentleman is aware, there is no question before the body at this time. (Senate Journal Special Session of 1964, pages 50-51.)

Breach of Order to Discuss Actions by House or Its Members

11 (g). During debate on House Bill 1447, the Chair, Lt. Gov. Ernest P. Kline, ruled that Senator Duffield could discuss the bill as he pleased, but could not include in his remarks personal references nor intemperate remarks about what happened in the House. It is not in the dignity of the Senate for a Senator to berate what happened in the House on any measure. (Senate Journal, August 12, 1972, p. 758.)

Debate Proper on Motion — Not About Individuals

11 (h). The President, ruling on a point of order raised by Senator Kelley, held that the Rules of the Senate require that Senators debate the motion, not individuals. (Senate Journal, 1980, p. 1152.)

Motives of Senator Not Subject to Debate

11 (i). The President decided Senator Bell's point of order, that a Senator's motives are not subject to debate, was well-taken. (Senate Journal, 1980, p. 1685.)

No Provisions in the Rules for Yielding the Floor

11 (j). The President, after an attempt to yield the floor to another Senator was made by Senator Mellow, recognized another member and stated that there are no provisions in the Rules allowing for yielding. (Senate Journal, 1980, p. 1927.)

Motion to Limit Debate to a Definite Time May Later Be Extended by Motion or Unanimous Consent

11 (k). After a motion to limit debate to a definite hour had been made, the President, on parliamentary inquiry from Senator Smith, held that if the motion to limit debate should carry, the time set forth may be extended either by unanimous consent or by the adoption of a motion to that effect, and that it would be in order for a Senator to offer a motion for extension of that time. (Senate Journal, 1980, p. 1928.)

Member May Yield, But He May Not Yield to Other Members

11 (l). Senator Fumo raised a point of order that a motion made by Senator Hager was out of order because Senator Mellow still retained the floor even though his attempt to yield the floor to another Senator was not allowed. The President reiterated that it was not in order for a Senator to

yield specifically to another Senator. He also stated that he judged Senator Mellow was yielding the floor, and therefore recognition of Senator Hager and the making of a new motion was in order. The decision of the Chair was upheld on appeal (31-9). (Senate Journal, 1980, pp. 1928-31.)

No Senator Shall Speak More Than Once on a Question if it Prevents Another Who Has Not Yet Spoken

11.(m). On parliamentary inquiry from Senator Mellow, the President decided that under Senate Rule VII: No Senator shall speak more than once on one question to the prevention of another who has not yet spoken and is desirous to speak, nor more than twice without the leave of the Senate. (Senate Journal, 1981, p. 67.)

Senator May Speak More Than Twice on Same Question With Leave of The Senate

11 (n). Senator Street raised a point of order asking that a Senator who has already spoken twice on an issue be refrained from further debate (Rule 12, Section 3). The President decided that if the member has the leave of the Senate, he may speak more than twice. (Senate Journal, 1981, p. 587.)

Not in Order to Play Audio Tape

11 (o). Senator Jubelirer objected, by point of order, to an attempt by a member to play an audio tape during the debate on the adoption of a conference committee report. The President decided that the point of order was well-taken, and the use of the tape-recorded voice was out of order. (Senate Journal, 1982, p. 1662.)

No Member May Speak More Than Twice on an Issue

11 (p). Senator Street rose to a point of order to object to a member who had spoken more than twice on an issue. The President pro tempore ruled the member out of order for having spoken more than twice without the consent of the Senate. On appeal, the Senate (26-24) upheld the decision of the Chair. (Senate Journal, 1982, p. 1752.)

Comments About Qualifications, Personal Attributes, Motives, Actions or Characters of Members Are Always Out of Order

11 (q). A Member continued to speak after he had been called out of order, and the Chair then turned off the Member's microphone. Under Petitions and Remonstrances, the Member, expressing his dissatisfaction with the Chair, was repeatedly called out of order by the Chair and by other members on the grounds that comments about the qualifications, personal attributes, motives, actions, or characters of members are always out of order. (Senate Journal, 1982, pp. 2415-20.)

Quotations of Leaders of the House Out of Order

11 (r). During debate on a motion to revert to a prior printer's number, Senator Zemprelli rose and inquired about the Chair's decision that certain conversations that took place with the leadership of the House were outside the scope of proper debate. The President pro tempore held that based on the Senate Rules and the rules of debate, quotations of leaders of another body are not germane to the debate and are out of order. (Senate Journal, 1983, pp. 308-9.)

SECTION 12

DILATORY MOTIONS

Rule Against Dilatory Motions

12 (a). On parliamentary inquiry from Senator Lincoln, regarding frivolous motions, the President held that any regular parliamentary motion when improperly used for the purpose of delaying or obstructing business is a dilatory motion, but the Chair noted that he felt the rereferral motion in question was not dilatory. (Senate Journal, 1980, p. 1920.)

SECTION 13

DISCHARGE OF COMMITTEE

Request for Discharge by a Member of the Committee is Not A Prerequisite for Motion to Discharge

13 (a). In response to a parliamentary inquiry from Senator Coppersmith, the President held that Rule XVI, § 6(c), pertains only to the request for discharge by a member of the committee, and Rule XVI, § 17, the rule of discharge of a committee does not imply Rule XVI, § 6(c), as a prerequisite to a discharge motion on the floor of the Senate. Thus the discharge motion on the floor of the Senate was in order. (Senate Journal, 1980, p. 1357.)

SECTION 14

DIVISION OF THE QUESTION

When Not Divisible

14 (a). Mr. Hall submitted the point of order that the question was not divisible, for the reason that if the first proposition was defeated the remaining proposition would be incomplete. Decided well taken. (Senate Journal, 1883, p. 696.)

Mr. Wallace called for a division of the question, so that a vote could be had upon each of the several sections offered as an amendment to the bill. The President decided that the question was not divisible, because the amendment would be incomplete unless adopted as a whole. (Senate Journal, 1883, p. 1225.)

When Divisible

14 (b). Mr. Gordon called for a division of the question (on a resolution to appoint a conference committee, and instruct the same); so that a separate vote could be had upon each of the two propositions contained there. Mr. Adams submitted the point of order, that the resolution could not be divided without destroying the sense, and the call for a division of the question was, therefore, not in order. The President decided the resolution could be divided without destroying the sense, and the point of order, therefore, not well taken. (Senate Journal, extra session, 1883, p. 56.)

When a Part of a Divisible Question Cannot Be Considered

14 (c). And the question being: "Will the Senate agree to the second division?" Mr. McCracken submitted the point of order that the first division of the question having been ruled out of order, the second division is incomplete and unintelligible, and, therefore, not in order. The President decided the point of order well taken. (Senate Journal, extra session, 1883, p. 56.)

Final Passage — Not Divisible

14 (d). The Senate was considering House Bill No. 247 on final passage when Senator Nolan rose to divide the question. The Presiding Officer, Senator Kelley, ruled that the question could not be divided on the basis of the constitutional requirement that bills contain only one subject. To be divisible a question must have more than one subject and include points so distinct and separate that, one of them being taken away, the other will stand as a complete proposition.

The decision was appealed and the Senate sustained the Presiding Officer. (Senate Journal, November 14, 1977, p. 1071.) also (Senate Journal, April 18, 1977, p. 223.)

Division Matter of Right as to Multiple Executive Nominations

14 (e). The President held Senator Kelley's point of order, that the question of multiple executive nominations can be divided by request as a matter of right, was well-taken. (Senate Journal, 1981, p. 60.)

Unanimous Consent Not Required for Division of the Question

14 (f). Senator Zemprelli inquired whether there is a requirement of unanimous consent in order to divide the question. The President decided that the Rules of the Senate (Rule XXXIV) state that any Senator may call for division of the question in certain cases, so it does not require unanimous consent in such instances. (Senate Journal, 1981, p. 1107.)

Question of Concurrence in House Amendments Divisible

14 (g). The President pro tempore, on parliamentary inquiry from Senator Fisher, held that the question of concurrence in House Amendments is divisible. Thus, the Senate could divide the amendments, concur in part and nonconcur in part, then return the bill to the House with the amendments concurred in part and nonconcurred in part. (Senate Journal, 1984, p. 2662.)

SECTION 15

EXECUTIVE COMMUNICATIONS AND NOMINATIONS

Committee on Executive Nominations Not Subject to Senate Rule Regarding Notice of Meetings

15 (b).   Senator Ross reported several Executive nominations from the Committee on Rules and Executive Nominations. Senator Romanelli rose to a point of order that since the meeting was not held in compliance with the Senate Rule regarding "Notice of Meetings," the report was, therefore, not in order.

The Presiding Officer, Senator Zemprelli, ruled the point of order not well taken in as much as the rule referred to by Senator Romanelli dealt with the consideration of bills only. During debate mention was made that the report may also violate the Sunshine Law (1974, P.L. 486, No. 175).   The Chair ruled that the Sunshine Law did not apply to the consideration of Executive Nominations.

Senator Romanelli appealed the decision of the Chair. The Senate sustained the decision (33-3). (Senate Journal, April 19, 1978, p. 455) (Compilers note: The Pennsylvania Supreme Court handed down decisions stating the "Committee of State Senate which was meeting to consider executive nominations was not conducting a meeting 'where bills are considered' nor was it conducting a hearing 'where testimony was taken,' so that the meeting did not come within notice requirements of the Sunshine Law, even though the committee was an 'agency' and was, when it decided to refer the nomination to the Senate floor, taking 'formal action.' " Consumers Ed. and Protective Ass'n. Intern. Inc. v. Nolan, 346 A2d 871, 21 Pa. Cmwlth. 566, 1975, affirmed 368 A2d 675, 470 Pa. 372.

Unanimous Consent for Consideration Not Needed on Day After Reported from Committee

15..(c).   Senator Ross called up for consideration several nominations which were reported from committee the day before. A Senator raised the point of order that under Senate Rules, these nominations needed the unanimous consent of the Senate in order to be considered. The Presiding Officer, Senator Scanlon, ruled the point not well taken. He quoted Senate Rule 30, Sec. 3: "When the consideration of executive nominations is reached in the order of business, a Senator may make a motion to go into executive session for the purpose of confirming the nominations which have been reported from committee at a previous session and, if unanimous consent be given, also those which may be reported on the same day the motion is made." Since these nominations were reported on a previous Session day, they do not need unanimous consent (Senate Journal, November 15, 1978, p. 1116.)

Motion to Return Nominations to the Governor Debatable

15 (d).   On a point of order raised by Senator Zemprelli, the President held that a motion to return nominations to the Governor per his recall request was debatable. (Senate Journal, 1979, pp. 128-9.)

Debate on Executive Nominations Must Be Confined to Nominee in Question

15 (e).   The President, on repeated responses to points of order, decided that comments about persons other than the nominee during debate of executive nominations were out of order, and held that remarks must be confined to the nominee in question and relevant to his nomination. (Senate Journal, 1980, pp. 1573-81.)

Recall Messages Need Not Lie on the Table Before Action on Them

15 (f).   Senator Zemprelli rose to a point of order to object to the immediate action being taken on recall messages reported from the Committee on Rules and Executive Nominations. The President pro tempore held there is nothing in the rules or practice of the Senate which requires that the recalls must lie on the table before action on them is taken. (Senate Journal, 1981, p. 335.)

Unanimous Consent Required For Consideration of Executive Nominations Only If Considered on the Same Day They Are Reported From Committee

15 (g).   The President pro tempore, on parliamentary inquiry from Senator Zemprelli, held that unanimous consent is required for consideration of executive nominations only if the nominees are considered the same day they are reported from committee. (Senate Journal, 1984, p. 2240.)

SECTION 16

EXECUTIVE SESSION

Five Day Rule Not Applicable in Executive Session

16 (c).   The Senate being in executive session, Mr. Humes submitted the point of order that as more than five days had elapsed since the vote was had, under Rule 16 of the Senate, a motion to reconsider is not now in order. The President pro tempore (Mr. Reyburn in the Chair) decided the point of order not well taken, as the sixteenth rule, governing the Senate in regular session has not been applied to the Senate in executive session. (Senate Journal, 1883, p. 1056.)

Unanimous Consent For Consideration Must Be Made at Proper Time

16 (d).   Mr. Fleming asked and obtained unanimous consent for immediate consideration of the nominations reported from committee and read by the clerk. The motion to go into Executive Session was made and carried.

When the first nominee was called up for consideration, Mr. Weiner rose to a point of order and quoted a part of Senate Rule 38 which states, "....Which question (Shall the Senate advise and consent to this nomination) shall not be put on the day on which the nomination or nominations are reported from committee, unless by unanimous consent...." Mr. Weiner stated that Mr. Fleming should have asked unanimous consent for the immediate consideration just prior to the time when the first nominee was called up for consideration.

Mr. Berger then rose and stated that just prior to going into Executive Session Mr. Fleming had asked and obtained unanimous consent to consider the names reported from committee at today's session, and the unanimous consent was given and not objected to.

The Presiding Officer decided the point of order well taken and ruled that at the time when Senator Fleming asked for unanimous consent for the immediate consideration of nominations made by the Governor and reported from committee at today's session, there was a general consent given. Later on after we did go into Executive Session, and the nominees were brought up in individual order, the first one being Mr. McGlinchey, the Chair is of the opinion that unanimous consent again must be granted under the rules. The rules specifically say that the Chair ask that unanimous consent be given for the consideration of this nomination. Because there has been no unanimous consent given at this time for the consideration of this nomination, the Chair feels the point of order taken by Senator Weiner to be well taken. (Legislative Journal, 1959, pp. 5162-5164.)

Executive Session Not Required for Motion to Return Nominations to the Governor Per Recall Request

16 (e).   The President, on a point of order raised by Senator Fumo ruled that past precedence has been established whereby the Senate does not have to be in executive session to return nominations to the Governor. (Senate Journal, 1979, p. 128.)

Motion to Rise From Executive Session Out of Order When Combined With Another Motion

16 (f).   The President, on a point of order, held that it is not in order to have a motion for the executive session to rise together with a motion allowing for a nomination to come before the Senate. (Senate Journal, 1979, p. 439.)

SECTION 17

EXTRAORDINARY SESSION (RESERVED)

SECTION 18

INDEFINITE POSTPONEMENT

Motion for, not Capable of Amendment

18 . (b). The President decided that a motion to postpone, indefinitely, being already in its simplest form, is not capable of amendment. (Senate Journal, 1879, p. 868.)

Does Not Preclude Debate Upon the Original Subject

18 (c). The President ruled that the motion to postpone indefinitely does not preclude debate upon the original subject. (Senate Journal, 1879, p. 788.)

Motion for, of Motion to Reconsider Limitation of Debate in Rule 16 Does Not Apply to

18 (d). Mr. Hall submitted the point of order that the spirit of the rule prohibiting a Senator from speaking longer than five minutes on a motion to reconsider, requires the rule to be applied likewise to a motion to postpone indefinitely such motion to reconsider. The President decided the point of order not well taken. (Senate Journal, extra session, 1883, p. 172.)

SECTION 19

INTERROGATION

Question Out of Order as it Questions Motives of Member

19 (a). Senator Kelley rose to a point of order objecting to a query asked of a member in interrogation because the question went to the motives of the member. The President pro tempore held that the point of order was well-taken and asked that the question be restated. (Senate Journal, 1983, p. 41.)

SECTION 20

LAY ON THE TABLE

Not Debatable

20 . (a). The Chair, Lieutenant-Governor John Morgan Davis, decided that it was not in order to debate the motion to lay on the table. The Chair quoted from Mason's Manual, Sec. 335, p. 235, the following:

"It is a matter of importance to a body that consideration of a question may be put over to a later date without debate or delay. To permit debate on the motion to lay on the table would defeat this purpose. This motion is not debatable." (Legislative Journal, 1959, p. 5162.)

Motion in Order on Final Day of Five-Day Provision of Discharge Petition

20 (b). An executive nomination was before the Senate on the fifth and final day of the five-day period of a discharge petition, and a motion to lay the nomination on the table was made. On a point of order, the President decided that the discharge petition was still in force and ruled that the motion was out of order. The decision of the Chair was appealed and the Senate (22-26) voted not to sustain the decision of the Chair; thus the motion was in order and the nomination was laid on the table. (Two legislative days later, the nomination was taken from the table and returned to the Governor per his recall request (Senate Journal, 1979, p. 465). (Senate Journal, 1979, pp. 434-8.)

Motion to Lay on the Table Out of Order Once Bill Has Gone Over in Its Order

20 (c). Senator Kelley objected by point of order to a motion to lay a bill on the table after a motion for the bill to go over in its order had passed. The Presiding Officer (William J. Moore) held that the point of order was well-taken — the bill had been put over in order and was no longer before the Senate for consideration. (Senate Journal, 1983, p. 1359.)

SECTION 21

LEAVES OF ABSENCE

Leaves of Absence Granted Last For Entire Legislative Day

21 (a). Senator Zemprelli raised a point of order that under Rule 22, Section 4, debate of legislative leaves already granted was not permitted.

The President decided that a return to the order of business of Leaves of Absence was in order, but that those legislative leaves granted on that legislative day were still in effect for the entire day. (Senate Journal, 1980, pp. 1781-2.)

Senator on Legislative Leave Eligible to Be Voted on Resolution

21 (b). Senator Kelley rose to a point of order, stating that the name of a Senator on legislative leave should not be called during the roll call on a resolution because Rule XXXI, Section 7 says "all members present" vote on a resolution. The Presiding Officer (D. Michael Fisher) decided that the use of the word "present" in Rule XXXI, Section 7, is consistent with the provisions for legislative leave in Rule XXVII, Section 1(a), and the Senator on legislative leave is eligible to be voted on the resolution. (Senate Journal, 1984, pp. 1870-1.)

SECTION 22

LEGISLATIVE DAY

Ends When Senate Adjourns

22 (a). Mr. Dent raised the question that since the official time was after midnight the Senate could not act on the calendar for the previous day.

The Presiding Officer ruled that a legislative day ends when the Senate adjourns for that day. (Legislative Journal, December 13, 1951, p. 6187.) (Legislative Journal, 1959, p. 5225.)

SECTION 23

MAJORITY IS PREVAILING SIDE

Motion to Reconsider Made by Prevailing Side

23 (a). The following point of order made by the Senator from Fayette, Mr. Cavalcante:

"That under Rule 38 of the Senate which requires two members who voted *with majority* to make the motion to reconsider a vote on confirmation of executive nominations, the Senator from Tioga, Mr. Owlett, and the Senator from Blair, Mr. Mallery, having voted in the negative could not make the motion."

The Chair, Lieutenant-Governor Samuel S. Lewis, President of the Senate, ruled the point of order not well taken; and stated:

"In this case there were 26 votes for confirmation and 20 votes against confirmation which was 8 votes less than the constitutional majority required.

"The question to be determined is:

'What construction is to be given to the word *"majority"* as used in rule 38?'

"Jefferson's Manual, edition of the 76th Congress, page 374, Section 813, says:

'The provision of the rule that the motion may be made "by any member of the majority"; is construed to mean any member of the *prevailing side* either in the case of a tie vote or in the case of a two-thirds vote.'

"In Hind's *Precedents;* Vol. 11, page 1133, paragraph 1650, there appears the following:

'Where a two-thirds vote is required, a member of the prevailing side may move to reconsider, even though he may be one of an actual minority. A majority is required to reconsider a vote taken under conditions requiring two-thirds for an affirmative action.'

"*Mason's Manual of Legislative Procedure,* page 111, Sec. 87, reads:

'The general parliamentary law requires that a motion to reconsider is made only by a member who voted on the prevailing side of the question.'

"Reading further; this authority says:

'In practice, the motion to reconsider is often made by a member who first voted upon the losing side but who changed his vote to the prevailing side before the announcement of the vote, in order to qualify to move to reconsider.'

"It is clear to the Chair, after a careful examination of the question, that the motion to reconsider must be made by two members who were on the prevailing side — which is a majority within the meaning of the rule.

"Rule 38 does not say a *majority of the votes cast* — it requires any two Senators *voting with the majority.*

"It is plain that those who voted in the negative defeated the confirmation, and were in the majority on the question. This has been the interpretation in the Congress of the United States (which rules are identical in this respect with ours) and in all Legislative Bodies; therefore the Senator from Tioga, Mr. Owlett, and the Senator from Blair, Mr. Mallery, were qualified to make the motion to reconsider, both having voted in the negative." (Legislative Journal, 1939, p. 1266.)

SECTION 24

MOTIONS

Order of Disposal

24 (a).   Mr. Dent inquired whether or not his colleague was in order to make another motion while one he has just made is pending.

The Chair, Lieutenant-Governor Lloyd H. Wood, ruled the gentleman out of order. (Legislative Journal, November 27, 1951, p. 5779.)

SECTION 25

ORDER OF BUSINESS

Comments Not in Order Under the Reading of Bills in Place

25 (a).   On a point of order raised by Senator Hager, the President decided comments concerning bills were not in order under the Reading of Bills in Place. (Senate Journal, 1979, p. 222.)

SECTION 26

ORDERS OF THE DAY

A Single Objection Prevents Suspension of, at a Special Session or a Special Purpose

26 (a).   The President pro tempore decided that at a single session, for a special purpose, a single objection would prevent the suspension of the orders. (Senate Journal, 1875, pp. 460,589.)

The President decided that at a special session for a special purpose, a motion cannot be considered without the unanimous consent of the Senate. (Senate Journal, 1875, p. 586.)

Motion to Extend Session Pending Consideration of Bills not in Order

26 (b).   Mr. Hall submitted the point of order that a motion to extend session was not in order, pending the consideration of a bill. Decided well taken. (Senate Journal, 1883, p. 664.)

Suspended by Special Order

26 (e).   Mr. Cooper submitted the point of order, that, as the order for the offering of original resolutions was not completed, the special order fixed by the Senate for half past eleven o'clock was not in order. Decided not well taken. (Senate Journal, 1883, p. 780.)

Mr. Hughes, then submitted the point of order that, as the resolution was still pending and undisposed of, its consideration could not be interrupted by other business. Decided the point of order not well taken. (Senate Journal, 1883, p. 780.)

Take Precedence of Call for the Previous Question

26 (f).   The Chair having decided the call for the previous question in order, and an appeal taken, and the question being, "Shall the decision of the Chair stand as the judgment of the Senate?" The hour of one o'clock having arrived, and the orders of the day being called for the President was about to adjourn the Senate, when Mr. Hall submitted the point of order that the orders of the day cannot be called pending a call for the previous question. The President decided the point of order not well taken and adjourned the Senate. (Senate Journal, extra session, 1883, p. 172.)

SECTION 27

OVER IN ORDER

Once Bill Has Gone Over in Order, Decision Must be Reconsidered Not Merely Reversed

27 (a).   Senator Kelley made a parliamentary inquiry that once a bill is gone over in its order, this decision is not reversible by the Chair, but rather must be reconsidered by the Senate. The President proceeded to a vote on the reconsideration of the decision to go over the bill. (Senate Journal, 1979, pp. 1098-9.)

If Motion to Go Over in Order Made on Tenth Day, Bill is Automatically Recommitted to Committee From Which it Emanated

27 (b).   Upon parliamentary inquiry from Senator Kelley, regarding the status of a bill under consideration, the President pro tempore stated that when a bill goes over on the tenth day it has appeared on the calendar it is automatically recommitted to the committee from which it emanated. (Senate Journal, 1982, p. 1691.)

Debate on Motion for Bill Over in Order Confined to Whether or Not Bill Should Go Over That Day

27 (c).   Senator Jubelirer raised a point of order objecting to the debate on a motion for a bill to go over in its order. The President held the Senator's point well-taken and stated that debate should be confined to the limited area of whether or not the bill should go over in order that day. (Senate Journal, 1982, p. 2286.)

Motion to Go Over In Order Debatable Only as to Postponement

27 (d).   Upon inquiry from Senator Greenleaf, the President pro tempore held that the motion for a bill to go over in its order was debatable only insofar as the postponement of the issue is concerned; the issue is not debatable on the merits of the legislation. (Senate Journal, 1983, p. 1000.)

Motion For Whole Calendar to Go Over in Order Not Divisible

27 (e).   On parliamentary inquiry from Senators Lloyd and Zemprelli, the President decided that when the motion is to go over the entire calendar, there is no question which can be divided, and the motion to divide the question so as to except a certain bill would not be on order. (Senate Journal, 1983, p. 1066.)

SECTION 28

PERSONAL PRIVILEGE

Definition of

28 (a).   Mr. Fleming raised the point of order as to the nature of the question of personal privilege.

The Chair, Lieutenant-Governor John Morgan Davis, ruled that questions of personal privilege are questions affecting the rights, reputation and conduct of Members of the Senate in their representative capacity. They must relate to a person as a Member of the Senate or relate to charges against his character which would, if true, incapacitate him for membership of entitlement to the floor. (Legislative Journal, 1959, p. 2059.)

SECTION 29

POINTS OF ORDER

Cannot Be Raised Upon Another Pending Point of Order

29 (a).   The President pro tempore decided that a point of order could not be raised upon another point of order pending before the Senate for consideration. (Senate Journal, 1876, p. 884.)

Can Be Raised at Any Stage of a Bill

29 (b).   The President decided that a point of order can be submitted at any stage of a bill, and was always in order. (Senate Journal, 1879, p. 389.)

Cannot Be Raised Upon a Question After Other Business Has Intervened

29 (c).   The President pro tempore decided that as a recess had been taken (a motion to that effect having been made and carried in the

meanwhile), and as the Senate had come together after the recess had expired it was then too late for a point of order to be raised upon the resolution which had been passed previous to the recess. (Senate Journal, extra session, 1891, p. 487.)

Point of Order Not Debatable

29 (d).   A point of order having been ruled upon by the presiding officer, is not debatable. Exceptions to the ruling may be taken only by appeal. (Legislative Journal, March 14, 1949, pp. 1200, 1201.)

Chair Does Not Have to Give Reasons for Ruling

29 (e).   The President concurred in a point of order raised by Senator Bell stating that the Chair does not have to give reasons for the Chair's ruling on a point of order. (Senate Journal, 1981, p. 327.)

SECTION 30

PREVIOUS QUESTION

Call for, Can Be Renewed Same Day

30 (a).   The Senate decided that the previous question, having been called on the pending question of a bill and not sustained, could be called again on the same day. (Senate Journal, 1884, p. 690.)

Call for in Order While a Senator is Speaking

30 (d).   Mr. Cooper submitted a point of order that, as the Senator from Philadelphia (Mr. Adams) had the floor, the call for the previous question could not be recognized by the Chair at that time. The President decided the point of order not well taken. (Senate Journal, extra session, 1883, p. 172.)

Call For Prevents Member From Speaking Twice

30 (e).   Senator Weiner raised the point of order that since some Members had not spoken twice on a bill as provided under Senate Rules (Senate Rule 4) they should be entitled to continue debate even though the call for the previous question had been adopted. The Chair, Lieutenant-Governor Raymond P. Shafer, ruled that since the call for the previous question had been carried, debate is closed.

Motion Undebatable

30 (f).   A motion for the previous question was made by Senator Duffield and others on an amendment offered by Senator Nolan. Senator Nolan attempted to debate the motion. Senator Coppersmith raised a point of order the motion was undebatable. The President, Lieutenant Governor, Ernest P. Kline, ruled the motion undebatable. (Senate Journal, August 10, 1977, p. 819) (Compilers note: see Mason's Manual, sec. 349, p. 244.)

Motion for Adjournment or Recess Takes Precedence

30 (g).   While a motion for the previous question was pending, Senator Hager rose to a parliamentary inquiry as to whether the motion to adjourn would take precedence over the motion for the previous question. The President, Lieutenant Governor Ernest P. Kline, ruled the motion to adjourn would take precedence over the motion for the previous question. (Senate Journal, August 10, 1977, p. 819.) (Compilers note: see Senate Rule 13.2.)

On Amendments — Order of Consideration After Adoption of Motion

30 (h).   Senator Nolan had offered amendments to House Bill 1349. After much debate, Senator Duffield and others moved the previous question. Senator Kelley and others raised point of order as to what procedure would be followed upon adoption of the motion. The President, Lieutenant Governor Ernest P. Kline, ruled that all debate would cease and the Senate would vote first on the amendments, and then without debate vote immediately on the passage of the bill. He quoted from Senate Rule 13.9. (Senate Journal, August 10, 1977, p. 820.) (Senate Journal, November 16, 1977, p. 1128.)

Reconsideration — Not in Order

30 (i).   Senator Hager moved to have the vote on the motion for the previous question on House Bill 1349 reconsidered. The President, Lieutenant Governor Ernest P. Kline, ruled the motion out of order, quoting

a portion of Mason's Manual, Sec. 352.2, p. 246, "The previous question may not be reconsidered." (Senate Journal, August 10, 1977, p. 824.)

Motion to Reconsider Not in Order — Dilatory

30 (j).   On appeal from the decision of the Chair, the President presiding, the Senate (31-9) sustained the Chair's decision that the motion for the previous question may not be reconsidered, and that such a reconsideration motion is a dilatory motion improperly delaying or obstructing business. (Senate Journal, 1980, p. 1930.)

Motion Not Debatable

30 (k).   The President, on parliamentary inquiry from Senator Zemprelli, held that on the basis of Rule XIII, Section 3 of the Senate Rules, the motion for the previous question is a non-debatable motion. (Senate Journal, 1983, p. 832.)

SECTION 31

QUESTIONS OF PRIVILEGE

Do Not Take Precedence of Special Orders

31 (a).   During the consideration of the resolution — (Resolved, As the sense of the Senate, that the ruling of the temporary President on the appeal taken from the decision of the President of the Senate on the point of order raised by the Senator from Delaware that amendments inserted on the second reading could not be stricken out on the third reading of House Bill No. 289, known as the repeal of the recorder's act of 1878, was an error, a tie vote having been cast, and the proceedings subsequent to the decision of the President of the Senate be corrected upon the Journal and rescinded) — the hour fixed for a special order having arrived. Mr. Reyburn then submitted the point of order that the question before the Senate was one of the highest privilege, and as such its consideration was in order until finally decided. The President submitted the point of order to the Senate for its decision. Decided in the negative by the Senate. (Senate Journal, 1883, pp. 779, 780, 787.)

Do Not Take Precedence Over Roll Call

31 (b).   Mr. Lane interrupted a roll call by rising on question of personal privilege.

The Presiding Officer ruled the question of personal privilege does not take precedence over the roll call and the gentleman was out of order. (Legislative Journal, December 10, 1951, p. 5963.)

SECTION 32

QUORUM

Senators Announcing "Pairs" to Be Counted in Making Up

32 (a).   Mr. Lee submitted the point of order that those members of the Senate who responded to the call of the yeas and nays just taken by stating as a reason for not voting that they were paired with absent Senators, are to be counted to ascertain whether there was a quorum present when the vote was taken. The President pro tempore decided the point of order well taken and the resolution agreed to. (Senate Journal, extra session, 1883, p. 143.)

Senators Announcing "Pairs" and Signing Appeal to Be Counted in Making Up

32 (b).   An appeal having been taken from the foregoing decision, and the yeas and nays called and the five Senators who signed the appeal declining to vote, Mr. Reyburn (acting President pro tempore), decided that with twenty-three Senators voting the two Senators recorded as present and paired, and the records on the question, a quorum was present, and the question was decided in the affirmative. (Senate Journal, extra session, 1883, p. 145; appeal from decision of the Chair, p. 145.)

The Acting President pro tempore (Mr. Reyburn) directed the clerk to call the names of the Senators who signed the appeal from the decision of the Chair, viz.: Messrs. Gordon, Kennedy, Biddis, Ross and Hess, and make a record of the same; which was done. And the acting President pro tempore (Mr. Reyburn) decided that with the Senators voting, the Senators present and paired, and the record on the question, a quorum was present, and the question determined in the affirmative. (Senate Journal, extra session, 1883, p. 146.)

SECTION 33

RECESS

Amending Motion for

33 (a).　The President decided it not in order to amend a motion "that the Senate take a recess" by adding thereto an amendment fixing the order of business when again convened. An appeal was taken, and the decision reversed. (Senate Journal, 1877, p. 574.)

A motion "that the Senate take a recess until eleven o'clock," having been amended by adding thereto "and that the Senate then proceed to the consideration of House Bill No. 162," the President decided that the Senate having under consideration bills on third reading, and the bill proposed to be considered after the recess, being on second reading, it would require a two-thirds vote to pass the resolution. An appeal was taken, and the decision reversed. (Senate Journal, 1877, p. 576.)

Motion for, Not in Order After Motion to Adjourn has been Defeated, and Vote Shows a Quorum Voting

33 (b).　A call for the previous question having been made on the first division of a motion to fix an afternoon session for the consideration of a certain bill, and less than a quorum voting thereon, a motion was made to adjourn and negatived, the vote showing more than a quorum present. A motion was then made to take a recess until tomorrow morning when Mr. Cooper submitted the point of order that as the vote on the motion to adjourn, just taken, demonstrated the presence of a quorum of the Senate, the motion just made was not in order, and that the question recurred upon the first division of the question now pending. The President decided the point of order well taken. (Senate Journal, 1885, p. 334.)

Motion Not Debatable

33 (c).　Mr. Lane rose to debate the motion to recess.

The Presiding Officer ruled the motion to recess is not debatable and the gentleman was out of order. (Legislative Journal, December 10, 1951, p. 5963.)

Motion to Recess Takes Precedence Over Motion to Reconsider

33 (d).　On a point of order raised by Senator Hager, the President determined that a motion for recess takes precedence over a motion to reconsider. (Senate Journal, 1979, p. 623.)

Motion Amendable Only as to Length of Recess — Such Amendment is Not Debatable

33 (e).　On points of order from Senators Lloyd and Mellow, the President pro tempore held that the motion to recess was amendable only as to the length of recess and that any motion to amend the length of the time for the recess would not be debatable. (Senate Journal, 1984, p. 2240.)

Motion Not Debatable

33 (f).　On points of order from Senators Rocks and Lloyd, the President pro tempore held that, under the Rules of the Senate and *Mason's Manual*, a motion to recess is not debatable. (Senate Journal, 1984, p. 2240.)

SECTION 34

RECOMMITMENT

Bill May Be Recommitted Any Time Before Final Action

34 (a).　The question having been raised as to the entertainment of a motion to recommit a bill, which through a printer's error, was not before the Senate in its proper form, the presiding officer (Lieutenant-Governor Daniel B. Strickler) ruled that a bill may properly be recommitted for the purpose of amendment regardless of the condition of the bill as long as there is not final action on the bill. (Legislative Journal, April 13, 1949, p. 312.)

Motion to Recommit Subject to Reconsideration

34 (b).　On a point of order raised by Senator Coppersmith, the President decided that a motion to recommit a bill was subject to reconsideration. (Senate Journal, 1979, p. 672.)

Debate on Motion to Recommit Cannot Go Into Merits of Question

34 (c).　The President concurred, in a parliamentary inquiry, that during debate of a motion to recommit, getting into the substance or merits of the bill is not proper. (Senate Journal, 1979, p. 932.)

Motion to Recommit Debatable But Not on Merits of Bill

34 (d).　Following a motion to rerefer a bill to committee, a point of order was raised by Senator Scanlon, and the President ruled that the motion to rerefer was open to debate, but not to debate on the bill itself. (Senate Journal, 1980, p. 1470.)

Motion to Recommit Takes Precedence Over the Motion to Adopt

34 (e).　The Presiding Officer, upon parliamentary inquiry from Senator Coppersmith, held that a motion to recommit was actually made and that the motion to recommit takes precedence over the motion to adopt. (Senate Journal, 1980, p. 1686.)

Choice of Committees in Rereferral

34 (f).　A motion was made to rerefer a bill to a different committee than to which it was originally referred. On a point of order raised by Senator Romanelli, the President decided that the Senate has the power to rerefer a bill to any committee it pleases. (Senate Journal, 1980, p. 1921.)

Debate on Motion to Recommit Limited to Reasons for Recommittal

34 (g).　The President, on a point of order raised by Senator Fumo, reminded the speaker that debate on the motion to rerefer is limited to the reasons for rereferral and that debate on the substance of the bill was out of order. (Senate Journal, 1980, p. 1964.)

Motion to Recommit Debatable as to the Propriety of Reference, But Not as to the Main Question

34 (h).　On several points of order raised by Senator Jubelirer, the President held that the motion to commit or recommit is debatable as to the propriety of the reference, but the main question is not open to debate. However, the President found that the urgency of the bill being discussed is germane to the propriety of the reference. (Senate Journal, 1981, pp. 1010-1.)

If Bill Recommitted, Amendments Pending Go With the Bill

34 (i).　On parliamentary inquiry from Senator Jubelirer, the President ruled that if a bill were to go back to committee on rereferral, the amendments offered to the bill, but not yet adopted, would go back to the committee with the bill. (Senate Journal, 1982, p. 2779.)

Debate on Motion to Recommit Limited Solely to the Appropriateness of the Recommittal

34 (j).　Senator Jubelirer objected to the debate on a motion to recommit, stating that when a member suggests that anyone who votes for the motion will deny him an opportunity to offer an amendment, that member is out of order. The President found the point of order well-taken and ruled that the Senator should confine his comments solely to the appropriateness of the recommittal. (Senate Journal, 1983, p. 765.)

Executive Nomination Not Subject to Recommittal Until Taken From the Table

34 (k).　A motion was made to take a nomination from the table. Then, prior to a vote, the motion to recommit the nomination was made. On point of order from Senator Zemprelli, the Presiding Officer (William J. Moore) decided that the nomination could not be subject to a motion for recommittal until it had been removed from the table. (Senate Journal, 1984, p. 1974.)

SECTION 35

RECONSIDERATION

Not in Order After Five Legislative Days

35 (d).   Mr. Cooper submitted the point of order that, as five legislative days had elapsed since the vote was had by which the amendment was agreed to, under the provisions of the sixteenth rule of the Senate, the motion was not now in order. Decided well taken. (Senate Journal, 1883, p. 737.)

Of Final Vote on Bill, Must Be Made Within Five Legislative Days

35 (f).   A motion having been made to reconsider final vote on bill. Mr. Grady submitted the point of order that, as five legislative days had elapsed since the vote on final passage of the bill by the Senate, the resolution is not in order. The President decided that point of order well taken, and ruled the motion out of order. (Senate Journal, 1883, p. 1241.)

Motion for, on Second Reading Having Been Made and Lost, Not in Order a Second Time

35 (h).   The bill being on third reading and a motion to reconsider the vote by which it passed second reading having been made and lost, Mr. Shapiro submitted the point of order that a motion to reconsider again was not in order. The President decided the point of order well taken and ruled the motion out of order. (Legislative Journal, 1937, p. 6129.)

Necessary When Instructing a Conference Committee to Do That Which the Senate Has Already Refused to Do

35 (i).   Mr. Hughes submitted the point of order that it is proposed by the resolution instructing a conference committee to do something that the Senate has already refused to do, without reconsidering the previous action of the Senate, and is, therefore, not in order. The President decided the point of order well taken, and ruled the resolution out of order. (Senate Journal, extra session, 1883, p. 62.)

A Motion for, Always in Order

35 (j).   An objection having been made to the motion for the reconsideration of the vote by which a resolution was defeated, the President decided that a motion to reconsider is always in order. (Senate Journal, extra session, 1891, p. 404.)

Motion for, Opens Main Question to Debate

35 (k).   Mr. Weiner raised the point of order that under the motion to reconsider only that motion was debatable.

The Presiding Officer decided the point of order not well taken and quoted from Mason's Manual, Sec. 471, p. 322, the following:

". . .When the question to be reconsidered is debatable, the entire question is opened to debate by the motion to reconsider."

Motion for Reconsideration in Order on Final Day of Five-Day Discharge Petition

35 (l).   On the final day of a five-day requirement of a discharge petition, an executive nomination was defeated. A motion to reconsider was made, and on point of order, the President held that the motion to reconsider was in order on the fifth day of the discharge petition. (Senate Journal, 1979, p. 434.)

Motion for Reconsideration Permitted Twice

35 (m).   After a second, consecutive reconsideration motion was made, Senator Coppersmith raised a point of order, and the President ruled that (under Rule 12, Section 12) a second reconsideration motion was in order. (Senate Journal, 1979, p. 644.)

Motion to Reconsider Executive Nominations Need Not Occur While in Executive Session But Senate Must Still Maintain Custody

35 (n).   Senator Romanelli inquired whether a vote approving executive nominations can be reconsidered after executive session rises. The President decided that the motion to reconsider can be made at any time, and that the motion need not be made in Executive Session. The President added that in order to reconsider the matter, it must still be in the custody of the Senate, and he noted that nominations approved would leave Senate custody when they are sent to the Governor. (Senate Journal, 1981, p. 61.)

Any Action of the Senate, Positive or Negative, Can be Reconsidered

35 (o).   Senator Reibman inquired whether reconsideration can be asked for when a question is determined in the affirmative. The President pro tempore decided that any action of the Senate, positive or negative, may be reconsidered. (Senate Journal, 1981, p. 502.)

Bill Does Not Have to be on Desks of Senators For Reconsideration Motion

35 (p).   Senator Snyder rose to a point of order to object to the motion to reconsider a bill because the bill was not "on the desks" of the Senators. The President decided the motion to reconsider is in order without the bill being "on the desks," but that the motion to finally pass the bill would not be in order without the bill being on the desks. (Senate Journal, 1981, p. 609.)

Motion for Reconsideration Not in Order While the Senate is at Ease

35 (q).   Senator Lloyd rose to a point of order to object to his not being recognized on the floor for the purposes of offering a reconsideration motion. The President decided that the gentleman was not recognized because: the Majority Leader had asked for the Senate to be at ease; the President had put the Senate at ease; and it is not proper to recognize a member when the Senate is at ease. (Senate Journal, 1982, p. 2088.)

SECTION 36

RESOLUTIONS

Merits of Resolution Not to Be Debated When Presented

36 (c).   The point of order was raised by Mr. Huffman that it is a violation of the rules of the Senate for a debate to be presented by a Senator offering a resolution. President decided point of order well taken. (Legislative Journal, 1937, p. 129.)

Discharge Resolution Is Not a Privileged Resolution

36 (d).   Mr. Dent raised the question as to whether or not a discharge resolution was a privileged resolution.

The Chair, Lieutenant-Governor Lloyd H. Wood, ruled that it is not and quoted from Section 400 of Jefferson's Manual the following:

"The motion to discharge a committee from the consideration of an ordinary legislative proposition is not privileged." (Legislative Journal, May 7, 1951, p. 1873.)

Discharge Resolution, Vote on, Not a Vote For or Against a Bill

36 (e).   Mr. Van Sant inquired as to whether a vote on a discharge resolution constitutes a vote for or against a bill. The Chair, Lieutenant-Governor John Morgan Davis, ruled that the vote is to decide whether or not to discharge the committee from further consideration of the bill. The vote is on the resolution only, not the merits of the bill. (Legislative Journal, 1959, p. 4174.)

Discharge Resolution Not Debatable

36 (f).   The question was raised as to debate on a discharge resolution. The Presiding officer quoted the following from Section 491, p. 329, of Mason's Manual:

"It is not in order to discuss the merits of a bill upon a motion to discharge a committee or withdraw a bill from committee. Debate in such cases must be confined strictly to the purpose of the motion, for if this were not true, the merits of any question could be forced under discussion merely by such a motion."

(Senate Journal, June 21, 1977, p. 494.)

SECTION 37

RESOLUTIONS CONCURRENT

Necessary to Provide for Printing of Report of an Investigating Committee — Cannot Be Considered Until Referred to Proper Committee

37 (a).   Mr. Gobin submitted to the point of order, that a concurrent resolution is necessary to provide for the printing proposed in the resolution, and a concurrent resolution, which originated in the Senate, of the same character, having been defeated in the House, the resolution is not in order. The President pro tempore decided that the resolution was not in order. (Senate Journal, 1881, p. 860.)

A concurrent resolution creating a commission to be known as a commission to investigate the disbursement of the Commonwealth, having been introduced the President decided that under Rule 39 of the Senate, it must be referred to an appropriate committee before consideration by the Senate. (Legislative Journal, June 11, 1913, p. 4522.)

From House Recalling a House Bill Which Is on Second Reading Calendar Out of Order

37 (b).   A resolution having been presented to the Senate recalling a House Bill, Mr. Lyon submitted the point of order, that said bill having been regularly presented to the Senate as having passed the House of Representatives, committed to the proper Senate committee, considered by the same and reported to the Senate, and having passed first reading and now being on second reading calendar, the position of the bill is such that the request of the House contained in the resolution could not be complied with under the rules of the Senate. Whereupon, the President of the Senate decided the point of order well taken and ruled the resolution out of order. (Senate Journal, 1893, p. 1136. See also Legislative Journal, 1921, p. 1295.)

SECTION 38

REVERSION TO PRIOR PRINTER'S NUMBER

Debate on Motion Confined to the Amendments Involved

38 (a).   During debate of a motion that a bill on third consideration revert to a prior printer's number, Senator Jubelirer rose to a point of order to object to the debate as being out of order. The President held the point well-taken because debate on the motion to revert to a prior printer's number should be confined to the amendments involved. (Senate Journal, 1983, p. 323.)

SECTION 39

ROLL CALL

Verification Cannot Be Asked for After Vote Announced

39 (a.)   Mr. Reed submitted the point of order that after the roll call was announced by the Chair it was too late to ask the verification of the roll. The President decided the point of order well taken. (Legislative Journal, 1933, p. 5640.) (See also Legislative Journal, 1937, pp. 397, 398.)

Announcement of Roll Call Cannot be Delayed for a Day

39 (b).   A roll call having been completed and the announcement thereof being next in order, Senator Dent requested the results be postponed until the following day to allow Senator Barr, who was absent, to register his opposition to the bill.

The Chair, Lieutenant-Governor Lloyd H. Wood, ruled the only order of business in order is the announcement of the roll call and the request is out of order. (Legislative Journal, December 17, 1951, p. 6294.)

Suspension of Rules — Motion — Not to Interrupt

39 (c).   The clerk was calling the roll on House Bill 1349 when Senator Hager rose and moved to suspend the rules in regards to the previous question. The President, Lieutenant Governor Ernest P. Kline, ruled the gentleman out of order. Once a roll call has begun, it cannot be interrupted even by a motion to adjourn. (Senate Journal, August 10, 1977, p. 824.)

Members of Senate Not Supposed to be Near Tally Desk During Tabulation of Roll Call

39 (d).   On a point of order raised by Senator Kelley, the President decided it well-taken that the Rules of the Senate provide that members are not supposed to be near the tally desk when the roll call is being tabulated. (Senate Journal, 1979, p. 645.)

Does Not Officially Begin Until it is Responded to

39 (e).   Senator Zemprelli rose to a point of order to object to the Chair's entertaining of business once the roll had been called for. The President stated that the rule is that the roll call does not officially begin until it has been responded to; thus the roll call had not yet begun. (Senate Journal, 1984, p. 1731.)

Did Not Begin Because No Response Given to First Name Called

39 (f).   The President pro tempore, on point of order from Senator Zemprelli, held that a roll call had not begun because there had been no response to the first name called; thus, it was not improper to recognize a Senator for debate at that point. (Senate Journal, 1984, p. 2498.)

SECTION 40

SENATORS

Before Qualification, Cannot Present Papers

40 (a).   The Speaker decided that it was not in order for a Senator-elect to present a paper to the Senate before he was qualified. (Senate Journal, 1866, p. 6.)

The Speaker decided that it was not in order to receive a paper from persons elected as Senators previous to their being qualified. The Senate sustained the decision. (Senate Journal, 1867, p. 6.)

Constitutional Order in Organization of Senate

40 (b).   Senator Barr, at the meeting for the organization of the Senate, and after the Senators-elect from the even-numbered districts had been declared elected but prior to the roll call, asked leave to present a resolution.

The Chair, Lieutenant-Governor Samuel S. Lewis, ruled that the resolution was out of order and stated:

"Motions at this time are out of order because of the lack of a quorum as provided in Section 10, Article 2, of the Constitution, which reads as follows:

" 'A majority of each House shall constitute a quorum.'

"Until the oath of office has been administered to the Senators whose election has just been certified to the Senate by the Secretary of the Commonwealth, the required quorum of twenty-six (26) members is lacking.

"In the absence of a quorum, the only thing before the Senate is the administering of the oath of office to the certified newly elected Senators and the calling of the roll to ascertain if a quorum is present."

(Legislative Journal, January 5, 1943, pages 3 and 4.)

May Vote on Question Affecting Seat of

40 (c).   The Speaker decided that an amendment, directing that the name of a Senator, whose seat was contested, be omitted in calling the yeas and nays on the resolution before the Senate relating to the right of such Senator to a seat in that body, was not in order. An appeal was taken and laid on the table. (Senate Journal, 1871, p. 125.)

A question of order was raised that a Senator should not vote upon a question affecting his seat in the Senate. The Speaker submitted the question to the Senate, and it was decided that the question of order was not well taken. (Senate Journal, 1871, p. 127.)

Formal Resignation of, Necessary to Preclude Their Voting

40 (d).   The yeas and nays having been called and taken, before the result was announced, Mr. Gordon submitted the point of order that the two Senators from Allegheny (Messrs. Arnhold and Upperman) having resigned their seats, were not entitled to a vote, and their vote should not be counted in ascertaining the result of the pending question. The President pro tempore (Mr. MacFarlane in the Chair) decided the point of order not well taken, the Senate having no official knowledge of the resignation of the Senators named. (Senate Journal, extra session, 1883, p. 209.)

SECTION 41

SPECIAL ORDERS

Debate Limited

41 (a).   Mr. Walker raised the question that if a bill is made a special order of business at 2:45 o'clock and another bill is made a special order of business at 3:00 o'clock, are the proceedings, although unfinished, stopped at the termination of the time allotted to the bill which was made a special order of business at 2:45 o'clock when the Senate clock shows the hour of 3:00 o'clock.

The Chair, Lieutenant-Governor Lloyd H. Wood, ruled they very definitely would be. (Legislative Journal, September 25, 1951, p. 5356.)

Privilege of

41 (b).   Mr. Weiner raised the point of order that the motion to make Executive Nominations a Special Order of Business immediately, while the Senate was under the Order of Business of Original Resolutions was out of order.

The Presiding Officer decided the point of order not well taken, and quoted from Mason's Manual, Sec. 264, p. 203, the following:

"The purpose of a special order is to expedite important business and set a definite time for its consideration, which gives such a special order privilege over other pending business. Whenever the making of a special order sets aside the general rules regarding the order of business it requires the same vote as would be required to specifically suspend the rules."

The Chair is of the opinion that the motion made by Senator Fleming is in order at this time.

An appeal was taken and the decision of the Chair was sustained. (Legislative Journal, 1959, p. 5226.)

SECTION 42

SPECIAL SESSION

For a Special Purpose Being Fixed, a Two-thirds Vote Not Necessary to Pass Resolution for General Business

42 (a).   A special session of the Senate being already fixed for the afternoon, for taking the vote on United States Senator, the President decided that two-thirds vote was necessary to pass a resolution — "That when the Senate adjourns this A.M., it will be to meet at three o'clock this P.M." An appeal was taken and the decision reversed by the Senate. (Senate Journal, 1877, p. 521.)

SECTION 43

SUSPENSION OF THE RULES

Motion to Suspend Not Debatable

43 (b).   Senator Frame made a motion to suspend Senate Rule 15 so that the Senate could immediately consider the concurrence of amendments placed by the House in Senate Bill No. 765 without it appearing on the calendar. A question arose as to whether the motion to suspend a rule was debatable. The Chair, Lieutenant Governor Ernest P. Kline, ruled it was not and quoted from Mason's Manual, Section 283(6), page 214:

"A motion to suspend the Rules may not be amended, debated, laid on the table, referred to committee, postponed, nor have any other subsidiary motion applied to it." (Legislative Journal, 1973, p. 741.) also (Senate Journal, June 20, 1978, p. 665.)

Motion to Suspend Rules to Amend House Amendments to Senate Bill is in Order

43 (c).   The President, on inquiry from Senator Zemprelli, held that precedent and the Rules of the Senate indicated that a motion to suspend the rules to allow amendment of House amendments made to a Senate bill was in order. (Senate Journal, 1981, pp. 1522-3.)

Motion to Suspend Rules, Not in Order For Amendment of Conference Committee Report

43 (d).   Upon a motion to suspend the rules for the purposes of amending a report of a committee of conference, the President held that the motion to suspend the rules is not in order due to the fact that the motion to adopt the report of the committee of conference is a privileged motion and privileged motions take precedence over motions to suspend the rules. On appeal, the Senate (28-22) sustained the decision of the Chair. (Senate Journal, 1982, pp. 1672-4.)

Motion to Suspend Rules Not in Order for Amendment of Bill on Concurrence in House Amendments

43 (e).   Senator Bodack moved to suspend the rules in order to offer amendments to a bill on concurrence in House amendments. The President decided the motion was not in order because it was the intention of the Senator to amend the bill rather than the amendments placed in the bill by the House of Representatives. On appeal, the Senate (25-23) upheld the decision of the Chair. (Senate Journal, 1982, p. 2503.)

Motion to Suspend Rules Not Debatable

43 (f).   The President, on parliamentary inquiry from Senator Lloyd, held that it is not in order to speak on the motion to suspend the rules because it is a non-debatable motion. (Senate Journal, 1983, p. 832.)

Motion to Suspend Rules to Amend House Amendments to Senate Bill in Order Before Amendments Are Presented

43 (g).   A motion to suspend the rules to amend House amendments to a Senate bill was made. Senator Bell raised a point of order, stating that the motion is out of order because the maker had not first presented the amendments. The President held the motion to suspend the rules was in order. (Senate Journal, 1984, p. 1585.)

Motion Not Debatable

43 (h).   Senator Kelley inquired if the motion to suspend the rules was debatable in light of the difference between the list of non-debatable motions in the Senate Rules (Rule XIII, Section 3), the rule in *Mason's Manual*, and the constructive principle, *Expressio Unius Est Exclusio Alterius* (the expression of one thing is the exclusion of the other). The President pro tempore held the motion was non-debatable based on Rule XXVIII (adopting *Mason's Manual* as authority) and on established precedent of the Senate. (Senate Journal, 1984, p. 1861.)

SECTION 44

TAKE FROM THE TABLE

Motion to Take From the Table Not Debatable

44 (a).   The Presiding Officer, in response to a point of order raised by Senator Hager, held that the motion to take from the table is not subject to debate. (Senate Journal, 1980, p.1718.)

Motion to Take From the Table a Report of a Committee of Conference on a House Bill Not in Order

44 (b).   The Senate received the report of a committee of conference on a House bill. On a motion to take the report from the table, the President held the motion out of order stating that the House is in possession of the bill, and the Senate cannot act on the bill until the intentions of the House are communicated. (Senate Journal, 1982, p. 1772.)

SECTION 45

TIE VOTE

On Appeal Sustains Decisions of the President

45 (a).   An appeal having been taken from the decision of the President of the Senate, and the vote of the Senate on the question of sustaining the decision, resulted in a tie, the President directed that a decision of the Chair on a point of order stands until reversed by a majority vote of the Senate. (Senate Journal, 1877, p. 163.)

Chair Obligated to Break Tie Vote

45 (b). Mr. Shapiro raised the point of order that a majority of those present had not voted on the motion to go into Committee of the Whole and that the Chair therefore is not entitled to a vote. The President disagreed with Mr. Shapiro as the Senate was not voting in Committee of the Whole. The President, however, ruled that under the Constitution the Chair is obligated to break a tie vote whether there is a constitutional majority or not. (Legislative Journal, 1937, p. 5949.)

President Not Entitled to Vote to Break Tie on Final Passage of Bill

45 (c). The President is not entitled to cast a deciding vote in case of a tie where it means the passage of a bill. The Constitution requires a majority vote of the members elected to the Senate. (Legislative Journal, April 28, 1949, p. 4808.)

Previous Question — President May Vote

45 (d). The vote on a motion for the previous question resulted in a tie. The President cast his vote in the affirmative. Senator Nolan rose to a point of information as to what authority permitted the Chair to vote. The President, Lieutenant Governor Ernest P. Kline, stated that he was permitted to vote in accordance with provisions of Art. 4, Sec. 4 of the Pennsylvania Constitution, which is titled,

"Lieutenant Governor

......he shall be President of the Senate. As such, he may vote in case of a tie on any question except final passage of a bill or joint resolution, the adoption of a conference report or the concurrence of amendments made by the House of Representatives"

(Senate Journal, August 10, 1977, p. 822.)

SECTION 46

UNANIMOUS CONSENT

Movant Can Inquire as to Reason for Objection to Unanimous Consent, But Member Need Not Reply

46 (a). Senator Loeper objected to unanimous consent for a request to take nominations from the table. The President held that the member who requested unanimous consent may inquire as to the reasons for the Senator's objection, but it is not incumbent upon the objecting Member to give an answer. (Senate Journal, 1980, p. 2211.)

SECTION 47

VOTE

Cannot Be Recorded After Result is Announced by the Chair

47 (a). The yeas and nays having been called on the passage of a resolution the names of Senators voting for and against it having been read by the clerk, the result announced by the President pro tempore, a Senator demanded that his vote, which he alleged had been cast but not recorded, should be recorded and counted. The President pro tempore decided that the Senator should have corrected the vote after it was read by the clerk, and before announced by the President pro tempore, and it could not be recorded and counted now. (Senate Journal, 1878, p. 615.)

Can Be Changed on a Misapprehension of the Question

47 (c). The yeas and nays having been taken, and before the list of those voting had been read by the clerk, and the result announced by the Chair, two Senators asked leave to change their votes from the affirmative to the negative, whereupon the President pro tempore inquired of them whether they had voted under a misapprehension. Upon a point of order being raised, the Senate decided that the proper question to put to each of the two Senators is "Has the Senator voted under a misapprehension of the question?" (Senate Journal, 1879, p. 948.)

Change of Vote by Reason of Misapprehension Only

47 (d). Senator Crowe having requested permission to change his vote from "aye" to "no" upon a pending bill, Senator Shapiro raised the point of order that no Senator has a right to change his vote unless he states that he voted under a misapprehension.

The Chair, Lieutenant-Governor John C. Bell, ruled that the point of order was well taken and that, under Senate Decision No. 123, in the State Manual, a Senator cannot change his vote without stating that he voted under a misapprehension. (Legislative Journal, March 23, 1943, p. 1957.)

Of Twenty-six Senators in the Affirmative Necessary to Pass a Bill Finally

47 (e). The President decided that the constitutional requirements relative to the final passage of a bill is intended to apply to the whole number of Senators provided for by the Constitution, which would be fifty, and that the number required to be recorded in favor of a bill upon its final passage is a majority of the whole number of Senators elected, which would be twenty-six. (Senate Journal, 1881, p. 479.)

Too Late to Correct on Bill After Other Business Has Intervened

47 (f). Mr. Grady rose to a question of privilege and made the statement that the vote on House Bill No. 35, as taken, was incorrect; that the vote of Mr. Moyer, in the affirmative had not been recorded, and if recorded, the bill would have received twenty-six affirmative votes, and would have passed the Senate. He then, upon leave given, moved that the vote be again taken on said bill. Mr. Merrick raised the point of order that the motion of Mr. Grady was not in order, the vote having been already taken and the result of said bill announced, and that other business had intervened. The Chair decided the point of order well taken. (Senate Journal, 1897, p. 1799.)

Right to Change Vote

47 (g). After the verification of a roll call, but before announcement of the vote, Senator Geltz requested that his vote be changed from "aye" to "no." Senator Shapiro objected, raising the point of order that "since the Chair has already verified the negative vote and declared it to stand, there can be no change in the vote" and suggested that "nothing is in order until the vote has been counted and there is nothing before the Chair except an announcement of the vote. Anything else that comes up now, after the vote has been verified, is out of order."

The President (Lieutenant-Governor Samuel S. Lewis) ruled the point of order was not well taken and stated that "in the absence of a Senate Rule or a joint House and Senate Rule governing the question, the Chair, under Rule 34 of the Senate, quotes from the House Rules and Manual of the 76th Congress, Rule 15, Paragraph 766, page 349:

"Before the result of a vote has been finally and conclusively pronounced by the Chair, but not thereafter, a member may change his vote."

The Chair also quoted from page 193, Roberts Rules of Order:

"A member has the right to change his vote, up to the time the vote is finally announced." (Legislative Journal, May 10, 1941, pp. 2438 and 2449.)

Misapprehension on Confirmation

47 (h). Mr. Barr raised the question as to whether a member can vote under a misapprehension on the confirmation of a cabinet member.

The Chair, Lieutenant-Governor Lloyd H. Wood, ruled that a member may change his vote any time before it is announced. (Legislative Journal, February 19, 1951, p. 363.)

Senator Must Vote if Present

47 (i). Mr. Walker raised the point of order that since Senator Kephart was in his seat and had not voted when his name was called, he was obliged to vote under the rules of the Senate.

The Chair, Lieutenant-Governor Lloyd H. Wood, ruled the point of order well taken. (Legislative Journal, December 4, 1951, p. 5855.)

Senator Must Vote on Confirmation if Present

47 (j). Senator Barr asked if he was required to vote on a confirmation.

The Presiding Officer ruled that a Senator must vote if present. (Legislative Journal, December 21, 1951, p. 6747.)

Vote "Present" Allowed on Nomination of President Pro Tempore

47 (k). On a roll call vote on amendments, Senator Bell voted "present." The Lieutenant-Governor (John Morgan Davis) stated the vote of "present" is not considered a vote in the Senate. Senator Bell then

referred to a vote of "present" by Senator Anthony J. DiSilvestro on a roll call vote on the election of Senator DiSilvestro as President Pro Tempore. The Lieutenant-Governor ruled that this vote was entirely in order for the simple reason that Senator DiSilvestro did not wish to vote for himself (there being no other candidates for the office) and also the vote would have meant an increase in salary. On that basis, naturally, he was accorded the privilege of not voting for or against himself. (Legislative Journal, February 7, 1961, p. 354.)

Twenty-five ELECTED Senators in the Affirmative Necessary to Pass a Bill Finally

47 (l). On a roll call vote on HB 1152 the Chair announced it had passed by a vote of 25-20. A Constitutional Point of Order was raised that the bill needed 26 affirmative votes for passage. The President, Raymond J. Broderick, submitted the following to the Senate for its determination:

"In accordance with Article III, Section 4 of the Constitution, the last sentence reads, in part, as follows:

". . .no bill shall become law, unless on its final passage the vote be taken by yeas and nays, the names of the persons voting for and against the same be entered on the journal, and a majority of the members elected to each House be recorded thereon as voting in its favor."

"In view of the fact that no Senator has been elected from the Twenty-eighth Senatorial District and that this Senate, since convening this Session, has never had more than forty-nine Members elected, therefore, a majority of the "members elected," as that term is used in the Constitution, shall be, at the present time, twenty-five Members.

"The Chair wants to explain that those voting "aye" shall vote that twenty-five votes are all that are necessary under the present makeup of this Senate. Those voting "nay," shall vote that twenty-six votes are necessary." A majority of all the Senators having voted "aye" the question was decided in the affirmatve and the point of order was sustained.

Immediately upon the announcement of the vote an appeal was taken by Senator Sesler on the President's announcement that the bill had passed the Senate. The President, Raymond J. Broderick, ruled the appeal out of order because the Chair had made no ruling, the Senate itself decided that the bill had passed.

Senator Sesler then raised a point of order that a constitutional majority did not exist in the passage of House Bill No. 1152 as only 25 affirmative votes were recorded and verified and that the bill, having failed to receive the constitutional majority (26), had failed.

The President, Raymond J. Broderick, ruled the point of order not well taken as this question had already been decided by the Senate.

Senator Sesler then appealed from the Statement of the Chair in which he stated "...the "aye" votes having been 25 and the "nay" votes having been 20, this bill will be returned to the House of Representatives with the information that the Senate has passed the bill without amendment."

On the question of the appeal the Chair was sustained. (Senate Journal 1967, page 775.) (Senate Journal 1968, page 472.)

Constitutional Majority — Senators Elected, Living, Sworn and Seated

47 (m). Senator Scales submitted his resignation to the Senate. After reading the letter of resignation, the President, Lieutenant-Governor Ernest P. Kline, made the following statement:

"The Chair wishes to advise the Members that with the resignation of Senator Scales and the vacancies presently existing in the Senate, and, inasmuch as only forty-eight Senators are presently serving, it is the opinion of this Chair that under the Constitution, particularly Article III, Section 4, which reads, in part, "...No bill shall become a law, unless on its final passage the vote is taken by yeas and nays, the names of the persons voting for and against are entered on the journal, and a majority of the members elected to each House is recorded thereon as voting in its favor."

Under the Rules of the Senate, particularly under Rule XXII, "Voting," subsection 8, "A majority of the Senators elected shall mean a majority of the Senators elected living, sworn and seated," it is the opinion of this Chair that the current constitutional majority for final passage of legislation in this Senate is twenty-five.

That opinion is given for the purpose of notice. If the issue is ever raised, certainly an appeal would be in order." (Senate Journal, 1974, p. 1457.)

Personal Interest — Bank Stock Ownership — Rate of Interest Bill

47 (n). The Senate had under consideration Senate Bill 262 which regulated the rate of interest. Several Senators raised the question as to whether they should vote since they held bank stock.

The President, Lieutenant Governor Ernest P. Kline, stated that it would be the ruling of the Chair that the holders of bank stock would be members of a class and, under the rules of the Senate and are entitled to vote and are compelled to vote under the rules of the Senate. (Senate Journal, 1973, p. 841.)

Personal Interest — No-fault Insurance — Attorneys and Those Engaged in Insurance Business — Permitted to Vote

47 (o). The Senate had under consideration House Bill 1973 pertaining to no-fault insurance. Senator Kelley raised the point of order that since he was a practicing attorney and may or may not be affected by the results of his vote, would he be permitted to vote under the conflict of interest provisions of the rules and constitution.

The President, Lieutenant Governor Ernest P. Kline, ruled that as an attorney he was a member of a class of attorneys, and, therefore, as a Senator, he would have the right to vote, since it would not be a conflict of interest. The same ruling, for the general information of the members, would also apply to those who may be engaged in the insurance business. (Senate Journal, 1974, p. 2210.)

Personal Interest — Appropriation Bill — Member of Board of Trustees

47 (p). The Senate had under consideration House Bill 1012 which appropriated money to the Pennsylvania College of Podiatric Medicine in Philadelphia.

Senator Rovner raised a parliamentary inquiry as to whether he could vote on this bill since he was a Member of the Board of Trustees of this College.

The President, Lieutenant Governor Ernest P. Kline, ruled that he would be one of a class of trustees and, thereby, not only eligible to vote, but is required to vote or give an explanation as to why you do not vote. (Senate Journal, 1973, p. 1242.)

Absent — Statement of Vote If Present

47 (q). Senator Zemprelli was absent from the Senate attending a committee meeting. Several roll calls were voted and he was not recorded. A question was raised as to how he may be recorded.

The President, Lieutenant-Governor Ernest P. Kline, stated that under the Rules of the Senate if he was not on the floor at the time the roll calls were taken he may state his reasons for his absence and how he would have voted had he been on the floor. This would become part of the record. (Senate Journal, 1973, p. 1121.)

Absent Member Cannot Abstain From Voting

47 (r). Senator Zemprelli, voting for an absent Senator, entered the vote of abstention. On parliamentary inquiry from Senator Andrews, the President ruled that the absent Senator may not abstain from voting. The absent Member's vote was changed to "not voting." (Senate Journal, 1979, p. 866.)

Member May Leave the Floor Once He Has Voted Even Though Tally Not Complete

47 (s). In interpreting Rule XXII after an inquiry from Senator Lincoln, the President decided that once a Senator has voted, being physically present for the vote, the member may leave the floor before final tally and announcement of the vote. (Senate Journal, 1980, p. 1400.)

Refusal to Vote Deemed a Contempt

47 . (t). Upon parliamentary inquiry from Senator Lewis, the President, quoting Senate Rule XXII, decided that the refusal of any Senator to vote shall be deemed a contempt unless he be excused by the Senate or unless he has a direct, personal or pecuniary interest. But, he went on to state that the Senate would then have the power to: (1) vote the non-voting Member in contempt; (2) hold a hearing on the issue; or (3) overlook the issue entirely. (Senate Journal, 1980, p. 1931.)

Constitutional Majority Consists of Senators Elected, Living, Sworn, and Seated

47 (u). The President ruled that a constitutional majority of the Senate needed for confirming executive nominations was "a majority of Senators elected, living, sworn and seated." Senator Zemprelli objected and appealed this decision of the Chair, claiming that the Constitution of Pennsylvania and statutory provisions stated that a constitutional majority consisted of "members elected." The Senate (25-20) upheld the decision of the Chair. (Senate Journal, 1981, pp. 95-101.)

Several Senators, invoking the original jurisdiction of the Pennsylvania Supreme Court pursuant to 42 Pa. C.S.A. Section 721 (c) (Purdon 1981), then initiated a *quo warranto* action to oust eighteen nominated and confirmed state officials from their positions because they claimed the officials were not properly confirmed by a "constitutional majority" of the Senate.

O'BRIEN, C.J. delivered the opinion of the court:

The events giving rise to this action, which are not in dispute, took place on the Senate floor during the 1981 Session of the 165th General Assembly. Governor Thornburgh nominated Respondent Daniels by a letter to the Senate dated December 24, 1980. Initially, the nomination was tabled, but it was reconsidered on January 27, 1981, when a vote was taken. The affirmative votes of a majority of the members elected to the Senate were required to confirm her appointment under 71 P.S. Section 67.1(d) (4) (Purdon Supp. 1981). The nomination received 25 "yeas" and 22 "nays," and the President of the Senate, finding that a constitutional majority had been obtained, ruled the appointment confirmed.

Respondent Zemprelli objected to the Chair's ruling, arguing that the constitutional majority should be computed on the basis of the total number of members "elected" to the Senate rather than on the number then in office, 48, and that consequently the affirmative vote of 25 Senators was insufficient to seat Respondent Daniels. The President based his ruling on Senate Rule XXII, subparagraph 8, 104 PA. Code Section 11.22 (i), which provides "[a] majority of the Senators elected shall mean a majority of the Senators elected, living, sworn, and seated." Since 25 constituted a majority of the 48 Senators then in office, the President ruled that Respondent Daniels' nomination had achieved the majority vote mandated by Article IV, section 8(a) of the Pennsylvania Constitution. That section provides:

> "The Governor shall appoint a Secretary of Education and such other officers as he shall be authorized to appoint. The appointment of the Secretary of Education and of such other officers as may be specified by law, shall be subject to the consent of two-thirds or a majority of the members elected to the Senate as is specified by law."

Petitioner Zemprelli appealed the Chair's ruling and, after debate, the Senate sustained it by a vote of 25 to 22. Zemprelli's subsequent motion for reconsideration of the nomination was defeated. This *quo warranto* action ensued.

It is evident from the foregoing that the entire controversy before us turns on a single question of constitutional interpretation, namely the meaning of the phrase "a majority of the members elected to the Senate" in the context of Article IV, section 8. Before we may engage in such interpretation, however, we must first determine whether petitioners have standing to maintain this action. If we answer in the affirmative, we must then decide whether the dispute before this Court presents a "political question" not amenable to judicial review.

[The Court found that the petitioners had alleged sufficient interest in the outcome of the action and thus had standing to bring it before the Court. The Court then concluded that the petitioner's claim was not a non-justiciable political question and proceeded to decide the substantive issue.]

This Court has announced clear guidelines to aid in the interpretation of constitutional provisions. In *Commonwealth ex rel. Paulinski v. Issac*, 483 Pa. 467, 397 A.2d 760 (1979), we stated:

> "Constitutional provisions are not to be read in a strained or technical manner. Rather, they must be given the ordinary, natural interpretation the ratifying voter would give them.

Commonwealth v. Harmon, 469 Pa. 490, 366 A.2d 895 (1976); *Beradocco v. Colden*, 469 Pa. 452, 366 A.2d 574 (1976).

> "Where, as here, we must decide between two interpretations of a constitutional provision, we must favor a natural reading which avoids contradictions and difficulties in implementation, which completely conforms to the intent of the framers and which reflects the views of the ratifying voter."

Id. at 475, 477, 397 A.2d at 765, 766. We believe the reading petitioners would impose upon Article IX, section 8(a) enjoys none of the characteristics of such an interpretation.

Petitioners contend that the phrase "a majority of the members elected to the Senate" means a majority computed on the basis of the total number of Senators *elected* at a given time, whether or not such Senators are, in the words of Senate Rule XXII-8, "living, sworn [or] seated." Hence, in the instant action, they would have us rule that Respondent Daniels was put into office by less than a constitutional majority, and should be ousted, because 50 Senators were "elected," and her nomination received only 25 affirmative votes. Petitioners appear to be relying on the common or natural meaning of the word "elected" and the meaning of "member" as it is used elsewhere in the Constitution to arrive at this interpretation, disregarding the phrase as a whole and in the context of Article IV, section 8.

In our view, to compute a majority based on a number greater than the total voting group, even where, as here, the potential for ambiguity may exist, would be irrational. The purpose of Article IV, section 8(a) in requiring a majority of "members elected" would appear to ensure that the entire body of the Senate participates in the executive appointment confirmation process, rather than just a quorum. Thus, if in the instant situation the two persons not in office at the time of the vote on Respondent Daniels' nomination were instead merely absent, petitioners method of computing a majority would have been correct. To include among the number of individuals charged with the responsibility of reviewing the qualifications of the Governor's nominees, Senators-elect or former Senators, neither entitled to vote in the Senate, would in no way enhance the ability of the Senate to advise and consent. What it would do, however, is cause Article IV, section 8(a) to require *greater than a majority vote* whenever there was a vacancy in the Senate. This would place a proportionately greater burden on the executive branch when a vacancy or vacancies exist in the Senate, which could in turn encourage needless delay in filling appointive positions.

Additionally, under petitioners' interpretation, the number of "members elected" could be greater than the total number of Senators provided for in the Constitution. For example, both defeated incumbents and the successful candidates who have not yet replaced them in office would be "members elected." The same would presumably be true of Senators who die or resign and those elected to fill their seats. Both petitioners posit "doomsday" hypotheticals in which 25 of 50 Senators are killed in a disaster. While under respondents' interpretation of the phrase in question, a lesser number of Senators could override the Governor's veto then were originally required to pass the voted bill, under the same circumstances, the Senate would be incapable of taking any action requiring the vote of a majority of all members if petitioners' interpretation of Article IV, Section 8(a) were followed. The latter consequence is by far less desirable.

Petitioners' only support in Pennsylvania case law for their position appears to be the *Marshall Impeachment Case*, 363 Pa. 326, 69 A.2d 619 (1949), wherein petitioners find language of this court they assert is controlling in the instant action. In *Marshall*, President Judge Brown of the Philadelphia County Court of Common Pleas, on whose opinion we affirmed the trial court decision per curiam, stated:

> "Rule 4 of the Rules of Council, Manual of the City of Philadelphia for 1949, page 14, provides: 'a quorum shall consist of a *majority of the members elected to council*.' This number is twelve, and it governs even where variance exists in the Council membership of twenty-two. It also constitutes a majority of such membership. Therefore, it seems that twelve councilmen must concur in finding the accused guilty. . . ."

Id. at 345, A.2d at 629. (emphasis added). We do not consider that decision relevant to the instant action. First, the language quoted was entirely unnecessary to the determination of the case, and, in fact, all 22 councilmen were seated at the time the opinion was written. Secondly, and most importantly, a Rule of Philadelphia City Council, not the Pennsylvania

Constitution, is discussed. Finally, it is impossible to determine from the reported opinion whether this rule is being construed or whether, as is just as likely, the actual practice of the City Council is merely being described.

Petitioners find additional support in several decisions of the courts of other states, most notably, an advisory opinion of the Delaware Supreme Court, *Opinion of the Justices*, 251 A.2d 827 (Del. Sup. 1969). There the court was asked to determine whether a constitutional provision stating that "a majority of *all the members* elected to each House shall constitute a quorum to do business" (emphasis added), meant the majority as prescribed by law, regardless of whether vacancies have occurred. *Id.* Answering in the affirmative, the court used language which indicates that the Delaware Constitution has been interpreted along the lines urged upon us by petitioners. In light of the above discussion, however, we decline to follow such an interpretation.

Moreover, on the whole respondents' interpretation of the phrase "majority of the members elected" finds considerable support in the published decisions of American courts construing that phrase or portions thereof. *See e.g., State ex rel. Pickrell v. Myers*, 89 Ariz. 167, 359 P.2d 757 (1961); *State v. Penta*, 127 N.J. Super. 201, 316 A.2d 733 (1974); *Bailey v. Greer*, 63 Tenn. App. 13, 468 S.W.2d 327, 336 (1971); *Osburn v. Staley*, 5 W.Va. 95, 13 Am. Rep. 640 (1871); *State Bank of Drummond v. Nuesse*, 108 N.W.2d 283, 285, 13 Wis.2d 74 (1960). *But see Satterlee v. San Francisco*, 23 Cal. 214 (1863); *Smiley v. Commonwealth ex rel. Kerr*, 116 Va. 979, 83 S.E. 406 (1914).

We therefore adopt the interpretation of Article IV, section 8(a) placed upon it by the Senate in its Rule XXII-8, and hold that "a majority of the members elected to the Senate" as employed in that subsection means "a majority of the members elected, living, sworn, and seated." Accordingly, the appointments of Respondent Daniels and of the other nominees confirmed by a vote of 25 Senators are upheld as valid under the Constitution of the Commonwealth of Pennsylvania. The relief requested by petitioners is denied and their Petition for Review dismissed.

Zemprelli v. Daniels, 496 Pa. 247, 436 A.2d 1166 (1981) (footnotes omitted).

Vote of "Present" Not Allowed

47 (v). Two Senators voted "present" in protest. The President decided Senate Rule XXII, Section 3 required a "yea" vote or a "nay" vote only, and a vote of "present" is invalid. On appeal, the Senate (29-16) upheld the decision of the Chair. (Senate Journal, 1981, pp. 169-71.)

Duty to Vote on Executive Nominations Imposed by Rules and the Constitution of Pennsylvania

47. (w). Several Senators instituted a *quo warranto* action challenging the right of certain nominated and confirmed state officials to hold office. The nominations were submitted to the Senate after the constitutionally mandated ninety-day period. *See, Zemprelli v. Thornburgh*, 47 Pa. Commw. 43, 407 A.2d 102 (1979) (Zemprelli I); Pa. Const. Art. IV, Section 8 (b). The Senate, by roll-call vote, confirmed the nominations, and the nominees took office. During the vote in the Senate, the petitioning Senators protested the nominations, and voted not to confirm respondent officials. The respondents objected to the complaint in the form of a demurrer, challenging the Senator's standing to maintain the action. The respondents contended that the only alleged injury was to their right to vote, and having exercised that right, they have suffered no injury.

In relevant part, the Court, CRUMLISH, P.J., held:

Under Section 8 of Article IV, each state Senator has a constitutional **duty** to vote on executive nominations for appointive offices. *Wilt V. Beal*, 26 Pa. Commonwealth Ct. 298, 262 A.2d 876 (1976). This constitutional duty is implicit in the Article IV, Section 8 mandate that "[t]he Senate shall act on each executive nomination . . . ." A duty to vote on executive nominations is also imposed by the rules of the Senate of Pennsylvania. Senate Rule XXII, Section 3, provides as follows:

Every Senator shall be present within the Senate Chamber during the sessions of the Senate, unless duly excused or necessarily prevented, *and shall be recorded as voting on each question stated from the Chair which requires a roll call vote* unless excused by the Senate. *The refusal of any Senator to vote shall be deemed a contempt* unless he be excused by the Senate or unless he has a direct personal or pecuniary interest in connection with the pending question.

104 Pa. Code Section 11.22(c). (Emphasis added.) This duty is unqualified and, hence, must be performed regardless of whether the nominations were, as alleged, unconstitutionally submitted. A refusal to act, as indicated above, invites a citation for contempt. Thus a state Senator is compelled to participate in roll-call votes on executive nominations, no matter how justifiably he may contest the constitutionality of the nomination or the vote necessitated thereby. Thus, we disagree with the respondent's assertion that the exercise of the vote extinguishes these Senators' legal interest in this controversy. A compulsion to vote on executive nominations conveys upon these individual Senators an interest greater than, and distinguishable from, the general citizenry of this Commonwealth. . . . The Senators have standing; thus, respondents' objection is overruled.

Zemprelli v. Thornburgh, 73 Pa. Commw. 101, 457 A.2d 1326, 1329-30 (1983) (footnotes omitted).

Proper For Senators Not Standing For Reelection to Vote on Issue of Eligibility of Senatorial Candidate

47 (x). The Senate was considering a resolution declaring a candidate for Senator ineligible because of failure to meet residency requirements. Senator Lewis raised a point of order that certain Senators not standing for reelection would not be present in the new session and as such were not eligible to vote on the resolution. The Presiding Officer (D. Michael Fisher) decided that the Senators in question were duly elected and qualified, and if present, were qualified to vote on the issue. (Senate Journal, 1984, p. 1867.)

If Senator Present He Must Vote and Vote Only "Aye" or "Nay"

47 (y). On points of order from Senators Rocks and Zemprelli, the Presiding Officer (D. Michael Fisher) held that under Rule XXII, Section 3, if the Senator is present on the floor, he must vote unless excused, and each member must be recorded "Aye" or "Nay" — not "Present". (Senate Journal, 1984, p. 1875.)

SECTION 48

YEAS AND NAYS

Call of, Out of Order, When Senators Demanding Same Decline to Vote

48 (a). On the completion of the call of the yeas and nays, and before the result was announced by the Chair, it appearing that less than a quorum had voted, the President pro tempore ruled the call out of order, because the Senators requiring the same had not voted. (Senate Journal, 1883, p. 1228.)

Call of, Cannot Be Interrupted After First Senator's Name Is Called

48 (b). Mr. Humes submitted the point of order that the motion was not in order at this time, the Chair having ordered the call of the yeas and nays, and the clerk having called the name of Mr. Adams. The President decided the point of order well taken. (Senate Journal, extra session, 1882, p. 174.)

INDEX TO SENATE DECISIONS

Section

HOUSE OF REPRESENTATIVES
OFFICERS AND EXECUTIVE STAFF
1987 - 1988

SPEAKER
K. Leroy Irvis, 205 Tennyson Avenue, Pittsburgh 15213

CHIEF CLERK
John J. Zubeck, 18 Heatherwood Road, Middletown 17057

HOUSE COMPTROLLER
Ann M. Santinoceto, 435 Meadow Drive, Camp Hill 17011

PARLIAMENTARIAN
Clancy Myer, 6350 Stephen's Crossing, Mechanicsburg 17055

MAJORITY LEADER
James J. Manderino, 15 Pleasant Drive, Monessen 15062

MAJORITY WHIP
Robert W. O'Donnell, 3425 Conrad Street,
    Philadelphia 19129

MAJORITY CAUCUS CHAIRMAN
Ivan Itkin, 6954 Reynolds Street, Pittsburgh 15208

MAJORITY CAUCUS SECRETARY
Thomas J. Fee, 325 Lincoln Avenue, New Castle 16101

MAJORITY POLICY CHAIRMAN
David R. Wright, 1074 Sunset Drive, Clarion 16214

MAJORITY CAUCUS ADMINISTRATOR
Bernard J. Dombrowski, 1302 Wallace Street, Erie 16503

MAJORITY APPROPRIATIONS CHAIRMAN
Max Pievsky, 6230 Everett Avenue, Philadelphia 19149

REPUBLICAN LEADER
Matthew J. Ryan, One South Olive Street, Media 19063

REPUBLICAN WHIP
Samuel E. Hayes, Jr., R.D. #1, Box 274, Tyrone 16686

REPUBLICAN CAUCUS CHAIRMAN
Fred C. Noye, 15 West High Street, New Bloomfield 17068

REPUBLICAN CAUCUS SECRETARY
Richard J. Cessar, 1412 Mt. Royal Boulevard,
    Glenshaw 15116

REPUBLICAN POLICY CHAIRMAN
Kenneth E. Brandt, R.D. #1, Village of Falmouth,
    Bainbridge 17502

REPUBLICAN CAUCUS ADMINISTRATOR
Harry E. Bowser, 2200 North Brickyard Road,
    North East 16428

REPUBLICAN APPROPRIATIONS CHAIRMAN
Richard A. McClatchy, Jr., Haverford & Rugby Roads,
    Bryn Mawr 19010

ASSISTANT CHIEF CLERK
Nancy K. Grove, R.D. #2, Dillsburg 17019

ASSISTANT CHIEF CLERK
Jean E. Skrbin, 303 North 31st Street, Harrisburg 17109

EXECUTIVE SECRETARY TO THE CHIEF CLERK
H. Beryl Wickard, General Delivery, Plainfield 17081

EXECUTIVE DIRECTOR, BIPARTISAN MANAGEMENT COMMITTEE
Austin M. Lee, 131 Putney Lane, Malvern 19355

CO-EXECUTIVE DIRECTOR, BIPARTISAN MANAGEMENT COMMITTEE
Robert N. Hendershot, 250 Blacksmith Road,
    Camp Hill 17011

EXECUTIVE ASSISTANT TO THE SPEAKER
Cleo Pherribo, 6134 Spring Knoll Drive, Harrisburg 17111

LEGISLATIVE ASSISTANT TO THE SPEAKER
M. Susan Carduff, Towne House Apts., Harrisburg 17102

DIRECTOR OF THE REPUBLICAN STAFF
Roger E. Nick, 407 Deerfield Road, Camp Hill 17011

ASSISTANT TO THE REPUBLICAN LEADER
Susan A. Kistler, R.D. 1, Box 1067, Duncannon 17020

SPECIALIST TO THE REPUBLICAN LEADER IN INTERGOVERNMENTAL AFFAIRS
Franklin D. Linn, 800 Spring Garden Drive,
    Middletown 17057

CHIEF OFFICIAL REPORTER
Jane C. Salay, 406 Fifth Street, New Cumberland 17070

OFFICE SUPERVISOR
Jeanette Cohen, 3409 North Second Street,
    Harrisburg 17110

COMPUTER INPUT SUPERVISOR
Phyllis "Cookie" Durasky, 425 Meadow Drive,
    Camp Hill 17011

HOUSE OF REPRESENTATIVES
OFFICERS

K. LEROY IRVIS

Speaker of the House
Allegheny County — 19th District

K. Leroy Irvis (D) was born in Saugerties, N.Y., Dec. 27, 1919, the son of Francis H. and Harriet (Cantine) Irvis; grad., N.Y. St. Teachers Coll. (A.B., summa cum laude); Univ. of N.Y. (M.A.) 1939; Univ. of Pgh. Law Schl. (LL.B., J.D.) 1969; Doctor of Laws, Lincoln Univ., 1979; Doctor of Laws, St. Univ. of N.Y., Albany, 1986; Owens Fellowship in Law; Order of the Coif; Phi Beta Kappa; law clerk to Judges Anne X. Alpern and Loran Lewis, 1955-57; asst. dist. atty., Allegheny Co., 1957-68; civilian attache, War Dept. Aviation Training Div.; author, former teacher, steel chipper, news commentator; mem., Urban League of Pgh.; life mem., NAACP; bd. trustees, Univ. of Pgh.; advsry. bd., U. of Pgh. Med. Schl.; honored by NAACP, the Conf. on Black Basic Education, the Univ. of Pa., and the Pa. Jewish Coalition, among others; wood sculptor, painter, supporter of the arts; founder, Legislative School Art Exhibit, 1977; mem., Dem. Natl. Com.; delegate, Dem. Natl. Convention, 1968, 72, 76, 80, 84; v. chmn., PA. Delegation to Dem. Natl. Convention, 1980; co-chmn., Dem. Natl. Convention, 1980; mem., House of Representatives since 1958; Minority Caucus Chmn., 1963-64; Majority Caucus Chmn., 1965-66; Minority Whip, 1967-68, 1973-74; Majority Leader, 1969-72, 1975-77; Minority Leader, 1979-1982; elected Speaker of the House, May 23, 1977; reelected 1983, 1985 and 1987; married Cathryn L. Edwards; 2 children: Sherri and Reginald.

JOHN JOSEPH ZUBECK

Chief Clerk of the House

John J. Zubeck was born May 21, 1938, in Connellsville, the son of George and Carrie Bodas Zubeck; attended parochial and public schools, Connellsville; began State House service as a page boy in 1959 and served continually as messenger, calendar and amendment clerk; elected Chief Clerk, Pa. House of Representatives, Nov. 18, 1980, effective Jan. 6, 1981; mem., Seven Sorrows Ch., Middletown; married Margaret Jean Wilkinson; 3 children; home address: 18 Heatherwood Rd., Middletown.

ANN M. SANTINOCETO

Comptroller

Ann M. Santinoceto was born Nov. 15, 1931, in Clearfield, the daughter of Joseph and Mary T. Curtorillo Santinoceto; Clearfield H.S., 1949; Catholic; elected Comptroller of the House of Representatives, Jan. 1981; home address: 399 David Dr., Camp Hill.

CLANCY MYER

Parliamentarian

Clancy Myer was born May 24, 1949, in Lancaster, the son of Clarence and Iva Martin Myer; Pa. St. Univ. (B.S.) 1971; Dickinson Schl. of Law (J.D.) 1974; Capt., Judge Advocate General's Corps, U.S. Army, 1974-78; attorney; Meritorious Service Medal, U.S. Army; legal counsel, Democratic Caucus, 1979-82; appt. Parliamentarian, House of Representatives, June 1, 1978-79; reappt., 1983, 1985, 1987; married Anne-Marie Collier; home address: 6350 Stephen's Crossing, Mechanicsburg.

MEMBERS

RALPH ACOSTA   Philadelphia County — 180th District

Ralph Acosta (D) was born on Sept. 28, 1934, in Puerto Rico, the son of Felix and Cruz Maria Figueroa Acosta; grad. from high school in 1952; long-haul trucking; pres., Kensington Action Council, 1978; founder, Puerto Rican Alliance; mem., founder, Congresso Latino; rec., Good Citizen on Community Affairs fr. Old Timers' Softball Club, Phila.; good standing mem., P.R.A.; traveled extensively throughout Central America; Catholic; elected to the House of Representatives, Nov. 6, 1984; reelected 1986; married Sandy C. Acosta; 3 children: Harry, Nanette Damaris, Leslie; home address: 2527 North Palethorp St., Philadelphia.

PAUL J. ANGSTADT   Berks County — 126th District

Paul J. Angstadt (R) was born Feb. 12, 1939, in Reading, the son of Paul Angstadt and Mardell Royer; U.S. Navy, 1961-64; formerly with Angstadt and Wolfe Theatres; Exec. Gen. Mgr. and Dept. Head of Advertising, Fox Theatres, Inc.; frmr. pres., Muhlenberg Shopping Assn.; elected to the House of Representatives, Nov 2, 1982; reelected 1984, 1986; 1 child, Lisa Ann; home address: 102 Mayer St., Pennside, Reading.

DAVID G. ARGALL   Lehigh and Schuylkill Counties — 124th District

David G. Argall (R) was born Nov. 21, 1958, the son of Arthur J. and Miriam Miller Argall; grad., Tamaqua Area H.S., 1976; Lycoming Coll. (B.A., magna cum laude) 1980; rec., "Chieftain" award, highest award to graduating senior; pres., Student Assembly; Phi Kappa Phi; Alpha Sigma Phi; legislator; frmr. staff asst., state Rep. William Klingaman, Sr., and research analyst, House Rep. Research Staff; mem., Tamaqua Lodge #238, F. & A.M.; Tamaqua Area Jaycees; Lions; Lewistown Grange; dir., frmr. chmn., Schuylkill Co. Young Republicans; Schuylkill Co. Rep. Ex. Com.; Scout Troop 76, BSA, com.; chmn., Broad Mountain Dist., Hawk Mountain Council BSA; ex. bd., Lycoming Coll. Alumni; First United Methodist Ch.; lay speaker; rec., James A. Finnegan Fellowship Foundation Award, 1979; natl. symposium of center on the study of the presidency; youngest state rep. elected in Schuylkill Co. history; elected to House of Representatives, Nov. 6, 1984; reelected 1986; home address: Rush Township, Schuylkill Co.

MARY ANN ARTY   Delaware County — 165th District

Mary Ann Arty (R) was born Nov. 24, 1926, in Phila., the daughter of Henry J. (dec.) and Pearl Van Dike Scheid; Medical Coll. of Pa. R.N. 1947; West Chester Univ. (B.S.) 1966; grad. studies, Univ. of Pa.; certified health officer, registered nurse, lecturer; active in many St. and Natl. health organizations, including: Am. and Pa. Nurses Assns.; Delaware Co. Bds. of Hlth. Assn., bd. dir., 1969-76; Pa. Environ. Hlth. Assn., bd. dir., 1973-75; Am. and Pa. Public Hlth. Assns., bd. dir., 1974-76; Rgnl. Comprehensive Hlth. Plan. Council, S.E. Pa., 1969-73, Delaware Co. Govt. Rep., 1976-78; Hlth. Systems Agency of S.E. Pa., 1977-78; Grtr. Phila. Alliance for the Eradication of Venereal Diseases; Delaware Co. Mental Hlth./ Mental Retardation, bd. dir., since 1976; delegate, White House Conf. on Families, 1980; appt. to Gov.'s Council on Drug and Alcohol Abuse, 1980; Repub. Committeewoman, Springfield Twp., 1966-78; Delaware Co. Repub. Exec. Comm., sec. 1970-72, v. chmn. since 1976; delegate, Pa. Repub. Natl. Convention, 1972; mem., Natl. Repub. Convention; Delaware Co. Govt. Study Comm.; Springfield Twp. Bd. of Commissioners, since 1977; *Who's Who in American Politics;* numerous awards, including: Certificate of Merit, Am. Acad. of Pediatrics, 1980; Sigma Theta Tau, 1980; Certificate of Merit, Knights of Columbus, 1980, 1982; Award of the Yr. 1979, Chester/Delaware Co. Dental Society; Benjamin Rush Award, 1972; elected to the House of Representatives in 1978; reelected 1980, 1982, 1984, 1986; married to Thomas B. Arty; 3 children: James, Janis, John; home address: 527 LeHann Circle, Springfield.

WILLIAM E. BALDWIN   Northumberland and Schuylkill Counties — 125th District

William E. Baldwin (D) was born Mar. 6, 1948, in Pottsville; Lehigh Univ. (B.S.) 1970; Univ. of Maryland Law Schl. (J.D.) 1975; U.S.M.C.R., 1970-76; attorney; Schuylkill Co., Pa., Am. Bar Assns.; Pa., Am. Trial Lawyers Assns.; Phi Alpha Delta, Delta Tau Delta; elected to the House of Representatives, Nov. 2, 1982; reelected 1984, 1986; married Patricia Ann Musalavage; 3 children: Brian, Kelly, Kasey; home address: 1229 Howard Ave., Pottsville.

JOHN E. BARLEY   Lancaster County — 100th District

John E. Barley (R) was born December 6, 1945, in Lancaster, the son of Abram and Grace (Smith) Barley; Penn Manor H.S., 1963; Dale Carnegie Course, 1977; farmer, 1963-present; past chmn., Agricultural Com., mem., bd. dirs. and ex. com., Lancaster Chamber of Commerce and Industry, 1982-present; mem., bd. dirs., Commonwealth Natl. Bank, Lancaster Region; mem., Pa. Agricultural Lands Condemnation Approval Bd., 1980-84; chmn., Manor Twp. Planning Comm., 1978-85; frmr. mem., Lancaster Co. Solid Waste Adv. Com., 1980-85; Millersville Jaycees, 1977-82; co-chmn., Lancaster Co. Republican Primary Campaign, 1983; mem., Lancaster Co. Rep. Com., 1976-present; regional dir., Pa. Ag Republicans, 1978-present; pol. ed. com. mem., Lancaster Co. Farmers Assn., 1978-79; mem., bd., S.S. supt., Bethany E.C. Ch., Creswell; mem., bd. of trustees, Evangelical School of Theology, 1985-pres.; rec., Master Farmer Award, 1978; Outstanding Young Farmer of America, 1979; author, monthly article, *"Farm Forecast," PA Farmer Magazine;* elected to the House of Representatives, Nov. 6, 1984; reelected 1986; married Jane L. Reeder; 4 children: Robert, Tom, Susan, Cindy; home address: R.D. #2, Box 317, Conestoga.

JOSEPH W. BATTISTO   Monroe County — 189th District

Joseph W. Battisto (D) was born June 27, 1931, in Mt. Pocono, the son of Angelo and Jennie Santarsiero Battisto; East Stroudsburg Univ. (B.S.); Scranton Univ. (M.S.); U.S. Army, 1953-55; NEA; PSEA; NCTE; Mt. Pocono Councilman, 1970-73, Mayor, 1974-81; exec. comm., Monroe Co. Democratic Party; elected to the House of Representatives, Nov. 2, 1982, reelected 1984, 1986; married Virginia Mayer; 4 children: Joseph, Jr., James, Pamela, Jessica; home address: 91 Winona Rd., Mt. Pocono.

FRED BELARDI   Lackawanna and Wayne Counties — 112th District

Fred Belardi (D) was born Dec. 30, 1942, in Scranton, the son of Fred and Clara Taroli Belardi; att., Penn St. Scranton Campus, Wilkes Coll.; U.S. Naval Reserve, 1963-65; frmr. exec. dir., Scranton Redevelopment Authority, 1973-78; assoc. mem., Am. Institute of Planners; bd. mem., sec./treas., Lackawanna Co. Regional Planning Comm., 1973-78; adv. comm., 1975 Scranton Community Development Program; past pres., mem., Dante Literary Society; 20th Ward Social and Athletic Club; East Scranton Athletic Assn.; Hill Neighborhood Assn.; Minooka Lions Club; Immaculate Conception Ch.; Who's Who in High Schools of Am.; Italian-Am. League, Lackawanna Co. award; elected to the House of Representatives in 1978; reelected 1980, 1982, 1984, 1986; married Pamela Buscarini; 2 children: Jeffrey and Jennifer; home address: 838 North Irving Ave., Scranton.

ROBERT E. BELFANTI, JR.   **Columbia, Montour, and Northumberland Counties**
107th District

Robert E. Belfanti, Jr. (D) was born Oct. 15, 1948, in Danville, the son of Robert, Sr. and Rose Marie Rich Belfanti; Mt. Carmel H.S., 1966; att., Univ. of N. Carolina, 1970-71; U.S. Marine Corps, 1967-71; Marine Corps League; Journeyman Wireman Local #607 Internatl. Brotherhood of Electrical Workers; Pa. Rifle and Pistol Assn.; N.E. Economic Development Council; Lions Club; B.P.O.E.; K. of C.; V.F.W.; Am. Legion; UNICO; NRA; Sons of Poland; Jan Sobieski Club; West End Fire Co.; chmn., Northumberland Co. Parks and Rec. Comm., 1975-81; Shamokin Area Jt. Schl. Auth., 1977-79; Democratic St. Comm., 1976-80; bd. chmn., 1972-74, St. v. pres., 1974-78, St. pres., Pa. Young Democrats, 1978-80; scouting coordinator, Cub Scout Pack 3178; Boy Scout Netami Dist. v. chmn.; *Who's Who in American Politics;* 1980 Outstanding Young Men of Am.; Natl. Young Democrat of 1980; Natl. Leadership Award, 1971-78; 6 decorations, Vietnam, 1968-69; United Way; Am. Cancer Society; Red Cross Coordinator; elected to the House of Representatives, Nov. 1980; reelected 1982, 1984, 1986; married Cecilia Ann Saduskie; 2 children: Robert III, Eric; home address: 49 E. Ave., Mt. Carmel.

JERRY BIRMELIN   **Pike, Susquehanna, and Wayne Counties**
139th District

Jerry Birmelin (R) was born on April 18, 1949, in New York City; the son of Freidrich and Carolyn Heinsohn Birmelin; grad., Lake Ariel H.S., 1967; Univ. of Scranton (B.S.) 1973; teacher; mem., Canaan Bible Chapel; elected to the House of Representatives, Nov. 6, 1984; reelected 1986; married Elaine Lesher; 3 children: Janice, Julie, Jennifer; home address: 12 Wood St., Honesdale.

RONALD E. BLACK   **Venango County — 64th District**

Ronald E. Black (R) was born Sept. 23, 1935, in Oil City, the son of Lucy (Lane) Black and James W. Black (dec.); Slippery Rock Univ. of Pa. (B.S.) 1957; Officer's Candidate Schl., Newport; Defense Information Officer's Course, Fort Benjamin; Defense Language Institute, Anacostia; cmdr., U.S. Navy, 1958-79; ex. dir., Oil City Area Retail Merchant's Assn., 1980-81; chmn., "911 Emergency Number" Task Force; Goodwill Industries Board; Industrial Develop. Corp. Board, Venango Co.; Oil City Economic Develop. Corp., Incorporator/Board Promotions Task Force Chmn.; General Advis. Com., Venango Co. VO-Tech Schl.; v. pres., advisory council, Div. of Nursing, Clarion Univ. of Pa., Venango Campus; pastor-Parish Com., Grace United Methodist Ch.; chmn., Young Life, Oil City Area; div. chmn., United Way, 1983-84; Oil City Hosp. Critical Care Capital Campaign, 1984; rec., Bronze Star; Vietnam Honor Medal, 2nd class; elected to the House of Representatives, Nov. 5, 1984; reelected 1986; married Patricia Symosko; 3 children: Ann, Susan, Ronald, Jr.; home address: 113 Wyllis St., Oil City.

KEVIN BLAUM   **Luzerne County — 121st District**

Kevin Blaum (D) was born June 4, 1952, in Wilkes-Barre, the son of Dr. Louis C. and Kathleen Fisher Blaum; Coughlin H.S., 1970; Univ. of Scranton (B.S.) 1974; faculty, Bishop Hoban H.S., 1975-80; Wilkes-Barre City Council, 1976-81; Wilkes-Barre Catholic Youth Center, bd. dir., 1985; Bishop Hoban H.S., bd. devel., 1985; elected to the House of Representatives, Nov. 1980; reelected 1982, 1984, 1986; married Elizabeth Ann McDermott; home address: 78 Laurel St., Wilkes-Barre.

RAYMOND T. BOOK — Allegheny County — 41st District

Raymond T. Book (R) was born Feb. 14, 1925; Robert Morris Bus. Coll.; Univ. of Pgh.; U.S. Army, 1943-45; J. & L. Steel Corp., Real Estate Broker/Appraiser; Grtr. Pgh. Bd. of Realtors, 1960-80; v. pres., S. Hills Uni-List, 1970; councilman, Whitehall Boro., 1980-82; Allegheny Co. Adv. Council, 1981-82; committeeman, Whitehall Boro., 1978-80; past pres., Pleasant Hills Rotary, 1974 (active mem.); dist. rep., Rotary Club, 1974-75; mgr., S. Whitehall Baseball Assn., 1970-74; elected to the House of Representatives, Nov. 2, 1982; reelected 1984, 1986; married Mary Ann Schriner; 6 children; home address: 4534 W. Barlind Dr., Pittsburgh.

MICHAEL E. BORTNER — York County — 95th District

Michael E. Bortner (D) was born Feb. 11, 1949, in York, the son of Marlet E. and Alice Marie Schrum Bortner; Susquehanna Univ. (B.A.) 1971; Ohio Northern Univ. (J.D.) 1976; attorney; instructor, Pa. State Univ., 1983; mem., York Co., Pa. and Am. Bar Assns.; Lions Club, Viking Athletic Club; Vigilant Fire Co.; 13th Ward Political Club; asst. dist. atty., York Co., 1978-81; asst. public defender, York Co., 1981-83; exec. com., York Co. Dem. Party, 1982-pres.; bd. dir., York Area Transp. Auth., 1979-86, v. chmn., 1980-86; bd. dir., York Alcohol and Drug Service, 1981-85; bd. dir., York Boys Club, 1979-pres.; bd. dir., York Co. Blind Center, 1984-pres.; Young Men's and Women's Dem. Club; Western York Co. Dem. Club; Springettsbury Dem. Club; Outstanding Young Men of America, 1984; Peace Corps Volunteer, Ghana, 1971-72; elected to the House of Representatives, Nov. 6, 1984; reelected 1986; married Valerie Ann Fisher; 2 sons: Nathan and Seth; home address: 155 W. Springettsbury Ave., York.

CURTIS SCOTT BOWLEY — Forest, Venango, and Warren Counties — 65th District

Curtis Scott Bowley (D) was born Aug. 10, 1954, in Warren, the son of Herbert and Jean Jones Bowley; grad., Sheffield H.S., 1972; Slippery Rock Univ. of Pa. (B.S., recreation) 1976; Pa. State Univ. (M.S. recreation) 1979; owner, Renewable Forest Products Co.; auditor, Sheffield Twp., 1980-84; mem., Sheffield Rod & Gun Club, Warren Co. Chamber of Commerce, PA Forestry Assn., NRA, Warren Co. League of Women Voters, Natl. Eagle Scout Assn.; Barnes United Methodist Ch.; elected to the House of Representatives, Nov. 6, 1984; reelected 1986; address: P.O. Box 813, Sheffield.

HARRY EUGENE BOWSER — Republican Caucus Administrator
Erie County — 4th District

Harry Eugene Bowser (R) was born Sept. 13, 1931, in Brookville; grad., Brookville H.S., Supply Schl. USMC; att., barber schl.; USMC, Sept. 1949 to Dec. 1952; grape grower; PFA; Masonic Lodge; North East Boro Council, 1969-73; past pres., North East Jaycees; Protestant; elected to the House of Representatives in 1978; reelected 1980, 1982, 1984, 1986; married Carol Lee MacTarnaghan; 3 children: Timothy, Dennis, Andrew; home address: 2200 N. Brickyard Rd., North East.

KARL WILLIAM BOYES   Erie County — 3rd District

Karl William Boyes (R) was born Mar. 1, 1936, in Erie, the son of W. Boyes (dec.) and Florence Smith Boyes; Edinboro Univ. (B.S.) 1959; grad. studies, Allegheny and Union Colls., 1961-62; supervisor, Millcreek Twp., 1965-70; Erie Co. Commissioner, 1976-79; Disting. Service Award, Jaycees; *Who's Who in the East* (govt.) 1975; Mercyhurst Coll. Law Enforcement Award, 1973; elected to the House of Representatives, Nov. 1980; reelected 1982, 1984, 1986; married Sue Clark; 2 sons: Brian and Bradley; home address: 3036 W. 38th St., Erie.

KENNETH E. BRANDT   Republican Policy Chairman
                                                        Lancaster County — 98th District

Kenneth E. Brandt (R) was born Nov. 17, 1938, in Lancaster Co., the son of Amos F. and Anna M. Brandt; grad., Elizabethtown Area H.S.; Elizabethtown Area Schl. Bd.; Elizabethtown Jaycees, past pres.; past area v. pres., past natl. dir., U.S. Jaycees; JCI Senator; Elizabethtown Rotary; F.&A.M. Lodge 286, Corinthian Royal Arch. Ch. 224, Columbia; Elizabethtown C. of C.; honry mem., Am. War Mothers; First Ch. of God; elected to the House of Representatives in 1972; reelected 7 successive terms; married Jean Marie Brandt; 5 children; home address: Village of Falmouth, R.D. #1, Bainbridge.

JOHN H. BROUJOS   Adams, Cumberland, and York Counties
                                                                           199th District

John H. Broujos (D) was born Feb. 12, 1929, in Wilmington, Del., the son of Nicholas and Jennie Pavoni Broujos; Univ. of Delaware (B.A.) 1954; Dickinson Schl. of Law (J.D.) 1958; colonel, ret., U.S Marines; attorney; Pa., Am. Bar Assns.; Navy League; Marine Corps Assn.; Pa. Trial Lawyers Assn.; VFW; Am. Legion; Exchange Club; solicitor, Cumberland Co., 1976-82; St. John's Episcopal Ch.; rec.: Purple Heart, Silver Star, Navy Commendation Medal; authored: "Joint Bond Bidding," "Stormwater Management," "Evacuation Planning for TMI," "National Defense"; elected to the House of Representatives, Nov. 2, 1982; reelected 1984, 1986; married Louise Davis; 4 children: Melanie, Nicholas, Gregory, Lisa; home address: 78 E. Ridge St., Carlisle.

RAYMOND BUNT, JR.   Montgomery County — 147th District

Raymond Bunt, Jr. (R) was born May 19, 1944, in Aquadillia, P.R., the son of Raymond and Victoria Marcantonio Bunt; att. Ursinus Coll., 1965-68; small businessman; Am. Numismatic Assn.; Montgomery Co. Historical Society; Pike Twp. Sportsmen's Assn.; Natl. Rifle Assn.; Lower Frederick Fire Co.; frmr. Dir. of Elections, Montgomery Co., 1979-82; bd. mem., Montgomery Co. Planning Comm., 1976-83; Lower Frederick Twp.: chmn., Planning Commission, 1976, chmn., Municipal Authority, 1979-80; Montgomery Co. Republican Comm., 1972-79; Chapel of the Four Chaplains Award; rec., Perkiomen Valley Watershed Assn. Conservation Award; elected to the House of Representatives, Nov. 2, 1982; reelected 1984, 1986; married Alexis Marie Thomas; 3 children: Raymond, III, Linda, Alexis Marie; home address: 222 Fulmer Rd., Spring Mount.

JAMES M. BURD   Butler and Lawrence Counties — 12th District

James M. Burd (R) was born March 31, 1931, in Butler Co., the son of William and Pearl E. Miller Burd; grad., Winfield-Clinton H.S., Montreal Schl. of Underwriting; legislator; frmr. small businessman, 22 yrs.; U.S. Army Signal Corps, 7th Inf. Div.; Korean War, 1952-54; past pres., dir., Saxonburg Fire and Relief Assn.; past pres., Southeast Area C of C; Republican committeeman, Area Five chmn., mem., Butler Co. Rep. Exec. Bd.; Am. Legion Post 683; VFW Post 7376; Butler Co. Law Enforcement Officers' Assn.; Butler Co. Assn. of Clubs; FOP Brady Paul Lodge 54; Saxonburg Sportsman Club; Wm. H. Miller Lodge 769, F.&A.M.; Valley of New Castle Consistory; Syria Shrine; Saxony Shrine Club; Syria Caravan #14; rec., Keystone Farmer Award, 1951; mem., elder, Saxonburg Meml. Presbyterian Ch.; elected to the House of Representatives in 1976; reelected 5 successive terms; married Mary Joan Schenkel; 2 sons, James E. and Mark D.; home address: 2348 Freeport St., Saxonburg.

EDWARD F. BURNS, JR.   Bucks County — 18th District

Edward F. Burns, Jr. (R) was born Jan. 28, 1931, in Branchdale, Pa., the son of Edward and Regina Larkin Burns; LaSalle Coll. (B.A.) 1952; Temple Univ. (M.Ed.) 1957; U.S. Navy, Korean Conflict; U.S. Naval Reserve; elected, Bensalem Twp. Schl. Bd., 1971 (resigned June 1974); St. Eprems Ch.; elected to the House of Representatives in 1972; reelected 7 successive terms; married Joan Friel on Aug. 20, 1955; 3 children; home address: 3480 Felton Ave., Bensalem.

ALVIN C. BUSH   Lycoming County — 84th District

Alvin C. Bush (R) was born Jan. 22, 1924, in Philipsburg, the son of frmr. Cong. Alvin R. and Lucinda Mattern Bush; att. Williamsport Public Schools; Univ. North Carolina (B.S.); Northwestern Univ. Midshipman's School; Phi Gamma Delta; U.S. Navy, 1942-46; frmr. business executive; Rep. Caucus Sec., 1967-70; Dir. Legislative Reference Bureau, 1972-73; Exec. Asst. to Senate President Pro Tempore, 1980-84; Rep. Senate Staff Administrator, 1976-80; rec., first Lycoming County Conservation Award; mem., F. & A.M. Lodge #755; Williamsport Consistory; First United Methodist Church of Muncy; elected to the House of Representatives, 1961-70; reelected in 1984, 1986; married Elizabeth Crooks Bush; 4 children: A. Charles, Jr., Cindalyn, Karen, Michael; home address: R.D. #2, Muncy.

THOMAS R. CALTAGIRONE   Berks County — 127th District

Thomas R. Caltagirone (D) was born Oct. 30, 1942, in Reading, son of Raymond and Stella Julian Caltagirone, both dec'd.; Frederick Coll., Portsmouth, Va. (B.A.) 1967; Temple Univ. (courses for M.A.) 1971; full-time legislator; first pres., Reading Model Cities Neighborhood Council; elected to Charter Study Comm., 1970, City of Reading; Americus Club; Colored Political Club; E. End Athletic Club; Jackson Dem. Social Club; Knights of St. Casimir; Liberty Firemen's Relief Assn.; Reading Liederkranz; Lions; 1900 Beneficial Assn.; N. Berks Dem. Club; Oakbrook & Reading Fire Co.'s; Orioles Home Assn.; Orioles; Polish Am. Citizen's Political Assn.; Falcon's Alliance; Roosevelt-Garner Dem. Club; Slovak Catholic Sohol Home Assn.; Gr. Lodge of Pa.; S. End Social Club; Ukrainian Am. Beneficial Assn., & Social Club; Victor Emmanuel II; Young Men's Dem. Assn., Inc.; 1st, 3rd, 12th, 13th, 14th, 15th, 17th, & 18th Ward Dem. Assns.; Spartaco Society; Puerto-Rican Civic Society; Travelers Protective Assn.; Reading Berks Automobile Club; Holy Name Society; Neversink Gun Club; Pa. Society; Italian Heritage Council; Polka Squires; Amanda Stoudt Home Schl. Assn.; Pa. Realtors; Gr. Reading Bd. of Realtors (assoc.); Alpha Phi Omega; Sigma Phi Alpha; Reading Lodge 549 Free & Accepted Masons; Dean's List; DAR, 1967; Jr. C of C, Outstanding First Year Man, 1968; Holy Rosary Ch.; elected to the House of Representatives in 1976; reelected 5 successive terms; married Ruth L. Santoro; 4 children: Stella, Thomas, Samuel, John; home address: 2521 Hill Rd., Reading.

ITALO S. CAPPABIANCA   Erie County — 2nd District

Italo S. Cappabianca (D) was born Dec. 19, 1936, in Erie, the son of John B. and Luisa Barboni Cappabianca; Gannon Univ. (B.A., pol. sci.) 1968; U.S. Army, 1956-58; travel agent; Professional Mens Club; Univ. Club; YMCA; Tourist Convention Bureau; past v. pres., Erie Civic Music Assn.; frmr. Airport Authority Treas., 1967-72; coordinator, 1963 Winter Carnival; commissioner, Housing Authority, City of Erie, 1975 to 1978; Eagles; Elks; Sportsmens; E. Erie Turners; Roman Catholic; elected to the House of Representatives in 1978; reelected 1980, 1982, 1984, 1986; home address: 1216 West 26th St., Erie.

EDGAR A. CARLSON   Potter and Tioga Counties — 68th District

Edgar A. Carlson (R) was born Sept. 2, 1929, in Harwick, the son of Edwin and Effie Haglund Carlson (dec.); grad., Morris Run H.S., 1946; att., Lycoming College (pol. sci.); legislator; mem., Bloss Lodge #350 F.&A.M.; Williamsport Consistory; Irem Temple; Hillside Rod & Gun Club; Covington Grange; life mem., Blossburg Fireman/ Ambulance Assn.; treas., Tioga Co., 1966-1984; Rep. Co. Chmn., 1972-present; delegate to Natl. Conv., 1980; Lutheran; elected to the House of Representatives, Nov. 1984; reelected 1986; married Margaret J. Jenkins; 3 children: James, Ann Lee, Janis; home address: 144 Morris St., Blossburg.

ANDREW J. CARN   Philadelphia County — 197th District

Andrew J. Carn (D) was born Aug. 25, 1950, in Phila., the son of Reggie and Evonia Herrington Carn; Howard Univ. (B.S.) 1973; electrical engineer and housing developer; bd. mem., Clara Baldwin Neighborhood House, Inc.; Committee for a Better North Phila.; Community Service Awards: City of Phila., Clara Baldwin Neighborhood House, Inc., Adelphos Civic Assn., Crises Intervention Network, Inc., Junior Achievement, Inc.; elected to the House of Representatives, Nov. 2, 1982; reelected 1984, 1986; married Dorothy Sims; 1 child, Imani; home address: 3407 Ridge Ave., Philadelphia.

GAYNOR CAWLEY   Lackawanna County — 113th District

Gaynor Cawley (D) was born June 19, 1941, in Scranton, the son of Gaynor (dec.) and Margaret McHale Cawley; St. Patrick's H.S., 1960; att., Univ. of Scranton, 1964; store manager, F.W. Woolworth, Co., 1964-69; mem., Professional Baseball Players of Am.; Knights of Columbus; dep. mayor, Scranton, 1977-80; supt. of recreation, 1974-75; dir. of public works, 1978-79; business admn., 1976-77; dir. of community development, 1980; Scranton Area Athlete of the Year, 1957-60; Life Underwriters Sportsman of the Yr., 1978; Scranton Area Hall of Fame, 1979; Pa. Hall of Fame Northeast Div., 1984; 3 yrs. prof. baseball, Houston & Detroit organizations; rec., U. of Scranton Cyrano De Bergerac Award, 1985; elected to the House of Representatives, Nov. 1980; reelected 1982, 1984, 1986; married Kathryn Karam; 5 children: Lynn, Tara, Claudine, Jennifer, Kate; home address: 807 N. Lincoln Ave., Scranton.

RICHARD J. CESSAR
**Republican Caucus Secretary
Allegheny County — 30th District**

Richard J. Cessar (R) was born Dec. 1, 1928, in Etna, the son of Helen Savor Bursich; att., Rio Grande Coll., OH.; legislator; former Republican chmn., Boro. of Etna 1970-84; past Exalted Ruler BPOE 932; life mem., FOP Lodge 91; Etna Hose Co. 2, Allegheny Co. Firemen's Assn., Allegheny Co. Fire Chief's Assn., Western Pa. Firemen's Assn.; advisor dir., North Hills Passavant Hospital; bd. dir., People's Savings Assn.; bd. dir., Pgh. Wind Symphony; mem., Etna Civic Assn.; hon. mem., Etna-Shaler Rotary Club; elected to the House of Representatives in 1970; reelected 8 successive terms; elected Minority Policy Chairman 1977-78, Majority Policy Chairman 1979-80, Majority Whip 1981-82, Republican Caucus Secretary 1983-84, 1985-86; married Dolores P. Whitehill; 5 children: Richard R., Christine C., Candace A., Robert S., Scott D.; home address: 39-B Bethany Drive, Pittsburgh.

JON SCOT CHADWICK
Bradford County — 110th District

Jon Scot Chadwick (R) was born Sept. 13, 1953, in Troy, the son of Harold H. and Wanda M. Rooks Chadwick; Towanda Area H.S., 1971; Bucknell Univ. (B.S., pol. sci.) 1975; Villanova Univ. Schl. of Law (J.D.) 1978; legislator; mem., Pa. Bar Assn.; asst. dist. atty., Bradford County, 1980-81; mem., Towanda Lions Club; bd. mem., General Sullivan Council, Boy Scouts of America; Wysox Presbyterian Ch.; elected to the House of Representatives, Nov. 6, 1984; reelected 1986; home address: P.O. Box 215, Wysox.

ANTHONY J. CIMINI (deceased)*
Lycoming County — 83rd District

Anthony J. Cimini (R) was born Feb. 12, 1922, in DuBois, the son of Alex and Catherine Cimini; grad., Lycoming Coll. (B.A.), Bucknell Univ. (M.A.); U.S. Army Air Force, W.W. II vet., European Theater (1942-1945); educator (20 yrs.) Williamsport Area Schl. Dist.; So. Williamsport 1st Ward Volunteer Fire Dept.; Am. Legion Post #617; VFW Post #844; Sons of Italy Lodge #138; General Adv. Comm., Williamsport Area Comm. Coll.; 40-8 #382; Consolidated Sportsmen of Lycoming Co.; K of C #366; Holy Name Society, Mater Dolorosa parish; frmr. mem., officer, Young Republicans of Lycoming Co.; frmr. mem., Lycoming Co. Rep. Comm.; dir., Lycoming Co. 4-H Development Fund; Williamsport Kiwanis; Bottle Run Grange; bd. of trustees, N. Central Pa. Chptr., Natl. Multiple Sclerosis Society; mem., Pa. Assn. for Retarded Citizens; Jr. League of Williamsport, Inc.; Community Advisory Bd.; Central Pa. Constables Assn. Inc. (Hon. Constable); W. Branch Valley Chptr., Pa. Sports Hall of Fame; elected to the House of Representatives in 1974; reelected 6 successive terms; married native Doris E. Johnson; 3 children: Judith R. Cimini, Lisa M. Newcomer, Anthony, Jr.; home address: 361 E. Mountain Ave., South Williamsport.

*August 25, 1987

MARIO J. CIVERA, JR.
Delaware County — 164th District

Mario J. Civera, Jr. (R) was born June 19, 1946, in Phila., the son of Mario J. and Josephine Pepe Civera; grad., Upper Darby H.S., 1965; att. Indoctrination course, Delaware Co. Bd. of Realtors; Delaware Co. Community Coll.; Polley Associates for Real Estate Fundamentals; U.S. Air Force, Staff Sgt., 1966; Delaware Co. Real Estate Prof. Bd.; Upper Darby Italian-Am. Club; appt. Upper Darby Councilman, Commissioner 1974, reelected 1975 and still serving; chmn., Public Safety Comm.; mem., Leisure Services, Rules and Procedures Comm., Public Works Comm., Upper Darby Twp. Fire Dept. Comm.; St. Dorothy's Roman Catholic Ch.; committeeman, Upper Darby Republican Party; Fire Safety Award, 1976, 1978, Upper Darby Fire Dept.; v. pres., 69th St. Athletic Assn., 1972-78, bd. dir., 1978-80; Delaware Co. "911" Task Force, 1979; CETA Manpower Bd.; elected to the House of Representatives in special election, March 1980; reelected Nov. 1980, 1982, 1984, 1986; married Elaine D. Gallagher; one child, Mario, III; home address: 4501 Dermond Ave., Drexel Hill.

BRIAN D. CLARK   **Allegheny County — 31st District**

Brian D. Clark (D) was born June 12, 1956, in Natrona, the son of John F. R. and Madeline P. Collignon Clark; att. Indiana Univ. of Pa.; legislator; elected to the House of Representatives in 1978; reelected 1980, 1982, 1984, 1986; Allegheny Valley Industrial Develop. Auth.; married Jayne Lower; 3 children: Jason, Matthew, Sarah; home address: 141 Oak Manor Drive, Natrona Heights.

PAUL IRVIN CLYMER   **Bucks County — 145th District**

Paul Irvin Clymer (R) was born July 8, 1937, in Sellersville, the son of Franklin S. (dec.) and Anna Marie Duch Clymer; Pennridge H.S., 1955; Muhlenberg Coll. (B.A.) 1959; U.S. Army, 1960-62; credit manager, Lankenau Hospital, Phila., 1967-80; Faith Baptist Ch.; mem. Republican Party, 21st ward, 1964-76; Comm. of Seven to elect Barry Goldwater President, 1964; Judge of Election, 30th Division, 1967-72; committeeman, 1972-76; Repub. Exec. Comm., 21st Ward, 1972-76; 21st Ward Community Council, v. pres., 1966-67, pres., 1967-69; organizer, mem., Roxborough, Manayunk, Wissahicken Historical Society, 1969-71; chmn., July 4th Fireworks Comm., 1967-69, 1976; co-chmn., "Operation Yuletide," 1967-76; chmn., "Operation Not Forgotten," 1970-71; pres., Upper Roxborough Civic Assn., 1971-74, v. pres., 1974-76; bd. mem., American Red Cross, Bucks County Chapter; mem., Civ. Adv. Bd., Guard, Sellersville Unit; lifetime mem., Paletown Rod and Gun Club; Pennridge Republican Club, 1978; Upper Bucks Rep. Club, 1979; Palisades Re. Club, 1982; "Good Citizenship" award, V.F.W., 1971; "Good Citizenship" award, 1977, from Mayor Frank Rizzo; elected to the House of Representatives, Nov. 1980; reelected 1982, 1984, 1986; home address: 12 Farmers Lane, Sellersville.

MARK B. COHEN   **Philadelphia County — 202nd District**

Mark B. Cohen (D) was born June 4, 1949, in New York City, the son of David and Florence Herzog Cohen; Univ. of Pa. (B.A.) 1970; grad. studies: in law, Antioch Schl. of Law; political science, Temple Univ.; history, Gratz Coll.; and regional planning, Pa. State Univ.; Congressional intern, 1967; U.S. Senatorial intern, 1968; staff mem., numerous political campaigns, 1968-73; Oxford Circle Jewish Comm. Center; assoc. bd. mem., Charles Drew Mental Health/Mental Retardation Community Policy Bd.; chmn., House Labor Relations Com., (3 terms); chmn., Central Pa. Chapter, Industrial Relations Research Assn.; bd. mem., Associated Alumni of Central H.S.; mem., political, civic, educational & service orgs.; Dem. committeeman, ward chmn., 17th ward, Dem. Exec. Com.; mem., Dem. State Com.; mem., House Dem. Policy Com.; Phila. Council, Boy Scouts of Am.; author, several "Laws of Politics" in Paul Dickson's *The Official Rules* (Praeger, 1978) and *The Official Explanations* (Praeger, 1980); two awards, Gratz Coll., for essay in Phila. history, and awards and certificates of apprec. from Chapel of Four Chaplains, St. Martin of Tours Cub Scout Pack #455, LaSalle Coll. Student Gov. Assn., Charles Drew Mental Health/Mental Retardation Center; elected to House of Representatives in special election, May 21, 1974; reelected 7 successive terms; chmn., Labor Relations Com.; single; home address: 6001 N. 5th St., Philadelphia.

NICHOLAS A. COLAFELLA   **Beaver County — 15th District**

Nicholas A. Colafella (D) was born Jan. 13, 1939, in West Aliquippa, the son of Domenic and Domenica Sonsino Colafella; Youngstown Univ. (B.S.) 1962; Duquesne Univ. (M.Ed.) 1965; Univ. of Pgh. (Ph.D.) 1977; U.S. Navy, 1956-58; college administrator; Pa. Assn. of Continuing Education Deans; Roman Catholic; Hopewell Jaycees "Educator of Year - 1969"; author, "The Role of Continuing Education in a Community College," *Catalyst,* 1975; elected to the House of Representatives, Nov. 1980; reelected 1982, 1984, 1986; married Frances Gorman; 3 children: Nick, Stephen, Douglas; home address: 111 Shadyside Dr., Aliquippa.

KENNETH JOSEPH COLE — Adams County — 91st District

Kenneth Joseph Cole (D) was born Feb. 13, 1936, in Gettysburg, the son of Richard and Catherine Codori Cole; att. Gettysburg Coll.; Korean War vet.; U.S. Navy (4 yrs.); active in vet. affairs; life mem., Am. Legion; VFW; state VFW legislative comm.; lifetime mem. Amvets; CWV; Elks; Moose; Eagles; Democratic committeeman (20 yrs.); pres., Adams Co. Young Democrats; state committeeman (2 terms); Co. Chmn. (6 terms); frmr. Congressional aide, 19th District; bd. of dirs., Adams Co. Cerebral Palsy Comm.; Eagle Scout; appt. by Governor as Pa. commissioner, Potomac River Basin Interstate Comm., 1976; commissioned colonel, staff of Kentucky governor, 1975; chmn., Adams Co. Cancer Crusade; special House-Senate task force, PUC reform; chmn., York-Adams-Franklin Special Olympics; 1986 v. chmn., 1987 chmn., Chesapeake Bay Comm.; rec., Golden Sword Award and Natl. Service Award by the Am. Cancer Society; Adv. Council, BSA, York-Adams Area Council; mem., ex. com., Natl. Conf. State Legislators, 1983-86; select House Comm. on Three Mile Island; elected to the House of Representatives in 1974, reelected 6 successive terms; married to Marilyn Spear Cole; resides with children Kenneth Casey & Kathryn; home address: R.D. #1, Orrtanna.

ROY W. CORNELL — Bucks and Montgomery Counties — 152nd District

Roy W. Cornell (R) was born Dec. 5, 1943, in Abington, the son of the late Warren M. and Helen Hopkins Cornell; att., Santa Ana Jr. Coll., Santa Ana, Calif., Temple Univ., North Phila. Bd. of Realtors Schl.; legislator; frmr. pres., Sovereign Title Searches Inc.; frmr. salesman, Bailey and Assoc.; pres., Hatboro Borough Council, 2 yrs., mem., 6 yrs.; v. chmn., 3 yrs., Hatboro Republican Organization, mem., 10 yrs.; Assn. of Title Examiners; Eastern Montgomery Co. Bd. of Realtors; W.K. Bray Lodge ★ 410 F. & A.M.; Lehigh Consistory; frmr. mem., Montgomery Co. Republican Comm., Hatboro Planning Comm.; elected to the House of Representatives in 1978; reelected 1980, 1982, 1984, 1986; married Sandi Holkey; 2 daughters: Wendy L. and Susan E.

THOMAS C. CORRIGAN, SR. — Bucks County — 140th District

Thomas C. Corrigan, Sr. (D) was born Feb. 26, 1938, in Bristol, the son of John J. (dec.) and Dorothy Leyers Corrigan; grad., Bristol H.S., 1956; PAANG, 1959-60; real estate salesman; mem., Bucks Co. bd. of realtors; Ancient Order of Hibernians; Loyal Order of Moose; borough councilman, 1966-69, 1972-86; council pres., 1972-73; chmn., Wash. Crossing Park Comm., 1972-74; Dem. committeeman, Bristol Twp. 1964-65; founder, 1st solid waste study comm. in Bucks County, 1983; elected to the House of Representatives, Nov. 4, 1986; married Annabelle McClafferty; 3 children: Mary Jo Harris, Thomas, Jr. and Matthew; home address: 211 Monroe St., Bristol.

RONALD RAYMOND COWELL — Allegheny County — 34th District

Ronald Raymond Cowell (D) was born Dec. 14, 1946, in Philipsburg, the son of Stephen and Lucille Przybylek Cowell; Univ. of Pgh. (B.A., pol. sci.); completed coursework, admn. of higher ed. and public admn.; housing admin., Univ. of Pgh. (6 yrs.); pres., Young Democratic Club of Allegheny Co. (1971 and 1973); speakers bureau and v. pres., (1974) Group Against Smog and Pollution (GASP); citizens adv. comm., Churchill Area Schl. Dist. (1972); Wilkins Twp. rep., Churchill Area Ecology Comm. (1973-77); pres., Wilkinsburg Community Action Assn., Inc., 1979-80; pres., East Suburban Pgh. Kiwanis (1980); mem., bds. of dirs.: Allegheny East MH/MR Cntr., Emergency Medical Services Council; PHEAA; Forbes Emergency Medicine Inst.; Generations Together; United Mental Health; Woodland Hills Task Force on Drug and Alcohol Abuse; Leg. Rep. to MILRITE Council and Legislative Office of Research Liaison; Kiwanis; listed, *Who's Who in American Government, Outstanding Young Men of America;* rec., 1984-85 Lay Leader Award, Univ. of Pgh. Chptr. of Phi Delta Kappa; elected to the House of Representatives, 1974; reelected 6 successive terms; married Virginia Segin on June 1, 1968; 2 children; home address: 30 Thorncrest Drive, Pittsburgh.

JEFFREY W. COY   **Franklin County — 89th District**

Jeffrey W. Coy (D) was born Oct. 6, 1951, in Chambersburg, the son of Wayne and Dorothy Upperman Coy; Shippensburg Univ. (B.A.) 1973; Cumberland Valley Lodge, F.&A.M.; Harrisburg Consistory, A.A.S.R.; Phi Sigma Epsilon; bd. trustees, Shippensburg Univ., 1975-82, chmn., 1981-82; pres., Pa. Assn. of St. Coll. & Univ. Trustees, 1981-82; pres., W. End Fire & Rescue Co., 1972-1986; bd. dir., WITF TV-Radio, PBS; Franklin Co. Democratic Comm.; bd. dir., Orrstown Bank; Outstanding Young Man of the Year, Shippensburg Jaycees, 1974; Outstanding Young Man, 1980; mem., Memorial Lutheran Church, Shippensburg; mem., Rotary Club, Elks, Shippensburg; elected to the House of Representatives, Nov. 2, 1982; reelected 1984, 1986; married Jo Anne Rasmussen; home address: 9620 Forest Ridge Rd., Shippensburg.

PETER J. DALEY, II   **Fayette and Washington Counties — 49th District**

Peter J. Daley, II (D) was born Aug. 8, 1950, in Brownsville, the son of Peter and Gladys Moyer Daley; California Univ. of Pa. (B.S.) 1972, (M.A.) 1975; Univ. of Pgh. (M.P.A.) 1983; att., Univ. of Pa.; Robert Morris Coll., Real Estate Certificate Program; Pa. State Education Assn.; Monongahela Valley Board of Realtors; Natl. Realtors Assn.; Sons of Italy; Mayor, California Borough, 1974-82; Lions International; Outstanding Young Men of America, 1972, 1975, 1977; Disting. Service Award, California Univ., 1972; Devotion to Public Service, Veterans of Foreign Wars, 1979; elected to House of Representatives, Nov. 2, 1982; reelected 1984, 1986; home address: East Malden Drive, California.

JOHN S. DAVIES   **Berks and Lebanon Counties — 129th District**

John S. Davies (R) was born Sept. 4 in Springmont, Berks Co., the son of William M. and Caroline Boas Davies; Gettysburg Coll. (A.B., pol. sci.); advanced studies, Kutztown Univ.; U.S. Navy, WW II vet.; teacher of economics and government, Kutztown and Wilson Schl. systems; frmr. pres., Eastern Region, PSEA; frmr. bd. mem., PSEA; frmr. pres., WEA; frmr. state treas., PSEA; elected to the House of Representatives in 1974; reelected 6 successive terms; married Marguerite Sprankle on March 11, 1950; 1 daughter and 1 son; home address: 2422 Cleveland Ave., West Wyomissing.

MICHAEL MATHEW DAWIDA   **Allegheny County — 36th District**

Michael Mathew Dawida (D) was born in Pgh., the son of Mathew and Edna Robert Dawida; Univ. of Pgh. (B.A.) 1971; Hamline Law Schl. (J.D.) 1976; neighborhood attorney; Pa. Bar Assn.; Eagles; I.S.D.A.; mem., Polish Falcons and Greek Catholic Union; Parish Council, St. Basil's Ch.; Roman Catholic; elected to the House of Representatives, 1978; reelected 1980, 1982, 1984, 1986; married Audrey Mielcuszny; 2 children: Sara Marysa and Peter Michael; home address: 7 Overbrook Blvd., Pittsburgh.

ALPHONSO DEAL (deceased)*　　　　Philadelphia County — 181st District

Alphonso Deal (D) was born April 15, 1923, in Watertown, Fla., the son of Freddie and Estella Fair Deal; Staton H.S., Fla.; Fells Instit., Wharton Schl., Univ. of Pa.; U.S. Army, 1941-45; Frat. Order of Police; financial sec., Natl. Black Police Assn.; frmr. v. pres., Council of Police Societies; police officer, Phila. Police Dept., 1954-78; pres., North "Action" Branch, N.A.A.C.P.; pres., The Urbanites; founder, The Guardian Civic League; frmr. chmn., N. Central Dist. Health and Welfare Council; exec. comm., N. City Congress; Deacon, St. Paul's Baptist Ch.; frmr. bd. dir., Phila. Baptist Assn.; numerous awards for dedication and service to the community, in addition to some 50 awards from the Natl., State and City N.A.A.C.P. Branches (including those presented to N. Phila. "Action" branch); numerous commendations from the Phila. Police Dept.; bd. dirs., bd. trustees, Temple Univ.; mem., Pa. Comm. on Crime and Delinquency; Dem. Maj. Policy Com.; elected to the House of Representatives, Nov. 1980; reelected 1982, 1984, 1986; married Ruth D. Lewis; 3 children: Casandra, Michelle, Alphonso; home address: Apt. 1407, 1220 N. Broad St., Philadelphia.

*June 3, 1987

ANTHONY M. DeLUCA　　　　Allegheny County — 32nd District

Anthony M. DeLuca (D) was born June 3, 1937, in Pgh., the son of Lawrence and Catherine Noschese DeLuca; Allegheny Comm. Coll.; ISDA; Elks; Moose; Eagles; Penn Hills Government Study Comm., 1974-76, councilman, 1976-80, 1981-82, Dep. Mayor, 1978-80; chmn., Public Safety, Finance and Public Works Comm., 1978-80; elected to the House of Representatives, Nov. 2, 1982; reelected 1984, 1986; married Constance Harrity; 4 children: Debbie, Larry, Michele, Anthony, Jr.; home address: 1416 Barbara Dr., Verona.

WALTER F. DeVERTER　　　　Juniata, Mifflin, and Perry Counties — 82nd District

Walter F. DeVerter (R) was born Aug. 25, 1934, in Hershey, the son of Walter A. and Esther L. (Moore) DeVerter; att. Central Pa. Business Coll., Williamsport Tech. Inst., George Washington Univ.; U.S. Marine Corps, 1953-56; practiced public accounting 8 yrs.; apptd. by Gov. Scranton as Register of Wills, Recorder of Deeds for Mifflin Co., 1965, reelected in 1965 and 1969; past dir., Lewistown YMCA, Young Republicans of Mifflin Co.; Republican committeeman; past pres., State Coll. chptr., Pa. Society of Public Accountants; past chmn., Mifflin Co. Industrial Development Corp.; Fund Drive; dir., Mifflin-Juniata United Fund; bd. of trustees, Lewistown Hospital; past regnl. v. pres., Pa. Jaycees; past st. treas., Pa. Jaycees; J.C.I. senator; BPOE 663; past campaign dir., Mifflin Co. March of Dimes; past dir., Hemlock Girl Scout Council; dir., AAA Lewistown Motor Club; Holy Communion Lutheran Ch., Yeagertown, and frmr. council mem.; elected to the House of Representatives in 1972; reelected to 7 successive terms; married Joyce L. Folk; 3 children; home address: R.D. #1, Box 84, McClure.

H. WILLIAM DeWEESE　　　　Greene, Fayette, and Washington Counties
50th District

H. William DeWeese (D) was born April 18, 1950, in Pittsburgh, the son of J. Victor and Frances Baily DeWeese; Wake Forest Univ. (B.A., history), 1972; U.S. Marines — 1st Lt. (1972-75); full-time legislator; chmn., House Judiciary Com. (appt. Jan. 1986, reappt. Jan. 1987); elected to the House of Representatives on April 27, 1976; reelected 6 successive terms; never married.

SCOTT DIETTERICK   Luzerne County — 120th District

Scott Dietterick (R) was born Feb. 10, 1941, in Wilkes-Barre, the son of Gordon S. Dietterick and Marjorie Honeywell Cummins; grad., Kingston H.S., 1958; att. Wilkes Coll.; U.S. Navy, 1959-63; independent ins. agent/ real estate sales associate; mem., Pa. Assn. of Indep. Ins. Agents, Pa. Realtors Assn.; Kingston Municipal Council, 1977-86; mem: Independent Fire Co., Am. Legion, King David Lodge F & AM, Caldwell Consistory, Irem Temple, Church of Christ Uniting, Grtr. Wilkes-Barre Chamber of Commerce, Am. Red Cross, Dial A Driver; rec., Jaycees International Senatorship; elected to the House of of Representatives, Nov. 4, 1986; married Nancy Carol Learn; 2 children: Jennifer and Julie; home address: 100 S. Maple Ave., Kingston.

RUDOLPH DININNI   Dauphin — 106th District

Rudolph Dininni (R) was born Oct. 19, 1926, in Rutherford Heights, the son of Valentine and Assunta Pagano Dininni; att. Swatara Twp. schls.; farmer; frmr. pres., R. Dininni Construction Co.; Electra Realty Co.; pres., Farmer's Bank and Trust Co., Hummelstown; Dauphin Co. Farmers Assn.; Harrisburg Builders' Exchange; life mem., Harrisburg Home Builders Assn.; past pres. and charter mem., Rutherford Heights Lions Club; St. Highway & Bridge Auth.; past pres., Reliance Hose Co. #1; Pa. Transportation Commission; Harrisburg Chptr., Sons of Italy; 40/8 of The Am. Legion; Dininni-Santoni Post 1213 of V.F.W.; elected to the House of Representatives in 1966; reelected to 10 successive terms; married Arlene M. Keiser; 3 children; home address: 435 69th St., Swatara Township.

JAMES T. DISTLER   Clearfield and Elk Counties — 75th District

James T. Distler (R) was born May 22, 1934, in St. Marys, the son of Wallace and Florence (Taylor) Distler; St. Marys Public High; Univ. of Buffalo; DuBois Bus. Coll., 1958; U.S. Air Force, 1953-57; mgr., Mfg. Control Systems; mem., Am. Legislative Exchange Council, Pa. Farmers, Elk Co. Sportsmen; Legion; Elks; Twp. Supr., 1977-84; mem., St. Marys Catholic Ch.; elected to the House of Representatives, Nov. 6, 1984; reelected 1986; married Joan Gabler; 4 children: James, Thomas, Frank, Diane; home address: 126 Edward Rd., St. Marys.

BERNARD J. DOMBROWSKI   Democratic Caucus Administrator
                                              Erie County — 1st District

Bernard Joseph Dombrowski (D) was born May 11, 1929, in Erie, the son of the late Boleslaus and Michalene Rutecki Dombrowski (dec'd. Mar. 20, 1976); att. Tech H.S.; coordinator, Am. Sterilizer Co.; U.S. Air Force, Sgt., 1950-53; Polish Professional Businessmen Organization; financial secy., Foreters Ben. Assn.; UAW Local 832; dir., M.A.C.O. Erie, 1970; secy., East Side Boys Club, 1969; East Side Federation, Model Cities; Holy Name Society, St. Stanislaus Parish; elected to the House of Representatives in 1970; reelected 8 successive terms; elected Majority Administrator, Jan. 4, 1983; reelected 1985; married Eleanor M. Lukaszewski on Nov. 27, 1952; 3 children; 7 grandchildren; home address: 618 East 14th St., Erie.

ROBERT C. DONATUCCI   **Delaware and Philadelphia Counties — 185th District**

Robert Charles Donatucci (D) was born May 3, 1952, in Phila., the son of Thomas F. (dec'd.) and Yolanda D'Amico Donatucci; grad., Bishop Neumann H.S. 1970; Temple Univ. (B.A., pol. sci.) 1974; frmr. Adm. Asst. to Dir. of Section 8, Phila. Housing Auth. 1974-80; elected Democratic Committeeman, 26th Ward, 15th Division 1972-74; elected to the House of Representatives in a special election, March, 1980; reelected Nov., 1980, 1982, 1984, 1986; married Maria Patelmo; 1 son, Thomas F.; home address: 2336 S. 21st St., Philadelphia.

DONALD W. DORR   **York County — 193rd District**

Donald W. Dorr (R) was born June 19, 1939, in Falls City, Ne., the son of Russell E. and Marjorie Dorr; Nebraska Wesleyan Univ. (B.A., with distinction) 1961; George Washington Univ. (J.D.) 1964; attorney; York Co., Pa., Am. Bar Assns.; Lions, Masonic Lodge; Methodist Ch.; elected to the House of Representatives in 1972; reelected 7 successive terms; married Helen Pfeffer of Gettysburg, Sept. 8, 1963; 1 son, Erik; home address: 305 Charles St., Hanover.

ROGER F. DUFFY   **Allegheny County — 33rd District**

Roger F. Duffy (D) was born Nov. 19, 1925, in Pgh., the son of Charles John and Elizabeth Carlton Duffy; grad. Taylor Allderice H.S., 1945; Duquesne Univ. (B.A., bus. admin.) 1951; U.S. Army, 1944-46; Mayor, Boro. of Oakmont, 1970-74; Councilman, Oakmont 1974-77; rec., Bronze Star Medal for Valor — WW II; Roman Catholic; St. Irenaeus Ch.; elected to the House of Representatives 1976; reelected 5 successive terms; married Dorothy Minutolo; 6 children: Suzanne Duffy Hannon, Roger Jr., Diane, Charles, John, Cristina; home address: 636 6th St., Oakmont.

KATHRYNANN DURHAM   **Delaware County — 160th District**

Kathrynann Durham (R) was born July 29, 1951, in Chester, the daughter of Glenn S. and Catherine Talarico Walrath; Widener Univ. (B.A.) 1973; Delaware Law Schl. of Widener Univ. (J.D.) 1982; mem.: Order of Women Legislators; St. Paul's Episcopal Ch.; married Stephen A. Durham; 1 child, Stephen Jr.; elected to the House of Representatives in 1978; reelected 1980, 1982, 1984, 1986; home address: 16 Pond's View Dr., Glen Mills.

DWIGHT EVANS   Philadelphia County — 203rd District

Dwight Evans (D) was born May 16, 1954, in Phila., the son of Henry and Jean Odoms Evans; grandson of Bernard & Katherine Odoms; Germantown H.S., 1971; Comm. Coll. of Phila. (A.A.) 1973; LaSalle Coll. (B.A.) 1975; grad. studies, Temple Univ., 1976-78; urban planner; City-Wide Political Alliance; frmr. pres., Concerned Cit. of 10th Ward; frmr. pres., Concerned Neigh. Assn.; N.W. Political Coalition; Phila. Council of Neighborhoods; consultant: N. Central Comm. Mental Health Ctr., House of Umoja, Council of Labor & Industry; 10th Ward Dem. Ex. Com.; Mt. Airy Baptist Ch.; Stenton Food Co-op Prog.; Political Ed. seminars; Voter Regis. Drive; Com. to rebuild West Oak Lane Lib.; Community Drive to Aid Fire Victims; Opposition to Further Issuance of Liquor Licenses in Community; seminar, Resources for Sr. Cit. Services; youth seminars, Employ. & Higher Ed.; Admissions Procedure Comm.; Black Student League; Student Govt. Assn.; Political Sci. Assn.; World-Wide Famine Comm., LaSalle Coll.; Pa. Minority Bus. Council; bd. mem., Urban League of Phila.; Operation PUSH; mem., Kiwanis Club of Germantown; Steering Com., Phila. Dem. Party, 1985; bd. dir., Anne Frank Inst. of Phila.; rec., "Citizen of the Month (1978) and of the Year (1979)," The Philadelphia *Tribune*/Pepsi Cola; Certificate of Appreciation, U.S. Military Acd.; "80 People to Watch in 1980," *Philadelphia Magazine*; "City-Wide Parents Council and Community Service Award," Dept. of Public Welfare; Certificate of Achievement, City-Wide Political Alliance, 1980; Chapel of Four Chaplains Award, 1980; finalist, Jaycees Award for Outstanding Young Leader, 1980; nominated Outstanding Leader of the Year by *Who's Who*, 1981; sec., Pa. Legis. Black Caucus, 1981-82; chmn., Task Force for the Pa. Legis. Black Caucus on Reapportionment, 1981-82; Democratic 10th Ward Leader; 2nd Vice-Chmn., Black Ward Leaders; 2nd Vice-Chmn., Black Elected Officials; co-chmn., Phila. Delegation, H.R.; elected to House of Representatives, Nov. 4, 1980; reelected 1982, 1984, 1986; home address: 2101 Homer St., Philadelphia.

HOWARD L. FARGO   Butler and Mercer Counties — 8th District

Howard L. Fargo (R) was born Apr. 18, 1928, in Clearfield, the son of W. Blair and Edna Fargo; Indiana Univ. at Indiana, Pa. (B.S.) 1952; Pa. St. Univ. (M.Ed.) 1957; U.S. Navy, 1946-48; public school teacher, 1952-57; Certified Public Accountant; Am. and Pa. Institute of CPA's; Grove City Kiwanis; Masonic bodies; Methodist; elected to the House of Representatives in a special election, June 23, 1981; reelected 1982, 1984, 1986; married June Uncles; 2 children: Doug, Mrs. Linda Imler; home address: 313 Elm Street, Grove City.

ELAINE F. FARMER   Allegheny County — 28th District

Elaine F. Farmer (R) was born March 14, 1937, the daughter of John R. (dec.) and Pearle A. McLure Frazier; grad., Case Western Reserve Univ., Cleveland (B.A., bus. admin.) 1958, (M.A., educ.) 1964; former teacher; businesswoman; legislator; mem.: Am. Legislative Exchange Council, Natl. Assn. of Realtors, St. Bd. of Realtors, Grtr. Pgh. Bd. of Realtors, Andron Epiphanon Frat., Theta Phi Omega Sor.; mem., McCandless Town Council, 1980-86; bd. mem., Northland Public Lib., 1981-85; mem., North Hills Area Chamber of Commerce; trustee-elder, Northmont Presbyterian Church; elected to the House of Representatives, Nov. 4, 1986; married Sterling N. Farmer Jr.; 2 children: Heather and Drew; home address: 1200 Prince Andrew Ct., Pittsburgh.

CHAKA FATTAH   Philadelphia County — 192nd District

Chaka Fattah (D) was born Nov. 21, 1956, in Phila., the son of David and Falaka Fattah; Phila. Comm. Coll.; Wharton Schl., Univ of Pa.; John Kennedy Schl. of Govt., Harvard Univ.; Fels Inst. for State and Local Govt. (M.G.A.) 1986; special asst. to Phila. Managing Dir.; asst. to dir., Office of Housing and Community Development; policy asst., Greater Phila. Partnership; asst. dir., House of Umoja; trustee, Temple Univ.; mem., PHEAA Bd.; chair., Black Caucus Ed. Com.; mem., Natl. Task Force on Ed. (NCSL); charter mem., Legislative Black Caucus Foundation Bd. of Dirs.; exec. com., Phila. Black Elected Officials Org.; Pa. Adv. Co. for the Special Olympics; bd. mem., Phildanco; chmn., Sunset Review Co. on Private Trade Schools; rec. numerous awards including: NAACP Outstanding Achievement Award, 1981; "Fifty Future Leaders," *Ebony Magazine;* "Who's Who in Black America," "Outstanding Young Men in America," and "Who's Who in American Politics"; mem., 59th Street Baptist Ch.; elected to the House of Representatives, Nov. 2, 1982; reelected 1984, 1986; married Michelle Renee Wingfield, 2 children: Frances Ellen, Chaka Jr.; home address: 5783 Nassau Rd., Philadelphia.

THOMAS J. FEE

Democratic Caucus Secretary
Lawrence County — 9th District

Thomas J. Fee (D) was born Jan. 6, 1931, in New Castle, the son of Thomas R. and Frances Quinn Fee; grad., New Castle H.S.; frmr. plasterer; legislator; mem., past pres., Fraternal Order of Eagles 455; mem., Democratic State Comm., 1958-60; New Castle City Council, 1966; past pres., St. Mary's Holy Name Society, 1962; elected to the House of Representatives in 1968; reelected 9 successive terms; sub-committee chmn., Youth & Aging Comm., 1975-76; chmn., Conservation Comm., 1977-80; Joint Legislative Air & Water Pollution Control Comm., 1979; Game & Fisheries Comm., 1979-82; Environmental Quality Bd., Dept. of Envir. Resources, 1980-82; chmn., Liquor Control Comm., 1981-84; Majority Caucus Secretary, 1985-86, 1987-88; married Lucretia Fuleno, Feb. 23, 1952; 6 children; 9 grandchildren; home address: 325 Lincoln Ave., New Castle.

ROGER RAYMOND FISCHER

Washington County — 47th District

Roger Raymond Fischer (R) was born June 1, 1941, in Washington, Pa., the son of Louise and Raymond Fischer; Washington and Jefferson Coll. (B.A., math and physics) 1963; grad. work, Carnegie Inst. of Tech.; grad., U.S. Air Force Command and Staff Coll.; Pa. Air Natl. Guard; Lt. Col.; frmr. research engineer; legislator; dir., Washington Schl. Dist., 1965-71; bd. of dirs., City Mission; Boy Scout Merit Badge Counselor; lay assist., Lutheran Ch. in Am.; Am. Legion; 40 & 8; F&AM; Washington Royal Arch Chap. 150; Jacques DeMolay Commander; Washington Council 1; Washington-Green Shrine Caravan; Syria Temple AAONMS; Joint St. Govt. Commission Task Forces on veterans benefits, prison reform, miner's black lung and education; chmn., police sub-committee, Pa. Crime Commission's Regnl. Planning Council, 1970; Warrior's Trail Assn.; Keystone Trail Assn.; Washington Road Runners; mem., State Board of Education; elected to the House of Representatives in 1966; reelected 10 successive terms; minority chmn., House Comm. on Ed.; Triathalon Federation/USA; mem., Pa. Appalachian Trail Comm.; Gov. Council on Physical Fitness; finisher, Ironman Triathlon; life mem., Pa. Appalachian Trail Conf.; married Catherine Louise Trettel on Aug. 13, 1972; 3 children: Roger Raymond II, Steven Gregory, Catherine Elizabeth; home address: Overlook Drive, Washington.

ROBERT J. FLICK

Chester and Delaware Counties — 167th District

Robert J. Flick (R) was born Oct. 27, 1944, in Bryn Mawr, the son of Lawrence and Margaret McDevitt Flick; Villanova Univ. (B.S.) 1966; Univ. of Pa., Certificate of Real Estate, 1971; U.S. Army Reserve, 1966-72; v. pres., Roach Bros., Inc.; Main Line Bd. of Realtors; Chester Co. Bd. of Realtors; Pa. Assn. of Realtors; Natl. Assn. of Realtors; Realtor Natl. Marketing Inst.; Chester Co. Republican Comm., 1971-1981; C of C; Concerned Residents of E. Whiteland; Great Valley Little League Assn.; Outstanding Young Men of America, 1973; elected to the House of Representatives, Nov. 2, 1982; reelected 1984, 1986; married Patricia A. Fitzpatrick; 3 children: Christopher, Michael, Jeffrey; home address: 13 James Thomas Rd., Malvern.

A. CARVILLE FOSTER, JR.

York County — 93rd District

A. Carville Foster, Jr. (R) was born Oct. 21, 1932, in Parkton, Md., the son of A. Carville Sr. and Dorothy Early Foster; grad. from Sparks H.S. in 1949 prior to moving to Shrewsbury, York Co.; U.S. Navy, 1955-57; Shrewsbury Borough Council, 1962-68; pres., York Co. Boroughs Assn., 1965; frmr. mem., New Freedom Jaycees; Seven Valleys Lions Club; Lay Leader, Cedar Grove United Methodist Ch.; Republican Exec. Comm. since 1964; elected to the House of Representatives in 1972; reelected 7 successive terms; home address: R.D. 2, Seven Valleys, Springfield Township.

JON D. FOX   Montgomery County — 153rd District

Jon D. Fox (R) was born April 22, 1947, in Phila., the son of William L. and Elainne B. Brickman Fox; Pa. State Univ. (B.A.) 1969; Delaware Law Schl. of Widener Univ., 1975; rec., Lindsay law prize for excellence in legal research; Reservist E-6 Tech. Sgt., U.S. Air Force, 1969-75; attorney; mem., Golden Slipper Club; Kiwanis Club; VFW; Montco. asst. dist. atty., 1976-80; commissioner, Abington Twp., 1980-1984; dir., Twp. Public Affairs Dept., 1982-1984; bd. dir., Eastern Montgomery Co. Red Cross; bd. dir., Am. Cancer Soc., 1981; chmn., Abington Joint Town Watch Council, 1982; sustaining bd., Abington Memorial Hosp.; elected to the House of Representatives, Nov. 1984; reelected 1986; home address: 523 Benson Manor, Jenkintown.

ROBERT L. FREEMAN   Northampton County — 136th District

Robert L. Freeman (D) was born March 9, 1956, in Easton, the son of Jacob and Joyce Styers Freeman; grad., Easton Area H.S., 1975; Moravian Coll. (B.A., magna cum laude) 1978; Lehigh Univ. (M.A., history) 1984; frmr. Shop Steward, United Food and Commercial Workers Union, Local 1357; Easton NAACP; Young Democrats of Northampton Co.; mem., Lehigh Valley Democratic Assn.; bd. mem., Easton Area Neighborhood Center; bd. mem., Turning Point; Phi Alpha Theta Historical Society; Triangle Honor Society; Elton Stone History Award, 1975; Moravian Coll. History Prize, 1978; authored *"Light Rail and the Lehigh Valley," New Valley Press*, April 1981; elected to the House of Representatives, Nov. 2, 1982; reelected 1984, 1986; single; home address: 138 S. 10th St., Easton.

STEPHEN F. FREIND   Delaware County — 166th District

Stephen F. Freind (R) was born April 22, 1944, in Phila., son of John and Elizabeth Taylor Freind; Villanova U. (B.A.) 1966, student body pres., full acad. schlrship.; Temple U. Law Schl. (J.D.) 1969; attorney; law partner, Freind and Willman; Am., Phila., Fed. Bar Assns.; Pa. Trial Lawyers' Assn.; Assn. of Trial Lawyers of Am.; spec. agent, Milwaukee & Detroit divs., FBI, 1969-72; asst. DA, spec. invest. div., Phila., 1972-74; spec. counsel, Select Comm. on State Contract Practices, Pa. H of R, 1974; spec. counsel, Min. Appro. Comm., Senate of Pa., 1974-76; author: "Staff Report, House Select Comm. on State Contract Practices," Senate Minority Approp. Comm., 1974; Phila. Spec. Investigating Grand Jury Presentments: 10th Presentment, Pa. Dept. of Treasury (co-author); 11th Presentment, Pa. Bureau of Cigarette & Beverage Taxes; 13th Presentment, Pa. Liquor Control Bd.; 24th Presentment, Pa. St. Bd. of Pharmacy; light humor articles, *Phila. Inquirer, Today Magazine, Phila. Bulletin, Discover Magazine*; author, novel *God's Children*, May 1987; FBI Dir's. Letters of Commendation, 1970, 1971; Annunciation B.V.M. Ch.; elected to the House of Representatives, April 1976, reelected 6 successive terms; married Judith Ritchie; 6 children; home address: 241 Brookline Blvd., Havertown.

JAMES J. GALLEN   Berks County — 128th District

James J. Gallen (R) was born Aug. 15, 1928, in Reading, the son of A. Joseph and Anna V. Strain Gallen; Villanova Univ. (B.S.); U.S. Army, Korean Conflict; legislator; chmn., Berks Co. Comm. on Problems of Older Workers; Am. Legion; Shillington Keystone Fire Co.; Young Republican Club; chmn., Republican Comm. of Berks Co.; cubmaster; elected to the House of Representatives in 1964; reelected 11 successive terms; married Sara C. Boyle; 8 children; 5 grandchildren; home address: 302 Hendel St., Shillington.

RON GAMBLE

Allegheny County — 44th District

Ron Gamble (D) was born Jan. 2, 1933, in Oakdale, the son of Dale (dec'd.) and Gertrude McGuane Gamble; grad. West Allegheny H.S., 1951; U.S. Marine Corps, 1953-56; airport manager and grocery store owner; Justice of the Peace, 1961-69; Oakdale Borough Secy., 1962-64; pres., Oakdale Borough Council, 1970-76; Oakdale Volunteer Fire Dept.; Oakdale Sportsmen; Am. Legion Post 171; VFW Post 7070; W. Allegheny Lions Club; chmn. Chartiers Valley Democrats; Christian; elected to the House of Representatives in 1976; reelected 5 successive terms; married Brenda Josey; 4 children: Cindi, Pam, Dale, Lynn; home address: 1 Highland Ave., Oakdale.

THOMAS P. GANNON

Delaware County — 161st District

Thomas P. Gannon (R) was born May 5, 1943, in Phila., the son of Michael J. and Elizabeth M. Barnes Gannon; Temple Univ. (B.A.), 1968; Delaware Law Schl. of Widener Coll. (J.D.), 1976; legislator/attorney; Pa. Bar Assn.; Pa. Trial Lawyers Assn.; Del-Chester Claims Assn.; Our Lady of Peace Home and Schl. Assn., v. pres., 1975-76, pres. 1976-78; Man of the Year Award, Del-Chester Claim Assn.; elected to the House of Representatives in 1978; reelected 1980, 1982, 1984, 1986; married Kathleen Patricia Kelley; 4 children: Christopher, Kelley Ann, Gregory, Patricia; home address: 1518 Grant Ave., Woodlyn.

RICHARD ALLEN GEIST

Blair County — 79th District

Richard Allen Geist (R) was born Nov. 21, 1944, in Altoona, the son of James Dysart and Catharine Wiggins Geist; att. Penn St. (Assoc. Drafting, Design Tech.) 1965; Kellogg Fellowship and Public Affairs Leadership Program; frmr. consulting engineer; legislator; commissioner/manager/coach, George B. Kelley Jr. Federation, 1971 to present; v. pres., 1975, pres., 1976-78, Neighborhood Housing Program; Blair Co. Republican Committeeman, sec./treas.; P.I.A.A. Wrestling Officials, Blair Chapter; bd. dir., AAA; Railroaders; Memorial Museum; Outstanding Young Men in Am. Award, 1976 edition; has written many articles on marketing engineering services; chmn., Exploring Task Force; Penns Woods Council; prime sponsor of legislation that created the High Speed Intercity Rail Passenger Comm.; elected 1st chmn., High Speed Rail Compact States; MILRITE Council; Ben Franklin Partnership Bd.; elected to the House of Representatives in 1978; reelected 1980, 1982, 1984, 1986; married Jean Elizabeth Dillen; home address: 1100 27th Ave., Altoona.

CAMILLE GEORGE

Clearfield County — 74th District

Camille George (D) was born Dec. 23, 1927, in Houtzdale, son of Jacob and Emily George; att. Houtzdale H.S., Am. Schl. of Chicago; U.S. Navy, 1945-46; businessman, partner in Jacob George Ford Sales Inc., auto agency; mayor, Houtzdale Borough, 1966-70; Democratic chmn., Clearfield Co., 1968-70; frmr. councilman, Houtzdale Borough; admin. officer, Pa. Dept. of Transportation, District 2-0, Clearfield, 1972-74; v. pres., Moshannon Valley Democratic Club; Operating Engineers, Local 66, Pgh.; Am. Legion Post 591; Cooper Twp. Democratic Club; Curwensville Area Democratic Women's Club; Clearfield Area Democratic Women's Club; Southern Democratic Club; Moran Gun and Rod Club; Moshannon Valley Knights Booster Club; Mosquito Creek Sportsman's Assn.; Fraternal Order of Eagles, Aerie, #812; Environmental Quality Bd., 1983; reappointed 1985; Joint Leg. Air and Water Pollution Control Comm.; elected to House of Representatives in 1974; reelected 6 successive terms; married Edna Mae Brobeck of Tyrone; 6 children: Edwina, Candace, Kim, Jacob, Edmond, Susan; home address: 512 Harry Street, Houtzdale.

JOSEPH M. GLADECK, JR.   Montgomery County — 61st District

Joseph M. Gladeck, Jr. (R) was born on Aug. 2, 1950, in Phila., the son of Joseph M., Sr. and Ellen Pittinger Gladeck; Temple Univ. (B.A., pol. sci.) 1972; Pa. Nat'l. Guard, 1972-1978; staff, U.S. Congressman Larry Coughlin; Lutheran; elected to the House of Representatives in 1978; reelected 1980, 1982, 1984, 1986; home address: 525 Butler Pike, Whitpain Twp.

ROBERT W. GODSHALL   Montgomery County — 53rd District

Robert W. Godshall (R) was born May 15, 1933, in Souderton, the son of Enos and Bessie Wambold Godshall; Juniata Coll. (B S.) 1955; Univ. of Pa., Wharton Schl., 1956; pres., Godshall's Hatchery, Inc.; Montgomery Co. Controller, 1980-83; Republican Committeeman, 1962-present; Area Leader, 1970-present; Souderton Area Schl. Bd., 1963-80; Montgomery Co. Schl. Bd. Legislative Comm., 1974-80; Pa. Schl. Bd. Assn., 1963-80; Indian Valley C of C; bd. dir., Harleysville Sr. Adult Activity Center; pres., Perkiomen Valley Watershed Assn.; elected to the House of Representatives, Nov. 2, 1982; reelected 1984, 1986; married Sara Fell; 5 children: Brad, Jamie, Grey, Tanya, Shanin; home address: 316 Godshall Rd., Souderton.

MICHAEL C. GRUITZA   Mercer County — 7th District

Michael C. Gruitza (D) was born May 2, 1951, in Sharon, the Univ. of John and Aurelia Vulcan Gruitza; Gannon Univ. (B.A.) 1973; Ohio N. Univ. (J.D.) 1977; attorney; Mercer Co., Pa. Bar Assns.; St. John's Byzantine Catholic Ch.; bd. dir., Mercer Co. Community Action Agency; elected to the House of Representatives, Nov. 1980; reelected 1982, 1984, 1986; married Joan Shaw; 3 children: Rebecca Jean, William John, David Michael; home address: 229 Fairmont Dr., Hermitage.

LEONARD QUIRICO GRUPPO   Northampton County — 137th District

Leonard Quirico Gruppo (R) was born Oct. 6, 1942, in Phila., the son of Leonard and Concetta Castone Gruppo; Moravian Coll. (B.A., business, pol. sci.), 1977; fulltime legislator; frmr. auditor, chairman, Washington Twp., 1966-1971; Knights of Columbus; Our Lady of Good Counsel Parish, Bangor; elected to the House of Representatives in 1978; reelected 1980, 1982, 1984, 1986; married Lucille Torcivia; 4 children: Leonard Jr., Christopher, Danielle, Salvatore; home address: 268 Oak Rd., Bangor.

LOIS SHERMAN HAGARTY
Montgomery County — 148th District

Lois Sherman Hagarty (R) was born Sept. 28, 1948, in Phila., the daughter of Daniel and Evelyn Wolpert Sherman; Harriton H.S., 1966; Temple Univ. (B.S., cum laude) 1970, (M.Ed.) 1973; Temple Univ. Schl. of Law (J.D.) 1976; atty.; Montgomery Co., Pa. Bar Assns.; 1st asst. dist. atty., Montgomery Co., 1979-80; Neighborhood Club of Bala Cynwyd; Lwr. Merion/Narberth Council, Republican Women; elected to the House of Representatives, in a special election Mar. 11, 1980; reelected Nov. 1980, 1982, 1984, 1986; married John Joseph Hagarty, Jr.; 2 children: Matthew and Seth; home address: 112 Colwyn Lane, Bala Cynwyd.

EDWARD J. HALUSKA
Cambria County — 73rd District

Edward J. Haluska (D) was born Aug. 18, 1916, in Patton, the son of John and Mary Jane Palko Haluska; Univ. of Pgh. (B.S. and D.D.S.); military service, 1943-46; dentist/D.D.S. businessman; Am. Dental Assn.; VFW; Moose; Am. Legion; Patton Fire Co.; Sons of Italy; Slovak Citizens Club; Patton Sr. Citizens; past pres., bd. dir., Cambria Hgts. (24 yrs.); past pres., Cambria Co. Bd. of Schl. Dirs., Intermediate Bd. of Schl. Dirs.; chmn., Patton Area Chamber of Commerce (past pres.); Johnstown Area Regional Industries Eco. Bd.; Bd. of Pa. Attractions Assn.; v. pres., Cambria Co. Tourist Council; pres., Seldom Seen Valley Mine; frmr. mem. and dir., Cambria Health and Man Power System; v. pres., Area Realty Corp.; pres., Paradise Point Develop. Corp.; Knights of Columbus; Victory Medal, Distinguished Unit Badge, American Theater Service Medal, Asiatic Pacific Service Medal; elected to the House of Representatives, Nov. 1980; reelected 1982, 1984, 1986; married Louise Buck; 4 children: George, Gary, Margie, Wayne; home address: 303 6th Ave., Patton.

RUTH B. HARPER
Philadelphia County — 196th District

Ruth B. Harper (D) was born Dec. 24, 1927, in Hinesville, Ga., daughter of Thomas and Sally Brant DeLoach; grad., Cuyler-Beach H.S., Savannah, Ga.; Berean Inst. Schl. Cosmetology and Business; Flamingo Modeling and Charm Schl.; The Phila. Miniversity; att., LaSalle College; Moore College of Art; owner-director, Ruth Harper's Modeling and Charm Schl., Phila.; instructor, Gratz H.S.; Strawberry Mansion Jr. H.S.; producer, Miss Ebony Pa. Scholarship Pageant; bd. mem., Columbia North Branch YMCA; Women of Grtr. Phila.; mem., Natl. Council of Negro Women; Fellowship Comm.; Tioga Civic League; NAACP (life mem.); Urban League; Timberly Lake Charities; frmr. mem., bd. dirs., Red Cross, Northwest Branch; founder, frmr. pres., North Central Women's Poli. Caucus; Dem. Women's Forum; Dem. Committeewoman, 23rd div., 13th Ward leader; Pa. Women's Legis. Exchange; frmr. treas., Pa. Legislative Black Caucus; frmr. mem., Pa. Council on the Arts; mem., Natl. Conf. of State Legislatures; Natl. Dem. Committeewoman; achieve., service awards: Phila. Women's Political Caucus; NAACP; Bright Hope Baptist Ch.; Phila. *Tribune*, Citation of Honor; Variety Club Tent 13; Cosmopolitan Club; Third World 76 Inc. Black Expo; Tribune Charities; YMCA; Elks Pyramid; World Culture Ctr., Cheyney St. Coll.; Mabel M. Keys Chptr. #99, O.E.S.-P.H.A.; Lambda Kappa Mu Kopelles; Theta Ne Sorority, Gamma Chptr. award; Zion Baptist Ch.; elected to the House of Representatives in 1976; reelected 5 successive terms; married James E. Harper; 2 children: Catherine, DeLoris (dec.).

GEORGE C. HASAY
Columbia and Luzerne Counties — 117th District

George C. Hasay (R) was born Feb. 7, 1948, in Nanticoke, the son of John A. and Anne Orzechoski Hasay; att. Huntington Twp. Schl.; grad., Northwest Area H.S.; att. Morehead St. Univ., KY; grad., Wilkes-Barre Business Coll., Jan. 1968, and Husson Coll., ME, 1971; Mu Sigma Chi Fraternity; N.E. Pa. Regl. Antique Auto. Club; Natl. Rifle Assn.; Pa. Rifle & Pistol Assn.; Slovak League of Am.; Eagles; Elks; AMVETS; Catholic War Vets.; Appreciation Awards: Lion's Club of Plymouth, 1978; Lion's Club of Wilkes-Barre, 1975; Rotary Club of Plymouth; Civil Air Patrol, United States Air Force, 1980; Certificates of Merit, AMVETS, 1974, 1975, and 1978; Kathleen Jones Memorial Award, 1979; United Cerebral Palsy of Luzerne Co. Humanitarian Service Award, 1981; Hampton House Health Group Care Center Disting. Service Award, 1982; David L. Lawrence Public Service Award, 1982; Honorary Member of the Penn Mountains Council of the Boy Scouts of America, 1982; Susquehanna Environmental Advocates Award for Outstanding Dedication to Environmental Issues, 1983; Susquehanna River Watch Festival, Cert. of Apprec., 1986; AMVETS of World War II, Korea and Vietnam Dist. Service Award, 1986; Military Order of Purple Heart Meritorious and Conspicuous Service Citation, 1986; Ascension Church, Mocanaqua; Roman Catholic; elected to the House of Representatives 1972; reelected 7 successive terms; frmr. chmn., House Federal-State Relations Com.; presently min. chmn., House Conservation Com.; married Nancy Cortright; home address: 63 W. Union St., Shickshinney.

RICHARD HAYDEN   **Philadelphia County — 194th District**

Richard Hayden (D) was born July 25, 1956, in Phila., the son of Thomas Jr. and Joan Theurkauf Hayden; grad., Archbishop Carroll H.S., 1974; Boston Coll. (B.A.) 1978; Villanova Law Schl. (J.D.) 1981; lawyer; mem., Pa. and Phila. Bar Assns.; elected to House of Representatives, Nov. 4; 1986; married Kathleen Hogan; home address: 4712 Fowler St., Philadelphia.

SAMUEL E. HAYES JR.   **Republican Whip**
Blair and Huntingdon Counties — 81st District

Samuel Elwood Hayes Jr. (R) was born Sept. 3, 1940, the son of Samuel E. and Helen Fisher Hayes; Pa. St. Univ. (B.S.) 1964, (M.Ed.) 1965; teacher; U.S. Army, active duty in Vietnam (Bronze Star); Am. Legion; VFW; Kiwanis; selected as an outstanding young man of Am.; elected to the House of Representatives in 1970; reelected to 8 successive terms; Minority Caucus Chairman 1977-78; Majority Whip, 1979-80; Majority Leader, 1981-82; Minority Whip 1983-; married Elizabeth Keister on July 27, 1963; 3 sons: Samuel III, Lee Hamilton, Erick Paul Madison; home address: R.D. 1, Tyrone.

DAVID W. HECKLER   **Bucks County — 143rd District** .

David W. Heckler (R) was born March 7, 1947, in Abington, the son of Jacob W. and Grace Jones Heckler; grad., Yale Univ. (B.A.) 1969; Univ. of Va. Schl. of Law (LL.B.) 1972; attorney, state legislator; mem., Bucks Co. and Pa. Bar Assns.; former counsel, Pa. District Attys.' Assn.; mem., Doylestown Lions Club; former counsel, Pa. Senate Finance Com., 1983-86; former asst. dist. atty., Bucks Co., 1972-79; author, *Manual for Pennsylvania Prosecutors*, 1981; instr., Bucks Co. Community Coll., 1973-82; Bucks Co. Constables; Bucks Co. Fire Schl. & Pa. State Fire Academy; elected to the House of Representatives, Nov. 4, 1986; married Susan Kruger; 2 children: Betsy and Matthew; home address: 2373 Turk Road, Doylestown.

LYNN B. HERMAN   **Centre and Clearfield Counties — 77th District**

Lynn B. Herman (R) was born Oct. 30, 1956, in Philipsburg, the son of Frederick and Barbara Briggs Herman; Univ. of Pgh., Johnstown (B.A., magna cum laude) 1978; Univ. of Pgh., (M.P.A.); frmr. admin. asst., Pa. Dept. of Ed. personnel; frmr. admin. analyst, Pa. Dept. of Trans.; mem., Kiwanis Int'l., Fraternal Order of Police, B.P.O. Elks, Penn State Club, Port Matilda-Grange, Toastmasters Int'l.; Outstanding Young Men of America; Who's Who Among American Colleges and Universities; Univ. of Pgh. Ambassadors, 1977-78; Am. Hist. Society, 1977-78; elected to the House of Representatives, Nov. 2, 1982; reelected 1984, 1986; home address: 99 Fifth St., Philipsburg.

ARTHUR D. HERSHEY

Chester County — 13th District

Arthur D. Hershey (R) was born Nov. 14, 1937, in Lancaster Co., the son of M. Clair and Anna Hauck Hershey; att. Pa. St. Univ.; farmer; Pa. Farmers' Assn.; Chester/Delaware Farmers' Assn.; past pres., Russleville Grange; Natl. Fed. of Ind. Businesses; Pa. Holstein Assn.; Pa. Farm Products Show Comm., 1981-1986; chmn., W. Fallowfield Planning Comm., 1975-82; Lions Club; Pa. Ag/Republicans; Young Farmers Community Service Award, 1977; elected to the House of Representatives, Nov. 2, 1982; reelected 1984, 1986; married Joyce E. Hoober; 4 children: Beverly, Duane, Brad, Julie; home address: Box 191, R.D. 1, Cochranville.

DICK LEE HESS

Bedford, Fulton and Huntingdon Counties 78th District

Dick Lee Hess (R) was born Sept. 12, 1938, in Pgh., the son of Thomas L. (dec.) and Pauline Wenrick Hess; grad., Saxton Liberty H.S., 1958; prothonotary, clerk of courts, 1972-87; bd. of trustees, Bedford Co. Memorial Hosp.; past mem., Jaycees; Bedford Moose; NRA member; twice pres., Bedford Rep. Club; mem., Yardley Woodside Fish & Game; United Methodist Ch., Bedford; Jaycee of Year, 1963-64; elected to the House of Representatives on Nov. 4, 1986; married Shirley Cornelius; 1 child, Jeffrey Lee; home address: 734 Preston St., Bedford.

JUNE N. HONAMAN

Lancaster County — 97th District

June N. Honaman (R) was born May 24, 1920, in Lancaster, the daughter of Lester W. and Maud Stauffer Newcomer; Beaver Coll. (BFA) 1941; Lancaster Bus. Schl.; housewife; Business and Professional Women; Am. Assn. of Univ. Women, Federated Women's Club; Pa. Council of Republican Women; Pa. Farmers Assn.; Conestoga Valley Assn.; Lancaster Co. Conservancy; platform comm., delegate-at-large, Republican Natl. Convention, 1964, 1968, 1972; v. chmn., Republican Party of Pa., 1964-75; St. Andrew's Episcopal Ch.; elected to the House of Representatives in 1976; reelected to 5 successive terms; married to Peter K. Honaman; home address: Landisville.

JOSEPH HOWLETT

Philadelphia County — 184th District

Joseph Howlett (D) was born on Aug. 4, 1943, in Phila., the son of Albert P. and Viola McCue Howlett; Bok Vocational; Sacred Heart of Jesus; Dible Management Development Seminar; longshoreman; mem., AFL-CIO; Phila. Allied Action Com., 1979; elected to the House of Representatives, Nov. 1984; reelected 1986; married Rita Henderson; 4 children: Joe, Jr., Viola, Dolores, and Danielle; home address: 437 Hoffman Street, Philadelphia.

VINCENT HUGHES   Philadelphia County — 190th District

Vincent Hughes (D) was born Oct. 26, 1956, in Phila., the son of James and Ann Adams Hughes; Temple Univ.; legislator; bd. mem.: Walnut Hill Community Development Corp., Welfare Pride, Pa. Public Interest Coalition, Citizen Action; rec., Human Rights Award, Natl. AFL-CIO, 1985; elected to House of Representatives, Nov. 4, 1986; 1 daughter, Ariell; mailing address: P.O. Box 13031, Philadelphia.

AMOS K. HUTCHINSON   Westmoreland County — 57th District

Amos K. Hutchinson (D) was born Jan. 1, 1920, in Greensburg, the son of Walter and Mary Hutchinson; grad., Greensburg H.S., 1938; U.S. Marine Corp., 1941-45; dir., Greensburg Schl.; elected to the House of Representatives in 1968; reelected 9 successive terms; married Louise Bompiani on Dec. 10, 1949; 3 children; home address: 308 Alexander Avenue, Greensburg.

IVAN ITKIN   Democratic Caucus Chairman
Allegheny County — 23rd District

Ivan Itkin (D) was born March 29, 1936, in New York City, the son of Abraham A. and Eda Kreger Itkin; Polytechnic Inst. of Brooklyn (B.Ch.E.) 1956; N.Y. Univ. (M.Nuc.E.) 1957; Univ. of Pgh. (Ph.D., math.) 1964; nuclear scientist and applied mathematician; past Democractic chmn., 14th Ward, Pgh.; frmr. judge of election; mem. and frmr. chmn., 14th Ward Dem. Club; mem., Pgh. Neighborhood Alliance; 15th Ward C. of C.; Squirrel Hill Urban Coalition; Am. Jewish Congress; B'nai B'rith; Group Against Smog & Pollution (GASP); Am. Nuclear Soc.; Nat'l. Assn. of Jewish Legislators; v. chmn., Science, Technology and Resource Planning Com., Nat'l. Conf. of State Legislatures; delegate, Dem. Nat'l. Convention, 1984; elected to the House of Representatives in 1972; reelected 7 successive terms; elected Majority Caucus Chmn., 1982; reelected 1984, 1986; appt., Speaker Pro Tempore, 1987-88 session; married Joyce Hudak; 3 children; home address: 6954 Reynolds St., Pittsburgh.

GEORGE W. JACKSON   Lebanon County — 101st District

George W. Jackson (R) was born Sept. 19, 1924, in Phila., the son of George W. and Ethel M. Dissiner Jackson (both dec.); Lebanon H.S., 1943; Lebanon Business Coll., 1949; U.S. Marine Corps. 1943-45, 1950-51; admn. asst.; Mt. Oliver Lodge No. 704, F. & A.M.; Harrisburg Consistory; Tall Cedars; Am. Legion Post 559; Vets. of Foreign Wars Post No. 23; Military Order of the Cottie of the U.S.; Rotary Club of Lebanon (Paul Harris Fellow); adv. bd., Salvation Army; Travelers Protection Assn. of Am.; Fraternal Order of Police, Lodge 42; Easter Seal Society; United Cerebral Palsy (life mem.) bd. mem.; Cancer bd. mem.; American Assn. of Retired Persons; Quittapahilla Rod and Gun Club; Mount Gretna Volunteer Fire Co.; Marine Corp. League; DAV Distinguished Service Award; Better Life Award, Pa. Health Care Assn., 1983; Grace United Ch. of Christ; Lebanon Co. Chmn., Republican Party (8 yrs.); Young G.O.P. Pres., (4 yrs.); Finance Comm., Exec. Comm., Republican Co. Comm.; committeeman, Mt. Gretna Borough; elected to the House of Representatives, Nov. 1980; reelected 1982, 1984, 1986; married Esther Miller; 1 child, Beth Renee; home address: Box 11, Lebanon Ave., Mt. Gretna.

KENNETH M. JADLOWIEC   McKean, Cameron, and Clearfield
67th District

Kenneth M. Jadlowiec (R) was born Jan. 12, 1951, in Pgh., the son of Edward J. and Stella D. Przygucki Jadlowiec; grad., North Hills H.S., 1968; Edinboro Univ., 1971; state representative; district justice, 1982-86; mem., Rotary, St. Bernard's Church; pres., Special Court Judges Dist. 2; bd. dirs., Univ. of Pgh.-Bradford, McKean Co. Bd. of Assist.; elected to the House of Representatives, Nov. 4, 1986; married Denise E. Mackowski; 2 children: Kenneth E. and Brian M.; home address: 5 Constitution Ave., Bradford.

STANLEY J. JAROLIN   Luzerne County — 119th District

Stanley J. Jarolin (D) was born in Nanticoke, the son of Emil and Victoria Struzinski Jarolin; U.S. Air Force Personnel & Guidance Schl.; U.S. Air Force, 1951-55; plumbing and heating contractor; Luzerne Co. Contractors Assn.; Plumbers Local #90; treas., Nanticoke, 1978-present; Holy Name Society; Catholic War Vets; Am. Legion; C of C (past pres.); Lions (past pres.); elected to the House of Representatives, Nov. 2, 1982; reelected 1984, 1986; married Theresa Raymond; 4 children: Michael, Kathleen, Brenda, Robert; home address: 1001 Kosciuszko St., Nanticoke.

EDWIN GEORGE JOHNSON   Blair County — 80th District

Edwin George Johnson (R) was born Feb. 15, 1922, in Altoona, the son of George A. and Dorothy Brubaker Johnson; att. Pa. St. Univ.; grad., Univ. of Pa. (B.S., econ.), 1948; U.S. Army Air Force, 1942-45; retired supervisor Internal Revenue agents, U.S. Treasury Dept.; Grace Brethren Ch.; Christian Businessmen's Comm.; Nat'l. Rifle Assn.; Altoona C. of C.; Am. Legion and Disabled Am. Vets.; elected to the House of Representatives in 1978; reelected 1980, 1982, 1984, 1986; married Eleanor M. McCurdy; 2 children: Sandra Johnson Eshelman, Kenneth P. Johnson; home address: R.D. 5, Box 712, Altoona.

BABETTE JOSEPHS   Philadelphia County — 182nd District

Babette Josephs (D) was born Aug. 4, 1940, the daughter of Egene S. and Myra Josephs; Queens Coll. (B.A.) 1962; Rutgers - Camden Schl. of Law (J.D.) 1976; attorney; mem., Phila. Bar Assn.; League of Women Voters; Am. Civil Liberties Union; Am. for Dem. Actions; Nuclear Freeze Campaign; Natl. Org. for Women; Am. Jewish Congress; League of Conservation Voters; Consumer Adv. Comm. of Blue Cross of Grtr. Phila; auth., *See How She Runs: A Manual for Committeepersons*; elected to the House of Representatives, 1984; reelected 1986; married Herbert B. Newberg; 2 children: Lee Aaron and Elizabeth; home address: 1939 Waverly St., Philadelphia.

RICHARD A. KASUNIC   Fayette County — 52nd District

Richard A. Kasunic (D) was born Jan. 8, 1947, in (Monarch) Dunbar, the son of Walter A. and Gertrude Bashinsky Kasunic; Dunbar Twp. H.S., 1964; Robert Morris Jr. Coll., Pgh. (A.A., bus. admin.); Youngstown St. Univ. (B.S., bus. admin.); Pa. Natl. Guard, 1970-76; full-time legislator; chief assessor, Fayette Co., 1971-82; mem., St. Vincent DePaul Roman Catholic Ch.; Monarch Volunteer Fire Dept.; Fayette Co. Firemen's Assn.; Dunbar Twp. Democrat Club; ex. mem., Fayette Co. Democrat Com.; Dunbar Twp. Fraternal Order of Eagles; Dunbar Sportsman's Club; N.R.A.; Ducks Unlimited Inc.; Adv. Council, Pa. Pistol & Rifle Assn.; Yough Fisherman's Assn.; B.P.O. Elks #370, Uniontown; Independent Slovak Citizens Club, Connellsville; Polish Independent Club, Connellsville; Fayette Co. Realtors Assn.; Natl. Assn. of Realtors; bd. dirs., Fay-West Baseball League; com. mem., Fayette Co. Headstart; Sponsoring Com., Penn's Southwest Assn.; elected to the House of Representatives, Nov. 2, 1982; reelected 1984, 1986; married Laura Gannon (dec.); 1 child, Richard A .,Jr.; home address: R.D. #1, Dunbar.

JOHN KENNEDY   Cumberland County — 88th District

John Kennedy (R) was born Mar. 22, 1938, in Youngstown, Oh., the son of Lawrence William and Elizabeth J. Nicklin Kennedy; grad., Youngstown N. H.S.; att., Youngstown Coll.; hon. discharge, U.S. Army, 1962; pres., Kennedy Railroad Builders, Inc.; bd., Grtr. W. Shore Area Chamber of Commerce, Camp Hill; Cumberland Co. Governor's Club; elected to the House of Representatives, Nov. 1980; reelected 1982, 1984, 1986.

GEORGE T. KENNEY, JR.   Philadelphia County — 170th District

George T. Kenney, Jr. (R) was born on Oct. 29, 1957, in Phila., the son of George T. Kenney, Sr., and the late Anne Meissler Kenney; LaSalle College H.S.; LaSalle College (B.S.) 1982; pharmaceutical sales, McNeil Pharmaceutical; elected Rep. Committeeman 58th Ward, 41st Div., 1976-present; treas., 58th Ward Rep. Ex. Com., 1978-1980; frmr. mem., Somerton Youth Organization; St. Christopher's Church; mem., Somerton Lions Club; Knights of Columbus; Shaare Shamayim Mens Club; Phila. Emerald Soc.; Com. to Benefit the Children; elected to the House of Representatives, Nov. 6, 1984; reelected 1986; married Elizabeth Tomlinson; 1 daughter, Caroline; home address: 125 Overhill Ave., Philadelphia.

GERARD A. KOSINSKI   Philadelphia County — 175th District

Gerard A. Kosinski (D) was born July 22, 1954, in Phila., the son of Edward and Stephany Grochowina Kosinski; Pa. St. Univ. (B.A., magna cum laude) 1976; Phi Beta Kappa; att. Dickinson Schl. of Law, 1976; Temple Univ. Schl. of Law (J.D.) 1981, class valedictorian; attorney; Bar mem.: Supreme Court of Pa., U.S. District Court for the Eastern Dist. of Pa.; Democratic exec. comm., 45th Ward; Polish-American Citizens League of Pa.; Harmonia Club; Josef Pilsudski Frat. Assn.; Lions; Polish American Congress, Eastern Dist. of Pa.; St. John Cantius Holy Name Society; Special Admissions and Curriculum Experiments Comm., Temple Univ. Schl. of Law, 1979-81; Pre-Trial Services Div., Phila. Court of Common Pleas, Municipal Court, 1977-82; elected to the House of Representatives, Nov. 2, 1982; reelected 1984, 1986; single; home address: 4479 Almond St., Philadelphia.

ALLEN GALE KUKOVICH

Westmoreland County — 56th District

Allen Gale Kukovich (D) was born Sept. 5, 1947, in Greensburg, the son of Albert and Catherine Heasley Kukovich; Kent St. Univ., Oh. (B.A., poli. sci.), 1969; Duquesne Univ. Law Schl. (J.D.), 1973; elected to the House of Representatives, Nov. 1977; reelected 5 successive terms; home address: Box 521, Rt. 993 Manor.

FRANK LaGROTTA

**Beaver, Lawrence, and Mercer Counties
10th District**

Frank LaGrotta (D) was born Nov. 25, 1958, in Ellwood City, the son of Francis and Loretta DeThomas LaGrotta; grad., Univ. of Notre Dame (B.A.) 1980, (M.A.) 1981; legislator; elected to the House of Representatives, Nov. 4, 1986; home address: P.O. Box 842, Ellwood City.

ALICE S. LANGTRY

Allegheny County — 40th District

Alice S. Langtry (R) was born June 29 in Massachusetts, the daughter of Daniel and Ethel Whitman Santini; North Quincy H.S.; att., Boston Coll. (Intown); Pa. State Univ.; corporate administration; mem., Pa. Elected Women's Assn.; League of Women Voters; Traffic Safety Bd., Upper St. Clair Twp., 1979-80; Principals' Adv. Comm., Upper St. Clair H.S., 1980-81; Rep. Committeewomen, 1977-81; past pres., Arts Council of Erie; Upper St. Clair Twp. Commissioner, 1982-84; Chair of Budget & Finance Com.; delegate, South Hills Area Council of Governments; mem., St. Pauls Church; Parent-Teachers-Student Org.; Upper St. Clair Rep. Club; elected to the House of Representatives in 1984; reelected 1986; married Alfred Leigh Langtry, Jr.; 3 children: Martha Whitman, Emilia Blair, Alfred Leigh, III; home address: 418 Manordale Rd., Upper St. Clair.

JOSEPH A. LASHINGER, JR.

Montgomery County — 150th District

Joseph A. Lashinger, Jr. (R) was born Aug. 7, 1953, the son of Joseph A. and Elizabeth M. Radvansky Lashinger; Univ. of Pa. (B.A.) 1975, (M.A.) 1975; Delaware Law Schl. (J.D.) 1981; associated with the law firm of Fox, Differ, Callahan, Ulrich and O'Hara, Norristown; fac. mem., Montgomery Co. Community Coll.; founder, Greater Norristown Corp.; (Private Development Corp.); charter mem.: Greater Norristown Am. Business Club; Norristown Jaycees; bd. mem.: Montgomery Co. Protection of Persons Task Force; Montgomery Co. Assn. for Retarded Citizens; Children's Aid Society of Montgomery Co.; Central Montgomery MH/MR Center; Pathway Schl.; Adv. Comm. of Pa. Evaluation Network, Inc.; chmn., 1979-80 Montgomery Co. Drive, Am. Heart Assn.; Visitation B.V.M. Roman Catholic Ch.; Jaycees "Ten Outstanding Young Men of the Year" Award, 1979; named "Outstanding Citizen of the Yr.-1983" by Greater Valley Forge Chamber of Commerce; bd. mem., Central Montgomery Co. YMCA; bd. mem., Norristown Police Athletic League; author of thesis, *Decision Making in the Highway Planning Process: A Case Study Approach to the Crosstown Expressway, Philadelphia, Pa.,* the Univ. of Pa.; youngest Republican elected to the House of Representatives in 1978; reelected 1980, 1982, 1984, 1986; married Maria R. Donofrio; 2 children: Joseph, Kristen.

CHARLES P. LAUGHLIN   Beaver County — 16th District

Charles P. Laughlin (D) was born Nov. 19, 1931, in Ambridge, the son of Lawrence Joseph, Sr. and Rosella Zink Laughlin; att. parochial and public schls.; former councilman, Conway; volunteer fireman; financial sec., Beaver Co. Labor Council; formerly worked in public relations; elected to the House of Representatives, 1972; reelected 7 successive terms; presently chairman, House Committee on Consumer Affairs; mem., Legislative Budget & Finance Committee; married Susan Bogosian, May 12, 1952; 1 son, Thomas, of New Jersey; home address: 1305 Sampson St., Conway.

DENNIS E. LEH   Berks County — 130th District

Dennis E. Leh (R) was born Jan. 4, 1946, in Pottstown, the son of R. Elwood and Mildred Thomas Leh; grad., Pottstown H.S., 1964; journeyman, Tool & Diemaker, 1972; U.S. Army, military police, 1965-67; tool & diemaker, small businessman; mem., Am. Legislative Exchange Council; mem: Covenant Presbyterian Ch., Amity Athletic Club, Daniel Boone Optimus, Daniel Boone National Foundation, Amity Rep. League, Longswamp Rep. League; elected to the House of Representatives, Nov. 4, 1986; married Columbia Ricci; 3 children: Christine, Dennis, Jr. and Robert; home address: 3 Magnolia Ct., Douglassville.

VICTOR JOHN LESCOVITZ   Beaver and Washington Counties — 46th District

Victor John Lescovitz (D) was born Mar. 18, 1953, in Canonsburg, the son of Victor and Inez Sprando Lescovitz; Fort Cherry H.S., 1971; Washington and Jefferson Coll. (B.A.) 1975; (MGA) Univ. of Pa.; Lions Club; pres., Midway Borough Council, 1980; Roman Catholic; elected to the House of Representatives in a special election, Mar. 11, 1980; reelected Nov. 1980, 1982, 1984, 1986; married Nancy Fowler; home address: P.O. Box 543, Midway.

RUSSELL P. LETTERMAN   Centre, Clinton, Clearfield, and Lycoming Counties
76th District

Russell P. Letterman (D) was born March 8, 1933, in Milesburg, the son of Russell and Savilla Heltman Letterman; grad. Bellefonte H.S., 1951; played professional baseball with St. Louis Browns at Pgh., Kansas; U.S. Navy; professional barber; mem., Lewistown Loyal Order of Moose #143; Mosquito Creek Sportsmen's Club; Pa. Rifle & Pistol Assn.; Three Point Sportsmen's Club; State Vets. of Foreign Wars Leg. Com.; Joint Air and Water Pollution Control and Conservation Comm.; Milesburg Am. Legion; Milesburg Fire Co. (life mem.); Southern Clinton Co. Sportsmen's Assn., Inc.; Western Clinton Co. Sportsmen's Assn.; Bellfonte VFW Post 1600; Bellefont Elks — Lodge #1094; Clarence Democratic Club; Milesburg Methodist Ch.; elected to House of Representatives, 1970; serving 9th term; Joint Legislative Air & Water Pollution Control & Conservation Com.; chmn., Game and Fisheries; married Janice G. Mapes, June 28, 1963; 1 son, Tor; home address: Turnpike St., Milesburg.

DAVID K. LEVDANSKY
Allegheny County — 39th District

David K. Levdansky (D) was born on Oct. 16, 1954, in Monongahela, the son of Walter R. and Irene A. Tabory Levdansky; Pa. State Univ. (B.A., pol. sci., labor studies) 1978; Notre Dame Univ. (M.A., econ.) 1980; economic analysis/organizer; mem., National Slovak Society; Croatian Fraternal Union; Elrama Sportsman's Club; elected to the House of Representatives in Nov. 1984; reelected 1986; home address: 294 Grouse Dr., Elizabeth.

GORDON J. LINTON
Philadelphia County — 200th District

Gordon J. Linton (D) was born March 26, 1948, in Phila., the son of James and Alberta James Linton; Peirce Junior Coll. (A.S., bus. mgt.) 1967; Lincoln Univ. (B.A., economics) 1970; Antioch Univ. (M. Ed., counseling psych.) 1973; regional dir., Pa. Dept. of the Auditor General; psycho-educational spec., Phila. Child Guidance Clinic; dir. of ed., Baptist Children's House; community consultant, Schl. Dist. of Phila.; Dem. Comm. 50th Ward, 1978-pres.; frmr. chmn., 50th Ward ex. comm.; Region II pres., Conf. of Minority Transportation Officials; Mayor's Economic Roundtable; trustee, Lincoln Univ.; Disadvantage Business Advisory Council, Pa. Dept. of Transportation; bd. mem., Downingtown Industrial; Lincoln Univ. Alumni Assn.; NAACP; Northwest Political Alliance; Chapel of Four Chaplains Community Service Award; Ivy Hill Youth Assn. Com. Ser. Award; Leeds Middle Schl. Com. Ser. Award; Crisis Intervention Network Inc. and Citywide Parents Council Com. Ser. Award, 1984; rec., New Penn Del Minority Purchasing Council Apprec. Award, 1985; Indep. Minority Businessmen of Central Pa. Apprec. Award, 1985; Entreprenurial Club, Bus. and Tech. Center, Outstanding Civic Leadership Award, 1985; Johnstown NAACP Apprec. Award, 1985; Lincoln Univ. Dedicated Service to Higher Ed. 1986; *Outstanding Young Men of America*; *Who's Who Among Black Americans*; *Who's Who in Black America*; *Who's Who in American Politics*; elected to the House of Representatives, Nov. 2, 1982; reelected 1984, 1986; married Jacqueline Flynn; 2 children: Sharifah and Sabriya; home address: 913 E. McPherson Street, Philadelphia.

HENRY LIVENGOOD
Armstrong County — 60th District

Henry Livengood (D) was born Sept. 16, 1933, in Manor Twp., the son of Glenn M. (dec.) and Helen Lukehart Livengood; grad., Ford City H.S., 1951; U.S. Navy, Korean War vet., 1951-53; elected Manorville Borough councilman, 1970; elected Armstrong Co. Register and Recorder, 1971, reelected 1975, 1979, 1983; past pres., Ford City Kiwanis Club, 1973-74 and 1976-77; past campaign chmn., pres., Middle Armstrong Co. United Way; pres., Social Progress for Retarded Citizens (S.P.A.R.C.); mem., Armstrong Co. Chptr. Pa. Assn. for Retarded Citizens; Am. Legion Post 654; Parks Twp. Sportsmen's Assn.; Armstrong Co. Farmers' Assn.; V.F.W. Post 4843; BPO Elks #203; Armstrong Co. Chamber of Commerce; Armstrong Co. Historical Society; Cowanshannock Creek Watershed Assn.; Crooked Creek Watershed Assn.; Armstrong Co. Orphans of the Storm, Inc.; selected Outstanding Young Man of Greater Kittanning-Ford City Area, 1968-69; mem., Church Council, Grace Lutheran Ch., Manorville; elected to the House of Representatives, 1976; reelected 5 successive terms; married Donna Shott; 6 children, 2 stepchildren; home address: 1239 4th Ave., Ford City.

WILLIAM R. LLOYD, JR.
Somerset County — 69th District

William R. Lloyd, Jr. (D) was born Oct. 30, 1947, in Somerset, the son of W. Robert and Lillian Saler Lloyd; Somerset Area H.S., 1965; Franklin and Marshall Coll. (B.A.) Phi Beta Kappa 1969; Harvard Law Schl. (J.D., cum laude) 1972; U.S. Naval Justice Schl., 1973; Lieut., U.S. Navy, Judge Advocate General's Corps. 1972-76; legislative asst., Pa. Dept. of Education, 1972; legislative atty., U.S. Navy Office of Leg. Affairs, 1973-76; asst. Consumer Advocate, Pa. Dept. of Justice, 1976-78; Admn. Law Judge, Pa. Public Utility Comm., 1979-80; Asst. Prof., Political Sci., Indiana Univ. of Pa., 1979-80; Instructor of Business Mgmt., Point Park Coll., 1979-80; lecturer in pol. sci., St. Vincent Coll., 1980; elected to the House of Representatives, Nov. 1980; reelected 1982, 1984, 1986; single; home address: 645 E. Main St., Somerset.

EDWARD J. LUCYK   Columbia and Schuylkill Counties — 123rd District

Edward J. Lucyk (D) was born July 29, 1942, in Mahanoy City, the son of Edward J. (dec.) and Lucy Wowak Lucyk; Mahanoy Area H.S., 1960; U.S. Military Academy (B.S.) 1964; George Washington Univ. (M.B.A.) 1968; U.S. Army, 1964-72; elected to the House of Representatives, Nov. 1980; reelected 1982, 1984, 1986; married Patricia Guinan; 2 children: Matthew and Tara; home address: Box 216, Barnesville.

NICHOLAS J. MAIALE   Philadelphia County - 183rd District

Nicholas J. Maiale (D) was born Aug. 1, 1951, in Phila., the son of Albert and Clementine Falcone Maiale; Central H.S., 1969; Pa. St. Univ. (B.A.) 1973; Temple Univ. Law Schl. (J.D.) 1976; attorney; Phila., Pa., N.J. Bar Assns.; Justinian Society; Phi Beta Kappa; Phi Kappa Phi; asst. city solicitor, Phila., 1978-80; asst. counsel, Pa. House of Rep., 1976-78; Knights of Columbus; bd. dir., C.A.T.C.H.; author, "The Tenant as Consumer," *Temple Law Quarterly*, Spring 1975; elected to the House of Representatives in a special election, March 1980; reelected Nov. 1980, 1982, 1984, 1986; single; home address: 1538 Emily St., Philadelphia.

CONSTANCE G. MAINE   Crawford County - 6th District

Constance G. Maine (D) was born Oct. 28, 1942, in Brownsville, the daughter of Dr. Ralph M. and Constance Pedicino Glott; grad., Calif. of Pa. H.S., 1960; Calif. St. Univ., 1960-62; Indiana Univ. of Pa. (B.S., ed.) 1964; grad. work, Univ. of Pgh. and Penn State; Indiana Univ. of Pa. (M.A.) 1986; consultant, counselor, lecturer; mem.: ZONTA Internl., Bus. & Prof. Women's Club, Natl. Ed. Assn., Natl. Assn. of Female Executives, Am. Soc. of Prof. Consultants, Women's Services, Peace Links, Gray Panther, Farmer's Union, PA Elected Women's Assn., Capitol Hill Dem. Women's Club, Crawford Co. Dem. Exec. Com.; author, booklet, *"Tornado Aftermath"*; booklet, *"Starting Up: Tips for Beginning Businesswomen"*; elected to the House of Representatives, Nov. 4, 1986; married Gary D. Maine; 6 children: Pamela, Robert, Aaron, Tuan, Marc, Daniel; home address: R.D. #1, Dingman Rd., Townville.

JAMES J. MANDERINO   Democratic Floor Leader
Westmoreland County — 58th District

James J. Manderino (D) was born May 6, 1932, in Monessen, the son of Anthony and Angeline Reda Manderino; St. Vincent Coll. (B.A.) 1954; Univ. of Michigan Law Schl. (LL.B.) 1956; attorney; Westmoreland Co., Pa. and Am. Bar Assns.; BPOE Lodge 773; Fraternal Order of Eagles; Sons of Italy; Italian Society of Mutual Aid; Ravens Athletic Assn.; Monessen Lions Club; LOOM; NIPA; Monessen C. of C.; past mem., bd. of dirs., Monessen Industrial Development Corp.; frmr. pres., Monessen Community Chest; mem., bd. of dirs., Mon Valley United Fund; Mon Valley United Health Service, Inc., Building Comm.; chmn., Monessen Code Review Bd.; chmn., Westmoreland Co. Bar Assn. Legislative Comm.; mem., v. chmn., Bd. of the Westmoreland Water Authority; Joint State Govt. Commission Task Force on Escheat Laws; elected to House of Representatives in 1966; reelected to 10 successive terms; House Majority Whip, 1975-76; Majority Leader, 1977-78; Minority Whip 1979-82; Majority Leader 1983-86, reelected Jan., 1987; married Constance Myers (dec.); 5 children; home address: 15 Pleasant Drive, Monessen.

JOSEPH C. MANMILLER   **Dauphin County — 105th District**

Joseph C. Manmiller (R) was born Nov. 28, 1925, in Steelton, the son of Joseph C. and Ethel Glass Manmiller; grad., Steelton H.S.; Lock Haven Univ. (B.S.); Penn St. Univ. (med. & doctoral work); WW II, Normandy invasion; educator, frmr. coach & official; Harrisburg Lodge 629, Harrisburg Consistory; Tall Cedars; Zembo Shrine; VFW Post 710; Am. Legion Post 272; West Hanover Lions, West Hanover, Linglestown and Colonial Park Fire Cos.; West Side Fire Co.; The Pa. Society; Skyline View Civic Assn.; Old Timers Athletic Assn.; Pa. Sports Hall of Fame; past pres., West Hanover PTA; NEA; Steelton 5th Ward Republican Club; v. chmn., Dauphin Co. Republican Comm. (4 yrs.), past pres. (3 yrs.) and committeeman (6 terms); chmn., W. Hanover Republican Comm. (14 yrs.), dist. chmn. (3 yrs.); chmn., Dauphin Co. Candidates Screening Comm., 1969; Mount Calvary Un. Methodist Ch.; elected to House of Representatives in 1974; reelected 6 successive terms; married Nada Mircheff; 4 children: Constance, Nadine, JoLynn, Nada; home address: 7865 Valleyview Ave., Harrisburg.

JOSEPH F. MARKOSEK   **Allegheny and Westmoreland Counties — 25th District**

Joseph F. Markosek (D) was born Jan. 27, 1950, in Pgh., the son of Frank and Lucy Markosek; Univ. of Notre Dame (B.A.) 1972; Duquesne Univ. Grad. Schl. of Bus.; frmr. Sr. Engineer, Westinghouse Electric Co.; Monroeville Planning Comm., 1981; Kiwanis; Jaycees; Knights of Columbus; Big Brothers of America; 1983 Jaycees "Young Public Servant of the Year Award," 1983; 1985 Monroeville Chamber of Commerce Citizen Service Award; elected to the House of Representatives, Nov. 2, 1982; reelected 1984, 1986; home address: 436 Blackberry Dr., Monroeville.

DAVID J. MAYERNIK   **Allegheny County — 29th District**

David J. Mayernik (D) was born June 15, 1952, in Pgh., the son of Joseph and Ludmilla Mayernik; Community Coll. of Alleg. Co. (A.A.) 1972; Univ. of Pgh. (B.A.) 1974, (M.Pub. Admn.); Alpha Kappa Honor Society, 1972; F.O.P.; frmr. councilman (2 terms), frmr. committeeman, West View Boro.; Most Outstanding Law Enforcement Officer, 1979; NRA Police Firearms Instructor; Alleg. Co. Police Acad. instructor, 1977-present; chrt. mem., Ross/West View Emergency Medical Service; exec. bd. of dir., Pa. St. Councilman's Assn.; bd. gov., North Hills Art Festival; mem., Pgh. Adv. Council on Regional Development; rec., 1984 North Hill's Jaycees Good Gov. Award; 1983 Outstanding Young Man in America; elected to the House of Representatives, Nov. 2. 1982; reelected 1984, 1986; single; address: Pittsburgh.

KEITH R. McCALL   **Carbon and Monroe Counties — 122nd District**

Keith R. McCall (D) was born Dec. 16, 1959, in Coaldale, the son of the former Representative Thomas J. and Mary Ann Guardiani McCall; att. Pa. St. Univ., 1977-78; H.A.C.C., 1979-81; Dept. of Auditor General, 1978-82; Elks; Italian Club; Lehighton Area Jaycees; Summit Hill Diligence Fire Co.; pres., Irish American Assn.; Natl. Rifle Assn.; C of C; American Legion Award, 1973; elected to the House of Representatives, Nov. 2, 1982; reelected 1984, 1986; single; home address: 336 W. Ludlow St., Summit Hill.

RICHARD A. McCLATCHY, JR.

Republican Appropriations Chairman
Montgomery County — 149th District

Richard A. McClatchy, Jr. (R) was born Nov. 6, 1929, in Ardmore, the son of Richard A. McClatchy, Sr., and Gertrude Wilson McClatchy; Malvern Preparatory Schl., 1948; Coll. of the Holy Cross, 1949; Univ. of Pa. (B.S.) 1952; Navy, Lieut. j.g., 1952-54; worked in family home-building and land-developing business since 1954; commissioner, Lower Merion Twp., 1965-69; Ardmore Rotary since 1967; Main Line C. of C.; elected to House of Representatives, 1968; reelected to 9 successive terms; married Marianne Gorham; 2 children: Marianne and Brian; home address: 647 Heatherwood Road, Rosemont.

PAUL McHALE

Lehigh County — 133rd District

Paul McHale (D) was born July 26, 1950, in Bethlehem, the son of Paul and Mary Wynne McHale; Lehigh Univ. (B.A., highest honors); Phi Beta Kappa; Georgetown Univ. Law Center (J.D.); Capt., U.S. Marine Corps Active: 1972-74, Reserve: 1974-present; attorney; admitted to practice: Pa. Supreme Court, U.S. Court of Appeals (3rd Circuit); American Legion; Fountain Hill Exchange Club; Lehigh Co. Historical Society; Marine Corps Assn.; Marine Corps League; Reserve Officers Assn. of America; Marine Corps Reserve Officers Assn.; Pa. Sierra Club; Lehigh Univ. Alumni Assn., 1972-present; Fountain Hill Planning Comm., 1977-80; Lehigh Co. Young Democrats, 1978-present; Lehigh Co. Executive Democratic Com., 1980-82; Democratic Coordinator, 133rd Dist., 1980-82; Pi Sigma Alpha; adjunct professor, Northampton Co. Community Coll., 1981; Pa. Commission on Sentencing, 1983-1987; elected to the House of Representatives, Nov. 2, 1982; reelected 1984, 1986; married Katherine Pecka; 1 child, Matthew Cornwell; home address: 523 Eighth Avenue, Bethlehem.

TERRENCE F. McVERRY

Allegheny County — 42nd District

Terrence F. McVerry (R) was born on Sept. 16, 1943, in Pgh., the son of Thomas L. and Anna A. Fritch McVerry; Duquesne Univ. (B.A.) 1965, Duquesne Univ. Schl. of Law (J.D.) 1968; U.S. Army Reserves, 1968-69; Capt., Pa. Air Natl. Guard, 1969-74; attorney, private practice 1968-present; Allegheny, Pa. and Am. Bar Assns.; Am. Arbitration Assn.; Duquesne Univ. Alumni Assn.; frmr. asst. dist. attny., Allegheny Co., 1969-73; mem., Pa. Comm. of Sentencing; elected to the House of Representatives in 1978; reelected 1980, 1982, 1984, 1986; married Judith M. Kausek; 3 children: Erin Kathleen, Bryan James, Bridget Anne; home address: 46 Ordale Blvd., Mt. Lebanon.

ANTHONY J. MELIO

Bucks County — 141st District

Anthony J. Melio (D) was born May 13, 1932, in Trenton, N.J., the son of Joseph A. Melio (dec.), Dorothy Tabilio Melio Trauagline and Leonard Trauagline, Sr. (stepfather); grad., Trenton Central H.S.; U.S. Naval Reserve, 1949-59; steelworker; appt. by Gov. Shapp, Southeast Regional Planning Council, Gov.'s Justice Comm.; reappt. to Council and Pa. Crime & Delinquency by Gov. Thornburgh; 4th Deg. Knights of Columbus; St. Michael the Archangel Ushers Soc., Levittown; elected to the House of Representatives on Nov. 4, 1986; married Anna May Muha; 3 children: Mark, Jay, Sheri; home address: 25 Begonia Lane, Levittown.

JAMES R. MERRY   **Crawford and Erie Counties — 5th District**

James R. Merry (R) was born in Andover, Ohio, the son of Ralph S. and Verna Crom Merry; grad., Linesville H.S.; General Motors Inst. of Tech., 1949; U.S. Army, 1945-46; business, Western Auto Store, Linesville; Pymatuning Sportsman Club; Franklin Club; N. Shore Boat Club; Zem Zem Shrine AAONMS; Valley of Erie Consistory; Northwestern Commandry No. 25; Pine Lodge 498 F. & A.M.; Samuel Wright Post 462 Am. Legion; Linesville Grange 694; Co. 38 St. Police of Crawford and Erie Cos.; Linesville Borough Council, 1959-71; Crawford Co. Industrial Auth., 1972-85; dir., Sr. Citizen Housing Devel. (PALFUND) 1969-85; dir., Linesville Area C. of C., 1958-59, 1979-80; elected to the House of Representatives, Nov. 1980; reelected 1982, 1984, 1986; married June A. Robinson; 3 children: Jill, Jan, Jon; home address: 316 S. Mercer St., Linesville.

THOMAS A. MICHLOVIC   **Allegheny County — 35th District**

Thomas A. Michlovic (D) was born Feb. 21, 1946, in Braddock, the son of Peter A. and Elizabeth Metrisin Michlovic; Univ. of Pgh., (B.A., pol. sci.) 1972, (M.P.A., public admn.) 1976; U.S. Army, July 1967-April 1969; Purple Heart, Combat Infantry Badge; Catholic; Amnesty International; Braddock Rotary; Common Cause; Vietnam Veteran's Inc.; bd. mem., Eastern Area Adult Services; Braddock Field Historical Soc.; President's Award, Pa. Assn. MH/MR Providers; elected to the House of Representatives, 1978; reelected 1980, 1982, 1984, 1986; married Gwen Thomas; home address: 515 Verona St., North Braddock.

NICHOLAS ANTHONY MICOZZIE   **Delaware County — 163rd District**

Nicholas Anthony Micozzie (R) was born Sept. 7, 1930, the son of Camillo and Josephine Maffei Micozzie; St. Joseph's Coll. (B.S., business) 1963; att. Villanova Univ.; U.S. Air Force, 1950-54; engineer, real estate; Knights of Columbus, Council #590; Italian Am. Club; Westbrook Park Boy's Club; Holy Cross CYO; Upper Darby commissioner (councilman), 1971-present; Knight of the Year Award, K of C; editor, Council #590 monthly newspaper; Grand Knight, DeLaSalle Council; pres., Home Assn. of DeLaSalle; elected to the House of Representatives in 1978; reelected 1980, 1982, 1984, 1986; married June Marie Howard; 3 children: Kathleen M. Micozzie O'Conner, Thomas N. Micozzie, Kelley Ann Micozzie; home address: 278 Westpark Lane, Clifton Heights.

MARVIN E. MILLER JR.   **Lancaster County — 96th District**

Marvin E. Miller Jr. (R) was born Dec. 13, 1945, in Lancaster, the son of Marvin E. and Arlene L. Miller; att. Manheim Twp. H.S., 1963; Temple Univ., 1972; U.S. Air Force, 1964-68; resident counselor, Lancaster Cleft Palate Clinic and H. K. Cooper Research Inst.; bd. dir., Goodwill Industries of Lancaster Co., chmn., Bd. Rehabilitation Com., 1972-82; bd. dir., Pa. Higher Ed. Assistance Agency, chmn.-Need Analysis Com., mem.-Executive Nominations Com., 1975-pres.; bd. dir., Urban League Guild of Lancaster, mem.-Public Relations Com., 1978-pres.; bd. trustees, Linden Hall Academy for Women, 1982-pres.; bd. dir., Lancaster Co. Chap., Natl. Council for the Prevention of Child Abuse, 1985-pres.; Millersville Univ. Award, 1975; H.K. Cooper Ser. Award, 1980; Lancaster Jaycees Good Govt. Award, 1981; Natl. Adoption Exchange Award, 1984; elected to the House of Representatives in 1972; reelected 7 successive terms; 1 son, Russell Hamilton; home: Lancaster.

NICHOLAS B. MOEHLMANN   **Lancaster and Lebanon Counties**
                                                              102nd District

Nicholas B. Moehlmann (R) was born July 26, 1938, in Reading, the son of Ernst O. and Helen Moehlmann; Yale Univ. (B.A.) 1960; Dickinson Law Schl. (J.D.) 1970; attorney; U.S. Army Intelligence Corps, NCO, Am. Consulate General, Bremen, Germany, 1961-64; staff mem., Speaker's Office, Pa. House of Representatives, 1964, 1968, 1969; industrial sales, SCM Corp., Reading, 1965-66; auditor, Richland Borough, 1968-74; frmr. solicitor, Millcreek Twp.; frmr. solicitor, Millcreek-Richland Regl. Police Dept.; Newmanstown Fire Co., Post 880 Am. Legion, v. pres., and frmr. pres., Lebanon Co. Young Republicans; Republican committeeman, Richland Borough, 1971-73; 1983, Natl. Conf. of State Leg. Task Force on Refugees and Immigration; 1981-82, bd. dir., Gen. State Auth.; elected to the House of Representatives, 1974; reelected 6 successive terms; home address: 16 Chestnut St., Richland.

SAMUEL W. MORRIS   **Chester County — 155th District**

Samuel W. Morris (D) was born Aug. 21, 1918, in Atlantic City, N.J., the son of Samuel W. and Barbara Warden Morris; Harvard Coll. (B.S.) 1940; Univ. of Pa. Law Sch. (J.D.) 1949; U.S. Army, WW II, Capt., Corp of Engineers; farmer, lawyer; Chester Co. Bar Assn.; Episcopalian; exec. bd., Chester Co. Council, BSA; dir., French & Pickering Creeks Conservation Trust; bd. mem., Project Together; dir., Kimberton Farms Sch.; mem. of the House of Representatives, 1971-78; reelected 1980, 1982, 1984, 1986; married Eleanor May Jones; 7 children, 10 grandchildren; home address: Box 360, R.D. 2, Pottstown.

HAROLD F. MOWERY, JR.   **Cumberland County — 87th District**

Harold F. Mowery, Jr. (R) was born Jan. 4, 1930, in Chambersburg, the son of Harold F. and Mary Strohm Mowery; Dickinson Coll. (B.A.) 1954; Chartered Life Underwriter, 1966; insurance business; Camp Hill Schl. Dir. (past pres.), 1969-76; past pres.: Estate Planning Council, Genl. Agents and Managers Assn.; Phi Delta Theta natl. fraternity; Masonic order, Zembo Temple; Trinity Evangelical Lutheran Ch.; articles published in various insurance journals; Tri-Co. Chmn., Am. Cancer Society; Bd. of Adv., West Shore, Commonwealth Natl. Bank; prime sponsor, legis. that created Public Employee Retirement Comm.; elected to the House of Representatives, 1976; reelected 5 successive terms; married Phyllis Shearer; 3 children: Harold F. III, Theodore W., Phyllis Denise; home address: 2849 Vista Circle, Camp Hill.

EMIL MRKONIC   **Allegheny and Westmoreland Counties — 37th District**

Emil Mrkonic (D) was born in McKeesport, the son of Mr. and Mrs. Matthew Mrkonic; Univ. of Pgh. (B.A., pol. sci.); Natl. Honor Society and Phi Eta Sigma hnry. fraternity; overseas veteran, WW II; McKeesport Democratic Comm. chmn., 1970 to present; Alumnus, McKeesport Boys Club; past mem., Un. Steelworkers of Am., Local #1408; v. pres., Sacred Heart Ch. Choir; Am.-Croatian Beneficial Club Dobrotvor; Am. Legion Post #361; Am. Vets Post #8; Loyal Order of Moose; K of C #955; Catholic War Vets #1559; 11th Ward Welfare Assn. of McKeesport; 6th Ward Athletic Club of McKeesport; bd. dir., Boys Club of W. Pa.; rec., McKeesport Athletic Sportsmen's Assn. Award; the Good Govt. Award by Phi Alpha Delta Law Fraternity of Duquesne Univ.; Natl. Commanders Disting. Service Award by Am. Veterans of World War II, Korea and Vietnam; the Knights of Columbus merit award; elected to the House of Representatives in 1974; reelected 6 successive terms; home address: 516 Rebecca St., McKeesport.

THOMAS J. MURPHY, JR.   **Allegheny County — 20th District**

Thomas J. Murphy, Jr. (D) was born Aug. 15, 1944, in Pgh., the son of Thomas and Rose Scanlon Murphy; John Carroll Univ. (B.S., biology) 1967; Hunter Coll. (M.S., urban studies) 1973; legislator; Alpha Sigma Nu (Jesuit Hon. Frat.); Knights of Equity; trustee, St. John's Hospital; bd. dir., Northside Civic Council; bd. dir., Buhl Science Center; bd. dir., Am. Wind Symphony; bd. mem., Ben Franklin Partnership; bd. mem., Lawrenceville Development Corp.; trustee, The Carnegie; Lawrenceville Meal on Wheels; frmr. Peace Corps volunteer; elected to the House of Representatives in 1978; reelected 1980, 1982, 1984, 1986; married Mona McMahon; 2 children: Shannan, Molly; home address: 2210 Perrysville Ave., Pittsburgh.

CHARLES F. NAHILL, JR.   **Montgomery County — 154th District**

Charles F. Nahill, Jr. (R) was born Nov. 12, 1938, in Phila., the son of Charles F. (dec'd.) and Eleanor Newnham Nahill; Germantown Acad. 1956; Coll. of William & Mary (A.B.) 1960; Temple Univ. (M.B.A.) 1966; U.S. Army, 1961-63; elected treas., Cheltenham Twp., 1970-78; Natl. Municipal Treasurer's Assn.; Kappa Sigma; Lions Club, bd. mem., Charter mem., since 1979; Cancer Society-Cheltenham Unit, bd. mem., 1974-81, pres., 1974-78; Wyncote Mens Club, pres., 1975-76; William & Mary Alumni Society, pres., 1970-72; Outstanding Young Men of Am. Award, 1972; coach, Old York Road Little League, 1971-74; Northwoods Community Assn., 1963-79; bd. mem., 1976-77; bd. mem., Montgomery Co. Comm. Services Planning Council 1979-86; Presbyterian; elected to the House of Representatives in 1978; reelected 1980, 1982, 1984, 1986; married Joanne C. Buggy; 3 children: Julie L., Kristin G., G. Bradley; home address: 26 Poe Ave., Wyncote.

FRED C. NOYE   **Republican Caucus Chairman**
Cumberland and Perry Counties — 86th District

Fred Charles Noye (R) was born May 13, 1946, in Duncannon, the son of Charles A. and Marie H. Noye; H.A.C.C. (A.A.) 1966; Mansfield Univ. (B.S.) 1968; Mansfield Univ. Alumni Exec. Comm.; Shippensburg Univ. (M.Ed.) 1970; frmr. mem., Shippensburg Univ. Alumni Assn.; bd. of managers, Holy Spirit Hospital; bd. dir., Carson Long Institute; sec., New Bloomfield Lions Club; Perry County Historians; frmr. teacher, Cumberland Valley Schl. Dist.; full time legislator; Republican Caucus Chmn.; bd. dirs., Perry Co. Cancer Soc.; nat'l. bd. dirs., Am. Legislative Exchange Council; Perry Co. Historical Soc.; Masonic bodies; Perry Co., Pa. Farmers Assn.; Shermanata, Perry Co. Pomona Grange; Tressler Lutheran Ch., Loysville; elected to the House of Representatives in 1972; reelected to 7 successive terms; married Debra Kay Freeman; 2 sons: Jeremy Wade and Andrew Charles; home address: 15 West High St., New Bloomfield.

DENNIS M. O'BRIEN   **Philadelphia County — 169th District**

Dennis M. O'Brien (R) was born June 22, 1952, in Phila., the son of Elmer and Patricia Cunningham O'Brien; LaSalle Coll. (B.S.); Fraternal Order of Police Assn.; Knights of Columbus; Irish Society; Phila. Emerald Society; Catholic Historical Society; adv. bd., Cora Services; adv. bd , Frankford Hospital; elected to the House of Representatives, 1976; reelected 1978, 1982, 1984, 1986; home address: 9805 Academy Rd., Philadelphia.

ROBERT W. O'DONNELL
Democratic Whip
Philadelphia County — 198th District

Robert W. O'Donnell (D) was born Sept. 25, 1943, in Phila., the son of Robert H. and Ruth Durand O'Donnell; Temple Univ. (B.A.) 1966; Temple Univ. Law School (J.D.) 1969; att. Hague Academy of Intl. Law, Netherlands; Milrite Council, 1979-82; Public Empl. Retire. Study Comm., 1982-84; Phila. Criminal Justice Coordinating Comm., 1984-85; Phila. Port Corp., bd. of dirs., 1984-85; Bipartisan Mgt. Com., 1983-87; General State Authority, 1983-85; Chesapeake Bay Comm., 1986-87; chmn., House Select Com. to Investigate the Problems of Teenage Pregnancies and Parenting in Pa., 1986; co-chair, New Member Orientation Prog., 1984, 1986; chmn., Legis. Organization and Mgmt. Com., Law and Justice Com., Task Force on State Housing Policies, Natl. Conf. of State Legislatures, 1985-87; chmn., Dem. Caucus, 1981-82; Majority Whip, 1983-87; elected to the House of Representatives in May, 1974; reelected to 7 successive terms; married Louise Ellen D'Alessandro; 2 children; home address: 414 W. Chelten Ave., Philadelphia.

RICHARD D. OLASZ
Allegheny County — 38th District

Richard D. Olasz (D) was born June 14, 1930, in Homestead, the son of John S. (dec.) and Helen Masters Olasz; Univ. of Pgh. (B.S.) 1958; U.S. Coast Guard, 1951-54, Disabled Vet., Korean War; West Mifflin Borough Council, 1972-80; past pres., West Mifflin Police Pension Bd.; mem., D.A.V., Elks; exec. bd., Resurrection Ch.; bd. dir., West Mifflin North Boosters; elected to the House of Representatives in 1980; reelected 1982, 1984, 1986; married Marie Dugan; 4 children: Mary Ann, Helen, Danny, Elizabeth; home address: 105 Fifth Ave., West Mifflin.

FRANK L. OLIVER
Philadelphia County — 195th District

Frank L. Oliver (D) was born in Phila., the son of James and Lessie Palmer Oliver; grad., Dobbins Vocatl. Schl.; frmr. supervisor, Food Service Division, Phila. Bd. of Education; frmr. dpty. sheriff; frmr. electrician, Phila. Dept. of Welfare; frmr. chmn. for Democratic registration; Democratic Ward Leader - 29th Ward, Phila. County; life-time mem., NAACP; trustee, Wayland Temple Baptist Ch.; internatl. pres., Emblem Club, YMCA; treas., Model Cities Neighborhood Council 13; elected to the House of Representatives in special election, Nov. 6, 1973, took office Nov. 15, 1973; reelected 7 successive terms; chmn., Pa. Legislative Black Caucus, 1981-82; majority chmn., State Government Comm., 1983-present; married Wilma Wooden; 3 children: Shawn, Frank Jr., Donna (deceased); home address: 1319 N. 29th St., Philadelphia.

JOHN MICHAEL PERZEL
Philadelphia County — 172nd District

John Michael Perzel (R) was born Jan. 7, 1950, in Phila., the son of Michael J. and Susan Mary DeLaTour Perzel; Enterprise St. Jr. Coll., Ala. (A.A.) 1972; Troy St. Univ., Ala. (B.S.); Gettysburg Coll.; Temple Univ.; Auburn Univ.; 64th Ward Rep. Ex. Comm., 1972; ward chmn., 1975; ward leader, 1978-85; Catholic; rec., Highest Repub. Registration in Phila. Award, 1974, 1975; v. pres., Jr. Coll.; pres., Inter Club Council; elected to the House of Representatives in 1978; reelected 1980, 1982, 1984, 1986; married Sheryl Stokes, Feb. 12, 1984; 3 children: Andrew, David, John Jr.; home address: 7810 Brous Ave., Philadelphia.

JOSEPH A. PETRARCA   Westmoreland County — 55th District

Joseph A. Petrarca (D) was born in Vandergrift, the son of Ercole and Marie Petrarca; att. Vandergrift H.S.; grad., Carnegie Coll., Cleveland, Oh., 1955; medical technologist; steelworker; U.S. Army, Korean Conflict; United Steelworkers Union, Local 1388; local COPE Comm.; North Westmoreland Co. Labor Council; life mem., Am. Legion; DAV; Lions Club; BPOE; ISDA; Thomas Jefferson Lodge, Am. Club; SOI, Marconi Club; Sportsman's Club; NRA; George G. McMurtry Vol. Fire Co.; Vandergrift Fire Co. #2; Westmoreland Co. Firemen's Assn.; 7th degree mem., Grange, Bell Twp.; trustee, United Way of Pa.; United Fund Bd. of Dirs., Citizen of the Year; VFW of the No. Westmoreland Co. Dist.; Distinguished Serv. Award, Disabled Am. Vets.; chmn., Pa. Legis. Italian - American Caucus; elected to House of Representatives in 1972; reelected 7 successive terms; married Madeline Biagoni; son and daughter.

THOMAS CHARLES PETRONE   Allegheny County — 27th District

Thomas Charles Petrone (D) was born July 31, 1937, in Pgh., the son of Frank A. (dec.) and Julia Visco Petrone; Crafton H.S., 1955; Carnegie Tech. and Pgh. Playhouse, 1955-56; Industrial Water Treatment, 1965; U.S. Navy, 1956-58; sales management and public relations, 20 yrs.; World Water Society; ISDA; PNA; V-PAC; Am. Legion; Olympic Club; Pulaski Club; Crafton Hgts. Athletic Assn.; Crafton Hgts. Community Council; Allegheny Co. Democratic Comm., 16 yrs.; rec., Hearst Newspaper Oration Award, Sales and Merchandising Man of the Year 1975; elected to the House of Representatives, Nov. 1980; reelected 1982, 1984, 1986; married Marlene Ricchiuto; 2 children: Dean Thomas, Christa Marie; home address: 1462 Barr Ave., Pittsburgh.

MERLE H. PHILLIPS   Montour, Northumberland and Snyder Counties
                                                                    108th District

Merle H. Phillips (R) was born Sept. 21, 1928, the son of Fred A. and Maude Witmer Phillips; Lower Mahanoy Twp. H.S.; att. Susquehanna Univ.; Marine Corp., over 4 yrs. active duty, 2 yrs., Reserves; pres., Irish Valley Food Processing, Inc.; treas., chmn., Emmanuel Bible Fellowship Ch.; mem. bd. trustees, Sunbury Community Hospital; bd. dirs., YMCA; mem., Gideon Int'l., Kiwanis; bd. of trustees, Lung Assn.; elected to the House of Representatives in special election, April 1980; reelected Nov. 1980, 1982, 1984, 1986; married Helen L. Heckert; 5 children; home address: R.D. 2 - Box 326, Sunbury.

JEFFREY E. PICCOLA   Dauphin County — 104th District

Jeffrey E. Piccola (R) was born May 16, 1948, in Harrisburg, the son of Anthony J. and Betty Jane Early Piccola; Gettysburg Coll. (B.A.) 1970; George Washington U. Law Schl. (J.D.) 1973; AFROTC, 1968-70; USAF Reserves, 1970-74; attorney; Pa., Dauphin Co. Bar Assns.; Susquehanna Twp. Lions Club; Sons of Italy, Capital City Lodge; mem., Progress Immanuel Presbyterian Ch., ruling elder; elected to the House of Representatives, 1976; reelected to 5 successive terms; married Denise Jane Naill; 2 children: Jason E. and Jenny N.; home address: 3817 Hillcrest Rd., Harrisburg.

MAX PIEVSKY   Democratic Appropriations Chairman
                                                  Philadelphia County — 174th District

Max Pievsky (D) was born July 4, 1925, in Phila., the son of Morris and Bessie Dockler Pievsky; att. Phila. public schls., Central H.S. and the Schl. of Business Administration; legislator; Equity Lodge; F&AM; Ludwig Lodge; B'nai B'rith; Steuben Lodge, Knights of Pythias; Circle Square Club; Pannonia Beneficial Assn.; frmr. Constable, 54th Ward, elected in 1957, reelected 1963; frmr. special investigator, Pa. Dept. of Revenue; committeeman, 4th Division, 54th Ward; Ward Leader, 54th Ward Democratic Exec. Comm.; Temple Sholom Congregation and the Men's Club; elected to House of Representatives in 1966; reelected to 10 successive terms; Democratic chmn., House Appropriations Comm., 1977 to present; married Shirley Rabinowitz on June 3, 1945; 2 children; home address: 6230 Everett St., Philadelphia.

FRANK J. PISTELLA   Allegheny County — 21st District

Frank J. Pistella (D) was born April 22, 1951, son of Rita B. Kineavy Pistella and Frank J. Pistella Jr. (dec'd); John Carroll Univ., Ohio, 1973; legislator; Allegheny Co. Democratic Comm.; Italian Sons and Daughters of Am.; adv. bd., Ursuline Center, Inc.; bd. dir., Louise Child Care Center; bd. dir., Bach Choir; Loyal Order of Moose; Lions Club; Orpheus Singing Society; Outstanding Young Men of America, 1982, 1984; St. Lawrence O'Toole Parish; elected to the House of Representatives in 1978; reelected 1980, 1982, 1984, 1986; home address: 231 S. Pacific Ave., Pittsburgh.

JOSEPH R. PITTS   Chester County — 158th District

Joseph R. Pitts (R) was born Oct. 10, 1939, in Lexington, Ky., the son of Joseph and Pearl Jackson Pitts; Asbury Coll. (A.B.) 1961; West Chester Univ.(M.Ed.) 1972; legislator; U.S. Air Force, Captain, 6 yrs.; Strategic Air Command; Vietnam Veteran, awarded Air Medal with five Oak Leaf Clusters; high schl. science teacher, 5 yrs.; Kennett Square Rotary; Willowdale Chapel; legislative founder, Keystone State Games; 1st chmn. Capitol Preservation Committee; elected to House of Representatives in 1972; reelected 7 successive terms; married Virginia M. Pratt; 3 children; home address: 905 Mitchell Farm Lane, Kennett Square.

JOHN F. PRESSMANN   Lehigh County — 132nd District

John F. Pressmann (D) was born Sept. 6, 1952, in Salisbury, Md., the son of Edward F. and Patricia Bartholemew Pressmann; Allentown Central Catholic; Lehigh Co. Comm. Coll.; Cedar Crest Coll.; v. pres., Allentown Sertoma Club; Travelers Protective Assn.; Dem. Committeeman, 1974-78; Constable, 1980-81; Co. Commissioner, 1982-84; st. v. pres., Young Democrats; sec., Lehigh Valley Dem. Assn.; rec., Young Democrats Leadership Award; elected to the House of Representatives in 1984; reelected 1986; married Deborah Couto; 3 children: Sean, Laura, Daniel; home address: 405 Washington St., Allentown.

JOSEPH PRESTON, JR.   Allegheny County — 24th District

Joseph Preston, Jr. (D) was born May 28, 1947, in New Kensington, the son of Joseph and Therese Mae Buckner Preston; att. Wilberforce Univ; grad., Univ. of Pgh. (B.A., pol. sci., psych.) 1979; bd.mem., Allegheny Academy; Pittsburgh Water and Sewer Auth.; bd. dirs., Homewood Brushton Revitalization Corp.; mem., Pgh. Elks Lodge, IBPOE of W; mem., adv. council, Adoption Council; mem., Natl. Conf. of Black St. Legislators, Natl. Conf. of St. Legislators; mem., NAACP and many more; elected to the House of Representatives, Nov. 2, 1982; reelected 1984, 1986; married Odelfa Smith; 2 children: Joseph, III and Diana; home address: 732 Dunmore St., Pittsburgh.

TERRY PUNT   Franklin and Fulton Counties — 90th District

Terry Lee Punt (R) was born Aug. 13, 1949, in Waynesboro, foster son of Raymond and Pearl Newcomer Sharrah; att. Waynesboro schls., Univ. of Maryland; U.S. Army, 1967-70; legislator; Franklin Co. Assn. for Retarded Children; Am. Legion; VFW; Waynesboro Sportsman Assn.; Loyal Order of Moose; chmn., Waynesboro Bicentennial Comm.; past pres., Waynesboro Lions Club; bd. of dirs., YMCA; First Christian Ch.; Pa. Assn. Retarded Children; Outstanding Young Man of 1979; Future Business Leaders of America-Natl. Repub. Comm.; bd. of dirs., OSI for Physically Handicapped; chmn., Waynesboro Youth Activities Assn.; Protestant; elected to the House of Representatives in 1978; reelected 1980, 1982, 1984, 1986; home address: Waynesboro.

RONALD C. RAYMOND   Delaware County — 162nd District

Ronald C. Raymond (R) was born on May 10, 1951, in Chester, the son of Ollie Eggers Raymond and Don Raymond (dec.); Sharon Hill H.S., 1969; Widener Univ.; real estate agent; mem., Del. Co. Board of Realtors; Rep. Committeeman, Folcroft Boro., 1973-76; frmr. councilman, Folcroft Boro., 1976; mem., Sharon Hill Rep. Com., 1978-81; chmn., Rep. Com., Sharon Hill; mem., Sharon Hill Boro. Council, 1978-81; Mayor of Sharon Hill, 1981-84; frmr. chmn., Southeastern Del. Co. Young Republicans; alternate delegate to Republican National Convention, 1976; elected to the House of Representatives in Nov. 1984; reelected 1986; married Michelle Homyak; 2 children: Jennifer and Ron, Jr.; home address: 900 Chester Pike, Sharon Hill.

ROBERT DOUGLASS REBER, JR.   Montgomery County — 146th District

Robert Douglass Reber, Jr. (R) was born June 19, 1947, in Pottstown, the son of Robert D. (dec.) and Virginia Stetler Reber; Pottsgrove H.S., 1965; Susquehanna Univ. (B.A.) 1969; Univ. of Akron Schl. of Law (J.D.) 1972; Akron Law Review; attorney; Montgomery Co., Pa., Am. Bar Assns.; Lambda Chi Alpha; past pres., Pottsgrove Lions Club; St. James Lutheran Ch.; author, "Right of Indigent Juvenile to Transcript at State Expense," Akron Law Review; elected to the House of Representatives, Nov. 1980; reelected 1982, 1984, 1986; home address: 715 Norbury Ct., Pottstown.

ROY REINARD   **Bucks County — 178th District**

Roy Reinard (R) was born Nov. 23, 1954, in Phila., the son of Roy and Ethel Walters Reinard; West Chester Univ. (B.S.) 1977; Certified Insurance Counselor; Reinard Insurance Agency; auditor, Northampton Twp., 1982; elected to the House of Representatives, Nov. 2, 1982; reelected 1984, 1986; married Cynthia Miller; 1 child, Roy IV; home address: 32 Pond View Drive, Richboro.

DAVID P. RICHARDSON, JR.   **Philadelphia County — 201st District**

David P. Richardson, Jr. (D) was born April 23, 1948, in Phila., son of Elaine and David P. Richardson, Sr.; Grmntwn. Sr. H.S., 1965; frmr. printing apprentice, insurance agent, anesthe. aide, recreation spec.; exec. dir., bd. mem. Grtr. Grmntwn. Youth Corp., 1968-72; past bd. mem: Grmntwn. branch, Young Afro-Americans; Grmntwn. Settlement; E. Grmntwn. Adv. Council; Northwest Polit. Caucus; bd. mem.: LaSalle Urban Studies Ctr.; Martin Luther King Scholarship Fund; Minority Ed. and Group Training Laboratories Inc.; Natl. Assn. Blacks in Criminal Justice; ADA; exec. comm. 12th ward, 2nd div.; Governor's Justice Comm., Comm. on Crime Preven.; bd. chmn., Camp Timerlake Charities Inc.; Natl. Caucus of Black St. Legislators; affiliated, Black United Front and Natl. Black Independent Party; numerous service, appre. awards: Outstanding Young Man of America, 1976; Phila. Ministry; Omega Psi Phi Man of Year; Citi. Comm. on Public Ed.'s Outstanding Alum.; NAACP; Wm. H. Gray Jr. Outstanding Service; "Hell No to Charter Change" Lewisburg branch NAACP; Mantu; House of Umoja Comm. Involvement, all 1978; Shiloh Apostolic Temple cert. of appre., 1979; Women in Education, 1983; Cafe D'Elegance, 1984; Alliance of Black Social Workers, 1984; Valiante, Inc., 1984; Mary David Balto Award, Pa. Black Conf. on Higher Ed., 1984; Black United Fund, 1983; Urban League of Phila., 1985; "Child Safety Week" award, Holy Cross Lutheran Day Care Center, 1985; Respect Yourself Class Award (Blackness at its Best), Westpark Hospital, 1985; exception volunteer contribution, Pa. Farmworker Opportunities; Certificate of the Elect, House of Representatives, 1985; Hon. Lieut. Col. Aide-de-Camp, Gov. of Alabama, 1984; Men's Fellowship Club award, St. Simon The Cyrenian P.E. Ch., 1985; Harriet Tubman Humanitarian Service award, Original Black Caucus PFT, 1985; Cub Pac 186; African Kings Plaque, 1985; Pa. Social Services Union; elected to the House of Representatives in 1973; reelected 7 successive terms; unmarried; home address: 5811 Chew Ave., Philadelphia.

WILLIAM W. RIEGER   **Philadelphia County — 179th District**

William W. Rieger (D) was born Nov. 2, 1922, in Phila., the son of Charles and Hannah Frances Rieger; grad., Simon Gratz H.S.; U.S. Army, WW II; Democratic committeeman, 43rd Ward, Phila. (26 yrs.); chmn., bd. of dirs., 43rd Ward Dem. Exec. Comm.; San Antonio Society; Am. Legion, Cpl. John Loudenslage Post 366; Franklin Delano Roosevelt Club; Civic Award, 43rd Ward Community Assn.; elected to House of Representatives in 1966, reelected to 10 successive terms; married Lucy Yacovetti on Oct. 24, 1942; 2 children: William J. Rieger, DDS; Mrs. Patricia Vittorelli; 2 grandchildren: Donna Lynn, Donald; home address: 1141 Rising Sun Ave., Philadelphia.

KAREN A. RITTER   **Lehigh County — 131st District**

Karen A. Ritter (D) was born Feb. 28, 1953, in Shirley, Ma., the daughter of James P. and Faye E. Morrissey Ritter; grad., L. E. Dieruff H.S. (Natl. Merit Scholar) 1971; Northampton Co. Area Comm. Coll. (paralegal cert.) 1978; legislator; formerly managed title insurance agencies; mem., Allentown City Council, 1982-86; mem.: Allentown Art Museum, Allentown League of Women Voters, Pa. Elected Women's Assn., Pa. Fed. of Democratic Women, Lehigh Valley Dem. Assn., Lehigh Valley Young Democrats; mem., past pres., Altrusa Club of Lehigh Valley; bd. dir., Girls Club of Allentown; mem., lector, Trinity Memorial Luthern Church; first daughter to follow father into legislature from same district; elected to the House of Representatives, Nov. 4, 1986; home address: 250 E. Elm St., Allentown.

ROBERT D. ROBBINS   Crawford and Mercer Counties — 17th District

Robert D. Robbins (R) was born Aug. 27, 1944, in Greenville, the son of Leo (dec.) and Twila Uber Robbins; U.S. Military Academy (B.S.) 1966; Masters work, East Stroudsburg Univ.; Geneva Coll., teaching certificate; U.S. Army, 1966-71; C of C; VFW, American Legion, B.P.O.E.; Fraternal Order of Eagles; Loyal Order of Moose; Masonic Lodge; Grange; Pa. Farmers Assn.; elected to the House of Representatives, Nov. 2, 1982; reelected 1984, 1986; married Cynthia Ann Duell; home address: 160 Sheakleyville-Greenville Road, Greenville.

JAMES R. ROEBUCK, JR.   Philadelphia County — 188th District

James Randolph Roebuck, Jr. (D) was born Feb. 12, 1945, in Phila., the son of James Randolph, Sr. and Cynthia Compton Roebuck; grad., Central H.S., 1963; Va. Union Univ. (B.A., with honors) 1966; Univ. of Va. (M.A.) 1969, (Ph.D.) 1977; lecturer, asst. prof., Drexel Univ., 1970-1984; legis. asst., Office of the Mayor, Phila., 1984-85; bd. dirs.: Am. Red Cross; Associated Alumni Assn. of Central H.S.; BSA (Conestoga Dist. Chmn., 1984-pres.); Southern Home; Spruce Hill Comm. Assn. (1st v. pres., 1984-85); Garden Court Comm. Assn.; Univ. of Va. Alumni Bd.; mem.: Marshall L. Shepard, Sr. Chap., Va. Union Univ. Alum. Assn. (pres., 1971-78); Mount Olivet Tabernacle Baptist Ch. (chmn., Bd. of Deacons, 1980-84 and 1987); Va. Club of Phila. (pres., 1984-86); rec. of awards fr: Va. Union Univ. Alum. Assn., 1973; United Negro Coll. Fund Alum., 1978; Chapel of Four Chaplains, 1980; Who's Who Among Black Americans, 1980-81; BSA, Conestoga Dist., 1982; Phila. Council BSA, 1986; rec., Pa. House of Rep.'s Cit., 1970; Phila. Art Alliance; Soc. for Historians of Am. Foreign Relations; Southern Historical Assn.; mem., Dem. Ward Ex. Comm., 60th Ward, 7th Div. (1974-76), 46th Ward, 25th Div. (1978-88), (lst v. chmn. 1984-86); Dem. State Com., 1984-88; elected to the Pa. House of Representatives in special election, May 21, 1985; reelected 1986; home address: 435 South 46th St., Philadelphia.

RUTH CORMAN RUDY   Centre and Mifflin Counties — 171st District

Ruth C. Rudy (D) was born Jan. 3, 1938, in Millheim, the daughter of Orvis and Mabel Stover Corman; Carnegie Inst. (x-ray tech.); Pa. St. Univ.; Bellefonte Bus. & Prof. Women's Club; Altrusa Club of St. Coll.; Prothonotary, Clerk of Cts., Centre Co., 1976-83; Democratic Natl. Comm. Women, 1980; reelected 1984; treas., Natl. Fed. of Democratic Women, 1981-1983; 1st v. pres., Nat'l. Fed. of Democratic Women, 1985, pres., 1987-; 2nd v. pres., Pa. Fed. of Democratic Women, 1980, pres., 1985-; delegate, Democratic Natl. Convention, 1980; Woman of the Year, Pa. Fed. of Democratic Women, 1982; elected to the House of Representatives, Nov. 2, 1982; reelected 1984, 1986; married C. Guy Rudy; 3 children: Douglas, Donita Rudy Koval, Dianna; home address: R.D. 1, Centre Hall.

MATTHEW J. RYAN   Republican Floor Leader
Delaware County — 168th District

Matthew J. Ryan (R) was born April 27, 1932, in Phila., the son of Thomas F. and Kathleen Mullin Ryan; att., St. Joseph's Preparatory Schl.; Villanova Univ. (B.S.) 1954, (J.D.) 1959; U.S. Marine Corps. 1st Lieut. 1954-56; attorney; elected to the House of Representatives in 1962; reelected to 12 successive terms; elected Minority Policy Comm. Chmn., 1970; elected Majority Whip, 1972; elected Minority Whip, 1974-1976; elected Majority Leader, 1978; elected Speaker of the House, 1981; elected Minority Leader, 1982, 1984, 1986; address: One S. Olive St., Media.

WILLIAM C. RYBAK   **Lehigh and Northampton Counties — 135th District**

William C. Rybak (D) was born Mar. 2, 1921, in New York City, the son of John and Katie Revotskie Rybak; Liberty H.S., 1942; Temple Univ. (B.S.) 1945; Univ. of Mississippi Schl. of Law (LL.B.) 1949, (J.D.) 1968; attorney; Northampton Co., Pa., Miss. Bar Assns.; St. Bernards R.C. Beneficial Society; Frat. Order of Eagles; Grover Cleveland Democratic Club; Hungarian Catholic Club; Bethlehem Schl. Dir., 1953-59, bd. pres., 1958-59; active mem., Grtr. Bethlehem Area Comm. for Employment of Handicapped, chrtr. mem. since 1956, chmn. 6 yrs. including 1980; founder and chmn., William C. Rybak Handicapped Childrens Fund Comm. (to provide prothesis or scholarships to needy area handicapped children); chmn., Heart Fund, 1970; Holy Name Society of St. Josephat's Ukranian Catholic Ch.; Northampton City Democratic Comm.; Pa. Handicapped Citizen of the Year, 1966; Benjamin Rush Award, 1967, by Northampton Co. Medical Society; 1983 Golden Charity Award for "Operation Overcome"; mem. of the House of Representatives, 1966-72; Nov. 1980, 1982, 1984, 1986; appt., chmn., House Insurance Com., 1985; reappt., 1987; married Louise D. Golab; 6 children: John, Mary, Margaret, Susan, Lucy, Anthony; home address: 1337 Easton Ave., Bethlehem.

EUGENE G. SALOOM   **Westmoreland County — 26th District**

Eugene G. Saloom (D) was born, Sept. 22, 1943, in Mt. Pleasant; the son of the late George and Isabelle Karfelt Saloom; grad., Pgh. Inst. of Mortuary Science, 1955; grad., Elon Coll., 1958; funeral director; mem.: B.P.O.E., L.O.O.M., C.S.A. and F. & A.M.; elected to the Pa. House of Representatives, 1966; served from 1967-76; mem., Mt. Pleasant Area Schl. Bd., 1980-83; reelected to House of Representatives, 1982; served from 1983 to pres.; chmn., Liquor Control Com., 1985-86, 1987-88; married Nancy Newill; two children: Charlene and Charles.

GEORGE E. SAURMAN   **Montgomery County — 151st District**

George E. Saurman (R) was born Jan. 15, 1926, in Houston, Tx., the son of Benjamin Franklin and Marcelene Borst Saurman; Upper Darby H.S., 1943; Ursinus Coll. (A.B.) 1950; U.S. Combat Infantryman, 1943-46; v. pres., Sellers, Kirk and Co., In.; Kiwanis Club; Ambler Borough Council, 1965-69; Mayor, Ambler Borough, 1969-80; Wissahickon Schl. Authority, 1965-80; Calvary Un. Methodist Ch.; Wissahickon Valley and Phila. Div. A.C.S.; Eagle Review Bd., B.S.A.; Disting. Service Award, Jaycees; Volunteer Achievement Award, A.C.S.; Wiss. Ed. Assn. Outstanding Service to Children; Chapel of Four Chaplains Award; Wiss. Schl. Dist. Community Service Award, 1983; Keystone Award, AAOP, 1983, 1984; Citizen of the Yr., Wissachickon Valley C of C, 1986; elected to the House of Representatives, Nov. 1980; reelected 1982, 1984, 1986; married Mary Ewen; 4 children: Nancy, Richard, George W., Robert; home address: 360 Mattison Ave., Ambler.

TERRY R. SCHEETZ   **Lancaster County — 99th District**

Terry R. Scheetz (R) was born Dec. 10, 1941, in Lancaster, the son of Edwin A. Scheetz and Mary Lilly; Delaware Valley Coll. (B.S.); farmer; Cocalico Area Schl. Bd., 1964-71; Republican Committeeman, 1978-82; W. Cocalico Twp. Planning Comm., 1978-present; PFA; elected to the House of Representatives, Nov. 2, 1982; reelected 1984, 1986; married Sandra Y. Bartsch; 1 child, Penny; home address: Box 65, Stevens.

JERE W. SCHULER   Lancaster County — 43rd District

Jere W. Schuler (R) was born Mar. 26, 1934, in Lancaster, the son of Charles E. and Reba Waddell Schuler; Millersville Univ. (B.S.) 1956; Westminster Coll., 1965; Temple Univ. (M.Ed.) 1962; Widener Univ., 1967; Univ. of Pa., 1968; U.S. Army Reserves, 1956-62; frmr. teacher; Phi Delta Kappa; chmn., E. Lampeter Twp. Planning Comm., 1970-73; chmn., W. Lampeter Twp. Planning Comm., 1975-77; sec./treas., bd. of supervisors, W. Lampeter Twp., 1977-82; sec., Inter-Municipal Gov. Comm., 1979-82; v. pres., Twp. Supervisors Assn. of Lancaster Co., 1980-82; Republican Area Chmn., 1978-82; v. chmn. Education, Lancaster Co. Republican Comm., 1979-82; admin. asst., Republican Co. Chmn., 1965-67; Teacher of the Year, Lampeter/Strasburg schl. dist., 1963; Baseball Coach of the year, Lancaster/Lebanon League, 1980, 1982; elected to the House of Representatives, Nov. 2, 1982; reelected 1984, 1986; married Margaret Newman; 2 children: Jere, Stephanie; home address: 1759 Pioneer Rd., Lancaster.

PAUL W. SEMMEL   Berks and Lehigh Counties — 187th District

Paul W. Semmel (R) was born Nov. 6, 1939, in Schnecksville, the son of Steward and Florence Heintzelman Semmel; Pa. St. Univ., (B.S.) 1961 Ag. Ed.; Delta Theta Sigma Fraternity; grad. studies, Pa. State Univ., Temple Univ.; farmer; educator; Pa. Farmers' Assn.; past pres., Lehigh Farmers; Holstein and Dairy Herd Assns.; bd. of dir., Northampton - Lehigh Co. Herd Improvement Assn.; frmr. St. dir., Pa. Holstein Assn.; frmr. co-chmn., Farm - City Activities Allentown - Lehigh Co. C of C; frmr. Leg. Coordinator, Lehigh Co. Farmers' Assn; frmr. mem., Farm & Home Admn. Comm.; frmr. teacher, Catasauqua Area Schl. Dist., CAEA; PSEA; frmr. mem., N. Whitehall Twp. Zoning Hearing Bd.; frmr. v.p., Parkland Area Jaycees; frmr. Councilman, Neffs Union Lutheran Ch.; Kutztown Univ. Nursing Dept. Advisory Comm.; elected to the House of Representatives, Nov. 2, 1982; reelected 1984, 1986; married Nancy J. Kemmerer; 3 children: Lisa, Andrea, Shannon; home address: 49 Excelsior Road, Schnecksville.

FRANK A. SERAFINI   Lackawanna County — 114th District

Frank A. Serafini (R) was born Feb. 15, 1945, in Taylor, the son of Louis and Dolores Ghigarelli Serafini; grad., Scranton Central H.S.; Univ. of Scranton (B.S., accounting) 1966; Bucknell Univ. (M.B.A., finance) 1968; New York Univ., Pa. St. Univ., Integrated Machines Bureau; U.S. Army Reserves, 1966-72; accountant; mem.: Nat'l. Assn. of Accountants; Elks Club; Rotary Club; author of *"Reflecting General Price Level Adjustments in Financial Statements";* elected to the House of Representatives in 1978; reelected 1980, 1982, 1984, 1986; home address: 603 Main St., Moosic.

STEVE SEVENTY   Allegheny County — 22nd District

Steve Seventy (D) was born June 12, in Pgh., son of Stefan Seventy and Mary Olesak; att. St. Matthew's and St. Michael's, Pgh.; Duquesne Univ.; U.S. Army, 1945-46, 179 AGF Band; bd. mem., Brashear Assn.; Am. Federation of Musicians; Pgh. Local; S.K. Sokol; Kollar Club; Polish Falcons; Moose; VFW; St. Matthew's Ch.; elected to the House of Representatives in 1978; reelected 1980, 1982, 1984, 1986; home address: 1910 Carson St., Pittsburgh.

JOHN SHOWERS   Snyder and Union Counties — 85th District

John Showers (D) was born April 12, 1952, in Danville, the son of Harlan F. and Jean Klase Showers; Mifflinburg Area H.S., 1970; American Univ. (B.A.) 1974; Univ of Pgh. (M.P.A.) 1980; elected Union Co. Commissioner, 1975; reelected 1979; mem: Messiah Evangelical Lutheran Ch.; New Berlin Lions Club; elected to the House of Representatives in 1980; reelected 1982, 1984, 1986; married Nancy Ross on May 28, 1983; resides with Nancy and her 3 children at 317 Vine St., New Berlin.

CARMEL A. SIRIANNI   Bradford, Susquehanna, Sullivan, and Wyoming Counties
111th District

Carmel A. Sirianni (R) was born Sept. 14, 1922, in Carbondale, daughter of John and Amelia Sirianni; moved to Hop Bottom, Susquehanna Co., 1927; Bloomsburg Univ. (bachelor's in business ed., English & social studies); Bucknell Univ. (master's in ed. and guidance); teacher (23 yrs.); guidance dir., asst. to principal, Mt. View Schl. Dist.; adm. asst. to House Speaker, 1967-74; v. chmn., 10th and 11th Congressional Dists. for Reagan-Bush '84 Campaign Com.; Fin. Com. for Pa. Republican State Committee; ex. bd., Pa. Rep. State Com.; past chmn., Susquehanna Co. Rep. Com.; past chmn., v. chmn., sec., Susquehanna Co. Rep. Com.; Hop Bottom Civic Club; Hop Bottom Planning Comm.; St. Patrick's Altar and Rosary Society; Susquehanna Co. Rep. Women; bd. of dirs., Northeastern Pa. Crippled Children's Society; bd. of dirs., Susquehanna Co. Cancer Society; bd., United Nations of Northeastern Pa.; Montrose Business and Professional Women; elected to House of Representatives in 1974; reelected 6 successive terms; home address: R.D. #1, Box 1A1, Montrose.

BRUCE I. SMITH, JR.   York County — 92nd District

Bruce I. Smith, Jr. (R) was born Feb. 19, 1934, in Harrisburg, the son of Bruce I. and Margaret M. Zerbe Smith; Elizabethtown Coll. (B.A.) 1956; Pa. St. Univ. (M.Ed.) 1961; U.S. Army, 1956-58; U.S. Army Reserves, 1958-62; frmr. teacher, Cedar Cliff H.S.; chmn., Recreation Bd., 1971-77, Planning Comm., 1978-80, chmn., Bd. of Supervisors, 1978-83, Newberry Twp.; Repub. Committeeman, 1976-80; pres., Newberry Twp. Repub. Club, 1974-75, 1977-78; dir., Salem Un. Methodist Ch., 1984-85; pres., Camp Hill Jaycees, 1966; York Men's Repub. Club; Junior Chamber Internatl. Senator, 1969; Outstanding Young Educator, 1968; Outstanding Young Man of Am., 1967; Goldsboro and Newberrytown Volunteer Fire Cos.; Brunner Island Public Adv. Comm.; N. York Co. Game and Fish Assn.; Greater West Shore Area Chamber of Commerce; dir., Red Land Sr. Citizens Center, 1982-87; Dillsburg Lions Club; dir., Dillsburg Senior Citizens Center, 1987; elected to the House of Representatives, Nov. 1980; reelected 1982, 1984, 1986; married Patricia A. Ninkovich; 2 children: Rhonda J., Renee N.; home address: 417 S. Baltimore St., Dillsburg.

SAMUEL H. SMITH   Indiana and Jefferson Counties
66th District

Samuel H. Smith (R) was born Aug. 10, 1955, in Punxsutawney, the son of L. Eugene and Jean Huey Smith; grad., Punxsutawney Area H.S., 1973; Pa. St. Univ. (B.A., adv.) 1978; mem.: YMCA, Chamber of Commerce, First Methodist Ch. of Punxsutawney; elected to the House of Representatives on Nov. 4, 1986; married Donna M. Bruder; home address: 247 Jenks Ave., Punxsutawney.

DONALD WILLIAM SNYDER   Lehigh County — 134th District

Donald William Snyder (R) was born Dec. 24, 1951, in Allentown, the son of Merritt W. J. and Marion E. Schneck Snyder; Parkland H.S., 1969; Lehigh Co. Comm. Coll. (A.A.) 1971; Pa. St. Univ. (B.A.) 1973; Lehigh Univ. (M.B.A.) 1976; Villanova Univ. Sch. of Law (J.D.) 1981; accountant, Mack Trucks, Inc., 1973-76; project accountant, Air Products and Chemicals, 1977-80; attorney; Lehigh Co., Pa., Am. Bar Assns.; S. Whitehall Twp. Planning Comm., chmn. (1974-78); pres. bd. commissioners (1977-81); asst. Scoutmaster, Greenawalds; past pres., St. dir., Parkland Area Jaycees; pres., LCCC Alumni Council; past chmn., Lehigh Co. Republican Comm.; Friends of Parkland Community Library; bd. dir., Friends of Channel 39; Young Republicans of Lehigh Co.; Eagle Scout; Outstanding Business Student, Lehigh Co. Comm. Coll.; Student Leadership Award, Pa. St. Univ.; Jaycees Internatl. Senator; Outstanding Young Pennsylvanian; mem., state com.; elected to the House of Representatives, Nov. 1980; reelected 1982, 1984, 1986; married Nancy A. Schelly; 1 child, Schelly; home address: 32 Cobbler Lane, RD #8, Allentown.

GREGORY M. SNYDER   York County — 94th District

Gregory M. Snyder (R) was born Apr. 11, 1953, in York Co., the son of Robert and Doris Keeler Snyder; Dickinson Coll. (B.A.) 1975; Valparaiso Univ. Schl. of Law (J D.) 1978; attorney; York Co., Pa. Bar Assns.; elected to the House of Representatives, Nov. 2, 1982; reelected 1984, 1986; married Mary Ann Paradise; 2 children: Marissa and Robert; home address: 4140 Stone Run Dr., York.

EDWARD G. STABACK   Lackawanna and Wayne Counties — 115th District

Edward G. Staback (D) was born July 2, 1937, in Olyphant, the son of Adolph and Irene Zipay Staback; St. Patrick's High; King's College (B.A., bus. econ.); dist. mgr., Commercial Credit Savings & Loan, 24 yrs.; full time legislator; Dem. Boro. Chmn., Archibald; Dem. Leg. Chmn., 115th (2 yrs.); Youth of Eynon & Sturges; Italian American Dem. League; American Slovak Soc.; pres., Vol. Hose Co. #5, Sturges (4 yrs.); "Ducks Unlimited"; elected to the House of Representatives, Nov. 1984; reelected 1986; married Angeline Berardi; 3 children: Sharon, Ed. Jr., Randy; home address: R.D. #1, Olyphant.

JESS STAIRS   Fayette and Westmoreland Counties — 59th District

Jess Stairs (R) was born June 5, 1942, in Mt. Pleasant, the son of Lawrence and Ann Hayes Stairs; Pa. St. Univ. (BSc) 1964, (M.Ed.) 1968; farmer; Delta Theta Sigma; Pa. Farmer Assn., Holstein Fresion Assn.; Mt. Pleasant Area Schl. Bd., 1973-76; IFYE Program, India, 1964; Rotary Group Study Exchange, Australia, 1973; trustee, H. C. Frick Hospital, Mt. Pleasant; Methodist; elected to the House of Representatives, 1976; reelected 5 successive terms; married Joan McQuaide; 2 children: Jennifer, Brian; home address: R.D. 1, Acme.

JOSEPH ALAN STEIGHNER   **Butler County — 11th District**

Joseph Alan Steighner (D) was born Sept. 28, 1950, in New Castle, the son of Harold J. and Beatrice Turk Steighner; att. Butler Co. Comm. Coll., Slippery Rock Univ.; frmr. dist. admn., Dept. of Revenue; mem.: Butler Moose Lodge #64; Knights of Columbus; Butler Sons of Italy Lodge #1664; American Heart Association, Butler Chapter; Pa. Federation of Sportsmen; Butler Hunting and Fishing Club; elected to Dem. St. Comm., 1974; reelected 1976; ex. bd., Dem. St. Comm., 1976-78; rec., Butler City Dem. Award, 1974 through 1984; 1980 Who's Who in Am. Politics; 1982 Lay Honor Award, Pa. State Park Soc.; Natl. Conf. St. Legislatures; St. Paul's Roman Catholic Ch.; elected to the House of Representatives in 1978; reelected 1980, 1982, 1984, 1986; youngest representative ever elected from Butler Co.; married Joan Eileen Criley; 2 children: Christopher and Bethann.

CORREALE F. STEVENS   **Luzerne County — 116th District**

Correale F. Stevens (R) was born Oct. 6, 1946, in Hazleton, the son of Joseph and Natalie Correale Stevens; Wyoming Seminary Prep. Schl.; Pa. St. Univ. (A.B.); Dickinson Schl.. of Law (J.D.) 1972; atty.-at-law; Am., Pa., Luzerne Co. Bar Assns.; Wilkes-Barre Law and Library Assn., frmr. exec. comm.; Natl. Rifle Assn.; Natl. Pilots Assn.; B.P.O.E.; Kiwanis; F.O.E.; Jaycees; Chamber of Commerce; Columbus Club; Sons of Italy; chmn., Young Lawyers Comm., Luzerne Co. Bar Assn., 1976-79; city solicitor, Hazleton, 1976-79; solicitor, Hazleton City Auth., 1979-81; one of Three Outstanding Young Pennsylvanians, Distinguished Service Award, Greater Hazleton Jaycees; Executive of the Year 1980, Hazleton Chptr. Natl. Secretaries Assn.; assoc. ed., *Dickinson Law Review*, 1970-72; elected to the House of Representatives, Nov. 1980; reelected 1982, 1984, 1986; married Joyce Slovak; 2 children: Brody Correale and Ryan John; home office address: Bldg. B, 29th & N. Church St., Hazleton.

TED STUBAN   **Columbia and Montour Counties — 109th District**

Ted Stuban (D) was born July 13, 1928, in Berwick, the son of John and Mary Onufrak Stuban; att. Berwick H.S., Wyoming Seminary, Reppert Schl. of Auctioneering; auctioneer; Northeastern Pa. Auctioneers' Assn.; Elks; Westend Hose Co. of Berwick; Dem. Exec. Comm. of Columbia Co.; St. Cyril Ch.; Berwick Boro Council, 1954-58 and 1970-76; Mayor of Briar Creek, 1960-64; pres., Col. COG Govt., 1972-76; Dem. St. Comm., 1974-76; elected to the House of Representatives in 1976; reelected 5 successive terms; married Charlotte Vee Hetler; 2 children: Kathy Ann and John II; home address: 1335 Second Ave., Berwick.

DAVID W. SWEET   **Washington County — 48th District**

David W. Sweet (D) was born Oct. 8, 1948, in Pgh., the son of Charles G. and Margaret Gibson Sweet; U. of Pa. (B.A.) 1970; U. of Chicago (M.A.) 1971; Dickinson Schl. of Law, 1981; legislator, attorney, coll. professor; Washington and Allegheny Co. Bar Assns.; exec. dir., Mon-Valley Council of Govts., 1974-76; author: "Plans and Program in Corrections: The Cave of the Blind," *Crime and Delinquency,* July 1973; Episcopalian; elected to the House of Representatives in 1976; reelected 5 successive terms; married Eveline Bulatovic, May 1984; home address: 438 Hunting Creek Road, Canonsburg.

ELINOR ZIMMERMAN TAYLOR
Chester County — 156th District

Elinor Zimmerman Taylor (R) was born April 18, 1921, in Norristown, the daughter of Harold I. and Ruth A. Rahn Zimmerman; W. Chester Univ. (B.S.) 1943; Temple U. (M.Ed.) 1958; att. U. of Delaware and Columbia U.; educator, assoc. professor, W. Chester Univ.; Pa. St. Assn. for Health Physical Ed. and Recreation, PSEA/APSCUP; Delta Kappa Gamma; AAUW; W. Chester Borough Council, 1974-77; W. Chester Recreation Comm.; Valley Forge Council, Rep. Women; Upper Main Line League of Women; Honor Award, Pa. St. Assn. for Health, Phys. Ed. and Recreation; Honor Award, Phila. Bd. of Women's Officials; Natl. Honorary U.S. Field Hockey Official; U.S. Field Hockey Umpiring Ch. (2 yrs.); chmn., Girl's and Women's Sports in Pa. (2 yrs.); 1st woman elected to W. Chester Borough Council; organized 1st women's intercollegiate athletic program, W. Chester Univ.; hnry. chmn., Mothers March on Polio, 1981; bd. mem., Big Brothers/Big Sisters; Order of Women Legislators; Women Helping Women Honoree presented by Soroptimist Internatl. of W. Chester; bd. mem., Robert Struble Foundation; Westminster Presbyterian Ch.; Presidential Award, Pa. St. Assn. for Health, Physical Education, Recreation and Dance, 1982; Sec., United Ways of Chester County, 1982; rec'd. *Order of the Owl* award Temple Alumni, 1982; West Chester Outstanding Citizen Award, 1984; Gov. Comm. on Higher Ed. Financing, 1984; Immaculata's President's Advisory Council, 1984; bd. mem., PA Higher Ed. Asst. Agency (PHEAA), 1976-88; founding trustee on bd., Chester Co. Ed. Foundation, 1985; Select Com. for Long Term Care, 1986; mem., Children's Caucus; chmn., Children's Caucus Task Force on Day Care and Latchkey Children, 1986; dir., Women in Politics PAC, 1986; elected to the House of Representatives in 1976; reelected 5 successive terms; married to William M. Taylor; 1 daughter, Barbara R. Taylor (Mrs. Edward L. Osborn); home address: 859 Spruce Ave., West Chester.

FRED TAYLOR
Fayette County — 51st District

Fred Taylor (D) was born Aug. 30, 1931, in Adah, the son of Clifton and Helen Moats Taylor; att. Fayette Co. public schls. and Murray Hill Bus. Schl.; U.S. Army, Alaskan Ski Command; owner/operator Taylor Insurance Agency; BPO Elks, Lodge #370; Am. Legion Post 51; Adah Sportsmen Club; Fairchance Rod and Gun Club Inc.; Natl. Assn. of Mutual Ins. Agents; Tri-State Mutual Agents Assn.; exec. comm., Fayette Co. Democratic Party; legislative dir., Outdoor Sportsmen of Pa.; past mem.: bd. of dirs., Fayette Co. Assn. for the Blind; Grtr. Uniontown C. of C.; legislative Comm., Fayette Co.; Society of Crippled Children & Adults; Fayette Co. Chap., Pa. Assn. of Retarded Children Inc.; mem., House of Representatives, 1967-1972; reelected 1974, 1976, 1978, 1980, 1982, 1984, 1986; married Gloria Cipoletti on April 19, 1952; 5 children; home address: 643 Morgantown Rd., Uniontown.

JOHN J. TAYLOR
Philadelphia County — 177th District

John J. Taylor (R) was born April 9, 1955, in Phila., the son of Martin and Gladys Taylor; Northeast Catholic H.S.; Univ. of Central Fla. (B.A.) 1980; Temple Univ. Schl. of Law (J.D.) 1984; legislator; elected to the House of Representatives, Nov. 6, 1984; reelected 1986; married Evelyn Frosch; 2 children: Sean and Sheila; home address: 2847 Almond St., Philadelphia.

WILLIAM TELEK
Cambria and Somerset Counties — 70th District

William Telek (R) was born Jan. 6, 1924, in Slickville, the son of the late Frank and Anna Kali Telek; Potomac St. Coll., W. Va., 1949; Univ. of Miami, Fla. (B.Ed.) 1951; Penn St. Univ. (M.Ed.) 1952; U.S. Army, 1943-46; educator; frmr. coll. Dir. of Admissions; frmr. coll. Assoc. Prof. of Ed.; frmr. high schl. guidance dir.; frmr. dir. of ESEA 4 County Ed. Program; frmr. high schl. teacher; past mem., P.S.E.A., N.E.A., A.F.T., A.S.C.A.; fellowship, Syracuse Univ., 1960; Johnstown Sportsmen's Assn., Somerset Co. Oldtimers Baseball Assn.; Am. Legion; Lions; K of C; Windber Polish Club; Am. Carpathian Society; adv. bd., Univ. of Pgh. at Johnstown; bd., Johnstown Area Regional Industries; Natl. Rifle Assn.; Windber Slovak Club; St. Benedict's Catholic Ch.; St. Adv. Council of Pa. Rifle and Pistol Assn., Inc.; elected to the House of Representatives in 1978; reelected 1980, 1982, 1984, 1986; married Leona G. Podgorney; 7 children; home address: 301 Metzler St., Johnstown.

THOMAS M. TIGUE **Lackawanna and Luzerne Counties — 118th District**

Thomas M. Tigue (D) was born Aug. 24, 1945, in Pittston, the son of Michael F. and Joan Walsh Tigue; St. John's H.S., 1964; Kings Coll. (B.A., govt.) 1968; candidate for M.P.A., Marywood Coll.; U.S. Marine Corps (1968-71 active, 1971-pres. Reserve), Vietnam vet. (awarded Silver Star), current rank, Lt. Col.; V.F.W.; Am. Legion; Marine Corps League; Lions Club; K. of C.; Hughestown Boys League; schl. dir., Pittston Area Schl. Dist., 1977-81; elected to the House of Representatives, Nov. 1980; reelected 1982, 1984, 1986; married Dianne Walsh; 4 children: Thomas, Tracy, Kristin, Colleen; home address: 172 Rock St., Hughestown.

FRED A. TRELLO **Allegheny County — 45th District**

Fred A. Trello (D) was born in Coraopolis, the son of Patsy and Emelia (Valera) Trello (both dec.); att. Coraopolis H.S.; Robert Morris Coll.; U.S. Air Force Vet.; Allegheny Co. Democratic Comm. (20 yrs.); Democratic Chmn., Borough of Coraopolis (12 yrs.); Coraopolis Borough Council (9 yrs.); chmn., Public Safety Comm. (6 yrs.); chmn., Housing and Redevelopment (3 yrs.); VFW; I.S.D.A. Vance Fort Lodge; Lions Club Chapter 14; Moose; Knights of Columbus; Catholic Knights of St. George; appt., chmn. House Finance Com., 3 consecutive terms; elected to the House of Representatives in 1974; reelected 6 successive terms; married Betty Meanor; 3 children: Mark, Fred, Jr. and Lilly Beth; home address: 1719 Vance Ave., Coraopolis.

PETER D. TRUMAN **Philadelphia County — 191st District**

Peter D. Truman (D) was born Jan. 13, 1935, in Phila., the son of Daniel and Silonia Adams Truman; Florida St. Christian Coll. (B.B.A.); N.Y. St. Univ. (criminal justice); Phila. Police Officer, 1959-67; asst. to Chief Clerk, House of Representatives, 1968-71; dir., Bureau of General Services, 1971-72; reg. dir., Pa. Dept. of Commerce, 1972-73; admn. asst., Sheriff of Phila., 1973-75; dep. chief clerk, Traffic Court, 1979-82; elected Constable, 3rd Ward (Phila.) 1968; pres., 3rd Ward Committeeman Assn., 1970-82; elected Ward Leader, 3rd Ward, 1982; elected to the House of Representatives, Nov. 2, 1982; reelected 1984, 1986; 4 children: Kimberly, Eric, Michael, Debra; home address: 5832 Whitby Ave., Philadelphia.

TERRY E. VAN HORNE **Allegheny and Westmoreland Counties — 54th District**

Terry E. Van Horne (D) was born Feb. 24, 1946, in Pgh., the son of Eugene H. and Rena Lorant Van Horne; Duquesne Univ. (B.A.) 1968; councilman, City of Arnold, 1978-80; past pres., Arnold Lions Club; past pres., Arnold C. of C.; Methodist; appt., Pa. Public Employee Retirement Study Comm., 1985, elected to the House of Representatives, Nov. 1980; reelected 1982, 1984, 1986; married Jacqueline Mondale; 1 child, Jason; home address: 658 Vance Dr., Lower Burrell.

MICHAEL R. VEON   **Beaver County — 14th District**

Michael R. Veon (D) was born Jan. 19, 1957, in Beaver Falls, the son of Robert and Donna Caruso Veon; Beaver Fall H.S., 1975; Allegheny Coll. (B.A., pol. sci.) 1979; frmr. legis. dir. to U.S. Cong. Joseph P. Kolter; elected to the House of Representatives, Nov. 6, 1984; reelected 1986; home address: 2535 7th Ave., Beaver Falls.

PETER R. VROON   **Chester and Montgomery Counties — 157th District**

Peter R. Vroon (R) was born in Grand Rapids, Mich., the son of Anthony and Marchien Vroon; U.S. Navy, WW II, 1943-46; New York Univ., Schl. of Commerce, (B.S., magna cum laude, acctng. and econ.) 1952; Beta Gamma Sigma award for outstanding scholarship and seriousness of purpose; bus. exec. over 25 yrs. as corporate tax expert, controller, treas., financial v. pres., exec. v. pres., pres., and bd. chmn. in various corps.; Financial Executives Institute; Beta Gamma Sigma (commerce honor society); past pres., Valley Forge Mountain Assn.; past trustee, Malone Coll., (12 yrs); dir., Community Christian Fellowship Center, Phila.; dir., Operation Mobilizaton (Christian Youth movement); past dir. and treas., World Relief Comm.; frmr. trustee, Great Valley Presbyterian Ch.; past bd. supervisor., Tredyffrin Twp. (Chester Co.); frmr. trustee, Wyckoff, N.J. Schl. Bd.; past mem., Industrial Relations Comm. of N.J. Manufacturers Assn.; elected to the House of Representatives in 1974; reelected 6 successive terms; married Isabelle Williamson; 3 sons: Donald R., Robert P., Richard A.; home address: 1754 S. Forge Mountain Dr., Valley Forge.

PETER C. WAMBACH   **Dauphin County — 103rd District**

Peter C. Wambach (D) was born May 12, 1946, in Harrisburg, the son of Peter C., Sr. and Margherita C. Zarbo Wambach; Bishop McDevitt H.S., 1964; Harrisburg Area Community Coll. (A.A.) 1966; Pa. St. Univ. (B.S.) 1970; United Steelworkers of Am., 1967; Grtr. Harrisburg Bd. of Realtors, 1973-74; Order Sons of Italy Lodge #272; chpt. chmn., bd. mem., (outstanding volunteer, 1975) Central Pa. March of Dimes; Greater Hbg. Branch NAACP; Midtown Sq. Action Council, Historic Harrisburg Assn., Community Task Force for Revitalization & Rehabilitation; bd. mem., Uptown Late Start Senior Citizen Center; bd. mem., YMCA, Camp Curtin Branch; advisory bd. mem., Program for Female Offenders, 4-H Clubs, Metro Arts, MADD; Central Cabinet Mem., Nursing Foundation of Pa.; parish adv. council, St. Lawrence Ch.; St. Adv. Council; Dauphin Co. Young Democrats; elected to the House of Representatives, Nov. 4, 1980; reelected 1982, 1984, 1986; married Nancy Virginia Barnes; 2 children: Heather and Peter III; home address: 108 Boas St., Harrisburg.

PAUL WASS   **Indiana County — 62nd District**

Paul Wass (R) was born July 9, 1925, in Young Twp., Indiana Co., the son of Metro and Sophia Casella Wass; grad. Elders Ridge Vocation H.S.; courses in local govt., Indiana U. of Pa.; public service; Indiana Co. Auditor, 1965-68; Treas., Indiana Co., 1968-76; mem., Pa. Farmers' Assn.; past pres. and mem., Indiana Lions Club; Indiana Co. Fish and Game Assn.; Indiana Co. Tourist Promotion Bur.; Indiana Co. United Fund; dir., Indiana Co. YMCA; past 1st v. pres., Co. Treasurers' Assn. of Pa.; Indiana Co. C of C; Pa. Horse and Mule Assn.; Burrel Twp. Rod and Gun Club; C and Y Sportsman Club, Shelocta Sportsman Club; past pres., Indiana Co. Repub. Men's Club; served as Rep. St. Committeeman, Indiana Co. Rep. Comm. chmn., precinct committeeman, Indiana Co. Rep. Finance Comm.; Zion Lutheran Ch.; Rep. v. chmn., Agriculture & Rural Affairs Com.; elected to the House of Representatives, 1976; reelected 5 successive terms; married V. Ilean Mears; 1 child, Vicky Wass-Steinhauer; home address: R.D. #5, Box 51, Indiana.

FRANCES WESTON   **Philadelphia County — 173rd District**

Frances Weston (R) was born Sept. 1, 1954, in Phila., the daughter of Alfred W. and Patricia Morgan Peteraf; St. Hubert's H.S.; Temple Univ. (B.A., pol. sci.); Am. Legion Oxley Post Women's Auxiliary; Pa. Polish American Citizen's League; Catholic; elected to the House of Representatives, Nov. 1980; reelected 1982, 1984, 1986; married Edward J. Weston; home address: 5924 Ditman St., Philadelphia.

EDWARD A. WIGGINS   **Philadelphia County — 186th District**

Edward A. Wiggins (D) was born March 13, 1933, in Phila., the son of Ed and Clara MaeDukes Wiggins; John Bartram Sr. High, 1951; Temple Univ., 1952-54; U.S. Army, 1954-56; bldg. admn., Phila. State Office Bldg., 1971-75; Equal Employment Opportunity Supervisor, Phila. Redevelop. Auth., 1975-76; clerk, Phila. Bd. of Revision of Taxes, 1979-80; past pres., Kings Village Comm. Assn.; mem., Holy Trinity Baptist Ch., Democrat Ex. Com. (20 yrs.); rec., Am. Legion Scholarship; mem., House of Representatives, 1976-78; reelected 1980, 1982, 1984, 1986; married Joyce V. Brown; 3 children: Clarena, Edmon, and Charles; home address: 2608 Federal St., Philadelphia.

BENJAMIN H. WILSON   **Bucks County — 144th District**

Benjamin H. Wilson (R) was born Jan. 25, 1925, in Mt. Carmel, the son of Benjamin H. and Esther Marshall Wilson; Pa. St. Univ. (B.A.) 1949; U.S. Air Force, S. Pacific, 1943-46; elected to the House of Representatives in 1966 and reelected to 10 successive terms; married Jean Terry; 2 daughters and 3 grandchildren; legislative office: 300 W. Street Rd., Warminster.

CHRIS R. WOGAN   **Philadelphia County — 176th District**

Chris R. Wogan (R) was born Feb. 15, 1950, in Phila., the son of Chris R., Jr., and Eleanor D. Futchko; Cardinal Dougherty H.S.; La Salle Coll. (B.A.) 1972; Temple Univ. Law Schl. (J.D.) 1975; major, Army Reserve, Judge Advocate General's Corps; trial attorney; Brehon Law Society; Phila. Bar Assn.; Emerald Society, Historical Soc. of Pa.; Cannstatter Volkfest Verein; Reserve Officers' Assn.; Burholme Civic Assn.; Lawncrest Kiwanis Club; Assumpta Council, Knights of Columbus; elected to the House of Representatives, Nov. 1980; reelected 1982, 1984, 1986; married Susan McAnany; home address: 878 Morefield Rd., Philadelphia.

JOHN N. WOZNIAK
Cambria County — 71st District

John N. Wozniak (D) was born Mar. 21, 1956, in Fort Knox, Ky., the son of John and Ann Ondreyik Wozniak; Johnstown H.S., 1974; Univ. of Pgh. at Johnstown (B.A.) 1978; adv. bd., Univ. of Pgh. at Johnstown; Plumbers and Pipefitters Local 354; sec., Delta Chi Alumni Bd. of Trustees; Boy Scout Commissioner; Daisytown and Conemaugh Volunteer Fire Depts.; mem., Moxham Citizens Assn.; Christ the Savior Cathedral; Elks; Eagle Scout; adv. bd., U. of Pgh., Johnstown; rec., Alpha Omega Religious Award; elected to the House of Representatives, Nov. 1980; reelected 1982, 1984, 1986; married Vanessa A. Vargo; home address: 320 Park Ave., Johnstown.

DAVID R. WRIGHT
Democratic Policy Chairman
Armstrong and Clarion Counties — 63rd District

David R. Wright (D) was born Dec. 24, 1935, in Springfield, Mo., the son of Clarence A. and Ruby Archer Wright; Southwest Baptist Coll. (A.A.) 1955; Univ. of Missouri (B.J.) 1961, (M.A.) 1962; Ohio Univ. (Ph.D.) 1971; U.S. Army, 1955-58; professor; Internatl. Communication Assn.; American Business Communications Assn.; Speech Communication Assn.; Kiwanis Club of Clarion; First United Methodist Ch.; elected to the House of Representatives, 1976; reelected 5 successive terms; Majority Policy Comm. Chmn., 1982, 1984, 1986; married Carolyn Golemon; 2 children: Douglas, Daniel; home address: 1074 Sunset Drive, Clarion.

JAMES L. WRIGHT, JR.
Bucks County — 142nd District

James L. Wright, Jr. (R) was born March 10, 1925, in New York City, the son of James and Rose Fitzsimmons Wright; Univ. of Michigan (B.S.E.) 1951; U.S. Air Force, European Campaign, WW II, Capt. Navigator; awarded Air Medal with cluster and 2 battle stars; registered professional engineer; co-founder, Bucks Co. Mental Health-Mental Retardation Dept.; supervisor, Middletown Twp., 1962-65, chmn., 1964; frmr. Repub. Committeeman and Asst. Co. Chmn., 1963-64; mem. of bd., Pa. Historical and Museum Comm.; Capitol Preservation Comm.; Governor's Energy Council; Pa. Energy Development Authority; Assn. for Retarded Children, Valley Day Schl. and Red Cross; elected to the House of Representatives in 1964; reelected to 11 successive terms; 4 children; home address: 116 Hollow Road, Levittown.

ROBERT C. WRIGHT
Delaware County — 159th District

Robert C. Wright (R) was born Nov. 5, 1944, in Chester, the son of Robert and Mary Maloney Wright; George Washington Univ. (B.A.) 1966; Villanova Univ. Law Schl. (J D.) 1969; attorney; Delaware Co., Pa. Bar Assns.; Tau Epsilon Phi; bd. dir., Chester Water Auth., 1975-82; adv. bd., Chester Lead Poisoning Program; ex. bd., NAACP; Concord Day Care Center; Republican Council of Delaware Co.; frmr. mem., Citizens for Action NOW; YMCA; rec., Chester Branch NAACP Gold Shield Award; NAACP Mary Thomas Freedom Award; 2 Man of the Year Awards, Chester Scholarship Fund; Humanitarian Award, Chester Black Expo; Community Service Award, Eastern Light Lodge; Achievement Award, Who's Who Club; Outstanding Community Service Award, Republican Council of Delaware Co.; Community Service Award, Chester Housing Auth.; Outstanding Community Service Award, Jeffery Manor Civic Assn., 1985; elected to the House of Representatives in a special election, Sept. 15, 1981; reelected 1982, 1984, 1986; married Florence Fletcher; 2 children: Josie, Robert, Jr.; home address: 1919 Providence Ave., Chester.

FRANK W. YANDRISEVITS   **Monroe and Northampton Counties — 138th District**

Frank W. Yandrisevits (D) was born Sept. 12, 1954, in Northampton, the son of Frank J. and Ethel Temmel Yandrisevits; St. Joseph's Univ. (A.B.) 1976; Villanova Univ. Law Schl. (J.D.) 1979; legislator/attorney; mem., Pa., Northampton Co. Bar Assns.; school dir., Northampton Area Schl. Dist., 1981-84; Our Lady of Hungary Roman Catholic Ch.; elected to House of Representatives, Nov. 6, 1984; reelected 1986; married Janet Pammer; home address: 550 E. 12th St., Northampton.

ALPHABETICAL LIST OF REPRESENTATIVES

Name	District	Mailing Address	Home County	Occupation	Previous Service
ACOSTA, Ralph D. (D)	180	2455 N. 5th St., Philadelphia 19133	Philadelphia	Truck driver	HR 1985-86
ANGSTADT, Paul J. (R)	126	102 Mayer St., Reading 19606	Berks	Legislator-Businessman	HR 1983-86
ARGALL, David G. (R)	124	237 W. Broad St., Tamaqua 18252	Schuylkill / Lehigh	Legislator	HR 1985-86
ARTY, Mary Ann (R)	165	312 S. Bishop Ave., Springfield 19064	Delaware	Prof. Nurse-Legislator	HR 1979-86
BALDWIN, William E. (D)	125	302 Mahantongo St., Pottsville 17901	Schuylkill	Attorney-Legislator	HR 1983-86
BARLEY, John E. (R)	100	1754 Columbia Ave., Lancaster 17603	Lancaster	Farmer	HR 1985-86
BATTISTO, Joseph W. (D)	189	Box 151, Tannersville 18372	Monroe	Legislator	HR 1983-86
BELARDI, Fred (D)	112	Geneva House, 325 Adams Ave., Scranton 18503	Lackawanna	Legislator	HR 1979-86
BELFANTI, Robert E., Jr. (D)	107	2nd & Vine Sts., Municipal Bldg., Mt. Carmel 17851	Northumberland	Legislator	HR 1981-86
BIRMELIN, Jerry (R)	139	214 Ninth St., Honesdale 18431	Wayne	Teacher	HR 1985-86
BLACK, Ronald E. (R)	64	Franklin City Hall, Franklin 16323	Venango	Executive Vice Pres., Chamber of Commerce	HR 1985-86
BLAUM, Kevin (D)	121	65 Public Sq., Wilkes-Barre 18701	Luzerne	Legislator	HR 1981-86
BOOK, Raymond T. (R)	41	Caste Village Shopping Center, Baptist & Grove Rds., Suite 128, Pittsburgh 15236	Allegheny	Legislator	HR 1983-86
BORTNER, Michael E. (D)	95	122 W. Philadelphia St., York 17401	York	Legislator-Attorney	HR 1985-86
BOWLEY, Curt (D)	65	301 S. Main St., P.O. Box 813, Sheffield 16347	Warren	Legislator	HR 1985-86
BOWSER, Harry E. (R)	4	2200 N. Brickyard Rd., North East 16428	Erie	Grape Grower-Legislator	HR 1979-86
BOYES, Karl W. (R)	3	5071 Peach St., Erie 16509	Erie	Legislator	HR 1981-86
BRANDT, Kenneth E. (R)	98	Village of Falmouth, Bainbridge 17502	Lancaster	Self-employed	HR 1973-86
BROUJOS, John H. (D)	199	6 N. Hanover St., Carlisle 17013	Cumberland	Attorney	HR 1983-86
BUNT, Raymond, Jr. (R)	147	1289 Bridge Rd., Rts. 73 & 113, Schwenksville 19473	Montgomery	Legislator	HR 1983-86
BURD, James M. (R)	12	Cranberry Twp. Municipal Bldg., 2700 Rochester Rd., Mars 16046	Butler	Legislator	HR 1973-86
BURNS, Edward F., Jr. (R)	18	3480 Felton Ave., Bensalem 19020	Bucks	Legislator	HR 1961-70
BUSH, Alvin C. (R)	84	24 W. 3rd St., Williamsport 17701	Lycoming	Legislator	HR 1965-86
CALTAGIRONE, Thomas R. (D)	127	744 Franklin St., Reading 19602	Berks	Legislator	HR 1977-86
CAPPABIANCA, Italo S. (D)	2	1216 W. 26th St., Erie 16508	Erie	Legislator	HR 1979-86
CARLSON, Edgar A. (R)	68	109½ Main St., Box 307, Wellsboro 16901	Tioga	Legislator	HR 1985-86
CARN, Andrew J. (D)	197	2015 N. 29th St., Philadelphia 19121	Philadelphia	Electrical Engineer-Developer	HR 1983-86
CAWLEY, Gaynor (D)	113	807 N. Lincoln Ave., Scranton 18504	Lackawanna	Legislator	HR 1981-86
CESSAR, Richard J. (R)	30	1412 Mt. Royal Blvd., Glenshaw 15116	Allegheny	Legislator	HR 1971-86
CHADWICK, J. Scot (R)	110	P.O. Box 215, Wysox 18854	Bradford	Legislator	HR 1985-86
CIVERA, Mario J., Jr. (R)	164	232 Long Lane, Upper Darby 19082	Delaware	Legislator	HR 1980-86
CLARK, Brian D. (D)	31	323 E. 10th Ave., Tarentum 15084	Allegheny	Legislator	HR 1979-86
CLYMER, Paul I. (R)	145	311 N. 7th St., Perkasie 18944	Bucks	Legislator	HR 1981-86
COHEN, Mark B. (D)	202	6001 N. 5th St., Philadelphia 19120	Philadelphia	Legislator	HR 1974-86
COLAFELLA, Nicholas A. (D)	15	111 Shadyside Dr., Aliquippa 15001	Beaver	Legislator	HR 1981-86
COLE, Kenneth J. (D)	91	Box 210, H of R, Harrisburg 17120	Adams	Legislator	HR 1975-86
CORNELL, Roy W. (R)	152	19 Byberry Ave., Hatboro 19040	Montgomery	Legislator	HR 1979-86

Name	Party	Dist.	Address	County	Occupation	Service
CORRIGAN, Thomas C., Sr.	(D)	140	211 Monroe St., Bristol 19007	Bucks	Rigger	HR 1975-86
COWELL, Ronald R.	(D)	34	789 Penn Ave., Pittsburgh 15221	Allegheny	Legislator	HR 1983-86
COY, Jeffrey W.	(D)	89	Ft. Chambers Bldg., 70 W. King St., Chambersburg 17201	Franklin	Legislator	HR 1983-86
DALEY, Peter J.	(D)	49	657 McKean Ave., Donora 15033	Washington	Legislator	HR 1975-86
DAVIES, John S.	(R)	129	2422 Cleveland Ave., West Wyomissing 19609	Berks	Legislator	HR 1979-86
DAWIDA, Michael M.	(D)	36	314 East 8th Avenue, Homestead, 15120	Allegheny	Legislator	HR 1983-86
DeLUCA, Anthony M.	(D)	32	1416 Barbara Dr., Verona 15147	Allegheny	Legislator	HR 1973-86
DeVERTER, Walter F.	(R)	82	R.D. 1, Box 84, McClure 17841	Mifflin	Legislator	HR 1976-86
DeWEESE, H. William	(D)	50	Ft. Jackson Hotel, Waynesburg 15370	Greene	Legislator	
DIETTERICK, Scott	(R)	120	1265 Wyoming Ave., Forty Fort 18704	Luzerne	Legislator	HR 1967-86
DININNI, Rudolph	(R)	106	5090 Franklin St., Swatara 17111	Dauphin	Legislator-Banker-Farmer	HR 1985-86
DISTLER, James T.	(R)	75	126 Edward Rd., St. Marys 15857	Elk	Legislator	HR 1971-86
DOMBROWSKI, Bernard J.	(D)	1	1302 Wallace St., Erie 16503	Erie	Legislator	HR 1980-86
DONATUCCI, Robert C.	(D)	185	2336 S. 21st St., Philadelphia 19145	Philadelphia	Legislator	HR 1973-86
DORR, Donald W.	(R)	193	305 Charles St., Hanover 17331	York	Legislator-Attorney	HR 1977-86
DUFFY, Roger F.	(D)	33	636 6th St., Oakmont 15139	Allegheny	Legislator	HR 1979-86
DURHAM, Kathrynann W.	(R)	160	Brookhaven Rd. & Edgmont Ave., Brookhaven 19015	Delaware	Legislator	HR 1981-86
EVANS, Dwight	(D)	203	210 South Office Bldg., H of R, Harrisburg 17120	Philadelphia	Legislator	HR 1981-86
FARGO, Howard L.	(R)	8	315 Elm St., Grove City 16127	Mercer	C.P.A.-Legislator	HR 1983-86
FARMER, Elaine F.	(R)	28	9600 Perry Hwy., Suite 200, Pittsburgh 15237	Allegheny	Legislator	HR 1969-86
FATTAH, Chaka	(D)	192	1845 N. 59th St., Philadelphia 19151	Philadelphia	Legislator	HR 1967-86
FEE, Thomas J.	(D)	9	325 Lincoln Ave., New Castle 16101	Lawrence	Legislator	HR 1983-86
FISCHER, Roger Raymond	(R)	47	Overlook Dr., Washington 15301	Washington	Legislator	HR 1973-86
FLICK, Robert J.	(R)	167	229 West Lancaster Avenue, Devon 19333	Chester	Legislator	HR 1985-86
FOSTER, A. Carville, Jr.	(R)	93	P.O. Box 31, H of R, Harrisburg 17120	York	Legislator	HR 1983-86
FOX, Jon D.	(R)	153	Easton and Edge Hills Rds., Abington 19001	Montgomery	Legislator-Attorney-Novelist	HR 1985-86
FREEMAN, Robert	(D)	136	65 N. 4th St., Easton 18042	Northampton	Legislator	HR 1965-86
FREIND, Stephen F.	(R)	166	2 Brookline Blvd., Havertown 19083	Delaware	Legislator	HR 1977-86
GALLEN, James J.	(R)	128	302 Hendel St., Shillington 19607	Berks	Legislator	HR 1979-86
GAMBLE, Ron	(D)	44	1 Highland Ave., Oakdale, 15071	Allegheny	Legislator-Attorney	HR 1979-86
GANNON, Thomas P.	(R)	161	552 Kelly Ave., Woodlyn 19094	Delaware	Consulting Engineer-Legislator	HR 1975-86
GEIST, Richard A.	(R)	79	1126 8th Ave., Suite 402, Altoona 16602	Blair	Legislator	HR 1979-86
GEORGE, Camille	(D)	74	512 Harry St., Houtzdale 16651	Clearfield	Legislator	HR 1975-86
GLADECK, Joseph M., Jr.	(R)	61	1166 Dekalb Pike, Blue Bell 19422	Montgomery	Legislator	HR 1983-86
GODSHALL, Robert W.	(R)	53	316 Godshall Rd., Souderton 18964	Montgomery	Hatchery Pres.	HR 1981-86
GRUITZA, Michael C.	(D)	7	P.O. Box 652, 487 S. Dock St., Sharon 16146	Mercer	Legislator-Attorney	HR 1979-86
GRUPPO, Leonard Q.	(R)	137	15 S. Main St., Nazareth 18064	Northampton	Legislator	HR 1980-86
HAGARTY, Lois Sherman	(R)	148	201 Whiteside Bldg., Heather Rd. & Highland Ave., Bala Cynwyd 19004	Montgomery	Legislator	
HALUSKA, Edward J.	(D)	73	809 N. 5th Ave., Patton 16668	Cambria	Dentist	HR 1981-86
HARPER, Ruth B.	(D)	196	1427 W. Erie Ave., Philadelphia 19140	Philadelphia	Legislator	HR 1977-86
HASAY, George C.	(R)	117	2261 Sans Souci Pkwy., Wilkes-Barre 18702	Luzerne	Legislator	HR 1973-86
HAYDEN, Richard	(D)	194	3978 Terrace St., Philadelphia 19127	Philadelphia	Lawyer	
HAYES, Samuel E., Jr.	(R)	81	P.O. Box 2, H of R, Harrisburg 17120	Huntingdon	Legislator	HR 1971-86
HECKLER, David W.	(R)	143	76 East State Street, Doylestown 18901	Bucks	Lawyer-Legislator	
HERMAN, Lynn B.	(R)	77	99 Fifth St., Philipsburg 16866	Centre	Legislator	HR 1983-86

Name	Party	Dist.	Address	County	Occupation	House Service
HERSHEY, Arthur D.	(R)	13	P.O. 69, Cochranville 19330	Chester	Owner-Operator of Ar-Joy Farms	HR 1983-86
HESS, Dick L.	(R)	78	734 Preston St., Bedford 15522	Bedford	Legislator	HR 1977-86
HONAMAN, June N.	(R)	97	Box 415, Landisville 17538	Lancaster	Legislator-Housewife	HR 1985-86
HOWLETT, Joseph	(D)	184	500 Ritner St., Philadelphia 19148	Philadelphia	Longshoreman	
HUGHES, Vincent	(D)	190	5241 Chestnut St., Philadelphia 19139	Philadelphia	Legislator	
HUTCHINSON, Amos K.	(D)	57	308 Alexander Ave., Greensburg 15601	Westmoreland	Legislator	HR 1969-86
IRVIS, K. Leroy	(D)	19	205 Tennyson Ave., Pittsburgh 15213	Allegheny	Attorney	HR 1959-86
ITKIN, Ivan	(D)	23	6954 Reynolds St., Pittsburgh 15208	Allegheny	Legislator	HR 1973-86
JACKSON, George W.	(R)	101	307 Municipal Bldg., 400 S. 8th St., Lebanon 17042	Lebanon	Legislator	HR 1981-86
JADLOWIEC, Kenneth M.	(D)	67	15 Main St., P.O. Box 144, Bradford 16701	McKean	Legislator	HR 1983-86
JAROLIN, Stanley J.	(D)	119	230 W. Main St., Plymouth 18651	Luzerne	Legislator	HR 1979-86
JOHNSON, Edwin G.	(R)	80	326 Allegheny St., Hollidaysburg 16648	Blair	Accountant	HR 1985-86
JOSEPHS, Babette	(D)	182	1229 Chestnut St., Box B, Philadelphia 19107	Philadelphia	Attorney	HR 1983-86
KASUNIC, Richard A.	(D)	52	R.D. 1, Dunbar 15431	Fayette	Legislator	HR 1981-86
KENNEDY, John.	(R)	88	304 E. Main St., P.O. Box 3176, Shiremanstown 17011	Cumberland	RR Contractor-Legislator	HR 1985-86
KENNEY, George T., Jr.	(R)	170	125 Overhill Ave., Philadelphia 19116	Philadelphia	Legislator-Pharmaceutical Sales	HR 1983-86
KOSINSKI, Gerard A.	(D)	175	2319 Margaret St., Philadelphia 19137	Philadelphia	Legislator	HR 1983-86
KUKOVICH, Allen.	(D)	56	Manor Valley Plaza, Rt. 993, Manor 15665	Westmoreland	Legislator	HR 1977-86
LaGROTTA, Frank	(D)	10	P.O. Box 842, Ellwood City 16117	Lawrence	Legislator	
LANGTRY, Alice S.	(R)	40	1750 N. Highland Rd., Pittsburgh 15241	Allegheny	Legislator-Homemaker	HR 1985-86
LASHINGER, Joseph A., Jr.	(R)	150	317 Swede St., Norristown 19401	Montgomery	Legislator-Attorney	HR 1978-86
LAUGHLIN, Charles P.	(D)	16	1305 Sampson St., Conway 15027	Beaver	Legislator	HR 1973-86
LEH, Dennis E.	(R)	130	3 Magnolia Ct., Douglassville 19518	Berks	Tool & Diemaker	
LESCOVITZ, Victor John.	(D)	46	11 N. Main St., Burgettstown 15021	Washington	Legislator	HR 1980-86
LETTERMAN, Russell P.	(D)	76	P.O. Box 120, Main Capitol Bldg., Harrisburg 17120	Centre	Legislator	HR 1971-86
LEVDANSKY, David K.	(D)	39	117 2nd Ave., Elizabeth 15037	Allegheny	Legislator	HR 1985-86
LINTON, Gordon J.	(D)	200	1521 E. Wadsworth Ave., Philadelphia 19150	Philadelphia	Legislator	HR 1983-86
LIVENGOOD, Henry.	(D)	60	Armstrong Co. Court House, Kittanning 16201	Armstrong	Legislator	HR 1977-86
LLOYD, William R., Jr.	(D)	69	S. Lynn Avenue & Plank Road, Somerset 15501	Somerset	Legislator	HR 1981-86
LUCYK, Edward J.	(D)	123	38 E. Centre St., Mahanoy City 17948	Schuylkill	Legislator	HR 1981-86
MAIALE, Nicholas J.	(D)	183	1420 Walnut St., Suite 1107, Philadelphia 19102	Philadelphia	Attorney	HR 1980-86
MAINE, Connie G.	(D)	6	254 Arch St., Meadville 16335	Crawford	Consultant-Counselor	
MANDERINO, James J.	(D)	58	444 Schoonmaker Ave., Monessen 15062	Westmoreland	Legislator-Attorney	HR 1967-86
MANMILLER, Joseph C.	(R)	105	7865 Valleyview Ave., Harrisburg 17112	Dauphin	Legislator	HR 1975-86
MARKOSEK, Joseph F.	(D)	25	3960 Monroeville Blvd., Monroeville 15146	Allegheny	Legislator	HR 1983-86
MAYERNIK, David J.	(D)	29	440 Perry Hwy., Pittsburgh 15229	Allegheny	Legislator	HR 1983-86
McCALL, Keith R.	(D)	122	124 W. Ridge St., Lansford 18232	Carbon	Legislator	HR 1983-86
McCLATCHY, Richard A.	(R)	149	Haverford & Rugby Rds., Bryn Mawr 19010	Montgomery	Businessman	HR 1969-86
McHALE, Paul	(D)	133	915 W. Broad St., Bethlehem 18018	Lehigh	Legislator	HR 1983-86
McVERRY, Terrence F.	(R)	42	46 Ordale Blvd., Mt. Lebanon 15228	Allegheny	Legislator-Attorney	HR 1983-86
MELIO, Anthony J.	(D)	141	1439 Haines Rd., Levittown 19057	Bucks	Legislator	HR 1979-86
MERRY, James R.	(R)	5	R.D. 1, Box 1-A, Linesville 16424	Crawford	Former Retailer	HR 1981-86

Name	Party	Address	Dist.	Occupation	County	Term
MICHLOVIC, Thomas A.	(D)	930 Penn Ave., Turtle Creek 15145	35	Legislator	Allegheny	HR 1979-86
MICOZZIE, Nicholas A.	(R)	100 W. Providence Rd., Aldan 19018	163	Legislator	Delaware	HR 1979-86
MILLER, Marvin E., Jr.	(R)	129 E. Orange St., Lancaster 17602	96	Legislator	Lancaster	HR 1973-86
MOEHLMANN, Nicholas B.	(R)	16 Chestnut St., Richland 17087	102	Legislator	Lebanon	HR 1975-86
MORRIS, Samuel W.	(D)	R.D. 2, Box 360, Pottstown 19464	155	Legislator	Chester	HR 1971-78; 1981-86
MOWERY, Harold F., Jr.	(R)	1023 Mumma Rd., Pennsboro Ctr., Lemoyne 17043	87	Legislator-Insurance	Cumberland	HR 1977-86
MRKONIC, Emil	(D)	126 Fifth Ave., McKeesport 15132	37	Legislator	Allegheny	HR 1975-86
MURPHY, Thomas J., Jr.	(D)	3935 Perrysville Ave., Pittsburgh 15214	20	Legislator	Allegheny	HR 1979-86
NAHILL, Charles F., Jr.	(R)	115 E. Glenside Ave., Glenside 19038	154	Legislator	Montgomery	HR 1979-86
NOYE, Fred C.	(R)	15 W. High St., New Bloomfield 17068	86	Legislator	Perry	HR 1973-86
O'BRIEN, Dennis M.	(R)	9805 Academy Rd., Philadelphia 19114	169	Legislator	Philadelphia	HR 1977-80; 1983-86
O'DONNELL, Robert W.	(D)	3425 Conrad St., Philadelphia 19129	198	Legislator	Philadelphia	HR 1974-86
OLASZ, Richard D.	(D)	105 5th Ave., West Mifflin 15122	38	Legislator	Allegheny	HR 1981-86
OLIVER, Frank L.	(D)	1205 N. 29th St., Philadelphia 19121	195	Legislator	Philadelphia	HR 1973-86
PERZEL, John M.	(R)	7330 Frankford Ave., Philadelphia 19136	172	Legislator-Auditing Clerk	Philadelphia	HR 1979-86
PETRARCA, Joseph A.	(D)	210 Longfellow St., Vandergrift 15690	55	Legislator	Westmoreland	HR 1973-86
PETRONE, Thomas C.	(D)	179 Steuben St., P.O. Box 8557, Pittsburgh 15220	27	Legislator	Allegheny	HR 1981-86
PHILLIPS, Merle H.	(R)	R.D. 2, Box 326, Sunbury 17801	108	Pres., Irish Valley Food Processing Inc.-Legislator	Northumberland	HR 1980-86
PICCOLA, Jeffrey E.	(R)	P.O. Box 104, H of R, Harrisburg 17120	104	Attorney	Dauphin	HR 1977-86
PIEVSKY, Max	(D)	P.O. Box 30, H of R, Harrisburg 17120	174	Legislator	Philadelphia	HR 1967-86
PISTELLA, Frank J.	(D)	506 S. Millvale Ave., Pittsburgh 15224	21	Legislator	Allegheny	HR 1979-86
PITTS, Joseph R.	(R)	905 Mitchell Farm Ln., Kennett Square 19348	158	Legislator	Chester	HR 1973-86
PRESSMANN, John F.	(D)	850 N. 5th St., Allentown 18102	132	Legislator	Lehigh	HR 1985-86
PRESTON, Joseph, Jr.	(D)	501 Larimer Ave., Pittsburgh 15206	24	Legislator	Allegheny	HR 1983-86
PUNT, Terry L.	(R)	P.O. Box 27, 57 E. Main St. Waynesboro 17268	90	Legislator	Franklin	HR 1979-86
RAYMOND, Ronald C.	(R)	1337 Chester Pike, Sharon Hill 19079	162	Real Estate Salesman	Delaware	HR 1985-86
REBER, Robert D., Jr.	(R)	424 King St., Pottstown 19464	146	Legislator-Attorney	Montgomery	HR 1981-86
REINARD, Roy	(R)	1260 Bustleton Ave., Feasterville 19047	178	Legislator	Bucks	HR 1983-86
RICHARDSON, David P., Jr.	(D)	5811 Chew Ave., Philadelphia 19138	201	Legislator	Philadelphia	HR 1973-86
RIEGER, William W.	(D)	1141 Rising Sun Ave., Philadelphia 19140	179	Legislator	Philadelphia	HR 1967-86
RITTER, Karen A.	(D)	932 Union Blvd., Allentown 18103	131	Legislator	Lehigh	HR 1985-86
ROBBINS, Robert D.	(R)	259 Main St., Greenville 16125	17	Legislator	Mercer	HR 1983-86
ROEBUCK, James R., Jr.	(D)	5746 Baltimore Ave., Philadelphia 19143	188	Legislator-Educator	Philadelphia	HR 1985-86
RUDY, Ruth C.	(D)	P.O. Box 405, Centre Hall 16828	171	Legislator	Centre	HR 1983-86
RYAN, Matthew J.	(R)	One S. Olive St., Media 19063	168	Legislator-Attorney	Delaware	HR 1963-86
RYBAK, William C.	(D)	408 Adams St., Bethlehem 18015	135	Legislator-Attorney	Northampton	HR 1967-72; 1981-86
SALOOM, Eugene G.	(D)	P.O. Box 14, Mt. Pleasant 15666	26	Funeral Director	Westmoreland	HR 1967-76; 1983-86
SAURMAN, George E.	(R)	360 Mattison Ave., Ambler 19002	151	Legislator	Montgomery	HR 1981-86
SCHEETZ, Terry R.	(R)	Rt. 272 & Creek Rd., R.D. 2, P.O. Box 1, Stevens 17578	99	Farmer	Lancaster	HR 1983-86
SCHULER, Jere W.	(R)	852 Village Rd., P.O. Box 268, Lampeter 17537	43	Legislator	Lancaster	HR 1983-86

Name	Party	Dist.	Address	County	Occupation	Service
SEMMEL, Paul W.	(R)	187	3 Spring Hill Drive, P.O. Box 235, Schnecksville 18078	Lehigh	Legislator	HR 1983-86
SERAFINI, Frank A.	(R)	114	421 S. State St., Clarks Summit 18411	Lackawanna	Farmer-Educator	HR 1979-86
SEVENTY, Steve	(D)	22	1910 Carson St., Pittsburgh 15203	Allegheny	Legislator	HR 1979-86
SHOWERS, John	(D)	85	204 Vine St., P.O. Box 398, New Berlin 17855	Union	Legislator	HR 1981-86
SIRIANNI, Carmel	(R)	111	28 Maple St., Montrose 18801	Susquehanna	Legislator	HR 1975-86
SMITH, Bruce	(R)	92	417 S. Baltimore St., Dillsburg 17019	York	Guidance Counselor	HR 1981-86
SMITH, Samuel H.	(R)	66	125A Main St., Brookville 15825	Jefferson	Legislator	HR 1981-86
SNYDER, Donald W.	(R)	134	228 State Ave., Emmaus 18049	Lehigh	Legislator	HR 1983-86
SNYDER, Gregory M.	(R)	94	4140 Stone Run Dr., York 17402	York	Attorney-Legislator	HR 1985-86
STABACK, Edward G.	(D)	115	307 Betty St., P.O. Box 305, Archbald-Eynon 18403	Lackawanna	Legislator	HR 1977-86
STAIRS, Jess	(R)	59	R.D. 1, Acme 15610	Westmoreland	Legislator	HR 1979-86
STEIGHNER, Joseph A.	(D)	11	138 East Jefferson St., Butler 16001	Butler	Legislator	HR 1981-86
STEVENS, Correale F.	(R)	116	Bldg. B 29th & N.Church St., Hazleton 18201	Luzerne	Legislator-Attorney	HR 1977-86
STUBAN, Ted.	(D)	109	1335 Second Ave., Berwick 18603	Columbia	Auctioneer	HR 1977-86
SWEET, David W.	(D)	48	Room 206, Borough Bldg., Canonsburg 15317	Washington	Legislator-Attorney	HR 1977-86
TAYLOR, Elinor Z.	(R)	156	13 W. Miner St., West Chester 19382	Chester	Legislator	HR 1967-72 1975-86
TAYLOR, Fred	(D)	51	643 Morgantown Rd., Uniontown 15401	Fayette	Businessman	
TAYLOR, John J.	(R)	177	3352 Kensington Ave., Philadelphia 19134	Philadelphia	Legislator	HR 1985-86
TELEK, William	(R)	70	301 Metzler St., Johnstown 15904	Cambria	Legislator	HR 1979-86
TIGUE, Thomas M.	(D)	118	42 Center St., Hughestown 18640	Luzerne	Legislator	HR 1981-86
TRELLO, Fred A.	(D)	45	1004 5th Ave., Coraopolis 15108	Allegheny	Legislator	HR 1975-86
TRUMAN, Peter D.	(D)	191	5832 Whitby Ave., Philadelphia 19143	Philadelphia	Legislator	HR 1983-86
VAN HORNE, Terry E.	(D)	54	1625 5th Ave., Arnold 15068	Westmoreland	Legislator	HR 1981-86
VEON, Michael R.	(D)	14	1414 7th Ave., Beaver Falls 15010	Beaver	Legislator	HR 1985-86
VROON, Peter R.	(R)	157	1754 S. Forge Mountain Dr., P.O. Box 471 Valley Forge 19481	Chester	Legislator	HR 1975-86
WAMBACH, Peter C.	(D)	103	108 Boas St., Harrisburg 17102	Dauphin	Legislator	HR 1981-86
WASS, Paul.	(R)	62	R.D. 5, Box 51, Indiana 15701	Indiana	Legislator	HR 1977-86
WESTON, Frances	(R)	173	5924 Ditman St., Philadelphia 19135	Philadelphia	Legislator	HR 1981-86
WIGGINS, Edward A.	(D)	186	1447 Point Breeze Ave., Philadelphia 19146	Philadelphia	Legislator	HR 1976-86
WILSON, Benjamin H.	(R)	144	300 West Street Rd., Warminster 18974	Bucks	Legislator	HR 1967-86
WOGAN, Christopher R.	(R)	176	6533 Rising Sun Ave., Philadelphia 19111	Philadelphia	Legislator	HR 1981-86
WOZNIAK, John N.	(D)	71	1100 Confer Ave., Johnstown 15901	Cambria	Legislator	HR 1981-86
WRIGHT, David R.	(D)	63	21 N. 6th Ave., Clarion 16214	Clarion	Legislator-Professor	HR 1977-86
WRIGHT, James L., Jr.	(R)	142	116 Hollow Rd., Levittown 19056	Bucks	Legislator-Engineer	HR 1965-86
WRIGHT, Robert C.	(R)	159	19 W. 5th St., Chester 19013	Delaware	Attorney	HR 1981-86
YANDRISEVITS, Frank W.	(D)	138	550 E. 12th St., Northampton 18067	Northampton	Legislator	HR 1985-86

RECAPITULATION

Democrats	101
Republicans	99
Vacancies	3
Total	**203**

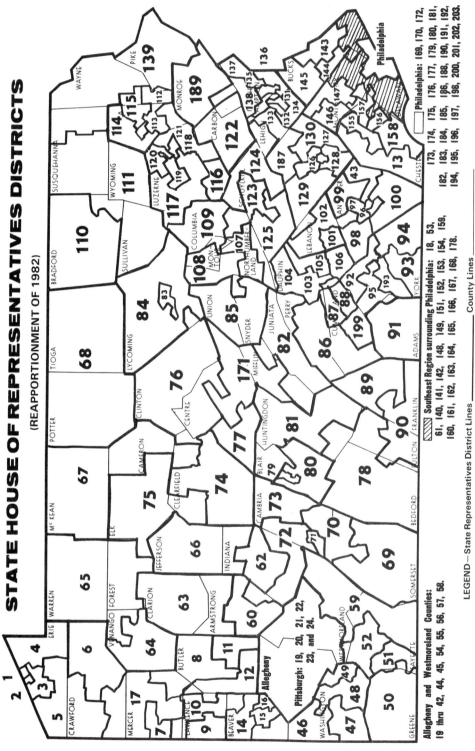

STATE HOUSE OF REPRESENTATIVES DISTRICTS

(REAPPORTIONMENT OF 1982)

Philadelphia: 169, 170, 172, 173, 174, 175, 176, 177, 179, 180, 181, 182, 183, 184, 185, 186, 188, 190, 191, 192, 194, 195, 196, 197, 198, 200, 201, 202, 203.

Southeast Region surrounding Philadelphia: 18, 53, 61, 140, 141, 142, 148, 149, 151, 152, 153, 154, 159, 160, 161, 162, 163, 164, 165, 166, 167, 168, 178.

Allegheny and Westmoreland Counties:
19 thru 42, 44, 45, 54, 55, 56, 57, 58.

Pittsburgh: 19, 20, 21, 22, 23, and 24.

LEGEND—State Representatives District Lines ———— County Lines

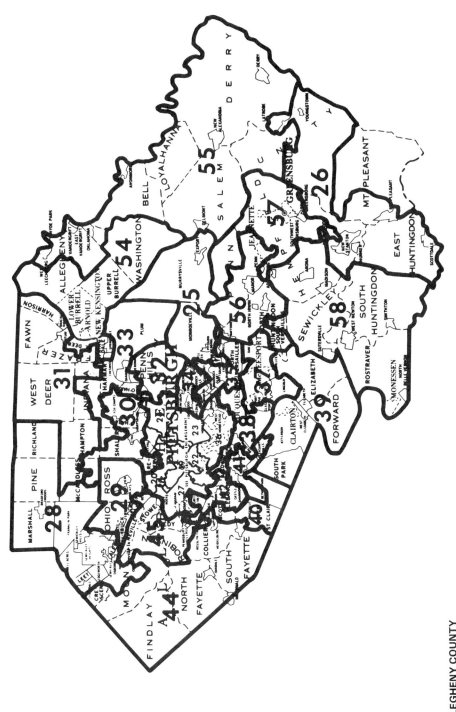

ALLEGHENY COUNTY
1982 REAPPORTIONMENT
HOUSE SUPPLEMENT

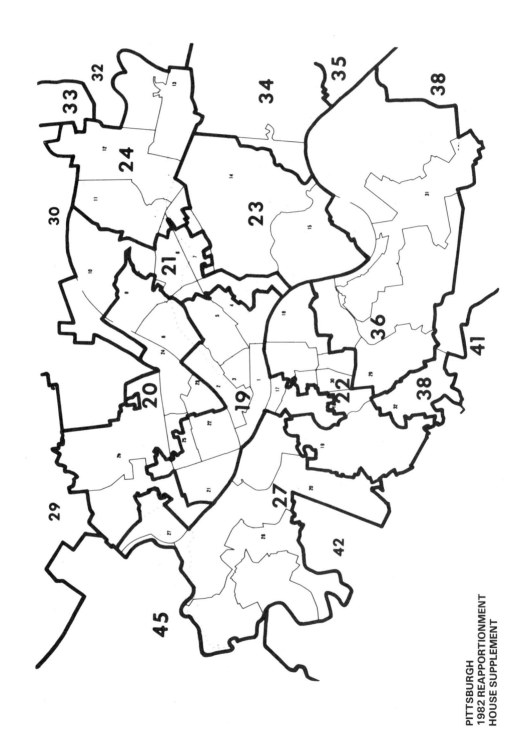

PITTSBURGH
1982 REAPPORTIONMENT
HOUSE SUPPLEMENT

PHILADELPHIA
1982 REAPPORTIONMENT
HOUSE SUPPLEMENT

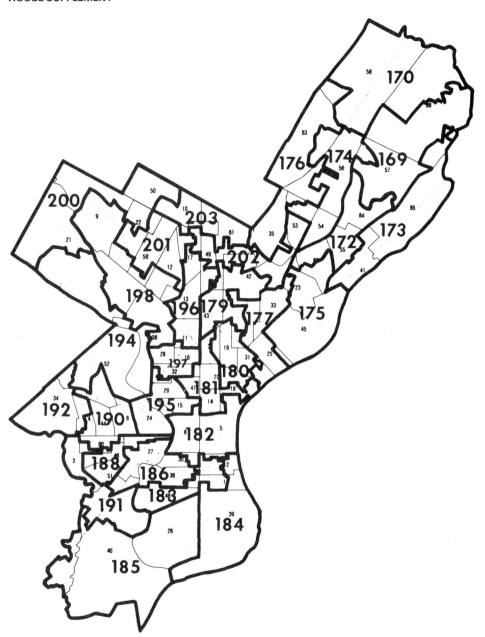

LEGISLATIVE DISTRICTS
HOUSE OF REPRESENTATIVES

Dist. 1 Erie County. Part of **Erie** County consisting of the *City* of Erie (part, wards 01, 02, and 05 [part, divisions 04, 05, 06, 07, 08, 09, 10, 12, 13, 14, 15, 16, 17, 18 and 19]) and the *Borough* of Wesleyville (part, District 03). Total population: 58,395

Dist. 2 Erie County. Part of **Erie** County consisting of the *City* of Erie (part, wards 03, 04 [part, divisions 01, 02, 03, 04 and 07], 05 [part, divisions 01, 02, 03, 11, 20 and 21] and 06). Total population: 58,220

Dist. 3 Erie County. Part of **Erie** County consisting of the *City* of Erie (part, Ward 04 [part, divisions 06, 08 and 09]) and the *Townships* of McKean, Millcreek and Summit and the *Borough* of McKean. Total population: 58,643

Dist. 4 Erie County. Part of **Erie** County consisting of the *City* of Corry and the *Townships* of Amity, Concord, Greene, Greenfield, Harborcreek, Lawrence Park, North East, Union, Venango and Wayne and the *Boroughs* of Elgin, North East, Union City, Wattsburg and Wesleyville. (part, District East) Total population: 58,207

Dist. 5 Crawford and **Erie** Counties. Part of **Crawford** County consisting of the *Townships* of Beaver, Conneaut, Cussewago, Pine, Spring, Summerhill, Summit and Venango and the *Boroughs* of Conneautville, Linesville and Springboro and part of **Erie** County consisting of the *Townships* of Conneaut, Elk Creek, Fairview, Franklin, Girard, Le Boeuf, Springfield, Washington and Waterford and the *Boroughs* of Albion, Cranesville, Edinboro, Fairview, Girard, Lake City, Mill Village, Platea and Waterford. Total population: 58,351

Dist. 6 Crawford County. Part of **Crawford** County consisting of the *Cities* of Meadville and Titusville and the *Townships* of Athens, Bloomfield, Cambridge, East Fairfield, East Mead, Hayfield, Oil Creek, Randolph, Richmond, Rockdale, Rome, Sparta, Steuben, Troy, Union, Wayne, West Mead and Woodcock and the *Boroughs* of Blooming Valley, Cambridge Springs, Centerville, Hydetown, Saegertown, Spartansburg, Townville, Venango and Woodcock. Total population: 58,500

Dist. 7 Mercer County. Part of **Mercer** County consisting of the *Cities* of Farrell and Sharon and the *Townships* of Delaware, Hermitage, Pymatuning and South Pymatuning (part, districts 02 and 03) and the *Borough* Sharpsvil1e. Total population: 57,951

Dist. 8 Butler and **Mercer** Counties. Part of **Butler** County consisting of the *Townships* of Allegheny, Brady, Center, Cherry, Clay, Concord, Connoquenessing, Fairview, Franklin, Marion, Mercer, Parker, Slippery Rock, Venango and Washington and the *Boroughs* of Bruin, Cherry Valley, Connoquenessing, Eau Claire, Fairview, Harrisville, Karns City, Petrolia, Prospect, Slippery Rock, West Liberty and West Sunbury and part of **Mercer** County consisting of the *Townships* of Findley, Liberty, Pine, Sandy Lake, Springfield (part, District East), Wolf Creek and Worth and the *Boroughs* of Grove City, Mercer and Sandy Lake. Total population: 58,251

Dist. 9 Lawrence County. Part of **Lawrence** County consisting of the *City* of New Castle and the *Townships* of Little Beaver, Mahoning, North Beaver, Pulaski, Taylor and Union and the *Boroughs* of Bessemer, Enon Valley, New Beaver and Snpj. Total population: 58,588

Dist. 10 Beaver, Lawrence and **Mercer** Counties. Part of **Beaver** County consisting of the *Townships* of Franklin, Marion and North Sewickley (part, district 01) and the *Borough* of Ellwood City (Beaver County Portion); part of **Lawrence** County consisting of the *Townships* of Hickory, Neshannock, Perry, Shenango, Washington, Wayne and Wilmington and the *Boroughs* of Ellport, Ellwood City (Lawrence County Portion), New Wilmington, South New Castle, Volant and Wampum and part of **Mercer** County consisting of the *Townships* of Shenango, Springfield (part, District West) and Wilmington and the *Boroughs* of West Middlesex and Wheatland. Total population: 58,651

Dist. 11 Butler County. Part of **Butler** County consisting of the *City* of Butler and the *Townships* of Buffalo, Butler, Clearfield, Donegal, Oakland, Summit and Winfield and the *Boroughs* of Chicora and East Butler. Total population: 58,560

Dist. 12 Butler and **Lawrence** Counties. Part of **Butler** County consisting of the *Townships* of Adams, Clinton, Cranberry, Forward, Jackson, Jefferson, Lancaster, Middlesex, Muddycreek, Penn and Worth

and the *Boroughs* of Callery, Evans City, Harmony, Mars, Portersville, Saxonburg, Valencia and Zelienople and part of **Lawrence** County consisting of the *Townships* of Plain Grove, Scott and Slippery Rock. Total population: 58,595

Dist. 13 Chester County. Part of **Chester** County consisting of the *Townships* of East Nantmeal, East Nottingham, Elk, Highland, Honeybrook, London Grove (part, District South), Londonderry, Lower Oxford, North Coventry, Penn, Sadsbury, Upper Oxford, Valley, Wallace, Warwick, West Caln, West Fallowfield, West Nantmeal, West Nottingham and West Sadsbury and the *Boroughs* of Atglen, Elverson, Honey Brook, Oxford and Parkesburg. Total population: 58,360

Dist. 14 Beaver County. Part of **Beaver** County consisting of the *City* of Beaver Falls and the *Townships* of Chippewa, Darlington, Daugherty, New Sewickley, North Sewickley (part, districts 02 and 03), Pulaski and South Beaver and the *Boroughs* of Big Beaver, Darlington, Eastbale, Fallston, Homewood, Koppel, New Brighton, New Galilee, Patterson Heights and West Mayfield. Total population: 58,616

Dist. 15 Beaver County. Part of **Beaver** County consisting of the *Townships* of Brighton, Center, Hopewell, Patterson, Potter, Vanport and White and the *Boroughs* of Beaver, Bridgewater, East Rochester, Industry, Monaca and South Heights. Total population: 58,981

Dist. 16 Beaver County. Part of **Beaver** County consisting of the *Townships* of Harmony and Rochester and the *Boroughs* of Aliquippa, Ambridge, Baden, Conway, Economy, Freedom and Rochester. Total population: 58,707

Dist. 17 Crawford and **Mercer** Counties. Part of **Crawford** County consisting of the *Townships* of East Fallowfield, Fairfield, Greenwood, North Shenango, Sadsbury, South Shenango, Vernon, West Fallowfield and West Shenango and the *Boroughs* of Cochranton and Conneaut Lake and part of **Mercer** County consisting of the *Townships* of Coolspring, Deer Creek, East Lackawannock, Fairview, French Creek, Greene, Hempfield, Jackson, Jefferson, Lackawannock, Lake, Millcreek, New Vernon, Otter Creek, Perry, Salem, Sandy Creek, South Pymatuning (part, district 01), Sugar Grove and West Salem and the *Boroughs* of Clark, Fredonia, Greenville, Jackson Center, Jamestown, New Lebanon, Sheakleyville and Stoneboro. Total population: 58,257

Dist. 18 Bucks County. Part of **Bucks** County consisting of the *Townships* of Bensalem, Lower Southampton (part, district West [part, divisions 01, 03 and 05]) and Middletown (part, District Lower [part, division 01]). Total population: 58,228

Dist. 19 Allegheny County. Part of **Allegheny** County consisting of the *City* of Pittsburgh (part, wards 01, 02, 03, 04 [part, divisions 02, 03, 04, 05, 06, 11, 13 and 14], 05 [part, divisions 01, 02, 03, 04, 05, 06, 07, 08, 10, 11, 12, 13, 14, 15, 16, 17, 18, 19, 20, 21, 22, 23, 24 and 25], 17 [part, division 07], 18 [part, divisions 02, 03, 04, 05, 06, 10 and 11], 21, 22, 25 [part, divisions 01, 02, 03, 04, 05, 10 and 11] and 26 [part, division 16]). Total population: 58,563

Dist. 20 Allegheny County. Part of **Allegheny** County consisting of the *City* of Pittsburgh (part, wards 06, 09 [part, divisions 01, 02, 03, 04, 05, 06, 07, 08, 09, 10 and 11], 23, 24, 25 [part, divisions 06, 07, 08 and 09], 26 [part divisions 01, 02, 03, 04, 05, 06, 07, 08, 09, 10, 11, 13, 14, 15 and 17] and 27 [part, divisions 01, 02, 05, 06, 09, 10, 11, 12, 13, 14, 15 and 16]). Total population: 58,853

Dist. 21 Allegheny County. Part of **Allegheny** County consisting of the *City* of Pittsburgh (part, wards 04 [part, divisions 01, 07, 08, 09, 10, 12, 15 and 16], 05 [part, division 09], 07 [part, divisions 02, 03, 04, 07 and 12], 08 [part, divisions 01, 02, 03, 04, 05, 06, 07, 08, 09, 10, 11, 12 and 14], 09 [part, division 12] and 10) and the *Township* of Shaler (part, ward 01 [part, division 02]) and the *Borough* of Millvale. Total population: 58,931

Dist. 22 Allegheny County. Part of **Allegheny** County consisting of the *City* of Pittsburgh (part, wards 16 [part, divisions 01, 02, 03, 04, 05, 06, 07, 08, 09 and 10], 17 [part, divisions 01, 02, 03, 04, 05, 06, 08, 09 and 10], 18 [part, divisions 01, 07, 08 and 09], 19 [part, divisions 10, 11, 12, 13, 14, 15, 16, 17, 18, 19, 20, 21, 22, 23, 24, 25, 26, 27, 29, 30 and 31] and 30) and the *Borough* of Mt. Oliver. Total population: 58,344

Dist. 23 Allegheny County. Part of **Allegheny** County consisting of the *City* of Pittsburgh (part, wards 07 [part, divisions 01, 05, 06, 09, and 13], 14 [part, divisions 01, 02, 03, 04, 05, 06, 07, 08, 09, 10, 13, 14, 15, 16, 17, 18, 19, 20, 21, 22, 23, 24, 25, 26, 27, 28, 29, 30 and 31] and 15 [part, divisions 01, 02, 03, 04, 05, 06, 07, 08, 09, 10, 11, 12, 13, 15, 17 and 18]). Total population: 58,950

Dist. 24 Allegheny County. Part of **Allegheny** County consisting of the *City* of Pittsburgh (part, wards 07 [part, division 08, 10 and 11], 08 [part, division 13], 11, 12 and 13) and the *Township* of Penn Hills (part, ward 01 [part, divisions 03, 04 and 05]). Total population: 58,558

Dist. 25 Allegheny and **Westmoreland** Counties. Part of **Allegheny** County consisting of the *Boroughs* of East McKeesport, Monroeville, Pitcairn, Wilmerding and part of **Westmoreland** County consisting of the *Boroughs* of Export and Murrysville. Total population: 57,692

Dist. 26 Westmoreland County. Part of **Westmoreland** County consisting of the *Townships* of East Huntingdon, Hempfield (part, Districts New Stanton, University, Weavers Old Stand and West Point), Mt. Pleasant (part, Districts Heccla and Spring Garden) and Unity (part, Districts Baggaley, Dennison, Dorothy, Gravel Hill, Marguerite, Mutual, Pleasant Unity and Whitney) and the *Boroughs* of Hunker, Latrobe, Mt. Pleasant, New Stanton, Scottdale and Youngstown. Total population: 58,506

Dist. 27 Allegheny County. Part of **Allegheny** County consisting of the *City* of Pittsburgh (part, wards 19 [part, divisions 02, 03, 04, 05, 06, 07, 08, 09 and 28], 20, 27 [part, divisions 03, 04 and 07] and 28) and the *Boroughs* of Crafton and Ingram. Total population: 59,196

Dist. 28 Allegheny County. Part of **Allegheny** County consisting of the *Townships* of Aleppo, Crescent, Leet, Marshall, McCandless (part, wards 02, 03, 04 and 05), Moon (part, Districts 01, 02, 03 and 11), Pine and Richland and the *Boroughs* of Bell Acres, Bradford Woods, Edgeworth, Franklin Park, Haysville, Leetsdale, Osborne, Sewickley, Sewickley Heights and Sewickley Hills. Total population: 57,999

Dist. 29 Allegheny County. Part of **Allegheny** County consisting of the *Townships* of Kilbuck, Ohio and Ross and the *Boroughs* of Avalon, Ben Avon, Ben Avon Heights, Emsworth, Glenfield and West View. Total population: 58,313

Dist. 30 Allegheny County. Part of **Allegheny** County consisting of the *Townships* of Hampton (part, district 05), McCandless (part, wards 06 and 07), O'Hara (part, wards 02, 03 and 04), Reserve and Shaler (part, wards 01 [part, divisions 01 and 03], 02, 04 [part, divisions 02 and 03], 05, 06 [part, division 03] and 07 [part, divisions 01, 02 and 03]) and the *Boroughs* of Aspinwall, Etna, Fox Chapel and Sharpsburg. Total population: 58,601

Dist. 31 Allegheny County. Part of **Allegheny** County consisting of the *Townships* of Fawn, Frazer, Hampton (part, districts 01, 02, 03, 04, 06, 07, 08 and 09), Harrison, Indiana (part, districts 01 and 03), McCandless (part, ward 01) and West Deer and the *Boroughs* of Brackenridge and Tarentum. Total population: 58,115

Dist. 32 Allegheny County. Part of **Allegheny** County consisting of the *Township* of Penn Hills (part, wards 01 [part, divisions 01 and 02], 02, 03, 04, 05, 06, 07, 08 and 09) and the *Boroughs* of Blawnox and Wilkinsburg (part, ward 01 [part, divisions 04 and 05]). Total population: 58,947

Dist. 33 Allegheny County. Part of **Allegheny** County consisting of the *Townships* of Harmar, Indiana (part, districts 02, 04 and 05), O'Hara (part, wards 01 and 05) and Shaler (part, wards 03, 04 [part, division 01], 06 [part, divisions 01 and 02] and 07 [part, division 04]) and the *Boroughs* of Oakmont, Plum and Verona. Total population: 58,344

Dist. 34 Allegheny County. Part of **Allegheny** County consisting of the *City* of Pittsburgh (part, ward 14 [part, divisions 11, 12 and 32]) and the *Township* of Wilkins and the *Boroughs* of Chalfant, Churchill, Edgewood, Forest Hills, Swissvale (part, districts 03, 04, 05, 06, 07, 09, 10, 11, 12, 13 and 15) and Wilkinsburg (part, wards 01 [part, divisions 01, 02, 03 and 06], 02 and 03). Total population: 58,680

Dist. 35 Allegheny County. Part of **Allegheny** County consisting of the *City* of Duquesne and the *Township* of North Versailles and the *Boroughs* of Braddock, Braddock Hills, East Pittsburgh, North Braddock, Rankin, Swissvale (part, districts 01, 02, 08 and 14), Trafford (Allegheny County Portion), Turtle Creek, Wall and White Oak (part, districts 01 and 03). Total population: 59,085

Dist. 36 Allegheny County. Part of **Allegheny** County consisting of the *City* of Pittsburgh (part, wards 15 [part, divisions 14 and 19], 16 [part,

divisions 11, 12, 13, 14 and 15], 29 and 31) and the *Boroughs* of Baldwin (part, Districts 01, 02, 03, 12 and 16), Homestead, Munhall, West Homestead and Whitaker. Total population: 58,847

Dist. 37 Allegheny and **Westmoreland** Counties. Part of **Allegheny** County consisting of the *City* of McKeesport and the *Boroughs* of Dravosburg, Liberty, Lincoln, Port Vue, Versailles and White Oak (part, districts 02, 04, 05, 06 and 07) and part of **Westmoreland** County consisting of the *Township* of North Huntingdon (part, ward 05). Total population: 58,186

Dist. 38 Allegheny County. Part of **Allegheny** County consisting of the *City* of Pittsburgh (part, ward 32) and the *Boroughs* of Baldwin (part, districts 04, 05, 09, 11, 13 and 15), Brentwood (part districts 01, 02, 03, 04, 05 and 06), Glassport and West Mifflin. Total population: 58,719

Dist. 39 Allegheny County. Part of **Allegheny** County consisting of the *City* of Clairton and the *Townships* of Elizabeth, Forward, South Park and South Versailles and the *Boroughs* of Elizabeth, Jefferson and West Elizabeth. Total population: 58,095

Dist. 40 Allegheny County. Part of **Allegheny** County consisting of the *Townships* of Scott (part, wards 01, 02, 03, 04, 05, 07 and 08) and Upper St. Clair and the *Borough* of Bethel Park (part, wards 01, 02, 03, 04 [part, division 01], 06, and 09). Total population: 58,114

Dist. 41 Allegheny County. Part of **Allegheny** County consisting of the *Boroughs* of Baldwin (part, districts 06, 07, 08, 10 and 14), Bethel Park (part, wards 04 [part, division 02], 05, 07 and 08), Brentwood (part, districts 07, 08 and 09), Castle Shannon, Pleasant Hills and Whitehall. Total population: 58,769

Dist. 42 Allegheny County. Part of **Allegheny** County consisting of the *Townships* of Baldwin, Mt. Lebanon and Scott (part, wards 06 and 09) and the *Boroughs* of Dormont, Green Tree, Rosslyn Farms and Thornburg. Total population: 59,154

Dist. 43 Lancaster County. Part of **Lancaster** County consisting of the *Townships* of Caernarvon, East Earl, East Lampeter (part, districts 01 and 02), Lancaster (part, districts 01, 03, 05, 06 and 07), Leacock, Manheim (part, District 11, Salisbury, Upper Leacock and West Lampeter and the *Boroughs* of Millersville and Terre Hill. Total population: 58,779

Dist. 44 Allegheny County. Part of **Allegheny** County consisting of the *Townships* of Collier, Crescent, Findlay, Moon (part, districts 04, 05, 06, 07, 08, 09 and 10), North Fayette and South Fayette and the *Boroughs* of Bridgeville, Carnegie (part, wards 01 [part, division 04] and 02), Heidelberg, McDonald (Allegheny County Portion) and Oakdale. Total population: 57,704

Dist. 45 Allegheny County. Part of **Allegheny** County consisting of the *Townships* of Kennedy, Neville, Robinson and Stowe and the *Boroughs* of Bellevue, Carnegie (part, ward 01), [part, divisions 01, 02 and 03]), Coraopolis, McKees Rocks and Pennsbury Village. Total population: 58,062

Dist. 46 Beaver and **Washington** Counties. Part of **Beaver** County consisting of the *Townships* of Greene, Hanover, Independence and Raccoon and the *Boroughs* of Frankfort Springs, Georgetown, Glasgow, Hookstown, Midland, Ohioville and Shippingport and part of **Washington** County consisting of the *Townships* of Cecil, Chartiers (part, districts 01, 03, 05 and 06), Cross Creek, Hanover, Independence, Jefferson, Mt. Pleasant, Robinson and Smith and the *Boroughs* of Burgettstown, McDonald (Washington County Portion), and Midway. Total population: 58,766

Dist. 47 Washington County. Part of **Washington** County consisting of the *City* of Washington and the *Townships* of Blaine, Buffalo, Canton, Donegal, East Finley, Hopewell, Morris, North Franklin, South Franklin, South Strabane and West Finley and the *Boroughs* of Claysville, East Washington, Green Hills, West Alexander and West Middletown. Total population: 57,669

Dist. 48 Washington County. Part of **Washington** County consisting of the *Townships* of Amwell, Chartiers (part, districts 02, 04 and 07),North Bethlehem, North Strabane, Nottingham, Peters, Somerset and West Bethlehem and the *Boroughs* of Beallsville, Bentleyville, Canonsburg, Centerville (part, districts 01, 04 and 05), Cokeburg, Deemston, Ellsworth, Houston and Marianna. Total population: 58,492

Dist. 49 Fayette and **Washington** Counties. Part of **Fayette** County consisting of the *Borough* of Newell and part of **Washington** County consisting of the *City* of Monongahela and the *Townships* of Carroll, Fallowfield, Union and West Pike Run and the *Boroughs* of Allenport,

California, Charleroi, Coal Center, Donora, Dunlevy, Elco, Finleyville, Long Branch, New Eagle, North Charleroi, Roscoe, Speers, Stockdale, Twilight and West Brownsville. Total population: 58,457

Dist. 50 Fayette, Greene and **Washington** Counties. Part of **Fayette** County consisting of the *Townships* Luzerne and Nicholson and the *Borough* of Masontown; all of **Greene** County and part of **Washington** County consisting of the *Township* of East Bethlehem and the *Borough* of Centerville (part, districts 02, 03 and 06). Total population: 58,341

Dist. 51 Fayette County. Part of **Fayette** County consisting of the *City* of Uniontown and the *Townships* of Georges, German, Menallen, Redstone, South Union and Springhill and the *Boroughs* of Fairchance, Point Marion and Smithfield. Total population: 59,160

Dist. 52 Fayette County. Part of **Fayette** County consisting of the *City* of Connellsville and the *Townships* of Brownsville, Dunbar, Franklin, Jefferson, North Union, Perry and Washington and the *Boroughs* of Belle Vernon, Brownsville, Dawson, Dunbar, Fayette City, Perryopolis and Vanderbilt. Total population: 58,587

Dist. 53 Montgomery County. Part of **Montgomery** County consisting of the *Townships* of Franconia (part, District South), Hatfield, Montgomery and Upper Gwynedd (part, districts 01, 03, 04 and 05) and the *Boroughs* of Hatfield, Lansdale, North Wales and Souderton. Total population: 58,967

Dist. 54 Allegheny and **Westmoreland** Counties. Part of **Allegheny** County consisting of the *Townships* of East Deer and Springdale and the *Boroughs* of Cheswick and Springdale and part of **Westmoreland** County consisting of the *Cities* of Arnold, Lower Burrell and New Kensington and the *Townships* of Allegheny (part, districts 01 and 02), Upper Burrell and Washington (part, districts Beamers, North Washington and Oakland X Roads). Total population: 58,911

Dist. 55 Westmoreland County. Part of **Westmoreland** County consisting of the *Townships* of Allegheny (part, districts 03, 04 and 05), Bell, Derry, Loyalhanna, Salem, Unity (part, Districts Beatty, Crabtree, Kuhns, Lloydsville and Roble) and Washington (part, District Paulton) and the *Boroughs* of Avonmore, Delmont, Derry, East Vandergrift, Hyde Park, New Alexandria, Oklahoma, Vandergrift and West Leechburg. Total population: 58,290

Dist. 56 Westmoreland County. Part of **Westmoreland** County consisting of the *City* of Jeannette and the *Townships* of North Huntingdon (part, wards 01, 02, 04, 06 and 07) and Penn (part, wards 01 [part, division 01], 02, 04 and 05) and the *Boroughs* of Irwin, Manor, North Irwin and Trafford (Westmoreland County Portion). Total population: 58,920

Dist. 57 Westmoreland County. Part of **Westmoreland** County consisting of the *City* of Greensburg and the *Townships* of Hempfield (part, Districts Alwine, Bovard, Carbon, Eastview, Fort Allen, Foxhill, Gayville, Grapeville, Hannastown, Haydenville, High Park, Lincoln Heights, Lincoln Heights West, Luxor, Maplewood, North Carbon, Todd, Valley and Wegley) and Penn (part, ward 01 [part, division 02] and 03) and the *Boroughs* of Penn, South Greensburg, Southwest Greensburg and Youngwood. Total population: 57,945

Dist. 58 Westmoreland County. Part of **Westmoreland** County consisting of the *City* of Monessen and the *Townships* of Hempfield (part, Districts East Adamsburg, Middletown, Sibel, Wendel Herm and West Adamsburg), North Huntingdon (part, ward 03), Rostraver, Sewickley and South Huntingdon and the *Boroughs* of Adamsburg, Arona, Madison, North Belle Vernon, Smithton, Sutersville and West Newton. Total population: 58,245

Dist. 59 Fayette and **Westmoreland** Counties. Part of **Fayette** County consisting of the *Townships* of Bullskin, Connellsville, Henry Clay, Lower Tyrone, Saltlick, Springfield, Stewart, Upper Tyrone and Wharton and the *Boroughs* of Everson, Markleysburg, Ohiopyle and South Connellsville and part of **Westmoreland** County consisting of the *Townships* of Cook, Donegal, Fairfield, Ligonier, Mt. Pleasant (part, Districts Bridgeport, Duncan, Laurel Run, Mammoth, Pleasant Valley, Ridgeview, United and Westmoreland) and St. Clair and the *Boroughs* of Bolivar, Donegal, Ligonier, New Florence and Seward. Total population: 58,159

Dist. 60 Armstrong County. Part of **Armstrong** County consisting of the *Townships* of Bethel, Burrell, Cadogan, Cowanshannock, East Franklin, Gilpin, Kiskiminetas, Kittanning, Manor, North Buffalo, Parks, Rayburn, South Buffalo and Valley and the *Boroughs* of Apollo, Applewold, Atwood, Ford City, Ford Cliff, Freeport, Kittanning, Leechburg, Manorville, North Apollo, Rural Valley and West Kittanning. Total population: 58,642

Dist. 61 Montgomery County. Part of **Montgomery** County consisting of the *Townships* of East Norriton, Plymouth (part, districts 01, 02, 03 and 04 [part, division 02]), Whitpain and Worcester and the *Borough* of Norristown (part, districts 03 [part, division 02], 04, 05, 06 [part, divisions 02 and 03], 08 [part, division 01] and 09). Total population: 58,475

Dist. 62 Indiana County. Part of **Indiana** County consisting of the *Townships* of Armstrong, Brush Valley, Center, Cherryhill, East Mahoning, Green, Rayne, Washington and White and the *Boroughs* of Cherry Tree, Clymer, Creekside, Ernest, Homer City, Indiana, Marion Center and Shelocta. Total population: 58,097

Dist. 63 Armstrong and **Clarion** Counties. Part of **Armstrong** County consisting of the *Townships* of Boggs, Bradys Bend, Hovey, Madison, Mahoning, Perry, Pine, Redbank, Sugarcreek, Washington, Wayne and West Franklin and the *Boroughs* of Dayton, Parker City, South Bethlehem and Worthington and all of **Clarion** County. Total population: 58,528

Dist. 64 Venango County. Part of **Venango** County consisting of the *Cities* of Franklin and Oil City and the *Townships* of Canal, Clinton, Cornplanter, Cranberry, Frenchcreek, Irwin, Jackson, Mineral, Pinegrove, Plum, Richland, Rockland, Sandycreek, Scrubgrass and Victory and the *Boroughs* of Barkeyville, Clintonville, Cooperstown, Emlenton, Polk, Rouseville, Sugar Creek and Utica. Total population: 58,483

Dist. 65 Forest, Venango and **Warren** Counties. All of **Forest** County; part of **Venango** County consisting of the *Townships* of Allegheny, Cherrytree, Oakland, Oil Creek and President and the *Borough* of Pleasantville and all of **Warren** County. Total population 58,482

Dist. 66 Indiana and **Jefferson** Counties. Part of **Indiana** County consisting of the *Townships* of Banks, Canoe, Grant, Montgomery, North Mahoning, South Mahoning and West Mahoning and the *Boroughs* of Glen Campbell, Plumville and Smicksburg and all of **Jefferson** County. Total population: 58,229

Dist. 67 Cameron, Clearfield and **McKean** Counties. All of **Cameron** County; part of **Clearfield** County consisting of the *Townships* of Covington and Girard and all of **McKean** County. Total population: 58,669

Dist. 68 Potter and **Tioga** Counties. All of **Potter** County and all of **Tioga** County. Total population: 58,699.

Dist. 69 Somerset County. Part of **Somerset** County consisting of the *Townships* of Addison, Allegheny, Black, Brothers Valley, Elk Lick, Fairhope, Greenville, Jefferson, Jenner, Larimer, Lincoln, Lower Turkeyfoot, Middlecreek, Milford, Northampton, Shade, Somerset, Southampton, Stonycreek, Summit and Upper Turkeyfoot and the *Boroughs* of Addison, Berlin, Boswell, Callimont, Casselman, Central City, Confluence, Garrett, Hooversville, Indian Lake, Jennerstown, Meyersdale, New Baltimore, New Centerville, Rockwood, Salisbury, Seven Springs, Shanksville, Somerset, Ursina and Wellersburg. Total population: 58,683

Dist. 70 Cambria and **Somerset** Counties. Part of **Cambria** County consisting of the *Townships* of Adams, Croyle, Richland, Stonycreek and Summerhill and the *Boroughs* of Ehrenfeld, Geistown, Scalp Level, Summerhill and Wilmore and part of **Somerset** County consisting of the *Townships* of Conemaugh, Ogle, Paint and Quemahoning and the *Boroughs* of Benson, Paint, Stoystown and Windber. Total population: 58,607

Dist. 71 Cambria County. Part of **Cambria** County consisting of the *City* of Johnstown and the *Township* of Upper Yoder and the *Boroughs* of Daisytown, Dale, East Conemaugh, Ferndale, Franklin, Lorain, Southmont and Westmont. Total population: 58,637

Dist. 72 Armstrong, Cambria and **Indiana** Counties. Part of **Armstrong** County consisting of the *Townships* of Plumcreek and South Bend and the *Borough* of Elderton; part of **Cambria** County consisting of the *Townships* of Barr, Blacklick, Conemaugh, East Taylor, Jackson, Lower Yoder, Middle Taylor and West Taylor and the *Boroughs* of Brownstown, Nanty Glo, South Fork and Vintondale and part of **Indiana** County consisting of the *Townships* of Blacklick, Buffington, Burrell, Conemaugh, East Wheatfield, Pine, West Wheatfield and Young and the *Boroughs* of Armagh, Blairsville, Jacksonville and Saltsburg. Total population: 57,649

Dist. 73 Cambria County. Part of **Cambria** County consisting of the *Townships* of Allegheny, Cambria, Chest, Clearfield, Cresson, Dean, East Carroll, Elder, Gallitzin, Munster, Portage, Reade, Susquehanna, Washington, West Carroll and White and the *Boroughs* of Ashville, Barnesboro, Carrolltown, Cassandra, Chest Springs, Cresson,

Ebensburg, Gallitzin, Hastings, Lilly, Loretto, Patton, Portage, Sankertown, Spangler and Tunnelhill (Cambria County Portion). Total population: 59,148

Dist. 74 Clearfield County. Part of **Clearfield** County consisting of the *Townships* of Beccaria, Bell, Bigler, Boggs, Bradford, Burnside, Chest, Cooper, Decatur, Ferguson, Goshen, Graham, Greenwood, Gulich, Huston, Jordan, Knox, Lawrence, Morris, Penn, Pike, Pine and Woodward and the *Boroughs* of Brisbin, Burnside, Clearfield, Coalport, Curwensville, Glenhope, Grampian, Houtzdale, Irvona, Lumber City, Mahaffey, New Washington, Newburg, Ramey, Wallaceton and Westover. Total population: 58,618

Dist. 75 Clearfield and **Elk** Counties. Part of **Clearfield** County consisting of the *City* of Dubois and the *Townships* of Bloom, Brady, Sandy and Union and the *Boroughs* of Falls Creek (Clearfield County Portion) and Troutville and all of **Elk** County. Total population: 58,787

Dist. 76 Centre, Clearfield, Clinton and **Lycoming** Counties. Part of **Centre** County consisting of the *Townships* of Boggs, Burnside, Curtin, Howard, Liberty, Miles, Snow Shoe, Union and Walker and the *Boroughs* of Howard, Milesburg, Snow Shoe and Unionville; part of **Clearfield** County consisting of the *Township* of Karthaus; all of **Clinton** County and part of **Lycoming** County consisting of the *Township* of Limestone. Total population: 57,647

Dist. 77 Centre and **Clearfield** Counties. Part of **Centre** County consisting of the *Townships* of Ferguson, Halfmoon, Huston, Rush, Taylor and Worth and the *Boroughs* of Philipsburg, Port Matilda, South Philipsburg and State College and part of **Clearfield** County consisting of the *Boroughs* of Chester Hill and Osceola. Total population: 58,056

Dist. 78 Bedford, Fulton and **Huntingdon** Counties. All of **Bedford** County; part of **Fulton** County consisting of the *Townships* of Bethel, Brush Creek, Dublin, Licking Creek, Taylor, Todd, Union and Wells and the *Borough* of McConnellsburg and part of **Huntingdon** County consisting of the *Townships* of Carbon, Hopewell, Lincoln, Todd and Wood and the *Boroughs* of Broad Top City, Coalmont and Dudley. Total population: 59,207

Dist. 79 Blair County. Part of **Blair** County consisting of the *City* of Altoona and the *Township* of Logan (part, district 03). Total population: 58,582

Dist. 80 Blair County. Part of **Blair** County consisting of the *Townships* of Allegheny, Blair, Catharine, Frankstown, Freedom, Greenfield, Huston, Juniata, Logan (part, districts 01, 02, 04, 05, 06 and 07), North Woodbury, Taylor and Woodbury and the *Boroughs* of Duncansville, Hollidaysburg, Martinsburg, Newry, Roaring Spring, Tunnelhill (Blair County Portion) and Williamsburg. Total population: 57,954

Dist. 81 Blair and **Huntingdon** Counties. Part of **Blair** County consisting of the *Townships* of Antis, Snyder and Tyrone and the *Boroughs* of Bellwood and Tyrone and part of **Huntingdon** County consisting of the *Townships* of Barree, Brady, Cass, Clay, Cromwell, Dublin, Franklin, Henderson, Jackson, Juniata, Lincoln, Logan, Miller, Morris, Oneida, Penn, Porter, Shirley, Smithfield, Springfield, Spruce Creek, Tell, Union, Walker, Warriors Mark and West and the *Boroughs* of Alexandria, Birmingham, Cassville, Huntingdon, Mapleton, Marklesburg, Mill Creek, Mt. Union, Orbisonia, Petersburg, Rockhill, Saltillo, Shade Gap, Shirleysburg and Three Springs. Total population: 58,860

Dist. 82 Juniata, Mifflin and **Perry** Counties. All of **Juniata** County; part of **Mifflin** County consisting of the *Townships* of Bratton, Decatur, Derry, Oliver and Wayne and the *Boroughs* of Burnham, Kistler, Lewistown, McVeytown and Newton Hamilton and part of **Perry** County consisting of the *Townships* of Buffalo, Greenwood, Howe, Liverpool, Oliver, Tuscarora and Watts and the *Boroughs* of Liverpool, Millerstown, New Buffalo and Newport. Total population: 58,715

Dist. 83 Lycoming County. Part of **Lycoming** County consisting of the *City* of Williamsport and the *Townships* of Loyalsock, Old Lycoming and Susquehanna and the *Boroughs* of Duboistown and South Williamsport. Total population: 58,282

Dist. 84 Lycoming County. Part of **Lycoming** County consisting of the *Townships* of Anthony, Armstrong, Brady, Brown, Cascade, Clinton, Cogan House, Cummings, Eldred, Fairfield, Franklin, Gamble, Hepburn, Jackson, Jordan, Lewis, Lycoming, McHenry, McIntyre, McNett, Mifflin, Mill Creek, Moreland, Muncy, Muncy Creek, Nippenose, Penn, Piatt, Pine, Plunketts Creek, Porter, Shrewsbury, Upper Fairfield, Washington, Watson,

Wolf and Woodward and the *Boroughs* of Hughesville, Jersey Shore, Montgomery, Montoursville, Muncy, Picture Rocks and Salladasburg. Total population: 58,295

Dist. 85 Snyder and **Union** Counties. Part of **Snyder** County consisting of the *Townships* of Adams, Beaver, Center, Chapman, Franklin, Penn, Perry, Spring, Union, Washington, West Beaver and West Perry and the *Boroughs* of Beavertown, Freeburg, McClure, Middleburg and Selinsgrove and all of **Union** County. Total population: 58,735

Dist. 86 Cumberland and **Perry** Counties. Part of **Cumberland** County consisting of the *Townships* of Hopewell, Lower Frankford, Lower Mifflin, North Middleton (part, precincts 02 and 03), North Newton, Shippensburg, South Newton, Southampton, Upper Frankford, Upper Mifflin and West Pennsboro and the *Boroughs* of Newburg, Newville and Shippensburg (Cumberland County Portion) and part of **Perry** County consisting of the *Townships* of Carroll, Centre, Jackson, Juniata, Miller, North East Madison, Penn, Rye, Saville, South West Madison, Spring, Toboyne, Tyrone and Wheatfield and the *Boroughs* of Blain, Bloomfield, Duncannon, Landisburg and Marysville. Total population: 58,470

Dist. 87 Cumberland County. Part of **Cumberland** County consisting of the *Townships* of East Pennsboro, Hampden, Middlesex, North Middleton (part, precinct 01) and Silver Spring and the *Boroughs* of Camp Hill, West Fairview and Wormleysburg. Total population: 58,103

Dist. 88 Cumberland County.Part of **Cumberland** County consisting of the *Townships* of Lower Allen, Monroe, South Middleton (part, precincts 01 and 02) and Upper Allen and the *Boroughs* of Lemoyne, Mechanicsburg, New Cumberland and Shiremanstown. Total population: 58,272

Dist. 89 Franklin County. Part of **Franklin** County consisting of the *Townships* of Fannett, Greene, Guilford, Hamilton, Letterkenny, Lurgan, Metal, Southampton and St. Thomas (part, district 03) and the *Boroughs* of Chambersburg, Orrstown and Shippensburg (Franklin County Portion). Total population: 58,784

Dist. 90 Franklin and **Fulton** Counties. Part of **Franklin** County consisting of the *Townships* of Antrim, Montgomery, Peters, Quincy, St. Thomas (part, districts 01 and 02), Warren and Washington and the *Boroughs* of Greencastle, Mercersburg, Mont Alto and Waynesboro and Part of **Fulton** County consisting of the *Townships* of Ayr, Belfast and Thompson. Total population: 58,742

Dist. 91 Adams County. Part of **Adams** County consisting of the *Townships* of Butler, Conewago, Cumberland, Franklin, Freedom, Germany, Hamiltonban, Highland, Huntington, Liberty, Menallen, Mt. Joy, Mt. Pleasant, Oxford, Strabane, Tyrone and Union and the *Boroughs* of Arendtsville, Bendersville, Biglerville, Bonneauville, Carroll Valley, Fairfield, Gettysburg, Littlestown, McSherrystown and New Oxford. Total population: 58,780

Dist. 92 York County. Part of **York** County consisting of the *Townships* of Carroll, Conewago, East Manchester, Fairview, Hellam, Monaghan, Newberry, Springettsbury (part, districts 02 and 07) and Warrington and the *Boroughs* of Dillsburg, Goldsboro, Hallam, Lewisberry, Manchester, Mt. Wolf, Wellsville, Wrightsville and York Haven. Total population: 59,294

Dist. 93 York County. Part of **York** County consisting of the *Townships* of Codorus, Manheim, North Codorus, Shrewsbury, Springfield, West Manheim and York and the *Boroughs* of Dallastown, Glen Rock, Jacobus, Jefferson, Loganville, New Freedom, Railroad, Seven Valleys, Shrewsbury, Spring Grove and Yoe. Total population: 58,578

Dist. 94 York County. Part of **York** County consisting of the *Townships* of Chanceford, East Hopewell, Fawn, Lower Chanceford, Lower Windsor, North Hopewell, Peach Bottom, Springettsbury (part, districts 01, 03, 04, 05, 06 and 08), and Windsor and the *Boroughs* of Cross Roads, Delta, East Prospect, Fawn Grove, Felton, Red Lion, Stewartstown, Windsor, Winterstown and Yorkana. Total population: 57,901

Dist. 95 York County. Part of **York** County consisting of the *City* of York and the *Township* of Manchester and the *Boroughs* of North York and West York. Total population: 58,537

Dist. 96 Lancaster County. Part of **Lancaster** County consisting of the *City* of Lancaster and the *Townships* of East Lampeter (part, district 01a), (part, districts 02, 03a and 04) and Manheim (part, districts 07a, 08a and 11a). Total population: 58,471

Dist. 97 Lancaster County. Part of **Lancaster** County consisting of the *Townships* of East Hempfield, Manheim (part, districts 01, 02, 03, 04, 05,

06, 07, 08, 09, 10, 12 and 13) and Warwick and the *Boroughs* of East Petersburg and Lititz. Total population: 58,280

Dist. 98 Lancaster County. Part of **Lancaster** County consisting of the *Townships* of Conoy, East Donegal, Mt. Joy, Rapho, West Donegal and West Hempfield and the *Boroughs* of Columbia, Elizabethtown, Marietta and Mt. Joy. Total population: 58,877

Dist. 99 Lancaster County. Part of **Lancaster** County consisting of the *Townships* of Brecknock, Clay, Earl, East Cocalico, Elizabeth, Ephrata, West Cocalico and West Earl and the *Boroughs* of Adamstown (Lancaster County Portion), Akron, Denver, Ephrata and New Holland. Total population: 58,791

Dist. 100 Lancaster County. Part of **Lancaster** County consisting of the *Townships* of Bart, Colerain, Conestoga, Drumore, East Drumore, East Lampeter (part, district 03), Eden, Fulton, Little Britain, Manor, Martic, Paradise, Pequea, Providence, Sadsbury and Strasburg and the *Boroughs* of Christiana, Mountville, Quarryville and Strasburg. Total population: 58,268

Dist. 101 Lebanon County. Part of **Lebanon** County consisting of the *City* of Lebanon and the *Townships* of Annville, North Cornwall, North Londonderry, South Annville, South Londonderry and West Cornwall and the *Boroughs* of Cleona, Mt. Gretna and Palmyra. Total population: 58,278

Dist. 102 Lancaster and **Lebanon** Counties. Part of **Lancaster** County consisting of the *Township* of Penn and the *Borough* of Manheim and part of **Lebanon** County consisting of the *Townships* of Cold Spring, East Hanover, Heidelberg, Jackson, Millcreek, North Annville, North Lebanon, South Lebanon, Swatara, Union and West Lebanon and the *Boroughs* of Cornwall, Jonestown Myerstown and Richland. Total population: 58,389

Dist. 103 Dauphin County. Part of **Dauphin** County consisting of the *City* of Harrisburg and the *Township* of Swatara (part, districts 01 and 03) and the *Borough* of Steelton (part, ward 04). Total population: 58,633

Dist. 104 Dauphin County. Part of **Dauphin** County consisting of the *Townships* of Halifax, Jackson, Lykens, Middle Paxton, Mifflin, Reed, Susquehanna, Swatara (part, districts 02 and 04), Upper Paxton, Washington, Wayne, Wiconisco and Williams and the *Boroughs* of Berrysburg, Dauphin, Elizabethville, Gratz, Halifax, Lykens, Millersburg, Paxtang, Penbrook, Pillow and Williamstown. Total population: 58,020

Dist. 105 Dauphin County. Part of **Dauphin** County consisting of the *Townships* of Derry (part, precincts 02, 03 and 04), East Hanover, Jefferson, Lower Paxton, Rush, South Hanover, and West Hanover and the *Borough* of Hummelstown. Total population: 57,868

Dist. 106 Dauphin County. Part of **Dauphin** County consisting of the *Townships* of Conewago, Derry (part, precincts 01, 05, 06, 07, 08 and 09), Londonderry, Lower Swatara and Swatara (part, districts 05, 06, 07, 08 and 09) and the *Boroughs* of Highspire, Middletown, Royalton and Steelton (part, wards 01, 02 and 03). Total population: 57,796

Dist. 107 Columbia, Montour and **Northumberland** Counties. Part of **Columbia** County consisting of the *Township* of Conyngham (part, Districts South East and South West) and the *Borough* of Centralia; part of **Montour** County consisting of the *Township* of Mayberry and the *Borough* of Danville and part of **Northumberland** County consisting of the *City* of Shamokin and the *Townships* of Coal, Jackson, Little Mahanoy, Lower Augusta, Mt. Carmel, Ralpho, Rush, Shamokin, Washington, West Cameron and Zerbe and the *Boroughs* of Herndon, Kulpmont, Marion Heights, Mt. Carmel, Riverside and Snydertown. Total population: 58,487

Dist. 108 Montour, Northumberland and **Snyder** Counties. Part of **Montour** County consisting of the *Townships* of Anthony, Derry, Liberty, Limestone and Valley and the *Borough* of Washingtonville; part of **Northumberland** County consisting of the *City* of Sunbury and the *Townships* of Delaware, East Chillisquaque, Lewis, Point, Rockefeller, Turbot, Upper Augusta and West Chillisquaque and the *Boroughs* of McEwensville, Milton, Northumberland, Turbotville and Watsontown and part of **Snyder** County consisting of the *Townships* of Jackson, Middlecreek and Monroe and the *Borough* of Shamokin Dam. Total population: 58,841

Dist. 109 Columbia and **Montour** Counties. Part of **Columbia** County consisting of the *Townships* of Beaver, Briar Creek, Catawissa, Fishing Creek, Greenwood, Hemlock, Jackson, Madison, Main, Mifflin,

Montour, Mt. Pleasant, North Centre, Orange, Pine, Scott and South Centre and the *Town* of Bloomsburg and the *Boroughs* of Berwick, Briar Creek, Catawissa, Millville, Orangeville and Stillwater and part of **Montour** County consisting of the *Townships* of Cooper, Mahoning and West Hemlock. Total population: 59,043

Dist. 110 Bradford County. Part of **Bradford** County consisting of the *Townships* of Albany, Armenia, Asylum, Athens, Burlington, Canton, Columbia, Franklin, Granville, Herrick, Leroy, Litchfield, Monroe, North Towanda, Orwell, Overton, Pike, Ridgebury, Rome, Sheshequin, Smithfield, South Creek, Springfield, Standing Stone, Stevens, Towanda, Troy, Ulster, Warren, Wells, West Burlington, Windham and Wysox and the *Boroughs* of Alba, Athens, Burlington, Canton, Leraysville, Monroe, New Albany, Rome, Sayre, South Waverly, Sylvania, Towanda and Troy. Total population: 59,086

Dist. 111 Bradford, Sullivan, Susquehanna and **Wyoming** Counties. Part of **Bradford** County consisting of the *Townships* of Terry, Tuscarora, Wilmot and Wyalusing and the *Borough* of Wyalusing; all of **Sullivan** County; part of **Susquehanna** County consisting of the *Townships* of Apolacon, Auburn, Bridgewater, Brooklyn, Choconut, Dimock, Forest Lake, Franklin, Harford, Jessup, Lathrop, Lenox, Liberty, Middletown, New Milford, Rush, Silver Lake and Springville and the *Boroughs* of Friendsville, Hop Bottom, Little Meadows, Montrose and New Milford and all of **Wyoming** County. Total population: 59,217

Dist. 112 Lackawanna and **Wayne** Counties. Part of **Lackawanna** County consisting of the *City* of Scranton (part, wards 07, 09, 10, 11, 12, 13 [part, divisions 01 and 02], 16, 17, 18, 19, 20 and 24) and the *Townships* of Elmhurst, Madison, Roaring Brook and Spring Brook and the *Borough* of Dunmore (part, wards 02 [part, divisions 02, 03 and 04], 03 and 05) and part of **Wayne** County consisting of the *Townships* of Dreher, Lehigh, Salem and Sterling. Total population: 58,858

Dist. 113 Lackawanna County. Part of **Lackawanna** County consisting of the *City* of Scranton (part, wards 01, 02, 03, O4, 05, 06, 13 [part, divisions 03 and 04], 14, 15, 18, 21, 22 and 23) and the *Boroughs* of Dunmore (part, wards 01, 02 [part, division 01], 04 and 06) and Taylor (part, ward 06 [part, division 01]). Total population: 58,657

Dist. 114 Lackawanna County. Part of **Lackawanna** County consisting of the *Townships* of Abington, Benton, Fell, Glenburn, Greenfield, La Plume, Newton, North Abington, Ransom, Scott, South Abington and West Abington and the *Boroughs* of Blakely (part, ward 02), Clarks Green, Clarks Summit, Dalton, Moosic, Old Forge, Taylor (part, wards 01, 02, 03, 04, 05 and 06 [part, division 02]) and Vandling. Total population: 58,071

Dist. 115 Lackawanna and **Wayne** Counties. Part of **Lackawanna** County consisting of the *City* of Carbondale and the *Townships* of Carbondale and Jefferson and the *Boroughs* of Archbald, Blakely (part, wards 01 and 03), Dickson City, Jermyn, Jessup, Mayfield, Olyphant and Throop and part of **Wayne** County consisting of the *Townships* of Canaan, Lake and South Canaan and the *Borough* of Waymart. Total population: 58,615

Dist. 116 Luzerne County. Part of **Luzerne** County consisting of the *City* of Hazleton and the *Townships* of Black Creek, Butler, Hazle, Hollenback, Nescopeck and Sugarloaf and the *Boroughs* of Conyngham, Jeddo, Nescopeck and West Hazleton. Total population: 58,327

Dist. 117 Columbia and **Luzerne** Counties. Part of **Columbia** County consisting of the *Townships* of Benton and Sugarloaf and the *Borough* of Benton and part of **Luzerne** County consisting of the *Townships* of Conyngham, Dorrance, Fairmont, Fairview, Hanover, Huntingdon, Lake Lehman (part, District Southwest), Rice, Ross, Salem, Slocum, Union, Wilkes-Barre and Wright and the *Boroughs* of Ashley, Harveys Lake, New Columbus, Nuangola, Shickshinny, Sugar Notch and Warrior Run. Total population: 58,088

Dist. 118 Lackawanna and **Luzerne** Counties. Part of **Lackawanna** County consisting of the *Townships* of Clifton, Covington and Lehigh and the *Borough* of Moscow and part of **Luzerne** County consisting of the *City* of Pittston and the *Townships* of Bear Creek, Buck, Dennison, Foster, Jenkins, Pittston and Plains (part, wards 01, 05 and 06) and the *Boroughs* of Avoca, Dupont, Duryea, Freeland, Hughestown, Laflin, Laurel Run, Penn Lake Park, White Haven and Yatesville. Total population: 58,336

Dist. 119 Luzerne County. Part of **Luzerne** County consisting of the *City* of Nanticoke and the *Townships* of Hunlock, Jackson, Newport and Plymouth and the *Boroughs* of Courtdale, Edwardsville, Larksville, Luzerne, Plymouth, Pringle, Swoyersville and West Wyoming. Total population: 58,425

Dist. 120 Luzerne County. Part of **Luzerne** County consisting of the *Townships* of Dallas, Exeter, Franklin, Kingston and Lehman (part, Districts Middle and Northeast) and the *Boroughs* of Dallas, Exeter, Forty Fort, Kingston, West Pittston and Wyoming. Total population: 58,974

Dist. 121 Luzerne County. Part of **Luzerne** County consisting of the *City* of Wilkes-Barre and the *Township* of Plains (part, wards 02, 03, 07, 08, 09 and 10). Total population: 58,208

Dist. 122 Carbon and **Monroe** Counties. All of **Carbon** County and part of **Monroe** County consisting of the *Townships* of Eldred and Polk. Total population: 58,068

Dist. 123 Columbia and **Schuylkill** Counties. Part of **Columbia** County consisting of the *Townships* of Cleveland, Conyngham (part, Districts East North, West and West North), Franklin, Locust and Roaring Creek and part of **Schuylkill** County consisting of the *City* of Pottsville (part, ward 06) and the *Townships* of Blythe, Butler (part, Districts Englewood and Northeast), Cass, Delano, East Norwegian, Mahanoy, New Castle, Norwegian, Reilly, Ryan and West Mahanoy and the *Boroughs* of Frackville, Gilberton, Girardville, Mahanoy City, Middleport, Minersville, Mt. Carbon, New Philadelphia, Palo Alto, Shenandoah and St. Clair. Total population: 57,977

Dist. 124 Lehigh and **Schuylkill** Counties. Part of **Lehigh** County consisting of the *Townships* of Heidelberg, Lynn and Washington (part, District Western) and part of **Schuylkill** County consisting of the *Townships* of East Brunswick, East Union, Kline, North Manheim, North Union, Rush, Schuylkill, South Manheim, Union, Walker, West Brunswick and West Penn and the *Boroughs* of Auburn, Coaldale, Cressona, Deer Lake, Landingville, McAdoo, New Ringgold, Orwigsburg, Port Clinton, Ringtown, Schuylkill Haven and Tamaqua. Total population: 58,089

Dist. 125 Northumberland and **Schuylkill** Counties. Part of **Northumberland** County consisting of the *Townships* of East Cameron, Jordan, Lower Mahanoy and Upper Mahanoy and part of **Schuylkill** County consisting of the *City* of Pottsville (part, Wards 01, 02, 03, 04, 05 and 07) and the *Townships* of Barry, Branch, Butler (part, Districts Fountainsprings, Germanville and Lavelle), Eldred, Foster, Frailey, Hegins, Hubley, Pine Grove, Porter, Tremont, Upper Mahantongo, Washington and Wayne and the *Boroughs* of Ashland, Gordon, Mechanicsville, Pine Grove, Port Carbon, Tower City and Tremont. Total population: 58,698

Dist. 126 Berks County. Part of **Berks** County consisting of the *City* of Reading (part, wards 14 [part, divisions 06 and 07], 15 [part, divisions 02, 04, 06, 07 and 09], 17 and 19) and the *Townships* of Alsace, Bern, Centre, Lower Alsace and Muhlenberg and the *Boroughs* of Centerport, Laureldale, Mt. Penn and Temple. Total population: 58,121

Dist. 127 Berks County. Part of **Berks** County consisting of the *City* of Reading (part, wards 01, 02, 03, 04, 05, 06, 07, 08, 09, 10, 11, 12, 13, 14 [part, divisions 01, 02, 03, 04 and 05], 15 [part, divisions 01 and 08], 16 and 18). Total population: 58,188

Dist. 128 Berks County. Part of **Berks** County consisting of the *Townships* of Brecknock, Caernarvon, Cumru (part, districts 01, 02, 03 and 06), Exeter and Robeson and the *Boroughs* of Birdsboro, Kenhorst, Shillington, St. Lawrence, West Reading and Wyomissing. Total population: 58,199

Dist. 129 Berks and **Lebanon** Counties. Part of **Berks** County consisting of the *Townships* of Bethel, Cumru (part, district 05), Heidelberg, Jefferson, Lower Heidelberg, Marion, North Heidelberg, Penn, South Heidelberg, Spring, Tulpehocken, Upper Bern and Upper Tulpehocken and the *Boroughs* of Adamstown (Berks County Portion), Bernville, Mohnton, Robesonia, Sinking Spring, Strausstown, Wernersville, West Lawn, Womelsdorf and Wyomissing Hills and part of **Lebanon** County consisting of the *Township* of Bethel. Total population: 57,681

Dist. 130 Berks County. Part of **Berks** County consisting of the *Townships* of Amity, Colebrookdale, District, Douglass, Earl, Hereford, Longswamp, Maidencreek, Oley, Ontelaunee, Pike, Richmond, Rockland, Ruscombmanor, Union and Washington and the *Boroughs* of Bally, Bechtelsville, Boyertown, Fleetwood, Leesport and Topton. Total population: 58,193

Dist. 131 Lehigh County. Part of **Lehigh** County consisting of the *City* of Allentown (part, wards 12, 13, 14, 15, 16, 18 and 19) and the *Township* of Salisbury (part, wards 03, 04 and 05). Total population: 58,380

Dist. 132 Lehigh County. Part of **Lehigh** County consisting of the *City* of Allentown (part, wards 01, 02, 03, 04, 05, 06, 07, 08, 09, 10, 11 and 17) and the *Township* of South Whitehall (part, districts 03, 04 and 05 [part, division 134 Ld]). Total population: 58,337

Dist. 133 Lehigh County. Part of **Lehigh** County consisting of the *City* of Bethlehem (Lehigh County Portion) (part, wards 10, 12 and 13) and the *Townships* of Hanover, Salisbury (part, wards 01 and 02) and Whitehall (part, districts 01, 02, 03, 04, 05, 06, 08, 09 and 11) and the *Boroughs* of Catasauqua, Coplay and Fountain Hill. Total population: 58,272

Dist. 134 Lehigh County. Part of **Lehigh** County consisting of the *Townships* of Lower Macungie, Lower Milford, South Whitehall (part, district 06), Upper Macungie, Upper Milford and Upper Saucon and the *Boroughs* of Alburtis, Coopersburg, Emmaus and Macungie. Total population: 58,545

Dist. 135 Lehigh and **Northampton** Counties. Part of **Lehigh** County consisting of the *City* of Bethlehem (Lehigh County Portion) (part, ward 11) and part of **Northampton** County consisting of the *City* of Bethlehem (Northampton County Portion) and the Township of Hanover. Total population: 57,955

Dist. 136 Northampton County. Part of **Northampton** County consisting of the *City* of Easton and the *Townships* of Lower Saucon, Palmer (part, Districts Eastern and Middle [part, division 02]) and Williams and the *Boroughs* of Freemansburg, Glendon, Hellertown, West Easton and Wilson. Total population: 58,078

Dist. 137 Northampton County. Part of **Northampton** County consisting of the *Townships* of Bethlehem, Forks, Lower Mt. Bethel, Lower Nazareth, Palmer (part, Districts Middle [part, division 01], Upper and Western), Upper Mt. Bethel, Upper Nazareth and Washington and the *Boroughs* of Bangor, East Bangor, Nazareth, Portland, Roseto, Stockertown and Tatamy. Total population: 58,789

Dist. 138 Monroe and **Northampton** Counties. Part of **Monroe** County consisting of the *Townships* of Chestnuthill and Ross and part of **Northampton** County consisting of the *Townships* of Allen, Bushkill, East Allen, Lehigh, Moore and Plainfield and the *Boroughs* of Bath, Chapman, North Catasauqua, Northampton, Pen Argyl, Walnutport and Wind Gap. Total population: 58,515

Dist. 139 Pike, Susquehanna and **Wayne** Counties. All of **Pike** County; part of **Susquehanna** County consisting of the *Townships* of Ararat, Clifford, Gibson, Great Bend, Harmony, Herrick, Jackson, Oakland and Thompson and the *Boroughs* of Forest City, Great Bend, Hallstead, Lanesboro, Oakland, Susquehanna Depot, Thompson and Uniondale and part of **Wayne** County consisting of the *Townships* of Berlin, Buckingham, Cherry Ridge, Clinton, Damascus, Dyberry, Lebanon, Manchester, Mt. Pleasant, Oregon, Palmyra, Paupack, Preston, Scott and Texas and the *Boroughs* of Bethany, Hawley, Honesdale, Prompton and Starrucca. Total population: 57,913

Dist. 140 Bucks County. Part of **Bucks** County consisting of the *Townships* of Bristol (part, ward 05 [part, divisions 01 and 02]) and Falls (part, wards 01 [part, divisions 01, 02, 03, 05, 06 and 07], 02, 03 and 04) and the *Boroughs* of Bristol, Morrisville and Tullytown. Total population: 58,904

Dist. 141 Bucks County. Part of **Bucks** County consisting of the *Townships* of Bristol (part, wards 01, 02, 03, 04, 05 [part, divisions 03 and 04], 06, 07, 08, 09, 10 and 11) and Falls (part, ward 01 [part, division 04]). Total population: 58,901

Dist. 142 Bucks County. Part of **Bucks** County consisting of the *Townships* of Lower Makefield and Middletown (part, Districts Lower [part, divisions 02, 03, 04, 05, 06, 07, 08, 09, 10, 11, 12 and 13] and Upper) and the *Boroughs* of Hulmeville, Langhorne, Langhorne Manor, Penndel and Yardley. Total population: 58,338

Dist. 143 Bucks County. Part of **Bucks** County consisting of the *Townships* of Buckingham, Doylestown, Newtown, Plumstead, Solebury, Tinicum, Upper Makefield, Warwick and Wrightstown and the *Boroughs* of Doylestown, New Hope and Newtown. Total population: 58,196

Dist. 144 Bucks County. Part of **Bucks** County consisting of the *Townships* of Hilltown (part, Districts Fairhill, Fairhill 2 and Hilltown),

New Britain, Warminster (part, districts 02, 03, 04, 05, 06, 07, 08, 09, 10, 12, 15 and 16) Warrington and Warwick and the *Boroughs* of Chalfont, Dublin and New Britain. Total population: 59,001

Dist. 145 Bucks County. Part of **Bucks** County consisting of the *Townships* of Bedminster, Bridgeton, Durham, East Rockhill, Haycock, Hilltown (part, District Blooming Glen), Milford, Nockamixon, Richland, Springfield and West Rockhill and the *Boroughs* of Perkasie, Quakertown, Richlandtown, Riegelsville, Sellersville, Silverdale, Telford (Bucks County Portion) and Trumbauersville. Total population: 58,610

Dist. 146 Montgomery County. Part of **Montgomery** County consisting of the *Townships* of Douglass, Limerick, Lower Pottsgrove, New Hanover, Upper Frederick, Upper Pottsgrove and West Pottsgrove and the *Boroughs* of Green Lane, Pottstown and Royersford (part, districts 01, 02 and 03). Total population: 58,237

Dist. 147 Montgomery County. Part of **Montgomery** County consisting of the *Townships* of Franconia (part, District North), Lower Frederick, Lower Salford, Marlborough, Perkiomen, Salford, Skippack, Towamencin, Upper Hanover and Upper Salford and the *Boroughs* of Collegeville, East Greenville, Pennsburg, Red Hill, Schwenksville, Telford (Montgomery County Portion) and Trappe. Total population: 58,726

Dist. 148 Montgomery County. Part of **Montgomery** County consisting of the *Townships* of Lower Merion (part, wards 01 [part, divisions 01 and 02], 02, 03, 07 [part, divisions 01 and 02], 09, 12 and 13), Plymouth (part, district 04 [part, division 01]) and Whitemarsh and the *Boroughs* of Conshohocken, Narberth and West Conshohocken. Total population: 58,647

Dist. 149 Montgomery County. Part of **Montgomery** County consisting of the *Townships* of Lower Merion (part, wards 01 [part, division 03], 04, 05, 06, 07 [part, division 03], 08, 10, 11 and 14) and Upper Merion (part, Districts Belmont [part, divisions 02 and 03], Candlebrook, Gulph, King, Roberts, Swedeland and Swedesburg) and the Borough of Bridgeport. Total population: 58,339

Dist. 150 Montgomery County. Part of **Montgomery** County consisting of the *Townships* of Lower Providence, Upper Merion (part, District Belmont [part, divisions 01 and 04]) and West Norriton and the Borough of Norristown (part, districts 01, 02, 03 [part, division 01], 06 [part, division 01], 07, 08 [part, division 02], 10, 11 and 12). Total population: 58,734

Dist. 151 Montgomery County. Part of **Montgomery** County consisting of the *Townships* of Abington (part, district 09 [part, divisions 01(151) and 02]), Horsham, Lower Gwynedd, Springfield (part, district 07), Upper Dublin, Upper Gwynedd (part, district 02) and the Borough of Ambler. Total population: 58,812

Dist. 152 Bucks and **Montgomery** Counties. Part of **Bucks** County consisting of the *Township* of Upper Southampton (part, Districts East, North [part, division 01], South and West) and part of **Montgomery** County consisting of the *Townships* of Lower Moreland and Upper Moreland and the *Boroughs* of Bryn Athyn and Hatboro. Total population: 57,930

Dist. 153 Montgomery County. Part of **Montgomery** County consisting of the *Township* of Abington (part, districts 01, 02, 03, 04, 05, 06, 07, 08, 09 [part, division 01(153)], 10, 11, 12, 13, 14 and 15) and the Borough of Rockledge. Total population: 58,595

Dist. 154 Montgomery County. Part of **Montgomery** County consisting of the *Townships* of Cheltenham and Springfield (part, districts 01, 02, 03, 04, 05 and 06) and the Borough of Jenkintown. Total population: 58,496

Dist. 155 Chester County. Part of **Chester** County consisting of the *City* of Coatesville and the *Townships* of Caln, East Brandywine, East Coventry, East Pikeland, East Vincent, South Coventry, Upper Uwchlan, West Brandywine and West Vincent and the *Boroughs* of Downingtown and Spring City. Total population: 58,721

Dist 156 Chester County. Part of **Chester** County consisting of the *Townships* of East Goshen, Uwchlan, West Goshen and West Whiteland and the Borough of West Chester (part, districts 01, 02, 03, 04, 05, 06 [part, divisions 01 and 02], 07, 08 and 09). Total population: 58,302

Dist. 157 Chester and **Montgomery** Counties. Part of **Chester** County consisting of the *Townships* of Charlestown, Schuylkill, Tredyffrin and West Pikeland and the Borough of Phoenixville and part of **Montgomery** County consisting of the *Township* of Upper Providence and the Borough of Royersford (part, district 04). Total population: 58,204

Dist. 158 Chester County. Part of **Chester** County consisting of the *Townships* of Birminhgam, East Bradford, East Caln, East Fallowfield, East Marlborough, Franklin, Kennett, London Britain, London Grove (part, District Chatham), New Garden, New London, Newlin, Pennsbury, Pocopson, Thornbury, West Bradford and West Marlborough and the *Boroughs* of Avondale, Kennett Square, Modena, South Coatesville, West Chester (part, district 06 [part, division 03]) and West Grove. Total population: 58,205

Dist. 159 Delaware County. Part of **Delaware** County consisting of the *City* of Chester and the *Townships* of Chester (part, precincts 03 and 05) and Ridley (part, ward 01 [part, divisions 01 and 02]) and the *Boroughs* of Eddystone, Trainer and Upland. Total population: 58,563

Dist. 160 Delaware County. Part of **Delaware** County consisting of the *Townships* of Aston, Bethel, Chester (part, precincts 01, 02 and 04), Concord, Lower Chichester and Upper Chichester and the *Boroughs* of Brookhaven, Marcus Hook and Parkside. Total population: 58,239

Dist. 161 Delaware County. Part of **Delaware** County consisting of the *Townships* of Darby (part, wards 03 and 05 [part, division 02]), Nether Providence (part, wards 01, 02 and 05), Ridley (part, wards 01 [part, division 03], 02, 03, 04, 05, 06, 07, 08 and 09) and Springfield (part, ward 03 [part, division 02(161)]) and the *Boroughs* of Morton, Ridley Park, Rutledge and Swarthmore. Total population: 58,198

Dist. 162 Delaware County. Part of **Delaware** County consisting of the *Township* of Tinicum and the *Boroughs* of Collingdale, Darby (part, wards 01 [part, division 01], 02 and 03), Folcroft, Glenolden, Norwood, Prospect Park and Sharon Hill. Total population: 58,243

Dist. 163 Delaware County. Part of **Delaware** County consisting of the *Townships* of Darby (part, wards 04 and 05 [part, division 01]) and Upper Darby (part, districts 01 [part, division 04], 02 and 05 [part, divisions 08 and 09]) and the *Boroughs* of Aldan, Clifton Heights, Darby (part, ward 01 [part, division 02]), Lansdowne and Yeadon. Total population: 58,364

Dist. 164 Delaware County. Part of **Delaware** County consisting of the *Township* of Upper Darby (part, districts 01 [part, divisions 01, 02 and 03], 03 [part, divisions 01, 03, 04, 05, 06, 07, 08, 09 and 10], 04, 05 [part, divisions 02, 04 and 05], 06 and 07) and the *Boroughs* of East Lansdowne and Millbourne. Total population: 58,252

Dist. 165 Delaware County. Part of **Delaware** County consisting of the *Townships* of Marple (part, wards 01 [part, divisions 01 and 02], 02, 03, 04, 05 [part, divisions 01 and 03], and 07 [part, divisions 02 and 03]), Springfield (part, wards 01, 02, 03 [part, divisions 01 and 02(165)], 04, 05, 06 and 07) and Upper Darby (part, districts 01 [part, divisions 05, 06, 07, 08, and 09], 03 [part, division 02] and 05 [part, divisions 01, 03, 06 and 07]). Total population: 58,604

Dist. 166 Delaware County. Part of **Delaware** County consisting of the *Townships* of Haverford, Marple (part, ward 01 [part, division 03]) and Radnor (part, ward 05). Total population: 58,400

Dist. 167 Chester and **Delaware** Counties. Part of **Chester** County consisting of the *Townships* of East Whiteland, Easttown, Westtown and Willistown and the Borough of Malvern and part of **Delaware** County consisting of the *Township* of Radnor (part, wards 01, 02, 03, 04, 06 and 07). Total population: 58,342

Dist. 168 Delaware County. Part of **Delaware** County consisting of the *Townships* of Birmingham, Edgemont, Marple (part, wards 05 [part, division 02] and 07 [part, division 01]), Middletown, Nether Providence (part, wards 03, 04 and 06), Newtown, Thornbury and Upper Providence and the *Boroughs* of Chester Heights, Media and Rose Valley. Total population: 58,244

Dist. 169 Philadelphia County. Part of **Philadelphia** County consisting of the *City* of Philadelphia (part, wards 57 [part, divisions 01, 02, 03, 04, 08, 09, 10, 11, 12, 13, 14, 15, 16, 17, 18, 19, 20, 21, 22, 23, 24, 25] and 66 [part, divisions 01, 03, 06, 10, 14, 16, 17, 18, 19, 20, 22, 24, 25, 30, 31, 32, 33, 34, 35, 36, 37, 38, 39, 40, 44, 45, 46, 49 and 50]. Total population: 58,134

Dist. 170 Philadelphia County. Part of **Philadelphia** County consisting of the *City* of Philadelphia (part, wards 58 [part, divisions 01, 02, 03, 04, 05, 06, 07, 08, 10, 11, 12, 14, 15, 16, 18, 19, 20, 21, 22, 23, 24, 25, 26, 27, 28, 29, 30, 31, 32, 33, 34, 35, 36, 37, 38, 39, 40 and 41] and 66 [part, divisions 02, 04, 05, 07, 08, 09, 11, 12, 13, 15, 23, 41, 42, 43 and 48]). Total population: 58,883

Dist. 171 Centre and **Mifflin** Counties. Part of **Centre** County consisting of the *Townships* of Benner, College, Gregg, Haines, Harris, Marion, Patton, Penn, Potter and Spring and the *Boroughs* of Bellefonte, Centre Hall and Millheim and part of **Mifflin** County consisting of the *Townships* of Armagh, Brown, Granville, Menno and Union and the Borough of Juniata Terrace. Total population: 58,199

Dist. 172 Philadelphia County. Part of **Philadelphia** County consisting of the *City* of Philadelphia (part, wards 23 [part, divisions 13], 55, 62 [part, divisions 07, 10, 11, 12, 14, 15, 16, 20, 21, 22, 23, 24, 25 and 27] and 64). Total population: 58,347

Dist. 173 Philadelphia County. Part of **Philadelphia** County consisting of the *City* of Philadelphia (part, wards 41, 65 and 66 [part, divisions 21, 26, 27, 28, 29 and 47]). Total population: 58,257

Dist. 174 Philadelphia County. Part of **Philadelphia** County consisting of the *City* of Philadelphia (part, wards 53 [part, divisions 14, 15, 16, 17, 18, 19, 20 and 22], 54 and 56 [part, divisions 01, 02, 05, 11, 12, 13, 15, 16, 17, 18, 20, 21, 22, 23, 24, 25, 26, 27, 28, 29, 30, 31, 32, 34, 35, 36, 37, 38, 39 and 40]). 57 [part, divisions 05, 06 and 07] and 63 [part, divisions 15, 22 and 27]. Total population: 58,055

Dist. 175 Philadelphia County. Part of **Philadelphia** County consisting of the *City* of Philadelphia (part, wards 23 [part, divisions 01, 02, 05, 06, 07, 08, 09, 14, 15, 16, 17, 18, 19, 20, 21, 22, 23 and 24], 25 [part, divisions 01, 02, 03, 04, 05, 06, 08, 09, 13, 17, 18, 19, and 26]). Total population: 58,236

Dist. 176 Philadelphia County. Part of **Philadelphia** County consisting of the *City* of Philadelphia (part, wards 35 [part, divisions 01, 02, 03, 04, 05, 06, 07, 08, 09, 10, 11, 12, 13, 17, 18, 19, 20, 21, 25, 27 and 31], 53 [part, division 20 and 21], 56 [part, divisions 03, 04, 06, 07, 08, 09, 10, 14, 19 and 33], 58 [part, divisions 09, 13, and 17] and 63 [part, divisions 01, 02, 03, 04, 05, 06, 07, 08, 09, 10, 11, 12, 13, 14, 16, 17, 18, 19, 20, 21, 23, 24, 25, 26, 28 and 29]). Total population: 58,742

Dist. 177 Philadelphia County. Part of **Philadelphia** County consisting of the *City* of Philadelphia (part, wards 07 [part, divisions 09, 10, 16, 19, 20, 21, 22, 23 and 24], 23 [part, divisions 03 and 04], 25 [part, divisions 04, 05, 06, 07, 08, 09, 10, 11, 12, 13, 14, 15, 16, 17, 18, 19, 20, 21, 22, 23, 24, 25 and 27], 31 [part, divisions 06, 15, 16, 17, 19, 23 and 24] and 33). Total population: 58,221

Dist. 178 Bucks County. Part of **Bucks** County consisting of the *Townships* of Lower Southampton (part, Districts East and West [part, divisions 02, 04, 05 and 06]), Northampton, Upper Southampton (part, District North [part, divisions 02, 03 and 04]) and Warminster (part, districts 01, 11, 13 and 14) and the Borough of Ivyland. Total population: 57,975

Dist. 179 Philadelphia County. Part of **Philadelphia** County consisting of the *City* of Philadelphia (part, wards 07 [part, divisions 06, 07, 08, 11, 12, 13, 14 and 15], 42 [part, divisions 01, 02, 03, 04, 05, 06, 07, 08, 09, 10, 11, 12, 13, 16, 17, 22 and 23], 43 [part, divisions 01, 02, 03, 04, 05, 06, 07, 08, 09, 10, 12, 13, 14, 15, 16, 17, 18, 19, 20, 21, 22, 23, 24, 25 and 26] and 49 [part, divisions 01, 03, 07, 08, 09 and 13]). Total population: 58,475

Dist. 180 Philadelphia County. Part of **Philadelphia** County consisting of the *City* of Philadelphia (part, wards 07 [part, divisions 01, 02, 03, 04, 05, 17, and 18], 18 [part, divisions 04, 07, 10, 11, 14, 15, 16, 17, 18, 19, 20 and 21], 19, 31 [part, divisions 01, 02, 03, 04, 05, 07, 08, 09, 10, 11, 12, 13, 14, 18, 20, 21 and 22]). 37 [part, divisions 13, 14, 15, 16, 17, 18, 19, 20 and 23] and 43 [part, division 11]). Total population: 58,370

Dist. 181 Philadelphia County. Part of **Philadelphia** County consisting of the *City* of Philadelphia (part, wards 05 [part, divisions 20 and 23], 14, 18 [part, divisions 01, 02, 03, 05, 06, 08, 09, 12, and 13], 20, 32 [part, divisions 05, 06 and 07], 37 [part, divisions 01, 02, 03, 04, 05, 06, 07, 08, 09, 10, 11, 12, 21 and 22] and 47). Total population: 58,253

Dist. 182 Philadelphia County. Part of **Philadelphia** County consisting of the *City* of Philadelphia (part, wards 02 [part, divisions 21, 22, 23, 24 and 25], 05 [part, divisions 01, 02, 03, 04, 05, 06, 07, 08, 09, 10, 11, 12, 13, 14, 15, 16, 17, 18, 19, 21, 22, 24, 25 and 26], 08 and 30 [part, divisions 01, 02, 03, 04, 05, 06, 07, 19, 20 and 21]). Total population: 58,573

Dist. 183 Philadelphia County. Part of **Philadelphia** County consisting of the *City* of Philadelphia (part, wards 01 [part, divisions 01, 02, 03, 04, 05, 06, 07, 08, 09, 10, 11, 12, 13, 14, 15, 16, 18 and 23], 02 [part, divisions 03, 04, 05, 06, 07, 08, 09, 10, 11, 12, 17, 18, 19 and 20], 36 [part, divisions 10, 11, 29, 31, 34, 36, 37, 38 and 41] and 48). Total population: 58,338

Dist. 184 Philadelphia County. Part of **Philadelphia** County consisting of the *City* of Philadelphia (part, wards 01 [part, divisions 17, 19, 20, 21 and

22], 02 [part, divisions 01, 02, 13, 14, 15, 16, 26 and 27] and 39). Total population: 58,253

Dist. 185 Delaware and **Philadelphia** Counties. Part of **Delaware** County consisting of the *Township* of Darby (part, wards 01 and 02) and the Borough of Colwyn and part of **Philadelphia** County consisting of the *City* of Philadelphia (part, wards 26 and 40 [part, divisions 25, 28, 29, 30, 31, 32, 34, 35, 36, 37, 38, 40, 41, 43, 44, 46, 47, 48, 49, 50, 52, 54, 55 and 56]). Total population: 58,047

Dist. 186 Philadelphia County. Part of **Philadelphia** County consisting of the *City* of Philadelphia (part, wards 27 [part, divisions 02, 04, 05, 07, 08, 10, 12, 15, 16, 17, 18, and 19], 30 [part, divisions 08, 09, 10, 11, 12, 13, 14, 15, 16, 17 and 18], 36 [part, divisions 01, 02, 03, 04, 05, 06, 07, 08, 09, 12, 13, 14, 15, 16, 17, 18, 19, 20, 21, 22, 23, 24, 25, 26, 27, 28, 30, 32, 33, 35, 39 and 40] and 51 [part, divisions 03, 08, 09, 22, 23, 24 and 25]). Total population: 58,315

Dist. 187 Berks and **Lehigh** Counties. Part of **Berks** County consisting of the *Townships* of Albany, Greenwich, Maxatawny, Perry, Tilden and Windsor and the *Boroughs* of Hamburg, Kutztown, Lenhartsville, Lyons and Shoemakersville and part of **Lehigh** County consisting of the *Townships* of Lowhill, North Whitehall, South Whitehall (part, districts 01, 02, 05 [part, division 132 Ld] and 07), Washington (part, Districts Eastern and Southern), Weisenberg and Whitehall (part, districts 07 and 10) and the Borough of Slatington. Total population: 58,422

Dist. 188 Philadelphia County. Part of **Philadelphia** County consisting of the *City* of Philadelphia (part, wards 27 [part, divisions 01, 03, 06, 09, 11, 13 and 14], 46, 51 [part, divisions 01, 02, 04, 05, 06, 07, 10, 11, 12, 13, 14, 15, 16, 17, 18, 19, 20, 21, 26, 27, 28, 29 and 30] and 60 [part, divisions 01, 09 and 24]). Total population: 58,439

Dist. 189 Monroe County. Part of **Monroe** County consisting of the *Townships* of Barrett, Coolbaugh, Hamilton, Jackson, Middle Smithfield, Paradise, Pocono, Price, Smithfield, Stroud, Tobyhanna and Tunkhannock and the *Boroughs* of Delaware Water Gap, East Stroudsburg, Mt. Pocono and Stroudsburg. Total population: 58,035

Dist. 190 Philadelphia County. Part of **Philadelphia** County consisting of the *City* of Philadelphia (part, wards 04 [part, divisions 01, 02, 03, 07, 08, 12 and 19], 06, 44, 52 [part, divisions 01 and 21] and 60 [part, divisions 02, 03, 04, 05, 06, 07, 08, 12, 13, 14, 15, 16, 17 and 23]). Total population: 58,562

Dist. 191 Philadelphia County. Part of **Philadelphia** County consisting of the *City* of Philadelphia (part, wards 03, 40 [part, divisions 01, 02, 03, 04, 05, 06, 07, 08, 09, 10, 11, 12, 13, 14, 15, 16, 17, 18, 19, 20, 21, 22, 23, 24, 26, 27, 33, 39, 42, 45, 51 and 53] and 60 [part, divisions 10, 11, 18, 19, 20, 21 and 22]). Total population: 58,008

Dist. 192 Philadelphia County. Part of **Philadelphia** County consisting of the *City* of Philadelphia (part, wards 04 [part, divisions 04, 05, 06, 09, 10, 11, 13, 14, 15, 16, 17, 18, 20 and 21], 34 and 52 [part, divisions 20, 27 and 28]). Total population: 58,585

Dist. 193 York County. Part of **York** County consisting of the *Townships* of Heidelberg, Jackson, Paradise, Penn, Spring Garden and West Manchester and the *Boroughs* of Hanover and New Salem. Total population: 58,989

Dist. 194 Philadelphia County. Part of **Philadelphia** County consisting of the *City* of Philadelphia (part, wards 21 [part, divisions 01, 02, 03, 04, 05, 06, 07, 08, 09, 10, 11, 12, 13, 14, 15, 16, 17, 18, 19, 20, 21, 22, 27, 28, 29, 31, 32, 36, 37, 40, 41 and 42], 38 [part, divisions 09 and 19] and 52 [part, divisions 02, 03, 04, 05, 06, 07, 08, 09, 10, 11, 12, 13, 14, 15, 16, 17, 18, 19, 22, 23, 24, 25, 26, 29 and 30]). Total population: 58,477

Dist. 195 Philadelphia County. Part of **Philadelphia** County consisting of the *City* of Philadelphia (part, wards 15, 24, 29 and 32 [part, divisions 01, 04, 23, 24, 25, 27, 31 and 32]). Total population: 58,652

Dist. 196 Philadelphia County. Part of **Philadelphia** County consisting of the *City* of Philadelphia (part, wards 11 [part, divisions 01, 02, 03, 04, 05, 06, 07, 08, 09, 10, 11, 12, 13, 14, 15, 16, 17, 18, 19, 22, 23 and 24], 13 [part, divisions 06, 07, 08, 09, 10, 11, 12, 13, 14, 15, 16, 17, 18, 19, 20, 21, 22, 23, 24 and 25], 17 [part, divisions 18, 21, 22, 23, 24 and 25] and 49 [part, divisions 02, 04, 05, 06, 10, 11, 12, 14, 15, 16, 17, 18, 19 and 21]). Total population: 58,820

Dist. 197 Philadelphia County. Part of **Philadelphia** County consisting of the *City* of Philadelphia (part, wards 11 [part, divisions 20 and 21], 16, 28 and 32 [part, divisions 02, 03, 08, 09, 10, 11, 12, 13, 14, 15, 16, 17, 18, 19, 20, 21, 22, 26, 28, 29 and 30]). Total population: 58,535

Dist. 198 Philadelphia County. Part of **Philadelphia** County consisting of the *City* of Philadelphia (part, wards 09 [part, divisions 03, 09, 10, 11, 12, 13, 14 and 15], 12 [part, divisions 15, 16, 17, 18, 19, 20, 22, 23, 24, 25 and 26], 13 [part, divisions 01, 02, 03, 04 and 05], 21 [part, divisions 23, 24, 25, 26 and 35], 22 [part, divisions 01, 02 and 03], 38 [part, divisions 01, 02, 03, 04, 05, 06, 07, 08, 09, 10, 11, 12, 13, 14, 15, 16, 17, 18, 20, 21, 22, 23 and 24] and 59 [part, divisions 17, 18, 20 and 26]). Total population: 58,479

Dist. 199 Adams, Cumberland and **York** Counties. Part of **Adams** County consisting of the *Townships* of Berwick, Hamilton, Latimore and Reading and the *Boroughs* of Abbottstown, East Berlin and York Springs; part of **Cumberland** County consisting of the *Townships* of Cooke, Dickinson, Penn and South Middleton (part, Precincts Upper and 03) and the *Boroughs* of Carlisle and Mt. Holly Springs and part of **York** County consisting of the *Townships* of Dover, Franklin and Washington and the *Boroughs* of Dover and Franklintown. Total population: 58,286

Dist. 200 Philadelphia County. Part of **Philadelphia** County consisting of the *City* of Philadelphia (part, wards 09 [part, divisions 01, 02, 04, 05, 06, 07, 08, 16 and 17], 21 [part, divisions 30, 33, 34, 38 and 39], 22 [part, divisions 12, 16, 17, 18, 19, 20, 21, 23, 24, 25 and 26] and 50). Total population: 58,423

Dist. 201 Philadelphia County. Part of **Philadelphia** County consisting of the *City* of Philadelphia (part, wards 12 [part, divisions 01, 02, 03, 04, 05, 06, 07, 08, 09, 10, 11, 12, 13, 14 and 21], 17 [part, divisions 08, 09, 10, 11, 14, 15, 16, 17 and 28], 22 [part, divisions 04, 05, 06, 07, 08, 09, 10, 11, 13, 14, 15, 22, 27, 28 and 29] and 59 [part, divisions 01, 02, 03, 04, 05, 06, 07, 08, 09, 10, 11, 12, 13, 14, 15, 16, 19, 21, 22, 23, 24, 25, 27 and 28]). Total population: 59,047

Dist. 202 Philadelphia County. Part of **Philadelphia** County consisting of the *City* of Philadelphia (part, wards 17 [part, divisions 04, 05, 12, 13, 19, 20, 26, 27 and 29], 23 [part, divisions 10, 11 and 12], 35 [part, divisions 14, 15, 16, 22, 23, 24, 26, 28, 29 and 30], 42 [part, divisions 14, 15, 18, 19, 20, 21, 24 and 25], 49 [part, divisions 20, 22, 23, 24, 28 and 29], 53 [part, divisions 01, 02, 03, 04, 05, 06, 07, 08, 09, 10, 11, 12, 13 and 23] and 61 [part, divisions 01, 02, 03, 04, 05, 08, 10 and 30]). Total population: 58,820

Dist. 203 Philadelphia County. Part of **Philadelphia** County consisting of the *City* of Philadelphia (part, wards 10, 17 [part, divisions 01, 02, 03, 06 and 07], 49 [part, divisions 25, 26 and 27] and 61 [part, divisions 06, 07, 09, 11, 12, 13, 14, 15, 16, 17, 18, 19, 20, 21, 22, 23, 24, 25, 26, 27, 28, 29, 31, 32, 33, 34 and 35]). Total population: 59,011

Population of all districts: 11,866,728

LEGISLATIVE DISTRICTS BY COUNTY
HOUSE OF REPRESENTATIVES
1987-1988

ADAMS COUNTY
91st District — Kenneth J. Cole (D)

ADAMS, CUMBERLAND AND YORK
199th District — John H. Broujos (D)

ALLEGHENY COUNTY
19th District — K. Leroy Irvis (D)
20th District — Thomas J. Murphy, Jr. (D)
21st District — Frank J. Pistella (D)
22nd District — Steve Seventy (D)
23rd District — Ivan Itkin (D)
24th District — Joseph Preston, Jr. (D)
27th District — Thomas C. Petrone (D)
28th District — Elaine F. Farmer (R)
29th District — David J. Mayernik (D)
30th District — Richard J. Cessar (R)
31st District — Brian D. Clark (D)
32nd District — Anthony M. DeLuca (D)
33rd District — Roger F. Duffy (D)
34th District — Ronald R. Cowell (D)
35th District — Thomas A. Michlovic (D)
36th District — Michael M. Dawida (D)
38th District — Richard D. Olasz (D)
39th District — David K. Levdansky (D)
40th District — Alice S. Langtry (R)
41st District — Raymond T. Book (R)
42nd District — Terrence F. McVerry (R)
44th District — Ron Gamble (D)
45th District — Fred A. Trello (D)

ALLEGHENY AND WESTMORELAND COUNTIES
25th District — Joseph F. Markosek (D)
37th District — Emil Mrkonic (D)
54th District — Terry E. Van Horne (D)

ARMSTRONG COUNTY
60th District — Henry Livengood (D)

ARMSTRONG, CAMBRIA AND INDIANA COUNTIES
72nd District — (Vacant)

ARMSTRONG AND CLARION COUNTIES
63rd District — David R. Wright (D)

BEAVER COUNTY
14th District — Michael R. Veon (D)
15th District — Nicholas A. Colafella (D)
16th District — Charles P. Laughlin (D)

BEAVER, LAWRENCE AND MERCER COUNTIES
10th District — Frank LaGrotta (D)

BEAVER AND WASHINGTON COUNTIES
46th District — Victor John Lescovitz (D)

BEDFORD, FULTON AND HUNTINGDON COUNTIES
78th District — Dick L. Hess (R)

BERKS COUNTY
126th District — Paul J. Angstadt (R)
127th District — Thomas R. Caltagirone (D)
128th District — James J. Gallen (R)
130th District — Dennis E. Leh (R)

BERKS AND LEBANON COUNTIES
129th District — John S. Davies (R)

BERKS AND LEHIGH COUNTIES
187th District — Paul W. Semmel (R)

BLAIR COUNTY
79th District — Richard A. Geist (R)
80th District — Edwin G. Johnson (R)

BLAIR AND HUNTINGDON COUNTIES
81st District — Samuel E. Hayes, Jr. (R)

BRADFORD COUNTY
110th District — J. Scot Chadwick (R)

BRADFORD, SULLIVAN, SUSQUEHANNA AND WYOMING COUNTIES
111th District — Carmel Sirianni (R)

BUCKS COUNTY
18th District — Edward F. Burns, Jr. (R)
140th District — Thomas C. Corrigan, Sr. (D)
141st District — Anthony J. Melio (D)
142nd District — James L. Wright, Jr. (R)
143rd District — David W. Heckler (R)
144th District — Benjamin H. Wilson (R)
145th District — Paul I. Clymer (R)
178th District — Roy Reinard (R)

BUCKS AND MONTGOMERY COUNTIES
152nd District — Roy W. Cornell (R)

BUTLER COUNTY
11th District — Joseph A. Steighner (D)

BUTLER AND LAWRENCE COUNTIES
12th District — James M. Burd (R)

BUTLER AND MERCER COUNTIES
8th District — Howard L. Fargo (R)

CAMBRIA COUNTY
71st District — John N. Wozniak (D)
73rd District — Edward J. Haluska (D)

CAMBRIA, ARMSTRONG AND INDIANA COUNTIES
72nd District — (Vacant)

CAMBRIA AND SOMERSET COUNTIES
70th District — William Telek (R)

CAMERON, CLEARFIELD AND McKEAN COUNTIES
67th District — Kenneth M. Jadlowiec (R)

CARBON AND MONROE COUNTIES
122nd District — Keith R. McCall (D)

CENTRE AND CLEARFIELD COUNTIES
77th District — Lynn B. Herman (R)

CENTRE, CLEARFIELD, CLINTON AND LYCOMING COUNTIES
76th District — Russell P. Letterman (D)

CENTRE AND MIFFLIN COUNTIES
171st District — Ruth C. Rudy (D)

CHESTER COUNTY
13th District — Arthur D. Hershey (R)
155th District — Samuel W. Morris (D)
156th District — Elinor Zimmerman Taylor (R)
158th District — Joseph R. Pitts (R)

CHESTER AND DELAWARE COUNTIES
167th District — Robert J. Flick (R)

CHESTER AND MONTGOMERY COUNTIES
157th District — Peter R. Vroon (R)

CLARION AND ARMSTRONG COUNTIES
63rd District — David R. Wright (D)

CLEARFIELD COUNTY
74th District — Camille George (D)

CLEARFIELD, CAMERON AND McKEAN COUNTIES
67th District — Kenneth M. Jadlowiec (R)

CLEARFIELD AND CENTRE COUNTIES
77th District — Lynn B. Herman (R)

CLEARFIELD, CENTRE, CLINTON AND LYCOMING COUNTIES
76th District — Russell P. Letterman (D)

CLEARFIELD AND ELK COUNTIES
75th District — Jim Distler (R)

CLINTON, CENTRE, CLEARFIELD AND LYCOMING COUNTIES
76th District — Russell P. Letterman (D)

COLUMBIA AND LUZERNE COUNTIES
117th District — George C. Hasay (R)

COLUMBIA AND MONTOUR COUNTIES
109th District — Ted Stuban (D)

COLUMBIA, MONTOUR AND NORTHUMBERLAND COUNTIES
107th District — Robert E. Belfanti, Jr. (D)

COLUMBIA AND SCHUYLKILL COUNTIES
123rd District — Edward J. Lucyk (D)

CRAWFORD COUNTY
6th District — Connie G. Maine (D)

CRAWFORD AND ERIE COUNTIES
5th District — James R. Merry (R)

CRAWFORD AND MERCER COUNTIES
17th District — Robert D. Robbins (R)

CUMBERLAND COUNTY
87th District — Harold F. Mowery, Jr. (R)
88th District — John Kennedy (R)

CUMBERLAND, ADAMS AND YORK COUNTIES
199th District — John H. Broujos (D)

CUMBERLAND AND PERRY COUNTIES
86th District — Fred C. Noye (R)

DAUPHIN COUNTY
103rd District — Peter C. Wambach (D)
104th District — Jeffrey E. Piccola (R)
105th District — Joseph C. Manmiller (R)
106th District — Rudolph Dininni (R)

DELAWARE COUNTY
159th District — Robert C. Wright (R)
160th District — Kathrynann W. Durham (R)
161st District — Thomas P. Gannon (R)
162nd District — Ron Raymond (R)
163rd District — Nicholas A. Micozzie (R)
164th District — Mario J. Civera, Jr. (R)
165th District — Mary Ann Arty (R)
166th District — Stephen F. Freind (R)
168th District — Matthew J. Ryan (R)

DELAWARE AND CHESTER COUNTIES
167th District — Robert J. Flick (R)

DELAWARE AND PHILADELPHIA COUNTIES
185th District — Robert C. Donatucci (D)

ELK AND CLEARFIELD COUNTIES
75th District — Jim Distler (R)

ERIE COUNTY
1st District — Bernard J. Dombrowski (D)
2nd District — Italo S. Cappabianca (D)
3rd District — Karl W. Boyes (R)
4th District — Harry E. Bowser (R)

ERIE AND CRAWFORD COUNTIES
5th District — James R. Merry (R)

FAYETTE COUNTY
51st District — Fred Taylor (D)
52nd District — Richard A. Kasunic (D)

FAYETTE, GREENE AND WASHINGTON COUNTIES
50th District — H. William DeWeese (D)

FAYETTE AND WASHINGTON COUNTIES
49th District — Peter J. Daley (D)

FAYETTE AND WESTMORELAND COUNTIES
59th District — Jess M. Stairs (R)

FOREST, VENANGO AND WARREN COUNTIES
65th District — Curt Bowley (D)

FRANKLIN COUNTY
89th District — Jeffrey W. Coy (D)

FRANKLIN AND FULTON COUNTIES
90th District — Terry L. Punt (R)

FULTON, BEDFORD AND HUNTINGDON COUNTIES
78th District — Dick L. Hess (R)

FULTON AND FRANKLIN COUNTIES
90th District — Terry L. Punt (R)

GREENE, FAYETTE AND WASHINGTON COUNTIES
50th District — H. William DeWeese (D)

HUNTINGDON, BEDFORD AND FULTON COUNTIES
78th District — Dick L. Hess (R)

HUNTINGDON AND BLAIR COUNTIES
81st District — Samuel E. Hayes, Jr. (R)

INDIANA COUNTY
62nd District — Paul Wass (R)

INDIANA, ARMSTRONG AND CAMBRIA COUNTIES
72nd District — (Vacant)

INDIANA AND JEFFERSON COUNTIES
66th District — Samuel H. Smith (R)

JEFFERSON AND INDIANA COUNTIES
66th District — Samuel H. Smith (R)

JUNIATA, MIFFLIN AND PERRY COUNTIES
82nd District — Walter F. DeVerter (R)

LACKAWANNA COUNTY
113th District — Gaynor Cawley (D)
114th District — Frank A. Serafini (R)

LACKAWANNA AND LUZERNE COUNTIES
118th District — Thomas M. Tigue (D)

LACKAWANNA AND WAYNE COUNTIES
112th District — Fred Belardi (D)
115th District — Edward G. Staback (D)

LANCASTER COUNTY
43rd District — Jere W. Schuler (R)
96th District — Marvin E. Miller, Jr. (R)
97th District — June N. Honaman (R)
98th District — Kenneth E. Brandt (R)
99th District — Terry R. Scheetz (R)
100th District — John E. Barley (R)

LANCASTER AND LEBANON COUNTIES
102nd District — Nicholas B. Moehlmann (R)

LAWRENCE COUNTY
9th District — Thomas J. Fee (D)

LAWRENCE, BEAVER AND MERCER COUNTIES
10th District — Frank LaGrotta (D)

LAWRENCE AND BUTLER COUNTIES
12th District — James M. Burd (R)

LEBANON COUNTY
101st District — George W. Jackson (R)

LEBANON AND BERKS COUNTIES
129th District — John S. Davies (R)

LEBANON AND LANCASTER COUNTIES
102nd District — Nicholas B. Moehlmann (R)

LEHIGH COUNTY
131st District — Karen A. Ritter (D)
132nd District — John F. Pressmann (D)
133rd District — Paul McHale (D)
134th District — Donald W. Snyder (R)

LEHIGH AND BERKS COUNTIES
187th District — Paul W. Semmel (R)

LEHIGH AND NORTHAMPTON COUNTIES
135th District — William C. Rybak (D)

LEHIGH AND SCHUYLKILL COUNTIES
124th District — David G. Argall (R)

LUZERNE COUNTY
116th District — Correale F. Stevens (R)
119th District — Stanley J. Jarolin (D)
120th District — Scott Dietterick (R)
121st District — Kevin Blaum (D)

LUZERNE AND COLUMBIA COUNTIES
117th District — George C. Hasay (R)

LUZERNE AND LACKAWANNA COUNTIES
118th District — Thomas M. Tigue (D)

LYCOMING COUNTY
83rd District — Vacant
84th District — Alvin C. Bush (R)

LYCOMING, CENTRE, CLEARFIELD AND CLINTON COUNTIES
76th District — Russell P. Letterman (D)

McKEAN, CAMERON AND CLEARFIELD COUNTIES
67th District — Kenneth M. Jadlowiec (R)

MERCER COUNTY
7th District — Michael C. Gruitza (D)

MERCER, BEAVER AND LAWRENCE COUNTIES
10th District — Frank LaGrotta (D)

MERCER AND BUTLER COUNTIES
8th District — Howard L. Fargo (R)

MERCER AND CRAWFORD COUNTIES
17th District — Robert D. Robbins (R)

MIFFLIN AND CENTRE COUNTIES
171st District — Ruth C. Rudy (D)

MIFFLIN, JUNIATA AND PERRY COUNTIES
82nd District — Walter F. DeVerter (R)

MONROE COUNTY
189th District — Joseph W. Battisto (D)

MONROE AND CARBON COUNTIES
122nd District — Keith R. McCall (D)

MONROE AND NORTHAMPTON COUNTIES
138th District — Frank W. Yandrisevits (D)

MONTGOMERY COUNTY
53rd District — Robert W. Godshall (R)
61st District — Joseph M. Gladeck, Jr. (R)
146th District — Robert D. Reber, Jr. (R)
147th District — Raymond Bunt, Jr. (R)
148th District — Lois Sherman Hagarty (R)
149th District — Richard A. McClatchy, Jr. (R)
150th District — Joseph A. Lashinger (R)
151st District — George E. Saurman (R)
153rd District — Jon D. Fox (R)
154th District — Charles F. Nahill, Jr. (R)

MONTGOMERY AND BUCKS COUNTIES
152nd District — Roy W. Cornell (R)

MONTGOMERY AND CHESTER COUNTIES
157th District — Peter R. Vroon (R)

MONTOUR AND COLUMBIA COUNTIES
109th District — Ted Stuban (D)

MONTOUR, COLUMBIA AND NORTHUMBERLAND COUNTIES
107th District — Robert E. Belfanti, Jr. (D)

MONTOUR, NORTHUMBERLAND AND SNYDER COUNTIES
108th District — Merle H. Phillips (R)

NORTHAMPTON COUNTY
136th District — Robert Freeman (D)
137th District — Leonard Q. Gruppo (R)

NORTHAMPTON AND LEHIGH COUNTIES
135th District — William C. Rybak (D)

NORTHAMPTON AND MONROE COUNTIES
138th District — Frank W. Yandrisevits (D)

NORTHUMBERLAND, COLUMBIA AND MONTOUR COUNTIES
107th District — Robert E. Belfanti, Jr. (D)

NORTHUMBERLAND, MONTOUR AND SNYDER COUNTIES
108th District — Merle H. Phillips (R)

NORTHUMBERLAND AND SCHUYLKILL COUNTIES
125th District — William E. Baldwin (D)

PERRY AND CUMBERLAND COUNTIES
86th District — Fred C. Noye (R)

PERRY, JUNIATA AND MIFFLIN COUNTIES
82nd District — Walter F. DeVerter (R)

PHILADELPHIA COUNTY
169th District — Dennis M. O'Brien (R)
170th District — George T. Kenney, Jr. (R)
172nd District — John M. Perzel (R)
173rd District — Frances Weston (R)
174th District — Max Pievsky (D)
175th District — Gerard A. Kosinski (D)
176th District — Christopher R. Wogan (R))
177th District — John Taylor (R)
179th District — William W. Rieger (D)
180th District — Ralph Acosta (D)
181st District — (Vacant)
182nd District — Babette Josephs (D)
183rd District — Nicholas J. Maiale (D)
184th District — Joseph Howlett (D)
186th District — Edward A. Wiggins (D)
188th District — James R. Roebuck (D)
190th District — Vincent Hughes (D)
191st District — Peter Daniel Truman (D)
192nd District — Chaka Fattah (D)
194th District — Richard Hayden (D)
195th District — Frank L. Oliver (D)
196th District — Ruth B. Harper (D)
197th District — Andrew J. Carn (D)
198th District — Robert W. O'Donnell (D)
200th District — Gordon J. Linton (D)
201st District — David P. Richardson, Jr. (D)
202nd District — Mark B. Cohen (D)
203rd District — Dwight Evans (D)

PHILADELPHIA AND DELAWARE COUNTIES
185th District — Robert C. Donatucci (D)

PIKE, SUSQUEHANNA AND WAYNE COUNTIES
139th District — Jerry Birmelin (R)

POTTER AND TIOGA COUNTIES
68th District — Edgar A. Carlson (R)

SCHUYLKILL AND COLUMBIA COUNTIES
123rd District — Edward J. Lucyk (D)

SCHUYLKILL AND LEHIGH COUNTIES
124th District — David G. Argall (R)

SCHUYLKILL AND NORTHUMBERLAND COUNTIES
125th District — William E. Baldwin (D)

SNYDER, MONTOUR AND NORTHUMBERLAND COUNTIES
108th District — Merle H. Phillips (R)

SNYDER AND UNION COUNTIES
85th District — John Showers (D)

SOMERSET COUNTY
69th District — William R. Lloyd, Jr. (D)

SOMERSET AND CAMBRIA COUNTIES
70th District — William Telek (R)

SULLIVAN, BRADFORD, SUSQUEHANNA AND WYOMING COUNTIES
111th District — Carmel Sirianni (R)

SUSQUEHANNA, BRADFORD, SULLIVAN AND WYOMING COUNTIES
111th District — Carmel Sirianni (R)

SUSQUEHANNA, PIKE AND WAYNE COUNTIES
139th District — Jerry Birmelin (R)

TIOGA AND POTTER COUNTIES
68th District — Edgar A. Carlson (R)

UNION AND SNYDER COUNTIES
85th District — John Showers (D)

VENANGO COUNTY
64th District — Ronald E. Black (R)

VENANGO, FOREST AND WARREN COUNTIES
65th District — Curt Bowley (D)

WARREN, FOREST AND VENANGO COUNTIES
65th District — Curt Bowley (D)

WASHINGTON COUNTY
47th District — Roger Raymond Fischer (R)
48th District — David W. Sweet (D)

WASHINGTON AND BEAVER COUNTIES
46th District — Victor John Lescovitz (D)

WASHINGTON AND FAYETTE COUNTIES
49th District — Peter J. Daley (D)

WASHINGTON, FAYETTE AND GREENE COUNTIES
50th District — H. William DeWeese (D)

WAYNE AND LACKAWANNA COUNTIES
112th District — Fred Belardi (D)
115th District — Edward G. Staback (D)

WAYNE, PIKE AND SUSQUEHANNA COUNTIES
139th District — Jerry Birmelin (R)

WESTMORELAND COUNTY
26th District — Eugene G. Saloom (D)
55th District — Joseph A. Petrarca (D)
56th District — Allen G. Kukovich (D)
57th District — Amos K. Hutchinson (D)
58th District — James J. Manderino (D)

WESTMORELAND AND ALLEGHENY COUNTIES
25th District — Joseph F. Markosek (D)
37th District — Emil Mrkonic (D)
54th District — Terry E. Van Horne (D)

WESTMORELAND AND FAYETTE COUNTIES
59th District — Jess M. Stairs (R)

WYOMING, BRADFORD, SULLIVAN AND SUSQUEHANNA COUNTIES
111th District — Carmel Sirianni (R)

YORK COUNTY
92nd District — Bruce Smith (R)
93rd District — A. Carville Foster, Jr. (R)
94th District — Gregory M. Snyder (R)
95th District — Michael E. Bortner (D)
193rd District — Donald W. Dorr (R)

YORK, ADAMS AND CUMBERLAND COUNTIES
199th District — John H. Broujos (D)

HOUSE OF REPRESENTATIVES
STANDING COMMITTEES OF THE SESSION OF 1987-1988

AGRICULTURE AND RURAL AFFAIRS

Majority	Minority
MORRIS, *Chairman*	SIRIANNI, *Chairwoman*
RUDY, *Vice Chairman*	WASS, *Vice Chairman*
BALDWIN, *Secretary*	
Battisto	Bush
Bowley	Chadwick
Broujos	DeVerter
Coy	Fargo
Haluska	Hershey
LaGrotta	Honaman
Lloyd	Johnson
Maine	Semmel
Mayernik	
Showers	
Yandrisevits	

APPROPRIATIONS

Majority	Minority
PIEVSKY, *Chairman*	McCLATCHY, *Chairman*
CAPPABIANCA, *Vice Chairman*	ARTY, *Subcommittee Chairwoman on Health and Welfare*
BELARDI, *Subcommittee Chairman on Health and Welfare*	MOWERY, *Subcommittee Chairman on Education*
WIGGINS, *Subcommittee Chairman on Education*	GRUPPO, *Subcommittee Chairman on Capital Budget*
STEIGHNER, *Subcommittee Chairman on Capital Budget*	
STUBAN, *Secretary*	
Belfanti	Book
Blaum	Boyes
Caltagirone	Clymer
Cawley	Cornell
Clark	Flick
Colafella	Perzel
Donatucci	Phillips
Duffy	Schuler
Evans	
Gruitza	
Kukovich	
Petrone	
Pistella	
Seventy	

BUSINESS AND COMMERCE

Majority	Minority
TAYLOR, F., *Chairman*	GALLEN, *Chairman*
DONATUCCI, *Subcommittee Chairman on Banking and Savings and Loan Associations*	HAGARTY, *Subcommittee Chairwoman on Banking and Savings and Loan Associations*
SEVENTY, *Subcommittee Chairman on Housing*	SERAFINI, *Subcommittee Chairman on Housing*
LIVENGOOD, *Subcommittee Chairman on Industrial Development, Recreation and Tourism*	GEIST, *Subcommittee Chairman on Industrial Development, Recreation and Tourism*
OLASZ, *Secretary*	
Cappabianca	Burd
Duffy	Dininni
Haluska	Dorr
Lescovitz	Godshall
Linton	McVerry
Maiale	Wright, J. L.
Pistella	
Preston	
Van Horne	

COMMITTEE ON COMMITTEES

Majority	Minority
HUTCHINSON, *Chairman*	GALLEN, *Chairman*
Blaum	Dininni
Dombrowski	McVerry
Duffy	Sirianni
Fee	Wright, J. L.
George	
Irvis	
Itkin	
Linton	
Pievsky	
Rieger	

CONSERVATION

Majority	Minority
GEORGE, *Chairman*	HASAY, *Chairman*
WOZNIAK, *Vice Chairman*	REBER, *Vice Chairman*
BOWLEY, *Secretary*	
Belardi	Argall
Bortner	Barley
Broujos	Jadlowiec
Freeman	Reinard
Hayden	Saurman
Jarolin	Scheetz
Levdansky	Smith, S.
Lucyk	Wass
Michlovic	
Murphy	
Steighner	

CONSUMER AFFAIRS

Majority	Minority
LAUGHLIN, *Chairman*	BURNS, *Chairman*
KUKOVICH, *Subcommittee*	DURHAM, *Subcommittee*
Chairman on Public Utilities	*Chairwoman*
FREEMAN, *Secretary*	*on Public Utilities*

Blaum	Bush
Coy	Civera
DeLuca	Fox
Lloyd	Hershey
Maine	Jadlowiec
McCall	Leh
McHale	Punt
Steighner	Weston
Truman	
Van Horne	
Wambach	

EDUCATION

Majority	Minority
COWELL, *Chairman*	FISCHER, *Chairman*
EVANS, *Subcommittee*	TELEK, *Subcommittee Chairman*
Chairman	*on Basic Education*
on Basic Education	TAYLOR, E. Z., *Subcommittee*
COLAFELLA, *Subcommittee*	*Chairwoman*
Chairman	*on Higher Education*
on Higher Education	
TIGUE, *Secretary*	

Battisto	Burns
Clark	Davies
Coy	Fox
Daley	Freind
Fattah	Herman
Kosinski	Stairs
Lescovitz	Wass
Linton	
Livengood	
Wiggins	

ETHICS COMMITTEE

RIEGER, *Chairman*
McVERRY, *Vice Chairman*
FEE, *Secretary*

Dombrowski	Honaman
Donatucci	Jackson
	Reber

FEDERAL-STATE RELATIONS

Majority	Minority
COLE, *Chairman*	BURD, *Chairman*
DALEY, *Vice Chairman*	JACKSON, *Vice Chairman*
YANDRISEVITS, *Secretary*	

Blaum	Distler
Corrigan	Farmer
Fattah	Hess
Hayden	Robbins
Hughes	Smith, B.
LaGrotta	Smith, S.
Maine	Taylor, J.
Mayernik	Weston
McHale	
Melio	
Roebuck	

FINANCE

Majority	Minority
TRELLO, *Chairman*	WILSON, *Chairman*
PETRONE, *Vice Chairman*	CORNELL, *Vice Chairman*
BATTISTO, *Secretary*	

Carn	Bunt
Colafella	Fargo
DeLuca	Foster
Evans	Gallen
Maiale	Gannon
Mayernik	Kenney
Preston	Robbins
Seventy	Smith, B.
Showers	
Van Horne	
Wiggins	

GAME AND FISHERIES

Majority	Minority
LETTERMAN, *Chairman*	DAVIES, *Chairman*
GRUITZA, *Vice Chairman*	PHILLIPS, *Vice Chairman*
MARKOSEK, *Secretary*	

Belfanti	Birmelin
Bowley	Carlson
Gamble	Distler
Kasunic	Fischer
Levdansky	Gruppo
McCall	Hess
Olasz	Merry
Petrone	Smith, B.
Seventy	
Staback	
Tigue	

HEALTH AND WELFARE

Majority	Minority
RICHARDSON, *Chairman*	DORR, *Chairman*
PISTELLA, *Subcommittee*	GLADECK, *Subcommittee*
Chairman on Health	*Chairman on Health*
DAWIDA, *Subcommittee*	CLYMER, *Subcommittee*
Chairman on Welfare	*Chairman on Welfare*
KUKOVICH, *Subcommittee*	LASHINGER, *Subcommittee*
Chairman on Youth and Aging	*Chairman*
KASUNIC, *Secretary*	*on Youth and Aging*

Cawley	Arty
Howlett	Jadlowiec
Hughes	Leh
Josephs	Saurman
Lucyk	Snyder, D.
Pressmann	Taylor, E. Z.
Stuban	
Tigue	
Wiggins	

INSURANCE

Majority	Minority
RYBAK, *Chairman*	DeVERTER, *Chairman*
MAIALE, *Vice Chairman*	GANNON, *Vice Chairman*
CARN, *Secretary*	

Cawley	Durham
Collafella	Godshall
Dawida	Mowery
Gamble	O'Brien
Josephs	Piccola
Lescovitz	Reinard
Michlovic	Snyder, G.
Murphy	Vroon
Truman	
Wambach	
Yandrisevits	

LIQUOR CONTROL

Majority	Minority
SALOOM, *Chairman*	MANMILLER, *Chairman*
CAWLEY, *Vice Chairman*	MICOZZIE, *Vice Chairman*
JAROLIN, *Secretary*	

Acosta	Civera
Belardi	Farmer
Carn	Gladeck
Clark	Moehlmann
Duffy	Perzel
Howlett	Punt
McCall	Stevens
Olasz	Wogan
Roebuck	
Tigue	
Wambach	

JUDICIARY

Majority	Minority
DeWEESE, *Chairman*	MOEHLMANN, *Chairman*
KOSINSKI, *Subcommittee Chairman on Courts*	McVERRY, *Subcommittee Chairman on Courts*
BLAUM, *Subcommittee Chairman on Crime and Corrections*	PICCOLA, *Subcommittee Chairman on Crime and Corrections*
MAYERNIK, *Secretary*	

Baldwin	Birmelin
Bortner	Hagarty
Caltagirone	Heckler
Dawida	Lashinger
Fattah	Reber
Gruitza	Wogan
Josephs	Wright, R. C.
Kukovich	
Maiale	
McHale	

LOCAL GOVERNMENT

Majority	Minority
SWEET, *Chairman*	FOSTER, *Chairman*
DUFFY, *Subcommittee Chairman on Boroughs*	SNYDER, D., *Subcommittee Chairman on Boroughs*
SHOWERS, *Subcommittee Chairman on Townships*	MERRY, *Subcommittee Chairman on Townships*
GAMBLE, *Subcommittee Chairman on Counties*	KENNEDY, *Subcommittee Chairman on Counties*
COY, *Secretary*	

Baldwin	Barley
Broujos	Distler
DeLuca	Nahill
Haluska	Raymond
Jarolin	Scheetz
Livengood	Telek
Melio	
Stuban	
Wozniak	

LABOR RELATIONS

Majority	Minority
COHEN, *Chairman*	PITTS, *Chairman*
BELFANTI, *Vice Chairman*	PUNT, *Vice Chairman*
DeLUCA, *Secretary*	

Belardi	Carlson
Carn	Chadwick
Donatucci	Flick
Freeman	Gladeck
Howlett	Heckler
Hughes	Jackson
Kasunic	Merry
Kosinski	Sirianni
Levdansky	
Pressmann	
Veon	

MILITARY AND VETERANS AFFAIRS

Majority	Minority
MRKONIC, *Chairman*	VACANT, *Chairman*
McCALL, *Vice Chairman*	JOHNSON, *Vice Chairman*
STABACK, *Secretary*	

Baldwin	Black
Broujos	Book
Cappabianca	Dietterick
Daley	Durham
Evans	Fargo
Hughes	Jackson
LaGrotta	Manmiller
Mayernik	Robbins
Petrone	
Showers	
Veon	

MINES AND ENERGY MANAGEMENT

Majority	Minority
PETRARCA, *Chairman*	WRIGHT, J. L., *Chairman*
HALUSKA, *Vice Chairman*	STAIRS, *Vice Chairman*
LEVDANSKY, *Secretary*	

Belardi	Angstadt
Belfanti	Argall
Daley	Black
Kasunic	Carlson
Lucyk	Semmel
Markosek	Smith, S.
McCall	Snyder, D.
Michlovic	Stevens
Olasz	
Wozniak	

PROFESSIONAL LICENSURE

Majority	Minority
RIEGER, *Chairman*	VROON, *Chairman*
LLOYD, *Vice Chairman*	BOYES, *Vice Chairman*
VEON, *Secretary*	

Acosta	Book
Cappabianca	Farmer
Corrigan	Herman
Donatucci	Langtry
Jarolin	Micozzie
Markosek	Miller
Pressmann	Saurman
Preston	Serafini
Ritter	
Rudy	
Staback	

RULES COMMITTEE

MANDERINO, *Chairman*

Dombrowski	Bowser
Hutchinson	Brandt
Irvis	Cessar
Itkin	Hayes
Letterman	McClatchy
O'Donnell	Noye
Pievsky	Ryan
Rieger	
Taylor, F.	

STATE GOVERNMENT

Majority	Minority
OLIVER, *Chairman*	MILLER, *Chairman*
MICHLOVIC, *Sub-committee Chairman on Telecommunications*	HONAMAN, *Subcommittee Chairman on Telecommunications*
VACANT, *Secretary*	

Battisto	Argall
Corrigan	Bunt
Freeman	Hasay
Hughes	Kennedy
Linton	Leh
Livengood	Raymond
McHale	Schuler
Melio	
Preston	
Ritter	
Rudy	
Truman	

TRANSPORTATION

Majority	Minority
HUTCHINSON, *Chairman*	DININNI, *Chairman*
LESCOVITZ, *Subcommittee Chairman on Aviation*	WILSON, *Subcommittee Chairman on Aviation*
MURPHY, *Subcommittee Chairman on Highways*	O'BRIEN, *Subcommittee Chairman on Highways*
LINTON, *Subcommittee Chairman on Public Transportation*	NAHILL, *Subcommittee Chairman on Public Transportation*
CLARK, *Subcommittee Chairman on Transportation Safety*	CIVERA, *Subcommittee Chairman on Transportation Safety*
LUCYK, *Secretary*	

Caltagirone	Dietterick
Gamble	Geist
Gruitza	Hess
Lloyd	Pitts
Markosek	Snyder, G.
Steighner	
Stuban	
Wozniak	

URBAN AFFAIRS

Majority	Minority
HARPER, *Chairman*	FREIND, *Chairman*
TRUMAN, *Acting Subcommittee Chairman on First Class Cities, Counties*	PERZEL, *Subcommittee Chairman on First Class Cities, Counties*
PRESTON, *Subcommittee Chairman on Second Class Cities, Counties*	WRIGHT, *Subcommittee Chairman on Second Class Cities, Counties*
VAN HORNE, *Subcommittee Chairman on Third Class Cities, Counties*	ANGSTADT, *Subcommittee Chairman on Third Class Cities, Counties*
WAMBACH, *Secretary*	

Acosta	Black
Bortner	Kenney
Caltagirone	Langtry
Dawida	Taylor, J.
Hayden	Weston
Murphy	Wogan
Pressmann	
Ritter	
Roebuck	

HOUSE COMMITTEE ASSIGNMENTS

Acosta, Ralph (D)
Liquor Control
Professional Licensure
Urban Affairs

Angstadt, Paul J. (R)
Urban Affairs,
   Sub-Committee Chairman
   (Third Class Cities, Counties)
Mines and Energy Management

Argall, David G. (R)
Conservation
Mines and Energy Management
State Government

Arty, Mary Ann (R)
Appropriations
   Sub-Committee Chairwoman
   (Health and Welfare)
Health and Welfare

Baldwin, William E. (D)
Agriculture and Rural Affairs, Secretary
Judiciary
Local Government
Military and Veterans Affairs

Barley, John E. (R)
Conservation
Local Government

Battisto, Joseph W. (D)
Finance, Secretary
Agriculture and Rural Affairs
Education
State Government

Belardi, Fred (D)
Appropriations,
   Sub-Committee Chairman
   (Health and Welfare)
Conservation
Labor Relations
Liquor Control
Mines and Energy Management

Belfanti, Robert (D)
Labor Relations, Vice Chairman
Appropriations
Games and Fisheries
Mines and Energy Management

Birmelin, Jerry (R)
Game and Fisheries
Judiciary

Black, Ronald E. (R)
Military and Veterans Affairs
Mines and Energy Management
Urban Affairs

Blaum, Kevin (D)
Judiciary
   Sub-Committee Chairman
   (Crime, Corrections)
Appropriations
Consumer Affairs
Federal-State Relations

Book, Ray (R)
Appropriations
Military and Veterans Affairs
Professional Licensure

Bortner, Michael E. (D)
Conservation
Judiciary
Urban Affairs

Bowley, Curt (D)
Conservation, Secretary
Agriculture and Rural Affairs
Game and Fisheries

Bowser, Harry (R)
Minority Caucus Administrator
Rules

Boyes, Karl W. (R)
Professional Licensure, Vice Chairman
Appropriations

Brandt, Kenneth E. (R)
Minority Policy Committee, Chairman
Rules

Broujos, John (D)
Agriculture and Rural Affairs
Conservation
Local Government
Military and Veterans Affairs

Bunt, Raymond, Jr. (R)
Finance
State Government

Burd, James M. (R)
Federal-State Relations, Chairman
Business and Commerce

Burns, Edward F., Jr. (R)
Consumer Affairs, Chairman
Education

Bush, Alvin C. (R)
Agriculture and Rural Affairs
Consumer Affairs

Caltagirone, Thomas R. (D)
Appropriations
Judiciary
Transportation
Urban Affairs

Cappabianca, Italo (D)
Appropriations, Vice Chairman
Business and Commerce
Military and Veterans Affairs
Professional Licensure

Carlson, Edgar A. (R)
Game and Fisheries
Labor Relations
Mines and Energy Management

Carn, Andrew J. (D)
Insurance, Secretary
Finance
Labor Relations
Liquor Control

Cawley, Gaynor (D)
Liquor Control, Vice Chairman
Appropriations
Health and Welfare
Insurance

Cessar, Richard J. (R)
Minority Caucus Secretary
Rules

Chadwick, J. Scot (R)
Agriculture and Rural Affairs
Labor Relations

Civera, Mario J. (R)
Transportation,
   Sub-Committee Chairman
   (Transportation Safety)
Consumer Affairs
Liquor Control

Clark, Brian (D)
Transportation,
   Sub-Committee Chairman
   (Transportation Safety)
Appropriations
Education
Liquor Control

Clymer, Paul I. (R)
Health and Welfare,
   Sub-Committee Chairman
   (Welfare)
Appropriations

Cohen, Mark B. (D)
Labor Relations, Chairman

Colafella, Nicholas A. (D)
Education,
    Sub-Committee Chairman
    (Higher Education)
Appropriations
Finance
Insurance

Cole, Kenneth J. (D)
Federal-State Relations, Chairman

Cornell, Roy W. (R)
Finance, Vice Chairman
Appropriations

Corrigan, Thomas (D)
Federal-State Relations
Professional Licensure
State Government

Cowell, Ronald R. (D)
Education, Chairman

Coy, Jeffrey W. (D)
Local Government, Secretary
Agriculture and Rural Affairs
Consumer Affairs
Education

Daley, Peter J. (D)
Federal-State Relations, Vice Chairman
Education
Military and Veterans Affairs
Mines and Energy Management

Davies, John S. (R)
Game and Fisheries, Chairman
Education

Dawida, Michael M. (D)
Health and Welfare,
    Sub-Committee Chairman
    (Welfare)
Insurance
Judiciary
Urban Affairs

DeLuca, Anthony M. (D)
Labor Relations, Secretary
Consumer Affairs
Finance
Local Government

DeVerter, Walter (R)
Insurance, Chairman
Agriculture and Rural Affairs

DeWeese, H. William (D)
Judiciary, Chairman

Dietterick, Scott (R)
Military and Veterans Affairs
Transportation

Dininni, Rudolph (R)
Transportation, Chairman
Business and Commerce

Distler, James (R)
Federal-State Relations
Game and Fisheries
Local Government

Dombrowski, Bernard J. (D)
Majority Caucus Administrator
Ethics
Rules

Donatucci, Robert (D)
Business and Commerce,
    Sub-Committee Chairman
    (Banking and Savings and Loan Assn.)
Appropriations
Ethics
Labor Relations
Professional Licensure

Dorr, Donald W. (R)
Health and Welfare, Chairman
Business and Commerce

Duffy, Roger F. (D)
Local Government,
    Sub-Committee Chairman
    (Boroughs)
Appropriations
Business and Commerce
Liquor Control

Durham, Kathrynann (R)
Consumer Affairs,
    Sub-Committee Chairman
    (Public Utilities)
Insurance
Military and Veterans Affairs

Evans, Dwight (D)
Education,
    Sub-Committee Chairman
    (Basic Education)
Appropriations
Finance
Military and Veterans Affairs

Fargo, Howard L. (R)
Agriculture and Rural Affairs
Finance
Military and Veterans Affairs

Farmer, Elaine F. (R)
Federal-State Relations
Liquor Control
Professional Licensure

Fattah, Chaka (D)
Education
Federal-State Relations
Judiciary

Fee, Thomas J. (D)
Majority Caucus Secretary
Ethics, Secretary

Fischer, Roger Raymond (R)
Education, Chairman
Game and Fisheries

Flick, Robert J. (R)
Appropriations
Labor Relations

Foster, A. Carville, Jr. (R)
Local Government, Chairman
Finance

Fox, Jon D. (R)
Consumer Affairs
Education

Freeman, Robert (D)
Consumer Affairs, Secretary
Conservation
Labor Relations
State Government

Freind, Stephen F. (R)
Urban Affairs, Chairman
Education

Gallen, James J. (R)
Business and Commerce, Chairman
Finance

Gamble, Ron (D)
Local Government,
    Sub-Committee Chairman
    (Counties)
Game and Fisheries
Insurance
Transportation

Gannon, Thomas P. (R)
Insurance, Vice Chairman
Finance

Geist, Richard A. (R)
Business and Commerce
    Sub-Committee Chairman
    (Industrial Development, Recreation
    and Tourism)
Transportation

George, Camille (D)
Conservation, Chairman

Gladeck, Joseph M., Jr. (R)
Health and Welfare,
    Sub-Committee Chairman
    (Health)
Labor Relations
Liquor Control

Godshall, Robert W. (R)
Business and Commerce
Insurance

Gruitza, Michael C. (D)
Game and Fisheries, Vice Chairman
Appropriations
Judiciary
Transportation

Gruppo, Leonard Q. (R)
Appropriations,
    Sub-Committee Chairman
    (Capital Budget)
Game and Fisheries

Hagarty, Lois S. (R)
Business and Commerce,
Sub-Committee Chairwoman
(Banking and Savings
and Loan Assn.)
Judiciary

Haluska, Edward J. (D)
Mines and Energy Management,
Vice Chairman
Agriculture and Rural Affairs
Business and Commerce
Local Government

Harper, Ruth B. (D)
Urban Affairs, Chairman

Hasay, George C. (R)
Conservation, Chairman
State Government

Hayden, Richard (D)
Conservation
Federal-State Relations
Urban Affairs

Hayes, Samuel E., Jr. (R)
Minority Whip
Rules

Heckler, David W. (R)
Judiciary
Labor Relations

Herman, Lynn B. (R)
Education
Professional Licensure

Hershey, Art (R)
Agriculture and Rural Affairs
Consumer Affairs

Hess, Dick L. (R)
Federal-State Relations
Game and Fisheries
Transportation

Honaman, June N. (R)
State Government,
Sub-Committee Chairman
(Telecommunications)
Agriculture and Rural Affairs
Ethics

Howlett, Joseph (D)
Health and Welfare
Labor Relations
Liquor Control

Hughes, Vincent (D)
Federal-State Relations
Health and Welfare
Labor Relations
Military and Veterans Affairs
State Government

Hutchinson, Amos K. (D)
Transportation, Chairman
Rules

Irvis, K. Leroy (D)
Speaker
Rules

Itkin, Ivan (D)
Majority Caucus Chairman
Rules

Jackson, George W. (R)
Federal-State Relations,
Vice Chairman
Ethics
Labor Relations
Military and Veterans Affairs

Jadlowiec, Kenneth (R)
Conservation
Consumer Affairs
Health and Welfare

Jarolin, Stanley (D)
Liquor Control, Secretary
Conservation
Local Government
Professional Licensure

Johnson, Edwin G. (R)
Military and Veterans Affairs,
Vice Chairman
Agriculture and Rural Affairs

Josephs, Babette (D)
Health and Welfare
Insurance
Judiciary

Kasunic, Richard A. (D)
Health and Welfare,
Secretary
Game and Fisheries
Labor Relations
Mines and Energy Management

Kennedy, John (R)
Local Government,
Sub-Committee Chairman
(Counties)
State Government

Kenney, George T. (R)
Finance
Urban Affairs

Kosinski, Gerard A. (D)
Judiciary,
Sub-Committee Chairman
(Courts)
Education
Labor Relations

Kukovich, Allen G. (D)
Consumer Affairs,
Sub-Committee Chairman
(Public Utilities)
Health and Welfare,
Sub-Committee Chairman
(Youth and Aging)
Appropriations
Judiciary

LaGrotta, Frank (D)
Agriculture and Rural Affairs
Federal State Relations
Military and Veterans Affairs

Langtry, Alice S. (R)
Professional Licensure
Urban Affairs

Lashinger, Joseph (R)
Health and Welfare,
Sub-Committee Chairman
(Youth and Aging)
Judiciary

Laughlin, Charles (D)
Consumer Affairs, Chairman

Leh, Dennis E. (R)
Consumer Affairs
Health and Welfare
State Government

Lescovitz, Victor J. (D)
Transportation,
Sub-Committee Chairman
(Aviation)
Business and Commerce
Education
Insurance

Letterman, Russell P. (D)
Game and Fisheries,
Chairman
Rules

Levdansky, David K. (D)
Mines and Energy Management,
Secretary
Conservation
Game and Fisheries
Labor Relations

Linton, Gordon J. (D)
Transportation,
Sub-Committee Chairman
(Public Transportation)
Business and Commerce
Education
State Government

Livengood, Henry (D)
Business and Commerce,
Sub-Committee Chairman
(Industrial Development,
Recreation and Tourism)
Education
Local Government
State Government

Lloyd, William R., Jr. (D)
Professional Licensure,
Vice Chairman
Agriculture and Rural Affairs
Consumer Affairs
Transportation

Lucyk, Edward J. (D)
Transportation, Secretary
Conservation
Health and Welfare
Mines and Energy Management

Maiale, Nicholas J. (D)
Insurance, Vice Chairman
Business and Commerce
Finance
Judiciary

Maine, Connie G. (D)
Agriculture and Rural Affairs
Consumer Affairs
Federal-State Relations

Manderino, James J. (D)
Majority Floor Leader
Rules, Chairman

Manmiller, Joseph C. (R)
Liquor Control, Chairman
Military and Veterans Affairs

Markosek, Joseph (D)
Game and Fisheries, Secretary
Mines and Energy Management
Professional Licensure
Transportation

Mayernik, David J. (D)
Judiciary, Secretary
Agriculture and Rural Affairs
Federal-State Relations
Finance
Military and Veterans Affairs

McCall, Keith (D)
Military and Veterans Affairs,
Vice Chairman
Consumer Affairs
Game and Fisheries
Liquor Control
Mines and Energy Management

McClatchy, Richard A., Jr. (R)
Appropriations, Chairman
Rules

McHale, Paul (D)
Consumer Affairs
Federal-State Relations
Judiciary
State Government

McVerry, Terrence F. (R)
Ethics, Vice Chairman
Judiciary,
Sub-Committee Chairman
(Courts)
Business and Commerce

Melio, Anthony (D)
Federal-State Relations
Local Government
State Government

Merry, James R. (R)
Local Government,
Sub-Committee Chairman
(Townships)
Game and Fisheries
Labor Relations

Michlovic, Thomas A. (D)
State Government,
Sub-Committee Chairman
(Telecommunications)
Conservation
Insurance
Mines and Energy Management

Micozzie, Nicholas B. (R)
Liquor Control, Vice Chairman
Professional Licensure

Miller, Marvin E. (R)
State Government,
Chairman
Professional Licensure

Moehlmann, Nicholas B. (R)
Judiciary, Chairman
Liquor Control

Morris, Samuel W. (D)
Agriculture and Rural Affairs,
Chairman

Mowery, Harold F., Jr. (R)
Appropriations,
Sub-Committee Chairman
(Education)
Insurance

Mrkonic, Emil (D)
Military and Veterans Affairs,
Chairman

Murphy, Thomas J. (D)
Transportation,
Sub-Committee Chairman
(Highways)
Conservation
Insurance
Urban Affairs

Nahill, Charles F., Jr. (R)
Transportation,
Sub-Committee Chairman
(Public Transportation)
Local Government

Noye, Fred C. (R)
Minority Caucus Chairman
Rules

O'Brien, Dennis M. (R)
Transportation,
Sub-Committee Chairman
(Highways)
Insurance

O'Donnell, Robert W. (D)
Majority Whip
Rules

Olasz, Richard D. (D)
Business and Commerce,
Secretary
Game and Fisheries
Liquor Control
Mines and Energy Management

Oliver, Frank (D)
State Government, Chairman

Perzel, John M. (R)
Urban Affairs,
Sub-Committee Chairman
(First Class Cities, Counties)
Appropriations
Liquor Control

Petrarca, Joseph A. (D)
Mines and Energy Management,
Chairman

Petrone, Thomas C. (D)
Finance, Vice Chairman
Appropriations
Game and Fisheries
Military and Veterans Affairs

Phillips, Merle H. (R)
Game and Fisheries, Vice Chairman
Appropriations

Piccola, Jeffrey E. (R)
Judiciary, Sub-Committee Chairman
(Crime and Corrections)
Insurance

Pievsky, Max (D)
Appropriations, Chairman
Rules

Pistella, Frank J. (D)
Health and Welfare,
Sub-Committee Chairman
(Health)
Appropriations
Business and Commerce

Pitts, Joseph (R)
Labor Relations, Chairman
Transportation

Pressmann, John F. (D)
Health and Welfare
Labor Relations
Professional Licensure
Urban Affairs

Preston, Joseph, Jr. (D)
Urban Affairs,
Sub-Committee Chairman
(Second Class Cities, Counties)
Business and Commerce
Finance
Professional Licensure
State Government

Punt, Terry (R)
Labor Relations, Vice Chairman
Consumer Affairs
Liquor Control

Raymond, Ron (R)
Local Government
State Government

Reber, Robert D. (R)
Conservation, Vice Chairman
Ethics
Judiciary

Reinard, Roy (R)
Conservation
Insurance

Richardson, David P., Jr. (D)
Health and Welfare, Chairman

Rieger, William W. (D)
Ethics, Chairman
Professional Licensure, Chairman
Rules

Ritter, Karen (D)
Professional Licensure
State Government
Urban Affairs

Robbins, Robert D. (R)
Federal-State Relations
Finance
Military and Veterans Affairs

Roebuck, James R. (D)
Liquor Control
Federal-State Relations
Urban Affairs

Rudy, Ruth C. (D)
Agriculture and Rural Affairs,
Vice Charman
Professional Licensure
State Government

Ryan, Matthew J. (R)
Minority Floor Leader
Rules

Rybak, William C. (D)
Insurance, Chairman

Saloom, Eugene G. (D)
Liquor Control, Chairman

Saurman, George E. (R)
Conservation
Health and Welfare
Professional Licensure

Scheetz, Terry R. (R)
Conservation
Local Government

Schuler, Jere W. (R)
Appropriations
State Government

Semmel, Paul (R)
Agriculture and Rural Affairs
Mines and Energy Management

Serafini, Frank A. (R)
Business and Commerce,
Sub-Committee Chairman
(Housing)
Professional Licensure

Seventy, Steve (D)
Business and Commerce,
Sub-Committee Chairman
(Housing)
Appropriations
Finance
Game and Fisheries

Showers, John R. (D)
Local Government,
Sub-Committee Chairman
(Townships)
Agriculture and Rural Affairs
Finance
Military and Veterans Affairs

Sirianni, Carmel (R)
Agriculture and Rural Affairs,
Chairwoman
Labor Relations

Smith, Bruce (R)
Federal-State Relations
Finance
Game and Fisheries

Smith, Sam (R)
Conservation
Federal-State Relations
Mines and Energy Management

Snyder, Donald W. (R)
Local Government,
Sub-Committee Chairman
(Boroughs)
Health and Welfare
Mines and Energy Management

Snyder, Gregory M. (R)
Insurance
Transportation

Staback, Edward G. (D)
Military and Veterans Affairs, Secretary
Game and Fisheries
Professional Licensure

Stairs, Jess M. (R)
Mines and Energy Management,
Vice Chairman
Education

Steighner, Joseph A. (D)
Appropriations,
Sub-Committee Chairman
(Capital Budget)
Conservation
Consumer Affairs
Transportation

Stevens, Correale F. (R)
Liquor Control
Mines and Energy Management

Stuban, Ted (D)
Appropriations, Secretary
Health and Welfare
Local Government
Transportation

Sweet, David W. (D)
Local Government, Chairman

Taylor, Elinor Z. (R)
Education, Sub-Committee
Chairwoman (Higher Education)
Health and Welfare

Taylor, Fred (D)
Business and Commerce,
Chairman
Rules

Taylor, John (R)
Federal-State Relations
Urban Affairs

Telek, William (R)
Education,
Sub-Committee Chairman
(Basic Education)
Local Government

Tigue, Thomas (D)
Education, Secretary
Game and Fisheries
Health and Welfare
Liquor Control

Trello, Fred A. (D)
Finance, Chairman

Truman, Peter D. (D)
Urban Affairs,
Sub-Committee Chairman
(First Class Cities, Counties)
Consumer Affairs
Insurance
State Government

Van Horne, Terry E. (D)
Urban Affairs,
Sub-Committee Chairman
(Third Class Cities, Counties)
Business and Commerce
Consumer Affairs
Finance

Veon, Michael R. (D)
Professional Licensure, Secretary
Labor Relations
Military and Veterans Affairs

Vroon, Peter R. (R)
Professional Licensure, Chairman
Insurance

Wambach, Peter C. (D)
Urban Affairs, Secretary
Consumer Affairs
Insurance
Liquor Control

Wass, Paul (R)
Agriculture and Rural Affairs,
Vice Chairman
Conservation
Education

Weston, Frances (R)
Consumer Affairs
Federal-State Relations
Urban Affairs

Wiggins, Edward A. (D)
Appropriations,
Sub-Committee Chairman
(Education)
Education
Finance
Health and Welfare

Wilson, Benjamin H. (R)
Finance, Chairman
Transportation, Sub-Committee
Chairman (Aviation)

Wogan, Christopher R. (R)
Judiciary
Liquor Control
Urban Affairs

Wozniak, John N. (D)
Conservation, Vice Chairman
Local Government
Mines and Energy Management
Transportation

Wright, David R. (D)
Majority Policy Chairman

Wright, James L., Jr. (R)
Mines and Energy Management,
Chairman
Business and Commerce

Wright, Robert C. (R)
Urban Affairs,
Sub-Committee Chairman
(Second Class Cities, Counties)
Judiciary

Yandrisevits, Frank W. (D)
Federal-State Relations, Secretary
Agriculture and Rural Affairs
Insurance

RULES OF THE HOUSE OF REPRESENTATIVES
As Adopted January 6, 1987

DEFINITIONS

A. "Day" shall mean any Calendar Day.

B. "Legislative Day" shall mean any day that the House shall be in session.

C. "Hall of the House" shall be the floor space within its four walls and does not include the adjoining conference rooms, the lobbies or the upper gallery of the House.

D. "Floor of the House" shall be that area within the Hall of the House between the Speaker's rostrum and the brass rail behind the Members' seats.

E. "Press Gallery" shall be within that area known as the Hall of the House as designated by the Speaker.

F. "Roll Call Vote" shall be a vote taken and displayed by and on the electric roll call board or in the event of a malfunction of the electric roll call board, by such method as shall be determined by the Speaker.

G. "Formal Action" shall mean any vote or motion of a member of a standing committee, Standing sub-committee, select committee or rules committee of the House of Representatives to report or not report, amend, consider or table a bill or resolution and the discussion and debate thereof.

RULE 1 — Speaker Presiding

The Speaker shall preside over the sessions of the House. He may name a member to preside, but the substitution shall not extend beyond an adjournment. He may appoint a member as Speaker Pro Tempore to act in his absence for a period not exceeding ten consecutive legislative days.

In case of failure to make an appointment, the House shall elect a Speaker Pro Tempore to act during the absence of the Speaker.

The Speaker Pro Tempore shall perform all the duties of the Chair during the absence of the Speaker.

RULE 2 — Taking the Chair

The Speaker shall take the Chair and call the members to order on every legislative day at the hour to which the House adjourned at the last sitting. On the appearance of a quorum, the Speaker shall proceed to the regular order of business as prescribed by the rules of the House.

RULE 3 — Order and Decorum

The Speaker shall preserve order and decorum. In case of any disturbance or disorderly conduct in the galleries or lobbies, he shall have the power to order the same to be cleared.

The Speaker shall have the right to summon State Police to assist in the preservation of order and decorum.

The Sergeant-at-Arms under the direction of the Speaker shall, while the House is in session, maintain order on the floor and its adjoining rooms. He shall enforce the rule with respect to the conduct of visitors.

RULE 4 — Questions of Order

The Speaker shall decide all questions of order subject to an appeal by two members. The Speaker may, in the first instance, submit the question to the House. Questions involving the constitutionality of any matters shall be decided by the House. On questions of order there shall be no debate except on an appeal from the decision of the Speaker or on reference of a question by him to the House. In either case, no member shall speak more than once except by leave of the House.

Unless germane to the appeal, a second point of order is not in order while an appeal is pending; but, when the appeal is disposed of, a second point of order is in order and is subject to appeal.

RULE 5 — Conference and Select Committee Appointments

All Committees of Conference shall be appointed by the Speaker and shall be composed of three members, two of whom shall be selected from the majority party and one from the minority party.

The Speaker shall appoint the members of Select Committees, unless otherwise ordered by the House.

RULE 6 — Signature of the Speaker

The Speaker shall, in the presence of the House, sign all bills and joint resolutions passed by the General Assembly after their titles have been publicly read immediately before signing, and the fact of signing shall be entered on the Journal.

Resolutions, addresses, orders, writs, warrants and subpoenas issued by order of the House, shall be signed by the Speaker and attested by the Chief Clerk.

RULE 7 — Oath to Employees

The Chief Clerk shall administer an oath or affirmation to the employees of the House that they will severally support, obey and defend the Constitution of the United States and the Constitution of Pennsylvania, and that they will discharge the duties of their offices with fidelity.

Each employee of the House, after taking the oath of office, shall sign his name in the Oath Book in the presence of the Chief Clerk.

RULE 8 — Supervision of Hall of the House and Committee Rooms

Subject to the direction of the Speaker, the Chief Clerk shall have supervision and control over the Hall of the House, the caucus and committee rooms and all other rooms assigned to the House.

During the sessions of the Legislature the Hall of the House shall not be used for public or private business other than legislative matters except by consent of the House. During periods of recess of the House such use may be authorized by the Speaker without the consent of the House.

RULE 9 — Decorum

While the Speaker is putting a question or addressing the House and during debate or voting, no member shall disturb another by talking or walking up and down or crossing the floor of the House.

RULE 9 — (a) Smoking

No smoking of cigarettes, cigars, pipes and other tobacco products shall be allowed in the Hall of the House.

RULE 10 — Debate

When a member desires to address the House, he shall rise and respectfully address himself to "Mr. Speaker." Upon being recognized, he may speak, confining himself to the question under consideration and avoiding personal reflections.

When two or more members rise at the same time and ask for recognition, the Speaker shall designate the member who is entitled to the floor.

No member, except the Majority and Minority Leaders, may speak more than twice on any question, without the consent of the House.

With the unanimous consent of the House a member may make a statement not exceeding ten minutes in length concerning a subject or matter not pending before the House for consideration, providing the Majority and Minority Leaders have agreed on a time the member is to ask for recognition.

RULE 11 — Interruption of a Member Who Has the Floor

A member who has the floor may not be interrupted, except for questions of order or by a motion for the previous question.

With his consent, a member may yield the floor for questions related to the subject before the House.

RULE 12 — Personal Privilege

Any member may by leave of the Speaker rise and explain a matter personal to himself, but he shall not discuss a pending question in his explanation. Questions of personal privilege shall be limited to questions affecting the rights, reputation and conduct of members of the House in their respective capacities.

RULE 13 — Transgression of House Rules

If any member in speaking or otherwise transgresses the Rules of the House, the Speaker or any member through the Speaker shall call him to order, in which case he shall immediately sit down unless permitted by the House to explain.

The House upon appeal shall decide the case without debate. If the decision is in favor of the member, he may proceed. If the case requires it, he shall be liable to censure or other punishment as the House deems proper.

RULE 14 — Members' and Employees' Expenses

A member who attends a duly called meeting of a standing or special committee of which he is a member when the House is not in session or who is summoned to the State Capitol or elsewhere by the Speaker, or the Majority or Minority Leader of the House, to perform legislative services when the House is not in session shall be reimbursed per day for each day of service, plus mileage to and from his residence, at such rates as are provided herein established from time to time by the Committee on Rules but not in excess of the applicable maximum per diem and mileage rate authorized by the Federal Government for travel. These expenses shall be paid by the Chief Clerk from appropriation accounts under his exclusive control and jurisdiction, upon a written request approved by the Speaker of the House, or the Majority or the Minority Leader of the House.

An employee of the House summoned by the Speaker or the Majority or Minority Leader of the House to perform legislative services outside of Harrisburg shall be reimbursed for actual expenses and mileage to and from his residence. Such expenses may be paid by the Speaker, Majority or Minority Leader, if they agree to do so, or shall be paid by the Chief Clerk from appropriation accounts under his exclusive control and jurisdiction, upon a written request approved by the Speaker of the House, or the Majority or the Minority Leader of the House.

Members and employees traveling outside the Commonwealth of Pennsylvania who receive any reimbursement for expenses or travel which reimbursement is from public funds shall file with the Chief Clerk a statement containing his name and the name, place and date of the function.

Money appropriated specifically to and allocated under a specific symbol number for allowable expenses of members of the House of Representatives shall be reimbursed to each member upon submission of vouchers and any required documentation by each member on forms prepared by the Chief Clerk of the House. No reimbursement shall be made from this account where a member receives reimbursement for the same purpose from any other appropriation account.

Such allowable expenses of members may be used for any legislative purpose or function, including but not limited to the following:

(1) Travel expense on legislative business.

(a) Mileage on session or nonsession days at a rate as may be approved from time to time by the Committee on Rules, but not in excess of the maximum mileage rate authorized by the Federal Government for travel; voucher only.

(b) Miscellaneous transportation on legislative business (taxi, airport limousine parking, tolls), and expenses of a similar nature; voucher only for any single expense not in excess of ten dollars ($10).

(c) Travel on legislative business by common carrier other than taxi and airport limousine; voucher and receipt from common carrier.

(d) Car rental; voucher and receipt from rental agency but reimbursement not to exceed three hundred fifty dollars ($350) in any month. Any amount in excess of the said amount shall be paid by the person renting the car. In no event shall other than American manufactured cars be rented.

(e) Lodging, restaurant charges and other miscellaneous and incidental expenses while away from home. Vouchers only for per diem allowance approved from time to time by the Committee on Rules, but not in excess of the applicable maximum per diem rate authorized by the Federal Government or for actual expenses not in excesss of such per diem rate.

(2) Administrative, clerical and professional services for legislative business, except for employment of spouses or any relatives, by blood or marriage.

(a) Administrative and clerical services; voucher and receipt from person employed.

(b) Professional services; voucher and receipt and copy of agreement or contract of employment.

(3) Rent for legislative office space; purchase of office supplies; postage; telephone and answering services; printing services and rental only of office equipment; voucher and vendor's receipt, except for postage expense. No reimbursement or expenditure shall be made out of any appropriation account for any mass mailing including a bulk rate mailing made at the direction or on behalf of any member which is mailed or delivered to a postal facility within sixty (60) days immediately preceding any primary or election at which said member is a candidate for public office.

Mass mailing shall mean a newsletter or similar mailing of more than fifty (50) pieces in which the content of the matter is substantially identical. Nothing in this rule shall apply to any mailing which is in direct response to inquiries or requests from persons to whom matter is mailed, which is addressed to colleagues in the General Assembly or other government officials or which consists entirely of news releases to the communications media.

(4) Official entertainment — restaurant and beverage charges; voucher only for expenses. Receipts for entertainment expenses, together with a statement of the reason for the expense, shall be submitted with the request for reimbursement.

(5) Purchase of flags, plaques, publications, photographic services, books, and other similar items in connection with legislative activities; voucher and vendor's receipt.

(6) Communications and donations in extending congratulations or sympathy of illness or death; voucher only on expenses not in excess of thirty-five dollars ($35).

No money appropriated for members' and employees' expenses shall be used for contributions to political parties or their affiliated organizations or to charitable organizations or for charitable advertisements.

All disbursements made, debts incurred or advancements paid from any appropriation account made to the House or to a member or non member officer under a General Appropriation Act or any other appropriation act shall be recorded in a monthly report and filed with the Chief Clerk by the person authorized to make such disbursement, incur any debt or receive any advancement on a form prescribed by the Chief Clerk.

The Chief Clerk shall prescribe the form of all such reports and make such forms available to those persons required to file such reports. Such report form shall include:

(1) As to personnel:

(a) The name, home address, social security number, job title, brief description of duties and where they are performed, department or member or members to whom assigned, the name of immediate supervisor and minimum hours of employment per week of each employee.

(b) The appropriation account from which such employee is compensated, the amount of compensation and whether such person is on salary, per diem or contract.

(2) As to all other expenditures:

(a) To whom it was paid, the amount thereof, and the nature of the goods, services or other purpose for which the expenditure was made.

(b) The appropriation account from which the expenditure was made and the name or names of the person or persons requesting and/or authorizing the same.

A copy of each such report shall also be filed with the special committee on internal affairs and House administration for use in the performance of its duties under Rule 47(a).

The reporting requirements as to personnel may be, fulfilled by the maintenance in the Office of the Chief Clerk of the House of an alphabetical file containing the current information for each employee as set forth above. In such event, however, the Chief Clerk shall supply annually, on or before February 1, a list of all employees appearing in said file together with the required information as to each as of January 1 of such year to the Special Committee on Internal Affairs and House Administration. The committee shall also be supplied with copies of all payroll changes as they occur.

All monthly reports filed on disbursements made or debts incurred by any officer or member or employee from appropriations made to the House under any General Appropriation Act shall be public information and shall be available for public inspection during regular business hours in the office of the Chief Clerk. The Chief Clerk shall prescribe reasonable rules and regulations for inspection of such reports but in no case shall inspection be denied to any person for a period exceeding forty-eight hours (excluding Saturdays and Sundays) from the time a written request has been submitted to the Chief Clerk. Photocopies of such reports shall be made available upon request to a member at no charge or to the public for a duplication fee as may be fixed by the Chief Clerk. Such reports shall be made available to a member or to the public on or before the last day of the month next succeeding the month in which the report was filed.

All requests for reimbursement out of any appropriation shall be accompanied by a voucher, or other documents where required, evidencing payment or approval. The voucher form shall be approved and supplied by the Chief Clerk. Receipts or documentation of every expenditure or disbursement which is in excess of the maximum amount as set forth herein shall be attached to the voucher. Where a request for payment is made in advance of an expense actually incurred, the Chief Clerk, before making such advance payment shall require a description satisfactory to the Chief Clerk of the item or service to be purchased or the expense to be incurred, and a receipt or other documentation shall be given to the Chief Clerk after the item or service has been purchased or expense incurred as evidence that such advancement was in fact expended for such purpose.

All reports, vouchers and receipts from which reports are prepared and filed shall be retained by the Chief Clerk, officer or member, as the case may be, for such period of time as may be necessary to enable the Legislative Audit Advisory Commission created pursuant to the act of June 30, 1970 (P.L. 442, No. 151), to conduct, through certified public accountants appointed by it, annual audits to assure that such disbursements made or debts incurred were in accordance with Legislative Audit Advisory Commission guidelines and standards, as approved by the Committee on Rules or for a minimum of three years whichever is longer. All annual audit reports shall be available for public inspection. Photocopies of such reports shall be available for a fee established by the Chief Clerk not to exceed the cost of duplication.

All expenditures of funds appropriated to the House or to a member or nonmember officer shall be subject to the expenditure guidelines established by the Rules Committee.

RULE 15 — Time of Meeting

The House shall convene on the first legislative day of the week at 1:00 P.M. prevailing time, and adjourn not later than 11:00 P.M. prevailing time, unless otherwise ordered by a roll call vote of the majority of those elected to the House.

On other days the House shall convene at the discretion of the House and adjourn not later than 11:00 P.M. prevailing time unless otherwise ordered by a roll call vote of the majority of those elected to the House.

RULE 16 — Quorum

A majority of the members shall constitute a quorum, but a smaller number may adjourn from day to day and compel the attendance of absent members. (Constitution, Article II, Section 10).

When less than a quorum vote on any question, the Speaker shall forthwith order the doors of the House closed and the names of the members present shall be recorded. If it is ascertained a quorum is present, either by answering to their names or by their presence in the House, the Speaker shall again order the yeas and nays. If any member present refuses to vote, his refusal shall be deemed a contempt. Unless purged, the House may order the Sergeant-at-Arms to remove the member or members without the bar of the House. All privileges of membership shall be refused the member or members so offending until the contempt is purged.

RULE 17 — Order of Business

The daily order of business shall be:

1. Prayer by the Chaplain.
   (a) Pledge of Allegiance.
2. Correction and approval of the Journal.
3. Leaves of Absence.
4. Master Roll Call.
5. Reports of Committees.
6. First consideration bills.
7. Second consideration bills.
8. Final passage bills recalled from the Governor.
9. Final passage bills (bills on final passage postponed calendar may be called up under this order of business).
10. Third consideration bills (bills on third consideration postponed calendar may be called up under this order of business).
11. Resolutions (House and concurrent).
12. Messages from the Senate and communications from the Governor.
13. Reference to appropriate committees of bills, resolutions, petitions, memorials, remonstrances and other papers.
14. Unfinished business on the Speaker's table.
15. Announcements.
16. Adjournment.

Any question may, by a majority vote of the House, be made a special order of business. When the time arrives for its consideration, the Speaker shall lay the special order of business before the House.

RULE 18 — Introduction and Printing of Bills

Bills shall be introduced in quadruplicate, signed and dated by each member who is a sponsor of the bill, and filed with the Chief Clerk. A sponsor may be added or withdrawn upon written notice to the Speaker, Majority Leader, Minority Leader and the prime sponsor. In the case of withdrawals, the names shall be withdrawn if and when the bill is reprinted. Additional sponsors may be added only by the prime sponsor by providing written notice to the Speaker, Majority Leader and Minority Leader. Such notice shall include the signatures of those members desiring to be additional sponsors.

Bills introduced when received at the Chief Clerk's desk shall be numbered consecutively and delivered to the Speaker, who shall refer each bill to an appropriate committee. The Speaker shall report to the House the committees to which bills have been referred, either on the day introduced or received or on the next two legislative days the House is in session.

If the Speaker neglects or refuses to refer to committee any bill or bills (whether House or Senate) as above after introduction or presentation by the Senate for concurrence, any member may move for the reference of the bill to an appropriate committee. If the motion is carried, said bill or bills shall be immediately surrendered by the Speaker to the committee designated in said motion.

The first copy of each bill introduced shall be for the committee, the second copy shall be for the printer, the third copy shall be for the news media and the fourth copy shall be for the Legislative Reference Bureau.

Every bill, after introduction and reference to committee, shall be printed. Bills may not be withdrawn after reference to committee.

RULE 19 — Bills Referred to Committees

No bill shall be considered unless referred to a committee, printed for the use of the members and returned therefrom. (Constitution, Article III, Section 2).

RULE 19 (a) Fiscal Notes

(1) No bill, except a General Appropriation bill or any amendments thereto, which may require an expenditure of Commonwealth funds or funds of any political subdivision or which may entail a loss of revenues overall, or to any separately established fund shall be given second consideration reading on the calendar until it has first been referred to the Appropriations Committee for a fiscal note, provided however that the Rules Committee may by an affirmative vote of three-quarters of the entire membership to which such committee is entitled:

(a) Waive the recommittal to the Appropriations Committee and provide that the fiscal note be attached to the bill while on the active calendar. The providing of such note shall be priority item for the Appropriations Committee; or

(b) Waive the necessity of a fiscal note on any bill which it deems to have a de minimis fiscal impact or which merely authorizes, rather than mandates, an increase in expenditures or an action that would result in a loss of revenue.

(2) Nothing herein shall preclude any member from moving, at the proper time, the recommittal of any bill to the Appropriations Committee for a fiscal note.

(3) The Appropriations Committee shall be limited in its consideration of any such bill to the fiscal aspects of the bill and shall not consider the substantive merits of the bill nor refuse to report any such bill from committee for reasons other than fiscal aspects. The fiscal note shall accompany the bill and provide the following information in connection with the Commonwealth and its political subdivisions:

(a) The designation of the fund out of which the appropriation providing for expenditures under the bill shall be made;

(b) The probable cost of the bill for the fiscal year of its enactment;

(c) A projected cost estimate of the program for each of the five succeeding fiscal years;

(d) The fiscal history of the program for which expenditures are to be made;

(e) The probable loss of revenue from the bill for the fiscal year of its enactment;

(f) A projected loss of revenue estimate from the bill for each of the five succeeding fiscal years; and

(g) The line item, if any, of the General Appropriation bill out of which expenditures or losses of Commonwealth funds shall occur as a result of the bill;

(h) The recommendation, if any, of the Appropriations Committee and the reasons therefor relative to the passage or defeat of the bill;

(i) A reference to the source of the data from which the foregoing fiscal information was obtained, and an explanation of the basis upon which it is computed.

(4) No bill which may result in an increase in the expenditure of Commonwealth funds shall be given second consideration reading on the

calendar until the Appropriations Committee has certified that provision has been made to appropriate funds equal to such increased expenditure. Whenever the Appropriations committee cannot so certify, the bill shall be returned to the committee from which it was last reported for further consideration and/or amendment.

(5) No amendment to a bill, concurrences in Senate amendments, or adoption of a conference report which may result in an increase in the expenditure of Commonwealth funds or those of a political subdivision or which may entail a loss of revenues in addition to that originally provided for in the bill prior to the proposed changes nor any bill requiring a fiscal note for which re-referral to the Appropriations Committee has been waived by the Rules Committee shall be voted upon until the day following the distribution of a fiscal note to the members with respect to such changes or to such bill showing the fiscal effect of the changes with respect to the bill, and containing the information set forth by subsection (3) of this rule.

(6) In obtaining the information required by these rules, the Appropriations Committee may utilize the services of the Budget Bureau and any other State agency as may be necessary.

(7) Any bill proposing any change relative to the retirement system of the Commonwealth or any political subdivision thereof, funded in whole or in part out of the public funds of the Commonwealth or any political subdivision, shall have attached to it an actuarial note. Except for the provisions pertaining to the content of fiscal notes as set forth in paragraphs (a) through (i) of subsection (3), all the provisions pertaining to and procedures required of bills containing fiscal notes, shall, where applicable, also be required for bills containing actuarial notes. The actuarial notes shall contain a brief explanatory statement or note which shall include a reliable estimate of the financial and actuarial effect of the propsed change in any such retirement system.

RULE 20 — Bills Confined to One Subject

No bill shall be passed containing more than one subject, which shall be clearly expressed in its title, except a general appropriation bill or a bill codifying or compiling the law or a part thereof. (Constitution, Article III, Section 3).

RULE 21 — Consideration of Bills

Every bill and every joint resolution shall be considered on three different days. All amendments made thereto shall be printed for the use of the members before the final vote is taken thereon, and before the final vote is taken, upon written request addressed to the presiding officer by at least twenty-five per cent of the members elected to the House, any bill shall be read at length. No bill shall become law and no joint resolution adopted unless, on its final passage, the vote is taken by yeas and nays, the names of the persons voting for and against it are entered on the Journal, and a majority of the members elected to the House is recorded thereon as voting in its favor. (Constitution, Article III, Section 4).

RULE 22 — First Consideration Bills

Bills reported from committees shall be considered for the first time when reported and shall then be automatically removed from the calendar and laid on the table, except House bills reported from committees after the first Monday in June until the first Monday in September which shall then be automatically recommitted to the Committee on Rules.

After the first Monday in September, any bill which was automatically recommitted to the Committee on Rules pursuant to this Rule 22 shall automatically be re-reported to the floor of the House and laid on the table.

The Rules Committee shall not in any instance have the power to amend a bill that has already gone through another committee.

Any bill which was automatically laid on the table pursuant to this Rule 22 and has remained on the table for fifteen legislative days shall automatically be removed from the table and returned to the calendar for second consideration the next legislative day.

Any bill which was automatically laid on the table pursuant to this Rule 22 may be removed from the table by motion of the Majority Leader, or his designee, acting on a report of the Committee on Rules. Such report shall be in writing and a copy thereof distributed to each member. Any bill so removed from the table shall be placed on the second consideration calendar on the legislative day following such removal. Nothing herein shall affect the right of any member to make a motion to remove a bill from the table.

Amendments shall not be proposed, nor is any other motion in order on first consideration.

Bills shall not be considered beyond first consideration until the latest print thereof is on the desk of the members.

Any noncontroversial bill, which is defined as any bill, other than an appropriations bill, approved by a committee with no negative votes or abstentions, shall be placed on an uncontested calendar. Bills on the uncontested calendar calendar shall be voted upon by a single roll call vote. Each bill listed on the uncontested calendar will be printed separately in the journal with the vote recorded on the approval of the uncontested calendar as the vote on final passage of each bill contained therein.

If any member should object to the placement of a bill on the uncontested calendar, the bill shall be automatically removed from the uncontested calendar and placed on the regular calendar the next legislative day.

RULE 23 — Second Consideration Bills

Bills on second consideration shall be considered in their calendar order and be subject to amendment.

No House bill on second consideration shall be considered until called up by a member.

RULE 24 — Third Consideration and Final Passage Bills

Bills on third consideration and final passage shall be considered in their calendar order.

A bill on third consideration may be amended.

After a bill is agreed to on third consideration, the Speaker shall state the question as follows:

"This bill has been considered on three different days and agreed to and is now on final passage."

"The question is, shall the bill pass finally?"

"Agreeable to the provision of the Constitution, the yeas and nays will now be taken."

When more than one bill shall be considered at the same time, the Speaker shall state the question as follows:

"These bills have been considered on three different days and agreed to and are now on final passage."

"The question is, shall the bills on the Uncontested Calendar pass finally?"

"Agreeable to the provisions of the Constitution, the yeas and nays will now be taken."

RULE 25 — Defeated Bills

When a bill or resolution has been defeated by the House, it shall not be re-introduced, or except as provided in rule 26, be reconsidered, nor shall it be in order to consider a similar one, or to act on a Senate bill or resolution of like import, during the same session.

RULE 26 — Reconsideration

A motion to reconsider the vote by which a bill, resolution or other matter was passed or defeated shall be made in writing by two members. The motion shall be in order only under the order of business in which the vote proposed to be reconsidered occurred and shall be decided on a roll call vote by a majority vote of the members elected to the House. No motion to reconsider shall be in order when the bill, resolution or other matter is no longer in the possession of or is not properly before the House.

A motion to reconsider any such vote must be made on the same day on which the initial vote was taken or within the succeeding five days in which the House is in session, provided such bill, resolution or other matter is still in the possession of or is properly before the House.

When a motion to reconsider any such vote is made within the aforesaid time limits and is decided by the affirmative vote prescribed herein, the question immediately recurs on the bill, resolution or other matter reconsidered.

Where a bill, resolution or other matter has been initially defeated and a motion to reconsider is not timely made, then such bill, resolution or other matter shall carry the status of "defeated finally" and not properly before the House. Therefore, it shall not be in order to entertain a motion to reconsider any such vote.

Where a timely made motion to reconsider is lost, it shall not be in order to again entertain a motion to reconsider any such vote, even though such second motion to reconsider is timely made.

Where a bill, resolution, or other matter has been initially defeated, and a timely made motion to reconsider the vote is lost, or if no motion to reconsider the vote was timely made, then it shall not be in order for the House thereafter to receive or consider a new bill, resolution or other matter embracing therein a subject or purpose basically identical to or of similar import to the subject matter or purpose of the bill, resolution or matter initially defeated.

The vote on a bill or resolution recalled from the Governor may be reconsidered at any time after the bill or resolution has been returned to the House.

Where a timely made motion to reconsider is lost, it shall not be in order to again entertain a motion to reconsider any such vote, even though such second motion to reconsider is timely made.

Where a bill, resolution, or other matter has been initially defeated, and a timely made motion to reconsider the vote is lost, or if no motion to reconsider the vote was timely made, then it shall not be in order for the House thereafter to receive or consider a new bill, resolution or other matter embracing therein a subject or purpose basically identical to or of similar import to the subject matter or purpose of the bill, resolution or matter initially defeated.

The vote on a bill or resolution recalled from the Governor may be reconsidered at any time after the bill or resolution has been returned to the House.

RULE 27 — Amendments

No bill shall be amended so as to change its original purpose. (Constitution, Article III, Section 1).

No motion or proposition on a subject different from that under consideration shall be admitted under color of amendment.

Any member may move to amend a bill or resolution, provided the proposed amendment is germane to the subject. Questions involving whether an amendment is germane to the subject shall be decided by the House.

No amendment to an amendment shall be admitted nor considered.

The sponsor of the amendment shall explain the amendment prior to consideration by the House.

Before consideration, eight typewritten copies of a proposed amendment signed by its sponsor shall be presented to the Speaker, one copy of which shall be delivered to the news media and a printed copy in typewritten form prepared by the Legislative Reference Bureau shall be placed on the desk of each member.

Amendments adopted or defeated may not be considered again without first reconsidering the vote.

RULE 28 — Bills Amending Existing Law

Bills amending existing law shall indicate present language to be omitted by placing it within brackets and new language to be inserted by underscoring. (Constitution, Article III, Section 6).

RULE 29 — Form for Printing Amendments

In printing amendments to bills and resolutions, all new matter added shall be in CAPITAL LETTERS and matter to be eliminated shall be indicated by strike-out type.

In reprinting House bills previously amended by the House and in reprinting Senate bills previously amended by the Senate, but not in Senate bills previously amended by the House, all matters appearing in strike-out type shall be dropped from the new print and all matter appearing in CAPITAL LETTERS shall be reset in lower case Roman type.

RULE 30 — House Bills Amended by the Senate

When a House bill or joint resolution has been amended by the Senate and returned to the House for concurrence, it shall not be considered until placed on the calendar and copies thereof are on the desks of the members.

When acting on bills or joint resolutions amended by the Senate, the amendments shall be read and the question put on the concurrence in the amendments.

The House shall not consider any proposed amendment to any amendment made by the Senate to a House bill or joint resolution.

A majority vote of the members elected to the House taken by yeas and nays shall be required to concur in amendments made by the Senate, except for appropriations to charitable and educational institutions not under the absolute control of the Commonwealth, where a vote of two-thirds of all the members elected to the House shall be required to concur. (Constitution, Article III, Sections 5 and 30).

RULE 31 — Bills Vetoed by the Governor

When the Governor has returned a bill to the House with his objections, the veto message shall be read and the House shall proceed to reconsider it. (Constitution, Article IV, Section 15).

RULE 32 — Hospital and Home Appropriations or Acquiring Lands of the Commonwealth

No bills appropriating moneys to State-aided hospitals or State-aided homes shall be introduced in the House, except such as appropriate in single bills the total sum to be appropriated to all of the institutions within the same class or group. Requests for appropriations for particular State-aided hospitals or State-aided homes shall be filed with the Chairman of the Committee on Appropriations on forms to be furnished by the said Committee on Appropriations, and shall be signed by the member requesting the appropriation.

No bill granting or conveying Commonwealth lands or taking title thereto shall be reported by any Committee to the House unless there has been filed with the Chief Clerk and the Chairman of the reporting committee a memorandum from the Department of General Services indicating the use to which the property is presently employed, the full consideration for the transfer, if any, a departmental appraisal of the property, including its valuation and a list of recorded liens and encumbrances, if any, the use to which the property will be employed upon its transfer, the date by which the land is needed for its new use, and the legislative district or districts in which the land is located. The memorandum shall contain a statement by a responsible person in the Department of General Services indicating whether or not the administration favors the transfer which is the subject of the bill under consideration.

RULE 33 — Special Legislation

No local or special bill shall be passed by the House unless notice of the intention to apply therefor has been published in the locality where the matter or the thing to be affected may be situated, which notice shall be at least thirty days prior to the introduction into the General Assembly of such bill and in the manner provided by law; the evidence of such notice having been published shall be exhibited in the General Assembly before the act shall be passed. (Constitution, Article III, Section 7).

No local or special bill shall be considered in violation of Article III, Section 32, of the Constitution.

RULE 34 — Non-Preferred Appropriations

No bill shall be passed appropriating money to any charitable or educational institution not under absolute control of the Commonwealth, except by a vote of two-thirds of all members elected. (Constitution, Article III, Section 17).

RULE 35 — House and Concurrent Resolutions

Members introducing resolutions other than concurrent resolutions shall file five copies thereof; seven copies of concurrent resolutions shall be filed. All resolutions shall be signed by their sponsors, dated and filed with the Chief Clerk. After being numbered, one copy of all resolutions shall be given to the news media and all other copies delivered to the Speaker. A sponsor may not be added or withdrawn after a resolution has been printed. Resolutions may not be withdrawn after reference to a committee.

Unless privileged under Rule 36 for immediate consideration, the Speaker shall refer House resolutions (except Discharge Resolutions) and Senate resolutions presented to the House for concurrence to appropriate committees.

The Speaker shall report to the House the committees to which resolutions have been referred, either on the day introduced or received or the next two legislative days the House is in session.

A resolution introduced in the House and referred to committee shall be printed and placed in the House files.

When a resolution (House or Senate) is reported from committee, it shall be placed on the calendar and may be called up by a member for consideration by the House under the order of business of resolutions. A House resolution other than a concurrent or joint resolution shall be adopted by a majority of the members voting.

RULE 36 — Privileged Resolutions

Resolutions privileged for the immediate consideration of the House are those:

- a. Recalling from or returning bills to the Governor.
- b. Recalling from or returning bills to the Senate.
- c. Originated by the Committee on Rules.
- d. Providing for a Joint Session of the Senate and House and its procedure.
- e. Placing bills negatived by committees on the calendar.
- f. Adjournment or recess.

RULE 37 — Legislative Citation

A member making a request that a Legislative Citation be issued to a particular person or on a specified occasion shall provide the Legislative Reference Bureau with the facts necessary for the preparation of the Citation on a suitable form.

The Citation request shall be filed with the Chief Clerk and automatically referred to the Speaker who may approve and sign such citation on behalf of the House of Representatives.

One original Citation shall be issued by the Chief Clerk.

RULE 38 — Sine Die and Final Introduction of Bills

Resolutions fixing the time for adjournment of the General Assembly sine die and the last day for introduction of bills in the House shall be referred to the Committee on Rules before consideration by the House.

RULE 39 — Petitions, Remonstrances and Memorials

Petitions, remonstrances, memorials and other papers presented by a member shall be signed, dated and filed with the Chief Clerk to be by him handed to the Speaker for reference to appropriate committees.

The Speaker shall report to the House the committees to which petitions, remonstrances, memorials and other papers have been referred, not later than the next day the House is in session following the day of filing.

RULE 40 — Messages

Messages from the Senate and communications from the Governor shall be received and read in the House within one legislative day thereafter.

All House and Senate Bills shall be delivered to the Senate with appropriate messages no later than the close of the next legislative day of the Senate which follows the fifth legislative day after which the House acted on such bill.

All House bills returned by the Senate after final passage therein without amendment, and all conference committee reports on House bills received from the Senate and adopted by the House, shall be signed by the Speaker within one legislative day after receipt or adoption, respectively, and shall be delivered to the Senate before the close of the next legislative day of the Senate.

All House bills and all conference committee reports on House bills signed by the Speaker shall be delivered to the Governor within twenty-four hours after return from the Senate with the signature of the appropriate Senate officer.

RULE 41 — Kind and Rank of Committee

The Committees of the House shall be of four kinds and rank in the order named:

Committee of the Whole House
Standing Committees
Select Committees
Conference Committees

RULE 42 — Committee of the Whole

The House may resolve itself into a Committee of the Whole at any time on the motion of a member adopted by a majority vote of the House.

In forming the Committee of the Whole, the Speaker shall leave the chair, after appointing a Chairman to preside.

The rules of the House shall be observed in the Committee of the Whole as far as applicable, except that a member may speak more than once on the same question.

A motion to adjourn, to lay on the table, or for the previous question cannot be put in the Committee of the Whole; but a motion to limit or close debate is permissible.

A motion that the Committee of the Whole "do now rise and report back to the House," shall always be in order, and shall be decided without debate.

Amendments made in the Committee of the Whole shall not be read when the Speaker resumes the Chair, unless so ordered by the House.

RULE 43 — Standing Committees and Sub-Committees

The Committee on Committees shall consist of the Speaker and fifteen members of the House, ten of whom shall be members of the Majority Party and five of whom shall be members of the Minority Party, whose duty shall be to recommend to the House the names of members who are to serve on the Standing Committees of the House.

The Speaker shall appoint the Chairman and Vice-Chairman of each Standing Committee when such Standing Committee has no Standing Sub-committees as prescribed herein; when the Standing Committee has Standing Sub-committees, the Speaker shall appoint a Sub-committee Chairman for each Standing Sub-committee. The Speaker shall appoint a secretary for each Standing Committee. The Minority Leader shall appoint the Minority Chairman and Minority Vice-Chairman of each Standing Committee and the Minority Sub-committee Chairman for each Standing Sub-committee.

The Speaker of the House, Floor Leader of the Majority Party and the Floor Leader of the Minority Party shall be ex-officio members of all Standing Committees, without the right to vote and they shall be excluded from any limitation as to the number of members on the Committees or in counting a quorum.

Twenty-one Standing Committees of the House, each to consist of twenty-four members except the Committee on Appropriations, which shall consist of thirty-two members, are hereby created. In addition, there is hereby created twenty-six Standing Sub-committees.

All Standing Committees shall consist of fourteen members of the Majority Party and nine members of the Minority Party, except the Committee on Appropriations which shall consist of nineteen members of the Majority Party and ten members of the Minority Party. The quorum for each of the Standing Committees and Sub-committees shall be no less than the majority of said committees. The following are the Standing Committees and Sub-committees thereof:

1. Agriculture and Rural Affairs
    a. Sub-committee on Rural Affairs
2. Apppropriations
    a. Sub-committee on Health and Welfare
    b. Sub-committee on Education
    c. Sub-committee on Capital Budget
3. Business and Commerce
    a. Sub-committee on Banking and Savings and Loan Associations
    b. Sub-committee on Housing
    c. Sub-committee on Industrial Development, Recreation and Tourism
4. Conservation
5. Consumer Affairs
    a. Sub-committee on Public Utilities
6. Education
    a. Sub-committee on Basic Education
    b. Sub-committee on Higher Education
7. Federal-State Relations
8. Finance
9. Game and Fisheries
10. Health and Welfare
    a. Sub-committee on Health
    b. Sub-committee on Welfare
    c. Sub-committee on Youth and Aging
11. Insurance

12. Judiciary
    a. Sub-committee on Crime and Corrections
    b. Sub-committee on Courts
13. Labor Relations
14. Liquor Control
15. Local Government
    a. Sub-committee on Boroughs
    b. Sub-committee on Counties
    c. Sub-committee on Townships
16. Mines and Energy Management
17. Professional Licensure
18. State Government
    a. Sub-committee on Telecommunications
19. Transportation
    a. Sub-committee on Highways
    b. Sub-committee on Public Transportation
    c. Sub-committee on Transportation Safety
    d. Sub-committee on Aviation
20. Urban Affairs
    a. Sub-committee on Cities, Counties — First Class
    b. Sub-committee on Cities, Counties — Second Class
21. Military and Veterans Affairs

RULE 44 — Organization of Standing Committees and Sub-Committees

The membership of each Standing Committee shall first meet upon the call of its Chairman and perfect its organization. A majority of the members to which each Standing Committee is entitled shall constitute a quorum for it to proceed to business. Each Standing Committee shall have the power to promulgate rules not inconsistent with these rules which may be necessary for the orderly conduct of its business.

Where a Standing Committee has Standing Sub-committees as prescribed by Rule 43, the membership on such Standing Sub-committees shall be appointed by the Committee on Committees after consultation with each Chairman of a Standing Committee of which the Standing Sub-committee is a part. Each Standing Sub-committee shall consist of the Chairman of its parent Standing Committee, as an ex-officio member, the Chairman of the Standing Sub-committee, and five other members from the parent Standing Committee to be appointed by the Committee on Committees three from among the majority party after consultation with the Majority Leader, and two from among the minority party after consultation with the Minority Leader. Where it is deemed advisable that the membership of any Standing Sub-committee be of greater number than that prescribed herein, the Committee on Committees may appoint additional members of the Standing Committee from the majority or minority party to serve on such Standing Sub-committee. The number of additional members selected should be such as to maintain, as far as is practicable, a ratio in majority and minority party membership which affords a fair and reasonable representation to the minority party on the Standing Sub-committee.

The Chairman and the Minority Chairman of each Standing Committee shall be ex-officio members of each Standing Sub-committee which is part of the parent Standing Committee, with the right to attend Standing Sub-committee meetings and vote on any matter before such Standing Sub-committee.

A majority of the members of each Standing Sub-committee shall constitute a quorum for the proper conduct of its business. Each Standing Sub-committee may promulgate such rules necessary for the conduct of its business which are not inconsistent with the rules of its parent Standing Committee or the Rules of the House.

When the Chairman of a Standing Committee has referred a bill, resolution or other matter to a Standing Sub-committee, the power and control over such bill, resolution or other matter shall then reside in such Sub-committee for a reasonable period of time thereafter in order that such Sub-committee may consider the bill, resolution or other matter and return the same to its Standing Committee with its recommendations as to the action which ought to be taken on such bill, resolution or other matter.

Each Standing Sub-committee, within a reasonable time after it has received a bill, resolution or other matter, shall meet as a committee for the purpose of considering the same and returning the bill, resolution or other matter back to its parent Standing Committee with a Sub-committee report as to what action it recommends. The report of the Sub-committee on a bill, resolution or other matter being returned to the Standing Committee shall contain one of the following recommendations:

a. that the bill, resolution or other matter in its present form be reported to the House.

b. that the bill, resolution, or other matter not be reported to the House,

c. that the bill, resolution or other matter be reported to the House, with recommendations for amendments,

d. that the bill, resolution or other matter is returned without recommendations.

When a Standing Committee receives reports from its Sub-committees, it shall consider the same and by majority vote of the members of the Standing Committee either approve or disapprove such report. If disapproved, the Standing Committee may then determine by a majority vote of its members what further action, if any, should be taken on such bill, resolution or other matter.

Where no action has been taken by a Standing Sub-committee on a bill, resolution or other matter referred to it, and the chairman of the Standing Committee considers that such Sub-committee has had reasonable time to consider the bill, resolution or other matter and return the same to its parent Standing Committee. The Sub-committee Chairman shall then forthwith surrender and forward the same, together with all documents or papers pertaining thereto, to the Standing Committee.

In the event that a Chairman of a Standing Committee is absent, the following rules shall apply:

1. If such Standing Committee has no Sub-committee prescribed by Rule 44, the Vice-Chairman of the Standing Committee shall act as Chairman of the Committee meetings;

2. If such Standing Committee has only one Sub-committee, the Sub-committee Chairman shall act as Chairman of the Standing Committee; and

3. If the Standing Committee has more than one Sub-committee, the Sub-committee Chairman with the longest consecutive legislative service shall act as Chairman of the Standing Committee, except where the Sub-committee Chairmen have equal legislative service, in which case the Speaker of the House shall designate one of the Sub-committee Chairmen to act as Chairman of the Standing Committee.

In case of absence of a Sub-committee Chairman, the Chairman of the appropriate Standing Committee shall designate one member from either the Standing Committee or Sub-committee to act as Chairman of the Sub-committee.

RULE 45 — Powers and Duties of Standing Committees and Sub-Committees

The Chairman of each Standing Committee and Sub-committee shall fix regular weekly, biweekly or monthly meeting days for the transaction of business before the Committee or Sub-committee. The Chairman of the Committee or Sub-committee shall notify all members, at least twenty-four hours in advance of the date, time and place of regular meetings, and, insofar as possible, the subjects on the agenda. In addition to regular meetings, special meetings may be called from time to time by the Chairman of the Committee or Sub-committee as they deem necessary. No committee shall meet during any session of the House without first obtaining permission of the Speaker. During any such meeting, no vote shall be taken on the Floor of the House on any amendment, recommittal motion, final passage of any bill, or any other matter requiring a roll call vote. Any Committee meeting called off the Floor of the House shall meet in a committee room. In addition to the specific provisions of this Rule 45, all provisions of the act of July 19, 1974 (P.L. 486, No. 175) relative to notice of meetings shall be complied with.

At regularly scheduled meetings, or upon the call of the chairman, or sub-committee chairman, for special meetings, the membership of such committees shall meet to consider any bill, resolution, or other matter on the agenda. The secretary of each standing committee, or in case of subcommittees a secretary designated by the subcommittee chairman, shall record:

(1) the minutes of the meeting,

(2) all votes taken,

(3) a roll or attendance of members at standing committee or subcommittee meetings showing the names of those present, absent or excused from attendance, and

(4) dispatch of bills and resolutions before the committee.

Such records shall be open to public inspection. On the first legislative day of each week the House is in session, the chairman of each standing committee shall submit to the Chief Clerk for inclusion in the House Journal only, the roll or record of attendance of members at standing committee or subcommittee meetings held prior thereto and not yet reported, along with the record of all votes taken at such meetings. All reports from standing committees shall be prepared in writing by the secretary of the committee. Members of a standing committee may prepare in writing and file a minority report, setting forth the reasons for their dissent. Such committee reports shall be filed with the Chief Clerk within five days of the meeting. All meetings at which formal action is taken by a standing committee or subcommittee shall be open to the public, making such reports as are required under Rule 44. When any member, except for an excused absence, fails to attend five consecutive regular meetings of his committee, the chairman of that committee or subcommittee shall notify him of that fact and, if the member in question fails to reasonably justify his absences to the satisfaction of a majority of the membership of the standing committee of which he is a member, his membership on the committee or subcommittee shall be deemed vacant and the chairman of the standing committee shall notify the Speaker of the House to that effect. Such vacancy shall then be filled in the manner prescribed by these rules.

Whenever the chairman of any standing committee shall refuse to call a regular meeting, then a majority of the members of the standing committee may vote to call a meeting by giving two days written notice to the Speaker of the House, setting the time and place for such meeting. Such notice shall be read in the House and the same posted by the Chief Clerk in the House Chamber. Thereafter, the meeting shall be held at the time and place specified in the notice. In addition, all provisions of the act of July 19, 1974 (P.L. 486, No. 175) relative to notice of meetings shall be complied with.

Records, bills and other papers in the possession of committees and subcommittees, upon final adjournment of the House shall be filed with the Chief Clerk.

No committee report, except a report of the Appropriations Committee, shall be recognized by the House, unless the same has been acted upon by a majority vote of the members of a standing committee present at a committee session actually assembled and meeting as a committee, provided such majority vote numbers at least 11 members, and provided further a quorum is present. No committee report for the Appropriations Committee shall be recognized by the House, unless the same has been acted upon by a majority vote of the members of such committee present at a committee session actually assembled and meeting as a committee, provided such majority vote numbers at least 14 members, and provided further a quorum is present.

When the majority of the members of a standing committee believe that a certain bill or resolution in the possession of the standing committee should be considered and acted upon by such committee, they may request the chairman to include the same as part of the business of a committee meeting. Upon failure of the chairman to comply with such request, the membership may require that such bill be considered by written motion made and approved by a majority vote of the entire membership to which such committee is entitled.

Whenever the phrase "majority of members of a standing committee or sub-committee" is used in these rules, it shall mean majority of the entire membership to which a standing committee or subcommittee is entitled, unless the context thereof indicates a different intent.

To assist the House in appraising the administration of the laws and in developing such amendments or related legislation as it may deem necessary, each standing committee or subcommittee of the House shall exercise continuous watchfulness of the execution by the administrative agencies concerned of any laws, the subject matter of which within the jurisdiction of such committee or subcommittee; and, for that purpose, shall study all pertinent reports and data submitted to the House by the agencies in the executive branch of the Government.

The Committee on Appropriations shall have the power to issue subpoenas under the hand and seal of its chairman commanding any person to appear before it and answer questions touching matters properly being inquired into by the committee, which matters shall include data from any fund administered by the Commonwealth, and to produce such books, papers, records, documents and data and information produced and stored by any electronic data processing system as the committee deems necessary. Such subpoenas may be served upon any person and shall have the force and effect of subpoenas issued out of the courts of this Commonwealth. Any person who willfully neglects or refuses to testify before the committee or to produce any books, papers, records, documents or data and information produced and stored by any electronic data processing system shall be subject to the penalties provided by the laws of the Commonwealth in such case. Each member of the committee shall have power to administer oaths and affirmations to witnesses appearing before the committee. The committee may also cause the deposition of witnesses either residing within or without the State to be taken in the manner prescribed by law for taking depositions in civil actions.

RULE 46 — Committee on Rules

The Committee on Rules shall consist of the Speaker, the Majority Leader, the Majority Whip, the Minority Leader, the Minority Whip, the Majority Appropriations Chairman, the Minority Appropriations Chairman, six members of the majority party appointed by the Speaker, and four members of the minority party appointed by the Minority Leader. The Majority Leader shall be Chairman.

The Committee shall make recommendations designed to improve and expedite the business and procedure of the House and its committees, and to propose to the House any amendments to the Rules deemed necessary. The Committee shall also do all things necessary to fulfill any assignment or duty given to the Committee by any resolution, or other rule of the House of Representatives.

The Committee shall be privileged to report at any time.

The Committee shall, until or unless superseded by law, adopt guidelines for the expenditure of all funds appropriated to the House or to any member or nonmember officer by any appropriation act.

Such guidelines shall include a detailed statement of the general and specific purposes for which the funds from that appropriation account may be used, as well as uniform standards of required documentation, accounting systems and record keeping procedures.

RULE 47 — Ethics Committee

As used in the context of this rule, the word "Committee" shall mean the Committee on Ethics of the House of Representatives, and the phrase "majority of the committee": shall mean a majority of the members to which the Committee is entitled:

The Committee shall consist of eight members: four of whom shall be members of the Majority Party appointed by the Speaker, and four of whom shall be members of the Minority Party appointed by the Minority Leader. The Speaker shall appoint from the members a Chairman, Vice Chairman and Secretary for the Committee. The Chairman shall be a member of the majority party and the Vice Chairman shall be a member of the minority party.

The Chairman shall notify all members of the Committee at least twenty-four hours in advance of the date, time and place of a regular meeting. Whenever the Chairman shall refuse to call a regular meeting, a majority of the Committee may vote to call a meeting by giving two days' written notice to the Speaker of the House setting forth the time and place for such meeting. Such notice shall be read in the House and posted in the House Chamber by the Chief Clerk, or his designee. Thereafter, the meeting shall be held at the time and place specified in such notice.

The Committee shall conduct its investigations, hearings and meetings relating to a specific investigation or a specific member, officer or employee of the House in closed session and the fact that such investigation is being conducted or to be conducted or that hearings or such meetings are being held or are to be held shall be confidential information unless the person subject to investigation advises the Committee in writing that he elects that such hearings shall be held publicly. In the event of such an election, the Committee shall furnish such person a public hearing. All other meetings of the Committee shall be open to the public.

The Committee shall receive complaints against members, officers and employees of the House, and persons registered or carrying on activities regulated by the act of September 30, 1961 (P.L. 1778, No. 712), known as the "Lobbying Registration and Regulation Act," alleging illegal or unethical conduct. Any such complaint must be in writing verified by the person filing the complaint and must set forth in detail the conduct in question and the section of the "Legislative Code of Ethics" or House rule violated. The Committee shall make a preliminary investigation of the complaint, and if it is determined by a majority of the Committee that a violation of the rule or law may have occurred, the person against whom the complaint has been brought shall be notified in writing and given a copy of the complaint. Within fifteen days after receipt of the complaint, such person may file a written answer thereto with the Committee. Upon receipt of the answer, by vote of a majority of the Committee, the Committee shall either dismiss the complaint within ten days or proceed with a formal investigation, to include hearings, not less than ten days nor more than thirty days after notice in writing to the persons so charged. Failure of the person charged to file an answer shall not be deemed to be an admission or create an inference or presumption that the complaint is true, and such failure to file an answer shall not prohibit a majority of the committee from either proceeding with a formal investigation or dismissing the complaint.

A majority of the Committee may initiate a preliminary investigation of the suspected violation of a Legislative Code of Ethics or House rule by a member, officer or employee of the House or lobbyist. If it is determined by a majority of the Committee that a violation of a rule or law may have occurred, the person in question shall be notified in writing of the conduct in question and the section of the "Legislative Code of Ethics," the "Lobbying Registration and Regulation Act" or House rule violated. Within fifteen days, such person may file a written answer thereto. Upon receipt of the answer, by vote of a majority of the Committee, the Committee shall either dismiss the charges within ten days or proceed with a formal investigation, to include hearings, not less than ten days nor more than thirty days after notice in writing to the person so charged. Failure of the person charged to file an answer shall not be deemed to be an admission or create an inference or presumption that the charge is true, and such failure to file an answer shall not prohibit a majority of the Committee from either proceeding with a formal investigation or dismissing the charge.

In the event that the Committee shall elect to proceed with a formal investigation of the conduct of any member, officer or employee of the House, the Committee shall employ independent counsel who shall not be employed by the House for any other purpose or in any other capacity during such investigation.

All constitutional rights of any person under investigation shall be preserved, and such person shall be entitled to present evidence, cross-examine witnesses, face his accuser, and be represented by counsel.

The Chairman may continue any hearing for reasonable cause, and upon the vote of a majority of the Committee or upon the request of the person subject to investigation, the Chairman shall issue subpoenas for the attendance and testimony of witnesses and the production of documentary evidence relating to any matter under formal investigation by the Committee. The Committee may administer oaths or affirmations and examine and receive evidence.

All testimony, documents, records data, statements or information received by the Committee in the course of any investigation shall be private and confidential except in the case of public hearings or in a report to the House. No report shall be made to the House unless a majority of the Committee has made a finding of unethical or illegal conduct on the part of the person under investigation. No finding of unethical or illegal conduct shall be valid unless signed by at least a majority of the Committee. Any such report may include a minority report. No action shall be taken on any finding of illegal or unethical conduct nor shall such finding or report containing such finding be made public sooner than seven days after a copy of the finding is sent by certified mail to the member, officer or employee under investigation.

The Committee may meet with a Committee of the Senate to hold investigations or hearings involving employees of the two houses jointly or officers or employees of the Legislature Reference Bureau, the Joint State Government Commission, Local Government Commission, Legislative Budget and Finance Committee and the Legislative Data Processing Committee; provided, however, that no action may be taken at a joint meeting unless it is approved by a majority of the Committee.

In the event that a member of the Committee shall be under investigation, such member shall be temporarily replaced on the Committee in a like manner as said member's original appointment.

The Committee, whether or not at the request of a member, officer or employee concerned about an ethical problem relating to himself alone or in conjunction with others, may render advisory opinions with regard to questions pertaining to legislative ethics or decorum. Such advisory opinions, with such deletions and changes as shall be necessary to protect the identity of the persons involved or seeking them, may be published and shall be distributed to all the members of the House.

Any member of the Committee breaching the confidentiality of materials and events as set forth in this rule shall be removed immediately from the Committee and replaced by another member of the House in a like manner as said member's original appointment.

The Committee may adopt rules of procedure for the orderly conduct of its affairs, investigations, hearings and meetings, which rules are not inconsistent with this rule.

The Committee shall continue to exist and have authority and power to function after the sine die Adjournment of the General Assembly and shall so continue until the expiration of the then current term of office of the members of the Committee.

RULE 47(a) — Special Committee on Internal Affairs and House Administration

(1) The Committee shall consist of the Speaker, Majority Leader, Minority Leader, four members of the Majority Party to be elected by the caucus, one of whom shall be named by the Speaker as Chairperson, and five members of the Minority Party to be elected by the caucus.

(2) The powers and duties of the Committee shall include, but not be limited to the following:

(a) To review all public payroll accounts under the control or jurisdiction of the Chief Clerk, Secretary, Comptroller, Minority Staff Administrator, Majority and Minority Committee Chairpersons, all members elected by the respective caucuses and any other member or person elected by the membership of the House.

(b) Such review shall be conducted at least quarterly and at such other times as the Committee may choose.

(c) The findings of each review shall be published in a Committee report and shall be available for public inspection. A copy of said report shall be furnished to any interested person upon request and payment of the actual cost to duplicate the same.

(d) The Committee may promulgate rules and regulations to carry out the purview of this Rule which shall be distributed to the members of the House and which shall remain in effect unless voided by a majority vote of the members elected to the House.

(3) No employee shall be assigned, hired or otherwise engaged to regularly perform duties outside the City of Harrisburg unless specifically authorized in writing by the person responsible for their performance and a copy of said authorization is filed with the Committee. Such person shall have thirty days after adoption of this rule to comply initially with such written authorization requirement.

(4) Before an employee is assigned to a member or members, said member or members shall receive a written statement of the employee's job related qualifications. Any member or members assigned an employee shall thereafter be responsible for the faithful performance by the employee of his or her designated duties.

(5) (a) Any member or nonmember having funds under his or her control or jurisdiction who intentionally provides any remuneration to another person in an apparent violation of this Rule or any employee who intentionally accepts any remuneration without providing the required services or otherwise receives public funds to which he or she is not entitled in any other apparent violation of this Rule, shall be notified in writing by the Committee of such alleged violation. Immediately following such notice, the Committee shall turn over all pertinent information on the matter to the House Ethics Committee, which shall conduct an immediate investigation of the allegations and report to the House within sixty days. The Ethics Committee shall make a recommendation to the House for appropriate action by the House which may include a recommendation that the person or persons so involved shall be discharged from employment and said person or persons shall not thereafter be eligible for further employment by the House and/or a recommendation to the House or respective caucus that said member be removed from his or her leadership position and the House or respective caucus shall then act on said recommendation within five legislative days.

(b) Whenever a determination is made that a violation has occurred, the Committee shall utilize all available means to recover the moneys disbursed in violation of this Rule.

(6) The Committee is authorized to employ the services of an Executive Director and a secretary. Said employees shall be compensated in the same manner and pay range as comparable employees of the several Standing House Committees.

(7) All meetings of the Committee shall be open to the public and the votes of the members recorded. No action may be taken without a quorum present and without a majority vote of those members present. A quorum shall consist of at least seven members. The Committee may meet in executive session from time to time subject to the limitations of the act of July 19, 1974 (P.L. 486, No. 175), referred to as the Public Agency Open Meeting Law.

RULE 48 — Conference Committee

All Committees of Conference shall be appointed by the Speaker and shall be composed of three members, two of whom shall be selected from the Majority Party and one from the Minority Party.

The conferees shall confine themselves to the differences which exist between the House and Senate.

The presentation of reports of Committees of Conference shall be in order after having been signed by a majority of members of the Committee of each House.

Consideration of a report of a Committee of Conference by the House shall be in order when it has been printed, placed on the desks of the members and listed on the calendar.

RULE 49 — Committee Action

Whenever a bill, resolution or other matter has been referred by the Speaker of the House to a Standing Committee, and such Committee has one or more Standing Sub-committees, the Chairman of the Standing Committee may either refer it to an appropriate Sub-committee or retain it for consideration by the entire Standing Committee. If it is retained, such Standing Committee shall have full power and control over such bill, resolution or other matter, except that such Committee shall not change the subject nor any amendments adopted by the House. Where the Chairman of the Standing Committee refers such bill, resolution, or matter to a Sub-committee, such Sub-committee, except as hereinafter provided, shall have full power over the same.

The recommendations by a commitee that a bill or resolution be reported negatively shall not affect its consideration by the House. The words "negative recommendation" shall be printed conspicuously on a line above the title of this bill.

All Standing Sub-committees shall be subject to the will of the majority of their parent Standing Committee and shall not promulgate any rules or take any action inconsistent with the rules of their parent Standing Committee or the Rules of the House.

RULE 50 — Public Hearings

Each Standing Committee, Sub-committee or Select Committee to which a proposed bill, resolution or any matter is referred shall have full power and authority to study said bill, resolution or other matter before it, as such committee, shall determine is necessary to enable it to report properly to the House thereon. To this end, a Standing Committee, Sub-committee or Select Committee, may as hereinafter provided, conduct public hearings. No Standing Committee, Sub-committee or Select Committee shall hold any public hearings without prior approval by a majority vote of the members of the Standing Committee and the Speaker or the Majority Leader of the House. The Speaker or the Majority Leader of the House shall withhold approval of public hearings based only on budgetary consideration.

When a public hearing has been authorized as aforesaid, the Chairman of the Standing Committee, Sub-committee Chairman, or Select Committee Chairman as the case may be, shall instruct the Chief Clerk to give written notice thereof to each House member not less than five calendar days before the proposed hearings and post the same in or immediately adjacent to the House Chambers. Such notice, which shall contain the day, hour, and place of the hearing and the number or numbers of bills or other subject matter to be considered at such hearing, shall also be given the supervisor of the news room, and to the news media. In addition, all provisions of the act of July 19, 1974 (No. 175), relative to notice of meetings shall be complied with.

Public hearings held by a Standing Committee shall be chaired by the Chairman of such Committee, unless absent, in which case an acting Chairman shall be selected in the manner prescribed by these rules to serve in his stead. Public hearings held by Standing Sub-committees shall be chaired by the Sub-committee Chairman thereof, but the Chairman of the parent Standing Committee, as an ex-officio member of the Sub-committee, shall have the right to attend and participate in the hearing proceedings. In the absence of the Sub-committee Chairman, an acting Chairman shall be appointed in the manner prescribed by these rules.

All public hearings shall be open to the public and reasonable opportunity to be heard shall be afforded to all interested parties who have requested an appearance before the Committee. In addition, it shall be the responsibility of the Committee in conducting its hearing to request the presentation of testimony by any person who, in the opinion of the Committee, is qualified to present pertinent and important testimony.

Such Committee shall, so far as practicable, request all witnesses appearing before it to file written statements of their proposed testimony. The Chairman shall have the right to fix the order of appearance and the time to be allotted to witnesses. Witnesses may submit brief pertinent statements in writing for inclusion in the record. The Committee is the sole judge of the pertinency of testimony and evidence adduced at its hearings.

The Chairman, in presiding at such public hearings, shall preserve order and decorum, in and adjacent to his committee room while the hearing is being conducted and he shall have the authority to direct the removal from the Committee room of any person who fails to comply with order and decorum of the committee.

Proceedings of all public hearings shall be either stenographically or electronically recorded. The Committee shall determine which parts of such recorded proceedings, if any, shall be transcribed and the distribution thereof. Except as hereinafter provided, no more than four (4) copies of any transcript shall be made. Such stenographic or electronic records and at least one copy of any transcription shall be preserved by the Chief Clerk until he is authorized to dispose of same by an affirmative vote of three-quarters of the entire membership of the Rules Committee and shall be made available to any member upon written request for the purpose of copying or transcription at that member's expense. Any transcribed records and any reports of the Committee shall be filed with the Chief Clerk or his designee and shall be made available to any person in accordance with reasonable rules and regulations prescribed by the Chief Clerk. Upon payment of a reasonable cost to be determined by the Chief Clerk, a person may obtain a copy of such transcribed record or reports.

The Chief Clerk shall not make payment of any expenses incurred as a result of a public hearing without the prior written approval of either the Speaker and the Majority Leader of the House.

RULE 51 — Investigations

Any standing Committee, Sub-committee or Select Committee, upon resolution introduced and approved by majority vote of the House, may be authorized and empowered to conduct hearings at any place in the Commonwealth to investigate any matter provided for in such resolution. When authorized by such a resolution, such Committee shall be empowered to issue subpoenas under the hand and seal of the Chairman thereof commanding any person to appear before it and answer questions touching matters properly being inquired into by the Committee and produce such books, papers, records, accounts, reports, and documents as the Committee deems necessary. Such subpoenas may be served upon any person and shall have the force and effect of subpoenas issued out of the courts of this Commonwealth. Where any person willfully neglects or refuses to comply with any subpoena issued by the Committee or refuses to testify before the Committee on any matter regarding which he may be lawfully interrogated, it shall be the duty of the Committee to report such disobedience or refusal to the House of Representatives, and such person shall be subject to the penalties provided by the laws of the Commonwealth in such cases. All such subpoenaed books, papers, records, accounts, reports, and documents shall be returned to the person from whom such material was subpoenaed when the Committee has completed its examination of such material, but in no event later than the date on which

the Committee completes its investigation. Such material, or any information derived therefrom not a part of public sessions of the Committee, shall not be turned over to any person or authority without the consent of the person from whom such material was subpoenaed. Each member of the Committee shall have power to administer oaths and affirmations to witnesses appearing before the Committee. The Sergeant-at-Arms of the Legislature or other person designated by the Committee shall serve any subpoenas issued by the Committee, when directed to do so by the Committee. The subpoena shall be addressed to the witness, state that such proceeding is before a Committee of the House at which the witness is required to attend and testify at a time and place certain and be signed by the Chairman of the Committee commanding attendance of such witness. Mileage and witness fees shall be paid to such witness in an amount prescribed by law.

The Chairman of the investigative hearing shall call the Committee to order and announce in an opening statement the subject or purposes of the investigation.

A copy of this rule shall be made available to the witnesses at least three calendar days prior to his or her scheduled testimony. Witnesses at investigative hearings, may be accompanied by their own counsel for the purpose of advising them concerning their constitutional rights. The Chairman, for breaches of order or decorum or of professional ethics on the part of counsel, may exclude him from the hearing. Counsel may interpose legal objection to any and all questions which in the opinion of counsel may violate the civil or constitutional rights of his clients.

If the Committee determines that evidence or testimony at an investigative hearing may tend to defame, degrade or incriminate any person, it shall:

    a.   receive such evidence or testimony in executive session;

    b.   afford such person an opportunity voluntarily to appear as a witness; and

    c.   receive and dispose of requests from such person to subpoena additional witnesses.

No evidence or testimony taken in executive session may be released to any person or authority or used in public sessions without the consent of the Committee.

Proceedings of all public hearings shall be either stenographically or electronically recorded. The Committee shall determine which parts of such recorded proceedings, if any, shall be transcribed and four copies thereof shall be distributed and additional copies made available as provided in Rule 50. Such stenographic or electronic records shall be preserved by the Chief Clerk until he is directed to dispose of same by an affirmative vote of three-quarters of the entire membership of the Rules Committee and shall be made available to any member upon written request for the purpose of transcription at that member's expense. Any transcribed records and any reports of the Committee shall be filed with the Chief Clerk or his designee and shall be made available to any person in accordance with reasonable rules and regulations prescribed by the Chief Clerk.

Upon payment of a reasonable cost to be determined by the Chief Clerk, a person may obtain a copy of the transcript of any testimony given at a public session or, if given at an executive session when authorized by the Committee. All standing committees, subcommittees, special committees or commissions which are authorized to hold public hearings and investigations shall file a final report before being discharged of delegated responsibilities.

RULE 52 — Possession of Bills by Committee

When a committee has ordered that a bill, resolution or other matter be reported to the House, the member to whom it is assigned shall make the report thereof to the House either on the same day or at the next meeting of the House.

Failure of a member to comply with this rule shall be reported to the House by the Committee, provided the official copy of the bill, resolution or other matter has not been obtained. Upon a motion agreed to by the House, a duplicate certified copy of a House bill, House resolution or other House matter shall be furnished to the committee by the Chief Clerk.

A committee or Sub-committee shall not consider a bill, resolution or other matter which is not in its possession.

When a committee reports to the House that a House bill, House Resolution or other House matter referred to it is lost, upon a motion agreed to by the House, a duplicate certified copy thereof shall be furnished by the Chief Clerk.

If the Senate bill, Senate resolution or other Senate matter received from the Senate is lost, upon a motion agreed to by the House, a request shall be made to the Senate to furnish the House with a duplicate certified copy thereof.

If a bill, resolution or other matter is lost before it has been referred to a committee, the fact shall be reported to the House and the procedure provided by this rule shall be followed.

RULE 53 — Discharge of Committees

A member may present to the Chief Clerk a resolution in writing to discharge a committee from the consideration of a bill or resolution which has been referred to it fifteen legislative days prior thereto (but only one motion may be presented for each bill or resolution). The discharge resolution shall be placed in the custody of the Chief Clerk, who shall arrange some convenient place for the signature of the members. A signature may be withdrawn by a member in writing at any time before the discharge resolution is entered in the Journal. When twenty-five members of the House shall have signed the resolution, it shall be entered in the Journal and the title of the bill or resolution and the name of the committee to be discharged shall be printed on the calendar.

Any member who has signed a discharge resolution which has been on the calendar at least one legislative day prior thereto and seeks recognition, shall be recognized for the purpose of calling up the discharge resolution and the House shall proceed to its consideration without intervening motion except one motion to adjourn; however, no discharge resolution shall be considered during the last six legislative days of any session of the House. A majority vote of all the members elected to the House shall be required to agree to a resolution to discharge a committee. When any perfected discharge resolution has been acted upon by the House and defeated it shall not be in order to entertain during the same session of the House any other discharge resolution from that committee of said measure, or from any other committee of any other bill or resolution substantially the same, relating in substance to or dealing with the same subject matter.

RULE 54 — Presentation and Withdrawal of Motions

When a motion which is in order has been made, the Speaker shall state it or (if it is in writing) cause it to be read by the Clerk. It shall then be in the possession of the House, but it may be withdrawn by the maker at any time before decision or amendment.

The Speaker shall put the question in the following form, viz: ''those in favor of the motion will say 'aye'.'' After the affirmative is expressed, ''those who are opposed will say 'no'.''

All motions, except for the previous question and a motion for reconsideration, may be made without a second.

No dilatory motion shall be entertained by the Speaker.

RULE 55 — Privileged Motions

When a question is under debate or before the House, no motion shall be received but the following, which shall take precedence in the order named:

1. To adjourn, or recess
2. A call of the House
3. To lay on the table
4. For the previous question
5. To postpone
6. To commit or recommit
7. To amend

Debate on the motion to postpone shall be confined to the question of the postponement and shall not include discussion of the main question.

The motion to commit or recommit is open to debate only as to the reasons for or against reference to committee and shall not include a discussion of the merits of the main question.

Debate on the motion to amend shall be limited to the amendment and shall not include the general merits of the main question.

RULE 56 — Adjourn

A motion to adjourn or recess is not debatable, cannot be amended and is always in order, except: (a) when another member has the floor; (b) when the House is voting.

When a motion to adjourn is made, it shall be in order for the Speaker, before putting the question, to permit the Majority and Minority Leaders and/or one member designated by each of them to state to the House any fact relating to the condition of the business of the House which would seem to render it inadvisable to adjourn. These statements shall be limited to two minutes and shall not be debatable.

RULE 57 — Call of the House

If a question of the absence of a quorum is raised by a member, the Speaker shall order the Sergeant-at-Arms to close the doors of the House. No member shall be permitted to leave the House, except by permission of the House. The names of the members present shall be recorded and absentees noted. Those for whom no leave of absence has been granted or no sufficient excuse is made may, by order of a majority of the members present, be sent for and taken into custody by the Sergeant-at-Arms and his assistants appointed for that purpose, and brought before the bar of the House where, unless excused by a majority of the members present, they shall be censured or punished for neglect of duty as the House may direct.

Further proceedings under a call of the House may be dispensed with at any time after the completion of the roll call and the anouncement of the result.

These proceedings shall be without debate, and no motion, except to adjourn, shall be in order.

RULE 58 — Persons Admitted Under a Call of the House

Members who voluntarily appear during a call of the House shall be admitted to the House. Upon recognition by the Speaker they shall announce their presence and their names shall be recorded on the roll.

Officers of the House, accredited correspondents and employees designated by the Chief Clerk shall be admitted to the House during a call.

Visitors shall not be admitted to the House after the doors are closed and until the proceedings under the call are terminated, but they shall be permitted to leave.

RULE 59 — Lay on the Table

A motion to lay on the table is not debatable, is not subject to amendment and carries with it the main question and all other pending questions which adhere to it, except when an appeal is laid on the table.

RULE 60 — Motion to Take from the Table

A motion to take from the table a bill or other subject is in order under the same order of business in which the matter was laid on the table. It shall be decided without debate or amendment.

RULE 61 — Previous Question

A motion for the previous question, seconded by twenty members and sustained by a majority of the members present, shall put an end to all debate and bring the House to an immediate vote on the question then pending, or the questions on which it has been ordered.

A motion for the previous question may be made to embrace any or all pending amendments or motions and to include the passage or rejection of a bill or resolution.

RULE 62 — Call for Yeas and Nays — Reasons for Vote

The yeas and nays of the members on any question shall, at the desire of any two of them, be entered on the Journal. (Constitution, Article II, Section 12).

When the Speaker or any member is not satisfied with a voice vote on a pending question, the Speaker may order a roll call vote; or, upon request of two members, before the result of the vote is announced, he shall order a roll call vote.

A member may submit a written explanation of his vote immediately following the announcement of the result of the vote and have it printed in the Journal.

RULE 63 — Division of a Question

Any member may call for a division of a question by the House, if it comprehends propositions so distinct and separate that one being taken away, the other will stand as a complete proposition for the decision of the House.

A motion to strike out and insert is indivisible, but a motion to strike out being lost shall neither preclude amendment nor a motion to strike out and insert.

RULE 64 — Members Required to be Present and Vote

Every member shall be present within the Hall of the House during its sittings, unless excused by the House or unavoidably prevented, and shall vote for or against each question put, unless he has a direct personal or pecuniary interest in the determination of the question, or unless he is excused by the House.

No member shall be permitted to vote and have his vote recorded on the roll unless he is present in the Hall of the House during the roll call vote.

The Legislative Journal shall show the result of each roll call by yeas and nays and those absent and not voting.

RULE 64.1 — Chronic Absenteeism

For purposes of this rule the term ''chronic absenteeism'' shall mean the unexcused absence of a representative for a period of five consecutive legislative days from official sessions of the House of Representatives or the absence of a committee member for a period of five consecutive days from their assigned committee meetings which meetings qualify as regular committee meetings under the rules of the House of Representatives and the Sunshine Law of the Commonwealth.

Any representative who is absent without excuse from regular House sessions for a period of five consecutive legislative days or is absent for a period of five consecutive committee meetings shall be deemed a chronic absentee and may, on a vote of the full House, be held in contempt of this House upon motion of five members of the House for chronic absence from regular House sessions and by motion of three members of the standing committee of the House to which such representative is assigned for chronic absence from regularly scheduled committee meetings.

The term ''chronic absenteeism'' shall not include:

(1) Absence due to the personal illness or bodily injury of a representative.

(2) Absence due to personal illness or bodily injury of a member of the immediate family of the representative.

(3) Death to a member of the immediate family of a representative.

(4) Any excused absence approved by the House pursuant to its rules.

RULE 65 — Member Having Private Interest

(a) A member who has a personal or private interest in any measure or bill proposed or pending before the House shall disclose the fact to the House and shall not vote thereon. (Constitution, Article III, Section 13).

(b) A member who, for remuneration, represents any organization required to register under the Lobbying Registration and Regulation Act shall file a statement of that fact with the Chief Clerk.

RULE 65(a) — Professionals-Legislators

(1) Except as hereinafter provided, any member or employee of the House or its agencies shall not be retained for compensation to appear in his or her professional capacity to represent the interest of any client in any proceeding before any Commonwealth department, board, agency, bureau or commission, except that such member or employee is authorized to represent the interest of a client at any stage of a proceeding before the Commonwealth or its agencies where such proceeding was initially taken or brought as a ministerial action, as defined by this rule, and as originally taken was not initially adverse in nature to the interest of the Commonwealth or its agencies.

(2) The provisions of this rule shall not be applicable to professionals-legislators:

(a) Representing clients on criminal matters before the courts of the Commonwealth.

(b) Representing clients on civil matters before the courts of the Commonwealth.

(c) Representing clients in all stages of a proceeding before the Commonwealth or its agencies which was initially commenced as a ministerial action. The term ''ministerial action'' means and includes any proceeding or action before the Commonwealth or its agencies where the proceeding, as initially commenced involved solely:

(i) The uncontested or routine action by the Commonwealth's administrative officers or employees in issuing or renewing licenses, charters, certificates or any other documents of a similar nature; or

(ii) The preparation, filing and review of tax returns and supporting documents required by law; or

(iii) The preparation, filing and review of engineering and architectural plans, drawings,specifications and reports; or

(iv) Any other initially routine or uncontested preparation, filing, review or other action not enumerated above and considered and normally handled by the Commonwealth or its agencies as a ministerial action.

(3) This rule shall not apply to the other members of the firm of such member and/or employee.

RULE 66 — Electric Roll Call

The names of the members shall be listed on the electric roll call boards by party affiliation in alphabetical order, except the name of the Speaker shall be last.

On any question requiring the ''yeas'' and ''nays'', the electric roll call system shall be used. On all other questions to be voted upon, the Speaker may, in his discretion, order the yeas and nays taken by the electric roll call system or voice vote or, upon demand of two members before the result of a vote has been declared, the yeas and nays shall be taken by the electric roll call system.

In the event the electric roll call system is not in operating order, the Speaker shall order all yea and nay votes be taken by calling the roll, as provided in the Rules of the House.

The vote of any member which has not been recorded because of mechanical malfunction of the electric roll call system shall be entered on the Journal, if said member was in the Hall of the House at the time of the vote and did cast his vote at the appropriate time, and the fact of such malfunction is reported to the Speaker of the House prior to the announcement of the result of the vote.

When the House is ready to vote upon any question requiring the yeas and nays and the vote is to be taken by the electric roll call system, the Speaker shall state: ''The question . . . . (Designating the matter to be voted upon.)'' The Speaker shall then unlock the voting machine and announce. ''The members shall now proceed to vote.'' Once the voting has begun, it shall not be interrupted, except for the purpose of questioning the validity of a member's vote or, if the voting switch of a member present in the Hall of the House is locked or otherwise inoperative, a request that such switch be rendeered operative or such member's vote be officially recorded, before the result is announced.

When, in the judgment of the Speaker, reasonable time has been allowed all members present in the House to vote (in no event shall such time exceed ten minutes) he shall ask the question: ''Have all members present voted?'' After a pause, the Speaker shall lock the machine and instruct the Clerk to record the vote, and the Speaker shall announce the result of the vote.

No member or other person shall be allowed at the Clerk's desk while the yeas and nays are being recorded, or the vote counted.

After the voting machine is locked, no member may change his vote and the votes of tardy members will not be recorded.

The vote as electrically recorded on the roll of members shall not in any manner be altered or changed by any person.

No member shall vote for another member, nor shall any person not a member vote for a member. Any member who shall vote or attempt to vote for another member, or a person not a member who shall vote or attempt to vote for a member, may be punished in such manner as the House determines.

Any member or other person who willfully tampers with or attempts to disarrange, deface, impair, or destroy in any manner whatsoever the electrical voting equipment used by the House, or who instigates, aids or abets with the intent to destroy or change the record of votes thereon shall be punished in such manner as the House determines.

A member who has been appointed by the Speaker to preside as Speaker Pro Tempore may designate either the Majority or Minority Whip to cast his vote on any question while he is presiding in accordance with his instructions from the Chair.

RULE 67 — Verification and Challenge

Upon completion of a roll call and before the result is announced, if there appears to be need for verification, the Speaker may direct the Clerk to verify it, or three members may demand a verification.

Any member may challenge in writing the yea or nay or electrically recorded vote of other members. The allegations made shall be investigated by a committee composed of the Speaker, a majority member and a minority member appointed by the Speaker, who shall submit a report to the House not later than its next session. The House shall then decide whether the challenged vote shall be recorded or not.

If the challenged vote would change the result, the announcement of the vote shall be postponed until the House decides the case.

RULE 68 — Changing Vote

No member may change his vote, or have his vote recorded after the result of a roll call vote has been announced, nor after an affirmative or negative roll has been declared verified.

RULE 69 — Journal

The Chief Clerk shall keep a Journal of the proceedings of the House, which shall be printed and shall be made available to the members.

The Journal of the proceedings of the last day's session shall not be read unless so ordered by a majority vote of the House.

RULE 70 — History of House Bills and House Resolutions

A weekly History, showing the title and action on House bills and the text and action on non-privileged resolutions, shall be compiled and indexed under the direction of the Chief Clerk and shall be printed and placed on each member's desk.

The House History shall include a cumulative index of laws enacted during the session and the text of vetoes by the Governor.

RULE 71 — House Calendar

Bills and non-privileged resolutions reported from committees to the House with an affirmative recommendation shall be listed on the calendar in such manner as prescribed by the Rules Committee and any other rule of the House. House bills and House resolutions shall precede Senate bills and Senate resolutions.

Bills and non-privileged resolutions shall be listed on the House calendar for no more than fifteen consecutive legislative days. At the end of the fifteenth consecutive legislative day the said bill or non-privileged resolution shall be automatically recommitted to the committee from which it was reported to the floor of the House.

Any bill or non-privileged resolution on the calendar which cannot, by its status, be recommitted shall be removed from the calendar and laid on the table, unless the House shall otherwise direct.

RULE 72 — Journal, Transcribing and Documents Rooms

No person, except members and employees of the House having official business, shall be permitted in the Transcribing, the Legislative Journal, and the Bills and Documents Rooms of the House without the consent of the Chief Clerk.

RULE 73 — Correspondents

Admission to and administration of the Press Galleries of the Senate and House of Representatives shall be vested in a Committee on Correspondents consisting of the President Pro Tempore of the Senate, or his designee; the Speaker of the House of Representatives, or his designee; the Supervisor of the Capitol Newsroom; the President of the Pennsylvania Legislative Correspondents' Association, or his designee and the Executive Director of the Pennsylvania Association of Broadcasters, or his designee.

Persons desiring admission to the press sections of the Senate and House of Representatives shall make application to the Chairman of the Committee on Correspondents. Such application shall state the newspaper, press association or licensed radio or television station, its location, times of publication or hours of broadcasting, and be signed by the applicant.

The Committee on Correspondents shall verify the statements made in such application, and, if the application is approved by the Committee, shall issue a correspondent's card signed by the members of the Committee.

The gallery assigned to newspaper correspondents or recognized press association correspondents or representatives of licensed radio and television stations, systems or newsgathering agencies shall be for their exclusive use and persons not holding correspondents' cards shall not be entitled to admission thereto. Employees of the General Assembly, representatives and employees of state departments, boards, commissions and agencies, visitors and members of the families of correspondents entitled to admission to the press gallery shall, at no time, be permitted to occupy the seats or be entitled to the privileges of the press gallery.

Accredited representatives of newspapers, wire, newsreel services and licensed radio or television stations, systems or newsgathering agencies, may be authorized by the Speaker of the House to take photographs, make audio or video recordings or tapes, and to broadcast or televise in the House of Representatives. Applications to take photographs, make audio or video recordings or tapes, or to broadcast or televise at public hearings of committees shall be approved by the Committee Chairman or Co-chairmen conducting such hearing. However, the Committee Chairman conducting the hearing may make such orders to such representatives as may be necessary to preserve order and decorum.

No photographs shall be taken nor any recordings or tapes made, nor any broadcasting or televising done in the House of Representatives during sessions, being at ease or recessed, without prior notice to the Representatives. When possible, such notice shall be given at the beginning of the session, at ease or recess, during which the photographs, recordings or taping, broadcasting or televising are scheduled to be taken or made.

No more than one representative of each newspaper, press association or licensed radio or television station, systems or newsgathering agency shall be admitted to the press gallery at one time. Members of the Pennsylvania Legislative Correspondents' Association and representatives of licensed radio and television stations, systems or newsgathering agencies, assigned to the House of Representatives on a daily basis shall have permanent assigned seating in the press gallery with identification plates. Visiting representatives of daily newspapers, press associations, Sunday newspapers as well as radio and television stations, systems or newsgathering agencies shall coordinate seating accommodations with the supervisor of the Capitol Newsroom.

Persons assigned to the press gallery on a permanent or temporary basis, shall at all times, refrain from loud talking or causing any disturbance which tends to interrupt the proceedings of the House of Representatives.

Persons assigned to the press gallery on a permanent or temporary basis shall not walk onto the floor of the House of Representatives nor approach the rostrum or the clerks' desks during session or while being at ease.

Persons assigned to the press gallery on a permanent or temporary basis wishing to confer with a Representative shall disclose this fact by having a message delivered by a page to the Representative. Such conversation shall be conducted off the floor of the House of Representatives.

Representatives of the Pennsylvania public broadcasting system may, subject to regulations of the Speaker, televise or make video tapes of proceedings of sessions of the House of Representatives and meetings of all committees of the House of Representatives.

RULE 74 — Visitors

Visitors shall be admitted to the Hall of the House only when sponsored by a member. The Chief Clerk shall issue an appropriate pass to any visitor so sponsored.

Persons admitted to the Hall of the House other than members and attaches, shall not be permitted to stand while the House is in session but shall be seated in chairs provided for them. At no time shall visitors be permitted on the Floor of the House while the House is in Session unless so permitted by the Speaker.

RULE 75 — Lobbyists

No registered lobbyist shall be admitted to the Hall of the House.

RULE 76 — Soliciting Prohibited

No officer or employee of the House shall solicit any member, other officer or employee of the House for any purpose.

RULE 77 — Suspending and Changing Rules

Any rule of the House, which is not required by the Constitution, may be temporarily suspended at any time for a specific purpose only by a majority vote of the members elected to the House by a roll call vote.

A motion to suspend the rules may not be laid on the table, postponed, committed or amended.

The existing rules of the House shall not be changed, added to, modified or deleted except by written resolution and the same approved by a majority vote of the members elected to the House by a roll call vote.

Except where such resolution originates with the Committee on Rules, no resolution proposing any change, addition, modification or deletion to existing House rules shall be considered until such resolution has been referred to the Committee on Rules, reported therefrom, printed, filed on the desk of each member and placed on the calendar.

Any proposed change, addition, modification or deletion offered by a member on the floor of the House to such resolution shall be considered, in effect, a change, addition, modification or deletion to existing House rules and shall require for approval a majority vote of the members elected to the House by a roll call vote.

RULE 78 — Parliamentary Authority

Jefferson's Manual supplemented by Mason's Manual of Legislative Procedure shall be the parliamentary authority of the House if applicable and not inconsistent with the Constitution of Pennsylvania, the laws of Pennsylvania, the laws of Pennsylvania applicable to the General Assembly, the rules of the House and the established precedents of the House and the established customs and usages of the House.

INDEX TO THE HOUSE RULES

DECISIONS OF THE HOUSE OF REPRESENTATIVES
POINTS OF ORDER

SECTION 1

ADJOURN

Not in Order to Entertain Two Consecutive Motions to

1 (a). The Speaker decided that it is not in order to entertain two consecutive motions to adjourn, if no other business of the House has intervened at the time the motion is made. (Journal H. R. 1843, p. 361.) (See also Journal H. R. 1885, p. 920.)

Motion to, in Order Immediately Following a Motion for Recess

1 (b). A motion that the House take a recess having been defeated, a motion was immediately made to adjourn. The point of order was raised that no other business having intervened, a motion to adjourn is not in order. The Speaker decided the point of order not well taken, stating the previous motion was for a recess. (Legislative Journal, April 17, 1913, pp. 2019 and 2020; Journal H. R., p. 2724.)

Motion to, Pending No Other in Order

1 (c). A motion to suspend the rules was made while a motion to adjourn was pending. The point of order was raised that no motion is in order while a motion to adjourn is before the House. The Speaker ruled the point of order well taken — motion to suspend a rule is not in order while a motion to adjourn is pending and a motion to adjourn takes precedence of all others; the House cannot be kept sitting against its will. (House Journal 1936, p. 318. Also Legislative Journal May 7, 1956, p. 7837.)

Motion to, Takes Precedence Over Motion to Adjourn to a Stated Time

1 (d). The point of order was raised that a motion to adjourn takes precedence over a motion to adjourn to a stated time. The Speaker decided the point of order well taken. (Journal H. R., 1889, p. 938.)

From Wednesday Until the Following Monday, Not In Contravention of Constitution

1 (e). A motion was made that when the House adjourns this Wednesday evening, it be to meet on next Monday evening at 9 o'clock. The point of order was submitted that it was unconstitutional for the House to adjourn for more than three days without the consent of the Senate. The Speaker decided the point of order well taken; that an adjournment of the House from Wednesday till the succeeding Monday was not an adjournment for more than three days as provided by the Constitution of Pennsylvania, Sunday being a dies non. See Buckalew on the Constitution of Pennsylvania, edition 1883, p. 52. Construction: It has been long held that the three days' limitation in this section (Section 14, Art. 2) is exclusive of Sundays, and such is the settled construction. Therefore, whether natural or secular days were intended by the authors of the limitation is not now a question of practical importance. Judical Opinion: West Philadelphia Passenger Ry. Co. v. Union Passenger Ry. Co., and Bancroft v. Same, 29 Legal Intel. 196, 4 Leg. Gaz., 193. (Journal H. R., 1897, p. 114. House Journal 1872, pp. 156-7. See also Senate Journal, 1913, p. 1127.)

Motion to Amend Resolution for Final

1 (f). The Speaker decided that a motion to amend a resolution for the final adjournment of the Legislature by adding thereto the following: "Provided, that in order to avoid the expense attendant upon the meeting of the convention of the two Houses, in October next, to which it stands adjourned, the members of the two Houses shall assemble previous to the final adjournment of the Legislature, for the purpose of electing a person to represent this Commonwealth in the Senate of the United States, in accordance with the Constitution of the United States, and the laws of the Commonwealth" was in order. The House overruled the decision of the Speaker. (Journal H. R., 1885, p. 826, p. 1086.)

Amendment to Resolution Fixing Date of Final, in Order

1 (g). On the question of agreeing to an amendment to a resolution fixing the date for adjustment sine die, the point of order was raised that the amendment to the resolution is out of order. The Speaker decided the point of order was not well taken for the reason that the amendment provides for a recess and not for an adjournment. (Legislative Journal, 1913, 4168; Journal H. R., p. 4729.) (Also Legislative Journal, August 30, 1961, pp. 3918-3919.)

Date of Final, Must be specific

1 (h). On the question of adopting a resolution relative to final adjournment of the House, the point of order was raised that the resolution is out of order because the date of final adjournment is not specific. The Speaker decided the point of order well taken. (Legislative Journal, June 5, 1913, p. 3951.)

SECTION 2

AMENDMENTS

Amendments, Germane

2 (a). A point of order was raised as to the germaneness of amendments. The Speaker ruled that: "In keeping with a long line of precedents on the part of the House and in conformity with an expressed decision made by the attorney general's office in times past in accordance with Mason's Manual which established legislation precedents, the Chair would be compelled to hold that these amendments are germane, that the subject of the bill is the vehicle code. The subject is not a particular amendment to the vehicle code, but the subject is the vehicle code and, therefore, the amendments are germane. Perhaps for the sake of precedent, the Chair will submit for the record the following:

(Legislative Journal July 10, 1961, pp. 2818-2819)

Article 3, Section 1 of the Constitution of Pennsylvania reads as follows:

"No law shall be passed except by bill and no bill shall be so altered or amended on its passage through either house as to change its original purpose."

In an opinion recently written by Deputy Attorney General Harrington Adams on the question of germaneness of proposed amendments to a bill, he quoted from authorities as follows:

In 82 Corpus Juris Secundum Statues, Section 30, it is said:

"A constitutional provision that a bill shall not be so altered or amended, in the course of its enactment, as to change its original purpose does not prevent the insertion of amendments germane to, and within the scope of, the original.

"A constitutional provision that a bill shall not be so altered or amended, in the course of its enactment, as to change its original purpose is not to be so construed as to prevent the introduction of matter merely extending the purpose or scope of operation of the bill, or limiting it, or the substitution of a measure or insertion of amendments having the same purpose as the original or germane to, and within the scope of, the original; and a bill thus limited and extended by the amendments of the two houses in its scope or purpose, or otherwise amended, but embracing no matter not germane to the original purpose or the subject of legislation as expressed in the title of the act which it purports to amend, may become a valid law. Also, such a restriction should not be so embraced as to prevent the substitution for a bill which is essentially amendatory in character of another related to the same subject and having the same general effect on existing laws, although some changes may be proposed by the substitute which would not have resulted from the passage of the original.

"The 'purpose' contemplated in such a constitutional provision is the general purpose of the bill, and not the mere details through which and by which that purpose is manifested and effectuated. Such a constitutional provision should be given a reasonable construction so as not unnecessarily to embarrass proper legislation...."

In 158 American Law Report in the annotation appearing at page 421, in discussing constitutional provisions against changing the purpose of the bill during passage, it is said:

"III Types of alterations or amendments which do not change original purpose:

"a. Immaterial Changes, 424.

"b. Extension of scope, 426.

"c. Limitations of scope, 428.

"d. Changes in Time, 428.

"e. Substitution of other measures having the same purpose as original measures, 429.

"f. Additions of matters germane to original purpose, 429."

In the case of Black Hawk Consol. Mines Co. v. Gallegos, 191 Pacific 2d 996 (1948), the Court at page 1005 said:

"The purpose of Article 4, Section 15 of the New Mexico Constitution prohibiting the altering or amending a bill on its passage so as to change its purpose is, solely to prohibit amendments not germane to subject of legislation expressed in the title of act purported to be amended.

"See Stein v. Leeper, 78 Ala. 517; Hall v. Steel, 82 Ala. 562, 2 So. 650; Alabama State Bridge Corp. v. Smith, 217 Ala. 311, 116 So. 695."

(Emphasis supplied)

In Cone v. Garner, 3 S.W. 2d 1 (1927), the Constitution of the State of Arkansas, which is identical with Article III, Sec. 1 of the Constitution of Pennsylvania, reads:

"No law shall be passed except by bill, and no bill shall be so altered or amended on its passage through either house as to change its purpose."

At page 4 the Court said:

"It is said that the object of this section of the Constitution was that the Senate and House of Representatives of the state might not be hampered or embarrassed in amending and perfecting their bills and thus be driven to accomplish by a number of bills that which might well be accomplished by one bill, but the purpose of the section was to forbid amendments which should not be germane to the subject of legislation expressed in the title of the act which it purports to amend, Hickey v. State, 114 Ark, 526, 170 S.W. 562."

In a later case, the Supreme Court of Arkansas, in Pope v. Oliver, 117 S.W. 2d 1072 (1938), said, in speaking of an alleged violation of Section 21 of Article V of the Constitution, that:

".... The purpose of this provision in our Constitution is to prevent amendments to a bill which would not be germane to the subject of the legislation expressed in the title of the Act, which it purports to amend. Loftin v. Watson, 32 Ark. 414; Hickey v. State, 114 Ark. 526, 170 S.W. 562; Cone v. Garner, 175 Ark. 860, 3 S.W. 2d 1; Matthews v. Byrd, 187 Ark. 458, 60 S.W. 2d 909."

(Emphasis supplied)

Rule 57 of the House reads, in part, as follows:

"No motion or proposition on a subject different from that under consideration shall be admitted under color of amendment."

ALSO:

"Any member may move to amend a bill provided the proposed amendment is germane to the subject."

Mason's Manual, Section 402, Section 3, defines "germane" as follows:

"To be germane, the amendment is required only to relate to the same subject it may entirely change the effect of the measure and still be germane to the subject. This article is supported by the established precedents of the House." Legislative Journal, May 25th, 1931, p. 5401 and numerous others.

Amendments Germane — Therefore Constitutional

2(b). On the question of agreeing to a bill on third reading the point of order was raised; that, inasmuch as the subject and purpose of the Senate bill, as it passed the Senate, was the express declaration restricted to amending the Public Service Company Law in the matter only of changes in utility rates and charges, the further amendments incorporated in the said bill by the House Committee on Public Utilities are reported and contained in a House bill, divesting the Senate from its present authority in the matter of removals of Public Service Commissioners from office; conferring new powers and imposing new duties on the Superior Court in

appeals from Commission orders; and requiring Commission approval as conditions precedent to utility security issues, a subject entirely new and not comprehended in any degree in the original of any amendatory provision of the Public Service Company Law, the Senate bill, as reported by the House Committee, was further amended as to the title thereof. The bill, which is now before this House for third reading and final passage, violates Articles 3, Section 1, of the State Constitution ordaining that:

"No law shall be passed except by bill, and no bill shall be so altered or amended, on its passage through either House, as to change its original purpose."

And violates 46 of the Rules of the House of Representatives, providing that:

"No bill or resolution shall at any time be amended by annexing thereto, or incorporating therewith, any other bill or resolution pending before the House, nor shall a motion or proposition be entertained under color of such an amendment, nor shall any bill or resolution be amended by substituting therefore, under a motion to strike out, or otherwise any other bill or resolution on a subject different from that under consideration, as required by the Constitution, Art. III, Sec. 1."

And accordingly the point of order is made that the said bill, being unconstitutional, it is improperly on the calendar and that for the Speaker to call for a yea and nay vote thereon would be to call upon a member of this House to violate his oath to observe and obey the Constitution.

In further explanation of the point of order, under the Rules of the National House of Representatives a rule similar in substance to that of the Pennsylvania House of Representatives provides:

"And no motion or proposition on a subject different from that under consideration shall be admitted under color of amendment."

Under this section it was ruled by Speakers Reed, Clark and Cannon that an amendment must be germane to the particular section of the law to which it is offered and that an amendment relating to the terms of the laws rather than to the terms of the bill, was not germane to a bill amending a general law upon a specific point. In reading such decision, the Speaker quoted "Hind's Precedent," Vol. 5, page 441, 5506, which provided:

"To a bill amendatory of an existing law as to one specific particular, and amendment relating to the terms of the law rather than to those of the bill was held not to be germane."

The Speaker stated that five members having requested in writing that the point of order be submitted to the House for its decision, and that Rule 4 of the House provides that all questions of order involving the determination of a constitutional question shall be submitted to the House upon request — the Chair therefore submits for decision by the House, this point of order. The Point of order was not sustained by the House (Legislative Journal, May 25, 1931, p. 5401.)

Not Germane, Out of Order

2 (c). The Speaker decided that it was not in order to amend a bill by adding to it matter different from the subject matter of the bill. (Journal H. R., 1858, p. 340.)

The Speaker decided that the first section being under consideration, it was not in order to strike out all after the enacting clause, and insert a new bill containing several different sections, which are not germane to the first section of the bill under consideration. The House sustained the decision. (Journal H. R., 1858, p. 592.)

A question of order was raised that "An act to revise, amend and consolidate existing laws for the assessment and collection of State taxes and county and township rates and levies," being under consideration, a motion to go into Committee of the Whole for special amendment for the purpose of taxing petroleum, coal and whiskey, articles that, by the present laws, are not now subject to taxation, the amendment, being for the purpose of revenue alone, is not germane to the subject before the House. The Speaker submitted the question to the House, and it was decided in the negative. (Journal H. R., 1869, p. 1093.)

(See also Journal H. R. 1879, p. 926; Journal H. R., 1883, p. 1098; Journal H. R. 1889, p. 1284; Journal H. R., 1893, p. 1016; Legislative Record, January 23, 1893, p. 321; Legislative Record, February 8, 1906, p. 439; Journal H. R., p. 200; Legislative Record, February 13, 1906, p. 579; Journal H. R., p. 246; Legislative Record, April 10, 1907, pp. 2413, 2414.)

Delegating Legislative Powers to a Third Person is Unconstitutional

2 (d). Amendments were offered to a Senate bill which was on second reading. The point of order was raised that the amendments offered were unconstitutional and entirely out of order because they seek to delegate legislative power and responsibility upon a third person or persons who are in no manner answerable for their conduct to the people. The Speaker decided the point of order well taken, stating the amendment violates Article II, Sections 1 and 15 of the Constitution of Pennsylvania. An appeal was taken from the decision of the Chair. The House sustained the ruling of the Speaker (Legislative Journal, February 13, 1917, p. 202; Journal H. R., p. 413.)

Changing Original Purpose of Bill, Not in Order

2 (e). The point of order was raised that an amendment proposed was not in order, as it would change the original purpose of the bill; also that the amendment contained more than one subject. The Speaker submitted the point of order to the House for decision. The House decided the point of order well taken. (Journal H. R., 1876, p. 196; see also Journal H. R., February 13, 1901, p. 430; Legislative Record, March 21, 1901, p. 954; Journal H. R., p. 841); (Legislative Record, April 10, 1907, p. 2445.)

Striking Out All After Enacting Clause and Inserting Different Bill, Not in Order

2 (f). The Speaker decided that it is not in order to strike from a bill all after the enacting clause, and insert another bill different from the subject contained in the original bill. The House sustained the decision. (Journal H. R., 1853, pp. 931, 932.)

To Amend on Final Passage, Vote on Third Reading Must First Be Reconsidered

2 (g). On the question whether a bill which has passed third reading and being, as required by the Constitution upon final passage, is subject to amendment, the Speaker pro tempore decided "that when a bill has passed three separate readings, and been agreed to each time, the only thing which remains is to take the vote required by the Constitution, unless postponed, and the vote agreeing to the bill the third time must be reconsidered in order to amend the bill." (Journal H. R., 1878, p. 424; see also, Legislative Record, February 8, 1909, p. 351.)

Defeated Cannot Be Offered Again

2 (h). The point of order was raised that "the amendment is out of order, because it had been offered and voted down when the section was under consideration, April 29." Decided well taken by the Speaker. (Journal H. R. 1885, p. 903; House Journal, 1891, p. 961.) (See also Legislative Record, May 14, 1907, p. 5429; Legislative Journal, April 4, 1911, p. 1152.)

Similar to One Defeated, But Not to Same Section Is in Order

2 (i). The point of order was raised that inasmuch as this amendment is similar to one already voted down and provides for the very same thing, it is out of order. The Speaker decided the point of order not well taken because the amendment offered is to another section of the Bill (Legislative Record, March 28, 1907, p. 1845.)

Striking Out a Portion of Bill Does Not Require Reprinting

2 (j). A House bill, having been amended on third reading by striking out a portion of the bill, the point of order was raised that the bill having been amended must lie over for printing. The Speaker decided the point of order not well taken, the amendment being a strike out, the bill is properly before the House for consideration on final passage. (Legislative Record, April 5, 1909, p. 2477; Legislative Journal, 1923, p. 4120.)

Rejected Not in Order to Discuss

2 (k). The point of order was raised that the amendments having been rejected by the House, a discussion of the same is not in order. The Speaker decided the point of order well taken. (Legislative Journal, April 12, 1915, p. 1492.)

Withdrawn and Presented at a Later Time Is in Order

2 (l). Amendments were offered on second reading to a House bill. The point of order was raised that the amendments offered had been previously withdrawn, therefore, the offering of them at this time is out of order. The Speaker decided the point of order not well taken. (Legislative Journal, June 3, 1913, p. 3819.)

Consistency of Amendments for House to Decide

2 (m). The Speaker ruled that the House, rather than the Speaker, should decide on the consistency of amendments and their legislative effect. It is not a question of order. He quoted Jefferson's Manual, Section 459. The question as to the consistency of the amendments was submitted to the House. (Legislative Journal, April 24, 1935, p. 2716.)

Amendment Defeated, Cannot be Offered Again Unless Vote be Reconsidered

2 (n). A point of order was raised that an amendment defeated cannot be again offered. The Speaker ruled that when an amendment has been defeated, the same amendment may not be proposed again without first reconsidering the vote by which the amendment lost. (Legislative Journal, August 31, 1961, p. 4075.)

SECTION 3

AMENDMENTS BETWEEN THE HOUSES

To Senate Amendments, Must Be Printed Before Senate Amendments Are Concurred in

3 (a). A House bill having been returned from the Senate with amendments in which the concurrence of the House is requested, said amendments were amended by the House and upon the question of concurring in the Senate amendments as amended, the point of order was raised "that the question could not be considered at this time." The Speaker decided that the amendments made by the House to the bill must first be printed and placed on the files of the House before the final vote on concurrence in the amendments made by the Senate as amended by the House could be taken. (Journal H. R., 1893, p. 1473.)

Motion to Concur in Senate, Not in Order After House Has Non-Concurred

3 (b). On a motion to concur in the amendments made by the Senate to a House bill, the point of order was raised that this motion is out of order because the House has already non-concurred. The Speaker decided that point of order well taken. (Legislative Journal, June 27, 1913, p. 5409; Journal H. R., p. 5834.)

Not in Order to Discuss Bill Not Properly Before the House

3 (c). On bill not properly before the House, the point of order was raised that a House bill which was amended in Senate, returned and House declined to concur in amendments, is not properly before the House. The Speaker ruled point well taken. (Legislative Journal, June 14, 1932, p. 5144.)

A Motion to Recede from Non-Concurrence in, After Notice Given to Senate, Not in Order

3 (d). After information has been given to the Senate, that the House insists upon its non-concurrence in an amendment by the Senate, a motion to recede from the non-concurrence is not in order. (Journal H. R., 1827-8, p. 781.) (The same principle is decided in Journal 1816-17, p. 708.)

Receding from, Requires a Constitutional Majority Vote

3 (e). The Speaker having decided a motion that the House recede from amendments, non-concurred in by the Senate was defeated, the point of order was raised that the motion just decided was defeated, did have the required number of votes to pass it. The Speaker decided the point of order not well taken inasmuch as to recede from the amendments made by the House, it requires a constitutional majority. (Legislative Record, June 26, 1901, p. 3895.)

Amended House Bill Returned for Concurrence — Motion to Refer to Committee in Order

3   (f). In reply to a parliamentary inquiry as to whether a motion to recommit is in order when a House Bill is before the House on the question of concurrence in Senate amendments, the Speaker read a parliamentary authority, as follows: 'It is proper for a House upon receiving an amended bill with the request to concur, to refer the message with the bill to a committee.' The Speaker added that it was also a privilege motion under the House Rules." (Legislative Journal, August 1, 1963, Page 2280).

In reply to a parliamentary inquiry as to whether a motion to recommit is in order when a House Bill is before the House on the question of concurrence in Senate amendments, the Speaker replied that such a motion is proper and cited Chapter 72 of Mason's Manual, Section 766, Sub-section 3, as follows: 'It is proper for a House, upon receiving an amended bill with a request to concur, to refer the message with the bill to a committee for consideration and a report upon concurrence.' (Legislative Journal, October 31, 1979, Page 2254).

SECTION 4

APPEAL

Not Entertained from Response to Parliamentary Inquiry

4   (a). A parliamentary inquiry having been made as to the reading of section reading.

The Speaker stated that the Journal shows that the section was read. That could mean nothing other that it was read at length.

An appeal was taken and the Speaker ruled that the question was a parliamentary inquiry made to the Speaker from which there is no appeal and quoted as follows from Jefferson's Manual:

"The rights of appeal insures the House against the arbitary control of the Speaker and cannot be taken away from the House; but appeal may not be entertained from responses to parliamentary inquires." (Legislative Journal, May 2, 1939, p. 2318.)

Speaker Pro-Tem, Not to Interpret Question Which Has Been Referred to House

4   (b). In reply to a parliamentary inquiry, the Speaker pro-tempore stated it was not proper for him to interpret a question of parliamentary law, which has been specifically referred to the House as a result of an appeal. (Legislative Journal, May 1, 1939, p. 2194.)

SECTION 5

BILLS

Under Control of Speaker While in the Possession of the House

5   (a). The Speaker decided that all bills were under his control while in the possession of the House. An appeal was taken, which was laid on the table. (Journal H. R., 1859, pp. 292, 293, 294.) (Legislative Journal, July 27, 1955, p. 2961.)

Passed Finally, Messaged to Senate

5   (b). The point of order was raised that it was not within the province of the House to hold a bill, inasmuch as it passed finally. The Speaker ruled the point of order not well taken, inasmuch as the Senate would not be in session until the next Tuesday and therefore, the bill would remain in the possession of the House until that time. (House Journal, 1931, pp. 1262-63.)

Defeated in House, Not in Order to Consider Similar One from Senate

5   (c). The House decided that when a bill has been considered and defeated in the House, it is not in order subsequently to consider a similar bill which had passed the Senate, and introduced into the House. (Journal H. R., 1865, pp. 802-894); House Journal, 1870, p. 1197. (See also Journal H. R., 1887, p. 1434; Journal H. R., 1891, p. 1694; House Journal, 1893, p. 507; Legislative Record, 1891, p. 2749; Legislative Journal, May 24, 1911, p. 3500. (Legislative Journal, August 30, 1961, pp. 3958-3960.)

Defeated, Not in Order to Consider Another Bill Containing Same Provisions

5   (d). A point of order was raised that a bill before the House for consideration was the same as one which was previously defeated.

The Speaker ruled that. . .

"When a bill has been defeated by the House, it shall not be re-introduced, nor shall it be in order to consider a similar one or to act on a Senate bill of like import during the same session."

The purpose of this rule, of course, is to prevent perhaps endless voting on questions upon which the judgment of the House has been expressed during a current session.

It is equally essential, however, that the discretion of the House should not be confined by its rules so as to prevent it from changing its mind when such change is proper and necessary.

This is precisely what the House had done with respect to House Bill No. 460, Printer's No. 499, when it reconsidered the vote on April 5th, by which this bill was defeated on final passage and placed it on the postponed calendar.

When the vote was reconsidered, that vote canceled completely the vote defeating House Bill 460 as though it has never been taken.

It is therefore the opinion of the Chair that House Bill 460, having been revived by the action of the House, does not come within the scope of a defeated bill under the provision of House Rule 49 and that House Bill 1496, being identical with House Bill 460, Printer's No. 499, is properly before the House for its consideration. (Legislative Journal June 13, 1961, p. 2268.)

Defeated Bill, May Not be Considered

5(e). The point of order was raised that a House Bill containing the same provisions as one previously defeated could not be considered. The Speaker decided the point of order well taken. (House Journal, 1911, p. 4122)

Negatived by a Committee, Similar One Cannot be Considered

5   (f). The point of order was raised whether a bill which was substantially the same as another bill which had been negatived was out of order. The Speaker submitted the question to the House, and it was decided in the affirmative. (Journal H. R., 1873, p. 624.)

Subject Matter Which Is Part of a Bill Negatived by Committee, Can be Considered

5   (g). The point of order was raised "that the bill cannot be further considered the subject matter being similar to that of another bill which had been negatived by the committee." The Speaker decided that the subject matter of the bill under consideration being only a part of the bill referred to the point of order was well taken. (Journal H. R., 1893, p. 507.)

Notations on Headings of Bills Only for Convenience of Members

5   (h). Under a parliamentary inquiry the question was asked whether it is required that the print of a bill, which was recommitted to a committee, must show that it was before the committee. The Speaker stated that notations printed on bills are for the information of the members and are not required either by law or rule. The Journal which is the official record of the House shows the course of the bill. (Legislative Journal, April 27, 1939, p. 2079.)

Printing of Senate, Not a Question for House to Decide

5   (i). On the question of agreeing to a resolution requiring the Senate to have printed all bills introduced in the Senate, the point of order was raised that it is not within the power of the House to direct the Senate what to do with their bills. The Speaker decided the point of order well taken. (Legislative Record, January 31, 1907, p. 352.)

Senate, Referred and Reported with Amendments, Must be Reprinted before Considered

5   (j). The Speaker decided that a bill introduced into the House from the Senate, referred to a committee, and reported from the committee with amendments must be reprinted as amended before it can be considered in the House (Journal H. R. 1874, p. 218.)

Not Properly Before the House Until Printed and in the Files of Members

5 (k). On a motion to recommit a House bill to committee, the point of order was raised that this bill is not properly before the House, as it has not been printed, it is not in the calendar or the files of the House and under the rules of the House cannot be recommitted at this time. The Speaker decided the point of order well taken for the reason that the bill is not properly before the House. (Legislative Record, March 8, 1901, p. 735, Journal H. R., p. 669.) (See also, Legislative Record, March 18, 1901, p. 855; Legislative Record, March 18, 1909, pp. 1278, 1281, 1282.)

Second Reading Bills, Constitutional Majority Vote Not Required

5 (l). Under a parliamentary inquiry the question was asked does it require a constitutional majority vote to agree to a bill on second reading. The Speaker replied that a constitutional majority was not required, only a simple majority was necessary to agree to a bill on second reading. (Legislative Journal, July 7, 1953, p. 2903.)

Appropriation to University of Pennsylvania, Requires a Two Thirds Vote

5 (m). On a motion to reconsider the vote by which a House bill was defeated on final passage, the point of order was raised that the University of Pennsylvania being a State institution the majority required by the Constitution of Pennsylvania to pass this bill is 103 votes. The Speaker decided the point of order not well taken. (Legislative Record, June 20, 1901, p. 3615, Journal H. R., p. 2544.)

Amended, Final Passage Same Day

5 (n). Under a parliamentary inquiry the question was asked whether a bill amended on third reading could be considered on final pasage on the same day. The Speaker replied the requirements for passage of bills is that amendments be printed in the bill as provided in the Constitution of Pennsylvania. Article III, Section 4. (Legislative Journal, September 19, 1951, p. 5121.)

Re-reported from Committee as Committed May Be Passed Finally on Same Day

5 (o). Under a question of parliamentary inquiry, as to whether a bill reported from committee on one legislative day could be considered the same day. The Speaker decided that the House by unanimous consent had dispensed with printing the title of the bill on the Calendar, the bill having been read twice before it was recommitted and was printed and on files of the members; therefore, the House could consider it on third reading and final passage the same day it was re-reported in compliance with Article III, Sections 2 and 4 of the Constitution of Pennsylvania. (Legislative Journal, 1941, pp. 5595 and 5596.) (See House Decision 55.)

SECTION 6

CALENDAR

Proceedings Placing Bill Upon, Regular

6 (a). A Senate bill was on final passage. The point of order was raised that this bill is improperly and illegally on the third reading calendar for the reason that the doors of this House were locked and members on the outside were unable to gain entrance to the hall during the time that action was taken on the resolution discharging the Committee on Municipal Corporations from further consideration of the bill, and the first reading thereof. The Speaker ruled that the proceedings, when that motion was adoped, were entirely regular in the opinion of the Chair, and the proceedings of that meeting have been approved by the House, and ratified by the refusal of a majority of the members elected to expunge from the records the proceedings referred to, therefore, the point of order is not well taken. (Legislative Journal, April 27, 1921, pp. 3132, 3137.)

Bill Carrying an Appropriation Is Properly on the Appropriation Calendar

6 (b). A Senate bill was on final passage. The point of order was raised that the Senate bill, not being an appropriation bill, is falsely placed upon the third reading calendar. The Speaker decided the point of order not well taken, as the bill carries an appropriation and is properly placed upon the calendar. (Legislative Journal, April 19, 1921, p. 2317.)

Bill Out of Place on, Cannot be Considered

6 (c). A House bill was on third reading. The point of order was raised that the bill is out of place on the calendar and objected to its consideration. The Speaker decided the point of order well taken. (Legislative Journal, June 20, 1917, p. 4002.)

Bill Must be Considered in Committee, before Appearing on

6 (d). The Speaker decided that a bill would be improperly on the calendar, if not having been considered in committee. (Journal H. R., 1875, p. 317.)

Calendar, Not in Print

6 (e). A point of order was raised that there not being any calendar for this day or file of bills on the desks, this bill was not in order.

The Speaker Pro Tempore decided the point of order well taken, whereupon an appeal was taken from the ruling of the Speaker. The question was determined in the negative and the decision of the Chair reversed. (House Part IV, 1911; pp. 4294-4295.)

Second Reading Bills Must Be Called up from, before Action Can be Taken

6 (f). On the question of recommitting a House bill to committee, the point of order was raised that his bill not having been called up from the second reading calendar, a motion to postpone for the present or recommit is not in order. The Speaker decided the point of order well taken. (Legislative Record, March 2, 1903, p. 1100; Journal H. R., p. 770.)

Defective Title On

6 (g). In reply to a parliamentary inquiry that the title of a bill as printed on the calendar, was defective at the time of passage, the Speaker stated the calendar does not govern. It is the bill placed on the Members' desks that governs. The members vote on the bills not on the titles as they appear on the calendar. (House Journal, 1937, p. 4912.)

SECTION 7

CALL OF THE HOUSE

When Quorum Present, Speaker to Order Vote to Be Again Taken

7 (a). The Speaker decided that when a call of the House is made, and a quorum appears to be present, it is the duty of the Speaker to order the vote to be again taken. The House sustained the decision. (Journal H. R., 1864, p. 1024.)

Members Actually Present Will be Recorded as Being Present Whether Answering to His Name Or Not

7 (b). Under a question of information concerning members not answering to a call of the House, when present in the House, the point of order was raised that when a session of the House is called and a member is present when the roll is called to ascertain the presence of a quorum, that gentleman should be recorded whether he votes or not. The Speaker pro tem, decided the point of order well taken, and ruled that when any member of the House is actually present in the House on the call of the House, he will be recorded as being present. (Legislative Journal, April 25, 1921, p. 2859.)

Quorum Call, Member Response

7 (c). Under a parliamentary inquiry, the question was asked: "What is the correct response for a member to make on a quorum roll call?"

The Speaker replied, "Present."

(Legislative Journal, Nov. 12, 1959, p. 4578.)

Quorum Call, Members Granted Leave of Absence Not Recorded

7 (d). Under a parliamentary inquiry the question was asked whether the names of members had been properly recorded on the roll.

The Speaker replied those members granted a leave of absence should not be recorded on the quorum roll. (Legislative Journal, Nov. 12, 1959, pp. 4571-4572.)

SECTION 8

COMMITTEES

Select, Appointed by House, Must Report to House
8 (a). The Speaker decided that a select committee appointed by the House was required to report to the House by which the committee was appointed. (Journal H. R., 1857, p. 131.)

Select, in Order to Instruct to Report at a Specified Time
8 (b). The House decided that it was in order to instruct a select committee not to make a report until a specified time. (Journal H. R. 1857, p. 201.)

Select, Having Been Ordered by Joint Resolution to Report within Three Days of Final Adjournment, House Cannot Extend the Time
8 (c). The Speaker decided that the Senate and House having by joint resolution determined that the Legislature would adjourn sine die on the eleventh day of April, instant, and that all select committees of each House shall report within three days of that time, and this committee having made their report, it is not now in order for this House to extend the power and function of the committee for a longer time, or for any such committee to sit longer than the time specified in the joint resolution above referred to. (Journal H. R., 1862, p. 803.)

Select, Has Right to Proceed After Final Adjournment if Instructed by the House
(Note: Pa. Supreme Court Decisions supersede Ruling 8 (d). 321 Pa. 54-61, Brown vs. Brancato; 401 Pa. 310 (1960 McGinley vs. Scott); 331 Pa. 165, Scutter vs. Smith.)

8 (d). On a motion to discharge an investigating committee authorized by the House, the point of order was raised that this motion is out of order. The investigating committee has been authorized under a resolution of the House and ceases to exist after this House adjourns sine die. "In a ruling of the Catlin Commission it was held that a Committee acting under a resolution of one of the Houses of Assembly would have no right to subpoena witnesses and no right to insist upon that subpoena being obeyed during the recess or interim of the General Assembly. Therefore, the Committee would be without power," and the motion would be futile. The Speaker overruled the point of order for this reason: There is no parallel between the Catlin Commission and the Committee. The Catlin Commission was appointed to investigate matters over which the Senate has no particular jurisdiction above or other than the jurisdiction of the House. This committee is solely and exclusively within the jurisdiction of the House. The question is whether or not the House shall prefer charges. The Attorney General has given an opinion in which he says: "There is no doubt of the right of the committee to proceed with the investigation after the adjournment of the House," and it is likewise the opinion of the chair. (Legislative Journal, June 27, 1913, pp. 5372 and 5373; Journal H. R., p. 5773.)

On Rules, Can Designate Bills as Special Orders of Business
8 (e). On the question of adopting a report from the Committee on Rules making bills Special Order of Business, the point of order was raised that the Committee on Rules has not the right to make any single bill a special order in advance of other bills. The Speaker decided the point of order not well taken under rules of the House. (Legislative Record, May 21, 1901, p. 2544.)

Standing, Power of, To Amend Bills
8 (f). The point of order was submitted that in line sixteen, of section three, the word "ten" is improperly in the section, for the reason that on second reading the word "ten" was stricken out, and the word "five" inserted by the House. The bill was afterwards recommitted, and the committee improperly restored the word "ten" and so reported it. An amended inserted by the House is direct instructions to a committee and should not be disobeyed by such committee. Decided well taken. (Journal H. R., 1885, p. 543.)

The point of order was raised that as when the bill under consideration was recommitted to the Committee on Agriculture it contained several amendments, inserted on the floor of the House, which were stricken out afterwards, by the Committee without authority, the House must insist on the amendments being replaced before proceeding with the further consideration of the bill. Decided well taken. (Journal H. R., 1893, p. 585.)

Power of, to Amend Appropriation Bills
8 (g). Under a parliamentary inquiry the question was asked whether the Committee on Appropriations has the power to amend the amount in a bill. The Speaker replied that it had, if the amendment had not been placed in the bill by the House. (Legislative Journal, May 6, 1957, p. 1598.)

Has Right to Reserve Its Original Recommendations
8 (h). A House bill was re-reported from Committee with a negative recommendation. The point of order was raised that when a committee has reported a bill affirmatively to the House and it is placed on the calendar of the House, and read, then is recommitted to the committee for the purpose of a hearing, the committee cannot thereafter report the bill with a negative recommendation. The Speaker decided the point of order not well taken, a committee has full power over any bill committed to it except when such bill is committed with specific instruction from the House. Further, the committee has the right to reverse its original recommendation based upon additional information obtained at a hearing or otherwise. (Legislative Record, April 22, 1907, p. 3066; Legislative Record, April 17, 1907, p. 2810, Journal H.R., p. 1925.)

Powers of Subpoena
8 (i). Under a parliamentary inquiry the question was asked whether a clause specifically conferring the power of subpoena is necessary in a resolution, or does a committee have that power? The Speaker replied that the House must confer power of subpoena on any of its committees. The House itself has the power to compel witnesses to appear and testify before any of its committees, to punish for contempt for refusal to do so, but only if the matter of inquiry is properly in connection with legislative business. The Speaker cited Article II, Section 2, of the Constitution of Pennsylvania. (Legislative Journal, January 28, 1947, p. 253.)

To Report Bills from, When Not the Order of Business, a Suspension of the Rules Necessary
8 (j). A motion being made to permit the reporting of a bill after the order, "Reports of Committees" has been passed, the point of order was raised that to permit such report the rules would have to be suspended. The Speaker decided the point of order well taken. (Journal H. R., 1891, p. 1712.)

Proceedings of, Not to be Divulged on the Floor of the House
8 (k). On a motion to discharge a committee from further consideration of a House bill, point of order was raised that the gentleman divulged to the House the conduct or action of the committee, which took place in the committee room. The Speaker ruled that it is out of order to divulge the proceedings that take place within the doors of a committee room, and decided the point of order well taken. (Legislative Journal, March 16, 1921, p. 705.) The Speaker also ruled that whatever occurs before a committee at a public hearing is proper to be considered on the floor of the House. (Legislative Journal, March 16, 1921, p. 705.) (See also Legislative Record, 1907, p. 4174, and Legislative Journal, 1919, pp. 3258, 3259.) (See also House Journal, 1927, p. 3044.) (Legislative Journal August 2, 1932, p. 779.) (Legislative Journal, April 10, 1933, pp. 2445, 2594 and 2595.)

Not Permitted to Sit During Sessions of the House without Leave
8 (l). A bill was reported from committee. The point of order was raised that the action of the committee in reporting the bill is irregular and out of order for the reason that the meeting yesterday was held during the session of this House. The Speaker decided the point of order well taken, stating that under the Rules of the House, no committee shall sit during the session of the House without leave. The bill was ordered returned to the committee with the recommendaion that they consider it in the regular way. (Legislative Record, April 4, 1907, p. 2144.)

Bill Reported by, Not Competent for Chair to Go Behind the Records Concerning Action in

8 (m). The Speaker decided that a bill having been regularly reported to a committee, it is not competent for the Chair to go behind the records for the purpose of inquiring how it was acted upon in committee. The House sustained the decision. (Journal H. R., 1868, pp. 713, 714; also Journal H. R., 1901, p. 303.)

Merits of Bill Cannot be Discussed Under Motion to Discharge

8 (n). On a motion to discharge a committee from further consideration of a bill, the point of order was raised that the member was speaking on the bill and not the motion. The Speaker decided the point of order well taken and ruled that the merits of a bill could not be discussed when a motion was made to discharge a committee. (Legislative Journal, May 5, 1931, p. 3067.)

Legally Constituted Whether Organized or Not

8 (o). A member inquired of the Speaker whether a standing committee of the House which had never organized was a legal committee of the House. The Speaker stated that under Rule 27 of the House, the committee is a duly constituted standing committee of the House, and that all its members were regularly elected by the committee of the House. The Speaker House. The fact that it had not organized had nothing to do with it being a legally constituted committee. (Legislative Journal, April 25, 1945, p. 3022.)

Responsibility for Consideration of Bills

8 (p). Replying to a question of information with reference to a standing committee and considering bills referred to it, the Speaker read Article 3, Section 2 of the Constitution of Pennsylvania:

"No bill shall be considered, unless referred to a committee, returned therefrom and printed for the use of the members."

Also Rule 30 of the House:

"Rule 30 of the House provides that, Each Committee shall have full power over the bill, resolution or other paper committed to it,. . ."

The Speaker stated:

"The responsibility for the consideration of bills before being acted upon by this House is placed under the provisions of the Constitution and Rules of this House directly upon the Committees of the House and not upon the Chairmen. The Chairman acts only as the organ of the Committee in precisely the same manner as the Speaker of the House acts as the instrument of the House. It is the function of both to carry out the will of the body over which they respectively preside."

(Legislative Journal, April 25, 1945, p. 3032.)

Meetings, Call of

8 (q). Replying to a question of information as to what action the members of a committee should take to compel a meeting where the Chairman refuses to call a meeting, the Speaker stated that:

"There are only two methods; one is a call by the Chairman, the other is a request signed by the majority of the members of the Committee asking for a meeting of the Committee."

(Legislative Journal, April 30, 1945, p. 3032.)

Meetings, Call of

8 (r). Under a question of parliamentary inquiry, it was asked in the event a Chairman declines to convene his committee and the members themselves fail to call a meeting, what is the jurisdiction of the House to require the committee to meet and act, or if the committee declines to act, to gain possession of the bills in the Chairman's keeping. The Speaker stated the only method would be for the House to discharge the Committee from consideration of the bill. (Legislative Journal, April 25, 1945, p. 3032.)

Chairman, Removal of

8 (s). Under a question of parliamentary inquiry it was asked whether a committee Chairman could be replaced if there was reason to question his conduct. The Speaker stated the appointment of Committee Chairmen is in the control of the Speaker and the power to appoint carries with it the power to remove. (Legislative Journal, April 25, 1945, p. 3032.)

SECTION 9

COMMITTEE ON CONFERENCE

Proceedings of, Not to be Discussed

9 (a). In reply to a parliamentary inquiry whether a member of a Committee of Conference could be interrogated relative to matters that have taken place in a Conference Committee. The Speaker stated that it would be out of order to interrogate a member of a Committee of Conference relative to proceedings of the committee. (House Journal, 1936, pp. 573-4)

Report of, Must be Printed before Action

9 (b). The Speaker decided that a report of a committee of conference must be printed before action can be taken by the House. (Journal H. R., 1874, p. 436.)

Cannot be Appointed Until Senate Has been Notified of the Non-concurrence of the House in Senate Amendments

9 (c). The point of order was raised that a committee of conference could not be appointed until after the Senate had been notified that the House had not concurred in the Senate amendments. The Speaker decided the point of order well taken. (Journal H. R., 1891, p. 876.)

Motion to Appoint, Cannot Include Instructions Not to Agree to Matters in Dispute

9 (d). The Speaker decided that it was not in order to couple with a motion to appoint a committee of conference, instructions for the said committee not to agree to certain matters in dispute. (Journal H. R., 1871, p. 1294.)

Proper Time to Instruct — Must be in Writing

9 (e). Under a parliamentary inquiry, the question was asked at what time would it be proper for the House to give specific instructions to a Conference Committee on the part of the House. The Speaker advised that the motion to instruct managers should be offered after the vote to ask for or agree to a conference and before the managers are appointed. Jefferson's Manual, Section 541, cited as authority. (Legislative Journal, July 2, 1980, p. 2025.)

House Can Instruct Its Own Conferees

9 (f). On a motion to instruct a Conference Committee to make certain amendments to a House bill, the point of order was raised that this motion is out of order because the House cannot instruct the conferees. This is a joint conference committee of the House and Senate and this body has no power to instruct such conferees. It can reject their report and the House has the power to name new conferees or the present conferees can be requested to reconsider the matter but this House cannot instruct joint conferees. The Speaker ruled that the question is not whether this House can instruct the joint conferees, but whether this House can instruct its own conferees to express its wishes, therefore, the point of order is not well taken. (Legislative Journal, June 28, 1917, p. 4734.)

Instructions of

9 (g). In response to a parliamentary inquiry as to whether the House can instruct its own conferees, the Speaker stated that the House has power to instruct its own conferees by written motion. (Legislative Journal, 1941, p. 3388.)

Not in Order for a Standing Committee to Act as a Committee of Conference

9 (h). The conference committee having failed to agree and the House Committee having been discharged, a motion was made that the bill be referred for any further conference to the Committee on Labor and Industry. The point of order was raised that the motion was out of order, as it changed the joint rule, and the rule must first be suspended. The Speaker decided the point of order well taken. (Journal H. R., 1903, p. 2337.)

Conference Report Rejected

9 (i). Under a parliamentary inquiry the question was asked: "What happens should a conference report be rejected?"

The Speaker Pro-Tempore replied that the question of concurring in the amendment placed in the bill by the Senate would again be before the House. (Legislative Journal, Nov. 20, 1959, p. 4930.)

Confined to Differences between House and Senate

9 (j). Under a question of parliamentary inquiry as to whether a conference committee was confined only to the consideration of the questions of difference between the House and Senate. The Speaker stated that under Rule 33 of the House, a Conference Committee is confined to consideration of the amendments which are in disagreement between the Houses. (Legislative Journal, 1941, pp. 5152-5153.)

Vote Required from House Prior to Senate on Conference Reports on House Bills

9 (k). Under a parliamentary inquiry, the question was asked whether the House was required to vote upon a Report of a Conference Committee prior to the Senate taking action on the same report. The Speaker replied that the Conference Report being on a House bill, the House should first act upon the Report. (Legislative Journal, December 12, 1951, p. 6127.)

SECTION 10

COMMITTEE OF THE WHOLE

Report of, Embracing Subjects Not Appertaining to Bill, Out of Order

10 (a). The Speaker decided that a report of the Committee of the Whole, embracing subjects not appertaining to the original bill, is out of order. (Journal H. R., 1850, p. 1120.)

Reconsideration of Vote, Refusing Leave to Sit Again Not in Order

10 (b). The House having refused the Committee of the Whole House leave to sit again upon a bill, the bill again before the House, pending the question "Will the House agree to the first section?" a motion was made to reconsider the vote refusing the Committee of the Whole leave to sit again. The Speaker ruled the motion out of order. (Journal H. R. 1885, p. 1015.)

Amendments Made in, Fall When Committee Reports Progress and Leave to Sit Again is Refused

10 (c). Amendments made in Committee of the Whole are not parts of bills when the committee reports progress, and leave to sit again is not granted by the House. (Journal H. R., 1820-21, p. 913)

Made in Committee of the Whole, Fall When Leave to Sit Again is Refused

10 (d). The Speaker decided that when the Committee of the Whole rises, reports progress, and is refused leave to sit again, the amendments made in Committee of the Whole are not parts of the bill, unless so ordered by a vote of the House. (Journal H. R., 1858, p. 463.)

Special Amendment, Offered in, Can be Amended

10 (e). That when a motion is made that the House go into Committee of the Whole for special amendment, the amendment is indicated, and is not subject to amendment. The Speaker decided the point of order to be not well taken. (Journal H. R., 1881, p. 984.)

Motion to Go Into, Is Debatable

10 (f). On the question of agreeing to a motion to go into the Committee of the Whole House for the purpose of special amendment to a Senate bill, the point of order was raised that this motion is not debatable. The Speaker decided the point of order not well taken. (Legislative Record, May 13, 1907, p. 5228.)

Motion to Go Into, Immediately Following Defeat of Like Motion, Not in Order

10 (g). A motion that the House resolve itself into a Committee of the Whole for the purpose of special amendment to a House bill, was offered immediately following the defeat of a similar motion. The point of order was

raised that the House having refused to go into the Committee of the Whole we cannot entertain the same motion a second time. The Speaker decided the point of order well taken. (Legislative Record, March 6, 1907, p. 1044; Journal H. R., p. 825.)

Motion to Go Into, Is a Privileged Motion

10 (h). On the question of agreeing to a motion to go into the Committee of the Whole for the purpose of special amendment to a Senate bill, the point of order was raised that this being a Senate bill it cannot be considered for the reason that the orders for the day have been fixed by the House. The Speaker decided the point of order not well taken as this is a privileged motion. (Legislative Record, May 8, 1901, p. 2288.)

Motion to Go Into, Not in Order After Bill Has Been Agreed to on Third Reading

10 (i). A House bill was being considered on final passage, and when a motion was made that the House resolve itself into Committee of the Whole, for special amendment, the point of order was raised that this bill having been agreed to on third reading and now being under consideration on final passage, the House cannot go into the committee of the Whole. The Speaker decided the point of order well taken. (Legislative Journal, April 12, 1915, p. 1492.)

Recess May Be Taken Only With Consent of the House

10 (j). A motion was made that the Committee of the Whole recess for the purpose of having printed amendments for the information of the Members to a bill which the Committee had under consideration.

The Chairman declared the motion out of order, when the point of order was raised, that the Chair erred in his ruling.

The chairman of the Committee of the Whole ruled the point of order not well taken. An appeal was taken from the ruling of the Chair. The Committee of the Whole sustained the ruling of the chairman. (Legislative Journal, Nov. 21, 1933, pp. 139-140.) (Note: Chairman of the Committee of the Whole stated the Committee could not recess, but must proceed with the business before it and report to the House or report that it cannot finish the business referred to it.) (Legislative Journal, Nov. 21, 1933, p. 157.)

Motion to Recommit to Committee of the Whole May Only Be Made in the House

10 (k). A motion was made in the Committee of the Whole that the Committee rise and report to the House a bill as amended.

An amendment was offered to add to this motion, that the bill be recommitted to the Committee of the Whole, for the purpose of taking up further amendments.

The chairman ruled the amendment to the original motion out of order for the reason that it was not within the power of the Committee to pass upon such a motion. The House alone has the power to resolve itself into Committee of the Whole. (Legislative Journal, Nov. 12, 1933, p. 159.)

Reprinting Bill Not Required to Pass on Second Reading

10 (l). The report of the Committee of the Whole having been adopted by the House, the Committee having inserted amendments in the bill referred to them.

A question of parliamentary inquiry was raised, as to whether the House could pass on the bill as amended before it was reprinted and distributed to the Members.

The Speaker stated it was in order under Rules of the House to consider the bill on second reading after which it would be printed. (Legislative Journal, Nov. 21, 1933, p. 129.)

SECTION 11

COMMIT AND RECOMMIT

Motion to, Not in Order When Reports from Committee Are Being Made

11 (a). Reports of committees being in order, the Speaker decided that it would require a suspension of the rules to make a motion to recommit a bill. (Journal H. R., 1870, p. 343.) (Legislative Journal, March 16, 1925, p. 1611.)

Motion to, With Instruction to Change Character of Bill, Not in Order

11 (b). A point of order was raised that a motion to recommit a bill, with instructions to amend so as to change the object of the bill, was not in order. The Speaker decided the point to be well taken. The House sustained the decision. (Journal H. R., 1875, pp. 314, 315.)

To Another Committee, When Motion to, in Order

11 (c). On the question whether a motion to recommit a bill to a different committee from the one which reported it is in order, the Speaker decided that the rule permits a motion to be made to recommit a bill which means that it be returned to the committee which reported it and a motion to commit to another committee should be made as an independent motion, when original resolutions are in order, or when the bill is properly before the House. (Journal H. R., 1879, p. 295.)

Motion to, Not in Order Until Bill is Before the House

11 (d). A bill being on the postponed calendar and a motion to recommit to committee having been made, the point of order was raised that the motion was not in order as the bill was not before the House. The Speaker decided the point of order well taken. (Journal H. R., 1901, p. 843.) (See also Legislative Record, February 13, 1905, p. 458, Journal H. R., p. 464.)

Motion to, Not in Order, Until Vote on Third Reading Is Reconsidered

11 (e). On a motion to recommit a House bill to committee, the point of order was raised that the bill could not be recommitted until the vote by which the bill passed third reading be reconsidered. The Speaker decided the point of order well taken. (Legislative Journal, May 1, 1913, p. 2528; Journal H. R., p. 3183.)

Motion to, Not in Order, When Bill Is Not on File

11 (f). The point of order was raised that the bill is not on file, and, therefore, under the rules it cannot be recommitted. Decided well taken. (Journal H. R., 1901, p. 669; see also Legislative Record, 1901, p. 855.)

Motion to, Not in Order on First Reading

11 (g). On the question of agreeing to a motion to recommit Senate bill to committee, the point of order was raised that a bill cannot be recommitted until it has been read before the House for the first time, this bill has not been read before the House at all. The Speaker decided the point of order well taken. (Legislative Record, June 3, 1901, p. 2862; Journal H. R., p. 1976.)

An appeal was taken from the decision of the Chair. The House sustained the ruling of the Speaker. (Legislative Record, June 3, 1901, p. 2862.)

Motion to, Precludes Amendment

11 (h). A motion was made to recommit a House bill while an amendment to the bill was under consideration. The point of order was raised that a motion to recommit precludes action on the question before the House. The Speaker decided the point of order well taken. (Legislative Journal, February 15, 1915, p. 207.)

Motion to, Carries With It Bill and Pending Amendments

11 (i). On a motion to recommit a bill on second reading, together with the amendments, the point of order was raised that the motion should apply solely to the bill as it appears on the calendar and does not affect the amendments which the House has not adopted; because if the House has not adopted the amendments, they do not appear in the record as anything that can be referred to committee. The Speaker ruled that under Rule 15 of the House, the motion to recommit takes precedence over the question on the amendment. The only thing that can be done with the amendments is to allow them to be recommitted with the bill, if the House decides to recommit the bill. The motion to recommit facilitates the motion to amend. (Legislative Journal, April 1, 1947, p. 1088.)

Merits of Bill Cannot be Discussed Under Motion to

11 (j). The point of order was raised that a member was discussing the merits of the bill under a motion to recommit. The Speaker ruled that the merits of a bill are not open to discussion on a motion to recommit. (House Journal, 1929, p. 4369.) (Legislative Journal, April 27, 1931, p. 2541; also Legislative Journal, April 29, 1931, p. 2738.) (Legislative Journal, March

31, 1931, p. 1393.) (Legislative Journal Jan. 31, 1933, p. 352; also April 3, 1933, p. 1926.)

Motion to, Stops Debate on the Merits of the Main Question

11 (k). A motion had been made to recommit a bill to committee on the second reading; in debate on the motion, a member was discussing the merits of the bill, when the point of order was raised that he was not limiting his debate to the motion to recommit.

The Speaker ruled:

"When a motion to recommit is made it stops debate on the main question and the debate is limited to the propriety of committing the bill. It has been uniformly held by former Speakers of this House that the merits of the main question cannot be debated when a motion to recommit is before the House.

"Rule 54 of the House specifically shuts out the original question when a motion to recommit is made.

"Rule 15 of the House provides that a motion to recommit is privileged and interrupts the question before the House. The motion to recommit must, therefore, be first decided by the House before consideration or debate of the main question is resumed." (Legislative Journal, 1943, p. 2031.)

Unanimous Consent Given to Recommit Precludes Any Other Action

11 (l). The point of order was raised that the House having given its unanimous consent for the purpose of recommitting a bill to Committee, the motion stopped there, and, therefore, further consideration of the bill for any other purpose is out of order. The Speaker ruled that the point of order well taken for the reason that the unanimous consent of the House was given only for the purpose of recommitment. (Legislative Journal, April 29, 1931, pp. 2740-2741.)

SECTION 12

CONSTITUTION

Advertisement of Notice of Local Or Special Bills Must Be Published in Two Papers in Each of Counties Affected, as Required by

12 (a). The point of order was raised that advertisement of local or special bills shall be in at least two newspapers, published in each of the counties to be affected. The Speaker submitted the question to the House for its decision. The House decided the point of order well taken. (Journal H. R., 1876, p. 190.)

On a third reading of a House bill the point of order was raised that the bill affects the counties of Allegheny, Westmoreland, Fayette, Greene, and Washington; that the notice of this bill was only advertised in Allegheny, in one paper, and in two papers in Washington, and not published in Westmoreland, Fayette or Greene, and, therefore, not properly advertised, the principal office of the corporation being situated in the city of Pittsburgh. The Speaker decided the point of order well taken. The House sustained the decision of the Chair. (Journal H. R., 1876, pp. 825, 826, 827.)

The Speaker ruled that a bill is not properly before the House, if affecting two counties, when notice for the proposed application has not been advertised in the two counties (the locality affected thereby), as required by section eight of the third article of the Constitution. (Journal H. R., 1878, p. 837.)

(See also Legislative Record, April 16, 1901, p. 1504; Journal H. R., p. 1247; Legislative Record, March 16, 1905, p. 1183; Journal H. R., p. 914; Legislative Record, April 13, 1909, p. 3491; Journal H. R., p. 3053; Legislative Record, April 13, 1909, p. 3504; Legislative Journal, May 22, 1911, p. 3256; Legislative Journal, May 27, 1913, p. 3518; Journal H. R., p. 4160.)

Proof of Publication of Advertisement, Must be Exhibited Before Final Vote Is Taken on Local Bill

12 (b). A local bill being under consideration on second reading, the point of order was raised that the bill could not be considered as it had never been advertised. The Speaker decided that before the bill passed finally, proof of advertisement must be shown, but that he could not rule it off the calendar on second reading, (Journal H. R., 1887, p. 1256.) (See also, Legislative Journal, March 29, 1915, p. 978; Journal H. R., p. 1234.)

Special or Local Legislation Violates Article III, Section 7

12 (c). On the final passage of a House bill the point of order was raised that this bill is unconstitutional being special and local legislation prohibited by Article III, Section 7, of the Constitution of Pennsylvania. The Speaker submitted the point of order to the House. The House sustained the point of order. (Legislative Journal, March 31, 1913, pp. 1301, 1302, 1303, and 1304; Journal H. R., p. 2009.) (See also Legislative Record, May 5, 1907, p. 963, Journal H. R., p. 782; Legislative Journal, May 5, 1915, p. 2845; Journal H. R., p. 3098.)

Seal of the Court Not Necessary to Verify Signatures of Justice to Affidavit of Publication of Advertisement

12 (d). The speaker decided that the signature of the justice, or other persons before whom affidavit of the publisher of the notice required in the case of local or special bills is made, is not necessary to be verified by the seal of the Court. (Journal H. R., 1879, p. 490.)

Amending Local Bill, Unconstitutional

12 (e). A constitutional point of order was raised that a local bill which had been introduced as advertised could not be amended, being a violation of Article III, Section 8 of the Constitution.

The House sustained the point of order. (Legislative Journal, June 13, 1961, pp. 2288-2290.)

Bill Amending Local Laws, Unconstitutional

12 (f). The point of order was submitted that this Act is in conflict with article three, section seven of the Constitution, in that it is a supplement of a local law regulating the opening and preparing of roads and bridges. A local law, the enactment of which is prohibited, cannot be amended. Decided well taken by the House. (Journal H. R., 1885, p. 972.)

Amendments to, Proposed by One Legislature, Not Subject to Amendment by Succeeding

12 (g). The Speaker decided that the proposed amendments to the Constitution agreed to by one Legislature, were not subject to amendment in the Legislature next afterwards chosen. (Journal H. R., 1857, p. 891.)

Proposing Amendments to

12 (h). Joint resolution of the State proposing amendments to the Constitution of the Commonwealth, being before the House, a question of order was raised, as follows, viz.: The Second part, or section nine, of the amendment now under consideration, having been before the House on the 2nd day of March, and on the call of the yeas and nays, a majority of the members elected not having agreed to the same, it was negatived, it is in order for this House again to consider and again to determine the question, whether it will agree to or negative the same question or part of said amendment. The Speaker decided that it was in order, and assigned for the decision the following reasons, viz.: "The manner of agreeing to or negativing amendments to the Constitution is prescribed by that instrument itself. It directs that any proposed amendment or amendments, to be operative, shall be agreed to by a majority of the members elected to each House. When the proposed amendments to the Constitution were before this House, on the 2nd day of March, the gentleman from Philadelphia (Mr. Smith), being temporarily in the chair, directed that the yeas and nays should be called, not only on the second amendment, but upon its separate parts severally. This the House had no power to do under the Constitution. It could take no constitutional action, only in obedience to the specific requirements of that instrument. The action of the House in this voting separately on two parts of one amendment, being without authority, was void and of no effect and could not affect the right of this House to do that which was its duty to do — to vote on the amendments. The amendment now before the House has not been negative. The vote now demanded of this House, is on the whole amendment, and not on a part of it, and is not the same proposition as that which was negatived on the second day of March by this House. It is, therefore, in order for the House to proceed to consider and vote upon the proposed amendment now before the House." The House sustained the decision. (Journal H. R., 1864, p. 371.)

Requires That Bill Must Recite Acts Proposed to Revise or Amend

12 (i). The point of order was raised that a House bill is in violation of section six, article three, of the Constitution, as it attempts to revise or amend a law without reciting the bill amended. The Speaker decided the point of order to be well taken. (Journal H. R., 1881, p. 1080.)

To Repeal a Law by Its Title Is a Constitutional Act

12 (j). The point of order was raised that section two of a House bill is not constitutional, if being in violaiion of section six, article three, of the Constitution, as follows, viz: "No law shall be recieved, amended, or the provisions thereof extended, or conferred by reference to its title only, but so much thereof as is revived, amended, extended or conferred, shall be reenacted and published at length." The Speaker decided the point of order not well taken, as the second section merely repealed an act, but did not revive, amend, or extend the provisions of any law. (Journal H. R., 1881, p. 291.)

Bill Repealing Local and Enacting General Laws, Constitutional

12 (k). The point of order was raised that the amendments was out of order, because an act to repeal an act could not be amended. The Speaker pro tempore decided the point not well taken, as the bill not only repealed an act, but enacted a new law. (Journal H. R., 1885, p. 940.)

Right of Eminent Domain Under Provisions of, Can Only Be to Public or Quasi Public Corporations

12 (l). A Senate bill was under consideration on second reading. The point of order was raised that this bill is unconstitutional because it is against the provisions of the Constitution of Pennsylvania to grant the right of eminent domain to any one but public or quasi public corporations. The Speaker submitted the point of order to the House. The House sustained the point of order. (Legislative Journal, May 18, 1915, p. 3703.)

Bill Exempting Private Property from Taxation, Unconstitutional

12 (m). The point of order was raised that this bill is unconstitutional in that it exempts from taxation real estate, in conflict with article nine, sections one and two, of the Constitution. Decided well taken by House. (Journal H. R., 1885, p. 918.)

Bill Falls When Declared Unconstitutional By the House

12 (n). Under a parliamentary inquiry the question was asked if by majority vote, a bill is decided to be unconstitutional, does the House then vote on the bill? The Speaker replied, if a bill is declared unconstitutional by the House, the bill falls. (Legislative Journal, July 7, 1953, p. 2908.)

Bill Unconstitutional, House Competent to Amend, Making Constitutional

12 (o). A point of order raised that a bill "to increase the revenue and impose a tax on all crude petroleum shipped outside the Commonwealth," was unconstitutional, could not be amended, and should be stricken from the calendar. The Speaker decided that while the bill might be unconstitutional it was certainly competent for the House to amend it so as to make it constitutional. (Journal H. R. 1883, p. 1085.)

Bills Providing for Settlement of Private Claims, Unconstitutional

12 (p). The point of order was raised that a bill which confers the right upon certain persons of presenting a claim against the Commonwealth in the courts of Dauphin county, which right is now possessed by other citizens of the State, confers a special privilege upon said persons, and is, therefore, contrary to section seven, article three, of the Constitution. The Speaker decided the point of order to be not well taken, as the bill confers simply the right to test the validity of an individual claim against the Commonwealth, which is not provided for by law. The House reversed the decision. (Journal H. R. 1881, p. 833.)

Constitutional Question Not in Order When Bill is Not in Possession of the House

12 (q). The Speaker ruled that a question of constitutionality of bills which had passed the House could not be submitted to the House, nor was it in order to discuss the bills. (Legislative Journal, May 27, 1931, p. 5978.)

Bill Prescribing New Duties for Public Officers of a Single County, Unconstitutional

12 (r). The point of order was raised that the bill was unconstitutional in that it prescribed new duties for public officers of a single county. Speaker pro tempore decided point well taken. (Journal H. R. 1885, p. 917; Legislative Record, 1885, p. 1654.)

Bill Regulating Duties of Judges Constitutional

12 (s). The point of order was raised that a: "House bill entitled 'An act to permit the judges of the several courts of common pleas in all counties in which there are two or more such courts, at the request of any of the other courts of common pleas in the same county, to perform judicial duties in the other courts,' is unconstitutional, because contrary to article five, section six of the Constitution, which says: "In Philadelphia all suits shall be instituted in the said courts of common pleas without designating the number of said court, and the several courts shall distribute and apportion the business among them in such manner as shall be provided by rules of court, and each court, to which any such suit shall be assigned shall have exclusive jurisdiction thereof, subject to change of venue, as shall be provided by law. In Allegheny each court shall have exclusive jurisdiction of all proceedings at law and in equity, commencing therein, subject to change of venue as may be provided by law." Decided not well taken. (Journal H. R., 1885, p. 111.)

Legal Classification of Cities, Necessary to Legislate for, Under Provision of

12 (t). The point of order was submitted that the present amendment to the amendment proposes to legislate for all the cities and towns of this Commonwealth upon the basis of population, without first being classified as required by the Constitution, in order to make it general, in place of special legislation. Point sustained by the House. (Journal H. R., 1885, p. 757.)

Delegating Legislative Powers to People Is in Violation of

12 (u). On the question of going into the Committee of the Whole for the purpose of special amendment, the point of order was raised that the special amendment is unconstitutional for the reason that it proposes to delegate legislative powers to the people. The Speaker Pro Tempore decided the point of order well taken. (Legislative Record, April 1, 1903, p. 2652; Journal H. R., p. 1606.)

Right of Jury Trial Not Limited by Bill, Therefore Not in Violation of

12 (v). A House bill was being considered on final passage; the point of order was raised that this bill is unconstitutional because it puts limitations upon the right of trials by jury. The Speaker submitted the point of order to the House. The House did not sustain the point of order. (Legislative Journal, April 27, 1915, pp. 2223 and 2224.)

Payment of Expenses Incurred by Members for Extra Services, Not Unconstitutional

12 (w). On the question whether the section of a bill to provide for the ordinary expenses of executive, legislative and judicial departments of the Commonwealth, et cetera, is unconstitutional, the Speaker decided the point of order not well taken, the section not providing compensation, but only making an appropriation for the expense of the commission, which had been directed to act by prior provisions of law. (Journal H. R., 1879, p. 743.)

Providing for Centennial Buildings, Constitutional

12 (x). The point of order was raised that under section eighteen article three, of the Constitution, a bill to provide for a permanent centennial exposition building is unconstitutional. The Speaker decided the point of order not well taken. The House sustained the decision. (Journal H. R., 184, p. 556.)

Reading of Bills by Short Title, Constitutional

12 (y). Acting on a motion that the reading of bills by short title is in compliance with the Constitution (Art. II, Sec. 4) "in every respect," the House voted in the affirmative. (Legislative Journal, June 15, 1965, p. 926.)

SECTION 13

DEBATE

Member May Not Criticize Senate

13 (a). A member was criticizing the action of the Senate in defeating a bill.

When the point of order was made that comment on the part of any member of the House concerning the deliberations of the Senate are distinctly out of order. The Speaker sustained the point of order, stating while the Senate may be referred to properly in debate, it is not in order to discuss its functions or criticize its acts or to refer to a Senator in terms of personal criticism or read a paper making such criticism. The Chair cited Jefferson's Manual as authority for his ruling. (Legislative Journal, December 20, 1933, p. 949.)

Senate Proceedings, May Not Be Read in

13 (b). Amendments were being considered to a section of a bill on second reading, when a member in debate proceeded to read from the Legislative Journal record of the Senate a statement by a member of the Senate on the same subject. The Speaker stated that the member was out of order in reading from the record of the Senate, which is an independent body and its proceedings should not be read into the record of the House. In support of his ruling, the Speaker quoted the following from Jefferson's Manual:

> "It is a breach of order in debate to notice what has been said on the same subject in the other House, the particular votes or majorities on it there; because the opinion of each House should be left to its own independency, not to be influenced by the proceedings of the other; and the quoting of them might beget reflections leading to a misunderstanding between the two Houses." (Legislative Journal, May 1, 1939, p. 2193.)

Executive Officers May Be Criticized but Personal Abuse Not Permitted

13 (c). In response to a Parliamentary inquiry —

The Speaker stated that it was in order for a member to criticize the official acts of the Governor and executive officers, but that personal abuse is not permitted in debate — quoting from Jefferson's Manual. (Legislative Journal, February 13, 1933, p. 583.)

Criticizing Federal Official

13 (d). The point of order was raised that a member in debate was criticizing a member of the President's Cabinet. The Speaker ruled that a member was within his right in criticizing a public official. (Legislative Journal, 1941, p. 4044.)

On Second Reading in Order

13 (e). The point of order was raised that a bill was being debated on second reading. The Speaker ruled that it was in order to debate a bill on second reading, the question before the House being "Will the House agree to the bill on second reading as amended?" (Legislative Journal, 1941, p. 1365.)

On a Bill on Second Reading in Order

13 (f). A bill was being considered on second reading when the point of order was raised that debate should take place on the third reading of the bill. The Speaker ruled that bills may be debated on second reading. (Legislative Journal, 1943, p. 476.) April 2, 1907, p. 2014. See also Pennsylvania Manual, Legislative Practice and Procedure under heading Action on Bills.

Confined to Question Before the House

13 (g). An amendment was being debated to section one of a bill on second reading. The point of order was raised that the member who has the floor was not confining his remarks to the amendment — which the Speaker sustained. After ruling the member out of order, during his debate on the amendment, the Chair stated that our House Rule was similar to that of the National House of Representatives and he read the following as an interpretation of the rule:

"He shall confine himself to the question under debate. Much meat is packed into this simple statement, and if the discussion is to be kept from aimless wanderings over an indefinite territory, this rule must be observed. If it is not, the debate ceases to be logical discussion on the particular subject and becomes a rambling and incoherent medley of unrelative statements. Of course, discretion is called for. Where there is plenty of time for debate and it's of a general character more leeway is necessarily expected and allowed." (Legislative Journal, 1943, pp. 1702-1703.)

Under Unanimous Consent

13 (h). A point of order was raised that once a member received unanimous consent to address the House, no rule would preclude him from speaking on any subject.

The Speaker stated that, under House Rule 63, a bill or resolution not reported from committee could not be debated. (House Journal, February 18, 1963, pp. 160-161.)

SECTION 14

DIVISIBLE QUESTIONS

When Not Divisible

14 (a). The Speaker decided that a question although embracing different propositions, could not be divided after these propositions had been amended and acted upon separately and independently, and the question thus blending them together, was presented for the final action of the House. The House sustained the decision. (Journal H. R., 1853, pp. 655, 656, 657.)

SECTION 15

JOURNAL

Reading and Approval of

15 (a). The point of order was raised that it is contrary to parliamentary practice for the House to approve the preceding day's Journal before it was in print and an opportunity to inspect it. The Speaker ruled that the question of the approval of the Journal, is for the House to decide. (Legislative Journal, February 7, 1951, p. 260.)

Motion to Expunge

15 (b). A motion was made to expunge remarks from the record. The Speaker stated a motion to expunge from the record is not in order until the main question is disposed of. (House Journal, 1906, p. 407.)

Proceedings Relative to, May Be Expunged from Record

15 (c). The question was raised whether the House could expunge from the record, proceedings relating to a resolution under consideration. The Speaker stated that all proceedings relating to the resolution could be expunged from the record by action of the House. (Legislative Journal, February 14, 1933, p. 253.)

SECTION 16

LAY ON THE TABLE

To Consider Resolution Placed on the Table, Motion Must Be Made to Take It from the Table

16 (a). The point of order was raised that inasmuch as the resolution was placed on the table by a vote of the House, that a motion to now proceed to its consideration is not in order for the reason that a motion must first be made to take it from the table. Decided well taken. (Journal H. R., 1893, p. 977.)

SECTION 17

LEAVE OF ABSENCE

Objected to

17 (a). An objection was made to a request for a leave of absence and, in reply to a parliamentary inquiry, the Speaker stated that if the House refused to grant a leave of absence to Members who are absent without leave and in contempt, it would also be for the House to decide whether the Member shall be brought before the House at the earliest possible moment. (Legislative Journal, September 12, 1955, pp. 3575-77.)

May Be Revoked

17 (b). Under a question of parliamentary inquiry the Speaker was asked if it was within the power of the House to revoke, rescind or recall leaves of absence granted? The Speaker stated that it is within the power of the House to revoke, rescind or recall leaves of absence. (Legislative Journal, April 11, 1945, p. 2329.)

SECTION 18

LEGISLATIVE INTENT

Could be Construed from Debate

18 (a). In reply to a parliamentary inquiry, the Speaker Pro-Tempore stated that legislative intent could be construed from debate before the House. (Legislative Journal, June 23, 1959, p. 1964.) (Legislative Journal, April 25, 1961, p. 1416.)

EXTRACTS FROM AN ADDRESS BY FORMER SPEAKER OF THE HOUSE, W. STUART HELM AT THE 1958 NATIONAL LEGISLATIVE CONFERENCE, BOSTON, MASSACHUSETTS.

The great weight of authority is, that the courts may ex-officio take judicial notice of the Legislative Journals.

The Courts have held — "That Journals of the Legislature may be considered even though not offered in evidence, being not only the official records of the coordinate branch of government, kept under requirement of law, but also important as bearing on the construction, validity and meaning of a statute law."

The second question that arises is — Are Legislative Journals always considered by the Courts in construing the statute?

The Pennsylvania Courts have repeatedly held that resort may not be had to the Legislative Journals when the language of a statute is plain.

In a case as recent as 1957, the Chief Justice of our Supreme Court said: "The intention and meaning of the Legislature must primarily be determined from conjectures. When the language of a statute is plain and unambiguous and conveys clear and definite meaning, there is no occasion for resorting to the rules of statutory interpretation and construction; the statute must be given its plain obvious meaning."

The third question that arises is — If the language of a statute is not plain and is ambiguous and resort is authorized to the Legislative Journals, what if any limitations are put upon their use by the Courts?

"The Supreme and Superior Courts of Pennsylvania, in considering this question, have frequently stated the rule to be that what is said in debate is not relevant, although reports of a Legislative Commission or Committee may, if obscurity or ambiguity exists, be considered. Moreover, a report of a Commission appointed to codify the law on a given subject is entitled to greater weight then a report of a Committee."

Recently, however, there has been a tendency of Pennsylvania Courts to recognize that while the Legislative debates are not controlling, they are a factor to be considered as indicating the Legislature's intent; that is what the Courts have said:

a. "In order to get at the old law, the mischief and the remedy and properly to understand and construe a statute — the history of the enactment in question may always be considered."

b. "In interpreting the Legislation before us, it is our duty to ascertain, if we can, the Legislative intent and give effect to it. The history of this Legislation is illuminating. The sponsor of the amendment, when it was before the Legislature, said:

'This bill proposes to cure something that was recently decided by the Supreme Court. The purport of the decision, as I take it, is to tax the proceeds of life insurance, left with the company by the assured and make it subject to a county tax'."

No doubt can be entertained that the amendment in question was intended to change the laws as then existing and to exempt life insurance proceeds on deposit with the company from being taxed for county purposes.

The Court said: "We are mindful that contemporary history is not controlling, but it is a factor which may be considered as indicative of legislative intent."

It is important to remember in reading the more recent decisions of the Supreme and Superior Courts of Pennsylvania, that Pennsylvania adopted a Statutory Construction Act May 28, 1937, P.L. 1019, 46 P.S. 551.

Included among its provisions is a section frequently quoted and referred to in the recent decisions of the Supreme and Superior Courts, namely Section 551 which reads as follows:

"The object of all interpretation and construction of laws is to ascertain and effectuate the intention of the Legislature. Every law shall be construed, if possible, to give effect to all its provisions.

When the words of a law are clear and free from all ambiguity, the letter of it is not to be disregarded under the pretext of pursuing its spirit.

When the words of a law are not explicit, the intention of the Legislature may be ascertain by considering among other matters:

1. The occasion and necessity for the law.
2. The circumstances under which it was enacted.
3. The mischief to be remedied.
4. The object to be attained.
5. The former law, if any, including other laws upon the same or similar subjects.
6. The consequences of a particular interpretation.
7. The contemporaneous legislative history.
8. Legislative and administrative interpretations of such law."

Thus, you see that the Legislature has now authorized the ascertainment of the intention of the Legislature when the words of a law are not explicit by considering the Legislative history and interpretation of such law.

CASE CITATIONS
ON FIRST QUESTION:

In Green's Dairy, et al., v. Pa. Milk Control Commission, 48 Dauphin 385. 23 Corpus Juris. Evidence 1885.

16 Corpus Juris. Sec. 982.

ON SECOND QUESTION:

Biddle Appeal, 390 Pa. 460, decided November 11, 1957, Chief Justice Jones, p. 466.

In Lancaster City Annexation Case (★5). 374 Pa. 546, Justice Musmanno, speaking for the Supreme Court, p. 549.

ON THIRD QUESTION:

Mr. Justice Bell in Martin's Estate, 365 Pa. 280, at p. 283:

National Transit Company v. Boardman, 328 Pa. 450, 197 A. 238; Tarlo's Estate, 315 Pa. 321, 172 A. 139.

In Tarlo's Estate, 315 Pa. 321, the Supreme Court, speaking through Mr. Justice Schaffer, pp. 324-325.

In Commonwealth v. W. Phila. Fidelio Mannerchor, 115 Pa. Superior Ct. 241, the Court, pp. 246-247.

In Scarborough v. Pa. R. R. Co., 154 Pa. Superior Ct. 129, the Court, pp. 132-133.

In Loeb v. Benham, 153 Pa. Superior Ct., 601, the Court.

SECTION 19

MEMBER

What Regarded as a Certificate of Election by the House, in Case of Contested Election

19 (a). On a resolution which recited that "it appears from the certified copy of the record of the court of common pleas, of Westmoreland county, duly transmitted to this House in accordance with the Act of 1874; that W. N. Porter and A. D. Hunter were duly elected members of the House of Representatives insead of Eli Waugaman and W. R. Barnhart, who, on the face of the returns, appear to be elected, and resolved that the said W. N. Porter and A. D. Hunter be sworn in as members of the House in conformity with the decision of the court, and that their names be placed on the roll of members." During the debate on the resolution a number of points of order were submitted to the effect that the resolution could not at that time be considered, as the court record was not a certificate of election, et cetera. The Speaker decided the points of order not well taken, for the reason that the record presented is regarded as a certificate of election under the Act of 1874, and under the decision of the court the contestants, in whose favor the decision has been made, are prima facie entitled to their seats. (Journal H. R., 1893, p. 666, and Legislative Record, 1893, p. 855.)

The Sitting Member is Entitled to Vote During Contest

19 (b). A resolution having been offered that neither the contestants nor respondent in the contested election case of Higby vs. Andrews be entitled to vote until a decision is reached by the House as to which is the member elected and qualified, to the end that legislation may not be imperiled thereby, the point of order was raised "that the resolution was 'res judicata' and would invalidate the whole proceedings of the organization of the House." the speaker decided the point of order well taken for the reason that the right of a member to be called and cast a vote was a constitutional right, which he could not be deprived of except for actions in violation of the Constitution or laws of this Commonwealth (Journal H. R., 1893, p. 397.)

Subpoenaed Before Contested Election Committee, Witness Must Be Paid

19 (c). The Speaker decided that witnesses regularly subpoenaed, before a contested election committee, must be paid according to law. (Journal H. R., 1869, p. 597.)

Expulsion of, in Order to Reconsider Vote for

19 (d). The Speaker submitted to the House for decision: Whether a motion to reconsider the vote given for the expulsion of a member by the constitutional majority, and his seat declared vacant, is in order? The House decided in the affirmative. (Journal H.R., 1840, pp. 859-61.)

Qualification of Members

19 (e). Proceedings with relation to, under Article II, Section 5, of the Constitution of Pennsylvania. (Legislative Journal, 1949, pp. 55, 113, 114, 321 and 322.)

Under Arrest for Contempt of the House Nothing in Order Until Purged

19 (f). The Speaker decided that when a member of the House was under arrest for contempt, nothing was in order until the contempt was purged, or the matter otherwise disposed of by the House. The House sustained the decision. (Journal H. R., 1875, p. 177.)

Motives of, Not to Be Questioned

19 (g). During the debate on Senate bill, the point of order was raised that the gentleman is impunging the motives of another member of the House, without any evidence, and furthermore, he is saying that which is to be the derogation of a member's private character, and he should, therefore be stopped. The Speaker decided the point of order well taken, and directed the gentleman to confine his remarks to the issue. (Legislative Journal, April 27, 1921, p. 3118; (Legislative Journal, 1935, p. 4141; Legislative Journal, March 21, 1956, p. 7053.)

Of Previous House not to be Referred to by Name by Committee in Report

19 (h). The Speaker decided that it is not in order for a committee, in a report, when referring to a report made at a previous session of the Legislature by a member of this House to call said member by name. The House sustained the decision. (Journal H. R., 1843, p. 594.)

Not Permitted to Speak More Than Twice on Same Subject Without Consent of the House

19 (i). A House bill was being debated on second reading. The point of order was raised that the gentleman has spoken twice on this subject. The Speaker decided the point of order well taken, stating that under the rules the gentleman cannot proceed without the consent of the House. (Legislative Record, April 2, 1907, p. 2014.)

Cannot Be Excluded from the House

19 (j). A request was made during the verification of the roll that the Sergeants-at-Arms be placed at the doors of the House and that no member be allowed to enter. The point of order was raised that a member cannot be excluded from the House. The Speaker ruled the point of order

well taken, stating that it is a member's constitutional right to come into the House at any time. (Legislative Journal, 1943, p. 1764.)

Member Being a Member of a Commission, Not Considered Personal Interest

19 (k). On the question of agreeing to amendments offered to a House bill, the point of order was raised that the gentleman has personal interests in the bill and is, therefore, not entitled to vote. The Speaker decided the point of order not well taken, stating that being a member of a Commission is not a personal and private interest. (Legislative Journal, June 3, 1913, p. 3819; Journal H. R., p. 4503.)

Member Himself Must Determine Whether He Has Private Interest in a Bill

19 (l). Under a question of parliamentary inquiry, a member asked whether the House rule prevented a member having a private interest in a bill to vote thereon. The Speaker stated that it was a matter entirely within the conscience of the individual member as to his right to vote. (Legislative Journal, December 12, 1933, p. 574.)

Entitled to Recognition before Call of Roll

19 (m). The point of order was raised that nothing was in order but the calling of the roll. The Speaker decided the point of order not well taken. A member is entitled to recognition before the roll call has actually begun. (House Journal, 1937, p. 2943; July 28, 1938, p. 440.)

Personal Interest in Member Voting Defined Under Provisions of Article III, Section 33, of Constitution

19 (n). Honorable Presely N. Jones, a member of the House of Representatives from the County of Lawrence, duly elected to the General Assembly for the Session of 1941 and 1942, on February 3, 1941, presented Resolution Number Nine to the House of Representatives alleging that the Honorable Don Wilkinson, a duly elected member of the House of Representatives from the County of Luzerne for the Session of 1941-1942, did while serving as a member of the House of Representatives during the Session of 1939 and 1940, introduce and sponsor legislation defining the rights, powers and duties of County Tax Collectors as will be found in Act No. 277, approved the 20th day of June, 1939, P. L. 508, and that said Don Wilkinson, at the time of introduction of said bill, was a Tax collector, that the bill introduced by the said Don Wilkinson for his private and pecuniary profit and that the said Don Wilkinson voted upon the said piece of legislation and that after passage of same received contracts from certain school districts, townships and boroughs of the Commonwealth of Pennsylvania for the collection of taxes under said Act.

On February 10, 1941, the Resolution was returned to the House of Representatives by the Committee on Rules and referred to the House Judiciary General Committee for action. The House Judiciary General Committee there upon appointed a sub-committee composed of the following members of the Judiciary General Committee, Honorable Homer S. Brown, Honorable John H. McKinney, Honorable John R. Bently, Honorable William L. Shaffer, and Honorable George W. Cooper.

Subsequent to the appointment of the sub-committee, the Petitioner, Presley N. Jones, submitted a Bill of Particulars to the Committee, which Bill of Particulars stated in substance that said Don Wilkinson as a Tax Collector, had secured certain contracts from the School Board of the City of New Castle for the collection of delinquent per capita taxes, which contracts provided for the payment to the said Don Wilkinson of fees and charges set forth in the Act of 1939 above referred to. To the Bill of Particulars the Respondent, Don Wilkinson, filed a demurrer alleging that the present Session of the House of Representatives had no jurisdiction in that the House of Representatives is not a continuous body and that Article 3, Section 33 of the Constitution of Pennsylvania dealing with the question of personal or private interest had not been violated. To the demurrer, the aforesaid Petitioner filed an answer stating that the Respondent had violated Article 7, Section 1, of the Constitution of Pennsylvania dealing with the oath of Senators, Representatives, the Judiciary and State and County Officers, and Article 3, Section 33, the personal and private interest section of the Constitution of Pennsylvania, as it applies to members of the General Assembly.

1. The first question raised by the demurrer filed by the Honorable Don Wilkinson is that the present House of Representatives has no authority to take jurisdiction of the matter alleged in the Resolution and in support of this question the Respondent cited a number of precedents recorded in Hinds' Precedents of the House of Representatives of the National Congress to the effect that the House of Representatives not being "a continuous body but an entity that dies at the expiration of the term of each of its members":

"It is a rule of the House of Representatives of Congress that a House may not try to punish one of its members for an offense alleged to have been committed against a preceding House." See Hinds' Precedents of the House of Representatives, Vol. 2, section 1283; also sections 1284 and 1285.

Our Committee, while not attempting to overrule the Hinds' Precedents, are of the opinion that the better view is to effect that misconduct on the part of a member of the House of Representatives in a previous term may constitute grounds for his removal and impeachment in a succeeding term, especially where the offending party is his own successor and that re-election would not condone the offense. See State v. Welsh, 109, Iowa, 19, 79, N. W., 369:

"The very object of removal is to rid the community of a corrupt, incapable, or unworthy official. His acts during his previous term quite as effectively stamp him as much as those of that he may be serving. Re-election does not condone the offense. Misconduct may not have been discovered prior to election, and, in any event, had not been established in the manner contemplated by the statute * * * The commission of any of the prohibited acts the day before quite as particularly stamps him as an improper person to be intrusted with the performance of the duties of the particular office as those done the day after."

See also the case of Throop Borough's School Directors, 298 Pennsylvania, 453, page 357:

"Wrong doing cannot be overlooked and approved by the act of the people in reelecting them to office for the ensuing term, and such attempted condonation does not prevent the legally constituted authorities from visiting on the offending persons the results of conduct expressly prohibited by the Act of Assembly." and on pages 458, 459:

"Offenses committed during a previous term are generally held not to furnish cause for general removal, but where removal carries with it a disqualification to hold office in the future, the rule is otherwise, 45 Corpus Juris 96."

II. The offense alleged in the Bill of Particulars submitted by the Petitioner, primarily charges the Respondent with violating Article 3. Section 33 of the Constitution of Pennsylvania, which article reads as follows:

"A member who has a personal or private interest in any measure or bill proposed or pending before the General Assembly shall disclose the fact to the House of which he is a member, and shall not vote thereon."

Believing that this Session of the legislature has jurisdiction over the subject involved in the pending Resolution, we now proceed to discuss whether or not the Respondent, Don Wilkinson, is guilty of violating Article 3, Section 33, aforementioned and it becomes necessary to discuss the important provision of this Section of the Constitution in order to define and explain the meaning of the words: "personal or private interest."

A perusal of the debates of the Constitutional Convention that concluded its work November 3, 1873, reveals that it not only failed to adopt a sanction of penalty for Article 3, Section 33, but likewise omitted to make clear the meaning of the important language embodied in this Section. Much was said about the practice of individuals representing corporations seeking special and local legislation and special favors, but the Section was finally adopted without a clear distinction as to its meaning.

The Committee is fortunate to cite as an authority in defining the aforementioned words, the interpretation of the able Parliamentarian of the House of Representatives of Pennsylvania, the Honorable S. Edward Moore, and quotes in its entirety his review of this subject, which has been handed to the Committee:

"The Constitution of Pennsylvania, Article 3, Section 33 provides: 'That a Member who has a personal or private interest in any measure or bill proposed or pending before the House shall disclose the fact to the House and shall not vote thereon.'

The right of a Member to represent his constituency, is of such major importance that a Member should be barred from voting on matters of direct personal interest only in clear cases and when the matter is to be voted upon is particularly personal.

When the matters under consideration affect a cause rather than individuals, the personal interest belongs to that cause and is not such as to disqualify a Member from voting.

As for instance a Member may have a personal interest in a particular hospital seeking an appropriation. The Pennsylvania Commission on Constitutional Revisions said 'It was not the intent of Article III, Section 33, that a Member should expose such personal interest to the House of which he is a Member.'

Rule VIII of the National House of Representatives reads in part: 'Every Member shall vote on each question put unless he has a personal or pecuniary interest.'

In interpreting this rule of Congress which is similar to our own it has been held that the disqualifying interest must be such as affects the Member directly and not as one of a class (Hinds' Precedents, Vol. V, Section 5952, 5954, 5955 and 5963.)

Senator Robert C. Winthrop of the Massachusetts House discussed the subject of Personal Interest exhaustively in 1840 and was of the opinion: 'That an interest which a Member holds in common with thousands of others could hardly be regarded as a private interest.'

Speaker James G. Blaine when the matter of personal interest came up in 1893 in the National House, said: 'You can go through the whole round of business and find upon this floor gentlemen, who in common with many citizens outside of this House, have an interest in questions before this House. But they do not have that interest separate and distinct from a class.'

Speaker Talbot of the Pennsylvania House in 1933, in response to a parliamentary inquiry stated: 'That the right of a Member to vote where a question of personal interest was involved was a matter entirely within the conscience of the individual member.'

In conclusion the question is definitely one upon which each individual Member must satisfy his conscience. He must settle it for himself.''

The view of the able Parliamentarian is supported by many authorities. See Luce-Legislative Procedure, Section 323 and Jefferson's Manual on Rules of the House of Representatives, 651. For the purpose of brevity, we quote only the following:

"In one or two instances the Speaker has decided that because of personal interest, a member should not vote (V.5955, 5958); but usually the Speaker has held that the Member himself should determine this question." (V.5950, 5951.) "And one Speaker denied his own power to deprive a member of the constitutional Right to Vote." (V.5956.)

"It is a principle of immemorable observance' that a member should withdraw when a question concerning himself arises (V.5949); but it has been held that the disqualifying interest must be such as affects the member directly (V.5952)." Jefferson's Manual on Rules of the House of Representatives, Section 651.

The committee finds that this matter has been the subject of interpretation by the Supreme Court of Pennsylvania, as will be found in the case of Wilson v. New Castle City, 301 Pa. 359, pages 362 and 363. The Court saying in this case:

"The question hinges upon what is known as personal or private interest. The 'interest' in a matter which will disqualify a public official acting in an executive capacity must be certain pecuniary or proprietary acts and capable of proof. It must be direct, not contingent nor depending on an indirect benefit as that of contract may or may not effect other independent transactions. A sentimental interest or a general interest is not enough."

III. The petitioner, Presley N. Jones, in his argument asking for explusion of the Respondent, Don Wilkinson, contends that the said Respondent violated Article 7, Section 1, of the Constitution of Pennsylvania, said Article having to do with the Oath of Senators, Representatives and all Judicial, State and County Officers; and provides inter alia the following:

"And any person who shall be convicted of having sworn or affirmed falsely or of having violated said oath or affirmation, shall be guilty of perjury, and be forever disqualified from holding any office of trust or profit within this Commonwealth."

and in support of his argument asserts, that under this Section, the Respondent could be found guilty without trial by jury; citing as his authority the opinion of the learned Chief Justice in the case of Commonwealth v. Walter, 83 Pa. 103, where the Court in construing Article 8, Section 9, of our Constitution, used the following language:

"The world 'guilty' is defined by our lexicographers to meaning 'having guilt'; 'chargeable with a crime'; 'not innocent'; 'criminal.' Hence we say a man is guilty of an offense when he has commited an offense. We say he has been convicted of an offense when he has been found guilty by the verdict of a jury."

Article 8, Section 9, supra, cannot be interpreted in the same manner as Article 7. Section 1; and we believe the latter Article presupposes that a person must be convicted of perjury in Court of proper jurisdiction before being disqualified from holding any office of trust or profit within this Commonwealth. However, a member violating his oath of office could be punished by the Legislature under Article 2, Section 2 of our Constitution, without first having been tried in Court of proper jurisdiction:

"Each House shall have power to determine the rules of its proceedings and punish its members or other persons for contempt or disorderly behavior in its presence to enforce obedience to its process, to protect its members against violence or offers or bribes or private solicitations, and, with the concurrence of two-thirds, to expel a member, but not a second time for the same cause, and shall have all other powers necessary for the Legislature of a free State. A member expelled for corruption shall not thereafter be eligible to either House, and punishment for contempt or disorderly behavior shall not bar an indictment for the same offense." Article 2, Section 2.

CONCLUSION

Your Committee is of the opinion from the argument above given that the House of Repesentatives of the Session of 1941 has jurisdiction to punish a member for an offense committed in the 1939 Session provided that offense is one which affects the right of the member to hold office in the present term and that if such offense were established it would be a violation of the oath of the member to the extent that the present Session of the House of Representatives would have the power to punish said member under Article 2, Section 2, of the constitution. However, we find that the matters alleged in the Petitioner's Bill of Particulars and Brief do not come within the meaning of the "personal and private interest" section contained in Article 3. Section 33 of the Constitution of Pennsylvania for the following reasons:

1 The matters alleged, namely the voting upon legislation in Act 277, approved the 20th day of June, 1939, P. L. 508, affected the Respondent, Don Wilkinson, as a member of a class, to wit, Tax Collectors.

2 The passage of said Act 277, by the House of Representatives in the absence of bribery, fraud or corruption would not make the Respondent's vote a violation of the Constitution notwithstanding the fact that he may have received a pecuniary benefit from the results of the Act of Assembly.

We have omitted in argument any discussion concerning paragraph ten (10) of the Petitioner's Bill of Particulars which charges the Respondent with violating Section 895 of the Act of 1939, P. L. 872, of the General Assembly of Pennsylvania, making it a misdemeanor to disperse any paper purporting to be a legal process or summons of a Court of the Commonwealth of Pennsylvania. It is our opinion that charges of this nature should be made in the Court of proper jurisdiction where the Respondent would have the constitutional protection offered Defendants charged with violating our Criminal Laws. If the legislature undertook to try each member on matters submitted to it of this nature, the accused member might be at the mercy of a Legislature unsympathetic to his political views, which alone might be the factor in determining his guilt or innocence. We believe that except in the case of impeachment and for crimes of bribery, perjury, corruption in office and closely related matters, the Legislature should not invade the field of Criminal Law to invoke the provisions of Article 2, Section 2 of State Constitution.

The procedure asked for by the Petitioner, Presley N. Jones, is a most extraordinary one and should not be used in a case or cases where the evidence admits of no doubt as to guilt of the Respondent. To hold otherwise would turn an orderly, and free House of Representatives into a chaotic and despotic body; and members might be allowed to hold office only by the will of two-thirds (2/3) of its membership. In this connection, we quote with approval the able argument presented in the dissenting opinion of Mr. Justice Dean in Commonwealth v. Moir, 199 P. 534:

"The time is not very remote in the past in English politics when the victorious political party, as soon as it was seated in power, promptly proceeded to cut off the physical heads of their leading antagonists and confiscate their property, it is not very remote in the future when the victorious political party will promptly proceed to cut off the political heads of their opponents where they held office by the municipal vote of cities."

Your Committee therefore urges that the Prayer of the Petitioner that the House of Representatives authorize the speaker to appoint a committee of five members of the House of Representatives to inquire into the matter concerning the official conduct of Don Wilkinson and further inquire whether he is guilty of misconduct as grounds for expulsion from the House of Representatives, be refused.

This is a Report of the Judiciary General Committee submitted to the House of Represenatatives by the Honorable Homer S. Brown, Chairman, June 2, 1941. The Report was unanimously adopted by the House of Representatives. (Legislative Journal, 1941, pp. 3114 to 3124, inclusive) Note: Exhibit A of the Report is House Resolution No. 9, introduced in the House January 28, 1941.

SECTION 20

ORDER OF BUSINESS

Unanimous Consent to Divert From

20 (a). Under a parliamentary inquiry, the question was asked whether it is within the province of a member to call any bill at any time.

The Speaker Pro-Tempore replied it was not. Only by unanimous consent or action taken by the House can we divert from the regular order of the calendar. (Legislative Journal #11, 1959, pp. 4568-4569.)

Objections to, Must Be Made Before Decision is Given to Proceed With

20 (b). The Chair decided that after an agreement to proceed with certain orders had been partially carried out, it was too late to make objections. The House sustained the decision. (Journal H. R., 1868, pp. 960, 907.)

Bill Under Consideration at Time of Last Adjournment No Quorum Being Present Not the First Order at the Next Session

20 (c). The point of order was submitted that when the House adjourned Friday last it had under consideration a Senate bill and there was no quorum present, that said bill should be the first order of business for this evening. The Speaker decided the point of order to be not well taken, as he had exhausted all available means of procuring a quorum and was, therefore, compelled to adjourn the House and that said bill would come up in its order with Senate bills on second reading. (Journal H. R., 1895, p. 2295.)

SECTION 21

ORDER OF BUSINESS, SPECIAL

Resolutions Fixing Special Orders of Business Are Privileged

21 (a). A resolution was presented, fixing as a special order of business, a time for the House to resolve itself into a Committee of the Whole to hear the Governor and department heads, etc., submit a plan on unemployment relief.

Unanimous consent having been denied its immediate consideration.

The point of order was made that this resolution did not come within the preview of the rule of the House requiring certain resolutions to lie over for printing, for the reason that it is in effect a motion regulating the business of the House permitted at any time.

The Speaker sustained the point of order, the rules provide that the House may resolve itself into a Committee of the Whole at any time, further Rule 14 provides that any subject may by a majority vote, be made a special order of business, the resolution is, therefore, privileged for the reason that it established an order of business for the House and its immediate consideration is in order. (Legislative Journal, July 25, 1932, p. 580)

Motion Fixing, in Order

21 (b). On a motion to make a House bill a Special Order of Business, on second reading, the point of order was raised that this motion being in the nature of a resolution, is out of order. The Speaker ruled that the motion being a mere motion, is in order. (Legislative Journal, February 19, 1913, p. 362; Journal H. R., p. 917.)

House by a Majority Vote on Recommendation of Committee on rules Can Fix for One Bill in Advance of Others

21 (c). Mr. Bedford submitted the point of order that the Committee on Rules had not the power to take out any single bill and make it a special order in advance of other bills. The Speaker read for the information of the gentleman, the rule and decided the point of order not well taken. (Legislative Record 1901, p. 2544.)

Committee of Whole Report Having Been Made Special Order for Second Reading

21 (d). The report of the Committee of the Whole having been adopted, the House proceeded to the second reading of the bill.

When a motion was made to fix a later time for its second reading.

The Speaker ruled the motion out of order, for the reason it should have been made before the House proceeded to the consideration on second reading of the bill and the rule requires that the House immediately proceed to the one reading of a bill after it has acted upon the report of the Committee of the Whole. (Legislative Journal, November 21, 1933, pp. 129-130.)

Hour for, Having Arrived, Must Proceed With

21 (e). The Speaker decided that the House having agreed to "proceed to the final vote upon a resolution at ten o'clock this evening," and that hour having arrived, nothing was in order but the vote on the final passage of the resolution. (Journal H. R., 1869, p. 767.)

Day Fixed for Consideration of, Cannot be Called Up Prior to

21 (f). The point of order was raised that the House having fixed a day for the consideration of a bill, that bill cannot be called up before the time fixed upon by the House for its consideration. The Speaker decided the point of order to be well taken. The House sustained the Speaker. (Journal H. R., 1876, pp. 612, 613, 614.)

Of a Bill, Adoption of a Resolution to Proceed to, at Certain Time in Order

21 (g). The Speaker decided that the House having, on yesterday, adopted a resolution by a vote of two-thirds, that it would proceed to the reconsideration of a certain bill when it met the next morning, the bill is, therefore, in order. The House sustained the decision (Journal H. R., 1840, pp. 946-50.)

Consideration of, in Order Even Though the Time Fixed for, Has Passed

21 (h). Consideration of a House bill was resumed on second reading, as a Special Order of Business. The point of order was raised that the special hour of eight-thirty fixed for consideration of this bill having passed there is now nothing in order but the regular order of business. The Speaker decided the point of order not well taken. (Legislative Record, April 7, 1909, p. 2968.)

Special, Takes Precedence Until Disposed of

21 (i). The Speaker decided that the House having, by a vote of two-thirds, determined that it would, at a certain specified hour upon a particular day, proceed to the consideration of a certain question and the time having arrived, the House must proceed to its consideration, and any

other business before the House stands postponed until the question is disposed by the House, either by adoption, rejection of postponement (Journal H. R., 1861, p. 131.)

One Special Order Must Be Rescinded before Making Another for Same Proposition

21 (j). A motion was made to suspend the rules for the specific purpose of considering a resolution.

The point of order was made that the House had fixed as a special order of business for the consideration of a bill today which this resolution proposes a public hearing for a later time, therefore, the special order would have to be rescinded before the resolution could be considered.

The Speaker sustained the point of order, the proper procedure being for the House first to rescind its action fixing the bill as a Special Order of Business. (Legislative Journal, July 13, 1932, p. 352.)

SECTION 22

PERSONAL PRIVILEGE

Must be Confined to Integrity of the Member of the House

22 (a). A member rose to a question of personal privilege and the speaker ruled that unless the question of personal privilege related to the integrity of the member or the integrity of the House, it is not in order. (Legislative Journal, May 20, 1931, p. 4677.)

Question Confined to Rights of the House or of the Member

22 (b). A member rose to question of personal privilege.

The point of order was raised that the gentleman was not speaking on a question of personal privilege.

The Speaker ruled that questions of privilege are first, those affecting the rights of the House collectively, its safety, dignity and the integrity of its proceedings; second, the right, reputation and conduct of its members individually in their representative capacity only. (Legislative Journal, March 20, 1933, p. 1251; also January 23, 1933, p. 247.)

Member Not to Discuss Merits of a Bill Under Question of Personal Privilege

22 (c). The Speaker ruled that a decision of the merits of a bill is not permitted under a question of personal privilege. (Legislative Journal, April 23, 1935, p. 2598.)

Confined to Remarks Concerning Himself

22 (d). A member was addressing the House under a question of personal privilege, when the point of order was made, that the gentleman was not speaking on a question of personal privilege.

The Speaker ruled the point of order well taken and in response to a parliamentary inquiry states the following:

"Questions affecting the rights, reputation and conduct of members of the House in their representative capacity are questions of personal privilege."

"Questions of privilege of a member must relate to a person as a member of the body, or relate to charges against his character, which therefore he is not entitled to the floor on a question of personal privilege unless the subject which he proposes to present relates to him in his representative capacity."

"A person who raises the question of personal privilege must confine himself to remarks which concern himself personally, and when speaking under personal privilege a member has no right to defend any person other than himself."

"If the gentleman from Allegheny will confine himself to a question of personal privilege, he has a right to be heard." (Legislative Journal, March 13, 1939, p. 611.)

SECTION 23

POINTS OF ORDER

Question for Speaker to Decide and Not the House Unless Submitted to It

23 (a). On the question of adopting a resolution, declaring subjects not enumerated in the Governor's proclamation out of order the point of order was raised that the resolution is not in order because under parliamentary rules a point of order is a question for the Speaker and not for the House to decide unless submitted to the House. The Speaker ruled the point of order well taken. (Legislative Record, January 22, 1906, p. 60; Journal H. R., p. 36.)

Members May Raise Constitutional Point of Order Whether or Not a Personal Interest in Bill

23 (b). The point of order was made that a member could not raise a question as to the constitutionality of a bill until he declared to the House whether or not he had any personal interest in the bill, Rule 72 of the House makes it obligatory for members to declare whether they have a personal interst. Speaker ruled that point of order not well taken, stating that any member of the House whether he has a personal interest or not has the right to raise a constitutional question. (Legislative Journal, April 1, 1939, pp. 1345 and 1346.)

Members May State Reasons for Raising

23 (c). A point of order having been raised that amendments to a bill were unconstitutional was being debated when another point of order was raised that the gentleman is debating the point of order which he has raised and, therefore, is out of order until the Chair has given his decision. The Speaker decided the point of order not well taken as a gentleman has a right to give his reasons for raising a point of order and refer to authorities. (Legislative Journal, February 13, 1917, p. 202.)

Decision on, Postponed for Purpose of Obtaining Information

23 (d). The Speaker postponed making a decision on a point of order for several days in order to obtain information upon which to make his decision. (Legislative Record, March 19, 1907, p. 1450. Decision made March 28, 1907. pp. 1834-35. Also Legislative Record, April 17, 1907, p. 2810. Decision made April 22, 1907, p. 3066.)

Constitutional Points of Order for House to Decide

23 (e). A bill was on final passage when the point of order was raised, that it was unconstitutional in violation of Art. III, Sec. 7.

The Speaker stated that it was his opinion that any question affecting the constitutionality of a bill is for the House itself to determine and not for the Speaker to decide.

This principle is supported by uniform rulings of Speakers of the House of Representatives of the United States and Pennsylvania, which will be found in Hinds' Precedents, Vols. 2 and 5. (See also Legislative Journal of Pa., 1913, pp. 1301, 1304.)

Cooley's Constitutional Limitations, Vol. 1, Chap. 4, p. 99, says: "The decisions for the construction of the Constitution must be made by the body upon whom the duty is imposed, or from whom the act is required."

The rules of this House give the Speaker the authority to submit the question to the House, which he does.

The bill was declared unconstitutional by the House. (Legislative Journal, Dec. 13, 1933, pp. 638, 639.) (Legisaltive Journal, June 5, 1935, p. 4805.) (Legislative Journal, 1949, April 27, p. 4703.)

Point of Order Must Be Made at Time Offense is Committed

23 (f). A point was raised that a bill was considered out of its regular order. The Speaker decided that the question was not subject to a point of order because it is business that has already passed. A point of order must be made at the time the offense is committed. (Legislative Journal, March 1, 1955, p. 537.)

Constitutionality of Bills, Question for House to Decide

23 (g). Under parliamentary inquiry the question was asked whether the House may determine the question of the constitutionality of legislation before it? The Speaker replied that it could. (Legislative Journal, July 7, 1953, p. 2098.)

Constitutionality of Bills, Attorney General May Not be Summoned to Decide Upon

23 (h). Under a parliamentary inquiry the question was asked could the House summon the Attorney General to appear before it for an opinion on the constitutionality of a bill? The speaker replied — it could not — the Attorney General being the legal advisor to the Governor of the Commonwealth and not the advisor to the House. (Legislative Journal, July 7, 1953, p. 2909.)

Constitutional Point of Order

23 (i). The House decided that a member given its unanimous consent could discuss a bill he was about to introduce without violating Article III, Section 2 of the Constitution, which reads:

"No bill shall be considered unless referred to a committee, returned therefrom, and printed for the use of the members."
(Legislative Journal, May 6, 1959, pp. 1196-1199.)

SECTION 24

POSTPONEMENT

Bill Properly on Regular Calendar and Not on Calendar of Postponed Bills When Reported by Committee

24 (a). A Senate bill was on second reading. The point of order was raised that when this bill was recommitted to committee it was on the postponed calendar, it should, therefore, go on the postponed calendar when re-reported from committee. The Speaker decided the point of order not well taken as the vote of the House to recommit took the bill from the postponed calendar and when re-reported from committee would properly be placed on the regular calendar. (Legislative Record, April 4, 1905, p. 2349; Journal H. R., p. 1494.)

Bill Not on Calendar, Motion for is Not in Order

24 (b). On a motion to postpone a House bill, the point of order was raised that the bill is not on the calendar, therefore, it cannot be postponed. The Speaker decided the point of order well taken. (Legislative Record, April 4, 1905, p. 2291.)

Bills on Postponed Calendar Must be Called Up Under Their Regular Order of Business

24 (c). A request was made to call up from the postponed calendar a House bill. The point of order was raised that the order of business is bills on first reading, therefore, consideration of this bill is out of order. The Speaker decided the point of order well taken (Legislative Record, March 29, 1909, p. 1843.)

Senate Postponed Bills Do Not Require Extension of Time

24 (d). The point of order was raised that Senate bills remain on the postponed calendar without an extension of time. The Speaker ruled that Senate bills would not be dropped from the House Postponed Calendar under the rule. (Legislative Journal, March 18, 1931, p. 1084.)

Must be by Action of the House

24 (e). In response to a parliamentary inquiry as to whether the House could proceed to act upon a bill which was on the calendar before the report of a Select Committee had made its report to the House appointed to investigate this subject. The Speaker stated that the question of postponement of the bill was for the House to decide — the Chair has no jurisdiction and cannot stop consideration of a bill on the Calendar. It must be done by motion from the floor. (Legislative Journal, 1941, p. 750.)

SECTION 25

PREVIOUS QUESTION

Call for, in Order During Pendency of an Appeal

25 (a). The Speaker decided that a call for the previous question is in order during the pendency of an appeal from the decision of the Speaker. The House sustained the decision. (Journal H. R. 840, pp. 946-8.)

Call for, While Member is Addressing the House, in Order

25 (b). The Speaker decided that the previous question could be called while a member was addressing the House. (Journal H. R., 1858, p. 347; also p. 539.)

When Exhausted

25 (c). The point of order was raised that the previous question having been ordered, no further amendments are in order to the bill, and the previous question is not exhausted until the bill is gone through with. The Speaker decided the point of order to be not well taken, for the following reasons, viz.: The previous question having been called on an amendment to the third section of the bill, and the main question ordered to be put, the previous question exhausted itself on the amendments to subsequent sections are in order. (Journal H. R. 1881, p. 1414.)

When Moved on Third Reading, Final Passage of Same Is a Part of the Main Question

25 (d). The bill on third reading and motion made to go into Committee of the Whole for special amendment, the previous question was moved. Upon the bill being agreed to on third reading, the point of order was submitted that the previous question had been exhausted on agreeing to the bill on third reading. The Speaker decided the point of order to be not well taken, and that the main question was on agreeing to the bill on third reading and final passage. (Journal H. R. 1895, p. 2013.)

Cuts off Motion to Go Into Committee of the Whole

25 (e). The point of order was raised that as a motion had been made to go into Committtee of the Whole for special amendments that said motion took precedence over a motion for the previous question which had been previously offered. Decided not well taken. (Legislative Record, 1901, p. 581.)

Debate May Continue Only if Previous Question is Voted down

25 (f). The point of order was raised that the House having given a member permission to speak, the previous question is not in order. The Speaker ruled that the previous question having been moved and seconded, this question would have to be voted down to permit the gentleman to continue in debate. (Legislative Journal, March 4, 1935, p. 799; also June 11, 1935, p. 5212.)

Previous Question Is Not Debatable

25 (g). Under a question of parliamentary inquiry, the Speaker stated that the motion for the previous question was not debatable and having been made, nothing is in order but the question "Shall the main question be now put?" It is for the House itself to determine whether it wants the main question. Rule 68 of the House, and Jefferson's Manual, Section 454, were cited as authority. (Legislative Journal, June 11, 1935, p. 5212; also pp. 5219, 5220.) (See Jefferson's Manual, Section 785; also Hinds, Precedents, Vol. V, Sections 5410-5411.)

May Not be Laid Upon Table

25 (h). The previous question having been moved and seconded. A motion was made to lay the motion for the previous question on the table. The Speaker ruled that the motion for the previous question could not be laid upon the table. (Legislative Journal, May 2, 1939, p. 2317.)

Interrogation Not Permitted, Is a Form of Debate

25 (i). A motion was made and seconded for the previous question, a member under a question of parliamentary inquiry asked if it was permissible under the rules to interrogate the gentleman who made the motion for the previous question. The speaker stated that he was of the opinion that an interrogation would be a form of debate and read for the information of the House Rule 68, relative to interrogation on an undebatable motion. (Legislative Journal, 1943, p. 2295)

SECTION 26

RECONSIDERATION

Omnibus Motion to Reconsider Vote to Reinstate Bills Not in Order

26 (a). A motion was offered to reconsider the vote by which several bills had been dropped from the calendar. The point of order was raised

that the bills could not be reinstated by an omnibus motion, but that the motion should designate the number of each bill and the page of the calendar. The Speaker decided the point of order well taken, stating that each individual bill should be acted upon separately. (Legislative Journal, April 5, 1925, p. 3766.)

Of Bill by Senate After Being in Possession of the House Not in Order

26 (b). After a bill incorporating a railroad company had passed the Senate had been received by the House, the Senate reconsidered the vote on its final passage and notified the House of the same. The bill being on the House private calendar of Senate bills, a question of order was raised that inasmuch as the Senate had reconsidered its vote on the final passage, and notified the House thereof, the bill was, therefore, not in order. The Speaker submitted the question to the House. The House decided the question of order not well taken. (Journal H. R., 1870, p. 1173.)

After Bill Has Passed House and Is Messaged to Senate Not in Order to

26 (c). A motion was made to reconsider the vote by which a House bill passed finally. The point of order was raised that this bill has already passed the House and sent to the Senate for concurrence and is no longer the property of the House. The Speaker pro tempore decided the point of order well taken. An appeal was taken from the decision of the Chair. The House sustained the decision of the Speaker pro tempore. (Legislative Journal, March 21, 1917, p. 732; Journal H. R., p. 948.)

Of Vote on Indefinite Postponement of Motion to Reconsider, Not in Order

26 (d). The Speaker decided that a motion to reconsider the vote on indefinitely postponing a motion to reconsider the vote on the final passage of a bill, was not in order. The House sustained the decision. (Journal H. R., 1862, p. 778.)

Of Vote Defeating Bill, May be Made within Five Days of Actual Session

26 (e). The point of order was raised that five legislative days had not intervened since the bill was defeated. The speaker ruled that the bill was defeated on the seventeenth instant, last Monday. The House was in session Tuesday, Wednesday and Thursday of last week. This will be the fourth day in which the House is in session. The point of order is not sustained. (Journal H. R. 1913, p. 6045, and Legislative Journal, 1913, p. 3072.)

Motion for, in Order Until Defeated

26 (f). On a motion to reconsider the vote by which a Senate bill was defeated on final passage, the point of order was raised that a motion has once been made for the reconsideration of this bill. The Speaker ruled that a motion to reconsider is always in order until the motion to reconsider has been defeated. (Legislative Record, April 15, 1909, p. 4096.)

Resolution Must be in Possession of the House to Reconsider

26 (g). A motion was made to reconsider the vote by which a resolution passed the House. The speaker ruled the motion out of order for the reason that the resolution was not in the possession of the House. (Legislative Journal, Jan. 23, 1933, p. 247.)

Of Motion by Which House Bill was Recommitted Not in Order

26 (h). A motion was made to reconsider the vote by which a House bill was recommitted to committee. Following the vote to reconsider the question was raised that the same could not be done because the House having voted to recommit the bill, the bill was no longer in the possession of the House so that action could be taken upon the motion to reconsider. The Chair ruled the point of order to be well taken and that the motion to reconsider the vote by which the bill was recommitted was out of order. (Legislative Journal — House, June 8, 1971, p. 699.)

Motion to take from Table Cannot be Reconsidered

26 (i). On the question of renewing a motion to take from the table, the speaker ruled that although this motion Cannot be reconsidered, it can be renewed after intervening business. (Legislative Journal — House, February 19, 1987, p. 342.)

SECTION 27

RESOLUTIONS

Placing Bill not Reported from Committee on Calendar, Not in Order

27 (a). On the question of adopting a resolution to place a Senate bill on the calendar not withstanding the negative recommendation to the Committee, the point of order was raised that this bill has not been reported to the House, and is not in the possession of the House, therefore, this resolution cannot be entertained. The Speaker decided the point of order well taken. (Legislative Record, May 6,1907, p. 176; Journal H. R., p. 2597.)

Laid Upon the Table by a Majority Vote by the House Cannot be taken from the Table Except by a Majority Vote

27 (b). A resolution which was laid on the table was called up by a member. The point of order was raised that the resolution was laid on the table by a vote of the House, therefore, must be taken off by a vote of the House. The Speaker decided the point of order well taken, stating that it will require a motion agreed to by a majority of the members present to take the resolution from the table. (Legislative Record, February 11, 1907, p. 513; Journal H. R., p. 498.)

Act of Assembly Cannot be Changed or Repealed by

27 (c). On a motion to refer a Concurrent Resolution abolishing the printing of the Legislative Record to the Committee on Printing the point of order was raised that the publishing of the Legislative Record is provided for by an Act of Assembly and an Act of Assembly cannot be repealed by a Concurrent Resolution. The Speaker decided the point of order well taken. (Legisaltive Record, April 2, 1907, pp. 1941 and 2034; Journal H. R., p. 1385.) (See also Legislative Record, March 12, 1901, p. 785; Journal H. R., p. 727; also Legislative Record, Feb. 15, 1906, p. 695; and Journal H. R., p. 303.)

Acts of Assembly Cannot be Amended by Concurrent

27 (d). On the question of adopting a concurrent resolution, the point of order was raised that this resolution is unconstitutional. The speaker decided the point of order well taken, holding that an Act of Assembly cannot be amended by a concurrent resolution. (Legislative Journal, June 7, 1917, p. 3273; Journal H. R., p. 3143.)

Not Concerning a Member of the House, Out of Order

27 (e). On the question of adopting a concurrent resolution, the point of order was raised that the House is not concerning in this resolution because there is no charge in it affecting a member of this House but the charge relates entirely to a Senator. The Speaker submitted the point of order to the House. The House sustained the point of order. (Legislative Record, May 6, 1907, p. 4180; Journal H. R., p. 2600.)

Requesting Certain Information from the Banking Department, Not in Order

27 (f). On the question of adopting a resolution requesting information from a department, the point of order was raised that the Banking Commission or any deputy officer or employe of this department shall not divulge the contents of the reports called for in this resolution. The Speaker suspended decision of the point of order until he has had a consultation with the Banking Department. (Legislative Record, March 19, 1907, p. 1450.) The Speaker decided the point of order well taken. (Legislative Record, March 28, 1907, p. 1384.) (See Decision of Attorney General, Legislative Record, 1907, p. 1835; Journal H. R., p. 1298.)

Requesting a Clerk in a Department to Furnish Information, Not in Order

27 (g). On a motion to commit a House Resolution to the Committee on Ways and Means, the point of order was raised that the resolution is out of order, because Mr. Lewis, being an employe and not an officer of the Auditor General's Department, cannot be called upon to furnish information from that Department. The Speaker decided the point of order well taken, and declared the resolution out of order. (Legislative Journal, April 13, 1921, p. 1836, and April 18, 1921, p. 2037.)

Recalling Bill from Senate Must be Acted upon by the Senate

27 (h). On a motion to reconsider the vote by which the resolution recalling a House bill from the Senate was adopted, the point of order was raised that the House cannot recall a bill from the Senate after it has passed second reading in the Senate. The Speaker ruled that the Resolution recalling the House bill is a Concurrent Resolution, therefore, the question of returning the bill to the House is for the Senate itself to determine. (Legislative Journal, April 5, 1921, p. 1308.)

Reconsideration of Vote Adopting, After Bill Has Been Messaged to Senate, Not in Order

27 (i). On a question to reconsider the vote by which the House adopted a Resolution to return a House bill to the Governor, the point of order was raised that the resolution authorizing the return of this bill to the Governor, was adopted by the House and messaged to the Senate before the gentleman presented his motion to reconsider the vote or the resolution, therefore, his motion is out of order, the resolution no longer being in the possession of the House. The Speaker decided the point of order well taken, stating that the resolution has already been messaged to the Senate and is not in the House, therefore, the motion is out of order. (Legislative Journal, June 16, 1919, pp. 3110 and 3111.)

Recalling Bill from Governor Is in Order After Bill Has Been Signed by Presiding Officers of Both Houses

27 (j). On the question of concurring in a resolution of the Senate to recall a Senate bill from the Governor, the point of order was raised that this bill has not yet been messaged to the Governor, therefore, the House cannot consider a resolution to recall it. The Speaker ruled that this bill has been signed by the speaker and is no longer in the possession of the House. (Legislative Journal, June 19, 1917, p. 3842.)

Consideration of a Similar, Previously Acted Upon, Not in Order

27 (k). On the question of adopting a resolution, the point of order was raised that the House has acted upon a similar resolution yesterday and that this resolution was not in order. The Speaker decided the point of order well taken. (Journal H. R., Feburary 15, 1901, p. 458.)

Consideration of, Not in Order Until Printed

27 (l). A concurrent resolution was offered and ordered laid over for printing when the point of order was raised that the resolution is out of order. The Speaker decided that until the resolution is printed its consideration is not in order and until its consideration is in order a point of order cannot be raised against it. (Legislative Journal, May 5, 1913, p. 2604.)

Amendment to, Restraining Persons from Leaving the State, Not in Order

27 (m). An amendment was offered to a resolution restraining certain persons from leaving the State, the point of order was raised that the amendment undertakes to give powers that the Legislature does not have. No legislative body has the power to restrain any person from leaving the jurisdiction of the Commonwealth before process is served. The speaker decided the point of order well taken. (Legislative Record, January 28, 1907, p. 267; Journal H. R., p. 303.)

Discharging a Committee from Further Consideration of a Bill, in Order

27 (n). On the question of adopting a resolution discharging a committee from further consideration of a bill, the point of order was raised that the committee did not report the bill when that order of business was reached and under the rules of the House, no such order will be reached until tomorrow, therefore, the resolution is out of order. The Speaker decided the point of order not well taken. An appeal was taken from the decision of the Chair. The House sustained the ruling of the Speaker. (Legislative Record, March 20, 1905, p. 1205; Journal H. R., p. 938)

Concurrent, Continuing an Old Commission, Is in Order

27 (o). A concurrent resolution was offered providing that the school code be referred to the Educational Commission, and providing for the continuance of the commission. The point of order was raised that a commission cannot be recreated in this manner and further the House cannot refer any bills to a commission which has no existence. The Speaker ruled that inasmuch as the resolution merely continues the old commission it is proper, therefore, the point of order is not well taken. (Legislative Record, March 31, 1909, p. 2065.)

Concurrent, Does Not Require Three Readings

27 (p). The point of order was raised that a concurrent resolution required three readings under Rule 32 of the House and is, therefore, not properly before the House. The Speaker decided the point of order not well taken for the reason that the resolution before the House is a concurrent resolution and not a joint resolution and does not take the course of the bill (Legislative Journal, February 3, 1931, p. 219.)

Motion to Adopt Negatived, Not in Order

27 (q). A motion was offered to adopt a resolution which had been reported by committee with the negative recommendation. The Speaker ruled the motion out of order, stating that the proper parliamentary practice is to offer a motion to have this resolution (which is in the nature of a bill) placed upon the calendar notwithstanding the negative recommendation of the committee. An appeal was taken from the decision of the Chair. The House sustained the ruling of the Chair. (Legislative Journal, February 7, 1911, pp. 176, 179 and 180; Journal H. R., pp. 450 and 453.)

A Majority of All the Members Elected Not Necessary to Pass Concurrent Resolution Entailing Expense to the State

27 (r). The speaker decided that a concurrent resolution to appoint a commission, which read: "The expenses of said commission shall be paid upon warrants drawn by the chairman upon the State Treasurer and approved by the Auditor General, and each of said commissioners shall be allowed the sum of ten dollars per day, said expenses and compensation to be paid out of such moneys as may by law be hereafter appropriated for such purposes" did not require one hundred and one votes (a majority of all the members of the House) to pass, as the resolution did not appropriate money. On an appeal, the House sustained the decision. (Journal H. R., 1878, p. 1394.)

House May Print Senate Resolutions for Its Own Use

27 (s). A question of parliamentary inquiry was submitted, whether the House could require a Senate resolution under consideration printed. The Speaker replied that it was within the power of the House to have the resolution printed if it so decided (Legislative Journal, February 20, 1933, p. 674.)

Resolutions Required to be Submitted to Governor

27 (t). The point of order was raised that the resolution under consideration is out of order, for the reason that the resolution it proposes to recall is improperly in the hands of the Governor and is, therefore, not subject to recall.

The Speaker. In ruling on the point of order raised by the gentleman from Cambria. Mr. Andrews, the Chair read for the information of the House Article III, Section 26, of the Constitution of Pennsylvania:

"Every order, resolution or vote, to which the concurrence of both Houses may be necessary, except on questions of adjournment, shall be presented to the Governor and before it shall take effect, be approved by him."

In Commonwealth v. Griest, 196, Pa. 396, it was held that the orders, resolutions and votes which must be submitted to the Governor are, and only can be such as relate to and are a part of the business of legislation, as provided for and regulated by the terms of Article III of the Constitution. The same principle is supported in Armstrong v. King, 281 Pa. 207; also Taylor v. King, 284 Pa. 235.

In an opinion by Attorney General Brown, 1915, page 2, he stated:

"That not all joint or concurrent resolutions passed by the Legislature must be submitted to the Governor for his approval, but only such as make legislation or have the effect of legislation, i. e., enacting, repealing or amending laws or statues, or which have the effect of committing the State to a certain action or which provide for the expenditure of public money. Resolutions which are passed for any other purpose, such as the appointment of a committee by the Legislature to obtain information on legislative matters for its future use or to investigate condition in order to assist in future legislation are not required to be presented to the Governor for action thereon."

Attorney General Woodruff approved the conclusions of Attorney General Brown above cited in 7 D & C 672.

In Resolution 143, Printer's No. 965, the first resolve clause, Section (a), provides that two members of the proposed committee shall be appointed by the Governor.

The second resolve clause proposes a committee of three members of the House, and three members of the Senate, together with the Executive Director of the Emergency Relief Board (who is an administrative officer appointed by the Governor), to perform administrative duties of passing on salary increases and personnel and all other matters pertaining to the State Emergency Relief Administration.

The last resolution commits the General Assembly to a definite course of legislative action. Unless the Governor were in accord with this resolution, the Assembly could have no assurance that this course to which it pledged itself could be carried out.

The Chair is, therefore, of the opinion that Resolution 143 very definitely commits the State to certain action pertaining to the administration of relief and directly affects the administrative branch of Government; furthermore it requires the Governor to appoint members of a committee which could not be done without his consent, and that the resolution is legislative in character for these reasons this resolution was properly submitted to the Governor for his approval and the point of order is not well taken. (Legislative Journal, May 8, 1935, pp. 3346-3347.)

SECTION 28

ROLL CALL

Call of, Under Call for Previous Questions in Order

28 (a). The Speaker decided that calling of the roll, under the call for the previous question is in order. (Journal H. R., 1875, p. 343.)

Not in Order After Question Has Been Determined

28 (b). On a motion to reconsider the vote by which a resolution recalling a House bill from the Senate, was adopted, a viva voce vote was taken, and the Speaker decided the motion was not agreed to. The point of order was raised that several members of the House called for a division of a yea and nay vote before the final decision of the Chair was made, but were not heard by the Speaker, therefore, they are entitled to the privilege of a roll call on the question. The Speaker ruled the original question has been determined, and the only question is the point of order on the decision of the Chair, as to the yeas and nays, on a viva voce vote. (Legislative Journal, April 5, 1921, p. 1308.)

Call for Roll Not in Order After Decision is Announced

28 (c). A motion having been decidedly agreed to on a viva voce vote, a request was made by a member that the Chair withdraw his decision and permit a roll call. The point of order was made that the Speaker having announced his decision in the vote, a request for a roll call is out of order. The Speaker sustained the point of order. (Legislative Journal, August 9, 1932, p. 868.)

Nothing in Order but the Calling of

28 (d). The roll having been ordered called after which an attempt was made to open discussion of the question, the point of order was raised that there is nothing in order but the calling of the roll. The Speaker decided the point of order well taken, stating that discussion of the question cannot be permitted. (Legislative Journal, March 19, 1913, p. 920; Journal H. R. p. 1553) (See also Legislative Journal, February 24, 1919, pp. 288-289.) (Legislative Journal, June 23, 1919, p. 3715.) (Legislative Journal, March 17, 1925, p. 1741.)

Roll Call May Not be Delayed to Permit Absent Member to Vote

28 (e). A request was made that the calling of the roll be delayed to give a member who had temporarily left his seat an opportunity to vote. The point of order was raised there was nothing before the House except voting on the question of concurring in the amendments of the Senate. Whether or not a member has absented himself from the House is of no moment. The Speaker decided the point of order well taken. (Legislative Journal, May 4, 1933, p. 5844.)

Terminates Upon Announcement of Vote

28 (f). Under a parliamentary inquiry the question was asked, does the calling of the name "Mr. Speaker" terminate the roll call? The Speaker replied that the termination of the roll call does not take place until the announcement of the vote. (Legislative Journal, July 21, 1953, p. 4008.)

Yeas and Nays May be Demanded in Joint Session

28 (g). The point of order was raised that when a joint assembly is not governed by any rules, the yeas and nays could not be ordered by a majority vote. The President ruled the Chair is bound by the Constitutional requirement to order the yeas and nays upon the call of two members. (House Journal, 1881, pp. 1613-14; House Journal, January 7, 1941, p. 1943.)

Motion to Recall Roll Not in Order

28 (h). The point of order was raised that a motion for recalling the roll is not in order. The Speaker ruled the point of order well taken. (Legislative Journal, April 30, 1935, p. 2937.)

Member May Question Affirmative Roll After It is Read, Then the Negative Roll

28 (i). The point of order was raised that a member is privileged only to question the affirmative roll under a verification after the affirmative roll is read and to question the negative roll only after the negative roll is read. The Speaker ruled the point of order well taken. (Legislative Journal, April 30, 1935, pp. 2938-2939.)

Challenging Vote of Members in Absentia

28 (j). The vote having been challenged on the charge that certain members were voted in absentia, and upon interrogation it was established that said members were not present nor in the Hall of the House, the Speaker declared the vote to be null and void, and ordered a new vote. Upon appeal taken, the decision of the Chair was sustained. (Legislative Journal, April 21, 1965, pp. 496-99.)

SECTION 29

RULES

Of Last House Do Not Continue in Force

29 (a). On motion to proceed to the election of a chief clerk, the point of order was raised that the nomination and election of an officer on the same day was a transgression of the rules of the House. The Speaker decided the point of order was not well taken, as the House was not yet organized, and there were not rules in force. (Journal H. R. 1889, p. 10.)

Organization of the House, before Adoption of

29 (b). Under a parliamentary inquiry during the organization of the House, the question was asked whether there were any rules governing debate. The Speaker replied there were no rules except those rules which by usage and custom have prevailed in the House. (Legislative Journal, January 3, 1939, p. 44.)

Organization of the House, before Adoption of

29 (c). Under a parliamentary inquiry during the organization of the House, the question was asked that since the House was preceeding without having yet adopted rules, are we not in the status of a committee of the whole. The Speaker replied we were not in the committee of the whole, but were members who had been elected and sworn, organizing the House, having selected a Speaker, and proceeding with selection of other officers. (Legislative Journal, January 3, 1939, p. 44.)

Joint Rules Not Binding on Succeeding House Unless Adopted

29 (d). Joint rules adopted by a former Senate and House were included in a current issue of a Legislative Directory.

A question of parliamentary inquiry was raised, asking whether they were binding on the present House.

The Speaker stated that they were not binding on the present House, for the following reasons:

Under the Constitution of Pennsylvania Art. II, Sec. 2. "Each House shall power to determine the rules of its proceedings."

Quoting from Jefferson's Manual. "It has been determined that one House may not continue its rules in force and over its successor. ...."

The Speaker further stated, "That the principle is well settled that it is not within the province of one House to adopt rules which are binding upon a subsequent House and the same principle applies to joint rules." (Legislative Journal, March 6, 1933, p. 925.)

Report from Committee on, Has Preference at All Times

29 (e). On the question of adopting a report of the Committee on Rules, the point of order was raised that the report should lie over one day. The Speaker decided the point of order not well taken, stating that a report of the Committee on Rules has preference at all times. (Legislative Journal, May 22, 1911, p. 1227.)

Motion to Suspend Must State a Specific Purpose

29 (f). On a motion to suspend House Rule No. 57 for the remainder of the session, the point of order was raised that the motion is out of order for the reason that it violates House Rule No. 43, which requires that a motion to suspend a rule of the House must state a specific purpose. The Speaker decided the point of order well taken. (Legislative Journal, April 20, 1921, p. 2645.)

Suspension of, for a Specific Purpose Is in Order

29 (g). A Senate bill was being considered on third reading. The point of order was raised that Rule No. 3 was suspended under the motion offered which rule provides for the method of suspending rules. That motion did not suspend Rule No. 8, which is, therefore, in force and there is no provision for the consideration of third reading bills at this time. The Speaker decided the point of order not well taken, the purpose of the motion was clearly stated, that it was for the purpose of proceeding to the consideration of this bill. (Legislative Journal, June 25, 1917, p. 4131) (Legislative Journal, April 13, 1925, p. 3460.)

Suspension of, for a Specific Purpose Is in Order

29 (h). Rule No. 43 of the House was suspended for the specific purpose of consideration on third reading of a Senate bill. The House proceeded to the consideration of the bill the point of order was raised that the consideration of this bill is out of order at this time, for the reason that Rule No. 8 of the House does not provide for consideration on Monday nights of bills upon third reading. The Speaker decided the point of order not well taken, stating that the rules of the House provide that the majority of those voting can at any time alter the rules of the House. (Legislative Journal, June 25, 1917, p. 4131.)

Suspension of, Required before Motion to Place Bill on Calendar after Five Days Have Elapsed Can be Considered

29 (i). On a motion to place a House bill on the calendar notwithstanding the fact that it has been dropped therefrom by reason of not having been called up from the postponed calendar within five days of such postponement, the point of order was raised that before this motion can be considered, the rule must be suspended. The Speaker decided the point of order well taken. (Legislative Journal, May 21, 1913, p. 3274; Journal H.R. p. 3866.)

Debate Not Allowed On Motion To Suspend The Rules

29 (j). Under a parliamentary inquiry, a question was raised of the Speaker as to what Rule provides that the Motion to Suspend the Rules is not debatable.

The Speaker replied that governing provisions are found in *Mason's Legislative Manual*, Section 82, Subsection (g). (Legislative Journal, October 26, 1983, p. 1738).

SECTION 30

SESSION

Continued after Midnight, Competent to Proceed with Business Pending before the House

30 (a). The session of the House having continued after twelve o'clock midnight, the Speaker decided that it was in order to proceed with the business before the House. An appeal was taken. The House sustained the decision. (Journal H. R., 1864, p. 1025.)

The hour of midnight having arrived, the Speaker decided that it was in order to proceed with the business under consideration. (Journal H. R., 1872, pp. 622, 623.)

The hour of midnight having passed the Speaker ruled that a legislative day extends until the House is adjourned (Legislative Journal, April 27, 1931, p. 2543) (Legislative Journal, Nov. 27, 1933, p. 230.)

Extends Until House is Adjourned

30 (b). The point of order was made that the House is governed by Eastern Standard Time, we are, therefore, in a new legislative day. (The hour of twelve midnight having passed.)

The Speaker ruled the point of order not well taken:

"A Legislative day is not govereened by the hour of the day or the day of the week, but extends until the House adjourns. The Chair will refer the gentleman to decisions of the House as follows:

'The session of the House having continued after midnight, the Speaker decided it was in order to proceed with the business before the House. An appeal was taken and the House sustained the decision. Journal of the House of Representatives, 1864, page 1025.

'The hour of midnight having passed, the Speaker decided it was in order to proceed with the business then under consideration, Journal of the House, 1872, pp. 622 and 623.

'The hour of midnight having passed, the Speaker ruled that the legislative day extends until the House is adjourned. Legislative Journal, April 27, 1931, page 2453.'

In addition the Chair would read to the gentleman from Cambria, from Jefferson's Manual, Section 6:

'Legislative rather than calendar days are observed by the House of Congress.' "

The Speaker further stated that the rule of the House referred to governs the convening of the House but not the adjourning of the House. (Legislative Journal, May 25, 1939, p. 4524.)

Special, for a Special Purpose, No Other Business Can be Considered

30 (c). The point of order was raised that this being a special session for a special purpose, no other business could be considered. The Speaker decided the point of order well taken. (Journal H. R., 1891, p. 1443.) (See also, House Journal, 1879, p. 788.)

Special, Subject Not Enumerated in Governor's Proclamation, Out of Order

30 (d). A point of order was raised that the subject of the bill was not germane to the proclamation of the Governor. The House sustained the point of order. (House Journal, 1906, p. 70.)

Fiscal

30 (e). Limitations defined in report of a Select Committee adopted.
REPORT AND SUGGESTIONS OF THE SELECT COMMITTEE APPOINTED TO STUDY THE AMENDMENT TO ARTICLE 11, SECTION 4, OF THE CONSTITUTION, PROVIDING FOR ANNUAL SESSION OF THE GENERAL ASSEMBLY

Presented pursuant to House Resolution No. 132, Printer's No. 2070 (Serial No. 138), which directed the committee to define the types of legislation to be considered and limitations thereon for the 1960 annual session and the "fiscal" sessions occurring in even-numbered years thereafter; and to make a report of its findings, together with its recommendations for appropriate rules to the General Assembly.

Pursuant to the provisions of House Resolution No. 132, Printer's No. 2070, the committee held several meetings. At the first meeting the committee directed the Joint State Government Commission and the Legislative Reference Bureau to conduct a study of the legal authorities and the experience of other states which have similar constitutional provisions and to make a report to the committee. The Governor was requested to direct the Attorney General to conduct a similar study. At subsequent meetings, the committee discussed these reports and the legal authorities cited therein.

As a result of these meetings, the committee drafted a rule which is designed to define the area within which the General Assembly may enact legislation during regular session convening in an even-numbered year.

A copy of this rule drawn for the House of Representatives, is made a part of this report.

It is suggested by the committee that the House of Representatives adopt this rule and that the Senate adopt a rule incorporating the definitions of "bills raising avenue" and "bills making appropriations" contained in this rule.

The Senate members of the committee preferred that this committee make no suggestions concerning procedural matters in the Senate.

The committee agrees that the limitation contained in the constitutional amendment applies only to legislation and that any other action which the General Assembly, or either House thereof, may lawfully take or consider, may also be taken nor considered during a "fiscal" session.

House Rule 38

All bills introduced during a regular session convening in an even-numbered year shall be either bills raising revenue or bills making appropriations.

A bill is a bill raising revenue when its primary purpose is to produce income to the State Treasury for use by the State, through taxation, license fees, regulatory fees, special assessments, rentals, royalties or from any other source through which the State may lawfully exact revenue. It may increase or decrease the revenue derived from any source, eliminate any source of revenue, or provide for a new source of revenue. It may contain such provisions of a regulatory character, or provisions making changes in existing law, which are incidental to its primary purpose.

A bill is a bill making an appropriation when its primary and specific purpose is to make expenditure of money from the State Treasury, and which contains no provisions of law other than those which may be lawfully imposed as conditions upon which such money may be expended.

Bills introduced during a regular session convening in an even-numbered year shall be numbered consecutively and those which are bills raising revenue or bills making appropriations shall be referred by the Speaker to an appropriate committee during the next ensuing five days during which the House is in session, at which time they shall be printed for the use of the members. All other bills shall remain in the possession of the Speaker, unless upon motion made and carried, the Speaker shall be directed to refer a bill to committee.

This rule shall be deemed to abrogate all other rules of the House to the extent that such other rules are inconsistent herewith. (Legislative Journal, January 25, 1960, pp. 38-39.)

SECTION 31

SPEAKER

Viva Voce Decision by, Not in Error

31 (a). The point of order was raised that several members of the House called for a division of a yea and nay vote before the final decision of the Chair was made, but were not heard by the Speaker, therefore, they are entitled to the privilege of a roll call on the question. The Speaker ruled the original question has been determined and the only question is the point of order on the decision of the Chair as to the yeas and nays on a viva voce vote. (Legislative Journal, April 5, 1921, pp. 1308-1310.) (The House sustained the decision of the Speaker on viva voce vote and over-ruled the point of order that the Speaker had erred.)

Interrogation of

31 (b). Under a parliamentary inquiry, the question was asked whether it would be in order to interrogate the Speaker of the House. The Speaker replied that if the interrogation was a proper one, it would be in order. (Legislative Journal, February 9, 1956, p. 5927.)

SECTION 32

VETO MESSAGE

Motion to Postpone Consideration of, for the Present, in Order

32 (a). A motion having been made to postpone consideration of the veto message for the present, the point of order was raised "that under the provisions of the Constitution the House could not postpone the consideration of the communication." The Speaker pro tempore decided the point of order not well taken. (Journal H. R., 1893, p. 530.) (See also similar decision, same Journal, p. 532.)

Reconsideration of Governor's Veto Message

32 (b). On a Point of Order raised regarding whether a Veto Message by the Governor can be reconsidered, the Speaker ruled that, by virtue of House Rule 26, just as a bill or resolution or other substantive matter may be reconsidered, a Governor's veto can, likewise, be reconsidered. Section 458 of *Mason's Manual of Legislative Procedure* is also supportive of this decision. (Legislative Journal, June 27, 1978, p. 2516).

SECTION 33

VISITORS

Attention Not to be Directed to, During Debate

33 (a) A member was addressing the House, when he paused in his remarks to ask a visiting constituent, whom he had invited to the Hall of the House, to rise and face the members to emphasize a point he was making in debate. The Speaker interrupted and advised the member that such procedure was out of order. (Legislative Journal, April 24, 1939, p. 1708.)

SECTION 34

VOTE

Challenge of Members, When Result is Affected Announcement of the Vote Is Withheld

34 (a). A House bill was on final passage, the roll was taken and on verification of the roll, a member's vote was challenged which changed the result of the vote. The Speaker pro temp decided under Rule 65 of the House, the result of the vote will be withheld until the challenge is investigated. (Legislative Journal, May 7, 1913, pp. 2763-4, also Journal H. R., p. 3344.)

After investigation by the Speaker the challenge was not sustained as the gentleman was present and voted. (Legislative Journal, 1913, p. 2764.)

Challenge of Vote Must be Made before Vote Is Announced

34 (b). Under parliamentary inquiry the question was asked whether the challenge of a member's vote must be made in writing before the vote is announced? The Speaker stated that under House Rule 80, the challenge must be submitted before the result of vote is announced. (Legislative Journal, April 14, 1953, p. 1285.)

Challenge of Member's Vote Must Be in Writing

34 (c). A member stated that another member who was recorded as voting was not present. When the point of order was made, that under the rules of the House the challenge of a member's vote must be in writing, the Speaker sustained the point of order. (Legislative Journal, July 19, 1932, p. 507.) (House Journal, 1935, p. 2699.)

Member Cannot be Recorded after Result of, Is Announced

34 (d). On a motion to reconsider the vote by which a bill was defeated on final passage, a roll was taken, verified and the result announced, and when a member asked to be recorded, the point of order was raised that the roll had been called, the verification made; and vote announced. The Speaker decided the point of order well taken, and the member's vote was not recorded. (Legislative Journal, May 5, 1913, p. 2618; (Journal H. R., p. 3238.)

Member's Right to, Defined

34 (e). Under a parliamentary inquiry the question was asked as to the interpretation of the rules governing a member's right to vote? The Speaker replied that a member was entitled to vote if he was in the Hall of the House during the first call of the roll and had asked to be recorded prior to the affirmative or negative roll being verified under the provisions of House Rule 80. (Legislative Journal, July 21, 1953, p. 4009.)

Absentee Voting

34 (f). Under a parliamentary inquiry, the question was asked whether or not under the Constitution the House can permit absentee voting.

The Speaker replied either by unanimous consent or the suspension of the Rules requiring members to be present to vote would permit an absentee vote. (Legislative Journal, January 26, 1961, pp. 190-191.)

Member Entitled to, If Within the Hall of the House When Roll Is Called

34 (g). On the final passage of a House bill, the point of order was raised that when an objection is raised to a member voting, after his name has been passed on the roll, under the rules of the House, he shall then not be permitted to vote, whether he is in the House or not. The Speaker decided the point of order not well taken, stating that if the gentleman desiring to be recorded, is within the Hall of the House when the roll is called, he is entitled to vote. (Legislative Journal, March 31, 1913, p. 1291; Journal H. R., 2004.)

Member Entitled to Vote if Within the Hall of the House

34 (h). Under a question of parliamentary inquiry, whether members who have not answered to their names will be recorded on the roll. The Speaker stated that every member who is within the Hall of the House has the constitutional right to vote. He may rise and state to the Chair that he did not hear his name called or that he voted under a misapprehension whatever statement or reason the gentleman sees fit to give, the Chair must accept that statement. (Legislative Journal, December 6, 1933, p. 465.)

Member Entitled to, If Present in the House

34 (i). The speaker was asked whether a member who had been granted leave of absence after a stated hour was officially present and entitled to vote on questions before the House after that hour. The Speaker stated that the member's presence in the House determines that he is officially present and entitled to vote. (Legislative Journal, April 11, 1945, p. 2336.)

Member Required to, Unless Excused by the House

34 (j). A member asked to be excused from voting, which was objected to.

Under a question of parliamentary inquiry as to what is the parliamentary procedure requiring a member to vote, the Speaker read Rule 71 of the House as follows:

"Every member shall be present within the Hall of the House during its sittings, unless excused by the House or necessarily prevented, and shall vote for or against each question, unless he has a direct personal or pecuniary interest in the determination of such question or unless he be excused by the House."

The Speaker also read to the House the following precedents in which the House had acted when members declined to vote:

"House Competent to Excuse a Member from Voting. The Speaker decided that it was at all times competent for the House to excuse a Member from voting." Journal of the House of Representatives 1858, p. 813.

The Chair also read Article 2, Section 11, of the Constitution of Pennsylvania.

"Powers of Each House-Expulsion. Each House shall have power to determine the rules of its proceedings and punish its Members or other persons for contempt or disorderly behavior in its presence, to enforce obedience to its process, to protect its members against violence or offers of bribes or private solicitations.

The Speaker stated that if every Member of this House should decide to refuse to vote it would stop the legislative process of this House."

A point of order was then raised that there being no rule prescribing penalties to be imposed and no process established under the rules by which a member can be disciplined for not voting, it is without the province of the House under the rules to require the gentleman to vote.

The Speaker decided the point of order not well taken. Under a question of parliamentary inquiry as to what the course of procedure would be and under what rule would a penalty be imposed upon a member refusing to vote.

The Speaker replied that House Rule 71 and Article 2, Section 11, of the Constitution of Pennsylvania established the procedure and that it would be for the House to decide the penalty to be imposed. (Legislative Journal, March 27, 1945, p. 1702.)

Member Required to Under Provisions of the Constitution and House Rules

34 (k). In reply to a parliamentary inquiry, the Speaker recited the following provisions of the Constitution and House Rules requiring Members to vote on questions before the House:

With the help of the Parliamentarian we have assembled the following information which the Chair thinks will be of interest to all the members, and in the opinion of the Chair this information should be made a part of the record of the House.

The Constitution of Pennsylvania prescribes the method of voting on the passage of bills in Article 3, Section 4, which reads:

(a) "...the vote be taken by yeas and nays, the names of the persons voting for and against the same be entered on the journal..."

This is a Constitutional provision.

Article 2, Section 12, provides that:

"...the yeas and nays of the members on any question shall, at the desire of any two of them be entered on the journal."

Article 2, Section 11, of the Constitution confers upon the House the power to determine the Rules of its proceedings and punish members for contempt.

Rule 71 provides, "Every Member shall vote for or against each question put, unless he has a direct personal or pecuniary interest in the determination of such question, or unless he be excused by the House."

Rule 78 provides, "The Legislative Journal shall show the result of each roll call by Yeas and Nays and not voting."

Rule 10 provides, "When less than a quorum vote on any subject under the consideration of the House, it shall be the duty of the Speaker forthwith to order the doors of the House to be closed, and that the roll of Members be called by the Clerk, and if it is ascertained that a quorum is present, either by answering to their names or by their presence in the House the Yeas and Nays shall again be ordered by the Speaker, and if any Member present refuses to vote, such refusal shall be deemed a contempt, and unless purged, the Speaker shall order the Sergeant-at-Arms to remove said Member or Members without the bar of the House, and all privileges of membership shall be refused the person so offending until the contempt be duly purged."

Rule 10 in its present form was first adopted, so the Parliamentarian tells me, by the House April 2, 1858, over a hundred years ago, to prevent the stoppage of legislative processes by Members refusing to vote. It has continued all through the years without any change to be a Rule of the House. It is interesting to note that at the time of the adoption of this Rule, an amendment to it was rejected by the House, and the proposed amendment reads, "Such Member shall be noted on the Journal as present; and not voting, and be considered a portion of a quorum." (The House Journal, April 2, 1958.)

In the Legislative Journal of the House of Representatives of June 7, 1935, in response to a question of parliamentary inquiry, the Speaker replied that a Member could not be recorded as voting "present" on a bill, for the reason that the Constitution requires the vote be taken and recorded by yeas and nays.

Incidentally, Jefferson's Manual, one of the parliamentary authorities, states. "Every member must give his vote one way or the other."

If a Member is not prepared to vote, the correct parliamentary recourse to him, under the rule, is to request the House to excuse him. He should not willfully and deliberately violate the Rule, by keeping silent or to refuse to vote and subject himself to possible contempt.

It should be also noted when a fixed number of votes is required to take action, such as is the case under our Constitution, a failure to vote reduces by one the vote available to take action as in the case of private institution bills where a two thirds majority of the House in order to approve the appropriation and, therefore, the vote "present" would have the effect of being a vote "no."

It is true the members of the House are bound by their oath which they take initially to obey the constitutional mode of proceedings, which, under the Rules adopted by the House, do not permit a member to be recorded as voting "present" where the Yeas and Nays are required or where the Yeas and Nays are demanded.

The Speaker. There is another aspect of the general problem which perhaps deserves some consideration. That is, a member strictly speaking is not voting as an individual, he is not primarily an individual he is a voice; a voice which presumably expresses the wishes of the constituency which he represents. So if one voted "present," the particular constituency which he represented would have no voice in the proceedings of this body. (Legislative Journal, August 2, 1955, pp. 3204-5.)

Member Cannot Be Recorded as Voting Present on a Bill

34 (l). Under a question of parliamentary inquiry, the Speaker stated a member cannot be recorded as voting present on a bill for the reason that the Constitution. Article III, Section 4, requires that the votes be taken by yeas and nays. (Legislative Journal, June 17, 1935, p. 5750.)

House Competent to Excuse Members from

34 (m). The Speaker decided that it was at all times competent for the House to excuse a member from voting. (Journal H. R., 1857, p. 813.)

Call for a Division of, Must be Made Before Speaker Renders Decision

34 (n). An amendment to a House bill was declared not agreed to by the Speaker, and when a division was called for, the point of order was raised that the call came too late as the Chair had already rendered its decision. The Speaker decided the point of order well taken. (Legislative Journal, March 22, 1911, p. 947.)

Tie Vote, Defeats Bill

34 (o). A roll call was taken on agreeing to a bill on second reading which resulted in a tie vote. A point of order was raised, that since the bill did not receive a majority of all the votes cast, it was lost. The Speaker decided the point of order well taken. (Legislative Record, March 12, 1907.) (Also Dec. 1951.)

INDEX TO DECISIONS OF THE HOUSE OF REPRESENTATIVES

Section

STATISTICS OF BILLS PRESENTED BY
THE LEGISLATURE — 1985-86

Number of bills introduced in House 2896
Number of bills introduced in Senate 1725
Total number of bills introduced **4621**

	1985			**1986**	
Number of House bills passed	116		Number of House bills passed	198	
Number of Senate bills passed	63		Number of Senate bills passed	77	
Total number of bills passed		**179**	**Total number of bills passed**		**275**
Number of General bills approved	120		Number of General bills approved	212	
Number of Appropriation bills approved	57		Number of Appropriation bills approved	56	
Number of bills vetoed	0		Number of bills vetoed	6	
Number of vetoes overridden by the General Assembly	0		Number of vetoes overridden by the General Assembly	1	
Number of Joint Resolutions amending the Constitution approved	2		Number of Joint Resolutions amending the Constitution approved	0	
Total		**177**	**Total**		**268**
Number of Legislative days (House)	80		Number of Legislative days (House)	72	
Number of Legislative days (Senate)	79		Number of Legislative days (Senate)	64	

LEGISLATIVE COMMISSIONS

Joint State Government Commission

Chairman: Senator Roger A. Madigan
Senate Members: Robert C. Jubelirer, F. Joseph Loeper, William J. Moore, John Stauffer (Vice Chairman), J. William Lincoln, Robert J. Mellow, Edward P. Zemprelli
House Members: K. Leroy Irvis, James J. Manderino, Robert W. O'Donnell, Ivan Itkin, Jeffrey E. Piccola, Samuel E. Hayes, Jr., Fred C. Noye
Research Director: Donald C. Steele

Legislative Budget and Finance Committee

Chairman: Senator Clarence D. Bell
Senate Members: John E. Peterson, John J. Shumaker, Michael A. O'Pake, Patrick J. Stapleton (Vice Chairman), William J. Stewart
House Members: David R. Wright, Charles P. Laughlin, Henry Livengood, Ron Raymond, Joseph R. Pitts, Howard L. Fargo
Executive Director: Richard D. Dario

Joint Legislative Air & Water Pollution Control & Conservation Committee

Senate Members: James C. Greenwood, Roger A. Madigan, John E. Peterson, James J. Rhoades, Roy W. Wilt, J. William Lincoln, Robert J. Mellow, Raphael Musto
House Members: Bernard J. Dombrowski, John Showers, Thomas J. Fee, Camille George, Russell P. Letterman, Terry R. Scheetz, James L. Wright, Jr., Arthur D. Hershey, Jess M. Stairs
Executive Secretary: Barbara M. Reeher

Local Government Commission

Chairman: Senator J. Doyle Corman
Senate Members: James J. Rhoades, Noah W. Wenger, Roy C. Afflerbach, J. Barry Stout
House Members: Joseph A. Petrarca, David W. Sweet, Ted Stuban, A. Carville Foster, Charles F. Nahill, Jr.
Executive Director: Virgil F. Puskarich

Legislative Audit Advisory Commission

Chairman: Representative George F. Pott, Jr.
Senate Members: William J. Moore, J. William Lincoln
House Members: Gerard A. Kosinski, Howard L. Fargo
Public Members: D. L. Wallace (Senate), Hon. George F. Pott, Jr. (Senate), Wendell Freeland (House), Loretta Benson Brown (House)

LEGISLATIVE REFERENCE BUREAU

POWERS AND DUTIES

The Legislative Reference Bureau was created by the Act of April 27, 1909, P. L. 208. It was reorganized as a legislative agency by the Act of May 7, 1923, P. L. 158. The bureau was created for the use of the members of the General Assembly, the Governor, the heads of agencies of the state government, and in certain cases, such citizens of the Commonwealth as desire to consult it.

The primary purpose was to provide an agency, with trained personnel, to draft and pass upon the legislative bills and resolutions for introduction in the General Assembly; to advise members of the Legislature and legislative committees; from time to time to prepare for adoption or rejection by the General Assembly, codes, by topics, of the existing general statutes; and to engage in research work on legislative questions and the history of legislation. The bureau does not give legal advice to private citizens, but upon request furnishes copies of statutory laws on particular subjects where available.

Under the Commonwealth Documents Law, all documents as defined therein shall not be valid unless filed with the bureau. The bureau edits, compiles and supplements these in the Pennsylvania Code and the Pennsylvania Bulletin, both of which are administered by the bureau.

Since the legislative session of 1969, the bureau has had the responsibility of editing and overseeing the publication of the slip laws and Pamphlet Laws. In 1974, the bureau was also given statutory authority to edit and issue an official publication of the Pennsylvania Consolidated Statutes.

The bureau is headed by the director who is elected by the Senate and House of Representatives in joint session. The director must be qualified by experience, knowledge and ability to conduct the work of the bureau. He appoints the assistant director and all other legal assistants and employes of the bureau and fixes their salaries.

CARL L. MEASE

Acting Director, Legislative Reference Bureau

Carl L. Mease was born June 3, 1932, in Hershey, the son of Ivan L. and Minnie D. Mease; Trinity Coll. (A.B.) 1954; Dickinson Schl. of Law (J.D.) 1959; U.S.A.F., Formosa, 1954-56; attorney; mem. of the bar, Pa. Supreme Ct., Commonwealth Ct., Dauphin Co. Cts., and U.S. District Ct.; mem., Dauphin Co. Bar and Pa. Bar Assns.; mem., Statutory Law Com., Pa. Bar Assn.; frmr. editor and asst. editor, Dauphin Co. Legal Reporter; mem., Trinity Evangelical Lutheran Ch., Camp Hill; appt. Assistant Director, Legislative Reference Bureau in 1981; Acting Director, Jan. 1987; married Rose Ann Sorber; 2 children: David and Kevin; home address: 411 Parkside Rd., Camp Hill.

PENNSYLVANIA LEGISLATIVE CORRESPONDENTS' ASSOCIATION

The Pennsylvania Legislative Correspondents' Association is the oldest legislative correspondents' association in the nation. It was organized by 25 reporters at the Capitol in January 1895.

The late Colonel Henry Hall, of the old Pittsburgh Times, was the first presiding officer of the association.

Official recognition is given to the association in the Rules of the Senate and House of Representatives. Press galleries in the House and Senate Chambers are restricted to accredited correspondents and photographers of daily newspapers and radio and TV stations.

The Capitol Newsroom is maintained by the Commonwealth for the use and convenience of the reporters who represent Pennsylvania's daily newspapers and press associations in the state's Capitol. It is located at the rear of E floor in the central wing of the Capitol and is room number 524.

BOARD OF GOVERNORS

PRESIDENT: Harry Stoffer, Pittsburgh Post Gazette, 703 5th St., New Cumberland, 17070

VICE PRESIDENT: David Morris, Associated Press, R.D. #2, Box 988, Duncannon, 17020

GOVERNORS: Thomas Cole, UPI, 60 Hummel Ave., Lemoyne, 17043
Stephen Drachler, Allentown Morning Call, 3751 Montour St., Harrisburg, 17111
Rich Kirkpatrick, Associated Press, 523 Coolidge Ave., New Cumberland, 17070

SECRETARY-TREASURER: Jack Nagle, 5006 Locust Lane, Harrisburg, 17109

CORRESPONDENTS

ASSOCIATED PRESS
Michael Blood, 923 N. Third St., Harrisburg, 17102
Rich Kirkpatrick, 523 Coolidge Ave., New Cumberland, 17070
Steve Liddick, R.D. #2, Newport, 17074
Dave Morris, R.D. #2, Duncannon, 17020
Rod Snyder, 610 N. Second St., Harrisburg, 17101
Paul Vathis, 4612 Surrey Rd., Harrisburg, 17109

UNITED PRESS INTERNATIONAL
Deborah Baker, 60 Hummel Ave., Lemoyne, 17043
Thomas Cole, 60 Hummel Ave., Lemoyne, 17043
Anne McGraw, 19 S. Pine St., York, 17401
Vince Piscopo, 232 Forster St., Harrisburg, 17101
Justin Supon, 931 N. Front St., Harrisburg, 17101
Terry Way, R.D. #5, Elizabethtown, 17022

ALLENTOWN CALL
Steve Drachler, 3751 Montour St., Harrisburg, 17111

CALKINS GROUP
Don Wolf, 223 Briggs St., Harrisburg, 17101

DELAWARE COUNTY DAILY TIMES
Harold D. Ellis, 1519 Embassy Drive, Harrisburg, 17109

GANNETT NEWS SERVICE
Lois Fecteau, 605 N. Front St., Harrisburg, 17101

GREENSBURG TRIBUNE REVIEW
Dennis Barbagello, 204 Parkway Rd., Harrisburg, 17110
J. R. Freeman, 22 E. Simpson St., Mechanicsburg, 17055

HARRISBURG PATRIOT
Carmen Brutto, 33 Circle Place, Camp Hill, 17011
Eric Conrad, 421 Plaza Apts., Lebanon, 17042
Kenn Marshall, Briarcrest Gardens, Hershey, 17033

OTTAWAY NEWS SERVICE
R. B. Swift, 920 Grantham Rd., Grantham, 17027

PA NETWORK
Tony Romeo, 5234-B Wynnewood Rd., Harrisburg, 17109

PHILADELPHIA DAILY NEWS
John Baer, 1704 Kathryn St., New Cumberland, 17070

PHILADELPHIA INQUIRER
Fred Cusick, 10 N. Market St., Lancaster, 17603
Russ Eshleman, 1504 Duffland Dr., Landisville, 17538
Dan Meyers, 3308 W. Penn St., Philadelphia, 19129

PITTSBURGH POST GAZETTE
Al Neri, 6479 Stanton Ave., Pittsburgh, 15206
Harry Stoffer, 703 5th St., New Cumberland, 17070

PITTSBURGH PRESS
Gary Warner, 219 E. Orange St., Lancaster, 17602

PPTN — THE PEOPLE'S BUSINESS
Gary Froseth, 1547 Creekbed Drive, Harrisburg, 17110
Jerome Kambic, 370 S. 2nd St., Steelton, 17013
Carol Kokoski, 3613 Lisburn Rd., Mechanicsburg, 17055
Mark Stultz, 1409 N. Front St., Harrisburg, 17102
Kate Megargee, 2311 N. Front St., Harrisburg, 17110
Jeff Pickering, 2918 Wilson Parkway, Harrisburg, 17104

THOMSON NEWSPAPERS
Albert Sterner, 303 Park Heights Blvd., Hanover, 17331

WILKES-BARRE TIMES-LEADER
Mary Ellen Alu, 89 Tompkins St., Pittston, 18640

WPVI-TV
James Murtha, 4611-A Florence Ave., Mechanicsburg, 17055

WESTINGHOUSE RADIO - KDKA - KYW
Sanford Starobin, 225 Glenn Road, Camp Hill, 17011

WESTINGHOUSE TV - KDKA - KYW
William Martin, 15 Clover Lane, Mechanicsburg, 17055
Dave Sollenberger, R.D. #2, Palmyra, 17078

WGAL-TV
Jim Sinkovitz, 3400 Cloverfield Rd., Harrisburg, 17109

WHTM-TV
Michael Ross, 214 N. 32nd St., Harrisburg, 17111

WITF-TV
Nell McCormack, 660 Boas St., Harrisburg, 17101

YORK DAILY RECORD
Gary Dutery, 4940 Harmony Grove Rd., Dover, 17315

MEMBERS OF THE GENERAL ASSEMBLY
1950 — 1987

For list of members prior to 1950 see 1978-1979 edition of the PENNSYLVANIA MANUAL

SENATORS

By Section 2, Article II, of the Constitution of 1873, the term of service of members of the General Assembly begins on the first day of December after their election. The term of service, as given in this table, is from the date of taking the oath of office, which is usually on the first Tuesday of January succeeding their election.

The county following each name is that of residence.

	Term of Service		Term of Service
Afflerbach, Roy C. (D) Lehigh.	1987-	Duffield, William E. (D) Fayette	1971-78
Ammerman, Joseph S. (D) Clearfield (resigned Jan. 4, 1977).	1971-77	Dwyer, R. Budd (R) Crawford (resigned Jan. 20, 1981) (deceased Jan. 22, 1987)	1971-81
Andrews, W. Thomas (R) Lawrence	1973-80		
Andrezeski, Anthony B. (D) Erie	1981-	Early, Edward M. (D) Allegheny	1975-86
Arlene, Herbert (D) Philadelphia.	1967-80	Ehrgood, Thomas A. (R) Lebanon	1957-64
Armstrong, Gibson E. (R) Lancaster	1985-	Elliott, Douglas H. (R) Franklin (resigned May 4, 1960, deceased June 19, 1960)	1957-60
Bailey, Daniel A. (R) Centre, (deceased June 4, 1970)	1963-70	Ewing, Edwin C. (R) Allegheny (deceased May 3, 1967)	1965-67
Bane, Eustace H. (D) Fayette (resigned December 31, 1955).	1951-55	Ewing, Wayne S. (R) Allegheny (seated Nov. 29, 1967, vice Edwin C. Ewing, deceased)	1967-76
Barr, Joseph M. (D) Allegheny (elected November 5, 1940, vice Thomas E. Kilgallen, resigned)	1941-60		
Barrett, Thomas E. (D) Allegheny (deceased Nov. 17, 1969)	1949-52	Farrell, Louis H. (R) Philadelphia (deceased Jan. 27, 1953)	1939-50
Beers, Robert O. (R) York	1963-70	Fetterolf, Morton H., Jr. (R) Montgomery (elected April 28, 1964, vice Henry J. Propert, deceased) (resigned July 2, 1964).	1964
Bell, Clarence D. (R) Delaware	1961-		
Berger, James S. (R) Potter (deceased April 18, 1984)	1945-66	Fisher, D. Michael (R) Allegheny	1981-
Blass, C. Arthur (R) Erie (deceased Nov. 14, 1970).	1945-60	Flack, Harold E. (R) Luzerne (deceased July 15, 1984)	1955-66
Bodack, Leonard J. (D) Allegheny	1979-	Fleming, Robert D. (R) Allegheny	1951-74
Brightbill, David J. (R) Lebanon	1983-	Fleming, Wilmot E. (R) Montgomery (deceased May 20, 1978)	1965-78
Brumbaugh, D. Emmert (R) Blair (deceased April 22, 1977).	1963-66	Frame, Richard C. (R) Venango (deceased Feb. 24, 1977).	1963-77
Byrne, John F., Jr. (D) Philadelphia.	1967-70	Frazier, Bertram G. (R) Philadelphia	1927-34,1947-50
Byrne, John F., Sr. (D) Philadelphia (resigned 1952, deceased Aug. 6, 1965).	1951-52	Freed, Tilghman A. (R) Lehigh	1951-54
		Fumo, Vincent J. (D) Philadelphia (seated April 3, 1978, vice Henry J. Cianfrani, resigned)	1978-
Camiel, Peter J. (D) Philadelphia	1953-64		
Casey, Robert P. (D) Lackawanna.	1963-66	Gaydos, Joseph M. (D) Allegheny (resigned Nov. 5, 1968).	1967-68
Chapman, Leroy E. (R) Warren (deceased July 16, 1967)	1931-62	Gekas, George W. (R) Dauphin (resigned Dec. 31, 1982).	1977-82
Cianfrani, Henry J. (D) Philadelphia (resigned Dec. 15, 1977)	1967-77	Geltz, James A. (R) Allegheny	1939-50
Confair, Zehnder H. (R) Lycoming (deceased Jan. 25, 1982) .	1959-72	Gerhart, Robert R., Jr. (D) Berks.	1969-72
Coppersmith, W. Louis (D) Cambria (seated May 26, 1969)	1969-80	Good, John G., Jr. (R) Beaver (seated June 21, 1971, vice Ernest P. Kline, resigned)	1971-72
Corman, J. Doyle (R) Centre (seated June 7, 1977, vice Joseph S. Ammerman, resigned)	1977-	Green, Richard J., Jr. (R) Cambria	1965-68
Coughlin, R. Lawrence (R) Delaware	1967-68	Greenleaf, Stewart J. (R) Montgomery	1979-
Crowe, Montgomery F. (R) Monroe	1939-54	Greenwood, James C. (R) Bucks	1987-
		Gurzenda, Joseph E. (D) Schuylkill	1977-80
Davis, Preston B. (R) Northumberland (elected Feb. 19, 1963, vice Samuel B. Wolfe, deceased)	1963-72	Hager, Henry G. (R) Lycoming	1973-84
Davis, William H. (R) Luzerne (elected Nov. 8, 1955 vice Patrick J. Toole, deceased) (deceased Dec. 5, 1955)	1955	Hall, Lyle Gillis (D) Elk.	1963-66
Dengler, Clyde R. (R) Delaware	1967-74	Haluska, John J. (D) Cambria.	1937-56,1961-64
Dent, John H. (D) Westmoreland (resigned Jan. 27, 1958)	1937-58	Hankins, Freeman (D) Philadelphia (seated Nov. 29, 1967, vice Charles R. Weiner, resigned)	1967-
Derk, Miles R. (D) Lycoming (deceased July 2, 1970).	1955-58	Hare, Fred P., Jr. (R) Somerset (resigned Sept. 15, 1953)	1947-53
Devlin, John H. (D) Allegheny (deceased July 20, 1967)	1961-67	Harney, Thomas P. (R) Chester (deceased July 17, 1960).	1953-60
Diehm, G. Graybill (R) Lancaster (deceased March 19, 1970)	1949-56	Hawbaker, D. Elmer (R) Franklin.	1961-72
DiSilvestro, Anthony J. (D) Philadelphia (deceased May 3, 1969).	1937-66	Hays, Jo (D) Centre	1955-62
Doehla, Theodore H. (R) Allegheny	1947-50	Helfrick, Edward W. (R) Northumberland	1981-
Donlan, Fraser P. (R) Lackawanna	1947-50	Hess, Ralph W. (R) York	1971-
Donolow, Benjamin R. (D) Philadelphia (deceased Nov. 27, 1972).	1955-72	Hill, Louis G. (D) Philadelphia (resigned Jan. 2, 1978)	1967-78
		Hobbs, Frederick H. (R) Schuylkill	1967-76
Dougherty, Charles F. (R) Philadelphia (resigned Jan. 15, 1979).	1973-79	Holl, Edwin G. (R) Montgomery	1967-
		Holland, Elmer J. (D) Allegheny (resigned Feb. 7, 1956).	1943-56

Term of Service

Homsher, Frederick L. (R) Lancaster (elected Nov. 8, 1938, vice John G. Homsher, deceased) (deceased May 3, 1950) 1939-50
Hopper, John D. (R) Cumberland 1977-
Howard, Edward L. (R) Bucks 1971-86

Jirolanio, Justin D. (D) Northampton (elected Nov. 3, 1964 vice Gus P. Verona, deceased) 1965-66
Johanson, Louis C. (D) Philadelphia. 1965-66
Johnson, Robert P. (R) Montgomery. 1965-66
Jones, Roxanne H. (D) Philadelphia. 1985-
Jubelirer, Robert C. (R) Blair 1975-

Kalman, Thomas J. (D) Fayette (seated Dec. 17, 1956, vice Eustace Bane, resigned) 1956-70
Keller, Marvin V. (R) Bucks (deceased Oct. 20, 1976) 1959-70
Kelley, James R. (D) Westmoreland (seated June 17, 1974, vice John Scales, resigned) 1974-
Kephart, A. Evans (R) Philadelphia (elected Nov. 7, 1939, vice Herbert S. Levin, not seated) 1940-54
Kessler, Edward J. (R) Lancaster (elected Nov. 7, 1950, vice Frederick L. Homsher, deceased) (resigned Sept. 1962, deceased Nov. 29, 1969). 1951-62
Kline, Ernest P. (D) Beaver (resigned Jan. 5, 1971) 1965-71
Kopriver, Frank, Jr. (R) Allegheny 1953-60
Kratzer, Guy M. (R) (Lehigh) 1983-86
Kromer, Arthur E. (R) Jefferson (deceased March 4, 1962) . . . 1957-62
Kury, Franklin L. (D) Northumberland. 1973-80
Kusse, Robert J. (R) Warren (seated June 7, 1977, vice Richard C. Frame, deceased) 1977-84

Lamb, Thomas F. (D) Allegheny 1967-74
Lane, W. J. (D) Washington (elected May 21, 1946, vice Wallace S. Gourley resigned) (deceased July 7, 1976) . . 1946-70
Leader, George M. (D) York 1951-54
Leader, Guy A. (D) York (elected Nov. 2, 1943, vice Henry E. Lanius, deceased) 1944-50
Lemmond, Charles D., Jr., (R) Luzerne (seated Nov. 20, 1985, vice Frank J. O'Connell, resigned) 1985-
Lentz, William B. (D) Dauphin (deceased Sept. 18, 1977) 1965-76
Letzler, A. H. (R) Clearfield (deceased May 28, 1972) 1939-54
Lewis, H. Craig (D) Bucks 1975-
Lincoln, J. William (D) Fayette 1979-
Lloyd, James R. Jr. (D) Philadelphia (seated April 23, 1979, vice Charles F. Dougherty, resigned) 1979-84
Loeper, F. Joseph (R) Delaware 1979-
Lord, John W., Jr. (R) Philadelphia 1947-50
Lynch, Francis J. (D) Philadelphia (seated March 26, 1973, vice Benjamin R. Donolow, deceased) 1973-

Madigan, Albert E. (R) Bradford (deceased August 22, 1984) . . 1953-66
Madigan, Roger A. (R) Bradford. 1985-
Mahady, Paul W. (D) Westmoreland (elected Nov. 4, 1958, vice John H. Dent, resigned) (deceased Oct. 7, 1973) . . 1959-72
Mahany, Rowland B. (R) Crawford 1947-66
Mallery, Charles R. (R) Blair (deceased 1968). 1935-62
Manbeck, Clarence R. (R) Lebanon 1967-82
Mazzei, Frank (D) Allegheny (seated Nov. 29, 1967, vice John H. Devlin, deceased) (service terminated June 2, 1975) (deceased Sept. 26, 1977). 1967-75
McCormack, Thomas J. (D) Philadelphia (seated April 3, 1978, vice Louis G. Hill, resigned) 1978
McCreesh, John J. (D) Philadelphia (deceased Sept. 9, 1959). 1935-46,1951-58
McCreesh, Thomas P. (D) Philadelphia 1959-74
McCusker, Francis P. (R) Philadelphia (elected April 22, 1952, vice John F. Byrne, Sr. resigned) (deceased Jan. 28, 1978). 1952-54
McGinnis, Bernard B. (D) Allegheny (deceased May 8, 1972) 1935-46,1951-66

Term of Service

McGlinchey, Herbert J. (D) Philadelphia. 1965-72
McGregor, Jack E. (R) Allegheny 1963-70
McKinney, Paul (D) Philadelphia 1975-82
McLaughlin, William J., III (R) Philadelphia (elected Nov. 2, 1965, vice Martin Silvert, deceased). 1965-66
McMenamin, Hugh J. (D) Lackawanna 1951-62
McPherson, Donald P., Jr. (R) Adams (resigned May 31, 1956) 1949-56
Meade, John R. (R) Philadelphia 1949-52
Mellow, Robert J. (D) Lackawanna. 1971-
Messinger, Henry C. (D) Lehigh 1971-82
Miller, John C. (D) Beaver. 1953-64
Moore, William J. (R) Perry. 1973-
Morris, Walter E. (R) Jefferson (elected Nov. 6, 1962, vice Arthur E. Kromer, deceased) 1963-64
Mullin, William V. (D) Philadelphia (deceased Feb. 3, 1966) . . 1955-66
Murphy, Austin J. (D) Washington (resigned Jan. 4, 1977) . . . 1971-77
Murray, Martin L. (D) Luzerne. 1957-64,1967-82
Musto, Raphael J. (D) Luzerne. 1983-
Myers, Robert L. III (D) Cumberland (seated June 11, 1974, vice George N. Wade, deceased). 1974-76

Neff, Samuel G. (D) Lawrence 1949-52
Nolan, Thomas M. (D) Allegheny 1971-78
Noszka, Stanley M. (D) Allegheny 1967-78

O'Connell, Frank J. (R) Luzerne (resigned, Aug. 31, 1985). . . 1979-85
Oesterling, Donald O. (D) Butler. 1965-72
O'Pake, Michael A. (D) Berks 1973-
Orlando, Quentin R. (D) Erie. 1973-80

Pechan, Albert R. (R) Armstrong (deceased Sept. 11, 1969). . 1949-69
Pecora, Frank A. (R) Allegheny 1979-
Peelor, Murray (R) Indiana 1949-56
Peterson, John E. (R) Venango 1985-
Piasecki, Arthur A. (R) Lackawanna 1967-70
Price, Philip, Jr. (R) Philadelphia. 1979-82
Propert, Henry J. (R) Montgomery (deceased Jan. 9, 1964). . 1951-64

Regoli, John W. (D) Westmoreland 1987-
Reibman, Jeanette F. (D) Northampton 1967-
Rhoades, James J. (R) Schuylkill 1981-
Ripp, Joseph D. (D) Allegheny (deceased April 2, 1966) 1959-62
Robinson, Guy B. (R) Susquehanna. 1949-52
Rocks, M. Joseph (D) Philadelphia. 1983-
Romanelli, James A. (D) Allegheny (seated Nov. 17, 1975, vice Frank Mazzei) 1975-
Rooney, Fred B. (D) Northampton (resigned Aug. 6, 1963). . . 1959-63
Rosenfeld, Maxwell S. (D) Philadelphia 1945-52
Ross, James E. (D) Beaver. 1973-
Rovner, Robert A. (R) Philadelphia 1971-74
Ruth, Frank W. (D) Berks (elected April 28, 1936, vice James E. Norton, deceased) (deceased March 6, 1968) 1936-60

Salvatore, Frank A. (R) Philadelphia 1985-
Sarraf, George J. (D) Allegheny (seated Dec. 17, 1956, vice Elmer Holland, resigned) (deceased Sept. 9, 1966) 1956-66
Scales, John N. (D) Westmoreland (resigned Feb. 4, 1974) . . 1973-74
Scanlon, Eugene F. (D) Allegheny 1975-
Scanlon, Joseph J. (D) Philadelphia (deceased Sept. 13, 1970). 1967-70
Scarlett, George B. (R) Chester (deceased Dec. 17, 1952) . . . 1937-52
Schaefer, Michael P. (D) Allegheny 1977-80
Schmidt, Theodore H. (D) Allegheny 1955-58
Scott, William Z. (R) Carbon 1955-66
Sesler, William G. (D) Erie 1961-72
Seyler, Harry E. (D) York 1955-62
Shafer, Raymond P. (R) Crawford 1959-62
Shaffer, Tim (R) Butler. 1981-

	Term of Service		Term of Service
Shumaker, John J. (R) Dauphin (seated April 11, 1983, vice George W. Gekas, resigned)	1983-	VanSant, John T. (R) Lehigh (deceased Oct. 2, 1972)	1955-70
Silvert, Martin (D) Philadelphia (deceased June 10, 1965)	1951-65	Verona, Gus P. (D) Northampton (elected Nov. 6, 1963, vice	
Singel, Mark S. (D) Cambria (resigned Jan. 20, 1987)	1981-87	Fred B. Rooney, resigned) (deceased March 6, 1964)	1963-64
Smith, Joseph F. (D) Philadelphia (resigned July 28, 1981)	1971-81		
Snowden, John G. (R) Lycoming	1939-54	Wade, George N. (R) Cumberland (deceased Jan. 9, 1974)	1941-74
Snyder, Richard A. (R) Lancaster (seated Nov. 11, 1962, vice		Wagner, Paul L. (R) Schuylkill	1945-64
Edward J. Kessler, resigned)	1962-84	Walker Ernest F. (R) Cambria (deceased May 2, 1965)	1957-60
Staisey, Leonard C. (D) Allegheny	1961-66	Walker, John M. (R) Allegheny (deceased Dec. 9, 1976)	1939-54
Stampone, Nicholas P. (D) Philadelphia (seated Nov. 16, 1981		Ware, John H. III (R) Chester (resigned Aug. 28, 1970)	1961-70
vice Joseph F. Smith, resigned)	1981-82	Watkins, G. Robert (R) Delaware (deceased)	1949-60
Stapleton, Patrick, J. (D) Indiana (seated June 8, 1970, vice		Watson, Edward B. (R) Bucks (deceased June 21, 1960)	1947-58
Albert R. Pechan, deceased)	1970-	Weiner, Charles R. (D) Philadelphia (resigned June 28, 1967).	1953-67
Stauffer, John (R) Chester (seated Nov. 17, 1970, vice John H.		Wenger, Noah W. (R) Lancaster	1983-
Ware III, resigned)	1970-	Whalley, J. Irving (R) Somerset (elected Nov. 2, 1954, vice	
Stevenson, George B. (R) Clinton (deceased March 10, 1964)	1939-62	Fred P. Hare Jr., resigned) (resigned Aug. 18, 1960)	1955-60
Stewart, William J. (D) Cambria (seated April 7, 1987, vice		Willard, James E. (R) Mercer	1967-70
Mark S. Singel, resigned)	1987-	Williams, Hardy (D) Philadelphia	1983-
Stiefel, Israel (D) Philadelphia (deceased June 27, 1966)	1937-64	Wilt, Roy W. (R) (seated April 21, 1981, vice R. Budd Dwyer,	
Stout, J. Barry (D) Washington (seated June 7, 1977, vice		resigned)	1981-
Austin J. Murphy, resigned)	1977-	Wolfe, Samuel B. (R) Union (elected May 21, 1946, vice	
Street, T. Milton (R) Philadelphia	1981-84	William I. Troutman, resigned) (deceased Dec. 12, 1962)	1946-62
Stroup, Stanley G. (R) Bedford (elected Nov. 5, 1960, vice J.		Wood, Lloyd H. (R) Montgomery (elected May 21, 1946, vice	
Irving Whalley, resigned) (deceased March 1, 1977)	1961-74	Franklin S. Edmonds, deceased) (deceased Feb. 15,	
Sweeney, John James (D) Delaware	1975-78	1964)	1946-50
		Wood, T. Newell (R) Luzerne (deceased Oct. 18, 1982)	1947-54,1967-78
Tallman, Oscar Jacob (R) Lehigh (deceased Nov. 30, 1967)	1939-50		
Tarr, Burton E. (D) Fayette	1947-50	Yatron, Gus (D) Berks	1961-68
Taylor, M. Harvey (R) Dauphin (deceased May 15, 1982)	1941-64	Yosko, Joseph J. (D) Northampton (deceased Sept. 19, 1958)	1949-58
Tilghman, Richard A. (R) Montgomery	1969-		
Toole, Patrick J. (D) Luzerne (deceased Aug. 5, 1955)	1949-55	Zemprelli, Edward P. (D) Allegheny	1969-

MEMBERS OF THE HOUSE OF REPRESENTATIVES

By Section 2, Article II, of the Constitution of 1873, the term of service of members of the General Assembly begins on the first day of December after their election. The term of service, as given in this table, is from the date of taking the oath of office, which is usually on the first Tuesday of January succeeding their election.

The county following each name is that of residence.

	Term of Service		Term of Service
Aaronson, Alfred (R) Philadelphia	1947-50	Arlene, Herbert (D) Philadelphia	1959-66
Abraham, Donald A. (D) Allegheny (deceased)	1975-78	Armstrong, Gibson E. (R) Lancaster	1977-84
Acosta, Ralph D. (D) Philadelphia	1985-	Armstrong, Joseph J. (D) Philadelphia	1965-66
Adam, Robert R. (D) Berks	1953-56	Arthurs, Jack, R. (D) Butler	1971-78
Adams, Richard L. (R) Berks (deceased)	1957-58,1961-62	Arty, Mary Ann (R) Delaware	1979-
Afflerbach, Roy C. (D) Lehigh	1983-86	Ashton, William H. (R) Chester	1953-68
Agnew, Willard F., Jr. (R) Allegheny (died March 14, 1961)	1955-61	Auker, Charles A. (R) Blair	1938-44,1953-64
Alden, John (R) Delaware	1979-82	Austin, Robb (D) Allegheny	1979-80
Alderette, Barry L. (D) Beaver	1983-84	Bachman, William T. (D) Luzerne	1961-70
Alexander, George W. (R) Clarion	1963-72	Backenstoe, John E. (R) Lehigh	1961-64
Alexander, Jane M. (D) York	1965-68	Bair, Donald O. (R) Allegheny (deceased)	1963-70
Alexander, Scholley P. (D) Philadelphia	1953-54	Baldwin, William E. (D) Schuylkill	1983-
Allen, Frank M. (R) Schuylkill	1967-72	Balthaser, Wayne L. (D) Berks	1959-60
Allen, William W. (R) Warren	1967-72	Bane, Eustace H. (D) Fayette	1947-50
Alley, Amin A. (R) Columbia	1963-64	Banker, Maurice (R) Huntingdon	1951-56
Allison, Gilbert J. (D) Schuylkill	1965-66	Barber, James (D) Philadelphia	1969-86
Altshuler, Benjamin S. (R) Philadelphia	1949-50	Barkdoll, Wilbur F. (R) Franklin	1949-54
Amarando, Louis J. (D) Philadelphia	1949-58	Barley, John E. (R) Lancaster	1985-
Anderson, John Hope (R) York	1961-82	Barnatovich, Anthony J. (D) Sullivan	1955-56
Anderson, Matt S. (D) Allegheny	1955-58	Barton, Carl M. (R) Perry (deceased)	1957-60
Anderson, Sarah A. (D) Philadelphia	1955-72	Battisto, Joseph W. (D) Monroe	1983-
Andrews, Hiram G. (D) Cameron	1933-36,1939-40,1945-62	Baumunk, Walter (R) Sullivan	1945-54
Angstadt, Paul J. (R) Berks	1983-	Bazin, Marvin (D) Philadelphia	1953-56
Appleton, William M. (R) Allegheny	1965-70	Bear, Luther L. (R) York	1951-54
Argall, David G. (R) Schuylkill	1985-	Beaver, H. Clayton (D) Columbia	1949-52

	Term of Service
Bednarck, George J. (R) Luzerne.	1949-50
Beech, Albert E. (R) Allegheny	1947-48, 1951-52
Belardi, Fred (D) Lackawanna	1979-
Belfanti, Robert E., Jr. (D) Northumberland.	1981-
Bell, Albert M. (R) Allegheny (deceased Feb. 28, 1953)	1953
Bell, Clarence D. (R) Delaware.	1955-60
Bellomini, Robert E. (D) Erie (resigned June 13, 1978)	1965-78
Beloff, Leland (R) Philadelphia	1967-70, 1977-84
Bennett, Reid L. (D) Mercer	1965-80
Beren, Daniel E. (R) Montgomery.	1967-76
Berkes, Milton (D) Bucks	1967-73
Berkstresser, Ralph E. (D) Fulton	1951-52
Berlin, Theodore (D) Bucks	1975-78
Berson, Norman S. (D) Philadelphia.	1967-82
Birmelin, Jerry (R) Wayne.	1985-
Bittinger, Adam (D) Cambria.	1977-78
Bittle, R. Harry (R) Franklin	1968-82
Bixler, Denny J. (D) Blair (deceased).	1968-73
Black, Ronald E. (R) Venango	1985-
Blackwell, Lucien E. (D) Philadelphia	1973-76
Blair, John Ellis (R) Mercer	1967-68
Blair, Russell J. (D) Fayette	1967-71
Blair, Stanley L. (R) Erie (deceased)	1949-68
Blaum, Kevin (D) Luzerne	1981-
Bloom, Louis A. (R) Delaware.	1947-52
Boies, David M. (D) Allegheny (deceased May 3, 1963)	1937-63
Bolton, William A. (R) Montgomery.	1951-54
Bomberger, Walter L. (R) Lancaster	1947-54
Bonetto, Joseph F. (D) Allegheny	1965-76
Bonner, John F. (D) Carbon (deceased Feb. 27, 1966)	1955-56, 1959-66
Book, Raymond T. (R) Allegheny	1983-
Boorse, Howard F. (R) Montgomery	1939-52
Boory, Benjamin (D) Philadelphia.	1943-46, 1953-58
Boris, John (R) Schuylkill (deceased)	1959-60, 1962-64
Borski, Robert A., Jr. (D) Philadelphia.	1977-82
Bortner, Michael E. (D) York	1985-
Bossert, W. Max (R) Clinton	1961-70
Bower, Adam T. (R) Northumberland (deceased)	1939-66
Bowley, Curt (D) Warren	1985-
Bowman, James S. (R) Dauphin (resigned Sept. 9, 1963) (deceased).	1957-63
Bowser, Harry E. (R) Erie	1979-
Boyes, Karl W. (R) Erie	1981-
Bradley, Joseph P. Jr. (D) Northumberland	1975-76
Braig, Joseph, P. (D) Philadelphia.	1971-72
Branca, Ernest O. (D) Philadelphia.	1955-56, 1959-66
Brand, William H. (R) Lycoming	1957-58
Brandon, Albert D. (D) Allegheny.	1949-50
Brandt, Kenneth E. (R) Lancaster	1973-
Breisch, Wayne M. (R) Schuylkill.	1945-58, 1962-64
Brennan, A. Patrick (D) Bucks	1955-58
Brennan, Joseph J. (D) Erie	1955-56
Brenninger, Floyd K. (R) Montgomery (resigned Jan. 12, 1961).	1955-61
Breon, Robert H., Jr. (R) Centre	1957-58
Breth, Harris G. (D) Clearfield	1941-42, 1949-62
Brice, James C. (R) Lawrence	1943-50
Broujos, John (D) Cumberland.	1983-
Brown, Harold L. (D) Berks	1977-82
Brown, Homer S. (D) Allegheny (resigned Dec. 31, 1949)	1935-50
Brown, William E. (R) Chester.	1949-60
Brucker, John W. (R) Philadelphia.	1957-58
Brugger, Jeanne D. (R) Montgomery	1965-66
Brunner, Charles H., Jr. (R) Montgomery	1939-50
Brunner, John L. (D) Washington (deceased Jan. 1, 1980)	1965-80
Bucchin, Francis W. (D) Northampton	1947-58
Buchanan, William G. (R) Indiana.	1953-54, 1957-67
Bullen, J. Warren, Jr. (R) Delaware	1953-56
Bunt, Raymond, Jr. (R) Montgomery	1983-
Burd, James M. (R) Butler	1977-
Burkhardt, Robert F. (R) Allegheny.	1969-73
Burns, Edward F. Jr. (R) Bucks	1973-
Burns, Howard M. (D) Lycoming	1959-60
Bush, Alvin C. (R) Lycoming.	1961-70
Butera, Robert J. (R) Montgomery (resigned Dec. 14, 1977)	1963-77
Byerly, Chester H. (R) Clarion (deceased).	1973
Byrne, James A. (D) Philadelphia.	1951-52
Cadwalader, Lambert (R) Montgomery	1937-50
Caldwell, Thomas D., Jr. (R) Dauphin	1965-66
Caltagirone, Thomas R. (D) Berks	1977-
Cantoni, Frank H. (D) Washington	1965-66
Capano, A. V. (D) Washington.	1947-48, 1953-64
Capitolo, Vincent (D) Philadelphia	1959-64
Cappabianca, Italo S. (D) Erie	1979-
Caputo, Charles N. (D) Allegheny (deceased)	1967-78
Carlson, Edgar A. (R) Tioga	1985-
Carn, Andrew J. (D) Philadelphia	1983-
Carson, Daniel (R) Philadelphia (deceased Dec. 4, 1957).	1957
Cassidy, Michael E. (D) Blair.	1977-78
Cauley, Thomas H. (D) Allegheny.	1961-62
Cavender, John C. (R) Susquehanna	1963-66
Cawley, Gaynor (D) Lackawanna.	1981-
Cella, Frank (R) Philadelphia	1951-52
Cessar, Richard J. (R) Allegheny	1971-
Chadwick, J. Scot (R) Bradford	1985-
Checchio, I. Harry (R) Philadelphia.	1973-78
Chess, Richard B. (D) Allegheny	1979-80
Cianciulli, Matthew, Jr. (D) Philadelphia	1976-79
Cianfrani, Henry (D) Philadelphia	1953-62
Cianfrani, Henry J. (D) Philadelphia (deceased)	1963-66
Cimini, Anthony J. (R) Lycoming (deceased Aug. 25, 1987).	1975-87
Cioffi, Dominick E. (D) Lawrence	1953-68
Civera, Mario J., Jr. (R) Delaware	1980-
Clapper, Robert R. (R) Bedford.	1949-54
Clark, Brian D. (D) Philadelphia	1979-
Clark, James E. (D) Armstrong (deceased Dec. 6, 1965)	1965
Clark, Rita (R) Cambria	1979-80
Clarke, James F. (D) Allegheny.	1959-67
Clarke, Robert E. (R) Blair (deceased)	1963-67
Clay, Curtis J. (D) Washington	1967-68
Claypoole, William H. (R) Armstrong (deceased)	1967-71
Clendening, Robert J. (R) Delaware.	1949-52
Cleveland, Hanford L. (R) Monroe	1957-58
Clymer, Paul I. (R) Bucks	1981-
Cochran, Harry (D) Fayette (deceased)	1913-14, 1935-36, 1941-42, 1947-56
Cochran, Harry Young (D) Fayette	1979-82
Cohen, Mark B. (D) Philadelphia	1974-
Colafella, Nicholas A. (D) Beaver	1981-
Cole, James D. (D) Greene	1947-50
Cole, Kenneth J. (D) Adams.	1975-
Coleman, Chester A. (D) Monroe	1943-46, 1949-50
Comer, Harry R. J. (D) Philadelphia	1953-73
Connelly, M. Joseph (R) Delaware (deceased April, 1956)	1953-56
Conner, Lawrence A. (D) Delaware	1953-54
Conway, Edward J. (D) Philadelphia	1949-52
Cooley, J. Woodrow (D) Fayette	1961-64
Cooper, George W. (R) Allegheny	1939-60
Coppolino, Matthew F. (R) Philadelphia	1967-72
Cordisco, John F. (D) Bucks.	1981-86
Cornell, Roy W. (R) Montgomery	1979-
Corr, Patrick J. (D) Allegheny	1951-52
Corrigan, Thomas C., Sr. (D) Bucks	1987-
Coslett, Franklin (R) Luzerne	1979-86
Costa, Frank A. (R) Philadelphia.	1943-52

Term of Service

*Term of
Service*

Coughlin, R. Lawrence (R) Montgomery	1965-66
Cowell, Ronald R. (D) Allegheny	1975-
Coy, Jeffrey W. (D) Franklin	1983-
Coyle, Josephine (D) Philadelphia	1945-46,1951-54
Coyne, William J. (D) Allegheny	1971-72
Crawford, Evelyn G. Henzel (R) Montgomery (deceased)	1955-62
Crawford, Patricia (R) Chester	1969-76
Crossin, Frank P. (D) Luzerne	1959-64
Crowley, Paul F. (D) Lackawanna	1969-72
Cumberland, James L. (R) Clarion	1975-76
Cummins, J. Blatch (D) Washington	1957-58
Cunningham, Gregg L. (R) Centre	1978-82
Curwood, William B. (D) Luzerne	1953-66
Dager, Charles H. (R) Montgomery	1967-73
Daikeler, Bert C. (R) Montgomery	1981-82
Daley, Peter J. (D) Washington	1983-
Dalrymple, Delbert W. (R) Erie	1939-52,1957-58
Dardanell, Edward L. (D) Allegheny	1965-68
Davies, John S. (R) Berks	1975-
Davis, Donald M. (D) Fayette (deceased Oct. 23, 1976)	1969-76
Davis, Erroll B. (D) Allegheny	1971
Davis, James K. (R) Forest	1951-66
Davis, Robert O. (R) Beaver	1967-73
Dawida, Michael M. (D) Allegheny	1979-
Deal, Alphonso (D) Philadelphia (deceased June 3, 1987)	1981-87
DeJoseph, Dominick (R) Philadelphia (deceased)	1969-70
De Long, Paul A. (R) Lehigh	1947-50,1957-58
DeLuca, Tony (D) Allegheny	1983-
DeMedio, A. J. (D) Washington	1967-82
DeMeo, Salvatore (R) Philadelphia	1967-68
Dengler, Clyde R. (R) Delaware	1957-66
Dennis, Ralph M. (D) Philadelphia (resigned Jan. 4, 1960)	1959-60
Dennison, Samuel B. (R) Jefferson (deceased Nov. 24, 1962)	1941-52,1957-62
Depuy, Warner M. (R) Pike	1943-50
DeVerter Walter F. (R) Mifflin	1973-
Devlin, John H. (D) Allegheny	1957-60
DeWeese, H. William (D) Greene	1976-
DiCarlo, David C. (D) Erie	1973-80
DiDonato, Anthony Jr. (D) Philadelphia	1975-76
Dietterick, Gordon S. Jr. (R) Luzerne	1957-58
Dietterick, Scott (R) Luzerne	1987-
Dietz, Clarence E. (R) Bedford	1975-86
Dininni, Rudolph (R) Dauphin	1967-
Distler, James T. (R) Elk	1985-
Dombrowski, Bernard J. (D) Erie	1971-
Donaldson, Lee A., Jr. (R) Allegheny	1955-70
Donatucci, Robert C. (D) Philadelphia	1980-
Donatucci, Ronald R. (D) Philadelphia	1977-80
Donehue, Ruth S. (R) Clinton	1955-60
Donnelly, Thomas J. (D) Warren	1965-66
Dorr, Donald W. (R) York	1973-
Dorsey, Joseph W. (R) Delaware	1967-73
Dougherty, James J. (D) Philadelphia (deceased May 3, 1964)	1949-64
Doughten, John V. (D) Philadelphia (deceased)	1961-62
Dowling, Huette F. (R) Dauphin	1951-52
Down, Ralph J. (R) Mercer	1953-64
Downey, John J. (D) Schuylkill	1933-40,1953-54
Doyle, Joseph T. (D) Delaware	1971-78
Dreibelbis, Galen E. (D) Centre	1971-76
Driscoll, Edward J. (R) Philadelphia	1949-50
DuBois, John E., Jr. (R) Clearfield	1951-54
Duffy, Edward, (D) Philadelphia	1941-46,1949-52
Duffy, Mary Alice (D) Philadelphia	1957-58
Duffy, Roger F. (D) Allegheny	1977-
Dumas, Alija (D) Philadelphia	1968,1976-80
Dumbauld, Peter T. (D) Somerset	1965-66
Dunn, Edward (R) Northumberland	1950-54,1957-58
Durham, Kathrynann (R) Delaware	1979-
Dwyer, R. Budd (R) Crawford (deceased Jan. 22, 1987)	1965-70
Earley, Arthur F. (R) Delaware (deceased June 9, 1981)	1979-81
Earley, Edward M. (D) Allegheny	1971-73
Eckensberger, William H., Jr. (D) Lehigh	1965-76
Edwards, Joseph R. (R) Somerset (deceased)	1963-64
Edwards, William (R) Lackawanna	1957-64
Ehrgood, Thomas A. (R) Lebanon	1955-66
Eilberg, Joshua (D) Philadelphia	1955-66
Elder, W. Henry (R) Lycoming	1941-50
Elvey, Harry M. (R) Fulton (deceased)	1961-66
Emerson, Junius M. (D) Philadelphia	1965-68, 1981-82
Englehart, Harry A. Jr. (D) Cambria (deceased)	1965-78
Erb, Daniel H. (R) Blair	1943-58
Eshback, J. Russell (R) Pike (deceased)	1959-70
Eshleman, Edwin D. (R) Lancaster (deceased)	1955-66
Esler, James A. (R) Allegheny (elected May 16, 1961, vice Williard F. Agnew deceased)	1961-64
Evans, Dwight (D) Philadelphia	1981-
Evans, Lewis E. (D) Cambria	1947-50
Ewing, Edwin C. (R) Allegheny	1939-40,1943-64
Farabaugh, E. J. (D) Cambria	1953-64
Fargo, Howard (R) Mercer (elected June 22, 1981)	1981-
Farmer, Elaine F. (R) Allegheny	1987-
Fattah, Chaka (D) Philadelphia	1983-
Fawcett, Charlotte, D. (R) Montgomery	1971-76
Fee, Thomas J. (D) Lawrence	1969-
Felton, William W. (R) Philadelphia	1949-50
Fenrich, Andrew T. (D) Allegheny	1949-54,1963-73
Ferster, Ellis E. (R) Snyder	1949-54
Fetterolf, Morton H., Jr. (R) Montgomery	1957-64
Filip, Leo A. (D) Luzerne	1951-52
Filo, Jules (D) Allegheny	1949-68
Fineman, Herbert (D) Philadelphia (resigned May 23, 1977)	1955-77
Firmstone, George W. (R) Wayne	1949-52
Fischer, Roger R. (R) Washington	1967-
Fisher, D. Michael (R) Allegheny	1975-80
Flack, Harold E. (R) Luzerne (deceased)	1943-54
Flaherty, Thomas E. (D) Allegheny	1975-78
Fleck, Daniel R. (R) Allegheny	1981-82
Fleischamn, Alfred J. (R) Elk	1953-54
Fleming, Robert D. (R) Allegheny	1939-50
Fleming, Wilmot E. (R) Montgomery	1963-64
Flick, Robert J. (R) Chester	1983-
Flint, Robert J. (D) Potter	1955-56
Floyd, Samuel (D) Philadelphia	1949-50,1953-60
Flynn, Michael R. (D) Washington	1953-64
Foerster, Thomas J. (D) Allegheny	1959-67
Foor, Percy G. (R) Bedford	1961-73
Foster, A. Carville, Jr. (R) York	1973-
Foster, John H. (R) Delaware	1955-58
Foster, William W. (R) Wayne	1971-84
Fox, Donald W. (R) Lawrence	1957-74
Fox, Jon D. (R) Montgomery	1985-
Fox, Ira M. (R) Forest	1919-22,1949-50
Frank, J. Calvin (R) Dauphin	1949-50
Frank, Samuel W. (D) Lehigh (deceased April 17, 1973)	1955-56,1959-60,1965-73
Frankenburg, Richard J. (R) Allegheny	1971-73
Frascella, Thomas A. (D) Philadelphia	1955-66
Frazier, Robert F. (R) Allegheny	1981-82
Freeman, Robert (D) Northampton	1983-
Freind, Stephen F. (R) Delaware	1976-

	Term of Service
Frost, Preston A. (R) Centre	1945-56
Fry, Walter C. (D) Montgomery	1961-62
Fryer, Lester K. (D) Berks	1963-86
Fuelhart, William C. (R) Warren	1967
Fulmer, Eugene M. (R) Centre (deceased)	1959-71
Gaffney, James L. (D) Northampton	1945-46,1949-52,1955-56
Gailey, John R. Jr., (D) York	1957-68
Gallagher, Edward T., Jr. (R) Philadelphia	1945-50
Gallagher, James J. A. (D) Bucks	1959-86
Gallen, James J. (R) Berks	1965-
Gamble, Ronald (D) Allegheny	1977-
Gannon, Thomas P. (R) Delaware	1979-
Garlock, Marl H. (D) Fulton	1955-60
Garzia, Ralph A. (D) Delaware	1975-78
Gatski, Ronald (D) Luzerne	1977-80
Geer, Thomas P. (R) Allegheny	1951-54
Geesey, Eugene R. (R) Cumberland	1969-80
Geisler, Robert A. (D) Allegheny	1967-78
Geist, Richard A. (R) Blair	1979-
Gekas, George W. (R) Dauphin	1967-73
Gelfand, Eugene (D) Philadelphia (deceased)	1955-73
George, Arthur (R) Cumberland (deceased)	1949-50,1955-62
George, Camille (D) Clearfield	1975-
George, Lourene W. (R) Cumberland	1963-70
George, Margaret H. (D) Bucks	1977-80
Gerhart, Robert R., Jr. (D) Berks	1967-68
Giammarco, Henry J. (D) Philadelphia	1975-80
Gibb, Laurence V. (R) Allegheny	1955-66
Gibbons, D. Barry (R) Delaware	1961-62
Gibson, Allen M. (R) Warren (deceased May 25, 1959)	1945-59
Gillespie, Patrick B. (D) Delaware	1975-76
Gillette, Helen D. (D) Allegheny	1967-78
Gladeck, Joseph M., Jr. (R) Montgomery	1979-
Gleason, James J. (R) Lycoming	1951-54
Gleason, Patrick A. (D) Cambria (deceased)	1971-76
Gleeson, Francis E., Jr. (D) Philadelphia	1969-78
Glembocki, Victor R. (D) Erie	1949-50
Glick, George J. (D) Philadelphia	1953-54
Godshall, Robert W. (R) Montgomery	1983-
Goebel, Ronald P. (D) Prev. (R), Allegheny	1977-80
Gola, Thomas J. (R) Philadelphia	1967-70
Goldstein, Joseph H. (R) Warren (elected Nov. 3, 1959, vice Allen Gibson, deceased May 25, 1959)	1959-64
Goldstein, Maurice H. (R) Allegheny	1955-64
Good, Elwood M. (D) Northampton	1949-52
Good, Wendell R. (R) Erie (deceased)	1967-71
Goodling, George A. (R) York (deceased)	1943-54,1957-58
Goodman, James A. (D) Schuylkill	1965-66,1969-80
Goodrich, Ray C. (R) Potter	1957-66
Grabowski, Stephen S. (D) Allegheny	1979-82
Gramlich, Harry S. (R) Venango	1953-64
Gray, Clifford (D) Philadelphia	1977-82
Gray, William (D) Philadelphia (elected April 26, 1960, vice Mary Varallo, resigned) (deceased Dec. 26, 1963)	1960-63
Graybill, Henry J. (R) Juniata	1947-52
Green, Clarence (R) York	1949-50
Green, James A. (D) Butler	1975-76
Green, Richard J., Jr. (R) Cambria	1963-64
Greenberg, Melvin J. (D) Philadelphia	1965-66
Greenfield, Roland (D) Philadelphia	1967-82
Greenleaf, Stewart J. (R) Montgomery	1977-78
Greenlee, James W. (D) Philadelphia (elected May 16, 1961, vice Francis X. Muldowney, deceased)	1961-64
Greenwood, James C. (R) Bucks	1981-86
Greenwood, Ray W. (R) Wyoming	1941-56
Greer, Thomas H., Jr. (R) Butler	1945-52
Gremminger, John E. (D) Delaware	1961-62,1965-66

	Term of Service
Grieco, Joseph V. (R) Lycoming	1973-84
Gring, Harry H. (R) Lancaster	1967-76
Gross, Bernard M. (D) Philadelphia	1967-70
Gross, Stanley H. (R) York	1957-58,1961-64
Gruitza, Michael C. (D) Mercer	1981-
Gruppo, Leonard Q. (R) Northampton	1979-
Guesman, Arthur O. (D) Allegheny	1961-62
Guss, Karl B. (D) Juniata	1953-56
Gutendorf, Vincent F. (R) Luzerne	1951-54
Guthrie, W. Mack (R) Armstrong (elected Nov. 4, 1943, vice Herbert G. Gates, resigned)	1943-62
Hagarty, Lois Sherman (R) Montgomery	1980-
Hagerty, Eugene J. (D) Philadelphia	1935-38,1949-52
Hall, Wrayburn R. (R) Potter	1937-54
Haluska, Edward J. (D) Cambria	1981-
Halverson, Kenneth S. (R) Somerset	1967-80
Hamilton, John H., Jr. (R) Philadelphia (deceased)	1965-78
Hamilton, Robert K. (D) Beaver (deceased)	1941-46,1949-72
Hamilton, Wilbur H. (R) Philadelphia (resigned Dec. 31, 1955)	1951-56
Hammock, Charles P. (D) Philadelphia	1973-76
Hankins, Freeman (D) Philadelphia	1961-67
Harney, Thomas P. (R) Chester	1949-52
Harper, Ruth B. (D) Philadelphia	1977-
Harrier, Austin M. (R) Clearfield	1963-64,1967-73
Harris, Garfield B., Sr. (D) Philadelphia	1953-54
Harris, J. Mervyn (R) Delaware	1965-66
Harris, Lewis (D) Fulton	1941-44,1949-50
Hartley, George B. (D) Philadelphia	1961-66
Hasay, George C. (R) Luzerne	1973-
Haskell, H. Harrison, II (R) Crawford	1971-78
Hass, Richard O. (D) York	1955-56
Haudenshield, George K. (R) Allegheny (elected Nov. 3, 1959, vice John R. Haudenshield, deceased)	1959-70
Haudenshield, John R. (R) Allegheny (deceased July 28, 1959)	1939-40,1943-59
Hayden, Richard (D) Philadelphia	1987-
Hayes, David S. (R) Erie	1969-80
Hayes, Samuel E., Jr. (R) Blair	1971-
Headlee, Russell (D) Greene (deceased)	1951-52,1963-70
Heatherington, Thomas J. (D) Allegheny	1941-46,1949-50
Heckler, David W. (R) Bucks	1987-
Heffner, George Wm. (R) Schuylkill	1957-66
Heiser, Lori (R) Allegheny	1981-82
Helfrick, Edward (R) Northumberland	1977-80
Helm, W. Stuart (R) Armstrong (deceased)	1941-64
Hennihan, James W. (D) Luzerne	1945-56
Hepford, H. Joseph (R) Dauphin	1963-76
Herman, Lynn B. (R) Centre	1983-
Herman, R. Dixon (R) Dauphin	1949-50
Hersch, Joseph J. (D) Philadelphia	1941-46,1949-54
Hershey, Arthur D. (R) Chester	1983-
Hess, Dick L. (R) Bedford	1987-
Hetrick, W. Brady (R) Mifflin	1963-71
Hewitt, Earl E., Sr. (R) Indiana	1933-34,1939-56
Hill, Sherman L. (R) Lancaster (deceased)	1965-76
Hippel, Elwood H. (R) Philadelphia	1967-68
Hocker, Blaine C. (R) Dauphin	1947-66
Hoeffel, Joseph M. III (D) Montgomery	1977-84
Hoffman, Mark W. (R) Lehigh	1949-50
Hoggard, Dennie W. (D) Philadelphia	1943-46,1949-54
Hoh, Paul J. (D) Berks	1965-66
Holl, Edwin G. (R) Montgomery (elected May 16, 1961, vice Floyd K. Brenninger, resigned)	1961-66
Holliday, Joseph R. (R) Blair	1957-62
Holman, Allan W., Jr. (R) Perry	1961-70
Holt, Herbert (D) Philadelphia	1955-60

	Term of Service			Term of Service
Homer, Max H. (D) Allegheny	1965-73		Kelly, William J. (D) Philadelphia (deceased July 15, 1963)	1961-63
Honaman, June N. (R) Lancaster	1977-		Kemp, William L. (R) Northumberland	1947-50
Hopkins, Forest W. (R) Erie (deceased April 27, 1978)	1967-78		Kennedy, H. Francis (R) Butler	1963-73
Horgos, Robert P. (D) Allegheny	1981-82		Kennedy, John (R) Cumberland	1981-
Horn, Harold A. (R) Lancaster (deceased)	1971-72		Kenney, George T., Jr. (R) Philadelphia	1985-
Horner, Jack B. (R) Lancaster	1965-72		Kent, Robert F. (R) Crawford	1947-56
Horst, Enos H. (R) Franklin (deceased)	1955-67		Kerlin, Merrill W. (R) Fulton	1953-54
Houk, Clyde B. (R) Lawrence	1955-56		Kernaghan, Mae W. (R) Delaware	1957-70
Hovis, Raymond L. (D) York	1969-71		Kernick, Phyllis T. (D) Allegheny	1975-80
Howlett, Joseph (D) Philadelphia	1985-		Kessler, Harry A. (R) Montour (deceased)	1959-66
Hughes, Vincent (D) Philadelphia	1987-		Kester, Stanley R. (R) Delaware	1965-73
Humes, James C. (R) Lycoming	1963-64		King, Thomas W., Jr. (R) Butler	1961-62, 1967-68
Hunter, B. Frank (D) Allegheny	1943-46, 1949-52		Kirley, Thomas J. (D) Allegheny	1943-50
Hutchinson, Amos K. (D) Westmoreland	1969-		Kistler, Guy A. (R) Cumberland	1961-76
Hutchinson, William D. (R) Schuylkill	1973-82		Klein, H. Beryl (D) Beaver	1961-66
			Klepper, John W. (D) Lycoming	1971
Ide, Joseph A. (R) Northampton	1953-54, 1957-58		Kline, G. Edgar (R) Schuylkill	1937-56
Irvis, K. Leroy (D) Allegheny	1959-		Klingaman, William K., S. (R) Schuylkill	1973-84
Isaacs, Joseph W. (R) Delaware	1955-66		Klingensmith, Marion C. (R) Fayette	1967-68
Itkin, Ivan (D) Allegheny	1973-		Klunk, Fred G. (D) Adams	1971
			Knecht, William K. (R) Schuylkill	1955-62
			Knepper, James W., Jr. (R) Allegheny	1971-80
Jackson, George W. (R) Lebanon	1981-		Knight, William W. (D) Allegheny (deceased)	1979-80
Jadlowiec, Kenneth M. (R) McKean	1987-		Kohl, William P. (R) Luzerne (resigned Jan. 15, 1954)	1947-54
Jarolin, Stanley J. (D) Luzerne	1983-		Kolankiewicz, Leon J. (D) Philadelphia	1941-46, 1949-56
Jenkins, Frank W. (R) Montgomery	1965-66		Kolter, Joseph P. (D) Beaver	1969-82
Jenkins, George E. (D) Allegheny	1949-56, 1959-62		Kondrath, Andrew (D) Berks	1949-50
Jenkins, Samuel (R) Allegheny	1957-58		Kooker, Margarette S. (R) Bucks	1955-66
Jennings, Edwin K. (R) Tioga	1947-50		Kornick, Nicholas (D) Fayette	1951-66
Jennings, W. Worth (R) Bradford			Korns, William R. (R) Somerset	1957-64
	1917-20, 1949-50, 1953-54, 1957-62		Kosinski, Gerard A. (D) Philadelphia	1983-
Johnson, Albert W. (R) McKean (resigned Nov. 27, 1963)	1947-63		Kovolenko, William (D) Beaver	1959-60
Johnson, Edwin G. (R) Blair	1979-		Kowalyshyn, Russell (D) Northampton	1965-84
Johnson, George R. (R) Delaware (deceased)	1967-72		Kradel, John F. (D) Westmoreland	1965-66
Johnson, Joel J. (D) Philadelphia	1969-80		Krakow, Benjamin J. (D) Philadelphia	1957-58
Johnson, Robert A. (D) Philadelphia	1967-68		Kramer, Harry A. (D) Allegheny	1961-64
Johnson, Robert P. (D) Montgomery	1959-64		Kratz, Raymond C. (R) Montgomery	1947-56
Johnson, Theodore (D) Allegheny	1965-70		Kromer, Arthur E. (R) Jefferson	1953-56
Johnston, William P. H. (R) Allegheny	1947-48, 1957-58		Kubacki, John C. (D) Berks (resigned Dec. 31, 1955)	1951-55
Jones, Edmund (R) Delaware	1973		Kubitsky, Leo (R) Luzerne	1959-60
Jones, Frances (D) Philadelphia (elected May 19, 1959, vice			Kukovich, Allen G. (D) Westmoreland	1977-
Granville Jones, deceased)	1959-66		Kurtz, Samuel G. (R) Lebanon	1945-50
Jones, George E. (R) Blair	1938-42, 1953-54		Kury, Franklin L. (D) Northumberland	1967-72
Jones, Granville E. (D) Philadelphia (deceased March 7,			Kusse, Robert J. (R) Warren (resigned June 7, 1977)	1973-77
1959)	1949-59			
Jones, James F. Jr. (D) Philadelphia	1977-80		Lafore, John A., Jr. (R) Montgomery	1951-58
Jones, John A. (R) Northampton	1943-44, 1947-48		LaGrotta, Frank (D) Lawrence	1987-
Jones, John M. (D) Northampton	1945-46, 1949-52		Lain, Joseph W. (R) Philadelphia	1967-68
Jones, Paul F. (D) Allegheny (resigned Jan. 5, 1953)	1951-53		LaMarca, Russell J. (D) Berks	1965-76
Jones, Thomas H. W. (R) Montgomery	1951-60		Lamb, Thomas F. (D) Allegheny	1959-66
Josephs, Babette (D) Philadelphia	1985-		Langtry, Alice S. (R) Allegheny	1985-
Jump, James J. (R) Luzerne	1947-60		Lashinger, Joseph A. (R) Montgomery	1978-
			Laudadio, John F., Sr. (D) Westmoreland (deceased June 6,	
Kahle, Alvin (R) Venango (deceased)	1965-73		1977)	1963-77
Kamyk, Walter T. (D) Allegheny (resigned Sept. 10, 1963)			Laughlin, Charles P. (D) Beaver	1973-
(deceased)	1949-63		Lawson, Paul M. (D) Philadelphia (elected April 26, 1960, vice	
Kanuck, George J. (R) Lehigh	1979-82		Ralph Dennis, resigned)	1960-70
Kasunic, Richard A. (D) Fayette	1983-		Lawyer, Clarence M. J. (D) York (deceased May 17, 1956)	1955-56
Katz, Alvin (D) Philadelphia	1970-78		Leberknight, Cecil K. (R) Cambria	1953-64
Kaufman, Gerald (D) Allegheny	1967-72		Lederer, Miles W. (D) (deceased Dec. 25, 1953)	1949-54
Kee, John (R) Philadelphia	1959-60		Lederer, Raymond F. (D) Philadelphia	1974-76
Kehler, H. Franklin (R) Schuylkill (deceased)	1955-58		Lederer, William J. (D) Philadelphia	1965-73
Keiser, Russell C. (R) Dauphin	1959-62		Lee, Austin M. (R) Philadelphia	1957-64
Keller, Marvin V. (R) Bucks	1949-58		Lee, Kenneth B. (R) Sullivan	1957-73
Kelly, Anita Palermo (D) Philadelphia (elected Nov. 5, 1963,			Lee, Thomas H. (R) Philadelphia	1941-50
vice Wm. J. Kelly, deceased)	1963-78		Leh, Dennis E. (R) Berks	1987-
Kelly, James B. III (R) Allegheny	1971-76		Lehr, Stanford I. (R) York	1969-84

	Term of Service		Term of Service
Leiby, Mary E. (D) Lehigh	1955-56	McCandless, Albert L. (R) Butler	1959-64
Leisey, Amos M. (R) Chester	1937-56	McCann, Stephen (D) Greene	1953-62
Lench, Ronald G. (D) Beaver	1965-68	McClatchy, Richard A., Jr. (R) Montgomery	1969-
Leonard, Louis (D) Allegheny (deceased)	1941-46, 1949-66	McClure, Harvey D. (R) Erie	1963-64
Leonard, William C. (R) Delaware	1951-52	McConnell, George F. (R) Mercer	1951-52
Lescovitz, Victor John (D) Washington	1980-	McCormack, John R. (R) Philadelphia	1945-52
Letterman, Russell P. (D) Centre	1971-	McCormack, Thomas J. (D) Philadelphia	1953-62
Levdansky, David K. (D) Allegheny	1985-	McCue, John B. (R) Armstrong	1963-64, 1971-76
Leven, Albert (D) Philadelphia	1951-56	McCullough, W. H. (R) Lawrence	1947-54
Levi, Joseph II (R) Venango	1975-84	McCurdy, Donald M. (R) Delaware	1967-73
Levin, Stephen E. (D) Philadelphia	1977-86	McDermit, Raymond E. (D) Cambria	1951-54
Lewis, Marilyn S. (R) Montgomery	1979-82	McDevitt, Daniel F. (D) Berks	1961-64
Light, John H. (R) Lebanon	1951-60	McDonald, John J. (D) Schuylkill	1959-62
Limper, William (D) Philadelphia	1949-66	McGee, Joseph A. (D) Philadelphia	1949-58
Lincoln, J. William (D) Fayette	1973-78	McGinnis, Patrick J. (R) Montgomery	1973-78
Linton, Gordon J. (D) Philadelphia	1983-	McGraw, Andrew J. (D) Allegheny	1967-76
Lippincott, Edwin E., II (R) Delaware	1952-62	McHale, Paul (D) Lehigh	1983-
Livengood, Henry (D) Armstrong	1977-	McInroy, Harry R. (R) Tioga	1951-62
Lloyd, William R., Jr. (D) Somerset	1981-	McIntyre, James M. (D) Philadelphia	1975-84
Lofus, Cornelius J. (R) Philadelphia	1945-52	McKeever, Leo A. (D) Philadelphia (deceased Nov. 12, 1963)	1955-63
Logue, Charles (D) Allegheny	1976-78	McKelvey, Gerald J. (R) Philadelphia	1979-80
Long, William James (D) Fayette	1961-64	McKinney, John H. (R) Venango	1917-18, 1933-52
Long, William Joseph (D) Schuylkill	1961-62	McLane, William J. (D) Lackawanna	1975-78
Lopresti, Philip (D) Cambria	1937-38, 1951-60	McLaughlin, Leo J. (D) Allegheny (deceased)	1955-64
Lovett, James E. (D) Westmoreland	1933-58	McMillen, William R. (R) Indiana	1941-52
Lucyk, Edward J. (D) Schuylkill	1981-	McMonagle, Gerald F. (D) Philadelphia	1979-84
Luger, Charles (R) Lackawanna	1967-68	McMonagle, John I. (D) Allegheny	1967-73
Luigard, Charles F. (D) Berks (deceased Dec. 30, 1960)	1959-60	McNally, Edward W. (D) Cambria	1961-68
Lutty, Paul F. (D) Allegheny	1951-71	McNally, Thomas V. (D) Allegheny	1945-46, 1949-52
Lynch, E. Raymond (R) Chester	1979-80	McVerry, Terrence F. (R) Allegheny	1979-
Lynch, Francis J. (D) Philadelphia (resigned March 25, 1973)	1967-73	McWherter, James L. (D) Westmoreland	1953-56
Lynch, Frank J. (R) Delaware (deceased)	1967-80	Mebus, Charles F. (R) Montgomery	1965-78
Lyons, C. Blair (R) Westmoreland	1947-48, 1951-52	Meholchick, Stanley (D) Luzerne	1955-56, 1959-71
		Melio, Anthony J. (D) Bucks	1987-
Maack, Herbert R. (R) Montgomery	1965-68	Melton, Mitchell W. (D) Philadelphia	1969-72
Mackowski, William D. (R) McKean	1977-86	Meluskey, Frank J. (D) Lehigh (deceased Nov. 22, 1978)	1977-78
Machmer, Lawrence C. (D) Berks	1959-60	Menhorn, Harry G., Jr. (D) Allegheny	1975-76
Maden, John R. (R) Westmoreland	1938-40, 1945-48, 1951-52	Merry, James R. (R) Crawford	1981-
Madigan, Albert E. (R) Bradford	1943-52	Merry, Ralph S. (R) Crawford	1957-64
Madigan, Roger A. (R) Bradford	1977-84	Metz, August, Jr. (R) Pike	1951-58
Magee, George C., Jr. (R) Crawford	1955-64	Michlovic, Thomas A. (D) Allegheny	1979-
Maguire, Charles (D) Philadelphia	1953-54	Micozzie, Nicholas A. (R) Delaware	1979-
Mahan, Samuel (R) Butler	1953-60	Mifflin, Edward B. (R) Delaware (deceased Jan. 2, 1971)	1963-71
Maine, Connie G. (D) Crawford	1987-	Mihm, Martin C. (D) Allegheny	1937-62
Malady, Regis R. (D) Allegheny (deceased)	1969-73	Mikula, John J. (R) Luzerne	1945-58
Maiale, Nicholas J. (D) Philadelphia	1980-	Milanovich, Fred R. (D) Beaver	1975-80
Malinzak, Frank L. (D) Fayette	1965-66	Miller, Beatrice Z. (R) Philadelphia	1957-60
Maloney, Thomas J. (R) Northampton	1973	Miller, Harold G. (R) Blair	1945-52, 1955-62
Manbeck, Clarence F. (R) Lebanon	1961-66	Miller, Harry E. (R) Philadelphia	1953-54
Manbeck, Joseph H. (R) Schuylkill	1963-64, 1967-72	Miller, John C. (R) Beaver	1951-52
Manderino, James D. (D) Westmoreland	1967-	Miller, Marvin E. (R) Lancaster	1967-76
Manmiller, Joseph C. (R) Dauphin	1975-	Miller, Marvin E. Jr., (R) Lancaster	1973-
Markley, Marian E. (R) Lehigh (deceased)	1951-68	Miller, Paul W. (D) Allegheny (elected Nov. 5, 1963 vice W. T. Karnyk, resigned)	1963-64, 1967-70
Markosek, Joseph (D) Allegheny	1983-	Miller, Wendell H. (R) Butler	1957-58
Markovitz, Harry (R) Allegheny	1965-66	Milliken, William H., Jr. (R) Delaware (elected Nov. 2, 1943 vice Thomas W. Linn, resigned)	1943-46, 1949-50
Marmion, Frank J., Jr. (R) Allegheny	1981-84	Milliron, John P. (D) Blair	1975-78
Marsh, Ralph A. (R) Clearfield	1957-58, 1961-64	Mills, Charles J. (D) Westmoreland (deceased)	1945-66
Martino, Leonard L. (D) Allegheny	1969-73	Mintess, Lewis M. (R) Philadelphia	1943-44, 1947-52
Mastrangelo, Adriano (R) Philadelphia	1971-72	Miscevich, George (D) Allegheny	1975-78, 1981-84
Matthews, William T. (R) Philadelphia	1953-54	Moehlmann, Nicholas B. (R) Lebanon	1975-
Maxwell, H. J. (D) Westmoreland	1941-44, 1951-64	Monroe, Susie (D) Philadelphia (deceased)	1949-67
May, Arthur J. (R) Snyder (deceased Sept. 1, 1963)	1961-63	Moody, John H. (D) Dauphin	1953-58
Mayernik, David J. (D) Allegheny	1983-	Moore, Clarence (R) Clinton	1943-54
Mazza, John (R) Washington	1947-48, 1951-52	Moore, Frank E. (D) Indiana	1969-70
McAneny, Joseph J. (D) Cambria	1965-70	Moore, Harvey A. (R) Butler	1947-52
McCall, Keith R. (D) Carbon	1983-		
McCall, Thomas J. (D) Carbon (deceased)	1975-81		

	Term of Service
Moore, William J. (R) Perry	1971-72
Moran, Cyril J. (D) Lackawanna	1963-66
Moran, J. P. (D) Allegheny	1935-46,1949-56,1959-60
Morley, Walter H. (D) Philadelphia	1961-66
Morris, Samuel W. (D) Chester	1971-78,1981-
Moscrip, Andrew S. (R) Bradford (deceased)	1953-58,1968-72
Mowery, Harold F. Jr. (R) Cumberland	1977-
Moyer, Russel S. (R) Northampton	1957-58
Mrkonic, Emil (D) Allegheny	1975-
Muldowney, Francis X. (D) Philadelphia (deceased Feb. 11, 1961)	1951-61
Mullen, Martin P. (D) Philadelphia	1955-82
Mullen, Michael M. (D) Allegheny (deceased Feb. 19, 1978)	1971-72,1974-78
Munley, Marion L. (D) Lackawanna (deceased)	1947-64
Murphy, Austin J. (D) Washington	1959-70
Murphy, Peter J. (R) Delaware	1955-60
Murphy, Thomas J. Jr., (D) Allegheny	1979-
Murray, Erwin L. (D) Cameron (deceased)	1963-66
Murray, Harvey P. (R) Snyder	1955-60
Murray, Harvey P., Jr. (R) Snyder (elected Nov. 5, 1963, vice A. J. May, deceased)	1963-68
Murray, John J. (D) Allegheny	1953-56,1959-64
Murray, Martin L. (D) Luzerne	1945-56
Murray, Paul G. (R) Lancaster	1945-60
Murtha, John P., Jr. (D) Cambria	1969-73
Musto, James (D) Luzerne (deceased)	1949-71
Musto, Raphael (D) Luzerne	1971-80
Myers, Michael (D) Philadelphia	1971-76
Nagel, Reuben A. (D) Beaver (deceased Nov. 15, 1950)	1935-38,1941-42,1945-46,1949-50
Nahill, Charles F., Jr. (R) Montgomery	1979-
Najaka, Leonard A. (R) Luzerne	1947-52
Naugle, Harry A. (R) Somerset	1951-60
Needham, Michael J. (D) Lackawanna (deceased)	1947-56,1959-71
Neff, Joseph H. (R) Huntingdon	1947-50
Nelson, Carl W. (D) York	1959-60
Nicholson, Charles G. (R) Montgomery	1965-70
Nitrauer, Harvey L. (R) Lebanon	1967-70
Nixon, Michael J. (D) Washington	1949-50
Nolan, Thomas M. (D) Allegheny	1970
Novak, Bernard R. (D) Allegheny	1969-80
Noye, Fred C. (R) Perry	1973-
O'Brien, Bernard F. (D) Luzerne	1963-80
O'Brien, Dennis M. (R) Philadelphia	1977-80,1983-
O'Brien, Frank W. (D) Allegheny	1968-70
O'Brien, Joseph M. (D) Philadelphia	1936-46,1957-58
O'Connell, Frank J., Jr. (R) Luzerne	1967-78
O'Dare, James J. (R) Philadelphia	1937-50
O'Dell, Ford E. (R) Erie	1957-66
O'Donnell, James A. (D) Northampton	1959-66
O'Donnell, James P. (D) Philadelphia	1959-72
O'Donnell, Michael J. (R) Philadelphia	1947-50
O'Donnell, Robert W. (D) Philadelphia	1974-
Odorisio, Helen (R) Delaware	1967-68
Odorisio, Rocco A. (R) Delaware (deceased April 5, 1967)	1959-67
Ogilvie, Robert S. (R) Dauphin (deceased)	1953-66
O'Keefe, Peter J. (D) Delaware	1975-78
Olasz, Richard D. (D) Allegheny	1981-
Oliver, Frank Louis (D) Philadelphia	1973-
Olsen, Olaf E. (D) Allegheny	1949-56
O'Neil, Frank M. (D) Clearfield	1955-56,1959-60,1965-66
O'Pake, Michael A. (D) Berks	1969-72
Orban, Frank A., Jr. (R) Somerset (resigned Jan. 2, 1950)	1947-50
Otto, Henry P. (R) Allegheny	1963-66

	Term of Service
Pacchioli, Joseph (D) Northampton	1955-56
Packroni, Telio (D) Fayette	1965-66
Pancoast, G. Sieber (R) Montgomery	1965-78
Parker, Ben L. (D) Greene	1971-72
Parker, H. Sheldon, Jr. (R) Allegheny	1967-78
Parlante, Alphonse (D) Philadelphia	1953-54,1959-66
Parry, Roy W. (R) Luzerne	1955-58
Pashley, Kathryn G. (D) Philadelphia (deceased)	1955-66
Pattern, William B. (R) Philadelphia	1947-48
Paulhamus, Perry M. (D) Lycoming	1955-56
Peifly, Clair H. (R) Northampton	1953-54
Pendleton, William W. (D) Allegheny	1981-82
Penglase, George A. (D) Philadelphia	1949-52
Pentrack, Frank J. (D) Cambria	1945-46,1949-50
Perri, Fortunato N. (R) Philadelphia	1973-76
Perry, Howard H. (D) York (deceased)	1959-60
Perry, Peter E. (D) Philadelphia	1959-76
Perzel, John M. (R) Philadelphia	1979-
Peta, Thomas P. (D) Philadelphia	1949-54
Peterson, John E. (R) Venango (elected Nov. 28, 1977)	1977-84
Petrarca, Joseph A. (D) Westmoreland	1973-
Petrone, Thomas C. (D) Allegheny	1981-
Petrosky, Anthony J. (D) Westmoreland	1941-64
Pettigrew, J. Thompson (D) Philadelphia	1945-46,1949-56
Pezak, John (D) Philadelphia	1965-72
Pfaff, Albert L. (D) Philadelphia (deceased Nov. 4, 1953)	1935,1949-53
Phillips, Merle H. (R) Northumberland	1980-
Phillips, J. Russell (R) Lackawanna	1935-36,1953-54,1957-58
Piccola, Jeffrey E. (R) Dauphin	1977-
Pichney, Harry (R) Philadelphia	1947-48,1951-52
Pievsky, Max (D) Philadelphia	1967-
Piper, William G. (R) Berks (deceased)	1957-58,1961-73
Pistella, Frank J. (D) Allegheny	1979-
Pittenger, John C. (D) Lancaster	1965-66,1969-70
Pitts, Joseph R. (R) Chester	1973-
Pitzer, H. Earl (R) Adams	1951-52
Polaski, Frank (D) Erie	1965-70
Polaski, Julian (D) Erie	1941-48,1951-64
Polen, J. Dean (D) Washington (deceased)	1941-42,1945-46,1949-56,1959-66
Polite, Roosevelt I. (R) Montgomery (deceased)	1973-80
Poltenstein, Jerome (D) Philadelphia	1953-54
Pomeroy, John N., Jr. (R) Philadelphia	1955-58
Post, James B., Jr. (R) Luzerne	1957-58
Posta, James A. (D) Westmoreland	1949-50
Pott, George F., Jr. (R) Allegheny	1977-86
Powers, James J., Sr. (D) Philadelphia	1963-64
Pratt, Ralph D. (D) Lawrence	1975-86
Prendergast, James F. (D) Northampton (deceased)	1959-78
Pressmann, John F. (D) Lehigh	1985-
Preston, Joseph, Jr. (D) Allegheny	1983-
Price, Harry W., Jr. (R) Mifflin	1947-62
Price, Robert A. (D) Lackawanna	1949-52
Propert, Henry J. (R) Montgomery	1945-50
Pucciarelli, Nicholas A. (D) Philadelphia (deceased)	1979-82
Punt, Terry L. (R) Franklin	1979-
Purnell, Karl H. (R) Union	1963-66
Pursley, Louis A. (R) Union	1955-62
Pyles, Vern (R) Montgomery	1975-80
Quest, William J. (D) Allegheny (sworn in June 5, 1978)	1978
Quiles, German (D) Philadelphia	1969-70
Quisenberry, James A. (R) Erie	1953-54
Ragot, Henry E. (R) Northampton	1947-48,1953-54,1957-58
Rappaport, Samuel (D) Philadelphia	1971-84
Rasco, Albert (R) Allegheny	1980-82

Term of Service

	Term of Service
Ravenstahl, Robert P. (D) Allegheny	1975-78
Raymond, Ronald C. (R) Delaware	1985-
Readinger, Albert S. (D) Berks	1937-58
Reagan, Charles R. (R) Union	1939-54
Reber, Robert D., Jr. (R) Montgomery	1981-
Reed, Stephen R. (D) Dauphin	1975-80
Reese, Russell E. (D) Washington	1937-52
Reibman, Jeanette F. (D) Northampton	1955-56,1959-66
Reidenbach, William J. (D) Lackawanna	1945-46,1949-62
Reilly, John M. (R) Montour	1943-52
Reinard, Roy (R) Bucks	1983-
Renninger, John S. (R) Bucks	1965-76
Renwick, William F. (D) Elk (deceased)	1955-78
Reynolds, Benjamin J. (R) Chester (deceased)	1965-69
Reynolds, Maurice L. (D) Allegheny	1941-46,1949-50
Rhodes, Joseph Jr. (D) Allegheny	1973-80
Richardson, David P. (D) Philadelphia	1973-
Richter, F. Garrett (R) Allegheny	1947-48,1953-54
Ridinger, Harry D. (R) Adams	1963-64
Rieger, William W. (D) Philadelphia	1967-
Rigby, Joseph P. (R) Allegheny	1950-52,1955-60,1963-68
Riley, Hampton (D) Philadelphia	1959-64
Riley, Raymond L. (R) Lycoming	1939-52
Ritter, James P. (D) Lehigh	1965-82
Ritter, Karen A. (D) Lehigh	1987-
Robbins, Charles M. (R) Luzerne	1947-50
Robbins, Robert D. (R) Mercer	1983-
Robertson, James N. (R) Delaware	1949-52
Rocks, M. Joseph (R) Philadelphia	1979-82
Rodgers, John M. (D) Bucks	1979-80
Roebuck, James R. (D) Philadelphia (elected May 21, 1985, vice James D. Williams, deceased)	1985-
Romanelli, James A. (D) Allegheny (resigned Nov. 17, 1975)	1973-75
Rose, Samuel (D) Philadelphia	1941-46,1949-52
Rosen, Morris (D) Philadelphia	1949-56
Ross, Samuel A. (D) Philadelphia	1975-76
Rovansek, Louis (D) Cambria	1949-62
Rowe, Robert C. (R) Lebanon	1971-73
Royer, Baker (R) Lancaster	1937-66
Ruane, Paul G. (R) Northumberland	1965-73
Rubin, Arthur (D) Philadelphia	1951-56,1961-68
Rudisill, Harold B. (D) York (deceased)	1955-69
Rudy, Ruth C. (D) Centre	1983-
Ruggiero, Philip S. (D) Northampton	1967-78
Rush, Francis J. (D) Philadelphia	1967-71
Rutherford, Eugene S. (R) Lancaster (deceased)	1961-64,1967-68
Ryan, Matthew J. (R) Delaware	1963-
Rybak, William C. (D) Northampton	1967-72,1981-
Sakulsky, Barnet (D) Westmoreland	1959-62
Saloom, Eugene G. (D) Westmoreland	1967-76, 1983-
Salvatore, Frank A. (R) Philadelphia	1973-1984
Sarraf, George J., M.D. (D) Allegheny (deceased)	1935-56
Saurman, George E. (R) Montgomery	1981-
Savitt, David M. (D) Philadelphia	1969-73
Sax, Louis (R) Philadelphia	1947-52
Scanlon, Agnes M. (D) Philadelphia	1977-78
Scanlon, Eugene F. (D) Allegheny	1968-73
Scanlon, Joseph A. (D) Philadelphia	1935-52
Scarcelli, Vincent F. (D) Philadelphia	1955-66
Schaaf, Peter G. (D) Erie	1959-62
Scheaffer, John E. (R) Cumberland	1971-80
Scheetz, Terry R. (R) Lancaster	1983-
Schmidt, Theodore H. (D) Allegheny	1949-54
Schmitt, C. L. (D) Westmoreland	1965-80
Schuler, Jere W. (R) Lancaster	1983-
Schulze, Richard (R) Chester	1971-73
Schuster, Edward A., Sr. (D) Allegheny	1943-64

	Term of Service
Schwartz, George X. (D) Philadelphia	1953-54,1957-60
Schweder, J. Michael (D) Northampton	1975-80
Scirica, Anthony J. (R) Montgomery	1971-80
Scott, William Z. (R) Carbon	1947-54
Seltzer, H. Jack (R) Lebanon	1957-80
Semanoff, Joseph (R) Carbon	1967-73
Semmel, Paul W. (R) Lehigh	1983-
Serafini, Frank A. (R) Lackawanna	1979-
Seventy, Steve (D) Allegheny	1979-
Seyler, Harry E. (D) York	1949-54
Shadding, David L. (D) Philadelphia	1979-80
Shane, William Rodger (D) Indiana	1971-76
Shelhamer, Kent D. (D) Columbia	1965-76
Shelton, Ulysses (D) Philadelphia (resigned May 23, 1978) (deceased)	1961-78
Sherman, Louis (D) Philadelphia	1955-72
Shields, Jesse J. (D) Philadelphia	1957-58
Shoemaker, George C. (R) Schuylkill (deceased Sept. 15, 1953)	1945-53
Shotwell, John S. (R) Monroe	1950-54
Showers, John R. (D) Union	1981-
Shuman, William O. (D) Franklin (deceased Aug. 30, 1978)	1965-78
Shupnik, Fred J. (D) Luzerne	1959-82
Sieminski, Edmund J. (R) Northampton	1979-82
Sigman, Abraham N. (R) Philadelphia	1955-56
Silverman, Louis (D) Philadelphia	1957-60,1969-70
Simmons, James C. (R) Allegheny (deceased June 26, 1963)	1961-63
Sirianni, Carmel (R) Susquehanna	1975-
Skale, Joseph (D) Philadelphia	1937-46,1965-66
Slack, Timothy (R) Chester (deceased)	1961-70
Smith, Bruce I., Jr. (R) York	1981-
Smith, Charles C. (R) Philadelphia (elected vice Edwin A. Lee, deceased)	1944-56
Smith, Clark S. (R) Adams	1973
Smith, Earl H. (R) Chester (deceased)	1973-82
Smith, James K. K. (R) Allegheny	1965-66
Smith, L. Eugene (R) Jefferson	1963-86
Smith, Samuel H. (R) Jefferson	1987-
Smith, William B. (D) Beaver	1949-50,1953-58
Snare, Orville E. (R) Huntingdon	1957-70
Snider, E. Gadd (D) Fayette	1943-60
Snyder, Donald W. (R) Lehigh	1981-
Snyder, Gregory (R) York	1983-
Sollenberger, D. Raymond (R) Blair	1937-52
Sorg, Herbert P. (R) Elk	1941-52
Spencer, Henry C. (R) Lackawanna (deceased Nov. 3, 1955)	1949-56
Spencer, Warren H. (R) Tioga	1963-84
Spitz, Gerald J. (R) Delaware	1977-84
Spray, Lester E. (R) Allegheny	1957-58
Staback, Edward G. (D) Lackawanna	1985-
Stahl, Harold J., Jr. (R) Berks	1973-76
Stairs, Jess M. (R) Westmoreland	1977-
Stank, John F. (D) Northumberland (deceased)	1933-56,1959-64
Stapleton, Thomas J., Jr. (D) Delaware	1975-78
Stauffer, John (R) Chester	1965-70
Stebbins, Herman E. (D) York	1955-56
Steckel, William A. (R) Lehigh	1955-64,1970
Steele, C. Doyle (D) Armstrong	1967-71
Steighner, Joseph A. (D) Butler	1979-
Stemmler, Gust L. (D) Westmoreland (deceased)	1963-72
Stephens, Paul A. (D) Somerset	1955-56
Sternberg, Louis A. (D) Philadelphia	1949-50
Stevens, Correale F. (R) Luzerne	1981-
Stevens, Dennis O. (R) Allegheny	1957-60
Stevenson, DeWitt (R) Butler	1953-56
Stewart, John, Jr. (R) Philadelphia	1959-60

	Term of Service		Term of Service
Yaffe, Herman H. (R) Philadelphia	1949-50	Zeitz, William L. (D) Philadelphia	1953-54
Yahner, Paul J. (D) Cambria	1965-80	Zeller, Joseph R. (D) Lehigh	1971-80
Yandrisevits, Frank W. (D) Northampton	1985-	Zember, Gerald S. (R) Berks (elected Feb. 7, 1961, vice Charles F. Luigard, deceased)	1961-62
Yarnell, Victor R. H. (D) Berks	1963-64		
Yatron, Gus (D) Berks	1957-60	Zemprelli, Edward P. (D) Allegheny (elected Nov. 5, 1963, vice D. M. Boies, deceased)	1963-68
Yeakel, Wilson L. (R) Bucks	1929-54		
Yester, William J. (D) Allegheny	1941-52	Zettelmoyer, William S. (R) Lehigh	1963-64
Yetter, Van D., Jr. (D) Monroe	1955-56, 1959-66	Ziegler, Nolan F. (R) Dauphin	1949-56
Yetzer, Harold A. (D) Berks	1947-56	Zimmerman, Lester H. (R) Juniata (deceased)	1957-66
Yohn, William H., Jr. (R) Montgomery	1969-80	Zimmerman, Miles B., Jr. (R) Dauphin	1967-73
Young, Edward M. (R) Mercer (deceased)	1947-56	Zitterman, Frank J. (D) Lackawanna	1977-80
		Zord, Joseph V., Jr. (R) Allegheny	1965-80
Zearfoss, Herbert K. (R) Delaware	1969-78	Zwikl, Kurt D. (D) Lehigh	1973-84

PRESIDENTS PRO TEMPORE
OF PENNSYLVANIA SENATE

PRESIDENTS PRO TEMPORE
*(The office of Speaker abolished and
President Pro Tempore created by Constitution of 1874.)*

George H. Cutler, Erie	Jan.	5, 1875	A. E. Sisson, Erie	May	16, 1907
E. W. Davis, Philadelphia	Mar.	18, 1875	Reelected	Jan.	5, 1909
Reelected	Jan.	4, 1876	Reelected	April	15, 1909
John C. Newmyer, Allegheny	May	5, 1876	William E. Crow, Fayette	Jan.	3, 1911
Reelected	Jan.	2, 1877	George W. Wertz, Cambria	May	25, 1911
Thomas V. Cooper, Delaware	Mar.	23, 1877	Daniel P. Gerberich, Lebanon	Jan.	7, 1913
Reelected	Jan.	1, 1878	Charles H. Kline, Allegheny	June	27, 1913
Andrew Jackson Herr, Dauphin	May	4, 1878	Reelected	Jan.	5, 1915
Reelected	Jan.	7, 1879	Edward E. Beidleman, Dauphin	May	20, 1915
John Lamon, Philadelphia	June	6, 1879	Reelected	Jan.	2, 1917
William J. Newell, Philadelphia	Jan.	4, 1881	Clarence J. Buckman, Bucks	June	28, 1917
Hugh McNeil, Allegheny	June	9, 1881	Reelected	Jan.	7, 1919
John Edgar Reyburn, Philadelphia	Jan.	2, 1883	Frank E. Baldwin, Potter	June	26, 1919
Amos H. Mylin, Lancaster	June	6, 1883	Reelected	Jan.	4, 1921
Reelected	Jan.	6, 1885	T. Lawrence Eyre, Chester	April	28, 1921
George Handy Smith, Philadelphia	June	12, 1885	Reelected	Jan.	2, 1923
Reelected	Jan.	4, 1887	John G. Homsher, Lancaster	June	14, 1923
John C. Grady, Philadelphia	May	19, 1887	Reelected	Jan.	6, 1925
Reelected	Jan.	1, 1889	Samuel W. Salus, Philadelphia	April	16, 1925
Boies Penrose, Philadelphia	May	9, 1889	Reelected	Jan.	4, 1927
Reelected	Jan.	6, 1891	Horace W. Schantz, Lehigh	April	14, 1927
J. P. S. Gobin, Lebanon	May	28, 1891	Reelected	Jan.	1, 1929
Reelected	Jan.	3, 1893	Augustus F. Daix, Jr., Philadelphia	April	18, 1929
C. Wesley Thomas, Philadelphia	June	1, 1893	Reelected	Jan.	6, 1931
Reelected	Jan.	1, 1895	James S. Boyd, Montgomery	May	28, 1931
Samuel J. M. McCarrell, Dauphin	June	8, 1895	Reelected	Jan.	3, 1933
Reelected	Jan.	5, 1897	Harry B. Scott, Centre	May	6, 1933
Daniel S. Walton, Greene	July	1, 1897	John G. Homsher, Lancaster	Jan.	1, 1935
William P. Snyder, Chester	Jan.	3, 1899	Reelected	June	21, 1935
Reelected	April	20, 1899	Harvey Huffman, Monroe	Jan.	5, 1937
Reelected	Jan.	1, 1901	Reelected	June	3, 1937
John M. Scott, Philadelphia	June	27, 1901	John S. Rice[1], Adams	Nov.	30, 1938
Reelected	Jan.	6, 1903	Frederick T. Gelder, Susquehanna	Jan.	3, 1939
William C. Sproul, Delaware	April	16, 1903	Reelected[2]	May	29, 1939
Reelected	Jan.	3, 1905			
Cyrus E. Woods, Westmoreland	April	13, 1905			
Reelected	Jan.	1, 1907			

[1]Senator Rice succeeded Senator Huffman (deceased, Nov. 30, 1938, the day his term was to expire).

[2]Term as Senator expired Dec. 1, 1940. Chairman of Judiciary General Committee, Charles R. Mallery, Acting President Pro Tempore until Jan. 7, 1941.

Charles H. Ealy, Somerset	Jan.	7, 1941		Martin L. Murray, Luzerne	Jan.	5, 1971
Reelected[3]	July	14, 1941		Reelected	Jan.	4, 1972
Reelected	Jan.	5, 1943		Reelected	Jan.	2, 1973
Reelected	May	8, 1943		Reelected	Jan.	1, 1974
M. Harvey Taylor, Dauphin	Jan.	2, 1945		Reelected	Jan.	7, 1975
Weldon B. Heyburn[4], Delaware	Jan.	7, 1947		Reelected	Jan.	4, 1977
M. Harvey Taylor, Dauphin	Mar.	17, 1947		Reelected	Jan.	2, 1979
Reelected	Jan.	4, 1949		Reelected	Jan.	1, 1980
Reelected	Jan.	2, 1951		Henry G. Hager, Lycoming	Jan.	6, 1981
Reelected	Jan.	6, 1953		Reelected	Jan.	5, 1982
Reelected	Jan.	4, 1955		Reelected	Jan.	4, 1983
Reelected	Jan.	1, 1957		Robert C. Jubelirer, Blair	Jan.	1, 1985
Reelected	Jan.	6, 1959		Reelected	Jan.	7, 1986
Anthony J. DiSilvestro, Philadelphia	Jan.	3, 1961		Reelected	Jan.	6, 1987
M. Harvey Taylor, Dauphin	Jan.	1, 1963				
James S. Berger, Potter	Jan.	5, 1965				
Robert D. Fleming, Allegheny	Jan.	3, 1967				
Reelected	Jan.	6, 1969				
Reelected	Jan.	6, 1970				

[3]Term as Senator expired Dec. 1, 1942. Acting Chairman of Judiciary General Committee, Thomas B. Wilson, Acting President Pro Tempore until Jan. 5, 1943.

[4]Resigned as President Pro Tempore March 17, 1947.

SECRETARIES OF THE SENATE
1950 — 1987

	Date of Term
G. Harold Watkins	1945-56
Alfons H. Letzler	1957-58
Edward B. Watson	1959-60
Paul Moomaw	1961-62
Mark Gruell, Jr.	1963-80
W. Thomas Andrews	Jan. 1981-June 1981
Mark R. Corrigan	June 1981-

CHIEF CLERKS OF THE SENATE
1950 — 1987

	Date of Term
William J. Ridge	1939-51
Vera L. Froberg (Acting Chief Clerk)	1951-53
J. Fred Thomas	1953-56
G. Graybill Diehm	1957-60
Dennis J. Mulvihill	1961-62
Alfons H. Letzler	1963-67
Albert E. Madigan	1967-70
Thomas J. Kalman	1971-80
Stanley I. Rapp	Jan. 1981-June 1981
W. Russell Faber	June 1981-May 1986
Gary E. Crowell	May 1986-

SPEAKERS OF THE PROVINCIAL ASSEMBLY
1682 — 1790

	When Elected		When Elected
———————[1]	1682	David Lloyd	1706
Thomas Winn	1682/1683[2]	Richard Hill	1710
Nicholas More	1684	Isaac Norris	1712
John White	1685	Joseph Growdon	1713
Arthur Cook	1689	David Lloyd	1714
Joseph Growdon	1690	Joseph Growdon	1715
———————[3]	1691	Richard Hill	1716
William Clark	1692	William Trent	1717
Joseph Growdon	1693	Jonathan Dickinson	1718
David Lloyd	1694	William Trent	1719
Edward Shippen	1695	Isaac Norris	1720
John Simcock	1696		
John Blunston	1697		
Phineas Pemberton	1698		
John Blunston	1699		
Joseph Growdon	1700		
David Lloyd	1703		
Joseph Growden	1705		

[1]Records of the session are incomplete. Probably the Speaker was either Thomas Winn or Nicholas More.

[2]The election occurred March 12, 1682, Old Style, which some Quakers calculated as 1682, others as 1683.

[3]No public record extant.

	When Elected		When Elected
Jeremiah Langhorne	1721	Isaac Norris (II)	1764
Joseph Growdon	1722	Joseph Fox	1764
David Lloyd	1723	Joseph Galloway	1766
William Biles	1724	Joseph Fox	1769
David Lloyd	1725	Joseph Galloway	1769
Andrew Hamilton	1729	Edward Biddle	1774
Jeremiah Langhorne	1733	John Morton	1775
Andrew Hamilton	1734	John Jacobs	1776
John Kinsey	1739	John Bayard	1777
John Wright	1745	Frederick Augustus Muhlenberg	1780
John Kinsey	1745/1746[4]	George Gray	1783
Isaac Norris (II)	1750	John Bayard	1784
Thomas Leech	1758	Thomas Mifflin	1785
Isaac Norris (II)	1758	Richard Peters	1788
Thomas Leech	1759	William Bingham (under the new constitution)	1790
Isaac Norris (II)	1759		
Benjamin Franklin	1764		

[4]The election occurred January 6, 1745, Old Style, which some Quakers calculated as 1745, others as 1746.

SPEAKERS OF THE PENNSYLVANIA HOUSE OF REPRESENTATIVES — 1791 to 1987

	When Elected		When Elected
William Bingham (Philadelphia)	1791	Findley Patterson (Washington)	1846
Geradus Wynkoop (Philadelphia)	1793	James Cooper (Adams)	1847
George Latimer (Philadelphia)	1794	William F. Packer (Lycoming, Clinton)	1848
Cadwalader Evans (Montgomery)	1799	William F. Packer (Potter, Sullivan)	1849
Isaac Weaver, Jr. (Greene)	1800	John S. McCalmont (Venango)	1850
Simon Snyder (Northumberland)	1804	John Cessna (Bedford)	1851
Charles Porter (Fayette)	1806	John S. Rhey (Armstrong, Cambria)	1852
Simon Snyder (Northumberland)	1807	William P. Schnell (Bedford)	1853
Nathaniel Boileau (Montgomery)	1808	E. B. Chase (Susquehanna, Wyoming)	1854
James Engle (Philadelphia)	1809	Henry K. Strong (Philadelphia)	1855
John Weber (Montgomery)	1810	Richard L. Wright (Philadelphia)	1856
John Todd (Bedford)	1812	J. Lawrence Getz (Berks)	1857
Robert Smith (Franklin) (resigned Feb., 1814)	1813	A. B. Longaker (Montgomery)	1858
John St. Clair (vice Smith) (Fayette)	1814	W. C. A. Lawrence (Dauphin)	1859
Jacob Holgate (Philadelphia)	1815	W. C. A. Lawrence (Dauphin)	1860
Rees Hill (Greene)	1816	Elisha W. Davis (Philadelphia, Venango)	1861
William Davidson (Fayette)	1818	John Rowe (Franklin)	1862
Rees Hill (Greene)	1819	John Cessna (Bedford)	1863
Joseph Lawrence (Washington)	1820	Henry C. Johnson (Crawford)	1864
John Gilmore (Allegheny, Butler)	1821	Arthur G. Olmstead (Potter)	1865
Joseph Lawrence (Washington)	1822	James R. Kelley (Fulton)	1866
Joel B. Sutherland (Philadelphia)	1825	John P. Glass (Allegheny)	1867
Joseph Ritner (Washington)	1826	Elisha W. Davis (Philadelphia)	1868
Ner Middleswarth (Union)	1828	John Clark (Washington)	1869
Frederick Smith (Franklin)	1830	Butler B. Strang (Tioga)	1870
John LaPorte (Bradford, Tioga)	1832	James H. Webb (Bradford)	1871
James Findley[1] (Westmoreland)	1833	William Elliott (Philadelphia)	1872
Samuel Anderson (Delaware)	1833	H. H. McCormick (Allegheny)	1874
William Patterson (Washington)	1834	Samuel F. Patterson (Allegheny)	1875
James Thompson (Venango, Warren)	1835	E. Reed Myer (Bradford)	1877
Ner Middleswarth (Union)	1836	Henry M. Long (Allegheny)	1879
Lewis Dewart (Northumberland)	1837	Benjamin L. Hewitt (Blair)	1881
William Hopkins (Washington)	1839	John E. Faunce (Philadelphia)	1883
William A. Crabb (Philadelphia)	1841	James L. Graham (Allegheny)	1885
J. Ross Snowden (Venango, Clarion)	1842	Henry K. Boyer (Philadelphia)	1887
H. B. Wright (Luzerne, Wyoming)	1843	Henry K. Boyer (Philadelphia)	1889
J. Ross Snowden (Venango, Clarion)	1844	Caleb C. Thompson (Warren)	1891
Findley Patterson (Washington)	1845		

[1]Resigned and appointed Secretary of the Commonwealth.

	When Elected		*When Elected*
Caleb C. Thompson (Warren)	1893	Ira T. Fiss (Snyder)	1945
Henry F. Walton (Philadelphia)	1895	Franklin H. Lichtenwalter[4] (Lehigh)	1947
Henry K. Boyer (Philadelphia) (resigned Jan. 17, 1898)	1897	Herbert P. Sorg (Elk)	1949
John R. Farr (Lackawanna)	1899	Herbert P. Sorg (Elk)	1951
William T. Marshall (Allegheny)	1901	Charles C. Smith (Philadelphia)	1953
Henry F. Walton (Philadelphia)	1903	Hiram G. Andrews (Cambria)	1955
Henry F. Walton (Philadelphia)	1905	W. Stuart Helm (Armstong)	1957
Frank B. McClain (Lancaster)	1907	Hiram G. Andrews (Cambria)	1959
John F. Cox (Allegheny)	1909	Hiram G. Andrews (Cambria)	1961
John F. Cox (Allegheny) (deceased Nov. 6, 1911)	1911	W. Stuart Helm (Armstong)	1963
Milton W. Shreeve[2] (Erie)	1911	Robert K. Hamilton (Beaver)	1965
George E. Alter (Allegheny)	1913	Kenneth B. Lee (Sullivan)	1967
Charles A. Ambler (Montgomery) (deceased Aug. 29, 1940)	1915	Herbert Fineman (Philadelphia)	1969
Richard J. Baldwin (Delaware)	1917	Herbert Fineman (Philadelphia)	1971
Robert S. Spangler (York)	1919	Kenneth B. Lee (Sullivan)	1973
Robert S. Spangler (York) (unseated April 26, 1921)	1921	Herbert Fineman[5] (Philadelphia)	1975, 1977
Samuel A. Whitaker (Chester) (elected April 26, 1921)	1921	K. Leroy Irvis (Allegheny) (elected May 23, 1977)	1977
C. J. Goodnough (Cameron)	1923	H. Jack Seltzer (Lebanon)	1979
Thomas Bluett (Philadelphia)	1925	Matthew J. Ryan (Delaware)	1981
Thomas Bluett (Philadelphia)	1927	K. Leroy Irvis (Allegheny)	1983
James H. McClure[3] (Allegheny)	1927	K. Leroy Irvis (Allegheny)	1985
Aaron B. Hess (Lancaster)	1929	K. Leroy Irvis (Allegheny)	1987
C. J. Goodnough (Cameron)	1931		
Grover C. Talbot (Delaware)	1933		
Wilson G. Sarig (Berks) (deceased March 14, 1936)	1935		
Roy E. Furman (Greene)	1936		
Roy E. Furman (Greene)	1937		
Ellwood J. Turner (Delaware)	1939		
Elmer Kilroy (Philadelphia)	1941		
Ira T. Fiss (Snyder)	1943		

[2]As Chairman of Judiciary General Committee of House of Representatives, succeeded John F. Cox, deceased, as Speaker, on Dec. 5, 1911.

[3]As Chairman of Judiciary General Committee of the House of Representatives, succeeded Thomas Bluett, who was elected judge of the Municipal Court of Philadelphia.

[4]Resigned Oct. 5, 1947, after elected to U.S. Congress.

[5]Resigned May 23, 1977.

SECRETARIES OF THE HOUSE OF REPRESENTATIVES
1950 — 1980

	Term of Service
William P. Roan	1943-54
Paul C. Moomaw	1955-56
	1959-60
W. W. Waterhouse	1957-60
	1963-64
Philip Lopresti	1961-62
Marion L. Munley	1965-66
R. P. Stimmel	1967-68
	1973-74
Thomas F. Sullivan	1969-72
	1975-78
Robert M. Scheipe	1979-80

CHIEF CLERKS OF THE HOUSE OF REPRESENTATIVES
1950 — 1987

	Term of Service
William E. Habbyshaw	1943-54
Benjamin L. Long	1955-56
Lloyd H. Wood	1957-58
Joseph Ominsky	1959-62
R. P. Stimmel	1963-64
Anthony J. Petrosky	1965-66
Adam T. Bower	1967-68
Vincent F. Scarcelli	1969-72
	1975-78
Robert M. Scheipe	1973-74
Charles F. Mebus	1979-80
John J. Zubeck	1981-

COMPTROLLERS OF THE HOUSE OF REPRESENTATIVES
1950 — 1987

	Term of Service
Harry A. Wagenheim	1947-66
Jean Francis	1967-78
Ann M. Santinoceto	1979-

DIRECTORS OF THE LEGISLATIVE REFERENCE BUREAU

(Director elected by Members of the General Assembly)

	When Elected		When Appointed
James N. Moore		**Assistant Directors:**	
(deceased Oct. 17, 1930)	July 22, 1909	James McKirdy	1910
John H. Fertig	Jan. 6, 1931	John H. Fertig	Jan. 1, 1917
Harry Hershey (acting)	Jan. 1, 1938	Robert S. Frey	Mar. 3, 1931
Robert S. Frey	Jan. 3, 1939	Harry Hershey	Feb. 3, 1935
Herbert B. Cohen	Jan. 6, 1941	S. Edward Hannestad	Jan. 3, 1939
Robert S. Frey		William H. Wood	Aug. 1, 1941
(deceased Sept. 1, 1946)	Jan. 5, 1943	S. Edward Hannestad	Jan. 5, 1943
S. Edward Hannestad (consultant,		Burt R. Glidden	Jan. 7, 1947
Jan. 1, to Dec. 31, 1957)	Jan. 7, 1947	Theodore S. Gutowicz	June 1, 1955
Burt R. Glidden	Jan. 1, 1957	Frank P. Garber	Jan. 1, 1959
Harry Hershey	Jan. 3, 1961	*Carl L. Mease	July 1, 1981
Edwin W. Tompkins	Jan. 1, 1963		
Martin L. Murray	Jan. 5, 1965		
James S. Berger	Jan. 17, 1967		
John Gailey	Jan. 14, 1969		
Alvin C. Bush	Jan. 2, 1973	*Incumbent	
Robert C. Wise	Jan. 20, 1975		
Russell J. LaMarca	Jan. 4, 1977		
Joseph Ted Doyle	Feb. 13, 1979		
Robert L. Cable	Jan. 6, 1981		

POLITICAL DIVISION OF GENERAL ASSEMBLY SINCE 1906

1906:	R	D	Vac		1914:	R	D	*K	**W	Vac
Senate	40	10	—		Senate	34	13	—	—	3
House	185	18	1		House	119	54	9	14	11
	225	28	1			153	67	9	14	14

1907:	R	D	Ind	Vac		1915:	R	D	**W	Soc
Senate	40	10	—	—		Senate	38	11	1	—
House	154	50	1	2		House	164	41	1	1
	194	60	1	2			202	52	2	1

1908:	R	D	Ind	Vac		1916:	R	D	**W	Soc	Vac
Senate	37	9	—	4		Senate	37	11	1	—	1
House	146	50	1	10		House	153	40	1	1	12
	183	59	1	14			190	51	2	1	13

1909:	R	D	Vac		1917:	R	D	**W	Soc	Vac
Senate	39	11	—		Senate	36	10	1	—	3
House	173	34	—		House	167	37	—	1	2
	212	45	—			203	47	1	1	5

1910:	R	D	Vac		1918:	R	D	**W	Soc	Vac
Senate	36	11	3		Senate	33	10	1	—	6
House	161	31	15		House	165	37	—	1	4
	197	42	18			198	47	1	1	10

1911:	R	D	Soc	Vac		1919:	R	D	Vac
Senate	38	12	—	—		Senate	42	6	2
House	159	44	1	3		House	176	21	10
	197	56	1	3			218	27	12

1912:	R	D	Soc	Vac		1920:	R	D	Vac
Senate	36	12	—	2		Senate	41	6	3
House	155	42	1	9		House	175	21	11
	191	54	1	11			216	27	14

1913:	R	D	*K	**W	Vac		1921:	R	D	Vac
Senate	34	15	—	1	2		Senate	44	3	3
House	125	55	9	14	4		House	181	14	12
	159	70	9	15	6			225	17	15

1923-24:

	R	D	Vac
Senate	41	7	2
House	162	40	6
	203	47	8

1925-26:

	R	D	Vac
Senate	42	8	—
House	194	14	—
	236	22	—

1927-28:

	R	D	Vac
Senate	45	5	—
House	190	17	1
	235	22	1

1929-30:

	R	D	Vac
Senate	44	6	—
House	192	16	—
	236	22	—

1931-32:

	R	D	Vac
Senate	46	4	—
House	184	22	2
	230	26	2

1933-34:

	R	D	Ind	Soc	Vac
Senate	43	7	—	—	—
House	139	65	2	1	1
	182	72	2	1	1

1935-36:

	R	D	Soc	Vac
Senate	31	19	—	—
House	88	117	2	1
	119	136	2	1

1937-38:

	R	D	Vac
Senate	16	34	—
House	54	154	—
	70	188	—

1939-40:

	R	D	Vac
Senate	25	23	2
House	129	79	—
	154	102	2

1941-42:

	R	D	Vac
Senate	34	18	—
House	82	126	—
	114	144	—

1943-44

	R	D	Vac
Senate	32	18	—
House	132	76	2
	164	94	2

1945-46:

	R	D	Vac
Senate	32	18	—
House	109	99	—
	141	117	—

1947-48:

	R	D	Vac
Senate	34	16	—
House	168	37	3
	202	53	3

1949-50:

	R	D	Vac
Senate	35	15	—
House	117	91	—
	152	106	—

1951-52:

	R	D	Vac
Senate	30	20	—
House	120	87	1
	150	107	1

1953-54:

	R	D	Vac
Senate	32	18	—
House	110	98	—
	142	116	—

1955-56:

	R	D	Vac
Senate	26	24	—
House	98	112	—
	124	136	—

1957-58:

	R	D	Vac
Senate	27	23	—
House	126	83	1
	153	106	1

1959-60:

	R	D	Vac
Senate	28	22	—
House	102	108	—
	130	130	—

1961-62:

	R	D	Vac
Senate	25	25	—
House	101	109	—
	126	134	—

1963-64:

	R	D	Vac
Senate	26	22	2
House	108	98	4
	134	120	6

1965-66:

	R	D	Vac
Senate	27	22	1
House	93	116	—
	120	138	1

1967-68:

	R	D	Vac
Senate	27	22	1
House	103	99	1
	130	121	2

1969-70:

	R	D	Vac
Senate	27	23	—
House	96	106	1
	123	129	1

1971-72:

	R	D	Vac
Senate	24	25	1
House	90	112	1
	114	137	2

1973:

	R	D	Vac
Senate	24	26	—
House	107	94	2
	131	120	2

1974:

	R	D	Vac
Senate	23	27	—
House	108	95	—
	131	122	—

1975:

	R	D	Vac
Senate	20	29	1
House	89	114	—
	109	143	1

1976:

	R	D	Vac
Senate	20	30	—
House	89	114	—
	109	144	—

1977:

	R	D	Vac
Senate	20	30	—
House	84	116	3
	104	146	3

1978:	R	D	Vac
Senate.	19	30	1
House.	84	118	1
	103	148	2

1979:	R	D	Vac
Senate.	22	28	—
House.	103	100	—
	125	128	—

1980:	R	D	Vac
Senate.	22	28	—
House.	101	99	3
	123	127	3

1981:	R	D	Vac
Senate.	26	23	1
House.	102	100	1
	128	123	2

1982:	R	D	Vac
Senate.	26	24	—
House.	101	98	4
	127	122	4

1983:	R	D	Vac
Senate.	27	23	—
House.	100	103	—
	127	126	—

1984:	R	D	Vac
Senate.	27	23	—
House.	99	103	1
	126	126	1

1985:	R	D	Vac
Senate.	27	23	—
House.	100	103	—
	127	126	—

1986:	R	D	
Senate.	27	23	—
House.	100	101	2

1987:	R	D	
Senate.	26	24	—
House.	100	101	2

* K - Keystone Party
** W - Washington Party

SPECIAL SESSIONS OF THE SENATE, 1791-1972

1791 — Thomas Mifflin convoked the General Assembly in special session on August 23, 1791, and in his address gave as the purpose: To plan internal improvements and provide for a loan to the Commonwealth; also to make appropriations for repelling invaders committing depredations on the western frontiers of the State, and to take action on claims of Pennsylvania against the United States. The General Assembly met in Philadelphia and adjourned September 30, 1791.

1793 — Thomas Mifflin, in his address to the Legislature, met in special session, beginning August 27, 1793, outlined the purpose of the session. The message was read August 30. He urged providing for defraying the expense of "defending the port and river Delaware," as well as an appropriation to pay deficiencies. The General Assembly adjourned September 5, 1793.

1794 — The General Assembly was convened in extraordinary session, September 1, 1794, by Governor Thomas Mifflin in a call issued August 7, for the purpose of deriving means to maintain peace and dignity in the Commonwealth and providing more effectually for organizing, arming and equipping the militia in order to ensure a prompt and faithful compliance with government orders and such requisitions as the President might make. This was the proclamation convoking the General Assembly to take action in connection with the Whiskey insurrection. The session was held at the State House, in the City of Philadelphia, and was adjourned September 23, 1794.

1797 — The General Assembly was convened in extraordinary session on August 28, 1797. Governor Mifflin, in a message to the General Assembly, read on August 29, 1797, gave the purpose of the session. To enable surer compliance with requisition of United States for 10,000 militia from Pennsylvania and to effect regulations reforming the military system, for regulating bankruptcy, to obtain better prison management and to make appropriations for the Land Office and also for the Health Office to further its fight against a malignant fever. The session was adjourned August 29, 1797, having consumed but two legislative days.

1800 — Governor Thomas McKean issued a proclamation, October 18, 1800, calling the General Assembly into special session, to lay before that body certain Federal obligations, viz.: Providing for the choice of electors

for President and Vice-President. The session was convened at the Borough of Lancaster, November 5, 1800 and ran into the regular session which began in December.

1829 — The General Assembly was convoked in extra session for the consideration of matters pertaining to the Pennsylvania Canal and Railroad, by Governor John Andrew Shulze, on October 15, 1829, at the State Capitol. It adjourned December 1, 1829.

1840 — From a message convening the General Assembly in extra session, it is found that the purpose was for consideration of certain financial matters of the Commonwealth. The General Assembly was called to meet on April 17, 1840, the day after the regular session had adjourned. Governor David Rittenhouse Porter issued the call on April 16, 1840. The session adjourned June 12, 1840.

1857 — Governor James Pollock issued a proclamation on September 28, 1857, convening the General Assembly in special session to adopt measures of financial relief under circumstances threatening the credit of the Commonwealth. The session held at the State Capitol was adjourned on October 13, 1857.

1861 — Governor Andrew G. Curtin called a special session of the General Assembly to meet at the Capitol on April 30, 1861, "to adopt such measures as seem best with the appearance of the rebellion." The General Assembly adjourned May 16, 1861.

1864 — Governor Curtin also issued a proclamation on August 1, 1864, for a special session of the General Assembly in the Capitol, August 9, 1864, to make greater military power of the Commonwealth immediately available for State and National defense. The session was called fourteen days before the date fixed for reconvening on August 23, in adjourned session by reason of war condition. It was adjourned on August 25, 1864.

1883 — As set forth in the executive's message, Governor Robert Emory Pattison convened the General Assembly in extra session June 7, 1883, to apportion the State into Senatorial and Representative districts in accordance to the provisions of the Constitution. The General Assembly adjourned on December 6, 1883.

1891 — Governor Pattison also called an extra session of the Senate to begin on October 13, 1891, to investigate charges involving the Auditor General and State Treasurer and reflecting upon the manner in which their official duties had been performed and also to ascertain whether "reasonable cause" existed for their removal. A supplementary proclamation included in this extra session the charges concerning the conduct of several magistrates and constables in Philadelphia. The latter was issued October 12, 1891. The Senate adjourned on November 11, 1891.

1906 — The General Assembly was called in extraordinary session, January 15, 1906, at 2 o'clock by Governor Samuel W. Pennypacker to consider legislation upon the following subjects: To adopt such measures as may be necessary for the handling of the public moneys; to reapportion the State into Senatorial and Representative districts; to provide for the personal registration of voters and for the government of cities of the first class; to designate the amount to be expended each year in the erection of county bridges; to abolish fees in the offices of the Secretary of the Commonwealth and the Insurance Commissioner. The General Assembly adjourned on February 15, 1906.

1926 — Governor Gifford Pinchot, in a proclamation issued December 14, 1925, convening the General Assembly to meet in extraordinary session on January 13, 1926, gave as the purpose of the following: To revise the election and registration laws; to regulate, through an appropriate State agency, the Anthracite coal industry for domestic use in Philadelphia; to revise laws concerning banks, trust companies and building and loan associations; to provide additional means for enforcing the Eighteenth Amendment to the United States Constitution; to adjust differences between New Jersey and Pennsylvania delaying the completion of the Philadelphia-Camden bridge; to provide for and define the powers and duties of a Giant Power Board; to enter into a compact with the States of New York and New Jersey for the regulation of the flow of the Delaware River. The extra session adjourned on February 18, 1926.

1931 — The General Assembly was convened in extraordinary session, November 9, 1931, by Governor Pinchot in his proclamation of October 31, 1931, for the purpose of considering measures for unemployment relief. A supplementary proclamation, issued November 9, 1931, included additional appropriations to the Department of Welfare for nonsectarian, medical and surgical hospitals and to the Department of Military Affairs for the State Veterans' Commission. It also provided for new appropriations to any department, board or commission of the State Government to enable additional projects to be undertaken for unemployment relief. The extra session adjourned December 30, 1931.

1932 — The General Assembly was convened by extraordinary session, June 27, 1932, by Governor Pinchot in his proclamation of June 22, 1932, for the purpose of reducing appropriations previously made to balance the deficiency; unemployment relief, to authorize political subdivisions; to negotiate emergency loans, increase their taxing powers and revise the method of collecting delinquent taxes; to expand the powers of the Secretary of Banking; to authorize building and loan associations; to borrow from the Reconstruction Finance Corporation, to regulate payment of compensation of county employes in cities of the first class and proposing certain constitutional amendments. The extra session adjourned August 19, 1932.

1933 — Governor Pinchot, in a proclamation dated November 9, 1933, convened the General Assembly in extraordinary session, November 13, 1933, to consider the following subjects: taxation and control of alcoholic beverages, old age pensions, unemployment relief, cooperation with Federal agencies, permanent registration in cities, relief for financially distressed property owners and taxpayers, modification of the banking laws, milk control, and legislation necessary to give effect to any constitutional amendments adopted by the people on November 7, 1933. The session adjourned December 21, 1933.

1934 — Governor Pinchot, in a proclamation dated September 8, 1934, convened the General Assembly in extraordinary session, September 12, 1934, to consider the following subject: Relief for the unemployed and indigent aged, financing necessary to provide therefor, and payment of expenses of the extraordinary session. The session adjourned September 20, 1934.

1936 — Governor Earle, in a proclamation dated April 27, 1936, and a supplemental proclamation dated April 30, 1936, convened the General Assembly in extraordinary session, May 4, 1936 to consider the following subjects: Flood relief and control; unemployment relief; relief of overcrowding and correction of fire and safety hazards in State hospitals, asylums, sanitoria and other institutions; legislation to enable Pennsylvania to participate in the benefits of the Federal Social Security Acts; abatement of the penalties on real estate taxes; legislation to permit refunding of certain existing bonded indebtedness at lower rates of interest; appropriations for financially distressed school districts; an amendment to the State Constitution permitting amendments to be submitted to the electors more frequently than is now permitted; legislation to provide revenue for the above enumerated subjects. The session adjourned August 6, 1936.

1936 — Governor Earle, in a proclamation dated November 25, 1936, convened the General Assembly in extraordinary session December 1, 1936, to consider the following subjects: Unemployment insurance and appropriations incident thereto, and appropriations for the expenses of the special session. The session adjourned December 5, 1936.

1938 — Governor Earle, in a proclamation dated July 22, 1938, convened the General Assembly in extraordinary session July 25, 1938, to consider the following subjects: Investigation of criminal charges against persons holding office under the Commonwealth; regulation of investigations of charges involving misdemeanor in office by the General Assembly and the courts; defining and regulating powers and duties of Attorney General and district attorneys; appropriation for public assistance and revision of laws relating to social security and public projects in order to obtain additional Federal grants; enlarging the scope of the General State Authority and municipal subdivisions in relation thereto; powers of school districts in the levy and collection of taxes; abatement of certain tax penalties; sale and exposure of fireworks; widening of approaches to the Delaware River Bridge; change in venue of criminal cases; regulating use of devices for transmission of information in furtherance of gambling; amendment of the Public Utility Law; creation of commission to investigate the oil industry; invalidating certain commissioners; action on report of the Anthracite Coal Industry Commission; appropriations for flood purposes; revision of laws relating to exits from buildings; acquisition of real estate from housing authorities; additional care for the mentally ill and feeble-minded; and appropriations for the social session. The session adjourned November 30, 1938.

1940 — Governor James, in a proclamation dated April 29, 1940, convened the General Assembly in extraordinary session May 6, 1940, to consider the following subjects: Appropriations for payment of public assistance and for payment of administrative, auditing and disbursement expenses relating thereto; appropriations to provide aid to financially handicapped school districts; appropriations to pay expenses of extraordinary session; appropriation to the Joint State Government Commission for the continuance of its work; to make funds available in General Fund for foregoing appropriations; to transfer moneys from various special funds in State Treasury and subsequent reimbursement of such special funds out of the General Fund and reductions in such appropriations made by the General Assembly in its 1939 session; legislation necessary to conform to the provisions of the Unemployment Compensation Law to the new definition of "wages," contained in the provisions of the Federal Internal Revenue Code, as amended, which now relate to and impose, the Federal Unemployment Tax; legislation necessary to conform the provisions of the Public Assistance Law to the new definition of the term "dependent" children contained in Title IV of the

Federal Social Security Act, as amended; legislation necessary to permit the Pennsylvania Turnpike Commission to construct a turnpike from a point at or near Middlesex in Cumberland County, to the Delaware River, at or near Philadelphia, and to issue turnpike revenue bonds, payable solely from tolls to pay the cost of such construction; legislation providing for the transfer of such moneys from the Veterans' Compensation Fund to the Sinking Funds as may be available to meet the interest and Sinking Fund requirements of the Veterans' Compensation Bonds issued under authority of the act, approved January 5, 1934; legislation necessary to permit the Department of Property and Supplies to supervise and operate the Northwest Office Building; an amendment to the Pennsylvania Election Code to provide for the filling of vacancies occurring in the membership of either branch of the General Assembly when it is not in session or has not been called into extraordinary session. The session adjourned May 16, 1940.

1942 — Governor James, in a proclamation dated February 10, 1942, and a supplemental proclamation dated February 17, 1942, convened the General Assembly in extraordinary session February 17, 1942, to consider the following subjects: Congressional reapportionment; postponement of the operation of the new parole law; suspension or modification of existing laws that interfere with the prosecution of any war in which this nation engages; authorizing political subdivisions to make appropriations to local district Councils of Defense; confirming and validating appropriations heretofore made for defense purposes permitting political subdivisions to acquire funds for these purposes by borrowing or by taxation; prevention of sabotage; mobilization and use of fire-fighting forces and equipment for National defense purposes; air-raid precautions and blackouts; liberalization of Unemployment Compensation Law; appointment of substitute fiduciaries where existing fiduciaries are in military service, or allowing remaining fiduciaries to act where co-fiduciaries are in military service; cessation by the Commonwealth to the United States of America of jurisdiction of certain lands in Eddystone for the establishment of a plant to produce steel forgings and other articles necessary for the National defense; revision of benefits payable to dependents under the provisions of the Act of June 7, 1917, P. L. 600, as amended; authorizing the Department of Highways to construct, replace or repair bridges in cities of the third class which form connecting links on State highways necessary for national defense in cases where Federal funds and city funds are available for such purposes; authorizing building and loan associations to act as fiscal agents of the United States Government for the sale of United States Defense Bonds and Stamps; extending the time within which writs of election may issue for holding special elections to fill vacancies occurring in either House of the General Assembly, and the time within which nominations thereof may be filed; appropriation to the Department of Justice for the conduct of parole work of the Board of Pardons; appropriation for the expenses of the Legislative Committee on Congressional Reapportionment; and appropriation for the expenses of the extraordinary session. The session adjourned April 10, 1942.

1944 — Governor Martin, in a proclamation dated April 19, 1944, convened the General Assembly in extraordinary session May 1, 1944, to consider the following subjects: Enabling persons serving in the armed forces of the United States or in the Merchant Marines of the United States, or serving in the American Red Cross, the Society of Friends, the Women's Auxiliary Service Pilots or the United Service Organizations attached to and serving with the armed forces of the United States, to vote by military ballot in any primary, special or general election held in time of war and six months thereafter, and authorizing the appropriation of funds and appropriating funds therefor; conferring certain powers and duties upon the State, local and district Councils of Defense, and others, county boards of election and election boards, with respect to obtaining, utilizing and disseminating information concerning persons serving in the armed forces of the United States or in the Merchant Marine of the United States, or serving in the American Red Cross, the Society of Friends, the Womens' Auxiliary Service Pilots or in the United Service Organizations attached to and serving with the armed forces of the United States, and authorizing the appropriations of funds and appropriating funds therefor; appropriation for the expenses of the Governor's Conference to be held in Harrisburg in the year one thousand nine hundred forty-four; appropriation for the

expenses of the extraordinary session. The session adjourned May 5, 1944.

1962 — Governor David L. Lawrence, in a proclamation dated January 16, 1962, convened the General Assembly in a special session January 22, 1962, to consider legislation upon the subject of Congressional Reapportionment. The session adjourned Janaury 29, 1962.

1963 — Governor William W. Scranton, in a proclamation dated September 11, 1963, convened the General Assembly in a special session November 12, 1963, to consider legislation upon the subject of Reapportionment. The session adjourned December 14, 1963. Governor William W. Scranton, in a proclamation dated December 6, 1963, convened the General Assembly in a special session December 9, 1963, to consider action on appropriations to charitable and educational institutions which under Article 3, Section 17, of the Constitution require a vote of two-thirds of all members elected to each house. The session adjourned December 14, 1963.

1964 — Governor William W. Scranton, in a proclamation dated February 4, 1964, convened the General Assembly in a special session February 11, 1964, to consider legislation upon the following subjects; (1) Codifying, amending, revising and consolidating the laws relating to eminent domain, (2) Implementation of the authority granted by Article IX, Section 24, of the Constitution of Pennsylvania, otherwise known as "Project 70," (3) Stabilization of the unemployment compensation fund by amending the provisions of the Unemployment Compensation Law relating to benefits, contributions and procedures, (4) Amending and clarifying the definition of "blind veteran" as defined in Act No. 17 of the 1963 sessions, (5) Providing for institutional care and treatment of aged patients of the State Mental Institutions who do not require treatment for mental disease.

1966 — Governor William W. Scranton, in a proclamation dated February 24, 1966, convened the General Assembly in a special session February 28, 1966, to consider legislation upon the following subjects: (1) To protect the safety of the public by prohibiting the mining of bituminous coal in such a manner as to cause cave-ins, collapses or subsidences, (2) Implementation of the amendment to Article V, Section 15, of the Constitution of Pennsylvania, adopted November 2, 1965, with respect to judicial service of former judges; (3) Authorizing the Governor of the Commonwealth of Pennsylvania to enter into an Interstate Mining Compact to assure sound mining practices, (4) Increasing the maximum authorized complement of officers and members of the Pennsylvania State Police Force, (5) Providing protection to consumers against unfair credit practices, (6) Empowering the State Public School Building Authority to construct, improve, maintain and operate buildings and facilities created and established pursuant to the Community College Act of 1963, (7) Postponing the date of establishment of those reorganized school districts which presently have judicial appeals pending until the final disposition thereof, (8) Providing for the purchase of social security offsets by retired members of the State Employes' Retirement System and the Public School Employes' Retirement System who retired prior to July 1, 1962.

1966 — Governor William W. Scranton, in a proclamation dated March 2, 1966, convened the General Assembly in a special session March 2, 1966, to consider legislation upon the subject of Congressional Reapportionment.

1966 — Governor William W. Scranton, in a proclamation dated April 15, 1966, convened the General Assembly to meet April 18, 1966 in an extraordinary session to consider legislation (1) Providing for advance payments of subsidies to school districts, (2) Providing for highway scenic improvement and beautification, (3) Amending the Higher Education Assistance Agency Law with respect to eligibility of borrowers and the time and period of repayment of student loans, (4) The establishment and operation of the University of Pittsburgh as a State-related university in the higher education system of the Commonwealth, (5) A comprehensive program relating to mental health and retardation, (6) Redefining and increasing the penalty for rape.

1972 — Governor Milton J. Shapp, in a proclamation dated August 7, 1972, convened the General Assembly to meet August 14, 1972 in an extraordinary session to consider legislation upon the following subjects: (1) Reimbursement of volunteer fire companies for equipment and building losses sustained as a result of flood waters, (2) Municipal tax abatement for property lost or damaged by flood waters, (3) Flood plain zoning, (4) Authorization of an emergency bond issue for rehabilitation in areas affected by the flood of June, 1972, (5) Unemployment compensation problems created by the flood of June, 1972, (6) Allowing local governments to participate in or to obtain the benefit of any state contracts appropriate to their operations, (7) Creation of a Pennsylvania Housing Assistance Agency and definition of its powers, (8) Site development planning by the Commonwealth, (9) Consideration of the final report of the Commonwealth Compensation Commission issued June 22, 1972, (10)

Amendments to the Industrial Development Authority Act to expand the provisions of the present act and make it applicable to Disaster Relief Projects, (11) Amendments to the Constitution of Pennsylvania to enable the Commonwealth to give grants to and guaranty loans for individuals, including farmers, who suffered major damage as a result of the flood of June, 1972.

1972 — Governor Milton J. Shapp, in a proclamation dated August 7, 1972, convened the General Assembly to meet August 14, 1972 in an extraordinary second and special session to consider legislation (1) To reform the Pennsylvania Election and Registration Laws to bring them into conformity with the Federal Voting Rights Act Amendments of 1970, (2) To enact any additional Election and Registration legislation.

LENGTH OF LEGISLATIVE SESSIONS, 1776-1986

CONSTITUTION OF 1776

No.		From		To		Days		No.	From		To		Days
1	1.	Nov.	28, 1776	Sept.	18, 1777	295		18	Dec.	3, 1793	April	22, 1794	41
	2.	Sept.	25, 1777	Oct.	13, 1777	19			¹Sept.	1, 1794	Sept.	23, 1794	23
2	1.	Oct.	27, 1777	April	21, 1778	177		19	Dec.	2, 1794	April	20, 1795	140
	2.	May	13, 1778	Sept.	11, 1778	122		20	Dec.	3, 1795	April	4, 1796	123
3	1.	Oct.	26, 1778	Dec.	5, 1778	41		21	Dec.	6, 1796	April	5, 1797	121
	2.	Feb.	1, 1779	Oct.	10, 1779	252			¹Aug.	28, 1797	Aug.	29, 1797	2
4	1.	Oct.	25, 1779	Mar.	25, 1780	152		22	Dec.	5, 1797	April	5, 1798	122
	2.	May	10, 1780	Sept.	23, 1780	137		23	Dec.	4, 1798	April	11, 1799	129
5	1.	Oct.	23, 1780	April	10, 1781	170		24	Dec.	3, 1799	Mar.	17, 1800	105
	2.	May	24, 1781	June	26, 1781	34			¹Nov.	5, 1800	Dec.	, 1800	
	3.	Sept.	4, 1781	Oct.	2, 1781	29		25	Dec.	, 1800	Feb.	27, 1801	
6	1.	Oct.	22, 1781	Dec.	28, 1781	68		26	Dec.	1, 1801	April	6, 1802	127
	2.	Feb.	11, 1782	April	16, 1782	65		27	Dec.	7, 1802	April	4, 1803	119
	3.	Aug.	1, 1782	Sept.	20, 1782	51		28	Dec.	6, 1803	April	3, 1804	119
7	1.	Oct.	28, 1782	Dec.	4, 1782	38		29	Dec.	4, 1804	April	4, 1805	122
	2.	Jan.	15, 1783	Mar.	22, 1783	67		30	Dec.	3, 1805	Mar.	31, 1806	119
	3.	Aug.	14, 1783	Sept.	26, 1783	44		31	Dec.	2, 1806	April	13, 1807	133
8	1.	Oct.	27, 1783	Dec.	9, 1783	44		32	Dec.	1, 1807	Mar.	28, 1808	118
	2.	Jan.	13, 1784	April	1, 1784	79		33	Dec.	6, 1808	April	4, 1809	120
	3.	July	20, 1784	Sept.	29, 1784	72		34	Dec.	5, 1809	Mar.	20, 1810	106
9	1.	Oct.	25, 1784	Dec.	24, 1784	64		35	Dec.	4, 1810	April	2, 1811	120
	2.	Feb.	1, 1785	April	8, 1785	67		36	Dec.	3, 1811	Mar.	31, 1812	119
	3.	Aug.	23, 1785	Sept.	23, 1785	32		37	Dec.	1, 1812	Mar.	29, 1813	119
10	1.	Oct.	24, 1785	Dec.	22, 1785	60		38	Dec.	7, 1813	Mar.	28, 1814	112
	2.	Feb.	25, 1786	April	8, 1786	43		39	Dec.	6, 1814	Mar.	13, 1815	98
	3.	Aug.	22, 1786	Sept.	27, 1786	37		40	Dec.	5, 1815	Mar.	19, 1816	105
11	1.	Oct.	25, 1786	Dec.	30, 1786	67		41	Dec.	3, 1816	Mar.	25, 1817	113
	2.	Sept.	20, 1787	Mar.	29, 1788	38		42	Dec.	2, 1817	Mar.	24, 1818	113
	3.	Sept.	4, 1787	Sept.	29, 1787	26		43	Dec.	1, 1818	Mar.	30, 1819	120
12	1.	Oct.	22, 1787	Nov.	29, 1787	39		44	Dec.	7, 1819	Mar.	28, 1820	112
	2.	Feb.	19, 1788	Mar.	29, 1788	39		45	Dec.	5, 1820	April	3, 1821	120
	3.	Sept.	2, 1788	Oct.	4, 1788	33		46	Dec.	4, 1821	April	2, 1822	120
13	1.	Oct.	27, 1788	Nov.	22, 1788	27		47	Dec.	3, 1822	April	1, 1823	120
	2.	Feb.	3, 1789	Mar.	28, 1789	54		48	Dec.	2, 1823	Mar.	30, 1824	119
	3.	Aug.	18, 1789	Sept.	30, 1789	44		49	Dec.	7, 1824	Mar.	12, 1825	96
14	1.	Oct.	26, 1789	Dec.	9, 1789	45		50	Dec.	6, 1825	April	11, 1826	96
	2.	Feb.	2, 1790	April	6, 1790	65		51	Dec.	5, 1826	April	17, 1827	134
	3.	Aug.	24, 1790	Sept.	3, 1790	11		52	Dec.	4, 1827	April	15, 1828	133
								53	Dec.	2, 1828	April	24, 1829	144
									¹Nov.	3, 1829	Dec.	1, 1829	29
		CONSTITUTION OF 1790						54	Dec.	1, 1829	April	7, 1830	128
								55	Dec.	7, 1830	April	5, 1831	120
15		Dec.	7, 1790	April	13, 1791	128		56	Dec.	7, 1831	April	12, 1832	127
		¹Aug.	23, 1791	Sept.	30, 1791	39		57	Dec.	4, 1832	April	9, 1833	127
16		Dec.	6, 1791	April	10, 1792	126		58	Dec.	3, 1833	April	15, 1834	134
17		Dec.	4, 1792	April	11, 1793	129		59	Dec.	2, 1834	April	15, 1835	135
		¹Aug.	27, 1793	Sept.	5, 1793	10		60	Dec.	1, 1835	June	16, 1836	198
								61	Dec.	6, 1836	April	4, 1837	120
								62	Dec.	5, 1837	April	17, 1838	134

CONSTITUTION OF 1838

No.	From		To		Days
63	Dec.	4, 1838	June	25, 1839	204
64	Jan.	7, 1840	April	16, 1840	131
	¹April	17, 1840	June	12, 1840	67
65	Jan.	1, 1841	May	4, 1841	124
66	Jan.	4, 1842	July	26, 1842	204
67	Jan.	3, 1843	April	18, 1843	106
68	Jan.	2, 1844	April	29, 1844	118
69	Jan.	7, 1845	April	16, 1845	100
70	Jan.	6, 1846	April	22, 1846	107
71	Jan.	5, 1847	Mar.	16, 1847	71
72	Jan.	4, 1848	April	11, 1848	98
73	Jan.	2, 1849	April	10, 1849	99
74	Jan.	1, 1850	May	15, 1850	135
75	Jan.	7, 1851	April	15, 1851	99
76	Jan.	6, 1852	May	4, 1852	119
77	Jan.	4, 1853	April	19, 1853	106
78	Jan.	3, 1854	May	9, 1854	127
79	Jan.	2, 1855	May	8, 1855	127
80	Jan.	1, 1856	April	22, 1856	112
81	Jan.	6, 1857	May	22, 1857	137
	¹Oct.	6, 1857	Oct.	13, 1857	8
82	Jan.	5, 1858	April	22, 1858	108
83	Jan.	4, 1859	April	14, 1859	101
84	Jan.	3, 1860	April	3, 1860	91
85	Jan.	1, 1861	April	18, 1861	108
	¹April	30, 1861	May	16, 1861	17
86	Jan.	7, 1862	April	11, 1862	95
87	Jan.	6, 1863	April	15, 1863	100
88	Jan.	5, 1864	April	25, 1864	111
	¹Aug.	9, 1864	Aug.	25, 1864	17
89	Jan.	3, 1865	Mar.	24, 1865	81
90	Jan.	2, 1866	April	12, 1866	101
91	Jan.	1, 1867	April	11, 1867	101
92	Jan.	7, 1868	April	14, 1868	98
93	Jan.	5, 1869	April	16, 1869	102
94	Jan.	4, 1870	April	7, 1870	94
95	Jan.	3, 1871	May	27, 1871	145
96	Jan.	2, 1872	April	4, 1872	93
97	Jan.	7, 1873	April	10, 1873	94
98	Jan.	6, 1874	May	15, 1874	130

CONSTITUTION OF 1874

No.	From		To		Days
99	Jan.	5, 1875	Mar.	18, 1875	73
100	Jan.	4, 1876	May	5, 1876	122
101	Jan.	2, 1877	Mar.	23, 1877	81
102	Jan.	1, 1878	May	24, 1878	144
103	Jan.	7, 1879	June	6, 1879	151
104	Jan.	4, 1881	June	9, 1881	157
105	Jan.	2, 1883	June	6, 1883	156
	¹June	7, 1883	Dec.	6, 1883	183
106	Jan.	6, 1885	June	12, 1885	158
107	Jan.	4, 1887	May	19, 1887	136
108	Jan.	1, 1889	May	9, 1889	129
109	Jan.	6, 1891	May	28, 1891	143
	²Oct.	13, 1891	Nov.	11, 1891	30
110	Jan.	3, 1893	June	1, 1893	150
111	Jan.	1, 1895	June	8, 1895	159
112	Jan.	5, 1897	July	1, 1897	178
113	Jan.	3, 1899	April	20, 1899	108
114	Jan.	1, 1901	June	27, 1901	178
115	Jan.	6, 1903	April	16, 1903	101

No.	From		To		Days
116	Jan.	3, 1905			
	¹Jan.	15, 1906	Feb.	15, 1906	32
117	Jan.	1, 1907	May	16, 1907	136
118	Jan.	5, 1909	April	15, 1909	101
119	Jan.	3, 1911	May	25, 1911	143
120	Jan.	7, 1913	June	27, 1913	172
121	Jan.	5, 1915	May	20, 1915	136
122	Jan.	2, 1917	June	28, 1917	178
123	Jan.	7, 1919	June	26, 1919	171
124	Jan.	4, 1921	April	28, 1921	115
125	Jan.	2, 1923	June	14, 1923	164
126	Jan.	6, 1925	April	16, 1925	101
	¹Jan.	13, 1926	Feb.	18, 1926	37
127	Jan.	4, 1927	April	14, 1927	101
128	Jan.	1, 1929	April	18, 1929	108
129	Jan.	6, 1931	May	28, 1931	143
	¹Nov.	9, 1931	Dec.	30, 1931	52
	¹June	27, 1932	Aug.	19, 1932	54
130	Jan.	3, 1933	May	5, 1933	123
	¹Nov.	13, 1933	Dec.	21, 1933	39
	¹Sept.	12, 1934	Sept.	20, 1934	9
131	Jan.	1, 1935	June	21, 1935	172
	¹May	4, 1936	Aug.	6, 1936	95
	¹Dec.	1, 1936	Dec.	5, 1936	5
132	Jan.	5, 1937	June	5, 1937	152
	¹July	25, 1938	Nov.	30, 1938	149
133	Jan.	3, 1939	May	29, 1939	147
	¹May	6, 1940	May	16, 1940	11
134	Jan.	7, 1941	July	15, 1941	196
	¹Feb.	17, 1942	April	10, 1942	53
135	Jan.	5, 1943	May	8, 1943	124
	¹May	1, 1944	May	5, 1944	5
136	Jan.	2, 1945	May	7, 1945	126
137	Jan.	6, 1947	June	16, 1947	162

Beginning with the 138th Session, the number of Legislative Days are listed, rather than calendar days.

No.	From		To		Days
138	Jan.	4, 1949	April	28, 1949	54
139	Jan.	2, 1951	Dec.	22, 1951	109(S) 99(HR)
140	Jan.	6, 1953	July	27, 1953	66(S) 72(HR)
141	Jan.	3, 1955	May	22, 1956	159(S) 168(HR)
142	Jan.	1, 1957	June	20, 1957	65(S) 71(HR)
143	Jan.	6, 1959	Jan.	5, 1960	114(S) 120(HR)
144	*Jan.	5, 1960	Nov.	14, 1960	16(S) 15(HR)
145	Jan.	3, 1961	Sept.	1, 1961	83(S) 89(HR)
146	Jan.	2, 1962	Feb.	28, 1962	17(S) 15(HR)
	¹Jan.	22, 1962	Jan.	29, 1962	4(S) 3(HR)

No.	From	To	Days
147	Jan. 1, 1963	Aug. 1, 1963	74(S) 78(HR)
148	Jan. 7, 1964	June 16, 1964	34(S) 30(HR)
	¹Feb. 11, 1964	June 16, 1964	25(S) 24(HR)
149	Jan. 5, 1965	Jan. 4, 1966	115(S) 112(HR)
150	Jan. 4, 1966	Nov. 15, 1966	58(S) 52(HR)
	¹Feb. 28, 1966	Nov. 15, 1966	47(S) 46(HR)
	¹Mar. 2, 1966	Mar. 8, 1966	5(S) 5(HR)
	¹April 18, 1966	Nov. 15, 1966	37(S) 40(HR)
151	Jan. 2, 1967	Dec. 21, 1967	103(S) 101(HR)
152	Jan. 1, 1968	Nov. 22, 1968	61(S) 54(HR)

CONSTITUTION OF 1968-69

No.	From	To	Days
153	Jan. 7, 1969	Dec. 31, 1969	98(S) 91(HR)
154	Jan. 6, 1970	Nov. 19, 1970	57(S) 57(HR)
155	Jan. 5, 1971	Dec. 28, 1971	108(S) 102(HR)
156	Jan. 4, 1972	Nov. 30, 1972	78(S) 78(HR)
	Aug. 14, 1972	Nov. 30, 1972	27(S) 25(HR)
	Aug. 14, 1972	Nov. 30, 1972	25(S) 25(HR)

No.	From	To	Days
157	Jan. 2, 1973	Jan. 1, 1974	87(S) 93(HR)
158	Jan. 1, 1974	Nov. 30, 1974	70(S) 77(HR)
159	Jan. 7, 1975	Jan. 6, 1976	71(S) 92(HR)
160	Jan. 6, 1976	Nov. 17, 1976	54(S) 69(HR)
161	Jan. 4, 1977	Jan. 3, 1978	94(S) 115(HR)
162	Jan. 3, 1978	Nov. 30, 1978	55(S) 51(HR)
163	Jan. 2, 1979	Jan. 1, 1980	
	Jan. 2, 1979	Dec. 12, 1979	71(S) 89(HR)
164	Jan. 1, 1980	Nov. 19, 1980	65(S) 70(HR)
165	Jan. 6, 1981	Jan. 5, 1982	
	Jan. 6, 1981	Dec. 16, 1981	75(S) 81(HR)
166	Jan. 5, 1982	Nov. 30, 1982	59(S) 64(HR)
167	Jan. 4, 1983	Jan. 3, 1984	93(S) 99(HR)
168	Jan. 3, 1984	Nov. 30, 1984	65(S) 70(HR)
169	Jan. 1, 1985	Jan. 7, 1986	79(S) 80(HR)
		Dec. 12, 1985	
170	Jan. 7, 1986	Nov. 26, 1986	64(S) 72(HR)
171	Jan. 6, 1987		

¹Extra or special session.
²Extra session of Senate.
*First annual session.

EXECUTIVE

SECTION 4 — EXECUTIVE

EXECUTIVE BRANCH

The Executive branch of state government is responsible for administering the laws of the Commonwealth. Along with the Judiciary and the Legislature, it is one of the three branches of state government as defined in the Constitution.

Organization:

Article IV of the Constitution establishes the "Executive Department" and its composition, and grants power to the Legislature to approve "such other officers as the General Assembly may from time to time prescribe." Other laws and statutes — particularly the Administrative Code of 1929 — more specifically delineate the organization and responsibilities of the Executive branch.

The Executive branch consists of the Governor, Lieutenant Governor, Attorney General, Auditor General, Treasurer, and numerous departments, agencies, boards and commissions. As head of the Executive branch, the Governor is the chief executive officer of the Commonwealth. All executive or administrative agencies are under his jurisdiction, except for such elected officers as the Attorney General, Auditor General and Treasurer.

There are several executive departments, each headed by an official — usually called a Secretary — who is appointed by the Governor and confirmed by the Senate, and who sits as a member of the Cabinet. Some agencies have advisory boards or commissions, many of whose members are also appointed by the Governor. Other executive boards and commissions are independent agencies. Although their members may also be appointed by the Governor, with or without Senate confirmation, the Governor has only limited responsibility over them.

In addition, there are several other agencies which do not fall within the Governor's jurisdiction. These include several public corporations, such as the General State Authority and the State Highway and Bridge Authority, on whose boards the Governor sits by law.

Administrative Code of 1929:

The Administrative Code of 1929 — which has been frequently updated — defines the organization, powers and duties of the Executive branch, including the creation and organization of divisions and bureaus within individual agencies; the appointment, employment and compensation of the Commonwealth's officers and employees; the issuance of rules and regulations; and the financial, budgetary and purchasing responsibilities of various agencies.

The Code is supplemented by laws passed by the General Assembly. Such state agencies as the Pennsylvania Turnpike and the Civil Service Commission, the Milk Marketing Board and the Liquor Control Board were established by statutes not included in the Administrative Code.

Executive Board:

The Executive Board is established by Section 204 of the Administrative Code of 1929 and is empowered to establish uniform standards and regulations within the Executive branch. It sets standard qualifications for employment, job classification and compensation; approves the establishment of divisions and bureaus within administrative departments; authorizes bonding of state officials; and sets other personnel regulations such as the hours and days for official business.

The Governor is chairman of the Executive Board and he appoints the heads of six administrative departments to fill the other positions.

Salaries:

The salaries of the Governor, Lieutenant Governor, Attorney General, Auditor General, State Treasurer, heads of departments and members of some commissions and boards are set by law. Legislation effective July 3, 1987, set new salaries for persons assuming certain offices after that date. Where applicable, the salary for the incumbent's successor is indicated in parentheses.

Offices are listed in order of their creation.

Governor	$85,000	($105,000)
Lieutenant Governor	67,500	(83,000)
Secretary of the Commonwealth	58,000	(72,000)
Attorney General	65,000	(84,000)
Auditor General	58,000	(84,000)
State Treasurer	58,000	(84,000)
Secretary of Education	65,000	(80,000)
Adjutant General	58,000	(72,000)
Insurance Commissioner	58,000	(72,000)
Secretary of Banking	58,000	(72,000)
Secretary of Agriculture	58,000	(72,000)
Secretary of General Services	61,500	(76,000)
Secretary of Environmental Resources	65,000	(80,000)
Secretary of Transportation	65,000	(80,000)
Secretary of Health	65,500	(80,000)
State Police Commissioner	61,500	(76,000)
Secretary of Labor and Industry	65,000	(80,000)
Secretary of Public Welfare	65,000	(80,000)
Secretary of Revenue	61,500	(76,000)
Secretary of Commerce	61,500	(76,000)
Secretary of Community Affairs	58,000	(72,000)
Secretary of Aging	61,500	(76,000)
Corrections Commissioner	61,500	

Neither the Governor, Lieutenant Governor nor the head of any administrative department can receive any additional compensation for any services rendered to the Commonwealth in any capacity.

Salaries of members of the following boards and commissions are set by statute:

Chairman, Public Utility Commission	$42,500
Four members, each	40,000
Chairman, Board of Probation and Parole	30,000
Four members, each	27,500
Chairman, Milk Marketing Board	13,000
Two members, each	12,500
Chairman, Liquor Control Board	25,000
Two members, each	24,000
Chairman, Pennsylvania Turnpike Commission	17,000
Three members, each	15,000

Chairman, State Tax Equalization Board	14,000
Two members, each	13,000
Chairman, Pennsylvania Labor Relations Board	12,000
Two members, each	11,000
Chairman, Pennsylvania Securities Commission	13,000
Two members, each	12,000
To the members of the Board of Pardons, other than the Lieutenant Governor and the Attorney General	7,500

Members of many independent boards and commissions, as well as members of departmental advisory boards, do not receive an annual salary, although they are reimbursed for expenses or may receive a per diem compensation. For members of boards and commissions who do not receive reimbursement by law, the Executive Board establishes compensation.

ELECTED OFFICES

ROBERT P. CASEY GOVERNOR

Robert Patrick Casey was elected Governor of Pennsylvania in 1986. His campaign platform and his first months in office have focused on three areas vital to the state's future: economic development, education, and the environment. In each, he has quickly established his mark as a Governor not content to conduct business as usual.

He recruited a cabinet widely acclaimed as one of the most diverse, able and accomplished in Pennsylvania history.

He placed a new emphasis on tough environmental enforcement and pumped new resources into the long-delayed effort to clean up toxic waste.

He issued a challenge to teachers and students alike to be great, and proposed an unprecedented increase in educational funding in order to achieve that goal.

Most importantly, he established the Pennsylvania Economic Development Partnership to create jobs for Pennsylvania workers and opportunity for Pennsylvania businesses. The Partnership for the first time brings the energy, expertise and entrepreneurial spirit of the private sector into the state's economic development effort. The result is a fresh, interdepartmental and strategic approach to fostering economic growth in the Commonwealth. It is the prime example of what Governor Casey calls, "the new Pennsylvania Partnership."

"A partnership," Casey says, "which recognizes that the policies of the past can't build Pennsylvania's future. A partnership which brings a concern for people to the task of rebuilding the economy and a business-like efficiency to helping our citizens to help themselves. A partnership which sees that Pennsylvania works when Pennsylvanians work together."

Robert P. Casey was born on January 9, 1932, in Jackson Heights, N.Y., where his father Alphonsus was practicing law after graduating from Fordham University Law School. He was raised by Alphonsus and Marie Casey in Scranton, where he was senior class president and valedictorian, class of 1949, at the Scranton Preparatory School.

An accomplished athlete, Casey was named to the Scranton Times' 1949 All-Regional Basketball Team. He attended Holy Cross College in Worcester, Massachusetts on an athletic scholarship. He played on nationally-ranked Holy Cross basketball teams during the era of Bob Cousey and Tom Heinsohn.

After earning his bachelor of arts degree in English, *cum laude,* in 1953, Casey attended the George Washington University Law School on a scholarship awarded by the university's trustees. A member of the Order of the Coif and research editor of the law review, he received his J.D. in 1956.

After graduation, Casey worked as an associate with the prestigious Washington, D.C. firm of Covington & Burling. Two years later, he returned to Scranton to begin his own law practice.

In 1962, Casey won election to represent Lackawanna County in the Pennsylvania State Senate. Senator Casey distinguished himself by authoring landmark environmental legislation.

Casey was also elected to serve as a delegate to the 1967 Pennsylvania State Constitutional Convention. He was chosen by his fellow delegates to serve as First Vice President of the convention and played a leading role in the writing and ratification of the Commonwealth's current constitution.

A year later, Casey won election to the first of two consecutive terms as Pennsylvania's Auditor General. From 1969 until 1977 he revolutionized the office of the Auditor General, turning it into a model of professionalism and corruption-fighting efficiency. According to one commentator, he took a backwater agency long known as a haven for patronage and turned it into "a rushing current of reform."

In 1978 he joined the law firm of Dilworth, Paxson, Kalish & Kauffman, where he later became a senior partner. For ten years leading up to his election as Governor, he remained active in Scranton civic affairs, as well as state and national politics. He unsuccessfully sought the Democratic nomination for Governor in 1978, as he had in 1966 and 1970. His community activities include service as a trustee of Scranton's Mercy Hospital and Marywood College.

He is the recipient of numerous awards, among them: Honorary Doctor of Law degrees from St. Francis College, the University of Scranton and College Misericordia; Philadelphia Emerald Society Man of the Year; the Distinguished Service Award from the Federal Government Accountants Association; and Distinguished Pennsylvanian from the William Penn Society of Gannon University.

In 1953, Casey was married to Ellen Theresa Harding, a Scranton native and graduate of Marywood College. The Caseys have eight children: Margi Casey McGrath, Mary Ellen Casey Philbin, Kate Casey Brier, Robert Jr., Christopher, Erin, Patrick, and Matthew; and five grandchildren.

OFFICE OF THE GOVERNOR
225 Main Capitol
Harrisburg, PA 17120

EXECUTIVE OFFICE

WILLIAM KEISLING　　　　　　**Executive Assistant to the Governor**
Chief of Staff

William Keisling was born May 14, 1936, in Scranton; grad., Univ. of Scranton (B.A., pol. sci.) 1957; newspaper reporter and editor, 1957-60; asst. to Congressman and Governor William W. Scranton, 1960-65; consultant, public relations, advertising, and public affairs, 1965-68; exec. dir., Greater Harrisburg Movement, 1968-74; exec. vice pres., chief exec. officer, Harristown Development Corp., 1974-87; appointed Executive Assistant to the Governor and Chief of Staff, Jan. 20, 1987; resides in Camp Hill.

JAMES W. BROWN　　　　　　**Executive Secretary to the Governor**

James W. Brown was born Oct. 2, 1951, in Scranton, the son of Paul M. (dec.) and Genevieve Reedy Brown; grad., Scranton Preparatory Schl.; Villanova Univ. (B.A., magna cum laude) 1973; Univ. of Virginia Law Schl. (J.D.) 1976; editor, *Virginia Journal of International Law;* counsel (1977-81), staff dir. and counsel (1981-82), Subcommittee on General Oversight and Renegotiation, Committee on Banking, Finance and Urban Affairs, U.S. House of Representatives, Washington, D.C.; attorney, Dilworth, Paxson, Kalish & Kauffman, Scranton, 1982-87; counsel, The Real Bob Casey Committee, 1985-86; mem., Pa. and Dist. of Columbia Bars; author of several articles on politics and government; appointed Secretary of General Services, Jan. 20, 1987, and Executive Secretary to the Governor on Dec. 1, 1987; married Lynne Liquori; 1 child, James Patrick; resides in Camp Hill.

WALTER W. GIESEY　　　　　　**Deputy Chief of Staff for Programs**

Walter W. Giesey was born March 20, 1924, in Utica, NY, the son of Wilfrid M. and Genevieve Turner; grad., Mars H.S.; attd., Univ. of Pgh.; U.S. Army Air Force, 1942-45; editor/public relations, 1945-50; exec. sec. to Mayor of Pgh., 1950-59; exec. sec. to Governor of Pa., 1959-63; sec. of admin., 1959; staff dir., President's Com. on Equal Opportunity in Housing, 1963-68; exec. asst. to chmn., Dem. Natl. Com., 1968; consultant, Ford Foundation, 1968-69; public affairs consultant, 1969-87; appointed Senior Special Assistant to the Governor, Feb. 16, 1987, and Deputy Chief of Staff for Programs on Dec. 1, 1987; resides in Harrisburg.

DAVID M. STONE　　　　　　**Deputy Chief of Staff for Communications**

David M. Stone was born April 13, 1958, in New York City, the son of James (dec.) and Elaine Stone; grad., Fieldston Schl.; Princeton Univ. (A.B., history, summa cum laude) 1980; Harvard Law Schl. (J.D.) 1985; mem., Pa. and Dist. of Columbia Bar Assns.; researcher, "The MacNeil/Lehrer Report," 1979-80; TV producer, Independent Network News, "From the Editor's Desk," 1981-82; law clerk, *The New York Times,* 1984; atty., Drinker, Biddle & Reath, Phila., 1985-86; author, *Nixon and the Politics of Public Television,* (Garland, 1985); appointed Special Assistant to the Governor, Jan. 20, 1987, and Deputy Chief of Staff for Communications on Dec. 1, 1987; married Wendy Horwitz; resides in Loganville.

JOHN T. TIGHE, III   Deputy Chief of Staff for Operations and Administration

John T. Tighe, III, was born April 16, 1955, in Scranton, the son of John T., Jr. and Wanda Jean Stephens Tighe; grad., Dunmore Jr./Sr. H.S.; Univ. of Pgh. (B.S., pharmacy) 1978; Villanova Univ. (M.B.A.) 1986; post-grad. work at George Washington Univ. (bus., econ., and public policy); staff mem., 1980 White House Conf. on Small Business, 1980; asst. to exec. v. pres., Natl. Assn. of Retail Druggists, 1981-84; asst. dir., Parenteral Drug Assn., 1984-87; exec. dir., 1987 Inaugural Com., Inc., 1987; appointed Secretary of Administration, Jan. 20, 1987, and Deputy Chief of Staff for Operations and Administration, Dec. 1, 1987; married Mary Grace Cukas; resides in Merion.

DAVID J. BAKO   Administrative Assistant
to the Governor

David J. Bako was born Feb. 26, 1952, in Johnstown, the son of Victor B. and Mary Agnes Kacur Bako; grad., Bishop McCort H.S., Johnstown, 1970; Univ. of Pgh. (B.A., economics) 1974; post-grad. work in public admin., Shippensburg Univ.; project coordinator, Treasury Dept., 1977; bank relations officer, Treasury Dept., 1978-79; manager, Cash Management Group, Treasury Dept., 1980-81; pres., Young Democratic Clubs of Pa., 1982; financial officer, Sen. Dem. Com. on Appropriations, 1981-84; exec. asst., Sen. H. Craig Lewis (6th Dist.) 1984-87; mem., Am. Management Assn.; Am. Soc. for Public Admin.; Eastern States' Legislative Fiscal Officers' Assn.; appointed Administrative Assistant to the Governor, Jan. 20, 1987; resides in Johnstown.

HELEN DICKERSON WISE   Secretary to the Cabinet

Helen Dickerson Wise was born Sept. 11, 1928, in Sussex, NJ, the daughter of Russell B. and Josephine Miles Dickerson; grad., State Coll., 1945; Pa. State Univ. (B.A.) 1949, (M.Ed.) 1952, (D.Ed.) 1968; junior high schl. teacher, 1949-76; mem., Pa. House of Rep., 1976-78; pres., PSEA, 1969; pres., NEA, 1973; exec. dir., Delaware St. Educ. Assn., 1979-86; mem., Penn St. Bd. of Trustees, 1969-pres.; Alumni Fellow, Penn State, 1987; appointed Secretary for Legislative Affairs, Jan. 20, 1987, and Secretary to the Cabinet, Dec. 1, 1987; married Howard E. Wise; 3 sons: Dan, David, Dirk; 5 grandchildren; resides in Spring Mills.

CHARLES BACAS   Secretary for Public Liaison

Charles Bacas was born Dec. 7, 1939, in Weymouth, MA, the son of Andrew and Theadora Bacas; grad., Brockton H.S.; attd. Boston Univ., Univ. of Mass.; former chmn., York Redevelopment Auth.; reporter/editor, York Gazette and Daily; writer/director, Documentary Film, PEACE Corp, 1970-71; exec. asst. to sec., 1964-68, dep. sec., Community Affairs, 1973-78; chief of staff, House Majority Leader, 1978-87; honor roll — Best Short Stories of 1965; appointed Secretary for Policy and Planning, Feb. 24, 1987, and Secretary for Public Liaison, Dec. 1, 1987; married Mary Anne Blais; 2 sons: Christopher E. and Alexander K.; resides in York.

VINCENT P. CAROCCI   Secretary for Government Operations

Vincent P. Carocci was born Dec. 5, 1936, in Scranton, the son of Roy (dec.) and Sophie Carocci; grad., Scranton Central Schl.; Pennsylvania State University (B.A. journalism) 1958; Capital Correspondent, Associated Press, 1961-1968; Philadelphia Inquirer, 1970-71; senior staff, Senate of Pennsylvania, 1971-84; Dir. of Government Relations, State System of Higher Education, 1985-86; appointed Deputy Secretary, Legislative Affairs, Feb. 16, 1987, and Secretary for Government Operations, Dec. 1, 1987; married Antoinette Winseck of Erie; 4 children: Patricia, Thomas, David, Stephen; resides in Hampden Township.

JAMES R. LLOYD, JR.   Special Assistant to the Governor

James R. Lloyd, Jr., was born Jan. 27, 1950, in Phila., the son of James R., Sr., and Margaret Mary Lloyd; grad., Father Judge H.S., 1967; St. Joseph's Univ. (A.B., English) 1971; grad. work in English, Villanova Univ., 1971-72; twice elected to Senate of Pa., first in a special election in March 1979 and reelected to a full four-year term in Nov. 1980; Dem. nominee for Lt. Gov. in 1982; co-author of Pace Prescription Drug Plan for Pa.'s elderly; appointed Special Assistant to the Governor, Aug. 25, 1987; married Victoria Regina Dombrowski; 2 children: James R., III, and John P.; resides in Philadelphia.

HENRY JOSEPH SALLUSTI   Special Assistant to the Governor

Henry Joseph Sallusti was born Dec. 1, 1956, in Scranton, the son of Henry C. and Pauline M. Sallusti; grad., Scranton Preparatory Schl.; Univ. of Scranton (B.S., bus. admin.) 1978; owner, Imperial Baking Co., 1979-85; investment banking, Butcher & Singer, 1985-87; appointed Special Assistant to the Governor, Jan. 20, 1987; married Margaret Elizabeth Jordan; resides in Dunmore.

BRIAN P. WALSH   Special Assistant to the Governor

Brian P. Walsh was born June 11, 1963, in Scranton, the son of Richard M. and Jean M. Walsh; grad., Scranton Central H.S.; Ithaca Coll. (B.S., communications) 1985; public relations specialist, Greater Scranton Chamber of Commerce, 1985-86; assistant producer, WVIA-TV Channel 44, Pittston, 1985-86; appointed Special Assistant to the Governor, Jan. 20, 1987; resides in Harrisburg.

DANIEL B. WOFFORD   Special Assistant to the Governor

Daniel B. Wofford was born June 25, 1955, in Washington, D.C., the son of Harris L. and Clare Lindgren Wofford; grad., Harriton H.S., Rosemont, 1973; Yale Univ. (B.A.) 1977; Georgetown Univ. Law Center (J.D.) 1983; atty., Ballard, Spahr, Andrews & Ingersoll, Phila., 1983-86; legis. aide to Cong. Peter H. Kostmayer, 1978-80; Gov.-elect Casey's Transition Staff, 1986-87; mem., Pa. and Dist. of Columbia Bars; appointed Special Assistant to the Governor, Jan. 21, 1987; married Sarah E. Peck; resides in Philadelphia.

G. BONITA SEAMAN   Personal Secretary to the Governor

G. Bonita Seaman was born Jan. 5, 1952, in Rebuck, the daughter of Lester L. and Alma L. Straub Geist; grad., Line Mountain H.S.; Indiana Univ. of Pa. (B.S.Ed., summa cum laude) 1980; teacher, Anne Arundel Schl. Dist., Annapolis, MD, 1980-81; admin. asst., Pa. AAA Federation, 1981-84; sec. to chief counsel, Senate Democratic Caucus, 1984-86; appointed Personal Secretary to the Governor, January 1987; married Thomas F. Seaman; resides in Lewisberry.

The Constitution of the Commonwealth of Pennsylvania provides that "the supreme executive power shall be vested in the Governor, who shall take care that the laws be faithfully executed." In addition to serving as chief officer of the executive branch of state government, the Governor is Commander-in-Chief of the Military Forces of the Commonwealth, except when they are called into the actual service of the United States.

To be eligible for election as Governor, a person must be at least 30 years old, a citizen of the United States, and a resident of the Commonwealth for a minimum of seven years before the election, unless he or she has been absent on the public business of the state or the nation.

The Governor holds office for a four-year term beginning on the third Tuesday of January following the gubernatorial election and is eligible to serve one additional four-year term.

Among the Governor's numerous duties are the following:

Appointments. With the consent of a two-thirds majority of the Pennsylvania Senate, the Governor appoints the secretaries of departments and heads of other cabinet-level agencies. The Governor also appoints members of state boards, commissions, and councils. Under the Administrative Code, some of these appointments are subject to Senate approval, mostly by a simple majority. The Governor also appoints justices of the peace, which a majority of the Senate must confirm, and he appoints other judicial officers, which two-thirds of the Senate must confirm.

The Senate has 25 legislative days to act upon nominations. Should the Senate fail to act upon a nomination within the required time, the nominee takes office as if the appointment has gained the Senate's consent.

In a similar manner, the Governor fills vacancies in the offices of the Auditor General, the State Treasurer, the Attorney General, justices of the peace and other offices. In the case of a vacancy in an elective office, a special election is held the next appropriate election day, unless the first day of the vacancy is within two calendar months before election day. In this case, the election is held on the second succeeding election day appropriate to the office.

Budget. The Governor must annually present to the General Assembly a balanced operating budget and a capital budget for the ensuing fiscal year, as well as a financial plan for not less than the next five succeeding fiscal years.

The General Assembly must initiate and pass a budget bill. If the estimated revenues and available surplus are less than the proposed expenditures, the Governor can disapprove of any individual item in the budget bill or recommend additional revenue sources. The General Assembly may override a Governor's veto and repass the vetoed items by a two-thirds vote. The Legislature also must initiate any measure to provide additional revenue.

Executive Department Management. The Governor approves the appointment and compensation of all deputies and employees in administrative departments and boards and commissions, as well as his own staff. Through his chairmanship of the Executive Board, as well as administrative and policy statements contained in Executive Orders or by Management and other Directives, the Governor establishes policies and practices for all employees and agencies under his jurisdiction. The Governor also issues emergency and other proclamations.

He may require information in writing from Executive Department officers, as well as request the head of any department, board or commission to submit for his approval estimates of the amount of money required for each activity or function to be carried on during any period of time. If the Governor does not approve the estimate, it must be revised in accordance with his wishes and resubmitted for approval. Should any agency not submit an estimate after it was requested, the Governor may notify the Treasurer not to draw any warrant in favor of the department until the Govenor has received and approved the estimate.

The Governor approves or disapproves of all investments by departments, boards or commissions. In addition, he appoints and determines the compensation for a comptroller and the comptroller's staff in each administrative department and independent board and commission.

With the consultation of the Auditor General, the Governor can require the installation of a uniform system or systems of bookkeeping, accounting and financial reports for administrative agencies.

Legislation. The Governor delivers messages to the General Assembly and suggests measures that the legislature may want to introduce in bill form.

On extraordinary occasions, the Governor may convene the General Assembly when it is not in session. In the case of disagreement between the Senate and the House with respect to adjournment, he can adjourn them at any time not exceeding four months. He may convene the Senate, as well, in extraordinary session by proclamation for the transaction of executive business.

Any bills and concurrent resolutions passed by the General Assembly except for adjournment must be submitted to the Governor for approval. If any bill is not returned by the Governor within 10 days after it has been submitted, it becomes law. If the General Assembly prevents the bill's return due to its adjournment, the bill becomes law, unless the Governor files it with his objections in the office of the Secretary of the Commonwealth and gives public notice of his actions within 30 days after the adjournment. If the Governor returns the bill, vetoing the measure, the General Assembly needs a two-thirds majority to override the veto.

Military. The Governor is the Commander-in-Chief of the Commonwealth's military forces, except when they are called into the service of the United States. He may order for service as many of the Militia as are needed in the case of war or invasion, or to prevent invasion, suppress riots, or aid civil officials in the execution of the laws of the Commonwealth.

Other Powers and Duties. The Governor can remit fines and forfeitures and grant reprieves. If the Board of Pardons has first held a public hearing and made a recommendation, the Governor can also commute sentences and pardon persons, except in cases of impeachment. He may demand fugitives from states or territories, as well as issue warrants for the arrest of persons in Pennsylvania upon the request of other Governors.

The Governor serves as an *ex officio* member of many state boards and commissions, several state colleges and universities and other state-related institutions, as well as a number of private institutions. He can appoint accountants to audit the Auditor General and his office, he approves applications for letters patent of corporations for profit, and he can grant commissions to pilots for aeronautical work.

The Governor certifies elections for Presidential Electors in the Electoral College and provides Congressional election returns to U.S. officials. He also issues commissions to persons for Judge of the Supreme Court or Superior Court and for every court of record.

OFFICE OF THE GOVERNOR
EXECUTIVE OFFICE STAFF

PATRICK BOLES
Deputy Administrative Assistant to the Governor
SONDRA MYERS
Cultural Advisor to the Governor
ELIZABETH MILDER BEH
Advisor to the Governor on Child Care Policy

JEANNE H. SCHMEDLEN
Press Secretary and Executive Assistant to Ellen Casey
ANN F. McCANN
Personnel/Fiscal Officer

Bessie F. Brenizer	Barbara J. Husic
Mary T. Cray	Norma P. Kirkpatrick
Andrea Faber	Dolores T. Lynch
Nancy C. Fink	John P. O'Boyle
Vicki Flohr	Clara E. Sienkiewicz
Terri Jo Foust	Lucinda H. Smyser
Sally A. Hitz	Patricia Stringer
Marilyn B. Howard	

EXECUTIVE SECRETARIAT

Karen L. Bailey	Frana A. Kane
Charlotte M. Cobb	Terry L. Moroz
Deborah J. Cox	Christa K. Scheidegger
Martin Goldwasser	Kelley L. Spotz
Earl C. Horner	Charles H. Troutman
Andrea M. Kalinchak	Donald Yohe

OFFICE OF ADMINISTRATION

JOSEPH L. ZAZYCZNY
Secretary of Administration

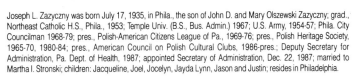

Joseph L. Zazyczny was born July 17, 1935, in Phila., the son of John D. and Mary Olszewski Zazyczny; grad., Northeast Catholic H.S., Phila., 1953; Temple Univ. (B.S., Bus. Admin.) 1967; U.S. Army, 1954-57; Phila. City Councilman 1968-79; pres., Polish-American Citizens League of Pa., 1969-76; pres., Polish Heritage Society, 1965-70, 1980-84; pres., American Council on Polish Cultural Clubs, 1986-pres.; Deputy Secretary for Administration, Pa. Dept. of Health, 1987; appointed Secretary of Administration, Dec. 22, 1987; married to Martha I. Stronski; children: Jacqueline, Joel, Jocelyn, Jayda Lynn, Jason and Justin; resides in Philadelphia.

The Office of Administration was established within the Governor's Office in 1955. Its purpose is to serve as staff support to the Governor in providing policy direction and administrative support to all agencies under the Governor's jurisdiction. In January of 1979, it was combined with the Office of Budget. Effective January 18, 1983, the Office of Budget and Administration was again divided into separate offices. The Office of Administration is managed by the Secretary of Administration. There are three basic operational areas — computer operations, employee relations, and management consulting services — which are divided into the following management subunits:

Bureau of Affirmative Action encourages and promotes Commonwealth-wide programs directed at ending discrimination against protected groups in all state agencies under the Governor's jurisdiction. This bureau develops programs to involve these individuals at all levels of employment.

Division of State Employment is responsible for establishing policies and procedures for the selection and appointment of candidates to Non-Civil Service positions. The division receives and evaluates applications and refers qualified applicants to agencies for consideration for vacant positions in accordance with established procedures and EEOC guidelines.

Bureau of Labor Relations plans and directs all labor relations activities for the Commonwealth as employer under the Public Employe Relations Act of 1970 and the Policemen's and Firemen's Collective Bargaining Act of 1968. The bureau negotiates collective bargaining agreements with state employe unions and provides direction and assistance to state agencies in the administration and interpretation of such agreements.

Bureau of Personnel has responsibility for all of the personnel policy and programs that are designed to support the Governor's management objectives. The bureau reviews personnel policy and recommends necessary legislative or executive action to improve the personnel operation. It gives direction to the agencies in the application of human, management and employe relations. It provides development programs for top executives, managers and supervisors. The bureau administers the job system, which includes the development of job classification standards and recommends statewide pay policies. In addition, the bureau is responsible for the administration of the Commonwealth's management benefits program.

Central Management Information Center provides systems analysis, computer programming and the computer operational support for Commonwealth-wide computer-based information, processing and reporting systems, including Payroll, Personnel, Central Accounting, and the new Integrated Central Systems Program. The center is also the Commonwealth's Computer Services center and provides Data Processing Resources to other agencies which either lack EDP capabilities within their own organization or require specialized services.

Bureau of EDP Policy and Planning provides for the development and implementation of a Commonwealth Master Plan for electronic data processing (EDP). The bureau develops, promulgates and evaluates statewide policies, procedures and standards for data processing. It provides technical assistance on EDP planning to the agencies. In addition, the bureau is responsible for the development of the Integrated Commonwealth Data Communications Network.

Integrated Central Systems (ICS) Project is responsible for the design, development, and implementation of the Commonwealth's on-line integrated administrative management system. This system will promote decentralization of operations and improved central controls, by making available to Commonwealth managers timely, accurate, compatible administrative information across functional lines.

Bureau of Management Services provides internal consulting services for the Secretary of Administration on management and administrative policy issues. The bureau conducts management improvement and organization studies designed to help solve single agency and inter-agency problems. It also manages the Executive Board and the Directives Management System.

SECRETARIES	Appointed Since 1950
James C. Charlesworth	Jan. 18, 1955
John H. Ferguson[1]	Sept. 14, 1956
Walter W. Giesey	Jan. 20, 1959
David H. Kurtzman	Sept. 29, 1959
John W. Ingram	Jan. 15, 1963
Arthur F. Sampson[1]	Jan. 17, 1967
David O. Maxwell[1]	June 2, 1969
Dominick J. Pastore[1]	Nov. 5, 1970
Ronald G. Lench (resigned Jan. 9, 1974)	Mar. 25, 1971
Frank S. Beal	Feb. 19, 1974
James N. Wade	Jan. 6, 1975
Robert C. Wilburn[1]	Jan. 16, 1979
Murray G. Dickman	Jan. 18, 1983
John T. Tighe, III	Jan. 20, 1987
*Joseph L. Zazyczny	Jan. 4, 1988

[1] *Secretary of Budget and Administration*

* *Incumbent*

OFFICE OF ADMINISTRATION

CHARLES T. SCIOTTO
  Deputy Secretary for Employee Relations
Polly Kirkpatrick
Lori J. Salinger

OFFICE OF THE BUDGET

MICHAEL H. HERSHOCK — Secretary of the Budget

Michael H. Hershock was born in Lancaster, the son of Anna L. (dec.) and Howard L. Hershock; grad., Springfield H.S., 1963; Pa. State Univ. (B.A., pol. sci.) 1967; Inst. of Public Admin., Pa. State Univ. (M.P.A.) 1969; Gov. Budget Office, 1968-69; exec. dir., House of Rep. Appropriations Com., 1971-86; taught graduate seminars in budgeting, legislative process, and program evaluation methodology for Penn State and Univ. of Pa.; guest lecturer for the Hubert Humphrey Fellowship at Penn State; appointed Secretary of the Budget, Jan. 20, 1987; married Joan Ann DiLucia; 3 children: Michael Duane, Chad David, Lara Gretchen; resides in Boiling Springs.

The Office of the Budget is authorized by the Administrative Code of 1929. It is under the direct supervision of the Secretary of the Budget, who reports to the Governor. The Budget Secretary has overall responsibility for preparation of the Governor's budget and its implementation after legislative enactment and also for maintenance of the Commonwealth's uniform accounting, payroll, and financial reporting systems. The Budget Secretary is responsible for evaluating special policy issues and providing other senior officials with information to change existing policy or formulate new policy.

The Office of the Budget is divided into two operational areas managed by the Deputy Secretary for Budget and by the Deputy Secretary for Comptroller Operations.

DEPUTY SECRETARY FOR BUDGET

The Deputy Secretary for Budget oversees the preparation and implementation of the Governor's budget each year, coordinates the capital budget, and maintains liaison between the Governor's Office and the several state authorities. The

Budget Office maintains a continuing evaluation of the progress and effectiveness of state programs in meeting program objectives.

Each year, it is the duty of the Budget Secretary to obtain and prepare information necessary for the preparation of a state budget. The Budget Office oversees this preparation of budget estimates for all institutions and agencies seeking state appropriations. These budget estimates are returned to the Budget Secretary who, at the direction of the Governor, may make further inquiries regarding the financial needs of any department, board, commission, institution or other agency. After each group is given an opportunity to be heard, the Governor may approve, disapprove or alter the budget estimates.

On or before January 1 of each year, the Budget Secretary is required to submit to the Governor in writing the information which will serve as the basis for the Governor's budget. Not later than the first full week in February of each year, except the year when a Governor has been elected to his first term of office, the Governor shall submit to the General Assembly the state budget, which includes the recommended amounts for all public purposes together with the established revenues and receipts from all sources and an estimated amount to be raised by taxation or otherwise. The Governor also must transmit with the state budget the various estimates of receipts with expenditures received by the Budget Secretary from officers in the executive, legislative and judicial branches.

The Deputy Secretary for Budget meets these responsibilities by directing an organization comprised of a Bureau of Administrative Services, Bureau of Budget Analysis, Bureau of Fiscal Policy Analysis, Bureau of Program Planning and Evaluation, Bureau of Legislative and Regulatory Analysis and Bureau of Revenue, Cash Flow and Debt.

DEPUTY SECRETARY FOR COMPTROLLER OPERATIONS

Comptroller Operations, headed by the Deputy Secretary for Comptroller Operations, provides assistance to the Secretary of the Budget in the development, implementation, maintenance, review, monitoring and control of uniform accounting, payroll, auditing, operating and financial reporting policies, procedures and systems to ensure accountability of funds and the efficiency, effectiveness and economy of financial operations throughout Commonwealth agencies under the Governor's jurisdiction.

The Deputy meets this responsibility by directing an organization comprised of a Bureau of Financial Management, Bureau of Audits, Bureau of Operations Review and seven Comptroller Offices. The bureaus provide central support and technical services to Comptrollers and, on occasion, to Commonwealth agencies. Comptrollers serve as chief financial accounting officers for the agencies to which they are assigned and are authorized to approve or disapprove agency financial transactions, contracts and payment requisitions on behalf of the Governor.

SECRETARIES	Appointed Since 1950	
Andrew M. Bradley	Jan.	18, 1955
John H. Ferguson[1]	July	18, 1957
David R. Baldwin	Jan.	20, 1959
Martin H. Brackbill	Jan.	15, 1963
Joseph J. McHugh	Sept.	15, 1966
Arthur F. Sampson[1]	Jan.	17, 1967
David O. Maxwell[1]	June	2, 1969
Dominick J. Pastore[1]	Nov.	5, 1970
Charles P. McIntosh	Jan.	19, 1971
Robert C. Wilburn[1]	Jan.	16, 1979
Robert A. Bittenbender	Jan.	18, 1983
*Michael H. Hershock	Jan.	20, 1987

Deputy Secretaries

Robert A. Bittenbender	May	10, 1979
William F. Schless	Feb.	9, 1981
*Harvey C. Eckert	Mar.	14, 1983
Kant Rao	Apr.	1, 1983
*Steven Rosskopf	Jan.	20, 1987
Karl R. Ross	Jan.	20, 1987
*Lori F. Fehr[2]	Jan.	20, 1987

[1] Also Secretary of Administration
[2] Director, Bureau of Budget Analysis

* Incumbent

OFFICE OF THE BUDGET

STEVEN ROSSKOPF
    Deputy Budget Secretary
HARVEY C. ECKERT
    Deputy Secretary for Comptroller Operations
LORI F. FEHR
    Director, Bureau of Budget Analysis
Carol A. Johnson
    Executive Assistant to Budget Secretary
Theresa M. Schiffhauer

OFFICE OF GENERAL COUNSEL

MOREY M. MYERS   General Counsel to the Governor

Morey M. Myers was born Aug. 5, 1927, in Scranton, the son of Samuel Z. (dec.) and Libby E. K. Myers; grad., Scranton Central H.S., 1945; Syracuse Univ. (A.B.) 1949; Yale Univ. Law Schl. (LL.B.) 1952; active practitioner in civil rights movement for over 20 years, including affiliation with Lawyers Com. for Equal Rights under Law and civil rights representation throughout Mississippi, Florida and other jurisdictions; visiting lecturer at Yale Univ. (1986), Hamilton Coll. (1982-84); Marywood Coll., Grad. Schl. of Social Work (1970-72); fellow, Am. Bar Foundation; chmn., mem., Hearing Com. 3.03 of the Disciplinary Bd. of the Supreme Ct. of Pa., 1978-84; consultant, President's Comm. on Campus Unrest, 1970; chief counsel, Milk Control Comm., 1963; asst. atty. gen., 1962-63; asst. solicitor, City of Scranton, 1955-60; bd. gov., Scranton Area Foundation, 1983-; bd. of trustees, Univ. of Scranton, 1985-; pres., Scranton-Lackawanna Jewish Fed., 1968-71; general chmn., Lackawanna United Fund, 1968; former mem., Natl. Cabinet, United Jewish Appeal; appointed General Counsel to the Governor, Jan. 20, 1987; married Sondra Gelb; 2 children: Jonathan and David; resides in Scranton.

CHRISTOPHER A. LEWIS

Executive Deputy General Counsel

Christopher A. Lewis was born Sept. 16, 1955, in Phila., the son of Charles E. and Florence Scott Lewis; grad., Harvard Coll. (B.A.) 1975; Univ. of Michigan Law Schl. (J.D.) 1978; lawyer; mem., Am. and Phila. Bar Assns.; Barristers' Assn. of Phila.; Sigma Pi Phi; Kappa Alpha Psi; Episcopalian; appointed Executive Deputy General Counsel, Jan. 21, 1987; married Sheilah Vance; resides in Philadelphia.

RICHARD D. SPIEGELMAN

**Chief Deputy General Counsel
for Agency Liaison**

Richard D. Spiegelman was born Oct. 12, 1948, in Phila., the son of Jay and Edith Bowman Spiegelman; grad., Williams Coll. (B.A.) 1970; Univ. of Pa. Law Schl. (J.D.) 1974; Univ. of Pa. Wharton Schl. (M.A.) 1976; lawyer; mem., Pa. Bar Assn.; Chief Deputy General Counsel for Agency Liaison; appointed Chief Deputy General Counsel, Jan. 21, 1987; married Kathi Bernhardt; 2 children: Alexander and Margaret; resides in Harrisburg.

In 1978, Pennsylvania voters approved a constitutional amendment that made the office of Attorney General an elected position, independent of the chief executive. In 1980, the General Assembly passed and the Governor signed into law the Commonwealth Attorneys Act. This Act set forth the duties of the elected Attorney General and created a new office of General Counsel, to be appointed by the Governor.

The Act seeks to distribute properly four important legal functions. The first is the interest in insuring that the Commonwealth has an independent and vigorous law enforcement effort. The second is the need of the Governor and other executive branch officials to be assured of ready access to legal counsel in the daily performance of their duties. The third is the interest in having an attorney with an independent perspective reviewing the numerous civil cases in which the Commonwealth is involved. The fourth is the right of the Governor and executive agency heads to obtain legal counsel when necessary to represent their interests, present their points of view and defend their programs in certain civil cases.

Under the Act, which took effect on January 21, 1981, the Attorney General has responsibility for enforcing the state's criminal laws and has primary responsibility for representing the state in civil court cases. The General Counsel serves as the legal advisor to the Governor and directs the legal activities of the executive branch. The act permits the General Counsel to intervene in civil litigation on behalf of the Governor and executive branch.

The Office of General Counsel is headed by the General Counsel who is appointed by the Governor and who serves as the chief legal advisor to the Governor. Additionally, the General Counsel is empowered to:

- Appoint deputy general counsel, as well as chief counsel and assistant counsel for the operation of each executive agency, and to supervise, coordinate and administer the legal services provided by the deputy general counsel and the chief counsel and assistant counsel for each executive agency.

- Render legal advice and representation prior to initiation of any action, as are required concerning every matter and issue arising in connection with the exercise and performance of the official powers and duties in the operation of executive agencies and, upon request, independent agencies.

- Upon request, assist and cooperate fully with the Attorney General and the counsel of each independent agency in the futherance of the performance of their duties.

- Initiate appropriate proceedings or defend the Commonwealth or any executive agency when an action or matter has been referred to the Attorney General and the Attorney General refuses or fails to initiate appropriate proceeding or defend the Commonwealth or executive agency.

- Represent the Governor or an executive agency if the Attorney General has initiated litigation against him or it.

- Upon the request of the Governor, appeal certain decisions adverse to an executive agency rendered by the Attorney General concerning deeds, leases, contracts and fidelity bonds.

- Issue rules, guidelines, standards and regulations as are necessary to carry out the duties of the General Counsel provided for in the Commonwealth Attorneys Act.

- Review and approve for form and legality all proposed rules and regulations of executive agencies before they are deposited with the Legislative Reference Bureau as required by the "Commonwealth Documents Law."

- Review for form and legality all Commonwealth deeds, leases and contracts to be executed by executive agencies, and may prepare uniform instrument forms and preapprove all such documents which are prepared in accordance with such forms and applicable instructions.

- Provide, through the Office of Legislative Counsel within the Office of General Counsel, advice and recommendations to the Governor concerning the constitutionality and legal effects of bills enacted by the Legislature and presented to him for his signature, as well as to provide legal counsel to the executive departments and agencies on pending legislation.

Whenever any action is brought by or against any executive branch agency, the Governor or other executive branch official, the Governor may request in writing, setting forth his reasons, the Attorney General to authorize the General Counsel to supersede the Attorney General and represent the agency, the Governor or other executive branch official.

If the Attorney General does not grant the request, the Governor may authorize the General Counsel to intervene in the litigation. Such intervention shall be a matter of right and, when exercised, confers upon the General Counsel the obligation to represent the Governor and his interests as Chief Executive Officer of the Commonwealth and its Executive Department. The Attorney General shall at all times continue to represent the Commonwealth.

BOARDS AND COMMISSIONS. The General Counsel serves

as chief administrative officer of the following administrative agencies of the Office of General Counsel: Juvenile Court Judges' Commission, Administrator for Arbitration Panels for Health Care, Crime Victim's Compensation Board, Board of Commissioners on Uniform State Laws, and State Health Facility Hearing Board.

EX-OFFICIO DUTIES. The General Counsel serves as a member of the Board of Commissioners on Uniform State Laws, the Pennsylvania Emergency Management Agency, the Joint Committee on Documents, the Board of Property, the Commission on Charitable Organizations, the Local Government Records Committee, the Medical Advisory Board, the Board of Finance and Revenue and the Civil Disorder Commission.

	Appointed
GENERAL COUNSELS	*Since 1980*
Jay C. Waldman..........................	Jan. 27, 1981
Henry G. Barr	Apr. 7, 1976
*Morey M. Myers.........................	Jan. 20, 1987

* *Incumbent*

OFFICE OF LEGISLATIVE AFFAIRS

THOMAS F. LAMB   Secretary for Legislative Affairs

Thomas F. Lamb was born Oct. 22, 1922, in Pittsburgh, the son of James Lamb (dec.) and Agnes Dunne Lamb (dec.); grad. from St. James H.S., 1940; grad., Duquesne Univ., 1948; grad., Duquesne Univ. Schl. of Law, 1952; elected to Pa. House of Representatives, 1958; served four terms; elected to Pa. Senate in 1966; Majority Leader (Democratic) of Senate 1970-74; mem., Governing Board of Joint State Government Commission; dir., Governmental Relations Office, Univ. of Pittsburgh, 1976-87; associated with Pittsburgh law firm of Gromer, Reinbold & Lamb; appointed Secretary of Legislative Affairs, Dec. 15, 1987; married Barbara Joyce; four children: Thomas, James, Michael, and Barbara; resides in Mt. Lebanon.

The Office of Legislative Affairs serves as the principal representative of the Office of the Governor in all issues and activities related to the legislative process of the General Assembly.

Its primary role is to serve as a major participant in the identification and development of the Governor's legislative initiatives; to serve as the administration's principal advocate with the General Assembly in pursuit of those legislative objectives; to coordinate the development and introduction of legislative initiatives by the various departments and agencies of the Executive Branch; and to serve as the principal point of contact between the members of the General Assembly and the Office of the Governor.

The Office of Legislative Affairs, as personified by the Secretary for Legislative Affairs, also serves as a senior policy

counselor to the Governor and is afforded cabinet status within the executive branch structure.

OFFICE OF LEGISLATIVE AFFAIRS

JOHN M. HOHENWARTER
    Deputy Secretary for Legislative Affairs
PATRICK T. BEATY
    Deputy General Counsel for Legislative Affairs
ANDREW SISLO
    Deputy General Counsel for Legislative Affairs
Neil P. Malady
    Assistant to Deputy Secretary for Legislative Affairs
Zara Waters

OFFICE OF POLICY AND PLANNING

VACANT   **Secretary for Policy and Planning**

The development and coordination of program plans and policy is under the direction of the Secretary for Policy and Planning. In carrying out these responsibilities, the Secretary works closely with the secretaries for Budget and Legislative Affairs in examining the fiscal, legislative and programmatic aspects of the Governor's plans and policy options. The Secretary works with all of the Executive branch departments, agencies, boards and commissions to insure their active participation in the Administration's program planning and policy development processes and reviews the implementation of policy initiatives. Through these various coordinated efforts, the Secretary develops integrated approaches for the Governor that span the jurisdiction of individual organizations. The Secretary also works closely with the Economic Development Partnership assisting in the creation of economic development policy.

The Secretary for Policy and Planning is assisted in his responsibilities by a Deputy Secretary and the Office of Policy Development.

The Office of Policy Development assists the Secretary for Policy and Planning in establishing Commonwealth policies relating to the environment, energy, human services, housing, job training and other issues. The Office of Policy Development works closely with the Economic Development Partnership and other departments in responding to issues which involve more than one agency or programmatic area.

The primary duties of the Office of Policy Development are:

- To support the Secretary for Policy and Planning.
- To develop new program initiatives and suggest changes to existing Commonwealth programs which will improve the efficiency and effectiveness of service.
- To assess the feasibility and desirability of ideas and proposals for improvements to programs and services, particularly those ideas affecting multiple agencies.
- To coordinate the implementation of Commonwealth policies and to assess the effectiveness of those policies.

- To monitor and develop responses to federal actions affecting the Commonwealth.

The Office of Policy Development also provides staff support to the Governor in identifying and examining long-term trends affecting Pennsylvania's future and in identifying policy objectives and alternative methods for achieving those objectives. The Office also provides the staff support for the Governor in his role as a member of the National Governors' Association and the Coalition of Northeastern Governors.

The Office of Policy Development, originally named the Office of Policy and Planning, was established by Executive Order of the Governor on September 18, 1979.

		Appointed
SECRETARIES		*Since 1980*
Frank Wright	Apr.	7, 1983
Charles Bacas	Feb.	24, 1987

Deputy Secretary

George F. Grode	Apr.	7, 1983
Robert G. Benko	Jan.	15, 1986
*R. David Myers	Feb.	24, 1987

Policy Development Directors

Robert G. Benko	Apr.	7, 1983
Harold D. Miller	Jan.	15, 1986
*W. Roy Newsome, Jr	Mar.	11, 1987

* *Incumbent*

OFFICE OF POLICY DEVELOPMENT

W. ROY NEWSOME, JR.
    Director, Office of Policy Development
Susan L. McBride
Elizabeth A. Rowe

GOVERNOR'S PRESS OFFICE

ROBERT W. GROTEVANT, JR.   **Press Secretary to the Governor**

Robert W. Grotevant, Jr. was born Nov. 24, 1950, in Erie, the son of Robert W. and Rita Galvin Grotevant; grad., Mt. Lebanon H.S., 1968; Pa. State Univ. (B.A., journalism) 1972; reporter, Beaver Co. (Pa.) Times, 1972-79; United Press International, 1979-83 (Hbg. bureau chief, 1982-83); Philadelphia Daily News, 1983-87; pres., Pa. Legislative Correspondents Assn., 1985-86; appointed Press Secretary to the Governor, Jan. 20, 1987; married Claire Sandra Miner; 3 daughters: Jessica, Sarah, Rebecca; resides in Harrisburg (Susquehanna Township).

ANTHONY J. MAY   Secretary of Public Information

Anthony J. May was born Sept. 27, 1942, in Canton, Ohio, the son of Joseph M. and Margaret M. May; grad., Lehman H.S., Canton, 1960; Kent State Univ., Kent, Ohio, (B.A., journalism) 1964, graduate study, interpersonal communications, Kent State, 1975-77; reporter, photographer and editor, the Lima (OH) *Citizen,* Ravenna (OH) *Record-Courier,* Akron (OH) *Beacon-Journal,* Dover (NJ) *Daily Advance,* and The Associated Press, 1962-1970; Press Secretary to Governor Milton J. Shapp, 1970-72; advertising, marketing and public relations executive, 1972-1980; Director of Legislative Information and Research, Pa. House of Representatives, Democratic Caucus, 1980-87; deputy chairman, Pa. Democratic State Committee, 1981-83; appointed Secretary of Public Information, Dec. 15, 1987; three children: Amy May Shestack, Cybele May and Crispin David May; resides in Harrisburg.

The task of the Governor's press office is to provide accurate, complete and timely information concerning the Commonwealth and the state government to the people of Pennsylvania through the news media. The press office responds to inquiries from the media and the public and undertakes initiatives in matters of public urgency such as health information, economic development promotion and crisis response.

The Secretary of Public Information supervises the public information efforts of the many executive department press offices. The goal is to maintain a coordinated and cost-effective communications operation throughout the executive branch of state government.

The office also provides a news clipping service which distributes and catalogues items of significance to state government from every daily and weekly newspaper published in Pennsylvania, as well as leading national dailies.

PRESS OFFICE

JOHN TAYLOR
    Deputy Press Secretary
RON JURY
    Deputy Press Secretary
RITA C. FREALING
    Deputy Press Secretary
Rene I. Brenner
Ruth Fox
Laura A. Hocker
Barry P. Johnston
Virginia R. Rosen

GOVERNOR'S WASHINGTON OFFICE

PHILIP F. JEHLE   Director, Governor's Washington Office

Philip F. Jehle was born in Lima, Ohio, the son of Herman J. and Dorothy Elvin Jehle; grad., Joliet Catholic H.S.; Joliet Junior Coll.; Stanford Univ.; Catholic Univ. of Am.; Catholic Univ. of Am. Law Schl. (J.D.) 1951; mem., Business-Gov. Relations Council; Assn. of Former Senate Aides; Am., Fed., and D.C. Bar Assns.; Natl. Health Lawyers Assn.; chief counsel, U.S. Senate Small Business Com., counsel to Sen. Hubert Humphrey on Sen. Subcom. on Retailing, Distribution and Fair Trade Practices, 1952-59; Washington representative/assoc. general counsel, Natl. Assn. of Retail Druggists, 1959-65; vice pres., SmithKline Beckman in Washington, 1965-87; appointed Director, Governor's Washington Office, April 1, 1987; married Marcelle Auclair; 5 children: Philip F., Jr., Patricia Anne, Kathleen Marie, Christopher Alan, Lawrence Arthur; resides in Washington, D.C.

The Governor's Washington Office represents and promotes Pennsylvania's interests in the nation's capital. The office works to ensure that Pennsylvania's citizens, local governments, business firms and non-profit institutions benefit to the fullest extent from federal programs. The office also serves as an important communications link between the state agencies in Harrisburg and the legislative and regulatory arms of the federal government. The office was recently reorganized to assign priorities to the numerous federal/state issues affecting the Commonwealth. In addition, the office serves as a liaison between the Governor and the Pennsylvania congressional delegation.

WASHINGTON OFFICE

LESLIE M. PETERSON
    Deputy Director
JOHN H. DIMSDALE
    Senior Legislative Analyst
CELIA M. FISCHER
    Senior Legislative Analyst
CYNTHIA A. KENNY
    Senior Legislative Analyst

Andrew Beaver
    Legislative Assistant
Michael Burns
    Legislative Assistant
Mara A. Gavin
    Legislative Assistant
Pamela Perry
Kathleen O'Connor

GOVERNORS OF PENNSYLVANIA SINCE 1790

Name	Political Affiliation	County of Birth	County from which Elected	Term of Service	Born	Died
Under the Constitution of 1790						
Thomas Mifflin	(No Party)	Philadelphia	Philadelphia	Dec. 21, 1790—Dec. 17, 1799	Jan. 10, 1744	Jan. 20, 1800
Thomas McKean	(D-R)	Chester	Philadelphia	Dec. 17, 1799—Dec. 20, 1808	Mar. 19,1734	June 24, 1817
Simon Snyder	(D-R)	Lancaster	*Northumberland	Dec. 20, 1808—Dec. 16, 1817	Nov. 5, 1759	Nov. 9, 1819
William Findlay	(D-R)	Franklin	Franklin	Dec. 16, 1817—Dec. 19, 1820	June 20, 1768	Nov. 12, 1846
Joseph Hiester	(D-R)	Berks	Berks	Dec. 19, 1820—Dec. 16, 1823	Nov. 18, 1752	June 10, 1832
John Andrew Shulze	(D-R)	Berks	Lebanon	Dec. 16, 1823—Dec. 15, 1829	July 19, 1775	Nov. 18, 1852
George Wolfe	(D-R)	Northampton	Northampton	Dec. 15, 1829—Dec. 15, 1835	Aug. 12, 1777	Mar. 11, 1840
Joseph Ritner	(Anti-Mason)	Berks	Washington	Dec. 15, 1835—Jan. 15, 1839	Mar. 25, 1780	Oct. 16, 1869
Under the Constitution of 1838						
David Rittenhouse Porter	(D-R)	Montgomery	Huntingdon	Jan. 15, 1839—Jan. 21, 1845	Oct. 31, 1788	Aug. 6, 1867
Francis Rawn Shunk[1]	(D)	Montgomery	Allegheny	Jan. 21, 1845—July 9, 1848	Aug. 7, 1788	July 20, 1848
William Freame Johnston[2]	(Whig)	Westmoreland	Armstrong	July 26, 1848—Jan. 20, 1852 (Vice Shunk, resigned)	Nov. 29, 1808	Oct. 25, 1872
William Bigler	(D)	Cumberland	Clearfield	Jan. 20, 1852—Jan. 16, 1855	Jan. 11, 1814	Aug. 9, 1880
James Pollock	(Whig)	Northumberland	Northumberland	Jan. 16, 1855—Jan. 19, 1858	Sept. 11, 1810	Apr. 9, 1890
William Fisher Packer	(D)	Centre	Lycoming	Jan. 19, 1858—Jan. 15, 1861	Apr. 2, 1807	Sept. 27, 1870
Andrew Gregg Curtin	(R)	Centre	Centre	Jan. 15, 1861—Jan. 15, 1867	Apr. 22, 1817	Oct. 7, 1894
John White Geary	(R)	Westmoreland	Westmoreland	Jan. 15, 1867—Jan. 21, 1873	Dec. 30, 1819	Feb. 8, 1873
John Frederick Hartranft	(R)	Montgomery	Montgomery	Jan. 21, 1873—Jan. 18, 1876	Dec. 16, 1830	Oct. 17, 1889
Under the Constitution of 1874						
John Frederick Hartranft	(R)	Montgomery	Montgomery	Jan. 18, 1876—Jan. 21, 1879	Dec. 16, 1830	Oct. 17, 1889
Henry Martyn Hoyt	(R)	Luzerne	Luzerne	Jan. 21, 1879—Jan. 16, 1883	June 8, 1830	Dec. 1, 1892
Robert Emory Pattison	(D)	Quantico Co., Maryland	Philadelphia	Jan. 16, 1883—Jan. 18, 1887	Dec. 8, 1850	Aug. 1, 1904
James Addams Beaver	(R)	Perry	Centre	Jan. 18, 1887—Jan. 20, 1891	Oct. 21, 1837	Jan. 31, 1914
Robert Emory Pattison	(D)	Quantico Co., Maryland	Philadelphia	Jan. 20, 1891—Jan. 15, 1895	Dec. 8, 1850	Aug. 1, 1904
Daniel Hartman Hastings	(R)	Clinton	Centre	Jan. 15, 1895—Jan. 17, 1899	Feb. 26, 1849	Jan. 9, 1903
William Alexis Stone	(R)	Tioga	Allegheny	Jan. 17, 1899—Jan. 20, 1903	Apr. 18, 1846	Mar. 1, 1920
Samuel Whitaker Pennypacker	(R)	Chester	Philadelphia	Jan. 20, 1903—Jan. 15, 1907	Apr. 9, 1843	Sept. 2, 1916
Edwin Sydney Stuart	(R)	Philadelphia	Philadelphia	Jan. 15, 1907—Jan. 17, 1911	Dec. 28, 1853	Mar. 21, 1937
John Kinley Tener	(R)	County Tyrone, Ireland	Washington	Jan. 17, 1911—Jan. 19, 1915	July 25, 1863	May 19, 1946
Martin Grove Brumbaugh	(R)	Huntingdon	Philadelphia	Jan. 19, 1915—Jan. 21, 1919	Apr. 14, 1862	Mar. 14, 1930
William Cameron Sproul	(R)	Lancaster	Delaware	Jan. 21, 1919—Jan. 16, 1923	Sept. 16, 1870	Mar. 21, 1928
Gifford Pinchot	(R)	Simsbury, Conn.	Pike	Jan. 16, 1923—Jan. 18, 1927	Aug. 11, 1865	Oct. 4, 1946
John Stuchell Fisher	(R)	Indiana	Indiana	Jan. 18, 1927—Jan. 20, 1931	May 25, 1867	June 25, 1940
Gifford Pinchot	(R)	Simsbury, Conn.	Pike	Jan. 20, 1931—Jan. 15, 1935	Aug. 11, 1865	Oct. 4, 1946
George Howard Earle	(D)	Chester	Montgomery	Jan. 15, 1935—Jan. 17, 1939	Dec. 5, 1890	Dec. 30, 1974
Arthur Horace James	(R)	Luzerne	Luzerne	Jan. 17, 1939—Jan. 19, 1943	July 14, 1883	Apr. 27, 1973
Edward Martin[3]	(R)	Greene	Washington	Jan. 19, 1943—Jan. 3, 1947	Sept. 18, 1879	Mar. 19, 1967
John C. Bell, Jr.[4]	(R)	Philadelphia	Philadelphia	Jan. 2, 1947—Jan. 21, 1947	Oct. 25, 1892	Mar. 21, 1974
James H. Duff	(R)	Allegheny	Allegheny	Jan. 21, 1947—Jan. 16, 1951	Jan. 21, 1883	Dec. 20, 1969
John S. Fine	(R)	Luzerne	Luzerne	Jan. 16, 1951—Jan. 18, 1955	Apr. 10, 1893	May 21, 1978
George Michael Leader	(D)	York	York	Jan. 18, 1955—Jan. 20, 1959	Jan. 17, 1918	Living
David Leo Lawrence	(D)	Allegheny	Allegheny	Jan. 20, 1959—Jan. 15, 1963	June 18, 1889	Nov. 21, 1966
William Warren Scranton	(R)	Madison, Conn.	Lackawanna	Jan. 15, 1963—Jan. 17, 1967	July 19, 1917	Living
Raymond P. Shafer	(R)	Lawrence	Crawford	Jan. 17, 1967—Jan. 19, 1971	Mar. 5, 1917	Living
Under the Constitution of 1968						
Milton J. Shapp	(D)	Cuyahoga, Ohio	Montgomery	Jan. 19, 1971—Jan. 16, 1979	June 25, 1912	Living
Dick Thornburgh	(R)	Allegheny	Allegheny	Jan. 16, 1979—Jan. 20, 1987	July 16, 1932	Living
Robert P. Casey	(D)	Jackson Heights, NY	Lackawanna	Jan. 20, 1987—	Jan. 9, 1932	Living

[1] Resigned July 9, 1848.
[2] There was an interregnum from July 9, 1848 to July 26, 1848. Johnston did not take the oath of office until July 26, 1848.
[3] Resigned January 2, 1947 to take seat in United States Senate.
[4] Became Governor upon resignation of Edward Martin.
* Now Snyder County.

LIEUTENANT GOVERNOR
200 Main Capitol
Harrisburg, PA 17120

MARK STEPHEN SINGEL   **LIEUTENANT GOVERNOR**

Mark S. Singel, son of Stephen and Jean Mertle Singel, was born on September 12, 1953, in Johnstown, Pennsylvania. He is a graduate of Westmont Hilltop High School and The Pennsylvania State University, graduating magna cum laude with a B.A. degree in English literature and a minor in political science.

During college, Singel spent his summers in the intern program of the Pennsylvania House of Representatives. He worked for then Majority Leader K. Leroy Irvis and for the Law and Justice Committee of the Pennsylvania House. After graduation, Singel accepted an assistantship with the doctoral program of higher education and worked for a term at the Penn State Capital Campus in Harrisburg. He served as a research consultant to the National Advisory Commission on Education Professions Development Education where he contributed to a Commission report to the Congress.

In August 1975, Singel joined the staff of U.S. Representative Helen S. Meyner (D-NJ) as a legislative assistant and became her chief of staff in November 1976. When Congresswoman Meyner left office, Singel accepted the position of chief of staff with U.S. Representative Peter A. Peyser (D-NY), where he assisted in coordinating all legislative and casework functions and in administering an 18-member Congressional staff. During that time, Singel also attended George Washington University working on a Master's degree in Legislative Affairs.

In April of 1980, he won the Democratic nomination for the 35th District seat in the Pennsylvania Senate. The 35th District includes all of Cambria County, most of Clearfield County, and the Borough of Windber in Somerset County. In November of 1980, he became one of the youngest members ever elected to the Pennsylvania Senate. He was reelected in 1984 with over 75 percent of the vote.

Singel served for six years as Minority Chairman of the Senate Committee on Community and Economic Development and is the founder and former co-chairman of the Commonwealth Coal Caucus. During his six years in the Senate he served as a member of the Senate Education Committee, the Senate Finance Committee, the Senate Committee on Local Government, the PA Public Television Network Commission, the Local Government Commission, the PA MILRITE Council, the Senate Committee on Labor and Industry and the Senate Aging and Youth Committee.

He established a 98 percent vote attendance record in the legislature and sponsored or co-sponsored over 50 pieces of legislation which were signed into law. Those initiatives include the nation's first Emergency Mortgage Foreclosure Assistance program, a pharmaceutical assistance program for the elderly, a nine-point program for economic development, and a statewide ban on so-called "tough-man" contests.

Singel is a member of the Knights of Columbus, the Greek Catholic Union, the Italian Sons and Daughters of America, the Cambria County Young Democrats, the Johnstown Sportsmen's Association, the Travelers' Protective Association, the Elks (B.P.O.E. #175), the Johnstown Lions' Club, and the Greater Johnstown Jaycees.

He is the recipient of the 1982 Man of the Year Award from the Archdiocese of Pittsburgh - Byzantine Rite, the 1984 Outstanding Citizen Award from the Greater Johnstown Chapter of Morality in Media, the 1985 Labor Award at the Sixth Annual Labor Celebration in Johnstown, the 1986 Special Award from the Archdiocese of Pittsburgh - Byzantine Rite, the 1986 Community Achievement Award from the Johnstown Lodge #214, Order Italian Sons and Daughters of America, PA Economic Development Association Award for his work on the Industrial Development Bond and Mortgage Program 1986, and the 1986 Public Service Award from the Greater Johnstown Regional Central Labor Council AFL-CIO.

Singel is married to Jacqueline Lynn (Schonek) of Johnstown; the couple has three children: Allyson Jean (born October 17, 1982), Jonathan Albert (born July 25, 1984), and Christopher Mark (born January 23, 1986).

In May of 1986, Singel won a hard-fought primary to capture the Democratic nomination for Lieutenant Governor over his two opponents. On the Democratic ticket with Governor Robert P. Casey, Singel - at age 33 - won the 1986 November general election to become the 27th Lieutenant Governor of the Commonwealth of Pennsylvania.

As Lt. Governor, Singel presides over the state Senate and serves as the Chairman of the PA Board of Pardons. By the Governor's appointment, he also serves as Chairman of the Pennsylvania Energy Office, the PA Emergency Management Agency, and the PA Emergency Response Commission.

Singel also represents the Governor on the Board of Trustees, Pennsylvania State University, and is a member of the PA Economic Development Partnership Board.

LIEUTENANT GOVERNOR'S OFFICIAL STAFF

JOSEPH R. POWERS   **Executive Assistant to the**
                                                        Lieutenant Governor

Joseph R. Powers was born July 10, 1949, in Harrisburg, the son of Paul J. and Henrietta Didion Powers (both dec.); grad., Bishop McDevitt H.S.; St. Joseph's Univ. (B.S., pol. sci.) 1971; public servant; mem., Irish Heritage Soc.; legislative aide, 1975-76; dir., Senate Military Affairs and Aeronautics Com., 1977-78; staff asst., Senate Labor and Industry Com., 1979; dir., Senate Consumer Protection Com., 1980; min. dir., Senate Community and Economic Development Com., 1981-86; campaign coordinator, Wambach for Representative, 1980; campaign manager, Singel for Lt. Gov., 1986; appointed Executive Assistant to the Lieutenant Governor, Jan. 20, 1987; home address: 3503 N. Third St., Harrisburg.

VERONICA VARGA

**Press Secretary to the
Lieutenant Governor**

Veronica Varga was born Nov. 13, 1955, in Johnstown, the daughter of Basil and Helen Jugan Varga; grad., Greater Johnstown H.S., 1973; Northwestern Univ., Medill Schl. of Journalism (B.S.) 1977; Cantor's degree (1982), Archdiocese of Pgh., Byzantine Rite; free-lance reporter, news anchor and general assignment reporter, WICU-TV, Erie; Gamma Phi Beta; admin. asst. and press secretary, State Sen. Mark S. Singel, 1981-86; campaign manager, Singel for Senate, 1980; press secretary, Singel for Lt. Governor campaign, 1986; appointed Press Secretary to the Lieutenant Governor, Jan. 20, 1987; home address: 86 Beacon Drive, Harrisburg.

JENNIFER L. GLASS

**Administrative Assistant/Scheduling
Lieutenant Governor's Office**

Jennifer L. Glass was born May 9, 1960, in Johnstown, the daughter of Donald and Betty Crum Ellis; sec./ bookkeeper, Stagers Chevrolet Co., 1979-82; exec. sec. to Senator Mark Singel, 1982-87; appointed Administrative Assistant/Scheduling, Lieutenant Governor's Office, July 15, 1987; married Eric C. Glass; home address: 44 Winter Lane, Enola.

JEAN E. BRANNON

**Personal Secretary to the
Lieutenant Governor**

Jean E. Brannon was born Nov. 12, 1940, in Newton, W.Va., the daughter of Lee and Nannie Nester Ellis; grad., Charleston Schl. of Commerce, 1960; Firestone Tire & Rubber Co., Akron, 1963-72; personal sec. to Sen. Franklin L. Kury, 1974-80; personal sec. to Sen. Mark S. Singel, 1981-87; appointed personal secretary to the Lieutenant Governor, Jan. 20, 1987; married Paul Brannon; 1 child, David; home address: 116 Locust Lane, Dillsburg.

LIEUTENANT GOVERNOR

The Lieutenant Governor is elected for a term of four years. He is President of the Senate and Chairman of the Board of Pardons. He presides over the Senate, but has no vote unless the Senate is equally divided. The Constitution provides that he shall be chosen at the same time, in the same manner, for the same term, and subject to the same provisions as the Governor, and that in case of the death, conviction on impeachment, failure to qualify, resignation or other disability of the Governor, the powers, duties and emoluments of the office for the remainder of the term or until the disability be removed shall devolve upon the Lieutenant Governor.

LIEUTENANT GOVERNORS

Under the Constitution of 1874

Name	Term of Service	Born	Died
John Latta	Jan. 19, 1875—Jan. 21, 1879	Mar. 2, 1836	Feb. 15, 1913
Charles Warren Stone	Jan. 21, 1879—Jan. 16, 1883	June 29, 1843	Aug. 15, 1912
Chauncey Forward Black	Jan. 16, 1883—Jan. 18, 1887	Nov. 24, 1839	Sept. 2, 1904
William T. Davies	Jan. 18, 1887—Jan. 20, 1891	Dec. 20, 1831	Sept. 21, 1912
Louis Arthur Watres	Jan. 20, 1891—Jan. 15, 1895	Apr. 21, 1851	June 28, 1937
Walter Lyon	Jan. 15, 1895—Jan. 17, 1899	Apr. 27, 1853	1933
John Peter Shindel Gobin	Jan. 17, 1899—Jan. 20, 1903	Jan. 21, 1837	May 1, 1910
William M. Brown	Jan. 20, 1903—Jan. 15, 1907	Sept. 20, 1850	Jan. 31, 1915
Robert S. Murphy	Jan. 15, 1907—Jan. 17, 1911	Oct. 18, 1861	June 24, 1912
John Merriman Reynolds	Jan. 17, 1911—Jan. 19, 1915	May 5, 1848	Sept. 14, 1933
Frank C. McClain	Jan. 19, 1915—Jan. 21, 1919	Apr. 14, 1864	Oct. 11, 1925
Edward Ensinger Beidelman	Jan. 24, 1919—Jan. 16, 1923	July 8, 1873	Apr. 9, 1929
David J. Davis	Jan. 16, 1923—Jan. 18, 1927	Nov. 22, 1870	Nov. 19, 1942
Arthur H. James	Jan. 18, 1927—Jan. 20, 1931	July 14, 1883	Apr. 27, 1973
Edward C. Shannon	Jan. 20, 1931—Jan. 15, 1935	June 24, 1870	May 20, 1946
Thomas Kennedy	Jan. 15, 1935—Jan. 16, 1939	Nov. 2, 1887	Jan. 19, 1963
Samuel S. Lewis	Jan. 17, 1939—Jan. 19, 1943	Feb. 17, 1874	Jan. 15, 1959
John C. Bell, Jr.	Jan. 19, 1943—Jan. 2, 1947	Oct. 25, 1892	Mar. 21, 1974
Daniel B. Strickler	Jan. 21, 1947—Jan. 16, 1951	May 17, 1897	Living
Lloyd H. Wood	Jan. 16, 1951—Jan. 18, 1955	Oct. 25, 1896	Feb. 15, 1964
Roy E. Furman	Jan. 18, 1955—Jan. 20, 1959	Apr. 16, 1901	May 18, 1977
John Morgan Davis	Jan. 20, 1959—Jan. 15, 1963	Aug. 9, 1906	Living
Raymond P. Shafer	Jan. 15, 1963—Jan. 17, 1967	Mar. 5, 1917	Living
Raymond J. Broderick	Jan. 17, 1967—Jan. 19, 1971	May 29, 1914	Living

Under the Constitution of 1968

Name	Term of Service	Born	Died
Ernest P. Kline	Jan. 19, 1971—Jan. 16, 1979	June 20, 1929	Living
William W. Scranton III	Jan. 16, 1979—Jan. 20, 1987	July 20, 1947	Living
Mark S. Singel	Jan. 20, 1987—	Sept. 12, 1953	Living

OFFICE OF ATTORNEY GENERAL
16th Floor, Strawberry Square
Harrisburg, PA 17120

LeROY S. ZIMMERMAN   Attorney General

LeRoy S. Zimmerman (R) was born Dec. 22, 1934, in Harrisburg, the son of LeRoy and Amelia A. Magaro Zimmerman; Villanova Univ. (B.S., econ.) 1956; The Dickinson School of Law (J.D.) 1959; U.S. Air Force Reserves and Headquarters Staff, Pa. Air Natl. Guard, 1959-65; lawyer; asst. dist. atty. (1963-65) Dauphin Co.; dist. atty. (1965-80) Dauphin Co.; elected Attorney General, Nov. 4, 1980; reelected Nov. 6, 1984; Am., Pa. & Dauphin Co. Bar Assns.; pres., Pa. Dist. Attys. Assn. (1970-71); Criminal Procedural Rules Comm. of Pa. Supreme Court (1971-86); bd. trustees, The Dickinson School of Law (1981-); Villanova Univ. Development Council (1982-); chmn., Criminal Law and Law Enforcement Comm., Natl. Assn. of Attorneys General; chmn., Executive Working Group for Federal-State-Local Prosecutorial Relations (1983-84), mem. (1982-); K. of C., Council 869; Sons of Italy in Am., Lodge 272; Sons & Daughters of Italy, Pittsburgh Lodge; Our Lady of the Blessed Sacrament Roman Catholic Ch.; rec. Disting. Service Awards from: Junior Chamber of Commerce (1963), Cosmopolitan Club (1977), Dauphin Co. Chiefs of Police Assn. (1977), Crime Clinic of Grtr. Harrisburg (1979); Pa. Hall of Fame Award for Outstanding Leadership, Young Repubs. of Pa.; Public Service Award for Outstanding Leadership in the Field of Law Enforcement and Criminal Justice in Pa., Pa. Co. Detectives Assn., 1974; Dedicated Service to the Cmwlth. and the Profession, Justice Lodge Award, Philadelphia B'nai B'rith, 1978; President's Award, Pa. Trial Lawyers Assn., 1981; The Dickinson School of Law Alumni Award, 1982; "Man of the Year" Award, Police Chiefs Assn. of Southeastern Pa., 1982; The John Price Lecturer Award, Natl. College of D.A.'s, 1982; co-author, Annual Survey of Criminal Law, Pa. Bar Assn. Quarterly, 1974-81; married Mary A. Jaymes; 3 children: Susan, Mark, Amy.

The Office of Attorney General is an independent department. In 1978, voters approved a constitutional amendment establishing an elected Attorney General effective with the general election in 1980. Prior to January 20, 1981, the Attorney General was appointed by the Governor and headed the Department of Justice.

The Attorney General is the Commonwealth's chief legal and law enforcement officer.

The duties and responsibilities of the elected Attorney General were established by the Commonwealth Attorneys Act of 1980.

The Office of Attorney General is divided into three divisions: the Criminal Law Division, the Civil Law Division, and the Public Protection Division.

Each division is rendered administrative and logistic support by the Office of Management Services.

The *fundamental duties* of the Attorney General's Office are:

To furnish upon request legal advice concerning any matter or issue arising in connection with the exercise of the official powers or performance of the official duties of the Governor or agency.

To represent the Commonwealth and all Commonwealth agencies and upon request the Auditor General, State Treasurer, and Public Utility Commission in any action brought by or against the Commonwealth or its agencies.

To represent the Commonwealth and its citizens in any action brought for violation of the Antitrust Laws of the United States and the Commonwealth.

To collect, by suit or otherwise, all debts, taxes, and accounts due the Commonwealth which shall be referred to and placed with the Attorney General.

To administer the provisions relating to Consumer Protection as well as appoint the Advisory Committee.

To review for form and legality, all proposed rules and regulations of Commonwealth agencies.

To review for form and legality all Commonwealth deeds, leases, and contracts to be executed by Commonwealth agencies.

To be the Commonwealth's chief law enforcement officer charged with the responsibility for the prosecution of organized crime and public corruption. This law enforcement program includes a criminal investigations unit and drug law enforcement program as well as direction of statewide and multi-county investigating grand juries and a Medicaid Fraud Control Unit.

The Attorney General also serves as a member of the Board of Pardons, the Joint Committee on Documents, the Hazardous Substances Transportation Board, the Board of Finance and Revenue, the Pennsylvania Commission on Crime and Delinquency, the Pennsylvania Emergency Management Agency, the Civil Disorder Commission, the Municipal Police Officers Education and Training Commission, and the Deputy Sheriffs' Education and Training Board.

Consumer Advocate is appointed by the Attorney General and this appointment is subject to the approval of a majority of the members elected to the Senate. The Office of the Consumer Advocate was established through Act 161 of 1976. Its purpose is to represent consumers in matters before the Public Utility Commission. At the Advocate's discretion, he/she may determine the consumer concern and initiate legal or administrative action.

ATTORNEYS GENERAL	Appointed Since 1950	
Charles J. Margiotti	July	5, 1950
Robert E. Woodside	Mar.	7, 1951
Frank F. Truscott	Oct.	13, 1953
Herbert B. Cohen	Jan.	18, 1955
Thomas D. McBride	Dec.	17, 1956
Harrington Adams	Dec.	16, 1958
Anne X. Alpern	Jan.	20, 1959
David Stahl	Aug.	29, 1961
Walter E. Alessandroni	Jan.	15, 1963
Edward Friedman	May	11, 1966
William C. Sennett	Jan.	17, 1967
Fred Speaker	July	4, 1970
J. Shane Creamer	Jan.	25, 1971
Israel Packel	Jan.	2, 1973
Robert P. Kane	Jan.	6, 1975
Gerald Gornish	June	7, 1978
Jay Justin Blewitt, Jr.	Jan.	1, 1979
Edward G. Biester, Jr.	Jan.	16, 1979
Harvey Bartle III	May	20, 1980

Elected

*LeRoy S. Zimmerman 1980-

(The elected Office of Attorney General was created by the Commonwealth Attorneys Act of 1980.)

First Deputy Attorney General	Appointed Since 1950	
Gaylor Dissinger	Jan.	20, 1981
*Thomas G. Saylor, Jr	Dec.	5, 1983

Consumer Advocate

Mark Widoff	Nov.	25, 1976
Walter Cohen	July	10, 1979
*David M. Barasch	Apr.	11, 1984

* *Incumbent*

AUDITOR GENERAL
229 Finance Building
Harrisburg, PA 17120

DON BAILEY   **Auditor General**

Don Bailey (D) was born July 21, 1945, in Pittsburgh, the son of Glenn B. and Anna Mabel (Cox) Bailey; Univ. of Michigan (B.A., pol. sci.) 1967; Duquesne Univ. Law Schl. (J.D.) 1976; U.S. Army 1967-70; attorney; Pa. and Westmoreland Co. Bar Assns.; Eagles; Elks; Moose; American Legion; VFW; in Vietnam decorated 4 times for Bravery receiving Silver Star, 2 Bronze Stars with "V", and Army Commendation Medal with "V" and the Air Medal; rec. Bronze Star and Army Commendation Medal for meritorious achievement; Outstanding Patriots Award from American Legion; Silver Medal of Merit from VFW of the USA; Outstanding Americanism Award, County Detectives Assn.; as Auditor General established Pa. government's first work-site child daycare facility, replaced manual recordkeeping and auditing functions with electronic data processing and established mandated minimum educational standards as condition for employment as auditor; all-star collegiate athlete, played in 1965 Rose Bowl and North/South All Star game; elec. to Pa. Sports Hall of Fame, Westmoreland Chptr.; mem., U.S. House of Representatives, 1978-1982, served on House Ways & Means Comm., sponsor of fundamental trade and tax savings legislation; elected Auditor General, Nov. 6, 1984; home address: Greensburg.

Basically, the duties of the Auditor General are designed to ensure that all money to which the Commonwealth is entitled is deposited in the State Treasury and to ensure that public money is disbursed legally and properly. This is the basis for the Auditor General's designation as the "Watchdog of the State Treasury."

As the chief auditing officer of the Commonwealth, the Auditor General reviews virtually every financial transaction of the state, except those of the Pennsylvania Turnpike Commission, State Public School Building Authority, State Highway and Bridge Authority, the General Assembly and the Judicial Departments.

The Act of 1811, The Administrative Code, and The Fiscal Code of 1929 empower the Auditor General to institute investigations, hold hearings, subpoena documents, books and papers, and subpoena witnesses.

Each year the department performs thousands of audits. Among them are audits of all state departments; state-owned hospitals, state universities, penal, correctional and other institutions; welfare recipients; state-aided hospitals, homes, universities, colleges and other educational institutions and training schools; municipal employee and police pension funds; firemen's relief and pension funds; district justices of the peace; certain county officials; and the many local public and private agencies and authorities receiving state aid.

Special audits may be made at any time when, in the Auditor General's judgment, they appear to be necessary. Special examinations must also be made when the Governor calls upon the Auditor General to do so. Copies of all audit reports prepared by the department are transmitted promptly to the Governor.

Another duty of the Commonwealth's chief auditor is to make all audits which may be necessary in connection with the financial affairs of the Pennsylvania Liquor Control Board and the more than 700 stores operated by the Board.

The department is also responsible for auditing an estimated 501 local public school districts, 66 area vocational schools and 29 intermediate units each year.

Under law, the Auditor General authorizes and distributes to firemen's relief and pension funds the entire net amount received by the Commonwealth from the two percent tax paid upon premiums collected in Pennsylvania by out-of-state fire insurance companies. Approximately 2,500 municipalities receive over $23 million annually from this tax.

Another statute authorizes the Auditor General to distribute for police and municipal pension funds purposes the entire amount realized from the two percent tax upon premiums by out-of-state casualty insurance companies. Approximately 1,000 police pension funds receive a total of over $70 million annually.

An important responsibility of the department, and one which carries great power of discretion, is the audit and approval of all corporation tax settlements and resettlements made by the Department of Revenue.

If any settlement is disapproved by the Department of the Auditor General, specific reasons for such action must be stated. It is then the duty of the Department of Revenue to reconsider it, to confer with the Department of the Auditor General and to attempt to agree with the Auditor General upon the settlement to be made.

In cases where the two departments fail to agree on a settlement, the question is submitted to the Board of Finance and Revenue for decision. The Auditor General is one of the five members constituting the board.

In addition to the Auditor General's fiscal duties, there are other responsibilities imposed by law.

The Auditor General is also a member of the State Highway and Bridge Authority, State Public School Building Authority, Delaware River Port Authority, Delaware River Joint Toll Bridge Commission, Board of Trustees to Invest Funds of the Pennsylvania Historical Commission, the Pennsylvania Higher Educational Facilities Authority, Local Government Records Committee, Pennsylvania Transportation Assistance Authority, Joint Inter-State Bridge Commission — Pennsylvania and New York, Resettlement Board, Board of Trustees to the Conrad Weiser Memorial, State Council of Civil Defense, and Bushy Run Battlefield Commission.

By statute, the administrative services for the Board of Claims is provided by the department. (See Board of Claims.)

Taxpayer Information Program (TIP). TIP is a toll-free hotline instituted in 1977 to augment the Auditor General's constitutional role of "fiscal watchdog." The program is intended as a public service to all Pennsylvanians who wish to report specific instances of fraud, waste or mismanagement of state funds. Interested citizens may call toll-free 1-800-692-7391 or write: TIP, Department of the Auditor General, 319 Finance Building, Harrisburg, Pennsylvania 17120.

AUDITOR GENERAL	Elected Since 1950
Weldon B. Heyburn	1949-1953
Charles R. Barber	1953-1957
Charles C. Smith	1957-1961
Thomas Z. Minehart	1961-1965
Grace M. Sloan	1965-1969
Robert P. Casey	1969-1977
Al Benedict	1977-1985
*Don Bailey	1985-

Deputies Auditor General	Appointed Since 1950	
Horace H. Eshbach	May	5, 1953
Alfred T. Novella	May	8, 1957
Martin H. Brackbill	Dec.	1, 1957

Deputies Auditor General	Appointed Since 1950	
John M. McHale	May	2, 1961
James R. Berry	May	4, 1965
Harry L. Rossi	Aug.	1, 1966
John M. Lynch (dec. Sept. 29, 1974)	May	6, 1969
C. Paul Brubaker, Jr.	May	10, 1972
William H. Smith	Jan.	16, 1973
John M. Kerr	Jan.	18, 1977
Lester Eisenstadt	Jan.	18, 1977
Harry I. Yaverbaum	Aug.	5, 1977
Arthur R. Martinucci	Aug.	12, 1977
Joseph L. Theurer, Jr.	Mar.	30, 1979
Mario Maffeo	Jan.	17, 1983
*Mowry Mike	Jan.	15, 1985
*Harold Imber	Jan.	15, 1985
*Joseph Brimmeier	Jan.	15, 1985
*Gregory Naylor	Jan.	15, 1985
*Anthony McNeil	Jan.	15, 1985

* Incumbent

STATE TREASURER
129 Finance Building
Harrisburg, PA 17120

G. DAVIS GREENE, JR.   **State Treasurer**

G. Davis Greene, Jr. was born March 22, 1931, in Phila., the son of G. Davis and Leola Helmer Greene; grad., Coll. of Liberal Arts, Univ. of Pa. (B.A., economics) 1953; Wharton Schl., Univ. of Pa. (M.B.A.) 1957; U.S. Navy, 1953-55; investment counselor; exec. trainee, Federal Reserve Bank of Phila., 1955-57; mem., Financial Analysts Federation; mem., Inst. of Chartered Financial Analysis; v. pres., Lionel D. Edie & Co., Inc., 1957-69; financial consultant to State Auditor General, 1970-77; pres., principal and owner, Greene Associates, Inc., 1977-87; elder, Summit Presbyterian Ch.; trustee, Presbytery of Phila., 1972-86; appointed State Treasurer, January 23, 1987; married Ann F. Norcott; 5 children; home address: 725 N. Mt. Pleasant Road, Philadelphia.

The Office of State Treasurer, created by the Constitution of 1776, is the oldest elective office in state government. State Treasurers were elected by the Legislature until the Constitution of 1873 required their direct election by the people.

The State Treasurer is elected to a term of four years at the general state election following the election of a Governor. The Constitution provides that the State Treasurer may stand for reelection to one succeeding four-year term.

As well as serving as chief executive officer of the Treasury Department, the State Treasurer is the statutory custodian of the Public School Employees' Retirement Fund, State Employees' Retirement Fund, Municipal Employees' Retirement Fund, State Workmen's Insurance Fund, Unemployment Compensation Fund and some 12 others.

The State Treasurer is Chairman of the Board of Finance and Revenue and a member of the Board of Commissioners of Public Grounds and Buildings, State Workmen's Insurance Board, Public School Employees' Retirement Board, State Employees' Retirement Board, Municipal Employees' Retirement Board, Municipal Police Retirement Board, State Public School

Building Authority, State Highway and Bridge Authority, Pa. Transportation Assistance Authority, Pa. Higher Education Facilities Authority, Delaware River Port Authority, Delaware River Joint Toll Bridge Commission, Board of Trustees to invest funds of the Pennsylvania Historical and Museum Commission, Coal and Clay Mine Subsidence Board and the New York-Pennsylvania Joint Commission on Bridges over the Delaware River.

The **fundamental duties** of the Treasury Department are:

Receipt of all Commonwealth monies from state agencies; deposit of such monies (together with funds not belonging to the Commonwealth but for which the State Treasurer is custodian) in state depositories approved by the Board of Finance and Revenue; investment in short-term securities of all Commonwealth monies exceeding the daily needs of some 73 separate funds; management of securities within its custody; pre-auditing all requisitions for the expenditure of Commonwealth funds as to accuracy, legality and reasonableness, and payment of state monies, upon proper authorization, to those entitled to receive them.

Treasury officers reporting to the State Treasurer with agencies and responsibilities under their jurisdiction:

DEPUTY STATE TREASURER — Represents State Treasurer in chairing the Board of Finance and Revenue, which handles over 400 tax cases monthly, and serves as the State Treasurer's designee to other boards and commissions.

CHIEF COUNSEL — Counsels State Treasurer, represents Treasury Department in all legal matters and reviews Commonwealth real estate leases.

PRESS SECRETARY — Coordinates Treasury Department information to the public.

EXECUTIVE DEPUTY TREASURER FOR ADMINISTRATION

Bureau of Unemployment Compensation Disbursements: Processes Unemployment Compensation requisitioned by the federal-state Bureau of Employment Security. Jobless pay checks cashed and returned are filed for three years, kept on microfilm for four more.

Bureau of Public Assistance Disbursements: Processes and pre-audits Public Assistance checks requisitioned by the Department of Public Welfare, then reconciles them after they have been cashed and returned.

Bureau of Investigations: Investigates loss, theft or fraud involving all Commonwealth checks except Unemployment Compensation.

Bureau of Personnel Services: Handles personnel matters for Treasury Department employes from employment to retirement and administers the Commonwealth's U.S. Savings Bond participation.

Bureau of Contract Information: Repository for all Commonwealth contracts over $5,000; contracts are open to public inspection, with copies available at cost.

Bureau of Purchasing and Maintenance: Responsible for providing furniture, equipment, supplies, a mail and messenger service and verifies Treasury Department invoices preceding payment procedures.

EXECUTIVE DEPUTY TREASURER FOR FINANCIAL OPERATIONS

Bureau of Audits and Administration: Performs Treasury's exclusive power of pre-auditing Commonwealth expenditures as to accuracy and legality. Proposed expenditures challenged as to legality or propriety are returned to the requesting state agencies; those approved by auditors are paid within four days.

Bureau of Treasury Automated Bookkeeping Systems (TABS): Processes all daily revenues and expenditures for the Commonwealth, using computers to ensure that payments from each of more than 3,500 separate accounts do not exceed appropriation balances. The bureau also reconciles daily cash,

receipts and disbursements by fund with the Bureau of Cash Management.

Bureau of Cash Management and Investments: Invests annually in short-term securities over $24 billion of funds not needed immediately for state government operating expenses. The bureau maintains 27 active bank accounts for payment of state bills and keeps inactive or time deposit accounts in 186 additional depositories.

Comptroller: As fiscal housekeeper of Treasury, the Comptroller prepares the departmental budget and is responsible for reconciling more than 10 million Commonwealth checks annually as well as reconcilement daily of state accounts in 27 active depository banks.

Bureau of Information Services: The computer center for Treasury, the bureau writes an average 45,000 Commonwealth checks each working day and supports TABS Bureau in providing integrated fund and appropriation accounting for the entire Commonwealth.

Bureau of Securities: Safeguards over $11 billion worth of Commonwealth stocks, bonds, and various fiscal documents for which the Treasurer is custodian. Also manages the Treasury vault which is one of the largest "working" vaults in the world.

BOARD OF FINANCE AND REVENUE

The Board of Finance and Revenue is comprised of the State Treasurer as Chairman, the Attorney General, General Counsel, Auditor General, Secretary of the Commonwealth and Secretary of Revenue.

The board's duties are:
1. Selection of depositories for Commonwealth funds and the fixing of interest rates on interest-bearing deposits.
2. Administration of the State Sinking Fund and reporting to the Governor and General Assembly on public debt.
3. Review and decision on appeals from settlements or resettlements made with persons, associations or corporations by the Department of Revenue, Auditor General, Attorney General or Treasury Department, and the hearing and determination of petitions for refund of monies received by the Commonwealth from licenses, fees, taxes, fines, penalties and miscellaneous overpayments to which the Commonwealth is not legally or equitably entitled.

STATE TREASURERS	*Elected Since 1950*
Weldon B. Heyburn	1953-1957
Robert F. Kent	1957-1961
Grace M. Sloan	1961-1965
Thomas Z. Minehart	1965-1969
Grace M. Sloan	1969-1977
Robert E. Casey	1977-1981
R. Budd Dwyer (dec.)	1981-1987
*G. Davis Greene, Jr. (appointed)	1987-

* *Incumbent*

CABINET LEVEL AGENCIES

DEPARTMENT OF AGING
Barto Building
231 State Street
Harrisburg, PA 17101

LINDA M. RHODES   **Secretary of Aging**

Linda M. Rhodes was born June 13, 1949, in Erie, the daughter of John W. Colvin and Shirley Sommerhof; grad., Mercyhurst Coll. (B.A., sociology); Edinboro Univ. (M.E.); Columbia Univ. Teachers Coll. (Doctorate in Gerontology) 1980; gerontologist; mem., Zonta Internatl.; Adv. Bd. of Aging, Natl. Health Policy Forum; past mem., Urban League of Pgh.'s Bd. of Dir.; author, "Blueprints on Aging — A Strategic Plan on Aging for Allegheny County" — 30 publications on aging; pres., Rhodes & Brennan, consulting firm; delegate to NGO Forum on aging, Vienna; spoke before United Nations Conf. on Women and Aging; testified before presidentially-appointed Federal Council on Aging; appointed Secretary of Aging, Jan. 20, 1987; married Joseph Rhodes, Jr.; 2 children: Matthew and Brennan; home address: 4501 Terrace Place, Harrisburg.

The Department of Aging was created by the General Assembly in June of 1978, with the passage of Act 70. This Cabinet-level state agency was established to advance the well-being of Pennsylvania's older citizens; to affect coordination in the administration of federal and state aging programs; to promote the creation and growth of organizations designed to maximize independence and involvement of older Pennsylvanians.

ADMINISTRATION

Executive Office. The Secretary of Aging is the chief executive officer of the department. The Deputy Secretary of Aging is responsible for the department's day-to-day administration and supervises all of its bureaus and field offices. The Secretary also has an Executive Staff comprised of a Chief Counsel, Public Information Officer, and Legislative Liaison.

Bureau of Administrative Services. This bureau provides central management services to the department, including personnel management, fiscal management, office services, mail and messenger service, and management information systems.

Bureau of Pharmaceutical Assistance. This bureau administers the Pharmaceutical Assistance Contract of the Elderly (PACE) Program. It directs the computerized operations of a private contractor for enrollment of eligible persons and claims processing. In addition to oversight and monitoring responsibilities for the program, the bureau staff coordinates utilization review efforts and investigates fraud and abuse by providers and participants. The bureau has additional responsibilities for the fair hearings and appeals process and drug education programs.

Bureau of Program and Field Operations. This bureau is responsible for all aspects of program development, monitoring and technical assistance. It monitors program and fiscal reports of Area Agencies on Aging and provides technical assistance to departmental Field Staff, Area Agencies on Aging and other aging providers.

Bureau of Policy, Planning and Monitoring. This bureau is responsible for the development of the Administration on Aging State Plan, Title XX Aging Plans, and the conceptual development of demonstration projects. It coordinates and conducts social research and special studies as well. Additionally, the bureau develops, for the Secretary's review, departmental policy and reviews proposed regulations of other state agencies.

Bureau of Advocacy. This bureau develops advocacy programs for the department which will ensure that a level of advocacy is provided consistent with the mandates of the Older Americans Act. It provides individual and class advocacy for older citizens and the adult handicapped. It also reviews the activities of state agencies and other governmental units that provide services to older citizens to ensure that the rights and needs of older citizens are being served by their programs.

Bureau of Lamp. The bureau is responsible for administering the Long Term Care Assessment and Management Program, an inter-departmental effort funded in part by the Office of Medical Assistance. The program combines pre-admission assessment of nursing home applicants with a range of case-managed community-based care options designed to assure that institutionalization of older persons only happens when other less restrictive options have been examined and found inadequate to meet their needs.

Pennsylvania Council on Aging. The council is appointed by the Governor and shall consist of nineteen (19) persons, at least ten (10) of whom shall be 55 years of age or older. It shall establish at least four (4) Regional Councils on Aging. The council is to assist the Secretary of Aging in the preparation of the State Plan, to prepare an annual report evaluating level and quality of programs for the aging, to hold public hearings on matters affecting the aging and to consult with the Secretary of Aging on the operations of the department.

SECRETARIES OF AGING	Appointed Since 1950	Deputy Secretaries	Appointed Since 1950
Gorham L. Black, Jr.	Feb. 27, 1979	Hugh H. Jones	Apr. 1, 1979
Alma R. Jacobs	Jan. 2, 1985	William A. Hawkins	Jan. 28, 1985
*Linda M. Rhodes, Ed.D.	Jan. 20, 1987	*Richard Browdie	Mar. 9, 1987

Incumbent

DEPARTMENT OF AGRICULTURE
211 Agriculture Office Building
and Laboratories
2301 North Cameron Street
Harrisburg, PA 17110-9408

BOYD E. WOLFF   **Secretary of Agriculture**

Boyd E. Wolff was born May 17, 1931, in New Alexandria, the son of James K. and Mabel Seanor Wolff; grad., Penn State Univ. (B.S., agricultural, animal husbandry) 1953; Pa. Cooperative Directors' Schl., 1986; owner/operator, family farm since 1953; mem., bd. of trustees, Penn State Univ.; past state dir., Pa. Farmer's Assn. (PFA), 1967-72 and 1978-81; honors: 1970, Pa. Master Farmer; Outstanding Grassland Award; American Forage and Grassland Council, 1976; Outstanding Farm Conservationist Award, 1975; Westmoreland County Conservation District; Kellog Fellow, 1972; former dir. and past pres., Westmoreland Co. Farmers' Assn.; past chmn., West Central Federal Land Bank; past pres., and treas., Westmoreland Co. Cooperative Extension Service; former chmn., Pa. Farmers' Assn., Dairy Com.; Am. Farm Bureau Dairy Com. and com. mem. of the Atlantic Breeder's Cooperative; appointed Secretary of Agriculture, January 20, 1987; married to Margaret A. Wolff; 3 children: Patricia, Corrinne, Margaret; home address: R.D. 2, New Alexandria.

The Department of Agriculture was established in 1895 as an administrative agency in the Executive Department of the Commonwealth.

The Secretary of Agriculture is charged with the responsibility to "encourage and promote agriculture and related industries throughout the Commonwealth." This primary responsibility is accomplished through numerous programs and services, mostly mandated by law. These programs/services range from animal/plant disease control and eradication programs, agricultural product inspection and regulatory programs, marketing and agricultural promotional services to grants and subsidies.

The overall goals of the department include preservation of the family farm, improved marketing and promotion of Pennsylvania agricultural products, and supporting rural economic development.

EXECUTIVE OFFICE

Three deputies assist the Secretary in determining departmental policy, program development and overall administration.

Departmental programs/services are furnished from the headquarters building in Harrisburg and seven regional offices serving the entire Commonwealth; each regional office is responsible for providing all departmental services within a specified area containing from eight to ten counties.

Three departmental administrative commissions are assigned in the Department of Agriculture: the State Harness Racing Commission, the State Horse Racing Commission, and the State Farm Products Show Commission.

Legal Office serves as legal advisor to the Secretary and to department supervision in the performance of their duties.

Legislative Relations Office coordinates the department's legislative program, assigns priorities and responsibilities for specific legislation.

Press Office conducts the department's public information program and advises officials of the public relations implications of departmental programs and initiatives.

DEPUTY SECRETARY FOR PROGRAMS

Office of Planning and Research coordinates statewide planning and research within the department and with other governmental agencies.

Bureau of Agricultural Development helps expand business and marketing opportunities for Pennsylvania's agribusinesses and works to protect and preserve our farm resources. Working directly with agriculture/agribusiness, the bureau provides technical assistance, funds and liaison services to encourage economic expansion and promote export marketing of Pennsylvania farm and food products.

Bureau of Farm Show operates and maintains the Farm Show Complex, consisting of approximately 80 acres, 450,000 square feet of exhibition area and a large arena, for the promotion of Pennsylvania's agriculture and agricultural products. More than 150 other shows and exhibits are accommodated on an "as available" basis at the complex.

Bureau of Marketing assists the state's food production, distribution and marketing industries in promotion and sale of Pennsylvania agricultural commodities. The bureau coordinates public-private promotional programs, two statewide product identification programs, as well as market grading and information services for livestock, poultry and eggs, fruits and vegetables.

DEPUTY SECRETARY FOR REGIONAL PROGRAMS

Bureau of Animal Industry protects and promotes the livestock and poultry industries of the Commonwealth through prevention, control and eradication programs toward dangerous transmissible diseases. The bureau maintains animal diagnostic laboratories and administers licensing programs for animal-related services and industries.

Bureau of Dog Law Enforcement licenses dogs, kennels, pet shops and dealers, insures the humane treatment of dogs and reimburses owners of livestock and poultry for dog-related damages.

Bureau of Foods and Chemistry protects the public health, prevents deception and fraud in food products and other agricultural materials. The bureau provides inspection, certification and licensing programs, and operates chemical and analytical laboratories for matters relating to the food industry.

Bureau of Plant Industry protects and promotes agriculture and consumers through prevention and control of plant pests and diseases. The bureau regulates sales and labeling of agricultural, horticultural and nursery products, pesticides, feeds and fertilizers to protect producers and consumers.

Bureau of Standard Weights and Measures tests and certifies all standards for accuracy of commercial weighing and measuring devices in the state. The bureau inspects and tests accuracy of small and large capacity weighing devices, packaged commodities and other devices used for measurement in the marketplace.

DEPUTY SECRETARY FOR ADMINISTRATION

Bureau of Administrative Services provides administrative, logistical, fiscal, personnel and data processing services for headquarters and regional operations.

Bureau of Government Donated Food, in cooperation with the U.S. Department of Agriculture, administers federal surplus donated food programs for public and private schools, institutions, elderly feeding programs and other non-profit human service organizations. The bureau also oversees state and federal emergency food assistance programs.

Bureau of Amusement Rides and Attractions is responsible for registration and licensing of amusement parks and carnivals

and for certifying safety inspectors for these rides and attractions.

State Horse Racing Commission regulates thoroughbred racing and pari-mutuel betting in the state; administers the Pennsylvania Breeders Fund, licenses horse racing corporations, track officials, employees, horsemen and others who are involved in horse racing. The three-member commission is appointed by the Governor.

State Harness Racing Commission regulates harness racing and pari-mutuel betting in the state; administers the Pennsylvania State Sire Stakes Fund, licenses harness racing corporations, track officials, employees, horsemen and others who are involved in harness racing. The three-member commission is appointed by the Governor.

Agricultural Statistics is a cooperative crop and livestock reporting service between the department and the Statistics Reporting Service of the U.S. Department of Agriculture, which collects, analyzes and publishes primary agricultural statistical information for Pennsylvania.

Weather Modification Board regulates and licenses rain making activities pursuant to Act 449 of 1968. Its seven members include the Secretary of Agriculture, Secretary of Commerce, Secretary of Health, Dean of the College of Earth Sciences of The Pennsylvania State University, and three members appointed by the Governor.

SECRETARIES OF AGRICULTURE	Appointed Since 1950	
Miles Horst (resigned June 30, 1954)	Jan.	19, 1953
W. S. Hagar	Nov.	19, 1954
William L. Henning	Jan.	18, 1955
Leland H. Bull	Jan.	15, 1963
James A. McHale	Jan.	25, 1971
Raymond J. Kerstetter (resigned Jan. 14, 1977)	Mar.	23, 1976
Kent D. Shelhamer	Feb.	14, 1977
Penrose Hallowell (resigned Apr. 3, 1985)	Jan.	16, 1979
Richard E. Grubb (acting)	May	8, 1985
*Boyd E. Wolff	Jan.	20, 1987

Deputies

W. S. Hagar[1]	Mar.	7, 1939
Leland H. Bull	Feb.	4, 1955
D. Richard Wenner (acting)	Oct.	8, 1958
Appointed	June	9, 1960
Jack H. Grey	Feb.	1, 1963
Raymond J. Kerstetter[2] (resigned Mar. 22, 1976)	Feb.	17, 1971
Arlo Swanson	Apr.	12, 1971
Jane M. Alexander	Dec.	1, 1972
Kent D. Shelhamer	Dec.	1, 1976
Raymond J. Kerstetter	Jan.	15, 1977
Neal R. Buss	July	26, 1977
Frank Bertovich	Sept.	6, 1977
E. Chester Heim	Feb.	26, 1979
J. Luther Snyder	Feb.	28, 1979
Michael L. McGovern	Oct.	19, 1983
*J. Fred King	Mar.	16, 1987
*Neal R. Buss	Apr.	1, 1987

Harness Racing Commissioners

L. B. Sheppard (resigned July 29, 1963) (dec.)	Jan.	26, 1960

	Appointed Since 1950
Edward J. Kane (reappt. June 17, 1964)	Jan. 26, 1960
Martin E. Cusick.	Jan. 26, 1960
John B. H. Carter (reappt. June 17, 1964) (dec.)	Aug. 8, 1963
Matthew A. Powers	Dec. 16, 1963
William E. Park.	Jan. 3, 1969
Philip Ahwesh	Dec. 29, 1971
James L. Douds.	Nov. 30, 1972
Wilbur E. Schonek (Interim)	Jan. 4, 1972
P. H. Liscastro	Jan. 6, 1977
*Francis J. Fitzpatrick, Jr..	Apr. 24, 1979
*Jesse L. Crabbs (Chairman).	Oct. 17, 1979
*James B. Eckenrode	Mar. 31, 1980

Executive Secretaries

Joseph M. Lynch.	July 18, 1960
Paul G. Secoy	Mar. 7, 1962
Maj. Ralph D. Gardner.	Apr. 29, 1963
Edward R. Gikey	July 1, 1966
John P. Cowan.	May 17, 1971
Bernard Hammer.	Dec. 20, 1972
John P. McCord (acting).	July 28, 1980
Charles R. Ord.	Dec. 31, 1980
Ralph P. Jones, Jr. (acting)	May 18, 1981
Ben F. Mader	Sept. 23, 1981
*Richard E. Sharbaugh	Mar. 23, 1987

Horse Racing Commissioners

	Appointed Since 1950
Roy Wilkinson, Jr., Esq. (Chairman)	May 28, 1968

	Appointed Since 1950
A. Marlyn Moyer, Jr.	May 28, 1968
Thomas A. Livingston, Esq.	May 22, 1968
William F. Martson, Esq.	Dec. 31, 1969
Joseph L. Lecce (Chairman)	Dec. 29, 1971
William P. Minnotte	Dec. 1, 1972
Andrew R. Johnson (Chairman)	Jan. 6, 1975
Harris Lipez	Jan. 6, 1975
William D. Gross.	Nov. 16, 1976
Hart Stotter (Chairman)	Nov. 27, 1979
Joan F. Pew	Jan. 8, 1981
Frank Ursomarso (Chairman).	Nov. 17, 1982
Robert P. Horton	May 24, 1983
*Fred D. Tecce.	Feb. 13, 1985
*F. Eugene Dixon.	Jun. 18, 1986
*Russell B. Jones, Jr.	Nov. 25, 1986

Executive Secretaries

Donald Shanklin.	Jan. 6, 1969
Billy Lee Hart	Mar. 12, 1970
Robert W. Schmidt	Dec. 17, 1970
James A. LaJohn.	Jan. 12, 1972
Robert B. Glass	Oct. 7, 1974
Gail E. Hayward.	Nov. 1, 1976
*Charles R. Trimmer.	Apr. 21, 1982

[1] *Acting Secretary, July 1-Nov. 18, 1954.*
[2] *Acting Secretary, Jan. 8-Mar. 22, 1976.*

* *Incumbent*

DEPARTMENT OF BANKING
333 Market Street
1651 Harristown 2
Harrisburg, PA 17101-2290

SARAH W. HARGROVE   **Secretary of Banking**

Sarah W. Hargrove was born Nov. 24, 1946, in Winston-Salem, N.C., the daughter of Carol Glenn and John Henry Winder; Mary Baldwin Coll.; Univ. of N.C. (B.A., psych.) 1968; Wharton Schl., Grad. Div., Univ. of Pa. (M.B.A., finance) 1976; chartered financial analyst, 1980; investment banker; marathon runner; mem., Inst. of Chartered Financial Analysts; Financial Analysts of Phila.; Forum of Exec. Women (former pres. & dir.); UNC Pi Beta Phi Sorority; PSI CHI Natl. Psychology Hon. Soc.; bd. of trustees, Walnut St. Theatre; bd. of trustees, Germantown Theatre Guild; Junior League of Phila.; Wharton Alumni Club Adv. Bd.; Business Volunteers for the Arts; appointed Secretary of Banking, March 27, 1987; home address: 423 Walnut St., Harrisburg.

The Department of Banking was originally created by the act of June 8, 1891, P.L. 217. However, that act and several subsequent acts have been repealed and the department currently operates under the "Department of Banking Code," approved May 15, 1933, P.L. 565, as amended. The department is responsible for chartering, licensing, regulating and supervising depository and lending institutions in Pennsylvania, and for administering the provisions of most laws authorizing lending and deposit taking activities.

ADMINISTRATION

The Secretary of Banking is the chief officer of the department, appointed by the Governor with the advice and consent of the Senate for a term of four years.

The department is organized into the bureaus of Banking, Savings Associations, Consumer Credit and Administrative Services.

Bureau of Banking regulates and supervises state-chartered banks, trust companies, bank and trust companies, savings banks and private banks, and is responsible for administering the provisions of the Banking Code of 1965, approved November 30, 1965, P.L. 847. That statute provides for the safe and sound conduct of the business of institutions subject to the Code, conservation of their assets, the maintenance of public confidence in them, the protection of the interests of depositors, creditors and shareholders and the interest of the public in the soundness and preservation of the banking system. The bureau is required to examine all institutions at least once every two calendar years, may also examine affiliated organizations of institutions, has the power to subpoena information from witnesses or records, and regulates establishment of new branch offices of institutions, mergers and chartering of new institutions.

Bureau of Savings Associations regulates and supervises state-chartered savings associations and is responsible for administering the provisions of the Savings Associations Code of 1967, approved December 14, 1967, P.L. 746. The bureau is required to examine all associations at least once every two calendar years and is charged with responsibilities relative to savings associations similar to those of the Banking Bureau.

Bureau of Consumer Credit regulates and supervises consumer discount companies, credit unions, installment sellers, finance companies, collector-repossessors, money transmitters, pawnbrokers and secondary mortgage lenders, and administrates the Consumer Discount Company Act, approved April 8, 1937, P.L. 262; the Credit Union Act, approved September 30, 1961; the Motor Vehicle Sales Finance Act, approved June 28, 1947; the Pawnbrokers License Act, approved April 6, 1937; the Money Transmitter Act, approved September 2, 1965; and the Secondary Mortgage Loan Act, approved December 12, 1980. Examinations of entities under the jurisdiction of the Consumer Credit Bureau are carried out in a manner similar to those of banks and savings associations.

Bureau of Administrative Services provides all staff and office services to the several bureaus in the form of budgetary expertise, personnel management and training, administrative supervision and recruitment programs.

SECRETARIES OF BANKING		Appointed Since 1950
L. Merle Campbell	Mar.	5, 1951
Robert L. Myers, Jr.	Jan.	18, 1955
G. Allen Patterson	Jan.	15, 1963
Carl K. Dellmuth (resigned June 1, 1976)	Jan.	2, 1973
William E. Whitesell	June	23, 1976
Ben McEnteer	Feb.	13, 1979
*Sarah W. Hargrove	Mar.	27, 1987

Deputy Secretaries

Frank W. Poe	Oct.	17, 1955
William M. Steinbach	Jan.	12, 1961
Fred Wigfield, Jr.	May	3, 1963
John B. Toppin	May	12, 1969
James G. Novinger	May	1, 1975
*William J. Beatty	Aug.	5, 1980

Incumbent

PENNSYLVANIA ECONOMIC DEVELOPMENT PARTNERSHIP/ DEPARTMENT OF COMMERCE
433 Forum Building
Harrisburg, PA 17120

RAYMOND R. CHRISTMAN

Secretary of Commerce
Executive Director, Economic Development Partnership

Raymond R. Christman was born June 13, 1949, in Pittsburgh, the son of William T. and Mary C. Carlmark Christman; grad., Lakewood H.S., St. Petersburg, FL, 1967; Florida State Univ., 1971; Univ. of Pgh. (Masters in Urban and Regional Planning) 1974; urban and regional planner; industrial developer; v. pres., Natl. Council on Urban Economic Development; mem., Urban Land Institute; appointed Secretary of Commerce and Executive Director, Economic Development Partnership, Nov. 9, 1987; married Eileen S. Hoffman; two children: Margot and Nicholas; home address: 7152 Reynold St., Pittsburgh.

On February 4, 1987, Governor Robert P. Casey signed an executive order creating the Pennsylvania Economic Development Partnership, which is responsible for directing the Commonwealth's economic development strategy and coordinating programs and initiatives to create and retain jobs.

This public-private Partnership is chaired by the Governor and includes representatives from Pennsylvania's business, labor, educational and governmental communities. The Partnership administers the majority of established economic development programs through the Department of Commerce.

Enabling Legislation. The following is a list of the laws under which the department operates, including a short description of each law.:

1. *The Commerce Law,* Act No. 51, May 10, 1939 (P.L. 111) as amended, created the Department of Commerce and

charged it with the duty of "the promotion and development of business, industry and commerce in the Commonwealth."

2, *PIDA,* Act No. 537, May 17, 1956 (P.L. 1609) as amended, created the independent lending agency which has financed new facilities and expanded older facilities with low interest financing totaling in excess of a billion dollars.

3. *PENNTAP,* Act No. 119-A, December 17, 1965, enables the state to finance research and information dissemination projects to be conducted by state institutions for the benefit of Pa. industry to insure more jobs for Pa.

4. *IDA Law,* Act No. 102, August 23, 1967 (P.L. 251) as amended, is the basic Revenue Bond and Mortgage Act which provides a method for low interest loans to be given to help industry become established and/or expanded in the state, thereby helping to support a high rate of employment for Pennsylvanians.

5. *Site Development,* Act No. 61, May 6, 1968, as amended, provides for grants to municipalities, municipal authorities, industrial development agencies or state agencies for the construction rehabilitation, alteration, expansion or improvement of water facilities, sewage collection lines, channel realignment and access roads.

6. *Tourist Promotion,* Act No. 50 (P.L. 111), April 28, 1961, as amended, enables the Bureau of Travel Development to make grants to eligible tourists promotion agencies for the promotion, attraction, stimulation, development and expansion of all business, industry and commerce within the Commonwealth through the planning and promoting of programs designed to stimulate and increase the volume of tourism in the Commonwealth.

7. *Pennsylvania Industrial Development Assistance Act,* Act No. 635, May 31, 1956, provides for grants to industrial development agencies engaged in promoting the development and expansion of business, industry and commerce in the respective counties of the Commonwealth.

8. *Appalachia Program,* Public Law 89-4, 89th Congress, S.3, March 9, 1955; and Governor's Directive, dated April 12, 1967. The Governor has designated the Executive Deputy Secretary of Commerce as the alternate Pa. member to the Appalachian Regional Commission; the basic purpose of this legislation is to promote the economic development of that portion designated as Appalachia.

9. *Nursing Home Loan Agency Law,* Act No. 207, July 22, 1974 (P.L. 610) as amended, created an independent lending agency to provide financing for the repair, reconstruction and rehabilitation of nursing homes in order for them to comply with state and federal safety standards. Act No. 141 (1984) provides financing for the repair, reconstruction and rehabilitation of personal care boarding homes in order for them to comply with state and local Fire and Panic Standards.

10. *Pennsylvania Minority Business Development Authority Act,* Act No. 206, July 26, 1974, creates an independent lending agency to provide low-interest financing to business enterprises owned or controlled by one or more socially or economically disadvantaged persons. PMBDA is housed in the Bureau of Minority Business Development. Technical assistance is also provided by qualifying minority business through the authority.

11. *Ben Franklin Partnership Board.* Act 223, December 6, 1982, created the Ben Franklin Partnership Board which is authorized to promote, stimulate and encourage applied research and development in Pennsylvania, including providing grant assistance for the establishment and operation of Advanced Technology Centers throughout the Commonwealth.

12. *Pennsylvania Energy Development Agency and Emergency Powers,* Act No. 280, December 14, 1982, created the agency to provide financial assistance for energy developments and conservation projects in the Commonwealth which will use or save Pennsylvania energy resources.

13. *Business Infrastructure Development (BID) Program,* Act No. 105, July 2, 1984, provides communities across the state with the resources necessary to fund infrastructure improvements needed for the location or expansion of private firms.

14. *Pennsylvania Capital Loan Fund Program,* Act No. 109, July 2, 1984, to expand the Capital Loan Fund Program to meet the financing needs of a wide range of growing firms, not just those with energy-related projects.

15. *Engineering School Equipment Program,* Act No. 110, July 2, 1984, to award grants to engineering degree granting colleges and universities and to purchase new engineering equipment or to upgrade existing engineering equipment.

16. *Small Business Incubators Program,* Act No. 111, July 2, 1984, to encourage the development of facilities that provide small units of manufacturing/R & D space and to provide business development services by making available loans and loan guarantees for small business incubators.

17. *Employee Ownership Assistance Program,* Act No. 113, July 2, 1984, to assist, through the provision of loans for technical and financial assistance, employee ownership groups in their efforts to convert an existing firm into an employee-owned enterprise or to improve an existing employee-owned enterprise.

18. *Minority Economic Development Program,* Act No. 114, July 2, 1984, to focus financial and technical assistance on minority business enterprises that create net new jobs by increasing Pennsylvania's share of domestic and international markets, and to assist minority businesses to obtain contracts with state agencies.

EXECUTIVE

The Secretary, appointed by the Governor, by and with the consent of the Senate, administers and maintains executive authority over all phases of departmental activities. The Secretary also is chairman ex officio of the Pennsylvania Industrial Development Authority (PIDA), the Pennsylvania Minority Business Development Authority (PMBDA) and the Nursing Home Loan Agency (NHLA). Additionally, the Secretary of Commerce is a member of various other boards and commissions.

Legislative Liaison. The Legislative Liaison serves as liaison between the Legislature, the Governor's Office, and the department, and is responsible for monitoring and analyzing legislation that will affect the business community and the department.

Office of Chief Counsel. Acts as Chief Counsel for the Secretary and supervises the department's legal activities and provides support to the Governor's General Counsel. This is accomplished by drafting, monitoring and reviewing legislation and contracts, monitoring grant and loan applications, and providing advice when required on legal issues. Legal Support is also provided for the department's grant and loan programs.

Office of Communications. This office is responsible for the external communication of the department, and directs and controls the management and administration of the operations and activities of the Press Office and Bureau of Promotion and Marketing. Responsible for the direction and management of the industrial and tourism marketing programs.

Press Bureau. Directs and controls the agency's public relations functions and acts as media consultant and advisor. Writes, directs and manages the distribution of news releases to the media and the public and responds to oral and written requests from media and the public. Maintains a liaison with the media and the other bureaus of the department and arranges interviews between department personnel and news media. Prepares speeches for the Secretary and press releases and briefings for the Governor's Press Office upon request.

Bureau of Promotion and Marketing. Responsible for directing and controlling all phases of the advertising and promotion programs in the department including the industrial and travel marketing programs. Directs and controls the activities of the Tourism, Economic/Industrial, and Film divisions.

Tourism Division. Responsible for the promotion of travel and tourism within the department. Includes the management and administration of trade and consumer advertising marketing plan development, and travel publication activities. Administers the Tourism Matching Fund Program (Act 200).

Economic/Industrial Division. Directs and controls the economic and industrial advertising and promotion efforts.

Film Division. Directs and controls the promotion of the Commonwealth as a location for filming motion pictures, television shows, commercials and documentaries. Activities include location scouting, preproduction coordination, liaison services, assistance in film production and encouraging use of Pennsylvania companies affiliated with the industry.

DEPUTY SECRETARY FOR PLANNING, ADMINISTRATION, AND PROGRAM MANAGEMENT

Deputy Secretary for Planning, Administration, and Program Management directs and controls all phases of the department's planning, research, program management and administrative functions. This includes the management and administration of the operations and activities of the Office of Administrative Services, Office of Economic Policy, Planning and Research and the Office of Program Management.

Office of Administration. Directs and controls all phases of the department's administrative services, including personnel administration, employe services, fiscal services, affirmative action, computer services, program and management analysis, office services and contract compliance. Support services are also administered through the bureau, including supply and inventory control, mail/messenger service, reproduction services, automotive fleet maintenance and information distribution. Responsible for the management and administration of the operations and activities of the Budget and Fiscal, Personnel, Support Services, Executive and Computer Systems' divisions.

Budget and Fiscal Division. Responsible for all budget and fiscal activities of the agency and for contract compliance.

Personnel Division. Responsible for all personnel, affirmative action, and related activities in the agency.

Support Services Division. Responsible for the operation of the agency's mail room and print shop, and all automotive activities.

Computer-Systems Division. Responsible for all data and word processing activities of the agency.

Office of Economic Policy, Planning & Research. Directs and controls all phases of the agency's economic policy analysis, planning, and research activities. Directs and controls the management and administration of the Bureau of Economic Policy Analysis and Development and the Bureau of Economic Research and Legislative Analysis.

Bureau of Economic Policy Analysis and Development. Directs and controls the agency's policy analysis, economic planning and program design and evaluation activities. Will provide support to strategic planning and development units.

Bureau of Economic Research and Legislative Analysis. Directs and controls the agency's economic research and legislative analysis activities. Prepares required statistical reports and maintains research library.

Office of Program Management. Directs and controls the delivery of the categorical economic development programs. Manages and administers the activities of the Bureaus of Technology, PMBDA, Bond and Loan Programs and Small Business. Directly coordinates and controls the Financial Analysis operation.

Bureau of Pennsylvania Minority Business Development. Director serves as Executive Director to PMBDA and administers the minority business technical assistance program. Responsible for the administration of business opportunities for economically disadvantaged minority business persons, and serves as an information source for the minority business community. Provides loans, technical assistance and business information services to minority businesses throughout the state.

PMBDA Division. Directs the PMBDA activities. The program activities include loans, technical assistance, and business information services for minority businesses throughout the state, and maintain regional offices in Pittsburgh, Philadelphia, and Harrisburg.

Bureau of Bond and Loan Program. Directs and controls the department's bond and loan activities including management and administration of the Pennsylvania Industrial Development Authority (PIDA), the Revenue Bond and Mortgage Program (RBMP), the NHLA, Site Development, Business Infrastructure Development, and special appropriation programs through the divisions of PIDA, NHLA, Revenue Bond, and Grants and Loans.

PIDA Division. Director serves as Executive Director to Pennsylvania Industrial Development Authority, and directs the staff support services to the Pennsylvania Industrial Development Authority (Act 537 of 1956), including the preparation and presentation of loan applications to the Board, processing of loan documents, maintenance of Authority files and other related duties.

NHLA Division. Provides low-interest loans to nursing homes and personal care boarding homes for the repair, rehabilitation, or reconstruction of facilities to comply with the Life Safety Code and/or fire and panic safety standards.

Revenue Bond and Mortgage Division. Administers the Agency's Revenue Bond and Mortgage Program (Act 102 of 1967) and other related duties.

Grants and Loans Division. Administers the Site Development, Business Infrastructure Development and special appropriation programs.

Pennsylvania Economic Development Finance Authority Division. Administers the authorities and duties granted to the authority and executive decisions issued by its governing body, the Financing Board.

Bureau of Small Business. Administers the PCLF and EOAP Programs.

PCLF Division. Directs and controls the PCLF program and other related duties.

Office of Regional/Community Initiatives. Responsible for directing targeted assistance and planning for impacted communities and regions of the state; identification and development of high yield facilities; and the design of sector initiative proposed by the Partnership Board, Governor or Secretary.

DEPUTY SECRETARY OF DEVELOPMENT

Directs and controls all phases of the department's development efforts including the Offices of Technology, Enterprise Development, Business Assistance, Development Packaging and the Response Team.

Office of Technology Development. Director serves as Executive Director of the Ben Franklin Partnership (BFP).

Directs all phases of the department's scientific and technological activities including the management and administration of Ben Franklin Partnership challenge and Seed Grants programs and the Small Business Incubator, Engineering Equipment grant and Seed Capital programs, coordination of the Pennsylvania Technical Assistance Program (PENNTAP), and the monitoring of advanced technology initiatives and growth throughout the state.

Research Grants Division. Directs and controls the activities of the Ben Franklin Challenge and Small Business Research Seed Grant, to stimulate technical research at small companies to develop new products or processes.

Office of Enterprise Development. Directs and controls the functional activities of the Small Business Action Center and Technical Assistance to promote and assist the start up of new small and minority/women businesses. Provides technical assistance, advice and information from various existing programs. Serves as liaison with small and minority/women business organizations and responsible for advocacy of their interests in policy and legislative matters in a support role.

Technical Assistance Division. Responsible for conducting all of the annual project development activities of the Appalachian Development Highway and non-Highway Programs.

Small Business Action Center. Assists small businesses in cutting through bureaucratic red tape by providing them with a centralized source of information and answers. The center utilizes a statewide network of information sources to obtain information on permits, regulations, and items of interest to the small business person, and responds to the caller.

Office of Business Assistance. Directs and controls all phases of the Department's Economic Development activities both domestic and international.

Bureau of Domestic Commerce. Directs and controls all phases of the domestic economic development activities of the Field Services and Marketing divisions. This includes the business outreach program, field representative staff, preparation of proposals, climate calls, marketing missions and other related activities.

Marketing Division. Directs and administers the economic development activities of the Marketing Division including preparation of proposals, business outreach, marketing missions and other related activities.

Field Services Division. Directs and administers the field representatives and the business outreach programs within the bureau including climate calls.

Bureau of International Commerce. Directs and controls the economic development activities of the bureau. Promoting Pennsylvania as an ideal location for foreign reverse investments joint ventures and assists foreign investors in identifying suitable locations within the Commonwealth as well as identifying public and private funding sources. Supervises and monitors the foreign representatives under contract to the Department.

Office of Development Packaging. Directs and controls the responsibility to participate/lead, on behalf of the Partnership and Commonwealth, the packaging of large scale development projects.

Office of Response Team. Accountable to and works closely with the Governor and Secretary. Provides quick response to priority projects involving plant shutdowns, move-outs, expansions, and recruitment. Responsible for maintaining a confidential communications network and reporting system. Directs a support team of assigned personnel in other agencies.

Regional Offices. Prepare and execute specific actions to service the Office of Response Team directions.

SUB-AGENCIES
BOARDS AND COMMISSIONS

Pennsylvania Minority Business Development Authority Board. Sixteen members: secretaries of Commerce (chairman), Community Affairs, Labor and Industry, and Banking, two appointed by the President Pro Tempore of the Senate, two appointed by the Speaker of the House and eight appointed by the Governor.

Pennsylvania Industrial Development Authority Board.

Twelve members: secretaries of Commerce (chairman), Community Affairs, Banking, Agriculture and Labor and Industry, and seven appointed by the Governor.

Nursing Home Loan Agency Board.

Ten members: secretaries of Commerce (chairman), Health, Public Welfare, Labor and Industry, Environmental Resources, Banking, and Aging and three appointed by the Governor.

SECRETARIES OF COMMERCE	Appointed Since 1950	
Andrew J. Sordoni	Jan.	20, 1951
John P. Robin (resigned Sept. 1, 1955)	Jan.	18, 1955
William R. Davin (dec. Oct. 21, 1961	Sept.	13, 1955
Thomas J. Monaghan	Nov.	29, 1961
John K. Tabor	Jan.	22, 1963
Clifford L. Jones	Jan.	17, 1967
Robert Mumma	Apr.	28, 1969
William Schmidt	Mar.	6, 1970
Will L. Ketner (acting)	Sept.	8, 1970
Daniel S. Buser, Jr.	Nov.	19, 1970
Elwood S. Hochstetter (acting)	Jan.	28, 1971
Walter G. Arader	Apr.	19, 1971
John J. O'Connor	Dec.	26, 1974
Nancy B. Mawby (acting)	Sept.	16, 1976
Norval D. Reece	Apr.	28, 1977
James F. Bodine	Feb.	13, 1979
Geoffrey Stengel, Jr.	Jun.	6, 1980
James O. Pickard	Mar.	16, 1983
Donald F. Mazziotti (acting)	Feb.	17, 1987
*Raymond R. Christman	Nov.	9, 1987

Deputies

William W. Behrens	Feb.	1, 1951
John R. Hertzler	Apr.	18, 1955
John T. Gross	Sept.	18, 1956
J. Eric Jones	June	30, 1959
Harold A. Swenson	Mar.	1, 1962
Clifford L. Jones	Apr.	15, 1963
Edward Smith	Jan.	19, 1967
Robert Mumma	Mar.	27, 1969
William Schmidt	Apr.	1, 1969
Will L. Ketner	Feb.	4, 1970
Elwood S. Hochstetter	Jan.	28, 1971
Victor Yarnell	Jan.	10, 1972
Richard G. Watson	Feb.	16, 1972
George E. Bartol, III	Oct.	22, 1973
Charles Welsh	Aug.	7, 1974
Nancy Mawby	Mar.	3, 1975
Frank Brooks Robinson	Mar.	19, 1979
Franklin H. Mohney	Feb.	11, 1981
Walter H. Plosila	Feb.	21, 1983
Robert E. Baker, Jr.	Feb.	22, 1983
Douglas W. Reeser	Feb.	22, 1983
*Joseph Rhodes, Jr.	May	4, 1987
*Brenda K. Mitchell	May	11, 1987

The Pennsylvania Industrial Development Authority
(Created by Act of Legislature, No. 537 of May 17, 1956)

Board Members	Appointed Since 1950	
William R. Davlin, ex-officio	May	17, 1956
Genevieve Blatt	May	17, 1956
Robert L. Myers, Jr., ex-officio	May	17, 1956
John Torquato, ex-officio	May	17, 1956
J. Robert Baldwin	July	24, 1956
Victor C. Diehm	July	24, 1956
Asbury W. Lee, III	July	24, 1956
Thomas L. Moran	July	24, 1956
Ralph C. Swartz	July	24, 1956
Arthur T. Chapman	Aug.	20, 1956

	Appointed Since 1950	
J. Dean Polen	Dec.	1, 1956
Max. F. Balcom	Mar.	19, 1957
William L. Batt, Jr., ex-officio	Mar.	4, 1957
R. Warren Grigg	Aug.	14, 1957
Robert G. MacDonald	Aug.	20, 1958
A. Allen Sulcowe, ex-officio	June	12, 1961
John K. Tabor, ex-officio	Jan.	22, 1963
G. Allen Patterson, ex-officio	Jan.	15, 1963
William P. Young	Jan.	15, 1963
Louis H. Roddis	Jan.	11, 1961
Max F. Balcom	Aug.	20, 1959
Frank E. Hemelright	May	28, 1963
William W. Ward	Mar.	1, 1966
Clifford L. Jones, ex-officio	Jan.	17, 1967
William J. Hart, ex-officio	Jan.	17, 1967
Rolland W. Britt	Dec.	9, 1968
Paul J. Smith, ex-officio	Jan.	20, 1971
William H. Wilcox, ex-officio	Feb.	1, 1971
Walter G. Arader, ex-officio	Mar.	8, 1971
G. William Ward	Jan.	27, 1970
Charles H. Whittum	Jan.	1, 1972
James A. McHale, ex-officio	June	16, 1972
Dr. Thomas J. Ritter	Oct.	4, 1972
Carl K. Dellmuth, ex-officio	Dec.	15, 1972
John J. O'Connor, ex-officio	Dec.	26, 1974
Henry A. Satterwhite	Jan.	2, 1974
Raymond J. Kerstetter, ex-officio	Jan.	1, 1976
Andrew G. Freeman	Nov.	16, 1976
Arthur J. Gardner	Jan.	7, 1976
Timothy A. Durkin, III	Jan.	7, 1976
Edward M. Petsonk	Nov.	16, 1976
William E. Whitesell, ex-officio	June	23, 1976
Nancy B. Mawby, ex-officio	Sept.	16, 1976
Norval D. Reece, ex-officio	Apr.	28, 1977
Albert L. Hydeman, Jr., ex-officio	Oct.	25, 1977
Kent D. Shelhamer, ex-officio	Jan.	15, 1977
Richard A. Doran	Dec.	12, 1978
James F. Bodine, ex-officio	Feb.	13, 1979
Penrose Hallowell, ex-officio	Feb.	13, 1979
Ben McEnteer, ex-officio	Feb.	13, 1979
William R. Davis, ex-officio	Feb.	23, 1979
Myron L. Joseph, ex-officio	Mar.	6, 1979
Shirley M. Dennis, ex-officio	Oct.	31, 1979
Charles J. Lieberth, ex-officio	Nov.	27, 1979
*Maurice A. Lawruk	Mar.	18, 1980
Geoffrey Stengel, Jr., ex-officio	June	6, 1980
*David Tressler	June	17, 1980
Leonard Goldfine	Apr.	18, 1981
*Lawrence F. Klima	May	5, 1981
Mil Hallan	May	27, 1981
Barry H. Stern, ex-officio	Jan.	19, 1982
*Nate Smith	Apr.	5, 1983
James O. Pickard, Chairman	Mar.	16, 1983
James W. Knepper, ex-officio	Nov.	28, 1984
*Ralph Evans	Nov.	28, 1984
*Joseph Yencho	June	24, 1986
*John C Schmidt	Nov.	24, 1986
*Harris L. Wofford, Jr.	Jan.	20, 1987
*Boyd E. Wolff	Jan.	20, 1987
*Karen A. Miller	Jan.	26, 1987
Donald F. Mazziotti (acting)	Feb.	17, 1987
*Sarah W. Hargrove	Mar.	27, 1987
*Raymond R. Christman	Nov.	9, 1987

Executive Directors

John T. Gross	Sept.	18, 1956
J. Eric Jones	June	30, 1959
Clifford L. Jones	Sept.	17, 1963
John S. Cole	July	18, 1967
Nicholas J. S. Stevens	Jan.	7, 1976
*Gerald W. Kapp, Jr.	Oct.	12, 1977

* Incumbent

Pennsylvania Minority Business Development Authority
(Created by Act of Legislature, No. 206 of July 22, 1974.)

Board Members	*Appointed Since 1950*	
Uvelia S. A. Bowen	June	2, 1975
John L. Braxton (reappt. Sept. 27, 1977)	June	2, 1975
Alex Thompson (reappt. Nov. 14, 1978)	June	2, 1975
Nathan H. Waters, Jr.	June	2, 1975
Paul D. Nelson	May	25, 1976
Carlos E. Graupera	Mar.	22, 1977
*Eugene Smith, Jr.	Nov.	15, 1978
Ronald P. Goebel	Feb.	1, 1979
William R. Davis, ex-officio	Feb.	7, 1979
James F. Bodine, ex-officio	Feb.	13, 1979
Ben McEnteer, ex-officio	Feb.	13, 1979
Philip Price, Jr.	Feb.	13, 1979
Myron L. Joseph, ex-officio	Mar.	29, 1979
Paul McKinney	Apr.	24, 1979
Alija Dumas	May	10, 1979
Doris Williams	Mar.	4, 1980
Shirley Dennis, ex-officio	Apr.	28, 1980
Charles Lieberth, ex-officio		
Geoffrey Stengel, ex-officio	June	6, 1980
*Frank Oliver	Feb.	4, 1981
John Dykes	Apr.	28, 1981
*Robert C. Wright	Oct.	26, 1981
Barry H. Stern, ex-officio	Jan.	19, 1982
William Andrews	Feb.	2, 1982
Edith Benson	June	1, 1982
*Freeman Hankins	Jan.	27, 1983
James O. Pickard, Chairman	Mar.	16, 1983
T. Milton Street	Mar.	21, 1983
*James Corum, Jr.	July	23, 1983
*Tim Shaffer	Apr.	16, 1985
*Robert Hubbard, Jr.	Jan.	28, 1986
*Ronald Reese	May	28, 1986
*Charles Pittman	June	30, 1986
*Millicent Hooper	June	30, 1986
*Sheila Bass	Nov.	24, 1986
*Julio Tio	Nov.	25, 1986
*Harris Wofford	Jan.	20, 1987
*Karen Miller	Mar.	4, 1987
*Sarah W. Hargrove	Mar.	27, 1987
Donald F. Mazziotti	Mar.	31, 1987
*Raymond R. Christman	Nov.	9, 1987

Executive Directors

Robert H. Byrd	June	25, 1973
Owen H. Montague, Jr.	July	1, 1975
Frederick Reed	Sept.	1, 1977
Antoinette Harris	Feb.	20, 1979
William Foster	Aug.	7, 1980
*William F. Peterson	Jan.	14, 1982

Pennsylvania Nursing Home Loan Agency
(Created by Act of Legislature, No. 207 of July 22, 1974)

Board Members

Maurice Goddard, ex-officio	Jan.	19, 1971
Paul J. Smith, ex-officio	Jan.	25, 1971
Walter G. Arader, ex-officio	Apr.	19, 1971
Carl K. Dellmuth, ex-officio	Jan.	2, 1973
Ralph Buchanan (reappt. Oct. 10, 1975)	Oct.	10, 1974
Rev. Dean Shetler (reappt. Jan. 31, 1978)	Oct.	10, 1974
Rev. William Gray III (reappt. Mar. 14, 1977)	Oct.	10, 1974
John J. O'Connor, ex-officio	Dec.	26, 1974

	Appointed Since 1950	
Dr. Leonard Bachman, ex-officio	Jan.	3, 1975
Frank S. Beal, ex-officio	Jan.	6, 1975
William E. Whitesell, ex-officio	June	23, 1976
Nancy Mawby, ex-officio	Sept.	16, 1976
John Brandeburg	Apr.	19, 1977
Norval D. Reece, ex-officio	Apr.	28, 1977
Maxine T. Segal	Oct.	19, 1977
Aldo Colautti, ex-officio	May	1, 1978
*Marvin Finkelstein	Nov.	15, 1978
James F. Bodine, ex-officio	Feb.	13, 1979
Ben McEnteer, ex-officio	Feb.	13, 1979
Clifford L. Jones, ex-officio	Feb.	16, 1979
Helen B. O'Bannon, ex-officio	Feb.	16, 1979
Dr. Myron Joseph, ex-officio	Mar.	6, 1979
Dr. Gordon MacLeod, ex-officio	Mar.	16, 1979
Dr. H. Arnold Muller, ex-officio	Nov.	26, 1979
Geoffrey Stengel, Jr., ex-officio	Nov.	27, 1979
Carl Weiss	Mar.	4, 1980
Charles J. Lieberth, ex-officio	June	6, 1980
*S. Murray Rust, III (reappt. Sept. 29, 1986)	Apr.	18, 1981
Barry H. Stern, ex-officio	Jan.	19, 1982
Walter W. Cohen, ex-officio	Mar.	16, 1983
*Bruce E. Toll (reappt. June 30, 1986)	June	1, 1983
Nicholas DeBenedictis, ex-officio	Feb.	7, 1984
James O. Pickard, ex-officio	Mar.	16, 1984
James W. Knepper, ex-officio	Sept.	10, 1984
Alma Jacobs, ex-officio	Jan.	2, 1985
F. Rogers Tellefsen (acting), ex-officio	Jan.	20, 1987
*Linda M. Rhodes, ex-officio	Jan.	20, 1987
William J. Beatty (acting), ex-officio	Jan.	20, 1987
*Harris Wofford, ex-officio	Jan.	20, 1987
*John F. White, Jr., ex-officio	Jan.	20, 1987
*N. Mark Richards, ex-officio	Jan.	20, 1987
*Arthur A. Davis, ex-officio	Jan.	21, 1987
Donald F. Mazziotti (acting), ex-officio	Feb.	17, 1987
*Sarah W. Hargrove, ex-officio	Mar.	27, 1987
*Raymond R. Christman	Nov.	9, 1987

Executive Directors

Alan H. Rauzin	Aug.	15, 1974
Joseph A. Fanone	Mar.	4, 1976
George Charney, Jr.	Feb.	17, 1977
Richard P. Johnson	Aug.	1, 1979
*Barbara A. Musko	Dec.	2, 1980

Ben Franklin Partnership

Board Members

*Odgen C. Johnson, Ph.D.	Jan.	20, 1987
*Charles Bacas	Jan.	21, 1987
*Arthur Davis	Jan.	21, 1987
*Jan Freeman	Jan.	21, 1987
*Boyd Wolff	Jan.	21, 1987
*Michael A. O'Pake	Jan.	27, 1987
*Richard A. Geist	Feb.	17, 1987
*Thomas J. Murphy	Feb.	17, 1987
*Howard Grossman	Feb.	20, 1987
*Theodore Kirsch	Feb.	20, 1987
*Timothy Parks	Feb.	20, 1987
*James A. Ream	Feb.	20, 1987
Donald F. Mazziotti	Mar.	31, 1987
*Roy W. Wilt	June	29, 1987
*Raymond R. Christman	Nov.	9, 1987

* *Incumbent*

DEPARTMENT OF COMMUNITY AFFAIRS
317 Forum Building
Harrisburg, PA 17120

KAREN A. MILLER   Secretary of Community Affairs

Karen A. Miller was born Jan. 8, 1942, in Evanston, IL, the daughter of Samuel and Betty Feddersen Anderson; B.A. cum laude with departmental honors in English, Indiana Univ., Bloomington, IN (1964); Ford Foundation Fellowship; Woodrow Wilson Fellowship Finalist; Mortar Bd., women's activities and scholarship honorary; Mayor, City of Reading, 1980-87; councilwoman, dir. of accounts/finance, City of Reading, 1976-79; Natl. League of Cities, former mem., Steering Com. on Finance, Admin. and Intergov. Relations; Telecommunications Task Force and Steering Com. on Human Development; U.S. Conf. of Mayors, former mem., Steering Com. on Urban Economic Policy; chmn., Municipal Pension Adv. Com. of the Pa. Public Employment Retirement Study Comm., 1985-87; mem., President's Adv. Council, Albright Coll.; bd. of dirs., League of Women Voters, Phila., 1969-70, and Reading, 1972-74; Reading 8th Ward Dem. Committeewoman, 1974-77; Berks Co. Dem. Com. Ex. Bd., 1974-75; st. govt.: chmn., Pa. Housing Finance Agency; sec., Pa. Industrial Development Auth.; sec., Governor's Energy Council; mem., Pa. Emergency Mgt. Council; bd. of dirs., Pa. Minority Bus. Development Auth.; Environmental Quality Bd.; Governor's Small Business Council; State Planning Bd.; State Highway and Bridge Auth.; State Transp. Adv. Com.; Bd. of Properties; appointed Secretary of Community Affairs, January 26, 1987; confirmed by Senate, March 4, 1987; married Barry E. Miller; 1 child, Joshua; home address: 120 N. 11th St., Reading.

The Department of Community Affairs (DCA) was created by the General Assembly in 1966 to be the principal advocate within Pennsylvania state government for the more than 2,600 municipalities throughout the Commonwealth. DCA was the first state agency of its kind in the nation.

The department provides a broad range of financial and technical assistance and comprehensive training to local governments and community-based organizations. These funds and programs are designed to help local governments and nonprofit agencies operate more effectively on behalf of all Pennsylvanians, urban and rural, and to encourage the use of local resources and expertise toward that goal.

As the leading advocate for local government and community agencies, the department maintains communications with members of the General Assembly, local government and related associations, and the municipalities on relevant issues and legislation. The department also plays a key role in the development and implementation of policies and programs within state government to promote and strengthen the development of all areas of the state. In support of these objectives, the department staffs five regional offices in Pittsburgh, Erie, Harrisburg, Scranton and Philadelphia, providing more direct service to the municipalities.

EXECUTIVE

The Secretary, appointed by the Governor, by and with the consent of the State Senate, administers and maintains executive authority over all phases of departmental activities. The Secretary is also chairman of the Pennsylvania Housing Finance Agency and is secretary of the Pennsylvania Industrial Development Authority. In addition, the Secretary of Community Affairs is a member of numerous other state boards and commissions.

The executive office includes the Press Office, Office of Legal Services, Office of Policy Development and the Office of Legislative Relations.

Press Office oversees statewide media relations for the department. Its staff coordinates public information activities concerning the department's objectives, programs and services. The office also supervises departmental communications; designs, writes and edits publications; and develops multi-media materials for dissemination to the department's diverse publics.

Office of Legal Services acts as chief counsel for the Secretary and supervises the department's legal activities. It reviews and monitors contracts and provides advice on legal issues, especially those affecting local government.

Office of Policy Development conducts research for the department, undertakes special projects, and evaluates departmental policies and programs. It also provides analysis of federal programs and policies which affect the department.

Office of Legislative Relations develops departmental legislation, monitors and analyzes legislation that will affect local government and the department. It acts as a department liaison with the members and staff of the General Assembly.

DEPUTY SECRETARIES

The Department of Community Affairs is responsible for a diversity of programs and services that are administered through five bureaus and five regional offices. The department's two deputy secretaries, administration and programs, oversee these bureaus and regional offices.

DEPUTY SECRETARY FOR ADMINISTRATION

Bureau of Management Services provides central management services, including financial management, audit services, contract administration, and other office services.

Governor's Heritage Affairs Commission promotes greater awareness, understanding and appreciation of Pennsylvania's ethnic traditions and cultures.

Governor's Council on the Hispanic Community acts as a liaison between Pennsylvania state government and the Hispanic neighborhoods statewide.

DEPUTY SECRETARY FOR PROGRAMS

Bureau of Local Government Services — This bureau provides a direct, comprehensive consulting, information, and training services program to all local governments, covering virtually every phase of municipal operation. Consultants in each of the department's regional offices are primary contacts for local officials and provide assistance in areas of general, financial and public works management, and policy and personnel administration. The bureau maintains annual municipal statistics and financial, budgetary, and tax records. The bureau also administers the state's Council of Governments (COGs) grants program and the Matching Assistance Program (MAP) for financially disadvantaged municipalities. The bureau also administers the Distressed Communities Grant/Loan programs.

Bureau of Housing and Development — One of the highest priorities for the department is decent and affordable housing for all Pennsylvanians. The bureau provides professional expertise and funding to Pennsylvania communities for various housing and community revitalization and economic development activities.

Additionally, the bureau is responsible for the administration of building standards for factory produced industrial housing and inspection and building standards conformance for factory-produced manufactured housing units. The bureau works with municipalities in disaster recovery projects and has been involved in the Centralia Mine Fire relocation project. The bureau administers the department's Main Street program, as well as the federal Small Communities Block Grant program.

Bureau of Recreation and Conservation — The bureau administers programs of grant funding to help local governments acquire, develop, and rehabilitate public park, recreation, and community center facilities and areas. Technical assistance is also available to help local governments with the operation, maintenance, and management of areas and facilities and the provision of recreation programs and services to residents of neighborhoods and communities. The bureau is an active participant in the statewide recreation planning process and a co-sponsor of the Pennsylvania Senior Games with the Department of Aging.

Bureau of Community Planning — Local planning activities are encouraged and supported by this bureau, which offers planning expertise and financial assistance to municipalities, regional agencies and counties in the preparation and updating of community development plans. Funding is provided through several state-sponsored planning grants programs.

The bureau's technical assistance expertise is provided in various ways, including planning training, publications and professional advice to local government officials and planning commissions.

Also of importance are efforts by this bureau to provide technical assistance to nearly 2,400 flood-prone municipalities in Pennsylvania to help them meet eligibility requirements for the National Flood Insurance Program.

This bureau also administers the Enterprise Zone Program and the Municipal Tax Exemption Reimbursement Program.

Bureau of Human Resources — This bureau is the conduit through which the department serves Pennsylvania's low-income population. The bureau coordinates state and federal resources to 44 community action and limited purpose agencies, 48 weatherization agencies and more than 200 other local non-profit agencies that work toward alleviating the causes and effects of poverty in their communities. The types of services provided to urban and rural residents include weatherization, community action, employment training, community conservation and urban assistance activities.

The bureau administers five grant programs: the federal Community Services Block Grant, Low Income Home Energy Assistance, Department of Energy Weatherization, Community Conservation and Development and the state-funded Employment and Community Conservation program. In addition, the bureau administers the Neighborhood Assistance Act which provides corporate contributors with credit against the state corporate tax. Technical assistance is provided to non-profit agencies throughout the state. The bureau also oversees the Weatherization Training Center which is designed to improve the technical skills of weatherization personnel throughout Pennsylvania.

Regional Offices — The department has regional offices in Philadelphia, Scranton, Erie, Pittsburgh and Harrisburg. Each office is headed by a regional director, with at least one specialist in each of the department's program bureaus at every office. These offices offer assistance with the development of applications for funding and project proposals and provide close personal contact with local government officials and community organizations.

SECRETARIES OF COMMUNITY AFFAIRS	Appointed Since 1950	
Joseph W. Barr, Jr.	July	26, 1966
William H. Wilcox	Jan.	25, 1971
A. L. Hydeman, Jr.	Oct.	25, 1977
William R. Davis	Feb.	23, 1979
Shirley M. Dennis	Oct.	30, 1979
*Karen A. Miller	Jan.	26, 1987

Executive Deputy Secretaries

Daniel Rogers	Dec.	8, 1966
A. L. Hydeman, Jr.	Jan.	27, 1977
James G. Shultz	Nov.	3, 1977
Karl C. Smith	Jan.	16, 1979
Shirley Dennis	July	10, 1979
William A. Hawkins	July	22, 1980

Deputy Secretaries

George G. Freeman	July	14, 1969
James N. Wade	Jan.	20, 1971
Gregory L. Coleman	Jan.	5, 1976
Charles Bacas	May	15, 1978
Shirley M. Dennis	July	2, 1979
W. N. Walters, Jr.	Mar.	3, 1980
William A. Hawkins	June	16, 1980
Maria A. Keating	Feb.	17, 1983
John T. Martino	Mar.	24, 1983
Robert W. Brown	Dec.	17, 1984
*Ronald L. Jackson	Mar.	6, 1987
*Earl F. Gohl	Mar.	6, 1987

* Incumbent

DEPARTMENT OF CORRECTIONS
Lisburn Road
P.O. Box 598
Camp Hill, PA 17011

DAVID S. OWENS, JR.   Commissioner, Department of Corrections

David S. Owens, Jr., was born March 10, 1935, in Anderson, SC, the son of Catherine Akins and David S. Owens, Sr.; Temple Univ. (A.S., criminal justice) 1976, (B.S., educ.) 1977, (M.E.) 1985; mem., Am. Correctional Assn.; Natl. Assn. of Blacks in Criminal Justice; Northeastern Assn. of Corrections Administrators; correctional officer, Phila. prisons, 1964; dep. warden, Phila. Detention Center, 1978; warden, Detention Center, 1979; Superintendent of Phila. Prisons, May 1980; mem., Young Men's Christian Alliance; Men of Malvern; bd. mem., Methodical Jaycees; v. pres., West Oak Lane Assn.; pres., John L. Kinsey Home and Schl. Assn.; rec., 1985 "Excellence in Public Administration" Award from Am. Soc. of Public Administration; Disting. Unit Award, Phila. Dept. of Welfare, 1975; Disting. Service Award, U.S. Jaycees, 1972; instructor, lecturer, Holy Family Coll. and St. Joseph's Univ.; appointed Commissioner, Department of Corrections, April 20, 1987; married Dolores Yeager; 2 sons: David S., III and Dean F.; home address: Philadelphia.

Created by Act 245 of 1984, the Department of Corrections is responsible for the management and supervision of the Commonwealth's adult correctional system. Included are all state correctional institutions and regional facilities, as well as community-oriented pre-release facilities, known as community service centers.

Pennsylvania's correctional system played a major role in the development of corrections throughout the world. Solitary confinement and religious penitence were primary components of the early "Pennsylvania System." The "penitentiary" was the embodiment of this philosophy. It was born in 1790 when reformers experimented with a limited penitentiary program at the Walnut Street Jail in Philadelphia. In 1829, the first true penitentiary in the world — Eastern State Penitentiary — was opened near what is now Fairmount Park in northwestern Philadelphia. Until the latter part of the 19th century, the Pennsylvania System was the model for corrections throughout the nation and widely copied by countries overseas. "Old Eastern," also known as Cherry Hill, was ultimately closed by the Commonwealth in 1970.

In the 1920's, Pennsylvania's major prison facilities were placed under the jurisdiction of the old Department of Welfare, along with mental health facilities and juvenile institutions. A legislative investigation into major prison riots at Pittsburgh and Rockview in 1952 led to legislation which established a separate Bureau of Correction within the state Department of Justice to oversee reforms and operate the system. Governor John S. Fine signed the bill on August 31, 1953.

In 1980, the state attorney general became an elected, rather than appointed, position, and the bureau was transferred from the Justice Department to the newly created Office of General Counsel within the Governor's Office. Four years later, on December 30, 1984, corrections was elevated to departmental status through legislation proposed and signed by Gov. Dick Thornburgh.

ADMINISTRATION

The department is headed by a commissioner and three deputy commissioners. There are nine bureaus within the agency supervised by bureau directors who serve as resource staff to the commissioner and to the various administrators in the field.

Office of the Commissioner

The Commissioner of Corrections is responsible for the supervision and management of the entire adult correctional system, including 14 institutions and 15 community service centers. This office is responsible for coordination of inmate transfer vans, the Interstate Corrections Compact and Consolidated Inmate Grievance System.

Chief Counsel provides legal representation and advice to the department.

Press Office coordinates dissemination of information on the department to the news media and general public. The department's Legislative Liaison is also based here.

Human Resources Bureau reports directly to the Commissioner and is responsible for activities relating to payroll, benefits, recruitment, labor relations and position classification as well as the department's employe training programs. Training is provided in two training centers and onsite at each facility.

Special Services Bureau also reports to the Commissioner and has two primary functions: inspection and evaluation of all state and county correctional facilities, and the investigation of alleged crimes or misconduct within the department. This bureau must approve new construction or major renovation plans for county jails and prisons, as well as requests for temporary transfer of prisoners from county facilities to department-operated institutions.

Deputy Commissioner for Programs

This Deputy Commissioner is legally responsible for approval of all inmate transfers within the state correctional system and supervises the following four bureaus:

Classification Services Bureau supervises the three diagnostic and classification centers, inmate records and the hearing examiners who deal with inmate disciplinary hearings.

Community Services Bureau supervises the residential treatment services provided to offenders housed in the department's 15 community service centers. Community services represents a part of the correctional system's efforts to provide effective supervision of the process of reintegrating the offender with society. It is one aspect of the "pre-release program" mandated under Act 173 of 1968.

Correctional Industries Bureau operates without support of the state General Fund. It is self-sustaining through the sale of inmate-made goods and services. Its production centers manufacture or process literally hundreds of items, ranging from clothing to furniture, from printing to dental products.

Treatment Services Bureau serves a wide range of areas grouped under the term "treatment." Included are health care, psychological and counseling services, recreation and leisure-time activities, religious programs and academic and vocational education. The latter category involves coordination with the state Department of Education's Division of Correction Education, which operates education programs in the state correction system.

Deputy Commissioner for Administration

This Deputy Commissioner oversees planning, research and statistical reporting and supervises two bureaus:

Data Processing Bureau provides computer support to the department through a central mainframe computer. The agency's use of personal computers is also coordinated by this bureau.

Fiscal Management Bureau oversees financial activities of the department, including budget preparation and expenditure monitoring.

Deputy Commissioner for Correctional Services

This Deputy Commissioner supervises the agency's institutions and one bureau:

Bureau of Facility Services coordinates maintenance and construction projects throughout the correctional system, monitors security systems and fire safety planning, and supervises food services within the institutions.

State Correctional Institutions (SCI)

SCI Camp Hill, Cumberland County, opened 1941, adult males.

SCI Cresson, Cambria County, opened 1987, adult males.

SCI Dallas, Luzerne County, opened 1960, adult males.

SCI Frackville, Schuylkill County, opened 1987, adult males.

SCI Graterford, Montgomery County, opened 1929, adult males.

SCI Greensburg, Westmoreland County, opened 1969 as a regional correctional facility, redesignated "SCI" in 1986, adult males.

SCI Huntingdon, Huntingdon County, opened 1889, adult males.

SCI Muncy, Lycoming County, opened 1920, adult females, some adult males.

SCI Pittsburgh, Allegheny County, opened 1882, adult males.

SCI Retreat, Luzerne County, scheduled to open 1987, adult males.

SCI Rockview, Centre County, opened 1915, adult males.

SCI Smithfield, Huntingdon County, scheduled to open 1987, adult males.

SCI Waynesburg, Greene County, opened 1984, adult females.

State Regional Correctional Facilities (SRCF)

SRCF Mercer, Mercer County, opened 1978, adult males.

Community Service Centers (CSC) (for males except where indicated for females)

Region I (Regional Office, Philadelphia)
    Philadelphia — (4) males, (1) females

Region II (Regional Office, Harrisburg)

Harrisburg	Scranton
York	Allentown
Johnstown	

Region III (Regional Office, Pittsburgh)
    Pittsburgh — (2) males, (1) females

Sharon	Erie

STATE CORRECTIONS COMMISSIONERS	Appointed Since 1950	
Arthur T. Prasse	Aug.	31, 1953
Allyn Sielaff	Oct.	8, 1970
Stewart Werner	July	24, 1973
William B. Robinson	Aug.	1, 1975
Ronald J. Marks	Jun.	16, 1980
Glen R. Jeffes (acting)	July	5, 1983
Glen R. Jeffes	Mar.	29, 1985
*David S. Owens, Jr.	Apr.	20, 1987

Deputy Commissioners

Kenneth Taylor	Oct.	16, 1953
Allyn Sielaff	May	8, 1969
Stewart Werner	Dec.	31, 1970
*Erskind DeRamus	Oct.	1, 1973
*Erskin DeRamis (Programs)	Apr.	4, 1986
*Lee T. Bernard II (Administration)	Apr.	4, 1986
*Lowell D. Hewitt (Correctional Services)	Apr.	4, 1986

* *Incumbent*

DEPARTMENT OF EDUCATION
333 Market Street
Harristown 2
Harrisburg, PA 17126-0333

THOMAS K. GILHOOL   **Secretary of Education**

Thomas K. Gilhool was born Sept. 10, 1938, in Ardmore, the son of Thomas M. and Frances Kane Gilhool; grad., St. Paul's H.S., Scranton; Lehigh Univ. (B.A.) 1960; Yale Law Schl. (LL.B.) 1964; Yale Univ. (M.A., pol. sci.) 1964; lawyer; mem., Bar of the U.S. Supreme Court; lecturer, LaSalle Coll., Temple Univ., Univ. of Pa., and City Planning Dept.; Community Legal Services, Inc., 1966-69; co-dir., Natl. Legal Services Training Program, 1971; assoc. prof. of law, Univ. of Southern Cal., 1972-75; chief counsel, Public Interest Law Center of Phila., 1975-87; Phila. Tutorial Project, founder (1961), chair (1964-68); Natl. Adv. Com., O.E.O. Legal Services Program, 1968-72; Adv. Hon. Bd., Natl. Soc. for Children & Adults with Autism, 1972; Professional Adv. Bds., Assn. for Children and Adults with Learning Disabilities, 1981-82; Professional Adv. Com., Natl. Easter Seal Soc., 1975-82; Natl. Academy of Science's Panel on Selection and Placement of Students in Programs for the Mentally Retarded, 1980-82; Council of Chief State School Officers Working Group on Children At Risk of School Failure, 1986; Natl. Merit Scholar, 1956; Woodrow Wilson Fellow, 1960; Fulbright Scholar, 1964; Pa. Co. Detectives Award, 1972; United Cerebral Palsy Associates Award, 1979; appointed Secretary of Education, Feb. 18, 1987; married Gillian Russell; 2 children: Bridget R. and Nicholas K.; home address: 625 West Upsal Street, Philadelphia.

The state Constitution declares "The General Assembly shall provide for the maintenance and support of a thorough and efficient system of public schools wherein all the children of the Commonwealth above the age of six years may be educated."

To carry out this mandate the General Assembly has established a public school system and authorized the Department of Education to administer school laws and assist school districts in conducting their educational programs. The present organization and status of the Pennsylvania Department of Education are the result of many years of evolution.

Following passage and signing of the Free School Law on April 1, 1834, the Secretary of the Commonwealth acted as head of the Common School System until 1837. In that year a separate department of schools was created with a Superintendent of Common Schools as its chief officer. In 1873, the title was changed to Superintendent of Public Instruction, and greater responsibilities were assigned to that official and to the department. In 1969, the name of the Department of Public Instruction was changed to the Department of Education, with the Superintendent of Public Instruction changed to the Secretary of Education. The department's broad responsibilities in the field of education are to:

- Administer the school laws of Pennsylvania.
- Administer rules and regulations of the State Board of Education.
- Assist local school districts in their educational programs.
- Evaluate programs of instruction and prescribe minimum courses of study.
- Apportion state appropriations for education to local school districts.
- Contract with and distribute funds to nonpublic schools for the purchase of secular educational services.
- Promote and assist in the establishment of community colleges and provide services to other institutions of higher education.
- Conduct educational research projects.
- License and regulate private schools.
- Approve programs of proprietary post-secondary institutions.

- Administer and supervise cooperative programs with private and other state and federal agencies.
- Collect and publish information about education in the Commonwealth.
- Administer the state program for public libraries.

The department also cooperates with independent groups concerned with public education: State Tax Equalization Board, State Public School Building Authority, Pa. Higher Education Assistance Agency, Pa. Public School Employes Retirement Board and the Pennsylvania Public Television Network.

ADMINISTRATION

Executive Office. The Secretary of Education, the only cabinet officer established by the Constitution of the Commonwealth, is the chief executive officer of the department. The Secretary serves as a member or official of various boards, commissions, authorities and councils.

State Board of Education is the regulatory and policy-making board for basic and higher education in the Commonwealth. There are 21 members of the State Board. Seventeen members are appointed by the Governor and confirmed by the state Senate for six-year terms, and they serve without pay. Four members of the board are members of the General Assembly. They serve as long as they hold majority and minority chairs of the House and Senate Education Committees. Ten members comprise the Council of Basic Education with ten also on the Council of Higher Education, with the chairman of the board and the chairman of each council designated by the Governor. The 21 members of the board also serve as the State Board for Vocational Education.

The board has the power and duty to review and adopt regulations that govern educational policies and principles and establish standards governing the educational programs of the Commonwealth, upon recommendation of its councils.

The Pennsylvania Department of Education provides administrative services for the board, and the Secretary of Education is the chief executive officer of the board.

The State Board of Education is supported by a staff consisting of an executive secretary and two administrative assistants.

Comptroller is the chief financial officer of the department. He aids the Secretary of Education and Governor in enforcing established policies and standards regulating the expenditure of public funds, and advises on the formulation of financial policy. He is assisted by three assistant comptrollers for Accounting, Auditing, and Systems.

Legal Office in the Department of Education is staffed by attorneys appointed by the General Counsel in the Governor's Office. It provides legal counsel to the Secretary of Education, Executive Deputy Secretary, Commissioners and other department officials and the State Board of Education. It provides legal representation to the department at certain judicial and administrative proceedings; provides opinions on questions of law; reviews contracts and regulations for legality; provides legal counsel to the Scranton State School for the Deaf; Scotland School for Veterans' Children and the Thaddeus Stevens Trade School of Technology.

State Library of Pennsylvania is the agency of the Commonwealth charged with developing, improving and coordinating library services and systems. It provides statewide leadership in the development of libraries as informational, recreational and educational contributors to the enrichment of the citizenry of all ages. As one of the largest research libraries in the Commonwealth, the State Library has holdings in almost every area of human concern. It provides information and materials from its collections and automated resources to state government, state institutions and the general public. It also provides rapid access to other library collections around the state and the nation through the use of various computerized systems, networks and databases. The State Library coordinates a network of state-aided local, district and regional public libraries established under the provisions of the Library Code. The State Library also provides support to instructional television, to Instructional Material Services units at the IUs, to the school library media program in the public and non-public schools and operates the Resource Center which provides information on education programs and practices in the vocational, adult as well as general education fields. The State Library has three divisions — Library Services, Library Development, and School Library Media Educational Resource Services.

EXECUTIVE DEPUTY SECRETARY

The Office of the Executive Deputy Secretary is responsible for all administrative and managerial staff functions of the department. These include budget, fiscal management, basic instructional subsidy, personnel, information systems and data resource management.

This office is headed by the Executive Deputy Secretary who functions as the chief aide to the Secretary in matters of administration and management. The bureaus reporting to the Executive Deputy Secretary are: Information Systems, Budget and Management, Personnel and Basic Education Fiscal Administration.

Bureau of Budget and Management directs the development, formulation and control of the department's budget and fiscal management program, Pennsylvania Management Assistance Resource Team, and supports the department by providing services in internal administrative and support operations.

Bureau of Basic Education Fiscal Administration coordinates all basic education fiscal management programs including subsidies, the administration of state and federal grants and subsidies, and acquisitions, construction and renovation, financing and planning of school plant facilities.

Bureau of Personnel provides technical support services to the department in management functions associated with: classification, compensation, organizational design, recruitment, employe benefits, staff development, transactions, affirmative action and labor relations.

Bureau of Information Systems provides data processing, word processing and decision-support services to the Department of Education; collects, processes, analyzes and disseminates education data maintained by field activities; provides information to state and federal agencies for use in research, planning, evaluation budgeting, school reimbursement, and occupational supply and demand functions; provides department-wide leadership in state-of-the-art technology and techniques in such areas as data base management systems, on-line query and report generating, distributed data processing, computer-based statistical analysis and word processing.

EXECUTIVE ASSISTANT TO THE SECRETARY

Office of the Executive Assistant to the Secretary of Education is responsible for assisting the Secretary in the review, analysis and implementation of objectives and priorities of the Department of Education. The office also assists in the development of new priorities and initiatives of the department and the Governor. The office manages special projects of interest and importance to the Secretary of Education, represents the Secretary in matters and issues involving inter-agency cooperation, and recommends appropriate options and strategies which are in the best interest of the department. The office also oversees the policy and budgetary workings of the State Library.

COMMISSIONER FOR BASIC EDUCATION

Office of Basic Education is responsible for statewide development, administration and improvement of the public and non-public schools. The major components are general education, vocational education, special education and support services — kindergarten through basic adult education — and correction education.

The office is headed by a deputy secretary/commissioner for basic education. A special assistant is chief aide to the commissioner in administrative and executive matters.

Bureau of Special Education provides professional leadership and management in the operation of the statewide program of special services for exceptional persons in public and private schools of the Commonwealth; administers and is responsible for planning, developing, promoting and coordinating appropriate special education programs, including clinical, remedial and guidance services for exceptional children; provides consultation and advice to school authorities in educational agencies, including program approval for state and federal budgets and coordinates services with appropriate local, state and federal agencies.

Bureau of Educational Planning and Testing is responsible for a statewide program of school planning. This involves districts completing Long Range Plans and implementing and evaluating their outcome. The bureau also has responsibility for in-service and staff development, school equity and student testing programs.

Bureau of Curriculum and Instruction functions as a consultative and facilitative agency in specific curriculum areas, classroom instruction strategies, correction education and compensatory education. Major activities of the bureau include the development of curriculum and instructional materials and guidelines; provision of technical assistance to school districts, intermediate units, institutions which prepare teachers, and other administrative units of the department; provision of program and administrative service for correction education and federal programs and projects.

Bureau of Vocational Education is responsible for the administration and supervision of the vocational and adult education programs. Additional responsibility includes the administration of the job-training programs under the state and federal acts. The bureau provides leadership and consultative services in the vocational areas of agriculture, business education, distributive education, health occupations, consumer and homemaking, trade and industrial education, industrial arts, as well as the special emphasis areas of disadvantaged, handicapped, work study, cooperative education, vocational-technical adult and postsecondary programs.

Bureau of Basic Education Support Services is responsible for the direction and administration of diverse educational programs in support of basic education in the public and non-public schools. The major areas are providing advisory services regarding the School Code and the laws affecting basic education; providing leadership in the area of pupil personnel services; administration of the state's non-public and private school services.

COMMISSIONER FOR HIGHER EDUCATION

Office of Higher Education provides evaluation of program approval requests for two-year, four-year, graduate and professional degrees; conducts studies of programs and services of colleges and universities, reviews and processes budgets for state-related and state-aided colleges and universities, and the State System of Higher Education; provides support services to postsecondary institutions for equal educational opportunity; participates in long range planning for higher education and assisting institutions develop programs needed in the Commonwealth.

Act 188 of 1982, which took effect on July 1, 1983, created the State System of Higher Education (SSHE), comprised of fourteen universities, the Board of Governors, the Chancellor's Office, the local councils of trustees and the institutional presidents. The Chancellor serves as the chief executive officer of the Board of Governors. Prior to this action by the Pennsylvania General Assembly, these institutions were under the administrative jurisdiction of the Department of Education.

Bureau of Academic Programs consults with degree-granting institutions, consortia and professional associations in developing new programs; recommends the approval of programs to the Secretary of Education for the awarding of degrees at private junior colleges, colleges and universities with restricted charters, professional schools, and the specialized technical and business degree programs at private, licensed schools; consults with the State Board of Education on developing regulations to assure quality postsecondary and higher education programs in Pennsylvania; manages the licensing and administrative functions for the Board of Private Licensed Schools; consults with citizens who wish to develop institutions of higher education on legislative and incorporation processes; provides training to law enforcement officers in the use of equipment and techniques for detection of those driving under the influence of chemical substances; provides advising services to institutions in the process of professional development for faculty and administrators; and approves and supervises "On-the-Job Training" programs, educational institutions, and training establishments for the education and training of veterans; works with organizations wishing to be approved as degree-granting colleges, universities and seminaries to effect this approval; amendment, merger of charters/articles of incorporation of degree-granting institutions.

Bureau of Teacher Preparation and Certification evaluates and certifies all professional staff in the Commonwealth's basic schools; issues certificates of preliminary education for professional licensure; cooperates with all teacher education institutions, basic education offices, and professional associations in developing standards for program approval of teacher education programs; coordinates the evaluation activities in program approval of teacher education programs; provides staff assistance to the Professional Standards and Practices Commission.

Bureau of Higher Education Planning and Research is responsible for supporting the conduct of planning activities in higher education and the subsequent development of plans for the future direction of higher education; and for conducting research projects and coordinating research activities with institutions of higher education and other agencies which interact with the higher education community.

Office of Equal Educational Opportunity coordinates and monitors equal educational opportunities at institutions of higher education as stated in the Commonwealth's Plan for Equal Opportunity.

BOARDS AND COMMISSIONS

Board of Governors of the State System of Higher Education is composed of sixteen members which includes two ex officio members — the Governor and the Secretary of Education. The fourteen members, including one student, are appointed by the Governor with the consent of the Senate.

The Board of Governors has overall responsibility for planning and coordinating the development and operation of the State System of Higher Education. It establishes broad fiscal, personnel and educational policies, as well as policies and procedures, for the fourteen state-owned universities.

Council of Trustees of the State Universities reviews all matters pertaining to the welfare of each respective institution; recommends to the Governor through the Board of Governors the appointment of a president and reviews and forwards a budget to the Board of Governors. The council members are appointed by the Governor with the consent of the Senate. A student member sits on each council.

Scranton State School for the Deaf Board of Trustees. Nine members appointed by the Governor with the consent of the Senate; ex officio member is the Secretary of Education. The board has general direction and control of the property and management of the institution. Reimbursement for expenses.

Scotland School for Veterans' Children Board of Trustees. Nine members appointed by the Governor with the consent of the Senate; ex officio member is the Secretary of Education. The board has general direction and control of the property and management of the institution. Reimbursement for expenses.

Thaddeus Stevens School of Technology Board of Trustees. Nine members appointed by the Governor with the consent of the Senate; ex officio member is the Secretary of Education. The board has general direction and control of the property and management of the institution. Reimbursement for expenses.

Advisory Panel for Special Education. Fifteen members appointed by the Governor. The panel advises the Secretary of Education and the Department of Education on met and unmet needs in the education of exceptional persons. Mandated by federal law. Reimbursement for expenses.

State Advisory Committee for Chapter 2, Education Consolidation and Improvement Act of 1981. Twenty-eight members appointed by the Governor. The committee assists the Department of Education in fulfilling its responsibilities under this Chapter. Reimbursement for expenses.

State Board of Private Schools. Seven members, appointed by the Secretary of Education, on the State Board of Private Academic Schools; fifteen members, fourteen of whom are appointed by the Secretary of Education and one by the director of the Office of Consumer Protection or his designee, on State Board of Private Licensed Schools; members receive per diem allowance and reimbursement for expenses.

Advisory Council on Library Development. Fourteen members; twelve appointed by Governor, who designates one as chairman; Secretary of Education and State Librarian ex officio; reimbursement for expenses.

Advisory Council for Vocational Education. Twenty-nine members appointed by Governor.

Professional Standards and Practices Commission. Sixteen members appointed by Governor; reimbursement for expenses.

Board of Trustees of the Pennsylvania State University. Thirty-two members. Six members appointed by Governor; ex officio members are the Governor, President of the University, Secretary of Education, Secretary of Agriculture, and Secretary of Environmental Resources.

Commonwealth Trustees Boards. Temple University, Lincoln University and the University of Pittsburgh. Thirty-six members (Lincoln University, thirty-nine members); four appointed by the Governor, eight appointed by General Assembly; ex officio members: Governor, Secretary of Education and Mayor of Philadelphia (Temple), Mayor of Pittsburgh (University of Pittsburgh) or President of Lincoln University; remainder of trustees are elected annually under such terms and conditions as may be provided by the universities' by-laws.

SECRETARIES OF EDUCATION (Created July 23, 1969, Act 74)		*Appointed Since 1950*
Dr. David H. Kurtzman	July	23, 1969
John C. Pittenger	Jan.	1, 1972
Robert N. Hendershot (acting)	Jan.	6, 1977
Caryl M. Kline	Apr.	28, 1977
Robert G. Scanlon	Jan.	16, 1979
Robert C. Wilburn	Jan.	18, 1983
Margaret A. Smith	Nov.	27, 1984
D. Kay Wright (acting)	July	30, 1986
William Logan (interim)	Jan.	22, 1987
*Thomas K. Gilhool	Feb.	18, 1987

Deputy Commissioners

Neal Musmanno	July	23, 1969
Donald M. Carroll[1]	Mar.	1, 1972
David C. Hornbeck	Sept.	19, 1972
Jerome M. Ziegler[2]	Oct.	2, 1972
Frank S. Manchester[1]	Sept.	15, 1975
Robert N. Hendershot	July	8, 1976
Edward C. McGuire[2]	May	6, 1977
Warren E. Ringler[2]	Sept.	6, 1978
Ronald H. Lewis[1]	June	1, 1979
Clayton L. Sommers[2]	Sept.	6, 1979
James P. Gallagher[2]	Nov.	1, 1981
Michael A. Worman	Jan.	18, 1983
Margaret A. Smith[1]	June	16, 1983
D. Kay Wright	Nov.	29, 1984
James O. Hunter	Nov.	29, 1984
William Logan (acting)	Nov.	3, 1986
*Donna Wall	Aug.	10, 1987

[1] *Dual capacity as Commissioner for Basic Education.*
[2] *Dual capacity as Commissioner for Higher Education.*

* *Incumbent*

DAVID R. HOFFMAN   Acting State Librarian

David R. Hoffman was born Sept. 28, 1934, in Brownwood, TX, the son of Albert W. and Adelaide Hoffman; grad., Davis and Elkins Coll. (B.A.) 1954; Western Reserve Univ. (MSLS) 1955; librarian; mem., Am. and Pa. Lib. Assns.; bd. mem., Market Square Concerts, Harrisburg Civic Opera Assn.; dir., Library Services Div. of State Library since 1981; named Acting State Librarian, March 1, 1987; home address: 1108 Green Street, Harrisburg.

State Librarians[1]	Appointed Since 1950	
Ralph Blasingame (resigned Jan. 17, 1964)	Apr.	1, 1957
Ernest E. Doerschuk, Jr. (acting)	Jan.	20, 1964
Ernest E. Doerschuk, Jr.	Aug.	20, 1964
Patricia Broderick (acting)	Mar.	21, 1978
Elliot Shelkrot	Mar.	10, 1980
*David Hoffman (acting)	Mar.	7, 1987

(The Act of Jan. 25, 1854, placed the power of appointment in the hands of the Governor.)

[1] Prior to the Act of February 28, 1816, there were three distinct libraries — that of the Executive Department, the Senate, and the House. By this Act the three libraries were consolidated, making a single library, and the appointment of a librarian by the joint library committee of the General Assembly, was authorized. The Act of May 23, 1919, reorganizing the State Library, changed the title of the office of State Librarian to State Librarian and Director of the Museum. The Code of 1923 continued this title. In the 1929 Code the title of State Librarian was restored.

* Incumbent

DEPARTMENT OF ENVIRONMENTAL RESOURCES
Fulton Building
P.O. Box 2063
Harrisburg, PA 17120

ARTHUR ALEXANDER DAVIS   Secretary of Environmental Resources

Arthur A. Davis was born June 20, 1922, in New York City, the son of Emanuel S. Davis and Betty Alexander; grad., Univ. of Maine (B.S.) 1947; Yale Univ. Schl. of Forestry (Master in Forestry) 1948; U.S. Army 1943-46; forestry, wildlife conservation, land & water management; former v. pres. for operations, Conservation Foundation in Washington, D.C.; former dir. of resource policy and land policy project, Western Pennsylvania Conservancy; Goddard Professor of Forestry and Environmental Resources, 1984-87; bd. of trustees, Pa. State Univ.; appointed Secretary of Environmental Resources, Jan. 20, 1987; married Lillian L. Davis; 5 children; home address: 25 West Circle, Camp Hill.

Created by Act 275 of 1970, the Department of Environmental Resources is charged with the responsibility for development of a balanced ecological system incorporating social, cultural and economic needs of the Commonwealth through development and protection of our environmental and natural resources. The department is responsible for the state's land and water management programs, all aspects of environmental protection and the regulation of mining operations. The Secretary of Environmental Resources heads the department.

Environmental Hearing Board holds hearings and issues opinions and orders and adjudications upon appeals on final action of the department.

The board is composed of three (3) members nominated by the Governor, and confirmed by majority vote of the State Senate. The Governor designates the chairman of the board.

Water Facilities Loan Board administers a $300 million program authorized under Act 167 of 1982 to provide low interest loans to the owners or operators of community water supply systems, flood control facilities and port facilities to finance repairs, construction, reconstruction, rehabilitation and improvement projects. Funds for the loans are made available through issue of periodic General Obligation Bonds to the Commonwealth. The board meets quarterly to consider applications and approve qualified loans; special meetings can be called by the Chairman to consider emergency situations.

The board is composed of eleven members: Secretary of Environmental Resources, who serves as chairman; the secretaries of Commerce, Community Affairs, General Services, Transportation, and Budget; the Chairman of the Public Utility Commission; two senators, appointed by the President Pro Tempore, one from the majority party and one from the minority party; and two members of the House of Representatives, appointed by the Speaker, one from the majority party and one from the minority party.

DEPUTY SECRETARY FOR PUBLIC LIAISON

Responsible for coordinating departmental response to environmental problems of a highly sensitive nature involving the General Assembly, local governments, and other interests.

COMMUNICATIONS OFFICE

Communications Office prepares and distributes information releases to news media explaining department activities, plans and objectives; analyzes public reaction to the department's programs and makes appropriate recommendations; maintains liaison with representatives of the news media; coordinates the department's public information programs, including films, exhibits and brochures or other publications, as developed by Resources Management and Environmental Protection Deputates.

The Community Relations function within this office develops, implements, evaluates and coordinates statewide programs designed to promote statewide communication and citizen participation and understanding of the Department of Environmental Resources. It maintains liaison with statewide community, environmental and other groups, makes recommendations for incorporating public concerns into departmental programs, presents departmental programs to the public, analyzes public reaction to departmental policies, and directs statewide community relations program.

SECRETARY'S OFFICE OF POLICY

Director, Secretary's Office of Policy is responsible for developing and coordinating departmental policy, preparing budget initiatives, coordinating strategic long-range planning, managing the department's regulatory development and review process; reviewing and analyzing Federal legislation, providing administrative support to the Environmental Quality Board and serving as the department's liaison with the Citizens Advisory Council.

Environmental Quality Board formulates, adopts and promulgates rules and regulations for the performance of the department. Receives and reviews reports from the department and the Secretary on matters of policy. Establishes rules and regulations for environmental protection, mining, water management, and lands and resources of State Parks and Forests.

The board is composed of twenty-one members: secretaries of Environmental Resources, Health, Commerce, Transportation, Agriculture, Labor and Industry, and Community Affairs; executive directors of Fish Commission, Game Commission, State Planning Board, and the Historical and Museum Commission; Chairman of the Public Utility

Commission; five members of the Citizens Advisory Council; and four members of the General Assembly.

Citizens Advisory Council reviews all environmental laws of the Commonwealth and makes appropriate suggestions for their revision, modification, and codification; annually reports to the Governor and the General Assembly; reviews the work of the department and makes recommendations for improvements.

The council is composed of nineteen members: Secretary of Environmental Resources and six members (each) appointed by the Governor, the President Pro Tempore of the Senate, and the Speaker of the House of Representatives.

DEPUTY SECRETARY FOR ADMINISTRATION

The Deputy Secretary for Administration reports directly to the Secretary. The areas of responsibility under the deputy secretary include: Fiscal Management, Automated Technology, Personnel and Office Systems Services.

Bureau of Fiscal Management reviews department funding proposals; prepares budget documents; monitors implementation of spending plans; and advises Executive Staff on fiscal aspects of agency programs.

Bureau of Automated Technology is charged with the planning, development, and implementation of agency mainframe and microprocessor based production systems and end user office automation tools; manages systems maintenance contracts and custom develops automated applications through the specialized uses of networks, mainframe executive software tools, data base administration, and scientific and commerical application programming languages.

Bureau of Personnel develops, implements, and administers the full range of personnel management and administrative programs for the department, including job classification, compensation, recruitment and placement; labor/employe relations; safety; training; employe benefits and services; personnel systems, transactions, and records.

Bureau of Office Systems and Services manages DER's office automation, word processing, office equipment, records, forms, publications management, space, leases, telecommunications, automotive equipment, procurement, capital inventory, surplus property, building services, internal stores, duplicating, and mail.

DEPUTY SECRETARY FOR ENVIRONMENTAL PROTECTION

Bureau of Waste Management administers statewide programs for hazardous waste management, municipal and residual solid waste management, resource recovery, municipal waste planning and abandoned site investigation and cleanup. Provides expert advice and guidance to industry, private enterprise and municipal government regarding facility design, construction and operation. Administers grant programs for solid waste management planning and resource recovery projects, responsible for statewide solid waste enforcement, investigation and inspection activities, responsible for state activities related to Federal Resource Conservation and Recovery Act and the Comprehensive Environmental Response Compensation and Liability Act of 1980 (Superfund).

Bureau of Mining and Reclamation administers an environmental regulatory program for all mining activities, mine subsidence regulation, mine subsidence insurance, and coal refuse disposal. Conducts a program to ensure underground bituminous mining and protects certain structures from subsidence; conducts a program to provide, at the lowest possible cost, insurance protection from damage caused by subsidence; administers a regulatory program for the manufacture and use of explosives; provides for training, examination, and certification of applicants for blaster's licenses and is responsible for a statewide program for determination and designation of areas unsuitable for mining.

Bureau of Oil and Gas Management is responsible for statewide oil and gas conservation and environmental programs as provided under the provisions of the Oil and Gas Act, the Coal and Gas Resources Coordination Act, the Oil and Gas Conservation Law, the Natural Gas Policy Act as amended, and those portions of the Clean Streams Law and Solid Waste Management Act as they apply to oil and gas well operations and natural gas storage fields. This program regulates oil and gas development and production, underground natural gas storage, and waste disposal activities and their associated safety, conservation and environmental impacts, as well as certain natural gas pricing and certain coal mining activities.

Bureau of Radiation Protection is responsible for regulating and inspecting users of radiation sources throughout the Commonwealth; conducts a comprehensive environmental radiation monitoring program throughout the state; conducts a nuclear safety review and continuing evaluation of nuclear power plants; carries out an emergency radiation response program; carries out a statewide radon monitoring program, plans for regulating low-level radioactive waste disposal.

Bureau of Community Environmental Control plans, develops, and administers statewide programs for public drinking water supplies; food protection at public eating and drinking places and shellfish establishments; and environmental sanitation at public facilities such as organized camps and campgrounds, public bathing places, schools, and seasonal farm labor camps. The agency also administers a vector control program which identifies and resolves insect and rodent problems which may affect public health.

Bureau of Water Quality Management carries out its duties and responsibilities under the state's Clean Streams Laws, Sewage Facilities Act, Sewage Treatment Plant and Waterworks Operators Certification Act, and Act 339 (State Grants for Operation of Sewage Treatment Plants) and delegated responsibilities under the Federal Clean Water Act, and other Federal legislation. This program is responsible for developing water quality standards for surface and groundwater quality monitoring program and regulating water pollution control facilities through its planning, permitting, surveillance and monitoring, enforcement, grants administration, and certification activities.

Bureau of Laboratories provides analytical services to environmental, regulatory, planning, and advisory programs of the department; provides organic and inorganic chemical, microbiological, radiological, biological and physical testing of environmental samples in Harrisburg and Erie. Provides technical consultation to programs as in the Blackfly Eradication Program, provides expert witnesses in enforcement actions, develops and implements quality assurance programs for the various tests performed; develops new or modified analytical techniques and methods of laboratory analysis; provides laboratory certification services required by state and federal law; provides emergency laboratory services during occurrences of natural or man-made disasters.

Bureau of Air Quality Control provides for the well-being of citizens through development and implementation of programs for control of air pollution within the geographic confines of the state; assures compliance with the State Air Pollution Control Act and the Federal Clean Air Act by an aggressive monitoring, educational and enforcement policy; investigates complaints and initiates remedial action to abate air pollutant sources; provides guidance to industry and citizen groups and coordinates with local, state and federal agencies to establish effective clean air control programs.

Bureau of Deep Mine Safety is responsible for enforcement of anthracite and bituminous coal mining laws of the Commonwealth; provides for the health and safety of persons employed in and about coal mines and for the protection and preservation of property connected therewith. These responsibilities are also undertaken for all metal and non-metal underground mining operations in the state; responsible for maintaining an index of abandoned mine maps on record in the Commonwealth.

State Board for Certification of Sewage Treatment Plant and Waterworks Operators reviews and passes on application for certification of Sewage Treatment Plant & Waterworks Operators, administers examinations, holds hearings, and issues adjudications.

State Board of Certification of Sewage Enforcement Officers reviews and acts upon applications for certification of sewage enforcement officers, administers examinations, holds hearings and issues adjudications.

Coal and Clay Mine Subsidence Insurance Board sets policy and administers the Coal and Clay Mine Subsidence Insurance Fund.

Seasonal Farm Labor Committee reviews existing and proposed rules and regulations concerning seasonal farm labor; provides commentary to the Environmental Quality Board.

The committee consists of the Secretary of Environmental Resources or his designee, who shall be chairman; secretaries of Agriculture, Labor and Industry, and Health, or their designees; and six persons appointed by the Governor.

DEPUTY SECRETARY FOR RESOURCES MANAGEMENT

Bureau of Water Resources Management directs and

coordinates water resource management activities for the department and the Commonwealth by planning and managing the Commonwealth's water and related land resources. This includes water conservation, water allocations, hydropower feasibility, coastal zone management and scenic rivers preservation. The Bureau provides Commonwealth representation in comprehensive water resources studies, river basin commissions, and operational planning of federal and other agencies in areas affecting Pennsylvania.

Bureau of Water Projects plans, designs, inspects and maintains DER dams, flood protection and desilting projects. Conducts engineering investigations and feasibility studies for proposed dams and flood protection projects; designs projects which are to be constructed by the department for control of surface water; and investigates, designs and constructs stream clearance and channel improvement projects.

Bureau of Abandoned Mine Reclamation administers and oversees the Abandoned Mine Reclamation Program in Pennsylvania. Responsible for resolving environmental degradation problems such as mine fires, mine subsidence and mining pollution which has resulted from past mining practices.

Bureau of State Parks administers the overall operation, maintenance, planning, development and management of the Pennsylvania State Park system; provides year-round recreational opportunities and experiences for Pennsylvania residents and visitors; engages in the interpretation of State Park ecological systems; utilizes, protects and perpetuates as a principal heritage the natural environment and recreational opportunities of the State Parks system.

Bureau of Topographic and Geologic Survey plans, administers and conducts comprehensive and detailed surveys of the geology, mineral resources, topography and ground water resources of Pennsylvania. The results of all geologic, topographic, water and mineral investigations and surveys are made available to the public through publications, technical services and a geologic library which is maintained by the bureau. This bureau is the only agency in Pennsylvania which is systematically mapping the geologic resources of the Commonwealth.

Bureau of Dams and Waterway Management administers and enforces laws and regulations related to flood plain management, storm water management, dams and water obstructions. Administers grant programs to counties for storm water management planning and processes permits for regulated facilities in flood plain management, dam safety and water obstructions.

Bureau of Forestry is responsible for the protection of over two million acres of forest land in the Commonwealth from forest fire, insects and disease. They also protect water resources; aid in soil erosion control; provide recreational opportunities, timber and other forest products, and wildlife food and cover.

Bureau of Soil and Water Conservation carries out mandated responsibilities of the Soil Conservation Law including PL 566 small watershed projects, establishes

priorities for watershed project installations, and implements erosion and sedimentation control regulations. Also provides advisory and financial assistance to the 66 conservation districts within the state.

State Conservation Commission assists local conservation districts by providing financial assistance to employ professional help, provides financial assistance for the support of small watershed projects and supports local conservation districts in soil and water conservation efforts.

OFFICE OF CHIEF COUNSEL

Bureau of Regulatory Counsel is responsible for the substantive review of department regulations and policies and procedures, for legal comment upon legislation introduced in the General Assembly and the U.S. Congress, the drafting of legislation which the department wishes to advance, occasional major or other important litigation assignments, the legal interpretation of state and federal statutes, the development of delegation agreements and the development and coordination of enforcement policy and mechanisms in conjunction with the field offices.

Litigation services are provided by three field offices: Harrisburg, Philadelphia and Pittsburgh. These offices initiate all enforcement actions, defend appeals from department actions, supervise department personnel when conducting investigations and tests for use in enforcement actions; and provide counsel to the regional offices of the department on daily enforcement, inspections and policy problems to assure statewide uniformity of actions. Issues of administrative policy and procedure are coordinated with the Bureau of Regulatory Counsel.

Bureau of Legal Services has a wide variety of responsibilities on behalf of the Department of Environmental Resources, similar to those of a general law firm with the exception that this bureau does not enforce or counsel with respect to statutes and regulations within the department's jurisdiction directed to the alleviation of nuisances, pollution and other damage to the environment, which responsibilities are those of the field offices and the Bureau of Regulatory Counsel.

SECRETARIES OF ENVIRONMENTAL RESOURCES (Created on Dec. 3, 1970, Act 275)	*Appointed Since 1950*	
Maurice K. Goddard[1]	Jan.	19, 1971
Clifford L. Jones	Feb.	16, 1979
Peter Duncan (acting)	Oct.	19, 1981
Nicholas DeBenedictis	Feb.	7, 1983
*Arthur A. Davis	Jan.	20, 1987

Deputy Secretaries

Louis F. Waldmann	Mar.	22, 1971
Edward M. Seladones	June	7, 1971
Wesley E. Gilbertson	June	7, 1971
William M. Eichbaum	June	7, 1971
Clifford H. McConnell	June	7, 1971
Donald O. Osterling	Jan.	1, 1973
Clifford H. McConnell	Feb.	23, 1979

* *Incumbent*

	Appointed Since 1950	
William B. Middendorf	Feb.	23, 1979
Peter S. Duncan	Feb.	23, 1979
Edward J. Miller	Apr.	2, 1979
Walter A. Lyon	May	3, 1979
Mary T. Webber	June	19, 1980
Isadore R. Lenglet	Mar.	7, 1983
R. Harry Bittle	Feb.	4, 1983
*Patrick J. Solano	Feb.	4, 1983
William J. Green	Nov.	4, 1983
*Mark M. McClellan	Feb.	17, 1987
*Gregg Robertson	Feb.	20, 1987
*James R. Grace	Feb.	20, 1987

State Geologist

Stanley H. Cathcart (dec. Mar. 19, 1953)	Jan.	1, 1947
Carlyle Gray (acting)	Oct.	1, 1953
Carlyle Gray	Oct.	1, 1955
Dr. Arthur A. Socolow	Dec.	4, 1961

	Appointed Since 1950	
*Dr. Donald Hoskins	Jan.	8, 1987

(This office was within the Department of Internal Affairs, under the Administrative Code of 1929. Upon the abolition of Internal Affairs, the position was transferred to the Department of Environmental Resources.)

(Under Code, Act of June 7, 1923. The Department of Forests and Waters was abolished by the Act of Dec. 3, 1970, Act 275, which created the Department of Environmental Resources.)

State Forester

Samuel S. Cobb	Oct.	27, 1966
Richard R. Thorpe	Oct.	20, 1977

[1] *Dr. Goddard was Secretary of the Dept. of Forests and Waters and has uninterrupted service with the creation of this department.*

* *Incumbent*

DEPARTMENT OF GENERAL SERVICES
515 North Office Building
Harrisburg, PA 17125

DAVID L. JANNETTA

**Acting Secretary of General Services
Executive Director, General State Authority**

David Lynn Jannetta was born June 1, 1952, in Altoona, the son of Phillip A. and Betty Sellers Jannetta (dec.); grad., Altoona Area H.S., 1970; att., Pa. State Univ., 1971; U.S. Air Force Academy (B.S., International Relations) 1975; Webster Coll., St. Louis, Mo. (M.A., Public Admin.) 1979; Univ. of Arkansas (M.S., Operations Mgt.) 1981; active duty, USAF, 1975-81; Capt., PA Air National Guard, 1981-pres.; rec., Air Medal, AF Commendation Medal; mem., Pi Lambda Phi; Mayor, City of Altoona, Jan. 1984-Dec. 21, 1987; part-time instructor, St. Francis Coll., Loretto, Pa.; former natl. dir., Air Force Assn. (AFA); state pres., PA Air Force Assn., 1987, 1988; 1st v.p., Pa. League of Cities, 1987; chmn. of bd., PENN Prime Trustees, 1987; gen. chmn., Blair Co. United Way Campaign, 1984; mem.: Sons of Italy Lodge #958, K. of C., American Legion, A&J Iaia Post #827, The Army and Navy Club; FRAM/Autolite Sparkplug of Year Award; Outstanding Young Man of America; Presidential Classroom for Young Americans; appointed acting Secretary of General Services, Dec. 21, 1987; married Heather Poppke; 4 children: Aaron, David, Elizabeth, Ian; home address: 312 Logan Boulevard, Altoona.

The Department of General Services is the central maintenance, purchasing, publishing and building construction agency for departments and other agencies of the Commonwealth. It was created by Act 45 of 1975, which amended the Administrative Code by providing for a merger of the powers and duties of the Department of Property and Supplies and the General State Authority (GSA). (The Authority will continue to exist as a public corporation until 1998, however, when its bond obligations will be satisfied. See also GSA powers and duties, this section.)

The Secretary of General Services, the chief executive officer, is appointed by the Governor with the advice and consent of the majority of the Senate. He is ex officio, a member of the governing bodies of the General State Authority, the State Public School Building Authority, the Pennsylvania Transportation Assistance Authority and the Pennsylvania Higher Educational Facilities Authority. He is Insurance Broker of Record for the Commonwealth and Secretary to the Board of Commissioners of Public Grounds and Buildings.

The organizational units of the department are grouped into five functional areas: executive, administration,

procurement, central services, and public works. These areas report to, respectively, the Secretary, and the deputy secretaries for Administration, Procurement, Central Services, and Public Works.

EXECUTIVE

Executive Office includes the Secretary's immediate staff, the departmental press secretary, legislative liaison and the editor of *The Pennsylvania Manual.* Also reporting to the Secretary are the four departmental deputy secretaries and the following organizational units:

Office of Chief Counsel serves as legal advisor to the Secretary and to other officers of the department.

Office of State Inspector General initiates, supervises, and coordinates investigative activities relating to fraud, waste, misconduct, or abuse in executive agencies.

Public Events Office is responsible for scheduling public events, demonstrations, news conferences and cultural activities occurring in the Capitol Rotunda, Forum and other locations within the Capitol Complex, and arranges for appropriate support services; operates Capitol Tours program.

Bureau of Risk and Insurance Management maintains insurance and self-insurance on Commonwealth-owned property and on Commonwealth construction projects whose bond obligations are still outstanding; underwrites the state's torts liability, employe liability and workers' compensation liability insurance; maintains coverage for approximately 25,875 state vehicles; contracts for state employes' group life insurance; and formulates comprehensive policies for the management of the state's insurance and loss prevention program.

DEPUTY SECRETARY FOR ADMINISTRATION

Bureau of Management Services provides administrative support services to the department, including organizational studies, forms control, records management, systems analysis, data processing, telecommunications, pre-audit and coordination of procurement requests with Bureau of Purchases and Comptroller and mail and messenger services; compiles the Commonwealth Telephone Directory.

Bureau of Personnel administers the department's personnel program, including recruitment, placement, classification, payroll and employe training and counseling services.

Bureau of Publications and Paperwork Management administers a centralized management program for all government communications in the print medium, including publishing, printing, forms management; manages the State Bookstore, the State Records Center, in-house printing and micrographic services.

Financial Administration Office formulates the departmental budget and coordinates budgetary activities between the department and the Governor's Office of the Budget.

Office of Minority and Women Business Enterprise coordinates efforts to prevent discriminatory practices in hiring and contracting.

Commonwealth Media Services centrally accommodates state agencies' needs for audio, video and photographic services, operating the central television studio, the Capitol media center, and the central photographic laboratory.

DEPUTY SECRETARY FOR PROCUREMENT

Bureau of Purchases is the Commonwealth's central purchasing coordinator and exercises control over the acquisition of commodities for state agencies, selection of bidders and awarding of contracts to vendors; develops standards and specifications for all materials and commodities purchased by state agencies; inspects and tests purchased goods for compliance with specifications; offers technical advice to all state agencies.

Bureau of Telecommunications and Information Technology Services operates the Commonwealth telephone network and centrally manages the planning and acquisition of data processing, radio and telephone equipment.

Bureau of Supplies and Surplus Operations warehouses and distributes bulk supplies, including office supplies, forms and automotive supplies; is responsible for two distinct programs: first, the Surplus Federal Property Program, in which surplus federal property is made available to eligible health, education and civil defense organizations and to state and local governmental agencies; second, the Surplus State Property program, in which surplus state property is made available at no charge to other state agencies and to school districts, or is sold to the public through auctions or private sales.

Bureau of Vehicle Management is the central Commonwealth agency responsible for the purchase, maintenance, inspection, registration and disposition of all Commonwealth-owned motor vehicles, except PennDOT vehicles.

DEPUTY SECRETARY FOR CENTRAL SERVICES

Bureau of Buildings and Grounds is responsible for the maintenance, operation, repair and housekeeping functions for state buildings, facilities and grounds in the Capitol Complex as well as the Altoona, Philadelphia, Pittsburgh, Reading and Scranton State Office Buildings.

Bureau of Police and Safety, through its Capitol Police force, provides protection, security and enforcement of order at the Capitol Complex and other buildings and grounds under the jurisdiction of the department. Its Fire and Accident Prevention division inspects these facilities to ensure their compliance with the Fire Safety and Panic Act.

Bureau of Real Estate contracts for rental of office space and other accommodations for state agencies not housed in state-owned facilities, such as state police barracks, state liquor stores and county boards of assistance; conducts appraisals and sells state property as specified by the Legislature.

Bureau of Space and Facilities Management is responsible for the planning and assignment of office space in the Capitol Complex and other facilities under the jurisdiction of the department and for the maintenance and operation of an inventory program of all state-owned and state-leased land and buildings.

DEPUTY SECRETARY FOR PUBLIC WORKS

The Deputy Secretary for Public Works oversees all state-funded and bond-financed construction projects in excess of $25,000. Those projects and related services include: new construction, alteration and repair of Commonwealth properties; capital improvement projects (as provided for by the General Assembly in successive Capital Budgets); project land acquisition; project management and design; establishment of specifications and standards for construction projects; providing architectural and engineering services to other state agencies; providing project specifications to state agencies for projects under $25,000; and correction and repair to existing General State Authority projects.

Bureau of Engineering and Architecture provides and oversees professional engineering and architectural services for all state agencies; reviews designs for Capital Construction projects and recommends their approval, disapproval or modification.

Bureau of Construction is responsible for the supervision, coordination and inspection of all construction projects under the department's jurisdiction.

Bureau of Contract and Support Service provides support services to the public works sector, including gathering of bid proposals, letting of bids, and maintenance of the master project file.

BOARDS AND COMMISSIONS

State Art Commission, consisting of five citizens appointed by the Governor, examines and approves or disapproves the design or location of a wide variety of public structures, including monuments, memorials, buildings and other structures acquired by the Commonwealth, funded by the State Treasury or by any political subdivision, or structures for which the site is furnished either by the Commonwealth or by any of its subdivisions. No private structures may be erected over any state or local public place without commission approval. Exceptions to the commission's jurisdiction are cities of the first and second class.

Board of Commissioners of Public Grounds and Buildings consists of the Governor and State Treasurer; the Secretary of General Services serves as secretary to the board. The board is responsible for final action on state lease negotiations, sale of Commonwealth-owned automotive equipment, purchases where there is an absence of competitive bidding and claims by state agencies against the State Insurance Fund for loss or damage to state property.

Joint Committee on Documents administers the Commonwealth Documents Law (Act 240 of 1968) and is responsible for the policy supervision of the Legislative Reference Bureau in connection with its publication of the *Pennsylvania Bulletin* (the official gazette of the Commonwealth) and the *Pennsylvania Code,* which contains agency administrative regulations, court rules and other official (but non-statutory) documents having the force and effect of law. Members of the committee are the President Pro Tempore of the Senate, Speaker of the House of Representatives, Attorney General, Secretary of General Services, Director of the Legislative Reference Bureau and two members from the general public appointed by the Governor.

Architects and Engineers Selection Committee consists of five members appointed by the Governor, none of whom may be Commonwealth employes or elected officials. The membership consists of architects, engineers or other persons knowledgeable in the field of building construction.

The committee reviews the work, experience and qualifications of architects and engineers and submits three recommendations for each Capital Construction project, in order of preference, to the Secretary of General Services. An appointment is then made by the Secretary for each project based on restrictions imposed by the Administrative Code.

Committee on Construction Contract Documents consists of not more than five nor less than three members selected from associations representing contractors doing business with the department; appointed by the Secretary of General Services; the committee serves in an advisory capacity to the department and its Public Works staff, bringing to their attention issues of concern among state contractors and recommending changes or improvements to contract documents, related procedures, paperwork and other contractural proceedings.

GENERAL STATE AUTHORITY

The General State Authority was created by the Act of March 31, 1949, P.L. 372. (A GSA was created earlier by the Act of June 28, 1935, P.L. 452, but subsequently was repealed by the Act of May 18, 1945, P.L. 641.)

Under the 1949 Act, the authority was created for the purpose of "constructing, improving, equipping, furnishing, maintaining, acquiring and operating" a wide range of public works, including all state buildings, institutions and airports, state-aided schools, and municipal exhibition halls. Projects were financed by the sale of general obligation bonds sold in accordance with the Capital Facilities Debt Enabling Act of 1968. Bond proceeds were repaid from the lease or rental of such buildings.

The Act of July 22, 1975, No. 45, effective October 20, 1975, created the Department of General Services and transferred to the new department the powers and duties of the former Department of Property and Supplies and of the General State Authority. However, the authority continues to function as an independent public corporation until the outstanding debt from bond proceeds spent on earlier projects is satisfied in 1998.

SECRETARIES OF GENERAL SERVICES	Appointed Since 1950	
Ronald G. Lench[1]	Oct.	20, 1975
William H. McKenzie (acting)	Mar.	20, 1978
Ronald G. Lench (reappt.)	June	20, 1978
Walter Baran	Jan.	16, 1979
James W. Brown	Jan.	20, 1987
*David L. Jannetta (acting)	Dec.	21, 1987

Deputies

Edmund C. Kulpa	Oct.	20, 1975
William H. McKenzie	Oct.	20, 1975
William M. McLaughlin	Feb.	5, 1976
Edward J. Smith	Sept.	9, 1976
Gary E. Crowell (reappt. Mar. 14, 1979)	Feb.	24, 1977
*Thomas J. Topolski	Mar.	14, 1979
John F. Lawlis, Jr.	Apr.	16, 1979
Patrick J. Solano	May	29, 1979
Donald E. Smith	Feb.	15, 1983
Charles F. Mebus	Mar.	11, 1983
Merle H. Ryan	Aug.	12, 1983
*Harold P. Anderson	July	20, 1987
*Richard E. Barber	July	24, 1987

[1] *Resigned Mar. 20, 1978 to seek Lieutenant Governor nomination; reappt. Deputy May 26, 1978; reappt. Secretary June 20, 1978; resigned Jan. 16, 1979.*

* *Incumbent*

GENERAL STATE AUTHORITY

Members	Appointed Since 1950
John S. Fine.	Jan. 16, 1951
Charles C. Smith (reappt. May 7, 1957)	Feb. 7, 1951
Alan D. Reynolds	Feb. 26, 1951
Rowland B. Mahany.	Jan. 14, 1953
Albert W. Johnson	Feb. 9, 1953
Frank C. Hilton.	Nov. 2, 1953
Rowland B. Mahany.	Jan. 6, 1955
Albert S. Readinger	Jan. 6, 1955
George M. Leader	Jan. 18, 1955
Wm. D. Thomas.	Jan. 18, 1955
Francis J. Myers.	Feb. 11, 1955
Genevieve Blatt	May 3, 1955
John S. Rice.	Jan. 1, 1956
Michael Lawler.	July 24, 1957
W. Stuart Helm	Jan. 1, 1957
Robert F. Kent	May 6, 1957
Andrew M. Bradley	July 19, 1957
Charles R. Weiner	Jan. 6, 1959
Stephen McCann.	Jan. 6, 1959
James S. Berger	Jan. 6, 1959
David L. Lawrence.	Jan. 20, 1959
Grace M. Sloan	May 1, 1961
Thomas Z. Minehart.	May 2, 1961
Anthony J. DiSilvestro	Jan. 3, 1961
William W. Scranton	Jan. 15, 1963
Richard M. Hornbeck.	Jan. 15, 1963
Anthony J. Petrosky.	Jan. 7, 1963
General Milton Baker	Mar. 1, 1963
Kenneth B. Lee	Dec. 6, 1963
John H. Devlin (dec.)	Jan. 5, 1965
Robert K. Hamilton	Jan. 5, 1965
Stanley G. Stroup.	Jan. 5, 1965
Joshua Eilberg.	Jan. 5, 1965
Raymond P. Shafer.	Jan. 17, 1967
Perrin C. Hamilton	Jan. 17, 1967
John K. Tabor	Jan. 17, 1967
Herbert Fineman	Jan. 17, 1967
Robert D. Fleming	Jan. 24, 1967
Lee A. Donaldson	Jan. 24, 1967
Ernest P. Kline	Aug. 1, 1967
K. Leroy Irvis	Jan. 12, 1969
Robert P. Casey	June 3, 1969
Milton J. Shapp	Feb. 3, 1971
Martin L. Murray	Feb. 3, 1971
Paul J. Smith	Feb. 3, 1971
Frank C. Hilton.	Feb. 3, 1971
Kenneth B. Lee	Feb. 3, 1971
Thomas F. Lamb	Feb. 3, 1971
Richard A. Doran.	Apr. 28, 1971
Robert J. Butera.	Jan. 24, 1973
Richard C. Frame.	Jan. 24, 1973
Stanley G. Stroup.	Apr. 3, 1974
Ronald G. Lench	Oct. 1, 1974
Thomas M. Nolan	Jan. 7, 1975

	Appointed Since 1950
T. Newell Wood	Jan. 7, 1975
William B. McLaughlin III	Mar. 26, 1975
Henry G. Hager	Jan. 4, 1977
Al Benedict	Jan. 18, 1977
Robert E. Casey.	Jan. 18, 1977
T. Newell Wood (reappt.)	July 27, 1977
Dick Thornburgh	Jan. 16, 1979
Walter Baran	Jan. 16, 1979
Matthew J. Ryan	Jan. 29, 1979
Edward P. Zemprelli	Apr. 2, 1979
*Fred Taylor.	May 2, 1979
Samuel E. Hayes, Jr.	May 7, 1979
Eugene F. Scanlon	May 23, 1979
Myron L. Joseph	Mar. 6, 1979
H. Jack Seltzer.	July 10, 1979
Robert S. Ross, Jr.	July 11, 1979
Charles J. Lieberth.	Nov. 27, 1979
R. Budd Dwyer (dec.).	Jan. 20, 1981
*Ralph W. Hess	Mar. 3, 1981
Nicholas B. Moehlmann.	Jan. 19, 1981
Barry H. Stern	Jan. 19, 1982
*Robert J. Mellow	Feb. 2, 1983
K. Leroy Irvis	Jan. 4, 1983
John J. Shumaker	June 3, 1983
Robert O'Donnell.	Feb. 9, 1983
Murray Dickman	June 12, 1984
James W. Knepper.	Dec. 10, 1984
*Ralph W. Hess (reappt.)	Jan. 7, 1985
*Don Bailey.	Jan. 15, 1985
*Robert J. Mellow (reappt.)	Jan. 28, 1985
*Peter C. Wambach.	Feb. 22, 1985
*Robert P. Casey	Jan. 20, 1987
James W. Brown	Jan. 20, 1987
*Harris L. Wofford, Jr.	Jan. 20, 1987
*G. Davis Greene, Jr.	Feb. 11, 1987
*Joseph C. Manmiller	May 8, 1987
*John T. Tigue, III.	May 18, 1987
*Robert A. Bittenbender	July 7, 1987
*David L. Jannetta (acting)	Dec. 21, 1987

Executive Directors

Warren W. Holmes (acting)	May 13, 1952
John N. Forker.	Jan. 6, 1954
A. J. Caruso.	June 1, 1957
John J. Lynam.	July 12, 1961
A. J. Caruso (reappt.).	Mar. 5, 1963
R. L. Kunzig.	Jan. 24, 1967
James D. Logan	Mar. 24, 1969
Robert H. Jones.	Jan. 19, 1971
Ronald G. Lench	Oct. 22, 1975
Walter Baran	Jan. 16, 1979
James W. Brown	Jan. 20, 1987
*David L. Jannetta (acting)	Dec. 21, 1987

* *Incumbent*

DEPARTMENT OF HEALTH
802 Health and Welfare Building
Harrisburg, PA 17120

N. MARK RICHARDS, M.D.   **Secretary of Health**

N. Mark Richards, M.D., was born June 20, 1939, in Warren, Ohio; grad., Oberlin Coll. (A.B.) 1961; Univ. of Wisconsin (M.S.) 1964, (M.D.) 1966; internship, Rush Presbyterian-St. Luke's Hosp., Chicago, 1966-67; residency, Duke Univ. Medical Center, 1969-70; chief resident in medicine, Univ. of Ill., 1970-71; surgeon, USPHS, Center for Disease Control, 1967-69; instructor in medicine and asst. prof. of medicine, Univ. of Ill., 1970-78; clinical asst. prof., Schl. of Medicine, and adj. asst. prof., Graduate Schl. of Public Health, Univ. of Pittsburgh, 1979 to present; dep. dir. for med. services, Allegheny Co. Health Dept., 1979-87; dir., 1979-87; Am. Assn. for Advancement of Science; Am. Public Health Assn.; Western Pa. Public Health Council; Pa. Public Health Assn.; Health Systems Agency of Southwestern Pa.; Allegheny Co. Medical Soc.; Health Education Center; Natl. Assn. of Co. Health Officers; participant in various Pa. public service and univ. activities; author of numerous medical publications; appointed Secretary of Health, Jan. 20, 1987; married Barbara Geisler; 2 children: Jennifer and Gretchen; home address: 884 Old Hickory Rd., Mt. Lebanon.

The Department of Health has the duty and power to protect the health of the people of the Commonwealth. It is responsible for employing the most efficient and effective means for the prevention and suppression of disease and injury. In addition, the department has the responsibility to ensure the accessibility of high quality health care at a reasonable cost. The department provides the leadership and assistance necessary to plan, coordinate and support a total statewide public health effort.

The Department of Health was created by the Act of April 27, 1905, P.L. 312, which has been somewhat modified by the Administrative Code of 1929. The department has authority to enforce all statutes pertaining to public health and the rules and regulations of the Advisory Health Board. It acts indirectly through local boards of health in cities, boroughs and first and second class townships. In 1951 the State General Assembly authorized county commissioners to establish county departments of health.

The Secretary of Health is appointed by the Governor and confirmed by the Senate for a term of four years, with full executive control of public health affairs in the Commonwealth. The Secretary is, by virtue of office, a member of the Commission on Charitable Organizations, Nursing Home Loan Agency Board, chairperson of the Council on Drug and Alcohol Abuse and Executive Director of the Statewide Health Coordinating Council. By statute, the Secretary of Health is chairperson of the Advisory Health Board, Drug, Device and Cosmetic Board, Health Care Policy Board and the Vietnam Herbicides Information Commission, and a member of the Advisory Committee on Organ and Tissue Donation, Humanities Gift Registry Board, Cancer Control, Prevention and Research Advisory Board, State Board of Medical Education and Licensure, State Dental Council and Examining Board, Emergency Management Council, State Board of Examinations of Nursing Home Administrators, and the Commission of Public Welfare.

EXECUTIVE

Office of Chief Counsel advises the Secretary of Health and all units of the department on the interpretation of state and federal statutes, regulations, policy directives and all formal legal documents so as to guide and assist the department in carrying out its mission and mandates in a lawful manner. It also

reviews proposed legislation, in conjunction with the Office of Legislative Programs and specifically affected program offices.

Office of Legislative Programs is the liaison between the state and federal legislative branches and the department. It develops, coordinates and comments on proposed and pending legislation after consultation with department staff, other agencies and organizations and the Governor's Office. It collects, analyzes and disseminates information regarding health legislation and regulations.

Office of Press Secretary is responsible for maintaining free access by the public and news media to all information regarding the department's programs and services within the confines of existing mandates. It is also responsible for liaison between the Department of Health and the Governor's Office for all facets of communication policy through the news media.

Office of Policy, Planning and Evaluation is the central coordinating point for inter- and intradepartmental strategic planning, policy development and evaluation. It prepares departmental policy analysis, develops short and long-range plans and systems for implementing policies and designs monitoring and evaluation strategies. Recommends final distribution of departmental resources to enable goal achievement.

Advisory Board of Arthritis assesses the magnitude of the arthritis problem in the Commonwealth and develops a control plan which will define the impact of arthritis and its complications in Pennsylvania. There are nine members appointed by the Governor.

Advisory Health Board is responsible for adopting rules and regulations necessary for the prevention of disease, for the protection of lives and health, and for the health services of counties or other political subdivisions. The board has twelve members; the Secretary of Health, chairperson, and eleven members appointed by the Governor.

Cancer Control, Prevention and Research Advisory Board advises the Secretary of Health on cancer control matters and each year approves a program for cancer control, prevention and research to be known as the Pennsylvania

Cancer Plan. It also recommends to the Secretary the awarding of grants and contracts to qualified associations or governmental agencies in order to plan, establish or conduct programs in cancer control or prevention, cancer education and training and cancer clinical research. The board has eleven members; the Secretary of Health and ten members appointed by the Governor.

Drug, Device and Cosmetic Board advises the Secretary of Health on matters pertaining to the manufacture and distribution of drugs, devices and cosmetics. The board also recommends rules and regulations that might be required to administer the Controlled Substance, Drug, Device and Cosmetic Act (P.L. 233) and the Generic Drug Law. There are ten members appointed by the Governor and the Secretary of Health is the chairperson.

Health Care Policy Board reviews rules and regulations prepared by the Department of Health relating to the policies, procedures and criteria used for Certificate of Need Reviews and for licensing health care facilities. There are thirteen members; the Secretary of Health, chairperson, and twelve members appointed by the Governor.

Humanity Gifts Registry Board controls the distribution and delivery of cadavers to and among persons and institutions specified under P.L. 119 and its amendments. The board, composed of medical and dental institutional representatives and the Secretary of Health, establishes rules and regulations for registry operations.

Council on Drug and Alcohol Abuse advises the Secretary of Health concerning the development and implementation of the State Plan for the control, prevention, intervention, treatment, rehabilitation, research, education and training aspects of drug and alcohol abuse and dependency problems. The council has seven members; the Secretary of Health and six members appointed by the Governor.

Council on Physical Fitness and Sports promotes and improves physical fitness programs in the Commonwealth. The council works with state and local officials to develop community-centered and school-based physical education programs to include the physically handicapped. The council has fifteen members appointed by the Governor.

State Health Coordinating Council advises the Department of Health on health planning and development matters and reviews health service plans, annual implementation plans, and grant applications submitted by areawide health systems agencies. The council adopts a State Health Plan, oversees its implementation and reviews certain statewide health grant applications submitted to the federal government. There are twenty-four members appointed by the Governor.

Advisory Committee on Organ and Tissue Donation advises the Secretary of Health regarding the availability and coordination of securing organs for transplantation, with emphasis on encouraging public and professional awareness. The committee consists of persons involved in organ donation and transplantation within the state.

Vietnam Herbicides Information Commission obtains information relating to the health effects of exposure to "Vietnam Herbicides" by Vietnam Veteran residents of Pennsylvania. It determines medical, administrative and social assistance needed by veterans who were exposed to "Vietnam Herbicides," conducts outreach and disseminates information about epidemiological or other studies relating to "Vietnam Herbicides" exposure to those veterans. The commission has fifteen members; the Secretary of Health, chairperson, and fourteen other members.

Diabetes Task Force is responsible for surveying the effects of diabetes and developing a control plan which defines the impact of diabetes and its complications. It has thirteen members and an executive director who is appointed by the Governor.

DEPUTY SECRETARY FOR PUBLIC HEALTH PROGRAMS

Deputy Secretary for Public Health Programs administers public health programs to deliver effective health services to the citizens of the Commonwealth.

Bureau of Epidemiology and Disease Prevention administers investigatory and educational health programs as well as the development of preventive programs to reduce morbidity and mortality of chronic acute infectious, occupational and environmental disease of man. In addition, it conducts epidemiologic studies and research programs to address major public health issues within the Commonwealth.

Bureau of Maternal/Child and Preventive Health Programs administers programs and services with major goals of health promotion, disease prevention and early intervention that can ameliorate diseases and health problems of childbearing women, their infants and children. The WIC Program provides supplemental nutrition and food and nutrition education to pregnant and post-partum women, infants and children during critical times of growth and development.

Bureau of AIDS directs, coordinates and monitors the implementation of health education, counseling, testing, surveillance and other efforts related to the prevention, control and epidemiology of acquired immunity deficiency syndrome (AIDS).

Bureau of Special Public Health Services directs, coordinates and monitors the implementation of public health preventive and medical programs. These include Children's Rehabilitative Programs, Emergency Health Services and School Health Programs.

DEPUTY SECRETARY FOR ADMINISTRATION

Deputy Secretary for Administration is responsible for providing administrative support to all units in the department. This office is also responsible for developing all management and administrative policies and procedures for the department.

Equal Opportunity Office is responsible for monitoring the personnel management system for compliance with federal and state laws. Other civil rights activities include coordination of all activities relating to the Rehabilitation Act of 1973; review of all health services for compliance with Title 6 of the Civil Rights Act of 1964; and monitoring of the department's contracting process to ensure that minorities and women are awarded contracts. In addition, the office develops the procedures and provides civil rights related technical assistance to the 44 Single County Authorities responsible for drug and alcohol programs.

State Health Data Center, as the designated state center for health statistics, is responsible for collecting, processing, and disseminating health information to appropriate users throughout the Commonwealth. The center also develops information systems, provides statistical and research assistance and is the repository for all vital statistics in the Commonwealth.

Bureau of Administrative Services is responsible for forms and publications management, procurement, office services, graphics and reproduction, word processing, facilities management, administrative methods and automotive functions of the department.

Bureau of Financial Management is responsible for budgeting and budgetary control. It also develops financial processes and procedures for federal grant administration and state funds that ensure contracts are properly written and executed.

Bureau of Personnel is responsible for employment activities from pre-hiring to retirement by maintaining personnel records, providing in and out-service training for employes, and performing all aspects of manpower planning and review, recruitment, certification and classification. It also is responsible for handling labor relations activities.

DEPUTY SECRETARY FOR PLANNING AND QUALITY ASSURANCE

Deputy Secretary for Planning and Quality Assurance administers regulatory and programmatic quality assurance programs, public health laboratory services, health planning and health care financing and development programs.

Bureau of Health Financing and Program Development administers state regulatory programs to ensure quality of care provided by and through Health Maintenance Organizations and Professional Health Service Corporations. It supports the development of alternative and competitive health delivery systems and promotes the use of health financing systems to enhance competition and improve quality and access. It also administers federal health manpower programs and develops primary care resources in medically underserved areas.

Bureau of Laboratories serves as the public health laboratory for the Commonwealth and is responsible for a comprehensive program that includes clinical laboratory improvement and support for department activities in disease prevention and control. It also provides to both the public community and the medical profession the laboratory support essential for timely and appropriate diagnosis, prevention, and treatment of diseases.

Bureau of Planning makes determinations of statewide health needs, conducts statewide health planning activities and coordinates the development and implementation of the State Health Plan. It also administers a Certificate of Need program to promote an equitable and efficient allocation of health resources and cost containment through review of major capital expenditures proposed by health care facilities.

Bureau of Quality Assurance administers state and federal regulatory programs to ensure compliance with minimum health and safety standards in licensed health care facilities as mandated by law. It also provides policy and direction for the development of educational, consultative, and technical assistance programs to licensed health care facilities in order to encourage and facilitate compliance with health care standards.

DEPUTY SECRETARY FOR DRUG AND ALCOHOL PROGRAMS

Deputy Secretary for Drug and Alcohol Programs administers a statewide drug and alcohol prevention, intervention and treatment service system.

Office of Policy and Planning provides developmental and compliance planning, regulatory coordination and policy analysis activities concerning drug and alcohol service programs. It coordinates statewide drug and alcohol planning, develops an annual management plan and coordinates rules and regulations development.

Bureau of Community Assistance monitors the performance of drug and alcohol service delivery system and provides technical assistance to Single County Authorities (local administrative units) and projects concerning the implementation of agency policy, regulations and procedures. The bureau is responsible for all project approval/licensure of drug and alcohol programs.

Bureau of Program Services develops and coordinates alcoholism and drug occupational programs for business, government and industry, develops and conducts a training program for service delivery personnel and recommends prevention strategies for use by county drug and alcohol programs and other state agencies. Coordinates the Alcohol Highway Safety Program in association with the Pennsylvania Department of Transportation. Also, the bureau is responsible for the distribution of films, brochures and pamphlets on a statewide basis as well as a toll free hotline service.

DEPUTY SECRETARY FOR COMMUNITY HEALTH

Deputy Secretary for Community Health administers statewide implementation of the department's public health programs and coordinates departmental program direction with community needs through local units: six district offices, including state health centers, county/municipal independent health departments and local health departments.

District Offices direct and coordinate public health programs of the department in a multi-county area. The District Offices provide specialized consultative services and administrative support to state health centers and local health jurisdictions in their district.

State Health Centers are located in sixty-two counties in the Commonwealth. They provide public health services, referrals, counseling and epidemiological investigations to meet community needs through home visits and scheduled clinics. Staff support is provided through public health nurses, and on a referral basis through physicians and other public health professionals.

County and Municipal Health Departments serve five counties and two cities by providing referral, clinic services and staff support to specialized department-sponsored clinics. They also conduct disease surveillance through community investigations, data collection and analysis, laboratory support services and appropriate control measures. Financial support for these health departments are provided by the Commonwealth and their activities are monitored.

SECRETARIES OF HEALTH		Appointed Since 1950
Russell E. Teague, M.D.	Feb.	26, 1951
Berwyn F. Mattison, M.D. (resigned Nov. 18, 1957)	Feb.	1, 1955
C. L. Wilbar, Jr., M.D.	Nov.	19, 1957
Thomas W. Georges, Jr., M.D. (acting)	Jan.	17, 1967
Thomas W. Georges, Jr., M.D.	July	13, 1967
Richard J. Potter, M.D., M.P.H. (acting)		
Dr. John R. Clark, D.D.S. (acting)		
Ellsworth R. Browneller, M.D.	Jan.	5, 1970
J. Finton Speller, M.D.	Mar.	2, 1971
Leonard Bachman, M.D.	Jan.	3, 1975
Buford S. Washington, M.D. (acting)	Feb.	6, 1979
Gordon K. MacLeod, M.D. (resigned Nov. 1, 1979)	Mar.	16, 1979

		Appointed Since 1950
Donald Reid, M.D. (acting)	Nov.	1, 1979
H. Arnold Muller, M.D.	Nov.	26, 1979
*N. Mark Richards, M.D.	Jan.	20, 1987

Deputies

C. L. Wilbar, Jr., M.D.	Apr.	15, 1953
C. Earle Albrecht, M.D.	Jan.	15, 1958
Ralph E. Dwork, M.D.	Apr.	18, 1963
Richard J. Potter, M.D., M.P.H.	Aug.	28, 1968
Col. Paul A. Rittlemann.	Jan.	13, 1969
John R. Clark, D.D.S.	Oct.	8, 1969
John W. Simmons, M.D.	Nov.	8, 1972
Trin F. Dumlao, Jr.	Apr.	5, 1973
Brydon M. Lidle	Apr.	5, 1973
Morton D. Rosen	Jan.	15, 1975
William R. Montgomery, Ph.D.	Mar.	3, 1975
Milton Berkes.	Feb.	5, 1975
Robert E. Wallace.	Mar.	20, 1978
Buford S. Washington, M.D. (acting)	Feb.	6, 1979
Emmett E. Welch	Mar.	29, 1979
Donald Reid, M.D.	Aug.	3, 1979
William J. Saltzer	Apr.	1, 1980
Rhea R. Singsen	Sept.	15, 1980
Gary F. Jensen (acting).	July	1, 1981
Alexander B. Rakow, D.O.	July	1, 1981
Luceille E. Fleming.	Mar.	24, 1982
Jennifer Riseon	Jan.	1, 1983
Paul A. Zuidema	Mar.	2, 1983
Maria A. Keating	Nov.	1, 1985
*Robert Zimmerman (acting)	Apr.	1, 1987
*Victor Greco, M.D.	May	1, 1987
*Jeannine Peterson.	Aug.	13, 1987
*John Clem	Aug.	14, 1987

* *Incumbent*

INSURANCE DEPARTMENT
13th Floor, Strawberry Square
Harrisburg, PA 17120

CONSTANCE B. FOSTER   Insurance Commissioner

Constance B. Foster was born Dec. 5, 1946, in Slayton, MN, the daughter of Donald Adrian and Rosina Luft Boudreau; grad., Univ. of Calif. at Los Angeles (B.A., cum laude) 1968; Rutgers Univ. Schl. of Law (J.D., magna cum laude) 1975; attorney; mem., Am., Pa. and Phila. Bar Assns.; pres., Eman Child Care Center, Phila., 1983-85; panelist, "Women and the Law," Rutgers Camden Law Schl., 1983-84; author, "Medical Treatment and Human Experimentation: Introducing Illegality, Fraud, Duress and Incapacity to the Doctrine of Informed Consent," 6 *Rutg. L.J.* 538 (Winter 1975); appointed Insurance Commissioner on Jan. 20, 1987; married Frederick L. Foster; 3 children; home address: 1079 Beach Ave., Hershey.

The Insurance Department, established under the Act of Assembly of April 4, 1873, P.L. 20 and reorganized under the Insurance Department Act of May 17, 1921, P.L. 789, is responsible for administering the laws of the Commonwealth as they pertain to the regulation of the insurance industry and the protection of the insurance consumer. It ensures that the industry is responsive to the needs of the consumer by making available to the consumer reliable insurance coverage at reasonable rates.

EXECUTIVE

The Chief Executive of the department is the Insurance Commissioner. In addition to overseeing the daily administration of the department, the Commissioner chairs the Catastrophic Loss Trust Fund Board; supervises the Workmen's Compensation Security Fund; and serves as a member of the Anthracite and Bituminous Coal Mine Subsidence Board and the State Workmen's Insurance Fund.

In addition to three Deputy Insurance Commissioners who report to the Commissioner, the Executive Office includes the Commissioner's immediate staff and the following organizational units:

Press Office coordinates the department's public information program through preparation of news releases, newsletters, speeches and printed materials.

Legislative Office serves as liaison between the legislature and the department and monitors and analyzes legislation effecting the department and its programs.

Office of Chief Legal Counsel provides legal advice and assistance to the Insurance Commissioner and other department staff, initiates actions to enforce the insurance laws, and represents the department before state and federal courts.

Administrative Hearings Office conducts and prepares proposed adjudications of formal administrative hearings in matters affecting departmental interpretation and enforcement of insurance laws and regulations.

Office of Executive Director, Catastrophic Loss Trust Fund provides programmatic direction and administrative support to the Catastrophic Loss Trust Fund.

DEPUTY INSURANCE COMMISSIONER FOR CONSUMER AFFAIRS, POLICY AND ADMINISTRATION

Bureau of Consumer Affairs and Enforcement directs a program to investigate and resolve consumer complaints and to enforce state laws and regulations pertaining to insurance agents, brokers and companies.

Policy and Program Development Division coordinates a program to develop, implement and evaluate Insurance Department policies consistent with laws and regulations, administrative requirements, and department objectives.

Budget and Administrative Services Division provides administrative support to the department in the areas of budget and fiscal management, computer systems management, procurement, telecommunications and related functions; provides administrative support to the Workers Compensation Security Fund; and provides fiscal management support to the Catastrophic Loss Trust Fund.

Personnel Management and Affirmative Action Division coordinates the personnel management program, including recruitment, classification and pay, labor relations, employee training and development, employee benefits and personnel transactions and records; and coordinates the department's affirmative action program.

DEPUTY INSURANCE COMMISSIONER FOR RATE AND POLICY FORM REGULATION

Bureaus of Property and Casualty Rate and Policy Form Review, Life Rate and Policy Form Review, and Accident and Health Rate and Policy Form Review administer laws and regulations relating to the review and analysis of insurance rates to determine whether they conform with statutory requirements that they not be excessive, unjust, or unfairly discriminatory; and direct programs to review and approve or disapprove insurance policies and related forms in accordance with laws and regulations.

DEPUTY INSURANCE COMMISSIONER FOR REGULATION OF COMPANIES

Bureau of Examinations examines the financial conditions and operations of insurance companies to determine their compliance with insurance laws and regulations, their solvency and their ability to pay claims.

Audit Division conducts audits of the annual statements of insurance companies licensed to do business in Pennsylvania to determine the solvency, profitability and compliance with insurance laws and regulations.

Agents and Brokers Division coordinates the written examination programs for insurance agents and brokers and public adjusters; and issues and renews insurance licenses.

Company Licensing Division reviews and analyzes applications for formation of new domestic insurance companies and related entities; reviews and approves or disapproves applications of foreign insurance companies seeking licensure in Pennsylvania; and reviews the corporate activities of presently authorized insurance companies.

Liquidation Division coordinates the liquidation of insolvent insurance companies pursuant to orders of court.

INSURANCE COMMISSIONERS	Appointed Since 1950	
Artemas C. Leslie	Apr.	8, 1950
Francis R. Smith	Jan.	18, 1955
Theodore S. Gutowicz	July	16, 1962
Audrey R. Kelly	Jan.	15, 1963
David O. Maxwell	Jan.	17, 1967
George F. Reed	Sept.	11, 1969
Dr. Herbert S. Denenberg (resigned Mar. 29, 1974)	Jan.	25, 1971
William J. Sheppard (resigned Dec. 31, 1978)	Apr.	30, 1974
John J. Sheehy (acting)	Jan.	2, 1979
Harvey Bartle, III (resigned May 20, 1980)	Feb.	23, 1979
James R. Farley (acting)	May	21, 1980
Michael L. Browne	July	24, 1980
Anthony A. Geyelin (acting)	Sept.	26, 1983
William R. Muir (acting)	May	1, 1984
George F. Grode	July	23, 1985
*Constance B. Foster	Jan.	20, 1987

DEPUTY INSURANCE COMMISSIONERS

Luther H. Williams	Mar.	3, 1953
Thomas R. Balaban	Mar.	16, 1955
Bernard J. Kelley	Mar.	16, 1955
Forrest J. Henry	May	19, 1955
William V. Fox, Jr	Feb.	1, 1956
Theodore S. Gutowicz	Apr.	10, 1958
Charles V. Walsh	June	1, 1961
Robert C. Davies	Feb.	13, 1963
John A. Skelton	Mar.	7, 1963
Paul Silverstein	Mar.	21, 1963
C. S. Lazarus	Nov.	1, 1963

* Incumbent

	Appointed Since 1950			Appointed Since 1950
A. John Smither	Jan. 25, 1967	Gaele M. Barthold	Apr. 2, 1979
Richard W. Krimm	Aug. 14, 1967	Jonathan P. Neipris	May 15, 1980
David P. Trulli	Oct. 23, 1967	J. Alan Lauer	June 4, 1981
Herbert Goldstein	May 25, 1971	Linda L. Lanam	Mar. 18, 1983
Andrew F. Whitman	July 26, 1971	Alexander Bratic	Sept. 17, 1984
Kimber A. Wald	Nov. 1, 1971	*Ronald Chronister	Oct. 5, 1985
John J. Sheehy	Sept. 21, 1972	*Thomas S. Buzby	May 22, 1987
William J. Sheppard	Sept. 10, 1973	*Michael R. Powers	May 22, 1987
Gerald J. Mongelli	June 4, 1974		
A. Moore Lifter	Mar. 13, 1975	*Incumbent	

DEPARTMENT OF LABOR AND INDUSTRY
1700 Labor and Industry Building
Harrisburg, PA 17120

HARRIS L. WOFFORD, JR.   Secretary of Labor and Industry

Harris L. Wofford, Jr., was born April 9, 1926, in New York City, the son of Harris L. Wofford, Sr. and Estelle Gardner; grad., Univ. of Chicago (B.A.) 1948; Yale Law Schl. (LL.B.) 1954; Howard Univ. Law Schl. (J.D.) 1954; rec., honorary degrees from Tufts Univ., Wake Forest Univ., and King's Coll.; U.S. Army Air Force (1944-45); attorney; mem., Am. Bar Assn.; assoc. dir., Peace Corps (1964-66); Peace Corps Special Representative to Africa (1962-64); special asst. to Pres. Kennedy and chmn., White House Subcabinet Group on Civil Rights (1961-62); counsel, U.S. Comm. on Civil Rights; trustee, Martin Luther King, Jr. Center for Non-violent Social Change; sec., Phila. Martin Luther King, Jr. Assn. for Nonviolence; bd. of dirs., Public Interest Law Center of Phila.; mem., Council of Foreign Relations; Phila. Drum Major Award for Social Justice; Eleanor Roosevelt Humanities Award; Howard Univ. Alumni Award for Postgraduate Achievement; author of four books, including *Of Kennedys and Kings; Making Sense of the Sixties;* several other articles and writings on politics, education and law; appointed Secretary of Labor and Industry, March 23, 1987; married Clare Lindgren; 3 children: Susanne, Daniel and David; home address: Bryn Mawr.

In 1889, the Legislature first established an Office of Factory Inspector to administer safety inspections of industrial plants. This office became the Department of Factory Inspection in 1905, whose powers and responsibilities were assumed by the Department of Labor and Industry (L&I) with its creation in 1913. The department currently administers programs involving building inspection, unemployment compensation, workers' compensation and vocational rehabilitation.

EXECUTIVE OFFICE

The department Secretary is appointed by the Governor and confirmed by the Senate. The Secretary is assisted by four deputies. Several department agencies report either directly to the Secretary or to special assistants designated by the Secretary. They include:

Bureau of Mediation mediates disputes between unions and employers in the public sector, under Act 195, and the private sector, under the Mediation Act of 1937. The bureau also furnishes names of arbitrators for arbitration panels upon the request of either party to a collective bargaining agreement under Act 195.

Office of the Deaf, created by the Legislature in 1986, is an advocacy agency for the deaf and hearing impaired in Pennsylvania. The office ensures that state services and programs are accessible to the deaf. It also monitors and coordinates sign language training and interpreter programs.

Press Office is the spokesman for the department, providing information on L&I activities and policy to representatives of the news media and members of the public. The office responds to queries and initiates public information programs. The office also generates or coordinates the development of informational materials that facilitate communications within the department.

Chief Counsel serves as the legal advisor to the Secretary and represents the department in legal matters.

Legislative Liaison monitors Legislative activity affecting the department, works with the secretary and deputies to develop departmental legislative activity, and coordinates inquiries from legislators on behalf of their constituents.

EXECUTIVE DEPUTY SECRETARY, ADMINISTRATION

Responsible for general administration of the department through the bureaus of Budget, Personnel and Administrative Services. Acts on all department matters in the Secretary's absence, and frequently represents the Secretary in dealings with other state agencies.

Office of Workers' Compensation oversees the operation of two agencies:

Bureau of Workers' Compensation administers the Workmen's Compensation and Occupational Disease Laws to assure that proper benefits are paid to injured workers or their dependents. These functions include the regulation of insurers and self-insurers' claims handling. The bureau has the authority to prosecute employers or carriers who fail to comply with the provisions of the Act. By reviewing all claim documents concerning compensation, the bureau monitors the compliance feature of the law. A petition may be filed with the bureau for adjudication before a referee. In addition, the bureau provides information to injured employees of their rights under the Act and operates a toll-free telephone service to respond to questions concerning the law. This number is (800) 482-2383.

State Workmen's Insurance Fund provides workers' compensation insurance and employers' liability to employers, including those refused policies by private insurance firms. The fund is subject to underwriting rules, classifications and rates which are promulgated by rating bureaus and approved by the State Insurance Commissioner. Overseeing operations is the State Workmen's Insurance Board.

DEPUTY SECRETARY OF EMPLOYMENT SECURITY

Administers the State Unemployment Compensation Law providing weekly benefits to the unemployed, and also is responsible for providing employment services to applicants and employers. Office of Employment Security is federally funded and it draws revenues from the Federal Unemployment Tax Act and the Social Security Act. Office of Employment Security, in addition to its Labor Exchange Function, jointly administers the Work Incentive Program (WIN) with the Department of Public Welfare in which training and work experience are made available to public assistance recipients, and handles work registration under Welfare Reform Program; coordinates certain activities under the Job Training Partnership Act and prepares and disseminates labor market information.

DEPUTY SECRETARY FOR LABOR AND INDUSTRY

Is responsible for programs that ensure a Pennsylvania workforce is ready to meet the challenges and opportunities of a changing economy. Also is the department's representative in cooperative jobs and training initiatives with other state agencies, such as the departments of Public Welfare and Education. The deputy is responsible for the following department programs:

Bureau of Job Training Partnership administers statewide employment and training programs with funds received through the Job Training Partnership Act.

Bureau of Apprenticeship and Training aids in providing maximum opportunities for unemployed and employed persons to improve and modernize work skills through development of training and apprenticeship programs.

DEPUTY SECRETARY FOR LABOR AND INDUSTRY

Oversees several key department regulatory functions affecting the well-being of workers and the general public. They include:

Bureau of Community and Worker Right to Know implements 1984 legislation requiring that information be made available to employees and community residents about hazardous substances introduced into the workplace and into the general environment.

Bureau of Occupational and Industrial Safety is primarily responsible for administering and enforcing the Fire and Panic Act and Regulations, which mandate minimum fire safety standards in public buildings except for the cities of Philadelphia, Pittsburgh and Scranton. The bureau is also responsible for administering laws relating to the operation of elevators, boilers, liquified petroleum gas bulk plants, and private employment agencies, and the licensing of manufacturers and suppliers of bedding and upholstery materials, and the communication of information regarding hazardous substances in the workplace.

Bureau of Labor Standards administers the state's Minimum Wage Law, the Wage Payment and Collection Law, the Child Labor Law, the Equal Pay Law, the Medical Pay Law, Industrial Homework Law, and the Personnel File Act. The bureau also administers the Seasonal Farm Labor Act (Act 93), which requires the registration of farm labor contractors, provides minimum wages for laborers, and allows for inspection of farm labor camps.

Prevailing Wage Division is required to establish the crafts and classifications, and wages to be paid construction workers on public work projects valued at $25,000 or more that are wholly or partly funded by state, county and local government bodies.

EXECUTIVE DIRECTOR
OFFICE OF VOCATIONAL REHABILITATION

The Office of Vocational Rehabilitation is responsible for providing vocational rehabilitation services to eligible handicapped persons to enhance their employability. The bureau also operates the Hiram G. Andrews Center in Johnstown which provides therapeutic medical/occupational services and vocational training. The Disability Determination Division with the office adjudicates claims on behalf of the SSA for Social Security Disability Insurance benefits and for Supplemental Security Income benefits to the blind and disabled.

BOARDS AND COMMISSIONS

Advisory Council on Unemployment Compensation. Thirteen members; eight appointed by the Governor and the Secretary of Labor and Industry is an ex officio member; members select chairman; reimbursement for expenses.

Industrial Board. Five members; four appointed by the Governor and confirmed by the Senate; the Secretary of Labor and Industry is ex officio member and chairman; reimbursement for expenses and per diem compensation.

Labor Relations Board. Three members appointed by the Governor and confirmed by the Senate; Governor designates chairman; Salaries: chairman, $12,000; members, $11,000; administers the Public Employe Relations Act of 1970 (Act 195) governing labor relations between public employes and their employers; the Pennsylvania Labor Relations Act of 1937 which covers small private sector employers over which the National Labor Relations Board does not exercise jurisdiction; and since 1977, Act 111 of 1968 which regulates bargaining between policemen and firemen and their public employers.

In implementing these statutes, the board conducts formal hearings and renders decisions on representation disputes and unfair labor practice charges, conducts elections to determine if employes desire union representation, and in certain public sector cases, may appoint fact finders to help resolve bargaining impasses and may assist in the selection of arbitrators to resolve contract disputes.

State Board of Vocational Rehabilitation. Eight members; Secretary of Labor and Industry (chairman) and seven appointees of Governor; reimbursement for expenses.

State Apprenticeship and Training Council. Eleven members appointed by the Governor, and five ex officio members; per diem compensation and reimbursement for expenses; examines and approves apprenticeship programs and issues journeymen certificates upon completion of such training.

State Job Training Coordinating Council recommends statewide goals and priorities to the Governor on employment and training programs, primarily those established under the Job Training Partnership Act.

Unemployment Compensation Board of Review. Three members appointed by the Governor and confirmed by the Senate; Governor designates chairman; Salary: chairman, $14,000; members, $13,000; is composed of three members who hear appeals of decisions made on unemployment compensation eligibility. The referees decide appeals on OES determinations at de novo hearings and the board independently reviews the appeals made from the referees' decisions.

Workmen's Compensation Appeal Board. Four members appointed by the Governor and confirmed by the Senate; Governor designates chairman; Secretary of Labor and Industry ex officio; Salary: set by the Secretary and approved by the Governor; hears appeals on decisions of worker's compensation referees concerning claims for compensation for occupational injuries and diseases, and renders decisions on petitions by claimants and insurers affecting compensation agreements.

State Workmen's Insurance Board. Three members: State Treasurer, Insurance Commissioner, and the Secretary of Labor and Industry serves as chairman.

SECRETARIES OF LABOR AND INDUSTRY
(Under Code, Act of June 7, 1923)

Appointed Since 1950

David M. Walker	Jan.	16, 1951
John R. Torquato	Jan.	18, 1955
William L. Batt (resigned May 22, 1961)	Mar.	4, 1957
A. Allen Sulcowe	June	12, 1961
William P. Young	Jan.	15, 1963
William J. Hart	Jan.	17, 1967

Appointed Since 1950

John K. Tabor	June	3, 1968
Clifford L. Jones	Mar.	28, 1969
Theordore Robb	June	22, 1970
Paul J. Smith	Jan.	25, 1971
Myron L. Joseph (resigned Nov. 1, 1979)	Mar.	6, 1979
Charles J. Lieberth	Nov.	27, 1979
Barry H. Stern	Aug.	3, 1981
James W. Knepper, Jr.	Sept.	10, 1984
*Harris L. Wofford, Jr.	Jan.	21, 1987

Deputy Secretaries

James A. Sipe	Mar.	9, 1953
Milton Weisberg (dec. Jan. 16, 1958)	Apr.	19, 1955
David E. Glavin	May	11, 1955
Joseph H. Sabel	June	3, 1958
Louis Ginsburg	Sept.	25, 1958
John T. Garvey	July	1, 1959
John Curtin, Jr.	Feb.	14, 1963
Pasquale Jiuliano	Feb.	18, 1963
George C. Guenther	Sept.	13, 1967
William C. Diosegy	Mar.	15, 1968
William E. Coyle	July	8, 1968
H. Ward Adams	Sept.	15, 1969
Joseph J. Marino	Feb.	3, 1971
C. Ted Dombrowski	Feb.	3, 1971
George A. DeLong	Feb.	18, 1971
James M. Weaver	Sept.	24, 1973
Barry H. Stern	Feb.	11, 1979
Thomas Breslin	Aug.	15, 1979
John T. J. Kelly, Jr.	July	29, 1980
*Earl Brown	Mar.	17, 1982
Mary Webber	Feb.	24, 1983
*Herbert C. Thieme	June	1, 1983
Francis Carey	July	11, 1983
William Hawkins	Feb.	10, 1986
Michael Acker	Mar.	10, 1986
*Thomas P. Foley	Mar.	2, 1987
*Franklin G. Mont	Mar.	17, 1987
*Patricia Halpin-Murphy	Mar.	23, 1987
*Larry J. Hockendoner	Mar.	25, 1987

Workmen's Compensation Appeals Board

Frank B. Brennan, Esq.	Jan.	20, 1950
L. Pat McGrath	Jan.	15, 1952
Dr. John L. Dorris (resigned Apr. 17, 1961)	Feb.	8, 1955
Hugo J. Parente	May	5, 1955
Thomas B. Nognan, Esq. (resigned Dec. 4, 1961)	May	5, 1955
John T. Welsh	Apr.	25, 1961
Eugene J. Mirachi	Dec.	15, 1961
Edwin M. Kosik	Aug.	12, 1963
Thomas P. Geer	Aug.	13, 1963
Wilbur C. Creveling, Jr.	Aug.	7, 1963
James J. Ligi	Aug.	8, 1963
Horace J. Culbertson	Jan.	3, 1972
Edward McCullough	Jan.	3, 1972
Arthur S. Herskovitz (chairman)	Jan	3, 1972
Arthur H. Reede	Dec.	4, 1975
William Brady	Feb.	8, 1980
*Harold F. Fergus (chairman Dec. 24, 1980)	June	16, 1980
*Anthony Cognetti	Apr.	14, 1981
William R. Hagner	June	30, 1981
*Thomas Breslin	July	13, 1983
*Robert P. Fohl	Dec.	4, 1984

* Incumbent

Manager, State Workmen's Insurance Fund	Appointed Since 1950	
Samuel Gunnett Neff	Feb.	8, 1955
Edward J. Reider	Aug.	25, 1959
Robert S. Tkatch	Oct.	9, 1961
Joseph L. Carrigg	Feb.	7, 1963
Robert A. Loftus	June	16, 1971
Anthony Cognetti	June	20, 1979
William Westington	Feb.	9, 1983

Labor Relations Board

Michael J. Crosetto	Feb.	8, 1955
C. P. Bowers	June	24, 1955
John T. Halesky	Mar.	9, 1956
Malcolm B. Petriken	Aug.	12, 1963

	Appointed Since 1950	
William J. Hart	June	22, 1965
Daniel H. Huyett III	Dec.	8, 1965
Joseph Licastro	June	24, 1968
George Stuart	Jan.	2, 1969
Raymond Scheib	Jan.	4, 1972
James A. Jones	Jan.	4, 1972
Kenneth F. Kahn	June	15, 1977
*Ralph F. Scalera (chairman)	June	30, 1981
*Dennis Martire	June	6, 1983
*John Hope Anderson	June	8, 1983

Incumbent

DEPARTMENT OF MILITARY AFFAIRS
Fort Indiantown Gap
Annville, PA 17003

GERALD T. SAJER   **Adjutant General**

Major General Gerald T. Sajer enlisted in the Army on Sept. 16, 1946; att. Officers Candidate Schl., Fort Benning, GA; Engineer Schl., Fort Belvoir, VA; Airborne Schl. and Ranger Training, Fort Benning; grad., Tufts Univ. (bachelors) 1946; Harvard Univ. (law degree) 1959; U.S. Army Command and General Staff Coll., 1972; U.S. Army Reserve, 1953-59, 1980-87; Army National Guard, 1959-1980, retired as Brigadier General; former mem., law firm of Stone, Sajer, and Stewart; awards and decorations include: Legion of Merit, Soldiers Medal, Meritorious Service Medal, American Campaign Medal, World War II Victory Medal, Natl. Defense Service Medal, Korean Service Medal, Armed Forced Reserve Medal, Army Reserve Components Achievement Medal, United Nations Service Medal, Gen. Thomas J. Stewart Medal, Pa. Service Ribbon, and Parachute Badge; Pa. and Cumberland Co. Bar Assns.; Phi Beta Kappa (Tufts Chapt.); Natl. Guard Assns. of the U.S. and Pa.; Harrisburg City Grays; Camp Hill Athletic Booster Club; past. pres., Lincoln Home and Schl. Assn.; Military Order of World Wars; pres., Blue Mountain Chapt., Assn. of the U.S. Army; appt. Adjutant General, Jan. 20, 1987; married Helen Sajer; 6 children: Captain Marsha A. (U.S. Army), Mark S., Dr. Susan A., 1st Lt. Scott A. (U.S. Army), 2nd Lt. Frank M. (PAARNG), Peter J.; address: Quarters 1, Fort Indiantown Gap.

The Adjutant General's Office, established by the Act of April 11, 1793, is the headquarters of the Department of Military Affairs. It is the office of permanent record for all personnel papers and documents of the Pa. National Guard since the post World War II era. The Adjutant General, as head of this department, is chairman of the State Armory Board.

Pennsylvania National Guard. Of the various duties and responsibilities of the Adjutant General the most important is the administration of the Pa. National Guard.

Authorized by federal and state laws, the Pa. National Guard is organized into Army and Air units and consists of members voluntarily enlisted therein, and of commissioned officers and warrant officers, armed, equipped, and federally recognized by the departments of the Army and Air Force, respectively. The Adjutant General administers the National Guard through two deputies, one for Air, one for Army.

When not in the service of the United States, the National Guard is a state force, the command of which is vested in the Governor as Commander-in-Chief.

In time of national emergency or at other periods when authorized by law, the President of the United States orders units of the Pa. Army and Air National Guard into the active military service of the United States; the Governor releases these units from the Pa. National Guard for such service.

Administration of the Pa. National Guard includes management, supervision and logistical and facility support of all units. The U.S. Department of Defense, through the Chief, National Guard Bureau, and the Commanding General, First U.S. Army, and the commanders of the major Air Force commands furnish advisors and members of the active military forces to assist and advise in accomplishment of the required training.

The Adjutant General designates the commanders and the regional and/or sector responsibility in the event the Pa. National Guard, Army and/or Air, is ordered to State Active Duty by the Governor for employment in emergency situations within the Commonwealth. During such periods the command and deployment of National Guard forces is exercised through the Adjutant General.

In accordance with their federal mission, the units of the Pa. National Guard, Army and Air, are required to participate in field training, or active duty for training in lieu thereof, and armory drill assemblies.

The troops list of the Pa. Army National Guard includes all types of units; infantry, armor, armored cavalry, field artillery, engineer, military police maintenance, ordnance, transportation, aviation, public affairs, and medical. The units authorized to the Pa. Air National Guard include missions assigned to the Strategic Air Command, Military Airlift

Command, Tactical Air Command, and Air Force Communications Command. Moreover, equipment issued to the various Army and Air units enables them to render many types of service to local communities; emergency equipment, strategically stored throughout the state, could be issued in a very short period of time and transported to any section of the state in a matter of hours.

State Maintenance Facilities for the Pa. Army National Guard come under the direct control and supervision of the Adjutant General and include the Directorate of Surface Maintenance, Combined Support Maintenance Shop, Unit Training Equipment Site and the Organizational Maintenance Shops (OMS). These facilities insure proper utilization, maintenance and repair of all federal equipment assigned to the Pa. Army National Guard. The Directorate of Surface Maintenance (DSM) is responsible for the maintenance and operational readiness of federal military equipment assigned to the Pa. Army National Guard.

The DSM provides the Adjutant General with technical staff assistance on matters pertaining to maintenance and inspection of equipment, performs liaison activities with other agencies and is responsible for the establishment and operation of an efficient statewide maintenance program.

The Combined Support Maintenance Shop (CSMS), located at Fort Indiantown Gap, provides support maintenance for all Army National Guard equipment except aircraft. Command Maintenance Evaluation Teams (COMET) are sent out from the CSMS to evaluate each unit in the Pa. Army National Guard on an 18-month cycle. Three full-time Missile Repair Teams with the responsibility of repairing TOW/Dragon anti-tank missiles are located at OMS #10 in Philadelphia, OMS #17 in Lock Haven and OMS #22 in Pittsburgh.

These teams come under the control of Electronics Foreman of the CSMS. Calibration of Test Measurement and Diagnostic Equipment (TMDE) to include nuclear instruments also performed at the CSMS.

The Unit Training Equipment Site, also located at Fort Indiantown Gap, is responsible for receiving, maintaining and storing heavy items of equipment that are used in training exercises, and for which storage facilities at home station are inadequate.

The 30 Organizational Maintenance Shops are located at armories throughout the Commonwealth. Repair of equipment beyond the capability of these shops is performed by the Combined Support Maintenance Shop.

Bureau for Veterans Affairs is responsible for the administration and management of all veterans' programs within the Department of Military Affairs. The Bureau for Veterans Affairs by legislative mandate is the official liaison between federal, state and local government agencies on all matters concerning veterans' benefits.

Pennsylvania Soldiers' and Sailors' Home, located in Erie, was established by authority of the State Legislature P.L. 62 on June 3, 1885. The Home's bed capacity is 75 nursing, 52 personal care and 48 domiciliary beds. Its purpose is to provide multi-levels of care for indigent, invalid and disabled Pennsylvania veterans. The Adjutant General through his Bureau for Veterans Affairs, is responsible for management of the Home. An eleven member Advisory Council advises the

Adjutant General as to the management, operation and the adequacy of facilities and services at the Home.

Hollidaysburg Veterans Home, located in Hollidaysburg, was established by authority of the State Legislature P.L. 211 on September 28, 1976. The Home's bed capacity is 200 nursing, 64 personal care and 115 domiciliary beds. Its purpose is identical to the Soldiers' & Sailors' Home (described above).

Southeastern Pennsylvania Veterans Center, located in Spring City, was established by authority of the State Legislature Act 1986-7 on February 14, 1986. The Home's bed capacity is currently 70 domiciliary beds; however, eventually the facility will be authorized 140 domiciliary and 450 nursing care beds. Its purpose is identical to the Soldiers' & Sailors' Home (described above).

State Veterans' Commission shall have the power, and its duties shall be:

   a. to advise the Adjutant General upon such matters as the Adjutant General may bring before it.

   b. to investigate the work of the department and make recommendations to it regarding administration of the laws providing for the payment of pensions and relief, for the marking of graves of veterans, and for selection, acquisition and maintenance of a state military cemetery.

   c. to investigate and compile data concerning veterans of the United States, and all state and municipal activities relating thereto, and to recommend to the Governor legislation for submission to the General Assembly concerning veterans and their activities.

   d. to expend funds, appropriations to or for it, for the purpose of providing the necessities of life, and to otherwise assist such Pennsylvania veterans of any war or armed conflict, or the widows and infant children or dependents of such veterans who are sick, disabled or indigent, and who are without means for planning and providing for the rehabilitation and care of veterans.

   e. to certify for payments of gratuities for the children of certain disabled veterans and veterans who die or have died of service-connected disabilities, to attend any state or state-aided education or training institution of secondary or college grade or other institution of higher learning.

There are 17 members: the Adjutant General, Ex-Officio or his designee, and the State Commander, Commandant or head, or his designee of the following veterans' organizations: the American Legion; AMVETS; Blinded Veterans Association; Catholic War Veterans; Disabled American Veterans; Jewish War Veterans of the United States; Marine Corps League; Military Order of the Purple Heart; State Association of County Directors of Veterans Affairs; Veterans of Foreign Wars of the United States; Veterans of World War I of the USA, Inc.; Italian-American War Veterans of the U.S., Inc.; and four members-at-large appointed by the Governor each of whom shall be a veteran and a member in good and regular standing of a Pennsylvania branch, post, lodge or club of a recognized national veterans' organization active in the Commonwealth and at least one shall be a female veteran and at least one shall be a veteran of the Vietnam Era. The Director of the Bureau of

Veterans Affairs serves as the Executive Secretary to the Commission.

Army Guard Aviation. The Aviation Program in the Pennsylvania Army National Guard is funded 100 percent by the federal government. All aircraft, support equipment, building maintenance and construction funds, repair parts and civil service military technician payrolls are provided to Pennsylvania through the National Guard Bureau. Three Army Aviation Support Facilities (AASF) support one of the largest aviation programs in the Army National Guard. The AASF at Muir Army Airfield, Fort Indiantown Gap, is the largest of its kind in the country. Ninety aircraft, 196 aviators and 110 crewmembers and noncrewmembers are assigned to this facility. Another AASF is located at Washington County Airport, Washington, PA. This facility supports 36 aircraft, 71 aviators and 39 crewmembers and noncrewmembers. The newest AASF, organized in November 1985, is temporarily located at the Wilkes-Barre/Scranton International Airport. This facility maintains 12 aircraft and has 40 aviators and 19 crewmembers and noncrewmembers. Overall, these facilities provide training to personnel of 7 aviation units, and maintenance support of aircraft and ground equipment.

The Eastern Army National Guard Aviation Training Site (EAATS) is also located at Fort Indiantown Gap. The mission of the EAATS is to provide aviation training to soldiers from ARNG units throughout the United States. This training is no longer available to the National Guard from the U.S. Army Training and Doctrine Command. The objective of the centralized approach for individual training is to provide an alternative resource, thereby allowing more time for unit level training. Through the effective use of the EAATS, aviation unit commanders can concentrate all efforts toward attaining the principal goal of unit level combat readiness.

A Synthetic Flight Training Facility (SFTF) and an AH-1 Flight and Weapons Simulator (AH-1FWS) are under control of the EAATS. The SFTF is a highly sophisticated, 2.8 million dollar computerized flight simulator, which provides initial and advanced instrument training at a substantial cost savings per hour, versus using aircraft for this purpose. The AH-1FWS is currently under construction and is expected to be operational by January 1988. It will be used to train approximately 530 aviators annually, in the skills and techniques necessary to operate an attack helicopter in a combat environment during both day and night. The AH-1FWS will have a cost avoidance of $3,387,000 yearly, which does not include ammunition costs.

The Governor's Veterans Outreach and Assistance Centers (GVOAC) were placed under the aegis of the Department of Military Affairs effective July 1, 1982, in order that the services rendered the Commonwealth's 1.5 million veterans may be better coordinated with other veterans' programs. The GVOAC program is intended to serve as a bridge or link between the individual veteran requiring information or assistance and the public or private agency which can best meet the veterans' needs. The procedure of the centers is designed to provide advice and counseling in a one-stop mode using a one-on-one peer-oriented approach. The program functions at the grass-roots level, a feature that is not found in any other veterans' service organizations.

The Pennsylvania Air National Guard is made up of 47 units which are subordinated to the Adjutant General and come under the managerial and operational control of the State Headquarters which is located at Fort Indiantown Gap. The force structure includes four major flying units: the 171st Air Refueling Wing, 112th Tactical Fighter Group, 111th Tactical Air Support Group and 193rd Special Operations Group. Each of these units includes a mission squadron, aircraft maintenance, resource management, medical, security, communications, engineering and combat support elements. In addition, three communications-electronics squadrons, one radar squadron, an air traffic control flight, a heavy engineering flight and three weather flights operate as separate units and are based at five locations throughout Pennsylvania.

PaANG units are located at Ft. Indiantown Gap, Harrisburg and Pittsburgh International Airports, Willow Grove Naval Air Station and State College, Pennsylvania. These units are gained in wartime by US Air Force Major Commands, namely Strategic Air Command (SAC), Military Airlift Command (MAC), Tactical Air Command (TAC), Air Force Communications Command (AFCC) and the Air Weather Service (AWS). Day-to-day involvement in Air Force missions and in readiness training requires that all PaANG units work closely with both their Air Force parent commands and the State Headquarters on a continual basis. To be immediately responsible to its two-fold mission to the state and federal governments, the Pennsylvania Air National Guard must maintain its forces and equipment in a constant state of readiness to provide the capability and professionalism necessary to fulfill all assigned tasks, while at the same time continuing its training of personnel to maintain the peak of proficiency which is vital to its operation.

Support Personnel Management. Full-time Manning — The federal government, through the National Guard Bureau, provides full-time manning for day-to-day support and operating continuity in the administration, training and equipment maintenance requirement of National Guard units.

At the state level these federally funded full-time resources are managed by the Support Personnel Management Office of the Department of Military Affairs.

The full-time manning program consists of a mixed force of Excepted Federal Civil Service Military Technicians and National Guard members on full-time military duty tours.

All the full-time military personnel and the majority of the Excepted Federal Civil Service Military Technicians are required to be members of the Guard. As such they must maintain compatible military skill qualifications and meet all other standards for military membership.

State Armory Board consists of the Adjutant General, who acts as chairman, and five members appointed by him. Three of the appointed members shall also be members of the Pa. National Guard. The Director of Facilities serves as the Secretary of the State Armory Board in an ex-officio capacity. Four voting members of the board constitute a quorum.

Originally constituted in 1905, the board provides, equips, maintains, manages and regulates armories for the use of Pa. National Guard units and the Pa. Guard when organized.

The board may, with the approval of the Governor, accept gifts of land, with or without buildings thereon, to be used for National Guard purposes. Title to such land and facilities shall be taken in the name of the Commonwealth. The board may expend funds appropriated to it to purchase suitable buildings or sites. The board may, in accordance with the law, sell any buildings, armory sites, or other real estate owned by the

Commonwealth when no longer needed for military services due to changes in population or to the needs of the military service. Money derived from such sales shall be paid into the State Treasury Armory Fund. These funds shall be expended solely for the purchase of equipment, furniture and fixtures, and for the construction of new armories in the Commonwealth.

Facilities Directorate is responsible for providing all needed architectural and engineering services for the department. Its prime function is to assist the State Armory Board in the preparation of plans and specifications, receiving bids, issuing contracts, and inspecting construction, maintenance and repair work.

Similar services are rendered to the Bureau of Veterans Affairs for Veterans Homes projects and to the United States Property and Fiscal Officer for projects paid with federal funds.

Office of the United States Property and Fiscal Officer for PA. The organization and administration of this office is the responsibility of the U.S. Property and Fiscal Officer under the general direction of the Adjutant General. Support of the Army National Guard program is handled directly from this office. There are nine designated assistants to handle the administration of the Air National Guard program on decentralized basis. An Assistant USPFO for Air (Fiscal), Assistant USPFO for Air (Property), and Assistant USPFO for Air (Real Property), each maintains offices at Willow Grove Naval Air Station, Harrisburg International Airport and Greater Pittsburgh International Airport, respectively.

The responsibilities of the United States Property and Fiscal Officer are contained in Section 708 of Title 32, United States Code.

The USPFO is detailed for duty with the National Guard Bureau for administrative purposes. He is responsible for complying with laws; implementing regulations and instructions issued by the National Guard Bureau and applicable regulations of the departments of the Army and the Air Force; receipting and accounting for all federal funds and property, including real property, of the United States in the possession of the Pennsylvania Army and Air National Guard; and making returns and reports concerning those funds and that property, as required by the Secretary concerned.

ADJUTANTS GENERAL	Appointed Since 1950	
Maj. Gen. A. J. Drexel Biddle, Jr. (resigned April 4, 1961)	Apr.	19, 1955
Maj. Gen. Malcolm Hay	Apr.	11, 1961
Maj. Gen. Thomas R. White, Jr. (dec. Feb. 20, 1968)	Jan.	15, 1963
Maj. Gen. Richard Snyder	May	6, 1968
Maj. Gen. Harry J. Mier, Jr.	Apr.	19, 1972
Maj. Gen. Nicholas P. Kafkalas	Apr.	28, 1977
Maj. Gen. Richard M. Scott	Feb.	16, 1979
*Maj. Gen. Gerald T. Sajer	Jan.	21, 1987

Deputy Adjutants General

Brig. Gen. Richard Snyder	Jan.	22, 1952
Col. Robert C. Boden	Jan.	22, 1952
Col. William B. Freeland	Feb.	1, 1955
Maj. Gen. Richard B. Posey	June	7, 1956
Lt. Col. Anthony R. Flores	May	1, 1963
Daniel Shaub	Sept.	15, 1965
Maj. Gen. Nicholas P. Kafkalas	July	8, 1968
Maj. Gen. William J. Gallagher	May	18, 1972
Harold Wells	Aug.	25, 1972
Brig. Gen. Robert M. Carroll	July	7, 1977
Maj. Gen. Frank H. Smoker, Jr.	Apr.	30, 1979
Brig. Gen. Francis E. Jones, Jr.	May	13, 1980
*Brig. Gen. Robert E. Harris	Sept.	1, 1984
Brig. Gen. Pasquale J. Macrone	Nov.	14, 1984

* Incumbent

DEPARTMENT OF PUBLIC WELFARE
Box 2675
333 Health and Welfare Building
Harrisburg, PA 17105

JOHN F. WHITE, JR.   **Secretary of Public Welfare**

John F. White, Jr. was born March 25, 1949, in Phila., the son of John F. White, Sr. and Sylvia Lewis; att., Lincoln and West Chester Univ.; hon. Doctor of Humane Letters, Coll. of Podiatry; mem., Am. Public Welfare Assn.; chair, Social Services Com.; Natl. Assn. of Human Service Directors; Campbell-Washington-Joppa Lodge #37 Prince Hall Afffiliated; Free and Accepted Masons; King Hiram Chapter Holy Royal Arch Masons; State Representative, 1976-81, 200th Dist.; Phila. City Council, 1981-87, 9th Dist.; leader, 50th Ward Democratic Exec. Com.; v. chair, Black Ward Leaders and elected officials; rec., Man of the Year, Big Brothers and Big Sisters Assn.; Natl. Assn. Negro Business and Prof. Women of Am.; Master Mason of the Year, CWJ Lodge; mem., Salem Baptist Ch., Jenkintown; mem., Deacon Bd. and Inspirational Choir; mem., bd. dirs., Cora Services, Child Welfare Adv. Council, Phila. Urban League, Salba Corp.; appointed Secretary of Public Welfare, Jan. 20, 1987; married Deborah Ragland; 3 sons: John III, Levan and Kellan; home address: 8016 Gilbert Street, Mt. Airy, Philadelphia.

The state Department of Public Welfare administers a vast array of human services programs; promotes local social services and planning activities; distributes federal and state funds to local agencies and develops programs to respond to the human services needs of the Commonwealth's residents.

Annually, the budget for department programs totals more than $5 billion — the largest among state agencies in Pennsylvania and one of the largest in the nation. Programs provide basic needs including cash, food, shelter, health care, heat, and job-funding assistance for individuals and families. The department also provides treatment, care and support services in state-operated facilities and in the community for the mentally ill and retarded, and children and families.

What was then called the Department of Welfare was first established by the Act of May 25, 1921 (P.L. 1144). This legislation drew together in one agency activities previously performed by the Board of Public Charities, the Commission of Lunacy, the Prison Labor Commission and others. The Administrative Code of 1929 further defined the powers of the new department.

Acts of June 24, 1937 (P.L. 2003 and P.L. 2015) established a Department of Public Assistance and centralized relief and money distribution elements of state government. These acts also established the 67 county boards of assistance.

The Act of July 29, 1953, (P.L. 1428) transferred supervision of penal and correction institutions from the Department of Welfare to the Department of Justice.

The former Departments of Welfare and Public Assistance became the Department of Public Welfare on June 1, 1958, as authorized by the Act of July 13, 1957, (P.L. 852).

Specialized institutions for juvenile offenders were established by the Act of November 21, 1959, (P.L. 1579); also restoration centers for older people were authorized by the Acts of June 19, 1964 (Special Session, P.L. 75 and 77). The legislative base for the department's programs for the mentally impaired was greatly expanded and codified by the Act of October 20, 1966, (Third Special Session, P.L. 96).

All existing public welfare laws were consolidated and codified in the Public Welfare Code, and Act of June 13, 1967 (P.L. 31), which has largely become the legal base of the department's operation.

Mission of the Department. The Department of Public Welfare's mission is to promote, improve and sustain the quality of family life; break the cycle of dependency; promote respect for employees; and protect and serve Pennsylvania's most vulnerable citizens.

The overall policy direction of the department is toward financial independence for those who are able and community living in the least restrictive settings for those in need of assistance in daily living. When institutional care and treatment are necessary, the goal is to deliver high quality services in settings which are safe and responsive to human needs.

Federal funds are employed to the greatest possible extent. Local private and public funds expand the impact of state-appropriated dollars.

Citizen participation is an essential ingredient in helping the Department of Public Welfare to define service needs and develop programs to address these needs.

EXECUTIVE

The chief executive of the department is the Secretary of Public Welfare, who is responsible for overall policy and operation of programs and services.

Deputy secretaries who have operational, program development or management support functions provide direction to the major activities of the department. The areas of responsibility of the deputy secretaries include administration; income maintenance; medical assistance; mental health; mental retardation; children, youth and families; and fraud and

abuse investigation and recovery.

Program offices are responsible for statewide planning for their respective programs, policy and program development, implementation, monitoring, supervision, program evaluation, and the securing of resources through the state budget process and federal grants.

Office of Communication provides information about the department to news media outlets statewide, coordinates publication and distribution of pamphlets and brochures about the department's services and coordinates the dissemination of information and other promotional and advertising activities within the department and with the executive branch. It also advises the Secretary and deputy secretaries on media relations, speeches, public appearances and the effect of policy decisions.

Office of State and Federal Relations provides the Secretary with information on actions under consideration by the Pennsylvania General Assembly and provides members of the Legislature with information about the department's programs, policies and regulations. The office assists in coordinating and directing the department's initiatives with the legislative and executive branches, answers legislative inquiries, and monitors legislative bills and the General Assembly's reaction to department regulations.

Office of Legal Counsel provides legal advice to the senior staff of the department, participates in and reviews regulations and contracts, represents the interests of the department in administrative hearings, where appropriate — including the department's Office of Hearings and Appeals, Civil Service Commission, Pennsylvania Human Relations Commission and related offices — represents the department in state and federal courts where responsibility is delegated by the state Attorney General, and provides liaison between the department and the Office of General Counsel.

Office of Client Rights assists the Secretary of Public Welfare in assuring that the department's mental health and mental retardation programs operate in a manner which protects the rights of the clients they serve.

Office of Hearings and Appeals has responsibility for conducting administrative appeal hearings for clients and injured employes of the department who dispute actions taken by DPW program offices.

DEPUTY SECRETARY FOR ADMINISTRATION

The deputy secretary for administration reports to the Secretary of Public Welfare and is responsible for the day-to-day administration of the department. Staffing, budget, personnel and other internal administration and management actions are among those reviewed, initiated or authorized through the office. The department's other separate offices including fiscal management, personnel services and information systems report to this office. The deputy secretary also directs the Office of Operations Review in its functions.

Office of Operations Review is responsible for reviewing operations of the department and conducting internal audits. It is responsible for reporting to the executive deputy secretary any department non-compliance with state and federal policies and identifying any circumstances or situations which could be changed to promote greater efficiency. In addition, the office is responsible for the coordination of outside, both federal and state, audit resolution and follow-up.

Office of Fiscal Management provides technical support to the Secretary and program offices for the fiscal administration of the department's programs. These activities are frequently coordinated with the federal government, the Governor's Office of Budget, Office of Administration, other state departments, the General Assembly, county officials and service providers.

Office of Personnel Services is the department's liaison with the state Civil Service Commission and the Bureaus of Personnel and Labor Relations in the Governor's Office of Administration. This office's responsibilities include the administration of employe development; recruiting; personnel transactions and complement control; classification and position management; personnel planning; staffing and organizational studies; employe benefits and assistance; labor relations contract management; grievance administration; and discipline and leave management. It also provides guidance and assistance to program offices in these areas.

Office of Information Systems provides data processing and word processing for the department. To carry out its responsibilities, the office relies on a specialized staff who provide technical expertise in systems design, telecommunications, data base development and computer operations.

DEPUTY SECRETARY FOR FRAUD AND ABUSE INVESTIGATION AND RECOVERY

The Office of Fraud and Abuse Investigation and Recovery combines the activities of the Bureau of Claims Settlement (BCS) and Bureau of Special Investigations. BCS administers the child support collections operations for the state of Pennsylvania. It also collects overpayments and payments made under the Medical Assistance program when a third-party insurer is liable for health care received by a recipient. BSI, which operates a fraud and abuse tip line, 1-800-932-0582, investigates any suspected recipient or worker abuse of the welfare system. Its work serves as a significant deterrent to those who would seek to defraud the system. In addition, the Office of FAIR works closely with the Office of Medical Assistance and state and local law enforcement officials in investigating and prosecuting medical assistance fraud and abuse by recipients and providers.

DEPUTY SECRETARY FOR INCOME MAINTENANCE

Eligibility for and the administration of the income maintenance, medical assistance, and food stamp programs is regulated by the Office of Income Maintenance.

Income maintenance programs provide cash and other assistance to eligible individuals and families.

The Commonwealth totally funds the State Blind Pension and General Assistance programs. State Blind Pension provides cash assistance for legally blind persons whose income level excludes them from participation in the federal

Supplemental Security Income program. General Assistance provides cash assistance for persons who do not meet eligibility requirements for federally-funded programs for the disabled or families with dependent children.

The state and federal governments share the costs for Aid to Families with Dependent Children, a cash assistance program for families with children who are deprived of the support of a parent for reasons of incapacity, desertion or unemployment.

The federally-funded Low Income Home Energy Assistance Program (LIHEAP) is administered through the office. LIHEAP provides assistance for thousands of Pennsylvania families to help pay for winter heating bills each year. A crisis component of LIHEAP provides 24-hour-a-day emergency assistance to households, while another portion of LIHEAP funds is channeled to the state Department of Community Affairs, through the Office of Income Maintenance, for weatherization of low income families' homes.

The Supplemental Security Income program is a cash assistance program, administered by the federal government through the Social Security Administration, for elderly, blind and disabled persons. Pennsylvania supplements the basic SSI grant.

The Food Stamp program provides additional in-kind assistance to individuals and families who are eligible for income maintenance programs or who have limited incomes. The program is financed by the U.S. Department of Agriculture and is administered by the Department of Public Welfare.

DEPUTY SECRETARY FOR MEDICAL ASSISTANCE

The Office of Medical Assistance administers the joint state/federal Medicaid program, under which more than a million Pennsylvania residents can receive health care. Services include inpatient hospital care, prescription drugs, home health care, nursing home care, outpatient psychiatric care, drug and alcohol clinic visits, physician, dental, and other medical services.

Eligibility for the program is determined by the county assistance offices. Persons who are eligible for cash assistance also qualify for the medical assistance program, as do other low income families and individuals if they meet certain income and resource standards.

The office is responsible for enrolling providers for participation in the program, establishing rates or fees, and reviewing and approving invoices submitted by providers. Reimbursement for services is made directly to providers.

The office is responsible for taking administrative actions, including suspending from the program or seeking restitution against providers who abuse or overutilize Medicaid.

DEPUTY SECRETARY FOR CHILDREN, YOUTH, AND FAMILIES

The department works through county children and youth agencies and the juvenile courts to provide an array of services to troubled children and their families. The major emphasis is to assure that all children have an opportunity for healthy development, preferably in their own homes. If this is not possible, the aim is to provide a permanent alternative home as quickly as possible. To accomplish this, county children and youth agencies make available services designed to assist parents in caring for their children. These include counseling, homemaker services, life skills education and day treatment services. If a child must be removed from his or her home, efforts are made to provide temporary residential care such as a foster family or small group home in a family and community setting similar to the child's own. Other placement options include institutional care for children in need of a more structured setting, and adoption for those children for whom a new family is to be legally obtained.

In all but the most serious criminal cases, the major thrust is to divert juvenile offenders away from institutionalization and imprisonment close to adult criminals. The department directly operates residential programs in Youth Development Centers across the state, and Youth Forestry Camps. In addition, it provides funding to county and private agencies for the operation of neighborhood group homes, day treatment centers and other community-based treatment programs.

Under the state Child Protective Services Act of 1975, the department launched a major initiative aimed at fighting the problem of child abuse. The act requires physicians, teachers, social service professionals and others to report instances of suspected child abuse to the department for investigation. Also, a toll-free hotline (800-932-0313) has been established which receives reports of child abuse on a 24-hour-a-day basis and refers them for investigation by the county children and youth agencies.

DEPUTY SECRETARY FOR MENTAL HEALTH

Mental health services range from community to hospital programs, with the emphasis on helping people to remain in their communities. Community residential services for former hospital patients are emphasized, with the aim to develop more services to help the chronically mentally ill to break the cycle of repeated hospital admissions.

The state's 15 hospitals for mentally ill persons provide special intensive services for patients needing psychiatric rehabilitation. Long-term care for older persons who no longer require intensive psychiatric services but who need nursing care is also provided.

A wide range of community-based services is provided including short-term inpatient, outpatient and partial hospital care, emergency "crisis intervention" services, counseling, information, and referral.

A restoration center provides care for geriatric patients, all of whom are former residents of state hospitals. The goal of the centers is to move residents into appropriate community programs whenever possible and to provide long-term care for the others.

DEPUTY SECRETARY FOR MENTAL RETARDATION

Pennsylvania operates 18 facilities for mentally retarded persons including 11 state centers and 7 units on the grounds of state mental hospitals. The objectives of the institutional program are to prepare residents for placement in community programs and to provide care for those who, because of multiple handicaps or severity of retardation, are unlikely to move into community programs.

There are a variety of community residential mental retardation facilities to accommodate persons with differing levels of ability and need. Supportive services, for both retarded persons and their families, help to maintain individuals in community settings. These support services include respite care, in-home therapy, transportation, homemaker service and recreation for families with a retarded member living at home. Other community services available to retarded individuals residing in their own homes or licensed community residential mental retardation facilities include vocational services, social rehabilitation, and early intervention.

OFFICE OF POLICY, PLANNING AND EVALUATION

The Office of Policy, Planning and Evaluation provides a wide range of services including development and coordination of department policy, planning and analysis of issues critical to the department's decision-making process; administration of local Title XX funds through programmatic block grants to counties and providers; management of the operation of and the divestiture of the six state general hospitals; technical assistance to county government; and research and evaluation of major program and impact studies.

Through the federal Title XX program, augmented by state funds, the department provides the resources to operate a substantial network of day care facilities available to parents who work and meet certain income eligibility standards.

This office is also responsible for licensing personal care boarding homes. These homes provide care for those who require assistance with dressing, bathing, diet or medication but who do not require hospitalization or care in a skilled nursing home or intermediate care facility.

The office is responsible for administering the Refugee Assistance Program. Through state and federal funds, including Title XX, adult social services are made available for legal services, domestic violence, rape crisis and family planning programs.

BOARDS AND ADVISORY COMMITTEES

County Assistance Offices
Boards of Trustees of State Institutions
Public Assistance Advisory Committee
Medical Assistance Advisory Committee
Mental Health/Mental Retardation Advisory Committee
Children, Youth, and Families Advisory Committee
Developmental Disabilities Planning Council
Advisory Committee for the Blind
Business Enterprises Program Committee (BVS)

SECRETARIES OF PUBLIC WELFARE	Appointed Since 1950	
Harry Shapiro	June	2, 1958
Ruth Grigg Horting	Jan.	20, 1959
Arlin M. Adams	Jan.	15, 1963
Max Rosenn	Mar.	1, 1966
Thomas W. Georges, Jr., M.D.	July	13, 1967
Stanley A. Miller	Jan.	5, 1970
Helene Wohlgemuth	Jan.	25, 1971
Frank S. Beal	Jan.	6, 1975
Aldo Colautti	May	1, 1978
Helen B. O'Bannon	Feb.	16, 1979
Walter W. Cohen	Mar.	17, 1983
*John F. White, Jr.	Jan.	20, 1987

* Incumbent

Deputy Secretaries	Appointed Since 1950				Appointed Since 1950	
Norman V. Lourie (retired Sept. 6, 1979)	June	2, 1955	Gerald F. Radke	Aug.	4, 1976
John E. Davis, M.D. (resigned July 13, 1963)	July	18, 1958	Peter P. Polloni	Mar.	21, 1977
William P. Camp, M.D.	Oct.	14, 1963	John C. Cuddy	Mar.	15, 1979
Joseph A. Adelstein, M.D.	July	25, 1967	John Pazour	June	8, 1979
John H. Jones	Mar.	6, 1968	Donna A. Jeffers	Aug.	6, 1979
Frank S. Beal	Apr.	12, 1971	Jennifer L. Howse, Ph.D.	Jan.	14, 1980
William McLaughlin	Apr.	12, 1971	Scott H. Nelson, M.D.	Jan.	14, 1980
William B. Beach, Jr., M.D.	Dec.	1, 1971	Frank D. Wilson, Jr.	Aug.	8, 1980
Richard G. Farrow	Dec.	24, 1971	Richard L. Addison	Dec.	1, 1980
Irene F. Pernsley	Dec.	24, 1971	Brian T. Baxter	Feb.	7, 1983
Jeffrey N. Ball	Aug.	28, 1972	Margaret Jean Sosnowski, Ph.D.	Feb.	18, 1983
Norman J. Taylor	Dec.	1, 1972	Patricia S. Jacobs	Aug.	5, 1983
Kathryn McKenna	Jan.	19, 1973	Kathryn McKenna	July	26, 1984
Gregory L. Coleman	May	1, 1973	*Gilbert M. Branche	Nov.	19, 1984
Stanley Meyers	Oct.	1, 1973	*Eileen M. Schoen	Apr.	6, 1987
Anna Belle Calloway	Apr.	11, 1975	*Harry D. Sewell	Apr.	20, 1987
Ford S. Thompson, Jr.	Apr.	11, 1975	*Jerry Friedman	Apr.	20, 1987
Wilbur E. Hobbs	May	23, 1975	*Julia Danzy	May	11, 1987
Aldo Colautti	Sept.	15, 1975	*Steven M. Eidelman	May	11, 1987
Thomas L. Hooker	Nov.	7, 1975			
Robert M. Daly, M.D.	Feb.	2, 1976	*Incumbent		

DEPARTMENT OF REVENUE
11th Floor, Strawberry Square
Harrisburg, PA 17127

BARTON A. FIELDS
Secretary of Revenue

Barton A. Fields was born May 22, 1930, in Philadelphia, the son of Archibald A. and Daisy B. Fields; Penn State Univ. (B.A.) 1954; state government service since 1957 as Director of Municipal Pension and Fire Relief Audits in the Department of Auditor General; exec. dep. sec. and Secretary of the Commonwealth, Pa. Dept. of State; chief of manpower planning, recruitment and placement, Pa. Dept. of Ed.; public utility analyst, Pa. Public Utility Commission; dir. of administrative services, Pa. Dept. of Property and Supplies; supervising personnel analyst, principal personnel analyst, and personnel analyst, Governor's Office of Admin.; U.S. Army; 1954-56; former pres. and bd. chmn., Harristown Development Corp.; former pres., Harrisburg Area Branch NAACP; appointed Secretary of Revenue, February 16, 1987; married to Lorraine Robinson Brown, 6 children: Lynn, Barton, Clifton, Raymond, Sherman, Lorraine; home address, 912 N. 16th St., Harrisburg.

The Department of Revenue originated in 1927 and was reorganized on a functional basis in 1975. It administers the Commonwealth's revenue collection activities as well as special programs such as the Senior Citizen Property Tax/Rent Rebate, Public Utility Realty Tax, and the Pennsylvania State Lottery.

The department is responsible for collecting personal income tax, sales and use tax, hotel occupancy tax, all corporate taxes, inheritance tax, realty transfer tax, cigarette tax, malt beverage tax, spirituous and vinous liquors tax, thoroughbred and harness racing taxes, liquid fuels tax, fuel use tax, motor carriers road tax, the interstate bus compact, writ tax, fines, costs and marriage license tax.

EXECUTIVE

The chief executive of this department is the Secretary of Revenue who is appointed by the Governor and confirmed by the Senate. The Secretary is a member of the Governor's cabinet and of the Board of Finance and Revenue.

Reporting directly to the Secretary are the Internal Investigations Office, the Press Secretary, the Pennsylvania State Lottery and the Legislative Office. In addition, four Deputy Secretaries directly report to the Secretary and assist him in directing the functions of various bureaus of the department.

DEPUTY SECRETARY FOR TAXATION

The Deputy Secretary for Taxation oversees the Board of Appeals, the bureaus of Individual Taxes, Business Trust Fund Taxes, Receipts and Control, and Corporation Taxes.

Board of Appeals is a quasi-judicial body that receives, hears, considers, and renders decisions on administrative appeals filed with the department and referred to the board.

Bureau of Corporation Taxes administers all corporate related taxes including corporate net income, capital stock/ foreign franchise, Pennsylvania "S," banks, insurance and utility gross receipts, and public utility realty taxes. It conducts all corporate tax report processing, settlement, accounting, and corporate clearance functions.

Bureau of Individual Taxes is responsible for the administration of tax programs related to individuals, personal income tax, and the inheritance tax. It is also responsible for administering the Lottery funded Property Tax/Rent Rebate Program. Miscellaneous responsibilities of the bureau include the administration of the realty transfer tax and the reporting of writ and marriage license taxes and Commonwealth fines.

Bureau of Business Trust Fund Taxes administers the sales/use tax and employer withholding. It is also responsible for the administration of the malt beverage tax, cigarette tax, and pari-mutuel tax.

Bureau of Receipts and Control receives, processes, controls, accounts for, transmits and deposits monies submitted in payment of taxes administered by the department.

DEPUTY SECRETARY FOR ADMINISTRATION

The Deputy Secretary for Administration is responsible for the bureaus of Administrative Services, Data Reduction, Personnel, and the Affirmative Action Office.

Bureau of Administrative Services is responsible for Procurement, Form Design, Commodity Supply, Capital Inventory, Printing/Duplicating, Mail Services, Building Maintenance/Renovation, control of all major tax records, Building Leases, Telecommunications, Parking, Automotive and the collection and holding in custody of Abandoned and Unclaimed Property.

Bureau of Data Reduction has two divisions: one to process information onto tape to be entered in the department's main computer, the second division to provide word processing, secretarial services and clerical assistance to department bureaus.

Bureau of Personnel is responsible for the implementation and administration of the Commonwealth's personnel policies, programs and procedures. The bureau supplies technical support services to the department in a number of management functions.

Affirmative Action Office is responsible for working with management to ensure equality of opportunity to department employes as well as persons applying for work to the department. This includes preparing, administering, and monitoring the department's Affirmative Action Plan.

DEPUTY SECRETARY FOR ENFORCEMENT

The Deputy Secretary for Enforcement supervises the activities of the bureaus of Audit, Compliance, Motor License Funds, Office of Criminal Tax Investigations, and Field Operations.

Bureau of Audits enforces compliance with various tax laws by conducting a comprehensive audit program.

Bureau of Compliance administers enforcement and compliance programs and collects delinquent corporate taxes.

Office of Criminal Tax Investigations identifies areas of non-compliance and methods used to evade taxes and conducts criminal tax case investigations recommending, when warranted, criminal prosecution.

Bureau of Field Operations operates twenty-four district offices throughout the state which investigate taxpayer accounts owing delinquent monies and/or tax returns. It administers the Inheritance Tax Program and provides assistance to taxpayers for annual tax filings and the Property Tax/Rent Rebate Program.

Bureau of Motor License Funds functions include licensing of new accounts, examination of quarterly and monthly returns, account maintenance, as well as delinquency, assessment and enforcement programs for liquid fuels, fuel use, motor carrier and related taxes.

DEPUTY SECRETARY FOR FISCAL POLICY AND ANALYSIS

The Deputy Secretary for Fiscal Policy and Analysis oversees the duties and functions of the Office of Policy Evaluation and Analysis, the Office of Systems and Operational Analysis, and the bureaus of Computer Services and Fiscal Management.

The Office of Policy Evaluation and Analysis is responsible for forecasting and reporting General Fund, Motor License Fund and other special fund revenues, and estimating the state fiscal impacts of legislative proposals or changes in economic conditions.

The Office of Systems and Operational Analysis is responsible for reviewing all tax systems and operational priorities to enhance productivity and efficiency throughout the department.

The Bureau of Computer Services provides Information Systems Support for the Tax Administration, Lottery, and Property Tax/Rent Rebate functions of the Department of Revenue. The bureau provides a full range of data processing services including Information Systems and Consulting, System Development, Computer Operations, Technical Support functions, and Information Center Services.

The Office of Fiscal Management is responsible for the preparation and execution of the budget. It also has responsibility to be the official repository of all departmental contracts.

SECRETARIES OF REVENUE	Appointed Since 1950
Gerald A. Gleeson (resigned Jan. 27, 1958)	Jan. 18, 1955
Vincent G. Panati (dec. Apr. 22, 1958)	Jan. 27, 1958
A. Allen Sulcowe (acting)	Apr. 23, 1958
Charles M. Dougherty	Jan. 20, 1959
Theodore B. Smith	Jan. 15, 1963
Warner M. Depuy	Jan. 17, 1967
Robert P. Kane	Jan. 25, 1971

	Appointed Since 1950				Appointed Since 1950	
Vincent X. Yakowicz	Feb.	4, 1974	Vincent X. Yakowicz	Mar.	24, 1971
George J. Mowod	Jan.	6, 1975	Julius N. Rothman	Dec.	18, 1972
Charles S. Seligman (acting)	Apr.	6, 1976	Abe L. Yablon	Sept.	24, 1973
Milt Lopus	June	30, 1976	Charles S. Seligman	Jan.	21, 1974
Stanley M. Weiss, Jr. (acting)	Jan.	15, 1979	Marco S. Sonnenschein	Mar.	18, 1975
Howard A. Cohen	Feb.	13, 1979	Darleen J. Fritz (acting)	June	23, 1978
Robert K. Bloom (acting Dec. 2, 1980)	Jan.	5, 1982	Patrick A. Philbin	June	25, 1979
James I. Scheiner (acting Jan. 20, 1983)	Mar.	23, 1983	Robert E. Matson	Sept.	4, 1979
Eileen Healy McNulty (acting)	Jan.	20, 1987	Robert K. Bloom	Sept.	10, 1979
*Barton A. Fields	Feb.	16, 1987	Daniel S. Nagin	July	13, 1981
			William A. Hawkins	Feb.	22, 1983
Deputy Secretaries of Revenue			W. Michael Trant (acting)	May	13, 1983
			Harold J. Walker	Aug.	1, 1983
William J. Lederer (resigned Feb. 19, 1957)	Feb.	17, 1955	James L. Nelligan	Nov.	9, 1983
Joseph Andrews	Apr.	1, 1955	Kenneth D. Henderson	June	16, 1985
Charles S. Seligman	Nov.	13, 1956	Carl W. Back, Jr. (acting)	July	5, 1985
A. Allen Sulcowe	Apr.	16, 1957	Frank R. Booth	Nov.	7, 1985
Edward R. Devlin (dec. June 12, 1960)	Mar.	11, 1959	*Eileen Healy McNulty	Jan.	20, 1987
Mrs. Edward R. Devlin	June	23, 1960	*James W. Harris	June	1, 1987
Warner M. Depuy	Apr.	29, 1963	*Stephen H. Stetler	June	11, 1987
James A. Armstrong, Jr.	Mar.	15, 1963	*Trudy A. Fraas	June	15, 1987
Michael J. Bednarek	Mar.	18, 1963			
George E. Gold	Sept.	9, 1966	*Incumbent		
Edward S. Hineman	Jan.	20, 1967			
Abraham D. Cohn	Mar.	4, 1971			

DEPARTMENT OF STATE
302 North Office Building
Harrisburg, PA 17120

JAMES J. HAGGERTY

Secretary of the Commonwealth

James J. Haggerty was born June 12, 1936, in Scranton, the son of Margaret W. Cummings and the late James J. Haggerty; Holy Cross Coll. (A.B.) 1957; Georgetown Univ. Law Center (J.D.) 1960; mem., The Georgetown Law Journal, 1959-60; Univ. of Scranton, Honorary Doctor of Laws degree, 1987; attorney; mem., Scranton law firm, Haggerty, McDonnell and O'Brien, 1970-87; mem., Casey, Haggerty and McDonnell, 1965-70; law clerk to Judge William J. Nealon, Chief Justice, U.S. Dist. Ct., Middle Dist. of Pa., 1963-64; frmr. mem., bd. of dirs., and solicitor, First Natl. Bank of Dunmore; past pres., dir., Lackawanna Bar Assn.; mem.: Pa. Bar Assn., Am. Bar Assn.; Pa. Trial Lawyers Assn.; Assn. of Trial Lawyers of America; Hearing Com. on No. 3.03 Disciplinary Bd. of the Supreme Ct.; permanent mem., Judicial Conf. of the U.S. Third Judicial Circuit; pres., dir., Shamrock Communications Corp.; frmr. dir., Specialty Plastics Products, Inc.; chmn., bd. of trustees, Univ. of Scranton, 1982-86, mem. since 1979; Natl. Disting. Service Award in Trusteeship, 1986, Univ. of Scranton Nominee; T. Donald Reinfret S.J. Award, 1985, Outstanding Alumnus of the Year, Scranton Preparatory Alumni Assn.; Outstanding Alumnus of the Year, 1982, Holy Cross Coll. Alumnus of Northeastern Pa. Award; chmn., "The Real Bob Casey Committee," 1985-86; dir., former v. pres., Grtr. Scranton Chamber of Commerce; frmr. dir., Lackawanna United Way; past pres., Friendly Sons of St. Patrick of Lackawanna Co.; active duty, U.S. Army, Infantry; frmr. mem., Pa. Natl. Guard; mem., St. Paul's Parish, Scranton; appointed Secretary of the Commonwealth, Jan. 20, 1987; married Cecelia Ellen Lynett; 7 children: Jean Margaret, Mauri Elizabeth, James Joseph, Jr., Matthew Edward, Cecelia Ellen, Daniel Patrick and Kathleen Mary; home address: 1524 Adams Avenue, Dunmore.

The Secretary of the Commonwealth, head of the Department of State, is appointed by the Governor and confirmed by the Senate. By appointment of the Governor, the Secretary is a member of the Governor's Executive Board and administers the Bureau of Commissions, Elections and Legislation, the Bureau of Professional and Occupational Affairs, the Corporation Bureau and the Bureau on Charitable Organizations. By statutory provision, he is a member of the Board of Property, the Board of Finance and Revenue, the State Athletic Commission and the Pennsylvania Municipal Retirement Board.

The Secretary is the keeper of the Great Seal of the Commonwealth and has the duty of authenticating government documents through the seal's use.

Nearly all the official transactions of the Governor pass through the Secretary's hands. He is custodian of the laws and resolutions passed by the General Assembly and of all proclamations issued by the Governor. Veto messages of the Governor are prepared for publication under his signature.

The Secretary examines and approves or disapproves all types of voting systems used in the 67 counties of the state. (See Elections)

All commissions, appointments and proclamations issued by the Governor are countersigned and recorded by the Secretary of the Commonwealth.

The Department of State — A record of all official acts of the Governor is kept in the Department of State, as is a record of all death warrants, respites, pardons, remittances of fines and forfeitures and commutations of sentences.

The department registers and issues licenses to notaries public and keeps their bonds. The official bonds and recognizances of county offices whom the Governor commissions are kept in the department.

The department further furnishes, upon request and payment of fees as fixed by law, certificates of matters of public record in the department or certified copies of public papers or documents on file, and authenticates the official capacity of state, judicial and county officers and notaries public appointed or elected who are commissioned by the Governor.

BUREAU OF COMMISSIONS, ELECTIONS AND LEGISLATION

Commissions. The department issues commissions to all state officials who are elected by popular vote, including judges of the various courts, certain county officers and district justices.

Appointed officials such as departmental officers, trustees of state hospitals, State board members, commissioners of deeds, police officers, officers appointed by the Governor to fill vacancies in elective offices, etc., are commissioned only upon written order from the Governor for a term fixed by law.

Notaries public are commissioned by the Secretary of the Commonwealth under Act No. 373, approved August 21, 1953 (P.L. 1323).

Extraditions. Warrants for the extradition and return of fugitives are issued upon requisitions from governors of other states when approved by the Attorney General, and upon written order by the Governor. Requisitions issued on governors of other states for the return of fugitives are based on applications when made by a district attorney, and approved by the Governor and Attorney General.

Legislation. The department is in charge of recording and filing all legislation enacted by the General Assembly. All acts and resolutions are filed and recorded in this department. The department prepares bond issues certified under the Great Seal to be sent through Budget to Treasury.

Elections. The Secretary of the Commonwealth:

(a) is the custodian of the election returns for national, state, judicial, legislative and such county officers as receive commissions, and he compiles and publishes the returns of the general elections; (b) prescribes the forms of nomination petitions and papers, expense accounts and all other forms and records required by the Pennsylvania Election Code; (c) examines and re-examines voting machines and approves or disapproves them for use in this Commonwealth; (d) certifies to the county boards of elections for primaries and elections the names of the candidates for President and Vice President of the United States, presidential electors, United States Senators, Representatives in Congress and all State officers, including Senators and Representatives, Judges of all courts of records, delegates and alternate delegates, committees; (e) receives

and determines the sufficiency of nomination petitions, certificates and papers of these candidates; (f) issues certificates of election to successful candidates unless otherwise prescribed by law; (g) receives reports from county boards of elections and may demand such additional reports on special matters as he may deem necessary; (h) prescribes the form and wording of constitutional amendments to be submitted to the electors of the state at large.

The bureau administers the Pennsylvania Voter Hall of Fame which was established in October 1986 to honor citizens who have exemplary voting records (voted in every November election for which they were eligible for 50 years or more consecutive years).

Professional and Occupational Affairs Bureau. Twenty-five licensing boards and commissions within the bureau have powers to perform under the licensure laws of the Commonwealth. Among these are such matters as processing of applications for licenses, authorizing the issuance of licenses, monitoring licenses, suspending and revoking licenses of licensees for unethical or incompetent behavior, approval and disapproval of professional schools and authorizing examinations. The names of the licensing boards are: Board of Accountancy, Architects Licensure Board, Board of Auctioneer Examiners; Board of Barber Examiners, Board of Chiropractic, Board of Cosmetology, Board of Dentistry, Board of Funeral Directors, Board of Landscape Architects, Board of Medicine, Navigation Commission, Board of Nursing, Board of Nursing Home Administrators, Board of Occupational Therapy Education and Licensure, Board of Optometry, Board of Osteopathic Medicine, Board of Pharmacy, Board of Physical Therapy, Board of Podiatry, Board of Professional Engineers, Board of Psychology, Real Estate Commission, Board of Speech-Language and Hearing Examiners, Board of Vehicles and Board of Veterinary Medicine.

Corporation Bureau. Under the several corporation laws of the Commonwealth, every proceeding for the organization of corporations, both for profit and not-for-profit, and every ancillary transaction relating to such corporations including, but not limited to amendment of articles, restatement of articles, merger or consolidation, division, change in principal office, change in share structure, increase or decrease in capital stock, conversion, dissolution or reorganization, and change in corporate officers, is under the jurisdiction of the Department of State and is required to be filed therein.

Those businesses registering with the department include: for profit business corporations, professional corporations, not-for-profit corporations, municipal authorities, limited partnerships, foreign corporations qualifying to do business in Pennsylvania and individuals and corporations conducting business under an assumed or fictitious name.

Trade marks or service marks may be registered in the office of the Secretary of the Commonwealth. The department is in the central filing agency for secured transactions under the Uniform Commercial Code. Financing statements and subsequent ancillary transactions are recorded in the department.

Bureau on Charitable Organizations. The bureau is charged with the registration and regulation of more than 7,000 charities in the Commonwealth through enforcement of the Charitable

Organization Reform Act. The Act requires organizations soliciting for charitable purposes to register with the Commonwealth and file financial disclosure reports, providing documentation that the money donated is used for the purpose for which it was intended.

In carrying out its responsibility, the bureau consults regularly with the five-member Charities Advisory Board which represents charitable organizations as well as the general public.

The State Athletic Commission. This is a departmental commission in the Department of State which consists of three members appointed for terms of two years, and the Secretary of the Commonwealth, ex-officio. The commission regulates professional and amateur boxing, kick boxing, and professional and non-scholastic amateur wrestling. There are offices in Harrisburg, Philadelphia, Pittsburgh and Scranton. The Medical Advisory Board to the commission consists of nine members appointed by the Governor.

SECRETARIES OF THE COMMONWEALTH	Appointed Since 1950	
Gene D. Smith	May	31, 1950
James A. Finnegan (resigned Dec. 15, 1955)	Jan.	18, 1955
Henry E. Harner (resigned Dec. 28, 1956)	Jan.	3, 1956
James A. Finnegan (dec. Mar. 26, 1958)	Dec.	28, 1956
John S. Rice (resigned Mar. 31, 1961)	June	9, 1958
E. James Trimarchi, Jr.	Apr.	10, 1961
George I. Bloom	Jan.	14, 1963
Jerry Rich (acting)	May	3, 1965
W. Stuart Helm	June	23, 1965
Craig Truax	Jan.	17, 1967
Joseph J. Kelley, Jr.	Jan.	1, 1968

	Appointed Since 1950	
C. DeLores Tucker	Jan.	25, 1971
James D. Golden (acting)	Sept.	21, 1977
Barton A. Fields	Oct.	25, 1977
Barton A. Fields (acting)	Jan.	16, 1979
Ethel D. Allen, D.O.	Feb.	13, 1979
William R. Davis	Nov.	27, 1979
Richard E. Anderson (acting)	Sept.	27, 1985
Robert A. Gleason, Jr.	Nov.	25, 1985
*James J. Haggerty	Jan.	20, 1987

Deputy Secretaries

Richard R. Samuel	Aug.	21, 1953
Henry F. Harmer	Feb.	1, 1955
C. William Trout	Aug.	1, 1956
Henry E. Harner (resigned Feb. 27, 1957)	Dec.	29, 1956
Albert E. Eberman	Mar.	19, 1963
Jerry Rich	Mar.	19, 1963
Verna Z. Bennett	June	22, 1966
C. Russell Welsh, Jr.	Mar.	6, 1968
Barton A. Fields	Jan.	27, 1971
Ronald J. Pettine	Jan.	27, 1971
James D. Golden	May	29, 1975
Edward W. Robinson, Jr.	Nov.	1, 1977
James A. Green	July	6, 1978
Barton A. Fields	Jan.	16, 1979
Edward W. Robinson, Jr.	Jan.	16, 1979
Patricia A. Crawford	Mar.	19, 1979
John T. Martino	Sept.	21, 1981
John T. Martino	Dec.	17, 1984
LeGree S. Daniels	Oct.	26, 1986
*Robert N. Grant	Feb.	11, 1987

* Incumbent

PENNSYLVANIA STATE POLICE
1800 Elmerton Avenue
Harrisburg, PA 17110

RONALD M. SHARPE
State Police Commissioner

Ronald M. Sharpe was born April 16, 1940, in Phila., the son of Elizabeth M. and the late Cornelius W. Sharpe; grad., Northeast H.S., 1958; Northwest Univ. Traffic Inst., Evanston, IL, 1968; Elizabethtown Coll. (B.A., soc., anthrop.) 1975; St. Francis Coll. (M.A., indust. rel.) 1978; enlisted in the State Police, 1962; mem., Alpha Phi Alpha Fraternity; mem., bd. of trustees, Bethel African Methodist Episcopal Ch., Harrisburg; appointed Commissioner of the State Police, August 7, 1987; married Jessie L. Sowell; 3 children: Martin L., Tracey E. and Jennifer A.; home address: 6781 Chambers Hill Road, Harrisburg.

The Pennsylvania State Police was created as an executive department of the state government by the Act of May 2, 1905.

The department was the first organization of its kind in the United States.

The department is headed by a Commissioner of State Police, appointed by the Governor, with the advice and consent of the Senate, and by a Deputy Commissioner appointed by the Governor.

By special acts of the legislature, the State Police Force and its members are authorized and empowered to make arrests without warrant for all violations of the law which they may witness; to serve and execute warrants issued by the proper local authorities. These powers are extended throughout all the political subdivisions of the Commonwealth. Members of the force have all the powers and prerogatives conferred by law upon members of the police force of cities of the first class and upon constables of the Commonwealth; to act as game protectors, and as forest, fish or fire wardens.

In addition, the Pennsylvania State Police shall have the power and duty:

1. to assist the Governor in the administration and enforcement of the laws of the Commonwealth;
2. with the approval of the Governor, to assist any administrative department, board or commission of state government to enforce the laws applicable to such department, board or commission, or any organization hereof;
3. whenever possible, to cooperate with counties and municipalities in the detection of crime, the apprehension of criminals and the preservation of law and order throughout the state;
4. to aid in the enforcement of all laws relating to game, fish, forests and waters;
5. to collect and classify information useful for the detection of crime, and identification and apprehension of criminals. Such information shall be available for all police officers within the Commonwealth, under such regulations as the Commissioner may prescribe;
6. to enforce the laws regulating the use of the highways of this Commonwealth, and to assist the Department of Revenue in the collection of motor license fees, fees for titling vehicles and tractors, operator's license fees, the taxes on cigarettes and liquid fuels, and the issuance of certificates of title and motor and operator's licenses;
7. to search without warrant any boat, conveyance, vehicle or receptacle, or any place of business when there is good reason to believe that any law has been violated, the enforcement or administration of which is imposed or vested in the Department of Revenue.

The present authorized strength of the Pennsylvania State Police is 3,940, plus an additional 217 assigned to the Pennsylvania Turnpike Commission to patrol the toll road.

ADMINISTRATION

The command staff of the Commissioner includes the Deputy Commissioner, the Chief of Staff and the Bureau of Professional Responsibility. The Deputy Commissioner has direct authority over the field forces, the Bureau of Criminal Investigation and the Bureau of Patrol. The field forces consist of five Area Commands and 17 State Police Troops. The area commanders and the bureau directors are Majors; troop commanders are Captains.

The Chief of Staff has direct authority over the staff function of the State Police, consisting of the following seven bureaus, each directed by a Major or an equivalent civilian ranking: Bureau of Research and Development, Bureau of Personnel, Bureau of Laboratory and Communications Services, Bureau of Records and Information Services, Bureau of Staff Services, Bureau of Community Services and Bureau of Training and Education.

The facilities, manpower, equipment and expertise of the Pennsylvania State Police are available to all police departments in Pennsylvania.

Bureau of Patrol directs traffic law enforcement and patrol activities; directs operation of drivers' examination and testing facilities; maintains a safety program that develops vehicle regulations, manuals, and inspection station programs.

Bureau of Criminal Investigation directs and coordinates the department's criminal investigation activities, including general investigations, narcotics, gambling and fire investigations, polygraph examination and criminalistic processing of crime scenes.

Bureau of Liquor Control Enforcement is responsible for the investigation and enforcement of the provision of Act 14, Liquor Code, and such rules and regulations promulgated by the Liquor Control Board.

Bureau of Research and Development develops department policies, procedures and organizational structure; develops standards and systems of operation for staff and line functions; compiles and prepares statistical data; administers the Uniform Crime Reporting program for the Commonwealth.

Bureau of Laboratory and Communications Services operates six crime laboratories throughout the state and maintains the radio system and telephone facilities of the department.

Bureau of Records and Information Services classifies and maintains fingerprint records, furnishes information to requesting agencies concerning persons charged with criminal activity; operates the Pennsylvania State Police computer system (CLEAN) with access to computers at the Department of Transportation and the FBI computer system NCIC.

Bureau of Professional Responsibility investigates allegations of misconduct by department personnel and all instances of the use of physical force or shooting incidents involving members; conducts in-depth inspections of department personnel and installations and evaluates department policies and procedures to determine their effectiveness.

Bureau of Community Services maintains liaison with community agencies to devise an ongoing plan to eradicate tension-inducing conditions, crime, traffic accidents, and juvenile delinquency, and administers the departments' crime prevention activities.

Bureau of Personnel develops standards and procedures for personnel management, maintains and processes all personnel records, maintains liaison with various agencies and boards; administers the department recruiting and cadet processing programs, and includes the Affirmative Action Office.

Bureau of Staff Services develops fiscal plans; the budget; coordinates the department's application for Federal Funds; prepares requisitions; maintains supplies; maintains the department's automotive fleet; coordinates and plans space allocation, leases, bid proposals and specifications for facilities.

Bureau of Training and Education directs the administration of state and municipal police training at the Academy in Hershey, and at four regional training centers located throughout the Commonwealth.

The Municipal Police Officers' Education and Training Commission is a 19-member commission created by Act 120, June 18, 1974, and amended by Act 227, December 20, 1984. This act requires all political subdivisions of the Commonwealth (other than a city of the first class) or groups of political subdivisions acting in concert, to train all members of their police departments hired by them after the effective date of this Act.

The commission is composed of the Secretary of Community Affairs; the Attorney General; the Commissioner of the Pennsylvania State Police (chairman); a member of the Senate of Pennsylvania, appointed by the President Pro Tempore; a member of the House of Representatives, appointed by the Speaker; gubernatorial appointments are: four elected officials of political subdivisions, four incumbent chiefs of police from political subdivisions, one Federal Bureau of Investigation special agent-in-charge, one educator qualified in the field of law enforcement, one member representing the public at large, two noncommissioned police officers, and the police commissioners of a city of the first class or his designee.

The powers and duties of the commission are: to establish the minimum courses of study and training for municipal police officers; to establish courses of study and in-service training for municipal police officers appointed prior to the effective date of the Act; to approve or revoke the approval of any school which may be utilized to comply with the educational and training requirements as established by the commission; to establish the minimum qualifications for instructors; to promote the most efficient and economical program for police training by utilizing existing facilities, programs and qualified state, local and federal police personnel; to make an annual report to the Governor and to the General Assembly on administration of the program and the activities of the commission, together with recommendations for executive or legislative action necessary

for the improvement of law enforcement and the administration of justice.

(Act 52 approved April 28, 1943, changed name of Pennsylvania Motor Police to Pennsylvania State Police.)

STATE POLICE COMMISSIONERS	Appointed Since 1950
Col. E. J. Henry	Mar. 28, 1955
Col. Frank G. McCartney	Feb. 26, 1959
Col. E. Wilson Purdy (resigned Apr. 8, 1966).	Jan. 29, 1963
Lt. Col. Paul A. Rittelmann (acting)	Apr. 8, 1966
Col. Frank McKetta	Jan. 17, 1967
Col. Rocco P. Urella	Jan. 25, 1971
Col. James D. Barger.	Jan. 2, 1973
Col. Paul J. Chylak.	Feb. 15, 1977
Col. Daniel F. Dunn	Mar. 1, 1979
Lt. Col. Cyril J. Laffey (acting)	Aug. 14, 1984
Lt. Col. Nicholas G. Dellarciprete (acting)	Dec. 1, 1984
Col. Jay Cochran, Jr.	Mar. 6, 1985
Col. John K. Schafer (dec.).	Jan. 20, 1987
*Lt. Col. Ronald M. Sharpe	Aug. 7, 1987

Deputy Commissioners

Lt. Col. Jacob C. Mauk.	June 1, 1943
Lt. Col. Albert Dahlstrom	June 16, 1956
Lt. Col. Charles Hartman	Feb. 4, 1960
Lt. Col. George M. Sauer	Apr. 13, 1962
Lt. Col. Frank McKetta	May 29, 1963
Lt. Col. Joseph Dussia	Jan. 19, 1967
Lt. Col. Roy O. Wellendorf	Jan. 19, 1973
Lt. Col. George Evan	Aug. 19, 1976
Maj. George Evan (acting)	Jan. 11, 1979
Lt. Col. Cyril J. Laffey	June 29, 1979
Lt. Col. Richard C. Weatherbee	May 30, 1985
Lt. Col. Ronald M. Sharpe	Jan. 30, 1987

* Incumbent

DEPARTMENT OF TRANSPORTATION
1200 Transportation and Safety Building
Harrisburg, PA 17120

HOWARD YERUSALIM   **Secretary of Transportation**
Chairman, Pennsylvania Turnpike Commission

Howard Yerusalim was born Jan. 2, 1940, the son of Joseph and Edith Stupchanski Yerusalim; Drexel Univ. (B.S., civil eng.) 1962; professional engineer, Pa. Dept. of Transp., 1968; dep. sec. for admin., 1983-86; chmn., Pa. Transp. Comm.; chmn., Gov. Traffic Safety Council; chmn., Pa. Turnpike Comm.; mem., Am. Society of Civil Engineers; v. chmn., sub-committee on highway transport, Am. Assn. of State Highway and Transp. Officials; Secretary of Transportation, Mar. 13, 1987; married Barbara Perfler; 2 children: Davie E. and Eli D.; home address: 2206 Dover Rd., Harrisburg.

Act 120 of 1970 created the Department of Transportation, effective July 1, 1970.

The department was given the responsibility to develop programs to assure adequate, safe and efficient transportation facilities and services at the lowest reasonable cost to the citizenry. Coordination of transportation services by local

government and private enterprise is encouraged as is cooperation of federal, state and local government bodies in the achievement of transportation goals. These goals include providing needed facilities for the movement of people and goods, stimulating technological advancement in transportation facilities, providing leadership to identify and solve transportation problems, and developing and applying inter and multi-modal approaches to transportation policy and programs.

The department assumed all of the powers and duties formerly performed by the Department of Highways, the Bureaus of Motor Vehicles and Traffic Safety in the Department of Revenue, the High-Speed Rail Demonstration Programs in the Department of Commerce, the Mass Transit Division in the Department of Community Affairs and the Aeronautics Commission in the Department of Military Affairs. Of special importance among these responsibilities are those relating to certificates of title, licensing of operators, registration and licensing of motor vehicles, administrative enforcement of the Motor Vehicle Code including the Point System, and administration of aviation and airport development programs within the Commonwealth.

ADMINISTRATION

The Secretary. The Secretary of Transportation is the chief executive officer of the department. His responsibilities include the development, maintenance and operation of a balanced transportation system that includes highways, mass transit, rail service, aviation and various forms of assistance to municipalities.

The Secretary is assisted by a work force of 12,600 men and women in the department's central office and 11 engineering districts.

As representatives of the Secretary, they are custodians of 43,000 miles of highways (the fourth largest state maintained network in the nation), 25,000 bridges, three state-owned airports, 450 buildings, and 25,000 pieces of equipment.

They are responsible for administering 7.5 million motor vehicle registrations and 7.5 million operator licenses.

They play a direct role in the administration of financial and management assistance to 17 major transit authorities, 50 private transit companies, 2,572 local municipalities and 67 county governments.

All of these activities are financed from a budget which derives its principal sources of revenue from liquid fuel taxes, motor license fees and federal aid.

Organizationally, the department is composed of six major offices headed by six deputy secretaries. These offices, in turn, include 17 bureaus and approximately 58 divisions, the 11 engineering districts, and the 52 county maintenance offices.

Reporting directly to the Secretary are: Office of Research and Special Studies, Press Office, and Office of Legislative Affairs.

Deputy Secretary for Administration is directly responsible for the Fiscal and Systems Management Center; Bureau of Equal Opportunity; Operations eview Group; Bureau of Office Services; and Bureau of Personnel.

Deputy Secretary for Planning is directly responsible for the Center for Program Development and Management, and the Bureau of Strategic Planning.

Deputy Secretary for Local and Area Transportation is directly responsible for the Bureau of Public Transit and Goods Movement Systems, and Bureau of Municipal Services.

Deputy Secretary for Safety Administration is directly responsible for the Bureau of Motor Vehicles, Bureau of Driver Licensing, and the Center for Highway Safety.

Deputy Secretary for Highway Administration is directly responsible for the bureaus of Design, Construction and Materials, Maintenance and Operations, and Bridge and Roadway Technology; the 11 engineering districts; and county maintenance offices.

Deputy Secretary for Aviation, established by Act 1982-66, is directly responsible for the department's programs for airport development, aviation planning, operation of state-owned airport and flight services, and such other related duties as assigned by the Secretary of Transportation.

POWERS

Powers and Duties of the Department:

- To develop and maintain a continuing comprehensive and coordinated transportation planning process.
- To foster efficient and economical public transportation services.
- To prepare plans for preservation and improvement of commuter railroad systems.
- To develop more efficient bus transportation services.
- To develop plans and programs for all modes of urban transportation, including (in addition to commuter rail and motor bus) rapid rail, trolly coach, surface rail, corridor rail, and other innovative modes of urban transportation.
- To coordinate the activities of the department with those of other public agencies.
- To plan, build, and maintain state-designated highways, bridges and other transportation facilities.
- To enter into contracts for designing, constructing, repairing, or maintaining state-designated highways, bridges and other transportation facilities.
- To prepare and submit every even-numbered year to the State Transportation Commission a recommended program for the next 12 fiscal years. Each two years thereafter, the department reviews and adjusts its construction program.
- To appear or intervene as a party before the Public Utility Commission when transportation problems are being considered by the commission.
- To consult with appropriate officials regarding the environmental hazards and the construction, sanitary, recreation and social considerations that may arise in the location, design or reconstruction of any transportation facility.
- To represent the transportation interests of the Commonwealth before any federal agency or commission which determines national or regional transportation rates, routes or policies.

Upon the submission of the preliminary plan or design to the department for any transportation route or program requiring the acquisition of right-of-way, the department follows hearing procedures required by the federal government for federal-aid transportation programs. At these hearings the department considers the following effects of the transportation route or program: Residential and neighborhood character and location; conservation, noise, air and water pollution; multiple use of space; replacement housing; displacement of families and businesses; recreation and parks esthetics; public health and safety; fast, safe and efficient transportation; civil defense; economic activities; employment; fire protection; public utilities; religious institutions; and the conduct and financing of government. Additional considerations include natural and historic landmarks; property values; education; engineering right-of-way and construction costs; maintenance and operating costs; and operation and use of existing transportation routes and programs during construction and after completion.

State Transportation Advisory Committee consults with and advises the State Transportation Commission and the Secretary of Transportation in planning, development and maintenance programs and technologies for transportation systems. It includes 30 members; eight ex officio members, Secretary of Transportation, Director of the Governor's Office of Policy Development, Chairman of Public Utility Commission, Secretary of Commerce, Secretary of Education, Secretary of Environmental Resources, Secretary of Agriculture and Secretary of Community Affairs; two members appointed by the Speaker of the House and two members by the President Pro Tempore of the Senate; eighteen additional members appointed by Governor.

State Transportation Commission holds regular meetings throughout the state and holds public hearings to set transportation program priorities.

The commission gathers and studies information relating to the needs of highway construction or reconstruction, rapid transit, railroad, omnibus and other mass transportation facilities and services, and aviation and airport facilities and services, to determine the need and the recommended order of priority for their construction or reconstruction.

To accommodate local mass transportation needs, the commission coordinates its mass transit recommendations with the plans of local instrumentalities such as regional and county planning commissions.

Each two years, the commission recommends a 12-year transportation program to the Governor and the General Assembly.

It includes 13 members: Secretary of Transportation (ex officio and chairman), Chairmen of House and Senate Transportation Committees (ex officio), one member of Minority party appointed each by President Pro Tempore of Senate and Speaker of the House of Representatives; remaining eight members appointed by Governor. They receive per diem compensation and reimbursement for expenses.

Hazardous Materials Transportation Advisory Committee recommends regulations for the highway transportation of hazardous substances. Created by Act 99 of 1984, the committee is composed of representatives of the Department of Transportation, Office of Attorney General, the Department of Health, the Department of Environmental Resources, the Pennsylvania Emergency Management Agency and the Pennsylvania Public Utility Commission and nine representatives of the hazardous materials industry and the public.

STATE HIGHWAY AND BRIDGE AUTHORITY

Originally created by the Act of April 18, 1949, P.L. 604, the State Highway and Bridge Authority was authorized to sell bonds to provide funds for the acquisition or construction of highways, bridges and related facilities.

After the Constitution of the Commonwealth of Pennsylvania was amended in 1968 to provide for an itemized capital budget and to allow the Commonwealth to incur debt, Pennsylvania General Obligation Highway Bonds have been issued with the proceeds appropriated to the authority.

Act 1982-91 transferred all the functions, powers and duties of the State Highway and Bridge Authority to the department and further provided for the continued existence of the authority "until all State Highway and Bridge Authority bonds, together with the interest thereon, are fully met and discharged . . . ." Members are the Governor, the State Treasurer, Auditor General, Secretary of Transportation, Secretary of Community Affairs, the Speaker of the House of Representatives, President pro tempore of the Senate, the minority leader of the Senate, the minority leader of the House of Representatives, and three appointed members, one each by the Governor, the Speaker, and the President pro tempore. Once the authority's financial obligations are met, which will be in the 1991-92 fiscal year, the act abolishes the authority.

(Created May 6, 1970, by Act 120, P.L. 356)

SECRETARIES OF TRANSPORTATION	Appointed Since 1950	
Victor Anckaitis	July	1, 1970
Jacob Kassab	May	4, 1971
George S. Pulakos (acting)	Jan.	1, 1976
William H. Sherlock	Apr.	1, 1976
George S. Pulakos (acting)	Feb.	25, 1977
James B. Wilson	Apr.	28, 1977
George S. Pulakos	Nov.	14, 1978
Thomas D. Larson	Feb.	13, 1979
*Howard Yerusalim	Mar.	3, 1987

Deputy Secretaries	Appointed Since 1950	
Jack Kinstlinger	July	1, 1970
William B. Polk	July	1, 1970
David C. Sims	July	1, 1970
William B. Blake	Feb.	9, 1971
George S. Pulakos	Feb.	3, 1971
Edson L. Tennyson	Jan.	3, 1972
Louis Keefer	Nov.	27, 1975
Thomas H. May (acting)	Feb.	18, 1977
James B. Chiles	Oct.	13, 1977
George Wenick (acting)	July	1, 1978
Seymore G. Heyison	Oct.	5, 1978
*John J. Zogby	Feb.	19, 1979
*Harvey Haack	Mar.	5, 1979
James I. Scheiner	Mar.	12, 1979
Don Bryan	May	11, 1979
Howard Yerusalim	Apr.	22, 1983
*David E. Zazworsky	Mar.	11, 1987
*Parker F. Williams	Mar.	13, 1987
*Cheryl Y. Spicer	Mar.	13, 1987
*Bradley L. Mallory	July	28, 1987

STATE HIGHWAY AND BRIDGE AUTHORITY

Executive Directors	Appointed Since 1950	
Warren W. Holmes (acting)	May	13, 1952
John N. Forker (dec. Sept. 19, 1956)		
Kenneth R. Burks (acting)	Sept.	6, 1954
A. J. Caruso	June	1, 1957
John J. Lynam	July	12, 1961
A. J. Caruso	Apr.	30, 1963
R. L. Kunzig	Jan.	17, 1967
James D. Logan	Mar.	24, 1969
Robert H. Jones	Feb.	3, 1971
William H. Sherlock	Apr.	6, 1976
James B. Wilson	Apr.	28, 1977
George S. Pulakos	Nov.	14, 1978

Executive Directors	Appointed Since 1950	
Thomas D. Larson	Feb.	13, 1979
*Howard Yerusalim (acting)	Jan.	20, 1987

Chief Engineers		
John G. Gruener	Apr.	30, 1963
John Swanger, Jr.	Oct.	25, 1967
David C. Sims	Aug.	25, 1976
Robert R. Meuser	Nov.	21, 1979
Alfred F. Lyng	July	1, 1980
*William R. Moyer (acting)	June	2, 1986

* Incumbent

OTHER STATE AGENCIES

GOVERNOR'S ACTION CENTER
402 Finance Building
Harrisburg, PA 17120

EDWARD F. DEMPSEY   Executive Director, Governor's Action Center

Edward F. Dempsey was born Feb. 22, 1951, in Scranton, the son of Thomas A. Jr. and Nancy Ann White Dempsey; grad., Lackawanna Junior Coll (A.B.A.) 1971; Univ. of Scranton (B.S., basic admin.) 1973; appt. Executive Director, Governor's Action Center, April 13, 1987; married Barbara Ann O'Hara; 1 child, Edward, Jr.; home address: 1709 Electric St., Dunmore.

The Governor's Action Center (GAC) serves to provide the citizens of Pennsylvania with an easily accessible source of information or referral, and a channel for mediation of their complaints. Requests for assistance are received primarily through a toll-free statewide telephone network (1-800-932-0784). The Center will attempt to respond to any request made by: providing information on programs and services, referring citizens in need to the appropriate agencies, mediating inappropriate denials of service. The Center will also conduct follow-up to assure that suitable responses are made to inquiries.

In extraordinary circumstances, the GAC has been assigned additional functions as they relate to the dissemination of information during crisis or disaster situations.

The Center also provides data regarding trends in activity to other Commonwealth agencies.

PENNSYLVANIA COUNCIL ON THE ARTS
216 Finance Building
Harrisburg, PA 17120

JUNE BATTEN AREY   Executive Director, Council on the Arts

June Batten Arey was born in Norfolk, Va., the daughter of Gilmer Randolph and Flaura Mae Burch Batten; Salem Coll.; Arts Administration, Foundation Program Director; Natl. Endowment for the Arts, 1965-71; rec., Arts Council Award, Disting. Service to the Arts, 1963; Assn. of American Dance Companies, Disting. Service to Am. Dance, 1972; author, *State Art Agencies in Transition,* 1975; *Purpose, Financing and Governance of Museums,* 1979; consultant to private foundations and corps. in natl. and internatl. programming in the arts, 1972-80; appt. Executive Director, Pa. Council on the Arts, Jan. 1, 1981; formerly married to Robert Francis Arey; 3 children: Robert, Dana, David; home address: 218 Herr St., Harrisburg.

Chairman: Joseph J. Stevens; **Members:** Joan Apt, Flora L. Becker, Esq., Marjorie Broderick, Louise Curl Adams, Frank H. Goodyear, Jr., Lois Grass, June N. Honaman, Robert C. Jubelirer, James P. McBrier, Nancy S. Price, Jeanette F. Reibman, David P. Richardson, Lyn M. Ross, Carol D. Sides, Dr. Bernard Watson.

On January 26, 1966, Governor William D. Scranton signed enabling legislation for the Pennsylvania Council on the Arts. Under the provisions of the act (No. 538), the council is charged with "the encouragement and development of the various arts" in the Commonwealth. The council is directly responsible to the Governor.

The council responds to requests for support of projects initiated by non-profit art groups, institutions, and, in some cases, artists. This work is carried on through the council's grants program. Where special needs exist, the council has taken direct action and originated projects such as the Artists-in-Schools and Communities Program, Minority Arts

Program, and sponsored workshops and seminars on specific topics such as arts management, small press publishing, and community arts planning.

All meetings of the council and its various committees and panels are open to the public. The council is specifically directed to avoid actions which would interfere with the freedom of artistic expression, or with established or contemplated cultural programs in any local community.

The council consists of 19 members — 15 private citizens and four members of the General Assembly. The citizen members are appointed to three-year terms by the Governor, with the advice and consent of the Senate, and serve without compensation. From these members, the Governor also appoints the chairman and vice chairman of the council, who serve at his pleasure.

Citizen members hold office until their successors have been appointed and confirmed. No member is eligible for re-appointment during a one-year period following the expiration of his/her second successive term.

Two of the legislative members are appointed from the House of Representatives by the Speaker, and two from the Senate by the President Pro Tempore. Legislative members are selected equally from the major political parties. For the purposes of Act 538, such members of the legislature constitute a joint interim legislative committee on the arts, the council, and its appropriation.

In order to receive the best and most complete information in making decisions on the awarding of grants, the council appoints expert advisory panels whose members include professional artists, administrators and others with specialized knowledge. Each grant program is served by such a panel.

More than 100 private citizens serve on these panels which evaluate approximately 2,000 applications yearly. These advisory panels are responsible for reviewing grant applications and making recommendations for action and funding. The panels may also advise the council on policy matters.

Panel members serve without compensation. A portion of each panel's membership rotates each year. The chairman of each panel is a member of the council; co-chairmen may be selected from among the panel membership.

A professional staff, headed by an executive director, administers the council's decisions. The staff advises applicants on the council's grant programs, provides technical assistance to individuals and arts organizations, and serves as a resource for arts-related information. Program directors are specialists in various art disciplines or art fields.

The council has adopted the following objectives:

1. To make arts programs of the highest quality available throughout Pennsylvania.
2. To encourage and enable individual creative artists to do their work and bring their work to public attention.
3. To assist organizations which produce or sponsor quality arts programs.
4. To preserve the rich cultural heritage of the Commonwealth and to stimulate greater public awareness of the unique and varied contributions made to our society by Pennsylvania arts and artists.
5. To encourage community involvement and participation in the arts at every level.

In pursuing these objectives, the council sees its role as one of partnership with local arts activities, locally initiated and locally supported.

CIVIL SERVICE COMMISSION
State Street Building
P.O. Box 569
Harrisburg, PA 17120

THERESE LeMELLE MITCHELL   **Chairman, State Civil Service Commission**

Therese LeMelle Mitchell was born Feb. 12, 1952, in Harrisburg, the daughter of Leonard J. LeMelle and Jewell M. Dillon; grad., Xavier Univ. of Louisiana (B.A.) 1976; Natl. Judicial Coll., Reno, NV, 1987; public relations/journalist; mem.: Natl. Assn. of State Civil Service Commissioners; Internatl. Personnel Mgt. Assn.; Delta Sigma Theta Sorority, Inc.; Jinx Club of Harrisburg; Council of Minority Republican Women; Capitol Hill Council of GOP Women; articles published in *Essence Magazine, New Black South, Black Collegian;* asst. press sec. to Gov. Thornburgh, 1981-83; dep. press secretary, 1983-86; appt. Chairman, State Civil Service Commission, Aug. 12, 1986; 3 children: Randall, Dillon, Elise; home address: Harrisburg.

DAVID M. ZURN

Member, State Civil Service Commission

David M. Zurn was born May 24, 1938, in Erie, the son of Melvin A. and Marian Schmid Roberts; grad., Williams Coll. (A.B.) 1960; Columbia Univ. Schl. of Law (J.D.) 1963; served with Zurn Industry Inc. in various capacities, 1960-84, pres. and chief exec. officer, 1973-84; mem., Pa. and Erie Co. Bar Assns.; Gannon Univ.; mem., bd. of corporators, Hamot Health Systems, Inc.; chmn. (Emeritus) St. Vincent Foundation; mem., bd. of corporators, Hamot 20th Century Foundation; chmn., Northwestern Pa. Chapter of the Natl. Multiple Sclerosis Assn.; appt. member, State Civil Service Commission, July 15, 1986; married Barbara St. John; 3 children: Rena Zurn Fulweiler, Ameli Susan, Christopher Fredrick; home address: 1850 S. Shore Dr., Erie.

JOHN E. MILLETT

Executive Director, State Civil Service Commission

John E. Millett was born Feb. 27, 1934, in New York City, the son of Russell C. and Christine Cavaliere Millett; Univ. of Ga. (B.S.); Fels Inst., Wharton Schl. of Univ. of Pa. (M. Govt. Admn.); career employe in state govt. since 1957; entomologist, Pa. Dept. of Ag., 1957-63; pers. analyst, Dept. of Public Welfare, 1963-64; asst. personnel dir., St. Police, 1964-67, personnel dir., 1967; personnel dir., Dept. of Banking, 1968-69; dep. dir., St. Civil Service Comm., 1969-77; Am. Society for Public Admn.; Internatl. Personnel Mgt. Assn.; Natl. Assn. of St. Personnel Executives; charter mem., bd of dirs., Harrisburg Area Chapt. IPMA; frmr. pres., St. Training Council; frmr. v. pres., St. Personnel Council; has served on numerous task forces studying state personnel and training functions; frmr. evening faculty, Pa. St. Univ. Capitol Campus, grad. courses in public personnel admn.; staff mem., St. Francis Coll. Grad. Schl. of Industrial Relations, Harrisburg Ctr., grad. courses in personnel admn.; appt. Executive Director, State Civil Service Commission, Jan. 6, 1977.

The State Civil Service Commission, a three-member, bipartisan, independent adminstrative Commission, was created by the Act of June 6, 1939, P.L. 250, as amended; by the Acts of August 5, 1941, P.L. 781; May 21, 1943, P.L. 600; March 20, 1945, P.L. 44; and June 25, 1947, P.L. 930. The Act of August 5, 1941, P.L. 752, known as the Civil Service Act, created the State Civil Service Commission agency to administer the merit system in the Commonwealth.

Purpose. The purpose of the Civil Service Act of August 5, 1941, P.L. 752, as amended, is to provide greater efficiency and economy in the government of the Commonwealth by (1) establishing conditions of employment which will attract to the service of the Commonwealth qualified persons of character and ability, and (2) appointing and promoting said persons on the basis of merit and fitness.

Administration. The commission is the administrative agency for the Pennsylvania Merit System. It is a bipartisan three-member body appointed by the Governor for six-year terms or until a successor is appointed and qualified. Not more than two members are of the same political affiliation. The Governor designates one of the members as chairperson.

The Act provides that the executive director direct and supervise all administrative work and exercise certain powers and duties under the direction of the commission. As the administrative head of the agency, he reports to the commission and supervises the office of the Deputy Director.

Powers and Duties. The commission is required to establish and adopt rules for making the provisions of the Civil Service Act effective; to require observance of the provisions of the Act and of the rules and regulations thereunder; and to make

investigations requested by the Governor, the Legislature, or on matters relating to the enforcement and effect of provisions of the Act. It has the authority to conduct investigations, hold public hearings, render decisions on appeals and record findings and conclusions, upon request or on its own motion, in cases of demotion, furlough, suspension, or removal.

Bureau of Employment Services plans and implements a recruitment program to attract an adequate supply of qualified personnel from which Merit System agencies can select employes. It also coordinates agency activities to include recruitment assistance and provides comprehensive employment services for positions in the classified service.

Bureau of Personnel Assessment develops and administers the merit system examination program, supervises statewide, local, and special test administration; and conducts basic and applied research in personnel selection.

Bureau of Document Control provides computer input and output pertaining to examination scheduling and scoring, lists of eligibles, certifications, and veterans' preference claims; creates, maintains, and retrieves data from computer files; develops or modifies requirements for central computer support and monitors quantity and quality of output.

Bureau of Audit and Technical Services administers and interprets the Civil Service Act and Commission Rules and investigates alleged violations; trains agency personnel staff in proper personnel practices; provides examination, employe, and certification information; verifies personnel documents and maintains a manual of certification policies and procedures.

Bureau of Management Services administers programs for fiscal control, program planning and evaluation, personnel and training, management improvement services, publications control, distribution and dissemination of examination-related materials; monitors the directives management system and coordinates labor relations activities as they pertain to the merit system.

Agencies and Offices Served. Initially, civil service procedures were applied only to personnel in the Department of Public Assistance, Bureau of Employment Security, Liquor Control Board and the State Civil Service Commission. This application was mandatory in the Act. On September 10, 1956, the Executive Board of the Commonwealth, by resolution and amendments thereto during the next six years, added approximately 13,000 professional and technical positions to the civil service program. On August 26, 1963, the Civil Service Act was amended, increasing coverage to approximately 45,000 employes and providing a single, uniform, modern legislative system for all civil service employes. As of January 9, 1985, there were approximately 70,818 civil service employes. The following state agencies now participate in the commission's program of personnel services: departments of Aging, Agriculture, Banking, Commerce, Community Affairs, Corrections, Education, Environmental Resources, General Services, Governor's Office, Health, Insurance, Labor and Industry, Military Affairs, Public Welfare, Revenue, State, State Police and Transportation; Liquor Control Board, Milk Marketing Board, Board of Probation and Parole, State Tax Equalization Board; Civil Service Commission, Crime Commission, Fish Commission, Game Commission, Historical and Museum Commission, Governor's Justice Commission, Public Utility Commission, Securities Commission; Governor's Council on Drug and Alcohol Abuse, Emergency Management Agency, State Employes' Retirement System, Municipal Employes' Retirement System, Public School Employes' Retirement System.

Local offices receiving contractual personnel services from the commission include: Emergency Management Agencies, Housing Authorities, Mental Health/Mental Retardation County Agencies, Children and Youth County Agencies, Drug and Alcohol County Units, Area Agencies on the Aging, and CETA Prime Sponsors.

COMMISSION MEMBERS		Initial Appointment Date
Ruth Glenn Pennell (reappt. 1946, 1952)	Apr.	9, 1942
John A. M. McCarthy (reappt. 1944, 1950, 1963, 1969, 1976 chairman)	Apr.	9, 1942
George Young (chairman) (reappt. 1948, 1954)	Sept.	18, 1945
Elmer D. Graper (chairman)	May	28, 1956
Susan H. Baker	Aug.	6, 1956
C. Herschel Jones (reappt. 1970 chairman)	Aug.	5, 1963
Mary D. Barnes (reappt. 1966, 1976, chairman 1981)	Aug.	5, 1963
Grace S. Hatch (chairman).	Dec.	1, 1972
Ethel S. Barnett (reappt. 1978)	May	7, 1976
Fred E. Bryan.	Jan.	9, 1981
*David M. Zurn	July	15, 1986
*Therese L. Mitchell (chairman)	Aug.	1, 1986

* Incumbent

BOARD OF CLAIMS
707 Transportation and Safety Building
Harrisburg, PA 17120

FRED C. PACE   Chief Administrative Judge —
                                   Chairman, Board of Claims

Fred C. Pace, B.A. L.L.B., J.D., was born Dec. 28, 1919, in Phila.; att. Phila. public schl. system, Drexel Inst. of Tech.; 108th Field Artillery, Feb. 1941-June 1942; Corps of Engineers, Officers Schl.; commissioned Lieut. Sept. 1, 1942, retired due to instrumentality of war, Oct. 1945; Duke Univ. (B.A.) 1947; Duke Univ. Law Schl. (LL.B) 1950 (J.D.); private practice of law, 1951, Gallagher and Gallagher; Noonan and Pace, 1955; Noonan, Pace and Lavelle, 1961; Noonan, Pace and Noone, 1973-78; dpty. atty. genl., Workmen's Compensation Bd., 1955-63; Commonwealth atty., 1971-74; former chancellor, Schuylkill Co. Bar Assn.; Pa. Appellate, Schuylkill Co. Courts, Federal Dist. Court, 3rd Circuit Court of Appeals, Am. Trial Lawyers Assn.; appt. and confirmed Chief Administrative Judge — Chairman, Board of Claims, Nov. 15, 1978; married Peggy L. Leach; 3 daughters; home address: 1601 Oak Road, Pottsville.

CHARLES F. MEBUS   Member, Board of Claims

Charles F. Mebus was born June 15, 1928, in Abington, the son of George and Estelle Claxton Mebus; Pa. St. Univ. (B.S., chemistry) 1949, (B.S. San. Engr.) 1951; 1st Lt., U.S. Army Corps of Engineers, 1951-53; U.S. Army Reserve, 1949-62; engineer; Am. Society of Civil Engineers; Natl. Society of Professional Engineers; The Franklin Inst.; chmn., Young Republicans, Cheltenham Twp.; bd. dir., Young Republican Federation, Montgomery Co., 1960-62; frmr. mem., House of Representatives, 1965-78; elected Chief Clerk, House of Representatives, Jan. 2, 1979-81; Dep. Sec. for Admin., Dept. of Revenue, 1982-83; Dep. Sec. for Public Works, Dept. of General Services, 1983; v. pres., Sigma Alpha Epsilon; Scabbard of Blade (Military Honorary Fraternity); appt. Engineer Member, Board of Claims, May 24, 1983; married Kathleen Ann Carlson; 1 child, Lisa Jane; home address: Ten Dogwood Ct., Camp Hill.

STANLEY A. MILLER   Member, Board of Claims

Stanley A. Miller was born Aug. 3, 1928, in Harrisburg, the son of Sigmund and Molly Miller; grad. of Harrisburg Academy; att., University of Pennsylvania Wharton School; frmr. pres., Miller's Auto Supplies, Incorporated; frmr. Special Assistant on Human Affairs to Gov. Raymond Shafer; frmr. sec. of Pa. Human Relations Commission; frmr. sec. of Pa. Dept. of Public Welfare; frmr. chmn., Pa. Securities Commission; frmr. chmn. and mem., Health Insurance Benefits Advisory Council, Dept. of Health, Education & Welfare; frmr. Commissioner, Professional and Occupational Affairs, Comm. of Pa.; appt. Citizen Member, Board of Claims, June 25, 1984; married Shirley Tuck; 1 child, Elliott R.; home address: 4713 Galen Rd., Harrisburg.

Board of Claims is both a judicial and an independent administrative agency. The board was created October 5, 1978 according to Legislative Act 260 and supercedes the former Board of Arbitration of Claims. By statute, the administrative services for the Board of Claims shall be provided by the Department of Auditor General. (See "Powers and Duties" of the Auditor General.) An executive secretary, counsel and supporting staff are appointed by the board.

Administration. The board is composed of three members: an attorney, who serves as Chief Administrative Judge and chairman; a civil engineer; and a citizen of the Commonwealth. Appointments to the board are made by the Governor with the advice and consent of the Senate. Each member shall be appointed for a term of eight years.

The powers and duties of the board are set forth in the Act of May 20, 1937, as amended. The most recent and important amendment is the Act of October 5, 1978, which, among other provisions, repealed the authority of the Auditor General and State Treasurer to settle and adjust certain claims against the Commonwealth and combined such duties with those of the former Board of Arbitration of Claims.

The Board of Claims has exclusive jurisdiction to hear and determine claims against the Commonwealth arising from contracts to which the Commonwealth is a party where the amount in controversy is $300 or more, and exclusive jurisdiction to hear and determine those claims against the Commonwealth formerly submitted to the Auditor General and State Treasurer. Appeal from decisions of the board is to the Pennsylvania Commonwealth Court.

PENNSYLVANIA CRIME COMMISSION
1100 E. Hector Street, Suite 470
Conshohocken, PA 17428

MICHAEL J. REILLY　　　　　　　　　**Chairman, Crime Commission**

Michael J. Reilly, Pittsburgh; grad., Georgetown, Univ., 1964; rec., law degree, Duquesne Univ.; frmr. detective, Pittsburgh Police Dept., and homicide detective, District Attorney's Office; frmr. deputy dir., Public Safety, Pittsburgh; frmr. First Assistant District Attorney, Allegheny Co.; frmr. chief counsel, investigation into organized crime and public corruption, Pa. House of Representatives, 1978; served on Thornburgh's transition team for state Dept. of Justice, Pa. State Police and Pa. Crime Commission; appt. to the Commission by Gov. Dick Thornburgh on March 15, 1985; elected Chairman, June 3, 1985.

FREDERICK T. MARTENS　　　　　　　**Executive Director, Crime Commission**

Frederick T. Martens was born May 7, 1944, in Paterson, NJ, the son of Fred and Ruth Martens; grad., Fairleigh Dickinson Univ. (B.A.); City Univ. of New York (M.A.); Fordham Univ. (M.A.); U.S. Air Force, 1962-66; Lieutenant, New Jersey State Police, 1967-87; trustee, Internatl. Assn. for Study of Organized Crime; mem., Am. Soc. of Criminology; exec. bd., Rahway Lifers Assn.; author, *Police Intelligence in Crime Control;* consultant, Scotland Yard; appt. Executive Director, Pennsylvania Crime Commission, March 1, 1987; 3 children: Jeff, Scott, Heather.

Chairman: Michael J. Reilly; **Members:** Thomas F. Lamb, Trevor Edwards, James Manning, Charles H. Rogovin.

The Pennsylvania Crime Commission is mandated to investigate organized criminal activity and public corruption within the Commonwealth and to report the results of its investigations to the General Assembly, along with recommendations for legislative or administrative action to remedy problems uncovered.

The commission produces public reports for consumption by other branches of government, the business sector, and the Commonwealth's citizenry. It collects, analyzes and disseminates intelligence information relating to organized crime activity to other law enforcement agencies, as well as refers numerous cases for prosecution.

The commission was restructured by the General Assembly in 1978 as an independent agency of the Legislature with law enforcement powers. There are five commissioners, one appointed by the Governor and the other four by the majority and minority leaders of the House and Senate. Not more than three commissioners can be members of the same political party. They serve three-year terms.

The commission is headquartered in Conshohocken, also the site of one of four regional offices. The others are located in Pittsburgh, Harrisburg and Scranton.

The commission is unique in that often its investigations are proactive, rather than reactive in nature, concentrating on complex, unexplored patterns of organized criminal activity, including white collar, financial crime.

One of the commission's major programs is the collection and analysis of criminal intelligence information. Not only is this program vital to the commission in carrying out its own investigative work, but over the years the commission has proved to be an important repository for data useful to other agencies in the criminal justice system.

In addition to the dissemination of such information, the commission is mandated to disclose its findings to the Legislature and the public via public hearings and public reports. The purpose of this program is to increase awareness of organized crime and public corruption and to deter such activity through its exposure.

The commission refers to other law enforcement agencies numerous cases for prosecution, both civil and criminal, tracking them as they move through the criminal justice system.

The Crime Commission is a member of the Leviticus Project Association, a multi-state network of law enforcement and regulatory agencies formed in 1978 in response to a dramatic rise in crime associated with the Appalachian coal industry.

It is the founding member of MAGLOCLEN (Middle Atlantic, Great Lakes Organized Crime Law Enforcement Network), and serves as the host agency and administrator of this multi-state intelligence gathering unit that monitors organized criminals who continually cross jurisdictional boundaries.

Both Leviticus and MAGLOCLEN are federally funded.

Upon completion of investigations, the Crime Commission formulates recommendations for remedial legislation or administrative action to deal with the abuses it uncovers. Crime Commission personnel testify frequently at legislative and congressional hearings about their findings and about ways to strengthen the criminal justice system. They also present evidence at trials, hearings and other judicial proceedings and conduct seminars for representatives from regulatory and other law enforcement agencies on such subjects as white collar crime.

CHAIRMEN	Appointed Since 1950[1]
Alvin B. Lewis, Jr., Esq.	May 3, 1979
Malcolm L. Lazin, Esq.	April 26, 1982

	Appointed Since 1950[1]
Dean Wm Roach	April 26, 1983
Charles F. Scarlata, Esq.	Aug. 15, 1984
Dean Wm Roach	Dec. 20, 1984
*Michael J. Reilly	June 3, 1985

Executive Director

William Anderson	1979
Wallace P. Hay	Nov. 3, 1980
*Frederick T. Martens	Mar. 1, 1987

[1] Prior to 1979, the Commonwealth's Attorney General served as Committee Chairman.

* Incumbent

PENNSYLVANIA COMMISSION ON CRIME AND DELINQUENCY
Second and Chestnut Streets
Executive House, Fourth Floor
P.O. Box 1167, Federal Square Station
Harrisburg, PA 17108-1167

ALFRED BLUMSTEIN   Chairman, Pennsylvania Commission on Crime and Delinquency

Alfred Blumstein was born June 3, 1930, in New York City; grad. Cornell Univ. (B.S.) 1951; Univ. of Buffalo (M.A.) 1954; Cornell Univ. (Ph.D.) 1960; J. Erik Jonsson Professor of Urban Systems and Operations Research; dir., Urban Systems Inst. and Dean, Schl. of Urban and Public Affairs; Carnegie-Mellon Univ.; Operations Reserach Soc. of Am. (pres., 1977-78); The Institute of Management Sciences (pres., 1987-88); chmn., Comm. on Research on Law Enforcement and Admin. of Justice, Natl. Acad. of Sciences (chmn., Panel on Research on Deterrent and Incapacitative Effects and Panel on Sentencing Research); Sigma Xi and Phi Kappa Phi; Cosmos Club; dir., Science and Tech. Task Force, President's Comm. on Law Enforcement and Admin. of Justice, 1966-67; Pa. Sentencing Comm.; numerous publications on operations reserach, transportation, law enforcement, and criminal justice; assoc. ed., Journal of Criminal Justice; Socio-Economic Planning Sciences; Operations Research; Journal of Environmental Sciences; and Journal of Research in Crime and Delinquency; appt. Chairman, Pennsylvania Commission on Crime and Delinquency, April 2, 1979; married Dolores Reguera Blumstein; 3 children: Lisa, Ellen, Diane; home address: 1455 Wightman St., Pittsburgh.

JAMES O. THOMAS, JR.   Executive Director, Pennsylvania Commission on Crime and Delinquency

James O. Thomas, Jr. was born Aug. 21, 1948, in McKeesport, the son of James and Anna Marks Thomas; Indiana Univ. of Pa. (B.A.) 1970; Univ. of Pgh. Grad. Schl. of Public and Internatl. Affairs, Public Admin./Justice Admin., 1974; Natl. Criminal Justice Assn.; Pa. Assn. of Probation, Parole and Correction; Am. Correctional Assn.; Criminal Justice Systems Planner, 1971-75; Chief of Planning Unit, 1975-78; Governor's Justice Comm., Pa. Dept. of Justice; Chief of Plan Development Div. (1979-82); Principal Investigator, Governor's Panel to Investigate Hostage Incident at Graterford St. Correctional Inst. (1982), Asst. to Exec. Dir., (1983), Comm. on Crime and Delinquency; State Academic Sabbatical, 1973-74; Am. Legion Keystone Boys State, 1965; appt. Executive Director, Commission on Crime and Delinquency, Apr. 11, 1983; married Rosemarie Akers; 3 children: Tressa, Kristin, Bradley; home address: New Cumberland.

Chairman: Dr. Alfred Blumstein; **Members:** Charlotte S. Arnold, Jay R. Bair, Kenneth G. Biehn, Kevin Blaum, David J. Brightbill, Walter W. Cohen, Daniel P. Elby, D. Michael Fisher, Ian H. Lennox, Robert N. C. Nix, Jr., Michael A. O'Pake, David S. Owens, Jr., Jeffrey E. Piccola, Ernest D. Preate, Jr., Sallyanne Rosenn, Ronald M. Sharpe, Nancy M. Sobolevitch, John Q. Stranahan, David W. Sweet, David Varrelman, Clarie Walker, Arthur M. Wallenstein, John F. White, Jr., LeRoy S. Zimmerman.

The Pennsylvania Commission on Crime and Delinquency is authorized under State Act 274 of 1978 and has general responsibility to examine criminal justice problems, propose solutions and monitor and evaluate the impact these solutions have on the criminal justice system. The commission meets on a regular basis to award funds under the Federal Juvenile Justice and Delinquency Prevention Act, the Justice Assistance Act, the Victims of Crime Act, and the Narcotics Control Assistance Act. It also administers the Deputy Sheriffs' Education and Training Act (State Act 1984-2) with the advice of the Deputy Sheriffs' Education and Training Board. The victim services grant and technical assistance functions mandated by state Act 1984-96 are also provided by the commission. A Juvenile Advisory Committee counsels the commission on juvenile justice matters.

Other commission duties are to prepare and periodically update a state criminal justice and juvenile justice plan; provide statewide criminal statistical analysis services; render technical assistance and training to components of the justice system; advise the legislative and executive branches on justice policies, plans, programs and budgets; develop priorities and strategies for responding to justice system problems and serve as a forum for the continuing examination of criminal justice issues. The commission also manages the statewide crime prevention program known as Pennsylvania Crime Watch and provides assistance to counties in dealing with jail overcrowding.

EXECUTIVE DIRECTORS

		Appointed Since 1950
J. Shane Cramer	Mar.	27, 1967
Charles F. Rinkevich	Nov.	7, 1969
E. Drexel Godfrey, Jr.	Sept.	15, 1971
Robert E. Frederick (acting)	Jan.	5, 1974
John T. Snavely	Mar.	6, 1974
Thomas J. Brennan	Apr.	15, 1976
Martin V. Walsh (acting)	June	11, 1979
George F. Grode	Oct.	1, 1979
James O. Thomas, Jr. (acting)	Apr.	11, 1983
*James O. Thomas, Jr.	Oct.	3, 1983

* Incumbent

PENNSYLVANIA EMERGENCY MANAGEMENT AGENCY
Transportation and Safety Building
Harrisburg, PA 17120

JOSEPH L. LaFLEUR   Director, Pennsylvania Emergency Management Agency

Joseph Leo LaFleur was born March 31, 1951, in Sheboygan, Wisconsin, the son of Jerry A. and Monica R. LaFleur; University of Wisconsin — Stevens Point (B.S., bus. and econ.) 1973; University of Wisconsin — Whitewater (M.B.A., marketing) 1976; mem., Eisenhower Society, National Emergency Management Assn., Future Society, Lewistown Volunteer Fire Department; Roman Catholic; appointed Director, Pennsylvania Emergency Management Agency, July 20, 1987; wife, Shauna M.; children: Michael J. and Jacqueline R.

Chairman: Mark S. Singel; **Members:** Gerald T. Sajer, N. Mark Richards, LeRoy Zimmerman, Morey M. Myers, Karen A. Miller, Arthur A. Davis, Howard Yerusalim, Boyd E. Wolff, John F. White, Jr., Ronald M. Sharpe, William Shane, Frank Yandrisevitz, William Moore, John Kennedy, James E. Ross.

The Pennsylvania Emergency Management Agency is an emergency preparedness and response agency, under the direction of the Governor and is responsible for the judicious planning, assignment and coordination of all Commonwealth available resources in an integrated program of prevention, mitigation, preparedness, response, and recovery from emergencies of any kind, whether from attack, man-made or natural sources. The agency was first established by the Act of March 19, 1951, P.L. 28, and was known as the State Council of Civil Defense. The present agency was established by the Act of November 26, 1978, P.L. 1332.

Administration. The agency consists of a council whose primary responsibility is for overall policy and direction of a statewide civil defense and disaster program and response capability. The council consists of 17 members: Governor, Lieutenant Governor, Adjutant General, Secretary of Health, Attorney General, General Counsel, Secretary of Community Affairs, Secretary of Environmental Resources, Secretary of Transportation, Secretary of Agriculture, Secretary of Public Welfare, Commissioner of the Pennsylvania State Police, Chairman of the Public Utility Commission, Speaker of the House of Representatives, President Pro Tempore of the Senate, Minority Leaders of the Senate and House of Representatives. The Governor may designate a member to serve as chairman and has historically designated the Lieutenant Governor to do so.

To provide for the effective discharge of its legally assigned powers and duties, and to coordinate emergency preparedness and response activities within the various political subdivisions of the Commonwealth, the Pennsylvania Emergency Management Agency employs a small staff of both technical and clerical personnel. These individuals staff and operate one state, three area headquarters, and the State Fire Academy, through which the agency's administrative, training and emergency operations responsibilities are discharged.

DIRECTORS

	Appointed Since 1950	
Richard Gerstell	Mar.	28, 1951
Craig A. Williamson (acting)	Aug.	5, 1975
Oran K. Henderson	Aug.	19, 1976
DeWitt C. Smith	Sept.	2, 1980

	Appointed Since 1950	
Craig A. Williamson (acting)	Jan.	18, 1983
John L. Patten	Oct.	31, 1983
Carl C. Kuehn, II (acting)	Mar.	13, 1987
*Joseph L. LaFleur	July	20, 1987

State Fire Commissioner

*Charles A. Henry	Dec.	1, 1976

* Incumbent

PENNSYLVANIA ENERGY OFFICE
P.O. Box 8010
116 Pine Street
Harrisburg, PA 17105

JAN H. FREEMAN

Executive Director, Pennsylvania Energy Office

Jan H. Freeman was born on Sept. 3, 1948, in Williamsport, the son of John H. and Frances R. Freeman; grad., Duke Univ. (B.A., econ.) 1970; public utility consultant, Weber, Fick and Wilson, Inc., 1970-79, exec. v. pres., 1977; assoc. dir. for policy, Governor's Energy Council, 1979-83; dep. dir. for policy, 1983-87; appointed Executive Director, April 1987; project director for the 1981 and 1984 state energy policies; author of numerous energy reports and studies and a member of many task forces on utility-related issues; married Cynthia Lynn Freeman; 2 daughters: Leah and Samantha; home address: 266 North 24th St., Camp Hill.

Chairman: Lieutenant Governor Mark S. Singel.

The Pennsylvania Energy Office was established by Executive Order on July 23, 1987. The office, previously known as the Governor's Energy Council, administers the Pennsylvania Energy Development Authority. Lieutenant Governor Mark S. Singel serves as the office chairman. The goal of the Energy Office is to ensure energy security for the Commonwealth through planning, development and conservation. The office develops energy policy and supports the implementation of policy recommendations through legislation, program initiatives and federal grants activities.

The office is active in the areas of coal, natural gas and oil development, renewable energy projects, utility and low income energy issues and energy efficiency in buildings, industries, commercial establishments, and local government.

The office is the primary recipient of federal and private energy funds assigned to Pennsylvania, and distributes these funds for energy conservation, development and research, policy planning, and the development of new energy using technologies. The office is also responsible for monitoring petroleum supplies and implementing allocation measures during declared emergency petroleum product shortages.

Pennsylvania Energy Development Agency
(Created by Act of Legislature, No. 280 of December 14, 1982)

Board Members	Appointed Since 1950	
Sandra A. Beynon	June	16, 1984

	Appointed Since 1950	
*Richard C. Waybright	June	16, 1984
Malcolm B. Petriken, Esq.	June	26, 1984
*Thomas P. Gordon	June	26, 1984
*Robert A. Shinn	June	26, 1984
*Joseph F. Welch	June	26, 1984
*Lawrence B. Abrams, III, Esq., Chairman	June	26, 1984
*Joseph Levi, II	May	28, 1985
*Franklin H. Mohney	June	24, 1986
*Daniel S. Nagin	June	30, 1986
*Werner Fricker	Nov.	24, 1986
*Boyd E. Wolff	Jan.	20, 1987
*Arthur Davis	Jan.	23, 1987
Donald F. Mazziotti (acting)	Feb.	17, 1987
*Sarah W. Hargrove	Mar.	27, 1987
*David M. Barasch, Esq.		
*D. Michael Fisher		
*Joseph A. Petrarca		
*William Shane		
*James L. Wright		

Executive Director

*William A. Roth, P.E.	June	14, 1984

* Incumbent

STATE ETHICS COMMISSION
308 Finance Building
P.O. Box 11470
Harrisburg, PA 17108-1470

G. SIEBER PANCOAST   Chairman, State Ethics Commission

G. Sieber Pancoast was born June 16, 1914, in Audubon, NJ, the son of Gargield and Frances Mae Rood Pancoast; grad., Camden H.S., 1932; Wenonah MJ Acad., 1933; Ursinus Coll. (B.S.) 1937; Univ. of Pa. (M.A.) 1940, (Ph.D.) 1956; Ursinus Coll. (LL.D.) 1984; U.S. Naval Reserve Lt. (jg), 1944-46; retired college prof.; mem., Am. Political Science Assn., Natl. Municipal League; Pi Gamma Mu; Collegeville Borough Council, 1957-61; Mayor, Borough of Collegeville, 1961-64; mem., House of Representatives, 1964-78; bd. mem., Visiting Nurse Assn., Norristown; bd. mem., Perkiomen Valley Watershed Assn.; pres. of congregation, Trinity Reformed (UCC); University Scholar, Univ. of Pa., 1940; Ursinus Coll. Hall of Fame for Athletes, 1980; dissertation, Second Class Townships in Pennsylvania; appointed Commissioner, State Ethics Commission, May 21, 1984; reappointed February 12, 1986; currently serving as Chairman, State Ethics Commission; married Muriel Elva Brandt; 2 daughters; home address: 122 W. 7th Ave., Collegeville.

JOHN J. CONTINO   Executive Director, State Ethics Commission

John J. Contino was born Jan. 3, 1953, in Phila., the son of Thomas J. and Mary DiSciascio Contino; grad., Brandywine Coll., Widener Univ. (A.A.) 1972; Villanova Univ. (B.A., cum laude) 1974; Univ. of Miami, FL (J.D.) 1977; continuing education, Am. Univ., Cornell Univ., Temple Univ., Villanova Univ.; Pi Sigma Alpha Honor Soc.; asst. dist. atty., Phila., 1977-78; asst. atty. gen., Pa., 1978-79; counsel, Pa. Crime Comm., 1979-85; general counsel, State Ethics Comm., 1985-87; appointed Executive Director, State Ethics Commission, Feb. 3, 1987; married Donna M. Cappuccio; 2 children: Christopher and Timothy; home address: Wynnewood.

Chairman: G. Sieber Pancoast; **V. Chairman:** Joseph W. Marshall, III; **Members:** Robert W. Brown, Dennis C. Harrington, Helena G. Hughes, Paul J. Smith.

The Commission was created by Act 170 of 1978, the Ethics Act, to administer and enforce the provisions of the Act, particularly that "the financial interests of holders of or candidates for public office present neither a conflict of interest nor the appearance of a conflict of interest with the public trust."

The commission is composed of seven members: President Pro Tempore of the Senate, the Minority Leader of the Senate, the Speaker of the House, and the Minority Leader of the House shall each appoint one member. Three members shall be appointed by the Governor without confirmation.

The commission's powers and duties include the following:

- Render opinions to present or former public officials and public employees as to their obligations under the Ethics Act.
- Investigate alleged violations of the Ethics Act.
- Receive and review Financial Interest Statements of persons required to file.
- Prescribe rules and regulations to implement the provisions of the Ethics Act.
- Prescribe forms for filing.
- Make statements available for public inspection and copying.
- Maintain a master index of statements filed with the commission.
- Prepare and publish an annual report.

- Accept and file information voluntarily supplied that exceeds the requirements of the Act.

COMMISSION MEMBERS	Appointed Since 1950
John Butera	Jan. 1, 1979
Robert Myers	Jan. 3, 1979
Donetta Ambrose	Jan. 11, 1979
Msgr. John P. Foley	Jan. 11, 1979
James Doran	Jan. 12, 1979
Ralph Scalera	Feb. 5, 1979
*Paul J. Smith	Feb. 5, 1979
Harold Horn	Oct. 26, 1979
Joseph F. Welch	June 23, 1980
Dr. Leon L. Haley	Jan. 19, 1979
Everett Keech	Jan. 26, 1981
Ralph Evans	Feb. 29, 1980
Carl Weiss	Oct. 7, 1981
Sherman Hill	Jan. 6, 1982
Roy Wilkinson	Mar. 2, 1982
Herbert Conner	Jan. 13, 1983
Rita Resick	Feb. 3, 1984
*G. Sieber Pancoast	May 21, 1984
*W. Thomas Andrews	Aug. 15, 1984
*Helena G. Hughes	Feb. 11, 1986

* Incumbent

	Appointed Since 1950	Executive Directors	Appointed Since 1950
*Joseph W. Marshall, III	Mar. 26, 1986	Edward M. Seladones	Apr. 26, 1979
*Robert W. Brown	Sept. 24, 1986	*John J. Contino	Feb. 3, 1987
Michael J. Acker	Jan. 19, 1987		
*Dennis C. Harrington	Mar. 3, 1987	* Incumbent	

FISH COMMISSION
3532 Walnut Street (Progress)
P.O. Box 1673
Harrisburg, PA 17105-1673

EDWARD R. MILLER   **Executive Director, Pennsylvania Fish Commission**

Edward R. Miller was born April 22, 1934, in Bellefonte, the son of Edward R. and S. Marjory Hill Miller; grad., State Coll. Area H.S., 1952; Penn State Univ. (B.S., civil eng.) 1956; active duty, U.S. Army Corps of Engineers, 1956-58; Professional Registration (Pa.): Public Land Surveyor, P.L.S. (Aug. 1959); engineer, P.E. (May 1961); Am. Soc. of Civil Engineers; Natl. and Pa. Soc. of Prof. Engineers; Am. Fisheries Soc. — Fish Culture Sec., Fisheries Admin. Sec., and Bio-Engineering Sec. (pres., 1985); treas., Steering Com., AFS Bio-Engineering Workshop (1979) and Fish Culture/Fish Management Workshop (1985); Northeast Soc. of Conservation Engineers (dir. and past pres.); mem.: St. Paul's Methodist Ch.; Benevolent and Protective Order of the Elks; Hawk Mountain Sanctuary Assn.; Beta Theta Social Frat. (dir., past pres. Alumni Bd.); lifetime mem., Penn State Alumni Assn.; Northeast Soc. of Conservation Engineers "Conservation Engineer of the Year" award (1978); employed by Penn State Univ., 1958-60; employed by Pa. Fish Comm., 1960-pres.; mem.: Environmental Qualtiy Bd.; Pa. Wild Res. Cons. Bd.; Mid-Atlantic Fishery Management Council; Atlantic State Marine Fisheries Comm.; ex-officio mem., Boating Adv. Bd., and Schuylkill River Greenway Assn.; appointed Executive Director, Pennsylvania Fish Commission, June 1, 1987; married Cheryl Davis; 2 children: Nina and Scott; home address: 510 North Burrowes St., State College.

President: Joan R. Plumly; **Members:** Marilyn Black, David D. Coe; R. Mark Faulkner, Leonard A. Green, Ross J. Huhn, Calvin J. Kern, T. T. (Ted) Metzger, Jr., Leon H. Reed, J. Wayne Yorks.

The Pennsylvania Fish Commission is one of the oldest governmental conservation agencies in the nation, dating back to 1866. Today, ten members make up the commission and they serve eight-year terms. Eight members represent specific geographic locations, while the ninth and tenth are members-at-large and must be experienced boaters.

The commission sets rules and regulations governing fishing and boating in and on all inland and boundary waters of the Commonwealth. In addition to managing and protecting the state's aquatic resources, the commission also is mandated with the responsibility for all of the state's reptiles, amphibians and salamanders.

As an independent state agency, the commission is supported by anglers' and boaters' dollars generated through the sale of fishing licenses and boat registrations.

ADMINISTRATION

Executive Director is appointed by the ten-member commission. The Executive Director is the commission's chief administrative officer as well as chief waterways conservation officer. He is a member of the Atlantic States Marine Fisheries Commission, Mid-Atlantic Fishery Management Council, Pennsylvania Environmental Quality Board, Water Resources Council, Wild Resources Conservation Board, and an Ex-officio member of the Boating Advisory Board.

Bureau of Property and Facilities Management directs the planning, survey, design, construction, and maintenance of Fish Commission facilities and property.

Bureau of Fisheries directs the research, propagation, management, and protection of fish, fisheries, habitat, reptiles, amphibians, and certain threatened and endangered species in the Commonwealth.

Bureau of Administrative Services provides support services for all Commission operations, including computer services, labor relations, communication, affirmative action, duplicating, warehousing, fedeal aid, personnel, budget and procurement. The bureau is also responsible for the issuance of fishing licenses (over 1 million) and special permits required by the fish law and regulations.

Bureau of Boating monitors the expenditures of Boat Fund monies; serves as the Assistant Executive Director for Watercraft Safety pursuant to the provisions of 30 Pa. Consolidated Statutes, 303 (b); directs the boating registration program; directs statewide training and information programs on safe boating practices; boating accident prevention, and water survival and rescue techniques; directs a statewide navigational aids program; supervises the inspection and licensing of commercial passenger-carrying vessels and operators.

Bureau of Law Enforcement directs the enforcement of fish laws, boating laws, and certain water pollution laws of the Commonwealth. In addition, within the scope of Fish Commission activities, directs the enforcement of Title 18 (relating to crimes and offenses) and laws relating to misdemeanors and felonies; directs review of permits for mine drainage, stream encroachments; highway and bridge construction; enforces laws and conducts other Fish Commission programs.

Bureau of Education and Information plans and directs a statewide fishing, boating, and conservation education program; develops and implements electronic media capabilities; produces special publications such as brochures, booklets, maps, and pamphlets; supervises the magazine circulation unit and the sale and collection of monies for promotional items; edits and produces two magazines: "Pennsylvania Angler" (monthly) and "Boat Pennsylvania" (bi-monthly).

	Appointed Since 1950
COMMISSION MEMBERS	
Philip E. Angle	Dec. 14, 1950
Wallace Dean	June 8, 1953
R. Stanley Smith	June 1, 1955
Gerard R. Adams	June 1, 1955
Charles C. Houser	June 1, 1955
Albert R. Hinkle, Jr.	June 1, 1955
John W. Grenoble	July 11, 1955
Joseph M. Critchfield	Nov. 29, 1955
Maynard M. Bogart	Feb. 29, 1956
Raymond M. Williams	Aug. 18, 1959
Joseph M. Critchfield	Oct. 14, 1959
Howard R. Heiny	Dec. 16, 1963
Robert M. Rankin	Aug. 2, 1963
Douglas E. McWilliams, Jr.	June 17, 1964

	Appointed Since 1950
Clarence E. Dietz	Sept. 20, 1966
Frank E. Masland, Jr.	Dec. 21, 1967
*Calvin J. Kern	July 17, 1968
Sam Guaglianone	Dec. 31, 1971
William O. Hill	Dec. 31, 1971
William Cox	Dec. 31, 1971
James Stumpf	Dec. 31, 1971
John A. Hugya	Jan. 9, 1975
*Leonard A. Green	Jan. 9, 1975
*Jerome E. Southerton	Jan. 9, 1975
*Walter F. Gibbs	June 20, 1975
*Robert L. Martin	May 7, 1980
*J. Wayne Yorks	Apr. 29, 1980
*Ross J. Huhn	June 17, 1980
*Marilyn Black	Feb. 23, 1982
*Theodore T. Metzger, Jr.	June 7, 1983
*Joan R. Plumly	June 28, 1984
*D. Mark Faulkner	June 18, 1986
*David D. Coe	June 18, 1986
*Leon H. Reed, Jr.	July 1, 1986

Executive Directors

	Appointed
C. A. French	Apr. 25, 1949
William Voigt, Jr.	Sept. 12, 1955
Albert M. Day	July 18, 1960
Robert J. Bielo	Jan. 1, 1965
Ralph W. Abele	Jan. 3, 1972
*Edward R. Miller	June 1, 1987

* Incumbent

(Act No. 180, approved April 25, 1949, provides for a Pennsylvania Fish Commission with power to appoint an Executive Director. C. A. French, the Commissioner of Fisheries at the time of the approval of this Act was appointed Executive Director of the new commission, April 25, 1949.)

GAME COMMISSION
8000 Derry Street (Rutherford)
P.O. Box 1567
Harrisburg, PA 17105-1567

PETER S. DUNCAN   **Executive Director, Pennsylvania Game Commission**

Peter S. Duncan was born May 1, 1944, in Hollidaysburg; grad. Pa. St. Univ., 1966; U.S. Army, 1967-69 (recipient, Bronze Medal, Vietnamese Cross of Gallantry, and Army Commendation Medal); frmr. park naturalist for Arlington Co., Va.; frmr. pres., Pa. Forestry Assn.; field representative (1970), Asst. Exec. Secretary (1971), Exec. Secretary (1972), Legislative Joint Committee on Air and Water Pollution and Conservation; appt. Special Deputy Secretary for DER, Feb. 23, 1979; appt. Deputy Secretary, Resources Management, July 1, 1981; appt. Acting Secretary, Oct. 19, 1981; appt. Secretary DER, Jan. 6, 1982; appt. Exec. Dir., Pa. Game Comm., Jan. 19, 1983; married to Rebecca Albright; 2 sons; home address: Millerstown.

President: Taylor A. Doebler, Jr. **Commissioners:** C. Dana Chalfant, Clair W. Clemens, Donald R. Craul, Thomas P. Greenlee, Paul E. Hickes, Jr., Elmer M. Rinehart, Roy J. Wagner, Jr.

The Pennsylvania Game Commission, an independent administrative agency created by legislative action June 25, 1895, is responsible for the scientific management of all wildlife in the Commonwealth. As an independent agency, its authority stems from The Game and Wildlife Code.

ADMINISTRATION

The commission is composed of eight members, each of whom serves an eight-year term without compensation, following appointment by the Governor and confirmation by the Senate. Each member is appointed from one of eight geographical districts in the Commonwealth. The terms of two commissioners expire every two years.

The Game Commission is not supported by tax money. The primary source of income is the sale of hunting licenses. Annually, more than one million sportsmen purchase licenses to hunt in Pennsylvania.

The commission maintains a central office in Harrisburg and six regional offices throughout the state.

The Harrisburg office contains an executive office and six administrative bureaus.

Executive Office consists of the Executive Director and one Deputy Executive Director, who are the chief administrators of the commission.

Bureau of Administrative Services is responsible for the commission's training programs, personnel, the procurement of all materials and supplies, the sale of hunting licenses, labor relations, and automotive.

Bureau of Game Management employs trained wildlife biologists holding advanced degrees in wildlife management. They study the state's wildlife species to develop the most effective management practices, and prepare guidelines that are reviewed by the executive office and presented to the commission for adoption. This division also is responsible for propagating game birds.

Bureau of Law Enforcement is responsible for enforcing The Game and Wildlife Code.

District game protectors carry out the respective programs on a local basis. Most districts have approximately 300 square miles. One game protector, assigned to each district, is responsible for enforcing the game laws and public relations activities.

The deputy game protector force assists district game protectors in executing their duties. They are volunteers and very few receive compensation for their work.

Bureau of Land Management manages State Game Lands to provide the highest possible sustained yield of wildlife and timber and to furnish outdoor recreation in the form of sport hunting and compatible outdoor recreational activities for the enjoyment of all segments of the population.

The land manager, responsible for an area of two or more counties, supervises habitat management programs for development of commission lands and privately owned land under lease by the commission and provides training, guidance and supervision of the commission's Food and Cover Corps.

The Game Commission has several programs to provide lands for public hunting. Foremost is the acquisition of State Game Lands. This program began in 1920 and more than 1.02 million acres had been purchased by 1987.

This division also coordinates leasing and management of mineral, oil and gas resources under State Game Lands.

Bureau of Information and Education provides information for sportsmen and the general public on Game Commission programs and wildlife management practices. This is accomplished through the publication of the *Game News* magazine, news releases, television public service spot announcements, educational television programs, displays and exhibits, and personal presentations. The Hunter Education Training Program is coordinated by the Information & Education Division.

Bureau of Management Information Systems provides data processing and office automation support for all operating bureaus and regional offices. The bureau is an electronic storehouse of information for the agency.

Field Administration. The state is divided into six regions for the administration of field duties. The Northwest region office is located in Franklin, the Southwest Office in Ligonier, the Northcentral Office in Jersey Shore, the Southcentral Office in Huntingdon, the Northeast Office in Dallas and the Southeast Office in Reading.

COMMISSION MEMBERS	Appointed Since 1950
Herbert L. Buchanan	June 8, 1953
Andrew C. Long	June 25, 1953
Tom L. McDowell	May 19, 1954
C. Ellwood Huffman	July 25, 1955
Dewey H. Miller	May 9, 1956
Russell M. Lucas	July 25, 1956
James A. Thompson	June 28, 1957
Carroll F. Hockersmith	Nov. 5, 1958
R. G. Smith	Aug. 29, 1961
Loring H. Cramer	Mar. 11, 1963
Frederick M. Simpson	Aug. 2, 1963
Robert E. Fasnacht	Oct. 5, 1965
E. J. Brooks	Apr. 29, 1969
Andrew C. Long	Jan. 1, 1970
Marshall E. Jetty	Nov. 9, 1970
*Elmer M. Rinehart	Jan. 7, 1972
C. Clair Winter	Jan. 7, 1972
Robert E. Sutherland	Dec. 31, 1973
David L. Drakula	Feb. 3, 1976
*Paul E. Hickes, Jr.	Mar. 24, 1980
*Donald R. Craul	Mar. 24, 1980
*Thomas P. Greenlee	Feb. 23, 1982
*Taylor A. Doebler, Jr.	May 5, 1982
*C. Dana Chalfant	May 24, 1983
*Roy J. Wagner, Jr.	May 24, 1983
*Clair W. Clemens	Dec. 10, 1985

Executive Directors

Dr. Logan J. Bennett (dec. Sept. 12, 1957)	Oct. 1, 1953
Merton J. Golden	Jan. 3, 1958
Glenn L. Bowers	Oct. 18, 1965
*Peter S. Duncan	Jan. 18, 1983

* Incumbent

PENNSYLVANIA HERITAGE AFFAIRS ADVISORY COMMISSION
309 Forum Building
Harrisburg, PA 17120

SHALOM DAVID STAUB   **Executive Director,**
Pennsylvania Heritage Affairs Advisory Commission

Shalom David Staub was born Jan. 28, 1956, in Brooklyn, the son of Daniel Marvin Staub and Miriam Rosen Staub; grad., Wesleyan Univ. (B.A.) 1977, (M.A.) 1978; Univ. of Pa. (Ph.D.) 1985; folklorist; mem.: Am. Folklore Soc.; Am. Anthropological Assn.; Soc. of Ethnomusicology; Congress on Research in Dance; Middle Atlantic Folklife Assn.; Pa. Folklore Soc.; author, *Yemeni Folklore and Ethnic Identity in New York City* (Phila.: The Balch Inst. Press, forthcoming); "Folklore and Authenticity: A Myopic Marriage in Public Sector Programs," in *The Conservation of Culture:Folklorists and the Public Sector* (Burt Feintuch, editor, Univ. of Kentucky Press, in press); editor, *Jewish Folklore and Ethnology Review;* dir., State Folklife Programs, Pa. Heritage Affairs Comm., 1982-87; appointed Executive Director, Pennsylvania Heritage Affairs Advisory Commission, June 1, 1987; married Janet Frankel; 2 children: Eli Solomon and Rena Yael; home address: 212 Montrose St., Harrisburg.

Chairman: Charles Bojanic; **Members:** Russell Angermann, George Batyko, Michael Blichasz, Charles Blockson, Ronald Bryan, Ivar Christensen, Elias Dungca, Gim Eng, John Fabec, Joseph Garay, Merlin Jenkins, Do Shick Joe, Rev. Dr. Michael Kovach, Krishna Lahiri, Thomson Leiper, Froso Manakos, Daniel Maxymuik, Joseph Monte, Annie Morgalis, Truong Ngoc Phuong, John Plesh, Judy Reedman, Perry Shertz, Russell Simms, Armindo Sousa, Joseph Stefka.

The Pennsylvania Heritage Affairs Advisory Commission was created by Executive Order in January 1980 and renewed in 1983 and 1986. The commission seeks to conserve Pennsylvania's diverse cultural heritages and to promote greater public awareness and understanding of the Commonwealth's ethnic diversity. The commission monitors governmental and nongovernmental programs relating to or affecting ethnic communities, including their social, cultural, and economic concerns. Through its Folklife Program, the commission develops public programs which document, present, and perpetuate ethnic and folk cultural traditions. Commission staff provides technical assistance to individuals, organizations and communities which seek to preserve their cultural traditions, and in cooperation with other state agencies,

seeks to provide grant funds to support these projects. The commission co-administers the Apprenticeships in Traditional Arts program with the Pennsylvania Council on the Arts.

Composed of up to 27 members appointed by the Governor for one-year terms, the commission is broadly representative of the ethnic diversity within the Commonwealth. Advising the commission's Folklife Program is the Pennsylvania Folklife Advisory Council, a group of up to 17 professionals representing various fields and types of institutions appointed by the Commission.

The executive director of the commission, appointed by the Governor, develops and implements the commission's policies and programs and maintains liaison activities with federal, state and local agencies on matters of cultural concern.

STATE SYSTEM OF HIGHER EDUCATION
301 Market Street
Harrisburg, PA 17108

JAMES H. McCORMICK   **Chancellor, State System of Higher Education**

James H. McCormick was born Nov. 11, 1938, in Indiana, Pa., the son of Harold Clark and Mary Blanche Truby McCormick; Ind. Univ. of Pa (B.S.) 1959; Univ. of Pgh. (M.Ed.) 1961, (Ed.D.) 1963; post doctoral study, Univ. of Michigan, Columbia Univ. Teachers' Coll.; J. F. Kennedy Schl. of Gov., Harvard Univ.; mem., Academy of Political Science; Am. Assn. of Schl. Administrators; Am. Assn. of Univ. Administrators; Natl. Heads of Higher Ed.; Honor Soc. of Phi Kappa Phi; Pa. Assn. of Coll. and Univ.; Phi Delta Kappa; Planning Council for Comprehensive Plan for Library Service in Pa.; Pa. Ed. Policy Seminar; faculty, v. pres. for Adm., Shippensburg St. Coll., 1963-73; pres., Bloomsburg State Coll., 1973-83; mem., Pine Street Presbyterian Ch., Harrisburg; frmr. mem., bd. of dirs., Bloomsburg Kiwanis; frmr. mem., adv. bd., Columbia-Montour Boy Scouts; frmr. pres., Bloomsburg Ch. of Commerce; rec., Disting. Alumnus, Ind. Univ., 1981; Outstanding Alumnus, Bloomsburg Univ., 1984; rec., Young Leaders in Ed., Phi Delta Kappa, 1981; Outstanding Alumnus, Univ. of Pgh., 1985; Falk Intern in Politics; author of several articles in professional journals; President Emeritus, Bloomsburg Univ. of Pa.; James H. McCormick Center for Human Services, Bloomsburg, ded., 1984; Interim Chancellor, July 1, 1983-July 1, 1984; appointed Chancellor, State System of Higher Education, July 1, 1984; married Maryan Kough Garner; 2 children: Douglas Paul, David Harold; home address: Box 28, 825 Indiana Ave., Lemoyne.

The State System of Higher Education, created by Act 188 of 1982, is comprised of 14 publicly-owned universities in the Commonwealth of Pennsylvania. Established on July 1, 1983, the State System is guided by a sixteen-member Board of Governors, all of whom are appointed by the Governor of Pennsylvania and confirmed by the Senate.

The Chancellor is the chief executive officer of the State System of Higher Education. The Chancellor, appointed by the Board of Governors, is responsible to the board for the overall administration of all facets of the system. Under the Chancellor's direction, the university presidents, line officers, and support staff provide system-wide management in such areas as academic policy and planning, business affairs, faculty and staff affairs, legislative policy, institutional research, legal affairs, capital planning, and equal educational opportunities.

As established by the founding legislation, the primary mission of the State System of Higher Education ''. . . is the provision of instruction for undergraduate and graduate students to and beyond the master's degree in the liberal arts and sciences, and in the applied fields, including the teaching profession.''

The state universities spent the first 100 years of existence training teachers for Pennsylvania's schools. The Normal School Act of 1857 established regional teacher training institutions throughout the Commonwealth. The School Code of 1911 called for the state purchase of all normal schools, and by 1921 the present configuration of 14 publicly-owned universities was established. The 14 normal schools evolved from state normal schools, to state teachers colleges, to state colleges. On November 12, 1982, Act 188 was signed into law creating on July 1, 1983 the Pennsylvania State System of Higher Education. Thus, the 13 former state colleges joined Indiana University of Pennsylvania to achieve university status. The universities have a cumulative history of 1,600 years.

The 14 universities and 3 branch campuses (and the McKeever Environmental Center) are located throughout the Commonwealth. The system has a combined university campus of 4,000 acres. The physical plant is comprised of 655 buildings for classroom, residential and administrative purposes.

The 86,000 students who attend the State System of Higher Education universities study in associate, baccalaureate, masters, and doctoral programs. The universities are fully accredited by the Middle States Association of Colleges and Secondary Schools and by the National Council for Accreditation of Teacher Education. Academic programs are also individually accredited by appropriate national professional organizations.

PENNSYLVANIA HIGHER EDUCATION ASSISTANCE AGENCY
660 Boas Street
Towne House Apartments
Harrisburg, PA 17102

KENNETH R. REEHER

Executive Director, Pennsylvania Higher Education Assistance Agency

Kenneth R. Reeher graduated from Villanova Univ. (B.S.) 1948; Westminster Coll. (M.S., guidance, counseling) 1952; Doctor of Laws (Honorius Causa) Allegheny Coll., 1975; Doctor of Humane Letters (Honorius Causa) Duquesne Univ., 1984; enlisted in Navy, Nov. 1942, discharged as Lieut., Jan. 1946; teacher and director of guidance, Sharon School District, 1948-60; guidance specialist and coordinator, Testing Div., Pa. Dept. of Public Instruction, 1960-64; appt., ex. dir., Pa. Higher Education Assistance Agency, 1964; past pres., Natl. Assn. of State Scholarship Directors; past pres., Natl. Council of Higher Education Loan Programs; Natl. Task Force on Student Aid Problems (the Keppel Task Force); Natl. Student Aid Coalition; Commissioner, Natl. Comm. on Student Financial Aid.

The Pennsylvania Higher Education Assistance Agency is a government instrumentality established for the purpose of improving higher education opportunities for residents of the Commonwealth by guaranteeing private loans, issuing State Higher Education Grants, making alternative loans and administering work-study programs and a program of institutional assistance grant aid. In 1974, the agency was given legislative authority to market its loan servicing system to other states and lenders, enabling the agency to earn income with which to fund additional student aid programs and fund its costs to administer the Commonwealth's programs of student aid. The Information Technology Education Act was assigned to PHEAA in 1984 and the agency developed fourteen Regional Computer Resource Centers throughout Pennsylvania in 1984 to expand the use of computers in the elementary and secondary school classrooms.

Administration. The agency is governed and all its corporate powers exercised by a board of directors. It is administered by a staff headed by an executive director who is appointed by the Board of Directors. The board consists of 20 members: Secretary of Education, three appointed by the Governor, eight by the President Pro Tempore of the Senate, and eight by the Speaker of the House; members serve without pay but are reimbursed for actual and necessary expenses.

Students are able to obtain low-interest educational loans from private lenders under the State Student Guaranty Loan program; repayment of these loans is guaranteed by the agency. In 1981 the agency was given legislative authority to administer PLUS loans, an auxiliary program of loans to parents and students. Legislation enacted in 1982 allowed the agency to sell tax-exempt bonds to provide additional programs of direct loans to students and parents who were ineligible for federally subsidized loans or needed relief of interest charges. These programs, which are alternatives to the guaranty programs, include: Family Partnership Loans, PHEAA Supplemental Loans, and Health Education Assistance Loans.

Using funds appropriated by the General Assembly, the agency determines grant awards to students based on the students' demonstrated financial need. By authority of the Veterans Education Act of 1971, the agency was given the responsibility of administering a program of educational benefits for veterans of the Vietnam Conflict. Authority was given in 1972 for a program to provide scholarship aid to dependents of service people who were or are missing in action or were prisoners of war.

In cooperation with educational institutions and the federal government, work-study programs enable students who require further assistance to earn money to help with their educational costs.

The passage of the Institutional Assistance Grants Act in 1974 allowed eligible private institutions of higher education to receive state funds for the payment of educational costs based on the number of state grant students in attendance at the institution.

Revenue generated through the servicing of student loans throughout the country funds a major portion of the agency's administrative costs and the Scholars in Education Award Program, the Loan Forgiveness Program and the Science Teacher Education Program. These programs were developed to help meet Pennsylvania's need for highly proficient science and math teachers.

The agency, using funds appropriated by the General Assembly, sponsors teacher training programs, grants to school districts and loans equipment to non-public schools to purchase or access computer equipment and software through the fourteen Regional Computer Resource Centers established in 1984 or the Commonwealth's Intermediate Units.

EXECUTIVE DIRECTORS

	Appointed Since 1950
Jack Critchfield (acting)	Mar. 13, 1964
*Kenneth R. Reeher	July 20, 1964

Incumbent

PENNSYLVANIA HIGHER EDUCATIONAL FACILITIES AUTHORITY[1]
101 South 25th Street
Kline Village
Harrisburg, PA 17105-3161

President: Robert P. Casey; **Members:** Donald Bailey, James W. Brown, G. Davis Greene, Jr., Thomas K. Gilhool, Matthew J. Ryan, K. Leroy Irvis, Edward P. Zemprelli, Robert C. Jubelirer.

The Pennsylvania Higher Educational Facilities Authority (PHEFA) was created by the Act of December 6, 1967 (P.L. 678), for the purpose of acquiring, constructing, improving, maintaining and operating educational facilities for any nonprofit college or university within the Commonwealth. The Act excludes facilities to be used for sectarian study or religious activity, and further excludes use of PHEFA by colleges or universities which have admission restrictions based on race, creed, or national origin.

Administration. PHEFA is a separate body corporate and politic constituting a public corporation and governmental instrumentality. By specific provisions of the Act, PHEFA is administered by an executive director and a staff. Accounting

[1]See State Public Building Authority for biographical information.

records of PHEFA are audited by a certified public accounting firm.

Financing. PHEFA is authorized to sell issues for the purpose of undertaking college/university projects. The college/university decides the type of debt instrument and the structure of financing that suites its individual needs. The issue will be paid for by the college/university by payments made under terms of loan agreements, tax exempt leases, notes and other debt instruments entered into between PHEFA and the college/university. Issuing costs can be included in the financing. Administrative costs are funded partly from administrative fees.

Projects. College/university projects financed by PHEFA are designed by architects or engineers selected by the college/university. The college/university enters into the construction contracts or purchase agreements and maintains and operates the facility upon completion.

AUTHORITY MEMBERS	Appointed Since 1950	
Raymond P. Shafer	Dec.	6, 1967
Thomas Z. Minehart	Dec.	6, 1967
Grace M. Sloan	Dec.	6, 1967
David H. Kurtzman	Dec.	6, 1967
Perrin C. Hamilton	Dec.	6, 1967
Robert D. Fleming	Dec.	6, 1967
Kenneth B. Lee	Dec.	6, 1967
Ernest P. Kline	Dec.	6, 1967
Herbert Fineman	Dec.	6, 1967
*Robert P. Casey (reappt. Jan. 20, 1987)	May	6, 1969
Martin L. Murray	Jan.	4, 1971
Milton J. Shapp	Jan.	19, 1971
Frank C. Hilton	Jan.	19, 1971
Richard C. Frame	Jan.	2, 1972
John C. Pittenger	Jan.	8, 1972
Ronald G. Lench	Sept.	14, 1974
Robert J. Butera	Jan.	7, 1975
Henry G. Hager	Nov.	15, 1976
Robert N. Hendershot	Jan.	6, 1977
Al Benedict	Jan.	18, 1977
Robert E. Casey	Jan.	18, 1977
Caryl M. Kline	Apr.	28, 1977
*K. Leroy Irvis	May	23, 1977

	Appointed Since 1950	
H. Jack Seltzer	Dec.	14, 1977
Dick Thornburgh	Jan.	16, 1979
Walter Baran	Jan.	16, 1979
Robert G. Scanlon	Jan.	16, 1979
*Matthew J. Ryan	Jan.	6, 1981
*Edward P. Zemprelli	Jan.	6, 1981
R. Budd Dwyer	Jan.	20, 1981
Robert C. Wilburn	Jan.	18, 1983
Margaret A. Smith	Nov.	29, 1984
*Robert C. Jubelirer	Jan.	1, 1985
*Donald Bailey	Jan.	15, 1985
*James W. Brown	Jan.	20, 1987
*G. Davis Greene, Jr.	Jan.	29, 1987
*Thomas K. Gilhool	Feb.	18, 1987

Executive Directors

W. Stuart Helm	Jan.	31, 1968
Robert R. Gerhart	Dec.	1, 1972
Charles J. Lieberth	June	21, 1979
Edward W. Mills (acting)	Nov.	14, 1979
Wayne D. Gerhold	Mar.	26, 1980
Robert K. Bloom	Jan.	20, 1983
*Donald W. Bagenstose	Mar.	11, 1987

* Incumbent

GOVERNOR'S COUNCIL ON THE HISPANIC COMMUNITY
378 Forum Building
Harrisburg, PA 17120

MERCEDES ROLDAN   Director, Governor's Council on the Hispanic Community

Mercedes Roldan was born Sept. 24, 1932, in San Juan, Puerto Rico, the daughter of Felix del Valle and Rafaela Campis; Univ. of Puerto Rico; over 25 years experience in business and public relations; former life skills specialist and dir. of English as a Second Language Program, Harrisburg Spanish Community-Center; professional English/Spanish translator; mem., bd. dirs., Tri-County United Way; The Girl's Club of Harrisburg; Urban League of Metropolitan Harrisburg; Business and Professional Women's Club of Harrisburg; Hispanic-American Women for the Arts; Community Adv. Com. of the Junior League of Harrisburg; rec., Citizen of the Year Award, New Cumberland Army Depot, 1979; active community volunteer; mem., Panel 9, Admissions Com.; adv. bd. of Gaudenzia; adv. bd., HACC's Hispanic Project; mem., Task Force on Women, the Synod of The Trinity; asst. dir., Governor's Council on the Hispanic Community, 1980-86; appt. Director, 1986; married Julian Roldan; 4 children: Maria, Julian Jr., David, Alberto; 9 grandchildren.

Members: Manuel Lorenzo, Wilfredo Seda, Loida Esbri-Amor, MHS, Eduardo Robreno, Esq., Rosa Herting, Rose Marie Herrero, Jose R. Cox, II, Maria de la Luz Lopez-Nix, Margarita Kearns, Camilo A. Rincon, Rebeca Gonzalez-Briody, Eron de Leon-Soto, Ives Thillet, Lydia Carbonell de Garcia, Graciela de Garcia, Adamino Ortiz, Manuel Recio, Marta Velazquez-Loescher, Delma Rivera, Patricia M. Louque, Sister Mary Consuela, Ana Bartash, Iris M. Sanchez-Cintron, Lydia Reyna DiCio, Mario A. Candal, MD, Efrain Colon.

The Governor's Council on the Hispanic Community was created to be the Commonwealth's advocate agency for its Hispanic citizens. The council consists of 21-27 members, appointed by the Governor for two-year terms and functions in an advisory capacity to the Executive Director, also appointed by the Governor.

Among its functions are: to assist in insuring the Hispanic community equal opportunities and equal treatment; to assist in designing, developing, and coordinating effective policies and programs impacting Hispanics; advise and encourage the development and coordination of bicultural programs and activities; encourage interagency cooperation and coordination; conduct liaison activities with federal, state and local agencies on behalf of Hispanic issues; and evaluate the effectiveness of programs affecting Hispanics. The Council also serves as an information clearinghouse to a number of Hispanic organizations and individuals across the state. The council publishes a quarterly newsletter, *El Forum.*

HISTORICAL AND MUSEUM COMMISSION
Box 1026
Harrisburg, PA 17108

VIVIAN WEYERHAEUSER PIASECKI   Chairman, Historical and Museum Commission

Vivian Weyerhaeuser Piasecki was born Oct 20, 1930, in Chicago, Ill., the daughter of Frederick K. and Vivian O'Gara Weyerhaeuser; Visitation Convent; Miss Porter's Schl.; Vassar Coll., 1953; regional representative of Trustees Comm., American Assn. of Museums; chmn., Franklin Inst. Museum and Planetarium; bd. mem.: Balch Inst., Beaver Coll., Groton Schl.; bd. mem., Mutual Assurance Co. (1983); bd. mem., Fidelcor, Inc. (1981) and The Fidelity Bank, Phila. (1981); bd. mem., First Natl. Bank of Palm Beach, Fla. (1983); Roman Catholic; appt. Chairman of the Historical and Museum Commission, Apr. 29, 1980; married Frank Nicholas Piasecki; 7 children; home address: Turnbridge Rd., Haverford.

BRENT D. GLASS   Executive Director, Historical and Museum Commission

Brent D. Glass was born Sept. 27, 1947, in Brooklyn, NY, the son of Joseph H. and Corinne Bernstein Glass; grad., Lafayette Coll. (B.A., history) 1969; New York Univ. (M.A., American Civilization) 1971; Univ. of North Carolina, Chapel Hill (Ph.D., history) 1980; bd. of dirs.: Chapel Hill Historical Soc., 1975-77; Chapel Hill Preservation Soc., 1976-78; Soc. for Industrial Archeology, 1978-80; Assoc. for Retarded Citizens/Durham Co., 1987; sec.-treas., Historic Preservation Foundation of N.C., 1977-81; chmn., Public History Com., Organization of Am. Historians, 1985-; mem: Am. Assoc. for State and Local History, Natl. Trust for Historic Preservation, and Soc. for the History of Technology; rec.: Citation for Architectural Conservation, Historic Preserv. Soc. of Durham, 1983; Award of Merit, Historic Preserv. Foundation of N.C., 1983; Travel to Collections Grant, Natl. Endowment for the Humanities, 1986; Exemplary Project Award, co-dir. of "The Way We Lived in North Carolina" 1986; Historic Preserv. Award, Historic Salisbury (N.C.) Foundation, 1987; authored various books, articles and papers; appointed Executive Director, Historical and Museum Commission, Aug. 20, 1987; married Barbara Martin; 1 child, Loren Evan; home address: 524 Orrs Bridge Road, Camp Hill.

Chairman: Vivian W. Piasecki; **Members:** Clarence D. Bell, William H. Combs, D. David Eisenhower, James A. Fisher, Thomas K. Gilhool, Mrs. J. Welles Henderson, Samuel W. Morris, LeRoy Patrick, Mrs. Russell D. Robison, Mrs. Robert S. Ross, Hardy Williams, Mrs. F. Karl Witherow, James L. Wright, Jr.

The Pennsylvania Historical and Museum Commission was created by Act No. 446, approved June 6, 1945, amending the Administrative Code to consolidate the functions of the Pennsylvania Historical Commission, the State Museum and the State Archives. The commission is an independent administrative board, consisting of nine citizens of the Commonwealth appointed by the Governor, the Secretary of Education ex officio, two members of the Senate appointed by the President Pro Tempore, and two members of the House of Representatives appointed by the Speaker. The Chairman, who is designated by the Governor, is an ex officio member of the Washington Crossing Park Commission and the Brandywine Battlefield Park Commission. The Executive Director, appointed by the commission to serve at its pleasure, is an ex officio member of the Environmental Quality Board, County Records Committee and the Local Government Records Committee.

As "the official agency of the Commonwealth for the conservation of Pennsylvania's historic heritage," the powers and duties of the commission fall into these principal fields: care of historical manuscripts, public records, and objects of historic interest; museums; archaeology; publications; historic sites and properties; historic preservation; geographic names and the promotion of public interest in Pennsylvania history.

ADMINISTRATION

Powers and Duties are executed through the Executive Office with the Division of Management Services and through four bureaus: the Bureau of Archives and History includes the Division of Archives and Manuscripts (the State Archives), the Division of History and the Division of Land Records; the Bureau of Historic Sites and Museums administers the State Museum and some eight other museums throughout the Commonwealth and is responsible for 19 historic sites; the Bureau for Historic Preservation includes a Division for Preservation Services and a Division for Protection Services; and the Bureau of Historical and Museum Services includes four divisions for Collection Services, Architectural Services, Marketing Sales and Publications, and Exhibits Management.

Executive Office consists of the Executive Director, Assistant Executive Director and a Division of Management Services which are together responsible for the overall administration and policy implementation of the agency as directed by commission actions. The Division of Management Services includes two sections responsible for Budget and Personnel Management, and Administrative Services.

Bureau of Archives and History is responsible for the collection, care, preservation, interpretation, promotion and publication of the documentary history of Pennsylvania. It provides services and publications for the general public, for the scholarly community, and in support of other commission activities as well as in support of regional, county and local historical organizations. The bureau provides administrative and professional support for the State Historical Records Advisory Board, the Commonwealth's County Records Committee and the State's Municipal Records Committee. It coordinates activities with the National Archives, the National Historical Publications and Records Commission, the American Association for State and Local History, the National Conference of State Historical Records Coordinators, the Society of American Archivists, the National Association of State Archivists and Record Administrators, the Pennsylvania Historical Association and the United States Board on Geographic Names. The director of the bureau serves as the Pennsylvania State Archivist. Activities of the bureau are carried-out by three operating divisions: Division of History; Division of Archives and Manuscripts; Division of Land Records. Cooperation activities are maintained with the County Records Committee, the Local Government Records Committee, the Bureau of Publications and Paperwork Management of the Department of General Services, the U.S. Geographic Board, and historical societies throughout the Commonwealth.

Division of History researches, writes and publishes popular and scholarly works pertaining to the history of Pennsylvania. It also reviews manuscripts for publication by the commission or in cooperation with other academic or scholarly organizations or institutions. The division publishes an Oral History Newsletter, and related materials to promote and assist historical interests and conducts conferences and seminars at various locations throughout the state to stimulate research in Pennsylvania history. The Division of History provides technical assistance for local and statewide historical organizations, interest groups and individuals. Administrative support is provided by the division to the Pennsylvania Federation of Historical Societies, the Pennsylvania Junior Historians, and to historical organizations in general. It cooperates with various organizations in promoting and fulfilling research in ethnic studies; answers inquiries on Pennsylvania history and provides assistance to scholars and researchers. The division erects historical markers throughout the state to call public attention to persons, places and events significant in Pennsylvania history. A research library in support of all commission programs and an up-to-date bibliography on Pennsylvania history is maintained by the division. By initiating oral history projects and providing a clearing house for history programs, the Division of History expands the collection of data concerning Pennsylvania's social, ethnic and community history.

Division of Archives and Manuscripts maintains the State Archives and acquires, maintains and describes public records and private papers relating to the history of the Commonwealth. It provides reference services to the public, scholars and students including the preparation and publication of manuscript collection and record group guides. The division microfilms records and historical papers originating at state, county and municipal levels of government as well as records of

private industry and individuals in order to preserve historical data and provide greater access for research. It provides records management expertise to county and municipal governments and to historical societies and contributes to the development of records disposal schedules on behalf of the County Records Committee and the Local Government Records Committee. The Division of Archives and Manuscripts plans, directs, coordinates and evaluates a record management system for county and municipal offices and examines and evaluates all public records to determine their historical value and rules upon the retention of such records.

Division of Land Records is the Commonwealth's Land Office, tracing its functional origins to the days of William Penn. The major functions of the division are to preserve documents relating to the early history of the Commonwealth, and to preserve land titles and boundary documents to protect the legal claims of land owners. The division also maintains real estate titles and other records on all state-owned land to establish the legal rights of the Commonwealth. Upon request, the division searches land records and plots tracts of land on maps to provide tax assessors, engineers, title searchers, property owners and others with information on individual land tracts. The division also oversees the Commonwealth's Land Patent process, processing a few patent applications for vacant land each year.

County Records Committee consists of the Chief Justice of Pennsylvania or his judicial representative, the executive director of the commission, a prothonotary, a clerk of courts, a county commission, a county controller or auditor, a district attorney, a county treasurer, a sheriff, a register of wills, a recorder of deeds, an attorney, a jury commissioner, a coroner and a member from the general public, who are appointed by the Governor. It prepares and adopts schedules for the retention and disposition of records in county offices in counties from the second to the eighth class. The Chief Justice or his representative serves as chairman of the committee, and the commission's executive director as secretary.

Local Government Records Committee consists of the Auditor General, the State Treasurer, the Attorney General, the Secretary of Community Affairs, the executive director of the commission and five other members appointed by the Governor to represent the various municipal associations. The ex officio members may designate representatives to act in their place. The Secretary of Community Affairs is chairman, and the executive director of the commission is secretary. The commission has studies made of municipal public records in order to prepare proposed retention and disposition schedules for the Local Government Records Committee. Such schedules do not become operative until they are approved by the committee, nor are they effective in any municipality until accepted by ordinance or resolution of its governing body.

Public Records: Section 524 of the Administrative Code provides that departments, boards and commissions may dispose of records not needed for current or anticipated future operations only with the approval of both the Executive Board and the Historical and Museum Commission; the Executive Board may then direct that any records of permanent value of historical interest be turned over to the commission for preservation in the Archives in cooperation with the Bureau of Publications and Paperwork Management in the Department of General Services. Schedules for the retention and disposition of records have been developed and approved to systematize this process. Staff of the State Archives administer the work of the State Historical Advisory Board in implementing in Pennsylvania the records grant program of the National Historical Publications and Records Commission. College and university archives, church archives, local historical societies, and similar institutions and organizations in Pennsylvania have benefited considerably from this program.

Geographic Names: In cooperation with the U.S. Geographic Board, the commission determines all unsettled questions concerning geographic names which arise in the administrative departments of state government; and to determine, charge and fix the names of mountains, rivers, creeks and other topographic features within the Commonwealth. Such decisions involve careful review not only of historical origin but also of local usage, the wishes of residents and public policy.

Historical Societies: Numerous Pennsylvania historical societies and agencies have gathered and preserved manuscripts, books and other materials of importance for writing and presenting state and local history. Many have developed outstanding museums, others have preserved and restored historic homes. This important contribution of historical societies in promoting interest in Pennsylvania's historical heritage was recognized by Act No. 394 of 1961, which authorized the commission to cooperate with any qualified historical society in historical or archeological investigations relating to Pennsylvania, in the care of historical papers and museum pieces, and otherwise in encouraging their activities whenever the commission feels that such cooperation will serve the historic interests of the Commonwealth.

Bureau of Historic Sites and Museums is responsible for the operation, management and interpretation of the State Museum, a Mobile Museum, eight topical museums, and 19 historic sites located throughout the Commonwealth. The bureau, through the State Museum, its field museums, and historic sites administers three regional offices, acquires, maintains, conserves and catalogues artifact objects for the state collections illustrating Pennsylvania history, culture, art, flora and fauna, prehistory and archaeology. The commission makes and enforces regulations for the visitation of the sites; it may also charge admission fees, which are paid into the Historical Preservation Fund of the State Treasury.

State Museum, housed within the William Penn Memorial Museum and Archives Building, is the main repository for the state collection of museum artifacts. Its major curatorial sections include: Archaeology, Decorative Arts, Fine Arts, Military History, Technology, Natural History, and Earth Science. Collections are acquired and preserved for both exhibition and study purposes. The museum presents long-term and changing exhibitions, all relating to the history of Pennsylvania. The works of past and contemporary Pennsylvania artists are exhibited and special programs, lectures, festivals and performances are provided on its own initiative and in cooperation with other organizations and institutions. Visitor and interpretation services are provided through the Education Section. The museum operates a planetarium as well as a mobile museum which takes museum exhibits to communities throughout the state. An Archaeology Section is responsible for coordinating archaeological activities throughout the state; conducting and causing to be conducted archaeological investigations, surveying and identifying archaeological resources; preserving and exhibiting the archaeology collection of the commission; and assisting and cooperating with other bureaus of the commission in fulfilling program responsibilities which require knowledge and expertise in archaeology.

Eastern Regional Division includes Washington Crossing Historical Park, Hope Lodge, Graeme Park, the Anthracite Museums at Scranton and Ashland, Eckley Miners' Village, Pennsbury Manor and the Brandywine Battlefield Park.

Central Regional Division includes the Pennsylvania Farm Museum, Daniel Boone Homestead, Pottsgrove Mansion, Cornwall Iron Furnace, Joseph Priestley House, Conrad Weiser Homestead, Ephrata Cloister, and the Railroad Museum of Pennsylvania.

Western Regional Division includes the Drake Well Museum, Flagship Niagara, the Pennsylvania Lumber Museum, Pennsylvania Military Museum, the Fort Pitt Museum, Bushy Run Battlefield and Old Economy Village.

Bureau of Historical and Museum Services provides a variety of technical services to the Bureau of Historic Sites and Museums particularly as well as to the other operational bureaus. These services are provided through four divisions.

Collections Services Division is responsible for the registration of artifacts and museum collections for all museums as well as historic sites owned by the commission. Moreover, this division operates the Commonwealth Conservation Center in cooperation with the Capitol Conservation Committee of the General Assembly. The Commonwealth Conservation Center provides the necessary technical expertise to preserve Pennsylvania's material culture for the enjoyment of future generations.

Architectural Services Division provides the commission's construction planning and project supervision; maintains over 1400 historical markers; and provides oversight of placed properties which are under the custody of the commission but administered by local organizations. The placed properties include: Curtin Village, Centre County; Old Mill Village, Susquehanna County; Judson House, Old Custom House and Cashier's House, Erie County; Robert Fulton Birthplace, Lancaster County; Fort Augusta and Warrior Run Church, Northumberland County; French Azilum, Bradford County; Old Tuscarora Academy, Juniata County; McCoy House, Mifflin County; Brown's Mill School, Franklin County; Admiral Perry Monument, Cambria County; Captain Phillips' Rangers Memorial, Bedford County; Peace Church, Cumberland County; Searights Tollhouse, Fayette County; David Bradford House, Washington County; Hughes House, Greene County; Old Stone House, Butler County; and Johnston Tavern, Mercer County.

Marketing Sales and Publications Division publishes the commission's quarterly magazine *Pennsylvania Heritage*. In addition, this division provides marketing and promotional expertise for commission programs including its publication sales efforts.

Exhibits Management Division designs and fabricates exhibits for both the State Museum and historic sites and museums in the field.

Bureau for Historic Preservation develops, coordinates and administers the Pennsylvania Historical and Museum Commission's comprehensive program to identify, protect and enhance buildings, structures, districts and neighborhoods of historic and architectural significance in public and private ownership throughout the Commonwealth. The bureau provides federally mandated professional staff to support the activities of the State Historic Preservation Officer designated by the Governor to receive federal historic preservation funds and implement the National Historic Preservation Program throughout the Commonwealth. Program and policy matters pertaining to historic preservation are coordinated with the National Conference of State Historic Preservation Officers, the National Trust for Historic Preservation, the Advisory Council on Historic Preservation, the U.S. Department of the Interior; interested citizens, and with numerous non-profit community based historic preservation organizations throughout the Commonwealth.

Division for Preservation Services provides for the enhancement of significant historic properties through the administration of a variety of state and federal preservation programs. Program responsibilities include: administration of National Register of Historic Places Program; administration of the federal matching grant program authorized by the National Historic Preservation Act of 1966; administration of other federally-mandated preservation programs such as certifications of eligible properties under the Tax Reform Act of 1976 and the HUD historic preservation loan program; provides advice and technical assistance to the public on preservation and restoration techniques; maintenance of the Pennsylvania Register of Historic Places which involves a comprehensive survey to record historic buildings and sites in each of Pennsylvania's 67 counties.

Historic Preservation Board: Created by the Historic Preservation Act of 1978, this body of nine citizens is designated by the commission on the basis of individual competency in the fields of architecture, archaeology, architectural history, history, or historic preservation. The board advises the commission on the criteria of significance for inclusion of historic resources in the Pennsylvania Register of Historic Places; reviews and recommends nomination to the National Register of Historic Places; and comments upon the commission's comprehensive preservation plan for historic resources within the Commonwealth.

Brandywine Battlefield Park Commission. Ten members appointed by Governor and Chairman of Historical and Museum Commission ex officio.

Washington Crossing Park Commission. Ten members appointed by Governor and Chairman of Historical and Museum Commission ex officio.

State Historical Records Advisory Board. Eleven members appointed by Governor.

Drake Well Memorial Advisory Board. Seven members, residents of Pennsylvania, appointed by American Petroleum Institute.

28th Division Shrine Advisory Board. Three members appointed by Pennsylvania Historical and Museum Commission and Adjutant General ex officio.

COMMISSION MEMBERS	Appointed Since 1950
Leroy E. Chapman[2]	Oct. 4, 1951
Israel Stiefel[2]	Oct. 4, 1951
John R. Haudenshield[3]	Oct. 4, 1951
Norman Wood[3]	Oct. 4, 1951
James B. Stevenson[4]	Dec. 17, 1952
Frank W. Melvin[5]	Jan. 24, 1956
Miss Grace A. Rankin	Jan. 24, 1956
Mrs. Lawrence M. C. Smith	Jan. 24, 1956
Maurice Mook	Jan. 24, 1956
J. Bennett Nolan	Jan. 24, 1956
E. Gadd Snider[3]	Feb. 7, 1956
Charles H. Boehm[1]	Apr. 15, 1956
John G. Carney	July 27, 1959
Leon G. Kennedy	June 7, 1960
J. Dean Polen[3]	Feb. 6, 1961
Gilbert Cassidy	Oct. 27, 1961
Herman Blum	Nov. 7, 1963
Edward B. Coddington	Nov. 7, 1963
Ralph Hazeltine	Nov. 7, 1963
Mrs. Ferne Smith Hetrick[6]	Nov. 7, 1963
Mrs. Henry Hoffstot	Nov. 7, 1963
Charles G. Webb	Nov. 7, 1963
Thomas Elliott Wynne	Nov. 7, 1963
John H. Ware, III[2]	Nov. 7, 1963
James Kepler Davis[3]	Feb. 16, 1965
Paul W. Mahady[2]	Apr. 7, 1965
J. R. Rackley[1]	Sept. 16, 1965
Sarah Anderson[3]	Feb. 13, 1967
William Ashton[3]	Feb. 13, 1967
David H. Kurtzman[1]	Aug. 24, 1967
Mark S. Gleeson	Dec. 26, 1968
*James L. Wright, Jr.[3]	Feb. 23, 1971
Stanley T. Brosky	Jan. 4, 1972
Albert W. Gendebien	Jan. 4, 1972
John M. Gibson	Jan. 4, 1972
Mrs. James John	Jan. 4, 1972
Irvin G. Schorsch, Jr.	Jan. 4, 1972
Mrs. Nathan Schwartz	Jan. 4, 1972
Edwin G. Warman	Jan. 4, 1972
Maxwell Whiteman	Jan. 4, 1972
John C. Pittenger[1]	Jan. 4, 1972

[1] Ex officio
[2] Appointed from the Senate by the President pro tempore
[3] Appointed from the House of Representatives by the Speaker
[4] Chairman, 1962-1971
[5] Chairman, 1956-1961
[6] Chairman, 1972-1975

* Incumbent

Appointed Since 1950				*Appointed Since 1950*		
Frederick H. Hobbs[2]	Feb.	10, 1972	*William H. Combs	May	22, 1984
Iso Briselli	Dec.	5, 1972	*James A. Fisher	May	22, 1984
Homer T. Rosenberger	Dec.	5, 1972	Margaret A. Smith	Nov.	27, 1984
Clarence D. Bell[2]	Feb.	13, 1973	*Clarence D. Bell[2]	Feb.	5, 1985
Joseph S. Ammerman[2]	Mar.	21, 1973	*Samuel W. Morris[3]	Feb.	22, 1985
Philip S. Klein	Sept.	23, 1974	*Thomas K. Gilhool	Feb.	18, 1987
Jacob W. Gruber[7]	Jan.	6, 1975			
Mrs. Irvin G. Schorsch, Jr.	Jan.	6, 1975			
Samuel W. Morris[3]	Jan.	23, 1975	**Executive Directors**		
James R. Kelley[2]	Mar.	17, 1975	(Appointed by the Commission)		
Mrs. Rhoten A. Smith	May	25, 1976			
Mrs. Carly M. Kline[1]	Apr.	20, 1977	Sylvester K. Stevens	Feb.	9, 1956
R. Budd Dwyer[2]	Nov.	30, 1977	William J. Wewer	Dec.	13, 1972
Robert G. Scanlon[1]	Feb.	13, 1979	Larry E. Tise	Apr.	9, 1981
Kurt D. Zwikl[3]	Mar.	7, 1979	*Brent D. Glass	Aug.	20, 1987
*Mrs. Robert S. Ross	May	7, 1980			
*Mrs. F. Karl Witherow	May	7, 1980	[1] *Ex officio*		
Arthur P. Zeigler, Jr.	May	13, 1980	[2] *Appointed from the Senate by the President pro tempore*		
*Mrs. Frank N. Piasecki[8]	May	20, 1980	[3] *Appointed from the House of Representatives by the Speaker*		
*LeRoy Patrick	June	12, 1980	[4] *Chairman, 1962-1971*		
*Mrs. J. Welles Henderson	Dec.	15, 1980	[5] *Chairman, 1956-1961*		
*D. David Eisenhower	Dec.	24, 1980	[6] *Chairman, 1972-1975*		
Richard A. Snyder[2]	Feb.	4, 1981	[7] *Chairman, 1976-1980*		
*Mrs. Russell D. Robison	Mar.	19, 1981	[8] *Chairman, 1980-*		
Robert C. Wilburn	Jan.	18, 1983			
*Hardy Williams[2]	Feb.	15, 1983	* *Incumbent*		

PENNSYLVANIA HOUSING FINANCE AGENCY
2101 North Front Street
P.O. Box 8029
Harrisburg, PA 17105-8029

KARL SMITH   **Executive Director,**
Pennsylvania Housing Finance Agency

Karl Smith was born on December 10, 1933, in Omaha, Nebraska, the son of Ivan Thomas and Irma Abbot Smith; Univ. of Wisconsin (B.A., M.A.); U.S. Air Force 1952-56; Acting Secretary of Community Affairs, 1979, 1987; Mortgage Bankers Assn.; Natl. Assn. of Housing and Redevelopment Officials; Council of State Housing Agencies; Pa. Assn. of Housing and Redevelopment Authorities Distinguished Service Award, 1971; Pa. Homebuilders Assn. Service Award, 1984; married Lois Dilg; 2 children: Kimberly, Stephanie; home address; Camp Hill.

Chairman: Karen A. Miller; **Members:** J. Roger Glunt, G. Davis Greene, Jr., Sarah W. Hargrove, Hillard Madway, Donald F. Mazzioti, Ronald S. Mintz, Esq., David A. Murdoch, Esq., Kenny Ross, Herman Silverman.

The Pennsylvania Housing Finance Agency (PHFA) is a public corporation and governmental instrumentality created in 1972 to finance the development of multi-family rental housing for elderly citizens, families of low and moderate income and handicapped persons. In 1981, the agency's enabling legislation was amended to include a single-family home mortgage loan program. In 1983, Act 91 established the Homeowners' Emergency Mortgage Assistance Program,

administered by PHFA. This initiative provides loans to homeowners who, through no fault of their own, are threatened with the loss of their homes to foreclosure.

Administration. The members of the agency are the secretaries of Community Affairs, Commerce and Banking, and the State Treasurer, as well as six additional members appointed by the Governor with the advice and consent of a majority of the

Senate. Each appointed member serves for a term of six years or until a successor is appointed and qualified.

The agency staff includes an executive director and specialists in the fields of finance, market analysis, architecture, engineering, housing management, loan underwriting, construction and law. PHFA fair housing practices are a matter of agency policy.

Programs. The agency operates three major programs: the Single-Family Home Ownership Program, the Multi-Family Development Program, and the Homeowners' Emergency Mortgage Assistance Program.

The Single-Family Home Ownership Program provides mortgage loans at interest rates substantially lower than conventional rates to individual qualified home buyers throughout the Commonwealth. Both new and existing homes may be purchased using this program.

The Multi-Family Development Program provides qualified project sponsors with mortgage loans for the interim and permanent financing of new construction or substantial rehabilitation or rental housing developments.

The Homeowners' Emergency Mortgage Assistance Program provides loans to families who are unable to make mortgage payments and are in danger of losing their homes to foreclosure. Loans are used to cure mortgage delinquencies and make payments for up to 36 months.

Both the Single-Family Home Ownership and the Multi-Family Development Programs are financed with the proceeds of bond issues. No tax dollars are used for their operation. An appropriation from the Commonwealth finances the Homeowners' Emergency Mortgage Assistance Program.

Total agency financings amount to approximately $2 billion.

HUMAN RELATIONS COMMISSION
101 South Second Street, Suite 300
Harrisburg, PA 17101

HOMER C. FLOYD   Executive Director, Human Relations Commission

Homer C. Floyd is a native of Massillon, Ohio; grad., Univ. of Kansas; received many honors in football, high school and college; played professional football one year; exec. dir., Topeka, Kansas Human Relations Comm., 1964-65; consultant to U.S. Equal Employ. Opportunity Comm., 1964-65; exec. dir., Omaha, Nebraska Human Relations Comm., 1965-66; exec. dir., Kansas Comm. on Civil Rights, 1966-70; consultant to U.S. Civil Rights Comm., 1967-70; appointed exec. dir., Pa. Human Relations Comm., 1970; treas. and bd. mem., Internatl. Assn. of Official Human Rights Agencies; NAACP; Natl. Assn. of Human Rights Workers; bd. mem., Tri-Co. United Way; past pres., Boys Club of Harrisburg; Kansas Univ. Alumni Assn.; bd. mem., Tri-Co. Volunteer Action Center; pres., Susquehanna Township Midget Basketball Assn.; married Mattie Longshore; 3 children; home address: 507 Clinton Rd., Harrisburg.

Chairperson: Thomas L. McGill, Jr.; **Vice Chairperson:** Rita Clark; **Members:** John P. Wisniewski, Raquel Otero de Yiengst, Carl E. Denson, Alvin E. Echols, Esq., Robert Johnson Smith, Gregory J. Celia, Jr., Russell S. Howell, Elizabeth Coles Umstattd, Aubra Gaston, Esq.

The Pennsylvania Human Relations Commission enforces the civil rights laws of the Commonwealth. Created in 1955, the commission administers two laws, the Pennsylvania Human Relations Act (originally the Pennsylvania Fair Employment Practice Act) and the Pennsylvania Fair Educational Opportunities Act.

Commission policy is established by eleven Commissioners who are appointed by the Governor with the advice and consent of a majority of the members of the Senate. The commission is non-partisan in composition, with no more than six of its eleven members being from any one political party. Commissioners also appoint staff and adopt rules and regulations to effectuate the purpose of the law.

The commission's goal is to eliminate discrimination in employment, housing, commercial real estate, places of public accommodation and education, where based upon race, color, religion, ancestry, age (40 and above), sex, national origin, handicap or disability, use of a guide dog or support animal because of blindness, deafness, or physical disability, or willingness or refusal to participate in abortion or sterilization procedures.

The commission conducts two principal programs: a compliance program in which discrimination cases are investigated and resolved, and a technical assistance program in which staff provides information and guidance to employers, owners and managers of housing, business proprietors, educators and others to comply with the law.

Executive offices of the commission are located in Harrisburg. Complaints are received and investigated at regional offices located in Pittsburgh, Harrisburg and Philadelphia.

INDEPENDENT REGULATORY REVIEW COMMISSION
22-A Harristown 2
333 Market Street
Harrisburg, PA 17101

IRVIN G. ZIMMERMAN Chairman, Independent Regulatory Review Commission

Irvin G. Zimmerman was born Jan. 24, 1918, in Harrisburg, the son of William and Mahala Graybill Zimmerman; Gettysburg Coll. (A.B.) 1940; Temple Univ. (M.A.) 1941; U.S. Navy, 1943-46; retired from The Bell Telephone Co.; pres., Zimmerman Assoc., Inc. (consultants to management); Phila. Advertising Golf Assn.; Union League; Elder, Swarthmore Presbyterian Ch.; bd. trustees, Gettysburg Coll.; bd. dir., Central Penn Natl. Bank; appt. Chairman, Independent Regulatory Review Comm., Feb. 4, 1983; reelected Chairman, Feb. 7, 1985; married Caroline Fetherolf; 3 children: Carol Z. Taylor, Karl, William; home address: 513 Cedar Lane, Swarthmore.

FRANK J. ERTZ Executive Director, Independent Regulatory Review Commission

Frank J. Ertz was born Feb. 3, 1925, in West Nanticoke, the son of John and Mary Daugherty Ertz; Michigan State Univ., 1946-48; U.S. Army Air Corps, 1943-46; retired as Director of Public Affairs from The Bell Telephone Co.; pres., Trinity Athletic Board; mem., Pa. Council on Aging; bd. mem., American Red Cross; mem., Pa. Green Thumb Advisory Board; appt. Executive Director, Independent Regulatory Review Comm., May 16, 1986; married Gatha Ruoff; 5 children: Steve, Kathy Massarand, Vinson, Jeff, Gregory; home address: 723 Hilltop Drive, New Cumberland.

Chairman: Irvin G. Zimmerman; **Members:** John R. McGinley, Jr., Robert J. Harbison, III, Arthur V. Harris, Mark P. Widoff.

The Independent Regulatory Review Commission was created by Act 181 of 1982 (the Regulatory Review Act) to provide oversight and review of all proposed and existing rules and regulations issued by all departments, boards, commissions, agencies or other authorities of the Commonwealth, excluding the Legislature, Fish and Game Commissions, and any court, political subdivision or municipal or local authority.

The commission exercises its authority to ensure that regulations are in the public interest and to determine whether regulations are cost justifiable, minimal in inflationary impact, non-duplicative of other regulations, and conform to legislative intent. The commission maintains a system of accountability to ensure that affected agencies properly justify their use of regulatory authority so that rules and regulations are not unduly burdensome nor adverse to the best interests of the private and public sectors of the Commonwealth.

The commission also acts as a clearinghouse for complaints, comments, and other input regarding existing regulations, proposed regulations and administrative procedures.

COMMISSIONERS	Appointed Since 1980	
*Robert J. Harbison, III (reappt. 8/16/84)	Sept.	17, 1982
*Arthur V. Harris (reappt. 9/28/84)	Sept.	27, 1982
*Irvin G. Zimmerman, Chrm. (reappt. 9/25/84)	Sept.	30, 1982
Michael D. Hanna, Jr.	Nov.	23, 1982
Lawrence B. Abrams, III	Jan.	28, 1983
Richard A. Stafford	May	12, 1983
*John R. McGinley, Jr. (reappt. 2/24/86)	Jan.	27, 1984
Robert S. Ross, Jr.	Feb.	26, 1986
*Mark P. Widoff	Feb.	19, 1987

Executive Director

Gary E. Crowell	June	16, 1983
*Frank J. Ertz	May	16, 1986

* Incumbent

LIQUOR CONTROL BOARD
518 Northwest Office Building
Harrisburg, PA 17124-0001

DANIEL W. PENNICK   Chairman, Liquor Control Board

Daniel W. Pennick was born Jan. 16, 1915, in Coaldale; grad., LaSalle Coll.; Federal Bureau of Investigation Acad.; frmr. dist. sales manager, metropolitan Phila., 5-county area, Peter Ballantine and Sons; frmr. sales supervisor, Scott and Grauer Wholesale Beer Distributors, Phila.; frmr. special agent, FBI, Wash., D.C.; frmr. supervisor of security and communications and labor relations representative, Ford Motor Co., Detroit; frmr. purchasing administrator, Wright Aeronautical Co., Detroit; frmr. regional agent representative, Harness Track Security, metropolitan Phila., Wash., D.C.; Society of Former Agents of the Federal Bureau of Investigation; Pa. Sports Hall of Fame; Circus Saints and Sinners; appt. to Liquor Control Board, Jan. 4, 1972; married Helen Mack; 3 children: Daniel Jr., Gary, and Bruce; home address: 3506 Margo Lane, Chestnut Hills, Camp Hill.

RALPH O. BARNETT   Member, Liquor Control Board

Ralph O. Barnett was born Mar. 20, 1915, in Pgh., the son of Abraham and Daisy Bruce Barnett (both decd.); att. West Penn Tech. Schl. of Drafting, Carnegie Tech. Univ.; Univ. of Pgh. (B.A.) 1976; U.S. Army, 1943-46, WW II, France D+21 w/3rd U.S. Army, inducted as pvt., promoted to 1st Sgt.; rec'd. battlefield commission as 2nd Lt., March 1945, Luxenbourg; promoted to 1st Lt., Co. Cmndr., 3510 QM Truck Transp. Co., Sept. 1945; discharged from active duty, Apr. 1, 1946; Pgh. Police Dept.; appt. Sept. 23, 1938, as sub-patrolman (svc. interrupted by Army, 1943-46); walked "beat" as patrolman, 1946-55; Detective Div., Robbery and Burglary Squads; Desk Officer, 1955-64; appt. Inspector of Police, 1964, commanded 1+2 stations (Downtown and Hill Dist.; No. 9 Northside; and 5+6 E. Liberty and Squirrel Hill); retired Apr. 1966; architectural draftsman, Blumcraft Co., Pgh., 1966-69; dpty. dir., Allegheny Co. Police Training Acad., 1970-76; dep. dir. of investigations, Pa. Dept. of Justice, Feb. 5, 1976-Sept. 28, 1976; Kappa Alpha Psi Frat.; Pgh. Alumni Chaptr.; FOP Fort Pitt Lodge No. 1; Weslley Center AME Zion Ch., Pgh.; appt. mem., Pa. Liquor Control Board, Sept. 29, 1976; married Anna Lene Bell; 2 sons: Ralph O. Jr. and Gregory A.; home address: 3761 Evergreen Dr., Monroeville.

MARIO MELE   Member, Liquor Control Board

Mario Mele was born June 27, 1941, in Cosenza, Italy, the son of Frank M. and Jenny Arnone Mele; LaSalle Coll. (B.A.) 1964; Temple Univ. (M.A.) 1967; N.Y. Inst. of Finance, 1969; pres., Dental Delivery Systems, Inc.; American Inst. of Physics; Sons of Italy; Graduate Club of Phila.; Union League of Phila.; Governor Thornburgh's Transition Team, 1978-79; chmn., Grtr. Phila. Young Republicans, 1974-75; chmn., Friends of Wistar Inst., 1981; President's Council, LaSalle Coll., 1975-77; American-Italy Society of Phila., since 1968; bd., Phila. Art Alliance, since 1972; bd. of managers, Wistar Inst.; bd., Cardiovascular Inst. of Hahnemann Hospital; single; home address: 1240 Pinetown Rd., Fort Washington.

The Pennsylvania Liquor Control Board was created and organized by various acts of Assembly upon the repeal of National Prohibition in 1933. The board was officially organized on December 1, 1933, four days before the sale of liquor became legal in Pennsylvania. The numerous laws related to alcoholic beverage control were later consolidated to form the present Pa. Liquor Code (Act 21 of April 12, 1951, P.L. 90, as amended). The Liquor Code serves as the basis for all operations of the Pa. Liquor Control Board under essentially the same basic tenets originally established by the Legislature in 1933.

The board operates a system of over 700 State Liquor Stores and employs 4,100 salaried personnel in its administrative, compliance and merchandising activities, as well as a fluctuating complement of part-time employes within the store system as required by cyclical sales demands. Virtually all Pennsylvania Liquor Control Board employes have Civil Service status. Pennsylvania is the largest of the 18 control or monopoly states in the nation and as such, is the largest single purchaser of liquors and wines in the entire world.

The Pa. Liquor Code governs the three main functions of the board: the enforcement of the laws and regulations of the Commonwealth related to alcoholic beverages, the issuing of licenses and permits, and the buying and selling of distilled spirits and wines. The Code is an exercise of the police power of the Commonwealth designed to protect the public welfare, health, peace and morals of the people. As of 1987, the enforcement of the Liquor Code was transferred to the jurisdiction of the Pennsylvania State Police.

Subject to the specific provisions of the Act, and in accordance with all other laws of the Commonwealth, the Liquor Code invests the Pa. Liquor Control Board with the duty and power to:

- Buy, import or have in its possession for sale, and sell distilled spirits and wines with all purchases subject to the approval of the State Treasurer.
- Control the manufacture, possession, sale, consumption, importation, use, storage, transportation and delivery of alcohol and malt and brewed beverages, and fix the retail and wholesale prices at which liquors and alcohol are sold in State Liquor Stores.
- Determine the municipalities and the locations within these municipalities where Pennsylvania Liquor Stores shall be established subject to local option decisions by citizens regarding whether their community will be "wet" or "dry."
- Grant, issue, suspend and revoke authorized licenses and impose fines on licensees.
- Lease, furnish and equip accommodations required for the operation of the Pa. Liquor Control Board through the agency of the Department of General Services.
- Appoint, fix the compensation and define the powers and duties of employes as required in the operation of the Pa. Liquor Control Board subject to the requirements of the Civil Service Act and the Administrative Code of 1929.
- Determine the nature, form and capacity of all packages and original containers for liquor, alcohol and malt or brewed beverages in the Commonwealth.
- Make regulations not inconsistent with the Liquor Code necessary for the efficient administration of the Code. Such regulations have the force of law.
- Do all other things and perform all acts as are deemed necessary to carry out the provisions of the Liquor Code and the regulations made thereunder.

There are currently eleven *Liquor Control Board Hearing Examiners,* appointed by the Governor.

BOARD MEMBERS	Appointed Since 1950
Patrick E. Kerwin (chairman)	Feb. 8, 1955
John S. Rice	Feb. 8, 1955
Donald A. Behney	Feb. 8, 1955
A. D. Cohn (chairman)	Jan. 26, 1956
Daniel B. Swaney	Dec. 2, 1957
Dean R. Fisher	Sept. 6, 1961
James E. Staudinger	Jan. 13, 1964
Edwin Winner (chairman)	Nov. 22, 1966
William Z. Scott (chairman)	Dec. 20, 1966
George R. Bortz	Jan. 2, 1968
*Daniel W. Pennick (chairman)	Jan. 1, 1972
Gene F. Roscioli (chairman)	Dec. 1, 1972
Henry H. Kaplan (chairman)	Jan. 6, 1975
*Ralph O. Barnett	Sept. 29, 1976
*Mario Mele	May 13, 1980

* Incumbent

MILK MARKETING BOARD
110 Agriculture Building
2301 North Cameron Street
Harrisburg, PA 17110

J. ROBERT DERRY   **Chairman, Milk Marketing Board**

J. Robert Derry was born Mar. 3, 1923, in Lancaster, Ohio, the son of Lawrence and Florence Stephens Derry; Ohio St. Univ. (B.S.) 1947; 1st Lt., U.S. Air Force, 1943-45; exec. dir., United Way of Indiana Co.; Rotary Club; bd. mem., Health Systems Agency of Southwest Pa.; appt. to Milk Marketing Bd., Nov. 17, 1982; married Jane Mitchell; 3 children; home address: R.D. 1, Box 7-C, Penn Run.

GEORGE R. BRUMBAUGH   **Member, Milk Marketing Board**

George R. Brumbaugh was born May 29, 1923, in James Creek, the son of Randall L. and Elizabeth Donelson Brumbaugh; Juniata Coll. (B.S.) 1942; U.S.N.R., 1944-45; frmr. dairy farmer; Lincoln Grange; Woodcock Valley Lions Club; Pa. Farmers Assn.; James Creek Methodist Ch.; Marklesburg Vol. Fire Co.; appt. Chairman, Milk Marketing Board, May 7, 1980; married Jean Entriken; 2 children: Bernice and Brett; resides in James Creek.

PAUL A. O'HOP, SR. — Member, Milk Marketing Board

Paul A. O'Hop, Sr., was born June 26, 1939, in Avoca, the son of William and Estelle Cofferan O'Hop; grad., George Washington Univ. (B.S. 1969 and M.B.A. 1973); frmr. ex. asst. to Sec. of Defense (Health and Environment); retd. U.S.A.F. officer (1976); educator/author/ consultant/entrepreneur; asst. prof., Marywood Coll.; pres., P.A. O'Hop Associates; bd. mem., Pa. Intl. Trade Conference; officer, World Trade Club of Northeast Pa.; chmn., CAB, Channel 44 (PBS); mem., North Pocono Health Task Force; mem, Neighbor Assistance (Region II) Advisory Council, Pa. Dept. of Community Affairs; Academy of Management; Assn. of Pa. Economists; Natl. Fed. of Independent Businessmen; Data Processing Management Assn.; Organizational Behavior Teaching Society; Lions Intl.; Elks; American Legion; Am Vets; co-chmn., Reagan-Bush Reelection Com. (Lackawanna Co.) 1984; appt. to Milk Marketing Bd., Nov. 15, 1983; married to Florentine Wroblewski; 3 children: Lynne Marie, Paul, Jr., and Suzanne; home address: Janette Circle, Moscow.

LEON H. WILKINSON — Member, Milk Marketing Board

Leon H. Wilkinson was born Aug. 17, 1921, in West Grove, the son of Walter L. and Beatrice Hocking Wilkinson; grad., Kennett H.S., 1939, retired dairy farmer; chmn., Bd. of Assessment Appeals, Chester Co., 1976-86; mem., Pa. Farmers Assn.-Pa. Grange; mem., bd. of gov., Southern Chester Co. Medical Center; elder, New London Presbyterian Ch.; finance sec., Chester Co. Republican Com.; Member, Pennsylvania Milk Marketing Board, May 16, 1986; married Edna Wickersham; 4 children: Lawrence, Charles, Thomas, Lewis; home address: Box 185, RD #1, Landenberg.

Regulation of the milk industry in Pennsylvania was originally organized on a temporary basis by Act No. 37 of 1934, and Act No. 43 of 1935. This regulation was made permanent under Act No. 105, P.L. 417, April 28, 1937, as amended. In 1968, the Milk Control Commission became the Milk Marketing Board.

On July 10, 1980, the board's scope was broadened by addition of Act 104 of 1980 (Milk Producers' Security Fund Act).

The board was created to supervise and regulate the entire milk industry of the Commonwealth, including production, manufacture, processing, storage, transportation, disposal, distribution and sale of milk and milk products for the protection of the health and welfare of the inhabitants.

Administration. Milk Marketing Board consists of three members, one of whom is designated as chairman by the Governor. The members are appointed by the Governor with the consent of the Senate.

The board is charged with all aspects of marketing milk from cow to consumer. Thus, it licenses milk haulers and handlers, certifies milk weighers and samplers, verifies laboratory procedures as well as establishing prices. With the advent of the Commonwealth Attorney's Act (Act No. 164 of 1980), the board has exercised its option and retained a chief counsel. Producer security is now provided under Act 104.

Three bureaus are maintained to properly supervise these varied functions; they are as follows:

Enforcement Bureau receives and investigates complaints of violation of the law and orders of the board. A staff of auditors and examiners, located in each of the three districts in the state, inspects and audits records of milk dealers to insure timely and proper payments to milk producers; investigates and prosecutes violation of the law in connection with Milk Marketing Board orders and regulations; tests milk samples to insure proper payment to producers; and issues licenses and requires bonds of milk dealers.

Bureau of Accounts and Statistics requires monthly reports and annual financial statements from dealers to be used in the administration of the law; compiles statistical data on the movement of milk within the Commonwealth and in interstate commerce; examines data representing the operation of dealers in all milk marketing areas of the Commonwealth and presents this information to the board through public hearings in order that all interested parties may have information concerning dealers' profits.

Bureau of Consumer Affairs consults with representatives of consumer groups, disseminates information on board and related activities to news media and other interested parties; makes recommendations arising from consultations with consumer groups.

BOARD MEMBERS	Appointed Since 1950	
P. Stephen Stahlnecker	Mar.	5, 1952
Joab K. Mahood	Mar.	5, 1952
John A. Smith	May	31, 1956
Simon K. Uhl (chairman)	Aug.	20, 1956
G. Emerson Work	Nov.	18, 1960
J. Lin. Huber	July	1, 1963
Joab K. Mahood	Aug.	7, 1963
Mary T. Denman	June	30, 1966
Robert J. Johnson	June	6, 1968
Albert G. Slocum	Jan.	4, 1971

		Appointed Since 1950	Executive Secretaries		Appointed Since 1950
Nina Gowell	Jan.	4, 1972	Robert Brewington		1956
Harry E. Kapleau	Jan.	4, 1972	Maurice M. Martin		1963
Peter Elish (chairman)	Dec.	31, 1973	Morris Blanding		1972
Donald E. Lanius	Nov.	9, 1976	Harry E. Kapleau (resigned June 20, 1975)	Jan.	2, 1974
Marianne Olson	Oct.	3, 1977	Earl B. Fink, Jr.	Jan.	14, 1976
*George R. Brumbaugh	May	7, 1980	Gene G. Veno	Mar.	7, 1984
*J. Robert Derry	Nov.	17, 1982	*John C. Pierce	Oct.	30, 1985
*Paul A. O'Hop, Sr.	Nov.	15, 1983			
*Leon H. Wilkinson	May	15, 1986	* Incumbent		

PENNSYLVANIA MILRITE COUNCIL
513 Finance Building
Harrisburg, PA 17120

Chairman: Ogden C. Johnson; **V. Chairman:** Robert T. McIntyre; **Members:** William E. Cockerill, Ronald R. Cowell, Richard A. Geist, Elmer G. Grant, Charles Lukens Huston, III, Clifford L. Jones, Richard L. Reinhardt, James J. Rhoades, James W. Smith, Edward Steinmetz, William J. Stewart, John L. Weaver, Harris L. Wofford.

The Pennsylvania MILRITE Council is an independent agency created by the Pennsylvania General Assembly in June 1978 to foster the economic development of the Commonwealth through the cooperative efforts of labor, business and government. Members first were appointed to the council by Governor Dick Thornburgh in December 1979.

The acronym "MILRITE" stands for "Make Industry and Labor Right in Today's Economy" and derives from the millwright, who in earlier days designed, erected and equipped the mills and factories of America, paving the way for the nation's industrial growth and prosperity.

The council seeks to identify the key barriers and opportunities for economic development and job creation in Pennsylvania, and to develop solutions through the cooperation of labor, business and government.

The council is comprised of fifteen members. Five members are nominated by the Pennsylvania Chamber of Commerce. Five members are nominated by the Pennsylvania AFL-CIO. Two members are nominated by the President Pro Tempore of the Senate, one each from the majority and minority parties. Two members are nominated by the Speaker of the House, one each from the majority and minority parties. One member is selected by the Governor. Members are appointed by the Governor and serve terms of three or six years.

		Appointed Since 1950
*James W. Smith	Dec.	14, 1979
Clifton C. Caldwell	Dec.	14, 1979
*William E. Cockerill	Dec.	14, 1979
*Clifford L. Jones	Dec.	14, 1979
*Robert T. McIntyre	Dec.	14, 1979
William L. Mobraaten	Dec.	14, 1979
*Richard L. Reinhardt	Dec.	14, 1979
Richard M. Smith	Dec.	14, 1979
*John L. Weaver	Dec.	14, 1979
Edward P. Zemprelli	Dec.	14, 1979
*Richard A. Geist	Jan.	19, 1981
D. Michael Fisher	July	14, 1981
Harry C. McCreary	Sept.	22, 1981
*James J. Rhoades	Jan.	10, 1983
*Ronald R. Cowell	Feb.	9, 1983
Mark S. Singel	Feb.	9, 1983
*Charles Lukens Huston, III	June	12, 1984
*Ogden C. Johnson	Mar.	6, 1985
*Elmer G. Grant	Dec.	11, 1985
*Edward Steinmetz	Apr.	8, 1986
*William J. Stewart	May	4, 1986
*Harris L. Wofford	Feb.	20, 1987

Executive Director

Gregg E. Robertson	June	19, 1980
*Carlton R. Berger (acting)	July	1987

* Incumbent

COUNCIL MEMBERS		Appointed Since 1950
Robert W. O'Donnell	May	10, 1979
Robert C. Milsom	Dec.	14, 1979

PENNSYLVANIA MUNICIPAL RETIREMENT BOARD
605 Executive House
101 South Second Street
Harrisburg, PA 17108

JAMES B. ALLEN   Secretary, Pennsylvania Municipal Retirement Board

James B. Allen was born March 20, 1952, in New Kensington, the son of Jack B. and Veronica Peck Allen; Indiana University of PA (B.A., Political Science) 1973; research analyst, Local Government Commission 1974-1976; assistant director 1976-1978, executive director 1978-1984, PA State Assn. of County Commissioners; appt. Secretary, Pennsylvania Municipal Retirement System, September 20, 1984; married Barbara Kerlick; 3 children: Jessica, Kimberly, and Cassandra; home address: 3524 Schoolhouse Lane, Susquehanna Township.

Chairman: Aurel M. Arndt; **Vice Chairman:** George E. Gift, Jr.; **Members:** James B. Bonner, Roy C. Bridges, John G. Brown, III, Jeffrey L. Chamberlain, G. Davis Greene, Jr., James J. Haggerty, Harry H. Wonderland.

Established in 1974 by Act 15, the Pennsylvania Municipal Retirement Board took the nucleus of the Municipal Employees' Retirement System (1943) and the Municipal Police Retirement System (1968) to formulate an independent state agency responsible for administering, at the option of the political subdivisions, public employee pension plans. Fiduciary and management responsibility rests with an 11 member board.

Ex officio members of the board are the State Treasurer and the Secretary of the Commonwealth. The remaining nine individuals are nominated by the PA State Association of County Commissioners, the PA League of Cities, PA State Association of Township Commissioners, PA State Association of Township Supervisors, PA State Association of Boroughs, PA Municipal Authorities Association, PA Chiefs' of Police Association and the PA Fire Fighters' Association. The official appointments are made by the Governor. One of the nine must be a retired member of the system.

The Secretary is responsible for the daily management of the system. The organization is divided into three divisions: Municipal and Membership Services Division, Accounting Division, and Operations Division.

BOARD MEMBERS	Appointed Since 1950	
William J. Ganster	Apr.	17, 1961
Arthur K. Fickling	Oct.	17, 1961
Henry C. Lamparski	Oct.	17, 1961
Hon. Grace M. Sloan	Oct.	17, 1961
Hon. E. James Trimarchi, Jr.	Oct.	17, 1961
William G. Willis	Oct.	17, 1961
Charles R. Witmer	Oct.	17, 1961
Hon. George I. Bloom	May	15, 1963
Frank N. Happ	Mar.	10, 1964
Hon. Thomas Minehart	July	28, 1965
Hon. W. Stuart Helm	July	28, 1965
Hon. Craig Truax	Feb.	8, 1967
Hon. Joseph J. Kelley, Jr.	Mar.	29, 1968
Hon. Grace M. Sloan	May	22, 1969
Joseph W. Barr, Jr.	Apr.	7, 1970

	Appointed Since 1950	
Hon. Barton A. Fields	Feb.	2, 1971
Hon. C. DeLores Tucker	Feb.	2, 1971
William H. Wilcox	Apr.	6, 1971
Joseph Abate	May	1, 1974
Joseph Banta	May	1, 1974
John R. Caldwell	May	1, 1974
Hon. Eugene Fike	May	1, 1974
R. Paul Lessy	May	1, 1974
Clarence J. Randolph	May	1, 1974
Robert W. Ruddy	May	1, 1974
Hon. Gordon B. Mowrer	Dec.	16, 1976
Hon. Robert E. Casey	Jan.	17, 1977
Marjorie I. Hansen	Aug.	18, 1977
Hon. Mark Vrahas	Dec.	15, 1977
Michael K. M. Galomb	Apr.	21, 1978
Michael K. Grim	Sept.	21, 1978
Frederick W. Wahl, Sr.	Dec.	14, 1978
Hon. Ethel Allen	Jan.	16, 1979
Walter C. Stevens	Sept.	20, 1979
Charles R. Feindler	Sept.	20, 1979
Hon. William R. Davis	Feb.	21, 1980
Hon. Patricia Crawford	Feb.	21, 1980
Hon. Paul M. Marcincin	Sept.	18, 1980
Hon. R. Budd Dwyer	Jan.	17, 1981
David L. Smith	Feb.	21, 1981
David W. Black	June	6, 1982
*Aurel M. Arndt	June	16, 1982
Dale L. Metzger	June	16, 1982
N. James Fluck	Mar.	15, 1983
Howard Eckert	Dec.	15, 1983
Robert E. Burke	Oct.	10, 1984
*James B. Bonner	Mar.	12, 1985
*George E. Gift, Jr.	Sept.	9, 1985
*John G. Brown, II	July	3, 1986
*Jeffrey L. Chamberlain	July	3, 1986
*Roy C. Bridges	Dec.	22, 1986
*Harry H. Wonderland	Dec.	22, 1986
*Hon. James J. Haggerty	Jan.	20, 1987
*Hon. G. Davis Greene, Jr.	Feb.	11, 1987

* Incumbent

Secretaries	Appointed Since 1950		Secretaries	Appointed Since 1950	
Fred G. Klunk	Oct.	17, 1961	Robert C. Rossman	June	13, 1974
Fred Davies, Jr.	May	15, 1963	*James B. Allen	Sept.	20, 1984
Gordon R. Bender (acting)	May	22, 1969			
Richard L. Witmer	Sept.	6, 1969	* Incumbent		
Margaret A. Bateman (acting)	May	1, 1974			

PENNSYLVANIA BOARD OF PROBATION AND PAROLE
3101 North Front Street
P.O. Box 1661
Harrisburg, PA 17105-1661

FRED W. JACOBS   Chairman, Board of Probation and Parole

Fred W. Jacobs was born Dec. 10, 1942, in Sunbury, the son of Fred W. (dec.) and Sara Byerly Jacobs of Sellinsgrove; Susquehanna Univ. (B.A., psych.) 1964; W. Va. Univ. (M.S.W.) 1967; Loysville Youth Development Center, caseworker, cottage supervisor, unit supervisor, director of staff development, 1964-65, 1967-71; Pa. Board of Probation and Parole, director of staff development, 1971-73, ex. asst. to the chmn., 1973-76; appt. Chairman of Board of Probation and Parole, April 2, 1976; reappt. April 20, 1977, June 2, 1982 and Nov. 25, 1986; current and past professional activities include: Natl. Assn of Social Workers (chmn. certif. comm. Central Pa. Chptr. and mem. higher ed. and public relations comms.); steering committee, PCCD's Task Force on Prison/ Jail Overcrowding; legis. comm., Pa. Assn. of Probation, Parole and Corrections; advsry. bd., Hbg. Area Community Coll. Urban Dvlpmnt. Instit.; Residential Svcs. Bd. Mem. Cumberland Co. Assn. for Retarded Citizens; adv. bd., Pa. Adult Correctional Training Program, Pa. St. Univ.; bd of dir., Consilium Inc.; Gov's. Rehabilitation Task Force; Acad. of Certified Social Workers; Am. Correctional Assn.; Public Personnel Assn.; Middle Atlantic States Corrections Assn.; Natl. Council on Crime and Delinquency; Pa. Prison Wardens' Assn.; Natl. Criminal Justice Assn.; Internatl. Chiefs of Police, Inc.; Assn. of Paroling Authorities; married Patricia Sparrow; 2 daughters: Melissa and Amy.

RAYMOND P. McGINNIS   Member, Board of Probation and Parole

Raymond P. McGinnis was born July 10, 1947, in Carbondale, the son of Raymond and Anne Nolan McGinnis; Temple Univ. (B.A.) 1969; Marywood Coll. (M.S.W.) 1977; U.S. Army, 1969-71; adult probation officer, Lycoming County, 1971-72; parole agent, Pa. Board of Probation and Parole, 1972-83; instructor (part time) Lycoming College, 1982; appt. mem., Board of Probation and Parole, June 1, 1983; Am. Correctional Assn.; Assn. of Paroling Authorities; Pa. Assn. on Probation, Parole and Corrections; Natl. Assn. of Social Workers; Academy of Certified Social Workers; Middle Atlantic States Correctional Assn.; Natl. Co. on Crime and Delinquency; Pa. Law Officers Assn.; Pa. Chiefs of Police Assn.; Fraternal Order of Police; Pa. Prison Wardens Assn.; Pa. Am. Legion Parole Agent of the Year Award, 1975; married Diane Hollingshead; 2 children: Colin and Kyle; home address: Williamsport.

WALTER G. SCHEIPE   Member, Board of Probation and Parole

Walter G. Scheipe was born June 22, 1924, in Schuylkill Haven, the son of Walter H. and Anna M. Scheipe; Bloomsburg St. Coll. (B.S., educ.) 1951; schl. admn., Bethlehem Steel Corp., Venezuela, S.A., 1952-57; parole agent, Pa. Bd. of Probation and Parole, 1958-61; chief probation and parole officer, Berks Co., 1961-69; warden, Berks Co. Prison, 1969-80; appt. mem., Pa. Bd. of Probation and Parole, Nov. 19, 1980; reappt. Nov. 24, 1986; Pa. Prison Wardens Assn. (exec. comm.); Berks Co. Chiefs of Police Assn. (past pres.); Pa. Chiefs of Police Assn.; Am. Correctional Assn.; Assn. of Paroling Authorities; Pa. Assn. on Probation, Parole, and Correction; Middle Atlantic States Correctional Assn.; Natl. Council on Crime and Delinquency; Swatara Lodge #267 F&A.M.; B.P.O. Elks Lodge 207, Pottsville; W. Reading Lions Club; Travelers Protective Assn., Reading; Americanism Award, 1975, B'nai B'rith Lodge 768, Reading; Am. Legion; U.S. Coast Guard (1943-46); Adv. Council, Governor's Task Force on Criminal Justice Systems; delegate, Governor's Convention on Criminal Justice, 1975; consultant, Council on Education and Science Jail Health Project, Pa. Medical Society, 1976-80; married Judith C. Mahle; home address: Snyder Drive, Route 1, Leesport.

WALTER L. CROCKER   Member, Board of Probation and Parole

Walter L. Crocker was born Nov. 16, 1927, in Pgh., grad., Lincoln Univ. (B.A.) 1949; Univ. of Pgh. (M.Ed.) 1957; U.S. Army (active duty) 1951-52, reserves 1952-56; mem., Am. Correctional Assn.; Assn. of Paroling Authorities; Pa. Assn. on Probation, Parole and Correction; Natl. Council on Crime and Delinquency; Pa. Chiefs of Police Assn.; Pa. Prison Wardens Assn.; Middle Atlantic States Correctional Assn.; Crime Prevention Officers of Western Pa.; dir. of physical education, Pgh. Y.M.C.A., Centre Branch, 1953-58; Allegheny Co. Juvenile Ct. probation officer, intake officer, supervisor, sr. supervisor, 1958-71; community relations civilian coordinator, Pgh. Bureau of Police, 1971-75; regional coordinator, Pa. Commission on Crime and Delinquency, 1975-83; parole agent, Pa. Board of Probation and Parole, 1985-85; appt. member, Bd. of Probation and Parole, Nov. 13, 1985; married Marcella Crocker; 2 daughters, 1 son; home address: Pittsburgh.

MARY ANN STEWART   Member, Board of Probation and Parole

Mary Ann Stewart was born Dec. 12, 1937, in Rochester, Pa., the daughter of Israel Wagner, Sr. and Helene Theresa Cusack; grad., Univ. of Southern Mississippi (B.S.) 1960; Univ. of Pittsburgh (M.S.W.) 1973; mem., Am. Correctional Assn.; Assn. of Paroling Authorities; Pa. Assn. on Probation, Parole and Correction; Natl. Council on Crime and Delinquency; Pa. Chiefs of Police Assn.; Pa. Prison Wardens Assn.; Middle Atlantic States Correctional Assn.; Natl. Assn. of Social Workers; social worker, Am. Red Cross (Korea and Europe) 1960-64; juvenile probation officer, Indianapolis, 1965-68; Allegheny Co., 1968; social worker, Gilmary School, 1968-70; parole agent, Pa. Bd. of Probation and Parole, 1971-78; staff development specialist, Bd. of Probation and Parole, 1978-85; appt. member, Bd. of Probation and Parole, Nov. 13, 1985; home address: Pittsburgh.

The Pennsylvania Board of Probation and Parole, an independent state correctional agency was established by the Act of August 6, 1941, P.L. 861, amended by the Act of May 27, 1943, P.L. 767, Act 501, December 27, 1965, P.L. 1230 and Act 134, October 9, 1986, P.L. 1424. This legislation established a uniform parole system and provided for assistance in the improvement of adult probation services in the Commonwealth.

Administration. The board consists of five full-time members, appointed by the Governor, with the consent of the majority of the Senate members, to serve staggered, renewable, six-year terms. Board members are prohibited from engaging in any other employment or political activities.

Power. The board is authorized to grant parole and supervise all offenders sentenced by the courts to a maximum sentence of two years or more; revoke parole of technical parole violators and those convicted of new crimes; and release from parole, persons under supervision who have fulfilled their sentences in compliance with the conditions governing their parole.

Guidelines have been established to structure the board's discretion in making parole decisions, and consideration is given to the extent of risk to the community, the nature of the offense, prior criminal history, employment potential, emotional stability, history of family violence, adjustment to prison, and input from victims.

The board's power to revoke parole and return an individual to prison is taken very seriously, and extensive hearing procedures have been established to ensure that the parolee is afforded adequate due process rights consistent with U.S. Supreme Court and Pennsylvania Supreme Court decisions.

EXECUTIVE

The chief executive of the board is the chairman who is responsible for the overall administration of program operations and services. The Office of Chief Counsel serves as the legal advisor to the board. The Affirmative Action Officer advises the board on compliance with Equal Opportunities Laws. The Office of the Executive Assistant to the Chairman is responsible for the board's public information function, day-to-day oversight of the Division of Staff Development, agency accreditation and special projects.

Bureau of Pre-Parole Services is responsible for the scheduling and preparation of material for the board's parole release interviews, conducting due process hearings; responding to inquiries relative to decisions and policies of the board; reviewing sentence structures for accuracy and compliance with current laws; recording official case decisions of the board; and reviewing parole violation actions to insure compliance with board policy. To fulfill its function, hearing examiners are located throughout the state and an institutional parole staff is maintained at most state correctional institutions.

Bureau of Supervision is responsible for the supervision of the persons paroled by the board, parolees from other states residing in the Commonwealth, and at the request of the court, persons placed on probation. The parole supervision staff, located in ten district offices and twelve sub-offices also makes investigations for, and recommendations to, the Board of Pardons.

Bureau of Probation Services is responsible for the board's mandate to give assistance in the improvement of adult probation services in the Commonwealth. This is accomplished by providing funds to county probation departments through a grant-in-aid program, establishment of standards for the departments, and the provision of technical assistance and in-service training to county probation staff members. A nine-member Advisory Committee on Probation provides guidance to the board in its work of improving adult probation services.

Bureau of Administrative Services provides administrative support to the board and its staff. The bureau's principal functions relate to budget and fiscal control, office services and purchasing, personnel, and the board's management information system.

BOARD MEMBERS
(Act of May 27, 1943, P.L. 767)

	Appointed Since 1950
E. Washington Rhodes	Oct. 15, 1953
Paul J. Gernert (reappt. Aug. 4, 1964)	May 7, 1956
Richard T. S. Brown	June 1, 1956

	Appointed Since 1950
William F. Butler (reappt. June 12, 1969)	Jan. 4, 1965
Ralph J. Phelleps	Dec. 11, 1967
Harry W. Poole	Dec. 27, 1967
Richard W. Lindsey	Jan. 6, 1968
William C. Boor	Dec. 9, 1970
Ernest R. Conley	Dec. 31, 1971
John H. Jefferson (reappt. Apr. 20, 1977)	Dec. 3, 1971
Paul J. Descano (reappt. Apr. 20, 1977)	Dec. 31, 1973
Verdell Dean, Esq. (reappt. Apr. 20, 1977)	Aug. 13, 1975
*Fred W. Jacobs (reappt. Apr. 20, 1977, June 2, 1982, Nov. 25, 1986) (chairman)	Mar. 18, 1976
William Forbes (reappt. Apr. 20, 1977)	Nov. 19, 1976
*Walter G. Scheipe (reappt. Nov. 24, 1986)	Dec. 27, 1980
*Raymond P. McGinnis	June 1, 1983
*Walter L. Crocker	Nov. 13, 1985
*Mary Ann Stewart	Nov. 13, 1985

* *Incumbent*

STATE PUBLIC SCHOOL BUILDING AUTHORITY
P.O. Box 3161
101 South 25th Street
Kline Village
Harrisburg, PA 17105-3161

DONALD W. BAGENSTOSE

Executive Director,
State Public School Building Authority,
Higher Educational Facilities Authority

Donald W. Bagenstose was born Feb. 18, 1919, in West Reading, the son of Harry W. and Margaret E. Foster Bagenstose; grad., Franklin and Marshall Coll. (B.S., econ.) 1942; Notre Dame Midshipman's School, 1943; U.S. Navy, 1943-53; rec., Silver and Bronze Star medals for Conspicuous Gallantry in Action Against Enemy Forces; general manager and treas. of retail chain for 18 years; employed in accounting field, 8 years; West Reading Borough Council, 1959-71; Berks Co. Commissioner, 1971-87; delegate to the Constitutional Convention; mem., Mason Lodge 62, Rajah Temple Tall Cedars of Lebanon; Pagota Club; Legion of Honor; appt. Executive Director, State Public School Building Authority, Higher Educational Facilities Authority, March 11, 1987; married Mabel G. Herr; 1 son, Thomas H.; home address: 416 Spruce St., West Reading.

President: Robert P. Casey; **Members:** James. W. Brown, Donald Bailey, G. Davis Greene, Jr., Thomas K. Gilhool, Matthew J. Ryan, K. Leroy Irvis, Edward P. Zemprelli, Robert C. Jubelirer.

The State Public School Building Authority (SPSBA) is a public corporation and governmental instrumentality of the Commonwealth of Pennsylvania, created by the Act of July 5, 1947 (P.L. 1217) for the purpose of constructing, improving, furnishing, equipping, maintaining and operating buildings and other facilities and equipment for public schools, vocational/technical schools, community colleges, and educational broadcasting facilities. Legislation has expanded SPSBA's financing ability by allowing SPSBA to enter into loan agreements and mortgages as well as agreement and leases. SPSBA has been granted and may exercise all powers necessary or convenient for carrying out the foregoing purpose. When a school has used an agreement and lease to

finance a project, SPSBA also has the right to reconvey the property to the schools when the bonds issued to construct the projects have been redeemed and retired.

Administration. SPSBA is a separate body corporate and politic constituting a public corporation and governmental instrumentality. It is administered by an Executive Director and a staff of experienced professionals. All books of account are audited by a certified public accounting firm.

Financing. SPSBA is authorized to issue bonds for the purpose of financing capital projects for public schools, vocational/technical schools and community colleges. Issuing costs can be included in the financing. SPSBA is considered the issuer of the bonds, with the school as the underlying credit. When a school finances through SPSBA, it has the flexibility to structure an issue to suit its individual needs while taking advantage of SPSBA's reputation, expert staff and services. The school maintains control of its building program. SPSBA also has the ability to refinance prior issues of its own or others.

Bonds may be sold by competitive bids after public advertisement, or by private negotiated sale, if the board so directs. Bonds issued by SPSBA are repaid under terms of loan agreements, agreements and leases or other debt instruments which are entered into between the school and SPSBA. Administrative costs are funded partly from investment earnings, and partly from service fees charged in connection with some types of financing.

Projects. School projects financed by SPSBA are designed by architects or engineers selected by the school. The school enters into the construction contracts or purchase agreements and maintains and operates the facility upon completion. Under the provisions of the SPSBA Act and the Public School Code, all new school projects must be approved by the Pennsylvania Department of Education (PDE). PDE establishes certain criteria that must be met, and approves the financial ability of the local school to make the payments which will be due to SPSBA. In the event of default of payments by the local school, PDE must by law withhold any subsidy due the school in an amount equal to the unpaid payment, and must then pay such amount to SPSBA. Projects financed for longer than five years and more than $50,000 must also be approved under the Local Government Unit Debt Act of the Department of Community Affairs.

AUTHORITY MEMBERS
(Created by Act of July 5, 1947)

	Appointed Since 1950
Hiram G. Andrews (reappt. Dec. 12, 1957)	Apr. 20, 1949
John S. Fine	Jan. 16, 1951
Charles C. Smith (reappt. May 7, 1957)	Feb. 7, 1951
Alan D. Reynolds	Feb. 26, 1951
Frank C. Hilton (reappt. Jan. 19, 1971)	Nov. 2, 1953
Albert S. Readlinger	Jan. 6, 1955
George M. Leader	Jan. 18, 1955
William D. Thomas	Jan. 18, 1955
Ralph C. Swan	Jan. 19, 1955
John S. Rice	Jan. 3, 1956
Charles H. Boehm	Apr. 15, 1956
W. Stuart Helm	Jan. 1, 1957
Robert F. Kent	May 6, 1957
Andrew M. Bradley	July 18, 1957
Charles R. Weiner	Jan. 3, 1959
Albert W. Johnson	Jan. 3, 1959
David L. Lawrence	Jan. 20, 1959
Anthony J. DiSilvestro	Jan. 3, 1961
James S. Berger (reappt. Jan. 5, 1965)	Jan. 3, 1961
Grace M. Sloan	May 1, 1961
Thomas Z. Minehart	May 2, 1961

	Appointed Since 1950
Richard M. Hornbeck	Feb. 6, 1963
W. Stuart Helm	Feb. 6, 1963
Anthony J. Petrosky	Feb. 6, 1963
William W. Scranton	Jan. 15, 1963
M. Harvey Taylor	Feb. 6, 1963
Charles R. Weiner	Feb. 6, 1963
John H. Devlin	Jan. 5, 1965
Robert K. Hamilton	Jan. 5, 1965
Kenneth B. Lee (reappt. Jan. 4, 1971)	Jan. 5, 1965
J. R. Rackley	Oct. 8, 1965
Raymond P. Shafer	Jan. 17, 1967
Perrin C. Hamilton	Jan. 17, 1967
Herbert Fineman	Jan. 17, 1967
Dr. David H. Kurtzman	Aug. 24, 1967
Robert D. Fleming	Jan. 3, 1967
Ernest P. Kline	Aug. 1, 1967
Lee A. Donaldson	Jan. 7, 1969
*Robert P. Casey (reappt. Jan. 20, 1987)	May 6, 1969
Milton J. Shapp	Jan. 19, 1971
Martin L. Murray	Jan. 4, 1971
Richard C. Frame	Jan. 2, 1972
John C. Pittenger	Jan. 8, 1972
Ronald G. Lench (reappt. May 26, 1978)	Sept. 14, 1974
Robert J. Butera	Jan. 7, 1975
Henry G. Hager	Nov. 15, 1976
Robert N. Hendershot	Jan. 6, 1977
Al Benedict	Jan. 18, 1977
Robert E. Casey	Jan. 18, 1977
Caryl M. Kline	Apr. 28, 1977
*K. Leroy Irvis	May 23, 1977
H. Jack Seltzer	Dec. 14, 1977
William H. McKenzie	Mar. 20, 1978
Dick Thornburgh	Jan. 16, 1979
Robert G. Scanlon	Jan. 16, 1979
Walter Baran	Jan. 16, 1979
*Matthew J. Ryan	Jan. 6, 1981
*Edward P. Zemprelli	Jan. 6, 1981
R. Budd Dwyer	Jan. 20, 1981
Robert C. Wilburn	Jan. 18, 1983
Margaret A. Smith	Nov. 29, 1984
*Robert C. Jubelirer	Jan. 1, 1985
*Donald Bailey	Jan. 15, 1985
*James W. Brown	Jan. 20, 1987
*G. Davis Greene, Jr.	Jan. 29, 1987
*Thomas K. Gilhool	Feb. 18, 1987

Executive Directors

Elliott Falk	June 23, 1961
W. Stuart Helm	Jan. 17, 1967
Robert R. Gerhart, Jr.	Dec. 1, 1972
Charles J. Lieberth	June 21, 1979
Edward W. Mills (acting)	Nov. 14, 1979
Wayne D. Gerhold	Mar. 26, 1980
Robert K. Bloom	Jan. 20, 1983
*Donald W. Bagenstose	Mar. 11, 1987

* Incumbent

PUBLIC SCHOOL EMPLOYES' RETIREMENT SYSTEM
5 North Fifth Street
P.O. Box 125
Harrisburg, PA 17108

JAMES A. PERRY

Executive Director, Public School Employes' Retirement System

James A. Perry was born in Renovo, Clinton Co.; Williamsport Community Coll. (A.A., bus. adm.); Elizabethtown Coll. (B.A., bus. adm.); Univ. of Pa. (M.G.A., public adm.); joined the agency in 1971 as fiscal asst., then accountant; named Asst. Executive Dir. in 1978; appt. Executive Director, Public School Employes' Retirement System, 1984; married; 2 sons; residence: West Hanover Twp.

Chairman: Samuel A. McCullough; **Members:** Thomas K. Gilhool, G. Davis Greene, Jr., Joseph V. Oravitz, Albert Fondy, Jacque D. Angle, Bernard J. Freitag, Dennis Ciani, Dorothy B. Taylor, James McCann, Richard C. Harris, Peter R. Vroon, Max Pievsky, M. Joseph Rocks, Roger A. Madigan.

The Public School Employes' Retirement Board was originally created by the Act of July 18, 1917 and reenacted by the Public School Employes' Retirement Code of 1959. The board gained its present status as an independent administrative board when the Code was revised and reenacted as the Public School Employes' Retirement Code of 1975 (P.L. 298, Act 96).

The board consists of 15 members: the Secretary of Education, State Treasurer and executive secretary of the Pennsylvania School Board Association (all ex officio); two members appointed by the Governor, at least one of whom shall not be a school employe or an officer or employe of the state; three members elected by the active professional members of the retirement system from their number; one member elected by the system's annuitants from among their number; one elected by the active nonprofessional members of the system from among their number; and one elected by members of public school boards from among their number. Four other nonvoting members of the Legislature, two appointed by the Speaker of the House and two appointed by the President Pro Tempore of the Senate, complete the board. The terms of members are three years; the chairman of the board is elected by its members. Legislative members serve for the duration of their terms.

As trustee of the fund, the board has exclusive control and management of the fund, including the power of investment.

Four bureaus within the agency report directly to the Executive Office which consists of the executive director. The Bureau of Information Systems plans, administers and controls all electronic data processing activities; the Bureau of Contributor Services manages, directs and administers all activities related to the system's membership; the Bureau of Fiscal Control plans, organizes and directs a complete accounting system; and the Bureau of Administrative Services includes personnel, purchasing, and office services. Legal services are provided through the Office of General Counsel.

SECRETARIES OF THE BOARD

Appointed Since 1950

J. Y. Shambach	1944-1950
George H. Richwine[1]	1950-1953
Rex T. Wrye	1953-1970
Frank R. Cashman	1970-1977
M. Andrew Sheffler[2]	1977-1984
*James A. Perry	1984-

[1] *Served as Acting Secretary during the interim between Mr. Shambach's resignation and Mr. Wrye's appointment.*

[2] *Served as Acting Secretary Apr.-Oct. 1977; appointed Executive Director Oct. 1977.*

* *Incumbent*

PENNSYLVANIA PUBLIC TELEVISION NETWORK COMMISSION
169 West Chocolate Avenue
Hershey, PA 17033

PHILIP I. BERMAN

Chairman, Pennsylvania Public Television Network

Philip I. Berman was born June 28, 1915, in Pennsburg; att. Pennsburg H.S., Ursinus Coll.; honors: Ursinus Coll. (LL.D.) 1968; Lehigh Univ. (Doctor of Humane Letters) 1969; Hebrew Univ. (Ph.D., Honoris Causa) 1979; bd. chmn., exec. officer, Hess's Inc. and Hess Brothers Inc.; pres., treas., founding bd. mem., Lehigh Valley Educational TV (pres., 1973-77); founding comm. mem., mem. first commission, Pa. Public Television Network Commission (chmn., 1970); Friends of Scouting Dinners, Lehigh Co. Boy Scout Council; hon. chmn., Pa. chptr., Am. Jewish Comm.; bd. mem., Pennsylvanians for Effective Government, 1978; participant in various missions throughout the world for organizations, the U.S., and U.N.; mem. of many art museums, art. assns., social, fraternal and philanthropic organizations; Beta Gamma Sigma Honorary Business Frat.; recipient of many awards; married to Muriel M. Berman; 3 children: Nancy, Nina, and Steven; home address: "20 Hundred" Nottingham Rd., Allentown.

H. SHELDON PARKER JR.

General Manager
Pennsylvania Public Television Network

H. Sheldon Parker Jr. was born April 14, 1938, in Pgh., the son of H. Sheldon and Elizabeth Matthews Parker; Williams Coll. (B.A.) 1960; Univ. of Pgh. (M.A.) 1965; U.S. Army; mem., Pa. House of Representatives, 1967-78; frmr. investment broker, Parker/Hunter Inc., Pgh.; general manager, PPTN, Hershey; Pi Sigma Alpha (natl. pol. sci. honor society); honorary dir., The Performing Arts-For-Children; trustee, Eastern Ed. Television Network Inc.; bd. mem., Jt. Council on Ed. Telecommunications; exec. bd., Keystone Area Co. of B.S.A.; bd. dirs., Am. Lung Assn. of Pa.; bd. dirs., State YMCA of Pa.; bd. dirs., Central Pa. Lung and Health Service Assn.; bd. of adv., Pa. St. Capitol Campus; author, *The State of Allegheny* and *The Securities Industry and Public Office: A Review;* married Sallie Lawler on March 26, 1969; 3 boys; home address: 522 Cedar Avenue, Hershey.

Chairman: Philip I. Berman; **Members:** Roy C. Afflerbach, Bart H. Cavanagh, Sr., Helen B. Craig, D. Michael Fisher, Thomas K. Gilhool, Lois Lehrman Grass, Joseph D. Hughes, Herman Niebuhr, Jr., Louis I. Pollock, Louise P. Ross, Robert J. Scannell, John Scotzin, Paul W. Semmel, Sheldon P. Siegel, Richard A. Stafford, Joseph J. Stevens, Emily Sunstein, Patrick Toole, Albert C. Van Dusen, Peter C. Wambach.

The Pennsylvania Public Television Network Commission is a 22-member commission created by Act 329, November 20, 1968.

Its duties are to operate, on behalf of the Commonwealth, a public television network system interconnecting all noncommercial television stations in the state; to make grants to them to aid in the improvement of their broadcast operations, programming and capital facilities; to apply for and distribute federal, state, public or private funds from any source whatsoever; insure diversity, freedom, objectivity, and initiative in programming, and prevent misuse of the network for political or other unconstitutional propaganda purposes.

Organization. The Governor appoints six commissioners, subject to Senate confirmation; each serves for six years. They are selected to provide broad representation of appropriate professions, occupations, talents, and experience useful to television network operations. The Governor also appoints a representative of private and public education, respectively, and designates the commission chairman. The Secretary of Education, the chairmen of the Pennsylvania Council on the Arts and the Network Operations Committee are ex officio members. One board member from each of the seven public TV stations in the state serves on the commission. The other four members are appointed by the President Pro Tempore of the Senate, the Speaker of the House of Representatives and

the Minority Leaders of each house in the General Assembly.

Network members are: WLVT-TV, Allentown/Bethlehem; WQLN-TV, Erie; WITF-TV, Harrisburg; WHYY-TV, Philadelphia; WVIA-TV, Scranton/Wilkes-Barre; WQED-TV/WQEX-TV, Pittsburgh; WPSX-TV, University Park.

COMMISSIONERS	Appointed Since 1950	
Valla Amsterdam	Dec.	1968
*Philip I. Berman[1]	Dec.	1968
George S. DeArment	Dec.	1968
Edward D. Eddy	Dec.	1968
Herbert Fineman	Dec.	1968
Floyd D. Fischer	Dec.	1968
Fred Gualtieri	Dec.	1968
Theodore Hazlett	Dec.	1968
B. Anton Hess[2]	Dec.	1968
Edwin G. Holl	Dec.	1968
Harold M. Friedman	Dec.	1968
John O. Hershey	Dec.	1968
*Joseph D. Hughes	Dec.	1968
Warren A. Kraetzer	Dec.	1968
David H. Kurtzman	Dec.	1968
J. Harry LaBrum	Dec.	1968
Albert Nesbitt	Dec.	1968
Henry F. Paterson	Dec.	1968

* Incumbent

	Appointed *Since 1950*			*Appointed* *Since 1950*
Mary Jane Scully	Dec. 1968	David L. Phillips	Jan. 1979
William G. Sesler	Dec. 1968	Robert G. Scanlon	Jan. 1979
George L. Sterns	Dec. 1968	Harold F. Mowery	Mar. 1979
Eric A. Walker	Dec. 1968	W. Louis Coppersmith	Mar. 1979
Maurice Kolpein	May 1969	David W. Sweet	May 1979
Lourene George	Dec. 1969	Ann Witmer[2]	Sept. 1979
Clyde R. Dengler	Feb. 1970	Marlowe Froke	Jan. 1980
Elkins Wetherill	May 1970	Diana Rose	Jan. 1980
Edward P. Junker	July 1970	Donald Y. Clem	Feb. 1980
J. Muir Crosby	Nov. 1970	Frank A. Ursomarso	Jan. 1981
John W. Oswald	Nov. 1970	Mark S. Singel	Mar. 1981
H. Harrison Haskell	Jan. 1971	*Albert C. VanDusen	Oct. 1981
Eugene M. Dougherty	Nov. 1971	*Lois Lehrman Grass	Nov. 1981
Jay C. Leff	Dec. 1971	Vivian W. Piasecki	Sept. 1982
John C. Pittenger	Dec. 1971	*Patrick Toole	Nov. 1982
Lee J. Gray	May 1972	Robert C. Wilburn	Mar. 1983
David Hornbeck[2]	June 1972	*Robert J. Scannell	July 1983
Lloyd E. Kaiser	Dec. 1972	James O. Hunter	Nov. 1983
Frederick Leuschner	Dec. 1972	Margaret A. Smith	Sept. 1984
Mary Lou Murray	Dec. 1972	*Richard A. Stafford	Dec. 1984
Leonard B. Williams	Dec. 1972	William R. Lloyd	Feb. 1985
Stanley G. Stroup	Jan. 1973	*Paul W. Semmel	Mar. 1985
Louis G. Hill	Apr. 1973	Edward L. Howard	Apr. 1985
Andrew Bradley	Dec. 1973	D. Kay Wright	Aug. 1986
Taylor Grant	Dec. 1973	*Bart H. Cavanagh	Nov. 1986
Ralph Tive	Dec. 1973	*Louise P. Ross	Nov. 1986
John Christopher[2]	May 1973	*John Scotzin	Nov. 1986
*Sheldon P. Siegel	Dec. 1974	*Joseph J. Stevens	Dec. 1986
Thomas J. Fee	Jan. 1975	*Emily Sunstein	Dec. 1986
Andrea Mitchell	Jan. 1975	*Peter C. Wambach	Feb. 1987
Richard A. Snyder	Jan. 1975	*Thomas K. Gilhool	Mar. 1987
John J. Sweeney	Apr. 1975	*Roy C. Afflerbach	Apr. 1987
Hiram R. Hershey	June 1975	*D. Michael Fisher	May 1987
*Helen B. Craig	May 1976		
*Louis I. Pollock	Aug. 1976	**General Managers**	
George H. Strimel	Jan. 1977		
James A. Goodman	Jan. 1977	David H. Leonard	Mar. 1969
Robert N. Hendershot	Jan. 1977	*H. Sheldon Parker, Jr.	Jan. 1979
Donald H. Tollefson	Mar. 1977		
Caryl M. Kline	Apr. 1977	[1] *Incumbent Chairman*	
Philip Klein	Sept. 1977	[2] *Nominees of Secretary of Education*	
*Herman Niebuhr	Sept. 1977		
Gerald J. Specter	Apr. 1978	* *Incumbent*	
Edward W. Arian	Jan. 1979		

PUBLIC UTILITY COMMISSION
North Office Building
P.O. Box 3265
Harrisburg, PA 17120

WILLIAM R. SHANE   **Chairman, Public Utility Commission**

William R. Shane was born Oct. 1, 1935, in Indiana, Pa., the son of Joseph S. and Jean Bell Shane; Harvard Coll. (B.A.) 1957; Univ. of Pa. Law Schl. (J.D.) 1961; attorney; Dean of Admissions and Financial Aid, Univ. of Pa. Law Schl., 1962-67; Professor and Asst. Dir. of Admissions, Indiana Univ. of Pa., 1967-71; v. chmn., Education Com. and chmn., Higher Education Sub-Committee, Pa. House of Rep., 1971-76; participated in writing of Public Utility Code, proposed Public School Code and Commonwealth University Bill, Chief Admin. Law Judge, Pa. Public Utility Commission, 1977-83; Admin. Law Judge, Pa. Public Utility Commission, 1983-84; appt. Public Utility Commissioner, May 7, 1984; designated chairman, May 18, 1987; married Esther McGeoch; 3 children: Susan, Mark, Joseph; home address: 440 School Street, Indiana.

LINDA CHERYL TALIAFERRO   Commissioner, Public Utility Commission

Linda Cheryl Taliaferro was born Nov. 13, 1947, in Springfield, Ma., the daughter of Ernest and Julia Addison Taliaferro; Skidmore Coll. (B.A.) 1969; Boston Univ. School of Law (J.D.) 1973; attorney; chmn., Comm. on Administration and mem., ex. com., Natl. Assn. of Regulatory Commissioners; Pa., Am., and Natl. Bar Assns.; founding officer, Am. Assn. of Blacks in Energy, Inc.; NAACP, Pgh. Branch; Links, Inc.; Energy Policy Task Force to U.S. Dept. of Energy Sec. James B. Edwards, 1981; Technical Hazardous Liquids Pipeline Safety Standards Comm., U.S. Dept. of Trans. Sec. Elizabeth H. Dole, 1984; Pa. Prof. & Business Women's Assn. Achievement Award, 1979; Pa. Co. of Rep. Women Achievement Award, 1980; Outstanding Young Women of Am., 1980, 1981; Nat. Co. of Negro Women, Pgh. Chptr. Award, 1981; Natl. Assn. of Negro Bus. & Prof. Women of Phila. & Vicinity Professional Achievement Award, 1982; American Foundation for Negro Affairs Disting. American Award, 1984; appt. Public Utility Commissioner, Nov. 13, 1979; appt. Chairman, April 28, 1983 and served through May 18, 1987; home address: 330 Lopax Rd., Harrisburg.

FRANK FISCHL   Commissioner, Public Utility Commission

Frank Fischl was born Oct. 25, 1926, in Allentown, the son of Frank (dec.) and Helen Gehringer Fischl; USMA, West Point (B.S.) 1951; Syracuse Univ. (M.S.) 1964; Industrial Coll. of the Armed Forces, 1971; U.S. Army Occupation Europe, PFC, 1946; USAF 1951-1974: Command Pilot, Korea and Vietnam Conflicts, Decorations, Silver Star, Two Disting. Flying Crosses, 11 Air Medals, Legion of Merit; Retired Colonel; Mayor of Allentown, 1978-82; Phila. Chamber of Commerce Disting. Pennsylvanian Award, 1981; VP Natl. Football Foundation and Hall of Fame, Lehigh Valley Chptr.; appt. Public Utility Commissioner, May 7, 1984; married Anne Eckert Wanish; 3 children: Dianne, Nancy, and Donna; home address: 119 South 21st Street, Allentown.

WILLIAM H. SMITH   Commissioner, Public Utility Commission

William H. Smith was born Oct. 14, 1928, in Aliquippa, the son of William B. Smith and Rose Agatha Dougherty; grad., Aliquippa H.S., 1946; Univ. of Pgh., 1951; Univ. of Pgh. Law Schl., 1954; 11th Airborne Div., U.S. Army, 1946-47; attorney; mem., Beaver Co. and Pa. Bar Assns.; Knights of Columbus (Harrisburg Council #869); V.F.W. — Aliquippa Post 3577; American Legion — Harrisburg Post 998; dep. auditor gen., 1973-77; chief admin. law judge, Public Utility Commission, 1984-86; former state advocate of Knights of Columbus; past pres., Knights of Columbus, Educ. Loan Foundation; nominated Commissioner, Pa. Public Utility Commission, April 20, 1987; confirmed June 29, 1987; sworn in July 14, 1987; married Veronica Bolinsky; 1 child, Maria; home address: 988 Blue Jay Road, Swatara Township.

The Pennsylvania Public Utility Commission is an independent, quasi-judicial agency created by the legislature in 1937 to establish and maintain reasonable rates and safe, adequate service in the regulation of the state's public utilities.

The commission, one of the nation's largest, is comprised of five full-time members appointed by the Governor for staggered five-year terms, and subject to confirmation by a majority vote of the Senate.

The Public Utility Commission's predecessor was the Public Service Commission (PSC). The PSC was created in 1913, and started to operate in 1914, after the Legislature found it could no longer administer or control rapidly increasing public utility services.

Two major structural and procedural changes have occurred since 1937. The first changes were made under Acts 215 and 216 of 1976. The second, following an extensive legislative review of the Commission's functions pursuant to the "Pennsylvania Sunset Act," culminated in Act 114 of 1986.

The PUC has an authorized complement of 590 employees, including attorneys, rate and service analysts, auditors, economists, engineers, motor transit and railroad specialists, safety inspectors and enforcement investigators. They work, together with administrative, fiscal, computer, stenographic and clerical personnel in thirteen offices and bureaus: Director of Operations; Trial Staff; Special Assistants; Intergovernmental Affairs; Public Information; Safety and Compliance; Audits; Law; Transportation; Secretary; Administrative Law Judge; Consumer Services; and Conservation, Economics and Energy Planning (CEEP).

The latter three bureaus were created under the 1976 reorganization legislation, which also made attorneys appointees of the commission rather than the Attorney General. Act 114-1986 established the Office of Trial Staff, effective September 8, 1986.

In order to further increase its responsiveness to the public, the commission formed consumer and utility advisory councils and also established an office of Intergovernmental Affairs.

The PUC has its headquarters and a regional office in Harrisburg; and other regional offices in Philadelphia, Pittsburgh, Scranton and Altoona where written and telephone inquiries are acted on or sent to the Harrisburg offices for processing and action.

In maintaining close scrutiny over utility service and facilities, the PUC is especially concerned with safety and reliability of natural gas pipelines, water and telephone lines, and railroad grade crossings. Utilities must report accidents to the commission, which regularly inspects facilities to determine whether they are safe and adequate. Gas explosions and railroad grade crossing accidents are promptly and thoroughly investigated in an effort to prevent recurrences.

The PUC, in a joint Federal-State effort and with federal funding places priority on the elimination of hazardous rail-highway grade crossings. In the further interest of rail safety, the commission also examines the structural strength of railroad bridges and underpasses.

In addition to its railroad safety inspectors, the PUC has a force of motor transportation investigators who check on safety, cargo, and certificated routes of truck, taxi, and bus operators.

The commission annually processes thousands of applications and other documents, including numerous consumer complaints and questions about such things as size of bills, fuel surcharges, billing procedures, late payments, penalties, meter readings and general service problems. A meter testing laboratory is maintained in Harrisburg to help settle disputes over gas, electric, and water meter readings and tamperings.

The Consumer Services Bureau was established in an effort to make consumers aware of their rights and responsibilities, provide timely procedural information, and speed efforts to settle customer-utility controversies informally to avoid the cost and delay of formal litigation.

The commission, through its Bureau of Conservation, Economics and Energy Planning has a legislative mandate to research and study all utility matters within PUC jurisdiction; including long range forecasting of energy needs and conservation. Electric and gas companies are required to file annual reports on energy conservation measures.

With the enactment of Act No. 33 (P.L. 90) House Bill No. 1180 on March 3, 1972, the commission became fully funded by assessment of the regulated public utilities. Subject to budgetary approval, the PUC may assess utilities up to three-tenths of one percent of gross intra-state revenue to cover the cost of regulation. Each utility is billed in advance by the commission for its share of an approved estimate of expenditures for the following fiscal year. All assessments and fees received, collected or recovered under Act NO. 33 are paid into the General Fund of the State Treasury through the Department of Revenue for use solely by the commission.

The commission's budget for the fiscal year 1987-88 is $26,549.000. It is a substantially lower budget than permissible through the assessment process; and an austere approach to control expenses and to direct spending wisely in consonance with the achievement of commission responsibilities and operational objectives.

As a member of the National Association of Regulatory Utility Commissioners (NARUC), the PUC cooperates with other State and Federal regulatory agencies in fulfilling its regulatory role. Since its reorganizations in 1976 and 1986, the commission has pursued the legislative intent that it become an effective force in serving the public interest.

COMMISSION MEMBERS	Appointed Since 1950	
Henry Houck (reappt. Apr. 15, 1953)	Aug.	16, 1943
Leon Schwartz (chairman)	Mar.	4, 1952
P. Stephen Stahlnecker	Jan.	2, 1953
Thomas C. Egan	Jan.	5, 1953
Joseph Sharfsin (chairman)	May	29, 1956
Robert Anthony	Jan.	5, 1960
William F. O'Hara	Feb.	1, 1960
Dr. John L. Dorris	Apr.	10, 1961
Maurice H. Claster	Aug.	5, 1963
George I. Bloom (chairman)	Apr.	27, 1965
James McGirr Kelly	May	23 1967
Daniel H. Huyett, III	Dec.	27, 1968
Louis J. Sparvero	Dec.	31, 1968
Robert K. Bloom	Nov.	19, 1970
Louis J. Carter (former chairman)	Nov.	10, 1971
Herbert S. Denenberg (interim appt.)	Jan.	6, 1975
Helen B. O'Bannon	Dec.	8, 1975
Michael Johnson	Dec.	16, 1975
W. Wilson Goode (chairman)	Feb.	21, 1978
Susan M. Shanaman (chairman)	Nov.	16, 1979
James H. Cawley	Nov.	16, 1979
*Linda C. Taliaferro (former chairman)	Nov.	16, 1979
Clifford Jones	Oct.	19, 1981
*Frank Fischl	May	7, 1984
*William R. Shane (chairman)	May	7, 1984
*William Smith	Apr.	20, 1987

* Incumbent

PENNSYLVANIA SECURITIES COMMISSION
333 Market Street
14th Floor
Harrisburg, PA 17101

ROBERT M. LAM   Chairman, Securities Commission

Robert M. Lam was born Sept. 8, 1925, in Phila., the son of Julius and Beatrice Kahn Lam; att. Temple Univ. and Southwest Texas St. Univ.; U.S. Air Force, 1944-45; realtor-natl., state and local real estate bds.; bd. of dir. & exec. com., Home Unity Savings Bank; pres., Lam and Buchsbaum Realtors; Pa. Securities Comm., 1965-71, 1980, elected chmn., 1981; bd. mem., North American Sec. Admin. (NASAA); former chmn., NASAA Real Estate Comm.; pres., Philmont C.C.; hon. trustee, Congregation Keneseth Israel; former: bd. mem., Holy Redeemer Hosp., Cheltenham Twp. Commissioner, v. chmn., Chelt. Twp. Govt. Study Comm., chmn., Chelt. Twp. Plan. Comm. & Lib. System; 4 children: Jane, Stephen, Bradford, Richard; home address: 1336 Red Rambler Rd., Rydal.

FREDERICK H. PLANK   Member, Securities Commission

Frederick H. Plank was born Feb. 23, 1923, in Pgh., the son of Harry and Katharine K. Plank; att., Carnegie Mellon, Univ. of Pgh., Pa. St. Univ.; U.S. Army, 1943-46, 69th Inf. Div., Bronze Star; frmr. group vice pres., McGraw-Edison; frmr. Governor, Div. Chmn., Std.'s Co. Chmn., Natl. Electrical Mfgr.'s Assn. (NEMA); pres., Nomad Enterprises; vice pres., gen. mgr., Superior Concrete Products; Managing Partner, Resource Assoc.; frmr. Officer/Dir., founder, United Way, Southwestern Pa.; dir., Canonsburg Hospital (5 years); Canonsburg "Man of the Year" 1965; appt. Commissioner, Securities Commission, June 13, 1983; married Kathleen W. King; 2 children: Stephen, Lisa; home address: 202 Center Church Rd., McMurray.

LORI HEISER   Member, Securities Commission

Lori Heiser was born in Chicago, the daughter of Michael and Helen Rams; grad., Northern Illinois Univ. (B.S.); frmr. home economist, teacher, Chicago public schools; mem., Zonta Internatl., Am. Assn. of Univ. Women; PA House of Representatives, 1980-82; past pres., NH/McKnight AAUW; founder & frmr. pres., Crisis Center North; chair, adv. com., Lutheran Services of W. Pa.; mem., bd. of trustees, Recovery Hall Nursing Home; frmr. mem., bd. dirs.: S.W. Pa. Council of Girl Scouts, Women's Crisis Center & Shelter of Greater Pgh.; frmr. pres., N.H. Arts Center; delegate, Gov. Shapp's Conf. on Libraries; Government/Public/Civic Leadership Award, Pgh. YWCA "Tribute to Women," 1987; Who's Who of American Women, 1983-84; "Woman of the Year," 1981; BPW Who's Who in Politics, 1982; Good Government Award, Jaycees, 1979; "Outstanding Woman," AAUW, 1978; alt. delegate, Republican Natl. Conv., 1976; frmr. chair, Ross Twp. Rep. Com.; appt. Member, Securities Commission, June 1986; married Richard S. Heiser; 2 children: James and Clair; home address: 108 S. Harleston Dr., Ross Twp., Pittsburgh.

The Pennsylvania Securities Commission is an administrative board, having obtained independent status by virtue of Acts Nos. 171 and 172 enacted on February 17, 1976.

Administration. The commission consists of three commissioners appointed by the Governor with the advice and consent of the Senate who hold office at the pleasure of the Governor and until their successors are duly appointed and qualified.

The commission is responsible for administering the Pa. Securities Act of 1972 (up P.S. §§1-101, et seq.; Act No. 284, adopted December 5, 1972). The Act of May 15, 1933, (Act No. 113, P.L. 788; P.S. §§6051, et seq.) and the Takeover Disclosure

Law of Pennsylvania (70 P.S. §§71-85; Act No. 19 of March 3, 1976).

The primary purpose of the regulatory responsibilities and objectives described below is to protect the public from fraudulent practices in connection with the offer, sale and purchase of securities in Pennsylvania while, at the same time, to encourage the financing of legitimate business and industry in the Commonwealth.

Office of the Secretary is responsible for the overall administration and management of the agency. The secretary provides support services to the commissioners, maintains official documentation and custody of records, provides legislative liaison, liaison with other state and federal agencies, press and public relations, as well as policy and planning. Division of Management Services provides support services to the commission. Principal functions include personnel management, computer services, budget, financial management, revenue management, purchasing, affirmative action, and general administrative services.

The Chief Accountant is responsible for the accounting review and financial analysis of all records and documents associated with the commission programs as well as the development of accounting policy and professional accounting advice to the commission.

Chief Counsel is responsible for all legal matters involving the commission and the statute which it administers, as well as the supervision of the commission's legal staff.

Division of Corporation Finance is responsible for the review and analysis of all securities offered and sold in Pennsylvania or to Pennsylvania residents. The Pennsylvania Securities Act of 1972 requires the registration of all securities offered for sale in Pennsylvania, unless there is an applicable exemption. The Act provides a series of exemptions to cover situations where, because of the nature of the security or the character of the transaction, registration is not deemed to be in the public interest or necessary for the protection of investors.

This division is also responsible for the review and analysis of Takeover Disclosure Law filings. This law requires the filing of a registration statement or exemption notice in certain cases involving persons seeking to acquire equity securities for the purpose of changing or influencing the control of a Pennsylvania corporation or a corporation which has its principal place of business and substantial assets in Pennsylvania. The purpose of this statute is to ensure full and fair disclosure to all offerees of material information in regard to a takeover offer and is designed for the protection of Pennsylvania corporations, shareholders, employees and the public in order to prevent fraud and deception by persons making such offers.

Division of Licensing and Compliance

Licensing Section is responsible for the review and analysis of all applications for registration submitted by persons seeking to engage in business in Pennsylvania as broker-dealers, agents (salesmen) or investment advisers.

The Pennsylvania Securities Act of 1972 requires that all such persons must be registered by the commission prior to engaging in such activities. The Act gives the commission the authority to deny, suspend or revoke any registration where the commission deems it not to be in the public interest to permit such person to conduct business in Pennsylvania.

The division is responsible for conducting background research on all applicants to determine the business conduct of such persons prior to seeking registration in Pennsylvania.

Compliance Section was initially established within the commission during FY 84-85 and is responsible for the field examinations of broker-dealer and investment adviser offices located in Pennsylvania in order to determine whether a registrant is in compliance with the requirements of the Pennsylvania Securities Act of 1972. Major emphasis in the

examination is to ascertain whether Pennsylvania investors have been subject to abusive sales practices.

The division's primary activity is directed to examinations of offices in this state which are not examined by any other federal or self-regulatory agency. The division also participates in joint-cooperative examinations conducted by other state and federal regulatory agencies.

In cases of non-compliance, the commission may consider taking administrative action against a registrant which includes a censure, suspension, or revocation of registration.

Division of Enforcement and Litigation institutes public and private investigations to determine whether any person has violated or is about to violate the Act or any rule or order thereunder. Administrative actions taken in the public interest and to protect investors include the issuance of orders to show cause, orders to cease and desist, and orders to cease and desist false advertising. Judicial actions include the institution (with the approval of the Attorney General) of civil suits to enjoin violators of the Act or to enforce compliance. In certain instances recommendations are made that cases be referred to other agencies for criminal investigation and prosecution. This division also advises and represents the commission in all matters involving litigation.

Leviticus. In 1982 the commission became the second Pennsylvania state agency to be voted membership in the Leviticus Project Association, a multi-state federally funded law enforcement network created to combat crimes related to the coal industry. Cases investigated and prosecuted range from fraudulent tax shelters and "boiler room" sales deferred delivery contracts to fraud on financial institutions and theft of heavy equipment.

(By the Act of April 13, 1927, The Securities Bureau was abolished and the Pennsylvania Securities Commission was created. The commission was a departmental board in the Banking Department until it was designated an independent board by Acts 171 and 172 of 1976.)

	Appointed
COMMISSIONERS	*Since 1950*
Frank N. Happ (chairman)	Feb. 8, 1955
J. Warren Mickle (resigned Sept. 5, 1961)	Feb. 8, 1955
Elizabeth G. Zeidman (resigned Aug. 15, 1959)	June 1, 1956
John R. Torquato	Nov. 23, 1960
James J. Connor	Sept. 6, 1961
Elkins Wetherill	Aug. 2, 1963
Edward L. Flaherty	Aug. 2, 1963
Joseph W. Bullen, Jr.	Aug. 2, 1963
*Robert Lam (reappt. May 14, 1980; elected chairman Jan. 13, 1981)	Nov. 3, 1965
Stanley A. Miller (chairman)	Jan. 5, 1971
James P. Breslin (chairman)	Jan. 3, 1972
Ralph M. Fratkin (appt. chairman Dec. 23, 1974)	Jan. 3, 1972
Samuel Meyers (resigned Aug. 16, 1975)	Jan. 3, 1972
Walter G. Arader	Jan. 6, 1975
Warren G. Terhorst	Feb. 3, 1976
Frank A. Ursomarso (resigned May 1, 1981)	Jan. 9, 1981
Cole B. Price, Jr. (resigned June 30, 1985)	Jan. 9, 1981
John C. Tuten (resigned Mar. 1, 1983)	Dec. 28, 1981
*Frederick H. Plank	June 13, 1983
*Lori Heiser	June 4, 1986

* *Incumbent*

STATE EMPLOYES' RETIREMENT SYSTEM
Boas School Building
909 Green Street
Harrisburg, PA 17102-2999

JOHN R. BROSIUS

**Executive Director, State Employes'
Retirement System**

John R. Brosius was born Feb. 22, 1946, in Danville, the son of Russell B. and Pauline Wetzel Brosius; Bloomsburg Univ. (B.S.) 1968; Bucknell Univ. (M.B.A.) 1971; certified public accountant; mem., American Institute of CPA's; Pa. Institute of CPA's; dir., Office of Financial Management, State Employes' Ret. System, 1981-84; appt. Acting Secretary, State Employes' Retirement System, Nov. 29, 1984; appt. Secretary, March 20, 1985; married Donna Bohner; 2 children: Jennifer and Justin; home address: 253 Indian Creek Drive, Mechanicsburg.

Chairman (acting): William J. Moran; **Members:** Anthony B. Andrezeski, Robert A. Bittenbender, G. Davis Greene, Jr., Charles J. Lieberth, F. Joseph Loeper, Nicholas Maiale, Harold F. Mowery, Jr., K. Paul Muench, James I. Scheiner.

The State Employes' Retirement System, established in 1923, has been recodified and amended in 1959; and comprehensively revised by Act 31 in 1974.

The State Employes' Retirement Board is an independent administrative board of the Commonwealth. The board consists of 11 members: the State Treasurer, ex officio, and six members appointed by the Governor for terms of four years, subject to confirmation by the Senate, two Senators and two members of the House of Representatives. At least five board members shall be active members of the system, and at least two shall have ten or more years of credited state service. The Governor designates the chairman of the board from among the members.

Under Act 31, the board possesses the power and privileges of a corporation. The members of the board are the trustees of the state employes' retirement fund; the State Treasurer is the custodian of the fund. The board has exclusive control and management of fund accounts; has the power to invest the fund; adopts and promulgates all rules and regulations for the uniform administration of the system.

BOARD MEMBERS

	Appointed Since 1950
Charles R. Barber	1949-53
Katherine G. Murdock	June 8, 1949
Gene D. Smith (chairman, Acting Secy. of Commonwealth; appt. Secy. May 31, 1950)	Oct. 26, 1949
Weldon B. Heyburn	1953-57
Kevy K. Kaiserman	Apr. 21, 1954
James A. Finnegan (chairman)	Jan. 18, 1955
Frank N. Happ	Mar. 15, 1955
Henry E. Harner (chairman)	Jan. 3, 1956
James A. Finnegan (chairman)	Dec. 28, 1956
Robert F. Kent	1957-61
Grace M. Sloan	Apr. 29, 1958
John S. Rice (chairman)	June 9, 1958
E. James Trimarchi, Jr. (chairman)	Apr. 10, 1961
Grace M. Sloan	1961-65
Louise M. John	June 27, 1961
George I. Bloom (chairman)	Jan. 14, 1963

BOARD MEMBERS

	Appointed Since 1950
Hannah Y. Cooke	June 17, 1964
W. Stuart Helm (chairman)	June 23, 1965
Thomas Z. Minehart	1965-69
J. Warren Bullen, Jr.	Nov. 18, 1965
Craig Truax (chairman)	Jan. 17, 1967
Helen Corson	Nov. 14, 1967
Joseph J. Kelley, Jr. (chairman)	Jan. 1, 1968
Grace M. Sloan	1969-77
Judge Robert Lee Jacobs	Dec. 9, 1970
C. DeLores Tucker (chairman)	Jan. 25, 1971
Sol E. Zubrow	Jan. 3, 1972

(Act 31 of 1974, created the State Employes' Retirement Board as an independent board; Judge Robert Lee Jacobs was voted Acting Chairman; other two members were J. Warren Bullen, Jr., and Hon. Grace M. Sloan, then State Treasurer.)

BOARD MEMBERS

	Appointed Since 1950
Sole E. Zubrow	Jan. 6, 1975
C. DeLores Tucker	Jan. 6, 1975
*William J. Moran	Jan. 6, 1975
Paul J. Smith	Jan. 6, 1975
Vincent X. Yakowicz	Jan. 6, 1975
Robert E. Casey	1977-81
William J. Moran (reappt.; acting chairman)	Mar. 22, 1977
William J. Sheppard (to fill unexpired term of C. DeLores Tucker)	June 27, 1978
Milton Melman	Sept. 26, 1978
Gilbert Teitel	Sept. 26, 1978
*K. Paul Muench	Feb. 12, 1980
Harvey Bartle III	May 13, 1980
*Robert A. Bittenbender	May 13, 1980
*Charles J. Lieberth	Nov. 19, 1980
*James I. Scheiner (to fill unexpired term of Harvey Bartle)	Jan. 8, 1981
R. Budd Dwyer	Jan. 20, 1980

* Incumbent

		Appointed Since 1950	Secretaries to the Board		Appointed Since 1950
Samuel Rappaport		May 25, 1982	Maynard M. Small		May 22, 1957
Stephen F. Freind		May 25, 1982	H. S. Cannon		Apr. 29, 1958
*Edward L. Howard		Apr. 1, 1982	Fred G. Klunk		July 28, 1959
*Anthony B. Andrezeski		Feb. 9, 1983	Fred Davies, Jr.		June 13, 1963
*Nicholas Maiale		Jan. 6, 1985	Richard L. Witmer		June 27, 1969
Christine M. Crist		Feb. 4, 1985	Robert L. Cusma		Sept. 4, 1979
*F. Joseph Loeper		Jan. 6, 1987	*John R. Brosius		Nov. 29, 1984
*Harold F. Mowery, Jr.		Jan. 6, 1987			
*G. Davis Greene, Jr.		Feb. 11, 1987	* Incumbent		

STATE TAX EQUALIZATION BOARD
705 Transportation and Safety Building
P.O. Box 1294
Harrisburg, PA 17108

MARTHA B. SCHOENINGER   Chairman, State Tax Equalization Board

Martha B. Schoeninger was born Sept. 15, 1914, in Philadelphia, the daughter of William and Ella May Stein Kelly; Overbrook H.S.; Berte Art School; Purdue Univ.; sales, designer; mem., Commonwealth Bd. of the Medical Coll. of Pa.; v. chmn., Republican State Committee, 1976-80; chmn., Rep. State Com., 1980-83; Ladies Comm. Union League; v. pres., Council of Rep. Women; pres., Church Choir & Women's Assn.; Pa. chmn., Women for Reagan-Bush '84; mem., Rep. Natl. Com., 1980-83; mem., Electoral College, 1984; rec., Four Chaplains Award; Who's Who in American Politics; appt., mem., State Tax Equalization Board, Dec. 12, 1983; married John W. Schoeninger; 3 sons: John, Thomas, Richard; home address: 245 Valley Stream Lane, Wayne.

JOHN T. MARTINO   Member, State Tax Equalization Board

John T. Martino was born Dec. 13, 1951, in the Bronx, NY, the son of Thomas and Marion Martino; grad., Franklin and Marshall Coll. (B.S., govt.) 1974; Millersville Grad. Study (masters program); former Dep. Sec. of Community Affairs; Dep. Sec. of the Commonwealth, 1981-86; pres., Keystone Data Marketing Firm; volunteer, Big Brothers of America; founder, Lancaster Lacrosse Assn.; appointed member, State Tax Equalization Board; married Susan Geis; 2 children: Melissa Lee and John Scott; home address: 925 Virginia Ave., Lancaster.

GUS A. PEDICONE   Member, State Tax Equalization Board

Gus A. Pedicone was born Feb. 6, 1926, in Phila.; Palmer Business Coll., Wharton Schl., Univ. of Pa.; U.S. Navy, WWII and Korean Conflict; pres., Flite Line Service, Inc.; South Phila. Lions Club; appt. member, Tax Equalization Board, Apr. 14, 1980; 3 children: Constance, Valerie, Thomas; home address: 2222 S. 17th St., Philadelphia.

The State Tax Equalization Board (STEB) is an independent administrative board created by Act 447 of 1947, P.L. 1046, as amended. The board consists of three members appointed by the Governor for terms of four years. The chairman is designated by the Governor. The board performs several functions:

Market Value: The primary function of the board is to determine annually the aggregate market value of taxable real property in each political subdivision and school district throughout the Commonwealth of Pennsylvania. Legislative restrictions as stipulated in Section 7 (3) and Section 14 of Act 447, determine the computation procedure to be used in an odd or even year.

The market values are certified annually to the Department of Education and the respective school districts on or before July 1 of each year. These market values are used by the Department of Education as one factor in a legislative formula for the distribution of state subsidies to each school district.

School districts aggrieved by any findings or conclusions of the board may appeal said findings through appropriate board hearings as set forth in Section 13 of Act 447, as amended. Objections are to be filed on or before October 1 in the year certified according to Regulation No. 1 of the State Tax Equalization Board. The board conducts informal and formal hearings.

Common Level Ratio: This function of the board is to establish a common level ratio of assessed value to selling price for each county for the prior calendar year.

Act 267 of 1982, requires the State Tax Equalization Board to use statistically acceptable techniques, to make the methodology for computing ratios public and to certify the ratio to the chief assessor of each county each year.

Common Level Ratios appeals may be filed with the STEB. Fixed Asset Accounting and Reporting Management Directive 310.4 designates STEB personnel as the appraisal staff for administering and maintaining, on an as needed basis, a continuing program of valuation services for Commonwealth General Fixed Asset Real Property.

Certification of Assessors: Act 192 of 1986 mandates the certification and recertification by STEB of Pennsylvania Assessors of Real Property for ad valorem taxation purposes.

Since the inception of the State Tax Equalization Board of 1947, the General Assembly from time to time has broadened the use of the board's findings.

BOARD MEMBERS
(Created by Act 447 of 1947, P.L. 1046)

	Appointed Since 1950
Walter J. Kress (reappt. Sept. 25, 1952)	Nov. 15, 1947
John N. O'Neil (reappt. Sept. 25, 1952)	Mar. 8, 1948
Paul C. Kaestner	July 7, 1950

	Appointed Since 1950
Cornelius S. Deegan, Jr.	Sept. 14, 1952
Frank K. Cochran	Dec. 14, 1955
John Bevec	Jan. 19, 1956
Herbert J. McGlinchey	Jan. 24, 1956
James L. McWherter	Nov. 17, 1960
Frank J. Tiemann	Sept. 23, 1963
Ruth Glenn Pennell	Jan. 6, 1964
Walter J. Scheller	Jan. 6, 1964
C. V. Afflerback	May 23, 1967
Warner DePuy	Dec. 31, 1970
Jack I. Greenblat	Jan. 3, 1972
Earl P. McNair	Jan. 3, 1972
Robert J. Tullio	Jan. 3, 1972
James H. J. Tate (resigned Feb. 28, 1979)	Jan. 6, 1975
Martin D. Bookbinder	Jan. 6, 1975
David J. Batdorf	Mar. 22, 1977
*Gus A. Pedicone	Apr. 14, 1980
Jean E. Kistler	May 20, 1980
LeGree S. Daniels	Jan. 28, 1981
Mary Ann Meloy	May 24, 1983
*Martha Bell Schoeninger	Dec. 12, 1983
*John T. Martino	Jan. 21, 1987

* Incumbent

PENNSYLVANIA TURNPIKE COMMISSION
P.O. Box 8531
Harrisburg, PA 17105

HOWARD YERUSALIM Chairman, Pennsylvania Turnpike Commission

See Department of Transportation for photograph and biographical information.

JAMES J. DODARO Vice Chairman, Pennsylvania Turnpike Commission

James J. Dodaro was born March 8, 1944, in Blawnox, the son of John and Evelyn Vitori Dodaro; grad., Univ. of Pgh. (B.A., pol. sci.) 1966; Duquesne Univ. (J.D.) 1969; attorney; mem., Zappala, Dodaro & Cambest, 1970-79; exec. sec., Allegheny Co. Auth. for Improvements in Municipalities (AIM), 1970-79; admin., Allegheny Co. Hosp. Develop. Auth. (HDA), 1974-79; dir., Allegheny Co. Dept. of Develop., 1979; solicitor, Allegheny Co. Dept. of Law, 1984; solicitor, Comm. Coll. of Allegheny Co., 1985; mem.: bd. dirs., Allegheny Co. Redevelop. Auth.; bd. dirs., McKeesport Area Conf., Inc.; bd. dirs. Pauline Auberle Foundation; bd. dirs., Mon-Yough River Entertainment Cultural Council; Allegheny Co. Bar Assn.; Allegheny Co. Planning Comm.; ISDA Verity Lodge; Italian Cultural & Heritage Soc.; McKeesport Educ. Consortium; White Oak Advisory Com.; Univ. of Pgh., Varsity Letter Club; St. Angela Merici Building Com.; exec. dir., ISDA Cultural Heritage Foundation; confirmed as member, Turnpike Commission, March 27, 1984, and commissioned March 30, 1984; elected Vice Chairman, June 5, 1987; married Carol E. Pogyor; 3 children: James J. Jr., Daniel Louis, and Carolyn Margaret; home address; 119 Victoria Drive, White Oak.

PETER J. CAMIEL Member, Pennsylvania Turnpike Commission

Peter J. Camiel was born Jan. 30, 1910, in Phila., the son of Joseph and Anna Nagurny Camiel; businessman and farmer; mem., Senate of Pennsylvania, 1953-64; chmn., Democratic Co. Exec. Comm. of Phila.; confirmed as mem., Turnpike Commission, July 8, 1975, and commissioned July 11, 1975; married Nina Guman; 3 children: Peter J, Valentine Richard, and Nina Christina; home address: St. James House, 13th & Walnut Sts., Apt. 808, Philadelphia.

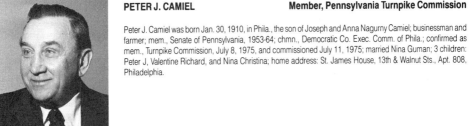

FRANK A. URSOMARSO   Member, Pennsylvania Turnpike Commission

Frank A. Ursomarso was born Sept. 19, 1942, in Phila., the son of Anthony and Agelina Ursomarso; grad., Gettysburg Coll. (B.A. in philosophy) 1964; U.C.L.A. (J.D.) 1967; U.S. Army, military policy officer, Vietnam Vet., awarded Bronze Star Medal, 1967-69; automobile business, 1969-73; staff asst. for Presidents Nixon and Ford, 1973-76; television production coordinator for 1976 Presidential debates; television prod. coordinator/ advance coordinator for Gov. Reagan, Presidential debates, 1980; dir., White House Off. of Communications, 1981; appt. to PA Public Television Network and PA Securities Comm., 1981; appt. chmn., Horse Racing Comm., 1982; advisor to V.P. Bush for V.P. debates, 1984; commissioned as member, Turnpike Commission on Sept. 6, 1984; married former Catherine Sanders; three sons; home address: 476 Cossart Rd., Chadds Ford.

JAMES FRANCIS MALONE, III   Member, Pennsylvania Turnpike Commission

James Francis Malone, III, was born Sept. 12, 1943, in Pgh., the son of James Francis Jr. and Helen Black Malone; grad., Pa. State Univ. and Univ. of Pgh. Schl. of Law; atty., firm of Dickie, McCamey & Chilcote; mem., Allegheny Co., Pa., and Am. Bar Assns.; Allegheny Co. Academy of Trial Lawyers; appointed PA Turnpike Commissioner, Oct. 1, 1985; married Sherry Helfant; 2 children: Robin and Jamie; home address: 24 Edgewood Road, Pittsburgh.

LOUIS R. MARTIN   Executive Director, Pennsylvania Turnpike Commission

Louis R. Martin was born May 10, 1943, in Monongahela, the son of Robert C. and Inez K. Grandy Martin; grad., Monongahela H.S., 1961; Univ. of Pgh. (B.S.M.E.) 1965; Duquesne Univ. Night Schl. (J.D.) 1974; engineer/ lawyer/administrator; mem., Allegheny Co. Bar Assn.; Internatl. Bridge, Tunnel & Turnpike Assn., Inc.; Cumberland Co. Redevelopment Auth., 1978-pres.; Cumb. Co. Housing Auth., 1980-pres; P.I.A.A. and small coll. football official; asst. chief counsel, Pa. Turnpike Comm., 1975; dep. chief counsel, 1977; acting chief counsel, 1980; chief counsel, 1983; appointed Executive Director, Oct. 1, 1985; married Lynda A. Black; 3 children: Robert Edward, Thomas Louis, Jennifer Lynda; home address: 117 Allendale Way, Camp Hill.

The Pennsylvania Turnpike Commission was created by Act No. 211 of 1937 with authority to construct, finance, operate and maintain a toll highway from Middlesex, Cumberland County, to Irwin, Westmoreland County, a distance of 160 miles, opened to traffic October 1, 1940. Today the Turnpike stretches 470 miles across the state from Gateway Interchange at the Ohio Line to the Delaware River Bridge at the New Jersey Line; Northeast Extension from Junction at Norristown to the Scranton Terminus. Act 61 of 1985 authorized the commission to construct, and prioritize, twenty (20) additions and improvements to the existing system.

ADMINISTRATION. The commission consists of five members, four of whom are appointed by the Governor for terms of four (4) years each, while the fifth is the Secretary of Transportation, a member ex-officio. Act 61 temporarily expanded membership of the commission from five to six members. On June 5, 1987, the commission reverted to five members.

POWERS. To determine the line of the Turnpike, with the approval of the Governor; to construct, operate and maintain the same, to issue Turnpike revenue bonds to finance cost of construction, to be paid solely out of revenues; to make necessary rules and regulations for its own government, including traffic rules and regulations; to acquire, lease and dispose of real and personal property; to condemn, if necessary, the land upon which to construct the Turnpike; to enter into all necessary contracts, except that construction contracts shall be approved by the Department of Transportation; to employ engineers, attorneys, and all other personnel and fix their compensation; to fix tolls; to provide for the policing of the Turnpike; and to provide necessary services for its patrons; to sue and be sued.

OPERATIONS. A Turnpike cadre functions on a twenty-four-hour basis under the Executive Director. Overnight and weekend staffing is supervised by a Deputy Executive Director, serving as duty officer, and/or the Executive Director and the necessary operating staff to meet specific weather and traffic conditions. Deputy Executive Directors and other operating staff officers maintain twenty-four-hour contact throughout the Turnpike on an in-house microwave radio system via ten relay towers and controlled from Highspire headquarters at four consoles.

Engineering, supervised by a Deputy Executive Director and Chief Engineer, directs all planning, construction, mapping and electrical operations.

Maintenance, supervised by a Deputy Executive Director with superintendents of an eastern division and a western division, has day-to-day charge of the physical quality of the roadbed, buildings and bridges. Its chief winter function is the swift removal of snow and ice from the roadway and such activity begins immediately upon the onset of a storm. Maintenance operations are localized in nineteen sheds across the Turnpike.

A Deputy Executive Director supervises *Fare Collections* at thirty-eight toll plazas operating through superintendents in eastern, central and western divisions.

Administration is supervised by a Deputy Executive Director whose operations include Administrative Services, Purchasing, Electronic Data Processing, Fare Audit, Safety, Traveler Services and the Communications System. Safety operations include EMT-staffed ambulances at three maintenance locations and First-Responder-staffed units at the other sixteen maintenance locations, all of which are located within twelve minutes of all Turnpike points. The above are supported by contracted, off-Turnpike ambulance, fire and rescue services throughout the Turnpike System. In addition, helicopter ambulance services are available over the entire System.

Traveler Services encompasses supervision, inspection and price monitoring of twenty-two restaurant/gasoline station/tourist service plazas.

Other staff functions under the Executive Director are managed by a Chief legal Counsel, a Comptroller, a Director of Human Resources, and Directors of Public Information and Public Affairs.

Police functions on the Turnpike are managed by Troop "T" of the Pennsylvania State Police which enforces the laws of Pennsylvania and regulations of the Turnpike; all police services are compensated to the state by the non-tax funds collected from Turnpike tolls.

An Operations Review Staff, operating independently as an inhouse "watchdog" is comprised of auditors and accountants and reports directly to the Commission Chairman.

Turnpike bondholders are represented by a fiduciary trustee and by a consulting engineer.

COMMISSION MEMBERS[1]	Appointed Since 1950
David E. Watson.	Mar. 1, 1952
G. Frank McSorley.	Feb. 21, 1955
John B. Byrne.	May 23, 1956
Merrit A. Williamson.	Jan. 29, 1957
Joseph J. Lawler.	Oct. 2, 1957
E. James Trimarchi, Jr.	Oct. 2, 1957
Roy E. Furman.	July 14, 1959
Patrick E. Kerwin.	Aug. 22, 1961
Lester F. Burlein.	Aug. 2, 1963
William A. Meehan.	Nov. 21, 1966
Ray M. Bollinger.	Feb. 7, 1968
Abraham D. Cohn.	Oct. 4, 1972
Egidio Cerilli.	Dec. 11, 1974
Jack I. Greenblat.	Jan. 3, 1975
*Peter J. Camiel.	July 8, 1975
*James J. Dodaro (vice chairman).	Mar. 27, 1984
*Frank A. Ursomarso.	Mar. 27, 1984
*James F. Malone, III.	Oct. 1, 1985
*Howard Yerusalim.	June 5, 1987

[1] *Since the creation of the Pennsylvania Turnpike Commission, secretaries of the Department of Transportation have always served as commission members ex officio.*

* *Current commission members serving ten-year terms, and until successor is qualified.*

THE COMMISSION FOR WOMEN
209 Finance Building
P.O. Box 1323
Harrisburg, PA 17105

Chair: Alma Jacobs; **Vice Chair:** Harriet McGeehan; **Members:** Elizabeth Milder Beh, Dr. Muriel Berman, Ruby Bowe, Mimi Unger Coppersmith, Carol Coren, Faye Z. Dissinger, Pat Halpin, Rose Mary Herrero, Leslye Herrmann, Issie Jenkins, Esq., Christine B. Lang, Dr. Jacinta Mann, Veronica McDonough, Senator Jeanette Reibman, Juilet C. Rowland, Doris A. Smith, Connie Soldano, Pat Waddington.

The Commission for Women, in cooperation with other state and nongovernmental agencies, works to ensure that Pennsylvania women have equal opportunities and treatment in all areas of life.

The director is appointed by the Governor to act as state government's advocate for women, to develop and implement policies, to cooperate with and enlist the support of appropriate agencies, and widely to disseminate information concerning women.

Commission members, numbering 15 to 21, are appointed by the Governor to one or two-year terms and serve without salary. They meet at least four times a year to advise the director on policy and to present the concerns of their constituency.

INTERSTATE AGENCIES

In order to promote shared interests and encourage mutual cooperation with other states, Pennsylvania has entered into a number of interstate compacts and agreements. Such arrangements serve to foster the continued planning and protection of joint resources and to discourage the fragmentation and duplication of the respective states' programs.

Brandywine River Valley Compact. The Department of Environmental Resources is authorized to act on behalf of the Commonwealth.

Delaware River Basin Compact. Governors of Signatory states ex officio (Delaware, New Jersey, Pennsylvania and New York) and one commissioner appointed by the President of the United States.

Delaware River Joint Toll Bridge Commission. Auditor General, State Treasurer, Secretary of Transportation and two members appointed by Governor.

Delaware River Joint Commission. Eight Pennsylvania members: Auditor General and State Treasurer ex officio, and six members appointed by Governor.

Delaware Valley Urban Area Compact. Eleven Pennsylvania members: Secretary of Transportation, ex officio; Executive Director of State Planning Board, ex officio; an appointee of Governor; two legislative members, one from the House of Representatives and one from the Senate; each of whom must reside within the Delaware Valley urban area; representative each from counties of Bucks, Chester, Delaware and Montgomery and the cities of Philadelphia and Chester.

Atlantic States Marine Fisheries Compact. Three members: Executive Director of Pennsylvania Fish Commission, ex officio; a member of the General Assembly jointly appointed by the President pro tempore of the Senate and the Speaker of the House of Representatives; and a citizen appointed by the Governor.

Interstate Compact for Education. (Education Commission of the States). Seven members: Governor, four members of the General Assembly and two appointees of Governor.

Great Lakes Basin Compact. Three members appointed by Governor; reimbursement for expenses.

Interstate Commission on the Potomic River Basin. Three members: Secretary of Environmental Resources, a member of the General Assembly, and a third member named by the Governor.

Interstate Compact to Conserve Oil and Gas. The Governor or his designated representative.

Ohio River Valley Water Sanitation Compact. Three members: Secretary of Health, ex officio, and two members appointed by Governor.

Susquehanna River Basin Compact. The Governor or his designated representative (presently the Secretary of Environmental Resources).

Wheeling Creek Watershed Protection and Flood Prevention District Compact. Pennsylvania members: two appointed by each of the Boards of County Commissioners of Greene and Washington Counties, one to be selected from the members of each board and one to be appointed by Governor from membership of the Water and Power Resources Board and a non-resident of either of those two counties.

Appalachian Regional Commission. A 13-state compact entered into by: Alabama, Georgia, Kentucky, Maryland, Mississippi, New York, North Carolina, Ohio, Pennsylvania, South Carolina, Tennessee, Virginia and West Virginia. Pennsylvania representative on the commission is the Governor or his designee. (Each state member shall be the Governor who may appoint a single alternate from his cabinet or staff.)

Interstate Civil Defense and Disaster Compact. The directors of civil defense of all party states constitute a committee.

Interstate Compact for Supervision of Parolees and Probationers. Governor designates an officer.

Interstate Corrections Compact. Attorney General is authorized and directed to do all things necessary to carry out the compact.

Interstate High Speed Inter-City Rail Passenger Network Compact. Three representatives from Pennsylvania: One appointed by Speaker of House, one appointed by President pro tempore of Senate and an ex officio representative appointed by the Governor.

JUDICIARY

SECTION 5 - JUDICIARY

COURTS OF THE COMMONWEALTH OF PENNSYLVANIA

Brief History
Composition
Powers and Duties

The history of Pennsylvania courts is one of long evolution and has its roots in England's judicial system.

Prior to the State Constitution of 1776, there existed in Pennsylvania a collection of courts, some inherited from the rule of the Duke of York (1664-1673), some established by William Penn, and some — such as the Pennsylvania Supreme Court — created by Pennsylvania's Provincial Assembly. Although attempts were made from time to time to create a unified system which would define and organize the powers and jurisdictions of the several courts, these attempts were often nullified in England. It was not until the Constitution of 1776, which established in each county courts of sessions, common pleas and orphans' courts, that Pennsylvania saw the beginning of a statewide framework for the development of its judicial system.

The Constitution of 1790 furthered this development, grouping the counties into judicial districts and providing president judges for the common pleas courts in those districts to ease the burden of the Supreme Court. In addition to the common pleas courts, the Constitution also vested the judicial powers of the Commonwealth in the Supreme Court, Courts of Oyer and Terminer and General Jail Delivery, Orphans' Courts, Courts of the Quarter Sessions of the peace, and in justices of the peace. This Constitution also made the judiciary appointive in nature.

The Constitutions of 1838 and 1874 effected changes in the jurisdiction, tenure and election or appointment of members of the judiciary, but the basic structure created by the Constitution of 1790 remained essentially unchanged.

The Constitution of 1968 initiated many judicial reforms and reorganized the judiciary under a Unified Judicial System consisting of the Supreme, Superior and Commonwealth Courts, Courts of Common Pleas, Community Courts, Philadelphia Municipal Court, Pittsburgh Magistrates Court, Traffic Court of Philadelphia, Justices of the Peace (now called "District Justices") and "such other courts as may be provided by law." Thus the stage was set for coordinated management, by the Supreme Court, of all courts as a part of a single, integrated system.

The 1968 Constitution also established, for the first time in the state's history, a constitutional right of appeal in all cases, whether they involve courts of record, the minor judiciary or state agencies.

The new Constitution also provided for the composition of each court and for the qualifications, election, tenure and compensation of justices, judges and district justices.

Judges: Qualifications, Election, Tenure, Vacancies

In addition to certain basic requirements such as citizenship and residency, judges are subject to strict standards of conduct and may be removed, suspended or otherwise disciplined for misconduct in office. All major court judges within the system are elected to ten-year terms. Lower court judges, including Philadelphia's Municipal and Traffic Courts and district justices, are elected to terms of six years, and judges of Pittsburgh Magistrates Court, are appointed to four-year terms by the mayor. Other vacancies are filled by gubernatorial appointment, subject to Senate confirmation; appointees are required to run for election in the first municipal election ten or more months after their appointment.

The "merit retention" provision allows judges to run for reelection on a "yes - no" vote, without ballot reference to political affiliation. This provision was designed to remove them from pressures of the political arena once they serve their first term of office.

Mandatory retirement age for judges is 70, although retired judges may continue to serve in a "retired active" status in order to ease court backlogs.

Chief Justice and President Judges

The Chief Justice of Pennsylvania and the president judges of all other courts of seven or fewer judges shall be those judges in longest continuous service on those courts. The one exception to this is the president judge of the Philadelphia Traffic Court, who is appointed to this position by the Governor. In courts of eight or more judges, the judges select from their ranks a president judge, who serves in that capacity for five years.

Jurisdiction

A court's jurisdiction refers to those cases falling within the court's right to hear. Original jurisdiction refers to those cases heard in the first instance; appellate jurisdiction, to those cases heard on appeal from a lower court.

The new Judicial Code (42 Pa. C.S.) provides for the organization and jurisdiction of all courts within the system.

Additionally, under the Constitution of 1968, the Supreme Court is empowered to assign or reassign classes of actions or appeals among the several courts "as the needs of justice shall require."

SUPREME COURT

History

Established by the Provincial Assembly's Judiciary Act of May 22, 1722, the Supreme Court of Pennsylvania is the oldest appellate court in the nation, predating the United States Supreme Court by sixty-seven years.

It is the highest court of the Commonwealth and the repository of the supreme judicial power of the state.

Since its creation, the Court has experienced changes in the number of justices, their qualifications and tenure. The 1722 Act established a court composed of one chief justice and two associate justices who would hold two sessions a year in Philadelphia and go on circuit to try cases throughout the state. In 1767, the number of justices was increased to a total of four; in 1809, the number was reduced from four to three; in 1826, the Court was increased to five justices, and in 1874 to seven, the present number.

The Supreme Court was given constitutional status under the Constitution of 1776, which also provided for appointment of justices by the president of the Provincial Council to seven-year terms, removable for "misbehavior." The Constitution of 1790 provided for life tenure based on "good behavior." The Constitution of 1838 fixed tenure at fifteen years. An 1850 Constitutional amendment made the entire judiciary elective, a standard which prevails today. The Constitution of 1874 assured minority party representation on the Court by designating the method of electing justices, increased their tenure to 21 years, and established a limited original jurisdiction for the Court.

The Constitution of 1968, in establishing the Unified Judicial System, gave the Supreme Court broad supervisory and administrative powers over that system. (See Court Administration.) Additionally, it fixed the tenure of justices at ten-year terms.

Composition

The Supreme Court of Pennsylvania is composed of seven justices, elected to terms of ten years; the justice with the longest continuous service presides as Chief Justice. Vacancies on the Court are filled by gubernatorial appointment, subject to Senate confirmation.

Jurisdiction

The Judicial Code establishes the original and appellate jurisdictions of the Supreme Court.

The Supreme Court holds *original* (but not exclusive) *jurisdiction* in cases of habeas corpus, mandamus or prohibition to courts of inferior jurisdiction, and cases of quo warranto (questions of authority) as to any officer of statewide jurisdiction.

The Supreme Court's *appellate jurisdiction* includes those cases it hears as a matter of right and those it hears upon its own discretion. Cases which may be appealed to the Court as a matter of right are those from Commonwealth Court originating in that court; appeals from final orders of common pleas courts in certain classes of cases (listed below); and appeals from final orders of certain constitutional and judicial agencies (listed below).

Appeals heard from final orders of Common Pleas Court include cases involving: (1) matters prescribed by general rule; (2) the right to public office; (3) matters where the qualifications; tenure or right to serve or the manner of service of any member of the judiciary is in question; (4) review of death sentences; (5) supersession of a district attorney by the attorney general or by a court; (6) matters where the right or power of the Commonwealth or any political subdivision to create or issue indebtedness is in question; (7) statutes and rules held unconstitutional by the courts of common pleas; and (8) matters where the right to practice law is involved.

The Supreme Court has exclusive jurisdiction of appeals from final orders of the following agencies: (1) Legislative Reapportionment Commission; (2) Judicial Inquiry and Review Board; (3) the agency empowered to certify members of the Minor Judiciary; (4) the agency empowered to admit or recommend the admission of persons to the bar and the practice of law (Pennsylvania Board of Law Examiners) and (5) the agency vested with the power to discipline or recommend discipline of attorneys-at-law (Disciplinary Board of the Supreme Court of Pennsylvania); also within its appellate jurisdiction, in the Court's discretion, there may be allowances of appeal to review certain determinations by the Superior and Commonwealth Courts.

Under its power of *extraordinary jurisdiction,* the Court may, on its own motion or upon petition of any party, assume jurisdiction of a case pending before any court or district justice involving an issue of immediate public importance.

SUPERIOR COURT

History and Composition

Pennsylvania's Superior Court was created by the General Assembly in 1895 in order to ease the burden of the Supreme Court, thus giving Pennsylvania two appellate courts with separate jurisdictions. In 1980 an amendment was passed which increased the number of judges sitting on this Court from seven to fifteen. The judges are elected to ten-year terms. In January 1986, Judge Vincent A. Cirillo was elected President Judge, by vote of the Court, for a five-year term.

Jurisdiction

The Superior Court has limited original jurisdiction. Its appellate jurisdiction extends to appeals from final orders of Common Pleas Courts in those matters not within the jurisdiction of either the Supreme or Commonwealth Courts.

COMMONWEALTH COURT

History

The Commonwealth Court, which came into existence on January 1, 1970, was created by the Constitution of 1968. The Constitutional Convention intended to create a court which would not only serve as a third appellate court, reducing the workload of the Supreme and Superior Courts, but also a court which would hear and try initial jurisdiction cases involving actions by or against the Commonwealth.

Since 1870, such cases had been heard by the Dauphin County Court of Common Pleas, sitting in Harrisburg. Over the years, however, the growth of state agencies and the corrresponding rise in litigation involving the Commonwealth created an increasingly heavy caseload for the Commonwealth docket of Dauphin County Court. The need for a new and separate court to handle such matters, as well as provide an appellate court for government-related appeals, became apparent, and so the Constitutional Convention provided for the creation of a Commonwealth Court, leaving its structure and jurisdiction to the General Assembly.

Composition

The Constitution of 1968 provided that Commonwealth Court "shall consist of the number of judges . . . as provided by law," thus allowing for addition of judges, as needed, by the Legislature.

The Commonwealth Court Act of 1970 (P.L. 1969) originally provided for a court of seven judges, elected to ten-year terms. The Judicial Code now provides for a court of nine judges.

Jurisdiction

Commonwealth Court is possessed of both original and appellate jurisdiction. The Court has exclusive original jurisdiction of Election Code matters as well as matters arising in the Office of the Secretary of the Commonwealth relating to statewide office except nomination and election contests which are within the jurisdiction of another tribunal. *Original jurisdiction* includes civil actions against the Commonwealth, with the exception of writs of habeas corpus; eminent domain proceedings and actions in which sovereign immunity has been waived; and civil actions by the Commonwealth (concurrent with Common Pleas Courts), except eminent domain proceedings.

The Court's *appellate jurisdiction* encompasses primarily direct appeals from final decisions of state administrative agencies (unless the Courts of Common Pleas have jurisdiction), and also appeals from Courts of Common Pleas (unless the Supreme Court has jurisdiction) in cases involving: 1) civil actions to which the Commonwealth is a party with certain exceptions; 2) criminal actions arising from violations of regulations of state administrative agencies, or from violations of regulatory statutes administered by a state agency subject to the Administrative Agency Law; 3) secondary review (after a Court of Common Pleas) of certain appeals from Commonwealth agencies; 4) interpretation of home rule charters, local ordinances and legislative acts governing local political subdivisions, and appeals from local administrative agencies; 5) certain nonprofit corporation matters; and 6) eminent domain proceedings.

Also within the Court's appellate jurisdiction is review of arbitrators' awards in disputes between the Commonwealth and its employees.

COURTS OF COMMON PLEAS

History

Courts of Common Pleas have existed in Pennsylvania at least since the Constitution of 1776, under which they were given constitutional status.

Prior to the Constitution of 1968, there existed in addition to Courts of Common Pleas — Courts of Oyer and Terminer and General Jail Delivery, Quarter Sessions of the Peace and Orphans' Courts. The new Constitution abolished these latter separate courts and incorporated them into existing Common Pleas Courts as divisions therein.

Composition

Pennsylvania's 67 counties are divided into 60 judicial districts. Each district has a Court of Common Pleas consisting of a number of judges and divisions as determined by the Legislature. The Legislature, with the consent of the Supreme Court, also has the latitude to establish new districts as deemed appropriate. Judges are elected to terms of ten years.

Jurisdiction

Under the Constitution of 1776, the Courts of Common Pleas were given the powers "usually exercised by such courts," a recognition that such a jurisdiction existed and was commonly accepted at that time.

Under the 1968 Constitution, the Courts of Common Pleas have "unlimited original jurisdiction in all cases except as may otherwise be provided by law." The exceptions are the limited original jurisdictions of Supreme and Commonwealth Courts described above.

Appellate jurisdiction of the Common Pleas Courts extends to appeals from final orders of the minor judiciary and appeals from certain state and most local governmental agencies.

SPECIAL COURTS

Special Courts

At the first level in the court system are the special courts. In counties other than Philadelphia, these courts are presided over by district justices, formerly known as justices of the peace. District justices have jurisdiction over summary criminal cases, landlord-tenant matters and other civil actions where the amount claimed does not exceed $4,000. They may also accept guilty pleas of misdemeanors of the third degree under certain circumstances. District justices also have jurisdiction to issue warrants and to hold arraignments and preliminary hearings in all criminal cases.

Although district justices do not have to be lawyers, they must take a course and pass a qualifying examination before taking office. They also must take one week of continuing education each year while they remain in office.

As of 1985, there were 527 (complement — 550) district justices on the payroll.

In Philadelphia, the special courts are the Municipal Court and the Traffic Court. The Municipal Court is the only special court of Pennsylvania which is a court of record. It has 22 judges, all of whom must be lawyers. The Municipal Court has jurisdiction over all criminal offenses (other than summary traffic offenses) which are punishable by a term of imprisonment not exceeding five years. Otherwise, the Municipal Court has the same jurisdiction as the district justices, except that civil actions in that court are limited to those cases where the amount claimed does not exceed $1,000.

The Philadelphia Traffic Court is composed of six judges who need not be lawyers. It has jurisdiction over all summary offenses under the Motor Vehicle Code (Title 75 of the Pennsylvania Consolidated Statutes) and offenses under city ordinances enacted pursuant to the Vehicle Code.

The City of Pittsburgh has six police magistrates in addition to the county district justices. These justices are appointed by the Pittsburgh Mayor. They are the only non-elective judiciary in Pennsylvania. These magistrates, who need not be lawyers, have jurisdiction to issue arrest warrants and hold arraignments and preliminary hearings for all criminal offenses occurring within the city. They also have jurisdiction over criminal cases brought by the city police for the violations of city ordinances and other specified offenses, including claims for fines and penalties imposed by any city ordinance or by any ordinance or regulation relating to health and housing and enforced by a county health department. In addition, they may hear summary cases arising under any such ordinances or regulations. The police magistrates also sit on the Pittsburgh Housing Court and on the Pittsburgh Traffic Court which has the same jurisdiction as the Philadelphia Traffic Court.

There are no jury trials in the special courts. However, appeals from special court judgments may be taken to the county Common Pleas Court where the case is heard *de novo.*

District Justices

The office of justice of the peace existed as early as 1776, when the State Constitution of that year first provided for their election.

The Constitution of 1968 effected a major reorganization of the minor judiciary, especially with respect to justices of the peace.

The reorganization called for establishment of the number and classes of magisterial districts, replacement of the fee system with salaried positions, compulsory education and training for prospective district justices (see Minor Judiciary Education Board, below), a reduction in the number of district justices and their supervision by the Supreme Court.

The 1968 Constitution mandated the classification of magisterial districts solely on the basis of population and population density; districts may be added or eliminated as needed for the efficient administration of justice. There are no district justices in the City and County of Philadelphia, their jurisdiction being exercised by Philadelphia's Municipal and Traffic Courts. Each district contains one district justice who is elected to a six-year term, and whose salary is determined by law. Vacancies are filled by gubernatorial appointment, subject to Senate confirmation.

Minor Judiciary Education Board

Article V of the Constitution of the Commonwealth of Pennsylvania and the Judicial Code require individuals seeking to take office as District Justices to be certified as qualified to perform the duties of the office.

The Minor Judiciary Education Board is responsible for prescribing and approving the subject matter and the examination for the courses of instruction which prospective district justices must successfully complete. The Administrative Office of Pennsylvania Courts serves as the staff of the Board and, as such, administers the courses of instruction and conducts the certifying examination as directed by the Board.

The basic District Justice course of instruction is four weeks in duration. General subject areas covered are: criminal law, civil law, evidence, judicial procedure and administration, motor vehicle law, the Controlled Substance, Drug, Device and Cosmetic Act, ethics and moot courts. The basic Philadelphia Traffic Court Judge course of instruction is twenty hours in length. General subject areas covered are: evidence, judicial procedure and administration, motor vehicle law, and ethics. In addition, the Board revises yearly the curriculum for the mandated continuing education program for all district justices.

The Board is composed of seven members appointed by the Governor with the consent of two-thirds of the Senate.

COURT ADMINISTRATION

Administrative Office of Pennsylvania Courts

Under Article V of the Constitution of 1968, the Supreme Court was given powers of general supervision and administrative authority over all courts and district justices, including the power to temporarily assign judges and district justices from one court or district to another; to assign or reassign classes of actions or appeals among the several courts; to prescribe the practice, procedures and conduct of all courts and officers thereof; and to appoint a court administrator.

As supervisor of the Administrative Office of Pennsylvania Courts, the Court Administrator of Pennsylvania is responsible for the prompt and proper disposition of the business of all courts, including district justices. Among the functions of the Administrative Office are: review of the operations of the entire court system for efficiency, and formulation of recommendations for its improvement; review of the administrative and business methods employed by all courts; collection of financial and statistical data on the courts; examination of court dockets with recommendations for expedition of litigation; budget preparation and authorization of expenditures; purchasing; central record-keeping; preparation of educational and training materials for the system's personnel; and investigation of complaints from the public regarding the courts' operations.

Related Court Agencies

Also within the aegis of the Supreme Court are the court committees and related court agencies, which help establish judicial policy, formulate rules of court procedure, investigate charges of misconduct and establish standards for the practice of law. These agencies are: the Judicial Council; Civil, Criminal and Minor Court Civil Procedural Rules Committees; Pennsylvania Board of Law Examiners; the Disciplinary Board of the Supreme Court; Judicial Inquiry and Review Board (a constitutional agency); Supreme Court Committee for Proposed Standard Jury Instruction; Supreme Court Orphans' Court Rules Committee; and the Advisory Committee on Appellate Court Rules. In addition, the Supreme Court created the Pennsylvania Client Security Fund Board which aids in ameliorating losses caused to individuals by defalcating attorneys.

Independent of the Supreme Court is the Judicial Auditing Agency which periodically audits the financial affairs of the unified judicial system.

PENNSYLVANIA JUDICIARY

SUPREME COURT

Name	Year Commissioned	Expiration Date, 1st Monday in January
Robert N.C. Nix, Jr., C.J.	1972	1992
Rolf Larsen	1978	1988
John P. Flaherty, Jr.	1979	1990
James T. McDermott	1982	1992
William D. Hutchinson	1982	1992
Stephen A. Zappala	1983	1993
Nicholas P. Papadakos	1984	1994

Full Complement 7

COMMONWEALTH COURT

Name	Year Commissioned	Expiration Date, 1st Monday in January
James Crumlish, Jr., P.J.	1978	1988
David W. Craig	1980	1990
John A. MacPhail	1980	1990
Joseph T. Doyle	1982	1992
Francis A. Barry	1983	1994
J. Gardner Colins	1984	1994
Madaline Palladino	1984	1994

Complement 9
Vacancy 2

Senior Judge

Genevieve Blatt

SUPERIOR COURT

Name	Year Commissioned	Expiration Date, 1st Monday in January
Vincent A. Cirillo, P.J.	1982	1992
James R. Cavanaugh	1980	1990
John G. Brosky	1980	1990
James E. Rowley	1982	1992
Donald E. Wieand	1982	1992
Stephen J. McEwen, Jr.	1982	1992
Peter Paul Olszewski	1984	1994
Joseph A. Del Sole	1984	1994
Frank J. Montemuro, Jr.	1984	1994
Phyllis W. Beck	1984	1994
Patrick R. Tamilia	1984	1994
Zoran Popovich	1980	1996
Justin M. Johnson	1980	1996
John T. J. Kelly, Jr.	1986	1996

Complement 15
Vacancy 1

Senior Judges

G. Harold Watkins
Harry M. Montgomery
J. Sydney Hoffman
William F. Cercone
John P. Hester

COURTS OF COMMON PLEAS

FIRST JUDICIAL DISTRICT

Court of Common Pleas
PHILADELPHIA COUNTY (Philadelphia)

Name	Year Commenced	Expiration Date, 1st Monday in January
Edward J. Bradley, P.J.	1965	1996
Nicholas A. Cipriani, A.J.	1970	1990
Edward J. Blake, A.J.	1971	1994
Edmund S. Pawelec, A.J.	1972	1992
Juanita K. Stout	1959	1990
Theodore S. Gutowicz	1965	1996
Joseph C. Bruno	1968	1990

Name	Year Commissioned	Expiration Date, 1st Monday in January
Robert A. Latrone	1969	1994
Julian F. King	1971	1994
Joseph P. McCabe, Jr.	1971	1996
Norman A. Jenkins	1971	1994
Lisa A. Richette	1971	1994
Calvin T. Wilson	1971	1994
Jerome A. Zaleski	1971	1994
Paul Ribner	1971	1994
Curtis C. Carson, Jr.	1971	1994
William Porter	1971	1994
Armand Della Porta	1971	1994
Charles P. Mirarchi, Jr.	1972	1992

Name	Year Commis-sioned	Expiration Date, 1st Monday in January
Samuel M. Lehrer	1973	1992
Lawrence Prattis	1974	1996
Albert F. Sabo	1974	1994
Alex Bonavitacola	1974	1994
Judith J. Jamison	1974	1994
Marvin R. Halbert	1974	1994
David N. Savitt	1974	1994
Angelo A. Guarino	1974	1994
Francis A. Biunno	1974	1994
Charles A. Lord	1974	1994
Levan Gordon	1974	1990
Berel Caesar	1974	1988
Charles L. Durham	1974	1996
Joseph P. Braig	1976	1996
Richard B. Klein	1976	1996
Murray C. Goldman	1976	1996
Alfred J. Dibona, Jr.	1976	1996
Kenneth S. Harris	1976	1994
Bernard J. Goodheart	1976	1996
Lynne M. Abraham	1976	1990
Abraham J. Gafni	1977	1988
Nicholas M. D'Alessandro	1977	1990
I. R. Kremer	1977	1988
Ricardo C. Jackson	1978	1992
Louis G. Hill	1978	1990
Thomas A. White	1978	1988
Michael E. Wallace	1978	1988
John J. Chiovero	1980	1990
Mitchell S. Lipschutz	1980	1996
James D. McCrudden	1980	1992
Leon Katz	1980	1992
Eugene H. Clarke, Jr.	1980	1992
Leonard A. Ivanoski	1980	1992
Victor J. Dinubile, Jr.	1981	1992
John L. Braxton	1981	1992
Nelson A. Diaz	1981	1992
William J. Mazzola	1982	1992
Eugene E. Maier	1982	1992
Bernard J. Avellino	1982	1992
Michael R. Stiles	1983	1994
William J. Manfredi	1983	1994
Joseph D. O'Keefe	1984	1994
Albert W. Sheppard, Jr.	1984	1994
Thomas D. Watkins	1984	1994
Tama M. Clark	1984	1994
John J. Poserina, Jr.	1984	1994
Sandra M. Moss	1984	1994
Theodore A. McKee	1984	1994
Frederica A. Massiah-Jackson	1984	1994
Carolyn E. Temin	1984	1994
Frank M. Jackson	1984	1996
Mary Rose F. Cunningham	1986	1996
Abram F. Reynolds	1986	1996
Esther R. Sylvester	1986	1996
Stephen E. Levin	1986	1996
Edward R. Summers	1987	1988
Jane C. Greenspan	1987	1990
Mark I. Bernstein	1987	1988

Complement 85
Vacancies 8

Municipal Court
PHILADELPHIA

Name	Year Commis-sioned	Expiration Date, 1st Monday in January
Alan K. Silberstein, P.J.	1976	1988

Name	Year Commis-sioned	Expiration Date, 1st Monday in January
Joseph R. Glancey	1969	1988
Charles J. Margiotti, Jr.	1969	1992
Michael J. Conroy	1969	1992
J. Earl Simmons, Jr.	1970	1988
Francis P. Cosgrove	1974	1992
Edward G. Mekel	1974	1992
Meyer Charles Rose	1976	1988
Arthur S. Kafrissen	1978	1990
Thomas J. McCormack	1980	1992
William J. Brady, Jr.	1980	1988
Matthew F. Coppolino	1982	1990
Louis J. Presenza	1982	1990
Morton Krase	1984	1992
Ronald B. Merriweather	1984	1990
Thomas E. Dempsey	1984	1992
Barbara S. Gilbert	1986	1992
Lydia Y. Kirkland	1986	1992
Harvey W. Robbins	1986	1988
William A. King, Jr.	1986	1988

Complement 22
Vacancies 2

Traffic Court
PHILADELPHIA

Name	Year Commis-sioned	Expiration Date, 1st Monday in January
George Twardy, P.J.	1969	1990
Salvatore DeMeo	1969	1988
Raymond A. Malone	1969	1988
Charles H. Cuffeld	1982	1988
Lillian H. Podgorski	1982	1988
Dominic M. Cermele	1982	1988

Full Complement 6

SECOND JUDICIAL DISTRICT

Court of Common Pleas
LANCASTER COUNTY (Lancaster)

Name	Year Commis-sioned	Expiration Date, 1st Monday in January
D. Richard Eckman, P.J.	1978	1988
Ronald L. Buckwalter	1980	1990
Wayne G. Hummer, Jr.	1980	1990
Michael J. Perezous	1982	1992
Michael A. Georgelis	1986	1996
Louise G. Herr	1986	1996
Louis J. Farina	1986	1996

Full Complement 7

THIRD JUDICIAL DISTRICT

Court of Common Pleas
NORTHAMPTON COUNTY (Easton)

Name	Year Commis-sioned	Expiration Date, 1st Monday in January
Alfred T. Williams, Jr., P.J.	1968	1988
Richard D. Grifo	1968	1990
Michael V. Franciosa	1970	1990
Franklin S. Van Antwerpen	1979	1992
Robert A. Freedberg	1980	1990

Complement 6
Vacancy 1

Name	Year Commenced	Expiration Date, 1st Monday in January

FOURTH JUDICIAL DISTRICT

Court of Common Pleas
TIOGA COUNTY (Wellsboro)

Name	Year Commenced	Expiration
Robert M. Kemp, P.J.	1972	1992

Full Complement 1

FIFTH JUDICIAL DISTRICT

Court of Common Pleas
ALLEGHENY COUNTY (Pittsburgh)

Name	Year Commenced	Expiration
Michael J. O'Malley, P.J.	1971	1994
Robert E. Dauer, A.J.	1972	1996
Paul R. Zavarella, A.J.	1974	1994
R. Stanton Wettick, Jr., A.J.	1976	1988
Ralph J. Cappy, A.J.	1978	1990
Ralph H. Smith, Jr.	1960	1992
Joseph H. Ridge	1962	1992
I. Martin Wekselman	1962	1988
J. Warren Watson	1966	1996
Silvestri Silvestri	1968	1990
John L. Musmanno	1970	1992
Robert A. Doyle	1970	1992
James F. Clarke	1971	1994
Marion K. Finkelhor	1972	1992
John W. O'Brien	1972	1992
Eunice Ross	1972	1994
Livingstone M. Johnson	1973	1996
James R. McGregor	1974	1996
George H. Ross	1975	1996
S. Louis Farino	1975	1988
Bernard J. McGowan	1976	1996
Richard G. Zeleznik	1976	1996
Gerard M. Bigley	1978	1988
Lawrence W. Kaplan	1978	1990
Eugene B. Strassburger, III	1978	1990
Leonard C. Staisey	1980	1990
Raymond A. Novak	1980	1992
William L. Standish	1980	1992
Bernard L. McGinley	1982	1992
David S. Cercone	1982	1996
Alan S. Penkower	1983	1984
Robert P. Horgos	1983	1994
James H. McLean	1984	1996
Robert A. Kelly	1984	1996
Walter R. Little	1986	1996
Donna J. McDaniel	1986	1996
Joseph A. Jaffe	1986	1996
Judith L. Friedman	1986	1996
Patrick McFalls	1986	1996

Complement 41
Vacancies 2

SIXTH JUDICIAL DISTRICT

Court of Common Pleas
ERIE COUNTY (Erie)

Name	Year Commenced	Expiration
William E. Pfadt, P.J.	1970	1994

Name	Year Commenced	Expiration
Fred P. Anthony	1972	1992
Richard L. Nygaard	1981	1994
Jessamine S. Jiuliante	1981	1992
Roger M. Fischer	1983	1994
Michael T. Joyce	1986	1996
George Levin	1986	1996
Shad F. Connelly	1986	1996

Full Complement 8

SEVENTH JUDICIAL DISTRICT

Court of Common Pleas
BUCKS COUNTY (Doylestown)

Name	Year Commenced	Expiration
Isaac S. Garb, P.J.	1966	1988
Paul R. Beckert	1964	1996
William Hart Rufe, III	1971	1994
Oscar S. Bortner	1977	1990
George T. Kelton	1977	1988
Kenneth G. Biehn	1979	1992
Edward G. Biester, Jr.	1980	1992
Leonard B. Sokolove	1981	1992
Ward F. Clark	1986	1996
Michael J. Kane	1986	1996

Complement 11
Vacancy 1

EIGHTH JUDICIAL DISTRICT

Court of Common Pleas
NORTHUMBERLAND COUNTY (Sunbury)

Name	Year Commenced	Expiration
Samuel C. Ranck, P.J.	1976	1986
James J. Rosini	1986	1988

Full Complement 2

NINTH JUDICIAL DISTRICT

Court of Common Pleas
CUMBERLAND COUNTY (Carlisle)

Name	Year Commenced	Expiration
Harold E. Sheely, P.J.	1978	1988
George E. Hoffer	1980	1990
Edgar B. Bayley	1984	1994
Kevin A. Hess	1986	1996

Full Complement 4

TENTH JUDICIAL DISTRICT

Court of Common Pleas
WESTMORELAND COUNTY (Greensburg)

Name	Year Commenced	Expiration
Gilfert M. Mihalich, P.J.	1972	1992
Joseph A. Hudock	1978	1988
Charles H. Loughran	1978	1988
Charles E. Marker	1980	1990
Daniel J. Ackerman	1980	1992
Bernard F. Scherer	1982	1992
Donetta W. Ambrose	1982	1992
John E. Blahovec	1986	1996
Gary P. Caruso	1986	1996

Full Complement 9

Name	Year Commenced	Expiration Date, 1st Monday in January	Name	Year Commenced	Expiration Date, 1st Monday in January

ELEVENTH JUDICIAL DISTRICT

Court of Common Pleas
LUZERNE COUNTY (Wilkes-Barre)

Robert J. Hourigan, P.J.	1968	1988
Bernard C. Brominski	1958	1990
Arthur D. Dalessandro.	1971	1994
Bernard J. Podcasy.	1972	1992
Patrick J. Toole, Jr.	1978	1990
Chester B. Muroski	1982	1992
Gifford S. Cappellini	1986	1996

Full Complement 7

TWELFTH JUDICIAL DISTRICT

Court of Common Pleas
DAUPHIN COUNTY (Harrisburg)

Lee F. Swope, P.J.	1961	1992
Warren G. Morgan.	1970	1992
John C. Dowling	1970	1992
Clarence C. Morrison	1980	1992
Herbert A. Schaffner	1984	1994
Sebastian D. Natale	1986	1996

Full Complement 6

THIRTEENTH JUDICIAL DISTRICT

Court of Common Pleas
GREENE COUNTY (Waynesburg)

H. Terry Grimes, P.J.	1986	1996

Full Complement 1

FOURTEENTH JUDICIAL DISTRICT

Court of Common Pleas
FAYETTE COUNTY (Uniontown)

Richard D. Cicchetti, P.J.	1974	1994
Fred C. Adams	1975	1996
Conrad B. Capuzzi	1977	1990
William J. Franks.	1978	1988

Full Complement 4

FIFTEENTH JUDICIAL DISTRICT

Court of Common Pleas
CHESTER COUNTY (West Chester)

Leonard Sugerman, P.J.	1973	1994
Robert S. Gawthrop, III	1978	1988
Lawrence E. Wood	1980	1992
M. Joseph Melody, Jr.	1981	1992
Charles B. Smith	1981	1992
Alexander Endy.	1984	1996
Thomas C. Gavin	1986	1996
J. Curtis Joyner	1987	1988

Full Complement 8

SIXTEENTH JUDICIAL DISTRICT

Court of Common Pleas
SOMERSET COUNTY (Somerset)

Norman A. Shaulis, P.J.	1972	1994
Eugene E. Fike II.	1986	1996

Full Complement 2

SEVENTEENTH JUDICIAL DISTRICT

Court of Common Pleas
UNION & SNYDER COUNTIES
(Lewisburg, Middleburg)

James F. McClure, Jr., P.J.	1984	1996
Wayne A. Bromfield.	1986	1996

Full Complement 2

EIGHTEENTH JUDICIAL DISTRICT

Court of Common Pleas
CLARION COUNTY (Clarion)

Merle E. Wiser, P.J.	1980	1990

Full Complement 1

NINETEENTH JUDICIAL DISTRICT

Court of Common Pleas
YORK COUNTY (York)

Joseph E. Erb, P.J.	1974	1996
Emanuel A. Cassimatis.	1978	1988
John T. Miller.	1980	1992
John F. Rauhauser, Jr.	1982	1992
Richard H. Horn	1986	1996
John H. Chronister	1987	1988

Complement 7
Vacancy 1

TWENTIETH JUDICIAL DISTRICT

Court of Common Pleas
HUNTINGDON COUNTY (Huntingdon)

Newton C. Taylor, P.J.	1980	1992

Full Complement 1

TWENTY-FIRST JUDICIAL DISTRICT

Court of Common Pleas
SCHUYLKILL COUNTY (Pottsville)

George W. Heffner, P.J.	1968	1988
Wilbur H. Rubright.	1957	1994
John E. Lavelle	1972	1992
Joseph F. McCloskey	1975	1988
Donald D. Dolbin.	1978	1988

Full Complement 5

Name	Year Commenced	Expiration Date, 1st Monday in January

TWENTY-SECOND JUDICIAL DISTRICT

Court of Common Pleas
WAYNE COUNTY (Honesdale)

Robert J. Conway, P.J.	1980	1990

Full Complement 1

TWENTY-THIRD JUDICIAL DISTRICT

Court of Common Pleas
BERKS COUNTY (Reading)

Forrest G. Schaeffer, Jr., P.J.	1976	1988
W. Richard Eshelman	1968	1990
Thomas J. Eshelman	1978	1988
Elizabeth G. Ehrlich	1984	1994
Calvin Lieberman	1984	1994
Calvin E. Smith	1986	1996

Complement 7
Vacancy 1

TWENTY-FOURTH JUDICIAL DISTRICT

Court of Common Pleas
BLAIR COUNTY (Hollidaysburg)

Thomas G. Peoples, Jr., P.J.	1980	1990
R. Bruce Brumbaugh	1980	1990
David B. Smith	1984	1996
Bertram B. Leopold	1987	1988

Full Complement 4

TWENTY-FIFTH JUDICIAL DISTRICT

Court of Common Pleas
CLINTON COUNTY (Lock Haven)

Carson V. Brown, P.J.	1974	1994

Full Complement 1

TWENTY-SIXTH JUDICIAL DISTRICT

Court of Common Pleas
COLUMBIA & MONTOUR COUNTIES
(Bloomsburg, Danville)

Jay Walter Myers, P.J.	1972	1992

Full Complement 1

TWENTY-SEVENTH JUDICIAL DISTRICT

Court of Common Pleas
WASHINGTON COUNTY (Washington)

Thomas D. Gladden, P.J.	1971	1994
John F. Bell	1976	1996
Thomas J. Terputac	1978	1990
Samuel L. Rodgers	1978	1990

Name	Year Commenced	Expiration Date, 1st Monday in January
David L. Gilmore	1984	1994

Full Complement 5

TWENTY-EIGHTH JUDICIAL DISTRICT

Court of Common Pleas
VENANGO COUNTY (Franklin)

Vacant

Complement 1
Vacancy 1

TWENTY-NINTH JUDICIAL DISTRICT

Court of Common Pleas
LYCOMING COUNTY (Williamsport)

Thomas C. Raup, P.J.	1974	1996
Clinton W. Smith	1981	1992
Robert J. Wollet	1982	1992

Full Complement 3

THIRTIETH JUDICIAL DISTRICT

Court of Common Pleas
CRAWFORD COUNTY (Meadville)

P. Richard Thomas, P.J.	1964	1996
Robert L. Walker	1978	1990

Full Complement 2

THIRTY-FIRST JUDICIAL DISTRICT

Court of Common Pleas
LEHIGH COUNTY (Allentown)

John E. Backenstoe, P.J.	1972	1992
Maxwell E. Davison	1971	1994
David E. Mellenberg	1976	1996
James N. Diefenderfer	1979	1990
James K. Gardner	1981	1992
Robert K. Young	1984	1996
Carol K. McGinley	1986	1996

Full Complement 7

THIRTY-SECOND JUDICIAL DISTRICT

Court of Common Pleas
DELAWARE COUNTY (Media)

Francis J. Catania, P.J.	1963	1996
Howard F. Reed, Jr., A.J.	1969	1990
Domenic D. Jerome, A.J.	1970	1992
R. Barclay Surrick, A.J.	1978	1988
Clement J. McGovern, Jr.	1974	1994
Robert A. Wright	1970	1992
William R. Toal, Jr.	1974	1994
Joseph T. Labrum, Jr.	1976	1996
Robert F. Kelly	1976	1996
Rita E. Prescott	1976	1996

Name	Year Commenced	Expiration Date, 1st Monday in January
Melvin G. Levy	1978	1988
Frank T. Hazel	1981	1992
Charles C. Keeler	1981	1992
Anthony R. Semeraro	1982	1992

Complement 15
Vacancy 1

THIRTY-THIRD JUDICIAL DISTRICT

Court of Common Pleas
ARMSTRONG COUNTY (Kittanning)

Name	Year Commenced	Expiration
Roy A. House, Jr., P.J.	1972	1992

Full Complement 1

THIRTY-FOURTH JUDICIAL DISTRICT

Court of Common Pleas
SUSQUEHANNA COUNTY (Montrose)

Name	Year Commenced	Expiration
Donald O'Malley, P.J.	1968	1988

Full Complement 1

THIRTY-FIFTH JUDICIAL DISTRICT

Court of Common Pleas
MERCER COUNTY (Mercer)

Name	Year Commenced	Expiration
Albert E. Acker, P.J.	1968	1990
Francis J. Fornelli	1982	1992
Thomas T. Frampton	1986	1996

Full Complement 3

THIRTY-SIXTH JUDICIAL DISTRICT

Court of Common Pleas
BEAVER COUNTY (Beaver)

Name	Year Commenced	Expiration
Robert C. Reed, P.J.	1974	1994
Joseph S. Walko	1978	1988
Thomas C. Mannix	1978	1990
Robert E. Kunselman	1982	1994
Peter O. Steege	1986	1996

Full Complement 5

THIRTY-SEVENTH JUDICIAL DISTRICT

Court of Common Pleas
WARREN & FOREST COUNTIES
(Warren, Tionesta)

Name	Year Commenced	Expiration
Robert L. Wolfe, P.J.	1970	1990

Full Complement 1

THIRTY-EIGHTH JUDICIAL DISTRICT

Court of Common Pleas
MONTGOMERY COUNTY (Norristown)

Name	Year Commenced	Expiration Date, 1st Monday in January
William W. Vogel, P.J.	1968	1988
Richard S. Lowe	1968	1990
Louis D. Stefan	1970	1992
Joseph H. Stanziani	1971	1994
Horace A. Davenport	1976	1996
Lawrence A. Brown	1976	1988
William T. Nicholas	1980	1990
Samuel W. Salus, II	1980	1990
William H. Yohn, Jr.	1981	1992
Anita B. Brody	1981	1992
Albert R. Subers	1983	1994
Paul W. Tressler	1983	1994
Joseph A. Smyth, Jr.	1984	1996
S. Gerald Corso	1985	1996

Complement 15
Vacancy 1

THIRTY-NINTH JUDICIAL DISTRICT

Court of Common Pleas
FRANKLIN & FULTON COUNTIES
(Chambersburg, McConnellsburg)

Name	Year Commenced	Expiration
John W. Keller, P.J.	1968	1990
John R. Walker	1986	1996
William H. Kaye	1987	1990

Full Complement 3

FORTIETH JUDICIAL DISTRICT

Court of Common Pleas
INDIANA COUNTY (Indiana)

Name	Year Commenced	Expiration
Robert C. Earley, P.J.	1976	1996
W. Parker Ruddock	1983	1994

Full Complement 2

FORTY-FIRST JUDICIAL DISTRICT

Court of Common Pleas
JUNIATA & PERRY COUNTIES
(Mifflintown, New Bloomfield)

Name	Year Commenced	Expiration
Keith B. Quigley, P.J.	1976	1988

Full Complement 1

FORTY-SECOND JUDICIAL DISTRICT

Court of Common Pleas
BRADFORD COUNTY (Towanda)

Name	Year Commenced	Expiration
Jeffrey A. Smith, P.J.	1983	1996

Full Complement 1

Name	Year Commenced	Expiration Date, 1st Monday in January

FORTY-THIRD JUDICIAL DISTRICT

Court of Common Pleas
MONROE COUNTY (Stroudsburg)

Name	Year Commenced	Expiration Date
James R. Marsh, P.J.	1971	1994
Ronald E. Vican	1981	1992
Peter J. O'Brien.	1986	1996

Full Complement 3

FORTY-FOURTH JUDICIAL DISTRICT

Court of Common Pleas
SULLIVAN & WYOMING COUNTIES
(Laporte, Tunkhannock)

Name	Year Commenced	Expiration Date
Roy A. Gardner, P.J.	1971	1994

Full Complement 1

FORTY-FIFTH JUDICIAL DISTRICT

Court of Common Pleas
LACKAWANNA COUNTY (Scranton)

Name	Year Commenced	Expiration Date
James J. Walsh, P.J.	1971	1994
James M. Munley	1978	1988
S. John Cottone	1980	1992

Complement 5
Vacancies 2

FORTY-SIXTH JUDICIAL DISTRICT

Court of Common Pleas
CLEARFIELD COUNTY (Clearfield)

Name	Year Commenced	Expiration Date
John K. Reilly, Jr., P.J.	1974	1994
Joseph S. Ammerman.	1986	1996

Full Complement 2

FORTY-SEVENTH JUDICIAL DISTRICT

Court of Common Pleas
CAMBRIA COUNTY (Ebensburg)

Name	Year Commenced	Expiration Date
H. Clifton McWilliams, Jr., P.J.	1964	1994
Francis J. Leahey	1966	1988
Joseph F. O'Kicki	1971	1992
Caram J. Abood	1976	1996
Gerard Long	1986	1996

Full Complement 5

FORTY-EIGHTH JUDICIAL DISTRICT

Court of Common Pleas
McKEAN COUNTY (Smethport)

Name	Year Commenced	Expiration Date
John M. Cleland, P.J.	1984	1996

Full Complement 1

FORTY-NINTH JUDICIAL DISTRICT

Court of Common Pleas
CENTRE COUNTY (Bellefonte)

Name	Year Commenced	Expiration Date
Charles C. Brown, Jr., P.J.	1980	1990
David E. Grine.	1981	1992

Full Complement 2

FIFTIETH JUDICIAL DISTRICT

Court of Common Pleas
BUTLER COUNTY (Butler)

Name	Year Commenced	Expiration Date
Floyd A. Rauschenberger, P.J.	1982	1992
John H. Brydon	1982	1992
Martin J. O'Brien.	1986	1988

Full Complement 3

FIFTY-FIRST JUDICIAL DISTRICT

Court of Common Pleas
ADAMS COUNTY (Gettysburg)

Name	Year Commenced	Expiration Date
Oscar F. Spicer, P.J.	1978	1988
John D. Kuhn	1986	1996

Full Complement 2

FIFTY-SECOND JUDICIAL DISTRICT

Court of Common Pleas
LEBANON COUNTY (Lebanon)

Name	Year Commenced	Expiration Date
G. Thomas Gates, P.J.	1960	1992
John A. Walter.	1975	1996
Robert J. Eby	1981	1992

Full Complement 3

FIFTY-THIRD JUDICIAL DISTRICT

Court of Common Pleas
LAWRENCE COUNTY (New Castle)

Name	Year Commenced	Expiration Date
Glenn McCracken, Jr., P.J.	1979	1990
Francis X. Caiazza	1982	1992
Ralph D. Pratt	1986	1996

Full Complement 3

FIFTY-FOURTH JUDICIAL DISTRICT

Court of Common Pleas
JEFFERSON COUNTY (Brookville)

Name	Year Commenced	Expiration Date
Edwin L. Snyder, P.J.	1972	1992

Full Complement 1

	Year Commenced	Expiration Date, 1st Monday in January		Year Commenced	Expiration Date, 1st Monday in January
Name			*Name*		

FIFTY-FIFTH JUDICIAL DISTRICT

Court of Common Pleas
POTTER COUNTY (Coudersport)

Harold B. Fink, Jr., P.J. 1978   1988

Full Complement 1

FIFTY-SIXTH JUDICIAL DISTRICT

Court of Common Pleas
CARBON COUNTY (Jim Thorpe)

John P. Lavelle, P.J. 1978   1988

Full Complement 1

FIFTY-SEVENTH JUDICIAL DISTRICT

Court of Common Pleas
BEDFORD COUNTY (Bedford)

Daniel L. Howsare, P.J. 1986   1996

Full Complement 1

FIFTY-EIGHTH JUDICIAL DISTRICT

Court of Common Pleas
MIFFLIN COUNTY (Lewistown)

Francis A. Searer, P.J. 1982   1992

Full Complement 1

FIFTY-NINTH JUDICIAL DISTRICT

Court of Common Pleas
CAMERON & ELK COUNTIES
(Emporium, Ridgway)

Gordon J. Daghir, P.J. 1986   1996

Full Complement 1

SIXTIETH JUDICIAL DISTRICT

Court of Common Pleas
PIKE COUNTY (Milford)

Harold A. Thomson, Jr., P.J. 1978   1988

Full Complement 1

COURTS OF COMMON PLEAS
JUDICIAL DISTRICTS AND THEIR JUDICIAL COMPLEMENTS
Act of July 9, 1976, P.L. 586, No. 142, as amended; 42 Pa. C.S.A. § 901, et seq.

The following are the current judicial districts and their judicial complements:

First District shall be composed of the City and County of Philadelphia; Complement of 85 Common Pleas Court Judges — 8 vacancies; Philadelphia Municipal Court — Complement of 22 judges — 2 vacancies.

Second District, Lancaster County — Full complement of 7 judges.

Third District, Northampton County — Complement of 6 judges — 1 vacancy.

Fourth District, Tioga County — Full complement of 1 judge.

Fifth District, Allegheny County — Complement of 41 judges — 2 vacancies.

Sixth District, Erie County — Full complement of 8 judges.

Seventh District, Bucks County — Complement of 11 judges — 1 vacancy.

Eighth District, Northumberland County — Full complement of 2 judges.

Ninth District, Cumberland County — Full complement of 4 judges.

Tenth District, Westmoreland County — Full complement of 9 judges.

Eleventh District, Luzerne County — Full complement of 7 judges.

Twelfth District, Dauphin County — Full complement of 6 judges.

Thirteenth District, Greene County — Full complement of 1 judge.

Fourteenth District, Fayette County — Full complement of 4 judges.

Fifteenth District, Chester County — Full complement of 8 judges.

Sixteenth District, Somerset County — Full complement of 2 judges.

Seventeenth District, Union and Snyder Counties — Full complement of 2 judges.

Eighteenth District, Clarion County — Full complement of 1 judge.

Nineteenth District, York County — Complement of 7 judges — 1 vacancy.

Twentieth District, Huntingdon County — Full complement of 1 judge.

Twenty-First District, Schuylkill County — Full complement of 5 judges.

Twenty-Second District, Wayne County — Full complement of 1 judge.

Twenty-Third District, Berks County — Complement of 7 judges — 1 vacancy.

Twenty-Fourth District, Blair County — Full complement of 4 judges.

Twenty-Fifth District, Clinton County — Full complement of 1 judge.

Twenty-Sixth District, Columbia and Montour Counties — Full complement of 1 judge.

Twenty-Seventh District, Washington County — Full complement of 5 judges.

Twenty-Eighth District, Venango County — Complement of 1 judge — 1 vacancy.

Twenty-Ninth District, Lycoming County — Full complement of 3 judges.

Thirtieth District, Crawford County — Full complement of 2 judges.

Thirty-First District, Lehigh County — Full complement of 7 judges.

Thirty-Second District, Delaware County — Complement of 15 judges — 1 vacancy.

Thirty-Third District, Armstrong County — Full complement of 1 judge.

Thirty-Fourth District, Susquehanna County — Full complement of 1 judge.

Thirty-Fifth District, Mercer County — Full complement of 3 judges.

Thirty-Sixth District, Beaver County — Full complement of 5 judges.

Thirty-Seventh District, Warren and Forest Counties — Full complement of 1 judge.

Thirty-Eighth District, Montgomery County — Complement of 15 judges — 1 vacancy.

Thirty-Ninth District, Franklin and Fulton Counties — Full complement of 3 judges.

Fortieth District, Indiana County — Full complement of 2 judges.

Forty-First District, Juniata and Perry Counties — Full complement of 1 judge.

Forty-Second District, Bradford County — Full complement of 1 judge.

Forty-Third District, Monroe County — Full complement of 3 judges.

Forty-Fourth District, Wyoming and Sullivan Counties — Full complement of 1 judge.

Forty-Fifth District, Lackawanna County — Complement of 5 judges — 2 vacancies.

Forty-Sixth District, Clearfield County — Full complement of 2 judges.

Forty-Seventh District, Cambria County — Full complement of 5 judges.

Forty-Eighth District, McKean County — Full complement of 1 judge.

Forty-Ninth District, Centre County — Full complement of 2 judges.

Fiftieth District, Butler County — Full complement of 3 judges.

Fifty-First District, Adams County — Full complement of 2 judges.

Fifty-Second District, Lebanon County — Full complement of 3 judges.

Fifty-Third District, Lawrence County — Full complement of 3 judges.

Fifty-Fourth District, Jefferson County — Full complement of 1 judge.

Fifty-Fifth District, Potter County — Full complement of 1 judge.

Fifty-Sixth District, Carbon County — Full complement of 1 judge.

Fifty-Seventh District, Bedford County — Full complement of 1 judge.

Fifty-Eighth District, Mifflin County — Full complement of 1 judge.

Fifty-Ninth District, Cameron and Elk Counties — Full complement of 1 judge.

Sixtieth District, Pike County — Full complement of 1 judge.

PENNSYLVANIA SUPREME COURT AND THE SUPERIOR COURT OF PENNSYLVANIA

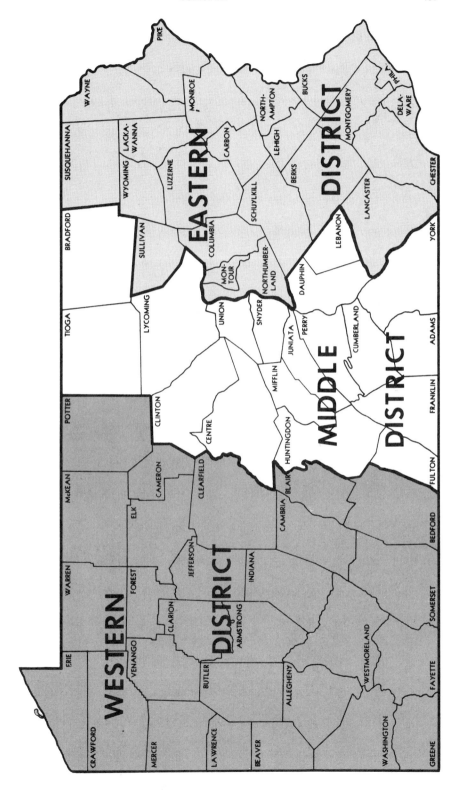

JUDICIAL DISTRICTS

AS APPORTIONED BY ACT OF 1951
AS AMENDED*

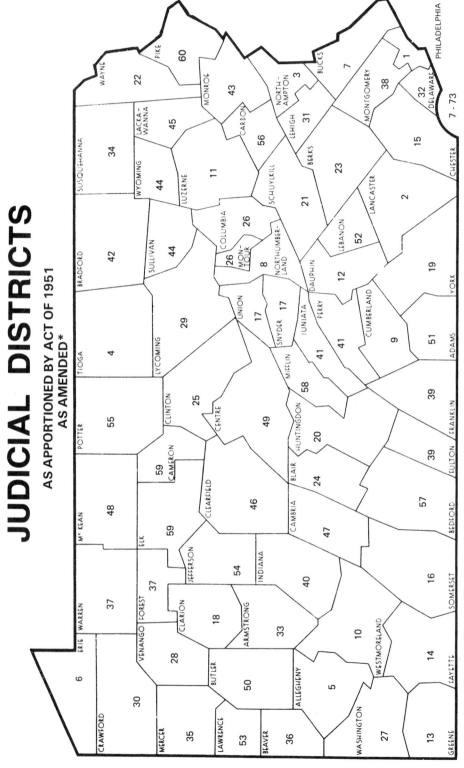

*April 8, 1982, PL. 292, No. 82, Section 1

JUDICIAL DISTRICTS AND THEIR PRESIDENT JUDGES
by County and in Numerical Order

COUNTY	JUD. DIST.	PRESIDENT JUDGE		Judicial Districts in Numerical Order
ADAMS	51	Oscar F. Spicer	01	Philadelphia
ALLEGHENY	05	Michael J. O'Malley	02	Lancaster
ARMSTRONG	33	Roy A. House, Jr.	03	Northampton
BEAVER	36	Robert C. Reed	04	Tioga
BEDFORD	57	Daniel Lee Howsare	05	Allegheny
BERKS	23	Forrest G. Schaeffer	06	Erie
BLAIR	24	Thomas G. Peoples, Jr.	07	Bucks
BRADFORD	42	Jeffrey A. Smith	08	Northumberland
BUCKS	07	Isaac S. Garb	09	Cumberland
BUTLER	50	Floyd A. Rauschenberger, Jr.	10	Westmoreland
CAMBRIA	47	H. Clifton McWilliams, Jr.	11	Luzerne
CAMERON-ELK	59	Gordon J. Daghir	12	Dauphin
CARBON	56	John P. Lavelle	13	Greene
CENTRE	49	Charles C. Brown, Jr.	14	Fayette
CHESTER	15	Leonard Sugerman	15	Chester
CLARION	18	Merle E. Wiser	16	Somerset
CLEARFIELD	46	John K. Reilly, Jr.	17	Snyder-Union
CLINTON	25	Carson V. Brown	18	Clarion
COLUMBIA-MONTOUR	26	Jay Walter Myers	19	York
CRAWFORD	30	P. Richard Thomas	20	Huntingdon
CUMBERLAND	09	Harold E. Sheely	21	Schuylkill
DAUPHIN	12	Lee F. Swope	22	Wayne
DELAWARE	32	Francis J. Catania	23	Berks
ELK-CAMERON	59	Gordon J. Daghir	24	Blair
ERIE	06	William E. Pfadt	25	Clinton
FAYETTE	14	Richard D. Cicchetti	26	Columbia-Montour
FOREST-WARREN	37	Robert L. Wolfe	27	Washington
FRANKLIN-FULTON	39	John W. Keller	28	Venango
FULTON-FRANKLIN	39	John W. Keller	29	Lycoming
GREENE	13	H. Terry Grimes	30	Crawford
HUNTINGDON	20	Newton C. Taylor	31	Lehigh
INDIANA	40	Robert C. Earley	32	Delaware
JEFFERSON	54	Edwin L. Snyder	33	Armstrong
JUNIATA-PERRY	41	Keith B. Quigley	34	Susquehanna
LACKAWANNA	45	James J. Walsh	35	Mercer
LANCASTER	02	D. Richard Eckman	36	Beaver
LAWRENCE	53	Glenn McCracken, Jr.	37	Forest-Warren
LEBANON	52	G. Thomas Gates	38	Montgomery
LEHIGH	31	John E. Backenstoe	39	Franklin-Fulton
LUZERNE	11	Robert J. Hourigan	40	Indiana
LYCOMING	29	Thomas C. Raup	41	Juniata-Perry
McKEAN	48	John M. Cleland	42	Bradford
MERCER	35	Albert E. Acker	43	Monroe
MIFFLIN	58	Francis A. Searer	44	Sullivan-Wyoming
MONROE	43	James R. Marsh	45	Lackawanna
MONTGOMERY	38	William W. Vogel	46	Clearfield
MONTOUR-COLUMBIA	26	Jay Walter Myers	47	Cambria
NORTHAMPTON	03	Alfred T. Williams, Jr.	48	McKean
NORTHUMBERLAND	08	Samuel C. Ranck	49	Centre
PERRY-JUNIATA	41	Keith B. Quigley	50	Butler
PHILADELPHIA	01	Edward J. Bradley	51	Adams
PIKE	60	Harold A. Thomson, Jr.	52	Lebanon
POTTER	55	Harold B. Fink	53	Lawrence
SCHUYLKILL	21	George W. Heffner	54	Jefferson
SNYDER-UNION	17	James F. McClure, Jr.	55	Potter
SOMERSET	16	Norman A. Shaulis	56	Carbon
SULLIVAN-WYOMING	44	Roy A. Gardner	57	Bedford
SUSQUEHANNA	34	Donald O'Malley	58	Mifflin
TIOGA	04	Robert M. Kemp	59	Cameron-Elk
UNION-SNYDER	17	James F. McClure, Jr.	60	Pike
VENANGO	28	Vacancy		
WARREN-FOREST	37	Robert L. Wolfe		
WASHINGTON	27	Thomas D. Gladden		
WAYNE	22	Robert J. Conway		
WESTMORELAND	10	Gilfert M. Mihalich		
WYOMING-SULLIVAN	44	Roy A. Gardner		
YORK	19	Joseph E. Erb		

SENIOR JUDGES
As of June 1987

Senior judges are defined by the Judicial Code, Act of July 9, 1976, P.L. 586, as amended by the Act of April 28, 1978, P.L. 202, 42 Pa. C.S.A. §101 et seq., as both retired and former judges who, with their consent, are assigned to temporary judicial service by the Supreme Court of Pennsylvania, pursuant to Section 4121(b) of the Code. That Section is marked reserved and reference must be made to the Pennsylvania Rules of Judicial Administration No. 701, which prescribes the procedures for the assignment of such judges. Such assignment is authorized by Section 16(c) of Article V of the Pennsylvania Constitution.

All judges seeking assignment must have served at least ten years and not have been defeated for reelection or, in the case of judges who retired mandatorily at age seventy, must have served at least six years.

Therefore, the term "senior judge" is reserved for those judges who make themselves available for assignment as opposed to other retired judges of any age who are not available for such service.

Anderson, Hon. Levy
Appel, Hon. Anthony R.
Barbieri, Hon. Alexander F.[1]
Bednarek, Hon. Michael
Bigelow, Hon. Richard L.
Blatt, Hon. Genevieve
Bloom, Hon. Louis A.
Blount, Hon. Lynwood
Boyle, Hon. Hugh C.
Breene, Hon. William
Bucher, Hon. Wilson
Buckingham, Hon. James
Cadran, Hon. Francis
Canuso, Hon. Vito. F.
Cercone, Hon. William Franklin
Cherry, Hon. John A.
Coffroth, Hon. Charles
Creany, Hon. Eugene
Diggins, Hon. John V.
Doty, Hon. Ethan Allen
Dwyer, Hon. James B.
Edenharter, Hon. Frederick
Forer, Hon. Lois G.
Geisz, Hon. John A.
Greevy, Hon. Charles F.
Greiner, Hon. Paul
Handler, Hon. Earl R.

Hess, Hon. Warren K.
Hester, Hon. John P.
Hirsh, Hon. Ned L.
Hoffman, Hon. J. Sydney
Ivins, Hon. George J.
Kalish, Hon. Jacob[1]
Kiester, Hon. George P.
Klein, Hon. Charles
Kohler, Hon. Richard E.
Kubacki, Hon. Stanley
Lederer, Hon. William J.
Lehman, Hon. Paul S.
Lewis, Hon. Loran L.
Lipez, Hon. Abraham H.[2]
Lipsitt, Hon. William
Louik, Hon. Maurice
Macones, Hon. Alexander
McCormick, Hon. Richard
Meade, Hon. John R.
Monroe, Hon. Lawrence A.
Montgomery, Hon. Harry M.
Murphy, Hon. Joseph T.
Narick, Hon. Emil
O'Neill, Hon. Jerome A.
Penetar, Hon, Daniel
Rahauser, Hon. William S.
Rodgers, Hon. Theodore

Rosenberg, Hon. Edward B.
Rosenwald, Hon. Edward
Salmon, Hon. J. Quint
Sawyer, Hon. John
Scheib, Hon. Raymond L.
Schwartz, Hon. Nathan
Shoyer, Hon. Kendall H.
Silverstein, Hon. Paul
Smillie, Hon. Frederick B.
Smith, Hon. Henry
Stively, Hon. John
Stranahan, Hon. John
Strauss, Hon. Samuel
Sweet, Hon. Charles G.
Takiff, Hon. Harry
Taxis, Hon. Alfred L.
Tranchitella, Hon. Paul A.
Trommer, Hon. Evelyn M.
Van Horn, Hon. Ellis
Watkins, Hon. G. Harold
Weir, Hon. Frederic G.
Wesner, Hon. Grant E.
Williams, Hon. Arlington W.
Williams, Hon. Evan
Wright, Hon. Charles

[1]By special assignment to Commonwealth Court
[2]By special assignment to Superior Court

JUDICIAL BIOGRAPHIES
SUPREME COURT
THE CHIEF JUSTICE

ROBERT N.C. NIX, JR., Chief Justice, was born July 13, 1928; grad., Villanova Univ. (A.B.) 1950; Univ. of Pa. (J.D.) 1953; Hon. Doctor of Laws degrees: Villanova Univ., June 1976; Delaware Law Schl. of Widener Coll., Jan. 1980; Chestnut Hill Coll., May 1983; Dickinson Law Schl., June 1983; Scranton Univ., May 1984; LaSalle Coll., May 1984; St. Charles Seminary, June 1985; dep. atty. gen., Common. of Pa., 1956-58; partner in law firm of Nix, Rhodes and Nix, 1958-68; judge, Court of Common Pleas, First Judicial Dist., 1968-71; mem.: Am., Pa., Phila., and Natl. Bar Assns.; mem., bd. trustees, Villanova Univ.; Knight Commander of the Order of Saint Gregory issued by The Vatican; assumed office January 2, 1984, having served as associate justice of the Pennsylvania Supreme Court since 1972; widower; 4 children.

THE JUSTICES

JOHN P. FLAHERTY was born Nov. 19, 1931, in Pgh., the son of J. Paul and M.G. McLaughlin Flaherty; Duquesne Univ. (B.A.) 1953; Univ. of Pgh. Schl. of Law (J.D.) 1958; commissioned, U.S. Army, 1953; served 2 yrs., separated with rank of 1st lieut.; professor, Carnegie-Mellon Univ., 1958-1973; private practice of law, 1958-1973; chief counsel, Pa. Milk Marketing Bd., 1971; chmn., Advisory Bd., Pa. Academy of Science; honorary Kentucky Colonel; Freedom For All Ireland Award, Ancient Order of Hibernians, 1977; "Man of the Year" award, law and government, Greater Pgh. Jaycees, 1978; Distinguished Alumni Award, Pa. Academy of Science, 1978; Humanitarian Award, Irish Natl. Caucus, 1978; Fellow Military History Society of Ireland; Pa. Society; Irish Society of Pgh.; Counselor Emeritus; Ancient Order of Hibernians; Knights of Equity; Friendly Sons of St. Patrick; Gaelic Art Society; Irish-American Cultural Institute; American Legion; hon. mem., Philippine Natl. Bar Assn.; U.S.I.A. sponsored speaker in Japan, Thailand, the Philippines, Australia, Korea and Hong Kong, 1985 and 1986; listed in *Who's Who in the East; Who's Who in American Law; Who's Who in America; Who's Who in the World; Personalities of America;* elected judge, Court of Common Pleas, Nov. 6, 1973; elected administrative (chief) judge, Civil Division of the Court of Common Pleas, Feb. 1978; justice, Supreme Court, June 16, 1979; home address: 901 William Penn Court, Pittsburgh (Wilkinsburg).

WILLIAM D. HUTCHINSON was born June 20, 1932, in Minersville, the son of Elmer and Elizabeth Price Hutchinson; Moravian Coll. (B.A., magna cum laude) 1954; Harvard Law Schl. (J.D.) 1957; Schuylkill Co., Pa., Am. Bar Assns.; Am. Judicature Society; Cressona Lodge, F&AM; Caldwell Consistory; Rajah Shrine; Tall Cedars; St. Davids Society, Schuylkill and Carbon Cos.; mem. Pa. House of Representatives, 1973-81; solicitor, Schuylkill Co., 1969-71; asst. dist. atty., Schuylkill Co., 1963-69; Lay Leader, chm., bd. of trustees, First Un. Methodist Ch.; John Amos Comenius Award, Moravian Coll., 1982; authored Pa. Jury Selection and Compensation Act; Pomeroy Comm. on Unified Judicial System in Pa.; chmn., Joint St. Gov. Comm., 1981; Task Force on Elected Atty. Gen. and Commonwealth Atty. Act; elected justice, Pennsylvania Supreme Court, Nov. 3, 1981; married Louise Meloney; 4 children: Kathryn Barone, William, Jr., Louise, Andrew.

ROLF LARSEN was born Aug. 26, 1934, in Pgh., the son of Thorbjorn Ruud and Mildren Young Larsen; attd., Penn State Univ., Univ of Pgh., Duquesne Univ. Schl. of Philosophy, Univ. of Santa Clara Schl. of Law, Dickinson Schl. of Law (LL.B.) 1960; U.S. Army, active duty, 1954-56; sole practitioner 13 years; lecturer, Duquesne Univ. Schl. of Law; mem., various Masonic bodies including Syria Temple; rec., Humanitarian Award; Outstanding Jurist Award, Pa. Dist. Attorneys Assn., 1985; Judicial Excellence Award, Pa. State AFL-CIO, 1986; Pa. Trial Lawyers Assn. Annual Award, 1986; Justice Michael A. Musmanno Award, Phila. Trial Lawyers Assn., 1986; elected judge, Court of Common Pleas, Allegheny Co. for a term of 10 years beginning Jan. 7, 1974; elected to Supreme Court, 1977; office address: Grant Building, Pittsburgh.

JAMES THOMAS McDERMOTT was born Sept. 22, 1926; St. Joseph's Univ. (B.S.C.) 1947; Temple Univ. Schl. of Law (LL.B.) 1950; instructor, Instit. of Indus. Relations, Legal Evidence, St. Joseph's Univ., Am. Institute of Banking; past chmn., Criminal Justice Comm., Bd. of Judges and City Chrt. Revision Comm.; various posts, Pa. St. Trial Judges; Phila., Pa. Bar Assns.; Law Alumni Assn. of St. Joseph's Univ., Temple Univ.; St. Patrick's Day Assn.; Brehon Law Society; Emerald Society; various civic activities; appt. judge, Court of Common Pleas, Aug. 1965; elected to justice, Pennsylvania Supreme Court, Nov. 3, 1981; widower; 6 children: James, John, Suzanne, Thomas, Michael, Matthew.

NICHOLAS P. PAPADAKOS was born Jan. 24, 1925, in Hoboken, N.J., the son of Rev. Petros and Olga Christopoulou Papadakos; grad., McKeesport Area H.S.; Dickinson College (B.A.) 1949; Columbus Law Schl., Catholic Univ. (LL.B.) 1952; veteran, U.S. Air Corps, South Pacific Theater, 1943-46; mem., Pa. State Trial Judges Conf.; Masonic Order; McKeesport Elks; bd. dir., Mendelssohn Choir; solicitor: Versailles Schl. Dist. (1964-65), Port Vue Borough (1969-75), City of McKeesport (1973-75); judge, Ct. of Common Pleas of Allegheny Co., 1976-83; mem., Greek Am. Progressive Assn.; Am. Hellenic Ed. and Progressive Assn.; Grtr. Phila. Spartan-Hercules Chptr. 26; rec., Commendation, Borough of Greentree; Citation from Pa. House of Representatives; Pan Laconian Society Mystras No. 50 Award; Southwestern PA Building and Construction Trades Council Award; Pgh. Chapter #38 Am. Soc. of Appraisers Award; elected justice, Supreme Court of Pa., Nov. 1983; married Roula Sakellariou; 3 children: Peterclyde N., James N., and Thomas N.; home address: 109 Lindberg Drive, McKeesport.

STEPHEN A. ZAPPALA was born Sept. 26, 1932, in Pgh., the son of Frank J. and Josephine M. Andolina Zappala; Univ. of Notre Dame, 1950-51; Duquesne Univ. Law Schl. (J.D.) 1956-58; U.S. Army, 1954-56, hon. dis.; lawyer; hon. natl. pres., Italian Sons & Daughters of Am.; bd., Multiple Sclerosis Society, Alleg. Chapt.; dir., Allegheny Co. Dept. of Planning and Development, 1973; mem., Justinian Soc.; solicitor, Allegheny Co. Comm. Coll., 1974; solicitor, Allegheny Co., 1974-76; elected judge, Court of Common Pleas, Dec. 26, 1979; elected justice, Pennsylvania Supreme Court, Dec. 30, 1982; married Phyllis M. Koleno; 4 children: Stephen A., Jr., Esq., J. Michele Zappala Peck, Gregory R., Dana Lynn; home address: 1200 Lancaster St., Pittsburgh.

PROTHONOTARY OF THE SUPREME COURT

MARLENE F. LACHMAN was born June 27, 1946, in Phila., the daughter of Sidney and Bertha Thalheimer Lachman; Temple Univ. (B.A.) 1968; Univ. of Pa. Law Schl. (J.D.) 1970; private practice, 1970-81; Dep. Gen. Counsel for the Governor, 1981; Phila., Pa., Am. Bar Assns.; House of Delegates, Pa. Bar Assn.; Phila., Pa., Am. Trial Lawyers Assn.; Natl. Conf. of Appellate Court Clerks; Pa. Supreme Court, Disciplinary Bd., Hearing Panel, 1973-80; *Who's Who in American Women;* bd. mgrs., Univ. of Pa. Law Alumni Society, 1972-80; bd. trustees, Gratz Coll.; various bds. of social and community assns.; appt. Prothonotary, Pennsylvania Supreme Court, Eastern District, Jan. 1982; home address: Park Towne Place, Philadelphia.

MEMBERS, THE SUPREME COURT OF PENNSYLVANIA

left to right
Seated: Rolf Larsen, Robert N. C. Nix, Jr. (Chief Justice), John P. Flaherty
Standing: Stephen A. Zappala, James Thomas McDermott, William D. Hutchinson, Nicholas P. Papadakos

THE SUPERIOR COURT

THE PRESIDENT JUDGE

VINCENT A. CIRILLO was born Dec. 19, 1927, in Ardmore, the son of Francesco and Victoria Cirillo; served in Korean Conflict; Villanova Univ., (B.A., cum laude) 1951; Temple Univ. Schl. of Law (LL.B.) 1955, (J.D.) 1969; asst. dist. atty., Montgomery Co. 1958-62; Catholic War Veterans; Phi Alpha Delta Law Fraternity; law clerk to Pres. Judge Harold G. Knight, 1955-58; served on awards jury, Freedoms Foundation, Valley Forge, 1966; listed *Who's Who in America, Who's Who in American Judicial System;* Catholic War Vets Man of the Year, 1976; Man of the Year Award — Catholic War Veterans, 1974-75; Certificate of Appreciation — Optimist Club of City Line, 1959; Man of the Year Award — Optimist Club of Norristown, 1978; Certificate of Appreciation — Pa. State Police Arson School, 1978; Phi Alpha Delta — Distinguished Service Award, 1955; Mendel Associate of Villanova Univ., 1978; Maria SS. Del Soccorso Di Sciacca — Certificate of Appreciation, 1979; Italian Am. Press Medal of Honor, 1979; exec. bd., Temple U. Law Schl.; asst. solicitor, Montgomery Co. 1966-71; commissioner, Lower Merion Township; v-chmn., Judicial Education Comm. of Pa. Conf. of St. Trial Judges; St. Judicial Assn. of Am. Bar Assn.; hon. mem. of FOP; appt. to Court of Common Pleas, Dec. 31, 1971; elected to Superior Ct. of Pa., Nov. 3, 1981, to a 10 yr. term; elected President Judge of the Superior Court, Jan. 8, 1986, to a 5 yr. term; married Beatrice D'Orazio; 3 children.

JUDGES

PHYLLIS W. BECK grad. from Brown Univ. (magna cum laude, Phi Beta Kappa); Temple Univ. Law Schl. (evening division) (1st in class); grad. studies, Bryn Mawr Coll.; v. dean, Univ. of Pa. Law Schl., 1976-81; assoc. professor, Temple Univ. Law Schl., 1974-76; private law practice, 1967-74; Fellow Am. Law Institute, Am. Bar Foundation; Am., Pa., Montgomery Co., Phila. Bar Assns.; Pa. Humanities Council; overseer, Univ. of Pa. Nursing Schl.; assoc. trustee, Univ. of Pa.; dir., Harcum Junior College; v-pres., Montgomery Co. Emergency Services; pres., Center for Cognitive Therapy and Research, Univ. of Pa.; founder, v. pres., bd. dir., Grtr. Phila. Community Develop. Corp.; Lindbach lecturer, Bryn Mawr Coll., 1984; Phi Beta Kappa lecturer, Brown Univ., 1984; author of numerous publications; editorial bd., *Family Law Quarterly; Who's Who in American Women; Who's Who in American Law;* judge, Superior Court of Pa.; married to Aaron T. Beck, M.D.; 4 children: Roy, Judith, Daniel, Alice; office: Suite 800, GSB Bldg., Bala Cynwyd.

JOHN G. BROSKY was born Aug. 4, 1920; Univ. of Pgh. (A.B.), Univ. of Pgh. Law Schl. (LL.B. & J.D.); Am., Pa. Allegheny Co. Bar Assns.; Am. Judicature Society; Pa. Conf. of St. Trial Judges, past state pres.; American Academy Matrimorial Lawyers Faculty, Pa. Coll. of Judiciary; Asst. Co. Solicitor, Alleg. Co. 1951-56; Major General, Pa. Air Natl. Guard and U.S. Air Force; World War II, Capt. Artillery, 39 months in South Pacific; numerous civic, sportsmen and military organizations, including President's Award, Natl. Guard Assn.; Pa. Distinguished Service Medal; Legion of Merit, Air Force; Philippine Liberation Ribbon with Bronze Star; past natl. pres., Air Force Assn.; past pres., Pa. Natl. Guard Assn.; past State Commander, Military Order of World Wars; Past Dept. Commander, Pa. Disabled Am. Vets.; Am. Legion, Man of the Year Award, 1978; Civil Air Patrol Award, 1972; Distinguished Judicial Service, Pa. Mason Juvenile Court Inst.; Juvenile Court Judges Comm., 1972-79; subcomm. on military affairs, Jt. St. Govt. Commission; VFW Loyalty Day Award, 1960; Natl. Certificate of Merit, DAV, 1958; Man of the Year, Catholic War Vets, 1960, 1984; Humanitarian Award, New Light Men's Club; Dapper Dan Award; Variety Club Award, Handicapped Children; cited for outstanding Americanism programs in resolution adopted by Pa. House of Representatives, June 22, 1965; Patriotic Civilian Service Award, Army Air Defense Command, 1965; Distinguished Citation, Military Order of World Wars; Varsity Letterman of Distinction, Univ. of Pgh., 1968; past pres., Varsity Letter Club, Univ. of Pgh., Western Pa. Sports Hall of Fame, 1972; State Humanitarian Award Domestic Relations Assn. of Pa., 1978; Alleg. Co. Family Law Award, 1979; certificate of commendation, Masonic, Sir Knights of Pgh. Commandery, 1980; award of outstanding service in the field of law, Chartiers Valley Jr. C of C, 1956; Man of the Year, Field of Law, Pgh. Jr. C of C, 1960; Internatl. Platform Society; Historical Society of Western, Pa.; the Pa. Society; Exceptional Service Award, USAF, 1982; Disting. Service Award, Arnold Air Society, AFROTC, 1984; Meritoroius Service Award, Air National Guard, 1984; Man of the Year, Family Law Section, Allegeny Co. Bar Assn., 1986; *Who's Who in America; Who's Who in American Law; International Who's Who of Intellectuals; Two Thousand Notable Americans,* First Edition; *Men of Achievement,* Eighth Edition; Honorary Advisor, Natl. Bd. of Advisors, Am. Biographical Inst.; apptd. to Alleg. Co. Court, May 24, 1956; elected to full term, Nov. 1957; apptd. to 5th Judicial Dist. Court of Common Pleas, Sept. 12, 1960; elected full term, 1961; reelected, 1971; Administrative Judge, Family Division, Court of Common Pleas, Feb. 13, 1970; elected to Superior Court of Pa., 1980; married Rose Fyderek; 3 children: John, Carol, and David; home address: 29 Greenview Dr., Carnegie.

JAMES R. CAVANAUGH was born Aug. 26, 1931, in Phila., the son of Joseph and Margaret Stapleton Cavanaugh; St. Joseph's Coll. (B.S.) 1953; Univ. of Pa. Law Schl. (J.D.) 1956; Am. Bar Assn.; Am. Judicature Society; exec. comm., Pa. St. Conf. Trial Judges; chmn., advsry. comm., Prisoner's Family Welfare Assn.; dir., Counseling or Referral Agency; State Court Standard Jury Charges Comm.; perm. secy., James Wilson Law Club; dir., Phila. Bicenntennial Comm., The Mummer's Museum, Phila., and Gaudenzia House; chmn., adv. comm., Self-Help Movement, dir., St. Thomas More Society; pres., St. Joseph's Coll. Law Alumni; dir., Phila. Boosters Assn.; dir., Catholic Philopatrian Literary Inst.; teacher, St. Joseph's Coll., Phila.; Gov.'s Justice Commission Regnl. Bd.; Pa. Bd. of Judicial Inquiry and Review; pres., Brehon Law Society; bd. dir., Community Coll. of Phila.; adv. bd., Learning — Plus; commissioned judge, Court of Common Pleas, Jan. 6, 1969; appt. to the Superior Court, Aug. 1, 1979; elected Nov. 1979 for term beginning Jan. 1980; married Patricia Malloy, Aug. 27, 1955; 3 children; home address: 1000 Clinton St., Philadelphia.

JOSEPH A. DEL SOLE was born Nov. 16, 1940, in Pittsburgh, the son of Joseph and Mildred Visnich Del Sole; Carnegie Inst. of Tech. (B.S.M.E.); Duquesne Univ. Sch. of Law (LL.B.) 1965; mem., Alleghency Co. Bar Assn.; PA Defense Inst.; Academy of Trial Lawyers of Allegheny Co.; mem., Italian Sons & Daughters of America; Serb Natl. Federation; St. Louise deMarillac Roman Catholic Ch., Religious Ed. Instructor, mem., Parish Council; Century Club Duquesne Univ.; co-auth., ''The Demise of Fair Trade in Pennsylvania,'' Duquesne Univ. Law Review; appt. judge, Court of Common Pleas, Allegheny Co., 1978; elected full term, Nov. 1979; elected judge, Superior Court, Nov. 8, 1983; married Karen M. Yesnick; 3 children: Joseph M., Kristen M., Stephen J.; home address: 2427 Kings Lane, Pittsburgh.

MEMBERS, SUPERIOR COURT OF PENNSYLVANIA

Standing Left to Right:
Zoran Popovich, Patrick R. Tamilia, Peter Paul Olszewski, Stephen J. McEwen, Jr., Joseph A. Del Sole, John T. J. Kelly, Jr., Justin M. Johnson
Seated Left to Right:
James W. Rowley, James R. Cavanaugh, Vincent A. Cirillo (President Judge), John G. Brosky, Donald E. Wieand
Missing From Photo:
Phyllis W. Beck, Frank J. Montemuro, Jr.

JUSTIN MORRIS JOHNSON was born Aug. 19, 1933, in Wilkinsburg, the son of Oliver L. (dec.) and Irene Olive Morris Johnson; Univ. of Chicago (A.B.) 1954, (J.D.) 1962, Univ. of Virginia Law Schl., 1982, 1983, no degree; U.S. Air Force, active duty, 1954-59; active reserve, 1963-73; Am., Natl., Pa., Allegheny Co. Bar Assns.; Fellow, Am. Bar Foundation; Natl. Conf. of Bar Examiners; Homer S. Brown Law Assn.; Alpha Delta Phi; Pa. Crime Commission, 1977-80; Pa. Bd. of Law Examiners, 1969-pres.; ruling elder, Bethesda U.P. Ch.; Permanent Judicial Comm., Gen. Assembly, Presbyterian Ch. (U.S.A.); vice moderator, Pgh. Presbytery, 1983; bd. trustees: Mercy Hospital of Pgh., Robert Morris Coll., South Side Hospital, Carnegie-Mellon Univ., Pgh. Theological Seminary; bd. dir., United Way of Alleg. Co., HWPA; rec.: Dr. Martin Luther King Citizen's Award, 1971, Humanitarian and Community Service Award, COMPA, 1978, PTLA President's Award, 1983; St. Thomas More Award, Pgh. Diocese, 1985; Public Service Award, Pgh. Chap. ASPA, 1986; Bond Medal, Univ. of Chicago, 1954; Disciplinary Bd. of the Pa. Supreme Court, chmn., Hearing Comm., 4.11, 1976-80; appt. judge, Superior Court of Pennsylvania, Nov. 19, 1980; elected Nov. 5, 1985; married Florence Elizabeth Lester; 3 children: William Oliver, Justin Llewellyn, Elizabeth Irene; home address: 4136 Bigelow Blvd., Pittsburgh.

JOHN T. J. KELLY, JR., was born December 29, 1930, the son of John T. J. and Frances Yetman Kelly; grad., LaSalle Univ., 1956; Creighton Law Schl., 1961; U.S. Army, 1954-55; mem., The Pa. Soc.; YMBA Soc.; asst. atty. gen. and chief counsel, Pa. Dept. of Public Welfare, 1963-66; exec. dir., "Committee for 5 Yes Votes"; chief of staff, Pa. Delegation to the Rep. Natl. Convention of 1968; appt. asst. to Lt. Gov. Broderick, 1967-71; exec. dir., Pa. Inaugural Com. for Gov. Thornburgh, 1978-79; natl. field dir., John B. Connally Rep. Presidential Campaign, 1979-80; dep. sec. for industry, Dept. of Labor and Industry, 1980-85; judge, Superior Court, Jan. 1986.

STEPHEN J. McEWEN, JR. was born Oct. 8, 1939, in Phila.; St. Joseph's Coll. (A.B.); Univ. of Pa. Law Schl. (J.D.); Univ. of Va. Law Schl. (LL.M.); Pa. and Delaware Co. Bar Assns.; Pa. Dist. Attys. Assn.; Natl. Dist. Attys. Assn.; St. Joseph's Coll. Law Alumni, (bd. dir., since 1978), (v. pres., 1981, pres. 1983); dist. atty., Delaware Co., 1967-76; professor of Trial Advocacy, Villanova Univ. Law Schl., since 1975; general counsel, Pa. Dist. Attys. Assn., 1976-79; solicitor: Delaware Co. (asst., 1966-67; controller, 1962-65), Collingdale Schl. Dist. (1964-67), Milbourne Schl. Dist. (1962-67), Borough of Collingdale (1962-67), Borough of Millbourne (1960-67), Delaware Co. Police Chiefs (1961-67); frmr. counsel to several volunteer fire cos.; frmr. lecturer, F.B.I. Police Schls.; Pa. Law and Justice Institute (bd. dir., 1971-75); Defender Assn. of Phila.; rec., Man of the Yr. Award, Delaware Co. Lawyers Club, 1974; Disting. Service Award, Pa. Dist. Attys., Assn., 1976; Univ. of Pa. James Wilson Law Society Annual Disting. Service Award, 1968; Outstand. Service Award, Ancient Order of Hibernians, 1972; Man of the Yr., Delaware Co. Friendly Sons of St. Patrick, 1981; St. Joseph's Coll. Law Alumni, McClonaghan Award, 1981; appt. judge, Superior Court of Pa., 1980, elected to a ten year term Nov. 1981; appt. to Judicial Inquiry & Review by Supreme Ct., 1983, reappt. 1985; married to Marguerite McEwen; 3 children: Mary Ann, Maureen, Happy.

FRANK J. MONTEMURO, JR. was born Oct. 27, 1925, in Phila., the son of Frank J., Sr. and Catherine Montemuro; att. Temple Univ. Law Schl.; Duke Univ. Law Schl. (LL.B.); Phi Alpha Delta Legal Frat.; Alpha Phi Delta undergrad. frat.; Phila., Pa. Bar Assns.; Pa. Conf. of St. Trial Judges; Pa. Natl. Council of Juvenile Court Judges; Natl. Juvenile Court Foundation; dpty. trial commissioner for Criminal Listings, 1959-63; frmr. mem., Phila. Co. Bd. of Law Examiners and sec., ward realignment commission; Natl. Pres., Order Sons of Italy in Am.; bd. of dir., Bustleton Lions Club; assoc. capt., St. Jude's Group, Men of Malvern; Rhawnhurst-Castor Mem'l. Post., Am. Legion; frmr. mem., Phila. Judicial Council; Annual Award of Excellence, Phila., Police, Firemen and Police Officers, Custodes Pacis Lodge No. 2085, Order Sons of Italy in Am., 1970; decoration, rank of "Knight of the Order of Merit of the Republic of Italy" conferred by his excellency, the pres. of the Italian Republic, 1968; in August of 1982, His Holiness, Pope John Paul II, conferred upon Judge Montemuro the Papal Honor of Knight Commander of the order of St. Gregory the Great; apptd. judge, Court of Common Pleas, Jan. 4, 1965; elected to full term, Nov. 2, 1965; elected to a second 10-yr. term, Nov. 1975; reelected administrative judge, family court division, for third 5-year term; apptd. to Superior Court on Nov. 19, 1980; elected to Superior Court of Pa. for a ten-year term, Nov. 8, 1983; married Margaret Gigliotti on June 26, 1954; 3 children; home address: 3 Pine Place W., Philadelphia.

PETER PAUL OLSZEWSKI was born May 12, 1925, in Plains, Pa., the son of Alexander J. and Sophie Mohelska Olszewski; Wyoming Seminary, 1942; Lafayette Coll. (A.B.) 1948; St. John's Univ. Schl. of Law (J.D.) 1952; U.S. Army, China-Burma-India, 1943-46; law clerk to Judge Thomas M. Lewis, Ct. of Common Pleas, Luzerne Co., 1955; city solicitor, City of Wilkes-Barre, 1955-62; county solicitor; solicitor, Redevelopment Authority, 1958-67, Parking Authority and Recreation Authority; judge, Court of Common Pleas of Luzerne Co., 1968-83; elected to Superior Court of Pa., Nov. 1983; mem., Am. Pa., Luzerne Co. Bar Assns.; Pa. Conf. of St. Trial Judges; Appellate Judges Conf.; ABA Long Range Planning Com.; mem., Veterans of Foreign Wars, Am. Legion, AmVets; bd. mem., Pa. State Univ., Wilkes-Barre Campus; bd. of trustees, College Misericordia, Dallas; rec., Pa. State Aerie, Fraternal Order of Eagles "Liberty Under Law" award; "Man of the Year," Polish Am. Citizens League of Pa.; "Distinguished Law & Justice Award," Deputy Sheriffs' Assn. of Pa.; lifetime dir., St. John's Univ. Law Schl. Alumni Assn.; hon. mem., Sigma Pi Mu; lifetime mem., YMPA; Catholic chmn., Interfaith Council; married June Swantko; 4 children: Peter Paul, Jr., Paul Peter, II, John Alexander, and Mary June; home address: 56 Riverside Dr., Wilkes-Barre.

ZORAN POPOVICH was born Feb. 4, 1931, in Akron, Ohio, the son of the late Rev. Dr. Milan and Zoritza Popovich; Univ. of Pgh. (B.A.) 1954; Univ. of Pgh. Law Schl. (LL.B.) 1957; U.S. Air Force, active duty, 1951-53, enlisted, achieved rank of Airman First Class; Allegheny Co. Bar Assn.; elected judge, Court of Common Pleas, Nov. 1973; appointed to the Superior Court, Dec. 16, 1980; married Helen Bodnar; 4 children; home address: 416 Beckman Dr., McKeesport.

JAMES E. ROWLEY was born April 8, 1926, in Tarentum, the son of Myron E. and Ethelwyn M. Beatty Rowley; att. Geneva Coll., Carnegie Instit. of Tech.; Washington and Jefferson Coll. (A.B.) 1949; Univ. of Pgh. Law Schl. (LL.B.) 1952; U.S. Army, 1944-46; Beaver Co., Pa., Am. Bar Assns., Am. Judicature Society; Pa. Conf. of St. Trial Judges; First Presbyterian Ch., Beaver; apptd. judge, Court of Common Pleas, June 11, 1966; elected to full term, 1967; reelected 1977 to second full term; elected to Pa. Superior Court, 1981; appt. to Judicial Inquiry & Review Bd., Dec. 1984; married Ruth A. Agnew on June 14, 1949; 1 son, Daniel A.; home address: 113 Maplewood Dr., Beaver.

PATRICK R. TAMILIA was born in Pgh., the son of Louis and Catherine Mareno Tamilia; Duquesne Univ. (B.A.) 1952; Duquesne Univ. Law Schl. (J.D.) 1959; post-grad., Duquesne Univ. (psych., sociol.) 1952-1955; U.S. Marine Corps, 1946-1948; commiss. off., U.S. Army Artillery, 1952; over 17 year period, worked in Juvenile Detention, Juvenile Probation; dir., Domestic Relations of Allegheny Co.; mem., Allegheny Co., Pa. Bar Assns.; Am. Judicature Soc.; Am. Justinian Soc. of Jurists; consultant, Dept. of Psychiatry Forensic Service, Univ. of Pgh. Schl. of Medicine; Glen Mills Schl.; chmn., Pa. Bar Assn., Family Law Section; chmn., Allegheny Co. Family Law Section; chmn., Juvenile Judges Section, Pa. Trial Judges; frmr. v. pres., Natl. Order Italian Sons and Daughters of Am.; advisor, "Positive Outcome Project" Natl. Center Juvenile Justice; Primary Prevention Prog., St. Francis Hosp.; Parenting Program, Salvation Army; Circle "C" Group Homes; South Hills Outreach; Task Force on Mental Health, Pa. Office of Mental Health; bd. chmn., Parental Stress Center (child abuse); Valley Community Services; Abraxas Foundation; Child Sexual Abuse Task Force; Prison Bd., Allegheny Co. Prison; led in creation of Neuropsychiatric Assessment Unit for Violent Children (Shuman Center program), faculty mem., Family Law, Duquesne Univ. Schl. of Law; Judicial Coll. Pa. Supreme Ct.; Natl. Council of Family and Juvenile Ct. Judges; author of numerous articles on juvenile delinquency, mental health, and family court; mem., Joint Family Law Council, participated in creating Domestic Relations Manual with Domestic Relations Com., Supreme Ct. Admin. Offices; rec. Disting. Alumnus Award, Duquesne Univ.; charter mem., Duquesne Univ. Century Club; meritorious service award, Pgh. Jaycees; Allegheny Co. Youth Council, Annual Recognition Award; Phi Delta Kappa Lay Leader Award in Ed.; recognition awards fr. Glen Mills Schl., Holy Family Inst., Circle "C" Group Homes, Abraxas Foundation, Juvenile Detention Bd., Pa. Coll. of the Judiciary, and the Italian Sons and Daughters of Am.; elected judge, Common Pleas Court, 1969, retained in 1979; served in Juvenile, Family and Criminal Court, 1970-84; elected to Superior Court for ten-year term in 1983; married Betty Jane Koffler, two children: Mark, Arthur; resident of Rosslyn Farms.

DONALD E. WIEAND was born Sept. 18, 1926, in Allentown, the son of Earl and Bernetta Frey Wieand; att. Muhlenberg Coll.; Villanova Univ. (A.B.) 1948; Dickinson Schl. of Law (LL.B.) 1950; editor-in-chief, Dickinson Law Review, 1950; U.S. Naval Reserve, WW II; Lehigh Co., Pa., Am. Bar Assns.; bd. of trustees, Dickinson Schl. of Law; service award, Pa. Trial Lawyers Assn., 1979; Am. Judicature Soc.; bd. dir., Allentown Osteopathic Hosp.; bd. dir., YMCA of the USA, 1978-83; pres., Middle Atlantic Region of YMCAs, 1978-83; pres., Allentown YMCA, 1970-71; bd. dir., State YMCA, pres., 1984-86; YMCA Member of the Year Award, 1971; adv. bd., Minsi Trails Co., BSA (v. pres., 1971-73); Service to Scouting Award, 1968, 1970; adv. bd., Allentown Salvation Army; bd., Allentown Police Athletic League; past pres., Kiwanis Club of W. Allentown; F&AM; Lehigh Consistory; Rajah Temple Shrine; Mason of the Year Award, 1974; Order of AHEPA, Lehigh Chpt.; bd. of assoc., Muhlenberg Coll.; Pa. Soc.; Sons of the Am. Revolution; Citizenship Award, Exchange Club of Allentown, 1979; Distinguished Service Award, Liberty Bell Shrine, 1979; elder, First Presbyterian Ch. of Allentown; elected judge, Court of Common Pleas, commencing Jan. 1964; reelected, 1973; appt. to the Superior Court of Pa., Sept. 19, 1978; reappt. Nov. 19, 1980; elected Nov. 3, 1981; married Wilma C. English; 2 children; home address: 50 Park Blvd., Allentown.

EXECUTIVE ADMINISTRATOR OF THE SUPERIOR COURT

NICHOLAS L. DiLORENZO was born July 28, 1949, in Phila., the son of Nicholas J. and Lucy Paradise DiLorenzo; grad., Villanova Univ. (B.S.) 1971; Drexel Univ. (M.S.) 1977; faculty, St. Gabriel's Hall, 1972-73; budget officer, Phila. Criminal Justice Coordinating Comm., 1977-80; appt. fiscal admin., Superior Court of Pa., 1981; appt. exec. admin., Superior Court, 1986; v. pres., Main Line Lodge Order Sons of Italy in America; sec., Overbrook Lions Club; Man of the Year, Order Son of Italy in American District 4, 1985; married Kathleen M. Nagurny, Esq.; home address: 31 St. Rd., Newtown Square.

PROTHONOTARY OF THE SUPERIOR COURT

DAVID A. SZEWCZAK was born June 19, 1956, in Phila.; grad., Villanova Univ. (B.A., pol. sci.) 1978; Villanova Univ. Schl. of Law (J.D.) 1981; admitted to the Bar of the Supreme Court of Pa., Nov. 6, 1981; admitted to Bar of the U.S. Dist. Court for the Eastern Dist. of Pa., Aug. 2, 1983; admitted to the Bar of the U.S. Court of Appeals for the Third Circuit, March 26, 1986; frmr. law clerk and admin. asst. to President Judge Vincent A. Cirillo; frmr. supervising staff atty. at Central Legal Staff; Prothonotary of the Superior Court of Pa., Nov. 3, 1986; mem., Montgomery Co. and Pa. Bar Assn.; resides in Hatfield.

THE COMMONWEALTH COURT

THE PRESIDENT JUDGE

JAMES C. CRUMLISH was born May 5, 1920, in Phila., son of the late Ruth Hardy Crumlish and the late Common Pleas Court Judge James C. Crumlish; Georgetown Univ. (B.S.) 1941; Univ. of Pa. (LL.B.) 1948; entered Navy as an ensign, Sept. 1941, served in Atlantic and Pacific areas and left service as a Lieut. Comm., 1946; Phila. Registration Commission, 1952-61; dist. attorney, Phila., 1961-66; private practice, 1966-70; commissioned judge, Commonwealth Court, April 15, 1970; president judge, Commonwealth Court, February 19, 1980; married Rosemary C. McCarthy, 1946; 5 children: Rosemary Crumlish Lord, Patricia R. Murphy, Frances R. Keating, James C. III, Thomas Sean; 9 grandchildren; home address: The Presidential Apartments, City Line Ave. & Presidential Blvd., Philadelphia.

JUDGES

FRANCIS A. BARRY was born Jan. 9, 1920, in Pgh., the son of Francis A. and Mary Agnes Kennedy Barry; Duquesne Univ., (B.A., magna cum laude); Duquesne Univ. Schl. of Law (LL.B.) 1951, (later awarded J.D. degree); grad., Natl. Judicial Coll., Univ. of Nevada; 4 years, U.S. Army Air Corps, Africa and Middle East; asst. co. solicitor, (1954-58), first asst. co. solicitor, (1958-70), solicitor, 1972-74, Allegheny Co.; solicitor, Allegheny Co.

MEMBERS, COMMONWEALTH COURT OF PENNSYLVANIA

left to right
Seated: Joseph T. Doyle, David W. Craig, James Crumlish, Jr. (President Judge), John A. MacPhail, Francis A. Barry
Standing: James Gardner Colins, Madaline Palladino
Not present: Genevieve Blatt (Senior Judge), Alexander F. Barbieri (Senior Judge), Jacob Kalish (Senior Judge), Emil E. Narick (Senior Judge)

Community Coll., 1972-74; solicitor, Boroughs of West Mifflin, Baldwin, Carnegie and Plum in Allegheny Co. and solicitor, 4 authorities; participated in many landmark cases in municipal litigation field: elected, 45th Congressional District representative, 1967-68 Pa. Constitutional Convention; subcomm. co-chmn., Judiciary Comm.; Ancient Order of Hibernians; various volunteer fire companies (former solicitor); Pa. Conf. of St. Trial Judges; adm. to all St., Fed. courts and U.S. Supreme Court; Adjunct Professor of Law, Duquesne Univ. Law Schl., 1972-80; Adjunct Prof. of Law, Univ. of Pgh., 1983-84; Pa. and Allegheny Co. Bar Assns.; recommended for appointment to Common Pleas Court by Allegheny Co. Bar Assn. and citizens Judicial Qualifications Commission; appt. judge, Court of Common Pleas of Allegheny Co., March 1974; elected to full term commencing January 1976; appt. to Commonwealth Court, July 12, 1983; elected for full term commencing Jan. 1984; married Ruth Goddard; 4 daughters and 4 sons: Margaret Agnes, Walter Timothy, Thomas Shannon, Mary Sheila Rose, Francis A. III, Rita Claire, Patrick Goddard, and Eileen Marie; home address: 1020 Fidelity Drive, Pittsburgh (West Mifflin Borough).

JAMES GARDNER COLINS was born June 9, 1946, in Philadelphia, the son of Charles and Florence Gardner Colins; grad., Northeast H.S., 1964; Univ. of Pa. (B.A.) 1968; Villanova Univ. Schl. of Law (J.D.) 1971; Sigma Chi Alumni Fraternity; Captain, U.S. Army Reserve; mem., Pa., Phila. Bar Assns.; asst. dist. atty., Phila. Co., 1971-75; judge, Phila. Municipal Ct., 1980; bd. gov., Hercules-Spartan Chptr. Am. Hellenic Ed. & Progressive Assn.; bd. gov., Phila. Boosters' Assn.; Order of Sons of Italy in Am.; Univ. of Pa. Alumni Affairs; rec., Italian/American Press Award; elected judge, Commonwealth Court of Pa., Nov. 1983; married Mary diGiacomo; 3 children: Sarah Jane, Alexander, Leah.

DAVID W. CRAIG was born Feb. 17, 1925, in Pgh., the son of David and Ella M. Williamson Craig; Univ. of Pgh. (A.B.) 1948, (J.D.) 1950; USAAF, 1943-45, 1st lieut. (bomber pilot), Disting. Flying Cross, 1944; Am., Pa. Bar Assns.; Pgh. City solicitor, 1961-65; Pgh. Dir. of Public Safety, 1965-69; author, *Pennsylvania Building and Zoning Laws*, 1951; adjunct professor, grad. schools of pub. admin., city planning at Univ. of Pgh., Carnegie-Mellon, Yale Universities (to 1978); appointed judge, Commonwealth Court, June 21, 1978; elected Nov. 1979; married Ella Van Kirk; 2 children: Linda Craig Mooser and Muriel Craig Lagnese; home address: Allison Park.

JOSEPH T. DOYLE was born Oct. 6, 1931, in Ridley Park, the son of Frank and Mary Bellwoar Doyle; LaSalle Coll. (B.S., cum laude) 1953; Villanova Univ. Law Schl. (J.D.) 1958; U.S. Army, 1953-55; Delaware Co., Pa., Am. Bar Assns.; dir., Legislative Reference Bureau, 1979-80; State Representative, 1970-78; Knights of Columbus; Am. Legion; elected judge, Commonwealth Court, Nov. 3, 1981; married Elizabeth Kavanaugh; 4 children: Louise, Meghan, Kimberly, Rebecca; home address: 129 W. Providence Rd., Aldan.

JOHN A. MacPHAIL was born Jan. 20, 1924, in Johnstown, the son of Donald C. and Marie Trapp MacPhail; Washington and Jefferson Coll. (A.B.) 1948; Dickinson Schl. of Law (LL.B.) 1951; U.S. Army, field artillery, 1942-45; Honorary Doctor of Laws, Gettysburg Coll., 1971; Disting. Service Award, Washington and Jefferson Coll., 1971; Adams Co., Pa., Am. Bar Assns.; Freedoms Foundation Award for Public Address, 1977; Masonic Bodies; Am. Legion; VFW; appointed judge, Court of Common Pleas, Nov. 1966; elected Nov. 1967; appointed judge, Commonwealth Court of Pa., June 21, 1978; elected to full term 1979; married Jeanne A. Spangler on Dec. 28, 1946; 4 children; home address: 721 Lincolnway West, Gettysburg.

MADALINE PALLADINO was born May 5, 1924, in Allentown, the daughter of Joseph and Angelena Trentalange Palladino; Univ. of Pa. (A.B.) 1944; Columbia Univ. Schl. of Law (J.D.) 1947; Phi Beta Kappa; asst. solicitor, City of Allentown; 1959-1960; asst. dist. atty., Lehigh Co., 1960-64; solicitor, Register of Wills, 1952-56, 1965-79; Fellow, Am. Bar Foundation; Natl. Assn. of Women Judges; Am., Pa., and Lehigh Co. Bar Assns.; Am. Arbitration Assn.; bd. trustees, Cedar Crest Coll.; Sacred Heart Hosp.; President's Council, Allentown Coll. of St. Francis De Sales; adv. bd., Muhlenberg Coll.; Our Lady of Mt. Carmel Church, Allentown; Supreme Ct. Appointee, v. chmn., Civil Procedural Rules Com.; lecturer, Continuing Legal Ed. Program, Pa. Bar Inst.; founder, past pres., Conf. of County-Legal Journal Officers, Pa. Bar Assn.; chmn., Public Relations Com., Pa. Bar Assn., appointed judge, Commonwealth Court, May 15, 1980; elected for full ten-year term, Nov. 1983; home address: 226 North 27th St., Allentown.

EXECUTIVE ADMINISTRATOR OF THE COMMONWEALTH COURT

G. RONALD DARLINGTON was born June 16, 1947, in Phila., the son of George W. and Alice Turner Darlington; grad., Princeton Univ. (B.A.) 1969; Dickinson Schl. of Law (J.D.) 1972; private law practice, York, 1972-73; admin. asst. to James S. Bowman, President Judge, Commonwealth Court, 1973-76; appt. Prothonotary of the Commonwealth Court, Oct. 27, 1976; appt. Executive Administrator of the Commonwealth Court, Oct. 13, 1986; Pa. Bar Assn.; Natl. Conf. of Appellate Ct. Clerks; frmr. trustee, Dickinson Schl. of Law; pres., Princeton Alumni Assn. of Central Pa.; frmr. pres., Dickinson Schl. of Law Alumni Club of Cumberland, Dauphin and Perry Cos.; lecturer, Pa. Bar Assn., Pa. Bar Institute, Dauphin Co. Bar Assn.; author, *Pennsylvania Appellate Practice;* married Diane Ashbock; 2 children; home address: 119 Slover Rd., Mechanicsburg.

PROTHONOTARY OF THE COMMONWEALTH COURT

DANIEL R. SCHUCKERS was born Feb. 24, 1943, in Pittsburgh, the son of Raymond R. and Monica Horak Schuckers; Colgate Univ. (B.A.) 1965; Stanford Univ. (M.A.) 1966; Peace Corps Vol. (Uganda) 1966-68; teacher, Rose Tree Media Schl. Dist., 1969-70; Dickinson Schl. of Law (J.D.) 1973; history instructor, Penn State Univ.-York, 1971-76; law clerk to Judge (later Justice) Roy Wilkinson, Jr., 1973-74; asst. atty. gen., Dept. of Labor and Industry, 1974-80; dep. chief counsel, Dept. of Labor and Industry, 1980-82; dep. atty. gen., litigation sec., 1982-84; dep. prothonotary for law, Commonwealth Ct., 1984-87; Prothonotary, Commonwealth Court, 1987- ; Pa. Bar Assn.; author of numerous articles on unemployment compensation; co-author, *Pennsylvania Appellate Practice* (1986); married Sara LeCleire; 3 children; home address: 3817 Hearthstone Road, Camp Hill.

DISTRICT COURTS
COURTS OF COMMON PLEAS

ABOOD, CARAM J. (47th District) was born Oct. 25, 1937, in Windber, the son of Joseph and Josephine Shaddy Abood; U. of Notre Dame (B.S.) 1960, U. of Notre Dame Law Schl. (J.D.) 1961; Pa. Natl. Gd., 1961-64; Pa. Bar Assn., Pa. St. Trial Judges Assn.; Cambria Co. Dist. Atty., 1972-76; elected to Court of Common Pleas, 1975; married Judith M. Dettor; 2 children: Anne Marie, Karen Therese; home address: 103 Colgate Ave., Johnstown.

ABRAHAM, LYNNE MARSHA (1st District) was born Jan. 31, 1941, in Phila.; Temple Univ. (B.A.) 1962, Temple Univ. Law Schl. (J.D.) 1965; Phila., Pa., Am. Bar Assns.; Lawyer's Club of Phila.; Justice Lodge; B'nai B'rith; Am. Judicature Society; Pa. Conf. of State Trial Judges; N.O.W.; exec. comm., B'nai B'rith; Boy Scouts; American-Italy Society; asst. dist. atty., Phila., 1967-72; exec. dir., Phila. RDA, 1972-73; Woman of the Year Award, B'nai B'rith; married Edward Felbin; home address: 296 St. James Pl., Philadelphia.

ACKER, ALBERT E. (P.J. — 35th District) was born July 25, 1925, in Sharon, the son of Kemp G. and Leah Mitchell Acker; attd. Allegheny Coll.; Dickinson Schl. of Law (LL.B.) 1951; U.S. Army Infantry during WW II 1943-46, 1951-52; lawyer; Pa., Mercer Co. Bar Assns., Pa. St. Trial Judges Conf.; v.chmn., Masonic Lodge No. 250, Sharon; BPOE, Sharon Lodge; commissioned judge, Court of Common Pleas, Jan. 1, 1968; elected to full term, Jan. 1, 1970; retained, Jan. 1, 1980; Pres. Judge, Jan. 3, 1986; First Presbyterian Ch. of Sharon; Buhl Trustees; married Helen Cartwright, April 14, 1951; 5 children; home address: 656 Carley Ave., Sharon.

ACKERMAN, DANIEL J. (10th District) was born Apr. 18, 1939, in Pgh., the son of James L. and Vivian C. Bomer Ackerman; Thiel Coll. (B.A.) 1961; Univ. of Pgh. Law Schl. (J.D.) 1964; Pa. Conf. of St. Trial Judges; asst. public def., Westmoreland Co., 1970-73; Denmark Manor Un. Ch. of Christ; appt. judge, Court of Common Pleas, May 9, 1980; elected, Nov. 1981; married Rebecca R. Robinson; 2 children; home address: R.D. 3, Export.

ADAMS, FRED C. (14th District) was born May 17, 1924, in Philippi, W. Va., the son of Randall and Bertha Adams; California St. Coll., (B.S.) 1948; Duquesne Law Schl., (LL.B.) 1956; entered private practice, 1957; Fayette Co., Pa., Am. Bar Assns.; Am. Trial Lawyers' Assns.; Pa. Trial Lawyers' Assn.; Pa. Commonwealth, Superior, Supreme Courts; U.S. District Court; commissioned judge, Court of Common Pleas, Jan. 1975; elected 1976; married Catherine Nebraska; 1 child, Fred C., Jr.; home address: 71 Eighth Street, Uniontown.

AMBROSE, DONETTA W. (10 District) was born Nov. 5, 1945, in New Kensington, the daughter of Chester J. and Mary Groza Wypiski; Duquesne Univ. (B.A.) 1967, and its law schl. (J.D.); Westmoreland Co., Pa., Am. Bar Assns.; William Penn Fraternal Assn.; Italian Sons and Daughters of Am.; Polish Nat. Alliance; Pa. asst. atty. gen., 1972-74; St. Ethics Comm., 1978-81; asst. dist. atty., Westmoreland Co., 1978-82; elected judge, Court of Common Pleas, Nov. 3, 1981; married J. Raymond Ambrose, Jr.; 1 child, J. Raymond, III; home address: 180 Glenview Dr., New Kensington.

AMMERMAN, JOSEPH S. (46th District). Judge, Court of Common Pleas.

ANTHONY, FRED P. (6th District) was born Aug. 26, 1935, in Erie, the son of Fred P. and Marion S. Scharrer Anthony; att. Cathedral Prep. (awarded Ford Foundation 4-year scholarship as junior); Univ. of Louisville (A.B.); Univ. of Louisville Law Schl. (J.D.) 1958; Judge Advocate, U.S. Air Force; Erie Co., Pa., Kentucky, Am. Bar Assns.; Pa. St. Trial Judges; Natl. Conf. of Juvenile Court Judges; appointed to Pa. Juvenile Court Judges Commission, May 1973; chmn., Juvenile Court Judges' Comm. 1975 to 1980; elected judge, Court of Common Pleas of Erie County, Nov. 1971;

appointed admin. judge, Juvenile Court of Erie Co., June 1972; co-founder, Youth Svcs. Coordinating Council & Youth Svcs. Bureau; 1st v.p., PA Conf. of State Trial Judges; married Maureen Von Hoven, Aug. 25, 1956; father of 5 children.

AVELLINO, BERNARD J. (1st District) was born Sept. 10, 1937, in Phila., the son of Benjamin and Josephine Della Selva Avellino; Villanova Univ. (B.S.) 1959; Villanova Law Schl. (J.D) 1962; Natl. Judicial Coll., 1982; attorney; Phila., Pa. Bar Assns.; Phila., Pa., Am. Trial Lawyers Assns.; UNICO; Dem. Leader, Ward 40A, 1975-81; Dem. Exec. Comm., 40th Ward, 1963-81; Dem. Natl. Convention, 1978; v. pres., S.W. Phila. C of C; Adv. Comm., Eastwick Project; Towne Gardens Civic Assn.; Man of the Year, 40th Ward Dem. Women's Aux., 1976; Patriot's Bowl, City of Phila., 1978; Sons of Italy, 1981; Justinian Society, 1982; *Who's Who in Am. Politics;* elected judge, Court of Common Pleas, Nov. 3, 1981; married Oramae Hester; 1 child, Lauren: business address: 692 City Hall, Philadelphia.

BACKENSTOE, JOHN EDWIN (P.J. — 31st District) was born Nov. 25, 1932, in Allentown, the son of Gerald S. and Harriet S. Backenstoe; Trinity Coll. (A.B.) 1954; Univ. of Pa. (LL.B.) 1957; frmr. capt., U.S. Army Reserve; Lehigh Co., Pa., Am. Bar Assns.; state rep. from Allentown, 1961-64; Emmaus Moravian Ch.; elected judge, Court of Common Pleas, 1971; retained, 1981; pres. judge, Jan. 1, 1984; married Lois Benner, Aug. 6, 1959, 3 sons; home address: 3955 Azalea Rd., Allentown.

BAYLEY, EDGAR B. (9th District) was born May 18, 1939, in Bayshore, N.Y., the son of Edgar and Dorothy Melhorn Bayley; St. Lawrence Univ. (B.A.) 1961; Dickinson Schl. of Law (LL.B.) 1964; U.S. Army, 1965-66; mem., Pa. Bar Assn.; chief public defender, 1968, 1st asst. dist. atty., 1969-75, dist. atty., 1976-83, Cumberland Co.; adjunct asst. prof. of law, Dickinson Schl. of Law, 1974-80; supervising judge, fifth statewide Invest. Grand Jury, 1986-; elected judge, Court of Common Pleas, Nov. 1983; married Mary K. Bayley; 2 children: Anne K. and Mark F.; home address: 118 N. 33rd St., Camp Hill.

BECKERT, PAUL REPPELLE (7th District) was born Dec. 16, 1921, in Pgh., the son of Paul M. and Mary R. Blacksmith Beckert; Drexel Institute of Tech. (B.S.) 1944; Temple Law Schl. (LL.B.) 1949; U.S. Navy, WW II, Lt. (j.g.); asst. dist. atty., Bucks Co., 1954-58; dist. atty., Bucks Co. 1958-64; commissioned judge, Court of Common Pleas, Jan. 6, 1964; elected to full term commencing Jan. 3, 1966; reelected Nov. 1975; elected pres. judge, Oct. 1977; married Norma Jean Smith, May 25, 1945; 3 children; home address: 601 Station Ave., Langhorne.

BELL, JOHN F. (27th District) was born June 24, 1936, in Pgh., son of Winfield Scott and Rosanna Cronaure Bell; Washington and Jefferson Coll. (A.B.) 1959; Univ. of W. Va. (LL.B.) 1961; U.S. Army, JAGC, active duty 1961-1964, Captain; Pa. Bar Assn.; active member of various civic assns.; asst., 1st asst. dist. atty., Washington Co., 1966-75; elected judge, Court of Common Pleas, 1976; married; home address: 1198 Sunnybrook Dr., Washington.

BERNSTEIN, MARK ISRAEL (1st District) was born Aug. 18, 1947, in New York City, the son of Harry and Edith Bernstein; grad., St. John's Coll., Annapolis (B.A.) 1969, Univ. of Pa. Law Schl. (J.D.) 1973; Pa. Army Natl. Guard, 1969-75; attorney; mem.: Pa. and Am. Bar Assns., Tort and Insurance Practice Section; Am. Trial Lawyers Assn.; Pa. Trial Lawyers Assn.; Pa. Civil Judicial Procedure Com.; Dep. City Commissioner, Phila., 1984, 1985, 1986; mem.: U.S. Service Academy Selection Com., Second Congressional Dist.; Philadelphians for Recycling; ex. com., Phila. Lawyers Against Apartheid; Affirmative Action Com., Dem. State Com.; West Mt. Airy Neighbors Bd. of Dirs. (v. chmn., 1980); bd. dirs., Help, Inc. (chmn., 1980); adv. council, Sudden Infant Death Resource Center; bd. dirs., Friends of Phila. Parks; appointed judge, Court of Common Pleas, April 6, 1987; married Linda Torcaso; 3 children: David, Joseph, and William; home address: 506 Westview St., Philadelphia.

BIEHN, KENNETH G. (7th District) was born July 10, 1939, in W. Rockhill Twp., Bucks Co., the son of Claire G. and Vivian Brown Biehn; Lafayette Coll. (A.B.) 1961, Phi Beta Kappa; Duke Law Schl. (LL.B.) 1964, honors; Pa. St. Trial Judges Assn.; Bucks Co. Bar Assn.; asst. dist. atty., 1966-69; 1st asst. dist. atty., 1962-72; dist. atty., 1972-79; State D.A.'s Assn., 1977-78; NOVA; one of the "Outstanding Young Men in Pa.," 1972, Pa. Jaycees; appt. judge, Court of Common Pleas, Dec. 1979; appt. supervising judge, Bucks Co. Investigating Grand Jury, 1982; chmn., Victim/Witness Advisory Group, P.C.C.D., 1983-present; married Julia Gibson; 3 children: Christopher, Alexander, Stephen; home address: 90 Buttonwood Lane, Doylestown.

BIESTER, EDWARD GEORGE, JR. (7th District) was born Jan. 5, 1931, in Phila., the son of Edward George and Muriel Worthington Biester; George School, 1948; Wesleyan Univ. (B.A.) 1952; Temple Law Schl. (LL.B.) 1955; Delaware Vlly. Coll. (hon. Doctor of Law) 1977; attorney; Pa. St. Trial Judges Assn.; Phila. Racquet Club; asst. dist. atty., Bucks Co., 1958-64; U.S. Congressman, 1967-77; Atty. Gen., Comm. of Pa., Jan. 1979 - May 1980; Reformed Ch. in Am., Dutch; Natl. Governing Bd. of Common Cause, 1977-79; bd. dir., Overseas Develop. Council, 1977-81; bd. dir., World Affairs Council of Phila.; appt. judge, Court of Common Pleas, May 19, 1980; married Elizabeth Lauffer; 4 children: Ann Meredith, Edward G., III, James Paul, David Robertson; home address: Lower Mountain Rd., Furlong.

BIGLEY, GERARD M. (5th District) was born on Aug. 24, 1939, in Pgh., the son of Paul E. (dec'd) and Julia Coffey Bigley; Univ. of Pgh. (BBA) 1961; Duquesne Univ. Schl. of Law, (J.D., cum laude) 1970; lawyer; Allegheny Co., Pa., Am. Bar Assns.; Pa. Coll. of the Judiciary; F.O.E.; B.P.O.E.; L.O.O.M.; Knights of Equity; Knights of Columbus; Police Legal Adv., Pgh. (July 1970-Dec. 1975; Sept. 1977-Dec. 1977); asst. dist. atty., Allegheny Co. (1976-77); Am. Academy of Trial Lawyers Prize for excellence in Torts; Am. Jurisprudence award of excellence in criminal law; West Publishing Co. Prize for scholastic excellence (4 yrs.); Duq. Law Wives Scholarship Award; Allegheny Co. Bar Assn. scholarship; elected judge, Court of Common Pleas, 1977; married E. Maureen Ward; 6 children: Julie, Maureen, Colleen, Kelly, Gerard, Jr. and Daniel; home address: 2451 Rosegarden Rd., Pittsburgh.

BIUNNO, FRANCIS A. (1st District) was born on April 4, 1925, in Phila., the son of Henry E. and Margherita Galasso Biunno; Univ. of Pa. (A.B.) 1947; Univ. of Pa. Law Schl. (LL.B.) 1950; U.S. Naval Reserve, active duty, 1943-45, and organized reserve until 1970, with several periods of recall to active duty; retired Commander; asst. dist. atty., Phila., 1953-55; tax conferee, Phila., Bd. of Ed.; Phila. and Am. Bar Assns.; Am. Legion; Catholic War Vet.; K. of C.; Sons of Italy; Justinian Society; UNICO; elected judge, Court of Common Pleas, Nov. 1973; married Jule C. Kleinz; 2 children: Regina Marie and Francis Henry; home address: 7337 Boreal Place, Philadelphia.

BLAHOVEC, JOHN EDWARD (10th District) was born Oct. 13, 1951, in Greensburg, the son of John G. and Margaret Muchoney Blahovec; grad., Univ. of Pgh. (B.A.) 1973, School of Law (J.D.) 1976; mem., Pa. and Westmoreland Co. Bar Assns.; Juvenile Court Master, 1983-85; mem., Our Lady of Grace Ch.; Westmoreland Mental Health Assn. Bd.; Outstanding Young Man in America, 1986; Who's Who in the East, 1983; author, "Role of Masters in Child Custody," Pa. Child Advocate, 1986; elected judge, Court of Common Pleas, Nov. 1985; married Mary Louise Grabowski; 2 children; home address: 128 Cheshire Dr., Greensburg.

BLAKE, EDWARD J. (A.J. — 1st District) was born May 18, 1926, in Phila., son of Philip and Agnes Dunleavy Blake; St. Joseph's Coll. (B.S.) 1950; pres., class of 1954, Univ. of Pa. Law Schl.; contributing ed., Wolffe on Zoning; co-author, "Computer Streamlines Caseload at Philadelphia Common Pleas Court"; private law practice, 1955-61; USNR, 1946-72; Lt. Comm., ret.; admitted to practice, U.S. Supreme Ct.; U.S. Ct. of Military Appeals; and Supreme Ct. of Pa.; mem., Lawyers' Club of Phila. pres.,

St. Joseph's Coll. Alumni 1969, past pres. exec. comm., Pa. Scholarship Assn.; chief dpty. court admin. 1962-64; court admin., Court of Common Pleas and Quarter Sessions of Phila., 1964-72; Phila., Pa. Bar Assn.; Am. Judicature Society; St. Joseph's Coll. Advsry. Council; Brehon Law Soc.; The Irish Soc.; U. of Pa. Schl. Honor Comm.; mem., editor'l. staff Dean Fordham's Municipal Law Letter, Americanism Award, 1976; Phila. Judicial Council, 1965-68; Lecturer in crim. law. St. Joseph's Coll. eve. div.; past pres., St. Patrick's Day Observance Assn., 1983-84; Cruiser Olympia Assn., Inc.; Professional Automative Data Systems Inc.; chmn., Self Help Movement, Inc.; appt. judge, Court of Common Pleas, Phila., Dec. 31, 1971; elected to full term, Nov. 6, 1973; retained Nov. 8, 1983; married Marian J. Blankley, June 1953; 4 children; office address: 658 City Hall, 1400 Market St., Philadelphia.

BONAVITACOLA, ALEX (1st District) was born June 23, 1931, in Phila., son of Fiore C. and Helen Guarente Bonavitacola; Temple Univ. (B.S.) 1953; Temple Law Schl. (J.D.) 1956, (LL.M.) 1964; admitted to practice of law, 1957; asst. city solicitor, Phila., 1957-62; chmn., Phila. Zoning Bd. of Adjustment, 1962-73; Phila., Pa. Bar Assns.; Phila. Bar Comm. of Censors, 1970-71; St. Disciplinary Hearing Bd., 1972-73; mem., officer, UNICO Charities Inc.; Bd. of Man., YMCA (Central Phila.) 1977-79; chmn., Juvenile Justice Center of Pa., 1975-79; Unico Village Inc.; Lions Club; Order Sons of Italy; Phi Theta Kappa; Phi Delta Phi (legal); Ch. of the Holy Spirit (R.C.); elected judge, Court of Common Pleas, Phila., Jan. 7, 1974, retained Nov. 1983; attended Natl. Coll. of the St. Judiciary, now known as National Judicial College 1974-78, and faculty advisor 1982 (Natl. Judical Coll.); mem., Judicial Inquiry and Review Bd., 1985; married Flora Jane Catalano; 2 children; office address: 686 City Hall, Philadelphia.

BORTNER, OSCAR S. (7th District) was born Sept. 3, 1920, in Phila.; Temple Univ. (A.B.) 1946; Univ. of Pa. Law Schl. (LL.B.) 1949; appt. judge, Court of Common Pleas, Sept. 1977; elected, Nov. 1979.

BRADLEY, EDWARD J. (P.J. - 1st District) was born May 22, 1928, in Phila., the son of Michael J. and Emilia Angiuli Bradley; Univ. of Pa. Wharton Schl. (B.S.) 1950; Univ. of Pa. Law Schl. (LL.B.) 1953; U.S. Navy, Lieut. (jg), 1953-57; dep. city solicitor, City of Phila., 1957-65; Phila. Bar Assn.; Judicial Council of Pa.; Am. Bar Assn.; Am. Judicature Soc.; Am. Judges Assn.; Pa. Conf. of State Trial Judges; Natl. Conf. of Metropolitan Courts; Justinian Soc.; Friendly Sons of St. Patrick; exec. com., St. Patrick's Day Observance Assn.; Order Sons of Italy (Comm. Lodge); bd. dirs., Assn. of Retarded Citizens; adv. council, Natl. Multiple Sclerosis Soc.; awards: recipient Distinguished Pennsylvanian Award, 1980; decoration, rank of "Cavalieri Ufficiale in the Order of Merit of the Italian Republic" conferred by the President of the Italian Republic, 1982; appt. judge, Court of Common Pleas, Aug. 9, 1965; elected to full term 1965; retained Nov. 1975 and Nov. 1985; elected pres. judge, April 11, 1975; reelected April 11, 1980, and Jan. 6, 1986; married Jane de C. Hill; 6 children; home address: 6390 Drexel Rd., Philadelphia.

BRADY, WILLIAM J., JR. (1st District — Municipal Court) was appt. judge, Municipal Court of Philadelphia, June 12, 1980; elected, Nov. 3, 1981.

BRAIG, JOSEPH P. (1st District) was born April 6, 1937, in Phila., the son of George and Marie Palmer Braig; LaSalle Coll. (B.A.) 1959, Temple U. Law Schl. (LL.B.) 1962; Lt. j.a.g., Pa. Ntl. Gd.; Lt., USNR; asst. U.S. Atty., E. Dist. of Pa., U.S. Dept of Justice, 1963-66; mem., Pa. House of Representatives, Nov. 1970-Jan. 1971; dpty. mayor, City of Phila., 1973-74; P.A.L. Hall of Fame, 1976; Internatl. Accessibility Award for helping handicapped, 1973; Outstanding Young Amer. Award, 1970; articles published: "U.S. Dist. Ct. Criminal Procedure," "A Meaningful Response to Victims Rights," 1976; elected to Court of Common Pleas, Nov. 1975; 2 children; residence: Philadelphia.

BRAXTON, JOHN L. (1st District) was born Feb. 6, 1945, in Phila., the son of John and Sylvia Trotman Braxton; Penn St. Univ. (B.S.) 1966; Howard Univ. Schl. of Law, 1971; U.S. Army, 1966-68; Am., Natl. Bar Assns.; Barristers Club; Pi Lamda Phi; bd. mem., Pa. Minority Bus. Devel. Auth., 1975-81; Penn St. Alumni; Howard Univ. Alumni; Phila. Council, Boy Scouts of America; The Child Psychiatry Center at St. Christopher's Hosp. for Children; Homemaker Service of Metropolitan Area, Inc.; v. pres., Fellowship Comm.; Union League Award; Am. Legion; appt. judge, Court of Common Pleas, July 1981; home address: 15 Randolph Court, Philadelphia.

BRODY, ANITA B. (38th District) was born May 25, 1935, in New York City, the daughter of David T. and Rita Sondheim Blumstein; Wellesley Coll. (A.B.) 1955; Columbia Law Schl. (J.D.) 1958; lawyer; Montgomery Co., Pa., Am. Bar Assns.; mem., Domestic Relations Panel, Civil Proc. Rules Com.; mem., Dep. Sheriff's Ed. & Training Bd., Pa. Comm. on Crime & Delinq.; Judicial Ed. Com., Pa. Conf. of St. Trial Judges; appt. judge, Court of Common Pleas, May 5, 1981; elected, Jan. 4, 1982; married Jerome I. Brody, M.D.; 3 children: Lisa, Marion, Timothy; home address: Bala Cynwyd.

BROMFIELD, WAYNE ALLAN (17th District) was born May 16, 1947, in Kingston, the son of Malcolm Poad and Edna Louise Price Bromfield; grad., Duke Univ. (A.B., econ.) 1969; Dickinson Schl. of Law (J.D., magna cum laude) 1974; mem., Union Co., Snyder Co., Pa. and Am. Bar Assns.; Union Co. public defender, 1975; Union Co. solicitor, 1976-85; New Berlin Lions Club; bd. dirs., Union Co. United Fund; bd. dirs., Union Co. Cancer Soc.; Messiah Evangelical Lutheran Ch.; Walter Harrison Hitchler Award, Dickinson Schl. of Law, 1974; Woolsack Soc. Award, 1974; editor-in-chief, Dickinson Law Review; judge, Court of Common Pleas, Jan. 6, 1986; married Kathleen Joyce Butler; 3 children: Kelly Nicole, James Malcolm, Devon Butler; home address: P.O. Box 415, New Berlin.

BROMINSKI, BERNARD CURTIS (11th District) was born on Oct. 4, 1922, in Swoyerville, the son of John and Josephine Hudock Brominski; attended F&M Coll., Dickinson Coll. (B.A.), Dickinson Law Schl. (LL.B.); hon. degree, Dickinson (J.D.) 1970; admitted to practice in Luzerne Co., Supreme, Superior Courts; Lieut. (jg) U.S. Navy 1943-46, U.S.S. Allen, Pacific Theater; bd. of adv., Kings Coll.; adv. bd., Office of Community Services, Wilkes Coll.; VFW Forty-Fort Post, Am. Legion; former special dpty. atty. genl., Comm. of Pa., Am., Pa., Luzerne Co. Bar Assns.; exec. bd., St. Trial Judges Assn.; past pres., Pulaski Day Comm.; Assumpta Council, K of C (4th Degree); appt. to Luzerne Co. Bench, Dec. 1958; elected to full term, 1959; reelected, Nov. 5, 1969, 1979; married Dorothea Stevens, Dec. 28, 1945; 1 child, Elizabeth Sieminski; home address: 618 Church St., Swoyerville.

BROWN, CARSON V. (P.J. — 25th District) was born May 29, 1938, in Manns Choice, Bedford Co., the son of Victor L. and Sara K. Merringer Brown; Lock Haven Univ. (B.S.) 1963; Dickinson Schl. of Law (J.D.) 1966; Natl. Coll. of the St. Judiciary (Univ. of Nevada) 1973; Clinton Co., Pa., Am. Bar Assns., Pa. Conf. of St. Trial Judges; Natl. Conf. of St. Trial Judges; Pa. Council of Juvenile Court Judges; Natl. Council of Juvenile Court Judges; Am. Judicature Soc. LaFayette Lodge No. 199, F&AM; AASR North. Masonic Jurisdiction (32°) Lions Club; Un. Methodist Ch.; elected judge, Court of Common Pleas, Jan. 7, 1974; retained for second term, Jan. 2, 1984; married Carol Rockey; 2 sons: Carson II and Jason; home address: 200 West Church St., Lock Haven.

BROWN, CHARLES CLIFFORD, JR. (P.J. — 49th District) was born June 22, 1937, in Bellefonte, the son of Charles Clifford and Laura Pearl Ritchie Brown; Bellefonte H.S., 1955; Juniata Coll. (B.A.) 1959; N.Y. Univ. Schl. of Law (L.D.) 1962; Centre Co., Pa., Am. Bar Assns.; Am. Judicature Society; dist. atty. Centre Co., 1966-78; St. John Lutheran Ch.; senator, Jr. Chamber Intnatl.; Root-Tilden Scholar, N.Y. Univ. Schl. of Law; Bd. of Trustees, Juniata Coll.; elected judge, Court of Common Pleas, Nov. 1979; married Sandra Sue Johnston; 4 children: Steven, Douglas, Christopher, Linda; home address: 505 E. Curtin St., Bellefonte.

BROWN, LAWRENCE A. (38th District) was born Sept. 20, 1925, in Phila., the son of Lawrence and Anne Fallon Brown; att. Bucknell U.; grad. Ohio Wesleyan U. (B.A.) 1948, U. of Michigan Law Schl. (J.D.) 1950; U.S. Navy, 1943-46; ensign, USNR; lawyer; Am., Pa., Montgomery Co. Bar Assns.; Am. Judicature Soc.; St. Thomas More Soc.; Sigma Chi; Friendly Sons of St. Patrick; Warminster Navy Flying Club; judge, Court of Common Pleas, July 1, 1976; married Inez V. McGough (decd. 1965); 4 children: Lawrence A. III, Claire M., Michael F., Kevin O'F.; residence: 44 Terrace Road, Norristown.

BRUMBAUGH, ROY BRUCE (24th District) was born Jan. 16, 1932, in Hilltop, Logan Twp., the son of Roy E. and Mary Books Brumbaugh; Phillips Acad., Mass., 1949; Princeton Univ. (B.A.) 1953; Dickinson Schl. of Law (LL.B.) 1959; U.S. Army, Security Agency, 1953-56; frmr. atty.-at-law; Pa., Blair Co. Bar Assns.; Pa. Conf. of St. Trial Judges; York Rite Bodies of Free Masonry; principal of 20th Masonic Dist. Schl. of Instruction, 1969-79; Dist. Dep. Grand High Priest of Grand Holy Royal Arch Chapt. of Pa., 1979; frmr. spec. asst. atty. gen., Cnwlth. of Pa., 1966-70; Fairview Un. Methodist Ch. (frmr. trustee, Youth Leader, Choir); Altoona City Zoning Bd. of Appeals (1961-70); Kiwanis; frmr. Altoona Jaycee-of-the-Month (twice); frmr. Altoona Sr. Men's Table Tennis Champ., Far Eastern/8th Army Table Tennis Champ., 1954-55; elected judge, Court of Common Pleas, Nov. 1979; married Patricia Louise Gery; 5 children: Jill, Mark, Grant, Brad, Jolene; home address: 308 28th Ave., Altoona.

BRUNO, JOSEPH C. (1st District) was born June 26, 1924, in Phila., the son of Charles J. and Emilia Marra Bruno; Temple Univ. (B.S.) 1948, Temple Univ. Schl. of Law (J.D.); pres., Alpha Phi Delta; U.S. Army, European Theater of Operation, 1943-46; ch. counsel, Pa. Public Utility Commission, 1963-68; Am. Legion; VFW; Union League of Phila.; B. S. of Am.; Justinian Society, Am. Justinian Society of Jurists; past pres., Rotary Club of Phila.; dist. gov. nominee, Rotary Internatl. Dist. 745, 1986-87; Phila., Pa. Bar Assns.; commissioned judge, Court of Common Pleas, Dec. 2, 1968; elected to full term commencing Jan. 1970; retained for 2nd 10 yr. term Nov. 1979.

BRYDON, JOHN H. (50th District) was born on Apr. 13, 1930, in Grove City, the son of Harold R. and Olive Carothers Brydon; Valley Forge Mil. Acad., 1949; Allegheny Coll., 1952; Univ. of Pa., (LL.B.) 1959; U.S. Army, 1954-56; Pa., Am. Bar Assns.; Mason; Moose; United Commercial Travelers; schl. bd., Slippery Rock Area, 1962-64; dist. atty., Butler Co., 1964-81; Phi Theta Kappa, Silver P.T., Valley Forge Mil. Acad.; elected judge, Court of Common Pleas; Nov. 3, 1981; married Norma Dee McCandless; 3 children: Karen A. Lytle, Yvonne, Harold; home address: R.D. 3, Slippery Rock.

BUCKWALTER, RONALD LAWRENCE (2nd District) was born Dec. 11, 1936, in Lancaster, the son of Noah Denlinger and Carolyn Marie Lawrence Buckwalter; Franklin and Marshall Coll. (A.B.) 1958; Coll. of Wm. and Mary (J.D.) 1962; U.S. Army, 1st Lieut. (PARNG, 1962-68); attorney; Pa., Lancaster Co. Bar Assns.; Pa. Conf. of St. Trial Judges; sec., City of Lancaster Auth. 1964-70; dist. atty., 1977-80; bd. dir., YMCA; bd. dir. Am. Cancer Society; exec. bd., B.S.A.; pres., Lancaster Co. Prison Bd.; pres. elect., Lancaster Co. Bar Assn.; elected judge, Court of Common Pleas, Nov. 1979; married Dolly Fitting; 2 children: Stephen Matthew, Wendy Susan; home address: 330 Spencer Ave., Lancaster.

CAESAR, BEREL (1st District) was born Oct. 21, 1927, in Phila.; Swarthmore Coll., 1948, Univ. of Pa. Law Schl., 1954; attorney and frmr. partner, Phila. firm of Rubin, Leib and Caesar; former v. chmn., and actng. chmn., first Phila. Mental Health and Mental Retardation Adv. Bd.; author, articles and textual material; lecturer and panelist on mental health law at various colleges; Clinical Assoc. Prof., Hahnemann Medical Coll., Dept. of Mental Health Sciences; Mental Health Assn., Southeastern Pa. and Pa. Mental Health, Inc.; Phila. Bar Assn. and past chmn. of its Mental Health Comm.; frmr. mem., Environmental Quality Comm., Corp., Banking and Real Estate Section, Probate and Trust Section; past pres., Congregation Melrose B'nai Israel; B'nai B'rith, Federation of Jewish Agencies, including past bd. mem., Rebecca Gratz Club, HIAS; past pres., Melrose Park Gardens Civic Assn.; frmr. ward chmn., 61st Ward Dem. Exec. Comm.; active in Dem. party, 17 years; approved by Phila. Bar Assn. Judiciary Comm. as qualified for Common Pleas Court Judge, 1973; recommended by Pa. Trial Court Nominating Comm., 1974 and 1975; appt. to Court of Common Pleas, Dec. 19, 1974; reapptd. Dec. 1975; married Joan Coleman; 2 sons, Neil and Robert; 1 daughter, Miriam; residence: 110 E. 64th Ave., Philadelphia.

CAIAZZA, FRANCIS X. (53rd District) was born Oct. 17, 1935, in New Castle, the son of Hugo and Anna Micco Caiazza; Duquesne Univ. (B.A.) 1958; Univ. of Pgh. (LL.B.); U.S. Army, 1961-63; Army Reserve, 1967; Pa. Conf. of State Trial Judges; Lawrence Co. Bar Assn.; ex. bd. mem., New Castle Labor Management Com.; mem., American Legion Post 343; sustaining mem., NAACP; board mem., Italian-American Heritage Festival; mass commentator, St. Vitus Church; elected judge, Court of Common Pleas, Nov. 3, 1981; married Roselee Morrone; 3 children: Matthew, Felicia, Christian; office address: Lawrence Co. Government Center, New Castle.

CAPPELLINI, GIFFORD S. (11th District) was born Dec. 10, 1925, in Plains, Pa., the son of Rinaldo and Marie Evan Cappellini; grad., Bucknell Univ. (B.A.) 1946; Cornell Law Schl. (LL.B.) 1951; U.S. Army, 1946-48; judge, Court of Common Pleas, Nov. 5, 1985; married Dorothy Dzialo; 5 children: Gifford, Jeffrey Dorothy, Jill Lester, and Kim Boyle; home address: 320 Academy St., Wilkes-Barre.

CAPPY, RALPH J. (A.J. — 5th District) was born on Aug. 25, 1943, in Pgh., the son of Joseph R. and Catherine Miljus Cappy; Univ. of Pgh. (B.S.) 1965; Univ. of Pgh. Schl. of Law (J.D.) 1968; Allegheny Co., Am., Pa. Bar Assns.; public defender, Allegheny Co., 1975-78; commissioned judge, Court of Common Pleas, June 1978; appt. admin. judge, 1985; married; home address: 1081 Shady Ave., Pittsburgh.

CAPUZZI, CONRAD B. (14th District) was born Mar. 6, 1939, in Uniontown, the son of Corrado and Ida Solary Capuzzi; Waynesburg Coll. (B.S.) 1961; W. Va. Univ. Law Schl. (J.D.) 1964; U.S. Army, active reserve, 1957; Fayette Co., Pa., Am. Bar Assns.; asst. dist. atty. (1968-75); dist. atty., (1975-77); appt. judge, Court of Common Pleas, Oct. 4, 1977; elected Nov. 1979; married Linda Simpson; 4 children: Nina, Lisa, Jon, James; home address: Uniontown.

CARSON, CURTIS C., JR. (1st Dsitrict) was born Feb. 5, 1920, in Cowpens, S.C., the son of Curtis and Mamie Hardy; Va. St. Coll. (A.B.) 1943, Univ. of Pa. Law Schl. (LL.B.) 1946; Natl. Judicial Coll., Reno, 1975; Pa., Phila. Bar Assns., Am. Judicature Society; Pa. Trial Judges; commissioned judge, Court of Common Pleas, Dec. 27, 1971; appt. faculty adv., Natl. Judicial Coll., Univ. of Nevada, Summer 1979, 1983; appt. observer, Conf. on "Prison Overcrowding," 1985; charter mem., Pa. Comm. on Sentencing, 1979-pres.; participant in training session, Natl. Inst. for Trial Advocacy; American Trial Lawyers and Moot Court; elder, Germantown Community Presbyterian Ch.; married Vida H. Timbers, June 7, 1947; 3 children; home address: 547 Pelham Rd., Philadelphia.

CARUSO, GARY P. (10th District) was born Oct. 22, 1948, in Monessen, the son of Herman and Alberta Jannotta Caruso; grad., Waynesburg Coll. (B.A., econ.) 1970; Duquesne Univ. (J.D.) 1973; mem., Pa. Conf. of St. Trial Judges; Roman Catholic; elected judge, Court of Common Pleas, Nov. 5, 1985; married Patricia Ann Hotz; 2 children.

CASSIMATIS, EMANUEL A. (19th District) was born Dec. 2, 1926, in Pottsville, the son of Andrew E. and Mary Calopedis Cassimatis; Dickinson Coll. (A.B.) 1949, Dickinson Schl. of Law (LL.B.) 1951; U.S. Army, Jan. 1945 to Sept. 1946; York Co., Pa. Bar Assns.; various Masonic bodies; 2nd v. pres., Pa. Conf. of St. Trial Judges, elected 1986; pres. elect., Juvenile Court Section, Pa. Conf. of St. Trial Judges, elected 1986; mem., Permanent Families Project Task Force, appt. 1984; Greek Orthodox Church of Annunciation of York, Pa., frmr. pres., Bd. of Trustees; various civic and charitable organizations; elected to the Hall of Fame, Wm. Penn Sr. H.S., York, 1981; elected judge, Court of Common Pleas, Nov. 1977; married Thecla Karambelas; 3 children: Mary Ann Maza, John E. and Gregory E.; home address: 176 Rathton Rd., York.

CATANIA, FRANCIS JAMES (P.J. — 32nd District) was born Mar. 26, 1920, in Woodlyn, the son of James V. and Mary Schlitsey Catania; Temple U. (B.S.) 1941; Temple U. Law Schl. (J.D.) 1949; capt. WW II, U.S. Army Air Corps; Delaware Co., Pa., Am. Bar Assns.; Phi Alpha Delta Law Frat., Lawyers Club of Delaware Co.; Pa. Council of Juvenile Ct. Judges; Pa. Trial Judges Conf.; Law Alumni of Temple U.; Am. Judicature Soc.; Delaware Co. coroner, 1957-63; dpty. atty. genl., Comm. of Pa., 1951-55; asst. atty. genl., Pa. Dept. of Revenue, 1963; former solicitor, Twp. of Chester, Boroughs of Brookhaven, Eddystone, Prospect Park and Folcroft (Del. Co.), 1950-63; former solicitor for sheriff, Del. Co. and co. controller; former solicitor, Woodlyn Fire Co., Eddystone Fire Co., Felton Hose and Chemical Co.; solicitor, Ridley Twp. Businessmen's Assn., 1949-63; former chmn., Delaware Co. Eagle Bd.of Review, B. S. of A., 1965-69; Bd. Trustees, Temple U.; active in many community fund drives; chmn., pres. elect., Pa. St. Trial Judges Conf.; grad., sentencing institute sponsored by Phila. Crime Comm. and St. Trial Judges Conf. (1968); appt. judge, Court of Common Pleas, 1963; elected to full term to commence Jan. 1966; retained, 1975; elected by board of judges to administrative judge, effective Dec. 1, 1970, and to pres. judge, eff. Jan. 5, 1976; reelected pres. judge Jan. 5, 1981 for 5 yrs.; married Elizabeth Ann Frandsen, July 29, 1950; 6 children.

CERCONE, DAVID STEWART (5th District) was born Nov. 24, 1952, in Stowe Twp., the son of Richard D. and Margaret Stewart Cercone; grad., Sto-Rox H.S., 1970; Westminster Coll. (B.A., magna cum laude) 1974; Duquesne Law Schl. (J.D.) 1977; attorney; mem., Allegheny Co. Bar Assn.; Pa. Conf. of State Trial Judges; ISDA; judicial law clerk in Common Pleas Ct., 1978; asst. dist. atty., Allegheny Co., 1979-81; dist. justice, 1982-85; mem., bd. dirs., Boys Club of Western Pa., Sto-Ken-Rox Unit; instructor, Univ. of Pgh., Legal Studies; elected judge, Court of Common Pleas, Nov. 1985; married Mary Ann Kraus (dist. justice); home address: 410 Phillips Ave., McKees Rocks.

CHIOVERO, JOHN J. (1st District) was born July 21, 1927, in Phila., the son of Joseph and Jennie Vitagliano Chiovero; Temple Univ. (B.S.) 1958; Temple Univ. Schl. of Law (LL.B.) 1963, (J.D.) 1968; clerk (1947-52), officer (1953-54), spec. agent, Intelligence Div. (1954-66), attorney (1966-77), U.S. Treas. Dept.; admn. law judge, Pa. Public Utility Comm., 1977-79; pres., dir., treas., counsel, Phila. I.R.S. Employees Fed. Credit Union, 1951-77; adjunct assoc. prof., Drexel Univ. 1974-present; "Special Commendation" from U.S. Atty. Walter E. Allesandroni and Reg. Commissioner of I.R.S.; "Special Commendation Award" from Robert F. Kennedy, U.S. Atty. Gen., 1964; numerous awards and honors from the U.S. Treas. Dept.; elected judge, Court of Common Pleas, Nov. 1979; married Bertha Lacopulos; home address: 3726 Conshohocken Ave., Philadelphia.

CHRONISTER, JOHN H. (19th District) was born July 21, 1944, in York, the son of Willard R. and Miriam V. Hughes Chronister; grad., York High, 1961; Dickinson Coll. (B.A.) 1965; Dickinson Schl. of Law (J.D.) 1968; Public Defender's Office of York Co., 1972-1987; Hayshire United Ch. of Christ, York; judge, Court of Common Pleas, March 16, 1987; married Nancy L. Hale; one child, Amy Jo; home address: 2181 Blenheim Ct., York.

CICCHETTI, RICHARD D. (P.J. — 14th District) was born Aug. 12, 1935, the son of Nazzareno (dec.) and Louise Cicchetti; att. Univ. of Notre Dame, Univ. of Pgh. (B.S.), Duquesne Univ. Schl. of Law (J.D.); adm. to practice law, Fayette Co. Dec. 11, 1961; elected district attorney, Fayette Co. 1971; elected judge, Common Pleas Court, Fayette County, Nov. 1973; sworn in pres. judge, June, 1978; married Erlene Nemish; 1 son, James.

CIPRIANI, NICHOLAS A. (A. J. — 1st District) was born July 1, 1919, in Phila., the son of Giacinto and Louisa Bozzuto Cipriani; Temple Univ. (B.S.) 1940, Temple Univ. Schl. of Law (J.D.) 1943; U.S. Army, 1943-46, released as 2nd Lt. M.A.C.; Phila., Pa., Am. Bar Assns.; mem., Juvenile Court Judges' Comm.; Lawyers Club of Phila.; bd. of trustees, Phila. Methodist Hospital; pres., Temple Gen. Alumni Assn.; bd. Crime Prevention Assn. of Phila.; Phila. Council, Boy Scouts of Am.; Order Sons of Italy in Am.; spec. asst. atty. genl., Comm. of Pa., 1965-69; certificate of merit, Big Brother Assn., Feb. 1956; decorated by the Republic of Italy, March 1961, June 1961, July 1978; Certificate of Honor, Temple Univ. Law Alumni Assn., April 1972; elected judge, Court of Common Pleas, Nov. 1969; married Catherine Campo, July 30, 1947; 2 children; home address: 1327 Wolf St., Philadelphia.

CLARK, TAMA MYERS (1st District) was born Dec. 24, in Boston, the daughter of Samuel Lloyd and Marion Rieras Myers; Morgan St. Univ. (B.S., summa cum laude) 1968; Univ. of Pa. (Gra. Schl. of Fine Arts (MCP)) 1972; Univ. of Pa. Law Schl. (J.D.) 1972; Alpha Kappa Alpha Sorority, Inc.; asst. dist. atty., 1973-80; deputy city solicitor, 1980-83; mem., Phila., Natl., D.C. Bar Assns.; Pa. Conf. of State Trial Judges; Pa. Supreme Ct., Civil Procedural Rules Com.; Barristers' Assn. of Phila.; Women & Girl Offenders Task Force, Mayor's Comm. for Women; bd. dirs., Prisoners' Family Welfare Assn.; bd. dirs., Community Services Planning Council of Southeastern Pa.; Am. Foundation for Negro Affairs: preceptor-legal div., "New Access Routes to Legal Careers" Program; Links, Inc., Penn Towne Chapter; Coalition of 100 Black Women, Phila. Chapt.; frmr., mem., Project Review Com. on Protection of Human Subjects; Corrections Task Force; Fee Disputes Com.; Big Brothers/Big Sisters Assn.; Women in Govt. Network; counsel, Phila. Prisons' Bd. of Trustees; awards received: Who's Who in American Coll. and Univ. Profile, 1967; Disting. Honor Scholar, Morgan State Coll., 1968; Achievement and Merit, Morgan Student Govt., 1968; Student Leadership, Parekh Memorial, 1968; 5,000th Membership, Phila. Bar Assn., 1972; Outstanding Young Woman of America Profile, 1976; Legion of Honor, Chapel of Four Chaplains, 1977; Disting. Alumnus, Phila. Chapt., Morgan State Univ. Alumni Assn., 1984; Outstanding Woman of the Community, Bright Hope Baptist Ch., Women's Com., 1984; 1984 Morgan State Univ. Disting. Alumni of the Year, Natl. Assn. for Equal Opportunity in Higher Education; Woman of the Year, Natl. Sports Foundation, 1985; elected judge, Court of Common Pleas, Nov. 8, 1983; married Peter Wellington Clark, Jr.

CLARK, WARD F. (7th District) was born Dec. 9, 1927, in Phila., the son of Frank Ward and Alice Cecelia McLane Clark; grad., Pa. State Univ. (B.S.) 1952; Univ. of Pa. (LL.B.) 1955; U.S. Army, 1946-47; mem., Bucks Co., Pa. and Am. Bar Assns.; mem., Hare Law Club; Bucks Co. Controller, 1978-86; Bucks Co. Dist. Atty., 1966-72; Presbyterian; author, "Scientific Evidence," Practicing Law Institute Sourcebook for Prosecutors, 1968; elected judge, Court of Common Pleas, Nov. 5, 1985; married Jonnye T. Clark; 5 children: Robert, Stephen, Amy, Beth, and Ward, Jr.; home address: 187 East Court St., Doylestown.

CLARKE, EUGENE H., JR. (1st District) was born July 26, 1920, in Phila., the son of Eugene H. and Mary E. Bell Clarke; Central H.S., Phila. 1936; Howard Univ. (A.B.) 1940; Howard Univ. Law Schl. (LL.B.) 1943; attorney; Am., Natl., Pa., Phila. Bar Assns.; Pa. Trial Lawyers Assn.; former pres., the Barristers; pres., Prisoner Family Welfare Assn.; adv. bd., the Academy of Advocacy; bd. dir., Women's Christian Alliance, 1947-49, 1979 to date; Phila. Boosters; Phila. Republican Policy Comm., 1977-80; chmn., Criminal Justice Section, Phila. Bar Assn., 1979; Voice Publication Community Service award, 1977; Phila. Business Assn. Law award, 1977; Howard Univ. Alumnus of Delaware Valley, 1978, and Disting. Alumni award, 1979; J. Austin Norris award, the Barristers, 1978; Phila. Electric Energy Debate Judge, 1978-79; appt. judge, Court of Common Pleas, May 13, 1980; married Annie Brown; home address: 2 Wissahickon Lane, Philadelphia.

CLARKE, JAMES F. (5th District) was born on Nov. 26, 1918, in Pgh., the son of John W. and Mary R. Clarke; Univ. of Pgh. and its law school (LL.B.) 1951; Natl. Coll. of the St. Judiciary (Univ. of Nevada) 1972; U.S. Army Air Corps, 1941-45, served in Africa and Italy as first sergeant; 20 years' law practice with firm of Cauley, Birsic & Clarke; admitted to practice before all state and county courts and U.S. Supreme Court; Allegheny Co., Pa., Am. Bar Assns., Pa. Conf. of St. Trial Judges; member, Pa. House of Representatives, 1958-68; Prothonotary, Com. Pleas Court, Alleg. Co., 1968-72; elected delegate, Dem. Natl. Convention, 1968; KC; Knights of Equity; Ancient Order of Hibernians; Am. Legion, Schenley Post 663, VFW, Post 223; appt. judge, Allegheny Co. Court of Common Pleas, Dec. 20, 1971; elected to full term, Nov. 1973; married, wife Miriam; home address: 104 Circle Dr., Pittsburgh.

CLELAND, JOHN MATTHEW (P.J. — 48th District) was born Dec. 24, 1947, in Kane, the son of Drs. Charles E. and Elizabeth Mason Cleland; Denison Univ. (B.A.) 1969; The National Law Center, Geo. Washington Univ. (J.D., with honors) 1972; appt. pres. judge, Court of Common Pleas, Oct. 5, 1984; married; 2 children; home address: R.D. #1, Kane.

CONNELLY, SHAD, F. (6th District). Judge, Court of Common Pleas.

CONROY, MICHAEL J. (1st District — Municipal Court) was born Nov. 4, 1928, in Phila., the son of Michael J. and Marie C. Conroy; St. Joseph's Coll. (B.S.) 1952; Temple Univ. Schl. of Law (LL.B.) 1958; Navy, 1946-48; member numerous civic organizations; Phila., Pa. Bar Assns.; Pa. Conf. St. Trial Judges; Pa. Assn. of Courts of Initial Jurisdiction; North Am. Judges Assn.; Am. Judges Assn.; Am. Judicature Society; civil and criminal rules comm.; Phila. Bar Assn.; Governor's Commission on Education of the Minor Judiciary; awards: Temple Law Alumni Assn. Certificate of Honor; Chapel of the Four Chaplains Disting. Service Award; Manayunk Neighborhood Council Man of the Year Award; North Light Boys' Club Disting. Service Award; co-author, Handbook of Phila. Courts and Admin. Offices (1962); operational adv. comm., Criminal Justice Agencies; Committee Distinguished Service, Commission on Merit Judicial Retention, Phila. Bar Assn.; former capt. of dpty. sheriffs, Sheriff's office, Phila.; elected magistrate, Phila. Co., Nov. 7, 1967; elected judge, Municipal Court, Phila., 1969; married Theresa Guidici, Pod. D., June 28, 1952; 3 children: Rosemary, Michael and Theresa; home address: 531 E. Gate St., Philadelphia.

CONWAY, ROBERT J. (P.J. — 22nd District) was born Dec. 21, 1938, the son of Joseph F. (dec.) and Helen Heneforth Conway; Univ. of Scranton, 1960; Brooklyn Law Schl., 1963; U.S. Army, 1963-65; maj., Natl. Guard; frmr. head of law firm; Pa., Am. Bar Assns.; Pa. Conf. of St. Trial Judges; Elks; Wayne Co. pub. def., 1970; Wayne Co. dist. atty., 1971-75; Texas Rod & Gun Club; elected president judge, Court of Common Pleas, 1979; married Maralyn A. Evans; 2 children: Holly Beth and Brent; home address: R.D. 2, Honesdale.

COPPOLINO, MATTHEW F. (1st District — Municipal Court) was born in Phila., the son of Domenick and Anna DeGrazia Coppolino; Villanova Univ. (A.B.); Temple Univ. Schl. of Law (LL.B., J.D.); U.S. Navy, Naval Reserves; attorney; Phila., Pa. Bar Assns.; Lawyer's Club of Phila.; St. Thomas More Society; Justinian Society; Sons of Italy; House of Representatives, 1967-72; frmr. chief counsel, House of Representatives, Liquor Control Bd.; Packer Park Civic Assn.; S. Health & Welfare Co.; Men of Malvern; Holy Spirit Holy Name Society; Holy Spirit Lectors Society; Filippo Palizzi Society; Jr. C of C of Phila.; while in the House, prime sponsor of the first bill passed in the U.S. to aid Non-Public Schls., and the Magistrate's Reform Act; appt. judge, Municipal Court, Dec. 12, 1981; married Amelia Capozzoli; 2 children: Lisa, Matthew, Jr.; home address: 3201 S. 17th St., Philadelphia.

CORSO, S. GERALD (38th District) — Judge, Court of Common Pleas.

COSGROVE, FRANCIS P. (1st District — Municipal Court) was born Jan. 19, 1929, in Phila., the son of Francis J. and Catherine Ksiazkiewicz Cosgrove; LaSalle Coll. (B.S.) 1956; Temple Univ. Schl. of Law (J.D.) 1963; U.S. Army, active duty, 1951-53; Phila. Bar Assn.; Pa. Conf. of St. Trial Judges; engaged in private practice, 1964-73; instructor, Law, community Coll. of Phila.; LaSalle Coll. Alumni; Temple Univ. Law Alumni; St. Thomas More Society; Am. Rowing Society; Dad Vail Rowing Assn.; Polish American Citizens League; Polish-American Congress; Brehon Law Society; Knights of Columbus; Catholic League for Religious and Civil Rights; Jagiellonian Law Society; elected judge, Municipal Court of Philadelphia, Nov. 6, 1973; commissioned, Jan. 7, 1974; sec. Bd. of Judges of Municipal Court; married Catherine M. Scanlon; 4 children: Christopher, Cathy, Francis, and Daniel; home address: 32 W. Hampton Rd., Philadelphia.

COTTONE, S. JOHN (45th District) was born Oct. 28, 1925, in Dunmore, the son of the late Salvatore and the late Antonina Colletti Cottone; Univ. of Scranton, 1943-44, 1946-48; Catholic Univ. of Am. Law Schl. (LL.B.) 1951; U.S. Air Force, 1944-46; lawyer, 1951-80; Am., Pa., Lackawanna Co. Bar Assn.; K. of C.; UNICO Natl. Service Club; Columbus Day Assn. of Lackawanna Co.; U.S. Atty., Mid. District of Pa., 1969-79; chmn., bd. dir., Catholic Youth Ctr., Scranton; appt. judge, Court of Common Pleas, Jan. 31, 1980; elected, Nov. 3, 1981; married Joan Marie Quinn; 4 children : John J., Anna M., Mary C., Paul G.; home address: 1505 Adams Ave., Dunmore.

CUNNINGHAM, MARY ROSE (1st District). Judge, Court of Common Pleas.

DAGHIR, GORDON J. (P.J. — 59th District) was born Feb. 9, 1933, in Dagus Mines; the son of Dr. N. M. and Katherine Louise Foster Daghir; grad., St. Marys H.S., 1951; Pa. State Univ. (B.A.) 1955; Univ. of Pgh. Law Schl. (LL.B.) 1958; U.S. Army, 1958-60; ; frmr. dist. atty., numerous solicitorships; mem., Presbyterian Ch., St. Marys; judge, Court of Common Pleas, Jan. 6, 1986; married Barbara Campbell; 1 child, Dianna Lynn; home address: 929 S. Michael Rd., St. Marys.

D'ALESSANDRO, NICHOLAS M. (1st District) was born Sept. 17, 1933, in Phila., the son of Nicholas and Nancy D'Alessandro; Temple Univ. (B.S.) 1956, Temple Univ. Law Schl. (J.D.) 1959; attorney; Phila., Pa. Bar Assns.; Am. Arbitration Assn.; Crime Comm. of Phila.; asst. city solicitor, Phila. 1967-72; Tax Review Bd., 1972-77 (chmn. 1974-77); atty. to frmr. 21st Wd. Dem. Exec. Comm.; Manayunk Neighborhood Council; Quaker City String Band; 21st Wd. Community Council; Sword Soc. (Temple U.); K of C; Order Sons of Italy in Am.; past venerable, Grtr. Roxborough Lodge; Justinian Soc.; St. Thomas More Soc.; bd. trustees, Roman Catholic H.S. Alumni Assn.; mgr., Yankees Little League Baseball Team, 1980-81, Padres Jr. League Baseball Team, 1982; Coach, Roxborough Eagles Baseball Team; awards rec'd.: Outstanding Service, Sons of Italy Dist. 1; Excellent Leadership, Sons of Italy Grtr. Roxborough Lodge; Hnry. Dpty. Sheriff, Phila. Co. Community Service; Outstanding Service, Am. Arbitration Assn.; Community Legal Services, Inc. - Volunteer Service to the Poor; Academic Achievement and Outstanding Service in Extracurricular Affairs, Sword Soc. (Temple U.); Highest Scholastic Academic Award, Alpha Phi Delta; Outstanding Performance Award, Am. Industrial Hygiene Assn. (Del. Valley); Excellence Award, Phila. Trial Lawyers Assn; Honry. Dist. Atty. in recognition of dedication; overcame polio to achieve present stature; John Boyce Mem. Award, 21st Ward Junior Baseball League; K of C Archbishop Ryan Gen. Assembly, 4th Deg. Silver Medal Award; appt. and elected, Municipal Court of Phila., 1977; elected, Court of Common Pleas of Phila., 1979; married Elizabeth M. McHenry; 3 children: Kara, Teresa, Nicholas; home address: 415 Ulmer St., Philadelphia.

DALESSANDRO, ARTHUR D. (11th District) was born Aug. 24, 1926, in Yatesville, the son of Dominick and Mary Dalessandro; Wilkes Coll. (B.S.) 1949; Dickinson Schl. of Law (J.D.) 1954; admitted to bar, 1954 and before U.S. Supreme Ct., 1965; aviation cadet, U.S. Army Air Force; Wilkes-Barre Law and Library Assn.; Pa. Conf. of St. Trial Judges; instructor, annual Dickinson Schl. of Law Trial Advocacy Seminar; Elks; Am. Legion 938; Luzerne Co. Mental Health Assn.; Luzerne Co. Assn. for Retarded Children; Sons of Italy; Italian-American Assn., Luzerne Co.; Am. Justinian Soc. of Jurists; honorary member, Penn Mts. Co., B.S.A.; active in civic and comm. affairs; mem.: *Pennsylvania Law Journal-Reporter,* Editorial Board; Penn State Club of Wyoming Valley; Our Lady of Mt. Carmel Ch., Pittston, Holy Name Soc.; rec., 1985 ATLA Outstanding St. Trial Judge Award, Assn. of Trial Lawyers of Am.; Dickinson Schl. of Law Alumni Assn. of Northeast Pa. Area recognition award; cert. of apprec., Wilkes-Barre Law & Library Assn. for outstanding service to assn.; honored by Italian Am. Assn. of Luzerne Co., "Man of the Year-1983"; recognized by Luzerne Co. Police Chiefs Assn. for exemplary service as juvenile judge; served in all divs. of Ct. of Common Pleas, Luzerne Co.; established Juvenile Court Week in Luzerne Co.; has spoken to more than 10,000 grade and high school students on courthouse tours; in charge of stale case terminations since 1976 and has terminated 8,083; appt. judge, Court of Common Pleas, Jan. 1972; reelected to full term commencing Jan. 1974; 1 child, David; home address: 19 Fordham Rd., Laflin, Wilkes-Barre.

DAUER, ROBERT EARL (A.J. — 5th District) was born Jan. 7, 1929; Georgetown Univ. Coll. of Arts and Sciences (B.S.) 1950; studied at Georgetown Univ. Schl. of Law, 1950; interrupted studies to serve in Army, Korean War; Univ. of South Carolina night school courses in economics, business finance; Univ. of Pgh. Schl. of Law (J.D.) 1956; admitted to practice before the Pa. Supreme and Superior Courts, U.S. Court of Appeals, Third Circuit, and U.S. Supreme Court; law clerk to Judge Harry M. Montgomery, Pa. Superior Court; successively, asst., special asst. and exec. city solicitor, Pgh.; chief magistrate city of Pgh., 1970-72; instructor, Inst. of Local Gov't., Univ. of Pgh.; Allegheny Co. Bar Assns.; appt. judge, Court of Common Pleas, Dec. 1, 1972; reappt., March 19, 1974; elected to full term commencing Jan. 5, 1976; elected admin. judge, Criminal Division, for 5 yr. term, Jan. 1978; married Mercedes McSorley; 4 children; home address: 714 Devonshire St., Pittsburgh.

DAVENPORT, HORACE ALEXANDER (38th District) was born Feb. 22, 1919, in Newberry, S.C., the son of William D. and Julia Green Davenport; Howard U. (B.A.) 1946; U. of Pa. (M.A.) 1947; U. of Pa. Law Schl. (LL.B.) 1950; U.S. Army Corps of Engrs., Capt., 1941-46; solicitorships: Central Mont. Co. Area Vo-Tech Schl. (1968-76), Norristown Area Schl. Dist. (1966-76), Norristown Area Schl. Authy. (1966-76), Mont. Co. Elec. Bd. (1958-76), Mont. Co. Tax Claim Bur. (1958-76), Mont. Co. Registration Comm. (1965-76); frmr. dir., Mont. Co. Bar Assn., chmn. and mem. of various comms.; Pa., Am. Bar Assns.; Am. Trial Lawyers Assn.; Civil Rights Comm., Pa. Bar Assn.; Natl. Advsry. Veterinary Medicine Comm., FDA (HEW); Estates Planning Council of Mont. Co.; mem. and frmr. v. chmn., Trial Lawyers Assn. of Mont. Co., dir. of Citizens Council of Mont. Co.; pres., Pa. Schl. Bd. Solicitors Assn., 1972-73, and frmr. dir.; dir., Natl. Schl. Bds. Solicitors Assn., 1969-1976; active in numerous civic and fraternal organizations; Norristown Schl. Bd.; frmr. dir. (6 yrs.), v. pres. (4 yrs.); trustee, Johnson C. Smith Univ., Charlotte, N.C., since 1978; teacher, Wm. Penn Bus. Inst. (1 yr.), practicing lawyer (24 yrs.); elect. judge, Court of Common Pleas, Nov. 4, 1975; married Alice I. Latney; 4 children: Alice K., Beverly A., Horace A., Jr. and Nina E.; home address: 118 S. Schuylkill Ave., Norristown.

DAVISON, MAXWELL E. (31st District) was born Sept. 4, 1932, in Shenadoah, the son of Leonard J. and Bessie Davison; Lafayette Coll. (B.A.) 1954; Dickinson Schl. of Law (LL.B. & J.D.) 1957; Lehigh Co., Pa., Am. Bar Assns.; Am. Judicature Society; City of Allentown Zoning Bd. of Adjustment, 1961-69; solicitor, Washington Twp., Lehigh Co., 1970-71; spec. asst. attny. genl., Comm. of Pa., 1971; mem. and dir., Kiwanis Club of Allentown; bd. of dir., United Fund of Lehigh Co.; Allentown Hosp.; Allentown Police Athletic League; pres., Jewish Community Center of Allentown; Boys Club of Allentown; Greenleaf Lodge F&AM; Temple Beth El; bd. of trustees, Cedar Crest Coll.; pres. elect., Pa. Conf. of Trial Judges; mem., past chmn., Juvenile Court Judges' Comm. of Pa.; Pa. Correction Education Vocational Adv. Comm.; Pa. Comm. Internatl. Year of the Child; part-time faculty, Cedar Crest Coll.; co-chmn., Task Force on Juvenile Certifications to Adult Court, Pa. Joint Council on the Criminal Justice System; co-chmn., comm. of 15; listed in *"Who's Who in Government, Who's Who in American Law,* Parents Anonymous of Pa.; appt. judge, Court of Common Pleas, 1971; elected to a full term, Nov. 1973; retained for additional term, 1983; married Barbara Seiden; 3 sons; home address: R.D. 2, Emmaus.

DELLA PORTA, ARMAND (1st District) was born Dec. 20, 1921, in Phila., son of Domenic and Louise Della Porta; Temple U. Liberal Arts Coll., Temple U. Schl. of Law (LL.B.) 1950; editor-in-chief, Temple Law Quarterly, author of "A Survey of Pennsylvania Law of Marriage & Divorce," "Goodrich-Amran Rules of Civil Procedures," 1950-52; frmr. asst. dist. atty. and general practitioner in small law firm; Pa., Phila. Bar Assns.; St. Thomas More Society; Justinian Society; Pa. Conf. of St. Trial Judges and Am. Justinian Society of Jurists; bd. of trustees, Phila. Free Library; bd. of trustees, Citizens for Ed. Freedom; chmn. of bd., Northwestern Corp.; pres., NW Community MH Center; Am. Judicature Society.; faculty, Pa. Coll. of the Judiciary; rec., 1977 Ignatian Award of St. Joseph's Prep. Sch.; Certificate of Honor, Temple U. Law Alumni Assn.; 2nd Annual St. Thomas More Society Award; commissioned judge, Court of Common Pleas, Dec. 30, 1971; elected to full term, Nov. 1973; reelected to 2nd full term, Nov. 1983; married Marie Cascarino; 4 children; home address: 8925 Crefeld St., Philadelphia.

DEMPSEY, THOMAS E. (1st District — Municipal Court) was born Oct. 22, 1945, in Phila., the son of Frank and Marie Halloran Dempsey; LaSalle Univ. (B.A.) 1967; Notre Dame Law Schl. (J.D.) 1970; mem., Brehon Law Society; Irish Society; appt. judge, Philadelphia Municipal Court, June 13, 1984; home address: 6103 Glenmore St., Philadelphia.

DIAZ, NELSON A. (1st District) was born May 23, 1947, in New York City, the son of Luis Diaz and Maria Cancel; St. John's Univ. (A.A.S.) 1967, (B.S.) 1969; Temple Univ. Law Schl. (J.D.) 1972; Natl. Judicial Coll., 1982; Honorary Doctor of Laws, LaSalle Coll., 1982; associate, Wolf, Block Schorr and Solis-Cohen, 1979-81; special asst., Vice President Mondale, 1977-78; exec. dir., Spanish Merchants Assn., 1973-77; chmn., Natl. Assn. for Spanish Speaking Elderly, 1978-present; bd. dir., Natl. Puerto Rican Coalition, 1978-present (founder 1978); bd. governors, Temple Univ. Hospital, 1976-present; bd. dir., Phila. Police Athletic League, 1981-present; White House Fellow Alumni Assn., 1977-present; bd. dir., exec. comm., Phila. Urban Coalition; bd. dir., Hispanic Assn. of Contractors and Enterprises, 1982-present; Grtr. Phila. Economic Devel. Coalition Task Force, 1982-present; delegate, White House Conf. on Aging, 1981; co-chair, Urban Affairs Partnership, 1977-pres.; bd. dir., William Penn Foundation 1977-pres.; Mayor's Comm. on Puerto Rican Latino Affairs; Phila. Leadership Prayer Breakfast; Implementation of Phila. Police Dept.; *Who's Who in American Lawyers; Who's Who in Hispanic America;* White House Fellows; 1977; Outstanding Young Leader, Phila. Jaycees, 1975; Outstanding Director, Phila. Urban Coalition, 1977; Leadership Mission to Israel, 1981-84; mission to Soviet Union on Soviet Jewry, 1985; appt. judge, Court of Common Pleas, July 20, 1981; elected Nov. 3, 1981; first Hispanic judge in Pa.; married Vilma Delia Ortiz; 3 children: Vilmarie, Nelson, Delia Lee; home address: 6730 N. 11th St., Philadelphia.

DiBONA, ALFRED J., JR. (1st District) was born Dec. 7, 1934, in Phila., the son of Catilda and Alfred DiBona; Temple Univ. (B.S.) 1957; Temple Univ. Law Schl. (LL.B.) 1960; Phila. Bar Assn.; Pa. Conf. of St. Trial Judges; Natl. Coll. of the Judiciary, Camp Gen. Douglas MacArthur Order of Brotherly Love, and Justinian Soc.; Temple Univ. Down Town Club.; asst. dist. atty., Phila., 1964-66; hrng. examiner, Pa. Liq. Control Bd., May 1974-Dec. 1975; Outstanding Undergraduate Award, Temple Univ. Alpha Phi Delta frat., 1957; past master Camp 43, O.B.L., 1966-68, 1974-76; Stella Maris R.C. Ch.; elec. judge, Court of Common Pleas, Nov. 1975; married Helen Hogan; 2 children: Alfred III and Barbara; home address: 2603 S. 11th Street, Philadelphia.

DIEFENDERFER, JAMES N. (31st District) was born Dec. 14, 1930, in Bethlehem, the son of Hon. John H. and Mildred Newhard Diefenderfer; Cornell Univ. (B.A.) 1952; Univ. of Pa. Law Schl. (LL.B.) 1957; U.S. Navy, 1952-54; St. Trial Judges Assn.; Masonic Lodge; Allentown Exchange Club; appt. judge, Court of Common Pleas, June 1979; elected Nov. 1979; 2 children: Allyn Jane, Jason James; home address: 1143 N. Wahneta St., Allentown.

DiNUBILE, VICTOR J., JR. (1st District) was born Apr. 16, 1938, in Phila., the son of Victor J. and Isabel DeVito DiNubile; Univ. of Pa. (B.A.) 1960; Temple Univ. Law Schl. (LL.B.) 1963; attorney; Phila. asst. dist. atty., 1966-73; Phila., Pa., Am. Bar Assns.; Am. Judicature Society; Lawyers' Club of Phila.; Defender Assn.; Phila. Citizens' Crime Comm.; Temple Univ. Law Alumni; Justinian Society; Phi Alpha Delta; frmr. mem., Fee Disputes Comm., Phila. Bar Assn., 1977-81; Alumni Society, Univ. of Pa.; chmn., Zoning Comm., Chestnut Hill Community Assn., 1976-1981; author of various articles for "Temple Law Quarterly;" appt. judge, Court of Common Pleas, June 19, 1981; elected, Nov. 3, 1981; married Mary Green; 3 children: Marybeth, Suzanne, Victor, III; home address: 301 Rex Ave., Philadelphia.

DOLBIN, DONALD DONGES (21st District) was born Nov. 7, 1920, in Hazleton, the son of Dr. Donald L. and Marie Umbenhen Dolbin; Pa. St. Univ. (A.B.); Univ. of Pa. Law Schl. (LL.B.); U.S. Air Force, 1943-46; Bd. of Ed., Pottsville Area Schl. Dist., 1955-77; rec., Silver Bayonet Award, St. Amvets; commissioned judge, Court of Common Pleas, 1977; married Patricia Suender; 3 children: Cyrus Palmer, Esq., Ellen Marie, and Jane Palmer; home address: 1 Cottage Hill, Pottsville.

DOWLING, JOHN C. (12th District) was born Sept. 3, 1923, the son of William B. and Beatrice Hilton Dowling; Univ. of Pgh. (B.S., cum laude) 1947; Dickinson Schl. of Law (LL.B.) 1950; mem., Woolsack Soc.; U.S. Army, 1943-46, Infantry Sgt., E.T.O., 4 Battle Stars; admitted to Bars of Dauphin Co., Commonwealth, Superior, Supreme Courts of Pa., U.S. District Ct., Middle Dist. of Pa., U.S. Third Circuit Ct. of Appeals; past chmn., Civil Service Comm., Susquehanna Twp.; bd. of managers, Harrisburg YMCA; trustee, Harrisburg Public Library; dir., Dauphin Co. Bar (1965-67); dir., B.S.A.; adj. prof. of political science, Lebanon Valley Coll.; supervising judge, Pa. Statewide Grand Jury; specially appointed to preside on the Superior Court; mem., Pa. Board of Probation and Parole Adv. Com. on Probation; appt. judge, Common Pleas Court, Dec. 3, 1970; married Barbara K. King, Sept. 17, 1949; 6 children; home address: 3620 Hillcrest Rd., Harrisburg.

DOYLE, ROBERT A. (5th District) was born in Latrobe, son of John J. and Mary Doyle; Univ. of Pgh. (A.B.) 1939; Univ. of Pgh. Sch. of Law, 1942; WW II, U.S. Army, Combat Infantryman (Private), Europe, P.O.W., Germany, commissioned 16 years; presently Major, U.S. Army Reserve (Judge Advocate), retired; Allegheny Co. (Bd. of Gov.), Pa., Am. Bar Assns.; Elks; Eagles; VFW; Am. Legion; K of C; dpty. atty. genl. Comm. of Pa., 1951-52; editor-in-chief, Univ. of Pgh. Law Review; various articles published in Pgh. Legal Journal; Pa. Constitutional Revision and Constitutional Implementation Committees; co-author, "The Judicial Code" 1976; House of Delegates, Pa. Bar Assn., lecturer, Law and Corporation Finance and Insurance, Univ. of Pgh. and Carlow Coll.; St. Basil's R. C. Ch. and Ch. Comm.; appt. judge, Court of Common Pleas, July 21, 1970; married Frances J. Parker, Aug. 7, 1943; 8 children; home address: 109 Hornaday Rd., Pittsburgh.

DURHAM, CHARLES L. (1st District) was born Oct 12, 1924, in Phila.; LaSalle Coll. (BA) 1952; Temple Univ. Law Schl. (LL.B.) 1955; adm. to Pa. Bar, 1956; legal asst. to pres., Phila. City Council, 1956-58; asst. dist. atty., Phila., 1958-62; private practice, Dashiell, Durham and Wilson, 1962-74; mem., City Council and chmn., License and Inspections, 1968-74; bd. mem., NAACP, 1962-65; YMCA, 1968-72; Boy Scouts of America, 1968-70; Mantua Community Planner, 1968-74; member, YGS, Cobbs Creek Civic Organization, Citizens for Progress; home address: 705 N. 39th St., Philadelphia.

EARLEY, ROBERT C. (P.J. — 40th District) was born Dec. 25, 1929, in Barnesboro, Cambria Co., the son of Samuel Lee and Evelyn Woodhead Earley; Washington Coll., Md. (B.S.) 1952; Dickinson Schl. of Law (LL.B.) 1957; 5th Reg., 1st Cavalry Div., Korea & Japan, 1952-54; attorney-at-law; Indiana Co., Pa. Bar Assns.; 1st asst. dist. atty., Indiana Co. 1961-75; Masons Consistory; Shrine; Allied Club of Indiana, Pa.; Univ. Club, Pittsburgh; Disting. Service Award, Co., Detectives Assn. of Pa.; elected judge, Court of Common Pleas, Nov. 1975; married Hazel Orem; 4 children: Evelyn, Robert, Stephen, and Samantha; home address: 125 South 6th Street, Indiana.

EBY, ROBERT J. (52nd District) was born Aug. 18, 1944, in Lebanon, the son of Robert L. and Lillian D. Boltz Eby; Dickinson Coll. (A.B.) 1966; Villanova Univ. Schl. of Law (J.D.) 1969; Lebanon Co., Pa., Am. Bar Assns.; Lebanon Co.: solicitor, 1980-81, Prothonotary & Tax Claim Bureau, 1971-76, MH/MR Adv. Bd., 1971-76, Domestic Relations Hearing Officer, 1978-80; bd. dir., Lebanon Co. chpt. Am. Red Cross; Easter Seal Soc.; Lions Club; appt. judge, Court of Common Pleas, June 24, 1981; elected Nov. 3, 1981; home address: 604 S. Sixth St., Lebanon.

ECKMAN, D. RICHARD (P.J. — 2nd District) was born Aug. 10, 1929, in Lancaster, the son of David E. and Florence S. Eckman; att. Pa. St. Univ.; Franklin & Marshall Coll. (B.A.) 1951; Dickinson Schl. of Law, (J.D.) 1956; private law practice, 1958-77; dist. atty., Lancaster Co., 1973-77; first asst. dist. atty., asst. dist. atty., Lancaster Co., 1968-73; solicitor, Lancaster Co. Tax Claim Bureau, 1964-67; solicitor, Lancaster Co. Recorder of Deeds Office, 1962-63; adjunct faculty, Franklin & Marshall Coll. 1965-67; Am., Pa., Lancaster Co. Bar Assns.; Pa. Trial Judges' Assn.; Supreme, Superior, Commonwealth Courts of Pa.; U.S. Supreme Ct., U.S. District Ct. for Eastern Dist. of Pa.; U.S. Tax Court; Southcentral Regional Advisory Co., Pa. Comm. on Crime and Delinquency, 1977-80; "Distinguished Service to Law Enforcement" award, and "Disting. Law & Justice Award;" County Detectives Assn. of Pa.; Lions Club (past pres.); Pa. Dist. Atty. Assn. (v. pres., sec., bd. of dir.) 1975-77; mem. Task Force on Crime and Juvenile Deliquency, 1969; elected judge, Court of Common Pleas, 1977; pres. judge since Jan. 6, 1986; married Mary Elizabeth Wohr; 2 sons, David and John; home address: 1022 Buchanan Ave., Lancaster.

EHRLICH, ELIZABETH (23rd District) was born May 27, 1930, in New York City; Hunter College H.S.; Bryn Mawr Coll. (A.B., magna cum laude) 1951; Yale Law Schl. (J.D.) 1954; mem., Berks Co., Pa. & Am. Bar Assns.; Wyomissing Area Schl. Bd., 1971-83; Berks Co. Intermed. Unit Bd., 1975-83; dir., Bank of Pa., 1971-83; bd. mem., United Way of Berks Co.; dir., The Reading Hosp.; Berks Co. Children & Youth Services; frmr. chmn., Juvenile Ct. Adv. Comm.; rec., Colby-Townsend Memorial Prize, Yale Law Schl.; elected judge, Court of Common Pleas, Nov. 1983; married Leon Ehrlich, Esq.; 4 children: Nathaniel E., William A., Steven A., Nancy J.; home address: 1114 Reading Blvd., Wyomissing.

ENDY, ALEXANDER (15th District) was born Oct. 18, 1922, in Coatesville, the son of Asher S. and Celia Hyman Endy; Univ. of Pgh. (B.S.) 1943; Univ. of Pa. Law Schl. (J.D.) 1962; U.S. Army, 1943-46; mem., Pa. & Chester Co. Bar Assns.; Natl. Inst. Munic. Law Offices; Pa. Conf. of State Trial Judges; Pi Lambda Phi Frat.; v. chmn., City Charter Comm., 1961; councilman, City of Coatesville, 1965-67; Coatesville City solicitor, 1967-84;

solicitor, City of Coatesville Authority, Borough of Kennett Square, Parkesburg Zoning Hearing Bd., hearing officer, Chester Co. Court of Common Pleas, 1980-84; mem., Coatesville Rotary Club; F. & A.M.; B'nai B'rith; Beth Israel Congregation; appt. judge, Court of Common Pleas, 1984; elected Nov. 1985; married Pauline B. Braveman; 3 children: Eric, Michael and Daryl; home address: 1220 Stirling St., Coatesville.

ERB, JOSEPH E. (P.J. — 19th District) was born Sept. 11, 1925, in Sunbury, the son of Joseph M. and Gertrude Buckley Erb; Gettysburg Coll. (A.B.) 1949; Univ. of Pa. (LL.B.) 1952; attorney; frmr. partner, Rudisill, Erb and Guthrie, Hanover; mem., Bars of Pa., Supreme, Superior Courts, York Co. Courts; Am., Pa., York Co. Bar Assns.; asst. dist. atty., York Co., 1953-1957, 1969-1973; appt. judge, Court of Common Pleas, Nov. 1974; elected judge, Jan. 1976; retained, Jan. 1986; pres. judge, Dec. 1986; married Jacquelyn March; 1 daughter, Andrea M. Erb, 1 son, Joseph E. Erb, Jr.; home address: 232 Broadway, Hanover.

ESHELMAN, THOMAS JACKSON (23rd District) was born Jan. 7, 1935, in West Reading, the son of Paul Richard and Vida Ellen Kutz Eshelman; Dickinson Coll. (A.B.) 1956; Dickinson Law Schl. (LL.B.) 1959; Pa. Bar Assn.; Pa. St. Trial Judges Assn.; Sigma Chi; Isaac Hiester Lodge No. 660, F&AM; Scottish Rite Bodies, Valley of Reading; Rajah Temple, A.A.O.N.M.S.; Rotary; register of wills, Berks Co., 1968-78; chmn., Domestic Relations Division; elected judge, Court of Common Pleas, Nov. 1977; home address: 3641 St. Lawrence Ave., Reading.

ESHELMAN, W. RICHARD (23rd District) was born Nov. 11, 1919, in Reading, the son of William L. and Beulah M. Leninger Eshelman; Dickinson Coll. (Ph.B.) 1941; Dickinson Schl. of Law (LL.B.) 1947; hon. degree, Albright Coll. (LL.D.) 1968; U.S. Navy, WW II; Lt. Comdr., USNR (ret.); Berks Co., Pa., Am. Bar Assns.; Am. Judicature Society; dist. atty., Berks Co., 1964-67; pres. bd. of trustees, Albright Coll.; bd. of dir., Community Gen. Hospital, Reading; YMCA of Reading; Berks Co. Lodge 227, F&AM; Reading Consistory, 33rd Degree; contributor to law journals; commissioned judge, Court of Common Pleas, Jan. 1, 1968; elected 1969; retained 1979; commissioned pres. judge, Jan. 1, 1973, resigned Dec. 31, 1980; married Mary P. Mackie, Oct. 4, 1947; 3 children; home address: R.D. 6, Sinking Spring.

FARINA, LOUIS J. (2nd District) was born May 5, 1943, in Pgh., the son of Aldo and Catherine Rosso Farina; grad., Pa. State Univ. (B.A.) 1965; Dickinson Schl. of Law (J.D.) 1968; Captain JAGC U.S. Army, 1969-73; mem., Lancaster and Pa. Bar Assns; Pa Conf. of State Trial Judges; frmr. pres., United Way of Lancaster Co., 1984-86; bd. dirs., United Way of Lancaster Co.; Leadership Lancaster; Children's Museum of Lancaster; Woolsack Honor Society; elected judge, Court of Common Pleas, Nov. 4, 1985; married Leevan Garvey; 2 children: Matthew B. and Ellen E.; home address: 525 Millcross Rd., Lancaster.

FARINO, SAL LOUIS (5th District) was born June 4, 1930, in Pgh., the son of Louis and Mary Farino; Duquesne Univ. (B.A.) 1953; George Washington Univ. Law Schl. (LL.B.) 1958; frmr. tax solicitor, city and schl. dist., Pgh., 1966-74; Bars, U.S. Supreme Court, Pa. Supreme, Superior, Commonwealth Courts, Allegheny Co. Courts; Pa., Allegheny Co. Bar Assns.; Am. Judicature Society; frmr. 1st Lt. U.S. Army Artillery; frmr. aide to the late Congressman Herman P. Eberhardter, 83rd, 84th Congress; Judge, Court of Common Pleas, Allegheny Co. 1975; married Catherine LeDonne; 2 children, Maureen and Stephen; home address: 122 High Park Place, Pittsburgh.

FIKE, EUGENE E., II (16th District) was born Dec. 8, 1939, in Uniontown, the son Eugene E. and Elsie Bender Fike; grad., Princeton Univ. (B.A.) 1961; Univ. of Pa. Law Schl. (LL.B.) 1964; U.S. Army (Artillery) 1965-66; judge, Court of Common Pleas, Jan. 1986; married Jessie Levering; 2 children: Colby and Eugene, III; home address: 580 W. Union St., Somerset.

FINK, HAROLD B., JR. (P.J. — 55th District) Judge, Court of Common Pleas.

FINKELHOR, MARION KAMIN (5th District) was born Aug. 5, 1918, in Pgh., the daughter of Dr. Philip Kamin and Ella Perelstine Kamin; Wells Coll. (B.A.) 1938; Univ. of Pgh. Schl. of Law (LL.B.) 1941; attorney, War Labor Bd., Washington, 1941-43; Am. Red Cross Field Service, Pacific War Theater, 1944-46; law practice, 1946-71; lecturer, Political Science Dept., Univ. of Pgh., 1946-58; asst. solicitor, city solicitor, Pgh., 1959-72; adjunct professor, Duquesne Univ. Schl. of Law, 1962-73; Bd. of Comm., Natl. Conf. of Comm. on Uniform State Laws, 1976; selected Disting. Daughter of Pa., Oct. 1978; elected judge, Court of Common Pleas, Nov. 1971; retained 1981; married to Dr. Howard Finkelhor; 4 children; home address: 118 Hastings St., Pittsburgh.

FISCHER, ROGER M. (6th District) was born June 28, 1934, in Erie, the son of Sebastian and Josephine Daubler Fischer; Pa. State Univ. (B.A.) 1955; Univ. of Pgh. Schl. of Law (J.D.) 1958; Natl. Judicial Coll., 1974; U.S. Army, 1958-60; mem., Am., Pa., Erie Co. Bar Assns.; Am. Judicature Society; Phi Alpha Delta Law Frat.; Register of Wills, Erie Co., 1964-80; chmn., Erie Co. Dem. Com., 1968-76; appt. judge, Court of Common Pleas, Sept. 2, 1983; elected judge, Nov. 8, 1983; married Gloria (Dee) Deegan; 3 children: Julie, Eric, Joan; home address: 353 East 41st St., Erie.

FORNELLI, FRANCIS J. (35th District) was born Aug. 1, 1941, in Sharon, the son of Louis and Quin Ruscio Fornelli; Univ. of Notre Dame (A.B., magna cum laude) 1963; New York Univ. Schl. of Law (J.D.) 1966; Univ. of Concepcion, 1965; frmr. solicitor: Mercer Co. Housing Auth., 1972-82, Hermitage Twp., 1970-82, F.O.P. (Sharon), 1968-72, Mercer Co. Recorder, 1970-80; v. pres., bd. dir., John XXIII Home for Sr. Citizens; Shenango Valley C of C; Christian Assoc., Shenango Valley; bd. dir., Bavarian Half Marathon; Kiwanis; bd dir., Mercer Co. Hall of Fame, 1981-present; Adv. Bds., Slippery Rock Univ., 1982-present; chmn., Leg. Comm. of Christian Assoc., Shenango Valley; H.S. C.C.D. instructor, St. Bartholomew's Ch., and St. Jospeh's Ch.; Headmaster's Adv. Bd., Kennedy Christian H.S.; instr., Penn State Univ. Shenango Valley Campus; *Who's Who in Am. Law; Who's Who in the East;* Outstanding Young Men of 1974; elected judge, Court of Common Pleas, Nov. 3, 1981; married Joann Lyden; 2 children: Jill, Nicholas; home address: 190 Todd Ave., Hermitage.

FRAMPTON, THOMAS THORNE (35th District) was born on May 26, 1948, in Pgh., the son of Frank E. and Helen A. Thorne Frampton; grad., Greenville H.S., 1966; Allegheny Coll. (B.A.) 1970; Univ. of Pittsburgh Law Schl. (J.D.) 1973; mem.: Am., Pa. & Mercer Co. Bar Assns.; American Judicature Soc.; Pa. Trial Judges Assn.; Lions Club; elder, First Presbyterian Ch., Greenville; dir., Penn Northwest Development Corp.; Greenville Area Economic Development Corp.; Greenville Reynolds Development; St. Paul Homes; elected judge, Court of Common Pleas, Nov. 1985; married Vanetta L. Miller; 3 children: Craig, Bethany and Launa; home address: 110 Hollywood Blvd., Greenville.

FRANCIOSA, MICHAEL V. (3rd District) was born Oct. 10, 1931, in Phila., the son of Frank E. and Letizia Cascioli Franciosa; Univ. of MD. (B.A.) 1953; Univ. of Pa. Law Schl. (J.D.) St. Trial Judges Coll.; officer, Strategic Air Command; attny.-at-law prior to being elevated to the Bench; Northampton Co., Pa., Am. Bar Assns.; Pa. Conf. of St. Trial Judges, Juvenile Court Judges Comm., Natl. Council on Crime and Delinquency, Northeast Regnl. Planning Council of Govs. Justice Comm.; Am. Arbitration Assn.; Kiwanis; P.A.L.; K. of C.; Moose; Minsi Trails Council - Exploring Division, BSA; Human Relations Comm.; asst city solicitor, 1960-62; city solicitor, 1962-67; first asst. dist. attny., 1967-69; elected judge, Court of Common Pleas, Nov. 4, 1969 and sworn in Jan. 4, 1970; retained for additional 10-yr. term, Jan. 1980; married Elaine Stroble on June 12, 1952; 1 child; home address: 3332 Sherwood Rd., Easton.

FRANKS, WILLIAM J. (14th District) was born Jan. 6, 1932, in Uniontown, the son of Ralph and Mary Jordan Franks; attended Univ. of Georgia; Univ. of Pgh. (B.A.) 1953, (LL.B.) 1956; U.S. Army, 1957-59; Am., Pa., Fayette Co. Bar Assns.; Am. Trial Lawyers Assn.; asst. dist. attny., 1960-68; pres., Church Council; elected judge, Court of Common Pleas 1978; married Lena Traficant; 1 child; home address: 131 Stockton Ave., Uniontown.

FREEDBERG, ROBERT A. (3rd District) was born Feb. 19, 1944, in Easton, the son of Morris and Bessie Weinberg Freedberg; Lafayette Coll. (B.A.) 1966; Columbia Univ. Schl. of Law (J.D.) 1969; Pa. St. Trial Judges Conf.; Pa., Northampton Co. Bar Assns.; asst. dist. atty., 1973-79; asst. city solicitor, Easton, 1976-80; grad., Natl. Judicial Coll., General Jurisdiction Session, 1980; elected, judge, Court of Common Pleas, Nov. 1979; married Ronnie Sue Meltzer; 2 children: Debra, Steven; home address: 434 Dogwood Terrace, Easton.

FRIEDMAN, JUDITH L. A. (5th District) was born Oct. 12, 1942, in New York, the daughter of May Lindquist and Harold Anderson; grad., Mt. Holyoke Coll. (A.B.) 1964; Univ. of Pgh. Schl. of Law (J.D.) 1973; Peace Corps Volunteer, 1964-66; mem., Allegheny Co. Bar Assn.; Pa. Conf. of State Trial Judges; Natl. Assn. of Women Judges; dep. coronor, 1980-85; Allied Activies Vice President Na'amat; bd. of trustees, Hebrew Institute of Pgh., mem., B'Nai Emunoh Cong.; Owens Fellowship, Univ. of Pgh.; elected judge, Court of Common Pleas, Nov. 5, 1985; married Edward B. Friedman, Esq.; 2 children; office address: 712 City County Building, Pittsburgh.

GAFNI, ABRAHAM J. (1st District) was born June 29, 1939, in Brooklyn, son of Reuben and Betty Feldman Gafni; Hebrew Univ. (Jerusalem) 1958-59; Yeshiva Univ. (B.A., magna cum laude, B.H.L.); Harvard Law Schl. (J.D.) 1963; dep. dist. atty., Phila., 1974-77; instructor, Temple Univ. Schl. of Law, Paralegal Instit., Phila.; lecturer, Pa. Coll. for the Judiciary, Pa. Dist. Atty.'s Assn.; Phila. Bar Assn.; Am., Pa., N.Y. U.S. Supreme Ct. Bar Assns.; Pa. Conf. of St. Trial Judges; numerous activities, Phila. Bar Assn.; Supreme Ct. Criminal Proced. Rules Comm., 1976-78; Comm. on Criminal Procedural Rules and Judicial Ed., Pa. Conf. of St. Trial Judges; Comm. on Appellate Procedures, Am. Bar Assn.; pres., West Mt. Airy Neighbors, 1973-74; chmn., Org. Div., Allied Jewish Appeal, 1975-76-77 campaigns; bd. of dir., Jewish Community Relations Coun. (chmn., Comm. on Anti-Semitism); Phila. Bd. of Jewish Ed.; Northwest Community Housing Assn. (1971-74); pres., Germantown Jewish Center; Am. Bar Assn., Judicial Admin. Bench Book Comm.; v. pres., Justice Lodge, B'nai B'rith, 1978-79; recipient: Pa. District Attys.' Assn., Outstanding Service, 1976; Phila. Bar. Assn. Disting. Service Award, 1976; Allied Jewish Appeal Disting. Service Award, 1975-76-77; Oak Lane Post, Jewish War Veterans, Outstanding Community Work, 1977; Fed. of Jewish Agenices Disting. Service Award, 1978; Mizrachi Woman's Org., Man of the Year, 1979; author: "Abolition of the Indicting Grand Jury Effects Many Procedural Changes," *The Retainer,* Jan. 9, 1976; "Guilty Plea Colloquies in Pa.," *Pa. Bar Association Quarterly,* April 1977; "Fifth and Sixth Amendments and Exclusionary Rules," St. Coll. of the Judiciary, 1978-79; "Criminal Trial Problems" Parts I, II, III, St. Coll. of the Judiciary, 1978-79; appt. judge, Court of Common Pleas, 1977; appt. State Court Administrator of Pa., Jan. 24, 1983; married Miriam L. Gafni, 2 children: Jonathan and Rachel; office address: 1000 One East Penn Square Building, Philadelphia.

GARB, ISAAC S. (P.J. - 7th District) was born June 19, 1929, in Trenton, N.J.; grad., Trenton Central H. S., 1947; att., Central Coll., Fayette, Mo., 1947-49; grad., Rutgers Univ. (A.B.) 1951; Univ. of Pa. Law Schl. (LL.B.) 1956; served with Counter Intelligence, Washington, D.C., 1951-53; mem., Pa. Trial Judges Assn.; Juvenile Court Judges Comm.; bd. mem., The Woods School, Langhorne; bd. mem., Doylestown Health Foundation; ex.bd.mem., Bucks Co. Council, Boy Scouts of America; adv. bd., Aid for Girls; trustee, Kildonan School; dir., TODAY, Inc.; asst. public defender, Bucks Co., 1960-63; asst. U.S. atty., Eastern Dist., 1963-65; appt. judge, Court of Common Pleas, Sept. 20, 1966; elected to 10-yr. term, Nov. 7, 1967; pres. judge, Jan. 3, 1983; married Joan Garb; 3 children.

GARDNER, JAMES K. (31st District) was born Sept. 14, 1940, in Allentown, the son of the Hon. Theodore and Margaret Schaeffer Knoll Gardner; Yale Univ. (B.A., magna cum laude) 1962; Harvard Law Schl. (J.D.) 1965; Capt., JAGC, USNR-R, active duty, 1966-69; Lehigh Co., Miss., Pa. Bar Assns.; solicitor, Lehigh Co. Treas., 1971-77; Lehigh Co.: asst. dist. atty., 1972-77, 1st asst. dist. atty., 1977-81; solicitor, E. Penn Area Jaycees, 1973-77; bd. dir., solicitor, Emmaus Bldg. and Loan Assn., 1973-81; chmn., E. Penn Schl. Dist. Year-Round Schl. Study Comm., 1972-74; solicitor, bd. dir., frmr. pres., E. Penn Center, Inc., 1971-78; solicitor,

P.H.O.N.E., Inc., 1971-79; asst. counsel, exec. comm., Lehigh Co. Repub. Comm., 1972-78; chmn., Lehigh Co. Young Repub., 1973-74; bd. dir., Boys Club of Allentown, Inc., 1985-; bd. dir., Police Athletic League, Inc., (PAL) 1984-; mem., Naval Reserve Trial Judiciary Activity (military judge), 1985-; Certificate of Merit, Chief of Naval Operations, 1982; Certificate of Recognition, Pa. Police Officer's Assn., 1981; Disting. Service Award, E. Penn Area Jaycees, 1972; author of "The Reservist and the U.C.M.J." (Uniform Code of Military Justice), Jan. 3, 1972; appt. judge, Court of Common Pleas, May 29, 1981; elected, Nov. 3, 1981; married Linda Kay Klenk; 4 children: Christine, Andrea, Victoria, Stephanie; home address: R.D. 2, Box 46, Emmaus.

GARDNER, ROY A. (P.J. — 44th District) was born Sept. 30, 1921, in Factoryville, the son of Roy A. and Edna Wademan Gardner; Univ. of Pa. (B.S., economics) 1943; Univ. of Pa. Law Schl. (LL.B.) 1949; U.S. Army, European Theater, 1943-46; Wyoming-Sullivan Co., Pa. (past pres.) Am. Bar Assns.; frmr. dist. atty., Wyoming Co. (11 years); admin. bd., Nicholson Methodist Ch.; frmr. dir., The Wyoming National Bank of Wilkes-Barre and Tunkhannock; adv. bd., Wyoming National Bank; Advry. Comm. on Probation, Pa. Bd. of Probation and Parole; Tunkhannock Rotary Club (past pres.); appt. pres. judge, Court of Common Pleas, Dec. 1971; elected to full term, Nov. 1973; commissioned for full term Jan. 1974; married Louise Pritchard on May 30, 1944; 2 children: Seth Frederick Gardner and Barbara Gardner Heller; home address: Clarendon Acres, R.D. 6, Tunkhannock.

GATES, GEORGE THOMAS (P.J. — 52nd District) was born Dec. 27, 1924, in Lebanon, the son of George W. and Etta M. DeWalt Gates; Brown Univ. (A.B.) 1946; Harvard Schl. of Bus. Admin., Univ. of Boston Schl. of Law (LL.B.) 1949, (J.D.) 1970; U.S. Naval Reserve, active duty, 1943-47, inactive duty, 1947-59; Lebanon Co., Pa., Am. Bar Assns.; Judicial Admin. Section, Pa. Conf. of St. Trial Judges; Am. Judicature Society; Am. Trial Lawyers' Assn.; asst. dist. atty., Lebanon Co., 1950-54; YMCA; part-time mem., faculty, Lebanon Valley Coll., Berks Campus, Pa. St. Univ., Dickinson Law Schl.; author, "History of Hangings for Homicide"; St. Luke's Episcopal Ch., Lebanon; appt. pres. judge of the Several Courts of Lebanon Co., Oct. 1, 1960; married Louise Mozier on May 14, 1946; 2 children; home address: 143 Hillside St., Lebanon.

GAVIN, THOMAS C. (15th District) was born Dec. 22, 1943, in Newark, N.J., the son of Gerald J. and Jean Cavanagh Gavin; grad., Scranton Preparatory H.S., 1961; Villanova Univ. (B.A.) 1965, (J.D.) 1971; captain, USMC, 1965-68; mem., Chester Co. Bar Assn.; Pa. Conf. of St. Trial Judges; bd. of supervisors, 1976-85; Lions Club, American Legion, VFW, Knights of Columbus; judge, Court of Common Pleas, Jan. 6, 1986; married Denise Marie Barbara; 5 children: Michael, Matthew, Thomas, Brian and Elizabeth; home address: 415 Goshen Ave., West Chester.

GAWTHROP, ROBERT S. III (15th District) was born Dec. 2, 1942, the son of Robert S., Jr. and Elizabeth Haldeman Campbell Gawthrop; Amherst Coll. (B.A.) 1964; Dickinson Schl. of Law (J.D.) 1970; U.S. Army 1964-67, field artillery OCS, Fort Sill, Okla., 1st lieut.; Am., Chester Co., Pa. Bar Assns; Am. Judicature Society; Pa. Conf. of St. Trial Judges; asst. dist. atty., Chester Co., 1971-78; asst. dist. atty., Wayne Co., 1977; elected judge, Court of Common Pleas, Nov., 1977; author "An Inquiry into Criminal Copyright Infringement," Columbia Univ. Press; co-author "Criminal Practice & Procedure," Pa. Bar Institute; bd. dir., Chester Co. Unit, Am. Cancer Society; Delta Kappa Epsilon; Phi Mu Alpha Sinfonia; Orpheus Club, The Savoy Company; Rose Valley Chorus; The Ardensingers (Gildmaster); Gilbert & Sullivan Players; unmarried; home address: 342 West Miner St., West Chester.

GEORGELIS, MICHAEL A. (2nd District) was born July 27, 1939, in Martins Ferry, Ohio, the son of Anthony D. and Irene A. Moustakas Georgelis; grad., Carnegie Mellon Univ. (B.S., met. eng.) 1961; Cleveland State Univ., Cleveland Marshall Coll. of Law (J.D., cum laude) 1974; 1st. Lt., U.S. Army, Corps of Engineers, 1961-63; mem., Pa.and Lancaster Bar Assns.; Pa. Conf. of St. Trial Judges; Greek Orthodox; judge, Court of Common Pleas, Jan. 6, 1986; married Diane Treires; 3 children: Anthony, George, and Stacey.

GILBERT, BARBARA S. (1st District — Municipal Court) was born March 13, 1946, in Wilmington, Del., the daughter of Frank and Ida Paul Spirer; grad., Univ. of Delaware (B.A.) 1968; Univ. of Pa. Law Schl. (J.D.) 1971; mem., Pa. Conf. of State Trial Judges; asst. city solicitor, 1972-74; chief asst./dep. city solicitor, 1975-85; Phi Beta Kappa Natl. Honor Soc.; Phi Kappa Phi Natl. Honor Soc.; author, Manual on Philadelphia Zoning Practice; elected judge, Municipal Court of Philadelphia, Nov. 5, 1985; married Alan H. Gilbert, Esq.; home address: 1920 Rittenhouse Sq., Philadelphia.

GILMORE, DAVID L. (27th District) was born Oct. 28, 1944, the son of Charles J. and Dorothy Beck Gilmore; California State Coll. (B.S.) 1966, Duquesne Univ. Schl. of Law (J.D.) 1970; USMRC, 1966-72; mem., Washington Co., Pa. Bar Assns.; Phi Alpha Delta Law Frat.; Delta Sigma Phi Social Frat.; Washington Co. Solicitor, 1973-76; commissioner, Washington Co., 1976-1983; managing editor, *Duquesne Univ. Law Review,* 1965-66; rec., Am. Jurisprudence Award in Labor Law; chmn., Washington Co. Government Study Comm., 1973-76; pres., Washington-Greene Community Action Bd., 1977-82; elected judge, Court of Common Pleas, Nov. 1983; married Janice Kughn; 2 children: Melissa, Thomas; home address: 351 East Beau St., Washington.

GLADDEN, THOMAS D. (P.J. — 27th District) was born Nov. 8, 1932, in Cecil Township, the son of George D. and Besse Stephenson Gladden; Allegheny Coll. (A.B.) 1954; Dickinson Schl. of Law (J.D.) 1957; U.S. Army, 1957-59; attorney at law; Washington Co., Pa. and Am. Bar Assns.; Phi Delta Theta, Pi Gamma Mu; East Washington Borough Council, 1969; Church of the Convenant, United Presbyterian; appt. judge, Court of Common Pleas, Jan. 4, 1971; elected to full term, 1973; retained 1983; pres. judge, 1984; married Rachel L. Hughey on Dec. 23, 1961; 2 children: Thomas and Laura; home address: 687 Elmhurst Dr., Washington.

GLANCEY, JOSEPH R. (1st District — Municipal Court) was born May 29, 1927, one of 9 children; Villanova Univ. (B.E.E.) 1950; Villanova Univ. Law Schl. (LL.D.) 1956; V.P., Natl. Student Law Assn.; rose from seaman to Lieut, U.S. Navy, 1950-52; taught business law, Villanova Univ., 1954-56; taught industrial electronics, Temple Univ., 1956-58; counsel, Phila. Dem. City Comm., 1967-68; Phila., Pa., Am. Bar Assns.; ed. bd., Villanova Law Review; Am. Judicature Society; editor, *Amran's Pa. Practice Book;* Natl. Trustee, Natl. Conf. of Christians and Jews; Pa. Conf. of St. Trial Judges; Phila. Fellowship Comm.; Phila. Judicial Council; Natl. Conf. of Special Court Judges; Historical Society of Pa.; v. chmn., Phila. Criminal Justice Coordinating Council; past pres., Natl. Conf. of Metro Cts.; chmn., Consumer Council of Grtr. Phila.; hon. dir., Community Service Corps.; dir., Brehon Law Society; chmn., Mayor's Drug and Alcohol Exec. Comm.; sworn in as pres. judge, Phila. Municipal Court, Jan. 2, 1969; married Mary A. King; 3 children; home address: 9101 Green Tree Rd., Philadelphia.

GOLDMAN, MURRAY C. (1st District) was born July 24, 1930, in Phila., the son of Herbert L. and Merle Rosenkoff Goldman; Pa. State Univ. (B.A.) 1952; Univ. of Pa. Law Schl. (LL.B.) 1959; Univ. of Pa. Law Schl. (J.D.); editor, U. of Pa. Law Review; U.S. Army, 1952-54; Phila., Pa., Am. Bar Assns.; lecturer, Univ. of Pa. Law Schl.; dep. city solicitor; mem., Am. Law Inst.; elected judge, Court of Common Pleas, Nov. 1975; married Rosemary R. Dolgert; 3 children: Amy, Lawrence and Eric; home address: 3452 Midvale Ave., Philadelphia.

GOODHEART, BERNARD J. (1st District) was born Dec. 25, 1930, in Phila., the son of Nathan and Rose Sudman Goodheart; Central H.S. (B.A.) 1948; Wharton Schl., U. of Pa. (B.S., econ.) 1952; U. of Pa. Law Schl. (J.D.) 1955; lawyer, 1955-75; asst. dist. atty., Phila. 1958-66; Phila., Pa. Bar Assns.; bd. of dirs., Phila. Assn. for Retarded Citizens, Golden Slipper; bd. of dirs., Phila. Urban League and Greenwich Home for Children; studied painting and sculpting, Fleischer Art Memorial, 1960-62; elec. judge, Court of Common Pleas, Nov. 1975; presiding over its Bus. Litigation Prog.; married Harriet Gay Kaufman; 3 children: Adam Kaufman, Harry Matthew, and Mark Bradley; home address: 730 W. Allens Lane, Philadelphia.

GORDON, LEVAN (1st District) was born Apr. 10, 1933, in Phila., son of Julius (dec'd) and Mary (dec'd) Gordon; attended Pa. St. Univ. 1951-53; Lincoln Univ. (A.B.) 1957; Howard Univ. Law Schl. (LL.B.) 1961; U.S. Army, 1953-55; USNR, 1958-61; hearing examiner, Pa. Labor Relations Bd., 1971-74; frmr. asst. city solicitor, counsel, Phila. Human Relations Comm.; exec. dir., Phila. Housing Info. Service, 1966-68; frmr. partner, firm of Schmidt, Williams, Gaskins and Gordon; Crime Prevention Assn. of Phila. Assn. for Youth, 1961-62; caseworker, Pa. Dept. of Public Assistance, 1957-60; assoc. counsel, Gov.'s Comm. to Investigate Police Brutality in Chester, 1964; World Assn. of Judges; instructor, Temple Univ. Schl. of Criminal Justice; Gov.'s Adv. Comm. on Probation, 1978 - present; Natl. Assn. of Blacks in Crim. Justice; AFNA Preceptor Program; Alpha Phi Alpha Fraternity Inc., Zeta Omicron Lambda Chapt.; Lincoln Univ. Alumni Assn.; West Phila. H.S. Alumni Assn.; Phila., Pa. Bar Assns. Barrister's Club of Phila.; Am. Judicature Society; Am. Arbitration Assn.; Project "IN"; Phila. Lawyers' Club of Phila.; Phila. Tribune Charities, past pres.; Natl. Bowling Assn.; General Alumni Assn., Lincoln U.; Men of Malvern; bd. of trustees, Lincoln Univ.; bd. dir., Natl. Assn. of Blacks in Criminal Justice (NABCJ); World Assn. of Judges; frmr. dist. chmn., Independence Dist., Phila. Council, BSA Disting. Service Award; Liberty Bell District, BSA, 1965; Meritorious Service Award, Strawberry Mansion Civic Assn.; appt. to Municipal Court of Philadelphia, Dec. 19, 1974; elected judge, Court of Common Pleas, Nov. 1979; married Vivian J. Goode; 1 child, Shari-Lyn.

GREENSPAN, JANE CUTLER (1st District) was born April 27, 1948, in Newark, NJ, the daughter of Gilbert G. and Lois Kahn Cutler; grad., Smith Coll. (A.B.) 1970; Rutgers Univ. Schl. of Law (J.D., magna cum laude) 1973; mem: Pa. Trial Judges, Phila. Bar Assn., Criminal Justice Section, Domestic Violence Task Force, Mayor's Comm. on Women, Attorney General's Family Violence Task Force; asst. dist. atty., 1976-1987; trustee, Child Psychiatric Center; Women's Way Corporate Campaign Com.; Pilot Project of Select Com. on Law Enforcement and Child Abuse; rec., Special Commendation Award, Attorney General's Family Violence Task Force, 1987; service to Board of Governors for 1986; Rutgers Univ. Fellowship; author, Case Note - Criminal Law - Sentencing - Application of the Rehabilitative Ideal in Sentencing First Time Marijuana Offender, 3 Rutgers, Camden, N.J. (1972); drafted Standards for Change in Treatment of Domestic Violence Cases adopted by Criminal Justice Coordinating Comm., Phila.; appointed judge, Court of Common Pleas, April 6, 1987; married Allan M. Greenspan, M.D.; 2 children: Katharine E. and Emily C.; home address: 7315 Elbow Lane, Philadelphia.

GRIFO, RICHARD DONALD (3rd District) was born Jan. 25, 1919, in Easton, the son of Antonio (dec'd.) and Biagia (dec'd.) Grifo; Lafayette Coll. (B.A.) 1940 class pres.; Univ. of Pa. Law Schl. (LL.B.), Wilson Law Club, 1943; Natl. Coll. of St. Trial Judges, Nevada, 1970; Northampton Co., Pa., Am. Bar Assns.; member, House of Delegates, Pa. Bar Assn.; Pa. Conf. of St. Trial Judges; bd. of dir. and past pres., Lehigh Delaware Development Council; bd. of dir. and past sec., Downtown Improvement Group, Easton; bd. of dir., Hospital and Health Council, Minor Judiciary Education Bd., Comm. of Pa.; pres., Northampton Co. Bar Assn., 1967-68; instructor, Lafayette Coll., Dept. of Gov't and Law, 1944-50; pres., Easton H.S. Class of 1936; pres., Lafayette Coll. Class of 1940; bd. of dir., past pres., Forks of the Delaware United Fund; bd. of dir., Am. Red Cross, Easton Chapter, and YMCA; solicitor, Borough of W. Easton Council, 1946-68; W. Easton Sewer Authority, Northampton Co., 1951-55; Easton Rod and Gun Club; L.O.O.M.; Pomfret Club; Union League of Phila.; Easton Anglers Assn.; Order Sons of Italy; Moravian Academy Bd. of Trustees; St. Anthony's Catholic Ch.; recipient, Distinguished Citizen Award, Am. Legion, Brown & Lynch Post, 1968; Disting. Service Award, Forks of the Delaware Un. Fund; Disting. Service Award, Inst. of Regional Affairs, Wilkes Coll., 1969; commissioned judge, Court of Common Pleas, Dec. 16, 1968; elected to full term Nov. 4, 1969 and Nov. 1979; married Leonarda T. Geraci; father of 3 children: Antonia, Francesca, and Carla; home address: 625 Paxinosa Ave., Easton.

GRIMES, H. TERRY (P.J. — 13th District) was born Sept. 2, 1942, the son of Halfred B. and Faye J. Stockdale Grimes; grad., California St. Univ. (B.S.); Ohio Northern Univ. (J.D.); major, U.S. Army, Artillery Branch, 1966-69; mem., Pa. Conf. of State Trial Judges; United Methodist Ch.; elected judge, Court of Common Pleas, 1985; married Carlyn Sue LaRoache; 4 children: Mark Allen, Kathy Lynn, Lori Beth, Jeffrey N.; home address: Star Route, Holbrook.

GRINE, DAVID E. (49th District) was born Mar. 7, 1945, in Washington, D.C., the son of Edward E. and Mildred Clary Grine; Pa. St. Univ. (B.S.) 1969; Dickinson Schl. of Law (J.D.) 1973; U.S. Army, 1964-66; attorney; Centre Co., Pa., Am. Bar Assns.; dist. atty., Centre Co., 1978-81; appt. judge, Court of Common Pleas, July 17, 1981; elected, Nov. 3, 1981; married Karen E. Nastase; 2 children.

GUARINO, ANGELO A. (1st District) was born Mar. 23, 1921, the son of Michael and Maria Guarino; Temple Univ. and Temple Law Schl. (LL.B.) 1950; U.S. Army, WW II, active duty in Italy and France, recipient of Purple Heart, Two Oak Leaf Clusters; Phila. trial lawyer for over 20 yrs.; elected judge, Court of Common Pleas, Nov. 1973; Phila. Bar Assn.; Pa. Conf. of Trial Judges; Justinian Society of Judges; Sons of Italy; ISDA; K of C; Lions Club; bd. of dirs., Parents Project on Drug Abuse; married Clorinda Fioravanti; 3 sons: Michael, Julius and Carl.

GUTOWICZ, THEODORE S. (1st District) was born May 3, 1920, in Phila., son of Frank and Sophia Dziakowska Gutowicz; Univ. of Pa. (A.B.) 1941; Dickinson Law Schl. (LL.B.) 1946; U.S. Naval Reserve, WW II; Phila. Professional Society; asst. dir., Legislative Reference Bureau, Comm. of Pa., 1955-57; spec. asst. atty. genl., Comm. of Pa., 1957-58; dep. insurance comm., Comm. of Pa., 1958-62; Insurance Comm., 1962-63; Men of Malvern, Polish Am. Citizens League of Pa., Polish Am. Congress — Polish Natl. Alliance; Bd. of Ed., Archdiocese of Phila.; Bd. of Adv., Holy Family Coll.; commissioned to the Bench Sept. 8, 1965; married LoRetta C. Basinski; 4 children; home address: 3808 Inwood Ln., Philadelphia.

HALBERT, MARVIN R. (1st District) was born Jan. 29, 1923, in Phila. the son of Samuel and Esther Halbert; Wharton Schl., Univ. of Pa. (B.S., economics) 1947; Univ. of Pa. Law Schl. (J.D.) 1950; in Feb. 1943, enlisted in U.S. Army Signal Corp, served 3 years active duty, received four Combat Battle Stars; Phila., Pa., Am. Bar Assns.; asst. dist. atty., 1952-62; chmn., Public Info. Comm., Pa. Conf. of St. Trial Judges; adjunct prof., Villanova Univ. and Community Coll. of Phila.; past co. commander, VFW; Am. Legion and Jewish War Vets.; Masonic bodies; past chmn., Polaris dist., BSA; past pres., Wm. Portner Lodge, B'nai B'rith; Congreg. Beth Zion-Beth Israel; author of a weekly column for *Pennsylvania Law Journal Reporter;* elected judge, Common Pleas Court, Jan. 7, 1974; married Marcia Oleve; 4 children: Andrew, Esther, Lisa and Lee-Ann; home address: Carlton House Apt. 2812, 1801 John F. Kennedy Blvd., Philadelphia.

HARRIS, KENNETH S. (1st District) Judge, Court of Common Pleas.

HAZEL, FRANK T. (32nd District) was born Dec. 17, 1941, in Darby, the son of Frank and Katherine McCabe Hazel; St. Joseph's Univ. (A.B.) 1964; Villanova Univ. Schl. of Law (J.D.) 1967; Natl. Judicial Coll., 1982; attorney; Delaware Co., Pa., Am. Bar Assns.; Dist. Justice of the Peace, 1969-75; dist. atty., Delaware Co., 1976-81; Pa. Supreme Ct.; frmr. pres., Pa. Dist Atty's. Assn., 1980-81; 1980 Man of the Year, Media Area Jr. C of C; elected judge, Court of Common Pleas, Nov. 3, 1981; married Frances E. Luke; 3 children: Janet, Jill, Kris; home address: 456 Irvington Rd., Drexel Hill.

HEFFNER, GEORGE WILLIAM (P.J. — 21st District) was born May 3, 1925, in Pottsville, the son of the late George S. and Helen Moyer Heffner; Dickinson Coll. (B.A.) Dickinson Schl. of Law (J.D.) 1951; U.S. Navy, 1943-46; Schuylkill Co., Pa. Bar Assn.; St. Trial Judges Assn.; Pa. House of Representatives, 1957-67; hnry. mem. of directors, Pottsville Children's Home; frmr. mem., bd. of trustees, Bloomsburg Univ., 1969-74; Lions Club; Pottsville Lodge F&AM; Trinity Lutheran Ch., Pottsville; elected judge, Court of Common Pleas, commissioned Jan. 1, 1968; reelected to 10 yr. term beginning Jan. 1, 1978; married Barbara Richards, Feb. 7, 1953; 2 children; home address: 1647 Oak Rd., Pottsville.

HERR, LOUISE GATLING (2nd District) was born Jan. 7, 1925, in Ahoskie, N.C., the daughter of Herman DeLoache Gatling, Sr. and Hilda Parsons Bailey; grad., Millersville Univ. (B.A.) 1968; Dickinson Schl. of Law (J.D.) 1971; mem., Pa. and Lancaster Bar Assns.; Pa. Conf. of State Trial Judges; mem., Blackstonian Club, Am. Assn. of Univ. Women; Lancaster Co. asst. dist. atty., 1973-85; bd. dirs., American Red Cross (10 yrs.); judge, Court of Common Pleas, Nov. 1985; married Carl G. Herr, Esq.; 4 children; home address: 1031 Woods Ave., Lancaster.

HESS, KEVIN A. (9th District) was born April 25, 1947, in Erie, the son of James M. Hess and Adele C. Francis; grad., Dickinson Coll. (A.B.), Dickinson Schl. of Law (J.D.) 1972; presently Adjutant 28th Inf. Div. Field Artillery, Natl. Guard; mem., county and Pa. Bar Assns.; frmr. asst. dist. atty.; frmr. crim. law instructor, Pa. Minor Judiciary; judge, Court of Common Pleas, Jan. 4, 1986; married Constance T.; 3 children: Caroline, Meredith and Emily; home address: 108 Burnt House, Carlisle.

HILL, LOUIS G. (1st District) was born Mar. 10, 1924, in Palm Beach, Fla., the son of Crawford and Ann Elizabeth Kaufman Hill; Harvard Univ. (B.S.) 1944; Univ. of Pa. Law Schl. (LL.B.) 1949; grad., Natl. Judicial Coll., Reno, Nev., Aug. 1980; U.S. Marine Corps, Lt., 1944-46, served in Pacific and China; Capt., 1950-51; prac. atty., 28 yrs., Phila.; Am. Bar Assns.; frmr. bd. mem. of Man.; St. Christopher's Hospital for Children; frmr. mem., bd. of Man., Overbrook Schl. for the Blind; Pa. St. Senator, 1966-78; chmn., Senate Judiciary Com., 1971-77; prime sponsor more than 60 acts of Pa. legislature, including Crimes Code, Judicial Code, Sentencing Code, Spouse Abuse Act, law compensating victims of violent crimes; elected judge, Municipal Court of Phila., Nov. 1977; elected judge, Common Pleas Court, Nov. 1979; married Marilyn Ashton; 7 children: Crawford, Leslie, Jessie, Thomas, Michael, Charlotte, Ann; office address: 1001 One East Penn Sq., Philadelphia.

HOFFER, GEORGE ERWIN (9th District) was born Nov. 18, 1935, in Carlisle, the son of Frank L. (dec.) and Dorothy Aldinger Hoffer; Carlisle H.S., 1953; Dickinson Coll. (A.B.) 1961; Dickinson Schl. of Law (J.D.) 1966; Intelligence, U.S. Army, 1957-60; private law practice, 1966-79; public def., 1968-75; 1st asst. dist. atty., 1976-79; admit. to practice, Cumberland Co., Pa. Commonwealth, Pa. Supreme, U.S. Supreme Cts.; trustee, Bosler Free Library; bd. dir., Am. Cancer Society; elected judge, Court of Common Pleas, Nov. 1979; married Ann Kramer; home address: 315 W. Willow St., Carlisle.

HORGOS, ROBERT P. (5th District) was born May 17, 1948, in Pgh., the son of Michael J. and Helen D. Takacs Horgos; Villanova Univ. (B.S.) 1970; Villanova Law Schl. (J.D.) 1973; Gamma Phi (highest natl. academic honor soc.); mem., Allegheny Co. Bar Assn.; Public Defenders Assn.; Natl. District Attorney's Assn.; Jednota; Natl. Slovak Soc., Croatian Fraternal Union; asst. public defender, 1974-75; solicitor, Clerk of Courts Office, 1975, asst., dist. atty, Allegheny Co., 1976-1980; mem., Pa. House of Representatives, 1981-82; elected judge, Court of Common Pleas, Nov. 8, 1983; home address: 709 East Ninth Ave., Munhall.

HORN, RICHARD H. (19th District) was born Nov. 10, 1932, in York; the son of Clarence H. and Edna J. Horn; grad., Gettysburg Coll. (A.B.) 1953; Washington & Lee Univ. (J.D.) 1959; USAF, 1954-56; Lt.Col. Ret. Res.; past pres., York Co. Bar Assn.; ABA; Pa. Bar Assn., delegate to House of Delegates; Phi Gamma Delta; asst. dist. atty., 1974-85; elected judge, Court of Common Pleas, Nov. 1985; married Sally A. Dunnick; 3 children: Tina, Gregory, and Richard, Jr.; home address: 41 Roselyn Dr., York.

HOURIGAN, ROBERT J. (P.J. — 11th District) was born Jan. 3, 1921, in Kingston; son of Joseph B. and Martha Hurley Hourigan; grad., Bucknell Univ. Jr. Coll., Dickinson Coll., Dickinson Law Schl.; Luzerne Co., Pa. Bar Assns.; spec. dpty. atty. genl., Comm. of Pa.; first asst. dist. atty., Luzerne Co.; asst. U.S. Atty., Middle District of Pa.; appt. judge, Court of Common Pleas, Dec. 7, 1966; elected Nov. 7, 1967; reelected 1977; appt. pres. judge, Sept. 25, 1981; married Augusta Wood, Feb. 3, 1949; 3 children; home address: 58 Grandview Ave., Dallas.

HOUSE, ROY ALEXANDER, JR. (P.J. — 33rd District) was born Mar. 31, 1925, in Buffalo, N.Y., the son of Roy Alexander and Ruby H. McCullough House; Allegheny Coll., Meadville, 1947 (A.B.); Univ. of Pgh. Schl. of Law, 1950 (LL.B., J.D.); U.S. Navy, lieut. (j.g.) 1943-46; private practice law, Kittanning (1950-71); elected judge, Common Pleas Court, Nov. 1971; married Jean Elizabeth Shaw on Sept. 10, 1949; 3 children; resides at 123 Hazel St., Kittanning.

HOWSARE, DANIEL LEE (P.J. — 57th District) was born Dec. 16, 1948, in Bedford Co., the son of Fred and Edna Mae Cessna Howsare; grad., Bedford School System, 1966; Pa. State Univ., 1971; Duquesne Schl. of Law, 1976; U.S. Army, 1971-1977; mem., Pa. and Bedford Co. Bar Assns.; dist. atty., Bedford Co., 1980-85; Rotary; elected judge, Court of Common Pleas, Nov. 5, 1985; married Joan Regan; 2 children: Brant Christopher and Ashley Regan; home address: 837 S. Juliana St., Bedford.

HUDOCK, JOSEPH A. (10th District) was born Nov. 21, 1937, in Greensburg, the son of Andrew J. and Rebecca Burke Hudock; St. Vincent Coll. (B.A.) 1959; Duquesne Law Schl. (J.D.) 1962; U.S. Navy, 1963-67; Pa. Bar Assn.; pres., Mt. View Rotary Club; v. chmn., adv. bd., Salvation Army; past pres., United Way of Central Westmoreland Co.; bd. of dir., United Way of Westmoreland Co.; frmr. mem., Regional Planning Council, Gov. Justice Comm.; mem. Am. Judicature Soc.; elected judge, Court of Common Pleas, Nov. 1977; married Rita Giegerich; 4 children: Joseph Jr., Ann, Daniel and Mary; home address: 3047 Ben Venue Dr., Greensburg.

HUMMER, WAYNE G., JR. (2nd District) was born Aug. 18, 1937, in Harrisburg, the son of Wayne G. and Ruth L. Lenker Hummer; Hershey Jr. Coll. (A.A.) 1957; Lebanon Valley Coll. (A.B.) 1959; Dickinson Schl. of Law (LL.B.) 1962; U.S. Navy, Lt., 1963-66; Lancaster Co., Pa., Bar Assns.; Pa. St. Trial Judges Assn.; Am. Business Club; Brownstone Lodge No. 666 F & AM; solicitor, Lancaster Co. Record. of Deeds Office, 1970-79; counsel, Lancaster Co. courts admn. office, 1977-79; asst. public def., Lancaster Co., 1968-70; Lititz Un. Methodist Ch.; mem., Natl. Council of Juvenile and Family Court Judges; elected judge, Court of Common Pleas, Nov. 1979; married Cynthia M. Deaven; 2 children: Elizabeth and Jennifer; home address: 318 Linden St., Lititz.

IVANOSKI, LEONARD A. (1st District) was born Sept. 16, 1928, in Shenandoah, the son of Stanley and Rose Zebrowski; Pa. St. Univ. (B.A.); Temple Schl. of Law (J.D.); 1st Lt., U.S.A.F. 1951-53; Pa. Conf. of St. Trial Judges; Pa., Phila., Am. Bar Assns.; Lawyer's Club; Polish-Am. Congress; Polish Heritage Society; mem., Oak Lane Improvement Assn.; Jagiellonian Law Soc.; Natl. Council, Juvenile Ct. Judges; Am. Legion Post #369; appt. judge, Court of Common Pleas, May 1980; elected to 10-yr. term, Jan. 2, 1982; married Mary T. Whalen; 4 children: Leonard A., Jr. (Esq.), Anthony (CPA), Christopher L. (Capt. USMC, res., eng.), Langon M. (comp. programmer); home address: Philadelphia.

JACKSON, FRANK M. (1st District) was born March 23, 1927, in Phila., the son of Matthew J. and Emma T. Maurer Jackson; St. Joseph's Univ. (B.S.) 1954; Univ. of Pa. Law Schl. (J.D.) 1957; U.S. Naval Reserve, 1945-47; U.S. Army, 1950-52; asst. dist. atty., Phila., 1963-64; mem., Fed. Bar Assn.; American Legion; Irish Society; Roman Catholic Church; Catholic Philopatrian Literary Society; judge, Court of Common Pleas, Oct. 2, 1984; married Roseann Montgomery; 6 children: Carolann (Esq.), Frank M., II, James (dec.), Joseph, William, Robert; home address: 6329 Woodbine Ave., Philadelphia.

JACKSON, RICARDO C. (1st District) was born Aug. 27, 1935, in Phila., son of Calvin and Virgina Smith Jackson; Virginia Union Univ. (B.A.) 1962; Howard Univ. Schl. of Law (J.D.) 1965; U.S. Army, 1958-61; lawyer; pres., Barristers' Assn. of Phila. (1970-74); Nat., Am., Pa., Phila. Bar Assns.; Pa. Trial Lawyers Assn.; Am. Arbitration Assn.; Am. Judicature Society; Pa. Conf. of St. Trial Judges; frmr. mem., Lawyers' Bi-Partisan Comm. to Support Sitting Judges; frmr. mem., Hearing Comm., Disciplinary Bd. of the Pa. Supreme Ct.; frmr. chmn., Judiciary Comm., Phila. Bar Assn.; frmr. mem., Judicial Retention and Election Comm., Phila. Bar Assn.; mem., Phila. Bar Assn.'s Lawyers' Com. to Invest. Criticism of Judges, 1976-77; mem., bd. of dirs., Public Interest law Center of Phila. (PILCOP), 1976-77; co-chmn., Phila. Bar Assn.'s Conf. on Community Legal Services, 1969; Sigma Tau (legal frat.); Judicial Council, Nat. Bar Assn.; numerous professional assns., civic activities, inc.: frmr. chmn., Crim. Justice Task Force, Phila. Urban Coalition, 1970-71; Judicial Council of Pa. 1973-76; Public Interest Law Center of Phila.; Phila. Fellowship Comm.; BSA, Phila. council; frmr. bd. dirs., Crime Prevention Assn. of Phila.; mem., World Assn., of Judges of the World Peace Through Law Center, 1980-pres.; appt. chmn., Com. on Juvenile Justice, World Peace Through Law Center, 1981; Judicial Ethics Com., Pa. Conf. of St. Trial Judges, 1983; co-author, "Racial Discrim. in Admin. of the Pa. Bar Examination," *Temple Law Quarterly,* Vol. 44, No. 2, Winter 1971; 1st elected Dem. Committeeman, 1970, 32nd Ward, 3rd Div.; 1st elected mem., Dem. St. Comm., 3rd Sen. Distr., 1970, 72, 74; Dem. Lawyers Comm., Dem. Co. Exec. Comm. of Phila.; elected judge, Municipal Court of Phila., 1978; mem., Civil Rules Comm.; Special Comm. on Elim. of De Novo Criminal Trials; chmn., Facilities Comm.; elected judge, Court of Common Pleas, 1981; 1 child, Terrence A.

JAFFE, JOSEPH ALLEN (5th District) was born Nov. 18, 1949, in Pgh., the son of Saul and Ida Holtzman Jaffe; grad., Univ. of Michigan (B.A.) 1971; Univ. of Pgh. (J.D.) 1974; mem., Allegheny Co. and Pa. Bar Assns. (family section); Big Brothers & Sisters of Greater Pittsburgh; Rodef Shalom Cong.; NAACP; B'nai B'rith; Univ. of Pgh. Golden Panther; Univ. of Mich. Alumni Club of Pgh.; judge, Court of Common Pleas, Nov. 1985; home address: 465 Peebles St., Apt. C, Pittsburgh.

JAMISON, JUDITH J. (1st District) was born Aug. 19, 1924, the daughter of Selig and Mary Salit Jaffe; Antioch Coll. (A.B.) 1946; attended Univ. of Chicago Law Schl.; Temple Univ. Law Schl. (LL.B.) 1948; Phila., Pa. Bar Assns.; Exec. Comm., Pa. Conf. of St. Trial Judges; Natl. Coll. of Probate Judges; asst. atty. gen. Comm. of Pa., 1956-63, 1971-73; bd. mem., officer, Auxiliaries of Children's Hospital and Graduate Hospital; Phila. Museum of Art; Phila. Orchestra Assn.; Dir., Institute for Cancer Research and Fox Chase Cancer Cntr.; Women's Leadership Bd., Commission on Aging; Fed. of Jewish Agencies; dir., Girls Coalition, S.E. Pa.; dir., O.A.R.; dir., Jenkins Law Library; dir., Congregation Rodeph Shalom; dir. Justice Lodge; B'nai B'rith; elected judge, Court of Common Pleas, Phila., Jan. 7, 1974; married I.I. Jamison, Esq.; 2 children: Seth and Sara Eve; home address: 2119 Delancey Place, Philadelphia.

JENKINS, NORMAN A. (1st District) was born Aug. 4, 1927, in Columbia, S.C., the son of Dr. and Mrs. Norman A. Jenkins; Morehouse Coll. (B.S.) 1950; Howard Univ. Law Schl. (LL.B.) 1953; Natl. Judicial Coll., 1972; Natl. Judical Coll., Speciality Session, Princeton Univ., 1975; U.S. Army, 1946-47; attorney; admitted to Phila. Bar (1954), Bar of U.S. Supreme Court (1967); exec. comm., Pa. Conf. of St. Trial Judges; Criminal Justice Comm., Judicial Ethics Comm., Criminal Justice Comm., Court of Common Pleas Bd. of Judges; Criminal Justice Section, Phila. Bar Assn.; participant in AFNA Preceptorship and AFNA Legal Scholars Program;

Phila. Barristers' Assn.; Commissioners Club; Omega Psi Phi; frmr. bd. dir., Natl. Co. on Alcoholism, Delaware Valley Area., Inc.; formerly served on Mayor's Drug and Alcohol Exec. Comm.; Co-Chmn., Sentencing Guidelines Comm., Court of Common Pleas Bd. of Judges; appt. judge, Court of Common Pleas, Dec. 29, 1971; elected to full term commencing Jan. 1974; retained for 10 yr. term commencing Jan. 1984; married Ella Dejoie; 4 children.

JEROME, DOMENIC D. (A.J. — 32nd District) was born Feb. 16, 1922, in Phila., the son of D. Jerry and Mary Celestino Jerome; Temple Law Schl. (LL.B.) 1952; U.S. Army, 1942-45; past solicitor, Haverford Twp.; past first asst. dist. atty., Delaware Co.; commissioned judge, Court of Common Pleas, Dec. 23, 1970; elected Nov. 2, 1971, retained Nov. 3, 1981; formerly admin. judge, Criminal Div.; formerly admin. judge, Civil Div.; mem., Supreme Ct. Civil Procedural Rules Com.; married Jean Randino on Oct. 13, 1945; 2 sons: Garry and Jeffrey; home address 513 Flora Circle, Springfield.

JIULIANTE, JESS S. (6th District) was born Nov. 20, 1925, in Erie, the son of Jess, Sr. and Rose Alfonso Jiuliante; Univ. of Pa. (B.A) 1949, and its law schl., 1952; military service, 1943-46; Pa. Bar Assn.; past Exalted Ruler of B.P.O.E.; bd. trustees, Millcreek Community Hospital; appt. judge, Court of Common Pleas, Nov.17, 1981; married Patricia A. Sicius; 2 children; home address: 210 W. 6th St., Erie.

JOHNSON, LIVINGSTONE M. (5th District) was born Dec. 27, 1927, in Wilkinsburg, the son of Oliver L. (dec'd.) and Irene Morris Johnson; Howard Univ. (A.B.) 1949; Air Force Navigation Schl., 1950; Univ. of Michigan Law Schl. (J.D.) 1957; Natl. Coll. of St. Judiciary, 1973; U.S. Air Force, 1949-54; navigator, radar bombardier; Korean War; Disting. Flying Cross, Commend. Medal, Air Medal, 3 Oak Leaf Clusters; hon. disch., 1st lieut.; Allegheny Co. Hall of Valor; disciplinary bd., Pa. Supreme Court, 1972-73; Am., Pa. Bar Assns.; Am. Bar Found.; Am. Judicature Soc.; Allegheny Co. Bar Assn., bd. of govs., 1969-74, public service comm., family law section; Assn. of Trial Lawyers in Criminal Court; asst. co. solicitor, 1962-73; mem., bds., NAACP (1962-68), life mem. Urban League; UNPC, 1963-68; bd. dirs., Am. Red Cross Alleg. Co., Pgh. Chptr., Boys Club of W. Pa.; Pa. Conf. of St. Trial Judges; Pa. Joint Coun. on Crim. Justice; bd., Metropolitan Broadcasting; Omega Psi Phi; YMCA; Golden Star Lodge 143, F&AM; Variety Club of Pgh.; Am. Legion Sportsmen's Post 913; VFW Angell Bolen Post 4040; judges panel, Louis Caplan Human Relations Award, 1975; BSA Eagle Badge, Order of Arrow, committeeman, Troop 174; appt. judge, Court of Common Pleas, 1973; married April 30, 1960; wife, LeeBrun; 5 children: Lee Carol, Oliver Morris II, Judith Lee, Livingstone James, Patricia Lee; Shannon, Irish Setter dog; home address: Calmwood Rd., Glenshaw.

JOYCE, MICHAEL T. (6th District) was born Feb. 24, 1949, in Pgh., the son of Mr. & Mrs. Joseph M. Cox; grad.; Pa. State Univ. (pol. science) 1973; Franklin Pierce Law Center (J.D.) 1977; U.S. Army, 1967-70; mem.: Pa. Trial Lawyer's Assn., Erie Co. and Pa. Bar Assns.; Phi Alpha Delta Law Frat.; Roman Catholic; appointed judge, Court of Common Pleas, July 1, 1985; elected Nov. 1985; married Cynthia Olsen; 2 children: Timothy and Robert; home address: 2533 Pandora Dr., Erie.

JOYNER, J. CURTIS (15th District) was born April 18, 1948, in Newberry, S.C., the son of George C. Joyner and Joan C. Glenn; grad., Central State Univ. (B.S.) 1971; Howard Univ. Schl. of Law (J.D.) 1974; mem.: Chester Co. Bar Assn., U.S. District Court (E. Dist. Pa.), Pa. Trial Judges Assn.; Omega Psi Phi Fraternity, Inc.; 1st asst. dist. atty., Chester Co., 1984-87; Trailblazers in Law Enforcement and numerous local civic awards; chmn., bd. of dirs., Student Services, Inc., West Chester Univ.; mem., NAACP; Counc. of Trustees, West Chester Univ.; judge, Court of of Common Pleas, Feb. 23, 1987; married Mildred Ann Carter; 3 children: Jennifer, Nicole, Jacqlyn; home address: 1270 Upton Circle, West Chester.

KAFRISSEN, ARTHUR S. (1st District — Municipal Court) was born Nov. 27, 1940, in Phila., the son of Ancel and Tessie Seffren Kafrissen; Temple Univ. (B.A.) 1964; Temple Univ. Law Schl. (J.D.); U.S. Army, hon. discharge 1961; Pa. Trial Lawyers Assn.; Tau Epsilon Rho (legal); elected judge, Municipal Court of Phila., Nov. 1977; married Carole F. Kafrissen, Esq.; 2 children: Samuel and Terri; home address: Philadelphia.

KANE, MICHAEL J. (7th District) was born Oct. 26, 1943, the son of James Joseph and Catherine Ann Swoyer Kane; Duke Univ. (J.D); mem., Pa. Bar Assn.; Bucks Co. dist. atty., 1979-86; judge, Court of Common Pleas, Jan. 6, 1986; 3 children: Richard, Christine, Jennifer; home address: 7-4 Aspen Way, Doylestown.

KAPLAN, LAWRENCE WILNER (5th District) was born Aug. 21, 1928, in Uniontown, the son of Edward and Libby Wilner Kaplan; Univ. of Pa. (B.A.) 1950; Univ. of Pgh. Schl. of Law (J.D.) 1953; U.S. Army, 1953-56, 1st lieut., Judge Advocate General's Corps; partner in Pgh. law firm; Am., D.C., Pa., Allegheny Co. Bar Assns.; Pa. Conf. of St. Trial Judges; v. pres., Assn. of Family & Conciliation Courts; mem., Pa. Bar Assn. House of Delegates; fellow, Am. Acad. of Matrimonial Lawyers; Domestic Relations Assn. of Pa.; Pgh. Estate Planning Council, hearing comm., Disciplinary Bd. of Supreme Ct. of Pa., 1973-78; Joint Family Law Council; Tau Epsilon Rho (legal); Pi Lambda Phi; B'nai B'rith; trustee, frmr. v. pres., Rodef Shalom Congreg.; bd., Carriage House Children's Cntr. and Natl. Conf. of Christians and Jews; founder, Squirrel Hill Urban Coalition; life trustee, Pgh. Chapt. Am. Jewish Comm. (past chmn.); bd., Alpha House, chmn., Community Relations Com., & Un. Jewish Fed.; Am. Legion; bd. dir., Pa. Bar Inst.; pres. emeritus, Family Mediation Co. of Western Pa.; bd. mem., Academy of Family Mediators; pres., Family Court Sec., Pa. Conf. of St. Trial Judges; bd. dir., Pgh. Mediation Center; case editor, Vol. XIV, Univ. of Pgh. Law Review; ed. bd., *Mediation Quarterly;* appt. judge, Court of Common Pleas, 1978; married Natalie Adler; 3 children: Thomas, Ellen, and Jon; home address: 6564 Lyndhurst Green, Pittsburgh.

KATZ, LEON (1st District) was born Dec. 25, 1921, in Phila., the son of Isadore and Jennie Epstein Katz; Temple Univ. (B.S.) 1943, (ED.M.) 1947; Temple Univ. Law Schl. (J.D.) 1950; U.S. Air Corps, 1943-46; admit. Pa. Bar, 1951; Lawyer; Fed., Am., Pa., Phila. Bar Assns.; Chancellor, Phila. Bar Assn., 1979; Assn. of Trial Lawyers of Am.; Am. Judicature Soc.; Lawyers Club of Phila.; ex. com., Pa. Conf. St. Trial Judges; Pa. Trial Lawyers Assn.; Tau Epsilon Rho; chancellor, Phila. grad. chapt., 1972-74; supreme natl V. chancellor, 1976-79; asst. dist. atty., 1952-54; appt. by Phila. Bd. of Judges to Bd. of Revision of Taxes, 1979; past pres., William Penn Lodge, B'nai B'rith; B'nai B'rith rep., Jewish Community Relations Council; gen. alumni bd. dir., Temple Univ.; Jewish War Vets., U.S.A.; Phila. Boosters Assn.; pres., Phila. Flag Day Assn., 1980-82; Certificate of Honor, Temple Univ. Schl. of Law, 1980; article, *Temple Alumni Review;* approx. 50 articles for the *Retainer,* Phila. Bar Assn.; appt. judge, Court of Common Pleas, May 7, 1980, elected, Nov. 3, 1981; married Irene Bernard; 2 children: Jean, Jack; home address: 1420 Locust St., F-20, Philadelphia.

KAYE, WILLIAM HERBERT (39th District) was born March 10, 1947, in Detroit, the son of Herbert R. Kaye and Doris M. Naugle; grad., Pa. State Univ. (B.A.) 1969; American Univ. (J.D.) 1972; mem.: Franklin Co., Pa. and Am. Bar Assns.; B.P.O. Elks, No. 600, Chambersburg; Falling Spring Presbyterian Ch.; Lions Club of Chambersburg; Chambersburg Little League, Inc.; Greater Chambersburg Chamber of Commerce; appointed judge, Court of Common Pleas, March 16, 1987; married Victoria A. Kendig; 2 children: Scott and David; home address: 1008 Byers Ave., Chambersburg.

KEELER, CHARLES C. (32nd District) was born Sept. 15, 1935, in Lansdowne, the son of Clement and Kathryn Gleason Keeler; Villanova Univ. (B.S.) 1957, and its law schl. (LL.B.) 1960; Law Review, 1958-60; U.S.A.F.R., 1960-66; Delaware Co., Pa., Am. Bar Assns.; Delaware Co.; Council, 1976-81, Govt. Study Comm., 1973-75; chmn., bd. trustees, Sacred Heart Medical Center; dir., Delaware Co. branch, Pa. Assn. for the Blind; appt. judge, Court of Common Pleas, Dec. 11, 1981; elected Nov. 2, 1982; married Patricia Ann Hogan; 4 children; home address: Box 26, Webb Road, Chadds Ford.

KELLER, JOHN WILLIAM (P.J. — 39th District) was born Mar. 15, 1927, in Waynesboro, the son of Niemond F. and Eva Nicodemus Keller (both dec.); Gettysburg Coll. (A.B.) 1948; Dickinson Schl. of Law (J.D.) 1951; U.S. Army, attorney, 1951-68; Pa., Am., Franklin Co. Bar Assns.; Masonic Orders, Am. Legion, Elks; borough solicitor, 1953-68; county solicitor, 1960-68; borough, county planning commissions solicitor; pres., Waynesboro Schl. Auth.; solicitor, Waynesboro Borough Auth.; pres., Waynesboro Chamber of Commerce; YMCA Bd.; Red Cross Bd.; Evangelical Lutheran Ch. Council, delegate, Pa. Constitutional Convention, 1967-68; commissioned judge, Court of Common Pleas, Dec. 17, 1968; elected Nov. 1969 and Nov. 1979; married Margaret L. Etchberger on Aug. 13, 1949; 2 sons: John N., Esq. and David S., Esq.; home address: 221 E. Third St., Waynesboro.

KELLY, ROBERT A. (5th District) was born July 6, 1944, in Pgh., the son of John J. and Mary J. Succop Kelly; South Hills Catholic H.S., 1962; Duquesne Univ. (B.A.) 1966; Duquesne Univ. Law Schl., 1969; Phi Alpha Delta Law Honor Frat.; mem., Pa. & Allegheny Co. Bar Assns.; Pa. Trial Lawyers Assn.; Western Pa. Trial Lawyers Assn.; mem., St. Agatha Parish Council, Bridgeville; St. Agatha's Men's Club, pres., 1979; Moot Court Honors, Duquesne Univ., 1968, 1969; assoc. editor, *Duquesne Univ. Law Review; Warden, Maryland Penitentiary v. Hayden* (1967); appt. judge, Court of Common Pleas, Oct. 9, 1984; married Joan Lorenzetti; 4 children: Sean, John, Laura and Maureen; home address: 1461 Old Meadow Road, Pittsburgh.

KELLY, ROBERT F. (32nd District) was born June 17, 1935, in Rosemont, the son of Owen Joseph and Sophie C. McCusker Kelly; Villanova Univ. (BS-econ) 1957; Temple Univ. Schl. of Law (LL.B.) 1960; prothonotary, Delaware Co., 1971-75; chmn., Del. Co. Rep. Exec. Comm., 1971-75; Del. Co., Pa., Am. Bar Assns.; St. Thomas Cath. Ch.; elec. judge, Court of Common Pleas, Nov. 1975; married Patricia J. Henkel; 4 children: Elizabeth, Robert F., Jr., Johanna, and Owen J.; home address: Villanova.

KELTON GEORGE T. (7th District) was born Jan. 10, 1922, in Bryn Mawr, the son of Stanton C. and Alice Twiss Kelton; Radnor Twp. public schls.; Harvard Coll. (A.B.) 1943; Harvard Law Schl. (LL.B.) 1948; U.S. Army, 1943-46; past pres., Bucks Co. Bar Assn.; appt. judge, Court of Common Pleas, 1977; elected 1977; married Fern Stehman; 2 children: Christopher, Jane; home address: 51 Rickert Dr., Yardley.

KEMP, ROBERT M. (P.J. — 4th District) was born Sept. 17, 1924, in Farmington Twp., Tioga Co., the son of Roscoe M. and Grena Chilson Kemp; Williamsport Technical Inst.; Army Univ. of Biarritz; Mansfield Univ. (B.S.) 1949; Dickinson Schl. of Law (J.D.) 1952; Natl. Coll. of St. Judiciary, 1972; U.S. Army, N. Africa, European Theatres, 45th Infantry Div., 3rd Infantry Div.; Tioga Co., Pa., Am. Bar Assns.; Judicial Administration Div.; dist. atty., 1959-71; Farmington Presbyterian Ch.; Lions Club; Am. Legion; VFW; General Sullivans Council, BSA; Friendship Lodge 247, F&AM; Williamsport Consistory (32nd Degree); Irem Temple Shrine, Wilkes-Barre; Natl. Council of Juvenile Court Judges; faculty, Pa. Coll. of the Judiciary; chmn., Domestic Relations Comm.; Pa. Conf. of Trial Judges; mem., Family Law Council; Domestic Relations Task Force; Supreme Court Domestic Relations Comm.; elected pres. judge, Court of Common Pleas, 1971; reelected, 1981; married Dorcas Lawton on June 29, 1946; 1 child; home address: R.D. 5, Wellsboro.

KING, JULIAN F. (1st District) was born May 20, 1931, in Phila., the son of Julian F. and Minnie Hines King; Lincoln Univ. (B.A., cum laude) 1953; Temple Univ. Schl. of Law (J.D.) 1956; Legal Spec., U.S. Army Signal Corps, 1956-58; v. chmn., bd. dir., Blue Cross of Grtr. Phila.; bd. man., Christian St. YMCA; Phila. Bar Assn.; Barristers' Assn.; Pa. Conf. of St. Trial Judges; bd. man., Assoc. Alumni of Central H.S. of Phila.; Law Alumni, Temple Univ.; Kappa Alpha Psi; Sigma Pi Phi; frmr. lecturer, Criminal Justice Dept., Comm. Coll. of Phila.; delegate, Pa. Constitutional Convention, 1967-68; commissioned judge, Court of Common Pleas, Dec. 30, 1971; elected, Nov. 6, 1973; retained Nov. 8, 1983; married Shirley A. Mackey; 1 child: Andrea Victoria; home address: 50 Hamilton Circle, Philadelphia.

KING, WILLIAM A., JR. (1st District — Municipal Court) was born April 25, 1926, in Eddystone, the son of William. A. and Ethel M. McKinley King; grad., Eddystone H.S., 1944; LaSalle Coll.; Temple Univ. Law Schl. (LL.B., J.D.) 1953; U.S. Navy, 1944-46 (signalman, 2nd class); admitted to practice before Pa. Supreme Ct. and Superior Ct., 1955; law clerk to Bd. of View, Phila.; mem., Lawyer Ref. Service of Phila. Bar Assn.; arbitrator for Am. Arbitration Assn., Phila. Common Pleas Ct. Arbitration System; private practice, 1955-70; register of wills, clerk of Orphans Ct. of Phila., 1970-1971; judge, Phila. Common Pleas Ct., 1971-73; regional counsel, Fed. Energy Admin., 1974-75; judge, U.S. Bankruptcy Ct., 1975-86; mem.: Natl. Conf. of Bankruptcy Judges, 1984-86; Am., Pa., and Phila. Bar Assns.; Natl. Conf. of St. Trial Judges, 1972-73; Pa. Conf. of St. Trial Judges, 1972-73; Natl. Conf. of Juvenile Ct. Judges, 1972-73; Juvenile Ct. Judges' Comm. of Pa., 1972-73; bd. of judges, Phila. Common Pleas Ct.; frmr. mem., Am. and Phila. Trial Lawyers Assns.; Lawyers Club of Phila.; mem., bd. gov., St. Thomas More Soc.; mem., bd. dirs., Frankford Hosp., 1979-84; mem., adv. council, LaSalle Coll. Alumni Assn., 1980-82; rec., commendation from State Sec. of Revenue, 1962; 25th Ward Man of Year Award, 1970; Northeast Phila. Young Republican Man of the Year Award, 1971; author, over 300 bankruptcy court opinions published from 1976 to 1986; appointed judge, Municipal Court, Dec. 1986; married: Marie Louise Rosato; 7 children: Marie Louise, Anne Louise, Margaret Mary, William A., III, Bridget A., Ernest R., Stephanie A.; home address: 410 E. Abington Ave., Phila.

KIRKLAND, LYDIA Y. (1st District — Municipal Court). Judge, Municipal Court of Philadelphia.

KLEIN, RICHARD B. (1st District) was born Dec. 24, 1939, in Phila., the son of Judge Charles and Rosalie Benson Klein; Amherst Coll. (B.A.-Phi Beta Kappa, magna cum laude) 1961; Harvard Law Schl. (LL.B.-honors grad.) 1964; faculty, Temple Univ. Schl. of Law, teaching trial advocacy, 1966-date; leader jazz orchestra commissioned by Pa. Council on the Arts to perform in prisons; v.pres., Prisoners' Family Welfare Assn.; Assoc. ed., contributor, *Shingle* (Phila. Bar Assn. magazine); mem., 10-person Am. Bar Assn. com. on Legal Writing; co-author, *Trial Communication Skills,* Shepard's/McGraw-Hill, 1986; author, *Legal Writing Techniques,* Inst. for Legal Communications; present., ed. activity leader, Prof. Seminar Consultants' legal study tours to Soviet Union, 1986, and China, 1987; *Opinion Writing,* Pa. Coll. of the Judiciary, 1985; planning com., panel moderator, Internatl. conf. on Compensation for Occupational Disability, 1984; present., author, "A Dozen Ways to Anger a Judge," *Litigation,* Winter 1987; "The Impaired Physician-Legal Aspects," Am. Soc. of Anesthesiologists, 1983; author, "Asbestos Case Termiology: A Glossary for Litigators," *The Legal Intelligencer,* 1982; rec., 1982 Friends' Central School Distinguished Alumni Award; attorney; spec. asst. atty. gen., 1967-71; Phi Beta Kappa, Phila. chptr.; Phila., Pa. Bar Assns.; St. Conf. of Trial Judges; chmn., Phila. Rep. Policy Comm., 1969-71; pres., chamber orchestra, "Concerto Soloists of Philadelphia," 1977-79; Trial Bd.; Musicians' Union Local No. 77, 1974-75; author: "A Practical Look at the New Juvenile Act," Duquesne Law Review, Vol. 12, No. 2, Winter, 1973; "The Juvenile Act of 1972 Revisited," Duquesne Law Review, Vol. 15, No. 3, Spring, 1977; apptd. judge, Court of Common Pleas, Dec. 29, 1971, served 1972-73; youngest Common Pleas Ct. Judge in history when apptd.; elected to full term, Nov. 1975; married Emanuela S. Miller; 2 children: Peter Grant Klein, Geoffrey Grant Klein, step-son, Alexander N. Miller; home address: 6408 Overbook Ave., Philadelphia.

KRASE, MORTON (1st District — Municipal Court) was born Oct. 5, 1934, in Phila., the son of Samuel and Sarah Cominsky Krase; Lincoln H.S., 1952; Temple Univ. (B.S.) 1956, Law Schl. (J.D.) 1962; attorney; mem., Phila. Bar Assn; T.E.R. Legal Fraternity; active in many civic organizations; rec., 1st prize, Legal Research and Writing, Temple Law Schl; Pa. Senate consumer protection award; published articles on consumer protection and related fields; coach, Youth Club (Bustleton Bengals); Jewish; appt. judge, Municipal Court, July 1983; reappt. June 1984; elected judge, Nov. 5, 1985; sworn in Jan. 6, 1986; married Vicki Rosenberg; 2 children: Sharon and Scott, home address: 9719 Laramie Rd., Philadelphia.

KREMER, I. RAYMOND (1st District) was born Jan. 28, 1921, in Phila., Temple Univ. (A.B.) 1942; Temple Univ. Law Schl. (J.D.) 1948; att. Indiana Univ. (constl. law); U.S. Army 1943-46; discharged as 1st Lt.j.a.g.; bd. of govs., Phila. Bar Assn.; Phila. Trial Lawyers Assn.; Sigma Pi; Tau Epsilon Rho (legal); 21 Jewel Square Club; B'nai B'rith; Justice Lodge; Variety Club; Fellowship Comm.; Temple Univ. Law Alumni Exec. Com.; 1972 B'nai B'rith Award of Distinction for "devotion to justice in the broadest sense"; 1978 Tau Epsilon Rho Law Frat. Appreciation Award for "dedicated service on behalf of all lawyers and the independence of the Judiciary"; Second Annual Musmanno Award; 1980 Pediatric Colitis Foundation honoree; 1985 21 Jewel Square Club Judiciary Award for Exemplary Service; appt. judge, Court of Common Pleas, Dec. 8, 1976; elected Nov. 1977; married Clare Rosof; 3 children: Dr. Cristine Kremer-Gusfa, Neil Atkinson Kremer, Andrea Kremer-Mongeluzzi; home address: Park Towne Place, Philadelphia.

KUHN, JOHN D. (51st District) was born Aug. 7, 1950, in Gettysburg, the son of Richard M. and Helen G. Small Kuhn; grad., Gettysburg Area H.S., 1968; Albright Coll. (B.A., history) 1972; Dickinson Schl. of Law (J.D.) 1975; mem., Lions, Gettysburg Presbyterian Ch.; elected judge, Court of Common Pleas, Nov. 5, 1985; married Laura Greenlee; 3 children: Kelli, Kristin, Kevin; home address: 90 Long View Dr., Gettysburg.

KUNSELMAN, ROBERT E. (36th District) was born June 21, 1937, in Summerville, the son of Harry E. and Priscilla Thomas Kunselman; Geneva Coll. (B.A.) 1959; Duquesne Univ. Schl. of Law (LL.B.) 1962; U.S. Army Reserve, 1962-68; Beaver Co., Pa. Bar Assns.; bd. mem., Beaver Co. Rehab. Center, Inc.; appt. judge, Court of Common Pleas, May 28, 1982; elected to full term, effective Jan. 1984; married E. Evonne Bilotto; 4 children; home address: 152 Laurel Dr., Beaver.

LABRUM, JOSEPH T., JR. (32nd District) was born Nov. 23, 1926, in Phila., the son of Joseph T. and Jane Schwab Labrum; Univ. of Pa. (A.B.) 1947; Univ. of Pa. Law Schl. (LL.B.) 1950; U.S. Navy, 1944-46, 1952-54; Del. Co. Bar Assn. pres. 1969, secy., mem. of bd. of dirs.; chmn of various comms., incl. grievance comm.; chmn. of bench-bar confrnce., comm. and specialization comm.; Pa. Bar Assn.; mem., House of Delegates, specialization comm.; past pres. Pa. Bar Assn., Conf. of Co. Bar Officers, Am. Judicature Soc.; bd. Governors, Pa. Bar Assn.; past pres., mem., Springfield Del. Co. Lions Club, advsry. bd. Dominican Convent; Award of Pa. Conf. of Co. Bar Officers, E. Chadwick Mem'l. Award, Del. Co. Bar Assn.; judge, Court of Common Pleas, Jan. 1976, married Rosemary Creamer; 7 children: Joseph T. III, Paula, Thomas, Anne, Maria, Carole and William; home address: 1901 Ridley Creek Rd., Media.

LATRONE, ROBERT A. (1st District) was born July 7, 1931, in Camden, N.J.; Central H.S. (B.A., cum laude) 1949; Temple Univ. (B.A., cum laude) 1952, and its Law Schl. (LL.B.) 1956, J.D. (1958); private law practice, 1957-67; asst. city solicitor 1960-67; elected magistrate, 1967, served until Dec. 1968; judge, municipal court, Jan. 1969 - Dec. 1971; recip.: Community Award for Outstanding Service from South Phila. News; Certificate of Honor, Temple Univ. Law Alumni Assn; Outstanding Service, Am. Arbitration Assn.; Award of Merit, Italian-Am. Press Assn.; Am. Judges Assn.; Phila. Bar Assn.; Justinian Society, Conf. of St. Trial Judges; completed following courses in judicial ed., Natl. Judicial Coll., Reno, Nevada: General Jurisdiction (1976), Evidence Graduate (1977), Judge and The Trial (1977), Decision Making Process (1978), Decision Making Skills & Techniques (1978), New Trends (1978); Search and Seizure (1979); adjunct prof., Temple Univ. and Villanova Univ.; faculty mem. of Natl. Inst. of Trial Advocacy; member, Jury Selection Comm., Criminal Justice Comm., Bd. of Judges of the Court of Common Pleas of Phila.; appt. judge, Phila. Court of Common Pleas, Dec. 1971; elected to full term commencing Jan. 1, 1974; reelected to 2nd full ten-year term commencing Jan. 1, 1984; home address: 2913 S. Juniper St., Philadelphia.

LAVELLE, JOHN E. (21st District) was born Jan. 23, 1920, in Connerton, the son of Edward and Mame McDonald Lavelle; Bloomsburg Univ. (B.S.) 1941; Temple Univ. (J.D.) 1948; Navy, 1942-46; Schuylkill Co., Pa., Am. Bar Assns.; Natl. Council Juvenile Court Judges; Pa. Conf. of St. Trial Judges; Phi Alpha Delta; Bd. of Gov. Fountain Springs Country Club; dir., Catholic Social Agency; mem., past dir., pres., Ashland C. of C.; dir., Ashland Public Library; dir., Good Samaritan Hosp.; member, P.E.R., Ashland Elks Lodge; Am. Legion, V.F.W., D.A.V., Washington Fire Co.; rec., Disting. Alumni Award, Bloomsburg Univ., 1973; elected judge, Court of Common Pleas, 1971; married Anne M. Cooke on Dec. 27, 1945; 7 children: home address: 1230 Centre Street, Ashland.

LAVELLE, JOHN PATRICK, (P.J. — 56th District) was born Feb. 18, 1931, in Phila., the son of John P. and Sarah McBride Lavelle; Niagara Univ. (A.B.) 1953; Villanova Law Schl. (LL.B.) 1958; U.S. Army, 1954-56; private practice, 1958-77; Pa. Bar Assn.; Pa. Trial Judges; Lehighton Rotary Club; dir., Lehigh Valley Motor Club; Carbon Co. solicitor, 1971-77; Shamrock Award, Irish Am. Society, 1983; Ss. Peter and Paul's R.C. Ch.; rec., Disting. Service to Law & Justice Award, County Detectives Assn., 1984; elected pres. judge, Nov. 1977; married Marianne Shutack; 4 children: Marianne P., John P., Jr., Jacqueline N., James M.; home address: 400 Beaver Run Rd., Lehighton.

LEAHEY, FRANCIS JOSEPH, JR. (47th District) was born Jan. 31, 1938, in Johnstown, the son of Francis J. and Kathern E. (Leffler) Leahey; grad., Univ. of Pgh. (B.A.) 1959; Dickinson Sch. of Law (J.D.) 1962; U.S. Navy, 1963-66; lawyer; mem.: Pa. and Am. Bar Assns., Pa. Conf. of State Trial Judges; Rotary Club of Ebensburg; past pres. (1985-86), Pa. Bar Inst.; examminer, Pa. Bd. of Law Examiners, 1966 to present; judge, Court of Common Pleas, March 25, 1987; married Irene M. Melnyk; 3 children: Stephen, Shane, Shawn; home address: 203 Charles St., Ebensburg.

LEHRER, SAMUEL MORRIS (1st District) was born Sept. 1, 1929, in Altoona, the son of Joseph and Bessie Lang Lehrer; Univ. of Pa., (B.S.) 1951; Univ. of Pa. Law Schl. (LL.B) 1954; Univ. of Paris, Certificate of Language, 1957; U.S. Army, 1st Lt., 1955-57; attorney, Richman & Richman (1956-58); Weiner, Basch, Lehrer & Cheskin (1965-67); individual practice (1967-73); Am., Pa., Phila. Bar Assns.; Am. Judicature Society; exec. bd., Conf. of St. Trial Judges, 1978-80; Child Welfare Adv. Bd., City of Phila.; bd. dir., Prisoners' Family Welfare Society; bd. trustees, Phila. Coll. of Art, 1974-1981; college instructor and lecturer; author of various legal articles, including ''The Preliminary Hearing in Pennsylvania,'' *Pennsylvania Bar Assn. Quarterly* Oct 1978, Vol. XLIX, No. 4, ''Report on National Seminar: Small Claims Court Suggestions,'' *Pennsylvania Law Journal,* August 25, 1980, Vol. III, No. 33; appt. judge, Municipal Court of Philadelphia, Dec. 1973; elected, 1975; elected to Court of Common Pleas, 1981; married Mary Josephine O'Shea; home address: Park Towne Place South, Philadelphia.

LEOPOLD, BERTRAM B. (24th District) was born July 12, 1940, in Altoona, the son of Emanuel S. and Mildred Bamberger Leopold; grad., Univ. of Pa. (B.A.) 1962; Dickinson Schl. of Law (J.D.) 1965; military service, 1966-69; mem., Am., Pa., and Blair Co. Bar Assns.; Rotary; appointed judge, Court of Common Pleas, March 30, 1987; married Susan Klatzkin; 4 children: Meg, Ann, Beth, David; home address: 3408 Baker Blvd., Altoona.

LEVIN, GEORGE (6th District) was born Oct. 15, 1925, in Erie, the son of Julius Louis and Rebecca Miller Levin; grad., Erie School System, 1943; Univ. of Pgh. (B.A.) 1948; Univ. of Pgh. Law School (LL.B.) 1950; U.S. Navy, 1944-46; mem., Pa., Am. and Erie Co. Bar Assns.; PUC Examiner, 1964-71; Phi Delta Kappa Educational Service Award; Lew Adler Friend of Education Award; appointed judge, Court of Common Pleas, 1972-73; elected judge, 1986; married Hy Beerman; 4 children: Lewis, Alan, Howard, Abby; home address: 311 Arlington Rd., Erie.

LEVIN, STEPHEN E. (1st District). Judge, Court of Common Pleas.

LEVY, MELVIN G. (32nd District) was born Oct. 20, 1923, in Chester, the son of George P. and Ada Blumberg Levy; Univ. of Pa. (B.S.) 1943; Univ. of Pa. Law Schl. (J.D.) 1950; att. Yale Univ., the Sorbonne (Paris); Natl. Judicial Coll., Univ. of Nevada; Am. Academy of Judicial Ed., Harvard Law Schl.; U.S. Army, 1943-46; Am., Pa., Del. Co. Bar Assns.; Am. Judicature Society; frmr. mem. bd. of dir., Del. Co. Bar Assn.; frmr. solicitor, controller, Delaware Co.; frmr. solicitor, City of Chester, Del. Co. Inst. Dist., Chichester, Ridley, Schl. Dist.; Boroughs of Trainer, Rutledge; frmr. special counsel, Upper Darby, Lower Merion, Wm. Penn Schl. Dist.; mem. (20 years), bd. dirs., pres., Congregation Ohev Shalom; frmr. trustee, Del. Valley Chapter, Natl. Hemophilia Society; adv. bd., The Academy of Advocacy; past pres., Pa. Schl. Bds. Solicitors Assn.; elected judge, Court of Common Pleas, Nov. 1977; 4 children; home address: 1000 Putnam Blvd., Wallingford.

LIEBERMAN, CALVIN (23rd District) was born Nov. 17, 1924, in Reading, the son of Max and Jennie Golden Lieberman; Albright Coll. (B.S.) 1949; Dickinson Schl. of Law (J.D.) 1953; U.S. Army, 1942-45, 501st Parachute Infantry Regiment, 101st Airborne Div.; general law practice (30 yrs.); mem., Berks Co., Am., Pa. Bar Assns.; State Trial Judges' Assn.; frmr., special asst. dep. atty. gen.; chief counsel, Dept. of Public Instruction; asst. dist. atty., Berks Co.; city solicitor, Reading; special asst. city solicitor, Civil Service Bds., and Zoning Hearing Bd., Reading; solicitor to Register of Wills, Berks Co.; solicitor to several twps. and schl. bds.; contribution drives: St. Joseph's Hosp., Community General Hosp., Albright Coll., Dickinson Schl. of Law; frmr. bd. dir., Olivet Boys' Club; frmr. solicitor to several fire companies, Fraternal Order of Police, Berks Co. Police Home Assn., Law Explorers Post; mem., bd. dirs., Reading-Berks Automobile Club; elected judge, Court of Common Pleas, Nov. 1983; married A. Jean Fehr; 3 children: Stephen B., Loren B., L. Stuart; home address: 2719 Park St., Reading.

LIPSCHUTZ, MITCHELL S. (1st Disrtict) was born Sept. 9, 1923, in Phila., the son of David and Amelia Lipschutz; Univ. of Pa., 1944, and its law schl. (LL.B.) 1946; Phi Beta Kappa; Order of the Coif; Law Review; attorney; Bar Assn. since 1947; Variety Club; Law Enforce. Sq. Club; 21 Jewel Sq. Club; Phila. Boosters; Masonic Lodge; Chapel of the Four Chaplains; Legion of Honor Membership Award, Chapel of the Four Chaplains; Honorary Citation, Phila. City Council; elected judge, Municipal Court, Nov. 6, 1979; elected judge, Court of Common Pleas, Nov. 5, 1985; home address: 419 N. 20th St., Philadelphia.

LITTLE, WALTER R. (5th District) was born Oct. 1, 1943, in Pgh., the son of George and Lillie Bell Henderson Little; grad., Allegheny Co. Comm. Coll. (A.A.) 1968; Univ. of Pgh. (B.A., pol. science) 1970; Univ. of Pgh. Schl. of Law (J.D.) 1973; U.S. Army, 1961-64; mem., Pa. Assn. Trial Court Judges; mem., Pa. and Am Bar Assns.; mem., Pgh. Branch NAACP, Legal Redress and Labor and Industry Committees; assoc. mem., Guardians of Greater Pgh., Inc.; mem., Natl. Assn. for the Study of Afro-American History; mem., Smith-Watkins Post #2 (Legion of Guardsmen); mem., Golden Star Lodge #143 F. & A. M.; bd. mem., Sickle Cell Soc., Inc.; mem., St. Benedict the Moor Ch.; magistrate, Ciy of Pgh., 1979-85; elected judge, Court of Common Pleas, Nov. 4, 1985; married Elizabeth Ross; 2 children: Karren Denise and Lisa; home address: 8522 Dersam Street, Pittsburgh.

LONG, GERARD (47th District) was born on Jan. 13, 1939, in Johnstown, the son of Benedict and Marie McDunn Long; grad., Brown Univ. (B.S.) 1963; Duquesne Univ. Law Schl. (J.D.) 1966; district attorney, Cambria Co., 1976-1986; Roman Catholic; elected judge, Court of Common Pleas, Nov. 1985; married Joan Fisanich; 3 children; home address: Box 294, R.D. 3, Ebensburg.

LORD, CHARLES A. (1st District) was born Oct. 29, 1919, in Phila., the son of Joseph S. and Irene Lord; grad. Colby Coll., 1942; Lt., U.S. Navy, 1942-46; Harvard Law Schl. (LL.B.) 1948; trial lawyer, 1948-73; mem., firm of Richter, Lord et al; bd. of dir., Prisoners' Family Welfare Assn.; Phila. and Pa. Bar Assns.; Pa. Conf. of St. Trial Judges; permanent delegate, Third Circuit Judicial Conference; commissioned judge, Phila. Court of Common Pleas, 1974; married Shirley Ellice; 5 children.

LOUGHRAN, CHARLES H. (10th District) was born Nov. 3, 1934, in Greensburg, the son of Joseph M. and Kathleen Hill Loughran; Univ. of Pa. (B.A.) 1957; Univ. of Pgh. (Doctorate of Law) 1960; U.S. Army, Army Reserve, 1960; Westmoreland Co., Pa. Bar Assns.; Westmoreland Academy of Trial Lawyers; Pa. Trial Lawyers Assn.; bd. dir., Westmoreland Co. Symphony; trustee, Westmoreland Museum of Art; trustee, Greensburg YMCA; exec. bd., State Assn. of Pa. Trial Judges; chmn., Civil Procedure Comm., State Assn. of Trial Judges, 1983; frmr. solicitor, Westmoreland Co. Controller; frmr. mem., Greensburg City Planning Comm.; Westmoreland Hospital Foundation Bd.; v. pres., Retired Sr. Volunteer Program, Westmoreland Co.; past mem., Co. Bd., Mental Health and Mental Retardation Program; author, *Westmoreland County Juvenile Hand Book;* past zone delegate, St. Cf. of Trial Judges; mem., Com. on Judicial Ethics for St. Trial Judges; elected judge, Court of Common Pleas, Nov. 1977; married Sarah Lyon; 2 children, Aimee C., Sydney C.; home address: 121 Morey Place, Greensburg.

LOWE, RICHARD S. (38th District) was born Dec. 14, 1924, in Phila., the son of Leroy S. and Margaret Edna Wolfe Lowe; Temple Univ. (B.S.) 1948; Temple Univ. Schl. of Law (LL.D.) 1951; U.S. Army, WW II, 1943-46; 18 months, European theater; Montgomery Co., Pa. Bar Assns.; Pa. Trial Judge Assn.; Council of Juvenile Court Judges; Masonic Order; spec. dpty. atty. genl., Comm. of Pa., 1952-55; asst. dist. atty., 1955-58; dist. atty., Montgomery Co. 1963-67; faculty, Natl. Judicial Coll., Reno, Nevada; Lutheran; numerous fraternal, civic organizations; commissioned judge, Court of Common Pleas, Jan. 1, 1968; elected Nov. 1969; elected pres. judge, Nov. 24, 1976; reelected pres. judge, Nov. 24, 1981; married Frances Evelyn Steeley on Aug. 28, 1948; 2 children; home address: 1961 Hemlock Rd., Norristown.

MAIER, EUGENE E.J. (1st District) was born July 22, 1937, in Phila., the son of Louis and Elizabeth Corcoran Maier; Temple Univ. (B.S.) 1968, and its law schl. (J.D.) 1971; Phila., Pa., Am. Bar Assns.; Brehon Law Society; Temple Law Alumni; The Irish Society; Phila. Urban League; chmn., city commissioners, Phila., 1973-81; Am. Catholic Hist. Society; Knights of Columbus; frmr. mem., Democratic St. & Natl. Comms.; Honor Awards, Temple Univ.: Constitutional Law, 1969, Constitutional History, 1970; author, "The Presidential Franchise," *Temple Law Quarterly;* while city commissioner, authored several voter registration bills and programs; elected judge, Court of Common Pleas, Nov. 3, 1981; married Constance Wambaugh; 4 children; home address: 1167 Bridge St., Philadelphia.

MANFREDI, WILLIAM J. (1st District) was born Aug. 15, 1943, in Phila., the son of William and Antoinette Leodori Manfredi; Univ. of Pa. (B.A.) 1965, (J.D.) 1968; mem., Phila. Bar Assn.; Justinian Society; Sons of Italy; Law Alumni Soc., Univ. of Pa.; judge, Court of Common Pleas; home address: 906 Spruce St., Philadelphia.

MANNIX, THOMAS C. (36th District) was born April 5, 1928, in Beaver Falls, the son of Thomas W. and Ellen Cavanaugh Mannix; Bucknell Univ. (A.B.) 1949; Dickinson Schl. of Law (LL.B.) 1952; U.S. Army, Corp of Engineers, 1952-54; practicing lawyer 1955-1978; Pa. Trial Lawyers Assn.; Am. Judicature Society; Pa. Conf. of Trial Judges; past pres., Pa. Assn. for the Blind; past pres., Beaver Co. Bar Assn.; mem., adv. bd., Pa. St. Univ., Beaver Campus; appt. judge, Court of Common Pleas, June 1978; elected to full ten-year term in 1979; married Jean McGonigle; 4 children: Tim, Kathy, Maura, and Paul; home address: 426 Fifth St., Patterson Heights, Beaver Falls.

MARGIOTTI, CHARLES J., JR. (1st District — Municipal Court) was born July 8, 1929, in Punxsutawney, the son of the Honorable Charles J. and Denise Wery Margiotti; Villanova Univ. (B.S.) 1952; Villanova Univ. Law Schl. (LL.B.) 1959; elected magistrate, city of Phila., 1967, appt. judge of the Municipal Court of Philadelphia, 1969; elected judge, 1973; and 1985; present term reelected in 1979, and 1985; present term expires Jan. 1992; married Anne Cunnane, Sept. 5, 1953; 3 children; home address: 3907 Vaux St., Philadelphia.

MARKER, CHARLES E. (10th District) was born Jan. 29, 1932, in Pitcairn, the son of Martin R. and Flora E. Whitehead Marker; Trafford H.S., 1949; Univ. of Pgh. (B.A.) 1953; Ohio N. Univ. Schl. of Law (J.D.) 1956; U.S. Army, 1957-59; attorney, 1957-79; Pa. Conf. of St. Trial Judges; B.P.O.E.; Family Court Admn., Westmoreland Co., 1969-79; Loyal Order of Moose; mem., Good Shepherd Lutheran Ch.; Democrat; hon. mem., adv. bd., Westmoreland Co. Special Olympics; life mem., Hempfield Hose Co., No. 2; Alternative Ed. Adv. Comm.; elected judge, Court of Common Pleas, Nov. 1979; married Adda Virginia Galloro; 4 children: Joyce, Teri J., Scott C., Melanie K.; home address: 809 Mt. Pleasant Rd., Greensburg.

MARSH, JAMES ROBERTSON (P.J. — 43rd District) was born Nov. 18, 1927, in Stroudsburg, the son of Fred and Janet Mildred Robertson Marsh; Muhlenberg Coll. (B.A.) 1950; Temple Univ. (JJ.D.) 1954; U.S. Navy, S1/C, 1945-46; Monroe Co. Bar; admitted to practice, U.S. District Court, Pa. Superior, Supreme Courts, U.S. Supreme Court, Commonwealth Court of Pa.; dist. atty., Monroe Co., 1960-67; solicitor, Barrett Twp., 1968-71; Borough of Stroudsburg, 1969-71; St. John's Lutheran Ch., Stroudsburg; Salvation Army Advsry. Bd.; Elks, Lehigh Consistory, Masonic Lodge, P.O.S. or A.; Jaycees Distinguished Service Award winner, 1963; appt. judge, Court of Common Pleas, Dec. 30, 1971; elected to full term, 1973; retained, 1983; married Helen Jolisok on March 10, 1961; 2 daughters; home address: 312 Wallace St., Stroudsburg.

MASSIAH-JACKSON, FREDERICA (1st District) was born Nov. 10, 1950, in Phila., the daughter of Frederick and Edith Lamarre Massiah; Chestnut Hill Coll. (A.B.) 1971; Univ. of Pa. Law Schl. (J.D.) 1974; mem., Pa., Phila. Bar Assns.; Barristers Assn; Lawyers Club; Univ. of Pa. Law Schl. Alumni Bd. of Mgrs.; Alpha Kappa Alpha Sorority; chief counsel, Com. to Investigate Business Closings, 1979-80, chief counsel, Pa. Senate Ins. Com., 1980-81; rec., Outstanding Young Leader of Phila., Jaycees, 1984; Ital.-Am. Press Club, 1984; Wharton Schl. Community Leadership Seminar Prog., 1980; elected judge, Court of Common Pleas, Nov. 8, 1983; married Thomas H. Jackson, III; two children.

MAZZOLA, WILLIAM J. (1st District) was born Jan. 8, 1945, in Phila., the son of Donato G. and Catherine Imbesi Mazzola; St. Joseph's Univ. (B.S.) 1966; Villanova Univ. (M.A.) 1967; Univ. of Baltimore (J.D.) 1970; U.S. Army Reserves, 1969-75; attorney; Phila., Pa. Bar Assns.; Phila. Trial Lawyers; Justinian Soc.; Sons of Italy; Grtr. Phila. Chapt., UNICO National; elected judge, Court of Common Pleas, Nov. 3, 1981; married Anne M. Rauch; 3 children; home address: 10835 Ellicott Rd., Philadelphia.

McCABE, JOSEPH PATRICK (1st District) was born July 19, 1927, the son of a professional Marine, and reared in Phila.; U.S. Navy, 1944-47, 1950-51, principally in submarines; Temple Univ. Schl. of Business and Public Admin. (B.S., cum laude) 1951, Schl. of Law (J.D.) 1956; Beta Gamma Sigma, honorary scholastic soc.; active in Legal Aid, locally and nationally; frmr. court clerk, probation officer, counsel and asst. chief of Probation Dept., Quarter Sessions Court, Phila.; Phila., Bar Assn.; Pa. St. Conf. of Trial Judges; Special Court Judges Assn. of Pa.; Friendly Sons of St. Patrick; Brehon Law Society; Phila. Emerald Society; The Irish Society; law judge, Phila. Municipal Court, 1971-85; elected Court of Common Pleas, 1985; married Dorothy Ann Ewald; 2 daughters: Shawn and Colleen; home address: 1303 Wakeling St., Frankford.

McCLOSKEY, JOSEPH F. (21st District) was born Oct. 9, 1929, in New Castle Twp., Schuylkill Co., the son of Peter V. (decd.) and Ethel Mills McCloskey; Shippensburg Univ. (B.S.) 1952; Villanova Univ. Law Schl. (J.D.) 1957; U.S. Navy, 2 yrs., Korean War; frmr. asst. atty. genl., Comm. of Pa.; Schuylkill Co., Pa., Am. Bar Assns.; admitted to practice before Schuylkill Cts., Pa. Superior, Supreme Cts., Fed. Dist. Ct.; workmen's comp. referee, Dist. 5, Comm. of Pa.; solicitor, City of Pottsville; Minersville Area Schl. Dist.; St. Clair Area Schl. Dist. Branch Twp. Bd. of Supervisors, New Castle Twp. Bd. of Supervisors; Grtr. Pottsville Area Sewer Auth.; Pottsville Housing Auth.; mem., bd. of mgrs., Pottsville Hosp.; The Pottsville Club; Pottsville Kiwanis; Pottsville Cath. War Vets; Am. Legion-Robt. B. Woodbury Post, F.O. Eagles; Am. Hose Co.; apptd. judge, Court of

Common Pleas, Oct. 6, 1975; elected, Nov. 8, 1977; appt. to Judicial Inquiry and Review Bd. by the Supreme Ct., March 30, 1982; married Joanne Charlton; 1 child, Patti Ann; home address: 16 Cottage Hill West, Pottsville.

McCLURE, JAMES FOCHT, JR. (P.J. — 17th District) was born April 6, 1931, in Danville, the son of James Focht and Florence Kathryn Fowler McClure; Lewisburg H.S., 1948; Amherst Coll. (A.B., magna cum laude, Phi Beta Kappa) 1952; Univ. of Pa. Law Schl. (J.D., cum laude, Law Review, Order of the Coif) 1957; U.S. Army, 1952-54; mem., Union Co. & Am. Bar Assns.; Pa Bar Assn. (frmr. mem., House of Delegates, Bd. of Governors, Long-range Planning Com., Com. to Study Disciplinary Bd.; Supreme Ct. of Pa.); frmr. mem., Pa. Appellate Ct. Nominating Comm.; frmr. lecturer, Pa. Bar Inst.; frmr. mem., Pa. Supreme Ct. Adv. Com., Appellate Ct. Rules; mem., Lewisburg Area Schl. Bd., 1967-74, pres., 1968-74; dist. atty., Union Co., 1974-75; frmr. elder, trustee, First Presbyterian Ch., Lewisburg; Susquehanna Valley Chorale; frmr. trustee and campaign chmn., Eastern Union Co. United Fund; trustee, Silver Bay Assn.; frmr. chmn., Lewisburg Planning Comm.; rec., Keedy Prize for most scholarly contribution to Law Review, Univ. of Pa. Law Schl.; appt. pres. judge, Court of Common Pleas, April 24, 1984; elected Nov. 1985; married Elizabeth Louise Barber; 5 children: Holly McClure Kerwin, Kimberly Ann Pacala, Jamee Martha Sealy, Mary Elizabeth Hudec, Margaret Louise McClure; home address: 63 University Ave., Lewisburg.

McCORMACK, THOMAS JOHN (1st District — Municipal Court) was born Sept. 28, 1922, in Phila., the son of John Patrick and Mary Jane Smyth McCormack; Temple Univ., 1949; Temple Univ. Law Schl., 1952; Sgt., U.S. Army, 1942-46; attorney; Phila. Bar Assn.; Brehon Law Society; Irish Society; mem., Pa. House of Representatives, 1953-62; House Parliamentarian, 1977-78; mem., Senate of Pa., 1978; Parliamentarian, Counsel, Special Ct. Judges' Assn. of Pa.; adv. bd., Catholic League for Religious and Civil Rights; Municipal Ct. Zone Rep., Pa. Cf. of St. Trial Judges; elected judge, Municipal Court of Philadelphia, Nov. 6, 1979; wife, Edith McCormack; 4 children: Molly, Nell, Will, Tom.

McCRACKEN, GLENN JR. (P.J. — 53rd District) was born May 16, 1935, in New Castle, the son of Glenn and Katherine Elizabeth McMillin McCracken; Westminster Coll. (B.A.) 1957; Univ. of Pgh. Law Schl. (J.D.) 1960; U.S. Army, 1960-62; Pa. Conf. St. Trial Judges; Sigma Nu; 1st asst. dist. atty., 1970, 1973; trustee, Westminster Coll.; Neshannock United Presbyterian Ch.; author, numerous legal opinions; elected judge, Court of Common Pleas, Nov. 6, 1979; married Julie Ann Myers; 3 children: Sharon Lynn, Susan Lynn, David Elliott; home address: R.D. 1, Orchard Terrace, New Wilmington.

McCRUDDEN, JAMES D. (1st District) was born May 19, 1921, in Phila., the son of John and Rose Liney McCrudden; att., St. Joseph's Univ.; Temple Univ. Schl. of Law (LL.B.) 1950; Naval aviator, 1943-46; Phila. Bar Assn.; asst. city solicitor, 1952-58; elected judge, Court of Common Pleas, May 1977; married Margaret F. Leighton; 6 children: Susan, John, Kathleen, Margaret, Maureen, James; home address: 6501 N. 8th St., Philadelphia.

McDANIEL, DONNA JO (5th District) was born June 29, 1946, in Sewickley, the daughter of Donald and Jo Wauro McDaniel; grad., Muskingum Coll. (B.A.) 1968; Ohio Northern Univ. (J.D.) 1973; judge, Court of Common Pleas, 1985; 2 children: Jaime, Lindsay; home address: 2015 Laurel Dr., Coraopolis.

McFALLS, PATRICK (5th District). Judge, Court of Common Pleas.

McGINLEY, BERNARD L., II (5th District) was born Jan. 7, 1946, the son of John R. and Marie Rooney McGinley; John Carroll Univ., 1967; Univ. of Pgh. Law Schl., 1970; Capt., Medical Svc. Corps, 1970-77, U.S. Army Reserve; Am. Bar Assn.; asst. dist. atty., 1970-74; chmn., bd. of Viewers of Allegheny Co., 1977-82; Knights of Equity; Ancient Order of Hibernians; Moose; Elks; elected judge, Court of Common Pleas, Nov. 3, 1981; married Denise Perrone; 4 children: Bernard, Joseph, Moira, Corinne; home address: 552 Glen Arden Dr., Pittsburgh.

McGINLEY, CAROL KAVANAGH (31st District) was born Jan. 31, 1948, in Evanston, Ill., the daughter of John Carroll and Maria Kirchman Kavanagh; grad., Manhattanville Coll. (B.A.) 1970; Georgetown Univ. (J.D.) 1973; mem., Pa. Conf. of State Trial Judges; Am., Pa., Lehigh Co., and D.C. Bar Assns.; Judicature Soc.; author, "Characterizing Police Encounters under the Fourth Amendment," Search & Seizure Law Report, Vol. 10, No. 8, Sept. 1983; elected judge, Court of Common Pleas, 1985; married Paul A. McGinley, Esq.; 3 children: Paige, Laura, and Paul; home address: 1805 Sherwood Road, Allentown.

McGOVERN, CLEMENT J., JR. (32nd District) was born Oct. 9, 1934, in Chester, the son of Madeline G. and Clement J. McGovern; St. Joseph's Coll. (A.B.) 1956; Univ. of Pa. Law Schl. (LL.B.) 1959; U.S. Air Force, 1960-63, rank of Captain; Delaware Co., Pa., Am. Bar Assns.; Pa. Conf. of St. Trial Judges; Am. Judicature Society; treas., city of Chester, 1967-70; elected councilman, city of Chester, 1970; ordained permanent deacon, Roman Catholic Ch., Phila. Archdiocese, May 1986; elected judge, Court of Common Pleas, Jan. 7, 1974; adjunct prof., Delaware Law Schl.; married Maureen Lee; 6 children: Terrance, Timothy, Valorie, Clement, Francis and Jonathan; home address: Box 76-C, Chadds Ford.

McGOWAN, BERNARD J. (5th District) was born Dec. 18, 1929, in McKeesport, the son of Bernard and Helen V. Hagerty McGowan; U. of Pgh. (A.B.) 1951; U. of Pgh. Law Schl. (J.D.) 1954; U.S. Marine Corps, 1954-57; Am. Judicature Society; St. Vet's. Comm., 1961; past St. Cmndr., Am. Vet's. WW II (Amvets); elect. judge, Court of Common Pleas, Nov. 1975; married Mary Aileen Truitt; 3 children: Kevin J., Brian J., and David A.; home address: 520 Chauncey Circle, McKeesport.

McGREGOR, JAMES R. (5th District) was born July 13, 1929, in Kittanning, the son of the late Russell A. and Leah Hampton McGregor; Washington and Jefferson Coll. (A.B.) 1951; Univ. of Pgh. Schl. of Law (J.D.) 1957; Natl. Coll. of the St. Judiciary; U. of Nev., Reno, 1974; U.S. Army, active duty, 1951-54, U.S. Army Intelligence Russian lang. interpreter-translator; Allegheny Co., Pa. and Am. Bar Assns.; Pa. Conf. of St. Trial Judges; legal counsel to Minority Leader, Pa. House of Representatives, 1966-67; solicitor, Allegheny Co. Controller, 1968-69; United Fund Chmn., 1965-66; frmr. mem., bd. gov's., Leukemia Society of W. Pa.; mem., bd. of gov's., Amen Corner (pres., 1976-77); mem., ex. bd., E. Valley Area Council, BSA; appt. judge, Court of Common Pleas, Allegheny Co., March 1974; served in Family Div., both adult and juvenile secs., Civil Div., currently in Criminal Div.; mem., Natl. Criminal Justice Task Force of the Urban Consortium; married Marguerite Ulrich; 5 children; home address: 1420 Walnut St., Edgewood, Pittsburgh.

McKEE, THEODORE A. (1st District) was born in Rochester, NY; grad., State Univ., N.Y.; Syracuse Univ. Coll. of Law; mem., bd. dir., Crisis Inter.; Crisis Intervention Network; judge, Court of Common Pleas, Nov. 1984.

McLEAN, JAMES H. (5th District) was born Nov. 10, 1930, in Homestead, the son of John J., Sr., and Margaret Graves McLean; Univ. of Notre Dame (A.B.) 1952; Univ. of Pgh. Law Schl. (J.D.) 1955; mem., Allegheny Co. Bar Assn.; Allegheny Co. Bench-Bar Com.; solicitor, Borough of Homestead, 1971-79; frmr. Mayor of Bethel Park, 1978-82; chief legal counsel, Comm. Coll. of Allegheny Co., 1979-84; solicitor, Allegheny Co., 1979-84; past chmn., Bethel Park Home Rule Study Comm.; past mem., St. Louise DeMarillac Parish Council; founding solicitor, Steel Valley Council of Governments; appt. judge, Court of Common Pleas, 1984; married Carolyn Kelver; 3 children: James G., David J. and Kathleen M.; home address: 3237 Postgate Dr., Bethel Park.

McWILLIAMS, HOWARD CLIFTON, JR. (P.J. — 47th District) was born in Ebensburg, son of Howard C. and Julia Jones McWilliams; Pa. St. Univ. (A.B.) 1940; Univ. of Pa. Law Schl. (LL.B.) 1943; Harvard Law Schl., 1946; lieut. U.S. Navy, WW II; Cambria Co., Pa. Bar Assns.; Gov's Justice Commission; past pres., Kiwanis; past pres. Johnstown Symphony Orchestra; Protestant; elected judge, Court of Common Pleas, 1963; retained 1973; named pres. judge, 1976; received U.S. Navy Citation for services; married Janice Sharbaugh; 3 children; home address: 510 Penn Ave., Johnstown.

MEKEL, EDWARD G. (1st District — Municipal Court) was born Aug. 29, 1933, in Philadelphia, the son of Jacob and Margaret Magee Mekel; LaSalle Coll. (B.A., cum laude) 1955; Villanova Univ. Law Schl. (J.D.) 1958; at Villanova was member, Law Review Staff; U.S. Air Force Reserves, 1958-64; member, Phila. Bar Assn., Pa. Conf. of St. Trial Judges, St. Thomas More Society; dpty. city commissioner, Philadelphia 1968-73; Legal House Counsel, Democratic County Exec. Committee, Philadelphia, 1960-67; elected judge, Municipal Court of Philadelphia, Nov. 1973; married Hilda Amoroso; 3 children; home address: Philadelphia.

MELLENBERG, DAVID EDWARD (31st District) was born May 27, 1926, in Detroit, the son of Edward F. (decd.) and Elsie A. Moyer Mellenberg (decd.); Pa. St. Univ. (B.A.) 1950; Dickinson Law Schl. (J.D.) 1957; U.S. Army, 1944-46; Lehigh Co., Am., Pa. Bar Assns.; Allentown Schl. Bd., 1966-71; Sigma Nu frat.; Kiwanis Club of West Allentown; Christ Lutheran Ch., Allentown; elected judge, Court of Common Pleas, Nov. 1975; retained Nov. 1985; married Eileen D. Derabasse; 2 children: David E., Jr. and Bryn R.; home address: 2727 Greenleaf St., Allentown.

MELODY, MICHAEL JOSEPH, JR. (15th District) was born March 11, 1932, in Phila., the son of Dr. M. Joseph and Helen Toomey Melody; grad., St. Joseph's Prep. Schl., 1950; St. Joseph's Coll. (B.S.) 1954; Georgetown U. Law Center (J.D.) 1957; U.S. Army 1957-59; general civil law practice; mem.: Chester Co., Pa., and Am. Bar Assns.; Pa. Conf. of State Trial Judges; Pa. Domestic Relations Assn.; K. of C.; Ancient Order of Hibernians; Italian Social Club (W.C.); frmr. Republican committeeman; Roman Catholic; appointed judge, Court of Common Pleas, April 28, 1981; elected judge, Nov. 1981; married: Mary Carrington Gawthrop; 3 sons: Michael, Brendan, Timothy; home address: 200 Kent Drive, Exton.

MERRIWEATHER, RONALD B. (1st District — Municipal Court) was born May 27, 1938, in Bridgeport, Ct., the son of Charles D. and Mildred A. Colley Merriweather; Morgan State Univ. (B.S., chem.) 1960; U.C.L.A. Schl. of Law (J.D.) 1971; U.S. Army, 1960-62; attorney; Phi Alpha Delta Legal Fraternity; Kappa Alpha Psi; elected judge, Municipal Court, Nov. 8, 1983; home address: 316 Crest Park Road, Philadelphia.

MIHALICH, GILFERT MATTHEW (P.J. — 10th District) was born July 12, 1926, in Monessen, Westmoreland Co., the son of Matt and Kathryn Mihalich; attended Antioch Coll., Yellow Springs, Oh., Pgh. Inst. of Aeronautics; grad. Duquesne Univ.; Univ. of Pgh. Schl. of Law; veteran of Army Air Force; taught Criminal Law, Indiana Univ. of Pa.; solicitor, City of Monessen; Westmoreland Co. Law Enforcement Officers Assn.; Police Chief Assn. of Westmoreland Co.; frmr. mem., Westmoreland Co., Pa. Bar Assns.; Am. Trial Lawyers Assn.; Am. Judicature Society; frmr. asst. dist. atty., Westmoreland Co., 1967-1971; served as law clerk for Court of Common Pleas of Westmoreland Co. and Pa. Supreme Court; elected to the Court of Common Pleas, 1971; member, Pa. Commission on Crime & Delinquency, since 1975; 1st elected pres. judge of Westmoreland Co.; elected pres. judge, Sept. 1985; reelected pres. judge, Jan. 6, 1986; married Pauline A. Razum; 3 children; home address: R.D. 1, Box 94A, Smithton.

MILLER, JOHN T. (19th District) was born Mar. 28, 1927, in Stewartstown, the son of J. Harvey and Sara Anderson Miller; Univ. of Pa. (A.B.) 1949; Univ. of Pa. Law Schl. (J.D.) 1952; U.S. Navy, 1945-46; York Co., Pa., Am. Bar Assns.; Pa. Conf. of St. Trial Judges; Delta Upsilon; James Wilson Law Club; Red Lion Lodge; F&AM; Hbg. Consistory; Tall Cedars; Zembo Shrine; 1st asst. dist. atty., York Co., 1962-70; Pa. asst. atty. gen., 1970-71; solicitor, Red Lion Boro, 1964-80; Fairview Twp., 1962-75; Elder, Round Hill Presbyterian Ch.; st. bd. dir., Am. Cancer Society; Devers Lions Club; Am. Legion; appt. judge, Court of Common Pleas, July 29, 1980; elected, Nov. 3, 1981; married Mary Auten; 4 children: John III, Susanna, David, Nan; home address: 510 E. Broadway Ext., Red Lion.

MIRARCHI, CHARLES P., JR. (1st District) was born Aug. 27, 1924, in Phila., son of Charles P. and Mary Caggliano Mirarchi Sr.; Temple Univ. (B.S.) 1944; Temple Univ. Schl. of Law (J.D.) 1948; Am., Pa., Phila. Bar Assns.; Am. Judicature Society; Justinian Society; Lawyers' Club of Phila.; St. Thomas More Society; pres., Pa. Conf. of St. Trial Judges; K. of C.

4th Degree; Knights of Malta; assoc. Capt. Caenaculum Group Men of Malvern; frmr. bd. of trustees, Phila. prisons; past mem. Cardinal's Advsry. Comm. on Diocesan H.S.; past general chmn., Annunciation B.V.M. Schl. Bd.; past grand master, Order of Brotherly Love; Venerable Msgr. John V. Tolino, P.A. Lodge, Order Sons of Italy in Am.; past dist. chmn., v. chmn., bd. mem., Boy Scouts of America; frmr. bd. of dir., Girl Scouts of America; Leukemia Society; Judicial Council of Pa.; frmr. v. chmn., Pa. Judicial Inquiry & Review Bd.; dir., Temple Univ. General Alumni Assn.; Catholic Philopatrian Literary Institute, Korean & Am. Friendship Soc.; adv. bd., Catholic League for Religions & Civil Rights; mem., President's Council, Manor Jr. Coll.; elected judge, Court of Common Pleas, 1971; commissioned Jan. 3, 1972; elected secretary, Board of Judges, Court of Common Pleas, Phila. Co., Nov. 1974; served to Nov. 1976; elected. Admin. Judge., Trial Div., Sept. 1976; adjunct prof., Delaware Law Schl. of Widener Coll., 1975-pres.; married Josephine Salvatore on June 4, 1949; 5 children; home address: 1329 Morris St., Philadelphia.

MORGAN, WARREN G. (12th District) was born Dec. 3, 1923, in Wilkes-Barre, the son of Winfield S. and Viola Williams Morgan; Dickinson Coll. (A.B.) 1947; Dickinson Law Schl. (J.D.) 1949; appt. judge, Court of Common Pleas, Dec. 1, 1970; elected to full term, Nov. 1971, retained Nov. 1981; married Pauline Culmann; 2 children: Paula and Scott; home address: 4709 N. Galen Road, Harrisburg.

MORRISON, CLARENCE E. (12th District) was born Feb. 17, 1930, in Charleston, S.C., the son of Ida Holmes Morrison; Howard Univ. (B.S.) 1954, (LL.B.) 1959; U.S. Army, 1954-56; law clerk, Dauphin Co., 1960-61; leg. asst. to Pa. State Aud. Gen., 1961-62; asst. atty. gen., Pa. Dept. of Revenue, 1962-65; asst. dist. atty., Dauphin Co.; staff counsel, Pa. St. Ed. Assn., 1969-76; lawyer; bd. dir., Hamilton Bank since 1972; frmr. bd. dir., pres., Harrisburg Housing Auth.; frmr. mem., Mayor's Comm. on Human Rel.; frmr. v. pres., Yoke Crest, Inc.; v. chmn., bd. trustees, adv., teacher, Tabernacle Baptist Ch.; co-chmn., Dauphin Co. Repub. Registration Drive, 1962, 63, 64; frmr. pres., Harrisburg Club of Frontiers Intrnatl.; bd. dir., Dauphin Co. NAACP; frmr. bd. dir., Dauphin Co. Young Repub. Club; charter mem., Optimist Club; Omega Psi Phi; Dauphin Co. (frmr. bd.), Pa. Bar Assns.; appt. judge, Court of Common Pleas, June 9, 1980, elected Nov. 3, 1981; married Grace Fulton; 2 children: Derricott M., Mark E.; home address: 4308 Beaufort Hunt Dr., Harrisburg.

MOSS, SANDRA MAZER (1st District) was born Oct. 10, 1942, in Vineland, N.J., the daughter of Marvin Ralph and Sylvia Levin Mazer; Temple Univ. (B.S.) 1964; Temple Univ. Schl. of Law, even. div. (J.D.) 1975; mem., Phila. & Am. Bar Assns.; Anti-Defamation League, Civil Rights Div.; Phila. Trial Lawyers Assn.; Tau Epsilon Rho; dep. city solicitor, 1980-83; counsel, Mayor's Comm. for Women, 1980-83; Fed. of Jewish Agencies; bd. dir., Temple Univ. Legal Aid Soc.; rec., Outstanding Woman of Delaware Valley, WIP (Radio); Outstanding Women Lawyers, *Philadelphia Magazine;* bd. governors, Phila. Bar Assn.; first woman major trial atty., city solicitors' off.; judge, Court of Common Pleas, Nov., 1983; 2 children: Deborah Ellen Picker, David Gilbert Picker; home address: #3 Lombard Mews, 812 Lombard St., Philadelphia.

MUNLEY, JAMES M. (45th District) was born June 28, 1936, in Scranton, the son of Robert W. and Marion Langan Munley (both members of Pa. Legislature); Univ. of Scranton (B.S.); Temple Law Schl. (LL.B.); Judicial Coll., Reno; Natl. Coll. of St. Trial Judges; U.S. Army, 1958-60; Am. Arbitration Assn.; Postal Service Expedited Arbitration Panel, Mid-Atlantic States; Mid. Atlantic Expedited Arbitration Assn.; Pa., Lackawanna Co. Bar Assns.; Scranton Lodge Elks; Ancient Order of Hibernians; Jermyn Lions Club; Veterans of Foreign Wars, Post 7963; past pres. and mem. exec. bd., Friendly Sons of Saint Patrick; past pres. and mem. exec. bd., Forest Lakes Council, Boy Scouts of America; Lackawanna Co. Fed. of Sportsmen's Club; frmr. Mid-Valley Coord., Lackawanna United Way Fund; frmr. mem., bd. dirs., St. Joseph's Hosp. Schl. of Nursing; frmr. dir., First Natl. Bank of Peckville; delegate, Dem. Natl. Convention, 1976; bd. of trustees, Everhart Museum; bd. dirs., Lourdesmont; law clerk, Chief Justice Michael J. Eagen, 1963-64; elected judge, Court of Common Pleas, Nov. 1977; appointed to Judicial Inquiry and Reveiw Bd. by Supreme Ct., 1986; bd. dirs., United Nations Assn. of Greater Scranton; married Dr. Kathleen P. Munley; 2 children: Julia and Gwendolyn; home address: 387 Main St., Archbald.

MUROSKI, CHESTER B. (11th District) was elected judge, Court of Common Pleas, Nov. 3, 1981.

MUSMANNO, JOHN L. (5th District) was born Mar. 31, 1942, in McKees Rocks, the son of John J. and Elizabeth Vecchio Musmanno; Washington & Jefferson Coll. (B.A., magna cum laude) 1963; Vanderbilt Univ. Schl. of Law (J.D.) 1966; Phi Beta Kappa (1963); pres., History Honorary Society, 1963; asst. ed., *Vanderbilt Law Review,* 1966; Allegheny Co. Bar Assn.; Pa. Trial Lawyers Assn.; Italian Sons and Daughters of Am.; dist. justice, 1970-81; solicitor, pres., Dist. Justices, Allegheny Co.; author of various articles in *Vanderbilt Law Review;* elected judge, Court of Common Pleas, Nov. 3, 1981; married Virginia Mary Farina; 1 child, Lisa Ann; home address: 5 Devon Ln., Pittsburgh.

MYERS, JAY WALTER (P.J. — 26th District) was born March 17, 1921, in Nescopeck, Luzerne Co., the son of Walter H. and Martha Hoag Myers; Pa. St. Univ. (A.B.) 1949; Duke Univ. Law Schl. (LL.B.) 1952; U.S. Marine Corps WW II, 1942-46; Bloomsburg Rotary Club; Am. Legion; Elks; Wesley United Methodist Ch., Bloomsburg; elected pres. judge, Court of Common Pleas, 26th Judicial District in 1971; married Joanne B. McCreary; 3 children: Kent, Kimberly, Kevin; home address: 424 Iron St., Bloomsburg.

NATALE, SEBASTIAN DAVID (12th District) was born Oct. 17, 1924, in Fossacesia, Italy, the son of Giovanni and Giovanna Polsoni Natale; grad., Bishop McDevitt H.S., 1942; Gettysburg Coll. (A.B.) 1950; Catholic Univ., Columbus Div. Schl. of Law (LL.B.) 1955; U.S. Air Force, 1943-45; attorney-at-law, 1962-1985; mem.: Sigma Alpha Epsilon, Jaycees, Sons of Italy, Navy League Exchange Club, Pa. Sports Hall of Fame (Capital Area Chapter); U.S. Commissioner (1966-1971), U.S. Magistrate (1971-1975); mem., St. Margaret Mary Ch.; involved in Democratic politics as a candidate, campaign manager, etc.; walked home from Washington, D.C., to Harrisburg, Pa., upon graduation from law school; elected judge, Court of Common Pleas, Nov. 5, 1985; married Rose Ametrano Natale; 3 children: Maria O'Donnell, Christine Dietz, Andrea Sullivan; home address: 2306 Chestnut St., Harrisburg.

NICHOLAS, WILLIAM T. (38th District) was born Sept. 3, 1938, in N.Y.C., the son of James Nicholas (dec.) and Anastasia Eliason Nicholas; City Coll. of N.Y. (B.A.) 1961; Temple Univ. Schl. of Law (LL.B.) 1964; dean's list; lawyer; adm. to practice, U.S. Supreme Ct., U.S. Ct. of Appeals, U.S. Dist. Ct., Supreme and Superior Cts. of Pa.; assoc. ed., *Temple Law Quarterly;* ch. justice, Moot Court; asst. dist. atty., Montgomery Co., 1968-71; 1st asst. dist. atty., 1971-76; dist. atty., 1976-80; lecturer: Montg. Co. Community Coll. (1969-76), Pa. State Police, Police Chiefs Assn., Montg. Co.; MBA; PBA; PDAA; NDAA; ABA; Order of AHEPA; St. George Gr. Ch.; Montg. Co. Emergency Service; Montg. Co. Histor. Society; Police Chiefs Assn.; rec., Disting. Service Award, Pa. Co. Detectives' Assn.; Disting. Service Award, F.O.P.; elected judge, Court of Common Pleas, Nov. 1979; married Catherine J. Demetris; 2 children: Stacey, Amelia; home address: 1700 DeKalb St., Norristown.

NOVAK, RAYMOND ANTHONY (5th District) was born Apr. 9, 1941, in Pgh.; St. Vincent Coll. (B.A.) 1964; St. Mary's Univ. (S.T.B.) 1966 (S.T.L.) 1967; Univ. of Pgh. (J.D.) 1973, (M.S.W.) 1974; Moot Ct. Honors, Univ. of Pgh.; Juvenile and Criminal Law; Bar of the Supreme Ct. of Pa.; Allegheny Co. Bar Assn.; Master, Court of Common Pleas, Juvenile Sect., 1976-1980; Am. Jurisprudence Award in Domestic Relations, 1974; Young Life Award for Outstanding Contribution to Children, 1977; author, *Eisenstadt v. Baird: A Return to the "Lochner" Era of Judicial Intervention?* (U. Pgh. Law Review 1972); *S. 439, The Proposed Pennsylvania Juvenile Act: A Two Edged Sword,* (U. Pgh. Law Review 1972); *The Incorrigible Child Under the New Pennsylvania Juvenile Act: An Unsound, Unsupportable and Unfortunate Policy Choice,* (U. Pgh. Law Review 1973); *Toward Effective Police Work with Juvenile Offenders,* (Chiefs of Police Bulletin 1978); *The Case for Retaining Juvenile Court Jurisdiction Over Dangerous Juvenile Offenders,* The Academy, Columbus, Ohio; Pa. Bar Inst., Book 1985-294, *Second Annual Criminal Law Symposium;* appt. judge, Court of Common Pleas, Apr. 2, 1980; elected to a 10-yr. term beginning Jan. 1, 1982; home address: 5539 Beacon Street, Pittsburgh.

NYGAARD, RICHARD L. (6th District) was born July 9, 1940, in Thief River Falls, Mn., the son of Leo B. and Amanda Arneson Nygaard; Univ. of Southern Calif., (B.S.) 1969; Univ. of Michigan (J.D.) 1971; U.S. Navy, 1958-64; Pa., Am. Bar Assns.; Pa. Conf. of St. Trial Judges; rep., Erie Co. Council, 1978-81; Erie Co. Bd. of Elections, 1978-80; chmn., Cerebral Palsy Telethon, 1980-81; v. chmn., NMSS, 1981-82; celebrity Host, March of Dimes, 1982; nominating chmn., French Creek Co. BSA, 1982; Am. Legion; Community Service award, 1982; Mayor's Certificate of Merit, 1982; Presidential appt. as only U.S. Judge to sit on the International Conf. of Free Elections, 1982; appt. judge, Court of Common Pleas, May 11, 1981; elected judge, Nov. 1983; married Martha J. Marks; 3 children: Jennifer, Richard, John.

O'BRIEN, JOHN W. (5th District) was born Aug. 22, 1921, in Pgh., the son of John W. O'Brien and Esther C. Lascheid O'Brien; Univ. of Pgh. (B.A.) 1948, (LL.B.) 1951; served in Infantry, WW II, 102nd Div.; retired mem., U.S.A.R.; pres. of council (1961-68); mayor (1969-70), Baldwin Borough; sec., v. pres., Pa. St. Conf. of Trial Judges; chmn., Pa. Comm. on Sentencing; elected judge, Nov. 1971; married Ruth Vollmer; 8 children.

O'BRIEN, MARTIN JOSEPH (50th District) was born Aug. 2, 1930, in Pgh., the son of Martin J., Sr. and Pauline Larkin O'Brien; grad. Butler H.S.; Coll. of Arts and Sciences, Georgetown Univ., 1952; Schl. of Law, Georgetown Univ., 1955; U.S. Army, 1956-58, 8th Infantry Div., 45th Field Artillery Battalion; mem.: Am., Pa. and Butler Co. (pres.,1981) Bar Assns.; staff, Pa. Constitutional Convention, 1967-68; Pa. Gov.'s Justice Comm., Southwest Region, 1969-76, chmn., 1970-73; Am. Arbitration Assn., Panel of Arbitrators, 1978-1986; Pa. Bar Assn., House of Delegates, 1979-81; awarded first hon. life membership, Butler Area Jaycees; Am. Red Cross, awarded life membership, 1986; appointed judge, Court of Common Pleas, 1986; home address: 505 North McKean St., Butler.

O'BRIEN, PETER J. (43rd District) was born Aug. 13, 1938, in Phila., the son of James M. and Catherine Reilly O'Brien; grad., Villanova Univ. (B.S., econ.) 1959, (Doctorate of Law) 1962; U.S. Army, judge advocate, General's Corps - 1963-66; mem., Am. Bar Assn.; Pa. Conf. of Trial Judges; elected judge, Court of Common Pleas, Nov. 1985; married Karin S. Maguire; 7 children: Kathleen, Peter, Kara, Daniel, Meghan, Sean and Elizabeth; home address: Knob Road, Mount Pocono.

O'KEEFE, JOSEPH DONALD (1st District) was born Jan. 13, 1944, in Phila., the son of Thomas F. O'Keefe and Elizabeth Galligan; grad., St. Joseph's Univ. (B.S) 1966; Duquesne Univ. (J.D.) 1973; U.S. Army, 1st Lieut. Ordnance, 1966-69; elected judge, Court of Common Pleas, Nov. 8, 1983.

O'KICKI, JOSEPH FRANCIS (47th District) was born Aug. 19, 1930, son of Joseph and Antonia Martincic O'Kicki; grad. Univ. of Pgh. and its law schl., 1957 (Law Review Staff); U.S. Navy, 1952-54; Cambria Co. Bar Assn., & U.S. Supreme Court; adj. assoc. prof., Univ. of Pgh. at Johnstown, St. Francis Coll.; ass't. co. solicitor, 1960-71; Law and Legislative Comm., Pa. Firemen's Assn.; pres., Am. Lung Assn. of Pa. 1975-77, 1984-85; Pa. Judicial Council; married Theresa Caroff; 7 children; elected judge, Court of Common Pleas, 1971; home address: 1515 Wm. Penn Ave., Johnstown.

O'MALLEY, DONALD (P.J. — 34th District) was born Feb. 24, 1918, in Susquehanna, the son of William and Ann Yourl O'Malley; att. Newark Coll. of Engineering; Temple Law Schl. (LL.B.) 1949; bombardier, 1st lieut., 15th Air Force, 499th Bombardment Group, WW II; Pa. Bar Assn.; Am. Legion; VFW; dist atty., Susquehanna Co., 1960-68; commissioned pres. judge, Court of Common Pleas, Jan. 1, 1968; married Elizabeth Reddon on Aug. 3, 1946; 7 children; home address: 10 Kelly St., Montrose.

O'MALLEY, MICHAEL J. (P.J. — 5th District) was born in Pgh., oldest of 6 children; enlisted U.S. Army Aviation Cadet, 1942; navigator of B-24's in 5th Air Force; combat, New Guinea, Philippines, Okinawa, occupation of Japan; 5 battle stars; hon. discharge, 1946; grad., Univ. of Pgh. and its law schl; former spec. asst. atty. genl.; former chm., Bd. of Viewers, Ct. of Common Pleas of Allegheny Co.; admitted to practice before all courts, incl. U.S. Supreme Court; Allegheny Co., Pa., and Am. Bar Assns.; Am.

Arbitration Assn., Pa. Conf. of St. Trial Judges; past pres. Natl. Conf. of Metropolitan Courts; Am. Bar Assn., adv. comm. on Metropolitan Delay; adv. bd., Natl. Center for St. Courts Study of Litigation Process; bd of dir., Natl. Conf. of Metropolitan Courts; Judicial Council of Pa; Comm. to Study Pa'.s Unified Judicial System; mem., Judicial Admin. Working Group on Asbestos Lit., 1983-84; Statewide Steering Com. on Automation of Pa. Cts.; Air Force Assn.; life mem., Pa. Assn. for Retarded Children; Variety Club of Pgh; Ancient Order of Hibernians and Knights of Equity; judge, Court of Common Pleas, 1972; married; 4 children.

PAWELEC, EDMUND S. (A.J. — 1st District) was born Oct. 23, 1930, in Phila., the son of the late Thomas and Catherine Pawelec; Villanova Coll. (B.S.) 1953; Univ. of Pa. Law Schl. (J.D.) 1956; Pa. Trial Judges; frmr. chmn., Supreme Ct. Orphans' Ct. Rules Com.; mem., Joint St. Gov. Comm. Adv. Com. on Decedents' Estate Laws; commissioned judge, Court of Common Pleas, Jan. 3, 1972, assigned to Orphans' Court Division; elect. admin. judge, Orphans' Court Div. commencing Jan. 5, 1976; married Joan K. Fetzer; 1 son.

PENKOWER, ALAN SCOTT (5th District) was born June 12, 1942, in Brooklyn, NY, the son of Jacob and Ida Albaum Penkower; Brandeis Univ. (B.A.) 1965; New York Univ. Schl. of Law (LL.B.) 1967; mem., ABA Special Com. on Housing & Urban Develop. Law; chief magistrate, Pittsburgh, 1978-83; Pgh. Housing Ct. Magistrate, 1972-83; appt. judge, Court of Common Pleas, June 1983; elected judge, Nov. 1983; married Lili Mandel; 2 children: Jessica, Jon; home address: 1548 Shady Ave., Pittsburgh.

PEOPLES, THOMAS G., JR. (P.J. — 24th District) was born Oct. 21, 1935, in Altoona, the son of Thomas G., Sr., and Alma M. Shoemaker Peoples; Univ. of Pa. (B.A.) 1958; Dickinson Schl. of Law (J.D.) 1964; attorney; Pa. Bar Assn.; Pa. Trial Lawyers Assn.; Rotary; dist. atty., Blair Co., 1976-80; bd. dir., United Way; bd. trustees, Garvey Manor, Hollidaysburg; rec., St. George Medal, B.S.A.; Domestic Abuse Program of Blair Co.; bd. of trustees, Mercy Hosp., Altoona; instructor, Criminology, Indiana U. of Pa.; elected judge, Court of Common Pleas, Nov. 1979; pres. judge, June 1, 1980; married Maureen McManus; 3 children: Thomas G., III, Amy M., Jennifer A.; home address: 3000 Union Ave., Altoona.

PEREZOUS, MICHAEL J. (2nd District) was born Aug. 1, 1936, in Lancaster, the son of John and Lucille Malamata Perezous; Franklin & Marshall Coll. (A.B.) 1958; Temple Univ. Law Schl. (J.D.) 1961; attorney; Lancaster Co., Pa , Am. Bar Assns.; Pa. Conf. of St. Trial Judges; asst. city solicitor, Lancaster, 1964-66; asst. solicitor, Lancaster Co., 1968-74; Certificate of Achievement, Natl. Judicial Coll.; orig. mem., Hearing Comm. of Disciplinary Bd., Pa. Supreme Ct.; elected judge, Court of Common Pleas, Nov 3, 1981; married Dolores Xakellis; 2 children: Jonathan, Mark; home address: 1750 Wicklawn Dr., Lancaster.

PFADT, WILLIAM E. (P.J. — 6th District) was born Mar. 1, 1919, in Erie, the son of Francis X. and Gertrude Gehrlein Pfadt; att. Univ. of Michigan; Univ. of Pgh. (B.S.) 1946; Univ. of Pgh. Schl. of Law (LL.B.) 1949; U.S. Air Force, Central Pacific Theatre, achieved rank of captain, Air Medal and DFC, with clusters; Erie Co., Am., Pa. Bar Assn.; Pa. Conf. of St. Trial Judges; asst. atty. genl., Cmwlth. of Pa., 1955; asst. city solicitor, Erie, 1961-64; asst. dist. atty., Erie Co., 1965-67; dist. atty., Erie Co., 1967-70; appt. judge, Court of Common Pleas, July 1970-71; elected, Jan. 1, 1974; retained Jan. 1, 1984; elected pres. judge, Jan. 1985; trustee, Boys Club of Erie; instructor, Gannon Univ.; past pres., Lake Erie Law Enforce. Assn.; Phi Alpha Delta (legal); Pi Gamma Mu (hon.); Erie Co. Prison Adv. Comm.; Joint Family Law Council of Pa.; Supreme Ct. Domestic Relations Com.; admitted, Pa. Supreme, Superior & Commonwealth Cts., U.S. Dist. Ct., Ct. of Appeals, Supreme Ct. of the U.S.; married Jeanne Maley; 4 daughters; home address: 4628 Homeland Blvd., Erie.

PODCASY, BERNARD J. (11th District) was born on Aug. 12, 1920, the son of the late Joseph and Catherine Pierozak Podcasy; Univ. of Toronto (B.A.) 1942; Georgetown Univ. Law Schl. 1948; 4 1/2 yr. service, 45th Infantry Division, Army, WW II, rose from private to captain, wounded in action three times, received Combat Infantryman's Badge; Luzerne Co. Bar Assn.; frmr. asst. dist. atty., solicitor of Ashley Borough, dpty. atty. genl.;

prothonotary of Luzerne Co. for 10 years; del., Dem. Natl. Conv., 1964; VFW, Kingston, Catholic War Vets, Ashley, DAV, Tatra Club; elected to full term as judge, Luzerne Co. Court of Common Pleas, Nov. 1971; retained, 1981; married Jane Ladner of East End, Wilkes-Barre; 3 children: Bernard, Susan and Melissa; home address: 120 Riverside Dr., Wilkes-Barre.

PORTER, WILLIAM (1st District) was born Jan. 24, 1928, in Phila., the son of Louis and Rose Porter; Univ. of Pa. (B.S.) 1951; Univ. of Pa. Law Schl. (LL.B.) 1954; Am., Phila. Bar Assns., Pa. Conf. of St. Trial Judges; Lawyers' Club of Phila.; Phila. Boosters Assn.; Variety Club; bd. of trustees, Justice Lodge; appt. judge, Court of Common Pleas, Dec. 29, 1971; elected to full term commencing Jan. 7, 1974; reelected to second full term commencing Jan. 2, 1984; address: 529 City Hall, Philadelphia.

POSERINA, JOHN J., JR. (1st District) was born Aug. 29, 1932, in Phila., the son of Judge John J. Poserina and Helen Lignare Poserina; La Salle H.S.; Temple Univ.; Temple Law Schl. (LL.B.) 1960; Temple Law Schl., Man of the Year, 1960; Dean's list, 1955-60; sgt., U.S. Army Infantry, 1953-55, hon. discharge; partner, Greenberg, Poserina and Sagot, 1961-62; partner, Ettinger, Poserina, Silverman, Dubin, Anapol & Sagot, 1962-76; mem., Pa. Supreme & Superior Ct., 1961; U.S. Supreme Ct., 1967; U.S. Dist. Ct., Ct. of Appeals, Customs Ct. and U.S. Tax Ct.; mem., State Conf. of Trial Judges; founding counsel, Vince Lombardi Lodge Sons of Italy; frmr. v. pres., counsel, Austrian Seacoast Soc.; Lower Kensington Environmental Drug Program; Knights of Columbus; mem., Phila. Bar Assn.; Phila. Trial Lawyers Assn.; Justinian Soc.; mem., Local 830 Teamsters Schmidt's Brewery; Local 252 Teamsters Inquirer Driver; atty., Transport Workers Union Local 234; Phila. Fed. of Teachers; rec., Community Leader Award; Port Richmond Civic Assn. 1973; Founders Award, Fishtown Recreation Center, 1975; contributing columnist, *Phila. Federation of Teachers Newspaper*, 1974-76; *Water Pollution Control Journal*, 1972-76; substitute lecturer, Temple Univ., 1983; Catholic; elected judge, Court of Common Pleas, Jan. 1, 1984; married Lillian Dwyer; 3 children: Susan, John and Mark; home address: 4600 Convent Lane, Phila.

PRATT, RALPH D. (53rd District) was born July 7, 1940, in New Castle, the son of Paul and Ann Morella Pratt; grad., Baldwin Wallace Coll. (B.S., chem.); U. of Pgh. Schl. of Law (J.D.); U. of Pgh. Grad. Schl. of Public Health (M.S., health law); trial judge; mem.: Pa. Conf. of State Trial Judges, Pa. and Lawrence Co. Bar Assns.; adv. bd., Pa. State Univ., Shenango Valley Campus; mem. Pa. House of Representatives, 1975-86; author, "Determining Legal Sanction for the Physician's Assistant, Physician's Associate," April 1972, Vol. II, Nov. 2; elected judge, Court of Common Pleas, Nov. 5, 1985; married Susan Chaundy; home address: 3304 Plank Rd., New Castle.

PRATTIS, LAWRENCE (1st District) was born June 16, 1926, in Phila.; Howard Univ. (A.B.) 1946; Temple Univ. Schl. of Law (J.D.) 1951; U.S. Marine Corps, 1951-59, active duty, 1951-53, Hdq. 1st Marine Div., (Korea) Sergeant; admitted to Pa. Bar, Nov. 1951; Phila., Am. Bar Assns.; asst. city solicitor, 1955-58; asst. U.S. atty., East. Dist. of Pa., Chief, Criminal Div., 1961-64; regional counsel, U.S. Dept. Housing & Urban Dev., 1964-67; exec. dir. Maple Corp., 1967-69; secy., Haas Community Fund, 1969-71; v. chmn., Phila. Housing Authority, 1969-71; director, Federal Home Loan Bank of Pgh., 1971-73; Civil Procedural Rules Comm., Pa. Supreme Court; trustee, Phila. Bar Foundation; lecturer in law, Villanova Univ. Law Schl.; member, Phila. Co. Bd. of Law Examiners, 1963-69; Alpha Phi Alpha; United Methodist Ch.; apptd. judge, Common Pleas Court of Phila., Dec. 31, 1973; elected 10-yr. term commencing Jan. 1976; retained for 10-yr. term, Jan. 1986; married Marie Bruen; 2 children: Susan M. and David H.; home address: 5209 Woodbine Ave., Philadelphia.

PRESCOTT, RITA ELIZABETH (32nd District) was born June 6, 1921, in Tonawanda, N.Y., the daughter of William Waldo and Marie Eleanore Dreyer Prescott; U. of Pa. (B.S.) 1943, (M.S.) 1944; Temple Univ. Law Schl. (LL.B.) 1949; public h.s. teacher, 1944-51; atty-at-law, 1951-75; Delaware Co., Pa., Am., Phila. (assoc. mem.) Bar Assns.; Am. Judicature Soc.; Pa. Council of Trial Ct. Administrators (charter mem.); Inst. of Judicial Admin.

Natl. Assn. of Women Lawyers; Natl. Assn. of Trial Ct. Administrators (pres. 1972-73; bd. dirs. 1971-75); Pa. Trial Lawyers Assn.; Assn. of Trial Lawyers of Am.; Cnwlth. Bd., Med. Coll. of Pa.; Natl. Fed. Business & Professional Women's Clubs Inc. (bd. dirs., 1972-74, 1975-77, 1984-85); Pa. Fed. Bus. & Prof. Women's Clubs, Inc. (St. pres., 1972-74); Alpha Xi Delta Frat.; "Woman of the Year," Lansdowne Bus. & Prof. Women's Club, 1970; Upper Darby Bus. & Prof. Women's Club, 1971; bd. of Overseers, Delaware Law Schl., 1982-; Woman of Distinction Award, Alpha Xi Delta, 1986; Donald J. Orlowsky Memorial Award, Del. Co. Bar Assn., 1985; Special Achievement Award, Temple Law Alumni/ae Assn., 1983; elect. judge, Court of Common Pleas, Nov. 1975; served as its adm. judge of Civil Div., 1981-84; business address: Court House, Media.

PRESENZA, LOUIS J. (1st District — Municipal Court) was born Oct. 15, 1945, in Phila., the son of Rocco and Angelina Castellotti Presenza; St. Joseph's Coll. (B.S.) 1967; Villanova Univ. Schl. of Law (J.D.) 1970; mem., Pa. Conf. St. Trial Judges; Criminal Coordinating Comm. Prelim. Arraignment Subcom.; Phila., Pa., Am. Bar Assns.; Phila. Trial Lawyers' Assn.; sec., Justinian Society; Sons of Italy; Basketball Club, Law Alumni Assn., St. Joseph's Univ.; Villanova Univ. Law Alumni Assn.; appt. judge, Municipal Court, Apr. 6, 1982; elected to full term, Nov. 1983; married Emily Rose DiBona; 3 children: Louis, Thomas, RitaMarie; home address: Philadelphia.

QUIGLEY, KEITH B. (P.J. — 41st District) was born April 3, 1939, in Harrisburg, the son of S. J. and Mary Leach Quigley; Gettysburg Coll. (B.S.) 1961; Dickinson Law Schl. (LL.B.) 1964; USMC Res., 1957-60; Pa. Bar Assn.; Perry Co. Dist. Atty., 1971-76; appt. pres. judge, Court of Common Pleas, May 11, 1976; elected, 1977; married Elizabeth Parker; 3 sons; home address: Box 446, New Bloomfield.

RANCK, SAMUEL C. (P.J. — 8th District) was born May 9, 1928, in Milton, son of Dale E. and L. Hilda Ranck; Bucknell Univ. (A.B.) 1950; Univ. of Pa. Law Schl. (J.D.) 1954; Northumberland Co., Pa. Bar Assns.; dist. atty., Northumberland Co., 1972-75; elected judge, Court of Common Pleas, Nov. 1975; retained Nov. 1985; married Sylvia Klock; 3 children; residence: R.D. 2, Milton.

RAUHAUSER, JOHN F., JR. (19th District) was born Dec. 7, 1918, in York, the son of John Sr. and Elsie Leas Rauhauser; Ursinus Coll. (B.A) 1941; Univ. of Pa. Law Schl. (LL.B.) 1948; Lt., U.S. Naval Reserve, 1943-46; attorney; York Co., Pa. Bar Assns.; York Co. solicitor, 1950-52; dist. atty., 1966-70; York Co. Bicentennial Comm., pres.; York Co. Hist. Society; York Twinning Assn.; Hall of Fame, William Penn H.S.; Service to Mankind award, Sertoma Club; Duke of York, York C of C; Distg. Pennsylvanian, Phila. C of C; Natl. D.A.R. citizenship medal; Doctor of Humane Letters, York Coll., 1978; author of various historical pamphlets; elected judge, Court of Common Pleas, Nov. 2, 1982; married Dorothy R. Landis; 3 children: Kathleen Rauhauser, Marjory Marsh, Elizabeth Stein; home address: 1608 Druck Valley Rd., York.

RAUP, THOMAS C. (P.J. — 29th District) was born Dec. 1, 1938, in Jersey Shore, the son of William L. and Eileen Kirby Raup; Columbia Coll. (A.B.) 1960; Columbia Schl. of Law (LL.B.) 1966; U.S. Navy, active duty, 1960-63; USNR, 1963-70; achieved rank of lieut. commander; Lycoming Pa., Am. Bar Assns.; Pa. Conf. of St. Trial Judges; first asst. dist. atty., Lycoming Co., 1968; sr. public defender, Lycoming Co., 1969-71; Criminal Procedural Rules Comm., Pa. Supreme Ct.; apptd. judge, Court of Common Pleas, March 19, 1974; elected to two 10-yr. terms, 1976 and 1986; married Barbara Jeanne Libby; 2 sons; home address: 821 Hawthorne Ave., Williamsport.

RAUSCHENBERGER, FLOYD A., JR. (P.J. — 50th District) was born Mar. 2, 1930, in Butler, the son of Floyd and Dorothy Huselton Rauschenberger; Univ. of Pgh. (A.B.) 1954, and its law schl. (LL.B.) 1957; U.S. Army, 1948-52; attorney; Butler Co., Pa., Bar Assn.; B.P.O.E.; Moose; Am. Legion; V.F.W.; Masonic Lodge; Consistory & Shrine; Kiwanis; elected judge, Court of Common Pleas, Nov. 3, 1981; married Agnes G. Raymond; 2 children: Floyd, III, Curtis; home address: 804 E. Pearl St., Butler.

REED, HOWARD F., JR. (A.J. — 32nd District) was born Dec. 20, 1920, in Niles, Oh., the son of Howard F. and Anna K. Bauroth Reed; resided Upper Darby from 1929; grad., Temple Univ., 1943; Univ. of Pa. Law Schl., 1949; U.S. Navy, WW II; adm., Del. Co. Bar, Supreme, Superior Courts of Pa., 1950; held elective offices, Del. Co. Bar Assn.; as prothonotary, Del. Co., 1956-63, and pres., St. Assn. of Prothonotaries, 1962-63; engaged in community services; appt. judge, Court of Common Pleas, Jan. 1969; elected to full term commencing Jan. 1, 1970; married Evelyn M. Bunnell of New York on April 22, 1950; 3 children.

REED, ROBERT C. (P.J. — 36th District) was born Nov. 19, 1932, in Beaver, the son of Clark and Ethel Reed; attended Lafayette Coll.; Dickinson Coll. (A.B.) 1954; Univ. of Pgh. (LL.B.) 1962; U.S. Army, active duty, 1954-56; reserve status, 1956-60; frmr. partner, Wallover, Reed and Steff; Bars of Pa. Supreme, Superior, Commonwealth Courts, Federal Courts; Pa., Beaver Co. Bar Assns.; Am. Judicature Society; asst. dist. atty., Beaver Co., 1968-70; dist. atty., Beaver Co., 1971; bd. of dirs. McGuire Memorial Home for Retarded Children; elected judge, Court of Common Pleas, Nov. 1973; retained, Nov. 1983; 1977-pres., Juvenile Judge; 1985-pres., pres. judge and admin. judge of Orphans' Court Div.; married Gretchen Sohn; 3 children: David, Cynthia and Grant Reed; home address: 1414 Midland/Beaver Road, Industry.

REILLY, JOHN K., JR. (P.J. — 46th District) was born Oct. 4, 1935, in Windber, the son of John K. and Winifred Dowler Reilly; Pa. St. Univ. (B.A.) 1957; Dickinson Schl. of Law (J.D.) 1960; U.S. Army, 1960-61, and U.S. Army Reserves, 1962-68; achieved rank of 1st Lieut.; Clearfield Co., Pa. Bar Assns.; Pa. Conf. of St. Trial Judges, past pres., Pa. Dist Attys. Assns.; elected 3 terms as Clearfield Co. dist. atty.; mem., chptr. chmn., Clearfield Co. Am. Red Cross; bd. of dir., BSA; Kiwanis; Eagles; BPOE; LOOM; Clearfield Co. Historical Society; various Masonic bodies, and was Jaycee Man of the Year; Presbyterian Ch.; elected judge, Court of Common Pleas, Nov. 6, 1973; pres. judge, Clearfield Co. Court of Common Pleas, Jan. 1974; retained, commenced 2nd term, Jan. 1984; married Mary Ann Wilson; 2 children; home address: Susquehanna Terrace, Clearfield.

REYNOLDS, ABRAM FRANK (1st District) was born March 15, 1938, in Binghamton, NY, the son of Joseph and Elizabeth Reynolds; grad., William & Mary Hampton Inst., L.S.U. Park Coll., Kansas City (B.A., history, cum laude) 1968; Univ. of Mo. (M.A., history); Rutgers Univ. Schl. of Law, 1973; Temple University Doctoral Program; U.S. Military, 1956-68; Disting. Unit Cit., 1966; Presidential Unit Cit., 1968; researcher, Mideast Research Inst., "Why Small Businesses Fail," 1969; information director, Model Cities, 1970; chief of operations, Rutgers Univ. Coll. Center, 1971-73; law clerk, pres. judge Joseph Glancey, Municipal Court, 1972-73; public defenders office, 1973; dist. atty., Felony Jury Unit (A.D.A.), 1974-75; legal services atty., Fraternal Order of Police, 1977-82; elected judge, Court of Common Pleas, Nov. 4, 1985; 2 children; home address: 2601 Pennsylvania Ave., Philadelphia.

RIBNER, PAUL (1st District) was born Aug. 1, 1928, in Shamokin, the son of Jack and Sadie Goodman Ribner; Univ. of Pa. (B.A.) 1949; Univ. of Pa. Law Schl. (J.D.) 1952; served as capt., U.S. Air Force, active duty 1952-54; Pa. Trial Judges, Phila. Bar Assn.; natl. commander, Jewish War Veterans, U.S.A., 1974-75, 1975-76; pres., 21 Jewel Square Club, 1974-75; pres., 1977-80, Justice Lodge 2552, B'nai B'rith; commissioned judge, Court of Common Pleas, Dec. 30, 1971; elected to full term, Nov. 1973; home address: 2009 Penn Center House, 1900 J. F. Kennedy Blvd., Philadelphia.

RICHETTE, LISA AVERSA (1st District) was born on Sept. 11, 1928, in Phila., the daughter of Domenico and Maria Giannini Aversa; Univ. of Pa. (B.A.) 1949; Yale Univ. Law Schl. (J.D.) 1952; Am., Pa., Phila. Bar Assns.; Am. Assn. of Univ. Women; winner of 1972 Gimbel Award; Medal of Honor & Outstanding Citizen Certif., Natl. Sons and Daughters of the Am. Rev. (1980); Pearl S. Buck Award, 1984; Alice B. Paul Centennial Award, 1985; prof. of law, Temple Univ.; commissioned judge, Court of Common Pleas, Dec. 30, 1971; 1 child, Lawrence A., II; home address: 1918 Lombard St., Philadelphia.

RIDGE, JOSEPH H. (5th District) was born in Pgh., the son of Joseph and Sarah McGonigle Ridge; Duquesne Univ. (B.S.) (J.D.); U.S. Army, 1943-46, elected judge, Allegheny Co. Ct., 1961; reelected judge, Court of Common Pleas, 1971 and 1981; married Ann Verzella; 2 children.

ROBBINS, HARVEY W. (1st District — Municipal Court) was born Feb. 18, 1945, in Phila., the son of Frank and Helen Tavelman Robbins; grad., Drexel Univ. (B.S., mech. eng.) 1967; Temple Univ. Schl. of Law (J.D.) 1973; former engineer; mem., Phila. Bar Assn.; Pa. Conf. of State Trial Judges; v. pres., Spring Garden Civic Assn.; bd. mem., Am. Technion Soc.; appointed judge, Philadelphia Municipal Court, June 30, 1986; married Susan Wenger; 1 child; home address: 639 North 22nd St., Philadelphia.

RODGERS, SAMUEL L. (27th District) was born Nov. 20, 1920, in Chartiers Twp., the son of Frank S. and Mary Cortese Rodgers; Univ. of Pgh. (B.A.) 1941; Univ. of Pgh. Law Schl. (LL.B.) 1948; att. Harvard Law Schl.; U.S. Navy, 1942-46; member, all Appellate Courts, Comm. of Pa.; Washington Co., Pa., Am. Bar Assns.; pres. (1976), Washington Co. Bar Assn.; past pres., Canonsburg-Houston Kiwanis Club; chmn., Peters Twp. Gov't. Study Comm., 1972-73; past pres., Canonsburg-Houston C. of C., 1960; appt. judge, Court of Common Pleas, June 28, 1978; elected 1979; married Mary Marchezak; 1 child, Marta K. Rodgers; home address: 101 Sherwood Dr., McMurray.

ROSE, MEYER CHARLES (1st District — Municipal Court) was born June 18, 1918, in Phila., the son of Isaac and Minnie Pearl Rose; Mich. Coll. of Tech.; Temple Univ.; Temple Univ. Law Schl. (LL.B.) 1953; Temple Univ. Grad. Law Schl.; U.S. Army, 1942-46; attorney; Phila. Bar Assn.; Pa. Conf. of State Trial Judges; B'nai B'rith; elected judge, Municipal Court, 1975; married Geraldine Dickman Gomer; 1 daughter, Marjorie Ellen; home address: 1806 Park Towne N. 2200 Benjamin Franklin Pkwy., Philadelphia.

ROSINI, JAMES J. (8th District) was born Jan. 31, 1946, in Danville, the son of Evoldo J. and Dorothy M. Persing Rosini; grad., Bloomsburg Univ. (B.S., ed.) 1967; Dickinson Schl. of Law (J.D.) 1971; mem., Am. and Pa. Bar Assns.; Pa. Judges Assn.; mem.: Elks, Moose, Knights of Columbus, Boy Scouts of America; asst. dist atty., 1974-76; dist. atty., 1976-84; Roman Catholic; appointed judge, Court of Common Pleas, May 12, 1986; married Patricia C. Dormer; 3 children: Paige, Marianne and Matthew; home address: 1755 Clinton Ave., Shamokin.

ROSS, EUNICE (5th District) was born Oct. 13, 1923, in Belleview, Allegheny Co., the daughter of Richard Kelly Latshaw and Eunice Weidner Latshaw; grad. first in her classes, from: Avonworth H.S., Univ. of Pgh. and its Schl. of Law; frmr. dir., family court, Allegheny Co., 1970-72; judicial asst. to pres. judge, orphans' court, 1954-70; law clerk, civil and criminal courts, 1952-54; Public Health Research Project, 1951-52; private practice, 1952-70; adjunct prof. of law, Univ. of Pgh. Schl. of Law, 1967-73; Order of COIF; Distinguished Alumna, Univ. of Pgh., 1973; Allegheny Co. Bar Assn., Pa. Bar Assn.; probate and trust section, St., Co., Bar Assns.; Orphans' Court Rules Comm.; Common Pleas Ct. Rules Comm.; Kappa Beta Pi, national sorority for women lawyers; Allegheny Conf. Gov.'s Justice Comm., 1972-79; ISDA, Pgh. History and Landmarks Foundation; West. Pa. Conservancy; Natl. Wildlife Fed.; Monday Luncheon Club; Business and Professional Women's Club; advsry. bd., Animal Friends; trustee, Univ. of Pgh. 1980-1986; Alumni Council, U. of Pgh., v. pres. 1978; pres. 1979; Pa. Conf. of Trial Judges; W. Pa. Historical Society; Zelienople Hist. Society; Womans City Club; mem., Judicial Inquiry & Review Bd. of Pa., 1985-present; co-author, *Survey of Pennsylvania Public Health Laws*, 1954; articles editor contribution, Univ. of Pgh. Law Review; apptd. judge, Allegheny Co. Common Pleas Court, Dec. 1, 1972; married John A. Ross (decd.) 1 daughter.

ROSS, GEORGE H. (5th District) was born Oct. 10, 1922, in Pgh., the son of J. A., Sr. and Mary H. McGaw Ross; Univ. of Pgh. (A.B., LL.B., J.D.); U.S. Army, 1943-46; asst. dist. atty., 1951-64; public defender, 1965-75; twp. solicitor, 8 years; appt. judge, Court of Common Pleas, 1975; elected, 1976; married Eleanore Gallagher; 1 child, Jo Lynne Petrini; home address: 2514 Springwood Dr., Glenshaw.

RUBRIGHT, WILBUR H. (21st District) was born April 11, 1922, in Frackville, the son of Harry A. and Eva S. White Rubright; Frackville public schools; Dickinson Coll. (Ph.B.); Dickinson Schl. of Law (J.D.); pilot, U.S. Naval Air Corps, 1942-46; mem., Schuylkill Co., Pa. & Am. Bar Assns.; F & AM Lodge 737; Rajah Temple Shrine; Valley of Reading Consistory; B.P.O.E. Lodge 1533; Am. Legion; Frackville Lions Club; various solicitorships; United Methodist Ch.; elected judge, Court of Common Pleas, Jan. 1984; married Sara R. Ingram; 3 children: Pamela Taylor, Wilbur H., Jr., Alison G.; home address: 620 Westwood Lane, Frackville.

RUDDOCK, W. PARKER (40th District) was born Sept. 17, 1928, in Indiana, the son of William M. and Dorothy Parker Ruddock; Kiski Prep Schl. (1946); Grove City Coll (A.B.) 1950; Univ. of Pgh. Schl. of Law (J.D.) 1953; U.S. Army, 1953-56; atty., Fisher, Ruddock & Simpson, 1956-83; mem., Indiana Co., Pa., Am. Bar Assns.; Pa. Conf. of State Trial Judges; Allied Club of Indiana; Indiana Borough solicitor, 1962-83; chief public defender, 1964-74; Indiana Area Schl. Dist. solicitor, 1977-83; Indiana Co. solicitor, 1980-83; appt. judge, Court of Common Pleas, June 7, 1983; elected judge, Nov. 1983; married Peggy Grafton; 3 children: Susan, William III and David P.; home address: 649 Shryock Ave., Indiana.

RUFE, WILLIAM HART, III (7th District) was born Sept. 6, 1932, in Sellersville, Bucks Co., the son of William H. and Frances Appenzeller Rufe Jr.; Lafayette Coll. (A.B.) 1955; Univ. of Pa. Law Schl. (LL.B.) 1958; Bucks Co., Pa. Bar Assns.; public defender, Bucks Co., 1961; solicitor, Sellersville Borough, 1965-69; Telford Borough, 1960-69; Telford Borough Authority (sewer and water) 1960-69; Pennridge Joint Elem. Schl. Auth., 1963-68; West Rockhill-Sellersville Joint Recreation Auth., (swimming pool) 1968-71; Telford Parking Auth., 1961-71; St. Paul's United Ch. of Christ; frmr. pres., Sellersville Kiwanis; bd., Bucks Co. Council, BSA; former dist. chmn, Tohpendel Dist., BSA; pres., Bucks Co. Audubon Society; bd., Bucks Co. chptr., Am. Red Cross; pres., Bucks Co. Conservancy; Disting. Service Award, Pennridge Jaycees, 1974; apptd. judge, Court of Common Pleas of Bucks Co., 1972; married Ivy B. Friesell on June 25, 1955; 4 children; home address: 146 Green St., Sellersville.

SABO, ALBERT F. (1st District) was born Dec. 21, 1920, in Phila., the son of Joseph A. Sr., and Rose Lipsack Sabo, both of Slovak heritage; Wharton Schl. Univ. of Pa. (B.S., econ.) 1942; Univ. of Pa. Law Schl. (J.D.) 1949; WW II veteran; one of organizers, first post commander, St. Agnes Post No. 1132, Catholic War Vets., Phila.; frmr. Under-Sheriff, Phila. Co., 16 yrs.; frmr. mem., Natl. Sheriff's Assn.; retired FOP; Police Chiefs' Assn. for S.E. Pa.; active mem., Phila., Pa. and Am. Bar Assns.; Am. Judicature Society; Pa. Conf. State Trial Judges; elected judge, Court of Common Pleas, Nov. 1973; elected to full term commencing Jan. 1974; first judge of Slovak heritage elected to the bench in Phila.; married Helen E. Komada on Oct. 14, 1961; 2 boys: Gregory and Mark Gerard; home address: 930 Woodbrook Lane, Philadelphia (Mt. Airy).

SALUS, SAMUEL WIEDER, II (38th District) was born July 11, 1933, in Phila., the son of Arthur Stuart and Eleanor Ritter Salus; Germantown Academy, 1951; Cornell Univ. (B.A.) 1955; Univ. of Pa. Law Schl. (LL.B.) 1960; U.S. Navy, 1955-57; attorney, 1961-79; Am., Pa., Montgomery Co. Bar Assns.; Montgomery Co. Trial Lawyers Assn.; chief public def., 1965-1979; bd. Hedgwig House for Mental Patients; comm., Cornell Secondary Schools; law clerk to Chief Judge of U.S. District Court, 1960-61; elected judge, Court of Common Pleas, Nov. 1979; married Kathryn L. Simon; 2 children: Eric Ritter, Christopher Jon; home address: 5 Haddon Place, Fort Washington.

SAVITT, DAVID N. (1st District) was born May 23, 1928, in Phila., the son of Jacob B. and Lillian Savitt; Rutgers Univ. (A.B.) 1950; Univ. of Pa. Law Schl. (LL.B.) 1953; U.S. Army, 1953-55; partner, law firm of Walsh & Savitt; elected to Pa. House of Representatives, 1968; reelected 1970, 1972; lecturer of law, Temple Univ. Law Schl. 1978-85; instruc., Temple Univ. Judicial and Bureaucratic Admin. of Justice Political Science, 1980; lecturer, Robert A. Taft Inst. of Govt. Judges and Politics, 1980; elected judge, Court of Common Pleas, Nov. 1973; Court Administrator, Dec. 1975 to Dec. 1982; lecturer, The Inst. for Paralegal Training, 1982-85; co-author, Penna. Grand Jury Practice, 1983; married Judith Cooper; 2 children; home address: 2316 Hopkinson House, 602 Washington Square So., Philadelphia.

SCHAEFFER, FORREST GRIM, JR. (P.J. — 23rd District) was born Sept. 9, 1927, in Allentown, the son of Forrest Grim (M.D.) and Elizabeth Gitt Schaeffer; Lehigh U. (B.A., with high honors) 1950; Harvard Law Schl. (LL.B.) 1953, (J.D.) 1968; USAAF, 1945-47; Am., Pa. Bar Assns.; Mayor, Borough of Kutztown, 1966-70; past pres., Reading Kiwanis Club; Kiwanis; Kutztown Lions Club; United Ch. of Christ; Phi Beta Kappa; apptd. judge, Court of Common Pleas, Nov. 15, 1976; elected to 10 yr. term Nov. 8, 1977; married Dorothea Lee; 5 children: Andrew Lee, Katharine Lee, D. Elizabeth, Phillip C., Forrest Grim III,; home address: R.D. 3, Box 337-25, Kutztown.

SCHAFFNER, HERBERT A. (12th District) was born July 22, 1934, in Hershey, the son of Herbert A. and Louise Koehll Schaffner; Hummelstown public schools; Franklin & Marshall Coll. (A.B.) 1956; Duke Univ. Schl. of Law (LL.B.) 1962; jet pilot, U.S. Air Force, 1956-59; Capt., Pa. Army Natl. Guard, 28th Div., Sr. Army Aviator, 1963-68; frmr. partner, Reynolds, Bihl & Schaffner; mem., Dauphin Co., Am. & Pa. Bar Assns.; Pa. Conf. of State Trial Judges; Hummelstown Rotary Club; elder, Hummelstown United Ch. of Christ; elected judge, Court of Common Pleas, Jan. 1, 1984; married Judith M. Schaffner; 4 children; home address: 145 Park Ave., Hummelstown.

SCHERER, BERNARD FREDERICK (10th District) was born Nov. 24, 1932, in Arnold, the son of Frederick F. Scherer and Ermine E. Hambene; grad., St. Vincent Coll. (A.B.); Duquesne Univ. (A.M.); Univ. of Pgh. (Ph.D.); Duquesne Univ. (J.D.); St. Vincent (D.H.L.) 1985; professor, St. Vincent Coll.; mem., A.B.A.; P.B.A.; Westmoreland Co. Bar Assn.; Medieval Acad. of America; Serra Club; chmn., Westmoreland Co. Commissioners, 1968-72; mem., Penn State Adv. Bd.; elected judge, Court of Common Pleas, 1982; married Norma Petrone; 2 children: Bernard C., M.D.; Christopher J.; home address: 3014 McClellan Dr., Greensburg.

SEARER, FRANCIS A. (P.J. — 58th District) was born May 21, 1939, in Lewistown, the son of John and Violet Young Searer; Lock Haven Univ. (B.S.) 1962; Dickinson Schl. of Law (J.D.) 1967; Pa. Bar Assn.; Elks; Mifflin Co.: pub. def., 1969-71, dist. atty., 1972-76, solicitor, 1976-81; elected judge, Court of Common Pleas, Nov. 3, 1981; home address: 53 Academy Hill, Lewistown.

SEMERARO, ANTHONY R. (32nd District) was born Aug. 16, 1932, in Chester, the son of Victor and Helen Lovari Semeraro; Mt. St. Mary's Coll. (B.S.) 1953; Georgetown Univ. Schl. of Law (A.B., J.D.) 1958; Natl. Judicial Coll., 1982; Amer. Acad. Jud. Ed., 1984; U.S. Army, 1953-55; Pa. Conf. of St. Trial Judges; Register of Wills, Clerk of the Orphan's Court, 1974-81; elected judge, Court of Common Pleas, Nov. 3, 1981; married Elizabeth Ann Reilly; 2 children: Anne, Victor; home address: 510 Springhaven Rd., Wallingford.

SHAULIS, NORMAN ALBERT (P.J. — 16th District) was born July 13, 1922, in Somerset, son of Harvey W. and Lucy M. Barndt Shaulis; Temple Univ. (B.S) 1949; Temple Univ. Law Schl. (J.D.) 1952; U.S. Army, European Theatre, 1942-45; Somerset Co., Pa., Am. Lawyer-Pilots Bar Assns.; Judicature Soc.; St. Paul's Presbyterian Ch.; 4 years, U.S. Commissioner; Air Force Assn.; lieut. colonel, Civil Air Patrol; Am. Legion; VFW; 32nd Mason, Noble Jaffa Temple; Legion of Honor, Jaffa Temple; Rotary International; Moose Club; apptd. judge, Court of Common Pleas, Feb. 1, 1972; elected to full term commencing Jan. 1974; retained 1984; married Janice L. Robbins; 2 children; home address: 707 Cannel Dr., Somerset.

SHEELY, HAROLD E. (P.J. — 9th District) was born Nov. 2, 1930, in Mechanicsburg, the son of Jacob C. and Ethel E. Harbold Sheely; Muhlenburg Coll. (A.B.) 1953; Dickinson Schl. of Law (LL.B.) 1958; U.S.M.C., June 1953-Aug. 1955; atty.; Masonic groups; dist. atty., Cumberland Co., 1968-76; elected judge, Court of Common Pleas, Nov. 1977; pres. judge since June 27, 1983; married Dolores M. Smith; 2 children: Stephen and Andrew; home address: 14 S. Stoner Ave., Shiremanstown.

SHEPPARD, ALBERT W., JR. (1st District) was born June 3, 1937, in Phila.; Villanova Univ. (B.S.) 1960; Temple Univ. Law Schl. (J.D.) 1968; U.S. Navy, 1960-63; attorney, 1968-83; judge, Common Pleas Court, Nov. 8, 1983.

SILBERSTEIN, ALAN K. (Acting P.J. — 1st District — Municipal Court) was born July 30, 1938, in Phila., the son of Isadore and Anne Brody Silberstein; grad., Central H.S., 1952-56 (B.A.); Temple Univ. (B.S., pre-law) 1960; Temple Univ. Schl. of Law (J.D.) 1963; Army Reserves, 1964-70; mem., Am. Trial Lawyers' Assn.; Phila. and Pa. Bar Assns.; Am. Arbitration Assn.; Pannonia Beneficial Assn.; Temple Univ. Law Alumni Assn.; B'nai B'rith, Justice Lodge; pres., bd.dirs., Northeast Community Center MH/MR; co-author, "The Nature and Extent of Appraisals Required Under Pennsylvania's New Divorce Code," published in Valuation, Vol. 28, No. 1, Am. Soc. of Appraisers; pres., Northeast Community Center MH/MR; elected Judge, Municipal Court, Nov. 75; reelected 1981; married Dveral Taylor; 1 child, Marisa Hope; home address: 9009 Pine Rd., Philadelphia.

SILVESTRI, SILVESTRI (5th District) was born March 7, 1920 ,in North Charleroi; Univ. of Pgh. Schl. of Pharmacy; Univ. of Pgh. Schl. of Law; captain, Air Force, 1941-45; appt. judge, Court of Common Pleas, Dec. 1968; elected Nov. 1969, retained Nov. 1979; home address: 220 N. Dithridge St., Apt. 907, Pittsburgh.

SIMMONS, J. EARL, JR. (1st District — Municipal Court) born Dec. 19, 1932, in Phila.; St. Joseph's Prep. Schl., 1950 (1st quintile of grad. class) St. Joseph's Coll. (A.B.) 1954 (1st quintile of grad. class); Alpha Sigma Nu, Natl. Jesuit Honor Society; Who's Who Among Am. Univ. Students; editor, student newspaper, student officer, Air Force ROTC; U. of Pa. (J.D.) 1957; pres., Kent Law Club; chmn., finalist, Moot Court Competition; practicing atty. in Phila. since 1958; engaged in genl. practice with civil, criminal trial, corp. and estate experience; Phila., Pa., Am. Bar Assns.; K. of C.; Holy Name Society; Friendly Sons of St. Patrick; BSA; bd. of govs., St. Joseph Prep. Schl. Alumni; pres., Alumni, 1979-81; bd. of govs., St. Joseph's Coll.; bd. trustees, St. Joseph's Prep.; McClanaghan Award, 1985, St. Joseph's Univ. Law Alumni; Achievement Award, 1986, Phila. Bar Assn. Crim. Law Section; bd. of advs., Law Enf. Ed. Program, St. Joseph's Coll.; frmr. secy., Unauthorized Practice of Law Comm.; Lawyer's Club of Phila.; St. Thomas More Society; apptd. magistrate, Dec. 5, 1968; apptd. judge, Municipal Court of Phila., Jan. 1, 1969; elected to 6 year term, Jan. 1, 1970; chmn., Municipal Court Civil Rules Committee; Pa. Conf. of St. Trial Judges; Judicial Ed. Comm., Criminal Sentencing Comm.; North Am. Judges Assn.; Am. Judicature Society; Am. Acad. of Judicial Ed.; Bd. of Adv., Catholic League for Religious and Civil Rights, Phila. Chpt.; assigned to Common Pleas Court criminal trial list on regular basis, 1969-72; recommended as "eminently well qualified" for appointment, election to Common Pleas Court by Judiciary Committee, Phila. Bar Assn., 1973, 1975, 1979; found qualified by bar plebiscite, Lawyers' Non-Partisan Committee for Election of Judges for retention as Municipal Court Sitting Judge, 1969, 1981, 1987; married; 4 children.

SMITH, CALVIN E. (23rd District) was born March 20, 1927, in Hamburg, the son of Edward C. and Mary R. Wagner Smith; grad., Hamburg H.S., 1945; Franklin & Marshall, 1947-50; Duke Univ. (J.D.) 1953; Headquarters & Headquarters Co. of Army Ground Forces in the Pentagon, 1945-46; Selective Service Bd. Official, 1946; U.N. Rehabilitation & Relief Org., 1947 (Sicily, Italy; Lipari Islands); mem., Am. and Pa. Bar Assns.; Endlich Law Club, Reading; Eastern Dist. Court Historical Soc.; mem., Bethany Childrens' Home Bd. of Managers, Womelsdorf; author, Berks County Bench and Bar - A Commentary; judge, Court of Common Pleas, Jan. 6, 1986; married Jacqueline Mitchell; 3 children: Cynthia Lee (Smith) Spotswood, C. Mitchell, Cabot M.; home address: 113 East Penn Ave., Wernersville.

SMITH, CHARLES B. (15th District) was born June 10, 1940, in Phila., the son of Charles and Dorothy Landis Smith; Dickinson Coll. (B.A.) 1962, and its law schl. (J.D.) 1965; U.S. Army, 1965-70; active in U.S.A.R.; attorney; Chester Co., Pa. Bar Assns.; Pa. Conf. of St. Trial Judges; Natl. Co. of Juvenile and Family Ct. Judges; Alpha Chi Rho; Juvenile Ct. Master,

MH Rev. Officer, 1976-81, Chester Co.; frmr. vestryman, Sr. Warden, Ch. of Good Samaritan; frmr. exec. dir., past pres., bd. dir., Legal Aid of Chester Co. Inc.; past pres., Chester Co. Community Action Bd.; elected judge, Court of Common Pleas, Nov. 3, 1981; married Cynthia Arndt; 3 children: Suzanne, Leigh, Benjamin; home address: 106 Grubb Rd., Malvern.

SMITH, CLINTON W. (29th District) was born Dec. 15, 1933, in Williamsport, the son of Edward B. and Dollie Wilcox Smith; Lycoming Coll., (summa cum laude) 1955; Dickinson Shl. of Law, 1958; U.S. Army, Pa. Natl. Guard, 1958-64; Lycoming Co., Pa., Am. Bar Assns.; Pa. Conf. of St. Trial Judges; Mason; F&AM; Williamsport Consistory; Ross Club; asst. dist. atty., Lycoming Co., 1963-64; bd. dir., Williamsport/Lycoming C of C; bd. trustees, Un. Methodist Home for Children; bd. dir., Loyalsock Little League; mem., bd. trustees, Lycoming Coll.; appt. judge, Court of Common Pleas, May 27, 1981; married Mary Johnson; 1 child, Christopher; home address: 1439 Grampian Blvd., Williamsport.

SMITH, D. BROOKS (24th District) was born Dec. 4, 1951, in Altoona, the son of William P. and Betsy Garman Smith; Franklin & Marshall Coll. (A.B.) 1973; Am. Univ. (Wash. Semester) 1971; Dickinson Schl. of Law (J.D.) 1976; mem., Am. & Pa. Bar Assns.; Pa. Conf. of St. Trial Judges, co-chmn., Economics and Finance Comm.; Supreme Ct. Criminal Proc. Rules Comm.; Lions Club; Masonic bodies; bd. mem., Salvation Army, St. YMCA of Pa., Inc.; frmr. dir., Altoona Symphony Soc., Blair Co. Legal Services Corp., Altoona Area Public Library, Family and Chilldrens' Service of Blair Co., Blair Co. Soc. for Crippled Children and Adults; frmr. mem., Governor's Advisory Comm. to Oversee Implementation of Com.'s Plan for Equal Opportunity in the State-Supported Institutions of Higher Ed.; instructor, Penn State Univ. and St. Francis Coll.; asst. dist. atty., 1977-79, and dist. atty., Blair Co., 1983-84, spec. asst. atty. gen. 1982-83; Lutheran, Central Pa. Synod transition team Comm. for New Luth. Ch.; appt. judge, Court of Common Pleas, Nov. 28, 1984; elected judge 1985; married Karen Hall; home address: 3008 Second Ave., Altoona.

SMITH, JEFFREY ALAN (P.J. — 42nd District) was born Jan. 31, 1953, in Sayre, the son of David Rahm, Jr., and Frances Rice Smith, Univ. of Pgh. (B.A.) 1974; Dickinson Schl. of Law (J.D.) 1979; mem., Pa. & Bradford Co. Bar Assns.; *Who's Who in American Law;* special prosecutor, 1979-81; asst. dist. atty., 1981-82; divorce master/juvenile master, 1982-85, Bradford Co.; Towanda Lions Club; Towanda Elks Lodge #2191; appt. pres. judge, Court of Common Pleas, Dec. 27, 1983; elected to 10-yr. term beg. Jan. 2, 1986.

SMITH, RALPH H., JR. (5th District) was born Sept. 16, 1928, in Pgh., the son of the late Judge Ralph H., Sr., and Florence E. Raber Smith; Univ. of Pgh. (B.A.) 1949; Univ. of Pgh. Schl. of Law (J.D.) 1952; admitted to practice in courts of Allegheny Co., Pa., Supreme, Superior Courts, U.S. District Court for Western Dist. of Pa., U.S. Cir. Ct. of Appeals, 3rd Cir., U.S. Supreme Court; Pa., Allegheny Co., Am. Bar Assns.; judge, Allegheny Co., 1960-62; solicitor to prothonotary, Allegheny Co., 4 yrs.; Order of Coif; mem., Univ. of Pgh. Law Review staff; elected judge, Court of Common Pleas, 1961; commissioned Jan. 1, 1962; reelected, 1971 & 1981; married Clara E. Jiles; 4 children.

SMYTH, JOSEPH A., JR. (38th District) was born April 7, 1945, in Norristown, the son of Dorothy Donovan Smyth (father dec.); Bishop Kenrick H.S., 1963; Notre Dame (B.A.) 1967; Villanova Law Schl (J.D.) 1971; Temple Law Schl. (Masters, law labor) 1979; mem., Montgomery Co. Trial Lawyers Assn.; Pa. Trial Lawyers Assn.; Montgomery Co. Bar Assn. Bench Bar Com.; district attorney, 1980-84; judge, Court of Common Pleas, Oct. 22, 1984; married Theresa Deloggie; 3 children: Tashya, Douglas, Randy; home address: 2304 Coles Blvd., Norristown.

SNYDER, EDWIN L. (P.J. — 54th District) was born April 22, 1925, in Homer City; Univ. of Michigan (A.B.) 1949; Univ. of Pgh. Law Schl. (LL.B.) 1952; Natl. Coll. of the Judiciary, 1972; Judicial Council of Pa., 1980; exec. comm., Pa. Conf. of Trial Judges, 1980; frmr. trustee, Indiana Univ. of Pa.; Presbyterian Ch.; WW II veteran, U.S. Navy; elected judge, Court of Common Pleas, Nov. 1971; married Virginia Carter of Homestead Park; 3 children; home address: 401 Rockland Ave., Punxsutawney.

SOKOLOVE, LEONARD B. (7th District) was born Dec. 24, 1925, in Phila., the son of William A. and Anna Berman Sokolove; Lehigh Univ.; Temple Univ. Law Schl. (LL.B.) 1951; U.S. Army, 1944-46; practice of law, 1951-81; Bucks Co. Bar Assn.; Zone Nine Delegate, Pa. Bar Assn.; NIMLO; (past chmn., Comm. on Intergovernment Cooperation); trustee Bucks Co. Comm. Coll.; frmr. comm. (1958-63), solicitor (1964-67, 1972-81) Bristol Twp.; frmr. mem. Levittown Library Bd.; past pres., Temple Shalom; 63rd Infantry Division Assn.; rec., Purple Heart, Bronze Star, Combat Infantry Badge; appt. judge, Court of Common Pleas, May 6, 1981; elected Nov. 1981; married Doris Kessler; 3 children: Robert, Michael, Nancy; home address: 2151 Bromley Common, Holland.

SPICER, OSCAR FRANKLIN (P.J. — 51st District) was born May 31, 1931, in Harlan, Ky., the son of Charles B. and Addie Neal Spicer; Univ. of Pa. (A.B.) 1953; Univ. of Pa. Law Schl. (LL.B.) 1959; U.S. Navy, 1953-56; public defender, Adams Co., 1965-67; dist. atty., Adams Co., 1968-77; elected pres. judge, Court of Common Pleas, Nov. 1977; married Barbara Yoder, 4 children: Nathan, Bruce, Wendy, Amy; home address: 685 Black Horse Tavern Road, Gettysburg.

STAISEY, LEONARD C. (5th District) was born Nov. 10, 1920, in Duquesne, the son of Daniel L. and Anna Kostelac Staisey; W. Pa. Schl. for Blind, 1940; Northwestern Univ. (B.S.S., highest distinction) 1944; Northwestern Univ. Law Schl. (J.D.) 1947; Am. Judicature Society; Am. Blind Lawyers Assn.; Theta Xi; Phi Alpha Delta; dir., Duquesne Schl., 1949-59; council, City of Duquesne, 1959-60; State Senator, 1960-66; Co. Commissioner, chmn., 1968-76; elected judge, Court of Common Pleas, Nov. 1979; married Emilie Sylvester; 2 children: Consuelo Emilie Woodhead, Esq., Nancy Lora Staisey, Ph.D.; home address: 500 Commonwealth Ave., Duquesne.

STANDISH, WILLIAM LLOYD (5th District) was born Feb. 16, 1930, the son of William Lloyd and Eleanor McCargo Standish; Yale Univ. (B.A.) 1953; Univ. of Va. (LL.B.) 1956; mem., frmr. gov., frmr. treas., Academy of Trial Lawyers of Allegheny Co.; Allegheny, Pa., Am. (Antitrust, Litigation and Family Law Sect.) Bar Assns.; Am. Judicature Society; P.A.D. (leg. frat.); solicitor, Edgeworth Borough Schl. Dist., 1963-66; trustee, Mary and Alexander Laughlin Children's Ctr.; corp., Sewickley Cemetery; natl. bd. trustees, frmr. trustee, Leukemia Society of Am.; frmr. trustee, frmr. pres., W. Pa. Chapt., Leukemia Society of Am.; dir., Stanton Farm Foundation; trustee, Western Pa. Schl. for the Deaf; elder, Presbyterian Ch.; President's Award, Leukemia Society of Am.; married Marguerite Oliver; 4 children; home address: 626 Pine Rd., Sewickley.

STANZIANI, JOSEPH H. (38th District) was born Nov. 9, 1930, in Phila., the son of Henry and Louise Stanziani; legal and deck officer, U.S. Coast Guard, 1955-58; lieut. aboard USCGC Spar during historic Northwest Passage of 1957; elected Phi Beta Kappa jr. yr. from Hobart Coll. (B.S.) 1952; Univ. of Pa. (J.D.) 1955; admitted to bars Pa. Supreme Court, Dec. 1955; Montgomery Co., Pa., Am. Bar Assns.; dir., Pa. Bar Institute; Montgomery Co. Juvenile Adm. Judge; pres., Pa. Conf. of St. Trial Judges, Juvenile Court Section; Pa. Juvenile Ct. Judges' Comm., 1984-85; solicitor, sheriff, Montgomery Co. and Montgomery Co. Community Coll. Auth.; active mem., past pres., Hobart and William Smith Club of Delaware Valley; St. Peter's Ch., Glenside; frmr. vestryman, solicitor, Ch. of Our Saviour, Jenkintown; frmr. dir., Abington YMCA; frmr. chmn., bd. of dir., Afro-Am. Federation Inc.; Rotary Club of Jenkintown; OSIA, Inter-County Chapter; charter mem., Cheltenham Jaycees; solicitor, LaMott Citizens for Action; auditor, Highland PTA; appt. judge, Court of Common Pleas, Dec. 30, 1971; elected to full term commencing Jan. 1, 1972; 2 daughters; home address: 1119 Meadow Dr., Norristown.

STEEGE, PETER O. (36th District) was born Nov. 9, 1933, in Hartford, Ct., the son of Otto P. and Cecelia Ostlin Steege; grad., Wesleyan (A.B.) 1955; Univ. of Chicago Law Schl. (J.D.) 1958; mem., Beaver Co. and Pa. Bar Assns.; Pa. Conf. of State Trial Judges; Rochester (Pa.) Elks Lodge; Ellwood City Moose; frmr., pres., Community Mental Health Center and Medical Center, Beaver; elder, Park U.P. Ch.; elected judge, Court of Common Pleas, Nov. 5, 1985; married Betty Tarazano; 5 children, 3 grandchildren; home address: 1150 Bank St., Beaver.

STEFAN, LOUIS DAMON (38th District) was born May 13, 1925, in Phila., the son of Louis and Helen E. Damon Stefan; Ursinus Coll. (B.A.) 1950; Temple Univ. Schl. of Law (LL.B.) 1953; U.S. Infantry, 1943-46; admitted to practice before Pa. Supreme, Superior Courts, U.S. District Court, Eastern Dist. of Pa., Montgomery Co. Courts; Montgomery Co., Pa. Bar Assns.; v. pres.; Montgomery Bar Assn., 1970; Montgomery Co. Bd. of Law Examiners, 1960-70; solicitor, Ambler, North Wales, Hatfield Boroughs, Hatfield Borough Auth., Ambler-Lower Gwynedd-Whitpain-Upper Dublin-Whitemarsh Sewer conglomerate; past pres., North Wales Rotary Club; Ambler Rotary Club; past pres., McCann Community Bldg.; dir., counsel, Community Ambulance Assn. of Ambler; active in various charitable undertakings; Fort Washington Lodge 308, F&AM; William Boulton Dixon Post 10, Am. Legion, Fort Washington; Phi Delta Phi legal frat., Sigma Rho Lambda frat.; appt. judge, Court of Common Pleas, Dec. 9, 1970; married Joan Kreinberg on Sept. 26, 1953; 2 children; home address: 11 Ramsgate Ct., Blue Bell.

STILES, MICHAEL RANKIN (1st District) was born Jan. 1, 1946, in Phila., the son of Carson A. and Jacqueline Jane Rankin Stiles; Univ. of Pa. (B.A.) 1967; Villanova Schl. of Law (J.D.) 1971; hon. discharge, U.S. Army Reserves, 1968-74; Phila. Bar Assn., Criminal Justice Section; Pa. Conf. of State Trial Judges; mem., Phila. Crim. Justice Coordinating Comm.; adj. prof., Temple Univ., Criminal Justice Dept.; bd. dir., Woodlynne School; trial asst., Motions and Homicide Units; 1971-74, chief, Major Trials Unit, 1975-76, chief, Appeals Unit, 1977, dep. dist. atty., 1978-82, 1st asst. dist. atty., 1982-83, Office of District Attorney, Philadelphia; author, *Constitutional Law-Equal Representation Requires Good Faith Effort to Achieve Absolute Equality: Kirkpatrick v. Preisler; Wells v. Rockefeller,* 15 Vill. L. Rev. 223 (1970); *The Indigents' Right To In Forma Pauperis Proceedings in Pennsylvania Divorce Litigation,* 16 Vill. L. Rev. 283 (1970); appt. judge, Court of Common Pleas, June 28, 1983; elected to 10 year term, Nov. 1983; married Leslie Simons; 2 children: Jacqueline and Eric Scott; home address: 3436 Warden Dr., Philadelphia.

STOUT, JUANITA KIDD (1st District) was born Mar. 7, 1919, in Wewoka, Okla. daughter of Henry M. and Mary Chandler Kidd; Univ. of Iowa (B.A.) 1939; Indiana Univ., Bloomington (J.D., LL.M.) 1948, 1954; 8 hrnry. degrees; Am., Pa., Phila. Bar Assns.; Delta Sigma Theta Sorority; asst. dist. atty., 1956-69; admin. secy., U.S. Court of Appeals, 1949-54; teacher-grade schl, high schl., coll., 1939-42, 1949-50; Episcopalian; Jane Addams Medal, Rockford Coll., Ill., 1966; 3rd Annual Educators Award, Phila. Teachers Assn., 1967; Centennial Gold Medal of Mid-City Branch YMCA, Phila., 1969; Special Ambassador to Kenyan Independence, 1963; Disting. Service Award, Univ. of Iowa; Henry G. Bennett Disting. Service Award, Oklahoma St. Univ.; Criminal Justice Section Award, Phila. Bar Assn., 1982; Oklahoma Hall of Fame, Nov. 16, 1981; participant, People-to-People Mission to China, Hong Kong and Japan, May 1983; author, "Executive Clemency in Pa.," *The Shingle,* May 1959 official pub. of Phila. Bar Assn.; *Shall We Recommend? The Eastern Echo,* Spring, 1960, 'The Suitable Home' — One Proposal for Preventing Juvenile Delinquency" *Temple Law Quarterly,* Winter, 1961; "The Life of Richard Allen," *The A.M.E. Review,* April-June, 1963; "Why Must the Taxpayer Subsidize Immorality?" *The Sunday Bulletin Magazine,* March 7, 1965; reprinted in the *Reader's Digest,* April 1967; "Troubled Children and Reading Achievement," *"Catholic Library World,* May-June, 1965; "Building for the Future," *Teen Times,* Sept.-Oct, 1965; "The Twentieth Century Frontier," *The Review,* pub. of Lebanon Valley Coll., March 1970; "Queries on Jury Confusion—A View from the Bench," *Verdict,* pub. of the Phila. Trial Lawyers Assn., May 1970; apptd. judge, Court of Common Pleas, 1959; elected to full term, 1959; reelected, Nov. 1969; married to Charles Otis Stout on June 23, 1942; home address: 1919 Chestnut St., Philadelphia.

STRASSBURGER, GENE (5th District) was born on Nov. 28, 1943, in Columbus, Oh., the son of Eugene B. and Jane Schanfarber Strassburger; Yale Coll., (B.A., summa cum laude) 1964; Harvard Law Schl., (J.D., cum laude) 1967; Am. Law Institute; Pa. Conf. of St. Trial Judges; Am. Acad. of Matrimonial Lawyers; Allegheny Co., Pa. Bar Assns.; Phi Beta Kappa; law clerk to Justice Henry X. O'Brien, Pa. Supreme Court (1967-70); asst., dep. city solicitor, City of Pgh. (1970-78); Rodef Shalom Congregation; appt.

judge, Court of Common Pleas, June 1978; married Dr. Phyllis Kitzerow; 3 children: David, Ellen and Sarah; home address: 241 Rosscommon Rd., Wexford.

SUBERS, ALBERT R. (38th District) was born April 20, 1929, in Elkins Park, the son of C. Van Artsdalen and Ruth Raigual Subers; Univ. of Pa. (B.S.) 1951; Univ. of Pa. Law Schl. (LL.B.) 1954; mem., Montgomery, Pa., Am. Bar Assns.; Pa. State Conf. of Trial Judges; Theta Xi; James Wilson Law Club; solicitor, Upper Gwynedd Twp., 1970-83; North Penn Water Auth., 1970-83; Lower Salford Twp. Auth., 1970-83; Upper Gwynedd-Towamencin Auth., 1970-83; mem., The Church of the Messiah; disting. graduate, Cheltenham H.S. Alumni Assn.; appt. judge, Court of Common Pleas, April 6, 1983; elected, Nov. 8, 1983; married Emmaneta Hepford; 4 children: Ruth, Emily, Janet and Elizabeth; home address: 1168 Kenyon Dr., Fort Washington.

SUGERMAN, LEONARD (P.J. — 15th District) was born Oct. 11, 1927, in Devault, the son of H. H. and Susan Fierman Sugerman; Pa. St. Univ. (B.A.) 1949; Univ. of Pa. Law Schl. (J.D.) 1955; U.S. Army, Korea-artillery, 1950-52; Chester Co., Pa. and Am. Bar Assns.; Am. Judicature Society; Mason; solicitor to various municipalities, authorities; elected judge, Court of Common Pleas, Nov. 1973; married Carol Lynne Desilvis; 1 child, Kimberly; home address: Raintree, Malvern.

SUMMERS, EDWARD R. (1st District). Judge, Court of Common Pleas.

SURRICK, R. BARCLAY (A.J. — 32nd District) was born Dec. 18, 1937, in Media, the son of John Earl and Florence Derbyshire Surrick; Dickinson Coll. (A.B.) 1960; Dickinson Schl. of Law (LL.B.) 1965; Univ. of Va. Schl. of Law, (Master of Laws in the Judicial Process) 1982; U.S.A.R. 1st lieut., 1961-67; Delaware Co., Pa., Am. Bar Assns.; Pa. St. Trial Judges Assn.; Am. Judicature Society; bd. dirs., Wallingford-Chester chap. Am. Red Cross, Helen Kate Furness Free Library, 1974-77; commissioner, Nether Providence Twp., 1974-77; elected judge, Court of Common Pleas, 1977; married Patricia Kelly; 3 children: Patricia Kelly, Maryann Powell, R. Barclay, Jr.; home address: 905 Winding Lane, Wallingford.

SWOPE, LEE F. (P.J. — 12th District) was born Feb. 9, 1921, in Harrisburg, the son of Guy J. and Mayme Gerberich Swope; att. Univ. of Puerto Rico; Univ. of Colorado; Duke Univ. (A.B.) 1943; Dickinson Schl. of Law (LL.B.) 1948; U.S. Naval Reserve, active duty, 1942-46; enlisted, achieved rank of lieut. (sg.); Dauphin Co., Pa. Bar Assns.; asst. atty. gen., Comm. of Pa., 1955; asst. dir., dir., Pa. Bureau of Corporations, Dept. of State, 1956-60; Pa. Bd. of Finance and Revenue, 1955-60; various Masonic bodies; Phi Beta Kappa (Duke U.); apptd. judge, Jan. 1, 1961; elected to full term, 1961; reelected, 1971, 1981; pres. judge since Jan. 3, 1972; married Jean Creager Swartzell; 2 children; home address: 1402 Regency Circle, Harrisburg.

SYLVESTER, ESTHER R. (1st District) was born June 19, 1939, in Norristown, the daughter of Lawrence (dec.) and Rose Evangelist Sylvester; grad., Rosemont Coll. (B.A.) 1961; Villanova Law Schl. (J.D.) 1964; mem.: Pa. Conf. of St. Trial Judges; Natl. Council of Juvenile & Family Court Judges; dep. dist. atty., Phila., 1970-77; chief counsel, Phila. Police Dept., 1978-80; judge, Court of Common Pleas, Nov. 1985; office address: 2005 One East Penn Square, Chambers.

TAYLOR, NEWTON C. (P.J.— 20th District) was born Mar. 10, 1935, in Huntingdon, the son of the late Atty. I. Newton, Jr. and Janet Campbell Taylor; Huntingdon H.S., 1953; Juniata Coll. (A.B.) 1957; Duke Univ. (LL.B.) 1960; private law practice, 1961-80; Huntingdon Co. (pres. 1963,77), Pa., Am. Bar Assns.; Pa. Conf. of St. Trial Judges; Natl. Council of Juvenile & Family Ct. Judges; past master, Mt. Moriah Lodge No. 300, F. & A.M.; past high priest, Standing Stone Chapt. No. 201 R.A.M.; past commander, Huntingdon Commandry No. 65 K.T.; Scottish Rite bodies, Altoona; Jaffa Shrine; dist. atty., Huntingdon Co , 1968-69; Un. Presbyterian Ch.; past pres., Lions Club; Republican St. Comm. of Pa., 1972-74, 1978-80; del., 1976 Rep. Natl. Convention; dir., Keystone Legal Services, 1976-80, v. pres., 1979-80; appt. pres. judge, Court of Common Pleas, Feb. 28, 1980, elected Nov. 3, 1981; married Nancy Louise Rosevear; 2 children: Mary Jane, David Newton; home address: Lions Back Dr., Huntingdon.

TEMIN, CAROLYN ENGEL (1st District) was born Nov. 3, 1934, in Phila., the daughter of David Morton and Ethel Berman Engel; Univ. of Pa. (B.F.A.) 1955; Univ. of Pa. (LL.B.) 1958; mem., Phila. Bar Assn.; Criminal Law Com., 1963; panel mem., Criminal Law Sec., Bench-bar Conf., 1969-73; Ad Hoc Com. on Juvenile Drug Abuse, 1970; sec., Com. on Prisons and Penology, 1972; planning com., Chancellor's Drug Comm., 1972; chmn., Juvenile Procedural Rules Com., 1973; sec., Criminal Law Section, 1974; panel mem., Constitutional Implications of the Right to Life Amendment, 1981; Family Law Section, 1981-present; Civil Rights Com.; Women in Legal Profession Com.; author, "Report on Post Conviction Services to the County Prisons," *The Legal Aid Briefcase*, Oct. 1966; "Criminal Sentencing Procedures — A Judical Strait Jacket," *The Shingle*, Oct. 1969; "The Indeterminate Sentence: The Muncy Experience," *The Prison Journal*, Spring 1972; "Discriminatory Sentencing of Women Offenders: The Argument for ERA in a Nutshell," *Americal Criminal Law Journal,* Winter 1973; "Post-Gideon Effects on the Practice of Criminal Law in Philadelphia," *The Shingle*, Dec. 1974; co-author, *Benchbook for Criminal Procedure*, 1986; mem., Natl. Assn. of Women Judges; mem., Pa., Fed. & Am. Bar Assns.; mem., Justice Lodge, B'nai B'rith; mem., Am. Jewish Congress; mem., Jewish Law Day Com., 1987; elected judge, Court of Common Pleas, Nov. 8, 1983; married Martin Heller, Esq.; 2 children: Aaron and Seth Temin.

TERPUTAC, THOMAS J. (27th District) was born Jan. 11, 1927, in Continental No. 2, Fayette Co., the son of John and Catherine Gerich Terputac; Duquesne Univ. (B.Ed., cum laude) 1950; Univ. of Pgh. Schl. of Law (J.D.) 1953; Law Review Bd.; Order of the Coif; U.S. Army, 1945-46; Am., Allegheny Co., Washington Co. Bar Assns.; Assn. of Trial Lawyers of Am.; Am. Legion Post 793; Optimist Club of Washington; VFW Post 191; Elks Lodge 776; Knights of Columbus; asst. dist. atty., Washington Co., 1956-59; asst. co. solicitor, 1959-60; atty. examiner, Public Util. Comm., 1961-75; appt. judge, Court of Common Pleas, March 1978; elected in 1979 for a 10-yr. term; married Caroline K. Ptak; 4 children: Leslie, Alan, Pamela, Sally; home address: 71 Samuel Dr., Washington.

THOMAS, P. RICHARD (P.J. — 30th District) was born Aug. 13, 1920, Meadville; son of Paul E. and Clarissa Smith Thomas; Cornell Univ. (B.A.) 1942; Dickinson Schl. of Law (LL.B.) 1948, Natl. Coll. of St. Trial Judges, 1964; asst. dist. atty., Crawford Co., 1949-55; elected dist. atty., 1955; reelected to second term, 1959 and served until Jan. 6, 1964; U.S. Army, Field Artillery, 1942-45; awarded Bronze Star, 1st lieut.; pres., Pa. Conf. of St. Trial Judges, 1971-72; dir., United Way of Western Crawford Co.; Round Table; established Meadville Area Red Cross Blood Program and chrmn. of same for 3 yrs. in the early 1950's; pres. Dist. Attny.'s Assn., 1960; secy. treas., Dist. Attny.'s Assn. of Pa., 1961-63; appt. judge, Court of Common Pleas, by Governor Wm. Scranton, Jan. 1964; elected, Nov. 2, 1965 full term, commissioned pres. judge on Jan. 28, 1966; retained for 2nd 10-yr. term, Nov. 1975 and 3rd. 10-yr. term, Nov. 1985; married Josephine Ingraham, Dec. 28, 1946; 3 children; home address: 738 Chestnut St., Meadville 16335.

THOMSON, HAROLD ARTHUR, JR. (P.J. — 60th District) was born Sept. 14, 1934, in Upper Darby, the son of Harold Arthur "Cappy" and Myrtle McCullam Thomson; Pa. St. Univ. (B.S.) 1959; Dickinson Law Schl. (J.D.) 1962; U.S. Army, 1953-56, Korea; Pa. Conf. of St. Trial Judges; Pa., Pike Co. Bar Assns.; dist. atty., Pike Co., 1971-77; pres., Pa. Dist. Attys. Assn., 1976; former special agent, FBI, 1962-64; adj. instructor, E. Stroudsburg St. Univ., "Criminal Process," 1984-85; St. Trial Judges Ed. Com.; Natl. Judicial Coll., Reno, 1981; mem., Am. Legion; Elks; Masons; Shriners; elected judge, Court of Common Pleas, 1977; married Sara Jane Sanderson; 6 children: Ingrid, Tracey, Laura, Heather, Holly, Margaret Belle; home address: Star Route, Box 18, Paupack.

TOAL, WILLIAM R., JR. (32nd District) was born Sept. 9, 1932, in Phila.; the son of Hon. William R. and Gertrude D. Gertz Toal; Bucknell Univ. (A.B.) 1954; Temple Univ. Schl. of Law (LL.B.) 1961; 1st lieut., U.S. Army Signal Corps, Germany, 1954-56; Delaware Co., Pa., Am. Bar Assns.; Phi Alpha Delta Law Frat.; Phi Gamma Delta Frat.; Lawyers Club of Delaware Co.

(past secy.); Pa. Trial Judges Assn.; Council of Juvenile Court Judges; Am. Judicature Society; Eagle Scout Bd. of Review; General Wayne Dist., BSA; Cassia Lodge, F&AM No. 273; asst. dist. atty., 1963-68; 1st asst. dist. atty., 1968-74; elected judge, Court of Common Pleas, Nov. 1973; retained for second term, 1983; married Lolita C. Bunnell; 3 children: William R. III, Robert B. and John A.; home address: 215 Green Briar Lane, Havertown.

TOOLE, PATRICK J., JR. (11th District) was born Sept. 16, 1933, in Wilkes-Barre, the son of Patrick J. and Catherine E. McKay Toole; att. St. Mary's H.S.; Kings Coll. (B.A.); Temple Univ. (LL.B.); U.S. Army, 1953-55; dist. atty., Luzerne Co., 1971-78; pres., Pa. Dist. Atty's Assn., 1976-77; solicitor, W-B Area Schl. Dist., 1969-75; rec., Co. Detective, Disting. Public Service Award, 1976; appt. judge, Court of Common Pleas, Feb. 1978; elected, Nov. 1979; married Betty Jane Mullen; 4 children: Patrick, Joseph, Michael, and Lisa; home address: 66 Mallery Place, Wilkes-Barre.

TRESSLER, PAUL W. (38th District) Judge, Court of Common Pleas.

VAN ANTWERPEN, FRANKLIN STUART (3rd District) was born Oct. 23, 1941, in Passaic, N.J., the son of Franklin John and Dorothy Hoedemaker Van Antwerpen; Newark Acad., 1960; Univ. of Me. (B.S.) 1964; Temple Univ. Schl. of Law (J.D.) 1967; Natl. Coll. of the Judiciary, Univ. of Nv., 1980; U.S. Army, R.O.T.C., 1960-62; Northampton Co., Pa., Am. (Comm. on Judicial Ed.) Bar Assns.; Pa. Conf. of Trial Judges; Am., Pa. Trial Lawyers Assns.; Sigma Pi Sigma (hon. soc.); Phi Alpha Delta; chf. counsel, Northampton Co. Legal Aid Society,1970-71; solicitor, Palmer Twp., 1971-79; active in numerous civic organizations; adjunct professor, Northampton Co. Area Community Coll., 1976-80; B.I.P. Booster Award, 1979; George Palmer Award, 1979; Northampton Co. Disting. Citizen of the Yr., 1981; author, *An Investigation of Electron Paramagnetic Resonance,* 1964; *Who's Who in the World; Who's Who in America; Who's Who in American Law;* appt. judge, Court of Common Pleas, Oct. 9, 1979; elected Nov. 3, 1981; temporarily appt. acting pres. judge, Bradford Co., 1983; married Kathleen O'Brien; 3 children: Joy, Franklin, Virginia; home address: Palmer Township, Easton.

VICAN, RONALD E. (43rd District) was born Sept. 12, 1946, the son of Edward and Mary Lee Somerville Vican; Dickinson Coll. (B.A.) 1968, and its law schl. (J.D) 1971; "Dist. Military Graduate," Dickinson Schl. of Law R.O.T.C.; Capt., U.S. Army Police Corps; Monroe Co., Pa. Bar Assns.; Pa Trial Lawyers Assn.; Sigma Chi; pub. def., 1973-75; chief pub. def., 1975-80; solicitor: Pleasant Valley Manor, Inc., Pocono Mts. Mun. Airport Auth., F.O.P.; Elks; adv. bd., Salvation Army; frmr. chmn., Zoning Hearing Bd., Paradise Twp.; authored an article in Dickinson *International Law Journal;* elected judge, Court of Common Pleas, Nov. 3, 1981; married Joan Teresa Kane; 2 children: Lindsay, Justin; home address: Henryville.

VOGEL, WILLIAM W. (P.J. — 38th District) was born Oct. 28, 1926, in Merion, the son of Adolph and Ann Whitten Vogel; Haverford Coll. (A.B.) 1950; Univ. of Pa. Law Schl., 1953; U.S. Navy, Pacific, 1944-46; Montgomery Co., Pa. and Am. Bar Assns.; chmn., Southeast Regional Planning Council, Pa. Criminal Justice Planning Bd., 1970-72; commissioner, Lower Merion Twp., 1958-64; commissioner, Montgomery Co. 1964-66; Overbrook Presbyterian Ch.; appt. judge, Court of Common Pleas, Nov. 15, 1966, elected judge, Nov. 1977; elected pres. judge, Nov. 24, 1986; married Sara Carter on Oct. 1, 1965; home address: 315 Kent Rd., Wynnewood.

WALKER, JOHN R. (39th District) was born June 2, 1943, in Chambersburg; the son of Robert and Floe Hartman Walker; grad., Chambersburg Area Senior H.S., 1961; Gettysburg Coll. (B.S.) 1965; Dickinson Schl. of Law (J.D.) 1969; att., University of Pa., Wharton Schl. of Finance and Commerce; asst. public defender, 1970-71; dist. atty., 1972-85; judge, Court of Common Pleas, Jan. 6, 1986; married Martha Baum; 2 children; home address: 2003 Philadelphia Ave., Chambersburg.

WALKER, ROBERT L. (30th District) was born May 5, 1924, in Erie, the son of Dr. Herman H. and Bertha L. McKean Walker; attd. Dickinson Coll.; Baylor Univ.; Dickinson Schl. of Law (LL.B.) 1948; U.S. Army, 1943-45; Am., Pa., Crawford Co. Bar Assns.; bd. of govs., PBA; Pine Lodge F&AM; Solomon Royal Arch Chapter, Northwestern Commandry; Zem Zem Temple; A.A.O.N.M.S.; appt. judge, Court of Common Pleas, June 26, 1978, elected to full term Nov. 1979; married Patricia A. Woods; 5 children; home address: 200 Beach St., Linesville.

WALKO, JOSEPH S. (36th District) was born Oct. 10, 1930, in Ambridge, the son of Joseph and Anna Tkatch Walko; Geneva Coll. (B.S.) 1952; Dickinson Schl. of Law (J.D.) 1955; Beaver Co., Pa., Am. Bar Assns.; Am. Judicature Society; Pa. Conf. of St. Trial Judges; Rotary; Eagles; Elks; Sons of Italy; Wolves; Knights of Columbus; asst. dist. atty., 1957-68; dist. atty., 1972-77; Outstanding Citizens Award, Jaycee's; Disting. Service to Law Enforcement, Co. Detectives Assn. of Pa.; elected judge, Court of Common Pleas, Nov. 1977; married Rosemary Rosatelli; 3 children: Joseph Jr., Jonathan, and James; home address: 1399 Adams Dr. Ambridge.

WALLACE, MICHAEL EMEDIO (1st District) was born July 11, 1941, in Phila., the son of Edward and Mary DeLaurentis Wallace; LaSalle Coll. (B.A.) 1963; Villanova Univ. Law Schl. (J.D.) 1966; hon. degrees: Cavalier Order of St. George, 1973 (society dates back to 14th cent.), Cavaliere Commendatore DiGrazia Magistiale-Order of St. George in Carinzia, 1975; Am. Judicature Society; Phila., Pa., Am., Fed. Bar Assns.; Justinian Law Society; Cr. Procedures Com. of Pa. Conf. of St. Judges; frmr. venerable, Judge Alessandroni Lodge, Sons of Italy; dep. to mayor, Phila., 1972-77; bd. of dirs., Civic Center Museum, since 1979, Phila. Assn. of Retarded Citizens; recipient: Puerto Rico Com. Awards, 1972, 1974, 1976; Torresdale Boys Club, 1974; Phila. Building Trades, 1973; Columbus Forum Lodge Sons of Italy, 1975; Berean Youth Center; Frankford Arsenal Management Assn.; Assn. Conf. of Registered Officials; Man of the Year Award and Alessandroni Lodge Award for Meritorious Service, 1977; Cuban Com. Award, 1976; Parkwood Boys Club, 1976; inducted, PAL Hall of Fame, 1980; 1980 Founders Award, UNICO — (Greater Phila. Chapt.); elected judge, Court of Common Pleas, 1977; married Judith Ann Barr; 2 children: Glenn Anthony and Gwyn Marie; home address: 9238 Hegerman St., Philadelphia.

WALSH, JAMES J. (P.J. — 45th District) was born October 12, 1930, in Scranton, son of Dorothy Gurrell Walsh and the late Edward J. Walsh; U.S. Army, 2 yrs. during Korean War incl. 18 mos. overseas; att. Washington and Lee Univ.; education interrupted by Korean war; Univ. of Scranton (B.S.); Georgetown Univ. Schl. of Law (J.D.); St. treas., Young Dem. of Pa., 1961-63; Scranton Schl. Bd. rep., P.I.A.A. 1963-65; Scranton Schl. Bd., 1960-65, pres., 1964; Mayor of Scranton, 1966-69; Pa., Lackawanna Co. Bar. Assns.; K. of C.; St. Patrick's R.C. Ch. and its Holy Name Soc.; Pa. Conf. St. Trial Judges Assn.; chmn. N.E. Regn. Pa. Crim. Justice Planning Council; Friendly Sons of St. Patrick, pres.; A.O.H.; DAV; chaplain, VFW; Friends of Scouting; bd.; March of Dimes; Scranton Elks; Lions Club; Pa. "Man of the Year," Catholic War Vets., 1980; Cyrano Award, Univ. of Scranton Grad. Schl., 1981; Scranton Area Sports Hall of Fame, 1982; apptd. judge, Lackawanna Co. Court of Common Pleas, December 1971, elected to full term, Nov. 1973; retained for another full term, Nov. 1983; elevated to pres. judge, Aug. 2, 1986; married Mary Frances McHugh; 2 children; home address: 731 North Main Avenue, Scranton.

WALTER, JOHN (52nd District) born Nov. 4, 1931, Lebanon; son of late Daniel E. and the late Edith Stager Walter; Lebanon Valley Coll. (B.S.) 1953; Univ. of Pa. Law Schl. (J.D.) 1960; USNR 1953-57 sep. as lt. j.g.; senior warden, St. Luke's Episcopal Ch., 1979-82; Pa., Lebanon Co. Bar Assns.; Pa. Conf. of Trial Judges; past pres., Lebanon Co. Workshop Inc.; Lebanon Co. Chptr., Am. Cancer Soc., bd. dir.; past co. chrmn., Heart Fund; Mt. Lebanon Lodge 226 F&AM, Valley of Reading Consistory, Tall Cedars, Rajah Shrine Temple, Northside Civic League, Lebanon Lions Club, Elks; Pi Gamma Mu (Natl. Soc. Sci. Hnry. Soc.) 1953; one of 4 Outstanding Young Men of Am. from Lebanon Co., Natl. Jaycees, 1965; potentate,

Rajah Shrine Temple 1972; mem., Bd. of Gov's Phila. Unit, Shriners Hospitals for Crippled Children; pres., Lebanon Valley Coll. Alumni Assn., 1980-82; Lebanon Valley Coll. Trustee; apptd. judge, Court of Common Pleas, Mar. 1975; elected Nov. 1975; retained Nov. 1985; married Patricia Ann Lutz; 4 children: Heather, John Daniel, Heidi, and Hope; home address: 400 Birch Ave., Mt. Gretna.

WATKINS, THOMAS D. (1st District) was born Jan. 25, 1942, in Phila., the son of Edmund Nash and Hope Brister Watkins; Columbia Univ. (B.A.) 1964; Univ. of Pa. Law Schl. (J.D.) 1968; mem., Pa. & Phila. Bar Assns.; Pa. Conf. of Trial Judges; asst. dist. atty., 1970-72, 1978-81; mem., Chestnut Hill Civic Assn.; Phila. Booster's; St. Paul's Episcopal Ch.; rec. of awards from Univ. of Pa. Alumni, Columbia Alumni, Penn Charter Alumni; judge, Court of Common Pleas, Nov. 1983; married Janet Iandola; 1 son, Llewellyn; home address: 8409 Navajo St., Philadelphia.

WATSON, J. WARREN (5th District) was born Feb. 20, 1923, in Pgh.; Duquesne Univ. (B.A.) 1949 (LL.B.) 1953; Unemp. Comp. Bur., 1953-54; Bur. of Workmen's Comp., 1956-62; asst. city solicitor, Pgh., 1962-66; Duquesne Univ. associate prof., Schl. of Bus. Admin., Dept. of Continuing Ed., 1965; lecturer, Duffs Bus. Inst., Penn St. Univ., Pgh. Tech. Inst., Robert Morris Coll., and Bus. and Job Development Corp., since 1967; Elks; Frogs; Omega Psi Phi.; Sigma Pi Phi Rho Boule; active in boy scouting; numerous social services groups; bd. dir., exec. bd., Business and Job Devel. Corp.; bd. dir., athlet. comm. chmn., Centre Ave. YMCA; plan. comm., Family Court; Health and Welfare Assn. Task Force on Services to Families and Children; legal counsel, adv., Homewood-Brushton Athletic Assn., Homewood-Brushton Community Imp. Assn.; bd. dirs.: Kay-Shadyside Boys Clubs; Leukemia Society, Mendelssohn Choir; Opp. Indust. Corp.; Urban League of Pgh.; Voc. Rehab. Center; pres. council, Carlow Coll.; Community Action, Pgh. Ile Elegba drug program; pres. Teen Exposure pres.; Three Rivers Youth; NAACP; DAV Man of Year, 1969; Allegheny Co., Pa., Natl. Bar Assns.; Pa. Assn. St. Trial Judges; Am. Judicature Soc.; bd. mem., Judicial Inquiry & Review Bd.; Roman Catholic; judge, orphans' court div., Court of Common Pleas of Allegheny Co.; married, Carole A. Watson; 6 children.

WEKSELMAN, I. MARTIN (5th District) was born Feb. 6, 1928, in Pgh., the son of Abe and Leah Fingeret Wekselman; Univ. of Pgh. (B.S.) 1947; Duquesne Univ. Law Schl. (J.D.) 1958; appt. judge, Court of Common Pleas of Allegheny Co., Jan. 2, 1973; elected to full term Nov. 1977; married Selma E. Finkelstein, May 29, 1949; 3 children; home address: 825 Morewood Avenue, Pittsburgh.

WETTICK, R. STANTON, JR. (A.J. — 5th District) was born Apr. 21, 1938, in New Castle, son of R. Stanton and Katharine Buchholz Wettick; Amherst Coll. (B.A., cum laude) 1960; Yale Law Schl. (LL.B.) 1963; Juvenile Court Judges' Comm.; assoc. in large Pgh. law firm, 1963-66; prof. of law, Univ. of Pgh., 1966-69; exec. dir., Neighborhood Legal Services Assn., 1969-76; adj. prof. of law, Univ. of Pgh. Law Schl., 1966-present; adj. prof. of law, Duquesne Law Schl., 1979-80; appt. judge, Court of Common Pleas, July 21, 1976; admin. judge, Family Div.; married to Nancy S. Hazlett; 3 children: Brett, Lissa, and Caroline; home address: 702 S. Linden Ave., Pittsburgh.

WHITE, THOMAS A. (1st District) was born Sept. 24, 1926, in County Derry, Ireland, the son of James A. and Ellen Millar White (both deceased); LaSalle Coll., dean's list (B.S.) 1950; Temple Univ. Schl. of Law, Criminal Law Award (LL.B.) 1958; military service, Jan. 1945 to July 1946; Pa., Phila. Bar Assns., Am. Judicature Society; St. Thomas More Society; past pres., Brehon Law Society; Dem. committeeman, 1947-65; 3rd div., 3rd ward; elected to General Assembly Nov. 1952; sec., Phila. Delegation under Chmn. Hon. Joseph Hersch until 1954; Our Lady of Calvary Roman Catholic Ch.; Regina Coeli Council; K. of C.; Torresdale Boys Club; Am. Legion Kensington Post No. 68; pres., Irish Society of Phila.; Friendly Sons of St. Patrick membership comm.; elected judge, Court of Common Pleas, Nov. 1977; married to Edna F. White; 6 children: Kevin, Katharine, Edna, James, Eileen, Leo; home address: 10800 Ellicott Rd., Philadelphia.

WILLIAMS, ALFRED T., JR. (P.J. — 3rd District) was born Nov. 13, 1930, in Bethlehem, the son of Alfred Thomas and Florence Grogg Williams; Moravian Coll. (A.B.) 1952; Univ. of Pa. Law Schl. (LL.B.) 1955; Northampton Co., Pa. Bar Assns.; Pa. Council of St. Trial Judges; solicitor, Northampton Co. Prison, 1960-67; general counsel, Pa. Jr. Chamber of Commerce, 1960-61; Bethlehem Rotary Club; Masonic organizations; Eagles; chmn., bd. of trustees, Moravian Coll.; mem., bd. of trustees, Moravian Theological Sem.; frmr. pres., Lehigh Valley Community Council, Moravian Coll. Alumni Assn.; Advsry. Bd. of Law, Univ. of Pa.; Bethlehem Outstanding Young Man of the Year, 1961; Outstanding Young Men of America, 1962; Moravian Coll. Alumni Medallion of Merit Award, 1966; DeMolay Legion of Honor Award, 1968; Lehigh Valley Com. Council's Lois Woodhull Barnum Award, 1983; Moravian Coll. Comenius Alumni Award, 1984; Co. Det. Assn. of Pa. Disting. Service to Law and Justice Award, 1985; elected judge, Court of Common Pleas, 1967; commissioned president judge, March 6, 1979; married Patricia A. Shelly on Jan. 24, 1987; 3 children; home address: 730 Chestnut St., Bethlehem.

WILSON, CALVIN T. (1st District) was born Feb. 25, 1928, in Phila., the son of the late Ernest and Beatrice Culbreath Wilson; Lincoln Univ. (B.S.) 1949; Howard Univ. Law Schl. (J.D.) 1952; Barristers Club, Pa. Trial Judges, SNAP, Dec. 1975; elect. secy., Phila. Bd. of Judges; Nov. 1975; elect. bd. mem., Metro. Hosp., Phila.; 1975, AFNA Law Preceptorial Program; Nov. 18, 1980, appt. pres., exec. comm., S.E. Pa. Area Chapt. Muscular Dystrophy Assn.; elected Natl. V. Pres., Muscular Dystrophy Assn., 1982; commissioned judge, Court of Common Pleas, Dec. 30, 1971; married Yvonne Garnett on Jan. 1, 1953; 1 child, Calvin II; home address: 1411 E. Cliveden St., Philadelphia.

WISER, MERLE E. (P.J. — 18th District) was born Dec. 24, 1919, in Sligo, the son of William H. Wiser; Clarion Univ. (B.S.) 1941; Dickinson Law Schl. (LL.B.) 1949; Army, 1941-46; Pa. Bar Assn.; Natl. Council of Juvenile Ct. Judges; St. Trial Judges Assn.; Domestic Relations Assn.; elected pres. judge, Nov. 1979; married Norma Sanesi; 1 child, Mark; home address: Applewood Valley, Clarion.

WOLFE, ROBERT LEA (P.J. — 37th District) was born Mar. 4, 1926, the son of Stanley B. and Almyra Myers Wolfe; St. Bonaventure Univ. (B.A.); Univ. of Buffalo Law Schl. (J.D.); U.S. Air Force, WW II; Pa. Bar Assn.; Pa. Conf. St. Trial Judges; 1st Presbyterian Ch. of Warren; elected pres. judge, Court of Common Pleas, Nov. 1969; appt. on February 15, 1978 to the Juvenile Court Judges' Commission; married Margaret E. Larson on Dec. 31, 1955; 6 children; home address: 410 Liberty St., Warren.

WOLLET, ROBERT J. (29th District) was born July 17, 1927, in Williamsport, the son of Harold E. and Sarah Snyder Wollet; Bucknell Univ. (B.S.) 1953; Univ. of Pa. Law Schl. (J.D.) 1956; U.S. Air Force, 1944-48, 1950-51; sec., Lycoming Law Assn., 1956; Pa., Am. Bar Assns.; Pa. Conf. of St. Trial Judges; Williamsport Wheel Club; Ross Club; Antlers Club; Lycoming Co. Law Librarian, 1959-63, Sheriff solicitor, 1959-63, Commissioner Solicitor, 1972-76; spec. asst. atty. gen., Pa. Liquor Control Bd., 1963-71; chmn., Lycoming Co. Bloodmobile, 1958-59; chmn., Lycoming Co. Blood Comm., 1961-62; dir., N. Central Heart Assn., 1967-69; elected judge, Court of Common Pleas, Nov. 3, 1981; married Marguerite DiSalvo; 4 children: Robert, Jr., Nancy, Christine, Kimberly; home address: 831 High St., Williamsport.

WOOD, LAWRENCE EYRE (15th District) was born July 26, 1936, in West Chester, the son of Harold K. and Kathryn Eyre Smith Wood; St. Andrews Schl., Middletown, Del., 1954; Colgate Univ. (B.A.) 1958; Univ. of Pa. (LL.B.) 1961; U.S. Naval Reserve (active duty) 1961-65; Chester Co., Pa., Am. Bar Assns.; Pa. Conf. of St. Trial Judges; A.T.O. frat.; Order of Coif; Phi Beta Kappa; asst. dist. attny., Chester Co., 1966-67; asst. public def., 1969-70; controller, 1974-80; Episcopalian (Vestry mem.); Republican (frmr. Co. Exec. Comm.); NAACP; Turk's Head Rugby Club; Wilmington Opera Society; Y.M.C.A.; appt. judge, Court of Common Pleas, Mar. 25, 1980; married Mary Reynolds Parke; 2 children: Lawrence E., Jr., Rebecca S.; home address: 165A Brinton's Bridge Rd., Chadds Ford.

WRIGHT, ROBERT A. (32nd District) Lincoln Univ. (B.A.); Temple Univ. Law Schl. (LL.B.); U.S. Army, WW II; Delaware Co., Pa., Am. Bar Assns.; Lawyers Club of Delaware Co. NAACP; Temple Law Alumni Assn.; John A. Watts Lodge IBPOE of W; Past Exalted Rulers Council No. 7, IBPOE of W; Adv. bd., Pa. St. Univ., Delaware Co. Campus; Pa. Conf. of St. Trial Judges; Pa. Council of Juvenile Court Judges; Am. Judicature Society; Am. Legion; VFW; frmr. mem. of Judicial Inquiry & Review Bd.; Phila. Crime Comm.; bd. dir., Health & Welfare Council of Delaware Co.; Delaware Co. Bd. of Assistance; Citizen's Adv. Comm. for Urban Renewal, City of Chester & Chester Township; Legal Services Adv. Bd.; dist. v. chmn. William Penn Dist., Valley Forge Council BSA; bd. of man., W. Branch YMCA; hon. mem. FOP, William Penn Lodge No. 19; Chester Youth League; Magistrates Assn. of Delaware Co.; Felton Hose & Chemical Co.; asst. dist. atty., Delaware Co., 1964-70; Episcopalian; awards from W. Branch YMCA; Chester Scholarship Fund; Who's Who Club; Central Rest Recreation Club, Inc.; John A. Watts Lodge IBPOE of W; 1st Annual Achiev. Award, Deputies Club IBPOE of W; Freedom Found. Fellowship House; appt. judge, Court of Common Pleas, Dec. 23, 1970; married Mary Maloney on Sept. 10, 1938; 1 child; home address: 2539 Green Street, Feltonville, Chester.

YOHN, WILLIAM H., JR. (38th District) was born Nov. 20, 1935, in Pottstown, the son of William H., Sr. and Dorothy Cornelius Yohn; Princeton Univ. (A.B) 1957; Yale Law Schl. (LL.B.) 1960; U.S. Marine Corps Reserves, 1960-65; Montgomery Co., Pa., Am. Bar Assns.; asst. dist. atty., Montgomery Co., 1962-65; frmr. mem., Pa. House of Representatives, 1968-80; chmn., bd. dir., Pottstown Memorial Medical Center; Phi Beta Kappa; Outstanding Young Man of the Year, Pottstown Jaycees, 1968; appt. judge, Court of Common Pleas, May 13, 1981; elected Nov. 3, 1981; married Jean Kochel; 3 children: William, III, Bradley, Elizabeth; home address: Crestwood Dr., Pottstown.

YOUNG, ROBERT K. (31st District) was born March 15, 1931, in Phila., the son of Donald R. and Ada Wise Young; Westtown Friends Schl., 1949; Haverford Coll. (B.A.) 1953; Univ. of Pa. Law Schl. (LL.B.) 1956; mem., Lehigh Co. & Pa. Bar Assns.; Pa. Conf. of State Trial Judges; East Penn Schl. Bd., 1962-66; Joint Planning Comm., 1962- ; Appeal Agent for Local Draft Bd., 1965; Lehigh Co. Charter Study Com, 1976; Trial Court Nominating Com., 1978-80; chmn., Macungie "Das Awkscht Fescht"; Boy Scouts of America; rec., Henry C. Laughlin Legal Essay Award, Univ. of Pa., 1956; President's Award, Lehigh Co. Bar Assn., 1983; author, Authority Financing, *Pa. Bar Quarterly*, Jan. 1970, pilot; judge, Court of Common Pleas, July 17, 1984; married Carolyn E. Stephen; 5 children: Donald, David, William, Paul, and Nancy; home address: 1250 Indian Creek Rd., Emmaus.

ZALESKI, JEROME A. (1st District) was born June 21, 1933, in Phila., the son of Anthony and Valeria Nowakoski Zaleski; LaSalle Coll. (B.S.) 1959; Temple Univ. Law Schl. (J.D.) 1963; Pa. Trial Judges; commissioned judge, Court of Common Pleas, Dec. 30, 1971; married Eileen Donnelly on Sept. 14, 1963; 6 children; home address: 1015 Welsh Rd., Philadelphia.

ZAVARELLA, PAUL R. (A.J. — 5th District) was born April 10, 1932, in Pgh., son of Ralph and Irene Bogaty Zavarella; Allegheny Coll. (A.B.) 1953; Univ. of Pgh. Schl. of Law (LLB. and J.D.) 1956; frmr. Dep. Register of Wills and Solicitor, Allegheny Co.; elected judge, Court of Common Pleas, Jan. 1974; admn. judge, Orphans' Court Division; home address: 14 Shangri-La Circle, Pittsburgh.

ZELEZNIK, RICHARD GEORGE (5th District) born Nov. 7, 1924, in Glassport, son of George and Sophie Petrusz Zeleznik; Duquesne Univ. (B.A.) 1954; and its Law Schl. (LL.B.) 1958; U.S. Army, F.A. Armored, 1943-46; solicitor, ch. legal counsel of W. Mifflin, Dravosburg, 1968-75; various civic, social, veterans' orgs.; rec'd. Disting. Citizen Achievement Award, Clairton Deanary Byzantine Ch., elect. judge, Court of Common Pleas, Nov. 1975; married Nellie Czura; 12 children; home address: 124 Holliday Dr., West Mifflin.

COURT ADMINISTRATION

COURT ADMINISTRATOR OF PENNSYLVANIA

NANCY M. SOBOLEVITCH was born March 3, 1938, in Phila., the daughter of Ada Bower and Walter D. Mayberry; att. St. Leonard's Academy; Univ. of Pa. (B.A.) 1960; asst. ed., A.S. Barnes & Co., Inc., NY; dir. pub. rel., Lenox Hill Hosp., NY, Doctor's Hosp., and Columbus Gallery of Fine Arts, Columbus, OH; asst. dir. devel., Thomas Jefferson Univ.; dir., commun. rel., West Phila. Corp.; dep. dir., Gov.'s Energy Council; exec. asst. to Speaker, Pa. House of Reps.; former bd. mem., Council of State Govts.-Eastern Reg., Y.M.C.A., Adult Basic Ed. Academy; currently Comm. of Pa. Commission on Crime & Delinquency; chmn., Lawyers Assessment Co.; appt. Court Administrator of Pennsylvania, March 31, 1986.

OFFICERS

Office of the State Court Administrator
1515 Market Street, Suite 1414, Philadelphia 19102
Court Administrator — Nancy M. Sobolevitch

Supreme Court
Prothonotary, Eastern District — Marlene F. Lachman, Esquire
Deputy Prothonotary — Eastern Office — Patrick Tassos
Deputy Prothonotary — Middle Office — Mildred E. Williamson
Deputy Prothonotary — Western Office — Irma T. Gardner

Superior Court
Executive Administrator — Nicholas L. DiLorenzo, #2 Bala Plaza, Bala Cywyd 19004
Prothonotary — David A. Szewczak, Esquire, 2044 Robert N.C. Nix, Sr. Federal Bldg., 9th & Chestnut Streets, Philadelphia 19107
Deputy Prothonotary — Eastern Office — Beatrice Curtiss
Deputy Prothonotary — Viola E. McClay
Deputy Prothonotary — Middle Office — Mildred E. Williamson
Deputy Prothonotary — Western Office — Eleanor T. Valecko

Commonwealth Court
Executive Administrator — G. Ronald Darlington, Esquire, 626 South Office Building, Harrisburg 17120
Prothonotary — Daniel S. Schuckers, Esquire
Deputy Prothonotary for Law — Kristen W. Brown, Esquire
Deputy Prothonotary/Chief Clerk — Charles R. Hostutler
Deputy Prothonotary for Administration — H. Ward Adams

COURTROOMS

Eastern Office
Supreme Court, Room 456, City Hall, Philadelphia 19107
Superior and Commonwealth Courts, 2nd Floor, Robet N.C. Nix, Sr. Federal Bldg., 9th & Chestnut Streets, Philadelphia 19107

Middle Office
Supreme and Superior Courts, Room 434, Main Capitol, Harrisburg 17120
Commonwealth Court, 5th Floor, South Office Building, Harrisburg 17120

Western Office
Supreme, Superior, and Commonwealth Courts, 8th Floor, City-County Building, Pittsburgh 15219

COURT SESSIONS

1986 Supreme Court Sessions

January 21 to 24	Philadelphia
January 28 to 29	Harrisburg
March 3 to 7	Pittsburgh
March 12 to 13	Harrisburg
April 14 to 18	Philadelphia
May 13 to 16	Harrisburg
June 17 to 18	Philadelphia
September 9 to 10	Harrisburg
September 15 to 19	Pittsburgh
October 20 to 24	Philadelphia
October 29 to 30	Harrisburg
December 1 to 5	Philadelphia

1987 Supreme Court Sessions

January 26 to 30	Philadelphia
March 9 to 13	Pittsburgh
March 19 to 20	Harrisburg
April 6 to 10	Philadelphia
May 12 to 15	Harrisburg
June 16 to 17	Philadelphia
September 9 to 10	Harrisburg
September 21 to 25	Pittsburgh
October 19 to 23	Philadelphia
December 7 to 11	Philadelphia

1986 Superior Court Sessions

January 13 to 14	Philadelphia
January 21 to 23	Philadelphia
January 28 to 30	Pittsburgh
February 4 to 6	Philadelphia
February 11 to 13	Philadelphia
February 18 to 20	Pittsburgh
February 25 to 27	Harrisburg
March 4 to 6	Philadelphia
March 11 to 13	Philadelphia
March 18 to 20	Pittsburgh
March 24 to 26	Pittsburgh
April 1 to 3	Philadelphia
April 8 to 10	Philadelphia
April 15 to 17	Pittsburgh
April 21 to 23	Harrisburg
April 29 to May 1	Pittsburgh
May 6 to 8	Philadelphia
May 13 to 15	Philadelphia
May 20 to 22	Pittsburgh
	Harrisburg
May 28 to 30	Philadelphia
June 3 to 5	Pittsburgh
June 9 to 11	Philadelphia
June 17 to 19	Philadelphia
June 24 to 26	Philadelphia
	Pittsburgh
	Harrisburg
September 3 to 5	Philadelphia
	Pittsburgh
September 9 to 11	Philadelphia
	Pittsburgh
September 16 to 18	Philadelphia
September 30 to October 2	Philadelphia
	Harrisburg
October 7 to 9	Pittsburgh
October 15 to 17	Doylestown
October 21 to 23	Philadelphia
October 28 to 30	Philadelphia
	Pittsburgh
November 5 to 7	Philadelphia
November 18 to 20	Philadelphia
	Harrisburg
December 2 to 4	Philadelphia
	Pittsburgh
December 16 to 18	Pittsburgh

1987 Superior Court Sessions

January 13 to 15	Philadelphia
January 21 to 23	Pittsburgh
January 27 to 29	Philadelphia
February 3 to 5	Pittsburgh
February 10 to 12	Philadelphia
February 18 to 20	Harrisburg
February 24 to 26	Philadelphia
March 3 to 5	Pittsburgh
March 10 to 12	Philadelphia
March 17 to 19	Pittsburgh
March 24 to 26	Philadelphia
March 31 to April 2	Harrisburg
April 21 to 23	Philadelphia
April 28 to 30	Philadelphia
	Pittsburgh
May 5 to 7	Philadelphia
May 12 to 14	Pittsburgh
May 19 to 21	Philadelphia
May 27 to 29	Philadelphia
June 2 to 4	Pittsburgh
June 9 to 11	Harrisburg
June 16 to 18	Philadelphia
	Pittsburgh
June 23 to 25	Philadelphia
September 1 to 3	Philadelphia
	Pittsburgh
September 9 to 11	Philadelphia
	Pittsburgh
September 14 to 16	Philadelphia
September 21 to 23	Philadelphia
	Harrisburg
September 29 to October 1	Philadelphia
	Pittsburgh
October 6 to 8	Philadelphia
October 14 to 16	Pittsburgh
	Philadelphia
October 27 to 29	Philadelphia
	Harrisburg
November 4 to 6	Philadelphia
	Pittsburgh
November 17 to 19	Philadelphia
	Pittsburgh
December 1 to 3	Philadelphia
	Harrisburg
December 8 to 10	Philadelphia
	Pittsburgh

1986 Commonwealth Court Sessions

February 3 to 7	Harrisburg
March 10 to 14	Pittsburgh
April 7 to 11	Philadelphia
May 12 to 16	Harrisburg
June 9 to 13	Philadelphia
September 8 to 12	Harrisburg
October 6 to 10	Pittsburgh
November 17 to 21	Harrisburg
December 8 to 12	Philadelphia

1987 Commonwealth Court Sessions

February 23 to 27	Philadelphia
March 23 to 27	Pittsburgh
April 20 to 24	Harrisburg
May 18 to 22	Pittsburgh
June 8 to 12	Philadelphia
September 14 to 18	Philadelphia
October 5 to 9	Pittsburgh
November 16 to 20	Harrisburg
December 14 to 18	Philadelphia

SPECIAL COURTS

(By County)

DISTRICT JUSTICES, PITTSBURGH MAGISTRATES,

AND

PHILADELPHIA TRAFFIC COURT JUDGES

The first two numbers following the district justice's name refer to the judicial district. The second number, which is either a one, two, three, or four, refers to the legislative classification of the magisterial district (See Magisterial Districts Act, Act of December 2, 1968, P.L. No. 352, and Magisterial Districts Act for Counties of the Second Class, Act of December 2, 1968, P.L. No. 359.) The third set of numbers represents the magisterial district number within the particular classification. For instance, Magisterial District 51-3-01 identifies the office of District Justice Donald G. Weaver, which is located in the 51st Judicial District (Adams County). It is a 3rd Class District, and it is number one of the 3rd Class Districts. In those cases where the last two numbers appear to be missing in a county's numerical order of districts, this is an indication that a previously existing district has been eliminated.

ADAMS COUNTY
FIFTY-FIRST JUDICIAL DISTRICT
District Justices

Thomas R. Carr   51-3-01
Adams County Courthouse, Baltimore Street, Gettysburg 17325
    Townships of Cumberland, Straban and Mt. Joy; Borough of Gettysburg

Samuel K. Frymyer   51-3-02
Bonneauville Borough Office, 46 East Hanover St., Gettysburg 17325
    Townships of Conewago, Union, Germany and Mt. Pleasant; Boroughs of McSherrystown, Littlestown and Bonneauville

John C. Zepp, III   51-3-03
P.O. Box 605, East Berlin 17316
    Townships of Huntingdon, Latimore, Tyrone, Reading, Hamilton, Berwick and Oxford; Boroughs of York Springs, East Berlin, Abbotstown and New Oxford

Harold R. Deardorff   51-3-04
P.O. Box 53, 16 E. Main St., Fairfield 17320
Box 325, Main St., Arendtsville 17303
    Townships of Highland, Hamiltonban, Liberty, Freedom; Boroughs of Fairfield, Carroll Valley

Harold R. Deardorff   51-3-04
Box 325, Main St., Arendtsville 17303
    Townships of Butler, Franklin and Menallen; Boroughs of Arendtsville, Biglerville and Bendersville

ALLEGHENY COUNTY
FIFTH JUDICIAL DISTRICT
District Justices

Donald H. Presutti, Esq.   05-2-01
617 Lincoln Avenue, Pittsburgh 15202
    Townships of Kilbuck and Ohio; Boroughs of Ben Avon, Ben Avon Heights, Emsworth, Bellevue and Avalon

Mark B. Devlin   05-2-02
439 Perry Highway, Pittsburgh 15229
    Township of Ross; Borough of West View

James H. Bowen   05-2-03
1330 Evergreen Avenue, Pittsburgh 15209
    Township of Shaler; Borough of Etna

Raymond L. Casper   05-2-04
707 Main Street, Pittsburgh 15215
    Townships of Indiana and O'Hara; Boroughs of Aspinwall, Blawnox, Sharpsburg and Fox Chapel

Anthony F. Clark   05-2-05
53 Garfield Street, Natrona 15065
    Townships of Harrison and Fawn; Boroughs of Brackenridge and Tarentum

Rinaldo J. Secola   05-2-06
15 Duff Rd., Pittsburgh 15235
    Township of Penn Hills

Eugene B. Yarnel   05-2-07
304 Jonnet Bldg., 4099 William Penn Highway, Monroeville 15146
    Boroughs of Monroeville and Pitcairn

Elverda J. Daw   05-2-08
110 Peffer Road, Turtle Creek 15145
    Township of Wilkins; Boroughs of Churchill, Forest Hills, Edgewood and Chalfant

Betty Lloyd   05-2-09
300 Rankin Blvd., Braddock 15104
    Boroughs of Braddock, North Braddock, Swissvale, Rankin and Braddock Hills

James B. Richard   05-2-10
612 S. Trenton Ave., Pittsburgh 15221
    Borough of Wilkinsburg

Georgina G. Franci   05-2-11
802 Lincoln Hwy., North Versailles 15137
    Township of North Versailles; Boroughs of East McKeesport, Wall, Wilmerding, Trafford (Allegheny Co.), East Pittsburgh and Turtle Creek

Ralph C. Freedman, Jr.   05-2-12
8150 Perry Hwy., Pittsburgh 15237
    Townships of McCandless, Marshall; Boroughs of Bradford Woods and Franklin Park

Howard D. Lindberg   05-2-13
339 Fifth Ave., McKeesport 15132
    City of McKeesport

Albert V. Belan   05-2-14
1800 Homeville Rd., West Mifflin 15122
    City of Duquesne; Boroughs of West Mifflin, Whitaker and Dravosburg

Richard J. Terrick 05-2-15
304-306 E. 8th Ave., Homestead 15120
    Boroughs of West Homestead, Homestead and Munhall

Mary Grace Boyle 05-2-16
Old S. Park Hosp. Bldg., Buffalo Dr., Library 15129
    Township of South Park; Boroughs of Jefferson and Pleasant Hills

Jules C. Melograne, Esq. 05-2-17
3609 Library Rd., Pittsburgh 15234
    Township of Baldwin; Boroughs of Whitehall and Castle Shannon

Robert R. Graff, Esq. 05-2-18
3505 Brownsville Rd., Pittsburgh 15227
    Boroughs of Baldwin and Brentwood

William J. Ivill, Esq. 05-2-19
710 Washington Rd., Pittsburgh 15228
    Township of Mt. Lebanon; Borough of Dormont

William D. Martin, Esq. 05-2-20
Bethel Pk., Mun. Bldg., 5100 W. Library Ave., Bethel Park 15102
    Borough of Bethel Park

Elaine M. McGraw 05-2-21
275 Millers Run Road, Bridgeville 15017
    Townships of Collier and South Fayette; Boroughs of Bridgeville and Heidelberg

Gary M. Zyra, Esq. 05-2-22
301 Lindsay Rd. Carnegie 15106
    Township of Scott; Borough of Greentree

Dennis R. Joyce, Esq. 05-2-23
11 East Crafton Ave., Crafton 15205
    Boroughs of Carnegie, Rosslyn Farms, Crafton, Ingram and Thornburg

Walter V. Casasanta 05-2-25
923 Fifth Ave., Coraopolis 15108
    Townships of Moon, Crescent and Neville; Borough of Coraopolis

Paul Komaromy, Jr. 05-2-26
5909 Smithfield St., McKeesport 15135
    Townships of Elizabeth and Forward; Boroughs of Elizabeth and West Elizabeth

Nicholas A. Diulus 05-2-27
218 Atwood St., Pittsburgh 15213
    City of Pittsburgh, Ward 4

Jacob H. Williams 05-2-28
West Penn Bldg., 14 Wood St., Pittsburgh 15219
    City of Pittsburgh, Wards 1,2,3,5

Douglas W. Reed, Esq. 05-2-29
4502 Liberty Ave., Pittsburgh 15224
    City of Pittsburgh, Wards 7,8

John R. DeAngelis, Esq. 05-2-31
5906 Bryant St., Pittsburgh 15206
    City of Pittsburgh, Wards 10,11

Lee J. Mazur, Esq. 05-2-32
4555 New Texas Rd., Pittsburgh 15239-1193
    Borough of Plum

Robert E. Tucker,Esq. 05-2-35
1831 Murray Ave., Pittsburgh 15217
    City of Pittsburgh, Ward 14

James J. Hanley 05-2-36
4375 Murray Ave., Pittsburgh 15217
    City of Pittsburgh, Wards 15,31

Nancy L. Longo 05-2-37
1320 East Carson St., Pittsburgh 15203
    City of Pittsburgh, Wards 16,17

Charles A. McLaughlin 05-2-38
736 Brookline Blvd., Pittsburgh 15226
    City of Pittsburgh, Ward 19

Charles M. Morrissey 05-2-40
1025 Western Ave., Pittsburgh 15233
    City of Pittsburgh, Wards 21,22,23,24,25

Bernard J. Regan 05-2-42
3872 Perrysville Ave., Pittsburgh 15214
    City of Pittsburgh, Wards 26,27

John E. Swearingen 05-2-43
5538 Steubenville Pike, McKees Rocks 15136
    City of Pittsburgh, Ward 28; Townships of Kennedy and Robinson; Borough of Pennsbury

Regis C. Welsh, Jr., Esq. 05-2-46
4773 Rt. 8, Barrister Ct., Allison Park 15101
    Townships of Pine, Richland and Hampton

James E. Russo 05-3-02
190 Ohio River Blvd., Box 153, Leetsdale 15056
    Townships of Aleppo and Leet; Boroughs of Leetsdale, Edgeworth, Osborne, Sewickley Hills, Sewickley Heights, Sewickley, Bell Acres, Haysville and Glenfield

Arthur Sabulsky 05-3-03
3 Beta Drive, Pittsburgh 15238
    Townships of Harmar and Springdale; Boroughs of Cheswick and Springdale

Suzanne R. Blaschak 05-3-04
P.O. Box 401, Main St., Russellton 15076-0401
    Townships of East Deer, Frazer and West Deer

Arthur P. Conn 05-3-05
1501 Lincoln Way, McKeesport 15131
    Township of South Versailles; Boroughs of White Oak and Versailles

Mary Anne Cercone 05-3-06
907 Valley Street, McKees Rocks 15136
    Township of Stowe; Borough of McKees Rocks

Andrew Kurta 05-3-07
539 Monogahela Ave., Glassport 15045
    Boroughs of Port Vue, Liberty, Glassport and Lincoln

Sarge Fiore 05-3-09
416 St. Clair Ave., Clairton 15025
    City of Clairton

Eileen H. Ambrose 05-3-10
3718 Penn Ave., Pittsburgh 15201
    City of Pittsburgh, Wards 6, 9

Edward A. Tibbs 05-3-11
1013 Lincoln Ave., Pittsburgh 15206
    City of Pittsburgh, Ward 12

Helen V. Hull   05-3-12
566 Brushton Ave., Pittsburgh 15208
    City of Pittsburgh, Ward 13

Regis C. Nairn, Esq.   05-3-13
635 Hillsboro Street, Pittsburgh 15204
    City of Pittsburgh, Ward 20

Leonard W. Boehm   05-3-14
1136 Brownsville Rd., Pittsburgh 15210
    City of Pittsburgh, Wards 29, 32

Anna Marie Scharding   05-3-15
500 Brownsville Rd., Pittsburgh 15210
    City of Pittsburgh, Wards 18, 30; Borough of Mt. Oliver

Sally A. Edkins   05-3-16
1751 McLaughlin Run Road, Pittsburgh 15241
    Township of Upper St. Clair

Lee G. Peglow, Esq.   05-3-17
220 Main St., Imperial 15126
    Townships of Findlay and North Fayette; Boroughs of Oakdale and
    McDonald (Allegheny County part)

Richard K. McCarthy   05-4-01
517 Lincoln Ave., Pittsburgh 15209
    Township of Reserve; Borough of Millvale

Vacant   05-4-02
364 Plum St., Oakmont 15139
    Boroughs of Oakmont and Verona

City Magistrates for the
City of Pittsburgh

Joan O. Melvin
Chief Judge for the City of Pittsburgh
541 Public Safety Bldg., Pittsburgh 15219

Angela Marasco, Chief Clerk
Public Safety Bldg.
Pittsburgh 15219

Donald G. Turner, Esq.
Public Safety Bldg.
Pittsburgh 15219

Edward Borkowski
Public Safety Bldg.
Pittsburgh 15219

Linda Cobb
Public Safety Bldg.
Pittsburgh 15219

ARMSTRONG COUNTY
THIRTY-THIRD JUDICIAL DISTRICT
District Justices

Eugene W. Shaeffer   33-3-01
402 O'Conner St., P.O. Box 306, Ford City 16226
    Townships of Manor, Cadogan, North Buffalo and South Buffalo;
    Boroughs of Ford Cliff, Ford City, Manorville and Freeport

Homer Crytzer   33-3-02
Armsdale Admin. Bldg., P.O. Box 2, R.D. 5, Kittanning 16201
    Townships of Rayburn, East Franklin, West Franklin, Washington,
    Sugarcreek, Bradys Bend, Perry and Hovey; Boroughs of Kittanning,
    Applewold, Worthington and Parker City

Louis E. Milks   33-3-03
P.O. Box 582, Leechburg 15656
    Townships of Gilpin, Parks, Kiskiminetas and Bethel; Boroughs of
    Leechburg, North Apollo and Apollo

Samuel Goldstrohm   33-3-04
608 Main St., Rural Valley 16249
    Townships of Madison, Mahoning, Redbank, Pine, Boggs, Wayne,
    Cowanshannock, Plumcreek, Kittanning, Valley, South Bend and
    Burrell; Boroughs of South Bethlehem, Dayton, Rural Valley, Atwood
    and Elderton

BEAVER COUNTY
THIRTY-SIXTH JUDICIAL DISTRICT
District Justices

Hugo R. Iorfido   36-1-01
1010 State St., Baden 15005
    Township of Harmony; Boroughs of Ambridge and Baden

Milton H. Richeal   36-1-02
37th St. Ext., West Mayfield, Beaver Falls 15010
    City of Beaver Falls; Townships of Patterson and White; Boroughs of
    Fallston, Patterson Heights, Eastvale and West Mayfield

Peter J. Loschiavo   36-1-03
484 Franklin Ave., Aliquippa 15001
    Borough of Aliquipppa

Lewis E. Kirchner   36-2-01
1121 - 11th St., Conway 15027
    Townships of New Sewickley and Rochester; Boroughs of Economy,
    Freedom, Conway, Rochester and East Rochester

Vacant   36-2-02
Allencrest Western Ave., Beaver 15009
    Boroughs of Beaver, Bridgewater, Midland, Industry, Ohioville,
    Glasgow and Vanport

Arthur L. Schlemmer   36-3-01
1035 5th Ave., New Brighton 15066
    Townships of Pulaski, Daugherty, Franklin, Marion and North
    Sewickley; Boroughs of New Brighton and Ellwood City (2nd Ward)

Ross M. Keefer, Jr.   36-3-02
2760 Constitution Rd., Beaver Falls 15010
    Townships of South Beaver, Darlington and Chippewa; Boroughs of
    Darlington, Big Beaver, New Galilee, Homewood and Koppel

Joseph V. Lakas   36-3-03
1093 Brodhead Rd., Monaca 15061
    Townships of Center, Potter, Raccoon and Greene; Boroughs of
    Monaca, Hookstown, Georgetown and Shippingport

Stephen D. Mihalic   36-3-04
1955 Maratta Rd., Aliquippa 15001
    Townships of Independence, Hanover and Hopewell; Boroughs of
    Frankfort Springs and South Heights

BEDFORD COUNTY
FIFTY-SEVENTH JUDICIAL DISTRICT
District Justices

Charles D. Ferguson   57-3-01
P.O. Box 58, Schellsburg 15559
     Townships of Union, Kimmell, Lincoln, King, West St. Clair, Napier, Harrison, Juniata and Londonderry; Boroughs of Pleasantville, New Paris, Schellsburg, Manns Choice and Hyndman

H. Cyril Bingham, Jr.   57-3-02
R.D. 5, Box 355, Bedford 15522
     Townships of Bedford, East St. Clair, Colerain and Cumberland Valley; Boroughs of Bedford, St. Clairsville and Rainsburg

Charles O. Guyer   57-3-03
Front & Mifflin Sts., Hopewell 16650
     Townships of Bloomfield, South Woodbury, Woodbury, Liberty, Hopewell and Broad Top; Boroughs of Woodbury, Saxton, Coaldale and Hopewell

Marion L. Morgret   57-3-04
State St., Everett 15537
     Townships of Snake Spring, West Providence, East Providence, Monroe, Southampton and Mann; Borough of Everett

BERKS COUNTY
TWENTY-THIRD JUDICIAL DISTRICT
District Justices

James M. Korch   23-1-01
2800 Shillington Rd., Box 2744, Sinking Spring 19608-0741
     Township of Spring; Boroughs of Sinking Spring and Adamstown

Felix V. Stacherski   23-2-01
130 Belvedere Ave., Reading 19611-2039
     City of Reading, Wards 1, 4, 5, and 18

Albert J. Gaspari   23-1-02
744 Franklin St., Reading 19602-1109
     City of Reading, Wards 2, 3, 10, and 16

Walley Scott   23-1-03
123 N. 8th St., Reading 19601-3609
     City of Reading, Wards 6, 7, 8, 9, and 11

Barbara A. Clark   23-1-04
1231-1233 Greenwich St., Reading 19604-2646
     City of Reading, Wards 12, 13, and 17

O. Andrew Farrara   23-1-05
700 Schuylkill Ave., Reading 19601-2335
     City of Reading, Wards 14, 15, and 19

Doris M. Dorminy   23-1-06
5400 Leesport Ave., Temple 19560-1248
     Township of Muhlenberg; Boroughs of Temple and Laureldale

John F. Dougherty   23-2-02
2320 Highland St., Box 2744, West Lawn 19609-0741
     Boroughs of Wyomissing, West Reading, Wyomissing Hills and West Lawn

Phyllis J. Kowalski   23-2-03
107 N. 23rd St., Mt. Penn, Reading 19606-1994
     Townships of Exeter and Lower Alsace; Boroughs of Mt. Penn and St. Lawrence

Charlotte F. Reber   23-2-04
310 W. Broad St., Shillington 19607-2402
     Township of Cumru; Boroughs of Kenhorst, Mohnton and Shillington

George L. Wenger   23-3-01
113 E. Main St., Birdsboro 19508-2095
     Townships of Robeson, Caernarvon, Union, Brecknock and Amity; Borough of Birdsboro

Roland H. Schock   23-3-02
P.O. Box 36, Route 73
Colebrookdale Twp. Bldg., Boyertown 19512-0036
     Townships of Earl, Douglass, Colebrookdale, Washington and Hereford; Boroughs of Boyertown, Bechtelsville and Bally

Wallace W. Wagonseller   23-3-03
Rt. 73, P.O. Box 36, Oley 19547-0018
     Townships of Longswamp, Rockland, District, Pike and Oley; Borough of Topton

Gail Greth   23-3-04
120 S. Richmond St., Fleetwood 19522-1514
     Townships of Maxatawny, Richmond, Ruscombmanor and Alsace; Boroughs of Kutztown, Lyons and Fleetwood

Douglas N. Heydt   23-3-05
R.D. 1 - Box 247, Leesport 19533-9743
     Townships of Maidencreek, Ontelaunee, Bern and Centre; Boroughs of Leesport and Centerport

Gloria N. Stitzel   23-3-06
407 S. 4th St., Hamburg 19526-1305
     Townships of Windsor, Perry, Albany, Greenwich and Tilden; Boroughs of Hamburg, Shoemakersville and Lenhartsville

Laura A. Keener   23-3-07
Main Street, Strausstown 19559-0224
     Townships of Penn, Upper Bern, Upper Tulpehocken, Bethel, Jefferson and Tulpehocken; Boroughs of Bernville and Strausstown

Opal W. Bodanza   23-3-08
154 E. Penn Ave., Robesonia 19551-1528
     Townships of Marion, North Heidelberg, Heidelberg, Lower Heidelberg and South Heidelberg; Boroughs of Womelsdorf, Robesonia and Wernersville

BLAIR COUNTY
TWENTY-FOURTH JUDICIAL DISTRICT
District Justices

Joseph Moran   24-1-01
1117-19 9th Ave., Altoona 16602
     City of Altoona, Wards 2, 3, 4, 5, 9 and 11

Todd Kelly   24-1-02
1117-19 9th Ave., Altoona 16602
     City of Altoona, Wards 6, 12 and 14

William G. Camberg   24-1-03
1117-19 9th Ave., Altoona 16602
     City of Altoona, Wards 1, 7, 8, 10 and 13

John Greene   24-3-01
1100 Logan Ave., Tyrone 16686
    Townships of Antis, Snyder and Tyrone (Part); Boroughs of Bellwood and Tyrone

Patrick T. Jones   24-3-02
Box 372, R.D. 2, Canan Station School, Altoona 16603-9316
    Townships of Allegheny, Logan and Tyrone (Part); Boroughs of Duncansville and Tunnehill (Part)

Frederick L. Klepser   24-3-03
Highland Hall Annex, Hollidaysburg 16648
    Townships of Blair, Catherine, Frankstown and Woodbury; Boroughs of Hollidaysburg, Newry and Williamsburg

Denver K. Ake   24-3-04
230 Spang St., Roaring Spring 16673
    Townships of Freedom, Greenfield, Huston, Juniata, North Woodbury and Taylor; Boroughs of Martinsburg and Roaring Spring

BRADFORD COUNTY
FORTY-SECOND JUDICIAL DISTRICT
District Justices

Jack Huffman, Jr.   42-3-01
35 Canton St., Troy 16947
    Townships of Wells, South Creek, Columbia, Springfield, Armenia, Canton, Granville and LeRoy; Boroughs of Sylvania, Troy, Canton and Alba

Fordham F. Wood   42-3-02
226 Desmond St. Sayre 18840
    Townships of Athens, Ridgebury and Litchfield; Boroughs of Athens, Sayre and South Waverly

James M. Cox   42-3-03
Bradford County Court House, Towanda 18848
    Townships of Overton, Albany, Franklin, Monroe, West Burlington, Burlington, Towanda, North Towanda, Smithfield and Ulster; Boroughs of New Albany, Monroe and Towanda

Daniel Aquilio, III   42-3-04
R.D. 2, Box 0, Wysox 18854
    Townships of Wilmot, Terry, Wyalusing, Tuscarora, Stevens, Asylum, Standing Stone, Herrick, Wysox, Rome, Pike, Orwell, Warren, Windham and Sheshequin; Boroughs of Wyalusing, Rome and LaRaysville

BUCKS COUNTY
SEVENTH JUDICIAL DISTRICT
District Justices

Catharine L. Ritter   07-1-01
2356 Galloway Rd., Bensalem 19020
    Townships of Bensalem - Lower East 1, 2, 3 and 4, Lower West 1 and 2, Lower Middle 1, 2, 3, 4 and 5, Upper West Upper 4

Michael J. Manto   07-1-02
3030 Bath Rd., Bristol 19007
    Township of Bristol, Wards 1 and 4; Borough of Bristol

Jennie I. Pekarski   07-1-03
3030 Bath Rd., Bristol 19007
    Township of Bristol, Wards 2, 3, 5, 6, and 10

Anne V. Huhn   07-1-04
7625 New Falls Rd., Levittown 19055
    Township of Bristol, Wards 7, 8, 9 and 11

Dorothy Ann Pollock   07-1-06
District Court Blvd., 1500 Desire Ave., Feasterville 19047
    Townships of Upper Southampton and Lower Southampton

Catherine Marks   07-1-07
389 W. Lincoln Hwy., Penndel 19047
    Townships of Bensalem - Upper 1, 2, 3, 5, 6, 7, 8, 9, Lower East 5, and Middletown - Upper 2, Lower 1; Boroughs of Langhorne, Langhorne Manor, Penndel and Hulmeville

Dominick C. Spadaccino   07-1-08
2661 Trenton Road, Levittown 19056
    Township of Middletown - Upper 1, Lower 2, 3, 4, 5, 6, 7, 8, 9, 10, 11, 12, and 13

James M. Kelly   07-1-09
Centennial Plaza, 202-6 Street Rd., Warminster 18974
    Township of Warminster; Borough of Ivyland

Dorothy Vislosky   07-1-10
9187 New Falls Rd., Fallsington 19054
    Township of Falls - Upper 1, 2, and 3

Anne E. Orazi   07-1-11
31 E. Cleveland Ave., Morrisville 19067
    Township of Lower Makefield; Boroughs of Yardley and Morrisville

Donald Nasshorn, Esq.   07-2-01
Rt. 332 & Terry Drive, Newtown 18940
    Townships of Newtown, Northampton, Wrightstown and Upper Makefield; Borough of Newtown

Oliver A. Groman   07-2-02
10 S. Clinton St., Doylestown 18901
    Townships of Doylestown, New Britain and Warrington; Boroughs of Chalfont, Doylestown and New Britain

J. Robert Hunsicker   07-2-03
80 N. Main St., Sellersville 18960
    Townships of Hilltown and West Rockhill; Boroughs of Perkasie, Sellersville, Telford and Silverdale

Kathryn L. Stump   07-2-05
515 S. West End Blvd., Quakertown 18951
    Townships of East Rockhill, Milford and Richland; Boroughs of Quakertown, Richlandtown and Trumbauersville

Joseph F. Basile   07-2-06
210 Main St., Tullytown 19007
    Township of Falls, Upper 4 District; Borough of Tullytown

Clyde C. Leaver, Jr.   07-3-01
3893 Rt. 202 N., Doylestown 18901
    Townships of Buckingham, Plumstead, Solebury and Warwick; Borough of New Hope

BUTLER COUNTY
FIFTIETH JUDICAL DISTRICT
District Justices

Vacant   50-1-01
County Office Annex, 710 Morten Ave., Room 101, Butler 16001
    City of Butler; Township of Butler

Robert Watson 50-3-01
306 E. Water St., Slippery Rock 16057
Townships of Worth, Slippery Rock, Franklin, Mercer, Center, Cherry, Clay, Brady, Marion, Muddycreek; Boroughs of Prospect, West Liberty, Portersville, Slippery Rock, West Sunbury, and Harrisville

Ruth E. Miller 50-3-02
P.O. Box 249, Chicora 16025-0249
Townships of Summit, Clearfield, Venango, Allegheny, Washington, Parker, Concord, Fairview, Oakland, and Donegal; Boroughs of Fairview, Karns City, Cherry Valley, Eau Claire, Bruin, Petrolia, Chicora and East Butler

Vacant 50-3-03
Borough Bldg., Main St., P.O. Box 463, Saxonburg 16056-0463
Townships of Penn, Middlesex, Clinton, Jefferson, Winfield and Buffalo; Borough of Saxonburg

Frank C. Wise 50-3-04
Borough Bldg., Wahl Ave., Evans City 16033
Townships of Lancaster, Jackson, Cranberry, Connoquenessing, Forward and Adams; Boroughs of Zelienople, Connoquenessing, Evans City, Mars, Valencia, Callery and Harmony

CAMBRIA COUNTY
FORTY-SEVENTH JUDICIAL DISTRICT
District Justices

Rick T. Farra 47-1-01
147 Clinton St., Johnstown 15901
City of Johnstown (by Neighborhood) Central Business District; Wds. 1, 2, 3, 4; Kernville, Wds. 5, 6; Conemaugh Borough, Wds. 9, 10; Woodvale, Ward 11; Prospect, Wds. 12, 13; Minersville, Ward 14; Cambria City, Wds. 15, 16; Morrellville, Wds. 18, 19; Oakhurst, Ward 20; Coopersdale, Ward 21; Township of Lower Yoder; Borough of Brownstown

James E. Mayer, Esq. 47-1-02
205 Suppes Ave., Johnstown 15902
City of Johnstown (by Neighborhood) Roxbury, Ward 8, Moxham, Ward 17; Township of Upper Yoder; Boroughs of Westmont, Conemaugh and Southmont

Julia Ann Rozum 47-1-03
1610 Bedford St., Johnstown 15902
Townships of Conemaugh and Stonycreek; Boroughs of East Conemaugh, Franklin, Daisytown, Dale, Ferndale, Lorain; City of Johnstown, Hornerstown, Ward 7 and Walnut Grove, Ward 17

Max F. Pavlovich 47-2-01
719 E. Oakmont Blvd., Johnstown 15904
Township of Richland; Boroughs of Geistown and Scalp Level

Stephen J. Yesenosky 47-3-01
1552 William Penn Ave., Conemaugh 15909
Townships of East Taylor, Jackson, Middle Taylor and West Taylor; Boroughs of Nanty Glo and Vintondale

Galen P. Decort 47-3-03
535 Main Street, Portage 15946
Townships of Portage, Summerhill, Washington; Boroughs of Cassandra, Lilly, Portage, and Wilmore

Kenneth Robine 47-3-04
718 2nd Street, Cresson 16630
Townships of Allegheny, Gallitzin, Cresson, and Munster; Boroughs of Gallitizin, Cresson, Sankertown, Loretto, Tunnelhill (part)

Anthony A. Carnicella 47-3-05
Hastings Boro Bldg., Hastings 16646
Townships of Elder, Susquehanna, and Barr; Boroughs of Barnesboro, Hastings, Patton and Spangler

William J. Shay 47-3-06
P.O. Box 22, Sidman 15955
Townships of Adams and Croyle; Boroughs of South Fork, Summerhill and Ehrenfield

Francis P. Brosius 47-3-07
722 E. Wm. Penn Hwy., Ebensburg 15931
Townships of Cambria, East Carroll, West Carroll and Blacklick; Boroughs of Ebensburg and Carrolltown

Alice M. Krug 47-3-08
Box 48, Ashville 16613
Townships of Chest, Clearfield, Dean, Reade and White; Boroughs of Ashville and Chest Springs

CAMERON COUNTY
FIFTY-NINTH JUDICIAL DISTRICT
District Justice

Alvin E. Brown 59-3-01
Cameron County Courthouse, Emporium 15834
Townships of Shippen, Portage, Lumber, Gibson and Grove; Boroughs of Emporium and Driftwood .

CARBON COUNTY
FIFTY-SIXTH JUDICIAL DISTRICT
District Justices

Edward M. Lewis 56-3-01
52 Broadway, Jim Thorpe 18229
Townships of Kidder, Penn Forest and Mahoning; Boroughs of Jim Thorpe, Lehighton and Weissport

Bruce F. Appleton 56-3-02
443 Delaware Ave., Palmerton 18071
Townships of Lower Towamensing, Towamensing, East Penn; Boroughs of Palmerton, Bowmanstown and Parryville

Irene M. Hudasky 56-3-03
171 W. Ridge St., Lansford 18232
Boroughs of Summit Hill, Lansford and Nesquehoning

Paul J. Hadzick 56-3-04
54 Broad St., Beaver Meadows 18216-0254
Townships of Lausanne, Lehigh, Packer and Banks; Boroughs of Weatherly, East Side and Beaver Meadows

CENTRE COUNTY
FORTY-NINTH JUDICIAL DISTRICT
District Justices

Clifford H. Yorks 49-2-01
137 S. Pugh St., State College 16801
Townships of College, Ferguson, Halfmoon and Patton; Borough of State College

Robert T. May 49-3-02
10 N. Spring St., Bellefonte 16823
Townships of Benner, Boggs, Spring, Union, Curtin, Howard, Liberty, Marion, Howard and Walker; Boroughs of Bellefonte, Milesburg, Unionville and Howard

Robert A. Shoff   49-3-03
Boro Bldg., 2nd Fl., Phillipsburg 16886-0095
6th St., Box 284, Snow Shoe 16874-0284
> Townships of Huston, Rush, Taylor, Worth, Burnside and Snow Shoe; Boroughs of Philipsburg, S. Philipsburg, Port Matilda and Snow Shoe

Vacant   49-3-04
R.D. 2, Box 61, Centre Hall 16828
> Townships of Gregg, Haines, Penn, Potter, Harris and Millheim; Borough of Centre Hall

CHESTER COUNTY
FIFTEENTH JUDICIAL DISTRICT
District Justices

Mitchell Crane   15-1-01
Barnard Bldg, Market St., & Westtown Rd., West Chester 19382
> Borough of West Chester

Armand A. Pomante   15-1-02
30 S. Valley Rd. - Suite 203, Paoli 19301
> Townships of Tredyffrin and Easttown

Paul L. Johnson   15-1-03
735 E. Lincoln Hwy., Coatesville 19320
> City of Coatesville; Township of Caln; Boroughs of Modena and South Coatesville

John T. Jeffers   15-2-01
221 Bridge St., Phoenixville 19460
> Townships of East Pikeland, Charlestown and Schuylkill; Borough of Phoenixville

Earl M. Heald   15-2-03
1101 Paoli Pike, West Chester 19380
> Townships of West Goshen, Birmingham, Westtown and Thornbury

John R. Blackburn, Jr.   15-2-05
28 S. Warren Ave., Malvern 19355
> Townships of Willistown and East Goshen; Borough of Malvern

C. Burtis Coxe   15-2-06
703 E. Lancaster Ave., Downingtown 19335
> Townships of East Caln, East Brandywine, East Bradford and West Bradford; Borough of Downingtown

Stanley Scott   15-2-07
446 Lancaster Ave., Frazer 19355
> Townships of West Pikeland, Uwchlan, Upper Uwchlan, West Whiteland, and East Whiteland

Robert G. Mull   15-3-01
Bucktown, R.D. 4, Rt. 23, Pottstown 19464
> Townships of North Coventry, South Coventry, East Coventry, Warwick, East Nantmeal, East Vincent and West Vincent; Borough of Spring City

Eugene J. DiFilippo, Jr   15-3-04
455-A Birch St., Kennett Square 19348
> Townships of Kennett, East Marlborough, West Marlborough, New Garden, Newlin, Pennsbury, Pocopson, London Britain and Franklin; Borough of Kennett Square

Donald C. Brown   15-3-05
113-115 S. Third St., Oxford 19363
> Townships of London Grove, Penn, Elk, East Nottingham, West Nottingham, Upper Oxford and Lower Oxford; Boroughs of West Grove, Avondale and Oxford

Susann E. Welsh   15-3-06
230 W. Main St., Honey Brook 19344
> Townships of Honeybrook, Wallace, West Brandywine, West Caln and West Nantmeal; Boroughs of Honey Brook and Elverson

Carl W. Henry   15-3-07
334 Strasburg Ave., Parkesburg 19365
> Townships of Valley, Londonderry, East Fallowfield, Sadsbury, West Sadsbury, West Fallowfield, and Highland; Boroughs of Atglen and Parkesburg

CLARION COUNTY
EIGHTEENTH JUDICIAL DISTRICT
District Justices

Alta Laverne Hamilton   18-3-01
Court House, Clarion 16214
> Townships of Clarion and Limestone; Boroughs of Clarion and Strattanville

Norman E. Heasley   18-3-02
R.D. 1, Shippenville 16254
> Townships of Farmington, Highland, Knox, Millcreek, Paint, Washington, Piney and Monroe; Borough of Sligo

Virginia C. Dibble   18-3-03
P.O. Box 519, Knox 16232
> Townships of Beaver, Licking, Perry, Salem, Ashland, Elk and Richland; Boroughs of Callensburg, Foxburg, St. Petersburg and Shippenville

Daniel P. George   18-3-04
237 Broad St., New Bethlehem 16242
> Townships of Madison, Porter, Redbank, Brady and Toby; Boroughs of East Brady, Hawthorn, New Bethlehem and Rimersburg

CLEARFIELD COUNTY
FORTY-SIXTH JUDICIAL DISTRICT
District Justices

Wesley J. Read   46-3-01
111 N. Brady St., DuBois 15801
> City of DuBois; Townships of Bloom, Brady, Huston, Penn, Pine, Sandy and Union; Boroughs of Falls Creek, Grampian and Troutville

William Daisher   46-3-02
416 Arnold Ave., Clearfield 16830
> Townships of Lawrence and Pike; Boroughs of Clearfield and Curwensville

Michael A. Rudella   46-3-03
P.O. Box 210, Kylertown 16847
> Townships of Boggs, Bradford, Cooper, Covington, Decatur, Girard, Goshen, Karthaus and Morris; Boroughs of Chester Hill, Osceola Mills and Wallaceton

Robert Vogle   46-3-04
Main St., Box 381, Coalport 16627
> Townships of Beccaria, Bell, Bigler, Burnside, Chest, Ferguson, Greenwood, Gulich, Jordan, Knox and Woodward; Boroughs of Brisbin, Burnside, Coalport, Glen Hope, Houtzdale, Irvona, Lumber City, Mahaffey, Newburg, New Washington, Ramey and Westover

CLINTON COUNTY
TWENTY-FIFTH JUDICIAL DISTRICT
District Justices

John B. Fraizer   25-3-01
151 Susquehanna Ave., Lock Haven 17745
> City of Lock Haven; Townships of Allison, Castanea, Colebrook, Crawford, Dunnstable, Gallagher, Pine Creek, Wayne and Woodward; Boroughs of Avis and Flemington

C. David Gilmore   25-3-02
P.O. Box 174, Mill Hall 17751
> Townships of Bald Eagle, Beech Creek, Green, Lamar, Logan and Porter; Boroughs of Beech Creek, Logantown and Mill Hall

Kevin R. Dwyer   25-3-03
130 3rd St., Renovo 17764
> Townships of Chapman, East Keating, Grugan, Leidy, Noyes and West Keating; Boroughs of Renovo and South Renovo

COLUMBIA COUNTY
TWENTY-SIXTH JUDICIAL DISTRICT
District Justices

Donna Coombe   26-2-01
1115 Old Berwick Rd., Bloomsburg 17815
> Townships of Bloomsburg, Montour and Scott

Delbert L. Pennypacker   26-3-01
Main St., Millville 17846
> Townships of Jackson, Sugarloaf, Benton, Pine, Greenwood, Orange, Mt. Pleasant, Madison, Hemlock and Fishingcreek; Boroughs of Benton, Stillwater, Millville and Orangeville

Vacant   26-3-02
210 W. 11th St., Berwick 18603
> Townships of Briar Creek, North Centre, South Centre; Boroughs of Berwick and Briar Creek

William L. Breech   26-3-03
304 Main St., Catawissa 17820
> Townships of Coyngham, Main, Catawissa, Franklin, Cleveland, Locust, Roaring Creek, Mifflin and Beaver; Boroughs of Catawissa, Ashland (part) and Centralia

CRAWFORD COUNTY
THIRTIETH JUDICIAL DISTRICT
District Justices

William D. Chisholm   30-2-01
984 Water St., Meadville 16335
> City of Meadville; Township of West Mead

Wayne E. Hanson   30-3-01
120 Erie St., P.O. Box 128, Linesville 16424
> Townships of Beaver, Spring, Conneaut, Summerhill, Pine, North Shenango, South Shenango, and West Shenango; Boroughs of Springboro, Conneautville and Linesville

Hubert E. Vogan   30-3-02
R.D. 9, Rt. 763A, Meadville 16335
> Townships of Summit, Sadsbury, East Fallowfield, Vernon, Union and Greenwood; Borough of Conneaut Lake

Robert J. Leonhart   30-3-03
182 Venango Ave., Cambridge Springs 16403
> Townships of Cussewago, Venango, Cambridge, Hayfield, Rockdale, Bloomfield, Richmond, Athens and Woodcock; Boroughs of Cambridge Springs, Saegertown, Blooming Valley, Woodcock and Venango

George W. Herzberger, III   30-3-04
106 S. Franklin St., Box 584, Cochranton 16314
> Townships of East Mead, Randolph, East Fairfield, Wayne and Fairfield; Borough of Cochranton

Ronald A. Cole, Sr.   30-3-06
106 E. Central Ave., Titusville 16354
> City of Titusville; Townships of Rome, Troy, Sparta, Steuben, and Oil Creek; Boroughs of Centerville, Spartansburg, Townville and Hydetown

CUMBERLAND COUNTY
NINTH JUDICIAL DISTRICT
District Justices

Robert B. Failor   09-1-01
1106 Carlisle Rd., Cedar Cliff Mall
Camp Hill 17011
> Township of Lower Allen; Boroughs of Shiremanstown, New Cumberland and Lemoyne

Edward J. Carl   09-1-02
1507 Market St., Camp Hill 17011
> Township of East Pennsboro; Boroughs of Camp Hill, West Fairview and Wormleysburg

Meade G. Lyons   09-2-01
112 W. High St., Carlisle 17013
> Township of North Middleton; Borough of Carlisle

Donald W. Daihl   09-3-01
R.D. 6, P.O. Box 361, Shippensburg 17257
> Townships of Hopewell, Shippensburg, Southampton and South Newton; Boroughs of Newburg and Shippensburg

Esther M. Cohick   09-3-02
17 S. High St., Newville 17241
> Townships of Upper Mifflin, Lower Mifflin, Upper Frankford, North Newton, West Pennsboro, Penn and Lower Frankford; Borough of Newville

Terry L. Keller   09-3-03
P.O. Box 167, 229 Mill St., Mt. Holly Springs 17065
> Townships of South Middleton, Dickinson and Cook; Borough of Mt. Holly Springs

Glenn R. Farner   09-3-04
5002 Lenker St., Mechanicsburg 17055
> Townships of Middlesex, Silver Spring and Hampden

Ronald E. Klair   09-3-05
1 S. Frederick St., Mechanicsburg 17055
> Townships of Upper Allen and Monroe; Borough of Mechanicsburg

DAUPHIN COUNTY
TWELFTH JUDICIAL DISTRICT
District Justices

Marlin E. Strohm   12-1-01
3540 N. Progress Ave., Harrisburg 17109
> Township of Susquehanna; Borough of Penbrook

Paul H. Hardy   12-1-02
2935 N. 7th St., Harrisburg 17110
> City of Harrisburg - Wards 10, 11, and 14

Joseph Solomon   12-1-03
1335 N. Front St., Harrisburg 17102
> City of Harrisburg - Wards 5, 6, 7, 12, and 15

Michael Stewart   12-1-04
112 Market St.,1st Fl., Harrisburg 17104
    City of Harrisburg - Wards 3, 4, 8, and 9

George Zozos   12-1-05
538 S. 29th St., Harrisburg 17104
    City of Harrisburg - Wards 1, 2, and 13

Mary E. Cross   12-2-01
1281 S. 28th St., Harrisburg 17111
    Townships of Swatara and Lower Swatara; Borough of Paxtang

Steven Semic   12-2-02
123 N. Front St., Steelton 17113
    Boroughs of Steelton and Highspire

William Heckman   12-2-03
28 N. Union St., Middletown 17057
    Townships of Londonderry and Conewago; Boroughs of Middletown
    and Royalton

Edward Williams   12-3-01
24 N. Callowhill St., Elizabethville 17023
    Townships of Upper Paxton, Mifflin, Washington, Lykens, Williams
    and Wiconisco; Boroughs of Millersburg, Berrysburg, Pillow,
    Elizabethville, Gratz, Lykens and Williamstown

Lawrence E. Alvord   12-3-02
206 Allegheny St., Dauphin 17018
    Townships of Halifax, Reed, Jackson, Wayne, Jefferson, Middle
    Paxton and Rush; Boroughs of Halifax and Dauphin

Samuel J. Magaro   12-3-03
7171 Allentown Blvd., Harrisburg 17112
    Townships of Lower Paxton and West Hanover

William P. Rathfon   12-3-04
475 West Governor Rd., Hershey 17033
    Townships of East Hanover, South Hanover and Derry; Borough of
    Hummelstown

DELAWARE COUNTY
THIRTY-SECOND JUDICIAL DISTRICT
District Justices

Charles G. Nistico, Esq.   32-1-20
Center City Bldg., 418 Ave. of the States, Chester 19013
    City of Chester - Wards 1, 2, and 3

William L. Brown, Jr.   32-1-21
Center City Bldg., 418 Ave. of the States, Chester 19013
    City of Chester - Wards 4, 5, 6, 7 and 8

Garland W. Anderson   32-1-22
Center City Bldg., 418 Ave. of the States, Chester 19013
    City of Chester - Wards 9, 10 and 11

William J. Dittert, Jr.   32-1-23
100 Clifton Ave., Collingdale 19023
    Boroughs of Collingdale and Sharon Hill

Robert W. Burton, Esq.   32-1-24
710 West Chester Pike, Havertown 19083
    Townships of Haverford - Wards 1, 3, 4, and 9

Gerald C. Liberace, Esq.   32-1-25
710 West Chester Pike, Havertown 19083
    Township of Haverford - Wards 2, 5, 6, 7 and 8

John J. Perfetti   32-1-26
7 S. Springfield Rd., Clifton Heights 19018
    Boroughs of Aldan, Clifton Heights and Lansdowne

Maureen Fitzpatrick, Esq.   32-1-27
Marple Newtown Jr., H.S., 30 Media Line Rd.,
1st Fl., Newton Sq. 19073
    Township of Marple and Broomall

Joseph V. Gessler   32-1-28
349 W. Baltimore Ave., Media 19063
    Townships of Nether Providence; Boroughs of Swarthmore and
    Media

Beverly H. Foster   32-1-29
771 E. Lancaster Ave., Villanova 19085
    Township of Radnor and Wayne

Vincent D. Gallagher, Jr.   32-1-30
Ridley Twnshp. Mun. Bldg.
Morton & McDade Blvd., Folsom 19033
    Township of Ridley - Wards 2, 3, 5, 7, and 8

Gregory M. Mallon, Esq.   32-1-31
1207 Chester Pike, Crum Lynne 19022
    Township of Ridley - Wards 1, 4, 6 and 9; Boroughs of Eddystone and
    Rutledge

Joseph L. DiPietro   32-1-32
50 Powell Rd., Springfield 19064
    Township of Springfield; Borough of Morton

Michael P. Ballezzi, Esq.   32-1-33
Upper Darby Magisterial Courts, Barclay Sq. Bldg.
1550 Garrett Rd., Upper Darby 19082
    Township of Upper Darby - Wards 1 through 5; Borough of Millbourne

Michael G. Cullen, Esq.   32-1-34
Upper Darby Magisterial Courts, Barclay Sq. Bldg.
1550 Garrett Rd., Upper Darby 19082
    Township of Upper Darby - Wards 6, 7, 8, 10, and 11

Albert J. Berardocco   32-1-35
Upper Darby Magisterial Courts, Barclay Bldg.
1550 Garrett Rd., Upper Darby 19082
    Township of Upper Darby - Wards 9, 12 through 15

George W. Paige   32-1-36
417-19 Marionville Rd., P.O. Box 2185, Aston 19014
    Townships of Lower Chichester and Upper Chichester; Boroughs of
    Marcus Hook, Linwood and Trainer

Thomas J. Lacey, Esq.   32-2-37
100 Clifton Ave., Collingdale 19023
    Boroughs of Darby and Colwyn

Henry J. Silva   32-2-38
417-19 Marionville Rd., P.O. Box 2185, Aston 19014
    Township of Aston; Borough of Chester Heights

C. Walter McCray, Jr.   32-2-39
Edgemont & Brookhaven Rd., Brookhaven 19015
    Township of Chester; Borough of Brookhaven

Leonard McDevitt   32-2-40
155 Elmwood Ave., Folcroft 19032
    Township of Darby

Anthony M. Truscello 32-2-41
155 Elmwood Ave., Folcroft 19032
    Township of Tinicum; Borough of Folcroft and Essington

Peter R. Tozer, Esq. 32-2-42
155 Elmwood Ave., Folcroft 19032
    Boroughs of Glenolden and Norwood

David T. Videon, Esq. 32-2-43
30 Media Line Rd., Newtown Sq. 19073
    Township of Newtown

Robert M. Shaffer 32-2-44
119 N. Swarthmore Ave., P.O. Box 129, Ridley Park 19078
    Boroughs of Prospect Park and Ridley Park

Kenneth N. Miller 32-2-45
2808 Edgemont Ave., Parkside 19015
    Boroughs of Upland and Parkside

Dewey LaRosa 32-2-46
211 W. Rose Tree Rd., Media 19063
    Township of Upper Providence; Borough of Rose Valley and Media

Francis J. Murnaghan, Esq. 32-2-47
100 Clifton Ave., Collingdale 19023
    Borough of Yeadonand East Landsdowne

Paul Ewaka 32-2-48
27 S. Pennell Rd., P.O. Box 93, Lima 19037
    Township of Middletown and Lima

Leon J. Mascaro 32-2-49
Concord Village Shops
Baltimore Pike and Cheyney Rd., Concordville 19331
    Townships of Birmingham, Concord and Bethel

Clarence B. Nesbitt, Jr. 32-4-01
1176 N. Middletown Rd., P.O. Box 179, Gradyville 19039
    Townships of Edgmont and Thornbury

ELK COUNTY
FIFTY-NINTH JUDICIAL DISTRICT
District Justices

Daniel T. Brahaney, Esq. 59-3-02
536 Market St., Johnsonburg 15845
    Townships of Millstone, Springcreek, Highland, Horton, Ridgway and Jones

Elizabeth J. Freidl 59-3-03
808 S. Michael Rd., P.O. Box 548, St. Marys 15857
    Townships of Benzinger, Fox, Jay and Benezette; Borough of St. Marys

ERIE COUNTY
SIXTH JUDICIAL DISTRICT
District Justices

Carmie Hogan Munsch 06-1-01
657 E. 5th St., Erie 16507
    City of Erie - Ward 1

Kathryn L. Pohl 06-1-02
913 Parade St., Erie 16503
    City of Erie - Ward 2

John A. Vendetti 06-1-03
708 W. 18th St., Erie 16502
    City of Erie - Ward 3

Rosalind Kightlinger 06-1-04
937 E. 26th St., Erie 16504
    City of Erie - Ward 5

Larry R. Fabrizi 06-1-05
657 W. 26th St., Erie 16508
    City of Erie - Ward 6

Arthur Joseph Weindorf 06-2-01
426 Cherry St., Erie 16502
    City of Erie - Ward 4

Charles R. Wise 06-2-02
3524 W. 26th St., Erie 16506
    Township of Millcreek

Joyce K. Dunn 06-2-03
4112 Main St., Lawrence Park 16511
    Township of Lawrence Park; Borough of Wesleyville

Patsy A. Nichols 06-2-04
103 E. Main St., Corry 16407
    City of Corry

Peter P. Nakoski, Jr. 06-3-01
211 E. Preston Ave., Erie 16511
    Township of Harborcreek

Frank Abate, Jr. 06-3-02
10300 W. Main Rd., North East 16428
    Township of North East; Borough of North East

Charles F. Smith 06-3-03
7910 Wattsburg Rd., Erie 16509
    Townships of Greenfield, Greene, Venango and Amity; Borough of Wattsburg

Mary Jane Fuller 06-3-04
29 S. Main St., Union City 16438
    Townships of Union, Concord and Wayne; Boroughs of Union City and Elgin

James J. Dwyer 06-3-05
201 High St., Waterford 16441
    Townships of Summit (Part), Waterford and LeBoef; Boroughs of Waterford and Mill Village

Ronald E. Stuck 06-3-06
8952 W. Main St., McKean 16426
    Townships of Franklin, McKean, Washington and Fairview; Boroughs of McKean, Fairview

Robert Saxton, Jr. 06-3-08
P.O. Box 5244, Rt. 215, East Springfield 16411
    Townships of Springfield, Conneaut, Girard and Elk Creek; Boroughs of East Springfield, Albion, Cranesville, Girard, Platea, and Lake City

FAYETTE COUNTY
FOURTEENTH JUDICIAL DISTRICT
District Justices

Lawrence Blair 14-1-01
32 Morgantown St., Uniontown 15401
    City of Uniontown

Charles F. Hartz 14-1-02
601 W. Crawford Ave., Connellsville 15425
    City of Connellsville; Township of Connellsville; Borough of South Connellsville

Rick Vernon   14-2-01
253 South Mt. Vernon Ave., Uniontown 15401
    Townships of South Union and Menallen

Eugene J. Simon   14-2-02
600 N. Gallatin Ave., Uniontown 15401
    Township of North Union

Oliver F. Battaglini   14-2-03
Second and High Sts., Brownsville 15417
    Townships of Brownsville and Luzerne; Borough of Brownsville

Paul Shenal   14-3-01
207 South Main St., Masontown 15461
    Townships of German and Nicholson; Borough of Masontown

Randy S. Abraham   14-3-02
7 N. Morgantown St., Fairchance 15436
    Townships of Georges and Springhill; Boroughs of Smithfield, Fairchance and Point Marion

Anthony A. Shuli   14-3-03
Capuzzi Bldg., P.O. Box 711, Republic 15475
    Townships of Redstone and Franklin

Jesse J. Cramer   14-3-04
207 Main St., P.O. Box 476, Fayette City 15438
    Townships of Washington and Jefferson; Boroughs of Belle Vernon, Fayette City and Newell

Michael Rubish   14-3-05
R.D. 1, Box 90 E, Perryopolis 15473
    Townships of Perry and Upper Tyrone; Boroughs of Perryopolis, Dawson and Lower Tyrone

Dwight Shaner   14-3-06
R.D. 1, Box 14BB, Dunbar 15431
    Township of Dunbar; Boroughs of Dunbar and Vanderbilt

Robert Breakiron   14-3-07
P.O. Box 2318, Connellsville 15425
    Townships of Bullskin, Saltlick and Springfield

Harry L. Glisan   14-3-08
U.S. 40 & Rt. 381 North, Farmington 15437
    Townships of Wharton, Stewart and Henry Clay; Boroughs of Ohiopyle and Markleysburg

FOREST COUNTY
THIRTY-SEVENTH JUDICIAL DISTRICT
District Justices

Michael Lee Fedora   37-4-02
P.O. Box 427, 150 Elm St., Tionesta 16353
    Townships of Harmony, Hickory and Tionesta; Borough of Tionesta

Curtis E. Carbaugh   37-4-03
108 S. Forest St., Box 425, Marienville 16239
    Townships of Kingsley, Green, Jenks, Barnett and Howe

FRANKLIN COUNTY
THIRTY-NINTH JUDICIAL DISTRICT
District Justices

J. William Stover   39-2-01
120 Lincoln Way East, Chambersburg 17201
    Township of Hamilton; Borough of Chambersburg

Bruce C. Ingels   39-3-02
57 E. Main St., Waynesboro 17268
    Townships of Washington and Quincy; Boroughs of Waynesboro and Mont Alto

James L. Campbell   39-3-03
3629 Orrstown Rd., Orrstown 17244
    Townships of Fannett, Metal, Lurgan, Southampton and Letterkenny; Boroughs of West End Shippensburg and Orrstown

Larry K. Meminger   39-3-04
181 Franklin Farm Lane, Chambersburg 17201
    Townships of Greene and Guilford

John R. Ommert   39-3-05
P.O. Box 262, Greencastle 17225
    Township of Antrim; Borough of Greencastle

David E. Hawbaker   39-3-06
113 S. Main St., Mercersburg 17236
    Townships of Peters, Montgomery, Warren and St. Thomas; Borough of Mercersburg

FULTON COUNTY
THIRTY-NINTH JUDICIAL DISTRICT
District Justices

Linda Hershey   39-4-01
P.O. Box 8, Fort Littleton 17223
    Townships of Wells, Taylor, Dublin and Licking Creek

Dorothy S. Brantner   39-4-02
208 N. 2nd St., McConnellsburg 17233
    Townships of Todd and Ayr; Borough of McConnellsburg

Carol Jean Johnson   39-4-03
P.O. Box171, Needmore 17238
    Townships of Union, Bethel, Thompson, Brush Creek and Belfast

GREENE COUNTY
THIRTEENTH JUDICIAL DISTRICT
District Justices

John C. Watson   13-3-01
121 E. High St., Waynesburg 15370
    Townships of Aleppo, Centre, Freeport, Gilmore, Gray, Morris, Richhill, Springhill, and Wayne; Borough of Waynesburg

Anne R. Hughes   13-3-02
R.D. 2, Box 50A, Waynesburg 15370
    Townships of Morgan, Franklin, Jefferson, Perry, Washington and Whiteley; Boroughs of Clarksville and Jefferson

Emil Bertugli   13-3-03
106 West George St., Carmichaels 15320
    Townships of Cumberland, Dunkard, Greene and Monogahela; Boroughs of Carmichaels, Greensboro and Rices Landing

HUNTINGDON COUNTY
TWENTIETH JUDICIAL DISTRICT
District Justices

Daniel S. Davis   20-3-01
Box 361, Alexandria 16611
    Townships of Barree, Franklin, Logan, Morris, Porter, Spruce Creek, Warriors Mark and West; Boroughs of Alexandria, Birmingham and Petersburg

James H. Kyper   20-3-02
231 Washington St., Huntingdon 16652
    Townships of Henderson, Hopewell, Jackson, Juniata, Lincoln, Miller, Oneida, Penn, Smithfield and Walker; Boroughs of Huntingdon and Marklesburg

Michael J. Colyer   20-3-03
50 S. Division St., P.O. Box 386, Mount Union 17066
    Townships of Brady, Shirley and Union; Boroughs of Mapleton, Mill
    Creek, Mount Union and Shirleysburg

N. Dale Wakefield   20-3-04
Cromwell St., Orbisonia 17243
    Townships of Carbon, Clay, Cromwell, Dublin, Springfield, Tell, Todd
    and Wood; Boroughs of Broad Top City, Cassville, Coalmont, Dudley,
    Orbisonia, Rockhill, Saltillo, Shade Gap and Three Springs

INDIANA COUNTY
FORTIETH JUDICIAL DISTIRCT
District Justices

Richard G. Orendorff   40-2-01
8th & Water Sts., Indiana 15701
    Township of White; Borough of Indiana

Geraldine M. Wilkins   40-3-01
6th & Franklin Sts., Clymer 15728
    Townships of West Mahoning, North Mahoning, Canoe, Banks, South
    Mahoning, East Mahoning, Grant, Montgomery, Washington, Rayne,
    Cherryhill, Pine and Green; Boroughs of Cherry Tree, Glen Campbell,
    Smicksburg, Plumville, Marion Center, Creekside, Clymer and Ernest

Michael K. Steffee   40-3-02
340 N. Main St., Homer City 15748
    Townships of Armstrong, Center, Brush Valley and Buffington;
    Boroughs of Shelocta and Homer City

Angelo C. Cravotta   40-3-03
12 W. Market St., P.O. Box 73, Blairsville 15717
    Townships of Young, Conemaugh, Blacklick, Burrell, West Wheatfield
    and East Wheatfield; Boroughs of Jacksonville, Saltsburg, Blairsville

JEFFERSON COUNTY
FIFTY-FOURTH JUDICIAL DISTRICT
District Justices

Guy M. Lester   54-3-01
East Mahoning St., Punxsutawney 15767
    Townships of Bell, Gaskill, McCalmont, Oliver, Perry, Porter and
    Young; Boroughs of Big Run, Punxsutawney and Timblin

Bernard E. Hetrick   54-3-02
315 Main St., Reynoldsville 15851
    Townships of Snyder, Henderson, Winslow and Washington;
    Boroughs of Brockway, Falls Creek, Sykesville and Reynoldsville

George B. Miller   54-3-03
Jefferson County Services Center
R. D. 5, Brookville 15825
    Townships of Barnett, Beaver, Clover, Eldred, Knox, Pinecreek, Polk,
    Ringgold, Rose, Union and Warsaw; Boroughs of Brookville, Corsica,
    Summerville and Worthville

JUNIATA COUNTY
FORTY-FIRST JUDICIAL DISTRICT
District Justices

Marian S. Mertz   41-3-01
Court House Annex, Mifflintown 17059
    Townships of Fermanagh, Fayette, Delaware, Monroe, Greenwood
    and Susquehanna; Boroughs of Mifflintown and Thompsontown

Betty G. Gingrich   41-3-02
Community Bldg., Port Royal 17082
    Townships of Milford, Walker, Turbett, Beale, Spruce Hill, Tuscarora
    and Lack; Boroughs of Mifflin and Port Royal

LACKAWANNA COUNTY
FORTY-FIFTH JUDICIAL DISTRICT
District Justices

Vacant   45-1-01
312 N. Main Ave., Old Forge 18518
    Boroughs of Old Forge, Taylor and Moosic

Carmen D. Minora, Esq.   45-1-02
Lackawanna Co. Admin. Bldg.
200 Adams Ave., Scranton 18510
    City of Scranton - Wards 9, 10, 16 and 17

Francis Eagen, Esq.   45-1-03
201 Prospect Ave., Scranton 18505
    City of Scranton - Wards 11, 12, 19, 20, and 24

Eugene T. Cadden   45-1-04
232 Railroad Ave., Scranton 18504
    City of Scranton - Wards 5, 6, 14, 15, 18, and 22

Daniel J. Kelleher, Esq.   45-1-05
1600 Farr St., Scranton 18504
    City of Scranton - Wards 2, 4, 7, and 21

James P. Kennedy   45-1-06
622 E. Market St., Scranton 18507
    City of Scranton - Wards 1, 3, 13, and 23

Michael S. Polizzi   45-1-07
425 S. Blakely St., Dunmore 18512
    Borough of Dunmore

John V. Pieski, Esq.   45-1-08
1057 Main St., Dickson City 18519
    Boroughs of Throop, Dickson City and Olyphant

Ferdinand A. Grunik   45-2-01
122 Constitution Ave., Jessup 18434
    Boroughs of Blakely and Jessup

George E. Clark, Jr.   45-3-01
415 S. State St., Clarks Summit 18411
    Townships of Benton, LaPlume, North Abington, West Abington,
    Glenburn, Abington, South Abington, Newton and Ransom;
    Boroughs of Dalton, Clarks Summit and Clarks Green

John J. Mercuri   45-3-02
115 N. Main St., Moscow 18444
    Townships of Jefferson, Roaring Brook, Elmhurst, Madison,
    Springbrook, Covington, Clifton and Lehigh; Borough of Moscow

Mary A. McAndrew   45-3-03
33 S. Main St., Carbondale 18407
    City of Carbondale; Townships of Fell, Greenfield and Carbondale;
    Borough of Vandling

Donald A. Yurgosky   45-3-04
299 S. Washington Ave., Jermyn 18433
    Township of Scott; Boroughs of Archbald, Jermyn and Mayfield

LANCASTER COUNTY
SECOND JUDICIAL DISTRICT
District Justices

Earle M. Schmuckie   02-1-01
225 W. King St., Lancaster 17603
    City of Lancaster - Wards 4 and 8

Murray Horton   02-1-02
2205 Oregon Pike, Lancaster 17601
    Township of Manheim

Robert A. Herman, Jr.   02-1-03
458 Locust St., Columbia 17512
    Township of West Hempfield; Boroughs of Columbia and Mountville

Louise B. Williams   02-2-01
225 W. King St., Lancaster 17603
    City of Lancaster - Wards 3 and 7

William A. Hull, Jr.   02-2-02
225 W. King St., Lancaster 17603
    City of Lancaster - Wards 1, 5, and 9

Doris R. James   02-2-03
225 W. King St., Lancaster 17603
    Township of Lancaster

Richard W. Musser   02-2-04
225 W. King St., Lancaster 17603
    City of Lancaster, Wards 2 and 6

Richard A. Sheetz   02-2-05
399 Camp Meeting, Rd., Landisville 17538
    Township of East Hempfield; Borough of East Petersburg

Stella V. Caldwell   02-2-06
R.D. 1, Stehman Rd., Millersville 17551
    Townships of Conestoga and Manor, Borough of Millersville

John W. Miller   02-2-07
24 E. Orange St., Ephrata 17522
    Townships of Clay and Ephrata; Boroughs of Akron and Ephrata

James L. Garrett   02-2-08
690 Furnace Hills Pike, Lititz 17543
    Townships of Elizabeth and Warwick; Borough of Lititz

William G. Reuter   02-3-01
775 Donegal Springs Rd., Mount Joy 17552
    Townships of East Donegal and Conoy; Boroughs of Marietta and
    Mount Joy

Arden I. Kopp   02-3-02
15 Geist Rd., Lancaster 17601
    Townships of East Lampeter, Upper Leacock and West Earl

Mary F. Wilkinson   02-3-03
852 Village Rd., P.O. Box 310, Lampeter 17537-0310
    Townships of Strasburg, Pequea and West Lampeter; Borough of
    Strasburg

Joseph W. Bledsoe   02-3-04
248 Maple Avenue, Quarryville 17566
    Townships of Providence, Colerain, Drumore, Little Britain, Eden,
    Fulton, and Martic; Borough of Quarryville

Gilbert R. Book   02-3-05
P.O. Box 307, Bellevue Ave., Gap 17527
    Townships of Leacock, Paradise, Sadsbury, Bart and Salisbury;
    Borough of Christiana

Richard L. Reeser   02-3-06
745-B East Main St., New Holland 17557
    Townships of Caernarvon, Earl and East Earl; Boroughs of New
    Holland and Terre Hill

Nancy G. Hamill   02-3-07
R.D. 3, Box 17, Denver 17517
    Townships of East Cocalico, West Cocalico and Brecknock; Boroughs
    of Adamstown and Denver

Marilyn E. Stoner   02-3-08
R.D. 5, P.O. Box 96
Manheim 17545
    Townships of Penn and Rapho; Borough of Manheim

Harold E. Greiner   02-3-09
905 S. Market St., Elizabethtown 17022
    Townships of Mount Joy and West Donegal; Borough of
    Elizabethtown

LAWRENCE COUNTY
FIFTY-THIRD JUDICIAL DISTRICT
District Justices

Ernest Crawford   53-1-01
Lawrence County Court House, New Castle 16101
    City of New Castle

Samuel Battaglia   53-3-01
607 Lawrence Ave., Ellwood City 16117
    Townships of Wayne and Perry; Boroughs of Ellwood City, New
    Beaver, Ellport and Wampum

Betty Lou Kradel   53-3-02
R.D. 2, Box 225, Route 224, Edinburg 16116
    Township of North Beaver, Little Beaver, Taylor, Union and Mahoning;
    Boroughs of Bessemer, Enon Valley, and S.N.P.J

Ruth E. French   53-3-03
2516 New Butler Rd., New Castle 16101
    Townships of Shenango, Slippery Rock, Scott, Hickory, Plain Grove
    and Washington; Borough of South New Castle

Robert L. Zedaker   53-3-04
3455 Wilmington Rd., New Castle 16105
    Townships of Pulaski, Wilmington, and Neshannock; Boroughs of
    Volant and New Wilmington

LEBANON COUNTY
FIFTY-SECOND JUDICIAL DISTRICT
District Justices

John F. Arnold   52-1-01
400 S. 8th St., Lebanon 17042
    City of Lebanon - Wards 1, 2, 3, and 6; Townships of North
    Cornwall and West Lebanon

Catherine M. Coyle   52-2-01
400 S. 8th St., Lebanon 17042
    City of Lebanon - Wards 4, 5, 7, 8, 9, and 10

Jo Ann Shultz   52-3-01
6 W. Main St., Myerstown 17067
    Townships of Jackson and Millcreek; Boroughs of Richland and
    Myerstown

Lucy A. Peitsch   52-3-02
1800 S. 5th Ave., Lebanon 17042
    Townships of South Lebanon, West Cornwall and Heidelberg;
    Borough of Cornwall

Mary M. Spannuth   52-3-03
Jonestown Boro Hall, Jonestown 17038
    Townships of Swatara, Bethel and North Lebanon; Borough of
    Jonestown

Betty Ann Smith   52-3-04
P.O. Box 2012, Cleona 17042-1322
    Townships of Annville, Cold Spring, East Hanover, Union and North
    Annville; Borough of Cleona

Lee R. Lehman   52-3-05
P.O. Box 408, 325 S. Railroad St., Palmyra 17078
    Townships of North Londonderry, South Londonderry and South
    Annville; Boroughs of Palmyra and Mt. Gretna

LEHIGH COUNTY
THIRTY-FIRST JUDICIAL DISTRICT
District Justices

Charles J. Trinkle   31-1-01
1201 Sumner Ave., Allentown 18102
    City of Allentown - Wards 8 and 10

John E. Dugan   31-1-02
1216 Turner St., Allentown 18102
    City of Allentown - Wards 4, 7, and 11

Janice B. Hettinger   31-1-03
2012 Reading Rd., Allentown 18104
    City of Allentown - Wards 13, 17, and 18

Ralph H. Beck   31-1-04
607 Cleveland St., Allentown 18103
    City of Allentown - Wards 12, 16, and 19

James E. Stahl   31-1-05
1525 E. Congress St., Allentown 18103
    City of Allentown - Wards 14 and 15; Township of Hanover; Borough
    of Catasaqua

Joseph J. Maura   31-1-06
431 W. Broad St., Bethlehem 18018
    City of Bethlehem, West Bethlehem - Wards 10, 11, 12, and 13

Joan Snyder   31-1-07
3311 Hobson St., Whitehall 18052
    Township of Whitehall; Borough of Coplay

Vacant   31-1-08
200 E. Emmaus Ave., Allentown 18103
    Township of Salisbury; Borough of Fountain Hill

Edward F. Pressmann   31-2-01
506 Court St., Allentown 18101
    City of Allentown - Wards 1, 2, 3, 5, 6, and 9

Theodore L. Russiano   31-2-02
13 S. Fairview Ave., Allentown 18104
    Townships of North Whitehall and South Whitehall

John J. Zettlemoyer, Jr.   31-2-03
14 S. 4th St., Emmaus 18049
    Township of Upper Milford; Borough of Emmaus

Edward E. Hartman   31-3-01
106 S. Walnut St., Slatington 18080
    Townships of Lynn, Heidelberg and Washington; Borough of
    Slatington

Marybeth Shankweiler   31-3-02
Rt. 100 North, P.O. Box C, Trexlertown 18087
    Townships of Weisenberg, Lowhill, Macungie; Borough of Alburtis

Charles A. Deutsch   31-3-03
Village Ctr., North Main St., Coopersburg 18036
    Townships of Lower Milford and Upper Saucon; Borough of
    Coopersburg

LUZERNE COUNTY
ELEVENTH JUDICIAL DISTRICT
District Justices

Michael J. Collins, Esq.   11-1-01
268 S. Main St., Wilkes-Barre 18701
    City of Wilkes-Barre - Wards 10, 12, 13, 14 and 15

Martin Robert Kane   11-1-02
53 N. Main St., Wilkes-Barre 18702
    City of Wilkes-Barre - Wards 1, 2, 3, 4, 5, 6, 8, 9, 16, 17, 18, 19 and 20

Michael T. Conahan, Esq.   11-1-03
City Hall Bldg., Church & Green Sts., Hazleton 18201
    City of Hazleton

Joseph M. Augello, Esq.   11-1-04
City Hall Bldg., Broad St., Pittston 18640
    City of Pittston; Boroughs of Avoca, Duryea, Dupont and Hughestown

Richard P. Adams   11-1-05
500 Wyoming Ave., Kingston 18704
    Borough of Kingston

Andrew Barilla, Jr.   11-1-06
Shoemaker & Main St., Swoyersville 18704
    Boroughs of Forty Fort, Swoyersville, Pringle, Luzerne and Courtdale

Carmen J. Maffei, Esq.   11-2-01
Municipal Bldg., 555 Exeter Ave., West Pittston 18643
    Township of Exeter; Boroughs of West Pittston, Exeter, Wyoming and
    West Wyoming

John Hopkins   11-2-02
470 Main St., Edwardsville 18704
    Boroughs of Edwardsville, Plymouth and Larksville

Patrick L. Cooney   11-2-03
104 Lee Park Ave., Wilkes-Barre 18702
    Township of Hanover; Boroughs of Ashley, Sugar Notch and Warrior
    Run

Vacant   11-3-01
33-35 W. Union St., Shickshinny 18655
    Townships of Huntingdon, Fairmount, Ross, Hunlock, Union, Salem
    and Nescopeck; Boroughs of Shickshinny, New Columbus and
    Nescopeck

Leonary C. Olzinski   11-3-02
30 E. Broad St., Nanticoke 18634
   City of Nanticoke; Townships of Newport, Slocum, Conyngham and
   Hollenback

Burton E. Balliet   11-3-03
Rt. 93, Brookhill Cntr., Sugarloaf 18249
   Townships of Black Creek, Sugarloaf and Butler; Borough of
   Conyngham

Edward Verbonitz   11-3-04
Calbeth Cntr., Rt. 309, Milnesville 18239
   Township of Hazle; Borough of West Hazleton

Gerald Feissner   11-3-05
Freeland Borough Municipal Bldg., Center & Walnut Sts.,
Freeland 18224
   Townships of Foster and Dennison; Boroughs of Freeland, Jeddo,
   Penn Lake Park and White Haven

Ronald W. Swank   11-3-06
321 S. Mountain Blvd., Mountain Top 18707
   Townships of Rice, Wright and Dorrance; Borough of Nuangola

Bernard J. Hendrzak   11-3-07
Mun. Bldg., 19 Ash St., Wilkes-Barre 18702
   Townships of Wilkes-Barre, Buck and Bear Creek; Borough of Laurel
   Run

Joseph Verespy   11-3-08
126 N. Main St., Plains 18705
   Townships of Plains, Jekins and Pittston; Boroughs of Laflin and
   Yatesville

Earl Sidney Gregory   11-3-09
172 N. Memorial Highway, Shavertown 18708
   Townships of Franklin, Kingston, Dallas, Lehman, Lake and Jackon;
   Boroughs of Dallas and Harveys Lake

LYCOMING COUNTY
TWENTY-NINTH JUDICIAL DISTRICT
District Justices

John M. McDermott   29-1-01
2117 W. 4th St., Williamsport 17701
   City of Williamsport - Wards 4 through 10 and 11

Allen P. Page III   29-1-02
48 W. Third Street, Williamsport 17701
   City of Williamsport - Wards 1, 2, 3, and 12 through 17

Robert Stack   29-3-01
216 Market St., Jersey Shore 17740
   Townships of Anthony, Bastress, Brown, Cummings, Limestone,
   McHenry, Nippenose, Piatt, Pine, Porter, Watson, Woodward and
   Salladasburg; Borough of Jersey Shore

Gerald A. McGee   29-3-02
2130 Northway Rd., R.D. 1, Box 2103, Williamsport 17701
   Townships of Cascade, Eldred, Gamble, Plunketts Creek, Upper
   Fairfield and Loyalsock-1, 2, 4, 5, 6, 7; Boroughs of South
   Williamsport and Montoursville

C. Roger McRae   29-3-03
R.D. 1, P.O. Box 118, Hughesville 17737
   Townships of Clinton, Brady, Franklin, Jordan, Mill Creek, Moreland,
   Muncy, Muncy Creek, Penn, Shrewsbury, Washington and Wolf;
   Boroughs of Hughesville, Montgomery, Muncy and Picture Rocks

James H. Sortman   29-3-04
1965 Lycoming Creek Rd., Williamsport 17701
   Townships of Armstrong, Cogan House, Hepburn, Jackson, Lewis,
   Lycoming, McIntyre, McNett, Old Lycoming, Susquehanna,
   Loyalsock-3; Borough of Duboistown

McKEAN COUNTY
FORTY-EIGHTH JUDICIAL DISTRICT
District Justices

Kenneth Jadlowiec   48-1-01
27 Bishop St., Bradford 16701
   City of Bradford

David Dar Feheley   48-3-01
155 Main St., Eldred 16731
   Townships of Annin, Otto, Ceres, and Eldred; Borough of Eldred

John Yoder   48-3-02
307 W. Main St., Smethport 16749
   Townships of Liberty, Norwich and Keating; Boroughs of Port
   Allegany and Smethport

John D. Geibel   48-3-03
14 N. 3rd St., Bradford 16701
   Township of Corydon, Bradford and Foster; Borough of Lewis Run

J. Alden Anderson   48-3-04
136 Fraley St., Kane 16735
   Townships of Hamilton, Wetmore, Hamlin, Lafayette and Sergeant;
   Boroughs of Kane and Mt. Jewett

MERCER COUNTY
THIRTY-FIFTH JUDICIAL DISTRICT
District Justices

William M. Coleman   35-2-01
528 Thornton St., Sharon 16146
   City of Sharon; Borough of Sharpsville

Frank J. Tamber   35-2-02
1119 Mercer Ave., R.D. 2, Hermitage 16148
   City of Farrell, Townships of Shenango and Hermitage; Boroughs of
   Wheatland and West Middlesex

Joseph V. Gabany   35-3-01
123 W. Market St., Mercer 16137
   Townships of Salem, Sandy Creek, Otter Creek, Perry, Delaware,
   Fairview, Lackawannock, East Lackawannock, Springfield,
   Jefferson, Coolspring, Findley and Wilmington; Boroughs of
   Sheakleyville, Fredonia and Mercer

George E. McCandless   35-3-02
R.D. 1, Box 218A, Jackson Center 16133
   Townships of Deer Creek, French Creek, New Vernon, Mill Creek,
   Lake, Sandy Lake, Jackson, Worth, Pine, Liberty and Wolf Creek;
   Boroughs of New Lebanon, Stoneboro, Sandy Lake, Jackson Center
   and Grove City

Francis Warren Brown   35-3-03
47 Clinton St., Greenville 16125
   Townships of Greene, Sugar Grove, West Salem, Hempfield,
   Pymatuning and South Pymatuning; Boroughs of Jamestown,
   Greenville and Clarks

MIFFLIN COUNTY
FIFTY-EIGHTH JUDICIAL DISTRICT
District Justices

Richard Williams   58-3-01
20 N. Wayne St., Lewistown 17044
    Townships of Granville, Bratton, Oliver, Wayne, Menno and Union; Boroughs of Lewistown, Juniata Terrace, Newton Hamilton, Kistler and McVerytown

Barbara A. Clare   58-3-02
513 Electric Ave., Lewistown 17044
    Townships of Derry, Decatur, Brown and Armagh; Borough of Burnham

MONROE COUNTY
FORTY-THIRD JUDICIAL DISTRICT
District Justices

Dale A. Keenhold   43-2-01
777 Main St., Stroudsburg 18360
    Borough of Stroudsburg

Eleanor K. Randolph   43-2-02
401 Prospect St., East Stroudsburg 18301
    Borough of East Stroudsburg

Clara Pope   43-3-01
303 Belmont Ave., Mt. Pocono 18344
    Townships of Coolbaugh, Tobyhanna and Tunkhannock; Borough of Mount Pocono

Thomas R. Shiffer, Jr.   43-3-02
1316 N. 5th St., Stroudsburg 18360
    Township of Stroud

Henry McCool   43-3-03
Rt. 611, Tannersville 18372
    Townships of Pocono, Jackson and Hamilton

Glenn A. Borger   43-3-04
P.O. Box 218, Brodheadsville 18322
    Townships of Chestnuthill, Polk, Eldred and Ross

John L. Davies   43-4-01
R.D. 2, East Stroudsburg 18301
    Townships of Smithfield and Middle Smithfield; Borough of Delaware Water Gap

Marjorie J. Shumaker   43-4-02
Box 213, Mountainhome 18342
    Townships of Barrett, Paradise and Price

MONTGOMERY COUNTY
THIRTY-EIGHTH JUDICIAL DISTRICT
District Justices

Elaine J. Adams   38-1-01
317 W. Germantown Pike, Norristown 19403
    Townships of East Norriton and West Norriton

Michael C. Richman, Esq.   38-1-02
8101 Old York Rd., Elkins Park 19117
    Townships of Cheltenham - Wards 5 through 7; Borough of Jenkintown

Loretta F. Leader   38-1-03
8230 Old York Rd., Elkins Park 19117
    Township of Cheltenham - Wards 1 through 4

M. William Peterson   38-1-04
1925 Old York Rd., Abington 19001
    Township of Abington - Wards 1-1, 1-2, 2, 5, 8, 10, 11-1, 11-2, 14, and 15; Borough of Rockledge

Henry Liss   38-1-05
1030 Old York Rd., Abington 19001
    Township of Abington - Wards 1-3, 3, 4, 6, 7, 9, 11-3, 12, and 13

Henry J. Schireson, Esq.   38-1-06
707 Montgomery Ave., Penn Valley 19072
    Townships of Lower Merion - Wards 1, 2, 3, 6, 9, 11-3, 12, and 13

Caroline Culley Stine   38-1-07
80 Rittenhouse Place, Ardmore 19003
    Township of Lower Merion - Wards 4, 5, 7, 8, 10, 11-1, 11-2, and 14; Borough of Narberth

George R. Eastburn, Jr.   38-1-08
1107 Bethlehem Pike, P.O. Box 223, Flourtown 19031
    Township of Springfield

Donald O. Riehl   38-1-09
1300 DeKalb Pike, King of Prussia 19406
    Township of Upper Merion Districts: Belmont 1, 2, 3, 4, King 1, 2, Roberts, Swedeland, Swedesburg, Candlebrook 1 and 2, Gulph 1 and 2

Albert T. Maynard, Jr.   38-1-10
1301 Bethlehem Pike, Ambler 19002
    Township of Upper Dublin; Borough of Ambler

Charles A. Dasch   38-1-11
262 King St., Pottstown 19464
    Townships of Upper Pottsgrove and West Pottsgrove; Borough of Pottstown - Wards 2, 3, 4, and 1-1

Richard E. Evans   38-1-12
100 Porter Rd., Pottstown 19464
    Township of Lower Pottsgrove; Borough of Pottstown - Wards 5, 6, 7, and 1-2

John T. Sachaczenski   38-1-13
625 W. Ridge Pike, Bldg B - Suite 101, Conshohocken 19428
    Township of Plymouth; Boroughs of Conshohocken and West Conshohocken

Gloria Morgan   38-1-14
221 Davisville Rd., Willow Grove 19090
    Township of Upper Moreland - Wards 2, 5, 3-2, and 7; Borough of Hatboro

Francis J. Lawrence   38-1-15
113 E. Main St., Norristown 19401
    Borough of Norristown, Wards 1, 2, 3, 7, 10, 11 and 12

Robert A. Saraceni   38-1-16
1947 New Hope St., Norristown 19401
    Borough of Norristown, Wards 4, 5, 6, 8 and 9

Grant Musselman   38-1-17
66 County Line Rd., Souderton 18964
    Townships of Salford and Franconia; Boroughs of Souderton and Telford

Robert Kulp   38-1-18
762 Main St., Lansdale 19446
    Townships of Hatfield and Montgomery; Boroughs of Hatfield and Lansdale

Walter Gadzicki, Jr.   38-1-19
838 Oak St., Royersford 19468
    Townships of Limerick and Upper Providence; Borough of
    Royersford

William K. Kurtz, Jr.   38-1-20
3938 Ridge Pike, Collegeville 19426
    Townships of Perkiomen and Lower Providence; Boroughs of Trappe
    and Collegeville

John S. Murray   38-1-21
Blue Bell West-Suite 101, Skippack Pike, Blue Bell 19422
    Townships of Lower Gwynedd, Towamencin, Upper Gwynedd and
    Whitpain; Borough of North Wales

Kenneth Nonnenman   38-1-22
617 Horsham Rd., Horsham 19044
    Township of Horsham

Catherine Speers   38-1-23
4002 Center Ave., Lafayette Hill 19444
    Township of Whitemarsh

Carroll A. Rosenberger   38-1-24
596 Main St., Schwenksville 19473
    Townships of Lower Frederick, Lower Salford, Skippack, Upper
    Salford and Worcester; Borough of Schwenksville

Elaine Berkoff   38-2-01
221 Davisville Rd., Willow Grove 19090
    Township of Upper Moreland - Wards 1, 3-1, 4, and 6

Leroy Oelschlager   38-2-02
307 Main Street, East Greenville 18041
    Townships of Marborough and Upper Hanover; Boroughs of Green
    Lane, Red Hill, East Greenville, Pennsburg

Nancy W. Moore   38-2-03
2020 Swamp Pike, Gilbertsville 19525
    Townships of Douglass, New Hanover and Upper Frederick

James B. Hunter   38-2-08
2351 Huntingdon Pike, Huntingdon Valley 19006
    Township of Lower Moreland; Borough of Bryn Athyn

MONTOUR COUNTY
TWENTY-SIXTH JUDICIAL DISTRICT
District Justices

Robert B. Geiger   26-3-04
Montour County Court House
Mill St., Danville 17821
    Townships of Anthony, Cooper, Derry, Liberty, Limestone, West
    Hemlock, Mayberry, Mahoning and Valley; Boroughs of Danville and
    Washingtonville

NORTHAMPTON COUNTY
THIRD JUDICIAL DISTRICT
District Justices

William Griffith   03-1-04
1414 Center St., Bethlehem 18018-2596
    Townships of Hanover; City of Bethlehem-Ward 14

James F. Stocklas   03-2-01
402 E. Broad St., Bethlehem 18018-6385
    City of Bethlehem - Wards 2, 6, 8 and 9

Dennis J. Monaghan, Esq.   03-2-03
4119 Nazareth Pike, Bethlehem 18017-9485
    Townships of Bethlehem and Lower Nazareth; Borough of
    Freemansburg

Diane S. Repyneck   03-2-04
800 Main St., Hellertown 18055-1535
    Township of Lower Saucon; Borough of Hellertown

Joseph N. Leo   03-2-05
731 Lehigh St., Easton 18042-4350
    City of Easton - Wards 1 through 6

Pat J. Maragulia   03-2-06
431 Center St., Easton 18042-6410
    City of Easton - Wards 9 through 12; Township of Williams; Borough of
    Glendon

Charles A. Kutzler   03-2-07
1065 Main St., Northampton 18067-1695
    Township of Allen; Boroughs of Northampton and North Catasauqua

Elmo L. Prey, Jr.   03-2-08
Industrial & Tatamy Rds., Nazareth 18064-0256
    Townships of East Allen and Upper Nazareth; Boroughs of Bath and
    Nazareth

Walter F. Auch, Jr.   03-2-09
3351 Rear, Nazareth Rd., Easton 18042-2097
    Townships of Forks and Palmer; Borough of Tatamy

John Gombosi   03-2-10
402 E. 4th St., Bethlehem 18015-1895
    City of Bethlehem-Wards 1, 2, 3, 4 and 5

Elizabeth A. Romig   03-2-11
1319 Stefko Blvd., Bethlehem 18017-6696
    City of Bethlehem-Wards 15, 16 and 17

Michael J. Koury   03-2-12
1710 Butler St., Easton 18042-4621
    City of Easton-Wards 7 and 8; Boroughs of Wilson and West Easton

Harold R. Weaver, Jr.   03-3-01
3935 Mountain View Dr., Danielsville 18038-0054
    Townships of Lehigh and Moore; Boroughs of Walnutport and
    Chapman

Adrianne Masut   03-3-02
31 C West First St., Wind Gap 18091-0175
    Townships of Bushkill and Plainfield; Boroughs of Wind Gap and Pen
    Argyl

Sherwood R. Grigg   03-3-03
305 Roseto Ave., Roseto 18013-1397
    Townships of Washington, Upper Mt. Bethel and Lower Mt. Bethel;
    Boroughs of Bangor, East Bangor, Roseto and Portland

NORTHUMBERLAND COUNTY
EIGHTH JUDICIAL DISTRICT
District Justices

Michael F. Mychak, Esq.   08-2-01
Mun. Bldg., 100 N. Vine St., Mt. Carmel 17851
    Townships of East Cameron, Ralpho and Mount Carmel; Boroughs of
    Mount Carmel, Kulpmont and Marion Heights

William Frede,ick Kear 08-3-01
195 Fourth St., Milton 17847
Townships of Delaware, Lewis, Turbot, East Chillisquaque and West Chillisquaque; Boroughs of Milton, McEwensville, Turbotville and Watsontown

Wade J. Brown 08-3-02
225 Market St., Sunbury 17801
City of Sunbury; Townships of Point, Rush, Upper Augusta, Rockerfeller, Lower Augusta, Little Mahanoy, Jackson, Washington, Lower Mahanoy and Jordan; Boroughs of Herndon, Northumberland, Riverside and Snydertown

Wilbur Reddinger 08-3-03
506 N. Shamokin St., Shamokin 17872
City of Shamokin; Townships of Coal, Shamokin, Zerbe, West Cameron and Upper Mahanoy

PERRY COUNTY
FORTY-FIRST JUDICIAL DISTRICT
District Justices

James R. Mayer, Jr. 41-3-03
415 High St., Duncannon 17020
Townships of Rye, Penn, Wheatfield, Watts and Miller; Boroughs of Marysville, Duncannon and New Buffalo

Donald F. Howell 41-3-04
120 Market St., Newport 17074-1593
Townships of Greenwood, Tuscarora, Juniata, Oliver, Howe, Buffalo, Centre and Liverpool; Boroughs of Millerstown, Liverpool, Newport and Bloomfield

Jane R. Dyar 41-3-05
P.O. Drawer H, Loysville 17047
Townships of Saville, Spring, Tyrone, Northeast Madison, Southwest Madison, Carroll, Jackson and Toboyne; Boroughs of Landisburg and Blain

PHILADELPHIA COUNTY
FIRST JUDICIAL DISTRICT
Philadelphia Traffic Court

George Twardy, President Judge
800 N. Broad St., Philadelphia 19130

Salvatore DeMeo, Judge
800 N. Broad St., Philadelphia 19130

Dominic M. Cermele, Judge
800 N. Broad St., Philadelphia 19130

Charles H. Cuffeld, Judge
800 N. Broad St., Philadelphia 19130

Raymond A. Malone, Judge
800 N. Broad St., Philadelphia 19130

Lillian H. Podgorski, Judge
800 N. Broad St., Philadelphia 19130

PIKE COUNTY
SIXTIETH JUDICIAL DISTRICT
District Justices

Carolyn H. Purdue 60-3-01
P.O. Box 632, Milford 18337
Townships of Westfall and Milford; Boroughs of Matamoras and Milford

Dore N. James 60-3-02
Star Rt. 2, Hawley 18428
Townships of Lackawaxen, Palmyra, Greene and Blooming Grove

Gudrun Quinn 60-3-03
R.R. 1, Box 70, Milford 18337
Townships of Dingman, Delaware, Lehman, Porter and Shohola

POTTER COUNTY
FIFTY-FIFTH JUDICIAL DISTRICT
District Justices

Edward L. Easton 55-3-01
110 N. East St., Coudersport 16915
Townships of Eulalia, Roulette, East Fork District of Eulalia, Homer, Keating, Portage, Summit, Sweden, Sylvania and Wharton; Boroughs of Coudersport and Austin

Donna J. Fetzer 55-4-01
Academy St., Shinglehouse 16748
Townships of Clara, Hebron, Oswayo, Pleasant Valley, Sharon and Shinglehouse; Borough of Oswayo

Jeanne M. Cole 55-4-02
Main St., Box 102, Ulysses 16948
Townships of Allegheny, Bingham, Genesee, Harrison and Ulysses; Borough of Ulysses

Katherine G. Garrote 55-4-03
11 Union St., Galeton 16922
Townships of Abbott, Hector, Pike, Stewardson and West Branch; Borough of Galeton

SCHUYLKILL COUNTY
TWENTY-FIRST JUDICIAL DISTRICT
District Justices

Bernard Brutto 21-2-03
126 1/2 N. Main St., Shenandoah 17976
Boroughs of Shenandoah, Gilberton and Girardville

Elizabeth M. Lurwick 21-3-01
26 Pike St., Port Carbon 17965
City of Pottsville, Wards 1, 2, 3 and 6; Townships of Blythe, East Norwegian and New Castle; Boroughs of New Philadelphia, Middleport, Port Carbon, Mechanicsville, St. Clair, Palo Alto and Mount Carbon

Catherine E. Thompson 21-3-02
206 N. Second St., Pottsville 17901
Ciy of Pottsville-Wards 4, 5 and 7; Townships of Norwegian, Cass, Branch, Foster, Keilly; Borough of Minersville

James R. Ferrier 21-3-03
Borough Hall, Orwigsburg 17961
Townships of North Manheim, South Manheim,West Brunswick and East Brunswick; Boroughs of Schuylkill Haven, Cressona, Auburn, Deer Lake, Landingville, Port Clinton, Orwigsburg and New Ringgold

Suzanne Subalusky-Lobichusky 21-3-05
1 W. Center St., Mahanoy City 17948
Townships of Delano, Mahanoy, East Union, West Mahanoy, Union and North Union; Boroughs of Mahanoy City and West Mahanoy

Norman H. Richards 21-3-06
Box 500-A, R.D. 2, Tamaqua 18252
Townships of Walker, West Penn, Schuylkill, Kline, Ryan and Rust; Boroughs of Tamaqua, McAdoo and Coaldale

Bernadette J. Nahas 21-3-07
1004 Center St., Ashland 17921
Townships of Butler, Barry and Eldred; Boroughs of Ashland, Gordon and Frackville

Earl H. Matz, Jr.   21-3-08
19 N. Pine St., Tremont 17981
> Townships of Hegins, Hubley, Upper Mahantongo, Porter, Pine Grove, Tremont, Frailey, Washington and Wayne; Boroughs of Tower City, Pine Grove and Tremont

SNYDER COUNTY
SEVENTEENTH JUDICIAL DISTRICT
District Justices

Harley M. Parker   17-3-03
R.D. 1, Box 13A, Selinsgrove 17870
> Townships of Penn, Monroe, Jackson, Union, Chapman and Washington; Boroughs of Shamokin Dam, Selinsgrove and Freeburg

William C. Saylor   17-3-04
Snyder County Court House, P.O. Box 217, Middleburg 17842
> Townships of West Beaver, Spring, Adams, Beaver, West Perry, Center, Franklin, Perry and Middlecreek; Boroughs of Beavertown, McClure and Middleburg

SOMERSET COUNTY
SIXTEENTH JUDICIAL DISTRICT
District Justices

William H. Roush   16-3-01
301 Main St., P.O. Box 55, Boswell 15531
> Townships of Conemaugh, Jenner and Quemahoning; Boroughs of Benson, Boswell, Jennerstown, Hooversville and Stoystown

Joseph Anthony Cannoni   16-3-02
1409 Somerset Ave., Windber 15963
> Townships of Paint, Ogle and Shade; Boroughs of Paint, Windber and Central City

Jon A. Barkman, Esq.   16-3-03
121 East Union St., P.O. Box 88, Somerset 15501
> Townships of Somerset, Jefferson, Lincoln, Allegheny and Stonycreek; Boroughs of Somerset, Indian Lake, New Baltimore and Shanksville

Frances L. Cornish   16-3-05
616 Logan Place, P.O. Box 72, Confluence 15424
> Townships of Middlecreek, Upper Turkeyfoot, Lower Turkeyfoot, Milford, Black and Addison; Boroughs of Confluence, New Centerville, Rockwood, Ursina, Casselman and Seven Springs

Robert M. Philson, Esq.   16-3-06
P.O. Box 203, 613 Second St., Meyersdale 15552
> Townships of Brothers Valley, Summit, Elk Lick, Northampton, Fairhope, Southampton, Larimer and Greenville; Boroughs of Berlin, Garrett, Meyersdale, Salisbury, Wellersburg and Callimont

SULLVIAN COUNTY
FORTY-FOURTH JUDICIAL DISTRICT
District Justices

Milo D. Clinton   44-3-03
R.D. 1, Box 75C, Dushore 18614
> Townships of Colley, Cherry, Laporte and Davidson; Boroughs of Dushore and Laporte

Francis M. McCarthy   44-4-03
P.O. Box 71, Forksville 18616
> Townships of Fox, Elkland, Forks, Hillsgrove and Shrewsbury; Boroughs of Forksville and Eagles Mere

SUSQUEHANNA COUNTY
THIRTY-FOURTH JUDICIAL DISTRICT
District Justices

Marjory A. Wheaton   34-3-01
Court House Annex, Montrose 18801
> Townships of Bridgewater, Franklin, Liberty, Silver Lake, Choconut, Apolacon, Forest Lake, Jessup, Middletown, Rush, Auburn, Dimock and Springville; Boroughs of Montrose, Little Meadows and Friendsville

Kenneth W. Seamans, Esq.   34-3-02
204 Main St., New Milford 18834
> Townships of Ararat, Great Bend, Harmony, Jackson, New Milford and Thompson; Boroughs of Great Bend, Hallstead, New Milford, Oakland, Susquehanna, Depot, Thompson and Lanesboro

Barbara Obelenus   34-3-03
P.O. Box 184, Harford 18823
> Townships of Brooklyn, Clifford, Gibson, Harford, Herrick, Lathrop and Lenox; Boroughs of Forest City, Hop Bottom and Uniondale

TIOGA COUNTY
FOURTH JUDICIAL DISTRICT
District Justices

William A. Buckingham   04-3-01
105 Parkhurst St., Elkland 16920
> Townships of Jackson, Brookfield, Clymer, Westfield, Deerfield, Elkland, Nelson, Farmington, Lawrence and Osceola; Boroughs of Westfield, Knoxville, Elkland and Lawrenceville

William G. Farrell   04-3-02
118 Main St., Wellsboro 16901
> Townships of Elk, Morris, Middlebury, Gaines, Duncan, Shippen, Delmar, Chatham and Charleston; Borough of Wellsboro

Eleanor Trask   04-3-03
P.O. Box 307, Mansfield 16933
> Townships of Richmond, Sullivan, Rutland, Tioga, Bloss, Ward, Union, Hamilton, Liberty, Covington and Putnam; Boroughs of Mansfield, Roseville, Tioga, Blossburg and Liberty;

UNION COUNTY
SEVENTEENTH JUDICIAL DISTRICT
District Justices

Leo S. Armbruster   17-3-01
Union County Court House, 103 S. Second St., Lewisburg 17837
> Townships of Gregg, White Deer, Kelly, East Buffalo and Union; Borough of Lewisburg

William D. Yohn   17-3-02
701 Walnut St., Mifflinburg 17844
> Townships of Buffalo, Limestone, West Buffalo, Lewis and Hartley; Boroughs of New Berlin, Mifflinburg and Hartleton

VENANGO COUNTY
TWENTY-EIGHTH JUDICIAL DISTRICT
District Justices

Mary E. Nosko 28-3-01
140 W. State St., P.O. Box 186, Pleasantville 16341
Townships of Plum, Cherrytree, Allegheny, Oakland and Cornplanter; Boroughs of Pleasantville and Rouseville

Charles R. Thurau 28-3-02
Riverside Dr., R.D. 2, Oil City 16301
City of Oil City; Townships of Cranberry, Pinegrove and President

Robert E. Billingsley, Sr. 28-3-03
1174 Elk St., Franklin 16323
City of Franklin; Townships of Jackson, Canal, Frenchcreek, Mineral, Victory and Sandycreek; Boroughs of Sugarcreek, Cooperstown, Utica and Polk

Walter Turk 28-3-04
601 Main St., Emlenton 16373
Townships of Irwin, Clinton, Scrubgrass, Rockland and Richland; Boroughs of Barkeyville and Emlenton

WARREN COUNTY
THIRTY-SEVENTH JUDICIAL DISTRICT
District Justices

Judy C. Lobdell 37-2-01
7 Oak St., Warren 16365
Borough of Warren

Ruth J. Mills 37-3-01
1733 Market St. Ext., Warren 16365
Townships of Conewango, Elk, Pine Grove, Glade and Farmington

Suzanne M. Hodges 37-3-02
29 Railroad St., Youngsville 16347
Abbott St., Sugar Grove 16350
Townships of Sugar Grove, Freehold, Columbus, Brokenstraw and Pittsfield; Boroughs of Sugar Grove, Bear Lake and Youngsville

Allan D. Carlett 37-3-04
104 S. Main St., Sheffield 16347
Townships of Mead, Pleasant, Cherry Grove and Sheffield; Borough of Clarendon

Dalton E. Hunter, Sr. 37-4-01
129 Main St., Tidioute 16351
Townships of Spring Creek, Eldred, Southwest, Triumph, Deerfield, Watson and Limestown; Borough of Tidioute

WASHINGTON COUNTY
TWENTY-SEVENTH JUDICIAL DISTRICT
District Justices

J. Albert Spence 27-1-01
Washington County Court House, Washington 15301
City of Washington; Township of North Franklin; Borough of East Washington

James N. Brady 27-1-02
614 Park Ave., Monongahela 15063
City of Monongahela; Township of Carroll; Boroughs of Donora and New Eagle

Lawrence P. Celaschi 27-1-03
404 Fallowfield Ave., Charleroi 15022
Boroughs of North Charleroi, Speers, Dunlevy, Elco, Roscoe, Twilight, Stockdale, Allenport, Long Branch and Charleroi

Walter A. Mark 27-2-01
20 N. Central St., Canonsburg 15317
Boroughs of Canonsburg and Houston

Michael J. Fagella, Esq. 27-3-01
501 Valley Brook Dr., McMurray 15317
Townships of Union, Peters, and Nottingham; Borough of Finleyville

Stephen J. Morgo 27-3-02
613 Main St., Bentleyville 15314
Townships of North Bethlehem, Fallowfield and Somerset; Boroughs of Bentleyville, Ellsworth and Cokeburg

Daryl A. Zeaman 27-3-03
218 Wood St., California 15419
Township of West Pike Run; Boroughs of West Brownsville, Coal Center, Beallsville, and California

Louis I. Quail 27-3-04
P.O. Bldg., P.O. Box 41, Richeyville 15358
Townships of East Bethlehem and West Bethlehem; Boroughs of Centerville, Marianna and Deemston

Henry Mavrich 27-3-05
P.O. Box 336, Strabane 15363
Townships of North Strabane and South Strabane

Paul Michael Pozonsky 27-3-06
104 E. Lincoln Ave., McDonald 15057
Townships of Cecil and Robinson; Borough of McDonald

Thomas McGraw 27-3-07
17 Railroad St., Burgettstown 15021
Townships of Smith, Jefferson and Hanover; Boroughs of Midway and Burgettstown

June B. Lilley 27-3-08
P.O. Box 395, Pike St., Meadow Lands 15347
Townships of Chartiers, Mt. Pleasant and Cross Creek

Marjorie L. Teagarden 27-3-09
2918 Jefferson Ave., Washington 15301
Townships of Canton, Hopewell and Independence; Borough of West Middletown

Richard L. Martin 27-3-10
Rt. 40 East, Box 422, Claysville 15323
Townships of Amwell, South Franklin, Buffalo, Blaine, East Finley, West Finley, Donegal and Morris; Boroughs of West Alexander and Claysville

WAYNE COUNTY
TWENTY-SECOND JUDICIAL DISTRICT
District Justices

Dorothy C. Laabs 22-3-01
Federal Building, 100 Main St., Hawley 18428
Townships of Lake, Salem, Sterling, Dreher, Lehigh, Palmyra and Paupack; Borough of Hawley

Bonnie Price Lewis   22-3-02
Wayne County Court House, Honesdale 18431
   Townships of Dyberry, Oregon, Berlin, Texas and Cherry Ridge;
   Boroughs of Honesdale, Bethany and Prompton

Jane E. Hauck-Farrell   22-3-03
239 Belmont St., Waymart 18472
   Townships of Clinton, Canaan and South Canaan; Borough of
   Waymart

Edward H. Dix   22-3-04
Old Railroad Station Building, Lakewood 18439
   Townships of Scott, Buckingham, Preston, Mt. Pleasant, Manchester,
   Lebanon and Damascus; Borough of Starrucca

WESTMORELAND COUNTY
TENTH JUDICIAL DISTRICT
District Justices

Donald C. Japalucci   10-1-01
305 Clay Avenue, Jeannette 15644
   City of Jeannette; Borough of Penn

John F. Billy   10-1-03
279 Shoonmaker Ave., Monessen 15062
   City of Monessen; Township of Rostraver

William S. Guido   10-1-04
3016 Leechburg Rd., Lower Burrell 15068
   Cities of Lower Burrell and New Kensington - 4th Ward; Township of
   Upper Burrell

Buddy P. Cipolla   10-1-05
419 10th St., New Kensington 15068
   Cities of Arnold and New Kensington, Wards 1, 2, 3, 5, 6, and 7

Ernest M. Johnson   10-2-01
403 S. 3rd St., Youngwood 15697
   Townships of Hemfield - Voting Districts: Middletown, New Stanton,
   Weavers Old Stand, Foxdale, Haydenville, Maplewood and
   University, Sibel, West Point, Todd-Eastview and Fort Allen; Borough
   of Youngwood

Bernice A. McCutcheon   10-2-02
229 Longfellow St., Vandergrift 15690
   Township of Allegheny; Boroughs of Vandergrift, East Vandergrift,
   Hyde Park, Oklahoma and West Leechburg

Frank Del Bene   10-2-03
R.D. 2, Sunrise Estates, Irwin 15642
   Township of Penn; Boroughs of Manor and Trafford

Martha Medich   10-2-04
227 Main St., Irwin 15642
   Township of North Huntingdon - Wards 1, 2 and 6; Boroughs of Irwin
   and North Irwin

Jeane C. Anderson   10-2-06
R.D. 2, Belle Vernon 15012
   Township of Rostraver (part); Boroughs of North Belle Vernon and
   West Newton

Anthony Angelo   10-2-08
1017 Court Yard Plaza, Latrobe 15650
   Borough of Latrobe

Raymond E. Tubbs   10-2-09
26 Buttermilk Hollow Rd., North Huntingdon 15642
   Township of North Huntingdon - Wards 3,4,5,and 7

Michael Moschetti   10-2-10
10 Court House Sq., Greensburg 15601
   City of Greensburg; Boroughs of Southwest Greensburg and South
   Greensburg

Lois L. Diehl   10-3-01
2999 Greengate Mall
Greensburg 15601
   Township of Hempfield - Districts: Carbon, Wegley, High Park, West
   Adamsburg, East Adamsburg, Lincoln Heights (East & West),
   Herminie, Grapeville, Valley, Alwine, Foxhill, Hannastown, Luxor,
   Bovard, Gayville and North Carbon; Borough of Adamsburg

Robert E. Scott   10-3-02
5819 Washington Ave., Export 15632
   Boroughs of Murrysville, Export and Delmont

Shirley A. Miller   10-3-03
422 Sewickley Ave., Herminie 15637
   Townships of Sewickley, South Huntingdon and Hempfield - Voting
   District: Wendel; Boroughs of Madison, Sutersville, Smithton, and
   Arona

Lawrence J. Franzi   10-3-05
731 - Rt. 66, Apollo 15613
   Townships of Washington, Bell, Loyalhanna and Salem; Borough of
   Avonmore

Michael R. Mahady   10-3-07
Colonial Mini-Plaza, Rt. 30, R.D. 6, Box 310-6
Latrobe 15650
   Township of Unity; Borough of Youngstown

Michael P. Giannini   10-3-08
125 N. Derry Rd., Loyalhanna 15661
   Township of Derry; Borough of Derry and New Alexandria

Vacant   10-3-09
210 W. Church St., Ligonier 15658
   Townships of Ligonier, Cook, Fairfield and St. Clair; Boroughs of
   Ligonier, New Florence, Seward and Bolivard

J. Bruce King   10-3-10
130 N. Broadway St., Scottdale 15683
   Townships of East Huntingdon and Hunker; Boroughs of Scottdale,
   Hunker and New Stanton

Margaret L. Tlumac   10-3-11
R.D. 1, Box 409-A, Mt. Pleasant 15666
   Townships of Mt. Pleasant and Donegal; Boroughs of Mt. Pleasant
   and Donegal

WYOMING COUNTY
FORTY-FOURTH JUDICIAL DISTRICT
District Justices

Leo P. Conway, Jr.   44-3-01
P.O. Box 276, Factoryville 18419
   Townships of Lemon, Nicholson, Clinton and Overfield; Boroughs of
   Nicholson and Factoryville

Marion J. Robinson   44-3-02
R.D. 5, Tunkhannock 18657
126 Warren St., Tunkhannock 18657
   Townships of Eaton, Noxen, Monroe, Northmoreland, Exeter and
   Falls; Borough of Tunkhannock

Patricia A. Robinson   44-3-04
R.D. 2, Box 26B, Meshoppen 18630
    Townships of Forkston, North Branch, Windham, Mehoopany, Braintrim, Meshoppen, Washington and Tunkhannock; Boroughs of Laceyville and Meshoppen

YORK COUNTY
NINETEENTH JUDICIAL DISTRICT
District Justices

Mildred H. Becker   19-1-01
204 E. King St., York 17403
    City of York - Wards 1, 2, 6, 7, 8, 10, 12, and 15

Chester D. Thomas, Jr.   19-1-02
907 Roosevelt Ave., York 17404
    City of York - Wards 3, 4, 5, 9, 11, 13, and 14

William Y. Naill, Jr.   19-1-03
200 Pleasant St., Hanover 17331
    Borough of Hanover

Roy L. Lam   19-2-01
110 Pleasant Acres Rd., York 17402
    Townships of Springettsbury and Hellam; Boroughs of Hellam and Wrightsville

Jack H. Barton, Esq.   19-2-02
2318 S. Queen St., York 17402
    Townships of Spring Garden and York; Boroughs of Dallastown and Yoe

Harold C. Dixon   19-2-03
1998 Carlisle Rd., York 17404
    Township of West Manchester; Borough of West York

Donald G. Rode   19-2-04
3281 N. George St., Emigsville 17318
    Townships of Manchester and East Manchester; Boroughs of North York, Manchester and Mount Wolf

James G. Wallace   19-3-01
146 W. Main St., Windsor 17366
    Townships of Windsor and Lower Windsor; Boroughs of Red Lion, Windsor, Yorkana and East Prospect

Lois Jean Mundorff   19-3-02
R.D. 1, Airville 17302
    Townships of Chanceford, Lower Chanceford and Peach Bottom; Boroughs of Felton and Delta

Vacant   19-3-03
Midtown Shopping Cntr., P.O. Box 296, Stewartstown 17363
    Townships of East Hopewell, North Hopewell, Hopewell and Fawn; Boroughs of Cross Roads, Winterstown, Stewartstown and Fawn Grove

James W. Reedy   19-3-04
R.D. 2, Seven Valleys 17360
    Townships of Springfield and Shrewsbury; Boroughs of Jacobus, Loganville, Glen Rock, Shrewsbury, Railroad and New Freedom

Margaret L. Klinedinst   19-3-05
33 Fairview Dr., Hanover 17331
    Townships of Penn, Codorus, Manheim and West Manheim; Borough of Jefferson

Paul M. Diehl, Jr.   19-3-06
R.D. 1, Spring Grove 17362
    Townships of Heidelberg and North Codorus; Boroughs of Seven Valleys and New Salem

Quentin R. Stambaugh   19-3-07
R.D. 1, Thomasville 17364
    Townships of Dover, Paradise and Jackson; Boroughs of Dover and Spring Grove

Roger A. Estep   19-3-09
520 Locust Road, New Cumberland 17070
    Townships of Fairview, Newberry and Conewago; Boroughs of Lewisberry, Goldsboro and York Haven

Paul A. Walters   19-3-10
Suite C, P.O. Box 415, 101 U.S. Rt. 15-South, Dillsburg 17019
    Townships of Monaghan, Carroll, Franklin, Warrington and Washington; Boroughs of Dillsburg, Franklintown and Wellsville

DISTRICT and DISTRICT JUSTICE
COURT ADMINISTRATORS

DISTRICT COURT ADMINISTRATORS	DISTRICT JUSTICE COURT ADMINISTRATORS	DISTRICT COURT ADMINISTRATORS	DISTRICT JUSTICE COURT ADMINISTRATORS
ADAMS		**ARMSTRONG**	
Overman, Betty D. Adams County Courthouse Gettysburg, PA 17325	Overman, Betty D. Adams County Courthouse Gettysburg, PA 17325	Lang, Gayle M. Armstrong County Courthouse Kittanning, PA 16201	Davidson, Martha J. Armstrong County Courthouse Kittanning, PA 16201
ALLEGHENY			
Starrett, Charles H., Jr. Allegheny County Courthouse Pittsburgh, PA 15219	Lawlor, John Gary, Esq. 14 Wood Street Pittsburgh, PA 15222		

DISTRICT COURT ADMINISTRATORS	DISTRICT JUSTICE COURT ADMINISTRATORS	DISTRICT COURT ADMINISTRATORS	DISTRICT JUSTICE COURT ADMINISTRATORS
	BEAVER		**CLARION**
Cabraja, Joseph Beaver County Courthouse Beaver, PA 15009	Cabraja, Joseph Beaver County Courthouse Beaver, PA 15009	Carrier, Emma Lou Clarion County Courthouse Clarion, PA 16214	Carrier, Emma Lou Clarion County Courthouse Clarion, PA 16214
	BEDFORD		**CLINTON**
Dorner, Paul Bedford County Courthouse Annex Bedford, PA 15522		Shoemaker, John Clinton County Courthouse P.O. Box 540 Lock Haven, PA 17745	Shoemaker, John Clinton County Courthouse Clerk of Courts-Prothonotary Lock Haven, PA 17745
	BERKS		**COLUMBIA**
Rhein, John H. Berks County Courthouse 33 N. 6th Street Reading, PA 19601	Shurr, Frank D. Sprecher, Jeffrey K. Berks County Courthouse 33 N. 6th Street Reading, PA 19601	Trump, Frederick T. Columbia County Courthouse P.O. Box 380 Bloomsburg, PA 17815	Trump, Frederick T. Columbia County Courthouse P.O. Box 380 Bloomsburg, PA 17815
			CRAWFORD
	BLAIR	Yetman, Imogene Crawford County Courthouse Meadville, PA 16335	
Reighard, Michael Blair County Courthouse Hollidaysburg, PA 16648	Gildea, Patricia Blair County Courthouse Hollidaysburg, PA 16648		**CUMBERLAND**
		Hollinger, Gary L. Cumberland County Courthouse P.O. Box 189 Carlisle, PA 17013	Johnson, Ronald E., Esq. Cumberland County Courthouse P.O. Box 189 Carlisle, PA 17013
	BRADFORD		**DAUPHIN**
Dunn, Mary Lou Bradford County Courthouse Towanda, PA 18648	Dunn, Mary Lou Bradford County Courthouse Towanda, PA 18648	Minnich, John E. Dauphin County Courthouse Harrisburg, PA 17101	Faiola, Herman J. Dauphin County Courthouse Harrisburg, PA 17101
	BUCKS		**DELAWARE**
Kester, H. Paul, Esq. Bucks County Courthouse Main & Court Streets Doylestown, PA 18901	Wiley, G. Thomas Bucks County Courthouse Main & Court Streets Doylestown, PA 18901	Montella, Gerald, Esq. Media County Courthouse Media, PA 19063	Guthrie, Donald J., Esq. Delaware County Courthouse 106 West Front Street Media, PA 19063
			ELK
	BUTLER	Masson, Martha Keller Elk County Courthouse P.O. Box 416 Ridgway, PA 15853	Masson, Martha Keller Elk County Courthouse P.O. Box 416 Ridgway, PA 15853
McAnany, Bette M. Butler County Courthouse Butler, PA 16001	McAnany, Bette M. Butler County Courthouse Butler, PA 16001		**ERIE**
		Lurker, Ralph L. Erie County Courthouse 140 W. 6th Street Erie, PA 16501	Agresti, Richard D., Esq. Erie County 39 West Tenth Street Erie, PA 16501
	CAMBRIA		**FAYETTE**
Allison, Robert Cambria County Courthouse Ebensburg, PA 15931	Romani, David A., Esq. 224 Swank Street Johnstown, PA 15901	Wetzel, Robert Fayette County Courthouse Uniontown, PA 15401	Wetzel, Robert Fayette County Courthouse Uniontown, PA 15401
	CARBON		**FOREST**
Rader, Elizabeth A. Carbon County Courthouse Jim Thorpe, PA 18229	Cassidy, Aileen Carbon County Courthouse Jim Thorpe, PA 18229	Reitz, Robert J. Forest County Courthouse Tionesta, PA 16353	Reitz, Robert J. Forest County Jail P.O. Box 425 Tionesta, PA 16353
	CENTRE		**FRANKLIN**
Bickford, Lawrence C. Centre County Courthouse Bellefonte, PA 16823	Bickford, Lawrence C. Centre County Courthouse Bellefonte, PA 16823	Sheaffer, William A. Franklin County Courthouse Chambersburg, PA 17201	Sheaffer, William A. Franklin County Courthouse Chambersburg, PA 17201
	CHESTER		**GREENE**
Huss, Jeffrey C., Sr. Chester County Courthouse High & Market Streets West Chester, PA 19380	Cox, Kathy Chester County Courthouse Room 7 West Chester, PA 19380	Smith, Wanda B. Greene County Courthouse Waynesburg, PA 15370	Smith, Wanda B. Greene County Courthouse Waynesburg, PA 15370

DISTRICT COURT ADMINISTRATORS	DISTRICT JUSTICE COURT ADMINISTRATORS

HUNTINGDON

Fultz, Alexa R.	Fultz, Alexa R.
Huntingdon County Courthouse	Huntingdon County Courthouse
Huntingdon, PA 16652	Huntingdon, PA 16652

INDIANA

Peck, Linda K.	Simpson, John S., Esq.
Indiana County Courthouse	Indiana County
Indiana, PA 15701	20 North Seventh Street
	Indiana, PA 15701

JEFFERSON

Brown, Norma R.	Brown, Norma R.
Jefferson County Courthouse	Jefferson County Courthouse
Brookville, PA 15825	Brookville, PA 15825

LACKAWANNA

Murray, William J.	Powell, James, J., III, Esq.
Lackawanna County Courthouse	Lackawanna County Courthouse
Scranton, PA 18503	Scranton, PA 18503

LANCASTER

Reedy, R. Ronald	Weaver, Thomas N., Esq.
Lancaster County Courthouse	Lancaster County Courthouse
50 N. Duke Street	50 N. Duke Street
Lancaster, PA 17602	Lancaster, PA 17602

LAWRENCE

Pagley, Micheline R.	Pagley, Micheline R.
Lawrence County Government Ctr.	Lawrence County Government Ctr.
New Castle, PA 16101	New Castle, PA 16101

LEBANON

Rutter, Edward J.	Rutter, Edward J.
Room 308, Municipal Building	Room 308, Municipal Building
400 S. 8th Street	400 S. 8th Street
Lebanon, PA 17042	Lebanon, PA 17042

LEHIGH

Sabetti, Daniel P., Esq.	Cirilli, Vincent J.
Lehigh County Courthouse	P.O. Box 1548
Allentown, PA 18105	455 Hamilton Street
	Allentown, PA 18101

LUZERNE

Mihalko, Andrew J.	Maffei, Carmen J., Esq.
Luzerne County Courthouse	Luzerne County Courthouse
200 N. River Street	200 N. River Street
Wilkes-Barre, PA 18711	Wilkes-Barre, PA 18711

LYCOMING

Holland, Raymond A.	Holland, Raymond A.
Lycoming County Courthouse	Lycoming County Courthouse
Williamsport, PA 17701	48 West Third Street
	Williamsport, PA 17701

McKEAN

Caldwell, Mark	Caldwell, Mark
McKean County Courthouse	McKean County Courthouse
Smethport, PA 16749	Smethport, PA 16749

MERCER

Webster, Michael	Webster, Michael
Mercer County Courthouse	Mercer County Courthouse
Mercer, PA 16137	Mercer, PA 16137

DISTRICT COURT ADMINISTRATORS	DISTRICT JUSTICE COURT ADMINISTRATORS

MIFFLIN

Vacant	Vacant
Mifflin County Courthouse	Mifflin County Courthouse
20 N. Wayne Street	20 N. Wayne Street
Lewistown, PA 17044	Lewistown, PA 17044

MONROE

Prevoznik, John	Prevoznik, John
Monroe County Courthouse	Monroe County Courthouse
Stroudsburg, PA 18360	Stroudsburg, PA 18360

MONTGOMERY

Lewis, Marvin J., Esq.	Borek, Harold D., Esq.
Montgomery County Courthouse	Montgomery County Courthouse
Swede & Airy Streets	Swede & Airy Streets
Norristown, PA 19401	Norristown, PA 19401

NORTHAMPTON

Marhefka, Al V.	Crumling, Debra
Northampton County Courthouse	Northampton County
7th & Washington Streets	Government Ctr.
Easton, PA 18042	7th & Washington Streets
	Easton, PA 18042

NORTHUMBERLAND

Diorio, Lawrence E.	Diorio, Lawrence E.
Northumberland County	Northumberland County
Courthouse	Courthouse
2nd and Market Streets	2nd and Market Streets
Sunbury, PA 17801	Sunbury, PA 17801

PERRY

Jones, Donna M.	Jones, Donna M.
Perry County Courthouse	Perry County Courthouse
New Bloomfield, PA 17068	New Bloomfield, PA 17068

PHILADELPHIA

Scally, Bernard A., III	Scally, Bernard A., III
Municipal Court	City Hall Annex
1224 City Hall Annex	12th Floor-Room 43
Philadelphia, PA 19107	Philadelphia, PA 19107

PIKE

Kellam, Colleen E.	Kellam, Colleen E.
Pike County Courthouse	Pike County Courthouse
Milford, PA 18337	Milford, PA 18337

POTTER

Downs, Bertha M.	Downs, Bertha M.
Potter County Courthouse	Potter County Courthouse
Coudersport, PA 16915	Coudersport, PA 16915

SCHUYLKILL

Johns, Frank G.	Vacant
Schuylkill County Courthouse	Schuylkill County Courthouse
2nd and Laurel Streets	2nd and Laurel Streets
Pottsville, PA 17901	Pottsville, PA 17901

SNYDER

Shambach, Ruth	Shambach, Ruth
Snyder County Courthouse	Snyder County Courthouse
P.O. Box 217	P.O. Box 217
Middleburg, PA 17842	Middleburg, PA 17842

SOMERSET

Trexell, Howard H.	Trexell, Howard H.
Somerset County Courthouse	Somerset County Courthouse
E. Union/N. Center Streets	E. Union/N. Center Streets
Somerset, PA 15501	Somerset, PA 15501

DISTRICT COURT ADMINISTRATORS	DISTRICT JUSTICE COURT ADMINISTRATORS	DISTRICT COURT ADMINISTRATORS	DISTRICT JUSTICE COURT ADMINISTRATORS

SUSQUEHANNA

Rydzewski, Barbara W.
Susquehanna County Courthouse
Montrose, PA 18801

Rydzewski, Barbara W.
Susquehanna County Courthouse
Montrose, PA 18801

WAYNE

Scamell, Vincent A., Jr.
Wayne County Courthouse
Honesdale, PA 18431

Scamell, Vincent A.
Wayne County Courthouse
Honesdale, PA 18431

TIOGA

Matteson, Carl L.
Tioga County Courthouse
118 Main Street
Wellsboro, PA 16901

Matteson, Carl L.
Tioga County Courthouse
118 Main Street
Wellsboro, PA 16901

WESTMORELAND

Kuntz, Paul
Westmoreland County
  Courthouse
Greensburg, PA 15601

Speicher, Lena M.
Westmoreland County
  Courthouse
Greensburg, PA 15601

UNION

Noll, Kathy A.
Union County Courthouse
Lewisburg, PA 17837

Noll, Kathy A.
Union County Courthouse
Lewisburg, PA 17837

WYOMING

Morgan, John R., Esq.
116-118 Warren Street
Tunkhannock, PA 18657

VENANGO

Hutchinson, Carol E.
Venango County Courthouse
Franklin, PA 16323

Hutchinson, Carol E.
Venango County Courthouse
Franklin, PA 16323

YORK

Krier, Barbara L.
York County Courthouse
28 E. Market Street
York, PA 17401

Myers, Russell A.
York County Courthouse
28 E. Market Street
York, PA 17401

WASHINGTON

Drewitz, Mary L.
Washington County Courthouse
Washington, PA 15301

Brady, Christine
Washington County Courthouse
Washington, PA 15301

PENNSYLVANIA SUPREME COURT JUSTICES
SINCE 1681

CHIEF JUSTICES[1]

	Assumed Office			Assumed Office
Capt. William Crispin,[2] appointed		1681	Ulysses Mercur	Jan. 1, 1883
Dr. Nicholas Moore	June	4, 1684	Isaac G. Gordon	June 6, 1887
James Harrison (declined)	July	14, 1685	Edward M. Paxson	Jan. 17, 1889
Arthur Cook	Jan.	31, 1686	James P. Sterrett	Feb. 21, 1893
John Simcock	Sept.	21, 1690	Henry Green	Jan. 1, 1900
Andrew Robeson	May	29, 1692	J. Brewster McCollum	Aug. 17, 1900
John Guest	June	20, 1701	James T. Mitchell	Oct. 5, 1903
William Clarke		1703	D. Newlin Fell	Jan. 3, 1910
John Guest		1705	J. Hay Brown	Jan. 4, 1915
Roger Mempesson	April	17, 1706	Robert von Moschzisker	Jan. 3, 1921
Joseph Growden	Nov.	20, 1707	Robert S. Frazer	Nov. 24, 1930
David Lloyd	Feb.	15, 1717	John W. Kephart	Jan. 6, 1936
Isaac Norris (declined)	April	3, 1731	William I. Schaffer	Jan. 2, 1940
James Logan	Aug.	20, 1731	George W. Maxey	Jan. 4, 1943
Jeremiah Langhorne	Aug.	13, 1739	James B. Drew	Mar. 21, 1950
John Kinsey	April	5, 1743	Horace Stern	Nov. 1, 1952
William Allen	Sept.	20, 1750	Charles Alvin Jones	Dec. 29, 1956
Benjamin Chew	April	9, 1774	John C. Bell, Jr.	July 31, 1961
Joseph Reed (declined)	Mar.	20, 1777	Benjamin R. Jones	Jan. 3, 1972
Thomas McKean, July 28, 1777;			Michael J. Eagen	Mar. 1, 1977
July 29, 1784	Jan.	31, 1791	Henry X. O'Brien	Sept. 23, 1980
Edward Shippen	Dec.	18, 1799	Samuel J. Roberts	Jan. 3, 1983
William Tilghman	Mar.	1, 1806	*Robert N.C. Nix, Jr.	Jan. 6, 1984
John Bannister Gibson, May 18, 1827	Nov.	19, 1838		
Jeremiah S. Black	Nov.	17, 1851		
Ellis Lewis, Dec. 1, 1854	Jan.	5, 1855		
Walter H. Lowrie	Dec.	7, 1857		
George W. Woodward	Dec.	7, 1863		
James Thompson	Dec.	2, 1867		
John Meredith Read	Dec.	2, 1872		
Daniel Agnew	Dec.	1, 1873		
George Sharswood	Jan.	6, 1879		

[1]Where three dates are given the first indicates appointment, second and third indicate elections, other dates indicate assuming of office of Chief Justice

[2]Named by William Penn in a letter to William Markham, dated at London, August 18, 1681; Crispin died at sea on way to Pennsylvania.

*Incumbent

JUSTICES

Assumed Office

Assumed Office

William Welsh	June 4, 1684
William Wood	June 4, 1684
Robert Turner	June 4, 1684
John Eckley	June 4, 1684
William Clarke	July 10, 1684
James Clapoole	July 14, 1685
Arthur Cooke	July 14, 1685
John Cann	Jan. 31, 1686
John Simcock	Jan. 20, 1686
James Harrison	Jan. 20, 1686
Joseph Growden	Feb. 2, 1690
Peter Alricks	May 7, 1690
Thomas Wynne	May 7, 1690
Griffith Jones	Sept. 21, 1690
Edward Blake	Sept. 21, 1690
William Salway	May 20, 1693
Anthony Morris	Aug. 10, 1694
Cornelius Empston	About 1698
Edward Shippen	About 1699
William Biles	About 1699
Robert French	June 20, 1701
Caleb Pusey	June 20, 1701
Thomas Masters	June 20, 1701
Samuel Finney	1702
John Guest	April 10, 1704
Jasper Yates	April 10, 1704
William Trent	April 10, 1704
Richard Hill	Mar. 16, 1711
Jonathan Dickinson	Mar. 16, 1711
George Roche	June 10, 1715
Robert Assheton	June 12, 1716
Jeremiah Langhorne	Sept. 20, 1726
Dr. Thomas Graeme	April 9, 1731
Thomas Griffitts	Aug. 13, 1739
William Till	April 5, 1743
Lawrence Growden	Sept. 20, 1750
Caleb Cowpland	Sept. 20, 1750
William Coleman	April 8, 1758
Alexander Steadman	Mar. 21, 1764
John Lawrence	Sept. 14, 1767
Thomas Willing	Sept. 14, 1767
John Morton	April 20, 1774
William Augustus Atlee, April 2, 1777; Aug. 16, 1777	Aug. 9, 1784
John Evans	Aug. 19, 1777
George Bryan	April 5, 1780
Jacob Rush	Feb. 26, 1784
George Bryan	April 4, 1787
Edward Shippen	Jan. 31, 1791
Jasper Yates	Mar. 21, 1791
William Bradford, Jr.	Aug. 20, 1791
Thomas Smith	Jan. 3, 1794
Hugh Henry Brackenridge	Dec. 18, 1800
John Bannister Gibson	June 27, 1816
Thomas Duncan	Mar. 14, 1817
Morton Cropper Rogers, April 15, 1826; Jan. 1, 1842	Jan. 25, 1842
Charles Huston	April 17, 1826
Horace Binney (declined)	May 18, 1827
John Tod	May 25, 1827
Frederick Smith	Jan. 31, 1828
John Ross	April 9, 1830
John Kennedy	Nov. 23, 1830
Thomas Sergeant	Feb. 3, 1834
Thomas Burnside, Jan. 2, 1845	Feb. 22, 1845
Richard Coulter, Sept. 17, 1846	Feb. 17, 1847
Thomas S. Bell, Nov. 10, 1846	Mar. 5, 1847
George Chambers	April 10, 1851
Ellis Lewis	Dec. 1, 1851
Walter H. Lowrie	Dec. 1, 1851
George W. Woodward, May 8, 1852	Dec. 6, 1852
John C. Knox, May 23, 1853	Dec. 5, 1853
Jeremiah S. Black	Dec. 4, 1854
James Armstrong	April 6, 1857
James Thompson	Dec. 7, 1857
William Strong	Dec. 7, 1857
William A. Porter	Jan. 20, 1858
Gaylord Church	Oct. 22, 1858
John M. Read	Dec. 6, 1858
Daniel Agnew	Dec. 7, 1863
George Sharswood	Dec. 2, 1867
Henry W. Williams, Oct. 1, 1868	Dec. 5, 1868
Henry W. Williams	Nov. 19, 1869
Ulysses Mercur	Dec. 2, 1872
Isaac G. Gordon	Dec. 8, 1873
Edward M. Paxson	Jan. 4, 1875
Warren I. Woodward	Jan. 4, 1875
James P. Sterrett	Feb. 26, 1877
John Trunkey	Dec. 6, 1877
James P. Sterrett	Dec. 6, 1878
Henry Green	Sept. 29, 1879
Henry Green	Dec. 2, 1880
Silas M. Clark	Dec. 21, 1882
Henry W. Williams	Aug. 19, 1887
Henry W. Williams	Dec. 22, 1887
Alfred Hand	July 31, 1888
J. Brewster McCollum	Dec. 18, 1888
James T. Mitchell	Dec. 18, 1888
Christopher Heydrick	Nov. 28, 1891
John Dean	Dec. 19, 1892
Samuel Gustine Thompson	Mar. 3, 1893
D. Newlin Fell	Jan. 1, 1894
J. Hay Brown	Sept. 25, 1899
J. Hay Brown	Jan. 1, 1900
S. Leslie Mestrezat	Jan. 1, 1900
William P. Potter	Sept. 25, 1899
William P. Potter	Jan. 6, 1902
Samuel Gustine Thompson	Nov. 25, 1903
John P. Elkin	Jan. 2, 1905
John Stewart	June 8, 1905
John Stewart	Jan. 1, 1906
Robert von Moschzisker	Jan. 3, 1910
Robert S. Frazer	Jan. 4, 1915
Emory A. Walling	Jan. 3, 1916
Emory A. Walling	Jan. 1, 1917
Alexander Simpson, Jr.	May 20, 1918
Alexander Simpson, Jr.	Jan. 6, 1919
Edward J. Fox	June 17, 1918
John W. Kephart	Jan. 6, 1919
Sylvester B. Sadler	Jan. 3, 1921
William I. Schaffer	Dec. 14, 1920
William I. Schaffer	Jan. 2, 1922
George W. Maxey	Nov. 24, 1930
James B. Drew	Sept. 28, 1931
William B. Linn	Feb. 23, 1932
William B. Linn	Jan. 2, 1933
Horace Stern	Jan. 6, 1936
H. Edgar Barnes, Aug. 12, 1935	Jan. 6, 1936
Marion D. Patterson	Jan. 2, 1940
William M. Parker	Dec. 13, 1941
Allen M. Stearne	Dec. 24, 1942
Howard W. Hughes	Dec. 30, 1943
Charles Alvin Jones	Jan. 3, 1945
John C. Bell	Mar. 24, 1950
Grover C. Ladner	July 6, 1950
Thomas McKeen Chidsey	July 6, 1950
Michal A. Musmanno	Jan. 7, 1952

	Assumed Office		Assumed Office
John C. Arnold	Jan. 5, 1953	*Robert N. C. Nix, Jr.	Jan. 3, 1972
Benjamin R. Jones	Jan. 7, 1957	Louis L. Manderino	Jan. 3, 1972
Herbert B. Cohen	Jan. 7, 1957	Israel Packel (appointed)	June 1, 1977
Thomas D. McBride	Dec. 6, 1958	*Rolf Larsen	Jan. 5, 1978
Curtis Bok	Jan. 1959	*John P. Flaherty, Jr.	June 15, 1979
Michael J. Eagen	Jan. 5, 1960	Bruce W. Kauffman	Feb. 29, 1980
Anne X. Alpern (appointed)	Sept. 6, 1961	Roy Wilkinson, Jr.	Mar. 19, 1981
Henry X. O'Brien	Jan. 1, 1962	*William D. Hutchinson	Jan. 4, 1982
Earl S. Keim (appointed)	Aug. 30, 1962	*James T. McDermott	Jan. 4, 1982
Samuel J. Roberts	Jan. 8, 1963	*Stephen A. Zappala	Jan. 3, 1983
Thomas W. Pomeroy, Jr.	Dec. 30, 1968	*Nicholas P. Papadakos	Jan. 2, 1984
Alexander F. Barbieri	Jan. 4, 1971		

*Incumbent

PENNSYLVANIA SUPERIOR COURT JUDGES SINCE 1895

PRESIDENT JUDGES

	Assumed Office		Assumed Office
Charles E. Rice	June 28, 1895	J. Colvin Wright	Jan. 1, 1968
George B. Orlady	Dec. 19, 1915	G. Harold Watkins	Jan. 7, 1974
William D. Porter	Dec. 18, 1925	Robert Lee Jacobs	Jan. 3, 1978
Frank M. Trexler	Feb. 10, 1930	William Franklin Cercone	Jan. 2, 1979
William H. Keller	Jan. 7, 1935	Edmund B. Spaeth, Jr.	Aug. 11, 1983
Thomas J. Baldridge	Jan. 16, 1945	*Vincent A. Cirillo	Jan. 8, 1986
Chester H. Rhodes	Mar. 1, 1947		
Harold L. Ervin	Jan. 4, 1965	*Incumbent	

JUDGES[1]

	Assumed Office		Assumed Office
James A. Beaver[2], 1895, 1906	June 28, 1895	William E. Hirt[2], 1940, 1950	Mar. 8, 1939
Howard I. Reeder[2], 1896	June 29, 1895	Charles E. Kenworthey[2], 1942	April 14, 1941
George B. Orlady[2], 1896, 1906, 1916	June 28, 1895	Claude T. Reno[2], 1944	Dec. 15, 1942
John J. Wickham[2], 1896	June 28, 1895	Arthur H. James[2]	Feb. 8, 1944
Edward N. Willard[2], 1896	June 28, 1895	F. Clair Ross	Jan. 18, 1945
Henry J. McCarthy[2]	June 28, 1895	W. Heber Dithrich[2], 1946	Dec. 29, 1945
Peter P. Smith	1896	John C. Arnold[2], 1946	April 2, 1945
William W. Porter[2], 1899	Sept. 14, 1897	John S. Fine[2], 1948	July 15, 1947
William D. Porter[2], 1899, 1909, 1919	July 1898	Blair F. Gunther	April 25, 1950
Dimmer Beeber[2]	Jan. 2, 1899	J. Colvin Wright, Jan. 4, 1954	Mar. 2, 1953
John I. Mitchell	1900	Robert E. Woodside, Jan. 4, 1954	Oct. 1, 1953
Thomas A. Morrison[2], 1904	Dec. 30, 1902	Harold L. Ervin	Jan. 4, 1954
John J. Henderson[2], 1904, 1914, 1924	Mar. 11, 1903	Philip O. Carr, Jan. 7, 1957	Mar. 5, 1956
John B. Head, 1916	1906	G. Harold Watkins	Jan. 7, 1957
John W. Kephart	1914	Harry M. Montgomery	Jan. 5, 1960
Frank M. Trexler[2], 1915, 1925	Feb. 6, 1914	Gerald F. Flood	Jan. 2, 1961
J. Henry Williams	1916	Robert Lee Jacobs	Jan. 4, 1965
William H. Keller (PJ, Jan. 7, 1935), 1929, 1939.		J. Sydney Hoffman	Jan. 4, 1965
	1919	Theodore O. Spaulding[2]	Mar. 27, 1966
William B. Linn[2], 1921	Nov. 5, 1919	John B. Hannum	Jan. 6, 1968
Robert S. Gawthrop[2], 1923	April 12, 1922	William Franklin Cercone	Jan. 6, 1969
Jesse E. B. Cunningham, 1936.	1926	Israel Packel[2]	Dec. 31, 1971
Thomas J. Baldridge[2] (PJ, Jan. 16, 1945), 1930, 1940.	Jan. 28, 1929	Edmund B. Spaeth, Jr.[2], Dec. 31, 1972.	Jan. 2, 1973
James B. Drew	1931	Gwilym A. Price, Jr.	Jan. 7, 1974
J. Frank Graff[2]	Feb. 18, 1930	Robert Van der Voort	Jan. 7, 1974
John G. Whitmore[2]	June 24, 1930	John P. Hester	Jan. 3, 1978
Joseph Stadfelt[2], 1933, 1943	Nov. 7, 1931	*Donald E. Wieand	Oct. 12, 1978
Arthur H. James	1933	*James R. Cavanaugh	July 31, 1979
William M. Parker[2], 1933	Feb. 23, 1932	*John G. Brosky	Jan. 7, 1980
Chester H. Rhodes, (PJ, Mar. 1, 1947) 1945, 1955.		*Frank J. Montemuro, Jr.	Dec. 16, 1980
		Richard B. Wickersham	Jan. 7, 1980
	1935	Richard DiSalle	Dec. 16, 1980

	Assumed Office	
Perry J. Shertz	Dec.	16, 1980
*Stephen J. McEwen, Jr.	May	15, 1981
*Phyllis W. Beck	June	23, 1981
*Zoran Popovich	Dec.	16, 1980
*Justin M. Johnson	Dec.	16, 1980
*Vincent A. Cirillo	Jan.	4, 1982
*James E. Rowley	Jan.	4, 1982
*Peter Paul Olszewski	Jan.	2, 1984

	Assumed Office	
*Joseph A. Del Sole	Jan.	2, 1984
*Patrick R. Tamilia	Jan.	2, 1984
*John T. J. Kelly, Jr.	Jan.	8, 1986

[1]Unless otherwise indicated Judges assumed or reassumed office on first Monday in January of years given.

[2]Appointed.

*Incumbent.

COMMONWEALTH COURT JUDGES SINCE 1970

PRESIDENT JUDGES

	Assumed Office	
James S. Bowman	April	15, 1970
*James Crumlish, Jr.	April	8, 1981

JUDGES

	Assumed Office	
Alexander F. Barbieri	April	15, 1970
Harry A. Kramer (dec'd. Aug. 4, 1977)	April	15, 1970
Roy Wilkinson, Jr.	April	15, 1970
Louis Lawrence Manderino	April	15, 1970
*James Crumlish, Jr.	April	15, 1970
Glenn E. Mencer	April	15, 1970
Theodore O. Rogers	Jan.	4, 1971
Genevieve Blatt	Jan.	3, 1972
Richard DiSalle	Nov.	28, 1977

	Assumed Office	
*John A. MacPhail	July	10, 1978
*David W. Craig	July	13, 1978
Robert W. Williams, Jr.	Jan.	7, 1980
*Madaline Palladino	Oct.	2, 1980
*Joseph T. Doyle	Jan.	4, 1982
*Francis A. Barry	July	12, 1983
*J. Gardner Colins	Jan.	2, 1984

*Incumbent

COURT ADMINISTRATORS OF PENNSYLVANIA COURTS SINCE 1968

	Appointed	
A. Evans Kephart	Dec.	23, 1968
Alexander F. Barbieri	Dec.	5, 1974
Abraham J. Gafni	Jan.	24, 1983
Donald J. Harris, Ph.D. (acting)	Feb.	8, 1985
*Nancy M. Sobolevitch	Mar.	31, 1986

*Incumbent

LOCAL
GOVERNMENT

SECTION 6 — LOCAL GOVERNMENT

PENNSYLVANIA LOCAL GOVERNMENT

Local government in Pennsylvania is a mosaic of 5,663 individual units. All were established by the State or provincial government and operate under laws of the Commonwealth. Each unit is distinct and independent of other local units, although they may overlap geographically and may act together to serve the public.

As of 1987, there were 67 counties, 54 cities, 967 boroughs, 1 incorporated town, 1,550 townships (91 first class, 1,459 second class), 501 school districts and 2,548 authorities (active and inactive). The number of local units remained fairly stable for the past few decades with two major exceptions. After passage of school district legislation in 1963 and 1965, the number of school districts diminished radically. Authorities, born as local units during the depression years of the 1930's, have proliferated at a phenomenal pace since then.

STATE AND LOCAL GOVERNMENT

Constitutional Provisions

The Constitution authorizes the state to enact laws regulating local units of government. It outlines basic requirements and rights. The Constitution requires periodic legislative apportionment, guarantees the right to select a home rule charter or an optional plan of government, and mandates uniform legislation establishing the procedure for consolidation, merger or change of municipal boundaries. The Constitution also prohibits special or local legislation by the General Assembly, sets up county government with elected row officers, permits classification of local governments according to population, and requires taxation to be uniform upon the same classes of subjects. The General Assembly is allowed to enact certain tax exemptions and special tax provisions because of age, disability, infirmity or poverty.

Classifications

Municipalities and school districts may be classified according to population, and the General Assembly can legislate separately for each class. There are four general types of municipalities in Pennsylvania: counties, cities, boroughs and townships. At the present time there are nine classes of counties, four classes of cities, two classes of townships and five classes of school districts. Boroughs are not classified. Legislation may be enacted for each class even though there is only one unit in a particular class, as is the case of Philadelphia as a city of the first class and Allegheny as the only county of the second class.

Each class of municipality operates under its own code of laws which sets forth the governmental structure as well as the general and specific powers of local government. Except for home rule municipalities, the codes are the most important source of legislative powers granted to a municipal governing body by the General Assembly. They are the County Code, Third Class City Code, Borough Code, First Class Township Code, Second Class Township Code and Public School Code.

Legislation

There is also extensive general legislation applying to local governments. Some examples of legislative provisions outside the local government codes are real property assessment, local non-property taxation, municipal borrowing, real estate tax collection, intergovernmental cooperation, municipal employes retirement, solid waste management, sewage facilities, and planning and zoning.

Significant general laws affecting local governments both grant powers and impose restrictions. The Pennsylvania Municipalities Planning Code empowers municipalities to plan their development and adopt zoning, subdivision and land development ordinances. The Pennsylvania Sewage Facilities Act regulates community and individual sewage disposal systems. The Solid Waste Management Act provides for solid waste collection and disposal.

The Local Government Unit Debt Act establishes debt limits for local government units based on municipal revenues. The Municipal Police Education and Training Act mandates training of all municipal police officers. The Intergovernmental Cooperation Act permits two or more municipalities to cooperate jointly in the exercise of any governmental functions and allows municipalities to delegate powers to other local units. The Sunshine Law requires public agencies to discuss and act upon agency business only at meetings open to the public. There are numerous other general laws affecting local government powers and procedures.

Taxes

The state gives local governments authority to levy taxes on inhabitants and property within their jurisdiction and provides for tax exemptions. Taxes are levied and collected under general laws. The two primary sources of tax revenue at the local level are the real estate tax, authorized under the respective municipal codes, and the earned income tax, authorized by the Local Tax Enabling Act. The Local Tax Enabling Act authorizes numerous other types of taxes.

Home Rule

The Home Rule Charter and Optional Plans Law grants Pennsylvania municipalities the power to determine for themselves what structure their government will take and what services it will perform. A home rule municipality no longer has its powers and organization determined by the state legislature. A home rule municipality drafts and amends its own charter and can exercise any power or perform any function not denied by the state Constitution, the General Assembly or its home rule charter. As of January 1987, 58 municipalities have adopted home rule charters, including 5 counties, 11 cities, 17 boroughs and 25 townships.

Between 1957 and 1972, third class cities could choose the mayor-council or council-manager form of government. The Home Rule Charter and Optional Plans Law extended to all municipalities the right to adopt optional plans of government. Adoption of an optional plan of government alters a municipality's structural form and administrative organization. The municipality continues to be subject to its particular municipal code regarding municipal powers.

Six optional plans are provided for under the law: (1) Executive (Mayor)-Council Plan A (department of administration optional); (2) Executive (Mayor)-Council Plan B (department of administration mandated); (3) Executive (Mayor)-Council Plan C (provides for the office of managing director); (4) Council-Manager Plan; (5) Small Municipality Plan (limited to any municipality having a population of less than 7,500 residents; and (6) Optional County Plan (limited to counties). As of January 1987, two cities, two boroughs and five townships have adopted optional plans of government. Fifteen cities continue to operate under the Optional Third Class City Charter Law.

NATIONAL GOVERNMENT AND LOCAL UNITS

Local government is one of the powers reserved to the states in Article X of the United States Constitution. However, since the 1930's when the big cities of the nation looked to the federal government for financial assistance to combat the problems brought on by the economic depression, the national government has taken an increasingly active role in local government, especially in the urban areas. Recent developments have also evidenced concern for rural areas. Through financial subsidies, grants and technical assistance, federal agencies have stimulated development of low-cost housing, urban renewal, improved educational facilities, modern highways, health and welfare services, and personal security. Federal programs, such as housing and community development, have strengthened direct links between federal and local government. There is a trend toward more local decision making in federal programs.

COUNTIES

There are 67 counties in Pennsylvania including the consolidated city-county of Philadelphia, and each inhabitant of the state lives in and comes under the jurisdiction of one of them. The largest in population is Philadelphia with over one and a half million people; the smallest is Forest with approximately five thousand. The Constitution establishes a basic organization, but counties can adopt their own form of government. Five counties have adopted home rule charters: Delaware, Erie, Lackawanna, Lehigh and Northampton.

County Functions

Counties continue to serve in their traditional role as agents of the state for law enforcement, judicial administration and the conduct of elections. The county is also responsible for the property assessment function. Counties become involved in regional planning, solid waste disposal and public health. They perform welfare functions, including mental health. Counties also can establish housing and redevelopment authorities and conduct community development programs. Counties maintain hospitals and homes for the aged. Counties may support local libraries and community colleges.

Legislation enacted in recent years has strengthened the policymaking role of boards of county commissioners, granting them greater control of and responsibility for county government. The geographic size of counties enables them to cope with functions that can be better performed on an area-wide basis, i.e., mass transportation and environmental protection.

County Government

County government, as provided for in the county codes, may be described as a "no-executive" type. The chief governing body is the three-member board of county commissioners. But there are also numerous other elected officials to a large extent independent of the county commissioners. These include the sheriff, district attorney, prothonotary, clerk of courts, register of wills, recorder of deeds and two jury commissioners whose duties are mostly concerned with the work of the county court. Additionally, there are the elective offices of the controller or three auditors and the treasurer who are county finance officers. A public defender is appointed as provided by law. The county commissioners, the elected officers and the county court individually or jointly appoint a number of other county officials and employes needed to carry out county functions by law.

Whereas the 11 elective county officers are enumerated in the Pennsylvania Constitution, their powers and duties are prescribed by statutes which are scattered throughout the county codes and general state laws. Consolidation of certain elective offices is provided by state law in the smaller class counties involving the offices of prothonotary, clerk of courts, register of wills and recorder of deeds.

MUNICIPALITIES

Municipal Powers

In addition to living under a county government, every Pennsylvanian also lives in a municipality. Municipal governing bodies make policy decisions, levy taxes, borrow money, authorize expenditures and direct administration of their governments by their appointees. The scope of their functions and responsibilities is broad.

Many powers given to local governments are not exercised, while others are shared with the state and even the national government. All of the various municipal units of Pennsylvania share the same basic responsibilities with respect to the provision of public services at the local level and have similar statutory powers for the most part. Although cities have more specifically enumerated powers than boroughs or townships, many of those powers may also be exercised by boroughs and townships under general grants of power. Home rule provides equal opportunity for all classes of municipalities to exercise new powers.

Municipal Functions

The main areas of local services include police and fire protection, maintenance of local roads and streets, water supply, sewage collection and treatment, parking and traffic control, local planning and zoning, parks and recreation, garbage collection, health services, libraries, licensing of businesses and code enforcement.

CITIES

First and Second Class Cities

The oldest and largest Pennsylvania city, Philadelphia, has had a strong-mayor home rule charter since 1952. There is a council of 17 members, one elected from each of the ten councilmanic districts of the city and seven elected at large. Each political party may nominate one candidate for each of the ten districts but only five for the seven at large places. This allows the minority party to elect at least two members. The mayor, also elected, has control over the administration of the city. He is assisted by a managing director who supervises ten major departments, a director of finance, a city representative and a city solicitor.

Pittsburgh and Scranton, second class and second class A cities respectively, also have strong mayors. These mayors, like the chief executive of Philadelphia, have broad appointive and removal powers, are responsible for the preparation of the annual budget, recommend measures for the consideration of council and may veto legislation which may be overridden by a two-thirds majority of the council. Home rule charters were adopted by Scranton and Pittsburgh in 1974. In all three cities, the mayor is the dominant force in city government.

Third Class Cities

The code establishes a commission form of government. Under this form, the mayor and four other members constitute the commission which is the governing body of the city. The mayor is one of the members of council and acts as president. Each councilman is in charge of one of the five major departments. These officials and the controller and treasurer are elected at large by the voters for a four-year term. Councilmanic terms overlap. Appointment of all other officers and employes is made by council. Twenty-five of the 50 third class cities operate under the commission form: Aliquippa, Altoona, Arnold, Beaver Falls, Bradford, Butler, Clairton, Connellsville, Corry, Duquesne, Greensburg, Jeannette, Lebanon, Lower Burrell, Monessen, Monongahela, Nanticoke, New Kensington, Pittston, Pottsville, Reading, Shamokin, Sunbury, Uniontown and Washington.

From 1957 to 1972, cities could adopt two other forms of government by referendum under the Optional Third Class City Charter Law. The mayor-council form has a five, seven or nine member council, elected at large for overlapping four-year terms. A mayor, treasurer and a controller also are elected for a four-year period. The mayor is the chief executive of the city and enforces the ordinances of council. The mayor may veto ordinances which can be overridden by a two-thirds majority of council. The mayor supervises the work of all city departments and submits the annual city budget to council. Cities operating under this plan include Allentown, Bethlehem, Easton, Erie, Harrisburg, Johnstown, Lancaster, New Castle, Sharon, Williamsport and York.

In the council-manager form, all authority is lodged with council which is composed of five, seven or nine members elected at large for a four-year term. A city treasurer and controller also are elected. A city manager is appointed by council. The manager is the chief administrative officer of the city and is responsible for executing the ordinances of council. The manager appoints and may remove department heads and subordinates. Cities operating under this plan include Lock Haven, Meadville, Oil City and Titusville.

Since 1972, eight cities have adopted home rule charters including Carbondale, Chester, Coatesville, Farrell, Franklin, Hermitage, McKeesport and Wilkes-Barre. Also, DuBois adopted the council-manager optional plan and Hazleton, the mayor-council optional plan, under the Home Rule Charter and Optional Plans Law.

BOROUGHS

The present type of borough government is the weak mayor form which governed all incorporated municipalities during the 19th century. Most of the present cities were boroughs first and became cities as their population increased. Boroughs have a strong and dominant council, a weak executive and other elected officers with powers independent of the council. The governing body of the borough is an elected council. The tax collector, tax assessor and the auditors also are elected. Many other officials are appointed by borough council.

The mayor is elected for a four-year term; councilmen are elected for four-year overlapping terms. A borough not divided into wards has seven councilmen; in boroughs divided into wards, at least one and not more than two are elected from each ward. The powers of council are broad and extensive, covering virtually the whole range of urban municipal functions.

In more than two hundred boroughs, the chief administrative officer is a manager appointed by council. The manager is responsible for carrying out the policies and enforcing the ordinances of council, relieving council from routine day-to-day administration.

Since 1972, seventeen boroughs have adopted home rule charters: Bellevue, Bethel Park, Bradford Woods, Green Tree, Monroeville, Whitehall, Tyrone, Chalfont, State College, Cambridge Springs, Edinboro, Kingston, Bryn Athyn, Norristown, Warren, Youngsville and Murrysville. The boroughs of Weatherly and Quakertown have adopted optional plans, selecting council-manager plans.

TOWNSHIPS

Pennsylvania has two classes of townships. The first numbers 91 and includes the more urban townships located in the state's metropolitan areas; the second class, numbering 1,459, is generally rural.

In townships of the first class, the governing body is made up of elected commissioners. There are either five commissioners elected at large or up to 15 elected by wards. The commissioners have four-year overlapping terms.

The governing body of second class townships is composed of three supervisors who are elected at large. Two additional supervisors may be elected if approved by referendum. All are elected at large for six-year terms.

Other elected township officials include the tax assessor, tax collector (second class), three auditors or controller, and a treasurer (first class). Appointive officers include the secretary, township manager if desired, chief of police, fire chief, engineer, solicitor and others.

To become a township of the first class, a second class township must have a population density of 300 persons per square mile, and voters must approve change of classification in a referendum. Many townships meeting the density requirement have remained second class.

Since 1972, twelve townships of the first class adopted home rule charters: McCandless, Mt. Lebanon, O'Hara, Penn Hills, Upper St. Clair, Haverford, Upper Darby, Whitehall, Wilkes-Barre, Cheltenham, Plymouth and Radnor. Thirteen townships of the second class have also adopted home rule charters: Richland, Hampton, Whitemarsh, West Deer, Ferguson, Elk, Tredyffrin, Middletown, Upper Providence, Hanover, Kingston, Horsham and Peters. Four townships of the second class adopted optional plans of government: Indiana, College, Washington and Lower Saucon. All of the townships adopted the council-manager form. Bristol, a first class township, has adopted the executive-council optional plan.

AUTHORITIES

The authority is a special kind of local unit. They are not general government entities as are cities, boroughs and townships. They are set up to perform a special service. An authority is a body corporate and politic authorized to acquire, construct, improve, maintain and operate projects, and to borrow money and issue bonds to finance them. Projects include public facilities such as buildings, including school buildings, transportation facilities, marketing and shopping facilities, highways, parkways, airports, parking places, waterworks, sewage treatment plants, playgrounds, hospitals and industrial development projects.

An authority can be organized by any county, city, town, borough, township or school district of the Commonwealth, acting singly or jointly with another municipality. An authority is established by ordinance by one or more municipalities. The governing bodies of the parent local unit or units appoint the members of the authority's board. If incorporated by one unit, the board consists of five members; if comprised of two or more local units, there is at least one member from each unit but no less than five. The board carries on the work of the authority, acquires property, appoints officers and employes, undertakes projects, makes regulations and charges, and collects revenue from services of the facilities or projects.

The original reason for the establishment of authorities was the restrictive provisions for incurring debt imposed by the Commonwealth prior to the 1968 constitutional amendments, but they have proven useful mechanisms particularly for joint municipal projects. As of January 1987, there were 2,548 authorities in Pennsylvania. They have continued to grow at a substantial rate from the 1962 figure of 1,398.

MUNICIPALITIES WHICH HAVE ADOPTED HOME RULE CHARTERS, OPTIONAL PLANS AND OPTIONAL CHARTERS AS OF JANUARY 1, 1987

A total of fifty-eight communities have adopted home rule charters, including five counties, eleven cities, twenty-five townships and seventeen boroughs. Nine have adopted optional plans; five townships, two boroughs and two cities. Fifteen cities continue to operate under optional charters.

County	Municipality	1980 Population	Form	Date Adopted
Allegheny	Bellevue Borough	10,128	Home Rule	Nov. 1974
	Bethel Park Borough	34,755	Home Rule	Nov. 1976

County	Municipality	1980 Population	Form	Date Adopted
	Bradford Woods Borough	1,264	Home Rule	May 1974
	Green Tree Borough	5,722	Home Rule	Nov. 1974
	Hampton Township	14,260	Home Rule	Nov. 1981
	Indiana Township	6,080	Optional Plan	Nov. 1974
	McCandless Township	26,191	Home Rule	Nov. 1974
	McKeesport City	31,012	Home Rule	Nov. 1973
	Monroeville Borough	30,977	Home Rule	May 1974
	Mount Lebanon Township	34,414	Home Rule	May 1974
	O'Hara Township	9,233	Home Rule	Nov. 1973
	Penn Hills Township	57,632	Home Rule	May 1973
	Pittsburgh City	423,938	Home Rule	Nov. 1974
	Richland Township	7,749	Home Rule	May 1974
	Upper St. Clair Township	19,023	Home Rule	Nov. 1973
	West Deer Township	10,897	Home Rule	May 1974
	Whitehall Borough	15,142	Home Rule	May 1974
Blair	Tyrone Borough	6,346	Home Rule	May 1982
Bucks	Bristol Township	58,773	Optional Plan	Nov. 1984
	Chalfont Borough	2,802	Home Rule	Nov. 1974
	Quakertown Borough	8,867	Optional Plan	May 1974
Cambria	Johnstown City	35,496	Optional Charter	Apr. 1972
Carbon	Weatherly Borough	2,891	Optional Plan	May 1974
Centre	College Township	6,239	Optional Plan	May 1974
	Ferguson Township	8,105	Home Rule	May 1974
	State College Borough	36,130	Home Rule	Nov. 1973
Chester	Coatesville City	10,698	Home Rule	May 1979
	Elk Township	750	Home Rule	Nov. 1974
	Tredyffrin Township	23,019	Home Rule	May 1974
Clearfield	DuBois City	9,290	Optional Plan	May 1978
Clinton	Lock Haven City	9,617	Optional Charter	Nov. 1969
Crawford	Cambridge Springs Borough	2,102	Home Rule	May 1974
	Meadville City	15,544	Optional Charter	Nov. 1965
	Titusville City	6,884	Optional Charter	Nov. 1962
Dauphin	Harrisburg City	53,264	Optional Charter	May 1969
Delaware	Delaware County	555,007	Home Rule	May 1975
	Chester City	45,794	Home Rule	April 1980
	Haverford Township	52,349	Home Rule	Apr. 1976
	Middletown Township	12,463	Home Rule	May 1975
	Radnor Township	27,676	Home Rule	Nov. 1976
	Upper Darby Township	84,054	Home Rule	May 1974
	Upper Providence Township	9,477	Home Rule	Nov. 1975
Erie	Erie County	279,780	Home Rule	Nov. 1976
	Edinboro Borough	6,324	Home Rule	May 1974
	Erie City	119,123	Optional Charter	Nov. 1959
	Washington Township	3,567	Optional Plan	Nov. 1973
Lackawanna	Lackawanna County	227,908	Home Rule	Apr. 1976
	Carbondale City	11,255	Home Rule	Nov. 1975
	Scranton City	88,117	Home Rule	May 1974
Lancaster	Lancaster City	54,725	Optional Charter	Nov. 1963
Lawrence	New Castle City	33,621	Optional Charter	Nov. 1965
Lehigh	Lehigh County	273,582	Home Rule	Nov. 1975
	Allentown City	103,758	Optional Charter	Nov. 1967
	Hanover Township	2,223	Home Rule	Nov. 1976
	Whitehall Township	21,538	Home Rule	Nov. 1974
Luzerne	Hazleton City	51,318	Optional	Nov. 1985
	Kingston Borough	15,681	Home Rule	Nov. 1974
	Kingston Township	6,535	Home Rule	May 1974
	Wilkes-Barre City	51,551	Home Rule	Nov. 1974
	Wilkes-Barre Township	4,244	Home Rule	May 1974
Lycoming	Williamsport City	33,401	Optional Charter	May 1970
Mercer	Farrell City	8,645	Home Rule	Nov. 1974
	Hermitage City	16,365	Home Rule	May 1974
	Sharon City	19,057	Optional Charter	Nov. 1959
Montgomery	Bryn Athyn Borough	947	Home Rule	Nov. 1977
	Cheltenham Township	35,509	Home Rule	Nov. 1976
	Horsham Township	15,959	Home Rule	Nov. 1975
	Norristown Borough	34,684	Home Rule	Nov. 1984
	Plymouth Township	17,168	Home Rule	May 1974

County	Municipality	1980 Population	Form	Date Adopted
	Whitemarsh Township.	15,101	Home Rule.	May 1982
Northampton	Northampton County	225,418	Home Rule.	Apr. 1976
	Bethlehem City	70,419	Optional Charter	Nov. 1959
	Easton City	26,027	Optional Charter	Nov. 1970
	Lower Saucon Township.	7,372	Optional Plan.	Nov. 1973
Philadelphia.	Philadelphia City.	1,688,210	Home Rule.	Apr. 1951
Venango.	Franklin City	8,146	Home Rule.	Nov. 1974
	Oil City	13,881	Optional Charter	Nov. 1969
Warren.	Warren Borough	12,146	Home Rule.	May 1975
	Youngsville Borough	2,006	Home Rule.	Nov. 1974
Washington	Peters Township	13,104	Home Rule.	Nov. 1973
Westmoreland	Murrysville Borough	16,036	Home Rule.	Apr. 1976
York	York City.	44,619	Optional Charter	Nov. 1959

COUNTIES, COUNTY SEATS AND NUMBER OF MUNICIPALITIES IN PENNSYLVANIA — 1987

County	County Seat	Total	Cities	Number of Municipalities Boroughs	Townships
TOTAL.		2,572	54	968	1,550
Adams.	Gettysburg.	34	—	13	21
Allegheny	Pittsburgh	128	4	82	42
Armstrong	Kittanning	45	1[1]	16	28
Beaver.	Beaver.	52	1	29	22
Bedford.	Bedford.	38	—	13	25
Berks.	Reading.	75	1	30	44
Blair.	Hollidaysburg	24	1	8	15
Bradford	Towanda	51	—	14	37
Bucks	Doylestown	53	—	22	31
Butler.	Butler.	57	1	23	33
Cambria.	Ebensburg.	64	1	33	30
Cameron.	Emporium.	7	—	2	5
Carbon.	Jim Thorpe	23	—	12	11
Centre	Bellefonte.	36	—	11	25
Chester.	West Chester.	73	1	15	57
Clarion.	Clarion.	34	—	12	22
Clearfield.	Clearfield.	50	1	19	30
Clinton.	Lock Haven	29	1	7	21
Columbia.	Bloomsburg.	33	—	9[2]	24
Crawford	Meadville.	51	2	14	35
Cumberland.	Carlisle	34	—	12	22
Dauphin.	Harrisburg.	40	1	16	23
Delaware.	Media.	49	1	27	21
Elk.	Ridgway.	13	—	3	10
Erie.	Erie.	39	2	15	22
Fayette	Uniontown.	42	2	16	24
Forest	Tionesta.	9	—	1	8
Franklin	Chambersburg	21	—	6	15
Fulton	McConnellsburg	13	—	2	11
Greene	Waynesburg.	26	—	6	20
Huntingdon	Huntingdon	48	—	18	30
Indiana.	Indiana.	39	—	15	24
Jefferson	Brookville.	34	—	11	23
Juniata.	Mifflintown.	17	—	4	13
Lackawanna	Scranton	40	2	17	21
Lancaster	Lancaster.	60	1	18	41
Lawrence.	New Castle	27	1	10	16
Lebanon	Lebanon	26	1	7	18
Lehigh	Allentown.	24	1	8	15
Luzerne	Wilkes-Barre	75	4	35	36

County	County Seat	Total	Cities	Number of Municipalities Boroughs	Townships
Lycoming	Williamsport	52	1	9	42
McKean	Smethport	22	1	6	15
Mercer	Mercer	48	3	14	31
Mifflin	Lewistown	16	—	6	10
Monroe	Stroudsburg	20	—	4	16
Montgomery	Norristown	62	—	24	38
Montour	Danville	11	—	2	9
Northampton	Easton	38	2	19	17
Northumberland	Sunbury	36	2	11	23
Perry	New Bloomfield	30	—	9	21
Philadelphia	Philadelphia	1	1	—	—
Pike	Milford	13	—	2	11
Potter	Coudersport	31	—	6	25
Schuylkill	Pottsville	67	1	30	36
Snyder	Middleburg	21	—	6	15
Somerset	Somerset	50	—	25	25
Sullivan	Laporte	13	—	4	9
Susquehanna	Montrose	40	—	13	27
Tioga	Wellsboro	40	—	10	30
Union	Lewisburg	14	—	4	10
Venango	Franklin	31	2	9	20
Warren	Warren	27	—	6	21
Washington	Washington	67	2	33	32
Wayne	Honesdale	28	—	6	22
Westmoreland	Greensburg	65	6	38	21
Wyoming	Tunkhannock	23	—	5	18
York	York	72	1	36	35

Dash (—) represents zero.

[1]Represents city of Parker City, created by special act of Legislature in 1873 and not classified.
[2]Includes only incorporated town in Pennsylvania — Bloomsburg.

THE ACT PROVIDING FOR THE
CLASSIFICATION OF COUNTIES

Section 210. Counties Divided Into Nine Classes.
Section 1. Section 210, act of August 9, 1955 (P.L. 323), known as "The County Code," amended Feb. 5, 1982, is amended to read:

Section 210. Counties Divided Into Nine Classes. — For the purposes of legislation and the regulation of their affairs, counties of this Commonwealth, now in existence and those hereafter created, shall be divided into nine classes as follows:

(1) **First Class Counties,** those having a population of 1,500,000 inhabitants and over.

(2) **Second Class Counties,** those having a population of 800,000 and more but less than 1,500,000 inhabitants.

(2.1) **Second Class A Counties,** those having a population of 500,000 and more but less than 800,000 inhabitants.

(3) **Third Class Counties,** those having a population of 225,000 and more but less than 500,000 inhabitants.

(4) **Fourth Class Counties,** those having a population of 150,000 and more but less than 225,000 inhabitants.

(5) **Fifth Class Counties,** those having a population of 95,000 and more but less than 150,000 inhabitants.

(6) **Sixth Class Counties,** those having a population of 45,000 and more but less than 95,000 inhabitants and those having a population of 35,000 and more but less than 45,000 inhabitants which by ordinance or resolution of the Board of County Commissioners elect to be a county of the sixth class.

(7) **Seventh Class Counties,** those having a population of 20,000 or more but less than 45,000 inhabitants and those having a population of 35,000 and more but less than 45,000 inhabitants which have not elected to be a county of the sixth class.

(8) **Eighth Class Counties,** those having a population of less than 20,000 inhabitants.

Section 2. Whenever a county advances in class under this act, the provisions of The County Code or any other law relating to the qualifications of district attorneys for the higher class county shall not be applicable to any district attorney of such county elected prior to January 1, 1972.

Section 211. Ascertainment, Certification and Effect of Change of Class.

(a) The classification of counties shall be ascertained and fixed according to their population by reference from time to time to the decennial United States census as hereinafter provided, deducting therefrom the number of persons residing on any lands that have been ceded to the United States.

(b) Whenever it shall appear by any such census that any county has attained a population entitling it to an advance in classification, or whenever it shall appear by the last two preceding censuses that a county has heretofore or hereafter decreased in population so as to recede in classification, as herein prescribed, it shall be in the duty of the Governor, under the great seal of this Commonwealth, to certify that fact accordingly, to the board of county commissioners on or before the first day of October of the year succeeding that in which the census was taken or as soon thereafter as may be, which certificate shall be forwarded by the commissioners to the recorder of deeds and be recorded in his office.

It is the intent of this section that the classification of any county shall not be changed because its population has decreased at the time of one United States decennial census, because it is recognized that a change in the form of local government is attended by certain expense and hardship, and such change should not be occasioned by a temporary fluctuation in population, but rather only after it is demonstrated by two censuses that the population of a county has remained below the minimum figure of its class for at least a decade.

(c) Changes of class ascertained and certified as aforesaid shall become effective on the first day of January next following the year in which the change was so certified by the Governor to the county commissioners but the salaries of county officers shall not thereby be increased or decreased during the term for which they shall have been elected. In the municipal election following such certification of change of class and preceding the effective date of such change, the proper number of persons shall be elected to fill any elective office which will exist in the county by the change in classification certified. No election shall be held for any office which will be abolished as a result of such change of classification. The County Code, (P.L. 323), Aug. 9, 1955; as last amended Act No. 478, Aug. 22, 1961.

CLASSIFICATION OF COUNTIES

Returns from the 1980 Census indicate three Pennsylvania counties grew sufficiently to move up in class. Dauphin and Northampton counties moved from fourth to third class and Wyoming moved from eighth to seventh class. In addition three seventh class counties surpassed the 35,000 population mark, making them eligible to become sixth class counties by election. They are Perry, Susquehanna and Wayne.

First Class (1) — Philadelphia (1,688,210).

Second Class (1) — Allegheny (1,450,085).

Second Class A (2) — Montgomery (643,621), Delaware (555,007).

Third Class (12) — Bucks (479,211), Westmoreland (392,294), Lancaster (362,346), Luzerne (343,079), Chester (316,660), York (312,963), Berks (312,509), Erie (279,780), Lehigh (273,582), Dauphin (232,317), Lackawanna (227,908), Northampton (255,418).

Fourth Class (6) — Washington (217,074), Beaver (204,441), Cambria (183,263), Cumberland (178,037), Schuylkill (160,630), Fayette (160,395).

Fifth Class (9) — Butler (147,912), Blair (136,621), Mercer (128,299), Lycoming (118,416), Franklin (113,629), Centre (112,760), Lebanon (109,829), Lawrence (107,150), Northumberland (100,381).

Sixth Class (23) — Indiana (92,281), Crawford (88,869), Clearfield (83,578), Somerset (81,243), Armstrong (77,768), Monroe (69,409), Adams (68,292), Venango (64,444), Bradford (62,919), Columbia (61,967), Carbon (53,285), McKean (50,635), Jefferson (48,303), Warren (47,449), Mifflin (46,908), Bedford (46,784), Clarion (43,362), Huntingdon (42,253), Tioga (40,973), Greene (40,355), Clinton (38,971), Elk (38,338), Susquehanna (37,876).

Seventh Class (5) — Perry (35,718), Wayne (35,237), Snyder (33,584), Union (32,870), Wyoming (26,433).

Eighth Class (8) — Juniata (19,188), Pike (18,271), Potter (17,726), Montour (16,675), Fulton (12,842), Cameron (6,674), Sullivan (6,349), Forest (5,072).

POPULATION OF COUNTIES: 1970-1980

The State Counties	Total Population 1980	Total Population 1970	Percent Change 1970-1980
THE STATE..............................	11,866,728	11,800,766	0.6
Adams.....	68,292	56,937	19.9
Allegheny	1,450,085	1,605,133	-9.7
Armstrong........................	77,768	75,590	2.9
Beaver	204,441	208,418	-1.9
Bedford......................	46,784	42,353	10.5
Berks.....	312,509	296,382	5.4
Blair.....	136,621	135,356	0.9
Bradford	62,919	57,962	8.6
Bucks	479,211	416,728	15.0
Butler	147,912	127,941	15.6
Cambria	183,263	186,785	-1.9
Cameron.....	6,674	7,096	-5.9
Carbon	53,285	50,573	5.4
Centre.....	112,760	99,267	13.6
Chester.....	316,660	277,746	14.0
Clarion	43,362	38,414	12.9
Clearfield	83,578	74,619	12.0
Clinton	38,971	37,721	3.3
Columbia	61,967	55,114	12.4
Crawford.....	88,869	81,342	9.3
Cumberland	178,037	158,177	12.6
Dauphin	232,317	223,713	3.8
Delaware.....	555,007	603,456	-8.0
Elk.....	38,338	37,770	1.5
Erie.....	279,780	263,654	6.1
Fayette	160,395	154,667	3.7
Forest	5,072	4,926	3.0
Franklin.....	113,629	100,833	12.7
Fulton	12,842	10,776	19.2
Greene	40,355	36,090	11.8
Huntingdon.....	42,253	39,108	8.0
Indiana	92,281	79,451	16.1
Jefferson.....	48,303	43,695	10.5
Juniata	19,188	16,712	14.8
Lackawanna	227,908	234,504	-2.8
Lancaster	362,346	320,079	13.2
Lawrence	107,150	107,374	-0.2
Lebanon	109,829	99,665	10.2
Lehigh.....	273,582	255,304	7.2
Luzerne.....	343,079	341,956	0.3
Lycoming	118,416	113,296	4.5
McKean.....	50,635	51,915	-2.5
Mercer	128,299	127,225	0.8
Mifflin	46,908	45,268	3.6
Monroe	69,409	45,422	52.8
Montgomery	643,621	624,080	3.1
Montour	16,675	16,508	1.0
Northampton.....	225,418	214,545	5.1
Northumberland	100,381	99,190	1.2
Perry.....	35,718	28,615	24.8
Philadelphia	1,688,210	1,949,996	-13.4
Pike.....	18,271	11,818	54.6
Potter	17,726	16,395	8.1
Schuylkill.....	160,630	160,089	0.3
Snyder	33,584	29,269	14.7
Somerset	81,243	76,037	6.8
Sullivan.....	6,349	5,961	6.5
Susquehanna	37,876	34,344	10.3
Tioga.....	40,973	39,691	3.2
Union	32,870	28,603	14.9
Venango	64,444	62,353	3.4
Warren	47,449	47,682	-0.5
Washington.....	217,074	210,876	2.9
Wayne.....	35,237	29,581	19.1
Westmoreland.....	392,294	376,935	4.1
Wyoming.....	26,433	19,082	38.5
York.....	312,963	272,603	14.8

PENNSYLVANIA COUNTIES*

ADAMS COUNTY (6th class, population 68,292) was created on January 22, 1800, from part of York County, and was named in honor of President John Adams. *Gettysburg,* the county seat, was incorporated as a borough on March 10, 1806. It was named for James Gettys, a local landowner.

Office	Name	Political Affiliation	Term Expires	Annual Salary
Commissioner, Chairman	Thomas L. Collins	R	Jan. 1988	$23,987
Commissioner, Vice Chairman	Robert W. Klunk	R	Jan. 1988	23,987
Commissioner, Secretary	Catherine W. Cowan	D	Jan. 1988	23,987
Sheriff	Bernard V. Miller	R	Jan. 1990	21,462
Coroner	Leah Maltland, MD	D	Jan. 1988	8,837
Recorder of Deeds and Register of Wills	Betty H. Pitzer	R	Jan. 1988	22,462
Clerk of Courts and Clerk, Orphans' Court	Peggy J. Breighner	R	Jan. 1990	22,462
Prothonotary	Parker D. Lerew	R	Jan. 1988	21,462
Treasurer	George W. Stock	R	Jan. 1990	21,462
District Attorney	Gary E. Hartman	D	Jan. 1988	22,725
Jury Commissioner	Rosalie K. Fitez	D	Jan. 1990	3,787
Jury Commissioner	Deborah Jacoby Grim	R	Jan. 1990	3,787
Clerk to Commissioners	Jeffrey L. Chamberlain	Appt.		20,592
Chief Assessor	Barbara Walter	Appt.		17,113
County Solicitor	John R. White, Esq	Appt.		22,296

ALLEGHENY COUNTY (2nd class, population 1,450,085) was created on September 24, 1788, from parts of Westmoreland and Washington Counties and named for the Allegheny River. *Pittsburgh,* the county seat, was named by General John Forbes in November 1758 in honor of William Pitt, a British statesman. It was incorporated as a borough on April 22, 1794, and as a city on March 18, 1816.

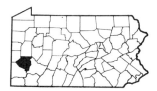

Office	Name	Political Affiliation	Term Expires	Annual Salary
Commissioner, Chairman	Tom Foerster	D	Jan. 1988	$41,540
Commissioner	Pete Flaherty	D	Jan. 1988	39,294
Commissioner	Barbara Hafer	R	Jan. 1988	39,294
Sheriff	Eugene L. Coon	D	Jan. 1990	30,000
Coroner	Joshua A. Perper, MD, LLB, M Sc	D	Jan. 1990	30,000
Recorder of Deeds	Michael Della Vecchia	D	Jan. 1988	30,000
Recorder of Wills and Clerk, Orphans' Court	Rita Wilson Kane	D	Jan. 1988	30,000
Prothonotary	John P. Joyce	D	Jan. 1988	30,000
Clerk of Courts	John Kyle	D	Jan. 1988	30,000
Controller	Frank Lucchino	D	Jan. 1988	30,000
Treasurer	Jay Costa	D	Jan. 1988	30,000
District Attorney	Robert Colville	D	Jan. 1988	44,000
Jury Commissioner	Jean A. Milko	D	Jan. 1990	25,700
Jury Commissioner	Jane McMullen	R	Jan. 1990	25,700
Clerk to Commissioners	Salvatore M. Sirabella	Appt.		44,000
Chief Assessor	Bill Dougherty	Appt.		38,000
County Solicitor	James J. Dodaro	Appt.		40,000

*All population figures are taken from ''Advanced Reports'' of U.S. Census Bureau 1980 tabulations.

ARMSTRONG COUNTY (6th class, population 77,768) was created on
March 12, 1800, from parts of Allegheny, Westmoreland and Lycoming Counties and was named for General John Armstrong. It was attached to Westmoreland County until 1805. *Kittanning,* the county seat, was incorporated as a borough on April 2, 1821, and derived its name from a Delaware Indian village at the same place.

Office	Name	Political Affiliation	Term Expires	Annual Salary
Commissioner, Chairman	Carl L. Culp	D	Jan. 1988	$24,907
Commissioner.......................	Harry M. Fox	R	Jan. 1988	24,907
Commissioner.......................	Grover Myers	D	Jan. 1988	24,907
Sheriff............................	John Kochman	R	Jan. 1990	21,848
Coroner...........................	Robert Bower	R	Jan. 1990	8,996
Recorder of Deeds, Register of Wills, and Clerk, Orphans' Court	Henry Livengood....................	D	Jan. 1988	23,596
Prothonotary and Clerk of Courts.....................	Mary Lou Mull	R	Jan. 1988	23,134
Controller	Timothy L. Pesci	D	Jan. 1988	22,285
Treasurer.........................	Ray G. Heilman.....................	D	Jan. 1988	22,285
District Attorney.....................	George R. Kepple	R	Jan. 1990	23,596
Jury Commissioner..................	Nancy Heilman	R	Jan. 1990	3,933
Jury Commissioner..................	Marion Crissman....................	D	Jan. 1990	3,933
Clerk to Commissioners	Dorothy C. Morris	Appt.		19,890
Chief Assessor	William Bruggeman..................	Appt.		17,404
County Solicitor.....................	Joseph A. Nickleach	Appt.		12,852

BEAVER COUNTY (4th class, population 204,441) was created on March 12,
1800, from parts of Allegheny and Washington Counties, and named for the Beaver River. It was attached to Allegheny County until 1803. *Beaver,* the county seat, was incorporated as a borough on March 29, 1802.

Office	Name	Political Affiliation	Term Expires	Annual Salary
Commissioner, Chairman	Joseph H. Widmer...................	D	Jan. 1988	$28,631
Commissioner.......................	Gerald J. LaValle...................	D	Jan. 1988	27,438
Commissioner.......................	Roger L. Javens	R	Jan. 1988	27,438
Sheriff............................	Frank Policaro, Jr...................	D	Jan. 1988	25,649
Coroner...........................	Dr. Joseph Tritschler	D	Jan. 1988	20,280
Recorder of Deeds	William B. O'Neil...................	D	Jan. 1988	25,649
Register of Wills	Lois Wood	D	Jan. 1988	26,842
Prothonotary.......................	Michael J. Jackson	D	Jan. 1988	25,649
Clerk of Courts	Evelyn Zigerelli	D	Jan. 1988	25,649
Controller	Richard W. Towcimak	D	Jan. 1988	28,167
Treasurer..........................	Kenneth E. Campbell	D	Jan. 1988	25,649
District Attorney.....................	Edward J. Tocci	D	Jan. 1988	28,035
Jury Commissioner..................	Betty DiCicco	D	Jan. 1988	5,964
Jury Commissioner..................	Nancy Loxley.......................	R	Jan. 1988	5,964
Chief Clerk	Robert W. Cyphert..................	Appt.		37,000
Chief Assessor	Michael P. Kohlman..................	Appt.		28,700
Court Administrator..................	Joseph Cabraja.....................	Appt.		38,970
Engineer	John Grant	Appt.		36,700

BEDFORD COUNTY (6th class, population 46,784) was created on March
9, 1771, from part of Cumberland County. It was named for Fort Bedford, which in turn
had been named in 1759 for the Duke of Bedford. *Bedford,* the county seat, on the site
of Fort Bedford, was incorporated as a borough on March 13, 1795.

Office	Name	Political Affiliation	Term Expires	Annual Salary
Commissioner, Chairman	Joseph H. Clapper, Jr.	D	Jan. 1988	$23,095
Commissioner	Jay B. Cessna	R	Jan. 1988	23,095
Commissioner	Gary W. Ebersole	D	Jan. 1988	23,095
Sheriff	Max H. Norris, Sr.	D	Jan. 1988	20,664
Coroner	Jack H. Geisel	R	Jan. 1988	8,508
Recorder of Deeds and Register of Wills	Gerald A. Yoder	R	Jan. 1990	19,845
Clerk, Orphans' Court, Prothonotary and Clerk of Courts	Vacant		Jan. 1988	21,879
Treasurer	Rowland A. Clark	R	Jan. 1988	20,664
District Attorney	Thomas Ling	R	Jan. 1988	21,879
Jury Commissioner	Edwin C. "Ted" Ickes	R	Jan. 1990	3,308
Jury Commissioner	Betty J. Weyant	D	Jan. 1990	3,308
Auditor	Ona Stouffer	R	Jan. 1988	54/day
Auditor	Colleen Hite	R	Jan. 1988	54/day
Auditor	Betty Diehl	D	Jan. 1988	54/day
Clerk to Commissioners	Patricia M. Chapin	Appt.		18,972
Chief Assessor and Tax Claim Director	Hubert K. Ross	Appt.		14,908
County Solicitor	Barry A. Scatton	Appt.		12,750

BERKS COUNTY (3rd class, population 312,509) was created on March 11,
1752, from parts of Philadelphia, Chester, and Lancaster Counties, and was named for
Berkshire in England. *Reading,* the county seat, was named for Berkshire's county
town. It was incorporated as a borough on September 12, 1783, and as a city on March
16, 1847.

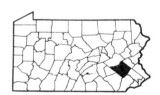

Office	Name	Political Affiliation	Term Expires	Annual Salary
Commissioner, Chairman	Donald W. Bagenstose	D	Jan. 1988	$41,744
Commissioner	Anthony J. Carabello	D	Jan. 1988	40,519
Commissioner	Vernon K. Shaffer	R	Jan. 1988	40,519
Sheriff	John H. Kramer	D	Jan. 1988	35,268
Coroner	Michael F. Feeney	D	Jan. 1990	28,514
Recorder of Deeds	Linda Hilgendorf Frey	R	Jan. 1988	35,268
Register of Wills and Clerk, Orphans' Court	Joseph G. Natale	D	Jan. 1988	36,493
Prothonotary	Thomas Gajewski	D	Jan. 1990	35,268
Clerk of Courts	Donald R. Dissinger	D	Jan. 1988	35,268
Controller	William J. Campbell	D	Jan. 1988	39,202
Treasurer	Stella Kompa	D	Jan. 1990	35,268
District Attorney	George Yatron	D	Jan. 1988	64,000
Jury Commissioner	LeRoy R. Gensemer	D	Jan. 1990	9,755
Jury Commissioner	Marianne Sutton	R	Jan. 1990	9,755
Clerk to Commissioners	Ronald R. Seaman	Appt.		33,074
Chief Assessor	Clarence Hess	Appt.		22,827
County Solicitor	C. Wilson Austin	Appt.		27,519
County Engineer	Ronald H. Weaver	Appt.		35,988

BLAIR COUNTY (5th class, population 136,621) was created on February 26, 1846, from parts of Huntingdon and Bedford Counties, and named for John Blair, a prominent citizen. *Hollidaysburg,* the county seat, was incorporated as a borough on August 10, 1836, and named for Adam and William Holliday, early settlers.

Office	Name	Political Affiliation	Term Expires	Annual Salary
Commissioner, Chairman	William C. Stouffer	R	Jan. 1988	$22,575
Commissioner	John J. Ebersole	R	Jan. 1988	22,575
Commissioner	Donna D. Gority	D	Jan. 1988	22,575
Sheriff	Albert E. Wegemer	R	Jan. 1990	25,406
Coroner	Charles R. Burkey	R	Jan. 1988	15,050
Recorder of Deeds and Register of Wills	James F. Shuman	R	Jan. 1988	21,500
Clerk of Courts and Prothonotary	Vernon D. Weicht	R	Jan. 1990	26,743
Controller	Robert A. Grove	R	Jan. 1988	20,425
Treasurer	William Collins, Jr.	R	Jan. 1988	20,425
District Attorney	William Haberstroh	R	Jan. 1990	27,411
Jury Commissioner	Jeanne M. Bolger	R	Jan. 1990	5,349
Jury Commissioner	Robert V. Cassidy	D	Jan. 1990	5,349
Clerk to Commissioners	Ralph T. Mangus	Appt.		25,848
Chief Assessor	Charles J. McGrain	Appt.		21,848
County Solicitor	Merle K. Evey	Appt.		21,846

BRADFORD COUNTY (6th class, population 62,919) was created on February 21, 1810, from parts of Luzerne and Lycoming Counties and named Ontario County for the lake of the same name. On March 24, 1812, it was formally organized, and renamed for William Bradford, second Attorney General of the United States. *Towanda,* the county seat, was incorporated as a borough on March 5, 1828, and named for Towanda Creek.

Office	Name	Political Affiliation	Term Expires	Annual Salary
Commissioner, Chairman	Marilyn A. Bok	R	Jan. 1988	$28,513
Commissioner	William A. Gannon	R	Jan. 1988	28,513
Commissioner	Robert P. Horton	R	Jan. 1988	28,513
Sheriff	Thomas Fairchild	R	Jan. 1988	25,512
Deputy Coroner	Eugene Farr	R	Jan. 1988	10,505
Recorder of Deeds and Register of Wills	Shirley Rockefeller	R	Jan. 1988	27,512
Clerk, Orphans' Court, Prothonotary and Clerk of Courts	Wanda Foulkrod	R	Jan. 1988	27,512
Treasurer	Michael N. Brutzman	R	Jan. 1988	25,512
District Attorney	Daniel Barrett	R	Jan. 1988	27,013
Jury Commissioner	John Stetz	D	Jan. 1988	4,502
Jury Commissioner	Freda H. Burleigh	R	Jan. 1988	4,502
Auditor	L. Alice Hunsinger	R	Jan. 1988	68/day
Auditor	Shirley B. Greenough	R	Jan. 1988	68/day
Auditor	Constantine J. Spentzas	D	Jan. 1988	68/day
Clerk to Commissioners	Gary L. Wood	Appt.		23,280
Chief Assessor	Klas Anderson	Appt.		25,085
County Solicitor	Jonathon Foster	Appt.		18,000
Director, Tax Claim Bureau	Michael N. Brutzman	Appt.		4,000

BUCKS COUNTY (3rd class, population 479,211) was one of the original
counties created by William Penn in November, 1682. Bucks is a contraction of
Buckinghamshire, an England shire where the Penns lived for generations. *Doylestown*
replaced Newtown as the county seat in 1812 and was incorporated as a borough on
April 16, 1838. It was named for William Doyle, an innkeeper.

Office	Name	Political Affiliation	Term Expires	Annual Salary
Commissioner, Chairman	Carl F. Fonash	D	Jan. 1988	$28,000
Commissioner	Lucille M. Trench	D	Jan. 1988	27,000
Commissioner	Andrew L. Warren	R	Jan. 1988	27,000
Sheriff	Lawrence R. Michaels	R	Jan. 1990	31,466
Coroner	Thomas Rosko, M.D.	R	Jan. 1990	19,000
Recorder of Deeds	Edward Gudknecht	R	Jan. 1990	31,466
Register of Wills and Clerk, Orphans' Court	Barbara Reilly	R	Jan. 1988	24,500
Prothonotary	Charles L. Worthington	R	Jan. 1990	31,466
Clerk of Courts	Richard Hoffman, Esq.	D	Jan. 1988	23,500
Controller	Daniel L. Lawler	R	Jan. 1990	31,466
Treasurer	William R. Snyder	R	Jan. 1988	23,500
District Attorney	Alan Rubenstein, Esq.	R	Jan. 1990	64,000
Jury Commissioner	Sydell Gross	D	Jan. 1990	8,703
Jury Commissioner	Keren McIlhinney	R	Jan. 1990	8,703
County Administrator	William H. Rieser	Appt.		44,935
County Solicitor	James McNamara, Esq.	Appt.		34,227
Public Information, Director	Bette Phelan	Appt.		23,507

BUTLER COUNTY (5th class, population 147,912) was created on March 12,
1800, from part of Allegheny County and named for General Richard Butler. It was
attached to Allegheny County until 1803. *Butler,* the county seat, was laid out in 1803,
incorporated as a borough on February 26, 1817, and chartered as a city on January 7,
1918.

Office	Name	Political Affiliation	Term Expires	Annual Salary
Commissioner, Chairman	R. M. Patterson	R	Jan. 1988	$21,000
Commissioner	Richard A. Huff	R	Jan. 1988	21,000
Commissioner	James A. Green	D	Jan. 1988	21,000
Sheriff	Dennis Rickard	R	Jan. 1990	24,792
Coroner	William Young, Jr.	R	Jan. 1990	18,268
Recorder of Deeds and Register of Wills	Jon Campbell	R	Jan. 1988	20,000
Clerk, Orphans' Court and Clerk of Courts	John H. Wise	R	Jan. 1990	26,097
Prothonotary	Glenna Walters	R	Jan. 1988	19,000
Controller	John B. Cranmer, Jr.	R	Jan. 1990	26,097
Treasurer	Joan T. Chew	R	Jan. 1988	19,000
District Attorney	David L. Cook	R	Jan. 1988	20,500
Jury Commissioner	Mary K. Stone	R	Jan. 1990	5,219
Jury Commissioner	Nancy Jane Oesterling	D	Jan. 1990	5,219
Clerk to Commissioners	Thomas D. Lavorini	Appt.		23,789
Chief Assessor	LaVern E. Dunbar	Appt.		25,372
County Solicitor	Frank P. Krizner	Appt.		45,900

CAMBRIA COUNTY (4th class, population 183,263) was created on March 26, 1804, from parts of Huntingdon, Somerset and Bedford Counties and named for Cambria Township of Somerset County. Cambria is an ancient name for Wales. It was attached to Somerset County until 1807. *Ebensburg,* the county seat, was incorporated as a borough on January 15, 1825 and named by Reverend Rees Lloyd for his eldest and deceased son, Eben.

Office	Name	Political Affiliation	Term Expires	Annual Salary
Commissioner, Chairman	Joseph P. Roberts	D	Jan. 1988	$31,841
Commissioner	Ron Stephenson	D	Jan. 1988	30,514
Commissioner	T. T. Metzger, Jr.	R	Jan. 1988	30,514
Sheriff	Jay Roberts	D	Jan. 1990	28,524
Coroner	John Barron	D	Jan. 1988	22,554
Recorder of Deeds	F. Joseph Link	D	Jan. 1988	28,524
Register of Wills and Clerk, Orphans' Court	Victor B. Bako	D	Jan. 1988	29,851
Prothonotary	Michael Tsikalas	D	Jan. 1988	28,524
Clerk of Courts	James McNulty	D	Jan. 1988	28,524
Controller	Robert J. McCormick, Jr.	D	Jan. 1988	28,524
Treasurer	Esther Donahue	D	Jan. 1988	28,524
District Attorney	Timothy Creany	D	Jan. 1988	31,178
Jury Commissioner	Joseph F. Pencek	D	Jan. 1990	6,633
Jury Commissioner	Marjorie Barnhart	R	Jan. 1990	6,633
Clerk to Commissioners	Robert W. Roseman	Appt.		23,738
Chief Assessor	Michael Jerome	Appt.		28,930
County Solicitor	George Raptosh	Appt.		23,153

CAMERON COUNTY (8th class, population 6,674) was created on March 29, 1860, from parts of Clinton, McKean, Elk, and Potter Counties and named for U.S. Senator Simon Cameron. *Emporium,* the county seat, was incorporated as a borough on October 13, 1864; its name is Latin for "market or trade center."

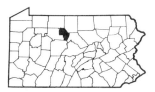

Office	Name	Political Affiliation	Term Expires	Annual Salary
Commissioner, Chairman	Mary J. Donovan	R	Jan. 1988	$15,298
Commissioner	Judd A. Schager	D	Jan. 1988	15,298
Commissioner	W. Anson Mason	NP	Jan. 1988	15,298
Sheriff	James J. Fragale	D	Jan. 1990	15,298
Coroner	Albert S. Metz	R	Jan. 1988	6,010
Recorder of Deeds, Register of Wills, Clerk, Orphans' Court, Prothonotary and Clerk of Courts	David J. Reed	R	Jan. 1990	16,390
Treasurer	Richard D. English	R	Jan. 1988	15,298
District Attorney	Russell F. D'Aiello, Jr.	D	Jan. 1988	16,390
Jury Commissioner	Dennis P. Fapore	R	Jan. 1990	2,185
Jury Commissioner	Roderick R. Shadman	D	Jan. 1990	2,185
Chief Clerk to Commissioners	George M. Obleski	Appt.	Jan. 1988	11,846
Chief Assessor	John Boswell	Appt.	Jan. 1988	14,752
County Solicitor	Edwin W. Tompkins II	Appt.	Jan. 1988	7,100

CARBON COUNTY (6th class, population 53,285) was created on March 13, 1843, from parts of Northampton and Monroe Counties. Its name alludes to its deposits of anthracite coal. *Jim Thorpe,* the county seat, was originally incorporated on January 26, 1850, as the borough of Mauch Chunk, an Indian name meaning "bear mountain." It was renamed in 1954 for the famous Indian athlete, who is buried there.

Office	Name	Political Affiliation	Term Expires	Annual Salary
Commissioner, Chairman	Albert U. Koch	D	Jan. 1988	$25,197
Commissioner	Charles E. Wildoner	D	Jan. 1988	25,197
Commissioner	Dean D. W. DeLong	R	Jan. 1988	25,197
Sheriff	Peter P. Hoherchak	D	Jan. 1988	22,545
Coroner	Robert G. Deibert	R	Jan. 1988	9,283
Recorder of Deeds	James F. Walker	R	Jan. 1988	22,545
Register of Wills and Clerk, Orphans' Court	Margaret O'Donnell	D	Jan. 1990	23,871
Prothonotary	Francis Cannariato	R	Jan. 1988	22,545
Clerk of Courts	Jeanette Scapura	D	Jan. 1990	22,545
Controller	John R. Williams	D	Jan. 1988	22,545
Treasurer	Gilbert Gerhard	R	Jan. 1990	22,545
District Attorney	Richard W. Webb	D	Jan. 1988	23,871
Jury Commissioner	Willard Hill	R	Jan. 1990	3,979
Jury Commissioner	Jeannette D. Coury	D	Jan. 1990	3,979
Clerk to Commissioners	Joseph P. Orsulak	Appt.		22,812
Chief Assessor	David R. Ratajczak	Appt.		20,000
County Solicitor	Joseph J. Velitsky	Appt.		21,000

CENTRE COUNTY (5th class, population 112,760) was created on February 13, 1800, from parts of Huntingdon, Lycoming, Mifflin and Northumberland Counties. Its name refers to its geographical location at the center of the state. *Bellefonte,* the county seat, was incorporated as a borough on March 28, 1806. Its name, French for "beautiful spring," alludes to a large spring there and is said to have been suggested by the famous French statesman, Talleyrand.

Office	Name	Political Affiliation	Term Expires	Annual Salary
Commissioner, Chairman	Jeffrey M. Bower	R	Jan. 1988	$28,142
Commissioner	Martin L. Horn	R	Jan. 1988	28,142
Commissioner	John T. Saylor	D	Jan. 1988	28,142
Sheriff	Garry G. Kunes	R	Jan. 1988	25,462
Coroner	W. Robert Neff	R	Jan. 1988	18,761
Recorder of Deeds	John W. Miles	D	Jan. 1988	25,462
Register of Wills and Clerk, Orphans' Court	Roger A. Bierly	D	Jan. 1988	26,462
Prothonotary and Clerk of Courts	David L. Immel	D	Jan. 1988	26,462
Controller	Donald A. Asendorf	R	Jan. 1988	25,462
Treasurer	Gino P. Fornicola	R	Jan. 1988	25,462
District Attorney	Ray F. Gricar	R	Jan. 1990	27,472
Jury Commissioner	Anna B. Lose	R	Jan. 1990	5,360
Jury Commissioner	Ruth M. DeWitt	D	Jan. 1990	5,360
Clerk to Commissioners	Sandra C. Baney	Appt.		17,154
Executive Assistant	James R. Eckert	Appt.		32,038
Chief Assessor	Gerald N. Dann	Appt.		32,429
County Solicitor	Robert K. Kistler	Appt.		25,200

CHESTER COUNTY (3rd class, population 316,660) was one of the three

original counties created by William Penn in November 1682. It did not become an inland county until 1789, when Delaware County was created from a part of it. Its name derives from Chesire (i.e. Chester-shire), England, from which many of its early settlers came. *West Chester,* the county seat since 1788, was incorporated as a borough on March 28, 1799. It was named for Chester, the original county seat (now in Delaware County), which in turn derived its name from the shire town of Cheshire.

Office	Name	Political Affiliation	Term Expires	Annual Salary
Commissioner, Chairman	Irene B. Brooks	R	Jan. 1988	$35,735
Commissioner........................	Earl M. Baker	R	Jan. 1988	34,459
Commissioner........................	Patricia Moran Baldwin	D	Jan. 1988	34,459
Sheriff.............................	Robert A. Erling.....................	R	Jan. 1988	29,992
Coroner............................	Donald E. Harrop, MD.................	R	Jan. 1990	29,992
Recorder of Deeds	Elaine S. Weil	R	Jan. 1988	29,992
Register of Wills and				
Clerk, Orphans' Court	James Dunworth.....................	R	Jan. 1988	31,268
Prothonotary (Acting)	Marian Bartlett	R	Jan. 1988	29,992
Clerk of Courts	Norman J. Pine.....................	R	Jan. 1990	29,992
Controller	E. Raymond Lynch	R	Jan. 1990	29,992
Treasurer..........................	Armand Taraschi	R	Jan. 1990	29,992
District Attorney.....................	James Paul MacElree	R	Jan. 1988	64,000
Jury Commissioner...................	Doris L. Boden......................	R	Jan. 1990	8,295
Jury Commissioner...................	Nancy D. Lewis.....................	D	Jan. 1990	8,295
Clerk to Commissioners	Molly Keim Morrison	Appt.		38,000
Chief Assessor	Harry T. Williams....................	Appt.		32,114
County Solicitor.....................	John S. Halsted.....................	Appt.		25,163
County Engineer.....................	R. P. Wilking	Appt.		47,944

CLARION COUNTY (6th class, population 43,362) was created on March

11, 1839, from parts of Venango and Armstrong Counties and named for the Clarion River. *Clarion,* the county seat, was incorporated as a borough on April 6, 1841.

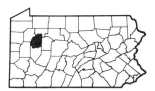

Office	Name	Political Affiliation	Term Expires	Annual Salary
Commissioner, Chairman	Fred C. McIlhattan....................	R	Jan. 1988	$25,462
Commissioner........................	Thomas M. Armagost	R	Jan. 1988	25,462
Commissioner........................	Keith F. Martin......................	D	Jan. 1988	25,462
Sheriff.............................	Vern E. Smith	R	Jan. 1990	22,782
Coroner............................	Frederick A. Goble	R	Jan. 1990	9,382
Recorder of Deeds,				
Register of Wills and				
Clerk, Orphans' Court	David E. Black......................	R	Jan. 1988	24,122
Prothonotary and				
Clerk of Courts......................	Yvonne E. Summerville................	D	Jan. 1988	24,122
Treasurer..........................	Walter A. Karg......................	D	Jan. 1988	22,782
District Attorney.....................	William M. Kern.....................	D	Jan. 1988	24,122
Jury Commissioner...................	Twila Wollaston	D	Jan. 1990	4,020
Jury Commissioner...................	Marian F. Master	R	Jan. 1990	4,020
Clerk to Commissioners	Donna R. Hartle	Appt.		18,340
Chief Assessor	Robert E. Lieberum..................	Appt.		18,535
County Solicitor.....................	H. Ray Pope III	Appt.		9,298

CLEARFIELD COUNTY (6th class, population 83,578) was created on
March 26, 1804, from parts of Huntingdon and Lycoming Counties and named for
Clearfield Creek. The creek's name alluded to openings or clear fields in its vicinity. For
many years Clearfield County functioned as part of Centre County, not electing its own
commissioners until 1812. It was organized for judicial purposes in 1822. *Clearfield,* the
county seat, was incorporated as a borough on April 21, 1840.

Office	Name	Political Affiliation	Term Expires	Annual Salary
Commissioner, Chairman	E. Jay Master	R	Jan. 1988	$25,461
Commissioner	Harry Fred Bigler	R	Jan. 1988	25,461
Commissioner	Tim Morgan	D	Jan. 1988	25,461
Sheriff	Chester A. Hawkins	R	Jan. 1990	22,781
Coroner	Michael Mowrey	D	Jan. 1988	9,380
Recorder of Deeds, Register of Wills, and Clerk, Orphans' Court	Michael Lytle	R	Jan. 1988	24,121
Prothonotary and Clerk of Courts	Raymond Witherow	D	Jan. 1990	25,171
Controller	Vacant		Jan. 1990	22,781
Treasurer	James W. Laing, Jr.	R	Jan. 1988	22,781
District Attorney	Tomas Morgan	R	Jan. 1988	24,121
Jury Commissioner	Hale Beck	D	Jan. 1990	4,019
Jury Commissioner	Margaret J. Gates	R	Jan. 1990	4,019
Clerk to Commissioners	Eleanor Ludwig	Appt.		15,250
Chief Assessor	John E. West	Appt.		21,707
County Solicitor	Carl Belin, Jr.	Appt.		20,000
Assistant County Solicitor	Cynthia Soult	Appt.		

CLINTON COUNTY (6th class, population 38,971) was created on June 21,
1839, from parts of Centre and Lycoming Counties and probably named for Governor
DeWitt Clinton of New York, a promoter of the Erie Canal. Actually, the name seems to
have been substituted, as a political maneuver, for the name "Eagle," first proposed,
thus thwarting opponents of the new county. *Lock Haven,* the county seat, derived its
name from its position on the West Branch Canal, which was completed to Lock Haven
in 1834. It was incorporated as a borough on May 25, 1840, and as a city on March 28,
1870.

Office	Name	Political Affiliation	Term Expires	Annual Salary
Commissioner, Chairman	Larry J. Kephart	D	Jan. 1988	$19,000
Commissioner	Earl L. Lentz, Jr.	R	Jan. 1988	19,000
Commissioner	James E. Bottorf	D	Jan. 1988	19,000
Sheriff	William M. Maggs	R	Jan. 1988	17,000
Coroner	Dean K. Wetzler	D	Jan. 1990	9,733
Recorder of Deeds, Register of Wills and Clerk, Orphans' Court	Donald L. Fague	R	Jan. 1988	18,000
Prothonotary and Clerk of Courts	Barbara L. Emery	D	Jan. 1988	18,000
Treasurer	Lee K. Marshall, Jr.	R	Jan. 1990	18,035
District Attorney	Merritt McKnight	R	Jan. 1988	18,000
Jury Commissioner	Rexford Taylor	D	Jan. 1990	3,183
Jury Commissioner	Louis McGill	R	Jan. 1990	3,183
Clerk to Commissioners	Linda K. Bickford	Appt.		18,144
Chief Assessor	Alfred Weaver	Appt.		19,826
County Solicitor	Lewis L. Steinberg	Appt.		18,000

COLUMBIA COUNTY (6th class, population 61,967) was created on March 22, 1813, from part of Northumberland County. Its name is a poetic allusion to America. *Bloomsburg,* the county seat since November 30, 1847, was incorporated as a town on March 4, 1870, and still is the only incorporated town in the state. Its name comes from Bloom Township, which was named for Samuel Bloom, a commissioner of Northumberland County. Danville, the county seat from 1813 to 1846, is now the seat of Montour county.

Office	Name	Political Affiliation	Term Expires	Annual Salary
Commissioner, Chairman	Lucille B. Whitmire	D	Jan. 1988	$22,800
Commissioner.........................	Kent D. Shelhamer	D	Jan. 1988	22,800
Commissioner.......................	George H. Gensemer	R	Jan. 1988	22,800
Sheriff............................	John R. Adler	R	Jan. 1990	23,664
Coroner...........................	Dr. D. Ernest Witt.....................	R	Jan. 1988	8,400
Recorder of Deeds and Register of Wills....................	Beverly J. Michael...................	D	Jan. 1988	21,600
Clerk, Orphans' Court, Prothonotary and Clerk of Courts....................	Tami B. Kline........................	R	Jan. 1988	21,600
Treasurer...........................	Shirley F. Drake......................	R	Jan. 1988	20,400
District Attorney......................	Elwood Harding, Jr....................	D	Jan. 1988	21,600
Jury Commissioner....................	Donna E. Whitenight..................	D	Jan. 1990	4,176
Jury Commissioner....................	Thelma Knorr	R	Jan. 1990	4,176
Auditor.............................	Lone Derr	D	Jan. 1988	9.00/hr.
Auditor.............................	Eugene A. Patterson..................	D	Jan. 1988	9.00/hr.
Auditor.............................	A. Delroy Fetterman	R	Jan. 1988	9.00/hr.
Clerk to Commissioners	Harry R. Faux	Appt.		22,423
Chief Assessor	D. Ode Henrie	Appt.		19,661
County Solicitor......................	Alvin J. Luschas	Appt.		12,000

CRAWFORD COUNTY (6th class, population 88,869) was created on March 12, 1800, from part of Allegheny County and named for Colonel William Crawford, a frontier hero. *Meadville,* the county seat, was named for its founder, David Mead, and incorporated as a borough on March 29, 1823, and as a city on February 15, 1866.

Office	Name	Political Affiliation	Term Expires	Annual Salary
Commissioner, Chairman	Ivan G. Rose	R	Jan. 1988	$26,696
Commissioner.......................	Gene G. Rumsey.....................	R	Jan. 1988	26,696
Commissioner.......................	David M. Glenn	D	Jan. 1988	26,696
Sheriff..............................	Howard N. Stewart	R	Jan. 1988	23,884
Coroner............................	G. Arden Hughes	R	Jan. 1988	9,834
Recorder of Deeds and Register of Wills....................	Esther Hill	R	Jan. 1988	23,884
Clerk, Orphans' Court and Clerk of Courts....................	Blake E. Adsit	R	Jan. 1990	23,884
Prothonotary........................	James F. Simmons	R	Jan. 1988	23,884
Treasurer...........................	Frederic A. Wagner...................	R	Jan. 1990	23,884
District Attorney......................	John Dawson	R	Jan. 1988	25,290
Jury Commissioner....................	Dorothy Kennedy	R	Jan. 1990	4,215
Jury Commissioner....................	Lucile Mae Kean	D	Jan. 1990	4,215
Clerk to Commissioners	H. Richard Hays	Appt.		20,638
Chief Assessor	Richard Frontz	Appt.		16,380
County Solicitor......................	James Irwin.........................	Appt.		11,500

CUMBERLAND COUNTY (4th class, population 178,037) was created on
January 27, 1750, from part of Lancaster County, and named for Cumberland County
in England. *Carlisle,* the county seat since 1752, was incorporated as a borough on
April 13, 1782. It was named for the county town of the English county. Shippensburg
was the county seat from 1750 to 1752.

Office	Name	Political Affiliation	Term Expires	Annual Salary
Commissioner, Chairman	Marcia L. Myers.	D	Jan. 1988	$27,540
Commissioner.	Robert A. Adams.	D	Jan. 1988	26,392
Commissioner.	Robert J. Moore	R	Jan. 1988	26,392
Sheriff	William C. Beck.	R	Jan. 1990	24,671
Coroner.	Michael Norris.	R	Jan. 1990	19,507
Recorder of Deeds	Patricia H. Vance.	R	Jan. 1990	24,671
Register of Wills and				
Clerk, Orphans' Court	Mary C. Lewis	R	Jan. 1990	24,818
Prothonotary	Larry E. Welker	R	Jan. 1990	24,671
Clerk of Courts	Robert C. Gwin	R	Jan. 1990	24,671
Controller	Alfred L. Whitcomb	R	Jan. 1990	24,671
Treasurer.	Jerry L. Nailor	R	Jan. 1988	24,671
District Attorney.	Michael Eaken	R	Jan. 1988	24,671
Jury Commissioner	Ralph Viehman	R	Jan. 1990	5,738
Jury Commissioner	Winnifred Williams	D	Jan. 1990	5,738
Clerk to Commissioners	Samuel L. Nedrow.	Appt.		33,430
Chief Assessor	James Woof	Appt.		26,193
County Solicitor.	Robert C. Saidis	Appt.		23,493
Assistant Solicitor	William Costopoulos	Appt.		10,947

DAUPHIN COUNTY (3rd class, population 232,317) was created on March
4, 1785, from part of Lancaster County and named for the Dauphin, the title of the eldest
son of the French King. *Harrisburg,* the county seat, named for its founder, John Harris,
was incorporated as a borough on April 13, 1791, and chartered as a city on March 19,
1860.

Office	Name	Political Affiliation	Term Expires	Annual Salary
Commissioner, Chairman	Frederick S. Rice.	R	Jan. 1988	$35,378
Commissioner.	Norman P. Hetrick	R	Jan. 1988	34,115
Commissioner.	Louis J. Adler*	D	Jan. 1988	34,115
Sheriff	William Livingston.	R	Jan. 1988	29,694
Coroner.	William Bush	R	Jan. 1990	24,007
Recorder of Deeds	Mary E. Baum	R	Jan. 1988	29,694
Register of Wills and				
Clerk, Orphans' Court	Sally S. Klein.	R	Jan. 1988	30,956
Prothonotary	Robert A. Farina	R	Jan. 1990	29,694
Clerk of Courts	Russell L. Sheaffer	R	Jan. 1988	29,694
Controller	Thomas E. Washic	R	Jan. 1988	29,694
Treasurer.	Robert F. Dick	R	Jan. 1988	29,694
District Attorney.	Richard A. Lewis	R	Jan. 1988	64,000
Jury Commissioner	Germaine S. Bowman	R	Jan. 1990	8,214
Jury Commissioner	Helen Y. Swope	D	Jan. 1990	8,214
Exec. Adm./Chief Clerk.	Jethro J. Davis	Appt.		31,900
Chief Assessor	William J. Collins.	Appt.		31,283
County Solicitor.	Robert L. Knupp	Appt.		31,900

*appointed

DELAWARE COUNTY (2nd class A, population 555,007) was created on September 26, 1789, from part of Chester County and named for the Delaware River, which in turn had been named for Lord de la Warr, governor of Virginia. *Media,* its county seat since 1850, was incorporated as a borough on March 11, 1850, and named for its central location in the county. Chester, its original county seat, was the county seat of Chester County before 1788, and the temporary capital of Pennsylvania, 1681-1682, before Philadelphia was laid out. The county adopted a home rule charter in May 1975.

Office	Name	Political Affiliation	Term Expires	Annual Salary
Council, Chairman	Edwin B. Erickson, III	R	Jan. 1988	$38,850
Council, Vice Chairman	Nicholas F. Catania	R	Jan. 1990	34,965
Councilman	Joseph F. Kelly	R	Jan. 1988	34,965
Councilman	John W. Taylor	R	Jan. 1988	34,965
Councilman	Edmund Jones	R	Jan. 1988	34,965
Sheriff	Joseph F. Battle	R	Jan. 1990	29,415
Coroner	Dimitri L. Contostavlos, M.D.	Appt.		91,000
Recorder of Deeds	James J. Ward	Appt.		36,031
Register of Wills	Peter J. Nolan	R	Jan. 1990	29,415
Office of Judicial Support, Director	Joseph W. Dorsey	Appt.		42,130
Controller	Thomas M. Hayward	R	Jan. 1988	29,415
Treasurer	Robert A. Judge	Appt.		31,100
District Attorney	John A. Reilly	R	Jan. 1988	64,000
Jury Commissioner	Mary Daisley	Appt		50/day
Jury Commissioner	Anne Nelson	Appt.		50/day
Clerk to Council	Carma M. Mullen	Appt.		23,836
Chief Assessor	John Deitch	Appt.		44,348
County Solicitor	Francis P. Connors	Appt.		44,902

ELK COUNTY (6th class, population 38,338) was created on April 18, 1843, from parts of Jefferson, Clearfield and McKean Counties and named for the herd of elk that used to roam the county. *Ridgway,* the county seat, was laid out in 1833 and named for Jacob Ridgway, a local landowner. It was incorporated as a borough on February 15, 1881.

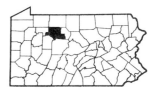

Office	Name	Political Affiliation	Term Expires	Annual Salary
Commissioner, Chairman	James C. Yetzer	D	Jan. 1988	$19,000
Commissioner	Gary Lee Kraus	D	Jan. 1988	19,000
Commissioner	Glenn W. Olson	R	Jan. 1988	19,000
Sheriff	Raymond J. Krasinski	R	Jan. 1988	17,000
Coroner	James Contanzo	D	Jan. 1988	7,000
Recorder of Deeds and Register of Wills	Louis Uhernick	R	Jan. 1988	18,000
Clerk, Orphans' Court, Prothonotary and Clerk of Courts	David Frey	D	Jan. 1988	18,000
Treasurer	John R. Kestler	D	Jan. 1988	17,000
District Attorney	Vernon D. Roof	D	Jan. 1990	15,000
Jury Commissioner	Earl Detwiler	R	Jan. 1990	2,000
Jury Commissioner	Allie Eckert	D	Jan. 1990	2,000
Clerk to Commissioners	Pat Butler	Appt.		15,000
Chief Assessor	Duane E. Duffy	Appt.		17,732
County Solicitor	David A. Whitney	Appt.		7,800

ERIE COUNTY (3rd class, population 279,780) was created on March 12, 1800, from part of Allegheny County and named for Lake Erie, which in turn had been named for the Indian tribe of the same name. It was attached to Crawford County until 1803. *Erie,* the county seat, was so named because it was Pennsylvania's port on Lake Erie. It was laid out in 1795, incorporated as a borough on March 29, 1805, and as a city on April 14, 1851. The county adopted a home rule charter in November 1976.

Office	Name	Political Affiliation	Term Expires	Annual Salary
County Executive	Judith M. Lynch	D	Jan. 1989	$40,100
Councilman, Chairman	Fiore Leone	D	Jan. 1988	4,000
Councilman, Vice Chairman	Paul M. Foust	D	Jan. 1988	3,500
Councilman	Robert C. Walkow	D	Jan. 1988	3,500
Councilman	Joseph F. Giles	D	Jan. 1989	5,500
Councilman	Barbara P. Mack	R	Jan. 1989	5,500
Councilman	Gary L. Bukowski	D	Jan. 1989	5,500
Councilman	Tracy Seyfert	R	Jan. 1988	3,500
Controller	A. Jake Gehrlein	D	Jan. 1988	32,000
Clerk of Records	David B. Wiley	D	Jan. 1989	34,200
District Attorney	Michael Veshecco	D	Jan. 1988	54,000
Sheriff	Robert N. Michel	R	Jan. 1989	30,900
Coroner	Merle E. Wood	R	Jan. 1988	25,000
Clerk to County Council	Florindo J. Fabrizio	Appt.		31,240
County Solicitor	Kenneth Chestek	Appt.		25,345
Chief Assessor	Howard Henning	Appt.		30,494

FAYETTE COUNTY (4th class, population 160,395) was created on September 26, 1783, from part of Westmoreland County and named in honor of the Marquis de la Fayette. *Uniontown,* the county seat, was laid out about 1776 as Beeson's-town and later renamed in allusion to the Federal Union. It was incorporated as a borough on April 4, 1796, and as a city on December 19, 1913.

Office	Name	Political Affiliation	Term Expires	Annual Salary
Commissioner, Chairman	Fred L. Lebder	D	Jan. 1988	$34,019
Commissioner	Carmine V. Molinaro, Jr.	D	Jan. 1988	33,019
Commissioner	Robert E. Jones, Jr.	R	Jan. 1988	33,019
Sheriff	Norma Jean Santore	D	Jan. 1988	30,864
Coroner	Dr. Phillip Reilly	D	Jan. 1988	24,406
Recorder of Deeds	David G. Malosky	D	Jan. 1990	30,864
Register of Wills and Clerk, Orphans' Court	John V. Schroyer	D	Jan. 1988	31,864
Prothonotary	Edward Brady	D	Jan. 1988	30,864
Clerk of Courts	Charles Baer	D	Jan. 1988	30,864
Controller	Edward T. Zimmerman	D	Jan. 1988	30,864
Treasurer	Nicholas Kornick	D	Jan. 1988	30,864
District Attorney	Gerald R. Solomon	D	Jan. 1988	33,738
Jury Commissioner	Walter Hager	R	Jan. 1990	7,178
Jury Commissioner	Mark Lepore	D	Jan. 1990	7,178
Chief Clerk	Joseph P. Korona, Jr.	Appt.	Jan. 1988	29,038
Chief Assessor	Richard Bitner	Appt.	Jan. 1988	23,153
County Solicitor	Philip T. Warman	Appt.	Jan. 1988	15,750

FOREST COUNTY (8th Class, population 5,072) was created on April 11, 1848, from part of Jefferson County; part of Venango County was added on October 31, 1866. It was named for its extensive forests. It was attached to Jefferson County until 1857 when Marienville became the county seat. *Tionesta,* the county seat after 1866, was incorporated as a borough on February 28, 1856, and was named for Tionesta Creek.

Office	Name	Political Affiliation	Term Expires	Annual Salary
Commissioner, Chairman	Samuel J. Wagner.....................	R	Jan. 1988	$18,761
Commissioner.......................	Donna J. Snyder	D	Jan. 1988	18,761
Commissioner.......................	Lee Allen Dunkle....................	R	Jan. 1988	18,761
Sheriff............................	Harry E. Tucker	R	Jan. 1990	17,761
Coroner............................	James K. Haslet	R	Jan. 1988	6,685
Recorder of Deeds, Register of Wills, Clerk, Orphans' Court, Prothonotary and Clerk of Courts....................	B. Jane Flick	R	Jan. 1988	19,761
Treasurer...........................	Elizabeth R. Mealy	R	Jan. 1988	18,761
District Attorney.....................	Paul Millin	R	Jan. 1988	20,101
Jury Commissioner...................	Anna Kincaid.......................	D	Jan. 1988	2,680
Jury Commissioner...................	Mary Lou Hale......................	R	Jan. 1988	2,680
Clerk to Commissioners	Virginia M. Call	Appt.		9,500
Chief Assessor	Patti J. Tucker	Appt.		11,025
County Solicitor......................	Joseph E. Altomare..................	Appt.		6,375

FRANKLIN COUNTY (5th class, population 113,629) was created on September 9, 1784, from part of Cumberland County and named for Benjamin Franklin. *Chambersburg,* the county seat, was founded in 1764 by Benjamin Chambers, for whom it was named. It was incorporated as a borough on March 21, 1803.

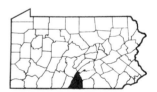

Office	Name	Political Affiliation	Term Expires	Annual Salary
Commissioner, Chairman	Fred J. Rock	R	Jan. 1988	$27,086
Commissioner.......................	Joe W. Ausherman	R	Jan. 1988	27,086
Commissioner.......................	Dennis A. Zeger	D	Jan. 1988	27,086
Sheriff.............................	Raymond Z. Hussack	R	Jan. 1988	24,508
Coroner............................	Herman P. Bender...................	R	Jan. 1988	18,057
Recorder of Deeds and Register of Wills.....................	David W. Bowers	R	Jan. 1988	25,796
Clerk, Orphans' Court and Clerk of Courts.....................	Robert J. Woods*....................	R	Jan. 1988	26,796
Prothonotary........................	John F. George	R	Jan. 1988	24,508
Controller	Thomas R. Swope....................	R	Jan. 1988	24,508
Treasurer...........................	Mary C. Hockenberry	D	Jan. 1990	24,508
District Attorney.....................	John F. Nelson*.....................	R	Jan. 1988	25,424
Jury Commissioner...................	Robert S. Little	R	Jan. 1990	5,158
Jury Commissioner...................	Paul Shatzer	D	Jan. 1990	5,158
Clerk to Commissioners	Linford S. Pensinger	Appt.		26,622
County Solicitor......................	Thomas H. Humelsine................	Appt.		20,009

*appointed

FULTON COUNTY (8th class, population 12,842) was created on April 19, 1851, from part of Bedford County and named for Robert Fulton, the inventor who pioneered in the use of the steamboat. *McConnellsburg,* the county seat, was laid out by Daniel McConnell in 1786 and incorporated as a borough on March 26, 1814.

Office	Name	Political Affiliation	Term Expires	Annual Salary
Commissioner, Chairman	Cecil F. Fraker	R	Jan. 1988	$16,220
Commissioner	Boyd R. Mellott	D	Jan. 1988	16,220
Commissioner	Donald N. Culler	R	Jan. 1988	16,220
Sheriff	Charles A. Waters	D	Jan. 1988	16,220
Coroner	Russell C. McLucas	D	Jan. 1988	6,372
Recorder of Deeds, Register of Wills, Clerk, Orphans' Court, Prothonotary and Clerk of Courts	Ruth M. Bolinger	R	Jan. 1990	17,379
Treasurer	David R. Wright	R	Jan. 1988	16,220
District Attorney	James M. Schall	D	Jan. 1988	17,379
Jury Commissioner	Doretta K. Mellott	D	Jan. 1990	2,317
Jury Commissioner	Mildred M. Fix	R	Jan. 1990	2,317
Clerk to Commissioners	Richard L. Wible	Appt.		21,003
Chief Assessor	Maynard C. Gordon	Appt.		59/day
County Solicitor	Stanley J. Kerlin	Appt.		12,000

GREENE COUNTY (6th Class, population 40,355) was created on February 9, 1796, from part of Washington County and named for General Nathanael Greene. *Waynesburg,* the county seat, named for Major General Anthony Wayne, was laid out in 1796, and incorporated as a borough on January. 29, 1816.

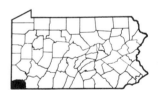

Office	Name	Political Affiliation	Term Expires	Annual Salary
Commissioner, Chairman	John R. Gardner	R	Jan. 1988	$19,000
Commissioner	Daniel E. Bailey	D	Jan. 1988	19,000
Commissioner	Leonard R. Santore	D	Jan. 1988	19,000
Sheriff	Remo E. Bertugli	D	Jan. 1990	17,000
Coroner	Frank J. Behm	D	Jan. 1990	7,000
Recorder of Deeds and Register of Wills	Thomas M. Headlee	D	Jan. 1988	18,000
Clerk, Orphans' Court and Clerk of Courts	Margaret S. Stockdale	D	Jan. 1988	18,000
Prothonotary	David Coder	D	Jan. 1988	17,000
Treasurer	Joseph R. Souders	D	Jan. 1988	17,000
District Attorney	Charles J. Morris	D	Jan. 1988	18,000
Jury Commissioner	Bernice Kuharcik	D	Jan. 1990	3,000
Jury Commissioner	Rosalind Laur	R	Jan. 1990	3,000
Clerk to Commissioners	Herbert A. Cox	Appt.		22,670
Chief Assessor	Perry Bavera	Appt.		16,254
County Solicitor	A. J. Marion	Appt.		13,917

HUNTINGDON COUNTY (6th class, population 42,253) was created on September 20, 1787, from part of Bedford County and named for its county seat, *Huntingdon.* Dr. William Smith, provost of the University of Pennsylvania, owned the land where the town was laid out in 1767 and named it for the Countess of Huntingdon, England. Huntingdon was incorporated as a borough on March 29, 1796.

Office	Name	Political Affiliation	Term Expires	Annual Salary
Commissioner, Chairman	Larry O. Sather	R	Jan. 1988	$22,013
Commissioner, Vice Chairman	Merle E. Steninger	R	Jan. 1988	22,013
Commissioner, Secretary	Louise H. Hetrick	D	Jan. 1988	22,013
Sheriff	Mark E. Leamer, Jr.	R	Jan. 1990	19,696
Coroner	Daniel Quarry	R	Jan. 1988	8,110
Recorder of Deeds, Register of Wills and Clerk, Orphans' Court	John P. Mills	D	Jan. 1988	20,854
Prothonotary and Clerk of Courts	Edwin S. Mansberger	R	Jan. 1988	20,508
Treasurer	Richard E. Kidd	R	Jan. 1988	19,696
Tax Claims Bureau, Director	Richard E. Kidd	R	Jan. 1988	3,696
District Attorney	Stewart L. Kurtz	R	Jan. 1988	20,854
Jury Commissioner	John Brewster	R	Jan. 1990	3,244
Jury Commissioner	Audrey Horton	D	Jan. 1990	3,244
Clerk to Commissioners	Louella C. Coons	Appt.		17,376
Chief Assessor	William Fagan	Appt.		12,199
County Solicitor	Scot D. Gill	Appt.		13,260
County Auditor	Thelma R. Shoop	R	Jan. 1988	52/day
County Auditor	G. Hobart Smith	R	Jan. 1988	52/day
County Auditor	Alice M. Lancaster	D	Jan. 1988	52/day
Public Defender, Chief	Robert B. Stewart, III	Appt.		18,200
Public Defender, Assistant Chief	Harvey B. Reeder	Appt.		16,640

INDIANA COUNTY (6th class, population 92,281) was created on March 30, 1803, from parts of Westmoreland and Lycoming Counties and probably named for the Territory of Indiana. It was attached to Westmoreland County until 1806. *Indiana,* the county seat, was laid out in 1805 and incorporated as a borough on March 11, 1816.

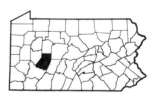

Office	Name	Political Affiliation	Term Expires	Annual Salary
Commissioner, Chairman	James E. McQuown	D	Jan. 1988	$19,000
Commissioner	Beatrice L. States	D	Jan. 1988	19,000
Commissioner	Anthony S. Hewitt	R	Jan. 1988	19,000
Sheriff	John R. Gondal	D	Jan. 1988	17,000
Coroner	Thomas Streams	R	Jan. 1990	7,000
Recorder of Deeds, Register of Wills and Clerk, Orphans' Court	Donald B. Shank	R	Jan. 1988	18,000
Prothonotary and Clerk of Courts	Linda Moore	R	Jan. 1988	18,000
Treasurer	Emma Ober	R	Jan. 1990	17,000
District Attorney	William J. Martin	R	Jan. 1988	18,000
Jury Commissioner	John Griffith	D	Jan. 1990	3,000
Jury Commissioner	Elsie T. Young	R	Jan. 1990	3,000
County Auditor	Annelise E. Shaffer	D	Jan. 1988	45/day
County Auditor	Sarah J. Bloom	R	Jan. 1988	45/day
County Auditor	Samuel J. Kelly	R	Jan. 1988	45/day
Clerk to Commissioners	Helen C. Hill	Appt.		18,554
Chief Assessor	David S. Wilson	Appt.		23,981
County Solicitor	James D. Carmella	Appt.		12,600

JEFFERSON COUNTY (6th class, population 48,303) was created on March 26, 1804, from part of Lycoming County and named for President Thomas Jefferson. It was attached to Westmoreland County until 1806 and then to Indiana County until 1830, when it was formally organized. *Brookville,* the county seat, was laid out in 1830 and incorporated as a borough on April 9, 1834. It is said to have been named for the numerous brooks and streams in the vicinity.

Office	Name	Political Affiliation	Term Expires	Annual Salary
Commissioner, Chairman	David W. Black	R	Jan. 1988	$25,462
Commissioner	Jere D. Pearson*	R	Jan. 1988	25,462
Commissioner	Andrew S. Laska	D	Jan. 1988	25,462
Sheriff	Harry E. Dunkle	R	Jan. 1990	22,782
Coroner	Christopher Burkett	D	Jan. 1990	9,381
Recorder of Deeds, Register of Wills and Clerk, Orphans' Court	Robert H. Lyle	D	Jan. 1988	23,782
Prothonotary and Clerk of Courts	Cadwallader M. Emery	R	Jan. 1990	23,782
Treasurer	Dale Corbin	R	Jan. 1990	22,782
District Attorney	A. Ted Hudock	D	Jan. 1990	24,122
Jury Commissioner	Diane Maihle Kiehl	R	Jan. 1990	4,020
Jury Commissioner	Donna Hoffman	D	Jan. 1990	4,020
Clerk to Commissioners	Julie Rhoades*	R		19,756
Chief Assessor	Delvin Kerr	Appt.		20,042
County Solicitor	John C. Dennison	Appt.		12,000

*appointed

JUNIATA COUNTY (8th class, population 19,188) was created on March 2, 1831, from part of Mifflin County and named for the Juniata River. The Indian name Juniata is said to mean "people of the standing stone." *Mifflintown,* the county seat, was laid out in 1791 and incorporated as a borough on March 6, 1833. It was named for Governor Thomas Mifflin.

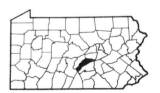

Office	Name	Political Affiliation	Term Expires	Annual Salary
Commissioner, Chairman	Ronald Clyde Shearer	D	Jan. 1988	$14,000
Commissioner	Richard P. Kerstetter	D	Jan. 1988	14,000
Commissioner	John P. Henry, Jr.	R	Jan. 1988	14,000
Sheriff	Douglas McKee	R	Jan. 1990	15,908
Coroner	Dr. Stephen F. Dodd	R	Jan. 1988	5,500
Recorder of Deeds, Register of Wills and Clerk, Orphans' Court	Ansel B. McNaight	D	Jan. 1990	18,180
Prothonotary and Clerk of Courts	Frances Lindenmuth	D	Jan. 1988	15,000
Controller and Treasurer	Betty S. Carter	D	Jan. 1990	15,908
District Attorney	Daniel F. Clark	R	Jan. 1988	15,000
Jury Commissioner	D. Michael Mertz	R	Jan. 1990	2,272
Jury Commissioner	Betty Kipp	D	Jan. 1990	2,272
Clerks to Commissioners	Pauline I. Mengel	Appt.		12,400
Chief Assessor	Clair Parson	Appt.		14,500
County Solicitor	Clyde R. Bomgardner	Appt.		9,500

LACKAWANNA COUNTY (3th class, population 227,908) created on

August 13, 1878, from part of Luzerne County, was the last county to be created. It was named for the Lackawanna River, a name meaning "stream that forks." *Scranton,* the county seat, was laid out in 1841, incorporated as a borough in 1856, and became a city on April 23, 1866. It was named for the Scranton family, its founders. The county adopted a home rule charter in April 1976.

Office	Name	Political Affiliation	Term Expires	Annual Salary
Commissioner, Chairman	Ray A. Alberigi.	D	Jan. 1988	$35,737
Commissioner........................	Joseph Corcoran.	D	Jan. 1988	34,460
Commissioner........................	Charles Luger	R	Jan. 1988	34,460
Sheriff..............................	John Syzmanski	D	Jan. 1990	29,998
Coroner.............................	William H. Sweeney	D	Jan. 1988	24,250
Recorder of Deeds	Ann Marie Regan	D	Jan. 1990	29,998
Register of Wills and Clerk, Orphans' Court	Jery Notarianni	R	Jan. 1990	29,998
Clerk of Judicial Records	William P. Rinaldi.....................	R	Jan. 1990	29,998
Controller	Joseph Profera	D	Jan. 1988	29,998
Treasurer...........................	Robert E. Payton......................	D	Jan. 1988	29,998
District Attorney......................	Ernest Preate	R	Jan. 1990	64,000
Administrative Director	Gerald Stanvitch	Appt.		27,600
Chief Assessor	Thomas Dunda	Appt.		21,600
County Solicitor......................	David Rinaldi, Esq.	Appt.		20,600

LANCASTER COUNTY (3rd class, population 362,346) was created on

May 10, 1729, from part of Chester County and named for Lancashire, England. *Lancaster,* the county seat, named for its England counterpart, was laid out in 1730. It was chartered as a borough on May 1, 1742, and as a city on March 10, 1818.

Office	Name	Political Affiliation	Term Expires	Annual Salary
Commissioner, Chairman	James E. Huber	R	Jan. 1988	$36,072
Commissioner........................	Robert C. Boyer.......................	R	Jan. 1988	34,788
Commissioner........................	Brad S. Fischer	D	Jan. 1988	34,788
Sheriff..............................	Thomas Williams......................	R	Jan. 1988	30,278
Coroner.............................	Dr. Barry D. Walp.....................	R	Jan. 1988	24,481
Recorder of Deeds	Isa J. Breineisen	R	Jan. 1990	30,278
Register of Wills and Clerk, Orphans' Court	Richard H. Witmer.....................	R	Jan. 1988	31,567
Prothonotary........................	Ethel M. Zook	R	Jan. 1988	30,278
Clerk of Courts	Gloria V. Goldy	R	Jan. 1988	30,278
Controller	James V. Fullmer......................	R	Jan. 1990	30,278
Treasurer...........................	Esther G. Holder	R	Jan. 1988	30,278
District Attorney......................	Henry S. Kenderine, Jr..................	R	Jan. 1988	32,211
Jury Commissioner....................	Harriet L. Lewis	D	Jan. 1990	6,825
Jury Commissioner....................	Jacob L. Brown	R	Jan. 1990	6,825
County Administrator and Clerk to Commissioners	John H. Hoober.......................	Appt.		40,262
Chief Assessor	Leo C. Grasser	Appt.		29,019
County Solicitor......................	Thomas Goodman	Appt.		26,250
County Engineer	Thomas F. Shirk	Appt.		45,308
Chief, Voter Registration and Election Board	Karen G. Axe.........................	Appt.		19,190
Personnel Director	William J. Brennan	Appt.		35,600
Purchasing Director	Charles R. Schatzman	Appt.		21,102
Prison Warden.......................	Vincent A. Guarini....................	Appt.		39,542

LAWRENCE COUNTY (5th class, population 107,150) was created on
March 20, 1849, from parts of Beaver and Mercer Counties and named for Perry's flagship, *Lawrence,* which had been named for Captain James Lawrence, a naval hero. *New Castle,* the county seat, was laid out in 1802, incorporated as a borough on March 25, 1825, and chartered as a city on February 25, 1869. It is not certain whether it was named for Newcastle, England, or New Castle, Delaware.

Office	Name	Political Affiliation	Term Expires	Annual Salary
Commissioner, Chairman	Roger M. DeCarbo	D	Jan. 1988	$25,813
Commissioner.	Paul L. Tanner	R	Jan. 1988	25,813
Commissioner.	Vern L. Eppinger	D	Jan. 1988	25,813
Sheriff	George Sigler	D	Jan. 1990	25,204
Coroner.	J. Russell Noga	D	Jan. 1988	17,209
Recorder of Deeds and Register of Wills.	Janet L. Kalajainen	D	Jan. 1990	26,204
Clerk, Orphans' Court, Prothonotary and Clerk of Courts.	Helen I. Morgan.	D	Jan. 1988	24,354
Controller	Robert E. Foht.	R	Jan. 1988	23,354
Treasurer.	Robert D. Shaffer	D	Jan. 1988	23,354
District Attorney.	William M. Panella.	D	Jan. 1990	27,194
Jury Commissioner.	Thomas George	D	Jan. 1990	5,305
Jury Commissioner.	Ann Daugherty	R	Jan. 1990	5,305
Clerk to Commissioners	Charleen T. Micco	Appt.		18,667
Chief Assessor	Mary Bullano.	Appt.		19,214
County Solicitor.	John W. Hodge	Appt.		18,000

LEBANON COUNTY (5th class, population 109,829) was created on
February 16, 1813, from parts of Dauphin and Lancaster Counties and named for old Lebanon Township. Lebanon is a Biblical name meaning "white mountain." *Lebanon,* the county seat, was laid out in 1750. It was first incorporated as a borough on March 28, 1799, but the citizens did not accept incorporation. It was finally chartered as a borough on February 20, 1821, and as a city in 1885.

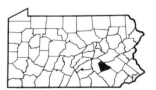

Office	Name	Political Affiliation	Term Expires	Annual Salary
Commissioner, Chairman	Daniel J. Kreider	R	Jan. 1988	$22,714
Commissioner.	Rose Marie Swanger.	R	Jan. 1988	22,714
Commissioner.	Edward L. Arnold.	D	Jan. 1988	22,714
Sheriff	Clifford A. Roland, Sr.	R	Jan. 1990	22,227
Coroner.	Dr. Robert M. Kline	R	Jan. 1988	15,142
Recorder of Deeds	Russell K. Light	R	Jan. 1988	20,550
Register of Wills and Clerk, Orphans' Court	Harold W. Risser, Jr.	R	Jan. 1990	23,397
Prothonotary/Clerk of Courts	Corwin C. Erdman.	R	Jan. 1990	21,632
Controller	Edward I. Wolfe	R	Jan. 1988	20,550
Treasurer.	Lois J. Bomberger.	R	Jan. 1990	20,550
District Attorney.	Thomas S. Long	R	Jan. 1990	23,982
Jury Commissioner.	Robert W. Rothermel.	D	Jan. 1990	4,679
Jury Commissioner.	Diane Shultz	R	Jan. 1990	4,679
Clerk to Commissioners	Donald J. Rhine.	Appt.		34,760
Chief Assessor	Norma J. P. Sando.	Appt.		22,563
County Solicitor.	Robert Sullivan, Jr.	Appt.		20,207

LEHIGH COUNTY (3rd class, population 273,582) was created on March 6, 1812, from part of Northampton County and named for the Lehigh River. The name Lehigh is derived from the German "Lecha," which comes from the Indian "Lechauwekink," meaning "where there are forks." *Allentown,* the county seat, was laid out about 1762 and named for Chief Justice William Allen of Pennsylvania, a local landowner. It was incorporated as the Borough of Northampton on March 18, 1811, renamed Allentown in 1838, and chartered as a city on March 12, 1867. The county adopted a home rule charter in November 1975.

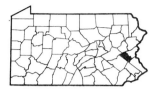

Office	Name	Political Affiliation	Term Expires	Annual Salary
County Executive	David K. Bausch	R	Jan. 1990	$37,000
Commissioner, Chairman	Kenneth H. Mohr, Jr.	D	Jan. 1990	2,800
Commissioner, Vice Chairman	John F. McHugh	R	Jan. 1988	2,500
Commissioner	Jane S. Baker	R	Jan. 1990	2,500
Commissioner	John W. Brosious	D	Jan. 1988	2,500
Commissioner	Donald H. Davies	R	Jan. 1988	2,500
Commissioner	Judith R. Diehl	D	Jan. 1988	2,500
Commissioner	Leon W. Eisenhard	D	Jan. 1990	2,500
Commissioner	Sterling H. Raber	R	Jan. 1990	2,500
Commissioner	Donald E. Wieand, Jr.	R	Jan. 1990	2,500
Sheriff	Ronald Neimeyer	R	Jan. 1988	25,850
Coroner	Robert C. Weir	D	Jan. 1988	20,900
Recorder of Deeds	George D. Black	R	Jan. 1988	25,850
Register of Wills	Charles J. Kistler	D	Jan. 1988	25,850
Clerk, Orphans' Court	Sandra Schantz	Appt.		26,790
Clerk of Courts	Doris A. Glaessmann	D	Jan. 1988	25,850
Controller	Frank Concannon	D	Jan. 1988	25,850
Fiscal Officer	Thomas J. Lazorik	Appt.		39,561
District Attorney	William Platt	R	Jan. 1988	64,000
Clerk to Commissioners	Mary T. Haney	Appt.		25,290
Chief Assessor	Robert A. Hanisits	Appt.		34,195
County Solicitor	Lawraence P. Brenner	Appt.		29,000

LUZERNE COUNTY (3rd class, population 343,079) was created on September 25, 1786, from part of Northumberland County and named for the Chevalier de la Luzerne, French minister to the United States. *Wilkes-Barre,* the county seat, was laid out in 1772 and named for two members of Parliament, John Wilkes and Isaac Barre, both advocates of American rights. It was incorporated as a borough on March 17, 1806, and as a city on May 4, 1871.

Office	Name	Political Affiliation	Term Expires	Annual Salary
Commissioner, Chairman	Frank J. Trinisewki, Jr.	R	Jan. 1988	$39,448
Commissioner	Frank P. Crossin, Jr.	D	Jan. 1988	38,448
Commissioner	Jim Phillips	R	Jan. 1988	38,448
Sheriff	Frank J. Jagodinski	D	Jan. 1988	33,268
Coroner	George E. Hudock, Jr., M.D.	D	Jan. 1988	26,898
Recorder of Deeds	Frank C. Castellino	D	Jan. 1988	33,268
Register of Wills	Helen A. O'Connor	D	Jan. 1990	34,268
Prothonotary	Eugene E. Duffy, Esq	D	Jan. 1990	33,268
Clerk of Courts	Eugene Hudak	D	Jan. 1988	33,268
Controller	Joseph S. Tirpak	D	Jan. 1990	33,268
Treasurer	Michael L. Morreale	D	Jan. 1988	33,268
District Attorney	Bernard Podcasy	D	Jan. 1988	64,000
Jury Commissioner	Daniel F. Blaine	D	Jan. 1990	6,500
Jury Commissioner	Martha Reese	R	Jan. 1990	6,500
Clerk to Commissioners	Eugene R. Klein	Appt.		27,070
Assessor	John J. Anstett	Appt.		24,420
County Solicitor	Richard Goldberg	Appt.		20,074

LYCOMING COUNTY (5th class, population 118,416) was created on April 13, 1795, from part of Northumberland County and named for Lycoming Creek. The name is derived from a Delaware Indian word meaning "sandy or gravelly creek." *Williamsport,* the county seat, was laid out in 1795, incorporated as a borough on March 1, 1806, and became a city on January 15, 1866. There are various theories about the origin of the city's name: that it was so called for Judge William Hepburn; that Michael Ross named it for his own son William; or that William Ross, a boatman, used it as a port years before the town was founded.

Office	Name	Political Affiliation	Term Expires	Annual Salary
Commissioner, Chairperson	Gene Smith	R	Jan. 1988	$25,075
Commissioner, Vice Chairperson	Lora P. Morningstar	R	Jan. 1988	25,075
Commissioner	Dolly M. Wilt	D	Jan. 1988	25,075
Sheriff	Charles Brewer	R	Jan. 1990	22,687
Coroner	George W. Gedon	R	Jan. 1988	17,041
Recorder of Deeds and Register of Wills	Mary G. Mosser	R	Jan. 1988	22,687
Prothonotary and Clerk of Courts	Thomas W. Dempsey	R	Jan. 1988	22,687
Controller	Hazel M. Follmer	R	Jan. 1988	22,687
Treasurer	Irene S. Migrath	R	Jan. 1988	22,687
District Attorney	Brett O. Feese	R	Jan. 1988	24,478
Jury Commissioner	Helen Sheffer	R	Jan. 1990	4,776
Jury Commissioner	H. Eugene Frey	D	Jan. 1990	4,776
Clerk to Commissioners	John Balog	Appt.		43,644
Chief Assessor	George McCormick	Appt.		24,930
County Solicitor	Paul W. Reeder	Appt.		25,000

McKEAN COUNTY (6th class, population 50,635) was created on March 26, 1804, from part of Lycoming County and named for Governor Thomas McKean. It was attached to Centre County until 1814, when it was combined with Potter County to elect commissioners jointly, and was also attached to Lycoming County for judicial and elective purposes. It was fully organized in 1826. *Smethport,* the county seat, was laid out in 1807, and named in honor of Raymond and Theodore de Smeth, Amsterdam bankers. It was incorporated as a borough on February 11, 1853.

Office	Name	Political Affiliation	Term Expires	Annual Salary
Commissioner, Chairman	Raymond J. Curtis	R	Jan. 1988	$28,513
Commissioner	Patrick J. Costello, Jr.	R	Jan. 1988	28,513
Commissioner	Sherwood Anderson	D	Jan. 1988	28,513
Sheriff	Donald Morey	R	Jan. 1990	25,512
Coroner	Francis D. (Frank) Cahill	R	Jan. 1988	10,505
Recorder of Deeds	Betty B. Comes	R	Jan. 1988	25,512
Register of Wills and Clerk, Orphans' Court	L. W. (Tom) Pendleton	R	Jan. 1988	26,512
Prothonotary and Clerk of Courts	Bonnie Moore	R	Jan. 1990	26,512
Controller	Joyce Carr	R	Jan. 1990	25,512
Treasurer	Connie Eaton	R	Jan. 1990	25,512
District Attorney	Jay Paul Kahle	R	Jan. 1988	27,013
Jury Commissioner	Kathryn L. Gorton	R	Jan. 1990	4,502
Jury Commissioner	Wanita H. Lane	D	Jan. 1990	4,502
Clerk to Commissioners	Audrey B. Irons	Appt.		18,700
Chief Assessor	Barry L. Hurley	Appt.		19,541
County Solicitor	Stanley E. Pecora, Jr.	Appt.		22,000

MERCER COUNTY (5th class, population 128,299) was created on March 12, 1800, from part of Allegheny County and named for General Hugh Mercer. It was attached to Crawford County until February 1804 when it was formally organized. *Mercer,* the county seat, was laid out in 1803 and incorporated as a borough on March 28, 1814.

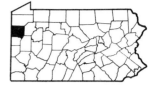

Office	Name	Political Affiliation	Term Expires	Annual Salary
Commissioner, Chairman	Harold E. Bell	D	Jan. 1988	$27,527
Commissioner........................	Les Cattron	D	Jan. 1988	27,527
Commissioner........................	William M. Reznor....................	R	Jan. 1988	27,527
Sheriff	Donald Marenchin.....................	R	Jan. 1988	24,905
Coroner............................	John K. Mohney	R	Jan. 1988	18,351
Recorder of Deeds	Marilyn Felesky......................	D	Jan. 1988	24,905
Clerk of Courts and Register of Wills.....................	Marie Forsyth	R	Jan. 1988	26,216
Prothonotary........................	Mary E. Griffin......................	R	Jan. 1988	24,905
Controller	Wanda McCamey	R	Jan. 1990	24,905
Treasurer...........................	Nettie Pantall.......................	R	Jan. 1990	24,905
District Attorney.....................	James Epstein.......................	D	Jan. 1988	26,871
Jury Commissioner	Marie Campman	R	Jan. 1990	5,243
Jury Commissioner	Betty J. Devito......................	D	Jan. 1990	5,243
Clerk to Commissioners	Jack S. Cardwell	Appt.		21,000
Chief Assessor and Director of Tax Claim	William Fagley.......................	Appt.		28,792
County Solicitor......................	Robert Tesone.......................	Appt.		16,692

MIFFLIN COUNTY (6th class, population 46,908) was created on September 19, 1789, from parts of Cumberland and Northumberland Counties and named for Governor Thomas Mifflin. *Lewistown,* the county seat, was laid out in 1790 and incorporated as a borough on April 11, 1795. However, this charter apparently was not accepted, for it was reincorporated on February 6, 1811. It was named for William Lewis, local ironmaster.

Office	Name	Political Affiliation	Term Expires	Annual Salary
Commissioner, Chairman	Bill Finkenbiner	R	Jan. 1988	$19,000
Commissioner........................	H. Kenneth Kochenderfer	R	Jan. 1988	19,000
Commissioner........................	Herbert K. Yingling	D	Jan. 1988	19,000
Sheriff	Jay R. Laub.........................	D	Jan. 1990	17,000
Coroner............................	Dr. A. Reid Leopold, Jr.	R	Jan. 1988	7,000
Recorder of Deeds, Register of Wills and Clerk, Orphans' Court	Charles E. "Yogi" Laub................	R	Jan. 1990	19,000
Prothonotary and Clerk of Courts.....................	Sue Ellen Saxton.....................	R	Jan. 1988	18,000
Treasurer...........................	Gerald R. Hepler.....................	R	Jan. 1990	17,000
District Attorney.....................	William A. Helm......................	D	Jan. 1988	18,000
Jury Commissioner	Donald E. Baggus	R	Jan. 1990	3,000
Jury Commissioner	Maxwell L. Hook	D	Jan. 1990	3,000
Clerk to Commissioners	Peggy G. Yoder	Appt.		15,250
Chief Assessor	David R. Fultz	Appt.		15,000
County Solicitor......................	Timothy S. Searer....................	Appt.		12,550

MONROE COUNTY

MONROE COUNTY (6th class, population 69,409) was created on April 1, 1836, from parts of Northampton and Pike Counties and named for President James Monroe. *Stroudsburg,* the county seat, was incorporated as a borough on February 6, 1815, and named for Jacob Stroud, a settler.

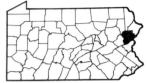

Office	Name	Political Affiliation	Term Expires	Annual Salary
Commissioner, Chairman	James E. Cadue	D	Jan. 1988	$24,249
Commissioner......................	John H. Parker, Sr....................	R	Jan. 1988	24,249
Commissioner......................	Thomas R. Joyce	D	Jan. 1988	24,249
Sheriff............................	Forrest B. Sebring...................	R	Jan. 1988	21,697
Coroner..........................	Robert M. Allen	R	Jan. 1990	15,193
Recorder of Deeds and Register of Wills....................	Dennis Deshler	D	Jan. 1988	22,973
Clerk, Orphans' Court, Prothonotary and Clerk of Courts....................	Joyce Reese	R	Jan. 1988	22,973
Treasurer.........................	Robert Coleman	D	Jan. 1990	22,848
District Attorney.....................	James F. Marsh	D	Jan. 1988	22,973
Jury Commissioner...................	Thomas J. Blewitt	D	Jan. 1990	4,032
Jury Commissioner...................	Fred Shoemaker	R	Jan. 1990	4,032
Clerk to Commissioners	Betsy Caprioli	Appt.		20,500
Chief Assessor	David Fenner........................	Appt.		24,000
County Solicitor.....................	Daniel Corveleyn.....................	Appt.		29,000

MONTGOMERY COUNTY

MONTGOMERY COUNTY (2nd class A, population 643,621) was created on September 10, 1784, from part of Philadelphia County. *Norristown,* the county seat, was laid out in 1784 and incorporated as a borough on March 31, 1812. It was named for Isaac Norris, who owned land there.

Office	Name	Political Affiliation	Term Expires	Annual Salary
Commissioner, Chairman	Paul B. Bartle	R	Jan. 1988	$36,420
Commissioner......................	Betty B. Linker......................	R	Jan. 1988	34,235
Commissioner......................	Rita C. Banning......................	D	Jan. 1988	34,235
Sheriff............................	Frank P. Lalley......................	R	Jan. 1988	28,985
Coroner..........................	Dr. Theodore A. Garcia	R	Jan. 1988	26,250
Recorder of Deeds	James L. Price	R	Jan. 1988	28,985
Register of Wills and Clerk, Orphans' Court	Sara E. Long........................	R	Jan. 1988	29,985
Prothonotary.......................	William E. Donnelly...................	R	Jan. 1988	28,985
Clerk of Courts	George J. Miller......................	R	Jan. 1988	28,985
Controller	William M. Bickel.....................	R	Jan. 1988	28,985
Treasurer.........................	Floriana M. Bloss	R	Jan. 1988	28,985
District Attorney.....................	Thomas E. Waters, Jr.................	Appt.	Jan. 1988	64,000
Jury Commissioner...................	Virginia R. Kanengeiser	R	Jan. 1990	10,500
Jury Commissioner...................	Claire B. Comalli	D	Jan. 1990	10,500
Clerk to Commissioners	Robert W. Graf......................	Appt.		48,500
Chief Assessor	William P. Wentz, Jr.	Appt.		43,250
County Solicitor.....................	Frederic M. Wentz....................	Appt.		44,000

MONTOUR COUNTY (8th class, population 16,675) was created on May 3, 1850, from part of Columbia County and named for Madame Montour, a woman of Indian and French descent, who was prominent in the Indian affairs. *Danville,* the county seat, was laid out in 1792 and incorporated as a borough on February 27, 1849. It was the county seat of Columbia from 1813 to 1846.

Office	Name	Political Affiliation	Term Expires	Annual Salary
Commissioner, Chairman	Thomas E. Herman	D	Jan. 1988	$15,800
Commissioner	Robert P. Burke	D	Jan. 1988	15,800
Commissioner	Edwin R. Kremer	R	Jan. 1988	15,800
Sheriff	Fred R. Shepperson	D	Jan. 1988	15,800
Coroner	James C. F. Rodenhaver	R	Jan. 1988	6,550
Recorder of Deeds and Register of Wills	Linda L. Weaver	D	Jan. 1988	16,800
Clerk, Orphans' Court, Prothonotary and Clerk of Courts	Suzanne M. Tinsley	D	Jan. 1988	16,800
Treasurer	Robert P. Love	D	Jan. 1990	14,600
District Attorney	George O. Wagner	R	Jan. 1988	16,800
Jury Commissioner	M. Jane Muffly	R	Jan. 1988	2,382
Jury Commissioner	Virginia Shultz	D	Jan. 1988	2,382
Clerk to Commissioners	Susan M. Kauwell	D	Jan. 1988	14,720
Chief Assessor	Esther Cotner	D	Jan. 1988	13,525
County Solicitor	Richard C. Brittain	D	Jan. 1988	7,600
Auditor	Clinton Buck	R	Jan. 1988	46/day

NORTHAMPTON COUNTY (3rd class, population 225,418) was created on March 11, 1752, from parts of Bucks County and named for Northamptonshire, England, where Thomas Penn's father-in-law, the Earl of Pomfret, lived. *Easton,* the county seat, was named for the Earl's estate. It was incorporated as a borough on September 23, 1789, and became a city on November 2, 1886. The county adopted a home rule charter in April 1976.

Office	Name	Political Affiliation	Term Expires	Annual Salary
County Executive	Eugene R. Hartzel	D	Jan. 1990	$48,500
Councilman	Gerald E. Seyfried	D	Jan. 1988	5,500
Councilman	Gordon T. Heller	D	Jan. 1988	5,500
Councilman	Dorothy M. Zug	D	Jan. 1990	5,500
Councilman	Richard T. Grucela	D	Jan. 1988	6,000
Councilman	Ralph R. Hartzell	D	Jan. 1990	5,500
Councilman	James A. Hemstreet	R	Jan. 1988	5,500
Councilman	James P. Mazza	D	Jan. 1988	5,500
Councilman	Joseph M. Saveri	D	Jan. 1990	5,500
Councilman	Ladd Siftar, Jr.	D	Jan. 1988	5,500
Controller	Kenneth A. Florey	D	Jan. 1988	30,500
District Attorney	Donald B. Corriere	D	Jan. 1988	30,500
Sheriff	Kenneth Stocker	Appt.		31,971
Coroner	Joseph Reichel	Appt.		26,828
Court Services Director	Maurice Dimmick	Appt.		31,971
Fiscal Affairs Director	Charles Houck	Appt.		45,003
Human Services Director	Jerry W. Friedman	Appt.		45,003
Public Works Director	John Giesen	Appt.		42,862
Warden	A. S. DiGiacinto	Appt.		42,862
Public Defender	Chester Reybitz	Appt.		29,808
Clerk to Council	Frank E. Flisser	Appt.		32,273
Solicitor to Council	Karl Longenbach	Appt.		18,899
County Solicitor	William F. Moran	Appt.		29,906
Administration Director	Joseph Zajacek	Appt.		45,003
Court Administrator	Al Marhefka	Appt.		42,862

NORTHUMBERLAND COUNTY (5th class, population 100,381) was

created on March 21, 1772, from parts of Lancaster, Cumberland, Berks, Bedford and Northampton Counties. It probably was named for the English county of the same name. *Sunbury,* the county seat, was laid out in 1772, incorporated as a borough on March 24, 1797, and became a city in 1921. It was named for an English village near London.

Office	Name	Political Affiliation	Term Expires	Annual Salary
Commissioner, Chairman	James P. Kelley	D	Jan. 1988	$26,511
Commissioner	Charles F. Lewis	D	Jan. 1988	26,511
Commissioner	Lester W. Blevins	R	Jan. 1988	26,511
Sheriff	Russell H. Wolfe	R	Jan. 1988	23,985
Coroner	Dr. George Dietrick	R	Jan. 1990	17,661
Recorder of Deeds, Register of Wills and Clerk, Orphans' Court	Frederick F. Reed	R	Jan. 1990	26,227
Prothonotary and Clerk of Courts	Suzanne V. Smith	R	Jan. 1990	26,227
Controller	Allen J. Cwalina	D	Jan. 1990	26,106
Treasurer	Ronald E. Schreffler	R	Jan. 1988	23,985
District Attorney	Robert Sacavage	D	Jan. 1988	25,874
Jury Commissioner	Lester Burgess	R	Jan. 1990	5,032
Jury Commissioner	George Dorko	D	Jan. 1990	5,032
Clerk to Commissioners	George J. Edwards	Appt.		35,984
Assistant Clerk	James M. Brennan	Appt.		22,476
Chief Assessor	Richard Martini	Appt.		21,612
County Solicitor	G. Robert Fitzpatrick	Appt.		19,982
Assistant Solicitor	Jeffrey Apfelbaum	Appt.		12,979
Assistant Solicitor	James Purcell	Appt.		12,979
County Engineer	Charles Hopta	Appt.		24,310
Chief Registrar	Albert Santor	Appt.		18,474

PERRY COUNTY (7th class, population 35,718) was created on March 22,

1820, from part of Cumberland County and named in honor of Oliver Hazard Perry, victor in the Battle of Lake Erie. *Bloomfield,* the county seat after 1827, bears the name given to the tract of land in the original patent; it is said that it was laid out in the month of June 1822, when clover was in bloom. It was incorporated as a borough on March 14, 1831. The post-office name is New Bloomfield.

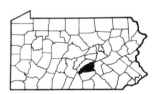

Office	Name	Political Affiliation	Term Expires	Annual Salary
Commissioner, Chairman	Ralph Elwood Mohler	R	Jan. 1988	$15,500
Commissioner, Vice-Chairman	Billy M. Roush	R	Jan. 1988	15,500
Commissioner, Secretary	Edward R. Kennedy	D	Jan. 1988	15,500
Sheriff	George W. Frownfelter	R	Jan. 1990	15,500
Coroner	Michael Shalonis	R	Jan. 1988	6,500
Register of Wills and Recorder of Deeds	David Magee	R	Jan. 1988	16,500
Prothonotary	William Templeton	R	Jan. 1988	16,500
Treasurer	Margaret M. Bolton	R	Jan. 1988	15,500
District Attorney	R. Scott Cramer	R	Jan. 1988	16,500
Jury Commissioner	Harry G. Sheaffer	D	Jan. 1990	2,500
Jury Commissioner	D. Ray Womer	R	Jan. 1990	2,500
Clerk to Commissioners	L. Dean McMillen*	R		14,000
Chief Assessor	Glenn Keller*	R		16,200
County Solicitor	William R. Bunt*	D		8,200

*appointed

PHILADELPHIA COUNTY was one of the three original counties created by William Penn in November, 1682, and its name to him signified "brotherly love," although the original Philadelphia in Asia Minor was actually "the city of Philadelphus." *Philadelphia* was laid out in 1682 as the county seat and the capital of the Province; it was chartered as a city on October 25, 1701, and rechartered on March 11, 1789. On February 2, 1854, all municipalities within the county were consolidated with the city. The county offices were merged with the city government in 1952.

**For Municipal Officials
See City of Philadelphia**

PIKE COUNTY (8th class, population 18,271) was created on March 26, 1814, from part of Wayne County and named for General Zebulon Pike. *Milford,* the county seat, was incorporated as a borough on December 25, 1874, and probably named for Milford Haven in Wales.

Office	Name	Political Affiliation	Term Expires	Annual Salary
Commissioner, Chairman	Willis J. Gilpin	R	Jan. 1988	$20,281
Commissioner	Donald C. Brink	R	Jan. 1988	20,281
Commissioner	H. James Crellin	D	Jan. 1988	20,281
Sheriff	Harry Geiger	R	Jan. 1990	20,281
Coroner	James J. Martin	R	Jan. 1988	7,967
Recorder of Deeds, Register of Wills, Clerk, Orphans' Court, Prothonotary and Clerk of Courts	Joyce Z. Helms	Appt.	Jan. 1988	21,730
Auditor	Shirley Basham	R	Jan. 1988	65/day
Auditor	Glenna Ryder	R	Jan. 1988	65/day
Auditor	Carol Haas	D	Jan. 1988	65/day
Treasurer	Edward Delling	R	Jan. 1988	20,281
District Attorney	Michael Weinstein	D	Jan. 1988	21,730
Jury Commissioner	Lloyd Nearing	R	Jan. 1988	2,771
Jury Commissioner	Catherine Steele	D	Jan. 1988	2,771
Chief Clerk	Centa T. Quinn	Appt.		28,150
Chief Assessor (Acting)	Walter Prigge	Appt.		20,900
County Solicitor	Jay R. Rose	Appt.		16,900

POTTER COUNTY (8th class, population 17,726) was created on March 26, 1804, from part of Lycoming County and named for General James Potter. It was attached to Lycoming County until 1814 when it was authorized to elect commissioners jointly with McKean County. McKean and Potter counties were separated in 1824 but Potter was still attached to McKean for judicial purposes. It was fully organized in 1835. *Coudersport,* the county seat, was laid out in 1807, and incorporated as a borough on February 7, 1848. It was named for Jean Samuel Couderc, an Amsterdam banker.

Office	Name	Political Affiliation	Term Expires	Annual Salary
Commissioner, Chairman	Thomas O. Bowman	R	Jan. 1988	$14,000
Commissioner........................	Carl H. Roberts	R	Jan. 1988	14,000
Commissioner........................	Susan S. Kefover	D	Jan. 1988	14,000
Sheriff	Dale W. Russell	R	Jan. 1988	14,000
Coroner............................	Thomas E. Fickinger	R	Jan. 1990	6,356
Recorder of Deeds and Register of Wills....................	Dale A. Jackson	R	Jan. 1988	15,000
Clerk, Orphans' Court, Prothonotary and Clerk of Courts.....................	Dean M. Dow........................	R	Jan. 1988	15,000
Treasurer...........................	Richard T. McCaigue.................	D	Jan. 1988	14,000
District Attorney......................	Jeffrey E. Leber......................	R	Jan. 1990	17,334
Jury Commissioner...................	Mildred E. Cowburn..................	D	Jan. 1990	2,311
Jury Commissioner...................	Jessie M. Palmatier..................	R	Jan. 1990	2,311
Clerk to Commissioners and Chief Assessor	F. W. Gunzburger.....................	Appt.		20,775
County Solicitor.......................	D. Bruce Cahilly	Appt.		19,500
Auditor.............................	Shirley M. Anderson	R	Jan. 1988	45/day
Auditor.............................	Helen Y. Kosa	D	Jan. 1988	45/day
Auditor.............................	Brenda M. White	R	Jan. 1988	45/day

SCHUYLKILL COUNTY (4th Class, population 160,630) was created on March 1, 1811, from parts of Berks and Northampton Counties and named for the Schuylkill River. Schuylkill is Dutch for "hidden stream." Parts of Columbia and Luzerne Counties were added on March 3, 1818. *Pottsville,* the county seat after December 1, 1851, was incorporated as a borough on February 19, 1828, and became a city in 1910. It was named for the Pott family, early settlers. The original county seat was Orwigsburg.

Office	Name	Political Affiliation	Term Expires	Annual Salary
Commissioner, Chairman	Paul Sheers........................	R	Jan. 1988	$24,000
Commissioner........................	Franklin L. Shollenberger	R	Jan. 1988	23,000
Commissioner........................	Richard F. Higgins...................	D	Jan. 1988	23,000
Sheriff	Timothy Holden......................	D	Jan. 1990	21,500
Coroner............................	John Mika, M.D......................	D	Jan. 1988	17,000
Recorder of Deeds	Richard Koch	R	Jan. 1988	21,500
Register of Wills	George Uritis........................	R	Jan. 1988	22,500
Prothonotary	Charles K. Heffner...................	R	Jan. 1988	21,500
Clerk of Courts	Mary C. Long.......................	R	Jan. 1988	21,500
Controller	Donald Kerns	D	Jan. 1988	21,500
Treasurer...........................	Gerald Lengel	D	Jan. 1988	21,500
District Attorney......................	Claude A. Lord Shields	D	Jan. 1990	64,000
Jury Commissioner...................	Harold Boyer	R	Jan. 1990	5,000
Jury Commissioner...................	Metro Litwak	D	Jan. 1990	5,000
Chief Clerk to Commissioners...........	Nancy Whitaker......................	Appt.		19,080
Chief Assessor (Acting)................	Lillian Bergan	Appt.		15,553
County Solicitor......................	Joseph H. Jones, Jr.	Appt.		21,000

SNYDER COUNTY (7th class, population 33,584) was created on March 2, 1855, from part of Union County and named for Governor Simon Snyder. *Middleburg,* the county seat, was laid out in 1800 and incorporated as a borough on September 25, 1860. It was on Middle Creek near the middle of former Centre Township, so its name became even more appropriate after the creation of the county.

Office	Name	Political Affiliation	Term Expires	Annual Salary
Commissioner, Chairman	Chester H. Troutman	R	Jan. 1988	$20,635
Commissioner	Michael L. Aumiller	D	Jan. 1988	20,635
Commissioner	Paul T. Heeter	R	Jan. 1988	20,635
Sheriff	Richard T. Nornhold	R	Jan. 1988	20,635
Coroner	Harold E. Hassinger	R	Jan. 1988	8,653
Recorder of Deeds and Register of Wills	Mariann L. Ernest	R	Jan. 1990	22,635
Clerk, Orphans' Court, Prothonotary and Clerk of Courts	Teresa J. Berger	R	Jan. 1990	22,635
Treasurer	Orpha M. Lyter	R	Jan. 1988	20,635
District Attorney	John T. Robinson	R	Jan. 1988	21,966
Jury Commissioner	Rae M. Bressler	R	Jan. 1990	3,328
Jury Commissioner	John W. Gift	D	Jan. 1990	3,328
Auditor	Clarence J. Middleswarth	R	Jan. 1988	60/day
Auditor	Marie G. Shaffer	R	Jan. 1988	60/day
Auditor	June E. Felker	D	Jan. 1988	60/day
Clerk to Commissioners	Lee E. Knepp	Appt.		23,221
Chief Assessor	Ned R. Dunkin	Appt.		18,222
County Solicitor	Karen L. Hackman	Appt.		12,731

SOMERSET COUNTY (6th class, population 81,243) was created on April 17, 1795, from part of Bedford County and named for Somersetshire, England. *Somerset,* the county seat, was laid out in 1795 and incorporated as a borough on March 5, 1804.

Office	Name	Political Affiliation	Term Expires	Annual Salary
Commissioner, Chairman	Paul L. O'Connor	D	Jan. 1988	$22,831
Commissioner	Douglas M. Bell	D	Jan. 1988	22,831
Commissioner	Brad Cober	R	Jan. 1988	22,831
Sheriff	John A. Watkins	R	Jan. 1988	20,428
Coroner	Wilbur D. Miller	R	Jan. 1990	8,411
Recorder of Deeds	Vera M. Lohr	R	Jan. 1988	20,428
Register of Wills and Clerk, Orphans' Court	Linda Jo Berkey	D	Jan. 1988	21,630
Prothonotary	Robert J. Will	D	Jan. 1990	20,428
Clerk of Courts	L. Jean Rice	R	Jan. 1988	20,428
Treasurer	Lois L. Brougher	R	Jan. 1990	20,428
District Attorney	James B. Yelovich	R	Jan. 1988	21,630
Jury Commissioner	Harold M. Knepper	R	Jan. 1990	3,605
Jury Commissioner	Helen V. Russian	D	Jan. 1990	3,605
Auditor	Thomas Brown, Jr.	R	Jan. 1988	9/hr.
Auditor	Ocie Lee Judy	R	Jan. 1988	9/hr.
Auditor	Donna M. Schmitt	D	Jan. 1988	9/hr.
Clerk to Commissioners	Kay F. Slope	Appt.		19,169
Chief Assessor	John Riley, Jr.	Appt.		17,224
County Solicitor	John M. Cascio	Appt.		18,388
Assistant County Solicitor	Kim R. Gibson	Appt.		626

SULLIVAN COUNTY (8th class, population 6,349) was created on March 15, 1847, from part of Lycoming County and named for Senator Charles C. Sullivan, Butler District, who took an active part in procuring passage of the bill. *Laporte,* the county seat, was laid out in 1850 and incorporated as a borough in 1853. It was named for John La Porte, surveyor general of Pennsylvania from 1845 to 1851.

Office	Name	Political Affiliation	Term Expires	Annual Salary
Commissioner, Chairman	Vivian McCarty	R	Jan. 1988	$14,856
Commissioner	George B. Miller, Jr.	R	Jan. 1988	14,856
Commissioner	John W. Potuck	D	Jan. 1988	14,856
Sheriff	Burton R. Adams	R	Jan. 1988	14,856
Coroner	Russell P. McHenry	R	Jan. 1988	5,836
Recorder of Deeds, Register of Wills, Clerk, Orphans' Court, Prothonotary and Clerk of Courts	Clair D. Johnson	R	Jan. 1988	15,918
Treasurer	Alice Taylor	R	Jan. 1988	14,856
District Attorney	Leonard R. Simpson	R	Jan. 1990	15,918
Jury Commissioner	Dorothy P. Schoch	R	Jan. 1990	2,122
Jury Commissioner	June C. Taylor	D	Jan. 1990	2,122
Auditor	Elizabeth Velardo	D	Jan. 1988	47/day
Auditor	Helen L. Pond	R	Jan. 1988	47/day
Chief County Clerk	Melanie Eddinger	Appt.		13,650
Chief Assessor	Donald Edkin	Appt.		13,685
County Solicitor	Kenneth R. Levitzky	Appt.		7,000

SUSQUEHANNA COUNTY (6th class, population 37,876) was created on February 21, 1810, from part of Luzerne County and named for the Susquehanna River. It remained attached to Luzerne County until 1812. *Montrose,* the county seat, was laid out in 1812, and incorporated as a borough on March 19, 1824. Its name is a combination of "mont," French word for "mountain," and Rose, for Dr. R. H. Rose, a prominent citizen.

Office	Name	Political Affiliation	Term Expires	Annual Salary
Commissioner, Chairman	Jack M. Masters	R	Jan. 1988	$20,947
Commissioner	Gary W. Marcho	R	Jan. 1988	20,947
Commissioner	Henry D. Prince	D	Jan. 1988	20,947
Sheriff	Richard Pelicci	D	Jan. 1990	20,742
Coroner	John Conarton	R	Jan. 1988	7,717
Recorder of Deeds, Register of Wills and Clerk, Orphans' Court	Shirley Rosendale	R	Jan. 1988	20,742
Prothonotary and Clerk of Courts	Donald C. Caterson	R	Jan. 1988	20,742
Treasurer	Ann M. Smith	R	Jan. 1988	20,742
District Attorney	Lawrence M. Kelly	R	Jan. 1988	19,845
Jury Commissioner	Edna H. Hadaway	R	Jan. 1990	3,307
Jury Commissioner	Eleanor Tompkins	D	Jan. 1990	3,307
Clerk to Commissioners	Evan A. Price	Appt.		28,290
Chief Assessor	James Holbert	Appt.		23,643
County Solicitor	Robert G. Dean	Appt.		18,015

TIOGA COUNTY (6th Class, population 40,973) was created on March 26, 1804, from part of Lycoming County and named for the Tioga River. Tioga is derived from an Indian word meaning "the forks of a stream." **Wellsboro,** the county seat, was laid out in 1806 and incorporated as a borough on March 6, 1830. It was named for the Wells family, prominent in the locality.

Office	Name	Political Affiliation	Term Expires	Annual Salary
Commissioner, Chairman	Oliver Richard Bartlett	R	Jan. 1988	$26,442
Commissioner	Brian W. Edgcomb	R	Jan. 1988	26,442
Commissioner	Van W. Emmons, Sr.	D	Jan. 1988	26,442
Sheriff	Richard M. Hastings	R	Jan. 1990	23,620
Coroner	Dr. James Wilson	R	Jan. 1988	9,617
Recorder of Deeds, Register of Wills and Clerk, Orphans' Court	Nancy C. Kimble	R	Jan. 1988	24,620
Prothonotary and Clerk of Courts	Harold Clark	R	Jan. 1990	24,620
Treasurer	Evalyn Moreal	R	Jan. 1990	23,620
District Attorney	James E. Carlson	R	Jan. 1988	25,009
Jury Commissioner	Christine Wakely	R	Jan. 1990	4,168
Jury Commissioner	Marie Cooper	D	Jan. 1990	4,168
Auditor	Helen West	R	Jan. 1988	9.63/hr.
Auditor	Julia Holmes	R	Jan. 1988	9.63/hr.
Auditor	Wilma Nagy	D	Jan. 1988	9.63/hr.
Clerk to Commissioners	Donald H. Blackwell	Appt.		26,000
Chief Assessor	John Greenfield	Appt.		18,650
County Solicitor	William A. Hebe	Appt.		16,000

UNION COUNTY (7th class, population 32,870) was created on March 22, 1813, from part of Northumberland County. Its name is an allusion to the Federal Union. **Lewisburg,** the county seat after 1855, was laid out in 1785 and named for Ludwig (i.e. Lewis) Derr, its founder. It was incorporated as a borough on March 21, 1822. New Berlin was the county seat from 1815 to 1855.

Office	Name	Political Affiliation	Term Expires	Annual Salary
Commissioner, Chairman	Robert W. Donehower	R	Jan. 1988	$20,771
Commissioner	W. Sherman Doebler	R	Jan. 1988	20,771
Commissioner	John R. Reichley	D	Jan. 1988	20,771
Sheriff	Donald N. Everitt	R	Jan. 1990	20,771
Coroner	James L. Schwartz	R	Jan. 1990	8,711
Recorder of Deeds and Register of Wills	Dorothy E. Dershem	R	Jan. 1988	22,112
Clerk, Orphans' Court, Prothonotary and Clerk of Courts	Bertha W. Boyer	R	Jan. 1990	23,213
Treasurer	Miriam H. Oberdorf	R	Jan. 1988	20,771
District Attorney	Graham C. Showalter	R	Jan. 1988	22,112
Jury Commissioner	Pauline A. Swank	R	Jan. 1990	3,350
Jury Commissioner	Beatrice L. Englehart	D	Jan. 1990	3,350
Chief Clerk	Diana L. Robinson	Appt.		21,313
Chief Assessor	Cathy Falck	Appt.		16,500
County Solicitor	Michael Hudock	Appt.		13,500

VENANGO COUNTY (6th class, population 64,444) was created on March 12, 1800, from parts of Allegheny and Lycoming Counties. Its name comes from the Indian name for French Creek. It was attached to Crawford County until April 1, 1805. *Franklin,* the county seat, was laid out in 1795 at Fort Franklin, which had been built in 1787 by United States troops. Both were named for Benjamin Franklin. Franklin was incorporated as a borough on April 14, 1828, and as a city on April 4, 1868.

Office	Name	Political Affiliation	Term Expires	Annual Salary
Commissioner, Chairman	Oscar W. Bodamer	R	Jan. 1988	$26,399
Commissioner	Raymond T. Mohnkern	R	Jan. 1988	26,399
Commissioner	Ralph H. Prichard	D	Jan. 1988	26,399
Sheriff	Eugene E. Prioe	R	Jan. 1990	23,620
Coroner	Jonathan H. Hutchinson	R	Jan. 1990	9,726
Recorder of Deeds, Register of Wills and Clerk, Orphans' Court	Jennie M. Brandon	R	Jan. 1990	26,070
Prothonotary and Clerk of Courts	Donald F. Fischer	R	Jan. 1988	26,070
Treasurer	Margaret Spence	R	Jan. 1988	23,620
District Attorney	William Martin	R	Jan. 1990	25,009
Jury Commissioner	Carol Hutchinson	R	Jan. 1990	4,168
Jury Commissioner	John Spence	D	Jan. 1990	4,168
Auditor	Linda Burchfield	R	Jan. 1988	62.54/day
Auditor	Mary Kay Johnson	R	Jan. 1988	62.54/day
Auditor	Thelma Graves	D	Jan. 1988	62.54/day
Clerk to Commissioners	Naomi L. Osborne	Appt.		22,932
County Solicitor	T. Gregory Williams	Appt.		13,200

WARREN COUNTY (6th class, population 47,449) was created on March 12, 1800, from parts of Allegheny and Lycoming Counties and named for General Joseph Warren. It was attached to Crawford County until 1805 and then to Venango County until 1819 when it was formally organized. *Warren,* the county seat, was laid out in 1795 and incorporated as a borough on April 3, 1832.

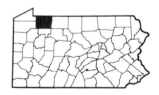

Office	Name	Political Affiliation	Term Expires	Annual Salary
Commissioner, Chairman	David K. Rice, VMD	R	Jan. 1988	$25,462
Commissioner	Raymond A. Marti	R	Jan. 1988	25,462
Commissioner	Timothy E. Greelund	D	Jan. 1988	25,462
Sheriff	Donnell E. Allen, Jr.	R	Jan. 1988	24,782
Coroner	Dr. Ronald Simonsen	R	Jan. 1990	8,934
Recorder of Deeds, Register of Wills and Clerk, Orphans' Court	Plummer F. Collins	R	Jan. 1988	24,075
Prothonotary and Clerk of Courts	Norma Mills	R	Jan. 1990	24,075
Treasurer	Bonnie J. Trawick	R	Jan. 1988	22,782
District Attorney	Richard A. Hernan, Jr., Esq.	R	Jan. 1990	22,973
Jury Commissioner	Geraldine Kusse	R	Jan. 1988	4,020
Jury Commissioner	Patricia Hecei	D	Jan. 1988	4,020
Auditor	Frederick A. Berry	R	Jan. 1988	60.29/day
Auditor	John R. Krupey	R	Jan. 1988	60.29/day
Auditor	Ruth Bleech	D	Jan. 1988	60.29/day
Clerk to Commissioners	Georgianna Shea	Appt.		20,961
Chief Assessor	I. Mark Sibert	Appt.		21,679
County Solicitor	William R. Mervine	Appt.		8,652

WASHINGTON COUNTY (4th class, population 217,074) was created on March 28, 1781, from part of Westmoreland County and named in honor of George Washington. *Washington,* the county seat, was laid out in 1781, incorporated as a borough on February 12, 1810, and chartered as a city in 1924.

Office	Name	Political Affiliation	Term Expires	Annual Salary
Commissioner, Chairman	Frank K. Mascara	D	Jan. 1988	$39,157
Commissioner	Metro Petrosky, Jr.	D	Jan. 1988	38,157
Commissioner	Edward M. Paluso	R	Jan. 1988	38,157
Sheriff	James Fazzoni	D	Jan. 1990	35,667
Coroner	Farrell Jackson	D	Jan. 1988	28,204
Recorder of Deeds	Olga O. Woodward	D	Jan. 1990	35,667
Register of Wills and Clerk, Orphans' Court	Kathleen Flynn Reda	D	Jan. 1988	36,667
Prothonotary	Bob A. Franks	D	Jan. 1988	35,667
Clerk of Courts	Barbara Gibbs	D	Jan. 1988	35,667
Controller	Patricia A. Beharry	D	Jan. 1990	35,667
Treasurer	John F. Yoney	D	Jan. 1988	35,667
District Attorney	John C. Pettit	D	Jan. 1988	38,988
Jury Commissioner	Mary Holleran	R	Jan. 1990	8,295
Jury Commissioner	Josephine Vincent	D	Jan. 1990	8,295
Clerk to Commissioners	Christine S. Dallatore	Appt.		24,024
Chief Assessor	C. Wayne Fleming	Appt.		31,766
County Solicitor	Melvin B. Bassi	Appt.		27,300

WAYNE COUNTY (7th class, population 35,237) was created on March 21, 1798, from part of Northampton County and named for General Anthony Wayne. *Honesdale,* the county seat after 1842, was laid out in 1827 and incorporated as a borough on January 28, 1831. It was named for Philip Hone, president of the Delaware and Hudson Canal Company. Earlier county seats included Wilsonville (1799-1802), Milford (1802-1805) and Bethany (1805-1841).

Office	Name	Political Affiliation	Term Expires	Annual Salary
Commissioner, Chairman	Earl J. Simons	R	Jan. 1988	$20,370
Commissioner	Donald E. Olsommer	R	Jan. 1988	20,370
Commissioner	Robert V. Carmody	D	Jan. 1988	20,370
Sheriff	William M. Bluff	R	Jan. 1988	20,370
Coroner	Young Woo Lee	D	Jan. 1988	8,542
Recorder of Deeds and Register of Wills	Lois K. Keen	R	Jan. 1988	21,684
Prothonotary and Clerk of Courts	Edmund J. Rose	R	Jan. 1988	21,684
Treasurer	Alfred H. Perkins	R	Jan. 1988	20,370
District Attorney	Raymond L. Hamill	R	Jan. 1988	20,370
Jury Commissioner	Barbara Giguere	R	Jan. 1990	3,285
Jury Commissioner	Doris L. Fries	D	Jan. 1990	3,285
Clerk to Commissioners	Reg Wayman	Appt.	Jan. 1988	26,259
Chief Assessor	Walter A. Beck	Appt.	Jan. 1988	23,276
County Solicitor	Lee C. Krause	Appt.	Jan. 1988	17,460

WESTMORELAND COUNTY (3rd Class, population 392,294) was

created on February 26, 1773, from part of Bedford County and named for a county in
England. *Greensburg,* the county seat after 1785, was incorporated as a borough on
February 9, 1799, and as a city in 1928. It was named for General Nathanael Greene.
Hannastown, the original county seat, was burned by the British and Indians on July 13,
1782.

Office	Name	Political Affiliation	Term Expires	Annual Salary
Commissioner, Chairman	Ted Simon	D	Jan. 1988	$36,702
Commissioner	Richard Vidmer*	D	Jan. 1988	35,391
Commissioner	Terry R. Marolt*	R	Jan. 1988	35,391
Sheriff	John W. Peck	D	Jan. 1988	30,803
Coroner	Leo Bacha	D	Jan. 1990	32,997
Recorder of Deeds	Jeanne C. Griffith	D	Jan. 1988	30,803
Register of Wills and Clerk, Orphans' Court	Earl S. Keim, II	D	Jan. 1988	32,114
Prothonotary	Stephen Mikosky	D	Jan. 1990	32,997
Clerk of Courts	Randolph V. Biller	D	Jan. 1990	32,997
Controller	Thomas A. Tangretti	D	Jan. 1988	30,803
Treasurer	Dick W. Myers	D	Jan. 1988	30,803
District Attorney	John Driscoll	D	Jan. 1990	64,000
Jury Commissioner	Kathalyn O'Brien	D	Jan. 1990	9,127
Jury Commissioner	Lowman S. Henry	R	Jan. 1990	9,127
Director, Administration	Jack W. Simon	Appt.		44,289
Clerk to Commissioners	Elaine Oravets	Appt.		28,358
Chief Assessor	H. John Wilt	Appt.		25,688
County Solicitor	Adam N. Aretz	Appt.		31,011

*appointed

WYOMING COUNTY (7th class, population 26,433) was created on April 4,

1842, from part of Luzerne County and named for the Wyoming Valley. Wyoming is
derived from an Indian word meaning "extensive meadows." *Tunkhannock,* the county
seat, was incorporated as a borough on August 8, 1841, and was named for
Tunkhannock Creek. The creek's name means "small stream."

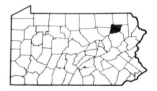

Office	Name	Political Affiliation	Term Expires	Annual Salary
Commissioner, Chairman	Robert V. Barziloski	R	Jan. 1988	$17,943
Commissioner	Richard Fitzsimmons	R	Jan. 1988	17,943
Commissioner	Harold A. Grow	D	Jan. 1988	17,943
Sheriff	Robert Truesdale	R	Jan. 1988	17,943
Coroner	Thomas Kukuchka	R	Jan. 1990	9,350
Recorder of Deeds and Register of Wills	Dennis Montross	R	Jan. 1988	19,100
Clerk, Orphans' Court, Prothonotary and Clerk of Courts	Victoria Stefanko	R	Jan. 1988	19,100
Treasurer	Carl W. Smith, Jr.	R	Jan. 1990	18,589
District Attorney	Brendan Vanston	R	Jan. 1990	19,789
Jury Commissioner	Robert Ferguson	R	Jan. 1990	2,998
Jury Commissioner	Thelma Shebby	D	Jan. 1990	2,998
Clerk to Commissioners	Janice Gay	Appt.		22,548
Chief Assessor	Jeff Summersgill	Appt.		16,920
County Solicitor	J. Joel Turrell	Appt.		15,000
Auditor	Willard Reese	R	Jan. 1988	52/day
Auditor	Elizabeth Drost	R	Jan. 1988	52/day
Auditor	Sharon Davis	D	Jan. 1988	52/day

YORK COUNTY (3rd class, population 312,963) was created on August 19, 1749, from part of Lancaster County and named either for the Duke of York, an early patron of the Penn Family, or for the city and shire of York in England. The name may have been suggested by the proximity to Lancaster County, as the names are linked in English history. *York,* the county seat, was laid out in 1741 and incorporated as a borough on September 24, 1787. It was chartered as a city on January 11, 1887.

Office	Name	Political Affiliation	Term Expires	Annual Salary
Commissioner, Chairman	William C. McKinley	R	Jan. 1988	$28,000
Commissioner........................	Jay R. Bair..........................	R	Jan. 1988	27,000
Commissioner........................	Lorraine B. Hovis.....................	D	Jan. 1988	27,000
Sheriff.............................	Oliver C. Nace.......................	R	Jan. 1988	23,500
Coroner............................	Kathryn Fourhman Olewiler	R	Jan. 1990	26,884
Recorder of Deeds	John Norris	R	Jan. 1990	26,884
Register of Wills and Clerk, Orphans' Court	William J. Walters	R	Jan. 1988	24,500
Prothonotary........................	Stacia N. Gates......................	D	Jan. 1988	23,500
Clerk of Courts	Marlyn L. Holtzapple	D	Jan. 1988	23,500
Controller	Michael R. Gingerich..................	R	Jan. 1990	26,884
Treasurer..........................	Betty J. Kinports	R	Jan. 1988	23,500
District Attorney......................	H. Stanley Rebert	R	Jan. 1990	64,000
Jury Commissioner...................	Glenn Gunnett.......................	D	Jan. 1990	7,436
Jury Commissioner...................	Edward H. Reever....................	R	Jan. 1990	7,436
Chief Assessor	Stanley Saylor.......................	Appt.	Jan. 1988	28,620
County Solicitor......................	J. Christian Ness.....................	Appt.	Jan. 1988	20,734

THE ACT PROVIDING FOR THE CLASSIFICATION OF CITIES

Section 1. Purpose of classification; division into classes.

For the purpose of legislation regulating their municipal affairs, the exercise of certain corporate powers, and having respect to the number, character, powers, and duties of certain officers thereof, the cities now in existence and those hereafter created in this Commonwealth shall be divided into four classes:

Those containing a population of one million or over shall constitute the first class.

Those containing a population of five hundred thousand and under one million shall constitute the second class.

Those containing a population of one hundred thousand and under five hundred thousand and which by ordinance elect to be a city of the second class A shall constitute the second class A.

Those containing a population under five hundred thousand and which have not elected to become a city of the second class A constitute the third class.

Section 2. The classification of said cities respectively, shall be ascertained and fixed by reference to the last two preceding United States decennial censuses, and whenever it shall appear by both of such censuses, that any city of the first, second or second A class has decreased in population below the minimum population figures prescribed for its current classification, or that any city of the second, second A or third class has increased above the maximum population figure prescribed for its current classification, it shall be the duty of the Governor, under the great seal of the Commonwealth, to certify the fact accordingly, which certificate shall be entered at large upon the minutes of the councils of such city and recorded in the office for recording the deeds of the proper county. No change in classification or in the existing form of government shall become effective until ten years after the certification of the fact of decrease or increase of population by the Governor: Provided, That the court of common pleas of the county in which the city is located shall appoint a charter commission to study and make recommendations on the adoption of a form of city government under sections 3, 4, 5, 6 and 7 of this act, and a form of government is adopted within the above ten year period. If a form of government is not adopted within the ten year period, the city shall automatically become classified according to the provisions of section 1 of this act and be subject to the provisions therein.

It is the intent of the preceding paragraph that the classification of any city of the first, second, second class A and third class shall not be changed because its population has changed at the time of one United States decennial census, because it is recognized that a change in the form of municipal government is attended by certain expense and hardship and such change should not be occasioned by a temporary fluctuation in population but rather only after it is demonstrated by two censuses that the population of a city has remained below the minimum figure or above the maximum figure of its class for at least a decade.

At the municipal election occurring not less than one month after the date of such certificate the proper officers shall be elected to which the said city will become entitled under the change in classification, and upon the first Monday of April next ensuing the terms of all officers of said city when in office whose offices are superseded by reason thereof shall cease and determine, and the city government shall be duly organized and shall thereafter be controlled and regulated by the laws of this Commonwealth applicable to the same under the classification hereby fixed and appointed.

Until otherwise provided by law, cities of the second class A shall continue to be governed, and shall have all the powers, privileges and prerogatives now provided by the laws of the Commonwealth relating to the cities of the second class. (1895 P.L. 275, Sections 1 and 2, as amended.)

CITIES CLASSIFIED, 1980 CENSUS

First Class (1) — Philadelphia (1,688,210).

Second Class (1) — Pittsburgh (423,938).

Second Class A (1) — Scranton (88,117).

Third Class (50) — Aliquippa (17,094), Allentown (103,758), Altoona (57,078), Arnold (6,853), Beaver Falls (12,525), Bethlehem (70,419), Bradford (11,211), Butler (17,026), Carbondale (11,255), Chester (45,794), Clairton (12,188), Coatesville (10,698), Connellsville (10,319), Corry (7,149), DuBois (9,290), Duquesne (10,094), Easton (26,027), Erie (119,123), Farrell (8,645), Franklin (8,146), Greensburg (17,558), Harrisburg (53,264), Hazleton (27,318), Hermitage (16,365), Jeannette (13,106), Johnstown (35,496), Lancaster (54,725), Lebanon (25,711), Lock Haven (9,617), Lower Burrell (13,200), McKeesport (31,012), Meadville (15,544), Monessen (11,928), Monongahela (5,950), Nanticoke (13,044), New Castle (33,621), New Kensington (17,660), Oil City (13,881), Pittston (9,930), Pottsville (18,195), Reading (78,686), Shamokin (10,357), Sharon (19,057), Sunbury (12,292), Titusville (6,884), Uniontown (14,510), Washington (18,363), Wilkes-Barre (51,551), Williamsport (33,401), York (44,619).

Unclassified (1) — Parker City (808).

PENNSYLVANIA CITIES*

PHILADELPHIA, 1st Class City, Population 1,688,210 (Home Rule)   Philadelphia County

Office	Name	Political Affiliation	Term Expires	Annual Salary
Mayor	W. Wilson Goode	D	Jan. 1988	$70,000
President, City Council	Joseph E. Coleman	D	Jan. 1988	57,500
Majority Leader	Joan Krajewski	D	Jan. 1988	43,000
Minority Leader	Joan Specter	R	Jan. 1988	42,000
Councilman at Large	W. Thacher Longstreth	R	Jan. 1988	40,000
Councilman at Large	Augusta A. Clark	D	Jan. 1988	40,000
Councilman at Large	Joan Specter	R	Jan. 1988	
Councilman at Large	Francis Rafferty	D	Jan. 1988	40,000
Councilman at Large	David Cohen	D	Jan. 1988	40,000
Councilman at Large	Angel L. Ortiz	D	Jan. 1988	40,000
Councilman at Large	Edward A. Schwartz	D	Jan. 1988	40,000
Councilman — 1st District	Vacant			
Councilman — 2nd District	Anna Cibotti Verna	D	Jan. 1988	40,000
Councilman — 3rd District	Lucien E. Blackwell	D	Jan. 1988	42,000
Councilman — 4th District	Ann J. Land	D	Jan. 1988	40,000
Councilman — 5th District	John F. Street	D	Jan. 1988	40,000
Councilman — 6th District	Joan Krajewski	D	Jan. 1988	
Councilman — 7th District	Patricia A. Hughes	D	Jan. 1988	40,000
Councilman — 8th District	Joseph E. Coleman	D	Jan. 1988	
Councilman — 9th District	Vacant	D	Jan. 1988	40,000
Councilman — 10th District	Brian J. O'Neill	D	Jan. 1988	42,000
Controller	Joseph C. Vignola	D	Jan. 1988	50,000
Sheriff	Ralph Passio	D	Jan. 1988	40,000
Clerk of Quarter Sessions	Edgar C. Campbell	D	Jan. 1988	40,000
City Commissioner, Chairwoman	Margaret M. Tartaglione	D	Jan. 1988	42,000
City Commissioner	Vacant	D	Jan. 1988	40,000
City Commissioner	John Kane	R	Jan. 1988	40,000
District Attorney	Ron Castille	R	Jan. 1990	60,000
Register of Wills	Ronald R. Donatucci	D	Jan. 1988	40,000
Prothonotary	John J. Pettit	Appt.		52,039
Treasurer	Eric Pookrum	Appt.		55,000
City Representative	Vacant	Appt.		62,500
Director of Commerce	Charles Pizzi	Appt.		62,500
City Solicitor	Handsel B. Minyard	Appt.		62,500
Managing Director	James S. White	Appt.		62,500
Director, Finance	Carlo R. Gambetta	Appt.		62,500
Chief of Staff	Shirley Hamilton	Appt.		60,000
Deputy Mayor	John E. Flaherty	Appt.		60,000
Press Secretary	Karen Warrington	Appt.		45,000
Personnel Director	Orville W. Jones	Appt.		50,000
Chairman, Civil Service Commission	Harry Bailey	Appt.		125/mtg.
Police Commissioner	Kevin Tucker	Appt.		55,000
Health Commissioner	Maurice Clifford	Appt.		55,000
Fire Commissioner	William S. Richmond	Appt.		55,000
Streets Commissioner	Harry M. Perks	Appt.		55,000
Recreation Commissioner	Harold Comfort	Appt.		55,000
Human Services Commission	Irene F. Pernsley	Appt.		55,000
Water Commissioner	William J. Marrazzo	Appt.		55,000
Licenses & Inspections Commissioner	Henry Herling	Appt.		55,000
Commissioner, Records	Florence Scott	Appt.		45,000
Revenue Commissioner	Christine Murphy	Appt.		55,000
Public Property Commissioner	David A. Dambly	Appt.		55,000
Procurement Commissioner	Angela Dowd Burton	Appt.		55,000
Chairman, Board of Revision of Taxes	Irvin F. Fineman	Appt.		45,000

*All population figures are U.S. Census Bureau 1980 tabulations.

PITTSBURGH, 2nd Class City, Population 423,938 (Home Rule)   Allegheny County

Office	Name	Political Affiliation	Term Expires	Annual Salary
Mayor	Richard S. Caliguiri	D	Jan. 1990	$59,280
Council President	Ben Woods	D	Jan. 1990	33,800
Councilmembers	James O'Malley	D	Jan. 1988	33,800
	Eugene DePasquale	D	Jan. 1990	33,800
	Richard E. Givens	D	Jan. 1988	33,800
	Stephen S. Grabowski	D	Jan. 1988	33,800
	Sophie Masloff	D	Jan. 1990	33,800
	Mark Pollock	D	Jan. 1990	33,800
	Jack Wagner	D	Jan. 1988	33,800
	Michelle Madoff	D	Jan. 1988	33,800
Controller	Tom Flaherty	D	Jan. 1988	37,440

SCRANTON, 2nd Class A City, Population 88,117 (Home Rule)   Lackawanna County

Office	Name	Political Affiliation	Term Expires	Annual Salary
Mayor	David J. Wenzel	R	Jan. 1990	$25,000
Council President	William J. Gerrity	D	Jan. 1990	7,000
Councilmembers				
Public Works	William J. Gerrity	D	Jan. 1990	7,000
Finance	Thomas P. Gilhooley	D	Jan. 1990	7,000
Public Safety	Vincent A. Manzo	D	Jan. 1988	7,000
Rules	Michael J. Melnick	D	Jan. 1988	7,000
Controller	Joseph A. Refice	D	Jan. 1988	18,000

ALIQUIPPA, 3rd Class, Population 17,094   Beaver County

Office	Name	Political Affiliation	Term Expires	Annual Salary
Mayor	Daniel Britza	D	Jan. 1988	$3,500
Councilmembers	Andy Dobo	D	Jan. 1988	2,400
	William Forbes	D	Jan. 1988	2,400
	Mabel Jarrett	D	Jan. 1988	2,400
	Vickie Frataugeli	D	Jan. 1988	2,400
	Mike Diaddigo	D	Jan. 1988	2,400
	Frank K. Atkinson	D	Jan. 1988	2,400
	Mary Alvini	D	Jan. 1988	2,400
Fiscal Officer (Part Time)	Mike Bobanic	Appt.		7,320
Secretary (Acting)	Josephine McKenna	Appt.		20,000
Tax Collector	James Mansueti	D	Jan. 1988	1% Comm.
Auditors	Hope Fuller	D	Jan. 1988	Hourly
	Gary Hickman	D	Jan. 1988	Hourly
	Harry Jarrett	Appt.	Jan. 1988	Hourly

ALLENTOWN, 3rd Class, Population 103,758 (Optional Charter)   Lehigh County

Office	Name	Political Affiliation	Term Expires	Annual Salary
Mayor	Joseph S. Daddona	D	Jan. 1990	$41,200
Council President	Watson W. Skinner	D	Jan. 1988	4,500
Council Vice President	Frank J. Palencar	D	Jan. 1990	4,000
Councilmembers	John E. Harry*	D	Jan. 1988	4,000
	Barbara C. Irvine	D	Jan. 1990	4,000
	Mark C. Van Horn	D	Jan. 1990	4,000
	Benjamin F. Howells, Jr.	D	Jan. 1990	4,000
	Emma D. Tropiano	D	Jan. 1988	4,000
Treasurer	Harry S. Diehl	R	Jan. 1988	1
Controller	Louis J. Hershman	D	Jan. 1988	24,000

*appointed

ALTOONA, 3rd Class, Population 57,078 — Blair County

Office	Name	Political Affiliation	Term Expires	Annual Salary
Mayor	David L. Jannetta	D	Jan. 1988	$29,355
Councilmembers	Raphael J. Voltz, II	R	Jan. 1990	25,527
	Theodore A. Beam, Jr.	D	Jan. 1988	25,527
	Karl R. King	R	Jan. 1990	25,527
	John L. Wingard	I	Jan. 1988	25,527
Treasurer	Mary A. Long	R	Jan. 1988	25,552
Controller	Travis B. Young	R	Jan. 1990	25,527
City Clerk	Francis E. Kuhn	Appt.	May 1988	21,787
City Solicitor	N. John Casanave	Appt.	May 1988	26,000
City Engineer	Bernard J. Joyce	Appt.	May 1988	29,815

ARNOLD, 3rd Class, Population 6,853 — Westmoreland County

Office	Name	Political Affiliation	Term Expires	Annual Salary
Mayor	William DeMao	D	Jan. 1988	$2,400
Councilmembers	Oscar S. Doutt, Jr.	D	Jan. 1988	1,000
	Anthony Santucci	D	Jan. 1990	1,000
	Walter Weber	D	Jan. 1990	1,000
	Carl Martz	D	Jan. 1988	1,000
Treasurer	Joseph G. Puet	D	Jan. 1990	10,105
Controller	Elias E. Moses	D	Jan. 1988	2,100

BEAVER FALLS, 3rd Class, Population 12,525 — Beaver County

Office	Name	Political Affiliation	Term Expires	Annual Salary
Mayor	Fred D. Leksell	D	Jan. 1990	$2,500
Councilmembers				
Accounts and Finance	Clifford V. Alford	D	Jan. 1990	2,000
Public Safety	Ted A. Krzemienski	D	Jan. 1988	2,000
Public Works	Eugene N. DeSimone	D	Jan. 1990	2,000
Parks and Buildings	Sammuel G. Wagner, Jr.	D	Jan. 1988	2,000
Treasurer	Daniel P. Cellini	D	Jan. 1990	11,646
Controller	Jerry T. Ford	D	Jan. 1990	2,000
City Clerk-Coordinator	Perry C. Wayne, Jr.	Appt.		25,694

BETHLEHEM, 3rd Class, Population 70,419 (Optional Charter) — Northampton and Lehigh Counties

Office	Name	Political Affiliation	Term Expires	Annual Salary
Mayor	Paul M. Marcincin	D	Jan. 1990	$37,500
Council President	Jack Lawrence	D	Jan. 1988	4,200
Councilmembers	Paul J. Calvo	D	Jan. 1988	3,700
	James A. Delgrosso	D	Jan. 1990	3,700
	Richard J. Szulborski	D	Jan. 1988	3,700
	Otto Ehrsam, Jr.	R	Jan. 1990	3,700
	George R. Karabin	D	Jan. 1990	3,700
	Michael Loupos	D	Jan. 1988	3,700
Treasurer	Theresa Bartholomew	D	Jan. 1988	25,000
Controller	Wallace DeCrosta	D	Jan. 1990	27,000

BRADFORD, 3rd Class, Population 11,211 — McKean County

Office	Name	Political Affiliation	Term Expires	Annual Salary
Mayor	Gregory A. Henry	R	Jan. 1988	$3,600
Councilmembers	James D. Leake	D	Jan. 1990	2,400
	Jack K. Burns	R	Jan. 1988	2,400
	Harrijane B. Hannon	R	Jan. 1990	2,400
	Dene Wesmiller	R	Jan. 1990	2,400

BUTLER, 3rd Class, Population 17,026 — Butler County

Office	Name	Political Affiliation	Term Expires	Annual Salary
Mayor and Council President	Richard J. Schontz	R	Jan. 1990	$20,000
Councilmembers	William M. Hulton, Jr.	R	Jan. 1990	3,500
	Leonard M. Pintell	D	Jan. 1988	3,500
	Peter Zissi	D	Jan. 1988	3,500
	Fred M. Vero	D	Jan. 1990	3,500
Treasurer	Marian L. Taylor	D	Jan. 1988	7,725
Controller	Bob Grigoletti	D	Jan. 1990	3,500

CARBONDALE, 3rd Class, Population 11,255 (Home Rule) — Lackawanna County

Office	Name	Political Affiliation	Term Expires	Annual Salary
Mayor	Charlotte Moro	D	Jan. 1988	$1,800
Council President	Andrew Leo	D	Jan. 1988	1,125
Council Vice President	James McMyne	D	Jan. 1988	1,125
Councilmembers	Frank Grecco	R	Jan. 1988	1,125
	John Moran	D	Jan. 1990	1,125
	Peter Kacer	R	Jan. 1988	1,125
	Donald McDonough	D	Jan. 1988	1,125
	Michael Tolerico	D	Jan. 1990	1,125

CHESTER, 3rd Class, Population 45,794 (Home Rule) — Delaware County

Office	Name	Political Affiliation	Term Expires	Annual Salary
Mayor	Willie Mae James Leake	R	Jan. 1988	$26,000
Councilmembers	Michael J. Koterba	R	Jan. 1988	23,000
	Stephen A. McKellar	R	Jan. 1988	23,000
	Timothy J. Gorbey	R	Jan. 1990	18,000
	William H. Waldron, Jr.	R	Jan. 1990	23,000
Treasurer	Samuel C. Poliafico	R	Jan. 1990	23,000

CLAIRTON, 3rd Class, Population 12,188 — Allegheny County

Office	Name	Political Affiliation	Term Expires	Annual Salary
Mayor and Council President	Nick C. Zumbo	D	Jan. 1988	$3,500
Councilmembers	Barbara Johnson	D	Jan. 1990	2,500
	Domenic J. Curinga	D	Jan. 1990	2,500
	John A. Hronakes	D	Jan. 1988	2,500
	Dr. Thomas B. Meade	D	Jan. 1988	2,500
Treasurer	George L. Laver	D	Jan. 1988	8,275
Controller	Ralph Imbrogo	D	Jan. 1990	2,500

COATESVILLE, 3rd Class, Population 10,698 (Home Rule) — Chester County

Office	Name	Political Affiliation	Term Expires	Annual Salary
President of Council	Rodger Johnson	D	Jan. 1990	$600
Vice President	Dominic Scamuffa	R	Jan. 1988	600
Councilmembers	Mark Milanese	R	Jan. 1990	600
	Charles Wilson	D	Jan. 1988	600
	William Chertok	D	Jan. 1988	600
	Frances Regener	D	Jan. 1988	600
	Harold Yost	D	Jan. 1988	600
City Manager	Dennis Paul Elko	Appt.		35,000
Director of Finance	Lewis J. Gay, III	Appt.		34,900
Codes Administrator	Everett K. Kimes	Appt.		27,000

CONNELLSVILLE, 3rd Class, Population 10,319   **Fayette County**

Office	Name	Political Affiliation	Term Expires	Annual Salary
Mayor	Thomas E. Duncan	D	Jan. 1990	$1,200
Councilmembers				
Accounts and Finance	Casimir Zabela	D	Jan. 1988	750
Public Safety	William E. Hughes	D	Jan. 1990	750
Streets & Public Improvements	Louis Schroyer	D	Jan. 1990	750
Parks & Public Property	Harry Cochran	D	Jan. 1988	750
City Clerk	Marsha A. Bower	Appt.	May 1988	21,048
City Solicitor	Michael J. Macko	Appt.	May 1988	9,000
City Controller	Peter J. Adams, Jr.	D	Jan. 1990	750
City Treasurer	H. L. Wrote	D	Jan. 1988	1,220
Tax Collector	H. L. Wrote	Appt.	Jan. 1988	4,295

CORRY, 3rd Class, Population 7,149   **Erie County**

Office	Name	Political Affiliation	Term Expires	Annual Salary
Mayor	Ivan G. Bennick	R	Jan. 1990	$1,200
Councilmembers				
Finance & Accounts	Danie R. McEldowney	R	Jan. 1990	900
Public Safety	G. Kenneth Nichols	D	Jan. 1988	900
Parks & Property	Anne S. Gould	R	Jan. 1990	900
Streets & Public Improvements	Jack S. Armitage	R	Jan. 1988	900
Treasurer	Mary S. Hubley	R	Jan. 1988	18,385
Controller	John E. Bliley	R	Jan. 1990	900

DuBOIS, 3rd Class, Population 9,290 (Optional Plan)   **Clearfield County**

Office	Name	Political Affiliation	Term Expires	Annual Salary
Mayor and Council President	Leo Karoleski	D	Jan. 1988	$2,400
Councilmembers	William Rieg	R	Jan. 1988	1,200
	Paul Begler*	D	Jan. 1988	1,200
	Douglas Kohlhepp	D	Jan. 1990	1,200
	Dominick Suplizio	R	Jan. 1990	1,200
Treasurer	Ralph J. Boyer	R	Jan. 1990	20,400
Controller	Francis Romeo	R	Jan. 1988	1,200

*appointed

DUQUESNE, 3rd Class, Population 10,094   **Allegheny County**

Office	Name	Political Affiliation	Term Expires	Annual Salary
Mayor	Raymond R. Terza	D	Jan. 1990	$3,000
Councilmembers	Edward Fagan	D	Jan. 1990	2,400
	George Tarczy*	D	Jan. 1988	2,400
	Melvyn Achitzehn	D	Jan. 1990	2,400
	Charlotte Jefferies	D	Jan. 1988	2,400
Treasurer	Carl R. Denne	D	Jan. 1988	15,000
Controller	George C. Adomitis	D	Jan. 1988	2,400

*appointed

EASTON, 3rd Class, Population 26,027 (Optional Charter)   Northampton County

Office	Name	Political Affiliation	Term Expires	Annual Salary
Mayor	Salvatore J. Panto, Jr.	D	Jan. 1988	$34,000
Council President	William D. Houston	D	Jan. 1990	6,500
Councilmembers	Thomas F. Goldsmith	R	Jan. 1988	6,000
	Michael P. McFadden*	D	Jan. 1988	6,000
	Edward P. Kennedy	D	Jan. 1990	6,000
	Joseph W. Grollman*	D	Jan. 1988	6,000
Treasurer	Pat Vulcano, Jr.*	D	Jan. 1988	18,500
Controller	Philip J. Altieri	D	Jan. 1988	18,500

*appointed

ERIE, 3rd Class, Population 119,123 (Optional Charter)   Erie County

Office	Name	Political Affiliation	Term Expires	Annual Salary
Mayor	Louis J. Tullio	D	Jan. 1990	$42,000
Council President	Patrick S. Cappabianca	D	Jan. 1988	7,000
Councilmembers	C. Ted Dombrowski	D	Jan. 1988	6,000
	Mario S. Bagnoni	D	Jan. 1988	6,000
	Gerald F. Mifsud	D	Jan. 1990	6,000
	Robert C. Brabender	D	Jan. 1990	6,000
	Joyce A. Savocchio	D	Jan. 1990	6,000
	Joseph A. Walcak, Jr.	D	Jan. 1988	6,000
Treasurer	Carl F. Cannavino	D	Jan. 1988	28,000
Controller	Philip S. English	R	Jan. 1990	25,000

FARRELL, 3rd Class, Population 8,645 (Home Rule)   Mercer County

Office	Name	Political Affiliation	Term Expires	Annual Salary
Mayor and Council President	Eugene C. Pacsi	D	Jan. 1988	$4,000
Councilmembers	Donna Egercic	D	Jan. 1990	2,400
	William F. Marks	D	Jan. 1990	2,400
	Anthony DeMartinis	D	Jan. 1990	2,400
	Peter Stephanopoulos	D	Jan. 1990	2,400
	Louis Falconi	D	Jan. 1988	2,400
	David DeMasy	D	Jan. 1988	2,400
Treasurer	James Kaikis	D	Jan. 1988	2,400

FRANKLIN, 3rd Class, Population 8,146 (Home Rule)   Venango County

Office	Name	Political Affiliation	Term Expires	Annual Salary
Mayor	Robert Olson	R	Jan. 1990	$2,400
Councilmembers	William G. Heller, Jr.	R	Jan. 1990	2,000
	Robert Culbertson	R	Jan. 1988	2,000
	Rosemarie Mattison	R	Jan. 1988	2,000
	Margaret Hamilton	D	Jan. 1988	2,000
	Gary Hutchison	D	Jan. 1990	2,000
	David Westerburg	R	Jan. 1990	2,000

GREENSBURG, 3rd Class, Population 17,558   Westmoreland County

Office	Name	Political Affiliation	Term Expires	Annual Salary
Mayor and Council President	Scott L. Brown	R	Jan. 1988	$4,800
Councilmembers	Emidio Peterinelli	D	Jan. 1988	3,600
	Ruth Gordon	D	Jan. 1988	3,600
	John B. DeFloria	D	Jan. 1990	3,600
	John R. Finfrock	D	Jan. 1990	3,600
Treasurer	Ruth B. Metz	D	Jan. 1988	7,645
Controller	Daniel J. Fajt	D	Jan. 1988	3,600

HARRISBURG, 3rd Class, Population 53,264 (Optional Charter)

Dauphin County

Office	Name	Political Affiliation	Term Expires	Annual Salary
Mayor	Stephen R. Reed	D	Jan. 1990	$27,500
Council President	Reizdan B. Moore	D	Jan. 1989	5,200
Council Vice President	O. Frank DeGarcia	D	Jan. 1988	4,800
Councilmembers	Harriet E. Braxton	D	Jan. 1988	4,800
	Calvin E. Gilchrist	D	Jan. 1988	4,800
	Paul P. Wambach	D	Jan. 1988	4,800
	Stanley H. Mitchell	D	Jan. 1990	4,800
	Leonora M. Smith	D	Jan. 1990	4,800
Treasurer	Bruce D. Foreman	D	Jan. 1988	15,000
Controller	James McCarthy	D	Jan. 1990	15,000

HAZLETON, 3rd Class, Population 27,318

Luzerne County

Office	Name	Political Affiliation	Term Expires	Annual Salary
Mayor	John Ford	R	Jan. 1988	$6,000
Councilmembers				
Accounts & Finance	Jacob Ripa III	D	Jan. 1990	4,800
Streets	Art Smith	R	Jan. 1990	4,800
Parks & Public Buildings	William Lockwood	D	Jan. 1988	4,800
Public Safety	John Tarone	D	Jan. 1988	4,800
Treasurer	Dr. John Degenhart	D	Jan. 1988	2,667*
Controller	Elizabeth J. Lukatch	D	Jan. 1990	4,800

*City share

HERMITAGE, 3rd Class, Population 16,365, (Home Rule)

Mercer County

Office	Name	Political Affiliation	Term Expires	Annual Salary
President, Commissioners	William E. Scanlon	D	Jan. 1988	$2,500
Vice President	Sylvia A. Stull	D	Jan. 1990	2,500
Commissioners	Mike Mudrak, Jr.	R	Jan. 1990	2,500
	James "Pat" White	D	Jan. 1990	2,500
	Albert J. Kuti	D	Jan. 1988	2,500

JEANNETTE, 3rd Class, Population 13,106

Westmoreland County

Office	Name	Political Affiliation	Term Expires	Annual Salary
Mayor	Jeffrey A. Pavetti	D	Jan. 1990	$1,200
Councilmembers				
Accounts & Finance	Glenn D. Hoak	D	Jan. 1988	1,125
Public Safety	James F. Solomon	D	Jan. 1990	1,125
Parks & Public Buildings	A. B. Elias	D	Jan. 1988	1,125
Streets & Improvements	Don Shirer	D	Jan. 1990	1,800
Treasurer	Dorothy Gaudi	D	Jan. 1990	6,000
Controller	Nicholas Priolo	D	Jan. 1990	2,400

JOHNSTOWN, 3rd Class, Population 35,496 (Optional Charter)   **Cambria County**

Office	Name	Political Affiliation	Term Expires	Annual Salary
Mayor	Herbert Pfuhl, Jr.	R	Jan. 1990	$20,000
Council President	James T. Malloy, Jr.	D	Jan. 1988	2,500
Council Vice-President	Owen W. Wissinger	R	Jan. 1990	2,200
Councilmembers	William S. Gentile, Jr.	D	Jan. 1988	2,200
	Fern Dorian	D	Jan. 1990	2,200
	William Stasko	D	Jan. 1988	2,200
	Albert M. Penksa	D	Jan. 1990	2,200
	Ron R. Stevens	D	Jan. 1988	2,200
	Anthony C. Truscello	D	Jan. 1990	2,200
	John Williams	D	Jan. 1990	2,200
Treasurer	Michael Musulin	D	Jan. 1988	18,000
City Controller	Edward P. Wojnaroski, Sr.	D	Jan. 1988	18,000

LANCASTER, 3rd Class, Population 54,725 (Optional Charter)   **Lancaster County**

Office	Name	Political Affiliation	Term Expires	Annual Salary
Mayor	Arthur E. Morris	R	Jan. 1990	$42,000
Council President	Gregory J. Scott	R	Jan. 1990	3,300
Councilmembers	Ronald E. Ford	D	Jan. 1988	3,000
	George D. Alspach	R	Jan. 1990	3,000
	Charles G. Cooke	R	Jan. 1990	3,000
	Jon C. Lyons	D	Jan. 1988	3,000
	Janice C. Stork	D	Jan. 1988	3,000
	Michele D. Madonna	R	Jan. 1990	3,000
Treasurer	Robert Raubenstine	R	Jan. 1990	8,500
Controller	Douglas G. Zellem	R	Jan. 1990	8,500

LEBANON, 3rd Class, Population 25,711   **Lebanon County**

Office	Name	Political Affiliation	Term Expires	Annual Salary
Mayor	Dr. Martin Schneider	R	Jan. 1988	$7,200
Councilmembers				
Accounts and Finance	Betty J. Eiceman	R	Jan. 1990	5,600
Public Safety	Michael J. Folmer	D	Jan. 1988	5,600
Public Works Department	Richard A. Bleistine	R	Jan. 1988	5,600
Parks and Public Property	George E. Gruber	D	Jan. 1990	5,600
City Treasurer	W. Lawrence Hess	R	Jan. 1988	8,000
Controller	Joyce M. Yingst	R	Jan. 1988	5,600

LOCK HAVEN, 3rd Class, Population 9,617 (Optional Charter)   **Clinton County**

Office	Name	Political Affiliation	Term Expires	Annual Salary
Mayor and Council President	Diann Stuempfle	R	Jan. 1988	$1,800
Council Vice President	George Hendricks	D	Jan. 1988	1,200
Councilmembers	Scott A. Smith	D	Jan. 1990	1,200
	Jerome E. Oecker	R	Jan. 1990	1,200
	June L. Houser	R	Jan. 1990	1,200
	Joseph J. Nevins*	R	Jan. 1988	1,200
	George Shade	D	Jan. 1988	1,200
Treasurer	Cambridge G. Beers	R	Jan. 1990	20,800
Controller	Ronald D. Suter	R	Jan. 1990	1,200

*appointed

LOWER BURRELL, 3rd Class, Population 13,200 — Westmoreland County

Office	Name	Political Affiliation	Term Expires	Annual Salary
Mayor	Dennis Kowalski	D	Jan. 1988	$2,400
Councilmembers	Jack Anderson	D	Jan. 1990	1,800
	Donald Kinosz	D	Jan. 1990	1,800
	Ernest Mrvan	D	Jan. 1988	1,800
	James Haley	D	Jan. 1988	1,800
Treasurer	Joseph Widmer	D	Jan. 1988	3,501
Controller	Ernest Fiorina	D	Jan. 1988	1,800

McKEESPORT, 3rd Class, Population 31,012 (Home Rule) — Allegheny County

Office	Name	Political Affiliation	Term Expires	Annual Salary
Mayor	Louis Washowich	D	Jan. 1988	$22,000
Council President	Samuel R. Vidnovic	D	Jan. 1990	1,800
Council Vice President	James S. Honick	D	Jan. 1988	1,800
Councilmembers	Charles D. Mikell	D	Jan. 1990	1,800
	Joseph P. Graziano	D	Jan. 1990	1,800
	William E. Campbell	D	Jan. 1988	1,800
	William P. Dougherty	D	Jan. 1988	1,800
	Carolyn O. Young	D	Jan. 1988	1,800
Controller	Harry C. Walsh	D	Jan. 1990	3,600

MEADVILLE, 3rd Class, Population 15,544 (Optional Charter) — Crawford County

Office	Name	Political Affiliation	Term Expires	Annual Salary
Mayor	James J. DiMaria	R	Jan. 1990	$1,800
Councilmembers	Charles Flynn	D	Jan. 1988	1,200
	Christine B. Lang	D	Jan. 1988	1,200
	Barrett Brewer	D	Jan. 1990	1,200
	Robert J. Rozell	R	Jan. 1990	1,200
Treasurer	Aundra Zack	R	Jan. 1988	8,000
Controller	Sandra Cheropovich	R	Jan. 1988	1,500

MONESSEN, 3rd Class, Population 11,928 — Westmoreland County

Office	Name	Political Affiliation	Term Expires	Annual Salary
Mayor and Council President	James A. Sepesky	D	Jan. 1990	$4,800
Councilmembers				
Accounts and Finance	Earnest S. Wisyanski	D	Jan. 1990	2,800
Public Safety	Dr. Thomas M. Persico	D	Jan. 1988	2,800
Streets and Public Improvement	Anthony Mascetta	D	Jan. 1988	2,800
Parks & Public Property	Joseph Cieply	D	Jan. 1990	2,800
Treasurer	Frank Rizzuto	D	Jan. 1990	3,200
Controller	William J. Bielawski	D	Jan. 1990	2,800

MONONGAHELA, 3rd Class, Population 5,950 — Washington County

Office	Name	Political Affiliation	Term Expires	Annual Salary
Mayor	John Moreschi	D	Jan. 1988	$3,000
Councilmembers				
Accounts and Finance	Joseph Jordan	D	Jan. 1990	1,500
Public Safety	Kenneth Cole	D	Jan. 1988	1,500
Streets and Improvements	James Harrison	D	Jan. 1990	1,500
Parks and Property	Scott Frederick	D	Jan. 1988	1,500
Treasurer	Helen Marie Doty	D	Jan. 1988	1,500
Controller	Joseph Inserra	D	Jan. 1990	1,500

NANTICOKE, 3rd Class, Population 13,044 — Luzerne County

Office	Name	Political Affiliation	Term Expires	Annual Salary
Mayor	John Haydock	D	Jan. 1990	$2,500
Councilmembers	Leonard Locke	D	Jan. 1988	2,400
	Joseph Berry	D	Jan. 1988	2,400
	John Gorka	D	Jan. 1990	2,400
	Mark Yeager	D	Jan. 1988	2,400
Treasurer	Al Szatkowski	D	Jan. 1990	2,167
Controller	Walter Sokolowski	D	Jan. 1990	2,400

NEW CASTLE, 3rd Class, Population 33,621 (Optional Charter) — Lawrence County

Office	Name	Political Affiliation	Term Expires	Annual Salary
Mayor	Dale W. Yoho	R	Jan. 1988	$20,000
Council President	John Russo, Jr.	D	Jan. 1988	2,700
Councilmembers	Nick DeRosa	D	Jan. 1990	2,400
	Richard A. Christofer	D	Jan. 1988	2,400
	Richard Costello	D	Jan. 1988	2,400
	Elizabaeth Verterano	D	Jan. 1990	2,400
Treasurer	Joseph J. Cozza	D	Jan. 1990	11,500
Controller	Anthony M. Toscano	D	Jan. 1988	10,688

NEW KENSINGTON, 3rd Class, Population 17,660 — Westmoreland County

Office	Name	Political Affiliation	Term Expires	Annual Salary
Mayor	John J. Monaco	D	Jan. 1990	$6,000
Councilmembers				
Accounts and Finance	David M. Hanna	D	Jan. 1990	3,600
Streets and Public Improvements	Bernard T. Kubiak	D	Jan. 1990	3,600
Parks and Buildings	Ronald S. Balla	D	Jan. 1988	3,600
Public Safety	Paul W. Schrecongost	D	Jan. 1988	3,600
Treasurer*	Frank J. Pallone, Jr.	D	Jan. 1990	5,512
Controller	Edward J. Chmiel	D	Jan. 1990	3,600

*City/School/County

OIL CITY, 3rd Class, Population 13,881 — Venango County

Office	Name	Political Affiliation	Term Expires	Annual Salary
Mayor	Leonard M. Abate	D	Jan. 1988	$2,400
Councilmembers	Michael Antkowiak	D	Jan. 1988	1,800
	Terrance L. Whitling	R	Jan. 1988	1,800
	Barbara F. Davison	D	Jan. 1990	1,800
	Max M. Serafin	R	Jan. 1990	1,800
Treasurer	Lillian L. Marvin	R	Jan. 1988	15,250
Controller	James A. Nelles	R	Jan. 1986	2,280

PITTSTON, 3rd Class, Population 9,930 — Luzerne County

Office	Name	Political Affiliation	Term Expires	Annual Salary
Mayor	Thomas A. Walsh	D	Jan. 1990	$3,000
Councilmembers	P. J. Melvin	D	Jan. 1988	2,000
	Maria Capolarella	D	Jan. 1988	2,000
	John S. Argo	D	Jan. 1990	2,000
	Carmen Falcone	D	Jan. 1990	2,000
City Solicitor	Joseph Castellino	Appt.	May 1988	4,500
City Clerk	Paul S. McGarry	Appt.	May 1988	23,000
Treasurer	Rosemary Dessoye	D	Jan. 1988	14,500
Controller	Ken Scaz	D	Jan. 1990	2,000

POTTSVILLE, 3rd Class, Population 18,195 — Schuylkill County

Office	Name	Political Affiliation	Term Expires	Annual Salary
Mayor	Anthony J. Pacenta, D.D.S.	D	Jan. 1990	$5,200
Councilmembers				
Streets and Public Improvements	Michael Smink*	D	Jan. 1988	2,600
Accounts and Finance	Thomas J. Pellish, Esq.	D	Jan. 1990	2,600
Parks and Public Property	Jack Dolbin	D	Jan. 1990	2,600
Public Safety	Edward Hampford	D	Jan. 1988	2,600
Treasurer	Margaret Purcell*	D	Jan. 1988	2,500
Controller	Jesse Achenbach	D	Jan. 1988	2,600

*appointed

READING, 3rd Class, Population 78,686 — Berks County

Office	Name	Political Affiliation	Term Expires	Annual Salary
Mayor	Warren H. Haggerty, Jr.*	D	Jan. 1988	$25,000
Councilmembers				
Accounts and Finance	Thomas Loeper	D	Jan. 1988	21,500
Streets and Public Improvements	Edward W. Leonardziak	D	Jan. 1990	21,500
Parks and Public Improvements	Ronald E. DiBenedetto	D	Jan. 1990	21,500
Public Safety	James A. Pollock*	D	Jan. 1988	21,500
Treasurer	Melvin I. Adams	D	Jan. 1988	21,500
Controller	William S. Hartranft	D	Jan. 1988	21,500

*appointed

SHAMOKIN, 3rd Class, Population 10,357 — Northumberland County

Office	Name	Political Affiliation	Term Expires	Annual Salary
Mayor	Harvey M. Boyer, Sr.	D	Jan. 1990	$1,200
Councilmembers	Lawrence J. Kinder	D	Jan. 1990	1,125
	Eleanor S. Wyscock	D	Jan. 1988	1,125
	M. C. Farrow, IV	R	Jan. 1988	1,125
	Betsy Richardson	R	Jan. 1988	1,125
Treasurer	Dorothy Bradley	R	Jan. 1990	2,000
Controller	Joanne C. Kaseman	R	Jan. 1990	1,125

SHARON, 3rd Class, Population 19,057 (Optional Charter) — Mercer County

Office	Name	Political Affiliation	Term Expires	Annual Salary
Mayor	Robert T. Price	D	Jan. 1990	$26,000
Council President	Vito Manilla	D	Jan. 1990	4,200
Councilmembers	Joseph F. Fragle	D	Jan. 1988	3,600
	Joseph L. Baldwin	D	Jan. 1988	3,600
	Raymond Fabian	D	Jan. 1988	3,600
	Harry E. Morrison	D	Jan. 1990	3,600
Treasurer	Leo A. Hanley	D	Jan. 1988	17,400
Controller	John A. Wareham	D	Jan. 1990	5,200

SUNBURY, 3rd Class, Population 12,292 — Northumberland County

Office	Name	Political Affiliation	Term Expires	Annual Salary
Mayor	Charles E. Moll	R	Jan. 1988	$1,550
Councilmembers				
Accounts & Finance	Scott A. Heintzelman	R	Jan. 1988	1,125
Public Safety	David Packer	R	Jan. 1990	1,125
Streets & Public Improvement	Charles E. Schlegel	R	Jan. 1990	1,125
Parks & Public Property	Daniel H. Filer	R	Jan. 1988	1,125
Treasurer	Edward M. Neff	R	Jan. 1990	6,425
Controller	Randi S. Buehner	R	Jan. 1988	1,125

TITUSVILLE, 3rd Class, Population 6,884 (Optional Charter)   Crawford County

Office	Name	Political Affiliation	Term Expires	Annual Salary
Mayor	Eugene C. Mitcham	R	Jan. 1988	$1,200
Deputy Mayor	Robert W. Schneider	R	Jan. 1990	900
Councilmembers	John D. Waychoff	R	Jan. 1990	900
	Carl R. Meinstereifel	R	Jan. 1988	900
	Robert R. Rhoades	R	Jan. 1988	900
Treasurer	Milton P. McCracken	R	Jan. 1988	9,300
Controller	David Edwards*	R	Jan. 1988	1,800

*appointed

UNIONTOWN, 3rd Class, Population 14,510   Fayette County

Office	Name	Political Affiliation	Term Expires	Annual Salary
Mayor	Paul H. Bortz	R	Jan. 1988	$3,000
Councilmembers	Charles D. Curry	R	Jan. 1988	1,200
	John Fisher	R	Jan. 1990	1,200
	Charles B. Smiley	R	Jan. 1990	1,200
	Harry J. Mulligan	R	Jan. 1988	1,200
Treasurer	Susan Maher	R	Jan. 1988	21,722
Controller	J. Vernon Crawford	R	Jan. 1988	1,200

WASHINGTON, 3rd Class, Population 18,363   Washington County

Office	Name	Political Affiliation	Term Expires	Annual Salary
Mayor	L. Anthony Spoosey	D	Jan. 1988	$9,000
Councilmembers	Robert Williams	D	Jan. 1990	7,000
	John A. Manning	D	Jan. 1988	7,000
	Susanne E. Gomez	D	Jan. 1990	7,000
	Bob Sabot	D	Jan. 1988	7,000
Treasurer	Edward W. Abel	D	Jan. 1988	11,100
Controller	Francis King	D	Jan. 1988	7,000

WILKES-BARRE, 3rd Class, Population 51,551 (Home Rule)   Luzerne County

Office	Name	Political Affiliation	Term Expires	Annual Salary
Mayor	Thomas V. McLaughlin	D	Jan. 1988	$30,000
Council Chairman	Thomas D. McGroarty	D	Jan. 1988	6,000
Vice Chairman	Philip C. McCabe	D	Jan. 1988	5,000
Councilmembers	Albert C. Boris	D	Jan. 1988	5,000
	Jack Jones	R	Jan. 1988	5,000
	Lee A. Namey	D	Jan. 1988	5,000
	Robert F. Reilly	D	Jan. 1988	5,000
	Edward White	D	Jan. 1988	5,000
City Controller	Mercedes J. Leighton	D	Jan. 1988	15,000

WILLIAMSPORT, 3rd Class, Population 33,401 (Optional Charter)   Lycoming County

Office	Name	Political Affiliation	Term Expires	Annual Salary
Mayor	Stephen J. Lucasi	R	Jan. 1988	$29,500
Council President	Randall F. Hipple	D	Jan. 1990	2,500
Councilmembers	Charles M. Pagana	R	Jan. 1990	2,200
	Carl M. Hunter	R	Jan. 1988	2,200
	Jessie Bloom	D	Jan. 1990	2,200
	Carl A. Curchoe	R	Jan. 1988	2,200
	John M. Confer	D	Jan. 1988	2,200
	Thomas E. Bailey	D	Jan. 1988	2,200
Treasurer	Leland J. Calistri	R	Jan. 1988	15,100
Controller	Robert Fox	R	Jan. 1988	14,000

YORK, 3rd Class, Population 44,619 (Optional Charter)   **York County**

Office	Name	Political Affiliation	Term Expires	Annual Salary
Mayor	William J. Althaus	R	Jan. 1990	$20,000
Council President	Gregory H. Gettle	D	Jan. 1988	3,000
Councilmembers	Helen E. Rohrbaugh	R	Jan. 1990	2,400
	Donald T. Murphy, Jr.	D	Jan. 1988	2,400
	Wm. Lee Smallwood	D	Jan. 1988	2,400
	Carl E. Jacobs	R	Jan. 1990	2,400
Treasurer	Valerie Bortner	D	Jan. 1988	9,250
Controller	John Peters	D	Jan. 1988	8,000

BOROUGHS OVER 10,000 POPULATION*

BALDWIN, Population 24,712   **Allegheny County**

Office	Name	Political Affiliation	Term Expires	Annual Salary
Mayor	Samuel L. McPherson	D	Jan. 1990	$4,500
President of Council	Donald E. Piel	D	Jan. 1990	3,300
Vice President of Council	Kenneth L. Guerra	D	Jan. 1988	3,300
Councilmembers	Dennis Lynn	D	Jan. 1990	3,300
	William J. Riley	D	Jan. 1988	3,300
	Robert M. Sable	D	Jan. 1988	3,300
	Victor M. Luncinski, Jr.	D	Jan. 1990	3,300
	David J. Kappert	D	Jan. 1988	3,300
Tax Collector	Marjorie L. Dobson	D	Jan. 1990	6,000

BELLEVUE, Population 10,128 (Home Rule)   **Allegheny County**

Office	Name	Political Affiliation	Term Expires	Annual Salary
Mayor	James M. Hirsch	D	Jan. 1990	$2,400
Council President	Rosemary Hefflin	D	Jan. 1988	1,800
Council Vice President	Raymond Capp	D	Jan. 1990	1,800
Councilmembers	Doris Connolly	D	Jan. 1988	1,800
	Thomas Myers	R	Jan. 1990	1,800
	Ella Reshko	R	Jan. 1990	1,800
	Doug Kunst	D	Jan. 1988	1,800
	Ed Fitzgerald	D	Jan. 1990	1,800
	Patrick Hirsch	D	Jan. 1990	1,800
	E. Gillott	R	Jan. 1990	1,800
Tax Collector	James Porch	R	Jan. 1990	Comm.
Secretary	Harry J. Mertz	Appt.		
Treasurer	E. W. Baker	Appt.		11,054

BERWICK, Population 12,189   **Columbia County**

Office	Name	Political Affiliation	Term Expires	Annual Salary
Mayor	Louis L. Biacchi	D	Jan. 1990	$2,000
Council President	James L. Hinckley	R	Jan. 1988	2,000
Council Vice President	Harold L. Peters	D	Jan. 1988	1,200
Councilmembers	Kirk Bower	R	Jan. 1988	1,200
	Pauline Hovanchak	D	Jan. 1988	1,200
	Michael Scala	D	Jan. 1988	1,200
	Andrew Soback	D	Jan. 1988	1,200
	Greg Green	D	Jan. 1988	1,200

* All population figures are U.S. Census Bureau 1980 tabulations.

BETHEL PARK, Population 34,755 (Home Rule) — Allegheny County

Office	Name	Political Affiliation	Term Expires	Annual Salary
Mayor	Reno Virgili	D	Jan. 1990	$3,000
Councilmembers	Richard Clossin	D	Jan. 1988	1,800
	Donald L. Harrison	R	Jan. 1990	1,800
	Wayne Wilson	R	Jan. 1990	1,800
	Alan F. Hoffman	R	Jan. 1990	1,800
	Reid W. McGibbeny	R	Jan. 1988	1,800
	Robert Hatch	D	Jan. 1988	1,800
	John A. Pape	D	Jan. 1990	1,800
	Glenn Trautman	D	Jan. 1988	1,800
	Samuel Ruta	R	Jan. 1990	1,800

BLOOMSBURG (town)*, Population 11,717 — Columbia County

Office	Name	Political Affiliation	Term Expires	Annual Salary
Mayor and Council President	Daniel J. Bauman	D	Jan. 1990	$3,000
Vice President	Edward Kitchen	R	Jan. 1990	1,800
Councilmembers	George Hemingway	R	Jan. 1988	1,800
	Angelo Scheno	D	Jan. 1990	1,800
	Florence Thompson	D	Jan. 1988	1,800
	Steve Beck	R	Jan. 1988	1,800
	Charles Learn	D	Jan. 1990	1,800

*Bloomsburg is the only incorporated town in Pennsylvania.

BRENTWOOD, Population 11,907 — Allegheny County

Office	Name	Political Affiliation	Term Expires	Annual Salary
Mayor	James H. Joyce	D	Jan. 1990	$3,399
Council President	Edward J. Haney	D	Jan. 1990	2,400
Vice President	James Flanigan	D	Jan. 1988	2,400
Councilmembers	Fred A. Swanson	D	Jan. 1990	2,400
	Sonya Vernau	R	Jan. 1990	2,400
	David K. Schade	D	Jan. 1990	2,400
	Scot Werner	R	Jan. 1988	2,400
	Patricia Larkin	D	Jan. 1988	2,400
Property Tax Collector	Katherine Gannis	D	Jan. 1990	5,000
Secretary	Elvina R. Nicola	Appt.		15,288
Treasurer	Geoffrey A. Brandon	Appt.		16,950
Solicitor	Lawrence G. Zurawsky	Appt.		*

*Retainer Fee

BRISTOL, Population 10,867 — Bucks County

Office	Name	Political Affiliation	Term Expires	Annual Salary
Mayor	Gary Tosri	D	Jan. 1990	$2,400
Council President	William Pezza	D	Jan. 1988	2,400
Vice President	David Clark	D	Jan. 1988	2,400
Councilmembers	Donald McCloskey	D	Jan. 1990	2,400
	Charles Caucci	D	Jan. 1990	2,400
	James Lutz	D	Jan. 1990	2,400
	Joseph Coffman	D	Jan. 1990	2,400
	George Pirollo	D	Jan. 1988	2,400
	Joseph Saxton	D	Jan. 1988	2,400
Tax Collector	James Nealis	D	Jan. 1990	5,100*

*Borough share

CANONSBURG, Population 10,459 — Washington County

Office	Name	Political Affiliation	Term Expires	Annual Salary
Mayor	Jack Passante	D	Jan. 1990	$2,400
Councilmembers	David Duda	D	Jan. 1990	2,400
	Manuel Pihakis	D	Jan. 1990	2,400
	James Gregorakis	D	Jan. 1988	2,400
	Joyce Farella	D	Jan. 1990	2,400
	Joseph D'Orazio	D	Jan. 1988	2,400
	John Alterio	D	Jan. 1990	2,400
	James Matrogran	D	Jan. 1988	2,400
	Frank Barbosky	D	Jan. 1988	2,400
	Frances Maceiko	D	Jan. 1990	2,400

CARLISLE, Population 18,314 — Cumberland County

Office	Name	Political Affiliation	Term Expires	Annual Salary
Mayor	Kirk R. Wilson	R	Jan. 1990	$2,500
Council President	William A. Duncan	D	Jan. 1988	1,500
Vice President	Blaine L. Shatto	R	Jan. 1988	1,200
Councilmembers	George W. Davidson, Jr.	D	Jan. 1988	1,200
	Richard K. Ocker	R	Jan. 1990	1,200
	Stephen Herman	R	Jan. 1990	1,200
	Harold E. Cline	R	Jan. 1988	1,200
	Roger C. Spitz	R	Jan. 1988	1,200

CARNEGIE, Population 10,099 — Allegheny County

Office	Name	Political Affiliation	Term Expires	Annual Salary
Mayor	Lawrence Harkovich	D	Jan. 1990	$2,400
Councilmembers	John DeFonso	D	Jan. 1990	1,800
	Albert Falcioni	D	Jan. 1988	1,800
	Lud Hanczar	D	Jan. 1988	1,800
	Christine Herman	D	Jan. 1988	1,800
	Robert Horak	D	Jan. 1990	1,800
	John Fisher	D	Jan. 1990	1,800

CASTLE SHANNON, Population 10,164 — Allegheny County

Office	Name	Political Affiliation	Term Expires	Annual Salary
Mayor	Thomas P. O'Malley	D	Jan. 1988	$2,400
Council President	Donald J. Baumgarten	D	Jan. 1988	2,400
Vice President	Rudolph M. Richtar	D	Jan. 1988	2,400
Councilmembers	Anthony J. Nedzesky	D	Jan. 1990	2,400
	Theodore H. Kirk	D	Jan. 1990	2,400
	Merle M. Michelucci	D	Jan. 1990	2,400
	Robert J. Carluzzi	D	Jan. 1988	2,400
	Michael Zheberenzhick	D	Jan. 1990	2,400
Borough Manager	Edward R. McFadden	Appt.		32,000

CHAMBERSBURG, Population 16,174 — Franklin County

Office	Name	Political Affiliation	Term Expires	Annual Salary
Mayor	Robert P. Morris	D	Jan. 1990	$3,900
Council President	Samuel W. Worley	R	Jan. 1990	3,900
Vice President	Robert K. Wasik	R	Jan. 1988	2,700
Councilmembers	Harold D. Kennedy	R	Jan. 1990	2,700
	Roy M. McLaughlin	D	Jan. 1990	2,700
	Walter E. Miner	R	Jan. 1990	2,700
	Quentin A. Naugle	D	Jan. 1988	2,700
	Gerald D. Shipp	R	Jan. 1988	2,700
	Bernard L. Washabaugh	D	Jan. 1990	2,700
	George W. Pentz	D	Jan. 1988	2,700
	Robert A. Wareham, Sr.	R	Jan. 1988	2,700

COLUMBIA, Population 10,466 — Lancaster County

Office	Name	Political Affiliation	Term Expires	Annual Salary
Mayor	Ross R. Nicholas	D	Jan. 1990	$1,200
Council President	Paul W. Myers	D	Jan. 1988	1,200
Council Vice President	Sylvester F. Devine	D	Jan. 1988	1,200
Councilmembers	Gordon Eck	D	Jan. 1990	1,200
	Ann Grubb	R	Jan. 1990	1,200
	Michael Halter	D	Jan. 1988	1,200
	Thomas Lawson	R	Jan. 1988	1,200
	George F. McGinness	R	Jan. 1990	1,200
Borough Manager	Gary L. Myers	Appt.		30,000

DARBY, Population 11,513 — Delaware County

Office	Name	Political Affiliation	Term Expires	Annual Salary
Mayor	Louis Saraullo	R	Jan. 1990	$3,000
Council President	Nicholas DiGregorio	R	Jan. 1990	2,400
Council Vice President	Wilbur Smith	R	Jan. 1988	2,400
Councilmembers	Robert Layden	R	Jan. 1990	2,400
	Robert Deaver	R	Jan. 1990	2,400
	Steven Del Guercio	R	Jan. 1988	2,400
	Armenta Carter	R	Jan. 1990	2,400
	Maury Millison*	R	Jan. 1988	2,400
	Margaret Griffith	R	Jan. 1988	2,400
	Robert Tyler	R	Jan. 1990	2,400
Tax Collector	John C. Maguire	Appt.	Jan. 1990	6,000

*appointed

DORMONT, Population 11,275 — Allegheny County

Office	Name	Political Affiliation	Term Expires	Annual Salary
Mayor	William H. Moreland, Jr.	R	Jan. 1990	$2,700
Council President	Thomas R. Lloyd	R	Jan. 1990	1,800
Vice President	Edgar C. Good	R	Jan. 1990	1,800
Councilmembers	James C. Morehead, III	D	Jan. 1988	1,800
	Pat Schmotzer	D	Jan. 1988	1,800
	Harry C. Luebbe	R	Jan. 1990	1,800
	Dale R. Hutchison	R	Jan. 1988	1,800
	Barry E. Wood	R	Jan. 1990	1,800

DUNMORE, Population 16,781 — Lackawanna County

Office	Name	Political Affiliation	Term Expires	Annual Salary
Mayor	Joseph J. Domnick	D	Jan. 1990	$4,200
Council President	Leonard Verrastro	D	Jan. 1988	4,200
Councilmembers	Michael Cummings	D	Jan. 1988	3,000
	Louis W. Beardell	D	Jan. 1988	3,000
	Louis O. Kelly	D	Jan. 1988	3,000
	Thomas Golden	D	Jan. 1990	3,000
	Martin F. Monahan	D	Jan. 1990	3,000
	Frank Padula	D	Jan. 1990	3,000
Controller	Joseph Tomko	D	Jan. 1990	3,600
Tax Collector	Eustachio Arduino	D	Jan. 1990	2,500

EMMAUS, Population 11,001 — Lehigh County

Office	Name	Political Affiliation	Term Expires	Annual Salary
Mayor	Linwood D. Nester	R	Jan. 1990	$2,820
Council President	Pierce E. Randall	D	Jan. 1988	2,400
Councilmembers	Dr. Richard P. Keim	D	Jan. 1990	2,001
	Harvey Eck	D	Jan. 1988	2,001
	John Shafer	D	Jan. 1990	2,001
	Greg Brittenburg	D	Jan. 1990	2,001
	Patricia M. Shirock	D	Jan. 1988	2,001
	Robert Wessner	D	Jan. 1990	2,001
Tax Collector	Chlorina Godusky	R	Jan. 1992	9,400
Auditors	ConCannon, Gallagher, Miller & Co.	Appt.	Jan. 1988	8,000
Borough Manager	Bruce E. Fosselman	Appt.		33,000

EPHRATA, Population 11,095 — Lancaster County

Office	Name	Political Affiliation	Term Expires	Annual Salary
Mayor	Clair L. Wolf	R	Jan. 1990	$300
Councilmembers	Richard McQuate	R	Jan. 1990	0
	Deloris Wingenroth	R	Jan. 1990	0
	Harlan J. Weit	R	Jan. 1988	0
	Ralph E. Mowen	R	Jan. 1988	0
	Kenneth Zimmerman	R	Jan. 1988	0
	Donald E. Suter	R	Jan. 1988	0
	Michael K. Worrall	R	Jan. 1990	0
	William V. Hecker	R	Jan. 1990	0
Borough Manager/Secretary	L. Victor Dickinson	Appt.		
Treasurer	Ronald M. Martin	Appt.		
Solicitor	David R. Eaby	Appt.		

HANOVER, Population 14,890 — York County

Office	Name	Political Affiliation	Term Expires	Annual Salary
Mayor	W. Roy Attlesberger	R	Jan. 1990	$2,334
Councilmembers	Ira A. Bitner	R	Jan. 1990	0
	Pete G. Keriazes	R	Jan. 1990	0
	David F. Humbert, III	R	Jan. 1990	0
	Wendell S. Felix	R	Jan. 1990	0
	Bryce B. Little	R	Jan. 1988	0
	Burnell L. Small	R	Jan. 1990	0
	Margaret Hormel	R	Jan. 1990	0
	Daniel E. Pittinger	R	Jan. 1988	0
	Carroll T. Mays	R	Jan. 1988	0
	Richard V. Hoke	R	Jan. 1988	0

INDIANA, Population 16,051 — Indiana County

Office	Name	Political Affiliation	Term Expires	Annual Salary
Mayor	Geo. E. Thompson	R	Jan. 1990	$4,000
Councilmembers	David Naylon	R	Jan. 1988	0
	John Barton	R	Jan. 1990	0
	Sumner Palmer	R	Jan. 1988	0
	Leonard Abrams	R	Jan. 1990	0
	Edward Petrosky	R	Jan. 1988	0
	Guy Creek	R	Jan. 1990	0
	Wallace Trusal	R	Jan. 1990	0
	Ross Bricklemyer	R	Jan. 1988	0
	Joseph Gatt, Jr.	R	Jan. 1988	0
	Kenneth E. Brown	R	Jan. 1990	0
	John Fetterman	R	Jan. 1990	0
	Patrick J. Ward	R	Jan. 1988	0

KINGSTON, Population 15,681 (Home Rule) — Luzerne County

Office	Name	Political Affiliation	Term Expires	Annual Salary
Mayor	Charles A. Bankes	R	Jan. 1990	$5,000
Councilmembers	Thomas Roberts	R	Jan. 1988	2,400
	Henry T. Billman	R	Jan. 1988	2,400
	James Fennell	R	Jan. 1990	2,400
	Charles Gommer, Jr.	R	Jan. 1988	2,400
	Frank Peterson	R	Jan. 1990	2,400
	Francis Sorochak	R	Jan. 1990	2,400
	Leslie Nicholas	R	Jan. 1988	2,400

LANSDALE, Population 16,526 — Montgomery County

Office	Name	Political Affiliation	Term Expires	Annual Salary
Mayor	Michael DiNunzio	R	Jan. 1990	$1,500
Council President	Charles R. Wall	R	Jan. 1988	1,500
Council Vice President	Robert A. DiDomizio	R	Jan. 1990	1,500
Councilmembers	Joan Y. Williams	R	Jan. 1988	1,500
	Carl W. Guenst	R	Jan. 1990	1,500
	Howard L. Cauffman	R	Jan. 1988	1,500
	James E. Hunt	R	Jan. 1990	1,500
	John H. Klock	R	Jan. 1990	1,500
	Robert Rosenberger	D	Jan. 1988	1,500
	Salvatore Serrao	R	Jan. 1990	1,500

LANSDOWNE, Population 11,891 — Delaware County

Office	Name	Political Affiliation	Term Expires	Annual Salary
Mayor	Jane K. Deshong	R	Jan. 1990	0
Council President	E. J. Meloney, Jr.	R	Jan. 1988	0
Council Vice President	John J. Rankin, Jr.	R	Jan. 1988	0
Councilmembers	George V. Bochanski, Jr.	R	Jan. 1990	0
	Mark DuFrayne	R	Jan. 1990	0
	Joseph Gorman	R	Jan. 1990	0
	Robert Alpigini	R	Jan. 1990	0
	Michael F. X. Coll	R	Jan. 1988	0
Tax Collector	Nancy A. Davies	R	Jan. 1990	$12,600
Auditors	William J. Mulgrew	R	Jan. 1992	250
	George E. Heinly, Jr.	R	Jan. 1990	250
	Joseph D. Clarke	R	Jan. 1988	250

LATROBE, Population 10,799 — Westmoreland County

Office	Name	Political Affiliation	Term Expires	Annual Salary
Mayor	Angelo Caruso	D	Jan. 1990	$2,400
Council President	Kenneth J. McCallen	D	Jan. 1988	1,200
Vice President	Oland Canterna	D	Jan. 1988	1,200
Councilmembers	Rudolph A. Prohaska, Jr.	D	Jan. 1988	1,200
	Ronald Smith	D	Jan. 1988	1,200
	Samuel D. DePasquale	D	Jan. 1990	1,200
	Paul M. Guter	R	Jan. 1988	1,200
	Gerald Atkins	R	Jan. 1990	1,200
	Donald G. Albert	D	Jan. 1990	1,200
	Richard Stadler	D	Jan. 1990	1,200
	Theodore E. Cawoski	D	Jan. 1988	1,200
	Doris Herald	D	Jan. 1990	1,200
	John Trout	D	Jan. 1990	1,200

MIDDLETOWN, Population 10,122 — Dauphin County

Office	Name	Political Affiliation	Term Expires	Annual Salary
Mayor	Robert G. Reid	R	Jan. 1990	$2,100
President	David H. Judy	D	Jan. 1988	2,100
Vice President	Barbara N. Layne	R	Jan. 1988	1,500
Councilmembers	Charles C. Benson	R	Jan. 1990	1,500
	Robert R. Louer	R	Jan. 1988	1,500
	Barry W. Goodling	R	Jan. 1990	1,500
	Richard B. Swartz	R	Jan. 1990	1,500
	Donald D. Smith	R	Jan. 1990	1,500
	George W. Elberti, III	R	Jan. 1988	1,500
	James H. Grim, Sr.	R	Jan. 1990	1,500
Tax Collector	Jean Kaylor	R	Jan. 1990	2,100

MONROEVILLE, Population 30,977, (Home Rule) — Allegheny County

Office	Name	Political Affiliation	Term Expires	Annual Salary
Mayor	Michael P. Lynch	D	Jan. 1990	$4,500
Councilmembers	George Dale	D	Jan. 1988	3,000
	Anthony LaGorga	D	Jan. 1990	3,000
	Thomas Schuerger	R	Jan. 1988	3,000
	Michael Kelly	D	Jan. 1990	3,000
	Miles Span	D	Jan. 1988	3,000
	Margaret Anderson	D	Jan. 1990	3,000
	Henry J. Itri	D	Jan. 1990	3,000
Tax Collector	Geneva McKee	R	Jan. 1990	10,000

MUNHALL, Population 14,532 — Allegheny County

Office	Name	Political Affiliation	Term Expires	Annual Salary
Mayor	William Knight	D	Jan. 1990	$3,000
Council President	Raymond Bodnar	D	Jan. 1990	2,400
Vice President	Clement Matta	D	Jan. 1988	2,400
Councilmembers	William Davis	D	Jan. 1990	2,400
	Ronald Watkins	D	Jan. 1990	2,400
	Lawrence Oieksa	D	Jan. 1990	2,400
	John Tichon	D	Jan. 1988	2,400
Tax Collector	Robert Olson	D	Jan. 1990	13,000

MURRYSVILLE, Population 16,036 (Home Rule)   **Westmoreland County**

Office	Name	Political Affiliation	Term Expires	Annual Salary
Mayor	Barbara B. Redding	R	Jan. 1988	$2,400
President of Council	Wilbert H. Ferguson	R	Jan. 1990	1,200
Vice President of Council	Harold A. Wright	R	Jan. 1988	1,200
Councilmembers	Robert J. Brooks	R	Jan. 1990	1,200
	Richard P. Kole	R	Jan. 1990	1,200
	Colleen Lloyd	R	Jan. 1988	1,200
	Betty J. Hoover	R	Jan. 1990	1,200
	James G. Earhart, Sr.	R	Jan. 1988	1,200
Secretary/Treasurer-Manager	John M. Lynch	Appt.		
Auditor — CPA	McKeever Varga Kokkila & Assoc.	Appt.		
Tax Collector	Calla W. Sabol	R	Jan. 1990	15,000
Tax Collector — Act 511	Calla W. Sabol	Appt.		

NORRISTOWN, Population 34,684 (Home Rule)   **Montgomery County**

Office	Name	Political Affiliation	Term Expires	Annual Salary
Mayor	John Marberger	R	Jan. 1990	$5,000
Council President	Samuel Vallone	R	Jan. 1988	4,000
Vice President	Paul Santangelo	R	Jan. 1988	4,000
Councilmembers:	Thomas C. Tornetta	R	Jan. 1988	4,000
	John Evans	R	Jan. 1988	4,000
	Nicholas Durante	R	Jan. 1990	4,000
	Russell Montalbano	R	Jan. 1988	4,000
	William Glass	R	Jan. 1988	4,000
	Thomas J. Murray	D	Jan. 1988	4,000
	Theodore LeBlanc	R	Jan. 1990	4,000
	Harry Falco, Jr.	R	Jan. 1990	4,000
	Dennis Caglia	R	Jan. 1990	4,000
	Thomas J. Murray	D	Jan. 1988	4,000

PHOENIXVILLE, Population 14,165   **Chester County**

Office	Name	Political Affiliation	Term Expires	Annual Salary
Mayor	Michael J. Basca	R	Jan. 1990	$2,500
Council President	Bonnie K. August	D	Jan. 1988	1,800
Councilmembers	John Fedora	D	Jan. 1988	1,200
	Theodore X. Beluch	D	Jan. 1990	1,200
	Loren B. Griffith	D	Jan. 1988	1,200
	Kevin H. Smith	R	Jan. 1990	1,200
	James A. McGuigan, Jr.	D	Jan. 1988	1,200
	John P. Horenci, Jr.	R	Jan. 1990	1,200
	Robert W. Mark	R	Jan. 1990	1,200
	Robert J. Gray	D	Jan. 1988	1,200
	Helen M. Rambo	R	Jan. 1990	1,200
	Alex C. Kovach	D	Jan. 1988	1,200
	Dominic V. Viola, Jr.	D	Jan. 1990	1,200
Tax Collector	Kevin McElroy	D	Jan. 1990	7,000

PLUM, Population 25,390 — Allegheny County

Office	Name	Political Affiliation	Term Expires	Annual Salary
Mayor	A. E. O'Block	D	Jan. 1990	$600
Council President	Richard B. Hereda	D	Jan. 1990	300
Vice President	Thomas White, Jr.	D	Jan. 1990	300
Councilmembers	Al Flickinger	D	Jan. 1990	300
	Stanley J. Caraher	D	Jan. 1990	300
	Alfred Franci	D	Jan. 1988	300
	Donald Knopfel	D	Jan. 1988	300
	Stephen M. Zelahy, Jr.	D	Jan. 1988	300
Auditors	David W. London	D	Jan. 1988	400
	Michael Kozar	D	Jan. 1988	400
	Marge McCafferty	D	Jan. 1990	400
Tax Collector	Matthew Churilla	D	Jan. 1990	1%

POTTSTOWN, Population 22,729 — Montgomery County

Office	Name	Political Affiliation	Term Expires	Annual Salary
Mayor	Edmund Skarbek	R	Jan. 1990	$2,000
Council President	Charles D. Garner, Sr.	R	Jan. 1990	1,500
Vice President	Douglas Breidenbach	R	Jan. 1988	1,200
Councilmembers	Doris M. Kohler	D	Jan. 1990	1,200
	Charles Barr	D	Jan. 1988	1,200
	James Smale, Jr.	R	Jan. 1988	1,200
	Frank J. Ciprero	D	Jan. 1988	1,200
	James Ottaviano	R	Jan. 1990	1,200
Tax Collector	Guy Sperat, Jr.	D	Jan. 1990	7,000

STATE COLLEGE, Population 36,130, (Home Rule) — Centre County

Office	Name	Political Affiliation	Term Expires	Annual Salary
Mayor	Arnold Addison	R	Jan. 1990	$6,600
Council President	John A. Dombroski	R	Jan. 1988	0
Councilmembers	Daniel Chaffee	D	Jan. 1988	0
	Mary Ann Haas	R	Jan. 1988	0
	James B. Bartoo	R	Jan. 1988	0
	R. Thomas Berner	R	Jan. 1988	0
	Ruth K. Lavin	R	Jan. 1990	0
	Fremont D. Winand	R	Jan. 1990	0

SWISSVALE, Population 11,345 — Allegheny County

Office	Name	Political Affiliation	Term Expires	Annual Salary
Mayor	Charles Martoni	D	Jan. 1990	$2,400
Council President	Thomas J. Kasardo	D	Jan. 1990	1,200
Council Vice President	Richard W. Abraham	D	Jan. 1988	1,200
Councilmembers	John P. Kennedy	R	Jan. 1990	1,200
	Anthony Russo	D	Jan. 1990	1,200
	Walter Eiseman	D	Jan. 1990	1,200
	Bernard C. Turley	R	Jan. 1988	1,200
	Joseph Valentino	R	Jan. 1988	1,200
Auditors	Thomas Barr	D	Jan. 1988	500
	Nancy Miller	R	Jan. 1990	500
	Barbara Rock	D	Jan. 1990	600
Tax Collector	Hugh E. Shields	D	Jan. 1990	8,000

WARREN, Population 12,146, (Home Rule) — Warren County

Office	Name	Political Affiliation	Term Expires	Annual Salary
Mayor and Council President	Susan N. McConnell	D	Jan. 1990	$1,800
Council Vice President	Lawrence Loughlin	R	Jan. 1990	1,000
Councilmembers	Ralph Papalia	R	Jan. 1990	1,000
	Merl Rice	D	Jan. 1990	1,000
	Robert Rice	R	Jan. 1990	1,000

WEST CHESTER, Population 17,435 — Chester County

Office	Name	Political Affiliation	Term Expires	Annual Salary
Mayor	Thomas A. Chambers	D	Jan. 1990	$2,000
Council President	W. Barry Wright	D	Jan. 1988	2,000
Council Vice President	Ann E. Aerie	D	Jan. 1990	2,000
Councilmembers	Steven K. Handzel	R	Jan. 1988	2,000
	Richard A. Fazio	D	Jan. 1990	2,000
	H. Kenneth Hagerty	R	Jan. 1988	2,000
	William B. Bowes	D	Jan. 1990	2,000
	A. Wayne Burton	D	Jan. 1990	2,000

WEST MIFFLIN, Population 26,279 — Allegheny County

Office	Name	Political Affiliation	Term Expires	Annual Salary
Mayor	Peter W. Richards	D	Jan. 1990	$3,000
Council President	Frank L. Stupar	D	Jan. 1988	3,000
Vice President	C. L. Jabbour	D	Jan. 1990	3,000
Councilmembers	George B. Miklos	D	Jan. 1990	3,000
	Richard D. Olasz, Jr.	D	Jan. 1990	3,000
	Robert L. Hess	D	Jan. 1988	3,000
	Irene Parkinson	D	Jan. 1988	3,000
	William Welsh	D	Jan. 1990	3,000
Tax Collector	Richard A. Allen	D	Jan. 1990	12,500

WHITEHALL, Population 15,142, (Home Rule) — Allegheny County

Office	Name	Political Affiliation	Term Expires	Annual Salary
Mayor	Edwin F. Brennan	R	Jan. 1990	$2,990
Councilmembers	Andrew Sakmar	R	Jan. 1990	2,380
	James F. Nowalk	D	Jan. 1988	2,380
	David Barton	D	Jan. 1990	2,380
	Raymond R. Miller	R	Jan. 1990	2,380
	Frank J. Mundy	R	Jan. 1988	2,380
	George C. Sites	R	Jan. 1990	2,380
	Jack Wright	D	Jan. 1988	2,380
Auditors	James R. Stoker	R	Jan. 1990	1,587
	George W. Cunningham	R	Jan. 1992	1,587
	Daniel K. Leonard	R	Jan. 1988	1,587
Tax Collector	James M. Kite	R	Jan. 1990	4,800

WILKINSBURG, Population 23,669 — Allegheny County

Office	Name	Political Affiliation	Term Expires	Annual Salary
Mayor	Richard C. Depperman	R	Jan. 1990	$5,000
Councilmembers	Patrick O'Leary	D	Jan. 1990	3,300
	Bernard J. McKenna	I	Jan. 1988	2,400
	Peter Mathis*	D	Jan. 1988	2,400
	William A. Chessman	R	Jan. 1990	3,300
	Ronald J. Hill	D	Jan. 1990	3,300
	Dennis O'Leary	D	Jan. 1988	2,400
	Ralph P. Watson	D	Jan. 1988	2,400
	Jean Kirkland	D	Jan. 1990	3,300
	Mark G. Weitzman	D	Jan. 1990	3,300
Tax Collector	Dominick J. Gambino	D	Jan. 1990	Comm.

*appointed

YEADON, Population 11,727 — Delaware County

Office	Name	Political Affiliation	Term Expires	Annual Salary
Mayor	James F. Mollan, Jr.	R	Jan. 1990	$1,800
Council President	John P. Capuzzi	R	Jan. 1990	1,800
Vice President	Frank Urso	R	Jan. 1988	1,080
Councilmembers	Jack Green	R	Jan. 1990	1,800
	Antoinette Rafferty	R	Jan. 1988	1,800
	Aris J. Karalis	R	Jan. 1988	1,080
	Allen P. Roberts	R	Jan. 1990	1,800
	Van Copeland	R	Jan. 1988	1,800

FIRST CLASS TOWNSHIPS OVER 10,000 POPULATION*

ABINGTON, Population 59,084 — Montgomery County

Office	Name	Political Affiliation	Term Expires	Annual Salary
President	William D. C. Dennis	R	Jan. 1988	$3,000
Vice President	Nicholas Turco	R	Jan. 1990	3,000
Commissioners	Jeffrey Albert	R	Jan. 1990	3,000
	Bruce Toll	D	Jan. 1988	3,000
	Randall L. Aiken	R	Jan. 1988	3,000
	Richard E. Fluge, Jr.	R	Jan. 1990	3,000
	Albert J. Cunningham	R	Jan. 1988	3,000
	James Hotchkiss	D	Jan. 1990	3,000
	Matthew J. Somers, Jr.	D	Jan. 1988	3,000
	Joseph Dougherty	R	Jan. 1990	3,000
	Edwin S. Eichert, III	R	Jan. 1988	3,000
	Bud Hannings	R	Jan. 1990	3,000
	Dolores (Dee) McGrath	R	Jan. 1990	3,000
	Betty S. Melville	R	Jan. 1988	3,000
Treasurer	George H. Snyder, III	R	Jan. 1990	10,000

*All population figures are U.S. Census Bureau 1980 tabulations.

ASTON, Population 14,530 — Delaware County

Office	Name	Political Affiliation	Term Expires	Annual Salary
President	James H. Persing	R	Jan. 1990	$2,600
Vice President	James W. McGinn	R	Jan. 1988	1,200
Commissioners	Lewis H. Fisher	R	Jan. 1990	2,600
	Edmund Kulesa	D	Jan. 1988	1,200
	Robert Parkinson	R	Jan. 1988	1,200
	Mercedes I. Buffington	D	Jan. 1988	1,200
	Robert P. Seefeldt	R	Jan. 1990	2,600
Treasurer, Tax Collector	Raymond J. Locke	R	Jan. 1988	5,000
Auditors	James Joyce	R	Jan. 1988	533
	Robert D. Ciunci	R	Jan. 1992	533
	Russell D. Replogle	R	Jan. 1990	533

BETHLEHEM, Population 12,094 — Northampton County

Office	Name	Political Affiliation	Term Expires	Annual Salary
Commissioners	William Berry	R	Jan. 1988	$2,600
	Joseph Gencarelli	D	Jan. 1990	2,600
	Francis Sitoski	D	Jan. 1988	2,600
	Stephen Lang	D	Jan. 1988	2,600
	Richard Seeds	D	Jan. 1988	2,600
Secretary/Manager	Carl F. DiCello	Appt.		32,000
Treasurer	Michael J. Symons	D	Jan. 1990	4,000

BRISTOL, Population 58,733 — Bucks County

Office	Name	Political Affiliation	Term Expires	Annual Salary
President of Council	Harold Saxton	R	Jan. 1990	3,500
Vice President of Council	James McCullen	R	Jan. 1990	3,500
Members of Council	Theresa Bradley	R	Jan. 1990	3,500
	Carl Cini	D	Jan. 1988	3,500
	David Hite		Jan. 1990	3,500
Tax Collector, Managing Director	Stanley P. Gawel	I		$48,509
Executive	Edna Roth	R	Jan. 1990	14,000

BUTLER, Population 18,651 — Butler County

Office	Name	Political Affiliation	Term Expires	Annual Salary
President	John A. Seezox	D	Jan. 1988	$2,400
Vice President	Joseph J. Hasychak	R	Jan. 1988	2,400
Commissioners	Paul L. Langland	R	Jan. 1990	3,300
	Joseph H. Matson	D	Jan. 1988	2,400
	Joseph C. Wiest	D	Jan. 1990	3,300
Treasurer	Robert M. Hunka	D	Jan. 1990	5,000

CHELTENHAM, Population 35,509 (Home Rule) — Montgomery County

Office	Name	Political Affiliation	Term Expires	Annual Salary
Commissioners	Robert J. Hannum	R	Jan. 1988	$5,500
	Bernard Borine	R	Jan. 1988	5,000
	Gordon G. Lawrence	R	Jan. 1990	5,000
	Allan H. Reuben	D	Jan. 1988	5,000
	Herbert Wile, Jr.	D	Jan. 1990	5,000
	Robert C. Gerhard, Jr.	R	Jan. 1988	5,000
	Stanley A. Casacio	R	Jan. 1990	5,000
Finance Officer	William David Webb	R	Jan. 1990	15,000

COAL, Population 10,984 — Northumberland County

Office	Name	Political Affiliation	Term Expires	Annual Salary
President	Sylvester Schicatano	R	Jan. 1988	$1,500
Vice President	Henry J. Negherbon	R	Jan. 1990	2,600
Commissioners	Thomas R. Williams	R	Jan. 1988	1,500
	Carl A. Petrovich	R	Jan. 1990	2,600
	Vince Purcell	D	Jan. 1988	1,500
Treasurer	Thelma Klinger	R	Jan. 1990	Comm.
Solicitor	Vincent V. Rovito, Jr.	Appt.		4,400
Engineer	John J. Levkulic	Appt.		1,200
Secretary	Joan E. Nelson	Appt.		18,050

CUMRU, Population 11,474 — Berks County

Office	Name	Political Affiliation	Term Expires	Annual Salary
Chairman	Richard F. Venne	R	Jan. 1988	$1,500
Vice Chairman	Edgar I. Zerbe	R	Jan. 1990	2,600
Commissioners	Wayne E. Bortz	R	Jan. 1990	2,600
	Carolyn L. Ramsey	R	Jan. 1990	2,600
	Theodore Starr	D	Jan. 1988	2,600
Manager	William S. Shea	Appt.		
Secretary	Carol J. Steffy	Appt.		
Treasurer	Wanda L. Quinter	D	Jan. 1990	10,000

DARBY, Population 12,264 — Delaware County

Office	Name	Political Affiliation	Term Expires	Annual Salary
President — Recreation	Lawrence Patterson	R	Jan. 1990	$2,592
	Lee Taliaferro	D	Jan. 1990	2,592
Safety	John B. Ryan, Jr.*	R	Jan. 1988	1,500
Controller	Martin Reape	R	Jan. 1990	2,500
Tax Collector/Treasurer	John McGowan	R	Jan. 1990	2,500

*appointed

EAST PENNSBORO, Population 13,955 — Cumberland County

Office	Name	Political Affiliation	Term Expires	Annual Salary
Commissioners	George A. DeMartyn, Jr.	D	Jan. 1990	$2,600
	Philip E. Sgrignoli	D	Jan. 1990	2,600
	William R. Fry, Jr.	R	Jan. 1990	2,600
	Bertram W. Olley*	R	Jan. 1988	1,500
	Mary Withington	R	Jan. 1988	2,600
Treasurer	Alicia D. Stine	D	Jan. 1990	5,000

*appointed

ELIZABETH, Population 16,269 — Allegheny County

Office	Name	Political Affiliation	Term Expires	Annual Salary
Commissioners	Charles J. Carlock, Jr.	D	Jan. 1988	$2,400
	Donald Similo	D	Jan. 1988	2,400
	Richard Maha	D	Jan. 1988	2,400
	Glenn Johnston, Sr.	D	Jan. 1990	2,400
	Michael Castine	D	Jan. 1988	2,400
	JoAnne Beckowitz	D	Jan. 1990	2,400
	Gerald Hinchey	D	Jan. 1990	2,400
	Fred A. Brassart	D	Jan. 1990	2,400
	Helen Kochan	D	Jan. 1988	2,400
Treasurer	James W. Knight	D	Jan. 1990	2,500
Auditor	William Blosel, CPA	Appt.		

HAMPDEN, Population 17,960   **Cumberland County**

Office	Name	Political Affiliation	Term Expires	Annual Salary
President................................	John V. Thomas........................	R	Jan. 1990	$3,300
Vice President..........................	Kenneth Hammaker	R	Jan. 1988	3,300
Commissioners.........................	Melvyn Finkelstein	R	Jan. 1990	3,300
	John B. Turo	R	Jan. 1988	3,300
	Isabell Stathas........................	R	Jan. 1990	3,300

HANOVER, Population 12,601   **Luzerne County**

Office	Name	Political Affiliation	Term Expires	Annual Salary
President................................	Robert Youngblood	R	Jan. 1988	$1,500
Vice President..........................	Joseph Mera	R	Jan. 1988	1,500
Commissioners.........................	George Bienias*	R	Jan. 1988	1,500
	Carl Palsha*	R	Jan. 1988	1,500
	Frank J. Ciavarella	R	Jan. 1990	1,500
	Robert Chesna	D	Jan. 1990	1,500
	Randolph S. Yanoshak	R	Jan. 1988	1,500
Treasurer, Tax Collector................	John Marut	R	Jan. 1990	5,200

*appointed

HARRISON, Population 13,252   **Allegheny County**

Office	Name	Political Affiliation	Term Expires	Annual Salary
President................................	George E. Conroy	D/R	Jan. 1988	$1,500
Commissioners.........................	J. Gracian Korpanty	D	Jan. 1990	1,500
	William R. Poston	D	Jan. 1988	1,500
	Fred C. Skwirut	D/R	Jan. 1988	1,500
	Craig A. Negley, Sr....................	D	Jan. 1990	1,500
Treasurer..............................	Michael D. McKechnie	D	Jan. 1990	1% Coll.
Township Secretary....................	Faith A. Payne........................	Appt.		24,872

HATFIELD, Population 13,411   **Montgomery County**

Office	Name	Political Affiliation	Term Expires	Annual Salary
Chairman	Raymond N. Masser	R	Jan. 1988	$1,200
Vice Chairman	Gary D. Wampole	D	Jan. 1988	1,200
Commissioners.........................	Stanley L. Ogden	R	Jan. 1990	1,200
	Clyde J Roberts.......................	R	Jan. 1988	1,200
	John F. Norman.......................	R	Jan. 1988	1,200
Secretary/Manager....................	Sydney C. Brittin	Appt.	Jan. 1988	30,000

HAVERFORD, Population 52,349 (Home Rule)   **Delaware County**

Office	Name	Political Affiliation	Term Expires	Annual Salary
President................................	Stephen W. Campetti	R	Jan. 1988	$3,000
Vice President..........................	Wilton A. Bunce.......................	R	Jan. 1988	3,000
Commissioners.........................	John R. Genthert......................	R	Jan. 1988	3,000
	Rick L. DeAntoniis....................	R	Jan. 1990	3,000
	Frederick C. Moran	R	Jan. 1990	3,000
	John W. MacMurray	R	Jan. 1988	3,000
	Joseph F. Kelly	R	Jan. 1990	3,000
	Benjamin Kapustin	D	Jan. 1990	3,000
	John D. McDonald.....................	D	Jan. 1988	3,000
Auditor................................	Stephen M. Campetti	R	Jan. 1990	3,600

HOPEWELL, Population 14,662 — Beaver County

Office	Name	Political Affiliation	Term Expires	Annual Salary
President	James Albert	D	Jan. 1990	$1,500
Vice President	Tim Force	D	Jan. 1990	1,500
Commissioners	Fred Bologna	D	Jan. 1990	1,500
	Ross Damaso	D	Jan. 1988	1,500
	Vince D'Eramo	D	Jan. 1988	1,500

LOWER ALLEN, Population 14,077 — Cumberland County

Office	Name	Political Affiliation	Term Expires	Annual Salary
President	Richard F. Schin	R	Jan. 1990	$2,600
Vice President	Robert B. Roth	R	Jan. 1990	2,600
Commissioners	John J. Paulding	R	Jan. 1988	1,500
	Frank X. Burke	D	Jan. 1988	1,500
	Ambrose Klain	D	Jan. 1988	1,500
Treasurer	Raymond B. Martin	R	Jan. 1990	5,300

LOWER MERION, Population 59,651 — Montgomery County

Office	Name	Political Affiliation	Term Expires	Annual Salary
President	Charles F. Ward	R	Jan. 1990	$3,000
Vice President	Frank Lutz	R	Jan. 1990	3,000
Commissioners	Lita Indzel Cohen, Esq.	R	Jan. 1990	3,000
	Richard B. Cuff	R	Jan. 1990	3,000
	Calvin S. Drayer, Jr., Esq.	R	Jan. 1990	3,000
	Mark D. Newberger, Esq.	D	Jan. 1990	3,000
	Aram K. Jerrehian	R	Jan. 1988	3,000
	Ora R. Pierce	R	Jan. 1988	3,000
	Joseph M. Manko, Esq.	R	Jan. 1988	3,000
	Hester R. McCullough	R	Jan. 1988	3,000
	Edith N. Phelan	R	Jan. 1988	3,000
	Senton J. FitzPatrick	R	Jan. 1990	3,000
	Howard L. West, Jr.	R	Jan. 1990	3,000
	Gloria P. Wolek	R	Jan. 1988	3,000
Township Treasurer	C. Dale McClain	R	Jan. 1990	

LOWER MORELAND, Population 12,472 — Montgomery County

Office	Name	Political Affiliation	Term Expires	Annual Salary
President	Kurt G. Mayer	R	Jan. 1990	$2,600
Vice President	Austin Morris	R	Jan. 1988	1,500
Commissioners	Anthony P. Tinari	R	Jan. 1988	1,500
	Sara-jane Nedl	R	Jan. 1988	1,500
	Bernard Kanefsky	D	Jan. 1990	2,600
	Franklin A. Terry	R	Jan. 1990	2,600
Treasurer	Robert Slauch	R	Jan. 1990	2,600

MANHEIM, Population 26,042 — Lancaster County

Office	Name	Political Affiliation	Term Expires	Annual Salary
President	John B. Heroux	R	Jan. 1988	$2,400
Vice President	Leonard A. Steiner, Jr.	R	Jan. 1988	2,400
Commissioners	Walter H. Offermann	R	Jan. 1990	2,400
	Marcelline A. Woodson	R	Jan. 1990	2,400
	John S. Shirk	R	Jan. 1990	2,400

MARPLE, Population 23,642   Delaware County

Office	Name	Political Affiliation	Term Expires	Annual Salary
President	Jeanne Marie Cella	R	Jan. 1988	$3,000
Vice President	Louis Guerrera	R	Jan. 1990	3,000
Commissioners	Robert G. Jordan	R	Jan. 1990	3,000
	Barry C. Dozor	D	Jan. 1988	2,400
	John L. Butler	D	Jan. 1988	2,400
	Patricia A. Keates	R	Jan. 1988	2,400
	James S. Phillips	R	Jan. 1988	3,000

Town of McCANDLESS, Population 26,191 (Home Rule)   Allegheny County

Office	Name	Political Affiliation	Term Expires	Annual Salary
Councilmembers	Richard E. Parsons	R	Jan. 1988	$2,400
	Merrill E. Kline	R	Jan. 1990	2,400
	Robert J. Powers	R	Jan. 1990	2,400
	J. Howard Womsley	R	Jan. 1988	2,400
	Gerard J. Aufman, Jr.	R	Jan. 1990	2,400
	Harold W. Moores	R	Jan. 1988	2,400
	Roger A. Anderson	R	Jan. 1988	2,400

MT. LEBANON, Population 34,414 (Home Rule)   Allegheny County

Office	Name	Political Affiliation	Term Expires	Annual Salary
Commissioners	June S. Delano	D	Jan. 1990	$2,400
	James M. Delsole	R	Jan. 1990	2,400
	Edward J. Daly, Jr.	R	Jan. 1988	2,400
	Gregory M. Drahuschak	R	Jan. 1988	2,400
	Carolyn Byham	R	Jan. 1988	2,400
Treasurer	John C. Ferguson, Jr.	R	Jan. 1990	19,000

MUHLENBERG, Population 13,031   Berks County

Office	Name	Political Affiliation	Term Expires	Annual Salary
President	Glenn A. Yeager	R	Jan. 1988	$1,500
Commissioners	Herbert F. Henry	D	Jan. 1988	1,500
	Stephen J. Geras	D	Jan. 1988	1,500
	Charles E. McCann	D	Jan. 1990	2,600
	Franklin R. Shalter	D	Jan. 1990	2,600
Treasurer, Tax Collector	Thelma S. Napoletano	D	Jan. 1990	5,500*

*Township share

NETHER PROVIDENCE, Population 12,730   Delaware County

Office	Name	Political Affiliation	Term Expires	Annual Salary
Commissioners	Eugene Monaco	R	Jan. 1988	$1,500
	John R. Larkin	R	Jan. 1990	2,600
	Daniel R. Butler	R	Jan. 1988	1,500
	Joseph F. Mulcahy, Jr.	R	Jan. 1990	2,600
	Marie A. Hosler	D	Jan. 1988	1,500
	Virgil J. Mills	R	Jan. 1990	2,600
Tax Collector, Treasurer	Alfred McNerney	R	Jan. 1988	6,000

NORTH HUNTINGDON, Population 31,517

Westmoreland County

Office	Name	Political Affiliation	Term Expires	Annual Salary
President........................	Gerald P. Hagan	D	Jan. 1990	$3,500
Vice President.....................	David L. Beeler	D	Jan. 1988	3,000
Commissioners.....................	Phil Abbott........................	D	Jan. 1988	3,000
	Fred Batley	D	Jan. 1988	3,000
	Chester E. Ludwicki	D	Jan. 1990	3,500
	James M. Tempero	D	Jan. 1988	3,000
Treasurer........................	Lucille A. Eresh	D	Jan. 1990	10,000 +Comm.

NORTH VERSAILLES, Population 13,294

Allegheny County

Office	Name	Political Affiliation	Term Expires	Annual Salary
President........................	Robert Vuyanich	D	Jan. 1988	$1,500
Commissioners.....................	Victor Milko.......................	D	Jan. 1990	2,600
	Armond J. Matarazzo	D	Jan. 1988	1,500
	Andrea M. Graziano	D	Jan. 1990	2,600
	Paul A. Homonai....................	D	Jan. 1988	1,500
	Edward R. McGuire..................	D	Jan. 1990	2,600
	Frank J. Bivins.....................	D	Jan. 1988	1,500
Tax Collector	Anna McKay	D	Jan. 1990	7,500*

*Township share

PENN, Population 16,153

Westmoreland County

Office	Name	Political Affiliation	Term Expires	Annual Salary
Commissioners.....................	John W. Beech	D	Jan. 1990	$3,300
	Robert E. Geiger....................	D	Jan. 1990	3,300
	James A. Cortazzo	D	Jan. 1988	2,400
	J. Robeart Dodds	D	Jan. 1988	2,400
	Laura Lee Painter	D	Jan. 1988	2,400

PENN HILLS, Population 57,632 (Home Rule)

Allegheny County

Office	Name	Political Affiliation	Term Expires	Annual Salary
Mayor	Roy C. Ritenour....................	R	Jan. 1988	$4,800
Deputy Mayor	Robert L. Chambers	R	Jan. 1988	3,600
Councilmembers....................	Daisy Altenburger*	R	Jan. 1988	3,600
	Donald J. Sanker....................	R	Jan. 1988	3,600
	George Brenick.....................	D	Jan. 1990	3,600
Controller	Charles D. Pagano*	R	Jan. 1988	4,200
Manager	Harry R. McIndoe	Appt.		42,000

*appointed

PLAINS, Population 11,338

Luzerne County

Office	Name	Political Affiliation	Term Expires	Annual Salary
Chairman	Paul Motsko	D	Jan. 1988	$1,500
Vice Chairman	Louise Pesotski.....................	D	Jan. 1990	1,500
Commissioners.....................	Benjamin Berrini, Jr.	D	Jan. 1988	1,500
	Thomas Kubicki	D	Jan. 1988	1,500
	Arthur Fanelli......................	D	Jan. 1988	1,500
	Mary Conway	D	Jan. 1990	1,500
	Ralph Macaravage	D	Jan. 1988	1,500
	Baldino Vinciarelli..................	D	Jan. 1990	1,500
	Joseph Parada	D	Jan. 1990	1,500
Treasurer, Tax Collector.................	Richard J. Lussi....................	D	Jan. 1990	1,700

PLYMOUTH, Population 17,168 (Home Rule)   Montgomery County

Office	Name	Political Affiliation	Term Expires	Annual Salary
Chairman	John J. Washeleski	D	Jan. 1988	$2,000
Vice Chairman	Joan M. Grohoski	D	Jan. 1988	2,000
Councilmembers	William Culp	R	Jan. 1990	2,000
	John Russo	D	Jan. 1990	2,000
	William G. Zimmerman, Jr.	R	Jan. 1990	2,000

RADNOR, Population 27,676 (Home Rule)   Delaware County

Office	Name	Political Affiliation	Term Expires	Annual Salary
President	Graham D. Andrews	R	Jan. 1990	$2,100
Vice President	Curtis R. Nase	R	Jan. 1988	2,100
Commissioners	James J. Marks	R	Jan. 1988	2,100
	James C. Higgins	D	Jan. 1988	2,100
	George M. Aman, III	R	Jan. 1988	2,100
	John L. Cappelli	R	Jan. 1990	2,100
	Clinton A. Stuntebeck	R	Jan. 1990	2,100
Treasurer, Tax Collector	James F. Merriman	R	Jan. 1990	15,000

RIDLEY, Population 33,771   Delaware County

Office	Name	Political Affiliation	Term Expires	Annual Salary
President	Joseph P. Cronin, Jr., Esq.	R	Jan. 1990	$3,000
Vice President	Paul G. Mattus	R	Jan. 1988	3,000
Commissioners	Fiore Peticca	R	Jan. 1988	3,000
	Timothy J. Murtaugh	R	Jan. 1988	3,000
	Nancy M. Collins	D	Jan. 1990	3,000
	William L. McCrossan	R	Jan. 1988	3,000
	James J. Pentimall	R	Jan. 1990	3,000
	Peter T. Maginnis	R	Jan. 1990	3,000
	Paul Graf	R	Jan. 1988	3,000
Treasurer	Eleanor Doperak	R	Jan. 1990	5,000
Controller	Daniel E. Mingis	R	Jan. 1990	4,800

ROSS, Population 35,102   Allegheny County

Office	Name	Political Affiliation	Term Expires	Annual Salary
President	Arthur F. White	R	Jan. 1990	$4,000
Vice President	J. Robert McAfee	R	Jan. 1990	4,000
Commissioners	Robert C. Raida	R	Jan. 1988	3,000
	Thomas G. Lawlor	D	Jan. 1988	3,000
	Dr. Donald J. Wessel	R	Jan. 1988	3,000
	Mark A. Purcell	R	Jan. 1990	4,000
	Dr. William Locher	R	Jan. 1988	4,000
	Harry G. Menhorn, Jr.	D	Jan. 1990	4,000
	Molly Daly	R	Jan. 1988	3,000
Treasurer	Theodore A. Bartlett	R	Jan. 1990	10,000*
Auditors	Steven E. Pohl	R	Jan. 1988	800
	Paul H. Rettger	R	Jan. 1988	800
	Raymond Wilt, III	R	Jan. 1990	800
Manager	Robert J. Novak	Appt.		32,000

*Township share

ROSTRAVER, Population 11,430
Westmoreland County

Office	Name	Political Affiliation	Term Expires	Annual Salary
Commissioners	Robert E. Sokol	D	Jan. 1990	$1,200
	Henry M. Indof, Jr.	D	Jan. 1990	1,200
	Dennis C. Manown	D	Jan. 1988	1,200
	Francis Barch	D	Jan. 1988	1,200
	Nicholas Lorenzo, Jr.	D	Jan. 1988	1,200
Tax Collector	Violet M. Winstone	D	Jan. 1990	Comm.
Secretary/Manager	Andrew H. Solan*	D	Jan. 1988	30,000

*appointed

SALISBURY, Population 12,259
Lehigh County

Office	Name	Political Affiliation	Term Expires	Annual Salary
President	Francis Walter, Jr.	D	Jan. 1988	$1,500
Vice President	Janet B. Keim	D	Jan. 1990	2,600
Commissioners	Lloyd M. Peters	D	Jan. 1990	2,600
	Michael Hanuschak	D	Jan. 1988	1,500
	Alton Slane	R	Jan. 1988	1,500
Tax Collector, Treasurer	Linda J. Minger	D	Jan. 1990	Comm.

SCOTT, Population 20,413
Allegheny County

Office	Name	Political Affiliation	Term Expires	Annual Salary
Commissioners	Gerald McNamara	D	Jan. 1990	$3,300
	Domenic Colarosa	D	Jan. 1988	2,400
	Donald Diebold	D	Jan. 1988	2,400
	Richard Barrett	D	Jan. 1988	2,400
	Gerald Heyl	D	Jan. 1990	3,300
	Gloria Westcott	R	Jan. 1988	2,400
	Richard Fallon	D	Jan. 1990	3,300
	Harry Tinney	D	Jan. 1990	3,300
	Bennie Komosinski	D	Jan. 1988	2,400
Treasurer	Edward E. Stevens	D	Jan. 1990	5,000

SHALER, Population 33,712
Allegheny County

Office	Name	Political Affiliation	Term Expires	Annual Salary
Commissioners	Joe Gally	D	Jan. 1990	$3,000
	Robert Marko	R	Jan. 1990	3,000
	William Neely	D	Jan. 1988	3,000
	A. John Koehler	R	Jan. 1990	3,000
	Frank Orga	R	Jan. 1988	3,000
	Henry Janikowski	R	Jan. 1988	3,000
	Richard R. Cessar	R	Jan. 1988	3,000
Treasurer, Tax Collector	Richard J. Starr	D	Jan. 1990	10,000
Auditors	Virginia Dowling	D	Jan. 1990	800
	Norbert McDermott, Jr.	D	Jan. 1988	800
	John Kenst	R	Jan. 1992	800

SOUTH WHITEHALL, Population 15,919   Lehigh County

Office	Name	Political Affiliation	Term Expires	Annual Salary
President	Charles E. Mackenzie	R	Jan. 1988	$2,400
Vice President	Steven M. Okun	R	Jan. 1990	2,400
Commissioners	Elwood M. Bernhard	R	Jan. 1988	2,400
	Ethel F. Lichtenwalner	R	Jan. 1988	2,400
	Martha Nolan	R	Jan. 1988	2,400
Treasurer	Albert P. Haines	D	Jan. 1990	10,000
Secretary	Ronnie Rice	Appt.	Sept. 1987	

SPRING GARDEN, Population 11,127   York County

Office	Name	Political Affiliation	Term Expires	Annual Salary
President	Clarence H. Gotwalt	R	Jan. 1988	$1,500
Vice President	Joseph K. Bath	R	Jan. 1990	2,600
Commissioners	Earl D. Pipher	R	Jan. 1988	1,500
	Richard G. Pennell	R	Jan. 1988	1,500
	John N. Ports	R	Jan. 1990	2,600
Treasurer	Georgianna H. Scholl	R	Jan. 1990	1,800

SPRINGFIELD, Population 25,326   Delaware County

Office	Name	Political Affiliation	Term Expires	Annual Salary
President	Robert M. DiOrio, Esq.	R	Jan. 1990	$3,500
Vice President	Lee J. Janiczek	R	Jan. 1988	3,000
Commissioners	William F. Adolph, Jr.	R	Jan. 1988	3,000
	George A. Pagano	R	Jan. 1990	3,500
	Anthony J. Grosso	R	Jan. 1988	3,500
	Bernard E. Stein	D	Jan. 1988	3,000
	JoAnn Hunn	R	Jan. 1990	3,500
Auditors	Joseph C. Bowers	R	Jan. 1992	1,600
	Thomas J. Reardon	R	Jan. 1990	1,500
	Frank D. Giardini	R	Jan. 1988	1,500
Tax Collector, Treasurer	Albert C. Young	R	Jan. 1990	14,500

SPRINGFIELD, Population 20,344   Montgomery County

Office	Name	Political Affiliation	Term Expires	Annual Salary
President	Richard E. Buck	R	Jan. 1988	$2,000
Vice President	John C. Sommar	R	Jan. 1990	2,000
Commissioners	Roy D. Hanshaw	R	Jan. 1988	2,000
	Gerald H. Bell	R	Jan. 1988	2,000
	Joseph P. Phelps, Jr.	R	Jan. 1990	2,000
	Gary L. Croskey	D	Jan. 1990	2,000
	Henry Z. Shelton, Jr.	R	Jan. 1986	2,000
Treasurer	Peter Leis	R	Jan. 1990	8,500*

*Township share

SUSQUEHANNA, Population 18,034 — Dauphin County

Office	Name	Political Affiliation	Term Expires	Annual Salary
Commissioners	Jack S. Pincus	R	Jan. 1988	$2,400
	Charles B. Zwally	R	Jan. 1990	3,300
	Stanley R. Lawson	R	Jan. 1988	2,400
	J. Ronald Mowery	R	Jan. 1990	3,300
	John M. Micka	R	Jan. 1988	2,400
	Graham S. Hetrick	R	Jan. 1990	3,300
	James M. Klein	D	Jan. 1988	2,400
	Bertram H. Goldberg	R	Jan. 1990	3,300
	James D. Ross	D	Jan. 1988	2,400
Treasurer	Frank A. Allen	R	Jan. 1990	6,500

SWATARA, Population 18,796 — Dauphin County

Office	Name	Political Affiliation	Term Expires	Annual Salary
President	Nicholas M. Dininni	R	Jan. 1988	$2,400
Vice President	Dominick J. Costanza	R	Jan. 1990	3,300
Commissioners	Frank M. Cibort	R	Jan. 1988	2,400
	Robert E. Wagner	D	Jan. 1990	3,300
	Patricia A. Macut	R	Jan. 1988	2,400
	Paul R. Johnson	R	Jan. 1988	2,400
	Howard F. Randolph	R	Jan. 1990	3,300
	Anthony T. Spagnolo	D	Jan. 1988	2,400
	Francis L. Cadden	D	Jan. 1990	3,300
Treasurer, Tax Collector	Joseph L. Donato, Jr.	R	Jan. 1990	10,000

UPPER ALLEN, Population 10,533 — Cumberland County

Office	Name	Political Affiliation	Term Expires	Annual Salary
Commissioners	Ray E. Trimmer	R	Jan. 1988	$1,500
	Virginia M. Anderson	R	Jan. 1989	2,600
	William F. Kane	R	Jan. 1989	2,600
	John F. Allison	R	Jan. 1988	1,500
	Gerald F. Koons	R	Jan. 1988	1,500
Secretary-Manager	George R. Easton	Appt.		37,580
Assistant Manager	Jan Dell	Appt.		27,500
Township Solicitor	William E. Miller, Jr. Esq.	Appt.		varies
Township Engineer	Warren R. Sullivan	Appt.		33,200
Treasurer/Tax Collector	Marlin A. Yohn, Sr.	R	Jan. 1989	3,800
Township Assessor	Carol Keefer	Appt.	Jan. 1988	
Chief of Police	Clyde R. King	Appt.		32,350

UPPER CHICHESTER, Population 14,377 — Delaware County

Office	Name	Political Affiliation	Term Expires	Annual Salary
President	Thomas C. Roberts	R	Jan. 1990	$2,600
Vice President	Anne M. Denney	R	Jan. 1988	2,600
Commissioners	William E. Burland	R	Jan. 1988	2,600
	Edward E. Moore	R	Jan. 1990	2,600
	James J. Curry	R	Jan. 1988	2,600
Treasurer, Tax Collector	Michael J. Baker	R	Jan. 1988	4,250

UPPER DARBY, Population 84,054 (Home Rule) — Delaware County

Office	Name	Political Affiliation	Term Expires	Annual Salary
Mayor	James J. Ward	R	Jan. 1988	$10,000
Council President	John E. Clark	R	Jan. 1988	5,000
Vice President	Rudolph A. D'Alesio	R	Jan. 1990	5,000
Treasurer	Anthony L. Milone	R	Jan. 1990	10,000

UPPER DUBLIN, Population 22,348 — Montgomery County

Office	Name	Political Affiliation	Term Expires	Annual Salary
President	Patrick J. Zollo	R	Jan. 1988	$2,400
Vice President	Harry Lenz	R	Jan. 1988	2,400
Commissioners	James Bockius	R	Jan. 1990	3,300
	Norton A. Freedman	D	Jan. 1988	2,400
	W. Richard Webster	R	Jan. 1988	2,400
	Judith Herold	R	Jan. 1990	3,300
	Richard R. Rulon	R	Jan. 1990	3,300
Treasurer	Jean E. Nester	R	Jan. 1990	5,000
Manager/Secretary	Gregory N. Kelmick	Appt.	Jan. 1988	50,935

UPPER MORELAND, Population 25,874 — Montgomery County

Office	Name	Political Affiliation	Term Expires	Annual Salary
President	William C. Seiberlich, Jr.	R	Jan. 1990	$2,500
Vice President	Ian A. McGain	R	Jan. 1990	2,500
Commissioners	Donald Brecker	D	Jan. 1990	2,500
	Ned R. Nelson	R	Jan. 1988	2,000
	James J. Gould	R	Jan. 1988	2,000
	Michael Weinrich	R	Jan. 1988	2,000
	John E. Tarman, Jr.	R	Jan. 1990	2,500

UPPER ST. CLAIR, Population 19,023 (Home Rule) — Allegheny County

Office	Name	Political Affiliation	Term Expires	Annual Salary
Commissioners	David W. Knapp	R	Jan. 1988	$1,200
	Russell L. Crane	R	Jan. 1990	1,200
	Charles R. Molzer	R	Jan. 1988	1,200
	David B. Rice	R	Jan. 1990	1,200
	Edward S. Long, Jr	R	Jan. 1988	1,200
	Samuel O. Lemon	R	Jan. 1990	1,200
	Richard D. Faytinger	R	Jan. 1988	1,200
Township Manager	Douglas A. Watkins	Appt.		
Township Attorney	Robert N. Hackett	Appt.		

WEST NORRITON, Population 14,034 — Montgomery County

Office	Name	Political Affiliation	Term Expires	Annual Salary
Commissioners	Mark Chalphin	R	Jan. 1990	$2,600
	James J. Flannery	R	Jan. 1990	2,600
	Joseph G. Koegel	R	Jan. 1990	2,600
	Margaret A. Bailey	R	Jan. 1988	1,500
	Aloysius S. Banmiller	R	Jan. 1988	1,500
Treasurer	Edward R. Coughey	R	Jan. 1990	7,500
Auditors	Vacant			
	William E. Lessig	R	Jan. 1990	300
	Vacant			

WHITEHALL, Population 21,538 (Home Rule) Lehigh County

Office	Name	Political Affiliation	Term Expires	Annual Salary
President.	Richard L. Fahringer	D	Jan. 1988	$2,000
Vice President.	Michael K. M. Galomb.	D	Jan. 1990	2,600
Secretary.	George C. Trively.	D	Jan. 1988	2,600
Commissioners.	Clair D. Hunsberger	D	Jan. 1988	2,000
	Gerald J. Fabian	D	Jan. 1988	2,000
	John C. Wieand.	D	Jan. 1990	2,600
	Elizabeth L. Buchmiller	D	Jan. 1990	2,600
Township Executive.	Michael P. Harakal, Jr.	D	Jan. 1988	31,689
Assistant Township Executive	John Marcarelli	Appt.		33,110
Treasurer.	Marion E. Gownaris.	D	Jan. 1990	10,170

YORK, Population 16,893 York County

Office	Name	Political Affiliation	Term Expires	Annual Salary
President.	Robert R. Jacobs	R	Jan. 1988	$2,400
Vice President.	John M. McCullough	R	Jan. 1988	3,300
Commissioners.	Paul E. Saylor	R	Jan. 1988	2,400
	Emerson T. Knaper	R	Jan. 1990	3,300
	Richard L. Reinhardt.	R	Jan. 1988	3,300
Treasurer.	Augusta S. Petron.	R	Jan. 1990	1,500

SECOND CLASS TOWNSHIPS OVER 10,000 POPULATION*

BENSALEM, Population 52,399 Bucks County

Office	Name	Political Affiliation	Term Expires	Annual Salary
Chairman	Paul W. Rauer, Esq.	R	Jan. 1988	$25/mtg.
Vice Chairman	Joseph Francano, Jr.	R	Jan. 1992	25/mtg.
Supervisors.	Patricia Zajac	D	Jan. 1990	25/mtg.
	John J. Maher, Jr.	R	Jan. 1992	25/mtg.
	Mary V. Komada	D	Jan. 1990	25/mtg.
Tax Collector	Ray Wall	R	Jan. 1990	11,500**
Auditors.	John Honofsky	D	Jan. 1990	
	Jane Faust	R	Jan. 1988	
	John O'Hara	R	Jan. 1992	

**Township share

CANTON, Population 10,311 Washington County

Office	Name	Political Affiliation	Term Expires	Annual Salary
Supervisor, Chairman	Eugene Foster.	R	Jan. 1992	$2,600
Supervisor, Vice Chairman	Leroy Cimino.	D	Jan. 1988	25/mtg.
Supervisor.	Mike Kopko.	I	Jan. 1990	25/mtg.
Auditor, Chairman	William Weirich	D	Jan. 1988	20/mtg.
Auditor, Secretary	Freda Brock.	D	Jan. 1990	30/mtg.
Auditor.	Cora Mitchell.	D	Jan. 1992	30/mtg.
Secretary/Treasurer	Rosemary Zanol	Appt.		

*All population figures are U.S. Census Bureau 1980 tabulations.

CENTER, Population 10,733 — Beaver County

Office	Name	Political Affiliation	Term Expires	Annual Salary
Chairman	James R. Huff	D	Jan. 1992	0
Vice Chairman	Anthony Amadio	D	Jan. 1990	0
Supervisors	Fred Taddeo	D	Jan. 1988	0
	Frank Vescio	D	Jan. 1988	0
	William DiCioccio	D	Jan. 1990	0
Tax Collector	Arnold Trombetta	D	Jan. 1990	$4,000
Auditors	Bernie Novotny	D	Jan. 1992	
	Harry Gromo	D	Jan. 1990	

CRANBERRY, Population 11,066 — Butler County

Office	Name	Political Affiliation	Term Expires	Annual Salary
Chairman	Barry R. Webster	R	Jan. 1990	$25/mtg.
Vice Chairman	Ronald Kozlowski	R	Jan. 1992	75/mtg.
Supervisors	John Frances	D	Jan. 1988	25/mtg.
	Dennis Yarian	R	Jan. 1992	75/mtg.
	John Gullo	D	Jan. 1988	25/mtg.
Tax Collector	Deanne Woodling	D	Jan. 1990	3% Comm.
Wage Tax Collector	Berkheimer Assoc.	Appt.		
Auditors	Wilbur Robinson	R	Jan. 1988	4/hr.
	Keith Weyman	R	Jan. 1990	4/hr.
	William Salsgiver	D	Jan. 1992	4/hr.
Township Manager/Secretary	Sheldon K. Williams	Appt.		
Township Solicitor	Tucker Arensburg, P.C.	Appt.		

DERRY, Population 18,115 — Dauphin County

Office	Name	Political Affiliation	Term Expires	Annual Salary
Chairman	Kathryn S. Taylor	R	Jan. 1990	$25/mtg.
Vice Chairman	Charles W. Staudenmeier	R	Jan. 1990	25/mtg.
Supervisors	Norman A. Fisher	R	Jan. 1991	25/mtg.
	Thomas R. Embich	R	Jan. 1988	25/mtg.
	Ralph G. Fisher	R	Jan. 1988	25/mtg.
Township Manager	Michael R. Schneider	Appt.		39,500

DERRY, Population 16,193 — Westmoreland County

Office	Name	Political Affiliation	Term Expires	Annual Salary
Chairman	Edward W. Ankney	D	Jan. 1990	$23,000
Supervisors	Steven Kozar	D	Jan. 1992	23,000
	Aldo Razza	D	Jan. 1988	23,000
Auditors	John Fiorina	D	Jan. 1992	1,200
	William Lipinsky	D	Jan. 1989	0
	Albert Matteo	D	Jan. 1989	0
Tax Collector	David Matrunick	D	Jan. 1990	11,000

DOVER, Population 12,589 — York County

Office	Name	Political Affiliation	Term Expires	Annual Salary
Supervisors	Fredrick E. Dentler	R	Jan. 1990	per mtg.
	Donald J. Deitz	D	Jan. 1988	per mtg.
	Donald L. Keener	R	Jan. 1992	1,500
Manager	Leon B. Lankford	Appt.		30,301
Secretary-Treasurer	Betty A. Shoemaker	Appt.		20,203
Zoning Officer & SEO	Gurney O. Gross	Appt.		21,042
Codes Enforcement Inspector	Carl D. Miller	Appt.		20,203
Auditors	Carl S. Fry, Sr.	R	Jan. 1988	per mtg.
	Charles A. Rauhauser	D	Jan. 1990	per mtg.
	Alice M. Snelbaker	D	Jan. 1992	per mtg.
Tax Collector	Wayne E. Spangler	R	Jan. 1990	Comm.

DOYLESTOWN, Population 11,824 — Bucks County

Office	Name	Political Affiliation	Term Expires	Annual Salary
Chairman	Walter J. Conti, Jr.	R	Jan. 1990	$2,600
Vice Chairman	John T. Carson, Jr.	R	Jan. 1992	2,600
Supervisors	C. Morell Brown	R	Jan. 1988	1,350
	Adelaide F. Coyle	R	Jan. 1990	1,350
	Jeffrey M. Williams	R	Jan. 1988	2,600
Manager, Secretary, Treasurer, Zoning Officer	David R. Jones	Appt.	Jan. 1988	40,000
Tax Collector	Margaret S. Hall	R	Jan. 1990	3,000
Auditor, Chairman	Joseph P. Hart	R	Jan. 1990	1,000
Auditor, Secretary	Rick Gaver	R	Jan. 1992	1,000
Auditor, Member	Anna Marie Walsh	R	Jan. 1988	1,000

EAST GOSHEN, Population 10,021 — Chester County

Office	Name	Political Affiliation	Term Expires	Annual Salary
Supervisors	E. Martin Shane	R	Jan. 1991	$650/qtr.
	Anthony G. Iacovelli	R	Jan. 1988	25/mtg.
	John Chatley, III.	R	Jan. 1988	25/mtg.
	Melvin C. Johnson	R	Jan. 1989	25/mtg.
	Thomas E. Tawney	R	Jan. 1989	25/mtg.
Auditors	Raymond Mikolajczyk	R	Jan. 1988	
	Gordon Whiting, Jr.	R	Jan. 1990	
	Robert H. Scott	R	Jan. 1992	
Tax Collector	Dolores Hassler	R	Jan. 1990	
District Justice 15-2-05	John R. Blackburn	R	Jan. 1988	

EAST HEMPFIELD, Population 15,152 — Lancaster County

Office	Name	Political Affiliation	Term Expires	Annual Salary
Supervisors	Edward G. Myers	R	Jan. 1990	$25/mtg.
	Fred G. Geiger, Jr.	R	Jan. 1992	3,300
	Jack A. Bidding	R	Jan. 1988	3,300
	Noel S. Dorwart*	R	Jan. 1988	3,300
	Philip E. Bomberger, III	R	Jan. 1990	25/mtg.
Tax Collector	Carol W. Etter	R	Jan. 1990	Comm.
Auditors	Kenneth Beard	R	Jan. 1990	20/day
	W. Scott Stoner	R	Jan. 1988	20/day
	Richard S. Yarnell	R	Jan. 1992	20/day

*appointed

EAST NORRITON, Population 12,711   **Montgomery County**

Office	Name	Political Affiliation	Term Expires	Annual Salary
Chairman	John B. Gourley	R	Jan. 1990	$25/mtg.
Vice Chairman	Herman J. Marks	R	Jan. 1988	2,600
Supervisor	John W. Fichter	R	Jan. 1992	2,600
Tax Collector	Louis J. Mincarelli	R	Jan. 1990	Comm.

EXETER, Population 14,419   **Berks County**

Office	Name	Political Affiliation	Term Expires	Annual Salary
Chairman	Jean M. Berg	D	Jan. 1988	$25/mtg.
Vice Chairman	John L. DeFrees	R	Jan. 1990	52/mtg.
Supervisors (Treasurer)	Harold E. Boone	D	Jan. 1988	25/mtg.
	Linda K. Buler	R	Jan. 1992	52/mtg.
	William H. Becker	D	Jan. 1990	25/mtg.
Tax Collector	Charles I. Diamond	D	Jan. 1990	Comm.
Auditors	Helen Weidner	R	Jan. 1988	30/day
	Marlene E. Moore	R	Jan. 1988	30/day
	Christine A. Jenkins	D	Jan. 1988	30/day

FAIRVIEW, Population 11,941   **York County**

Office	Name	Political Affiliation	Term Expires	Annual Salary
Supervisors	Charles J. Bender, Jr.	R	Jan. 1990	$25/mtg.
	Herbert C. Shoffner	R	Jan. 1988	25/mtg.
	Robert J. Seybold	R	Jan. 1992	200/mo.
Auditors	Edith M. Cline	R	Jan. 1992	30/mtg.
	Raymond W. Fisher	R	Jan. 1990	30/mtg.
	Elwood Wylie	R	Jan. 1988	30/mtg.
Tax Collector	Clifford M. Bailets	R	Jan. 1990	3.7% Comm.

FALLS, Population 36,083   **Bucks County**

Office	Name	Political Affiliation	Term Expires	Annual Salary
Chairman	Keith Gowton	D	Jan. 1992	25/mtg.
Vice Chairman	Holly A. Moyer	D	Jan. 1992	25/mtg.
Supervisors	Charles C. Chimera	D	Jan. 1988	25/mtg.
	Richard Goulding	D	Jan. 1990	25/mtg.
Secretary-Treasurer	Charles E. Kochersperger, III*	D	Jan. 1988	25/mtg.
Manager	David P. Cooper*	I	Jan. 1988	$43,200

*appointed

GREENE, Population 11,470   **Franklin County**

Office	Name	Political Affiliation	Term Expires	Annual Salary
Supervisors	Richard P. Kramer	R	Jan. 1990	$25/mtg.
	Charles D. Jamison, Jr.	D	Jan. 1992	25/mtg.
	Ralph D. Cook	D	Jan. 1988	25/mtg.
Auditors	Harold F. Gsell	R	Jan. 1990	200
	Frederick S. Kraiss	R	Jan. 1992	200
	Robert M. Hargleroad	R	Jan. 1988	200
Tax Collector	Kathy Frazer	R	Jan. 1988	0
Assessor	Harold L. Strock	D	Jan. 1992	0*

*Assessor is paid by County.

GUILFORD, Population 10,567 — Franklin County

Office	Name	Political Affiliation	Term Expires	Annual Salary
Supervisors	Michael A. Helman	D	Jan. 1990	$10/hr.
	James E. Bower	R	Jan. 1988	10/hr.
	John W. Rife	R	Jan. 1988	10/hr.
Secretary	Gregory L. Cook	Appt.		21,300

HAMPTON, Population 14,260 (Home Rule) — Allegheny County

Office	Name	Political Affiliation	Term Expires	Annual Salary
Councilmembers	James Hammer	R	Jan. 1988	$15/mtg.
	Gloria Newman	D	Jan. 1990	15/mtg.
	Arthur Secor	R	Jan. 1988	15/mtg.
	Frank Hardt	R	Jan. 1990	15/mtg.
	Donald Wolfe	R	Jan. 1990	15/mtg.
Controller	Marion G. King	R	Jan. 1988	500

HARBORCREEK, Population 14,644 — Erie County

Office	Name	Political Affiliation	Term Expires	Annual Salary
Supervisors	Donna L. Mindek	D	Jan. 1992	$28,202
	Marvin L. Akerly	R	Jan. 1988	7,463
	James Sonney	R	Jan. 1990	28,202
Auditors	Donald Burnett	R	Jan. 1988	30/mtg.
	Leonard E. Rodland	R	Jan. 1988	30/mtg.
	Susan Carver	D	Jan. 1988	30/mtg.

HEMPFIELD, Population 43,396 — Westmoreland County

Office	Name	Political Affiliation	Term Expires	Annual Salary
Supervisors	Joseph Svetkovich	D	Jan. 1992	$4,000
	Donald DeNezza	D	Jan. 1988	4,000
	A. Virginia Lohr	D	Jan. 1988	25/mtg.
	Robert Wile	D	Jan. 1990	25/mtg.
	Thomas Beaufort	R	Jan. 1990	25/mtg.

HORSHAM, Population 15,959 (Home Rule) — Montgomery County

Office	Name	Political Affiliation	Term Expires	Annual Salary
Council President	Gloria M. Calise	R	Jan. 1990	$2,000
Vice President	Alan C. Walter	R	Jan. 1988	1,500
Parliamentarian	Daren D. Miller	R	Jan. 1988	2,000
Treasurer	Joseph A. Hari	R	Jan. 1988	1,500
Council Secretary	Edward F. Lehr	R	Jan. 1990	2,000

LANCASTER, Population 10,833 — Lancaster County

Office	Name	Political Affiliation	Term Expires	Annual Salary
Chairman, Supervisors	Willard E. Landis	R	Jan. 1992	$2,400
Vice Chairman & Secretary	Clarence J. Randolph	R	Jan. 1990	2,400
Treasurer, Supervisors	Alice M. Bertzfield	R	Jan. 1989	2,400
Asst. Sec./Treas., Twp. Manager	Karen L. Koncle	Appt.	Jan. 1988	23,500
Tax Collector	County Treasurer's Office			
Auditor, Chairman	Harry Weisman	R	Jan. 1988	25/mtg.
Auditor, Secretary	Harry R. Frey	R	Jan. 1990	30/mtg.
Auditor, Member	Ruth Hawkins	R	Jan. 1992	30/mtg.

LOGAN, Population 12,183 — Blair County

Office	Name	Political Affiliation	Term Expires	Annual Salary
Supervisors	Joseph L. Lynch	R	Jan. 1990	$6,504
	Daniel D. Horner	R	Jan. 1988	6,504
	Vaul E. Rouzer	R	Jan. 1992	6,504

LOWER MACUNGIE, Population 12,958 — Lehigh County

Office	Name	Political Affiliation	Term Expires	Annual Salary
Chairman, Supervisors	Kenneth J. M. Dorney	R	Jan. 1988	$25/mtg.
Vice Chairman, Supervisors	Robert E. Lee, P.E.	R	Jan. 1992	216/mo.
Secretary, Supervisors	Marilyn L. Jones	R	Jan. 1990	25/mtg.

LOWER MAKEFIELD, Population 17,351 — Bucks County

Office	Name	Political Affiliation	Term Expires	Annual Salary
Supervisors	Henry S. Miiller	R	Jan. 1990	$1,350
	Ruth B. Hoyt	R	Jan. 1988	1,350
	Grace M. Godshalk	R	Jan. 1990	1,350
	Daniel F. Rattigan	R	Jan. 1988	1,350
	Sidney H. Lehmann	D	Jan. 1992	1,350

LOWER PAXTON, Population 34,830 — Dauphin County

Office	Name	Political Affiliation	Term Expires	Annual Salary
Supervisors	Jane D. Marfizo	R	Jan. 1988	$25/mtg.
	H. Michael Liptak	R	Jan. 1992	4,000
	Richard N. Koch	R	Jan. 1992	4,000
	James L. Snyder	R	Jan. 1990	25/mtg.
	Carl C. Lentz	R	Jan. 1988	25/mtg.

LOWER PROVIDENCE, Population 18,945 — Montgomery County

Office	Name	Political Affiliation	Term Expires	Annual Salary
Chairman	Charles J. Eskie	R	Jan. 1990	$25/mtg.
Vice Chairman	Richard Brown	R	Jan. 1988	25/mtg.
Supervisors	Mary Ralston	R	Jan. 1988	25/mtg.
	John C. Rafferty, Jr.	R	Jan. 1992	250/mo.
	Nancy McFarland	R	Jan. 1992	250/mo.
Tax Collector	Robert Love	R	Jan. 1990	9,000
Auditors	Thomas Ertell	R	Jan. 1990	30/mtg.
	Douglas H. Swart	R	Jan. 1992	30/mtg.
	Catherine P. Weigand	R	Jan. 1988	30/mtg.

LOWER SOUTHAMPTON, Population 18,305 — Bucks County

Office	Name	Political Affiliation	Term Expires	Annual Salary
Chairman	Daniel Fraley	R	Jan. 1988	$575
Vice Chairman	William Hull	R	Jan. 1992	3,100
Secretary-Treasurer	Charles Raudenbush, Jr.	R	Jan. 1992	3,850
Supervisors	Dennis M. O'Brien	R	Jan. 1990	575
	Susanne McKeon	R	Jan. 1990	3,100
Auditors	Sheila Barsky	R	Jan. 1992	0
	Nancy Reisig	R	Jan. 1988	0
	Robert Duggan	R	Jan. 1990	0
Tax Collector	Priscilla Lee	D	Jan. 1992	Comm.

LOYALSOCK, Population 10,763 — Lycoming County

Office	Name	Political Affiliation	Term Expires	Annual Salary
Supervisors	Richard C. Haas	R	Jan. 1990	$25/mtg.
	Bruce E. Henry	R	Jan. 1988	25/mtg.
	William C. Reighard	R	Jan. 1992	50/mtg.
	Donald L. Garver	R	Jan. 1992	50/mtg.
	Lynn C. Womer Jr.	R	Jan. 1990	25/mtg.
Auditors	Harold J. Mulliner	R	Jan. 1988	400
	Jack O. Bender	D	Jan. 1990	425
	George A. Richner, Jr.	R	Jan. 1992	400
Tax Collector	John P. Nittinger	R	Jan. 1990	1% Coll.

MANOR, Population 11,474 — Lancaster County

Office	Name	Political Affiliation	Term Expires	Annual Salary
Supervisors	Edward C. Goodhart III	R	Jan. 1992	$2,600
	Robert K. Aichele	R	Jan. 1988	25/mtg.
	Lester E. Eckman	R	Jan. 1988	2,600

MIDDLETOWN, Population 36,472 — Bucks County

Office	Name	Political Affiliation	Term Expires	Annual Salary
Supervisors	Robert J. Brann	D	Jan. 1990	$25/mtg.
	Thomas R. Kearns	D	Jan. 1990	25/mtg.
	Raymond P. Mongillo	D	Jan. 1988	25/mtg.
	Mark S. Schweiker	R	Jan. 1992	4,000
	George R. Marcellus	R	Jan. 1992	4,000
Auditors	Robert W. Hillis	D	Jan. 1990	0
	Howard Marx	D	Jan. 1992	0
	Paul E. Coleman, Jr.	D	Jan. 1988	0
Tax Collector	Robert H. Saunders	D	Jan. 1990	18,500

MIDDLETOWN, Population 12,463 (Home Rule) — Delaware County

Office	Name	Political Affiliation	Term Expires	Annual Salary
Chairman	John J. Laskas, Jr.	R	Jan. 1990	$1,000
Vice Chairman	Lawrence E. Hartley	R	Jan. 1988	1,000
Councilmembers	Kenneth C. Ferro	R	Jan. 1988	1,000
	Douglas Roger	R	Jan. 1990	1,000
	Thomas J. Butler	R	Jan. 1988	1,000
	Norman Shropshire	R	Jan. 1990	1,000
	Eva V. Beechler	R	Jan. 1988	1,000
Auditors	Cheston M. Gilday, Jr.	R	Jan. 1988	8/hr.
	Russell Waters	R	Jan. 1990	8/hr.
	J. Karl Thomas	R	Jan. 1992	8/hr.

MILLCREEK, Population 44,303 — Erie County

Office	Name	Political Affiliation	Term Expires	Annual Salary
Supervisors	Arthur F. Detisch	R	Jan. 1992	$30,090
	George S. Pulakos	D	Jan. 1990	30,090
	Paul J. Martin	R	Jan. 1988	31,860

MOON, Population 20,935   **Allegheny County**

Office	Name	Political Affiliation	Term Expires	Annual Salary
Chairman	Jack W. Wise	D	Jan. 1990	$25/mtg.
Vice Chairperson	Clara L. Shemmer	D	Jan. 1990	25/mtg.
Supervisors	Al Berardi	D	Jan. 1988	25/mtg.
	Edwin L. Nelson	R	Jan. 1988	25/mtg.
	Frank J. Mahr	D	Jan. 1992	3,300
Auditors	Bryce C. Billetdeaux	D	Jan. 1988	800
	Ellsworth Williams	D	Jan. 1990	1,200
	Joseph Falbo	D	Jan. 1990	1,200
Tax Collector	Martin T. Grogan	D	Jan. 1990	32,000
Township Manager	Gregory G. Smith	Appt.		42,000
Assistant Manager	Gerald F. Bunda	Appt.		33,000

MT. PLEASANT, Population 11,851   **Westmoreland County**

Office	Name	Political Affiliation	Term Expires	Annual Salary
Supervisors	Thomas E. Homulka	D	Jan. 1990	$25/mtg.
	Andrew L. Lipko	D	Jan. 1992	25/mtg.
	Walter W. Witek	D	Jan. 1988	25/mtg.
Auditor	Frank E. Tomechko	D	Jan. 1988	1,200
	Clarence E. Gorinski	D	Jan. 1988	1,200
	Stephen P. Mizak	D	Jan. 1992	1,200
Tax Collector	Helen B. Schachte	D	Jan. 1990	% Coll.
Secretary-Treasurer	Raymond E. Zimmerman	Appt.	Jan. 1988	25/mtg.

NEWBERRY, Population 10,047   **York County**

Office	Name	Political Affiliation	Term Expires	Annual Salary
Chairman	Reid Thomas	R	Jan. 1992	$25/mtg.
Vice Chairman	Marvin M. Brothers	R	Jan. 1988	25/mtg.
Supervisor	David T. Altland	R	Jan. 1990	25/mtg.
Tax Collector	Wayne Kohr	R	Jan. 1990	Comm.
Auditors	Paul S. Lentz	R	Jan. 1988	20/day
	Gethron Reeser	R	Jan. 1990	30/day
	Beatrice Wintrode	R	Jan. 1992	30/day
Manager	Henry W. Clemens	Appt.		29,300

NEWTOWN, Population 11,775   **Delaware County**

Office	Name	Political Affiliation	Term Expires	Annual Salary
Supervisors	Joseph L. Crawford	R	Jan. 1990	$25/mtg.
	Edward M. Corse	R	Jan. 1988	25/mtg.
	David E. Dunn	R	Jan. 1992	2,600
	Paul E. Russell*	R	Jan. 1990	2,600
	E. Coe Williams	R	Jan. 1992	2,600
Tax Collector	Diana Cucchi	R	Jan. 1992	5,800
Auditors	Robert O'Connel	R	Jan. 1990	20/mtg.
	Anne Mallon Curran	R	Jan. 1988	20/mtg.
	Sylvan Gatti	R	Jan. 1992	20/mtg.

*appointed

NORTHAMPTON, Population 27,392 — Bucks County

Office	Name	Political Affiliation	Term Expires	Annual Salary
Chairman	Peter F. Palestina	R	Jan. 1990	$25/mtg.
Vice Chairman	Steven H. Benner	R	Jan. 1992	1,200
Secretary	George F. Komelasky	R	Jan. 1992	1,200
Treasurer	Fred W. Little	R	Jan. 1988	25/mtg.
Supervisor	Albert Wiley, Jr.	R	Jan. 1990	25/mtg.
Tax Collector	Mildred Peterson	R	Jan. 1986	17,680
Auditors	James T. Devenney	R	Jan. 1992	0
	Paul Heise	R	Jan. 1990	0
	Susan Friedman	R	Jan. 1988	0
Township Manager	D. Bruce Townsend			

NORTH UNION, Population 13,561 — Fayette County

Office	Name	Political Affiliation	Term Expires	Annual Salary
Supervisors	Stanley Kumor	D	Jan. 1988	$25/mtg.
	Carmen Galderisi	D	Jan. 1990	25/mtg.
	John Mateosky	D	Jan. 1992	25/mtg.
Tax Collector	Robert Kouach	D	Jan. 1990	% Coll.
Auditors	Walter Matthews	D	Jan. 1992	1,200
	Robert Bodnar	D	Jan. 1990	1,200
	Donald Santore	D	Jan. 1988	800

PALMER, Population 13,926 — Northampton County

Office	Name	Political Affiliation	Term Expires	Annual Salary
Chairman	H. Robert Daws	R	Jan. 1990	$25/mtg.
Vice Chairman	Paul C. Kocher	D	Jan. 1992	650/qtr.
Supervisors	Charles W. Fuller	D	Jan. 1988	25/mtg.
	Eston Morgan	D	Jan. 1990	25/mtg.
Public Works Form	Donald E. Campbell	R	Jan. 1992	650/qtr.
Secretary/Treasurer	Virginia S. Rickert	Appt.		28,255
Auditors	Earl Snyder	D	Jan. 1992	20/mtg.
	Charles Trux	R	Jan. 1988	20/mtg.
	Jeff Young	D	Jan. 1990	30/mtg.
Tax Collector	William F. Voight, Jr.	R	Jan. 1990	% Coll.

PETERS, Population 13,104 (Home Rule) — Washington County

Office	Name	Political Affiliation	Term Expires	Annual Salary
Chairman	O. Forrest Morgan, Jr.	R	Jan. 1988	$25/mtg.
Vice-Chairman	Jacqueline L. Campbell	R	Jan. 1990	25/mtg.
Councilmembers	Henry S. Wacker	R	Jan. 1988	25/mtg.
	John L. Richards	R	Jan. 1988	25/mtg.
	Robert J. Lewis	R	Jan. 1990	25/mtg.
	Raymond L. Mason	R	Jan. 1990	25/mtg.
	Harry R. Obley	R	Jan. 1990	25/mtg.
Tax Collector	Edwin L. Snee, Jr.	R	Jan. 1990	24,948

RICHLAND, Population 12,899 — Cambria County

Office	Name	Political Affiliation	Term Expires	Annual Salary
Supervisors	Walter J. Mattern	R	Jan. 1988	$25/mtg.
	Paul J. Shiley	D	Jan. 1990	25/mtg.
	James E. Eyler, Jr.	R	Jan. 1992	52/mtg.
	Ralph E. Mulhollen	R	Jan. 1990	25/mtg.
	Melvyn D. Wingard	R	Jan. 1992	52/mtg.
Auditors	Stephen Seifert	D	Jan. 1990	1,200
	Barry Ott	R	Jan. 1992	1,200
	Donald Lehman	R	Jan. 1992	1,200
Tax Collector	Glenn O. Hershberger	R	Jan. 1990	Comm.

SOUTH PARK, Population 13,535 — Allegheny County

Office	Name	Political Affiliation	Term Expires	Annual Salary
Chairman	Joseph H. Ehrenberger	D	Jan. 1992	$2,600
Vice Chairman	William Obricki	R	Jan. 1988	25/mtg.
Member, Board of Supervisors	Susan Yablonsky	D	Jan. 1990	25/mtg.
Tax Collector	David Buchewicz	D	Jan. 1990	6,000
Auditors	John Caldwell		Jan. 1992	30/day
	Alan J. Caponi	D	Jan. 1990	30/day
	Robert Quinlan	D	Jan. 1988	30/day

SOUTH UNION, Population 10,992 — Fayette County

Office	Name	Political Affiliation	Term Expires	Annual Salary
Supervisor/Secretary-Treasurer	Thomas Frankhouser	D	Jan. 1990	$29,000
Supervisors	Rock Coville	D	Jan. 1988	27,000
Treasurer	Robert Schiffbauer	D	Jan. 1992	29,000
Auditors	John R. Gaddis	D	Jan. 1992	800
	Walter Boskovich	D	Jan. 1990	1,200
	William Arnold	D	Jan. 1988	800
Tax Collector	Robert Nichols	D	Jan. 1992	3% Comm.

SPRING, Population 17,193 — Berks County

Office	Name	Political Affiliation	Term Expires	Annual Salary
Supervisors	James E. Keiser	R	Jan. 1990	$25/mtg.
	John E. Leber	R	Jan. 1992	100/mo.
	Walter H. Diehm	R	Jan. 1990	25/mtg.
	William B. Myers	R	Jan. 1992	100/mo.
	Kevin G. Bitz	R	Jan. 1988	25/mtg.
Tax Collector	Lillian B. Cramsey	R	Jan. 1990	Comm.
Auditors	John S. Miller	R	Jan. 1992	30
	Alfred P. Large	R	Jan. 1992	30
	Robert W. Boltz	R	Jan. 1988	30

SPRINGETTSBURY, Population 19,687 — York County

Office	Name	Political Affiliation	Term Expires	Annual Salary
Supervisors	Albert H. Spinner	R	Jan. 1992	$3,300
	James A. Deitch	R	Jan. 1990	3,300
	Roger H. Shultz	R	Jan. 1992	3,300
	Robert A. Minnich	R	Jan. 1988	25/mtg.
	Donald L. Shultz	R	Jan. 1990	25/mtg.
Auditors	John R. Dorgan	R	Jan. 1991	30/day
	Edward P. Lyons	R	Jan. 1991	30/day
Tax Collector	Margaret Cousler	R	Jan. 1990	% Coll.

TOWAMENCIN, Population 11,112   Montgomery County

Office	Name	Political Affiliation	Term Expires	Annual Salary
Township Manager	Cecile M. Daniel	Appt.		$28,896
Secretary & Treasurer	Cecile M. Daniel	Appt.		
Building & Zoning Inspector	Bryon Law	Appt.		37,700
Chairman	Michael J. Becker	R	Jan. 1992	2,600
Supervisors	Colin Hannings	R	Jan. 1990	25/mtg.
	Thomas J. Ciesielka	R	Jan. 1988	25/mtg.
	Charles J. O'Reilly	D	Jan. 1992	2,600
	Edward J. Furman	R	Jan. 1990	2,600
Tax Collector	Marion Newman	R	Jan. 1988	2.3% Comm.
Auditors	Karl F. Trupp	Appt.	Jan. 1988	30/hr.
	Paul Caracciolo	Appt.	Jan. 1988	30/hr.
	Ron Curll	Appt.		30/hr.
Sewer Assessor	John L. Krupp	Appt.		7%
Solicitor	Frank Jenkins	Appt.		2,000/mo.

TREDYFFRIN, Population 23,019 (Home Rule)   Chester County

Office	Name	Political Affiliation	Term Expires	Annual Salary
Chairman	Tracy C. Massey	R	Jan. 1990	$1,500
Vice Chairman	Paul W. Olson	R	Jan. 1990	1,500
Supervisors	Herbert G. Keene, Jr.	R	Jan. 1988	1,500
	William Scott Magargee, III	R	Jan. 1988	1,500
	Herbert W. Greenwood	R	Jan. 1988	1,500
	Leonard A. Lubking	R	Jan. 1990	1,500
Auditor	Richard Veith	R	Jan. 1988	1,200

UNITY, Population 19,976   Westmoreland County

Office	Name	Political Affiliation	Term Expires	Annual Salary
Chairman	Thomas B. Yazvec	D	Jan. 1990	26,000
Vice Chairman	C. Tom Baughman	D	Jan. 1988	26,000
Supervisors	John E. Goodman	D	Jan. 1992	26,000
Auditors	Merle L. Musick	D	Jan. 1990	1,200
	Harry Miller	D	Jan. 1988	1,200
	Michael J. O'Barto	D	Jan. 1992	1,200
Tax Collector	Mark J. Burkardtl	D	Jan. 1990	Comm.

UPPER MERION, Population 26,138   Mongtomery County

Office	Name	Political Affiliation	Term Expires	Annual Salary
Chairman	Ralph P. Volpe	R	Jan. 1988	25/mtg.
Vice Chairman	William M. Smith	R	Jan. 1990	25/mtg.
Supervisors	Lydia Garcia	R	Jan. 1992	70/mtg.
	Hunter R. Robinson	R	Jan. 1988	25/mtg.
	Van Weiss	R	Jan. 1992	70/mtg.
Tax Collector	Edward T. Peterson	R	Jan. 1990	10,000
Auditors	John A. Paciello	R	Jan. 1990	0
	Maurice Levin	R	Jan. 1988	0
	Nathan L. Diamond	R	Jan. 1992	0

UPPER SOUTHAMPTON, Population 15,806 Bucks County

Office	Name	Political Affiliation	Term Expires	Annual Salary
Chairman	Charles H. Martin	R	Jan. 1990	$25/mtg.
Vice Chairman	Thomas L. Farrington	R	Jan. 1992	25/mtg.
Supervisors	Gerald Crandley	R	Jan. 1991	33/mtg.
	Frank Settle	D	Jan. 1988	25/mtg.
	David Shafter	R	Jan. 1990	25/mtg.
Auditors	A. Thomas Mitchell	R	Jan. 1992	800
	Emil Frank Dzara	R	Jan. 1992	800
	Geoffry Thompson	R	Jan. 1988	800
Tax Collector	Hanni Pozsky	R	Jan. 1988	6,050

WARMINSTER, Population 35,543 Bucks County

Office	Name	Political Affiliation	Term Expires	Annual Salary
Chairman	William Davis	R	Jan. 1988	$1,250
Vice Chairman	Thomas W. Lisowski	R	Jan. 1992	4,000
Secretary/Treasurer	Carl J. Messina	D	Jan. 1990	1,250
Supervisors	Christopher Staub	R	Jan. 1992	4,000
	Raymond J. Regan	D	Jan. 1990	1,250
Tax Collector	Kathleen Hodgkinson	D	Jan. 1990	10,000
Auditors	Joseph Swartz	R	Jan. 1992	30/yr.
	George Rounds	D	Jan. 1988	30/yr.
	Ethel Travis	R	Jan. 1990	30/yr.

WARRINGTON, Population 10,704 Bucks County

Office	Name	Political Affiliation	Term Expires	Annual Salary
Chairman	Randolph A. Scott*	R	Jan. 1988	$50/mtg.
Vice Chairman	Frank L. Shelly	R	Jan. 1988	25/mtg.
Supervisors	Carol M. Butterworth*	R	Jan. 1988	50/mtg.
	Ruth V. Ramins	D	Jan. 1992	50/mtg.
	John R. Paul	D	Jan. 1992	50/mtg.
Township Manager	Teresa S. Thomas	Appt.		37,500

*appointed

WEST DEER, Population 10,897 (Home Rule) Allegheny County

Office	Name	Political Affiliation	Term Expires	Annual Salary
Chairman	Thomas DeMartini	D	Jan. 1988	$ 0
Vice Chairman	Catherine Kurtiak	D	Jan. 1988	0
Supervisors	Nick DeVita	D	Jan. 1990	0
	James McCaskey	D	Jan. 1988	0
	Matthew Arena	R	Jan. 1988	0
	William Thomas	D	Jan. 1990	0
	Orlando Yaconis	D	Jan. 1990	0
Tax Collector	Michael Yaconis	D	Jan. 1990	9,478
Auditors	Shirley Catanese	D	Jan. 1990	1,200
	Barbara Catanese	D	Jan. 1992	1,200
	Vacant			

All West Deer officials are appointed.

WEST GOSHEN, Population 16,164 — Chester County

Office	Name	Political Affiliation	Term Expires	Annual Salary
Supervisors	Robert E. Lambert	R	Jan. 1990	$25/mtg.
	J. Leon Hagerty	R	Jan. 1992	1,600
	Richard Cloud	R	Jan. 1988	1,600
Tax Collector	Anne Cavanaugh	R	Jan. 1990	Comm.
Auditors	James L. Mosteller	R	Jan. 1990	20/mtg.
	John Crego	R	Jan. 1988	20/mtg.
	Gary D. See	D	Jan. 1992	20/mtg.

WEST MANCHESTER, Population 12,728 — York County

Office	Name	Political Affiliation	Term Expires	Annual Salary
Supervisors	Michael J. March	D	Jan. 1988	$100/mo.
	N. Christopher Menges	D	Jan. 1992	100/mo.
	Thomas Mitchell	D	Jan. 1990	100/mo.
Tax Collector	Robert W. Miller	D	Jan. 1990	.35/bill
Auditors	Benjamin LePore, Jr.	R	Jan. 1990	30/day
	Carl Smyser	D	Jan. 1988	20/day
	Lewis McCleaf	R	Jan. 1992	30/day

WHITE, Population 13,177 — Indiana County

Office	Name	Political Affiliation	Term Expires	Annual Salary
Chairman	Rocco Yanity	R	Jan. 1992	$50/mtg.
Supervisors	Robert V. Brady	R	Jan. 1988	25/mtg.
	Clyde Little	R	Jan. 1992	50/mtg.
	Luther Elkin	R	Jan. 1988	25/mtg.
	Clifford P. Fleming	R	Jan. 1990	25/mtg.
Secretary/Treasurer	Anna M. Willis*	R	Jan. 1988	24,154
Tax Collector	Robert L. Marker	R	Jan. 1990	
Auditors	Martha Yachisko	R	Jan. 1990	30/day
	Mona Beatty	R	Jan. 1992	30/day
	Ivan McGee	R	Jan. 1988	30/day
Township Manager	Ford Buterbaugh	R		33,123

*appointed

WHITEMARSH, Population 15,101 (Home Rule) — Montgomery County

Office	Name	Political Affiliation	Term Expires	Annual Salary
Chairman	Robert Wiser	R	Jan. 1988	$2,500
Vice Chairman	John S. Gabel	R	Jan. 1988	2,500
Supervisors	John P. McCarthy	R	Jan. 1990	2,500
	E. Charles Pellegrini	R	Jan. 1990	2,500
	Robert G. Gordon	R	Jan. 1988	2,500
Tax Collector/Finance Officer	John Donnelly			

WHITPAIN, Population 11,772 — Montgomery County

Office	Name	Political Affiliation	Term Expires	Annual Salary
Chairman, Supervisor	Leigh P. Narducci	R	Jan. 1990	$25/mtg.
Vice Chairman	Albert Lewullis	R	Jan. 1992	75/mtg.
Secretary	James Woods	R	Jan. 1988	25/mtg.
Treasurer	Martin Wurzer, Jr.	R	Jan. 1990	25/mtg.
Assistant Secretary	William Dewald	R	Jan. 1992	75/mtg.
Tax Collector	Susan Dunn	R	Jan. 1990	7,000
Auditors	Richard J. Schmalbach	R	Jan. 1990	20/mtg.
	Benedict Iarovetti	R	Jan. 1992	20/mtg.
	Anthony O. DeMarco	R	Jan. 1988	20/mtg.
Township Manager	Phyllis C. Lieberman	Appt.		44,000

ELECTIONS

SECTION 7 — ELECTIONS

ELECTION GUIDE
GENERAL INFORMATION

The Secretary of State, or as he or she has been called in Pennsylvania, the Secretary of the Commonwealth, is the chief election officer of the Commonwealth.

The Bureau of Elections, supervised by the Commissioner of Elections, performs the administrative election functions for the Secretary of the Commonwealth. These functions include duties related to campaign expense reporting, voter registration, absentee balloting, candidate requirements and election legislation. The Bureau of Elections has available an election guide which briefly describes the electoral process, a voter registration brochure which highlights important procedures as well as election calendars which list important dates.

Both the Constitution of the United States and the Constitution of Pennsylvania contain provisions concerning the voter and elections. Article XV of the United States Constitution declares: "The right of citizens of the United States to vote shall not be denied or abridged by the United States or by any state on account of race, color, or previous condition of servitude." Congress is given the power to enforce this article by appropriate legislation.

In the bill of rights, the Constitution of Pennsylvania states that elections are to be free and equal, and that no power, civil or military, shall interfere to prevent the free exercise of the right of suffrage. The Constitution also enumerates the qualifications for voting. Every citizen eighteen years of age is eligible to vote if he or she has been a citizen of the United States at least one month, has resided in the state thirty days immediately preceding the election and has resided in the appropriate election district thirty days preceding the election. In a 1971 opinion handed down by the Attorney General of Pennsylvania, college students are permitted under state law to vote in the locality at which they are attending a college or university.

Other constitutional provisions relate to election days, offices to be filled by election, rights of electors, bribery of electors, election and registration laws, voting machines, violation of election laws, election districts, election officers, contested elections, and absentee voting.

Outside of constitutional provisions, the General Assembly has the power to enact legislation on voting and elections. The substantial bulk of such legislation is contained in the Registration and Election Codes of the Commonwealth. A further amplification of election law is made by the courts in their interpretations of constitutional and statutory provisions in the light of actual cases of violation which comes before them.

REGISTRATION FOR PRIMARY ELECTION
May 20, 1986

COUNTIES	REPUBLICAN Women	Men	Total	DEMOCRATIC Women	Men	Total	CONSUMER Women	Men	Total
Adams...........	7,658	7,346	15,004	5,916	5,224	11,140	2	3	5
Allegheny	112,542	96,497	209,039	291,770	238,805	530,575	205	215	420
Armstrong.........	8,171	7,269	15,440	9,013	8,197	17,210	1	2	3
Beaver...........	14,644	12,756	27,400	36,896	32,618	69,514	87	78	165
Bedford..........	6,771	6,216	12,987	4,662	4,342	9,004	0	0	0
Berks............	27,464	25,484	52,948	39,291	35,830	75,121	62	37	99
Blair.............	16,598	14,577	31,175	11,051	8,878	19,929	7	7	14
Bradford	8,991	8,292	17,283	4,005	3,509	7,514	3	7	10
Bucks	63,093	61,324	124,417	57,512	48,032	105,544	21	41	62
Butler	16,425	15,042	31,467	17,527	15,449	32,976	10	23	33
Cambria	14,881	12,764	27,645	28,770	25,542	54,312	2	4	6
Cameron.........	985	865	1,850	808	714	1,522	0	0	0
Carbon	5,125	4,892	10,017	6,576	5,958	12,534	0	1	1
Centre...........	13,068	14,106	27,174	11,104	9,954	21,058	0	0	0
Chester..........	50,612	47,567	98,179	24,256	18,653	42,909	55	35	90
Clarion	4,870	4,432	9,302	4,690	4,197	8,887	0	3	3
Clearfield........	8,606	7,983	16,589	9,318	8,392	17,710	0	1	1
Clinton..........	3,285	3,182	6,467	3,206	3,004	6,210	3	2	5
Columbia.........	5,882	5,264	11,146	7,778	6,908	14,686	0	4	4
Crawford........	11,036	10,038	21,074	9,321	8,227	17,548	1	1	2
Cumberland	26,064	23,649	49,713	15,254	12,785	28,039	5	12	17
Dauphin	32,654	28,708	61,362	20,774	16,197	36,971	43	33	76
Delaware.........	114,137	102,098	216,235	48,086	34,412	82,498	111	75	186
Elk..............	3,017	2,921	5,938	5,389	4,974	10,363	0	1	1
Erie	24,252	22,576	46,828	41,139	35,850	76,989	5	8	13
Fayette	7,468	6,527	13,995	28,081	25,506	53,587	3	0	3
Forest	692	681	1,373	547	496	1,043	1	1	2
Franklin.........	12,826	11,891	24,717	9,029	8,450	17,479	2	5	7
Fulton	1,329	1,390	2,719	1,354	1,303	2,657	0	0	0
Greene	1,907	1,785	3,692	7,775	7,059	14,814	0	0	0
Huntingdon	5,486	5,006	10,492	3,529	3,141	6,670	4	4	8
Indiana	10,230	9,177	19,407	10,224	8,719	18,943	5	8	13
Jefferson.........	5,889	5,201	11,090	4,751	4,217	8,968	0	1	1
Juniata	2,603	2,425	5,028	1,983	1,907	3,890	0	0	0
Lackawanna	19,348	16,603	35,951	43,624	37,189	80,813	0	1	1
Lancaster	52,285	50,045	102,330	21,863	17,669	39,532	11	19	30
Lawrence	10,355	8,879	19,234	16,191	13,947	30,138	7	4	11
Lebanon	14,300	13,607	27,907	6,745	6,157	12,902	1	4	5
Lehigh...........	26,940	25,697	52,637	32,433	27,886	60,319	28	24	52
Luzerne..........	32,483	28,914	61,397	49,809	43,321	93,130	0	0	0
Lycoming	13,681	12,416	26,097	10,784	9,296	20,080	1	1	2
McKean..........	6,565	5,791	12,356	3,352	2,925	6,277	0	2	2
Mercer..........	12,696	11,195	23,891	16,499	14,495	30,994	5	9	14
Mifflin	4,452	4,010	8,462	3,792	3,337	7,129	0	0	0
Monroe	7,093	6,575	13,668	7,468	6,616	14,084	2	2	4
Montgomery	105,454	98,654	204,108	56,962	42,623	99,585	68	56	124
Montour..........	1,889	1,571	3,460	1,795	1,473	3,268	1	0	1
Northampton......	16,781	16,115	32,896	30,725	27,125	57,850	44	11	55
Northumberland	11,131	10,016	21,147	11,266	9,453	20,719	1	3	4
Perry...........	5,228	5,060	10,288	2,580	2,240	4,820	2	1	3
Philadelphia	102,935	92,921	195,856	455,481	364,465	819,946	2,068	1,421	3,489
Pike..............	3,194	2,974	6,168	1,993	1,824	3,817	0	0	0
Potter	2,665	2,441	5,106	1,509	1,377	2,886	0	0	0
Schuylkill.........	21,910	19,676	41,586	15,586	13,279	28,865	1	3	4
Snyder..........	4,959	4,687	9,646	1,697	1,645	3,342	0	0	0
Somerset.........	10,276	9,263	19,539	9,753	8,998	18,751	0	0	0
Sullivan	946	843	1,786	718	709	1,427	0	0	0
Susquehanna	5,730	5,300	11,030	3,210	2,893	6,103	1	1	2
Tioga............	6,523	5,877	12,400	2,700	2,383	5,083	0	1	1
Union	4,182	3,984	8,166	1,929	1,667	3,596	0	3	3
Venango	7,931	7,164	15,095	5,985	5,278	11,263	5	3	8
Warren	5,967	5,570	11,537	4,613	3,984	8,597	2	0	2
Washington........	13,818	12,241	26,059	38,822	34,021	72,843	0	0	0
Wayne...........	5,445	5,015	10,460	2,415	2,234	4,649	0	0	0
Westmoreland......	25,899	22,446	48,345	64,262	58,190	122,452	15	22	37
Wyoming..........	3,940	3,634	7,574	1,845	1,580	3,425	0	0	0
York.............	33,172	32,436	65,608	30,347	27,335	57,682	8	9	17
TOTALS	**1,249,434**	**1,141,551**	**2,390,985**	**1,740,118**	**1,455,063**	**3,195,181**	**2,909**	**2,212**	**5,121**

Official election results reported in this section were supplied by the Pennsylvania State Bureau of Elections.

REGISTRATION FOR PRIMARY ELECTION
May 20, 1986

| OTHER PARTIES | | | ALL PARTIES TOTAL | | | Total Voting Districts | Voting Machine Districts | Electronic Equipment Districts |
Women	Men	Total	Grand Total	Women	Men			
745	766	1,511	27,660	14,321	13,339	49	0	0
19,079	21,219	40,298	780,332	432,596	356,736	1,302	1,302	0
508	601	1,109	33,762	17,693	16,069	74	0	74
1,799	2,306	4,105	101,184	53,426	47,758	155	0	155
262	279	541	22,532	11,695	10,837	42	0	0
3,709	4,052	7,761	135,929	70,526	65,403	188	188	0
1,183	1,199	2,382	53,500	28,839	24,662	119	0	119
527	630	1,157	25,964	13,526	12,438	61	0	61
8,927	9,610	18,537	248,560	129,553	119,007	272	272	0
1,817	1,953	3,770	68,246	35,779	32,467	79	0	79
956	1,178	2,134	84,097	44,609	39,488	201	0	98
53	78	131	3,503	1,846	1,657	10	0	0
334	457	791	23,343	12,035	11,308	46	46	0
2,315	2,898	5,213	53,445	26,487	25,958	85	0	85
7,436	7,232	14,668	155,846	82,359	73,487	190	0	190
363	420	783	18,975	9,923	9,052	51	0	51
538	702	1,240	35,540	18,462	17,078	70	0	70
254	259	513	13,195	6,748	6,447	37	17	0
520	519	1,039	26,875	14,180	12,695	66	0	66
625	764	1,389	40,013	20,983	19,030	67	44	0
2,578	2,825	5,403	83,172	43,901	39,271	89	89	0
3,038	3,225	6,263	104,672	56,509	48,163	142	0	142
9,501	9,654	19,155	318,074	171,835	146,239	395	395	0
256	293	549	16,851	8,662	8,189	35	0	0
2,665	3,055	5,720	129,550	68,061	61,489	152	152	0
727	786	1,513	69,098	36,279	32,819	112	112	0
29	39	68	2,486	1,269	1,217	11	0	0
1,525	1,538	3,063	45,266	23,382	21,884	70	0	70
60	83	143	5,519	2,743	2,776	13	0	0
166	169	335	18,841	9,828	9,013	48	0	0
278	289	576	17,737	9,297	8,440	58	0	0
1,030	1,166	2,196	40,559	21,489	19,070	77	0	77
344	365	708	20,767	10,984	9,783	72	0	0
106	133	239	9,157	4,692	4,465	20	0	0
1,433	1,516	2,949	119,714	64,405	55,309	241	241	0
5,928	5,993	11,921	153,813	80,087	73,726	193	193	0
841	1,025	1,866	51,249	27,394	23,855	105	0	105
1,123	1,263	2,386	43,200	22,169	21,031	54	54	0
4,191	4,561	8,752	121,760	63,592	58,168	146	146	0
1,583	1,720	3,303	157,830	83,875	73,955	317	317	0
836	1,069	1,906	48,084	25,302	22,782	86	43	0
312	360	672	19,307	10,229	9,078	43	39	0
1,131	1,293	2,424	57,324	30,331	26,992	112	106	0
243	264	507	16,098	8,487	7,611	30	29	0
1,248	1,291	2,539	30,295	15,811	14,484	36	36	0
12,159	12,584	24,743	328,560	174,643	153,917	358	358	0
230	210	440	7,169	3,915	3,254	15	0	15
2,830	3,151	5,981	96,782	50,380	46,402	134	134	0
599	645	1,253	43,123	22,997	20,126	94	94	0
333	333	668	15,779	8,143	7,636	33	0	33
13,549	14,351	27,900	1,047,191	574,033	473,158	1,795	1,795	0
425	422	867	10,852	5,612	5,240	14	14	0
89	133	222	8,214	4,263	3,951	34	0	0
952	1,022	1,974	72,429	38,449	33,980	177	0	0
198	222	420	13,408	6,854	6,554	27	0	0
484	534	1,018	39,308	20,513	18,795	68	0	68
56	55	111	3,327	1,720	1,607	15	0	0
329	388	717	17,852	9,270	8,582	43	20	0
288	341	629	18,113	9,511	8,602	46	0	0
439	401	840	12,605	6,550	6,055	25	0	26
580	665	1,245	27,611	14,501	13,110	74	0	74
564	646	1,210	21,346	11,146	10,200	42	28	0
1,770	2,079	3,849	102,751	54,410	48,341	205	0	205
339	335	674	15,783	8,199	7,584	37	37	0
3,868	4,203	8,071	178,905	94,044	84,861	307	307	0
211	239	460	11,459	6,006	5,453	30	0	0
3,654	3,999	7,653	130,960	67,181	63,779	144	144	0
137,078	148,085	285,163	5,876,450	3,129,539	2,746,911	9,539	6,752	1,862

GOVERNOR OF PENNSYLVANIA
Primary Election, May 20, 1986

COUNTIES	REPUBLICAN William W. Scranton	DEMOCRATIC Edward G. Rendell	Steve Douglas	Bob Casey	CONSUMER Bill W. Thorn, Sr.
Adams............	3,334	567	257	1,774	0
Allegheny........	45,833	48,782	8,476	119,194	35
Armstrong........	4,622	2,151	282	3,571	0
Beaver...........	6,908	5,928	1,449	18,484	6
Bedford..........	4,739	753	141	1,919	0
Berks............	8,854	10,468	1,102	8,670	2
Blair............	9,311	2,643	293	3,934	3
Bradford	3,614	150	136	1,343	0
Bucks	28,125	18,123	761	9,964	0
Butler	6,763	1,921	585	5,060	0
Cambria	7,784	5,654	659	19,445	0
Cameron.........	587	174	29	349	0
Carbon	2,061	629	132	2,658	0
Centre...........	5,189	2,421	174	2,466	3
Chester..........	16,626	4,869	307	4,639	1
Clarion	2,573	861	190	1,774	0
Clearfield.........	4,856	2,134	235	4,280	0
Clinton...........	1,524	539	72	925	0
Columbia.........	2,377	492	174	3,586	0
Crawford.........	7,776	2,328	398	2,441	0
Cumberland	14,905	1,599	548	6,612	1
Dauphin	14,357	1,996	372	7,093	5
Delaware.........	47,342	17,223	1,403	9,165	29
Elk..............	1,924	1,279	301	2,924	0
Erie	9,645	9,064	1,524	9,357	0
Fayette	3,693	5,773	632	14,705	0
Forest	476	140	26	192	0
Franklin..........	2,758	327	258	1,694	0
Fulton	697	162	81	620	0
Greene	1,193	1,554	342	3,838	0
Huntingdon	2,861	690	70	1,167	0
Indiana	5,134	1,630	195	3,967	0
Jefferson.........	4,939	1,045	174	2,548	0
Juniata	1,209	198	92	851	0
Lackawanna	6,773	2,160	218	30,747	0
Lancaster	15,887	1,896	469	4,445	2
Lawrence	6,313	2,767	773	7,277	0
Lebanon	8,391	1,001	253	2,376	3
Lehigh...........	8,370	7,006	641	5,226	0
Luzerne..........	18,930	2,891	699	35,211	3
Lycoming	5,377	742	306	3,296	0
McKean..........	3,173	445	155	930	0
Mercer...........	5,630	2,321	512	5,211	0
Mifflin	1,807	369	123	967	0
Monroe	3,307	1,128	217	2,916	0
Montgomery	35,550	17,272	845	7,260	9
Montour..........	750	77	39	806	0
Northampton......	4,657	6,676	682	6,344	0
Northumberland ...	4,419	1,238	210	6,473	0
Perry............	2,404	188	97	990	0
Philadelphia	42,561	148,386	3,614	68,838	215
Pike.............	1,714	104	57	481	0
Potter	1,510	140	142	526	0
Schuylkill.........	8,944	1,388	273	6,229	0
Snyder...........	2,271	121	66	661	0
Somerset.........	5,774	1,604	206	5,094	0
Sullivan..........	520	85	27	461	0
Susquehanna	3,861	226	92	2,060	1
Tioga............	3,428	190	151	1,040	0
Union	1,805	198	46	657	0
Venango	3,639	803	187	1,827	2
Warren	2,718	672	183	1,205	0
Washington........	6,237	7,302	1,353	18,109	0
Wayne...........	3,885	180	59	1,517	0
Westmoreland......	10,751	17,087	1,795	28,393	3
Wyoming.........	3,088	97	39	1,317	0
York.............	18,258	4,512	1,896	9,277	0
TOTALS	**537,381**	**385,539**	**38,295**	**549,376**	**323**

LIEUTENANT GOVERNOR OF PENNSYLVANIA
Primary Election, May 20, 1986

COUNTIES	REPUBLICAN Mike Fisher	DEMOCRATIC Dwight Evans	DEMOCRATIC Tom Flaherty	DEMOCRATIC Mark Singel	CONSUMER Lance S. Haver
Adams............	3,048	474	1,385	594	0
Allegheny	44,099	17,580	65,792	84,528	31
Armstrong........	4,437	466	2,819	2,660	0
Beaver...........	6,643	2,552	11,459	11,501	8
Bedford..........	4,411	159	502	2,126	0
Berks............	8,899	3,353	9,617	3,972	2
Blair.............	6,199	464	1,534	4,569	3
Bradford	3,366	264	786	436	0
Bucks	25,367	7,824	10,194	5,276	0
Butler	5,050	674	3,512	3,329	0
Cambria	6,192	857	1,610	23,460	0
Cameron.........	531	44	229	262	0
Carbon	1,879	454	1,168	1,484	0
Centre...........	3,654	739	1,476	2,539	3
Chester..........	15,687	3,288	3,548	2,236	1
Clarion	2,383	211	1,404	1,156	0
Clearfield.........	4,428	223	1,273	5,133	0
Clinton...........	1,385	180	733	529	0
Columbia.........	1,355	721	1,376	1,799	0
Crawford.........	6,826	778	3,205	894	0
Cumberland	13,879	1,309	3,365	3,588	1
Dauphin	13,106	1,634	3,408	4,030	5
Delaware.........	43,304	7,733	8,760	6,197	18
Elk..............	1,826	246	1,940	2,252	0
Erie	8,840	3,106	12,185	3,559	0
Fayette	3,244	1,429	7,022	10,854	0
Forest	422	42	199	111	0
Franklin..........	1,767	403	987	779	0
Fulton	633	98	245	492	0
Greene	1,067	622	2,597	2,410	0
Huntingdon.......	2,609	187	574	1,054	0
Indiana	4,809	254	1,423	4,022	0
Jefferson.........	4,571	216	1,411	2,099	0
Juniata	1,145	177	597	310	0
Lackawanna	5,861	2,309	4,763	21,778	0
Lancaster	15,369	1,466	3,232	1,688	3
Lawrence	5,923	839	6,252	3,559	0
Lebanon	7,479	583	1,993	696	3
Lehigh...........	7,616	2,636	5,819	3,001	0
Luzerne..........	15,256	4,308	7,042	22,083	3
Lycoming	5,001	621	2,290	1,264	0
McKean..........	2,828	184	947	316	0
Mercer...........	5,282	883	4,208	2,555	0
Mifflin	1,637	168	666	571	0
Monroe	2,912	717	1,639	1,254	0
Montgomery	32,238	8,626	8,057	5,120	7
Montour..........	481	112	375	383	0
Northampton......	4,194	2,900	5,845	3,364	0
Northumberland	3,932	686	2,798	3,345	0
Perry............	2,070	203	661	344	0
Philadelphia	37,714	107,598	34,283	37,257	210
Pike.............	1,566	103	266	220	0
Potter	1,395	106	513	150	0
Schuylkill.........	8,371	1,299	3,210	3,068	0
Snyder...........	2,074	129	347	341	0
Somerset.........	5,305	235	763	5,880	0
Sullivan	482	92	220	209	0
Susquehanna	3,516	292	739	1,268	0
Tioga............	3,167	202	652	449	0
Union	1,551	163	378	304	0
Venango	2,615	259	1,648	836	2
Warren	2,461	257	1,384	315	0
Washington.......	5,875	2,036	11,173	12,940	0
Wayne...........	3,308	244	612	710	0
Westmoreland......	10,126	3,234	17,393	24,591	2
Wyoming.........	2,833	222	582	541	0
York.............	16,357	2,751	8,081	2,965	0
TOTALS	**483,856**	**205,224**	**307,166**	**363,605**	**302**

UNITED STATES SENATOR
Primary Election, May 20, 1986

COUNTIES	REPUBLICAN Richard A. Stokes	REPUBLICAN Arlen Specter	DEMOCRATIC Bob Edgar	DEMOCRATIC George R. H. Elder	DEMOCRATIC Cyril E. Sagan	DEMOCRATIC Don Bailey	CONSUMER Thelma R. Hambright
Adams.	1,271	2,116	1,421	136	47	1,054	0
Allegheny	11,579	36,400	63,327	6,768	4,176	95,565	28
Armstrong.	1,175	3,644	1,590	327	134	3,901	0
Beaver.	1,748	5,640	6,259	1,711	1,950	15,560	9
Bedford	1,092	3,750	589	129	53	1,959	0
Berks.	2,146	6,906	11,279	2,013	777	4,659	2
Blair.	2,013	7,788	2,778	303	122	3,524	3
Bradford	979	2,664	531	125	69	830	0
Bucks	5,754	23,651	19,351	767	425	6,343	1
Butler	2,435	5,084	2,321	878	639	3,589	0
Cambria	1,884	6,294	5,341	645	303	18,997	0
Cameron.	141	467	135	54	15	320	0
Carbon	451	1,745	1,051	112	96	2,052	0
Centre.	1,327	3,993	2,788	156	79	1,989	4
Chester	3,648	13,404	7,426	143	100	2,005	1
Clarion	842	1,847	760	438	76	1,453	0
Clearfield.	1,103	3,990	2,479	352	178	3,448	0
Clinton.	274	1,281	678	65	29	746	0
Columbia.	494	1,877	1,431	183	104	2,416	0
Crawford	1,730	6,318	1,588	1,060	129	2,404	0
Cumberland	5,757	9,988	3,853	271	153	4,549	1
Dauphin	3,652	11,396	4,194	332	197	4,549	6
Delaware.	10,599	41,579	25,112	702	457	2,813	27
Elk.	585	1,425	1,264	441	134	2,542	0
Erie	1,563	8,569	8,286	2,756	517	7,624	0
Fayette	870	2,957	4,150	543	356	14,667	0
Forest	101	388	110	63	7	170	0
Franklin.	1,038	1,748	769	198	95	1,172	0
Fulton	227	498	234	65	34	485	0
Greene	263	954	1,639	209	106	3,670	0
Huntingdon	584	2,094	545	87	35	1,196	0
Indiana	1,488	3,942	1,744	185	79	3,666	0
Jefferson.	1,356	3,808	923	327	80	2,349	0
Juniata	271	970	341	76	18	685	0
Lackawanna	1,372	5,801	8,473	968	953	17,407	0
Lancaster	6,495	10,614	3,426	298	198	2,980	2
Lawrence	1,952	4,707	2,395	785	3,589	4,059	0
Lebanon	2,387	6,630	1,623	193	76	1,777	3
Lehigh.	1,735	7,053	7,294	547	294	4,040	0
Luzerne	3,935	15,673	12,389	2,379	1,505	16,789	3
Lycoming	1,419	4,188	1,601	318	137	2,244	0
McKean.	1,063	2,163	595	261	78	566	0
Mercer.	1,741	4,113	1,813	2,445	478	3,073	0
Mifflin	434	1,430	534	112	31	780	0
Monroe	764	2,646	1,572	238	138	1,900	0
Montgomery	8,507	30,361	19,847	818	533	3,576	12
Montour.	184	590	257	47	24	544	0
Northampton.	972	3,855	7,448	635	360	4,409	0
Northumberland	1,205	3,549	2,242	453	214	4,059	0
Perry	902	1,523	340	56	26	817	0
Philadelphia	9,014	40,381	138,828	7,929	3,586	41,891	258
Pike.	526	1,235	245	46	24	297	0
Potter	459	1,071	239	141	37	346	0
Schuylkill.	1,895	7,430	2,391	284	235	4,652	0
Snyder.	573	1,782	275	51	17	495	0
Somerset.	1,566	4,304	1,084	125	68	5,488	0
Sullivan	119	404	197	28	16	313	0
Susquehanna	853	3,184	689	110	83	1,465	0
Tioga.	1,195	2,250	564	126	84	543	0
Union	423	1,412	448	44	19	399	0
Venango	971	2,815	905	617	116	1,102	2
Warren	831	2,005	765	386	114	803	1
Washington.	1,447	4,923	6,970	910	576	17,632	0
Wayne.	992	3,014	508	86	45	1,003	0
Westmoreland.	2,819	8,492	13,548	1,370	659	31,496	3
Wyoming.	569	2,712	526	55	40	727	0
York.	5,914	13,138	6,622	1,182	456	7,837	0
TOTALS	135,673	434,623	432,940	46,663	26,569	408,460	366

U.S. CONGRESS
Primary Election, May 20, 1986

Dist.	Party	Name	Votes
		Philadelphia	
1st	Rep.	Anthony J. Mucciolo	8,190
	Dem.	*Thomas M. Foglietta	40,443
		James J. Tayoun	25,253
		Bernard Salera	1,158
2nd	Dem.	*William H. Gray, III.	75,829
		Denise M. Henderson	2,455
3rd	Rep.	Robert A. Rovner	21,385
		Charles F. Dougherty	10,466
	Dem.	*Robert A. Borski	58,902
		Jack C. Holton	2,198

Armstrong, Beaver, Butler, Indiana, Lawrence and Westmoreland

Dist.	Party	Name	Votes
4th	Rep.	Al Lindsay	17,750
		Merle L. Pears	7,557
	Dem.	*Joseph P. Kolter	33,599
		Frank M. Clark	4,632
		Sam Blancato	3,208

Chester, Delaware and Montgomery

Dist.	Party	Name	Votes
5th	Rep.	*Richard T. Schulze	27,632
	Dem.	Tim Ringgold	8,058
		Donald Hadley	3,732

Berks, Carbon, Lancaster and Schuylkill

Dist.	Party	Name	Votes
6th	Rep.	Norm Bertasavage	17,431
	Dem.	*Gus Yatron	27,249

Delaware and Philadelphia

Dist.	Party	Name	Votes
7th	Rep.	Curt Weldon	40,156
	Dem.	Bill Spingler	14,067
		David Landau	12,903
		Bob Moran	1,918
		Wayne R. Long	359

Bucks and Montgomery

Dist.	Party	Name	Votes
8th	Rep.	David A. Christian	28,167
	Dem.	*Peter H. Kostmayer	26,861
		Beth Biancosino	1,789
		Richard M. Barnes	990

Bedford, Blair, Cambria, Clearfield, Cumberland, Franklin, Fulton, Huntingdon, Juniata and Mifflin

Dist.	Party	Name	Votes
9th	Rep.	*Bud Shuster	28,368
	Dem.	Bud Shuster	2,232

Bradford, Clinton, Lackawanna, Monroe, Pike, Potter, Susquehanna, Tioga, Wayne and Wyoming

Dist.	Party	Name	Votes
10th	Rep.	*Joseph M. McDade	30,632
	Dem.	Robert C. Bolus	21,561
		George Eddleston, Jr.	11,268

Carbon, Columbia, Luzerne, Monroe, Montour, Northumberland and Sullivan

Dist.	Party	Name	Votes
11th	Rep.	Marc Holtzman	22,185
	Dem.	*Paul E. Kanjorski	49,726
		Daniel Russell Fisher	3,013

Armstrong, Cambria, Somerset and Westmoreland

Dist.	Party	Name	Votes
12th	Rep.	Kathy Holtzman	18,577
	Dem.	*John P. Murtha	44,280
		Christopher G. Lewis	10,412

Montgomery and Philadelphia

Dist.	Party	Name	Votes
13th	Rep.	*Lawrence Coughlin	29,275
	Dem.	Joseph M. Hoeffel	22,744
		John E. Scheetz	3,337

Allegheny

Dist.	Party	Name	Votes
14th	Dem.	*William J. Coyne	56,581
		Gary T. Forrest	9,429

Lehigh, Monroe and Northampton

Dist.	Party	Name	Votes
15th	Rep.	*Don Ritter	13,485
	Dem.	Joe Simonetta	14,119
		Charles Buss	5,256
		William R. Logue	3,599

Chester, Lancaster and Lebanon

Dist.	Party	Name	Votes
16th	Rep.	*Robert S. Walker	26,902
	Dem.	James D. Hagelgans	7,340
		Michael T. Neal	3,455

Dauphin, Lycoming, Northumberland, Perry, Snyder and Union

Dist.	Party	Name	Votes
17th	Rep.	*George W. Gekas	28,669
	Dem.	Gene Stilp	14,400

Allegheny

Dist.	Party	Name	Votes
18th	Rep.	Ernie Buckman	24,916
	Dem.	*Doug Walgren	40,314

Adams, Cumberland and York

Dist.	Party	Name	Votes
19th	Rep.	*Bill Goodling	34,215
	Dem.	Richard F. Thornton	17,718
		Jonathan Kulp	4,008

Allegheny and Westmoreland

Dist.	Party	Name	Votes
20th	Rep.	Joseph M. Gaydos	1,036
	Dem.	*Joseph M. Gaydos	58,198
		Constance Brown Komm	8,955

Crawford, Erie, Lawrence and Mercer

Dist.	Party	Name	Votes
21st	Rep.	*Tom Ridge	24,953
	Dem.	Joylyn Blackwell	18,444

Allegheny, Beaver, Fayette, Greene and Washington

Dist.	Party	Name	Votes
22nd	Rep.	Austin J. Murphy	1,498
	Dem.	*Austin J. Murphy	57,312
		Donald A. Shapira	7,858

Armstrong, Cameron, Centre, Clarion, Clearfield, Clinton, Elk, Forest, Jefferson, McKean, Venango and Warren

Dist.	Party	Name	Votes
23rd	Rep.	*Bill Clinger	29,676
	Dem.	Bill Wachob	24,714
		Jerry A. McMurdy	4,487

STATE SENATE
Primary Election, May 20, 1986

Dist.	Party	Name	Votes
		Philadelphia	
2nd	Rep.	Joe O'Donnell	5,500
	Dem.	*Francis J. Lynch	13,943
		Carol Coady	9,922
4th	Rep.	Thomas Memmo	1,384
	Dem.	*M. Joseph Rocks	23,221
		Bucks	
6th	Rep.	Jim O'Brien	7,394
	Dem.	*H. Craig Lewis	11,486
		John F. Cordisco	9,183
		Philadelphia	
8th	Rep.	Cordell D. Jones	2,526
	Dem.	*Hardy Williams	20,971
		Bucks	
10th	Rep.	Jim Greenwood	9,751
		Charles R. Gerow	7,250
		Andrew L. Warren	4,767
	Dem.	John J. Rufe	5,614
		Montgomery	
12th	Rep.	*Stewart J. Greenleaf	14,210
		Luzerne	
14th	Rep.	Dale Walker	7,163
	Dem.	*Raphael Musto	24,610
		Lehigh	
16th	Rep.	David K. Bausch	5,593
		Alfred A. Siess, Jr.	1,660
	Dem.	Roy C. Afflerbach	8,966
		Monroe and Northampton	
18th	Rep.	Lawanda Givler	4,205
	Dem.	*Jeanette F. Reibman	11,761
		Luzerne, Monroe, Pike, Susquehanna, Wayne and Wyoming	
20th	Rep.	*Charles D. Lemmond, Jr	15,636
		Charlie Kirkwood	10,094
	Dem.	Joseph M. Bilbow	11,102
		Lackawanna and Monroe	
22nd	Rep.	Robert Castellani	6,495
	Dem.	*Robert J. Mellow	27,513
		Bucks and Montgomery	
24th	Rep.	*Edwin G. Holl	10,320
	Dem.	Steven G. Biddle	922
		Delaware	
26th	Rep.	*F. Joseph Loeper	18,505
	Dem.	Dai Williams	8,313
		York	
28th	Rep.	*Ralph W. Hess	11,211
		Bedford, Blair, Fulton and Huntingdon	
30th	Rep.	*Robert C. Jubelirer	17,311
		Fayette and Somerset	
32nd	Dem.	*J. William Lincoln	20,870
		Cameron, Centre, Clearfield, Clinton, Juniata and Mifflin	
34th	Rep.	*J. Doyle Corman	10,447
	Dem.	Al Brelo	7,843
		Chester and Lancaster	
36th	Rep.	*Noah W. Wenger	10,386
		Allegheny	
38th	Rep.	Bill Pendleton	5,074
	Dem.	*Leonard J. Bodack	21,940
		Allegheny, Armstrong and Westmoreland	
40th	Rep.	Bob Holste	9,396
	Dem.	John W. Regoli	12,254
		*Edward M. Early	9,156
		Ron Brown	4,554
		Allegheny	
42nd	Rep.	William R. Cordero	4,539
	Dem.	*Eugene F. Scanlon	21,701
		Don Walko	10,726
		Allegheny and Westmoreland	
44th	Rep.	*Frank A. Pecora	9,390
	Dem.	Ernest D'Achille	10,729
		Mark A. McKillop	10,313
		Beaver, Greene and Washington	
46th	Rep.	J. Barry Stout	1,063
	Dem.	*J. Barry Stout	26,167
		Berks, Lebanon and Lehigh	
48th	Rep.	*David J. Brightbill	11,786
	Dem.	John H. Anspach	6,592
		Crawford, Mercer and Venango	
50th	Rep.	*Roy W. Wilt	12,793

STATE HOUSE OF REPRESENTATIVES
Primary Election, May 20, 1986

Dist.	Party	Name	Votes
		Erie	
1st	Dem.	*Bernard J. Dombrowski	5,238
2nd	Dem.	*Italo S. Cappabianca	4,391
3rd	Rep.	*Karl Boyes	2,315
4th	Rep.	*Harry E. Bowser	2,714
		Crawford and Erie	
5th	Rep.	*Jim Merry	3,005
		Crawford	
6th	Rep.	Gene G. Rumsey	3,098
		*Tom Swift	2,918
	Dem.	Connie G. Maine	2,674
		Mercer	
7th	Rep.	David Desantis	1,481
	Dem.	*Mike Gruitza	4,646
		Butler and Mercer	
8th	Rep.	*Howard L. Fargo	3,366
	Dem.	Kathy W. James	1,995
		Lawrence	
9th	Rep.	Donald E. Williams	2,536
	Dem.	*Thomas J. Fee	5,040
		Beaver, Lawrence and Mercer	
10th	Rep.	Jim Gerlach	2,363
		Henry D. Karki	1,186
		Joe Mazzant	942
	Dem.	Frank LaGrotta	4,329
		Thomas J. Fee, Jr.	2,053
		Butler	
11th	Rep.	June M. Cannard	2,551
	Dem.	*Joseph A. Steighner	3,748
		Butler and Lawrence	
12th	Rep.	*James M. Burd	2,776
	Dem.	Ronald Goebel	2,284
		Chester	
13th	Rep.	*Art Hershey	2,644
	Dem.	James B. Norton, III	1,387
		Beaver	
14th	Rep.	Richard K. Pegg	2,236
	Dem.	*Michael R. Veon	4,890
		Ronald J. Brozich	1,089
15th	Rep.	Nicholas A. Colafella	303
	Dem.	*Nicholas A. Colafella	7,616
16th	Dem.	*Charles Laughlin	8,030
		Crawford and Mercer	
17th	Rep.	*Robert D. Robbins	3,085
		Bucks	
18th	Rep.	*Edward F. Burns	2,216
	Dem.	Gregory C. McCarthy	2,071
		Robert J. Jones	781
		Allegheny	
19th	Dem.	*K. Leroy Irvis	5,963
20th	Dem.	*Thomas J. Murphy	6,737
		Jimmy Steigerwald	1,895
		Robert Kennedy Griser	310
21st	Dem.	*Frank J. Pistella	5,894
22nd	Dem.	*Steve Seventy	6,587
		Pete Wagner	5,236
23rd	Rep.	Lawrence N. Paper	965
	Dem.	*Ivan Itkin	8,223
24th	Dem.	*Joe Preston	6,250
		Allegheny and Westmoreland	
25th	Rep.	Howard Ash	1,774
	Dem.	*Joseph F. Markosek	4,815
		Westmoreland	
26th	Dem.	*Eugene G. Saloom	5,007
		Allegheny	
27th	Rep.	Nancy Ann Moorhead	867
		Frank Liberatore	608
	Dem.	*Thomas C. Petrone	5,986
		Ben Caparelli	1,197
28th	Rep.	*George Pott	3,650
	Dem.	Dale Newman	2,695
29th	Rep.	John J. O'Brien, III	2,837
	Dem.	*David J. Mayernik	5,095
30th	Rep.	*Richard J. Cessar	2,855
		Thomas Plesco	685
	Dem.	Richard J. Cessar	1,681
31st	Rep.	Leonard V. Stanga	1,694
	Dem.	*Brian D. Clark	5,450
32nd	Rep.	Roy C. Ritenour	2,541
	Dem.	*Anthony M. DeLuca	5,171
33rd	Dem.	*Roger F. Duffy	4,665
34th	Dem.	*Ronald R. Cowell	4,971
35th	Dem.	*Tom Michlovic	5,731
		Edward R. McGuire	4,902
36th	Rep.	Gerard F. Dauginikas	780
	Dem.	*Michael M. Dawida	6,630
		William J. Davis	2,441
		JoAnn F. Herman	933
		Allegheny and Westmoreland	
37th	Rep.	Dennis W. Lion	1,191
	Dem.	*Emil Mrkonic	6,727

Allegheny

38th	Dem.	*Richard D. Olasz	5,590
		William J. Welsh	4,535
39th	Rep.	John J. Skalican	1,346
	Dem.	*David K. Levdansky	5,617
		George Miscevich	2,391
40th	Rep.	*Alice S. Langtry	2,759
	Dem.	Raymond C. McKelvey, Jr.	3,252
41st	Rep.	*Raymond T. Book	2,913
	Dem.	Nello N. Fiore	3,838
42nd	Rep.	*Terry McVerry	3,791
	Dem.	John Adams	3,715

Lancaster

43rd	Rep.	*Jere W. Schuler	2,349

Allegheny

44th	Rep.	William R. Harper	1,215
	Dem.	*Ron Gamble	5,106
45th	Dem.	*Fred A. Trello	9,467
		Michael Angelo	2,936

Beaver and Washington

46th	Dem.	*Victor John Lescovitz	5,580

Washington

47th	Rep.	*Roger Raymond Fischer	2,254
		Leo J. Trich, Jr.	2,560
48th	Rep.	Michael J. Schultz, Sr.	855
		David J. Martino	835
	Dem.	*David W. Sweet	4,962
		Frank A. Barbosky	2,057
		Bruce E. Krane	554

Fayette and Washington

49th	Dem.	*Peter J. Daley	8,482

Greene, Fayette and Washington

50th	Dem.	*Bill DeWeese	7,840

Fayette

51st	Rep.	Edward E. Olesh	533
	Dem.	*Fred Taylor	5,172
		Harry Young Cochran	2,760
52nd	Dem.	*Richard A. Kasunic	7,224
		James J. Hartz	1,308

Montgomery

53rd	Rep.	*Robert W. Godshall	2,528
	Dem.	Robert N. Rosenberger	1,104

Allegheny and Westmoreland

54th	Dem.	*Terry E. Van Horne	7,051

Westmoreland

55th	Dem.	*Joseph A. Petrarca	5,467
56th	Rep.	Lenny Santimyer	1,478
	Dem.	*Allen Kukovich	4,983
		John Abraham	2,419
57th	Dem.	*Amos K. Hutchinson	5,257

58th	Dem.	*James J. Manderino	7,317

Fayette and Westmoreland

59th	Rep.	*Jess Stairs	2,538
	Dem.	William A. Burd	2,431

Armstrong

60th	Rep.	Henry Livengood	945
	Dem.	*Henry Livengood	4,462

Montgomery

61st	Rep.	*Joseph M. Gladeck, Jr	3,207
	Dem.	Andre Moreno	1,164

Indiana

62nd	Rep.	*Paul Wass	3,001
	Dem.	George T. Sink	2,321

Armstrong and Clarion

63rd	Rep.	David E. Black	3,334
	Dem.	*David R. Wright	3,378

Venango

64th	Rep.	*Ronald E. Black	3,197
	Dem.	John Last	2,043
		Crystal D. Graham	552

Forest, Venango and Warren

65th	Rep.	Gary E. Olson	2,830
	Dem.	*Curt Bowley	2,571

Jefferson and Indiana

66th	Rep.	Sam Smith	2,920
		Robert H. Lyle	2,057
		Thomas A. Stojek	1,173
	Dem.	Joseph M. Betta	2,537
		Clayton D. Winebark	1,493

Cameron, Clearfield and McKean

67th	Rep.	*Kenneth M. Jadlowiec	3,226
	Dem.	William Kuhn	328

Potter and Tioga

68th	Rep.	*Edgar A. Carlson	5,041

Somerset

69th	Rep.	Clay Mankamyer	758
	Dem.	*William R. Lloyd, Jr.	3,904

Cambria and Somerset

70th	Rep.	*William Telek	2,876
	Dem.	Paul E. Danel	5,827

Cambria

71st	Rep.	Thomas Eugene Heider	2,736
	Dem.	*John N. Wozniak	4,793
		Rosalie Danchanko	2,313
		George Salem, Jr.	653

Armstrong, Cambria and Indiana

72nd	Rep.	Bob Kunkle	2,422
	Dem.	*William J. Stewart	6,272

Cambria

73rd	Rep.	Robert A. Etchells	1,428
	Dem.	*Edward J. Haluska	6,183
		Anthony P. Carnicella	2,169
		William Bill Demi	1,075

Clearfield

74th	Rep.	Camille George	1,449
	Dem.	*Camille George	4,888

Clearfield and Elk

75th	Rep.	*Jim Distler	3,113
	Dem.	Gary Lee Kraus	4,805

Centre, Clearfield, Clinton and Lycoming

76th	Dem.	*Russell P. Letterman	2,420

Centre and Clearfield

77th	Rep.	*Lynn B. Herman	2,366
	Dem.	George Field	1,840

Bedford, Fulton and Huntingdon

78th	Rep.	Dick L. Hess	2,062
		Roy A. Foor	1,942
		Dick M. Rice	1,910
	Dem.	Gary W. Ebersole	3,140

Blair

79th	Rep.	*Richard A. Geist	3,730
	Dem.	Richard A. Geist	467
80th	Rep.	*Edwin G. Johnson	4,133

Blair and Huntingdon

81st	Rep.	*Samuel E. Hayes, Jr	4,196

Juniata, Mifflin and Perry

82nd	Rep.	*Walter F. DeVerter	2,896
	Dem.	David S. Stetler	2,103

Lycoming

83rd	Rep.	*Anthony J. Cimini	2,488
84th	Rep.	*Alvin C. Bush	2,784
	Dem.	Richard D. Sheddy	1,723

Snyder and Union

85th	Rep.	Kenneth F. Mease	3,167
	Dem.	*John Showers	1,557

Cumberland and Perry

86th	Rep.	*Fred C. Noye	3,058

Cumberland

87th	Rep.	*Harold F. Mowery, Jr.	4,381
88th	Rep.	*John Kennedy	3,563
		Jack Murray	2,659
		William F. Kane	554
		Robert W. Farver	498
	Dem.	Paul S. Dlugolecki, Jr.	2,312

Franklin

89th	Rep.	Jeffrey W. Coy	429
	Dem.	*Jeffrey W. Coy	1,318

Franklin and Fulton

90th	Rep.	*Terry Punt	1,336

Adams

91st	Rep.	Shirley Reed	2,682
	Dem.	*Kenneth J. Cole	2,250

York

92nd	Rep.	*Bruce Smith	3,174
		Greg Reed	1,986
	Dem.	Paul E. Parsells	1,901
93rd	Rep.	*A. Carville Foster, Jr.	2,873
94th	Rep.	*Gregory M. Snyder	3,268
		Dean L. Graham	914
95th	Rep.	Charlene A. Vaught	1,585
	Dem.	*Michael E. Bortner	2,704

Lancaster

96th	Rep.	*Marvin E. Miller, Jr.	1,609
	Dem.	Jon C. Lyons	1,332
97th	Rep.	*June N. Honaman	3,325
	Dem.	Lou A. Kosmela	919
98th	Rep.	*Kenneth E. Brandt	2,408
99th	Rep.	*Terry Scheetz	2,566
100th	Rep.	*John E. Barley	2,267
	Dem.	William E. Bunce	724

Lebanon

101st	Rep.	*George W. Jackson	4,261
	Dem.	Judy D. Hoffman	1,505

Lebanon and Lancaster

102nd	Rep.	*Nicholas B. Moehlmann	3,243
	Dem.	Charles T. Jones	1,026

Dauphin

103rd	Rep.	Tom Pyne	2,041
	Dem.	*Pete Wambach	2,492
104th	Rep.	*Jeffrey E. Piccola	4,148
	Dem.	Jeffrey E. Piccola	360
105th	Rep.	*Joseph C. Manmiller	4,619
106th	Rep.	*Rudy Dininni	3,331

Columbia, Montour and Northumberland

107th	Dem.	*Robert E. Belfanti, Jr.	6,173

Montour, Northumberland and Snyder

108th	Rep.	*Merle H. Phillips	2,525

Columbia and Montour

109th	Rep.	Ted Stuban	601
	Dem.	*Ted Stuban	3,737

Bradford

110th	Rep.	*J. Scot Chadwick	3,299

Bradford, Sullivan, Susquehanna and Wyoming

111th	Rep.	*Carmel Sirianni	6,612
	Dem.	Carmel Sirianni	1,442

Lackawanna and Wayne

112th	Rep.	Aaron K. Jones	1,101
		Sydelle O'Neil	793
	Dem.	*Fred Belardi	6,369

Lackawanna

113th	Dem.	*Gaynor Cawley	7,907
114th	Rep.	*Frank A. Serafini	2,467
	Dem.	Frank A. Serafini	350

Lackawanna and Wayne

115th	Rep.	Robert J. Davis	1,254
	Dem.	*Edward G. Staback	8,491

Luzerne

116th	Rep.	*Correale F. Stevens	3,358
	Dem.	Neil Craig, Jr	2,068
		James P. Ferry	1,505

Columbia and Luzerne

117th	Rep.	*George C. Hasay	3,536
	Dem.	Stephanie G. Wychock	3,292

Lackawanna and Luzerne

118th	Dem.	*Thomas M. Tigue	7,899

Luzerne

119th	Rep.	Blythe H. Evans	2,327
	Dem.	*Stanley J. Jarolin	5,820
		Joseph Yeager	5,612
120th	Rep.	Scott Dietterick	5,119
		Robert L. Taylor	2,470
	Dem.	John J. Ruane	2,829
121st	Dem.	*Kevin Blaum	6,473

Carbon and Monroe

122nd	Dem.	*Keith R. McCall	3,496

Columbia and Schuylkill

123rd	Rep.	Arthur D. Kaplan	2,501
	Dem.	*Edward J. Lucyk	3,984

Lehigh and Schuylkill

124th	Rep.	*David G. Argall	3,590

Northumberland and Schuylkill

125th	Rep.	Craig R. Morgan	2,933
	Dem.	*William E. Baldwin	2,299

Berks

126th	Rep.	*Paul J. Angstadt	1,609
	Dem.	Mary H. Schmidt	3,675
127th	Rep.	Jeff Jefferson	749
	Dem.	*Thomas R. Caltagirone	3,935
128th	Rep.	*James J. Gallen	2,191

Berks and Lebanon

129th	Rep.	*John S. Davies	2,255
	Dem.	Zia Mahmood	1,625

Berks

130th	Rep.	Dennis E. Leh	1,093
		Lawrence D. Werst	1,035
	Dem.	John R. McCloskey	2,085
		Randy L. Pyle	2,064
		Levi M. Wegman	662
		Florence E. Kozak	189

Lehigh

131st	Rep.	Neil Polster	1,194
	Dem.	Karen A. Ritter	1,838
		Lou Hershman	1,285
		Art Beers	272
132nd	Rep.	William Kurt Malkames	1,239
	Dem.	*John F. Pressmann	2,377
133rd	Dem.	*Paul McHale	3,110
134th	Rep.	*Don Snyder	1,947
	Dem.	Fred Duke	1,413

Lehigh and Northampton

135th	Rep.	James V. Banks	1,008
	Dem.	*William C. Rybak	3,588

Northampton

136th	Rep.	Mark Chehi	799
	Dem.	*Robert Freeman	2,917
137th	Rep.	*Leonard Q. Gruppo	1,330
	Dem.	Gordon T. Heller	2,299

Monroe and Northampton

138th	Rep.	Jim Oakes	1,084
	Dem.	*Frank W. Yandrisevits	2,620

Pike, Susquehanna and Wayne

139th	Rep.	*Jerry Birmelin	5,493

Bucks

140th	Rep.	Kathy Waters	1,277
	Dem.	Thomas C. Corrigan	2,313
		George J. Galloway	1,784
		Amy Mcilvaine	1,646
		Edward T. Czyzyk	1,098
		Edgar W. Sprague	143
141st	Rep.	Ralph L. McClellan, Jr.	1,394
	Dem.	*James J. A. Gallagher	4,268
142nd	Rep.	*James L. Wright, Jr.	2,633
	Dem.	Vanya Tyrrell	2,661
143rd	Rep.	David W. Heckler	2,862
		Michael A. Smerconish	2,443
		E. Thomas Scarborough, Jr.	2,163
		David P. Snyder	570
	Dem.	Theodore F. Schneider, Jr.	1,785
144th	Rep.	*Benjamin H. Wilson	3,263
		Reginald B. Snyder	832
	Dem.	Benjamin H. Wilson	416
145th	Rep.	*Paul I. Clymer	3,441

Montgomery

146th	Rep.	*Robert D. Reber, Jr.	1,534
	Dem.	Edmund S. Zerbey	1,042
147th	Rep.	*Raymond Bunt, Jr.	3,310
148th	Rep.	*Lois Sherman Hagarty.	3,375
	Dem.	Tamara Steerman Gordon.	2,420
149th	Rep.	*Richard A. McClatchy, Jr.	3,573
	Dem.	Philip M. Andrews	2,241
150th	Rep.	*Joseph A. Lashinger, Jr.	2,930
151st	Rep.	*George E. Saurman	4,200

Bucks and Montgomery

152nd	Rep.	*Roy W. Cornell.	3,197
	Dem.	Thomas P. Murt	1,494

Montgomery

153rd	Rep.	*Jon D. Fox.	4,403
	Dem.	Jon D. Fox.	419
154th	Rep.	*Charles F. Nahill, Jr.	3,658
	Dem.	Phyllis Magerman	3,876

Chester

155th	Rep.	J. Barry Pignoli	2,483
	Dem.	*Samuel W. Morris	1,794
156th	Rep.	*Elinor Z. Taylor	2,955
	Dem.	Melva Mueller	567

Chester and Montgomery

157th	Rep.	*Peter R. Vroon	3,163

Chester

158th	Rep.	*Joseph R. Pitts	2,991

Delaware

159th	Rep.	*Robert C. Wright	4,927
	Dem.	Sheridan D. Jones, Jr.	1,030
160th	Rep.	*Kathrynann W. Durham.	4,363
	Dem.	Ralph A. Garzia.	1,365
161st	Rep.	*Thomas Gannon	5,085
	Dem.	James Barnes.	2,121
162nd	Rep.	*Ron Raymond	4,590
	Dem.	Dorothy Gallagher.	1,912
163rd	Rep.	*Nicholas A. Micozzie.	3,669
	Dem.	Nancy B. Baulis.	1,784
		Stephen Demarco.	1,233
164th	Rep.	*Mario J. Civera, Jr.	5,217
	Dem.	John M. Rybnik	2,061
165th	Rep.	*Mary Ann Arty	6,152
	Dem.	Roberta M. Timpko	2,363
166th	Rep.	*Stephen F. Freind	6,235
	Dem.	Allen R. Polsky	2,931

Chester and Delaware

167th	Rep.	*Robert J. Flick	4,817

Delaware

168th	Rep.	*Matthew J. Ryan	5,810
	Dem.	Jeff Nagorny	1,910

Philadelphia

169th	Rep.	*Dennis M. O'Brien.	4,115
	Dem.	Pat Gentile Owens	4,477
170th	Rep.	*George T. Kenney, Jr.	4,333
	Dem.	Elinda Fishman	4,180

Centre and Mifflin

171st	Rep.	Joyce Conklin Williamson	2,824
	Dem.	*Ruth C. Rudy.	2,634

Philadelphia

172nd	Rep.	*John M. Perzel	3,642
	Dem.	Robert V. O'Brien	6,247
173rd	Rep.	*Frances Weston	2,622
	Dem.	Alan D. Stasson	3,607
174th	Rep.	Joseph Kabo.	2,189
	Dem.	*Max Pievsky	9,965
175th	Rep.	Louis J. Koreck	2,145
	Dem.	*Gerard A. Kosinski	5,748
176th	Rep.	*Chris Wogan	4,828
	Dem.	Gary Chilutti	3,828
177th	Rep.	*John J. Taylor	1,755
	Dem.	Frank M. Felici, Jr.	4,454

Bucks

178th	Rep.	*Roy Reinard	3,475
	Dem.	Mark B. Dubowe	524

Philadelphia

179th	Rep.	Mary A. Houser.	868
	Dem.	*William W. Rieger	3,865
180th	Rep.	Lester A. Ketters	683
	Dem.	*Ralph Acosta.	3,422
		Edward J. Crompton	1,602
		Wilfredo P. Rojas	1,495
181st	Rep.	Iris Thompson	309
	Dem.	*Alphonso Deal.	3,904
		Charlie Duncan.	1,340
		Jimmie L. Smith	423
182nd	Rep.	John A. Kolody, Jr.	1,397
	Dem.	*Babette Josephs	6,201
		Stephen H. Skale	2,850
183rd	Rep.	Victor A. Desiderio.	1,668
	Dem.	*Nicholas J. Maiale.	5,580
184th	Rep.	Anthony N. Dipietro.	1,586
		Nicholas A. Marrandino	300
	Dem.	*Joseph Howlett	4,636

Delaware and Philadelphia

185th	Rep.	Robert J. Corcoran	1,329
	Dem.	*Robert C. Donatucci	4,709

Philadelphia

186th	Rep.	F. Malana Pettit	303
	Dem.	*Edward A. Wiggins	2,608
		David L. Shadding.	2,187
		Claudia S. Sherrod	1,767
		Jasper Baxter	636

Berks and Lehigh

187th	Rep.	*Paul Semmel	1,586
	Dem.	James J. Gaffney	1,704

Philadelphia

188th	Rep.	Daniel J. Callaghan	254
	Dem.	*James R. Roebuck	3,999
		Ronald J. Pugh	1,714

Monroe

189th	Rep.	Joseph W. Battisto	363
	Dem.	*Joseph W. Battisto	3,181

Philadelphia

190th	Rep.	Sandra R. Kellar	355
	Dem.	Vincent Hughes	5,115
		*James D. Barber	4,605
191st	Rep.	Joseph Tremarki	546
	Dem.	*Peter D. Truman	5,422
192nd	Rep.	Mary Bachetti	724
	Dem.	*Chaka Fattah	6,988
		John McClellan	1,608

York

193rd	Rep.	*Donald W. Dorr	3,184

Philadelphia

194th	Rep.	Carmela M. Lari	1,354
	Dem.	Richard Hayden	4,358
		John P. Hogan	3,787

195th	Rep.	Lowell Webb	538
	Dem.	*Frank L. Oliver	4,700
196th	Dem.	*Ruth B. Harper	3,548
		T. Milton Street	3,054
		Robert C. Gibson	1,739
197th	Rep.	Edward P. Bevans	244
	Dem.	*Andrew J. Carn	3,634
		Maurice Floyd	2,744
		Jewel Williams	2,459
198th	Dem.	*Robert W. O'Donnell	5,957
		John Connelly	1,048

Adams, Cumberland and York

199th	Dem.	*John H. Broujos	2,643

Philadelphia

200th	Dem.	*Gordon J. Linton	7,227
201st	Rep.	Werner F. Tillmann	334
	Dem.	*David P. Richardson, Jr.	7,061
		Leonard T. Tanzymore, Jr.	934
202nd	Rep.	James G. Wright	1,910
	Dem.	*Mark B. Cohen	6,436
203rd	Rep.	Larry S. Kramer	859
	Dem.	*Dwight Evans	6,644

REGISTRATION FOR GENERAL ELECTION
November 4, 1986

COUNTIES	REPUBLICAN			DEMOCRATIC			CONSUMER		
	Women	Men	Total	Women	Men	Total	Women	Men	Total
Adams............	7,789	7,473	15,262	6,026	5,297	11,323	2	3	5
Allegheny	113,873	97,880	211,752	297,057	242,058	539,115	212	224	436
Armstrong........	8,213	7,277	15,490	9,120	8,251	17,371	1	3	4
Beaver...........	14,489	12,597	27,086	36,984	32,486	69,470	82	74	156
Bedford..........	6,847	6,285	13,132	4,812	4,484	9,296	0	0	0
Berks............	27,981	26,043	54,024	39,821	36,071	75,892	62	37	99
Blair.............	16,989	14,840	31,829	11,228	8,982	20,210	8	7	15
Bradford	9,118	8,375	17,493	4,076	3,571	7,647	3	7	10
Bucks	65,488	63,592	129,080	59,238	49,171	108,409	0	0	0
Butler	16,732	15,317	32,049	17,799	15,646	33,445	11	24	35
Cambria	14,928	12,780	27,708	29,116	25,386	54,502	2	6	9
Cameron.........	1,020	894	1,914	811	708	1,519	0	0	0
Carbon	5,289	5,026	10,315	6,679	5,988	12,667	0	0	0
Centre...........	13,704	15,013	28,717	11,703	10,484	22,187	0	0	0
Chester..........	52,204	49,063	101,267	25,328	19,271	44,599	54	37	91
Clarion	5,009	4,556	9,565	4,828	4,327	9,155	0	2	2
Clearfield.........	8,712	8,091	16,803	9,427	8,445	17,872	0	2	2
Clinton...........	3,368	3,248	6,616	3,229	3,027	6,256	3	2	5
Columbia.........	6,343	5,603	11,946	8,127	7,104	15,231	0	2	2
Crawford	11,316	10,327	21,643	9,565	8,393	17,958	1	0	1
Cumberland	26,783	24,281	51,064	15,655	13,058	28,713	5	12	17
Dauphin	33,498	29,330	62,828	21,535	16,699	38,234	43	30	73
Delaware.........	116,248	103,952	220,200	48,954	34,933	83,887	106	84	190
Elk..............	3,094	2,991	6,085	5,499	5,045	10,544	0	1	1
Erie	24,623	22,946	47,569	41,741	36,153	77,894	5	8	13
Fayette	7,527	6,617	14,144	28,121	25,440	53,561	3	0	3
Forest	704	704	1,408	542	503	1,045	2	2	4
Franklin..........	13,220	12,104	25,324	9,177	8,567	17,744	2	5	7
Fulton	1,343	1,414	2,757	1,371	1,311	2,682	0	0	0
Greene	1,926	1,791	3,717	7,794	7,068	14,862	0	0	0
Huntingdon	5,535	5,067	10,602	3,606	3,192	6,798	4	3	7
Indiana	10,400	9,302	19,702	10,494	8,920	19,414	5	7	12
Jefferson.........	5,970	5,295	11,265	4,811	4,270	9,081	0	0	0
Juniata	2,643	2,456	5,099	1,987	1,913	3,900	0	0	0
Lackawanna	19,714	16,920	36,634	44,780	37,919	82,699	0	3	3
Lancaster	53,614	51,187	104,801	22,403	18,001	40,404	13	22	35
Lawrence	10,449	8,932	19,381	16,454	14,060	30,514	8	3	11
Lebanon	14,563	13,869	28,432	6,893	6,253	13,146	1	6	7
Lehigh...........	27,467	26,267	53,734	32,856	28,162	61,018	29	24	53
Luzerne..........	33,330	29,593	62,923	50,577	43,877	94,454	0	0	0
Lycoming	13,877	12,596	26,473	10,884	9,409	20,293	2	1	3
McKean..........	6,616	5,856	12,472	3,383	2,938	6,321	0	2	2
Mercer...........	12,992	11,479	24,471	16,704	14,612	31,316	7	11	18
Mifflin	4,583	4,096	8,679	3,855	3,389	7,244	0	0	0
Monroe	7,308	6,813	14,121	7,674	6,762	14,436	3	4	7
Montgomery	107,834	100,625	208,459	58,397	43,520	101,917	67	58	125
Montour..........	1,939	1,615	3,554	1,862	1,512	3,374	1	0	1
Northampton......	17,233	16,533	33,766	31,206	27,421	58,627	45	20	65
Northumberland	11,240	10,069	21,309	11,490	9,608	21,098	1	3	4
Perry............	5,339	5,150	10,489	2,643	2,287	4,930	4	1	5
Philadelphia	96,208	86,712	182,920	403,439	312,227	715,666	1,826	1,271	3,097
Pike.............	3,295	3,076	6,371	2,028	1,861	3,889	1	0	1
Potter	2,661	2,432	5,093	1,518	1,382	2,900	0	0	0
Schuylkill.........	22,176	19,820	41,996	15,822	13,439	29,261	2	5	7
Snyder...........	5,036	4,729	9,765	1,737	1,661	3,398	0	0	0
Somerset.........	10,476	9,479	19,955	10,073	9,234	19,307	0	0	0
Sullivan..........	972	859	1,831	743	743	1,486	0	0	0
Susquehanna	5,867	5,410	11,277	3,298	2,979	6,277	0	0	0
Tioga............	6,406	5,714	12,120	2,576	2,260	4,836	0	1	1
Union	4,263	4,029	8,292	1,970	1,706	3,676	0	3	3
Venango	8,029	7,257	15,286	6,086	5,328	11,414	5	3	8
Warren	6,146	5,732	11,878	4,702	4,044	8,746	2	0	2
Washington........	13,988	12,404	26,392	39,123	34,116	73,239	0	0	0
Wayne...........	5,534	5,098	10,632	2,488	2,285	4,773	0	0	0
Westmoreland......	26,195	22,693	48,888	64,831	58,433	123,264	5	12	17
Wyoming.........	3,995	3,690	7,685	1,883	1,606	3,489	0	0	0
York.............	33,833	33,018	66,851	30,776	27,594	58,370	10	9	19
TOTALS	**1,266,103**	**1,156,282**	**2,422,385**	**1,711,415**	**1,416,850**	**3,128,265**	**2,649**	**2,044**	**4,693**

Official election results reported in this section were supplied by the Pennsylvania State Bureau of Elections.

REGISTRATION FOR GENERAL ELECTION
November 4, 1986

COUNTIES	OTHER PARTIES			ALL PARTIES TOTAL			Total Voting Districts	Voting Machine Districts	Electronic Equipment Districts
	Women	Men	Total	Grand Total	Women	Men			
Adams............	762	787	1,549	28,139	14,579	13,560	49	0	0
Allegheny	19,627	21,844	41,471	792,774	430,768	362,006	1,302	1,302	0
Armstrong........	546	636	1,182	34,047	17,880	16,167	74	0	74
Beaver............	1,814	2,286	4,100	100,812	53,369	47,443	155	0	155
Bedford..........	267	295	562	22,990	11,926	11,064	42	0	0
Berks............	3,816	4,178	7,994	138,009	71,680	66,329	186	186	0
Blair.............	1,215	1,237	2,452	54,506	29,440	25,066	96	0	96
Bradford	540	650	1,190	26,340	13,737	12,603	61	0	61
Bucks	9,532	10,206	19,738	257,227	134,258	122,969	272	272	0
Butler	1,850	2,006	3,856	69,385	36,392	32,993	79	0	79
Cambria	981	1,196	2,177	84,396	45,028	39,368	201	0	98
Cameron..........	54	80	134	3,567	1,885	1,682	10	0	0
Carbon	345	477	822	23,804	12,313	11,491	46	46	0
Centre...........	2,606	3,230	5,836	56,740	28,013	28,727	85	0	85
Chester...........	7,793	7,558	15,351	161,308	85,379	75,929	190	0	190
Clarion..........	381	434	815	19,537	10,218	9,319	51	0	51
Clearfield.........	540	708	1,248	35,925	18,679	17,246	70	0	70
Clinton...........	259	265	524	13,401	6,859	6,542	37	17	0
Columbia.........	671	586	1,257	28,436	15,141	13,295	66	0	66
Crawford.........	643	799	1,442	41,044	21,525	19,519	67	44	0
Cumberland	2,704	2,954	5,658	85,452	45,147	40,305	89	89	0
Dauphin	3,165	3,399	6,564	107,699	58,241	49,458	142	0	142
Delaware..........	9,868	9,967	19,835	324,112	175,176	148,936	395	395	0
Elk...............	267	301	568	17,198	8,860	8,338	36	0	0
Erie..............	2,763	3,125	5,888	131,364	69,132	62,232	152	152	0
Fayette	735	806	1,541	69,249	36,386	32,863	112	112	0
Forest	32	40	72	2,529	1,280	1,249	11	0	0
Franklin..........	1,570	1,582	3,152	46,227	23,969	22,258	70	0	70
Fulton	62	83	145	5,584	2,776	2,808	13	0	0
Greene	165	167	332	18,911	9,885	9,026	48	0	0
Huntingdon	291	309	600	18,007	9,436	8,571	58	0	0
Indiana	1,080	1,199	2,279	41,407	21,979	19,428	77	0	77
Jefferson..........	344	376	720	21,066	11,125	9,941	72	0	72
Juniata	111	138	249	9,248	4,741	4,507	20	0	0
Lackawanna	1,523	1,618	3,141	122,477	66,017	56,460	241	241	0
Lancaster	6,100	6,155	12,255	157,495	82,130	75,365	195	195	0
Lawrence	870	1,059	1,929	51,835	27,781	24,054	105	0	105
Lebanon	1,159	1,298	2,457	44,042	22,616	21,426	54	54	0
Lehigh............	4,293	4,644	8,937	123,742	64,645	59,097	146	146	0
Luzerne...........	1,739	1,861	3,600	160,977	85,646	75,331	317	317	0
Lycoming	863	1,094	1957	48,726	25,626	23,100	86	43	00
McKean...........	318	372	690	19,485	10,317	9,168	43	39	0
Mercer............	1,198	1,365	2,563	58,368	30,901	27,467	112	106	0
Mifflin	258	278	536	16,459	8,696	7,763	30	29	0
Monroe	1,299	1,340	2,639	31,203	16,284	14,919	36	36	0
Montgomery	12,480	12,852	25,332	335,833	178,778	157,055	358	358	0
Montour..........	242	222	464	7,393	4,044	3,349	15	0	15
Northampton......	2,916	3,293	6,209	98,667	51,400	47,267	134	134	0
Northumberland	623	679	1,302	43,713	23,354	20,359	94	94	0
Perry	339	346	685	16,109	8,325	7,784	33	0	33
Philadelphia	12,071	12,841	24,912	926,595	513,544	413,051	1,795	1,795	0
Pike..............	457	464	921	11,182	5,781	5,401	14	14	0
Potter	89	137	226	8,219	4,268	3,951	34	0	0
Schuylkill..........	947	1,018	1,965	73,229	38,947	34,282	177	0	0
Snyder............	214	231	445	13,608	6,987	6,621	27	0	0
Somerset..........	505	544	1,049	40,311	21,054	19,257	68	0	68
Sullivan	57	59	116	3,433	1,772	1,661	15	0	0
Susquehanna	340	407	747	18,301	9,505	8,796	43	20	0
Tioga.............	250	340	590	17,547	9,232	8,315	46	0	0
Union	457	421	878	12,849	6,690	6,159	25	0	25
Venango	590	686	1,276	27,984	14,710	13,274	74	0	74
Warren	573	665	1,238	21,864	11,423	10,441	42	28	0
Washington........	1,847	2,146	3,993	103,624	54,958	48,666	205	0	205
Wayne............	352	354	706	16,111	8,374	7,737	37	37	0
Westmoreland......	3,957	4,284	8,241	180,410	94,988	85,422	307	307	0
Wyoming..........	224	243	467	11,641	6,102	5,539	30	0	0
York..............	3,756	4,107	7,863	133,103	68,375	64,728	144	144	0
TOTALS	**140,305**	**151,327**	**291,632**	**5,846,975**	**3,120,472**	**2,726,503**	**9,517**	**6,752**	**1,911**

GOVERNOR AND LIEUTENANT GOVERNOR OF PENNSYLVANIA
General Election, November 4, 1986

COUNTIES	REPUBLICAN Scranton/ Fisher	DEMOCRATIC Casey/ Singel	CONSUMER Hoover/ Brickhouse
Adams	10,511	7,277	200
Allegheny.	181,562	242,296	4,521
Armstrong	9,376	11,635	225
Beaver.	19,232	39,216	526
Bedford	8,180	6,874	127
Berks	43,849	36,147	1,038
Blair	17,509	15,135	380
Bradford.	9,100	5,547	141
Bucks.	83,492	55,729	1,532
Butler.	19,750	17,697	459
Cambria.	17,158	39,239	475
Cameron	1,245	1,109	10
Carbon.	6,617	8,839	144
Centre	17,294	13,029	273
Chester	58,518	28,572	821
Clarion.	6,464	6,022	149
Clearfield.	10,030	13,316	155
Clinton	4,196	4,373	85
Columbia	7,709	9,069	95
Crawford	12,546	10,859	183
Cumberland.	33,285	19,591	355
Dauphin	37,641	29,116	502
Delaware	113,628	75,218	1,596
Elk	4,818	7,523	110
Erie	37,583	35,727	1,385
Fayette.	11,704	26,540	412
Forest	966	813	18
Franklin	14,750	9,429	148
Fulton.	1,794	1,618	23
Greene.	3,748	7,476	78
Huntingdon	6,348	4,974	103
Indiana.	10,911	13,369	220
Jefferson	7,171	6,947	122
Juniata.	3,683	2,952	40
Lackawanna	26,775	55,979	140
Lancaster.	68,736	27,247	788
Lawrence.	12,189	19,235	307
Lebanon.	15,815	12,154	218
Lehigh	38,984	31,174	799
Luzerne	37,572	66,790	610
Lycoming.	15,080	13,505	277
McKean	6,976	4,579	113
Mercer	15,577	19,406	398
Mifflin.	5,788	4,683	95
Monroe	9,272	7,800	109
Montgomery	129,771	66,823	1,777
Montour	2,171	2,429	20
Northampton	27,723	29,482	628
Northumberland	12,660	16,337	236
Perry	6,005	3,819	126
Philadelphia.	172,718	307,233	5,161
Pike	3,529	2,304	39
Potter.	2,683	2,297	56
Schuylkill	23,824	25,854	459
Snyder.	6,000	3,150	99
Somerset	11,471	14,297	272
Sullivan	1,263	1,194	13
Susquehanna	6,668	5,237	60
Tioga	6,392	4,835	125
Union.	4,882	2,810	93
Venango.	8,530	8,480	200
Warren.	7,641	5,527	134
Washington	23,033	37,308	481
Wayne	5,718	4,886	92
Westmoreland	40,719	63,473	1,100
Wyoming	4,002	3,583	59
York	45,733	30,301	788
TOTALS.	**1,638,268**	**1,717,484**	**32,523**

UNITED STATES SENATOR
General Election, November 4, 1986

COUNTIES	REPUBLICAN Arlen Specter	DEMOCRATIC Bob Edgar	CONSUMER Lance S. Haver
Adams	11,121	6,730	119
Allegheny	216,279	207,814	3,619
Armstrong	11,854	9,188	141
Beaver	25,498	35,155	450
Bedford	9,890	5,214	70
Berks	49,113	30,990	616
Blair	22,616	10,240	245
Bradford	10,564	4,093	96
Bucks	91,209	49,703	818
Butler	23,163	14,363	312
Cambria	26,302	29,953	439
Cameron	1,580	764	9
Carbon	8,073	7,105	156
Centre	18,844	11,570	163
Chester	60,782	27,010	379
Clarion	7,937	4,624	98
Clearfield	12,970	10,346	147
Clinton	4,706	3,722	93
Columbia	10,229	6,567	107
Crawford	14,896	8,189	165
Cumberland	35,749	17,048	314
Dauphin	43,717	23,015	379
Delaware	107,922	83,779	952
Elk	6,639	5,787	68
Erie	42,267	30,701	1,071
Fayette	17,151	20,609	361
Forest	1,146	645	5
Franklin	16,174	8,117	124
Fulton	2,078	1,315	21
Greene	5,717	5,579	48
Huntingdon	7,562	3,835	69
Indiana	14,370	10,033	133
Jefferson	8,907	5,369	92
Juniata	4,114	2,538	21
Lackawanna	42,355	35,815	371
Lancaster	72,164	23,774	570
Lawrence	14,832	16,764	172
Lebanon	18,583	8,737	227
Lehigh	42,216	27,978	529
Luzerne	51,246	50,421	599
Lycoming	18,568	9,874	249
McKean	7,769	3,509	115
Mercer	18,560	15,230	420
Mifflin	6,466	3,846	96
Monroe	10,476	6,328	96
Montgomery	136,265	61,576	917
Montour	2,877	1,725	30
Northampton	30,465	25,958	521
Northumberland	16,427	12,094	273
Perry	7,144	2,924	90
Philadelphia	211,193	271,759	3,041
Pike	3,954	1,740	49
Potter	3,506	1,533	29
Schuylkill	30,429	19,273	316
Snyder	7,105	2,098	60
Somerset	15,297	10,477	199
Sullivan	1,497	949	16
Susquehanna	8,270	3,417	81
Tioga	8,102	3,260	76
Union	5,836	2,191	45
Venango	10,761	6,370	149
Warren	8,237	4,672	109
Washington	30,526	30,095	333
Wayne	7,487	2,794	97
Westmoreland	50,804	51,648	1,055
Wyoming	5,731	1,914	35
York	49,950	25,766	605
TOTALS	**1,906,537**	**1,448,219**	**23,470**

U.S. CONGRESS
General Election, November 4, 1986

Dist.	Party	Name	Votes
		Philadelphia	
1st	Dem.	*Thomas M. Foglietta	88,224
	Rep.	Anthony J. Mucciolo	29,811
2nd	Dem.	*William H. Gray	128,399
	Rep.	Linda R. Ragin	2,096
3rd	Dem.	*Robert A. Borski	107,804
	Rep.	Robert A. Rovner	66,693
		Armstrong, Beaver, Butler, Indiana, Lawrence and Westmoreland	
4th	Dem.	*Joseph P. Kolter	86,133
	Rep.	Al Lindsay	55,165
	Pop.	Emily C. Fair	1,296
		Chester, Delaware and Montgomery	
5th	Rep.	*Richard T. Schulze	87,593
	Dem.	Tim Ringgold	45,648
		Berks, Carbon, Lancaster and Schuylkill	
6th	Dem.	*Gus Yatron	98,142
	Rep.	Norm Bertasavage	43,858
		Delaware and Philadelphia	
7th	Rep.	Curt Weldon	110,118
	Dem.	Bill Spingler	69,557
		Bucks and Montgomery	
8th	Dem.	*Peter H. Kostmayer	85,731
	Rep.	David A. Christian	70,047
		Bedford, Blair, Cambria, Clearfield, Cumberland, Franklin, Fulton, Huntingdon, Juniata and Mifflin	
9th	Rep.	*Bud Shuster	120,890
	Dem.	Bud Shuster	
		Bradford, Clinton, Lackawanna, Monroe, Pike, Potter, Susquehanna, Tioga, Wayne and Wyoming	
10th	Rep.	*Joseph Michael McDade	118,603
	Dem.	Robert C. Bolus	40,248
		Carbon, Columbia, Luzerne, Monroe, Montour, Northumberland and Sullivan	
11th	Dem.	*Paul E. Kanjorski	112,405
	Rep.	Marc Holtzman	46,785
		Armstrong, Cambria, Somerset and Westmoreland	
12th	Dem.	*John P. Murtha	97,135
	Rep.	Kathy Holtzman	46,937
		Montgomery and Philadelphia	
13th	Rep.	*Lawrence Coughlin	100,701
	Dem.	Joseph M. Hoeffel	71,381
		Allegheny	
14th	Dem.	*William J. Coyne	104,726
	Lib.	Richard Edward Caligiuri	6,058
	Soc.	Mark Weddleton	3,120
	Pop.	Thomas R. McIntyre	1,487
	Wor.	Phyllis Gray	1,468
		Lehigh, Monroe and Northampton	
15th	Rep.	*Don Ritter	74,829
	Dem.	Joe Simonetta	56,972
		Chester, Lancaster and Lebanon	
16th	Rep.	*Robert S. Walker	100,784
	Dem.	James D. Hagelgans	34,399
		Dauphin, Lycoming, Northumberland, Perry, Snyder and Union	
17th	Rep.	*George W. Gekas	101,027
	Dem.	Michael S. Ogden	36,157
		Allegheny	
18th	Dem.	*Doug Walgren	104,164
	Rep.	Ernie Buckman	61,164
		Adams, Cumberland and York	
19th	Rep.	*Bill Goodling	100,055
	Dem.	Richard F. Thornton	37,233
		Allegheny and Westmoreland	
20th	Dem.	*Joseph M. Gaydos	136,638
	Wor.	Alden W. Vedder	2,114
	Rep.	Joseph M. Gaydos	
		Crawford, Erie, Lawrence and Mercer	
21st	Rep.	*Tom Ridge	111,148
	Dem.	Joylyn Blackwell	26,324
		Allegheny, Beaver, Fayette, Greene and Washington	
22nd	Dem.	*Austin J. Murphy	131,650
	Rep.	Austin J. Murphy	
		Armstrong, Cameron, Centre, Clarion, Clearfield, Clinton, Elk, Forest, Jefferson, McKean, Venango and Warren	
23rd	Rep.	*Bill Clinger	79,595
	Dem.	Bill Wachob	63,875

Party Abbreviations: Dem.—Democratic; Rep.—Republican; Ind.—Independent; Lib.—Libertarian; NA—New Alliance; Pop.—Populist; S/W—Socialist Workers; WL—Workers League

STATE SENATE
General Election, November 4, 1986

Dist.	Party	Name	Votes
		Philadelphia	
2nd	Dem.	*Francis J. Lynch	39,643
	Rep.	Joe O'Donnell	23,679
4th	Dem.	*M. Joseph Rocks	53,483
	Rep.	Thomas Memmo	16,847
		Bucks	
6th	Dem.	*H. Craig Lewis	35,608
	Rep.	Jim O'Brien	28,421
		Philadelphia	
8th	Dem.	*Hardy Williams	48,792
	Rep.	Cordell D. Jones	11,776
		Bucks	
10th	Rep.	Jim Greenwood	50,090
	Dem.	John J. Rufe	21,350
		Montgomery	
12th	Rep.	*Stewart J. Greenleaf	60,923
		Luzerne	
14th	Dem.	*Raphael Musto	52,339
	Rep.	Dale Walker	15,256
		Lehigh	
16th	Dem.	Roy C. Afflerbach	31,674
	Rep.	David K. Bausch	27,594
	Ind.	*Guy Kratzer	2,756
		Monroe and Northampton	
18th	Dem.	*Jeanette F. Reibman	37,365
	Rep.	Lawanda Givler	22,604
		Luzerne, Monroe, Pike, Susquehanna, Wayne and Wyoming	
20th	Rep.	*Charles D. Lemmond, Jr.	44,167
	Dem.	Joseph M. Bilbow	25,028
		Lackawanna and Monroe	
22nd	Dem.	*Robert J. Mellow	58,900
	Rep.	Robert Castellani	23,048
		Bucks and Montgomery	
24th	Rep.	*Edwin G. Holl	39,059
	Dem.	Steve Biddle	16,606

Dist.	Party	Name	Votes
		Delaware	
26th	Rep.	*F. Joseph Loeper	55,670
	Dem.	Dai Williams	25,326
		York	
28th	Rep.	*Ralph W. Hess	41,324
		Bedford, Blair, Fulton and Huntingdon	
30th	Rep.	*Robert C. Jubelirer	48,788
		Fayette and Somerset	
32nd	Dem.	*J. William Lincoln	46,642
		Cameron, Centre, Clearfield, Clinton, Juniata and Mifflin	
34th	Rep.	*J. Doyle Corman	43,185
	Dem.	Al Brelo	16,770
		Chester and Lancaster	
36th	Rep.	*Noah W. Wenger	43,819
		Allegheny	
38th	Dem.	*Leonard J. Bodack	43,380
	Rep.	Bill Pendleton	20,925
		Allegheny, Armstrong and Westmoreland	
40th	Dem.	John W. Regoli	39,928
	Rep.	George Pott	32,316
		Allegheny	
42nd	Dem.	*Eugene F. Scanlon	45,090
	Rep.	William R. Cordero	14,869
		Allegheny and Westmoreland	
44th	Rep.	*Frank A. Pecora	40,686
	Dem.	Ernest D'Achille	29,739
		Beaver, Greene and Washington	
46th	Dem.	*J. Barry Stout	59,346
	Rep.	J. Barry Stout	
		Berks, Lebanon and Lehigh	
48th	Rep.	*David J. Brightbill	35,033
	Dem.	John H. Anspach	26,176
		Crawford, Mercer and Venango	
50th	Rep.	*Roy W. Wilt	42,616

STATE HOUSE
General Election, November 4, 1986

Dist.	Party	Name	Votes
		Erie	
1st	Dem.	*Bernard J. Dombrowski.	11,500
2nd	Dem.	*Italo S. Cappabianca.	10,397
3rd	Rep.	*Karl Boyes.	14,729
4th	Rep.	*Harry E. Bowser	11,746
		Crawford and Erie	
5th	Rep.	*Jim Merry	11,965
		Crawford	
6th	Dem.	Connie G. Maine.	9,654
	Rep.	Gene G. Rumsey	6,099
		Mercer	
7th	Dem.	*Mike Gruitza	12,832
	Rep.	David DeSantis	3,918
		Butler and Mercer	
8th	Rep.	*Howard L. Fargo	10,260
	Dem.	Kathy W. James	4,625
		Lawrence	
9th	Dem.	*Thomas J. Fee	11,830
	Rep.	Donald E. Williams	4,587
		Beaver, Lawrence and Mercer	
10th	Dem.	Frank LaGrotta	9,720
	Rep.	Jim Gerlach.	8,589
		Butler	
11th	Dem.	*Joseph A. Steighner	11,469
	Rep.	James Cannard.	3,595
		Butler and Lawrence	
12th	Rep.	*James M. Burd	9,745
	Dem.	Ronald Goebel	5,237
		Chester	
13th	Rep.	*Art Hershey.	8,798
	Dem.	James B. Norton, III	3,969
		Beaver	
14th	Dem.	Michael R. Veon	12,476
	Rep.	Richard K. Pegg	4,204
15th	Dem.	*Nicholas A. Colafella.	18,285
	Rep.	Nicholas A. Colafella.	
16th	Dem.	*Charles Laughlin.	15,751
		Crawford and Mercer	
17th	Rep.	*Robert D. Robbins.	11,422
		Bucks	
18th	Rep.	*Edward F. Burns	9,036
	Dem.	Gregory C. McCarthy	5,370

Dist.	Party	Name	Votes
		Allegheny	
19th	Dem.	*K. Leroy Irvis	12,147
20th	Dem.	*Thomas J. Murphy	12,723
	Lib.	Charles Stutler	440
21st	Dem.	*Frank J. Pistella	11,372
22nd	Dem.	*Steve Seventy.	13,353
23rd	Dem.	*Ivan Itkin	13,701
	Rep.	Lawrence N. Paper	4,177
24th	Dem.	*Joseph Preston, Jr.	13,499
		Allegheny and Westmoreland	
25th	Dem.	*Joseph F. Markosek	12,076
	Rep.	Howard Ash	5,020
		Westmoreland	
26th	Dem.	*Eugene G. Saloom	10,193
		Allegheny	
27th	Dem.	*Thomas C. Petrone.	11,286
	Rep.	Nancy Ann Moorhead	3,780
	Pop.	Kathryn G. Meider.	162
28th	Rep.	Elaine F. Farmer	10,920
	Dem.	Dale Newman	7,911
29th	Dem.	*David J. Mayernik	13,417
	Rep.	John J. O'Brien, III	5,620
30th	Rep.	*Richard J. Cessar	18,673
	Dem.	Richard J. Cessar	
31st	Dem.	*Brian D. Clark	10,878
	Rep.	Leonard V. Stanga.	5,623
32nd	Dem.	*Anthony M. DeLuca	12,204
	Rep.	Roy C. Ritenour.	5,779
33rd	Dem.	*Roger F. Duffy	10,751
34th	Dem.	*Ronald R. Cowell	12,453
	Pop.	John F. Bright	459
35th	Dem.	*Tom Michlovic	13,064
36th	Dem.	*Michael Dawida.	14,782
	Rep.	Gerard F. Dauginikas	2,159
		Allegheny and Westmoreland	
37th	Dem.	*Emil Mrkonic.	12,793
	Rep.	Dennis W. Lion	2,910
		Allegheny	
38th	Dem.	*Richard D. Olasz.	13,161
39th	Dem.	*David K. Levdansky	12,409
	Rep.	John J. Skalican	3,431
40th	Rep.	*Alice S. Lantry.	12,396
	Dem.	Raymond C. McKelvey, Jr.	6,114
41st	Rep.	*Raymond T. Book	11,698
	Dem.	Nello N. Fiore	6,757
42nd	Rep.	*Terry McVerry	13,917
	Dem.	John Adams	6,421

Lancaster

| 43rd | Rep. | *Jere W. Schuler.................... | 12,659 |

Allegheny

44th	Dem.	*Ron Gamble	10,675
	Rep.	William R. Harper	3,674
45th	Dem.	*Fred A. Trello.....................	14,697

Beaver and Washington

| 46th | Dem. | *Victor John Lescovitz .... | 12,701 |

Washington

47th	Rep.	*Roger Raymond Fischer.............	9,165
	Dem.	Leo J. Trich, Jr.	6,131
48th	Dem.	*David W. Sweet....................	11,976
	Rep.	Michael J. Schultz.................	4,947

Fayette and Washington

| 49th | Dem. | *Peter J. Daley .... | 15,525 |

Greene, Fayette and Washington

| 50th | Dem. | *Bill DeWeese..................... | 14,152 |

Fayette

51st	Dem.	*Fred Taylor	9,416
	Rep.	Edward E. Olesh..................	4,503
52nd	Dem.	*Richard A. Kasunic	11,710

Montgomery

| 53rd | Rep. | *Robert W. Godshall................ | 11,695 |
| | Dem. | Robert N. Rosenberger............. | 3,852 |

Allegheny and Westmoreland

| 54th | Dem. | *Terry E. Van Horne .... | 13,204 |

Westmoreland

55th	Dem.	*Joseph A. Petrarca	11,796
56th	Dem.	*Allen Kukovich	9,030
	Rep.	Lenny Santimyer..................	7,124
57th	Dem.	*Amos K. Hutchinson	10,924
58th	Dem.	*James J. Manderino	13,355

Fayette and Westmoreland

| 59th | Rep. | *Jess Stairs .... | 10,562 |
| | Dem. | William A. Burd .... | 3,423 |

Armstrong

60th	Dem.	*Henry Livengood..................	15,229
	Pop.	Frank Habe.......................	832
	Rep.	Henry Livengood..................	

Montgomery

| 61st | Rep. | *Joseph M. Gladeck, Jr. .... | 12,084 |
| | Dem. | Stafford J. Keer................... | 4,643 |

Indiana

| 62nd | Rep. | *Paul Wass....................... | 10,513 |
| | Dem. | George T. Sink .... | 5,274 |

Armstrong and Clarion

63rd	Dem.	*David R. Wright...................	11,262
	Rep.	David E. Black.....................	5,500
	Pop.	Barbara Kammerdiener	127

Venango

| 64th | Rep. | *Ronald E. Black .... | 8,122 |
| | Dem. | John Last .... | 7,506 |

Forest, Venango and Warren

| 65th | Dem. | *Curt Bowley...................... | 10,985 |
| | Rep. | Gary E. Olson .... | 5,868 |

Indiana and Jefferson

| 66th | Rep. | Sam Smith .... | 8,677 |
| | Dem. | M. Joseph Betta .... | 8,069 |

Cameron, Clearfield and McKean

| 67th | Rep. | Kenneth M. Jadlowiec.............. | 9,041 |
| | Dem. | William Kuhn...................... | 4,758 |

Potter and Tioga

| 68th | Rep. | *Edgar A. Carlson.................. | 13,951 |

Somerset

| 69th | Dem. | *William R. Lloyd, Jr................ | 11,922 |
| | Rep. | Clay Mankamyer.................. | 6,400 |

Cambria and Somerset

| 70th | Rep. | *William Telek..................... | 9,807 |
| | Dem. | Paul E. Danel .... | 9,536 |

Cambria

| 71st | Dem. | *John N. Wozniak.................. | 12,298 |
| | Rep. | Thomas Eugene Heider .... | 5,926 |

Armstrong, Cambria and Indiana

| 72nd | Dem. | *William J. Stewart................. | 10,861 |
| | Rep. | Bob Kunkle .... | 5,656 |

Cambria

| 73rd | Dem. | *Edward J. Haluska .... | 13,656 |
| | Rep. | Robert A. Etchells................. | 3,611 |

Clearfield

| 74th | Dem. | *Camille George.................... | 15,618 |
| | Rep. | Camille George.................... | |

Clearfield and Elk

| 75th | Rep. | *Jim Distler....................... | 12,856 |
| | Dem. | Gary Lee Kraus.................... | 5,641 |

Centre, Clearfield, Clinton and Lycoming

| 76th | Dem. | *Russell P. Letterman .... | 9,699 |

Centre and Clearfield

| 77th | Rep. | *Lynn B. Herman .... | 8,734 |
| | Dem. | George Field .... | 4,937 |

Bedford, Fulton and Huntingdon

| 78th | Rep. | Dick L. Hess .... | 10,552 |
| | Dem. | Gary W. Ebersole .... | 8,139 |

Blair

79th	Rep.	*Richard A. Geist	12,672
	Dem.	Richard A. Geist	
80th	Rep.	*Edwin G. Johnson	11,778

Blair and Huntingdon

81st	Rep.	*Samuel E. Hayes, Jr.	12,766

Juniata, Mifflin and Perry

82nd	Rep.	*Walter F. DeVerter	10,618
	Dem.	David S. Stetter	5,889

Lycoming

83rd	Rep.	*Anthony J. Cimini	11,167
84th	Rep.	*Alvin C. Bush	10,339
	Dem.	Richard D. Sheddy	4,190

Snyder and Union

85th	Dem.	*John Showers	10,301
	Rep.	Kenneth F. Mease	4,743

Cumberland and Perry

86th	Rep.	*Fred C. Noye	10,839

Cumberland

87th	Rep.	*Hal Mowery	13,890
88th	Rep.	*John Kennedy	10,914
	Dem.	Paul S. Dlugolecki, Jr.	8,795

Franklin

89th	Dem.	*Jeffrey W. Coy	13,748
	Rep.	Jeffrey W. Coy	

Franklin and Fulton

90th	Rep.	*Terry Punt	9,382

Adams

91st	Dem.	*Kenneth J. Cole.	8,807
	Rep.	Shirley Reed	6,917

York

92nd	Rep.	*Bruce Smith	10,262
	Dem.	Paul E. Parsells.	4,860
93rd	Rep.	*A. Carville Foster, Jr.	12,054
94th	Rep.	*Gregory M. Snyder	10,641
	Ind.	Charles T. Johnson	1,419
95th	Dem.	*Michael E. Bortner	6,997
	Rep.	Charlene A. Vaught	4,470

Lancaster

96th	Rep.	*Marvin E. Miller, Jr.	7,381
	Dem.	Jon C. Lyons	5,307
97th	Rep.	*June N. Honaman.	16,459
	Dem.	Lou Kosmela	4,657
98th	Rep.	*Kenneth E. Brandt	12,436
99th	Rep.	*Terry Scheetz	11,966
100th	Rep.	*John E. Barley.	10,511
	Dem.	William E. Bunce.	4,261

Lebanon

101st	Rep.	*George W. Jackson.	8,928
	Dem.	Judy D. Hoffman	6,696

Lebanon and Lancaster

102nd	Rep.	*Nicholas B. Moehlmann	9,670
	Dem.	Charles T. Jones	4,339

Dauphin

103rd	Dem.	*Pete Wambach	8,420
	Rep.	Tom Pyne	4,731
104th	Rep.	*Jeffrey E. Piccola	17,572
	Dem.	Jeffrey E. Piccola	
105th	Rep.	*Joseph C. Manmiller	15,994
106th	Rep.	*Rudy Dininni	12,667

Columbia, Montour and Northumberland

107th	Dem.	*Robert E. Belfanti, Jr.	14,700

Montour, Northumberland and Snyder

108th	Rep.	*Merle H. Phillips	11,747

Columbia and Montour

109th	Dem.	*Ted Stuban	14,831
	Rep.	Ted Stuban	

Bradford

110th	Rep.	*J. Scot Chadwick	12,012

Bradford, Sullivan, Susquehanna and Wyoming

111th	Rep.	*Carmel Sirianni	17,454
	Dem.	Carmel Sirianni	

Lackawanna and Wayne

112th	Dem.	*Fred Belardi	13,834
	Rep.	Aaron K. Jones	5,368

Lackawanna

113th	Dem.	*Gaynor Cawley	15,418
114th	Rep.	*Frank A. Serafini	18,535
	Dem.	Frank A. Serafini	

Lackawanna and Wayne

115th	Dem.	*Edward G. Staback.	16,175
	Rep.	Robert J. Davis	5,274

Luzerne

116th	Rep.	*Correale F. Stevens.	11,198
	Dem.	Neil Craig, Jr..	4,937

Columbia and Luzerne

117th	Rep.	*George C. Hasay	10,420
	Dem.	Stephanie G. Wychock	7,087

Lackawanna and Luzerne

118th	Dem.	*Thomas M. Tigue	14,673

Luzerne

119th	Dem.	*Stanley J. Jarolin.	12,326
	Rep.	Blythe H. Evans.	7,446

120th	Rep.	Scott Dietterick	11,819
	Dem.	John J. Ruane	7,055
121st	Dem.	*Kevin Blaum	13,709

Carbon and Monroe

| 122nd | Dem. | *Keith R. McCall | 12,197 |

Columbia and Schuylkill

123rd	Dem.	*Edward J. Lucyk	11,792
	Rep.	Arthur D. Kaplan	5,926
	Ind.	Peter Paul Sarno, Jr	1,939

Lehigh and Schuylkill

| 124th | Rep. | *David G. Argall | 13,148 |

Northumberland and Schuylkill

| 125th | Dem. | *William E. Baldwin | 9,490 |
| | Rep. | Craig R. Morgan | 8,165 |

Berks

126th	Rep.	*Paul J. Angstadt	8,837
	Dem.	Mary H. Schmidt	7,625
127th	Dem.	*Thomas R. Caltagirone	8,910
	Rep.	Jeff Jefferson	2,819
128th	Rep.	*James J. Gallen	12,567

Berks and Lebanon

| 129th | Rep. | *John S. Davies | 11,458 |
| | Dem. | Zia Mahmood | 4,452 |

Berks

| 130th | Rep. | Dennis E. Leh | 7,547 |
| | Dem. | John R. McCloskey | 7,050 |

Lehigh

131st	Dem.	Karen A. Ritter	7,605
	Rep.	Neil Polster	6,814
132nd	Dem.	*John F. Pressmann	7,700
	Rep.	William Kurt Malkames	6,187
133rd	Dem.	*Paul McHale	9,896
134th	Rep.	*Don Snyder	13,537
	Dem.	Fred Duke	3,683

Lehigh and Northampton

| 135th | Dem. | *William C. Rybak | 9,130 |
| | Rep. | V. James Banks | 5,178 |

Northampton

136th	Dem.	*Robert Freeman	9,177
	Rep.	Edward A. Miller	4,321
137th	Rep.	*Leonard Q. Gruppo	12,073
	Dem.	Gordon T. Heller	5,095

Monroe and Northampton

| 138th | Dem. | *Frank W. Yandrisevits | 7,296 |
| | Rep. | James D. Oakes | 6,736 |

Pike, Susquehanna and Wayne

| 139th | Rep. | *Jerry Birmelin | 13,457 |

Bucks

140th	Dem.	Thomas C. Corrigan	8,840
	Rep.	Kathy Waters	6,297
141st	Dem.	Anthony Melio	8,224
	Rep.	Ralph L. McClelan	6,933
142nd	Rep.	*James L. Wright, Jr.	14,046
	Dem.	Vanya Tyrrell	6,174
143rd	Rep.	David W. Heckler	13,781
	Dem.	Theodore F. Schneider	5,999
144th	Rep.	*Benjamin H. Wilson	15,396
	Dem.	Benjamin H. Wilson	
145th	Rep.	*Paul I. Clymer	12,282

Montgomery

146th	Rep.	*Robert D. Reber, Jr.	8,692
	Dem.	Edmund S. Zerbey	3,901
147th	Rep.	*Raymond Bunt, Jr.	12,921
148th	Rep.	*Lois Sherman Hagarty	14,449
	Dem.	Tamara Steerman Gordon	6,324
149th	Rep.	*Richard A. McClatchy, Jr.	11,878
	Dem.	Philip M. Andrews	8,416
150th	Rep.	*Joseph A. Lashinger, Jr.	9,571
151st	Rep.	*George E. Saurman	15,717

Bucks and Montgomery

| 152nd | Rep. | *Roy W. Cornell | 12,793 |
| | Dem. | Thomas P. Murt | 5,413 |

Montgomery

153rd	Rep.	*Jon D. Fox	21,081
	Dem.	Jon D. Fox	
154th	Rep.	*Charles F. Nahill, Jr.	13,451
	Dem.	Phyllis Magerman	10,367

Chester

155th	Dem.	*Samuel W. Morris	8,823
	Rep.	J. Barry Pignoli	6,366
156th	Rep.	*Elinor Z. Taylor	12,879
	Dem.	Melva Mueller	3,989

Chester and Montgomery

| 157th | Rep. | *Peter R. Vroon | 14,385 |

Chester

| 158th | Rep. | *Joseph R. Pitts | 12,964 |

Delaware

159th	Rep.	*Robert C. Wright	8,891
	Dem.	Sheridan D. Jones, Jr.	5,034
160th	Rep.	*Kathrynann W. Durham	12,042
	Dem.	Ralph A. Garzia	5,439
161st	Rep.	*Thomas Gannon	14,843
	Dem.	James Barnes	6,501
162nd	Rep.	*Ron Raymond	11,828
	Dem.	Dorothy Gallagher	5,511
163rd	Rep.	*Nicholas A. Micozzie	13,313
	Dem.	Nancy B. Baulis	6,139

164th	Rep.	*Mario J. Civera, Jr.	15,181
	Dem.	John M. Rybnik	5,595
165th	Rep.	*Mary Ann Arty	18,260
	Dem.	Roberta M. Timpko	5,661
166th	Rep.	*Stephen F. Freind	15,543
	Dem.	Allen R. Polsky	7,323

Chester and Delaware

| 167th | Rep. | *Robert J. Flick | 16,754 |

Delaware

| 168th | Rep. | *Matthew J. Ryan | 15,790 |
| | Dem. | Jeff Nagorny | 6,224 |

Philadelphia

169th	Rep.	*Dennis M. O'Brien	12,166
	Dem.	Pat Gentile Owens	6,647
170th	Rep.	*George T. Kenney, Jr.	12,312
	Dem.	Elinda Fishman	6,713

Centre and Mifflin

| 171st | Dem. | *Ruth C. Rudy | 11,814 |
| | Rep. | Joyce Conklin Williamson | 5,530 |

Philadelphia

172nd	Rep.	*John M. Perzel	13,352
	Dem.	Robert V. O'Brien	8,857
173rd	Rep.	*Frances Weston	11,701
	Dem.	Alan D. Stasson	5,822
174th	Dem.	*Max Pievsky	16,174
	Rep.	Joseph Kabo	6,742
175th	Dem.	*Gerard A. Kosinski	11,381
	Rep.	Louis J. Koreck	6,552
176th	Rep.	*Chris Wogan	15,409
	Dem.	Gary Chilutti	5,528
177th	Rep.	*John Taylor	10,818
	Dem.	Frank M. Felici, Jr.	7,312

Bucks

| 178th | Rep. | *Roy Reinard | 14,376 |
| | Dem. | Mark B. DeBowe | 4,700 |

Philadelphia

179th	Dem.	*William W. Rieger	7,513
	Rep.	Mary A. Houser	2,940
	Con.	Cardell Johnson	157
180th	Dem.	*Ralph Acosta	7,547
	Rep.	Lester A. Ketters	2,969
181st	Dem.	*Alphonso Deal	10,542
	Rep.	Iris Thompson	1,468
182nd	Dem.	*Babette Josephs	12,021
	Rep.	John A. Kolody, Jr.	5,260
	Lib.	Ralph Mullinger	363
183rd	Dem.	*Nicholas J. Maiale	10,706
	Rep.	Victor A. Desiderio	5,369

| 184th | Dem. | *Joseph Howlett | 9,126 |
| | Rep. | Anthony N. Dipietro | 6,416 |

Delaware and Philadelphia

| 185th | Dem. | *Robert C. Donatucci | 9,106 |
| | Rep. | Robert Corcoran | 6,236 |

Philadelphia

| 186th | Dem. | *Edward A. Wiggins | 11,116 |
| | Rep. | F. Malana Pettit | 1,807 |

Berks and Lehigh

| 187th | Rep. | *Paul Semmel | 9,231 |
| | Dem. | James J. Gaffney | 5,154 |

Philadelphia

| 188th | Dem. | *James R. Roebuck | 11,008 |
| | Rep. | Daniel J. Callaghan | 1,194 |

Monroe

| 189th | Dem. | *Joseph W. Battisto | 14,019 |
| | Rep. | Joseph W. Battisto | |

Philadelphia

190th	Dem.	Vincent Hughes	13,428
	Rep.	Sandra R. Kellar	1,671
191st	Dem.	*Peter D. Truman	12,076
	Rep.	Joseph Tremarki	3,040
192nd	Dem.	*Chaka Fattah	13,282
	Rep.	Mary Bachetti	4,486

York

| 193rd | Rep. | *Donald W. Dorr | 11,849 |

Philadelphia

194th	Dem.	Richard Hayden	10,534
	Rep.	Carmela M. Lari	6,412
195th	Dem.	*Frank L. Oliver	11,639
	Rep.	Lowell Webb	2,354
196th	Dem.	*Ruth B. Harper	11,242
197th	Dem.	*Andrew J. Carn	12,876
	Rep.	Edward P. Bevans	853
198th	Dem.	*Robert W. O'Donnell	12,203

Adams, Cumberland and York

| 199th | Dem. | *John H. Broujos | 8,446 |

Philadelphia

200th	Dem.	*Gordon J. Linton	14,911
201st	Dem.	*David P. Richardson, Jr.	13,857
	Rep.	Werner F. Tillmann	1,365
202nd	Dem.	*Mark B. Cohen	11,187
	Rep.	James G. Wright	5,785
203rd	Dem.	*Dwight Evans	12,294
	Rep.	Larry S. Kramer	3,774

1986 GENERAL ELECTION
By Political Subdivision

	GOVERNOR/LT. GOVERNOR			U.S. SENATE		
	Republican Scranton/ Fisher	Democratic Casey/ Singel	Consumer Hoover/ Brickhouse	Republican Arlen Specter	Democratic Bob Edgar	Consumer Lance S. Haver
ADAMS COUNTY						
ABBOTTSTOWN BOROUGH	77	63		74	67	
ARENDTSVILLE BOROUGH	163	110	2	166	110	1
BENDERSVILLE BOROUGH	117	57		124	48	
BERWICK TOWNSHIP	137	88	3	134	91	3
BIGLERVILLE BOROUGH	242	99	2	239	101	3
BONNEAUVILLE BOROUGH	101	134	2	111	124	1
BUTLER TOWNSHIP	397	224	8	427	199	3
CARROLL VALLEY BOROUGH	164	107		164	105	
CONEWAGO TOWNSHIP	362	429	3	425	365	4
CUMBERLAND TOWNSHIP	1,026	666	13	1,045	648	6
EAST BERLIN BOROUGH	211	113	7	221	108	2
FAIRFIELD BOROUGH...............	98	90	1	109	75	1
FRANKLIN TOWNSHIP...............	571	440	9	596	416	6
FREEDOM TOWNSHIP..............	111	74	3	119	72	1
GERMANY TOWNSHIP	259	173	3	276	156	2
GETTYSBURG BOROUGH	1,041	681	25	1,037	697	14
WARD 01	411	270	10	421	267	4
WARD 02	233	184	9	220	204	5
WARD 03	397	227	6	396	226	5
HAMILTON TOWNSHIP..............	172	170	3	198	148	1
HAMILTONBAN TOWNSHIP	273	150	5	273	155	4
HIGHLAND TOWNSHIP	144	70	2	145	70	3
HUNTINGTON TOWNSHIP...........	334	179	4	346	159	2
LATIMORE TOWNSHIP..............	293	155	6	314	144	1
LIBERTY TOWNSHIP	100	78	3	115	66	1
LITTLESTOWN BOROUGH	490	367	11	521	339	5
WARD 01	225	170	6	241	156	3
WARD 02	265	197	5	280	183	2
MC SHERRYSTOWN BOROUGH........	221	436	7	300	357	4
MENALLEN TOWNSHIP..............	475	173	12	509	150	4
MT. JOY TOWNSHIP	382	224	7	397	208	5
MT. PLEASANT TOWNSHIP	366	315	11	415	266	6
NEW OXFORD BOROUGH	245	167	4	254	157	4
OXFORD TOWNSHIP	278	249	6	304	224	5
READING TOWNSHIP	393	265	14	427	230	11
STRABAN TOWNSHIP	696	417	11	726	387	6
TYRONE TOWNSHIP	216	93	2	220	89	2
UNION TOWNSHIP..................	254	178	8	274	162	6
YORK SPRINGS BOROUGH	101	43	3	107	37	1
ADAMS COUNTY TOTALS	**10,510**	**7,277**	**200**	**11,112**	**6,730**	**118**
ALLEGHENY COUNTY						
ALEPPO TOWNSHIP	187	148	7	214	125	3
ASPINWALL BOROUGH...............	649	470	13	752	364	12
AVALON BOROUGH	977	908	11	1,153	724	13
WARD 01	162	224	3	194	187	3
WARD 02	358	278	5	433	206	4
WARD 03	457	406	3	526	331	6
BALDWIN TOWNSHIP	420	438	5	519	320	6
BALDWIN BOROUGH..................	2,813	4,124	79	3,649	3,285	56
BELL ACRES BOROUGH..............	235	229	3	260	198	4
BELLEVUE BOROUGH	1,430	1,392	25	1,656	1,157	23
WARD 01	472	424	9	532	360	9
WARD 02	462	500	8	532	418	9
WARD 03	496	468	8	592	379	5
BEN AVON BOROUGH	439	276	7	468	246	3
BEN AVON HEIGHTS BOROUGH	147	18	4	137	28	2
BETHEL PARK BOROUGH.............	6,540	4,317	82	7,196	3,544	83
WARD 01	540	599	16	609	515	13
WARD 02	677	415	5	762	324	8
WARD 03	978	465	5	1,012	401	14
WARD 04	650	493	7	752	384	8
WARD 05	670	556	16	781	450	11
WARD 06	701	465	7	807	349	6

	GOVERNOR/LT. GOVERNOR			U.S. SENATE		
	Republican Scranton/ Fisher	Democratic Casey/ Singel	Consumer Hoover/ Brickhouse	Republican Arlen Specter	Democratic Bob Edgar	Consumer Lance S. Haver
WARD 07	752	420	10	785	370	9
WARD 08	842	476	9	888	402	9
WARD 09	730	428	7	800	349	5
BLAWNOX BOROUGH	227	413	8	299	344	5
BRACKENRIDGE BOROUGH	344	853	15	397	788	13
WARD 01	71	256	2	91	228	3
WARD 02	140	349	6	165	322	6
WARD 03	133	248	7	141	238	4
BRADDOCK BOROUGH.	204	1,065	27	290	984	26
WARD 01	23	218	3	42	202	5
WARD 02	36	225	6	59	203	4
WARD 03	50	251	11	68	235	11
WARD 04	95	371	7	121	344	6
BRADDOCK HILLS BOROUGH	242	548	13	312	496	8
BRADFORD WOODS BOROUGH	372	132	2	380	129	
BRENTWOOD BOROUGH	1,670	1,873	33	2,019	1,524	35
BRIDGEVILLE BOROUGH	680	1,088	8	778	954	26
CARNEGIE BOROUGH	1,016	1,655	33	1,280	1,362	31
WARD 01	376	870	16	483	749	16
WARD 02	640	785	17	797	613	15
CASTLE SHANNON BOROUGH	1,211	1,683	25	1,557	1,299	24
CHALFANT BOROUGH	93	189	5	114	164	5
CHESWICK BOROUGH	315	472	9	409	378	8
CHURCHILL BOROUGH	1,258	512	10	1,339	424	11
CLAIRTON CITY	750	2,635	32	1,099	2,252	32
WARD 01	245	530	9	345	436	9
WARD 02	505	2,105	23	754	1,816	23
COLLIER TOWNSHIP	532	857	19	604	772	9
WARD 01	74	78	1	75	74	
WARD 02	194	258	2	203	239	2
WARD 03	116	235	6	148	205	
WARD 05	58	118	2	73	96	2
WARD 06	90	168	8	105	158	5
CORAOPOLIS BOROUGH	642	1,552	19	813	1,363	19
WARD 01	130	400	6	165	359	7
WARD 02	90	322	1	116	294	1
WARD 03	250	414	7	311	356	4
WARD 04	172	416	5	221	354	7
CRAFTON BOROUGH	1,168	1,141	20	1,298	1,006	18
WARD 01	390	364	2	426	315	8
WARD 02	356	400	7	411	349	6
WARD 03	422	377	11	461	342	4
CRESCENT TOWNSHIP.	238	389	11	321	314	10
WARD 01	122	212	4	164	177	3
WARD 02	116	177	7	157	137	7
DORMONT BOROUGH	1,582	1,762	25	1,798	1,509	33
DRAVOSBURG BOROUGH	319	528	16	403	437	17
DUQUESNE CITY	786	1,950	28	1,033	1,681	35
WARD 01	297	670	4	384	574	10
WARD 02	274	625	11	360	518	14
WARD 03	215	655	13	289	589	11
EAST DEER TOWNSHIP.	95	478	4	127	442	4
WARD 01	37	189	2	56	172	2
WARD 02	58	289	2	71	270	2
EAST MCKEESPORT BOROUGH	320	519	11	428	400	13
EAST PITTSBURGH BOROUGH	161	658	5	240	563	5
WARD 01	45	179	2	71	146	3
WARD 02	57	205	2	94	161	2
WARD 03	59	274	1	75	256	
EDGEWOOD BOROUGH	963	504	27	916	554	16
EDGEWORTH BOROUGH	652	145	1	674	124	1
ELIZABETH TOWNSHIP	1,890	2,725	50	2,313	2,264	43
WARD 01	251	308	4	295	272	6
WARD 02	205	317	5	247	260	5
WARD 03	181	387	10	234	331	7
WARD 04	315	245	3	350	200	2
WARD 05	214	244	5	235	218	4
WARD 06	231	170	3	263	132	2
WARD 07	113	302	6	161	250	4
WARD 08	221	320	8	296	250	6

	GOVERNOR/LT. GOVERNOR			U.S. SENATE		
	Republican Scranton/ Fisher	Democratic Casey/ Singel	Consumer Hoover/ Brickhouse	Republican Arlen Specter	Democratic Bob Edgar	Consumer Lance S. Haver
WARD 09	159	432	6	232	351	7
ELIZABETH BOROUGH	215	352	7	272	282	5
EMSWORTH BOROUGH	437	451	12	517	371	5
ETNA BOROUGH	440	889	18	652	685	20
WARD 01	143	330	7	232	240	10
WARD 02	151	294	2	188	256	5
WARD 03	146	265	9	232	189	5
FAWN TOWNSHIP	240	398	8	304	334	10
FINDLAY TOWNSHIP	449	634	14	577	515	12
FOREST HILLS BOROUGH	1,648	1,273	31	1,783	1,130	26
FORWARD TOWNSHIP.	387	756	14	528	619	11
FOX CHAPEL BOROUGH	1,736	281	6	1,779	247	3
FRANKLIN PARK BOROUGH.	1,722	749	14	1,880	563	20
WARD 01	552	286	4	596	228	6
WARD 02	558	244	5	606	193	9
WARD 03	612	219	5	678	142	5
FRAZER TOWNSHIP	131	300	3	174	255	2
GLASSPORT BOROUGH.	396	1,437	25	594	1,247	31
GLENFIELD BOROUGH.	31	38		41	28	
GREEN TREE BOROUGH	1,223	862	18	1,377	690	22
HAMPTON TOWNSHIP.	1,826	1,289	26	2,109	991	27
HARMAR TOWNSHIP	250	757	12	375	626	9
HARRISON TOWNSHIP	1,304	2,710	36	1,537	2,447	48
WARD 01	85	527	9	123	485	4
WARD 02	163	495	2	190	462	6
WARD 03	374	732	9	449	646	18
WARD 04	273	498	10	312	458	10
WARD 05	409	458	6	463	396	10
HAYSVILLE BOROUGH	12	19		19	13	
HEIDELBERG BOROUGH	132	362	4	171	324	8
HOMESTEAD BOROUGH	230	1,278	18	289	1,241	20
WARD 01	86	416	6	99	416	4
WARD 02	68	447	5	84	424	5
WARD 03	76	415	7	106	401	11
INDIANA TOWNSHIP	740	815	24	857	695	24
INGRAM BOROUGH.	571	709	13	678	588	15
JEFFERSON BOROUGH	1,069	1,494	22	1,295	1,256	22
KENNEDY TOWNSHIP	1,011	1,800	25	1,306	1,485	16
KILBUCK TOWNSHIP	204	111	4	239	80	1
LEET TOWNSHIP	250	253	7	289	216	3
LEETSDALE BOROUGH	165	297	1	208	262	1
LIBERTY BOROUGH	359	710	17	493	578	11
LINCOLN BOROUGH	107	235	4	153	186	4
MARSHALL TOWNSHIP	573	366	14	635	306	12
MC CANDLESS TOWNSHIP.	5,782	3,061	79	6,553	2,264	67
WARD 01	831	497	11	984	348	12
WARD 02	946	417	12	1,049	308	12
WARD 03	991	406	10	1,087	299	13
WARD 04	696	442	8	757	382	4
WARD 05	855	495	16	986	359	12
WARD 06	727	494	12	866	341	11
WARD 07	736	310	10	824	227	3
MC DONALD BOROUGH	22	83		39	68	
(BALANCE IN WASHINGTON CO.)						
MC KEES ROCKS BOROUGH	635	1,732	22	934	1,431	18
WARD 01	83	333	4	134	290	1
WARD 02	170	601	8	268	514	7
WARD 03	382	798	10	532	627	10
MC KEESPORT CITY	2,219	5,324	97	2,970	4,593	113
WARD 01	1	6		2	3	1
WARD 02	21	85	4	30	79	2
WARD 03	45	275	4	43	276	7
WARD 04	46	96	1	60	77	5
WARD 05	61	190	5	77	175	5
WARD 06	93	370	4	133	331	5
WARD 07	550	1,345	22	752	1,152	21
WARD 08	470	975	13	622	811	24
WARD 09	316	657	14	400	598	6
WARD 10	158	361	9	209	317	16
WARD 11	185	513	9	262	439	10

	GOVERNOR/LT. GOVERNOR			U.S. SENATE		
	Republican Scranton/ Fisher	Democratic Casey/ Singel	Consumer Hoover/ Brickhouse	Republican Arlen Specter	Democratic Bob Edgar	Consumer Lance S. Haver
WARD 12	273	451	12	380	335	11
MILLVALE BOROUGH................	384	733	17	535	595	8
MONROEVILLE BOROUGH...........	4,345	4,622	91	5,382	3,560	80
WARD 01	499	671	14	612	560	6
WARD 02	1,005	556	6	1,136	416	6
WARD 03	816	691	15	980	509	16
WARD 04	497	690	15	665	519	17
WARD 05	434	525	13	557	406	10
WARD 06	549	672	14	724	508	13
WARD 07	545	817	14	708	642	12
MOON TOWNSHIP	2,663	2,363	35	2,974	2,033	29
MT. LEBANON TOWNSHIP.............	9,026	3,662	82	9,234	3,390	71
WARD 01	1,859	663	7	1,859	650	8
WARD 02	2,031	766	15	2,079	705	17
WARD 03	1,953	735	16	2,029	637	17
WARD 04	1,524	734	23	1,560	685	13
WARD 05	1,659	764	21	1,707	713	16
MT. OLIVER BOROUGH	335	827	11	474	682	11
MUNHALL BOROUGH	1,579	3,066	64	1,993	2,664	72
NEVILLE TOWNSHIP	208	340	5	230	322	3
WARD 01	54	122		66	116	
WARD 02	68	111	3	71	107	
WARD 03	86	107	2	93	99	3
NORTH BRADDOCK BOROUGH........	468	1,804	34	692	1,601	27
WARD 01	169	651	14	263	567	8
WARD 02	150	639	12	227	568	13
WARD 03	149	514	8	202	466	6
NORTH FAYETTE TOWNSHIP	723	1,123	16	913	942	14
NORTH VERSAILLES TOWNSHIP.......	1,213	2,720	48	1,608	2,310	35
WARD 01	275	462	11	356	384	7
WARD 02	184	323	7	235	262	1
WARD 03	201	320	3	271	231	1
WARD 04	166	393	9	233	330	6
WARD 05	113	328	6	154	296	4
WARD 06	207	542	7	290	458	10
WARD 07	67	352	5	69	349	6
O'HARA TOWNSHIP.................	1,994	1,169	34	2,182	989	22
WARD 01	355	252	9	410	199	6
WARD 02	386	212	4	430	170	3
WARD 03	278	344	12	328	301	8
WARD 04	536	162	1	536	156	2
WARD 05	439	199	8	478	163	3
OAKDALE BOROUGH	196	395	13	262	326	5
OAKMONT BOROUGH................	1,325	1,009	26	1,456	855	21
OHIO TOWNSHIP	387	341	13	473	262	8
OSBORNE BOROUGH................	156	55	1	166	48	
PENN HILLS TOWNSHIP	7,620	9,133	194	9,468	7,254	153
WARD 01	313	1,235	27	422	1,150	16
WARD 02	733	742	10	847	602	15
WARD 03	1,024	1,009	33	1,282	749	22
WARD 04	926	805	20	1,119	598	14
WARD 05	1,174	1,098	20	1,430	835	17
WARD 06	776	1,136	21	1,048	878	14
WARD 07	1,062	1,240	23	1,325	963	21
WARD 08	939	1,194	21	1,187	948	21
WARD 09	673	674	19	808	531	13
PENNSBURY VILLAGE BOROUGH......	135	81	5	140	81	2
PINE TOWNSHIP	752	524	12	891	388	9
PITCAIRN BOROUGH	382	707	14	501	571	20
PITTSBURGH CITY	37,392	76,758	1,330	45,102	69,749	777
WARD 01	104	310	6	134	288	4
WARD 02	216	256	2	247	232	1
WARD 03	172	1,085	12	212	1,035	6
WARD 04	1,534	2,689	62	1,691	2,559	28
WARD 05	502	4,317	49	650	4,192	29
WARD 06	405	1,217	20	514	1,108	14
WARD 07	2,382	1,624	43	2,233	1,752	17
WARD 08	1,132	2,036	37	1,282	1,870	28
WARD 09	843	2,183	35	1,111	1,920	34
WARD 10	1,893	4,077	62	2,453	3,521	42

	GOVERNOR/LT. GOVERNOR			U.S. SENATE		
	Republican Scranton/ Fisher	Democratic Casey/ Singel	Consumer Hoover/ Brickhouse	Republican Arlen Specter	Democratic Bob Edgar	Consumer Lance S. Haver
WARD 11	1,711	3,017	73	1,886	2,936	35
WARD 12	441	3,809	45	625	3,665	29
WARD 13	563	4,475	53	686	4,379	45
WARD 14	6,967	5,745	199	7,200	5,907	49
WARD 15	1,645	4,048	56	2,320	3,385	33
WARD 16	662	2,962	30	955	2,655	36
WARD 17	572	1,732	25	760	1,553	18
WARD 18	803	2,235	30	1,034	1,990	19
WARD 19	3,829	6,581	103	4,933	5,495	77
WARD 20	1,972	3,386	70	2,434	2,936	32
WARD 21	139	1,032	5	166	1,019	9
WARD 22	364	576	18	386	570	5
WARD 23	263	568	9	321	516	7
WARD 24	567	1,273	10	740	1,074	7
WARD 25	366	1,194	29	414	1,167	14
WARD 26	1,287	2,915	59	1,702	2,538	28
WARD 27	1,549	2,855	39	2,155	2,274	30
WARD 28	1,230	2,377	30	1,518	2,084	26
WARD 29	1,347	2,513	49	1,773	2,079	38
WARD 30	361	997	17	505	863	11
WARD 31	603	1,163	22	817	938	12
WARD 32	968	1,511	31	1,245	1,249	14
PLEASANT HILLS BOROUGH	1,906	1,238	31	2,154	997	27
PLUM BOROUGH....................	2,888	3,802	68	3,630	3,035	63
PORT VUE BOROUGH...............	399	1,155	22	586	977	24
RANKIN BOROUGH	122	754	38	199	674	13
RESERVE TOWNSHIP	569	853	12	800	633	13
WARD 01	124	185	4	178	137	2
WARD 02	144	231	4	213	167	2
WARD 03	140	197	1	193	148	3
WARD 04	161	240	3	216	181	6
RICHLAND TOWNSHIP	1,584	985	20	1,770	793	24
ROBINSON TOWNSHIP	1,293	1,791	29	1,583	1,483	31
ROSS TOWNSHIP..................	6,280	5,312	127	7,469	4,114	94
WARD 01	902	646	19	1,040	517	12
WARD 02	1,155	674	12	1,317	499	6
WARD 03	662	533	14	813	378	17
WARD 04	583	485	8	685	381	5
WARD 05	680	595	12	824	440	16
WARD 06	415	659	10	540	531	9
WARD 07	407	612	15	521	494	11
WARD 08	783	620	22	911	504	15
WARD 09	693	488	15	818	370	3
ROSSLYN FARMS BOROUGH	197	41	3	188	45	4
SCOTT TOWNSHIP..................	2,928	3,277	40	3,367	2,754	49
WARD 01	145	498	3	176	438	6
WARD 02	85	194	2	117	163	3
WARD 03	374	430	10	437	369	5
WARD 04	415	444	3	505	347	7
WARD 05	254	380	3	300	319	5
WARD 06	358	364	5	403	306	3
WARD 07	524	269	8	561	230	4
WARD 08	437	435	5	506	360	7
WARD 09	336	263	1	362	222	9
SEWICKLEY BOROUGH	866	575	18	940	500	12
WARD 01	178	206	4	204	177	2
WARD 02	395	178	7	430	146	3
WARD 03	293	191	7	306	177	7
SEWICKLEY HEIGHTS BOROUGH	304	54		311	42	3
SEWICKLEY HILLS BOROUGH	86	44	1	97	35	
SHALER TOWNSHIP	5,415	5,370	126	6,844	3,940	80
WARD 01	579	813	17	796	615	15
WARD 02	644	876	16	881	641	6
WARD 03	745	723	17	921	535	16
WARD 04	1,056	712	21	1,239	523	13
WARD 05	1,034	710	23	1,266	479	13
WARD 06	785	801	14	1,013	570	5
WARD 07	572	735	18	728	577	12
SHARPSBURG BOROUGH	336	1,013	7	427	915	10
SOUTH FAYETTE TOWNSHIP	842	1,229	13	969	1,060	14

	GOVERNOR/LT. GOVERNOR			U.S. SENATE		
	Republican Scranton/ Fisher	Democratic Casey/ Singel	Consumer Hoover/ Brickhouse	Republican Arlen Specter	Democratic Bob Edgar	Consumer Lance S. Haver
WARD 01	492	416	6	518	370	6
WARD 02	53	152	1	71	130	1
WARD 03	74	210	1	102	176	1
WARD 04	29	83		39	70	1
WARD 05	50	146	2	68	124	1
WARD 06	88	103	2	100	89	1
WARD 07	56	119	1	71	101	3
SOUTH PARK TOWNSHIP	1,471	1,958	32	1,776	1,619	30
SOUTH VERSAILLES TOWNSHIP	44	90	1	53	83	1
SPRINGDALE TOWNSHIP	146	423	7	225	344	3
SPRINGDALE BOROUGH	415	842	9	522	735	23
STOWE TOWNSHIP	844	2,531	34	1,234	2,132	35
WARD 01	66	333	1	90	312	
WARD 02	131	440	5	200	358	6
WARD 03	78	258	8	126	218	6
WARD 04	162	499	5	253	398	9
WARD 05	72	234		111	182	4
WARD 06	115	195	5	139	168	6
WARD 07	58	150	1	84	127	2
WARD 08	98	253	6	142	216	2
WARD 09	64	169	3	89	153	
SWISSVALE BOROUGH.	1,363	2,001	50	1,654	1,792	35
TARENTUM BOROUGH	434	897	16	530	788	21
WARD 01	224	320	9	256	289	10
WARD 02	110	184	4	139	157	6
WARD 03	100	393	3	135	342	5
THORNBURG BOROUGH	152	56		151	48	3
TRAFFORD BOROUGH	7	30	1	14	21	1
(BALANCE IN WESTMORELAND CO.)						
TURTLE CREEK BOROUGH	516	1,205	19	751	965	30
WARD 01	220	482	10	300	399	11
WARD 02	142	266	4	201	211	10
WARD 03	154	457	5	250	355	9
UPPER ST. CLAIR TOWNSHIP	5,448	1,599	30	5,553	1,422	36
WARD 01	1,015	254	6	1,035	227	7
WARD 02	1,068	399	8	1,137	321	7
WARD 03	1,127	342	3	1,103	346	9
WARD 04	1,175	313	4	1,222	247	6
WARD 05	1,063	291	9	1,056	281	7
VERONA BOROUGH	257	503	14	300	427	16
VERSAILLES BOROUGH.	169	378	6	211	334	9
WALL BOROUGH	38	219	2	65	196	2
WEST DEER TOWNSHIP	1,075	1,773	31	1,409	1,438	24
WEST ELIZABETH BOROUGH	61	142	1	91	110	3
WEST HOMESTEAD BOROUGH.	254	748	22	323	684	12
WEST MIFFLIN BOROUGH	2,381	5,598	123	3,386	4,685	89
WEST VIEW BOROUGH.	1,043	1,488	36	1,318	1,225	25
WHITAKER BOROUGH.	135	442	5	181	394	6
WHITE OAK BOROUGH	1,584	1,694	41	1,969	1,337	26
WHITEHALL BOROUGH	3,153	2,248	34	3,632	1,738	30
WILKINS TOWNSHIP	1,347	1,274	34	1,597	1,032	17
WARD 01	960	833	20	1,140	652	11
WARD 03	387	441	14	457	380	6
WILKINSBURG BOROUGH	2,488	3,362	53	2,627	3,240	53
WARD 01	874	1,356	12	937	1,312	9
WARD 02	828	959	18	908	880	21
WARD 03	786	1,047	23	782	1,048	23
WILMERDING BOROUGH	220	556	8	284	493	8
WARD 01	70	129	1	95	102	2
WARD 02	52	162		71	147	2
WARD 03	76	175	4	97	156	3
WARD 04	22	90	3	21	88	1
ALLEGHENY COUNTY TOTALS	**180,426**	**241,453**	**4,496**	**214,738**	**207,035**	**3,604**
ARMSTRONG COUNTY						
APOLLO BOROUGH.	217	271	4	251	241	3
WARD 01	126	111	2	143	96	1
WARD 02	91	160	2	108	145	2
APPLEWOLD BOROUGH.	60	67	4	68	59	5
ATWOOD BOROUGH	13	18		17	14	

	GOVERNOR/LT. GOVERNOR			U.S. SENATE		
	Republican Scranton/ Fisher	Democratic Casey/ Singel	Consumer Hoover/ Brickhouse	Republican Arlen Specter	Democratic Bob Edgar	Consumer Lance S. Haver
BETHEL TOWNSHIP	112	199	5	164	150	2
BOGGS TOWNSHIP	141	92	4	185	50	3
BRADYS BEND TOWNSHIP	105	172		134	145	
BURRELL TOWNSHIP	105	81	4	129	58	2
CADOGAN TOWNSHIP	37	137	1	65	108	2
COWANSHANNOCK TOWNSHIP	281	458	11	390	359	3
DAYTON BOROUGH	136	72	1	153	55	
EAST FRANKLIN TOWNSHIP	676	475	9	790	359	8
ELDERTON BOROUGH	58	39	3	60	38	1
FORD CITY BOROUGH	400	1,054	12	545	907	21
FORD CLIFF BOROUGH	57	121		65	114	
FREEPORT BOROUGH	242	404	9	296	354	4
GILPIN TOWNSHIP	280	620	6	388	522	7
HOVEY TOWNSHIP	9	14		15	7	
KISKIMINETAS TOWNSHIP	440	820	14	658	615	3
KITTANNING TOWNSHIP	270	230	11	319	180	12
KITTANNING BOROUGH	653	866	9	795	508	9
WARD 01	174	306	3	163	123	1
WARD 02	117	227	5	210	119	3
WARD 03	227	179		249	153	3
WARD 04	135	154	1	173	113	2
LEECHBURG BOROUGH	291	533	8	351	477	4
MADISON TOWNSHIP	139	89	5	185	44	6
MAHONING TOWNSHIP	217	290	4	307	191	2
MANOR TOWNSHIP	732	845	17	893	682	22
MANORVILLE BOROUGH	47	77	1	57	65	2
NORTH APOLLO BOROUGH	158	258	2	200	219	2
NORTH BUFFALO TOWNSHIP	391	388	7	490	290	12
PARKER CITY BOROUGH	114	104	4	131	82	2
WARD 01	50	47		52	41	2
WARD 02	64	57	4	79	41	
PARKS TOWNSHIP	219	533	7	321	432	5
PERRY TOWNSHIP	44	47	2	47	42	1
PINE TOWNSHIP	57	82	2	77	62	3
PLUMCREEK TOWNSHIP	215	265	6	287	193	6
RAYBURN TOWNSHIP	179	218	5	248	155	3
REDBANK TOWNSHIP	133	133	1	185	69	2
RURAL VALLEY BOROUGH	156	150	5	180	130	3
SOUTH BEND TOWNSHIP	158	144	4	191	109	5
SOUTH BETHLEHEM BOROUGH	106	61	1	121	47	
SOUTH BUFFALO TOWNSHIP	400	383	13	502	279	9
SUGARCREEK TOWNSHIP	209	188	10	265	133	9
VALLEY TOWNSHIP	101	97	4	131	67	1
WASHINGTON TOWNSHIP	103	109	5	135	81	6
WAYNE TOWNSHIP	186	123	1	234	73	3
WEST FRANKLIN TOWNSHIP	263	230	5	327	165	2
WEST KITTANNING BOROUGH	271	249	1	323	192	2
WORTHINGTON BOROUGH	157	84	5	179	66	1
ARMSTRONG COUNTY TOTALS	**9,338**	**11,890**	**232**	**11,854**	**9,188**	**198**
BEAVER COUNTY						
ALIQUIPPA BOROUGH	847	3,642	28	1,154	3,511	29
AMBRIDGE BOROUGH	556	2,319	24	873	2,104	29
BADEN BOROUGH	432	1,306	22	654	1,154	20
BEAVER BOROUGH	1,208	777	22	1,386	665	8
WARD 01	334	217	4	373	191	3
WARD 02	394	301	11	478	248	4
WARD 03	480	259	7	535	226	1
BEAVER FALLS CITY	851	2,316	25	1,145	2,203	28
WARD 01	50	225	1	77	221	1
WARD 02	68	243		107	222	3
WARD 03	101	282	3	135	270	5
WARD 04	47	149	2	60	152	2
WARD 05	168	439	5	222	421	3
WARD 06	91	302	1	109	307	3
WARD 07	326	676	13	435	610	11
BIG BEAVER BOROUGH	206	552	9	278	516	9
BRIDGEWATER BOROUGH	79	122	2	94	112	3
BRIGHTON TOWNSHIP	1,255	1,042	18	1,477	872	20
CENTER TOWNSHIP	1,014	2,475	29	1,354	2,259	22

	GOVERNOR/LT. GOVERNOR			U.S. SENATE		
	Republican Scranton/ Fisher	Democratic Casey/ Singel	Consumer Hoover/ Brickhouse	Republican Arlen Specter	Democratic Bob Edgar	Consumer Lance S. Haver
CHIPPEWA TOWNSHIP	1,106	1,359	24	1,411	1,094	18
CONWAY BOROUGH	226	695	10	347	606	9
DARLINGTON TOWNSHIP	214	276	6	264	244	3
DARLINGTON BOROUGH	36	47	2	48	35	2
DAUGHERTY TOWNSHIP	444	701	24	617	564	13
EAST ROCHESTER BOROUGH	67	177	1	99	149	2
EASTVALE BOROUGH	13	58	1	27	48	1
ECONOMY BOROUGH	989	1,747	34	1,322	1,504	19
ELLWOOD CITY BOROUGH . . . . (BALANCE IN LAWRENCE CO.)						
FALLSTON BOROUGH	29	70	1	38	65	
FRANKFORT SPRINGS BOROUGH	20	40		31	34	1
FRANKLIN TOWNSHIP	419	591	14	549	509	12
FREEDOM BOROUGH	126	410	11	174	398	2
WARD 01	39	126	5	59	118	
WARD 02	37	169	4	52	165	1
WARD 03	50	115	2	63	115	1
GEORGETOWN BOROUGH	25	38	2	37	31	1
GLASGOW BOROUGH	9	20		10	21	
GREENE TOWNSHIP	231	266	8	290	233	1
HANOVER TOWNSHIP	322	349	14	402	299	9
HARMONY TOWNSHIP	340	1,131	21	519	1,011	11
HOMEWOOD BOROUGH	2	39	1	5	38	
HOOKSTOWN BOROUGH	36	34		47	27	
HOPEWELL TOWNSHIP	1,460	3,543	34	1,974	3,183	44
INDEPENDENCE TOWNSHIP	234	274	7	279	245	2
INDUSTRY BOROUGH	255	500	2	301	472	3
KOPPEL BOROUGH	58	306	1	99	285	
MARION TOWNSHIP	135	134	1	169	111	3
MIDLAND BOROUGH	285	1,019	7	377	993	5
MONACA BOROUGH	582	1,531	20	797	1,410	15
WARD 01	45	123	1	57	114	2
WARD 02	102	188	2	142	170	1
WARD 03	63	210	6	78	208	5
WARD 04	235	644	5	325	591	4
WARD 05	137	366	6	195	327	3
NEW BRIGHTON BOROUGH	660	1,305	22	843	1,191	25
WARD 01	153	332	12	199	304	10
WARD 02	110	166	3	141	155	4
WARD 03	59	166	2	78	159	1
WARD 04	120	224	1	153	200	4
WARD 05	218	417	4	272	373	6
NEW GALILEE BOROUGH	35	122		53	107	1
NEW SEWICKLEY TOWNSHIP	713	1,044	28	955	858	23
NORTH SEWICKLEY TOWNSHIP	827	1,411	17	1,039	1,272	26
OHIOVILLE BOROUGH	312	660	13	446	567	4
PATTERSON TOWNSHIP	463	589	9	566	514	2
PATTERSON HEIGHTS BOROUGH	193	123	3	214	110	2
POTTER TOWNSHIP	54	98	2	81	81	2
PULASKI TOWNSHIP	109	359	6	164	327	7
RACCOON TOWNSHIP	309	475	13	418	396	13
ROCHESTER TOWNSHIP	307	683	4	456	575	6
ROCHESTER BOROUGH	358	703	12	492	611	10
WARD 01	91	157	3	126	131	3
WARD 02	96	179	3	127	158	3
WARD 03	87	199	3	136	162	3
WARD 04	84	168	3	103	160	1
SHIPPINGPORT BOROUGH	35	25	1	41	24	
SOUTH BEAVER TOWNSHIP	293	389	7	375	317	4
SOUTH HEIGHTS BOROUGH	45	126	2	71	107	
VANPORT TOWNSHIP	223	478	6	310	412	6
WEST MAYFIELD BOROUGH	69	402	4	128	352	2
WHITE TOWNSHIP	116	318	5	153	294	2
BEAVER COUNTY TOTALS	19,232	39,216	579	25,453	35,120	479
BEDFORD COUNTY						
BEDFORD TOWNSHIP	949	721	5	1,117	554	5
BEDFORD BOROUGH	786	519	14	922	394	8
WARD EAST	427	234	9	488	175	5
WARD WEST	359	285	5	434	219	3

	GOVERNOR/LT. GOVERNOR			U.S. SENATE		
	Republican Scranton/ Fisher	Democratic Casey/ Singel	Consumer Hoover/ Brickhouse	Republican Arlen Specter	Democratic Bob Edgar	Consumer Lance S. Haver
BLOOMFIELD TOWNSHIP	128	78	2	162	46	
BROAD TOP TOWNSHIP	170	373	7	213	337	4
COALDALE BOROUGH	10	55		14	50	
COLERAIN TOWNSHIP	203	163	3	241	128	2
CUMBERLAND VALLEY TOWNSHIP	201	212	4	255	150	3
EAST PROVIDENCE TOWNSHIP	313	196	4	366	141	3
EAST ST. CLAIR TOWNSHIP	408	360	9	516	260	3
EVERETT BOROUGH	326	224	3	380	172	4
HARRISON TOWNSHIP	191	136		224	100	1
HOPEWELL TOWNSHIP	233	262	8	309	197	2
HOPEWELL BOROUGH	32	34		32	32	
HYNDMAN BOROUGH	130	213	2	185	159	
JUNIATA TOWNSHIP	144	209	2	188	167	2
KIMMEL TOWNSHIP	129	245	3	170	207	1
KING TOWNSHIP	196	228	6	262	158	4
LIBERTY TOWNSHIP	225	209	5	268	167	2
LINCOLN TOWNSHIP	56	58		65	52	2
LONDONDERRY TOWNSHIP	286	220	4	335	170	2
MANN TOWNSHIP	56	52	1	62	49	
MANNS CHOICE BOROUGH	44	81		58	66	
MONROE TOWNSHIP	186	141	2	212	116	4
NAPIER TOWNSHIP	374	340	4	473	241	3
NEW PARIS BOROUGH	42	20	1	50	12	2
PLEASANTVILLE BOROUGH	48	46	1	53	39	
RAINSBURG BOROUGH	18	46		27	35	
SAXTON BOROUGH	166	83	3	167	82	1
SCHELLSBURG BOROUGH	80	37		88	26	
SNAKE SPRING TOWNSHIP	256	219	7	317	162	1
SOUTH WOODBURY TOWNSHIP	440	197	4	516	125	2
SOUTHAMPTON TOWNSHIP	109	94	3	139	65	1
ST. CLAIRSVILLE BOROUGH	14	15		19	10	
UNION TOWNSHIP	36	31		56	10	
WEST PROVIDENCE TOWNSHIP	651	384	15	745	302	3
WEST ST. CLAIR TOWNSHIP	242	197	5	299	138	5
WOODBURY TOWNSHIP	214	136		283	68	
WOODBURY BOROUGH	88	40		102	27	
BEDFORD COUNTY TOTALS	**8,180**	**6,874**	**127**	**9,890**	**5,214**	**70**
BERKS COUNTY						
ADAMSTOWN BOROUGH						
(BALANCE IN LANCASTER CO.)						
ALBANY TOWNSHIP	268	145	2	282	129	2
ALSACE TOWNSHIP	417	392	14	508	310	6
AMITY TOWNSHIP	974	550	14	1,080	449	11
BALLY BOROUGH	120	126	2	148	97	
BECHTELSVILLE BOROUGH	105	62	2	106	59	1
BERN TOWNSHIP	884	627	19	978	523	15
BERNVILLE BOROUGH	93	145		115	117	
BETHEL TOWNSHIP	316	212	8	370	156	1
BIRDSBORO BOROUGH	436	411	8	527	327	5
BOYERTOWN BOROUGH	709	484	12	794	395	11
BRECKNOCK TOWNSHIP	436	301	8	479	252	3
CAERNARVON TOWNSHIP	293	179	7	343	131	5
CENTERPORT BOROUGH	52	36	1	49	35	
CENTRE TOWNSHIP	333	310	9	379	260	4
COLEBROOKDALE TOWNSHIP	632	467	15	735	365	11
CUMRU TOWNSHIP	2,093	1,254	28	2,206	1,133	18
DISTRICT TOWNSHIP	131	100	3	142	84	2
DOUGLASS TOWNSHIP	417	280	11	476	222	5
EARL TOWNSHIP	338	272	17	380	239	12
EXETER TOWNSHIP	2,342	1,607	43	2,575	1,385	21
FLEETWOOD BOROUGH	535	442	9	627	351	11
GREENWICH TOWNSHIP	352	185	11	375	158	5
HAMBURG BOROUGH	717	568	14	820	465	5
HEIDELBERG TOWNSHIP	244	157	7	255	137	6
HEREFORD TOWNSHIP	299	169	1	322	144	2
JEFFERSON TOWNSHIP	183	108	10	214	92	
KENHORST BOROUGH	445	551	18	510	483	17
KUTZTOWN BOROUGH	568	419	22	615	384	12
LAURELDALE BOROUGH	577	637	18	649	549	13

	GOVERNOR/LT. GOVERNOR			U.S. SENATE		
	Republican Scranton/ Fisher	Democratic Casey/ Singel	Consumer Hoover/ Brickhouse	Republican Arlen Specter	Democratic Bob Edgar	Consumer Lance S. Haver
LEESPORT BOROUGH	213	165	6	239	146	1
LENHARTSVILLE BOROUGH	34	36	1	38	29	
LONGSWAMP TOWNSHIP	540	369	9	583	321	5
LOWER ALSACE TOWNSHIP..........	818	667	23	947	545	11
LOWER HEIDELBERG TOWNSHIP	363	248	10	420	197	3
LYONS BOROUGH	55	54	1	67	43	
MAIDENCREEK TOWNSHIP	293	317	19	357	245	10
MARION TOWNSHIP	142	97	8	170	68	2
MAXATAWNY TOWNSHIP.............	502	295	8	526	262	5
MOHNTON BOROUGH...............	381	250	6	394	232	4
MT. PENN BOROUGH	496	437	10	569	367	6
MUHLENBERG TOWNSHIP	2,152	1,887	45	2,464	1,591	31
NORTH HEIDELBERG TOWNSHIP	168	105	3	191	83	2
OLEY TOWNSHIP...................	484	316	13	545	261	7
ONTELAUNEE TOWNSHIP	170	186	6	191	163	1
PENN TOWNSHIP..................	190	157	2	208	135	1
PERRY TOWNSHIP	323	247	5	356	212	5
PIKE TOWNSHIP...................	200	105	6	199	109	4
READING CITY....................	6,642	9,903	238	7,648	9,008	154
WARD 01	95	243	2	94	246	3
WARD 02	112	355	7	143	327	7
WARD 03	208	385	7	219	351	5
WARD 04	83	135	3	88	119	4
WARD 05	40	117	4	44	118	4
WARD 06	157	480	6	173	466	2
WARD 07	150	97	4	154	91	5
WARD 08	186	199	4	206	176	3
WARD 09	193	371	11	233	324	8
WARD 10	146	426	14	194	395	6
WARD 11	183	439	13	232	402	11
WARD 12	293	468	15	346	524	4
WARD 13	411	678	16	521	564	10
WARD 14	721	800	22	792	732	10
WARD 15	681	959	27	767	873	21
WARD 16	603	997	26	734	862	14
WARD 17	1,268	1,322	33	1,425	1,191	23
WARD 18	765	1,045	15	899	895	8
WARD 19	347	387	9	384	352	6
RICHMOND TOWNSHIP..............	335	333	10	410	267	2
ROBESON TOWNSHIP...............	738	430	14	807	350	7
ROBESONIA BOROUGH	282	213	6	312	169	5
ROCKLAND TOWNSHIP..............	310	250	8	343	213	3
RUSCOMBMANOR TOWNSHIP........	414	266	8	451	227	5
SHILLINGTON BOROUGH............	1,224	745	17	1,319	632	13
SHOEMAKERSVILLE BOROUGH	178	178	5	224	129	3
SINKING SPRING BOROUGH	498	283	9	516	257	6
SOUTH HEIDELBERG TOWNSHIP	452	305	21	515	240	7
SPRING TOWNSHIP.................	3,336	1,887	61	3,703	1,516	32
ST. LAWRENCE BOROUGH...........						
STRAUSSTOWN BOROUGH	50	66		64	57	
TEMPLE BOROUGH.................	179	242	3	191	232	2
TILDEN TOWNSHIP	251	207	11	288	162	7
TOPTON BOROUGH.................	210	192	8	238	165	4
TULPEHOCKEN TOWNSHIP	237	203	5	293	147	5
UNION TOWNSHIP.................	459	344	11	523	281	11
UPPER BERN TOWNSHIP	208	138	3	227	129	4
UPPER TULPEHOCKEN TOWNSHIP	168	114	2	200	80	1
WASHINGTON TOWNSHIP............	301	214	11	346	181	2
WERNERSVILLE BOROUGH...........	353	249	4	417	185	5
WEST LAWN BOROUGH	344	214	9	375	182	3
WEST READING BOROUGH	574	562	13	667	462	10
WINDSOR TOWNSHIP...............	206	177	6	230	153	2
WOMELSDORF BOROUGH............	246	191	2	267	165	2
WYOMISSING BOROUGH	1,962	645	24	2,047	551	11
WYOMISSING HILLS BOROUGH........	634	291	8	676	240	3
BERKS COUNTY TOTALS	43,624	35,976	1,031	48,820	30,820	611
BLAIR COUNTY						
ALLEGHENY TOWNSHIP..............	883	735	20	1,162	471	9
ALTOONA CITY.....................	6,560	7,229	160	8,648	5,160	114

	GOVERNOR/LT. GOVERNOR			U.S. SENATE		
	Republican Scranton/ Fisher	Democratic Casey/ Singel	Consumer Hoover/ Brickhouse	Republican Arlen Specter	Democratic Bob Edgar	Consumer Lance S. Haver
WARD 01	212	196	9	246	165	2
WARD 02	245	372	5	305	309	10
WARD 03	250	383	12	348	283	10
WARD 04	308	529	12	440	387	8
WARD 05	211	468	4	335	342	10
WARD 06	989	1,117	20	1,358	742	11
WARD 07	188	223	6	247	173	4
WARD 08	302	390	7	399	290	3
WARD 09	167	257	6	246	176	5
WARD 10	482	615	8	685	415	6
WARD 11	703	626	15	920	410	11
WARD 12	630	671	17	837	464	13
WARD 13	772	639	20	987	445	13
WARD 14	1,101	743	19	1,295	559	8
ANTIS TOWNSHIP	696	551	10	902	352	7
BELLWOOD BOROUGH..............	296	189	5	358	136	1
BLAIR TOWNSHIP	597	340	5	716	222	6
CATHARINE TOWNSHIP	108	95	3	159	44	3
DUNCANSVILLE BOROUGH..........	219	113	2	257	73	1
FRANKSTOWN TOWNSHIP	1,146	660	30	1,408	425	8
FREEDOM TOWNSHIP...............	319	269	12	436	162	7
GREENFIELD TOWNSHIP	342	319	6	431	226	6
HOLLIDAYSBURG BOROUGH.........	1,047	661	20	1,259	467	16
WARD 01	94	90		119	62	4
WARD 02	181	116	4	224	72	3
WARD 03	66	61	3	89	44	
WARD 04	186	125	5	211	105	2
WARD 05	202	114	3	242	75	3
WARD 06	163	67	2	181	53	3
WARD 07	155	88	3	193	56	1
HUSTON TOWNSHIP	163	104	2	227	46	2
JUNIATA TOWNSHIP................	127	83	3	175	37	2
LOGAN TOWNSHIP.................	1,522	1,491	40	2,047	986	28
MARTINSBURG BOROUGH	426	167	7	489	118	3
NEWRY BOROUGH	22	61		44	33	1
NORTH WOODBURY TOWNSHIP	332	160		402	92	1
ROARING SPRING BOROUGH	737	423	11	664	191	4
SNYDER TOWNSHIP	375	311	14	513	192	6
TAYLOR TOWNSHIP	356	237	1	465	131	4
TYRONE TOWNSHIP	219	178	9	295	101	7
TYRONE BOROUGH	743	643	11	1,007	394	5
WARD 01	135	111	1	180	67	
WARD 02	102	93	1	142	54	1
WARD 03	100	104	1	142	65	1
WARD 04	62	59	1	77	48	1
WARD 05	71	59	1	104	28	
WARD 06	175	107	2	219	63	1
WARD 07	98	110	4	143	69	1
WILLIAMSBURG BOROUGH...........	248	143	5	288	103	2
WOODBURY TOWNSHIP	191	121	4	247	69	2
BLAIR COUNTY TOTALS.............	**17,674**	**15,283**	**380**	**22,599**	**10,231**	**245**
BRADFORD COUNTY						
ALBA BOROUGH	28	20	1	33	17	
ALBANY TOWNSHIP	121	62	1	139	48	
ARMENIA TOWNSHIP	28	11	1	30	7	
ASYLUM TOWNSHIP	158	97	4	176	80	3
ATHENS TOWNSHIP................	558	381	6	633	294	10
ATHENS BOROUGH.................	490	352	10	556	293	6
WARD 01	121	86	2	137	70	
WARD 02	91	69	4	100	63	4
WARD 03	111	88	2	132	70	
WARD 04	167	109	2	187	90	2
BURLINGTON TOWNSHIP	126	65	3	152	41	
BURLINGTON BOROUGH	36	20	1	42	15	
CANTON TOWNSHIP	277	123	3	319	84	4
CANTON BOROUGH	271	150	6	316	111	2
COLUMBIA TOWNSHIP	173	91	2	185	77	4
FRANKLIN TOWNSHIP...............	63	36		79	22	
GRANVILLE TOWNSHIP	146	72	1	143	73	2

	GOVERNOR/LT. GOVERNOR			U.S. SENATE		
	Republican Scranton/ Fisher	Democratic Casey/ Singel	Consumer Hoover/ Brickhouse	Republican Arlen Specter	Democratic Bob Edgar	Consumer Lance S. Haver
HERRICK TOWNSHIP................	92	57	4	110	40	3
LERAYSVILLE BOROUGH.............	65	44	1	69	40	2
LEROY TOWNSHIP.................	82	50	3	93	42	1
LITCHFIELD TOWNSHIP	185	86	4	206	63	5
MONROE TOWNSHIP	117	61	4	141	39	2
MONROE BOROUGH................	125	57	3	150	30	2
NEW ALBANY BOROUGH.............	49	29		56	23	
NORTH TOWANDA TOWNSHIP	208	106	1	244	68	2
ORWELL TOWNSHIP.................	199	75	4	237	42	1
OVERTON TOWNSHIP	29	31	2	46	17	1
PIKE TOWNSHIP..................	74	64		90	48	
RIDGEBURY TOWNSHIP	215	145	4	257	100	2
ROME TOWNSHIP	146	60	4	172	37	3
ROME BOROUGH	70	30		81	19	
SAYRE BOROUGH.................	686	824	11	797	700	5
WARD 01	109	131	4	132	107	1
WARD 02	310	361	2	374	290	1
WARD 03	33	49	2	36	48	
WARD 04	218	224	3	240	198	3
WARD 05	16	59		15	57	
SHESHEQUIN TOWNSHIP.............	182	87	3	213	57	1
SMITHFIELD TOWNSHIP	305	121	4	347	74	2
SOUTH CREEK TOWNSHIP	166	82	4	186	64	2
SOUTH WAVERLY BOROUGH	161	168	2	193	136	2
SPRINGFIELD TOWNSHIP.............	220	97	5	252	69	
STANDING STONE TOWNSHIP	73	57	1	78	51	2
STEVENS TOWNSHIP	81	29	1	93	17	1
SYLVANIA BOROUGH................	39	24		46	17	
TERRY TOWNSHIP..................	95	71		116	47	1
TOWANDA TOWNSHIP	146	67	2	156	55	1
TOWANDA BOROUGH	562	393	4	720	237	2
WARD 01	128	78	1	163	44	
WARD 02	160	123	2	204	83	1
WARD 03	274	192	1	353	110	1
TROY TOWNSHIP..................	308	130	9	348	99	4
TROY BOROUGH	265	111	4	303	77	
TUSCARORA TOWNSHIP	156	108		202	65	1
ULSTER TOWNSHIP	185	154	3	228	109	2
WARREN TOWNSHIP................	141	121	2	178	80	3
WELLS TOWNSHIP	113	72	4	136	51	2
WEST BURLINGTON TOWNSHIP	91	55		100	46	
WILMOT TOWNSHIP	164	78	1	203	37	3
WINDHAM TOWNSHIP...............	149	43	7	164	34	2
WYALUSING TOWNSHIP	193	93		211	69	2
WYALUSING BOROUGH	178	78	1	202	48	3
WYSOX TOWNSHIP	310	109		337	84	
BRADFORD COUNTY TOTALS.........	**9,100**	**5,547**	**141**	**10,564**	**4,093**	**96**
BUCKS COUNTY						
BEDMINSTER TOWNSHIP.............	899	335	15	966	289	8
BENSALEM TOWNSHIP...............	6,840	5,487	136	7,890	4,650	75
BRIDGETON TOWNSHIP	167	111	5	159	122	2
BRISTOL TOWNSHIP	6,540	8,556	171	7,894	7,290	142
WARD 01	646	689	24	774	575	16
WARD 02	456	572	11	548	478	12
WARD 03	499	948	10	623	830	11
WARD 04	652	800	17	798	666	15
WARD 05	410	683	18	489	607	19
WARD 06	562	740	10	659	650	8
WARD 07	625	793	12	738	693	8
WARD 08	504	622	16	577	547	15
WARD 09	897	1,143	18	1,113	944	14
WARD 10	642	749	22	796	604	9
WARD 11	647	817	13	779	696	15
BRISTOL BOROUGH	1,167	2,063	49	1,453	1,883	24
BUCKINGHAM TOWNSHIP	2,014	711	37	2,019	750	11
CHALFONT BOROUGH	549	231	7	574	202	7
DOYLESTOWN TOWNSHIP	2,780	1,031	33	2,786	1,064	14
WARD 01	590	251	7	599	241	4
WARD 02	301	67	2	296	74	1

	GOVERNOR/LT. GOVERNOR			U.S. SENATE		
	Republican Scranton/ Fisher	Democratic Casey/ Singel	Consumer Hoover/ Brickhouse	Republican Arlen Specter	Democratic Bob Edgar	Consumer Lance S. Haver
WARD 03	549	164	4	552	180	2
WARD 04	394	158	5	404	157	3
WARD 05	427	168	7	411	186	1
WARD 06	519	223	8	524	226	3
DOYLESTOWN BOROUGH	2,024	904	26	1,943	1,043	12
WARD 01	762	344	13	716	407	5
WARD 02	759	319	9	733	370	3
WARD 03	503	241	4	494	266	4
DUBLIN BOROUGH	238	95		244	87	
DURHAM TOWNSHIP................	176	90	2	187	73	
EAST ROCKHILL TOWNSHIP	499	242	15	528	228	6
FALLS TOWNSHIP	3,888	4,926	109	4,548	4,466	54
WARD 01	1,727	1,820	45	1,970	1,713	19
WARD 02	432	607	9	511	540	5
WARD 03	434	620	10	474	594	5
WARD 04	1,295	1,879	45	1,593	1,619	25
HAYCOCK TOWNSHIP	341	171	3	355	148	2
HILLTOWN TOWNSHIP...............	1,683	758	26	1,889	576	11
HULMEVILLE BOROUGH	185	130	5	185	130	4
IVYLAND BOROUGH	130	46	3	137	42	1
LANGHORNE BOROUGH	279	168	8	289	164	7
LANGHORNE MANOR BOROUGH	227	94	3	237	89	3
LOWER MAKEFIELD TOWNSHIP	5,112	2,110	53	5,134	2,121	24
LOWER SOUTHAMPTON TOWNSHIP....	3,419	2,318	71	4,063	1,743	26
MIDDLETOWN TOWNSHIP	6,273	4,838	118	6,708	4,529	58
MILFORD TOWNSHIP	993	488	17	1,058	421	9
MORRISVILLE BOROUGH.............	986	1,091	24	1,087	1,021	15
NEW BRITAIN TOWNSHIP	1,580	667	26	1,695	565	8
NEW BRITAIN BOROUGH	457	208	5	488	178	3
NEW HOPE BOROUGH	309	184	11	254	250	4
NEWTOWN TOWNSHIP	1,546	656	21	1,510	721	10
NEWTOWN BOROUGH	632	238	13	584	307	4
NOCKAMIXON TOWNSHIP	505	239	3	520	224	2
NORTHAMPTON TOWNSHIP..........	6,558	3,123	73	7,319	2,490	49
PENNDEL BOROUGH	381	356	12	467	288	5
PERKASIE BOROUGH	1,184	598	16	1,310	505	9
PLUMSTEAD TOWNSHIP.............	1,114	458	23	1,197	391	7
QUAKERTOWN BOROUGH............	1,425	762	19	1,476	729	7
RICHLAND TOWNSHIP	871	478	22	950	404	11
RICHLANDTOWN BOROUGH	141	77	3	157	63	2
RIEGELSVILLE BOROUGH	158	91	5	169	83	3
SELLERSVILLE BOROUGH............	594	348	16	657	298	7
SILVERDALE BOROUGH	140	49	2	151	38	2
SOLEBURY TOWNSHIP	1,289	511	23	1,230	606	7
SPRINGFIELD TOWNSHIP.............	816	415	13	828	406	8
TELFORD BOROUGH	197	88	4	220	69	1
(BALANCE IN MONTGOMERY CO.)						
TINICUM TOWNSHIP	763	326	13	750	338	6
TRUMBAUERSVILLE BOROUGH	131	69	2	138	62	2
TULLYTOWN BOROUGH	237	471	10	313	421	6
UPPER MAKEFIELD TOWNSHIP........	1,346	408	14	1,357	403	4
UPPER SOUTHAMPTON TOWNSHIP	3,849	2,101	62	4,325	1,715	39
WARMINSTER TOWNSHIP.............	5,655	3,707	104	6,477	2,988	51
WARRINGTON TOWNSHIP	1,744	1,042	35	1,868	937	16
WARWICK TOWNSHIP	774	261	8	758	274	8
WEST ROCKHILL TOWNSHIP	640	321	16	692	287	8
WRIGHTSTOWN TOWNSHIP	572	172	11	550	204	7
YARDLEY BOROUGH.................	475	311	11	466	328	7
BUCKS COUNTY TOTALS	**83,492**	**55,729**	**1,532**	**91,209**	**49,703**	**818**
BUTLER COUNTY						
ADAMS TOWNSHIP	489	353	10	584	260	10
ALLEGHENY TOWNSHIP..............	80	49	5	94	39	2
BRADY TOWNSHIP	101	113	2	121	95	
BRUIN BOROUGH	107	56		119	43	1
BUFFALO TOWNSHIP	717	796	21	889	632	12
BUTLER CITY.......................	1,937	2,312	53	2,275	1,982	38
WARD 01	402	600	6	474	517	6
WARD 02	224	280	4	280	234	2
WARD 03	198	400	6	242	352	10

	GOVERNOR/LT. GOVERNOR			U.S. SENATE		
	Republican Scranton/ Fisher	Democratic Casey/ Singel	Consumer Hoover/ Brickhouse	Republican Arlen Specter	Democratic Bob Edgar	Consumer Lance S. Haver
WARD 04	555	432	15	639	348	8
WARD 05	558	600	22	640	531	12
BUTLER TOWNSHIP	2,775	2,842	41	3,184	2,433	33
CALLERY BOROUGH.	48	41		61	28	2
CENTER TOWNSHIP	1,119	776	19	1,234	668	14
CHERRY TOWNSHIP	91	107	5	121	80	4
CHERRY VALLEY BOROUGH	18	12	1	18	12	1
CHICORA BOROUGH	143	165		184	119	2
CLAY TOWNSHIP	197	266	11	271	198	1
CLEARFIELD TOWNSHIP	147	290	5	214	225	2
CLINTON TOWNSHIP	318	250	6	383	189	5
CONCORD TOWNSHIP	156	161	5	192	125	5
CONNOQUENESSING TOWNSHIP	430	338	11	502	261	11
CONNOQUENESSING BOROUGH	84	79	2	95	68	1
CRANBERRY TOWNSHIP	1,552	1,163	35	1,802	933	17
DONEGAL TOWNSHIP	153	208	6	205	157	6
EAST BUTLER BOROUGH.	79	142	3	101	120	2
EAU CLAIRE BOROUGH	58	44	1	68	34	1
EVANS CITY BOROUGH	319	255	7	371	201	5
FAIRVIEW TOWNSHIP	286	217	6	330	172	3
FAIRVIEW BOROUGH	29	24	2	32	21	1
FORWARD TOWNSHIP.	311	251	11	355	207	7
FRANKLIN TOWNSHIP	323	264	10	396	195	7
HARMONY BOROUGH.	212	149	1	237	120	2
HARRISVILLE BOROUGH	159	128	3	183	100	4
JACKSON TOWNSHIP	390	311	7	450	249	5
JEFFERSON TOWNSHIP	622	482	23	728	387	9
KARNS CITY BOROUGH	37	29		46	19	
LANCASTER TOWNSHIP	330	204	8	376	162	3
MARION TOWNSHIP	99	203	4	151	152	3
MARS BOROUGH.	300	127	4	301	123	2
MERCER TOWNSHIP	105	137	3	148	92	3
MIDDLESEX TOWNSHIP	786	542	20	904	425	22
MUDDYCREEK TOWNSHIP	222	185	15	252	159	6
OAKLAND TOWNSHIP	247	364	3	323	285	4
PARKER TOWNSHIP	84	46	1	96	36	
PENN TOWNSHIP.	849	537	20	967	432	12
PETROLIA BOROUGH.	36	42	1	33	43	
PORTERSVILLE BOROUGH	46	31	1	54	23	
PROSPECT BOROUGH	160	126	4	196	89	2
SAXONBURG BOROUGH	240	154	5	277	121	2
SEVEN FIELDS BOROUGH	40	17	1	45	10	2
SLIPPERY ROCK TOWNSHIP	353	294	4	381	264	5
SLIPPERY ROCK BOROUGH	412	231	4	419	219	3
SUMMIT TOWNSHIP	417	603	12	593	431	8
VALENCIA BOROUGH	36	26		43	19	
VENANGO TOWNSHIP.	69	91		85	76	
WASHINGTON TOWNSHIP.	137	127	6	166	102	4
WEST LIBERTY BOROUGH.	59	51	1	69	39	
WEST SUNBURY BOROUGH	51	18		54	12	1
WINFIELD TOWNSHIP	422	368	9	532	261	7
WORTH TOWNSHIP	145	106	6	159	92	4
ZELIENOPLE BOROUGH.	618	394	14	694	324	6
BUTLER COUNTY TOTALS	**19,750**	**17,697**	**459**	**23,163**	**14,363**	**312**
CAMBRIA COUNTY						
ADAMS TOWNSHIP	683	1,511	15	1,027	1,159	14
ALLEGHENY TOWNSHIP.	81	283	5	189	174	5
ASHVILLE BOROUGH	22	130	1	42	112	
BARNESBORO BOROUGH	223	634	3	361	492	6
BARR TOWNSHIP.	144	561	9	387	312	3
BLACKLICK TOWNSHIP.	145	482	3	243	387	3
BROWNSTOWN BOROUGH	61	336	1	134	264	2
CAMBRIA TOWNSHIP	500	1,402	25	790	1,098	31
CARROLLTOWN BOROUGH	87	361	2	176	265	7
CASSANDRA BOROUGH.	16	60	1	32	43	1
CHEST TOWNSHIP.	34	48	3	56	27	
CHEST SPRINGS BOROUGH	9	57	3	29	36	2
CLEARFIELD TOWNSHIP	128	274	3	232	169	4
CONEMAUGH TOWNSHIP.	211	595	9	299	510	8

	GOVERNOR/LT. GOVERNOR			U.S. SENATE		
	Republican Scranton/ Fisher	Democratic Casey/ Singel	Consumer Hoover/ Brickhouse	Republican Arlen Specter	Democratic Bob Edgar	Consumer Lance S. Haver
CRESSON TOWNSHIP	149	467	6	286	329	7
CRESSON BOROUGH	211	472	6	361	338	3
CROYLE TOWNSHIP	267	582	14	401	450	14
DAISYTOWN BOROUGH	24	133	1	56	100	
DALE BOROUGH	217	288	4	296	207	6
DEAN TOWNSHIP	36	113	2	65	84	1
EAST CARROLL TOWNSHIP	111	405	8	234	281	5
EAST CONEMAUGH BOROUGH	167	535	4	206	497	2
EAST TAYLOR TOWNSHIP	293	803	9	446	652	9
EBENSBURG BOROUGH	502	942	9	775	662	12
WARD CENTER	144	270	2	223	192	4
WARD EAST	190	323	2	287	223	2
WARD WEST	168	349	5	265	247	6
EHRENFELD BOROUGH	9	86	1	22	72	1
ELDER TOWNSHIP	60	301	2	149	218	3
FERNDALE BOROUGH	330	428	3	437	318	3
FRANKLIN BOROUGH	34	278	1	49	264	
GALLITZIN TOWNSHIP	88	291	8	152	227	6
GALLITZIN BOROUGH	140	612	26	282	476	1
GEISTOWN BOROUGH	403	767	15	627	542	15
HASTINGS BOROUGH	96	428	7	223	298	2
JACKSON TOWNSHIP	610	1,078	14	919	775	9
JOHNSTOWN CITY	2,818	6,971	78	4,058	5,706	68
WARD 01	156	192	2	179	165	2
WARD 02	18	29		23	23	
WARD 03	10	10		11	9	
WARD 04	97	242	2	114	225	1
WARD 05	49	104	3	68	87	
WARD 06	84	309	8	141	260	4
WARD 07	252	588	7	331	500	4
WARD 08	502	776	10	719	549	8
WARD 09	35	227	5	81	179	7
WARD 10	53	252	1	88	209	1
WARD 11	57	221	2	74	198	2
WARD 12	22	180		37	165	1
WARD 13	4	71	1	14	62	
WARD 14	11	83	1	20	75	1
WARD 15	11	40		12	37	
WARD 16	45	187	3	75	158	3
WARD 17	700	1,242	18	971	980	20
WARD 18	105	453	3	209	342	3
WARD 19	218	437	4	291	374	3
WARD 20	314	1,072	6	469	913	5
WARD 21	75	256	2	131	196	3
LILLY BOROUGH	93	347	1	124	281	2
WARD 01	39	129		23	109	1
WARD 02	54	218	1	101	172	1
LORAIN BOROUGH	75	254	1	125	201	1
LORETTO BOROUGH	36	143	1	77	101	1
LOWER YODER TOWNSHIP	387	1,059	11	627	819	13
MIDDLE TAYLOR TOWNSHIP	137	259	7	198	194	7
MUNSTER TOWNSHIP	54	152	4	124	80	3
NANTY GLO BOROUGH	190	997	8	350	868	7
WARD 01	97	475	7	180	393	6
WARD 02	93	522	1	170	475	1
PATTON BOROUGH	238	624	10	372	496	7
WARD 01	122	294	7	176	235	6
WARD 02	116	330	3	196	261	1
PORTAGE TOWNSHIP	324	1,087	5	548	858	17
PORTAGE BOROUGH	304	848	9	492	664	2
WARD 01	199	494	3	322	371	1
WARD 02	105	354	6	170	293	1
READE TOWNSHIP	208	246	3	221	194	2
RICHLAND TOWNSHIP	1,741	2,343	31	2,396	1,678	30
SANKERTOWN BOROUGH	56	193		104	146	
SCALP LEVEL BOROUGH	42	293	2	84	248	5
SOUTH FORK BOROUGH	138	283	4	200	220	3
WARD 01	46	169	1	80	133	1
WARD 02	92	114	3	120	87	2
SOUTHMONT BOROUGH	505	550	9	672	378	8

	GOVERNOR/LT. GOVERNOR			U.S. SENATE		
	Republican Scranton/ Fisher	Democratic Casey/ Singel	Consumer Hoover/ Brickhouse	Republican Arlen Specter	Democratic Bob Edgar	Consumer Lance S. Haver
SPANGLER BOROUGH	113	590	5	268	435	5
STONYCREEK TOWNSHIP	612	875	10	861	621	12
SUMMERHILL TOWNSHIP	263	663	8	407	525	6
SUMMERHILL BOROUGH	85	191	1	141	136	2
SUSQUEHANNA TOWNSHIP	118	570	3	257	432	2
TUNNELHILL BOROUGH	39	85	1	52	73	
(BALANCE IN BLAIR CO.)						
UPPER YODER TOWNSHIP	915	1,251	10	1,350	812	12
VINTONDALE BOROUGH	47	183	4	82	156	
WASHINGTON TOWNSHIP	42	251	2	82	213	
WEST CARROLL TOWNSHIP	72	533	5	143	453	11
WEST TAYLOR TOWNSHIP	117	252	3	167	200	4
WESTMONT BOROUGH	1,198	1,277	13	1,615	822	21
WHITE TOWNSHIP	66	55	3	76	47	2
WILMORE BOROUGH	34	71		46	58	1
CAMBRIA COUNTY TOTALS	**17,158**	**39,239**	**475**	**26,302**	**29,953**	**439**
CAMERON COUNTY						
DRIFTWOOD BOROUGH	25	24		27	21	1
EMPORIUM BOROUGH	542	488	4	659	364	2
GIBSON TOWNSHIP	36	41	1	51	25	1
GROVE TOWNSHIP	45	42		61	25	
LUMBER TOWNSHIP	31	60	1	38	52	1
PORTAGE TOWNSHIP	49	42		64	26	1
SHIPPEN TOWNSHIP	517	412	4	680	251	4
CAMERON COUNTY TOTALS	**1,245**	**1,109**	**10**	**1,580**	**764**	**10**
CARBON COUNTY						
BANKS TOWNSHIP	133	467	10	181	401	10
BEAVER MEADOWS BOROUGH	117	243	2	159	193	1
BOWMANSTOWN BOROUGH	119	99	3	130	84	
EAST PENN TOWNSHIP	232	171	13	261	144	6
EAST SIDE BOROUGH	45	36		54	26	1
FRANKLIN TOWNSHIP	439	379	4	497	283	14
JIM THORPE BOROUGH	676	1,046	14	862	825	19
KIDDER TOWNSHIP	219	132	6	252	88	5
LANSFORD BOROUGH	548	1,121	19	773	865	14
LAUSANNE TOWNSHIP	14	39		19	29	1
LEHIGH TOWNSHIP	81	62		113	31	2
LEHIGHTON BOROUGH	684	777	8	819	619	7
LOWER TOWAMENSING TOWNSHIP	215	281	9	250	241	9
MAHONING TOWNSHIP	477	410	8	524	357	10
NESQUEHONING BOROUGH	373	775	9	512	613	7
PACKER TOWNSHIP	169	140		212	93	2
PALMERTON BOROUGH	709	421	12	777	701	21
PARRYVILLE BOROUGH	45	53		51	45	1
PENN FOREST TOWNSHIP	251	190	2	291	149	1
SUMMIT HILL BOROUGH	384	906	9	528	733	12
WARD 03	206	345	1	250	286	2
TOWAMENSING TOWNSHIP	232	217	8	254	197	7
WEATHERLY BOROUGH	423	433	7	507	340	6
WEISSPORT BOROUGH	32	61	1	47	46	2
CARBON COUNTY TOTALS	**6,617**	**8,459**	**144**	**8,073**	**7,103**	**158**
CENTRE COUNTY						
BELLEFONTE BOROUGH	1,281	836	11	1,406	691	15
BENNER TOWNSHIP	421	306	7	455	268	2
BOGGS TOWNSHIP	256	371	7	366	261	6
BURNSIDE TOWNSHIP	47	59		61	47	1
CENTRE HALL BOROUGH	306	194	2	340	164	
COLLEGE TOWNSHIP	1,490	815	25	1,465	848	21
CURTIN TOWNSHIP	45	99	2	47	100	
FERGUSON TOWNSHIP	1,690	1,083	22	1,844	934	15
GREGG TOWNSHIP	301	270	1	345	222	3
HAINES TOWNSHIP	174	184	2	210	146	2
HALFMOON TOWNSHIP	169	119	1	207	85	
HARRIS TOWNSHIP	909	531	14	957	486	7
HOWARD TOWNSHIP	102	152		122	131	1
HOWARD BOROUGH	130	128	2	146	112	1
HUSTON TOWNSHIP	192	135	5	224	108	3

	GOVERNOR/LT. GOVERNOR			U.S. SENATE		
	Republican Scranton/ Fisher	Democratic Casey/ Singel	Consumer Hoover/ Brickhouse	Republican Arlen Specter	Democratic Bob Edgar	Consumer Lance S. Haver
LIBERTY TOWNSHIP	130	177		151	152	1
MARION TOWNSHIP	72	107	1	92	88	
MILES TOWNSHIP	158	195	2	182	170	1
MILESBURG BOROUGH	153	172	1	193	130	
MILLHEIM BOROUGH	149	163	2	168	147	1
PATTON TOWNSHIP	1,544	856	25	1,577	840	13
PENN TOWNSHIP	111	126	3	126	115	2
PHILIPSBURG BOROUGH	548	471	6	673	345	3
PORT MATILDA BOROUGH	95	80	2	106	74	1
POTTER TOWNSHIP	412	330	3	485	262	2
RUSH TOWNSHIP	389	632	9	536	476	8
SNOW SHOE TOWNSHIP	151	315	1	231	231	1
SNOW SHOE BOROUGH	110	119	3	142	88	2
SOUTH PHILIPSBURG BOROUGH	51	120		75	86	4
SPRING TOWNSHIP	772	685	7	923	526	8
STATE COLLEGE BOROUGH	4,084	2,456	88	3,924	2,700	27
TAYLOR TOWNSHIP	117	80	4	123	72	3
UNION TOWNSHIP	141	136	5	188	94	2
UNIONVILLE BOROUGH	60	40	4	76	27	1
WALKER TOWNSHIP	449	388	4	564	275	4
WORTH TOWNSHIP	85	99	2	114	69	2
CENTRE COUNTY TOTALS	17,294	13,029	273	18,844	11,570	163
CHESTER COUNTY						
ATGLEN BOROUGH	103	54	4	115	46	2
AVONDALE BOROUGH	84	53	1	94	42	
BIRMINGHAM TOWNSHIP	614	123	5	595	144	1
CALN TOWNSHIP	1,201	959	21	1,325	848	11
CHARLESTOWN TOWNSHIP	575	168	7	540	205	6
COATESVILLE CITY	821	1,315	20	972	1,180	7
WARD 01	134	309	2	196	253	
WARD 02	215	235	8	227	227	
WARD 03	86	226	4	97	219	1
WARD 04	338	247	4	388	197	6
WARD 05	48	298	2	64	284	
DOWNINGTOWN BOROUGH	893	842	22	1,035	707	11
EAST BRADFORD TOWNSHIP	866	304	6	875	293	6
EAST BRANDYWINE TOWNSHIP	935	446	14	1,040	348	10
EAST CALN TOWNSHIP	344	126	5	342	128	5
EAST COVENTRY TOWNSHIP	763	339	10	820	291	5
EAST FALLOWFIELD TOWNSHIP	600	448	16	663	399	7
EAST GOSHEN TOWNSHIP	2,665	1,031	29	2,704	1,014	14
EAST MARLBOROUGH TOWNSHIP	916	275	13	906	289	6
EAST NANTMEAL TOWNSHIP	278	77	8	290	71	4
EAST NOTTINGHAM TOWNSHIP	340	230	4	385	187	3
EAST PIKELAND TOWNSHIP	918	489	22	1,012	414	6
EAST VINCENT TOWNSHIP	740	331	12	806	273	7
EAST WHITELAND TOWNSHIP	1,664	795	27	1,681	779	9
EASTTOWN TOWNSHIP	2,540	864	28	2,536	891	11
ELK TOWNSHIP	115	95	2	131	76	1
ELVERSON BOROUGH	99	38		97	38	
FRANKLIN TOWNSHIP	365	166	7	376	162	3
HIGHLAND TOWNSHIP	218	94	1	245	66	2
HONEY BROOK BOROUGH	201	67	2	214	61	1
HONEYBROOK TOWNSHIP	397	256	4	480	177	4
KENNETT TOWNSHIP	1,101	307	11	1,062	363	7
KENNETT SQUARE BOROUGH	662	355	10	694	323	7
LONDON BRITAIN TOWNSHIP	370	117	4	357	132	3
LONDON GROVE TOWNSHIP	534	214	11	565	191	4
LONDONDERRY TOWNSHIP	180	95	5	219	62	
LOWER OXFORD TOWNSHIP	267	264	5	313	219	1
MALVERN BOROUGH	539	212	5	534	225	3
MODENA BOROUGH	44	36		48	31	1
NEW GARDEN TOWNSHIP	512	233	6	545	203	3
NEW LONDON TOWNSHIP	254	130	3	299	88	4
NEWLIN TOWNSHIP	197	86	3	199	90	2
NORTH COVENTRY TOWNSHIP	1,191	526	19	1,265	458	7
OXFORD BOROUGH	514	272	6	542	243	10
PARKESBURG BOROUGH	340	286	4	405	228	2
PENN TOWNSHIP	267	125	5	293	105	1

	GOVERNOR/LT. GOVERNOR			U.S. SENATE		
	Republican Scranton/ Fisher	Democratic Casey/ Singel	Consumer Hoover/ Brickhouse	Republican Arlen Specter	Democratic Bob Edgar	Consumer Lance S. Haver
PENNSBURY TOWNSHIP	753	226	8	710	275	5
PHOENIXVILLE BOROUGH.	1,436	1,476	27	1,660	1,256	12
POCOPSON TOWNSHIP	500	148	7	509	144	3
SADSBURY TOWNSHIP.	300	247	6	375	178	2
SCHUYLKILL TOWNSHIP.	1,223	460	16	1,247	448	11
SOUTH COATESVILLE BOROUGH	89	141	5	118	123	3
SOUTH COVENTRY TOWNSHIP	343	267	8	371	247	3
SPRING CITY BOROUGH	537	263	18	601	207	9
WARD 01	145	83	4	160	67	3
WARD 02	75	25	2	81	21	
WARD 03	152	73	6	163	66	4
WARD 04	165	82	6	197	53	2
THORNBURY TOWNSHIP	277	121	7	279	122	2
TREDYFFRIN TOWNSHIP	6,803	2,309	70	6,716	2,436	39
UPPER OXFORD TOWNSHIP	232	86	6	242	82	4
UPPER UWCHLAN TOWNSHIP.	518	224	11	563	190	1
UWCHLAN TOWNSHIP	2,048	705	26	2,038	734	9
VALLEY TOWNSHIP	288	418	2	345	356	1
WALLACE TOWNSHIP	350	130	4	360	124	5
WARWICK TOWNSHIP	479	177	5	515	140	5
WEST BRADFORD TOWNSHIP	1,330	684	23	1,411	618	10
WEST BRANDYWINE TOWNSHIP.	633	398	12	664	365	7
WEST CALN TOWNSHIP	602	428	13	676	357	7
WEST CHESTER BOROUGH.	2,105	1,411	33	1,926	1,611	19
WEST FALLOWFIELD TOWNSHIP	345	151	8	374	125	4
WEST GOSHEN TOWNSHIP	3,192	1,561	36	3,264	1,504	21
WEST GROVE BOROUGH.	243	126	2	272	99	1
WEST MARLBOROUGH TOWNSHIP.	165	40	2	162	46	2
WEST NANTMEAL TOWNSHIP	247	124	3	298	69	3
WEST NOTTINGHAM TOWNSHIP	211	147	5	231	133	1
WEST PIKELAND TOWNSHIP	473	120	10	452	147	2
WEST SADSBURY TOWNSHIP	225	121	2	250	96	3
WEST VINCENT TOWNSHIP	631	181	20	601	224	3
WEST WHITELAND TOWNSHIP	1,616	854	18	1,702	794	7
WESTTOWN TOWNSHIP	1,759	738	18	1,822	705	7
WILLISTOWN TOWNSHIP	2,338	847	30	2,262	934	8
CHESTER COUNTY TOTALS.	58,518	28,572	848	60,635	26,979	416
CLARION COUNTY						
ASHLAND TOWNSHIP	221	154	4	271	108	3
BEAVER TOWNSHIP.	306	266	5	387	185	3
BRADY TOWNSHIP	15	11	1	23	4	1
CALLENSBURG BOROUGH	15	58	1	33	40	
CLARION TOWNSHIP.	428	371	10	540	265	5
CLARION BOROUGH.	835	538	10	900	477	7
EAST BRADY BOROUGH	181	173	7	210	151	2
ELK TOWNSHIP	284	183	5	325	145	2
FARMINGTON TOWNSHIP	280	298	6	369	215	6
FOXBURG BOROUGH	43	46	3	42	45	2
HAWTHORN BOROUGH	78	95	2	109	60	4
HIGHLAND TOWNSHIP	82	82	1	103	65	
KNOX TOWNSHIP.	151	249	2	210	191	1
KNOX BOROUGH.	323	172	2	319	173	3
LICKING TOWNSHIP	66	87	1	81	71	4
LIMESTONE TOWNSHIP	314	209	7	390	136	4
MADISON TOWNSHIP	109	276	3	183	199	2
MILLCREEK TOWNSHIP	83	61	5	93	55	2
MONROE TOWNSHIP	199	207	7	253	156	1
NEW BETHLEHEM BOROUGH	278	205	3	307	172	1
PAINT TOWNSHIP.	357	298	7	389	270	3
PERRY TOWNSHIP	116	230	5	191	158	7
PINEY TOWNSHIP	58	72	8	83	53	4
PORTER TOWNSHIP	237	207	4	302	147	1
RED BANK TOWNSHIP	225	219	8	328	126	5
RICHLAND TOWNSHIP	78	71	2	102	48	2
RIMERSBURG BOROUGH.	189	167	5	231	123	2
SALEM TOWNSHIP	177	132	6	210	105	1
SHIPPENVILLE BOROUGH	114	64	1	117	63	1
SLIGO BOROUGH	139	136	1	166	113	1
ST. PETERSBURG BOROUGH	56	63	2	74	46	2

	GOVERNOR/LT. GOVERNOR			U.S. SENATE		
	Republican Scranton/ Fisher	Democratic Casey/ Singel	Consumer Hoover/ Brickhouse	Republican Arlen Specter	Democratic Bob Edgar	Consumer Lance S. Haver
STRATTANVILLE BOROUGH	86	68	3	103	52	4
TOBY TOWNSHIP....................	113	237	6	189	165	4
WASHINGTON TOWNSHIP............	230	319	6	304	244	8
CLARION COUNTY TOTALS	**6,466**	**6,024**	**149**	**7,937**	**4,626**	**98**
CLEARFIELD COUNTY						
BECCARIA TOWNSHIP	226	379	10	309	293	13
BELL TOWNSHIP	81	130	1	123	87	1
BIGLER TOWNSHIP	156	318	2	228	239	5
BLOOM TOWNSHIP	79	61	3	105	34	1
BOGGS TOWNSHIP	158	283	1	214	212	4
BRADFORD TOWNSHIP..............	374	437	4	483	320	9
BRADY TOWNSHIP	247	266	10	321	185	7
BRISBIN BOROUGH.................	59	79	2	83	56	1
BURNSIDE TOWNSHIP	134	190	3	210	117	3
BURNSIDE BOROUGH	34	41		42	35	
CHEST TOWNSHIP.................	43	116		79	78	1
CHESTER HILL BOROUGH	119	171	1	151	140	1
CLEARFIELD BOROUGH.............	1,154	1,183	5	1,359	981	8
WARD 01	362	224	1	400	185	2
WARD 02	397	358	1	470	284	1
WARD 03	234	269	1	281	224	3
WARD 04	161	332	2	208	288	2
COALPORT BOROUGH	95	120		129	86	
COOPER TOWNSHIP................	258	436	3	352	339	6
COVINGTON TOWNSHIP	67	103	1	94	75	
CURWENSVILLE BOROUGH...........	364	504	2	418	453	3
DECATUR TOWNSHIP	313	550	5	461	405	6
DUBOIS CITY	1,408	1,342	12	1,650	1,099	9
WARD 01	167	298	1	214	253	1
WARD 02	389	300	3	449	244	3
WARD 03	454	301	5	497	254	3
WARD 04	215	169	1	238	144	2
WARD 05	183	274	2	252	204	
FALLS CREEK BOROUGH.............						
(BALANCE IN JEFFERSON CO.)						
FERGUSON TOWNSHIP	63	85		88	56	1
GIRARD TOWNSHIP.................	69	64		90	40	2
GLEN HOPE BOROUGH	34	52		45	41	
GOSHEN TOWNSHIP.................	56	75		87	44	
GRAHAM TOWNSHIP.................	139	144	4	186	99	2
GRAMPIAN BOROUGH	60	76	2	69	65	3
GREENWOOD TOWNSHIP	48	50	2	59	39	1
GULICH TOWNSHIP	100	358	3	155	302	4
HOUTZDALE BOROUGH..............	140	244	1	188	194	3
HUSTON TOWNSHIP	164	234	8	235	166	5
IRVONA BOROUGH	69	132	2	102	101	1
JORDAN TOWNSHIP	69	79	1	95	53	1
KARTHAUS TOWNSHIP...............	66	81	1	91	58	
KNOX TOWNSHIP....................	56	121	1	79	100	2
LAWRENCE TOWNSHIP...............	982	1,389	24	1,299	1,103	7
LUMBER CITY BOROUGH.............	11	23		17	18	
MAHAFFEY BOROUGH	33	72	1	56	48	2
MORRIS TOWNSHIP	213	503	7	291	426	5
NEW WASHINGTON BOROUGH	10	17		11	16	
NEWBURG BOROUGH	16	33		21	27	
OSCEOLA BOROUGH	228	284	2	277	231	2
PENN TOWNSHIP....................	193	221	4	269	141	3
PIKE TOWNSHIP	231	304	7	302	236	3
PINE TOWNSHIP	4	7		5	5	
RAMEY BOROUGH	83	130		102	110	
SANDY TOWNSHIP	1,088	1,070	13	1,343	815	11
TROUTVILLE BOROUGH.............	46	44		55	32	
UNION TOWNSHIP...................	122	132	2	165	91	3
WALLACETON BOROUGH.............	32	50	1	42	40	1
WESTOVER BOROUGH...............	59	105	1	74	87	1
WOODWARD TOWNSHIP.............	177	428	3	261	328	6
CLEARFIELD COUNTY TOTALS........	**10,030**	**13,316**	**155**	**12,970**	**10,346**	**147**

	GOVERNOR/LT. GOVERNOR			U.S. SENATE		
	Republican Scranton/ Fisher	Democratic Casey/ Singel	Consumer Hoover/ Brickhouse	Republican Arlen Specter	Democratic Bob Edgar	Consumer Lance S. Haver
CLINTON COUNTY						
ALLISON TOWNSHIP	20	30		17	32	1
AVIS BOROUGH	129	274	5	150	240	2
BALD EAGLE TOWNSHIP	136	169	2	169	138	1
BEECH CREEK TOWNSHIP	98	132		114	115	
BEECH CREEK BOROUGH	110	108		126	91	
CASTANEA TOWNSHIP	131	176	3	149	160	2
CHAPMAN TOWNSHIP.	82	137	2	94	113	4
COLEBROOK TOWNSHIP	16	31		17	28	1
CRAWFORD TOWNSHIP	84	95	2	107	74	
DUNNSTABLE TOWNSHIP.	114	124	2	128	108	3
EAST KEATING TOWNSHIP	7	5		12	1	
FLEMINGTON BOROUGH	226	211	5	254	166	8
GALLAGHER TOWNSHIP.	26	25		35	16	
GREENE TOWNSHIP	121	104	5	136	94	1
GRUGAN TOWNSHIP.	2	16		7	12	
LAMAR TOWNSHIP	292	230	5	300	194	8
LEIDY TOWNSHIP	41	48	1	61	28	
LOCK HAVEN CITY	899	740	11	950	656	22
WARD 01	96	131	1	109	112	4
WARD 02	49	71		58	58	3
WARD 03	283	152	3	281	149	7
WARD 04	340	265	3	359	235	8
WARD 05	131	121	4	143	102	
LOGAN TOWNSHIP	83	78	1	112	50	1
LOGANTON BOROUGH	58	93		74	76	2
MILL HALL BOROUGH.	222	182	7	239	153	6
NOYES TOWNSHIP	73	95		82	87	
WARD EAST	50	74		58	68	
WARD WEST	23	21		24	19	
PINE CREEK TOWNSHIP.	369	288	8	388	255	9
PORTER TOWNSHIP	171	138	7	181	122	7
RENOVO BOROUGH	125	228	2	159	181	5
WARD EAST	40	84	1	51	70	3
WARD MIDDLE	42	68	1	47	58	2
WARD WEST	43	76		61	53	
SOUTH RENOVO BOROUGH	74	110		94	87	
WAYNE TOWNSHIP.	80	117	3	103	92	3
WEST KEATING TOWNSHIP	10	2		10	3	
WOODWARD TOWNSHIP.	397	387	14	438	350	7
CLINTON COUNTY TOTALS	**4,196**	**4,373**	**85**	**4,706**	**3,722**	**93**
COLUMBIA COUNTY						
BEAVER TOWNSHIP.	71	142	3	97	115	
BENTON TOWNSHIP	149	143	2	201	90	2
BENTON BOROUGH	137	121	1	169	89	1
BERWICK BOROUGH	1,139	1,901	11	1,609	1,425	14
WARD 01	534	542	3	699	382	3
WARD 02	142	209	1	193	149	1
WARD 03	175	498	4	271	398	6
WARD 04	288	652	3	446	496	4
BLOOMSBURG INC. TOWN	1,334	1,285	20	1,561	1,061	15
BRIAR CREEK TOWNSHIP.	379	445	7	517	311	8
BRIAR CREEK BOROUGH.	50	62		65	47	
CATAWISSA TOWNSHIP	138	148		185	101	2
CATAWISSA BOROUGH	220	218	2	271	163	4
CENTRALIA BOROUGH.	33	101		61	74	
CLEVELAND TOWNSHIP	92	113	1	137	66	3
CONYNGHAM TOWNSHIP.	107	243	1	155	196	2
FISHING CREEK TOWNSHIP.	183	202	2	248	138	1
FRANKLIN TOWNSHIP.	75	79	1	103	52	1
GREENWOOD TOWNSHIP	250	292	1	356	183	4
HEMLOCK TOWNSHIP	223	267	3	311	178	7
JACKSON TOWNSHIP	78	87	1	118	43	
LOCUST TOWNSHIP	171	216	2	253	143	2
MADISON TOWNSHIP	184	179	1	236	128	
MAIN TOWNSHIP	162	164	4	219	109	4
MIFFLIN TOWNSHIP.	241	425	6	364	310	8
MILLVILLE BOROUGH	158	158	2	200	113	2
MONTOUR TOWNSHIP	188	228	3	271	142	4

	GOVERNOR/LT. GOVERNOR			U.S. SENATE		
	Republican Scranton/ Fisher	Democratic Casey/ Singel	Consumer Hoover/ Brickhouse	Republican Arlen Specter	Democratic Bob Edgar	Consumer Lance S. Haver
MT. PLEASANT TOWNSHIP	176	176	4	249	108	1
NORTH CENTRE TOWNSHIP	229	194	2	296	126	3
ORANGE TOWNSHIP.	136	116	3	187	66	3
ORANGEVILLE BOROUGH	80	57		94	44	
PINE TOWNSHIP	109	143	2	152	96	1
ROARING CREEK TOWNSHIP.	67	78		88	55	1
SCOTT TOWNSHIP.	789	697	5	969	526	3
SOUTH CENTRE TOWNSHIP	254	258	2	345	166	4
STILLWATER BOROUGH	28	38	2	31	35	2
SUGARLOAF TOWNSHIP.	80	93	1	108	68	3
COLUMBIA COUNTY TOTALS	**7,710**	**9,069**	**95**	**10,226**	**6,567**	**105**
CRAWFORD COUNTY						
ATHENS TOWNSHIP.	117	71	2	149	44	
BEAVER TOWNSHIP.	73	100	2	97	77	2
BLOOMFIELD TOWNSHIP	264	165	3	259	148	9
BLOOMING VALLEY BOROUGH	77	83		96	62	1
CAMBRIDGE TOWNSHIP.	233	204	2	291	141	
CAMBRIDGE SPRINGS BOROUGH	309	227	7	376	149	7
CENTERVILLE BOROUGH	59	38		70	29	
COCHRANTON BOROUGH	219	137	4	256	93	2
CONNEAUT TOWNSHIP	179	174	3	217	140	2
CONNEAUT LAKE BOROUGH.	128	97	3	137	79	6
CONNEAUTVILLE BOROUGH.	150	127	7	178	92	2
CUSSEWAGO TOWNSHIP	184	175	2	222	132	4
EAST FAIRFIELD TOWNSHIP.	129	146	3	172	108	2
EAST FALLOWFIELD TOWNSHIP	138	159	2	178	122	2
EAST MEAD TOWNSHIP	162	240	3	227	164	3
FAIRFIELD TOWNSHIP.	129	76	4	147	54	3
GREENWOOD TOWNSHIP	198	177	6	231	129	4
HAYFIELD TOWNSHIP	374	427	6	480	305	7
HYDETOWN BOROUGH	137	79		155	59	
LINESVILLE BOROUGH.	174	132		202	99	1
MEADVILLE CITY	2,045	1,840	28	2,634	1,634	29
WARD 01	700	517	5	1,106	557	10
WARD 02	951	776	13	1,057	620	10
WARD 03	311	382	8	374	319	5
WARD 04	49	104	1	54	92	2
WARD 05	34	61	1	43	46	2
NORTH SHENANGO TOWNSHIP	102	178	1	130	151	1
OIL CREEK TOWNSHIP	327	179	2	383	128	1
PINE TOWNSHIP	63	65	1	84	48	
RANDOLPH TOWNSHIP.	282	220	2	369	120	4
RICHMOND TOWNSHIP.	271	230	8	330	183	3
ROCKDALE TOWNSHIP.	138	164	5	172	131	1
ROME TOWNSHIP	163	80	1	193	62	3
SADSBURY TOWNSHIP.	397	274	3	441	216	7
SAEGERTOWN BOROUGH	152	140	4	182	101	3
SOUTH SHENANGO TOWNSHIP.	182	187	3	213	150	1
SPARTA TOWNSHIP	150	67	3	164	35	2
SPARTANSBURG BOROUGH	64	58	1	69	48	1
SPRING TOWNSHIP	188	186	2	221	159	1
SPRINGBORO BOROUGH.	59	63	4	83	42	
STEUBEN TOWNSHIP	119	93	2	147	79	1
SUMMERHILL TOWNSHIP.	149	175	6	208	119	3
SUMMIT TOWNSHIP	267	231	2	316	168	4
TITUSVILLE CITY	1,061	705	2	1,159	551	9
WARD 01	306	214		345	157	3
WARD 02	516	242	1	554	189	2
WARD 03	61	77	1	69	64	3
WARD 04	125	130		138	103	1
WARD 05	53	42		53	38	
TOWNVILLE BOROUGH.	92	51		108	29	1
TROY TOWNSHIP.	144	125	4	194	88	1
UNION TOWNSHIP	132	126	5	165	89	5
VENANGO TOWNSHIP.	111	101	5	145	72	2
VENANGO BOROUGH.	66	76	2	87	56	1
VERNON TOWNSHIP	766	813	13	948	598	11
WAYNE TOWNSHIP.	155	160	1	211	95	3
WEST FALLOWFIELD TOWNSHIP.	86	116	3	117	89	1

	GOVERNOR/LT. GOVERNOR			U.S. SENATE		
	Republican Scranton/ Fisher	Democratic Casey/ Singel	Consumer Hoover/ Brickhouse	Republican Arlen Specter	Democratic Bob Edgar	Consumer Lance S. Haver
WEST MEAD TOWNSHIP	851	752		991	575	
WEST SHENANGO TOWNSHIP	104	59		117	47	
WOODCOCK TOWNSHIP	400	284	9	459	215	8
WOODCOCK BOROUGH	27	27	2	39	17	1
CRAWFORD COUNTY TOTALS	**12,546**	**10,859**	**183**	**15,219**	**8,321**	**165**
CUMBERLAND COUNTY						
CAMP HILL BOROUGH	2,647	1,231	20	2,810	1,068	18
CARLISLE BOROUGH	2,909	1,672	44	2,895	1,630	43
WARD 01	276	185	7	294	166	7
WARD 02	177	147	8	183	136	7
WARD 03	1,506	727	18	1,506	703	15
WARD 04	396	234	3	362	262	5
WARD 05	554	379	8	550	363	9
COOKE TOWNSHIP	23	8		28	3	
DICKINSON TOWNSHIP	508	374	5	578	286	8
EAST PENNSBORO TOWNSHIP	1,953	1,829	22	2,321	1,441	22
HAMPDEN TOWNSHIP	4,065	2,193	34	4,444	2,044	32
HOPEWELL TOWNSHIP	251	172	7	244	177	3
LEMOYNE BOROUGH	956	461	10	805	327	8
LOWER ALLEN TOWNSHIP	3,317	1,687	41	3,626	1,370	23
LOWER FRANKFORD TOWNSHIP	149	123	3	154	117	1
LOWER MIFFLIN TOWNSHIP	175	128	1	173	120	2
MECHANICSBURG BOROUGH	1,860	1,194	18	2,034	987	16
WARD 01	197	121	1	214	105	1
WARD 02	884	591	10	987	483	9
WARD 03	251	175	2	279	148	2
WARD 04	179	102	3	196	82	2
WARD 05	349	205	2	358	169	2
MIDDLESEX TOWNSHIP	640	387	4	708	321	6
MONROE TOWNSHIP	903	489	10	979	401	9
MT. HOLLY SPRINGS BOROUGH	242	192	3			
NEW CUMBERLAND BOROUGH	1,946	1,160	12	2,089	948	19
WARD 01	534	365	5	553	300	9
WARD 02	1,412	795	7	1,536	648	10
NEWBURG BOROUGH	51	34	2	58	30	1
NEWVILLE BOROUGH	174	122	1	176	112	2
WARD NORTH	97	62		90	62	1
WARD SOUTH	77	60	1	86	50	1
NORTH MIDDLETON TOWNSHIP	1,425	834	15	1,506	738	13
NORTH NEWTON TOWNSHIP	268	149	5	270	145	2
PENN TOWNSHIP	270	186	3	283	164	5
SHIPPENSBURG TOWNSHIP	170	106		170	106	
SHIPPENSBURG BOROUGH	537	330	5	508	360	7
(BALANCE IN FRANKLIN CO.)						
WARD EAST	271	146	3	261	153	5
WARD MIDDLE	159	121	2	149	137	1
WARD WEST	107	63		98	70	1
SHIREMANSTOWN BOROUGH	421	206	4	437	173	
SILVER SPRING TOWNSHIP	1,240	715	17	1,354	588	13
SOUTH MIDDLETON TOWNSHIP	1,582	858	22	1,699	743	14
SOUTH NEWTON TOWNSHIP	127	124	3	150	102	2
SOUTHAMPTON TOWNSHIP	360	280	3	414	224	5
UPPER ALLEN TOWNSHIP	2,396	1,154	25	2,506	1,041	17
UPPER FRANKFORD TOWNSHIP	164	101	2	161	101	3
UPPER MIFFLIN TOWNSHIP	96	86	1	104	79	1
WEST FAIRVIEW BOROUGH	186	151	3	225	108	1
WEST PENNSBORO TOWNSHIP	686	433	5	710	396	9
WORMLEYSBURG BOROUGH	599	411	5	656	349	4
CUMBERLAND COUNTY TOTALS	**33,296**	**19,580**	**355**	**35,275**	**16,799**	**309**
DAUPHIN COUNTY						
BERRYSBURG BOROUGH	67	34		83	16	3
CONEWAGO TOWNSHIP	473	192	7	515	146	3
DAUPHIN BOROUGH	133	144	2	172	103	3
DERRY TOWNSHIP	3,518	1,937	28	3,924	1,535	19
EAST HANOVER TOWNSHIP	742	296	13	841	201	7
ELIZABETHVILLE BOROUGH	220	189	2	252	152	2
GRATZ BOROUGH	124	71	1	153	41	2

	GOVERNOR/LT. GOVERNOR			U.S. SENATE		
	Republican Scranton/ Fisher	Democratic Casey/ Singel	Consumer Hoover/ Brickhouse	Republican Arlen Specter	Democratic Bob Edgar	Consumer Lance S. Haver
HALIFAX TOWNSHIP	171	119	2	200	88	3
HALIFAX BOROUGH	506	297	9	602	205	3
HARRISBURG CITY	5,010	6,562	99	5,528	5,956	90
WARD 01	372	538	3	422	476	6
WARD 02	293	318	9	344	262	9
WARD 03	189	169	1	206	143	3
WARD 04	243	233	1	241	233	3
WARD 05	267	243	5	245	274	3
WARD 06	127	120	2	114	128	1
WARD 07	228	597	8	268	535	5
WARD 08	113	405	3	115	385	10
WARD 09	1,008	1,216	16	1,090	1,120	14
WARD 10	593	1,003	21	670	899	21
WARD 11	125	194	2	138	182	1
WARD 12	163	215	2	152	234	
WARD 13	866	791	14	1,043	613	7
WARD 14	351	336	11	398	303	4
WARD 15	72	184	1	82	169	3
HIGHSPIRE BOROUGH	372	370	4	458	287	5
HUMMELSTOWN BOROUGH	789	427	7	880	339	5
JACKSON TOWNSHIP	224	155	2	266	109	1
JEFFERSON TOWNSHIP	61	42	2	65	39	
LONDONDERRY TOWNSHIP	713	443	7	845	326	4
LOWER PAXTON TOWNSHIP	7,224	4,909	75	8,333	3,829	55
LOWER SWATARA TOWNSHIP	895	843	17	1,123	638	8
LYKENS TOWNSHIP	153	63	3	185	30	2
LYKENS BOROUGH	334	268	6	398	205	3
WARD 01	149	134	3	182	99	2
WARD 02	185	134	3	216	106	1
MIDDLE PAXTON TOWNSHIP	829	534	10	1,008	373	5
MIDDLETOWN BOROUGH	1,322	979	20	1,600	691	15
WARD 01	313	229	8	391	148	5
WARD 02	564	414	8	664	315	3
WARD 03	445	336	4	545	228	7
MIFFLIN TOWNSHIP	78	71	1	96	52	2
MILLERSBURG BOROUGH	477	296	11	570	218	4
PAXTANG BOROUGH	530	305	5	599	242	2
PENBROOK BOROUGH	564	398	7	663	296	4
PILLOW BOROUGH	71	40		76	32	2
REED TOWNSHIP	42	54		56	35	1
ROYALTON BOROUGH	103	75	2	118	61	1
RUSH TOWNSHIP	36	17	3	40	13	2
SOUTH HANOVER TOWNSHIP	927	472	16	1,050	351	11
STEELTON BOROUGH	852	981	6	1,039	773	7
WARD 01	152	155	1	182	119	
WARD 02	303	334	1	377	256	3
WARD 03	268	292	4	309	244	3
WARD 04	129	200		171	154	1
SUSQUEHANNA TOWNSHIP	3,986	2,737	31	4,498	2,218	32
SWATARA TOWNSHIP	3,340	3,065	59	4,137	2,257	45
UPPER PAXTON TOWNSHIP	492	268	6	574	183	5
WASHINGTON TOWNSHIP	294	157	2	335	114	2
WAYNE TOWNSHIP	139	93	1	170	59	3
WEST HANOVER TOWNSHIP	1,283	813	27	1,604	510	10
WICONISCO TOWNSHIP	161	116	3	180	95	5
WILLIAMS TOWNSHIP	160	81	4	190	50	3
WILLIAMSTOWN BOROUGH	226	203	2	282	145	
DAUPHIN COUNTY TOTALS	**37,641**	**29,116**	**502**	**43,708**	**23,013**	**379**
DELAWARE COUNTY						
ALDAN BOROUGH	1,052	655	13	1,042	676	6
ASTON TOWNSHIP	2,953	1,978	25	2,797	2,165	18
WARD 01	408	350	2	385	368	3
WARD 02	378	243	3	350	276	1
WARD 03	429	308	5	393	349	1
WARD 04	444	292	4	450	298	3
WARD 05	472	247	6	442	292	3
WARD 06	359	229	3	338	245	6
WARD 07	463	309	2	439	337	1
BETHEL TOWNSHIP	581	213	7	589	213	7

	GOVERNOR/LT. GOVERNOR			U.S. SENATE		
	Republican Scranton/ Fisher	Democratic Casey/ Singel	Consumer Hoover/ Brickhouse	Republican Arlen Specter	Democratic Bob Edgar	Consumer Lance S. Haver
BIRMINGHAM TOWNSHIP	599	164	3	584	187	1
BROOKHAVEN BOROUGH	1,747	1,235	21	1,666	1,382	20
CHESTER CITY	5,793	4,459	146	5,480	5,092	115
WARD 01	1,780	980	26	1,688	1,118	10
WARD 02	486	422	15	445	498	7
WARD 03	87	40	1	82	44	1
WARD 04	133	110	2	126	122	6
WARD 05	261	285	7	243	313	8
WARD 06	220	98	8	214	123	5
WARD 07	518	524	28	499	595	26
WARD 08	334	357	9	300	430	11
WARD 09	387	430	15	353	514	11
WARD 10	220	387	21	195	439	14
WARD 11	1,367	826	14	1,335	896	16
CHESTER TOWNSHIP	535	427	10	510	471	12
CHESTER HEIGHTS BOROUGH	295	107	3	259	149	
CLIFTON HEIGHTS BOROUGH	1,116	1,226	17	1,175	1,202	14
WARD 01	178	147	2	175	160	1
WARD 02	324	287	2	320	302	6
WARD 03	237	408	4	286	368	2
WARD 04	377	384	9	394	372	5
COLLINGDALE BOROUGH	1,844	1,267	24	1,836	1,329	18
COLWYN BOROUGH	398	367	2	391	386	2
CONCORD TOWNSHIP	1,462	569	10	1,422	622	11
DARBY TOWNSHIP	1,654	1,953	21	1,730	1,940	11
WARD 01	91	406	4	69	442	3
WARD 02	93	333	7	78	359	4
WARD 03	468	382	2	505	352	1
WARD 04	511	413	4	555	388	1
WARD 05	491	419	4	523	399	2
DARBY BOROUGH.	1,293	1,413	30	1,216	1,533	18
WARD 01	533	560	9	556	567	6
WARD 02	289	488	13	250	564	5
WARD 03	471	365	8	410	402	7
EAST LANSDOWNE BOROUGH	476	541	7	481	556	3
EDDYSTONE BOROUGH.	663	280	5	625	338	2
EDGEMONT TOWNSHIP	505	225	5	478	254	3
FOLCROFT BOROUGH	1,486	1,040	6	1,527	1,023	6
GLENOLDEN BOROUGH.	1,319	977	22	1,264	1,086	14
HAVERFORD TOWNSHIP.	12,066	8,419	211	12,111	8,788	122
WARD 01	1,390	1,032	24	1,494	944	8
WARD 02	1,086	940	21	1,162	864	18
WARD 03	1,513	762	23	1,502	997	19
WARD 04	1,490	795	18	1,395	899	13
WARD 05	1,269	734	21	1,075	971	10
WARD 06	1,116	967	24	1,053	1,067	19
WARD 07	1,309	1,130	39	1,517	969	15
WARD 08	1,471	1,078	24	1,445	1,118	9
WARD 09	1,422	981	17	1,468	959	11
LANSDOWNE BOROUGH	2,447	2,042	57	2,201	2,361	33
LOWER CHICHESTER TOWNSHIP	504	292	7	491	315	4
MARCUS HOOK BOROUGH	509	240	5	491	260	4
WARD 01	79	23		74	23	
WARD 02	90	45	3	84	53	1
WARD 03	156	83	1	152	94	1
WARD 04	184	89	1	181	90	2
MARPLE TOWNSHIP	5,726	3,606	70	5,411	4,042	50
WARD 01	1,019	529	8	952	604	8
WARD 02	737	439	8	666	523	9
WARD 03	704	557	10	678	598	6
WARD 04	635	627	9	705	576	7
WARD 05	896	526	9	816	622	10
WARD 06	834	449	15	731	571	6
WARD 07	901	479	11	863	548	4
MEDIA BOROUGH	1,413	879	33	1,123	1,215	9
MIDDLETOWN TOWNSHIP	3,380	1,286	43	3,001	1,752	25
MILLBOURNE BOROUGH	125	67	1	116	78	2
MORTON BOROUGH	404	400	8	372	437	4
NETHER PROVIDENCE TOWNSHIP	3,478	1,705	48	2,870	2,405	18
WARD 01	608	312	9	560	382	1

	GOVERNOR/LT. GOVERNOR			U.S. SENATE		
	Republican Scranton/ Fisher	Democratic Casey/ Singel	Consumer Hoover/ Brickhouse	Republican Arlen Specter	Democratic Bob Edgar	Consumer Lance S. Haver
WARD 02	597	216	9	470	361	5
WARD 03	530	253	9	357	449	1
WARD 04	657	268	7	542	393	3
WARD 05	615	408	8	552	480	5
WARD 06	471	248	6	389	340	3
NEWTOWN TOWNSHIP	3,134	1,511	21	3,085	1,623	14
NORWOOD BOROUGH	954	947	14	943	981	13
PARKSIDE BOROUGH	450	309	3	411	353	3
PROSPECT PARK BOROUGH	1,123	848	22	994	1,014	11
RADNOR TOWNSHIP	6,697	2,706	63	6,289	3,222	25
WARD 01	835	380	15	779	463	8
WARD 02	782	250	6	745	291	4
WARD 03	1,128	322	15	1,033	422	4
WARD 04	1,250	464	5	1,178	553	3
WARD 05	1,104	510	9	1,024	606	1
WARD 06	967	398	8	882	504	4
WARD 07	631	382	5	648	383	1
RIDLEY TOWNSHIP	7,050	5,148	71	6,834	5,483	48
WARD 01	551	407	1	522	442	2
WARD 02	798	522	7	786	555	6
WARD 03	827	695	11	804	733	5
WARD 04	690	620	11	678	645	5
WARD 05	994	613	10	975	652	3
WARD 06	738	616	9	722	650	5
WARD 07	948	502	4	912	554	8
WARD 08	736	524	8	679	585	7
WARD 09	768	649	10	756	667	7
RIDLEY PARK BOROUGH	1,521	1,182	20	1,432	1,305	10
ROSE VALLEY BOROUGH	367	120	6	301	204	
RUTLEDGE BOROUGH	187	128	5	171	150	4
SHARON HILL BOROUGH	1,198	895	15	1,164	952	9
SPRINGFIELD TOWNSHIP	7,291	4,182	72	6,595	5,034	37
WARD 01	1,079	567	11	952	713	9
WARD 02	1,062	615	14	985	705	9
WARD 03	929	605	10	828	740	2
WARD 04	1,001	610	8	885	761	4
WARD 05	1,128	583	10	1,024	714	7
WARD 06	995	624	8	941	687	3
WARD 07	1,097	578	11	980	714	3
SWARTHMORE BOROUGH	1,645	754	91	904	1,641	8
THORNBURY TOWNSHIP	700	322	6	634	407	2
TINICUM TOWNSHIP	907	614	14	809	768	8
WARD 01	188	134	3	160	164	2
WARD 02	161	87	2	140	111	1
WARD 03	154	122	2	138	145	3
WARD 04	227	121	4	218	151	1
WARD 05	177	150	3	153	197	1
TRAINER BOROUGH	341	213	6	310	243	4
UPLAND BOROUGH	612	311	6	591	345	3
UPPER CHICHESTER TOWNSHIP	2,114	1,419	19	2,169	1,407	16
WARD 01	426	262	3	432	271	1
WARD 02	297	242	3	296	246	3
WARD 03	379	292	4	373	298	6
WARD 04	621	332	8	656	319	4
WARD 05	391	291	1	412	273	2
UPPER DARBY TOWNSHIP	17,542	12,294	226	17,369	12,864	148
UPPER PROVIDENCE TOWNSHIP	2,523	1,152	28	2,218	1,568	16
YEADON BOROUGH	1,449	1,924	27	1,440	1,958	21
DELAWARE COUNTY TOTALS	**113,628**	**75,011**	**1,595**	**107,922**	**83,779**	**952**
ELK COUNTY						
BENEZETT TOWNSHIP	91	66	1	92	65	
BENZINGER TOWNSHIP	1,039	1,688	29	1,647	1,110	17
FOX TOWNSHIP	339	699	6	453	597	5
HIGHLAND TOWNSHIP	62	128	2	67	127	
HORTON TOWNSHIP	158	226		198	183	3
JAY TOWNSHIP	250	539	5	313	477	6
JOHNSONBURG BOROUGH	499	868	15	617	759	14
JONES TOWNSHIP	214	392	7	272	336	1
MILLSTONE TOWNSHIP	22	32		31	24	

	GOVERNOR/LT. GOVERNOR			U.S. SENATE		
	Republican Scranton/ Fisher	Democratic Casey/ Singel	Consumer Hoover/ Brickhouse	Republican Arlen Specter	Democratic Bob Edgar	Consumer Lance S. Haver
RIDGWAY TOWNSHIP.	340	439	10	435	349	4
RIDGWAY BOROUGH.	917	962	14	1,049	821	9
WARD 01	83	72	2	75	74	1
WARD 02	351	342	1	402	279	1
WARD 03	141	194	5	176	163	2
WARD 04	170	217	3	205	187	1
WARD 05	172	137	3	191	118	4
SPRING CREEK TOWNSHIP	42	53	3	60	38	
ST. MARYS BOROUGH.	845	1,431	24	1,401	898	12
WARD 01	136	236	2	272	103	1
WARD 02	198	292	4	315	177	2
WARD 03	118	160	8	167	115	4
WARD 04	152	294	2	240	204	2
WARD 05	150	226	3	232	154	1
WARD 06	91	223	5	175	145	2
ELK COUNTY TOTALS.	4,818	7,523	116	6,635	5,784	71
ERIE COUNTY						
ALBION BOROUGH	256	160	4	280	135	3
AMITY TOWNSHIP	144	76	8	157	64	7
CONCORD TOWNSHIP	158	122	6	185	98	6
CONNEAUT TOWNSHIP	281	213	10	329	161	3
CORRY CITY.	1,004	593	21	1,106	487	20
WARD 01	235	138	4	263	105	6
WARD 02	329	158	8	354	135	6
WARD 03	293	216	5	331	176	5
WARD 04	147	81	4	158	71	3
CRANESVILLE BOROUGH	86	76	1	103	57	3
EDINBORO BOROUGH	640	328	12	570	398	3
ELGIN BOROUGH	36	32	1	42	27	1
ELK CREEK TOWNSHIP.	228	199	4	254	165	5
ERIE CITY.	12,256	18,107	663	14,127	16,025	535
WARD 01	1,014	1,957	81	1,189	1,768	49
WARD 02	520	1,548	69	610	1,552	59
WARD 03	1,036	1,288	63	1,164	1,141	43
WARD 04	1,759	1,550	65	1,863	1,395	62
WARD 05	4,426	6,929	238	5,290	5,980	189
WARD 06	3,501	4,835	147	4,011	4,189	133
FAIRVIEW TOWNSHIP	1,745	717	36	1,918	537	22
FAIRVIEW BOROUGH	406	197	3	427	163	7
FRANKLIN TOWNSHIP.	200	141	12	203	136	8
GIRARD TOWNSHIP.	565	469	14	647	371	12
GIRARD BOROUGH.	474	304	15	533	243	5
GREENE TOWNSHIP	668	755	33	804	602	37
GREENFIELD TOWNSHIP	196	146	11	237	111	7
HARBORCREEK TOWNSHIP.	2,148	1,896	87	2,410	1,635	56
LAKE CITY BOROUGH.	284	242	12	326	194	5
LAWRENCE PARK TOWNSHIP.	811	635	27	887	656	12
LE BOEUF TOWNSHIP.	221	130	7	257	93	6
MC KEAN TOWNSHIP	584	467	18	669	365	14
MC KEAN BOROUGH.	103	46	3	117	30	3
MILL VILLAGE BOROUGH.	51	64	1	55	54	3
MILLCREEK TOWNSHIP	8,186	5,781	207	9,058	4,751	168
NORTH EAST TOWNSHIP	927	460	23	1,052	334	9
NORTH EAST BOROUGH	656	401	20	837	318	7
WARD 01	322	236	13	360	195	4
WARD 02	334	165	7	477	123	3
PLATEA BOROUGH	48	40	1	58	29	1
SPRINGFIELD TOWNSHIP.	400	266	11	464	199	8
SUMMIT TOWNSHIP	741	682	20	851	554	22
UNION TOWNSHIP.	282	159	6	290	140	10
UNION CITY BOROUGH	399	226	18	407	221	9
WARD 01	181	123	9	202	103	4
WARD 02	218	103	9	205	118	5
VENANGO TOWNSHIP.	288	194	4	322	148	8
WASHINGTON TOWNSHIP.	617	345	15	617	333	16
WATERFORD TOWNSHIP.	410	271	13	444	233	7
WATERFORD BOROUGH.	293	158	10	329	114	7
WATTSBURG BOROUGH.	80	43	2	72	48	5
WAYNE TOWNSHIP.	233	153	5	272	111	8

	GOVERNOR/LT. GOVERNOR			U.S. SENATE		
	Republican Scranton/ Fisher	Democratic Casey/ Singel	Consumer Hoover/ Brickhouse	Republican Arlen Specter	Democratic Bob Edgar	Consumer Lance S. Haver
WESLEYVILLE BOROUGH	475	433	21	548	361	13
ERIE COUNTY TOTALS	37,580	35,727	1,385	42,264	30,701	1,081
FAYETTE COUNTY						
BELLE VERNON BOROUGH	79	347	3	105	310	3
BROWNSVILLE TOWNSHIP..........	53	244	7	102	197	2
BROWNSVILLE BOROUGH...........	254	947	18	406	784	14
WARD 01	19	120	1	33	102	3
WARD 02	28	237	3	59	204	2
WARD 03	95	209	5	143	156	4
WARD 04	11	59	3	26	47	
WARD 05	27	85	1	56	55	1
WARD 06	55	99	1	67	90	
WARD 07	19	138	4	22	130	4
BULLSKIN TOWNSHIP	648	889	27	874	627	18
CONNELLSVILLE CITY	938	1,355	29	1,211	1,030	24
WARD 01	65	122	4	92	96	5
WARD 02	82	170	6	117	133	2
WARD 03	147	238	4	206	165	3
WARD 04	158	184	2	212	120	6
WARD 05	296	260	5	337	203	6
WARD 06	190	381	8	247	313	2
CONNELLSVILLE TOWNSHIP	308	383	8	428	249	7
DAWSON BOROUGH	52	103	3	77	69	3
DUNBAR TOWNSHIP	467	1,172	19	686	928	17
DUNBAR BOROUGH	105	287	7	174	215	5
EVERSON BOROUGH	49	171	2	84	134	3
FAIRCHANCE BOROUGH	123	407	5	211	314	2
FAYETTE CITY BOROUGH...........	52	207	2	79	173	3
FRANKLIN TOWNSHIP..............	192	455	12	282	365	5
GEORGES TOWNSHIP...............	344	1,163	18	595	897	18
GERMAN TOWNSHIP................	268	1,255	20	539	959	19
HENRY CLAY TOWNSHIP	191	170	4	230	130	3
JEFFERSON TOWNSHIP	183	464	7	266	366	5
LOWER TYRONE TOWNSHIP	119	187	4	150	160	
LUZERNE TOWNSHIP	298	1,408	12	579	1,108	20
MARKLEYSBURG BOROUGH..........	32	15		33	14	1
MASONTOWN BOROUGH.............	260	973	14	535	704	9
MENALLEN TOWNSHIP	320	955	14	476	768	13
NEWELL BOROUGH	51	164	4	88	125	4
NICHOLSON TOWNSHIP	123	355	3	207	264	4
NORTH UNION TOWNSHIP	757	2,200	33	1,225	1,732	23
OHIOPYLE BOROUGH...............	22	15		22	14	
PERRY TOWNSHIP	165	626	9	247	551	5
PERRYOPOLIS BOROUGH	149	516	8	227	435	5
POINT MARION BOROUGH...........	151	197	2	209	143	2
REDSTONE TOWNSHIP	319	1,505	19	597	1,192	18
SALTLICK TOWNSHIP	276	264	7	324	200	8
SMITHFIELD BOROUGH	105	139	7	143	105	3
SOUTH CONNELLSVILLE BOROUGH ...	178	333		309	198	4
SOUTH UNION TOWNSHIP	1,045	1,930	17	1,511	1,412	18
SPRINGFIELD TOWNSHIP............	273	311	6	368	200	9
SPRINGHILL TOWNSHIP.............	196	435	5	291	332	5
STEWART TOWNSHIP	122	87		149	55	
UNIONTOWN CITY	1,440	1,802	32	1,835	1,383	25
WARD 01	347	343	9	417	271	5
WARD 02	109	247	5	160	192	4
WARD 03	192	255	4	268	181	3
WARD 04	81	208	4	115	179	5
WARD 05	51	106	1	75	82	
WARD 06	208	169	6	238	137	2
WARD 07	155	121	1	184	89	
WARD 08	297	353	2	378	252	6
UPPER TYRONE TOWNSHIP	136	266	1	177	209	3
VANDERBILT BOROUGH	72	113		84	93	3
WASHINGTON TOWNSHIP...........	329	1,320	12	489	1,148	12
WHARTON TOWNSHIP	460	405	9	527	317	16
FAYETTE COUNTY TOTALS	**11,704**	**26,540**	**409**	**17,151**	**20,609**	**361**

	GOVERNOR/LT. GOVERNOR			U.S. SENATE		
	Republican Scranton/ Fisher	Democratic Casey/ Singel	Consumer Hoover/ Brickhouse	Republican Arlen Specter	Democratic Bob Edgar	Consumer Lance S. Haver
FOREST COUNTY						
BARNETT TOWNSHIP	76	80		86	52	
GREEN TOWNSHIP	64	51	1	81	33	
HARMONY TOWNSHIP	106	108	2	129	84	1
HICKORY TOWNSHIP	73	103	2	92	86	1
HOWE TOWNSHIP	27	41	2	41	28	
JENKS TOWNSHIP.................	246	211		285	174	2
KINGSLEY TOWNSHIP.	75	37	5	80	32	
TIONESTA TOWNSHIP	129	105	3	162	76	1
TIONESTA BOROUGH	170	97	2	190	80	1
FOREST COUNTY TOTALS	**966**	**833**	**17**	**1,146**	**645**	**6**
FRANKLIN COUNTY						
ANTRIM TOWNSHIP................	1,029	591	9	1,191	425	10
CHAMBERSBURG BOROUGH	2,414	1,832	28	2,642	1,648	19
FANNETT TOWNSHIP	321	223	3	339	205	3
GREENCASTLE BOROUGH	483	340	1	542	277	7
GREENE TOWNSHIP	1,519	988	12	1,744	790	8
GUILFORD TOWNSHIP	1,589	964	14	1,751	812	17
HAMILTON TOWNSHIP.............	787	529	8	918	396	15
LETTERKENNY TOWNSHIP	291	230	1	346	171	1
LURGAN TOWNSHIP	270	134	6	278	130	1
MERCERSBURG BOROUGH...........	239	120	5	244	119	4
METAL TOWNSHIP................	204	113		203	113	1
MONT ALTO BOROUGH.............	155	103		165	93	
MONTGOMERY TOWNSHIP	351	212	3	393	176	4
ORRSTOWN BOROUGH	25	22		26	21	
PETERS TOWNSHIP	522	245	3	555	218	4
QUINCY TOWNSHIP................	383	352	12	444	293	10
SHIPPENSBURG BOROUGH	257	122	5	236	146	2
(BALANCE IN CUMBERLAND CO.)						
SOUTHAMPTON TOWNSHIP..........	632	466	3	630	458	12
ST. THOMAS TOWNSHIP	601	400	8	698	304	8
WARREN TOWNSHIP	24	23		22	26	
WASHINGTON TOWNSHIP.............	1,319	683	12	1,405	609	11
WAYNESBORO BOROUGH	1,335	797	15	1,402	687	5
FRANKLIN COUNTY TOTALS	**14,750**	**9,489**	**148**	**16,174**	**8,117**	**142**
FULTON COUNTY						
AYR TOWNSHIP	245	148	2	243	140	3
BELFAST TOWNSHIP..............	153	193	7	199	149	1
BETHEL TOWNSHIP.................	126	124	4	160	90	2
BRUSH CREEK TOWNSHIP...........	112	119	1	136	97	1
DUBLIN TOWNSHIP	178	119	2	197	96	1
LICKING CREEK TOWNSHIP...........	191	189	1	221	161	
MC CONNELLSBURG BOROUGH.......	176	159		202	132	2
TAYLOR TOWNSHIP	179	160	2	226	113	3
THOMPSON TOWNSHIP	95	111	2	102	97	4
TODD TOWNSHIP...................	170	129	1	189	107	3
UNION TOWNSHIP..................	86	59		93	48	
VALLEY-HI BOROUGH	6	8		8	6	1
WELLS TOWNSHIP	77	100	1	100	77	
FULTON COUNTY TOTALS	**1,794**	**1,618**	**23**	**2,076**	**1,313**	**21**
GREENE COUNTY						
ALEPPO TOWNSHIP	46	112	1	63	95	
CARMICHAELS BOROUGH...........	81	119		106	91	1
CENTER TOWNSHIP	178	227	3	256	151	
CLARKSVILLE BOROUGH.............	31	58	1	40	47	
CUMBERLAND TOWNSHIP	489	1,533	10	932	1,093	7
DUNKARD TOWNSHIP...............	131	579	7	301	393	1
FRANKLIN TOWNSHIP.................	626	789	8	814	607	6
FREEPORT TOWNSHIP	19	88		27	81	
GILMORE TOWNSHIP	39	84	2	58	70	
GRAY TOWNSHIP..................	35	41		44	32	
GREENE TOWNSHIP	66	79	3	97	53	1
GREENSBORO BOROUGH.............	31	112	1	71	75	
JACKSON TOWNSHIP	71	89		92	68	1
JEFFERSON TOWNSHIP	194	636	5	346	493	5
JEFFERSON BOROUGH	44	97	1	60	87	1

	GOVERNOR/LT. GOVERNOR			U.S. SENATE		
	Republican Scranton/ Fisher	Democratic Casey/ Singel	Consumer Hoover/ Brickhouse	Republican Arlen Specter	Democratic Bob Edgar	Consumer Lance S. Haver
MONONGAHELA TOWNSHIP	110	394	4	262	287	
MORGAN TOWNSHIP	182	634	4	336	483	3
MORRIS TOWNSHIP	128	105	4	151	81	
PERRY TOWNSHIP	154	309	3	246	212	
RICES LANDING BOROUGH...........	50	104	2	87	70	2
RICHHILL TOWNSHIP	121	208	2	177	163	1
SPRINGHILL TOWNSHIP..............	44	62	3	46	60	5
WASHINGTON TOWNSHIP.............	143	145	1	195	99	1
WAYNE TOWNSHIP..................	115	232	3	170	177	3
WAYNESBURG BOROUGH	542	509	8	634	413	8
WARD 01	221	177	3	262	138	3
WARD 02	142	176	2	160	155	3
WARD 03	179	156	3	212	120	2
WHITELEY TOWNSHIP	78	131	2	110	98	2
GREENE COUNTY TOTALS............	3,748	7,476	78	5,721	5,579	48
HUNTINGDON COUNTY						
ALEXANDRIA BOROUGH	63	71	2	78	57	1
BARREE TOWNSHIP	73	27	1	77	22	1
BIRMINGHAM BOROUGH.............	25	12		28	10	
BRADY TOWNSHIP	108	78	6	135	52	5
BROAD TOP CITY BOROUGH	47	71		50	65	
CARBON TOWNSHIP	58	87		64	80	1
CASS TOWNSHIP...................	113	92	1	131	76	
CASSVILLE BOROUGH	35	35		52	20	
CLAY TOWNSHIP	124	102	1	145	83	2
COALMONT BOROUGH...............	9	29	2	12	28	
CROMWELL TOWNSHIP	177	202	2	234	145	4
DUBLIN TOWNSHIP	162	122		183	96	
DUDLEY BOROUGH	32	50		40	44	
FRANKLIN TOWNSHIP...............	126	41	3	145	26	2
HENDERSON TOWNSHIP	94	129		135	88	1
HOPEWELL TOWNSHIP...............	92	76	3	106	61	2
HUNTINGDON BOROUGH	1,161	744	13	1,264	643	9
WARD 01	129	81		134	71	3
WARD 02	133	116	3	167	83	1
WARD 03	203	131	4	212	123	1
WARD 04	204	159	3	239	123	1
WARD 05	214	117	3	207	124	2
WARD 06	278	140		305	119	1
JACKSON TOWNSHIP	121	93	3	159	57	2
JUNIATA TOWNSHIP.................	61	42	3	72	34	
LINCOLN TOWNSHIP.................	95	42		111	25	
LOGAN TOWNSHIP	113	84	2	140	56	2
MAPLETON BOROUGH	71	60	1	87	44	2
MARKLESBURG BOROUGH............	79	5		81	2	
MILL CREEK BOROUGH	28	29	2	32	30	
MILLER TOWNSHIP	83	41	3	90	35	1
MORRIS TOWNSHIP	53	66	1	75	44	
MT. UNION BOROUGH................	330	414	3	393	358	4
WARD 01	40	130	3	55	119	2
WARD 02	89	89		96	80	1
WARD 03	201	195		242	159	1
ONEIDA TOWNSHIP.................	223	135	4	255	111	1
ORBISONIA BOROUGH...............	64	59		69	51	
PENN TOWNSHIP..................	159	100	3	191	68	1
PETERSBURG BOROUGH	97	72	2	122	49	
PORTER TOWNSHIP	309	242	5	387	173	4
ROCKHILL BOROUGH................	83	62	3	100	50	1
SALTILLO BOROUGH.................	69	54	1	82	45	
SHADE GAP BOROUGH	15	20		19	15	
SHIRLEY TOWNSHIP	267	227	8	335	169	2
SHIRLEYSBURG BOROUGH...........	28	14		26	15	
SMITHFIELD TOWNSHIP	219	208		295	132	1
SPRINGFIELD TOWNSHIP.............	97	47	1	114	32	
SPRUCE CREEK TOWNSHIP..........	49	57		79	28	1
TELL TOWNSHIP	68	83	2	88	67	1
THREE SPRINGS BOROUGH	119	68	6	138	50	4
TODD TOWNSHIP..................	132	125	2	168	91	1
UNION TOWNSHIP.................	106	93	5	137	65	2

	GOVERNOR/LT. GOVERNOR			U.S. SENATE		
	Republican Scranton/ Fisher	Democratic Casey/ Singel	Consumer Hoover/ Brickhouse	Republican Arlen Specter	Democratic Bob Edgar	Consumer Lance S. Haver
WALKER TOWNSHIP	284	171	5	327	127	9
WARRIORS MARK TOWNSHIP	301	117	1	351	70	2
WEST TOWNSHIP	90	46	3	104	36	1
WOOD TOWNSHIP....................	36	130		56	110	1
HUNTINGDON COUNTY TOTALS.......	**6,348**	**4,974**	**103**	**7,562**	**3,835**	**71**
INDIANA COUNTY						
ARMAGH BOROUGH................	17	31		22	26	
ARMSTRONG TOWNSHIP.............	330	298	8	441	190	5
BANKS TOWNSHIP	106	98	2	140	66	2
BLACKLICK TOWNSHIP..............	199	169	14	252	115	8
BLAIRSVILLE BOROUGH	540	699	9	720	535	5
BRUSH VALLEY TOWNSHIP	245	265	4	335	171	3
BUFFINGTON TOWNSHIP	130	175	4	189	120	2
BURRELL TOWNSHIP	384	639	6	569	455	5
CANOE TOWNSHIP	204	300	6	273	233	1
CENTER TOWNSHIP	425	1,223	11	711	942	7
CHERRY TREE BOROUGH	43	70	1	60	55	
CHERRYHILL TOWNSHIP	365	364	11	448	281	10
CLYMER BOROUGH.................	166	414	5	224	359	4
CONEMAUGH TOWNSHIP.............	256	411	2	363	306	1
CREEKSIDE BOROUGH	50	70	2	64	56	2
EAST MAHONING TOWNSHIP.........	174	129	2	235	73	
EAST WHEATFIELD TOWNSHIP	313	505	9	445	373	9
ERNEST BOROUGH	38	150	3	70	120	1
GLEN CAMPBELL BOROUGH..........	32	92		44	79	
GRANT TOWNSHIP	98	100	2	140	58	1
GREEN TOWNSHIP	392	561	9	565	388	9
HOMER CITY BOROUGH.............	266	481	6	372	377	3
INDIANA BOROUGH	1,853	1,385	39	2,075	1,197	21
JACKSONVILLE BOROUGH	4	26	1	15	18	
MARION CENTER BOROUGH..........	93	83		124	52	
MONTGOMERY TOWNSHIP	168	262	4	254	176	4
NORTH MAHONING TOWNSHIP.......	216	107	1	237	84	2
PINE TOWNSHIP	129	399	4	220	310	3
PLUMVILLE BOROUGH..............	49	57	1	63	44	1
RAYNE TOWNSHIP.................	417	404	9	550	273	6
SALTSBURG BOROUGH	132	152	2	168	118	
SHELOCTA BOROUGH	23	24	4	31	17	4
SMICKSBURG BOROUGH............	17	11		19	9	
SOUTH MAHONING TOWNSHIP	187	211	2	264	134	2
WASHINGTON TOWNSHIP............	185	197	4	260	120	3
WEST MAHONING TOWNSHIP	83	33		95	21	
WEST WHEATFIELD TOWNSHIP.......	234	409	7	356	287	8
WHITE TOWNSHIP.................	2,189	1,912	39	2,660	1,451	28
YOUNG TOWNSHIP	159	453	6	278	337	4
INDIANA COUNTY TOTALS............	**10,911**	**13,369**	**239**	**14,351**	**10,026**	**164**
JEFFERSON COUNTY						
BARNETT TOWNSHIP	39	37	3	53	26	1
BEAVER TOWNSHIP..................	79	74		109	50	
BELL TOWNSHIP	312	268	5	396	188	3
BIG RUN BOROUGH	134	119	4	150	105	4
BROCKWAY BOROUGH................	308	494	3	420	379	8
BROOKVILLE BOROUGH	948	474	13	1,042	393	8
CLOVER TOWNSHIP	98	55	2	122	37	
CORSICA BOROUGH.................	63	45	1	63	43	4
ELDRED TOWNSHIP	218	173	3	276	118	2
FALLS CREEK BOROUGH.............	174	175	4	214	138	1
(BALANCE IN CLEARFIELD CO.)						
GASKILL TOWNSHIP	77	89	1	120	46	2
HEATH TOWNSHIP..................	32	15	2	38	12	1
HENDERSON TOWNSHIP	130	206	6	188	151	9
KNOX TOWNSHIP...................	174	106	2	197	81	5
MC CALMONT TOWNSHIP.............	149	149		195	105	2
OLIVER TOWNSHIP	152	206	1	247	114	1
PERRY TOWNSHIP	197	210	6	270	145	2
PINE CREEK TOWNSHIP.............	215	163	2	277	102	3
POLK TOWNSHIP....................	49	31	2	54	26	1
PORTER TOWNSHIP	50	45	2	74	25	

	GOVERNOR/LT. GOVERNOR			U.S. SENATE		
	Republican Scranton/ Fisher	Democratic Casey/ Singel	Consumer Hoover/ Brickhouse	Republican Arlen Specter	Democratic Bob Edgar	Consumer Lance S. Haver
PUNXSUTAWNEY BOROUGH	1,095	1,159	14	1,348	938	14
WARD 01	201	218	2	227	200	2
WARD 02	188	223	4	251	172	1
WARD 03	306	206	2	361	154	2
WARD 04	153	129	1	188	95	3
WARD 05	80	120	1	107	99	
WARD 06	167	263	4	214	218	6
REYNOLDSVILLE BOROUGH	406	542	7	497	464	2
WARD 01	119	207	2	160	172	1
WARD 02	151	145	2	168	128	1
WARD 03	96	122	2	117	104	
WARD 04	40	68	1	52	60	
RINGGOLD TOWNSHIP	107	104		145	68	
ROSE TOWNSHIP.................	220	130	6	280	77	1
SNYDER TOWNSHIP	296	341		361	298	2
SUMMERVILLE BOROUGH............	133	86		147	75	1
SYKESVILLE BOROUGH.............	117	291	1	154	257	
TIMBLIN BOROUGH..................	27	25		34	18	
UNION TOWNSHIP.................	121	81	2	148	55	
WARSAW TOWNSHIP................	233	124	3	278	84	4
WASHINGTON TOWNSHIP............	310	226	6	361	180	2
WINSLOW TOWNSHIP	274	365	5	333	306	6
WORTHVILLE BOROUGH	21	16	2	24	15	
YOUNG TOWNSHIP	213	323	4	292	250	3
JEFFERSON COUNTY TOTALS	**7,171**	**6,947**	**112**	**8,907**	**5,369**	**92**
JUNIATA COUNTY						
BEALE TOWNSHIP..................	88	104	1	108	83	1
DELAWARE TOWNSHIP	261	148	4	282	131	
FAYETTE TOWNSHIP	595	310	5	663	240	7
FERMANAGH TOWNSHIP	416	302	7	449	269	2
GREENWOOD TOWNSHIP	88	71	1	96	65	
LACK TOWNSHIP..................	91	111	1	100	105	
MIFFLIN BOROUGH.................	94	167	1	102	159	2
MIFFLINTOWN BOROUGH	205	147	2	231	120	1
MILFORD TOWNSHIP	278	287	1	297	270	
MONROE TOWNSHIP	293	317		379	228	
PORT ROYAL BOROUGH.............	196	148	2	205	142	1
SPRUCE HILL TOWNSHIP.............	126	80	3	133	74	2
SUSQUEHANNA TOWNSHIP...........	132	111	1	162	85	1
THOMPSONTOWN BOROUGH	133	109	2	159	84	
TURBETT TOWNSHIP	139	107	1	141	107	1
TUSCARORA TOWNSHIP	151	191	5	168	174	2
WALKER TOWNSHIP	397	242	3	439	202	1
JUNIATA COUNTY TOTALS............	**3,683**	**2,952**	**40**	**4,114**	**2,538**	**21**
LACKAWANNA COUNTY						
ABINGTON TOWNSHIP	459	236		539	139	
ARCHBALD BOROUGH	468	2,192	14	1,035	1,486	5
WARD 01	188	782	8	430	484	4
WARD 02	72	541	3	209	368	
WARD 03	41	242		93	174	
WARD 04	167	627	3	303	460	1
BENTON TOWNSHIP	258	268	3	362	141	4
BLAKELY BOROUGH	1,076	2,153	13	1,620	1,485	16
WARD 01	281	449	3	390	319	3
WARD 02	259	472	6	401	310	3
WARD 03	536	1,232	4	829	856	10
CARBONDALE CITY.................	992	2,736	5	1,773	1,713	15
WARD 01	289	645		471	405	2
WARD 02	60	169		122	94	1
WARD 03	242	648		406	425	3
WARD 04	94	477	1	226	292	4
WARD 05	146	436	3	312	261	2
WARD 06	161	361	1	236	236	3
CARBONDALE TOWNSHIP	120	368	3	206	256	5
CLARKS GREEN BOROUGH...........	345	379	3	520	212	1
CLARKS SUMMIT BOROUGH	1,137	1,055	7	1,556	562	8
CLIFTON TOWNSHIP	77	97	6	113	60	2
COVINGTON TOWNSHIP	260	312	1	377	179	

	GOVERNOR/LT. GOVERNOR			U.S. SENATE		
	Republican Scranton/ Fisher	Democratic Casey/ Singel	Consumer Hoover/ Brickhouse	Republican Arlen Specter	Democratic Bob Edgar	Consumer Lance S. Haver
DALTON BOROUGH	304	188	1	361	113	1
DICKSON CITY BOROUGH	709	2,012	4	1,243	1,293	12
WARD 01	262	725	3	486	429	6
WARD 02	87	380		169	265	2
WARD 03	360	907	1	588	599	4
DUNMORE BOROUGH	1,502	5,227	17	2,850	3,438	33
WARD 01	413	1,623	7	893	1,003	10
WARD 02	312	965	4	508	685	7
WARD 03	282	753	4	484	478	9
WARD 04	14	46		27	28	1
WARD 05	41	161		69	123	
WARD 06	440	1,679	2	869	1,121	6
ELMHURST TOWNSHIP	130	189	1	214	100	3
FELL TOWNSHIP	280	815	3	482	524	9
GLENBURN TOWNSHIP	264	195	2	348	88	2
GREENFIELD TOWNSHIP	176	340	5	275	207	2
JEFFERSON TOWNSHIP	382	588	2	533	390	
JERMYN BOROUGH	298	535	3	473	315	3
WARD 01	84	153		146	83	
WARD 02	114	188	3	166	116	2
WARD 03	100	194		161	116	1
JESSUP BOROUGH	442	1,878	5	802	1,338	14
WARD 01	66	286	2	148	179	2
WARD 02	154	695	2	298	491	5
WARD 03	222	897	1	356	668	7
LA PLUME TOWNSHIP	97	53	1	122	28	1
LEHIGH TOWNSHIP	49	82	2	72	55	2
MADISON TOWNSHIP	194	270	4	281	173	1
MAYFIELD BOROUGH	234	624	2	353	453	6
WARD 01	72	238		117	174	2
WARD 02	97	269	2	147	193	2
WARD 03	65	117		89	86	2
MOOSIC BOROUGH	660	1,499	13	1,033	947	13
WARD 01	158	266	1	209	183	1
WARD 02	42	182	2	78	130	2
WARD 03	115	280	3	188	168	2
WARD 04	345	771	7	558	466	8
MOSCOW BOROUGH	230	288		304	193	2
NEWTON TOWNSHIP	330	317	4	448	176	3
NORTH ABINGTON TOWNSHIP	143	95		179	54	
OLD FORGE BOROUGH	1,232	2,348	9	1,872	1,503	9
WARD 01	215	352		335	209	
WARD 02	143	301	3	215	194	2
WARD 03	256	513		410	308	
WARD 04	166	368	2	256	246	1
WARD 05	124	180		178	114	2
WARD 06	328	634	4	478	432	4
OLYPHANT BOROUGH	564	1,440	7	894	965	12
WARD 01	56	259	1	101	193	1
WARD 02	191	331	1	251	223	7
WARD 03	143	440	5	277	281	4
WARD 04	174	410		265	268	
RANSOM TOWNSHIP	147	252	2	216	261	3
ROARING BROOK TOWNSHIP	270	473	6	431	283	5
SCOTT TOWNSHIP	634	956		924	561	4
SCRANTON CITY	9,590	21,066	149	15,518	13,385	155
WARD 01	487	925	8	685	624	7
WARD 02	486	1,322	9	863	859	6
WARD 03	208	638	9	367	434	8
WARD 04	547	1,055	2	824	663	5
WARD 05	542	1,090	9	835	696	9
WARD 06	142	457	4	268	300	5
WARD 07	62	206	2	117	134	1
WARD 09	380	726	8	593	471	4
WARD 10	1,000	1,283	4	1,409	768	7
WARD 11	204	482	4	332	305	7
WARD 12	422	1,111	9	741	710	3
WARD 13	401	1,201	5	750	761	10
WARD 14	87	270	2	150	169	2
WARD 15	417	837	5	670	508	11

	GOVERNOR/LT. GOVERNOR			U.S. SENATE		
	Republican Scranton/ Fisher	Democratic Casey/ Singel	Consumer Hoover/ Brickhouse	Republican Arlen Specter	Democratic Bob Edgar	Consumer Lance S. Haver
WARD 16	108	215	5	162	135	4
WARD 17	553	838	13	815	534	8
WARD 18	36	74	1	32	70	2
WARD 19	888	1,754	13	1,480	1,037	10
WARD 20	593	1,356	12	977	849	12
WARD 21	873	1,920	17	1,394	1,229	14
WARD 22	327	756	3	534	486	7
WARD 23	667	1,749	5	1,174	1,107	11
WARD 24	160	801		346	536	2
SOUTH ABINGTON TOWNSHIP.........	1,112	920	5	1,485	479	6
SPRING BROOK TOWNSHIP...........	330	269	2	492	178	1
TAYLOR BOROUGH	829	1,634	12	1,260	1,040	11
WARD 01	13	63	2	33	37	2
WARD 02	77	127		98	91	1
WARD 03	126	162	2	176	96	1
WARD 04	118	269	1	191	229	
WARD 05	245	366	6	347	170	6
WARD 06	250	647	1	415	417	1
THROOP BOROUGH	332	1,268	3	593	882	3
WARD 01	74	375	3	144	275	2
WARD 02	115	349		170	250	
WARD 03	48	224		115	135	
WARD 04	95	320		164	222	1
VANDLING BOROUGH.................	71	170		117	108	2
WEST ABINGTON TOWNSHIP..........	36	83		72	45	
LACKAWANNA COUNTY TOTALS.......	**26,763**	**55,870**	**319**	**42,348**	**35,808**	**374**
LANCASTER COUNTY						
ADAMSTOWN BOROUGH	174	87	4	186	64	6
(BALANCE IN BERKS CO.)						
AKRON BOROUGH	907	307	15	948	267	9
BART TOWNSHIP	230	80	4	243	73	1
BRECKNOCK TOWNSHIP	582	162	7	637	99	5
CAERNARVON TOWNSHIP	374	142	5	428	94	2
CHRISTIANA BOROUGH..............	185	97		189	86	
CLAY TOWNSHIP	503	154	11	548	106	9
COLERAIN TOWNSHIP	324	124	2	356	93	1
COLUMBIA BOROUGH	1,225	1,406	21	1,374	1,220	23
WARD 01	56	82		58	77	
WARD 02	71	83	1	78	68	5
WARD 03	51	87	2	61	74	3
WARD 04	157	203	3	188	171	1
WARD 05	80	104	2	87	94	3
WARD 06	338	308	5	380	258	6
WARD 07	209	224	4	232	197	3
WARD 08	86	136	2	94	127	1
WARD 09	177	179	2	196	154	1
CONESTOGA TOWNSHIP	551	170	11	581	137	8
CONOY TOWNSHIP	370	144	7	400	108	5
DENVER BOROUGH	486	163	5	505	143	7
DRUMORE TOWNSHIP	313	101	3	319	95	1
EARL TOWNSHIP	737	156	7	772	105	6
EAST COCALICO TOWNSHIP	947	337	17	1,039	247	10
EAST DONEGAL TOWNSHIP...........	864	309	12	970	211	5
EAST DRUMORE TOWNSHIP..........	544	128	3	557	111	2
EAST EARL TOWNSHIP..............	670	140	6	702	103	4
EAST HEMPFIELD TOWNSHIP	3,961	1,422	43	4,199	1,216	29
EAST LAMPETER TOWNSHIP.........	2,247	716	19	2,365	603	10
EAST PETERSBURG BOROUGH	960	321	7	973	309	3
EDEN TOWNSHIP....................	184	63	2	196	52	2
ELIZABETH TOWNSHIP..............	502	138	6	526	111	6
ELIZABETHTOWN BOROUGH.........	1,675	684	13	1,755	591	12
WARD 01	364	144	4	389	113	6
WARD 02	493	187	3	506	176	2
WARD 03	818	353	6	860	302	4
EPHRATA TOWNSHIP.................	638	164	11	680	119	4
EPHRATA BOROUGH	2,178	766	25	2,346	626	13
WARD 01	475	129	5	513	103	2
WARD 02	478	215	6	530	173	2
WARD 03	693	276	12	759	222	6

	GOVERNOR/LT. GOVERNOR			U.S. SENATE		
	Republican Scranton/ Fisher	Democratic Casey/ Singel	Consumer Hoover/ Brickhouse	Republican Arlen Specter	Democratic Bob Edgar	Consumer Lance S. Haver
WARD 04	532	146	2	544	128	3
FULTON TOWNSHIP	315	112	4	337	90	3
LANCASTER CITY	6,565	4,909	107	6,639	4,811	84
WARD 01	100	73	1	87	85	1
WARD 02	400	262	8	396	253	8
WARD 03	160	137	10	145	158	6
WARD 04	152	160	4	149	158	5
WARD 05	500	304	6	475	326	5
WARD 06	1,807	1,046	20	1,854	975	23
WARD 07	553	908	16	579	885	11
WARD 08	1,851	1,414	23	1,987	1,283	17
WARD 09	1,042	605	19	967	688	8
LANCASTER TOWNSHIP	3,023	1,201	32	3,083	1,134	21
LEACOCK TOWNSHIP	494	112	6	508	87	4
LITITZ BOROUGH	1,818	664	20	1,904	559	22
WARD 01	521	202	7	566	155	9
WARD 02	535	224	6	548	199	9
WARD 03	762	238	7	790	205	4
LITTLE BRITAIN TOWNSHIP	278	147	5	310	112	3
MANHEIM TOWNSHIP	7,525	2,547	64	7,754	2,328	43
MANHEIM BOROUGH	1,025	375	13	1,044	356	9
WARD 01	597	210	4	615	192	3
WARD 02	428	165	9	429	164	6
MANOR TOWNSHIP	2,681	1,096	26	2,832	931	24
MARIETTA BOROUGH	341	275	4	379	236	3
WARD 01	168	138	2	192	117	2
WARD 02	173	137	2	187	119	1
MARTIC TOWNSHIP.................	548	189	8	567	158	10
MILLERSVILLE BOROUGH	1,187	533	8	1,202	493	4
MOUNTVILLE BOROUGH	348	130	4	375	106	3
MT. JOY TOWNSHIP	1,050	289	9	1,122	220	6
MT. JOY BOROUGH	1,163	404	8	1,225	328	7
WARD EAST	386	121		399	102	3
WARD FLORIN	409	163	7	435	134	3
WARD WEST	368	120	1	391	92	1
NEW HOLLAND BOROUGH...........	1,043	287	14	1,095	251	5
PARADISE TOWNSHIP...............	655	181	9	696	147	3
PENN TOWNSHIP..................	1,088	321	9	1,155	257	7
PEQUEA TOWNSHIP	750	254	13	791	198	9
PROVIDENCE TOWNSHIP............	654	287	8	686	251	7
QUARRYVILLE BOROUGH	392	124	4	406	104	2
RAPHO TOWNSHIP	1,280	359	15	1,350	299	6
SADSBURY TOWNSHIP..............	290	118	4	299	109	2
SALISBURY TOWNSHIP	838	251	12	898	195	13
STRASBURG TOWNSHIP	645	155	6	647	143	2
STRASBURG BOROUGH.............	643	189	5	651	172	4
WARD 01	122	38	1	117	41	2
WARD 02	265	71	3	273	60	2
WARD 03	256	80	1	261	71	
TERRE HILL BOROUGH	242	86	1	263	65	2
UPPER LEACOCK TOWNSHIP	1,109	333	2	1,184	254	8
WARWICK TOWNSHIP	2,074	563	20	2,100	528	17
WEST COCALICO TOWNSHIP.........	707	272	12	787	189	12
WEST DONEGAL TOWNSHIP	1,023	292	7	1,105	203	5
WEST EARL TOWNSHIP	840	281	13	899	223	6
WEST HEMPFIELD TOWNSHIP........	1,709	798	32	1,870	649	14
WEST LAMPETER TOWNSHIP	2,062	632	18	2,120	575	17
LANCASTER COUNTY TOTALS	**68,736**	**27,247**	**788**	**72,077**	**23,750**	**570**
LAWRENCE COUNTY						
BESSEMER BOROUGH..............	155	274	4	162	264	3
ELLPORT BOROUGH................	140	351	4	193	307	
ELLWOOD CITY BOROUGH...........	1,118	2,170	15	1,305	2,005	13
(BALANCE IN BEAVER CO.)						
WARD 01	160	385	2	187	362	3
WARD 02	85	344	2	121	312	2
WARD 03	152	279		166	264	
WARD 04	264	663	5	309	623	2
WARD 05	457	499	6	522	444	6
ENON VALLEY BOROUGH...........	61	78	1	71	69	1

	GOVERNOR/LT. GOVERNOR			U.S. SENATE		
	Republican Scranton/ Fisher	Democratic Casey/ Singel	Consumer Hoover/ Brickhouse	Republican Arlen Specter	Democratic Bob Edgar	Consumer Lance S. Haver
HICKORY TOWNSHIP	389	384	7	458	317	5
LITTLE BEAVER TOWNSHIP	125	119	2	145	100	1
MAHONING TOWNSHIP	285	718	13	382	630	6
NESHANNOCK TOWNSHIP	1,820	1,412	15	2,021	1,221	10
NEW BEAVER BOROUGH	161	236	7	210	196	1
NEW CASTLE CITY	2,850	6,528	82	3,745	5,642	49
WARD 01	252	449	4	294	403	6
WARD 02	1,405	1,449	33	1,658	1,200	17
WARD 03	262	866	10	364	761	7
WARD 04	464	1,568	24	697	1,348	7
WARD 05	187	792	8	279	702	9
WARD 06	59	333		78	316	
WARD 07	139	616	1	230	519	2
WARD 08	82	455	2	145	393	1
NEW WILMINGTON BOROUGH	431	120	4	423	131	4
NORTH BEAVER TOWNSHIP	646	689	19	733	611	10
PERRY TOWNSHIP	277	353	16	329	319	6
PLAIN GROVE TOWNSHIP	128	70	4	133	67	1
PULASKI TOWNSHIP	363	678	7	518	523	11
SCOTT TOWNSHIP	326	251	7	394	192	5
SHENANGO TOWNSHIP	844	1,420	27	1,096	1,186	14
SLIPPERY ROCK TOWNSHIP	405	402	17	476	336	15
SNPJ BOROUGH	6	3		7	2	
SOUTH NEW CASTLE BOROUGH	49	202	7	74	183	4
TAYLOR TOWNSHIP	65	320	3	100	283	1
UNION TOWNSHIP	510	1,330	22	683	1,167	12
VOLANT BOROUGH	31	35	2	32	36	
WAMPUM BOROUGH	77	189	3	98	171	1
WASHINGTON TOWNSHIP	104	113	2	111	106	1
WAYNE TOWNSHIP	337	513	17	405	452	8
WILMINGTON TOWNSHIP	486	277	6	523	246	3
LAWRENCE COUNTY TOTALS	**12,189**	**19,235**	**313**	**14,827**	**16,762**	**185**
LEBANON COUNTY						
ANNVILLE TOWNSHIP	634	431	6	704	330	14
BETHEL TOWNSHIP	483	410	9	631	263	6
CLEONA BOROUGH	400	258	4	463	178	9
CORNWALL BOROUGH	596	365	3	664	280	8
EAST HANOVER TOWNSHIP	419	257	5	515	157	4
HEIDELBERG TOWNSHIP	529	320	14	623	217	8
JACKSON TOWNSHIP	590	476	11	774	290	7
JONESTOWN BOROUGH	152	101	4	179	61	4
LEBANON CITY	2,979	3,283	48	3,704	2,464	58
WARD 01	496	499	12	635	339	12
WARD 02	868	741	8	1,047	545	15
WARD 03	71	116	4	85	98	2
WARD 04	130	112		156	92	1
WARD 05	435	608	11	575	446	13
WARD 06	65	130	2	86	100	1
WARD 07	120	148	2	135	130	2
WARD 08	388	325	1	470	231	2
WARD 09	143	259	3	193	206	2
WARD 10	263	345	5	322	277	8
MILLCREEK TOWNSHIP	266	208	4	308	170	3
MT. GRETNA BOROUGH	103	34	1	93	42	1
MYERSTOWN BOROUGH	476	333	5	585	220	6
NORTH ANNVILLE TOWNSHIP	405	196	2	470	129	6
NORTH CORNWALL TOWNSHIP	743	604	5	918	420	8
NORTH LEBANON TOWNSHIP	936	1,037	15	1,253	704	7
NORTH LONDONDERRY TOWNSHIP	1,143	586	10	1,280	430	8
PALMYRA BOROUGH	1,413	674	13	1,501	544	21
RICHLAND BOROUGH	246	172	3	285	126	4
SOUTH ANNVILLE TOWNSHIP	464	275	9	533	195	10
SOUTH LEBANON TOWNSHIP	1,035	898	16	1,241	661	16
SOUTH LONDONDERRY TOWNSHIP	746	405	12	820	325	9
SWATARA TOWNSHIP	347	306	5	457	193	7
UNION TOWNSHIP	307	256	13	395	161	6
WEST CORNWALL TOWNSHIP	319	151	1	365	101	3
WEST LEBANON TOWNSHIP	84	118	2	122	76	3
LEBANON COUNTY TOTALS	**15,815**	**12,154**	**220**	**18,883**	**8,737**	**236**

	GOVERNOR/LT. GOVERNOR				U.S. SENATE		
	Republican Scranton/ Fisher	Democratic Casey/ Singel	Consumer Hoover/ Brickhouse		Republican Arlen Specter	Democratic Bob Edgar	Consumer Lance S. Haver
LEHIGH COUNTY							
ALBURTIS BOROUGH	157	104	7		156	109	4
ALLENTOWN CITY	12,400	11,577	350		13,299	10,763	204
WARD 01	80	190	7		91	181	4
WARD 02	77	112	6		78	117	
WARD 03	114	144	7		115	136	3
WARD 04	113	101	6		110	107	6
WARD 05	61	101	4		74	89	
WARD 06	156	428	18		171	410	12
WARD 07	240	180	5		240	189	3
WARD 08	1,242	1,224	39		1,337	1,145	17
WARD 09	111	225	4		132	206	4
WARD 10	417	728	22		489	677	13
WARD 11	2,009	1,310	47		2,108	1,254	32
WARD 12	1,177	1,170	34		1,221	1,047	19
WARD 13	928	665	13		947	661	10
WARD 14	327	577	15		370	527	13
WARD 15	1,019	1,199	42		1,201	1,023	14
WARD 16	410	525	20		459	479	18
WARD 17	1,754	786	15		1,798	758	11
WARD 18	859	487	13		907	461	4
WARD 19	1,306	1,425	33		1,451	1,296	21
BETHLEHEM CITY	2,832	2,668	62		3,137	2,393	40
(BALANCE IN NORTHAMPTON CO.)							
WARD 10	141	185	7		153	184	2
WARD 11	129	136	6		149	125	2
WARD 12	331	375	12		360	365	6
WARD 13	2,231	1,972	37		2,475	1,719	30
CATASAUQUA BOROUGH	704	654	17		765	586	9
COOPERSBURG BOROUGH.	371	317	4		404	289	4
COPLAY BOROUGH.	260	601	10		354	509	3
EMMAUS BOROUGH	2,098	1,290	35		2,211	1,179	25
FOUNTAIN HILL BOROUGH.	455	785	20		511	725	14
WARD 01	166	240	9		176	235	5
WARD 02	289	545	11		335	490	9
HANOVER TOWNSHIP	203	163	4		221	146	1
HEIDELBERG TOWNSHIP	435	203	4		457	173	4
LOWER MACUNGIE TOWNSHIP	2,901	1,252	30		3,104	1,033	28
LOWER MILFORD TOWNSHIP.	505	294	11		571	230	7
LOWHILL TOWNSHIP.	231	131	2		252	107	4
LYNN TOWNSHIP	471	271	9		507	242	7
MACUNGIE BOROUGH	344	196	4		373	169	1
NORTH WHITEHALL TOWNSHIP	1,444	941	16		1,515	850	17
SALISBURY TOWNSHIP	1,976	1,676	36		2,143	1,496	30
WARD 01	253	347	8		253	342	4
WARD 02	232	397	9		242	391	6
WARD 03	247	305	3		288	260	4
WARD 04	551	274	7		601	231	5
WARD 05	693	353	9		759	272	11
SLATINGTON BOROUGH.	451	278	4		495	240	6
WARD 01	118	96	1		135	80	2
WARD 02	130	68	2		145	56	2
WARD 03	203	114	1		215	104	2
SOUTH WHITEHALL TOWNSHIP.	3,533	1,976	54		3,841	1,666	33
UPPER MACUNGIE TOWNSHIP	1,239	738	21		1,377	598	8
UPPER MILFORD TOWNSHIP	931	543	15		977	479	13
UPPER SAUCON TOWNSHIP	1,627	991	26		1,739	879	21
WASHINGTON TOWNSHIP.	586	395	10		648	327	3
WEISENBERG TOWNSHIP	402	232	8		448	197	11
WHITEHALL TOWNSHIP	2,428	2,898	50		2,711	2,593	44
LEHIGH COUNTY TOTALS	**38,984**	**31,174**	**809**		**42,216**	**27,978**	**541**
LUZERNE COUNTY							
ASHLEY BOROUGH.	313	832	6		475	545	10
WARD 01	148	283	2		204	213	5
WARD 02	77	188	3		111	145	3
WARD 03	88	361	1		160	187	2
AVOCA BOROUGH.	189	1,125	6		321	931	5
WARD 01	41	408	3		105	328	1
WARD 02	92	341	1		134	279	

	GOVERNOR/LT. GOVERNOR			U.S. SENATE		
	Republican Scranton/ Fisher	Democratic Casey/ Singel	Consumer Hoover/ Brickhouse	Republican Arlen Specter	Democratic Bob Edgar	Consumer Lance S. Haver
WARD 03	56	376	2	82	324	4
BEAR CREEK TOWNSHIP	376	475	9	487	351	9
BLACK CREEK TOWNSHIP	223	234	4	285	166	7
BUCK TOWNSHIP.	53	61		71	43	
BUTLER TOWNSHIP	606	545	6	787	322	8
CONYNGHAM TOWNSHIP.	188	334	5	269	239	5
CONYNGHAM BOROUGH.	504	232	2	578	146	2
COURTDALE BOROUGH.	112	158		131	124	
DALLAS TOWNSHIP.	1,198	762	12	1,402	519	5
DALLAS BOROUGH	601	348	11	713	252	5
DENNISON TOWNSHIP	106	110	1	134	82	
DORRANCE TOWNSHIP	204	274		252	211	4
DUPONT BOROUGH	261	1,020	8	437	813	9
WARD 01	70	342	1	120	287	2
WARD 02	104	419	4	172	339	3
WARD 03	87	259	3	145	187	4
DURYEA BOROUGH	426	1,419	4	597	1,183	5
WARD 01	70	292		103	259	
WARD 02	91	275	1	115	233	1
WARD 03	139	436	3	187	363	4
WARD 04	99	258		144	205	
WARD 05	27	158		48	123	
EDWARDSVILLE BOROUGH	542	1,214	12	750	953	14
WARD 01	133	442	2	199	354	5
WARD 02	156	219	3	196	174	4
WARD 03	38	94		53	66	
WARD 04	83	161	2	111	125	2
WARD 05	61	127	4	82	108	1
WARD 06	22	79	1	38	56	2
WARD 07	49	92		71	70	
EXETER TOWNSHIP	277	457	3	431	281	4
EXETER BOROUGH.	412	1,539	10	624	1,253	4
WARD 01	43	179		72	139	
WARD 02	98	321	1	139	261	
WARD 03	45	278	5	84	226	1
WARD 04	226	761	4	329	627	3
FAIRMOUNT TOWNSHIP	142	123	3	173	82	4
FAIRVIEW TOWNSHIP	460	469	5	589	329	5
FORTY FORT BOROUGH	1,059	942	7	1,338	626	13
WARD 01	435	313		533	205	2
WARD 02	255	234	2	314	160	3
WARD 03	369	395	5	491	261	8
FOSTER TOWNSHIP	182	532	4	318	378	3
FRANKLIN TOWNSHIP.	234	149	1	283	92	1
FREELAND BOROUGH	460	658	5	680	358	
WARD 01	114	116		158	70	
WARD 02	106	128	2	144	89	
WARD 03	43	111	2	81	66	
WARD 04	93	111	1	132	6	
WARD 05	66	109		99	71	
WARD 06	38	83		66	56	
HANOVER TOWNSHIP	1,245	2,515	36	1,925	1,840	30
WARD 01	253	349	7	351	258	8
WARD 02	159	400	5	233	310	8
WARD 03	27	64		50	48	
WARD 04	113	275	8	211	190	4
WARD 05	248	527	9	370	401	5
WARD 06	153	261	2	236	173	3
WARD 07	292	639	5	474	460	2
HARVEYS LAKE BOROUGH	360	411	6	465	299	6
HAZLE TOWNSHIP.	675	1,820	21	1,050	1,303	29
HAZLETON CITY.	2,882	4,633	50	3,861	3,191	41
WARD 01	50	141	2	87	94	3
WARD 02	48	115		74	92	
WARD 03	432	446	7	532	326	1
WARD 04	83	297	4	151	220	2
WARD 05	77	129	1	93	98	3
WARD 06	20	22		20	20	
WARD 07	69	102		95	70	2
WARD 08	153	147	1	185	96	2

	GOVERNOR/LT. GOVERNOR			U.S. SENATE		
	Republican Scranton/ Fisher	Democratic Casey/ Singel	Consumer Hoover/ Brickhouse	Republican Arlen Specter	Democratic Bob Edgar	Consumer Lance S. Haver
WARD 09	210	245	4	291	156	2
WARD 10	160	190		121	123	
WARD 11	251	242	6	325	158	3
WARD 12	551	983	8	815	654	4
WARD 13	274	468	4	398	292	6
WARD 14	259	644	6	320	475	6
WARD 15	245	462	6	354	317	7
HOLLENBACK TOWNSHIP	174	138	1	228	71	
HUGHESTOWN BOROUGH	169	625		244	536	2
WARD 01	129	363		182	304	1
WARD 02	40	262		62	232	1
HUNLOCK TOWNSHIP	249	257	4	345	161	3
HUNTINGTON TOWNSHIP	282	253		388	138	
JACKSON TOWNSHIP	429	414		524	289	6
JEDDO BOROUGH	21	20	1	28	13	1
JENKINS TOWNSHIP	405	1,158	8	629	902	5
WARD 04	46	167		75	133	
WARD 05	33	82	1	52	61	
WARD 06	35	61		64	33	
KINGSTON TOWNSHIP	1,116	891	14	1,266	613	12
KINGSTON BOROUGH	2,828	2,605	33	3,488	1,880	30
WARD 01	100	379	6	183	283	3
WARD 02	225	215	5	255	177	4
WARD 03	216	239	4	271	176	5
WARD 04	246	248	4	334	157	1
WARD 05	1,097	631	2	1,282	438	6
WARD 06	451	420	8	536	320	5
WARD 07	493	473	4	627	329	6
LAFLIN BOROUGH	229	390	2	342	260	1
LAKE TOWNSHIP	190	208		255	137	
LARKSVILLE BOROUGH	293	1,145	12	455	957	13
WARD 01	47	149	3	77	127	2
WARD 02	23	75	1	29	66	
WARD 03	17	98	2	25	90	1
WARD 04	17	118	1	41	93	2
WARD 05	43	243	2	75	205	1
WARD 06	30	124	1	38	110	3
WARD 07	116	338	2	170	266	4
LAUREL RUN BOROUGH	72	59	2	86	42	1
LEHMAN TOWNSHIP	517	420	11	643	277	7
LUZERNE BOROUGH	280	798	6	401	639	8
WARD 01	49	149		68	117	
WARD 02	67	140	1	89	110	2
WARD 03	110	264	1	144	217	1
WARD 04	54	245	4	100	195	5
NANTICOKE CITY	1,171	3,243	27	1,608	2,644	19
WARD 01	78	136		105	106	
WARD 02	55	149		71	125	
WARD 03	5	22		12	15	
WARD 04	57	275	1	83	243	3
WARD 05	225	415	5	286	344	4
WARD 06	89	111	1	106	85	
WARD 07	40	77	1	42	69	1
WARD 08	101	342	2	123	318	1
WARD 09	148	420	8	226	251	1
WARD 10	43	137	1	71	115	2
WARD 11	121	525	5	196	427	5
WARD 12	149	483	3	209	415	2
WARD 13	60	151		78	131	
NESCOPECK TOWNSHIP	84	62	2	105	46	3
NESCOPECK BOROUGH	196	158	6	275	88	4
NEW COLUMBUS BOROUGH	34	34		43	21	1
NEWPORT TOWNSHIP	442	1,452	14	676	1,187	10
WARD 01	112	407	3	183	316	3
WARD 02	70	305	1	112	246	2
WARD 03	60	204		93	179	
WARD 04	113	287	7	162	242	3
WARD 05	87	249	3	126	204	2
NUANGOLA BOROUGH	108	113	1	143	73	
PENN LAKE PARK BOROUGH	41	51	1	53	35	

	GOVERNOR/LT. GOVERNOR			U.S. SENATE		
	Republican Scranton/ Fisher	Democratic Casey/ Singel	Consumer Hoover/ Brickhouse	Republican Arlen Specter	Democratic Bob Edgar	Consumer Lance S. Haver
PITTSTON CITY	529	2,815	10	909	2,319	15
WARD 01	25	205		74	153	2
WARD 02	26	170	1	41	151	1
WARD 03	67	231	5	95	196	
WARD 04	30	209		67	165	1
WARD 05	68	212	1	86	189	
WARD 06	79	436	1	150	342	1
WARD 07	35	198		65	157	
WARD 08	20	119		34	101	1
WARD 09	20	100		33	84	
WARD 10	95	457		156	368	2
WARD 11	64	478	2	108	413	7
PITTSTON TOWNSHIP	256	952	9	383	784	9
PLAINS TOWNSHIP	1,008	2,387	22	1,381	1,983	17
WARD 01	249	386	3	305	323	4
WARD 02	167	451	7	225	387	3
WARD 03	101	238	1	161	177	2
WARD 05	103	321	3	156	266	2
WARD 06	89	228	3	120	197	1
WARD 07	69	148	2	96	124	1
WARD 08	34	80	2	49	59	1
WARD 09	72	202		104	171	
WARD 10	124	333	1	165	279	3
PLYMOUTH TOWNSHIP	274	548	6	355	443	5
PLYMOUTH BOROUGH	840	1,677	12	1,124	1,341	15
WARD 01	104	174	1	144	117	3
WARD 02	21	72		32	57	
WARD 03	48	90	2	68	69	1
WARD 04	54	125	2	75	99	2
WARD 05	97	110		112	89	
WARD 06	126	244	1	163	195	1
WARD 07	38	136	2	56	114	1
WARD 08	81	293	2	121	246	5
WARD 09	92	89	1	109	71	
WARD 10	48	67		60	59	
WARD 11	88	89		110	65	2
WARD 12	22	103	1	43	84	
WARD 13	21	85		31	76	
PRINGLE BOROUGH	57	406	4	108	351	6
WARD 01	33	206	3	57	181	2
WARD 02	24	200	1	51	170	4
RICE TOWNSHIP	162	198	2	229	124	2
ROSS TOWNSHIP	307	262	6	406	150	7
SALEM TOWNSHIP	651	468	9	756	346	12
SHICKSHINNY BOROUGH	205	209	1	233	171	2
WARD 01	63	48		60	40	
WARD 02	20	41		31	30	
WARD 03	85	63		96	55	1
WARD 04	37	57	1	46	46	1
SLOCUM TOWNSHIP	112	160	2	158	109	2
SUGAR NOTCH BOROUGH	68	337	1	111	281	3
SUGARLOAF TOWNSHIP	449	327	7	548	205	9
SWOYERSVILLE BOROUGH	525	1,708	14	822	1,395	10
WARD 01	172	652	1	311	497	5
WARD 02	265	775	8	395	642	4
WARD 03	88	281	5	116	256	1
UNION TOWNSHIP	231	259	5	320	166	2
WARRIOR RUN BOROUGH	74	179	3	106	143	
WEST HAZLETON BOROUGH	671	852	5	910	564	16
WARD 01	87	105		112	72	1
WARD 02	399	429	3	547	261	8
WARD 03	185	318	2	251	231	7
WEST PITTSTON BOROUGH	1,144	1,291	5	1,426	948	8
WEST WYOMING BOROUGH	281	991	3	458	786	2
WHITE HAVEN BOROUGH	137	134		190	71	3
WILKES-BARRE CITY	4,357	10,004	81	6,377	7,685	87
WARD 01	181	433	3	278	332	4
WARD 02	193	767	2	309	610	2
WARD 03	173	531	5	272	423	4
WARD 04	73	107	3	95	94	1

	GOVERNOR/LT. GOVERNOR			U.S. SENATE		
	Republican Scranton/ Fisher	Democratic Casey/ Singel	Consumer Hoover/ Brickhouse	Republican Arlen Specter	Democratic Bob Edgar	Consumer Lance S. Haver
WARD 05	47	51		59	35	
WARD 06	124	365	3	184	278	6
WARD 08	189	309		242	254	
WARD 09	169	397		224	331	8
WARD 10	380	370	4	435	310	4
WARD 12	492	748	10	680	533	6
WARD 13	376	1,224	10	608	977	12
WARD 14	425	1,158	7	612	944	9
WARD 15	677	1,218	13	991	837	15
WARD 16	351	914	10	610	625	6
WARD 17	143	396	3	223	296	3
WARD 18	161	403	4	243	318	4
WARD 19	94	316	3	146	258	
WARD 20	109	297	1	166	230	3
WILKES-BARRE TOWNSHIP	338	898	4	513	710	6
WARD 02	108	306	3	165	238	1
WARD 03	69	230		111	191	3
WARD 04	106	159		140	112	2
WARD 05	55	203	1	97	169	
WRIGHT TOWNSHIP	648	814	9	900	544	5
WYOMING BOROUGH	591	841	7	807	609	1
WARD 01	119	356	2	203	273	
WARD 02	148	213	1	197	159	
YATESVILLE BOROUGH	37	185		62	154	3
LUZERNE COUNTY TOTALS	**37,572**	**66,787**	**609**	**51,243**	**50,303**	**601**
LYCOMING COUNTY						
ANTHONY TOWNSHIP	120	67	2	141	47	2
ARMSTRONG TOWNSHIP	75	95	4	113	61	2
BASTRESS TOWNSHIP	39	100		88	49	
BRADY TOWNSHIP	57	59	2	91	27	1
BROWN TOWNSHIP	34	10	1	32	11	2
CASCADE TOWNSHIP	60	52		76	36	
CLINTON TOWNSHIP	278	229	3	342	170	1
COGAN HOUSE TOWNSHIP	134	66	4	164	40	1
CUMMINGS TOWNSHIP	52	56		77	33	
DUBOISTOWN BOROUGH	219	175	8	262	131	8
ELDRED TOWNSHIP	268	220		339	149	
FAIRFIELD TOWNSHIP	336	241	6	410	154	7
FRANKLIN TOWNSHIP	119	122	6	157	89	3
GAMBLE TOWNSHIP	101	74		123	51	
HEPBURN TOWNSHIP	303	299	8	416	194	
HUGHESVILLE BOROUGH	326	345	1	364	303	3
WARD 01	172	170		193	145	2
WARD 02	154	175	1	171	158	1
JACKSON TOWNSHIP	67	34		67	34	
JERSEY SHORE BOROUGH	491	449	7	599	358	3
WARD 01	102	111	2	120	94	2
WARD 02	103	126	3	139	93	
WARD 03	141	90		156	75	
WARD 04	145	122	2	184	96	1
JORDAN TOWNSHIP	86	100	4	116	74	2
LEWIS TOWNSHIP	118	123	2	149	94	
LIMESTONE TOWNSHIP	161	258	6	278	138	1
LOYALSOCK TOWNSHIP	1,990	1,139	32	2,206	890	26
LYCOMING TOWNSHIP	168	181	2	208	128	7
MC HENRY TOWNSHIP	44	42		60	25	
MC INTYRE TOWNSHIP	82	67		95	53	
MC NETT TOWNSHIP	26	27		37	19	
MIFFLIN TOWNSHIP	119	84	4	159	46	3
MILL CREEK TOWNSHIP	49	64	1	74	40	
MONTGOMERY BOROUGH	160	165	2	214	116	3
MONTOURSVILLE BOROUGH	930	841	17	1,183	583	16
WARD 01	290	232	5	354	169	7
WARD 02	265	229	2	334	160	2
WARD 03	375	380	10	495	254	7
MORELAND TOWNSHIP	117	146	7	152	113	3
MUNCY TOWNSHIP	203	155	3	249	111	3
MUNCY BOROUGH	443	289	4	521	202	5
MUNCY CREEK TOWNSHIP	428	352	4	516	259	6

	GOVERNOR/LT. GOVERNOR			U.S. SENATE		
	Republican Scranton/ Fisher	Democratic Casey/ Singel	Consumer Hoover/ Brickhouse	Republican Arlen Specter	Democratic Bob Edgar	Consumer Lance S. Haver
NIPPENOSE TOWNSHIP	79	75	2	104	52	
OLD LYCOMING TOWNSHIP	711	679	10	919	453	13
PENN TOWNSHIP.	106	95	1	125	78	
PIATT TOWNSHIP	149	118	2	191	78	2
PICTURE ROCKS BOROUGH	128	66	3	139	57	1
PINE TOWNSHIP	54	37	1	67	25	
PLUNKETTS CREEK TOWNSHIP	119	94	2	156	57	2
PORTER TOWNSHIP	178	154	2	226	114	2
SALLADASBURG BOROUGH	50	36		62	23	
SHREWSBURY TOWNSHIP.	65	70	3	86	52	1
SOUTH WILLIAMSPORT BOROUGH	894	896	18	1,041	722	26
WARD 01	280	286	7	322	247	5
WARD 02	312	295	4	358	235	12
WARD 03	302	315	7	361	240	9
SUSQUEHANNA TOWNSHIP.	125	157		164	118	1
UPPER FAIRFIELD TOWNSHIP	257	171	4	291	134	5
WASHINGTON TOWNSHIP.	201	197	6	289	117	1
WATSON TOWNSHIP	77	55	4	92	40	3
WILLIAMSPORT CITY	3,160	3,429	70	3,896	2,571	84
WARD 01	150	225	3	214	155	3
WARD 02	128	213	2	189	146	4
WARD 03	155	145	3	195	99	5
WARD 04	107	168	5	121	149	5
WARD 05	108	139	5	124	116	6
WARD 06	131	253	3	194	184	4
WARD 07	162	150	6	181	132	5
WARD 08	202	201	3	233	162	8
WARD 09	147	260	10	219	175	13
WARD 10	207	237	6	255	185	5
WARD 11	183	190	1	214	152	2
WARD 12	80	153	2	113	108	5
WARD 13	189	188	5	240	139	3
WARD 14	325	232	6	345	192	5
WARD 15	352	219	4	397	160	6
WARD 16	258	305	3	369	184	2
WARD 17	276	151	3	293	133	3
WOLF TOWNSHIP	297	250	11	341	210	5
WOODWARD TOWNSHIP.	224	200	3	281	139	4
LYCOMING COUNTY TOTALS.	**15,077**	**13,505**	**282**	**18,548**	**9,868**	**258**
MCKEAN COUNTY						
ANNIN TOWNSHIP	78	45	2	85	34	2
BRADFORD CITY	1,409	845	23	1,531	658	24
WARD 01	78	45		88	30	3
WARD 02	235	161	5	262	121	3
WARD 03	358	214	5	378	173	6
WARD 04	252	139	4	268	110	6
WARD 05	101	66	4	108	60	1
WARD 06	385	220	5	427	164	5
BRADFORD TOWNSHIP.	840	487	9	910	398	6
CERES TOWNSHIP	136	81	2	178	37	1
CORYDON TOWNSHIP	55	39	1	59	33	
ELDRED TOWNSHIP	193	131	2	225	87	4
ELDRED BOROUGH	137	79	1	150	63	2
FOSTER TOWNSHIP	820	341	9	872	266	9
HAMILTON TOWNSHIP.	100	95	2	108	75	7
HAMLIN TOWNSHIP.	118	138	1	136	116	4
KANE BOROUGH	626	756	15	751	565	18
WARD 01	215	236	7	263	163	7
WARD 02	90	148	6	96	125	3
WARD 03	220	184		254	136	
WARD 04	101	188	2	138	141	8
KEATING TOWNSHIP	403	274	15	484	184	9
LAFAYETTE TOWNSHIP.	94	81	2	98	74	2
LEWIS RUN BOROUGH	89	87	1	104	68	2
LIBERTY TOWNSHIP	218	100	3	221	83	
MT. JEWETT BOROUGH	190	174	6	216	153	3
NORWICH TOWNSHIP.	69	55	1	81	45	4
OTTO TOWNSHIP	283	116		302	81	7
PORT ALLEGANY BOROUGH	372	182	4	412	133	2

	GOVERNOR/LT. GOVERNOR			U.S. SENATE		
	Republican Scranton/ Fisher	Democratic Casey/ Singel	Consumer Hoover/ Brickhouse	Republican Arlen Specter	Democratic Bob Edgar	Consumer Lance S. Haver
SERGEANT TOWNSHIP.............	29	24	1	31	24	
SMETHPORT BOROUGH	447	160	8	485	122	4
WETMORE TOWNSHIP	270	289	5	330	210	5
MCKEAN COUNTY TOTALS	**6,976**	**4,579**	**113**	**7,769**	**3,509**	**115**
MERCER COUNTY						
CLARK BOROUGH..................	68	110		75	97	3
COOLSPRING TOWNSHIP............	297	187	5	304	127	5
DEER CREEK TOWNSHIP	56	43	2	70	27	2
DELAWARE TOWNSHIP	338	372	7	420	266	9
EAST LACKAWANNOCK TOWNSHIP.....	266	207	8	318	133	5
FAIRVIEW TOWNSHIP	112	91	1	137	54	2
FARRELL CITY	340	1,955	38	460	1,639	28
FINDLEY TOWNSHIP	194	200	7	247	155	1
FREDONIA BOROUGH	118	56	3	132	38	2
FRENCH CREEK TOWNSHIP	113	89	2	122	77	1
GREENE TOWNSHIP	152	117	8	180	82	5
GREENVILLE BOROUGH	938	798	18	1,067	615	25
GROVE CITY BOROUGH..............	1,344	742	15	1,519	551	9
HEMPFIELD TOWNSHIP	762	486	9	867	346	20
HERMITAGE CITY....................	2,004	3,027	50	2,451	2,382	55
JACKSON TOWNSHIP	161	124	5	195	83	3
JACKSON CENTER BOROUGH	35	44		38	38	2
JAMESTOWN BOROUGH	106	93	1	119	81	
JEFFERSON TOWNSHIP	286	293	6	355	213	9
LACKAWANNOCK TOWNSHIP..........	282	298	7	331	250	5
LAKE TOWNSHIP	99	51	2	111	39	
LIBERTY TOWNSHIP	210	142	3	248	103	
MERCER BOROUGH	432	325	10	497	250	9
MILLCREEK TOWNSHIP	112	64	1	130	42	5
NEW LEBANON BOROUGH	40	22		42	20	
NEW VERNON TOWNSHIP	100	70	1	114	49	3
OTTER CREEK TOWNSHIP	74	86	3	97	59	5
PERRY TOWNSHIP	215	191	5	256	145	6
PINE TOWNSHIP	591	424	11	687	314	15
PYMATUNING TOWNSHIP............	329	492	12	408	387	10
SALEM TOWNSHIP	108	81	1	124	59	1
SANDY CREEK TOWNSHIP	124	81	2	138	60	3
SANDY LAKE TOWNSHIP	232	148	2	260	123	
SANDY LAKE BOROUGH.............	188	107	3	213	80	1
SHARON CITY	1,636	3,465	50	2,048	2,830	72
SHARPSVILLE BOROUGH	565	1,248	25	700	1,005	29
SHEAKLEYVILLE BOROUGH	26	23	1	39	11	1
SHENANGO TOWNSHIP	404	708	12	518	578	13
SOUTH PYMATUNING TOWNSHIP	385	612	11	446	525	16
SPRINGFIELD TOWNSHIP............	206	239	6	250	178	6
STONEBORO BOROUGH	160	174	5	212	126	2
SUGAR GROVE TOWNSHIP	187	138	7	229	85	6
WEST MIDDLESEX BOROUGH.........	158	186	4	189	142	5
WEST SALEM TOWNSHIP	437	518	15	535	387	14
WHEATLAND BOROUGH.............	54	220	5	75	186	6
WILMINGTON TOWNSHIP	206	104	2	229	80	1
WOLF CREEK TOWNSHIP............	160	76	1	178	54	1
WORTH TOWNSHIP	167	79	6	191	59	3
MERCER COUNTY TOTALS	**15,577**	**19,406**	**398**	**18,571**	**15,230**	**424**
MIFFLIN COUNTY						
ARMAGH TOWNSHIP................	428	283	8	461	235	10
BRATTON TOWNSHIP	114	135	2	153	98	2
BROWN TOWNSHIP.................	464	329	6	452	324	8
BURNHAM BOROUGH...............	297	280	6	343	226	3
DECATUR TOWNSHIP	351	246	3	403	184	6
DERRY TOWNSHIP	949	905	13	1,056	772	13
GRANVILLE TOWNSHIP	586	555	14	668	452	15
JUNIATA TERRACE BOROUGH.........	70	153	1	86	131	2
KISTLER BOROUGH	27	31		27	31	
LEWISTOWN BOROUGH..............	1,343	1,103	20	1,464	928	20
WARD 01	282	307	1	313	273	2
WARD 02	68	49		69	39	
WARD 03	70	21	1	70	16	1

	GOVERNOR/LT. GOVERNOR			U.S. SENATE		
	Republican Scranton/ Fisher	Democratic Casey/ Singel	Consumer Hoover/ Brickhouse	Republican Arlen Specter	Democratic Bob Edgar	Consumer Lance S. Haver
WARD 04	139	124	4	155	101	2
WARD 05	352	320	6	394	260	4
WARD 06	99	81	4	94	84	3
WARD 07	333	201	4	369	155	8
MC VEYTOWN BOROUGH.	65	60	4	80	45	2
MENNO TOWNSHIP.	175	57		221	27	1
NEWTON HAMILTON BOROUGH.	37	35	1	46	24	
OLIVER TOWNSHIP	200	160	7	230	123	4
UNION TOWNSHIP.	493	185	6	536	131	7
WAYNE TOWNSHIP.	189	166	4	240	115	3
MIFFLIN COUNTY TOTALS	**5,788**	**4,683**	**95**	**6,466**	**3,846**	**96**
MONROE COUNTY						
BARRETT TOWNSHIP	535	337	5	563	288	5
CHESTNUTHILL TOWNSHIP	603	502	7	673	423	5
COOLBAUGH TOWNSHIP	561	540	10	666	405	7
DELAWARE WATER GAP BOROUGH.	107	64	3	93	75	2
EAST STROUDSBURG BOROUGH.	725	703	5	835	575	5
ELDRED TOWNSHIP	136	179		167	140	1
HAMILTON TOWNSHIP	596	578	9	667	498	4
JACKSON TOWNSHIP	377	290	5	421	238	7
MIDDLE SMITHFIELD TOWNSHIP.	400	363	5	458	281	5
MT. POCONO BOROUGH	187	232	4	241	168	3
PARADISE TOWNSHIP.	338	205	2	361	177	3
POCONO TOWNSHIP.	665	617	8	793	463	9
POLK TOWNSHIP.	371	409	5	429	341	4
PRICE TOWNSHIP	75	70	1	95	49	1
ROSS TOWNSHIP.	218	199	4	233	176	4
SMITHFIELD TOWNSHIP	517	415	11	566	358	6
STROUD TOWNSHIP	1,335	958	14	1,490	770	13
STROUDSBURG BOROUGH.	641	539	6	682	501	6
WARD 01	36	38		34	38	1
WARD 02	131	113	2	137	112	
WARD 03	134	98	2	130	109	2
WARD 04	121	120	1	130	105	2
WARD 05	219	170	1	251	137	1
TOBYHANNA TOWNSHIP	740	450	3	847	307	5
TUNKHANNOCK TOWNSHIP.	145	150	2	196	95	1
MONROE COUNTY TOTALS	**9,272**	**7,800**	**109**	**10,476**	**6,328**	**96**
MONTGOMERY COUNTY						
ABINGTON TOWNSHIP	13,731	7,851	197	14,941	6,828	91
AMBLER BOROUGH	1,042	661	23	1,088	600	20
BRIDGEPORT BOROUGH	417	546	9	511	432	9
BRYN ATHYN BOROUGH	464	46	2	466	48	
CHELTENHAM TOWNSHIP	8,989	5,296	143	9,136	5,394	47
COLLEGEVILLE BOROUGH	556	224	9	558	201	7
CONSHOHOCKEN BOROUGH	831	1,100	22	1,032	899	19
DOUGLASS TOWNSHIP.	805	430	8	878	352	5
EAST GREENVILLE BOROUGH	344	178	4	362	158	3
EAST NORRITON TOWNSHIP	2,243	1,376	28	2,556	1,055	25
FRANCONIA TOWNSHIP	1,336	435	14	1,435	331	12
GREEN LANE BOROUGH	83	64	2	100	49	3
HATBORO BOROUGH	1,409	582	17	1,448	551	11
HATFIELD TOWNSHIP	1,899	1,003	23	2,086	818	12
HATFIELD BOROUGH	361	178		401	139	5
HORSHAM TOWNSHIP	3,223	1,434	49	3,433	1,241	19
JENKINTOWN BOROUGH	1,177	822	18	1,230	772	9
LANSDALE BOROUGH	2,530	1,541	52	2,757	1,318	32
LIMERICK TOWNSHIP	939	493	13	1,032	414	7
LOWER FREDERICK TOWNSHIP	472	175	5	487	155	3
LOWER GWYNEDD TOWNSHIP	2,209	741	21	2,169	786	18
LOWER MERION TOWNSHIP	17,051	6,770	234	15,631	8,633	62
WARD 01	1,469	450	16	1,313	628	7
WARD 02	1,287	347	5	1,232	412	2
WARD 03	1,215	414	16	1,172	480	1
WARD 04	578	661	28	522	745	17
WARD 05	1,460	433	18	1,236	674	5
WARD 06	1,257	383	5	1,217	427	5
WARD 07	1,305	508	5	1,288	566	2

	GOVERNOR/LT. GOVERNOR			U.S. SENATE		
	Republican Scranton/ Fisher	Democratic Casey/ Singel	Consumer Hoover/ Brickhouse	Republican Arlen Specter	Democratic Bob Edgar	Consumer Lance S. Haver
WARD 08	1,249	517	30	1,122	697	
WARD 09	1,146	499	24	1,025	656	4
WARD 10	1,045	310	10	943	424	6
WARD 11	1,381	373	11	1,244	516	5
WARD 12	1,225	551	28	993	835	4
WARD 13	1,158	607	17	1,126	724	1
WARD 14	1,276	717	21	1,198	849	3
LOWER MORELAND TOWNSHIP	3,238	1,197	35	3,497	981	18
LOWER POTTSGROVE TOWNSHIP	1,117	560	18	1,240	441	10
LOWER PROVIDENCE TOWNSHIP	2,936	1,503	46	3,205	1,235	36
LOWER SALFORD TOWNSHIP	1,614	581	18	1,769	435	8
MARLBOROUGH TOWNSHIP	415	244	6	458	201	9
MONTGOMERY TOWNSHIP	1,669	641	16	1,692	613	9
NARBERTH BOROUGH...............	1,133	600	21	1,008	736	8
NEW HANOVER TOWNSHIP	802	397	13	862	343	7
NORRISTOWN BOROUGH	3,174	2,866	64	3,610	2,421	43
NORTH WALES BOROUGH	517	330	6	533	308	4
PENNSBURG BOROUGH	300	217		307	204	3
PERKIOMEN TOWNSHIP.............	636	233	10	682	196	3
PLYMOUTH TOWNSHIP	2,994	2,078	32	3,401	1,678	18
POTTSTOWN BOROUGH	2,482	2,024	32	2,726	1,775	25
RED HILL BOROUGH...............	214	153	2	253	109	
ROCKLEDGE BOROUGH	591	302	10	663	236	4
ROYERSFORD BOROUGH	590	292	5	623	261	6
SALFORD TOWNSHIP	330	165	6	372	126	1
SCHWENKSVILLE BOROUGH	224	92	6	235	84	4
SKIPPACK TOWNSHIP	726	319	8	798	255	5
SOUDERTON BOROUGH	1,075	398	10	1,131	340	6
SPRINGFIELD TOWNSHIP............	5,700	2,608	65	5,803	2,523	42
TELFORD BOROUGH .... (BALANCE IN BUCKS CO.)	401	225	4	445	178	2
TOWAMENCIN TOWNSHIP............	2,461	1,169	26	2,751	928	11
TRAPPE BOROUGH.................	380	156	5	391	142	2
UPPER DUBLIN TOWNSHIP	5,575	2,398	56	5,850	2,152	28
UPPER FREDERICK TOWNSHIP........	340	165	5	373	128	5
UPPER GWYNEDD TOWNSHIP........	2,242	934	23	2,363	828	10
UPPER HANOVER TOWNSHIP	667	369	12	699	332	9
UPPER MERION TOWNSHIP	5,145	3,083	88	5,523	2,758	43
UPPER MORELAND TOWNSHIP	4,940	2,468	59	5,389	2,100	33
UPPER POTTSGROVE TOWNSHIP.....	393	202	8	443	169	2
UPPER PROVIDENCE TOWNSHIP	1,485	659	22	1,546	601	10
UPPER SALFORD TOWNSHIP	448	217	12	497	175	6
WEST CONSHOHOCKEN BOROUGH....	162	149	4	174	132	3
WEST NORRITON TOWNSHIP.........	2,297	1,245	33	2,505	1,039	21
WEST POTTSGROVE TOWNSHIP.......	355	338	5	435	256	3
WHITEMARSH TOWNSHIP	3,520	1,542	35	3,666	1,407	17
WHITPAIN TOWNSHIP	3,248	1,336	36	3,366	1,224	16
WORCESTER TOWNSHIP	1,124	422	22	1,214	352	6
MONTGOMERY COUNTY TOTALS......	129,771	66,823	1,777	136,235	61,576	915
MONTOUR COUNTY						
ANTHONY TOWNSHIP................	144	149	3	182	115	2
COOPER TOWNSHIP.................	117	121		166	75	
DANVILLE BOROUGH	602	897	3	811	676	12
DERRY TOWNSHIP..................	106	104	2	141	71	
LIBERTY TOWNSHIP	173	175	4	231	117	2
LIMESTONE TOWNSHIP	109	69	2	137	46	1
MAHONING TOWNSHIP..............	551	546	3	730	367	9
MAYBERRY TOWNSHIP...............	31	29		39	21	
VALLEY TOWNSHIP	246	255	1	321	179	3
WASHINGTONVILLE BOROUGH........	35	34	1	43	26	1
WEST HEMLOCK TOWNSHIP	57	50	1	76	32	
MONTOUR COUNTY TOTALS..........	2,171	2,429	20	2,877	1,725	30
NORTHAMPTON COUNTY						
ALLEN TOWNSHIP..................	288	289	9	302	279	5
BANGOR BOROUGH	672	697	10	764	561	18
WARD 01	166	158	3	184	129	9
WARD 02	147	162	3	166	136	3
WARD 03	208	174	2	213	152	4

	GOVERNOR/LT. GOVERNOR			U.S. SENATE		
	Republican Scranton/ Fisher	Democratic Casey/ Singel	Consumer Hoover/ Brickhouse	Republican Arlen Specter	Democratic Bob Edgar	Consumer Lance S. Haver
WARD 04	151	203	2	201	144	2
BATH BOROUGH	209	182	3	221	154	5
BETHLEHEM CITY	5,499	6,673	117	5,779	6,297	91
(BALANCE IN LEHIGH CO.)						
WARD 01	199	434	12	208	431	9
WARD 02	70	176	5	70	178	4
WARD 03	37	202	4	44	194	2
WARD 04	63	347	7	81	324	3
WARD 05	81	439		94	410	
WARD 06	234	130	1	215	147	1
WARD 07	238	178	6	222	197	4
WARD 08	201	247	4	213	235	4
WARD 09	562	718	18	631	636	18
WARD 14	2,964	2,239	32	3,100	2,058	29
WARD 15	783	1,340	24	829	1,276	11
WARD 16	41	105	2	48	97	3
WARD 17	26	118	2	24	114	3
BETHLEHEM TOWNSHIP.	1,589	1,950	30	1,820	1,668	31
WARD 01	530	352	6	589	280	7
WARD 02	226	672	13	312	591	8
WARD 03	423	543	9	447	497	9
WARD 04	410	383	2	472	300	7
BUSHKILL TOWNSHIP	563	527	14	639	427	13
CHAPMAN BOROUGH.	34	25		34	24	
EAST ALLEN TOWNSHIP.	529	404	12	546	371	8
EAST BANGOR BOROUGH	108	96	4	129	66	4
EASTON CITY.	2,105	2,978	67	2,300	2,675	50
WARD 02	80	111	3	96	92	2
WARD 03	816	475	19	792	475	7
WARD 04	153	269	6	194	221	9
WARD 05	41	76	1	46	66	1
WARD 06	77	235	2	84	214	1
WARD 07	102	226	4	121	197	3
WARD 08	288	434	7	311	395	10
WARD 09	180	351	8	225	291	5
WARD 10	158	462	5	202	412	3
WARD 11	108	183	8	119	164	8
WARD 12	102	156	4	110	148	1
FORKS TOWNSHIP	897	581	15	943	516	11
FREEMANSBURG BOROUGH.	99	261	6	117	236	5
GLENDON BOROUGH	34	52	2	40	44	1
HANOVER TOWNSHIP.	1,314	801	14	1,444	653	10
HELLERTOWN BOROUGH	775	996	21	841	907	8
WARD 01	221	333	7	257	286	1
WARD 02	172	226	4	188	206	1
WARD 03	382	437	10	396	415	6
LEHIGH TOWNSHIP	799	766	28	878	671	19
LOWER MT. BETHEL TOWNSHIP	346	342	7	400	267	7
LOWER NAZARETH TOWNSHIP.	512	469	12	594	368	10
LOWER SAUCON TOWNSHIP	1,090	1,026	20	1,146	927	23
MOORE TOWNSHIP.	851	766	27	1,015	642	17
NAZARETH BOROUGH	717	817	22	789	727	18
WARD 01	349	284	4	373	252	4
WARD 02	249	256	9	259	236	12
WARD 03	119	277	9	157	239	2
NORTH CATASAUQUA BOROUGH	279	509	9	282	496	5
WARD 01	85	181	3	78	182	3
WARD 02	194	328	6	204	314	2
NORTHAMPTON BOROUGH.	741	1,384	22	821	1,285	18
WARD 01	223	325	4	238	305	3
WARD 02	244	371	9	255	355	7
WARD 03	221	494	9	262	449	6
WARD 04	53	194		66	176	2
PALMER TOWNSHIP	2,476	2,003	34	2,658	1,842	38
PEN ARGYL BOROUGH.	510	482	3	575	381	7
WARD 01	64	81	1	72	61	1
WARD 02	215	191	2	246	149	3
WARD 03	148	119		167	95	2
WARD 04	83	91		90	76	1
PLAINFIELD TOWNSHIP	612	674	18	726	556	8

	GOVERNOR/LT. GOVERNOR			U.S. SENATE		
	Republican Scranton/ Fisher	Democratic Casey/ Singel	Consumer Hoover/ Brickhouse	Republican Arlen Specter	Democratic Bob Edgar	Consumer Lance S. Haver
PORTLAND BOROUGH	97	55	1	104	39	2
ROSETO BOROUGH	307	283	4	370	205	2
STOCKERTOWN BOROUGH	73	82	2	79	69	2
TATAMY BOROUGH	152	119	1	159	104	3
UPPER MT. BETHEL TOWNSHIP	693	481	16	756	374	10
UPPER NAZARETH TOWNSHIP	358	437	2	390	383	8
WALNUTPORT BOROUGH	183	152	6	207	123	5
WASHINGTON TOWNSHIP.	512	362	12	558	292	10
WEST EASTON BOROUGH	91	165	6	104	150	3
WILLIAMS TOWNSHIP	492	382	12	570	293	9
WILSON BOROUGH	859	883	31	998	729	29
WARD 01	280	283	8	304	240	11
WARD 02	271	211	11	316	172	11
WARD 03	308	389	12	378	317	7
WIND GAP BOROUGH	258	331	10	326	245	7
NORTHAMPTON COUNTY TOTALS	**27,723**	**29,482**	**629**	**30,424**	**26,046**	**520**
NORTHUMBERLAND COUNTY						
COAL TOWNSHIP	1,040	2,652	30	1,562	2,047	
WARD 01	95	282	7	135	238	
WARD 02	86	210	3	140	155	
WARD 03	25	260		45	232	
WARD 04	214	275	5	284	198	
WARD 05	84	293	2	140	225	
WARD 06	35	288	2	65	241	
WARD 07	149	399	4	222	313	
WARD 08	75	129	2	104	93	
WARD 09	277	516	5	427	352	
DELAWARE TOWNSHIP	417	344	10	514	245	
EAST CAMERON TOWNSHIP	68	92	1	93	65	
EAST CHILLISQUAQUE TOWNSHIP	111	73		146	35	
HERNDON BOROUGH.	73	55		77	46	
JACKSON TOWNSHIP	130	65	2	150	47	
JORDAN TOWNSHIP	115	70	1	128	50	
KULPMONT BOROUGH.	288	1,275	16	485	1,043	
LEWIS TOWNSHIP	217	158	4	245	127	
LITTLE MAHANOY TOWNSHIP	50	27	1	50	26	
LOWER AUGUSTA TOWNSHIP	134	105	3	163	75	
LOWER MAHANOY TOWNSHIP.	305	118	3	334	86	
MARION HEIGHTS BOROUGH	131	244	3	185	178	
MC EWENSVILLE BOROUGH	43	48	3	59	35	
MILTON BOROUGH	819	649	15	1,006	446	
WARD 01	64	64		81	44	
WARD 02	230	140	2	266	103	
WARD 03	211	161	4	264	104	
WARD 04	136	105	4	162	78	
WARD 05	178	179	5	233	117	
MT. CARMEL TOWNSHIP	177	954	9	324	952	
MT. CARMEL BOROUGH	786	2,236	23	1,234	1,661	
WARD 01	165	417	2	242	317	
WARD 02	179	498	3	266	383	
WARD 03	234	758	11	408	549	
WARD 04	208	563	7	318	412	
NORTHUMBERLAND BOROUGH	624	384	8	764	276	
WARD 01	171	107	1	197	75	
WARD 02	243	102	6	294	94	
WARD 03	210	175	1	273	107	
POINT TOWNSHIP	510	291	7	596	197	
RALPHO TOWNSHIP	566	603	6	737	405	
RIVERSIDE BOROUGH	365	284	2	433	207	
ROCKEFELLER TOWNSHIP	287	159	1	348	85	
RUSH TOWNSHIP	191	107	4	223	74	
SHAMOKIN CITY	1,285	2,015	31	1,743	1,515	
WARD 01	62	125	1	90	93	
WARD 02	148	271	6	195	217	
WARD 03	139	98	2	159	78	
WARD 04	222	343	6	323	238	
WARD 05	132	501	4	229	397	
WARD 06	138	207	6	195	142	
WARD 07	157	197	1	200	151	

	GOVERNOR/LT. GOVERNOR			U.S. SENATE		
	Republican Scranton/ Fisher	Democratic Casey/ Singel	Consumer Hoover/ Brickhouse	Republican Arlen Specter	Democratic Bob Edgar	Consumer Lance S. Haver
WARD 08	129	85	3	148	66	
WARD 09	94	93	2	124	60	
WARD 10	64	95		80	73	
SHAMOKIN TOWNSHIP	281	263	4	378	156	
SNYDERTOWN BOROUGH	36	59		60	31	
SUNBURY CITY	1,524	1,101	18	1,832	755	
WARD 01	141	101		176	65	
WARD 02	206	121	1	220	105	
WARD 03	123	130	3	154	98	
WARD 04	67	61	2	92	35	
WARD 05	189	167	3	247	105	
WARD 06	125	144	2	160	107	
WARD 07	268	145	3	308	100	
WARD 08	265	142	3	310	85	
WARD 09	140	90	1	165	55	
TURBOT TOWNSHIP	299	217	5	379	140	
TURBOTVILLE BOROUGH	117	88	3	133	72	
UPPER AUGUSTA TOWNSHIP.........	491	282	1	591	164	
UPPER MAHANOY TOWNSHIP	124	83	2	142	63	
WASHINGTON TOWNSHIP.............	109	70	1	123	49	
WATSONTOWN BOROUGH	318	285	6	358	244	
WARD 01	108	114	3	128	87	
WARD 02	210	171	3	230	157	
WEST CAMERON TOWNSHIP.........	53	45		66	32	
WEST CHILLISQUAQUE TOWNSHIP	307	211	6	375	142	
ZERBE TOWNSHIP..................	269	414	7	371	310	
NORTHUMBERLAND COUNTY TOTALS .	12,660	16,126	236	16,407	12,081	
PERRY COUNTY						
BLAIN BOROUGH..................	59	43	2	63	38	2
BLOOMFIELD BOROUGH	275	96	2	303	71	3
BUFFALO TOWNSHIP	187	137	7	242	96	2
CARROLL TOWNSHIP	436	287	7	528	210	4
CENTRE TOWNSHIP	307	147	15	354	121	8
DUNCANNON BOROUGH	244	150	2	295	120	2
GREENWOOD TOWNSHIP	226	99	6	257	71	1
HOWE TOWNSHIP	104	51	4	119	43	
JACKSON TOWNSHIP	91	45		90	47	
JUNIATA TOWNSHIP................	204	137	2	242	112	2
LANDISBURG BOROUGH	53	20	5	61	18	1
LIVERPOOL TOWNSHIP	146	78	5	177	60	3
LIVERPOOL BOROUGH..............	121	110	4	152	88	1
MARYSVILLE BOROUGH	412	263	7	482	221	7
MILLER TOWNSHIP	66	60	2	87	43	1
MILLERSTOWN BOROUGH............	180	70	2	187	63	1
NEW BUFFALO BOROUGH	24	21		30	14	
NEWPORT BOROUGH................	295	171	4	349	123	2
NORTH EAST MADISON TOWNSHIP	103	58	1	117	41	1
OLIVER TOWNSHIP	244	240	6	300	186	7
PENN TOWNSHIP..................	427	237	5	533	152	8
RYE TOWNSHIP	245	195	7	314	128	7
SAVILLE TOWNSHIP................	296	211	5	362	155	9
SOUTH WEST MADISON TOWNSHIP	102	76	4	121	61	3
SPRING TOWNSHIP.................	218	166	2	256	135	1
TOBOYNE TOWNSHIP	71	49	2	77	41	2
TUSCARORA TOWNSHIP	153	88	3	188	59	4
TYRONE TOWNSHIP	207	190	3	251	157	3
WATTS TOWNSHIP	150	94	6	193	58	2
WHEATFIELD TOWNSHIP	359	230	5	414	192	3
PERRY COUNTY TOTALS	6,005	3,819	125	7,144	2,924	90
PHILADELPHIA COUNTY						
PHILADELPHIA CITY						
WARD 01	2,519	3,504	38	3,654	2,310	31
WARD 02	2,996	3,226	79	2,886	3,531	32
WARD 03	900	6,476	56	1,413	6,009	43
WARD 04	857	5,977	45	1,268	5,651	33
WARD 05	3,423	2,771	100	2,657	3,681	42
WARD 06	598	3,412	41	951	3,140	37
WARD 07	1,621	2,657	81	2,011	2,271	55

	GOVERNOR/LT. GOVERNOR			U.S. SENATE		
	Republican Scranton/ Fisher	Democratic Casey/ Singel	Consumer Hoover/ Brickhouse	Republican Arlen Specter	Democratic Bob Edgar	Consumer Lance S. Haver
WARD 08	5,783	3,677	177	4,508	5,299	72
WARD 09	3,779	2,649	101	2,995	3,537	18
WARD 10	1,022	7,105	47	1,614	6,565	30
WARD 11	726	3,957	40	1,054	3,631	40
WARD 12	1,238	4,554	111	1,314	4,664	39
WARD 13	1,073	4,578	90	1,418	4,288	48
WARD 14	386	1,894	19	480	1,775	20
WARD 15	2,409	2,823	82	2,134	3,163	39
WARD 16	423	4,402	92	731	4,223	81
WARD 17	1,047	6,313	62	1,590	5,991	37
WARD 18	1,206	2,237	48	1,528	1,950	29
WARD 19	441	2,537	59	565	2,303	69
WARD 20	215	2,113	57	334	2,035	33
WARD 21	7,575	7,166	121	8,716	5,747	83
WARD 22	2,480	6,144	179	2,122	6,366	31
WARD 23	2,731	3,603	60	3,317	3,056	49
WARD 24	878	2,950	71	734	2,981	26
WARD 25	2,634	3,959	78	3,437	3,033	49
WARD 26	3,389	3,750	57	4,179	2,929	32
WARD 27	1,491	1,887	105	927	2,597	12
WARD 28	557	4,190	39	807	3,942	28
WARD 29	452	3,726	86	650	3,447	67
WARD 30	1,053	2,758	56	987	2,862	40
WARD 31	2,263	3,143	54	2,838	2,552	49
WARD 32	582	5,900	129	910	5,727	135
WARD 33	2,941	4,860	74	4,084	3,745	55
WARD 34	4,206	8,420	93	5,217	7,549	56
WARD 35	5,188	5,142	114	6,610	3,972	63
WARD 36	1,815	8,105	107	2,703	7,312	87
WARD 37	601	3,770	38	748	3,478	54
WARD 38	1,677	4,464	64	1,904	4,076	32
WARD 39	5,823	7,386	85	7,820	5,477	91
WARD 40	4,914	8,739	63	6,186	7,648	46
WARD 41	3,387	4,137	79	4,755	2,985	43
WARD 42	2,879	3,339	40	3,592	2,633	26
WARD 43	904	3,876	37	1,204	3,564	34
WARD 44	682	4,275	37	909	3,965	24
WARD 45	3,496	4,624	107	4,326	3,837	69
WARD 46	1,548	4,856	150	1,262	5,231	28
WARD 47	242	2,526	47	306	2,488	43
WARD 48	2,442	3,770	34	3,128	3,200	28
WARD 49	1,408	4,852	94	1,882	4,425	32
WARD 50	1,390	8,171	67	2,271	7,490	32
WARD 51	654	5,801	48	984	5,510	40
WARD 52	2,686	6,758	80	3,378	6,038	45
WARD 53	4,263	4,757	86	5,612	3,496	38
WARD 54	3,476	4,748	96	4,902	3,598	47
WARD 55	4,676	5,730	72	6,270	4,097	48
WARD 56	7,015	7,327	123	8,948	5,130	66
WARD 57	5,165	5,065	98	6,481	3,668	56
WARD 58	9,114	7,008	112	11,576	4,746	81
WARD 59	1,454	4,969	103	1,694	4,809	31
WARD 60	775	5,907	39	1,086	5,568	29
WARD 61	3,736	4,355	110	4,590	3,313	41
WARD 62	4,406	5,174	85	5,456	3,901	55
WARD 63	5,256	3,907	78	6,361	2,788	45
WARD 64	3,419	3,253	50	4,178	2,385	23
WARD 65	3,685	4,040	62	4,646	3,092	40
WARD 66	8,124	7,290	119	10,675	4,996	85
PHILADELPHIA COUNTY TOTALS	172,194	307,439	5,151	210,473	271,466	3,042
PIKE COUNTY						
BLOOMING GROVE TOWNSHIP	248	217	1	298	159	3
DELAWARE TOWNSHIP	296	238	6	324	193	9
DINGMAN TOWNSHIP	366	179	4	375	151	7
GREENE TOWNSHIP	320	191	2	394	118	
LACKAWAXEN TOWNSHIP.............	362	331	2	456	207	4
LEHMAN TOWNSHIP	180	131	2	197	111	3
MATAMORAS BOROUGH..............	333	281	5	345	250	7
MILFORD TOWNSHIP	155	61	3	167	49	1

	GOVERNOR/LT. GOVERNOR			U.S. SENATE		
	Republican Scranton/ Fisher	Democratic Casey/ Singel	Consumer Hoover/ Brickhouse	Republican Arlen Specter	Democratic Bob Edgar	Consumer Lance S. Haver
MILFORD BOROUGH................	284	110	3	283	103	4
PALMYRA TOWNSHIP..............	483	199	6	541	130	3
PORTER TOWNSHIP	27	16	1	42	4	
SHOHOLA TOWNSHIP..............	218	164	1	246	121	4
WESTFALL TOWNSHIP	257	186	3	286	144	4
PIKE COUNTY TOTALS	**3,529**	**2,304**	**39**	**3,954**	**1,740**	**49**
POTTER COUNTY						
ABBOTT TOWNSHIP	53	38	3	63	29	1
ALLEGANY TOWNSHIP	44	65		68	44	
AUSTIN BOROUGH	76	114		97	95	
BINGHAM TOWNSHIP	94	43		106	30	2
CLARA TOWNSHIP.................	16	21	1	25	12	2
COUDERSPORT BOROUGH...........	546	394	10	675	275	5
WARD 01......................	216	158	5	270	109	1
WARD 02......................	330	236	5	405	166	4
EULALIA TOWNSHIP	128	70	4	166	38	1
GALETON BOROUGH	202	283	2	311	167	3
WARD 01......................	100	131		140	89	1
WARD 02......................	102	152	2	171	78	2
GENESEE TOWNSHIP	105	109	6	133	87	3
HARRISON TOWNSHIP	110	142	4	174	78	3
HEBRON TOWNSHIP	105	50	2	124	35	
HECTOR TOWNSHIP	44	45	3	61	29	
HOMER TOWNSHIP	28	46	1	42	32	2
KEATING TOWNSHIP	52	58	2	75	35	1
OSWAYO TOWNSHIP	36	18		47	8	
OSWAYO BOROUGH	18	21		26	14	
PIKE TOWNSHIP..................	36	40	1	54	22	1
PLEASANT VALLEY TOWNSHIP	19	10		23	7	
PORTAGE TOWNSHIP	37	42		50	26	
ROULETTE TOWNSHIP	185	126	4	212	105	1
SHARON TOWNSHIP	95	97	3	151	50	2
SHINGLEHOUSE BOROUGH	225	104	2	247	84	
STEWARDSON TOWNSHIP	28	22	1	36	13	
SUMMIT TOWNSHIP	48	22		66	8	
SWEDEN TOWNSHIP	94	69		114	52	
SYLVANIA TOWNSHIP	17	20	1	24	14	
ULYSSES TOWNSHIP................	89	78	1	118	50	1
ULYSSES BOROUGH................	82	74	2	105	56	
WEST BRANCH TOWNSHIP	50	61	2	87	27	1
WHARTON TOWNSHIP	21	15	1	26	11	
POTTER COUNTY TOTALS............	**2,683**	**2,297**	**56**	**3,506**	**1,533**	**29**
SCHUYLKILL COUNTY						
ASHLAND BOROUGH	639	790	6	817	595	9
AUBURN BOROUGH	105	56	1	116	43	3
BARRY TOWNSHIP	145	90	5	187	52	2
BLYTHE TOWNSHIP................	191	330	3	248	268	6
BRANCH TOWNSHIP	288	363	9	367	284	7
BUTLER TOWNSHIP	741	699	13	963	465	13
CASS TOWNSHIP..................	149	521	9	278	393	6
COALDALE BOROUGH	449	611	5	619	442	4
CRESSONA BOROUGH.............	297	164	6	365	96	5
DEER LAKE BOROUGH..............	109	73	4	140	45	
DELANO TOWNSHIP	70	181	2	135	117	
EAST BRUNSWICK TOWNSHIP	299	125	7	343	82	5
EAST NORWEGIAN TOWNSHIP	107	268	7	196	186	
EAST UNION TOWNSHIP..............	204	218	5	266	156	4
ELDRED TOWNSHIP	263	81		283	57	
FOSTER TOWNSHIP	47	68	3	62	54	2
FRACKVILLE BOROUGH..............	787	909	18	1,064	627	13
FRAILEY TOWNSHIP	91	48	1	110	28	3
GILBERTON BOROUGH	139	307	5	199	255	2
WARD EAST	72	105	2	84	100	1
WARD WEST...................	67	202	3	115	155	1
GIRARDVILLE BOROUGH.............	264	678	10	373	571	6
WARD EAST	103	216	4	144	175	4
WARD MIDDLE	88	252	3	121	220	1
WARD WEST...................	73	210	3	108	176	1

	GOVERNOR/LT. GOVERNOR			U.S. SENATE		
	Republican Scranton/ Fisher	Democratic Casey/ Singel	Consumer Hoover/ Brickhouse	Republican Arlen Specter	Democratic Bob Edgar	Consumer Lance S. Haver
GORDON BOROUGH.................	190	141	5	239	92	3
HEGINS TOWNSHIP.................	790	416	10	925	287	6
HUBLEY TOWNSHIP	210	87	4	237	61	3
KLINE TOWNSHIP	271	285	4	343	222	
LANDINGVILLE BOROUGH...........	38	10	1	40	7	
MAHANOY TOWNSHIP...............	140	304	5	206	244	1
MAHANOY CITY BOROUGH	816	1,465	10	1,180	1,088	15
WARD 01	78	201		127	148	3
WARD 02	61	228	1	124	167	1
WARD 03	107	249	2	171	180	5
WARD 04	94	135		131	97	
WARD 05	135	158		154	137	
WARD 06	175	243	5	248	167	5
WARD 07	166	251	2	225	192	1
MC ADOO BOROUGH	292	604	4	436	464	3
MECHANICSVILLE BOROUGH	100	74	5	116	63	2
MIDDLEPORT BOROUGH	85	131	1	118	94	2
MINERSVILLE BOROUGH............	725	1,100	9	1,043	763	14
MT. CARBON BOROUGH.............	26	17	2	21	23	
NEW CASTLE TOWNSHIP	63	127	2	90	97	4
NEW PHILADELPHIA BOROUGH	120	414	3	206	328	2
NEW RINGGOLD BOROUGH..........	70	31	2	84	17	3
NORTH MANHEIM TOWNSHIP	522	258	13	594	192	4
NORTH UNION TOWNSHIP	220	137	3	258	100	4
NORWEGIAN TOWNSHIP	228	387	4	330	289	1
ORWIGSBURG BOROUGH	542	213	17	606	156	8
PALO ALTO BOROUGH...............	136	345	5	201	279	5
WARD 01	62	192	5	95	159	4
WARD 02	74	153		106	120	1
PINE GROVE TOWNSHIP.............	394	382	9	530	250	8
PINE GROVE BOROUGH.............	388	253	6	436	210	2
PORT CARBON BOROUGH............	315	389	2	417	285	6
PORT CLINTON BOROUGH...........	51	58		72	36	1
PORTER TOWNSHIP	399	195	16	467	145	4
POTTSVILLE CITY	2,588	3,027	38	3,214	2,422	27
WARD 01	152	208	1	199	161	
WARD 02	268	248	3	323	190	4
WARD 03	441	537	7	541	435	9
WARD 04	326	359	3	387	297	
WARD 05	473	620	9	620	495	5
WARD 06	163	378	4	241	302	2
WARD 07	765	677	11	903	542	7
REILLY TOWNSHIP.................	68	158	3	99	126	1
RINGTOWN BOROUGH	203	121	5	246	81	
RUSH TOWNSHIP	655	527	7	797	378	7
RYAN TOWNSHIP	291	201	8	339	154	6
SCHUYLKILL TOWNSHIP.............	233	280	4	319	195	1
SCHUYLKILL HAVEN BOROUGH	995	506	15	1,137	376	11
WARD EAST	285	115	7	316	89	2
WARD NORTH.....................	190	134	5	233	96	2
WARD SOUTH.....................	272	135	1	307	100	4
WARD WEST	248	122	2	281	91	3
SHENANDOAH BOROUGH	744	1,701	18	1,070	1,354	20
SOUTH MANHEIM TOWNSHIP	184	88	5	211	68	
ST. CLAIR BOROUGH.................	533	853	12	731	651	8
WARD MIDDLE	144	233	6	190	189	3
WARD NORTH.....................	97	177	4	146	126	3
WARD SOUTH.....................	218	355	1	296	273	2
WARD WEST	74	88	1	99	63	
TAMAQUA BOROUGH	1,255	1,251	21	1,614	895	11
WARD EAST	476	526	4	619	382	2
WARD MIDDLE	301	224	4	357	161	3
WARD NORTH.....................	291	251	6	368	178	3
WARD SOUTH.....................	187	250	7	270	174	3
TOWER CITY BOROUGH.............	260	146	5	313	94	5
TREMONT TOWNSHIP...............	47	23		53	18	
TREMONT BOROUGH...............	327	243	4	416	156	2
WARD EAST	188	149	4	241	98	2
WARD WEST	139	94		175	58	
UNION TOWNSHIP..................	226	146	4	286	94	

	GOVERNOR/LT. GOVERNOR			U.S. SENATE		
	Republican Scranton/ Fisher	Democratic Casey/ Singel	Consumer Hoover/ Brickhouse	Republican Arlen Specter	Democratic Bob Edgar	Consumer Lance S. Haver
UPPER MAHANTONGO TOWNSHIP	208	101	2	240	68	2
WALKER TOWNSHIP	214	88		250	52	
WASHINGTON TOWNSHIP.	285	255	6	362	181	3
WAYNE TOWNSHIP.	556	330	5	653	232	4
WEST BRUNSWICK TOWNSHIP	461	191	15	515	150	4
WEST MAHANOY TOWNSHIP	405	942	12	578	760	10
WEST PENN TOWNSHIP	571	273	9	682	160	3
SCHUYLKILL COUNTY TOTALS.	23,824	25,854	459	30,451	19,273	316
SNYDER COUNTY						
ADAMS TOWNSHIP	183	90	4	210	64	3
BEAVER TOWNSHIP.	141	46		158	24	
BEAVERTOWN BOROUGH	249	100	2	272	77	1
CENTER TOWNSHIP	260	127	5	303	79	4
CHAPMAN TOWNSHIP.	125	105	2	166	65	2
FRANKLIN TOWNSHIP.	352	191	3	422	120	5
FREEBURG BOROUGH.	135	63	2	158	40	3
JACKSON TOWNSHIP	172	102	2	201	71	2
MC CLURE BOROUGH	258	153	6	296	114	5
MIDDLEBURG BOROUGH.	312	143	6	377	82	3
MIDDLECREEK TOWNSHIP.	320	150	10	396	77	4
MONROE TOWNSHIP	678	332	10	826	202	5
PENN TOWNSHIP.	344	192	6	409	129	4
PERRY TOWNSHIP	247	150	2	296	108	1
SELINSGROVE BOROUGH	888	449	18	1,025	319	7
SHAMOKIN DAM BOROUGH.	362	191		418	148	
SPRING TOWNSHIP.	292	168	7	343	121	3
UNION TOWNSHIP.	156	97	3	169	84	3
WASHINGTON TOWNSHIP.	194	107	3	244	53	2
WEST BEAVER TOWNSHIP	144	99	3	182	67	1
WEST PERRY TOWNSHIP	188	95	5	234	54	2
SNYDER COUNTY TOTALS.	6,000	3,150	99	7,105	2,098	60
SOMERSET COUNTY						
ADDISON TOWNSHIP	143	142	3	182	107	
ADDISON BOROUGH.	51	37		65	22	
ALLEGHENY TOWNSHIP.	86	95	1	112	69	1
BENSON BOROUGH	33	82		41	72	2
BERLIN BOROUGH	441	284	5	517	203	3
BLACK TOWNSHIP.	115	147	10	183	87	5
BOSWELL BOROUGH	107	394	3	175	326	3
BROTHERS VALLEY TOWNSHIP.	424	352	11	542	233	12
CALLIMONT BOROUGH	5	2		6	1	
CASSELMAN BOROUGH.	12	21		16	16	1
CENTRAL CITY BOROUGH.	120	355	1	214	259	1
CONEMAUGH TOWNSHIP.	1,124	1,836	30	1,573	1,389	24
CONFLUENCE BOROUGH	135	104	2	148	89	3
ELK LICK TOWNSHIP	324	169	5	365	128	4
FAIRHOPE TOWNSHIP.	8	19		16	13	
GARRETT BOROUGH	50	99	2	68	78	2
GREENVILLE TOWNSHIP	102	77	3	132	46	4
HOOVERSVILLE BOROUGH	77	191	3	108	155	5
INDIAN LAKE BOROUGH.	99	34	2	105	24	2
JEFFERSON TOWNSHIP	240	185	5	285	137	3
JENNER TOWNSHIP	501	828	24	705	635	17
JENNERSTOWN BOROUGH	116	122	1	150	86	2
LARIMER TOWNSHIP.	80	89	2	107	60	1
LINCOLN TOWNSHIP.	310	269	8	406	170	4
LOWER TURKEYFOOT TOWNSHIP	114	65	4	138	42	2
MEYERSDALE BOROUGH	305	369	5	391	280	5
MIDDLECREEK TOWNSHIP.	173	129	3	217	83	
MILFORD TOWNSHIP	302	242	11	388	156	6
NEW BALTIMORE BOROUGH	14	82		24	71	1
NEW CENTERVILLE BOROUGH	68	32		84	15	
NORTHAMPTON TOWNSHIP.	64	59	2	99	28	
OGLE TOWNSHIP.	56	114	3	82	86	4
PAINT TOWNSHIP.	485	677	11	687	478	9
PAINT BOROUGH.	78	322	5	128	271	7
QUEMAHONING TOWNSHIP.	280	467	8	398	348	
ROCKWOOD BOROUGH	199	228	5	241	187	4

	GOVERNOR/LT. GOVERNOR			U.S. SENATE		
	Republican Scranton/ Fisher	Democratic Casey/ Singel	Consumer Hoover/ Brickhouse	Republican Arlen Specter	Democratic Bob Edgar	Consumer Lance S. Haver
SALISBURY BOROUGH.............	147	102	1	170	78	
SEVEN SPRINGS BOROUGH	18	6		19	4	
SHADE TOWNSHIP	286	802	10	446	642	5
SHANKSVILLE BOROUGH	52	49	1	74	28	1
SOMERSET TOWNSHIP..............	1,228	1,225	21	1,653	807	21
SOMERSET BOROUGH..............	1,321	906	19	1,611	623	13
SOUTHAMPTON TOWNSHIP.........	55	65	1	70	51	
STONYCREEK TOWNSHIP	366	266	11	493	143	6
STOYSTOWN BOROUGH.............	102	99	4	121	81	2
SUMMIT TOWNSHIP	287	371	10	405	249	5
UPPER TURKEYFOOT TOWNSHIP......	241	157	4	312	85	3
URSINA BOROUGH	46	36		58	23	1
WELLERSBURG BOROUGH...........	40	14	1	43	13	
WINDBER BOROUGH	441	1,480	24	724	1,203	10
SOMERSET COUNTY TOTALS	**11,471**	**14,297**	**285**	**15,297**	**10,480**	**204**
SULLIVAN COUNTY						
CHERRY TOWNSHIP	243	426	4	322	339	3
COLLEY TOWNSHIP	85	116		92	93	
DAVIDSON TOWNSHIP..............	82	96	2	98	82	1
DUSHORE BOROUGH...............	122	141	2	116	96	1
EAGLES MERE BOROUGH	79	17		85	10	
ELKLAND TOWNSHIP	163	76		195	43	4
FORKS TOWNSHIP	101	69		115	52	2
FORKSVILLE BOROUGH..............	48	22		46	23	
FOX TOWNSHIP	69	66		83	55	
HILLSGROVE TOWNSHIP	65	37	1	72	28	2
LAPORTE TOWNSHIP	74	49	2	72	51	2
LAPORTE BOROUGH	82	41	1	86	38	1
SHREWSBURY TOWNSHIP............	50	38		49	39	
SULLIVAN COUNTY TOTALS	**1,263**	**1,194**	**12**	**1,431**	**949**	**16**
SUSQUEHANNA COUNTY						
APOLACON TOWNSHIP..............	77	70	2	95	50	3
ARARAT TOWNSHIP.................	86	54		100	43	
AUBURN TOWNSHIP	239	188	2	329	101	2
BRIDGEWATER TOWNSHIP............	492	268	4	556	183	5
BROOKLYN TOWNSHIP	177	99	2	196	80	1
CHOCONUT TOWNSHIP	136	82		155	62	
CLIFFORD TOWNSHIP...............	280	278		386	155	5
DIMOCK TOWNSHIP	200	162	1	251	107	2
FOREST CITY BOROUGH	279	560	2	418	365	3
WARD 01.........................	111	237	1	186	144	1
WARD 02.........................	168	323	1	232	221	2
FOREST LAKE TOWNSHIP	174	107		215	66	1
FRANKLIN TOWNSHIP...............	160	65	1	174	50	
FRIENDSVILLE BOROUGH	16	16	1	20	13	
GIBSON TOWNSHIP.................	166	132		229	70	1
GREAT BEND TOWNSHIP	293	147	3	323	105	4
GREAT BEND BOROUGH	91	121		126	80	1
HALLSTEAD BOROUGH	187	165	2	232	109	5
HARFORD TOWNSHIP...............	248	129	1	291	74	5
HARMONY TOWNSHIP	83	51	1	91	40	1
HERRICK TOWNSHIP................	94	111		132	71	2
HOP BOTTOM BOROUGH............	90	45	1	109	27	
JACKSON TOWNSHIP	148	73		177	44	1
JESSUP TOWNSHIP.................	116	45	3	133	29	3
LANESBORO BOROUGH..............	55	78	1	84	49	2
LATHROP TOWNSHIP	140	139	2	174	101	4
LENOX TOWNSHIP	262	200	4	344	125	2
LIBERTY TOWNSHIP	187	70		209	42	2
LITTLE MEADOWS BOROUGH.........	64	28		76	15	
MIDDLETOWN TOWNSHIP	40	77	2	80	36	2
MONTROSE BOROUGH	496	270	6	572	176	2
WARD 01.........................	308	156	2	353	96	
WARD 02.........................	188	114	4	219	80	2
NEW MILFORD TOWNSHIP...........	257	158	4	302	104	3
NEW MILFORD BOROUGH	162	118	3	191	87	2
OAKLAND TOWNSHIP	74	63	1	96	43	
OAKLAND BOROUGH	84	84	1	112	56	

	GOVERNOR/LT. GOVERNOR			U.S. SENATE		
	Republican Scranton/ Fisher	Democratic Casey/ Singel	Consumer Hoover/ Brickhouse	Republican Arlen Specter	Democratic Bob Edgar	Consumer Lance S. Haver
RUSH TOWNSHIP	173	158	1	241	89	2
SILVER LAKE TOWNSHIP	208	188	2	242	145	5
SPRINGVILLE TOWNSHIP	242	204	3	312	118	3
SUSQUEHANNA DEPOT BOROUGH	178	321	2	249	227	5
WARD 01	32	120	1	66	80	1
WARD 02	146	201	1	183	147	4
THOMPSON TOWNSHIP	73	36		84	26	
THOMPSON BOROUGH	59	38	1	65	29	1
UNIONDALE BOROUGH	82	39	1	99	25	1
SUSQUEHANNA COUNTY TOTALS	6,668	5,237	60	8,270	3,417	81
TIOGA COUNTY						
BLOSS TOWNSHIP	56	67		86	35	
BLOSSBURG BOROUGH	287	219	7	363	148	3
BROOKFIELD TOWNSHIP	65	76	3	92	52	
CHARLESTON TOWNSHIP	492	307	5	612	196	2
CHATHAM TOWNSHIP	115	99	5	152	68	3
CLYMER TOWNSHIP	88	125	7	136	80	3
COVINGTON TOWNSHIP	121	86	3	162	54	1
DEERFIELD TOWNSHIP	106	70	3	118	56	1
DELMAR TOWNSHIP	413	295	16	549	184	2
DUNCAN TOWNSHIP	19	54		30	44	
ELK TOWNSHIP	8	15		19	6	
ELKLAND TOWNSHIP	13	7		15	5	
ELKLAND BOROUGH	213	400	3	293	319	5
FARMINGTON TOWNSHIP	108	51	1	131	28	2
GAINES TOWNSHIP	119	104	1	157	65	3
HAMILTON TOWNSHIP	73	68	2	93	47	
JACKSON TOWNSHIP	241	150	4	285	110	3
KNOXVILLE BOROUGH	139	80	1	157	58	2
LAWRENCE TOWNSHIP	218	133	7	284	80	
LAWRENCEVILLE BOROUGH	94	53	2	115	32	
LIBERTY TOWNSHIP	175	99	1	205	69	1
LIBERTY BOROUGH	57	42	1	62	39	
MANSFIELD BOROUGH	355	321	3	443	237	4
MIDDLEBURY TOWNSHIP	201	98	6	261	51	3
MORRIS TOWNSHIP	125	70	2	149	52	1
NELSON TOWNSHIP	99	41	1	100	40	2
OSCEOLA TOWNSHIP	82	82		120	45	1
PUTNAM TOWNSHIP	77	49		103	22	1
RICHMOND TOWNSHIP	319	254	5	440	142	8
ROSEVILLE BOROUGH	28	19		33	14	
RUTLAND TOWNSHIP	95	62		110	48	
SHIPPEN TOWNSHIP	61	69	3	92	44	1
SULLIVAN TOWNSHIP	183	98	2	233	52	
TIOGA TOWNSHIP	118	121	3	162	78	6
TIOGA BOROUGH	76	71	1	95	53	
UNION TOWNSHIP	150	123	3	185	92	2
WARD TOWNSHIP	9	14		15	10	1
WELLSBORO BOROUGH	850	410	17	1,004	267	6
WARD 01	386	217	6	478	127	2
WARD 02	464	193	11	526	140	4
WESTFIELD TOWNSHIP	155	132	4	200	87	5
WESTFIELD BOROUGH	189	201	3	241	151	4
TIOGA COUNTY TOTALS	6,392	4,835	125	8,102	3,260	76
UNION COUNTY						
BUFFALO TOWNSHIP	372	242	6	498	155	
EAST BUFFALO TOWNSHIP	1,073	455	15	1,134	442	5
GREGG TOWNSHIP	117	95	3	134	81	1
HARTLETON BOROUGH	33	22	1	49	10	
HARTLEY TOWNSHIP	199	167	11	282	107	10
KELLY TOWNSHIP	375	244	6	482	168	4
LEWIS TOWNSHIP	123	77	2	165	47	2
LEWISBURG BOROUGH	736	385	21	743	431	9
WARD 01	138	83	9	135	110	2
WARD 02	219	91	5	196	123	2
WARD 03	122	61	4	126	67	2
WARD 04	257	150	3	286	131	3
LIMESTONE TOWNSHIP	182	81	1	196	73	1

	GOVERNOR/LT. GOVERNOR			U.S. SENATE		
	Republican Scranton/ Fisher	Democratic Casey/ Singel	Consumer Hoover/ Brickhouse	Republican Arlen Specter	Democratic Bob Edgar	Consumer Lance S. Haver
MIFFLINBURG BOROUGH	691	290	7	808	218	5
NEW BERLIN BOROUGH..............	149	146	4	209	101	1
UNION TOWNSHIP..................	191	120	5	233	89	3
WEST BUFFALO TOWNSHIP	179	121	3	262	52	
WHITE DEER TOWNSHIP	462	364	8	640	217	4
UNION COUNTY TOTALS	4,882	2,809	93	5,835	2,191	45
VENANGO COUNTY						
ALLEGHENY TOWNSHIP..............	41	27	2	54	15	1
BARKEYVILLE BOROUGH.	24	40	1	36	29	
CANAL TOWNSHIP...................	101	133	3	150	83	4
CHERRYTREE TOWNSHIP	195	137	3	233	96	1
CLINTON TOWNSHIP	95	97	6	129	70	4
CLINTONVILLE BOROUGH	86	66	3	114	41	2
COOPERSTOWN BOROUGH	79	60	2	85	55	1
CORNPLANTER TOWNSHIP	472	482	10	606	355	5
CRANBERRY TOWNSHIP	1,098	968	28	1,414	665	20
EMLENTON BOROUGH	191	89	3	217	65	2
FRANKLIN CITY	1,045	1,074	20	1,271	848	20
WARD 01	292	355	3	358	286	3
WARD 02	467	357	8	562	265	11
WARD 03	286	362	9	351	297	6
FRENCHCREEK TOWNSHIP	194	296	9	287	201	7
IRWIN TOWNSHIP	155	140	3	201	101	
JACKSON TOWNSHIP	110	115	2	144	87	1
MINERAL TOWNSHIP.................	53	90	2	87	55	4
OAKLAND TOWNSHIP	193	229	3	245	180	2
OIL CITY CITY.....................	1,809	1,901	40	2,181	1,578	34
WARD 01	209	303	6	268	251	4
WARD 03	26	33	1	32	30	
WARD 04	534	386	9	621	304	8
WARD 05	62	79	4	78	71	1
WARD 06	174	217	5	228	170	5
WARD 07	92	151	4	124	123	2
WARD 08	92	252	3	115	235	10
WARD 09	264	178	3	294	153	2
WARD 10	356	302	5	421	241	2
OIL CREEK TOWNSHIP	150	99	3	193	56	1
PINEGROVE TOWNSHIP	198	132	4	231	103	3
PLEASANTVILLE BOROUGH	218	90	3	232	77	1
PLUM TOWNSHIP....................	154	148	5	216	90	2
POLK BOROUGH	74	93	2	102	66	
PRESIDENT TOWNSHIP	94	88	6	125	62	1
RICHLAND TOWNSHIP	111	88	3	137	62	3
ROCKLAND TOWNSHIP..............	188	175	3	252	116	1
ROUSEVILLE BOROUGH	87	136	2	115	111	
SANDYCREEK TOWNSHIP	328	397	5	461	268	7
SCRUBGRASS TOWNSHIP	118	75	3	145	49	2
SUGAR CREEK BOROUGH............	781	921	20	994	712	20
UTICA BOROUGH	32	49		40	40	
VICTORY TOWNSHIP................	56	45	1	64	34	
VENANGO COUNTY TOTALS	8,530	8,480	200	10,761	6,370	149
WARREN COUNTY						
BEAR LAKE BOROUGH..............	32	30		34	29	
BROKENSTRAW TOWNSHIP...........	217	196	7	234	169	6
CHERRY GROVE TOWNSHIP	20	35	1	34	24	
CLARENDON BOROUGH	66	93	2	76	79	2
COLUMBUS TOWNSHIP	215	180	5	226	167	2
CONEWANGO TOWNSHIP.............	662	512	11	706	435	7
DEERFIELD TOWNSHIP..............	56	44	2	66	36	
ELDRED TOWNSHIP	79	89	2	106	62	2
ELK TOWNSHIP	81	49	2	91	42	1
FARMINGTON TOWNSHIP	239	103	5	225	107	6
FREEHOLD TOWNSHIP..............	159	111	5	186	87	2
GLADE TOWNSHIP.................	507	281	2	538	236	5
LIMESTONE TOWNSHIP	71	40		76	34	
MEAD TOWNSHIP	248	200	8	266	177	4
PINE GROVE TOWNSHIP.............	487	362	14	512	321	13
PITTSFIELD TOWNSHIP	183	164	3	207	141	1

	GOVERNOR/LT. GOVERNOR			U.S. SENATE		
	Republican Scranton/ Fisher	Democratic Casey/ Singel	Consumer Hoover/ Brickhouse	Republican Arlen Specter	Democratic Bob Edgar	Consumer Lance S. Haver
PLEASANT TOWNSHIP	545	351	5	594	291	8
SHEFFIELD TOWNSHIP	351	436	9	412	355	6
SOUTHWEST TOWNSHIP	69	43	2	80	33	2
SPRING CREEK TOWNSHIP	137	53		139	53	
SUGAR GROVE TOWNSHIP	199	162	4	200	145	2
SUGAR GROVE BOROUGH...........	138	75	2	134	72	2
TIDIOUTE BOROUGH	156	97	3	158	84	5
TRIUMPH TOWNSHIP	46	22	1	53	15	2
WARREN BOROUGH	2,293	1,505	34	2,467	1,236	23
WARD 01	310	138	5	311	128	3
WARD 03	139	59	5	148	53	
WARD 04	103	192		130	153	
WARD 05	435	226	6	470	173	3
WARD 06	329	283	7	371	217	9
WARD 07	138	120	3	148	107	2
WARD 08	211	186		245	133	
WARD 09	174	126	4	174	121	2
WARD 10	454	175	4	470	151	4
WATSON TOWNSHIP	16	47	2	20	43	2
YOUNGSVILLE BOROUGH	369	247	3	397	199	6
WARREN COUNTY TOTALS	**7,641**	**5,527**	**134**	**8,237**	**4,672**	**109**
WASHINGTON COUNTY						
ALLENPORT BOROUGH	28	208	2	64	175	
AMWELL TOWNSHIP	487	425	5	582	338	2
BEALLSVILLE BOROUGH	62	89	2	84	69	
BENTLEYVILLE BOROUGH............	193	685	6	310	568	7
BLAINE TOWNSHIP	100	86	1	117	69	1
BUFFALO TOWNSHIP	320	254	5	371	200	4
BURGETTSTOWN BOROUGH..........	211	322	6	274	264	3
CALIFORNIA BOROUGH	381	896	13	562	723	3
CANONSBURG BOROUGH............	704	2,319	20	998	2,020	15
WARD 01	167	921	9	270	822	5
WARD 02	325	681	7	411	590	4
WARD 03	212	717	4	317	608	6
CANTON TOWNSHIP	845	1,548	19	1,189	1,232	16
CARROLL TOWNSHIP	700	1,375	16	1,010	1,078	14
CECIL TOWNSHIP	581	1,488	21	855	1,225	13
CENTERVILLE BOROUGH	315	986	5	541	771	2
CHARLEROI BOROUGH	560	1,268	17	815	1,036	8
CHARTIERS TOWNSHIP	735	1,510	10	990	1,256	12
CLAYSVILLE BOROUGH	135	73	1	147	64	1
COAL CENTER BOROUGH	12	59		20	52	
COKEBURG BOROUGH	48	236		91	187	2
CROSS CREEK TOWNSHIP...........	175	295	1	206	260	2
DEEMSTON BOROUGH..............	74	135	2	113	99	2
DONEGAL TOWNSHIP...............	336	288	3	414	211	4
DONORA BOROUGH................	502	1,672	13	735	1,455	4
DUNLEVY BOROUGH	31	152	1	63	120	1
EAST BETHLEHEM TOWNSHIP	164	841	3	351	656	4
WARD 01	39	210		73	177	
WARD 02	59	275	2	121	214	1
WARD 03	29	154	1	73	108	2
WARD 04	37	202		84	157	1
EAST FINLEY TOWNSHIP	139	115	3	165	90	4
EAST WASHINGTON BOROUGH........	531	235	6	559	219	3
ELCO BOROUGH..................	32	100		47	85	
ELLSWORTH BOROUGH.............	71	286	4	134	224	1
FALLOWFIELD TOWNSHIP	550	1,235	13	812	976	8
FINLEYVILLE BOROUGH	45	67	1	59	53	
GREEN HILLS BOROUGH.............	5	2		7		
HANOVER TOWNSHIP	302	298	2	377	229	2
HOPEWELL TOWNSHIP..............	150	109	2	183	80	4
HOUSTON BOROUGH...............	164	301	5	222	246	1
INDEPENDENCE TOWNSHIP	156	259	3	213	205	
JEFFERSON TOWNSHIP	124	211	2	181	157	2
LONG BRANCH BOROUGH...........	42	133	3	75	101	2
MARIANNA BOROUGH	27	172	1	64	133	2
MC DONALD BOROUGH	203	283	7	256	242	6
(BALANCE IN ALLEGHENY CO.)						

	GOVERNOR/LT. GOVERNOR			U.S. SENATE		
	Republican Scranton/ Fisher	Democratic Casey/ Singel	Consumer Hoover/ Brickhouse	Republican Arlen Specter	Democratic Bob Edgar	Consumer Lance S. Haver
MIDWAY BOROUGH.................	108	201	2	159	153	1
MONONGAHELA CITY...............	460	1,276	7	704	1,040	4
WARD 01.......................	83	301	1	134	247	2
WARD 02.......................	166	509	4	264	414	1
WARD 03.......................	211	466	2	306	379	1
MORRIS TOWNSHIP	198	106	3	227	81	3
MT. PLEASANT TOWNSHIP	416	679	13	570	535	7
NEW EAGLE BOROUGH	159	507	5	263	410	2
NORTH BETHLEHEM TOWNSHIP.......	212	246	4	267	191	2
NORTH CHARLEROI BOROUGH	161	403	7	248	316	5
NORTH FRANKLIN TOWNSHIP	904	779	16	1,030	657	10
NORTH STRABANE TOWNSHIP	927	1,389	18	1,204	1,114	20
NOTTINGHAM TOWNSHIP	279	302	9	363	226	7
PETERS TOWNSHIP	2,892	1,287	36	3,212	962	32
ROBINSON TOWNSHIP	196	372	8	285	286	5
ROSCOE BOROUGH	98	260	2	140	217	2
SMITH TOWNSHIP	321	1,140	18	500	979	7
SOMERSET TOWNSHIP..............	329	518	6	441	411	5
SOUTH FRANKLIN TOWNSHIP	407	346	7	500	265	1
SOUTH STRABANE TOWNSHIP	1,336	1,078	19	1,582	831	13
SPEERS BOROUGH	221	284	2	294	213	1
STOCKDALE BOROUGH	27	171	1	43	157	1
TWILIGHT BOROUGH	30	58		30	56	
UNION TOWNSHIP.................	678	1,217	22	1,035	874	18
WASHINGTON CITY	1,781	2,396	40	2,223	2,084	22
WARD 01.......................	34	41	3	39	38	2
WARD 02.......................	111	197	3	151	158	4
WARD 03.......................	58	123	3	69	112	1
WARD 04.......................	71	79	4	82	75	1
WARD 05.......................	327	360	6	412	375	3
WARD 06.......................	377	413	5	427	365	4
WARD 07.......................	600	869	10	793	687	6
WARD 08.......................	203	314	6	250	274	1
WEST ALEXANDER BOROUGH	43	44		57	31	
WEST BETHLEHEM TOWNSHIP	146	313		230	225	2
WEST BROWNSVILLE BOROUGH	78	334	2	161	249	2
WEST FINLEY TOWNSHIP...........	181	81	3	194	71	2
WEST MIDDLETOWN BOROUGH	45	37		53	28	1
WEST PIKE RUN TOWNSHIP..........	155	463	7	253	367	3
WASHINGTON COUNTY TOTALS	**23,028**	**37,303**	**481**	**30,524**	**30,197**	**333**
WAYNE COUNTY						
BERLIN TOWNSHIP	258	194		344	105	2
BETHANY BOROUGH	69	37		88	16	
BUCKINGHAM TOWNSHIP	91	87	1	106	61	2
CANAAN TOWNSHIP	88	118	1	160	44	1
CHERRY RIDGE TOWNSHIP	191	163	4	257	85	6
CLINTON TOWNSHIP...............	217	323	4	317	204	2
DAMASCUS TOWNSHIP	481	237	7	537	161	7
DREHER TOWNSHIP	161	100		206	45	2
DYBERRY TOWNSHIP................	174	122	1	221	68	1
HAWLEY BOROUGH	171	172	2	233	96	1
HONESDALE BOROUGH..............	843	752	14	1,097	447	15
LAKE TOWNSHIP	367	347	6	550	141	8
LEBANON TOWNSHIP	73	53	1	87	36	
LEHIGH TOWNSHIP	133	156	5	179	98	4
MANCHESTER TOWNSHIP	124	69		146	36	1
MT. PLEASANT TOWNSHIP	166	241	6	233	158	7
OREGON TOWNSHIP................	94	52	1	113	31	1
PALMYRA TOWNSHIP	164	127	2	201	82	3
PAUPACK TOWNSHIP	319	232	6	385	152	5
PRESTON TOWNSHIP	196	140	5	217	113	3
PROMPTON BOROUGH.	69	43		74	27	3
SALEM TOWNSHIP	351	276	3	468	143	5
SCOTT TOWNSHIP.................	59	32	5	60	27	2
SOUTH CANAAN TOWNSHIP	148	200	7	257	85	5
STARRUCCA BOROUGH	65	26		74	15	
STERLING TOWNSHIP................	116	77	2	152	44	1
TEXAS TOWNSHIP.................	352	328	8	482	174	7
WAYMART BOROUGH	178	182	2	243	100	3
WAYNE COUNTY TOTALS	**5,718**	**4,886**	**93**	**7,487**	**2,794**	**97**

	GOVERNOR/LT. GOVERNOR			U.S. SENATE		
	Republican Scranton/ Fisher	Democratic Casey/ Singel	Consumer Hoover/ Brickhouse	Republican Arlen Specter	Democratic Bob Edgar	Consumer Lance S. Haver
WESTMORELAND COUNTY						
ADAMSBURG BOROUGH	27	35	2	43	18	2
ALLEGHENY TOWNSHIP	651	1,225	12	819	1,021	18
ARNOLD CITY	329	1,548	22	471	1,333	21
WARD 01	54	409	7	75	378	6
WARD 02	275	1,139	15	396	955	15
ARONA BOROUGH	36	60	3	47	46	2
AVONMORE BOROUGH	69	278	3	102	245	3
BELL TOWNSHIP	185	422	3	277	319	8
BOLIVAR BOROUGH	54	113		74	87	1
COOK TOWNSHIP	255	189	4	309	139	7
DELMONT BOROUGH	261	245	9	318	190	5
DERRY TOWNSHIP	929	2,458	38	1,298	2,036	26
DERRY BOROUGH	321	477	10	414	375	5
WARD 01	124	152	3	155	117	
WARD 02	74	141	3	103	112	1
WARD 03	64	94	1	80	74	2
WARD 04	59	90	3	76	72	2
DONEGAL TOWNSHIP	226	222	12	285	164	9
DONEGAL BOROUGH	21	24	1	26	17	
EAST HUNTINGDON TOWNSHIP	745	1,022	28	917	831	28
EAST VANDERGRIFT BOROUGH	39	253	3	74	216	2
EXPORT BOROUGH	78	266	4	111	231	4
FAIRFIELD TOWNSHIP	258	322	7	312	259	10
GREENSBURG CITY	2,190	2,283	36	2,625	1,783	40
WARD 01	342	341	4	410	265	2
WARD 02	890	635	10	1,031	481	6
WARD 03	79	84	1	88	72	2
WARD 04	76	88	1	94	63	4
WARD 05	197	381	8	256	310	10
WARD 06	35	95		41	88	2
WARD 07	351	387	6	438	290	12
WARD 08	220	272	6	267	214	2
HEMPFIELD TOWNSHIP	5,137	5,649	106	6,304	4,377	113
HUNKER BOROUGH	42	47	1	52	34	2
HYDE PARK BOROUGH	32	138	3	49	117	2
IRWIN BOROUGH	632	611	11	764	451	14
WARD 01	51	55		58	47	
WARD 02	48	72		67	46	5
WARD 03	67	71	1	89	50	
WARD 04	57	99	1	77	73	4
WARD 05	170	148	2	191	121	3
WARD 06	109	72		125	52	
WARD 07	130	94	7	157	62	2
JEANNETTE CITY	1,059	2,071	43	1,406	1,658	30
WARD 01	50	121	4	66	101	4
WARD 02	229	267	8	261	229	2
WARD 03	168	406	6	236	321	4
WARD 04	35	108	2	60	81	3
WARD 05	283	756	14	416	600	9
WARD 06	294	413	9	367	326	8
LATROBE BOROUGH	1,002	1,648	10	1,226	1,386	11
WARD 01	212	483	2	282	403	4
WARD 02	173	127	3	198	99	2
WARD 03	232	276	1	253	244	3
WARD 04	185	291	1	233	240	
WARD 05	129	259	1	168	209	
WARD 06	71	212	2	92	191	2
LAUREL MOUNTAIN BOROUGH	44	29	3	44	31	2
LIGONIER TOWNSHIP	1,263	832	13	1,355	713	16
LIGONIER BOROUGH	437	213	7	448	205	7
LOWER BURRELL CITY	1,244	2,574	41	1,512	2,205	46
WARD 01	510	902	17	589	796	19
WARD 02	394	822	9	481	698	11
WARD 03	258	592	9	319	498	14
WARD 04	82	258	6	123	213	2
LOYALHANNA TOWNSHIP	166	299	6	233	224	6
MADISON BOROUGH	87	79	2	104	61	1
MANOR BOROUGH	214	326	8	288	251	2
MONESSEN CITY	673	3,756	41	1,028	3,312	47

	GOVERNOR/LT. GOVERNOR				U.S. SENATE		
	Republican Scranton/ Fisher	Democratic Casey/ Singel	Consumer Hoover/ Brickhouse		Republican Arlen Specter	Democratic Bob Edgar	Consumer Lance S. Haver
WARD 01	320	1,529	12		458	1,352	11
WARD 02	83	517	9		114	471	10
WARD 03	97	765	11		163	689	18
WARD 04	173	945	9		293	800	8
MT. PLEASANT TOWNSHIP	1,060	1,825	35		1,365	1,442	44
MT. PLEASANT BOROUGH	434	960	22		600	776	20
WARD 01	131	241	9		184	188	3
WARD 02	189	424	9		262	338	11
WARD 03	114	295	4		154	250	6
MURRYSVILLE BOROUGH	3,241	1,737	34		3,421	1,406	32
NEW ALEXANDRIA BOROUGH	135	113	2		157	88	1
NEW FLORENCE BOROUGH	113	140	2		139	112	3
NEW KENSINGTON CITY..............	1,531	3,586	65		1,832	3,104	68
WARD 02	33	155	9		41	137	8
WARD 03	317	1,014	11		409	888	11
WARD 04	699	1,547	23		856	1,319	31
WARD 05	71	194	1		74	175	2
WARD 06	103	191	7		105	174	7
WARD 07	308	485	14		347	411	9
NEW STANTON BOROUGH	270	267	7		326	196	9
NORTH BELLE VERNON BOROUGH	176	545	10		249	465	2
NORTH HUNTINGDON TOWNSHIP	3,540	5,298	83		4,629	4,080	76
WARD 01	567	906	18		718	728	11
WARD 02	527	855	15		700	676	5
WARD 03	475	691	9		639	509	13
WARD 04	551	764	12		737	557	13
WARD 05	413	702	6		562	548	4
WARD 06	586	668	8		701	525	15
WARD 07	421	712	15		572	537	15
NORTH IRWIN BOROUGH.............	84	186	6		132	139	1
OKLAHOMA BOROUGH...............	80	187	3		112	140	5
PENN TOWNSHIP...................	1,752	2,440	46		2,227	1,908	44
WARD 01	307	403	9		394	298	9
WARD 02	358	611	12		435	539	7
WARD 03	301	472	6		399	364	7
WARD 04	337	437	8		413	348	8
WARD 05	449	517	11		586	359	13
PENN BOROUGH....................	27	113	2		44	86	4
ROSTRAVER TOWNSHIP..............	1,036	2,142	35		1,347	1,788	40
SALEM TOWNSHIP	872	1,208	18		1,103	945	20
SCOTTDALE BOROUGH	626	776	18		746	631	14
WARD 01	147	149	1		164	125	1
WARD 02	222	258	5		265	214	3
WARD 03	165	158	6		191	125	3
WARD 04	92	211	6		126	167	
SEWARD BOROUGH	42	119	3		77	81	1
SEWICKLEY TOWNSHIP	630	1,316	32		834	1,088	25
SMITHTON BOROUGH	61	104	1		80	87	
SOUTH GREENSBURG BOROUGH	219	467	11		321	362	9
SOUTH HUNTINGDON TOWNSHIP......	481	1,302	26		655	1,098	22
SOUTHWEST GREENSBURG BOROUGH	385	431	8		451	361	7
ST. CLAIR TOWNSHIP	140	278	2		165	238	7
SUTERSVILLE BOROUGH.............	63	153	3		86	129	3
TRAFFORD BOROUGH	410	825	17		555	642	19
(BALANCE IN ALLEGHENY CO.)							
UNITY TOWNSHIP	2,156	3,037	42		2,211	2,428	33
UPPER BURRELL TOWNSHIP..........	154	344	13		234	262	5
VANDERGRIFT BOROUGH	576	1,474	14		746	1,287	14
WARD 01	61	99	3		67	90	2
WARD 02	129	217	2		156	195	1
WARD 03	171	247	2		200	208	4
WARD 04	55	196	2		83	164	4
WARD 05	86	335	1		118	301	
WARD 06	74	380	4		122	329	3
WASHINGTON TOWNSHIP.............	805	875	15		969	692	9
WEST LEECHBURG BOROUGH........	92	378	8		114	354	8
WEST NEWTON BOROUGH	314	581	10		402	480	7
WARD 01	135	195	2		164	162	3
WARD 02	60	192	3		94	154	1
WARD 03	119	194	5		144	164	3

	GOVERNOR/LT. GOVERNOR			U.S. SENATE		
	Republican Scranton/ Fisher	Democratic Casey/ Singel	Consumer Hoover/ Brickhouse	Republican Arlen Specter	Democratic Bob Edgar	Consumer Lance S. Haver
YOUNGSTOWN BOROUGH............	40	45	1	49	33	1
YOUNGWOOD BOROUGH.............	468	507	14	567	382	12
WESTMORELAND COUNTY TOTALS ...	**40,719**	**63,473**	**1,100**	**50,280**	**51,645**	**1,055**
WYOMING COUNTY						
BRAINTRIM TOWNSHIP...............	83	61	1	117	33	
CLINTON TOWNSHIP.................	138	134	3	210	66	1
EATON TOWNSHIP...................	201	201	3	291	112	2
EXETER TOWNSHIP	92	120	140	73	2	
FACTORYVILLE BOROUGH............	194	143	2	263	72	3
WARD 01	103	65	2	134	36	
WARD 02	91	78		129	36	3
FALLS TOWNSHIP	282	269	8	410	150	1
WARD 01	104	103	5	151	59	
WARD 02	178	166	3	259	91	1
FORKSTON TOWNSHIP...............	54	46	63	34		
LACEYVILLE BOROUGH..............	111	55	3	143	28	
LEMON TOWNSHIP	165	146	3	250	68	1
MEHOOPANY TOWNSHIP	140	130	2	208	63	
MESHOPPEN TOWNSHIP	113	98	5	152	60	3
MESHOPPEN BOROUGH	59	42	77	23		
MONROE TOWNSHIP	249	203	5	338	124	4
NICHOLSON TOWNSHIP	185	152	4	273	67	
NICHOLSON BOROUGH	157	117	3	211	66	2
WARD 01	60	56	1	94	24	
WARD 02	97	61	2	117	42	2
NORTH BRANCH TOWNSHIP	43	29		53	17	
NORTHMORELAND TOWNSHIP	182	198	3	283	98	4
NOXEN TOWNSHIP	122	136	3	174	87	3
OVERFIELD TOWNSHIP..............	202	241	2	305	134	
TUNKHANNOCK TOWNSHIP...........	498	429	5	719	215	3
TUNKHANNOCK BOROUGH...........	413	351	4	577	188	4
WARD 01	58	80	2	94	44	1
WARD 02	149	105	1	195	60	
WARD 03	105	66		123	45	1
WARD 04	101	100	1	165	39	2
WASHINGTON TOWNSHIP............	173	179	1	276	82	
WINDHAM TOWNSHIP...............	146	103	2	198	54	2
WYOMING COUNTY TOTALS:..........	**4,002**	**3,583**	**62**	**5,731**	**1,914**	**35**
YORK COUNTY						
CARROLL TOWNSHIP	645	305	8	712	230	11
CHANCEFORD TOWNSHIP	573	398	9	633	332	2
CODORUS TOWNSHIP	431	284	13	475	229	14
CONEWAGO TOWNSHIP	506	396	19	573	322	10
CROSS ROADS BOROUGH...........	49	23		53	21	1
DALLASTOWN BOROUGH.............	515	376	10	555	339	7
DELTA BOROUGH...................	106	66	1	107	66	1
DILLSBURG BOROUGH..............	388	178	6	392	161	3
DOVER TOWNSHIP	1,703	1,260	33	1,939	1,030	28
DOVER BOROUGH	195	165	2	204	162	1
EAST HOPEWELL TOWNSHIP	190	121	6	209	103	5
EAST MANCHESTER TOWNSHIP	492	313	9	548	255	3
EAST PROSPECT BOROUGH..........	121	43	2	139	28	3
FAIRVIEW TOWNSHIP	2,084	1,157	31	2,363	879	21
FAWN TOWNSHIP...................	225	101	3	222	99	4
FAWN GROVE BOROUGH	83	57	5	91	46	3
FELTON BOROUGH	98	38		117	26	
FRANKLIN TOWNSHIP...............	455	188	3	468	150	6
FRANKLINTOWN BOROUGH..........	49	27	1	58	18	2
GLEN ROCK BOROUGH	225	143	3	220	143	1
GOLDSBORO BOROUGH	53	62		64	56	
HALLAM BOROUGH.................	180	130		188	114	2
HANOVER BOROUGH	2,320	1,338	35	2,427	1,228	21
WARD 01	456	252	8	490	220	2
WARD 02	776	358	7	796	328	5
WARD 03	391	259	11	412	247	7
WARD 04	307	221	4	327	205	4
WARD 05	390	248	5	402	228	3
HEIDELBERG TOWNSHIP............	287	220	6	298	211	2

	GOVERNOR/LT. GOVERNOR			U.S. SENATE		
	Republican Scranton/ Fisher	Democratic Casey/ Singel	Consumer Hoover/ Brickhouse	Republican Arlen Specter	Democratic Bob Edgar	Consumer Lance S. Haver
HELLAM TOWNSHIP	704	460	9	768	384	5
HOPEWELL TOWNSHIP.............	295	192	7	307	164	8
JACKSON TOWNSHIP	702	507	11	746	442	11
JACOBUS BOROUGH	275	189	5	334	137	3
JEFFERSON BOROUGH	130	81	5	139	66	5
LEWISBERRY BOROUGH	59	45		68	34	
LOGANVILLE BOROUGH.............	177	65	8	177	70	1
LOWER CHANCEFORD TOWNSHIP	296	235	7	331	203	2
LOWER WINDSOR TOWNSHIP	689	418	5	789	300	12
MANCHESTER TOWNSHIP	1,212	772	13	1,448	615	17
MANCHESTER BOROUGH	280	197	8	333	133	3
MANHEIM TOWNSHIP	243	190	10	264	167	6
MONAGHAN TOWNSHIP	369	189	3	401	150	7
MT. WOLF BOROUGH	282	176	1	307	154	2
NEW FREEDOM BOROUGH	359	186	8	387	145	9
NEW SALEM BOROUGH	115	80	5	125	68	2
NEWBERRY TOWNSHIP	1,311	874	26	1,475	694	25
NORTH CODORUS TOWNSHIP........	872	670	22	991	539	17
NORTH HOPEWELL TOWNSHIP.......	245	151	7	280	107	8
NORTH YORK BOROUGH	236	200	5	254	184	2
PARADISE TOWNSHIP...............	290	223	8	331	184	9
PEACH BOTTOM TOWNSHIP	260	185	12	294	145	13
PENN TOWNSHIP...................	1,156	810	22	1,232	731	12
RAILROAD BOROUGH...............	42	41	2	48	36	1
RED LION BOROUGH	875	585	13	925	505	15
SEVEN VALLEYS BOROUGH...........	77	52		82	44	
SHREWSBURY TOWNSHIP............	619	351	8	647	304	9
SHREWSBURY BOROUGH....	398	242	5	424	206	3
SPRING GARDEN TOWNSHIP.........	2,588	1,217	25	2,710	1,083	10
WARD 01	438	221	5	454	200	2
WARD 02	347	217	5	361	205	3
WARD 03	742	275	6	768	247	1
WARD 04	521	168	4	530	153	1
WARD 05	540	336	5	597	278	3
SPRING GROVE BOROUGH	246	214	2	247	196	5
SPRINGETTSBURY TOWNSHIP	3,920	2,513	66	4,340	2,078	46
SPRINGFIELD TOWNSHIP............	606	321	12	660	265	7
STEWARTSTOWN BOROUGH.........	226	130	3	221	130	3
WARRINGTON TOWNSHIP	569	327	4	615	268	7
WASHINGTON TOWNSHIP...........	327	201	12	363	175	4
WELLSVILLE BOROUGH	55	32	1	52	33	1
WEST MANCHESTER TOWNSHIP	2,252	1,552	31	2,488	1,296	28
WEST MANHEIM TOWNSHIP	663	363	6	698	327	8
WEST YORK BOROUGH	608	629	15	680	555	14
WINDSOR TOWNSHIP	1,331	815	20	1,523	610	15
WINDSOR BOROUGH	131	113	3	145	95	1
WINTERSTOWN BOROUGH	70	58	1	73	51	
WRIGHTSVILLE BOROUGH	330	222	4	376	175	3
WARD 01	69	61		89	44	
WARD 02	53	41	2	62	32	2
WARD 03	208	120	2	225	99	1
YOE BOROUGH	131	75	6	153	58	
YORK CITY	3,605	3,929	112	3,821	3,636	96
WARD 01	104	144	5	106	137	7
WARD 05	165	154	4	151	172	2
WARD 06	87	190	9	88	176	7
WARD 07	135	167	4	137	153	3
WARD 08	186	376	9	219	338	8
WARD 09	329	382	14	360	331	13
WARD 11	494	367	16	500	349	11
WARD 12	673	879	28	751	809	12
WARD 13	107	196	4	129	169	5
WARD 14	962	793	16	1,038	710	18
WARD 15	363	281	3	342	292	10
YORK TOWNSHIP.................	3,433	1,759	39	3,672	1,505	23
WARD 01	695	351	9	742	288	6
WARD 02	705	374	6	756	329	3
WARD 03	636	296	8	677	252	4
WARD 04	552	279	10	573	258	4
WARD 05	845	459	6	924	378	6
YORK HAVEN BOROUGH	47	52		62	33	2
YORKANA BOROUGH	54	24		54	22	
YORK COUNTY TOTALS	45,733	30,301	802	49,915	25,750	631
STATE TOTALS......................	1,636,500	1,716,234	32,809	1,902,770	1,446,775	23,441

POPULAR VOTE OF PENNSYLVANIA
FOR PRESIDENT SINCE 1952*

Tuesday, November 4, 1952

Dwight D. Eisenhower (Republican)	2,415,789
Adlai E. Stevenson (Democrat)	2,146,269
Stuart Hamblen (Prohibition)	8,771
Vincent Hallinan (Progressive)	4,200
Darlington Hoopes (Socialist)	2,684
Eric Hass (Indus. Gov.)	1,347
Farrell Dobbs (Militant Workers)	1,502

Tuesday, November 6, 1956

Adlai E. Stevenson (Democrat)	1,981,769
Dwight D. Eisenhower (Republican)	2,585,252
Eric Hass (Socialist Labor)	7,447
Farrell Dobbs (Militant Workers)	2,035

Tuesday, November 8, 1960

John F. Kennedy (Democrat)	2,556,282
Richard M. Nixon (Republican)	2,439,956
Eric Hass (Socialist Labor)	7,185
Farrell Dobbs (Militant Workers)	2,678

Tuesday, November 3, 1964

Barry Goldwater (Republican)	1,673,657
Lyndon B. Johnson (Democrat)	3,130,954
Clifton DeBerry (Militant Workers)	10,456
Eric Hass (Socialist Labor)	5,092
All Others (Scattering)	2,531

Tuesday, November 6, 1968

Hubert Humphrey (Democrat)	2,259,405
Richard M. Nixon (Republican)	2,090,017
George C. Wallace (Amer.-Ind.)	378,582
Dick Gregory (Peace & Freedom)	7,821
All Others	12,103

*For figures from 1789 to 1948, see Volume 101, 1972-73.

Tuesday, November 7, 1972

Richard M. Nixon (Republican)	2,714,521
George McGovern (Democrat)	1,796,951
Schmidt-Anderson (Const.)	70,593
Jenness-Pulley (Socialist Workers)	4,639
Hall-Tyner (Communist)	2,686
All Others	2,715

Tuesday, November 2, 1976

James E. Carter (Democrat)	2,328,677
Gerald R. Ford (Republican)	2,205,604
Maddox-Dyke (Const.)	25,344
Camejo-Reid (Socialist Workers)	3,009
Hall-Tyner (Communist)	1,891
LaRouche-Evans (Labor)	2,744
McCarthy-Wheaton (McCarthy '76)	50,584
All Others	2,934

Tuesday, November 4, 1980

Ronald Reagan (Republican)	2,261,872
Jimmy Carter (Democrat)	1,937,540
DeBerry-Zimmerman (Socialist Workers)	20,291
Commoner-Harris (Consumer)	10,430
Anderson-Lucey (Anderson Coalition)	292,921
Hall-Davis (Communist USA)	5,184
Clark-Koch (Libertarian)	33,263

Tuesday, November 6, 1984

Ronald Reagan (Republican)	2,584,323
Walter F. Mondale (Democrat)	2,228,131
Johnson-Thorn (Consumer)	21,628
Bergland-Lewis (Libertarian)	6,982
Hall-Davis (Communist, USA)	1,780
Winn-Halyard (Workers League)	2,059

ELECTORAL VOTE OF PENNSYLVANIA
SINCE 1957*

FORTY-THIRD TERM
January 20, 1957 to January 20, 1961   **(32 electors)**
President — Dwight D. Eisenhower, Pennsylvania. 32
Vice President — Richard M. Nixon, California 32
    Dwight D. Eisenhower reelected President, and Richard M. Nixon, Vice President.

FORTY-FOURTH TERM
January 20, 1961 to January 20, 1965   **(32 electors)**
President — John F. Kennedy, Massachusetts 32
Vice President — Lyndon B. Johnson, Texas. 32
    John F. Kennedy elected President, and Lyndon B. Johnson elected Vice President.

FORTH-FIFTH TERM
January 20, 1965 to January 20, 1969   **(29 electors)**
President — Lyndon B. Johnson, Texas. .29
Vice President — Hubert H. Humphrey, Minnesota 29
    Lyndon B. Johnson elected President, and Hubert H. Humphrey elected Vice President.

FORTY-SIXTH TERM
January 20, 1969 to January 20, 1973   **(29 electors)**
President — Hubert H. Humphrey, Minnesota 29
Vice President — Edmund Muskie, Maine 29
    Richard M. Nixon elected President, and Spiro T. Agnew elected Vice President.

FORTY-SEVENTH TERM
January 20, 1973 to January 20, 1977   **(27 electors)**
President — Richard M. Nixon, California 27
Vice President — Sprio T. Agnew, Maryland 27
    Richard M. Nixon reelected President, and Spiro T. Agnew, Vice President.

FORTY-EIGHTH TERM
January 20, 1977 to January 20, 1981   **(27 electors)**
President — James E. Carter, Georgia. 27
Vice President — Walter F. Mondale, Minnesota 27
    James E. Carter elected President, and Walter F. Mondale elected Vice President.

*For figures from First to Forty-Second Terms, see Volume 101, 1972-73.

FORTY-NINTH TERM
January 20, 1981 to January 20, 1985   (27 electors)
President — Ronald Reagan, California. 27
Vice President — George Bush, Texas. 27
    Ronald Reagan elected President and George Bush elected Vice
    President.

FIFTIETH TERM
January 20, 1985 to January 20, 1989   (25 electors)
President — Ronald Reagan, California. 25
Vice President — George Bush, Texas. 25
    Ronald Reagan reelected President and George Bush, Vice
    President.

VOTE FOR GOVERNOR OF PENNSYLVANIA
SINCE 1902*

Year	Candidate / Party	Votes
1902	Samuel W. Pennypacker	593,328
	Republican	592,867
	Citizens	461
	Robert E. Pattison	450,978
	Democrat	436,451
	Anti-Machine	9,550
	Ballot Reform	4,977
	Silas C. Swallow, Proh.	23,327
	William Adams, Soc. Lab.	5,155
	J. W. Slayton, Soc.	21,910
	Scattering	73
1906	Edwin S. Stuart	506,418
	Republican	501,818
	Citizens	4,600
	Lewis Emery Jr	458,054
	Democrat	301,747
	Commonwealth	6,194
	Lincoln	145,657
	Referendum	781
	Union Labor	3,675
	Homer L. Castle, Proh.	24,793
	James A. Maurer, Soc.	15,169
	John Desmond, Soc. Lab.	2,109
	Scattering	34
1910	John K. Tener	415,614
	Republican	412,658
	Workingmen's League.	2,956
	Webster Grim, Democrat	129,395
	Madison F. Larkin, Proh.	17,445
	John W. Slayton, Soc.	53,055
	George Anton, Indus.	802
	William H. Berry, Keystone	382,127
	Scattering	10
1914	Martin G. Brumbaugh	588,705
	Republican	532,902
	Keystone	30,847
	Personal Liberty	17,956
	Vance C. McCormick	453,380
	Democrat	313,553
	Washington	140,327
	Joseph B. Allen, Soc.	40,115
	Charles N. Brumm, Bull Moose	4,031
	William Draper Lewis, Rosvlt-Prog.	6,503
	Matthew H. Stevenson, Proh.	17,467
	Caleb Harrison, Indus.	533
	Scattering	18
1918	William C. Sproul	552,537
	Republican	547,923
	Washington	4,614
	Eugene C. Bonniwell	305,315
	Democrat	295,718
	Fair Play	9,597
	Charles Sehl, Soc.	18,714
	E. J. Fithian, Proh.	27,359
	Robert C. Macauley, S.T.	1,077
	Scattering	33
1922	Gifford Pinchot, Republican	831,696
	John A. McSparran, Democrat	581,625
	Lilith Martin Wilson, Soc.	31,748
	William Repp, Proh	14,151
	William H. Thomas, Indus.	3,137
	John W. Dix, S.T.	2,246
	Scattering	69
1926	John S. Fisher, Republican	1,102,823
	Eugene C. Bonniwell	365,280
	Democrat	349,134
	Labor	16,146
	John W. Slayton, Soc.	11,795
	George E. Pennock, Proh.	19,524
	Julian P. Hichok, Com. Land	922
	H. W. Hicks, W.	3,256
	Scattering	68
1930	Gifford Pinchot	1,068,874
	Republican	1,036,605
	Prohibition	31,909
	Independent	462
	John M. Hemphill	1,010,204
	Democrat	643,170
	Liberal	366,572
	Independent	462
	Frank Mozer, Com.	5,267
	James H. Maurer, Soc.	21,036
	Scattering	64
1934	George H. Earle, Democrat	1,476,467
	Wm. A. Schnader, Republican	1,410,138
	Jesse H. Holmes, Soc.	42,417
	Herbert T. Ames, Proh.	13,521
	Emmett Patrick Cush, Com.	5,584
	Bess Gyekis, Indus. Lab.	2,272
	Scattering	47
1938	Arthur H. James, Republican	2,035,340
	Charles Alvin Jones	1,756,192
	Democrat	1,745,377
	Royal Oak	10,748
	Non-Partisan	59
	No Party	8
	Jesse H. Holmes, Socialist	12,635
	Robert G. Burnham, Proh.	6,438
	Ella Bloor Omholt, Com.	1,273
	Scattering	89
1942	Edward Martin, Republican	1,367,531
	F. Clair Ross, Democrat	1,149,897
	Dale H. Learn, Prohibition	17,385
	Joseph Pirincin, Soc. Lab.	5,310
	John J. Haluska, United Pension	7,911
	Scattering	37

* For figures from 1802 to 1898, see Volume 101, 1972-73.

1946	James H. Duff, Republican	1,828,462
	John S. Rice, Democrat	1,270,947
	James A. W. Killip, Proh.	13,838
	George S. Taylor, Soc. Lab.	10,747
1950	John S. Fine, Republican	1,796,119
	Richardson Dilworth, Democrat	1,710,355
	Richard R. Blews, Proh.	12,282
	Reginald B. Naugle, G.I.'s Against Communism	7,715
	George S. Taylor, Ind. Gov.	1,645
	Herbert G. Lewin, Mili. Wk.	841
	Thomas J. Fitzpatrick, Prog.	6,097
	Robert Z. Wilson, Socialist	5,005
1954	George M. Leader, Democrat	1,996,266
	Lloyd H. Wood, Republican.	1,717,070
	Henry Beitscher, Prog.	4,471
	Louis Dirle, Soc. Lab.	2,650
1958	David L. Lawrence, Democrat.	2,024,852
	Arthur T. McGonigle, Republican	1,948,769
	Herman A. Johnson, Soc. Lab.	8,677
	Eloise Fickland, Workers.	4,556
1962	William W. Scranton, Republican	2,424,918
	Richardson Dilworth, Democrat	1,938,627
	George S. Taylor, Soc. Lab.	14,340
	Scattering	157

1966	Raymond P. Shafer, Republican	2,110,349
	Milton J. Shapp, Democrat	1,868,719
	Edward S. Swartz, Const.	57,073
	George S. Taylor, Soc. Lab.	14,527
1970	Milton J. Shapp, Democrat	2,043,029
	Raymond Broderick, Republican	1,542,854
	A. J. Watson, Const.	83,406
	Francis McGeever, Amer. Ind.	21,647
	George S. Taylor, Soc. Lab.	3,588
	Scattering	5,541
1974	Milton J. Shapp, Democrat	1,878,252
	Drew Lewis, Republican	1,578,917
	Stephen Depue, Const.	33,691
	Scattering	374
1978	Dick Thornburgh, Republican	1,966,042
	Pete Flaherty, Democrat	1,737,888
	Mark Zola, Independent	20,062
	Lee Frissell, Independent	17,593
1982	Dick Thornburgh, Republican	1,872,784
	Allen E. Ertel, Democrat	1,772,353
	Mark Zola, Socialist Workers.	15,495
	Lee Frissell, Consumer.	13,101
	Richard D. Fuerle, Libertarian.	10,252
1986	Robert P. Casey, Democrat	1,717,484
	William W. Scranton, III, Republican	1,638,268
	Heidi J. Hoover, Consumer	32,523

VOTE FOR UNITED STATES SENATOR
FROM PENNSYLVANIA SINCE 1950*

1950	James H. Duff, Republican	1,820,400
	Francis J. Myers, Democrat	1,694,076
	Earl N. Bergerstock, Proh.	12,618
	Jack Still, G.I.'s Against Com.	8,353
	Frank J. Knotek, Indus. Gov.	1,596
	Clyde A. Turner, Militant W.	1,219
	Lillian R. Narins, Prog.	5,516
	William J. Van Essen, Soc.	4,864
1952	Edward Martin, Republican.	2,331,034
	Guy K. Bard, Democrat.	2,168,546
	Ira S. Sassaman, Proh.	12,150
	William J. Van Essen, Soc.	3,538
	Frank Knotek, Indus. Gov.	1,897
	Anna Chester, Militant W.	2,258
1956	Joseph S. Clark, Democrat	2,268,641
	James H. Duff, Republican	2,250,671
	George S. Taylor, Soc. Lab.	7,922
	Herbert Lewin, Mil. Wkr.	2,640
1958	Hugh Scott, Republican	2,042,586
	George M. Leader, Democrat	1,929,821
	George S. Taylor, Soc. Lab.	10,431
	Ethel Peterson, Workers	5,742
1962	Joseph S. Clark, Democrat	2,238,383
	James E. Van Zandt, Republican	2,134,649
	Arla A. Albaugh, Soc. Lab.	10,387
	Scattering	56
1964	Hugh D. Scott, Republican	2,429,858
	Genevieve Blatt, Democrat.	2,359,223
	Morris Chertov, Mil. W.	7,317
	George S. Taylor, Soc. Lab.	6,881
	Scattering	473
1968	Richard S. Schweiker, Republican	2,399,762
	Joseph S. Clark, Democrat	2,117,662

	Frank W. Gaydosh, Const.	96,742
	Benson Perry, Soc. Lab.	7,198
	Pearl Chertov, Mil. W.	2,743
	Scattering	111
1970	Hugh D. Scott, Republican	1,874,106
	William G. Sesler, Democrat	1,653,774
	Frank Gaydosh, Const.	85,813
	W. Henry MacFarland, Amer. Ind.	18,275
	Herman A. Johansen, Soc. Lab.	4,375
	Robin Maisel, Soc. Work.	3,970
	William R. Mimms, Consumer.	3,932
	Scattering	60
1974	Richard S. Schweiker, Republican	1,843,317
	Pete Flaherty, Democrat	1,596,121
	George W. Shankey Jr., Const.	38,004
	Scattering	370
1976	H. John Heinz III, Republican	2,381,891
	William J. Green, Democrat	2,126,977
	Andrew J. Watson, Constitutional	26,028
	Frederick W. Stanton, Soc. Workers	5,484
	Frank Kinces, Communist.	2,097
	Bernard Salera, Labor.	3,637
	Scattering	239
1980	Arlen Specter, Republican.	2,230,404
	Pete Flaherty, Democrat	2,122,391
	Linda Mohrbacher, Socialist Workers	27,229
	Lee Frissell, Consumer	16,089
	Frank Kinces, Communist USA.	3,334
	David K. Walter, Libertarian.	18,595
1982	John Heinz, Republican	2,136,418
	Cyril H. Wecht, Democrat	1,412,965
	Kip Miriam Dawson, Socialist Workers	18,951
	Liane Norman, Consumer.	16,530
	Barbara I. Karkutt, Libertarian.	19,244
1986	Arlen Specter, Republican.	1,906,537
	Bob Edgar, Democrat	1,448,219
	Lance S. Haver, Consumer	23,470

*For figures from 1920 to 1946, see Volume 101, 1972-73.

DEMOCRATIC VOTER REGISTRATION IN PENNSYLVANIA COUNTIES FOR PRESIDENTIAL ELECTION YEARS: 1956 TO 1984

	1956	1960	1964	1968	1972	1976	1980	1984
Adams	9,857	11,391	10,862	10,099	10,217	11,645	11,031	11,861
Allegheny.	489,688	536,601	534,783	526,631	590,323	531,393	508,655	566,484
Armstrong	16,575	17,693	57,018	15,114	16,137	16,883	15,761	18,127
Beaver	41,563	51,380	16,843	56,606	58,735	63,211	63,259	73,126
Bedford	9,276	10,259	10,351	8,419	7,928	8,317	8,166	9,159
Berks	72,476	79,765	81,702	77,687	78,281	79,100	76,433	77,323
Blair	22,468	24,002	23,125	20,454	20,052	22,258	21,356	21,781
Bradford.	6,716	7,962	8,193	7,720	8,343	8,575	7,899	7,954
Bucks.	41,898	59,559	65,995	68,085	84,832	97,978	100,344	110,884
Butler	17,180	20,532	21,993	22,106	25,513	29,042	31,225	36,343
Cambria	61,460	61,216	56,192	52,394	54,750	53,091	51,759	56,291
Cameron	1,176	1,253	1,356	1,338	1,602	1,846	1,736	1,690
Carbon.	12,846	14,846	14,042	12,640	12,978	13,314	12,715	13,311
Centre	10,650	12,086	12,775	12,772	18,190	22,806	22,086	22,821
Chester	18,918	24,900	28,262	29,101	36,382	40,711	40,467	47,469
Clarion	8,474	8,760	8,775	7,726	9,180	9,385	8,943	9,476
Clearfield	18,719	19,943	19,116	16,158	16,220	17,453	17,508	18,730
Clinton	6,799	7,535	7,490	6,534	7,470	7,867	7,050	6,932
Columbia	14,463	15,666	15,273	13,945	15,310	16,515	15,912	16,074
Crawford	11,752	13,492	13,424	12,799	14,916	16,039	15,829	18,886
Cumberland.	18,509	23,793	23,348	20,494	25,673	31,697	29,893	30,387
Dauphin	29,235	35,541	30,466	23,462	35,768	43,367	37,760	40,131
Delaware	45,817	59,500	67,247	64,406	79,266	88,363	81,855	83,284
Elk	9,535	10,243	10,001	9,215	9,316	9,492	10,222	10,580
Erie	49,788	59,559	63,984	61,748	73,213	78,501	73,357	81,354
Fayette.	58,273	59,147	54,847	51,183	50,965	52,587	49,169	55,653
Forest	978	1,154	1,031	808	1,002	1,188	1,130	1,139
Franklin	16,005	18,690	18,467	17,949	18,513	18,754	18,337	18,903
Fulton.	2,728	2,885	2,695	2,458	2,643	2,678	2,688	2,932
Greene.	15,728	15,422	14,585	12,950	12,965	13,349	13,203	14,683
Huntingdon	5,489	6,162	6,192	5,263	6,176	6,341	6,506	7,125
Indiana.	15,573	16,720	15,583	13,156	15,656	17,378	17,311	20,350
Jefferson	9,705	11,380	9,910	8,563	9,348	9,339	9,180	9,263
Juniata.	3,909	4,073	3,956	3,483	3,808	4,045	3,764	4,020
Lackawanna	92,141	97,825	93,030	85,162	88,882	87,794	80,800	82,252
Lancaster.	29,657	34,144	36,178	35,315	38,706	40,138	40,505	47,235
Lawrence.	19,569	23,379	24,098	22,207	24,547	26,931	26,626	32,333
Lebanon.	12,287	13,738	12,739	11,567	11,736	13,173	13,272	14,014
Lehigh	44,902	52,079	55,207	55,438	58,302	60,556	59,867	64,247
Luzerne	59,701	81,763	81,948	77,571	89,679	101,550	101,715	99,632
Lycoming	19,119	23,413	22,499	20,749	21,895	23,197	21,657	21,891
McKean	5,750	7,177	7,389	6,238	7,033	8,269	6,420	6,958
Mercer	26,887	29,207	29,151	28,421	29,802	31,993	29,224	33,244
Mifflin	7,917	8,155	8,317	7,772	8,071	8,290	7,452	7,807
Monroe	11,144	11,720	11,720	10,961	12,084	13,077	13,844	14,879
Montgomery	46,006	61,654	72,734	75,496	92,633	101,853	101,510	104,793
Montour	3,099	3,353	3,344	3,009	3,974	3,886	3,430	3,577
Northampton	56,300	58,172	60,655	58,092	59,558	60,585	58,445	62,880
Northumberland	21,576	23,427	22,552	19,117	22,102	24,012	20,072	21,263
Perry	4,652	5,279	5,247	4,526	5,247	6,067	5,401	5,329
Philadelphia.	493,293	587,157	655,233	593,405	641,029	738,546	744,637	861,142
Pike	2,218	2,307	2,279	2,279	2,692	3,462	3,883	4,060
Potter.	3,091	3,509	3,017	2,485	2,994	3,810	3,420	3,237
Schuylkill	29,870	37,582	36,106	29,697	35,378	37,895	31,033	31,913
Snyder.	2,723	3,207	3,189	2,854	3,064	3,453	3,200	3,568
Somerset	18,756	19,871	18,051	15,819	15,869	16,300	15,890	19,114
Sullivan	1,617	1,632	1,483	1,296	1,421	1,615	1,527	1,545
Susquehanna	5,919	6,446	6,141	5,404	6,303	6,930	6,481	6,442
Tioga	3,617	4,337	4,929	4,211	5,264	5,530	5,325	5,162
Union	2,552	2,770	3,012	2,657	3,252	3,615	3,451	3,864
Venango.	7,930	9,684	9,191	7,943	8,774	9,339	8,782	11,891
Warren.	5,796	7,240	7,008	6,482	7,099	7,783	8,383	9,054
Washington	68,817	71,831	71,429	67,886	68,577	72,123	71,527	77,038
Wayne	4,533	5,477	4,488	3,730	4,116	4,980	4,806	4,825
Westmoreland	104,134	118,024	117,551	114,527	118,341	113,540	114,993	126,142
Wyoming	2,884	3,753	3,115	2,638	3,252	4,000	3,666	3,735
York	57,713	62,780	61,484	57,178	59,745	63,650	58,947	61,083
TOTALS.	**2,450,396**	**2,805,202**	**2,884,396**	**2,715,507**	**2,993,092**	**3,152,450**	**3,072,700**	**3,380,675**

REPUBLICAN VOTER REGISTRATION IN PENNSYLVANIA COUNTIES FOR PRESIDENTIAL ELECTION YEARS: 1956 TO 1984

	1956	1960	1964	1968	1972	1976	1980	1984
Adams	11,481	12,289	12,815	13,119	12,919	12,660	13,768	15,321
Allegheny	328,868	323,048	303,152	299,981	303,944	244,560	227,190	223,900
Armstrong	21,691	22,084	21,459	20,277	19,729	17,257	16,430	16,322
Beaver	45,817	43,340	39,515	37,041	34,702	31,847	29,746	29,442
Bedford	11,792	11,658	12,028	12,337	11,531	10,734	11,668	13,173
Berks	42,829	45,753	46,703	48,169	48,431	45,721	47,118	52,670
Blair	38,022	38,138	38,191	36,087	33,729	31,783	33,118	33,906
Bradford	17,446	17,589	16,893	17,001	16,377	15,641	16,287	17,496
Bucks	66,503	76,354	79,595	91,504	100,869	95,247	109,047	129,146
Butler	30,175	31,808	30,332	30,031	30,308	29,276	31,397	33,452
Cambria	43,093	40,808	39,901	40,107	36,279	31,503	29,860	28,817
Cameron	2,879	2,677	2,497	2,266	2,073	1,828	1,841	1,960
Carbon	14,054	13,346	12,710	12,243	11,687	10,285	10,065	10,369
Centre	16,215	17,947	18,541	19,911	21,325	21,326	25,921	28,871
Chester	58,122	66,170	72,320	80,175	87,845	86,451	92,920	103,361
Clarion	9,183	9,415	9,726	9,180	9,246	8,851	9,336	9,739
Clearfield	17,853	17,724	17,736	17,542	15,744	14,281	15,396	17,210
Clinton	9,922	9,368	9,409	9,266	8,651	7,585	7,888	7,006
Columbia	11,307	11,905	12,248	12,108	12,091	11,773	12,120	12,210
Crawford	21,531	21,671	20,757	20,735	20,195	19,173	20,040	21,586
Cumberland	32,301	35,650	36,940	40,839	42,737	42,218	46,687	51,726
Dauphin	80,810	77,228	76,480	74,490	63,921	55,759	59,755	64,660
Delaware	226,502	229,012	227,825	235,780	244,191	232,222	214,656	216,235
Elk	7,131	7,115	7,167	6,826	6,444	5,771	5,878	5,847
Erie	54,297	58,391	59,154	55,810	55,740	49,871	47,301	49,190
Fayette	26,991	23,642	23,600	23,666	19,633	16,001	14,868	14,911
Forest	1,549	1,546	1,565	1,473	1,425	1,427	1,495	1,458
Franklin	18,853	20,380	22,151	23,154	22,814	21,108	23,206	25,729
Fulton	2,226	2,231	2,366	2,326	2,247	2,137	2,407	2,795
Greene	5,152	4,626	4,589	4,293	4,073	3,618	3,873	3,754
Huntingdon	11,778	12,322	11,581	10,502	10,471	9,557	10,178	10,802
Indiana	19,836	20,329	20,212	20,623	19,670	18,473	19,185	20,393
Jefferson	13,555	14,581	14,053	13,346	12,132	10,991	10,915	11,291
Juniata	4,087	4,259	4,666	4,557	4,405	4,337	4,621	5,020
Lackawanna	60,407	50,601	55,801	48,895	47,165	43,600	38,425	36,961
Lancaster	80,882	87,010	85,098	87,483	87,938	85,412	95,124	113,906
Lawrence	32,444	29,991	28,143	27,294	25,631	22,209	21,200	20,344
Lebanon	25,021	26,687	26,721	27,243	26,535	24,648	26,882	29,029
Lehigh	47,695	51,760	51,862	53,050	52,627	48,437	50,190	54,091
Luzerne	133,524	115,050	109,016	97,184	77,432	64,179	63,184	62,345
Lycoming	28,267	30,475	30,696	29,905	29,111	25,573	25,692	27,434
McKean	17,677	17,133	15,841	14,623	13,586	12,487	12,135	12,549
Mercer	29,568	30,499	29,426	29,196	28,062	26,309	25,182	25,626
Mifflin	8,974	9,264	9,397	9,465	9,413	8,384	8,560	9,370
Monroe	7,977	8,054	8,227	9,818	10,682	10,781	12,209	14,084
Montgomery	169,052	189,550	199,307	213,239	217,273	203,934	203,320	213,333
Montour	3,788	3,991	3,960	3,917	3,810	3,421	3,650	3,717
Northampton	35,296	34,067	33,072	32,700	32,141	29,464	30,418	34,867
Northumberland	34,995	32,958	31,371	30,841	26,610	24,383	23,280	22,442
Perry	8,033	8,002	8,619	8,719	8,342	8,486	9,633	10,763
Philadelphia	523,055	408,694	382,561	386,360	338,997	232,848	205,084	195,321
Pike	4,277	4,003	4,262	4,507	4,800	4,824	5,333	6,227
Potter	5,482	5,316	5,296	4,953	4,608	4,318	4,866	5,431
Schuylkill	70,082	65,420	63,379	60,469	57,061	50,902	45,156	45,033
Snyder	7,950	8,402	8,305	8,140	8,229	8,115	8,943	10,019
Somerset	21,702	21,186	21,127	20,260	19,896	18,841	19,419	20,186
Sullivan	2,078	1,957	1,940	1,948	1,873	1,788	1,880	1,935
Susquehanna	11,523	11,471	11,455	11,128	11,144	10,785	11,183	11,304
Tioga	12,261	12,642	12,688	12,050	11,792	10,920	11,488	12,380
Union	7,395	7,843	8,207	7,851	7,615	7,712	8,103	8,543
Venango	18,660	19,110	17,859	17,051	16,245	14,888	14,879	15,729
Warren	12,864	12,977	13,130	12,841	11,786	10,698	10,846	11,795
Washington	34,774	33,424	33,127	31,815	30,844	28,746	28,047	27,920
Wayne	10,327	10,235	10,602	10,025	9,976	9,324	9,749	10,483
Westmoreland	56,221	58,078	56,948	57,490	56,784	48,808	49,357	50,472
Wyoming	6,538	6,403	6,600	6,868	7,155	7,138	7,285	7,968
York	44,567	45,580	46,645	51,363	54,953	53,563	57,420	66,177
TOTALS	**2,897,307**	**2,802,237**	**2,759,565**	**2,775,456**	**2,697,694**	**2,387,197**	**2,374,303**	**2,487,552**

THE FEDERAL
GOVERNMENT

SECTION 8 - THE FEDERAL GOVERNMENT

PRESIDENT OF THE UNITED STATES

RONALD WILSON REAGAN was born February 6, 1911, in Tampico, Illinois, the son of Nellie Wilson and John Reagan. He was educated in Illinois public schools and was graduated from Eureka College (Illinois) in 1932, with a degree in economics and sociology.

Following a brief career as a sports broadcaster and editor, Reagan moved to California to work in motion pictures. His film career, interrupted by three years of service in the Army Air Corps during World War II, encompassed 53 feature-length motion pictures. He served six terms as president of the Screen Actors Guild and two terms as president of the Motion Picture Industry Council.

In 1952 he married Nancy Davis. They have two grown children, Patricia Ann and Ronald Prescott. President Reagan has two other children, Maureen and Michael, by a previous marriage.

From motion pictures he went into television in the 1950's as production supervisor and host of "General Electric Theatre." In 1964-65 he was host of the television series "Death Valley Days."

In 1966 Ronald Reagan began his public service career with his election—by nearly a million-vote margin—as Governor of California. Mr. Reagan was Chairman of the Republican Governors Association in 1969. He was elected to a second term as Governor of California in 1970. After completing his second term, Mr. Reagan began a nationally syndicated radio commentary program and newspaper column and undertook an extensive speaking schedule, speaking to civic, business, and political groups. In 1974-75 he served as a member of the Presidential Commission investigating the CIA.

In November 1975 he announced his candidacy for the 1976 presidential nomination. He lost narrowly, but campaigned vigorously for the Republican ticket and for scores of local candidates in 1976. After the election, he renewed his radio commentary program, newspaper column, and national speaking schedule. He became a member of the Board of Directors of the Committee on the Present Danger and founded the Citizens for the Republic. In the 1978 elections he campaigned on behalf of 86 candidates.

In November 1979 Ronald Reagan announced his candidacy for the 1980 presidential nomination. At the Republican National Convention in July 1980 he was nominated unanimously on the first ballot. On November 4, 1980, Ronald Reagan was elected to the Presidency, by an electoral vote of 489-49, and on January 20, 1981, he was sworn in as the 40th President of the United States.

Mr. Reagan has received a number of awards, including: National Humanitarian Award from the National Conference of Christians and Jews; City of Hope "Torch of Life" Award for Humanitarian Service; Horatio Alger Award; American Newspaper Guild Award; Freedoms Foundation Awards; Distinguished American Award from the National Football Foundation Hall of Fame; American Patriots Hall of Fame; and Medal of Valor of the State of Israel.

UNITED STATES GOVERNMENT

Ronald Reagan, *President*

George Bush, *Vice President*

THE CABINET

Secretary of Agriculture . . . . .Richard E. Lyng
Secretary of Commerce. . . . . .C. William Verity, Jr. (nominee)
Secretary of Defense . . . . .Caspar W. Weinberger
Secretary of Education . . . . .William J. Bennett
Secretary of Energy . . . . .John S. Herrington
Secretary of Health and Human Services . . . . .Otis R. Bowen
Secretary of Housing and Urban Development . . . . .Samuel R. Pierce, Jr.
Secretary of the Interior . . . . .Donald P. Hodel
Attorney General. . . . . .Edwin Meese III
Secretary of Labor . . . . .William E. Brock
Secretary of State . . . . .George P. Shultz
Secretary of Transportation . . . . .Elizabeth H. Dole
Secretary of the Treasury . . . . .James A. Baker III
Chief of Staff to the President . . . . .Howard Baker
United States Representative to the United Nations. . . . . .Vernon A. Walters (nominee)
Director, Office of Management and Budget. . . . . .James C. Miller, III
Director of Central Intelligence . . . . .William Webster (nominee)
United States Trade Representative . . . . .Clayton Yeutter

The White House Office
1600 Pennsylvania Avenue NW 20500

Assistants to the President
Chief of Staff to the President . . . . .Howard Baker
Special Counsellor to the President . . . . .David M. Abshire
Assistant to the President for Legislative Affairs. . . . . .William L. Ball, III
Assistant to the President for Policy Development . . . . .Gary L. Bauer
Assistant to the President and Press Secretary . . . . .James S. Brady
Assistant to the President for National Security Affairs . . . . .Frank C. Carlucci
Assistant to the President for Political and Intergovernmental Affairs . . . . .Frank J. Donatelli
Assistant to the President for Press Relations . . . . .Max Marlin Fitzwater
Assistant to the President . . . . .William Henkel
Assistant to the President . . . . .Charles D. Hobbs
Assistant to the President and Director of Communications . . . . .John O. Koehler
Assistant to the President . . . . .Nancy J. Risque
Assistant to the President. . . . . .W. Dennis Thomas
Counsel to the President . . . . .Peter J. Wallison

Deputy Assistants to the President
Staff Secretary and Deputy Assistant to the President . . . . .David L. Chew
Deputy Assistant to the President and Chief of Staff to the First Lady . . . . .Jack L. Courtemanche
Deputy Assistant to the President. . . . . .Thomas C. Dawson
Deputy Assistant to the President and Director of Speechwriting . . . . .Anthony Dolan
Deputy Assistant to the President and Director of the Office of Intergovernmental Affairs . . . . .Gwendolyn S. King
Deputy Assistant to the President for Legislative Affairs (House) . . . . .Alan M. Kranowitz
Deputy Assistant to the President and Director of the Office of Public Liaison . . . . .Mari Maseng
Deputy Assistant to the President for Management and Administration . . . . .Jonathan S. Miller
Deputy Assistant to the President for National Security Affairs . . . . .Colin L. Powell, Lt. Gen., USA
Deputy Assistant to the President and Director of the White House Military Office. . . . . .Richard P. Riley
Deputy Assistant to the President and Director of Presidential Appointments and Scheduling,
  Director of Private Sector Initiatives. . . . . .Frederick J. Ryan, Jr.
Deputy Counsel to the President . . . . .Jay B. Stephens
Deputy Assistant to the President for Legislative Affairs . . . . .John C. Tuck
Deputy Assistant to the President for Legislative Affairs (Senate). . . . . .Pamela J. Turner
Deputy Assistant to the President and Director of Presidential Personnel . . . . .Robert H. Tuttle

THE 100th CONGRESS
STATE DELEGATIONS

ALABAMA

SENATORS
Howell T. Heflin (D)
Richard C. Shelby (D)

REPRESENTATIVES
(Democrats, 5; Republicans, 2)
1. Sonny Callahan (R)
2. William L. Dickinson (R)
3. Bill Nichols (D)
4. Tom Bevill (D)
5. Ronnie G. Flippo (D)
6. Ben Erdreich (D)
7. Claude Harris (D)

ALASKA

SENATORS
Theodore F. Stevens (R)
Frank Murkowski (R)

REPRESENTATIVE
(Republican, 1)
Representative-at-large
Don Young (R)

ARIZONA

SENATORS
Dennis DeConcini (D)
John McCain (R)

REPRESENTATIVES
(Democrats, 1; Republicans, 4)
1. John J. Rhodes III (R)
2. Morris K. Udall (D)
3. Bob Stump (R)
4. Jon L. Kyl (R)
5. Jim Kolbe (R)

ARKANSAS

SENATORS
Dale Bumpers (D)
David H. Pryor (D)

REPRESENTATIVES
(Democrats, 3; Republicans, 1)
1. Bill Alexander (D)
2. Tommy F. Robinson (D)
3. John Paul Hammerschmidt (R)
4. Beryl F. Anthony, Jr. (D)

CALIFORNIA

SENATORS
Alan Cranston (D)
Pete Wilson (R)

REPRESENTATIVES
(Democrats, 27; Republicans, 18)
1. Douglas H. Bosco (D)
2. Wally Herger (R)
3. Robert T. Matsui (D)
4. Vic Fazio (D)
5. Sala Burton (D)
6. Barbara Boxer (D)
7. George Miller (D)
8. Ronald V. Dellums (D)
9. Fortney H. (Pete) Stark (D)
10. Don Edwards (D)
11. Tom Lantos (D)
12. Ernest L. Konnyu (R)
13. Norman Y. Mineta (D)
14. Norman D. Shumway (R)
15. Tony Coelho (D)
16. Leon E. Panetta (D)
17. Charles Pashayan, Jr. (R)
18. Richard Lehman (D)
19. Robert J. Lagomarsino (R)
20. William M. Thomas (R)
21. Elton Gallegly (R)
22. Carlos J. Moorhead (R)
23. Anthony C. Beilenson (D)
24. Henry A. Waxman (D)
25. Edward R. Roybal (D)
26. Howard Berman (D)
27. Mel Levine (D)
28. Julian C. Dixon (D)
29. Augustus F. Hawkins (D)
30. Matthew G. Martinez (D)
31. Mervyn M. Dymally (D)
32. Glenn M. Anderson (D)
33. David Dreier (R)
34. Esteban Edward Torres (D)
35. Jerry Lewis (R)
36. George E. Brown, Jr. (D)
37. Alfred A. (Al) McCandless (R)
38. Robert K. Dorman (R)
39. William E. Dannemeyer (R)
40. Robert E. Badham (R)
41. Bill Lowery (R)
42. Dan Lungren (R)
43. Ron Packard (R)
44. Jim Bates (D)
45. Duncan Hunter (R)

COLORADO

SENATORS
William L. Armstrong (R)
Timothy E. Wirth (D)

REPRESENTATIVES
(Democrats, 3; Republicans, 3)
1. Patricia Schroeder (D)
2. David E. Skaggs (D)
3. Ben Nighthorse Campbell (D)
4. Hank Brown (R)
5. Joel Hefley (R)
6. Dan Schaefer (R)

CONNECTICUT

SENATORS
Christopher J. Dodd (D)
Lowell P. Weicker, Jr. (R)

REPRESENTATIVES
(Democrats, 3; Republicans, 3)
1. Barbara B. Kennelly (D)
2. Sam Gejdenson (D)
3. Bruce A. Morrison (D)
4. Christopher Shays (R)
5. John G. Rowland (R)
6. Nancy L. Johnson (R)

DELAWARE

SENATORS
William V. Roth, Jr. (R)
Joseph R. Biden, Jr. (D)

REPRESENTATIVE
(Democrat, 1)
Representative-at-large
Thomas R. Carper (D)

FLORIDA

SENATORS
Lawton Chiles (D)
Bob Graham (D)

REPRESENTATIVES
(Democrats, 12; Republicans, 7)
1. Earl Hutto (D)
2. Bill Grant (D)
3. Charles E. Bennett (D)
4. Bill Chappell, Jr. (D)
5. Bill McCollum (R)
6. Buddy MacKay (D)
7. Sam Gibbons (D)
8. C. W. Bill Young (R)
9. Michael Bilirakis (R)
10. Andy Ireland (R)
11. Bill Nelson (D)
12. Tom Lewis (R)
13. Connie Mack (R)
14. Dan Mica (D)
15. E. Clay Shaw, Jr. (R)
16. Lawrence J. Smith (D)
17. William Lehman (D)
18. Claude D. Pepper (D)
19. Dante B. Fascell (D)

GEORGIA

SENATORS
Sam Nunn (D)
Wyche Fowler, Jr. (D)

REPRESENTATIVES
(Democrats, 8; Republicans, 2)
1. Robert Lindsay Thomas (D)
2. Charles Hatcher (D)
3. Richard Ray (D)
4. Patrick L. Swindall (R)
5. John Lewis (D)
6. Newt Gingrich (R)
7. George (Buddy) Darden (D)
8. J. Roy Rowland (D)
9. Ed Jenkins (D)
10. Doug Barnard, Jr. (D)

HAWAII

SENATORS
Daniel K. Inouye (D)
Spark Matsunaga (D)

REPRESENTATIVES
(Democrats, 1; Republicans, 1)
1. Patricia F. Saiki (R)
2. Daniel K. Akaka (D)

IDAHO

SENATORS
Steven D. Symms (R)
James A. McClure (R)

REPRESENTATIVES
(Democrats, 1; Republicans, 1)
1. Larry E. Craig (R)
2. Richard H. Stallings (D)

ILLINOIS

SENATORS
Paul Simon (D)
Alan J. Dixon (D)

REPRESENTATIVES
(Democrats, 13; Republicans, 9)
1. Charles A. Hayes (D)
2. Gus Savage (D)
3. Marty Russo (D)
4. Jack Davis (R)
5. William O. Lipinski (D)
6. Henry J. Hyde (R)
7. Cardiss Collins (D)
8. Dan Rostenkowski (D)
9. Sidney R. Yates (D)
10. John Edward Porter (R)
11. Frank Annunzio (D)
12. Philip M. Crane (R)
13. Harris W. Fawell (R)
14. J. Dennis Hastert (R)
15. Edward R. Madigan (R)
16. Lynn Martin (R)
17. Lane Evans (D)
18. Robert H. Michel (R)
19. Terry L. Bruce (D)
20. Richard J. Durbin (D)
21. Melvin Price (D)
22. Kenneth J. Gray (D)

INDIANA

SENATORS
Dan Quayle (R)
Richard Lugar (R)

REPRESENTATIVES
(Democrats, 6; Republicans, 4)
1. Peter J. Visclosky (D)
2. Philip R. Sharp (D)
3. John Hiler (R)
4. Dan Coats (R)
5. James Jontz (D)
6. Dan Burton (R)
7. John T. Myers (R)
8. Frank McCloskey (D)
9. Lee H. Hamilton (D)
10. Andrew Jacobs, Jr. (D)

IOWA

SENATORS
Charles E. Grassley (R)
Tom Harkin (D)

REPRESENTATIVES
(Democrats, 2; Republicans, 4)
1. Jim Leach (R)
2. Thomas J. Tauke (R)
3. David R. Nagle (D)
4. Neal Smith (D)

5. Jim Lightfoot (R)
6. Fred Grandy (R)

KANSAS

SENATORS
Robert Dole (R)
Nancy L. Kassebaum (R)

REPRESENTATIVES
(Democrats, 2; Republicans, 3)
1. Pat Roberts (R)
2. Jim Slattery (D)
3. Jan Meyers (R)
4. Dan Glickman (D)
5. Bob Whittaker (R)

KENTUCKY

SENATORS
Mitch McConnell (R)
Wendell H. Ford (D)

REPRESENTATIVES
(Democrats, 4; Republicans, 3)
1. Carroll Hubbard, Jr. (D)
2. William H. Natcher (D)
3. Romano L. Mazzoli (D)
4. Jim Bunning (R)
5. Harold Rogers (R)
6. Larry J. Hopkins (R)
7. Carl C. Perkins (D)

LOUISIANA

SENATORS
John B. Breaux (D)
J. Bennett Johnson, Jr. (D)

REPRESENTATIVES
(Democrats, 5; Republicans, 3)
1. Bob Livingston (R)
2. Lindy (Mrs. Hale) Boggs (D)
3. W. J. (Billy) Tauzin (D)
4. Buddy Roemer (D)
5. Jerry Huckaby (D)
6. Richard H. Baker (R)
7. James A. Hayes (D)
8. Clyde C. Holloway (R)

MAINE

SENATORS
William S. Cohen (R)
George J. Mitchell (D)

REPRESENTATIVES
(Democrats, 1; Republicans, 1)
1. Joseph E. Brennan (D)
2. Olympia J. Snowe (R)

MARYLAND

SENATORS
Barbara A. Mikulski (D)
Paul S. Sarbanes (D)

REPRESENTATIVES
(Democrats, 6; Republicans, 2)
1. Roy Dyson (D)
2. Helen Delich Bentley (R)
3. Benjamin L. Cardin (D)
4. C. Thomas McMillen (D)

5. Steny H. Hoyer (D)
6. Beverly B. Byron (D)
7. Kweisi Mfume (D)
8. Constance A. Morella (R)

MASSACHUSETTS

SENATORS
Edward M. Kennedy (D)
John F. Kerry (D)

REPRESENTATIVES
(Democrats, 10; Republicans, 1)
1. Silvio O. Conte (R)
2. Edward P. Boland (D)
3. Joseph D. Early (D)
4. Barney Frank (D)
5. Chester G. Atkins (D)
6. Nicholas Mavroules (D)
7. Edward J. Markey (D)
8. Joseph P. Kennedy II (D)
9. Joe Moakley (D)
10. Gerry E. Studds (D)
11. Brian J. Donnelly (D)

MICHIGAN

SENATORS
Carl Levin (D)
Donald W. Riegle, Jr. (D)

REPRESENTATIVES
(Democrats, 11; Republicans, 7)
1. John Conyers, Jr. (D)
2. Carl D. Pursell (R)
3. Howard Wolpe (D)
4. Frederick S. Upton (R)
5. Paul B. Henry (R)
6. Bob Carr (D)
7. Dale E. Kildee (D)
8. Bob Traxler (D)
9. Guy Vander Jagt (R)
10. Bill Schuette (R)
11. Robert W. Davis (R)
12. David E. Bonior (D)
13. Geo. W. Crockett, Jr. (D)
14. Dennis Hertel (D)
15. William D. Ford (D)
16. John D. Dingell (D)
17. Sander M. Levin (D)
18. Wm. S. Broomfield (R)

MINNESOTA

SENATORS
Rudolph W. Boschwitz (R)
David Durenberger (R)

REPRESENTATIVES
(Democrats, 5; Republicans, 3)
1. Timothy J. Penny (D)
2. Vin Weber (R)
3. Bill Frenzel (R)
4. Bruce F. Vento (D)
5. Martin Olav Sabo (D)
6. Gerry Sikorski (D)
7. Arlan Stangeland (R)
8. James L. Oberstar (D)

MISSISSIPPI

SENATORS
Thad Cochran (R)
John C. Stennis (D)

REPRESENTATIVES
(Democrats, 4; Republicans, 1)
1. Jamie L. Whitten (D)
2. Mike Espy (D)
3. G. V. (Sonny) Montgomery (D)
4. Wayne Dowdy (D)
5. Trent Lott (R)

MISSOURI

SENATORS
Christopher (Kit) Bond (R)
John C. Danforth (R)

REPRESENTATIVES
(Democrats, 5; Republicans, 4)
1. William (Bill) Clay (D)
2. Jack Buechner (R)
3. Richard A. Gephardt (D)
4. Ike Skelton (D)
5. Alan Wheat (D)
6. E. Thomas Coleman (R)
7. Gene Taylor (R)
8. Bill Emerson (R)
9. Harold L. Volkmer (D)

MONTANA

SENATORS
Max Baucus (D)
John Melcher (D)

REPRESENTATIVES
(Democrats, 1; Republicans, 1)
1. Pat Williams (D)
2. Ron Marlenee (R)

NEBRASKA

SENATORS
J. James Exon (D)
David Karnes (R)

REPRESENTATIVES
(Republicans, 3)
1. Doug Bereuter (R)
2. Hal Daub (R)
3. Virginia Smith (R)

NEVADA

SENATORS
Chic Hecht (R)
Harry Reid (D)

REPRESENTATIVES
(Democrats, 1; Republicans, 1)
1. James H. Bilbray (D)
2. Barbara F. Vucanovich (R)

NEW HAMPSHIRE

SENATORS
Gordon J. Humphrey (R)
Warren Rudman (R)

REPRESENTATIVES
(Republicans, 2)
1. Robert C. Smith (R)
2. Judd Gregg (R)

NEW JERSEY

SENATORS
Bill Bradley (D)
Frank R. Lautenberg (D)

REPRESENTATIVES
(Democrats, 8; Republicans, 6)
1. James J. Florio (D)
2. William J. Hughes (D)
3. James J. Howard (D)
4. Christopher H. Smith (R)
5. Marge Roukema (R)
6. Bernard J. Dwyer (D)
7. Matthew J. Rinaldo (R)
8. Robert A. Roe (D)
9. Robert G. Torricelli (D)
10. Peter W. Rodino, Jr. (D)
11. Dean A. Gallo (R)
12. Jim Courter (R)
13. Jim Saxton (R)
14. Frank J. Guarini (D)

NEW MEXICO

SENATORS
Peter V. Domenici (R)
Jeff Bingaman (D)

REPRESENTATIVES
(Democrats, 1; Republicans, 2)
1. Manuel Lujan, Jr. (R)
2. Joe Skeen (R)
3. Bill Richardson (D)

NEW YORK

SENATORS
Alfonse M. D'Amato (R)
Daniel P. Moynihan (D)

REPRESENTATIVES
(Democrats, 20; Republicans, 14)
1. George J. Hochbrueckner (D)
2. Thomas J. Downey (D)
3. Robert J. Mrazek (D)
4. Norman F. Lent (R)
5. Raymond J. McGrath (R)
6. Floyd H. Flake (D)
7. Gary L. Ackerman (D)
8. James H. Scheuer (D)
9. Thomas J. Manton (D)
10. Charles E. Schumer (D)
11. Edolphus Towns (D)
12. Major R. Owens (D)
13. Stephen J. Solarz (D)
14. Guy V. Molinari (R)
15. Bill Green (R)
16. Charles B. Rangel (D)
17. Ted Weiss (D)
18. Robert Garcia (D)
19. Mario Biaggi (D)
20. Joseph J. DioGuardi (R)
21. Hamilton Fish, Jr. (R)
22. Benjamin A. Gilman (R)
23. Samuel S. Stratton (D)
24. Gerald B. H. Solomon (R)
25. Sherwood L. Boehlert (R)
26. David O'B. Martin (R)
27. George C. Wortley (R)
28. Matthew F. McHugh (D)
29. Frank Horton (R)
30. Louise McIntosh Slaughter (D)
31. Jack F. Kemp (R)
32. John J. LaFalce (D)
33. Henry J. Nowak (D)
34. Amory Houghton, Jr. (R)

NORTH CAROLINA

SENATORS
Jesse Helms (R)
Terry Sanford (D)

REPRESENTATIVES
(Democrats, 8; Republicans, 3)
1. Walter B. Jones (D)
2. Tim Valentine (D)
3. H. Martin Lancaster (D)
4. David E. Price (D)
5. Stephen L. Neal (D)
6. Harold Coble (R)
7. Charles Rose (D)
8. W. G. (Bill) Hefner (D)
9. J. Alex McMillan (R)
10. Cass Ballenger (R)
11. James McClure Clarke (D)

NORTH DAKOTA

SENATORS
Kent Conrad (D)
Quentin N. Burdick (D)

REPRESENTATIVE
(Democrat, 1)
Representative-at-large
Byron L. Dorgan (D)

OHIO

SENATORS
John Glenn (D)
Howard M. Metzenbaum (D)

REPRESENTATIVES
(Democrats, 11; Republicans, 10)
1. Thomas A. Luken (D)
2. Willis D. Gradison Jr. (R)
3. Tony P. Hall (D)
4. Michael G. Oxley (R)
5. Delbert L. Latta (R)
6. Bob McEwen (R)
7. Michael DeWine (R)
8. Donald E. "Buz" Lukens (R)
9. Marcy Kaptur (D)
10. Clarence E. Miller (R)
11. Dennis Eckart (D)
12. John J. Kasich (R)
13. Donald J. Pease (D)
14. Thomas C. Sawyer (D)
15. Chalmers P. Wylie (R)
16. Ralph Regula (R)
17. James A. Traficant, Jr. (D)
18. Douglas Applegate (D)
19. Edward F. Feighan (D)
20. Mary Rose Oakar (D)
21. Louis Stokes (D)

OKLAHOMA

SENATORS
David L. Boren (D)
Don Nickles (R)

REPRESENTATIVES
(Democrats, 4; Republicans, 2)
1. James M. Inhofe (R)
2. Mike Synar (D)
3. Wes Watkins (D)
4. Dave McCurdy (D)
5. Mickey Edwards (R)
6. Glenn English (D)

OREGON

SENATORS
Mark O. Hatfield (R)
Robert W. Packwood (R)

REPRESENTATIVES
(Democrats, 3; Republicans, 2)
1. Les AuCoin (D)
2. Robert F. (Bob) Smith (R)
3. Ron Wyden (D)
4. Peter A. DeFazio (D)
5. Denny Smith (R)

PENNSYLVANIA

SENATORS
Arlen Specter (R)
H. John Heinz III (R)

REPRESENTATIVES
(Democrats, 12; Republicans, 11)
1. Thomas M. Foglietta (D)
2. William H. Gray III (D)
3. Robert A. Borski (D)
4. Joe Kolter (D)
5. Richard T. Schulze (R)
6. Gus Yatron (D)
7. Curt Weldon (R)
8. Peter H. Kostmayer (D)
9. Bud Shuster (R)
10. Joseph M. McDade (R)
11. Paul E. Kanjorski (D)
12. John P. Murtha (D)
13. Lawrence Coughlin (R)
14. William J. Coyne (D)
15. Don Ritter (R)
16. Robert S. Walker (R)
17. George W. Gekas (R)
18. Doug Walgren (D)
19. William F. Goodling (R)
20. Joseph M. Gaydos (D)
21. Thomas J. Ridge (R)
22. Austin J. Murphy (D)
23. William F. Clinger, Jr. (R)

RHODE ISLAND

SENATORS
Claiborne Pell (D)
John Chafee (R)

REPRESENTATIVES
(Democrats, 1; Republicans, 1)
1. Fernand J. St. Germain (D)
2. Claudine Schneider (R)

SOUTH CAROLINA

SENATORS
Strom Thurmond (R)
Ernest F. Hollings (D)

REPRESENTATIVES
(Democrats, 4; Republicans, 2)
1. Arthur Ravenel, Jr. (R)
2. Floyd Spence (R)
3. Butler Derrick (D)
4. Elizabeth J. Patterson (D)
5. John M. Spratt, Jr. (D)
6. Robin Tallon (D)

SOUTH DAKOTA

SENATORS
Thomas A. Daschle (D)
Larry Pressler (R)

REPRESENTATIVE
(Democrat, 1)
Representative-at-large
Tim Johnson (D)

TENNESSEE

SENATORS
Albert Gore, Jr. (D)
James R. Sasser (D)

REPRESENTATIVES
(Democrats, 6; Republicans, 3)
1. James H. (Jimmy) Quillen (R)
2. John J. Duncan (R)
3. Marilyn Lloyd (D)
4. Jim Cooper (D)
5. William Hill Boner (D)
6. Bart Gordon (D)
7. Don Sundquist (R)
8. Ed Jones (D)
9. Harold E. Ford (D)

TEXAS

SENATORS
Phil Gramm (R)
Lloyd M. Bentsen (D)

REPRESENTATIVES
(Democrats, 17, Republicans, 10)
1. Jim Chapman (D)
2. Charles Wilson (D)
3. Steve Bartlett (R)
4. Ralph M. Hall (D)
5. John Bryant (D)
6. Joe Barton (R)
7. Bill Archer (R)
8. Jack Fields (R)
9. Jack Brooks (D)
10. J. J. Pickle (D)
11. Marvin Leath (D)
12. Jim Wright (D)
13. Beau Boulter (R)
14. Mac Sweeney (R)
15. E de la Garza (D)
16. Ronald D. Coleman (D)
17. Charles W. Stenholm (D)
18. Mickey Leland (D)
19. Larry Combest (R)
20. Henry B. Gonzalez (D)
21. Lamar S. Smith (R)
22. Tom Delay (R)
23. Albert G. Bustamante (D)
24. Martin Frost (D)

25. Michael A. Andrews (D)
26. Richard K. Armey (R)
27. Solomon P. Ortiz (D)

UTAH

SENATORS
Jake Garn (R)
Orrin Hatch (R)

REPRESENTATIVES
(Republicans, 3)
1. James V. Hansen (R)
2. Wayne Owens (D)
3. Howard C. Nielson (R)

VERMONT

SENATORS
Robert T. Stafford (R)
Patrick J. Leahy (D)

REPRESENTATIVE
(Republican, 1)
Representative-at-large
James M. Jeffords (R)

VIRGINIA

SENATORS
John W. Warner (R)
Paul S. Trible, Jr. (R)

REPRESENTATIVES
(Democrats, 5; Republicans, 5)
1. Herbert H. Bateman (R)
2. Owen B. Pickett (D)
3. Thomas J. Bliley, Jr. (R)
4. Norman Sisisky (D)
5. Dan Daniel (D)
6. Jim Olin (D)
7. D. French Slaughter, Jr. (R)
8. Stan Parris (R)
9. Frederick C. Boucher (D)
10. Frank R. Wolf (R)

WASHINGTON

SENATORS
Brock Adams (D)
Daniel J. Evans (R)

REPRESENTATIVES
(Democrats, 5; Republicans, 3)
1. John R. Miller (R)
2. Al Swift (D)
3. Don Bonker (D)
4. Sid Morrison (R)
5. Thomas S. Foley (D)
6. Norman D. Dicks (D)
7. Mike Lowry (D)
8. Rod Chandler (R)

WEST VIRGINIA

SENATORS
Jay Rockefeller (D)
Robert C. Byrd (D)

REPRESENTATIVES
(Democrats, 4)
1. Alan B. Mollohan (D)

2. Harley O. Staggers, Jr. (D)
3. Robert E. Wise, Jr. (D)
4. Nick Joe Rahall, II (D)

WISCONSIN

SENATORS
William W. Proxmire (D)
Robert W. Kasten, Jr. (R)

REPRESENTATIVES
(Democrats, 5; Republicans, 4)
1. Les Aspin (D)
2. Robert W. Kastenmeier (D)
3. Steve Gunderson (R)
4. Gerald D. Kleczka (D)
5. Jim Moody (D)
6. Thomas E. Petri (R)
7. David R. Obey (D)
8. Toby Roth (R)
9. F. James Sensenbrenner, Jr. (R)

WYOMING

SENATORS
Alan K. Simpson (R)
Malcolm Wallop (R)

REPRESENTATIVE
(Republican, 1)
Representative-at-large
Dick Cheney (R)

Non-Voting Delegates
to the U. S. House of Representatives

DISTRICT OF COLUMBIA

DELEGATE
(Democrat, 1)
Walter E. Fauntroy

AMERICAN SAMOA

DELEGATE
(Democrat, 1)
FoFo I.F. Sunia

GUAM

DELEGATE
(Republican, 1)
Ben Blaz

PUERTO RICO

RESIDENT COMMISSIONER
(Democrat, 1)
Jaime B. Fuster

VIRGIN ISLANDS

DELEGATE
(Democrat, 1)
Ron de Lugo

RECAPITULATION

SENATE
Democrats 54
Republicans 46
Total 100

HOUSE
Democrats 258
Republicans 177
Total 435

OFFICERS OF THE SENATE

Vice President of the United States and President of the Senate .... George H. W. Bush
President Pro Tempore of the Senate .... John Stennis
Secretary .... Walter Stewart
Sergeant at Arms .... Henry Giugni
Secretary for the Majority .... C. Abbott Saffold
Secretary for the Minority .... Howard O. Greene, Jr.
Parliamentarian .... Alan Frumin
Chaplain of the Senate .... Rev. Richard C. Halverson
Majority Leader .... Robert C. Byrd
Majority Whip .... Alan Cranston
Minority Leader .... Robert Dole
Minority Whip .... Alan Simpson

OFFICERS OF THE HOUSE

The Speaker .... Jim Wright
Clerk of the House .... Donald K. Anderson
Sergeant at Arms .... Jack Russ
Doorkeeper .... James T. Molloy
Postmaster .... Robert V. Rota
Chaplain of the House .... Rev. James David Ford, DD., L.H.D.
Majority Leader .... Thomas Foley
Majority Whip .... Tony Coelho
Chief Deputy Majority Whip .... David Bonior
Minority Leader .... Robert H. Michel
Minority Whip .... Trent Lott

PENNSYLVANIA DELEGATION TO THE 100th CONGRESS

THE SENATE

JOHN HEINZ

John Heinz (R) was born Oct. 23, 1938, in Pgh., the son of Henry John Heinz II and Joan Diehl McCauley; Phillips Exeter Academy (honors) 1956; Yale Univ. (B.A.) 1960; Harvard Grad. Schl. of Bus. Admin. (M.B.A.) 1963; staff sgt., U.S. Air Force, 1963; reserve duty, 1964-69; rec., U.S. Air Force Cost Reduction Program Citation, 1964; special asst., Office of U.S. Senator Hugh Scott, 1964; employed in the financial and marketing divisions of the H.J. Heinz Co., 1965-70; Lecturer, Grad. Schl. of Industrial Admin., Carnegie-Mellon Univ., 1970; delegate to Republican Natl. Convention, 1968, 1972, 1976, 1980, 1984; bd. mem., Children's Hospital of Pgh.; chmn., H. J. Heinz II Charitable and Family Trust; fellow of Carnegie Inst. Museum of Art; bd. mem., Yale Univ. Art Gallery; bd. visitors, Grad. Schl. Public & Internatl. Affairs and Grad. Schl. of Public Health, Univ. of Pgh.; bd. visitors, Grad. Schl. Bus. Admin., Harvard Univ.; bd. selectors, Am. Inst. for Public Service; Natl. Assn. for Advancement of Colored People (life mem.); Pennsylvania Society; Air Force Assn.; Friends of Independent Natl. Historical Soc. of Phila.; World Affairs Council of Pgh.; American Legion; Sons of Italy Award, 1968; Community Humanitarian Award, America; Co-chair: Senate Steel and Senate Coal Caucus; mem., Helsinki Commission; Committees: Finance; Banking; Housing and Urban Affairs; Government Affairs; and Aging (Ranking); elected to U.S. House of Representatives in a special election, Nov. 2, 1971; reelected 1974, 1976; elected to the U.S. Senate, 1976; reelected 1982; married Teresa Simoes-Ferreira; 3 children: John, Andre and Christopher; home address: 1950 Squaw Run Rd., Pittsburgh; office address: 277 Russell Building, Washington, D.C. 20510

ARLEN SPECTER

Arlen Specter (R) was born Feb. 12, 1930, in Wichita, Kansas, the son of Harry and Lillie Shanin Specter; Univ. of Pa. (B.A.) 1951, Phi Beta Kappa; Yale Law Schl. (LL.B.) 1956, Bd. of Editors, Yale Law Journal; Office of Special Investigations, U.S. Air Force, 1st Lt., 1951-53; Phila., Pa., Am. Bar Assns.; dist. atty. of Phila., 1966-74; Magisterial Investigation, Scranton Admn., 1965, spec. asst. to Atty. Gen. Walter Alessandroni; asst. counsel, Warren Commission, 1964; Society Hill Synagogue; rec., Outstanding Young Man of the Yr. 1964, Jr. Chamber of Commerce; B'nai B'rith Youth Services Award, 1966; Sons of Italy Award, 1968; Community Humanitarian Award, Baptist Ch., 1969; Man of the Yr. 1971, Temple Beth Ami; N.E. Catholic Outstanding Achievement Award, 1973; author, *Pension and Profit Sharing Plans: Close Corporations* (1962); "Censorship and Obsenity," *Dickinson Law Review,* 1962; "Mapp v. Ohio: Pandora's Problems for the Prosecutor," *University of Pennsylvania Law Review,* 1962; "Pollution: Are We Solving the Problem," *University of Pittsburgh Law Review,* 1971; "Philadelphia's Accelerated Rehabilitative Disposition Program," *American Bar Association Journal,* 1974; co-chmn., Senate Northeast-Midwest Coalition; co-chmn., Senate Children's Caucus; co-chmn., Congressional Crime Caucus; mem., Appropriations, Veterans' Affairs and Select Com. on Intelligence; Natl. Comm. on Criminal Justice; Peace Corps Natl. Advis. Council; White House Conf. on Youth; Pa. State Planning Bd.; elected to the U.S. Senate, Nov. 4, 1980; reelected 1986; married Joan L. Levy; 2 children: Shanin, Stephen.

THE HOUSE OF REPRESENTATIVES

ROBERT A. BORSKI, JR.　　　　　3rd District

Robert A. Borski, Jr. (D) was born Oct. 29, 1948, in Phila., the son of Robert A., Sr. (dec.) and Rita Savage Borski; Univ. of Baltimore (B.A.) 1971; frmr. mem., Phila. Stock Exchange; Roman Catholic; elected to the House of Representatives in 1976; reelected 1978, 1980; elected to the U.S. House of Representatives, 1982; reelected 1984, 1986; married Barbara Joniec; 3 children; home address: 3545 Emerald St., Philadelphia.

WILLIAM F. CLINGER, JR.　　　　　23rd District

William F. Clinger, Jr. (R) was born April 4, 1929, in Warren, the son of W. F. and Lella May Clinger; Johns Hopkins Univ. (B.A. - English) 1951; Univ. of Va. (LL.B.) 1965; U.S. Navy, 1951-55, Am. Spirit of Honor Medal as outstanding Seaman Recruit, USNR Lieut., inactive; attorney; Am., Pa., Warren Co. Bar Assns.; pres., Warren Jaycees, 1959-60 (Outstanding Chapter Pres. in Pa.) and Warren Library Assn., 1958-62, 1965-68; chmn., Kinzua Dam Dedication Comm., 1966; bd. of dir., Warren Co. Historical Society; chmn., Special Gifts Comm. and bd. of dir., Warren General Hospital; asst. to Rep. Co. Chmn., 1958-62; 1967 Pa. Constitutional Convention; Judiciary Comm. mem., appt. by Gov. Scranton to draft Judiciary Article with Dick Thornburgh and James Michener; State committeeman, Pa. Repub. Comm., 1968-75, Exec. Comm., 1972-75; delegate, 1972 Rep. Natl. Convention, Credentials Comm.; chmn., N.W. Pa. "Lewis for Governor" Comm.; chief counsel, Econ. Dev. Admin., U.S. Dept. of Commerce (1975-77) and was awarded Dept. Certificate of Appreciation, Feb. 1977, for work on Local Public Works Act; Phi Alpha Delta, legal frat.; elected to Congress, 1978; reelected 1980, 1982, 1984, 1986; mem., Public Works & Transportation and Gov't. Operations Coms.; former chmn., House Wednesday Group; co-chmn., House Rep. Task Force on Agriculture; married Julia Whitla; 4 children; home address: 510 W. Third Street, Warren.

LAWRENCE COUGHLIN　　　　　13th District

Lawrence Coughlin (R) of Villanova was born April 11, 1929, in Wilkes-Barre, the son of the late R. Lawrence and Evelyn Wich Coughlin; Yale Univ. (A.B.); Harvard Business Schl. (M.B.A.); Temple Univ. Evening Law Schl. (LL.B.); platoon leader and aide-de-camp to late U.S. Marine Corps Gen. L.B. (Chesty) Puller; U.S. Marine Corps, discharged as capt.; lawyer; frmr. partner, Saul, Ewing, Remick & Saul; mem., Phila., Pa., Am. Bar Assns.; rec., Union of Concerned Scientists Arms Control Award; First Human Rights Award of the Interreligious Task Force on Soviet Jewry; Norristown Jewish Community Center Men's Club Brotherhood Award; Outstanding Young Man, Main Line Jr. Chamber of Commerce; dir., Union of Councils for Soviet Jews; dir., Big Brother Assn., Montgomery Co. Opportunities Industrialization Center; mem., Am. Legion, Military Order of Foreign Wars, Charity Lodge No. 190, Marine Corps League; Episcopalian; elected to Pa. House of Representatives in 1964; elected to Pa. Senate in 1966; elected to Congress in 1968; reelected to 9 successive terms; married; 4 children; home address: 856 Mt. Moro Rd., Villanova; office address: 2467 Rayburn Bldg., Washington, D.C. 20515.

WILLIAM J. COYNE　　　　　14th District

William J. Coyne (D) was born Aug. 24, 1936, in Pgh., the son of Phillip and Mary Ridge Coyne; Robert Morris Coll. (B.S.) 1965; U.S. Army, 1955-57; accountant; Pa. House of Representatives, 1971-73; Pgh. City Council, 1974-81; Catholic; elected to Congress, Nov. 1980; reelected 1982, 1984, 1986; mem., House Ways & Means Com.; home address: 307 Halket St., Pittsburgh.

THOMAS M. FOGLIETTA   1st District

Thomas M. Foglietta (D) was born Dec. 3, 1928, in Phila., the son of Michael and Rose Butler Foglietta; St. Joseph's Coll. (B.A.) 1949; Temple Law Schl. (J.D.) 1952; attorney; Phila. City Council, 1955-75; regional dir., U.S. Dept. of Labor, 1976; Sons of Italy; Justinian Society; bd. member, St. Luke's Hospital Children's Medical Center, Easter Seal Society; sec., Pa. Coll. of Podiatric Medicine; chmn., S. Phila. Chpt., Cancer Society; elected to Congress, Nov. 1980; reelected 1982, 1984, 1986; mem., House Armed Services Com.; Merchant Marine Com.; home address: 708 Clymer St., Philadelphia.

JOSEPH M. GAYDOS   20th District

Joseph M. Gaydos (D), McKeesport; grad., Duquesne Univ.; Univ. of Notre Dame Law Schl. (LL.B.); WW II Veteran, USNR; elected to Pa. Senate in 1966; frmr. Dep. Atty. Gen., Pa.; frmr. Asst. Solicitor for Allegheny Co.; frmr. General Counsel to United Mine Workers of America, District 5; frmr. solicitor for various municipalities, school districts and authorities; seated in the 90th Congress to fill an unexpired term: elected to the U.S. House of Representatives in 1968; reelected 9 successive terms; married Alice Ann Gray; 5 children; office address: 2186 Rayburn House Office Building, Washington, D.C. 20515.

GEORGE W. GEKAS   17th District

George W. Gekas (R) was born April 14, 1930, in Harrisburg, the son of William and Mary Touloumes Gekas; Dickinson Coll. (B.A.) 1952; Dickinson Schl. of Law (Doctor of Laws) 1958; attorney; U.S. Army, 1953-55; Dauphin Co., Pa. Bar Assns.; Am. Judicature Society; Am. Legion; Ahepa; asst. dist. atty., Dauphin Co., 1960-66; Greek Orthodox Ch. of Greece, Hbg.; mem., House of Representatives, 1967-74; elected to the State Senate, 1976; reelected 1980; elected to the U.S. House of Representatives, 1982; reelected 1984, 1986; married Evangeline C. Charas.

BILL GOODLING   19th District

Bill Goodling (R) of Jacobus was born in Loganville, Dec. 5, 1927; Univ. of Maryland (B.S.) 1953; Western Maryland Coll. (M.Ed.) 1956; U.S. Army, 1946-48; educator and public school superintendent; schl. bd. dir., 1964-67; York County Mental Health Assn.; York/Adams Heart Assn.; Loganville United Methodist Church; elected to Congress in 1974; reelected 1976, 1978, 1980, 1982, 1984, 1986; married Hilda Wright in 1957; 2 children; office address: 2263 Rayburn House Office Building, Washington. D.C. 20515.

WILLIAM H. GRAY III
2nd District

William H. Gray III (D) was born Aug. 20, 1941, in Baton Rouge, La., son of the late Dr. William H. and Hazel Yates Gray; Franklin and Marshall Coll. (B.A. - History) 1963, Drew Theological Seminary (M. Div. - Church History) 1966, Princeton Theological Seminary (Th.M. - Am. Ch. History) 1970; grad. work, Univ. of Pa., Temple Univ.; pastor, Bright Hope Baptist Ch., Phila.; bd. of trustees, Berean Inst. and Martin Luther King Jr. Center, Atlanta; bd. of dir., Phila. Urban Coalition, Children's Hospital of Phila., Natl. Conf. of Christians and Jews Inc., Phila. O.I.C. and O.I.C. Internatl., Phila. Health and Welfare Council, Phila. United Fund; "Outstanding Citizens Award," Montclair Fair Housing Comm. Awards, The Reverend Martin Luther King Jr. Award for Disting. Humanitarian Service, Educator's Roundtable; Outstand. Service to the Community Award, Phila. Intercity YMCA; United Negro Coll. Fund Church Volunteer Leadership Award; Richard Allen Award for Religious & Civic Leadership; Mem. of the Yr. 1980, Natl. Federation of Housing Counselors; author, *"What Every White Clergyman Should Know About Black Clergymen," The Christian Ministry,* 1969; weekly columnist, *The Phila. Tribune;* elected to Congress, 1978; reelected 1980, 1982, 1984, 1986; chmn., House Committee on the Budget; mem., Appropriations and Dist. of Columbia Coms., Democratic Steering & Policy Com.; married Andrea Dash; 3 children; home address: 602 Vernon Road, Philadelphia.

PAUL EDMUND KANJORSKI
11th District

Paul Edmund Kanjorski (D) was born April 2, 1937, in Nanticoke, the son of Peter and Wanda Nebalski Kanjorski; Temple Univ.; Dickinson Schl. of Law; U.S. Army, 1960-61; lawyer; mem., Wilkes-Barre Law Lib. Assn.; Nanticoke Solicitor, 1967-82; Workman's Compensation Referee, 1972-80; Wyoming Sanitary Authority, 1972-84; Roman Catholic; elected to Congress, Nov. 6, 1984; reelected 1986; married Nancy Mary Hickerson; 1 child, Nancy Marie (Bitsy); home address: 103 South Hanover St., Nanticoke.

JOSEPH P. KOLTER
4th District

Joseph Paul Kolter (D) was born Sept. 3, 1926, in McDonald, Oh., the son of Stephen and Frances Shuster Kolter; Geneva Coll. (B.S.) 1950; additional studies at Pgh. Univ., Duquesne Univ.; U.S. Army Air Force; mem., RSROA; Natl. Assn. of Accountants; City Council, New Brighton, 1960-64; Beaver Valley Optimist Club, New Brighton Civil Serv. Comm.; past officer and baseball mgr., New Brighton Little-Pony-Colt League; Frat. Order of Eagles Aerie No. 1342; Am. Legion Anderson-Adkins Post 19; Vets of Foreign Wars Post # 48; BPO Elks Lodge No. 348; Sons of Italy Lodge 1883; elected to the House of Representatives in 1968; reelected 6 successive terms; elected to U.S. House of Representatives, 1982; reelected 1984, 1986; mem., Public Works & Transportation Com.; Gov't Operations Com.; 4 children; home address: 2185 Mercer Rd., New Brighton.

PETER H. KOSTMAYER
8th District

Peter H. Kostmayer (D) was born Sept. 27, 1946, in New York City, the son of John and Julia Carson Kostmayer; Columbia Univ. (B.A); U.S. Congress, 1977-81; reelected to Congress, 1982, 1984, 1986; married Pamela J. Rosenberg; home address: Solebury.

JOSEPH M. McDADE 10th District

Joseph M. McDade (R) was born Sept. 29, 1931, in Scranton, the son of John B. and Genevieve Hayes McDade; Univ. of Notre Dame (B.A.) 1953, and Univ. of Pa. (LL.B.) 1956; honorary degrees: Univ. of Scranton, Mansfield State Coll., King's Coll. (Wilkes-Barre, PA), Misericordia Coll. and St. Thomas Aquinas Coll.; lawyer; James Wilson Law Club; K. of C.; Elks; Scranton Chamber of Commerce; Lackawanna Co., Am. and Pa. Bar Assns.; clerkship in office of Chief Federal Judge John W. Murphy, Middle District of Pa.; Scranton City Solicitor, 1962; elected to Congress in 1962; reelected to each succeeding Congress; ranking minority mem., Defense Appropriations Subcom. and Small Business Committees; mem., Appropriations Subcom. on Interior and Related Agencies; married Mary Teresa O'Brien; 4 children; home address: 307 Clark Ave., Clarks Summit; office address: 2370 Rayburn House Office Building, Washington, D.C. 20515.

AUSTIN J. MURPHY 22nd District

Austin J. Murphy (D) was born June 17, 1927, in N. Charleroi, the son of Austin J. and Evelyn Spence Murphy; Duquesne Univ. (B.A.) and Univ. of Pgh. (LL.B.); Pvt., 1st Class, U.S. Marine Corps, 1944-46; USMA Reserve, 1948-50; attorney; Pa. Bar Assn.; adm. to practice before all state and federal courts; held offices of borough auditor, councilman, solicitor, and schl. bd. mem.; Democratic committeeman and asst. dist. atty., Washington Co., 1956-57; Univ. of Pgh. Law Review Staff; Local Government Comm.; Pa. State Assn. of Boroughs; chmn., Senate Local Government Comm.; Commission on Interstate Cooperation; Pa. House of Representatives, 1959-70; elected to the State Senate in 1970; reelected 1974; elected to Congress 1976; reelected 1978, 1980, 1982, 1984, 1986; office address: 2210 Rayburn House Office Building, Washington, D.C. 20515.

JOHN P. MURTHA 12th District

John P. Murtha (D) from Johnstown was born June 17, 1932; Kiskiminetas Spring Schl.; Univ. of Pgh. (B.A. econ.); grad. work at Indiana Univ. of Pa.; Mt. Aloysius Jr. Coll. (Hon. Doctor of Humanities); U.S. Marine Corps, Korean War; enlisted, commissioned as an officer, discharged as 1st Lt.; volunteered for 1 yr. active duty in Vietnam, Maj., 1966-67; awarded Bronze Star Medal with Combat ''V,'' 2 Purple Heart Medals and the Vietnamese Cross of Gallantry; Colonel, Marine Reserve; elected to Pa. House of Representatives, 1969; reelected 1970, 1972; rec., Pa. Distinguished Service Medal and Pa. Meritorious Service Medal; awards from Am. Legion, Adjutant General of Pa., Salvation Army, Vets. of Foreign Wars for work during 1977 Johnstown flood; John P. Murtha Award for student assistance at Univ. of Pgh., Johnstown; Man of the Yr., Johnstown Jaycees, 1978; Boy Scout Award, 1977; Person of the Yr., Grtr. Johnstown Rgnl. Central Labor Council, 1978; elected to Congress, Feb. 1974; reelected to each succeeding Congress; married Joyce Bell; 3 children: Donna Sue, John, Patrick; home address: 109 Colgate Ave., Johnstown; office address: 2423 Rayburn Bldg., Washington, D.C. 20515.

THOMAS J. RIDGE 21st District

Thomas J. Ridge (R) was born Aug. 26, 1945, the son of Thomas and Laura Sudimack Ridge; Harvard Coll., 1967; Dickinson Schl. of Law, 1972; U.S. Army, Infantry, 1968-70; attorney; Grtr. Erie Co. Community Action Comm.; Cathedral Prep Alumni Assn.; St. Mary's Home of Erie; Grtr. Erie Charity Golf Classic; part time asst. dist. atty., Erie Co.; Natl. Vietnam Vets Leadership Program; Northeast-Midwest Coalition; 92 Group; Wednesday Group; Cong. Coal Group; Cong. Steel Caucus; co-chair, Military Reform Caucus; Cathedral Prep.; Leadership Award; Dickinson Law Schl.'s Outstanding Advocate; Combat Infantry Badge; Army Commendation Medal; Bronze Star for Valor; Vietnamese Cross of Gallantry; elected to Congress, 1982; reelected 1984, 1986; married Michele Moore; 1 daughter, Lesley; home address: 3441 Breezeway Dr., Erie.

DON RITTER   15th District

Don Ritter (R) was born Oct. 21, 1940; Lehigh Univ. (B.S.-metallurgical eng.) 1961; Massachusetts Inst. of Tech. (M.S.-metallurgy) 1963; doctor of science in metallurgy, 1966; speaks French, Russian, Spanish, German; scientific exchange fellow, U.S. Natl. Acad. of Sciences/Soviet Acad. of Sciences, Baikov Instit. Moscow, 1967-68; asst. prof., California St. Polytechnic Univ. and contract consultant for General Dynamics, 1968-69; asst. prof., Dept. of Metallurgy and Materials Sciences, asst. to v. pres. for research, Lehigh Univ. 1969-76; manager of research program development, Lehigh Univ., 1976-78; Am. Society for Metals; Am. Inst. of Chemists; Natl. Society of Professional Engineers; Sigma Xi (excellence in research); Tau Beta Pi (excellence in engineering); Unitarian Ch.; ex officio mem., bd. of assoc. Muhlenberg Coll.; Elks; mem., Am. Security Council; Am. Assn. of Retired Persons; Lehigh Co. Farmers Assn.; Saucon Masonic Lodge; Hon. mem., Fraternal Order of Police; adv. bd., Combat Pilots Assn.; bd. dir., Greater Lehigh Valley Youth Symphony Orchestra and Lehigh Valley Ballet Guild; rec., ASM's Disting. Life Membership award, 1983; "Taxpayers' Best Friend," 1982, 1983, 1984, 1985, 1986; "Guardian of Small Business" award; "Golden Bulldog" Watchdogs of Treasury, Inc., award; Golden Age Hall of Fame; published in metallurgy-related journals; elected to Congress, 1978, despite 2:1 Democratic registration in district; 1st Repub. to hold seat since 1932; reelected 1980, 1982, 1984, 1986; Helsinki Commission; married Edith Duerksen; 2 children: Kristina and Jason; home address: 1208 Caterpillar Hill, Box 28, R.D. 1, Coopersburg.

DICK SCHULZE   5th District

Dick Schulze (R) of Malvern was born Aug. 7, 1929, in Phila., the son of John L., Jr. and Grace Taylor Schulze; att. Univ. of Houston, Villanova Univ. and Temple Univ.; U.S. Army, 1951-53; partner, retail electrical appliance business; register of wills, Chester Co. and clerk, Chester Co. Orphans' Court, 1968-70; pres., Upper Main Line Young Republicans and Chester Co. Federation of Young Republican Clubs; Chester Co. Repub. Exec. Comm.; chmn., Tredyffrin Twp. Repub. Comm.; active in scouting, received "Scoutmaster Key" and "district merit award" for outstanding service to boyhood; Great Valley Presbyterian Ch.; elected to Pa. House of Representatives, 1970; reelected 1972; elected to U.S. House of Representatives, 1974; reelected 1976, 1978, 1980, 1982, 1984, 1986; House Ways & Means Committee, subcommittees on Trade & Oversight; ex. com., Republican Study Com., mem, Cong. Caucus on Competitiveness; v. chmn., bd. dir, Cong. Steel Caucus; married Nancy Lockwood; 4 children; office address: 2201 Rayburn House Office Building, Washington, D.C. 20515.

BUD SHUSTER   9th District

Bud Shuster (R) of Everett was born Jan. 23, 1932, in Glassport; Univ. of Pgh. (B.S.), Duquesne Univ. (M.B.A.), American Univ. (Ph.D); served in U.S. Army (Infantry & Counterintelligence); computer industry exec. and founder (NYSE) software co.; Phi Beta Kappa; Sigma Chi (Significant Sig Award); ODK, Chowder & Marching Soc.; elected to Congress, 1972; pres., GOP Freshman Class; reelected to each successive Congress, winning both Republican & Democratic nominations (1976, 1980, 1986); del. Republican Natl. Conv. (1976, 1980, 1984); ranking mem., Surface Transportation Subcomm., Public Works & Transp.; mem., Select Intelligence Com.; chmn., Natl. Transp. Policy Study Comm., 1977-1980; chmn. House Republican Policy Committee, 96th Congress; authored award winning book, *Believing in America,* 1983; mem., The Authors Guild; married Patricia Rommell; 5 children: Peg, Bill, Deb, Bob and Gia; office address: 2268 Rayburn House Office Building, Washington, D.C. 20515.

DOUG WALGREN   18th District

Doug Walgren (D) was born Dec. 28, 1940; Dartmouth Coll. (B.A.) 1963; Stanford Law Schl. (LL.B.) 1966; adm. to the practice of law in Pa.; staff atty. Neighborhood Legal Services, 1967-68; private practice, 1969-72; corporate counsel, Behavorial Research Laboratories, Inc., Palo Alto, Calif., 1973-75; elected to Congress, 1976; reelected 1978, 1980, 1982, 1984, 1986; mem., Energy and Commerce Com., Science and Technology Com.; chmn., Subcom. on Science, Research and Technology; active member: Steel Caucus, Coal Caucus, Port Caucus, and Suburban Caucus; married Carmala Vincent of Canonsburg; 3 children; office address: 2241 Rayburn Office Building, Washington, D.C. 20515.

ROBERT S. WALKER   16th District

Robert S. Walker (R) was born Dec. 23, 1942, in Bradford, the son of Joseph E. and Rachael V. Smith Walker; att. Coll. of William and Mary; Millersville Univ. (B.S. - Ed.) 1964; Univ. of Delaware (M.A. - Pol. Sci.) 1968; Pa. Army Natl. Guard, 1967-73; frmr. public schl. teacher and Congressional aide; v. chmn., Lancaster Co. Republican Comm., 1973-74; Intnatl. Platform Assn.; Lancaster Co. Historical Soc'y.; Capitol Hill Club; Old Hickory Racquet Club; Eastern Lancaster Co. Republicans Inc.; Am. Legion; Elks; one of Outstanding Young Men of America, 1970 and 1976; Freedoms Foundation, 1973; Presidential Award, Pa. Jaycees, 1966; author, *Congress: The Pennsylvania Dutch Representatives, Can You Afford This House* (co-author) and numerous magazine articles; inaugural ball director, 1973 Presidential Inauguration; floor manager, 1980 Repub. Natl. Convention; Bethany Presbyterian Ch., trustee, 1975; Adv. Comm. on Intergovernmental Relations; elected to Congress, 1976; reelected 1978, 1980, 1982, 1984, 1986; married Sue Ellen Albertson; home address; 6065 Parkridge Drive, East Petersburg; office address: 2445 Rayburn House Office Building, Washington, D.C. 20515.

CURT WELDON   7th District

Curt Weldon (R) was born July 22, 1947, in Marcus Hook, the son of Stephen W. and Catherine Jones Weldon; grad., Media H.S., 1965; West Chester Univ. of Pa. (B.A.) 1969; grad. work: Cheyney Univ. of Pa., Temple Univ., St. Joseph, Cabrini Coll.; administrator/teacher, businessman, local official; mem., Certified Fire Protection Specialist, Assn. of Safety Professionals; mem: Lambda Chi Alpha, Lions Club, United Way, Red Cross, Marcus Hook Fire Co., Viscose Fire Co., Fraternal Order of Police; mem., chmn., Delaware Co. Council 1981-86; Mayor of Marcus Hook Borough, 1977-82; chmn., Delaware Valley Regional Planning Com., 1984-85; chmn., Partnership for Economic Development, 1983-87; bd. dir., Sacred Heart Medical Center; Community Action Agency, Neuman Coll. Development Council; Industrial Development Authority; Marcus Hook Development Corp.; Republican Leader, 160th Legis. Dist.; rec., Person of the Year, Delaware Co. Chamber of Commerce, 1987; Man of the Year, Chester Business Assn., 1984; Man of the Year, Delaware Co. Irish-Americans, 1984; Man of the Year, Chichester Rotary, 1983; Commitment Award, Delaware Co. Community Action Agency, 1986; twice nominated for Mayor of Marcus Hook by both political parties; elected to Congress, Nov. 4, 1986; married Mary Gallagher; 5 children: Karen, Kristin, Kimberly, Curt, Andrew; home address: 49 Weathervane Rd., Aston.

GUS YATRON   6th District

Gus Yatron (D) of Reading was born Oct 16, 1927, in Reading; grad., Kutztown Univ., where he was a member of the football team and a professional heavyweight boxer; businessman; elected to a six-year term, Reading Schl. Bd., 1955, service included work with the Reading Public Museum and Art Gallery; Bd. of Managers, Reading Hospital; elected to Pa. House of Representatives, 1956; reelected 1958; elected Pa. Senate, 1960; reelected 1964, 1966; elected to the U.S. House of Representatives in 1968; reelected to 9 successive terms; married Millie Menzies; 2 children, George and Theana; home address: 1908 Hessian Rd., Reading; office address: Room 2267, Rayburn House Office Bldg., Washington, D.C. 20515.

COMMITTEE ASSIGNMENTS OF PENNSYLVANIANS
IN THE 100th CONGRESS

SENATORS

Senator Heinz
Banking, Housing, and Urban Affairs
Finance
Government Affairs
Special Committee on Aging (Ranking)

Senator Specter
Appropriations
Judiciary
Intelligence
Veterans' Affairs

HOUSE MEMBERS

Representative Borski
Merchant Marine and Fisheries
Public Works and Transportation
Select Committee on Aging

Representative Clinger
Government Operations
Public Works and Transportation

Representative Coughlin
Appropriations
Select Committee on Narcotics Abuse and Control

Representative Coyne
Ways and Means

Representative Foglietta
Armed Services
Merchant Marine and Fisheries

Representative Gaydos
Education and Labor
House Administration
Joint Committee on Printing

Representative Gekas
Judiciary

Representative Goodling
Budget
Education and Labor

Representative Gray
Appropriations
Budget (Chmn.)
District of Columbia

Representative Kanjorski
Banking, Finance, and Urban Affairs
Veterans' Affairs

Representative Kolter
Government Operations
Public Works and Transportation

Representative Kostmayer
Foreign Affairs
Interior and Insular Affairs
Select Committee on Hunger

Representative McDade
Appropriations
Small Business

Representative Murphy
Education and Labor
Interior and Insular Affairs

Representative Murtha
Appropriations

Representative Ridge
Banking, Finance, and Urban Affairs
Select Committee on Aging
Veterans' Affairs

Representative Ritter
Energy and Commerce
Science and Technology

Representative Schulze
Ways and Means

Representative Shuster
Public Works and Transportation
Select Intelligence

Representative Walgren
Energy and Commerce
Science and Technology

Representative Walker
Government Operations
Science, Space and Technology

Representative Weldon
Armed Services
Merchant Marine and Fisheries

Representative Yatron
Foreign Affairs
Post Office and Civil Service

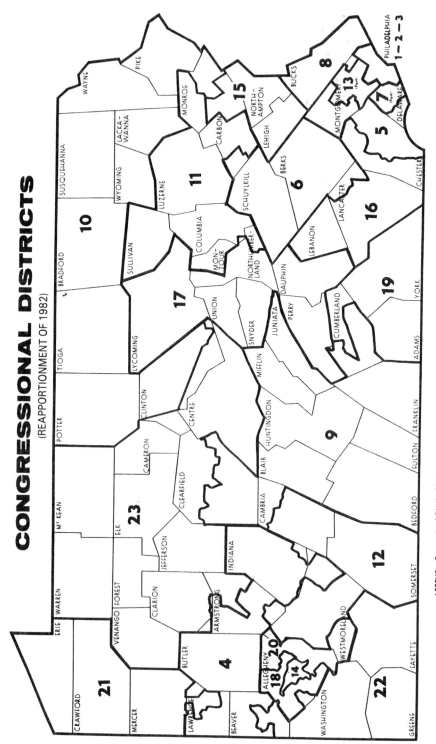

CONGRESSIONAL DISTRICTS
(REAPPORTIONMENT OF 1982)

LEGEND—Congressional District Lines _____ County Lines _____

PENNSYLVANIA'S CONGRESSIONAL DISTRICTS

U.S. SENATORS

John Heinz (R) 277 Russell Building, Washington, D.C. 20510.   Arlen Specter (R) 331 Hart Building, Washington, D.C. 20510.

U.S. REPRESENTATIVES
(Washington Address: House Office Building, 20515)

1st. Philadelphia: (part) wards 1, 2, 5, 7, 13, 14, 15, 18, 19, 20, 25, 26, 27, 30; (part) divisions 4, 5, 10, 11, 12, 13, 14, 15, 16, 17 and 18; (part) wards 31, 36, 37, 39, 42; (part) divisions 1, 2, 3, 4, 5, 6, 7, 8, 9, 10, 11, 12, 13, 14, 15, 16, 17, 18, 19, 20, 21, 22, 23 and 24; (part) wards 43, 47, 48 and 49. Total population: 515,707

2nd. Philadelphia (part) wards 3, 4, 6, 8, 9; (part) divisions 1, 2, 3, 14 and 15; (part) wards 11, 12, 16, 17, 22, 24, 28, 29, 30; (part) divisions 1, 2, 3, 6, 7, 8, 9, 15, 19, 20 and 21; (part) wards 32, 34; (part) divisions 1, 2, 3, 4, 5, 6, 7, 9, 10, 36, 38 and 43; (part) wards 38, 40; (part) divisions 2; (part) wards 44, 46, 50, 51, 52, 59 and 60. Total population: 515, 898

3rd. Philadelphia (part) wards 10, 23, 33,35, 41, 42; (part) division 25; (part) wards 45, 53, 54, 55, 56, 57, 58, 61, 62, 63, 64, 65 and 66. Total population: 516,154

4th. Armstrong (part) consisting of the *Townships* of Bethel, Burrell, Cadogan, East Franklin, Gilpin, Kittanning, Madison, North Buffalo, Parks, Plumcreek, South Bend, South Buffalo, Sugarcreek, Washington and West Franklin and the *Boroughs* of Applewold, Elderton, Freeport, Kittanning, Leechburg, West Kittanning and Worthington; **Beaver** (part) consisting of the *City* of Beaver Falls and the *Townships* of Brighton, Chippewa, Darlington, Daugherty, Franklin, Greene, Harmony, Marion, New Sewickley, North Sewickley, Patterson, Pulaski, South Beaver, Vanport and White and the *Boroughs* of Aliquippa, Baden, Beaver, Big Beaver, Bridgewater, Conway, Darlington, Eastvale, Economy, Ellwood City (Beaver County portion), Fallston, Georgetown, Glasgow, Homewood, Hookstown, Koppel, New Brighton, New Galilee, Ohioville, Patterson Heights and West Mayfield; all of **Butler** County; all of **Indiana** County; part of **Lawrence** County consisting of the *City* of New Castle and the *Townships* of Little Beaver, Mahoning, North Beaver, Perry, Plain Grove, Pulaski, Shenango, Taylor, Union, Wayne and Wilmington and the *Boroughs* of Bessemer, Ellport, Ellwood City (Lawrence County portion), Enon Valley, New Beaver, S.N.P.J., South New Castle, Volant and Wampum; and part of **Westmoreland** County consisting of the *Townships* of Fairfield and Ligonier and the *Boroughs* of Bolivar and Ligonier. Total population: 515,572.

5th. Chester County (part) consisting of the *City* of Coatesville and the *Townships* of Birmingham, Caln, Charlestown, East Bradford, East Brandywine, East Caln, East Fallowfield, East Goshen, East Marlborough, East Pikeland, East Whiteland, Easttown, Franklin, Kennett, London Britain, London Grove, New Garden, Newlin, Pennsbury, Pocopson, Schuylkill, Thornbury, Tredyffrin, Uwchlan, Valley, West Bradford, West Brandywine, West Goshen, West Marlborough, West Pikeland, West Whiteland, Westtown and Willistown and the *Boroughs* of Avondale, Downington, Kennett Square, Malvern, Modena, Phoenixville, South Coatesville, West Chester and West Grove; **Delaware** County (part) consisting of the *City* of Chester and the *Townships* of Bethel, Birmingham, Chester, Concord, Lower Chichester, Thornbury and Upper Chichester and the *Boroughs* of Marcus Hook and Trainer; and **Montgomery** County (part) consisting of the *Townships* of Douglass, East Norriton, Franconia, Hatfield, Limerick, Lower Frederick, Lower Pottsgrove, Lower Providence, Marlborough, New Hanover, Perkiomen, Salford, Skippack, Upper Frederick, Upper Hanover, Upper Pottsgrove, Upper Providence, Upper Salford, West Norriton and West Pottsgrove and the *Boroughs* of Collegeville, East Greenville, Green Lane, Hatfield, Pennsburg, Pottstown, Red Hill, Royersford, Schwenksville, Souderton, Telford (Montgomery County portion) and Trappe. Total population: 515,528

6th. Berks County, **Carbon** County (part) consisting of the *Townships* of Banks and Packer and the *Boroughs* of Beaver Meadows, Lansford, Nesquehoning and Summit Hill; **Lancaster** (part) County consisting of the *Townships* of Brecknock, Caernarvon, East Cocalico, East Earl and West Cocalico and the *Boroughs* of Adamstown (Lancaster County portion), Denver and Terre Hill; and **Schuylkill** County. Total population: 515,952

7th. Delaware County (part) consisting of the *Townships* of Aston, Darby, Edgemont, Haverford, Marple, Middletown, Nether Providence, Newtown, Radnor, Ridley, Springfield, Tinicum, Upper Darby and Upper Providence and the *Boroughs* of Aldan, Brookhaven, Chester Heights, Clifton Heights, Collingdale, Colwyn, Darby, East Lansdowne, Eddystone, Folcroft, Glenolden, Lansdowne, Media, Millbourne, Morton, Norwood, Parkside, Prospect Park, Ridley Park, Rose Valley, Rutledge, Sharon Hill, Swarthmore, Upland and Yeadon; and **Philadelphia** (part) ward 40 (part) divisions 1, 3, 4, 5, 6, 7, 8, 9, 10,11, 12, 13, 14, 15, 16, 17, 18, 19, 20, 21, 22, 23, 24, 25, 26, 27, 28, 29, 30, 31, 32, 33, 34, 35, 36, 37, 38, 39, 40, 41, 42, 43, 44, 45, 46, 47, 48, 49, 50, 51, 52, 53, 54, 55 and 56. Total population: 515,766

8th. Bucks County and **Montgomery** County (part) consisting of the *Townships* of Lower Moreland and Upper Moreland (part) districts 1, 2; (part) division 1; (part) districts 3, 4, 5, 6 and 7; and the *Borough* of Bryn Athyn. Total population: 516,296

9th. Bedford, Blair Counties, **Cambria** County (part) consisting of the *Townships* of Chest, Clearfield, Dean, Elder, Reade, Susquehanna and White and the *Boroughs* of Hastings and Patton; **Clearfield** County (part) consisting of the *Townships* of Beccaria, Bell, Bigler, Bloom, Boggs, Brady, Burnside, Chest, Cooper, Decatur, Ferguson, Greenwood, Gulich, Jordan, Knox, Morris, Penn, Pike and Woodward and the *Boroughs* of Brisbin, Burnside, Chester Hill, Coalport, Curwensville, Glenhope, Grampian, Houtzdale, Irvona, Lumber City, Mahaffey, New Washington, Newburg, Osceola, Ramey, Troutville, Wallaceton and Westover; **Cumberland** County (part) consisting of the *Townships* of Cooke, Dickinson, Hopewell, Lower Frankford, Lower Mifflin, Monroe, North Newton, Penn, Shippensburg, South Middleton, South Newton, Southampton, Upper Frankford and Upper Mifflin and the *Boroughs* of Mt. Holly Springs, Newburg, Newville and Shippensburg (Cumberland County portion); **Franklin, Fulton, Huntingdon, Juniata** and **Mifflin** Counties. Total population: 515,430

10th. Bradford County; **Clinton** County (part) consisting of the *Townships* of Chapman, Colebrook, Gallagher, Grugan, Leidy, Noyes and Woodward and the *Boroughs* of Renovo and South Renovo; **Lackawanna** County; **Monroe** County (part) consisting of the *Townships* of Jackson, Middle Smithfield, Paradise, Pocono, Price, Smithfield and Stroud and the *Boroughs* of Delaware Water Gap, East Stroudsburg and Stroudsburg; **Pike, Potter, Susquehanna, Tioga, Wayne** and **Wyoming** Counties. Total population: 515,442

11th. Carbon County (part) consisting of the *Townships* of East Penn, Franklin, Kidder, Lausanne, Lehigh, Lower Towamensing, Mahoning, Penn Forest and Towamensing and the *Boroughs* of Bowmanstown, East Side, Jim Thorpe, Lehighton, Palmerton, Parryville, Weatherly and Weissport; **Columbia, Luzerne** Counties; **Monroe** County (part) consisting of the *Townships* of Barrett, Coolbaugh and Tobyhanna and the *Borough* of Mt. Pocono; **Montour** County; **Northumberland** County (part) consisting of the *City* of Shamokin and the *Townships* of Coal, East Cameron and Mt. Carmel and the *Boroughs* of Kulpmont, Marion Heights and Mt. Carmel; **Sullivan** County. Total population: 515,729

12th. Armstrong County (part) consisting of the *Township* of Kiskiminetas and the *Boroughs* of Apollo and North Apollo; **Cambria** County (part) consisting of the *City* of Johnstown and the *Townships* of Adams, Allegheny, Barr, Blacklick, Cambria, Conemaugh, Cresson, Croyle, East Carroll, East Taylor, Gallitzin, Jackson, Lower Yoder, Middle Taylor, Munster, Portage, Richland, Stonycreek, Summerhill, Upper Yoder, Washington, West Carroll and West Taylor and the *Boroughs* of Ashville, Barnesboro, Brownstown, Carrolltown, Cassandra, Chest Springs, Cresson, Daisytown, Dale, East Conemaugh, Ebensburg, Ehrenfeld, Ferndale, Franklin, Gallitzin, Geistown, Lilly, Lorain, Loretto, Nanty Glo, Portage, Sankertown, Scalp Level, South Fork, Southmont, Spangler, Summerhill, Tunnelhill (Cambria County portion), Vihtondale, Westmont and Wilmore; **Somerset** County; **Westmoreland** County (part) consisting of the *Cities* of Greensburg and Jeannette and the *Townships* of Bell, Cook, Derry, Donegal, Hempfield, Loyalhanna, Mt. Pleasant, North Huntingdon, Penn, Salem, St. Clair, Unity and Washington and the *Boroughs* of Adamsburg, Arona, Avonmore, Delmont, Derry, Donegal, Export, Hunker, Irwin, Latrobe, Madison, Manor, Murrysville, New Alexandria, New Florence, New Stanton, North Irwin, Penn, Seward, South Greensburg, Southwest Greensburg, Youngstown and Youngwood. Total population: 515,915

13th. Montgomery County (part) consisting of the *Townships* of Abington, Cheltenham, Horsham, Lower Gwynedd, Lower Merion, Lower Salford, Montgomery, Plymouth, Springfield, Towamencin, Upper Dublin, Upper Gwynedd, Upper Merion, Upper Moreland (part) district 2, (part) division 2, Whitemarsh, Whitpain and Worcester and the *Boroughs* of Ambler, Bridgeport, Conshohocken, Hatboro, Jenkintown, Lansdale, Narberth, Norristown, North Wales, Rockledge and West Conshohocken; **Philadelphia** County (part) wards 9, (part) divisions 4, 5, 6, 7, 8, 9, 10, 11, 12, 13, 16 and 17; (part) wards 21 and 34; (part) divisions 8, 11, 12, 13, 14, 17, 18, 19, 20, 21, 22, 23, 24, 25, 26, 27, 28, 29, 30, 31, 32, 33, 34, 35, 37, 39, 40, 41 and 42. Total population: 515,707

14th. Allegheny County (part) consisting of the *City* of Pittsburgh and the *Townships* of Baldwin, Kennedy, Neville, Reserve and Stowe and the *Boroughs* of Castle Shannon, Coraopolis, Ingram, McKees Rocks, Millvale, Mt. Oliver, Sharpsburg and Wilkinsburg. Total population: 516,611

15th. Lehigh County; **Monroe** County (part) consisting of the *Townships* of Chestnuthill, Eldred, Hamilton, Polk, Ross and Tunkhannock; **Northampton** County. Total population: 516,492

16th. Chester County (part) consisting of the *Townships* of East Conventry, East Nantmeal, East Nottingham, East Vincent, Elk, Highland, Honeybrook, Londonderry, Lower Oxford, New London, North Coventry, Penn, Sadsbury, South Coventry, Upper Oxford, Upper Uwchlan, Wallace, Warwick, West Caln, West Fallowfield, West Nantmeal, West Nottingham, West Sadsbury and West Vincent and the *Boroughs* of Atglen, Elverson, Honey Brook, Oxford, Parkesburg and Spring City; **Lancaster** County (part) consisting of the *City* of Lancaster and the *Townships* of Bart, Clay, Colerain, Conestoga, Conoy, Drumore, Earl, East Donegal, East Drumore, East Hempfield, East Lampeter, Eden, Elizabeth, Ephrata, Fulton, Lancaster, Leacock, Little Britain, Manheim, Manor, Martic, Mt. Joy, Paradise, Penn, Pequea, Providence, Rapho, Sadsbury, Salisbury, Strasburg, Upper Leacock, Warwick, West Donegal, West Earl, West Hempfield and West Lampeter and the *Boroughs* of Akron, Christiana, Columbia, East Petersburg, Elizabethtown, Ephrata, Lititz, Manheim, Marietta, Millersville, Mountville, Mt. Joy, New Holland, Quarryville and Strasburg; **Lebanon** County. Total population: 515,832

17th. Dauphin, Lycoming Counties; **Northumberland** County (part) consisting of the *City* of Sunbury and the *Townships* of Delaware, East Chillisquaque, Jackson, Jordan, Lewis, Little Mahanoy, Lower Augusta, Lower Mahanoy, Point, Ralpho, Rockefeller, Rush, Shamokin, Turbot, Upper Augusta, Upper Mahanoy, Washington, West Cameron, West Chillisquaque and Zerbe and the *Boroughs* of Herndon, McEwensville, Milton, Northumberland, Riverside, Snydertown, Turbotville and Watsontown; **Perry, Snyder** and **Union** Counties. Total population: 515,900

18th. Allegheny County (part) consisting of the *Townships* of Aleppo, Crescent, Findlay, Hampton, Kilbuck, Leet, Marshall, McCandless, Moon, Mt. Lebanon, North Fayette, O'Hara, Ohio, Penn Hills, Pine, Richland, Robinson, Ross, Scott, Shaler, South Park and Upper St. Clair and the *Boroughs* of Aspinwall, Avalon, Bell Acres, Bellevue, Ben Avon, Ben Avon Heights, Bethel Park, Blawnox, Braddock Hills, Bradford Woods, Carnegie, Churchill, Crafton, Dormont, Edgewood, Edgeworth, Emsworth, Etna, Forest Hills, Fox Chapel, Franklin Park, Glenfield, Green Tree, Haysville, Jefferson, Osborne, Pennsbury Village, Pleasant Hills, Rosslyn Farms, Sewickley, Sewickley Heights, Sewickley Hills, Thornburg, West Elizabeth, West View and Whitehall. Total population: 516,068

19th. Adams County; **Cumberland** County (part) consisting of the *Townships* of East Pennsboro, Hampden, Lower Allen, Middlesex, North Middleton, Silver Spring, Upper Allen and West Pennsboro and the *Boroughs* of Camp Hill, Carlisle, Lemoyne, Mechanicsburg, New Cumberland, Shiremanstown, West Fairview and Wormleysburg; **York** County. Total population: 516,101

20th. Allegheny County (part) consisting of the *Cities* of Clairton, Duquesne and McKeesport and the *Townships* of East Deer, Elizabeth, Fawn, Forward, Frazer, Harmar, Harrison, Indiana, North Versailles, South Versailles, Springdale, West Deer and Wilkins and the *Boroughs* of Baldwin, Brackenridge, Braddock, Brentwood, Chalfant, Cheswick, Dravosburg, East McKeesport, East Pittsburgh, Elizabeth, Glassport, Homestead, Liberty, Lincoln, Monroeville, Munhall, North Braddock, Oakmont, Pitcairn, Plum, Port Vue, Rankin, Springdale, Swissvale, Tarentum, Trafford (Allegheny County portion), Turtle Creek, Verona, Versailles, Wall, West Homestead, West Mifflin, Whitaker, White Oak and Wilmerding; **Westmoreland** County (part) consisting of the *Cities* of Arnold, Lower Burrell, Monessen and New Kensington and the *Townships* of Allegheny, East Huntingdon, Rostraver, Sewickley, South Huntingdon and Upper Burrell and the *Boroughs* of East Vandergrift, Hyde Park, Mt. Pleasant, North Belle Vernon, Oklahoma, Scottdale, Smithton, Sutersville, Trafford (Westmoreland County portion), Vandergrift, West Leechburg and West Newton. Total population: 516,028

21st. Crawford, Erie Counties; **Lawrence** County (part) consisting of the *Townships* of Hickory, Neshannock, Scott, Slippery Rock and Washington and the *Borough* of New Wilmington; **Mercer** County. Total population: 516,645

22nd. Allegheny County (part) consisting of the *Townships* of Collier and South Fayette and the *Boroughs* of Bridgeville, Heidelberg, Leetsdale, McDonald (Allegheny County portion) and Oakdale; **Beaver** County (part) consisting of the *Townships* of Center, Hanover, Hopewell, Independence, Potter, Raccoon and Rochester and the *Boroughs* of Ambridge, East Rochester, Frankfort Springs, Freedom, Industry, Midland, Monaca, Rochester, Shippingport and South Heights; **Fayette, Greene** and **Washington** Counties. Total population:515,979

23rd. Armstrong County (part) consisting of the *Townships* of Boggs, Bradys Bend, Cowanshannock, Hovey, Mahoning, Manor, Perry, Pine, Rayburn, Redbank, Valley and Wayne and the *Boroughs* of Atwood, Dayton, Ford City, Ford Cliff, Manorville, Parker City, Rural Valley and South Bethlehem; **Cameron, Centre, Clarion** Counties; **Clearfield** County (part) consisting of the *City* of DuBois and the *Townships* of Bradford, Covington, Girard, Goshen, Graham, Huston, Karthaus, Lawrence, Pine, Sandy and Union and the *Boroughs* of Clearfield and Falls Creek (Clearfield County portion); **Clinton** County (part) consisting of the *City* of Lock Haven, and the *Townships* of Allison, Bald Eagle, Beech Creek, Castanea, Crawford, Dunnstable, East Keating, Greene, Lamar, Logan, Pine Creek, Porter, Wayne and West Keating and the *Boroughs* of Avis, Beech Creek, Flemington, Loganton and Mill Hall; **Elk, Forest, Jefferson, McKean, Venango** and **Warren** Counties. Total population: 515,976

Population of all districts: 11,866,728

UNITED STATES SUPREME COURT

First Court: 1790
Purpose: To exercise original jurisdiction in cases affecting ambassadors and other public ministers and consuls, and in cases in which the state is a party, and to exercise appellate jurisdiction in all other cases which fall within the judicial power of the United States as stated in the Constitution.

	Born	Year Appointed	Appointing President	Salary
CHIEF JUSTICE				
William H. Rehnquist Arizona	1924	1986	Reagan	$115,000
ASSOCIATE JUSTICES				
William J. Brennan Jr. New Jersey	1906	1956	Eisenhower	110,000
Byron R. White Colorado	1917	1962	Kennedy	110,000
Thurgood Marshall New York	1908	1967	Johnson	110,000
Harry A. Blackmun Minnesota	1908	1970	Nixon	110,000
John Paul Stevens Illinois	1920	1975	Ford	110,000
Sandra Day O'Connor Arizona	1930	1981	Reagan	110,000
Antonin Scalia Virginia	1937	1986	Reagan	110,000
RETIRED CHIEF JUSTICE				
Warren E. Burger Virginia	1907	1969	Nixon	115,000

UNITED STATES COURT OF APPEALS

Purpose: To provide a forum for review of the decisions of a case in a district court and to receive cases for review of action of various Federal Administrative Agencies for errors of law.

THIRD CIRCUIT
(Delaware, New Jersey, Pennsylvania and the Virgin Islands)
Clerk's Office: Philadelphia, Pa. 19106

Salary: $95,000

CIRCUIT JUDGES

Judge		Date Appointed
John J. Gibbons, Chief Judge	Newark, N.J.	December 18, 1969
Collins J. Seitz	Wilmington, Del	June 9, 1966
Joseph F. Weis Jr.	Pittsburgh, Pa.	March 15, 1973
A. Leon Higginbotham	Philadelphia, Pa.	October 13, 1977
Delores Korman Sloviter	Philadelphia, Pa.	June 21, 1979
Edward R. Becker	Philadelphia, Pa.	January 22, 1982
Walter K. Stapleton	Wilmington, Del.	April 4, 1985
Carol Los Mansmann	Pittsburgh, Pa.	April 4, 1985

SENIOR CIRCUIT JUDGES

Albert Branson Maris	Philadelphia, Pa.	June 24, 1938*
Francis L. Van Dusen	Philadelphia, Pa.	June 12, 1967
Ruggero J. Aldisert	Pittsburgh, Pa.	July 29, 1968
Max Rosenn	Wilkes-Barre, Pa.	October 7, 1970
James Hunter III	Camden, N.J.	September 23, 1971
Leonard I. Garth	Newark, N.J.	August 6, 1973

UNITED STATES DISTRICT COURTS

FOR THE EASTERN, MIDDLE, AND WESTERN DISTRICTS OF PENNSYLVANIA

Purpose: To exercise initial jurisdiction in cases in the states and territories. In each state and the District of Columbia, as well as the territories, there is at least one district court; many states have more than two districts.

Salary: $81,100

EASTERN DISTRICT
Clerk's Office: Philadelphia 19106

Judge		Date Appointed
John P. Fullam, Chief Judge	Philadelphia	August 11, 1966
Charles R. Weiner	Philadelphia	June 14, 1967
Daniel H. Huyett, 3rd	Reading	October 15, 1970
Clarence C. Newcomer	Philadelphia	November 30, 1971
Clifford Scott Green	Philadelphia	December 9, 1971
Louis Charles Bechtle	Philadelphia	March 7, 1972
Joseph L. McGlynn, Jr.	Philadelphia	March 8, 1974
Edward N. Cahn	Allentown	December 20, 1974
Louis H. Pollak	Philadelphia	July 12, 1978
Norma L. Shapiro	Philadelphia	August 11, 1978
James T. Giles	Philadelphia	November 27, 1979
Thomas N. O'Neill, Jr.	Philadelphia	August 5, 1983
James McGirr Kelly	Philadelphia	August 6, 1983
Marvin Katz	Philadelphia	August 6, 1983
Anthony J. Scirica	Philadelphia	September 18, 1984
Edmund V. Ludwig	Philadelphia	October 17, 1985

MIDDLE DISTRICT
Clerk's Office: Scranton 18501

William J. Nealon, Jr., Chief Judge	Scranton	March 27, 1963
Richard P. Conaboy	Scranton	August 6, 1979
Sylvia H. Rambo	Harrisburg	August 9, 1979
William W. Caldwell	Harrisburg	March 19, 1982
Edwin M. Kosik	Scranton	July 15, 1986

WESTERN DISTRICT
Clerk's Office: Pittsburgh 15230

Maurice B. Cohill Jr., Chief Judge	Pittsburgh	June 1, 1976
Hubert I. Teitelbaum	Pittsburgh	January 11, 1971
Gerald J. Weber	Erie	October 2, 1964
Paul A. Simmons	Pittsburgh	May 3, 1978
Gustave Diamond	Pittsburgh	May 24, 1978
Donald E. Ziegler	Pittsburgh	May 22, 1978
Alan N. Bloch	Pittsburgh	November 21, 1979
Glenn E. Mencer	Erie	April 16, 1982

SENIOR DISTRICT JUDGES

Rabe F. Marsh	Greensburg	June 8, 1950
Joseph P. Wilson	Smethport	July 14, 1953
Edward Dumbauld	Pittsburgh	August 3, 1961
Joseph S. Lord, III	Philadelphia	September 15, 1961
Louis Rosenberg	Pittsburgh	July 12, 1962
E. Mac Troutman	Reading	June 16, 1967
R. Dixon Herman	Harrisburg	December 11, 1969
John B. Hannum	Philadelphia	May 6, 1969
Malcolm Muir	Williamsport	October 14, 1970
Donald W. VanArtsdalen	Philadelphia	October 15, 1970
J. William Ditter, Jr.	Philadelphia	October 15, 1970
Barron P. McCune	Washington	December 18, 1970
Raymond J. Broderick	Philadelphia	April 23, 1971

PRESIDENTS, VICE PRESIDENTS, AND CONGRESSES
COINCIDENT WITH THEIR TERMS

President	Vice President	Service	Congress
George Washington	John Adams	Apr. 30, 1789—Mar. 3, 1797	1,2,3,4
John Adams	Thomas Jefferson	Mar. 4, 1797—Mar. 3, 1801	5,6
Thomas Jefferson	Aaron Burr	Mar. 4, 1801—Mar. 3, 1805	7,8
Thomas Jefferson	George Clinton	Mar. 4, 1805—Mar. 3, 1809	9,10
James Madison	George Clinton[2]	Mar. 4, 1809—Mar. 3, 1813	11,12
James Madison	Eibridge Gerry[2]	Mar. 4, 1813—Mar. 3, 1817	13,14
James Monroe	Daniel D. Tompkins	Mar. 4, 1817—Mar. 3, 1825	15,16,17,18
John Quincy Adams	John C. Calhoun	Mar. 4, 1825—Mar. 3, 1829	19,20
Andrew Jackson	John C. Calhoun[1]	Mar. 4, 1829—Mar. 3, 1833	21,22
Andrew Jackson	Martin Van Buren	Mar. 4, 1833—Mar. 3, 1837	23,24
Martin Van Buren	Richard M. Johnson	Mar. 4, 1837—Mar. 3, 1841	25,26
William Henry Harrison[2]	John Tyler	Mar. 4, 1841—Apr. 4, 1841	27
John Tyler		Apr. 6, 1841—Mar. 3, 1845	27,28
James K. Polk	George M. Dallas	Mar. 4, 1845—Mar. 3, 1849	29,30
Zachary Taylor[2]	Millard Fillmore	Mar. 5, 1849—July 9, 1850	31
Millard Fillmore		July 10, 1850—Mar. 3, 1853	31,32
Franklin Pierce	William R. King[2]	Mar. 4, 1853—Mar. 3, 1857	33,34
James Buchanan	John C. Breckinridge	Mar. 4, 1857—Mar. 3, 1861	35,36
Abraham Lincoln	Hannibal Hamlin	Mar. 4, 1861—Mar. 3, 1865	37,38
Abraham Lincoln[2]	Andrew Johnson	Mar. 4, 1865—Apr. 15, 1865	39
Andrew Johnson		Apr. 15, 1865—Mar. 3, 1869	39,40
Ulysses S. Grant	Schuyler Colfax	Mar. 4, 1869—Mar. 3, 1873	41,42
Ulysses S. Grant	Henry Wilson[2]	Mar. 4, 1873—Mar. 3, 1877	43,44
Rutherford B. Hayes	William A. Wheeler	Mar. 4, 1877—Mar. 3, 1881	45,46
James A. Garfield[2]	Chester A. Arthur	Mar. 4, 1881—Sept. 19, 1881	47
Chester A. Arthur		Sept. 20, 1881—Mar. 3, 1885	47,48
Grover Cleveland[3]	Thomas A. Hendricks[2]	Mar. 4, 1885—Mar. 3, 1889	49,50
Benjamin Harrison	Levi P. Morton	Mar. 4, 1889—Mar. 3, 1893	51,52
Grover Cleveland[3]	Adlai E. Stevenson	Mar. 4, 1893—Mar. 3, 1897	53,54
William McKinley	Garret A. Hobart[2]	Mar. 4, 1897—Mar. 3, 1901	55,56
William McKinley[2]	Theodore Roosevelt	Mar. 4, 1901—Sept. 14, 1901	57
Theodore Roosevelt		Sept. 14, 1901—Mar. 3, 1905	57,58
Theodore Roosevelt	Charles W. Fairbanks	Mar. 4, 1905—Mar. 3, 1909	59,60
William H. Taft	James S. Sherman[2]	Mar. 4, 1909—Mar. 3, 1913	61,62
Woodrow Wilson	Thomas R. Mashall	Mar. 4, 1913—Mar. 3, 1921	63,64,65,66
Warren G. Harding[2]	Calvin Coolidge	Mar. 4, 1921—Aug. 2, 1923	67
Calvin Coolidge		Aug. 3, 1923—Mar. 3, 1925	68
Calvin Coolidge	Charles G. Dawes	Mar. 4, 1925—Mar. 3, 1929	69,70
Herbert C. Hoover	Charles Curtis	Mar. 4, 1929—Mar. 3, 1933	71,72
Franklin D. Roosevelt	John N. Garner	Mar. 4, 1933—Jan. 20, 1941	73,74,75,76
Franklin D. Roosevelt	Henry A. Wallace	Jan. 20, 1941—Jan. 20, 1945	77,78
Franklin D. Roosevelt[2]	Harry S. Truman	Jan. 20, 1945—Apr. 12, 1945	79
Harry S. Truman		Apr. 12, 1945—Jan. 20, 1949	79,80
Harry S. Truman	Alben W. Barkley	Jan. 20, 1949—Jan. 20, 1953	81,82
Dwight D. Eisenhower	Richard M. Nixon	Jan. 20, 1953—Jan. 20, 1961	83,84,85,86
John F. Kennedy[2]	Lyndon B. Johnson	Jan. 20, 1961—Nov. 22, 1963	87,88
Lyndon B. Johnson		Nov. 22, 1963—Jan. 20, 1965	88
Lyndon B. Johnson	Hubert H. Humphrey	Jan. 20, 1965—Jan. 20, 1969	89,90
Richard M. Nixon	Spiro T. Agnew[4]	Jan. 20, 1969—Oct. 10, 1973	91,92,93
Richard M. Nixon		Oct. 10, 1973—Dec. 5, 1973	93
Richard M. Nixon[5]	Gerald R. Ford	Dec. 6, 1973—Aug. 8, 1974	93
Gerald R. Ford		Aug. 9, 1974—Dec. 18, 1974	93,94
Gerald R. Ford	Nelson A. Rockefeller	Dec. 19, 1974—Jan. 19, 1977	94
James E. Carter	Walter F. Mondale	Jan. 20, 1977—Jan. 19, 1981	95,96
Ronald Wilson Reagan	George Bush	Jan. 20, 1981—	97, 98, 99, 100

[1]Resigned Dec. 28, 1832, to become U.S. Senator
[2]Died in Office.
[3]Terms not consecutive.
[4]Resigned Oct. 10, 1973.
[5]Resigned Aug. 8, 1974.

U. S. GOVERNORS

State	Capital	Governor	Party	Term Years	Term Expires
Alabama	Montgomery	Guy Hurt	Rep.	4	Jan. 1991
Alaska	Juneau	Steve Cowper	Dem.	4	Dec. 1990
Arizona	Phoenix	Evan Meacham	Rep.	4	Jan. 1991
Arkansas	Little Rock	Bill Clinton	Dem.	4	Jan. 1991
California	Sacramento	George Deukmejian	Rep.	4	Jan. 1991
Colorado	Denver	Roy Romer	Dem.	4	Jan. 1991
Connecticut	Hartford	William A. O'Neill	Dem.	4	Jan. 1991
Delaware	Dover	Michael N. Castle	Rep.	4	Jan. 1989
Florida	Tallahassee	Bob Martinez	Dem.	4	Jan. 1991
Georgia	Atlanta	Joe Frank Harris	Dem.	4	Jan. 1991
Hawaii	Honolulu	John Waihee	Dem.	4	Dec. 1990
Idaho	Boise	Cecil Andrus	Dem.	4	Jan. 1991
Illinois	Springfield	James R. Thompson	Rep.	4	Jan. 1991
Indiana	Indianapolis	Robert D. Orr	Rep.	4	Jan. 1989
Iowa	Des Moines	Terry Branstad	Rep.	4	Jan. 1991
Kansas	Topeka	Mike Hayden	Rep.	4	Jan. 1991
Kentucky	Frankfort	Martha Lane Collins	Dem.	4	Dec. 1987
Louisiana	Baton Rouge	Edwin W. Edwards	Dem.	4	Mar. 1988
Maine	Augusta	John McKernan	Rep.	4	Jan. 1991
Maryland	Annapolis	Donald Schaefer	Dem.	4	Jan. 1991
Massachusetts	Boston	Michael S. Dukakis	Dem.	4	Jan. 1991
Michigan	Lansing	James J. Blanchard	Dem.	4	Jan. 1991
Minnesota	St. Paul	Rudy Perpich	Dem.	4	Jan. 1991
Mississippi	Jackson	William A. Allain	Dem.	4	Jan. 1988
Missouri	Jefferson City	John Ashcroft	Rep.	4	Jan. 1989
Montana	Helena	Ted Schwinden	Dem.	4	Jan. 1989
Nebraska	Lincoln	Kay Orr	Rep.	4	Jan. 1991
Nevada	Carson City	Richard H. Bryan	Dem.	4	Jan. 1991
New Hampshire	Concord	John H. Sununu	Rep.	2	Jan. 1989
New Jersey	Trenton	Thomas H. Kean	Rep.	4	Jan. 1990
New Mexico	Sante Fe	Garrey Carruthers	Rep.	4	Jan. 1991
New York	Albany	Mario Cuomo	Dem.	4	Jan. 1991
North Carolina	Raleigh	James G. Martin	Rep.	4	Jan. 1989
North Dakota	Bismarck	George Sinner	Dem.	4	Jan. 1989
Ohio	Columbus	Richard F. Celeste	Dem.	4	Jan. 1991
Oklahoma	Oklahoma City	Harry Bellman	Rep.	4	Jan. 1991
Oregon	Salem	Neil Goldschmidt	Dem.	4	Jan. 1991
Pennsylvania	Harrisburg	Robert P. Casey	Dem.	4	Jan. 1991
Rhode Island	Providence	Edward D. DiPrete	Rep.	2	Jan. 1989
South Carolina	Columbia	Carroll Campbell	Rep.	4	Jan. 1991
South Dakota	Pierre	George Mickelson	Rep.	4	Jan. 1991
Tennessee	Nashville	Ned McWherter	Dem.	4	Jan. 1991
Texas	Austin	Bill Clements	Rep.	4	Jan. 1991
Utah	Salt Lake City	Norman H. Bangerter	Rep.	4	Jan. 1989
Vermont	Montpelier	Madeleine M. Kunin	Dem.	2	Jan. 1989
Virginia	Richmond	Gerald L. Baliles	Dem.	4	Jan. 1990
Washington	Olympia	W. Booth Gardner	Dem.	4	Jan. 1989
West Virginia	Charleston	Arch A. Moore, Jr.	Rep.	4	Jan. 1989
Wisconsin	Madison	Tommy Thompson	Rep.	4	Jan. 1991
Wyoming	Cheyenne	Mike Sullivan	Dem.	4	Jan. 1991

Jurisdiction

Amer. Samoa	Pago Pago	A. P. Lutali	Dem.	4	Jan. 1989
Guam	Agana	Joseph Ada	Dem.	4	Jan. 1991
Northern Marianas Is.	Saipan	Pedro P. Tenorio	Rep.	4	Jan. 1990
Puerto Rico	San Juan	Rafael Hernandez-Colon	PDP	4	Jan. 1989
Virgin Islands	Charlotte Amalie	Alexander Farrelly	Ind.	4	Jan. 1991

APPENDIX

SECTION 9 - APPENDIX

ELLEN HARDING CASEY

Photo by Bachrach

Ellen Harding Casey was born February 11, 1932, in Scranton. Married to Governor Robert P. Casey, June 27, 1953, she and the Governor are the parents of eight children, including: Margaret Casey McGrath, Mary Ellen Casey Philbin, Kathleen Casey Brier, Robert Casey, Jr., Christopher Casey, Erin Casey Walsh, Patrick Casey, and Matthew Casey.

The Caseys have five grandchildren.

The Caseys' youngest child, Matthew, is 16 and lives at the Governor's Harrisburg residence with his parents, as does Mrs. Casey's mother, Mrs. Margaret Harding, who celebrates her 92nd birthday in March of 1988.

While Ellen Casey considers her career as wife and mother to be her most important role, she has taken an active interest in the problem of adult illiteracy, which she views as a crucial concern for Pennsylvania and the nation in the 1980s. As an advocate of literacy programs, she makes public appearances, appears in television public service announcements, and visits literacy councils, schools, libraries, and other sites throughout the Commonwealth to promote adult literacy.

A graduate of Marywood College with a degree in art, Mrs. Casey maintains the first floor of the Governor's Residence as art exhibition space and opens the residence to the public for regularly-scheduled tours.

JACQUELINE LYNN SINGEL

Jacqueline Lynn Singel, the wife of Lieutenant Governor Mark S. Singel, was born in Johnstown, Pennsylvania, on June 1, 1953. She is the daughter of Wilbur and Alice (G iffith) Schonek.

Jackie graduated from Westmount Hilltop High School, Johnstown, in 1971. She received her Bachelor of Arts degree from Albright College, Reading, in 1975, where she majored in home economics education.

A former home economics teacher and retail sales manager, Jackie has combined homemaking with a busy schedule supporting her husband's political career. Jackie is interested in volunteer work in the Central Pennsylvania area.

She is a member of the American Home Economics Association and the Pennsylvania Home Economics Association.

Jackie is the busy mother of three children: Allyson Jean (4), Jonathan Albert (2), and Christopher Mark (1).

The Singels reside at The State House, Fort Indiantown Gap, near Annville in Lebanon County.

U.S. POPULATION: 1980 and 1970

Region, Division and State	Population		Percent Change 1970 — 1980
	1980	1970	Percent
United States	226,504,825	203,302,031	11.4
Regions:			
Northeast	49,136,667	49,060,514	0.2
North Central	58,853,804	56,590,294	4.0
South.	75,349,155	62,812,980	20.0
West	43,165,199	34,838,243	23.9
Northeast:			
New England	12,348,493	11,847,245	4.2
Middle Atlantic	36,788,174	37,213,269	-1.1
North Central:			
East North Central	41,669,738	40,262,747	3.5
West North Central	17,184,066	16,327,547	5.2
South:			
South Atlantic	36,943,,139	30,678,826	20.4
East South Central	14,662,882	12,808,077	14.5
West South Central	23,743,134	19,326,077	22.9
West			
Mountain	11,368,330	8,289,901	37.1
Pacific	31,796,869	26,548,342	19.8
New England:			
Maine	1,124,660	993,722	13.2
New Hampshire	920,610	737,681	24.8
Vermont.	511,456	444,732	15.0
Massachusetts	5,737,037	5,689,170	0.8
Rhode Island.	947,154	949,723	-0.3
Connecticut.	3,107,576	3,032,217	2.5
Middle Atlantic:			
New York.	17,557,288	18,241,391	-3.8
New Jersey	7,364,158	7,171,112	2.7
Pennsylvania	11,866,728	11,800,766	0.6
East North Central:			
Ohio	10,797,419	10,657,423	1.3
Indiana	5,490,179	5,195,392	5.7
Illinois	11,418,461	11,110,285	2.8
Michigan.	9,258,344	8,881,826	4.2
Wisconsin	4,705,335	4,417,821	6.5
West North Central:			
Minnesota	4,077,148	3,806,103	7.1
Iowa.	2,913,387	2,825,368	3.1
Missouri	4,917,444	4,677,623	5.1
North Dakota.	652,695	617,792	5.6
South Dakota	690,178	666,257	3.6
Nebraska	1,570,006	1,485,333	5.7
Kansas	2,363,208	2,249,071	5.1
South Atlantic:			
Delaware.	595,225	548,104	8.6
Maryland.	4,216,446	3,923,897	7.5
District of Columbia	637,651	756,668	-15.7
Virginia	5,346,279	4,651,448	14.9
West Virginia.	1,949,644	1,744,237	11.8
North Carolina	5,874,429	5,084,411	15.5
South Carolina	3,119,208	2,590,713	20.4
Georgia.	5,464,265	4,587,930	19.1
Florida.	9,739,992	6,791,418	43.4

East South Central:			
Kentucky	3,661,433	3,220,711	13.7
Tennessee	4,590,750	3,926,018	16.9
Alabama	3,890,061	3,444,354	12.9
Mississippi	2,520,638	2,216,994	13.7
West South Central:			
Arkansas	2,285,513	1,923,322	18.8
Louisiana	4,203,972	3,644,637	15.3
Oklahoma	3,025,266	2,559,463	18.2
Texas	14,228,383	11,198,655	27.1
Mountain:			
Montana	786,690	694,409	13.3
Idaho	943,935	713,015	32.4
Wyoming	470,816	332,416	41.6
Colorado	2,888,834	2,209,596	30.7
New Mexico	1,299,968	1,017,055	27.8
Arizona	2,717,866	1,775,399	53.1
Utah	1,461,037	1,059,273	37.9
Nevada	799,184	488,738	63.5
Pacific:			
Washington	4,130,163	3,413,244	21.0
Oregon	2,632,663	2,091,533	25.9
California	23,668,562	19,971,069	18.5
Alaska	400,481	302,583	32.4
Hawaii	965,000	769,913	25.3

PERCENT CHANGE IN PENNSYLVANIA POPULATION, BY COUNTY
1970 TO 1980

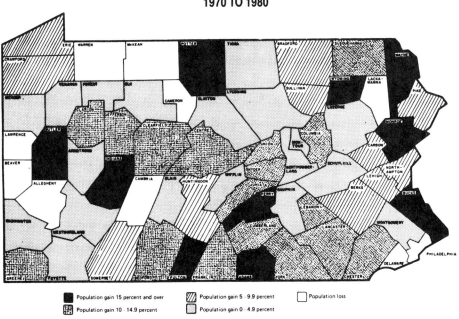

Population gain 15 percent and over
Population gain 10 - 14.9 percent
Population gain 5 - 9.9 percent
Population gain 0 - 4.9 percent
Population loss

Source   Chart prepared by Pennsylvania Department of Commerce. Data from U.S. Bureau of the Census,
Pennsylvania, (Final Population and Housing Unit Counts), PHC-80-V-40.

RECREATION

Pennsylvania offers unparalleled opportunities for enjoyment and appreciation of its natural beauty. Careful planning and construction of a system of state parks, preservation of waterways and virgin land within state forests utilize this natural beauty by providing citizens free or relatively inexpensive access to Pennsylvania's scenic, recreational and historic resources.

Beyond the simple enjoyment of nature, recreational activities include picnicking, boating, swimming, camping, fishing, hiking, hunting and winter sports. Continuing acquisition, development and maintenance of our State Parks and State Forest systems ensures increased availability and enjoyment of these facilities for tourists and all Pennsylvanians.

PENNSYLVANIA STATE PARKS

Park	County	Total Acreage	Water Area	
Archbald Pothole	Lackawanna	153.49		
Bald Eagle	Centre	5,900.00	Blanchard Reservoir	1,730.00 Acres
Beltzville	Carbon	2,972.39	Beltzville Reservoir	948.61 Acres
Bendigo	Elk	100.26	Pool	35' x 105'
Big Pocono	Monroe	1,306.40		
Big Spring	Perry	45.00		
Black Moshannon	Centre	3,394.12	Black Moshannon Lake	250.00 Acres
Blue Knob	Bedford	5,614.00	Pool (Group Camp)	25' x 75'
			Pool	42' x 82'
Buchanan's Birthplace	Franklin	18.50		
Bucktail	Cameron-Clinton	16,433.00	W. Br. Susquehanna River	
Caledonia	Franklin-Adams	1,130.00	Pool	75' x 190'
Canoe Creek	Blair	957.11		
Chapman	Warren	804.68	Chapman	68.00 Acres
Cherry Springs	Potter	48.00		
Clear Creek	Jefferson	1,209.00	Clear Creek Lake	1.30 Acres
Codorus	York	3,324.24	Lake Marburg	1,275.00 Acres
Colonel Denning	Cumberland	273.00	Doubling Gap	3.60 Acres
Colton Point	Tioga	368.00	Pine Creek	
Cook Forest	Jefferson, Forest, & Clarion	6,422.00	Pool	35' x 105'
Cowans Gap	Fulton	1,085.00	Cowans Gap Lake	42.00 Acres
Denton Hill	Potter	700.00		
Elk	Elk	3,192.00	E. Br. Clarion River Res.	1,160.00 Acres
Evansburg	Montgomery	3,349.00	Skippack Creek	
Fort Washington	Montgomery	493.90		
Fowlers Hollow	Perry	104.86	Fowlers Hollow Run	
Frances Slocum	Luzerne	1,005.61	Frances Slocum Lake	165.00 Acres
French Creek	Berks-Chester	7,344.88	Hopewell Lake	68.00 Acres
			Sixpenny Lake	2.50 Acres
			Scotts Run Lake	21.00 Acres
Gifford Pinchot	York	2,337.82	Gifford Pinchot Lake	340.00 Acres
Gouldsboro	Monroe-Wayne	2,800.04	Gouldsboro (Fish Comm.)	250.00 Acres
Greenwood Furnace	Huntingdon	349.00	Greenwood Lake	6.00 Acres
Hickory Run	Carbon	15,500.00	Sand Spring Lake	17.15 Acres
			Hickory Run Lake	4.20 Acres
			C.C.C. Dam	.90 Acres
			No. 5 Dam	0.10 Acres
			Stametz Lake	0.30 Acres
			Saylorville Lake	0.25 Acres
Hills Creek	Tioga	406.58	Hills Creek	137.00 Acres
Hyner Run	Clinton	180.00	Pool	33' x 105'
Hyner View	Clinton	6.00		
Jacobsburg	Northampton	1,166.49	Bushkill Creek	
Jennings	Butler	295.00	Big Run	
Kettle Creek	Clinton	1,793.23	Alvin R. Bush Reservoir	167.00 Acres
Keystone	Westmoreland	1,187.10	Keystone Lake	78.00 Acres
Kings Gap	Cumberland	1,432.99		
Kinzua Bridge	McKean	316.08	Kinzua Bridge	
Kooser	Somerset	170.00	Kooser Lake	4.00 Acres
Lackawanna	Lackawanna	1,410.99	Lackawanna Lake	210.00 Acres

Park	County	Total Acreage	Water Area	
Laurel Hill	Somerset	3,934.50	Laurel Hill	63.55 Acres
			Jones Mill	0.30 Acres
			Spruce Run	0.25 Acres
Laurel Mountain	Westmoreland	493.40		
Laurel Ridge	Fayette, Somerset, Westmoreland, Indiana & Cambria	15,333.70		
Laurel Summit	Westmoreland	15.00		
Leonard Harrison	Tioga	585.00	Pine Creek	
Linn Run	Westmoreland	612.77	Linn Run	
Little Buffalo	Perry	830.00	Little Buffalo Lake	88.00 Acres
Little Pine	Lycoming	2,159.00	Little Pine	93.70 Acres
Locust Lake	Schuylkill	1,143.51	Locust Lake	52.00 Acres
Lyman Run	Potter	595.00	Lyman Run Lake	40.00 Acres
Marsh Creek	Chester	1,705.35	Marsh Creek Lake	535.00 Acres
Maurice K. Goddard	Mercer	2,856.70	Lake Wilheim	1,440.00 Acres
McCalls Dam	Centre	7.50	White Deer Creek	
McConnell Mill	Lawrence	2,533.69	Slippery Rock Creek	
			McConnell Mill	.15 Acres
Memorial Lake	Lebanon	231.00	Memorial Lake	85.00 Acres
Milton	Northumberland	76.74	Susquehanna River	
Mont Alto	Franklin	23.57	W. Br. Antietam Creek	
Moraine	Butler	15,838.00	Lake Arthur	3,225.00 Acres
Mt. Pisgah	Bradford	1,302.29	Stephen Foster Lake & Pool	75.00 Acres 5,676.00 sq. ft.
Neshaminy	Bucks	330.27	Delaware River	
Nockamixon	Bucks	5,283.00	Nockamixon	1,450.00 Acres
Nolde Forest	Berks	665.82	Angelica Creek	
Ohiopyle	Fayette	18,719.35	Youghiogheny River	
Oil Creek	Venango	7,006.66	Oil Creek	
Ole Bull	Potter	117.53	Kettle Creek Lake	0.75 Acres
Parker Dam	Clearfield	968.00	Parker Lake	20.00 Acres
Patterson	Potter	10.00		
Penn Roosevelt	Centre	75.00	Penn Roosevelt Lake	5.00 Acres
Pine Grove Furnace	Cumberland	696.00	Laurel Lake	26.70 Acres
			Fuller Lake	1.70 Acres
Poe Paddy	Centre	10.00	Penn Creek	
Poe Valley	Centre	620.00	Poe Valley Lake	25.00 Acres
Point	Allegheny	36.00	Allegheny & Monongahela Rivers	
Presque Isle	Erie	3,202.00	Lake Erie	2,500.00 Acres
Prince Gallitzin	Cambria	6,249.00	Glendale Lake	1,602.00 Acres
Promised Land	Pike	5,808.60	Promised Land Lake	595.00 Acres
			Lower Lake	138.00 Acres
			Snow Hill Pond	3.00 Acres
			Egypt Meadow Lake	60.00 Acres
Prouty Place	Potter	5.00	Prouty Run	
Pymatuning	Crawford	21,122.00	Pymatuning Reservoir	13,716.00 Acres
Raccoon Creek	Beaver	7,299.88	Raccoon Lake	101.00 Acres
			Organized Group Camp Lake	4.00 Acres
Ralph Stover	Bucks	45.00	Stover Lake	2.30 Acres
Ravensburg	Clinton	78.00	Ravensburg Lake	.25 Acres
Raymond B. Winter	Union	695.00	Halfway Dam	6.00 Acres
Reeds Gap	Mifflin	220.00	Pool	35' x 105'
			Wading Pool	15' x 21'
Ricketts Glen	Luzerne-Sullivan	13,050.36	Lake Jean	245.00 Acres
			Lake Rose	25.00 Acres
Ridley Creek	Delaware	2,606.66	Ridley Creek	
			Sycamore Mills Dam	18.60 Acres
Roosevelt	Bucks-Northampton	528.89	Delaware Canal	275.00 Acres
Ryerson Station	Greene	1,164.15	Ryerson Station Reservoir	62.00 Acres
			Pool	50' x 120'

Park	County	Total Acreage	Water Area	
Sand Bridge	Union	3.00	Rapid Run	
Samuel S. Lewis	York	71.05		
S. B. Elliott	Clearfield	318.00		
Shawnee	Bedford	3,984.28	Shawnee Lake	451.00 Acres
Skilellamy	Union-Northumberland	130.25	Overlooks Susquehanna River — Lake Augusta	3,000.00 Acres
Sinnemahoning	Cameron	1,910.00	Geo. B. Stevenson	142.00 Acres
Sizerville	Potter-Cameron	386.00		
Susquehanna	Lycoming	19.59	W. Br. Susquehanna River	
Susquehannock	Lancaster	224.25	Overlooks Susquehanna River	
Tobyhanna	Monroe-Wayne	5,439.70	Tobyhanna Lake No. 2	170.00 Acres
Trough Creek	Huntingdon	541.00		
Tuscarora	Schuylkill	1,716.00	Tuscarora Lake	96.00 Acres
Tyler	Bucks	1,710.63	Neshaminy Creek Lake	12.50 Acres
			Spring Carden Mill	12.00 Acres
Upper Pine Bottom	Lycoming	4.00	Upper Pine Bottom Run	
Warriors Path	Bedford	296.01	Raystown Br. Juniata River	
Whipple Dam	Huntingdon	256.00	Whipple Dam	22.00 Acres
White Clay Creek Preserve	Chester	1,234.00	White Clay Creek	
Worlds End	Sullivan	780.00	Loyalsock Creek	
Yellow Creek	Indiana	2,926.80	Yellow Creek Lake	720.00 Acres

PENNSYLVANIA STATE PARKS
Under Acquisition, Design or Development

Park	County	Estimated Acreage
Allegheny Islands	Allegheny	43.00
Lehigh Gorge	Carbon	4,548.71
Prompton	Wayne	972.19
Swatara	Lebanon, Schuylkill	3,330.57
Salt Springs	Susquehanna	400.02
Benjamin Rush	Philadelphia	274.87

RECREATION AREAS OF PENNSYLVANIA
UNDER THE JURISDICTION OF THE
BUREAU OF STATE PARKS

SUMMARY

Number	Category	Acres
103	State Parks (Open to the Public)	262,378.91
4	Environmental Education Centers	3,560.30
107	SUBTOTAL — OPERATING AREAS	265,939.21
4	State Parks Undeveloped	1,690.08
2	State Parks Under Acquisition	7,879.28
113	GRAND TOTAL	275,508.57

ACTIVITIES IN PENNSYLVANIA STATE PARKS
(By County)

BOATING CODE
E = Electric Motors
NP = No Power Boating
UN = Unlimited Horsepower

SNOW SKIING D = Downhill   X = Cross Country

State Park	County	Address	Telephone	CAMPSITES	FISHING	SWIMMING (P-Pool / B-Beach)	BOATING Rental	Ramp	Mooring	Horsepower	Marina	SNOW SKIING	Hiking	Equestrian TRAILS	Snowmobile	HUNTING	PICNICKING	YOUTH GROUP TENTING	CABINS	FOOD CONCESSION	STORE (within 5 miles)	SANITARY DUMP STATION	LAUNDRY FACILITIES	INTERPRETIVE
Point	Allegheny	101 Commonwealth Place Pittsburgh 15222	412-471-0235	HISTORICAL PARK																				
Raccoon Creek	Beaver	Box 900, R.D. 1, Rt. 18, Hookstown 15050-9416	412-899-2200	176	x	B	x		x	E		Dx	x	x	x	x	x	x	x	x	x	x		x
Blue Knob	Bedford	R.D. 1, Box 449, Imler 16655	814-276-3576	75	x	P	x					x	x		x	x	x				x	x		x
Shawnee	Bedford	Box 67, Schellsburg 15559	814-733-4218	300	x	B	x	x	x	E		x	x		x	x	x			x	x	x		x
Warriors Path	Bedford	c/o Canoe Creek	814-695-7667		x							x	x			x				x	x			
French Creek	Berks	Box 448, R.D. 1, Elverson 19520	215-582-1514	260	x	P	x	x	x	E		x	x	x	x	x	x	x	x	x	x	x	x	x
Nolde Forest	Berks	Box 392, R.D. 1, Reading 19607	215-775-1411	ENVIRONMENTAL EDUCATION CENTER								x	x		x								x
Neshaminy	Bucks	263 Dunks Ferry Road, Bensalem 19020	215-639-4538		x	P	x	x	x	UN	x		x	x	x	x	x			x	x			x
Nockamixon	Bucks	Box 125A, R.D. 3, Quakertown 18951	215-538-2151		x	P	x	x	x	10	x			x	x	x	x	x	x	x	x			x
Ralph Stover	Bucks	6011 State Park Road, Pipersville 18947	215-297-5090		x								x			x			x					
Roosevelt	Bucks	Box 615A, R.R. 1, Upper Black Eddy 18972	215-982-5560				x		Canoeing	E		x	x	x	x	x	x			x		Bicycling		
Tyler	Bucks	Rt. 413, Bypass at Swamp Rd., Newtown 18940	215-968-2021		x		x		Canoeing	E		x	x	x	x	x	x			x				x
Jennings	Butler	R.D. 1, Slippery Rock 16057	412-794-6011	ENVIRONMENTAL EDUCATION CENTER								x	x		x	x							
Moraine	Butler	R.D. 1, Portersville 16051	412-368-8811		x	B	x	x	x	10	x	x	x		x	x	x			x	x		x	
Prince Gallitzin	Cambria	R.D. 1, Box 79, Patton 16668	814-674-3691	437	x	B	x	x	x	10	x	x	x	x	x	x	x	x	x	x	x	x	x	x
Sinnemahoning	Cameron	R.D. 1, Box 172, Austin 16720	814-647-8401	40	x	B	x	x	x	E		x	x	x	x	x	x	x	x	x	x	x	x	
Beltzville	Carbon	Box 242, R.D. 3, Lehighton 18235	215-377-3170		x	B	x		x	UN		x	x		x	x	x							x
Hickory Run	Carbon	Box 81, R.D. 1, White Haven 18661	717-443-9991	381	x	B	x		x	UN		x	x	x	x	x	x	x	x	x	x	x	x	x
Bald Eagle	Centre	Box 56, R.D. 1, Howard 16841	814-625-2775	70	x	B	x	x	x	UN	x	x	x	x	x	x	x	x	x	x	x	x	x	x
Black Moshannon	Centre	Box 183, R.D. 1, Philipsburg 16866	814-342-1101	80	x	B	x		x	E		Dx	x		x	x	x	x	x	x	x	x	x	x
McCalls Dam	Centre	c/o R. B. Winter	717-966-1455	15	x								x			x	x							x
Penn Roosevelt	Centre	c/o Greenwood Furnace	814-667-3808	15	x							x	x		x	x	x					x	x	
Poe Paddy	Centre	c/o Reeds Gap	814-349-8778	45	x							x	x		x	x	x					x	x	

ACTIVITIES IN PENNSYLVANIA STATE PARKS
(By County)

BOATING CODE
E = Electric Motors
NP = No Power Boating
UN = Unlimited Horsepower

SNOW SKIING D = Downhill X = Cross Country

State Park	County	Address	Telephone	CAMPSITES	FISHING	SWIMMING P-Pool B-Beach	Rental B-Beach	Ramp	Mooring BOATING	Marina	Horsepower	SNOW SKIING	Hiking	Equestrian TRAILS	Snowmobile	HUNTING	PICNICKING	YOUTH GROUP TENTING	CABINS	FOOD CONCESSION	STORE (within 5 miles)	SANITARY DUMP STATION	LAUNDRY FACILITIES	INTERPRETIVE
Poe Valley	Centre	c/o Reeds Gap, R.D. 1 Box 276A, Milroy 17063-9735	814-349-8778	79	x	B	x	x	x		E		x		x	x	x	x		x		x		
Marsh Creek	Chester	R.D. 2, Park Rd., Downingtown 19335	215-458-8515		x	P	x	x	x		E		x			x	x	x		x	x	x		x
White Clay Creek Preserve	Chester	P.O. Box 172, Landenberg 19350	215-255-5415		x								x			x					x			
Cook Forest	Clarion	P.O. Box 120, Cooksburg 16217	814-744-8407	226	x	P	x		Canoeing			x	x		x	x	x	x	x	x	x	x		x
Parker Dam	Clearfield	Box 165, R.D. 1, Penfield 15849	814-765-5082	110	x	B	x	x	x		E	x	x		x	x	x	x	x		x	x		x
S. B. Elliott	Clearfield	c/o Parker Dam	814-765-7271	25	x										x	x			x			x		x
Hyner Run	Clinton	c/o Little Pine, HC 63, Box 100, Waterville, 17776-9705	717-923-0257	30	x	P									x	x	x							
Hyner View	Clinton	c/o Hyner Run	717-923-0257												x	x	x							x
Kettle Creek	Clinton	HCR 62, Box 96, Renova 17764	717-923-0206	71	x	B		x	x		E		x		x	x	x	x	x			x		x
Ravensburg	Clinton	c/o R.B. Winter, R.D. 2, Box 377 Mifflinburg 17844	717-966-1455		x								x		x	x	x				x			
Pymatuning	Crawford	Box 425, Jamestown 16134	412-932-3141	807	x	B	x	x	x		10		x		x	x	x	x	x	x	x	x	x	x
Colonel Denning	Cumberland	R.D. 3, Box 2250, Newville 17241	717-776-5272	52	x	B	x					x	x			x	x	x			x	x	x	x
Kings Gap	Cumberland	500 Kings Gap Road, Carlisle 17013	717-486-5031						ENVIRONMENTAL EDUCATION CENTER				x			x	x				x		x	x
Pine Grove Furnace	Cumberland	R.D. 2, Box 399B, Gardners 17324	717-486-7174	74	x	B	x	x	x		E	x	x		x	x	x		x	x	x	x		x
Ridley Creek	Delaware	Sycamore, Mills Road, Media 19063	215-566-4800		x			x				x	x	x		x	x			x	x			x
Bendigo	Elk	P.O. Box A, Johnsonburg 15845	814-965-2646		x	P											x			x	x		x	
Elk	Elk	c/o Bendigo 15845	814-965-2646	75	x	B		x	x		UN		x		x	x	x	x		x	x	x	x	
Presque Isle	Erie	Box 8510, Erie 16505	814-871-4251		x	B	x	x	x	x	UN		x		x	x	x			x	x	x		x
Laurel Ridge	Fayette	Box 179, R.D. 3, Rockwood 15557	412-455-3744						Back Packing				x		x	x	x	x					Camping	
Ohiopyle	Fayette	Box 105, Ohiopyle 15470	412-329-8591	223	x				White Water				x		x	x	x			x	x	x		x
Buchanan's Birthplace	Franklin	c/o Cowens Gap Fort Loudon 17224	717-485-3948		x				HISTORICAL PARK								x				x			x

Park	County	Address	Phone	Acres	Notes
Caledonia	Franklin	40 Rocky Mountain Road, Fayetteville 17222	717-352-2161	185	
Mont Alto	Franklin	c/o Caledonia 17222	717-352-2161		P
Cowans Gap	Fulton	HC 17266, Fort Loudon 17224	717-485-3948	259	B, E
Ryerson Station	Greene	R.D. 1, Box 77, Wind Ridge 15380	412-428-4254	50	P, E
Greenwood Furnace	Huntingdon	R.D. 2, Box 118, Huntingdon 16652	814-667-3808	50	B
Trough Creek	Huntingdon	R.D. 1, James Creek 16657	814-658-3847	32	
Whipple Dam	Huntingdon	c/o Greenwood Furnace R.D. 2, Box 118, Huntingdon 16652	814-667-3808		B, E
Yellow Creek	Indiana	R.D. 1, Box 145D, Penn Run 15765	412-463-3850		B, 10
Clear Creek	Jefferson	R.D. 1, Box 82, Sigel 15860	814-752-2368	53	B, Canoeing
Archbald Pothole	Lackawanna	c/o Lackawanna, R.D. 1, Box 251, Dalton 18414	717-945-3239		
Lackawanna	Lackawanna	R.D. 1, Box 251, Dalton 18414	717-945-3239	96	P, E
Susquehannock	Lancaster	1880 Park Dr., Drumore 17518	717-548-3361		
McConnells Mill	Lawrence	R.D. 1, Portersville 16051	412-368-8091		
Memorial Lake	Lebanon	R.D. 1, Box 7045, Grantville 17028	717-865-5444 Ext. 2806		E
Frances Slocum	Luzerne	565, Mt. Olivet Road, Kingston Township, Wyoming 18644	717-696-3525		P, E
Ricketts Glen	Luzerne	R.D. 1, Box 251, Benton 17814	717-477-5675	120	B, E
Little Pine	Lycoming	HC 63, Box 100, Waterville 17776-9705	717-753-8209	105	B, E
Upper Pine Bottom	Lycoming	c/o Little Pine	717-753-8209		
Kinzua Bridge	McKean	c/o Bendigo, Box A Johnsonburg 15845	814-965-2646		
Maurice K. Goddard	Mercer	Box 74, R.D. 3, Sandy Lake 16145	412-253-4833		10
Reeds Gap	Mifflin	Box 276A, R.D. 1, Milroy 17063-9735	717-667-3622	14T	P
Big Pocono	Monroe	c/o Tobyhanna	717-894-8336		
Gouldsboro	Monroe	c/o Tobyhanna	717-894-8336		B, E
Tobyhanna	Monroe	P.O. Box 387, Tobyhanna 18466	717-894-8336	140	B, E
Evansburg	Montgomery	Box 258, Collegeville 19426	215-489-3729		
Fort Washington	Montgomery	500 Bethlehem Pike Fort Washington 19034	215-646-2942		HISTORICAL PARK
Jacobsburg	Northampton	435 Belfast Rd., Nazareth 18064	215-759-7616		
Milton	Northumberland	c/o Shikellamy 17801	717-286-7880		
Shikellamy	Northumberland	Bridge Ave., Sunbury 17801	717-286-7880		UN
Big Spring	Perry	c/o Colonel Denning, R.D. 3 Box 2250, Newville 17241	717-776-5272		

ACTIVITIES IN PENNSYLVANIA STATE PARKS
(By County)

BOATING CODE
E = Electric Motors
NP = No Power Boating
UN = Unlimited Horsepower

State Park	County	Address	Telephone	CAMPSITES	FISHING	SWIMMING (P-Pool / B-Beach)	Rental	Ramp	Mooring	Horsepower	Marina	SNOW SKIING (D=Downhill / X=Cross Country)	Hiking	Equestrian TRAILS	Snowmobile	HUNTING	PICNICKING	YOUTH GROUP TENTING	CABINS	FOOD CONCESSION	STORE (Within 5 miles)	SANITARY DUMP STATION	LAUNDRY FACILITIES	INTERPRETIVE
Fowlers Hollow	Perry	c/o Colonel Denning	717-776-5272	18	x							x	x		x	x	x							
Little Buffalo	Perry	Box 256, R.D. 2 Newport 17074	717-567-9255		x	P	x	x	x	E		x	x		x	x	x				x	x	x		x
Promised Land	Pike	R.D. 1, Box 96, Greentown 18426	717-676-3428	535	x	B	x	x	x	E		x	x		x	x	x		x	x	x	x	x		x
Cherry Springs	Potter	c/o Lyman Run	814-435-6444	50								x	x		x	x					x	x		x
Denton Hill	Potter	c/o Lyman Run	814-435-6444		x							Dx	x		x	x					x	x		
Lyman Run	Potter	P.O. Box 204, Galeton 16922	814-435-6444	50	x	B	x	x	x	E		x	x		x	x	x			x	x	x	x		x
Ole Bull	Potter	c/o Kettle Creek	814-435-2169	81	x	B						x	x		x	x	x			x	x	x	x		x
Patterson	Potter	c/o Lyman Run	814-435-6444	20								x			x	x	x							
Prouty Place	Potter	c/o Lyman Run	814-435-6444	10	x										x	x	x							
Sizerville	Potter/Cameron	Box 238A, R.D. 1 Emporium 15834	814-486-5605	23	x	P	x	x				x	x		x	x	x			x	x	x	x	x	x
Locust Lake	Schuylkill	c/o Tuscarora 18214	717-467-2404	282	x	B	x	x					x		x	x				x	x	x	x	x	x
Tuscarora	Schuylkill	R.D. Box 24A, Barnesville 18214	717-467-2404		x	B	x	x	x	E			x	x	x	x	x			x	x	x			x
Kooser	Somerset	Box 256, R.D. 4, Somerset 15501	814-445-8673	60	x	B	x	x				x	x		x	x	x		x	x	x	x			
Laurel Hill	Somerset	Box 130, R.D. 4, Somerset 15501	814-445-7725	270	x	B	x	x	x	E			x	x	x	x	x		x	x	x	x			
Worlds End	Sullivan	P.O. Box 62, Forksville 18616-0062	717-924-3287	70	x	B	x					x	x		x	x	x		x	x	x	x			x
Salt Springs	Susquehanna	c/o Lackawanna	717-945-3239		x								x			x								
Colton Point	Tioga	c/o Leonard Harrison 16901	717-724-3061	25									x		x	x	x							
Hills Creek	Tioga	P.O. Box 328, R.D. 2, Wellsboro 16901	717-724-4246	110	x	B	x	x	x	E		x	x		x	x	x		x	x	x	x	x	x	x
Leonard Harrison	Tioga	R.D. 6, Box 199, Wellsboro 16901	717-724-3061	30	x								x		x	x	x			x	x	x	x		x
R. B. Winter	Union	R.D. 2, Box 377, Mifflinburg 17844	717-966-1455	60	x	B	x	x					x		x	x	x			x	x	x	x		x
Sand Bridge	Union	c/o R.B. Winter	717-966-1455		x								x		x		x					x		
Oil Creek	Venango	Box 207, R.D. 1, Oil City 16301	814-676-5915		x			Canoeing				x	x	x	x	x	x			x	x	x		x
Chapman	Warren	Box 1610, R.D. 1, Clarendon 16313	814-723-5030	83	x	B	x	x	x	E		x	x		x	x	x		x	x	x	x	x	x	x
Keystone	Westmoreland	Box 101, R.D. 2, Derry 15627	412-668-2939	100	x	B	x	x	x	E		x	x	x	x	x	x		x	x	x	x	x	x	x

										Dx							
Laurel Mountain	Westmoreland	Box 527, Ligonier 15658	412-238-6623													x	
Laurel Summit	Westmoreland	c/o Linn Run	412-238-6623										x				
Linn Run	Westmoreland	Box 527, Ligonier 15658	412-238-6623	x					x		x	x	x		x		
Codorus	York	Box 118, R.D. 3, Hanover 17331	717-637-2816	198	x	P	x	x	x	10	x	x	x	x	x	x	x
Gifford Pinchot	York	2200 Rosstown Rd., Lewisberry 17339	717-432-5011	340	x	B	x	x	x	E	x	x	x	x	x	x	x
Samuel S. Lewis	York	c/o Gifford Pinchot	717-252-1134								x	x		x		

STATE FORESTS

STATE FOREST LAND IN ACRES*

County		County	
Adams	21,912	Lackawanna	6,024
Bedford	29,603	Lancaster	10
Berks	828	Luzerne	2,086
Blair	2	Lycoming	189,032
Bradford	3,838	McKean	3,449
Cambria	559	Mercer	44
Cameron	123,629	Mifflin	57,361
Carbon	997	Monroe	8,462
Centre	142,836	Northampton	55
Clarion	6	Northumberland	4
Clearfield	97,010	Perry	41,187
Clinton	255,949	Pike	65,937
Cumberland	35,079	Potter	264,037
Dauphin	7,257	Schuylkill	8,285
Elk	73,762	Snyder	28,683
Fayette	14,777	Somerset	29,273
Forest	2,247	Sullivan	39,989
Franklin	40,582	Tioga	149,384
Fulton	29,051	Union	64,140
Huntingdon	66,272	Westmoreland	14,561
Indiana	471		
Jefferson	9,488	**TOTAL**	**1,945,503**
Juniata	17,337		

*Based on deed descriptions as recorded in county courthouses.

STATE FOREST PICNIC AREAS

Park	County	Acres	Picnicking	Fishing	Boating	Camping
Asaph Run	Tioga	4.00	x	x		x
Babcock	Somerset	54.00	x			
Bear Gap	Mifflin	6.00	x	x		
Bear Valley	Franklin	8.00	x	x		
Blankley	Bedford	20.00	x			
Bradley Wales	Tioga	4.00	x			
Colerain	Huntingdon	33.00	x	x		
County Bridge	Tioga	9.00	x	x		x
Dry Run	Sullivan	13.00	x	x		
Fall Brook	Tioga	10.00	x			
Hairy Johns	Centre	48.00	x			
Jesse Hall	Clinton	6.00	x	x		
Karl B. Guss	Juniata	35.00	x	x		
Lambs Hill	Bradford	19.00	x			
Lick Hollow	Fayette	36.00	x			
Minnichs Springs	Dauphin	3.00	x			
Mount Davis	Somerset	21.00	x			
Old Forge	Franklin	78.00	x	x		
Pecks Pond	Pike	305.00	x	x	x	
Pine Hill	Huntingdon	12.00	x			
Rock Springs	Snyder	10.00	x	x		
Rowland	Dauphin	8.00	x			
Sideling Hill	Fulton	16.00	x			
Snow Hill	Monroe	25.00	x	x		
Sweet Root	Bedford	6.00	x			
Thornhurst	Lackawanna	15.00	x	x		
Ulsh Gap	Snyder	5.00	x			
Wayside Memorial	Cameron	1.70	x			

NATURAL AREAS ON STATE FOREST LANDS

Area	Acres	Forest	Location
Carbaugh Run	870	Michaux	Adams Co. South Rt. 30 near Caledonia.
Meeting of the Pines	611	Michaux	Franklin Co. End of Mont Alto Mountain east of Mont Alto.
Sweet Root	1,403	Buchanan	Bedford Co. 2 miles west of Chaneysville.
Pine Ridge	568	Buchanan	Bedford Co. south of Chaneysville.
Frank E. Masland	1,270	Tuscarora	Perry Co. 12 miles west of Landisburg on Laurel Run Road.
Box Huckleberry	10	Tuscarora	Perry Co. 2 miles south of New Bloomfield.
The Hemlocks	131	Tuscarora	Perry Co. 2 miles south of Big Spring State Park on the Hemlock Road.
Mt. Davis	581	Forbes	Somerset Co. 10 miles west of Meyersdale.
Roaring Run	3,090	Forbes	Westmoreland Co. south of Rt. 31 on west side of Laurel Ridge.
Bear Meadows	833	Rothrock	Centre Co. 6 miles south of Boalsburg.
Alan Seeger	118	Rothrock	Huntingdon Co. 6 miles south of McAlevy's Fort.
Big Flat Laurel	184	Rothrock	Huntingdon and Centre counties, intersection of Bear Gap and Gettis Ridge Roads.
Detweiler Run	185	Rothrock	Huntingdon Co. 2 miles north of Alan Seeger Natural Area along Detweiler Run.
Little Juniata	624	Rothrock	Huntingdon Co. west of Alexandria, a water gap in Tussey Mountain.
Dr. Charles F. Lewis	384	Gallitizin	Indiana Co. North side of Conemaugh Gap, west of Johnstown.
Joyce Kilmer	77	Bald Eagle	Union Co. 6 miles west of Hartleton on Paddy Mountain.
The Hook	5,119	Bald Eagle	Union Co., North branch Buffalo Creek, 3 miles north of Hartleton.
Mt. Logan	512	Bald Eagle	Clinton Co. Bald Eagle Mt. east of Castonea.
Rosecrans Bog	152	Bald Eagle	Clinton Co. North of Loganton along Cranberry Road.
Snyder-Middleswarth	500	Bald Eagle	Snyder Co. 5 miles west of Troxelville on the Swift Run Road.
Tall Timbers	660	Bald Eagle	Snyder Co. west of Snyder-Middleswarth along Swift Run.
Algerine Swamp	84	Tiadaghton	Lycoming Co. south of the Reynolds Spring Trail and Gamble Run Road intersection.
Bark Cabin	73	Tiadaghton	Lycoming Co. near Okoma on headwaters of Bark Cabin Run.
Miller Run	4,987	Tiadaghton	Lycoming Co. west of Pine Creek at Jersey Mills.
Lower Jerry Run	892	Elk	Headwaters of Lower Jerry Run near Cameron-Clinton Co. Line west of Dutchman Road.
Wykoff Run	1,215	Elk	Cameron at Junction of Wykoff and New Hoover Roads.
Marion Brooks	917	Moshannon	Elk Co. at intersection of Quehanna Highway and Losey Road.
Tamarack Swamp	86	Sproul	Clinton Co. east of Tamarack.
Pine Tree Trail	276	Elk	Between West Hicks Run Road and East Hicks Run Road near Pine Tree Trail.
Bucktail State Park	16,368	Sproul & Elk	Clinton-Cameron Co. Rim to rim along the Susquehanna River and Sinnemahoning Creek between Lock Haven and Emporium.
Johnson Run	216	Elk	Cameron Co. North of Driftwood on east side of Johnson Run.
East Branch Swamp	186	Sproul	Clinton Co. East Branch Big Run, Rt. 144 and Beech Creek Road.
Cranberry Swamp	144	Sproul	Clinton Co., Cranberry Run, 3 miles south of Renovo.
Forrest H. Dutlinger	1,521	Susquehannock	Clinton Co., Hammersley Fork, Beech Bottom Hollow.
Black Ash Swamp	308	Tioga	Tioga Co., Asaph Run.
Pine Creek Gorge	5,720	Tioga	Tioga Co. between Ansonia and Blackwell
Reynolds Springs	1,302	Tioga	Tioga Co. at intersection of Gamble Run and Reynolds Spring Road.
Pine Lake	67	Delaware	Pike Co., south of I-84, 2 miles north of Greentown.
Buckhorn	471	Delaware	Pike Co. 1 mile east of Pond Eddy.
Stillwater	1,931	Delaware	Pike Co. Delaware and Porter Twp. along Flat Ridge Road.
Pennel Run	936	Delaware	Pike Co. 2 miles west of Twelve Mile Pond.
High Knob	97	Wyoming	Sullivan Co. 4 miles west of the intersection of State Rt. 42 and the Dry Run Road.
Kettle Creek Gorge	774	Wyoming	Sullivan Co. 5 miles south of Hillsgrove on the Ogdania Road.

WILD AREAS ON STATE FOREST LANDS

Area	Acres	Forest	Location
Martin Hill	11,376	Buchanan	Bedord Co., Martin Hill.
Tuscarora	5,363	Tuscarora	Perry-Juniata Co. west of Millerstown on Tuscarora Mountain.

WILD AREAS ON STATE FOREST LANDS

Area	Acres	Forest	Location
Thickhead Mountain	4,886	Rothrock	Centre and Huntingdon Counties, Bear Meadows-Detweiler Run area.
Trough Creek	1,703	Rothrock	Huntingdon County adjoining the Raystown Dam.
Clear Shade	2,791	Gallitzen	Northeastern Somerset County, Southeastern corner of the Babcock Division.
Quehanna	48,186	Elk & Moshannon	Corner of Elk, Cameron and Clearfield Counties.
White Mountain	3,935	Bald Eagle	Union Co., west of Weikert along Penn's Creek.
Algerine	4,077	Tiadaghton	Lycoming Co. northwest of Slate Run.
Wolf Run	7,716	Tiadaghton	Lycoming Co. north of Cammal along Pine Creek.
McIntyre	7,279	Tiadaghton	Lycoming Co. east of Ralston.
Burn's Run	2,180	Sproul	Clinton Co. between Route 144 and the Susquehanna River.
Fish Dam	4,959	Sproul	Clinton Co. west on State Camp and Route 144.
Asaph	3,070	Tioga	Tioga Co. Asaph Run.

REPUBLICAN STATE COMMITTEE OFFICERS

CHAIRMAN
Earl M. Baker
112 State Street
Harrisburg 17105

VICE CHAIRMAN
Anne B. Anstine
Annlick Farm
325 Locust Grove Road
Mifflintown 17059

DEPUTY CHAIRMAN
Doris Carson Williams
1431 Pennsylvania Ave.
Pittsburgh 15233

TREASURER
Robert Taylor, Esq.
Eckert, Robb & Associates
#1 Plymouth Meeting
Plymouth Meeting 19462

NATIONAL COMMITTEEMAN
Hon. Drew Lewis
Rte. 113 & Skippack Pike
Schwenksville 19473

NATIONAL COMMITTEEWOMAN
Elsie H. Hillman
Morewood Heights
Pittsburgh 15213

SECRETARY
Grace Jesberger
506 S. St. Marys Street
St. Marys 15857

ASSISTANT SECRETARY
Nancy C. Kimble
R.R. #1, Box 234
Liberty 16930

LEGAL COUNSEL
E. Barclay Cale, Esq.
2000 One Logan Square
Philadelphia 19103

FINANCE CHAIRMAN
Timothy Carson, Esq.
Saul, Ewing, Remick & Saul
3800 Centre Sq. W.
Philadelphia 19102

REPUBLICAN STATE COMMITTEE MEMBERS

ADAMS
Nancy Hartzel
2444 Chambersburg Road
Biglerville 17307
Robert Monahan, Jr.
125 Carlisle Street
Gettysburg 17325

ALLEGHENY
Clara E. Bowen
1721 Grall Avenue
Pittsburgh 15209
John F. Casey
231 Thorn Street
Sewickley 15143
Vance P. Conard
116 Carrick Avenue
Pittsburgh 15210
Wilma Cottrell
120 Sheldon Avenue
Pittsburgh 15220
Charles W. Duffett, Jr.
1825 Village Road
Glenshaw 15116
Charles L. Engstrom
680 Moreland Drive
Pittsburgh 15243
Richard G. Haas
6869 Saltsburg Road
Pittsburgh 15235
Jean Hoelzel
918 Romine Avenue
McKeesport 15133
Margaret L. Jennings
460 Washington Road
Apt. 414
Pittsburgh 15228
Charles J. Lewis
115 Cowan Drive
Elizabeth 15037

Ronald W. Meehan
1821 Realty Avenue
Pittsburgh 15216
Mary Myers
115 McKenzie Drive
Pittsburgh 15235
Agnes Sakmar
611 E. Carson Street
Pittsburgh 15203
Robert S. Speicher
9325 Highmeadow Drive
Allison Park 15101
Kay W. Womsley
1453 Montgomery Road
Allison Park 15101

ARMSTRONG
James F. Heilman
1306-4th Avenue
Ford City 16226
Ruby A. Miller
Box 43
McGrann 16236

BEAVER
David J. Jackson
529 Cornell Drive
Aliquippa 15001
Nancy Loxley
355 Dravo Avenue
Beaver 15009

BEDFORD
Debbie Kovel
418 E. State Street
Everett 15537

BERKS
Jane E. Delong
Box 91
Bowers 19511
Arlyne Meyer
4324 Kutztown Road
Temple 19560
Earl F. Patterson
1155 Perry Street
Reading 19604
Leroy Reigel
56 E. Washington Avenue
Wernersville 19565

BLAIR
John H. Eichelberger, Jr.
R.D. #5, Box 408
Old Line Road
Altoona 16601
Bruce R. Erb
921 Walnut Street
Hollidaysburg 16648
Patricia L. Raugh
R.D. #4, Box 600
Altoona 16601

BRADFORD
Robert Storch
R.D. #3, Box 123
Troy 16947
Ellen E. M. Turrell
P.O. Box 277
Front Street
Wyalusing 18853

BUCKS
Peggy H. Adams
Box E
Bedminster 18910

Jane Frappier
55 Flamingo Road
Levittown 19053
Paul D. Guth, Esq.
R.D. #3, Box 110
Stoneyhill Road
New Hope 18938
John M. McClure
18 N. Main Street
Doylestown 18901
Leonard J. Oniskey
411 County Line Road
Huntingdon Valley 19006
Patricia K. Poprik
15 E. Elizabeth Lane
Richboro 18954
Betty Roach
74 Gough Avenue
Ivyland 18974
James C. Skillman
121 Chapel Road
New Hope 18938
Joseph Thompson
615 Belmont Avenue
Southampton 18966

BUTLER
Joan T. Chew
216 Center Avenue
Butler 16001
Thomas W. King, III
201 Cedar Road
Butler 16001
John H. Wise
151 N. Charles Street
Zelienople 16063

CAMBRIA
Robert Davis Gleason, Esq.
  Penn Traffic Bldg.
  Suite 350
  Johnstown 15901
Olive Wingard
  126 Ridgeview Avenue
  Johnstown 15904

CAMERON
Dennis P. Fapore
  323 E. Allegheny Avenue
  Emporium 15834

CARBON
Roger Nanovic, II
  Box 10 1M
  Star Route
  Jim Thorpe 18229

CENTRE
Jane A. Houser
  P.O. Box 186
  Bellefonte 16823
Albert F. Williams
  332 S. Gill Street
  State College 16801

CHESTER
Marilyn V. Baker
  1945 Fox Hill Lane
  Paoli 19301
Lillian K. Emery
  R.D. #2
  Birchrunville Road
  Chester Springs 19425
Richard Jones
  P.O. Box 398
  Coatesville 19320
Helen E. Martin
  329 Lamborntown Road
  West Grove 19390
Jesse T. Smith
  101 N. Barley Sheaf Road
  Coatesville 19320
Donald B. Stoughton
  P.O. Box 600
  Paoli 19301
Hon. John H. Ware, III
  55 S. Third Street
  Oxford 19363

CLARION
Gregory K. Mortimer
  204 N. Main Street
  Rimersburg 16248

CLEARFIELD
Donna L. Hallstrom
  113 E. DuBois Avenue
  DuBois 15801
C. Alan Walker
  P.O. Box 34
  Bigler 16825

CLINTON
Paul W. Houck
  R.D. #2
  Lock Haven 17745

COLUMBIA
Richard A. Benefield
  20 W. Main Street
  Hotel Magee
  Bloomsburg 17815

CRAWFORD
Mildred R. Merry
  R.D. 2
  Linesville 16424
Gaylord D. Wentworth
  R.D. 2
  Guys Mills 16327

CUMBERLAND
Anne Fry
  1938 Cooper Circle
  Camp Hill 17011
Patricia Saylor
  426 B West Simpson Street
  Mechanicsburg 17055
Richard W. Stewart
  1811 Warren Street
  New Cumberland 17070

DAUPHIN
Marion Alexander
  312 Maple Street
  Hummelstown 17036
Rosemary Chiavetta
  4424 Fargreen Road
  Harrisburg 17110
Robert McCloskey
  7925 Manor Drive
  Harrisburg 17112
Crawford W. Murdoch
  P.O. Box 286
  Hershey 17033
Patricia J. Myers
  1020 Collingswood Drive
  Harrisburg 17109

DELAWARE
William R. Armstrong
  1239 - 12th Street
  Eddystone 19013
Edward R. Boate, Jr.
  103 Cove Road
  Broomall 19008
Stephen W. Campetti
  2438 St. Denis Lane
  Havertown 19083
Richard J. Daisley
  202 E. Marshall Road
  Lansdowne 19050
Joanne M. Erb
  208 Scheivert Avenue
  Aston 19027
Lillian H. Griffin
  825 Eaton Road
  Drexel Hill 19026
Samuel S. Hoy
  210 Powell Road
  Springfield 19064
Robert A. Judge
  1054 Stratford Road
  Glenolden 19036
Willie Mae J. Leake
  N.E. Corner 10th & Pusey Sts.
  Chester 19013

Anna Mae B. Morley
  2121 Academy Avenue
  Morton 19070
Jane W. Nason
  72 Sweet Water Road
  Glen Mills 19342
Betty J. Nolan
  3361 Carter Lane
  Chester 19016
Marian P. Oliver
  501 N. Providence Road
  Media 19063
Harry J. Patterson
  7101 Llanfair Road
  Upper Darby 19082
Hugo N. Yannelli
  2611 Caranel Road
  Broomall 19008

ELK
Grace M. Jesberger
  506 South St. Marys Street
  St. Marys 15857

ERIE
Philip S. English
  2050 South Shore Drive
  Erie 16505
Robert W. Parker, Jr., Esq.
  MacDonald, Illig, Jones & Britton
  Erie 16501
Patricia S. Roberts
  241 W. 21st Street
  Erie 16502
Gail F. Sherred
  1616 Kuntz Road
  Erie 16510

FAYETTE
Dorothy J. Hawkins
  88 Greenwood Heights
  Connellsville 15425

FOREST
Paul H. Millin
  218 Elm Street
  Box 477
  Tionesta 16353

FRANKLIN
Carl R. Flohr
  25 Sheffield Drive
  Chambersburg 17201
Audrey L. Sipe
  509 S. Potomac Street
  Waynesboro 17268

FULTON
Merrill W. Kerlin
  125 North First Street
  McConnellsburg 17233

GREENE
John R. Gardner
  563 Bowlby Street
  Waynesburg 15370

HUNTINGDON
Fred B. Morgan
  HCR 60, Box 475
  Orbisonia 17243

INDIANA
Frank E. Moore
  695 Carter Avenue
  Indiana 15701
Elsie T. Young
  1012 Church Street
  Indiana 15701

JEFFERSON
William L. Henry
  340 Main Street
  Brookville 15825

JUNIATA
Timothy L. Foltz
  R.D. #2, Box 820
  Port Royal 17082

LACKAWANNA
Ralph R. Chase, Jr.
  210 E. Morton Street
  Old Forge 18517
Mary J. Dippre
  1622 E. Gibson Street
  Scranton 18510
C. Richard Marshall
  R.D. #2
  Dalton 18414

LANCASTER
Andrew Amway
  1046 Devonshire Road
  Lancaster 17603
Lynda J. Bowman
  220 N. Duke Street
  Lancaster 17602
Gerald G. Fischer
  658 Plane Street
  Columbia 17512
Lewis Fornoff, Jr.
  231 Memorial Drive
  Manheim 17545
Marilyn W. Lewis
  27 Conestoga Woods Road
  Lancaster 17602
Isabelle R. Rudisill
  3 Central Plaza
  P.O. Box 1231
  Lancaster 17603
Ruth A. Witman
  Box 85
  Goodville 17528
Douglas Zellum
  214 S. W. End Avenue
  Lancaster 17603

LAWRENCE
Florence E. Kildoo Brown
  208 West Winter Avenue
  New Castle 16101
Richard E. Flannery
  Classic Lane
  R.D. #5, Box 612
  New Castle 16103

LEBANON

Jane A. Aungst
559A East Penn Avenue
Cleona 17042

W. Lawrence Hess
729 S. 12th Street
Lebanon 17042

LEHIGH

Ann M. Black
4109 S. Church Street
Whitehall 18052

Wilbur C. Creveling, Jr.
828 N. Ott Street
Allentown 18104

Sally Meminger
932 Lawrence Drive
Emmaus 18049

Donald W. Snyder
32 Cobbler Lane
R.D. #8
Allentown 18105

LUZERNE

Leonard Falcone
519 Carverton Road
Wyoming 18644

Leonard Morgan
102 Maffett Street
Wilkes-Barre 18702

Margaret E. Snyder
541 S. Hanover Street
Nanticoke 18634

Joyce P. Steves
10 Hunter Road
Hazleton 18201

Carole Brent Williams
31 Forest Drive
Mountaintop 18707

LYCOMING

Betty S. Gardner
814 Weldon Street
Mountoursville 17754

L. Eugene Pauling
New Street
Muncy 17756

McKEAN

C. Russell Johnson
704 E. Main Street
Smethport 16749

MERCER

Wilda M. Boyd
R.D. #1
Stoneboro 16153

David O. King
208 Lynwood Drive
Greenville 16125

MIFFLIN

Clayton Canterbury
43 Long Drive
Lewistown 17044

MONROE

Edward A. Katz
1805 Laural Street
Stroudsburg 18360

MONTGOMERY

John Curtis Brewer
417 Toland Drive
Fort Washington 19034

Jo Rose Clifton
1149 Lafayette Road
Wayne 19087

Diane M. DeLong
1527 Swenk Road
Pottstown 19464

James N. Faust
Box 2557, R.D. 3
Pottstown 19464

John W. Fichter
210 Montgomery Avenue
Norristown 19401

Louis J. Guerra
1825 Holmes Road
Maple Glen 19002

Clay C. Hess
115 Hess Road
Collegeville 19426

Frank P. Lalley
103 Cardinal Way
North Wales 19454

Jane B. Markley
211 - 2nd St., Box 7
Schwenksville 19473

Luke F. McLauglin, III
312 Perkiomen Avenue
Oaks 19456

Eleanor G. Schneider
2473 Walton Road
Huntingdon Valley 19006

Thomas W. Scott
639 Lindley Road
Glenside 19038

Mary S. Shorley
1523 Sandy Hill Road
Norristown 19401

Sunnie R. Spiegel
1422 Carol Road
Meadowbrook 19046

Elizabeth Coles Umstattd
733 Stoke Road
Villanova 19085

MONTOUR

John F. Trowbridge
102 W. Mahoning
Danville 17821

NORTHAMPTON

Margaret L. Ferraro
134 El Reno Avenue
Nazareth 18064

James A. Hemstreet, Esq.
99 Lynnwood Avenue
Easton 18042

Charles H. Roberts
119 N. 2nd Street, Apt. 3A
Easton 18042

NORTHUMBERLAND

Hugh A. Jones
216 South Hickory Street
Mount Carmel 17851

Helen G. Rowe
1304 Susquehanna Avenue
Sunbury 17801

PERRY

Marlin C. Raffensperger
P.O. Box 125, Oak Road
New Bloomfield 17068

PHILADELPHIA

Stanley M. Bednarek
2607 E. Allegheny Avenue
Philadelphia 19134

Mary K. Bongiovanni
6426 Sherwood Road
Philadelphia 19151

Frank P. Buzydlowski
1118 Bingham Street
Philadelphia 19115

Constance J. Carlson
2910 S. Smedley Street
Philadelphia 19145

Suzanne D. Cohen
8A 1420 Locust Street
Philadelphia 19102

William Dunham
4313 Westminster Avenue
Philadelphia 19104

George Gershenfeld
417 Fourth Street
Philadelphia 19123

Henry J. Nimmons
1301 W. Lehigh Avenue
Philadelphia 19132

James J. O'Connell
4305 Howland Street
Philadelphia 19124

William Schaps
2049 S. 18th Street
Philadelphia 19145

Iris P. Thompson
1722 N. Willington Street
Philadelphia 19121

Theresa A. Tierney
3511 A Street
Philadelphia 19134

Elizabeth Walsh
121 Beth Drive
Philadelphia 19115

Angela P. Wechter
8943 Leonard Street
Philadelphia 19152

PIKE

Reid M. Bodine
406 Avenue 1
Matamoras 18336

POTTER

Martha Duvall
P.O. Box 429
Coudersport 16915

SCHUYLKILL

Robert E. Ames
129 Second Street
Coaldale 18218

Ernest Dilabio
701 E. Mahanoy Street
Mahanoy City 17948

Linda Klementovich
21 Hoffman Blvd.
Ashland 17921

Shirley R. Manbeck
Rt. #3, Box 235
Pine Grove 17963

SNYDER

Lee E. Knepp
17 N. Brown Street
P.O. Box 76
McClure 17841

SOMERSET

Nancy Friedline
356 Lincoln Street
Box 55
Somerset 15501

Michael D. Long
339 Stoystown Road
Somerset 15501

SULLIVAN

George B. Miller, Jr.
P.O. Box 8
Eagles Mere 17731

SUSQUEHANNA

Milton Bainbridge
R.D. #1, Box 1207
Carbondale 18407

TIOGA

William C. Bailey
70 E. Wellsboro Street
Mansfield 16933

UNION

Paul R. Wilson
520 Fairsom Drive
Lewisburg 17837

VENANGO

Beverly K. Snyder
315 Main St., Box 147
Emlenton 16373

G. Robert Thompson
32 Woodside Avenue
Oil City 16301

WARREN

Hon. Robert J. Kusse
390 Follett Run Road
Warren 16365

WASHINGTON

Edward M. Paluso
100 E. Beau Street
Washington 15301

Isobel R. Peterson
107 Scenery Circle
McMurray 15317

WAYNE
James R. O'Neill
R.D. 1, Box 577
Lake Ariel 18436

WESTMORELAND
Phil Davis
R.D. #6, Box 1516
Mt. Pleasant 15666
Dorothy Garland
46 Windhill
Greensburg 15601

Ronald Lee Kuhn
511 Jacks Street
Greensburg 15601
Sara S. Rugh
537 Hamel Avenue
Greensburg 15601

WYOMING
Russell O. Gunton
R.D. 2, Box 376
Dalton 18414

YORK
Patricia A. Bair
R.D. 2, Box 235
Wrightsville 17368
Nancy E. Blake
R.D. #5, Box 430
Red Lion 17356
Edward F. Hollinger
R.D. #1
Mt. Wolf 17347
Robert A. Minnich
1670 Northview Road
York 17402
Stanley Saylor
R.D. #2, Box 43
Red Lion 17356

Lifetime Voting Member
Hon. George I. Bloom
370 N. 26th Street
Harrisburg 17011
Honorary Lifetime Member
Louise Russell
95A Manor Road
Edwardsville 18704

REPUBLICAN COUNTY CHAIRMEN AND VICE CHAIRMEN

ADAMS
Chairman
Parker Lerew
232 Latimore Road
Gardners 17324
Vice Chairman
Doris Moul
1880 Pine Run Road
Abbottstown 17301

ALLEGHENY
Chairman
Lawrence Dunn
Suite 366, Box 110
Westin Wm. Penn Hotel
Pittsburgh 15219
Vice Chairman
Mary Myers
115 McKenzie Drive
Pittsburgh 15235

ARMSTRONG
Chairman
Jack Ludwig Miller
105 Ludwig Street
McGrann 16236
Vice Chairman
Helen Kerschbaumer
R.D. #1, Box 435
Chicora 16025

BEAVER
Chairman
Michael Stuban
44 Anthony Wayne Terrace
Baden 15005
Vice Chairman
Mary Jo McMahon
1401 Sampson Street
Conwaym 15027

BEDFORD
Chairman
Clarence Dietz
111 W. Pitt Street
Bedford 15522
Vice Chairman
John Foor, Jr.
R.D. #1, Box 683
Everett 15537

Gloria Goad
R.D. #1
New Paris 15554

BERKS
Chairman
Scott Keller, Esq.
536 Court Street Drive
P.O. Box 1538
Reading 19603
Vice Chairman
Jane C. Reber
132 N. 5th Street
Reading 19601

BLAIR
Chairman
Melvin L. Ellis
421 - 10th Avenue, Juniata
Altoona 16602
Vice Chairman
Margaret Burkett
Spruce Street
Roaring Spring 16673
Richard Carnicella
1418 Monroe Avenue
Altoona 16602
Dorothy L. Thomas
322 W. 21st Street
Tyrone 16686

BRADFORD
Chairman
F. Thomas Blackall
R.D. 1, Box 187
Monroeton 18832
Vice Chairman
Esther Birney
333 Chamung Street
Sayre 18840
Freda H. Burleigh
R.D. 3, Box 78
Columbia Cross Roads 16914

BUCKS
Chairman
Harry W. Fawkes
1017 Maryland Avenue
Croydon 19020

Vice Chairman
Karen McIlhinney
31 Meadow Lane
Doylestown 18901

BUTLER
Chairman
F. A. Rauschenberger, III
804 E. Pearl Street
Butler 16001
Vice Chairman
Martha Kennedy
R.D. #6
Butler 16001

CAMBRIA
Chairman
Robert A. Gleason, Sr.
543 Elknud Lane
Johnstown 15905

CAMERON
Chairman
Elona Brown
Box 215, R.D. 1
Emporium 15834
Vice Chairman
Donald Hoy
Star Route, Box 12A
Emporium 15834

CARBON
Chairman
John Faust
478 Columbia Avenue
Palmerton 18071
Vice Chairman
Esther Heartman
R.D. #5
Lehighton 18235

CENTRE
Chairman
H. B. Charmbury
420 S. Corl Street #8
State College 16801
Vice Chairman
Jeannie Suit
Centre Co. Republican
Committee, Suite 2C
State College 16801

CHESTER
Chairman
William H. Lamb
21 South Church Street
West Chester 19380
Vice Chairman
John A. Harding
3 Berrywood Road
Malvern 19355
Florence Hunt
31 Wood Lane
Malvern 19355

CLARION
Chairman
Donald L. Stroup
110 N. Fourth Avenue
Clarion 16214
Vice Chairman
Barbara Pope
River Hill
Clarion 16214

CLEARFIELD
Chairman
John R. Anderson
P.O. Box 606
Clearfield 16830
Vice Chairman
Susan Hayes
511 Wood Street
DuBois 15801

CLINTON
Chairman
Chris Dwyer
R.D. #2, Box 119
Mill Hall 17751

COLUMBIA
Chairman
Betty Broda
3750 Second St., Almedia
Bloomsburg 17815
Vice Chairman
Paul Thomas
R.D. 2
Berwick 18603

CRAWFORD
Chairman
Terrance Stover
P.O. Box 686
Hydetown 16328
Vice Chairmen
Genevieve Agnew
R.D. 3, Box 254
Linesville 16424
Charlotte Sweetland
R.D. #1
Cambridge Springs 16403

CUMBERLAND
Chairman
Robert C. Gwin
6030 Williams Drive
Mechanicsburg 17055
Vice Chairmen
Ginnie M. Anderson
503 Park Hills Drive
Mechanicsburg 17055
William Brandamore, Jr.
101 N. 30th Street
Camp Hill 17011
Mary C. Lewis
611 Park Avenue
New Cumberland 17070
LeAnn Long
481 State Street
West Fairview 17025
Jay McBride
1913 Esther Drive
Carlisle 17013
Patricia Saylor
426B W. Simpson St.
Mechanicsburg 17055
Gayle Walborn
405 Sixth Street
New Cumberland 17070
Hon. Kirk Wilson
433 "C" Street
Carlisle 17013

DAUPHIN
Chairman
Richard N. Koch
2224 Manchester Blvd.
Harrisburg 17112
Vice Chairmen
Albert B. Branch
58 Beale Street
Oberlin Heights
Steelton 17113
Thomas W. Helsel, Jr.
3141 N. 5th Street
Harrisburg 17110
Jack Minnich
702 Lente Avenue
Millersburg 17061
Danny Mosel
4903 Earl Drive
Harrisburg 17112
S. James Osprander
1038 Hillview Lane
Hershey 17033
Frank Pinto
2900 N. 2nd Street
Harrisburg 17110

Thomas L. Reider
808 N. Second Street
Steelton 17113
Keneth Rose, Jr.
R.D. #1
Lykens 17048
Martha K. Wolfgang
7708 Althea Avenue
Harrisburg 17112

DELAWARE
Chairman
Thomas J. Judge, Sr.
323 W. Front Street
Media 19063
Vice Chairman
Hon. Mary Ann Arty
527 LeHann Circle
Springfield 19064

ELK
Chairman
Victor C. Straub
121 Race Street
St. Marys 15857
Vice Chairman
Joan Distler
Edward Road
St. Marys 15857

ERIE
Chairman
Ann M. Grunewald
24 W. 8th Street
Erie 16508
Vice Chairman
Blaine Momeyer
2648 Lakeside Drive
Erie 16511

FAYETTE
Chairman
Richard C. Gomrick
109 Jane Lane
Uniontown 15401
Vice Chairman
Catherine Shearin
R.D. #1
Lake Lynn 15451

FOREST
Chairman
Robert M. Carringer
600 Elm Street
Tionesta 16353
Vice Chairman
Patricia Seybert
Box 442
Marienville 16239

FRANKLIN
Chairman
David C. Cleaver, Esq.
1035 Wayne Avenue
Chambersburg 17201
Vice Chairmen
Warren Elliott
4130 Main Street
Scotland 17254

Robert Felmlee
Dry Run 17220
Ruby Geiman
136 E. Baltimore
Greencastle 17225
William A. Martin, Jr.
832 Middle Street
Chambersburg 17201
Audrey Sipe
509 S. Potomac Street
Waynesboro 17268

FULTON
Chairman
Mildred Fix
Box 441, R.D. 1
Breezy Point Road
McConnellsburg 17233
Vice Chairmen
Bonnie Keefer
339 S. 2nd Street
McConnellsburg 17233
William Miller
Box 19, R.D. #2
Wardfordsburg 17267

GREENE
Chairman
Stephen Dragan
R.D. 1, Box 264
Clarksville 15322
Vice Chairman
Pauline Rice
R.D. 1
Holbrook 15341

HUNTINGDON
Chairman
Karl Lang
10th and Moore Streets
Huntingdon 16652
Vice Chairman
Helen Hicks
Three Springs 17264

INDIANA
Chairman
Robert W. Kunkle
712 Church Street
Indiana 16652
Vice Chairman
Laura Weaver
642 Philadelphia Street
Indiana 15701

JEFFERSON
Chairman
Maxine Zimmerman
R.D. 1, Box 464
Fuller Road
Brookville 15825
Vice Chairmen
Miriam Haag
429 Union Street
Big Run 15715
James L. Hinderliter
128 Taylor Avenue
Falls Creek 15840

JUNIATA
Chairman
Nora Ella Singer
620 Washington Avenue
Mifflintown 17059
Vice Chairman
Jean S. Groninger
R.D. #2
Port Royal 17082
David Kerstetter
R.D. #2
Millerstown 17062

LACKAWANNA
Chairman
John Roberts
619 W. Elm Street
Scranton 18504
Vice Chairman
Anne Smith
125 Main Street
Moscow 18444

LANCASTER
Chairman
John Martino
925 Virginia Avenue
Lancaster 17606
Vice Chairman
Bessie Ann Rabuck
304 Edge Hill Drive
Akron 17501

LAWRENCE
Chairman
Norman DeGidio
13 E. Addison
New Castle 16101
Vice Chairman
Marie M. Kauffman
R.D. #3, Box 1259
Volant 16156

LEBANON
Chairman
Michael S. Long
865 Lovers Lane
Lebanon 17042
Vice Chairman
Mary Alice Graybill
103 Hillside Road
Lebanon 17042

LEHIGH
Chairman
Charles E. Mackenzie
3808 Walnut Street
Allentown 18104
Vice Chairman
Ann I. Weinert
933 North 27th Street
Allentown 18104

LUZERNE
Chairman
Theodore Warkomski
Tilbury Terrace
West Nanticoke 18634

Vice Chairman
William Goss
    44 Furnace Street
    Shickshinny 18655

LYCOMING
Chairman
Richard C. Thomson
    Lycoming Co. Republican Com.
    P.O. Box 1986
    Williamsport 17703
Vice Chairman
Betty Gardner
    814 Weldon Street
    Montoursville 17754

McKEAN
Chairman
William D. Mackowski
    25 Abbott Road
    Bradford 16701
Vice Chairman
Betty Comes
    423 Minard Run
    Bradford 16701

MERCER
Chairman
Emil Koledin
    10 Pine Tree Lane
    Hermitage 16148
Vice Chairmen
Wilda Boyd
    R.D. 1
    Stoneboro 16153
Marie Campman
    1210 Carrol Lane
    Hermitage 16148
Cynthia Robbins
    Greenville-Sheakleyville Rd.
    Greenville 16125
Alice Spear
    R.D. 2
    New Wilmington 16142

MIFFLIN
Chairman
Ed Fike
    R.D. 1, Box 252
    Rt. 710
    Lewistown 17044
Vice Chairman
Barbara Bratton
    109 N. Brown Street
    Lewistown 17044

MONROE
Chairman
Margaret Butz
    104 Smith Street
    East Stroudsburg 18301
Vice Chairmen
William B. Cramer
    R.D. #4, Box 4098
    Stroudsburg 18360
Faye Cyphers
    LaFa Farms
    Henryville 18332

MONTGOMERY
Chairman
Frank Jenkins
    625 Swede Street
    P.O. Box 590
    Norristown 19404
Vice Chairman
Virginia Kanengeiser
    204 Godschall Road
    Collegeville 19426

MONTOUR
Chairmen
Connie Kuziak
    R.D. #8, Box 231
    Bush Road
    Danville 17821
James C. Rodenhaver
    R.D. #4, Box 240
    Danville 17821

NORTHAMPTON
Chairman
Larry Kisslinger
    Northampton Co. Republican Co.
    1st National Bank Bldg.
    Easton 18044
Vice Chairman
Edna Knerr
    671 W. Moorestown Road
    Bath 18016

NORTHUMBERLAND
Chairman
Daniel Strausser
    303 S. Market Street
    Shamokin 17872
Vice Chairman
Shirley Michaels
    290 Washington Avenue
    Sunbury 17801

PERRY
Chairman
Franklin Reidlinger
    R.D. #3
    Duncannon 17020
Vice Chairman
Suzanne Brown

PHILADELPHIA
Chairman
Donald Jamieson, Esq.
    Philadelphia City Com.
    The Windsor, 17th & Parkway
    Philadelphia 19103
Vice Chairman
Mary Tierney
    202 E. Indiana Avenue
    Philadelphia 19134

PIKE
Chairman
Carl Mulhauser, III
    Laurel Villa
    Milford 18337
Vice Chairman
Bernadette Frisbie
    R.D. 1
    Hawley 18428

POTTER
Chairman
Paul Herzig
    Laurelwood Inn
    R.D. #3, Box 132
    Coudersport 16915
Vice Chairmen
John Buckler
    R.D. #3, Box 255
    Coudersport 16915
Bruce Cahill, Esq.
    E. 2nd Avenue
    Coudersport 16915

SCHUYLKILL
Chairman
Clyde C. Holman
    Box 482, Locust Valley
    Barnesville 18214
Vice Chairmen
Donald R. Dillman
    37 S. Nice Street
    Frackville 17931
June E. Gressens
    124 E. Center Street
    P.O. Box 54
    Ashland 17921
Frank Schoeneman
    1220 Mahantongo Street
    Pottsville 17901
Gary J. Zerbe
    72 Clay Street
    Tremont 17981

SNYDER
Chairman
Marlin Inch
    54 N. Broad Street
    Selinsgrove 17870
Vice Chairmen
Luther A. Beaver
    R.D. 1
    Richfield 17086
Ann I. Shadel
    R.D. 1
    Mt. Pleasant 17853

SOMERSET
Chairman
Jerry Spangler, Esq.
    Box 702
    Somerset 15501
Vice Chairman
Nancy L. Aultz
    R.D. 2
    Somerset 15501

SULLIVAN
Chairman
Twila Starr
    R.D. 1
    Muncy Valley 17758
Vice Chairman
Richard McCarty
    R.D. 1, Box 159
    Forksville 18616

SUSQUEHANNA
Chairman
R. Lee Smith
    R.D. #5
    Montrose 18801
Vice Chairman
Carol Tripp
    R.D. #1, Trippsville
    Kingsley 18826

TIOGA
Chairman
Hon. Edgar A. Carlson
    144 Morris Street
    Blossburg 16912
Vice Chairman
Nancy C. Kimble
    R.R. #1, Box 234
    Liberty 19630

UNION
Chairman
William Haas
    Box 536, R.D. 2
    Lewisburg 17838
Vice Chairman
Thomas Rippon
    R.D. #1
    Mifflinburg 17844

VENANGO
Chairman
George A. Needle, Jr.
    27C National Transit Bldg.
    Oil City 16301
Vice Chairman
Mabel D. Bruner
    R.D. 3, Box 375
    Franklin 16323

WARREN
Chairman
Edward S. Ord
    3 Meadow Lane
    Warren 16356

WASHINGTON
Chairman
Donald Saxton
    63 S. Main Street
    Washington 15301
Vice Chairman
Julie J. Uram
    16 Wilmot Avenue
    Washington 15301

WAYNE
Chairman
Donald Olsommer
    P.O. Box 174
    Hamlin 18427
Vice Chairman
Sylvia Dewey
    R.D. #1, Box 292-H
    Hawley 18428

WESTMORELAND
Chairman
Lowman S. Henry
  Wellington Square
  1225 S. Main Street
  Greensburg 15601
Vice Chairman
Henry Jackson
  63 Soltis Drive
  North Huntingdon 15642

WYOMING
Chairman
Fran DeWitt
  61 College Avenue
  Factoryville 18419
Vice Chairman
Regina Husband
  R.D. #2
  Harveys Lake 18618

YORK
Chairman
John W. Thompson
  37 W. Market Street
  York 17402
Vice Chairman
Mabel Nell
  Box 10
  Rossville 17358

DEMOCRATIC STATE COMMITTEE OFFICERS
HEADQUARTERS: 510 N. Third St., Harrisburg 17101

CHAIRMAN
Lawrence J. Yatch
718 5th Avenue
Pittsburgh 15219

VICE CHAIR
Rena Baumgartner
R.D. #3
Kunkletown 18058

TREASURER
Frank McDonnell
Jordan Bldg.
203 Franklin Avenue
Scranton 18503

SECRETARY
Carolyn Ware Franklin
1151 Brintell Street
Pittsburgh 15201

MEMBERS OF THE DEMOCRATIC NATIONAL COMMITTEE

Lawrence J. Yatch
718 5th Avenue
Pittsburgh 15219

Rena Baumgartner
R.D. #3
Kunkletown 18058

Rita Wilson Kane
1009 Fidelity Drive
Pittsburgh 15236

Ruth Harper
1427 West Erie Avenue
Philadelphia 19140

Ruth C. Rudy
R.D. #1
Centre Hall 16828

Evelyn D. Richardson
6908 Kedron Street
Pittsburgh 15208

K. LeRoy Irvis
139 Main Capitol
Harrisburg 17120

Joseph F. Smith
1421 Walnut Street
Philadelphia 19102

Julius Uehlein
233 Winding Way
Camp Hill 17011

Andrew T. Dinniman
467 Spruce Drive
Exton 19341

A. Richard Gerber
One Montgomery Plaza-Suite 500
Norristown 19401

AT-LARGE
C. Delores Tucker
6700 Lincoln Drive
Philadelphia 19119

Leon Lynch
Five Gateway Center (USWA)
Pittsburgh 15222

Gerald McEntee
1625 L Street - N.W.
Washington, D.C. 20005

DEMOCRATIC STATE COMMITTEE MEMBERS

ADAMS
John Rarig, Chair
  247 Bottom Road
  Ortanna 17353
Gilbert J. Lupp
  347 Pickett Drive-Box 15
  Gettysburg 17325

ALLEGHENY
Edward E. Stevens, Chair
  546 Lindsay Road
  Carnegie 15106
Carol Ann Coyne
  410 Avon Drive
  Mt. Lebanon 15228
Art Komoroski
  525 Carothers Avenue
  Carnegie 15106

Myrona Little
  322 E. Garden Road
  Brentwood 15227
Mike Schaeffer
  5208 Library Road
  Bethel Park 15102
Marty Schmotzer
  4776 Rolling Hills Road
  Pittsburgh 15236
Eileen Wagner
  357 Rockfield Road
  Pittsburgh 15243
Connie Carlino
  415 Orwell Street
  Pittsburgh 15224
Jim Ferlo
  5517 Hays Street
  Pittsburgh 15206
Richard E. Givens
  229 S. Pacific Avenue
  Pittsburgh 15224

Linda E. Noszka
  5589 Bryant Street
  Pittsburgh 15206
Barbara Ann Parker
  7320 Race Street
  Homewood 15208
Mae Seeno
  110 Ramage Road
  Pittsburgh 15214
Mattie Stone
  7305 Hermitage Street
  Pittsburgh 15208
Zach Winston
  434 Wylie Avenue
  Pittsburgh 15219
Gay A. Amelio
  105 Glen-Da-Lough Court
  Pittsburgh 15237
Jennie Knox
  106 Red Bird Point
  Pittsburgh 15202

Shirley E. Lauth
  146 Buehner Drive
  Pittsburgh 15237
Jean Mastromatteo
  111 Marie Avenue
  Pittsburgh 15202
Carol Wolf
  900 Center Oak Drive
  Pittsburgh 15237
June M. Andrews
  138 Midway Drive
  Pittsburgh 15136
Jerri Cavalovitch
  1230 Oakmont Street
  Pittsburgh 15205
James R. Ellenbogen
  2327 Allender Avenue
  Pittsburgh 15220
Cathy Knoll
  1037 Chartiers Avenue
  McKees Rocks 15136

Robert Lutz
140 Connie Park Drive
McKees Rocks 15136
Sean J. McCurdy
228 Felician Drive
Coraopolis 15108
Carolyn C. Pilewski
2300 Whited Street
Pittsburgh 15226
Luvenia Richie
435 Cedar Avenue
Coraopolis 15108
Darlene Skosnik
1506 Chartiers Avenue Ext.
McKees Rocks 15136
Janice C. Vinci
612 Main Street
McKees Rocks 15136
Michael F. Coyne
5035 Glenwood Avenue
Pittsburgh 15207
John Dindak
3618 Pinewood Drive
West Homestead 15120
Angie Gialloreto
977 Elizabeth Street
Pittsburgh 15221
Cathy Irvis
P.O. Box 99811
Pittsburgh 15290
Joyce Lee Itkin
6954 Reynolds Street
Pittsburgh 15208
Sophie Masloff
Room 510 City County Bldg.
Pittsburgh 15219
Mark Pollock
1349 Beechwood Blvd.
Pittsburgh 15217
Ed Wuenschell
405 Ariston Avenue
Pittsburgh 15210
Sara Ann Wymard
1005 Lancaster Street
Pittsburgh 15218
George D. Braun
419 Center Road
Monroeville 15146
Eleanor Casciato
2420 Park Manor Drive
White Oak 15131
Elizabeth Keller
110 Brinton Street
Monroeville 15146
Jean A. Milko
2934 McKelvey Road
Pittsburgh 15221
Sarah Sansotta
1826 Monogahela Avenue
Apt. 910
Pittsburgh 15218
Frank Signore
229 Hazel Road
Pittsburgh 15235
Andy Butko
3610 Brinway Drive
West Mifflin 15122
Barbara Dansak
3541 O'Neil Blvd.
McKeesport 15132

Eleanor Fedor
1014 Burns Avenue
Duquesne 15110
Michael Horgos
6671 Dunlap Street
West Mifflin 15122
Susan A. Roach
1515 Manor Avenue
McKeesport 15132

ARMSTRONG
Earl Bowser, Chair
130 Vine Street
Kittanning 16201
Jack D. Heim
445 North Avenue
Kittanning 16201

BEAVER
Dan Donatella, Chair
311 Hice Avenue
Industry 15052
James Albert
2036 Circle Drive
Aliquippa 15001
Elizabeth McCurdy
599 8th Street
Freedom 15042
Betty H. Diciccio
18 Linden Drive
Industry 15052
Jim Corbett
133 Sherwood Drive
Monaca 15061
Charlotte Sommerville
120 Ridgeview Drive
Aliquippa 15001
Pauline Stanowich
1480 Ridge Road
Ambridge 15003

BEDFORD
Guy E. Ferguson, Chair
Box 103 Manns Choice
Manns Choice 15550
Wade Sigel
R.D. #1, Box 27A
Breezewood 15533

BERKS
Joseph Kuzminski, Chair
527 Park Avenue
Reading 19611
Thomas J. Diana
548 Perry Street
Reading 19601
Darlington Hoopes, Jr.
212 N. 6th St., Box 618
Reading 19603
Sheila Hume
38 Endlich Avenue
Mt. Penn 19606
Joan Kohl
1151 N. 11th Street
Reading 19604
Catherine Krause
2113 Peters Road
Greenfield
Reading 19601

Gary E. Lott
1021 North Tenth Street
Reading 19604
Gloria M. Strock
1103 Buttonwood Street
Reading 19604
Alice Swoyer Smolkowicz
1035 North 5th Street
Reading 19601

BLAIR
Bob Russell, Chair
1311 4th Avenue
Altoona 16602
Michael E. Cassidy
211 South St., Box 173
Newry 16665
Mary Gehrett
R.D. #3, Box 450
Duncansville 16635
Lois M. Sauers
503 East Walton Avenue
Altoona 16602

BRADFORD
John Sullivan, Chair
R.D. #2, Box 145A
Towanda 18848
David E. Ross
R.D. #1, Box 100
Milan 18831

BUCKS
Eugene Kellis, Esq., Chair
47 Briarwood Drive
Holland 18966
Isabel A. Godwin
144 Liberty Street
Newtown 19057
Cheryl W. Hoffman
151 Golf Club Drie
Langhorne 19047
Jack C. Holton
179 Willow Court
Bensalem 19020
Pamela S. Janvey
3348 Adams Court
Bensalem 19020
Jerome Mandell
41 Oval Turn Lane
Levittown 19055
Thomas Mellon
219 King Road
Doylestown 18901
Adele Miller
400 Cedar Avenue
Craydon 19020
Sandra A. Miller
Box 366
Washington Crossing 18977
Brian M. Rosenberg
511 Oxford Road
Morrisville 19067
Lucille Trench
158 Lowell Court
Langhorne 19047

BUTLER
Winifred James, Chair
R.D. #1, Box 386
Slippery Rock 16057
Helen Meaders
212 Kohler Avenue
Lyndora 16045
Robert Harvey
907 Center Avenue
Butler 16001
Marian L. Taylor
220 East Muntz Avenue
Butler 16001

CAMBRIA
William Joseph, Chair
221 Bridge Street
Conemaugh 15909
Martha Banda
233 Bossler Street
Johnstown 15902
David J. Bako
1063 McKinley Avenue
Johnstown 15905
Jerry Brant
609 1/2 Philadelphia Avenue
Barnesboro 15714
Barbara J. Kline
218 East Horner Street
Ebensburg 15931
Charles J. Vizzini
103 North Tanner Street
Ebensburg 15931

CAMERON
Ken Shaffer, Chair
R.D. #2-Box 313
Emporium 15834
Mary Ann Murray
417 Maple-Box 45
Emporium 15834
Elisabeth Griffith
R.D. #2 - Box 218
Emporium 15834

CARBON
John E. Erdman, Chair
R.D. #2-Box 266-C
Weatherly 18255
Peter A. Turko
222 Columbia Avenue
Palmerton 18071

CENTRE
Merle McCalips, Jr., Chair
716 Oak Hall Street
Boalsburg 16827
C. Guy Rudy
R.D. #1-Box 5770
Center Hall 16828

CHESTER
John Franco, Chair
1615 Boot Road
West Chester 19380
Barbara E. Cooper
931 South Walnut Street
West Chester 19382

John D. Fiore
334 Highland Avenue
Downingtown 19335
June Hamilton
610 Dogwood Drive
Downingtown 19335
Nancy Lewis
201 Long Lane
West Chester 19380

CLARION
Pearl Minich, Chair
R.D. #3
New Bethlehem 16242
Virginia G. Martin
731 Liberty Street
Clarion 16214

CLEARFIELD
David Wulderk, Chair
421 Eliza Street
Houtzdale 16651
Frederic J. Ammerman
23 North Second Street
Clearfield 16830

CLINTON
Joseph Berry, Chair
R.D. #1-Box 456
Beech Creek 16822
James S. Lovette
R.D. #1-Box 317
Lock Haven 17745

COLUMBIA
Richard S. Harter, Chair
319 East Street
Bloomsburg 17815
Lawrence Neach
9 East Park Street
Bloomsburg 17815

CRAWFORD
Richard Friedberg, Chair
Masonic Bldg.
Meadville 16335
Anna Larson
R.D. #8-Box 694
Meadville 16335

CUMBERLAND
Marianne McManus, Chair
312 Glenn Road
Camp Hill 17011
William Stone
705 Coolidge Street
New Cumberland 17070
Winnie Williams
251 West Willow Street
Carlisle 17013
Sandy Wolfe
614 York Circle
Mechanicsburg 17055

DAUPHIN
Bernard Hammer, Chair
660 Boas Street, Suite 1107
Harrisburg 17102
Marilyn Levin
101 Denison Drive
Dauphin 17018
Anthony M. Petrucci
523 Elm Avenue
Hershey 17033

Lena Schaefer
225 Poplar Street
Highspire 17111
Pete Wambach
2200 Walnut Street
Harrisburg 17103

DELAWARE
Dianne Merlino, Chair
2901 Armstrong Avenue
Secane 19018
Nancy B. Baulis
5112 Whitehall Drive
Clifton Heights 19018
Nancy Collins
2340 Cedar Lane
Secane 19018
Pat Donnelly
200 E. Township Line
Havertown 19083
Eileen Gannon
3933 Dennison Avenue
Drexel Hill 19026
James C. Leahan
79 Chester Avenue
Clifton Heights 19018
Nancy Lipsett
312 Harvard Avenue
Broomall 19008
Charles P. McLaughlin
1409 Willison Street
Chester 19013
Bob Rapp
265 Glenn Riddle Road
Glenn Riddle 19037

ELK
Gary Lee Kraus, Chair
330 Chestnut Street
St. Marys 15857
Darlene Barwin
First Avenue
Johnsonburg 15845
Gary Lee Kraus
330 Chestnut Street
St. Marys 15857

ERIE
Ian Murray, Chair
607 Powell Avenue
Erie 16505
Roy R. Bernardini
1102 Appletree Lane
Erie 16509
Thomas Carney
1322 West 31st Street
Erie 16508
Charles Casey
232 Norman Way
Erie 16508
Marjorie Christoph
205 Liberty Street
Erie 16507
Alice Cooney
124 West 22nd Street
Erie 16502
Kathryn Grimaldi
809 West Gore Road
Erie 16509

Terri Kaminski
3117 Hazel Street
Erie 16508

FAYETTE
Fred L. Lebder, Chair
14 Judith Street
Uniontown 15401
James T. Davis
107 East Main Street
Uniontown 15401
Gloria Dillon
108 Surrey Hill
Uniontown 15401
Margaret Molinaro
P.O. Box 725
Connellsville 15425
Joseph Vicites
14 Crestvue Drive
Uniontown 15401
Julia Williams
208 Second Street
Grindstone 15442

FOREST
Mary Remington, Chair
P.O. Box 31
West Hickory 16370
Zella Leonard
Box 103
Endeavor 16322

FRANKLIN
William H. Kaye, Esq., Chair
242 N. Main Street
Chambersburg 17201
Ronald K. Overcash
772 Cleveland Street
Chambersburg 17201

FULTON
A. Reed Shives, Chair
R.D. #2-Box 124
Big Cove Tannery 17212
Alice J. Mellott
R.D. #1-Box 881
Harrisonville 17228

GREENE
James Harris, Chair
60 Bonar Avenue
Waynesburg 15370
Pamela Snyder
R.D. #1-Box 153A
Jefferson 15344
John M. Stewart
R.D. #4-Box 269
Waynesburg 15370

HUNTINGDON
Harold Kann, Chair
R.D. #1-Warrior Oaks
Huntingdon 16652
John P. Mills
922 Mifflin Street
Huntingdon 16652

INDIANA
Thomas Huff, Chair
28 Overlook Drive
Indiana 15701

Beatrice States
913 Oak Street
Indiana 15701
William S. Tate
52 Morris Street
Clymer 15728

JEFFERSON
Gloria Rankus, Chair
563 Myrtle Street
Reynoldsville 15815
Henry Cook, Sr.
Star Route
Brookville 15825
Olga Cowan
43 Sykes Street
Sykesville 15865

JUNIATA
Larry Nemond, Chair
HCR-63 - Box 18
Richfield 17086
Hayes Eckard, Jr.
Jefferson Street-Apt. 13
Mifflintown 17059

LACKAWANNA
Patrick J. Mellody, Chair
1218 Woodlawn Street
Scranton 18509
Joseph Barrett
709 Crown Avenue
Scranton 18505
Theresa Barrett
816 Woodlawn Street
Scranton 18509
Frank McHale
321 Neptune Place
Scranton 18505
Linda Munley
920 Hilltop Drive
Jessup 18434
Todd O'Malley
R.D. #6-Box 20
Moscow 18444
Ann Opiel
48 Orchard Street
Carbondale 18407
Constance Payton
1508 Jefferson Avenue
Dunmore 18510
Marie A. Peperno
901 Glenwood Road
Old Forge 18518

LANCASTER
J. Richard Gray, Chair
53 North Duke Street
Lancaster 17602
Russell J. Hay
100 North 11th Street
Akron 17501
Gerald A. Nikolaus
1191 Ridge Avenue
Columbia 17512
Teresa Ruhle
133 Crystal Street
Lancaster 17603
Linda Todd
R.D. #2-Box 346
Quarryville 17566

LAWRENCE
Peter Vessella, Chair
317 Golf Avenue
Elwood City 16117
Marilyn J. Cook
913 Loraine Avenue
New Castle 16101
Thomas Costa
328 Shaw Street
New Castle 16101

LEBANON
Tom Horst, Chair
South Market Street
Schaefferstown 17088
Jacob Long
115 South King Street
Annville 17003

LEHIGH
Glenn R. Moyer, Chair
34 North 16th Street
Allentown 18102
Martha Falk
1921 East Columbia Street
Allentown 18103
Mary S. Jackson
1324 North Troxell Street
Allentown 18103
John B. Karoly, Jr
637 Washington Street
Allentown 18102
Minnie Marie Moyer
29 West State Avenue
Coopersburg 18036
Frank Palencar
2007 S. Delaware Street
Allentown 18103

LUZERNE
Joseph Tirpak, Chair
6 Terrace Drive
West Wyoming 18644
Tom H. Blaskiewicz
623 South Street
Avoca 18641
Jerry Bonner
48 Walden Drive
Mt. Top 18707
Leona Flannery
343 McLean Street
Wilkes-Barre 18702
Eileen Kolensky
R.D. #1
Middletown Jeddo
Freeland 18222
Lucille Maziarz
626 Main Street
Duryea 18642
James P. McCabe
562 Warren Avenue
Kingston 18704
Neil T. O'Donnell
886 S. Franklin Street
Wilkes-Barre 18702
Eileen Sorokas
14 Hurley Street
Wilkes-Barre 18705

Barbara Youngblood
489 East Northampton Street
Wilkes-Barre 18702
Rose S. Tucker
295 State Street
Nanticoke 18634

LYCOMING
Joseph Smith, Chair
R.D. #1
Williamsport 17701
Carol G. Armstrong
212 Pine Street
Williamsport 17701
Joan Flynn
338 Bastian Avenue
South Williamsport 17701
R. David Frey
1420 Pine Crest Drive
S. Williamsport 17701

McKEAN
J. Edward Carlson, Chair
Two Anderson Street
Mt. Jewett 16740
Eileen H. McKean
R.D. #1
Smethport 16749

MERCER
James Nevant, II, Chair
2030 Landy Lane
Farrell 16121
Harold E. Bell
388 Independence Court
Sharon 16146
Betty J. DeVito
307 West Market Street
Mercer 16137

MIFFLIN
John Leister, Chair
628 West Fifth Street
Lewistown 17044
Philip E. Gingerich
6 Summit Manor
Lewistown 17044

MONROE
Rena Baumgartner, Chair
R.D. #3
Kunkletown 18058
Melvin Solomon
R.D. #7-Box 7334
Stroudsburg 18360

MONTGOMERY
Philip Berg, Chair
706 Ridge Pike
Lafayette Hill 19444
Colleen Alexander
8804 Tyson Road
Wyndmoor 19118
Angela Badali
P.O. Box 460
Skippack 19474
Barbara G. Blum
P.O. Box 595
King of Prussia 19406

Michael L. Brint
1434 Remington Road
Penn Wynne 19151
Shirley P. Curry
250 Wyncote Road
Jenkintown 19406
Arline Lotman
526 Ott Road
Bala Cynwyd 19004
Jeanne M. Simon
1444 Welsh Road
Huntingdon Valley 19006
Art Wright
136 West Airy Street
Norristown 19401

MONTOUR
Thomas E. Herman, Chair
R.D. #4
Danville 17821
Elizabeth Bankes
204 Montgomery Village
Danville 17821
Glen A. Hagenbuch
P.O. Box 45
Danville 17821

NORTHAMPTON
Philip Ruggiero, Chair
920 North Main Street
Bangor 18013
Barbara Altemus
815 Walter Street
Bethlehem 18017
Joseph F. Leeson, Jr.
3355 Camelot Drive
Bethlehem 18017
Chester A. Reybitz
760 East Macade Road
Bethlehem 18017
Arlene Snyder
122 Mauch Chunk Street
Nazareth 18064
Anna A. Stofko
1954 Greenleaf Street
Bethlehem 18018

NORTHUMBERLAND
John Brennan, Chair
1709 Raven Avenue
Shamokin 17872
George A. Dorko
527 S. Seventh Street
Shamokin 17872
Eleanor Kovack Kuhns
R.D. #1-Box 766
Shamokin 17872

PERRY
Harry G. Sheaffer, Chair
Ickesburg 17037
Karl E. Kennedy
R.D. #1
Elliotsburg 17024

PHILADELPHIA
Robert A. Brady, Chair
1201 Kimberly Drive
Philadelphia 19151

Eleanor T. Bednarek
4388 Richmond Street
Philadelphia 19137
Emily Brozowski
2357 E. Dauphin Street
Philadelphia 19125
Margueritte Bukowski
6365 Ditman Street
Philadelphia 19135
Richard P. Cermele
1208 Tasker Street
Philadelphia 19148
Albert D'Intino
1208 Tasker Street
Philadelphia 19148
Milderd G. Kerns
636 Reed Street
Philadelphia 19147
Marie A. Lederer
1237 Shackamaxon
Philadelphia 19125
Dorothy Laudenslager
1919 E. Orleans Street
Philadelphia 19134
Matthew Myers
2429 South 5th Street
Philadelphia 19148
Dante J. Purifico
2338 South Hicks Street
Philadelphia 19145
Robert Rego
513 St. Michael Drive
Philadelphia 19148
Jean Smith
2513 Cedar Street
Philadelphia 19125
Lorraine Travelina
1208 Tasker Street
Philadelphia 19148
Maureen Wooten
1205 South 2nd Street
Philadelphia 19147
Patricia Dugan
3881 Dungan Street
Philadelphia 19124
Rose Jaffee
6138 Shisler Street
Philadelphia 19149
James P. McConville
958 Kenwyn Street
Philadelphia 19124
Jeffrey D. Moran
2100 Walnut Street-14C
Philadelphia 19103
Rita R. O'Donnell
4022 Magee Avenue
Philadelphia 19135
Gilbert Rochvarg
1444 Stirling Street
Philadelphia 19149
Lee Ruffin
743 North Uber Street
Philadelphia 19130
Mercedes Sanchez
2401 N. 4th Street
Philadelphia 19133
Anna S. Stinson
3951 L Street
Philadelphia 19124

Margaret M. Tartaglione
1407 VanKirk Street
Philadelphia 19149

Christine Tartaglione
1407 VanKirk Street
Philadelphia 19149

Joyce Ullman
2526 Aspen Street
Philadelphia 19130

Helen Campbell Yudizki
3425 Jasper Street
Philadelphia 19134

Bernice DeAngelis
876 N. Taylor Street
Philadelphia 19130

Herbert Arlene
1714 West Columbia Avenue
Philadelphia 19121

Helyn Cheeks
1705 North Willington Street
Philadelphia 19121

Hon. Mark B. Cohen
So. Office Bldg.-Room 106
Harrisburg 17120

Shirley Gregory
5803 North 12th Street
Philadelphia 19141

Beverly A. McCray
3039 North 23rd Street
Philadelphia 19132

Ann Moss
2315 West Cumberland Street
Philadelphia 19132

George Perez
2948 North 6th Street
Philadelphia 19133

Madeline Phillips
2246 North Van Pelt Street
Philadelphia 19132

Jesse Reason
3319 West Harold Street
Philadelphia 19132

John F. Street
1812 West Diamond Street
Philadelphia 19121

Linda Johnson
5024 N. 8th Street
Philadelphia 19120

Vergia Thomas
3511 N. Sydenham Street
Philadelphia 19132

Alice D. Blasi
863 Manaiawna Avenue
Philadelphia 19128

Dolores Cameron
7223 Pittville Avenue
Philadelphia 19126

Bruce Edward Caswell
1024 West Upsal Street
Philadelphia 19119

Donna Livingston
7247 Limekiln Pike
Philadelphia 19138

George J. Naulty
533 Sanger Street
Philadelphia 19120

Bridget A. Murray
6017 N. Water Street
Philadelphia 19120

Gail T. Petrofsky
900 Cathedral Road
Philadelphia 19128

Hon. M. Joseph Rocks
940 Cathedral Road
Philadelphia 19128

Andrew S. Ross
8407 Ardleigh Street
Philadelphia 19118

Arnold S. Storr
7916 Thouron Avenue
Philadelphia 19150

Marian B. Tasco
1000 East Vernon Road
Philadelphia 19150

Labora Mont Bennett
8114 Erdrick Street
Philadelphia 19136

Francis R. Conaway
9107 Ryerson Road
Philadelphia 19114

JoAnn Corrado
3327 Belgreen Road
Philadelphia 19154

Joan Dillon
3843 Violet Drive
Philadelphia 19154

Lorena S. Fagan
3034 Fairfield Street
Philadelphia 19136

Louis Farinella
12518 Chilton Road
Philadelphia 19154

Ruth Fisgaer
8616 Agusta Street
Philadelphia 19152

Elinda B. Fishman
428 Avon Place
Philadelphia 19116

Joan Krajewski
4107 Shelmire Avenue
Philadelphia 19136

Delores R. Micek
2310 Fuller Street
Philadelphia 19152

David Fine
458 Tomlinson Road
Philadelphia 19116

Lisa M. O'Mara
12540 Chilton Road
Philadelphia 19154

Abraham Siegel
7539 A Calvert Street
Philadelphia 19152

Obia Adams
201 East Price Street
Philadelphia 19144

Betty M. Carney
2201 Bryn Mawr Ave.-Apt. 511
Philadelphia 19131

Ella L. Dunn
27 North Peach Street
Philadelphia 19139

David Fineman
6006 Greene Street
Philadelphia 19144

Steven C. Greene
3500 Powelton Ave.-Apt. C008
Philadelphia 19104

James Harmon
407 North Salford Street
Philadelphia 19139

Marge Hipple Koral
3740 Country Club Road
Philadelphia 19401

Ann Land
3418 Coulter Street
Philadelphia 19129

James P. McMahon
3597 Indian Queen Lane
Philadelphia 19129

Marlene Marshall
2627 W. Westmoreland Street
Philadelphia 19129

Flora Pauling
1240 North 60th Street
Philadelphia 19151

Dianna L. Pierce
857 E. Stafford Street
Philadelphia 19138

Dorothy May Price
857 East Stafford Street
Philadelphia 19138

Phyllis Waters
2734 West Silver Street
Philadelphia 19132

Rita Avellino
7235 Mallard Place
Philadelphia 19153

Irene Bailey
5353 Osage Avenue
Philadelphia 19143

Lucien Blackwell
235 S. Melville Street
Philadelphia 19139

Frances B. Capetola
2022 S. 27th Street
Philadelphia 19145

Glenda Christopher
5900 Greenway Avenue
Philadelphia 19143

Mary Rita D'Allesandro
7913 Lindbergh Blvd.
Philadelphia 19153

Edward F. Dasilvio
5936 Chestnut Street
Philadelphia 19139

Thomas F. Gehrett
7119 Lindbergh Blvd.
Philadelphia 19153

Catherine A. Jenkins
2014 Latona Street
Philadelphia 19146

Hon. James R. Roebuck
435 S. 46th Street
Philadelphia 19143

Rita Rufo
2027 Mifflin Street
Philadelphia 19145

Ethel Saunders
2425 Pine Street
Philadelphia 19103

Isadore A. Shrager
4920 Locust Street
Philadelphia 19139

Sadie Tanker Smith
1542 South 15th Street
Philadelphia 19146

Patricia M. Walls
1016 South 60th Street
Philadelphia 19143

PIKE
Daniel Mazus, Chair
338 Lords Valley
Hawley 18428

Nancy Hiller
Lords Valley-Box 347
Hawley 18428

John E. Rose
R.D. #1, Box 114-58
Hawley 18428

POTTER
Warren White, Chair
R.D. #1
Coudersport 16915

Daniel F. Glassmire
R.D. #3
Coudersport 16915

SCHUYLKILL
Metro Litwak, Chair
127 North West Street
Shenandoah 17976

James A. Goodman
201 West Pine Street
Mahanoy City 17948

Jacqueline L. Shields
410 West Markert Street
Pottsville 17901

SNYDER
Donald Lauver, Chair
Box 26
Mt. Pleasant Mills 17853

Karen L. Hackman
604 North Orange Street
Selingsgrove 17870

SOMERSET
Harold E. Shepley, Chair
R.D. #1
Stoystown 15563

Helen Shepley
R.D. #1
Stoystown 15563

Robert B. Stahl
R.D. #6
Somerset 15501

SULLIVAN
James L. Rinker, Chair
R.D. #1-Box 105
Forksville 18616

Louise Rinker
R.D, #1-Box 105
Forksville 18616

Thomas J. Sick
R.D. #1
Dushore 18614

SUSQUEHANNA
Donald States, Chair
R.D. #1-Box 229
Springville 18844

Josephine Marshall
416 Jackson Avenue
Susquehanna 18847

TIOGA
Dayton Brown, Chair
108 Walnut Street
Elkland 16920
Marie Cooper
R.D. #2-Box 57
Tioga 16946

UNION
Miriam Landis, Chair
Kelly Courts-Apt. H6
R.D. #3
Lewisburg 17837
Cheryl D. Baker
R.D. #3-Box 321
Lewisburg 17837

VENANGO
Charles Kay, Chair
213 Second Avenue
Franklin 16323
Edward L Scurry
516 Elk Street
Franklin 16323
Nancy Troy
Box 8
Kennerdell 16374

WARREN
Merl Rice, Chair
707 Madison Avenue
Warren 16365

Catherine Donnelly Rice
707 Madison Avenue
Warren 16365

WASHINGTON
Olga Woodward, Chair
R.D. #1-Box 468
Charleroi 15022
George L. Eckert, Jr.
614 Ann Street
Monongahela 15063
Peter Elish
503 Bluff Avenue
Canonsburg 15317
Madge Finney
105 Gibson Road
Bentleyville 15314
Frances Lee
107 Burton Avenue
Washington 15301
Debbie O'Dell Seneca
333-335 N. Main Street
Washington 15301
John Solomon
189 Wilmont Avenue
Washington 15301
Marie Trozzo
612 8th Street
Donora 15033

WAYNE
Marcella Murray, Chair
308 Ridge Street
Honesdale 18431

Ann M. Bursis
415 - 15th Street
Honesdale 18431

WESTMORELAND
Dante G. Bertani, Chair
7553 Pennsylvania Avenue
North Huntingdon 15642
Sally Beene
1519 N. Front St.-Apt. 18
Harrisburg 17102
Bob Davis
502 North Maple
Greensburg 15601
Patrick J. Davis
303 N. Ninth Street
Jeannette 15644
Albert Kukovich
Box 21
Manor 15665
Patricia Lace
202 Washington Avenue
Vandergrift 15690
Marilyn Meriweather
516 Westchester Drive
Greensburg 15601
John W. Regoli
293 Elmtree Road
New Kensington 15068
Donna Sherry
R.D. #2-Box 453H
Greensburg 15601

Dana L. Testa
332 Third Street
Bovard 15619

WYOMING
James Byrnes, Chair
R.D. #2-Box 158
Mehoopany 18629
J.J. Bunnell
P.O. Box 302
Meshoppen 18630

YORK
Gloria L. Davis, Chair
375 Hill 'N Dale Drive N
York 17403
Lucille Breneman
60 Hillery Court
York 17402
Ruth F. Craley
839 McKenzie Street
York 17403
Donald Hughes
367 Norway Street
York 17403
Patricia Naftzger
550 Sundale Drive
York 17042
Carl Nelson
2800 Hialeah Court
York 17404

PENNSYLVANIA INSTITUTIONS OF HIGHER EDUCATION

STATE SYSTEM OF HIGHER EDUCATION
James H. McCormick, Chancellor

INSTITUTION	CHIEF EXECUTIVE OFFICER	LOCATION	1986 ENROLLMENT
Bloomsburg University of Pa.	Harry Ausprich	Bloomsburg 17815	6,757
California University of Pa.	John P. Watkins	California 15419	5,479
Cheyney University of Pa.	LeVerne McCummings,	Cheyney 19319	1,501
Clarion University of Pa.	Thomas A. Bond	Clarion 16214	6,112
East Stroudsburg University of Pa.	James E. Gilbert	East Stroudsburg 18301	4,320
Edinboro University of Pa.	Foster F. Diebold	Edinboro 16444	6,014
Indiana University of Pa.	John D. Welty	Indiana 15705	13,248
Kutztown University of Pa.	Lawrence M. Stratton	Kutztown 19530	6,647
Lock Haven University of Pa.	Craig D. Willis	Lock Haven 17745	2,725
Mansfield University of Pa.	Rod C. Kelchner	Mansfield 16933	2,670
Millersville University of Pa.	Joseph A. Caputo	Millersville 17551	7,166
Shippensburg University of Pa.	Anthony F. Ceddia	Shippensburg 17257	6,335
Slippery Rock University of Pa.	Robert N. Aebersold	Slippery Rock 16057	6,599
West Chester University of Pa.	Kenneth L. Perrin	West Chester 19383	10,101

TOTAL ENROLLMENT, STATE SYSTEM UNIVERSITIES: 85,674

BRANCH CAMPUSES	DIRECTOR	LOCATION
Clarion University of Pa.		
Venango Campus	Thomas J. Rookey	Oil City 16301
Indiana University of Pa.		
Armstrong Campus	Robert Doerr	Kittanning 16201
Punxsutawney Campus	Norman T. Storm	Punxsutawney 15767
Slippery Rock University of Pa.		
McKeever Environmental Center	Donna Bessken	Sandy Lake 16145

STATE-RELATED UNIVERSITIES

INSTITUTION	CHIEF EXECUTIVE OFFICER	LOCATION	1985 ENROLLMENT
Lincoln University	Donald L. Mullett	Lincoln University 19352	1,181
Pennsylvania State University, (The)	Bryce Jordan	University Park 16802	62,414
Temple University	Peter J. Liacouras	Philadelphia 19122	30,277
University of Pittsburgh	Wesley W. Posvar	Pittsburgh 15260	34,453

TOTAL ENROLLMENT, STATE-RELATED UNIVERSITIES: 128,325

BRANCH CAMPUSES

Pennsylvania State University (The)

Allentown Campus	John V. Cooney	Fogelsville 18051
Altoona Campus	James A. Duplass	Altoona 16601-3760
Beaver Campus	David B. Otto	Monaca 15061
Behrend College	John M. Lilley, Dean	Erie 16563
Berks Campus	Frederick Gaige	Reading 19608
Capitol Campus	Ruth Leventhal, Provost	Middletown 17057
Delaware Campus	Edward S. J. Tomezsko	Media 19063
DuBois Campus	Jacqueline L. Schoch	DuBois 15801
Fayette Campus	John D. Sink	Uniontown 15401
Hazleton Campus	James J. Staudenmeier	Hazleton 18201
King of Prussia Center for Graduate Studies	Helmut E. Weber	King of Prussia 19406
McKeesport Campus	Cash J. Kowalski	McKeesport 15132
Mont Alto Campus	Vernon L. Shockley	Mont Alto 17237
New Kensington Campus	Robert D. Arbuckle	New Kensington 15068
Ogontz Campus	Robert A. Bernoff	Abington 19001
Schuylkill Campus	Wayne D. Lammie	Schuylkill Haven 17972
Shenango Valley Campus	Vincent DeSanctis	Sharon 16146
Wilkes-Barre Campus	James H. Ryan	Lehman 18627
Worthington Scranton Campus	James D. Gallagher	Dunmore 18512
York Campus	John J. Romano	York 17403

Temple University

Ambler Campus	James H. Blackhurst	Ambler 19002

University of Pittsburgh

Bradford Campus	Richard E. McDowell	Bradford 16701
Greensburg Campus	George F. Chambers	Greensburg 15601
Johnstown Campus	Frank H. Blackington, III	Johnstown 15904
Titusville Campus	Samuel Johnson	Titusville 16354

COMMUNITY COLLEGES

INSTITUTION	CHIEF EXECUTIVE OFFICER	LOCATION	1985 ENROLLMENT
Bucks County Community College	Charles E. Rollins	Newtown 18940	9,233
Butler County Community College	Frederick W. Woodward	Butler 16001	2,150
Community College of Allegheny County	John W. Kraft	Pittsburgh 15233-1895	18,426
Community College of Beaver County	William K. Bauer	Monaca 15061-2588	2,373
Community College of Philadelphia	Judith S. Eaton	Philadelphia 19130	15,267
Delaware County Community College	Richard D. DeCosmo	Media 19063	7,638
Harrisburg Area Community College	Kenneth B. Woodbury, Jr.	Harrisburg 17110	6,598
Lehigh County Community College	Robert L. Barthlow	Schnecksville 18078-9372	3,287

Luzerne County Community College	Thomas J. Moran	Naticoke 18634	4,525
Montgomery County Community College	Edmond A. Watters, III.	Blue Bell 19422	7,047
Northampton County Area Community College	Robert J. Kopecek	Bethlehem 18017	4,041
Reading Area Community College	Gust Zogas	Reading 19603	1,279
Westmoreland County Community College	Daniel C. Krezinski	Youngwood 15697	3,312
Williamsport Area Community College	Robert L. Breuder	Williamsport 17701	3,589

TOTAL ENROLLMENT, COMMUNITY COLLEGES: 88,765

PRIVATE STATE-AIDED INSTITUTIONS

INSTITUTION	CHIEF EXECUTIVE OFFICER	LOCATION	1985 ENROLLMENT
Delaware Valley College of Science and Agriculture	Joshua Feldstein	Doylestown 18901	1,422
Drexel University	William Gaither	Philadelphia 19104	12,386
Hahnemann Medical College & Hospital (of Phila., The)	Bertram Brown	Philadelphia 19102	2,209
(The Woman's Medical College of Pennsylvania) Medical College of Pa., (The)	D. Walter Cohen	Philadelphia 19129	568
Pa. College of Optometry	Melvin D. Wolfberg	Philadelphia 19141	614
Pa. College of Podiatric Medicine	James E. Bates	Philadelphia 19107	477
Philadelphia College of Osteopathic Medicine	J. Peter Tilley	Philadelphia 19131	824
Philadelphia College of Textiles & Science	James P. Gallagher	Philadelphia 19144	2,974
Philadelphia Colleges of the Arts	Charles W. Raison	Philadelphia 19102	
Thomas Jefferson University	Lewis W. Bluemle Jr.	Philadelphia 19107	2,016
University of Pennsylvania (The Trustees of)	F. Sheldon Hackney	Philadelphia 19104	21,870

TOTAL ENROLLMENT, PRIVATE STATE-AIDED INSTITUTIONS: 45,360

PRIVATE COLLEGES, UNIVERSITIES AND SEMINARIES

INSTITUTION	CHIEF EXECUTIVE OFFICER	LOCATION	1985 ENROLLMENT
Academy of the New Church (The)	Rev. Peter M. Buss	Bryn Athyn 19009	155
Albright College	David G. Ruffer	Reading 19603	2,053
Allegheny College	Daniel Sullivan	Meadville 16335	1,905
Allentown College of St. Francis de Sales	Very Rev. Daniel G. Gambet O.S.F.S.	Center Valley 18034	1,407
(The Polish National Alliance School Corp.) Alliance College	James W. Gambart	Cambridge Springs 16403	277
Alvernia College	Sister Mary Dolorey	Reading 19607	779
American College, (The)	Edward G. Jordan	Bryn Mawr 19010	2,226
(Baptist Bible College of Pennsylvania) Baptist Bible College & School of Theology	Mark Evan Jackson	Clarks Summit 18411	694
Beaver College	Bette E. Landman	Glenside 19038	2,004
Biblical Theological Seminary	David G. Dunbar	Hatfield 19440	167
Bryn Mawr College	Mary P. McPherson	Bryn Mawr 19010	1,794
Bucknell University	Gary Sojka	Lewisburg 17837	3,296
Cabrini College	Sister Eileen Currie, M.S.C.	Radnor 19087	1,000

Calvary Baptist Theological Seminary	E. Robert Jordan	Lansdale 19446	102
Carlow College	Sister Mary Louise Fennell	Pittsburgh 15213	1,174
Carnegie-Mellon University	Richard M. Cyert	Pittsburgh 15213	6,621
Cedar Crest College	Gene S. Cesari	Allentown 18104	1,157
Chatham College	Rebecca Stafford	Pittsburgh 15232	565
Chestnut Hill College	Sister Matthew Anita McDonald, S.S.J.	Philadelphia 19118	925
Christ the Saviour Seminary (of Johnstown, Pa.)	Rev. John R. Martin, DD	Johnstown 15906	5
College Misericordia	Joseph R. Fink	Dallas 18612	1,268
Combs College of Music	Helen B. Braun	Philadelphia 19119	72
Curtis Institute of Music, (The)	Gary Graffman	Philadelphia 19103	158
Dickinson College	George Allan, Acting Pres.	Carlisle 17013	1,937
Dickinson School of Law	Hon. Dale F. Shughart	Carlisle 17013	561
Dropsie University, (The)	David Goldenberg	Philadelphia 19066	38
Duquesne University (of the Holy Ghost)	Rev. Donald S. Nesti	Pittsburgh 15282	6,528
(Eastern College: A Baptist Institution) Eastern College	Robert A. Seiple	St. Davids 19087	959
Eastern Baptist Theological Seminary, (The)	Robert A. Seiple	Philadelphia 19151	371
Elizabethtown College	Gerhard E. Spiegler	Elizabethtown 17022	1,608
Evangelical School of Theology (of the Evangelical Congregational Church, The)	Ray A. Seilhamer	Myerstown 17067	71
Faith Theological Seminary, (Inc.)	Rev. Carl McIntire	Elkins Park, Phila. 19117	45
Franklin & Marshall College	James L. Powell	Lancaster 17604	2,794
Gannon University	Joseph P. Scottino	Erie 16541	4,096
Geneva College	Joseph McFarland	Beaver Falls 15010	1,191
Gettysburg College	Charles E. Glassick	Gettysburg 17325	1,978
(The Hebrew Education Society of Philadelphia) Gratz College	Gary S. Schiff	Philadelphia 19141	246
Grove City College	Charles S. McKenzie	Grove City 16127	2,162
Gwynedd-Mercy College	Sister Isabelle Keiss, R.S.M.	Gwynedd Valley 19437	2,007
Haverford College, (The Corporation of)	Robert Bocking Stevens	Haverford 19041	1,101
Holy Family College	Sister M. Francesca, C.S.F.N	Philadelphia 19114	1,525
Immaculata College	Sister Marion William, IHM	Immaculata 19345	1,912
Juniata College	Robert W. Neff	Huntingdon 16652	1,127
King's College	Rev. James Lackenmier, C.S.C.	Wilkes-Barre 18711	2,327
Lafayette College	David W. Ellis	Easton 18042	2,375
Lancaster Bible College	Gilbert A. Peterson	Lancaster 17601	355
Lancaster Theological Seminary (of the United Church of Christ, The)	Peter M. Schmiechen	Lancaster 17603	254
LaRoche College	Sister Margaret Huber	Pittsburgh 15237	1,751
LaSalle University (in the City of Phila., The)	Brother F. Patrick Ellis, F.S.C.	Philadelphia 19141	6,340
Lebanon Valley College	Arthur Peterson	Annville 17003	1,210
Lehigh University	Peter Likins	Bethlehem 18015	6,396
Lutheran Theological Seminary (at Gettysburg, Pa.)	Rev. Herman G. Stuempfle, Jr.	Gettysburg 17325	243
Lutheran Theological Seminary (at Philadelphia, Pa.)	John W. Vannorsdall	Philadelphia 19119-1794	259
Lycoming College	Frederick E. Blumer	Williamsport 17701	1,208
Mary Immaculate Seminary	Rev. Thomas F. Hoar, CM	Northampton 18067	56
Marywood College	Sister M. Coleman Nee, I.H.M.	Scranton 18509-1598	3,194
Mercyhurst College	William P. Garvey	Erie 16546	1,653
Messiah College	D. Ray Hostetter	Grantham 17027	1,846
Moore College of Art	Edward C. McGuire	Philadelphia 19103	598
Moravian College*	Herman E. Collier Jr.	Bethlehem 18018	1,758
Muhlenberg College	Jonathan C. Messerli	Allentown 18104	2,133
Neumann College	Sister M. Margarella O'Neill, O.S.F.	Aston 19014	1,016
New School of Music, (The)	Tamara Brooks	Philadelphia 19103	46
Penna. College of Straight Chiropractic	William A. Volk	Langhorne 19047	97
Philadelphia College of Bible	W. Sherrill Babb	Langhorne 19047	544
Philadelphia College of Pharmacy and Science	Allen Misher	Philadelphia 19104	1,243

Pittsburgh Theological Seminary (of the United Presbyterian Church in the United States) of America	Carnegie Samuel Calain	Pittsburgh 15206	384
Point Park College	J. Matthew Simon	Pittsburgh 15222	2,762
Recontructionist Rabbinical College	Arthur Green	Wynecote 19095	65
Reformed Presbyterian Theological Seminary	Bruce C. Stewart	Pittsburgh 15208	70
Robert Morris College	Charles L. Sewall	Coraopolis 15108	5,545
Rosemont College (of the Holy Child Jesus)	Dorothy M. Brown	Rosemont 19010	519
(The Philadelphia Theological Seminary of) St. Charles Borromeo	Msgr. Francis X. DiLorenzo	Philadelphia 19151	504
St. Francis College (of Loretto, Pa.)	Rev. Christian R. Oravec, T.O.R.	Loretto 15940	1,604
St. Joseph's University (in the City of Phila., The)	Rev. Nicholas Rashford	Philadelphia 19131	5,705
St. Vincent College*	Rev. John F. Murtha, OSB	Latrobe 15650	1,237
Seton Hill College	Eileen Farrell	Greensburg 15601	892
Spring Garden College	Daniel N. DeLucca	Chestnut Hill, Philadelphia 19119	1,679
Susquehanna University (of the Evangelical Lutheran Church)	Joel Cunningham	Selinsgrove 17870	1,720
Swarthmore College	David W. Fraser	Swarthmore 19081	1,322
Theological Seminary of the Reformed Episcopal Church	Bishop Leonard W. Riches, D.D.	Philadelphia 19104	48
Thiel College	Louis T. Almen	Greenville 16125	854
Trinity Episcopal School for Ministry	John H. Rodgers, Jr.	Ambridge 15003	125
United Wesleyan College	John Ragsdale	Allentown 18103	187
University of Scranton	Rev. Joseph A. Panuska, S.J.	Scranton 18510	4,688
Ursinus College	Richard P. Richter	Collegeville 19426	2,127
Valley Forge Christian College (of the Assemblies of God)	Wesley W. Smith	Phoenixville 19460	610
Villa Maria College (of Erie, Pa.)	Sister M. Lawreace Antoun	Erie 16505	596
Villanova University (in the State of Pa.)	Rev. John M. Driscoll, O.S.A.	Villanova 19085	11,956
Washington & Jefferson College	Howard J. Burnett	Washington 15301	1,267
Waynesburg College, (The)	J. Thomas Mills	Waynesburg 15370	869
Westminster College	Jerry M. Boone	New Wilmington 16142	1,297
Westminster Theological Seminary	George C. Fuller	Philadelphia 19118	502
Widener University	Robert Bruce	Chester 19013	4,900
Brandywine College	Andrew A. Bushko	Wilmington, DE 19803	
Delaware Law School	Anthony J. Santoro, Dean	Wilmington, DE 19803	
Wilkes College	Christopher N. Briseth	Wilkes-Barre 18766	2,964
Wilson College	Mary Linda Merriam	Chambersburg 17201	328
York College of PA	Robert V. Iosue	York 17405	4,638

*Seminary Included

TOTAL ENROLLMENT, PRIVATE COLLEGES AND UNIVERSITIES: 160,927

PRIVATE JUNIOR COLLEGES

INSTITUTION	CHIEF EXECUTIVE OFFICER	LOCATION	1985 ENROLLMENT
Harcum Junior College	Norma Furst	Bryn Mawr 19010	1,003
Keystone Junior College	Margaretta B. Chamberlin	LaPlume 18440	1,198
Lackawanna Junior College	A. P. Mensky	Scranton 18503	1,191
Manor Junior College	Sr. Mary Cecilia Jurasinski, OSBM	Jenkintown 19046	515
Mt. Aloysius Junior College	Edward F. Peirce	Cresson 16630-1999	852

Northeastern Christian
  Junior College . . . . .Larry Roberts .Villanova 19085. 189
Peirce Junior College . . . . .Raymond C. Lewin . . . . .Philadelphia 19102 1,492
Pinebrook Junior College . . . . .Carl Cassel . . . . .Coopersburg 18036. 164
(Valley Forge Military Academy
  Foundation) Valley Forge Military . . . . .Lt. Gen. Alexander M. Weyland, ...Wayne 19087. 166
    Academy & Junior College   U.S.A., (Ret.)

TOTAL ENROLLMENT, PRIVATE JUNIOR COLLEGES: 6,770

PROPRIETARY SCHOOLS

INSTITUTION	CHIEF EXECUTIVE OFFICER	LOCATION	1985 ENROLLMENT
Altoona School of Commerce	Robert A. Halloran.	Altoona 16602	88
American Institute of Drafting, Inc.	Gail Zuckerman.	Philadelphia 19124	—
Antonelli Institute of Art and Photography	Gilbert Weiss	Plymouth Meeting 19462	355
Antonelli Institute of Art and Photography	Loren Kroh.	York 17405	199
Art Institute of Phila. (The).	John R. Knepper	Philadelphia 19103	1,422
Art Institute of Pitts. (The)	John T. Barclay	Pittsburgh 15222.	1,848
Berean Institute.	Lucille P. Blondin	Philadelphia 19103	154
Cambria-Rowe Business College	William M. Coward	Johnstown 15902	258
Center for Degree Studies.	Gerald E. Burns.	Scranton 18515.	5,821
Central Pa. Business School.	Bart A. Milano	Summerdale 17093.	699
Centre Business School, Inc.	Lois H. Campbell.	State College 16801	123
CHI Institute	Howard B. Patrick	Southampton 18966	—
Churchman Business School	Charles W. Churchman Jr.	Easton 18042	172
Clarissa School (The)	Penelope Smith.	Pittsburgh 15222.	36
Computer Systems Institute, Inc.	David J. Aber.	Meadville 16335	71
Computer Systems Inst., Inc.	Joseph Yorke.	Pittsburgh 15222.	189
Dean Institute of Technology.	James S. Dean	Pittsburgh 15226.	223
Douglas School of Business	Olga Plavko.	Monessen 15062.	61
DuBois Business College	Robert G. Flanagan.	DuBois 15801	284
Duff's Business Institute	Thomas W. Dillenburg, Jr.	Pittsburgh 15222.	657
Electronic Institutes.	William F. Margut.	Middletown 17057.	267
Electronic Institutes.	Philip M. Chosky	Pittsburgh 15217.	246
Erie Business Center	Charles P. McGeary.	Erie 16501	308
Erie Inst. of Tech., Inc.	Edward Grzelak, Jr.	Erie 16501	—
Hiram G. Andrews Center	Raymond Dalton, Jr.	Johnstown 15905	49
Hussian School of Art, Inc.	Ronald Dove	Philadelphia 19107	138
ICM School of Business	Wayne R. Zanardelli	Pittsburgh 15222.	280
Johnson School of Technology	John R. O'Hara	Scranton 18508.	510
Keystone Secretarial & Business Administration School	Alfred B. Smith	Swarthmore 19081	125
Lansdale School of Business	Marlon D. Keller.	Lansdale 19446.	103
Lansdale School of Business	(Vacant)	Pottstown 19464	65
Lincoln Technical Institute-Allentown	Donald R. Frey	Allentown 18104	1,000
Lincoln Technical Institute-Philadelphia	Douglas M. Johnson	Philadelphia 19114	127
Lyons Technical Institute	Craig Bickings.	Philadelphia 19134	62
Lyons Technical Institute.	William G. Mark.	Upper Darby 19082.	93
McCann School of Business	James F. Noone.	Mahanoy City 17948	199
McCarrie Schools, Inc.	Robert J. Walder	Philadelphia 19107	147
McCarrie Schools, Inc., Suburban Campus .	Robert J. Walder	Philadelphia 19115	—
Median School of Allied Health Careers	William B. Mosle, Jr.	Pittsburgh 15222.	69
Monroeville School of Business	Edward McNutt	Monroeville 15146.	74
National Education Center- Allentown Business School Campus.	Bettie H. Thomas.	Allentown 18103	492
National Education Center- Thompson Institute, Harrisburg Campus . .	Sherman Harlowe	Harrisburg 17111	440
National Education Center- Thompson Institute, Phila. Campus	Leon Yourgevidge	Philadelphia 19104	445
National Education Center- Vale Technical Institute Campus	Dwight L. Pierce	Blairsville 15717	341
National School of Health Technology, Inc.	William Lobel, C.D.T.	Philadelphia 19103	33

National Schools	William Lobel	Philadelphia 19107	—
New Castle School of Trades	Dale Ellgass	Pulaski 16143	258
New Kensington Commercial School	Robert J. Mullen	New Kensington 15068	205
Northeast Institute of Education	Gregory Walker	Scranton 18503	105
O. S. Johnson Technical Inst.	John R. O'Hara	Scranton 18508	—
Orthotics Technician Trng. Inst.	Frederick S. Blackburn	Pittsburgh 15238	68
Palmer School (The)	Ruth Hodge	Harrisburg 17111	114
Palmer School (The)	Pam McKinney	Philadelphia 19107	72
Penn Commercial, Inc.	Stanley Bazent	Washington 15301	127
Penn Technical Institute	Louis A. Dimasi	Pittsburgh 15222	461
Pennco Tech	John Long	Bristol 19007	454
Pa. Institute of Technology	John C. Strayer	Media 19063	403
Philadelphia School of Printing and Advertising	John S. McGowan	Philadelphia 19107	15
Philadelphia School of Office Technology	Diana M. Ross-Trachtman	Philadelphia 19103	349
Philadelphia School of Office Technology	Kenneth Collins	Chesterbrook 19087	—
Pittsburgh Beauty Academy	Arthur DeConciliis	Pittsburgh 15222	27
Pittsburgh Institute of Aeronautics	Ivan D. Livi	Pittsburgh 15236	568
Pittsburgh Institute of Mortuary Science	Emory S. James	Pittsburgh 15213	—
Pittsburgh Technical Institute	Leslie R. Valitutti	Pittsburgh 15222	295
PTC Career Institute	(Vacant)	Philadelphia 19103	—
Restaurant School (The)	Moira G. McGuire	Philadelphia 19103	—
RETS Electronic Schools	John S. Founds	Broomall 19008	—
Schuylkill Business Institute	James Tarity, Jr.	Pottsville 17901	124
Shenango Valley School of Business	Richard P. McMahon	Sharon 16827	253
Shenango Valley School of Business	Richard McMahon	New Castle 16101	78
South Hills Business School	Maralyn Mazza	Boalsburg 16827	170
Thaddeus Stevens School of Technology	Alan K. Cohen	Lancaster 17602	261
Tracey-Warner School	Lewis H. Warner	Philadelphia 19108	93
Triangle Tech.	James R. Agras	Pittsburgh 15214	246
Triangle Tech.	Peter Buckoski	Cambridge Springs 16403	
Triangle Tech.	Robert K. Bernini	DuBois 15801	192
Triangle Tech.	Raphael K. Chieke	Erie 16512	150
Triangle Tech.	Stanley R. Koper	Greensburg 15601	174
Welder Training & Testing Institute	Patrick F. Dorris	Allentown 18001	
Welder Training & Testing Institute	Raymond Moyer	Bridgeport 19405	
Welder Training & Testing Institute	Raymond Moyer	Philadelphia 19123	
Welder Training & Testing Institute	Richard Peterson	Wilkes-Barre 18702	
Welder Training & Testing Institute	Joseph P. Hughes	Selinsgrove 17870	
Williamson Free School of Mechanical Trades (The)	Howard B. Maxwell	Media 19063	92
Williamsport School of Commerce	Benjamin H. Comfort, III	Williamsport 17701	143
Yorktowne Business Institute	Maureen Chambers	York 17404	174

TOTAL ENROLLMENT, PROPRIETARY SCHOOLS: 23,944

OTHER

INSTITUTION	CHIEF EXECUTIVE OFFICER	LOCATION
Annenberg School of Communications	George Gerber	Philadelphia 19108
Antioch University	David A. Frisby, III	Philadelphia 19108

Drew University . . . . .Paul Hardin . . . . .Madison, N.J. 07940
Eastern Mennonite College & Seminary . . . .Richard C. Detweiler . . . . .Harrisonburg, VA 22801
Gordon-Conwell Theological Seminary. . . . .Robert E. Cooley. . . . . .South Hamilton, MA 01982
Nova University . . . . .Abraham S. Fischler . . . . .Ft. Lauderdale, FL 33314
  Delaware Valley Cluster . . . . .Edward J. Malloy . . . . .Essington 19029
  Philadelphia Cluster . . . . .James Gallagher. . . . . .Buckingham 18912
  Philadelphia Cluster . . . . .Phyllis Cooper . . . . .Philadelphia 19144
  South Park Cluster . . . . .Robert Piatt .Pittsburgh 15219
  Williamsport Cluster . . . . .Harry Sharp .Williamsport 15853
Touro College . . . . .Bernard Lander . . . . .New York, N.Y. 10036
University Center at Harrisburg. . . . . .Quay Snyder . . . . .Harrisburg 17110
Western Maryland .Richard H. Chambers . . . . .Westminster, MD 21157

PENNSYLVANIA MEDIA
NEWSPAPERS, RADIO, AND TELEVISION STATIONS

This listing includes, in order, publication or station, daily key or dial information (when available), address, city, zip code, publisher, editor, weekly key, approximate circulation, political leaning, and telephone number. Daily Key: E-evening; M-morning; S-Sunday; D-Daily; 1-daily except Sunday; 2-daily except Saturday and Sunday; 6-daily except Saturday; Weekly Key: Mo-Monday; Tu-Tuesday; We-Wednesday; Th-Thursday; Fr-Friday; Sa-Saturday; 3-biweekly; Other Keys: ME-managing editor; Ed-editor; EE-executive editor; Pub-publisher; GM-general manager; NE-news editor; ND-news director; PD-program director; PM-program manager; SM-station manager; R-Republican; D-Democrat; IR-Independent Republican; ID-Independent Democrat; I-Independent; NP-Non-Partisan; Rel-Religious; Fra-Fraternal; Shop-Shopper.

ADAMS COUNTY

DAILIES

GETTYSBURG TIMES, THE, (M-1), P.O. Box 370, 18 Carlisle St., Gettysburg 17325; James A. Kalbaugh (Ed & Pub); 8,841; (I); 717-334-1131

RADIO

WGET (1320 AM), P.O. Box 280, Gettysburg 17325; Roderick Burnham (GM); 717-334-3101

WGTY (107.7 FM), co-owned with WGET (AM)

ALLEGHENY COUNTY

DAILIES

DAILY NEWS, (E-1), P.O. Box 128, 401-409 Walnut St., McKeesport 15134; Thomas D. Mansfield (Ed & Pub); 30,219; (I); 412-664-9161

PITTSBURGH LEGAL JOURNAL, (E-2), 620 2nd Ave., Pittsburgh 15219; Robert L. Byer (Ed); (Leg.); 412-281-6556

PITTSBURGH PRESS, (E-Su), P.O. Box 566, 34 Blvd. of Allies, Pittsburgh 15230; Angus McEachran (Ed); Pittsburgh Press (Pub); 233,132, M-F; 560,714, Su; (I); 412-263-1100

POST GAZETTE, (M-1), P.O. Box 957, 50 Blvd. of Allies, Pittsburgh 15230; William E. Block (Pub); 168,961; (I); 412-263-1100

TARENTUM VALLEY NEWS DISPATCH, (E-1, Sa-M), P.O. Box 311, 210 4th Ave., Tarentum 15084; Harry Whipple (Pub); Paul Hess (Ed); 38,368; (I); 412-224-4321

WEEKLIES

ADVANCE LEADER, (We), 610 Beatty Rd., Monroeville 15146-1588; Robert Buckley (Pub); Edith Ladick (Ed); 4,837; (I); 412-856-7400

ALMANAC, THE, (We), P.O. Box 929, 3801 Washington Rd., McMurray 15317; Richard L. Barnes (Pub); Debbie Popp (Ed); 30,382; 412-561-0700

AMERICAN SRBOBRAN, (Mo, We, Fr), 3414 5th Ave., Pittsburgh 15213; Serb Nat'l Federation (Pub); Robert Stone (Ed); 9,450; (Fra); 412-621-6600

BRIDGEVILLE AREA NEWS, (We), P.O. Box 417, 316 Station St., Bridgeville 15017; Mary McCracken (Ed); Robert Buckley (Pub); 2,941; (I); 412-221-6397

BROOKLINE, (We), 610 Beatty Rd., Monroeville 15146; Edith Ladick (Ed); Robert Buckley (Pub); 2,000; (I); 412-856-7400

CITY AND SUBURBAN LIFE, (We), 705 5th Ave., Coraopolis 15108; Kevin Flowers (Ed); Robert Buckley (Pub); 816; (I); 412-264-4140

FREE PRESS, THE, (Th), 721 Talbot Ave., Braddock 15104; Braddock Free Press Pub. Co., Inc. (Pub); Marjorie Brandt (Ed); 20,000; (I); 412-271-0622

GAZETTE, (We), 610 Beatty Rd., Monroeville 15146; Edith Ladick (Ed); Robert Buckley (Pub); 2,500; (I); 412-856-7400

GREEN TAB, THE, (We), 2519 Universal Rd., Pittsburgh 15235; Green Tab (Pub); M. Eliza King (Ed); 42,000; (I); 412-795-3300

HERALD, THE, (We), 1024 Main St., Sharpsburg 15215; Thomas A. Bookstaver (Pub); Tim Trainer (Ed); 6,869; (I); 412-782-2121

JOURNAL, THE, (Th), 3623 Brownsville Rd., Pittsburgh 15227; Randy Shaffer (Ed); Robert Buckley (Pub); 1,605; (I); 412-884-3111

MARKET SQUARE, (We), 5620 Maple Heights Center, Pittsburgh 15232-2333; William J. Rasp (Pub); Michelle Pilecki (Ed); 15,000; 412-281-7378

MURRYSVILLE AREA STAR, (We), 610 Beatty Road, Monroeville 15146; Edith Hughes (ME); Robert Buckley (Pub); 4,419; 412-856-7400

NEW PITTSBURGH COURIER, (Sa), 315 E. Carson St., Pittsburgh 15219; John H. Sengstacke (Pub); Rod Doss (Ed); 30,000; (I); 412-481-8302

NORTH HILLS NEWS RECORD, (Tu & Fr), Box 11138, McKnight Branch, Pittsburgh 15237; Thomas Bookstaver (Pub); Ronald Wayne (Ed); 14,320; (I); 412-366-0545

OAKLAND NEWS, (Th), 234 Meyran Ave., Pittsburgh 15213; Margaret Kutz (Ed & Pub); 5,000; (I); 412-683-4500

PITT NEWS, (Mo, We, & Fr), 441 William Pitt Union, University of Pittsburgh, Pittsburgh 15260; Jim Urban (Ed); 16,000; (College); 412-624-5926

PITTSBURGH BUSINESS TIMES-JOURNAL, (We), 10 N. Gateway, Suite 2, Pittsburgh 15222-1402; John Beddow (Pub); Henry Lenard (Ed); 8,956; 412-391-7222

PITTSBURGH CATHOLIC, THE, (Fr), 100 Wood St., #500, Pittsburgh 15222; Pittsburgh Catholic Publishing Assoc., Inc. (Pub); Robert Melder (Ed); 117,558; (Rel-NP); 412-471-1252

PROGRESS, THE, (We), 610 Beatty Rd., Monroeville 15146; Edith Ladick (Ed); Robert Buckley (Pub); 7,175; (I); 412-856-7400

RECORD, THE, (We), 705 5th Ave., Coraopolis 15108; Robert Buckley (Pub); Ron Lowry (Ed); 5,278; (I); 412-264-4140

SEWICKLEY HERALD, (We), 514 Beaver St., P.O. Box 73, Sewickley 15143; Robert Buckley (Pub); Betty Shields (Ed); 4,203; (I); 412-741-8200

SIGNAL - ITEM, (We), 20 East Mall Plaza, Carnegie 15106-4499; Deborah Kades (Ed); Robert Buckley (Pub); 6,304; (I); 412-276-4000

SOUTH HILLS RECORD, (Th), 3623 Brownsville Rd., Pittsburgh 15227; Randy Shaffer (Ed); Robert Buckley (Pub); 4,942; (I); 412-884-3111

SOUTH PITTSBURGH REPORTER, (Tu), P.O. Box 4285, Pittsburgh 15203; Roberta Smith (Ed & Pub); 15,000; (I); 412-481-0266

SUBURBAN GAZETTE, (We), 421 Locust St., McKees Rocks 15136; Virginia Schramm (Pub); Ann Milles (Ed); 8,300; (I); 412-331-2645

TIMES EXPRESS, (We), 610 Beatty Rd., Monroeville 15146; Robert Buckley (Pub); Edith Ladick (Ed); 6,275; (I); 412-856-7400

UNIONE, (3), 1719 Liberty Ave., Pittsburgh 15222; James V. Tortola (Ed); Frediani Ptg. Co. (Pub); 13,500; (I); 412-281-8533

WEST MIFFLIN AREA RECORD, (Th), 3623 Brownsville Rd., Pittsburgh 15227; Randy Shaffer (Ed); Robert Buckley (Pub); 1,000; (I); 412-884-3111

WESTMORELAND STAR, (We), 610 Beatty Rd., Monroeville 15146; Robert Buckley (Pub); Edith Ladick (Ed); 6,100; (I); 412-856-7400

RADIO

KDKA (1020 AM), 1 Gateway Center, Pittsburgh 15222; Rick Starr (GM); Maureen Durkin (PM); 412-392-2200

KQV (1410 AM), 411 7th Ave., Pittsburgh 15219; Robert W. Dickey (GM); Carol Finelli (PD); B. J. McCrory (ND); 412-562-5900

WAMO (860 AM, 105.9 FM), 1500 Chamber of Commerce Building, Pittsburgh 15219; Roger Fairfax (VP, GM); Chuck Woodson (PD); 412-281-6747

WBZZ (93.7 FM), 1715 Grandview Avenue, Pittsburgh 15211; Tex Meyer (GM); Nick Ferrara (PD); 412-381-8100

WDSY (107.9 FM), 107 6th St., Pittsburgh 15222; Peter Casella (GM); Ron Antil (PD); John O'Malley (ND); 412-471-9950

WDUQ (90.5 FM), Duquesne University, Pittsburgh 15282; Judy Jankowski (GM); 412-434-6030

WDVE (102.5 FM), 200 Fleet Street, Pittsburgh 15220; Robert D. Schutt (VP, GM); Greg Gillispie (PD); 412-937-1441

WEDO (810 AM), 414 5th Avenue, Midtown Plaza Mall, McKeesport 15132; John James (GM); William Korch (ND); 412-664-4444

WEEP (1080 AM), Co-owned with WDSY (FM)

WHYW (1550 AM, 96.9 FM), 1233 Braddock Ave., Braddock 15104; Stu Cohen (GM); Don Wayne (ND); 412-351-1100

WIXZ (1360 AM), 400 Lincoln Hwy., E. McKeesport 15035; Alan Serena (Pres., GM); Brian Crocker (ND); 412-823-1100

WJAS (1320 AM), Broadcast Plaza, Crane Ave., Pittsburgh 15220; Anthony Renda (GM); 412-531-9500

WLTJ (92.9 FM), 1051 Brinton Rd., Pittsburgh 15222; C. Carroll Larkin (VP, GM); Jeff Long (ND); 412-244-7600

WPIT (730 AM, 101.5 FM), Suite 200, Gateway Towers, Pittsburgh 15222; Michael Komichak (GM); Michael Lee (ND); 412-281-1900

WPLW (1590 AM), 201 Ewing Ave., Pittsburgh 15205; Clay Shelton (GM); 412-922-0550

WPTS (98.5 FM), 411 William Pitt Union, Pittsburgh 15260; Mark Daniels (GM); Ron Asbury (NE); Dave Lawver (PM); 412-624-5932

WQED (89.3 FM), 4802 5th Ave., Pittsburgh 15213; Ceci Sommers (SM); 412-622-1436

WRCT (88.3 FM), 5020 Forbes Ave., Pittsburgh 15213; Bill Wrbican (GM); 412-621-9728

WSHH (99.7 AM), Broadcash Plaza, Crane Ave., Pittsburgh 15220; Anthony Renda (GM); 412-531-9500

WTAE (1250 AM), P.O. Box 1250, Pittsburgh 15230; Rich White (GM); Bob Kopler (ND); 412-731-1250

WTKN (970 AM), 1 Allegheny Sq., Pittsburgh 15212; Diane Sutter (GM); Scott Cassidy (PD); Dave Berner (ND); 412-323-5300

WWSW (94.5 FM), Co-owned with WTKN (AM)

WXKW (1470 AM), 1183 Mickley Road, Whitehall 18052; Rick Musselman (GM); Don Rutt (NE); Rich Holdsworth (PM); 215-434-9511

WXVX (1510 AM), 1 Sylves Lane, Monroeville 15146; Dale King (GM); 412-856-6827

WYDD (104.7 FM), 810 5th Ave., New Kensington 15068; Andrea Dudley (SM); Mike McQueen (GM); 412-362-2144

TELEVISION

KDKA-TV (Ch. 2), 1 Gateway Center, Pittsburgh 15222; Joe Berwanger (GM); Jayne Adair (PM); 412-392-2200

WPCB-TV (Ch. 40), Route 48, Signal Hill Drive, Wall 15148-1499; David F. Kelton (GM); David Skeba (PM); 412-824-3930

WPGH-TV (Ch. 53), 750 Ivory Ave., Pittsburgh 15214; Bill Saltzgiver (GM); Tom Peterson (NE); 412-931-8600

WPTT-TV (Ch. 22), Box 2809, Pittsburgh 15230; Chuck Hobbs (GM); Pamela Rhodes (PM); 412-856-9010

WPXI-TV (Ch. 11), 11 Television Hill, Box 1100, Pittsburgh 15230; John A. Howell III (VP, GM); Steve Riley (PM); 412-237-1100

WQED-TV (Ch. 13), 4802 5th Ave., Pittsburgh 15213; Lloyd Kaiser (Pres); 412-622-1300

WQEX-TV (Ch. 16), Co-owned with WQED-TV

WTAE-TV (Ch. 4), 400 Ardmore Blvd., Pittsburgh 15221; Fred Barber (GM); Judy Girard (PD); 412-242-4300

ARMSTRONG COUNTY

DAILIES

LEADER-TIMES, (E-1), 115-121 N. Grant Ave., Kittanning 16201; Toni Zucco (Ed); Ronald G. Masury (Pub); 10,975; (I); 412-543-1303

WEEKLIES

APOLLO NEWS-RECORD, (We), Box 308, 228 N. Warren Ave., Apollo 15613; Judy Laurina (Ed); Howard W. Grimes (Pub); 2,180; (IR); 412-478-3031

LEECHBURG ADVANCE, (We), P.O. Box 587, Second & Hicks Sts., Leechburg 15656; Jojo Bodnar (Ed); Howard Grimes (Pub); 1,328; (I); 412-842-1711

RADIO

WACB (1380 AM), RD 7, Bunkerhill Road, Kittanning 16201; R. A. Nicholas, III (VP); Becky Everson (ND); 412-543-1380

WAVL (910 AM), Box 277, Apollo 15613; Bob Dain (GM); 412-478-4020

BEAVER COUNTY

DAILIES

BEAVER COUNTY TIMES, (E & S), P.O. Box 400, 400 Fair Ave., Beaver 15009; F. Wallace Gordon (Pub); Leonard Brown (Ed); 45,995, E; 49,468, S; (I); 412-775-3200

WEEKLIES

NEWS, THE, (Th), 1181 Airport Rd., Aliquippa 15001; R.A. Palket (Pub); 74,500 (I); 412-375-6611

RADIO

WBVP (1230 AM), Box 719, Beaver Falls 15010; Chris Shovlin (GM); Sam Siple (PD, ND); 412-846-4100

WGEV (88.3 FM), Box 883, Geneva College, Beaver Falls 15010; Peter Croisant (Dir. of Bcstg.); 412-847-6674

WMBA (1460 AM), 291 4th St., Ambridge 15003; Diane Brown (GM); Rick Bergman (ND); 412-266-1110

WWKS (106.7 FM), Co-owned with WBVP (AM)

BEDFORD COUNTY

DAILIES

BEDFORD DAILY GAZETTE, (M-1), P.O. Box 671, 424 W. Penn St., Bedford 15522; Edward K. Frear (Pub & Ed); 8,418; (IR); 814-623-1151

WEEKLIES

BEDFORD/BLAIR COUNTY SHOPPER'S GUIDE, (S), 100 Masters Ave., Everett 15537; Nickolas Monico (Pub); Mike Coburn (Ed); 49,218; (I); 814-652-5191

BEDFORD INQUIRER, (Fr), Box 671, 424 W. Penn St., Bedford 15522; Edward K. Frear (Pub); Sharyn Maust (Ed); 585; (R); 814-623-1151

BROAD TOP BULLETIN, (We), 900 6th St., P.O. Box 188, Saxton 16678-0188; Jon D. Baughman (Ed & Pub); 2,900; (I); 814-635-2851

RADIO

WAYC (1600 AM), P.O. Box 1, Bedford 15522; John H. Cessna (GM); Keith Bagley (ND); 814-623-1000

WBFD (1310 AM), Box 672, Bedford 15522; Daniel R. Smouse (GM); 814-623-5131

WSKE (1040 AM), Box 187, Everett 15537; Melvin King Beckner (Pres.); Sandra King (GM); 814-652-2600

WRAX (100.9 FM), Co-owned with WBFD (AM)

BERKS COUNTY

DAILIES

READING EAGLE, (E & S), P.O. Box 582, 345 Penn St., Reading 19601; William S. Flippin (Pub); Edward A. Taggert (Ed); 35,188, E; 111,638, S; (I); 215-373-4221

READING TIMES, THE, (M-1), Box 582, 345 Penn St., Reading 19601; William S. Flippin (Pub); Edward A. Taggert (Ed); 44,950; (I); 215-373-4221

WEEKLIES

BIRDSBORO NEWS, THE, (We), P.O. Box 565, 124 N. Chestnut St., Boyertown 19512; Donald L. Webb (Pub); Sherry Herrlinger (Ed); 2,905; 215-367-6041

BOYERTOWN AREA TIMES, THE, (Th), P.O. Box 565, 124 N. Chestnut St., Boyertown 19512; Donald L. Webb (Pub); Mary Jane Schneider (Ed); 6,140; (I); 215-367-6041

EAST PENN VALLEY MERCHANDISER, (We), 6 N. 3rd St., Hamburg 19526; W. E. Mitten (Pub); 30,364; 215-562-2267

EL DIRECTORIO HISPANO, (Th), 850 Lancaster Ave., Reading 19607; Aaron G. Lopez (Ed & Pub); 9,000; (I); 215-775-3101

HAMBURG ITEM, THE, (We), 3rd & State St., P.O. Box 31, Hamburg 19526; Avery D. Piersons (Ed & Pub); 4,050; (I); 215-562-7515

NEWS OF SOUTHERN BERKS, THE, (We), 124 N. Chestnut St., Boyertown 19512; Donald L. Webb (Pub); Sherry Herrlinger (Ed); 3,500; (I); 215-367-6041

NORTHERN BERKS MERCHANDISER, (We), 6 N. 3rd St., Hamburg 19526; W. E. Mitten (Pub); 27,429; 215-562-2267

PATRIOT, THE, (Th), P.O. Box 346, 222 & Sharadin Rd., Kutztown 19530; Stephen Fellman (Ed); Jacob R. Esser (Pub); 3,800; (I); 215-683-7343

RADIO

WBYO (107.5 FM), Box 177, Boyertown 19512; David G. Hendricks (GM & PD); 215-369-1075

WEEU (850 AM), 34 N. 4th St., Reading 19601; Richard Schilpp (GM); Jack B. Gounder (PD); 215-376-7335

WHUM (1240 AM), 45 S. Front St., Reading 19603; Alan Beck (GM); Don Greth (ND); 215-376-3987

WRAW (1340 AM), 850 Lancaster Ave., Reading 19607; Aaron G. Lopez (prod.); 215-775-3101

WRFY (102.5 FM), 1265 Perkiomen Ave., Reading 19602; Tom Franko (GM); Connie Andrews (ND); 215-376-7173

WXAC (91.3 FM), P.O. Box 15234, Albright College, Reading 19612; David Nicholas (SM); Karen Opello (PD); 215-921-2217

TELEVISION

WTVE-TV (Ch. 51), 1729 N. 11th St., Box 3248, Reading 19604; Bob Pritchard (GM); Lisa Andrulevich (PD); 215-921-9181

BLAIR COUNTY

DAILIES

ALTOONA MIRROR, (E), P.O. Box 2008, 1000 Green Ave., Altoona 16603; Albert J. Holtzinger (Pub); David M. Cvzzolina (Ed); 34,012; (I); 814-946-7411

TYRONE DAILY HERALD, (E-1), P.O. Box 219, 1018 Pennsylvania Ave., Tyrone 16686; P. K. Miles, Jr. (Co-Pub); Dan Meckes (Ed); 3,047; (I); 814-684-4000

WEEKLIES

ALTOONA AMERICAN, (Th), 1114 12th St., Altoona 16603; Nat'l Dynamics Corp. (Pub); J. A. DeRenzo (Ed); (I); 814-943-1920

LABOR-TELEGRAM, (M), 1114 12th St., Altoona 16603; Nat'l Dynamics Corp. (Pub); J. A. DeRenzo (Ed); 814-943-1920

MORRISONS COVE HERALD, (Th), P.O. Box 277, 113 N. Market St., Martinsburg 16662-0277; David Snyder (Ed); Richard Barnes (Pub); 6,133; (I); 814-793-2144

RADIO

WFBG (1290 AM; 98.1 FM), Hilltop, Logan Blvd., Altoona 16603; Dick DiAndrea (GM); 814-943-1136

WHGM (103.9 FM), P.O. Box 2248, Altoona 16603; John R. Powley (GM); 814-943-2607

WHPA (104.9 AM), P.O. Box 464, Scotch Valley Rd., Hollidaysburg 16648; Louis Maierhofer (Pres.); Walter Frank (ND); 814-695-4441

WJSM (1110 AM, 92.7 FM), R.D. 2, Box 87, Martinsburg 16662; Sherwood B. Hawley (GM, ND); Larry S. Walters (GM, PD); 814-793-2188

WKMC (1370 AM), P.O. Box 229, Roaring Spring 16673; Louis J. Maierhofer (GM); E. Walter Frank (NE); 814-224-2151

WPRR (100.1 FM), 2727 W. Albert Dr., Altoona 16602; Dick Richards (GM); Darrell Ray (PD); 814-944-9456

WRTA (1240 AM), P.O. Box 272, Altoona 16603; D. Rod Wolf (GM); George Germann (ND); 814-943-6112

WTRN (1340 AM), P.O. Box 247, Tyrone 16686; William Moses (GM); Dennis Smith (PD); 814-684-3200

WVAM (1430 AM), Co-owned with WPRR (FM)

TELEVISION

WKBS-TV (Ch. 47), Route 48, Signal Hill Drive, Wall 15148-1499; David F. Kelton (GM); David Skeba (PM); 412-824-3930

WTAJ-TV (Ch. 10), 5000 6th Ave., Commerce Park, Altoona 16603; Donald F. Snyder (GM); Doug Parker (PD); 814-944-2031

WWCP-TV (Ch. 8); Evergreen Broadcasting Corp., 1450 Scalp Ave., Johnstown 15904; Sandy Benton (VP, GM); Chris Taylor (PD); 814-266-8088

WWPC-TV (Ch. 23); Evergreen Broadcasting Corp., 1450 Scalp Ave., Johnstown 15904; Sandy Benton (VP, GM); Chris Taylor (PD); 814-266-8088

BRADFORD COUNTY

DAILIES

DAILY REVIEW, THE, (M-1), P.O. Box 503, 116 Main St., Towanda 18848; Frank Blewitt (Ed & Pub); 8,611, (R); 717-265-2151

EVENING TIMES, THE (E-1), 201 N. Lehigh Ave., Sayre 18840; Steve Piatt (Ed); George Sample (Pub); 8,474; (I); 717-888-9643

WEEKLIES

CANTON INDEPENDENT-SENTINEL, (Th), P.O. Box 128, 43 Lycoming St., Canton 17714-0128; T. W. Shoemaker (Pub); Jane Cawley (ME); 1,707; (I); 717-673-5151

GAZETTE REGISTER, (Th), P.O. Box 126, 11 Canton St., Troy 16947; Troy Gazette Register, Inc. (Pub); Shirley Lewis (Ed); 1,003; (R); 717-297-3024

JOURNAL, (Th), P.O. Box 17, Bradford 16701; Grant & Katherine Nicholas (Ed & Pub); 5,000; (I); 814-362-6563

JOURNAL TOWN AND COUNTRY, (Th), P.O. Box 17, Bradford 16701; Nichols & Nichols (Pub); 10,200; (Shop); 814-362-6563

ROCKET COURIER, THE, (Th), Box 187, Wyalusing 18853; William Keeler (Ed); 5,500; (I); 717-746-1217

RADIO

WATS (960 AM), 204 Desmond St., Sayre 18840; Charles Carver (GM); 717-888-7745

WAVR (102.3 FM), Co-owned with WATS (AM)

WKAD (100.1 FM), Box 196, Canton 17724; John Callahan (GM); Sandra Johnson (PD); 717-673-3106

WTTC (1550 AM, 95.3 FM), 214 Main St., Towanda 18848; Jack Baker (GM); Joel Crayton (PD); 717-265-2165

BUCKS COUNTY

DAILIES

BUCKS COUNTY COURIER TIMES, (M-6, S), 8400 Route 13, Levittown 19057-5198; Michael Renshaw (Ed); Arthur Mathew (Pub); 63,229, M; 68,941, S; (I); 215-752-6701

FREE PRESS, (E-2), 312 W. Broad St., Quakertown 18951; Chas. M. Meredith III (Pub); Madeleine Mathias (Ed); 6,826; (I); 215-536-6820

INTELLIGENCER-RECORD, THE, (M-6, S), P.O. Box 858, 333 N. Broad St., Doylestown 18901; Charles P. Smith (Pub); James P. McFadden (Ed); 40,625, M; 43,876, S; (I); 215-345-3000

WEEKLIES

ADVANCE OF BUCKS COUNTY, THE, (Th), 211 Sycamore St., P.O. Box 68, Newtown 18940; Intercounty Publishing Co. (Pub); Robert Art Thompson (Ed); 6,000; (I); 215-968-2244

ADVISOR, (We), 661 Bristol Pike, Bensalem 19020; Intercounty Pub. Co. (Pub); Anne Devlin (Ed); 8,000; (I); 215-639-2271

BEACON NEWS, THE, (Th), Box 36, New Hope 18938; Joseph N. Hazen (Pub & Ed); 4,350; (I); 609-397-3000

BRISTOL PILOT, (Th), 113 Radcliffe St., Bristol 19007; Intercounty Pub. Co. (Pub); David Vasquez (Ed); 3,544; (I); 215-788-1682

BUCKS COUNTY MIDWEEK, (We), 1345 Old Lincoln Hwy., Levittown 19056; Kimberly Runk (Ed); William Smith (Pub); 104,000; (I); 215-547-4210

BUCKS COUNTY TELEGRAPH, (S), 390 Easton Rd., Horsham 19044-2592; Sandra L. Petersohn (Ed); Matthew H. Petersohn (Pub); 6,815; (I); 215-345-0820

BUCKS COUNTY TRIBUNE, (We), Box 375, Feasterville 19047-0958; Matthew H. Petersohn (Pub); Sandra L. Petersohn (Ed); 16,520; (I); 215-345-0820

CARRIER PIGEON, (We), 150 James Way, Southampton 18966-3857; Robert Seidman (Ed & Pub); 185,343; (Shop); 215-322-6920

FREE PRESS JOURNAL, (W & S), Box 100, 312 W. Broad St., Quakertown 18951; Charles Meredith III (Pub); M. Mathias (Ed); 14,833, We; 30,000, S; (I); 215-536-6820

NEW HOPE GAZETTE, (Th), P.O. Box 180, 170 Old York Rd., New Hope 18938; Intercounty Pub. Co., (Pub); Patrick Jardel (Ed); 4,600; (I); 215-862-9435

NEWS-HERALD, (We), P.O. Box 127, 320 S. 7th St., Perkasie 18944-0127; Charles W. Baum (Pub); John A. Gerner (Ed); 5,386; (I); 215-257-6839

NEWS & REPORTER, (Tu), Box 565, Bensalem 19020; B. M. Pearce (Ed & Pub); 9,000; (I); 215-638-8862

NORTHEAST ADVISOR, (Tu), 661 Bristol Pike, Bensalem 19020; Intercounty Pub. Co. (Pub); Anne Devlin (Ed); 20,000; (I); 215-639-2271

SPIRIT OF BUCKS COUNTY, (Tu), P.O. Box 157, 101 N. York Rd., Hatboro 19040; William E. Strasburg (Pub); Frederick S. Groshens (Ed); 40,199; (I); 215-675-3430

YARDLEY NEWS, (Th), P.O. Box 334, 45 E. Afton Ave., Yardley 19067; Intercounty Pub. Co. (Pub); Chris Verderame (Ed); 4,000; (I); 215-493-2794

RADIO

WBCB (1490 AM), 200 Magnolia Dr., Levittown 19054; Bob Burton (GM); 215-949-1490

WBUX (1570 AM), Box 2187, Doylestown 18901; George Pleasants (GM); Dan Taylor (PD); 215-348-3583

WRDV (89.3 FM), Box 2012, Warminster 18974; Charles Loughery (Pres.); Doug Gainor (GM); Scott Reinhard (PD); 215-672-3278

BUTLER COUNTY

DAILIES

BUTLER EAGLE, (E-1), P.O. Box 291, Butler 16003; Vernon L. Wise, Jr. (GM); John Laing Wise, Jr. (Ed); 30,955; (IR); 412-282-8000

WEEKLIES

BUTLER COUNTY NEWS, (We & Sa), P.O. Box 160, 101 E. Spring St., Zelienople 16063; Harry J. Whipple (Pub); Jeff Hoch (Ed); 3,296; (I); 412-452-7040

EAGLE II, (We), 114 W. Diamond St., Butler 16001; Eagle Printing Co., Inc. (Pub); John L. Wise, Jr. (Ed); 31,000; (Shop); 412-282-8000

TRI-COUNTY NEWS, (Sa), P.O. Box 97, Slippery Rock 16057; Strickler W. Pollock (Pub); K. D. Pollock (Ed); 43,000; 412-794-6857

RADIO

WBUT (1050 AM), P.O. Box 1645, Butler 16003; Robert C. Brandon (GM); Joyce Catt (ND); 412-287-5778

WISR (680 AM), P.O. Box 151, Butler 16001; Lorraine C. Laconi (GM); Dave Malarkey (NE); 412-283-1500

WLER (97.7 FM) Co-owned with WBUT (AM)

WSRU (90.1 FM), Slippery Rock Univ., Slippery Rock 16057; Tom Stewart (GM); 412-794-7469

CAMBRIA COUNTY

DAILIES

TRIBUNE DEMOCRAT, THE, (M), P.O. Box 340, 425 Locust St., Johnstown 15907; Richard H. Mayer (Pub); George Fattman (Ed); 51,080, M; 53,758, S; (I); 814-536-0711

WEEKLIES

BARNESBORO STAR, THE, (We), P.O. Box 158, 520 Phila. Ave., Barnesboro 15714; Frank K. Noll (Pub); 6,200; (R); 814-948-6210

CRESSON-GALLITZIN MAINLINER, (We), P.O. Box 777, Ebensburg 15931; Frank K. Noll (Pub); 3,220; (I); 814-472-9227

EBENSBURG NEWS LEADER, (We), P.O. Box 395, Portage 15946-0395; Frank K. Noll (Pub); Emily Stewart (Ed); 2,500; (I); 814-736-9666

MAINLINER, (We), P.O. Box 395, Portage 15946-0395; Frank K. Noll (Pub); Emily Stewart (Ed); 3,360; (I); 814-736-9666

MOUNTAINEER-HERALD, THE, (We), P.O. Box 113, S. Center St., Ebensburg 15931-0359; David E. Thompson (Pub & Ed); 3,450; (R); 814-472-8240

NANTY-GLO JOURNAL, (We), 709 Caldwell Ave., Portage 15946; Frank K. Noll (Pub); Emily Stewart (Ed); 2,910; (I); 814-736-9666

PORTAGE DISPATCH, (We), P.O. Box 395, Portage 15946-0395; Frank K. Noll (Pub); Emily Stewart (Ed); 5,200; (I); 814-736-9666

UNION PRESS-COURIER, (Th), P.O. Box 116, 452 Magee Ave., Patton 16668; Frank J. Cammarata (Ed & Pub); 5,900, (ID); 814-674-3666

RADIO

WAMQ (1400 AM), Box 103, Loretto 15940; Neil Hart (GM); Ken Williams (ND); Casey O'Day (PD); 814-886-5800

WBXQ (94.3 FM), Box FM 94, Cresson 16630; Neil Hart (GM); Ken Williams (ND); Casey O'Day (PD); 814-886-7777

WCRO (1230 AM), 407 Main St., Johnstown 15901; Doris Lichtenfels (GM); 814-536-5158

WEBG (1580 AM), P.O. Box 1580, Ebensburg 15931; Phillip P. Lenz (GM & PM); 814-472-9324

WGLU (92.1 FM), 516 Main St., Johnstown 15901; Ralph Lovette (GM); Allyson Saxx (PD); 814-536-7825

WIYQ (99.1 FM), 1240 Scalp Ave., Johnstown 15904; Helen Walker (SM); Kate Macowski (ND); 814-266-3691

WJAC (850 AM, 95.5 FM), P.O. Box 309, Plaza Dr., Johnstown 15905; Sandy D. Neri (GM); Rich Shepard (ND); 814-255-4186

WJNL (1490 AM, 96.5 FM), Tripoli St., Cover Hill, Johnstown 15902; John E. Gelormino (Pres.); David A. Smith (PD); Chauncey B. Ross (ND); 814-535-8554

WNCC (950 AM), 1015 Philadelphia Ave., Barnesboro 15714; Larry J. Sherwin (GM); Dennis Pompa (PD); 814-948-9200

WWML (1470 AM), 609 Main St., Portage 15946; Bill Henderson (GM & ND); Kim Henderson (PD); 814-736-8000

TELEVISION

WFAT-TV (Ch. 19), 108 Allen Bill Drive, Johnstown 15904; Timothy L. Crosby (GM); George Plenderleith (SM); 814-266-1919

CAMERON COUNTY

WEEKLIES

CAMERON COUNTY ECHO, (Tu), Box 308, Emporium 15834; Robert J. Brown (Ed & Pub); 4,000; (I); 814-486-3711

RADIO

WLEM (1250 AM), P.O. Box 310, Emporium 15834; Vito Lanzillo (GM); Jeannine Jones (PD); 814-486-3712

WQKY (FM), Co-owned with WLEM

CARBON COUNTY

DAILIES

TIMES-NEWS, THE, (E-1), P.O. Box 239, First & Iron Sts., Lehighton 18235-0239; Pencor Services (Pub); Robert Parfit (Ed); 16,580; (I); 215-377-2051

RADIO

WLSH (1410 AM), Box D, Lansford 18232; Mickey Angst (GM); 717-645-3123

WYNS (1150 AM), Box 115, Lehighton 18235; John Michaels (VP & GM); Betty Straubinger (VP & SM); Thom Tkach (PD); Mark Stine (ND); 215-377-1150

CENTRE COUNTY

DAILIES

CENTRE DAILY TIMES, (E-1), Box 89, 3400 E. College Ave., State College 16804; Christopher Harte (Pub); William Blair (Ed); 22,692; (I); 814-238-5000

COLLEGIAN, THE, (M-2), 126 Carnegie Bldg., Penn State Univ., University Park 16802; G. Hamilton (Ed & Pub); (Coll.); 814-865-2531

WEEKLIES

BARGAIN SHEET, (Th), P.O. Box 278, Pleasant Gap 16823; Joseph F. Shannon (Ed); Photoset, Inc. (Pub); 36,000; (Shop); 814-359-2918

CENTRE DEMOCRAT, (Th), P.O. Box 746, 106 N. Allegheny St., Bellefonte 16823-0746; Frank Gappa (Pub); Michael B. Sullivan (Ed); 2,800; (I); 814-355-4881

RADIO

WBLF (970 AM), P.O. Box 88, Bellefonte 16823; James F. Kerschner, Jr. (GM); T. Michaels (NE); 814-355-4751

WGMR (101.1 FM), Box 204, State College 16804; William E. Moses (GM); Kate Macowski (ND); Michael Thorn (PD); 814-238-0717

WMAJ (1450 AM), Box 888, State College 16801; Jim Eberly (GM); Roger Corey (PD); 814-237-4959

WPHB (1260 AM), R. D. 1 Box 38, Philipsburg 16866; C. Dean Sharpless (GM); Sheldon Sharpless (PD); 814-342-2300

WPSU (91.1 FM), 304 Sparks Bldg., University Park, State College 16802; James O'Brien (SM); Joan Osenback (PD); 814-865-9191

WQWK (96.7 FM), 160 Clearview Ave., State College 16801; Robert K. Zimmerman (GM); Mathew Haywood (PD); Bill Nichols (ND); 814-237-9736

WRSC (1390 AM), Co-owned with WQWK (FM)

WTLR (89.9 FM), 2020 Cato Ave., State College 16801; Kenneth R. Krater (Pres.); Garry T. Sutley (GM); 814-237-9857

WXLR (103.1 FM), Co-owned with WMAJ (AM)

CHESTER COUNTY

DAILIES

DAILY LOCAL NEWS, (E-1), 250 N. Bradford Ave., West Chester 19382; Daily Local News Co., Inc. (Pub); William H. Dean (Ed); 38,349; (I); 215-696-1775

EVENING PHOENIX, (E-1), 225 Bridge St., Phoenixville 19460; Mark Bulik (Ed); Patricia Crosson (Pub); 6,488; (I); 215-933-8926

RECORD, THE, (E-1), 204 E. Lincoln Hwy., Coatesville 19320; Rob McIlvaine (Ed); David C. Tomasini (Pub); 6,541; (I); 215-384-4900

WEEKLIES

CHESTER COUNTY PRESS, (We), P.O. Box H, Oxford 19363; Irvin S. Lieberman (Pub); Barbara Mastriania (Ed); 15,000; (I); 215-932-2444

MAIN LINE CHRONICLE, (We), 1560 McDaniel Dr., Box 2198, West Chester 19380; Nancy K. Colman (Ed); Ad Pro, Inc. (Pub); 21,000; (I); 215-692-0581

PARKESBURG POST, (Th), 411 First St., Parkesburg 19365; Morris Grace (Pub & ME); 2,200; (I); 215-857-5505

REPORTER, (We), Box 28, 842 Oak St., Royersford 19468; Bruce Fenstermacher (Pub); Shirley L. Elliott (Ed); 4,500; (I); 215-948-4850

SUBURBAN ADVERTISER, (Th), 134 N. Wayne Ave., P.O. Box 409, Wayne 19087; Marianne Schmitt (Ed); Deborah Shaw (Pub); 15,193; (I); 215-688-3000

VILLAGE NEWS, (We & S), 204 E. Lincoln Hwy., Coatesville 19320; Elene Crosson Brown (Ed); David Tomasini (Pub); 19,440; (I); 215-384-4900

RADIO

WCHE (1520 AM), 139 W. Gay St., West Chester 19380; William H. Gehlert (GM); Joan Pitt (NE); 215-692-3131

WCOJ (1420 AM), P.O. Box 1408, Coatesville 19320; Donald G. Kimes (GM); Colleen L. Leyden (ND); Art Douglas (PD); 215-384-2100

WCZN (1590 AM), 12 Kent Rd., Aston 19014; Lloyd Roach (GM); 215-358-1400

WDNR (89.5 FM), Box 1000, Widener Univ., Chester 19013; Jeff Buller (Tech.D); 215-499-4439

WLIU (88.7 FM), Lincoln University 19352; Anthony S. Bass (GM); 215-932-8300

WVCH (740 AM), Box 102, Springhouse 19477; Thomas Moffitt (GM); Lynne Gold (ND); 215-872-8861

WYIS (690 AM), 186 Bridge St., Phoenixville 19460; Jose L. Rivera (GM); 215-933-5819

CLARION COUNTY

WEEKLIES

CLARION NEWS, THE (Tu & Th), P.O. Box 110, 645 Main St., Clarion 16214; George M. Frasher (Ed); 3,915; (I); 814-226-7000

LEADER-VINDICATOR, THE, (We), P.O. Box 158, 435 Broad St., New Bethlehem 16242; Paul M. Hanke (Ed); James R. Shaffer (Pub); 5,147; (I); 814-275-3131

RADIO

WCCR (92.7 FM), Co-owned with WWCH

WCUC (91.7 FM), Clarion Univ., Clarion 16214; Henry Fueg (GM); Leanna Blouse (PD); Andy Mallison (ND); 814-226-2330

WWCH (1300 AM), 725 Wood St., P.O. Box 688, Clarion 16214; William Hearst (Pres. & GM); 814-226-8600

CLEARFIELD COUNTY

DAILIES

COURIER-EXPRESS, (E-1), P.O. Box 407, 50-58 W. Long Ave., DuBois 15801; J. S. Gray, Jr. (Pub); Paul R. Frederick (Ed); 11,294; (I); 814-371-4200

PROGRESS, THE, (E-1), P.O. Box 291, 206 E. Locust St., Clearfield 16830; William K. Ulerich (Pub); Leland D. Mather, Jr. (Ed); 17,201; (I); 814-765-5581

RADIO

WCED (1420 AM), 80 N. Park Place, DuBois 15801; George W. Williams (GM); Samuel Lewis Bundy (ND); 814-371-6100

WCPA (900 AM), P.O. Box 1032, Clearfield 16830; Carl A. Falvo (GM); Allan Moore (ND); Bob Day (PD); 814-765-5541

WDBA (107.3 FM), 28 W. Scribner Ave., DuBois 15801; Donald R. Shobert (GM); 814-371-1330

WOWQ (102.1 FM), Co-owned with WCED (AM)

WQYX (93.5 FM), Co-owned with WCPA (AM)

TELEVISION

WPSX-TV (Ch. 3), Wagner Annex, University Park, Clearfield 16802; Marlowe Froke (GM); 814-865-6535

CLINTON COUNTY

DAILIES

EXPRESS, THE, (E-1), P.O. Box 208, 9-11 W. Main St., Lock Haven 17745; Charles R. Ryan (Pub); Raymond Schaeter (Ed); 10,872; (I); 717-748-6791

WEEKLIES

RECORD, THE, (We), 129 5th St., P.O. Box 367, Renovo 17764; Ronald W. Dremel (Pub); 2,361; (I); 717-923-1500

RADIO

WBPZ (1230 AM), 738 Bellefonte Ave., Lock Haven 17745; John Lipez (GM); Mike Flanagan (NE); 717-748-4038

WWZU (92.1 FM), Co-owned with WBPZ

COLUMBIA COUNTY

DAILIES

PRESS ENTERPRISE, (M-1), 3185 Lackawanna Ave., Bloomsburg 17815; Carl E. Beck, Jr. (Ed); Paul Eyerly III (Pub); 21,934; (I); 717-784-2121

RADIO

WBRX (1280 AM), P.O. Box E, Berwick 18603; Paul Grimef (GM & PD); Bill Brady (ND); 717-752-4546

WBVQ (91.1 FM), Box 85, Bloomsburg Univ., Bloomsburg 17815; Ted Hodgins (GM); Mary Meneeley (NE); Chris Mingrone (PM); 717-389-4686

WCNR (930 AM), 125 W. Main St., Bloomsburg 17815; Joe Darlington (GM); Jack Morgan (ND); 717-784-1200

WHLM (550 AM, 106.5 FM), 107 W. Main St., Bloomsburg 17815; Robert W. Sweppenheiser (GM); Ron Williams (ND); Kim Rodkey (PD); 717-784-5500

CRAWFORD COUNTY

DAILIES

MEADVILLE TRIBUNE, THE, (M-1), 947 Federal Court, Meadville 16335; Robert W. Smith (Pub); 16,784; (I); 814-724-6370

TITUSVILLE HERALD, THE, (M-1), Box 328, 209 W. Spring St., Titusville 16354; James B. Stevenson (Pub); Holly Matthews (Ed); 4,833; (R); 814-827-3634

WEEKLIES

CONNEAUT LAKE BREEZE, (We), P.O. Box 385, Linesville 16424; David Schaef (Ed); John Lampson (Pub); 600; (R); 814-683-5444

CONNEAUTVILLE COURIER, (We), Box AC, Conneautville 16406; Jesse Haas (Ed); Herbert O. Haas (Pub); 1,800; (IR); 814-587-2033

CRAWFORD ADVISOR, (Tu), 947 Federal Court, Meadville 16335; Robert W. Smith (Pub); 12,000; (Shop); 814-724-6370

LINESVILLE HERALD, THE, (We), Box 385, Linesville 16424-0385; David Schaef (Ed); Penn Ohio Graphics (Pub); 1,400; (R); 814-683-5444

RADIO

WARC (90.3 FM), Box C, Allegheny College, Meadville 16335; Price Kirkendall (GM); Suzanne Simanaitis (PD); 814-724-3376

WEOZ (94.3 FM), 827 Park Ave., Meadville 16335; Thomas Osborne (GM); Kevin Nicholson (ND); Larry Baker (PD); 814-333-9494

WTIV (1230 AM), P.O. Box 184, Titusville 16354; Robert H. Sauber (GM); Jim Gross (NE); 814-827-3651

WVCC (101.7 FM), Box 307, Linesville 16424; A. Cervi, Sr. (GM); C. Stopp (NE); A. Cervi, Jr. (PD); 814-683-4000

CUMBERLAND COUNTY

DAILIES

SENTINEL, THE, (E-1), P.O. Box 130, 457 E. North St., Carlisle 17013; Wayne Powell (Pub); Carol L. Talley (Ed); 15,701; (I); 717-243-2611

WEEKLIES

CARLISLE SHOPPER, THE, (We), 4407-D Carlisle Pike, Camp Hill 17011; Charles Engle (Pub); 16,000; (NP); 717-243-9088

EAST SHORE SHOPPER, (We), 4407-D Carlisle Pike, Camp Hill 17011; Charles Engle (Pub); 61,500; (NP); 717-763-1337

GUIDE, THE, (We), 800 W. Church Rd., Mechanicsburg 17055; Henry Fry (Pub); Diane R. Miller (Ed); 145,742; 717-766-0211

MIDDLETOWN SHOPPER, THE, (We), 4407-D Carlisle Pike, Camp Hill 17011; Charles Engle (Pub); 8,500; (NP); 717-763-1337

NEWS-CHRONICLE, THE, (M & Th), P.O. Box 100, R.D. 1, Shippensburg 17257; Grace Schlichter (Pub); Galen Burkholder (Ed); 5,801; (IR); 717-532-4101

VALLEY TIMES-STAR, THE, (We), P.O. Box 158, 51 Big Spring Ave., Newville 17241; News Chronicle Co. (Pub); John Grane (Ed); 2,849; (I); 717-776-3197

WEST SHORE SHOPPER, (We), 4407-D Carlisle Pike, Camp Hill 17011; Charles Engle (Pub); 58,200; (NP); 717-763-1337

WEST SHORE TIMES, THE (Th), 13-15 W. Main St., Mechanicsburg 17055; Philip Clark (Ed & Pub); 3,000; (I); 717-766-9629

RADIO

WDCV (88.3 FM), Box 640, Dickinson College, Carlisle 17013; Brian J. Yost (GM); 717-245-1444

WHYL (960 AM, 102.3 FM), 1013 S. Hanover St., Carlisle 17013; Frank Kelley (GM); Delena Kelley (PD); Lynn Myers (ND); 717-249-1717

WIOO (1000 AM), P.O. Box 399, 180 York Rd., Carlisle 17013; Harold Swidler (GM); Rich Lewis (ND); 717-243-1200

WSHP (1480 AM), Box 1480, Shippensburg 17257; Arthur K. Greiner (GM); William Roesch (NE); 717-532-4105

WSYC (88.7 FM), Cumberland Union Bldg., Shippensburg 17257; Shawn Ambrose (PD); Bernie Capuscinski (ND); 717-532-6006

WTPA (93.5 FM), 107 E. Main St., Mechanicsburg 17055; Mike Brandon (GM); Simon Jeffries (PD); 717-697-1141

DAUPHIN COUNTY

DAILIES

EVENING NEWS, THE, (E-2), 812 Martin Luther King Blvd., P.O. Box 2265, Harrisburg 17105; Raymond L. Gover (Pub); Ronald Minard (Ed); 55,045; (I); 717-255-8100

PATRIOT, THE, (M-1), 812 Martin Luther King Blvd., P.O. Box 2265, Harrisburg 17105; Raymond L. Gover (Pub); Ronald Minard (Ed); 50,425, M; 92,740, Sa.; (I); 717-255-8100

WEEKLIES

CATHOLIC WITNESS, THE, (Fr), Box 2555, 4800 Union Deposit Rd., Harrisburg 17105; Most Rev. William H. Keeler (Pub); Father Thomas R. Haney (Ed); 54,750; (Rel); 717-657-4804

PATRIOT-NEWS, THE, (S), 812 Martin Luther King Blvd., P.O. Box 2265, Harrisburg 17105; Raymond L. Gover (Pub); Ronald Minard (Ed); 166,444; (I); 717-255-8100

PAXTON HERALD, THE, (We), 101 Lincoln St., P.O. Box 6310, Harrisburg 17112; Annette A. Antoun (Pub & Ed); 30,000; (I); 717-545-9540

PRESS & JOURNAL, (We), P.O. Box 310, 20 S. Union St., Middletown 17057; Joseph Sukle (Ed); Ben Graybill (Pub); 11,780; (R); 717-944-4628

SUN, THE, (We), 115-117 S. Water St., Hummelstown 17036; William S. Jackson (Ed); Rosemary K. Jackson (Pub); 7,000; (I); 717-566-3251

UPPER DAUPHIN SENTINEL, (We), P.O. Box 250, 510 Union St., Millersburg 17061-0250; Ben L. Kocher (Ed & Pub); 7,514; (I); 717-692-3171

RADIO

WCMB (1460 AM), P.O. Box 3433, Harrisburg 17105; Drian Danzis (GM); Michael Parks (ND); 717-763-7020

WHGB (1400 AM), 900 Martin Luther King Blvd., Harrisburg 17101; Jeffrey Scott (GM); David Herlihy (PM); 717-238-5122

WHP (58 AM, 97.3 FM), Box 1507, Harrisburg 17105; R. Max Mills (Pres., CEO); Chris Fickes (ND); 717-238-2100

WITF (89.5 FM), Box 2954, Harrisburg 17105; Stewart Cheifet (GM); John Blair (VP Bcstg.); Neil McCormack (SP); 717-236-6000

WKBO (1230 AM), 3211 N. Front St., Harrisburg 17110; John W. Dame (GM); David Madden (ND); 717-561-0710

WMSP (94.9 FM), 24 S. 2nd St., Harrisburg 17101; Bruce J. Holcombe (GM); Ray Lehman (PD); 717-257-1300

WMSS (91.1 FM), 214 Race St., Middletown 17057; John D. Cooper (GM); 717-948-3398

WNNK (104.1 FM), P.O. Box 104, Harrisburg 17108; Carol B. O'Leary (GM); Dennis Edwards (ND); 717-238-1402

WQIN (1290 AM), 316 Market St., Lykens 17048; Gordon Lockwood (GM); Barry Hersh (ND); 717-453-7125

WRKZ (Z107 FM), P.O. Box Z, Hershey 17033; Mike McGann (GM); Bob Dettrey (NE & PM); 1-800-932-0505

WSFM (99.3 FM), Co-owned with WCMB (AM)

WTPA (93.5 FM), P.O. Box 9350, Harrisburg 17108; Mike Brandon (GM); Simon Jeffries (ND); 717-697-1141

TELEVISION

WGAL-TV (Ch. 8), Lincoln Hwy. West, Lancaster 17604; David Dodds (GM); Nelson Sears (PD); Ed Wickenheiser (ND); 717-392-5851

WHP-TV (Ch. 21), P.O. Box 1507, Harrisburg 17105; R. Max Mills (Pres. & CEO); Chris Fickes (ND); 717-238-2100

WHTM-TV (Ch. 27), Box 2775, Harrisburg 17105; John Purcell (GM); John McCall (ND); Debra Adjan (PD); 717-236-2727

WITF-TV (Ch. 33), Box 2954, Harrisburg 17105; Stewart Cheifet (GM); John Blair (VP Bcstg.); Neil McCormack (SP); 717-236-6000

DELAWARE COUNTY

DAILIES

DELAWARE COUNTY DAILY TIMES, (E-6), 500 Mildred Ave., Primos 19018; Stuart Rose (Ed); Murray Schwartz (Pub); 61,884; (I); 215-284-7200

WEEKLIES

COUNTY PRESS, (We), 3732 West Chester Pike, P.O. Box 249, Newtown Square 19073; William Lawrence (Ed); Richard L. Crowe (Pub); 12,200; (I); 215-356-3820

HAVERFORD PRESS, THE (We), 3732 West Chester Pike, Newtown Square 19073; William Lawrence (Ed); Reese J. Crowe, Jr. & Richard L. Crowe (Pubs); 3,000; (NP); 215-356-6664

INTERBORO NEWS, (We), P.O. Box 70, Prospect Park 19076; Roger Wilks (Ed & Pub); 6,100; 215-532-0316

MARCUS HOOK PRESS, (Th), 3245 Garrett Rd., Drexel Hill 19026; Margaret M. Girard (Ed); Press Publishing Co. (Pub); 3,336; (R); 215-259-4141

NEWS OF DELAWARE COUNTY, (We), Manoa Shopping Center, West Chester Pike, Havertown 19083; Charlie Stricklen (Pub); Mark Bulik (Ed); 23,277; (I); 215-446-8700

RIDLEY PRESS, (Th), 3245 Garrett Rd., Drexel Hill 19026; P.A. Girard (Pub); T. B. Connon (Ed); 5,774; (IR); 215-259-4141

SPRINGFIELD PRESS, (We), P.O. Box 291, 204 Ballymore Rd., Springfield 19064; Ellen Simon (Ed); Reese Crowe (Pub); 6,700; (I); 215-544-6660

SUBURBAN ADVERTISERS, (Th), 134 N. Wayne Ave., Wayne 19087; Charles Stricklen (Pub); D. N. Ehart (Ed); 14,216; (I); 215-688-3000

SUBURBAN AND WAYNE TIMES, THE, (Th), P.O. Box 409, 134 N. Wayne Ave., Wayne 19087; Charles Stricklen (Pub); Jon Weaver (Ed); 14,703; (R); 215-688-3000

SWARTHMOREAN, THE, (Fr), 333 Dartmouth Ave., Swarthmore 19081; Marsha Mullan (Ed); Lewis Rinko (Pub); 2,010; (I); 215-543-0900

TOWN TALK, (We), P.O. Box 110, 39 State Rd., Media 19063; Edward Berman (Pub); Christina Parker (Ed); 120,000; (I); 215-566-6755

UPPER DARBY PRESS, (Th), 3245 Garrett Rd., Drexel Hill 19026; P. A. Girard (Ed); Press Publishing Co. (Pub); 4,275; (IR); 215-259-4141

YEADON TIMES, THE, (Th), 719 Church La., Yeadon 19050; Frank P. Davenport (Ed & Pub); 2,000; (R); 215-623-6088

RADIO

WHHS (89.3 FM), Mill Rd. & Leedom Ave., Havertown 19083; John Roberti (PD); Ross Katz (ND); 215-446-7111

WKSZ (100.3 FM), 1001 Baltimore Pike, Media 19063; Daniel M. Lerner (GM); 215-565-8900

WSRN (91.5 FM), Swarthmore College, Swarthmore 19081; Matt Wall (SM); 215-328-8000

ELK COUNTY

DAILIES

DAILY PRESS, THE, (E-1), P.O. Box 353, 245 Brussels St., St. Marys 15857; James A. Dippold (Ed & Pub); 5,371; (I); 814-781-1596

RIDGWAY RECORD, THE, (E-1), P.O. Box T, 20 Main St., Ridgway 15853; Joseph C. Piccirillo (Pub); William R. Peterson (Ed); 3,410; (I); 814-773-3151

WEEKLIES

JOHNSONBURG PRESS, THE, (Th), P.O. Box 10, 517 Market St., Johnsonburg 15845; Alva K. Gregory (Pub & Ed); 2,144; (I); 814-965-2503

RADIO

WKBI (1400 AM, 94.3 FM), P.O. Box 466, Melody Rd., St. Marys 15857; John Salter (GM); David Mazzaferro (PD); John Kuhn (ND); 814-834-2821

ERIE COUNTY

DAILIES

CORRY EVENING JOURNAL, (E-1), 28 W. South St., Corry 16407; George Sample (Ed & Pub); 4,006; (IR); 814-665-8291

ERIE DAILY TIMES, (E-1), Times Square, 12th & Sassafras Sts., Box 400, Erie 16534; Len Kholos (Ed); Edward & Michael Mead (Pub); 42,264; (I); 814-456-8531

MORNING NEWS, (M-1), Times Square, 12th & Sassafras Sts., Box 400, Erie 16534; Larie Pintea (Ed); Edward & Michael Mead (Pub); 28,426; (I); 814-456-8531

WEEKLIES

ALBION NEWS, THE, (We), P.O. Box 7, 16 Market St., Albion 16401; Robert McClymonds (Ed & Pub); 3,168; (I); 814-756-4133

COSMOPOLITE HERALD, (We), Box 151, W. High St. Ext., Union City 16438; Valerie Strubel (Ed); 4,365; (I); 814-438-7667

INDEPENDENT-ENTERPRISE NEWS, THE, (We), P.O. Box 704, 122 B Erie St., Edinboro 16412; Steve Brown (Pub); Lori M. Eason (Ed); 5,826; (I); 814-734-1234

LAKE SHORE VISITOR, (Fr), Box 4047, Erie 16512; Gary C. Loncki (Ed); 18,322; (R); 814-452-3610

MILLCREEK SUN, THE, (We), P.O. Box 151, W. High St. Ext., Union City 16438; Peter Strozniak (Ed); 2,915; (I); 814-438-7667

NORTH EAST BREEZE, THE, (We), P.O. Box 151, W. High St. Ext., Union City 16438; Roger Coda (Ed); 3,215; (I); 814-438-7667

TIMES LEADER, THE, (We), P.O. Box 151, West High St. Ext., Union City 16438; Harold Maynard (Ed); 4,601; (I); 814-438-7667

TIMES-NEWS, (Sa & S), 12th & Sassafras Sts., Box 400, Erie 16534; Edward & Michael Mead (Pub); Bill Rogosky (Ed); 96,220; (I); 814-456-8531

RADIO

WCCK (103.7 FM), P.O. Box 1184, Erie 16512; Howard Nemenz (GM); Michael Reilley (ND); Bill Shannon (PD); 814-456-7078

WCTL (106.3 FM), R.D. 3, Union City 16438; Rev. Bill Baker (GM & NE); 814-452-2041

WERG (89.9 FM), Box 236, Gannon University, Erie 16541; David Brennan (GM); Chris Scalise (PD); Erin Scully (ND); 814-459-9374

WEYZ (1450 AM), Co-owned with WCCK (FM)

WFSE (88.9 FM), Edinboro Univ., Edinboro 16444; Don Carraghan, Rob Starr (GM's); Rob O'Friell, Gary Smith (PD's); Lori Taylor (ND); 814-732-2889

WHYP (1530 AM, 100.9 FM), 10325 W. Main Rd., North East 16428; James D. Brownyard (GM); H. I. Brownyard (NE); Dusty Rhodes (PM); 814-725-9664

WJET (1400 AM), 1635 Ash St., Erie 16503; Myron Jones (Pres.); Jim Cook (PD); 814-455-2741

WLKK (1260 AM), 471 Robinson Rd., W. Erie 16509; Donald Kelly (GM); Darrell Edwards (ND); Dana Bolles (PD); 814-868-5355

WLVU (99.9 FM), Co-owned with WLKK (AM)

WQLN (91.3 FM), 8425 Peach St., Erie 16509; Robert Clark (GM); Thomas McLaren (PD); 814-864-3001

WSEG (102.3 FM), 3850 Walker Blvd., Erie 16509; Ronald Seggi (GM); Edie Marie (ND); 814-868-4627

WWCB (1370 AM), Box 4, Corry 16407; Bruce Lewis (GM & ND); Kathy Stolz (PD); 814-664-8694

TELEVISION

WICU-TV (Ch. 12), Box 860, 3514 State St., Erie 16508; John Speciale (ND); 814-454-5201

WJET-TV (Ch. 24), 8455 Peach St., Erie 16509; John Kanzius (GM); Ken Fanazini (PD); Eric Johnson (ND); 814-864-4902

WQLN-TV (Ch. 54), 8425 Peach St., Erie 16509; R. B. Clark (GM); Thomas J. McLaren (PM); 814-864-3001

WSEE-TV (Ch. 35), 1220 Peach St., Erie 16501; Jerry Montgomery (GM); George Stephenson (ND); 814-455-7575

FAYETTE COUNTY

DAILIES

DAILY COURIER, THE, (E-1), P.O. Box 864, 127 N. Apple St., Connellsville 15425; Lee Elby (Ed); Robert Lind (Pub); 12,634; (I); 412-628-2000

HERALD-STANDARD, THE, (M-6), P.O. Box 848, 8-18 E. Church St., Uniontown 15401; George Molesy (Pub); Donald P. Davis (Ed); 28,536; (I); 412-439-7500

TELEGRAPH, THE, (E-1), P.O. Box 570, 16-18 Bridge St., Brownsville 15417; Charles W. McKinley (Pub); Michael Zastudil (Ed); 6,242; (IR); 412-785-5000

WEEKLIES

MASONTOWN SENTINEL, (Th), P.O. Box 751, 211 N. Main St., Masontown 15461; Phyllis A. Hughes (Ed); E. E. Franks (Pub); 3,500; (I); 412-583-7741

RADIO

WASP (1130 AM), Box 270, Brownsville 15417; James J. Humes (GM); Joyce Smith (ND); David Bridges (PD); 412-785-3450

WCVI (1340 AM), 133 E. Crawford Ave., Connellsville 15425; Marlene Heshler (Pres.); Mike Manko (ND); 412-628-4600

WLSW (103.9 FM), Box 763, Connellsville 15425; Chris Moulton (GM); Doug McDonough (ND); Joe Brian (PD); 412-628-2800

WMBS (590 AM), 82 W. Fayette St., Uniontown 15401; Simon W. Rider (GM); Charles H. Underwood (ND); 412-438-3900

WPQR (99.3 FM), Drawer 639, Uniontown 15401; Edward E. Olesh (GM); Lorraine Livingston (SM); Jack McMullen (ND); 412-437-2813

WVCS (91.9 FM), 428 Hickory St., Univ. of Pa., California 15419; Tracy Behana (GM); John O'Malley (ND); J. R. Wheeler (Adv.); 412-938-3000

FOREST COUNTY

WEEKLIES

FOREST PRESS, (We), Box 366, Tionesta 16353; R. C. Clever (Ed & Pub); 5,000; (Con); 814-755-4900

FRANKLIN COUNTY

DAILIES

PUBLIC OPINION, (E-1), P.O. Box 499, 77 N. Third St., Chambersburg 17201; Jo-Ann Huff Albers (Pub & Ed); 19,123; (I); 717-264-6161

RECORD HERALD, (E-1), P.O. Box 271, 30 Walnut St., Waynesboro 17268; Paul F. Chalfant (Pub); Jesse F. Garber (Ed); 10,406; (IR); 717-762-2151

WEEKLIES

ECHO-PILOT, (Th), Box 159, 29 Center Square, Greencastle 17225; Wayne Baumbaugh (Pub); Sharon Baumbaugh (Ed); 2,500; (I); 717-597-2164

FRANKLIN SHOPPER, THE, (Tu), 25 Penn Craft Ave., Chambersburg 17201; Thomas D. Boock (Pub); Chambersburg Pub. Co., (Pub); 46,341; (R); 717-263-0359

MERCERSBURG JOURNAL, (We), P.O. Box 239, Mercersburg 17236; Vernon and Barbara Leese (Pub); Jim Hook (Ed); 2,500; 717-328-3223

NEWS CHRONICLE, (Mo & Th), R.D. 1, P.O. Box 100, Shippensburg 17257; Grace Schlichter (Pub); 5,951; (IR); 717-532-4104

RADIO

WAYZ (1380 AM, 101.5 FM), 33 E. Main St., Waynesboro 17268; Marge Martin (GM); Stacy Drake (ND & PD); 717-762-3138

WBZT (1130 AM), Old Airport Rd., Waynesboro 17268; Steven Berger (GM); Bill McCarrey (ND & PD); 717-762-7171

WCBG (1590 AM), P.O. Box U, Chambersburg 17201; Molly Darr Messner (GM); Lynne Newman (NE); 717-263-4131

WCHA (800 AM), Box 479, Chambersburg 17201; Thomas D. Boock (GM); Joyce Nowell (NE); 717-264-7121

WGLL (92.1 FM), Box 92, Mercersburg 17236; Pete Low (GM, NE & PM); Sue McLaughlin (ND); 717-597-9200

WIKZ (95.1 FM), Co-owned with WCHA (AM)

WKSL (94.3 FM), Box 10, 211 S. Antrim Way, Greencastle 17225; Benjamin F. Thomas (GM); Shelley Williams (PD & ND); 717-597-7151

WSHP (1480 AM), Box 1480, Shippensburg 17257; Arthur K. Greiner (GM); Bill Roesch (ND); Steve McDaniel (PD); 717-532-4105

FULTON COUNTY

WEEKLIES

FULTON COUNTY JOURNAL, (We), Box 716, McConnellsburg 17233; Lee Oakan (Ed & Pub); 3,350; (D); 717-485-3261

FULTON COUNTY NEWS, THE, (Th), Box 635, 417 E. Market St., McConnellsburg 17233; Jamie S. Greathead (Ed & Pub); 5,600; (I); 717-485-3811

RADIO

WVFC (1530 AM), Box 1530, McConnellsburg 17233; Arthur K. Greiner (GM); J. B. Nelson (ND); 717-485-3117

GREENE COUNTY

DAILIES

DEMOCRAT MESSENGER, (M-1), 32 Church St., Waynesburg 15370; Peter Rogers (Pub); Greg Brown (Ed); 5,200; (I); 412-627-7383

OBSERVER-REPORTER, (M), 32 Church St., Waynesburg 15370; Bob Eichenlaub (Ed); 8,500; (I); 412-627-6166

WEEKLIES

WAYNESBURG REPUBLICAN, (Fr), 122 S. Main St., Washington 15301; William & John Northrop (Pub); Robert M. Eichenlaub (Ed); 908; (R); 412-852-2602

RADIO

WANB (1580 AM, 103.1 FM), First Federal Bldg., Waynesburg 15370; John Loeper (GM); Lynn Marcuso (ND & PD); 412-627-5555

HUNTINGDON COUNTY

DAILIES

DAILY-NEWS, THE, (E-1), P.O. Box 384, 325 Penn St., Huntingdon 16652; Joseph F. Biddle II (Pub); James D. Hunt (Ed); 11,201; (I); 814-643-4040

WEEKLIES

MOUNT UNION TIMES, (Fr), 325 Penn St., Huntingdon 16652; Joseph F. Biddle, II (Pub); James D. Hunt (Ed); 122; (I); 814-643-4040

VALLEY LOG, (We), P.O. Box 219, Water St., Orbisonia 17243; C. Arnold McClure (Pub); George Bumgardner (Ed); 3,009; (I); 814-447-5506

RADIO

WHUN (1150 AM), Box 404, Huntingdon 16652; William E. Germann (GM); Joe Thompson (ND); 814-643-3340

WKVR (103.5 FM), Juniata College, Huntingdon 16652; Shelly Guest (GM); 814-643-5031

WQRO (1080 AM), Box 107, Huntingdon 16652; Tom Stevens (GM & PD); 814-643-5710

INDIANA COUNTY

DAILIES

INDIANA GAZETTE, (E-1), P.O. Box 10, 899 Water St., Indiana 15701; Lucilla R. & Joseph L. Donnelly (Pres., Pub & Ed); 20,429; (R); 412-465-5555

WEEKLIES

DISPATCH (We & Sa), P.O. Box 37, 101 W. Market St., Blairsville 15717; Richard M. Scaife (Pub); John M. Jennings (ME); 18,269; (D); 412-459-6100

RADIO

WCCS (1160 FM), Box 1020, Indiana 15701-1020; Mark Harley (GM); Bernie Smith (NE); David Goss (PM); 412-479-3523

WDAD (1450 AM), Box 668, Indiana 15701; Dick Sherry (GM); Ken Rich (ND); 412-349-1450

WIUP (90.1 FM), Indiana Univ. of Pa., Indiana 15705; Mary Beth Leidman (GM); 412-357-2492

WNQQ (106.3 FM), Routes 22 & 119, Blairsville 15717; Ray Gusky (GM); Hank Dale (PD & ND); 412-459-8888

WQMU (103 FM), Co-owned with WDAD (AM)

JEFFERSON COUNTY

DAILIES

SPIRIT, THE, (M-1), P.O. Box 444, 111 N. Findley St., Punxsutawney 15767; William C. Anderson (GM); David R. Divelbiss (Ed); 5,862; (I); 814-938-8740

WEEKLIES

BROCKWAY RECORD, THE, (We), P.O. Box K, 682 Main St., Brockway 15824; Joseph L. Donnelly (Ed); 1,603; (I); 814-265-0000

BROOKVILLE AMERICAN, (Tu), P.O. Box 249, 175 Main St., Brookville 15825; Bruce A. & Donald McMurray (Pub); Joseph McLaughlin (Ed); 5,132; (IR); 814-849-5338

JEFFERSONIAN DEMOCRAT, (Th), P.O. Box 249, 175 Main St., Brookville 15825; Bruce A. & Donald McMurray (Pub); Joseph McLaughlin (Ed); 5,485; (ID); 814-849-5338

REYNOLDSVILLE STAR, THE, (We), 511 Main St., P.O. Box 38, Reynoldsville 15851; Joseph Donnelly (Ed & Pub); 1,145; (I); 814-653-9300

SYKESVILLE POST-DISPATCH, (Fr), P.O. Box A, Sykesville 15865-0018; Terry J. Carlson (Ed & Pub); 1,150; (I); 814-894-2467

RADIO

WMKX (95.9 FM), 205 Main St., Brookville 15825; Jim Farley (GM); Robin Commons (ND); 814-849-8100

WPXZ (1540 AM, 105.5 FM), P.O. Box 458, Punxsutawney 15767; Al Anthony (GM); Robert L. Curry (NE); 814-938-6000

JUNIATA COUNTY

WEEKLIES

JUNIATA SENTINEL, (We), P.O. Box 127, Old Route 22, Mifflintown 17059; James R. Bauer (Ed); William A. Gilliland (Pub); 7,250; (I); 717-436-8206

RADIO

WJUN (1220 AM), Box 209, Mexico 17056; Richard C. Lyons (GM); Gary Ishler (NE); 717-436-2135

LACKAWANNA COUNTY

DAILIES

SCRANTON TIMES, THE, (E, S), P.O. Box 3311, 149 Penn Ave., Scranton 18505; Edward, William & George Lynett (Ed & Pub); 58,817, E; 60,835, S; (I); 717-348-9100

TRIBUNE, THE, (M-1), 338 N. Washington Ave., Scranton 18501; Nelson Goodman (Pub); Hal Lewis (Ed); 38,274; (R); 717-344-7221

WEEKLIES

ABINGTON JOURNAL, (We), P.O. Box 277, 406 S. State St., Clarks Summit 18411; J. Stephen Buckley (Pub); William Savage (Ed); 2,691; (I); 717-587-1148

CARBONDALE NEWS, (We), 41 N. Church St., Carbondale 18407-1991; Philip Heth (Pub); Rosemary Heth (Ed); 6,000; (I); 717-282-3300

CATHOLIC LIGHT, (3), P.O. Box 708, 300 Wyoming Ave., Scranton 18503; Catholic Light Pub. Co. (Pub); Arthur F. Perry (Ed); 52,597; (Rel); 717-346-8915

NARODNA VOLYA, (Th), 440 Wyoming Ave., Scranton 18509-0350; Roman Rychok (Ed); Ukrainian Fraternal Assn. (Pub); 3,500; (I); 717-342-8897

SCRANTONIAN, THE, (S), 338 N. Washington Ave., Scranton 18501; Nelson Goodman (Pub); Hal Lewis (Ed); 52,038; (R); 717-344-7221

STRAZ (Guard), (Th), 1004 Pittston Ave., Scranton 18505; Polish Nat'l Union of America (Pub); Wanda M. Cytowska (Ed); (Fra); 717-347-1911

TRIBORO BANNER, (Th), 105 S. Main St., Taylor 18517; Ruth Holder (Ed & Pub); 2,200; (I); 717-562-3511

VILLAGER, (Th), Wilson Dr., Box 362, Moscow 18444; C. Reed Kennedy (Ed & Pub); 6,700; (I); 717-842-8789

RADIO

WBQW (1320 AM), 1520 N. Keyser Ave., Scranton 18504; Nancy Sinclair (GM); Denny Talerico (NE); Jack Griswold (PM); 717-342-1320

WCDL (1440 AM, 94.3 FM), 127 Salem Rd., Carbondale 18407; Noble Blackwell (Pres. & GM); Jim Brando (PD); 717-282-2770

WEJL (630 AM), 149 Penn Ave., Scranton 18503; Tim Durkin (GM); John Hunter (PD); 717-346-6555

WEZX (107.1 FM), Co-owned with WEJL (AM)

WGBI (910 AM, 101.3 FM), 417 Lackawanna Ave., Scranton 18503; Madge Holcomb (GM); 717-344-9424

WICK (1400 AM), N. Sekol Rd., Scranton 18504; Douglas V. Lane (GM); Jean E. Wilding (ND); 717-344-1221

WLSP (94.3 FM), Co-owned with WCDL (AM)

WMGS (93 FM), Box 930, Avoca 18641; Philip Condron (GM); Carol Warholak (NE); Chris Norton (PM); 717-346-4646

WVIA (89.9 FM), Public Broadcasting Center, Pittston 18640; John Walsh (Pres & GM); Erika Funke (ND); 717-826-6144

WVMW (91.5 FM), Marywood College, Scranton 18509; Karen Howard (GM); Amelia Santaniello (PD); Lisa Nepersky (ND); 717-348-6202

WWDL (104.9 FM), Co-owned with WICK (AM)

TELEVISION

WBRE-TV (Ch. 28), 62 S. Franklin St., Wilkes-Barre 18773; Terry Baltimore (GM & PD); Bob Young (ND); 717-823-3101

WDAU-TV (Ch. 22), 415 Lackawanna Ave., Scranton 18503; Madge Holcomb (GM); Thomas Powell (NE); 717-961-2222

WNEP-TV (Ch. 16), Wilkes-Barre Scranton Airport, Avoca 18641; Elden A. Hale, Jr. (VP & GM); William Christian (PD); R. Paul Stueber (ND); 717-826-1616

WVIA-TV (Ch. 44), Public Broadcasting Center, Pittston 18640; John Walsh (Pres & GM); Karen Stone (PD); 717-826-6144

LANCASTER COUNTY

DAILIES

COLUMBIA NEWS, THE, (E-1), P.O. Box 191, 341 Chestnut St., Columbia 17512; S. S. Crist, Jr. (Pub); Cletus E. Aston (Ed); 4,380; (IR); 717-684-2125

INTELLIGENCER-JOURNAL, (M-1), P.O. Box 1328, 8 W. King St., Lancaster 17603; William R. Schultz (Ed); 43,950; (D); 717-291-8600

NEW ERA, (E-1), P.O. Box 1328, 8 W. King St., Lancaster 17603; Daniel L. Cherry (Ed); 57,150; (R); 717-291-8600

WEEKLIES

ELIZABETHTOWN CHRONICLE, (We), 9 N. Market St., Elizabethtown 17022; Ruth Ebersole (Ed); William S. Jackson (Pub); 5,200; (I); 717-367-7152

EPHRATA REVIEW, THE, (Th), 50 E. Main St., P.O. Box 527, Ephrata 17522; Michael Miller (Ed); The Ephrata Review, Inc. (Pub); 11,338; (IR); 717-733-2244

LANCASTER FARMING, (Sa), P.O. Box 366, 22 E. Main St., Lititz 17543; Robert G. Campbell (Pub); Everett R. Newswanger (Ed); (I); 717-626-1164

LITITZ RECORD-EXPRESS, (Th), 22 E. Main St., P.O. Box 366, Lititz 17543; Robert G. Campbell (Pub); Bonnie Szymanski (Ed); 7,162; (I); 717-626-2191

MERCHANDISER, (We), P.O. Box 500, Rt. 230 West, Mount Joy 17552; C. A. Engle (Ed); Pauline Engle (Pub); 56,673; (I); 717-653-1835

PENNY SAVER, (Tu), 200 Hazel St., Lancaster 17604; Betty Hostetter (Ed); James Weaver (Pub); 26,000; (I); 717-392-1321

SHOPPING NEWS OF LANCASTER COUNTY, (We), P.O. Box 456, 615 E. Main St., Ephrata 17522; John W. Hocking (Pub); 28,975; (R); 717-738-1151

STRASBURG NEWS, (Fr), Box 249, 140 W. Main St., Strasburg 17579; Gerald Lestz (Pub); Marjorie McCarthy (Ed); 850; (R); 717-687-7721

SUN LEDGER, THE, (We), P.O. Box 120, 19 S. Church St., Quarryville 17566; H. James Wolf (Ed); H. James Wolf & Donald A. Althouse (Pub); 14,000; (I); 717-786-2992

SUNDAY NEWS, (S), P.O. Box 1328, 8 W. King St., Lancaster 17603; David Hennigan (Ed); 97,436; (I); 717-291-8600

RADIO

WDAC (94.5 FM), Box 3022, Lancaster 17604; Paul R. Hollinger (GM); John MacAlarney (ND); 717-284-4123

WFNM (89.1 FM, 740 AM), Franklin & Marshall College, Lancaster 17604; Michael Benanti (GM); 717-291-4096

WGSA (1310 AM), 3 W. Main St., Ephrata 17522; Michael D. Rubright (GM); Julie Graham (ND); 717-733-1310

WIOV (105.1 FM), Co-owned with WGSA (AM)

WIXQ (91.7 FM), Millersville Univ., Millersville 17551; J. Nelson Keperling (CE); 717-872-3518

WLAN (1390 AM, 96.9 FM); 252 N. Queen St., Lancaster 17603; Samuel M. Altdoerffer (GM); Ellen Wascou (NE); 717-394-7261

WLPA (1490 AM), 24 S. Queen St., Lancaster 17603; William S. Baldwin (GM); William F. Richardson IV (ND); 717-397-0333

WNCE (101.3 FM), Co-owned with WLPA (AM)

WNZT (1580 AM), P.O. Box 270, Columbia 17512; Ted Byrne (GM); Don Yeager (NE & PM); 717-285-7290

WPDC (1600 AM), 939 Radio Rd., Elizabethtown 17022; Vince Grand (GM); John Hess (PD); Jane Hollinger (ND); 717-367-1600

WRKZ (106.7 FM), Box Z, Hershey 17033; Mike McGann (GM); Bob Dettrey (PD); Steve Wagner (ND); 717-367-7700

TELEVISION

WGAL-TV (Ch. 8), Lincoln Highway, Lancaster 17604; David Dodds (VP & GM); Nelson Sears (PM); Ed Wickenheiser (ND); 717-393-5851

WLYH-TV (Ch. 15), 1126 Park City Center, Lancaster 17601; Robert W. Eolin (GM); Cliff Eshbach (ND); 717-273-4551

LAWRENCE COUNTY

DAILIES

ELLWOOD CITY LEDGER, (E-1), P.O. Box 471, 835 Lawrence Ave., Ellwood City 16117; W. C. Kegel (Pub); Charles R. Moser (Ed); 7,612; (I); 412-758-5573

NEW CASTLE NEWS, (E-1), 27-35 N. Mercer St., P.O. Box 60, New Castle 16103; J. Fred Rentz (Ed); News Co., Inc. (Pub); 21,006; (I); 412-654-6651

WEEKLIES

GLOBE, (We), P.O. Box 226, 129 W. Neshannock Ave., New Wilmington 16142; Pat Leali (Ed); Guy Bongiovanni (Pub); 1,850; (I); 412-946-3501

RADIO

WBZY (1140 AM), Kennedy Square W., New Castle 16101; Robert McCracken (GM); Scott Burkett (GM); 412-656-1140

WFEM (92.1 FM), 219 Savannah-Gardner Rd., New Castle 16101; Angelo M. Lordi (GM); 412-654-5501

WKST (1280 AM), Co-owned with WFEM (FM)

WWNW (88.9 FM), Box 89, Westminster College, New Wilmington 16172; David L. Barner (GM); 412-946-8721

LEBANON COUNTY

DAILIES

DAILY NEWS, THE, (E & S), P.O. Box 600, S. 8th & Poplar Sts., Lebanon 17042; Richard Scaife (Pub); 24,760, E; 24,391, S; (I); 717-272-5611

WEEKLIES

LEBANON AREA MERCHANDISER, (We), 100 E. Cumberland St., P.O. Box 840, Lebanon 17042; George W. Kapp (Ed & Pub); (Shop); 717-273-8127

PALM ADVERTISER, (We), 11 E. Main St., Palmyra 17078; Lloyd A. Snell (Pub); 28,600; (Shop); 717-838-6345

RADIO

WAHT (1510 AM), P.O. Box 15, Lebanon 17042; Dorothy Sullivan (GM); Ken Meinhart (PD); Lelyn Perri (ND); 717-273-8547

WCTX (92.1 FM), Box 231, Palmyra 17078; Hugh Clinton (GM); Bob Moore (PD); 717-838-1318

WLBR (1270 AM), RT. 72 N., Lebanon 17042; Robert D. Etter (GM); Henry Hoffman (NE); 717-272-7651

WUFM (100.1 FM), Co-owned with WLBR (AM)

WVLV (940 AM), P.O. Box 940, Lebanon 17042; Donald Griffith (GM); Elaine Evans (PD); 717-273-2611

LEHIGH COUNTY

DAILIES

MORNING CALL, THE, (M & S), P.O. Box 1260, 6th & Linden Sts., Allentown 18105; Lawrence Hymans (Ed); Bernard C. Stinner (Pub); 132,806, M; 174,210, S; (I); 215-820-6500

WEEKLIES

CATASAUQUA DISPATCH, (Th), 420 Howertown Rd., Catasauqua 18032; Marlin E. Wolf (Ed); Dispatch Printery (Pub); 2,000; (I); 215-264-9451

EAST PENN FREE PRESS, THE, (We), Box 409, Emmaus 18049; Charles Meredith III (Pub); Julia Paxson (Ed); 3,000; (I); 215-965-6031

PENNY POWER, (We), 551 Station Ave., Coopersburg 18036; Penny Power Ltd. (Pub); 27,816; (Shop); 215-538-2454

RADIO

WAEB (790 AM, 104.1 FM), Box 2727, Lehigh Valley 18001; Jeff Frank (GM); Mathew Kerr (ND); 215-434-4424

WFMZ (100.7 FM), E. Rock Rd., Allentown 18103; Richard C. Dean (Pres.); Paul Brittin (NE); 215-797-4530

WHOL (1600 AM), 1125 Colorado St., Allentown 18105; Aaron G. Lopez (Prod.); 215-775-3101

WKAP (1320 AM), P.O. Box 246, Whitehall 18052; Ron Sotak (GM); Alan Raber (NE); 215-435-9572

WMUH (91.7 FM), Box 10-B, Muhlenberg College, Allentown 18104; Thomas A. Gillace (GM); Trudy Bottari (PD); Miryam Strassberg (ND); 215-433-5957

WXKW (1470 AM), 1183 Mickley Rd., Whitehall 18052; Rick Musselman (GM); Don Rutt (ND); 215-434-9511

TELEVISION

WLVT-TV (Ch. 39), Mountain Dr., Bethlehem 18015; Sheldon P. Siegel (Pres. & GM); Donald L. Robert (PD); 215-867-4677

LUZERNE COUNTY

DAILIES

CITIZENS VOICE, (M-1), 75 N. Washington St., Wilkes-Barre 18711; Paul Golias (Ed); Robert Manganiello (Pub); 45,952; 717-821-2091

STANDARD SPEAKER, (D-1), P.O. Box 578, 21 N. Wyoming St., Hazleton 18201; Jane & Paul Walser (Pub); Ramon Saul (Ed); 24,412; (I); 717-455-3636

TIMES-LEADER, (E-1), P.O. Box 730, 15 N. Main St., Wilkes-Barre 18711; Dale A. Duncan (Pub); Allison Walzer (Ed); 46,655; (I); 717-829-7100

WEEKLIES

DALLAS POST, THE, (We), Rt. 309-415 Plaza, Box 366, Dallas 18612; J. Stephen Buckley (Pub); Dotty Martin (Ed); 3,300; (I); 717-675-5211

DISPATCH, (S), 109 New St., Pittston 18640; William A. Watson (Ed); William A. Watson III (Pub); 14,000; (I); 717-655-1418

JOURNAL HERALD, THE, (Th), 211 Main St., White Haven 18661; Jay E. & Clara R. Holder (Ed & Pub); 1,475; 717-443-9131

MOUNTAINTOP EAGLE, (We), Box 10, 85 S. Main Rd., Mountaintop 18707; Stephanie Grubert (Ed & Pub); 1,550; (I); 717-434-6397

SUNDAY INDEPENDENT, (S), 90 E. Market St., Wilkes-Barre 18701-3599; T. F. Heffernan (Ed & Pub); 64,934; (I); 717-822-3111

RADIO

WARD (1550 AM), P.O. Box 1550, Pittston 18640; Samuel M. Liguori (PM); Robert R. Neyhard, Jr. (NE); James F. Ward (GM); 717-655-5521

WARM (590 AM), P.O. Box 590, Avoca 18641; Phil Condron (GM); Jerry Heller (NE); John Hancock (PM); 717-346-4646

WAZL (1490 AM), Hazleton Natl. Bank Bldg., Hazleton 18201; Ron Aughinbaugh (GM); Dave Becker (ND); Billy Waschko (PD); 717-454-3531

WBAX (1240 AM), 1 Broadcast Plaza, Wilkes-Barre 18703; Bob Maley (GM); Mike Kaye (PD); Mark Zimmerman (ND); 717-288-7575

WCLH (90.7 FM), Wilkes College, Wilkes-Barre 18706; Christine Bokarovic (GM); Cliff Bialkin (ND & PD); 717-825-7663

WGMS (92.9 FM), Co-owned with WARM (AM)

WILK (980 AM), 88 N. Franklin St., Wilkes-Barre 18711; James Morgan (GM); Bob Leidigh (NE); 717-824-4666

WKRZ (1340 AM, 98.5 FM), P.O. Box 1600, Wilkes-Barre 18773; Dave Stilli (GM); Bud Brown (ND); 717-823-5000

WMJW (92.1 FM), Box 92, Nanticoke 18634; Frank Stanley (GM); Joe Talmon (PD); 717-829-1957

WNAK (730 AM), 84 S. Prospect St., Nanticoke 18634; Robert W. Neilson (GM); Charmaine Grove (SM); 717-735-0730

WQEQ (103.1 FM), R. D. #1, Walnut St., Freeland 18224; Russell A. Caron (GM & PM); Andy Mehalshick (ND); 717-636-2346

WRKC (88.5 FM), King's College, Wilkes-Barre 18711; Thomas Carten (GM); Joe Ohrin (PD); Art Merchant (ND); 717-826-5821

WTLQ (Q-102 FM), 490 N. Main St., Pittston 18640; James F. Loftus (GM); Ben Smith (PM); 717-347-7102

WVIA (89.9 FM), Public Broadcasting Center, Scranton 18640; John Walsh (GM); Tom McHugh (PD); 717-655-2808

WXPX (1300 AM), P.O. Box 339, Hazleton 18201; Russell A. Caron (GM & PM); Andy Mehalshick (ND); 717-455-9979

TELEVISION

WBRE-TV (Ch. 28), 62 S. Franklin St., Wilkes-Barre 18773; Terry S. Baltimore (GM); Tom Rosing (SM); 717-823-3101

WNEP-TV (Ch. 16), Wilkes-Barre/Scranton Airport, Avoca 18641; Elven Held (GM); Paul Stueber (ND); Mary Cordaro (PD); 717-826-1616

WVIA-TV (Ch. 44), Public Broadcasting Center, Pittston 18640; John Walsh (Pres. & GM); Tom McHugh (ND); Karen Stone (PD); 717-826-6144

LYCOMING COUNTY

DAILIES

LOCK HAVEN EXPRESS, THE, (E-1), P.O. Box 208, 9-11 W. Main St., Lock Haven 17745; Charles R. Ryan (Pub); Raymond Schaefer (Ed); 11,999; (I); 717-748-6791

WILLIAMSPORT SUN-GAZETTE, (E-1), P.O. Box 728, 252 W. 4th St., Williamsport 17701; Cliford Thomas (Ed); John Person, Jr. (Pub); 33,906; (I); 717-326-1551

WEEKLIES

EAST LYCOMING SHOPPER, (Tu), 98 N. Main St., Hughesville 17737; V. Jud Rogers (Pub); 17,800; (Shop); 717-584-2134

LUMINARY, (Th), Box 267, Muncy 17756; Gene Winter (Pub); Eileen Winter (Ed); 9,000; (I); 717-546-8555

LYCOMING REPORTER, (We), 48 W. 3rd St., Williamsport 17701; William L. Knecht (Ed); (I); 717-326-5131

SUNDAY GRIT, THE, (S), 208 W. 3rd St., Williamsport 17701; Evan Anderson (Pub); Michael Rafferty (Ed); 575,124; (I); 717-326-1771

RADIO

WEUZ (97.7 FM), Box 354, Jersey Shore 17740; Dave McCormick (GM); Keith Kitchen (ND & PD); 717-398-4897

WFXX (1450 AM, 99.3 FM), P.O. Box 5057, S. Williamsport 17701; Warren Diggans, David Banks (GM); John Finn (NE); Ted Minier (PM); 717-323-3608

WILQ (105.1 FM), Box 1176, Williamsport 17701; Robert Cunnion (GM); 717-322-4676

WJSA (1600 AM, 93.5 FM), 262 Allegheny St., Jersey Shore 17740; John K. Hogg, Jr. (GM, NE & PM); 717-398-7200

WKSB (102.7 FM), 1559 W. 4th St., Williamsport 17701; George Gilbert (GM); Tom Turner (ND); Dan Demuro (PD); 717-327-9572

WLYC (1050 AM), Co-owned with WILQ (FM)

WRAK (1400 AM), Co-owned with WKSB (FM)

WRLC (91.7 FM), College Place, Williamsport 17701; Jack Buckle (Adv.); Ed Surdez (GM); Julie Hottle (PD); Katie Chadwick (ND); 717-323-1142

WWAS (88.1 FM), Williamsport Area Comm. College, Williamsport 17701; Janie Swartz (GM); 717-326-3761

WWPA (1340 AM), 230 Market St., Williamsport 17701; William Ott (GM & NE); 717-323-7119

McKEAN COUNTY

DAILIES

BRADFORD ERA, (M-1), P.O. Box 365, 43 Main St., Bradford 16701; Henry A. Satterwhite (Pub); John H. Satterwhite (Ed); 12,144; (I); 814-368-3174

KANE REPUBLICAN, THE, (E-1), P.O. Box 838, 200 N. Fraley St., Kane 16735; Joseph C. Piccirilli (Pub); Richard Coleman (Ed); 2,578; (R); 814-837-6000

WEEKLIES

ECHO, (Th), Box 17, Bradford 16701; Grant & Katherine Nichols (Ed & Pub); 1,075; (I); 814-362-6563

McKEAN COUNTY MINER, (Th), Box 17, Bradford 16701; Grant & Katherine Nichols (Ed & Pub); 1,075; (I); 814-362-6563

REPORTER-ARGUS, (Th), P.O. Box 129, 109 Maple St., Port Allegheny 16743; Dann M. Sholkowski & Charles F. Boller (Pub); Del Kerr (Ed); 2,300; (R); 814-642-2811

RADIO

WESB (1490 AM), 43 Main St., Bradford 16701; George H. Daggett, Jr. (SM); Kevin M. Kelley (ND); 814-368-4141

WIFI (103.9 FM), 95 Fraley St., Kane 16735; Skip Huber (GM); John McGuire (PM); 814-837-6500

WKZA (960 AM), P.O. Box 518, Kane 16735; Roger Collins (SM, ND & PD); 814-837-7100

MERCER COUNTY

DAILIES

HERALD, THE, (E-1), P.O. Box 51, 52 S. Dock St., Sharon 16146; Gregory H. Taylor (Pub); James Dunlap (Ed); 27,056; (I); 412-981-6100

RECORD-ARGUS, THE, (E-1), 10 Penn Ave., P.O. Box 711, Greenville 16125-0711; Larry Howsare (Ed); William A. Bright (Pub); 5,105; (I); 412-558-5000

WEEKLIES

ALLIED NEWS, (We), Box 190, 113 N. Broad St., Grove City 16127; Richard Calkins (Ed); 4,086; 412-458-5010

RADIO

WEDA (95.1 FM), 125 S. Broad St., Grove City 16127; James Perry (GM); Wayne Lightner (NE); 412-458-6500

WGRP (940 AM, 107.1 FM), Box 189, Greenville 16125; Merle G. Anderson (GM); William E. Shaffer (NE); 412-588-8900

WMGZ (95.9 AM, FM), P.O. Box 1470, Sharon 16148; Nick Corvello (GM); Jack Sandstrom (NE); Cornel Bogdan (PM); 412-981-9500

WPIC (790 AM), Box 211, Sharon 16146; Tom Klein (GM); Keith Corso (PD); 412-346-4113

WSAJ (1340 AM, 89.5 FM), Grove City College, Grove City 16127; Everett DeVelde (GM); Deena Snyder (PD); 412-458-9352

WTGP (88.1 FM), Thiel College, Greenville 16125; Charles Brown (GM); 412-588-7700

WWIZ (103.9 FM), Box 1120, Hermitage 16148; Karl Brandt (GM); 412-981-4580

WYFM (102.9 FM), Co-owned with WPIC (AM)

MIFFLIN COUNTY

DAILIES

COUNTY OBSERVER, THE, (We), P.O. Box 521, Reedsville 17084; David E. Semler (Pub); Joseph E. Cannon (Ed); 4,795; 717-667-2166

SENTINEL, THE, (E-1), Box 588, 6th & Summit Sts., Lewistown 17044; James E. Dible (Pub); 13,538; (I); 717-248-6741

RADIO

WIEZ (1490 AM), Co-owned with WMRF: 717-248-6757

WKVA (920 AM), P.O. Box 911, Lewistown 17044; David Wilson (GM); Tom Scott (ND); 717-242-1493

WMRF (95.9 FM), 12 1/2 E. Market St., Lewistown 17044; Frank Troiani (GM); 717-248-6757

MONROE COUNTY

DAILIES

POCONO RECORD, (M), 511 Lenox St., Stroudsburg 18360; Frances A. Perretta (Pub); Ronald F. Bouchard (Ed); 20,111; (I); 717-421-3000

RADIO

WESS (90.3 FM), Box 198, East Stroudsburg 18301; Dave Parsons (GM); Linda Geleta (ND); Bill Abramson (PD); 717-424-3512

WPCN (960 AM), Mountain Dr., Mt. Pocono 18344; Janet A. Buynak (GM); George Buynak (ND); 717-839-6796

WVPO (840 AM, 93.5 FM), 22 S. 6th St., Stroudsburg 18360; Sue Larose (GM); Bob Matthews (NE); 717-421-2100

MONTGOMERY COUNTY

DAILIES

MERCURY, THE, (M & S), P.O. Box 599, Hanover & King Sts., Pottstown 19464; H. L. Schwartz III (Pub); Terrence M. Brennan (Ed); 28,612, M; 28,570, S; (I); 215-323-3000

MONTGOMERY COUNTY RECORD, An edition of the Doylestown Daily Intelligencer, (M), 145 Easton Rd., Horsham 19044; Charles P. Smith (Pub); A. Stacy Briggs III (Ed); 18,000; (I); 215-443-5613

REPORTER, THE, (E-1), P.O. Box 390, 307 Derstine Ave., Lansdale 19446; William C. McKinney (Pub); Eric Wolferman (Ed); 18,359; (I); 215-855-8440

TIMES HERALD, THE, (E-1), P.O. Box 591, 410 Markley St., Norristown 19404; David S. John (Pub); Carroll Shelton (Ed); 31,357; (IR); 215-272-2500

WEEKLIES

AMBLER GAZETTE, THE, (We), P.O. Box 180, 95 E. Butler Ave., Ambler 19002; William E. Strasburg (Pub); Fred D. Behringer (Ed); 10,774; (I); 215-646-5100

BREEZE, THE, (Th), 54 Park Ave., Philadelphia 19111; George C. Beetham, Jr. (Ed); Intercounty Newspaper Group (Pub); 428; (I); 215-379-5500

BUCKS COUNTY TELEGRAPH, (S), 390 Easton Rd., Horsham 19044-2592; Sandra Petersohn (Ed); Matthew Petersohn (Pub); 6,800; (I); 215-345-0820

BUCKS-MONT COURIER, (Mo & Tu), P.O. Box 204, Harleysville 19438; Anne G. Thwaits (Ed); Donald E. Thwaits (Pub); 39,700; (I); 215-256-6556

GLENSIDE NEWS, (Th), P.O. Box 189, 12 E. Glenside Ave., Glenside 19038; Scott Weisenberger (Ed); William E. Strasburg (Pub); 3,185; (I); 215-884-4775

GLOBE, THE, (Th), P.O. Box 65, 413 Johnson St., Jenkintown 19046; William E. Strasburg (Pub); Scott Weisenberger (Ed); 3,845; (I); 215-884-4775

INDEPENDENT & MONTGOMERY TRANSCRIPT, (Tu), P.O. Box 39, 350 Walnut St., Collegeville 19426-0039; John Stewart (Pub); Lynne Nycee (Ed); 5,250; (I); 215-489-3001

INDIAN VALLEY ECHO, THE, (We), Box 39, Telford 18969; John Poisker (Pub); Gladys Amspacher (Ed); 9,971; (I); 215-723-3990

KING OF PRUSSIA COURIER, THE, (We), P.O. Box 409, 134 N. Wayne Ave., Wayne 19087; Deborah Shaw (Pub); Dennis F. Daylor (Ed); 8,389; (I); 215-688-3000

MAIN LINE TIMES, (Th), 311 E. Lancaster Ave., Ardmore 19003; Michael J. Murray (Pub); Joan Toenniessen (Ed); 17,046; (I); 215-642-4300

MARPLE NEWTON NEWS, (Th), 311 E. Lancaster Ave., Ardmore 19003; Michael J. Murray (Pub); Michael Caruso (Ed); 10,370; 215-642-4300

MONTGOMERY COUNTY OBSERVER, (We), 1079 DeKalb Pike, Center Square 19422; Francis Laping (Pub); Frank Bishop (Ed); 24,790; (I); 215-277-6342

MONTGOMERYVILLE SPIRIT, (We), P.O. Box 1628, Fort Washington 19034; William E. Strasburg (Pub); Fred D. Behringer (Ed); 30,772; (I); 215-646-5100

NEIGHBORS NEWS, (Th), 311 E. Lancaster Ave., Ardmore 19003; David B. Corr (Pub); Edward Peabody (Ed); 15,950; 215-642-4300

PEASTERVILLE SPIRIT, (Tu), 101 N. York Rd., P.O. Box C, Hatboro 19040; William Strasburg (Pub); Frederick Groshens (Ed); 7,033; (I); 215-675-3430

PENN VALLEY TIMES, (Th), Box 456, Souderton 18964; Bruce Fenstermacher (Ed); Souderton Independent, Inc. (Pub); 1,125; (I); 215-723-4801

PROGRESS, (We), 390 Easton Rd., Horsham 19044; Matthew H. Petersohn (Pub); Sandra L. Petersohn (Ed); 17,251; (I); 215-675-8250

RECORDER, THE, (Tu), 813 Fayette St., Conshohocken 19428; John Myers (Ed); Richard McCuen (Pub); 8,300; (I); 215-828-4600

REPORTER, (We), 842 Oak St., Box 28, Royersford 19468; Bruce Fenstermacher (Pub); Shirley Elliott (Ed); 4,500; (I); 215-948-4850

REPORTER EXTRA, THE, (We), 307 Dearstine Ave., Landsdale 19446; Eric Wolferman (Ed); William C. McKinney (Pub); 25,986; 215-885-8440

SOUDERTON INDEPENDENT, (We), 21 S. Front St., Box 459, Souderton 18964-0459; W. Brooke Moyer (Ed); Souderton Independent, Inc. (Pub); 6,700; (I); 215-723-4801

SPIRIT OF BUCKS COUNTY, (Tu), 101 N. York Rd., Hatboro 19040; William Strasburg (Pub); Frederick Groshens (Ed); 40,199; (I); 215-675-3430

SPRINGFIELD NEWS, (Th), 311 E. Lancaster Ave., Ardmore 19003; Michael J. Murray (Pub); Michael Caruso (Ed); 8,642; (I); 215-642-4300

SPRINGFIELD SUN, (Th), Commerce Drive, Ft. Washington 19034; Fred D. Behringer (Ed); William Strasburg (Pub); 2,613; (I); 215-646-5100

TIMES CHRONICLE, (Th), P.O. Box 140, 413 Johnson St., Jenkintown 19046; Scott Weisenberger (Ed); William S. Strasburg (Pub); 9,638; (I); 215-884-4775

TODAY'S POST, (We), P.O. Box 1310, 160 N. Gulph Rd., King of Prussia 19406; William E. Strasburg (Pub); Fred D. Behringer (Ed); 43,795; (I); 215-337-1700

TODAY'S SPIRIT, (Th), P.O. Box 157, 101 N. York Rd., Hatboro 19040; William E. Strasburg (Pub); Fred D. Groshens (Ed); 8,135; (I); 215-675-3430

TOWN AND COUNTRY, (We), P.O. Box 5, 4th St. & Main St., Pennsburg 18073; Ricki W. Smith (Pub); Jamie McCourt (Ed); 5,128; (I); 215-679-9561

WILLOW GROVE GUIDE, THE, (Th), P.O. Box N, Willow Grove 19090; William E. Strasburg (Pub); Fred S. Groshens (Ed); 2,097; (I); 215-659-5600

RADIO

WBMR (91.7 FM), 145 N. 3rd St., Telford 18969; Richard C. Dean (Pres.); Ed Feldman (ND); 215-723-7700

WGHW (1110 AM), 15 W. Carpenter Lane, Philadelphia 19119; John Grant (GM); 215-277-9449

WHHS (89.3 FM), 200 Mill Road, Havertown 19083; John Roberti (PD); Steve Fabiani (CE); 215-446-7111

WIBF (103.9 FM), Benson East Apartments, Jenkintown 19046; William L. Fox (GM); Donald Hess (NE); 215-887-5400

WNPV (1440 AM), P.O. Box 1440, Lansdale 19446; Phillip N. Hunt (GM); Darryl Berger (NE); 215-855-8211

WPAZ (1370 AM), Box 638, Pottstown 19464; Bob Eppeheimer (GM); Fred Williams (NE); 215-326-4000

MONTOUR COUNTY

DAILIES

DANVILLE NEWS, THE, (E-1), P.O. Box 200, 14 E. Mahoning St., Danville 17821; Martin Reddington (Ed); Stauffer Media, Inc. (Pub); 4,177; (I); 717-275-3235

RADIO

WPGM (1570 AM, 96.7 FM), 8 E. Market St., Danville 17821; George Vacca (GM); Terry M. Diener (ND); 215-275-1570

NORTHAMPTON COUNTY

DAILIES

EXPRESS, THE, (E, Sa & S), P.O. Box 391, 30 N. Fourth St., Easton 18042; Hal Neitzel (Pub); Bruce Frassinelli (Ed); 45,324; (I); 215-258-7171

GLOBE TIMES, (E), P.O. Box F, 202 W. Fourth St., Bethlehem 18015-1502; Donald Taylor (Pub); James R. Laubach, Jr. (Ed); 23,409; (I); 215-867-5000

NEWS, (E-2), 13-15 S. Main St., Bangor 18013; Nancy Freeman (Ed); Kathleen McFall (Pub); 3,000; (I); 215-588-2196

WEEKLIES

BULLETIN, (Th), 4th & Polk Sts., Bethlehem 18015; Bernard Fetsko (Pub & Ed); 11,850; (I); 215-866-3000

HOME NEWS, THE, (Th), P.O. Box 39, 120 S. Walnut St., Bath 18014-0039; William J. Halbfoerster, Jr. (Pub & Ed); 3,500; (I); 215-837-0107

RADIO

WEEX (1230 AM), Box 190, Easton 18042; Jim Shea (GM); Linda K. Schmidt (ND); 215-258-6155

WEST (1400 AM), 436 Northampton St., Easton 18044-0081; Larry Roberts (GM); Mike Moore (NE); 215-250-9600

WGPA (1100 AM), 528 N. New St., Bethlehem 18018; Henry Chadwick (GM); Mary Beth Chadwick (NE); J. J. Maura (PM); 215-866-8074

WJRH (90.5 FM), Lafayette College, Easton 18042; Illya D'Addezio (GM); Mat Rizzo (ND); 215-250-5316

WLEV (96.1 FM), Co-owned with WEST (AM): 215-250-9600

WLVR (91.3 FM), Lehigh University, Bethlehem 18015; Joe Nardone (GM); 215-861-3913

WQQQ (99.9 FM), Co-owned with WEEX (AM): 215-258-6155

WZZO (95.1 FM), Suite 205, Westgate Mall, Bethlehem 18017; Gordon Holt (GM); Tim Scott, Mark Devine (NE); Eugene Romano (PM); 215-694-0511

TELEVISION

WLVT-TV, See Lehigh County, Allentown

NORTHUMBERLAND COUNTY

DAILIES

DAILY ITEM, THE, (E-1), P.O. Box 607, 200 Market St., Sunbury 17801; Donald P. Micozzi (Pub); Robert E. Lauf (Ed); 26,634; (I); 717-286-5671

MILTON STANDARD, THE, (E-1), P.O. Box 259, 19 Arch St., Milton 17847-0259; W. P. Hastings (Pub); Catherine Hastings (Ed); 4,262; (I); 717-742-9671

NEWS-ITEM, (E-1), P.O. Box 587, 707 N. Rock St., Shamokin 17872; Thomas Brennan (Ed); John Reid (Pub); 14,293; (I); 717-648-4641

RADIO

WISL (1480 AM), Rock & Sunbury Sts., Shamokin 17872; Arthur M. Sherman (GM); Lena Haas (ND); 717-648-6831

WKOK (1070 AM), Box 1070, Sunbury 17801; Joseph McGranaghan (GM); Todd Brennan (ND); 717-286-5838

WMIM (1590 AM), 3rd & Oak Sts., Mount Carmel 17851; David Donlin (GM); 717-339-1600

WMLP (1380 AM), Box 334, Milton 17847; Don Steese (GM); 717-742-8705

WQEZ (100.9 FM), Co-owned with WMLP (AM): 717-742-8705

WQKX (94.1 FM), Co-owned with WKOK (AM): 717-286-5838

WSPI (95.3 FM), Box 428, Shamokin 17872; David Donlin (GM); 717-644-0834

PERRY COUNTY

WEEKLIES

DUNCANNON RECORD, (Th), Box A, 217 N. High St., Duncannon 17020; David R. Thompson (Pub & Ed); 2,400; (I); 717-834-4616

NEWS-SUN, THE, (We), 19 S. 3rd St., Newport 17074; Karen J. Green (Pub & Ed); 3,325; (I); 717-567-6226

PERRY COUNTY TIMES, (Th), Box 128, 51 N. Church St., New Bloomfield 17068; David R. Thompson (Pub & Ed); 5,307; (I); 717-582-4305

PHILADELPHIA COUNTY

DAILIES

DAILY NEWS, (E-1), Box 7788, 400 N. Broad St., Philadelphia 19101; Zackery Stalberg (Ed); 252,150; (I); 215-854-5905

INQUIRER, (M & S), P.O. Box 8263, 400 N. Broad St., Philadelphia 19101; Eugene Roberts, Jr. (EE); 504,946, M; 985,582, S; (I); 215-854-2000

WEEKLIES

CATHOLIC STANDARD AND TIMES, (Th), 222 N. 17th St., Philadelphia 19103; Rev. David G. Givey (Ed); 80,000; (REL); 215-587-3660

CHESTNUT HILL LOCAL, (Th), 8434 Germantown Ave., Philadelphia 19118; Chestnut Hill Community Assn. (Pub); Marie Reinhart Jones (Ed); 9,400; (I); 215-248-8800

COMMUNITY FOCUS OF THE DELAWARE VALLEY, (We), 160 W. Lippincott, Philadelphia 19133; Efrain Roche (Ed); 15,000; (I); 215-634-2843

FAR NORTHEAST CITIZEN SENTINEL, (We), 1102 Churchill Rd., Philadelphia 19118; Matthew H. Petersohn (Pub); Sandra L. Petersohn (Ed); 13,495; (I); 215-675-6600

FAR NORTHEAST NEWS, (We), 1612 Margaret St., Philadelphia 19124; Coulston R. Henry (Pub); Don Brennan (Ed); 18,000; (I); 215-535-4275

FAR NORTHEAST TIMES, (We), 8033 Frankford Ave., Philadelphia 19136; Eleanor Smylie (Pub); Marilyn Schaefer (Ed); 30,916; (I); 215-332-3300

FOCUS, (We), 1015 Chestnut St., Philadelphia 19107; Vijay Kothare (Ed); John W. Rorer (Pub); 17,500; (I); 215-925-8545

GERMANTOWN COURIER, (We), 156 W. Chelten Ave., Philadelphia 19144-3379; Rick Linsk (Ed); William Brown (Pub); 25,206; (I); 215-848-4300

GERMANTOWN PAPER, (We), 6220 Ridge Ave., Philadelphia 19128; Harold McCuen (Ed); Intercounty Newspaper Group (Pub); 13,000; (I); 215-483-7300

GIRARD HOME NEWS, (Th), 106 S. 7th St., Suite 600, Philadelphia 19106; Frank Silverman (Ed & Pub); 13,500; (I); 215-923-8087

GUIDE NEWSPAPERS, (Th), 2022 E. Allegheny Ave., Philadelphia 19134; H. Robert Jacobs (Ed); 47,000; (I); 215-288-2400

GWIAZDA (Star), (Th), 3800 Kensington Ave., Philadelphia 19134; Polish Star Publications Company (Pub); Gertrude Nowaczyk (Ed); 8,760; (Fra); 215-739-7571

JEWISH EXPONENT, (Fr), 226 S. 16th St., Philadelphia 19102; Albert Erlick (Ed); Jewish Exponent (Pub); 52,115; (I-REL); 215-893-5700

JEWISH TIMES, (Th), 2417 Welsh Rd., Philadelphia 19114; Jewish Times of Greater Northeast (Pub); Leon E. Brown (Ed); 32,500; 215-464-3900

JUNIATA NEWS, (Tu), 2241 N. 5th St., Philadelphia 19133; Gerald Lineman (Ed & Pub); 9,000; (I); 215-739-8197

LA ACTUALIDAD, (Th), 4953 N. 5th St., Philadelphia 19120; Carlos J. Morales (Ed); La Actualidad Corp. (Pub); 20,000; (I); 215-324-3838

LEADER, THE, (We), 2923 W. Cheltenham Ave., Philadelphia 19150; Harold McCuen (Ed); Intercounty Newspaper Group (Pub); 29,000; (I); 215-885-4111

MAYFLOWER NORTHEAST NEWS, (Th), 1612 Margaret St., Philadelphia 19124; Don Brennan (Ed); Coulston Henry (Pub); 25,000; (I); 215-535-4275

NATIONAL NEWS BUREAU, (Fr), 2019 Chancellor St., Philadelphia 19103; Andrea Diehl (Ed); Harry Jay Katz (Pub); 11,000,000; 215-569-0700

NEWS GLEANER PUBLICATIONS, (We), 1612 Margaret St., Philadelphia 19124; Don Brennan (Ed); 102, 484; (I); 215-535-4275

NORTHEAST ADVISOR, (We), 971 A Bristol Pike, Bensalem 19020; Intercounty Newspaper Group (Pub); Joseph Berkery (Ed); 20,000; (I); 215-639-2271

NORTHEAST BREEZE, THE, (Th), 54 Park Ave., Philadelphia 19111; George C. Beetham, Jr. (Ed); Intercounty Newspaper Group (Pub); 20, 000; (I); 215-379-5500

NORTHEAST TIMES, (We & Th), 8033 Frankford Ave., Philadelphia 19136, Eleanor Smylie (Pub); Louis Chimenti (Ed); 109,250; (I); 215-332-3300

OLNEY TIMES, (Th), 5703 N. 5th St., Philadelphia 19120; John Loomis (Ed); Thomas F. Reily (Pub); 22,254; (I); 215-424-0700

PA LAW JOURNAL-REPORTER, (Mo), 10th & Spring Garden Sts., Philadelphia 19123; Phillip J. Kendall (Pub); Howard Gibson (Ed); 2,420; (I); 215-236-2000

PHILADELPHIA BUSINESS JOURNAL, (We), 2401 Walnut St., Philadelphia 19103; David A. Pfanschmidt (Pub); Brian P. Sullivan (Ed); 10,783; (I); 215-569-0202

PHILADELPHIA CITY PAPER, 1307 Samson St., #3, Philadelphia 19107-4523; Bruce Schimmel (Pub); Chris Hill (Ed); 41,000; 215-735-8444

PHILADELPHIA GAY NEWS, (We), 254 S. 11th St., Philadelphia 19107; Mark Segal (Pub); Stanley Ward (Ed); 14,500; (I); 215-625-8501

PHILADELPHIA NEW OBSERVER, (Th), 511 N. Broad St., Philadelphia 19123; J. Hugo Warren III (Ed & Pub); 18,400; 215-922-5220

ROCKLEDGE BREEZE, THE, (Th), 54 Park Ave., Philadelphia 19111; George C. Beetham (Ed); Intercounty Newspaper Group (Pub); 400; (I); 215-379-5550

ROXBOROUGH REVIEW, (We), 6220 Ridge Ave., Philadelphia 19128; Richard McCuen (Pub); Charles Johnson (Ed); 23,000; (I); 215-483-7300

SONS OF ITALY TIMES, (3), 1520 Locust St., Philadelphia 19102; Grand Lodge of PA Order of Sons of Italy in America (Pub); Joseph L. Monte (Ed); 15,500; (Fra); 215-732-7501

SOUTHWEST GLOBE TIMES, (We), 6330 Paslhall Ave., Philadelphia 19142; Southwest Globe Times, Inc. (Pub); Lenora Iannuzzell (Ed); 18,500; (I); 215-727-7777

TRIBUNE, (Tu, Th & Fr), 524-526 S. 16th St., Philadelphia 19146; Waverly L. Easley (Pub); 33,887; (IR); 215-893-4050

WELCOMAT, (We), 1816 Ludlow St., Philadelphia 19103; Dan Rottenberg (Ed); Susan Seiderman (Pub); 30,000; (I); 215-563-7400

WEST OAK LAND LEADER, THE, (We), 2923 W. Cheltenham Ave., Philadelphia 19150; Harold McCuen (Ed); Intercounty Newspaper Group (Pub); 29,000; (I); 215-885-4111

RADIO

KYW (1060 AM), Independence Mall East, Philadelphia 19106; Roy Shapiro (GM); Steve Butler (ND); 215-238-4700

WCAU (1210 AM, 98.1 FM), City Line & Monument Aves., Philadelphia 19131; Alan Serxner (GM-AM); Vince Benedict (GM-FM); 215-581-5805

WDAS (1480 AM, 105.3 FM), Belmont Ave. & Edgely Dr., Philadelphia 19131; Cody Anderson (GM); Barbara Grant (ND); 215-581-2100

WDVT (900 AM), New Market, Philadelphia 19147; Jon Harmelin (GM); Stas Salwach (NE); Bill Davol (PM); 215-238-3905

WEAZ (101.1 FM), 10 Presidential Blvd., Bala Cynwyd 19004; James M. DeCaro (GM); Rod Phillips (ND); 215-667-8400

WFIL (560 AM), 400 Domino Lane, Philadelphia 19128; Bruce Holberg (Pres., GM); Jeff Collins (ND); 215-482-7000

WFLN (95.7 FM), 8200 Ridge Ave., Philadelphia 19128; Raymond F. Green (GM); Jules Rind (NE); 215-482-6000

WHAT (1340 AM), 3930 Conshohocken Ave., Philadelphia 19131; Dolly Banks (GM); Thomas Malloney (ND); 215-878-1500

WHYY (90.9 FM), 150 N. 6th St., Philadelphia 19106; William Siemering (GM); John Barth (ND); 215-351-9200

WIOQ (102.1 FM), 2 Bala Cynwyd Plaza, Bala Cynwyd 19004; Donald Pettibone (GM); Juan Varleta (ND); 215-667-8100

WIP (610 AM), 19th & Walnut Sts., Philadelphia 19103; Michael Craven (VP & GM); Bill Zimpfer (ND); Mikel Herrington (PD); 215-568-2900

WKDU (91.7 FM), 3210 Chestnut St., Philadelphia 19104; Diego Navarrete (GM); 215-895-2580

WMGK (102.9 FM), 1 Bala Cynwyd Plaza, Bala Cynwyd 19004; Larry Wexler (GM); Elaine Soncini (ND); 215-879-6000

WMMR (93.3 FM), 19th & Walnut Sts., Philadelphia 19103; Michael Crazer (GM); Mark Drucker (ND); 215-561-0933

WPEB (88.1 FM), 48th St., Philadelphia 19143; Robin Robinson (GM); 215-724-0161

WPEN (950 AM), Co-owned with WMGK (FM); 215-879-6000

WPGR (1540 AM), 1 Bala Cynwyd Plaza, Bala Cynwyd 19044; Michael Marder (GM); 215-668-0750

WPWT (91.7 FM), 1533 Pine St., Philadelphia 19147; Chuck Brutche (GM); 215-546-3324

WRTI (90.1 FM), 100 Annenberg Hall Univ., Philadelphia 19122; W. Theodore Eldredge (GM); Cassandra Stancil (ND); 215-787-8405

WSNI (104.5 FM), Co-owned with WRCP (AM); 215-668-0750

WTEL (860 AM), 1349 Cheltenham Ave., Philadelphia 19126; George D. Hopkinsin (Pres.); Quentin C. Sturm (GM); 215-276-0500

WTRK (106.1 FM), 555 City Line Ave., Bala Cynwyd 19004; Tony Davis (PD); 215-835-2350

WUSL (98.9 FM), Co-owned with WFIL (AM); 215-483-8900

WWDB (96.5 FM), 3930 Conshohocken Ave., Philadelphia 19131; Chuck Schwartz (GM); Betty Berneman (ND); Diane Raymond (PD); 215-878-1500

WXPN (88.9 FM), 3905 Spruce St., Philadelphia 19104; Peter Cuzzo (GM); 215-387-7950

WXTU (92.5 FM), 23 W. City Ave., Bala Cynwyd 19004; Lynne H. Adkins (ND); 215-667-9000

WYSP (94.1 FM), 1 Bala Cynwyd Plaza, Bala Cynwyd 19004; Ken Stevens (GM); Steve Trevelisi (ND); 215-668-9460

WZZD (990 AM), 117 Ridge Pike, Lafayette Hill 19444; Jennifer E. Lear (GM); 215-828-6965

TELEVISION

KYW-TV (Ch. 3), Independence Mall East, Philadelphia 19106; James Thompson (GM); Randy Covington (ND); 215-238-4700

WCAU-TV (Ch. 10), City Line & Monument Aves., Philadelphia 19131; Stephen J. Cohen (GM); Thomas Dolan (ND); 215-581-5600

WGBS-TV (Ch. 57), Grant Broadcasting of Phila., Inc., 420 N. 20th St., Philadelphia 19103; Milton Grant (Pres.); John Gardner (GM); 215-563-5757

WPHL-TV (Ch. 7), 5001 Wynnefield Ave., Philadelphia 19131; Eugene McCurdy (GM); 215-878-1700

WPVI-TV (Ch. 6), 4100 City Line Ave., Philadelphia 19131; Richard Spinner (Pres., GM); Ned Warwick (ND); 215-878-9700

WTAF-TV (Ch. 29), 330 Market St., Philadelphia 19106; Randall Smith (GM); Roger Lamay (ND); 215-925-2929

PIKE COUNTY

WEEKLIES

PIKE COUNTY DISPATCH, (Th), P.O. Box 186, 105 W. Catherine St., Milford 18337; Douglas N. Hay (Ed); 4,318; (I); 717-296-6641

POTTER COUNTY

WEEKLIES

POTTER COUNTY LEADER, THE, (We), P.O. Box 671, Coudersport 16915; Paul W. Heimel (Ed); Joseph A. Majot (Pub); 5,500; (I); 814-274-9372

POTTER ENTERPRISE, THE, (We), Box 29, 6 W. 2nd St., Coudersport 16915; Paul Heimel (Ed); Stauffer Media, Inc. (Pub); 8,056; (I); 814-274-8044

RADIO

WFRM (600 AM & FM), 9 S. Main St., Coudersport 16915; Cary Simpson (Pres.); Gerri Miller (ND); 814-274-8600

SCHUYLKILL COUNTY

DAILIES

EVENING HERALD, (E-1), Ringtown Rd., Shenandoah 17976; Molly Groody (Ed); Joseph Wallace (Pub); 10,317; (I); 717-462-2777

POTTSVILLE REPUBLICAN, (E-1), P.O. Box 209, 111 Mahantongo St., Pottsville 17901; Uzal H. Martz, Jr. (Pub); Douglas W. Costello (Ed); 28,718; (I); 717-622-3456

WEEKLIES

CALL, THE, (Th), Box 178, E. Main St., Schuylkill Haven 17972; La Jeune Steidle (Ed); Fred V. Knecht (Pub); 2,050; (I); 717-385-3120

CITIZEN-STANDARD, (We), 100 W. Main St., Box 147, Valley View 17983; Gregory J. Zyla (Ed & Pub); 4,500; (I); 717-682-9081

PRESS HERALD, (Th), 63 S. Tulpehocken St., Pine Grove 17963; Fred Knecht (Pub); Paula Schaeffer (Ed); 3,785; (I); 717-345-4455

WEST SCHUYLKILL HERALD, (Th), 613 E. Grand Ave., Tower City 17980; Fred V. Knecht (Pub); June Reibsane (Ed); 2,000; (I); 717-647-2191

RADIO

WAVT (101.9 FM), Box 540, Pottsville 17901; James A. Bowman (SM & NE); 717-622-1360

WMBT (1530 AM), Box 1530, Shenandoah 17976; Jeff Zuber (ND); Al Kovy (PD); 717-462-2759

WPAM (1450 AM), Box 629, Pottsville 17901; Roseann Cadau (ND); 717-622-1450

WPPA (1360 AM), Co-owned with WAVT (FM): 717-622-1450

SNYDER COUNTY

WEEKLIES

POST, THE, (Th), 29 W. Market St., P.O. Box 356, Middleburg 17842-0356; Irwin Graybill (Pub); Larry Bachman (Ed); 3,786; (I); 717-837-6065

TIMES-TRIBUNE, (Th), P.O. Box 30, Selinsgrove 17870; Barbara Mitchell (Pub); 2,000; (IR); 717-374-4408

RADIO

WYGL (1240 AM), R.D. 1, Box 1240, Selinsgrove 17870; David Bernstein (GM); 717-374-1155

SOMERSET COUNTY

DAILIES

DAILY-AMERICAN, THE, (M-1), P.O. Box 638, 334 W. Main St., Somerset 15501; David H. Reiley (Pub); Keith A. Curtis (Ed); 11,063; (R); 814-445-9621

WEEKLIES

REPUBLIC, THE, (Th), 301 North St., P.O. Box 239, Meyersdale 15552; Robert B. Wentworth (Pub); Fay Ohler Wentworth (Ed); 4,800; (I); 814-634-8321

SOMERSET COUNTY SHOPPER, (We), P.O. Box 638, 334 W. Main St., Somerset 15501; David H. Reiley (Pub); Keith A. Curtis (Ed); 31,500; (Shop); 814-445-9621

RADIO

WADJ (1330 AM), Box 1330, Somerset 15501; Ronald W. Lorence (Pres. & GM); Joe Henry (ND); 814-443-1677

WBEM (1350 AM), 1724 Scalp Ave., Johnstown 15904; Hank Baughman (GM); John Timko (PD); 814-467-6644

WVSC (990 AM, 97.7 FM), P.O. Box 231, Somerset 15501; I. Richard Adams (GM); Kevin Laird (ND); 814-445-4186

WWZE (101.7 FM), P.O. Box 100, Central City 15926; Mary Fetsko (SM); David Graham (ND); 814-754-4651

SULLIVAN COUNTY

WEEKLIES

SULLIVAN REVIEW, THE, (Th), P.O. Box 305, Dushore 18614-0305; Thomas Shoemaker & Stefana H. Shoemaker (Ed & Pub); 6,461; (I); 717-928-8403

SUSQUEHANNA COUNTY

WEEKLIES

FOREST CITY NEWS, THE, (Th), 636 Main St., Forest City 18421; John P. Kameen (Pub & Ed); 3,276; (I); 717-785-3800

SUSQUEHANNA COUNTY INDEPENDENT, (Th), P.O. Box 218, 10 Main St., Montrose 18801; Earle A. Wootton (Pub); Marcia K. Yoselson (Ed); 9,522; (I); 717-278-1141

SUSQUEHANNA COUNTY PRESS, (We), 113-115 Main St., Susquehanna 18847; Earle A. Wootton (Pub); Helen F. Foster (Ed); 717-853-3100

SUSQUEHANNA TRANSCRIPT, (Tu & Fri), 214-216 Exchange St., Susquehanna 18847; Charles Ficarro (Ed & Pub); 2,000; 717-853-3134

RADIO

WPEL (1250 AM, 96.5 FM), Locust & High Sts., Montrose 18801; Larry Souder (GM); Lloyd Sheldon (NE); 717-278-2811

TIOGA COUNTY

WEEKLIES

ELKLAND JOURNAL, THE, (We), 221 E. River St., P.O. Box 26, Elkland 16920; Deborah L. Watkins (Ed); H. Lorraine Stoddard (Pub); 12,000; (I); 814-258-5121

FREE PRESS-COURIER, (We), Box 515, Westfield 16950; Tioga Printing Corp. (Pub); Marie Pepero (Ed); 4,000; (I); 814-367-2230

PENNY SAVER, (Tu), 98 N. Main St., P.O. Box 37, Mansfield 16933; Max L. Colegrove (Ed & Pub); 9,000; (Shop); 717-662-3277

VALLEY DOLLAR SAVER, (We), Westfield 16950; Wilson A. Gridley (Pub); (Shop); 814-367-2622

WELLSBORO GAZETTE, THE, (We), 25 East Ave., Box 118, Wellsboro 16901-0118; Dianne Eaton (Ed); Tioga Printing Corp. (Pub); 6,615; (R); 717-724-2287

RADIO

WNBT (1490 AM, 104.5 FM), Box 98, Wellsboro 16901; David Burket (GM); Helen Roberts (ND); 717-724-1490

WNTE (89.5 FM), Box 84, South Hall, Mansfield Univ., Mansfield 16933; Robert Allen (GM); 717-622-2147

WRGN (88.1 FM, 100.1 FM), RD 3, Hunlock Creek 18621; Burl F. Updyke (GM); 717-477-3688

UNION COUNTY

WEEKLIES
MIFFLINBURG TELEGRAPH, THE, (Th), P.O. Box 189, 358 Walnut St., Mifflinburg 17844-0189; Harris Lemon (Pub); 929; (R); 717-966-2255
UNION COUNTY JOURNAL, (Th), P.O. Box 348, 337 Market St., Lewisburg 17837-0348; Mary Fleming (Ed); William Hastings (Pub); 2,622; (I); 717-523-1268

RADIO
WTGC (1010 AM), Colonial Park, R.D. 1, Lewisburg 17837; Nick Reed (GM & PD); 717-523-3271
WVBU (90.5 FM), Bucknell University, Lewisburg 17837; Vince Mehringer (GM); 717-524-3849
WWMC (98.3 FM), 333 Chestnut St., Mifflinburg 17844; Tony Sylvester (GM); Bill Starr (ND); 717-966-1777

VENANGO COUNTY

DAILIES
DERRICK, THE, (M-1), Box 928, 1510 W. First St., Oil City 16301; E. P. Boyle (Pub); P. C. Boyle (Ed); 16,449; (I); 814-676-7444
NEWS-HERALD, THE, (E-1), P.O. Box 911, 631 12th St., Franklin 16323; James W. Davis (Ed); 7,837; (I); 814-432-3141

WEEKLIES
PROGRESS NEWS, (Tu), Box A, 408 Main St., Emlenton 16373; David J. Staab (Pub & Ed); 15,000; (I); 412-867-1112

RADIO
WFRA (1450 AM), Box 908, Franklin 16323; Robert H. Stauber (GM); Susan Schuster (ND); 814-432-2188
WOYL (1340 AM), Box 1127, Oil City 16301; Sam Gordan (GM & PD); Frank Stacey (ND); 814-676-5744
WRJS (98.5 FM), Co-owned with WOYL (AM): 814-676-5744
WVEN (99.3 FM), Co-owned with WFRA (AM): 814-432-2188

WARREN COUNTY

DAILIES
WARREN TIMES OBSERVER, (M-1), P.O. Box 188, 205 Penna Ave. West, Warren 16365; Kevin Mead (Pub); Allen L. Anderson (Ed); 12,540; (I); 814-723-8200

WEEKLIES
VALLEY VOICE AND ECHO, THE, P.O. Box 825, 4 Leather St., Sheffield 16347; Susan R. Curtin (Pub & Ed); 3,100; (I); 814-968-3974
WARREN COUNTY TRI CITY GUIDE, (Mo), 400 E. Main St., Youngsville 16371; Barbara Pollard (Owner); 33,500; (Shop); 814-563-7546

RADIO
WNAE (1310 AM), P.O. Box 824, Warren 16365; W. LeRoy Schneck (Pres.); Robert Seiden (NE); 814-723-1310
WRRN (92.3 FM), Co-owned with WNAE (AM)

WASHINGTON COUNTY

DAILIES
OBSERVER-REPORTER, (M-1), 440 W. Main St., Monongahela 15063; John Crouse (Ed); W. B. & John Northrop (Pubs); 38,124; (I); 412-258-7000

WEEKLIES
ADVERTISER, THE, (We), Box 929, 3801 Washington Rd., McMurray 15317; Debbie Popp Gilbert (Ed); Richard L. Barnes (Pub); 37,415; (I); 412-561-0700
ALMANAC, THE, (We), Box 929, McMurray 15317; Debbie Popp Gilbert (Ed); Richard L. Barnes (Pub); 30,292; (I); 412-561-0700
BENTWORTH TIMES, THE, (Tu), 719 Main St., Bentleyville 15314; Douglas R. Teagarden (Pub & Ed); 1,449; (I); 412-239-4500
BURGETTSTOWN ENTERPRISE, (We), P.O. Box 191, 11 Main St., Burgettstown 15021; James T. Dallara (Ed); Eleanor M. Vosburg (Pub); 3,800; (R); 412-947-4700
RECORD-OUTLOOK, THE, (We), 115 Barr St., P.O. Box 117, McDonald 15057; James T. Dallara (Ed); Observer Publishing Co. (Pub); 3,300; (I); 412-926-2111
TODAY'S MAIL, (Mo), 440 W. Main St., Monongahela 15063; Glen L. Cobb (Ed & Pub); 104,000; (I); 412-258-7000

WEEKLY RECORDER, (Sa), 214 Main St., Claysville 15323; Elizabeth Henry Jones (Ed); William Carter Jones (Pub); 3,500; (I); 412-663-7742

RADIO
WARO (540 AM), Box 191, Canonsburg 15317; Joe D. Donato (GM); 412-531-8800
WESA (940 AM, 98.3 FM), Box 202, Charleroi 15022; Alan Murdoch (GM); Eric Hagman (ND); Brian Cleary (PD); 412-483-6551
WJPA (1450 AM, 95.3 FM), 98 S. Main St., Washington 15301; Michael S. Siegel (GM); Jim Jefferson (NE); 412-222-2110
WVCS (91.9 FM), 428 Hickory St., Univ. of Pa., California 15419; J. R. Wheeler (Adv.); 412-938-4330
WYTK (95.3 FM), Co-owned with WJPA (AM)

WAYNE COUNTY

WEEKLIES
NEWS-EAGLE, THE, (We & Fr), 522-24 Spring St., Hawley 18428; John C. Dyson, Jr. (Ed & Pub); 2,900; 717-226-4547
WAYNE INDEPENDENT, THE, (Tu, Th & Sa), P.O. Box 122, 220 8th St., Honesdale 18431; Coral A. Ripple (GM); 9,678; (I); 717-253-3055

RADIO
WDNH (1590 AM, 95.3 FM), 350 Erie St., Honesdale 18431; Robert Mermell (GM); George Schmidt (ND); Edward Histed (PD); 717-253-1616

WESTMORELAND COUNTY

DAILIES
LATROBE BULLETIN, (E-1), 1211 Ligonier St., Latrobe 15650; Thomas Whiteman (Pub); William J. Costanzo (Ed); 18,359; (IR); 412-537-3351
STANDARD OBSERVER, THE, (E-1), Box 280, Irwin 15642; Victor Ketchman (Pub); Virginia Kopas (Ed); 14,534; (I); 412-863-3601
TRIBUNE REVIEW, THE, (M & S), Cabin Hill Dr., Greensburg 15601; M. Scaife (Pub); George A. Beidler (Ed); 51,005, M; 78,603, S; (I); 412-834-1151
VALLEY INDEPENDENT, THE, (E-1), Eastgate 19, Monessen 15062; Frank Jaworski (Ed); R. J. Cooper (Pub); 17,227; (I); 412-684-5200

WEEKLIES
CATHOLIC ACCENT, 723 E. Pittsburgh St., Greensburg 15601; Alice Laurich (Ed); Bishop William G. Connore (Pub); 55,000; (Rel); 412-834-4010
INDEPENDENT-OBSERVER, THE, (We), P.O. Box 222, 229 Pittsburgh St., Scottdale 15683; H. Ralph Hernley (Pub); Charles B. Brittain (Ed); 3,010; (I); 412-887-7400
JEANNETTE SPIRIT, THE, (We), 310 Clay Ave., Jeannette 15644; H. Ralph Hernley (Pres. & Pub); Gregory L. Stock (Ed); 2,580; (I); 412-887-7400.
KISKI NEWS, (Sa), Box 90, Vandergrift 15690; Howard W. Grimes (Pub); Judy Laurinatis (Ed); 20,863; (Shop); 412-567-5656
LIGONIER ECHO, THE, (We), 112 W. Main St., Ligonier 15658 H. Ralph Hernley (Pub); Richard P. Schwab (Ed); 4,206; (I); 412-238-2111
MOUNT PLEASANT JOURNAL, THE, (We), 22-33 S. Church St., Mount Pleasant 15666; H. Ralph Hernley (Pub); Paul S. Brittain (Ed); 6,506; (I); 412-887-7400
NEWS-CITIZEN, THE, (We), 203 Walnut St., Box 90, Vandergrift 15690; Howard W. Grimes (Pub); Judy Laurinatis (Ed); 2,856; (I); 412-567-5656
PENN FRANKLIN NEWS, (Mo & We), 4021 Old Wm. Hwy., Box 73, Murrysville 15668; Georgia Boring (Ed); Charles K. Cooper (Pub); 3,565; (I); 412-327-3471
TIMES-SUN, THE, (We), 201-208 First St., West Newton 15089; H. Ralph Hernley (Pub); Gregg Kretchun (Ed); 3,022; (I); 412-887-7400
YOUNGWOOD ADVISER, THE, (We), P.O. Box 222, 229 Pittsburgh St., Scottdale 15683; H. Ralph Hernley (Pub); Charles B. Brittain (Ed); 2,914; (I); 412-887-7400

RADIOS
WBCW (1530 AM), 111 S. 4th St., Jeannette 15644; Verna M. Calisti (GM); 412-527-5656
WCNS (1480 AM), 317 Depot St., Latrobe 15650; John Longo (GM); Lynn Robbins (ND); 412-537-3338

WHJB (620 AM), 245 Brown St., Greensburg 15601; Barry Banker (OM); 412-834-0600

WKPA (1150 AM), 810 5th Ave., New Kensington 15068; Andrea Dudley (SM); Rick Pantale (PD); 412-337-3588

WOKU (107.1 FM), Co-owned with WHJB (AM)

WQTW (16Q), Box 208, Latrobe 15650; Chris R. Molton (GM); 412-539-2511

WYDD (104.7 FM), Co-owned with WKPA (AM)

TELEVISION

WPCB-TV (Ch. 40), Box 17220, Pittsburgh 15235; David F. Kelton (GM); David Skeba (PD); 412-824-3930

WYOMING COUNTY

WEEKLIES

NEW AGE EXAMINER, THE, (Tu & Fr), P.O. Box 59, 16 E. Tioga St., Tunkhannock 18657; James Dillon (Pub & Ed); 4,932; (I); 717-836-2123

ROCKET COURIER, (Th), P.O. Box 187, Wyalusing 18853; W. David Keeler (Ed); 5,500; (I); 717-746-1217

YORK COUNTY

DAILIES

EVENING SUN, THE, (E-1), Box 514, 135 Baltimore St., Hanover 17331; Marvin Roberts (Pub); Albert Sterner (Ed); 20,433; (I); 717-637-3736

YORK DAILY RECORD, (M-1), 1750 Industrial Hwy., York 17042; J. K. Spencer (Pub); Sam Fosdick (Ed); 40,185; (I); 717-757-4842

YORK DISPATCH, THE, (E-1), P.O. Box 2807, 15-21 E. Philadelphia St., York 17401; Robert L. Young (Pub); Henry R. Merges (Ed); 49,399; (IR); 717-854-1575

WEEKLIES

FREE PRESS, (We), 5-A 9 Main St., Shrewsbury 17361; Robert L. Young (Pub); 42,142; (I); 717-235-6835

RECORD ADVERTISER, (We), 549 S. Main St., Shrewsbury 17361; P. Gary Zarfoss (Pub); (I); 717-235-3811

STAR, (We), P.O. Box 47, 811 Main St., Delta 17314-0047; Star Printing Co. (Pub); Gilbert Sommer (Ed); 2,700; (R); 717-456-5692

WEEKLY BULLETIN, THE, (Tu), 2-4 N. Baltimore St., Dillsburg 17019-1228; Phillip Clark (Pub & Ed); 3,000; (I); 717-432-5211

RADIO

WGCB (1440 AM, 96.1 FM), Box 88, Red Lion 17356; Geneva Stamper (GM & PD); Steve Thompson (ND); 717-244-5360

WHTF (92.7 FM), R.D. 4, Box 312-B, York 17404; Douglas George (GM); Mike O'Ndyko (PD); Dave Powers (ND); 717-266-6606

WHVR (1280 AM), Box 234, Hanover 17331; Joan McAnall (GM); Rocky Spino (PD); 717-637-3831

WOBG (1250 AM), Box 2506, York 17405; Barry Bruce (GM); Craig Rhodes (NE); Joyce McSherry (PM); 717-755-1049

WOYK (1350 AM), 2 W. Market St., York 17401; Mike Leash (GM); Doug Walker (NE); Bill Hanson (ND); 717-846-5000

WQXA (1250 AM, 105.7 FM), P.O. Box 2506, York 17405; Barry Bruce (GM); Craig M. Rhodes (NE); Dick Fennessy (PM); 717-757-9402

WSBA (910 AM, 103.3 FM), P.O. Box 910, York 17405; Chris J. Huber, Jr. (VP & GM); Ron Corbin (ND); 717-764-1155

WVYC (88.1 FM), York College, York 17405; Carrie Tatem (GM); Tracey Leather (PD); Mike Roseberry (ND); 717-845-7413

WYCR (98.5 FM), Co-owned with WHVR (AM)

TELEVISION

WGCB-TV (Ch. 49), Box 88, Red Lion 17356; John Norris (Pres.); Jim Nicholls (ND); 717-246-1681

WPMT-TV (Ch. 43), P.O. Box 1868, York 17405; John A. Serrao, Sr. (GM); Lou Castriota (PD); 717-843-0043

PENNSYLVANIA JOURNALS AND MAGAZINES

Abbreviations:
mo. — monthly; bi-mo. — bi-monthly; bi-wkly. — bi-weekly; ti — times; quar. — quarterly

AGRICULTURE

Baer's Agricultural Almanac, Box 328, Lancaster 17603, 1 ti. a yr.

Baer's Garden Newsletter, P.O. Box 328, Lancaster 17603, quar.

Delicious, 328 S. Main St., New Hope 18938, 8 ti. a yr.

Farm Economics, Pa. State University, University Park 16801, mo.

Farm Economics, Cooperative Extension Service, 1 Weaver Bldg., State College 16801, mo.

Farm Journal, 230 Washington Sq., Philadelphia 19105, 14 ti. a yr.

Farm Museum Directory, Box 328, Lancaster 17603, 1 ti. a yr.

Food Industry Advisor, P.O. Box 1047, 224 Pine St., Harrisburg 17101, mo.

Food Trade News, 119 Sibley Ave., Ardmore 19005, mo.

Frozen Food Executive, 604 W. Derry St., P.O. Box 398, Harrisburg, mo.

Grange Advocate for Rural Pennsylvania, 1604 N. Second St., Harrisburg 17102, bi-wkly.

Harness Horse, P.O. Box 1831, Harrisburg 17105, Sat.

Inter-State Communicator, 125 Industrial Highway, Southampton 18966, bi-mo.

Lancaster Farming, P.O. Box 366, 22 E. Main St., Lititz 17543, wkly.

Natural Foods Merchandiser, 244 S. Main St., New Hope 18938, mo.

New Farm, The, 33 E. Minor St., Emmaus 18049, 7 ti. a yr.

Organic Gardening, 33 E. Minor St., Emmaus 18049, mo.

Pennmarva, 1225 Industrial Highway, Southampton 18966, mo.

Pennsylvania Farmer, 704 Lisburn Rd., Camp Hill 17011, bi-wkly.

Pennsylvania Forests (conservation), Pa. Forestry Assn., 401 E. Main St., Mechanicsburg 17055, bi-mo.

Server Pennsylvania, The, 2545-47 Brownsville Rd., Pittsburgh 15210, mo.

AUTOMOBILES/TRAVEL

AAA Today, Schuylkill County Motor Club, 340 S. Centre Street, Pottsville 17901, bi-mo.

AAA Traveler, 230 Lincoln Way East, Chambersburg 17201, quar.

AAA Traveler White Rose Motorist, 118 E. Market Street, P.O. Box 2387, York 17405, quar.

Aerospace Engineering, 400 Commonwealth Drive, Warrendale 15096, mo.

Antique Automobile, 501 W. Governor Road, P.O. Box 417, Hershey 17033, bi-mo.

Automotive Cooling Journal, Harleysville 19438, mo.

Automotive Engineering, 400 Commonwealth Drive, Warrendale 15096, mo.

Automotive Industries, Chilton Way, Radnor 19089, mo.

Automotive Litigation Reporter, P.O. Box 200, Edgemont 19028, mo. (2)

Automotive Marketing, Chilton Way, Radnor 19089, mo.

Commercial Carrier Journal, Chilton Way, Radnor 19089, mo.

Erie Motorist, The, 420 W. 6th Street, Erie 16507, bi-mo.

Gas Engine Magazine, 356 W. Orange Street, Box 328, Lancaster 17603, mo.

Happenings, Scranton 18411, mo.

Ke-Se Bi Ac Monthly, P.O. Box 247, 222 S. Easton Road, Glenside 19038, bi-mo.

Keystone Motorist, 2040 Market Street, Philadelphia 19103, bi-mo.

Lehigh Valley Motor Club News, 1020 Hamilton Street, Allentown 18105, 5 ti. a yr.

Motor Age, Chilton Way, Radnor 19089, mo.

Motorist, P.O. Box 186, 437 Vine Street, Johnstown 15907, bi-mo.

Owner Operator, Chilton Way, Radnor 19089, bi-mo.

Philadelphia Spotlite, The, 210 N. Broad Street, Philadelphia 19107, wkly.

Racing Digest, Box 101, Dover 17315, wkly.

Travelore Report, The, 1512 Spruce Street, Philadelphia 19102, mo.

Valley Motorist, Wilkes-Barre 18702, bi-mo.

Western Pennsylvania Motorist, 202 Penn Circle West, Pittsburgh 15206, mo.

Where and When, 403 S. Allen Street, State College 16801, mo.

COLLEGE JOURNALS

Advocate, The, U. of Pgh. at Johnstown, wkly.

Allegheny Magazine, Allegheny College, Meadville 16335, quar.

Altoona Collegian, Pa. State Univ., Altoona 16601, tri-wkly.

Ariel, Thomas Jefferson University, Philadelphia 19107

Beacon, Wilkes College, Wilkes-Barre 18766, Thurs.

Beaver Herald, Pennsylvania State University, Brodhead Road, Monaca 15061, mo.

Boyce Collegian, Community College of Allegheny Co., Monroeville 15146, bi-mo.

Brown and White, Lehigh University, Bethlehem 18015, Tues. and Fri.

Bryn-Mawr-Haverford College News, Haverford 19041, Fri.

Bucknell World, Bucknell U., Lewisburg 17837, 6 ti. a yr.

Bucknellian, Bucknell University, Box C-3059, Lewisburg 17837, wkly.

C.C. Reader, Pennsylvania State University, Middletown 17057

Cabrini College Loguitur, Radnor 19087

Campus Voice, Bloomsburg State University, Bloomsburg 17815, tri-wkly.

Capitol Times, The, Pennsylvania State University, Middletown 17057, bi-wkly.

Clarion Call, Clarion State University 16214, wkly.

Collegian, Grove City College, Grove City 16127, Fri.

Collegian, The, Pa. State Univ., State College 16802, morn. ex. Sat. & Sun.

College Reporter, Franklin and Marshall College, Lancaster 17604, Mon.

Comenian, The, Moravian College, Bethlehem 18108, Wed.

Crown, The, King's College, Wilkes-Barre 18711, bi-wkly.

Crusader, The, Box 772, Susquehanna University, Selinsgrove 17870, Fri.

Daily Pennsylvanian, The, University of Penna., 4015 Walnut Street, Philadelphia 19104, morn. ex. Sat. & Sun.

Dickinson Law Review, 150 S. College Street, Dickinson Law School, Carlisle 17013, quar.

Dickinson Magazine, Dickinson College, Carlisle 17013, bi-mo.

Dickinsonian, The, Dickinson College, Carlisle 17013, wkly.

Dome, Widener University, Box 1080, Chester 19013, wkly.

Drexel Triangle, Drexel University, 32nd and Chestnut Streets, Philadelphia 19104, Fri.

Duquesne Duke, Duquesne Univ., Pittsburgh 15282, Thurs.

Etownian, Elizabethtown College, Elizabethtown 17022, wkly.

First Edition, The, Chatham College, Box 87, Pittsburgh 15232, bi-mo.

Gannon Knight, The, P.O. Box 526, Gannon University, Erie 16541, wkly.

Geneva Alumnus, Geneva College, Beaver Falls 15010, quar.

Gettysburgian, Box 434, Gettysburg College, Gettysburg 17325, wkly.

Globe, 201 Wood Street, Point Park College, Pittsburgh 15222, Thurs.

Grove City College-Alumni News, Grove City 16127, bi-mo.

Holcad, Westminster College, New Wilmington 16142, Thurs.

Journal, The, Lebanon Valley College, Lebanon 17003

Keystone, The, Kutztown State University 19530, bi-wkly.

Lafayette Alumni Quarterly, Lafayette College, Easton 18042, 4 ti. a yr.

LaSalle (Coll. Alumni), LaSalle University, Philadelphia 19141, quar.

Lehigh Alumni Bulletin, Lehigh University, Bethlehem 18015, 4 ti. a yr.

Lehigh Horizons, Lehigh University, Bethlehem 18015, quar.

Lincolnian, The, Lincoln University 19352, 12 ti. a yr.

Lions Eye, Pennsylvania State University, Media 19063

Lycoming Ledger, The, Lycoming College, Williamsport 17701, bi-wkly.

Matrix, Chatham College, Pittsburgh 15232

Minuteman, The, Robert Morris College, 610 Fifth Ave., Pittsburgh 15219, mo.

Parameters-Journal of the U.S. Army War Coll., U.S. Army War College, Carlisle 17013, quar.

Penn, 319 Pratt Hall, Indiana University of Pa., Indiana 15705, Mon., Wed., Fri.

Penn Stater, 104 Old Main Bldg., State College 16802, bi-mo.

Pennsylvania Columns, Houston Hall, Univ. of Pa. 19104, quar.

Pennsylvania Gazette, University of Pennsylvania, Philadelphia 19104, mo.

Phoenix, 333 Dartmouth Ave., Swarthmore College, Swarthmore 19081, Fri.

Pioneer, The, Point Park College, Pittsburgh 15222, mo.

Pitt, University of Pittsburgh, Pittsburgh 15260, alumni, 6 ti. a yr.

Pitt News, University of Pittsburgh, Pittsburgh 15260, Mon., Wed., Fri.

Quad, The, West Chester University, West Chester 19380, Tues.

Rambler, Rosemont College, Rosemont 19010, bi-mo.

Red and Black, Washington and Jefferson College, Washington 15301, Thurs.

Rocket, Slippery Rock University, Slippery Rock 16057, Fri.

Setonian, Seton Hill College, Greensburg 15601, mo.

Slate, The, Shippensburg State University, Shippensburg 17257, wkly.

Susquehanna Alumnus, Susquehanna University, Selinsgrove 17870, quar.

Swarthmore College Bulletin, Swarthmore College 19081, 6 ti. a yr.

Tartan, The, Carnegie Mellon Univ., Pittsburgh 15213, Tues.

Temple Apothecary, Temple Univ. School of Pharmacy Alumni Assn., 3307 N. Broad Street, Philadelphia 19140, 4 ti. a yr.

Temple Review, Temple University, Philadelphia 19122, quar.

Temple Times, 302 University Services Bldg., Temple University, Philadelphia 19122, wkly.

Temple University News, Temple University, Philadelphia 19122, daily ex. Sat., Sun., and Mon.

Text, The, 4201 Henry Ave., Philadelphia 19144, bi-mo.

Thielensian, Thiel College, Greenville 16125, Tues.

Today, Peirce Jr. College, Philadelphia 19102, 4 ti. a yr.

University Record, Gannon University, Erie 16541, 4 ti. a yr.

Villanova Engineer, Villanova School of Engineering, Villanova 19085, 4 ti. a yr.

Villanovan, Villanova University, Villanova 19085, Fri.

Voice, The, Box 97 Kehr Union, Bloomsburg 17815, tri-wkly.

Washington & Jefferson Magazine, Washington & Jefferson College, Washington 15301, 4 ti. a yr.

Weekly Collegian, Pa. State Univ., State College 16802, wkly.

Westminster Magazine, Westminster College, New Wilmington 16172, quar.

Wharton Journal, The, 3733 Spruce Street, Philadelphia 19104, Thurs.

COMMERCIAL, PROFESSIONAL AND TRADE

Abrasive Engineering Society Magazine, Pittsburgh 15243, bi-mo.

Accent (wholesale jewelry), Radnor 19089, mo.

Advanced Office Concepts, Bala Cynwyd 19004, mo.

Advertising/Communications Times, 121 Chestnut Street, Philadelphia 19106, mo.

American Import and Export Bulletin, Philadelphia 19108, mo.

American Jewelry Manufacturer, Chilton Way, Radnor 19089, mo.

ASTM Standardization News, 1916 Race Street, Philadelphia 19103, mo.

Bio Cycle, P.O. Box 351, 18 S. 7th Street, Emmaus 18049, 10 ti. a yr.

Biological Abstracts, Biosciences Info. Service, Philadelphia 19103, mo.

Biomaterials Applications, Journal of, 851 New Holland Ave., Lancaster 17604, quar.

Business Digest, 2449 Golf Road, Philadelphia 19131, mo.

Business Forms and Systems, 401 N. Broad Street, Philadelphia 19108, bi-mo.

Cellular Plastics, Journal of, 851 New Holland Ave., Box 3535, Lancaster 17604, bi-mo.

Center City Office Weekly, 436 Regina Street, Philadelphia 19116, Tues.

CLU Journal, American Society of Chartered Life Underwriters, Pub., 270 Bryn Mawr Ave., Bryn Mawr 19010, bi-mo.

Cockshaw's Construction Labor News & Opinions, P.O. Box 427, Newtown Square 19073, mo.

Composite Material, Journal of, 851 New Holland Ave., Box 3535, Lancaster 17604, mo.

Construction Equipment Guide, 141 Glenside Ave., P.O. Box 156, Glenside 19038, bi-wkly.

Counselor, The, 1120 Wheeler Way, Langhorne 19047, mo.

CPCU Journal (insurance & economics), 720 Providence Road, Kahler Hall, CB #9, Malvern 19355, quar.

Dealerscope, (consumer electronics), 115 Second Avenue, Philadelphia 19113, mo.

DEC Professional, 921 Bethlehem Pike, Springhouse 19477, mo.

Delaware Valley Business Magazine, 404 Second Street, Philadelphia 19147, mo.

Directors and Boards, 229 S. 18th Street, Philadelphia 19103, quar.

Distribution, Chilton Way, Radnor 19089, mo.

Drexel Polymer Notes, Drexel University, Materials Eng. Dept., Philadelphia 19104, mo.

Dynamic Business, 339 Blvd. of the Allies, Pittsburgh 15222, 11 ti. a yr.

Elastomers & Plastics, Journal of, 851 New Holland Ave., Box 3535, Lancaster 17604, quar.

Electronic Component News, Chilton Way, Radnor 19089, mo.

Engineer's Digest, 2500 Office Center, Willow Grove 19090, mo.

Executive Report, Bigelow Square, Pittsburgh 15219, mo.

Focus (metro business), 1015 S. Chestnut Street, Philadelphia 19107, wkly.

Food Engineering, North American Edition, Chilton Way, Radnor 19089, mo.

Food Eng. Int'l., Chilton Way Radnor 19089, 10 ti. a yr.

Food Trade News (restaurants), 119 Sibley Ave., Ardmore 19005, mo.

FRI Monthly Portfolio, Box 365, Ambler 19002, mo.

Frozen Food Executive, P.O. Box 398, 604 W. Derry Road, Harrisburg 17032, mo.

Glass News, P.O. Box 7138, Pittsburgh 15213, mo.

Global Trade Executive, 401 N. Broad Street, Philadelphia 19108, mo.

Going Public - The IPO Reporter (business & finance), Philadelphia 19102, wkly.

Growth Capital, 1528 Walnut Street, Philadelphia 19102, mo.

Hardware Age, Chilton Way, Radnor 19089, mo.

Highway Builder, 800 N. Third Street, Harrisburg 17102, quar.

IEEE Almanack (elec'l eng'g), Moore School of EE, Univ. of Pa. 19104, mo.

In Business, Box 323, Emmaus 18049, bi-mo.

Industrial Distributor News, Chilton Way, Radnor 19089, bi-mo.

Industrial Heating, (thermal tech.), 1000 Killarney Drive, Pittsburgh 15234, mo.

Industrial Hygiene News, 8650 Babcock Blvd., Pittsburgh 15237, bi-mo.

Industrial Maintenance & Plant Operation, Chilton Way, Radnor 19089, mo.

Industrial Safety and Hygiene News, Chilton Way, Radnor 19089, mo.

In-Plant Reproductions (printing), 401 N. Broad Street, Philadelphia 19108, mo.

Instrument & Apparatus News, Radnor 19089, mo.

Iron Age, Chilton Way, Radnor 19089, 36 ti. a yr.

Iron Age (metalworking intl.), Chilton Way, Radnor 19089, mo.

Iron & Steel Engineer, 3 Gateway Center, Suite 2350, Pittsburgh 15222, mo.

Iron & Steelmaker, Iron & Steel Society, 410 Commonwealth Drive, Warrendale 15086, mo.

Jewelers' Circular - Keystone, Chilton Way, Radnor 19089, mo.

Journal of Coatings Technology (paint, varnish), 1315 Walnut Street, Suite 832, Philadelphia 19107, mo.

Journal of Commercial Bank Lending, 1616 PNB Bldg., Philadelphia 19107, mo.

Journal of Communications, P.O. Box 13358, Philadelphia 19101, quar.

Journal of Metals, P.O. Box 430, 420 Commonwealth Drive, Warrendale 15086, mo.

Journal of Protective Coatings and Linings, 4400 Fifth Ave., Pittsburgh 15213, mo.

Journal of Testing and Evaluation, 1916 Race Street, Philadelphia 19103, bi-mo.

Journal of the Society of Architectural Historians, 1700 Walnut Street, Room 716, Philadelphia 19103, quar.

Log Home & Alternative Housing Builder, 16 First Ave., Corry 16407, 9 ti. a yr.

Management World, 2360 Maryland Road, Willow Grove 19090, 8 ti. a yr.

Master Salesmanship, Concord Industrial Park, Concordville 19331, bi-wkly.

Measurements & Control, 2994 W. Liberty Ave., Pittsburgh 15216, bi-mo.

Mergers and Acquisitions, 229 S. 18th Street, Philadelphia 19103, bi-mo.

Mutual Magazine (railroad employes), Room 359 Amtrak Sta., 30th Street, Philadelphia 19104, mo.

National Clothesline, The, 717 E. Chelten Ave., Philadelphia 19144, mo.

National Coin-Operators Reporter, 717 E. Chelten Ave., Philadelphia 19144, bi-mo.

National Glass Budget, P.O. Box 7138, Pittsburgh 15213, semi-mo.

Northeast Business, 8601 E. Roosevelt Blvd., Philadelphia 19152, mo.

Nursing 87, 1111 Bethlehem Pike, Springhouse 19477, mo.

Nursing Life, 1111 Bethlehem Pike, Springhouse 19477, bi-mo.

Observer (alcol. bev. ind.), 226 N. 12th Street, Philadelphia, 19107, bi-wkly.

Package Printing, 401 N. Broad Street, Philadelphia 19108, mo.

Paper and Advertising Collector, Box 500, Mount Joy 17552, mo.

P.A.R.D. Bulletin, (retail drug trade), Philadelphia 19130, bi-mo.

Pennsylvania Contractor, 219 Pine Street, Harrisburg 17101, mo.

Pennsylvania CPA Journal, 1608 Walnut Street, Philadelphia 19103, 4 ti. a yr.

Pennsylvania Economy, No. 5 Station Sq., Pittsburgh 15219, mo.

Penntrux, P.O. Box 128, Camp Hill 17011, mo.

Personal & Professional, P.O. Box 114, Springhouse 19477, 6 ti. a yr.

Philadelphia Business Journal, 2401 Walnut Street, Philadelphia 19103, wkly.

Pittsburgh Business Journal, 7 Parkway Center, Suite 270, Pittsburgh 15220, Mon.

Pittsburgh Business Review, Univ. of Pittsburgh, Pittsburgh 15260, bi-mo.

Pittsburgh Business Times-Journal, 10 N. Gateway, Pittsburgh 15222, wkly.

Plant Energy Management, 2500 Office Center, Willow Grove 19090, bi-mo.

Plastic Film & Sheeting, Journal of, 1117 Talleyrand Road, West Chester 19382, quar.

Plastics in Building/Construction, 851 New Holland Ave., Lancaster 17604, mo.

PNPA PRESS (prntg. ind.) 2717 N. Front Street, Harrisburg 17110, 10 ti. a yr.

Pollution Equipment News, 8650 Babcock Blvd., Pittsburgh 15237, bi-mo.

Printing Impressions, 401 N. Broad Street, Philadelphia 19108, mo.

Product Design Development (durable goods), Chilton Way, Radnor 19089, mo.

PSA Journal (photography), 2005 Walnut Street, Philadelphia 19103, mo.

Rep World, (advertising), Box 2087, 806 Penn Ave., Sinking Spring 19608, quar.

Reuse/Recycle, 851 New Holland Ave., Lancaster 17604, mo.

Rodale's New Shelter, 33 E. Minor Street, Emmaus 18049, 9 ti. a yr.

RSTS Professional, P.O. Box 361, Fort Washington 19034-0361, bi-mo.

Seybold Report on Office Systems, P.O. Box 644, Media 19063, mo.

Seybold Report on Professional Computing, P.O. Box 644, Media 19063, 6 ti. a yr.

Seybold Report on Publishing Systems, P.O. Box 644, Media 19063, semi-mo.

Souvenirs and Novelties, 401 N. Broad Street, Philadelphia 19108, 7 ti. a yr.

Stack Sampling News, 851 New Holland Ave., Lancaster 17604, mo.

Stockholders & Creditors News Service, P.O. Box 200, Edgemont 19028, semi-mo.

Suburban West Business Magazine, 840 E. St. Rd., P.O. Box 31, Westtown 19395, mo.

Thermal Insulation, Journal of, 851 New Holland Ave., Lancaster 17604, quar.

Trade Association News (roof'g, metal & heat eng.), 167 W. Walnut Park Dr., Philadelphia 19120, mo.

Tri-State Food News, 610 Beatty Road, Monroeville 15146, mo.

Urethane Abstracts, 851 New Holland Ave., Lancaster 17604, mo.

Urethane Plastics & Products, 851 New Holland Ave., Lancaster 17604, mo.

Valley Gazette (coal mining), 102 W. Water Street, Lansford 18232, mo.

VAX Professional, The, P.O. Box 504, 921 Bethlehem Pike, Springhouse 19477, bi-mo.

Wharton Magazine (fin. & com., mgmt.), Univ. of Pa., Philadelphia 19104, 4 ti. a yr.

Words (data systems), 1015 N. York Road, Willow Grove 19090, bi-mo.

World Wide Printer/El Art Tipografico, 401 N. Broad Street, Philadelphia 19108, 6 ti. a yr.

Worldwide Business Opportunities, P.O. Box 7530, Pittsburgh 15213, mo.

Zip (target marketing), Philadelphia 19108, 12 ti. a yr.

EDUCATIONAL

American History Illustrated, Box 8200, Harrisburg 17105, 10 ti. a yr.
American Journal of Archaeology, Archaeological Institute, Bryn Mawr 19010
American Philosophical Society, Proceedings, 104 S. Fifth Street, Philadelphia 19106, quar.
American School & University (ed. facilities), 401 N. Broad Street, Philadelphia 19108, mo.
British Heritage, P.O. Box 8200, Harrisburg 17105, 6 ti. a yr.
Bulletin of the American School of Oriental Research, 4243 Spruce Street, Philadelphia 19104, quar.
Carnegie Magazine, Carnegie Institute, 4400 Forbes Ave., Pittsburgh 15213, 6 ti. a yr.
CEA Critic, Bucknell University, Lewisburg 17837, 4 ti. a yr.
CEA Forum, Bucknell University, Lewisburg 17837, 4 ti. a yr.
Civil War Times Illustrated, Box 8200, Harrisburg 17105, 10 ti. a yr.
Classical World, Classical Assn. of the Atlantic States, Duquesne University, Pittsburgh 15282, 6 ti. a yr.
Communication Quarterly, Penn State University, State College 16302, quar.
Computers in Nursing, E. Washington Square, Philadelphia 19105, bi-mo.
Current History, 4225 Main Street, Philadelphia 19127, 9 ti. a yr.
Cycles (econ.), 124 S. Highland Ave., Pittsburgh 15206, 9 ti. a yr.
D.C.A. Reports, (local govt.), Pa. Dept. of Community Affairs, Forum Bldg., Commonwealth Ave. & Walnut Streets, Harrisburg 17120, bi-mo.
Earth & Mineral Sciences, 116 Deike Bldg., University Park, State College 16802, quar.
Education and Training Exchange, 1015 N. York Road, Willow Grove 19090, quar.
Energy Management Technology, 2500 Office Center, Willow Grove 19090, 9 ti. a yr.
Entomological News, American Entomological Society, 1900 Race Street, Philadelphia 19103, 5 ti. a yr.
Ethnology, Dept. of Anthropology, Univ. of Pittsburgh 15260, quar.
General Linguistics, 215 Wagner Bldg., State College 16802, quar.
History of Photography, 249 Materials Research Lab, State College 16802, quar.
I & CS, Chilton Way, Radnor 19089, mo.
Isis (hist. of sci.), U. of Pa., 215 S. 34th Street, Philadelphia 19104, 5 ti. a yr.
Journal of the Air Pollution Control Ass'n., P.O. Box 2861, Pittsburgh 15230, mo.
Journal of Career Planning and Employment, 62 Highland Ave., Bethlehem 18017, quar.
Journal of Continuing Higher Education, 403 Grange Bldg., State College 16802, quar.
Journal of the History of Ideas, Temple Univ., 748 Humanities Bldg., Philadelphia 19122, quar.
Journal of Mammology, Shippensburg University 17257, quar.
Journal of Social History, Carnegie-Mellon Univ., Schenley Park, Pittsburgh 15213, quar.
Library and Information Science, 471 Park Lane, State College 16803, 5 ti. a yr.
Media and Methods (educ. media), 1511 Walnut Street, Philadelphia 19102, 5 ti. a yr.
Metals in the Environment, 2100 Arch Street, Philadelphia 19103, bi-wkly.
Military Images Magazine, 205 W. Miner Street, West Chester 19382, bi-mo.
Modern Age, 14 S. Bryn Mawr Ave., Bryn Mawr 19010; Intercollegiate Studies Inst., quar.
Newsletter of the Society of Architectural Historians, 1700 Walnut Street, Philadelphia 19103, bi-mo.
Nurse Educator, E. Washington Square, Philadelphia 19105, bi-mo.
Orbis (world affairs), 3508 Market Street, Suite 350, Philadelphia 19104, quar.
Pavlovian Journal of Biological Science, E. Washington Sq., Philadelphia 19105, quar.
Pennsylvania Heritage (historical), Box 1026, Harrisburg 17108, quar.
Pennsylvania History, 601 Liberal Arts Tower, State College 16802, quar.

Pennsylvania Magazine of History and Biography, 1300 Locust Street, Philadelphia 19107, quar.
Pennsylvanian (local govt.), 2941 N. Front Street, Harrisburg 17110, mo.
Philadelphia Museum of Art Bulletin, P.O. Box 7646, Philadelphia 19101, quar.
Poetry Newsletter, Temple Univ., Philadelphia 19122, quar.
Proceedings of the American Philosophical Society, 104 S. 5th Street, Philadelphia 19106, quar.
PSBA Bulletin (Pa. School Boards Assn.), 412 N. 2nd Street, Harrisburg 17101, bi-mo.
SIAM Journals (s) - Applied Math., Computing; Control & Optimization; Math. Analysis; Numerical Analysis; Algebraic & Discrete Methods; Scientific & Statistical Computing; News; Review; 117 S. 17th Street, Philadelphia 19103, quar.
Technical Book Review Index, 427 Wimer Dr., Pittsburgh 15237, mo.
Theory of Probability and Its Applications, 1400 Architects Bldg., 117 S. 17th Street, Philadelphia 19103, quar.
TLC Magazine, 1933 Chestnut Street, Philadelphia 19103, bi-mo.
Transactions of the American Entomological Soc'y., 1900 Race Street, Philadelphia 19103, quar.
Victorian, The, 219 S. 6th Street, Philadelphia 19106, quar.
Voice of PSEA, P.O. Box 1724, Harrisburg 17105, 12 ti. a yr.

ETHNIC, FRATERNAL, AND FOREIGN LANGUAGE
(see also Religious)

Black Careers, P.O. Box 8214, Philadelphia 19101, bi-mo.
Bratsvo (Brotherhood) (Slovak), 173 N. Main Street, Wilkes- Barre 18701, mo.
Constantian, The, (Journal of the Constantian Society), 123 Orr Road, Pittsburgh 15241, 6 ti. a yr.
Forum (a Ukrainian Review), Ukrainian Fraternal Assn., pub., 440 Wyoming Ave., Scranton 18509, quar.
Garsas (Lithuanian), P.O. Box 32, 71-73 S. Washington Street, Wilkes-Barre 18703, mo.
G.B.U. Reporter (German & English), 4254 Clairton Blvd., Pittsburgh 15227, bi-mo.
Junior Magazine (frat.), 100 Delaney Dr., Pittsburgh 15235, bi-mo.
Mission Herald, 701-03 S. 19th Street, Philadelphia 19146, bi-mo.
Naradna Volya (The People's Will), 440 Wyoming Ave., Scranton 18509-0350, wkly.
Narodne Noviny, 2325 E. Carson Street, Pittsburgh 15203, mo.
Slovak v. Amerike, P.O. Box 150, Middletown 17057, mo.
Sokol Polski, 615 Iron City Dr., Pittsburgh 15205, semi-mo.
Sons of Italy Times, 1520 Locust Street, Philadelphia 19102, bi-wkly.
Truth, The, 255 Hause Ave., Pottstown 19464, mo.
Zajednicar, 100 Delaney Dr., Pittsburgh 15235, wkly.

LABOR

McKean County Miner, Box 17, Bradford 16701, wkly.
Miner, The, 300 Parkview Circle, Wilkes-Barre 18702, mo.
Pennsylvania Labor News, P.O. Box 5197, Harrisburg 17110, Fri.
Steelabor, 5 Gateway Center, Pittsburgh 15227, mo.
U.I.U. Journal, Upholsterers' International Union, Pub., 25 N. 4th Street, Philadelphia 19106, quar.

LAW SCHOOL JOURNALS

Dickinson Law Review, Dickinson Law School, Carlisle 17103, quar.
University of Pa. Law Review, 3400 Chestnut Street, Philadelphia 19104, 6 ti. a yr.
Villanova Law Review, Villanova, 711 S. 50th Street, Philadelphia 19085, 5 ti. a yr.

LEGAL

ALI-ABA CLE Review, 4025 Chestnut Street, Philadelphia 19104, wkly.
ALI-ABA Course Materials Journal, 4025 Chestnut Street, Philadelphia 19104, bi-mo.
Altman and Weil Report to Legal Management, P.O. Box 472, Ardmore 19003, mo.
Andrews School Asbestos Alert, P.O. Box 200, Edgemont 19028, mo.

Animal Rights Law Reporter, 421 S. State Street, Scranton 18411, quar.

Asbestos Litigation Reporter, P.O. Box 200, Edgemont 19028, mo.(2)

Automotive Litigation Reporter, P.O. Box 200, Edgemont 19028, mo.(2)

Aviation Litigation Reporter, P.O. Box 200, Edgemont 19028, mo.(2)

Beaver County Legal Journal, 798 Turnpike Street, Beaver 15009, Sat.

Berks County Law Journal, 544-546 Court Street, P.O. Box 1058, Reading 19603, wkly.

Blair County Legal Bulletin, 115 Logan Blvd., Altoona 16002, wkly.

Bucks County Law Reporter, 135 E. State Street, P.O. Box 300, Doylestown 18901, wkly.

Chester County Law Reporter, Chester County Bar Assn. Bldg., 15 W. Gay Street, West Chester 19380, wkly.

CLE Register, 4025 Chestnut Street, Philadelphia 19004, ev. 6 wks.

Commodities Litigation Reporter, P.O. Box 200, Edgemont 19028, mo.(2)

Computer Industry Litigation Reporter, P.O. Box 200, Edgemont 19028, mo.(2)

Construction Industry Litigation Reporter, P.O. Box 200, Edgemont 19028, mo.(2)

Corporate Officers & Directors Liability Litigation Reporter, P.O. Box 200, Edgemont 19028, mo.(2)

Course Materials Journal (legal), 4025 Chestnut Street, Philadelphia 19087, bi-mo.

D.E.S. Litigation Reporter, P.O. Box 200, Edgemont 19028, mo.(2)

Delaware Corporate Law Litigation Reporter, P.O. Box 200, Edgemont 19028, mo.(2)

Failed Bank and Thrift Litigation Reporter, P.O. Box 200, Edgemont 19028, mo.(2)

Food and Drug Legislation, 2100 Arch Street, Philadelphia 19103, bi-wkly.

General Aviation Accident Report, P.O. Box 200, Edgemont 19028, wkly.

Hazardous Waste Litigation Reporter, P.O. Box 200, Edgemont 19028, mo.(2)

Insurance Industry Litigation Reporter, P.O. Box 200, Edgemont 19028, mo.(2)

Iranian Assets Litigation Reporter, P.O. Box 200, Edgemont 19028, mo.(2)

Lackawanna Jurist, Courthouse, Scranton 18503, Fri.

Lancaster Law Review, 11 N. Duke Street, Lancaster 17602, Fri.

Lawyer's Digest, 215 S. Broad Street, Suite 1008, Philadelphia 19107, mo.

Legal Intelligencer, The, 10th and Spring Garden Streets, Philadelphia 19123, 5 ti. a wk.

Lehigh Law Journal, Lehigh County Courthouse, Allentown 18105, Fri.

Monroe Legal Reporter, 729 Monroe Street, Stroudsburg 18360, wkly.

Montgomery County Law Reporter, P.O. Box 268, Norristown 19404, Thurs.

National Bankruptcy Reporter, P.O. Box 200, Edgemont 19028, wkly.

Ob/Gyn Litigation Reporter, P.O. Box 200, Edgemont 19028, mo.(2)

Pennsylvania Law Journal Reporter, 10th & Spring Garden Sts., Philadelphia 19123, wkly.

Personnel Directors' Legal Alert, P.O. Box 200, Edgemont 19028, mo.

Pittsburgh Legal Journal, 620 Second Ave., Pittsburgh 15219, 5 ti. a wk.

Practical Lawyer, The, 4025 Chestnut Street, Philadelphia 19104, 8 ti. a yr.

Practical Real Estate Lawyer, The, 4025 Chestnut Street, Philadelphia 19104, 6 ti. a yr.

Practical Tax Lawyer, The, 4025 Chestnut Street, Philadelphia 19104, 4 ti. a yr.

Racketeering Litigation Reporter, P.O. Box 200, Edgemont 19028, mo.

Toxic Chemicals Litigation Reporter, P.O. Box 200, Edgemont 19028, mo.(2)

Washington County Reports, 523 Washington Trust Bldg., Washington 15301, Thurs.

Westmoreland Law Journal, Courthouse Mezzanine Floor, Greensburg 15601, wkly.

Wrongful Discharge Litigation Reporter, P.O. Box 200, Edgemont 19028, mo.(2)

York Legal Record, 28 E. Market Street, York 17401, wkly.

MEDICAL AND SURGICAL
(Including Dentistry and Pharmacy)

Abstracts of Entomology, Biosciences Info. Service of Biological Abstracts, pub., 2100 Arch Street, Philadelphia 19103

Abstracts on Health Effects of Environmntl. Pollutants, Philadelphia 19103, mo.

Abstracts of Mycology, Biosciences Info. Service, 2100 Arch Street, Philadelphia 19103, mo.

Accomplishments in Oncology, E. Washington Square, Philadelphia 19105, 2 ti. a yr.

Allegheny County Pharmacist, Allegheny Co. Pharmaceutical Assn., 111 Two Parkway Ctr., Pittsburgh 15220, mo.

Allergy and Antiallergy, Biosis CAS Selects, 2100 Arch Street, Philadelphia 19103-1399, mo.

American College of Physicians Observer, 4200 Pine Street, Philadelphia 19104, mo.

American Journal of Cardiovascular Nursing, E. Washington Square, Philadelphia 19105, quar.

American Journal of Clinical Pathology, E. Washington Square, Philadelphia 19105, mo.

American Journal of the Medical Sciences, E. Washington Square, Philadelphia 19105, mo.

American Journal of Otolaryngology, W. Washington Square, Philadelphia 19105, bi-mo.

American Journal of Pharmacy, Philadelphia 19104, 1 ti. a yr.

American Surgeon, E. Washington Square, Philadelphia 19105, mo.

Anesthesiology, E. Washington Square, Philadelphia 19105, mo.

Annals of Internal Medicine, 4200 Pine Street, Philadelphia 19104, mo.

Annals of Surgery, E. Washington Square, Philadelphia 19105, mo.

ASA Refresher Course in Anesthesiology, E. Washington Square, Philadelphia 19105, 1 ti. a yr.

ASAIO Primers in Artificial Organs, E. Washington Square, Philadelphia 19105, bi-mo.

ASAIO Transactions, E. Washington Square, Philadelphia 19105, quar.

Bacterial & Viral Genetics, 2100 Arch Street, Philadelphia 19103, bi-wkly.

Biological Abstracts, Biosciences Information Service, 2100 Arch Street, Philadelphia 19103, mo.

Biological Clocks. Biosis/CAS Selects, 2100 Arch Street, Philadelphia 19103-1399, bi-wkly.

Bioresearch Today, Biosciences Information Service, 2100 Arch Street, Philadelphia 19103, mo.

Bulletin of Allegheny County Medical Society, 713 Ridge Ave., P.O. Box 6135, Pittsburgh 15212, bi-wkly.

Cancer, E. Washington Square, Philadelphia 19105, semi-mo.

Cancer and Nutrition Biosis/CAS Selects, 2100 Arch Street, Philadelphia 19103, bi-wkly.

Cancer Immunology: Biosis/CAS Selects, 2100 Arch Street, Philadelphia 19103, bi-wkly.

Cancer Research, Fels Research Inst., Temple Univ., Philadelphia 19140, semi-mo.

Cardiology Clinics, W. Washington Square, Philadelphia 19105, quar.

Catalyst, The (chemistry), Dept. of Chem., University of Pa., Philadelphia 19104, mo.

Clinical Nuclear Medicine, E. Washington Square, Philadelphia 19105, mo.

Clinical Obstetrics & Gynecology, E. Washington Square, Philadelphia 19105, quar.

Clinical Orthopaedics & Related Research, E. Washington Square, Philadelphia 19105, mo.

Clinical Pediatrics, E. Washington Square, Philadelphia 19105, mo.

Clinical Preventive Dentistry, E. Washington Square, Philadelphia 19105, bi-mo.

Clinics in Anaesthesiology, W. Washington Square, Philadelphia 19105, quar.

Clinics in Chest Medicine, W. Washington Square, Philadelphia 19105, quar.

Clinics in Dermatology, E. Washington Square, Philadelphia 19105, quar.

Clinics in Endocrinology and Metabolism, W. Washington Square, Philadelphia 19105, quar.

Clinics in Geriatric Medicine, W. Washington Square, Philadelphia 19105, quar.

Clinics in Laboratory Medicine, W. Washington Square, Philadelphia 19105, quar.

Clinics in Obstetrics and Gynecology, W. Washington Square, Philadelphia 19105, quar.

Clinics in Plastic Surgery, W. Washington Square, Philadelphia 19105, quar.

Clinics in Podiatry, W. Washington Square, Philadelphia 19105, quar.

Clinics in Sports Medicine, W. Washington Square, Philadelphia 19105, quar.

Computers in Nursing, E. Washington Square, Philadelphia 19105, bi-mo.

Current Surgery, E. Washington Square, Philadelphia 19105, bi-mo.

Dental Clinics of North America, W. Washington Square, Philadelphia 19105, quar.

Dermatologic Clinics, W. Washington Square, Philadelphia 19105, quar.

Digest of Philadelphia College of Osteopathic Medicine, Philadelphia 19131, quar.

Dimensions of Critical Care Nursing, E. Washington Square, Philadelphia 19105, bi-mo.

Diseases of the Colon and Rectum, (Proctology), E. Washington Square, Philadelphia 19105, mo.

DNA Replication, 2100 Arch Street, Philadelphia 19103, bi-wkly.

Emergency Medicine Clinics of North America, W. Washington Square, Philadelphia 19105, quar.

Endorphins: Biosis/CAS Selects, 2100 Arch Street, Philadelphia 19103, bi-wkly.

Enzyme Methods, 2100 Arch Street, Philadelphia 19103, bi-wkly.

Geriatric Pharmacology: Biosis/CAS Selects, 2100 Arch Street, Philadelphia 19103, bi-wkly.

Hand Clinics, W. Washington Square, Philadelphia 19105, quar.

Health Policy Quarterly, Univ. of Pittsburgh, Pittsburgh 15261, quar.

Health Devices Alerts, 5200 Butler Pike, Plymouth Meeting 19462, mo.

Histochemistry & Cytochemistry Biosis/CAS Selects, 2100 Arch Street, Philadelphia 19103-1399, bi-wkly.

HMO Practice, E. Washington Square, Philadelphia 19105, bi-mo.

Hormones & Gene Expression, 2100 Arch Street, Philadelphia 19103, bi-wkly.

Hormones & Hormone Receptor Interactions, 2100 Arch Street, Philadelphia 19103, bi-wkly.

Hospital Pharmacy, E. Washington Square, Philadelphia 19105, mo.

Human Pathology, W. Washington Square, Philadelphia 19105, mo.

Immunochemical Methods: Biosis/CAS Selects, 2100 Arch Street, Philadelphia 19103, bi-wkly.

Interferon: Biosis/CAS Selects, 2100 Arch Street, Philadelphia 19103, bi-wkly.

International Journal of Dermatology, E. Washington Square, Philadelphia 19105, 10 ti. a yr.

Investigative Radiology, E. Washington Square, Philadelphia 19105, mo.

Journal of the American Geriatrics Society, W. Washington Square, Philadelphia 19105, mo.

Journal of Andrology, E. Washington Square, Philadelphia 19105, bi-mo.

Journal of Dental Practice Administration, E. Washington Square, Philadelphia 19105, quar.

Journal of Diabetic Complications, E. Washington Square, Philadelphia 19105, quar.

Journal of Diagnostic Medical Sonography, E. Washington Square, Philadelphia 19105, bi-mo.

Journal of Nursing Administration, E. Washington Square, Philadelphia 19105, 11 ti. a yr.

Journal of Nursing Staff Development, E. Washington Square, Philadelphia 19105, bi-mo.

Journal of Obstetric Gynecologic & Neonatal Nursing, E. Washington Square, Philadelphia 19105, bi-mo.

Journal of Oral and Maxillofacial Surgery, W. Washington Square, Philadelphia 19105, mo.

Journal of Parenteral Science and Technology, Broad and Chestnut Streets, Philadelphia 19107, bi-mo.

Journal of Ultrasound in Medicine, W. Washington Square, Philadelphia 19105, mo.

Journal of Veterinary Internal Medicine, E. Washington Square, Philadelphia 19105, quar.

Leukotreines and Slow-Reacting Substances, 2100 Arch Street, Philadelphia 19103, mo.

Lymphokines: Biosis/CAS Selects, 2100 Arch Street, Philadelphia 19103, bi-wkly.

Mammalian Birth Defects: Biosis/CAS Selects, 2100 Arch Street, Philadelphia 19103, bi-wkly.

Medical Care, E. Washington Square, Philadelphia 19105, mo.

Medical Clinics of North America, W. Washington Street, Philadelphia 19105, bi-mo.

Medical Electronics/Products, 2994 West Liberty Avenue, Pittsburgh 15216, bi-mo.

Medical Malpractice Litigation Reporter, P.O. Box 200, Edgemont 19028, mo.(2)

Monoclonal Antibodies, 2100 Arch Street, Philadelphia 19103, bi-wkly.

Neurologic Clinics, W. Washington Square, Philadelphia 19105, quar.

Neuroreceptors, 2100 Arch Street, Philadelphia 19103, bi-wkly.

NITA, E. Washington Square, Philadelphia 19105, bi-mo.

Nursing 87, 1111 Bethlehem Pike, Springhouse 19477, mo.

Nursing Clinics of North America, W. Washington Square, Philadelphia 19105, quar.

Nurse Educator, E. Washington Square, Philadelphia 19105, bi-mo.

Nursing Life, 1111 Bethlehem Pike, Springhouse 19477, bi-mo.

Nursing Scan, E. Washington Square, Philadelphia 19105, bi-mo.

OB/GYN Litigation Reporter, P.O. Box 200, Edgemont 19028, mo.(2)

Observer, 226 N. 12th Street, Philadelphia 19107, bi-wkly.

Ophthalmology, E. Washington Square, Philadelphia 19105, mo.

Orthopedic Clinics of North America, W. Washington Square, Philadelphia 19105, quar.

Ostomy/Wound Management, 649 South Henderson Road, King of Prussia 19406, quar.

Otolaryngologic Clinics of North America, W. Washington Square, Philadelphia 19105, quar.

Pavlovian Journal of Biological Science, E. Washington Square, Philadelphia 19105, quar.

Pediatric Clinics of North America, W. Washington Square, Philadelphia 19105, bi-mo.

Pediatric Pharmacology: Biosis/CAS Selects, 2100 Arch Street, Philadelphia 19103, bi-wkly.

Pennsylvania Dental Journal, Pennsylvania Dental Assn., pub. Box 3341, Harrisburg 17105, 6 ti. a yr.

Pennsylvania Medicine, 20 Erford Road, Lemoyne 17043, mo.

Pennsylvania Message, 123 Forster Street, Harrisburg 17102, quar.

Pennsylvania Nurse, P.O. Box 8525, Harrisburg 17105, mo.

Pennsylvania Pharmacist, 508 N. 3rd St., Harrisburg 17101, mo.

Pharmaceutical Litigation Reporter, P.O. Box 200, Edgemont 19028, mo.

Philadelphia Medicine, 2100 Spring Garden Street, Philadelphia 19103, mo.

Physicians Washington Report, 1845 Walnut Street, Philadelphia 19103, mo.

Plant Genetics: Biosis/CAS Selects, 2100 Arch Street, Philadelphia 19103, bi-wkly.

Podiatry Management, 401 N. Broad Street, Philadelphia 19108, 8 ti. a yr.

Prevention, 33 E. Minor Street, Emmaus 18049, mo.

Primary Care, W. Washington Square, Philadelphia 19105, quar.

Problems in Anesthesia, E. Washington Square, Philadelphia 19105, quar.

Problems in Critical Care, E. Washington Square, Philadelphia 19105, quar.

Problems in General Surgery, E. Washington Square, Philadelphia 19105, quar.

Problems in Urology, E. Washington Square, Philadelphia 19105, quar.

Psychiatric Clinics, W. Washington Square, Philadelphia 19105, quar.

Radiologic Clinics of North America, W. Washington Square, Philadelphia 19105, quar.

Regional Anesthesia, E. Washington Square, Philadelphia 19105, quar.

Retina, The Journal of Retinal and Vitreous Diseases, E. Washington Square, Philadelphia 19105, quar.

Review of Optometry, Chilton Way, Radnor 19089, mo.

Schizophrenia: Biosis/CAS Selects, 2100 Arch Street, Philadelphia 19103-1399, bi-wkly.
Sexually Transmitted Diseases, E. Washington Square, Philadelphia 19105, quar.
Surgical Clinics of North America, W. Washington Square, Philadelphia 19105, bi-mo.
Temple Apothecary, Temple Univ. School of Pharmacy, Philadelphia 19140, 4 ti. a yr.
Transfusion, E. Washington Square, Philadelphia 19105, bi-mo.
Transplantation: Biosis/CAS Selects, 2100 Arch Street, Philadelphia 19103-1399, bi-wkly.
Urologic Clinics, W. Washington Square, Philadelphia 19105, quar.
Veterinary Clinics: Small Animal Practice, W. Washington Square, Philadelphia 19105, bi-mo.
Veterinary Surgery, E. Washington Square, Philadelphia 19105, quar.
Vitamins, 2100 Arch Street, Philadelphia 19103, bi-wkly.

Rola Boza, (God's Field), (English and Polish), 529 E. Locust Street, Scranton 18505, bi-wkly.
Russian Orthodox Journal, 10 Downs Drive, Wilkes-Barre 18705, mo.
Story Friends, 616 Walnut Street, Scottdale 15683, mo.
SVIT (The Light), 100 Hazel Street, Wilkes-Barre 18702, bi-mo.
United Evangelical, P.O. Box 186, 100 W. Park Ave., Myerstown 17067, mo.
United Lutheran, Ross Mt. Park Road, P.O. Box 947, Ligonier 15658, bi-mo.
U.R.O.B.A. Messenger, 333 Blvd. of Allies, Pittsburgh 15222, bi-mo.
US Catholic, 198 Allendale Road, King of Prussia 19406, mo.
Witness, Episcopal Church Pub'g. Co., P.O. Box 359, Ambler 19002, 11 ti. a yr.
World Encounter, 2900 Queen Lane, Philadelphia 19129, quar.
Your Church, 198 Allendale Road, King of Prussia 19406, bi-mo.

RELIGIOUS PUBLICATIONS

ACT, R.D. 9, Box 512, Gettysburg 15601, 10 ti. a yr.
American Baptist Publications, P.O. Box 851, Valley Forge 19842, bi-wkly.
American Presbyterians: Journal of Presbyterian History, 425 Lombard Street, Philadelphia 19147, quar.
Back to Godhead, P.O. Box 18928, Philadelphia 19119, mo.
Bible Standard and Herald of Christ's Kingdom, Chester Springs 19425, mo.
Biblical Archaeologist, Philadelphia 19104, quar.
Catholic Accent, 723 E. Pittsburgh Street, P.O. Box 850, Greensburg 15601, wkly.
Catholic Library World, 461 W. Lancaster Avenue, Haverford 19041, bi-mo.
Catholic Light, The, 300 Wyoming Avenue, P.O. Box 708, Scranton 18501, bi-wkly.
Catholic Register, The, Box 126C, Logan Blvd., P.O. Box 413, Hollidaysburg 16648, bi-wkly.
Catholic Standard and Times, 222 N. 17th Street, Philadelphia 19103, wkly.
Christian Living, 616 Walnut Avenue, Scottdale 15683, mo.
Church & Synagogue Libraries, P.O. Box 1130, Bryn Mawr 19010, bi-mo.
Episcopal Recorder, 4225 Chestnut Street, Philadelphia 19104, mo.
Episcopalian, The, Philadelphia 19103, mo.
Eternity, 1716 Spruce Street, Philadelphia 19103, mo.
Fraternal Leader, (Christian family), P.O. Box 13005, Erie 16512, bi-mo.
Friends Journal, 1501 Cherry Street, Philadelphia 19102, semi-mo.
Gospel Herald (Mennonite), 616 Walnut Street, Scottdale 15683, Tues.
Greek Catholic Union Messenger, 502 Eighth Street, Munhall 15120, bi-wkly.
Inside the Jewish Exponent, 226 S. 16th Street, Philadelphia 19102, quar.
Jednota (Union), (Slovak and English), (Catholic Frat.), P.O. Box 150, Middletown 17057, wkly.
Jewish Exponent, 226 S. 16th Street, Philadelphia 19102, Fri.
Jewish Quarterly Review, 250 N. Highland Ave., Philadelphia 19066, quar.
Jewish Times, 2417 Welsh Road, Philadelphia 19114, Thurs.
Lake Shore Visitor (Catholic); P.O. Box 4047, Erie 16512, Fri.
Lutheran, The, 2900 Queen Lane, Philadelphia 19129, semi-mo.
Lutheran Women, 2900 Queen Lane, Philadelphia 19129, 10 ti. a yr.
Mission Herald (Baptist), 701-03 S. 19th Street, P.O. Box 3873, Station D, Philadelphia 19146, bi-mo.
New Church Life (Swenenborgian), General Church of the New Jerusalem, pub., P.O. Box 278, Bryn Athyn 19009, mo.
New World Outlook, 198 Allendale Road, King of Prussia 19406, 10 ti. a yr.
North American Moravian, Moravian Church, P.O. Box 1245, Bethlehem 18018, mo.
Other Side, The, 300 W. Apsley Street, Philadelphia 19144, 10 ti. a yr.
Pendle Hill Pamphlets, 338 Plush Mill Road, Wallingford 19086, 6 ti. a yr.
Pioneer Woman, 198 Allendale Road, King of Prussia 19406, mo.
Presbyterian Layman, The, 1245 N. Providence, Media 19063, 6 ti. a yr.
Present Truth & Herald of Christ's Epiphany, Laymen's Home Missionary Movement, Chester Springs 19425, bi-mo.

MISCELLANEOUS

Access, 1015 N. York Road, Willow Grove 19090, mo.
Advance II, 6220 Ridge Avenue, Philadelphia 19128, mo.
Animaldom (S.P.C.A.), 350 E. Erie Avenue, Philadelphia 19134, mo.
Answers: Information Access Digest, 1102 McNeilly Avenue, Pittsburgh 15216, mo.
Area Advertiser, 65 W. Manila Avenue, Pittsburgh 15220-2840, bi-wkly.
A-V, The, American Anti-Vivisection Society, Pub., 801 Old York Road, Jenkintown 19046, mo.
Basenji, The, 789 Linton Hill Road, Newtown 18940, mo.
Best Sellers (Book Review), Univ. of Scranton 18510, mo.
Bicycle Guide, 128 N. 11th Street, Allentown 18102, 9 ti. a yr.
Bicycling, 33 E. Minor Street, Emmaus 18049, 10 ti. a yr.
Boat Pennsylvania, 3532 Walnut Street, P.O. Box 1673, Harrisburg 17105-1673, bi-mo.
Cable Guide, 309 Lakeside Drive, Horsham 19044, mo.
Cable Today, 911 Fox Pavillion, Jenkintown 19046, mo.
Come All Ye, P.O. Box 494, Hatboro 19040, quar.
Common Ground, Saint Peters 19470, quar.
Counter Pentagon, 2208 South Street, Philadelphia 19146, bi-mo.
County Lines, 840 East Street Road, P.O. Box 31, Westtown 19395, mo.
Country Journal, 2245 Kohn Road, P.O. Box 8200, Harrisburg 17105, mo.
Country Living, P.O. Box 8200, Harrisburg 17105, mo.
Dauphin Schuylkill Area Merchandiser, 100 East Cumberland Street, P.O. Box 840, Lebanon 17042, We.
Early American Life, P.O. Box 8200, Harrisburg 17105, bi-mo.
Erie Chautaugua Magazine, 1250 Tower Lane, Erie 16505, bi-mo.
Executive Fitness Newsletter, 33 E. Minor Street, Emmaus 18049, bi-wkly.
Fish Culturists, 1823 Dudley Street, Philadelphia 19145, 10 ti. a yr.
Fly Fisherman, P.O. Box 8200, Harrisburg 17105, 6 ti. a yr.
Format, 1015 N. York Road, Willow Grove 19090, mo.
FRI Monthly Portfolio, Box 365, Ambler 19002, mo.
General Aviation Accident Report, P.O. Box 200, Edgemont 19028, We.
German Sheperd Dog Review, German Shepherd Dog Club of America, 30 Far View Road, Chalfont 18914, mo.
Germantown Crier, 5214 Germantown Ave., Philadelphia 19144, quar.
Gettysburg Area Merchandiser, 100 E. Cumberland Street, P.O. Box 840, Lebanon 17042, We.
Greater Reading Area Merchandiser, Zone I, 100 E. Cumberland Street, P.O. Box 840, Lebanon 17042, We.
Greater Reading Area Merchandiser, Zone II, 100 E. Cumberland Street, P.O. Box 840, Lebanon 17042, We.
Greater Reading Area Merchandiser, Zone III, 100 E. Cumberland Street, P.O. Box 840, Lebanon 17042, We.
Green Revolution (alternative lifestyles), R.D. 7, Box 388, York 17402, 4 ti. a yr.
Guide, 131 N. York Road, Box N, Willow Grove 19090, wkly.
Hanover Area Merchandiser, 100 E. Cumberland Street, P.O. Box 840, Lebanon 17042, We.
Harness Horse, P.O. Box 1831, Harrisburg 17105, Sat.
Hershey Area Merchandiser, 100 E. Cumberland Street, P.O. Box 840, Lebanon 17042, We.

Himalayan News, Box 400, Honesdale 18431, bi-mo.

Hounds and Hunting, Box 372, 146 W. Washington Street, Bradford 16701, mo.

Idea Source Guide (gifts), Box 66, Fairless Hills 19030

Independent Press, P.O. Box 275, Lancaster 17603, mo.

Individual Liberty (civil liberties), P.O. Box 1147, Warminster 18974, mo.

Iron Men Album (hobby), Box 328, 356 W. Orange Street, Lancaster 17603, 6 ti. a yr.

ISAR, Int'l Society of Animal Rights, 421 S. State Street, Clarks Summit 18411, bi-mo.

ISAR Report, 421 S. State Street, Scranton 18411, quar.

Joel Sater's Antiques and Auction News, P.O. Box 500, Mount Joy 17552, bi-wkly.

Journal of Church Music, 2900 Queen Lane, Philadelphia 19129, mo.

Journal of the Lancaster County Historical Society, 230 N. President Avenue, Lancaster 19603, quar.

Lebanon Area Merchandiser, 100 E. Cumberland Street, P.O. Box 840, Lebanon 17042, We.

Market Square, 5620 Maple Heights Center, Pittsburgh 15232, Wed.

Marquee (theatre historical), 624 Wynne Road, Springfield 19064, quar.

Mercury Tri-County Market Place, King & Hanover Streets, Pottstown 19464, Wed.

Metals in the Environment: Biosis/CAS Selects, 2100 Arch Street, Philadelphia 19013-1399, bi-wkly.

Military Images Magazine, 205 W. Miner Street, West Chester 19382, bi-mo.

Muscular Development, Box 1707, York 17405, mo.

Music Article Guide, P.O. Box 27066, Philadelphia 19118, quar.

Myerstown Area Merchandiser, 100 E. Cumberland Street, P.O. Box 840, Lebanon 17042, We.

National Association of Watch and Clock Collectors Bulletin, 514 Popular Street, Columbia 17512, bi-mo.

Natvoa Bulletin, (terrain amphibious vehicles), P.O. Box 1272, Bristol Road, Bensalem 19020, bi-mo.

New Records, The, 128-130 Chestnut Street, Philadelphia 19106, mo.

Northeast Hunting and Fishing, 29 Reeder Road, New Hope 18938, mo.

Paper and Advertising Collector, The, Box 500, Mount Joy 17552, mo.

Pascal Press, 10 1/2 S. 8th Street, Allentown 18105, mo.

Peacelines, 145 S. 13th Street, Philadelphia 19107, bi-mo.

Pennsylvania Angler, 3532 Walnut Street, P.O. Box 1673, Harrisburg 17105-1673, mo.

Pennsylvania Game News, (Game Comm.), Box 1567, Harrisburg 17105, mo.

Pennsylvania Magazine, 1830 Walnut Street, P.O. Box 576, Camp Hill 17011, quar.

Pennsylvania Report, P.O. Box 97, Harrisburg 17108-0097, bi-wkly.

Pennsylvania Township News, 3001 Gettysburg Road, Camp Hill 17011, mo.

Pennsylvanian, 2941 N. Front Street, Harrisburg 17110, mo.

Philadelphia Gay News, 354 S. 11th Street, Philadelphia 19107, wkly.

Philadelphia Spotlite, The (local int.), 210 N. 13th Street, Philadelphia 19107, wkly.

Philadelphia Magazine (regional int.), 1500 Walnut Street, Philadelphia 19102, mo.

Philatelic Literature Review, P.O. Box 8338, State College 16803, quar.

Phillies Report, P.O. Box 157, Springhouse 19064, bi-wkly.

Pittsburgh Magazine, 4802 Fifth Avenue, Pittsburgh 15213, mo.

Playbill (theat. mag.), 210 N. 13th Street, Philadelphia 19107, mo.

Pony Express, (baseball), P.O. Box 225, Washington 15301, 4 ti. a yr.

Private Placements, Two Penn Center Plaza, Philadelphia 19102, 24 ti. a yr.

Rodale's New Shelter, 33 E. Minor Street, Emmaus 18049, mo.

Rowing USA, No. 4 Boathouse Row, Philadelphia 19130, bi-mo.

Runners World, 33 E. Minor Street, Emmaus 18049, mo.

Sewickley Magazine, P.O. Box 413, Sewickley 15143, mo.

Sing Out, Box 1017, Easton 18042, quar.

Spring, 33 E. Minor Street, Emmaus 18049, 9 ti. a yr.

Steam & Gas Slow Directory, Box 328, Lancaster 17603, 1 ti. a yr.

Susquehanna Magazine, R.D. 1, Box 75A, Marietta 17547, mo.

Technical Book Review Index, 427 Wimer Drive, Pittsburgh 15237, mo.

Theatrical Faces/Gallery Arts, 136 S. 4th Street, 2nd Floor, Allentown 18101, mo.

Today Magazine, 627 N. Glenwood Street, Allentown 18104, mo.

Topical Time, P.O. Box 630, Johnstown 15907, bi-mo.

Tourist Attractions & Parks (tourism), 401 N. Broad Street, Philadelphia 19108, 6 ti. a yr.

Town & Gown (reg'l int., central Pa.), 403 S. Allen Street, State College 16801, mo.

Transactions of the American Entomological Society, 1900 Race Street, Philadelphia 19103, quar.

Trottingbred, The, 575 Broadway, Hanover 17331, 8 ti. a yr.

TV Guide, (TV enter. & info.), 4 Radnor Corporate Center, Matsonford Road, Radnor 19088, wkly.

Univercity, 2019 Chancellor Street, Philadelphia 19103, Thurs.

Wordsworth Circle, The, 12th & Berks Streets, Philadelphia 19122, quar.

GENERAL INDEX

Abbreviations

THE PENNSYLVANIA MANUAL

INDIVIDUAL INDEX

ADDITIONS

ADDENDA

Elizabeth H. Dole resigned as Secretary of the U.S. Department of Transportation effective September 30, 1987, and James H. Burnley IV was named Acting Secretary of Transportation effective October 8, 1987. Burnley was approved by the Senate on November 30, 1987.

On October 14, 1987, Robert G. Garraty was appointed Executive Director of the Pennsylvania MILRITE Council.

On October 15, 1987, C. William Verity was sworn in as the Secretary of the U.S. Department of Commerce, replacing the late Malcolm Baldrige.

William E. Brock resigned as Secretary of the U.S. Department of Labor effective November 1, 1987, and Ann Dore McLaughlin, former Interior Undersecretary was nominated to succeed Brock as Secretary of Labor. McLaughlin was sworn in December 17, 1987.

In special elections, on November 3, 1987, Thomas W. Dempsey (R) won election to the seat held by the late State Representative Anthony Cimini; Shirley Kitchen (D) was elected to succeed the late State Representative Alphonso Deal; and Andrew Billow, Jr., (D) won the House seat vacated by Rep. William Stewart when he filled the Senate vacancy created by the election of Mark S. Singel as Lieutenant Governor.

On November 5, 1987, Caspar Weinberger resigned as Secretary of the U.S. Department of Defense effective upon Senate confirmation of Frank C. Carlucci III as defense secretary. On November 23, 1987, Carlucci was confirmed by the Senate. Lt. Gen. Colin L. Powell replaced Carlucci as National Security Adviser.

On November 24, 1987, Ethel S. Barnett was confirmed as a member of the State Civil Service Commission.

On December 15, 1987, James A. Goodman, Oliver Slinker and Robert P. Fohl were sworn in as members of the Liquor Control Board.

On December 16, 1987, James F. Malone, III, was elected Vice Chairman of the Pennsylvania Turnpike Commission.